Jon Courson's
APPLICATION
COMMENTARY

Jon Courson's
APPLICATION
COMMENTARY

NEW TESTAMENT

Foreword by
CHUCK SMITH

THOMAS NELSON PUBLISHERS
Nashville

FOREWORD

There are so many commentaries on the Bible that are available today. Even though most are expositional, or exegetical, they often seek to be so exacting with the letter of the law or the possible meaning of a particular word that they lack life and inspiration. It is hard to find a good devotional commentary on the Bible, one that brings both understanding and life to the passage, so that you are inspired to worship the Lord as you gain new insights into the truth of His love and grace toward us.

This commentary is one that does just that.

In Nehemiah chapter eight, we are told that the people were gathered together and they read in the book of the law of God distinctly, and gave the sense, and caused them to understand the meaning. I find that this perfectly describes what Jon has done in his commentaries, and is the greatest need in the church today. In Nehemiah's day, this method of commentary brought great conviction upon the people and a genuine turning to God. The ultimate result was that the people went their way rejoicing because they understood the words that were declared unto them.

I am convinced that you also will go your way rejoicing after reading the insights that the Holy Spirit has given to Jon on the scriptures.

Pastor Chuck Smith
Senior Pastor, Calvary Chapel
Costa Mesa, California

TABLE OF CONTENTS

TOPICAL TABLE OF CONTENTS

The Church

The Cross

End Times

Evolution

Faith

Ministry

Prayer

Salvation

Sin

Spiritual Growth

Spiritual Warfare

Trials & Suffering

The Word

Jon Courson's
APPLICATION
COMMENTARY

MATTHEW

Background to Matthew

About fifty years after Jesus ascended into heaven, one of His followers, a man named Matthew, picked up his pen and began to write about Him. Matthew had a great appreciation for Jesus—perhaps because of his occupation at the time Jesus called him. As a tax collector, Matthew would have been hated by the people of Israel, not only because he worked for the despised Romans, but because the Jews would have perceived him to be dishonest. Each tax collector was assigned to raise a certain amount of money from his particular region, and any amount he could raise above that figure was his to keep. So here is Matthew—looked down upon by some, hated by most, a pariah. And here comes Jesus saying to him, "Follow Me."

Matthew immediately left his desk and began to follow Jesus. Amazed that Jesus would reach out to a man like him, Matthew opened his heart to Jesus. We then read in the next verses how he opened his home. Immediately, he had all of his tax-collecting buddies and all of the prostitutes (the only people who would hang out with the tax collectors) over to his house to introduce them to Jesus. Seeing Jesus eating in the home of Matthew with prostitutes and tax collectors, the Pharisees were scandalized. But, of course, Jesus would begin to teach those self-righteous Pharisees that the Son of Man came to seek and save those who were lost.

It always interests me how sinners were very comfortable around Jesus as He taught them about the kingdom, about the love of the Father, and about Old Testament Scriptures. Sinners loved to be around Jesus. It was the religious people—the Pharisees and the scribes—who had such a tough time with Him that they eventually ordered Him to be crucified.

I am sometimes concerned because I find that we get too comfortable around religious people. But sinners? When they see us coming, they often run from us as fast as they can in fear that we're going to come down hard on them, preach at them, or turn our backs and walk away from them. Pray about spending a little more time with people who don't know the Lord. Share with them the things you're learning as though they are already believers. Do you know what you'll discover? Amazed that you're not judging them, they'll be attracted to Jesus just as they were in the days of Matthew. Let the Pharisees sniff and the scribes scoff, but you be like Matthew, a man who opened his heart and then his home. After opening his home, Matthew also opened his hand. A keeper of records by vocation, it's only fitting that he would grab the pen to which he was so accustomed, and use it to keep a new, important record of the teachings and deeds of Jesus, his Hero, and his Leader.

Truly, the Lord uses whatever is in one's hands presently to do His work in ministry. As God called Moses in the wilderness, He said, "Moses what's in your hand? A rod. That's what I'll use as an instrument of authority in your ministry."

"What's in your hand, David? A slingshot. Let's go get Goliath!"

"Peter, what's in your hand? A net. I will make you a fisher of men."

I think too often we wish we had other gifts, skills, or trades, and we think, *"If I could only play guitar, there would be no stopping me!"* But take it from one who's bought more than one guitar. It doesn't work that way, folks! Use what's in your hand right now, and the Lord will use you.

The Gospel Matthew recorded is essential. You see, if you went from Malachi to Mark, you would go from the Old Testament promises to the New Testament promises, but you would have some very great questions. "Wait a minute," you'd say. "What do I do with all of these promises in the prophets concerning the people of Israel, the apple of the Father's eye, the chosen people—the Jews? How do the promises of the kingdom—given throughout the Old Testament by God's prophets—work out?"

Matthew is a bridge-builder, spanning the gap between the Old Testament promises and the New Testament promises. How? By quoting the Old Testament constantly, much more than the other Gospel writers.

- In Matthew's Gospel, the Old Testament is quoted or alluded to 129 times.
- "The kingdom of heaven," a phrase used only by Matthew, is seen 32 times.
- The phrase, "that it might be fulfilled," used only by Matthew, appears 9 times.
- The phrase, "that which was spoken," in reference to the Old Testament, is used 14 times, only by Matthew.

What's Matthew doing? He's constantly drawing upon the Old Testament prophets and relating them to their fulfillment in a Person—Messiah—Jesus Christ. Matthew's Gospel was written primarily, though not exclusively, for the Jews.

Mark, on the other hand, written primarily to the Romans, is a very fast-moving book, only sixteen chapters long. The Roman attention span was somewhat limited, much like that of Americans. So there aren't a lot of long discourses in Mark's Gospel, not a whole lot of heavy teachings, but rather stories that catered to their "video mentality."

As Luke was written to the Greeks, and John was written to the whole world, we see each one of the Gospels has a different audience in mind. Matthew's audience was Jewish; thus, he addresses Jewish questions.

As you read through Matthew's Gospel, you will notice it does not unfold chronologically, but rather topically. There are five main sections in Matthew, each one consisting of a discourse, or body of teaching, a demonstration of how Jesus worked it out practically, and a debate with people questioning, wondering, and talking.

We'll see a discourse, a demonstration, and a debate in each of the following five sections:

- The King *revealed* in chapters 1 through 10, where Matthew writes about the kingdom and the King of the Jews.
- The King *resisted* in chapters 11 through 13, when opposition to Jesus begins to surface.
- The King *retreating* in chapters 14 through 20, where Jesus takes His disciples and pulls them aside to give them personal instruction.
- The King *rejected* in chapters 21 through 27, as the people say, "We will not have this Man to rule over us."
- And finally, the King *resurrected* in chapter 28.

MATTHEW

1 Because every Jewish king must have a record of his right to the throne, Matthew launches out by giving the genealogy of Jesus Christ—a genealogy so interesting that we could spend years studying it. In the interest of space, however, I will point out just one or two things in order that we can move through the first chapter of Matthew before the next millennium arrives!

Matthew 1:1
The book of the generation of Jesus Christ, the son of David, the son of Abraham.

Matthew begins by saying Jesus is the rightful Heir to the throne of Israel both racially and royally.

Racially, He is the Son of Abraham. In the Book of Genesis, God made a promise to Abraham that through his seed the entire world would be blessed. Paul would later say the word God used was "seed," not "seeds," and that the "Seed" was Christ Jesus.

Royally, He is the Son of David. One day David said to the prophet Nathan, "I want to build a house for God."

"Far out!" Nathan said.

But that night, the Lord spoke to Nathan, saying, "David can't build Me a temple because his hands are full of blood. He's a man of war, not a man of peace. Go tell David he can't build, but tell him this: Although he can't build Me a house, I will build him a house."

Our God has a way of tempering our disappointments with even greater blessings that we had no idea were coming, and that's exactly what happened with David. The house God built through him was the Messiah—One who will reign forever in a kingdom without end.

The Jews knew the Messiah must be of the seed of Abraham and a Son of David. Did you know there is only one Jew able to make such a claim? In A.D. 70, when the Romans sacked Jerusalem, all of the genealogical records of the Jewish people were destroyed. Thus, there is no Jew today who can claim with certainty and authority to be a Son of Abraham *and* a Son of David except Jesus. His genealogy recorded in this first chapter of Matthew is the only preserved genealogy that fits both requirements.

To the Jewish student, this is heavy. "You mean there is a Jew who can really trace His genealogy back to Abraham?" Yes. His name is Jesus of Nazareth. There is something in this genealogy that must have blown the mind of the Jew who studied this through. There are four women named: In verse 3, Tamar is mentioned; in verse 5, Rahab and Ruth are listed; in verse 6, we find Bathsheba.

This would be a mind-blower because, you see, Jewish men prayed this prayer daily: "God, I thank You that I was not born a Gentile, a dog, or a woman." It was a tremendously male-oriented kind of society, where women's names were never included in genealogies. What's the Lord doing? He's saying, "The kingdom I'm establishing is different from the kingdom the Jews are expecting." Paul would later write that in Christ there is neither male nor female, for Jesus is the great liberator of women (Galatians 3:28).

Study history. Wherever the gospel has been rejected, women have been treated poorly, even in sophisticated societies. Consider the Grecian culture, for example. The Greeks, perhaps the most sophisticated society in history, believed every man should have three women: a legitimate wife to bear his children, a woman to talk to so he wouldn't have to talk to his wife, and a lover to satisfy his physical needs. But wherever the gospel has gone, women have been elevated.

Because the Jews placed a high priority on *family responsibility,* much like the Mormons do today, Tamar's name in verse 3 would have been a real shocker to the mind of the Jewish reader. You might remember her from the thirty-eighth chapter of Genesis.

Judah, one of the twelve sons of Jacob, had three sons—Er, Onan, and Shelah. The oldest son, Er, married Tamar, and Scripture records that Er did wickedly before the Lord and was smitten, or killed. The cultural practice, which was later recorded in Deuteronomy 25, was such that if a man died and left a woman without child, the younger brother was to marry her and raise offspring in the name of the deceased brother. This happened in order that his heritage might continue and the property might be passed along. So when Er died, Onan was obligated to marry Tamar.

But Onan refused to impregnate her. Therefore, because of the hardness of his heart in saying, "I'm not going to allow her to raise children in my brother's name," the Lord smote him as well. Now Er is dead. Onan's gone, and Judah says, "I've got one son left. Do I want to give my last son to this gal? I mean, her record isn't very good." Understandably concerned as a father, he says, "Listen, Tamar, wait until Shelah gets a little bit older, and then I'll give him to you."

But the years went on, Shelah grew up, and Judah didn't keep his promise. So Tamar took matters into her own hands. She took off her widow's garments, veiled herself as a harlot, and sat beside the road Judah traveled frequently. Judah, noticing this harlot whom he hadn't seen before, approached her and sought to make a deal with her. He didn't have his wallet with him, so she said, "Give me your ring, your staff, and your bracelet, and that will do for now. You can give me the sheep you owe me later." They had sexual relations, and he left her with his ring, his bracelet, and his staff. He had no idea, of course, with whom he was dealing, since she was completely veiled.

A few months later, the news is out in the town and in the community: Tamar, the widow of Er and Onan, the daughter-in-law of Judah, has played the whore. She's pregnant. Judah said, "Let her be burned."

She answered him, "Do you know whose staff this is, whose ring this is, and whose bracelet this is?"

Judah's jaw must have dropped as he said, "Oh no! You mean that was *you?* I have done wrong in that I have not given you my son." Judah realized he was at fault in failing to care for his family in a way that was traditionally and customarily proper. In holding back his son, Judah had robbed Tamar of her rightful seed.

It's a sordid story to say the least. Can't you see the Lord saying, "Let's put Tamar in the genealogy for these Jews who are so proud of their male superiority and their sense of family responsibility"?

The Jews not only valued family responsibility, but they also valued *sexual purity.* And guess who is number two in the genealogy? A prostitute named Rahab. In the days of Joshua, when the spies came to scope out Jericho, it was Rahab who hid them and covered up for them. She is honored not only by appearing here in the genealogy of Jesus Christ, but in the listing of the Hall of Faith found in Hebrews 11. Rahab was a tremendous woman because, in spite of her limited knowledge and understanding, she risked everything, believing that the God of Israel was the True and the Living God.

Not only were the Jews concerned about family responsibility and moral purity, but the third big issue was *racial superiority.* So determined were they that their racial line remain free from pollution, they believed that if you, as a Jew, even accidentally brushed against a Gentile, you would have to go home immediately, take off your garments, burn them, take a bath, get dressed again, and go on your way. And guess who's in the genealogy—a Gentile, a Moabitess!

Third, Matthew draws attention to Bathsheba, referred to in verse 6 as "she that had been the wife of Uriah." To the Jews, so proud of their history and particularly of their great King David, this reminder of his affair with Bathsheba and his subsequent murder of her husband, Uriah, must have been a particularly painful one. But the inclusion of Bathsheba in this genealogy is further indication that the Holy Spirit, through the pen of Matthew, desired to shake the Jews out of their pseudo-spiritual complacency to alert them of the coming Messiah.

What does this say to me theologically? It says the stage is already set for the Lord to do a new work. "My kingdom is the kingdom of heaven, not the kingdom of the nation Israel." It's much broader than Israel. It's a whole new thing. The Lord declares, "Behold, I make all things new." But personally, it reminds me that these words should never pass from our lips again: "The Lord can't use me because I have sinned greatly, I've shirked my family responsibilities, and I've messed up my family."

The Pharisees may stick up their noses and say, "How can this be?" Let them! Know this: He does all things new, and He's included people like Rahab along with people like you and me. He's the Friend of Sinners. Your family may have had failures in the past, either thirty years ago or three minutes ago. Your morals may be questionable, you might be a Moabitess, feeling you haven't had the education theologically, or haven't been "Christianized" culturally.

So what? Join Tamar and Rahab. Join Ruth, who simply looked at Naomi and said, "Naomi, you're a child of Israel, and wherever you go, I'll go. Your God will be my God. Your people shall be my people. And where you die, I'll die there as well. I'm going to start traveling with you."

The names go on for fifteen verses—tracing the genealogy of Jesus through Abraham and David and on down to Joseph.

Matthew 1:16
And Jacob begat Joseph the husband of Mary, of whom was born Jesus, who is called Christ.

Notice, students, that Matthew doesn't say, "And Jacob begat Joseph of whom was born Jesus," which was the wording he used in the first fifteen verses. No, he specifically breaks the order by telling us very clearly that Jacob begat Joseph (not Joseph the father of Jesus, but Joseph the husband of Mary). Joseph was not the father of Jesus, but His foster-father.

Matthew 1:17
So all the generations from Abraham to David are fourteen generations; and from David until the carrying away into Babylon are fourteen generations; and from the carrying away into Babylon unto Christ are fourteen generations.

I am so grateful for the genealogy of Jesus. We can't pick our relatives, but Jesus did. He knew exactly who was going to be in His lineage before the foundation of the world. And He chose people like those listed here to give us great hope no matter who we are, no matter where we're at. I hope, if the Lord tarries, that we will saturate ourselves in the Gospel, the Good News, that Jesus takes people like Matthew the tax collector, and Mary Magdalene the streetwalker, Tamar and Rahab, David and Bathsheba. And He delights in rescuing and rebuilding them. And even after they fail yet again, as we will see in Matthew, He never gives up on them. Neither will He give up on you.

I once read an article that talked about a group of psychologists who were studying the victims of the Holocaust, including those who survived concentration camps like Auschwitz and Treblinka. They found that 40 percent of the survivors who had adjusted well and had gone on successfully in their lives versus the 60 percent who were still struggling shared one common denominator that set the world of psychology topsy-turvy. That is, the 40 percent who had adjusted well did not, when asleep, dream about their past experiences. Until this study, the traditional rap in psychology had been to follow this advice: If you want to get over your hurts, you need to dwell on, relive, and work out the past. Instead, because of what they called "the Auschwitz Studies," psychologists found that the people who were still working through the horrors of the holocaust were not doing well, while those who were healing were those who had been able to say, "That's a closed chapter in my life. That was then. This is now. I'm going on."

There is therefore now no condemnation to them which are in Christ Jesus, who walk not after the flesh, but after the Spirit.
Romans 8:1

The Cross completed the work. If you're reliving the failures of yesterday, last Monday, or last month, you're missing the Good News of the gospel. The genealogy of Jesus says, "I'm doing something new." Go your way rejoicing, saint. You have been included in His family.

Matthew 1:18
Now the birth of Jesus Christ was on this wise: When as his mother Mary was espoused to Joseph, before they came together, she was found with child of the Holy Ghost.

Joseph, the foster-father of Jesus, whose genealogy has just been given to us, was espoused to Mary. What does it mean to be espoused? An espoused couple was legally considered husband and wife, although the relationship would not be consummated until the marriage festival. During the espousal period, which lasted for one year, if either one felt, "Oh, I cannot live with her," or, "I can't stand him," they could divorce each other during that time. This is the period in which Joseph and Mary are right now. It is during this time that Mary, perhaps fifteen years of age, as most scholars believe, finds herself pregnant.

Matthew 1:19
Then Joseph her husband, being a just man, and not willing to make her a publick example, was minded to put her away privily.

When Mary came to Joseph and said, "I'm pregnant," he could have charged her with immorality. But Joseph showed mercy. This is why I like Joseph. He is a moral man who stands for rightness, but he is also merciful, which is a rare combination. Most people are either moral *or* merciful. God, make us men like Joseph! Give us his morality, but also his mercy.

Matthew 1:20 (a)
But while he thought on these things, behold, the angel of the Lord appeared unto him in a dream . . .

Joseph was also logical, yet mystical. Scripture says, "he thought on these things." He was a thinker, but when he went to sleep, he became a dreamer. Most men are logical; however, some are overly mystical. But here's Joseph with a beautiful balance of both. I personally think Joseph should get more press during the Christmas season! He's a tremendous example of being moral, but merciful, and logical, yet mystical.

Matthew 1:20 (b)
. . . saying, Joseph, thou son of David, fear not to take unto thee Mary thy wife: for that which is conceived in her is of the Holy Ghost.

Over and over again, we men, like Joseph, need to hear this message from the Lord: "Fear not." When the women we love become wise by growing in the Lord, something is conceived in them of the Holy Ghost. Perhaps they come back from a prayer meeting and they are just elated in the Lord. Perhaps they begin a new Bible study, where they become excited about the Lord. If we are not careful, we will "think on these things"

but then say, "I don't know if this is good for my wife, because she is getting a little too spiritual." And we'll begin to squirm a bit when our wives tell us that a passion for Jesus is being conceived within them because, although they don't express it and maybe haven't even articulated it, the fact remains that to some men, Jesus can be the other Man in his wife's life.

"You mean you're getting up early now and praying? When did *that* start?" we ask. "What about my oatmeal? You want to go to church *again?* We went last month!"

Somehow in women, who are oftentimes innately more spiritually sensitive than men, the Holy Spirit can begin to conceive something of Jesus. And we guys can start to fear. But the Lord would say to you and to me as husbands, "Fear not! Don't worry!" Husband, the more your wife falls in love with that other Man, the Son of Man, Jesus Christ, her capacity will expand exponentially to love you along with loving Jesus.

A couple had celebrated their golden anniversary with a big party. Presents were exchanged, and congratulations were expressed before they got in their car and drove home. When they got home, the woman made her way into the kitchen. As was her custom, she brewed some tea and took out a loaf of bread, one of which she had baked daily for years. She cut off the heel, warmed it, and buttered it for her husband before cutting another slice for herself. Then she served him the warm piece of bread.

Now this man, who had been married for fifty years, loved his wife greatly, but the stress of the day had taken its toll. He blew up and said, "Honey, I love you, and you know that, but quite frankly, this is the last straw. For more years than I can count, you have baked bread for me every day. But you always give me the heel. You always pass off that crusty piece of bread on me. I've had it! I won't take it anymore!"

She looked at him, blinked back the tears, and said, "But honey, that's my favorite piece."

She was giving him the best.

And, guys, if you want your wives to give you the best in any area, let them be expanded in the Lord. Don't fear!

Matthew 1:21 (a)
And she shall bring forth a son, and thou shalt call his name JESUS . . .

Jesus is the name of our Savior. This is His only name as far as His human name goes. Jesus is neither His first name, nor is Christ His last name. No, Jesus is His full human name, which was a common name in that day, probably the most common name in all of Israel. "Joshua" was the Hebrew form, and "Jesus" the Greek form.

We read that Christ is not His human name, but His official name. *Christos* is the Greek form and means "anointed." In the Old Testament, three groups of people were anointed with oil: prophets, priests, and kings. Jesus is the Prophet who came to declare the Word (Deuteronomy 18:18). He is our faithful High Priest (Hebrews 2:17). He is the King of kings (Revelation 17:14).

Matthew 1:21 (b)
... for he shall save his people from their sins.

Remember, Joshua was the successor of Moses, and Moses represented the Law. Because Moses could not lead the people of God into the Land of Promise, the responsibility was given to Joshua, or Jesus. It's the same name. So, too, the Law cannot bring people into the fullness of God's blessings. The Law was provided to prepare us and point out to us that we are sinners in need of a Savior who can save us from our sins and bring us into the Land of Promise.

Matthew 1:22, 23
Now all this was done, that it might be fulfilled which was spoken of the Lord by the prophet, saying, Behold, a virgin shall be with child, and shall bring forth a son, and they shall call his name Emmanuel, which being interpreted is, God with us.

Emmanuel is Jesus' name descriptively, but it was never spoken to Him directly. You'll never read in Scripture about someone saying, "Emmanuel, come over here please." You'll hear them say, "Jesus," "Rabbi," or "Master," but never Emmanuel. This name Emmanuel is a descriptive title of the earthly ministry of Jesus Christ—God *with* us. Jeremiah 33:16 tells us when we see Him in the kingdom, His name will be Jehovah-Tsidkenu. When you see Jesus, you're not necessarily going to call Him "Jesus" or "Christ" or "Emmanuel," but "Jehovah-Tsidkenu" or, "The Lord Our Righteousness." This is great! When I see Jesus, I'm not going to say, "Jesus! Here I am! Aren't I wonderful?" No, I'm going to say, "Jehovah-Tsidkenu, You are my righteousness. It's not me. I have failed miserably. I botch it constantly. *You* are my righteousness. It's *Your* blood that allows me to embrace You and sit beside you. I fall at Your feet and worship You because *You* are my righteousness." Jesus is His human name, Christ His official name, Emmanuel His descriptive name, and Jehovah-Tsidkenu His prophetic name.

Matthew 1:24, 25
Then Joseph being raised from sleep did as the angel of the Lord had bidden him, and took unto him his wife: And knew her not till she had brought forth her firstborn son: and he called his name JESUS.

Joseph married Mary, but he refrained from having sexual relations with her until after Jesus was born. To me, this absolutely refutes the Catholic teaching that Mary was a virgin perpetually. The word here is he knew her not *until* she had birthed Jesus. We know that at least two of the writers of the New Testament, James and Jude, were the offspring of Joseph and Mary. Mary was not a perpetual virgin. She was, however, an extremely special lady.

Regarding the life of Mary, there are two common views: She is either exalted too greatly, as I believe the Roman Catholic Church presents her, or not honored adequately, as I believe she appears in the Protestant Church. She is a blessed lady, indeed; but it is the One who came from her, Jesus, who is truly the Blessed One.

❧

2 If you followed the development of the Stealth Bomber, you know this aircraft, which looks like a bat, is really beautiful and quite impressive. With a price tag of five hundred million dollars, it had better be impressive! On its maiden test flight, the Stealth circled successfully for several hours, and preliminary tests indicated it would be able to slip through even the most sophisticated radar. There was an interesting footnote regarding these tests: Where the plane flew, dogs barked. The Stealth emitted a noise the frequency of which could be detected by any garden variety German shepherd. We spend half a billion bucks on these technological wonders, and all you have to do to detect them is get yourself a dog. When you hear him bark, you'll know the Stealth's flying by!

I appreciate our country, and I'm thankful to be an American, but I don't have a lot of confidence in any human government. Not only is the political process vulnerable to corruption, but even our most advanced technology is outdated as soon as it goes into mass production.

I am relieved that the answer is not the Stealth Bomber, but Jesus Christ, our Hope. He is the solid Rock upon which we stand. What we really need in this world is not more sophisticated military technology, but for Jesus to come back personally. When He returns, Scripture says He will rule with a rod of iron. This means He's going to rule rightly and effectively with authority.

Matthew's mission is to present Jesus as such a King. The question is, if Jesus had a right to the throne of Israel, did anyone acknowledge this? It's one thing for Him to say, "I am the King, and here is My heritage. But it is something else altogether to have someone else ratify and recognize such a right. Matthew chapter 2 answers this very concern. In chapter 1, we saw the heritage of the King. Now chapter 2 shows us homage to the King paid by those who did, in fact, recognize His royalty.

Matthew 2:1
Now when Jesus was born in Bethlehem of Judaea in the days of Herod the king, behold, there came wise men from the east to Jerusalem.

Jesus was born in the days when Herod was king of Judaea. Standing only four feet four inches tall, Herod was a short man who wanted to prove he was a big guy. He became a master builder, erecting palaces, fortresses, and entire cities. He built Masada, Herod's royal citadel; aqueducts; and remodeled the temple in Jerusalem. He made monuments of great grandeur to his name and to his legacy. However, he was also a cruel and vicious individual who murdered his wife and three sons in the same evening, prompting Caesar Augustus to say, "It is safer to be Herod's pig than his son."

Well into his seventies, and realizing no one would mourn his death, Herod ordered the arrest of one hundred of the leading men of Jerusalem. He put them in prison and demanded that the moment he died, those hundred men were to be killed instantly. In his reasoning, he stated, "If the city won't mourn for me, let it mourn for those who die with me." The men were arrested, and Herod eventually died, but his final order was never carried out.

Herod was actually an Edomite, and not a Jew at all. The Edomites were the descendants of Esau. Jacob and Esau, who began warring in their mother's womb, continued their battle throughout history. This war began between the sons of Jacob—Israel versus the sons of Esau— the Edomites. And here we find them still at war in Matthew chapter 2 as a son of Esau, Herod, is trying to slaughter a Son of Jacob, Jesus.

How did Herod become king? He was a conniver who gained political influence through his dealings with Mark Antony of Cleopatra fame. A powerful person in Rome at that time, Mark Antony appointed Herod king of Judaea. This enabled Herod to become the potentate of Judaea,

although in actuality, he was a puppet of Rome. It was during this period when Herod was king that the wise men, or magi, came from the East.

Matthew 2:2 (a)
Saying, Where is he that is born King of the Jews? for we have seen his star in the east . . .

Regardless of how many Christmas movies you've seen, or how many Nativity scenes you might have, there is no reason to believe there were only three wise men. There may have been three hundred. There's no way to know for sure. We do know, however, they came from the East. We know these magi were astrologers, studying the stars to determine the future. They were also interpreters of dreams. They were likely to have been residing in the area of Babylon when they saw a star and followed it, believing it to be the sign of the coming King of the Jews. What made them think this to be true? I suggest it was due to another man who resided in Babylon five hundred years prior to this who was also an interpreter of dreams.

His name? Daniel.

In the seventh chapter of the book that bears his name, Daniel wrote that "One would come, called the Ancient of Days, to rule and reign upon the earth; and that He would have everlasting dominion." In fact, Daniel gave the very date this One would ride into Jerusalem. So these wise men, these magi, were most likely very familiar with Daniel's writings, prophecies, and teachings. And no doubt they were watching for the Ancient of Days to appear.

Isn't it great the way the Lord appears to people wherever they're at? The magi studied the stars, and the Lord said, "Okay, I'll speak to them in the stars and reveal to them the true Star, the Star of Jacob, as Balaam declared Him to be in Numbers 24:17. Because the magi were into astrology, God used the stars to draw them to the Son.

Matthew 2:2 (b)
. . . and are come to worship him.

Notice the magi weren't coming to get something from Jesus. After all, He was only a baby, a toddler there in Bethlehem. Nor were they coming because of what He had done for them; for at that point, He had done nothing. They came to worship Him solely because of who He was.

Do you ever come to church saying, "Lord, I'm going to worship You because I've got this business deal coming down next week, and I need Your help," or, "I'm feeling depressed, and I know if I worship, I'll get high emotionally and spiritually"? There are, indeed, blessings to be found in worship, but they shouldn't be our motivation to worship. Why should we worship the Lord? Because He is the King of kings, the Creator of all things, the reason *for* life, the destiny *of* life. He is the smitten Rock, the Alpha and the Omega, the Lily of the Valley, the Fairest of Ten Thousand, the Bright and Morning Star. An understanding of who Jesus is should be motivation enough for us to worship Him. For truly, "Thou art worthy O Lord, to receive glory and honour and power" (Revelation 4:11).

Matthew 2:3
When Herod the king had heard these things, he was troubled, and all Jerusalem with him.

Herod was upset because he realized there might be a true King, a Son of David, a Jew around whom the nation of Israel could rally. Herod realized he could be dethroned, Edomite that he was. But why was all Jerusalem troubled? Because Jerusalem was aware of the political ramifications of what these magi were saying. The birth of a new king introduced the possibility that the people in Israel, and perhaps those in the entire eastern world, would have someone to support and to whom they would willingly submit. Intimidated by this, Caesar would send down his legions into Jerusalem. The city would be trampled, and blood would be shed. Recognizing the makings of a revolution, those closest to Herod foresaw terrifying consequences.

Matthew 2:4–6
And when he had gathered all the chief priests and scribes of the people together, he demanded of them where Christ should be born. And they said unto him, In Bethlehem of Judaea: for thus it is written by the prophet, and thou Bethlehem, in the land of Juda, art not the least among the princes of Juda: for out of thee shall come a Governor, that shall rule my people Israel.

These scribes were aware of Micah 5:2, which said that Jesus Christ would be born in an insignificant little city five miles outside of Jerusalem. Yet, it amazes me that they didn't even bother to make the short journey to Bethlehem to see what was happening. The wise men spent months, perhaps years, traveling across the desert—spending much money and expending great energy to seek the Lord. The scribes who knew the Word wouldn't even get on their feet to see what was happening a mere five miles away. Isn't there a warning for you and me in this? Sometimes we think knowing the Scriptures is good enough.

But it's doing, not merely knowing the Word, that counts. You and I can easily become like these scribes, saying, "Well, we know what is happening. We know what we should be doing, and that's good enough." No, the blessing is in *doing*, not just in knowing.

The scribes told Herod he would find the Christ in Bethlehem. Bethlehem today is a major disappointment for tourists because they go expecting to see something special, but when they get there, all they see is a typical Middle Eastern city.

They go into the church of the Nativity, assuming it will be awesome. But as they walk in, they see the church itself divided into three sections (Catholic, Eastern, and Russian Orthodox) because these three groups have been fighting for centuries over who should control the site. And there are objects hanging from the ceiling that look like Christmas tree ornaments in a garage sale. With church groups fighting and dusty relics hanging, no wonder Bethlehem appears to be disappointing.

But you know what? It's perfect!

You see, when Jesus was born in Bethlehem, He was born in a stable, or a cave, which was used as a stable. It wasn't the picturesque setting we often have in our minds. No doubt, it was dirty. There were cow pies on the ground and flies buzzing overhead. It had to be so. Jesus came to a real world as a real Man to help real people. And Bethlehem mirrors reality today.

Bethlehem—a very appropriate place for the Bread of Life to be born, for 'Bethlehem' means 'House of Bread.' Bethlehem was an unimpressive little city then and is an unimpressive little city still. But because Jesus was born there, more songs have been sung about, more poetry written about, more photographs taken of, more trips made to this insignificant little city than any other. Bethlehem is one of the best-known places in the world today for only one reason: Jesus was there.

And so too with you and me. Jesus comes into little people like us—people who are somewhat dusty and not at all that impressive—and He makes us great, not because of who we are, but because of *whose* we are. We are His.

Matthew 2:7, 8
Then Herod, when he had privily called the wise men, inquired of them diligently what time the star appeared. And he sent them to Bethlehem, and said, Go and search diligently for the young child; and when ye have found him, bring me word again, that I may come and worship him also.

"You wise guys, go ahead and find Him, and when you have located Him, come and tell me that I may go and worship Him as well." Herod said this, not because he sincerely desired to worship the Christ, but because he was determined to exalt his own position, to establish his own authority, to eliminate the Babe of Bethlehem.

Matthew 2:9–11 (a)
When they had heard the king, they departed; and, lo, the star, which they saw in the east, went before them, till it came and stood over where the young child was. When they saw the star, they rejoiced with exceeding great joy. And when they were come into the house . . .

Notice the magi came into the house, not the stable because Jesus was probably about a year and a half old by the time they made it all the way to Jerusalem. So when you set up your Nativity scene next Christmas, put your wise men four blocks away because it took them a long time to arrive!

Matthew 2:11 (b)
. . . they saw the young child with Mary his mother, and fell down, and worshipped him: and when they had opened their treasures, they presented unto him gifts; gold, and frankincense, and myrrh.

Worship is always costly. It might cost you your so-called dignity. It might cost you financially as you learn to tithe and to give. It might cost you your friends or your family. The magi came worshiping with costly gifts. Gold indicates they acknowledged Jesus as King, since gold is a metal associated with kingly rule. By bringing frankincense, the spice used by priests, the wise men not only acknowledged Jesus as a mighty King, but as a Priest. Myrrh being the spice used in burials, the wise men acknowledged Jesus would be a martyred Prophet. The three-fold office of Jesus, the Messiah, is seen in the gifts of the wise men: gold for a Mighty King, frankincense for a Ministering Priest, myrrh for a Martyred Prophet.

Matthew 2:12
And being warned of God in a dream that they should not return to Herod, they departed into their own country another way.

The wise men were students not only of stars but of dreams, so it was fitting that they were warned in a dream about Herod's true intentions. At Jesus' birth, Gentile magi acknowledged Him as King. At Jesus' death, Pilate, a Gentile, commanded a placard reading "King of the Jews" be posted on His Cross. Although the Jews said, "We will not have this man rule over us," and rejected His kingship, there were those who did indeed acknowledge Jesus as King.

Matthew 2:13, 14
And when they were departed, behold, the angel of the Lord appeareth to Joseph in a dream, saying, Arise, and take the young child and his mother, and flee into Egypt, and be thou there until I bring thee word: for Herod will seek the young child to destroy him. When he arose, he took the young child and his mother by night, and departed into Egypt.

Evidently, Mary and Joseph used the gifts of the wise men to finance their trip to Egypt, where Jesus would be protected from Herod's wrath.

Matthew 2:15
And was there until the death of Herod: that it might be fulfilled which was spoken of the Lord by the prophet, saying, Out of Egypt have I called my son.

Egypt being a type of the world, Jesus journeyed *into* Egypt that He might free us *from* Egypt.

Matthew 2:16–18
Then Herod, when he saw that he was mocked of the wise men, was exceeding wroth, and sent forth, and slew all the children that were in Bethlehem, and in all the coasts thereof, from two years old and under, according to the time which he had diligently inquired of the wise men. Then was fulfilled that which was spoken by Jeremy the prophet, saying, in Rama was there a voice heard, lamentation, and weeping, and great mourning, Rachel weeping for her children, and would not be comforted, because they are not.

After Jesus was born and then taken safely into Egypt, Herod ordered the extermination of all male children two years old and younger. Swords flashed, mothers screamed, blood flowed in the streets, and we see the other side of the Christmas story.

For topical study of Matthew 2:16–18 entitled "Bedlam in Bethlehem," turn to page 11.

Matthew 2:19
But when Herod was dead, behold, an angel of the Lord appeareth in a dream to Joseph in Egypt.

I wish the Lord would call me to the ministry of sleeping. Four times in two chapters, the Lord spoke to Joseph in his sleep!

Matthew 2:20–23
Saying, Arise, and take the young child and his mother, and go into the land of Israel: for they are dead which sought the young child's life. And he arose, and took the young child and his mother, and came into the land of Israel. But when he heard that Archelaus did reign in Judaea in the room of his father Herod, he was afraid to go thither: notwithstanding, being warned of God in a dream, he turned aside into the parts of Galilee: And he came and dwelt in a city called Nazareth: that it might be fulfilled which was spoken by the prophets, He shall be called a Nazarene.

Nazareth was not the most picturesque or prominent spot. In fact, the word Nazareth literally means "bean town" or "sprout town." We would call it "hick town" today, which is why Nathanael, upon hearing of a Messiah from Nazareth, asked, "Can any good thing come out of Nazareth? Is it possible that Messiah would actually come from a place like that?"

Isaiah writes that Messiah would come forth as "a rod out of the stem of Jesse" (11:1). In other words, Messiah would come as a "sprout" out of the stem of Jesse—from "sprout town," a Sprout. Wherever you're living, or wherever you're from, remember that Jesus can relate to your situation. He chose to be a Nazarene, to be from Sprout Town, to be one of us.

BEDLAM IN BETHLEHEM
A Topical Study of
MATTHEW 2:16–18

I n the second chapter of Matthew, we come, of course, to the birth of the King of kings, Jesus Christ.

> *Thus saith the LORD; A voice was heard in Ramah, lamentation, and bitter weeping; Rachel weeping for her children refused to be comforted for her children, because they were not.*   Jeremiah 31:15

> *Then Herod, when he saw that he was mocked of the wise men, was exceeding wroth, and sent forth, and slew all the children that were in Bethlehem, and in all the coasts thereof, from two years old and under, according to the time which he had diligently inquired of the wise men. Then was fulfilled that which was spoken by Jeremy the prophet, saying, in Rama was there a voice heard, lamentation, and weeping, and great mourning, Rachel weeping for her children, and would not be comforted, because they are not.*   Matthew 2:16–18

When the Babylonians invaded Judah in 586 B.C. and carried the Jews captive into Babylon, Jeremiah 40 tells us that the deportation headquarters were in Ramah, a city five miles north of Bethlehem. Inspired by the Spirit, Matthew refers to that event as a picture of its ultimate fulfillment here in the story of the Nativity, six hundred years later. For once again there was weeping in Ramah, as Rachel—the mothers of Israel—wept for the children a crazed Herod had ordered annihilated in his attempt to kill the Christ Child.

"Peace on earth, goodwill towards men" was sung by the angels in the heavens on the night of Jesus' birth. But there's another side to the Christmas story. No longer, "O Little town of Bethlehem, how still we see thee lie," but "O little town of Bethlehem, how deep we hear thy cry."

Soldiers marching in the streets replaced shepherds running through the streets. And piercing swords replaced "Peace on earth" when a Silent Night became a screaming night.

Picture yourself there, mothers. Roman soldiers marching through your town, grabbing your children, piercing swords through their hearts or decapitating them, while you scream and lament without help and without hope. That's the other side of Christmas, for the Babe of Bethlehem brought bloodshed to Bethlehem, fulfilling the prophecy of Jeremiah 31:15 concerning weeping and lamentation, sorrow and suffering. No wonder in Matthew 10, Jesus gives us these words concerning His ministry:

> *Think not that I am come to send peace on earth: I came not to send peace, but a sword. For I am come to set a man at variance against his father, and the daughter against her mother, and the daughter in law against her mother in law. And a man's foes shall be they of his own household. He that loveth father or mother more than me is not worthy of me: and he that loveth son or daughter more than me is not worthy of me. And he that taketh not his cross, and followeth after me, is not worthy of me.* Matthew 10:34–38

The coming of Christ still causes pain. When you open up your heart to the Babe of Bethlehem, understand that pain and separation are sure to follow.

> *And going on from thence, he saw other two brethren, James the son of Zebedee, and John his brother, in a ship with Zebedee their father, mending their nets; and he called them. And they immediately left the ship and their father, and followed him.* Matthew 4:21, 22

You who give your lives to Jesus Christ, know this: It may result in a division among family. I'm not talking about leaving them physically, but about the pain of their inability to understand where you're at or what you're doing. Many parents would rather have their children smoke pot than come to church. "You're not becoming a Jesus freak, are you?" they say. "Anything but that!" There will be a division among friends. The sword comes, and suddenly, the group you hung out with is no longer so inclined to include you in their plans. "Oh, you used to be so much fun," they'll say. "What happened?"

There will also be a division among the flesh. If you are truly sincere about following this Babe of Bethlehem, the flesh must die. And the flesh doesn't die easily. It screams and cries, "Satisfy me." But you who are serious must say, "The sword has come. I will no longer give in to my fleshly impulses and desires. I will not be dominated by my flesh and by the sins of society."

The story is told that in the first century, when Hadrian, emperor of Rome, waged war against the Christians in the empire, a group of forty believers gathered to worship. Soldiers surrounded them and said, "Upon order of the emperor, your worship of this so-called King of the Jews must cease immediately, or you will be executed."

"Do what you will," answered the forty, "even if it costs our lives."

So the Roman soldiers took them into a mountainous region. It was wintertime, and the small lake in the area was completely frozen over. The captain of the guard said, "Here is one more opportunity for you to deny Jesus Christ— or we will place you on that lake all night until your bodies freeze."

"It is better to freeze for a night than to burn in hell for eternity," answered the brave believers.

So the forty believers took their places on the ice. With teeth chattering and knees knocking, they sang "Forty Brave Soldiers for Christ" as the Romans looked on and mocked them. Occasionally, the captain would call out, "Come to your senses, men. Deny Jesus just for a moment. Come and be warmed by the fire and be saved." But the believers would not budge, and kept singing "Forty Brave Soldiers for Christ, forty Brave Soldiers for Christ." After an hour or so, one Christian stood up, able to endure the pain no longer. He ran toward the soldiers, saying, "I deny Jesus the Christ." And he was welcomed to be warmed by the fire. He couldn't pay the price, and he turned his back on the Babe of Bethlehem.

What about you? What would happen if suddenly you were absolutely forbidden to name the Name of Jesus Christ? Would you be willing to suffer, to be tortured, or to die?

> *Think not that I am come to send peace on earth: I came not to send peace, but a sword.*   Matthew 10:34

> *Remember the word that I said unto you, The servant is not greater than his lord. If they have persecuted me, they will also persecute you; if they have kept my saying, they will keep yours also.*   John 15:20

> *Thus saith the LORD; A voice was heard in Ramah, lamentation, and bitter weeping . . .*   Jeremiah 31:15 (a)

But wait! There's an asterisk, a footnote we must consider. You see, the Jews knew that even as Jeremiah wept over a nation about to be destroyed, he also gave Israel a hope imbedded in chapters 30—33.

Thus saith the LORD; Refrain thy voice from weeping, and thine eyes from tears: for thy work shall be rewarded, saith the LORD; and they shall come again from the land of the enemy. And there is hope in thine end, saith the LORD, that thy children shall come again to their own border.   Jeremiah 31:16, 17

"Don't cry," says the Lord. "I hear the weeping that is going on in Israel, but you don't see what's coming. Refrain from your crying. Your children shall return—stronger than ever. The nation shall survive, and it shall prosper. The kingdom shall be established. The desert shall blossom. And you will have peace and prosperity unlike any other nation in the history of the world."

And I say the same thing to you this day. Yes, sometimes following the Savior means sword, suffering, and sorrow. Yes, there is a cost. Yes, it can mean difficulties. But I also say, "Refrain from your weeping because the blessings to come are even greater."

You who have felt forsaken by your family because they think you're a fanatic, know this: You have a new family that is eternal—a family with the same values and heart and priorities as yours; brothers and sisters who care about you, older brothers and sisters who will be fathers and mothers to you. This is the meaning behind the dialogue in Mark 10.

Then Peter began to say unto him, Lo, we have left all, and have followed thee. And Jesus answered and said, Verily I say unto you, There is no man that hath left house, or brethren, or sisters, or father, or mother, or wife, or children, or lands, for my sake, and the gospel's, but he shall receive an hundredfold now in this time, houses, and brethren, and sisters, and mothers, and children, and lands, with persecutions; and in the world to come eternal life.
                                  Mark 10:28–30

A hundred fold? How can that be? This is how: If my house burned down today, I know there are a hundred people who would take us in—at least for a while! In my church family, I have a hundred houses. I have land. I have brothers. I have friends, sisters, and mothers. This is much better than me just having my own little trip. I have something much bigger. It's called the family of God.

Your Friend will be faithful. If my friends forsake me, so be it. I have exchanged friends who are fickle for a Friend who will never fail me—even when I fail Him. Jesus called Judas "friend" even in the moment of betrayal. That's the kind of Friend I want.

Your flesh? Let it die.

He that findeth his life shall lose it: and he that loseth his life for my sake shall find it.   Matthew 10:39

What good could you do dying, you ask? Remember the forty believers on the lake in northern Italy? After one of their brothers left and turned away, they still sang, only they changed their song to, "Thirty-nine Brave Soldiers for Christ." One of the Roman soldiers observing this scene was so moved that he ran out upon the lake and said, "No. Forty Brave Soldiers for Christ. Forty Brave Soldiers for Christ."

If you live for your family, your friends, or your flesh, you'll lose everything. But if you give up your life and say, "Lord, I'm following You. I'm dying to self. Let the sword strike where it will," you'll find life. That's the irony of Christianity: The more you die, the more you live. Follow the Babe of Bethlehem. Yes, there will be weeping; yes, there will be sorrow. That's what Jeremiah 31:15 prophesied. But don't forget verse 16. Good things are coming. You who have paid the price and taken up the Cross, refrain from weeping. There can be hurts and sorrows, but the blessings you have presently and those that lie ahead are oh so much greater.

They really are!

3 For four hundred years, the Jews had not heard a single prophet calling to them in the name of the Lord. Then, seemingly out of nowhere, came John.

Matthew 3:1–4
In those days came John the Baptist, preaching in the wilderness of Judaea, and saying, Repent ye: for the kingdom of heaven is at hand. For this is he that was spoken of by the prophet Esaias, saying, The voice of one crying in the wilderness, Prepare ye the way of the Lord, make his paths straight. And the same John had his raiment of camel's hair, and a leathern girdle about his loins; and his meat was locusts and wild honey.

John preached in the wilderness, which was appropriate because Israel was going through dry, desert times spiritually. He came on the scene wearing not the fine flowing robes of the priests in all their glory, but camel's hair—the equivalent of torn Levi's—big leather belt around his waist, grasshopper legs hanging out of his mouth.

Matthew 3:5, 6
Then went out to him Jerusalem, and all Judaea, and all the region round about Jordan, And were baptized of him in Jordan, confessing their sins.

Fearlessly and boldly John said, "Repent! Change direction. The kingdom is at hand. Get ready. The time is now!"

Verily I say unto you, Among them that are born of women there hath not risen a greater than John the Baptist . . .   Matthew 11:11 (a)

No wonder Jesus said of all those born of women, John was the greatest. People came from miles and miles, in those days no small feat, to hear him, sensing he spoke with accuracy and authority. But catch this—Jesus went on to say,

. . . notwithstanding he that is least in the kingdom of heaven is greater than he.
Matthew 11:11 (b)

Do you know whom Jesus is talking about? He's talking about you. Jesus said you're greater than John with all of his power and authority. Why? Because you have seen things John couldn't.

John would later question and wonder, "If You are truly the Messiah, Jesus, why don't You do something to establish Your authority?" John struggled and stumbled and didn't see things all that clearly. You do. You understand Jesus came as the Suffering Savior before He will come again as the Conquering King. The Lord has placed you in His kingdom, and Jesus Himself said the least in the kingdom is greater than this greatest of prophets.

What a privilege! I feel so honored that God would place us in this era and include us in His kingdom. He could have had us born centuries before Christ and made us great prophets calling down fire from heaven, raising the dead, healing the lepers. Instead, He said, "I'm going to do something greater. They're going to be part of My church."

Matthew 3:7
But when he saw many of the Pharisees and Sadducees come to his baptism, he said unto them, O generation of vipers, who hath warned you to flee from the wrath to come?

Now, I don't believe John was giving a word of condemnation here, but rather a word of surprise. Amazed, he asked, "Oh, generation of snakes. Who has brought *you* here, you proud legalists and you liberal intellectuals?" I can even hear a chuckle in John's voice as he said this.

Matthew 3:8
Bring forth therefore fruits meet for repentance.

"It's not simply a matter of getting dunked," John warned. "It's a way of living. If your repentance is sincere, fruit will be produced in your life."

Matthew 3:9–12
And think not to say within yourselves, We have Abraham to our father: for I say unto you, that God is able of these stones to raise up children unto Abraham. And now also the axe is laid unto the root of the trees: therefore every tree which bringeth not forth good fruit is hewn down, and cast into the fire. I indeed baptize you with water unto repentance: but he that cometh after me is mightier than I, whose shoes I am not worthy to bear: he shall baptize you with the Holy Ghost, and with fire: Whose fan is in his hand, and he will thoroughly purge his floor, and gather his wheat into the garner; but he will burn up the chaff with unquenchable fire.

Many people want the power of the Spirit, but they are not interested in the fire, the purity. Acts chapter 8 tells of a man named Simon, a sorcerer, or *magi* in Greek, who performed tricks before the people. When he saw the power of the Holy Spirit dispatched by the disciples, and when he saw people getting filled with the Holy Ghost, he approached Peter and said, "Could I buy that trick from you? Here's some money, tell me how you do that!"

Peter answered Simon, "I perceive you are in the gall of bitterness and in bondage to iniquity," as he gave him a very stern rebuke and a serious warning.

I sense there are still those two kinds of wise men: the wise, wise men and the foolish, wise

men. Some come to worship Jesus solely because of who He is. Others say, "I want the power to hold people captivated and spellbound." But the baptism of Jesus in the Spirit is a baptism of fire—which speaks of purity. It's a dying to self, a cleansing of motives. Many folks want that power, but they don't want a changed lifestyle.

Matthew 3:13–17
Then cometh Jesus from Galilee to Jordan unto John, to be baptized of him. But John forbad him, saying, I have need to be baptized of thee, and comest thou to me? And Jesus answering said unto him, Suffer it to be so now: for thus it becometh us to fulfil all righteousness. Then he suffered him. And Jesus, when he was baptized, went up straightway out of the water: and, lo, the heavens were opened unto him, and he saw the Spirit of God descending like a dove, and lighting upon him: And lo a voice from heaven, saying, This is my beloved Son, in whom I am well pleased.

In this passage, we see a perfect picture of the Trinity—the Holy Spirit descending upon the Son, while the voice of the Father is heard. The Trinity had been hinted at throughout the Old Testament, beginning with the first verse.

In the beginning God created the heaven and the earth.   Genesis 1:1

The Hebrew word translated "God" is "Elohim." "El" is the singular form of the word; "Elohim" is the plural form. Here in the baptism of Jesus, the Trinity is not only alluded to linguistically, but illustrated physically—the Son baptized, the Spirit descending, and the Father speaking. We see it, yet it is a great mystery. There are not three Gods. There is one God, one God in three Persons. How can this be?

Saint Patrick was one who tried to illustrate this idea in nature. He used the shamrock as a picture of the Trinity—three leaves, but one shamrock.

Others have said, "Look at man—body, soul, and spirit. One man can be father, son, and brother, yet he is still just one person."

Still others have said, "Look at water. It can be liquid, solid, or gas." And scientists tell us that at absolute zero degrees, for a split second, water can be all three at once.

Countless examples have been used throughout history in an attempt to explain the idea of three in one, the concept of the Trinity. Why is the

Trinity such an important concept? I struggled for many years with this question.

"Lord, why three?" I asked. "Why didn't You keep it real simple and avoid this confusing Trinity concept? We are accused of being polytheistic. We're confused in our prayers. We get all tangled up. Why didn't You keep it simple, just You, just One?"

In recent years, however, I have come into an understanding of the Trinity, which for me personally has made all the difference. God the Father, God the Son, and God the Spirit dwelled together in ages past—a billion years before years even began—perfectly content. The Father loved the Son. The Son honored the Father. The three of Them dwelled together in complete harmony, in total satisfaction. They are, and always will be, family. But they're only One.

What does this mean? Contrary to much of today's teaching, it means God didn't need me. God went through billions and zillions of years without man. And you know what? He got along just fine. He doesn't need us, folks. So great is God's love that He gave His only Son to die and plunge into hell in order to redeem you. He's in love with you to be sure, but He doesn't need you. And that takes all of the pressure off because when love is demanding, it isn't love.

- "I need you. I must have you."
- "Where have you been? Who were you talking to?"
- "Where are you going? Who are you going with? Can I come?"

When love is not "trinitarian" in nature, it becomes smothering and restrictive. It causes tension and anxieties, and you feel caged in and cooped up.

Many of us erroneously picture God wringing His hands, pacing the clouds, worried about whether we're going to make it. He's not. He's very happy, totally fulfilled, and perfectly content. Yet He is so magnanimous and expansive that He has chosen to create us, love us, and walk with us. It's not a demand. It's not a need. It's an invitation.

How this blesses me! "You didn't need me, Lord. You don't need me now. But You still love me. You still want me to live with You forever. Wow!"

Come unto me, all ye that labour and are heavy laden, and I will give you rest. Take my yoke upon you, and learn of me; for I am meek and lowly in heart: and ye shall find rest unto your souls.   Matthew 11:28, 29

There is One who loves you, who is not uptight about you, or burdensome upon you. He is meek and lowly. And the mystery of the Trinity gives me rest in my love relationship with Him.

For topical study of Matthew 3:13–17 see "The Baptism of Jesus" below.

THE BAPTISM OF JESUS
A Topical Study of
MATTHEW 3:13–17

Because John's mother and Jesus' mother were cousins, John knew Jesus quite well. And although he did not yet understand that his second cousin was the promised Messiah, he knew Jesus was without sin. That is why, in the midst of baptizing others, John was suddenly aware of his own sinfulness when Jesus approached him.

"There's no fault in you," declared John. "You should be baptizing me."

But Jesus immediately said, "Allow it to be so, for in so doing, we will fulfill all righteousness. It's the right thing to do." Why? If baptism was a sign of repentance, why would Jesus, who was sinless, say, "It's important for Me to be baptized by you"?

I suggest four reasons for your consideration.

1. Jesus' Baptism Was an Affirmation of John's Ministry

In joining the masses and coming to the Jordan to be baptized, Jesus was saying, "Even though John knows he's a sinner, even though John is aware of his inadequacies, I approve of his service for Me. And his message of repentance is a valid one." When Jesus began His public preaching, repentance was His message as well. In coming to the Jordan, Jesus was affirming John's ministry—both the man and the message.

2. Jesus' Baptism Is an Identification with Us Personally

He who knew no sin took our sin, died for us, and identifies with us in baptism. Jesus was immersed, and so are we. Consequently, there is an identification and a bonding.

3. Jesus' Baptism Was a Declaration to His Father Prophetically

In submission to the Father's plan, Jesus came to die. Romans 6 teaches that baptism is a picture of death and burial. In baptism, Jesus was saying, "I know I have come to die. And, Father, I am submitted to that plan of death and burial." But because baptism doesn't end in the water, because He was pulled out again, which speaks of resurrection, Jesus also declared this to His Father, "Yes, I am submitted to Your plan—I will die. But I will also rise again through Your power."

4. Jesus' Baptism Is an Illustration of the Trinity

After Jesus came out of the water, the Holy Spirit descended upon Him in the form of a dove, and the voice of the Father was heard from the heavens.

The baptism of Jesus was an affirmation of John's ministry, an identification with us personally, a declaration to the Father prophetically, and an illustration of the Trinity practically.

When I read of Jesus' baptism, my mind goes back about twenty-three hundred years earlier to the story of a man whose name means "Comforter." You know him by the name of Noah. Noah was surrounded by a world that was corrupt and defiled. But Scripture tells us that Noah found grace in the eyes of the Lord. And God told Noah, "I'm going to drown this corrupt, wicked world. I'm going to be merciful."

Merciful? Yes.

In sending the Flood, God was doing quickly and mercifully what man was doing slowly and painfully. Noah's society, immersed in the occult and caught up in perversion, was destroying itself. So God sent the Flood. For forty days it rained, and the world was drowned. At the end of forty days, the rain stopped, and Noah let out a raven and a dove. The raven, a scavenger, had plenty to pick on. Carcasses were everywhere, so the raven didn't come back. But the dove, a bird of purity, circled, and finding no place to set her foot, came back and landed on Noah.

The picture is incredible to me. A man called Comfort, surrounded by water, in which the polluted world has been drowned, and the dove comes upon him. Could this have registered in the minds of those who observed the baptism of Jesus? It certainly does for me, and through it, I understand something of the significance of baptism—a dying to the world around us and a resurrection to newness of life as Paul declared in Romans 6:4.

I am not stretching the analogy, because in 1 Peter 3:21, Peter writes that Noah and the Flood are a picture of baptism. But wait—there was another man who was submerged in water, baptized radically, whose name literally means "dove." You know him by his more familiar name of Jonah. Jonah was rebelling against the Lord when he went through a most interesting baptism. He wasn't only immersed in water. He was thrown in! For three days, he was at the bottom of the sea in the belly of a great fish, where he was broken as he cried out to God and repented from his sin. And suddenly, he was resurrected as the whale had the "urge to re-gurge" him on the beach at Assyria.

Jonah's baptism was not a drowning of the world around him. It was a drowning of the rebellion and selfishness within him. Jonah had his own agenda, but through his baptism, he surrendered it. That's also what baptism is about. Not only are you dying to the world that surrounds you, but to the selfishness within you. Baptism says, "Lord, I will go wherever You lead. Do whatever You desire. Whatever that might mean, I trust You. You are my God and my King."

You might be saying, "This is all very fine theoretically. But I was baptized six months ago, or six years ago, or sixty years ago, and I have failed miserably."

So did Noah. After emerging from the ark, Noah got drunk and exposed himself in a manner that caused a problem in his sons felt to this day. The sinfulness that should have been eradicated from Noah's world resurfaced when he was drunk in his tent.

What about Jonah? Jonah preached, and the greatest revival in history took place as the entire city of Ninevah turned to the Lord. Yet what did Jonah do? He went up on a hillside and pouted, angry because four hundred thousand Ninevites got saved. He failed miserably because the selfishness that should have been drowned in the belly of the whale re-emerged.

During Noah's baptism, it rained for forty days. After Jonah's baptism, he emerged and preached, "forty days until Ninevah is destroyed." Following Jesus' baptism, He was led into the wilderness for forty days. Although all three had times of trial, only One emerged victorious. Only One made it successfully. Only One was baptized and moved on to total and complete victory. Was it Jonah, the great prophet? No. Noah, the man of faith? No. Only Jesus.

Jesus, in His forty-day temptation, overcame Satan. He didn't fail. And because of His victory, baptism not only says, "I am dying to the sin *around* me, and

I am dying to the sin *within* me," but most importantly, it says, "I believe in the One who died *for* me."

You see, gang, when you are baptized, it doesn't mean you are going to be perfect from that point on. It means you acknowledge that you are perfectly forgiven and perfectly loved, that Jesus Christ paid the price for every sin you ever have done, are doing, or will ever do. The One who was baptized and was victorious through those forty days of trial and testing is now living in you.

Thus Paul writes,

> *I am crucified with Christ: nevertheless I live; yet not I, but Christ liveth in me: and the life which I now live in the flesh I live by the faith of the Son of God, who loved me, and gave himself for me.*　　　　　Galatians 2:20

That's the gospel—Jesus Christ victorious, living in me. I don't know when you were baptized, but I encourage you to reaffirm your baptism in your own heart. Be like Noah. Watch the world drown, and rise above it. Be like Jonah. Die to your selfishness, and walk in newness of life. And if you have failed like Noah did, like Jonah did, like we all have, know this: Jesus is your Victory. He who knew no sin became sin for you. You are perfectly forgiven. Enjoy your salvation, and live to that calling.

4 Chapter 3 closed with the account of the water baptism of Jesus Christ. Indeed, this was when He was baptized in the Holy Spirit as well, for although Jesus had been conceived *by* the Spirit, and had the Spirit residing *within* Him, at the time of His water baptism, the Spirit came *upon* Him to empower Him for ministry. This was a crucial moment in the life of Jesus, and I believe we need to experience such a moment in our lives if we want to minister and serve effectively. How? Simply by saying, "I need to be filled with Your Spirit, Lord. I need Your Spirit to come *upon* me, to empower me." And in faith we receive it at that time. Then we move on to minister effectively, for it is truly "not by might, nor by power, but by my spirit, saith the LORD of hosts" (Zechariah 4:6).

So here is Jesus. The Holy Spirit has come upon Him. He has heard a voice from heaven, and no doubt, He must have been on a real high. Then chapter 4 begins.

Matthew 4:1
Then was Jesus led up of the Spirit into the wilderness to be tempted of the devil.

It is often true that after the blessings come the battles. On the heels of His baptism, the Spirit led Jesus into the wilderness, where He would encounter the enemy.

Matthew 4:2 (a)
And when he had fasted forty days and forty nights . . .

Fasting for forty days was not unknown to those who studied the Scriptures and to the people of Israel familiar with their history. Exodus 34:28 says when Moses was given the Law on Mount Horeb, he neither ate nor drank for forty days. In 1 Kings 19, we read Elijah also fasted for forty days after the Lord sent an angel who gave him a certain kind of food that was able to sustain him for that period of time. Moses and Elijah both fasted forty days. Jesus fasted forty days, and later in Matthew's account, we will see how we are to act when we fast as well.

We live in a society addicted not only to alcohol and lust, but to all sorts of things. I suggest to you the reason could be because, as a society, we have ignored the simple principle of fasting, of saying no to the appetites of our bodies on a regular basis. If you feel an addictive pull in some area of your life, try saying no to your stomach's demands for a meal for a day or a week. When you deny the physical to concentrate on the spiritual, a dynamic occurs that I believe will very definitely help you overcome evil.

Matthew 4:2 (b)
. . . he was afterward an hungred.

After forty days in the wilderness seeking His Father and denying His flesh, Jesus was hungry. Physiologists tell us that when one fasts for that length of time, he loses his appetite completely. His hunger returns only when he is on the verge of death. Therefore, at this point, in His fortieth day, Jesus was literally starving to death. Physically, His body systems were crying out, and He was about to die if not nourished soon. It was at this point that Satan came to tempt Him. Now before we consider the temptation of Jesus, I want you to remember that it was the Spirit who led Him into the wilderness. Why would the Spirit lead Jesus into the place where temptation was certain? I believe there are two reasons, both important for us to understand.

Jesus was led into the wilderness to reveal who He is. First Corinthians 15:45 declares that Jesus is the last Adam. I am reminded of the first Adam in the Garden of Eden who was also tempted directly by Satan.

The first Adam was in a beautiful garden. The last Adam was in a barren, forsaken desert. The first Adam ate freely of things except one forbidden fruit. The last Adam ate nothing for forty days. The first Adam was physically strong. The last Adam was on the verge of death. The first Adam blew it. He was the ultimate "Adam Bomb." He gave in to the temptation of Satan and thereby plunged all of humanity into a lost and hopeless situation. The last Adam, Jesus Christ, did not bomb out. He came through, and in so doing, He reveals to us who He is, the One who conquered sin.

Jesus was led into the wilderness not only reveal to us who He is, but also to relate to us as we are. The Book of Hebrews puts it this way:

Wherefore in all things it behoved him to be made like unto his brethren, that he might be a merciful and faithful high priest in things pertaining to God, to make reconciliation for the sins of the people. For in that he himself hath suffered being tempted, he is able to succour them that are tempted. For we have not an high priest which cannot be touched with the feeling of our infirmities; but was in all points tempted like as we are, yet without sin.
Hebrews 2:17, 18; 4:15

No matter what sin you're struggling with, no matter what temptation seems to attack you constantly, Jesus is a merciful High Priest who prays for you effectively because He feels with you sympathetically. He is not shocked by your sin, for according to Hebrews 4:15, He has been tempted in all points as we are—and "all" in Greek means *all.* As our compassionate High Priest, Jesus says, "I understand why you are so critical or negative, lustful or cynical, hateful or vengeful, lazy or slothful." He understands because He was tempted in all points as we are— yet without sin. He became *like* us that He might relate *to* us, and be strength *for* us in time of temptation.

Matthew 4:3
And when the tempter came to him, he said, If thou be the Son of God, command that these stones be made bread.

In the wilderness, there are multiplied millions of round limestone rocks that look remarkably like little loaves of bread. No doubt, as Jesus fasted, those rocks must have taken on the appearance of bread. And now Satan comes to Him and says, "*If* You're the Son of God, turn these stones into bread."

What is the Enemy doing here? He's questioning the Father's provision. During Jesus' baptism, God identified Him as His beloved Son. Now Satan comes on the scene, challenging the very words God had spoken, saying, "*If* You really are the Son of God, why are You hungry? *If* You are the Son of God, why is this happening?"

Satan does the same thing in your life and mine when he comes to us and says, "*If* you are a child of God, where's the Father's provision? Why are those bills piling up? Why is there a lack in your life physically or materially?"

He comes to us and whispers in our ears, "Do something in your own power. Exercise your faith. Make it happen now." But God would have us be patient. We are His children. And He promises He will meet our needs as we pray for our daily bread. Most of us want to reach the Promised Land without ever going through the wilderness. We want to get there immediately, but the Father says, "No. There's a time of preparation. Wait. Don't panic. I will provide."

Like the man who prayed, "Lord, is it true that to You a million years is like a second?"

"Yes," the Lord answered.
"Wow. Is it also true that a million dollars is like a penny?"
"Yes."

"Well, Father, could I have a penny?"
"Sure. Just a second."

We need to realize the Lord's timing is different from ours. Jesus knew this. He would not push or rush the Father by taking things into His own hands. He would wait. And soon—perhaps only hours later—angels would come to Him. Instead of eating dry little loaves of bread, He would dine on angel food cake! How often I settle for bread because I try to do things in my own energy instead of waiting for the Father's perfect timing and the angel food cake.

Matthew 4:4
But he answered and said, It is written, Man shall not live by bread alone, but by every word that proceedeth out of the mouth of God.

"The issue," Jesus said, "is not the material realm. More important than physical food is the spiritual food I find in God's Word." Jesus said that it's not the material realm that is important. Man shall not live by bread alone. For you who are involved in the argument over inspiration of Scripture, please note that Jesus quoted Deuteronomy and said, "every *word* that proceedeth out of the mouth of God" (8:3). It's not just the thoughts that are inspired. Jesus quoted Deuteronomy and declared that *every word* proceeds out of the mouth of God and is inspired by God. *Every word* is God-breathed.

Matthew 4:5, 6
Then the devil taketh him up into the holy city, and setteth him on a pinnacle of the temple, and saith unto him, If thou be the Son of God, cast thyself down: for it is written, He shall give his angels charge concerning thee: and in their hands they shall bear thee up, lest at any time thou dash thy foot against a stone.

Quoting Psalm 91, verses 11 and 12, Satan now questions the Father's protection. "Do You believe Your Father will really protect You, Jesus? Prove it. Prove it to Yourself, prove it to me, and prove it to all of Israel. Go to the pinnacle of the temple and jump down. Doesn't Psalm 91 declare that God will give His angels charge over You to keep You from even stubbing Your toe?"

Satan quotes Scripture, but always omits a phrase or two in the process. Psalm 91, verse 11 actually says, "For he shall give his angels charge over thee, to keep thee *in all thy ways*"—in all *God's* ways. Jesus knew this and answered accordingly.

Matthew 4:7
Jesus said unto him, It is written again, Thou shalt not tempt the Lord thy God.

"The Father will provide for Me, and the Father will protect Me, but I'm not going to test Him in order to satisfy you or anyone else. Scripture says, Satan, that I am not to test God."

Don't take Scripture out of context. Don't test God. If you lie on the freeway saying, "I'm going to prove right now that God is with me and that He will keep me," He'll keep you, all right—in heaven!

Don't tempt the Lord. Don't say, "I wonder how far I can go and not get hurt. I wonder how much I can be like the world without really being in the world." Don't do it. Don't jump off the temple to prove your spirituality, your liberty, or your maturity. Jesus said, "I'm not going to give in to this temptation. I know My Father is with Me. I know He will protect Me. I don't have to prove it."

Matthew 4:8–10
Again, the devil taketh him up into an exceeding high mountain, and sheweth him all the kingdoms of the world, and the glory of them; and saith unto him, All these things will I give thee, if thou wilt fall down and worship me. Then saith Jesus unto him, Get thee hence, Satan: for it is written, Thou shalt worship the Lord thy God, and him only shalt thou serve.

Lastly, Satan questions the Father's promise. The Father had promised all things to His Son. But Satan came to Jesus saying, "The world is mine to give You if You worship me."

How did Satan gain control of the world? Originally, God gave man dominion over the earth, but when Adam sinned in the Garden of Eden, he turned the title deed of planet earth over to Satan. Satan, therefore, had the right to say to Jesus, "I'll give You the whole world right now. You don't have to go the way of the Cross. It isn't necessary for You to plunge into hell. I'll give the world to You if You'll simply fall down and worship me. Take a shortcut! The promise of the Father? Who knows when it will be fulfilled or even *if* it will be fulfilled. Fall down, and You can have it all now!"

And God promises to you, single brother, that He is going to bless you. He whispers the promise in your heart that at the right time, He is going to send someone with whom you can walk in the way of the Lord. But Satan comes to you and says, "Are you sure that promise is going to come to pass? Let me give it to you now. Oh, I know she isn't a Christian, but you can influence her in the right direction. She'll go to church with you. No big deal. It'll be fine."

Satan comes to us and begins to question whether we can trust the Father's promise that if we delight ourselves in Him, He will give us the desires of our heart. "Why are you hungry? Where is your Father's provision?" He says. "Jump! Or do you doubt your Father's protection? Make it happen now! Don't wait for your Father's promise."

If you analyze the temptations that come your way, I think you will find every one will fall into one of these three categories: you will be tempted to deny the Father's provision, to doubt the Father's protection, or to despair of the Father's promise.

Matthew 4:11
Then the devil leaveth him, and, behold, angels came and ministered unto him.

How did Jesus overcome Satan? First, He quoted Scripture. Whether He was dealing with questions of provision, protection, or promise, in all three cases, Jesus quoted Scripture. This encourages me because I can do the same thing. When the Enemy attacks, I can quote Scripture. So can you! You can do exactly what Jesus did. If you don't have one, I recommend *The Jesus Person Pocket Promise Book*, which contains eight hundred promises from the Word, written in categories to fit every situation. Eight hundred promises for you to utilize when the Enemy says, "The Father is not providing for you. He's not really going to protect you. That promise is not meant for you."

Quote Scripture. But notice when Jesus said, "Man shall not live by bread alone," He was saying, "*I* am not going to live by bread alone. The material realm is not going to have priority for Me." When He said, "Thou shalt not tempt the Lord thy God," He was saying, "*I* am not going to do it because the Word forbids it." When He said, "Thou shalt worship the Lord thy God, and him only shalt thou serve," He was saying, "*I* will serve My Father and Him alone."

Many Christians are under the mistaken impression that by simply quoting Scripture, Satan is going to run away. But Satan himself can quote Scripture. So can the demons. The power lies in submission to the Word, not in recitation of it. Satan flees when he hears us say, "I will *do* it," not, "I can *quote* it."

Notice the three Scriptures quoted are all from Deuteronomy 6 and 8—a relatively small portion of Scripture. Personally, I believe Jesus was having His devotions in that particular passage when the temptations came His way. Meditating upon the Word of God is crucial because Satan comes to me when I least expect him. He doesn't say, "Jon, I'm going to meet you in three days. Get ready." No, he watches and waits until he sees I am in a place of weakness, frustration, tension, fatigue, or transition, and—boom!—he'll strike. Ephesians 6 says the Word of God is the Sword of the Spirit. Learn the Word. Meditate upon the Word. Stay in the Word. And like Jesus, in submission to the Word, you'll beat back the Enemy.

Matthew 4:12
Now when Jesus had heard that John was cast into prison, he departed into Galilee. . . .

Galilee, located in northern Israel, was a province comprised of two hundred four villages and over fifteen thousand people. It was called "Region of Death" by the Jews in Jerusalem because, throughout Israel''s history, the Gentiles would constantly wage war in this area. Consequently, there were many mixed marriages and a great deal of Gentile influence within Galilee. The "cool" Jews went to Jerusalem. Jesus said, "I'm going to Galilee where all the outcasts are—the people who are looked down on, the people who have funny accents—that's where I'll be."

Matthew 4:13
And leaving Nazareth, he came and dwelt in Capernaum, which is upon the sea coast, in the borders of Zabulon and Nephthalim.

I don't blame the Lord for making His headquarters in Capernaum! Nestled on the edge of the Sea of Galilee, it's a beautiful beach town.

Matthew 4:14–16
That it might be fulfilled which was spoken by Esaias the prophet, saying, The land of Zabulon, and the land of Nephthalim, by the way of the sea, beyond Jordan, Galilee of the Gentiles; the people which sat in darkness saw great light; and to them which sat in the region and shadow of death light is sprung up.

Jesus set up His headquarters among those who were sitting in a darkened region, in the midst of the ones who were looked down upon by their countrymen. The same is still true today. Jesus looks for those who feel unworthy, on the periphery, in the dark. The person who feels most out of it is the one within whom Jesus is most ready to set up His headquarters.

Matthew 4:17
From that time Jesus began to preach, and to say, Repent: for the kingdom of heaven is at hand.

The phrase "the kingdom of heaven" appears thirty-two times in Matthew's Gospel, while "the kingdom of God" is used only five times. Since the two phrases are basically interchangeable, why would Matthew be the only one to use "the kingdom of heaven," while Mark, Luke, and John refer to the "kingdom of God"? The reason is because the Jewish people were looking for a literal, physical, temporal, material kingdom based in Israel. In writing about "the kingdom of heaven," Matthew is saying, "Jesus talked not about a physical kingdom, but a spiritual kingdom—the kingdom of heaven. It's bigger than just you Jews. It's larger in scope and entirely different in substance."

Matthew 4:18–22
And Jesus, walking by the sea of Galilee, saw two brethren, Simon called Peter, and Andrew his brother, casting a net into the sea: for they were fishers. And he saith unto them, Follow me, and I will make you fishers of men. And they straightway left their nets, and followed him. And going on from thence, he saw other two brethren, James the son of Zebedee, and John his brother, in a ship with Zebedee their father, mending their nets; and he called them. And they immediately left the ship and their father, and followed him.

Here we see the call of James, John, Peter, and Andrew. We know from John's Gospel that at this point, these men already knew Jesus. Here, however, He is calling them into ministry.

"Follow Me," Jesus said. He didn't say, "Take a course in evangelism." He didn't say, "Study this book, go to this seminar, or practice this technique." He said, "If you hang out with Me, I'm going to be changing you, and inevitably you'll become like Me—a fisher of men."

Notice what Peter was doing when he was called. He was casting his net into the sea because Peter was bold and evangelistic in orientation. On the Day of Pentecost, it was Peter who preached. As a result, three thousand were saved—"caught up" in his glorious net of the gospel. John, on the other hand, wasn't casting nets, but mending them when Jesus called him. John, who would later become known as the "apostle of love," would go on to write epistles that would mend the church and mend people. I believe the Holy Spirit inspired these vignettes to illustrate how the disciples' eventual ministries were al-

ready seen in what they were doing naturally. God has a way of turning the natural into the supernatural through His grace and for His glory.

Matthew 4:23
And Jesus went about all Galilee, teaching in their synagogues, and preaching the gospel of the kingdom, and healing all manner of sickness and all manner of disease among the people.

Note the order: teaching first, then preaching, and finally healing. Teaching consists of laying down principles and precepts. Preaching is for the purpose of stimulating and proclaiming. Healing is the manifestation, the outworking of teaching and preaching. I believe the reason so many healing ministries are unbalanced and harmful is because they lack foundational teaching. If Jesus is our example, teaching and preaching must precede healing.

Matthew 4:24
And his fame went throughout all Syria: and they brought unto him all sick people that were taken with divers diseases and torments, and those which were possessed with devils, and those which were lunatick, and those that had the palsy; and he healed them.

Those who were demonized, those who were paralyzed, those who were hurting—Jesus healed them all.

Matthew 4:25
And there followed him great multitudes of people from Galilee, and from Decapolis, and from Jerusalem, and from Judaea, and from beyond Jordan.

The towns named here cover a one hundred-mile radius. People would literally walk hundreds of miles to see Jesus. Next time you are tempted to complain about your long trip to church, remember this verse!

5 Matthew's Gospel presents Jesus as King, King of the Jews specifically, although not exclusively.

In chapter 1, Matthew outlined Jesus' heritage. As a descendant of David, Jesus was the rightful Heir to the throne of Israel. In chapter 2, we saw homage paid the King by wise men who came from the East to worship Him. Also in chapter 2, we saw hostility toward the King when Herod, feeling intimidated by the Babe of Bethlehem, sought to destroy Him. In chapter 3, we saw the heralding of the King as John the Baptist came on the scene, wearing camel skins, eating honey-coated locusts and saying, "Repent, for the kingdom of God is at hand." In chapter 4, we saw a challenge to the King when Satan tempted Him in the wilderness, a challenge that our King met head-on and from which He emerged victorious. Also in chapter 4, we saw the establishing of the headquarters of the King as Jesus taught and healed throughout Galilee. Here in chapter 5, as we continue seeing Jesus as King, we come to the constitution of His kingdom.

Matthew 5:1, 2
And seeing the multitudes, he went up into a mountain: and when he was set, his disciples came unto him: And he opened his mouth, and taught them, saying,

As the multitudes began hearing of Jesus, the last verse in chapter 4 says they came from one hundred miles or more to be with Him. Jesus, seeing the multitudes, climbed a hill, sat down, and prepared to teach. In Jewish culture, if you were preaching, you would stand. But if you were teaching or explaining, you would sit. That is why even today when a university wants to establish a certain teacher or course, it will call that position "the Chair," as in "the Chair of Philosophy" or "the Chair of Psychology." So, too, when the Pope speaks on doctrinal matters, he is always seated when he makes his proclamation. He is speaking "ex-cathedra," which literally means "from the chair."

So here, we see Jesus seated, ready to give an authoritative, important, significant teaching.

Matthew 5:3 (a)
Blessed . . .

Verse 3 introduces a well-known portion of Scripture called the Beatitudes. "Beatitude," literally *beātus* in Latin, means "happy," and every one of the following nine verses begins with the word "blessed" or "happy." Our United States Constitution guarantees the pursuit of happiness, but Jesus' constitution points out the pathway to happiness as He delineates the attitudes that lead to happiness. The Scriptures declare, "Blessed, or happy, is the people whose God is the Lord" (Psalm 33:12). David said, "Blessed, or happy, is the man whose sins are forgiven" (Psalm 32:1). I believe the Bible knows nothing of a dour, heavy Christianity. I believe Scripture indicates that the people of God should be the happiest, most joyful people on earth.

Matthew 5:3 (b)
. . . are the poor in spirit: for theirs is the kingdom of heaven.

The world says, "The first step to happiness is to be self-assertive and confident, to highly esteem yourself and feel good about who you are." That's not what Jesus said. He said, "Blessed, or happy, are those who are poor in spirit—who realize their own spiritual poverty." Anyone who truly sees the Lord will inevitably feel poor in spirit.

In the first five chapters of his book, Isaiah indicts the people of Judah and the surrounding nations, saying, "Woe unto you and you and you." But in chapter 6, when he saw the Lord high and lifted up, he said, "Woe is *me!*" When Peter realized who Jesus was on a boat in the Sea of Galilee, he said, "Depart from me; for I am a sinful man" (Luke 5:8). When John the revelator saw Jesus, he fell down as though he were dead (Revelation 1:17).

Matthew 5:4
Blessed are they that mourn: for they shall be comforted.

When you realize you're a sinner and when you mourn over your sin, the Lord will come to you and say, "I don't condemn you. Go your way and sin no more." That's what the woman caught in the act of adultery heard, as did the prostitute who fell at the feet of Jesus weeping. "Leave her alone, Pharisees," Jesus said. "The one who is forgiven much loves much." In the state of realizing our poverty and in our mourning, we truly enter into the kingdom and are comforted.

Matthew 5:5
Blessed are the meek: for they shall inherit the earth.

When you realize you're a sinner and when you mourn over your sin, the Lord will say to you, "I don't condemn you. Go your way and sin no more."

Meekness is not weakness. Meekness is strength under control. *Praus,* the Greek word translated "meek," is a term used to describe a powerful stallion broken and able to be ridden. Moses was known for his meekness in the Old Testament. Numbers 12:3 declares him to be the meekest man on the face of the earth. Jesus was known for His meekness in the New Testament. In the only autobiographical description of His personality, Jesus said, "I am meek and lowly in heart" (Matthew 11:29). So too, after a person realizing he is poor in spirit and begins mourning, he finds himself meek with his strength harnessed for the purposes of the King and for Him alone.

Matthew 5:6
Blessed are they which do hunger and thirst after righteousness: for they shall be filled.

Notice the order: First you're poor in spirit, then you're mourning over your sin, then you find yourself meek. Now that you've gotten rid of all that self-grandeur and self-glory, you find yourself hungering and thirsting because you're emptied of all that junk.

I am personally convinced the reason many people are not filled is because they have not been emptied. They are still full of themselves. Pride must go before you find yourself hungering and thirsting for righteousness.

My wife fixes me excellent meals, but if I stop off and score a couple of burgers before I head home (as I have been known to do on occasion), even though there's a wonderful meal spread on the table, I don't have an appetite for it because I'm full of burgers and shakes.

Some people have lost their appetite for the Word of God. They no longer desire to worship; they no longer crave rightness. They are no longer meek, or mourning, or poor in spirit because they are full of the burgers and shakes of self-importance. When you empty yourself of self, happy are you because you're going to hunger once more for righteousness.

Matthew 5:7
Blessed are the merciful: for they shall obtain mercy.

After you have gone through the emptying process and you're filled with God's love, you'll be merciful toward others—no longer judgmental, critical, or analytical. Truly, the more righteous a man is, the more merciful he will be. The more sinful a man is, the more harsh and critical he will be.

Matthew 5:8
Blessed are the pure in heart: for they shall see God.

There is a difference between having a clean heart and a pure heart. All of us who have embraced the Lord have clean hearts. But a pure heart is one not distracted by the things of the world. Think of it this way: All soap is clean. But only one is 99.44 percent pure. Ivory soap doesn't have deodorants, perfumes, additives, or colorings. Ivory is nothing but soap. Other soaps are clean, but they're not pure. The pure in heart shall see God.

- "Why don't I see God?" people ask. Could it be because you're no longer pure in heart?
- "Are you saying I'm lost?" No. But has your vision been obscured by a bunch of perfumes and additives, still clean, but no longer Ivory, deodorized and perfumed, but no longer pure?

Matthew 5:9
Blessed are the peacemakers: for they shall be called the children of God.

Being a peacemaker doesn't mean wearing a peace symbol, marching against nukes, or marching for whales. I suggest to you that the finest peacemaking activity in which you can engage is introducing people to the Prince of Peace—Jesus Christ. What happiness is there that can compare to the joy of seeing a friend, relative, or neighbor open his heart to Jesus? Truly, it is then that we are blessed indeed.

Matthew 5:10–12
Blessed are they which are persecuted for righteousness' sake: for theirs is the kingdom of heaven. Blessed are ye, when men shall revile you, and persecute you, and shall say all manner of evil against you falsely, for my sake. Rejoice, and be exceeding glad: for great is your reward in heaven: for so persecuted they the prophets which were before you.

What? Persecution? Maybe you thought if a person possessed a "beatitude mentality"—if he was aware of his own poverty, if he mourned over his sin, if he was meek, if he hungered and thirsted after righteousness, if he had a pure heart, if he showed mercy—he would be popular. But such is not the case, for if the attitudes of meekness and mercy, poverty of spirit and righteousness of heart are being worked out in you, you will encounter persecution. You will have enemies. You will be slandered and misunderstood because in 2 Timothy 3:12, Paul says this, "Yea, and all that will live godly in Christ Jesus shall suffer persecution." That's a promise.

Jesus said, "Happy is the one who is persecuted. You're joining a great company, the company of the prophets. And, indeed, you will have profit in heaven—exceedingly great reward."

"Be happy," Jesus said, "because your reward in heaven is going to be great when men persecute you—and they will!" Notice one more thing before we leave these verses. It says, "and shall say all manner of evil against you *falsely,* for my sake." Many times Christians are being persecuted not because they're living righteously, but because they're weird. Weirdness doesn't count!

These are the attitudes that will lead to happiness and fulfillment: poverty of spirit, mourning over sin, meekness that no longer struts, but submits, hungering and thirsting for righteousness, mercy, purity of heart, peacemaking, persecution—this is the pathway to happiness.

Matthew 5:13
Ye are the salt of the earth: but if the salt have lost his savour, wherewith shall it be salted? It is thenceforth good for nothing, but to be cast out, and to be trodden under foot of men.

Salt promotes thirst, and as the salt of the earth, we should be making those around us thirsty for the living water of Jesus Christ. People should say, "There's something about you that creates in me a thirst for what you're enjoying."

Salt also preserves and heals. Therefore, if our culture is putrefying and decaying, we then, as the church, should hold back from indicting our society or critiquing our political leaders and begin preserving by repenting. "Lord, have we lost our saltiness? Have we lost our flavor and our effectiveness?"

Second Chronicles 7:14 declares, "If my people, which are called by my name, shall humble themselves, and pray, and seek my face, and turn from their wicked ways; then will I hear from heaven, and will forgive their sin, and will heal their land." It begins with us, gang. We are the salt.

Matthew 5:14–16
Ye are the light of the world. A city that is set on an hill cannot be hid. Neither do men light a candle, and put it under a bushel, but on a candlestick; and it giveth light unto all that are in the house. Let your light so shine before men, that they may see your good works, and glorify your Father which is in heaven.

Whenever Jesus did a miracle, people didn't ask Him to pose for a picture or to embark on a speaking tour. They simply glorified the Father. How I respect and admire Jesus for being able to work in such a way that He didn't draw attention or glory to Himself, but only to His Father.

Matthew 5:17–19
Think not that I am come to destroy the law, or the prophets: I am not come to destroy,

but to fulfil. For verily I say unto you, Till heaven and earth pass, one jot or one tittle shall in no wise pass from the law, till all be fulfilled. Whosoever therefore shall break one of these least commandments, and shall teach men so, he shall be called the least in the kingdom of heaven: but whosoever shall do and teach them, the same shall be called great in the kingdom of heaven.

"I am not coming to destroy the law, but to fulfill it. I am not seeking to weaken it, but to establish it."

Wherefore the law was our schoolmaster to bring us unto Christ, that we might be justified by faith. But after that faith is come, we are no longer under a schoolmaster. For ye are all the children of God by faith in Christ Jesus.
Galatians 3:24–26

People think, "Well, I'm pretty good."
"Oh?" says the Law. "Here's your standard."
And suddenly, as they read through the Law, they realize they're sinners in need of a Savior.

Matthew 5:20 (a)
For I say unto you, That except your righteousness shall exceed the righteousness of the scribes and Pharisees. . . .

This statement would have shocked those who heard it because, according to a popular Jewish saying of the time, "If only two men made it into heaven, one would be a scribe, and the other a Pharisee." The scribes were scholars who studied, interpreted, and commented endlessly upon the Law. The word "pharisee" literally means "separated one." Numbering seven thousand, this company of men kept the minutest details of the Law.

We look at the scribes and Pharisees rather humorously today, but no one did then. They were the Billy Grahams, Chuck Swindolls, and Jack Hayfords—the spiritual giants of their day. And Jesus said even their righteousness wasn't good enough.

Matthew 5:20 (b)
. . . ye shall in no case enter into the kingdom of heaven.

This is the key to the Sermon on the Mount. Jesus is saying, "If you think you can make it into the kingdom without Me as your Savior, you'd better be awfully good. In fact, you'd better be perfect."

So when people say, "I live by the Sermon on

the Mount," I say, "Oh? Good luck, because Jesus told us in that sermon to be perfect, that unless our righteousness exceeds that of even the most holy men, we will never enter the kingdom."

The Sermon on the Mount, perhaps the most misunderstood passage in all Scripture, is meant to bring us to the realization that there is no way *anyone* can keep its lofty standards. It is meant to make everyone equally guilty. It is meant to drive us to Jesus.

And once it has driven us *to* Christ, the Sermon on the Mount directs us *in* Christ, causing us to pray, "Lord, I thank You that Your blood has cleansed me when I have failed. But the standard is now before me. Help me to live in Your kingdom mentality—in poverty of spirit and purity of heart; in mourning and meekness and mercy—through *Your* strength, for I have a long way to go."

Our tendency is to compare ourselves with each other. That's what the Pharisees did. Compared to everyone else, they might have thought they looked pretty good.

One day after a wedding, I walked out to greet some of the people, and there was a guy who was over seven feet tall. He was huge! I had forgotten how big a seven-footer really is! When I'm around toddlers, I'm pretty big. But when I was around this guy, I was a runt! So, too, compared to the standards Jesus presented, the Pharisees were spiritual runts just like everyone else. That is why this sermon would have been so shocking.

Matthew 5:21, 22 (a)
Ye have heard that it was said by them of old time, Thou shalt not kill; and whosoever shall kill shall be in danger of the judgment: But I say unto you, That whosoever is angry with his brother without a cause shall be in danger of the judgment. . . .

"Anger" is only one letter short of "danger" because danger always lurks beneath anger. You might be able to disguise it temporarily, but if anger is brewing inside you, it will lead to danger, for murder begins in the heart.

Matthew 5:22 (b)
. . . and whosoever shall say to his brother, Raca, shall be in danger of the council: but whosoever shall say, Thou fool, shall be in danger of hell fire.

Is anger ever right? Yes.

Be ye angry, and sin not: let not the sun go down upon your wrath.   Ephesians 4:26

There is a place for righteous anger, but there is only one appropriate way to vent it. What did David say concerning his enemies? He said, "Lord, may their bones be broken and their skull cracked open. May their teeth be kicked in" (see Psalm 58:6). Since everything in the Old Testament physically is a picture of things in the New Testament spiritually, we are to wage war with violence, but not against flesh and blood.

For we wrestle not against flesh and blood, but against principalities, against powers, against the rulers of the darkness of this world, against spiritual wickedness in high places.
     Ephesians 6:12

There is a place, indeed, to get angry and wage war against the demons. With fasting and prayer, we should come against the forces that pollute, pervert, and destroy. Watch out, though, for unrighteous anger, when you call people idiots and fools. Jesus said that's equivalent to murder, for when you speak angrily or judgmentally of people, you murder a part of them.

Matthew 5:23, 24
Therefore if thou bring thy gift to the altar, and there rememberest that thy brother hath ought against thee; leave there thy gift before the altar, and go thy way; first be reconciled to thy brother, and then come and offer thy gift.

Does this mean we should track down every person who has something against us? For some of us, that would be a full-time job! I believe the key to understanding this is found in the phrase, "Therefore if thou bring thy gift to the altar, and *there* rememberest . . ." When you are at the altar and *there,* in the place of prayer, the Lord says, "This man or that woman has something against you, go get it right," then you must do as the Spirit leads.

Matthew 5:25, 26
Agree with thine adversary quickly, whiles thou art in the way with him; lest at any time the adversary deliver thee to the judge, and the judge deliver thee to the officer, and thou be cast into prison. Verily I say unto thee, Thou shalt by no means come out thence, till thou hast paid the uttermost farthing.

The legal system in Jesus' day required the plaintiff to personally track down the defendant. In other words, if you had something against someone, it would be your job to find him and bring him in physically before the judge. This is why Jesus here says, "If you are on the road with your adversary—if he has captured you—cut a deal with him before you get to court. Apologize! Get it right because once the matter reaches court, you could get cast into prison and remain until you pay the last penny." But how can you pay the last penny when you're in prison? You have no way to make money. That's the point. If you let the incident become a big deal by not dealing with it immediately, promptly, in humility, and with transparency, you'll never escape it.

I think many of us have found this to be true at one point or another. When we had the opportunity to deal with a situation, we chose not to because of pride, and then it grew and grew over the days and months and years, until it became so complicated and confusing that there was no way out. Jesus said, "Avoid this. Be wise. When you are on the road, when you're talking with your adversary, when you're still communicating, be humble, lest you find yourself imprisoned with no way of escape."

Matthew 5:27, 28
Ye have heard that it was said by them of old time, Thou shalt not commit adultery: But I say unto you, That whosoever looketh on a woman to lust after her hath committed adultery with her already in his heart.

The issue isn't only what you're doing outwardly; it's what's going on in your heart internally. We have all been angry at some time or another, thus we're all murderers. We have all looked with lust in our heart, thus we're all adulterers. Truly, there is none righteous, no not one.

Matthew 5:29, 30
And if thy right eye offend thee, pluck it out, and cast it from thee: for it is profitable for thee that one of thy members should perish, and not that thy whole body should be cast into hell. And if thy right hand offend thee, cut if off, and cast it from thee: for it is profitable for thee that one of thy members should perish, and not that thy whole body should be cast into hell.

One of my friends, a wonderful Christian brother, is a blind man. Yet, his number one problem is lust. Therefore, Jesus is not talking about physically poking out an eye or chopping off a hand. Rather, He's saying, "Deal violently and directly with any part of your being—your activities, your hobbies, your schedule—that is leading you to sin. It's destructive, so deal with it decisively."

Matthew 5:31
It hath been said, Whosoever shall put away his wife, let him give her a writing of divorcement.

The Pharisees were basically divided into two camps: the school of Shammai and the school of Hillel. Those who followed Shammai were very conservative, saying that on the basis of Deuteronomy 24, divorce could be granted only in the case of uncleanness, which they interpreted to be sexual immorality or adultery. The followers of Hillel were very liberal, saying uncleanness is much broader than simply adultery or immorality. If a woman, for example, put too much salt and pepper on her husband's eggs, which made him lose his temper, she had made him sin, and therefore was unclean—a legitimate reason for divorce. Or, if a man saw a woman who was more righteous or virtuous than his wife, he had the right to divorce her because she was now unclean by comparison. The followers of Shammai said a written bill of divorce must be given. The followers of Hillel said all that was required was for the husband to look at his wife and say, "I divorce you," three times. Consequently, not unlike today, divorce was occurring for the most frivolous reasons.

Matthew 5:32
But I say unto you, That whosoever shall put away his wife, saving for the cause of fornication, causeth her to commit adultery: and whosoever shall marry her that is divorced committeth adultery.

Based on the original text, I strongly believe this verse means that, although God's plan is that two people remain married until death separates them, those who divorce and remarry, in effect, do commit adultery. However, they don't *live* in adultery. Therefore, God forbid that we should say, "All manner of sin is forgiven all man except for one: divorce." That's not what Jesus said. He said, "All manner of sin is forgiven all men except the blasphemy of the Holy Spirit—the rejection of Jesus Christ" (see Matthew 12:31). We're all sinners, gang. We've all missed the mark. Look around you and you'll see a murderer sitting next to you and a bunch of adulterers in front and behind you. We're *all* sinners. We *all* need a Savior.

Matthew 5:33–37
Again, ye have heard that it hath been said by them of old time, Thou shalt not forswear thyself, but shalt perform unto the Lord thine oaths: But I say unto you, Swear not at all; neither by heaven; for it is God's throne: Nor by the earth; for it is his footstool:

neither by Jerusalem; for it is the city of the great King. Neither shalt thou swear by thy head, because thou canst not make one hair white or black. But let your communication be, Yea, yea; Nay, nay: for whatsoever is more than these cometh of evil.

Your words should be so solid that a simple yes or no should be sufficient. The minute you have to say, "I swear!" they're not.

Matthew 5:38–42

Ye have heard that it hath been said, An eye for an eye, and a tooth for a tooth: But I say unto you, That ye resist not evil: but whosoever shall smite thee on thy right cheek, turn to him the other also. And if any man will sue thee at the law, and take away thy coat, let him have thy cloke also. And whosoever shall compel thee to go a mile, go with him twain. Give to him that asketh thee, and from him that would borrow of thee turn not thou away.

If you lived in Jesus' day, a Roman soldier could come to you at any time and tap you on the shoulder with his spear. You then would be required by law to carry his armor or baggage for up to one mile. Here, Jesus says, "Blow his mind. Go with him two miles. And if someone wants your coat, give him your undercoat as well. If they hit you on the cheek, turn the other cheek."

There have been those throughout history who have found that what Jesus was saying was potent and dynamic—that turning the other cheek actually puts one in control. The entire subcontinent of India was freed from the powerful British rule because Ghandi read this verse, and although he was not a believer, he believed in what Jesus said. He inspired an entire nation to turn the other cheek, and it blew the Brits away. After all, what can you do if someone won't fight back? You can beat them with clubs, you can fire guns on them, but the morale of your own army is destroyed in the process. So eventually, the British got on their ships and sailed home.

Martin Luther King, Jr. found the same thing to be true when he mobilized the Blacks in Alabama. If the protesters had fought back, the U.S. Marshals would have felt justified in firing their guns indiscriminately, and the Civil Rights movement would have died. But peaceful resistance won out, and an entire people experienced liberation.

In your family, at work, in your neighborhood—wherever you might be—take the words of Jesus literally. Don't fight back, for he who doesn't fight back controls the situation.

Matthew 5:43, 44 (a)

Ye have heard that it hath been said, Thou shalt love thy neighbour, and hate thine enemy. But I say unto you, Love your enemies . . .

If you've ever lashed out at someone who refused to fight back, you know how small it made you feel. Don't fight back. Love back. Nothing will disarm your enemy so easily.

But you say, "She has hurt me or has trampled on me. I can't love back."

In the next verse, Jesus tells you how.

Matthew 5:44 (b)

. . . bless them that curse you, do good to them that hate you, and pray for them which despitefully use you, and persecute you.

Bless them! When the person who bugs you the most comes down on you, look at him and say, "The Lord bless you. The Lord be with you. The Lord make His face to shine upon you and give you peace." Pronounce blessing upon him; do good to him; pray for him.

I'll tell you a secret: If you pray for your enemies—for the people who bug you the most—you will experience power in your life and an ability to love them that will blow you away. Why? When you pray for your enemies, two things happen: They change and you change. It might take some time, but slowly yet surely, you'll see a change. If I'm praying every day for the guy I can't stand, something amazing happens. I become involved with him and interested in him. As I pray for him, there is a linkage established through prayer.

Matthew 5:45–48

That ye may be the children of your Father which is in heaven: for he maketh his sun to rise on the evil and on the good, and sendeth rain on the just and on the unjust. For if ye love them which love you, what reward have ye? do not even the publicans the same? And if ye salute your brethren only, what do ye more than others? do not even the publicans so? Be ye therefore perfect, even as your Father which is in heaven is perfect.

"Be ye perfect? You mean never be angry because that's equivalent to murder? Never say anything more than yes or no without defending or explaining? Turn the other cheek when people are attacking me? Bless those who hurt me? Be *perfect?* "Rabbi, if what You say is true, if this is what was meant in the Old Testament Law, then no matter how I come across outwardly with my robes, my pious postures, and my religious activities, I'm lost. No wonder You said righteousness must exceed that of the scribes and Pharisees. I'm a Pharisee—and I'm a sinner."

"Great!" Jesus would answer. "That's right where I want you. I will now help you live the way of the kingdom constitution as I, the King, take up residence within you."

Soon we'll see Jesus face-to-face. He's coming back. And when we see Him, the Bible says we shall be like Him (I John 3:2). We shall indeed be perfect. And what a day that will be!

6 Jesus continues His Sermon on the Mount, the constitution of His kingdom. In chapter 5, He addressed inner attitudes. Here in chapter 6, He will discuss outward activities.

Matthew 6:1, 2
Take heed that ye do not your alms before men, to be seen of them: otherwise ye have no reward of your Father which is in heaven. Therefore when thou doest thine alms, do not sound a trumpet before thee, as the hypocrites do in the synagogues and in the streets, that they may have glory of men. Verily I say unto you, They have their reward.

In the area of praying, giving, and fasting, Jesus will talk about the *hupokrites,* or hypocrites. *Hupokrites* is a Greek word that means "mask-wearer." Hupokrites were actors in the Greek theater who wore masks, very exaggerated in form, with huge smiles and frowns so that even people in the back row could see what kind of emotion was being portrayed. We get the word two-faced from this same idea.

Jesus said, "Don't be hypocritical in your giving." How did the hypocrites give? Originally, there was an area at the side of the temple courtyard called the Chamber of the Secret. People would go there and drop gifts designated for the poor in a large chest called the Trumpet. Later, the poor would come to the Chamber of the Secret and receive gifts from the Trumpet. It was all done very discreetly, with humility and honesty. But as the years went on, the Pharisees decided it wasn't practical to go all the way to the temple to give alms to the poor. So instead, they tied a small brass or silver trumpet to their belts. Then, whenever they wanted to give to the poor, they stood on a street corner and blew their trumpets. Upon hearing this, the poor people in the area would gather around the generous Pharisee as he distributed his alms with great flourish, while everyone around said, "My! Look how righteous he is!"

Jesus called the Pharisees hypocrites because they gave not out of concern for the poor, but that they might be seen by men.

Matthew 6:3, 4
But when thou doest alms, let not thy left hand know what thy right hand doeth: That thine alms may be in secret: and thy Father which seeth in secret himself shall reward thee openly.

Notice, Jesus doesn't say, "*If* thou doest alms," but "*When* thou doest alms." The assumption is we will give. The only question is, how will we do it? Share secretly, and your Father will reward you openly.

Matthew 6:5
And when thou prayest, thou shalt not be as the hypocrites are: for they love to pray standing in the synagogues and in the corners of the streets, that they may be seen of men. Verily I say unto you, They have their reward.

The Pharisees designated the third hour, the sixth hour, and the ninth hour as times of prayer. In other words, at nine o'clock in the morning, at noon, and at three o'clock in the afternoon, they would faithfully gather in the synagogues or in the temple to offer their prayers. We are told in the Book of Daniel that he, a man of God, opened his windows toward Jerusalem and prayed three times a day. But the Pharisees were not doing it to seek the Lord, but rather to be seen by men. How do we know this? On their way to prayer meetings, the Pharisees would stop on the corner of the street and begin to offer long and verbose prayers. In so doing, they were saying, "We are so eager to pray, we can't wait to get to the synagogue."

And people would say, "Oh, wow! Look how righteous they are!"

We still do that in our own subtle ways, don't we? "Yes, as I was praying this morning at three o'clock, the Lord brought you to my heart." And we subtly let people know we are in a place of continual prayer. Jesus said, "Don't do it. That's hypocrisy."

Matthew 6:6
But thou, when thou prayest, enter into thy closet, and when thou hast shut thy door, pray to thy Father which is in secret; and thy Father which seeth in secret shall reward thee openly.

The Father, who sees in secret, will bless you openly and eternally.

Matthew 6:7
But when ye pray, use not vain repetitions, as the heathen do: for they think that they shall be heard for their much speaking.

Jesus encourages us to be short and concise in our prayers. To me, this is fantastically liberating because I fall prey to thinking, *The longer I pray, the more impressed God will be.*

In Ecclesiastes 5, Solomon says that God is in heaven. You are on earth. Therefore, let your words be few. You know, I crack up at my own prayers sometimes. "Well now, Father," I hear myself praying, "I just pray right now for my wife, Tammy. She has this particular need, and I just pray You would . . ." As if the Lord is up in heaven saying, "Tammy? Oh yeah, Tammy. Now what need does she have?" We don't need to inform the Lord, nor convince the Lord. We just need to connect with the Lord.

Matthew 6:8–13
Be not ye therefore like unto them: for your Father knoweth what things ye have need of, before ye ask him. After this manner therefore pray ye: Our Father which art in heaven, Hallowed be thy name. Thy kingdom come. Thy will be done in earth, as it is in heaven. Give us this day our daily bread. And forgive us our debts, as we forgive our debtors. And lead us not into temptation, but deliver us from evil: For thine is the kingdom, and the power, and the glory, for ever. Amen.

As we sing and pray this most famous of all prayers, are we, like the Pharisees, guilty of meaningless repetition? Yes—if we're saying it without thinking. But the Scriptures do not forbid meaningful repetition. Jesus is not saying repetition in and of itself is wrong. How do I know? In Matthew 26, when Jesus made the same request of His Father three times in the Garden of Gethsemane, Matthew writes, "And He spake the same words yet again" (see v. 44). Thus, I believe there is such a thing as meaningful repetition, and I believe this prayer prayed word for word can be potent and powerful, mystical and wonderful, if prayed with an engaged mind and a sensitive heart.

For topical study of Matthew 6:9–13 entitled "The Perfect Prayer," turn to page 34.

Matthew 6:14, 15
For if ye forgive men their trespasses, your heavenly Father will also forgive you: But if ye forgive not men their trespasses, neither will your Father forgive your trespasses.

When people fail, don't rub it in. Rub it out. Forgive them. How? I personally believe when you pray, "Forgive us our debts as we forgive our debtors," the very act of articulating, "as we forgive our debtors," releases forgiveness at that moment. That might sound a bit mystical, but many of us have found it to be very practical. When you say, "Father, I am now forgiving my debtors," in the very act of praying it, you'll experience it.

Matthew 6:16–18
Moreover when ye fast, be not, as the hypocrites, of a sad countenance: for they disfigure their faces, that they may appear unto men to fast. Verily I say unto you, They have their reward. But thou, when thou fastest, anoint thine head, and wash thy face; That thou appear not unto men to fast, but unto thy Father which is in secret: and thy Father, which seeth in secret, shall reward thee openly.

The Pharisees—the ones who blew the trumpet when they gave their gifts and prayed on street corners because they couldn't wait to get to church—fasted every Monday and Thursday. You could always tell when they were fasting because they walked around with long faces, drawn cheeks, unbrushed teeth, and uncombed hair.

Jesus said when you fast, comb your hair, wash your face, brush your teeth, and don't let people know. Your Father who sees in secret will reward you. Fasting is an important discipline often neglected by American Christians. In the Scriptures, we see fasting primarily for two reasons.

The first is for direction. Both examples in the Old Testament are found in the books of Ezra and Nehemiah. In the New Testament, we see the examples not only in the life of Jesus but also in the Book of Acts. When people desired to know God's will or direction, they fasted.

Physiologists tell us when there is no food in the stomach, there is greater blood flow to the brain. You can actually think clearer when you're not digesting burgers and fries. Once you overcome those first pangs of hunger, your thinking processes are more focused and clearer than ever. On the other hand, if you have two Whoppers and a couple of shakes, all you want to do is sleep!

Second, people fast not only for direction, but for liberation. When you feel oppressed, bound, or hassled by some sin or problem, fasting is a powerful weapon in your spiritual arsenal. Why? When you say no to your stomach and start praying instead, something dynamic begins to happen. Saying no to your physical appetites helps you say no to the other temptations that hassle you. If you are plagued by temptation, I encourage you to begin to explore the discipline of fasting. When your stomach starts demanding, just say "No," and start praying. You will find a power and a liberty that will help you overcome whatever temptations are seeking to enslave you. There's real power in fasting. If you need direction, if you hunger for liberation, skip lunch, and seek the Lord.

Matthew 6:19–21
Lay not up for yourselves treasures upon earth, where moth and rust doth corrupt, and where thieves break through and steal: But lay up for yourselves treasures in heaven, where neither moth nor rust doth corrupt, and where thieves do not break through nor steal: For where your treasure is, there will your heart be also.

Giving is not God's way of raising cash. It's God's way of raising kids. Every time I give, I am giving away part of my stinginess and selfishness. God doesn't need my money, but I need to give. The Lord wants my heart, not my money, and He knows that wherever my treasure is, that's where my heart will be. If I have financial investments, I will follow the stock market carefully. If I hold real estate, I will follow the housing market with genuine interest. If I have treasure in heaven, guess where my heart will be? It is profoundly interesting to me that Jesus didn't say, "Where your heart is, there your treasure will be." Instead, He said, "Put your treasure in heaven, and your heart will inevitably follow."

How can we be more heavenly-hearted? By sending our treasure ahead.

Matthew 6:22, 23
The light of the body is the eye: if therefore thine eye be single, thy whole body shall be full of light. But if thine eye be evil, thy whole body shall be full of darkness. If therefore the light that is in thee be darkness, how great is that darkness!

Because the eye is the channel through which comes illumination, if you have an evil eye, your whole body shall be full of darkness. Proverbs 28:22 says, "He that hasteth to be rich hath an evil eye, and considereth not that poverty shall come upon him." Who has an evil eye? The one who lives for riches. It's not wrong to have things, but if you live for things, your eye is evil, and your life will be dark.

Charge them that are rich in this world, that they be not highminded, nor trust in uncertain riches, but in the living God, who giveth us richly all things to enjoy.   1 Timothy 6:17

Paul didn't say, "Sell your goods." He said, "Don't trust in them."

Matthew 6:24
No man can serve two masters: for either he will hate the one, and love the other; or else he will hold to the one, and despise the other. Ye cannot serve God and mammon.

Mammon is more than just nickels, dimes, and dollar bills. Jesus identifies mammon as a master. I believe mammon is a god, a demonic force who wants you to be focused on him, in bondage to him, and all wrapped up in him. The entire monetary system in our world right now is incredible. Truly, it is a religion requiring great faith. I was reading an article some time ago that said if suddenly a whistle was blown in the economic community and all accounts had to be settled immediately, only 10 percent of the debts and 10 percent of the cash would be real. In other words, if the music stopped in the world of financial musical chairs, nine out of ten people would be left without a chair because 90 percent of the transactions that happen in the economic world are backed by nothing. Zip. Zero. It's all faith.

Even the dollar bill in your wallet, except for a very rare one, doesn't say Silver Certificate anymore. It's a U.S. Government Note, backed by nothing.

Economics is a risky religion. And Jesus said, "You cannot serve God and mammon. You've got to make a choice."

Matthew 6:25
Therefore I say unto you, Take no thought for your life, what ye shall eat, or what ye shall drink; nor yet for your body, what ye shall put on. Is not the life more than meat, and the body than raiment?

Does this verse mean we shouldn't care at all what we wear or about investments or monetary matters? No. The meaning here is that we are to take no *anxious* thought, or literally, "Take no worry." The word *worry* means literally "to strangle." If you're worried about what you're wearing, eating, or drinking—about what you have or don't have materially—your personality will be tied in knots and strangled.

I once read that it takes sixty trillion droplets of fog to cover seven city blocks. Now sixty trillion droplets, or seven city blocks' worth of fog, can close down airports and tie up cities. Yet, if you condensed those sixty trillion fog droplets, you would end up with only half a glass of water.

That's a good picture of what worry is all about. You begin with something little, only half a glass of water. But you start thinking about it and wrestling with it, wondering, *How is this going to work out? How am I going to do that?* And before long, you can't see straight, and your airport is shut down. You're not hearing from the Lord, and you're not soaring with the Lord as you once did because you're all fogged in. Jesus said, "Don't take any anxious thought whatsoever. Don't let worry strangle you. Don't end up in a fog."

Matthew 6:26

Behold the fowls of the air: for they sow not, neither do they reap, nor gather into barns; yet your heavenly Father feedeth them. Are ye not much better than they?

First Peter 5 says we are to cast all of our anxieties upon God. How?

Be careful for nothing; but in every thing by prayer and supplication with thanksgiving let your requests be made known unto God. And the peace of God, which passeth all understanding, shall keep your hearts and minds through Christ Jesus.   Philippians 4:6–7

Be anxious for nothing. Pray about everything. Be thankful in all things. That's the key. Jesus wants us to be a carefree people.

Matthew 6:27–31

Which of you by taking thought can add one cubit unto his stature? And why take ye thought for raiment? Consider the lilies of the field, how they grow; they toil not, neither do they spin: And yet I say unto you, That even Solomon in all his glory was not arrayed like one of these. Wherefore, if God so clothe the grass of the field, which to day is, and to-morrow is cast into the oven, shall he not much more clothe you, O ye of little faith? Therefore take no thought, saying, What shall we eat? or, What shall we drink? or, Wherewithal shall we be clothed?

Styles change quickly. I was thinking about this one day when I saw a couple walking through downtown Medford, Oregon. Their clothes were totally out of fashion, but walking hand in hand, there was a glow about them because of their radiant smiles. And I thought, *There goes one of the best-looking couples I have ever seen.* Don't get all hung up on fads and fashions. Jesus tells us to check out the flowers. Even Solomon couldn't rival their splendor.

Matthew 6:32–34

(For after all these things do the Gentiles seek:) for your heavenly Father knoweth that ye have need of all these things. But seek ye first the kingdom of God, and his righteousness; and all these things shall be added unto you. Take therefore no thought for the morrow: for the morrow shall take thought for the things of itself. Sufficient unto the day is the evil thereof.

Seek first the kingdom, and everything else will fall into place. Every one of you is proof of this, for truly God has provided. We may have spent nights worrying, and yet the Lord has been faithful even when we've been foolish. That's why Jesus told us not to worry about tomorrow. Today has enough challenges of its own. Just deal with today, and above all, seek first the kingdom.

THE PERFECT PRAYER
A Topical Study of
MATTHEW 6:9–13

As far as we know, the disciples never asked Jesus to teach them to preach, to prophesy, or to cast out demons. There is no record of them asking how to worship or witness or how to build a ministry or lead their families. The one thing the disciples asked of Jesus directly was, "Lord, teach us to pray."

Why? I believe it is because, after watching Jesus for several years, the disciples were convinced prayer was the secret of His ministry and the foundation of all He did.

In Luke 11, Jesus gave His disciples the same prayer, virtually word for word, that He had given two years earlier, recorded here in Matthew. He didn't say, "The prayer I taught two years ago was for the multitudes, but for you disciples, here's something heavier." Or, "The prayer I taught in the Sermon on the Mount was at the beginning of My ministry, but now two years later, here is something more meaty." It was as though He was saying, "Don't you recall what I taught you two years ago?" as He gave this prayer verbatim to them once again.

This revolutionized my thinking. I had always been under the impression that the Lord's Prayer was simply an example or a model that we could study and learn from, but it was not necessarily to be prayed verbatim. While I still believe the Lord's Prayer is a wonderful model and a perfect example, I have come to believe it is more than that. I believe it is actually sacramental.

"Sacrament" refers to that which comes from the outside and works its way in. Baptism, the Lord's Table, and the marriage ceremony are all sacraments because they are external demonstrations that signify internal transformation. I have discovered personally that the Lord's Prayer is sacramental—or close to it. That is, by praying the Lord's Prayer from memory word for word externally, something wonderful, mystical, and beautiful happens internally.

"Wait!" you say. "Didn't Jesus teach against meaningless repetitions?"

Yes, in Matthew 6:7, Jesus did warn about vain and meaningless repetitions. If I say the Lord's Prayer with my mind a million miles away and my heart not sensitive to the Spirit, it will profit me nothing. But, when I say it meaningfully—concentrating, thinking, contemplating, and meditating—when I pray this prayer as the Lord gave it to His disciples in Luke 11 and to the masses in Matthew 6, I have discovered it has a very powerful and potent effect upon me personally. I believe it will upon you as well.

Two characteristics of this prayer strike me. I am amazed first by its completeness. It is wonderful because it covers all of our needs and all of God's worthiness. Secondly, I am impressed with its conciseness. Sixty-five words long, it only takes thirty seconds to pray.

We have fallen into the fallacy of thinking the strength of prayer is in direct proportion to the length of prayer—even though Jesus went out of His way to say that we wouldn't be heard for our "much speaking." Jesus' prayers were complete, but concise. If I asked the Lord to teach me to pray, I would think He would give me a one hundred-page book at the very least. But He didn't. He simply gave a prayer sixty-five words long.

I am reminded of the time Moses' sister Miriam was struck with leprosy. Moses looked to the Lord and said, "Heal her now, O God, I beseech thee" (Numbers 12:13). Eight words, and the Lord healed her.

Now, we also know Moses was so in love with God that he spent forty days and forty nights seeking His face in the desert. Thus, I'm not discounting or diminishing the importance of those lengthy chunks of time when you seek the Lord. But in our daily prayer life, I think we need a readjustment in our thinking.

When I have repeatedly prayed the Lord's Prayer word for word, I have found a liberty, an empowering, and a joy that have been really special and refreshing to me. I can pause in my car before going to my next appointment (already late) and say,

> Our Father which art in heaven, Hallowed be thy name.
> Thy kingdom come. Thy will be done in earth, as it is in heaven.
> Give us this day our daily bread.
> And forgive us our debts, as we forgive our debtors.
> And lead us not into temptation, but deliver us from evil:
> For thine is the kingdom, and the power, and the glory, for ever. Amen.

Then it's out my door and into the meeting with the sense that the Lord is with me and the bases are covered. Notice six elements of this prayer. The first component, verse 9, concerns God's Person. The second, verse 10, concerns God's purpose. Third, God's provision is seen in verse 11. Fourth, God's pardon is in verse 12. Fifth, God's protection is in the first half of verse 13. And sixth, God's preeminence is in the last half of verse 13.

First, God's Person . . .

Our Father . . .

When Jesus taught this prayer, He must have shocked those who were listening to Him when He said, "Our Father." The word for "Father" is "Abba," meaning "Papa." Keep in mind that in the Old Testament, God was addressed as Elohim, the Strong One; El Shaddai, the Mighty One; and Yahweh, the unspeakable word that meant, "I AM THAT I AM."

Why did Jesus suddenly say, "When you pray, call God Daddy, Papa, Abba, Father?" Was He no longer the Powerful, Unspeakable, Omnipotent God of the Old Testament? Did God change? No. God didn't change. We did.

But as many as received him, to them gave he power to become the sons of God, even to them that believe on his name. John 1:12

We were adopted into His family. If you are truly a child of God, He is still the Unspeakable One, the Almighty One, the Omnipotent One, but because you have been adopted into His family, to you He is also Abba. Notice also, He's not just *my* Father, but He is *Our* Father. He's the Presbyterian's Father, the Pentecostal's Father, the Catholic's Father, and the Lutheran's Father. Regardless of their denomination, Christians, hand in hand, pray, "Our Father," not only now, but throughout the ages.

I can't hit like Babe Ruth, paint like Michelangelo, or sing like George Beverly Shea. But you know what? I can pray like John Knox, like Martin Luther, and like

Charles Spurgeon, because I can pray the same prayer they prayed. It is the perfect prayer because it came from the perfect Pray-er—Jesus Christ. You can pray this prayer daily, hourly, whenever you like. And you will find yourself in incredible company with the great saints of the ages, with believers of all other flavors, who all love God and address Him as Father because of their relationship to the Son.

. . . Which art in heaven . . .

As my Father, I relate to Him. But because He's in heaven, I reverence Him.

Be not rash with thy mouth, and let not thine heart be hasty to utter any thing before God: for God is in heaven, and thou upon earth: therefore let thy words be few.
                                                                    Ecclesiastes 5:2

I like that! Solomon reminds us we don't have to pray with lofty terminology or sanctimonious tones. Yes, we must be reverent because God is in Heaven. But we can be real because He's our Father.

. . . Hallowed be thy name . . .

"Hallowed" is a word that has been lost in our language because the concept has been lost from our lives. It means "to make holy, separated, transcendent."

"O Lord, hallowed, holy is Your Name. Everyone around me, everything that touches me, all that is within me has been tainted and eroded by sin. But You are holy. Hallowed is Your Name." Second, notice not only God's Person, but also His purpose.

Thy kingdom come. Thy will be done on earth as it is in heaven.

There are only two kinds of people: those who are in harmony with God's purpose, saying, "Thy will be done," and those who live for themselves, saying, "My will be done."

God is terrifyingly fair. If you say, "My will be done," He will allow that to happen. If you say, "I don't want God," He will allow you to be damned. If you say, "I want my way," He will give you your way.

We have a choice to make. We can either, as the Psalmist says, "Be still, and know that He is God," or we can say, "God, You be still and know that I am me."

The prophet Isaiah went to Hezekiah and said, "Hezekiah, the Lord wants you to know it's time for you to die. Prepare your house." The original text of Isaiah 38:2 tells us Hezekiah turned his face to the wall and chattered like a bird, "Let me live. Let me live." Finally, God said, "Okay, you got it. Your will be done." Hezekiah lived fifteen more years, and they were the fifteen most tragic years of his life. During that time, Hezekiah set the stage for the Babylonian invasion, and he fathered a son named Manasseh who grew up to be the most wicked king in the history of Israel.

Hezekiah would have been so much better simply praying, "*Thy* kingdom come, *Thy* will be done, Father, on earth as it is in heaven."

Do you pray in simplicity, "Father, Thy will be done"? Or do you pray with a demanding mentality, "You listen to me, God. I want this"?

Ruth Bell Graham has said she is glad God did not listen to her foolish demands in her younger years, or she would have married the wrong guy fifteen times. But she showed wisdom when she ended her prayers with the Lord's Prayer, saying, "Thy kingdom come. Thy will be done."

Third, God's provision . . .

Give us . . .

Notice Jesus did not pray, "Give Me *My* bread," but "Give us *our* bread." There are no singular pronouns in the Lord's Prayer. For me, it's so freeing to think of my needs as "our needs." If I'm feeling tired, I pray, "Lord, give us strength, my brothers and sisters who are feeling fatigued today." If I'm sad, I pray, "Lord, lift our spirits today." There's wonderful, continual intercession when a person prays, "*Our* Father, give *us* this day, forgive *us* our debts, lead *us* not into temptation."

. . . This day . . .

Give us *this day*—not this month, not this year. Why does the Lord want us to pray day by day? Why can't we just sort of blanket our requests by saying, "Lord, give us this month our monthly needs," or "Give us this year our yearly bread"?

The Lord wants us to pray for our daily needs because prayer in and of itself is our greatest need. If the Father gave things to us on a monthly basis, we wouldn't pray very frequently. The Lord wants you and me to come before Him every day. Is it because He's on an ego trip? No. Is it because He has need of us? No. Because we have need of Him. *He* is our Bread.

. . . Our daily bread.

I think it's rather foolish for people to pray, "Give us this day our daily bread," but fail to take Communion. It's like praying, "Lord, send light," while keeping our eyes closed. "For this cause," writes Paul, "many are weak and sick and even dying unnecessarily" (see 1 Corinthians 11:30). I believe the ultimate answer to this request is found at the Communion Table, for truly *He* is our Bread. Don't let the pendulum swing too far, fundamental Protestant. Don't diminish the mystery of the Lord's Table by saying, "I don't believe Communion is really mystical or miraculous. It's not really necessary. It's optional."

No. It's foundational. It's essential. Check out the Book of Acts. Communion

was a key component of the early church. Jesus Himself said, "Do this often in remembrance of Me. Be constantly fed and refreshed in Me."

Fourth, God's pardon . . .

And forgive us our debts . . .

"What is found in Christianity which is not found in any other religion?" This was
the question asked at a seminar featuring several prominent Christian theologians. C. S. Lewis, the brilliant thinker and gifted author, was caught in traffic
while the rest of the panel puzzled over this question. After about an hour, Lewis
arrived, and the question was posed to him. "That's simple," he replied. "The forgiveness of sin."

Our past is buried in the sea of God's forgiveness and forgetfulness. He does
not remember our sin anymore. And that is what makes Christianity absolutely
unique.

. . . As we forgive our debtors.

In the expression of this prayer is the explosion of forgiveness. I might begin
praying the Lord's Prayer with bitterness in my heart toward someone who hurt
me six years ago, eight weeks ago, or ten minutes ago. But as I pray, "Forgive us
our debts as we forgive our debtors," suddenly the resentment, the bitterness, the
ill-will dissipates from me as I pray this prayer meaningfully.

Fifth, God's protection . . .

And lead us not into temptation . . .

The word "temptation" does not mean a drawing into sin, but into testing. Although Scripture records Abraham was tempted with a knife in his hand and his
son on the altar (Genesis 22:1), the temptation was not to do evil. It was a testing.
James 1:13 says that God cannot be tempted with evil, neither tempts He any man
with evil. God does not tempt you.

What, then, is Jesus teaching us to pray here? "Lead us not into testing."

Wait a minute! Doesn't the Word declare that testing is *good?* Doesn't James
say to count it all *joy* when you fall into various tests and trials, knowing that testing
produces patience? Doesn't Peter say that tests purify us as gold purified in the
fire? Why would we pray, "Lead us not into testing"? The answer is humility. Which
of us would stand up today and say, "Lord, test me! I'm ready! Send testing my way,
and watch me flex my spiritual muscles." Foolish is the person who would say such
a thing! Thus, it's in humility that we constantly pray, "Lead us *not* into testing."
But if I have prayed, "Lord lead us not into temptation," then should God take me

through testing, I can embrace it joyfully, knowing He will not test me above what I am able (1 Corinthians 10:13).

> *. . . But deliver us from evil.*

Satan is real, and we need God's protection.

I once read a story about George Adam Smith, a wonderful preacher and author, who was on a mountain-climbing tour of the Alps. On one particularly high peak, he ran to the very precipice and looked out over Switzerland. Suddenly, a strong gust of wind came up that threatened to blow him over the edge. From several feet away, his guide called to him, "Mr. Smith! On your knees, sir! The only way you're safe up here is on your knees!"

It has been rightly said that Satan trembles when he sees the weakest saint upon his knees. Jesus taught us to pray, "God, protect us. Lead us not into trials and testing. And deliver us from the evil one."

Finally, we come to the last component—God's preeminence.

> *For thine is the kingdom, and the power, and the glory, for ever. Amen.*

This concise and potent prayer ends in an explosion of praise, literally reading, "For thine is the kingship, and the weight or substance. It's all Yours. You are King. You are powerful! Glory! So be it!"

When I consider,

- God's Person—that He's my Abba, my Papa,
- His purpose—which is right,
- His provision—daily bread and the Bread of Life,
- His pardon—I am forgiven, and can forgive others, and
- His protection—from temptation and the evil one,

I have no other choice but to worship Him. God does not need our worship, but we need to worship. When I'm at a place where I'm saying, "For *Thine* is the kingdom, and the power, and the glory for ever," with open heart and raised hands, suddenly I'm outside myself, lifted above my cares and worries, my hobbies and toys.

The Lord's Prayer is comprised of sixty-five profoundly simple and simply profound words. You can meditate on this prayer for hours, days, months, and years for the rest of your life. But I encourage you to appropriate it right now. Allow this sacrament to be worked into your life, and you'll find a whole new dimension of the Lord's Person and purpose, provision and pardon, protection and preeminence worked out through your life.

7 Matthew 7:1
Judge not, that ye be not judged.

The Greek word translated "judge" is *krino,* which means "to judge to the place of condemnation." It's when you're in someone's face, so to speak, pointing your finger at them, and condemning them.

In Romans 16:17, Paul instructs the early church to mark the man who causes division. And in Galatians 1:8, he writes, "But though we, or an angel from heaven, preach any other gospel unto you than that which we have preached unto you, let him be accursed." So there *is* a need to judge, but not to the place of condemnation. Rather, we are to judge for identification and for restoration. I am to love people enough that when I see them erring, I am to say to them lovingly, "Because I care about you, I want you to know that you're going in the wrong direction."

> Thou shalt not hate thy brother in thine heart: thou shalt in any wise rebuke thy neighbour, and not suffer sin upon him.   Leviticus 19:17

Don't hate your brother, but love him by not allowing him to continue in his sin.

> Brethren, if a man be overtaken in a fault, ye which are spiritual, restore such a one in the spirit of meekness; considering thyself, lest thou also be tempted.   Galatians 6:1

According to Scripture, I must make some judgments and identification. But I am not to have an attitude of condemnation. How do I know if I'm condemning people? If I am not willing to partake in restoration, then I am probably practicing condemnation. When Jesus walked into the Upper Room where His disciples were sitting, He noticed they had dirty feet. Did He point His finger and say, "You guys, why don't you wash your stinky feet? It's a mess up here." No. John 13 says He rose from supper, girded Himself with a towel, and began to wash their feet Himself. So, too, I do not believe I have the right to point out someone's dirty feet unless I'm willing to kneel down and wash them.

Matthew 7:2
For with what judgment ye judge, ye shall be judged: and with what measure ye mete, it shall be measured to you again.

The manner in which I judge is the way I will be judged. Is it the manner in which I will be judged by God? No. All my sins have been dealt

with on the Cross of Calvary. Then who is going to judge me? People will. If I am critical of others, pointing out dirt on their feet with no intention of restoring, healing, or helping, I am going to find that same kind of judgment hurled at me.

In the first chapter of the Book of Judges, the men of Judah said to the men of Simeon, "There's a camp of Canaanites over in this valley. Let's go take them on." After beating the Canaanites soundly, the Israelites captured Adoni-bezek, the Canaanite king, and chopped off his thumbs and big toes. Why? Adoni-bezek himself gave the answer when he said, "Threescore and ten kings, having their thumbs and their great toes cut off, gathered their meat under my table: as I have done, so God hath requited me" (Judges 1:7).

If you chop up someone, or cut down someone, watch out. Jesus said the way you judge is the way you'll be judged.

Matthew 7:3–5
And why beholdest thou the mote that is in thy brother's eye, but considerest not the beam that is in thine own eye? Or how wilt thou say to thy brother, Let me pull out the mote out of thine eye; and, behold, a beam is in thine own eye? Thou hypocrite, first cast out the beam out of thine own eye; and then shalt thou see clearly to cast out the mote out of thy brother's eye.

I find this fascinating because the words Jesus used imply that the speck—the splinter I see in my brother's eye—is of the same exact material as the beam in my own eye, only smaller in dimension. That's why I can spot certain sins in other people very easily. They're my sins. Whatever sins you struggle with personally are the sins you will point out in others most readily. David found this to be true. The prophet Nathan came to him and said, "David, we have a problem. There's a rich man who has all sorts of sheep. Someone came to visit him, and instead of going out to his own herds and taking one of his own lambs, this rich man went to his neighbor who was very poor, grabbed his neighbor's one and only lamb, and killed it to serve his guest."

Outraged, David said, "What? The man who has done this thing shall surely die!" The Old Testament Law never prescribed death as the penalty for this kind of transgression. Yet, with blood vessels bursting and finger pointing, David said, "Kill him!"

Then Nathan said, "David, thou art the man. It's you. You have many wives and concubines, yet you stole Uriah's wife, Bathsheba, and you took her into your house. Thou art the man."

Why was David so eager to mete out excessive judgment? Because we're always harshest with the sin in others that also lurks within our own hearts. The old saying is true: You can always tell a preacher's sins by what he preaches against. And Jesus is saying, "If you see splinters in others, realize it's a splinter off the beam that is in your own eye."

Jesus is not saying you shouldn't help the brother who has a splinter in his eye. Instead, He is saying to make sure you recognize and deal with the beam in your own eye first. "Create in *me* a clean heart, O God," David prayed. "*Then* will I teach transgressors thy ways" (see Psalm 51:10, 13, emphasis mine). "Once You deal with me, Lord, my attitude will be entirely different as I deal with others."

Matthew 7:6
Give not that which is holy unto the dogs, neither cast ye your pearls before swine, lest they trample them under their feet, and turn again and rend you.

To be effective in ministry, we must make judgments—not for condemnation, but for identification. Is this person open? Is he sensitive? Is he hungering? Or does he just want to argue and discuss endlessly? The Lord loves to see us effective, and Satan would love to see us sidetracked. How do we know what is wise in these matters? How can we know what we should do and where we should invest our time? How does this work out practically? Jesus gives the answer in the next verse.

Matthew 7:7–11
Ask, and it shall be given you; seek, and ye shall find; knock, and it shall be opened unto you: For every one that asketh receiveth; and he that seeketh findeth; and to him that knocketh it shall be opened. Or what man is there of you, whom if his son ask bread, will he give him a stone? Or if he ask a fish, will he give him a serpent? If ye then, being evil, know how to give good gifts unto your children, how much more shall your Father which is in heaven give good things to them that ask him?

Ask your Father! In the Greek language, it's written this way: Keep asking and it shall be given. Keep seeking and you shall find. Keep knocking and it will be opened. The tense used speaks of continual action. When you don't know what to do, *keep* asking, *keep* seeking, *keep* knocking.

Now, please bear in mind folks that God does not want us to keep asking and keep seeking and

keep knocking because He's playing hard to get. It's not as though He's holding a dog biscuit out to me, saying, "Speak, Jon. Speak." No, that's not the heart of our Father. Rather, He is determined to cultivate a relationship with me that will be as vital in the ages to come as it is presently. Thus, He says to us, "I want you to be continually asking, continually seeking, continually knocking because you need the exercise in developing spiritual communication skills. And as you do, I'll take care of you. I'm not going to allow you to bite into a rock or eat a snake. I'll guide you and give you wisdom."

Matthew 7:12
Therefore all things whatsoever ye would that men should do to you, do ye even so to them: for this is the law and the prophets.

When you come across the word "therefore," you should always stop and ask what it's "there for." In this verse, commonly known as the Golden Rule, it precedes a summation of verses 1 through 11.

Matthew 7:13, 14
Enter ye in at the strait gate: for wide is the gate, and broad is the way, that leadeth to destruction, and many there be which go in thereat: Because strait is the gate, and narrow is the way, which leadeth unto life, and few there be that find it.

I went down the Rogue River in Oregon in a jet boat one summer, and when we came to Hell's Gate, the water seemed so tranquil with rock canyons on either side. But our guide said, "The water below you right now is one hundred fifty feet-deep, and because the river is channeled into such a small area, it is incredibly powerful." When filming the John Wayne movie *Rooster Cogburn*, one of the scenes called for a guy to jump from one of the cliffs at Hell's Gate into this 150-feet deep pool of water. The stunt man studied the currents and found that about four or five feet below the seeming tranquility of the surface, there were whirlpools that could have sucked him straight down. Although this stunt man was paid $150,000 for one jump, afterward, he said he would never do it again.

Jesus said, "Narrow is the way that leads to life." When things get narrow, they get strong, deep, and powerful.

For topical study of Matthew 7:13–14 entitled "Why One Way?" turn to page 45.

Matthew 7:15
Beware of false prophets, which come to you in sheep's clothing, but inwardly they are ravening wolves.

In Acts 20, Paul said the same thing to the elders at Ephesus: "When I leave, men will rise up, and draw disciples to themselves." He called such men ravenous wolves, even as Jesus did here. How will you know them? Acts 20 says they will seek to draw men after themselves instead of pointing them to Jesus. Secondly, 2 Peter 2:3 says these ravenous wolves will make merchandise of you. They'll go for your pocketbooks, concerned not so much about feeding you as they are about fleecing you.

The writings that circulated among the early church, called the Didache, specifically stated that if a man said, "Thus saith the Lord. I have need of a steak dinner and a new garment," he was to be branded as a false prophet immediately. Beware of any man who preaches about his own needs.

One of Aesop's fables is about a hungry wolf that put a sheepskin over himself and cruised into the sheepfold. It just so happened that the same night, the shepherd also had a strange craving for mutton. So he went out to his sheepfold and plunged his knife into the biggest sheep within the flock, which, of course, turned out to be the wolf.

The wolf who was disguised as a sheep was eventually dealt with by the shepherd. So, too, our Good Shepherd watches out for His flock.

Matthew 7:16–20
Ye shall know them by their fruits. Do men gather grapes of thorns, or figs of thistles? Even so every good tree bringeth forth good fruit; but a corrupt tree bringeth forth evil fruit. A good tree cannot bring forth evil fruit, neither can a corrupt tree bring forth good fruit. Every tree that bringeth not forth good fruit is hewn down, and cast into the fire. Wherefore by their fruits ye shall know them.

We are not to be judges, but we are to look for fruit. The fruit we are to look for is not flawless, because we are all full of flaws and shortcomings. No, the issue is not flawlessness, but fruitfulness. The tree that has a lot of leaves but no real fruit is going to be dealt with severely when it is hewn down and cast into the fire.

Matthew 7:21, 22
Not every one that saith unto me, Lord, Lord, shall enter into the kingdom of heaven; but he that doeth the will of my Father which

is in heaven. Many will say to me in that day, Lord, Lord, have we not prophesied in thy name? and in thy name have cast out devils? and in thy name done many wonderful works?

Many of these wolves and false trees will come to Jesus and say, "But, Lord, didn't we prophesy? Didn't we cast out demons? Didn't we do miracles?" The question arises, "How could these wolves, these false leaders, these bogus trees do these things? How could they prophesy, cast out demons, and do miracles if they were fakes?" There are three possible answers.

One is that they were lying. They never did them. Maybe they just thought about doing them, or thought they were doing them. Second, it is possible they were doing these things in the power of the devil. The Book of Acts talks about Simon the Sorcerer, who did miracles, but not in the power of the Spirit. In Moses' day, Pharaoh's magicians copied, to a certain extent, the miracles of God, but it was by the power of the devil. Third, the Lord could have been simply using them in spite of themselves. The Lord used Balaam, even though Balaam was not right with Him. He prophesied through King Saul, even though Saul's heart was far from Him. He spoke prophetically through Caiaphas the high priest, saying, "Should not one man die for the nation?" although Caiaphas knew it not.

Notice that many will say, "Did not *we* prophesy?" Always be wary of people who promote themselves in ministry. Whenever I hear a ministry say, "Look what *we* are doing," bells ring, and red flags go up in my mind because Jesus taught humility and secrecy.

Matthew 7:23
And then will I profess unto them, I never knew you: depart from me, ye that work iniquity.

Engraved in a cathedral in Germany are these words: Thus speaketh Christ our Lord to us.

You Call Me Master

You call Me Master and obey Me not.
You call Me Light and see Me not.
You call Me the Way and walk Me not.
You call Me Life and choose Me not.
You call Me Wise and follow Me not.
You call Me Fair and love Me not.
You call Me Rich and ask Me not.
You call Me Eternal and seek Me not.
You call Me Noble and serve Me not.

You call Me Gracious and trust Me not.
You call Me Might and honor Me not.
You call Me Just and fear Me not.
If I condemn you, blame Me not.

For topical study of Matthew 7:21–23 entitled
"Sincerely Saved," turn to page 47.

Matthew 7:24–27
Therefore whosoever heareth these sayings of mine, and doeth them, I will liken him unto a wise man, which built his house upon a rock: And the rain descended, and the floods came, and the winds blew, and beat upon that house; and it fell not: for it was founded upon a rock. And every one that heareth these sayings of mine, and doeth them not, shall be likened unto a foolish man, which built his house upon the sand: And the rain descended, and the floods came, and the winds blew, and beat upon that house; and it fell: and great was the fall of it.

Here is the familiar story of two men building houses. Both men used the same material. Both built in the same geographical location. But one man's house stood while the other man's house collapsed. The difference was in the foundations. One built on the rock, the other on the sand. In Palestine, all land becomes parched in the summer, causing even the sandy and unstable areas to appear rock-solid. The true test doesn't come until the rain falls. Jesus here is saying, "Be careful where you build your house. Build on something tried and true. Build upon the Rock."

Who is the one who builds his house upon the rock? The one who hears the Words of the Lord and does them. Who is the one who builds on the sand? The one who hears His Words but doesn't do them.

One of the great dangers for we who love the Scriptures is to think hearing is equivalent to doing. You might say tonight, "Yeah, I agree with the teaching Jesus gave on judging. I shouldn't judge. I need to show mercy. Right on." But if you leave here and immediately turn to someone and start gossiping or analyzing, judging or critiquing, you're foolish, and your house will collapse.

We have such need to hear these words of Jesus because Bible students are in great danger of being foolish men who erroneously conclude that because they are hearing the truth and agreeing with the truth, they are automatically practicing the truth. The wise man not only hears Jesus' words but also puts them into practice. And his house stands when the storm comes.

For topical study of Matthew 7:24–27 entitled
"When Bad Things Happen to Good People,"
turn to page 53.

Matthew 7:28, 29
And it came to pass, when Jesus had ended these sayings, the people were astonished at his doctrine: For he taught them as one having authority, and not as the scribes.

After this thirty-minute sermon, the people were amazed, accustomed as they were to hearing teaching by scribes who did nothing more than quote other scribes. "Rabbi So-and-So says . . . but Rabbi So-and-So disagrees. So Rabbi So-and-So proposes."

After hearing all these rabbis, a person would say, "Wait a minute. This is crazy. What's the solution? Where's the authority? There's no conclusion!"

Jesus said, "You have heard it said of old, but I say unto you . . . ."

The crowds marveled, "Wow!" they said. "He speaks with authority, and what He says makes sense."

Did the masses then say, "We're going to follow Him! This is great! He's our Man!"? No. That's not what happened. Why? C. S. Lewis, in his classic book, *Mere Christianity,* gives this answer:

When I was a child I often had toothaches, and I knew that if I went to my mother she would give me something which would deaden the pain for that night and let me get to sleep. But I did not go to my mother—at least, not till the pain became very bad. And the reason I did not go was this. I did not doubt she would give me the aspirin; but I knew she would also do something else. I knew she would take me to the dentist next morning. I could not get what I wanted out of her without getting something more, which I did not want. I wanted immediate relief from pain: but I could not get it without having my teeth set permanently right. And I knew those dentists; I knew they started fiddling about with all sorts of other teeth which had not yet begun to ache. They would not let sleeping dogs lie.[1]

That's why I thank the Lord for the saints at Applegate Christian Fellowship. Because they, as a group of rag-tag disciples, say, "Lord, we have a toothache, and You are the dentist. Keep on drilling. Sleeping dogs notwithstanding, Father, do whatever it takes to make us right."

WHY ONE WAY?
A Topical Study of
MATTHEW 7:13, 14

Over and over again, I find myself dialoguing on this particular point with unbelievers who say, "We like Jesus, but we reject the exclusive mentality you propagate." Why do people feel this way? I suggest to you it is because our culture—our generation in particular—is more interested in equality than in truth. We are more afraid of being thought prejudiced or bigoted than of being wrong. We are scared to death of being labeled narrow-minded.

Yet, that is exactly what Jesus Christ calls us to. He came on the scene and said there is an exclusive mentality to Christianity. He was direct and straightforward when He said, "Enter ye in at the strait gate: for wide is the gate, and broad is the way, that leadeth to destruction, and many there be which go in thereat: Because strait is the gate, and narrow is the way, which leadeth unto life, and few there be that find it" (Matthew 7:13, 14).

Why is Christianity so exclusive and so narrow? First of all, narrowness is God's protection of us.

God is saying, "I understand the frailty of humanity and that you are but children. So I will keep it real simple. The options? Only two: Jesus Christ or eternal death. That's it."

There are those who say, "All paths lead to God. You can embrace any philosophy and follow any guru as long as you're sincere. They all lead to heaven, bliss, or nirvana." But I ask them, "Do you believe those who followed the teachings of Jim Jones in Guyana were following a godly path as they drank Kool-Aid laced with cyanide? Do you believe if you followed Charles Manson sincerely, you would end up in the right spot eternally? Do you believe sincerely following Adolf Hitler, who used Scripture and quoted theologians, would lead to heaven?"

You see, if the Lord had fifteen legitimate paths to heaven, the Enemy would still counter with fifteen thousand illegitimate destructive paths, and it would still be confusing. There will always be Adolf Hitlers, Charlie Mansons, and Jim Joneses who will be deceptive and manipulative, weird and destructive. So our Father, in His wisdom, says, "Kids, I'm going to keep it real simple. There are not fifteen paths or eighteen paths. No. There's only one Way: Jesus, My Son."

Second, God made Christianity exclusive not only as protection for us, but as a proclamation to us. Jesus said, "I am the way, the truth, and the life: no man cometh unto the Father, but by me" (John 14:6). In Greek, it is most clear that He is saying, "I am the only way. There is no other way to enter into the presence of the Father but by Me." God's proclamation is exceedingly clear to any and all who will listen.

Third, and most importantly, narrow is the gate because of God's provision for us. If, indeed, there are many paths to God and many routes to eternal life, then the sacrifice God made in becoming a Man—slaughtered before the foundation of the world, plunging into hell, suffering in ways we will never comprehend—was all unnecessary.

If you say, "Well, let's be open-minded about the way to heaven," you discount the provision of what God did on your behalf. Mohammed didn't die for you. Buddha wouldn't die for you.

Only Jesus gave everything to save you from your sins.

> Mohammed came on the scene and said, "Do not look at me. My teachings are my essence."
>
> Buddha never claimed to be anything of a godly man at all. In fact, his religion or philosophy is basically atheistic.
>
> Hinduism is pantheistic.
>
> Jesus alone says, "It's Me. I am the Way."

You will hear over and over again that "Spirituality is a journey up a holy mountain, and no matter which route you take, when you get to the top, you will find God. So just wander wherever you feel inclined and embrace the other pilgrims on their paths. Don't try to convert them, for every route leads to the top of the mountain, and they will find God just as you will." Bunk. The analogy is all wrong. You see, it is not any mountain upon which God sits and man meanders. It is El Capitan—a sheer face, a stone where there are no handholds and no toeholds—a rock that is insurmountable and un-climbable.

God is holy, folks. He is not some sort of portly gentleman sitting on top of a hill, saying, "Any Buddha or guru who can find Me is wonderful." Rather, He is high and holy on the top of a sheer face, and although man is sinful, God in His love reaches down to him. It is not man meandering up to God. It is God reaching down to man, saying, "I will elevate you and save you if you grab hold of Me through the Person of My Son."

Every religion is man trying to make it up the mountain. Christianity alone says, "You're out to lunch, off the wall, and hopelessly lost—but I love you. And I'm reaching down to you. Grab My hand."

> Before I mow the grass, suppose I see a group of ants headed for destruction, and wanting their lives to be spared from the mower, I say, "Ants, repent! Hide! Run from the judgment to come!"
>
> They would look at me and scratch their heads. They wouldn't comprehend what I was saying because I'm too big. So the only way I could communicate effectively with them would be to become one of them—to become an ant myself.

God declared His holiness and righteousness and love to us, but we didn't hear Him. In His awesomeness, we couldn't comprehend Him.

So God became a Man, an ant, if you would, in the Person of Jesus, and He dwelt among us, not only to communicate to us truth, but to die for us when we violated that truth.

No one else did that. No one else could. No one else would. Only Jesus.

I am narrow-minded because Jesus Christ said, "I am the Way, the Truth, and the Life."

Jesus is God's protection *of* me, God's proclamation *to* me, and God's glorious provision *for* me.

That's fact. That's reality.

SINCERELY SAVED
A Topical Study of
MATTHEW 7:21–23

It was his farewell gathering. Knowing he was on his way to Rome where he could be beheaded, Paul gave final instruction to a group of elders from the church in Ephesus. "For three years," he said, "I have taught you and warned you with many tears" (see Acts 20).

If a shepherd only warns the flock, but never feeds them, they will die of malnutrition. If he only feeds the flock and never warns them, he is simply fattening them up for the kill.

In the Sermon on the Mount, the Good Shepherd both fed and warned His flock as the masses gathered around Him on the hillside. He began by talking about the pathway to happiness. His first words were "Blessed, or happy, are the poor in spirit. Happy are they who mourn. Happy are the meek."

Then He talked about the highway of holiness. Many people thought they were pretty good and fairly holy because they didn't commit murder or adultery. But Jesus explained to them that if they were angry with their brother without a cause, they were guilty of murder. If they had looked at a woman with lust in their heart, they were adulterers. Such teaching would drive people to realize that no one is holy, that all are sinners, and that everyone needs a Savior.

Finally, He taught that the broad way is hazardous, concluding His Sermon with this sober exhortation: "There are choices you must make concerning the right way and the wrong way."

There are two gates. Narrow is the gate that leads to life and broad is the way that leads to damnation. You've got to make a choice, and the wrong choice will be hazardous to your eternal state.

There are two trees. When you're wondering whom you should listen to or receive from, check out the fruit. A good tree cannot bear bad fruit, and a bad tree cannot bear good fruit. Watch out for deception.

There are two foundations. The wise man builds his house upon the rock, and the foolish man builds his house upon the sand. The wrong choice will lead to destruction. You'll lose everything.

It is in this context that we find our text—an extremely sobering, heavy-duty warning. What does it mean, and does it apply to us? In Acts 8, we see an example of one who could say, "Lord, Lord, did I not prophesy? Cast out demons? Do wonderful works?" We see a man who had religion, but not relationship, activity, but not intimacy. Perhaps his story will make us think about our own situations personally.

And Saul was consenting unto his death. And at that time there was a great persecution against the church which was at Jerusalem; and they were all scattered abroad throughout the regions of Judaea and Samaria, except the apostles. And devout men carried Stephen to his burial, and made great lamentation over him. As for Saul, he made havoc of the church, entering into every house, and haling men and women committed them to prison.   Acts 8:1–3

Saul was a man who was radically devoted to God—a Pharisee and a scholar. Believing that Christians were a dangerous cult, Saul thought he was doing God a favor by pulling them from their houses, beating them, and imprisoning them.

Therefore they that were scattered abroad went every where preaching the word.   Acts 8:4

Fleeing persecution, the church spread out. Christians went everywhere, and as they went, they preached the Word.

Then Philip went down to the city of Samaria, and preached Christ unto them.
                                                                                                          Acts 8:5

One believer, a man named Philip, went to the city of Samaria, which is located between Jerusalem to the south and Galilee to the north. This must have totally confounded the Samaritans, who knew the Jews took great pains to avoid even traveling through their region.

And the people with one accord gave heed unto those things which Philip spake, hearing and seeing the miracles which he did. For unclean spirits, crying with loud voice, came out of many that were possessed with them: and many taken with palsies, and that were lame, were healed. And there was great joy in that city.   Acts 8:6–8

The Samaritans were confounded that Philip came, convicted by what he said, and convinced by what they saw. The lame were healed, the oppressed were delivered, and the entire city was filled with joy.

But there was a certain man, called Simon, which beforetime in the same city used sorcery, and bewitched the people of Samaria, giving out that himself was some great one: To whom they all gave heed, from the least to the greatest, saying, This man is the great power of God. And to him they had regard, because that of long time he had bewitched them with sorceries.   Acts 8:9–11

Simon had been on the scene for many years. He was fascinating to the people and had a certain power over them because of his magic tricks. He made himself out to be someone great, and the people thought he possessed the power of God.

But when they believed Philip preaching the things concerning the kingdom of God, and the name of Jesus Christ, they were baptized, both men and women.
Acts 8:12

Although the Samaritans were confounded that Philip came, convicted by what he said, convinced by what they saw, they were not converted until they heard the message concerning the kingdom of God and the Name of Jesus Christ. Miracles do not convert people. Deliverance from demons does not convert people. Good deeds and good works do not convert people. What converts people is the message of the kingdom of God in the Name of Jesus Christ.

In John 10, we read that many came to Jesus and said of John the Baptist, "John did no mighty miracles, but all things he spake concerning this Man are true" (see verse 41). Jesus called John the greatest of all Old Testament prophets not because John did miracles, but because John spoke about Him. This encourages me because, although I might not be able to confound people with my good works or convince people with signs and wonders, I can see the conversion of people as I share this simple Gospel: Jesus loves you. He died for you. He wants to live within you.

When the Samaritans heard the preaching of the kingdom in the Name of Jesus, they were baptized, which is an outward sign of an inward acceptance.

Then Simon himself believed also: and when he was baptized, he continued with Philip, and wondered, beholding the miracles and signs which were done. Now when the apostles which were at Jerusalem heard that Samaria had received the word of God, they sent unto them Peter and John: Who, when they were come down, prayed for them, that they might receive the Holy Ghost: (For as yet he was fallen upon none of them: only they were baptized in the name of the Lord Jesus.) Then laid they their hands on them, and they received the Holy Ghost. And when Simon saw that through laying on of the apostles" hands the Holy Ghost was given, he offered them money, saying, Give me also this power, that on whomsoever I lay hands, he may receive the Holy Ghost. But Peter said unto him, Thy money perish with thee, because thou hast thought that the gift of God may be purchased with money. Thou hast neither part nor lot in this matter: for thy heart is not right in the sight of God. Repent therefore of this thy wickedness, and pray God, if perhaps the thought of thine heart may be forgiven thee. For I perceive that thou art in the gall of bitterness, and in the bond of iniquity. Then answered Simon, and said, Pray ye to the Lord for me, that none of these things which ye have spoken come upon me.

Acts 8:13–24

Although Simon professed to believe and was baptized, in reality Peter said, "You are in the gall of bitterness, in the bond of iniquity." In other words, "Your conversion is not real. And you're in big trouble."

Why wasn't Simon's conversion real? What went wrong?

First, Simon had a wrong view of self. Verse 9 says he made himself out to be someone great. That's the first problem. Jesus said if you want to be great in the kingdom, become the servant *of* all. Simon wanted to be esteemed and noticed *by* all.

How are you doing in the area of servanthood? We sing the song, "Lord, make me a servant." But how do you react when people treat you like a servant—when they don't thank or compliment you on what you've done? A servant serves without expecting acknowledgment. Jesus said if you want to be great, become the servant of all.

Second, Simon had a wrong view of supernatural power. When he saw that the laying on of hands by the apostles gave the believers in Samaria power, he said, "Give me also this power, that on whomsoever I lay hands, he may receive the Holy Ghost" (see verse 19). He didn't want the power of the Spirit to change his character, only to fulfill his ambition. This is where King Saul, from the Old Testament, blew it. Saul used the things of God to exalt himself. David, on the other hand, allowed himself to be used to exalt God. That's why Saul fell tragically and David was used powerfully.

Do you have a wrong view of supernatural power? Do you pray, "Give me power that I might accomplish this task and fulfill that ambition"? Or do you pray, "Give me the power of Your Spirit to break me and make me more like Your Son"?

Third, notice in Simon a wrong view of the Spirit. In verse 20, Peter said, "You don't understand, Simon, that the gift of God is not purchased with money, nor is it earned by energy. It is a gift that is bestowed freely by God's grace and mercy. You don't earn it, you don't prove that you are worthy of it, and you can't buy it."

And yet people today, like Simon, say, "What can I do to earn the Spirit? I'll fast for thirty days. I'll go to church every week for three months. I won't kick the dog anymore. I'll give to the building fund. I'll do this, that, or the other, and maybe then God will bless me."

That's a wrong view of the Spirit. You cannot purchase Him with energy or with money. Jesus said, "If you then being evil know how to give good gifts to your children, how much more will the heavenly Father give the Holy Ghost to them that *ask*" (see Luke 11:13). You just ask for the Spirit in humility, with expectancy, and according to God's grace and mercy.

Fourth, Simon had a wrong view of sin. When told he was in sin, he said to Peter, "Pray ye to the Lord for me, that none of these things which ye have spoken come upon me" There was not confession, there was not repentance, there was only a concern about repercussions. Although Simon believed initially and was baptized physically, he was headed for damnation eternally because of his wrong view of self, of supernatural power, of the Spirit, and of sin.

There are those today who are in danger of the same thing. You might say, "Well, I believe in Jesus." But the Book of James says that even the demons believe. Intellectual belief isn't enough. Salvation takes place when you put your full trust in Jesus Christ and Him alone.

"But I work for Jesus," you might say. "I teach Sunday school," or "I'm a part of the worship team." You might even lead a Bible study, but that doesn't assure you a place in the kingdom. You might do many wonderful works, but if you're not walking with the Lord personally and intimately, you're in danger of damnation eternally.

No wonder Peter pleads in 2 Peter 1:10, "Make your calling and election sure." What does it mean to make your calling and election sure, to be truly saved? Let's look again at Acts 8.

> *And they, when they had testified and preached the word of the Lord, returned to Jerusalem, and preached the gospel in many villages of the Samaritans. And the angel of the Lord spake unto Philip, saying, Arise, and go toward the south unto the way that goeth down from Jerusalem unto Gaza, which is desert. And he arose and went: and, behold, a man of Ethiopia, an eunuch of great authority under Candace queen of the Ethiopians, who had the charge of all her treasure, and had come to Jerusalem for to worship, was returning, and sitting in his chariot read Esaias the prophet.*   Acts 8:25–28

After Philip left Samaria, the angel of the Lord told him to go south toward the desert where he would encounter an Ethiopian eunuch reading from the Book of Isaiah.

> *Then the Spirit said unto Philip, Go near, and join thyself to this chariot. And Philip ran thither to him, and heard him read the prophet Esaias, and said, Understandest thou what thou readest?*   Acts 8:29–30

Philip caught up with him and asked, "Do you understand what you're reading?"

And he said, How can I, except some man should guide me? And he desired Philip that he would come up and sit with him.   Acts 8:31

The eunuch "happened" to be reading Isaiah 53:7, 8, and he asked Philip of whom the passage was speaking.

Then Philip opened his mouth, and began at the same scripture, and preached unto him Jesus.   Acts 8:35

There can be no finer exposition, no higher teaching, no more effective preaching than using the Word of God to point to the Son of God.

And as they went on their way, they came unto a certain water: and the eunuch said, See, here is water; what doth hinder me to be baptized? And Philip said, If thou believest with all thine heart, thou mayest. And he answered and said, I believe that Jesus Christ is the Son of God. And he commanded the chariot to stand still: and they went down both into the water, both Philip and the eunuch; and he baptized him. And when they were come up out of the water, the Spirit of the Lord caught away Philip, that the eunuch saw him no more: and he went on his way rejoicing.   Acts 8:36–39

This is true conversion.

First, we see in this story the sovereign work of the Spirit. It was a sovereign work of the Spirit when He drew the Ethiopian to Jerusalem to worship. It was an equally sovereign work of the Spirit when He said to Philip, "Leave the revival of Samaria. Go to the desert. There's a man there I want you to meet."

Second, we see the seeking heart of a sinner. The eunuch was searching the Scripture, not watching a miracle.

Third, there was a Scriptural base for salvation. When Philip said, "Isaiah is talking about Jesus Christ," he based his witness upon the Word. James declares faith comes by hearing, and hearing by the Word of God.

Finally, there was a sincere expression by the servant. Unlike Simon the sorcerer, the Ethiopian eunuch didn't say, "Give me power." He said, "Baptize me."

Every one of us falls into one of these two categories: Either we are like Simon the Sorcerer, or we are like the Ethiopian eunuch. Both stories are in the same chapter of Acts. Both take place in a similar situation. But each has an entirely different conclusion.

You may have been baptized fifty times or more, but when you see God, you may hear Him say, "Depart from Me. I never knew you." You might be one who's hung around the church for years—maybe you even hold a prominent position. But familiarity alone is no guarantee. The most successful skydiver in history died when he took a jump and halfway down realized he forgot to pack his parachute.

Jesus talked more about damnation and hell than any other subject because He knew its reality. He was a Good Shepherd who said, "This is serious."

How do you know if your salvation is real?

If you are feeling like Simon the sorcerer—in the grasp and dominion of sin—then you are in jeopardy. Repent today, and be finally, truly, and eternally saved.

If, however, you are like the Ethiopian eunuch, you will go your way rejoicing. Romans 8 declares His Spirit bears witness with our spirit that we are the children of God. Thus, you will rejoice in your heart, and you will know that you know that you know you're born again. No one will have to talk you into it or convince you of it because you will have *His* witness in your heart.

WHEN BAD THINGS HAPPEN TO GOOD PEOPLE
A Topical Study of
MATTHEW 7:24–27

When a Congressman was killed in a plane crash after researching United States assistance in the Ethiopian famine, the words of the minister conducting his memorial service caught my attention. "Why good people experience tragedy, I can't say," he said. "Why bad things happen to good people, I don't know."

This statement has been stirring in my mind for some time now. Why do bad things happen to good people? Are there no answers? Whether concerning lives lost in Ethiopia, or your own situation of the past week or two, people always ask the question: Why do bad things happen to good people? A few years ago, a best-selling book was entitled just that: *Why Bad Things Happen to Good People*. The author concluded there are no real answers, even as the minister said there are no easy answers. I suggest to you, however, that there is a profoundly simple answer to this question. It is this: There are no good people.

> *As it is written, There is none righteous, no, not one: There is none that understandeth, there is none that seeketh after God. They are all gone out of the way, they are together become unprofitable; there is none that doeth good, no, not one.*   Romans 3:10–12

You see, the world thinks, "I'm Okay, you're Okay." But regardless of what psychologists tell us, this just isn't so, for those who look to worldly understandings and explanations miss the central truth: There are no good people. So the real question is not "Why do bad things happen to good people?" but "Why do good things happen to bad people?"

You might have had a bad day or a terrible time this last month or two. But what we deserve is to live in terror, in tragedy, in difficulty every day of our lives because there is none that is good, no, not one.

"Why, then," we sometimes wonder, "are good things happening to those people who live next to me? They're not in church today; they're out on the lake water-skiing. Yet they get the raises and promotions. Why do good things happen to them?"

The first verse my kids learned was Psalm 73:1, "God is good," followed by 1 John 4:16, "God is love," because I'm convinced that the first concepts we should teach our kids are the goodness and the love of God. He is a loving Father who causes His sun to rise on the just and on the unjust, sending rain upon the crops of the good and on the evil (Matthew 5:45). God loves to bless because He is good.

I once read a quote that said, "God is the victim of bad PR, usually propagated by those who know Him." Too often, believers and unbelievers alike generate the false idea that, although God occasionally does a good thing, He's basically mean. We hear sermons and testimonies to that effect, saying, "God got my attention when He broke my legs and took away my house and caused me to go bankrupt." That's not Father God, that's the Godfather!

One of the great frustrations I have in talking with unbelievers is their impression that they have to wait until their marriage is on the rocks, until their finances are crumbling, until cancer is eating them up before they will consider Christ. They think their lives have to fall apart before they turn to Jesus.

So to the person who's skiing on the lake today, behind his power boat, beside his cabin, having left his five-thousand-square-foot house in the city, we shouldn't say, "God's going to get you"—but, "Hasn't God been *good* to you?"

The Bible says God demonstrated His love for us all in that while we were yet sinners, Christ died for us (Romans 5:8), but people in the world today have lost this understanding. They don't realize that God demonstrated His love for all people when Jesus died for us, that God looked at us and desired to bless us, even while we were still sinners. Rain falls on the just and the unjust (Matthew 5:45). The sun shines on the believer and the unbeliever because God is good. Everything He gives us is because of grace—unmerited, undeserved, unearned favor. But if we don't recognize this, if we misinterpret the source of our blessings, we become narrow, bitter, and full of sorrow.

In our text, Jesus says a day is coming when the rains will fall and the winds shall beat on the house of every man. Of what storm is He speaking? Death. The statistics are conclusive: Ten out of ten people die. Every person who has ever lived since Jesus spoke these words has built his house and done his thing until the storm came, at which point it was determined whether he had built upon the rock or upon the sand.

Jesus ended His Sermon on the Mount speaking of—

- two roads: one unto life, one to destruction;
- two trees: one of fruitfulness, one of failure;
- two foundations: one to stand, one to collapse.

The choice is yours. Upon which foundation are you building?

"Wait," you say. "I have one more question. If God is our good Father, why does He allow the devil to inflict pain and disease, destruction and death, discouragement and difficulty? Can't God stop the devil and put an end to our misery?"

Yes, He can. And yes, He will. But presently, God allows storms to arise that test our foundation in order that we might see where we stand eternally.

Several years ago on the East Coast, cod fishermen began to experience a real demand for their product, and they began to ship frozen cod all over the country. They discovered one drawback, however. In the freezing process, the cod lost their flavor. To remedy this, the fishermen shipped their cod live in saltwater tanks to be processed once they reached their destination.

The fish arrived okay, but because they were sitting in these tanks, they became spongy and soft. For several years, the fishermen didn't know what to do. Then someone had a brilliant idea: Ship the fish in saltwater tanks, but throw in some catfish—the natural enemy of the codfish. They tried it. The catfish chased the cod all around the tank as they traveled cross-country, and when the cod arrived, those that made it alive were flavorful and were sold at premium prices.

The catfish were necessary to keep the cod moving, thereby enhancing their texture and flavor.

So, too, God says to us,

"Because I want the best for you both now and in eternity, I will allow an occasional catfish to come into your tank and chase you around for a little while. Otherwise, you'll just sit around and get soft."

- I will not test you above that which you are able (1 Corinthians 10:13).
- I will always be there for you (Matthew 28:20).
- Call upon Me in the day of trouble (Psalm 50:15).
- Cast your care upon Me (1 Peter 5:7).
- And remember, all things are working together for good (Romans 8:28).
- Trust Me (Psalm 37:3).

Build your life on the Rock, gang. Jesus is a sure foundation, and He won't let you down.

8Matthew is the gospel of the King. In the first four chapters, His Person is revealed. In chapters 5 through 7, His principles are recorded. But the question arises: Does Jesus have the power to carry out those principles? Or is He, like so many of our leaders, a nice person with good principles, yet impotent to really make a difference? In Matthew 8, 9, and 10, we find the answer as we see the power of Jesus released.

In the following three chapters, Matthew records ten miracles which show Jesus not only had the rhetoric, but He had the dynamic to make things happen.

Matthew 8:1, 2 (a)
When he was come down from the mountain, great multitudes followed him. And, behold, there came a leper . . .

I think it fitting that the first miracle recorded in the New Testament deals with the cleansing of a leper because Isaiah 1:5, 6 makes it clear that leprosy is a picture of sin. Leviticus 13 teaches that leprosy begins beneath the surface of the skin—just as sin does. What you see outwardly in people's lives is only the result of what is going on within them. We are not sinners because we sin. We sin because we're sinners. Leviticus 13 goes on to say that leprosy, like sin, spreads throughout the body. Like sin, one could control it for a season. But if he didn't destroy it, it would eventually destroy him. The Talmud taught that leprosy was second only to death in its list of sixty-one defilements. He who had leprosy was as good as dead because his disease would separate him from the rest of the community. When a person contracted leprosy, he was forced to live only with fellow lepers. If he had to come to the city, the Law required him to cry out, "Unclean, unclean," in order for everyone within a one hundred fifty-foot radius to back away and clear the area. In the beginning stages, the skin of a leper would take on a hard, glossy appearance. As it progressed, it caused his nerves to become numb, which in turn led to the loss of fingers and toes.

The rabbis felt strongly that leprosy was a direct judgment from God. In fact, the word "leprosy" means "smitten." They felt that those who had leprosy were being judged by God and therefore must be terrible people.

Matthew 8:2 (b)
. . . and worshipped him, saying, Lord, if thou wilt, thou canst make me clean.

This leper, whose sickness was a symbol of sin, saw Jesus and had the audacity to go right through the multitude following Him and say, "Lord, if You want, You can make me clean." He didn't doubt Jesus' ability to make him clean; he doubted Jesus' willingness to do so. And I suggest to you that, like this leper, there's not one of us who doubts Jesus' ability to do the miraculous in our lives. But I suggest every one of us at times doubts His willingness.

- "Lord, if You want, You can heal my marriage," we pray.
- "If You want, You can save my child."
- "If You want, Lord, You can take away this habit, free me from that bondage, deal with my leprosy."

We know He *can,* but we question if He *will.*

This leper had the courage, the tenacity, and the audacity to approach Jesus and to come right into His presence. But like you and me, when he got there, he wondered, "Do You really *want* to make me clean?"

Matthew 8:3 (a)
And Jesus put forth his hand, and touched him. . . .

To this one with gross, running sores, and a strained voice, odor emanating, and digits missing, Jesus could have said, "Be clean," and the guy would have been clean. But what did Jesus do? He touched him. Regardless of the sin you might be struggling with right now, don't make the mistake of countless thousands of lepers saying, "I need to stay away from Jesus. I'm unclean." Jesus can handle your sin. He's not shocked or horrified by it. He's not embarrassed of it. Jesus touched the leper, and He can handle your sin as well.

The biggest mistake people make concerning Jesus is thinking, "When I get it together, *then* I'll let the Lord come near me. When I deal with my leprosy, *then* I'll let the Lord touch me."

But they'll never get it together *until* the Lord touches them!

You who are faltering in faith, struggling in sin,

caught up in carnality, I have news for you. Jesus can handle it.

Not only are there those who say, "Don't touch me until I get it together," but there are those who say, "Touch me, Lord. I want to come into Your presence. I want to lift my hands and sing Your praise. But don't change me. I like myself just the way I am."

If the Lord touches you, you will inevitably be changed. If you don't want to be changed, it's vain to seek His touch.

Matthew 8:3 (b)
. . . saying, I will; be thou clean. And immediately his leprosy was cleansed.

How I love these words of Jesus. He said, "I will. I will! Be thou clean." Did you know our Lord never refused anyone who came to Him looking for help? He never said, "No, I don't have time for you." In every instance, He dealt with people graciously, mercifully, and compassionately.

Maybe you're saying, "Well, I've sought the Lord. I've asked Him for His help. I've asked Him to do this thing in my life, but it never happened. Why would He help the leper and not me?"

Ye ask, and receive not, because ye ask amiss, that ye may consume it upon your lusts.
James 4:3

The Greeks had a saying that when the gods wanted to punish a man, they answered all his prayers. Many times our requests are just plain wrong, and our Father loves us enough to say, "No," if "No" is the best answer. But He'll never turn you away. He'll always do what's best for you, and you'll see it sooner or later, if you'll just ask Him. There were multiplied thousands of lepers in this region, but only one came and asked Jesus to be healed, and only one went away clean.

Matthew 8:4 (a)
And Jesus saith unto him, See thou tell no man . . .

Why would Jesus say this? Jesus often told those whom He healed, "Don't tell anyone," because He knew the vulnerability of humanity. He knew our tendency to get excited about the physical, while missing the truly significant realm of the spiritual. Because He evidently didn't want people following Him merely to see what the next circuslike event would be, Jesus always downplayed the miraculous. He would send His disciples to share the gospel throughout the world, and He would preach before thousands. But when it came to miracles, it seems as though Jesus had a penchant for secrecy.

Matthew 8:4 (b)
. . . but go thy way, shew thyself to the priest, and offer the gift that Moses commanded, for a testimony unto them.

"Go show yourself to the priest," Jesus said, because in Leviticus 14, there was a prescribed cleansing ceremony for lepers who were healed. The interesting thing is, although the ceremony had been on the books for fifteen hundred years, never was one leper cleansed until this man.

Matthew 8:5–13
And when Jesus was entered into Capernaum, there came unto him a centurion, beseeching him, and saying, Lord, my servant lieth at home sick of the palsy, grievously tormented. And Jesus saith unto him, I will come and heal him. The centurion answered and said, Lord, I am not worthy that thou shouldest come under my roof: but speak the word only, and my servant shall be healed. For I am a man under authority, having soldiers under me: and I say to this man, Go, and he goeth; and to another, Come, and he cometh; and to my servant, Do this, and he doeth it. When Jesus heard it, he marvelled, and said to them that followed, Verily I say unto you, I have not found so great faith, no, not in Israel. And I say unto you, That many shall come from the east and west, and shall sit down with Abraham, and Isaac, and Jacob, in the kingdom of heaven. But the children of the kingdom shall be cast out into outer darkness: there shall be weeping and gnashing of teeth. And Jesus said unto the centurion, Go thy way; and as thou hast believed, so be it done unto thee. And his servant was healed in the selfsame hour.

Keep in mind that the Romans had conquered Israel and were therefore the despised occupiers of the land. Furthermore, to attain the position of centurion, one had to prove himself a valiant warrior in battle. Therefore, the centurion in this story was not merely a soldier in the occupying forces—he was a commanding officer. We also know, from Luke's account of the same incident, that he was wealthy.

So, in the passage before us, Matthew paints a picture of a wealthy Roman approaching a poor Galilean, a powerful centurion seeking out a meek Carpenter, a mighty man of war addressing the Prince of Peace.

For topical study of Matthew 8:10–13 entitled "God's Final Word," turn to page 60.

Matthew 8:14 (a)
And when Jesus was come into Peter's house . . .

Mark tells us that Peter's house was in Capernaum. Yet John points out in his Gospel that Peter was from Bethsaida. This caught my attention, and I realized that Peter moved lock, stock, and barrel—fishing business, in-laws, the whole thing. He moved from his hometown of Bethsaida, which means "House of Fishing," to Capernaum, where Jesus had His headquarters. Peter left the place of occupational prosperity to be closer to Jesus. I think it would do us well to remember Peter's example. I am concerned about the number of people who move because of business reasons without considering if there is a group of people with whom they can worship and grow in the Lord.

There was a man in the Old Testament who based the decision as to where he would live on economic conditions. He lifted up his eyes, saw green grass, and said, "This is a great place for my cattle." The man's name was Lot, and he got in a lot of trouble because the green grass was growing right outside of Sodom and Gomorrah. It was a great place to raise cattle, but a lousy place to raise kids. Lot lifted up his eyes, but he didn't lift them high enough.

Peter did just the opposite. He said, "I want to be in the place where Jesus is ministering, in the place most conducive for me to follow, serve, and walk with Him." May the Lord give us such hearts in these days.

Matthew 8:14 (b)
. . . he saw his wife's mother laid, and sick of a fever.

Notice Peter was married. This is interesting because our Catholic friends suggest that to be a good spiritual leader, one should take a vow of poverty and celibacy. But they also teach Peter was the first pope, and look at him! He had a wife, a mother-in-law, and a house.

Matthew 8:15
And he touched her hand, and the fever left her: and she arose, and ministered unto them.

You can always tell a person who has been touched by Jesus because he will begin to minister. When the Lord touches you, you can't help but say, "To whom can I reach out and help?"

Matthew 8:16
When the even was come, they brought unto him many that were possessed with devils: and he cast out the spirits with his word, and healed all that were sick.

The darkness was defeated by the light of His Word.

Matthew 8:17
That it might be fulfilled which was spoken by Esaias the prophet, saying, Himself took our infirmities, and bare our sicknesses.

Here, Matthew draws the attention of his Jewish readers back to Isaiah 53:4, "Surely he hath borne our griefs, and carried our sorrows." Based on this verse, there are those who teach that since Jesus bore our infirmities and our sicknesses, those who are sick are out of the will of God, or their faith is lacking. Please note that sin, sickness, and death were all defeated on the Cross. When the kingdom is established on earth, the power of sin will be eradicated. All will be healed. There will be no death. But until then, those who preach true believers should never be sick must also preach that true believers should never sin and never die.

Am I saying that Jesus doesn't heal? Of course He heals. Am I saying we shouldn't pray for the sick?" No. We are commanded to pray for the sick. What I am questioning is the dogma, propagated on Christian TV that says "God never intends anyone to be sick. All should be healed."

All *will* be healed. Some will be healed now, some a year from now, some will be healed when they get to heaven. Jesus bore our sicknesses and our infirmities, and all of these problems, hurts, and pains and diseases are going to be healed— sooner or eventually. That's a promise.

Matthew 8:18, 19
Now when Jesus saw great multitudes about him, he gave commandment to depart unto the other side. And a certain scribe came, and said unto him, Master, I will follow thee whithersoever thou goest.

Perhaps this scribe was one who sat on the hillside and listened to the Sermon on the Mount. After hearing Jesus' principles and seeing His power as He healed all who were sick, it's no wonder he said, "Count me in. I'll follow You." Who wouldn't? Who wouldn't follow the Lord? The words He spoke and still speaks are so right on. The work He's done is so obvious. The Lord has done a work among us. We're not perfect, but we're being perfected. We're not what we should be, but we're not what we once were, either. He's changing us. Who wouldn't want to follow Him, seeing the work He's doing in the midst of people?

Matthew 8:20
And Jesus saith unto him, The foxes have holes, and the birds of the air have nests;

but the Son of man hath not where to lay his head.

This man was stung by these words because Jesus knew he wanted a comfortable life.

It's sort of like when my son Peter-John was younger. Watching a parade, he was really into seeing the soldiers marching in their uniforms with white gloves on their hands, shiny guns on their shoulders, and huge tanks rolling behind.

"Daddy, I want to be a soldier like those guys!" he said. I smiled because we who are older know it's not all marching in starched uniforms before cheering crowds. There's blood, dismembered bodies, and death. Yes, it's fun to see the parade go by, but the price of battle is an entirely different issue.

Watching the parade, this scribe said, "Wow. It'll be fun to be Your disciple." And Jesus said, "Wait. There's a price."

Matthew 8:21, 22
And another of his disciples said unto him, Lord, suffer me first to go and bury my father. But Jesus said unto him, Follow me; and let the dead bury their dead.

The second man wasn't hindered so much by riches as by relationships. "I'll follow You, Lord, just as soon as I bury my dad." Now, please don't misunderstand. It's not as though his father died and was lying in the front room while this guy was saying, "Let me go home and bury my dad, and I'll come right back." No, he was saying, "As soon as my dad passes away, then I'll really start following You. But right now I feel obligated to that relationship. Plus, I get part of the inheritance."

"Let the dead bury the dead, and you follow Me," Jesus answered because no relationship can stand in the way of those who are serious about following Jesus.

It's still those two issues, I believe, that keep people today from following Jesus. Following Him might mean some changes in business practices. Or it might mean letting go of that unbelieving boyfriend or girlfriend. It might cost riches. It might cost relationships. And like these two men, people today still conclude that they like the parade, but not the price.

Matthew 8:23, 24 (a)
And when he was entered into a ship, his disciples followed him. And, behold, there

arose a great tempest in the sea, insomuch that the ship was covered with the waves . . .

The word translated "tempest" is *seismos* in Greek, from which we get our word "seismology"—the study of earthquakes. This storm was really a shaker!

Keep in mind that the Sea of Galilee, where this story takes place, is six hundred eighty feet below sea level. Directly to the north, 9,280 feet above sea level, is Mount Hermon, which gets so cold it can be skied in the winter. So what happens is this: Cold air descends from Mount Hermon through a small ravine in the northern part of the valley, which funnels into the Sea of Galilee. As the cold air strikes the hot air below, it creates turbulence, and storms can erupt in seconds. Waves mount up, which in recent times have been recorded at higher than twenty-five feet. As you surfers know, waves are measured from the back, so we're talking about a face of perhaps forty feet. Thus, this wasn't a little drizzle on a lake. We're talking about a sea that terrorized even these salty fishermen.

Matthew 8:24 (b)
. . . but he was asleep.

I love this because it shows the humanity of Jesus. He was tired because He was a Man. In fact, He refers to Himself as the Son of Man eighty times in the New Testament, identifying with His humanity more than any other element in His personality. Next time you feel totally exhausted, remember Jesus can relate to you. In Jesus sleeping, we see His humanity. In His speaking to the storm, we see His deity.

If you sense Jesus is asleep in the storm you're going through—relax! If He's not doing anything, it means He's not pacing. He's not anxious. He's not worried. He's resting. You can rest as well if you remember that at any given moment, Jesus can stand up, speak a word and—boom—the storm will stop.

Matthew 8:25–27
And his disciples came to him, and awoke him, saying, Lord, save us: we perish. And he saith unto them, Why are ye fearful, O ye of little faith? Then he arose, and rebuked the winds and the sea; and there was a great calm. But the men marvelled, saying, What manner of man is this, that even the winds and the sea obey him!

"O ye of little faith." Why did Jesus say this to these men at this time? Mark tells us that Jesus previously had said to His disciples, "Come let us go over to the other side of the sea." He hadn't said, "Come let us sink to the bottom of the sea." He said, "Let us go over. We're going to make it." And He says to you,

> . . . And, lo, I am with you always, even unto the end of the world. Amen.   Matthew 28:20

> Fear thou not; for I am with thee: be not dismayed; for I am thy God: I will strengthen thee; yea, I will help thee; yea, I will uphold thee with the right hand of my righteousness.
> Isaiah 41:10

> Being confident of this very thing, that he which hath begun a good work in you will perform it until the day of Jesus Christ.
> Philippians 1:6

Matthew 8:28, 29
And when he was come to the other side into the country of the Gergesenes, there met him two possessed with devils, coming out of the tombs, exceeding fierce, so that no man might pass by that way. And, behold, they cried out, saying, What have we to do with thee, Jesus, thou Son of God? art thou come hither to torment us before the time?

To what time are the demons referring? To the day they would be cast into the bottomless pit.

Notice that these demons had fairly solid theology. They understood eschatology, the study of end times. And they called Jesus the Son of God—which is more than the scribes or Pharisees did. In his Epistle, James says, "You say that you believe? So what? The demons believe and tremble" (see James 2:19). It's not enough to believe Jesus is the Son of God intellectually. Bunches of people will miss heaven by eighteen inches—the distance between their brain and their heart.

Matthew 8:30–33
And there was a good way off from them a herd of many swine feeding. So the devils

besought him, saying, If thou cast us out, suffer us to go away into the herd of swine. And he said unto them, Go. And when they were come out, they went into the herd of swine: and, behold, the whole herd of swine ran violently down a steep place into the sea, and perished in the waters. And they that kept them fled, and went their ways into the city, and told every thing, and what was befallen to the possessed of the devils.

Note that the demons could not even go into a pig without permission from Jesus. People are saying, "Ooh, the *Medford Mail Tribune* has a horoscope on page 14, and if I have that newspaper in my house, the demon of horoscopes is going to come into me." Not true. It seems one of the biggest problems we have in the church today, at least here in America, is not demon possession, but demon obsession. Remember, gang, He that is in you is greater than he that is in the world.

Why would the demons want to enter pigs? I believe it was an attempt by these demons to drive Jesus out of the area. You see, pig farming was the number one industry there, and the demons knew that if Jesus interfered with business, the people would drive Him out. Keep in mind that pork was absolutely forbidden for Jews, making these pork ranchers the "marijuana farmers" of their day—hanging out on the rocks in Eastern Galilee, raising an illegal "crop."

Matthew 8:34
And, behold, the whole city came out to meet Jesus: and when they saw him, they besought him that he would depart out of their coasts.

"Leave, Lord. We care more about pigs than we do about people."

Jesus doesn't stay where He's not wanted, so He left. But in chapter 9, Matthew will continue to portray Jesus the King revealing His power to radically change those who were open to Him.

GOD'S FINAL WORD
A Topical Study of
MATTHEW 8:10–13

Put yourself in this setting: You are in Capernaum, observing an encounter between Jesus and a Roman centurion. You hear Jesus commend the centurion, saying,

"I have not found such great faith in all of Israel. And I say to you that men like you are going to be sitting at the table with Abraham, Isaac, and Jacob. But many of the religious people, the Jewish people who have so much, are going to be in outer darkness."

And you stand there absolutely amazed.

We have been exposed to this gospel story for so long, we begin to think,

"Big deal. So Jesus is commending a Roman centurion's faith as the greatest faith He had found in the land. So He's saying that Gentiles are going to be sitting at the table, and many Jews will be cast into outer darkness. So what?"

But at the time Jesus said this, those hearing Him would have scratched their heads in utter disbelief.

The reason Jesus' contemporaries would have been shocked by what He said was because in this culture, there were three groups of people who were absolutely, irrefutably looked down upon.

The first group was lepers. Lepers were believed to have been smitten by God. Lepers were banished from society. Leprosy was the AIDS of that day.

The second group was women. Jewish men felt that women were necessary for the propagation of the race, but outside of that, they didn't have a whole lot of value. In fact, if you were living in Jesus' day and were giving birth to a baby, your friends and relatives would gather in your house with presents in hand, anxiously waiting for the news of the baby's birth. If the midwife came out and said, "It's a boy!" celebration would follow. Gifts would be exchanged, and your friends and relatives would stay at your home for three days in celebration and feasting. But if the midwife came out and said, "It's a girl," your friends and relatives would immediately leave, taking their presents with them.

The third group looked down upon was Gentiles—everyone who was not a Jew. The Jews basically believed that Gentiles existed only as fuel for the fires of hell. With this in mind, check out Matthew 8, where the first three healing miracles Matthew recorded involved a leper, a Gentile, and a woman. Matthew's readers must have said, "What are you trying to tell us, Matthew, that the kingdom of God includes *lepers*, *Gentiles*, and *women?* This thing is more inclusive and more expansive than anything we've ever heard."

And Matthew would have said, "That's the point. The kingdom Jesus is building is a lot different from what the religious people think it is."

Let me tell you, folks, the message for us is that we must be so careful in our evaluations. We who feel like we've been blessed because we have the Word and we know the Lord need to be careful because the kingdom is bigger than our own theological niche. It's more expansive than our own flavor. It's big—much bigger than any of us think. "Well, it can't include Communists, can it?"

You who are old enough might remember Nikita Khrushchev, who banged the table of the United Nations with his shoe, saying, "We will bury you." I remember as a little boy that whenever I saw his face on TV, my heart was filled with terror, for he represented the Russian menace. I can recall many times during a school year when sirens would go off and we would get under our desks and cover our eyes with one hand and the back of our necks with the other to "protect" ourselves from Russian A-bombs.

"A Russian can't be part of the kingdom—not a guy like Khrushchev!"

Guess what happened to Khrushchev? The Lord included him in His kingdom.

Nikita Khrushchev memorized the entire New Testament word-for-word. And in his later years, he would sit in Gorky Park reciting it to Russians who recognized him. Although he was politically defamed and dethroned largely due to his faith, he gave his comments on New Testament teachings to all who would listen. Nikita Khrushchev became a teacher of the Word in his last days.

Furthermore, once, when Gorbachev came to America, he requested that Billy Graham travel in his entourage. Gorbachev's mother is a born-again believer—a Baptist. When Gorbachev was asked directly if he too was a believer, he hedged the question and didn't answer it directly. I'm not saying he's a brother, but I am suggesting that something could be happening in his heart.

I've listened to the prayers of Presbyterians and have been deeply touched. The prayers of some Catholic priests have penetrated my heart. I've listened to Christians who worship with rock and roll, and I've said, "Far out!" The kingdom is big. And I encourage you, as I remind myself, to be careful in our evaluations.

Jesus marveled and said, "This Roman-Gentile-Occupier-Centurion has the greatest faith I've found in Israel thus far." Only twice does Scripture say that Jesus marveled—here in Matthew 8, and in Mark 6, where He marveled at the unbelief of those in His home city who had been in the synagogue, who had journeyed to the temple, and who knew the Torah. Jesus marveled at Gentile faith and at Jewish unbelief.

Let us be big people, realizing the kingdom is more expansive and inclusive than what our flavor might be philosophically, or what our theology might be dogmatically. May God give us eyes to see what He's doing in churches other than ours, in fellowships flavored far differently than ours. Be embracive. Be a lover of people. See what the Lord is doing.

The second thing I glean from this simple story is not just to be careful in my evaluations, but to be confident in His articulation.

The centurion said, "Lord, I'm not worthy. Speak the word only."

I have heard messages on this verse that sound like this: "Speak the word, brother. Speak the word, sister. God said let there be light, and there was light, so name it and claim it." But the issue is not God *said,* "Let there be light." The issue is: *God* said, "Let there be light." It's not what was said. It's Who said it.

> *In the beginning was the Word, and the Word was with God, and the Word was God. The same was in the beginning with God. All things were made by him; and without him was not any thing made that was made. In him was life; and the life was the light of men.*   John 1:1–4

The Word is not an activity, not an exercise, not a theology. It's a Person. It's Jesus. *He* is the Word.

> *God, who at sundry times and in divers manners spake in time past unto the fathers by the prophets, hath in these last days spoken unto us by his Son . . .*
>   Hebrews 1:1, 2

God's final Word is His Son, Jesus Christ. Anything I want to know about life—the way to treat people, the way to handle various situations, the way to go through storms, the way to receive blessings—I find in Jesus Christ.

I am freed from having to pretend to be some kind of a spiritual prophet, guru, or wise master because I can move with great assurance in simplicity and confidence, saying, "My friend, dear sister, precious brother, God's final Word concerning anything you want to know about any situation you're in is Jesus Christ. What did *He* do? What did *He* teach? How did *He* respond? How did *He* act? Get to know the Savior, for the entire Bible speaks of *Him.*"

After Jesus rose from the dead, Luke tells us that as He walked with His disciples on the road to Emmaus, He opened the Scriptures and explained how they all spoke of Him. Everything God has to say is summed up in the Person of Jesus Christ.

"How can that be," you ask, "when Jesus was only here for three years?"

The speaker preceding him talked an hour and fifty-six minutes. Then Lincoln stood up and began, "Four score and seven years ago . . ."

Within three minutes, his speech was over. The audience was stunned. No one clapped. No one moved. The profundity of his words had silenced them.

So, too, God said, "I'm going to speak to you, humanity, through prophets and through the written Word. But My final Word, My most profound speech is the Logos, the Word—Jesus. Anything you want to know can be found in what He said, taught, and did in those three profound years He was on earth."

Jesus Christ is God's final Word to man. Therefore, throughout the Word, I look for Jesus.

• The Old Testament pointed to Him.

- The epistles of Paul looked back at Him.
- The Book of Revelation watches for Him.

Hermeneutics is the science of Biblical interpretation. But, gang, it's not hermeneutics that we need. It's *Him*-aneutics. We need to look for Jesus in every story and on every page. Whatever your need is, whatever your question might be, the answer is Jesus Christ.

He *is* God's final Word.

9 In chapters 8 and 9, writing of the King and the release of His power, Matthew enumerates ten miracles. In the first three, Jesus showed grace to the outcasts. In the next two, He gave peace to the troubled—the disciples in the storm and those tormented by demons. Now we will see peace extended once again to a man with a very real problem.

Matthew 9:1, 2
And he entered into a ship, and passed over, and came into his own city. And, behold, they brought to him a man sick of the palsy, lying on a bed: and Jesus seeing their faith said unto the sick of the palsy; Son, be of good cheer; thy sins be forgiven thee.

The other Gospel writers tell us the man stricken with palsy was brought by four friends who, because of the crowd, broke through the roof of the home in which Jesus was teaching in order to lower him down in front of the Master. Seeing this man lowered in front of Him, Jesus said, "Be of good cheer! Your sins are forgiven." But I wonder if at this point, the four friends were a bit disappointed. I wonder if they thought, *That's great, but we didn't lug him all this way and break open the roof just to hear some kind of spiritual statement.* I wonder if they were hoping to hear, "Be healed," instead of "Be of good cheer."

In reality, however, the most important need of the hurting man was forgiveness. In Romans 4, the apostle Paul, quoting David, said, "Blessed are they whose iniquities are forgiven, and whose sins are covered. Blessed is the man to whom the Lord will not impute sin." In other words, the happiest man is the man who knows he's forgiven. And I suggest to you that, although his friends may have been disappointed to hear those words, they were exactly what this guy was craving to hear due to the fact that, according to early tradition, this man was paralyzed because an im-

moral lifestyle had taken its toll on him physically.

So, too, I suggest to you that there are people today who are not walking because they are paralyzed by guilt over a sin or a series of sins that took place in their lives previously. And although they can walk physically, they cannot walk with the Lord in good cheer because they think, *I've gone too far. I've sinned too greatly.*

Matthew 9:3–5
And, behold, certain of the scribes said within themselves, This man blasphemeth. And Jesus knowing their thoughts said, Wherefore think ye evil in your hearts? For whether is easier, to say, Thy sins be forgiven thee; or to say, Arise, and walk?

Which is easier—physical healing or redemption from iniquity? For Jesus to physically heal the paralyzed man, He simply had to speak a word. But to forgive him, He had to die.

Matthew 9:6, 7
But that ye may know that the Son of man hath power on earth to forgive sins, (then saith he to the sick of the palsy,) Arise, take up thy bed, and go unto thine house. And he arose, and departed to his house.

The man took up his bed and cruised out of there, walking physically, but more importantly, walking spiritually. Notice verse 2 says that it was after seeing *their* faith that Jesus said to this man, "Your sins are forgiven." Seeing whose faith? Seeing the faith of the friends who brought their paralyzed buddy to Jesus.

Many times, Jesus would say to the person who was sick, "According to your faith, be made whole," and the person was healed. Other times, seeing other people's faith, Jesus would allow healing to be released. Still other times, at the tomb of Lazarus, for example, it was no one's faith. Mary and Martha were weeping in unbelief, and Lazarus was dead. So whose faith was it?

To so-called faith healers who say to the sick, "The reason you aren't healed is because you just didn't have enough faith," I would like to say, "What about *your* faith? Don't *you* have enough faith for him to be healed?"

Matthew 9:8
But when the multitudes saw it, they marvelled, and glorified God, which had given such power unto men.

Note this, students. Every time Jesus did a miracle, people who saw it glorified the Father. Jesus was able to move in such a way that when people saw His miracles, they praised God.

A man living in Taiwan who was really in love with a certain lady wrote her seven hundred flowery and lengthy letters in one year, sixty-two of which included proposals of marriage. The letters worked. The lady did indeed get married—but not to him. She married the mailman.

When I read that, I thought, *Isn't that just like us? Here the Father loves us and sends good gifts to us, but we're so dumb we exalt the mailman instead of the author of the letter.* If you're used by the Lord, people will either have a tendency to exalt you unrealistically, or to rail on you radically. Our goal should be to do what Jesus did— turn all the attention, all the glory back to the Father.

Matthew 9:9 (a)
And as Jesus passed forth from thence, he saw a man, named Matthew, sitting at the receipt of custom . . .

Matthew, the author of this Gospel, was also named Levi, which meant he sprang from the Levites, the priestly class, the tribe dedicated to worshipping and ministering. Matthew was a Levite, but instead of worshiping at the temple, he was working for the Romans, sitting at the receipt of custom collecting taxes. The Lord, however, has a way of seeing good in people, and He saw potential even in a man like Matthew.

Matthew 9:9 (b)
. . . and he saith unto him, Follow me. And he arose, and followed him.

"Follow Me, Matthew. I'll take you. Others might spit on you, turn their backs on you, and avoid you. But I'm willing to work with you and to work in you." Luke's Gospel tells us Matthew arose and left all to follow Jesus. Matthew, how-ever, doesn't mention this in his own writings. He simply says, "He arose, and followed him."

Proverbs 27:2 says, "Let another man praise thee, and not thine own mouth; a stranger, and not thine own lips." Matthew models this beautifully.

Matthew 9:10–13
And it came to pass, as Jesus sat at meat in the house, behold, many publicans and sinners came and sat down with him and his disciples. And when the Pharisees saw it, they said unto his disciples, Why eateth your Master with publicans and sinners? But when Jesus heard that, he said unto them, They that be whole need not a physician, but they that are sick. But go ye and learn what that meaneth, I will have mercy, and not sacrifice: For I am not come to call the righteous, but sinners to repentance.

There are none righteous, but the Lord says, "I am coming particularly to those who recognize their need—to the publicans, the prostitutes, the sinners, and the street people."

I wonder if we as the church today are like that. I wonder if the church, which should be representing Jesus, is now comfortable with the religious people, but is turning off the sinners, the street people, and the common folks. Jesus said, "I don't want sacrifice. I want mercy—compassion and concern for everyone."

I hope unbelievers relate to you well. I hope they don't look at you as being holier-than-thou. I hope people enjoy your company because you represent life and joy, that there's a quality about you that attracts people—believers and sinners alike. Such was true of Jesus. And such was true of Matthew, as he said to his friends, "Come on over to my house and meet the One who has shown such grace and mercy to me." We need more "Matthew parties," where people open their hearts and homes, saying, "I want you to be exposed to the One who's changed me."

Matthew 9:14–16
Then came to him the disciples of John, saying, Why do we and the Pharisees fast oft, but thy disciples fast not? And Jesus said unto them, Can the children of the bride-chamber mourn, as long as the bridegroom is with them? but the days will come, when the bridegroom shall be taken from them, and then shall they fast. No man putteth a piece of new cloth unto an old garment, for that which is put in to fill it up taketh from the garment, and the rent is made worse.

You don't put a new denim patch on old Levi's®, because when you wash them, it won't hold. The cloth will shrink, the stitching will rip, and the hole you were trying to patch will become even bigger.

Matthew 9:17
Neither do men put new wine into old bottles: else the bottles break, and the wine runneth out, and the bottles perish: but they put new wine into new bottles, and both are preserved.

Old wineskins, which are hard and rigid, aren't able to flex like new ones. Therefore, it would be foolish to put new wine in old wineskins because as the wine fermented, the wineskins would burst. Wine is a symbol of the Spirit, and I believe the Lord continually pours new wine. The problem is, the old structures and traditions can't contain it. Therefore, it seems as though the Lord raises up new wineskins in every generation— new vessels to hold the new work of the Spirit.

Matthew 9:18 (a)
While he spake these things unto them, behold, there came a certain ruler . . .

In the eighth chapter of his Gospel, Dr. Luke records this same miracle with much greater detail. He tells us the man's name was Jairus, a ruler of the synagogue. Before the year 586 B.C., virtually all Jews lived within one hundred miles of the temple, so they all worshiped there. But in 586 B.C., the Jews were carried away into Babylon and held hostage for seventy years. No longer able to worship in the temple, they established synagogues in every neighborhood with ten or more Jewish men. The synagogue then became the place of assembly for the Jews where they would worship and study the Scriptures. Each synagogue had ten leaders, called elders. Of those ten, one was elected by the other nine to be the ruler. The ruler of the synagogue was a man of tremendous importance. Not only was he in charge of the synagogue, but he would also settle civic disputes within the neighborhood. Synagogue rulers had power and prosperity, influence and impact. Jairus was such a man. Yet he was willing to risk it all and come to Jesus because death had crept into his family.

Matthew 9:18 (b), 19
. . . and worshipped him, saying, My daughter is even now dead: but come and lay thy hand upon her, and she shall live. And Jesus arose, and followed him, and so did his disciples.

Luke also tells us that Jairus' daughter was twelve years old. For twelve years, his daughter had brought light and laughter into his home, until suddenly, she was taken with sickness and was at the point of death.

Much can be learned from the way people react to death closing in on themselves or on someone close to them. Fifteen years before his death, Mahatma Ghandi wrote: "I must tell you in all humility, that Hinduism as I know it entirely satisfies my soul. It fills my whole being, and I find a solace in it that I find nowhere else." Three weeks before he died, however, he made this last journal entry: "My days are numbered. I am not likely to live very much longer. Perhaps a year, maybe a little more. For the first time in my fifty years, I find myself in the slough of despond and in total depression."

When Jairus came face-to-face with death, he knew what to do. He went to Jesus. He ran the risk of losing his prominent position, his wealth, and his reputation in order to save his daughter's life.

Matthew 9:20 (a)
And, behold, a woman, which was diseased with an issue of blood twelve years, came behind him . . .

Because this woman was hemorrhaging, she would have been unable to go to the temple to worship, and she would have been considered unclean and defiled by her community. Notice the parallel: A twelve-year-old girl, full of life, light, and laughter, was suddenly dying, and a woman, who, for the same twelve years, full of darkness, disease, and depression, was on the verge of being healed. Perhaps for the past twelve years you have had things go relatively well. Life has been good. God has been gracious. But you don't know what the next hour holds. You can't guarantee that in the next hour you won't meet with the greatest tragedy, the biggest challenge of your life. Like Jairus, you who perhaps for twelve years have been doing so well, might suddenly find yourself face-to-face with despair. So, too, for the past twelve years if you have been battling discouragement, depression, and disease, know this: You don't know what the next moment holds. The Lord can do something suddenly that will blow your mind and bring an end to your despair.

Matthew 9:20 (b), 21
. . . and touched the hem of his garment: For she said within herself, If I may but touch his garment, I shall be whole.

In Matthew's day, it was believed that there was certain power in the hem of a garment belonging to a rabbi or spiritual leader. "If I could just touch the hem of his garment." This woman probably didn't have the strength to wrestle Him in faith, or to grab hold of Him in belief. Yet she knew if she could even just lightly touch Jesus, she would be healed.

Matthew 9:22
But Jesus turned him about, and when he saw her, he said, Daughter, be of good comfort; thy faith hath made thee whole. And the woman was made whole from that hour.

Perhaps you say, "I would love to have Jesus touch me, but I don't feel His touch." Then be like this woman. If you're not feeling His touch upon you, reach out and touch Him. Have you made the effort to press through the crowd of unbelief, of busyness, of entertainment, of activities—the crowd of all that stands between you and the Lord? Press through and say, "I just want to touch the hem of His garment. I know if I can touch Him, I'll be helped."

This woman expended the energy to break through the crowd and touch Jesus. Was her theology correct? No. Was her knowledge complete? No. She was acting out of superstition. But the Lord didn't say, "Since your theology is all messed up, I won't help you." No! He's a Savior who heeds the cries of His children, even though their phrases are amiss, or their theology's not right. God honors the person who in desperation is seeking to touch Him.

Now, do you suppose by this time, Jairus was growing a little impatient? "Come on, Lord. My daughter is dying, and You're talking to some lady who's touched Your garment?"

Do you ever feel that way? "Lord, I see You're blessing this person and You're blessing that person. Great! But, Lord, what about me?" I suggest to you that in seeing the healing of this woman, Jairus was being prepared for the healing of his own daughter. You see, whenever the Lord delays in moving and seems to be working in other people or in other places, be observant of where He is working and what He is doing because therein lies lessons for you as well. Keep your antennae up, your eyes wide, and your journal open to record information the Lord knows you will need shortly.

Matthew 9:23–26
And when Jesus came into the ruler's house, and saw the minstrels and the people making a noise, he said unto them, Give place: for the maid is not dead, but sleepeth. And they laughed him to scorn. But when the people were put forth, he went in, and took her by
the hand, and the maid arose. And the fame hereof went abroad into all that land.

Whenever Jesus wants to work in your situation, there will be mockers, saying, "It's not going to happen. What a joke. The Lord's not going to help you. He's not even real to you. He doesn't care anything about you." And these little voices inside of us, the voices of unbelief, of demons, or even of well-meaning friends, say, "Grow up. Don't expect a miracle."

The laughers, the scorners, and the mockers were moved out before Jesus went in. Move out the mockers, gang. Believe the promises of God, quote Scripture, rejoice in advance, and anticipate His blessing.

For topical study of Matthew 9:18–26 entitled "Moving Out the Mockers," turn to page 68.

Matthew 9:27
And when Jesus departed thence, two blind men followed him, crying, and saying, Thou Son of David, have mercy on us.

"Son of David" was a title used for "Messiah." In reality, these blind men had better vision than anyone else, for they saw Jesus as Messiah.

Matthew 9:28 (a)
And when he was come into the house, the blind men came to him . . .

How did the blind men follow Jesus and come to Him? After all, they couldn't see! I suggest there's a spiritual principle here. John 1:9 says, "[Jesus] was the true Light, which lighteth every man that cometh into the world." The ministry of Messiah was to open the eyes not only of those physically blind, but of the spiritually blind. Therefore, the blindest of men can follow Him because Jesus, the true Light, lights every man. He makes Himself known to every person.

Romans 1 makes it clear that, both by instinct and observation, every man knows there's a God. But what do men do? They suppress the truth. People don't want to admit there's a Creator, because if there's a Creator, they are accountable to that Creator, and people want to sin. So they conveniently, illogically, and unscientifically bury the truth in the theory of evolution in order to say, "Hey, we're only animals. Let's party."

But even the blindest of men at some point will realize the truth in his heart. When he faces Jesus, no man will be able to say, "I never knew. I never heard. I had no idea." John 1:9 says He is the Light that lights *every* man.

Matthew 9:28 (b)–30

. . . and Jesus saith unto them, Believe ye that I am able to do this? They said unto him, Yea, Lord. Then touched he their eyes, saying, According to your faith be it unto you. And their eyes were opened; and Jesus straitly charged them, saying, See that no man know it.

Why did Jesus say, "Don't tell anyone?" Again, I believe the reason is because He knew the tendency of people to focus on the miraculous more than the Message, on the gifts more than the Giver. Also, perhaps Jesus was saying, "If you guys aren't careful spreading this news around this region at this time, you'll get in a lot of trouble." As opposition to Him was mounting, maybe He was protecting those who believed in Him.

Matthew 9:31

But they, when they were departed, spread abroad his fame in all that country.

These guys couldn't help spreading the word. I can understand that. I mean, they were blind and now they could see. They wanted people to know!

Matthew 9:32–35

As they went out, behold, they brought to him a dumb man possessed with a devil. And when the devil was cast out, the dumb spake: and the multitudes marvelled, saying, It was never so seen in Israel. But the Pharisees said, He casteth out devils through the prince of the devils. And Jesus went about all the cities and villages, teaching in their synagogues, and preaching the gospel of the kingdom, and healing every sickness and every disease among the people.

People ask, "Why aren't blind eyes opened, AIDS victims healed, and the paralyzed walking today? It happened then. Why can't it happen now?"

God still heals, but not in the same way. At this point, Jesus was giving the Jews the opportunity to acknowledge Him as their Messiah. Had they received Him, they could have moved right into the kingdom, but they rejected Him when they nailed Him to the Cross. Consequently, although we do see miracles today, they're not the same as the ones He performed physically when He walked the earth. The miracles we read about in the Gospels are "sneak previews of coming attractions" when He will rule and reign, when all will be right, when everyone will be healed.

Matthew 9:36–38

But when he saw the multitudes, he was moved with compassion on them, because they fainted, and were scattered abroad, as sheep having no shepherd. Then saith he unto his disciples, The harvest truly is plenteous, but the labourers are few; Pray ye therefore the Lord of the harvest, that he will send forth labourers into his harvest.

Looking at the multitudes, Jesus said to His boys, "Pray. The harvest is plenteous." He didn't say, "It's time for planting." He said, "It's ready for picking."

I sense the same thing is true today, don't you? The harvest is ready. Don't let Satan whisper in your ear, "Your neighbors won't listen. Your relatives won't respond." No, the harvest is *ready*.

MOVING OUT THE MOCKERS
A Topical Study of
MATTHEW 9:18–26

F unerals are normally very serious and very sobering. But I want us to look at a funeral where there were no quiet organ chords, no hushed whispers, no silent tears.

This funeral is unique because it was filled with laughter.

And when Jesus came into the ruler's house, and saw the minstrels and the people making a noise, He said unto them, Give place: for the maid is not dead, but sleepeth. And they laughed him to scorn.   Matthew 9:23, 24

Who were these minstrels? In Jesus' day, when someone died, the bereaved would hire professional mourners and wailers. Even the poorest of families would hire two minstrels, two flute players, and one screamer. But the wealthier one was, the more mourners he would hire. Because Jairus was so wealthy, there were perhaps twenty, fifty, perhaps even one hundred people at his home weeping, wailing, and mourning. Then Jesus arrived. "Give place," He said. "Make way. The maid is not dead. She sleeps."

Matthew writes, "And they laughed him to scorn." It wasn't a chuckle; it was a deep belly laugh. It wasn't a giggle; it was a guffaw. After all, they had been with her. They had checked her pulse. They had watched her die. No doubt about it, she was gone.

The Bible speaks of death with different terminology than the world does. John 11, Acts 7, 1 Corinthians 15, and 1 Thessalonians 4 all say that for the believer, death is sleep. That is, our bodies go to sleep to be resurrected later on, while our spirits go immediately to be with the Lord.

Sleep! Who of us doesn't enjoy a nice nap or taking some time to lie in the sun now and then? Jesus put death in an entirely different context when He said, "Don't worry. She's not dead in the way you think. She's simply sleeping."

> Imagine a funeral taking place in the amphitheatre with hundreds of caterpillars all dressed in black marching slowly down the floor of the amphitheatre, carrying the cocoon of their beloved, departed brother. Meanwhile, a beautiful butterfly is fluttering above them, looking down in utter disbelief. "What are you guys mourning for?" he shouts. "I've been metamorphosed!"

In 1 Corinthians 15, when Paul says we shall be changed, "metamorphosed" is the Greek word he uses. When we die, we get rid of these caterpillar costumes and become the butterflies we long to be.

"Give place," Jesus said. "She's not dead. She's asleep." Then He went in and took her by the hand. To a Jew, touching a dead body was defiling. It was like touching a leper. But Jesus was not afraid to touch defiled people. And He's not afraid to touch you.

Scripture records three accounts of people who were raised from the dead by Jesus: Jairus' daughter, the widow of Nain's son, and Lazarus.

- Following her resurrection, Jairus' daughter was hungry.
- Following his resurrection, the widow's son began to speak.
- Following his resurrection, Lazarus came forth walking.

I suggest to you the same three characteristics are found in those who have been spiritually resurrected and born again.

- Like Jairus' daughter, they hunger for the Word.
- Like the widow's son, they talk differently. The things they enjoy talking about are no longer what they once were.
- Like Lazarus, they walk differently, no longer bound by sin.

I want you to see something else here, because I believe every one of us deals constantly with some area in our lives that is dying.

Perhaps it is in the area of parenting. "My kids are rebelling against God. They're not interested in spiritual things. My daughter is at the point of death even now."

Maybe it's your wife or your husband. Your marriage is collapsing.

Maybe financially or occupationally things seem at the point of death.

It might be ministry.

And we run to Jesus, crying, "Lord, this thing, this person, this plan is at the point of death. Come. Please!" And Jesus hears your prayer. And you leave that place of prayer saying, "Far out! The Lord is with me. Great!"

But then the news comes the next day.

- She left you.
- He moved out.
- Your kids are in juvenile hall.
- You're fired.

And you say, "What happened, Lord? I thought You were traveling with me. Where did You go?"

He is still with you. And He whispers in your heart. "Give place. It's not dead. It's just sleeping."

"No way," you say. "It's over. There's no possibility it will ever work out."

But when the people were put forth, he went in . . .   Matthew 9:25

When did Jesus go in?

When the mockers were put out.

In this, I am reminded of an account in 2 Kings . . .

And he went up from thence unto Bethel: and as he was going up by the way, there came forth little children out of the city, and mocked him, and said unto him, Go up, thou bald head; go up, thou bald head.   2 Kings 2:23

Interestingly the Hebrew word translated "mock" used here is essentially the same Greek word translated "mock" in Matthew 9. The word for "little children" is the Hebrew word *na'ar.* It is used to describe Isaac when he was twenty-eight years old and Joseph when he was thirty-nine years old. Thus, it doesn't mean little children in the sense of preschoolers or kindergarteners. Instead, it means those who were younger than the venerated elders in a community. So these guys could have easily been twenty, thirty, or perhaps even forty years old. They should have known better than to mock a man of God.

Now, who were these "little children"? They were those who had heard about Elijah's miraculous departure in a chariot of fire, but evidently didn't believe it. So they said to Elisha, "Get out of here, man. Go up like Elijah did, if you're such a hot prophet."

What happened next?

> *And he turned back, and looked on them, and cursed them in the name of the LORD. And there came forth two she bears out of the wood, and tare forty and two children of them. And he went from thence to mount Carmel, and from thence he returned to Samaria.*   2 Kings 2:24–25

Elisha said, "I won't stand for it. This is un-bear-able. In the name of the Lord, I will not allow these mockers, these scoffers to make fun of the ministry that God has entrusted to me." Suddenly, two female bears came out of the woods and began ripping on these scorners, devouring them. And we see the situation become very "grizzly."

Don't send your pit bulls after those who make fun of you, gang, but realize this: We in New Testament times wrestle not against flesh and blood, but against principalities and powers and spiritual wickedness in high places (Ephesians 6:12). Our battle is with those demonic forces and with our own sin natures that whisper within us, "Go up. Go up. You think things are going to happen? No they're not, bald head man."

In the Name of Jesus, we need to come against these scoffers, these laughers, these mockers, and say, "I will not give place to these voices of doubt and depression. I will not allow them to whisper in my ear that this is doomed to fail. I refuse to listen to the lies of the enemy or to the doubts of my sinful humanity. I will claim the promises the Lord has given to me in His Word, and I will cling to them and believe in Him."

Over three thousand promises have been given to you in the Word dealing with every single need you might have today. Search the Scriptures. Find the promise. And when circumstances say, "No way," call for the bears!

When Jesus went into His hometown of Capernaum, does Scripture say He could do no mighty miracle there because of their carnality? No. Was it because of their sin? No. Was it because He was tired? No.

He could do no mighty work there because of their unbelief (Matthew 13:58).

Without faith, Hebrews 11 says, it is impossible to please Him. There are many ways to please God, but without faith, none of them mean a thing. Have faith. Give place. Move out the mockers.

"Eat 'em up, bears of belief. Go get 'em in the Name of the Lord. I'm quoting, claiming, believing, and standing on this Book. Devour those doubts, O Lord."

As the scorners make their exit, the Lord then moves in, and things begin to happen. May you be one who puts out the scorners and stands on Scripture.

Move out the mockers. Make way for Jesus. And let Him bring resurrection into your life.

10

The story is told of Jesus' return to heaven. After dying for the sins of humanity, He was greeted by the angel Gabriel.

"An awesome thing You did, Lord," Gabriel said. "Incredible! Does the world know?"

Jesus answered, "Not really. As a matter of fact, only a few guys in Palestine understand what I did."

"Well, how is the rest of the world going to understand?"

"I'm entrusting those guys with the message. I'm trusting they will carry My message throughout the world."

"But what if they don't?" Gabriel asked. "What if they decide to return to fishing? Or what if they get afraid? Or what if they get tangled up in relationships? What happens if they don't do it? What is Your plan then?"

And Jesus replied, "I have no other plan."

This story, although it is just a story, is reality. The Lord entrusted the gospel of the kingdom to men and left it with them, sending them out to propagate the Good News that men's sins are forgiven because of His death on the Cross. That was His only plan.

And here in Matthew 10, we see the beginning of this plan unfolding as we see Him training His disciples. After learning *from* Jesus and hanging out *with* Jesus, now they are sent forth *by* Jesus.

Matthew 10:1 (a)
And when he had called unto him his twelve disciples . . .

We saw in Luke 6 that, after spending the night in prayer, Jesus chose from among the many disciples who followed Him twelve to be *apostolos*, or "sent out ones."

Matthew 10:1 (b)
. . . he gave them power against unclean spirits, to cast them out, and to heal all manner of sickness and all manner of disease.

After seeing Jesus' principles recorded and His power revealed, here in chapter 10, we see His people released as He sends forth His disciples. Jesus was so radical. He entrusted His message not to the well-educated and impeccably trained, but to a rag-tag bunch of renegades made up of a tax collector, political rabble-rousers, and fishermen. The Lord will never ask you to do anything He does not enable you to do by the power of His Spirit. Since the greatest concerns of the culture in which they ministered were demon possession, sickness, and disease, Jesus specifically gave His disciples the power to meet those very needs.

Matthew 10:2 (a)
Now the names of the twelve apostles are these; The first, Simon, who is called Peter . . .

Luke 6 tells us that after Jesus spent a full night in prayer, He came down the mountain and chose twelve disciples from among the many who surrounded Him. "Mathetes," or "learner," is the Greek word for disciple. These men had been traveling with Jesus, listening to Jesus, and hanging out with Jesus. They were learners. Jesus called them disciples and transformed them into "apostles" or "sent out ones."

In the listing of the apostles, Peter always comes first and Judas is always at the end. Judas, of course, was the betrayer of Jesus, and Peter was one who had a special place in the apostolic order. Here we see that the Lord does have leaders among leaders. And Peter, indeed, was a leader amongst these leaders.

Nonetheless, Peter was the apostle with the foot-shaped mouth, often saying the wrong thing at the wrong time. Maybe you enjoy talking and your heart is as big as the world, but you have a tendency to speak and to think later. Peter was like this.

The Lord changed Simon from one who was shifting and unstable into "Petros," or "Rock." The Lord renamed Peter because He transformed him from one who was shifting and unstable to one who would become solid and reliable.

Matthew 10:2 (b)
... and Andrew his brother ...

Andrew was known as the younger brother of Peter. Maybe some of you feel like Andrew—always in someone else's shadow. Your older brother, your older sister, or someone else is always the star. Jesus chose someone you can perhaps relate to—Andrew—who was always in Peter's shadow.

Matthew 10:2 (c)
... James the son of Zebedee, and John his brother.

James and John were called the "sons of thunder" because of their volatile tempers. When one of the cities did not respond to the message of the gospel, James and John said, "Jesus, shall we call down fire from heaven and destroy them?" So Jesus chose a guy who said the wrong things, a guy who lived in the shadow of his older brother, and a couple of guys with explosive tempers.

Matthew 10:3 (a)
Philip, and Bartholomew; Thomas, and Matthew the publican ...

Then there were Philip and Bartholomew. Remember that Bartholomew is another name for Nathanael, the skeptic who asked, "Can any good thing come out of Nazareth?" Add to this group Thomas, a doubter, and Matthew, a rip-off artist. Would *you* have chosen these guys?

Matthew 10:3 (b)–4 (a)
... James the son of Alphaeus, and Lebbaeus, whose surname was Thaddaeus; Simon the Canaanite ...

James, the son of Alphaeus, is an unknown, since there's nothing more we know about him from Scripture. Perhaps you feel that way. You're somewhat shy and retiring, and you don't make

your presence known. But the Lord sees you just as He saw James and says, "Yeah, I can use you."

Then there was Simon the Canaanite, a political rabble-rouser. The Gospel of Luke tells us that Simon was a zealot. He was involved in a group trying to overthrow the Roman government. If Simon the Zealot and Matthew, who was employed by the Romans, had met in any other circumstance, Simon would have put a knife in Matthew's back. But here Jesus brings them together. Just like us! We have some liberals and some conservatives, some Republicans, and some Democrats. And that's the way it should be. People who would normally not hang out together find commonality in Christ Jesus.

Matthew 10:4 (b)
... and Judas Iscariot, who also betrayed him.

Even a traitor was chosen by Jesus. Were the disciples superstars? Hardly. How I appreciate the quality—or the lack of quality—of these men because it gives me hope that Jesus can use someone like me.

Matthew 10:5, 6
These twelve Jesus sent forth, and commanded them, saying, Go not into the way of the Gentiles, and into any city of the Samaritans enter ye not. But go rather to the lost sheep of the house of Israel.

Right away, Jesus put restrictions on them. Why? Because He was establishing priorities for them, saying, "This is where you start—in your home country. Start where you're at," Jesus says. "Cross the street before you cross the ocean." In addition to establishing priority, there's another reason Jesus put this restriction on them. Had these apostles gone to the Samaritans—Gentiles—first, no one would have received them when they came back home because the Jews despised the Gentiles. In Romans we read that the gospel went to the Jew first and then to the Greeks, or the Gentiles, not because of priority, but because of precedence. The Jews were prepared by the prophets, by the covenants, and by the promises. So the Lord sent His boys to the Jews first.

Matthew 10:7 (a)
And as ye go, preach ...

The Greek word for preach is *kerusso.* Maybe you remember Enrico Caruso, the great opera singer who would shatter a glass from fifteen paces with his powerful tenor voice. Remember

Caruso. That's the word for preach. Sing it out. Sing out the gospel!

Matthew 10:7 (b)
. . . saying, The kingdom of heaven is at hand.

What had Jesus been preaching and teaching? This very message: "The kingdom of heaven is at hand." Consequently, He was able to say, "You've heard it from Me. Now go and tell others." Truly, there is power in the Word, for it speaks to any person in any place during any age.

Matthew 10:8
Heal the sick, cleanse the lepers, raise the dead, cast out devils: freely ye have received, freely give.

These would have been impossible tasks had not Jesus already empowered them to do these very things (verse 1). Whatever God has given you—gifts, abilities, money, talent—has been given to you freely by His grace. Now let these gifts freely flow through you to help those around you.

You might be saying, "I feel so bankrupt. I don't feel like I have a lot to give." But the Word tells us that we have not because we ask not (James 4:2). Maybe we should be spending a little more time in prayer, saying, "Lord, I need to be blessed. I need to be empowered so that I might be a blessing to others." Blessings are like the measles—you can't give 'em unless you got 'em!

Matthew 10:9, 10 (a)
Provide neither gold, nor silver, nor brass in your purses, nor scrip for your journey, neither two coats, neither shoes, nor yet staves . . .

"I'm sending you out. Now go with the flow, and trust Me to take care of you. You don't need to encumber yourselves with lots of gadgets and gizmos. I will provide."

Matthew 10:10 (b)
. . . for the workman is worthy of his meat.

When the disciples went out healing the sick, cleansing the lepers, and raising the dead, don't you think someone might have asked them over for dinner? I do. I think what the Lord is saying here is, "If you're going about doing good, preaching the gospel, healing the sick, and cleansing the lepers, the workman is worthy of his meat. I'll take care of you. The people will respond to you, and blessings will flow freely to you because you are giving freely." Whatever minis-

try you are involved in, know this: When God guides, God provides. People will be blessed, touched, and encouraged. And they will want to be a blessing in return.

Matthew 10:11–13 (a)
And into whatsoever city or town ye shall enter, inquire who in it is worthy; and there abide till ye go thence. And when ye come into an house, salute it. And if the house be worthy, let your peace come upon it . . .

Whatever house you go in, stay there. The problem is, we so often get into a place and say, "Well, this is fine for now." But we keep our eye open for a more influential or powerful place to stay.

When I was a youth pastor years ago, I noticed the message of so many youth seminars and books was "Get the quarterback and the cheerleader converted, and you've got it made." But in reality, it was the *common* people who heard Jesus gladly (Mark 12:37). We learned the hard way to focus not so much on the quarterback, but rather to go to the kids who sat by themselves, those whom everyone else ignored. When we went to these kids, there was an openness and a readiness to receive Jesus.

I believe that's essentially what Jesus was referring to when He said, "When you go into a house, be content to stay there. Don't try to move around and move up. Just go in, pronounce peace, and stay until you leave the city."

Matthew 10:13 (b)–15
. . . but if it be not worthy, let your peace return to you. And whosoever shall not receive you, nor hear your words, when ye depart out of that house or city, shake off the dust of your feet. Verily I say unto you, It shall be more tolerable for the land of Sodom and Gomorrha in the day of judgment, than for that city.

Have you ever been visited by some Jehovah's Witness missionaries? After closing the door, if you peek out the window, you see them shake the dust from their feet as they get to the edge of your sidewalk. They do this because they're taking this verse literally and pronouncing judgment. In Jesus' day, when the Jews would accidentally or unavoidably walk across Gentile territory, once they got back to Jewish soil, they would shake their feet. Everyone knew they were shaking off the defilement of Gentile dirt. Thus, when the apostles shook the dust from their feet, people watching would know exactly what was happening. They would know the apostles were sending this message: "You're lost, just like you think the Gentiles are lost. We come to you presenting the Good News, but if you reject it, you bring judgment upon yourselves."

Matthew 10:16
Behold, I send you forth as sheep in the midst of wolves: be ye therefore wise as serpents, and harmless as doves.

Do you remember this story from the past? A twenty-five-foot boa constrictor took up residence in the basement of a house in Florida. Although the owners knew he was down there from the skins he shed, they couldn't find him. He was tricky—twenty-five feet long and still able to hide completely in cracks and crevices. Think about it. A snake has severe handicaps. It has no arms, no legs, and yet it gets around. It wisely maneuvers and stealthily hides itself. Jesus is saying that even if you feel as though you're handicapped, be as wise as a serpent in how you get into places. But also be as harmless as a dove.

Matthew 10:17–20
But beware of men: for they will deliver you up to the councils, and they will scourge you in their synagogues; and ye shall be brought before governors and kings for my sake, for a testimony against them and the Gentiles. But when they deliver you up, take no thought how or what ye shall speak: for it shall be given you in that same hour what ye shall speak. For it is not ye that speak, but the Spirit of your Father which speaketh in you.

The religious system and the government are going to come against you. But it's for a purpose. "Opposition," Jesus is saying, "brings opportunity. You'll be brought before magistrates, judges, kings, and leaders as a representative of Me."
Whenever you're called on the carpet because you're serving the Lord, or because you're taking a stand for righteousness, know this: Jesus said opposition would occur. He also said He would use it for His sake. You will be brought before people who will persecute you or come down on you because, in that way, He can use you as a witness. So don't tense your shoulders and furrow your brow when you get called into your boss's office. Realize the Lord put you there as a witness for Him.

Matthew 10:21
And the brother shall deliver up the brother to death, and the father the child: and the children shall rise up against their parents, and cause them to be put to death.

This prophecy of Jesus came to pass as the church went through ten tragic waves of persecution under ten Roman emperors. During this time, perhaps as many as 175 million Christians were killed. Until the rule of Constantine, Christians were systematically scourged, beaten, and burned. Caesar Nero had believers dipped in hot wax so he could ignite them and use them as torches in his palace gardens.

Matthew 10:22–25
And ye shall be hated of all men for my name's sake: but he that endureth to the end shall be saved. But when they persecute you in this city, flee ye into another: for verily I say unto you, Ye shall not have gone over the cities of Israel, till the Son of man be come. The disciple is not above his master, nor the servant above his lord. It is enough for the disciple that he be as his master, and the servant as his lord. If they have called the master of the house Beelzebub, how much more shall they call them of his household?

Beelzebub, literally "lord of the flies," was a Philistine god, worshiped by people who lived in what is today known as the Gaza strip. There were those who said, "Jesus is using demonic powers to do His work. He's demon-possessed." So here Jesus is saying to His disciples, "If they're calling Me the lord of the flies, they're also going to come down on you."

Matthew 10:26
Fear them not therefore: for there is nothing covered, that shall not be revealed; and hid, that shall not be known.

A day is coming when all things will be made right.

Matthew 10:27
What I tell you in darkness, that speak ye in light: and what ye hear in the ear, that preach ye upon the housetops.

"What I am telling you in the dark, speak in the light. What I am telling you in the quiet times, in your morning devotions, in your evening watches, spread abroad."

Matthew 10:28–31
And fear not them which kill the body, but are not able to kill the soul: but rather fear him which is able to destroy both soul and

body in hell. **Are not two sparrows sold for a farthing? and one of them shall not fall on the ground without your Father. But the very hairs of your head are all numbered. Fear ye not therefore, ye are of more value than many sparrows.**

You might be treated unjustly at school, on the job, or in your family. But the Father is watching. Do you know this? When you feel like you're getting ripped on and put down, the Father sees. Jesus says He sees when even a sparrow falls to the ground.

Sparrows weren't worth a whole lot. Two sold for a farthing, or one-sixteenth of a denarius. A denarius was a day's wage for the poorest of people. So sparrows were sold very cheaply. In fact, in Luke's Gospel, Jesus tells us that five sparrows could be bought for two farthings. They were so common that you got an extra bird thrown in for free! Here, Jesus says the Father sees when even one of these birds fall. Are not you more valuable than they? You bet. So be assured that when you're falling, stumbling, or hurting, the Lord is watching and caring.

Matthew 10:32, 33
Whosoever therefore shall confess me before men, him will I confess also before my Father which is in heaven. But whosoever shall deny me before men, him will I also deny before my Father which is in heaven.

This verse is often misunderstood. People ask, "Does this mean the Lord will deny me if I don't stand up for Him?" No. The very night Jesus was led away to be crucified for Peter's sins, Peter was cursing, swearing, and denying Him. Yet after He died, Jesus found Peter and said, "Peter, feed My sheep. Feed My lambs. Keep going, Peter." Jesus did not damn Peter, disown Peter, or disqualify him from service.

We need to remember that when Jesus ascended into heaven, He became our High Priest who ever lives, Hebrews says, to make intercession for the saints. He's praying for us right now. If we deny Him—if we don't stand up for Him— we will miss the benefits He wants to bestow upon us, and we will be the poorer. Thus, in my opinion, this verse has nothing to do with our salvation. It has to do with the blessings God bestows upon us as we stand up for His Son.

Secondly, it has to do with eternal rewards, crowns, and benefits.

And they that be wise shall shine as the brightness of the firmament; and they that turn many to righteousness as the stars for ever and ever.   Daniel 12:3

Daniel declares that you who are soul-winners are wise because you're going to shine as stars forever. If you're standing for the Lord and sharing the gospel of Jesus Christ, you will be confessed by the Lord when you stand at the Bema Seat of Christ. The Bema Seat is not a place where sins are judged. Our sins were all judged at Calvary. We will never be judged for our sins and denials, our departures and backsliding. However, we will be rewarded for what we did in Christ's Name. If we confess Jesus before men, Jesus will confess us before the Father. And rewards will come our way eternally.

Matthew 10:34–37
Think not that I am come to send peace on earth: I came not to send peace, but a sword. For I am come to set a man at variance against his father, and the daughter against her mother, and the daughter in law against her mother in law. And a man's foes shall be they of his own household. He that loveth father or mother more than me is not worthy of me: and he that loveth son or daughter more than me is not worthy of me.

I talked with an Oregon county leader one day who said, "Jon, you gotta face it. Your group out there intimidates an awful lot of people. You're claiming Jesus is the only Way. That makes a bunch of people feel pretty uncomfortable. You're going to have some enemies." He's right! It's inevitable. If we are the light we should be, we're going to cause people who are living in darkness to feel uncomfortable.

Jesus says, "There's going to be some severance, some tension, some difficulty if you're standing up for Me and living for Me. But if you value family or friendship more than you value Me, you're not worthy of Me."

Matthew 10:38
And he that taketh not his cross, and followeth after me, is not worthy of me.

How our generation needs to hear this.

- In the '60s, the goal was to "Find Yourself." *We tried that and didn't like what we found.*
- In the '70s, the goal was to "Improve Yourself." *All kinds of courses were taken, and health spas abounded, but it didn't work. People were not happy.*
- In the '80s, the goal was to "Serve Yourself." *As our nation grew more and more materialistic, it became less and less fulfilled.*
- In the '90s, the goal was to "Express Yourself."

But even as communication grew by leaps and bounds, the messages we sent and received confused us.

- In every age, Jesus says, "Die to self."

Die to self. Take up the cross. Today it would be, "Take up the gas chamber," or "Take up the electric chair." We wear cross earrings and cross necklaces, but what if we started wearing miniature gas chamber earrings or electric chair necklaces? They would more fully capture the essence of what Jesus was saying.

We sing the hymn, "There's room at the Cross for you." But what if we sang, "There's room in the gas chamber for you"? You see, the Cross has lost its impact because it's so familiar. But to these people at this time who heard Jesus say, "If you want to come after Me, you've got to take up the Cross," it would be like us hearing, "If you want to follow Me, you must take up the electric chair and die a degrading death."

Matthew 10:39 (a)
He that findeth his life shall lose it . . .

Do you ever hear people say, "Man, I'm losing it"? The reason they say this is because they're living for themselves. If you find your life and live for yourself, you'll lose it.

Matthew 10:39 (b)
. . . and he that loseth his life for my sake shall find it.

If you want to be miserable, turn inward; but if you want to have life, Jesus—the Author of life—says, "Die to self. Live for Me."

Matthew 10:40–42
He that receiveth you receiveth me, and he that receiveth me receiveth him that sent me. He that receiveth a prophet in the name of a prophet shall receive a prophet's reward; and he that receiveth a righteous man in the name of a righteous man shall receive a righteous man's reward. And whosoever shall give to drink unto one of these little ones a cup of cold water only in the name of a disciple, verily I say unto you, he shall in no wise lose his reward.

"Anyone who honors you will be honored by Me. Even if they give you a cup of cold water, they are going to be profited and blessed presently and eternally."

In the Book of Hebrews, we are told the Lord is not unfaithful to forget our works of righteousness (6:10). When you do something for someone else, they might forget about it. But when you do something in the Name of the Lord for the people of the Lord, He promises He will not forget, and you will be rewarded. When? Perhaps now—but even better, in heaven.

Go for it, gang. Take the words of Matthew 10 to heart. Die to self. Live for Jesus.

---

11 As we have seen thus far, the Book of Matthew presents Jesus Christ as King—King of Israel primarily, but not exclusively, for we know that Jesus is the King of kings and the Lord of lords for all people inclusively. But Jesus, in harmony and agreement with what the prophets predicted, came on the scene and presented Himself to the people of Israel as their King and Messiah. In chapters 1 through 10, we've seen the revelation of the King—His Person, His Principles, His Power, His People. Here in chapters 11 and 12, we see rebellion against the King, where all of the revelations of chapters 1 through 10 will be challenged by His enemies.

Matthew 11:1
And it came to pass, when Jesus had made an end of commanding his twelve disciples, he departed thence to teach and to preach in their cities.

I find it interesting that after Jesus sent out the twelve, He taught in their home cities. Jesus would later say a prophet is not without honor except in his own country. In other words, a prophet can go anywhere and be listened to by everyone, except by those who grew up with him or those who thought they really knew him. When He returned to His hometown of Capernaum, Jesus' neighbors said, "Don't we know You? You're the carpenter's son. We know Your brothers and sisters." And they didn't believe in Him.

Here, Jesus goes into the apostles' home cities, knowing that if the disciples had been sent to those who knew them, the response would be, "You think you guys are apostles? What a joke!" Does this mean you shouldn't be a witness at home? No. We *must* witness there. But if the Lord leads you to Mexico, to the Philippines, or to the untamed jungle of Los Angeles, you just might find yourself enjoying an extra measure of fruitfulness.

Matthew 11:2, 3
Now when John had heard in the prison the works of Christ, he sent two of his disciples,

and said unto him, Art thou he that should come, or do we look for another?

Herod, the ruler of Israel, had taken his brother's wife as his own, and John the Baptist boldly and pointedly indicted him for his sin. Herod retaliated by imprisoning John. John probably wasn't worried initially. He probably thought, *That's okay. Messiah's on the scene. He'll spring me out of here in no time. Don't the prophecies declare He shall open prison doors and set the captive free? I won't be in here long! No problem!* But there he sat, week after week after month in that dingy, damp dungeon. And he sent word to Jesus: "What's going on? You're Messiah, aren't You? That's what I was preaching. I even saw the dove of the Spirit descend upon You. Why, then, haven't You established Your kingdom? Why am I still in prison?"

Do you ever feel like that? Do you ever ask, "Lord, why am I still imprisoned? Why haven't You set me free? Why haven't You worked it out, Lord? Week after month after year has gone by, and here I sit." John did. So he sent emissaries to ask Jesus if He was the Messiah. If not, they would start looking for another.

Matthew 11:4–6
Jesus answered and said unto them, Go and shew John again those things which ye do hear and see: The blind receive their sight, and the lame walk, the lepers are cleansed, and the deaf hear, the dead are raised up, and the poor have the gospel preached to them. And blessed is he, whosoever shall not be offended in me.

"Look around, guys," said Jesus. "And look it up. See that Isaiah prophesied the very things you are seeing: the blind receiving their sight, the lame walking, lepers being cleansed, the deaf hearing, and the dead rising. Look around, look it up, and tell John that the prophecies are being fulfilled and the kingdom is being seen—although in a different way than perhaps he expected. The political, material, physical kingdom John was hoping for *will* come eventually. But now I am establishing My kingdom spiritually, and touching people individually."

So John was gently rebuked here as his disciples returned to him, saying, "The blind are seeing, the deaf are hearing, the lame are walking, and Jesus said happy is the one who's not offended in Him." I bet when John heard this, his heart sank. "Oh, how could I be so dumb? Of course. He is fulfilling the prophecies. How could

I doubt Him?" At this point, John must have been very down on himself, but read the next verse to see Jesus' impression of him.

Matthew 11:7
And as they departed, Jesus began to say unto the multitudes concerning John, What went ye out into the wilderness to see? A reed shaken with the wind?

"Did you go out to see someone who was flimsy and floppy, blowing in the wind and reading the latest public opinion polls before deciding what stance he should take? No! Far from being a reed shaken by the wind, John was a wind shaking the reeds!"

Matthew 11:8 (a)
But what went ye out for to see? A man clothed in soft raiment?

No. John wore camel's hair and dined on grasshoppers.

Matthew 11:8 (b)–10
. . . behold, they that wear soft clothing are in kings' houses. But what went ye out for to see? A prophet? yea, I say unto you, and more than a prophet. For this is he, of whom it is written, Behold, I send my messenger before thy face, which shall prepare thy way before thee.

Neither flimsy reed nor pampered courtier, John is the one who was prophesied by Malachi four hundred years previously—the messenger who would come before Messiah.

Matthew 11:11 (a)
Verily I say unto you, Among them that are born of women there hath not risen a greater than John the Baptist . . .

In Jesus' estimation, John the Baptist was greater than Abraham, greater than Moses, greater than Elijah, greater than David. Here's what interests me: This was spoken to the crowd *after* the messengers were sent off to tell John, "Blessed is the one who is not offended in Me." In other words, after John's disciples left, Jesus told the crowd John was the greatest who had ever been born of women. But John's disciples didn't hear that. Nor did John. So, too, although Jesus often challenges us through the Holy Spirit and convicts us through the Word, there are times He says to His angels, "Look at My people at Calvary Chapel—aren't they impressive? Robed in

My righteousness and cleansed by My blood. They study My Word. They sing praises to My Name. They like to pray. They love Me. Aren't they special?"

I know this is going on because I've been reading the Song of Solomon. I know what my Lord's heart is toward me. But sometimes those things are out of earshot because He wants to change me and push me to be all I can be, all I should be here on earth that I might be all He wants me to be in eternity. He keeps challenging us, but at the same time, perhaps out of earshot, He commends us.

Like John, you might be saying, "I'm such a failure. I've erred so badly. I've blown it again. There's no hope for me, my ministry, my walk with the Lord, my relationship with Him." The Lord might convict and challenge you, yes, but at the same time know this: Even as He commended John, I'm confident He commends you.

Matthew 11:11 (b)
. . . notwithstanding he that is least in the kingdom of heaven is greater than he.

In this kingdom age in which we live, even the least of us is greater than John. Why? Because we have an understanding of things John and the Old Testament prophets could not know. Peter tells us the prophets of old tried to understand, asking, "How can these things be?" We, on the other hand, have greater insight because we have been allowed to live in this age where we understand the plan of God, where we have been forgiven of all our sins by the blood of Jesus, and where we have the indwelling Spirit.

Matthew 11:12
And from the days of John the Baptist until now the kingdom of heaven suffereth violence, and the violent take it by force.

In the original Greek language, this can be translated two ways. It could mean that the kingdom of heaven is being attacked by violent men—for indeed it was. John was in prison, and he was about to be beheaded. Herod had killed perhaps thousands of babies in his drive to murder the Christ Child. Bloodshed and violence abounded as the kingdom emerged, so it could be that this verse speaks of the kingdom of heaven suffering violence by enemies trying to overtake it with force.

Or, it could be rendered another way with equal accuracy. That is, that the kingdom of heaven is taken by men who are aggressively, en-thusiastically pressing in and laying hold. It is not for those who just sit back apathetically and say, "*Que sera sera*, whatever will be will be." Rather, it is taken by those who, with fervency in prayer, an exercise of faith, and an expenditure of energy lay hold of the promises of God violently and aggressively. Both meanings of this verse find illustration in John the Baptist.

Matthew 11:13–15
For all the prophets and the law prophesied until John. And if ye will receive it, this is Elias, which was for to come. He that hath ears to hear, let him hear.

In John 1, the Pharisees asked John directly, "Are you Elijah?" to which he replied, "I am not." And yet here Jesus is saying, "If you can receive it, this is Elijah." How do we reconcile this? Stick around. The answer appears in chapter 17.

Matthew 11:16–19
But whereunto shall I liken this generation? It is like unto children sitting in the markets, and calling unto their fellows, and saying, We have piped unto you, and ye have not danced; we have mourned unto you, and ye have not lamented. For John came neither eating nor drinking, and they say, He hath a devil. The Son of man came eating and drinking, and they say, Behold a man gluttonous, and a winebibber, a friend of publicans and sinners. But wisdom is justified of her children.

Continuing His discussion of John the Baptist, Jesus asks, "What can I say about this generation? John came as an ascetic, neither eating, nor drinking, but chomping on grasshoppers and living on honey, and you called him crazy. Then I came, eating and celebrating, and you call Me a glutton and a winebibber. You didn't receive John with his asceticism, and you do not receive Me with My celebration. You don't want to dance, and you don't want to mourn. Nothing makes you happy."

Matthew 11:20–22
Then began he to upbraid the cities wherein most of his mighty works were done, because they repented not: Woe unto thee, Chorazin! woe unto thee, Bethsaida! for if the mighty works, which were done in you, had been done in Tyre and Sidon, they would have repented long ago in sackcloth and ashes. But I say unto you, It shall be more tolerable for Tyre and Sidon at the day of judgment, than for you.

Tyre and Sidon were Gentile cities that had been judged. But Jesus says, "Woe unto you, Chorazin and Bethsaida"—cities near Galilee where Jesus had headquartered His ministry. "Woe unto you even more than Tyre and Sidon because, although I have done many mighty works among you, you did not respond to Me."

Matthew 11:23, 24
And thou, Capernaum, which art exalted unto heaven, shalt be brought down to hell: for if the mighty works, which have been done in thee, had been done in Sodom, it would have remained until this day. But I say unto you, That it shall be more tolerable for the land of Sodom in the day of judgment, than for thee.

In addition to Chorazin and Bethsaida, Jesus indicts His hometown of Capernaum. Those living in Capernaum saw His works, they heard His message, but they did not respond.

If you go to Israel, you can go to the sites of Capernaum, Bethsaida, and Chorazin. These cities, once hugely prosperous, are now nothing but archaeological digs. By all logic, these cities should be thriving today. The location is beautiful. The climate is primo. The water is abundant. The resources are many. But these cities were judged and destroyed not very long after this statement was made, and they were never rebuilt. It would be as if Balboa Island, Newport Beach, and San Diego were wiped out and never rebuilt. People would say, "Why not? Those are lovely spots geographically." Yet centuries have come and gone, and these three cities are still dead.

And so are we if we reject the words of Jesus Christ. If any of you say, "I don't believe in this Jesus stuff, not really," you're a dead city. If you refuse to respond to the mighty works of Jesus Christ all around you and to His Word constantly before you, judgment will come upon you.

Matthew 11:25, 26
At that time Jesus answered and said, I thank thee, O Father, Lord of heaven and earth, because thou hast hid these things from the wise and prudent, and hast revealed them unto babes. Even so, Father: for so it seemed good in thy sight.

Jesus' attention shifted from the rebellious to the faithful as He said, "Father, thank You that You have revealed truth to these babes. The Pharisees, the religious, the scholars—they're not responding. But, Father, thank You for the babes." In the Book of Acts, Luke writes that the Pharisees, Sadducees, and scribes marveled when they heard the wisdom of Peter and John. "How did these fishermen get such wisdom?" they wondered. The answer? Peter and John had been with Jesus (Acts 4:13). That's the key. Spend time with the Lord in the Word, and you'll be so wise that even Pharisees will wonder how you became so wise.

Matthew 11:27
All things are delivered unto me of my Father: and no man knoweth the Son, but the Father; neither knoweth any man the Father, save the Son, and he to whomsoever the Son will reveal him. How do you know the Father? Only one Way, through the Son— Jesus Christ.

God is so immense. The Milky Way galaxy is approximately 100,000 light years across. Traveling at the speed of light, 186,000 miles per second, it would take 100 million years just to get across the length of the Milky Way galaxy.

And yet the Word says our Lord spans the universe between His thumb and His little finger (Isaiah 40:12)! Big! Enormous! How do we know such a vast God? Oh, great is the mystery of godliness, Paul said, that God would become a Man, manifesting Himself in Christ Jesus (1 Timothy 3:16).

Our Christian faith is truly ingenious. I mean, this huge, vast God became a Man that we might know Him. But our sin stood in the way of a relationship with Him, so that same God died on a Cross at Calvary to provide atonement for our sin. Then He rose again to live inside of us by His Spirit. It's perfect! There's not a flaw in it!

Matthew 11:28–30
Come unto me, all ye that labour and are heavy laden, and I will give you rest. Take my yoke upon you, and learn of me; for I am meek and lowly in heart: and ye shall find rest unto your souls. For my yoke is easy, and my burden is light.

"Come to Me," Jesus says. "Yoke with Me. Learn of Me. And you'll find rest in your souls."

For topical study of Matthew 11:28–30 entitled "A Word to the Weary," turn to page 81.

A WORD TO THE WEARY
A Topical Study of
MATTHEW 11:28–30

Although it took place in the 1930s, it remains one of the most mystifying missing person cases in FBI files. After spending an evening eating out with friends, a forty-five-year-old New York judge hailed a taxi and was never seen or heard from again. The FBI immediately became involved. They suspected a kidnapping by someone who held a judicial grudge against him. But that didn't seem to pan out. They then suspected Mafia activity because he was an outspoken enemy of the Mafia. But again, that led nowhere. To this day, there is only one clue that remains. When his wife returned to their apartment the evening her husband disappeared, there on the table was a check for a large sum of money made out to her and a note attached to it in her husband's handwriting which simply said,

I am very, very tired. Love, Joe

The question remains—were those words merely a comment made at the end of a particularly trying day? Or was his note saying, "I'm tired; I'm fatigued; I'm weary; I give up"? To this day, we can't be sure. For lack of further evidence, it is presently believed he rode off in a taxicab to an unknown destination where he took his own life because weariness had weighted his soul. I think all of us from time to time can relate to that kind of weariness. I'm not speaking of physical fatigue—the kind of fatigue you feel after mowing the lawn or playing a set of tennis. No, I'm speaking of the weariness which comes from life itself.

If you are of average weight and height, here is what you will go through in an average twenty-four-hour period: Your heart will beat 103,689 times. Your blood will travel 168 million miles as your heart pumps approximately 4 ounces per beat. You will breathe 23,040 times, inhaling 438 cubic feet of air. Your stomach will take in three and a half pounds of food and 2.9 quarts of liquid. You will lose seven eighths of a pound of waste. If you are a man, you will speak 4,800 words, and if you are a woman, you will speak close to 7,000 words. You will move 750 muscles and exercise 7 million brain cells.

No wonder we're tired! But there is a weariness much more draining than physical fatigue. It's the kind of weariness you feel when you just don't know if you can go on another day. It's the weariness a father feels when his child is doing wrong, the weariness a friend feels who has been abandoned or misunderstood, and the weariness a wife feels whose husband has rejected her. It's the weariness that can take a toll on even the most seemingly successful individual—even on a successful judge.

There is One, however, who said, "Come to me, all you who are weary . . ." (see Matthew 11:28). How I appreciate that! The Lord of the universe invited anyone who is weary to come to Him. If I were the Lord, I don't know if I would make that kind of invitation. Keep in mind that at this point in Matthew's Gospel, Israel is rejecting His invitation to make Him King. Consequently, no longer is Jesus speaking to a nation corporately, saying, "Repent: for the kingdom of heaven is at hand."

No, now He is speaking to individuals personally, saying, "Come to Me, any who are weary, any who are laboring." Would you have called this group of people? I'm not sure I would. If I were giving an invitation, I don't think I would have said, "Come unto me all you who are laboring and weary—feeling as though you're depressed to the point of death, despairing because of divorce or disease, death or discouragement."

No, I think I would say, "Come unto me, all you who are happy—let's celebrate life together! Let's lift each other's spirits!" Or maybe I would have said, "Come unto me, all you who are wealthy. Come and share your prosperity!" Or maybe, "Come unto me all you who are wise. Let's dialogue and philosophize and interact intellectually." But the personal invitation Jesus extended to people individually as the nation rebelled against Him corporately was: "Anyone who is weary, come to Me. Those are My people—the weary ones."

Come unto me . . .

Jesus didn't say, "Run to Me." So often in my weariness, I can't run. I can only stumble to Him or crawl before Him. But that's okay. He just said *"Come"* any way we can.

Come unto *me* . . .

He didn't say, "Go to church." He didn't say, "Listen to a sermon." He didn't say, "Get some counseling." He didn't say, "Read a book." He said, "Come to *Me*."

Come unto me, all ye that *labour* . . .

What causes us to be weary in our labor? I believe the answer is found in Exodus 5.

The people of Israel were in Egypt. Four hundred years previously, they left the Land of Promise due to famine and headed south to Egypt where there was plenty to eat. They lived there for a while, enjoying the abundance and prosperity. But suddenly the situation changed when a new Pharaoh came on the scene, looked at the Jewish people, and said, "We've got to control these people. How? We'll enslave them." So for hundreds of years, the people of God were enslaved by the Egyptians, baking bricks in the blistering, burning sun for the construction of Pharaoh's monuments. It has been documented that the Israelites baked enough bricks to build a wall ten feet high and five feet thick from LA to New York City. When Moses said, "Let my people go," Pharaoh answered,

> *Ye shall no more give the people straw to make brick, as heretofore: let them go and gather straw for themselves. And the tale of the bricks, which they did make heretofore, ye shall lay upon them; ye shall not diminish ought thereof: for they be idle; therefore they cry, saying, Let us go and sacrifice to our God. Let there more work be laid upon the men, that they may labour therein; and let them not regard vain words.*   Exodus 5:7–9

The Hebrew word translated "labour" in verse 9 has the same meaning as the Greek word translated "labour" Jesus used in Matthew 11. Do you sometimes feel like you're stuck in Egypt, endlessly making bricks for Pharaoh under the blistering sun? Maybe you've said, "I'm going to Egypt. I'm going to labor to get ahead in my career," or, "I'm going to work hard for this material thing." And for a while, it seemed enjoyable. But then, just like Pharaoh, it turned against you, and the very thing you thought would be wonderful is now a taskmaster—cracking the whip and enslaving you.

"Come to Me," the Lord says. "All you who are weary from labor, all you who have realized Pharaoh is a fake and Egypt is a rip off, come to Me."

We have a tendency to think, *I'm going to be so happy when I accomplish this task, when I reach that goal, when I get this business or that toy.*

And we labor and labor until we finally say, "This isn't working out the way I thought it could, the way the commercials promised it would. I'm miserable. I'm tired. I'm weary."

Come unto Me, all ye that labour and
are heavy laden . . .

What does it mean to be heavy laden?

> *Ah sinful nation, a people laden with iniquity, a seed of evildoers, children that are corrupters: they have forsaken the LORD, they have provoked the Holy One of Israel unto anger, they are gone away backward. Why should ye be stricken any more? ye will revolt more and more: the whole head is sick, and the whole heart faint. From the sole of the foot even unto the head there is no soundness in it; but wounds, and bruises, and putrifying sores: they have not been closed, neither bound up, neither mollified with ointment.*
>
> Isaiah 1:4–6

The Lord says to His people, Israel, "You're beat up and bruised and hurting and desolate and destroyed because you have been laden, loaded with iniquity." You see, Pharaoh makes us labor, but sin makes us heavy laden. Sin weighs us down.

David went through a season of sin on more than one occasion. During one such time, he wrote,

There is no soundness in my flesh because of thine anger; neither is there any rest in my bones because of my sin. For mine iniquities are gone over mine head: as an heavy burden they are too heavy for me. My wounds stink and are corrupt because of my foolishness. I am troubled; I am bowed down greatly; I go mourning all the day long. For my loins are filled with a loathsome disease: and there is no soundness in my flesh. I am feeble and sore broken: I have roared by reason of the disquietness of my heart. Psalm 38:3–8

Sin will make you tired. What does Jesus say? He says, "Whether you've been seduced and sucked in by Pharaoh's mentality—working for the world and finding it to be nothing but bricks and weariness—or whether you've been heavy laden with iniquity, come unto Me."

Come unto Me, all ye that labour and are heavy laden,
and I will give you rest.

How?

Take my *yoke* upon you . . .

The Greek word translated "carpenter" used in Matthew 13 to describe Joseph refers to a finish carpenter rather than for a framer. Tradition has it that the carpenter shop where Jesus worked with His father, Joseph, specialized in making yokes. To yoke two oxen together, the skilled carpenter designed the yoke to fit each ox individually. Since there was always a lead ox yoked together with one who would follow, the yoke was designed in such a way that the lead ox would pull the greater weight. The follower, or assistant ox, was just to go with the flow.

Take *My* yoke upon you . . .

Jesus used an analogy well known to the people who listened to Him when He said not only, "Come unto Me," but, "Yoke with Me. Let Me be the lead ox. Go with My flow. Don't try to figure out or change My direction. Let Me lead you."

The story is told of a battleship cruising the Atlantic, off the northern coast of Maine. One stormy evening, the commander was notified, "Sir, there's a light ahead. Oncoming vessel."

"Signal the oncoming vessel: change your courses ten degrees to the west."

The message was sent.

But a light flashed back, "Change *your* course ten degrees to the east."

"Signal again," barked the commander. "Change *your* course ten degrees to the west. I am an admiral!"

The light flashed back, "Change *your* course ten degrees to the east. I am a Seaman Third Class."

By this time, the admiral was incensed as he thundered, "Signal again: Change *your* course ten degrees to the west. I am a battleship."

And the message came back, "Change *your* course ten degrees to the east. I am a lighthouse."

So, too, as we impudently and impetuously say to the Lord, "Lord, let's go my way," He answers, "No. We're going My way."

> *I am the Lighthouse.*
> *I am the Light of the world,*
> *The Rock of your salvation,*
> *the Creator and Sustainer of your soul.*
> *I am the Alpha and the Omega,*
> *The One who knows the beginning from the end.*
> *Trust Me.*

Come unto Me, all ye that labour and are heavy laden, and I will give you rest. Take my yoke upon you, and *learn of Me; for I am meek and lowly in heart . . .*

This is the only autobiographical statement Jesus ever made.

He didn't say, "Learn of Me because I am majestic and mighty," or "Learn of Me because I am powerful and prominent." He said, "That which you discover when you learn of Me will refresh you, for I am meek."

What is meekness? Meekness is strength under control. Picture a big, gentle Saint Bernard surrounded by yapping, snapping, little Chihuahuas. Now the Saint Bernard could open his mouth and chomp the Chihuahuas down in one gulp. He could take his paw and knock them away with one swipe. But the powerful Saint Bernard patiently puts up with the yappers and snappers at his feet. That's meekness.

When I study the Scriptures and learn of Jesus, I am always amazed at His goodness, His grace, His kindness, His gentleness, and His meekness.

Jesus says, "Come to Me—you who have been burned out by Pharaoh, you who have been wearied by the folly of sin. Yoke with Me—don't try to maneuver Me, steer Me, or demand of Me. Learn of Me, for I am meek and lowly."

The result?

. . . And ye shall find rest unto your souls.

You'll find what your heart is craving: Shabbat. Sabbath. Rest.

For my yoke is easy, and my burden is light.

In Acts 15, questions arose concerning Gentile converts and whether or not they should follow the laws and the rituals and be circumcised. Peter gave this response:

*Now therefore why tempt ye God, to put a yoke upon the neck of the disciples,
which neither our fathers nor we were able to bear?*   Acts 15:10

"My yoke," Jesus said, "is easy." It's not religion—it's relationship. It's not Judaism—it's Jesus. It's not the law—it's love.

Sometimes I hear people say, "I'm so burdened. It's so tough being a servant. It's so hard to be a brother, a musician, or a witness."

If it's heavy, it's not His burden because His burden is light. If what I'm doing is tough and wearisome to me, then I know it's not the Lord who has placed that burden upon me. His burden is easy. His load is light.

Jesus would say to you today, "Come to Me. Don't labor under the burdens of Pharaoh. You'll become weary if you do. Don't become heavy laden under the bondage of sin. It will rob you of your energy. Don't become enslaved by the laws of the Pharisees. You'll be weighed down. Just come to Me. Yoke with Me. Learn of Me. And you'll find rest in your souls."

12 The purpose of Matthew's Gospel is to present Jesus as King. In chapter 11, however, we saw the beginning of a rebellion against His authority as Israel failed to respond to His work among them. It is a rebellion that will lead to rejection and ultimately to Calvary.

Realizing that, as a nation, Israel would not acknowledge He was Messiah, Jesus began speaking to people individually, saying, "Come unto me all ye that labour and are heavy laden, and I will give you rest." Upon hearing this, the religious leaders would think, *We don't need His rest. We have our Sabbath. That is all the rest we need.* But in reality, the Sabbath day had become anything but a day of rest, for the scribes had encumbered it with so many rules and regulations that the Talmud devoted numerous chapters to instructions for keeping the Sabbath.

There remaineth therefore a rest to the people of God.   Hebrews 4:9

Even though the Sabbath day was established in the Book of Genesis, the author of Hebrews quotes Psalm 95, saying there *remains* a Sabbath for God's people. The argument of Hebrews 4 is that the ultimate Sabbath encompasses much more than a singular day. God's intent was much greater than just to give His people a vacation.

Other people say, "The Sabbath is not a vacation, it's location. It's not so much a day, it's a place." The Jews thought the perfect location would be the Promised Land. But Hebrews 4 goes on to say that even after they were in the Promised Land, the Lord still spoke of a rest that was to come. The Promised Land didn't satisfy the restlessness within them, and the Sabbath day didn't bring them the refreshment for which they longed. So Hebrews 4 concludes that true rest comes neither from vacation nor location. It's found in a Person. Jesus Christ is the Sabbath they sought.

Let no man therefore judge you in meat, or in drink, or in respect of an holyday, or of the new moon, or of the sabbath days: Which are a shadow of things to come; but the body is of Christ.   Colossians 2:16–17

In other words, don't let anyone tell you that what you are looking for can be found in meats and drinks and holy days and Sabbaths. No, these Old Testament pictures are only shadows describing the reality, which is Christ. We don't have a Sabbath day. We have a Sabbath God in Jesus Christ. *He* is our Rest. *He* is our Shabbat. But these were fighting words for the religious leaders and rabbis. And now the stage is set for chapter 12. The issue? The Sabbath.

Matthew 12:1
At that time Jesus went on the sabbath day through the corn; and his disciples were an hungred, and began to pluck the ears of corn, and to eat.

See now in your mind's eye Jesus walking with His disciples, flanked by fields of wheat. With roads in that day few and far between, travelers would walk on pathways that wound their way through fields. The law made provision in Deuteronomy 23 for the hunger of such travelers. If you walked on a path through a man's field, you could eat what grew along the path. Therefore, don't be mistaken. Jesus and His disciples were not robbing some poor farmer of his crops. They were well within the legal boundaries of the provision of God's Law.

Matthew 12:2
But when the Pharisees saw it, they said unto him, Behold, thy disciples do that which is not lawful to do upon the sabbath day.

Here's the question I have: What were these Pharisees doing in the field in the first place? They had broken their own rules by being more than three thousand feet away from their own homes on the Sabbath. But that's the way Pharisees always are. They would go out of their way to find fault with others, and in so doing, err themselves.

Matthew 12:3, 4
But he said unto them, Have ye not read what David did, when he was an hungred, and they that were with him; how he entered into the house of God, and did eat the shewbread, which was not lawful for him to eat, neither for them which were with him, but only for the priests?

"Haven't you been reading the Scriptures?" Jesus asked. "Don't you know the story of 1 Samuel 21? When David and his men became hungry while fleeing from Saul, the priests gave him the showbread, which was not lawful for them to eat. Don't you remember that story that shows love is more important than the law, relationship more important than ritual?" Jesus chose a particularly interesting illustration, for just as David was at that time rejected as king of Israel, so Jesus was also at this time rejected as King.

Matthew 12:5
Or have ye not read in the law, how that on the sabbath days the priests in the temple profane the sabbath, and are blameless?

Temple priests worked twice as hard on the Sabbath, their supposed day of rest, since twice as many sacrifices were offered to the Lord on that day. Jesus here is making an airtight case. "Don't you know history?" He said. "David ate the showbread and was held blameless. Don't you

know the law? It requires the priests to work doubly hard on the Sabbath day."

Matthew 12:6, 7
But I say unto you, That in this place is one greater than the temple. But if ye had known what this meaneth, I will have mercy, and not sacrifice, ye would not have condemned the guiltless.

"Finally," Jesus asks, "don't you know the Word?" as He quoted from the prophet Hosea. "Don't you know the heart of your Father? He desires mercy more than sacrifice, love more than law, and relationship more than ritual." Notice the ironclad case Jesus makes here. He points to David—a king they honored. He points to the priests—who worked on the Sabbath. He points to the prophet Hosea—who declared God loves mercy more than sacrifice. In validation of His own actions, Jesus identifies with a prophet, the priests, and a king. Jesus is ingeniously driving a point home to those who had ears to hear. "I am the King of kings, the great High Priest, the Prophet of God. I am the Anointed One. I am Messiah."

Matthew 12:8
For the Son of man is Lord even of the sabbath day.

"It all speaks of Me," declares Jesus. "It all points to Me." When you read the Scriptures, don't get hung up in the regulations, rituals, and technicalities. They are all shadows that point to Jesus. Look for Him and become enamored with Him as you see Him on every page. Jesus is Lord of all—even of the Sabbath day.

Matthew 12:9
And when he was departed thence, he went into their synagogue.

He went into *their* synagogue. Their synagogue was no longer *His* synagogue. What a tragedy when a church is no longer His church—where Jesus is no longer honored and loved, exalted and worshiped—but where He is simply a mascot. "Oh yeah. We believe in Jesus. Now let's get down to the real matters of the church. We must plan for our Christmas bazaar."

What a tragic loss. What tremendous love. Although it was no longer His synagogue, He still came in. I love the Lord for this. He doesn't give up. He continues on, time and time again.

Matthew 12:10–12
And, behold, there was a man which had his hand withered. And they asked him, saying,

Is it lawful to heal on the sabbath days? that they might accuse him. And he said unto them, What man shall there be among you, that shall have one sheep, and if it fall into a pit on the sabbath day, will he not lay hold on it, and lift it out? How much then is a man better than a sheep? Wherefore it is lawful to do well on the sabbath days.

Keep in mind that in their regulations, the Jews specifically said you could do no healing on the Sabbath day. Let's say a man was bleeding to death. You could put a tourniquet around him to prevent him from dying, but you could put no ointment on the wound that might bring healing. Jesus asks, "Why is it that your regulations say if a sheep falls into a pit on the Sabbath, it's okay to bring him out, but a man cannot be healed on the Sabbath?"

That's what the law always does. When you become all bound up in regulations, traditions, and religious rituals, your heart becomes cold and hardened towards people. You constantly judge them and find fault with them. Religion apart from relationship will make you a pompous, snooty, holier-than-thou Pharisee.

Matthew 12:13
Then saith he to the man, Stretch forth thine hand. And he stretched it forth; and it was restored whole, like as the other.

How I love this incident! "Stretch out your hand," said Jesus.

The man could have said, "I can't! It's paralyzed." But he didn't. He simply stretched it out; and as he obeyed, his hand was healed. There's power in the Word, gang. Dare to act, and you'll be able to act because God's commandments are God's enablements.

Matthew 12:14
Then the Pharisees went out, and held a council against him, how they might destroy him.

The problem with the Pharisees was jealousy. Nobody was noticing them anymore, and they didn't like the competition.

Matthew 12:15, 16
But when Jesus knew it, he withdrew himself from thence: and great multitudes followed him, and he healed them all; and he charged them that they should not make him known.

I think verse 16 should be written very boldly on the pulpits and in the margins of those who

have healing ministries. Jesus ministered in such a way that He was *not* trying to advertise His successes.

Matthew 12:17–19
That it might be fulfilled which was spoken by Esaias the prophet, saying, I will put my spirit upon him, and he shall shew judgment to the Gentiles. He shall not strive, nor cry; neither shall any man hear his voice in the streets.

Matthew quotes Isaiah 42, a beautiful prophecy wonderfully fulfilled in Jesus. God said, "This is the One in whom I am well pleased. My Spirit is upon Him. Justice will come to the Gentiles through Him. And He will not cry, neither shall any man hear His voice in the streets." Jesus was not like some men we see today, striving, crying, and being weird in the name of the Lord. Jesus didn't draw attention to Himself. In fact, He blended into His world so completely that in the Garden of Gethsemane, His enemies couldn't identify Him without a kiss. Here was a Man who had healed, fed, and taught thousands, yet He remained unidentifiable because He moved in such humility and such grace.

Matthew 12:20, 21
A bruised reed shall he not break, and smoking flax shall he not quench, till he send forth judgment unto victory. And in his name shall the Gentiles trust.

Reeds grow in marshes. They were, and still are, good for only one thing: musical instruments. If a reed became bruised or bent, it was good for nothing. Flax, too, was good for only one thing: to be used for wicks in lamps. Through the analogy of reeds and flax, Isaiah described the ministry of Jesus. Maybe you feel like nothing more than a squeaky reed or a smoking wick. I have good news for you: The Lord will not break you, throw water upon you, or give up on you. He'll strengthen you, rebuild you, and use you for His glory.

Matthew 12:22–24
Then was brought unto him one possessed with a devil, blind, and dumb: and he healed him, insomuch that the blind and dumb both spake and saw. And all the people were amazed, and said, Is not this the son of David? But when the Pharisees heard it, they said, This fellow doth not cast out devils, but by Beelzebub the prince of the devils.

As Jesus' ministry continued, the dumb began to talk, the blind began to see, and the Pharisees had no other choice but to accuse Him of working by the power of Satan himself. What else could they say? Jesus was healing and affecting so many that they had to come up with some explanation for His power. The same thing happens today whenever a person chooses to believe the work of the Holy Spirit is the result of brainwashing or manipulation, emotionalism or hypnotism, instead of attributing such power to God.

Matthew 12:25, 26
And Jesus knew their thoughts, and said unto them, Every kingdom divided against itself is brought to desolation; and every city or house divided against itself shall not stand: And if Satan cast out Satan, he is divided against himself; how shall then his kingdom stand?

"If I am casting out Satan by the power of Satan, then Satan's house is divided. He's fighting against himself. What you are saying is illogical," declared Jesus. Not only was their accusation illogical, but based on the following verses, it was hypocritical.

Matthew 12:27, 28
And if I by Beelzebub cast out devils, by whom do your children cast them out? therefore they shall be your judges. But if I cast out devils by the Spirit of God, then the kingdom of God is come unto you.

The Pharisees endorsed certain exorcists who went throughout the community casting out devils. Jesus said, "If you indict Me because I have freed a man of demonic power, then what about those whom you have endorsed? If, on the other hand, I cast out devils by the Spirit of God, you must acknowledge His kingdom is represented by Me, that it is here in your midst."

Matthew 12:29
Or else how can one enter into a strong man's house, and spoil his goods, except he first bind the strong man? and then he will spoil his house.

The enemy had to be bound through prayer and in faith before Jesus could release the one possessed by a demon.

Matthew 12:30
He that is not with me is against me; and he that gathereth not with me scattereth abroad.

Jesus says, "You're against Me, Pharisees," as He goes on to give them a scathing indictment.

Matthew 12:31, 32
Wherefore I say unto you, All manner of sin and blasphemy shall be forgiven unto men: but the blasphemy against the Holy Ghost shall not be forgiven unto men. And whosoever speaketh a word against the Son of man, it shall be forgiven him: but whosoever speaketh against the Holy Ghost, it shall not be forgiven him, neither in this world, neither in the world to come.

Follow the flow: A man has been released of a demon. The Pharisees attributed the miracle to the power of Satan, and Jesus now gives a heavy word to these Pharisees: "You are speaking illogically, acting hypocritically, and jeopardizing your own souls eternally." If they had not already done so, they were dangerously close to committing the blasphemy of the Spirit, which according to Jesus, is the only unpardonable sin.

When Jesus Christ died on the Cross of Calvary, He died not only for our sins but also for the sins of the whole world. That's the gospel. Jesus died for every sin every person who has ever lived on the face of this planet has committed or ever will commit. When He said, "It is Finished," the work was done. Every sin was paid for. That's great news! We can tell anyone, "My friend, your sins are forgiven! The price has been paid. You're free!"

But there is one sin that cannot be forgiven. There is one sin that will damn you eternally. It is the blasphemy of the Spirit. If you sin against the Father or against the Son, it's forgiven. But if you sin against the Spirit in this blasphemy, it will damn you eternally. That's the one sin that is unpardonable, the one sin that's unforgivable.

What is the blasphemy of the Holy Spirit? It is when you come to the wrong conclusion that the reason miracles are happening, people are changing, and the dumb are speaking is due to some kind of hypnotism, demonic activity, or mental delusion. And you begin to blaspheme what the Spirit speaks in your heart when He says, "No, it's real. It's Jesus."

If you ignore the Spirit's voice in your heart and say, "Those people at Calvary Chapel are being brainwashed, those Christians are drinking their bathwater, those believers are under some kind of delusion," there comes a point where you will have said, "No" one too many times to the Holy Spirit. There comes a point when the unpardonable sin has been committed. What does this mean? It means the Holy Spirit will no longer speak to you. You see, in Genesis 6, God declared, "My Spirit shall not always strive with man . . ." He's not always going to speak to you about your need for salvation.

Therefore, if you keep saying, "Those people are just being emotional; they just imagine they hear from God; they're off the wall," eventually you will commit the blasphemy of the Spirit, and you will be damned.

You can only hear the message and see the miracles so many times before God will finally say, "Okay, have your way. You don't want to acknowledge My reality? Very well. My Spirit will no longer speak to you." And then you're lost. At that point, you not only *will* not believe. At that point, you *cannot* believe.

In Jeremiah 7:16, God said to Jeremiah, "Don't pray any longer for this people. They are lost." Jeremiah was told to preach to them, but not to pray for them. It wouldn't do any good. There comes a time, we know not when, and a place, we know not where, when a man's fate is sealed between heaven and despair. You can't play games when the Spirit is drawing you.

During World War II, a United States battleship, aircraft carrier, and several other smaller boats were patrolling the waters of the Northern Atlantic in search of German U-boats. One evening, several pilots took off from the carrier and were told to be back by a certain hour. But the leader of the squadron of four planes purposefully stayed out longer, feeling with just a little more time, he could find the enemy and secure an impressive hit.

As the sun set, a German armada entered the area. The American fleet was in trouble for now they were outgunned, outmanned, and outnumbered. Unbeknownst to the pilots, radio silence was ordered between the ships in the water and aircraft still in flight. At this point, as their fuel was getting dangerously low, the pilots radioed to the American ships, but there was no reply. Again and again the pilots cried, "Turn on the lights. Turn on the landing lights." But the lights didn't go on, for to have done so would have jeopardized the lives of thousands of men.

Thus, the story is recorded how the men on that aircraft carrier stood by in horror as they watched four American planes crash into the icy waters of the Atlantic.

So, too, the Scriptures say, "Today is the day of salvation." The light is shining in your heart. You're hearing the Word of the Lord. But there will come a time when the Lord, the Commander-in-Chief, will order radio silence. The lights will be dimmed, and you will not be able to find your way home. You will have blasphemed the Spirit, and there will be no hope for you. The Lord offers you eternal and abundant life. He wants to for-

give your sins and fill you with joy. Only a fool would turn his back on such a gift. *Today* is the day of salvation. When you witness, pray passionately, and express yourself clearly. You need to be zealous in your witness because the stakes are high. A person doesn't have forever to make a decision. There is a point in time when the lights go off, when the communication stops. Such was the case with the Pharisees.

Matthew 12:33
Either make the tree good, and his fruit good; or else make the tree corrupt, and his fruit corrupt: for the tree is known by his fruit.

"Check out what I am doing," Jesus says. "The good fruit of people being healed and liberated will tell you something about Me. Check out the fruit."

Matthew 12:34–36
O generation of vipers, how can ye, being evil, speak good things? for out of the abundance of the heart the mouth speaketh. A good man out of the good treasure of the heart bringeth forth good things: and an evil man out of the evil treasure bringeth forth evil things. But I say unto you, That every idle word that men shall speak, they shall give account thereof in the day of judgment.

A news broadcast in Chicago was once interrupted by the once familiar song, "It's Howdy Doody Time, It's Howdy Doody Time . . ." when Howdy Doody broadcast waves hit some sort of an asteroid and bounced back thirty years later. So too, our words go on and on, and Jesus says we will give an account for them. Therefore, how thankful I am for the blood of Jesus. We have been forgiven, but those who blaspheme the Spirit, saying, "I don't want Jesus," must eventually answer to Him.

Matthew 12:37
For by thy words thou shalt be justified, and by thy words thou shalt be condemned.

Your words will either condemn you or justify you.

That if thou shalt confess with thy mouth the Lord Jesus, and shalt believe in thine heart that God hath raised him from the dead, thou shalt be saved. For with the heart man believeth unto righteousness; and with the mouth confession is made unto salvation.
Romans 10:9, 10

Matthew 12:38, 39
Then certain of the scribes and of the Phari-
sees answered, saying, Master, we would see
a sign from thee. But he answered and said
unto them, An evil and adulterous genera-
tion seeketh after a sign; and there shall no
sign be given to it, but the sign of the
prophet Jonah.

"The one sign I will give you is the sign of Jonah. Jonah preached judgment. I have come
preaching grace and mercy. Jonah was disobedient. I have come obediently. Jonah preached to
one city. I have come for the whole world. A
greater Prophet than Jonah is in your midst, yet
you do not respond."

Matthew 12:40, 41
For as Jonah was three days and three
nights in the whale's belly; so shall the Son
of man be three days and three nights in the
heart of the earth. The men of Nineveh shall
rise in judgment with this generation, and
shall condemn it: because they repented at
the preaching of Jonah; and, behold, a
greater than Jonah is here.

"The sign of Jonah" is resurrection—the one
and only sign Jesus promised as validation of His
words and ministry. That's why the Resurrection
is so important. It's the one sign upon which we
build our faith.

How do I know if the Cross really "took"? Was
God fully satisfied with the sacrifice of Jesus?
Are my sins really forgiven? Yea and amen! The
Resurrection proves Jesus is the Messiah and
that His work on the Cross was complete.

As valid as your testimony may be, in reality,
the most powerful prod to salvation you can provide is to talk to people about the Resurrection of
Jesus Christ. It's provable historically. It's undeniable philosophically and logically. Get the book,
Who Moved The Stone? by Frank Morison, an
Ivy League scholar who was determined to disprove the Resurrection. He studied for seven
years, and in the process, became a born-again
believer. Read *Evidence That Demands A Verdict* by Josh McDowell, or *Know Why You Believe* by Paul Little. Study the Resurrection and
make it the focal point of your witness.

Matthew 12:42
The queen of the south shall rise up in the
judgment with this generation, and shall
condemn it: for she came from the utter-
most parts of the earth to hear the wisdom
of Solomon; and, behold, a greater than Sol-
omon is here.

Jesus is referring to the account in 1 Kings 10,
wherein we read the Queen of Sheba cruised up
from Africa to see Solomon. Having heard about
his splendor, his majesty, and his wisdom, she
went away saying, "Amazing! The half wasn't
even told to me. What I've seen here is a mind
blower." Yet a greater King than Solomon was in
their midst.

• Solomon had wisdom from God. Jesus is the
  wisdom of God.
• Solomon was a great king. Jesus is the King
  of kings.
• Solomon spoke practically to his nation.
  Jesus spoke powerfully to all of creation.
• Solomon gave the Queen of Sheba gifts.
  Jesus is able to do exceedingly abundantly
  above all we can ask or think.

Matthew 12:43-45
When the unclean spirit is gone out of a
man, he walketh through dry places, seek-
ing rest, and findeth none. Then he saith, I
will return into my house from whence I
came out; and when he is come, he findeth it
empty, swept, and garnished. Then goeth he,
and taketh with himself seven other spirits
more wicked than himself, and they enter
in and dwell there: and the last state of that
man is worse than the first. Even so shall it
be also unto this wicked generation.

Again, think with me and follow the flow carefully. Jesus here is indicting this wicked generation, saying, "Although you might have cleaned
yourself up from the idolatry that once plagued
your country and have had reformation, you
haven't experienced regeneration. Although
you've swept your nation clean of idols, seven
times as many demons will flood you because you
are rejecting Me."

Jesus is speaking primarily of the nation of Israel. But He also speaks to me personally and to
us as a church corporately because we must be
careful that we do not seek to get people to
merely "clean up" their lives. There's a move today to try to bring reformation to our communities in the name of Jesus. Our communities do not
need reformation. Our communities need regeneration. People need to be born again. The work
of the gospel is from the inside out. Jesus called
us to be fishers of men, and you can't clean the
fish until you catch them.

People who try to clean up their lives or their
communities through reformation will sweep the
house clean, but seven times as many demons will
come back. The evil that follows will be greater
than the initial evil unless there is rebirth. Do you
really think we're going to stop drug abuse by

trying to eradicate the fields of coca in South America? Do you really feel that militarily or politically or through slogans like "Just Say No," we're going to rid ourselves of cocaine nationally?

We tried in Prohibition. "We'll sweep it clean," we said. "We'll close down the distilleries. We'll board up the breweries. We'll change this country through legislation." But do you know what followed? For a while, alcoholism seemed to ebb, but in its place came cocaine and heroin—seven times the greater evil.

We need to take the words of Jesus to heart. We must be about regeneration—not reformation; rebirth inwardly—not reform outwardly. Should we not then be involved in community activities and political undertakings? Of course. But as you are involved, you must realize your ultimate goal is to see people changed through the Gospel of Jesus Christ. You must be salt and light—drawing people to and reflecting *Him.*

Matthew 12:46
While he yet talked to the people, behold, his mother and his brethren stood without, desiring to speak with him.

Why did Jesus' family want to talk with Him? They were worried about Him. They knew one didn't call the Pharisees a brood of vipers and escape scot-free. According to a long list of rules and regulations concerning infidels and heretics, the Pharisees could stone someone for such an offense. So Jesus' mother and brothers, sensing confrontation, might have wanted to protect Him.

Matthew 12:47–49
Then one said unto him, Behold, thy mother and thy brethren stand without, desiring to speak with thee. But he answered and said unto him that told him, Who is my mother? and who are my brethren? And he stretched forth his hand toward his disciples, and said, Behold my mother and my brethren!

For those who say Mary has some kind of special influence on Jesus, this passage shows she didn't have a whole lot of pull. Jesus said, "Wait a minute. Who is My mother? My mother and My brothers are My disciples."

Matthew 12:50
For whosoever shall do the will of my Father which is in heaven, the same is my brother, and sister, and mother.

It is true we can't choose our family. But the Lord did. If you believe on Him whom the Father has sent, He embraces you as His family. He-

brews says He is not ashamed to call us brethren (Hebrews 2:11). He says, "Behold, My brothers, My sisters, My mother—those who hear My word, those who do the will of the Father, believing in Me—they are My family." Before the world began, Jesus chose *us* to live with Him eternally. Amazing!

13 In chapter 12, we saw mounting opposition to Jesus. Here in chapter 13, the last in this section that presents the King resisted, Jesus heads for the seashore.

Matthew 13:1, 2
The same day went Jesus out of the house, and sat by the sea side. And great multitudes were gathered together unto him, so that he went into a ship, and sat; and the whole multitude stood on the shore.

In the late 1800s, Charles Spurgeon, the "Prince of Preachers," who at the age of twenty had a congregation of thousands, told young seminarians they would have to weigh at least two hundred fifty pounds to be effective expositors. A big man himself, he believed ample girth allowed voice projection essential in the days before electric amplification.

Jesus employed a simpler technique. He spoke from a boat so His voice could bounce off the water and be amplified in the process. Creator of this principle, Jesus used it powerfully.

Matthew 13:3 (a)
And he spake many things unto them in parables . . .

The use of parables was the way people communicated when they wanted to arouse curiosity and excite interest. They wouldn't use guitars or humor, but rather they would use parables—little stories with big messages. The word "parable" comes from *parabole* in Greek. The Greek word *para* means "alongside," while *ballo* means "to cast, or to throw." Thus, the word "parable" means "casting alongside." Parabolic teaching places a story alongside a truth or a principle. As you study parables, realize this: The lost and the lazy will not understand them, but for those who are interested in truth, they are wonderfully illuminating.

Matthew 13:3 (b)–9
. . . saying, Behold, a sower went forth to sow; and when he sowed, some seeds fell by the way side, and the fowls came and

devoured them up: Some fell upon stony places, where they had not much earth: and forthwith they sprung up, because they had no deepness of earth: And when the sun was up, they were scorched; and because they had no root, they withered away. And some fell among thorns; and the thorns sprung up, and choked them: But other fell into good ground, and brought forth fruit, some an hundredfold, some sixtyfold, some thirty-fold. Who hath ears to hear, let him hear.

This parable has two applications. Primarily, it speaks of how we *hear* the Word. Secondarily, it gives understanding about how we *share* the Word. In verse 9, Jesus says, "Whoever has ears to hear, let him hear." Tune in! Think through. Listen up!

A former television news producer conducted a most intriguing survey. Following one broad-cast, he sent a crew to survey people who watched the show in its entirety, which at that time consisted of nineteen stories in the thirty-minute broadcast. Fifty-one percent of those who watched the entire half-hour broadcast could not remember a single story. His conclu-sion was that people don't listen, and a decision was made at that time to simplify news pro-gramming.

So, too, understanding the limited attention span of humanity, Jesus taught in simple, unforgetta-ble, powerful parables—one of His most well known being the Parable of the Sower.

For topical study of Matthew 13:3–9 entitled "Sowing the Seed," turn to page 99.

Matthew 13:10–12
And the disciples came, and said unto him, Why speakest thou unto them in parables? He answered and said unto them, Because it is given unto you to know the mysteries of the kingdom of heaven, but to them it is not given. For whosoever hath, to him shall be given, and he shall have more abundance: but whosoever hath not, from him shall be taken away even that he hath.

In other words, the one who receives and re-sponds will gain even more insight, but the one who doesn't respond, even the little understand-ing he has will be taken away.

Matthew 13:13–15
Therefore speak I to them in parables: be-cause they seeing see not; and hearing they hear not, neither do they understand. And in them is fulfilled the prophecy of Esaias, which saith, By hearing ye shall hear, and shall not understand; and seeing ye shall see, and shall not perceive: For this people's heart is waxed gross, and their ears are dull of hearing, and their eyes they have closed; lest at any time they should see with their eyes, and hear with their ears, and should understand with their heart, and should be converted, and I should heal them.

Here Jesus quotes a difficult passage from Isa-iah 6, in which Isaiah is commanded by the Lord to speak to a people who won't hear him or re-ceive from him. It was a prophecy fulfilled com-pletely in Jesus, as He spoke to a people whose hearts were hardened, whose hearing was dull, and whose eyes were closed.

Now, here's the question. Why would God send Isaiah to preach to people who wouldn't listen or respond to him? Because God is a perfect gentle-man, and He will not force His will on anyone. He will honor the decision of those who don't want to be saved. Jesus spoke in parables because if He spoke plainly, His presentation would have been so powerful that everyone would automatically be converted—many against their will.

Maybe you've seen films of Adolf Hitler speak-ing to the German masses, firing them up during World War II. That is nothing compared to what Jesus could have done. He could have mobilized the entire country. He could have swept everyone up in what He was saying. But He bowed to hu-manity's freedom of choice. "If I speak in para-bles, those who don't want to see, won't see. Those who don't want to hear won't hear."

A number of years ago a coal mine collapsed, and seven miners were trapped inside for three and a half days. Rescue workers dug feverishly, and when they finally broke through the caved-in mineshaft, the miners were whooping and holler-ing, obviously grateful they had been rescued—until one of the seven said, "Hey, why doesn't someone light a lantern?" The other six looked at their friend, and they realized he was blind. The light was on. The lanterns were lit. The rescue team had brought light into the darkened shaft, but he could not see because he had been blinded by the cave-in. Until the light came through, no one knew who was blind and who could see. The light had to shine on all seven before anyone could differentiate between those who could see and those who were blind.

So, too, Jesus taught believer and non-believer

alike in order to determine who was truly blind. The light was shining for those who wanted to see. But those who chose to be wicked wouldn't see the light, and it would only prove their blindness.

Matthew 13:16, 17
But blessed are your eyes, for they see: and your ears, for they hear. For verily I say unto you, That many prophets and righteous men have desired to see those things which ye see, and have not seen them; and to hear those things which ye hear, and have not heard them.

First Peter chapter 1 echoes this same truth. That is, prophets of old penned prophecies concerning the coming of Christ without understanding what they were writing or how it would work out practically. Thus, Jesus says, "You're blessed because you're seeing things come to pass that confused the prophets. You're blessed because you have the opportunity to hear, to see, and to understand."

Matthew 13:18–23
Hear ye therefore the parable of the sower. When any one heareth the word of the kingdom, and understandeth it not, then cometh the wicked one, and catcheth away that which was sown in his heart. This is he which received seed by the way side. But he that received the seed into stony places, the same is he that heareth the word, and anon with joy receiveth it; yet hath he not root in himself, but dureth for a while: for when tribulation or persecution ariseth because of the word, by and by he is offended. He also that received seed among the thorns is he that heareth the word; and the care of this world, and the deceitfulness of riches, choke the word, and he becometh unfruitful. But he that received seed into the good ground is he that heareth the word, and understandeth it; which also beareth fruit, and bringeth forth, some an hundredfold, some sixty, some thirty.

Jesus now explains the parable of the Sower to His disciples. The seed is the Scripture, which as it is sown, falls on four kinds of soil.

The first is the hard soil of paths that meandered through fields. It was soil packed down and which the seed could not penetrate at all. So the birds of the air swooped down and ate the seed for breakfast. So, too, sometimes people hear the Word, and their hearts are so hard, it makes no sense. It makes no impact.

The second soil represents those who say, "Yeah. All right! Wonderful!" as they receive the Word with joy. Maybe they received the Lord in a service, and they're caught up in the emotion of it. But when tribulation or persecution comes— when they are put down for their belief, or when they begin to understand what it means to take up the cross—they're offended, and they wither away.

The third type of soil is infested with weeds that choke the seed as it springs up. Jesus said the weeds represent the world and the deceitfulness of riches. Many people become excited about the things of the kingdom. They are into Bible study, enjoy prayer, and engaged in worship. But then they get involved in the things of this world. No longer do they have time for Bible study, worship, or prayer.

Lastly, Jesus said some seed falls on good ground and produces bunches of fruit—some thirty-fold, some sixty-fold, some a hundredfold. I find this intriguing because the ratio of seed to harvest is generally eight to one. But here, Jesus is saying when the seed is sown in cultivated soil, it's incredible what happens. Not eight to one, but thirty to one, sixty to one, or one hundred to one. We're talking fruit!

What is fruit? Scripture specifies six types.

- Romans 1:13 identifies soul-winning as a fruit.
- Romans 6:22 says holiness is a fruit.
- Romans 15:28 calls financial giving a fruit.
- Galatians 5:22, 23 lists the fruit of the Spirit as love, which results in joy, peace, longsuffering, gentleness, goodness, faith, meekness, temperance.
- Colossians 1:10 labels good works a fruit.
- Hebrews 13:15 names praise as a fruit.

Matthew 13:24–30
Another parable put he forth unto them, saying, The kingdom of heaven is likened unto a man which sowed good seed in his field: But while men slept, his enemy came and sowed tares among the wheat, and went his way. But when the blade was sprung up, and brought forth fruit, then appeared the tares also. So the servants of the householder came and said unto him, Sir, didst not thou sow good seed in thy field? From whence then hath it tares? He said unto them, An enemy hath done this. The servants said unto him, Wilt thou then that we go and gather them up? But he said, Nay; lest while ye gather up the tares, ye root up also the wheat with them. Let both grow together until the harvest: and in the time of harvest I will say to the reapers, Gather ye together first the tares, and bind them in

bundles to burn them: but gather the wheat into my barn.

Continuing His analogy of sowing, Jesus moved on to a subject very familiar to His listeners. When a farmer planted a field of wheat, anyone who had something against him would, under cover of night, sow tares in with the wheat. Tares have the same color, shape, and fragrance as wheat, but no heads of grain form. In other words, the tares soak up the nutrients, and they take up space, but they produce nothing in return and are unidentifiable until harvest time.

Matthew 13:31, 32

Another parable put he forth unto them, saying, The kingdom of heaven is like to a grain of mustard seed, which a man took, and sowed in his field: Which indeed is the least of all seeds: but when it is grown, it is the greatest among herbs, and becometh a tree, so that the birds of the air come and lodge in the branches thereof.

Follow the flow. Jesus is giving us insight about the kingdom. In verses 19–23, He talked about the sower sowing seed and how some of the seed falls upon good soil and produces fruit. In verses 24–30, He said in this field there will be some tares growing alongside the true wheat. Developing still further His seed / kingdom analogy, Jesus now likens the kingdom of heaven to the smallest seed sown—a mustard seed. Some commentators say this parable shows how the kingdom starts small and just grows beautifully. But wait—there is no example either in history or in botany where a mustard seed has grown into a tree large enough to support birds.

In reality, Jesus is talking about abnormal, unnatural growth. He's talking about something that begins small, like a mustard seed, but which grows abnormally to a size where birds can call it home. Bear in mind, students, that throughout the Bible, birds speak of evil. This is why I believe Jesus is talking about the kingdom becoming bureaucratic, losing its simplicity, and becoming too big organizationally as ministries have a propensity to do.

Matthew 13:33

Another parable spake he unto them; The kingdom of heaven is like unto leaven, which a woman took, and hid in three measures of meal, till the whole was leavened.

Leaven is mentioned ninety-eight times throughout Scripture. In every single case, it is linked with evil. So again, I disagree with those teachers who say these two parables describe the beautiful and mysterious growth of the kingdom. Leaven, symbolizing a puffing up, speaks of evil. In contrast, meal or bread in Scripture speaks of the Word; and I see a very tight connection between this parable and the last. Jesus is saying, "Watch out for outward organization that becomes good only for birds. Watch out for internal deception when leaven is hidden in the meal."

People knock on your door, saying, "May we hold a Bible study in your house? We have some wonderful things we want to share with you." And they come in and open their Bibles, but in addition, they show you the *Pearl of Great Price, The Book of Mormon,* or the *Watchtower Magazine.* What are they doing? They're inserting leaven into the meal of the Word.

Stick with the Scriptures. Don't let people add to the Word as they try to appeal to your spirituality. After all, when Satan came to Eve in the Garden, he didn't say, "Hey Eve, let's party!" No, he said, "Eve, you're so spiritual. You just want to be like God, and the day you eat this fruit, your eyes will be opened, and you will be more like Him."

Matthew 13:34–36

All these things spake Jesus unto the multitude in parables; and without a parable spake he not unto them: That it might be fulfilled which was spoken by the prophet, saying, I will open my mouth in parables; I will utter things which have been kept secret from the foundation of the world. Then Jesus sent the multitude away, and went into the house: and his disciples came unto him, saying, Declare unto us the parable of the tares of the field.

After Jesus sent the multitude away, the disciples came to Him asking for further instruction and greater illumination. So too, after receiving a teaching—perhaps at a Bible study, over the radio, in a book, or in your own devotions—have you discovered the dynamic of stopping and asking Jesus for further revelation and specific application? I'm convinced we lose much because once we hear a study, we split out the door and go our way without really taking the time to seek the Lord and say, "Father, what is in this for me today?"

Matthew 13:37–43

He answered and said unto them, He that soweth the good seed is the Son of man; The field is the world; the good seed are the children of the kingdom; but the tares are the children of the wicked one; the enemy that sowed them is the devil; the harvest is the end of the world; and the reapers are the

angels. As therefore the tares are gathered and burned in the fire; so shall it be in the end of this world. The Son of man shall send forth his angels, and they shall gather out of his kingdom all things that offend, and them which do iniquity; and shall cast them into a furnace of fire: there shall be wailing and gnashing of teeth. Then shall the righteous shine forth as the sun in the kingdom of their Father. Who hath ears to hear, let him hear.

Throughout chapter 13, Jesus has been teaching about the kingdom of God. In so doing, He is explaining we really don't know who's in the kingdom and who's not. In the kingdom, there are those who appear as though they're believers. They go to church regularly. They carry a Bible. They may even tithe. But they've never had a relationship with Jesus. They're counterfeit and bogus. They're tares. Satan has planted them within the kingdom to cause confusion and consternation.

The Bible speaks of false brethren in 2 Corinthians 11, a false gospel in Galatians 1, a false Christ in 2 Thessalonians 2, and a false church in Revelation 2.

When the church was born, Satan tried to destroy it through three hundred years of persecution. Ten Roman emperors ordered the systematic persecution of the church as Christians were dipped in hot wax and lit as candles, placed in boiling oil, skinned alive, and crucified upside down. But do you know what happened? The stronger the persecution, the more the church grew. It reminds me of Exodus.

Now there arose up a new king over Egypt, which knew not Joseph. And he said unto his people, Behold, the people of the children of Israel are more and mightier than we: Come on, let us deal wisely with them; lest they multiply, and it come to pass, that, when there falleth out any war, they join also unto our enemies, and fight against us, and so get them up out of the land. Therefore they did set over them taskmasters to afflict them with their burdens. And they built for Pharaoh treasure cities, Pithom and Raamses. But the more they afflicted them, the more they multiplied and grew. And they were grieved because of the children of Israel.   Exodus 1:8–12

So, too, concerning the church. The more Satan afflicted and burdened the church, the more she grew. That's always the way it is. Some years ago, when they were going through tremendous difficulty and very real persecution, a group of Russian Christians sent a letter to America, saying, "We are praying for you in America that you will have the opportunity to endure persecution and grow like us."

We pray, "Oh, Lord, don't allow persecution in Russia," but they pray, "Oh, Lord, persecute the church in America," because the Russian church has discovered that persecution brings about maturation and the propagation of the gospel. According to various reports, as of September 2002, there are anywhere between sixty and eighty million believers in China. Incredible! In persecution, the church grows.

Satan goofed in those first three hundred years. The church experienced persecution and began to spread throughout the whole world. So what did he do? He changed his tactics. In A.D. 313, with the edict of Constantine, Christianity was adopted as the national religion of Rome. Satan, in essence, joined the church. And the church has been suffering ever since. You see, the danger is not persecution. The real danger is infiltration. When Christianity becomes respectable and easy, tares pop up all over the place.

Is it our responsibility to rid the church of tares? No. This parable teaches separation will take place by the angels at the end of the world. If we try to figure out who's a believer and who's not, we're going to err and pull out the wrong people. It's our job to love, and it's God's job to judge. We are to love people, for "By this shall all men know that ye are my disciples, if ye have love one to another" (see John 13:35). Whether he's your brother or whether he's your enemy, whether he's wheat or a tare, it makes no difference. You are to love him and let God judge him. I really like this. I don't have to analyze, scrutinize, and criticize. I can just say, "Lord, thank You for this parable. And now I'm going to practice it. I get to love people and leave the judging to You. You see things perfectly. I don't."

Matthew 13:44

Again, the kingdom of heaven is like unto treasure hid in a field; the which when a man hath found, he hideth, and for joy thereof goeth and selleth all that he hath, and buyeth that field.

In this parable, a man finds some treasure and immediately buys the field in order to gain the treasure therein. You may have heard this parable taught like this: The treasure in the field is Jesus. We are the man. Like the man who found the treasure, when you discover Jesus, you should forsake everything to follow Him. But I believe this is an improper interpretation. I believe Jesus is the Man, and we are the treasure.

Think about it. When you were saved, how

many of you sold everything to follow Jesus? None of us did that. We were simply born again. How? Not by our will, not by our efforts, not even by our desire, but by God. God saved us; God elected us; God predestined us. We didn't sell anything to receive Him. He, on the other hand, gave His life to purchase us. Why was the field—the world—purchased? Did the Lord want another planet? No, He wanted the treasure that was buried in the world. He wanted you.

Matthew 13:45, 46
Again, the kingdom of heaven is like unto a merchant man, seeking goodly pearls: Who, when he had found one pearl of great price, went and sold all that he had, and bought it.

A pearl begins as nothing more than an irritating grain of sand stuck in the shell of an oyster. But the oyster surrounds the grain with a crystalline covering, which over years hardens and becomes precious and valuable. Those who study such things say the most beautiful pearls take seven years to form. During that seven-year period, the irritating piece of sand is hidden away—clothed and covered with beauty. That's us, gang—irritating pieces of sand. Yet, the Lord clothes us in His righteousness.

For he hath made him to be sin for us, who knew no sin; that we might be made the righteousness of God in him.   2 Corinthians 5:21

You are the pearl of great price. You have been clothed with the righteousness of Jesus Christ. And His righteousness is a thing of matchless beauty and unspeakable value in the eyes of God.

For topical study of Matthew 13:44–46 entitled "You are Treasured!" turn to page 103.

Matthew 13:47–50
Again, the kingdom of heaven is like unto a net, that was cast into the sea, and gathered of every kind: Which, when it was full, they drew to shore, and sat down, and gathered the good into vessels, but cast the bad away. So shall it be at the end of the world: the angels shall come forth, and sever the wicked from among the just, and shall cast them into the furnace of fire: there shall be wailing and gnashing of teeth.

The third illustration Jesus gave His disciples concerning the kingdom is that of a fisherman hauling in a great catch. In the net, there are some edible fish and some terrible fish. Now listen carefully, students. In these three mini-parables that deal with the kingdom—that is, the parables of the hidden treasure, the pearl of great price, and the net full of fish—Jesus outlines three major aspects of the kingdom.

The first concerns the treasure. In the Book of Exodus and throughout the Psalms, the nation of Israel is referred to as a peculiar, special treasure. Entrusted with the riches of God's heart and mind—the Word—Israel was placed *in* the world to be a light *for* the world. But what happened? Israel did not evangelize. She did not shine forth, but rather turned inward. The Jews hid themselves and their traditions, saying, "Gentiles? Don't talk to them. Don't look at them. Don't reach out to them. If you happen to even brush against one, take off your clothes and burn them. Gentiles are good for nothing but to keep hell hot."

Instead of enriching the world, the treasure became hidden in the world as Israel missed her calling. There are those who say Israel has no place in the kingdom. But in this parable, I believe Jesus teaches the treasure will indeed resurface and prove very valuable. Although Israel failed historically, she will succeed eventually. Revelation 7 says after the church is raptured, suddenly Israel will become a mighty instrument of evangelism in the world. She will enrich the world in the time of Tribulation. God is not through with Israel, gang. There are those who suggest Israel has no place in God's prophetic plan. Not true. Read your Bible: Romans 9—11 makes it very clear that although Israel has been set-aside for a while—hidden—she shall resurface as God's instrument.

Secondly, the church is a major aspect of the kingdom. Here, the church is likened unto a pearl. I find this intriguing. Where is a pearl formed? In the sea. What is the sea symbolic of scripturally and prophetically? In Daniel and Revelation, the sea is always symbolic of the Gentile nations. Where was the church formed? Although there are some believing Jews in the church, there aren't many. The church was formed from the Gentile nations.

A pearl is the only gem that does not need to be cut to bring out its beauty. Diamonds, rubies, sapphires, and amethysts—they all must be cut. But a pearl? If you even scratch it, you ruin it. So, too, in the church there is neither male nor female, Jew nor Gentile, bond nor free. The church is one—one Lord, one baptism, and one faith. The church finds her beauty in her unity—the unity of all kinds of people brought together in Christ. Divisions only mar her, and quite frankly, that is the biggest problem with denominations. There can be a tendency in denominationalism to start dividing the body of Christ instead of enjoying our commonality in Christ.

That they all may be one; as thou, Father, art in me, and I in thee, that they also may be one in us: that the world may believe that thou hast sent me.   John 17:21

Finally, end-time believers comprise the third aspect of the kingdom. Revelation 7 specifically talks about this group.

And one of the elders answered, saying unto me, What are these which are arrayed in white robes? And whence came they? And I said unto him, Sir, thou knowest. And he said to me, These are they which came out of great tribulation, and have washed their robes, and made them white in the blood of the Lamb. Therefore are they before the throne of God, and serve him day and night in his temple: and he that sitteth on the throne shall dwell among them.
                                Revelation 7:13–15

They are those who rejected the message of salvation in the church age, but after the church is raptured, they will refuse the mark of the beast and turn to the Lord. They are not the bride of Christ—sitting with Him, ruling and reigning with Him. No, these Tribulation believers will be allowed to enter into the kingdom, but in a different category than Israel or the Church. Maybe you know people who say, "Well, I'm not going to get saved now. I'm going to wait and see how things come down. *If* all of you Christians really do disappear, and *if* a guy really does come trying to brand my head—I won't take his mark, and I'll get saved."

Tell them this: "If you get saved at that time, it will probably cost you your life. If you choose to go that route, you will make it into the kingdom, but in a different position than if you receive Jesus today. Come to Him now."

So there is one kingdom made up of the treasure—Israel, the pearl, the church, and the fish—end-time believers. Three distinct groups, yet one kingdom.

Matthew 13:51, 52
Jesus saith unto them, Have ye understood all these things? They say unto him, Yea, Lord. Then said he unto them, Therefore every scribe which is instructed unto the kingdom of heaven is like unto a man that is an householder, which bringeth forth out of his treasure things new and old.

Jesus is saying, "If you understand these things, you're like a scribe who owns a house in which he has new innovations alongside old antiques." If you understand the kingdom, you can read the Old Testament and get blessed. You can look at history and marvel at the Lord's continuity

throughout the ages. You can draw from the old. And you can draw from the new if you understand what the Lord is doing creatively and powerfully in these last days.

The scribes, you see, were not originally as off the wall as we think of them today. Originally, in the days when Ezra brought a group of exiled Jews back to Jerusalem to rebuild the city after the captivity, the purpose of the scribes was to teach truth. Initially, the scribes were great seekers and teachers of truth. And Jesus is here saying, "You should be like scribes—drawing from the Old Testament and from the New Covenant."

If we get stuck in the old and are not open to what the Lord is doing presently, we'll miss what the Lord is doing creatively in this day. But if we're only into the new and fail to draw from our history and heritage, we'll become spiritual lightweights and airheads. Jesus said the one who receives from *both* old and new will be a rich man.

Matthew 13:53–57 (a)
And it came to pass, that when Jesus had finished these parables, he departed thence. And when he was come into his own country, he taught them in their synagogue, insomuch that they were astonished, and said, Whence hath this man this wisdom, and these mighty works? Is not this the carpenter's son? Is not his mother called Mary? And his brethren, James, and Joses, and Simon, and Judas? And his sisters, are they not all with us? Whence then hath this man all these things? And they were offended in him.

They thought they knew Him. A false sense of familiarity kept them from receiving what He wanted to do in their midst. "Oh, we know Him. We know His father." No, they didn't. "We know His brothers." No, they were His half brothers. Jesus' neighbors failed to recognize Him because they thought they knew all about Him.

The same holds true for us when, mistakenly thinking we know all about them, we fail to recognize His presence in our midst through our brothers and sisters in the Lord.

Matthew 13:57 (b), 58
But Jesus said unto them, A prophet is not without honour, save in his own country, and in his own house. And he did not many mighty works there because of their unbelief.

In writing of this same incident, Mark said, "He *could* not do many mighty works because of their unbelief." Jesus would have been able to heal them and to work radically among them, but because of unbelief, He was limited in what He could do for them.

Yea, they turned back and tempted God, and limited the Holy One of Israel.   Psalm 78:41

I encourage you to be open to the brother who talks with you after the service, to the sister who comes into your shop tomorrow. Jesus may be using them in a very real sense. Don't make the mistake of saying, "I know him. The Lord could never use *that* guy!" or "I know more than she does. How could the Lord possibly use *her* to

speak to me?" Wonderful things happen when you begin to say, "Lord, I'm looking for You. I believe You're going to work in my homeland in unexpected ways, at unexpected times, through unexpected people—all for *Your* glory."

For topical study of Matthew 13:54–58 entitled "Unbelief: Its Cause and Cure," turn to page 108.

SOWING THE SEED
A Topical Study of
MATTHEW 13:3–9

Jesus was a master communicator and a marvelous teacher. Although He was not the inventor of parabolic teaching, Jesus brought the form to unparalleled heights and to great depths of insight, the parable of the Sower being one of His most well known. When we talk about sowers, we're talking about farmers—people who sowed seed. Walking through a field, scattering seed as he went, the seed the farmer in this particular parable sowed fell on four types of soil.

Some seed fell on the hard soil by the wayside or in the pathways. It did not penetrate the ground, and the birds came and picked it off. Other seed fell on shallow, stony ground—ground with topsoil an inch or so deep, covering solid rock underneath. Such seed would spring up quickly, but lacking any real root system, it would wither away when the sun came out. Still other seed fell on ground infested with thorns that would choke the seed. Finally, some seed fell on good soil, and it brought forth fruit.

This parable has two primary applications. First, it speaks to us as hearers of the Word. Jesus said, "Take heed how ye hear," and "He that hath ears to hear, let him hear." In other words, "Listen up when the seed is being sown."

What is the seed? Jesus tells us the seed is the Scriptures, the Word of God, specifically the gospel. Peter picks up the same metaphor in his writings when he says we are born again not of corruptible seed, but of incorruptible seed, which is the Word of God. According to this parable, people receive the Word in one of four ways.

Some people have such hard hearts that the Word doesn't penetrate at all. Birds pluck it away before it can make any impact, and their hearts remain unchanged.

Others hear the Word and say, "Yeah, that sounds good!" And they get saved. They come forward, they raise their hands, and they get baptized, but there's no root; and when persecution and tribulation come, they dry up and check out.

In others, the cares of this world choke out the Word. They don't have time for Bible study anymore. They have to wax their cars, paint their houses, or dig their pools. They can't fit Scripture into their schedules.

Finally, some hear the Word and receive it because the soil is ready. Their hearts are right. They take it in, and it produces fruit—thirty-fold, sixty-fold, or a hundred-fold.

The parable is a powerful one, as it speaks to each of us concerning the condition of our hearts upon hearing the Word. But I want us to look at the second application—not just as hearers of the Word—but also as those who are distributing the seed. We have been called to share the gospel. We have been entrusted with this glorious, fabulous message. And this parable gives insight to some important principles about sharing the Word.

First, I understand from what Jesus is saying that not everyone is going to respond. In fact, if we look at this story, we see only one of four receive the Word and go on to fruitfulness. That's enlightening for me because it explains why some people seem so excited to receive the Word, but don't go on with the Lord. Jesus said this would be so. We shouldn't be surprised by it. Jesus said one of four would bear fruit—only one of four. But there *is* one of four. Think about this: Of all the people you have shared the gospel with—family, friends, schoolmates, neighbors— have one of four gone on to bear fruit? Or is it one of forty? One of four hundred? One of four thousand? Maybe you've never seen one neighbor, friend, family member, or colleague become fruitful in the Lord.

What can be done? I believe the answer lies within the parable itself. If indeed Jesus received the inspiration for this parable from Jeremiah 4, where God instructed Jeremiah to "Break up the fallow ground and sow seed not amongst the thorns," the question then becomes: How do we break up hard ground? Let me suggest to you something that is often overlooked with regard to hardened hearts and fallow ground. The problem is not with the seed, for the Word of God is powerful and real. The problem is with the soil. The soil has not been properly prepared. We have sown seed without preparing the soil.

Suppose on a 747 heading from San Francisco to Honolulu, the captain suddenly called the stewardess into his cabin and said, "We have a hole in the gas tank and only about thirty minutes of fuel left. We're two hours from Honolulu, but too far to turn back. This plane is going down. Distribute parachutes immediately to all passengers.

And suppose the stewardess comes out of the cabin, wipes the worried look from her face, and cheerfully says, "Ladies and gentlemen, who would like to wear a parachute? Try one on, and you will see how smooth a flight can be, how wonderful the trip can become." People listen to her, scratch their heads, and wonder. A few raise their hands and volunteer.

But after a while, the parachutes become cumbersome. And the people find they can't sit in their seats as comfortably as they previously did. They can't put their tray tables down to hold their Cokes and peanuts. Worst of all, they see the people around them snickering and making fun of them. So, tired of the snickering and tired of squirming, they remove their parachutes. No sooner do they throw them down, however, than the plane sputters and crashes into the ocean, where all lives are lost.

Oftentimes I hear presentations like this: "Come to Jesus. Christians have more fun." Really? Tell that to Paul, who was beaten, imprisoned, and shipwrecked and constantly in pain, suffering, and difficulty.

But if Christianity is "more fun," what did Jesus mean when He said, "In the world you will have much tribulation"? What did He mean when He said we would enter into the kingdom only through trials and difficulties? And what did the writer to the Hebrews mean when he said believers in his day were sawn in half, that they traveled in animal skins to keep warm, and that they lived in caves in poverty?

Others say, "Come to Jesus, and you won't be miserable," only to hear people respond, "I like my life. I enjoy watching the A's and the Giants. I enjoy my ski boat. I like my kids. I'm doing well, thank you."

We try so hard to convince people they're miserable without Jesus, or that they will be happy with Jesus. But sooner or later the sun comes out. People begin to make fun of them for becoming Christians. They begin to have difficulties and problems. They say, "I've been sold a bill of goods," as they throw off their parachutes. Then the inevitable happens. The plane crashes. Death comes. And they are dumped into hell eternally because they came to the gospel on a wrong set of presuppositions. Their commitment was shallow because the presentation was shallow.

Consider stewardess number two.

She returns from the captain's cabin, saying, "Ladies and gentlemen, listen carefully. There is a leak in the fuselage. We are losing fuel rapidly. We have thirty minutes before we will make an emergency landing. Who wants a parachute?" Suddenly, hands go up everywhere. Everyone straps a parachute on. And you know what? They're still uncomfortable, and they still can't get their tray tables down. But they don't care one whit. They know an event is coming for which they must be prepared.

Maybe some are skeptical. Perhaps some are cynical. They say, "Oh, this is just some kind of drill, some kind of test. I don't want a parachute." And they laugh. But they laugh nervously, wondering, "What if she's right?" as they ask for a second and third and fourth drink. Thirty minutes later, when the plane begins to sputter and the doors open, those who have the parachutes jump to safety. The others are lost.

Gang, we need to make a realistic presentation of the gospel. He that has the Son has life. He that has not the Son shall not see life, but the wrath of God abides on Him. For God so loved the world that He gave His only begotten Son, that whosoever believes in Him shall not perish, but have everlasting life. We need to say,

"Friend, what will you do with the Person of Jesus Christ? Your eternal state hinges upon your decision. If you receive Him and respond to Him, you'll be saved. If you reject or ignore Him, you'll crash."

"That type of presentation makes me uncomfortable," some might object. But that's what it takes to break up fallow ground. How did Jesus break up the hard ground of the hearts to which He ministered, of those who thought they were basically okay?

He said, "You have heard it said of old that you're not to kill, but I say unto you that if you have been angry with your brother, you are a murderer. You have heard it said of old that you're not to commit adultery, but I say to you, if you've looked with lust, you're guilty. You have heard it said of old that you're not to swear, but I say unto you let your 'yea' be 'yea' and your 'nay' be 'nay.' Anything more than yes or no is blasphemy. Be ye therefore perfect, as your Father in heaven is perfect." (see Matthew 5). And suddenly, people who thought they were basically okay are indicted by the law. The law was spoken of and expanded on by Jesus in order to bring people into an awareness of their sin. Gang, those of you who have family or friends who seem to be hardened to the gospel, have you really sat down with them and said,

- "Thou shalt have no other gods before me.
- Thou shalt not make unto thee any graven image . . .
- Thou shalt not take the name of the LORD thy God in vain . . .
- Remember the sabbath day, to keep it holy.
- Honour thy father and thy mother . . .
- Thou shalt not kill.
- Thou shalt not commit adultery.
- Thou shalt not steal.
- Thou shalt not bear false witness against thy neighbour.
- Thou shalt not covet . . ."?

Do we know the law? Do we even know the Ten Commandments? Do we know why they were given? Galatians 3 says the law was given as a schoolmaster to drive people to Jesus Christ (Galatians 3:24). The law is a schoolmaster who cracks the whip, a schoolmaster who raps the knuckles, a schoolmaster who makes people wake up and realize they're sinners.

The law is like a mirror (James 1:23). When I look into a mirror and see dirt on my face, I don't take the mirror off the wall and start scrubbing my face with the mirror. The mirror is simply to show me what's real. So, too, the Ten Commandments and the law give people a proper understanding of their dirtiness and sinfulness, their depravity and iniquity. Therefore, we who sow seed must have the integrity and the honesty to say to people, "You're a sinner. You're headed for destruction. According to the Law of God, you're not okay. We're all lost. That's why Jesus came."

People will not appreciate how wonderful Jesus is until they realize how lost they are. They"ll say, "Big deal. So Jesus died on the Cross. So you say God loves me. So what?"

But when they realize that God's standard of holiness and righteousness is so transcendent and so valuable that the price of sin is death, they say, "I get it. Salvation is not just a matter of having a better day, or joining a new club that meets on Sundays and Wednesdays. This is heavy."

I believe we will see a much higher percentage of people responding to Jesus and continuing in Him if we sow the seed where the ground has been broken by the plow of the law. May God help us to plow deep and to sow well that people might truly be converted and become fruitful in the glorious kingdom of God.

YOU ARE TREASURED!
A Topical Study of
MATTHEW 13:44–46

One morning years ago, when the first heavy dew of the season had fallen in Jacksonville, Oregon, my then three-year-old daughter, Mary Elizabeth, looked out the window and saw the wet grass. With excitement in her voice, she said, "Mommy, Mommy! God made the whole world wet!" Then her little forehead furrowed. Looking rather puzzled, she said, "But He forgot to dry it."

I think, like Mary, we sometimes look around with a smile on our face and say, "Wow! Look what God made!"

I was reading about the screech owl, which unlike our spotted owl, resides in cities and towns on the East Coast. They're very prolific, but little bugs and maggots can infect and devastate their entire population. To counteract the maggots and bugs, the screech owl ingeniously gathers little snakes called blind snakes and takes them to his nest. The blind snake just so happens to love maggots, larvae, and little bugs, so he lives inside the nest along with the screech owl. They dwell together symbiotically—mutually beneficial to each other.[2]

Who taught the screech owl to go after that particular snake and drop it in the tree trunk in which he is building his nest? I know owls are wise, but they're not *that* smart! Such understanding was programmed into the owl by an ingenious Master Maker, a Creator.

Consider also the Alaskan blackfish.

The Alaskan blackfish, which lives in ponds and streams that freeze over every winter, has the amazing ability to freeze right along with the pond or stream for up to forty-five minutes. Then he thaws out and continues with his life. These fish have been given the ability to go with the flow in a remarkable way!

Finally, consider the spider.

The spider spins a web made of a sticky substance that traps insects and bugs for his dinner. Why isn't the spider caught in his own web? Ingeniously built into his little spider feet are tiny oil glands that secrete a minuscule amount of oil, allowing him to move over his own web without being caught.

I watch the spider, I see the owl, and I hear about the blackfish, and I marvel and say, "Oh, Lord, You are a master Creator!" But sometimes I look around, and like Mary Elizabeth, my brow begins to furrow as I say, "God, You made this world—but did You forget to dry it?"

"Why did Hurricane Hugo slam through the Caribbean, causing death and misery for countless thousands? Why are there volcanoes that erupt and wipe out entire villages in the Polynesian Islands? Why are thousands of babies born addicted to crack cocaine each year alone? If You are a God who is so ingenious and powerful, why do these things happen?"

People look around and see tragedy, war, rape, disease, difficulty, and say, "If there is a God who made this world, then how come He doesn't dry it? Why doesn't He take better care of it? Why are these things allowed to happen?" To find the answer, you need to go back to the beginning—back to the Book of Genesis. Here we read of a man who literally had the Spirit of God breathed into him, a man who was never polluted by sin, a man born without a sin nature. He was, in a sense, a champion for you and me. His name was Adam.

God gave Adam the authority, the opportunity, and the responsibility to oversee, tend, and rule this planet. But Satan came to Adam to tempt him, and Adam submitted to Satan when he ate of the forbidden fruit. The Bible says to whom you submit, of him you become the servant. When Adam submitted to Satan, he became the servant of Satan and handed to him the title deed, the authority, and the dominion of this planet. Thus, the ownership of the world changed hands—from God to man to Satan.

Why are there rape and hatred? Why is there starvation in Ethiopia? Why is there AIDS? It's the enemy who has caused the problems, pollution, and plagues that descend upon us.

When Jesus stilled the storm in Luke's Gospel, He said, "Be still," or literally, "Be muzzled," which is the same phrase He used whenever He encountered demonic activity. Therefore, I suggest to you the implication is clearly that many of these storms that bring about devastation and destruction are not "Acts of God," as insurance companies refer to them, but acts of Satan. God gets a bad rap and gets blamed for what the Enemy does.

Will the title deed to earth remain in the devil's grasp forever? Revelation 5 gives us the answer . . .

> *And I saw in the right hand of him that sat on the throne a book written within and on the backside, sealed with seven seals.*   Revelation 5:1

Now, what is this book, or literally scroll? Jeremiah 32 identifies it as a title deed to a piece of property. The scroll sealed with seven seals is the title deed to planet earth.

Why is it written on the outside as well as the inside? In Old Testament times, if you lost your property due to hardship or bankruptcy, the deed would be scrolled and sealed with seven seals. On the outside would be written all of your financial obligations. You would have to meet them within seven years in order to regain your property. If those qualifications were met, the person who took possession of your property was required by law to return it to you. Such a transaction took place in the temple, where the qualifications on the outside of the scroll were read before the people. In heaven, the ultimate temple, there is a scroll sealed seven times. It is the title deed to the earth, which was given to Adam, who in turn, passed it on to Satan.

> *And I saw a strong angel proclaiming with a loud voice, Who is worthy to open the book, and to loose the seals thereof?*   Revelation 5:2

In other words, "Who can meet the requirements? Who is worthy to take back the title deed of earth from Satan?"

Notice it doesn't say, "Who is *willing*?" Many men have been willing to try to take control of the world—Alexander the Great, Genghis Khan, Napoleon, Hitler. They were all willing to take control, believing they could bring the world into a new level of glory or grandeur. The angel is not asking, "Who is willing?" The angel asks, "Who is *worthy*?"

> *And no man in heaven, nor in earth, neither under the earth, was able to open the book, neither to look thereon. And I wept much, because no man was found worthy to open the book, neither to look thereon.*   Revelation 5:3, 4

John wept at the thought of the world indefinitely in the hand and control and dominion of the Enemy so much so that the Greek word translated "wept" means "sobbing in agony."

You mean poverty will continue, hunger will abound, disease will persist, and hate will be perpetuated? There will be wars, anxiety, tension, trauma, death, disease, and destruction—*forever?* John wept because no one was found worthy to wrest the scroll from the hand of the Enemy. As you read the papers, the editorials, and the news magazines today, no doubt your heart breaks as well. This can't go on. Hurt, pain, sorrow, and evil can't go on forever.

> *And one of the elders saith unto me, Weep not: behold, the Lion of the tribe of Juda, the Root of David, hath prevailed to open the book, and to loose the seven seals thereof. And he came and took the book out of the right hand of him that sat upon the throne.*
>   Revelation 5:5–7

Jesus comes forward, the Lion of the tribe of Judah, saying, "I will redeem the scroll," and the rest of Chapter 5 is a glorious outpouring of praise, adoration, and thanksgiving that someone was able to take the title deed of the planet. Worthy is the Lamb. He alone is worthy.

How did He do it? Look back at Matthew 13, where Jesus gives a one-verse parable that explains the redemptive process.

> *Again, the kingdom of heaven is like unto treasure hid in a field; the which when a man hath found, he hideth, and for joy thereof goeth and selleth all that he hath, and buyeth that field.*
>   Matthew 13:44

In Jesus' day, if a man had wealth, he would bury it in a field to keep it safe from thieves. The man in this parable stumbled across one such treasure chest and realized, "Wow! Someone has left his treasure here." With joy, he bought the field in order to get the treasure. He gave everything he had because he knew within the field lay a treasure of great value.

- *What is the field?*
  In a previous parable, Jesus identified the field as the world.
- *Who is the Man?*
  Jesus Christ.

Think with me for a moment.

- *The first Adam sold us out.*
  Jesus Christ, the last Adam, bought us back.
- *The first Adam ate of a forbidden tree and handed humanity to the enemy.*
  The last Adam hung on a tree to redeem humanity *from* the enemy.
- *Through the first Adam, the ground was cursed.*
  For our sake, the last Adam became a curse.
- *Sin, through the first Adam, produced thorns.*
  God, through the last Adam, buried those thorns in His own brow.

Why? So He could, with His own pure blood, appear before the Father in the temple of heaven and declare, "I am worthy to take the scroll."

You see, the price for the redemption of the world was not a million dollars, not ten billion dollars, not a zillion dollars. It was death.

Why did Jesus want the world? He certainly doesn't need this planet, which in many places has been polluted beyond repair. He didn't want another planet just to camp out on. There are a million planets He has created and a billion more He could speak into existence.

- *What did He want?*
  He bought the planet for the treasure.
- *What was the treasure?*
  You.

Jesus came, gave everything He had, and was slaughtered like a lamb in order that He might pay the price for the title deed to this earth. Because He wanted this planet? No. Because He wanted you. You are His treasure. *You* are the treasure He purchased with His own blood.

When the Enemy whispers in your ear that you're not worth anything, please understand this: Jesus, walking through this world, saw you and was so excited about you and so in love with you that He sold everything to buy this whole world in order to take you—the treasure—out of it.

Maybe you're saying, "That might be true theologically, but I couldn't be much of a treasure to Him. I'm always messing up, missing the mark, and blowing it. I'm just an irritation to Him."

Look at the next verse.

Again, the kingdom of heaven is like unto a merchant man seeking goodly pearls: Who, when he had found one pearl of great price, went and sold all that he had, and bought it.   Matthew 13:45, 46

- *Who is the One who sold all He had to purchase the pearl?*
  Jesus.
- *Who is the pearl?*
  You are.

A pearl begins as nothing more than an irritating speck of sand in the shell of an oyster. The oyster coats this troublesome speck with layer upon layer of a crystalline substance called nacre, which hardens and becomes the actual pearl. Interestingly, the more irritating the grain of sand, the more beautiful the pearl.

You are the pearl of great price. When you asked the Lord to come into your life, you became robed with His righteousness and surrounded by His goodness. Although you might feel as though you're terribly irritating, you are actually a trophy of His glory. You are a gem of His grace. And all of the cosmos looks at you and says,

"Wow! Glory be to the Lamb. Worthy is the Lamb. Hallelujah to the Lamb, who took that little speck of sand and made it a pearl of great price!"

God loves you, gang. Paul said He demonstrated His love for us in that while we were yet sinners, Christ died for us (Romans 5:8).

When did Jesus die for us?

Not when we were going to church; not when we were reading the Word; not when we were praying. He looked at us when we were nothing more than an irritation and said, "I love you, and I'll give all I have to redeem you, My treasure."

There's one thing that will ruin a pearl. It's perspiration.

So, too, one thing will ruin your beauty in the Lord. Perspiring, sweating, or trying to prove you are worthy of His blessing. Trying to prove "it's *my* spirituality, *my* energy, *my* togetherness that makes me so wonderful." No, the pearl is destroyed, eaten away, decayed by sweat.

What you need is not to sweat it out, but just let it out. Release praise, thanksgiving, appreciation, and adoration, saying, "Thank You, Lord, for seeing me as a pearl. I'm not going to try to earn it, nor add to it. I don't even understand it. But I am forever grateful."

Be a pearl for His glory.

In Jesus' Name.

UNBELIEF: ITS CAUSE AND CURE
A Topical Study of
Matthew 13:54–58

After presenting a powerful teaching to His disciples concerning the kingdom, Jesus left Galilee and traveled twenty miles west—home to Nazareth. In Nazareth, unbelief filled the hearts of His countrymen. Matthew ends this chapter saying of Jesus, "He did not many mighty works there because of their unbelief."

In recording the same incident, Mark takes it a step further when he writes, "And he could there do no mighty work, save that he laid his hands upon a few sick folk, and healed them. And he marveled because of their unbelief." It is not simply that Jesus *would* do no mighty works in Nazareth. Mark tells us He *could* do no mighty works there. He was limited by their unbelief, even as the Old Testament declares that the people of Israel limited the Holy One of Israel through their unbelief (Psalm 78:41).

- Unbelief is hazardous to your health. In this passage, we see it affecting people in three ways.

- Unbelief blinds your eyes, and you become skeptical.
- Unbelief poisons your heart, and you become cynical.
- Unbelief robs your joy, and you become sterile.

First, look with me at the way unbelief blinds eyes.

And when he was come into his own country, he taught them in their syna-gogue, insomuch that they were astonished, and said, Whence hath this man this wisdom, and these mighty works?   Matthew 13:54

Miracles were happening—the dead were raised, the lame were walking, the blind were seeing, the deaf were hearing. It was obvious God was working. But unbelief blinds eyes to the obvious.

People are still blinded today, even though it is obvious God is real. Just look up. On a clear night, you can see the Milky Way galaxy, consisting of four hundred billion stars. Traveling at tremendous speed, the Milky Way swirls within itself as it is hurled across the universe—all four hundred billion stars. Astronomers tell us there are at least one hundred billion more galaxies each containing at least one hundred billion stars. If you compute that out, it comes to ten billion billion stars spinning around and moving through the universe. Ten billion billion—that's more Big Macs than McDonalds serves in a year! And when you add the planets that circle many of these stars, the figures get even more astronomical.

"My, it must be crowded up there," you say. Well, state your coordinates and choose a point. Even though there are ten billion billion stars with billions of planets around them, what are the chances of your point landing on a star, a planet, a comet, or an asteroid? The chances are one in ten to the thirty-eighth power, or one in a billion trillion trillion—not very good odds. Space is *huge*, gang—enormous beyond our comprehension. And yet people have the audacity, the stupidity, and the idiocy to say, "Well, it just sort of all happened." Ref?

Truly, "the fool hath said in his heart, There is no God" (see Psalm 14:1). I recently talked with an atheist who said, "Jon, I hear all of your statistics on space, and I hear all of your illustrations on creation, but it still doesn't prove God exists. I would believe in God if He would prove His existence."

"Well, we have a problem here," I said, "because if God proved His existence, you couldn't be a believer. You might be a follower, but you couldn't be a believer, for if God proved Himself, there would be no faith required."

God is interested in developing your faith because faith is what is going to move on with you in the ages to come. He has given you evidence and indications, but He has not given you proof because if He gave you proof, you could never be a believer.

Second, notice not only the blindness of their eyes, which resulted in skepticism, but the poison in their hearts, which resulted in cynicism.

Is not this the carpenter's son? Is not his mother called Mary? And his brethren, James, and Joses, and Simon, and Judas? And his sisters, are they not all with us? Whence then hath this man all these things? And they were offended in him . . .   Matthew 13:55–57

When a person will not believe, his heart will inevitably become poisoned toward the family of God.

"Isn't His dad a carpenter—just an ordinary carpenter? He's not a scholar or a rabbi, a mystic or a miracle worker. We know His dad; he's the carpenter. And Mary? We've heard about *her* problem. She was pregnant before she got married."

You see, the unbeliever will always attack the family of God. His heart will become poisoned as he points out the problems of fallen Christian pastors or this Christian neighbor. He will point out problems in the family, even though, like those in Nazareth, his facts may be wrong. Since no one—not even the most avowed atheist or skeptical cynic—has ever been able to find one single fault with Christ, he or she will attack His family.

"Can you believe what a joke that minister on TV is?"
  "Look at those hypocrites sitting in church."
  "Some Christian *she* is."

And their hearts become cynical, hardened, and bitter.
Third, unbelief robs you of your joy.

And he did not many mighty works there because of their unbelief.
                                                Matthew 13:58

When Jesus went to His hometown, He would have healed many if only they would have believed. Great joy would have filled that little hamlet of Nazareth. But God will not work outside the arena of faith. God has chosen to limit Himself in certain ways. And because they didn't believe, He couldn't work. As a result, miracles were missing. Healings weren't happening. Joy wasn't exploding.

   Unbelief is hazardous to your health. It blinds your eyes; it poisons your heart; it steals your joy. What is the antidote for unbelief? What would the Great Physician prescribe to you and to me who, although we are believers in Jesus, are also guilty of limiting Him?

First, the antidote for the unbelief, which results in blinded eyes, is simply to offer prayer to God. Paul did this when, in Ephesians 1, he prayed for the believers at Ephesus—that their *eyes* might be enlightened. You see, faith is not blind. Faith sees what unbelief never will.

I am reminded of the story of Elisha in 2 Kings 6.

As the Syrians waged war against the Jews, the king of Syria set an ambush for the Israelites. Elisha sent word to the king of Israel, saying, "Don't go through that pass. You'll walk into a Syrian ambush." The king of Syria then set a second ambush, and again the Lord spoke to Elisha the prophet. Finally, the king of Syria said, "Every time we set up an ambush, Israel suddenly changes directions to avoid it. Someone is spying, and I want his head."

One of his advisers said, "King, there's no spy in our midst. There's a prophet in their land. His name is Elisha. He knows everything you say—even what you say in your bedchamber."

"Where is this man Elisha?" barked the king.

"In Dothan," answered his advisers.

That same night, the Syrians surrounded the city of Dothan with soldiers, chariots, and armaments. The next morning, when Elisha's servant, Gehazi, woke up, he ran to his master, shouting, "Master! We're surrounded! We're through! We're history!"

And he answered, Fear not: for they that be with us are more than they that be with them. And Elisha prayed, and said, LORD, I pray thee, open his eyes, that he may see. And the LORD opened the eyes of the young man; and he saw: and, behold, the mountain was full of horses and chariots of fire round about Elisha.
                                                                         2 Kings 6:17

Elisha wasn't worried because faith sees what unbelief never will.

Second, the antidote for the unbelief that results in a bitter heart is to see people in God.

Paul said, "I know no man after the flesh" (2 Corinthians 5:16). In other words, "I see people in Christ—washed in His blood, robed in His righteousness. That's the way I choose to see people."

When you see people in God, suddenly you're not so cynical. You can just embrace, love, and enjoy them.

Third, to thwart the unbelief that robs you of joy, speak the promises of God.

But without faith it is impossible to please him: for he that cometh to God must believe that he is, and that he is a rewarder of them that diligently seek him.
                                                                         Hebrews 11:6

There are many ways to please God—but not one apart from faith.

The word is nigh thee, even in thy mouth, and in thy heart: that is, the word of faith, which we preach: That if thou shalt confess with thy mouth the Lord Jesus, and shalt believe in thine heart that God hath raised him from the dead, thou shalt be saved.

Romans 10:8, 9

Faith is worked into our lives by God's Word. It is released from our lives by our spoken word. It's not enough to have a quiet, internal faith. Faith is released via the mouth.

Jesus said, "When you see an obstacle in front of you, a mountain looming before you, a problem facing you, *say* to the mountain, 'Be removed' and it shall be removed" (see Matthew 17:20).

Speak the praises of God. Scripture is packed with promises—over three thousand in number—a promise for every situation. Perhaps you have a difficulty in your life, a problem in your family, a hardship financially or vocationally, tough times in school or in friendship. Jesus desires to work in those situations. He really does. But we limit Him by unbelief.

God wants us to speak His promises because it's too easy for us to say, "Well, I've got some ideas and thoughts, some hopes and dreams, but I'm not going to go on record verbally lest I seem foolish." Once you have the promise of God in your heart, you need to release it via your mouth. Speak *out* that which has been worked *in*.

Either you will venture out in faith, or you will vegetate. Your Christian life will either grow in faith as you see wonderful things happen in your family, in your ministry, in your life personally, or you will shrink into a "church-ianity." God forbid.

Through faith we understand that the worlds were framed by the word of God, so that things which are seen were not made of things which do appear.

Hebrews 11:3

Hebrews says the worlds were framed by the Word of God. Whenever someone builds a house, he doesn't put up one wall and then move in. No, he constructs all the walls in order that there might be protection, symmetry, and balance.

So, too with God. When He framed the world, it was framed in totality. Therefore, we need to be students of His Word so we don't just put up one wall in our house of faith and say, "Well now, this is the way it has to be. I'm claiming the promise." No, solid faith, real faith, balanced faith comes by hearing the Word—not simply an isolated verse here or there.

As I study the Word, my focus changes. It's no longer me clenching my fists and gritting my teeth, saying, "I'm gonna trust or bust." No, my focus shifts from my faith to the Faithful One—Jesus Christ.

I don't know what struggle you might have, what difficulty you might face, but I know where the answer lies. It lies in the Faithful One—Jesus Christ.

Begin to venture out radically and watch what the Lord does joyfully. He wants to come into your Nazareth and do a mighty work.

14 Thus far in our study, we have seen that the purpose of Matthew's Gospel is to present Jesus as King—King of Israel, King of kings, King of all creation. His Person is revealed in chapters 1 through 4; His principles are recorded in chapters 5 through 7; His power is released in chapters 8 through 10. In chapters 11 through 13, the focus shifts from a revelation of the King to a rebellion against the King. And here in chapter 14, we will see the retreat of the King as Jesus pulls away from the crowds to share essential principles with His disciples.

Matthew 14:1
At that time Herod the tetrarch heard of the fame of Jesus.

You remember Herod from Matthew 2. He was the one who slaughtered all of the male children in Israel when he heard a new King had been born. The Herod referred to here is Herod Antipas, his son. Herod Antipas wasn't as bloodthirsty as his father was, but he was not a great leader in any sense of the word. He loved luxury and lived licentiously.

Matthew 14:2
And said unto his servants, This is John the Baptist; he is risen from the dead; and therefore mighty works do shew forth themselves in him.

Hearing of the fame of Jesus, Herod thought John the Baptist had come back from the dead. Why? His conscience was pricking him, for he was the one who had put John to death.

Matthew 14:3–5
For Herod had laid hold on John, and bound him, and put him in prison for Herodias'' sake, his brother Philip's wife. For John said unto him, It is not lawful for thee to have her. And when he would have put him to death, he feared the multitude, because they counted him as a prophet.

Herodias was Herod's brother's wife. Herod took a liking to her, got rid of his own wife, and stole her from his brother. John confronted him,

saying, "This is not right. You are king of the country and in a position of authority. You can't live in this kind of immorality." Herod responded by imprisoning the bold and radical Baptist. But Mark tells us when John was in prison, Herod talked with him and began to develop a real affinity for him. Herod saw that John was a just man, a godly man, a wise man. Thus, although he felt convicted by John, he respected him.

Matthew 14:6–11
But when Herod's birthday was kept, the daughter of Herodias danced before them, and pleased Herod. Whereupon he promised with an oath to give her whatsoever she would ask. And she, being before instructed of her mother, said, Give me here John Baptist''s head in a charger. And the king was sorry: nevertheless for the oath's sake, and them which sat with him at meat, he commanded it to be given her. And his head was brought in a charger, and given to the damsel: and she brought it to her mother.

At Herod's birthday party, with wine flowing freely, Herodias told her daughter to dance. Herodias' daughter complied, dancing seductively and sensually. Herod, probably under the influence of much wine, said, "Whatever you want to the half of my kingdom, you've got it." Herodias, angry with John the Baptist, instructed her daughter to ask for John's head.

Hardly a week goes by that I don't hear, "I was at this party," or "I was down at the bar," or "I was at the office get-together and I said something I shouldn't have said, and then I did something I shouldn't have done." These statements always come from broken, devastated people whose lives are permanently scarred because they were playing the game, trying to get ahead. Watch out for an environment wherein alcohol is flowing, and seductive music is playing. I don't care what society says. I don't care what the demands from your boss might be. Watch out. Herodias is dancing. You'll get sucked in, and you'll regret it later.

Matthew 14:12
And his disciples came, and took up the body, and buried it, and went and told Jesus.

Distressed and discouraged, the disciples of John went to Jesus—a good thing to do. Communication with Jesus is always the best insulation against depression.

Matthew 14:13 (a)
When Jesus heard of it, he departed thence by ship into a desert place apart . . .

Jesus and John were close not only in ministry, but as family, being that John was a cousin of Jesus. Hearing John had been beheaded, Jesus withdrew to a quiet place.

Matthew 14:13 (b), 14
. . . and when the people had heard thereof, they followed him on foot out of the cities. And Jesus went forth, and saw a great multitude, and was moved with compassion toward them, and he healed their sick.

Jesus had need of solitude, but when He saw the crowd, Matthew writes He was "moved with compassion, and he healed their sick." This is always a tension in our walks. We feel the need to get away and seek the Lord in quietness, yet there are needs all around us. The question arises: How do I know when to get involved with the needs I see around me and when to seek the Lord in solitude and tranquility? How do I know when it's time to plunge in and get involved, versus time to retreat and be quiet before the Lord? I believe the answer lies in this passage. As with Jesus, compassion *within* you and anointing *upon* you are good indicators that you need to get involved in the situation *around* you.

Matthew 14:15–20 (a)
And when it was evening, his disciples came to him, saying, This is a desert place, and the time is now past; send the multitude away, that they may go into the villages, and buy themselves victuals. But Jesus said unto them, They need not depart; give ye them to eat. And they say unto him, We have here but five loaves, and two fishes. He said, Bring them hither to me. And he commanded the multitude to sit down on the grass, and took the five loaves, and the two fishes, and looking up to heaven, he blessed, and brake, and gave the loaves to his disciples, and the disciples to the multitude. And they did all eat, and were filled . . .

Jesus took limited resources—five loaves and two fish—blessed them, gave them out, and fed five thousand. Notice, however, that in between blessing and giving, there was breaking. You might say, "I don't have much. My talents are limited. My gifts aren't great." That's Okay. In the Lord's hand, a little goes a long way *if* you will let Him bless you and break you.

I think of Mary with the alabaster box, anointing Jesus and ministering to Him. The box had to be broken before ministry could flow (Mark 14:3). I think of Gideon, whose three hundred men put torches in clay pots as they surrounded the hosts of the Midianites. On a given signal, they broke the clay pots, and the light flooded out. Confused by the light, the Midianites fought one another and destroyed themselves. Israel was victorious because before the battle was fought, the clay pots were broken (Judges 7:19).

People often say, "God has been good to me, and I want to be used in ministry. Why then am I going through the pits and through such difficulty?" The answer is very simple. Before the Lord can use a person greatly, He must allow him to be hurt and broken deeply. There's no other way. Pride must go. Self-sufficiency must die to make way for the tenderness and compassion that come only through the breaking process.

Matthew 14:20 (b)–23
. . . and they took up of the fragments that remained twelve baskets full. And they that had eaten were about five thousand men, beside women and children. And straightway Jesus constrained his disciples to get into a ship, and to go before him unto the other side, while he sent the multitudes away. And when he had sent the multitudes away, he went up into a mountain apart to pray: and when the evening was come, he was there alone.

Now, after a time of ministry, Jesus at last had an opportunity to be alone with His Father. He sent His disciples across the sea and went to a mountain alone for contemplation and intercession.

Matthew 14:24–26 (a)
But the ship was now in the midst of the sea, tossed with waves: for the wind was contrary. And in the fourth watch of the night Jesus went unto them, walking on the sea. And when the disciples saw him walking on the sea, they were troubled . . .

"They were troubled"—that's putting it mildly! A more accurate translation would be, "They were scared to death!" Here they were, struggling against the storm, obedient to the command of Jesus to proceed to the other side, when suddenly, they saw a figure walking towards them.

For topical study of Matthew 14:22–33 entitled "Recognizing Our Redeemer," turn to page 116.

Matthew 14:26 (b)–29
. . . saying, It is a spirit; and they cried out for fear. But straightway Jesus spake unto them, saying, Be of good cheer; it is I; be not afraid. And Peter answered him and said, Lord, if it be thou, bid me come unto thee on the water. And he said, Come. And when Peter was come down out of the ship, he walked on the water, to go to Jesus.

The reason Peter could walk on water was not because he wanted to write a book about walking on water, or to send out publicity photos of himself surfing without a board. Peter's motivation was neither notoriety nor fame. He simply wanted to go to Jesus.

Matthew 14:30–32
But when he saw the wind boisterous, he was afraid; and beginning to sink, he cried, saying, Lord, save me. And immediately Jesus stretched forth his hand, and caught him, and said unto him, O thou of little faith, wherefore didst thou doubt? and when they were come into the ship, the wind ceased.

In extra-Biblical literature, Peter is referred to as "the Giant." Historical writings corroborate the fact that he was a man of good size. Yet, Jesus was able to lift him out of the water with one hand. Artists' renderings over the centuries portraying Jesus as a wimp are false. Jesus was a carpenter in the days before power tools and lumberyards, which means He logged trees and finished lumber before even beginning the building process. Anything but a weakling, Jesus was able to single-handedly lift a waterlogged Peter out of the sea and into the boat. And He does the same with us. We tire of our situation and become weary of the people in our boats, so we venture out upon the water and start to sink. Jesus pulls us out of the water and sets us back in the boat because there are yet lessons for us to learn there. He loves us enough to plop us back in the boat until the lesson is learned and His work is complete.

Matthew 14:33
Then they that were in the ship came and worshipped him, saying, Of a truth thou art the Son of God.

When you're in a storm with the wind raging and the waves pounding, and you feel like you're sinking, know this: The same Lord who stills the storm allows the storm. Why does God allow storms?

Scripturally, storms appear for two reasons. First, there are storms of correction. Ask Jonah about them. If we're out of the Lord's will, He will use a storm to get us back to where we need to be. Storms of correction discipline us. Second, there are storms of perfection that develop us. In this passage, the disciples were obeying Jesus' command to go to the other side. Thus, this was not a storm to correct them, but to perfect them. In this storm, Jesus was saying, "I want to test you now. I've been teaching you. I've been with you. And now I want you to exercise your faith to go through this storm."

You see, faith is developed through struggle. If you ask people what faith is, most will answer, "Faith is believing even though you don't have evidence." Not true. Faith is not "believing in spite of the evidence." Faith is obeying in spite of the consequence. Faith says, "I will do what the Lord says, even though it means a storm is headed my way. Even though it means there will be difficulties, obstacles, and challenges, even though it may be brutal and difficult, even though I must struggle, I will obey."

When Jesus came to His disciples, they thought He was a ghost. So, too, we can look around and say, "The Lord is nowhere." Or we can slow down and say, "Wait a minute. Is the Lord speaking to me through my sister, through my mother, through that preacher, or through the radio?"

And suddenly, "The Lord is nowhere" becomes "The Lord is *now here*" by adding a little space.

I find if I slow down and give the Lord a little space, He appears through my brother who shares with me, through my wife who gives encouragement to me, or through my children who challenge me. He sent you *into* the storm, He's praying for you *through* the storm, and He'll come to you *in* the storm—perhaps when you least expect Him.

Matthew 14:34–36
And when they were gone over, they came into the land of Gennesaret. And when the men of that place had knowledge of him, they sent out into all that country round about, and brought unto him all that were diseased; and besought him that they might only touch the hem of his garment: and as many as touched were made perfectly whole.

Throughout Scripture, blue is the color of heaven.

Speak unto the children of Israel, and bid them that they make them fringes in the borders of their garments throughout their generations, and that they put upon the fringe of the borders a ribband of blue.   Numbers 15:38

The color blue on the hem of the garments of the Jews was to be a reminder to them that they were a unique people, a heavenly people. As they dressed each morning and as they saw one another throughout the day, they were to remember they were pilgrims on this earth, headed for a heavenly city whose "Builder and Maker is God."

Maybe you've sought the Lord, but wonder, *Why aren't I healed?* I encourage you to touch the hem of the garment of Jesus Christ and be reminded of eternity. There is healing when you realize, "I might suffer for a few weeks, months, years, or even decades, but I'm going to Heaven. And when I see Him, I shall be like Him. And when I am like Him, I will have a body custom-made for space, the cosmos, and the ages to come. There will be no sickness, no infirmity, no weakness whatsoever."

The Scriptures from Genesis to Revelation call us to a heavenly perspective. I do not understand why we have fallen into this "I've got to have it all now—wealth and health, prosperity and healing" mentality. If God blesses you materially or if He heals you physically, great! But don't build your life on that. Set your heart on things above. Live for heaven. Touch the hem of His garment, and be reminded once again that it's blue.

RECOGNIZING OUR REDEEMER
A Topical Study of
Matthew 14:22–33

Fighting the Philistines in a brutal battle, as the Israelites' losses mounted, so did their despair. Then someone had a brilliant idea: "Let's bring in the ark of the Covenant!" The ark of the Covenant, a box about three feet long and two feet wide, was instrumental in tabernacle worship.

When the ark was brought into the Israelite camp, the Israelites cheered so loudly that their shout of triumph could be heard in the Philistine camp. But though the Israelites charged ahead with the Ark leading them, they were defeated resoundingly. And the Philistines captured the Ark (1 Samuel 4).

The lesson? An obvious one. The people of God should not have tried to put God in a box, saying, "This box will represent God, and we will have victory because of *it*." Instead of looking to the Lord, they looked to the box and were beaten badly. If there is one thing many of us are learning, it is that the Lord works in mysterious ways. You just can't box Him in. He is predictably unpredictable. He comes at the unexpected time, in the unexpected way.

Here in Matthew 14, the disciples are out in the storm, toiling at the oars, continuing obediently in the directive Jesus had given them to "Go across the sea." And while they were working and perspiring, Jesus was watching and praying. He was letting them go through the struggle, knowing the struggle would strengthen them. Finally, at four o'clock in the morning, knowing His disciples were feeling anxious and fearful, He came to them, walking on the water. He came to them at the unexpected time in an unexpected way, and they, thinking He was a ghost, freaked out.

So, too, I suggest to you that many times Jesus comes to us as well, but like the disciples, we don't recognize Him.

> When your boyfriend or girlfriend calls and says, "You know, I've been thinking. I really appreciate your personality. You've been a good friend, but . . ." Your heart stops, and you say, "This is frightening. It's a ghost."

> When your boss calls you into the office and says, "Don't bother to take off your coat," you know what's coming, and you think, "It's a ghost! I'm scared."

Oftentimes, when we, like the disciples, are obedient to the Lord and toiling for the Lord, we call out, "Lord, save me. I'm perishing. Lord, help me. I'm struggling." Then He comes to us—but in ways that are totally surprising, refusing to be boxed in by our preconceptions of how and when He should appear. I would like us to look at four obstacles that prevent us from seeing Jesus when He comes to us in the unexpected way, at the unexpected time.

Fear and Anxiety

When our hearts are full of fear and anxiety, what should we do? Look at Jesus' answer in the text before us. He said, "Be of good cheer. It is I." This intrigues me. He didn't say, "It is I. Be of good cheer." He said, "Be of good cheer. It is I." First, "Be of good cheer"—an exhortation; then, "It is I"—a revelation. The exhortation comes *before* the revelation.

Scripture says that in everything we are to give thanks, to rejoice evermore, for this is the will of God (1 Thessalonians 5:16–18). If you begin to rejoice—to be of good cheer—suddenly you will see that it isn't a ghost, but it's Jesus drawing near. He's freeing you from that job, or from that relationship that will drag you down. It's the Lord coming to you in the storm.

Next time fear and anxiety fill your heart, don't freak out—faith out. By faith, rejoice, and He will reveal Himself to you as He walks on the water in the midst of your storm.

False Familiarity

Jesus came into His hometown, and there the people said of Him, "Hey, isn't this the carpenter's son? And isn't Mary His mother? And don't we know His brothers and sisters?" They thought they knew Him, but their assumptions were mistaken. Matthew writes that Jesus could not do many mighty works there because of their unbelief (see Matthew 13:58).

So, too, Jesus will come to you, gang, in people you know very well. Our tendency, however, is to say,

- "That guy can't tell me anything. I know him."
- "I know her. She's my wife. She has nothing to say to me."

- "Him? He's only been a Christian six months. What could he possibly say to me?"

In reality, those people are Jesus coming to you. Jesus comes to us constantly, yet if we're not careful, we'll say, "I can't receive from her. I can't receive from him. I know them." Paul said, "I know no man after the flesh. I will no longer look at people with their faults, flaws, and failures. I will see people only in Christ" (see 2 Corinthians 5:16). When we begin to look at our husband, our wife, our friends, our kids, our brothers, and our sisters as people in Christ, realizing Jesus indwells them, suddenly we will lay hold of the most incredible understanding, profound revelation, and convicting challenges. Why is it that we are so ready to receive from someone we esteem highly—a Billy Graham, or a Chuck Swindoll? Wouldn't it be radical if we saw *every* man in Christ? Jesus will come to you through the people closest to you, but if you're not careful, you'll miss Him.

Personal Tragedy

It was Easter morning. Mary Magdalene stood outside the sepulcher weeping, thinking the One speaking to her was a gardener (John 20:15).

Sometimes the person who comes to us in time of tragedy, the person who ministers to us most effectively is not an angel or an apostle. In times of tragedy, Jesus will come to you in the most ordinary of people—the gardeners. Mary, no doubt, thought, *If anyone is going to give me understanding, it will be Peter, John, or the angels at the tomb. They will help me.* But Jesus came to Mary directly, and she mistook Him for a gardener.

Maybe you're going through a time of real personal tragedy. In those times of weeping and crying, be careful because sometimes you'll miss Jesus coming to you very personally. You will think He should come in Peter or in John or in an angel sent from heaven. But you know how He'll come? Through a very common person you wouldn't have expected. And if your antennae aren't up, you'll miss Him. You'll mistake Him as being insignificant and unimportant.

Too often we think we need to see the pastor, a staff member, an elder, or an angel, when we should really be looking for the gardener. Look for the person you thought wouldn't have much to say or much to offer. That's where the deep, beautiful ministry of Jesus will often flow most freely.

Despair and Despondency

In Luke 24, we read the account of two followers of Jesus walking on the road to Emmaus, depressed and despondent following the death of their Master. As Jesus joined them and asked the reason for their sorrow, they said, "Are You a stranger here? Don't You know what's happening? Where have You been?" Then Jesus began gently and lovingly rebuking them for their lack of faith. Beginning with Moses and going through the prophets, He told them how all of the Scriptures foretold His death and resurrection.

When you are depressed and despondent, the Lord will come to you. Initially, however, you might feel He's a stranger. Going through a time of emotional turmoil and great difficulty, unable to sleep, I turned on the television to a Christian station and watched a preacher who I had previously thought was very strange. He wasn't into heresy doctrinally, but his whole approach to the ministry was kind of weird. Normally, I wouldn't have given him the time of day, but in this instance, I listened to him, since his show was the only thing on at three o'clock in the morning. And guess what? His words spoke precisely and powerfully to my exact situation.

The Lord will often come through the person you might have previously thought strange. The eyes of the travelers on the Emmaus road were opened when Jesus broke bread with them. So too, when we break bread in Communion, we realize we are one body, all partaking of the same Lord, all cleansed by His blood. Our differences become irrelevant when we break bread, because suddenly our eyes are opened, and we see Jesus.

Fear and anxiety, false familiarity, personal tragedy, despair and despondency—all will keep you from recognizing your Redeemer. But if you say, "I will watch for You, Lord, in the storm. I will praise Your Name and embrace this difficulty, trusting You are revealing Yourself to me."

- I will receive from those who I think I know so well. I will take their words as Yours.
- I will listen for You in the common person, in the gardener, rather than waiting for an apostle or an angel to speak my name.
- I will embrace the stranger who walks alongside of me, and as we break bread at Your table, I will see Your face.

You will find Jesus will come to you in ways and through people you never expected.

---

15 Matthew 15:1–3
Then came to Jesus scribes and Pharisees, which were of Jerusalem, saying, Why do thy disciples transgress the tradition of the elders? For they wash not their hands when they eat bread. But he answered and said unto them, Why do ye also transgress the commandment of God by your tradition?

A delegation of scribes and Pharisees came from Jerusalem to ask Jesus why His disciples did not follow the hand-washing tradition of the elders. You see, although the Jews rightly taught

that the law was given to Moses on Mount Sinai, they also said that later on, the Lord gave further revelation to Moses that was not written in the Scriptures. This further revelation was passed down orally from generation to generation, and the Jews became so caught up in it, they actually went so far as to say that the word of the elders was weightier than the Word of God.

One such oral tradition dealt with the ceremonial washing of hands. The Rabbis taught that at night, the demon Shibna would often come and sit upon a man's hands as he slept. They went on to say that if anyone ate with hands that had been sat upon by a demon, the demon could enter into him through the food and take control of him. Therefore, the Rabbis concluded, before eating one needed to wash his hands in the following manner:

One was to take one and a half eggshells of water and pour it over his hands as they were pressed together uprightly, letting the water drip only to his wrists and no further. Then, he would flip his hands over, pointing them downward while yet another one-and-a-half eggshells of water was poured over them. Finally, he was to rub his right fist with his left palm, then his left fist with his right palm. This procedure was followed not only before every meal, but between each course of every meal.

Jesus' complete disregard of this tradition infuriated the scribes and Pharisees.

Matthew 15:4–6
For God commanded, saying, Honour thy father and mother: and, He that curseth father or mother, let him die the death. But ye say, Whosoever shall say to his father or his mother, It is a gift, by whatsoever thou mightest be profited by me; And honour not his father or his mother, he shall be free. Thus have ye made the commandment of God of none effect by your tradition.

The tradition of the elders stated specifically that if you had something in your house which was of great value, you could say it was "corban," or "dedicated," which then made that object a gift to God. You could still keep it in your house and use it for your purposes, but it was technically dedicated to God. It was a convenient way to refuse help to people in need—even to those in your own family. Jesus indicts the people for this practice, saying, "The Scriptures declare, honor your father and your mother. But you have made the commandment of God of none effect by your vain traditions."

Matthew 15:7–9
Ye hypocrites, well did Esaias prophesy of you, saying, This people draweth nigh unto me with their mouth, and honoureth me with their lips; but their heart is far from me. But in vain they do worship me, teaching for doctrines the commandments of men.

"Here's the problem," says Jesus—"People think they draw near to Me with their traditions and their songs, with their lips and with their words—but their hearts are far from Me. The issue is the heart."

For with the *heart* man believeth unto righteousness; and with the mouth confession is made unto salvation.
                    Romans 10:10 [emphasis mine]

Let the word of Christ dwell in you richly in all wisdom; teaching and admonishing one another in psalms and hymns and spiritual songs, singing with grace in your *hearts* to the Lord.
                    Colossians 3:16 [emphasis mine]

Jesus said unto him, Thou shalt love the Lord thy God with all thy *heart*, and with all thy soul, and with all thy mind. This is the first and great commandment.
                    Matthew 22:37, 38 [emphasis mine]

Every man according as he purposeth in his *heart*, so let him give; not grudgingly, or of necessity: for God loveth a cheerful giver.
                    II Corinthians 9:7 [emphasis mine]

The issue is the heart. But there's a problem, for as Jeremiah declares, "The heart is deceitful above all things, and desperately wicked" (17:9). What then is the solution? David gave the answer when he said, "Thy word have I hid in mine heart, that I might not sin against thee" (Psalm 119:11).

How is the heart cleansed? By the Word. If people criticize you for something you are doing or not doing in the area of religion, say to them, "Show me in the Word where it says I should or should not do that, for unless you can show me in the Word, I don't care what the traditions might have been previously, or what our culture dictates presently. I am free in Jesus Christ."

Matthew 15:10–12
And he called the multitude, and said unto them, Hear, and understand: Not that which goeth into the mouth defileth a man; but that which cometh out of the mouth, this defileth a man. Then came his disciples, and said unto him, Knowest thou that the Pharisees were offended, after they heard this saying?

"It's not what goes into your mouth; it's what comes out of your heart. That's the key." In so saying, Jesus offended the pious, religious leaders.

Matthew 15:13–20
But he answered and said, Every plant, which my heavenly Father hath not planted, shall be rooted up. Let them alone: they be blind leaders of the blind. And if the blind lead the blind, both shall fall into the ditch. Then answered Peter and said unto him, Declare unto us this parable. And Jesus said, Are ye also yet without understanding? Do not ye yet understand, that whatsoever enter-

eth in at the mouth goeth into the belly, and is cast out into the draught? But those things which proceed out of the mouth come forth from the heart; and they defile the man. For out of the heart proceed evil thoughts, murders, adulteries, fornications, thefts, false witness, blasphemies: These are the things which defile a man: but to eat with unwashen hands defileth not a man.

The issue is not washing of hands by the egg-shell, but washing of hearts by the Word. Be free in Jesus. Enjoy your liberty and extend it to others graciously.

Matthew 15:21, 22
Then Jesus went thence, and departed into the coasts of Tyre and Sidon. And, behold, a woman of Canaan came out of the same coasts, and cried unto him, saying, Have mercy on me, O Lord, thou Son of David; my daughter is grievously vexed with a devil.

The phraseology this Canaanite woman uses is most enlightening. She approaches Jesus using a phrase made popular by Jews who were in need of healing. "Have mercy on me, Son of David," they would cry whenever Jesus approached. Why did they refer to Jesus as "Son of David"? A thousand years earlier, a prophecy was given to David that he would have a Son, a descendant who would reign forever—Messiah. And when Messiah came, the lame would walk and blind eyes would be opened. Consequently, the Jews recognized Jesus as their Messiah called Him "Son of David." Now suddenly, this Canaanite lady, upon hearing of Jesus' coming, searched for the most appropriate way to address Him. Having heard Him referred to as "Son of David" by Jews lining His path, she borrowed the phrase from them.

Matthew 15:23 (a)
But he answered her not a word.

If ever there were a situation to which I would think Jesus would respond quickly, it would be to a mother crying helplessly over her child. Yet, here this crying woman came to Jesus, and He answered her not a word.

Matthew 15:23 (b)
And his disciples came and besought him, saying, Send her away; for she crieth after us.

Her tears, no doubt, were having an effect on the disciples, and they came to Jesus, saying, "Lord, send her away. She's bothering us."

Matthew 15:24
But he answered and said, I am not sent but unto the lost sheep of the house of Israel.

If I were this woman, I think at this point I would have slunk away in despair. After all, she had *nothing* going for her. Her race was against her. She was a Canaanite—an enemy of the Israelites. Her sex was against her. She was a woman—in a time where women were held in low esteem. Even the disciples were against her, as they begged Jesus to send her away. But you've got to admire this lady because she didn't give up. And Jesus knew she wouldn't. You see, Jesus was not trying to be difficult with her. Rather, He was drawing out an understanding from her that would be helpful not only in her situation specifically, but to us and to all generations historically. Watch what happens.

Matthew 15:25
Then came she and worshipped him, saying, Lord, help me.

No longer concerned about the right phraseology and the proper presentation, in desperation and openness, she worships Jesus. In simplicity, she says, "Lord, save me," and a miracle was underway.

Sometimes when we're going through tough times, we hear how someone else prays, and we think, *That must be the key. King James English is what moves the hand of God.* So we pray, "Father, I thankest Thee that Thou beholdest the cries of all of Thy creation. Now, Father, in Thy magnificence and benevolence, have mercy upon me in my situation." And nothing happens. Or we hear someone share how they lifted their hand to the Lord, and He reached down and pulled them out of their depression. And we say, "Now how high did you hold your hand? Was it your right hand or your left hand?"

This Canaanite woman was in that same situation. She had the formula, but she failed miserably until she threw her formula aside and came in brokenness and openness to worship Jesus. Worship works where formulas fail. The word "worship," or *proskuneo* in Greek means, "to turn and kiss." Guys, when you kiss your wives, hopefully you don't follow a ten-step program to better kissing. I mean, it needs to be spontaneous and expressive, simple and sincere. The same is true of worship. Worship is not a procedure we follow. It's creative and spontaneous, simple and sincere. In II Samuel 6:12, we see an account of one who understood this principle. The ark of the covenant had been in the house of Obed-Edom for some time. David was bringing it back to Jerusalem.

And it was told king David, saying, The Lord hath blessed the house of Obed-edom, and all that pertaineth unto him, because of the ark of God. So David went and brought up the ark of God from the house of Obed-edom into the city of David with gladness. And it was so, that when they that bare the ark of the Lord had gone six paces, he sacrificed oxen and fatlings. And David danced before the Lord with all his might; and David was girded with a linen ephod. 2 Samuel 6:12–14

There was a time when all the rage was dressing for success. Many years ago, I saw a picture of fifteen men standing with the then current President of the United States. Every single one had on a dark suit and a red tie. Evidently, they had all read the same book! In the things of God, however, it's not so much dressing for success, but undressing; not so much robing yourself in royalty and regality, but disrobing in humility and spontaneity. David laid aside his "Dress For Success" manual and danced in his underwear before the Lord with gladness and spontaneity, expressing his heart creatively, energetically, and sincerely.

So David and all the house of Israel brought up the ark of the Lord with shouting, and with the sound of the trumpet. And as the ark of the Lord came into the city of David, Michal Saul's daughter looked through a window, and saw king David leaping and dancing before the Lord; and she despised him in her heart. 2 Samuel 6:15, 16

Observing her husband dancing in his boxers, Michal said, "This is terrible. He's the king of Israel. Where's his dignity?"

Then David returned to bless his household. And Michal the daughter of Saul came out to meet David, and said, How glorious was the king of Israel to day, who uncovered himself to day in the eyes of the handmaids of his servants, as one of the vain fellows shamelessly uncovereth himself! 2 Samuel 6:20

"That was great, Dave," laughed Michal. "You made a big impression out there. You looked like a fool."

And David said unto Michal, It was before the Lord, which chose me before thy father . . . 2 Samuel 6:21 (a)

"Remember your father, Michal? God was against him because although Saul was royal and regal, he was not humble and open. He was a worker, not a worshipper. He didn't have a heart

after God." In other words, David is saying, "Michal, you're acting just like your dad."

. . . and before all his house, to appoint me ruler over the people of the Lord, over Israel: therefore will I play before the Lord. And I will yet be more vile than thus, and will be base in mine own sight: and of the maidservants which thou hast spoken of, of them shall I be had in honour. 2 Samuel 6:21 (b),22

"If you think I acted foolishly today, stick around," David declares. "What I have done, I have done unto the Lord as an act of worship. And those maidens you are worried about? They will see the honor of the Lord working in me."

Therefore Michal the daughter of Saul had no child unto the day of her death. 2 Samuel 6:23

The same is true today. People or churches who feel worship is not important, or that it's foolish to express one's heart to the Lord publicly and privately will, like Michal, experience a barrenness, a dryness, and a lack of fruitfulness in their lives. Those of you who feel like the Lord is "answering you not a word," try worshiping Jesus. Put away your royal robes and futile formulas and say, "Lord, help me express my heart to You today."

Matthew 15:26
But he answered and said, It is not meet to take the children's bread, and to cast it to dogs.

Jesus responds to the woman allegorically. In speaking of children, He is referring to the children of Israel, the Jews. In speaking of bread, He is referring to Himself, the Bread of Life. In speaking of dogs, using the Greek word for a pet dog, He is referring to the Gentiles. In other words, Jesus is saying, "Since I have come first and foremost to the house of Israel, my primary focus must be upon the Jews."

Matthew 15:27
And she said, Truth, Lord: yet the dogs eat of the crumbs which fall from their masters' table.

"I hear You," she says. "I understand You're working according to certain priorities. Yet even though the puppy dogs don't get the best bread, they still get the leftover crumbs that fall from the table." Can't you see in your mind's eye a smile break out on the face of Jesus? This is what He was after all along—not to destroy her, but to develop her.

Matthew 15:28 (a)
Then Jesus answered and said unto her,
O woman . . .

The word translated "woman" is *gune,* a term
of respect. Jesus used the same word when He
spoke of His mother.

Matthew 15:28 (b)
. . . great is thy faith: be it unto thee even
as thou wilt. And her daughter was made
whole from that very hour.

Jesus knew all along what He would be doing.
He knew He would indeed heal and bless. But in
the process, He taught this Canaanite woman, and
all who have studied her story, the power and reality of true worship. I encourage you this day,
precious people, to put away phrases and forms
and instead follow the example of the Canaanite
woman. Worship Jesus in simplicity and sincerity
and watch Him work powerfully and radically.

Matthew 15:29–39
And Jesus departed from thence, and came
nigh unto the sea of Galilee; and went up into
a mountain, and sat down there. And great
multitudes came unto him, having with them
those that were lame, blind, dumb, maimed,
and many others, and cast them down at
Jesus' feet; and he healed them: Insomuch
that the multitude wondered, when they saw
the dumb to speak, the maimed to be whole,
the lame to walk, and the blind to see: and they

glorified the God of Israel. Then Jesus called
his disciples unto him, and said, I have compassion on the multitude, because they continue with me now three days, and have
nothing to eat: and I will not send them
away fasting, lest they faint in the way. And
his disciples say unto him, Whence should
we have so much bread in the wilderness, as
to fill so great a multitude? And Jesus saith
unto them, How many loaves have ye? And
they said, Seven, and a few little fishes. And
he commanded the multitude to sit down on
the ground. And he took the seven loaves
and the fishes, and gave thanks, and brake
them, and gave to his disciples, and the disciples to the multitude. And they did all eat,
and were filled: and they took up of the broken meat that was left seven baskets full.
And they that did eat were four thousand
men, beside women and children. And he
sent away the multitude, and took ship, and
came into the coasts of Magdala.

In this passage, we see Jesus feeding over four
thousand people. Were these people praying?
Were they asking to be fed? Did the disciples believe Jesus would feed the multitude miraculously? No. The people didn't pray. And even the
disciples didn't have faith. Yet Jesus provided
abundantly, graciously, and compassionately.

*For topical study of Matthew 15:32–39, see
"The Key: His Compassion" below.*

THE KEY: HIS COMPASSION
A Topical Study of
Matthew 15:32–39

The passage before us is controversial. Many scholars suggest it is nothing more
than a retelling of the "feeding of the five thousand" story in Matthew 14. Why?
It's the only explanation they can offer for the seeming stupidity of the disciples. You
see, here in chapter 15, the disciples ask Jesus how they are to feed such a large crowd.
Why would the disciples wonder how to feed four thousand if only a mere chapter
earlier, they had seen Jesus feed over five thousand? "The only logical answer," conclude the scholars, "is that Matthew 14:14–21 and Matthew 15:32–39 are two different
accounts of the same event." I, however, reject their premise for the following reasons:

• There were five thousand men in chapter 14.
• There were four thousand men in chapter 15.

- There were five loaves and two fish in chapter 14.
- There were seven loaves and a few fish in chapter 15.
- The multitude sat on the grass in chapter 14—the implication being it was springtime.
- The multitude sat on the bare ground in chapter 15—the implication being it was summertime.
- Jesus was in Bethsaida, the northern side of the Sea of Galilee, in chapter 14.
- Jesus was in Decapolis (Mark 8), on the eastern side of Galilee in chapter 15.
- After He fed the multitude in chapter 14, they wanted to make Him King.
- After He fed the multitude in chapter 15, they made no such request.

Above all, however, the reason I know these two events are separate is because Jesus Himself referred to them as such in Matthew 16:9, 10. If the "scholars" are right in suggesting there was only one feeding with two accounts, then Matthew wasn't listening to the Spirit as he wrote his Gospel, and Jesus was mistaken and confused about His own miracles.

I find this hard to believe. Many read this story and struggle with it. "How can this be? How could the disciples forget about the miracle that happened only one chapter previously? Nobody's that dumb." I suggest to you that the answer to that very question is very applicable and helpful for me and for you. First, you must understand that Galilee and Decapolis were very different regions. Galilee was the "headquarters" of Jesus' ministry. Galilee was where He hung out, delivered significant teachings, and developed His disciples. Decapolis, on the other hand, was a confederation of ten Gentile cities with its own monetary system, judicial system, king, and army. Decapolis was financially prosperous and very worldly. Huge monuments to Zeus and Aphrodite dotted the landscape, and coliseums provided Roman-style entertainment.

I believe that's where the problem was. Here, the disciples were with Jesus in Decapolis. "Certainly Jesus won't do a miracle *here*," the disciples must have thought. "This is heathen territory. Most of this crowd is Gentile. The Lord isn't going to feed *these* people. Besides that, they've been with Him three days now. In Galilee, He fed the crowd after only one day. This is the wrong place. These are the wrong people. This is the wrong time."

The same thing happens to me and to you. The Lord blesses us. A miracle happens. Provision is made. Grace is shown. Then we get into a similar situation a month, a year, or a decade later. And we say, "Oh yeah, I know the Lord saw me through that previous difficulty. I know He provided for me graciously. But that was a different time. I was in Galilee then. I was having morning devotions. I was really close to Him. Now? I'm in the wrong place with the wrong people. This is the wrong time. Nothing is going to happen. The Lord isn't going to see me through this trouble. Not now. I'm out to lunch. I'm in Decapolis."

How easy it is to fall into the subtle trap of expecting the Lord to bless us because of our own worthiness or because we're in Galilee. "I'm praying. I'm studying. I'm close to the Lord. Of course He'll bless me!" But what we fail to factor into the equation is this very simple understanding. Jesus, we are told in verse 32, called His disciples and said, "I have *compassion* on the multitude." The word translated "compassion" is actually a Greek word that describes the retching of the intestines—something which one feels very deeply. Looking out upon the hungry people of Decapolis, Jesus said, "I hurt for them. Even though no one is asking Me to provide, even though no one is believing I can provide, I want to do something for these people because I have compassion upon them."

What a glorious day it is when you understand that Jesus, your Redeemer and your Friend, looks at you in your need and has compassion upon you—even when you're in Decapolis. What a freeing day it is when we finally learn that the blessings the Lord gives us are not based on anything we do, but just because He sees our hunger and has compassion upon us. There's only one prerequisite—just as there was only one prerequisite for the multitude to be fed with so much food that the Greek text says they were "glutted." They needed to be where Jesus was.

You see, the four thousand weren't making requests of Jesus. They weren't exercising faith in Him. They were merely where He was. They were "under the spout where the blessings come out." And that's the same place we need to be. I have found this to be so true in my own life. The Lord has blessed me above all I could ask or think. I wish I could say to you it was because of my powerful prayer life, my disciplined fasting, my great faith. But that's not true. The Lord has blessed me because He looked on me and said, "Wow. You're hurting. And I hurt for you." That's the way Jesus is—He's a compassionate, caring, loving, gracious, and giving Friend. And the only thing I need to do is hang around Him.

Spending time with God's people

As a three-year-old, I sat on the pew with my mom and dad at Calvary Temple in San Jose, California, as Pastor Kermit Jeffries gave a message on hell. Usually, when Pastor Jeffries preached, Mom would give me some cookies or Lifesavers, and I would lie down and fall asleep. But for some reason on this particular morning, when he started talking about the devil, my ears perked up, and I listened carefully. "Satan has a stopwatch in his hand," Pastor Jeffries said. "He realizes time is running out. He's grabbing every man and woman, boy and girl he possibly can, and he's pulling them into the fires of hell." As soon as Pastor Jeffries gave an invitation to those who wanted to escape Satan's grasp, I scooted down the aisle to the front as quickly as I could. I got saved. Why? Because I was seeking the truth? Exploring the philosophies of the Western mentality? Trying to determine esoterically if there is truth, or if existential thought was the conclusion of my pursuit? No. I wasn't seeking, pursuing, thinking, or working. I was just where Jesus was.

My heart breaks when I know people who are hurting are hanging out at the local tavern. They're missing relational, financial, emotional, and occupational blessings because they're not hanging out with Jesus. Those who were around Jesus were blessed just because He looked at them and had compassion on them.

Spending time in God's Word

Jesus is revealed not only through His people, but also in His Word. Often, I open the Scriptures and suddenly find something that answers the question for me, gives a solution to me, and satisfies the longing within me. Coming down from Highway 62 after the accident in which the Lord took my first wife Terry home, a word from the Lord was whispered in my heart that I didn't even know I knew:

> *For I know the thoughts that I think toward you, saith the Lord, thoughts of*
> *peace and not of evil, to give you an expected end.*   Jeremiah 29:11

As I listen to His still small voice revealed through His Word to my heart, as I hang out with Him in the multitude of His people, I experience miracle after miracle, blessing after blessing. And when I feel like I'm in the wrong place with the wrong people at the wrong time, I have learned that He can work even in Decapolis because He looks upon me with compassion. I so appreciate our Lord Jesus. He is truly good. As the multitudes left, they did so with full stomachs and healed bodies, with praises flowing from their lips and excitement filling their hearts amazed by the compassion and goodness of Jesus Christ. Hang around Him, precious people, and you'll do the same.

16 As we have seen, the Gospel of Matthew is a presentation of Jesus Christ as King. Written from this perspective, chapters 1 through 10 reveal the King: His Person, His prophet, His precepts, His power. Chapters 11 through 13 portray the rebellion against the King: against His Person, His prophet, His precepts, and His power. Chapters 14 through 20 present the retreat of the King as Jesus pulls His disciples away for times of instruction and fellowship. He will still have encounters with His enemies, and from time to time, the crowds will still surround Him, but this section of Matthew is primarily a record of Jesus retreating with His disciples.

Matthew 16:1
The Pharisees also with the Sadducees came, and tempting desired him that he would shew them a sign from heaven.

The Pharisees and Sadducees tracked Jesus down as He withdrew into Galilee. Attempting to test Him, they asked Him for a sign. Now, this absolutely blows my mind because only two chapters earlier, Jesus fed five thousand men with a few loaves and fishes. And then in the sequel, Loaves and Fishes II, He fed four thousand. The Pharisees and Sadducees simply refused to see what was happening all around them. In 2 Corinthians 3:14, Paul writes that Satan has blinded the minds of those who have willingly rejected the gospel. If a person desires to see the light and to know the Truth, however, it will be revealed to him regardless of his surroundings or his situation.

I read about a French woman who lived fifty years ago and had been blind from birth. One day, someone gave her the Gospel of Mark in Braille. She was so blessed by the story of Jesus that she read it over and over until her fingertips became callused and lost their sensitivity.

To regain feeling in her fingers, she cut off the calluses, and with bloody fingertips, read Mark's Gospel yet again. As she continued to cut away the skin and the calluses, however, she damaged her nerve endings so badly that soon she permanently lost all feeling in her fingertips. Devastated, she held her copy of the Gospel of Mark in her hands one last time and literally kissed it goodbye. It was then she discovered that her lips were more sensitive than her fingertips had ever been. She continued to study the Scriptures—with her lips—and went on to become a gifted teacher of the Word.

Those who are blind but want to see will see, regardless of the obstacles. Those who don't wish to see—Pharisees, scribes, and Sadducees, even though miracles are happening round about them—will not see because they don't want to see.

Matthew 16:2, 3
He answered and said unto them, When it is evening, ye say, It will be fair weather: for the sky is red. And in the morning, It will be foul weather to day: for the sky is red and lowring. O ye hypocrites, ye can discern the face of the sky; but can ye not discern the signs of the times?

In Jesus' day, the rabbis taught that a demon could perform earthly miracles, but only God could work miracles that related to the sky. Therefore, when these Pharisees said, "Show us a sign from heaven," they were actually saying, "Okay, so You fed five thousand, walked on water, and healed a leper. You might be a demon. Show us a sign from heaven to prove You're not."

Continuing with their line of reasoning, Jesus said, "Speaking of the heavens, you can predict the heavenly signs, why not the signs of the times?" Daniel prophesied precisely when Messiah would be on the scene (chapter 9). Thus, Jesus is saying, "Can't you discern the signs of the times? Don't you know Bible prophecy?" knowing that if the religious community of the day had been studying the Word like they should have been, they would have known that this was the exact time for Messiah to appear.

Matthew 16:4 (a)
A wicked and adulterous generation seeketh after a sign . . .

Miracles never convert a person. They can satisfy a person's curiosity, but they will never bring him into a born-again salvation experience.

- The world says, "If I can see it, then I'll believe it."
- The Bible says, "If you believe it, then you'll see it."

Signs and wonders can confirm the Scripture, but only faith can convert the sinner. Voltaire, the famous French infidel, was so bitter towards Christianity, it was claimed that he said,

"Even if a miracle should be wrought in the open marketplace before one thousand sober witnesses, I would rather mistrust my senses than admit a miracle took place."

Such is the mentality of the skeptic, of the sinner, of the non-believer. Interestingly, Voltaire also said, "In one hundred years from now, Christianity will be a thing of the past and the only Bibles will be in museums!"[3] "Twenty years after his death, the Geneva Bible Society purchased his house to be used to print the Bible. Later it became the Paris headquarters for the British and Foreign Bible society."[4]

Matthew 16:4 (b)
. . . And there shall no sign be given unto it, but the sign of the prophet Jonas. And he left them, and departed.

Jonah—the one who was thrown overboard in the sea and for three days was seemingly in hell itself in the belly of the great fish before being thrown out on the beach—was himself a symbol of resurrection. "Destroy this temple," Jesus declared referring to Himself, "and in three days I will raise it up" (John 2:19). That's the one sign Jesus promised.

Matthew 16:5-7
And when his disciples were come to the other side, they had forgotten to take bread. Then Jesus said unto them, Take heed and beware of the leaven of the Pharisees and of the Sadducees. And they reasoned among themselves, saying, It is because we have taken no bread.

When Jesus talked about the leaven of the Pharisees and Sadducees, His disciples assumed He was speaking on a material level about something physical rather than something spiritual. This happened throughout the Gospels. Whenever Jesus spoke of a spiritual realm, people always confused it with the material world.

In John 3, Jesus said, "You must be born again."

"How does a man enter into his mother's womb the second time?" asked Nicodemus. Jesus was speaking spiritually, but Nicodemus was trying to figure it out materially.

In John 4, Jesus said, "I have water to give you which if you drink you shall never thirst again."

"Give me this water," said the woman at the well, "so I won't have to keep drawing out of the well!" She was thinking materially, but Jesus was speaking of the water of the Spirit internally.

In John 6, Jesus said, "Unless you eat of My body and drink of My blood, you can have no part of Me."

The crowds, thinking He was talking about cannibalism, began to turn away from Him. Yet again, He was speaking of a spiritual realm, but the people couldn't see past the material world.

Jesus' desire is to free us from this material, physical world in which we're so caught up. He longs for us to gain an eternal, spiritual perspective. But, like the disciples, we so often get hung up in the material realm. Even in our spiritual walk, we often count our blessings only in corporeal terms, and recognize only those miracles we see physically. Only the spiritual realm is eternal. That's why church is so important to me. As I come here to meet with you, to sing songs of praise to the Lord, to study the Word, my focus shifts from the material to the spiritual, from the temporal to the eternal.

Matthew 16:8–12
Which when Jesus perceived, he said unto them, O ye of little faith, why reason ye among yourselves, because ye have brought no bread? Do ye not yet understand, neither remember the five loaves of the five thousand, and how many baskets ye took up? Neither the seven loaves of the four thousand, and how many baskets ye took up? How is it that ye do not understand that I spake it not to you concerning bread, that ye should beware of the leaven of the Pharisees and of the Sadducees? Then understood they how that he bade them not beware of the leaven of bread, but of the doctrine of the Pharisees and of the Sadducees.

The leaven of the Pharisees is legalism. The Pharisees kept scores of rules and regulations, but their hearts were not right with the Lord. The leaven of the Sadducees is not legalism, but liberalism. The Sadducees said, "There are no miracles. There are no angels. There is no resurrection. This whole thing is really just to help you become a better person."

Beware of the leaven of legalism and liberalism. Galatians deals with the subject of legalism and Colossians with the subject of liberalism.

Matthew 16:13
When Jesus came into the coasts of Caesarea Philippi, he asked his disciples, saying, Whom do men say that I the Son of man am?

Over eighty times throughout Scripture, Jesus refers to Himself as the Son of Man. I believe there is a two-fold reason He uses this term more than any other. First, it speaks of His humility and His ability to relate. He desires to be numbered among us. Second, it speaks of His position prophetically. Daniel 7:13 foretold that Messiah would be known as the Son of Man.

Matthew 16:14, 15
And they said, Some say that thou art John the Baptist: some, Elias; and others, Jeremias, or one of the prophets. He saith unto them, But whom say ye that I am?

This is the most important question ever asked any man. The door to eternity swings upon it: Who do *you* say Jesus is personally?

Matthew 16:16–18
And Simon Peter answered and said, Thou art the Christ, the Son of the living God. And Jesus answered and said unto him, Blessed art thou, Simon Barjona: for flesh and blood hath not revealed it unto thee, but my Father which is in heaven. And I say also unto thee, That thou art Peter, and upon this rock I will build my church; and the gates of hell shall not prevail against it.

Jesus uses two Greek words for "stone" in this passage. *Petros*, or "Peter," means small stone. *Petra* means massive stone. In other words, Jesus is saying, "Blessed are you, little stone. Upon the massive stone of your confession, I will build My church."

Hadn't Peter and others already confessed that Jesus was the Christ?

In John 1, when Jesus told Nathanael He had seen him under the fig tree, Nathanael responded, "Truly Thou art the Son of God, the King of Israel." Yet Jesus didn't say, "Blessed are you, Nathanael. Upon that rock I'll build My Church."

In Luke 5, after a miraculous haul of fish, Peter acknowledged Jesus' lordship when he said, "Depart from me, for I am a sinful man, O Lord." Yet at that point, Jesus didn't say, "Blessed are you, Peter. Upon that rock I will build My church."

In John 6, after five thousand were fed, Peter declared, "Truly thou art the Son of God. You alone have the words of eternal life." Yet Jesus didn't say, "Upon that rock I'll build My church."

Why? Because Jesus' disciples had acknowledged His deity previously; in every case their acknowledgements were an emotional response to a physical miracle . . .

- "You saw me under the fig tree? You must be the Son of God!"
- "Look at these fish! You must be the Son of God!"
- "Wow! Five thousand are fed! You must be the Son of God!"

Peter's statement here in Matthew 16, on the other hand, is not an emotional response. His is a carefully thought through conclusion based upon supernatural revelation. Why is this important? Because a lot of times people will make a vow, saying,

"My mom was healed of cancer. I'll start going to church." And they do—for about five months. Or, "My husband didn't get fired when everyone else did, so we'll go to church." And they go—for a few weeks.

But that isn't the foundation upon which Jesus builds. He's looking for a man or woman who will come to a rational, intellectual conclusion based upon deep, spiritual revelation. He's listening for those who say, "I have concluded that You're the Christ, not because I won the lottery, not because I feel better physically, but because You have revealed Yourself to my heart spiritually and to my mind rationally."

It is then Jesus says, "Blessed are you. You're not talking about an emotional response, or a five-month foray into Christianity. You have made a declaration, a decision, and I will build My church upon the reality, the rock of your confession."

True conversion is not based upon some emotion or some event. True conversion takes place when a man or woman says, "I have concluded that Jesus really is who He declared Himself to be. He is the Son of God. And I'm giving my life to follow Him totally."

Matthew 16:19
And I will give unto thee the keys of the kingdom of heaven: and whatsoever thou shalt

bind on earth shall be bound in heaven: and whatsoever thou shalt loose on earth shall be loosed in heaven.**

This binding and loosing is not a picture of heaven doing *our* bidding; rather, it portrays *us* in harmony with heaven. Jesus is not saying, "Here are some keys. Whatever you want to do, I'll make it happen." No, it's just the opposite. We are to be binding and loosing even as it is done in heaven. We are to be in harmony with Jesus.

For topical study of Matthew 16:13–19 entitled "Just Jesus," turn to page 130.

Matthew 16:20–22
Then charged he his disciples that they should tell no man that he was Jesus the Christ. From that time forth began Jesus to shew unto his disciples, how that he must go unto Jerusalem, and suffer many things of the elders and chief priests and scribes, and be killed, and be raised again the third day. Then Peter took him, and began to rebuke him, saying, Be it far from thee, Lord: this shall not be unto thee.

In verse 16, when Peter spoke of Jesus as the Christ, he was into it. But now in verse 20, when Peter sees Jesus on the Cross, he wants no part of it.

Matthew 16:23
But he turned, and said unto Peter, Get thee behind me, Satan: thou art an offence unto me: for thou savourest not the things that be of God, but those that be of men.

This verse tells me two things.

First, it disqualifies Peter as a candidate for pope. You see, one of the qualifications for the papacy is infallibility on spiritual matters. So fallible was Peter on this point that Jesus called him Satan.

"Well," some might say, "that was before Peter was filled with the Holy Spirit."

But in Galatians 2:11, Paul writes, "When I saw Peter I rebuked him to his face." Why? Because Peter was burdening Gentile believers with Jewish rules and regulations. Therefore, even after Peter was filled with the Spirit, he still blundered. I love Peter. But I acknowledge his fallibility.

Second, this verse answers the question, "How can a person speak a word of prophecy Sunday night when Sunday morning he kicked his cat and yelled at his wife? How can he speak with spiritual authority one minute and be so carnal the next?"

We see Peter doing the same thing. One minute he had revelation from the Father—genuine, true revelation, acknowledged by Jesus. The next, he spoke in the flesh. This teaches me to say, "I'm going to listen to what you're saying, even though two weeks ago you said something dumb." Gang, the frailty of humanity is such that we all can move into times of revelation and deep understanding—then moments later be off the wall and out to lunch.

Matthew 16:24
Then said Jesus unto his disciples, If any man will come after me, let him deny himself, and take up his cross, and follow me.

Taking up one's cross doesn't mean suffering from hay fever, foot problems, a heart murmur, or even cancer. Taking up your cross means that you identify with Jesus to the point of suffering and shame, rejection, and perhaps even death. Taking up your cross is something you choose to do, not something you put up with. It's a choice to deny yourself, a determination that, no matter what, you'll stand for Jesus.

Matthew 16:25, 26
For whosoever will save his life shall lose it: and whosoever will lose his life for my sake shall find it. For what is a man profited, if he shall gain the whole world, and lose his own soul? or what shall a man give in exchange for his soul?

Here's the irony: The more you live for yourself, the more miserable you'll be. But the more you say, "Lord, I'm going to live for You completely, wholeheartedly, and totally," the more abundant your life will be both now and eternally. If you think back on the happiest times of your life, you will most likely find they were when you were really going for it in Jesus—when He was the priority in your life and the passion of your heart.

Matthew 16:27
For the Son of man shall come in the glory of his Father with his angels; and then he shall reward every man according to his works.

If you take up your cross and follow Jesus, you'll be rewarded in the ages to come as well as presently.

Matthew 16:28
Verily I say unto you, There be some standing here, which shall not taste of death, till they see the Son of man coming in his kingdom.

"Wait," you say, "the disciples are all dead and Jesus' kingdom hasn't come yet. Did Jesus make a mistake?"
Stay tuned. The answer lies in chapter 17.

JUST JESUS
A Topical Study of
Matthew 16:13–19

As we did every year for his birthday, my son Peter John and I traveled to the Bay Area one August to see the Oakland A's battle the Cleveland Indians. Quite honestly, however, although taking in a ballgame had become a tradition for Peter and me, I wasn't sure I'd ever go again. You see, I had some big problems with big-league baseball.

Every time I went to the coliseum, I was asked for money. And none of the people sitting next to me introduced themselves. The manager never paid a call on me, never welcomed me to the coliseum, and didn't even know my name. And then there were all those hypocrites in the stands, like the ladies polishing their nails and talking about what everyone was wearing. Behind me were some fanatics who were worse than the hypocrites. Every time Jose Canseco got on base, they stood up, cheered, and looked silly. And the umpires? Some of their calls were ridiculous. I'm sure I know more about baseball than they do. As for Peter, I didn't want to force him to go to major-league baseball games any more. I thought I'd let him decide for himself when he got older.

Now, if someone said that, we would think he was crazy. Those reasons are all bogus. And yet, why is it that no one protests when those same objections are raised concerning church? Those are the exact reasons people give for not going to church: "People are too fanatical and too hypocritical; the pastor talks too much about money, and he didn't call on me; the people weren't friendly. I'll let my own kids decide eventually."

Our generation, it seems, has rejected church. In fact, I remember seeing a bumper sticker in the '60s that sort of summed up our generational mentality: "Jesus, Yes. Church, No." And a lot of people are in that place. "Yeah, I'm into Jesus, but I'm not into the church. No way."

I'm here to say that I am really into the Church. You might think, *Well of course you are. You're a pastor.* But let me tell you, I am not into the church because I'm a pastor. I am a pastor because I am into the church.

The passage before us in Matthew 16 is very important, for it is the first time Jesus Christ uses the word "church." There is a principle of hermeneutics called the Principle of First Mention, which says: You will usually find key foundational understandings about a subject in the first place it is mentioned. Thus, when Jesus first mentions the church in Matthew 16, we find three reasons why it is essential.

Jesus Takes Pride *in* His Church

. . . Upon this rock I will build my church . . .   Matthew 16:18

The language is important. It speaks of a possessiveness, of an intimacy with us. Jesus didn't say, "I will build a church," or "I'll put up with the Church." He said, "I will build *My* church." Jesus is proud of His people.

> *For both he that sanctifieth [Jesus] and they who are sanctified [us] are all of one: for which cause he is not ashamed to call them brethren, Saying, I will declare thy name unto my brethren, in the midst of the church will I sing praise unto thee.*   Hebrews 2:11, 12

The writer of Hebrews declares Jesus is proud of us. Not ashamed of us, He sings praise to the Father right along with us in the midst of the congregation. Why isn't He ashamed of us? Because He sees our potential. When Jesus first called Peter, He said, "I call you Petros, "Small Rock," because I'm going to change you from one who is unsteady to someone who's solid, stable, and useful." Jesus doesn't see us with our present flaws, but in our potential usefulness.

Secondly, He sees us prophetically. Because we are already seated with Christ in the heavenly places (Ephesians 2:6), He sees us as already perfected.

Thirdly, He sees us positionally. Jesus sees us robed in His righteousness and washed with His blood. Our sins, failures, and shortcomings are completely out of His sight and gone from His memory.

So He looks at us potentially, prophetically, and positionally, and He sees us as perfect. Incredible! This past week the Lord has dealt very deeply in my own heart along these lines, telling me to look not on the outward appearance, but on the heart—the way He looks at me. I have discovered I have a tendency to judge people according to their actions, but to judge myself according to my intentions. And the Lord spoke to my heart, saying, "Jon, your world would be a whole lot sweeter if you reversed that. Judge yourself by what you do, but judge others by what they meant." Wouldn't it be radical if we looked at people that way? At their intentions rather than their actions? That's the way Jesus looks at His church. He says, "I see your hearts, and I'm proud of you."

Jesus Prevails *Through* His Church

. . . And the gates of hell shall not prevail against it.   Matthew 16:18

For many years, a lot of us thought that the church was a refuge, a fortress where we could hole up until the Lord came back. The gates of hell would not prevail against us if we huddled together within the church singing, "Hold the Fort till the Lord Comes." But that's not what Jesus meant. Gates don't prevail in and of themselves. How many of you have ever been attacked by a gate?

No. Jesus is saying, "The gates of hell will not hold back My church. I am going to prevail through My church. I will storm the gates of hell, where people have been held in bondage, where there has been darkness, discouragement, disease, and death. I will prevail through My church." When Jesus wants to touch someone in love or talk to someone about salvation, He storms the gates of hell through us, His church.

Jesus Protects *by* His Church

And I will give unto thee the keys of the kingdom of heaven: and whatsoever thou shalt bind on earth shall be bound in heaven: and whatsoever thou shalt lose on earth shall be loosed in heaven.   Matthew 16:19

Dr. Kenneth Wuest gives this proper translation: "Whatever shalt be loosed on earth shalt be loosed even as it is in heaven." Jesus protects by His church, giving her the keys of His kingdom.

If you look at my wife's key chain, you will see keys identical to those on my key chain. I'm her bridegroom. She's my bride. And she has the same keys I do. Why? Because we share authority. We rule together over our Volkswagen fleet and our house. We are one.

So, too, Jesus Christ, the Head, has given His bride, the church, the keys to His kingdom. What does this mean? In Matthew 18 and John 20, this same concept is reiterated. Matthew 18 deals with relationships, while John 20 deals with the forgiveness and the retaining of sin. What Jesus is saying is, "I'm giving authority to the church, to bring together or to loosen, even as it is happening in heaven."

If people within the church are having problems with one another, they are to work them out individually. But if they can't, it's a matter for the church to deal with corporately. It's not that we make those decrees ourselves, but through the Word by the Spirit, the church can speak with authority, unlocking God's truth and revealing God's heart. You see, those who say, "I don't need church. I'll just do my own thing. I've got my own ideas about the gospel and about worship," are vulnerable to anyone who comes along saying, "Let's go to Guyana, or to Waco, and we'll start a whole new movement. Who cares about church history? Who cares about theology? Who cares about collegiality? We'll do our own thing."

That's what happened with Jim Jones and David Koresh. Hundreds were killed because they strayed from the protection that comes from the church, the authority of binding and loosing. And thus, there was death. Any Christian who ignores the church will become vulnerable to needless bruises and wounds. The question then arises, "Why have so many people in our generation rejected the church?" I suggest one reason:

Jesus Is Not the Priority *of* His Church

Whom do men say that I the Son of man am?   Matthew 16:13

Jesus had come to Caesarea Philippi, which is located twenty-five miles north of the Sea of Galilee. At Caesarea Philippi, where the waters of the Jordan begin, there is a massive rock face—sort of like a miniature El Capitan. It's one of the prettiest spots I've seen anywhere in the world. There, Jesus gathered His boys and asked this question: "Whom do men say I am?"

His disciples then repeated the theories concerning Him that were floating around Israel.

"Some say You're John the Baptist."

John the Baptist came on the scene, saying, "Repent! The kingdom of God is at hand. You soldiers, quit oppressing the people. You tax collectors, quit extorting from the people. You fathers, be good to your children. Get it together. Repent."

When Jesus appeared, He began His ministry with the same words: Repent, for the kingdom of Heaven is at hand. So, reasoned some, because of His moral teaching and call to repentance, Jesus must be John the Baptist, returned from the dead.

Others said, "No. He's Elijah, returned from heaven."

Haven't you seen the miracles He's done? The lepers are cleansed. The blind see. The lame walk. Miracles happen. He must be Elijah.

Others said, "No. He's Jeremiah."

Haven't you seen the care He shows to the lost, how they move His heart, how He weeps over them? He must be Jeremiah, the weeping prophet who cared so tenderly for the lost sheep of Israel.

"No," others said. "He must be *that* Prophet," referring to the prophet promised in Deuteronomy 18:15, who would come and fully explain the Law of Moses.

Scripture records that the people marveled at the gracious words of Jesus, saying, "No man speaks like this man." Truly, the common people heard Him gladly. Surely He must be "*that* Prophet."

As I look around the Rogue Valley in Oregon, the country, and the world, I see churches built upon one of those four misconceptions.

There are those who say, "We're going to build our church on John the Baptist. That's who Jesus is. We'll call it First Moral Majority Church. We'll tell our community to repent. We'll picket 7–11. We'll write our congressman. We'll organize and let our voice be heard in the community. We'll tell people to get it together morally. And we'll meet together to activate believers, to mobilize Christians, to get them going."

Others say, "No, no, no. Our church is going to be built upon Elijah. That's who Jesus is. We'll call our church Miracle Center. It will be filled with miracles, signs, and wonders. People will see the glory and power of God fall at every single meeting. It's going to be heavy!"

Others say, "No, no, no. Our church is going to be built upon Jeremiah. That's who Jesus is. We'll call our church The Evangelical Expression. We'll have a million-dollar mission budget. We'll offer classes in door-to-door evangelism. We'll spread throughout the community, expand throughout the world globally, and we'll reach the world evangelistically. Like Jeremiah, we'll weep over the lost."

"No, no, no," others say. "Our church is going to be built upon That Prophet. We'll have three-hour marathon Bible studies Monday, Tuesday, and Wednesday nights. We'll have seminars and syllabi. We'll become hermeneutically flawless, exegetically excellent. We'll offer Hebrew, Greek, Chaldean, and Aramaic. We'll parse each verb. We'll know each doctrine thoroughly. We'll become a great teaching center."

Look at our text. Jesus responded to none of these suggestions. It was only when Peter said, "Thou art the Christ—the Christos, the Anointed One, the Messiah, the Son of the living God,"—that Jesus said, "Upon *this* rock I'll build My church."

The church—not a platform for ministry, political activity, or intellectual curiosity—which simply says, "We want to know Jesus personally," is the church Jesus will build. When people say, "Jesus, You're not simply a motivator for us politically, a teacher to us intellectually, a power for us miraculously, or a program for us in mission ministry. You're everything. You're all there is. We just want to know You. We want to love You. We want to walk with You, learn about You, and become more like You," Jesus will build His church upon their confession.

And when a group of people come together and say, "Jesus, we love You. We're impressed with You. We want to learn of You and walk with You," guess what happens? The community around such a group begins to change.

A sheriff in Jackson County, Oregon, who was not a believer wrote me saying that as far as he is concerned, Applegate Christian Fellowship was the best thing that ever happened to curb the drug problem there in the Applegate Valley because so many of the top drug producers in the valley have become converts. Were we marching against marijuana? Were we politically active? No. It's just that wherever Jesus is, the surroundings will be influenced very definitely.

Where Jesus builds His Church, there will be signs and wonders. Power will be experienced—not with fanfare or for itself—but in a supernaturally, natural way.

Where Jesus is the Christos, loved and honored, there will be evangelism, not because of a need to be a part of some program for ego gratification, but rather because people will *want* to share what they have discovered in Christ. They will be in love with Him and will find themselves talking about Him, taking every opportunity to share the One who means so much to them.

The person who is rock-solid in this life and on into eternity will be the one who says, "Jesus, it's You personally. Not ministry. Not study. Not anything but You. I appreciate You, I love You, and I'm committing myself to You. Jesus, You're everything to me."

That's my prayer for us. That's my prayer for you.

In Jesus' Name.

17

At the close of chapter 16, Jesus told His disciples that some of them would see the Kingdom before they died. Over the centuries, many have suggested that since all of the disciples died without witnessing His return, Jesus was amiss when He said this. Thus, they conclude, Jesus was actually fallible. Of course, this is blasphemy, for chapter 17 opens with three of His disciples about to see the glory of the kingdom . . .

Matthew 17:1
And after six days Jesus taketh Peter, James, and John his brother, and bringeth them up into an high mountain apart.

Once again, we see Jesus calling His disciples apart. It has been often said that if we don't come apart, we'll fall apart. We need to get away from the trials and the daily routine of life to retreat into a "high mountain" where we can be apart with Jesus lest we fall apart under the pressures of the world. Jesus took Peter, James, and John up the mountain. Scripture records three times when Jesus took these same three and ministered to them in very unique ways. Interestingly, each of those occasions dealt with death.

The first time Jesus singled out Peter, James, and John, He took them into the house of a man whose daughter had died. After moving out the mockers, Jesus brought the young girl back to life, and Peter, James, and John saw that He was victorious over death (Luke 8:49–55).

On a second occasion, Jesus would take them into the Garden of Gethsemane. As He prayed, "Father, if it be possible, let this cup pass from Me; nevertheless, not My will but thine be done," Peter, James, and John would understand that He was submitted to death (see Matthew 26:37–39).

And here in Matthew 17, Jesus takes the three up the mountain where they will see Him glorified in death.

I believe Peter, James, and John needed these special times of instruction concerning death because these three disciples would each have a very unique encounter with death.

Peter would be the first disciple to be told of his death. In John 21, Jesus said, "Peter, they're going to stretch out your hands and carry you where you don't want to go." And that is exactly what happened when Peter was crucified upside down.

James would be the first disciple put to death, sawed in half lengthwise by his persecutors.

John would be the last of the disciples to die. Banished to the seemingly God-forsaken island of Patmos, it was a ninety-year-old John who received the Book of Revelation.

The Lord uniquely prepared Peter, James, and John for what each of them would face. And He will do the same for you. He will prepare you through Bible studies, radio programs, friends, and books for what lies ahead for you personally. It's amazing to me how I'll study or hear something only to discover a week later that a situation arises in which I need that exact information. Remain sensitive to His voice, and then see the Lord's faithfulness in preparing you for the future.

Matthew 17:2 (a)
And was transfigured before them . . .

The Greek word translated "transfigured" is *metamorphoo,* from which we get our word "meta-

morphosis"—the same word used to describe what happens to a caterpillar inside a cocoon.

Matthew 17:2 (b)
. . . and his face did shine as the sun, and his raiment was white as the light.

After Moses received the Law on Mount Sinai, his face began to shine. But as time went on, it began to fade because the glory of Moses was a reflected glory (2 Corinthians 3:13). Jesus, on the other hand, shone not with a reflected glory, but with a radiant glory. As the Light of the world, the light emanated from within Himself (John 8:12).

Matthew 17:3–4 (a)
And, behold, there appeared unto them Moses and Elias talking with him. Then answered Peter, and said unto Jesus, Lord, it is good for us to be here . . .

Days earlier, as Jesus talked about suffering and death, Peter said, "Lord, be it far from Thee. This shall not be" (see Matthew 16:21, 22). Here, however, as he sees the glory of the Transfiguration, even though death was again the topic of conversation (Luke 9:31), Peter says, "Wow! It's good that we're here."

Matthew 17:4 (b)
. . . if thou wilt, let us make here three tabernacles; one for thee, and one for Moses, and one for Elias.

This is one of many arguments against reincarnation. Moses and Elijah returned not as cows, butterflies, or someone else living in some other time. They returned as Moses and Elijah. It is also interesting to me that Peter recognized them instantly. There is no record of a formal introduction, no record of Jesus saying, "Peter, meet Moses. Moses, Peter. Elijah, Peter. Peter, Elijah." No, there was simply immediate recognition. This tells me that when we get to heaven, we'll recognize everyone there. No need for introductions, no need for nametags, and no forgetting of names. Won't that be wonderful?

Matthew 17:5
While he yet spake, behold, a bright cloud overshadowed them: and behold a voice out of the cloud, which said, This is my beloved Son, in whom I am well pleased; hear ye him.

"Peter, I'm going to interrupt you once again," said God the Father from the cloud over the mountain. "You want to build three booths, but you can't put the Law and the Prophets on the same plane as My Son."

Matthew 17:6, 7
And when the disciples heard it, they fell on their face, and were sore afraid. And Jesus came and touched them, and said, Arise, and be not afraid.

Whereas the voice of God knocks people down in brokenness, Jesus Christ—the Word made flesh—picks them up with tenderness. As I listen to the voice of God thundering from Mount Sinai, "Thou Shalt Not," I fall on my face in humility. Then Jesus comes and says, "Arise. Be not afraid." I'm so thankful for Jesus Christ. Were it not for Him, I would still be on my face. So would you. He is our salvation.

Matthew 17:8
And when they had lifted up their eyes, they saw no man, save Jesus only.

They saw Jesus only. That's the key. May we not try to keep the law. May we not try to follow the prophets. May we have eyes for Jesus only.
The Transfiguration verifies that for thirty-three years, Jesus moved through life flawlessly. He was tempted in all points as we are, yet remained without sin (Hebrews 4:15). And here He is, radiant in His transfiguration. I firmly believe that, had He so chosen, Jesus could have launched right off that mountain into heaven, saying, "So long, gang. I came and showed you that man can live sinlessly. Don't condemn or indict Me for giving you an impossible task. I came and proved it could be done." At that point, the world would have been damned, and God could not have been held accountable for being unfair. But instead of launching into heaven, what did Jesus do? He came down from Mount Hermon to climb Mount Calvary.

Matthew 17:9, 10
And as they came down from the mountain, Jesus charged them, saying, Tell the vision to no man, until the Son of man be risen again from the dead. And his disciples asked him, saying, Why then say the scribes that Elias must first come?

Malachi prophesied that Elijah would come before Messiah appeared (4:5). Believing Jesus to be Messiah, the disciples asked Him why Elijah hadn't yet made his appearance.

Matthew 17:11–13
And Jesus answered and said unto them, Elias truly shall first come, and restore all things. But I say unto you, That Elias is come already, and they knew him not, but have done unto him whatsoever they listed.

Likewise shall also the Son of man suffer of them. Then the disciples understood that he spake unto them of John the Baptist.

Elijah had already come—in the spirit and power of John the Baptist.

Matthew 17:14, 15 (a)
And when they were come to the multitude, there came to him a certain man, kneeling down to him, and saying, Lord, have mercy on my son: for he is lunatic, and sore vexed ...

The word "lunatic" literally means "smitten by the moon." People in Eastern cultures believed that the moon shining on one's face would drive a person crazy. Perhaps it was in reference to this belief that the Lord made a beautiful promise in Psalm 121:6 to be our covering by night.

Matthew 17:15 (b)
... for ofttimes he falleth into the fire, and oft into the water.

This man's son was falling into the fire and into the water in an attempt to kill himself. So too, we see a dramatic rise in teenage suicide today. The solution to teenage suicide begins with the understanding that it is a spiritual rather than a social problem.
Even *Woman's Day* magazine, a secular publication states: "For many teenagers, Satan has become part of their daily lives. Rock lyrics glorify him. Werewolves leer from T-shirts. Satanic symbols decorate jewelry. Some kids just want to shock adults, but for a disturbed many, the attraction to satanic ritual is great and deadly."

Matthew 17:16 (a)
And I brought him to thy disciples ...

Realizing his son was in trouble, this dad did a very wise thing. He brought his boy to Jesus.

Matthew 17:16 (b)
... and they could not cure him.

I appreciate this father because he didn't give up, even though the disciples were unable to help. So often people say, "I took my kid to see this therapist, that counselor, or that minister, but nothing's happening. I quit." This dad didn't. And his persistence was soon to be rewarded.

Matthew 17:17, 18
Then Jesus answered and said, O faithless and perverse generation, how long shall I be with you? how long shall I suffer you? bring him hither to me. And Jesus rebuked the

devil; and he departed out of him: and the child was cured from that very hour.

Mom and Dad, you have the responsibility to bring your child to Jesus. Pray for him constantly. Talk to him continually. Bring him to fellowship regularly. How many must die before we understand that the solution lies not in dealing with the drug lords in Columbia or banning music through legislation in Washington? The solution lies in bringing our kids to Jesus.

Matthew 17:19, 20

Then came the disciples to Jesus apart, and said, Why could not we cast him out? And Jesus said unto them, Because of your unbelief: for verily I say unto you, If ye have faith as a grain of mustard seed, ye shall say unto this mountain, Remove hence to yonder place; and it shall remove; and nothing shall be impossible unto you.

"Why couldn't *we* cast out the demon?" the disciples asked.

"Lack of faith," Jesus said. "If you had believed in your heart, spoken with your mouth, and expected things to happen, the landscape would have changed. Mountains would have moved."

Matthew 17:21

Howbeit this kind goeth not out but by prayer and fasting.

Mark this, Mom and Dad; remember this, Grandma and Grandpa next time your child or grandchild is in trouble: There is a powerful interaction between prayer and fasting. Prayer attaches us to God; fasting detaches us from the flesh. The disciples, no doubt, would have been thinking, *This kind does not go out but by prayer and fasting? How were we to know we would be faced with a lunatic? We didn't have time for prayer and fasting!* And that's exactly the point. Jesus is calling for a lifestyle of prayer and fasting, not an emergency session. Had the disciples been praying and fasting all along, they could have spoken the word of faith that would have resulted in deliverance and salvation.

Maybe you're smugly saying, "I'm glad my son, daughter, or grandchildren don't have problems." Please be wiser than that, dear people, because we do not know the battles they're facing or the strategy of the enemy being plotted in the boardroom of hell for their souls. Satan is a master strategist who invades the lives of our loved ones at the most opportune times—perhaps when we least expect it. Prayer and fasting should be a part of our lifestyle because we don't know what tomorrow holds.

If I hear Jesus right, He's saying, "It's too late to pray and fast when the emergency is before you. You must develop a life of prayer and fasting so that when the problem surfaces, you're already prepared." I am reminded of Job. Every morning, he sacrificed an ox for each one of his kids because "It may be that my sons have sinned, and cursed God in their hearts" (see Job 1:5).

What a glorious privilege we have as parents. We can do more than just hope our kids aren't sucked into drugs or into demonic activity. We can seek the Father fervently. We can fast and pray faithfully. We can take our kids to Jesus continually.

Why weren't the disciples praying and fasting? A possible answer is that they were jealous and had let down their guard, saying, "How come Peter, James, and John always get to see the miracles? Why should we even bother praying? It's obvious Jesus has His favorites." Maybe you feel the same way from time to time. Maybe you wonder why the Lord seems to use everyone else but you. And if you're not careful, that's when you stop praying and fasting. Then the moment comes when you need the power of the Spirit, faith in your heart, weaponry for warfare—and you come up empty.

Matthew 17:22, 23

And while they abode in Galilee, Jesus said unto them, The Son of man shall be betrayed into the hands of men: And they shall kill him, and the third day he shall be raised again. And they were exceeding sorry.

The disciples were "exceeding sorry" because they only heard part of the story. They heard Jesus say He would be betrayed and killed, but they didn't hear Him say the third day He would be raised again. All they heard was death, betrayal, and tragedy. And that's just like us. When someone dies, my first response is one of deep grief and sorrow. While that's understandable, it's only part of the story. If that person knew the Lord, he is in heaven. He is where we long to be. Sorrow and grief are completely understandable responses to tragedy. But if we take into account the whole story, there will also be glory.

Matthew 17:24

And when they were come to Capernaum, they that received tribute money came to Peter, and said, Doth not your master pay tribute?

As they entered Capernaum, tax collectors approached the disciples. They were not raising money for the Roman Empire or for the political system. They were collecting the temple tax. You see, in Jesus' day, the ministry of the temple was not supported by the tithes and offerings of the people. Rather, as outlined in Exodus 30, every man twenty years of age and older was to pay a half-shekel of silver for atonement lest plague come upon him. This has caused no little controversy in theological circles. Was the law suggesting that a person could buy his salvation? Isn't salvation a free gift? Salvation is indeed free to us, but it was costly for Jesus. Silver being the metal of redemption, the temple tax speaks of the fact that, although salvation is free to us, it cost Jesus His life.

Matthew 17:25 (a)
He saith, Yes. And when he was come into the house, Jesus prevented him . . .

When Peter was on the mountain, the voice of the Father interrupted him. Here in the house, he's interrupted by the Son. I hope you're "interruptable." I hope whether you're on the mountain or in the house, the Father and the Son can interrupt your thoughts and activities lest you become dogmatic and rigid.

Matthew 17:25 (b)
. . . saying, What thinkest thou, Simon? of whom do the kings of the earth take custom or tribute? of their own children, or of strangers?

"Tell me, Simon, who does a king tax?" Jesus asked Peter. "Does he tax the strangers—the citizens of the empire—or does he go through the castle knocking on his kids' doors, saying, 'Pay up, kids. We've got to keep this kingdom going'?" The answer is obvious. No king taxes his own children. He taxes the strangers, the citizens of the nation.

Matthew 17:26
Peter saith unto him, Of strangers. Jesus saith unto him, Then are the children free.

In other words, Jesus said to Peter, "Should we be taxed if I am the King and you are My child? Does that make sense?"

Matthew 17:27 (a)
Notwithstanding, lest we should offend them, go thou to the sea, and cast an hook . . .

"Peter, go throw your line in." This command in itself would have been most curious because professional fishermen like Peter didn't use a hook and line. That was rookie equipment. It would be like Jose Canseco using a batting tee. *Real* fishermen used nets and boats. But Peter humbly obeyed. And I can see him walking along the shore, carrying his little pole and tackle box, as his colleagues looked at each other and whispered, "What's he doing?"

Matthew 17:27 (b)
. . . and take up the fish that first cometh up; and when thou hast opened his mouth, thou shalt find a piece of money: that take, and give unto them for me and thee.

"Open the mouth of the first fish you catch, Peter, and you'll find a stater—a full shekel— enough tax for you and for Me," Jesus said. Thus, tucked away in this chapter that spans the heights of the Transfiguration and the depths of the Cross, we find this simple story about a fisherman, a fish, and a coin.

For topical study of Matthew 17:27, see "The Fisherman Casting His Care" below.

THE FISHERMAN CASTING HIS CARE
A Topical Study of
Matthew 17:27

The passage before us speaks to me in a number of ways and interests me on several levels. First of all, it is the only miracle Jesus ever did that dealt with money. Second, it is the only miracle through which He did something for Himself. All too often, Christian TV and current books on faith say, "Want your needs met? Plant a seed in our ministry and watch what will happen to you financially." Folks, that's the opposite of what Jesus said and did. Although He had the power and authority to turn stones to bread, He refused to cater to His own needs (Matthew 4:3, 4).

Third, this was the only miracle Jesus did that dealt with a single fish. Other times Jesus did miracles with fish, it was always with multitudes of fish as His disciples either hauled them in (Luke 5:6) or gave them out (Matthew 14:19). Many commentators try to explain away the feeding of the five thousand by saying that the multitude was fed simply by people sharing the lunches they had packed. So, too, had Peter used a net in the account before us, commentators would probably say, "As Peter was fishing, he caught some fish, an old boot, and a few coins in his net. Therefore, the miracle of the coin and the fish was nothing more than the beautiful miracle of God's provision in the commonplace." But because Peter used a hook and a line and caught one fish with one shekel in its mouth, there's no way to rationalize such a miracle.

Fourth, the Lord provided the coin in the fish solely for Peter. It was one of a number of miracles done specifically for him.

Healing of His Mother-in-Law

We read in Mark that so complete was Peter's mother-in-law's healing, she immediately began to minister to those around her (Mark 1:31). So, too, maybe you've seen a lot of activity at church—people directing traffic on rainy mornings, tending crying babies in the nursery; or counseling into the wee hours of the morning. "Are they crazy?" you wonder. No, they're not crazy. They've simply been touched by the Lord. He removed the fear and the fever of eternal damnation when He saved their souls. Thus, like Peter's mother-in-law, they have no other choice but to serve Him by ministering to others.

A Boatload of Fish

Luke tells us that when pressed by the crowds while teaching on the seashore, Jesus borrowed Peter's boat (Luke 5:3). Using the water as a natural amplifier, He spoke from the boat to the crowd gathered on the shore. When He had finished speaking, He said, "Here's your boat back, Peter. Launch out into the deep and let down your nets." So Peter sailed to the deep, let down his nets, and the haul was so large that the boat almost sank.

What does this tell me? First, it tells me we can't outgive God. If you give to Him of your resources, your energy, your ability, or your money, He'll never "owe you one." If you let Him borrow your boat, He'll fill it with fish. Second, it tells me that the Lord will sometimes whisper in my ear, "Launch out to the deep. Go deeper than you've gone before in faith, in understanding, in praise, and in prayer. Go deeper. That's where the fish are."

Could that be a word from the Lord for you? Could the Lord be saying to some of you right now, "Launch out into the deep water. Go deeper in Me"?

Walking on Water

Crossing the Sea of Galilee, Peter and the disciples were struggling in a storm when suddenly Someone came towards them, walking on the water.

"It's a ghost!" they cried.

"Be of good cheer," Jesus said. "It is I. Be not afraid."

"If that's You, Lord, bid me come," said Peter.

"Come, Peter," answered Jesus.

Peter climbed out of the boat and began to walk on water. But you know the story. As soon as he took his eyes off Jesus, he began to sink.

"Lord, save me," he cried. And Jesus stretched out His hand, grabbed Peter, and put him back in the boat (see Mark 14).

I like this story because sometimes I get tired of the boat I'm in and weary of the disciples with whom I'm rowing. "Lord, get me out of here," I cry. "Even if it means going out where the waves are pounding and the wind is howling, get me out of this boat. I'll go anywhere." Sometimes I step out on my own and sink down in the waves only to have the Lord pick me up and put me right back in the same boat. As a result, I'm beginning to learn that God puts us in fixes to fix us. And if I get out of the boat to try to fix the fix God put me in, He'll have to put me in another fix to fix the fix He wanted to fix in the first place!

A Sword and an Ear

Jesus had taken Peter, James, and John into the Garden of Gethsemane to pray with Him the night before His crucifixion. But having fallen asleep, they were awakened by the sounds of Roman soldiers marching. Before Jesus could say, "Peter, put away your sword," Peter had sliced off the ear of Malchus, the high priest's servant. Jesus then picked up the severed ear and placed it back on the side of Malchus' head (John 18).

I wonder how many times we use the sword of the Spirit and hurt people in the process. How many times do we quote Scripture and recite verses only to bloody and beat people with our spirituality? If you've unsheathed your sword to cause hurt and damage to others, put it away. The last miracle Jesus ever performed was to heal one who had been hurt by the sword of His own disciple.

Praise, Prayer, and Peace

Some time later, we meet Peter again in another very difficult situation. In Acts 12, we read that Herod had sawn James, the brother of John, in half lengthwise. When Herod saw that this pleased the Jews, he imprisoned Peter as well. In other words, Peter was about to die. Yet we read that he was asleep between two guards—sound asleep and at peace. How could this be when the next day he knew he would either be sawn in half or beheaded?

Peter would later pen these words: "Casting all your care upon him for He careth for you" (see 1 Peter 5:7). The Greek word translated "cast" is a word that describes the process of rolling a heavy object like a stone or a wheel up a hill. Thus, "casting our care" means rolling our care upon Him. Now, if you roll a rock up a hill, what will happen? The rock will roll down again. People say, "I've prayed about that problem. I've rolled it upon Him. Why does it keep returning?"

Listen carefully. Scripture declares that "casting" is a process that happens continually. That is, you roll your care upon Him, and then it comes rolling back. You roll it on Him again, and it comes rolling back. You have peace for an hour, a day, or a month, and then you're troubled, perplexed, and anxious again. Why does God want us to roll our cares upon Him if they're only going to roll back upon us?

The story is told that centuries ago, in the city of Athens, there lived a man named Milo who was the strongest man in the world. How did he get so strong? When he was a young man, one of his cows gave birth to a calf. Every day, Milo picked up that calf, put it on his shoulders, and walked around his property. At first, it was relatively easy. But every day the calf got bigger and bigger, until one day, Milo was carrying an ox on his shoulders. You see, as sure as the calf was growing, so was Milo's strength and stamina.

I'm convinced the Lord wants us to be spiritual Milos. He says, "I'm going to allow this problem to come rolling back on you after a day or two because I want you to keep pushing it toward Me. And every time you do—as you commune with Me, wait upon Me, and talk to Me—you will gain strength. So keep rolling."

> Clovis Chapman, a pioneer aviator, was one of the first men to attempt a solo flight around the world. During his journey, after a brief stop in Fremont, California, he heard the sound of gnawing directly behind him. Listening carefully, Clovis realized there was a rat in the cockpit, chewing on a cable. Knowing he couldn't leave the controls to catch the rat, he thought, "My cables will be destroyed. It's all over." But then he had an idea. Pulling the throttle back, the plane rose to five thousand feet and then to ten thousand feet. At twelve thousand feet, Clovis listened and heard nothing. You see, remembering rodents need a high proportion of oxygen, he took his plane where the oxygen was thin, and the rat died.

That's what it means to cast your care upon Him. When you feel a rat gnawing within you, an anxiety overwhelming you, or a concern or a burden pressing on you, kick back and cruise up. In the rarefied atmosphere of praise and prayer, the enemy can't survive. That's what Peter found as he lay sound asleep between two guards.

Truly the Lord does care for me, he must have thought. *My mother-in-law was sick and He healed her. I wasn't catching any fish, and He filled my boat. I gave the wrong answer to some tax collectors, and He got me out of that jam. I chopped off someone's ear when I shouldn't have, and He healed it. And now that I'm in prison, I'll just trust Him. He's seen me through time and time and time again. So I'll just cast my care upon Him.*

And so can you.

18 In chapter 17, the disciples saw Jesus shine miraculously with kingdom light. Here in chapter 18, they will hear Him speak practically about kingdom life.

Matthew 18:1
At the same time came the disciples unto Jesus, saying, Who is the greatest in the kingdom of heaven?

According to Luke 9:46, the disciples here are actually arguing about who is the greatest in the kingdom of which they had just been given a sneak preview.

Matthew 18:2
And Jesus called a little child unto him, and set him in the midst of them.

This shows me something of the personality and character of Jesus. He called a little child to Him, and the child came readily. If you go to the mall and watch parents lining up their kids to sit on Santa's lap, you will invariably see tears and terror on the faces of the children. Told to sit on the lap of a big man with a big beard and black boots, it's no wonder they're fearful! But there is never an indication that kids were afraid of Jesus. There was something pure, gentle, and lovely about Him that made children come to Him rather than run from Him.

Matthew 18:3
And said, Verily I say unto you, Except ye be converted, and become as little children, ye shall not enter into the kingdom of heaven.

"You're asking who is the greatest?" Jesus said. "Unless you become like a child, you will not enter into the kingdom." How were the disciples to be childlike? First, they were to be childlike in sincerity. The word "sincere" literally means "without wax" and referred to the practice of merchants in Bible times who patched broken or chipped pieces of pottery with wax. If a vessel was not "sincere," an unsuspecting buyer would take it home and put it on his front porch only to see the wax melt and the vessel break in the heat of the sun.

Second, the disciples were to be childlike in sincerity.

I remember once when Peter-John was about six, I was somewhat upset with him. Trying to control my feelings as best I could, I began to talk with him. "Daddy, you're mad," he said.
"No, I'm not, Peter," I argued.
"Well, your eyebrows, they're mad," he said.

Kids are sensitive indeed. They can read us like a book!

Finally, the disciples were to be childlike in simplicity.

I read about a kindergarten class on a field trip to the post office. As the postmaster pointed out the pictures of the Ten Most Wanted Men in America, one of the kids said, "Those are criminals?"
"Yes," answered the postmaster.
"Bad guys?"
"That's right."
"Well, then, why didn't you just keep them when you took their pictures?"

Those childlike qualities of sincerity, sensitivity, and simplicity are key ingredients of kingdom life. David wrote in Psalm 131, "I will not look into things that are too great for me, but will behave myself quietly as a weaned child." In other words, "I'm not going to get spun out or hung up on things that are too lofty or too great. Like a weaned child, I'll just keep it simple." A weaned child is neither an infant screaming for milk nor an adult checking out the refrigerator wondering who's going to pay the bills. A weaned child neither cries nor analyzes. He simply trusts that his father and mother will take care of him. And that quality is what Jesus held up to the disciples as a model.

Matthew 18:4
Whosoever therefore shall humble himself as this little child, the same is greatest in the kingdom of heaven.

We must guard against the tendencies of cynicism and sophistication and remain like children if we want to be great in the kingdom.

A distinguished elderly gentleman walked into a toy store and saw a Lionel train going around the track. With a sparkle in his eye, he said to the salesgirl, "I'll take one."
"Oh, your grandson will love it!" she replied.
"You know, you're absolutely right!" he said. "Make that two."

There is something good, Jesus is saying, about retaining a childlike mentality.

At a testimony meeting, a multimillionaire said, "When I was eighteen years old, I heard a missionary speak about the need in Africa. Having recently given my heart to Jesus, I was touched deeply and reached into my pocket for the last five dollars I had to my name. That was the turning point in my walk with God, and He has blessed me ever since."
"Ooh" and "Aaah," said the congregation, until one elderly sister stood up in the back row and said, "I dare you to do it again."

We might say, "Oh yes, there was a time when I was like a child. When I first heard the gospel, I approached Jesus simply and openly as I came forward at a meeting." Do it again! That's what Jesus is saying here. We need to be in the place where we're continually excited about the Word and enjoying the gospel in its simplicity and beauty. Jesus said if you want to be great in the kingdom, humble yourself as a child once again.

Matthew 18:5
And whoso shall receive one such little child in my name receiveth me.

A number of years ago, a Scottish pastor stood before his congregation and resigned, saying, "In the past two years, I have seen only one conversion in this congregation: wee Bobby Moffatt. With such little fruit, I can no longer serve in this ministry." And he walked away from the pulpit a broken man. Little did he know that wee Bobby Moffatt grew up to be Robert Moffatt, the missionary who opened the entire continent of Africa to the gospel of Jesus Christ.

If you are teaching Sunday school right now, it's very possible that you have a "wee Bobby Moffatt" in your class. If you work with kids, realize that Jesus places a very high value on children. He says if you receive them, you receive Him.

Matthew 18:6
But whoso shall offend one of these little ones which believe in me, it were better for him that a millstone were hanged about his neck, and that he were drowned in the depth of the sea.

I believe this verse should be written on every schoolteacher's desk. The word "offend" means "to throw off course." In other words, Jesus says, "If you cause one of these little ones to question Me or to be thrown off course in their walk with Me, it would be better for you to drown." This would have made a definite impact on Jesus' audience because the Jewish people of that time had a genuine fear of the open ocean. Yes, they were fishermen, but only on the Sea of Galilee. The Jews have never been a seafaring people. In fact, unlike other coastal countries of their day, they refused to use drowning as capital punishment because of their fear of the sea. Thus, Jesus was giving a very vivid and very real description of terror. "If you cause these little guys to stumble," He said, "you're in grave danger."

Matthew 18:7
Woe unto the world because of offences! for it must needs be that offences come; but woe to that man by whom the offence cometh!

The first "woe" is a lamentation. The second one is a condemnation. In other words, Jesus said, "Problems in this world are inevitable. But if people are being derailed in their faith because of your cynicism and unbelief, woe unto you."

Matthew 18:8, 9
Wherefore if thy hand or thy foot offend thee, cut them off, and cast them from thee: it is better for thee to enter into life halt or maimed, rather than having two hands or two feet to be cast into everlasting fire. And if thine eye offend thee, pluck it out, and cast it from thee: it is better for thee to enter into life with one eye, rather than having two eyes to be cast into hell fire.

"Take heed," Jesus said. "If something you are doing causes offense, deal violently with it. Get it away from you no matter what the price or how painful it may be."

Matthew 18:10
Take heed that ye despise not one of these little ones; for I say unto you, That in

heaven their angels do always behold the face of my Father which is in heaven.

Here is where we get the understanding that each child has a guardian angel. Paul points out that when we get to heaven, we will actually judge angels (I Corinthians 6:3). I wonder if part of that might include asking the angel who was "assigned" to you, "Where were you when that baseball hit me in the head?!"

Matthew 18:11
For the Son of man is come to save that which was lost.

Children are lost so easily and disoriented so quickly. Continuing on that theme, Jesus begins to talk about His concern for those who are truly lost—not those who pretend to know where they're going and what they're doing, but those who humbly acknowledge that they're lost and hurting.

Matthew 18:12–14
How think ye? if a man have an hundred sheep, and one of them be gone astray, doth he not leave the ninety and nine, and goeth into the mountains, and seeketh that which is gone astray? And if so be that he find it, verily I say unto you, he rejoiceth more of that sheep, than of the ninety and nine which went not astray. Even so it is not the will of your Father which is in heaven, that one of these little ones should perish.

This analogy provides some interesting insights into our Lord. First, it tells me that His love is absolutely unconditional. Notice that although the lost sheep was one who had strayed, the shepherd didn't say, "That dumb sheep was off wandering where he shouldn't be. Why wasn't he with the rest of the flock? Well, maybe he'll learn a lesson out there." No, his love was independent of the obedience of the sheep.

So, too, whether you are staying or straying, God's love for you is absolutely unconditional. Then why not stray? Because there are problems out there: wolves, poisonous weeds, and all kinds of dangers that could bruise and break us. Slowly but surely, we're learning that it's safest to stay close to the Shepherd.

Second, His love is individual. He loves each of us as if there were only one of us. I tend to think, "Lord, You have millions and millions of sheep. Billy's always talking to You and working on the next crusade. Mother Teresa, while alive, was up at four o'clock in the morning talking with You daily. And then there's me—the dumb sheep who's strayed." But I'm beginning to understand that the Lord sees people individually. He would have sent His prophets and apostles and recorded the Scriptures just for me. He would have sent His Son just for me. He would have died just for me.

Finally, His love is emotional. When He finds the wandering, straying sheep, what does He do? Does He rebuke him? Lecture him? Shake him? Skin him? No, the Word says He *rejoices.* When we wander away, and the Lord comes after us and finds us, there follows an emotional outburst not of anger but of joy. He gathers the straying sheep in His arms and rejoices greatly because He loves him deeply.

Keep in mind that this illustration is all in answer to the question: Who is the greatest? Jesus said, "Check out this little child." That's the key. You'll not only enter the kingdom, but you'll be elevated within the kingdom as you continue to humble yourself.

Humility confuses a lot of us because we mistakenly think it means thinking less of ourselves. It doesn't. Humility is not a matter of thinking less of yourself. It's a matter of not thinking of yourself at all. There's a big difference. My saying, "I can't sing. I can't play guitar. I can't fix my car. I can't do anything," is not humility. It's pride because it's egocentric. I'm talking and thinking about me, me, me.

When the Lord called him, Moses said, "No one will listen to me because I stutter."

"Who made your mouth, Moses?" asked the Lord. "I will be with you. Quit stuttering about yourself and look to Me" (see Exodus 4:10–12).

Matthew 18:15–17
Moreover if thy brother shall trespass against thee, go and tell him his fault between thee and him alone: if he shall hear thee, thou hast gained thy brother. But if he will not hear thee, then take with thee one or two more, that in the mouth of two or three witnesses every word may be established. And if he shall neglect to hear them, tell it unto the church: but if he neglect to hear the church, let him be unto thee as an heathen man and a publican.

The first aspect of kingdom life is humility. The second is honesty. If I say I love you, but don't talk with you in honesty when you trespass against me because I'm afraid you won't like me, my love is not real. That would be like a doctor who notices a lump on your body but doesn't want to hurt your feelings by telling you that you need surgery. Love without truth is hypocrisy. But truth without love is brutality. If I speak the truth without love, I leave folks bruised, blood-ied, and beaten.

The key is to speak the truth in love (Ephesians 4:15). If there's a trespass, a problem, or a difficulty between us, love requires me to lovingly speak to you about it personally. If you won't listen to what I say about the sin or the trespass, I am to come to you again, bringing one or two witnesses with me. If you won't hear them, I am to go to the church. And if you won't listen to the church, you are to be treated as an outcast. Why? It's not for punishment, but for reconciliation. It's not punitive, but restorative. In chapter 5 of Paul's first Epistle to the Corinthians, he gives the account of a man who, although he was living with his stepmother in immorality, refused to take correction. Paul told the church at Corinth to turn him over to Satan that his flesh might be destroyed but his spirit saved. In other words, "Let him live in the world for a while until he gets so sick of it that his flesh will be destroyed. Then, hopefully he'll come around again and be saved." And that's exactly what happened. He did indeed turn from his sin and return to the Church (2 Corinthians 7:11, 12). Why? Because the church took a strong stand and said, "This can't go on."

Matthew 18:18
Verily I say unto you, Whatsoever ye shall bind on earth shall be bound in heaven: and whatsoever ye shall loose on earth shall be loosed in heaven.

Jesus is saying, "Church, it's your job to bind sin. Sin is bound in heaven. Therefore you have authority to bind it on earth. Righteousness and holiness, mercy and forgiveness are released in heaven. Therefore you have been given authority to release them on earth." Binding and loosing speak of the authority the Church has in dealing with matters where sin is flagrantly, consistently, and obnoxiously practiced. As seen in 1 Corinthians 5, the church has the right to bind sin and then to release forgiveness and restoration following repentance.

Matthew 18:19
Again I say unto you, That if two of you shall agree on earth as touching any thing that they shall ask, it shall be done for them of my Father which is in heaven.

Private prayer is wonderful but I also believe that we need consistent times of prayer with others. Why? First of all, praying with others is motivating. You will pray more if you're involved in a prayer group than you would otherwise. It's like working out. If you work out by yourself, it's

real easy to miss week after week. But if three or four guys are working out with you, they provide motivation for you to continue. The same is true of prayer.

Second, praying with others is purifying. When I'm praying in a group, I don't pray selfishly as I can do in my private prayer. In a group, I can't pray, "Lord, smash that guy. Teach that jerk a lesson." That kind of thing just doesn't flow when I'm praying in a circle.

Third, praying with others is confirming. As I pray in a group, if my petition is correct, those around me will say, "Amen, Lord! That's right. Yes, Lord." But if my request is out to lunch, I'll know by their silence that maybe I should reconsider my petition.

Matthew 18:20
For where two or three are gathered together in my name, there am I in the midst of them.

Keep these words of Jesus in the context of dealing honestly with church matters, relationships, and kingdom life. The church should pulsate with power when it comes to dealing with sin and releasing God's mercy with authority. Too often, however, the church is impotent because she fails to recognize Jesus in her midst. Where the church is moving in the power of prayer and in the authority of binding and loosing, she will make an impact.

Matthew 18:21
Then came Peter to him, and said, Lord, how oft shall my brother sin against me, and I forgive him? till seven times?

In kingdom life, there is humility, honesty, and finally, forgiveness. The rabbis taught that one who had been wronged was to forgive the perpetrator two or perhaps three times at the most. So Peter felt noble and generous in asking, "Should I forgive him *seven* times?"

Matthew 18:22
Jesus saith unto him, I say not unto thee, Until seven times: but, Until seventy times seven.

Jesus said, "Peter, you are to forgive four hundred and ninety times." Peter must have thought, *Four hundred and ninety? How am I supposed to keep track?* And that was the point. We are to just keep forgiving and forgiving and forgiving and forgiving. Where there is binding and loosing, there must also be a free, unending flow of forgiveness.

Matthew 18:23–35
Therefore is the kingdom of heaven likened unto a certain king, which would take account of his servants. And when he had begun to reckon, one was brought unto him, which owed him ten thousand talents. But forasmuch as he had not to pay, his lord commanded him to be sold, and his wife, and children, and all that he had, and payment to be made. The servant therefore fell down, and worshipped him, saying, Lord, have patience with me, and I will pay thee all. Then the lord of that servant was moved with compassion, and loosed him, and forgave him the debt. But the same servant went out, and found one of his fellowservants, which owed him an hundred pence: and he laid hands on him, and took him by the throat, saying, Pay me that thou owest. And his fellowservant fell down at his feet, and besought him, saying, Have patience with me, and I will pay thee all. So when his fellowservants saw what was done, they were very sorry, and came and told unto their lord all that was done. Then his lord, after that he had called him, said unto him, O thou wicked servant, I forgave thee all that debt, because thou desiredst me: Shouldest not thou also have had compassion on thy fellowservant, even as I had pity on thee? And his lord was wroth, and delivered him to the tormentors, till he should pay all that was due unto him. So likewise shall my heavenly Father do also unto you, if ye from your hearts forgive not every one his brother their trespasses.

We all know people who are in torment and imprisoned because they will not forgive someone who's wronged them. They're small people in the sense that they're no longer embracive and free. Instead, they're restricted, tormented, uptight, tense, angry, bitter, and harsh. You see, the Lord tells us to forgive not for the sake of the offender, but for the sake of the one who has been offended. Regarding confronting problems, dealing with issues, binding and loosing, Jesus says, "Remember that you are to be a people known for forgiving over and over and over and over and over."

Maybe you see yourself in this story. Maybe you've been hurt so badly that you just can't forgive. Maybe you're imprisoned, robbed of joy and peace, but you don't know how to get out. The answer lies in this passage. The king commanded that the servant remain in prison until he paid his debt. But how could the servant earn money to pay his debt if he was in prison? The only way he

could get out of prison was to go to his master and ask for forgiveness.

If Jesus says we are to be people who forgive over and over again, how much more will our Father forgive us when we go to Him and say, "Forgive me for not forgiving, Lord. Change my heart." And the great thing is that He'll not only forgive, but He'll also forget (Jeremiah 31:34).

- Humility: Getting our eyes off ourselves.
- Honesty: Dealing with problems in a Biblical manner.
- Forgiveness: Forgiving and forgiving until we lose count.

Lord, help us. Be merciful to us in an even greater measure by causing us to live in humility, not as cynics or sophisticates, but as children. I pray that there might be honesty in our lives, that we would care about others in such a way that we might speak the truth in love. Help us, Lord, to be forgiving, even as You are. We confess our bankruptcy and our inability to forgive apart from Your work in our hearts. May the characteristics You spoke of in Galilee become real in our lives.

19 Thus far in Matthew's gospel, we have seen the revelation of the King and the rebellion against the King. Now we come to the retreat of the King as Jesus takes His disciples away for a season of intensive discipleship.

Matthew 19:1
And it came to pass, that when Jesus had finished these sayings, he departed from Galilee, and came into the coasts of Judaea beyond Jordan.

Jesus is headed toward Jerusalem, the city wherein He will be crucified, buried, and resurrected.

Matthew 19:2, 3 (a)
And great multitudes followed him; and he healed them there. The Pharisees also came unto him, tempting him . . .

As Jesus heals the multitudes, the Pharisees are only interested in arguing with Him. This should not be surprising, for the Pharisaical mentality always wants to debate rather than celebrate.

Matthew 19:3 (b)
. . . and saying unto him, Is it lawful for a man to put away his wife for every cause?

The issue of divorce and remarriage was the hot controversy of the day. Two schools of thought proposed by two influential rabbis fueled the debate. Hillel was the liberal rabbi who said that, according to the Law of Moses, there were many justifications for divorce. For example, saying anything negative about her husband's mother would render a wife unclean and justify her husband divorcing her. Or if a husband saw a woman fairer to look upon than his wife, his wife would be unclean by comparison and he would be justified in divorcing her. Needless to say, Hillel had a great following among those looking for a way out of their marriages. Shammai, on the other hand, was very conservative and said there were virtually no grounds for divorce. Thus, the debate concerning divorce and remarriage was as heated as it is in the church today.

Matthew 19:4–6
And he answered and said unto them, Have ye not read, that he which made them at the beginning made them male and female, and said, For this cause shall a man leave father and mother, and shall cleave to his wife: and they twain shall be one flesh? Wherefore they are no more twain, but one flesh. What therefore God hath joined together, let not man put asunder.

In answer to their question, Jesus said, "Go back further than the Law of Moses. Go back to the Garden of Eden, for there you will discover the root of the matter."

Matthew 19:7
They say unto him, Why did Moses then command to give a writing of divorcement, and to put her away?

In other words, the Pharisees are asking Jesus, "If the union of two who become one is to remain for as long as they live, why does the Old Testament offer the option of divorce at all?"

Matthew 19:8
He saith unto them, Moses because of the hardness of your hearts suffered you to put away your wives: but from the beginning it was not so.

Jesus answered by saying that the Law of Moses made provision for divorce not because God desired it, but because of the hardness of men's hearts. Divorce was never God's heart or God's intention. But because the people had become so hardened, the Law of Moses allowed this heathen custom of divorce to take place within prescribed boundaries (Deuteronomy 24). Notice, divorce is

not mandated in the event of adultery. It is simply allowed. While Jesus is not saying there must be divorce if there is infidelity, He acknowledges that it is possible for a relationship to be dealt a deathblow by infidelity, making it the one ground for divorce.

According to Old Testament Law, the penalty for adultery was not divorce but death. Then came Jesus. In John 8, the Pharisees brought Him a woman who was caught in the act of adultery and He said to her, "I don't condemn you. I forgive you and free you to a better way of living. Go your way and sin no more." Though the law came by Moses, grace and truth indeed came by Jesus (John 1:17).

Matthew 19:9
And I say unto you, Whosoever shall put away his wife, except it be for fornication, and shall marry another, committeth adultery: and whoso marrieth her which is put away doth commit adultery.

Jesus is saying, "Divorce, not the result of adultery results in adultery if there is remarriage." This raises all kinds of questions. What if a person falls into trouble and difficulty in his marriage when he's twenty years old, and, after going through twenty-five years of being single and walking with the Lord, he meets someone special and wants to get married? If he does so, will the couple live in adultery? Is adultery the unpardonable sin? Is divorce the unpardonable sin? To answer, look at perhaps the most famous marital failure in history, a man after God's own heart, a man named David.

After his affair with Bathsheba, David killed her husband to cover his sin. God dealt with David by allowing the child conceived to be short-circuited into eternity. His death greatly affected David. But once David was dealt with, the next child from his union with Bathsheba was Solomon, the subsequent king of Israel and part of the Messianic line. Of all David's wives, which were many, Bathsheba remained in a prominent place. Even at the end of his life, it was Bathsheba who had access to David and who was instrumental in establishing the next phase of his kingdom.

On the basis of David's life, in which we see the Lord dealing with the situation through chastening, adjusting, and correcting, I do not believe a person who has had a failure in a previous marriage lives in continual adultery in a second marriage. If such were the case, God would not have blessed Solomon. I do believe that where there is divorce and remarriage, there is inevitably a tearing away of a previous relationship and a coming together of a new relationship. Thus, there is in that act adultery. Jesus does not say, however, that although there is an *act* of adultery, the person who remarries *lives* in adultery.

I once talked with a young man about twenty-five years of age who was part of our church family and on leave from an elite branch of the air force. He had fallen in love with a lady who also loved the Lord but who had been married at age seventeen. After her marriage failed, she was, at age twenty-five, a single mom. This young pilot sat in my office weeping as he said, "I love this lady deeply. But if I marry her, I fear we'll be living in adultery all of our lives."

"I can't tell you what to do," I said. "But I do know this: I'm a bride and I have failed greatly. But my Bridegroom, Jesus Christ, was willing to absorb my pollution and iniquity to bring me into His love and into His family. Therefore, I do not believe it is against the heart of God for you to enter into a relationship to redeem that mother and child— even if it means absorbing pollution and bearing iniquity—because that's exactly what Jesus did for me."

I take time to address this issue because I believe it is important. On one hand, people are taking divorce far too lightly because they fail to realize its seriousness. On the other hand, the church too often mistakenly stands ready to judge and condemn couples who have admittedly failed, but who have sought the Lord and are now starting a new life together. There needs to be a balance in this very sober and serious matter of divorce.

Matthew 19:10
His disciples say unto him, If the case of the man be so with his wife, it is not good to marry.

The disciples said, "If what You say is true, Master, it's better not to get married at all. It's too tricky, too dangerous, and too troublesome."

Matthew 19:11, 12
But he said unto them, All men cannot receive this saying, save they to whom it is given. For there are some eunuchs, which were so born from their mother's womb: and there are some eunuchs, which were made eunuchs of men: and there be eunuchs, which have made themselves eunuchs for the kingdom of heaven's sake. He that is able to receive it, let him receive it.

Jesus answered that there are some who are born eunuchs. That is, they remain single because they were born without any desire for the opposite sex. Others were made eunuchs. That is, they were made eunuchs through castration, which was a common practice of conquering nations upon men placed in certain positions; for example, those in charge of the king's harem. Still others made themselves eunuchs by choosing to live a single lifestyle for the sake of the kingdom.

The apostle Paul would later write that the single state was a superior state (1 Corinthians 7:25, 26) because one could devote himself fully and completely to the work of the kingdom. On the other hand, Philip, the great evangelist who preached to the city of Samaria in Acts 8 and saw virtually the entire city get saved, had a wife and four daughters who grew up to be prophetesses.

So, if you're given the grace and the calling to remain single, rejoice in that and in the freedom it affords you to serve God with abandon. If you're not single, be like Philip and raise godly kids. And if there has been a failure in your past, know there is a redemptive plan for your future as you seek the Lord with sincerity.

Matthew 19:13 (a)
Then were there brought unto him little children . . .

I don't think it's coincidental that right after dealing with the issue of divorce, Jesus turns His attention toward the children, for children are always directly affected by the divorce of their parents. Of this same event, Luke writes: "And they brought unto him infants . . ." (18:15). The Greek pronoun he uses for "they" is masculine. In other words, it was the men who brought their kids to Jesus. I like that!

Matthew 19:13 (b)
. . . that he should put his hands on them, and pray . . .

Dad, how do you lay hands on your kids? While I think it's important that we discipline them, I do wonder sometimes if a lot of us aren't heavy on the laying on of hands in discipline and too light on the laying on of hands in blessing. When was the last time you pronounced a blessing on your child?

Matthew 19:13 (c)
. . . and the disciples rebuked them.

Whenever Jesus ministered, there was a release of His virtue so noticeable to Him that even in the midst of a crowd He was aware of it (Luke

8:46). No doubt, ministry exacted a toll on Jesus, which may explain why His disciples were trying to protect Him.

Matthew 19:14, 15
But Jesus said, Suffer little children, and forbid them not, to come unto me: for of such is the kingdom of heaven. And he laid his hands on them, and departed thence.

Contrary to what His disciples thought, Jesus is never too tired for anyone—especially children.

Matthew 19:16
And, behold, one came and said unto him, Good Master, what good thing shall I do, that I may have eternal life?

This one who came was rich; he was young; and he was a ruler. In other words, he had made it to the top occupationally; he was set financially; and he was young and healthy physically. In response to this encounter with the rich young ruler, throughout the rest of this chapter Jesus will contrast the poverty of riches with the richness of poverty.

Matthew 19:17 (a)
And he said unto him, Why callest thou me good? there is none good but one, that is, God . . .

Scripture records that there is none righteous, no not one (Romans 3:10). Only God is good. Thus, Jesus asks, "Since God alone is good, are you saying I am God?"

Matthew 19:17 (b), 18 (a)
. . . but if thou wilt enter into life, keep the commandments. He saith unto him, Which? Jesus said, Thou shalt do no murder . . .

There are those who declare that on the basis of the Seventh Commandment, we should never kill under any circumstance. However, Jesus' rendering of the Seventh Commandment, given here, is, "Thou shalt do no murder." You see, freedom and redemption often come only by the shedding of blood. Politically and historically, we are free today because many men shed blood and gave their lives for the freedom we enjoy in this country. The same is true spiritually and eternally. We are free because one Man shed His blood and paid the price for our salvation.

Matthew 19:18 (b)–20
. . . Thou shalt not commit adultery, Thou shalt not steal, Thou shalt not bear false witness, Honour thy father and thy mother: and, Thou shalt love thy neighbour as thyself. The young man saith unto him, All these things have I kept from my youth up: what lack I yet?

"What lack I yet?" That is the question still being asked. According to an article in a newsmagazine, in the '80s people made a living. In the '90s, they were to make a life. No longer would young executives arrive at the office at six o'clock in the morning and be the last to leave at night. Long weekends, family time, and recreation would be the order of the day. In going from one extreme to another, however, our generation found emptiness once again. The only way to be fulfilled in life is through a relationship with God through Jesus Christ.

Matthew 19:21, 22
Jesus said unto him, If thou wilt be perfect, go and sell that thou hast, and give to the poor, and thou shalt have treasure in heaven: and come and follow me. But when the young man heard that saying, he went away sorrowful: for he had great possessions.

Knowing his possessions were possessing him, Jesus' desire was to free this rich young ruler. "Simplify your life," He said, "and follow Me." Please understand that poverty does not produce automatic spirituality. That's not what Jesus is saying. Many of the greatest men in Scripture were exceedingly wealthy. Abraham, David, and Solomon; Nicodemus, Zacchaeus, and Joseph of Arimathea were all men of great possessions. Possessions are not inherently wrong. But when they begin to dictate how you spend your time and how you make decisions, you're in trouble. Jesus was dealing with the particular issue in this man's life that was holding him back. In your life, in my life, there might be another issue entirely.

Matthew 19:23
Then said Jesus unto his disciples, Verily I say unto you, That a rich man shall hardly enter into the kingdom of heaven.

It's hard for a rich man to enter the kingdom because riches can make one independent of God and intolerant of others. Riches can cause us to say, "Why should I pray or seek God when I can consult my banker or stockbroker?" Riches can cause us to ask, "Why is everyone so poor? Why don't they have the initiative, the industry, or the energy I do? What's wrong with them?" When you become independent of God and intolerant of others, you forfeit the kingdom. Riches can be dangerous indeed if they make us stiff of knee and hard of heart.

Matthew 19:24
And again I say unto you, It is easier for a camel to go through the eye of a needle, than for a rich man to enter into the kingdom of God.

The Talmud, the Jewish body of teaching present in Jesus' day, contained the similar phrase, "It is easier for an elephant to go through the eye of a needle." Elephants were common in Persia or Iran, where the Talmud was written, but not in Jerusalem. So Jesus modified the Talmud with something His Jerusalem audience could relate to: a camel. Was He talking about a literal needle and camel, or was He, as G. Campbell Morgan strongly suggests, speaking of something else?

In Jerusalem, all commerce would stop when the gates of the city of Jerusalem were closed on the Sabbath day and every evening at sunset. Commerce stopped because camels and caravans could no longer enter. But there was a little gate called the Needle Gate that was actually a gate inside of the main gate. It could be opened to allow access and egress to only one person at a time. The only way a camel could possibly get through this Needle Gate would be if all of the baggage was removed from his back and if he crawled through the gate on his knees.

I believe it is very possible that this is what Jesus was alluding to, saying, "There is a way for a rich man to enter the kingdom, but only if he places no priority on his possessions and is willing to fall to his knees in humility."

Matthew 19:25
When his disciples heard it, they were exceedingly amazed, saying, Who then can be saved?

The disciples were amazed because in those days, the rabbis taught that the closer one was to God, the richer he would be. Prosperity theology was around even back then. Here, however, Jesus totally shoots that theory down by saying, "Contrary to Jewish theology, riches can actually hinder one entering the kingdom."

Matthew 19:26
But Jesus beheld them, and said unto them, With men this is impossible; but with God all things are possible.

Even a rich man can be saved by the grace and power of God.

Matthew 19:27
Then answered Peter and said unto him, Behold, we have forsaken all, and followed thee; what shall we have therefore?

"We've left everything to follow You," Peter says. "What the rich young ruler wasn't willing to do, we've done. How will our faithfulness be rewarded?"

Matthew 19:28, 29
And Jesus said unto them, Verily I say unto you, That ye which have followed me, in the regeneration when the Son of man shall sit in the throne of his glory, ye also shall sit upon twelve thrones, judging the twelve tribes of Israel. And every one that hath forsaken houses, or brethren, or sisters, or father, or mother, or wife, or children, or lands, for my name's sake, shall receive an hundredfold, and shall inherit everlasting life.

Jesus answers Peter by saying, "Any who forsake land, wealth, or family to follow Me will be ushered into the kingdom with great rewards."

Big deal, you might be thinking. *Heaven's too far away to think about. I don't care about rewards there.* But you will definitely care then. Only what you do for the Lord will bring you eternal reward. Jesus will reward you greatly for whatever you're giving up for Him now.

Mark adds this promise to his account of the same story:

And Jesus answered and said, Verily I say unto you, There is no man that hath left house, or brethren, or sisters, or father, or mother, or wife, or children, or lands, for my sake, and the gospel's, But he shall receive an hundredfold now in this time, houses, and brethren, and sisters, and mothers, and children, and lands, with persecutions; and in the world to come eternal life.   Mark 10:29, 30

In other words, what you give up for the Lord and for His kingdom will not only be rewarded eternally but will be returned to you a hundred times over presently. What does this mean? Does it mean, as some suggest, that if I make a vow or "plant my seed," I'll get a whole bunch of money in the mail next month? I don't think so. I believe Jesus is saying that, as part of the kingdom, we have access to a hundred houses and a hundred families. I'm so thankful for the church—for people who love the Lord, who care about each other, who stand by one another, and who share with those in need. Those who are radically following Jesus will find not only rewards in Heaven, but benefits on earth. Our needs will be met a hundred times over because we're part of a community; we're part of a family; we're part of the Kingdom.

Matthew 19:30
But many that are first shall be last; and the last shall be first.

"Watch out, Peter," Jesus says. "You're proud of the fact that you have given much to follow Me. But many that are first shall be last, and many that are last shall be first. There will be some surprises in heaven."

---

20 Matthew 20 is the last chapter in the section dealing with the retreat of the King. It opens with a continuation of the dialogue that began in chapter 19 between Peter and Jesus concerning the rewards of service for the kingdom.

Matthew 20:1, 2
For the kingdom of heaven is like unto a man that is an householder, which went out early in the morning to hire labourers into his vineyard. And when he had agreed with the labourers for a penny a day, he sent them into his vineyard.

A penny, or a denarius, being the daily salary of a Roman soldier, Jesus was speaking of a day's fair wage.

Matthew 20:3–10
And he went out about the third hour, and saw others standing idle in the marketplace, And said unto them; Go ye also into the vineyard, and whatsoever is right I will give you. And they went their way. Again he went out about the sixth and ninth hour, and did likewise. And about the eleventh hour he went out, and found others standing idle, and saith unto them, Why stand ye here all the day idle? They say unto him, Because no man hath hired us. He saith unto them, Go ye also into the vineyard; and whatsoever is right, that shall ye receive. So when even was come, the lord of the vineyard saith unto his steward, Call the labourers, and give them their hire, beginning from the last unto the first. And when they came that were hired about the eleventh hour, they received every man a penny. But when the first came, they supposed that they should have received more; and they likewise received every man a penny.

The men who started work at nine o'clock in the morning received the same wage as those who started at five o'clock in the afternoon.

Matthew 20:11–16
And when they had received it, they murmured against the goodman of the house, saying, These last have wrought but one hour, and thou hast made them equal unto us, which have borne the burden and heat of the day. But he answered one of them, and said, Friend, I do thee no wrong: didst not thou agree with me for a penny? Take that thine is, and go thy way: I will give unto this last, even as unto thee. Is it not lawful for me to do what I will with mine own? Is thine eye evil, because I am good? So the last shall be first, and the first last: for many be called, but few chosen.

This account of the vineyard and the harvest would have been very familiar to the disciples. The grape harvest usually took place in August. Because August was also the beginning of the rainy season in Israel, foremen in charge of the vineyards were always watching for the rains that could ruin the crops. In the morning, if a foreman saw rain coming, he would quickly go to the town square and hire workers to harvest the grapes. If the skies became even more threatening, he would go yet again and hire more workers. This would continue until the foreman had all the workers he needed to beat the rain.

In this story, those who had been hired early in the morning were upset because the men who were hired an hour before quitting time were paid the same amount they were. "Unfair!" they protested.

"The terms upon which I hired you were met," countered the owner of the vineyard. "You received your denarius, didn't you? If I choose to be generous with those who came late, that is my business."

What meaning does this parable have for us? Keep in mind that the parable was given in response to Peter's question about rewards. Through it, Jesus is saying, "You'll have rewards eternally. You will have everything returned one hundred-fold presently. But because the first shall be last and the last shall be first, when payday comes and rewards are given, there will be some big surprises."

This tells me a couple of key things. First of all, we'll be surprised in heaven. We have a tendency to think that Billy Graham will receive all kinds of crowns and rewards. And no doubt he will.

However, I think there will be some cleaning ladies who worked in obscurity and during their
breaks went to their knees in a broom closet
somewhere to intercede on behalf of Billy Graham's ministry who will be brought to the front
and rewarded greatly. I believe sitting in this
group tonight are those who have worked quietly
and in anonymity who will be escorted to the
front when rewards are given. "We didn't do
much," they'll say. "We weren't hired until five
o'clock. We didn't make much of a mark." But because they were exceedingly faithful, in what the
Foreman assigned them to do—visiting rest
homes, chopping wood for those who are unable,
praying and doing battle in intercession, changing diapers in the nursery—they will be brought
to the front. And perhaps a lot of us who have vis-
ibility and prominence presently will be sitting in
the back. Truly, the last shall be first and the first
last.

The second lesson I see in this radical teaching
is that we are to watch out for jealousy. "Hey, we
were out here all day. These guys just worked for
an hour. Unfair!" cried the servants. So, too,
there can be a tendency for our flesh to say, "How
come *he's* getting blessed when I've been faithful
for years and years?"

In Numbers 12, Miriam asked why Moses was
always the one who got to say, "Thus saith the
Lord." "Why is Moses the one who gets to go up
the mountain and come down shining, and all I
get to do is play a tambourine?" she asked. The
result? She was stricken with leprosy. That's
what jealousy always does. Like leprosy, it starts
small, but consumes us in the end.

A third principle this story teaches me is that
it's never too late to start. You might be saying,
"I'm old. I'm *thirty*." Listen, gang—even though
sportscasters talk about thirty-year-olds as if
they're dinosaurs, such is not the case with ministry. You might be at five o'clock in your lifespan.
You might be fifty, sixty, seventy, or eighty years
old. You might be saying, "I've walked with the
Lord for ten years and haven't done a thing for
Him." Take heart! It's never too late. Those who
show up at five o'clock saying, "I'm ready—just
point me in the right direction," have a definite
job to fulfill in the vineyard.

Matthew 20:17–19
And Jesus going up to Jerusalem took the
twelve disciples apart in the way, and said
unto them, Behold, we go up to Jerusalem;
and the Son of man shall be betrayed unto
the chief priests and unto the scribes, and
they shall condemn him to death, And shall
deliver him to the Gentiles to mock, and to

scourge, and to crucify him: and the third
day he shall rise again.

Since Matthew 16, we have seen Jesus underscoring and repeating that He was going to die.
Yet I call your attention to the fact that Jesus
never spoke of the Cross without speaking of the
Resurrection. I point this out because I often
hear brothers and sisters talking about the
Cross, saying, "I'm going through this trial," or
"I'm dealing with this struggle," or I'm paying
this price," but I don't hear them talking about
the Resurrection. If you talk about the Cross, follow the example of Jesus and talk about the Resurrection as well.

Precious people, if you think it's tough following Jesus, try *not* following Him. *That's* what's
tough. Going through disease, death, divorce,
bankruptcy, being fired from your job, or being
prosperous on Wall Street but empty internally—*that's* what's tough! If you who are struggling and suffering weren't a Christian, you
would still go through difficult times. The difference is, you would go through them with no solution, no promise, and no hope. That is why every
time Jesus talked about the Cross, He never
failed to speak of Resurrection.

Menelik II, Emperor of Ethiopia from 1889–
1913, heard that in Europe and America, criminals were executed with an efficient new device
called an electric chair. He immediately ordered one for his country and was excited when
it arrived—until he realized it needed electricity. There was no electricity in Ethiopia at that
time. Undaunted, he said, "If the electric chair
can't be used for the execution of criminals, it
will be used for the execution of my commands." Thus, for fifteen years, Menelik II sat
in an electric chair when he issued his procla-
mations. He turned the electric chair into a
throne.

When Jesus went to the Cross, He did something infinitely greater. He turned an instrument
of death into the pinnacle of power as He transformed shame into salvation, rejection into redemption, and grief into glory.

Matthew 20:20
Then came to him the mother of Zebedee's
children with her sons, worshipping him,
and desiring a certain thing of him.

Mark's Gospel tells us James and John persuaded their mother to talk to Jesus on their behalf (10:35). So she went to Jesus and began to
worship Him because she wanted something

from Him. All too often I fear, like James, John, and their mother, we worship in order to get something. But that's not what worship is about. Worship is about *giving*, about offering the sacrifice of praise (Hebrews 13:15).

Matthew 20:21
And he said unto her, What wilt thou? She saith unto him, Grant that these my two sons may sit, the one on thy right hand, and the other on the left, in thy kingdom.

Why did James and John deal with this issue during this particular time? Perhaps they were attempting to demonstrate their faith and devotion. "Lord, You're talking about death, but don't You remember all Your teachings on the kingdom? We believe You're still going to make it, Lord. Let's not talk about death. Let's not talk about the Cross. Let's talk about the seating arrangement in the kingdom."

Matthew 20:22
But Jesus answered and said, Ye know not what ye ask. Are ye able to drink of the cup that I shall drink of, and to be baptized with the baptism that I am baptized with? They say unto him, We are able.

"Do you know what you're asking?" Jesus said. "The cup in the kingdom is the cup of death. The baptism is the baptism of suffering. Do you understand what you're asking?"
"Oh, we understand, Lord," insisted James and John.
But they didn't.

Matthew 20:23
And he saith unto them, Ye shall drink indeed of my cup, and be baptized with the baptism that I am baptized with: but to sit on my right hand, and on my left, is not mine to give, but it shall be given to them for whom it is prepared of my Father.

Jesus answers, "My Father is preparing positions of authority in the heavenly arena for those who are preparing for those places." You see, salvation is free but position and rewards in the kingdom are dependent upon what we're doing right now. We want more prestige, more prominence, more power, more toys and more trinkets in this life. But Jesus is ever desirous of lifting our eyes from the temporal to the eternal and from the physical to the spiritual.

Matthew 20:24
And when the ten heard it, they were moved with indignation against the two brethren.

Why were the other disciples upset with James and John? Because they were trying to get a jump on the good seats in the kingdom. Next time you feel moved with indignation, ask yourself if you're upset because there's been a spiritual violation or merely because someone's getting ahead of you in some way.

Matthew 20:25–28
But Jesus called them unto him, and said, Ye know that the princes of the Gentiles exercise dominion over them, and they that are great exercise authority upon them. But it shall not be so among you: but whosoever will be great among you, let him be your minister [servant]; And whosoever will be chief among you, let him be your servant [slave]; Even as the Son of man came not to be ministered unto, but to minister, and to give his life a ransom for many.

If you want to be great, don't seek prominence. Seek service. Don't say, "Who's praying for me? Who cares about me?" Instead ask, "Who can I serve?"
"Go here. Do that. Get me this." The way you feel when people treat you like a slave is a good indication of how you're doing in the arena of servanthood.

Matthew 20:29, 30 (a)
And as they departed from Jericho, a great multitude followed him. And, behold, two blind men sitting by the way side . . .

Jericho was a beautiful desert oasis located fifteen miles from Jerusalem. A certain bush grew there which was believed to have medicinal value for the treatment of blindness. Thus, there was a large population of blind people in Jericho.

Matthew 20:30 (b)
. . . when they heard that Jesus passed by, cried out . . .

The Greek word translated "cried out" is *krazo,* a word that refers to the cry of a woman in childbirth.

Matthew 20:30 (c)–34
. . . saying, Have mercy on us, O Lord, thou Son of David. And the multitude rebuked them, because they should hold their peace: but they cried the more, saying, Have mercy on us, O Lord, thou Son of David. And Jesus stood still, and called them, and said, What will ye that I shall do unto you? They say unto him, Lord, that our eyes may be opened. So Jesus had compassion on them, and touched

their eyes: and immediately their eyes received sight, and they followed him.

These two men without eyesight had remarkable insight. "Son of David," they cried, "we recognize You as Messiah."

"Quiet down," said the crowd. But the blind men cried out all the more until Jesus healed them.

This story shows me three things about the nature and character of Jesus. First, it's a demonstration of His compassion. He took time to care for two blind men in a huge crowd. Second, it's an illustration of coming attractions. When He returns, *all* blind eyes shall be opened and *all* sickness healed forever. Finally, it gives illumination concerning our salvation. We too were blind, but when we cried out to our Messiah, we received sight and were then able to follow Him.

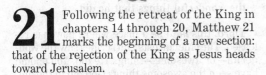

21 Following the retreat of the King in chapters 14 through 20, Matthew 21 marks the beginning of a new section: that of the rejection of the King as Jesus heads toward Jerusalem.

Matthew 21:1–3
And when they drew nigh unto Jerusalem, and were come to Bethphage, unto the mount of Olives, then sent Jesus two disciples, saying unto them, Go into the village over against you, and straightway ye shall find an ass tied, and a colt with her: loose them, and bring them unto me. And if any man say ought unto you, ye shall say, The Lord hath need of them; and straightway he will send them.

The city of Jerusalem was teeming with people, probably two million in number. They were there to commemorate Passover, an event that had taken place fifteen hundred years earlier . . .

While His people were being held captive, the hardness of Pharaoh's heart caused God to send a series of plagues upon Egypt, the tenth of which was the death of the firstborn in every home. The only way a family could escape this tragedy was to slaughter a lamb and mark the top, sides, and bottom of their door with blood, thereby painting a prophetic picture of the Cross that would one day save all mankind from the curse of sin and death.

Here, Jesus, the Passover Lamb, heads into Jerusalem, where He will orchestrate a massive public demonstration as He offers Himself to be King of Israel. Keep in mind that normally Jesus

moved quietly and preferred obscurity, many times charging those He healed to "tell no man" (see Matthew 8:4). Here, however, He organizes a huge crusade. Why? I suggest it was so the Jews would never be able to say, "If we had only had the opportunity to embrace You as our King, we certainly would have done so." He stripped away that excuse from the Jewish nation when He rode into Jerusalem and publicly offered Himself to them as their Messiah.

Matthew 21:4, 5
All this was done, that it might be fulfilled which was spoken by the prophet, saying, Tell ye the daughter of Sion, Behold, thy King cometh unto thee, meek, and sitting upon an ass, and a colt the foal of an ass.

Can't you hear the Roman soldiers garrisoned in Jerusalem snickering as they saw Jesus ride in on a donkey? When a Roman leader came cruising into a city, it wasn't on a donkey. No, Roman rulers rode black stallions followed by chariots and thousands of soldiers marching in step with shields gleaming. But I wonder what the Romans of this world will say when Jesus comes again, for next time He comes, it won't be on a donkey. He'll come back riding a white horse followed by ten thousands of His saints (Jude 14). You see, the first time Jesus came, He came as the suffering Servant. But the next time He comes, it will be as the conquering King.

Matthew 21:6–9
And the disciples went, and did as Jesus commanded them, and brought the ass, and the colt, and put on them their clothes, and they set him thereon. And a very great multitude spread their garments in the way; others cut down branches from the trees, and strawed them in the way. And the multitudes that went before, and that followed, cried, saying, Hosanna to the Son of David: Blessed is he that cometh in the name of the Lord; Hosanna in the highest.

Because the word "Hosanna" means "Save now," the crowd was essentially saying, "Overthrow the Roman yoke politically. Help us economically. Lead us militarily. Save Now!" No wonder that, as the week went on and they realized none of that was His intent, they turned against Jesus.

I see the same thing happen today, for there can be a tendency within the heart of each of us to cash it in when things don't work out. If you are expecting Jesus to be a "good luck charm" for you, if you expect Him to help you financially or physically, socially or vocationally, you will be disappointed when things don't go the way you thought they would.

We need to realize that Jesus Christ came to die for our sin and pay the price for our iniquity. If He never does anything else in this life presently, that is more than enough to merit our loyalty, our affection, and our devotion eternally. If He never does another thing for me, if He never gives another blessing to me, I owe Him my life because of what He did on Calvary.

Matthew 21:10, 11
And when he was come into Jerusalem, all the city was moved, saying, Who is this? And the multitude said, This is Jesus the prophet of Nazareth of Galilee.

The Greek word translated "moved" is *seio* from which we get our word "seismic." In other words, Matthew writes that the whole city was "quaking"—not physically, but mentally and emotionally— when Jesus made His entry.

Matthew 21:12 (a)
And Jesus went into the temple of God . . .

When Jesus came into the city, the multitude must have thought He would head straight for the fortress Antonia to deal with the Romans. Instead, He went into the temple to deal with the Jews.

Matthew 21:12 (b)
. . . and cast out all them that sold and bought in the temple, and overthrew the tables of the moneychangers, and the seats of them that sold doves.

Keep in mind that Jesus had already cleansed the temple at the outset of His public ministry (John 2:13–15). So, too, because I myself am a temple (1 Corinthians 3:16), the Lord has to come and overturn the tables of my life. And although I wish this were a one-time process, it's not. Just when I think I've learned a lesson, suddenly I find the old junk back in my temple once again. Then the Lord comes in faithfully and deals with it radically.

The Lord not only desires purity in our temples individually, but also corporately. In the following passage, I see four characteristics He is looking for in us, His corporate temple (1 Peter 2:5).

Matthew 21:13
And said unto them, It is written, My house shall be called the house of prayer; but ye have made it a den of thieves.

First of all, we are to be a house of prayer. I thank the Lord for times of corporate prayer. I continue to be blown away by the reports I hear from people, saying, "We prayed specifically for this and here is how the Lord answered our prayer. . . ."

Matthew 21:14
And the blind and the lame came to him in the temple; and he healed them.

Second, this is to be a place where people are helped. The blind and the lame came to Jesus in the temple and He healed them. So, too, we who have been spiritually blinded and we who are lame-brained should be able to come into this place and hear the Word, study the Scriptures, and receive help and healing.

Matthew 21:15 (a)
And when the chief priests and scribes saw the wonderful things that he did . . .

Third, this is to be a place where power is released. The chief priests and scribes saw the wonderful—or awesome—things He did. You should have seen the awesome things God did in the amphitheatre at Applegate Christian Fellowship one Sunday: On that cold and rainy day, eight or ten radical kids went on record, saying, "You can say we're all wet; you can call us drips; but we're taking the plunge. We're going for it. We're getting baptized. From this point on, Jesus Christ is our Savior and our Lord!"

Matthew 21:15 (b), 16
. . . and the children crying in the temple, and saying, Hosanna to the Son of David; they were sore displeased, And said unto him, Hearest thou what these say? And Jesus saith unto them, Yea; have ye never read, Out of the mouth of babes and sucklings thou hast perfected praise?

Finally, this is to be a place where praise is expressed. The old fuddy-duddies in our text were "sore displeased," but the kids were crying, "Hosanna." You see, when the kids cried "Hosanna" it wasn't for political reasons; it wasn't for economic reasons; it wasn't for vocational reasons. They cried "Hosanna" simply because they were excited about Jesus. I find that to be true with young Christians as well. It's often the young brother or sister who can lead the way in simple and sincere praise. This house must be a place where such praise is expressed. Following are four key Hebrew words that shed light on the meaning of true praise.

One Old Testament word for praise is *halal*

which literally means, "to acclaim or to glory in God who brings the deepest of satisfaction." I like that! Late at night when you think you're hungry, instead of making yourself a peanut butter and pickle sandwich, try worshiping. Over and over again, I have found that when I think I want to listen to some classical music, watch TV, read a book, or have a snack, if I get away and begin to worship, suddenly the deepest satisfaction overwhelms me and I realize that time with God was what I craved all along. If you have been frustrated or restless lately, try worshiping. *Halal* means you will find all you're longing for internally in the One who satisfies you totally.

The second word used for praise is *towdah* which means "acknowledging God's work and His character and commending it." *Towdah* says, "Yes, Lord, You are good. You are holy and righteous. At last, we have found Someone in this universe worthy of our commendation."

The third word is *zamar* which means "to break out in song." When you find yourself singing joyfully about something of the goodness of God, that is *zamar*.

The fourth word is *shabach*, which means, "to commend God with thanksgiving." *Shabach* is saying, "Lord, we commend You for the way You've seen us through our trials, the way You've answered our prayers, the way You purchased our salvation."

Matthew 21:17
And he left them, and went out of the city into Bethany; and he lodged there.

The day after Jesus entered Jerusalem, He departed for Bethany. Mark tells us that on His way to Bethany, He went through the tiny town of Bethphage, or "House of Figs" (Mark 11:1). It was in Bethany where His friends Mary, Martha, and Lazarus lived, and no doubt He stayed with them.

Matthew 21:18-20
Now in the morning as he returned into the city, he hungered. And when he saw a fig tree in the way, he came to it, and found nothing thereon, but leaves only, and said unto it, Let no fruit grow on thee henceforward for ever. And presently the fig tree withered away. And when the disciples saw it, they marvelled, saying, How soon is the fig tree withered away!

On the way from Bethany to Jerusalem, on the slopes of the Mount of Olives, Jesus saw a fig tree. Fig trees were common in Israel. Growing to heights of twenty-five feet and widths of

twenty to twenty-five feet, they covered the countryside. Because of their abundance, figs were a staple of the Hebrew diet. Here, Jesus—hungry for breakfast—saw a fig tree covered with leaves. Fig trees are unusual in that the appearance of fruit precedes the appearance of leaves. Jesus assumed, therefore, that since this particular tree was covered with leaves, it must surely contain fruit as well. But this fig tree was a hypocrite. It had leaves—the outward appearance of vitality and health—but no fruit. So Jesus cursed it. And it withered, Mark tells us, beginning with the roots (Mark 11:20).

Many people have a real problem at this point. Environmentalists say, "How could this be? What kind of person is this Jesus of Nazareth? Is He just venting His anger by cursing this poor, helpless tree?" Yet if Jesus and the disciples were cold and they used the tree for firewood to warm themselves, no one would think anything of it. Here, Jesus uses the tree not to warm the hands but to warn the hearts of His disciples.

To those who question the environmental correctness of Jesus' action, I say, "Consider what He could have done. Think of Elijah. When a group of soldiers came to get him, he called down fire from heaven and burned them up. Think of Elisha. When some young men were making fun of his bald head, he called a bear out of the woods and they became lunch." When you look at the Old Testament prophets and see the severity of the lessons they taught, cursing a fruitless fig tree should pose no problem for us. Seeing a barren fig tree, Jesus seized the moment to teach a lesson to His disciples, to you, and to me about hypocrisy, hope, and healing.

For topical study of Matthew 21:17–20 entitled "The Fate of the Figless Tree," turn to page 159.

Matthew 21:21, 22
Jesus answered and said unto them, Verily I say unto you, If ye have faith, and doubt not, ye shall not only do this which is done to the fig tree, but also if ye shall say unto this mountain, Be thou removed, and be thou cast into the sea; it shall be done. And all things, whatsoever ye shall ask in prayer, believing, ye shall receive.

In contrast to the impotent, barren state of the fig tree, here Jesus speaks of the power of prayer and the potency of faith.

Matthew 21:23
And when he was come into the temple, the chief priests and the elders of the people came unto him as he was teaching, and said, By what authority doest thou these things? and who gave thee this authority?

Upon His return from Bethany, Jesus taught in the Temple. With the cleansing of the Temple fresh in their minds, the chief priests and elders demanded to know by whose authority He overturned the tables and drove out the sheep and cows.

Matthew 21:24, 25 (a)
And Jesus answered and said unto them, I also will ask you one thing, which if ye tell me, I in like wise will tell you by what authority I do these things. The baptism of John, whence was it? from heaven, or of men?

Jesus answered their question with a question. "Remember John?" He said. "Was his ministry from God or simply done by his own energy?"

Matthew 21:25 (b)–27
And they reasoned with themselves, saying, If we shall say, From heaven; he will say unto us, Why did ye not then believe him? But if we shall say, Of men; we fear the people; for all hold John as a prophet. And they answered Jesus, and said, We cannot tell. And he said unto them, Neither tell I you by what authority I do these things.

Realizing they were backed into a corner, the chief priests and elders refused to answer. "If you won't answer Me, I have no obligation to answer you," Jesus said. Next, we see Him launch into a series of three parables in which He will answer them, but indirectly. "By whose authority did I cleanse the temple? He asked. "By the authority of the Father, the Son, and the Holy Spirit," He'll answer.

Matthew 21:28–32
But what think ye? A certain man had two sons; and he came to the first, and said, Son, go work to day in my vineyard. He answered and said, I will not: but afterward he repented, and went. And he came to the second, and said likewise. And he answered and said, I go, sir: and went not. Whether of them twain did the will of his father? They say unto him, The first. Jesus saith unto them, Verily I say unto you, That the publicans and the harlots go into the kingdom of God before you. For John came unto you in the way of righteousness, and ye believed him not: but the publicans and the harlots believed him:

and ye, when ye had seen it, repented not afterward, that ye might believe him.

First, Jesus cleansed the temple by the authority of the Father. Jesus likened the prostitutes and publicans to the first son. They seemed unlikely candidates to receive John's message, but receive it they did. On the other hand, like the second son, the pseudo-religious scribes and Pharisees gave only lip service to the preaching of John.

Matthew 21:33–41
Hear another parable: There was a certain householder, which planted a vineyard, and hedged it round about, and digged a winepress in it, and built a tower, and let it out to husbandmen, and went into a far country: And when the time of the fruit drew near, he sent his servants to the husbandmen, that they might receive the fruits of it. And the husbandmen took his servants, and beat one, and killed another, and stoned another. Again, he sent other servants more than the first: and they did unto them likewise. But last of all he sent unto them his son, saying, They will reverence my son. But when the husbandmen saw the son, they said among themselves, This is the heir; come, let us kill him, and let us seize on his inheritance. And they caught him, and cast him out of the vineyard, and slew him. When the lord therefore of the vineyard cometh, what will he do unto those husbandmen? They say unto him, He will miserably destroy those wicked men, and will let out his vineyard unto other husbandmen, which shall render him the fruits in their seasons.

Second, Jesus cleansed the temple by the authority of the Son. Taken from Isaiah 5, this parable speaks of Israel as a vineyard and of God as the owner who went to a far country, expecting to receive payment as the grapes were harvested. When the owner sent messengers to collect, the stewards killed the messengers just as the people of Israel had killed the prophets God had sent to them.

- *Did the Owner then say, "I'm going to send soldiers"?*
  No, He said, "I'll send My Son."
- *Did He say, "I'll send lightning to strike them"?*
  No, He said, "I'll send the Light of the world to instruct them."

Nonetheless, rather than respond to Him, they killed Him.

Matthew 21:42–44
Jesus saith unto them, Did ye never read in the scriptures, The stone which the builders rejected, the same is become the head of the corner: this is the Lord's doing, and it is marvellous in our eyes? Therefore say I unto you, The kingdom of God shall be taken from you, and given to a nation bringing forth the fruits thereof. And whosoever shall fall on this stone shall be broken: but on whomsoever it shall fall, it will grind him to powder.

This reference to Psalm 118, the very psalm sung during Jesus' triumphal entry into Jerusalem, speaks of the temple. When the temple was under construction, stones were quarried miles away and transported to the temple mount. Forty feet wide and twenty feet high, these stones were massive. Yet they fit together so perfectly that no mortar was needed, for not even a knife blade could fit between them. Tradition had it that one stone arrived on the scene but, because no one could figure out where it was supposed to go, the builders rolled it off a cliff into the Kidron Valley. Not until the foundation was complete did the builders discover they were one stone short. Sure enough, the stone they had rejected was none other than the cornerstone. Here, Jesus pulls from that tradition as well as from Psalm 118, and says, "Haven't you read? The One who was rejected, the One who was cast away is indeed the chief cornerstone, the foundation stone."

Truly, Jesus is our Rock. To the Jews, He is a stumbling stone (Romans 9:32, 33). To the Gentiles, He is a smiting stone (Daniel 2:34). To the believer, He is the foundation stone (Ephesians 2:20). Either you will fall on Him and be saved, or He will fall on you and you'll be crushed. It's your choice. I highly recommend the first. I recommend building your life upon the solid rock of Jesus Christ.

Matthew 21:45, 46
And when the chief priests and Pharisees had heard his parables, they perceived that he spake of them. But when they sought to lay hands on him, they feared the multitude, because they took him for a prophet.

At last, the chief priests and elders were getting the point that Jesus did what He did in the authority of the Father and of the Son. But, as we will see in chapter 22, He had one more parable left.

THE FATE OF THE FIGLESS TREE
A Topical Study of
Matthew 21:17–20

Jesus deals with the issue of hypocrisy in the miracle of the fig tree. You see, although this fig tree was covered with leaves, it was a hypocrite because it had no fruit. Why wasn't there fruit? To answer this question, consider three aspects of this miracle, each of which has practical application for us today....

Practical Application

Verse 19 says it was a lone fig tree. This tree bore no fruit because there was no cross-pollination. It's a matter of biology and a fact of life: A lone fig tree cannot bear fruit.

Not forsaking the assembling of ourselves together, as the manner of some is; but exhorting one another: and so much the more, as ye see the day approaching.   Hebrews 10:25

You see, gang, when we meet together, a spiritual "cross-pollination" takes place. There's a dynamic unlike any other when people come together corporately to praise, pray, and study the Word. This only makes sense, for our God is a Father who loves His family.

When my kids were all at home, I wanted them to sit around the table and eat together. We didn't serve Peter-John in his room, Jessie and Christy in their room, and Mary and Ben in their rooms because something special happened when we were all together. So, too, our Father desires that His children come together around His table, the table of Communion. Secondly, our Father calls us to come together to the table of Bible study, where the manna of the Word is opened for us to partake of its spiritual nutrition. If you are a lone fig tree, you might appear to be healthy for a while. You might have all the leaves of right theology. Others might be fooled by your outward appearance. But there will be no real fruit found on you. As "living stones being fit together for His glory" (see 2 Peter 2:4), we need each other.

Prophetic Illustration

Scripturally, historically, and presently, the fig tree is a symbol of the nation of Israel. Jeremiah, Amos, Ezekiel, Hosea, and Isaiah all liken Israel to the fig tree. Just as the eagle symbolizes America and the bear represents Russia, so Israel is portrayed by the fig tree. Like the fig tree in this account, Israel had lots of leaves. This nation appeared to be so religious—with temple worship, traditions, and the Torah; with Pharisees, scribes, and Sadducees—but Jesus found no fruit in her land. Forty years later, the Romans marched into Jerusalem, destroyed the temple, and slaughtered thousands. And the nation of Israel lost her identity until 1948. Thus, for almost two thousand years, the Jews, like the fig tree, shriveled and withered.

Personal Exhortation

When the first Adam came to a fig tree in the Garden of Eden, he was not looking for fruit. He was looking for leaves to cover his nakedness (Genesis 3:7). That's always the tendency of humanity. We cover up our nakedness with outward activity. We join Rotary. We volunteer for the Red Cross. We teach Sunday school. We do whatever it takes to cover our sinfulness because we know what lurks within us. The last Adam, as Paul calls Jesus in 1 Corinthians 15, came looking not for leaves, but for fruit. He didn't care about the leaves of outward demonstration. He desired fruit for inner satiation. And He still hungers for fruit. What fruit? The fruit of His Spirit: love, joy, peace, longsuffering, gentleness, goodness, faith, meekness, temperance (Galatians 5:22, 23); the fruit of our thanksgiving (Hebrews 13:15); the fruit of the gospel (Colossians 1:6); and the fruit of righteousness (James 3:18).

Jesus comes by your tree every day, saying, "I'm hungry."

What do you have for Him? A bunch of leaves?

"Oh, I'm doing fine," you might say. "I'm involved in this activity. I'm supporting that mission. I'm going to this meeting." Your tree may look healthy. Others might be attracted to it and impressed by it. But Jesus isn't fooled. What is there for Him?

When He comes morning by morning seeking satiation and satisfaction, does He find real fruit? Does He say, "It's such a joy being with you in the morning hour or in the cool of the day as we walk together. It's so wonderful that someone would take ten minutes to thank Me specifically for what I've done, that someone would worship Me for who I am"? Or does He see a tree filled with leaves but lacking fruit?

And seeing a fig tree afar off having leaves, he came, if haply he might find any thing thereon: and when he came to it, he found nothing but leaves; for the time of figs was not yet. And Jesus answered and said unto it, No man eat fruit of thee hereafter for ever. And his disciples heard it. Mark 11:13, 14

"No man eat fruit of thee." If we are not satisfying Jesus intimately and personally, we will not satisfy anyone else through service or ministry. What has He found in you today? What will He find in you tomorrow morning? Figs or leaves?

Maybe you're saying, "I don't know if there is any fruit in my life for Him to enjoy. What can I do?" Take a look at Luke 13 . . .

He spake also this parable; A certain man had a fig tree planted in his vineyard; and he came and sought fruit thereon, and found none. Then said he unto the dresser of his vineyard, Behold, these three years I come seeking fruit on this fig tree, and find none: cut it down; why cumbereth it the ground?
                                                                        Luke 13:6, 7

For three years this fig tree had been tended, cultivated, and watered even as Jesus had publicly ministered to the Jews for three years. But there was no fruit. And so the owner said, "Why should it continue to sap nutrients from the soil? Cut it down!"

And he answering said unto him, Lord, let it alone this year also, till I shall dig about it, and dung it: And if it bear fruit, well: and if not, then after that thou shalt cut it down.   Luke 13:8, 9

Here, the vinedresser pleads on behalf of the barren fig tree even as Jesus lives to make intercession for us (Hebrews 7:25). Jesus is our Advocate, our Defense Lawyer. Like the vinedresser, He says, "Give Me one more year to dig around it." In the parallel passage to Matthew 21, Mark 11 says the fig tree dried up from the roots. That's where dryness always begins. You see, it's what takes place in the quiet, secret, hidden time that matters. Is there a heart for God? Is there communication with the Lord? Is there an expression of thanks to the Lord? Or is there nothing beneath the surface because the roots are dry? The Vinedresser says, "Let Me dig it. Let Me expose sin. Let Me get to the heart of the matter."

What about your root system that was once so vibrant? What about your time with the Lord, your time in the Word, your time of praise and thanksgiving and adoration? Is it withered? Let Him dig it.

Secondly, let Him dung it. What is dung? Manure. In Philippians 3:4–6, speaking of past accomplishments, Paul wrote, "I have quite a record. I was born into a godly tribe, lived an upright life, worked zealously, and studied steadfastly." And then he added: "But what things were gain to me, those I counted loss for Christ" (see Philippians 3:7). Interestingly, the Greek word translated "loss" is "dung."

You might be saying, "I used to be a deacon" or "I used to be a pastor, gospel singer, or Sunday-school teacher." Gang, it doesn't matter what you *were*. You cannot live in the glory of what you were doing in 1942, the revival of 1964, or the spiritual high you felt three years ago. Only what you're doing presently matters. It is only where you're at with the Lord today that counts. When you allow the Vinedresser to dig and to dung, to expose sin and to expel self, fruit will come.

May the Lord make you fruitful. May Jesus come by your tree this week and eat of the abundance. May your goal not be to impress others, but to satisfy your Master. And may this be the fruitiest year of your whole life!

22 Chapter 21 ended with two parables illustrating that Jesus acted with the authority of the Father and the Son. Chapter 22 opens with the third and final parable in this series, a parable that illustrates He carried the authority of the Spirit as well.

Matthew 22:1–3 (a)
And Jesus answered and spake unto them again by parables, and said, The kingdom of heaven is like unto a certain king, which made a marriage for his son, And sent forth his servants to call them that were bidden to the wedding . . .

God the Father sent His Spirit to woo a bride for His Son. The ministry of the Spirit is to call people to the wedding, to win a bride for Jesus Christ. Who did He call first? Salvation is to the Jew first and then the Gentile (Romans 2:9, 10).

Matthew 22:3 (b)–6
. . . And they would not come. Again, he sent forth other servants, saying, Tell them which are bidden, Behold, I have prepared my dinner: my oxen and my fatlings are killed, and all things are ready: come unto the marriage. But they made light of it, and went their ways, one to his farm, another to his merchandise: And the remnant took his servants, and entreated them spitefully, and slew them.

Just as the Jews had rejected the authority of the Father and the Son, they rejected the ministry of the Spirit. They rejected Jesus when He came to Jerusalem just as they would reject the apostles when they ministered there after Pentecost.

Matthew 22:7–9
But when the king heard thereof, he was wroth: and he sent forth his armies, and destroyed those murderers, and burned up their city. Then saith he to his servants, The wedding is ready, but they which were bidden were not worthy. Go ye therefore into the highways, and as many as ye shall find, bid to the marriage.

"We're too busy. We're not interested," said the Jews. So the Father said to the Spirit, "Go to the highways and byways. Go to the Gentiles. Go to the Oregonians and tell *them* to come. The meal is ready. The doors are open. Whosoever will, let him come" (see Revelation 22:17).

Matthew 22:10
So those servants went out into the highways, and gathered together all as many as they found, both bad and good: and the wedding was furnished with guests.

Good and bad came. That's the church. That's us.

Matthew 22:11, 12
And when the king came in to see the guests, he saw there a man which had not on a wedding garment: And he saith unto him, Friend, how camest thou in hither not having a wedding garment? And he was speechless.

Jesus is telling us that in the church, there will be those traveling in our midst and sitting at the table who are not dressed properly. What does this mean?

I will greatly rejoice in the LORD, my soul shall be joyful in my God; for he hath clothed me with the garments of salvation, he hath covered me with the robe of righteousness, as a bridegroom decketh himself with ornaments, and as a bride adorneth herself with her jewels.   Isaiah 61:10

Who is dressed appropriately? Who is really saved? The one who says, "I need a Savior. I don't have the answer. I'm not righteous. Lord, I need You to robe me with Your robe of righteousness."

Matthew 22:13, 14
Then said the king to the servants, Bind him hand and foot, and take him away, and cast him into outer darkness; there shall be weeping and gnashing of teeth. For many are called, but few are chosen.

You see, it's not the person who sits in the pew or is dipped in the water who is saved. It's the one who says, "Lord I need You. You are my Savior. You are my Redeemer."

Matthew 22:15
Then went the Pharisees, and took counsel how they might entangle him in his talk.

The Pharisees and Sadducees decided to counterattack with a series of political, ethical, theological, and personal questions for Jesus. Why?

Unknowingly, they were fulfilling the prophecy of Exodus 12 which says that before the Passover lamb was sacrificed, it was to be inspected and observed for five days in order to make sure it was free of blemish or disease. So, too, before the Passover Lamb of God was sacrificed on the Cross, He underwent a period of scrutiny and examination by the most brutal inspectors of all: the Pharisees, Sadducees, scribes, and Herodians—His enemies.

Matthew 22:16 (a)
And they sent out unto him their disciples with the Herodians . . .

First came the Pharisees and Herodians. The Pharisees were those who kept the most minute details of the law. The Herodians, on the other hand, were a political party. It was an interesting combination because the two didn't normally get together. But political and philosophical enemies will often unite in opposition to Jesus Christ.

Matthew 22:16 (b), 17
. . . saying, Master, we know that thou art true, and teachest the way of God in truth, neither carest thou for any man: for thou regardest not the person of men. Tell us therefore, What thinkest thou? Is it lawful to give tribute unto Caesar, or not?

The Pharisees and Herodians thought they had Jesus cornered. If He said, "Yes, pay taxes to Caesar," that would be a most unpopular sentiment. You see, Caesar claimed to be God, and the Jews felt that by paying taxes to Caesar, they were in essence acknowledging him as such. On the other hand, if Jesus said, "No, don't pay taxes," He could be arrested for tax evasion and political rebellion.

Matthew 22:18–22
But Jesus perceived their wickedness, and said, Why tempt ye me, ye hypocrites? Shew me the tribute money. And they brought unto him a penny. And he saith unto them, Whose is this image and superscription? the things which are Caesar's; and unto God the things that are God's. When they had heard these words, they marvelled, and left him, and went their way.

In other words, Jesus said, "Because coins are stamped with the image of Caesar, they belong to Caesar. But because man is made in the image of God, man belongs to God."

Matthew 22:23–28
The same day came to him the Sadducees, which say that there is no resurrection, and asked him, Saying, Master, Moses said, If a man die, having no children, his brother shall marry his wife, and raise up seed unto his brother. Now there were with us seven brethren: and the first, when he had married a wife, deceased, and, having no issue, left his wife unto his brother: Likewise the second also, and the third, unto the seventh. And last of all the woman died also. Therefore in the resurrection whose wife shall she be of the seven? for they all had her.

The Sadducees brought the next question. As those who didn't believe in resurrection, they asked a question that inferred there were practical problems with a belief in life after death. "If a woman had seven husbands," they asked, "which one would she be married to in heaven?"

Matthew 22:29, 30
Jesus answered and said unto them, Ye do err, not knowing the scriptures, nor the power of God. For in the resurrection they neither marry, nor are given in marriage, but are as the angels of God in heaven.

Jesus simply said, "In heaven, relationships are different than they are on earth." But then He continued . . .

Matthew 22:31–33
But as touching the resurrection of the dead, have ye not read that which was spoken unto you by God, saying, I am the God of Abraham, and the God of Isaac, and the God of Jacob? God is not the God of the dead, but of the living. And when the multitude heard this, they were astonished at his doctrine.

God didn't say, "I *was* the God of Abraham, Isaac, and Jacob." He said, "I *am* the God of Abraham, Isaac, and Jacob." By quoting this verse, Jesus gave the Sadducees this message: God is the God of the living. Heaven is real.

Matthew 22:34–36
But when the Pharisees had heard that he had put the Sadducees to silence, they were gathered together. Then one of them, which was a lawyer, asked him a question, tempting him, and saying, Master, which is the great commandment in the law?

The scribes had determined that of the 613 commandments in the Old Testament, 248 were positive injunctions and 365 were negative prohibitions. No doubt hoping to spark a controversy, the lawyer asked Jesus which of the 613 was the greatest commandment.

Matthew 22:37, 38
Jesus said unto him, Thou shalt love the Lord thy God with all thy heart, and with all thy soul, and with all thy mind. This is the first and great commandment.

Jesus went right to the heart of the law: the Shemah. "And thou shalt love the LORD thy God with all thine heart, and with all thy soul, and with all thy might" (Deuteronomy 6:5). The Jews knew this was the Great Commandment. Orthodox Jews wrote it out and put it in their mezuzahs—the small, elongated boxes thy fastened to their front doorposts. They wrote it out and put it in their phylacteries—the leather pouches they wore on their foreheads in obedience to the command to keep the Word always on their minds. Thus, it would have been no surprise that Jesus named the Shemah, Deuteronomy 6:4, as the greatest commandment. But then He went on. . . .

Matthew 22:39
And the second is like unto it, Thou shalt love thy neighbour as thyself.

"Like unto it" means "linked to it." In other words, the First and Second Commandments are inextricably linked together. Using this commandment, there are those who say that in order to love our neighbor, we must first love ourselves. I don't believe that is what Jesus is saying here. Rather, I believe He is saying, "Just as you already love yourself, care for yourself, and think about yourself, you are to love your neighbor in the same way." You see, according to 1 John 4:20, loving my neighbor is not dependent upon loving myself. It is dependent upon loving God.

The ability to love God and to love people are inextricably linked. The problem is, most of us separate the two because of our "TV dinner" spirituality. In a TV dinner, the Salisbury steak, peas, mashed potatoes, and cherry cobbler are all in separate compartments. And that's just what we do spiritually. "Oh yes, I love God," we say. "I'm going to worship Sunday night." But on Monday we call our boss an idiot behind his back, and on Wednesday we complain about how our neighbor idles his car too early in the morning. Yet Sunday finds us worshiping the Lord once again. We compartmentalize our lives thinking that how we treat people has nothing to do with our relationship with God.

Jesus says our walk with God is not a TV dinner. Rather, if we really love God, we'll inevitably love people, and our lives will become like a chicken pot pie. No longer compartmentalized, the peas, potatoes, and chicken will all be mixed together. Truly, if our love for God is genuine, it will naturally flow into a love for people.

Matthew 22:40
On these two commandments hang all the law and the prophets.

The message of the Law and the Prophets, indeed the message of the entire Old Testament is summed up in one word: love. That is why Jesus says, "Love the Lord and love your neighbor and in so doing, you will exemplify the essence of all Old Testament teaching." I love the picture Jesus painted when He said that the Law and the prophets hang on loving God and loving our neighbor. As I look to heaven and love God; and as I look to my right and left and love people, I see the picture of a Cross. On these two *hang* all the Law and the Prophets. Who hung on the Cross? The One who loved His Father with all of His heart and soul, mind and strength; the One who loved us and gave Himself for us. Jesus is the Perfect One who loves His Father and who loves us.

Matthew 22:41–45
While the Pharisees were gathered together, Jesus asked them, saying, What think ye of Christ? whose son is he? They say unto him, The Son of David. He saith unto them, How then doth David in spirit call him Lord, saying, The LORD said unto my Lord, Sit thou on my right hand, till I make thine enemies thy footstool? If David then call him Lord, how is he his son?

Jesus quotes here from Psalm 110. We will see Peter use this same reference in his first sermon on the Day of Pentecost (Acts 2:34). This passage would have caused great consternation in the minds of the Pharisees who were so eager to confound and confuse Jesus. You see, in the Jewish culture, one would never call his offspring "Lord."

"Why, then," asked Jesus, "is David calling his own offspring Lord? Truly, David is referring to Someone greater than himself. If Christ be merely the Son of David as you suppose, David would never have called him Lord."

Matthew 22:46
And no man was able to answer him a word, neither durst any man from that day forth ask him any more questions.

The scribes and Pharisees, who prided themselves on their deep knowledge of Scripture, were stumped. Using the written Word, Jesus

Christ—the Living Word—had beaten them at their own game.

23 We now come to the last public sermon of Jesus Christ, given only days before His death. I would have thought this last message would have been one of salvation and invitation. On the contrary, it was a message of condemnation and denunciation against the religious hierarchy of the day. Calling the Pharisees blind guides, fools, and whitewashed tombs, Jesus didn't hold back but spoke pointedly and powerfully concerning their hypocrisy.

The apostle Paul wrote that it is the goodness of God that leads men to repentance (Romans 2:4). In other words, God's love and grace are a greater motivation to salvation than hellfire and damnation. But Paul went on to say that some will be saved by fire (1 Corinthians 3:15). That is, those who will not respond to God's grace and goodness need to hear a strong message of judgment. That is why, after spending three years preaching the grace and goodness of His Father, Jesus gave this final word of judgment.

So, too, as you share the gospel with people, I encourage you to approach them first on the basis of God's goodness and grace. But if they continually harden their hearts, it may be that they need to feel the heat of His judgment.

Matthew 23:1, 2
Then spake Jesus to the multitude, and to his disciples, saying, The scribes and the Pharisees sit in Moses'' seat.

Newer translations properly render this verse: "The scribes and the Pharisees have seated themselves in Moses' seat." In other words, the scribes and Pharisees had seized the position of authority, even though they were not called by God to do so. The first sign of false spiritual leadership is that it lacks God-given authority.

Matthew 23:3
All therefore whatsoever they bid you observe, that observe and do; but do not ye after their works: for they say, and do not.

Second, false spiritual leaders lack integrity. Although they may teach others to do right, they themselves only talk about it.

Matthew 23:4
For they bind heavy burdens and grievous to be borne, and lay them on men's shoulders; but they themselves will not move them with one of their fingers.

Third, false spiritual leaders lack sympathy. They bind heavy, legalistic burdens on others but won't lift a finger to help anyone bear them.

Matthew 23:5–7
But all their works they do for to be seen of men: they make broad their phylacteries, and enlarge the borders of their garments, love the uppermost rooms at feasts, and the chief seats in the synagogues, and greetings in the markets, and to be called of men, Rabbi, Rabbi.

Finally, false spiritual leaders lack humility. When the Pharisees went into the synagogue, they sat on the platform in large chairs in order to be seen by all. As time went on, they made phylacteries so big that some could hardly stand straight under the weight. They obeyed the command in Numbers 15 to place blue cloth on the hem of their robes as a reminder of their heavenly calling. But as their pride increased, so did the size of their blue borders.

Matthew 23:8–12
But be not ye called Rabbi: for one is your Master, even Christ; and all ye are brethren. And call no man your father upon the earth: for one is your Father, which is in heaven. Neither be ye called masters: for one is your Master, even Christ. But he that is greatest among you shall be your servant. And whosoever shall exalt himself shall be abased; and he that shall humble himself shall be exalted.

Jesus says the true spiritual leader does two things: He avoids elevated titles and he accepts lowly tasks. Jesus avoided the titles and honors that people wanted to heap upon Him in His early ministry, choosing instead to humble Himself, to eat with sinners, to wash feet, and to touch lepers. Jesus is the ultimate spiritual Leader.

Following His description of a true spiritual leader, Jesus did something I find intriguing. He ended His last sermon pronouncing eight woes. Bible students, think back. How did Jesus begin His public ministry? By pronouncing eight blessings in the form of the Beatitudes. Watch and see how the eight woes at the end of His preaching ministry correlate perfectly with the eight blessings given at the beginning of His ministry.

Matthew 23:13
But woe unto you, scribes and Pharisees, hypocrites! for ye shut up the kingdom of heaven against men: for ye neither go in yourselves, neither suffer ye them that are entering to go in.

Blessed are the poor in spirit: for theirs is the kingdom of heaven.   Matthew 5:3

Although the kingdom of heaven belongs to the poor in spirit, the Pharisees were proud in spirit. "I thank You, God, that I am not as other men," they prayed (see Luke 18:11). Their pride, Jesus said, would not only keep them from entering the kingdom, but would prevent others as well.

Matthew 23:14
Woe unto you, scribes and Pharisees, hypocrites! for ye devour widows'' houses, and for a pretence make long prayer: therefore ye shall receive the greater damnation.

Blessed are they that mourn: for they shall be comforted.   Matthew 5:4

Jesus promised that the mourners will be comforted. The Pharisees, however, manipulated those who mourned. You see, when a man died, the Pharisees would show up on his doorstep telling his widow that if she wanted to honor her husband's memory, she would make a donation to their ministry. Watch out for that, precious people. In this day when there's an abundance of fund-raising, be on guard against those who seek to manipulate rather than to comfort.

Matthew 23:15
Woe unto you, scribes and Pharisees, hypocrites! for ye compass sea and land to make one proselyte, and when he is made, ye make him twofold more the child of hell than yourselves.

Blessed are the meek: for they shall inherit the earth.   Matthew 5:5

The meek were to inherit the earth. The Pharisees, on the other hand, were trying to convert the earth to their legalistic, hypocritical, religious system. The tragedy is that when a legalist lays his trip on someone else, the convert or proselyte becomes more zealous than the teacher and the end result is damnation.

Matthew 23:16–22
Woe unto you, ye blind guides, which say, Whosoever shall swear by the temple, it is nothing; but whosoever shall swear by the gold of the temple, he is a debtor! Ye fools and blind: for whether is greater, the gold, or the temple that sanctifieth the gold? And, Whosoever shall swear by the altar, it is nothing; but whosoever sweareth by the gift that is upon it, he is guilty. Ye fools and blind: for whether is greater, the gift, or the

altar that sanctifieth the gift? Whoso therefore shall swear by the altar, sweareth by it, and by all things thereon. And whoso shall swear by the temple, sweareth by it, and by him that dwelleth therein. And he that shall swear by heaven, sweareth by the throne of God, and by him that sitteth thereon.

Blessed are they which do hunger and thirst after righteousness: for they shall be filled.
                                        Matthew 5:6

Blessed are those who hunger and thirst for righteousness—for integrity, truth, and simplicity. The Pharisees weren't hungering for righteousness. They were playing games with semantics and vocabulary. In Jesus' day, if one took an oath saying, "I swear by the temple," he could be lying through his teeth, and that would be acceptable. It was only when he said "I swear by the *gold* in the temple," that he was obligated to tell the truth. Thus, righteousness became a game.

Matthew 23:23, 24
Woe unto you, scribes and Pharisees, hypocrites! for ye pay tithe of mint and anise and cummin, and have omitted the weightier matters of the law, judgment, mercy, and faith: these ought ye to have done, and not to leave the other undone. Ye blind guides, which strain at a gnat, and swallow a camel.

Blessed are the merciful: for they shall obtain mercy.   Matthew 5:7

According to Leviticus 11, the largest unclean animal was a camel. The smallest was a gnat. Jesus said the Pharisees picked gnats out of their soup but missed the big camel swimming around. They had all the little details down—even tithing their spice seeds—but missed the big picture of love, faith, mercy and righteousness.

Matthew 23:25, 26
Woe unto you, scribes and Pharisees, hypocrites! for ye make clean the outside of the cup and of the platter, but within they are full of extortion and excess. Thou blind Pharisee, cleanse first that which is within the cup and platter, that the outside of them may be clean also.

Blessed are the pure in heart: for they shall see God.   Matthew 5:8

The purity of the true believer enables him to see God. The hypocrisy of the Pharisee blinds him to the things of God.

Matthew 23:27, 28
Woe unto you, scribes and Pharisees, hypocrites! for ye are like unto whited sepulchres, which indeed appear beautiful outward, but are within full of dead men's bones, and of all uncleanness. Even so ye also outwardly appear righteous unto men, but within ye are full of hypocrisy and iniquity.

Blessed are the peacemakers: for they shall be called the children of God.   Matthew 5:9

At the same time the Pharisees claimed to be men of peace, they were secretly plotting the murder of the Prince of Peace.

Matthew 23:29–35
Woe unto you, scribes and Pharisees, hypocrites! because ye build the tombs of the prophets, and garnish the sepulchres of the righteous, And say, If we had been in the days of our fathers, we would not have been partakers with them in the blood of the prophets. Wherefore ye be witnesses unto yourselves, that ye are the children of them which killed the prophets. Fill ye up then the measure of your fathers. Ye serpents, ye generation of vipers, how can ye escape the damnation of hell? Wherefore, behold, I send unto you prophets, and wise men, and scribes: and some of them ye shall kill and crucify; and some of them shall ye scourge in your synagogues, and persecute them from city to city: That upon you may come all the righteous blood shed upon the earth, from the blood of righteous Abel unto the blood of Zacharias son of Barachias, whom ye slew between the temple and the altar.

Blessed are they which are persecuted for righteousness; sake: for theirs is the kingdom of heaven.   Matthew 5:10

Jesus said, "Blessed are the persecuted and woe to the persecutors."
"If they had been alive in our day, we wouldn't have killed the prophets," boasted the Pharisees. But their claim was invalidated by the fact that at that very moment they sought to execute the One of whom the prophets spoke. From Abel to Zechariah—from A to Z—they killed the prophets.

Matthew 23:36
Verily I say unto you, All these things shall come upon this generation.

What will come upon them? The blood, the death, the scourging, the tribulation, the persecution that had befallen the prophets throughout history. "His blood be upon our heads and our sons' heads," the Jews cried a few days later when they demanded the crucifixion of Jesus (see Matthew 27:25). And His blood would indeed be on their heads, for less than forty years after this, the Romans annihilated Jerusalem and slit the throats of ten thousand Jews living in Damascus.

Matthew 23:37, 38
O Jerusalem, Jerusalem, thou that killest the prophets, and stonest them which are sent unto thee, how often would I have gathered thy children together, even as a hen gathereth her chickens under her wings, and ye would not! Behold, your house is left unto you desolate.

"O Jerusalem, Jerusalem . . ." Every time Jesus used a name twice, it was because His heart was breaking. . . .

And the Lord said, Simon, Simon, behold, Satan hath desired to have you, that he may sift you as wheat: But I have prayed for thee, that thy faith fail not: and when thou art converted, strengthen thy brethren.   Luke 22:31, 32

And Jesus answered and said unto her, Martha, Martha, thou art careful and troubled about many things: But one thing is needful: and Mary hath chosen that good part, which shall not be taken away from her.
Luke 10:41, 42

Saul, Saul, why persecutest thou me? Acts 9:4

"O Jerusalem, Jerusalem, how I wanted to gather you under My wings like a mother hen, to shield you from the heat, but you wouldn't let Me."

Matthew 23:39
For I say unto you, Ye shall not see me henceforth, till ye shall say, Blessed is he that cometh in the name of the Lord.

I love the way Jesus ends this sermon. What were the people crying when He first rode into Jerusalem on a donkey? "Blessed is He who comes in the name of the Lord." Now Jesus refers back to that cry and says, "You'll say it again, only next time you'll say it with new understanding."

Notice He didn't say, "Ye shall not see me henceforth *unless* ye say, Blessed is he that cometh in the name of the Lord." He said, "Ye shall not see me henceforth *until* ye shall say, Blessed is he that cometh in the name of the Lord." In other words, it's going to happen. The time is coming when the Jews will acknowledge Jesus as Lord.

There are three things of which the Bible says we are not to be ignorant: spiritual gifts (1 Corinthians 12:1), the Rapture (1 Thessalonians 4:13), and the salvation of Israel (Romans 11:25, 26). God is not finished with Israel, folks. The day is coming when Israel *will* say, "Blessed is he that comes in the name of the Lord." When will that happen? In Luke 21, Jesus said Jerusalem would be trodden down until the Gentile age was complete. Jerusalem was trodden down by the Gentiles from the time Rome destroyed the city in A.D. 70 until the return of Jewish control after the seven-day war. Thus, 1967 signaled the end of the Gentile age.

"Well," you say, "if the Gentile age ended in 1967, why haven't we been raptured yet?" According to Romans 11 and Luke 21, we're in overtime, the fifth quarter. Scripture says the Lord is longsuffering, not willing that any should perish (II Peter 3:9). Think of it this way: How many of you have been saved since June 1967? Aren't you glad we were given a "grace period"?

The time is at hand. Jesus will come and establish His throne in Jerusalem. Until then, His desire for us is the same as for the nation Israel. "Let Me gather you under My wings today," He says. "Come back to where you once were. Put away your worldly priorities, your backsliding, and your legalism. Time is short. It won't matter eternally how much money you saved, where you went to college, or how your career developed. What will matter is whether or not you were radical for Me, whether or not you lived to worship Me, whether or not you loved Me."

───────────── ✀ ─────────────

24 Matthew 24 and 25 comprise what is known as the Olivet Discourse, so named because it is a teaching Jesus gave to His disciples on the Mount of Olives overlooking Jerusalem. Chapter 24, the prophetic portion of the discourse, is basically a three-point message. In verses 1 through 14 Jesus speaks about the end times as they relate to the nations. In verses 15 through 36 He speaks about the end times as they relate to Israel specifically. In verses 37 through 42 He speaks about the end times as they relate to the church.

Matthew 24:1
And Jesus went out, and departed from the temple: and his disciples came to him for to shew him the buildings of the temple.

As the disciples showed Jesus the temple, perhaps they were thinking, *Wait a minute, Lord. Yes, the scribes and Pharisees are fools and hypocrites, but look at this temple! Surely there's* something *good here.* The temple was indeed an incredible building. The gates were brass. The courts were marble. The furnishings were gold. The stones were huge. The chipping and carving of these stones was done in a rock quarry miles away so that during construction not a sound was heard on the temple mount (I Kings 6:7). Since chiseling and shaping took place in the quarry, when the stones arrived at the temple mount, they fit together perfectly.

Peter tells us we are living stones (I Peter 2:5). All of us will fit together perfectly in heaven. So guess what this world is. It's the rock quarry. Do you ever feel like you're being hammered on? Worn down? Chipped away? Welcome to the rock quarry. The Lord is smoothing us and preparing us here so that when we get to heaven, the sound of a hammer will not be heard.

Matthew 24:2
And Jesus said unto them, See ye not all these things? verily I say unto you, There shall not be left here one stone upon another, that shall not be thrown down.

This would seem impossible in the minds of the disciples. After all, the stones Jesus was talking about were massive in size, measuring twenty feet high, twenty feet wide, and forty feet long. But guess what happened. Less than forty years after Jesus spoke these words, the Romans stormed Jerusalem and, although Titus commanded his soldiers not to desecrate or harm the temple, one of them threw a torch into it. The ensuing fire became so hot that the gold inside began to melt and run down the walls between the rocks. When it cooled and solidified, the Roman soldiers began to pull down the stones of the temple in order to get to the gold hidden in the crevices. They didn't quit until they had managed to pull down every single stone. Exactly as Jesus had prophesied, not one stone remained upon another. That is why if you go to Jerusalem today, all you will see is the Wailing Wall, a part of the temple foundation. It's a massive wall, but small in comparison to what the temple had been.

Matthew 24:3
And as he sat upon the mount of Olives, the disciples came unto him privately, saying, Tell us, when shall these things be? and what shall be the sign of thy coming, and of the end of the world?

Associating the destruction of the temple with the end of the world, the disciples asked Jesus specifically, "What will be the sign of Your coming and the end of the world?"

Matthew 24:4, 5
And Jesus answered and said unto them, Take heed that no man deceive you. For many shall come in my name, saying, I am Christ; and shall deceive many.

Although there were many Messianic promises and great expectation among the Jewish people, not one person came on the scene claiming to be Messiah until *after* Jesus came. Why? For the same reason no one counterfeits two hundred dollar bills. Counterfeiters only counterfeit that which is real.

Matthew 24:6, 7 (a)
And ye shall hear of wars and rumours of wars: see that ye be not troubled: for all these things must come to pass, but the end is not yet. For nation shall rise against nation, and kingdom against kingdom . . .

With forty tons of explosives and a sophisticated weapon for every person on this planet, mankind has armed himself to the proverbial teeth. One scientist was recently asked which weapons would be used in World War III. This atomic scientist gave an answer that I thought was insightful when he said, "I'm not sure exactly which weapons will be detonated in World War III. But I'll tell you which ones will be used in World War IV: rocks."

"Rocks?"

"Yes. Rocks will be all that's left if World War III ever takes place."

Matthew 24:7 (b)
. . . and there shall be famines . . .

Famine is the result of a population explosion. It took from the time of Adam until 1857 for the population of this planet to reach one billion. Since then, we add a billion people every twenty years. We now have seven billion people. It's getting crowded, folks. And the effects are felt particularly in the third world.

Matthew 24:7 (c)
. . . and pestilences . . .

The Greek word translated "pestilence" implies unusual pestilence. Consider the AIDS virus. As of May 2001, the Centers for Disease Control and Prevention (CDC) claimed that over one million Americans had been infected with AIDS. But the Brookings Institution and others dispute that figure, claiming the number of Americans infected is much higher, possibly three to four million.

Matthew 24:7 (d)
. . . and earthquakes, in divers places.

In 1976 a geological survey team discovered an interesting change happening in the tectonic plates upon which the earth rests. These gigantic plates are shifting in such a way that earthquakes now occur with greater frequency and intensity than at any time in recorded history. Jesus said when we begin to see pestilence, superpowers at war, famine, and earthquakes, we are to know the end is near.

Matthew 24:8
All these are the beginning of sorrows.

The Greek word translated "sorrows" is what we think of as "birth pangs." Like labor pains, war, famine, earthquakes, and pestilence will erupt and then subside. As we get closer to the time of "delivery," these "contractions" will intensify. I personally believe that the next birth pang will birth the kingdom. We're at eight centimeters, folks. Keep your eyes open and your ears tuned!

Matthew 24:9
Then shall they deliver you up to be afflicted, and shall kill you: and ye shall be hated of all nations for my name's sake.

Who shall be afflicted, killed and hated by all nations? The Jews. Yes, the Jews will experience a great revival during this time of tribulation. Yes, they will be saved by the millions. But they'll also be hated. All nations of the world will vent their anger and their hostility on one small nation, the nation of Israel.

Matthew 24:10, 11
And then shall many be offended, and shall betray one another, and shall hate one another. And many false prophets shall rise, and shall deceive many.

Although millions will be saved, false prophets will come on the scene and attempt to deceive the whole world.

Matthew 24:12 (a)
And because iniquity shall abound . . .

After Christians are removed from this planet in the Rapture, sin will run rampant. Part of the reason for the Tribulation is that, through it, sin will be exposed in all its grotesqueness. Then, when Jesus comes back seven years later, after experiencing the hideous results of unchecked sin, people will be ready to submit to His righteousness. Yet after one thousand years of living

in a virtual Garden of Eden during the millennium, those born during that time and raised in that environment will have one last opportunity to choose. Satan will be released and, incredible as it seems, many will choose to follow him. So much for the theories of B. F. Skinner and other psychologists who contend that environment is responsible for man's problems.

"If you change man's environment, man will be good," they say. Not so. Man will have a perfect environment for one thousand years. Yet he will still rebel against God. Why? Because people are born sinners (Psalm 51:5). The solution, therefore, is not political reformation. The solution is spiritual regeneration. You can try to reform the political system. You can try to change the environment. But those are not the ultimate solutions. "Ye must be born again," Jesus said (John 3:7). Man must be changed from the inside out. That's the only answer.

Matthew 24:12 (b), 13
. . . the love of many shall wax cold. But he that shall endure unto the end, the same shall be saved.

Because of sin, the love of people—both for God and for each other—will grow cold. But he who endures the Tribulation will be saved.

For topical study of Matthew 24:13 entitled "Enduring Through Tribulation," turn to page 170.

Matthew 24:14
And this gospel of the kingdom shall be preached in all the world for a witness unto all nations; and then shall the end come.

Sometimes I hear preachers say that, on the basis of this verse, we must evangelize the world so Jesus can come back. I personally don't believe that is a correct understanding of this Scripture. Jesus will come back at a time already appointed by the Father. Surely the gospel is to be preached, and surely we are to participate in the process. But the second coming is not dependent upon us, for the greatest explosion of evangelism this world has ever seen will not take place until after we're gone. Revelation 7 tells us that after the Rapture, 144,000 Jewish evangelists will be anointed. Moses and perhaps Elijah will come back on the scene, working miracles and calling down fire from Heaven. An angel will fly across the sky saying, "Don't be fooled by Antichrist's system. Don't take the mark of the beast."

Matthew 24:15, 16 (a)
When ye therefore shall see the abomina-
tion of desolation, spoken of by Daniel the
prophet, stand in the holy place, (whoso
readeth, let him understand:) Then let them
which be in Judaea flee . . .

Verse 15 begins the second section of Matthew
24. Jesus had spoken of the nations in verses 1–
14. In verses 15–36, He will speak of the Jews.
Speaking to the Jews, Jesus says very pointedly,
"When you see the event spoken of by the
prophet Daniel, called the abomination of desolation, run to the wilderness as fast as you can. Get
out! Things are coming down!" What is the abomination of desolation? There are two parts to this
cataclysmic event—one historic, one prophetic.

Daniel 11:31 speaks of the historic aspect of the
abomination of desolation in reference to a tragic
event in Jewish history. Following the reign of Alexander the Great, a king named Antiochus Epiphanes ruled Syria. He was an egomaniacal madman
who believed he was the embodiment of the Greek
god Zeus. When Antiochus realized that the Jews
in Israel were not acknowledging him as God, he
became enraged and ordered the destruction of
Jerusalem. Thus, on a single day in 170 B.C., one
hundred thousand Jewish males were slaughtered,
the women raped, the city looted. Then Antiochus himself entered the temple, butchered a
pig on the altar, and forced the priests to drink its
blood and eat the raw pork. Finally, he smeared the
remainder of the blood on the temple walls. It
was the abomination of desolation for it was
abominable and it left the people desolate.

The second aspect, an event yet to happen, is
prophesied in Daniel 9:27. In the last days, a man
will come on the scene who will make a seven-
year peace treaty with Israel. Appearing to be her
friend and protector, this leader will seem to de-
fuse all of the problems in the Middle East. He will
be charismatic and persuasive, an impressive intellectual, and a skilled orator. Called Antichrist
in Scripture, he will capture the attention of the
entire world. Although he will initially come across
as a man of peace, in the middle of his seven-year
peace treaty, 2 Thessalonians 2 tells us he will set
up his image in the temple and demand to be worshipped as God. This second abomination will result in desolation across this planet. Jesus said,
"When you see this happen—Run!" Where?

Matthew 24:16 (b)
. . . into the mountains.

Zechariah declares that following the abomination of desolation, the Jews will indeed flee.
But only one-third of them will make it to safety

(Zechariah 13:8, 9). Tragically, two-thirds of the
Jewish nation will be caught in the flood of persecution that will follow Antichrist's declaration of
war against them. The violence and bloodshed
will be staggering—beyond anything this world
has ever seen. Most Bible teachers believe the remainder of the Jews will run to the ancient city of
Petra. Located in present-day Jordan, Petra is a
mysterious, miraculous city indeed. . . .

In approximately 2000 B.C., Esau settled in a
volcanic crater that was approximately a mile
in length. It was an incredibly secure place, for
to get into the crater, one had to go through a
narrow canyon only twelve feet wide in many
places with a rock face between two hundred
feet and one thousand feet high on either side.
The entire city could be easily guarded by only
fifteen soldiers marching along the ridges above
its narrow entrance. Thus, the descendants of
Esau, called the Edomites, dwelt in this city of
Petra for centuries, believing they were invin-
cible. Over the years, they constructed an archi-
tectural phenomenon. Carved right into the rock
are amphitheatres, banks, temples, and an aq-
ueduct system that baffles scientists to this day.
With a population of one million, no one can
figure out how they got enough water into the
city to sustain the inhabitants. The Edomites
were a proud people who trusted in their for-
tress, rested in their cliff city, and had no need
of Jehovah. So Obadiah came on the scene in
the name of the Lord and said they would fall.
And guess what. They did. The city began to
weaken when it was struck with a plague. Even-
tually, the Edomites were wiped out entirely.

For many years, people heard stories about the
rock city of Petra. Bible teachers would talk about
it, but in most people's minds, it had been relegated
to the same status as the lost city of Atlantis—a
mythological place that never really existed.

In 1812, however, a Bible teacher/explorer/ad-
venturer named Johann Burckhardt was determined to find Petra. And when he finally did, he
couldn't believe what he saw, for although it had
been abandoned for centuries and remains desolate to this day, he was amazed by its grandeur
and splendor. Perhaps most arresting, however,
were the two huge eagles' wings carved into the
rock at the very entrance of the city, for the
Book of Revelation declares that the remnant
of Israel will be saved by the wings of an eagle
(Revelation 12:14). A number of years ago, W. E.
Blackstone, another Bible teacher, was so convinced that Petra will be the place in which the
Jews are kept safe, he purchased thousands of
Hebrew New Testaments, underlined passages

like Matthew 24 and Revelation 12, and left them in earthen jars throughout Petra. When the Jews get there, the Bibles will be waiting for them. I love it!

Matthew 24:17
Let him which is on the housetop not come down to take any thing out of his house.

You might be thinking, *What is this about a housetop? How many times are we on our roofs?* Remember, this section is speaking to the Jews, and in Israel even to this day, people relax on roof-top decks.

Matthew 24:18–21
Neither let him which is in the field return back to take his clothes. And woe unto them that are with child, and to them that give suck in those days! But pray ye that your flight be not in the winter, neither on the sabbath day: For then shall be great tribulation, such as was not since the beginning of the world to this time, no, nor ever shall be.

Pray that the abomination of desolation doesn't come on the Sabbath day. Why? Because in Israel, transportation comes to a standstill on the Sabbath. This is another indication that Jesus is speaking to the Jews. It wouldn't matter if the abomination of desolation came on the Sabbath in our country. Sadly, our nation treats the Sabbath no differently than any other day.

Matthew 24:22
And except those days should be shortened, there should no flesh be saved: but for the elect''s sake those days shall be shortened.

The final three -and -one-half years after Antichrist reveals his true nature in the temple and the Jews flee to the wilderness will be a time of disaster, destruction, and death unlike any other in history. Here, Jesus is saying that unless the days were shortened, no one would survive them. The entire world would be annihilated. But God will shorten those days for the elect's sake. And here is where controversy arises.

There are those who say that since the church is called "the elect," the church must be in the Tribulation period. Mark this down, students of prophecy: In passages such as Isaiah 45:4; 65:9; and Romans 11:28, God specifically calls Israel "His elect." It's not just Christians who are called "the elect." In fact, there are three groups in the Bible who are called by that name: Israel, the church, and those saved in the Tribulation. Keep in mind that in verses 15–36—with references to

Judaea, the Sabbath, and the temple—Jesus is still speaking to Israel.

Matthew 24:23–27
Then if any man shall say unto you, Lo, here is Christ, or there; believe it not. For there shall arise false Christs, and false prophets, and shall shew great signs and wonders; insomuch that, if it were possible, they shall deceive the very elect. Behold, I have told you before. Wherefore if they shall say unto you, Behold, he is in the desert; go not forth: behold, he is in the secret chambers; believe it not. For as the lightning cometh out of the east, and shineth even unto the west; so shall also the coming of the Son of man be.

False spiritual leaders will come on the scene, saying, "We have found Messiah. He's in the desert," or "He's over here," or "He's over there." Jesus said, "Don't believe any of them. When I truly come, it will be like lightning. It will be obvious to everyone." He didn't say, "I'm coming again to Brooklyn in 1921 to reveal Myself to the Watchtower Society." He didn't say, "I'm coming again in the late 1800s to reveal Myself through magic spectacles to Joseph Smith." No. He said, "When I come, it will be like lightning. *Everyone* will see Me."

Matthew 24:28
For wheresoever the carcase is, there will the eagles [vultures] be gathered together.

Here, Jesus makes an allusion to the battle of Armageddon that is further illuminated in Revelation 19. When the nations of the world come together for war in the Valley of Megiddo, carcasses will indeed abound and vultures will follow. So, too, the world system with all its pride, pomposity, and prowess will become nothing more than a dead carcass. No matter how much progress we might make politically, the system will always be corrupt because of depravity. Things are wrong in society, and the answer lies not in capitalism, socialism, or communism. The answer is not democracy, oligarchy, or anarchy. The only answer is the return of Jesus Christ.

Matthew 24:29, 30
Immediately after the tribulation of those days shall the sun be darkened, and the moon shall not give her light, and the stars shall fall from heaven, and the powers of the heavens shall be shaken: And then shall appear the sign of the Son of man in heaven: and then shall all the tribes of the earth mourn, and they shall see the Son of man coming in the clouds of heaven with power and great glory.

Why will the tribes of the earth mourn? Zechariah tells us that when Israel looks at Jesus and sees the wounds in His hands, the Jews will say, "Where did You get those wounds?"

"I received these in the house of My friends," He will answer (Zechariah 13:6).

And Israel will mourn as they look upon the One they have pierced.

Matthew 24:31
And he shall send his angels with a great sound of a trumpet, and they shall gather together his elect from the four winds, from one end of heaven to the other.

The angels shall gather the elect. Which elect? The Jews. Remember, Jesus is still dealing with Israel in this section. In 1948, something took place that had never before happened in history: a nation was re-birthed. A nation that hadn't existed for almost two thousand years was suddenly re-established exactly as the Old Testament prophesied when Jews from all over the world gathered in Israel once again. But their gathering has not been even close to complete. For example, more Jews live in New York City than live in the entire nation of Israel. And even though thousands of Russian Jews immigrated into Israel each week in the wake of the fall of the iron curtain, most of them immediately sought to leave Israel for New York. When Jesus comes back again, there will be a *complete* re-gathering. When will that happen? Look at verse 32.

Matthew 24:32–35
Now learn a parable of the fig tree; When his branch is yet tender, and putteth forth leaves, ye know that summer is nigh: So likewise ye, when ye shall see all these things, know that it is near, even at the doors. Verily I say unto you, This generation shall not pass, till all these things be fulfilled. Heaven and earth shall pass away, but my words shall not pass away.

The fig tree is the symbol of Israel nationally, historically, and scripturally. On May 14, 1948, the fig tree blossomed once again when the land of Israel was returned to the Jews. Jesus said the generation that sees that event take place will not pass away. Who is that generation? We are.

For topical study of Matthew 24:32–35 entitled "The Final Generation," turn to page 179.

Matthew 24:36
But of that day and hour knoweth no man, no, not the angels of heaven, but my Father only.

Jesus used the budding fig tree as an example of what to watch for regarding His return, for although no one will know the exact day and hour of His arrival, Paul tells us we will recognize the times and seasons (1 Thessalonians 5:1).

Matthew 24:37
But as the days of Noah were, so shall also the coming of the Son of man be.

Like Noah, you and I are end times believers. Noah lived before the Flood, we before the fire. Noah spoke of coming rain, we of the coming reign. And just as it was in Noah's day, so it will be in the day of Jesus' coming. What was it like in Noah's day? In Genesis 6, we see four parallels between Noah's day and the days in which we live.

In the days of Noah, there was a population explosion (Genesis 6:1). Due to the fact that in Noah's day, men lived for eight or nine hundred years, there were probably five to six billion people on the planet during the time of the Flood.

In the days of Noah, abnormal sexual practices abounded (Genesis 6:4). Most Bible scholars believe that Genesis 6:4 is a reference to fallen angels having sexual relationships with human women. So, too, we live in a time of abnormal sexual practices. Things that were unthinkable a generation ago are now commonplace and accepted.

When the hierarchy of the Episcopal Church is encouraging homosexual union as a pathway to personal holiness (*Newsweek: 2/90*), we are indeed living in dark, dark days.

In Noah's day, the imagination of man was evil continually (Genesis 6:5). Seeing that men's hearts were only evil continually, God decided to lovingly put them out of their misery. Thus, the Flood accomplished quickly and mercifully the destruction their sin and perversion would bring about inevitably. So, too, the imagination of people in our society is evil continually—as evidenced by the fact that in our country, legal pornography is now a multi-billion dollar industry.

In Noah's day, violence filled the earth (Genesis 6:11). I read recently that the high rate of suicide among policemen is attributed to the fact that of the thousands of violent crimes committed in this country, only a handful of criminals are brought to justice. No wonder policemen are frustrated and suicidal. Violence runs rampant, while justice is hamstrung.

Matthew 24:38
For as in the days that were before the flood they were eating and drinking, marrying

and giving in marriage, until the day that Noah entered into the ark.

Although Noah had been pounding on his ark and preaching to the people for one hundred and twenty years, they didn't listen. Since it had never rained on the planet before, they must have thought Noah was all wet.

Matthew 24:39–41
And knew not until the flood came, and took them all away; so shall also the coming of the Son of man be. Then shall two be in the field; the one shall be taken, and the other left. Two women shall be grinding at the mill; the one shall be taken, and the other left.

This is a controversial passage. Many say Jesus is speaking of the judgment that will take place when He comes back to rule and reign in Jerusalem. However, I join those who believe Jesus is speaking not of judgment but of the Rapture. You see, the Greek word translated "took" in verse 39 is *airo*. But in verses 40 and 41, the word translated "taken" is *paralombano*. Why? Looking through my concordance, I find three other times *paralombano* is used. In Matthew 1:20, the angel told Joseph not to be afraid to *take* Mary as his bride: In Matthew 17:1, Jesus *took* Peter, James, and John with Him up the Mount of Transfiguration. In John 14:3, Jesus said, "I will come again and *take* you unto Myself, that where I am there ye may be also." And I begin to see a pattern. Using *paralombano*, Jesus is not talking about judgment, punishment, and damnation.

He's talking about a bride, glory, and Heaven. In other words, He's talking about the Rapture.

Matthew 24:42–51
Watch therefore: for ye know not what hour your Lord doth come. But know this, that if the goodman of the house had known in what watch the thief would come, he would have watched, and would not have suffered his house to be broken up. Therefore be ye also ready: for in such an hour as ye think not the Son of man cometh. Who then is a faithful and wise servant, whom his lord hath made ruler over his household, to give them meat in due season? Blessed is that servant, whom his lord when he cometh shall find so doing. Verily I say unto you, That he shall make him ruler over all his goods. But and if that evil servant shall say in his heart, My lord delayeth his coming; and shall begin to smite his fellowservants, and to eat and drink with the drunken; the lord of that servant shall come in a day when he looketh not for him, and in an hour that he is not aware of, and shall cut him asunder, and appoint him his portion with the hypocrites: there shall be weeping and gnashing of teeth.

In light of the end times, Jesus instructs us to be faithful servants—to be watchful, wise, and warned concerning our Master's return.

For topical study of Matthew 24:42–51 entitled "Being Watchful, Wise, Warned," turn to page 184.

ENDURING THROUGH TRIBULATION

A Topical Study of
Matthew 24:13

Matthew 24:13 is not only applicable prophetically but also presently, for in this world, Jesus said we would have tribulations. Our Christian life is a race to be run (Hebrews 12:1). And that race, dear people, is not a one hundred-meter sprint. It's a marathon.

But he that shall endure unto the end, the same shall be saved.
Matthew 24:13

The Greek word translated "saved" is *sozo,* a word that refers to the full orb of God's blessing. In other words, according to Matthew 24:13, those who endure the marathon will experience the blessing of God upon themselves, their families, their ministries, their finances, and their vocations. They will experience the full orb of God's blessing in every area of their lives.

The Call to Endurance

In the fifth chapter of his book, James picks up on the theme of enduring to the end . . .

Behold, we count them happy which endure. Ye have heard of the patience of Job, and have seen the end of the Lord; that the Lord is very pitiful [compassionate], and of tender mercy.   James 5:11

This passage brings a question to our minds: "Lord, if You are merciful and compassionate, then why do You allow troubles to come against us and problems to plague us? Why don't You do something, Lord?"

James says, "Remember Job. Remember the heroes of the Old Testament. Don't lose sight of their example." There was one prophet who felt exceedingly weary. His name was Jeremiah. Jeremiah's problems were mounting on all sides, and he was about to throw in the towel as far as ministry was concerned. "Jeremiah," the Lord said to him, "you have run against the footmen and if you faint in running against the footmen, how will you run against the horses? You've been engaged in some battles. But if you're fainting now, what will you do when the horses come, when the big problems hit you?" (see Jeremiah 12:5). The Lord went on to tell him that the Babylonians were coming to carry the Jews out of their homeland. It's as if God said, "You think it's tough now, Jeremiah, but I see what's coming, and I am preparing you by allowing you to go through these difficulties and trials. I'm allowing you to go through hard times to prepare you for what I know lies ahead."

If God used hard times to prepare Jeremiah for the Babylonians, why didn't He save Himself and Jeremiah a lot of trouble and just destroy the Babylonians in the first place? For the same reason He doesn't destroy the problems in our lives: because this world has rejected His rule. Ever since the Garden of Eden, mankind has thumbed his nose at God and demanded liberation, saying, "We will do what we want."

It is because all of humanity throughout all of history has rebelled against God that we have disease and death, pollution and war, troubles and problems. Not only in the world generally, but in our worlds personally, whenever you and I rebel against the way of God, we reap devastation, destruction, and sadness. The Father does not promise to keep us *from* problems, but to be with us *in* them. Since He sees what is coming two years down the road, He says, "I see what's ahead and I'm going to work with you right now to get you ready. I'm going to have you race against the footmen so that when the horses come stampeding through, you'll be able to endure."

I think of Mama giraffe. When she gives birth, she does so from a standing position. This means when Baby giraffe is born, he immediately falls on his head ten feet to the ground. Mama then does something that absolutely intrigues me. After quickly stretching her neck down to check Baby's condition, she stands upright once again, swings her front leg, and kicks him. Baby then tries to stand up, wobbles, and falls to the ground in exhaustion. No sooner does Baby collapse than Mama winds up her leg and kicks him once more. This happens, three, four, or five times until Baby finally musters up enough strength—the adrenaline flowing and terror filling his heart—to stand up.

Once Baby gets up on all fours, Mama again swings her leg and kicks his legs out from under him. And the process is repeated two, three, or four more times. The result? Within the first hour of his life, Baby learns how to get up quickly and to move away from Mama readily. Why does Mama giraffe do this? She's not trying to be mean, but she instinctively understands that leopards, lions, hyenas, and jackals were watching the birth of her baby. Because giraffes are defenseless if they cannot move together in a pack, Baby must learn quickly how to stand up and get moving—even if it means getting mad at Mama and not understanding what she's doing.

Maybe you can relate. "What are you doing, God?" you might be asking. "I just barely get up and BAM! I'm down again. I just get going and BOOM! I'm flat on my face once more. What's happening?" The Lord is teaching you something. He loves you and me enough that even though we misunderstand Him, shake our fist at Him, or turn our back on Him, He says, "I know this is needed in your life in order that you might stand and be established, in order that you might be able to run with the horses, in order that you might endure."

The Key to Endurance

God is with us. That is the secret of endurance.

> *By faith Moses, when he was come to years, refused to be called the son of Pharaoh's daughter; choosing rather to suffer affliction with the people of God, than to enjoy the pleasures of sin for a season; esteeming the reproach of Christ greater riches than the treasures in Egypt: for he had respect unto the recompence of the reward.*   Hebrews 11:24–26

Having grown up in Pharaoh's court, Moses was in line to ascend the very throne of Pharaoh. Yet he chose instead to take on the reproach of Christ, for it was a greater treasure than the best Egypt had to offer. I like that! Sure, we go through suffering and reproach, tribulations and difficulties. But even they are better than the best the world has to offer us, with its heartache, disappointment, and disillusionment.

At forty years of age, Moses said, "I would rather be with God's people and suffer than remain in this place where the pleasures of sin are for but a season."

And he split the scene. Then he began to lead the people out of Egypt. For forty years, he led them through the wilderness. It wasn't easy. It was hot and dry. You think you're going through dry times? Think of Moses! You think people don't like you? Scripture says three million Jews rose up as a single man with rocks in hand, ready to stone him (Exodus 17:4).

How did Moses make it? How did he endure the rejection, dry times, and constant troubles from within and without? Look at verse 27: "By faith he forsook Egypt, not fearing the wrath of the king: for he endured as seeing him who is invisible." In other words, Moses saw God's hand in every situation.

> Several years ago, I talked with a lady who was devastated. She was ready to leave everything to marry a man who lived across the country. Although she hadn't known him very long, she felt it was providential. But the day before she was to leave, she discovered some things about him that indicated he had some serious problems. She had packed her goods, cut all her ties, and sold her business only to discover a day before the wedding that it wasn't going to happen. I understood her feeling of disappointment as she wondered, *What's the Lord doing? Where is He? Why is He allowing this to happen to me?*

In response, I told her it would be like if I had come home and seen my daughter Christy unwrapping a king-size Snickers bar. As she was just about to take a big bite, I lunged at her, grabbed the Snickers from her, and threw it to the floor, saying, "Christy, haven't you heard the news? Every Snickers in Oregon has been laced with arsenic. One bite will kill you!" Now, at that point, Christy would either have said, "Oh, Dad, I was just ready to enjoy that Snickers bar, and you took it from me. How mean!" Or she could say, "Oh, Daddy, thanks for rescuing me! You knew something I didn't. You saved my life!"

So, too, when the Father intervened in that lady's situation, she had a choice to make. She could have said, "Why is this happening to me?" Or she could have seen Him who is invisible, seen His hand in everything, and said, "Father, thank You for grabbing the Snickers from me. You caught me just in time!"

Dear saint, you have a choice to make right now in whatever you're going through. You can either shrivel up and fade away like the shallow seed in Mark 4, or you can endure, seeing God's hand in everything and everything in His hand.

Look at God's hand, and what will you see? A nail print. The invisible God became a visible Man in Christ Jesus. And as I see His nail-scarred hand, I have no choice but to say, "If You loved me enough to be pinned to the Cross for me and to plunge into hell for me, I will trust You, even though I may not understand what's happening presently."

What is faith? According to Hebrews 11, it is the substance of things hoped for, the evidence of things not seen. There is no such thing as "blind faith." On the contrary, faith sees more than unbelief ever will because it sees into an entirely different dimension. "Through faith we understand that the worlds were framed by the Word of God, so that things which are seen were not made of things which do appear" (see Hebrews 11:3).

The Hebrew word for create is *bara*, which means "to make something out of that which does not exist previously." In other words, God made everything from nothing. It wasn't that He refashioned material that already existed, but rather that He started "from scratch" when He spoke the worlds into existence. So, too, the world in which you live personally—your children, your job, your ministry, your marriage, and your finances—is presently being framed. You are framing your world, even as God framed this world by speaking the Word.

Think of a carpenter framing a house. The house is formed by how it's framed. Maybe you have framed your world with unbelief and griping, complaining and doubting, saying, "Why me? How come? Where's God?" Maybe you don't like the house you live in because the walls are falling down, the tiles are falling off, and it's a miserable place to live. Don't blame God. You built it. You framed it with complaints, cynicism and faltering faith. We have another option. We can say, "By faith I will frame my world with the Word of God. I will study the Scriptures. I will claim the promises and speak them in faith."

> And we know that all things work together for good to them that love God, to them who are the called according to his purpose.   Romans 8:28

> . . . For the joy of the LORD is your strength.   Nehemiah 8:10

> But my God shall supply all your need according to his riches in glory by Christ Jesus.   Philippians 4:19

Today I can build a house trusting God, seeing Him who is invisible, and believing His promises—or I can murmur to my wife when I get home. God judged the nation of Israel because they murmured in their tents (Deuteronomy 1:27). Husbands and wives got together, spoke words of complaint and unbelief to each other, and a great plague struck the land.

Speak the promises of God to each other. Go on record. Build a world that is in accordance with the Word of God as revealed in Scripture. Speak words of faith, and you'll endure.

Winston Churchill, 248 pounds of solid inspiration, saw England through Germany's blitzkrieg. As the Third Reich dropped thousands of bombs on London, Hitler felt, as did other international observers, that England would fall easily. But this bulldog of a man, Winston Churchill, went on the air time and time again, calling his nation to hang on and to believe. And England didn't go down.

Years later, one of his alma maters, an exclusive prep school, asked him to speak at graduation. When he accepted the invitation, the headmaster of the school was elated. For weeks he told the student body, "Soon Winston Churchill is coming. The most powerful orator in history is going to speak here. When he comes, bring your pencils and paper and take note of every word he says." Finally the day came. The graduation service began. The students, sitting behind the speakers' podium, had pencils and paper poised. The parents and guests settled in for a long, inspirational speech. After many flowery introductions, Churchill finally arose from his chair, took the podium, and turned around to address the young men behind him.

"Gentlemen," he said, "Never give up. Never give up. Never, never, never, never, give up."

Then he sat down. The students were stunned. The audience was amazed. And none of them ever, ever, ever forgot it.

That's what Jesus says to us. Never give up. He that endures to the end shall be saved.

So when the Father seems to be kicking your wobbly legs out from under you or when you seem to be running hard against the footmen, know this: It's all working for your ultimate salvation. Endure, gang, by seeing the invisible. Endure by framing your world with faith.

And never give up.

THE FINAL GENERATION
A Topical Study of
Matthew 24:32–35

Written by a then-unknown author named Hal Lindsay, *The Late Great Planet Earth* exposed an entire generation to the concepts of the Rapture of the church and the return of Jesus Christ. It was foundational to the Jesus Movement of the '70s, which started on the West Coast, spread across the country, and eventually circled the globe. Lindsay and other teachers of prophecy during that time stressed this teaching in Matthew 24. The parable of the fig tree enflamed the hearts of an entire generation—for Jesus said the budding of the fig tree signaled His impending return.

What is the budding of the fig tree? Scripture interprets Scripture. Thus, Jeremiah, Joel, Hosea, and others identify the fig tree as the nation Israel. For centuries, Israel seemed to be a dead tree. In the year A.D. 70, the Romans marched into Jerusalem, destroyed the city, and took over the country. The Jews scattered every direction in fulfillment of Deuteronomy 28:64–67. But in addition to saying the Jews would be scattered throughout the world, God also said, "But The Lord liveth, which brought up and which led the seed of the house of Israel out of the north country, and from all countries whither I had driven them; and they shall dwell in their own land" (Jeremiah 23:8).

You see, when the Jews were scattered, something happened historically that had never happened previously in world history. Without a homeland, the Jewish people kept their identity, religion, and ethnicity intact. No other nation in the history of the world has ever done that. Every other country swallowed by another has become assimilated by the conquering culture within two generations. That is why you never hear of Babylonians today and why none of you have Assyrian neighbors. The Jews kept their identity—not for two generations, but for two thousand years. Through wave after wave of persecution, prejudice and bigotry, Satan was relentless in his attempt to destroy them. But he failed.

Satan's plans always backfire. In the aftermath of the Holocaust, the world said, "The Jews deserve a land of their own. World sympathy was with the Jewish people for the first and only time in history. So it was that on May 14, 1948, Israel became a nation again. The fig tree that had appeared to be dead and hopeless suddenly sprang back to life and blossomed—just as Jesus prophesied. And, according to Matthew 24:34, the generation that saw that happen would be the final generation.

What constitutes a generation? Hal Lindsay and others taught that a Biblical generation could be a thirty-eight to forty-year time period.

And the Lord's anger was kindled against Israel, and he made them wander in the wilderness forty years, until all the generation, that had done evil in the sight of the LORD, was consumed.   Numbers 32:13

And the space in which we came from Kadesh-barnea, until we were come over the brook Zered, was thirty and eight years; until all the generation of the men of war were wasted out from among the host, as the LORD sware unto them.   Deuteronomy 2:14

Thus, anticipation grew. Excitement and expectancy filled the hearts of many, for if you add forty years to 1948—and if you believe the rapture of the Church takes place seven years before the return of Jesus, the Rapture would take place in 1980 or 1981. Truly the time was near! T-shirts, bumper stickers, and posters were printed. Maranatha—"Come quickly, Lord"—became the watchword of believers. 1981 came. So did 1982, '83, '84, '85, and '86. And then something began to happen. A whole bunch of radical Christians began to cool off, saying, "Maybe we're here for a while after all. Maybe we shouldn't be so committed to this kingdom thing."

Oh, they didn't say it in those exact words, but that's what they were thinking. And a dulling of expectancy swept over our generation.

What went wrong? Perhaps forty years is not the figure we should work with when looking at a Biblical generation. Take a look at Genesis 15 . . .

And he said unto Abram, Know of a surety that thy seed shall be a stranger in a land that is not theirs, and shall serve them; and they shall afflict them four hundred years; and also that nation, whom they shall serve, will I judge: and afterward shall they come out with great substance. But in the fourth generation they shall come hither again. . . .   Genesis 15:13, 14, 16

Here in Genesis 15, God refers to the four-hundred-year period the Jews were in Egypt as four generations. Therefore, in this model, a generation is not forty years but one hundred years. If a generation is one hundred years, am I suggesting that the Rapture will take place in 2048—one hundred years after the rebirth of the nation of Israel? No. I suggest it will be before then. You see, there is a principle in Bible interpretation called the Principle of First Mention that says foundational understanding about any given subject is usually found in the first place it is mentioned in Scripture. Where is the Greek term, "generation" first mentioned? In Matthew 1:17 we read: So all the generations from Abraham to David are fourteen generations; and from David until the carrying away into Babylon are fourteen generations; and from the carrying away into Babylon unto Christ are fourteen generations.

Sharpen your pencils and think with me: Christian and Jewish theologians alike agree that, based on Biblical genealogies, Abraham was called by God in the year 2085 B.C. Genesis 2 tells us he was seventy-five years old at that time, which means Abraham was born in 2160 B.C. Matthew 1:17 tells us there were forty-two generations (14x3) from Abraham to Christ. So, if you divide 2160—the year of Abraham's birth—by 42, you get 51.4. Thus, scripturally, there is validity for a Biblical generation to be 51.4 years.

Jesus told us that no man knows the day or the hour of His return. But of the times and season we are not to be ignorant (1 Thessalonians 5:1). Hebrews 10:25 says we are not to forsake assembling ourselves together so much the more as we see that day coming. 1 Thessalonians tells us that the return of Christ will surprise the world but not us (1 Thessalonians 5:5).

But, beloved, be not ignorant of this one thing, that one day is with the Lord as a thousand years, and a thousand years as one day.   2 Peter 3:8

From the Lord's perspective, one thousand years equals one day and one day equals one thousand years. This answers a lot of questions. For example, God told Adam that the day he ate of the forbidden fruit he would surely die. Yet Adam lived to be 938 years old. Why? From God's perspective, a day being a thousand years,

Adam died towards the end of the "day" in which he sinned. God kept His promise perfectly.

From this perspective, the early church fathers taught that the Genesis account of creation is not only history, but prophecy. God worked for six days. So, too, this world will work for six thousand years. On the seventh day of creation, God rested. So, too, in the seven thousandth year, there will come a one thousand-year period of time called the millennium when there will be rest and peace.

When is the seven thousandth year? When will Christ return?

In the year 1670, a brilliant thinker and theologian, Archbishop Usher, made some calculations that have withstood computer confirmation. By adding the years of the genealogy in Genesis, he calculated that Adam appeared on the scene in 4004 B.C.

"Wait a minute," you say. "It is well known that man has been on the earth for multiplied millions of years. How can you say that the first man appeared only six thousand years ago?"

Science is not at all committed to an ancient earth theory any longer.

Dr. Stuart Ross, a brilliant astronomer and thinker, but not a believer, wrote a book entitled *The Lunar Silence—A Post-Apollo View,* in which he makes a number of fascinating observations, among them the following. . . .

> In our first manned shot to the moon about twenty years ago Neil Armstrong stepped on to the moon's surface saying, "One small step for man, one giant leap for mankind." Did you ever wonder why it was that he had to climb so far down from the module to actually set foot on the moon? Why was the module perched twenty-five feet off the moon's surface? Ross writes that scientists, believing the moon to be 4.6 billion years old, were convinced that the accumulation of meteorite dust on the moon's surface would be at least two thousand and perhaps as much as twenty thousand feet deep. After all, if you didn't dust your house for 4.6 billion years, what would your house look like? So, twenty-five-foot legs with big cushions were constructed in order that the module could compact the dust as it landed and not sink indefinitely into a sea of meteorite powder. Imagine the scientists' surprise when they watched the lunar module set down without sinking a bit. In fact, the greatest depth of lunar dust measured thus far is two inches. Consequently, a number of scientists, including Dr. Stuart Ross, are now saying the moon can be no more than ten thousand years old.

On the other hand, even if you opt for an ancient earth, I still believe that the genealogies of Genesis take you back accurately to 4000 B.C.—or six thousand years ago. Genesis 1:1 says, "In the beginning God created the heaven and the earth." Genesis 1:2 says, "And the earth was without form, and void." The Hebrew translation of "without form and void" is *tohuw va bohuw,* which means "chaotic, turned upside-down, emptied."

Isaiah 45:18, however, says ". . . God himself that formed the earth and made it; he hath established it, he created it not in vain." In other words, He created the earth *with* form.

Is this a contradiction? No. Along with many Bible scholars, I believe a cataclysmic event occurred between Genesis 1:1 and Genesis 1:2. I believe it was between these two verses that Lucifer, the highest angel in Heaven, launched a rebellion against God and was cast out of Heaven. And it was when he fell to earth that the earth became "tohuw va bohuw." So God recreated the earth. That's why, in Genesis 1:28, He told Adam to replenish and subdue the earth (Genesis 1:28). Subdue it from whom? From Satan, who had set up his headquarters on this planet.

Whether you espouse an "old earth" theory or a much younger earth theory, the genealogies of Genesis meet with no scientific contradiction. Adam made his entrance in 4000 B.C. What does this mean? The answer is found in the Book of Hosea. . . .

> Come, and let us return unto the LORD: for he hath torn, and he will heal us; he hath smitten, and he will bind us up. After two days will he revive us: in the third day he will raise us up, and we shall live in his sight. Hosea 6:1, 2

Writing of the End Times, Hosea says for two days the Jewish people will go through hard, tearing, difficult times. But on the third day, they will be revived. Thus, the calculation is complete:

Day 1	Adam is created	4000 B.C.
Day 4	The coming of Jesus Christ	A.D. 1
Days 5–6	Israel goes through hard times	A.D. 1–2000
Day 7	Israel revived during millennium	A.D. 2000

I am not alone in this interpretation.

In A.D. 150, Iranius wrote concerning the Book of Genesis: "This is an account of things formerly created as it is also a prophecy of things which are yet to come, for the day of the Lord is as one thousand years. And in six days, created things were completed. It is evident, therefore, they will come to an end at the end of six thousand years." Lactanius said this in A.D. 300: "Because all the works of God were finished in six days, it is necessary that the world should remain in this state for six thousand years. Because having finished works, He rested on the seventh day and blessed it, it is necessary then, at the end of the six thousandth year, wickedness should be abolished out of the earth and righteousness should then reign

for one thousand years."God's week of human history is rapidly coming to completion. The return of Christ is nigh.

I believe you who are in your teens and early twenties are very possibly the
last generation. Set your heart on things above. Live for heaven. Seek first the kingdom, and you will be happy presently, rewarded eternally, and grateful constantly.

You who are older, continue setting an example for us who are younger. Continue to make the Lord top priority in your life. We're looking to you in a very real
sense. Please keep the fire hot.

Fellow baby boomers, we need to realize that Jesus Christ is coming soon. We
don't have time to play around. We don't have time to chase worldly pursuits any
longer. We need to return to ministry and service, worship and prayer, Bible study
and street witnessing. Whatever it was you used to do when you were fired up about
Jesus in the '70s, do it again.

Maranatha!

BEING WATCHFUL, WISE, WARNED
A Topical Study of
Matthew 24:42–49

After giving His disciples information concerning the end times, Jesus now
gives them inspiration for all times. You see, prophecy is not given to titillate
our curiosity. Rather, prophecy should motivate us to sobriety.

An Exhortation to Be Watchful

*Watch therefore: for ye know not what hour your Lord doth come. But know
this, that if the goodman of the house had known in what watch the thief would
come, he would have watched, and would not have suffered his house to be
broken up. Therefore be ye also ready: for in such an hour as ye think not the
Son of man cometh.*   Matthew 24:42–44

When will Jesus come?
If you're not watching, He'll come when you least expect Him.

The story is told of a lady in Czechoslovakia who was in great despair. Having
recently discovered that her husband had been seeing another woman, she
stood on her fifth-floor balcony, wondering whether she should kill him or

whether she should take her own life. She decided to do the latter. She jumped. Little did she know that at that very moment, her husband was walking on the sidewalk directly below. She landed right on top of him. He died. She lived.

Watch! You never know who will be dropping in! You who are feeling despondent, discouraged, defeated, and depressed, know this: The Lord *is* coming! Watch!

An Exhortation to Be Wise

Who then is a faithful and wise servant, whom his lord hath made ruler over his household, to give them meat in due season? Blessed is that servant, whom his lord when he cometh shall find so doing. Verily I say unto you, That he shall make him ruler over all his goods.   Matthew 24:45–47

What are we to be doing in Jesus' absence? We are not to be sitting around, goofing off, or kicking back. Jesus says the wise servant is the one who is doing good.

"But my doing good doesn't seem to be doing any good," you say.

I heard the story of a man who lived in the North Beach section of San Francisco—an area known for sin and carnality of the worst sort. As he watched the neighborhood begin to sink into sin, he went out on the streets and, while the barkers were trying to pull people into their topless bars, he talked to people about Jesus. In the early '40s and '50s he even wore a sandwich sign with a gospel message neatly lettered on both sides. A few years ago, this precious old man was asked, "Why do you keep doing this? It's not doing any good."

"I may not be changing them," he said. "But I'm doing this lest they change me."

Truly, this was a wise servant.

An Exhortation to Be Warned

But and if that evil servant shall say in his heart, My lord delayeth his coming; And shall begin to smite his fellowservants, and to eat and drink with the drunken . . .   Matthew 24:48, 49

The word "evil" here is interesting. *Kakos* in Greek, it means "something that was once good but has gone bad." It's a word used to describe an instrument out of tune or a piece of fruit gone bad. How did this servant go bad? He simply tired of waiting for his master's return. His sense of urgency and expectancy was replaced with brutality and carnality.

First, brutality. You can tell when you are falling into the "evil servant" mentality when you begin to "smite your fellowservants," when you begin to beat up on people verbally and treat them unkindly. You see, if I am truly looking for the Lord's coming today, it will affect how I treat every person with whom I come in contact. I will treat my wife differently if I believe Jesus is coming back within the hour. I'll talk to the guys at work differently if I believe Jesus will show up there any moment. You won't push people around; you won't put people down; you won't beat people up if you believe Jesus is coming back soon.

Second, carnality. The evil servant began to "eat and drink with the drunken." That's why almost one-third of the Bible deals with prophecy and why prophecy can never be over-emphasized. Speaking of the coming of Jesus, the apostle John said, "And every man that hath this hope in him purifieth himself" (1 John 3:3a). Truly, I am blessed as I look at Applegate Christian Fellowship and see the process of purification taking place. The Lord is changing the congregation there. Why? Because they are looking for His coming. They may have had setbacks. They might yet have struggles. But year after year, decade after decade, we who are looking for His coming find ourselves saying, "Lord, I want to be ready. I want to put away those things with which I once flirted. I want to keep looking for You."

Folks, heavenly rewards are not going to be little medals to pin on our shirts or flimsy trophies to put on our shelves. No, our rewards will affect our very beings for all of eternity (1 Corinthians 15:40, 41, Daniel 12:3). That's why the Lord talked so much about His coming. That's why He gave us the Book of Revelation. Heaven is *real*, gang. And when you get there, my prayer is that you will hear the words, "Well done, good and faithful servant."

How can that happen? One way. Priority is the key. Even though there were still millions of people who were physically diseased and spiritually lost, Jesus said, "Father I have glorified thee and *finished* the work which thou hast given Me to do" (see John 17:4). How could Jesus say this? Because He finished the work *the Father* gave Him to do.

To make your life meaningful presently and to prepare for eternity, you must hear what the Father tells you to do instead of listening to the pressures and demands of people. Burdens from people and preachers, churches and organizations are heavy. But Jesus says, "My yoke is easy. My burden is light" (see Matthew 11:30).

In Ezekiel 44, God told the priests they were to wear no wool, lest it cause them to perspire. They were to wear only linen because He didn't want them "sweating" in their service for Him. The same is true for us. It is not the heart of our Father that we frantically try to meet every need and minister to every problem. We'll burn out in the process. Rather, it is His desire that we are faithful in the work *He* gives us to do.

How do we find out what His work for us is? Moses went to the mountain to meet the Lord and came down with the Commandments (Exodus 19:20). A great while before morning, Jesus would go to a solitary place to pray (Mark 1:35). Follow the example of Moses and Jesus and daily enter the presence of the Lord, saying, "Lord, guide my thoughts right now as I spend time in Your Word and talk about the day ahead with You."

He might say, "I want you to mow your neighbor's lawn." He might whisper, "Can you take an hour away from TV tonight and pray for the mission in Carmen Serdan?" His answer might be, "Write a letter to your brother." The Lord isn't cracking the whip, saying, "Do more. Get busy." No, He's saying, "Let Me guide you and lead you day by day."

That is why I encourage you to take time to seek Him each and every day in a quiet, solitary place. Like Moses, go to the mountain with tablet in hand and write down whatever He places on your heart. You won't be burdened by His requests. You won't get an ulcer. You won't even sweat. Yours will be a beautiful ministry that will be rewarded eternally if you focus on the work *He* gives you to do.

25 In chapter 25, Jesus closes His Olivet Discourse with a practical exhortation. Hear His heart as He says, "In light of end times understanding, there are three things you must consider: personal salvation (verses 1–13), responsible stewardship (verses 14–30), and practical servanthood" (verses 31–46).

Matthew 25:1–13

Then shall the kingdom of heaven be likened unto ten virgins, which took their lamps, and went forth to meet the bridegroom. And five of them were wise, and five were foolish. They that were foolish took their lamps, and took no oil with them: But the wise took oil in their vessels with their lamps. While the bridegroom tarried, they all slumbered and slept. And at midnight there was a cry made, Behold, the bridegroom cometh; go ye out to meet him. Then all those virgins arose, and trimmed their lamps. And the foolish said unto the wise, Give us of your oil; for our lamps are gone out. But the wise answered, saying, Not so; lest there be not enough for us and you: but go ye rather to them that sell, and buy for yourselves. And while they went to buy, the bridegroom came; and they that were ready went in with him to the marriage: and the door was shut. Afterward came also the other virgins, saying, Lord, Lord, open to us. But he answered and said, Verily I say unto you, I know you not. Watch therefore, for ye know neither the day nor the hour wherein the Son of man cometh.

In Jesus' day, although the day of a wedding was known in a community, the exact hour was unknown. The bridegroom could show up at his bride's house any time during the day or night. He could come in the morning, at noon, even at midnight. But as soon as he arrived at the house of the bride, word passed quickly that the bridegroom had come and the marriage was about to begin. The community would then accompany the bride and the bridegroom as they made their way to the ceremony.

In this parable, there were ten maidens. Ten is the Jewish number of completion, as illustrated by the fact that there were ten Commandments and that ten Jewish males in a community warranted a synagogue. But of the ten maidens, only five had oil for their lamps. And when the bridegroom came at midnight, the other five were left out of the procession. What is Jesus saying? He's saying that when He, the Bridegroom, comes for His bride at an unknown hour, some will be ready to join the procession but others will not because they lack oil in their lamps. Scripturally, oil is a symbol of the Holy Spirit. Thus, those not born of the Spirit will be left behind.

If the Rapture occurred tonight, I fear some of you would still be sitting here while the rest of us went up. Yes, you've been hanging out with the wedding party—but there's no oil in your vessel. We must realize that many who think they are going up in the wedding party will be left behind for lack of oil. I believe the heartbeat of Jesus revealed in this parable is one which should sober every person. In Luke 21:36, Jesus said, "Pray that you might be found worthy to be kept from the hour of tribulation"—the implication being that some who mistakenly thought they were part of the procession will go through that terrible time of tribulation.

I would rather see my own family and my church family soberly on our knees, saying, "Please, Lord, fill us with the oil of Your Spirit and seal our salvation," than to give anyone false assurance and have him miss the wedding party, lulled to sleep by a false theology. I would rather see a person come forward fifty times to make sure of his salvation than to have him think that because he sits in a pew he's going to heaven.

The story is told of a meeting Satan held with his demons, trying to figure out how to trick people into eternal damnation . . .

One demon said, "I've got a plan. Let's whisper in people's ears that there is no God."

"No," Satan said, "creation declares the reality of God. People are too smart to deny His existence. A few idiots might be sucked in, but not the masses."

"I've got it," a second demon said. "We'll say there's no hell."

"No," said Satan. "People innately understand the need for retribution and judgment. People won't buy that."

A third demon said, "Let me suggest how we might trick them. Instead of saying 'No God' or 'No Hell,' we'll just say 'No Hurry.'"

"That's it!" Satan said gleefully. And he commissioned his demons to go throughout the world whispering, "No hurry."

Many have lost their sense of urgency. But the cry will soon go forth: behold the bridegroom cometh! Brethren, give diligence to make your calling and election sure (2 Peter 1:10). Don't miss the party.

Matthew 25:14–30

For the kingdom of heaven is as a man travelling into a far country, who called his own servants, and delivered unto them his goods. And unto one he gave five talents, to another two, and to another one; to every man according to his several ability; and straightway took his journey. Then he that had received the five talents went and traded with the same, and made them other five talents. And likewise he that had received two, he also gained other two. But he that had received one went and digged in the earth, and hid his Lord's money. After a long time the lord of those servants cometh, and reckoneth with them. And so he that had received five talents came and brought other five talents, saying, Lord, thou deliveredst unto me five talents: behold, I have gained beside them five talents more. His lord said unto him, Well done, thou good and faithful servant: thou hast been faithful over a few things, I will make thee ruler over many things: enter thou into the joy of thy lord. He also that had received two talents came and said, Lord, thou deliveredst unto me two talents: behold, I have gained two other talents beside them. His lord said unto him, Well done, good and faithful servant; thou hast been faithful over a few things, I will make thee ruler over many things: enter thou into the joy of thy lord. Then he which had received the one talent came and said, Lord, I knew thee that thou art an hard man, reaping where thou hast not sown, and gathering where thou hast not strawed: And I was afraid, and went and hid thy talent in the earth: lo, there thou hast that is thine. His lord answered and said unto him, Thou wicked and slothful servant, thou knewest that I reap where I sowed not, and gather where I have not strawed: Thou oughtest therefore to have put my money to the exchangers, and then at my coming I should have received mine own with usury. Take therefore the talent from him, and give it unto him which hath ten talents. For unto every one that hath shall be given, and he shall have abundance: but from him that hath not shall be taken away even that which he hath. And cast ye the unprofitable servant into outer darkness: there shall be weeping and gnashing of teeth.

As with the previous parable, this situation would have been familiar to Jesus' audience. When the owner of a house went on a long journey, he would give his servants the responsibility of caring for his property. In this case, the owner gave varying sums of money to his servants before he left, a talent being a year's wage. Upon his return, he learned that the five-talent servant had doubled his investment. The two-talent servant did the same. But the one-talent servant, afraid to invest his talent, buried it. And the owner of the house rebuked him radically.

So, too, Jesus has gone away to heaven to prepare a place for us. In the meantime, He has given us talents—money, energy, and abilities. It's interesting to me that the fellow who didn't show responsibility was the one with only one talent. That's often where the danger lies with us as well. The person who realizes he has a great musical gift will more often than not develop his gift and seek to use it. But the person who says, "I can't sing. I can't preach. I can't do miracles," often buries his one talent, whatever it might be.

Precious people, we all have been given at least one talent. "Not me," you say. "I have no talents and no abilities. I can't do anything." Can you change a diaper? Sign up to help in the nursery. Can you listen? Call on people at the rest home.

Can you feed a child? Spend a month at a mission. You can do so much. The problem is, the one-talent person has a tendency to bury it. Here, Jesus is telling us that we will give an account for that which has been entrusted to us. If you are one who doesn't think you have been given much, you are one who needs to be especially careful that you don't bury that which you do have.

Matthew 25:31–46

When the Son of man shall come in his glory, and all the holy angels with him, then shall he sit upon the throne of his glory: And before him shall be gathered all nations: and he shall separate them one from another, as a shepherd divideth his sheep from the goats: And he shall set the sheep on his right hand, but the goats on the left. Then shall the King say unto them on his right hand, Come, ye blessed of my Father, inherit the kingdom prepared for you from the foundation of the world: For I was an hungred, and ye gave me meat: I was thirsty, and ye gave me drink: I was a stranger, and ye took me in: Naked, and ye clothed me: I was sick, and ye visited me: I was in prison, and ye came unto me. Then shall the righteous answer him, saying, Lord, when saw we thee an hungred, and fed thee? or thirsty, and gave thee drink? When saw we thee a stranger, and took thee in? or naked, and clothed thee? Or when saw we thee sick, or in prison, and came unto thee? And the King shall answer and say unto them, Verily I say unto you, Inasmuch as ye have done it unto one of the least of these my brethren, ye have done it unto me. Then shall he say also unto them on the left hand, Depart from me, ye cursed, into everlasting fire, prepared for the devil and his angels: For I was an hungred, and ye gave me no meat: I was thirsty, and ye gave me no drink: I was a stranger, and ye took me not in: naked, and ye clothed me not: sick, and in prison, and ye visited me not. Then shall they also answer him, saying, Lord, when saw we thee an hungred, or athirst, or a stranger, or naked, or sick, or in prison, and did not minister unto thee? Then shall he answer them, saying, Verily I say unto you, Inasmuch as ye did it not to one of the least of these, ye did it not to me. And these shall go away into everlasting punishment: but the righteous into life eternal.

In this parable, Jesus refers to the judgment of nations that will take place at the end of the Tribulation. According to Zechariah 14:4, when Jesus comes back to earth, the Mount of Olives will split in half the moment His feet touch down upon it. I found it interesting that contractors were denied a permit to build a hotel on the Mount of Olives

because seismological studies indicated a major fault running through it. When Jesus comes, that fault will split the mountain in half, a great valley will open up, and a new stream will begin to flow from the Dead Sea to the Mediterranean. Joel refers to this valley as the valley of decision (Joel 3:14) because those who survive the Tribulation will be brought there to stand before the Lord at the judgment of the nations. The sheep will be allowed to enter into the millennium. The goats will be sent away to destruction. Who are the sheep? "The ones who clothed Me; fed Me; and cared about Me," answers Jesus.

"When did we do that, Lord?" the sheep ask.

"When you did it to the least of My brethren—the Jews," Jesus answers.

You see, midway through the Tribulation, Antichrist's determination to destroy the Jews will come to light. All over the world, anti-Semitism will run rampant. At that time, however, many will refuse to take the mark of the beast and will help the Jews, even as some did in Nazi Germany. They will visit those in prison. They will hide those in need of protection. They will reach out to those who are hurting. They will go on record, saying, "We will not take the mark of the beast. We will stand with these persecuted people." Jesus said in so doing, they will demonstrate outwardly their faith in Him.

Years ago, I sat on a hill outside Galilee and watched a single shepherd boy lead a flock of sheep. It was a beautiful sight. Goats, on the other hand, are impossible to lead. They would rather butt heads and eat trash than follow anyone. Goats do what they want. I know those of us who have embraced Jesus Christ as Lord are all sheep, but I fear sometimes there's too much goat in me. May we be like sheep who travel as a flock following the Lord's leading.

———— ✑ ————

26

Matthew 26:1 (a)
And it came to pass, when Jesus had finished all these sayings . . .

Chapter 25 marked the end of the preaching and teaching ministry of Jesus Christ.

Matthew 26:1 (b), 2
. . . he said unto his disciples, Ye know that after two days is the feast of the passover, and the Son of man is betrayed to be crucified.

The Passover feast was a yearly event in Jerusalem commemorating the delivery of God's people from Egypt. Josephus tells us that in Jesus' day, 250,000 lambs were slaughtered in commemoration of Passover. Since Exodus prescribed that one lamb be sacrificed for every ten people, we can conclude that there must have been at least 2.5 million people in Jerusalem for this festival.

Between the hours of three and five o'clock, the 250,000 lambs would be slaughtered in the temple in preparation for Passover. Blood would have flowed freely from the temple into the Kidron Valley below the temple mount, causing the Kidron brook to actually turn blood-red. Later in this chapter, we will see Jesus leaving Gethsemane and crossing over this creek. Its color must have been a graphic reminder to Him of what was to come as He, the Lamb of God, would shed His own blood for our sin.

Matthew 26:3–5
Then assembled together the chief priests, and the scribes, and the elders of the people, unto the palace of the high priest, who was called Caiaphas, and consulted that they might take Jesus by subtilty, and kill him. But they said, Not on the feast day, lest there be an uproar among the people.

Originally, the position of high priest was passed from father to son through the Levitical line. But when the Romans came into the area and seized control of the nation, they began appointing the high priest and he became their political puppet. Caiaphas was the son of Annas. Annas chose to remove himself from the office of high priest, allowing Caiaphas to serve in his place. This was because Annas had four other sons who were making money from temple concessions, and he didn't want to jeopardize their thriving business.

Think back with me. What did Jesus do with their concession tables? He overturned them (Matthew 21:12). Consequently, Caiaphas and Annas were determined to destroy Jesus. Not only were they jealous of His widespread fame and following among the people, but they were angry that He was upsetting their money-making operation and cutting into their profit margin.

Matthew 26:6
Now when Jesus was in Bethany, in the house of Simon the leper.

Simon the leper must have been one who had been healed by Jesus. Otherwise, he would have lived in a leper colony outside the city limits.

Matthew 26:7
There came unto him a woman having an alabaster box of very precious ointment, and poured it on his head, as he sat at meat.

We know from John's Gospel that this woman was Mary, the sister of Martha. Mary was a worshiper. She is mentioned three times in Scripture, each time at the feet of Jesus.

Mary found her blessing at Jesus' feet. Luke writes of the time Jesus was at the home of Mary and Martha. Martha was in the kitchen, saying, "Lord tell Mary to come here. She's just sitting at Your feet, listening to Your words, and I need help." Jesus, however, told Martha that Mary had chosen the better part (Luke 10:42).

Mary brought her burden to Jesus' feet. John writes that when Lazarus died, Mary ran out to meet Jesus, fell at His feet, and said, "Lord if You had been here, our brother would not have died" (John 11:21).

Mary gave her best at Jesus' feet. John writes that after she anointed Jesus with the oil in the alabaster box, she wiped His feet with her hair. John tells us that the ointment within the alabaster box was worth three hundred pence. This was Mary's dowry, her ticket to marriage (John 12:3).

Matthew 26:8, 9
But when his disciples saw it, they had indignation, saying, To what purpose is this waste? For this ointment might have been sold for much, and given to the poor.

John's Gospel tells us exactly which disciple was the most indignant. It was Judas who said, "This is a waste. You could have done something much more practical with this ointment."

"It's a waste," Judas said. Yet in a few hours, Jesus would call Judas himself the son of perdition, or literally, "the son of waste" (John 17:12). People who don't love God or understand His ways always see worship as a waste.

Please understand this about worship, fellow worshipers: As she broke the alabaster box and poured the ointment upon Jesus, Mary showed us that worship often comes through breaking,. When do you really become a worshiper? When you're broken. When finally you're at your wits' end, you humble yourself before the Lord and worship Him. Worship comes from brokenness.

Worship not only comes from brokenness, but true worship is often costly. It cost Mary her dowry. What does worship cost you and me? Our image. "There's no way I'm going to sing those songs. I'm too cool for that," some say.

"I don't care if Scripture declares lifting hands is a sign of submission and adoration, I'll never lift mine. People will think I'm weird."

Worship is often misunderstood. There will always be those in Judas' corner who say, "Quit trying to be so holy. Do something more practical." But although worship comes through brokenness and although worship is sometimes costly, worship is always beneficial. After Mary wiped the feet of Jesus with her hair, her hair took on the same fragrance as Jesus' feet. That's what worship does. When you're worshiping the Lord, you take on the fragrance of the Lord.

John goes on to tell us that after Mary broke the alabaster box, the entire house was filled with the aroma of the ointment (John 12:3). Mom and Dad, does your house stink? Do you find there's tension in the air? Do you feel your marriage is on the rocks? Do you worry your kids are falling apart? Let me tell you the secret of Mary: The whole house took on the fragrance of Jesus because she was at His feet. Take Mary's mindset. Dad, when your house "stinks," gather your wife and your kids around you and say, "Let's stop and seek the Lord's blessing for a few minutes." You will be amazed how this will affect the aroma of your house. I suggest that perhaps the key isn't always counseling or child-rearing classes. As helpful as those things might be, the real power lies at Jesus' feet. Mary discovered this and the whole world knows her story.

Matthew 26:10–13
When Jesus understood it, he said unto them, Why trouble ye the woman? for she hath wrought a good work upon me. For ye have the poor always with you; but me ye have not always. For in that she hath poured this ointment on my body, she did it for my burial. Verily I say unto you, Wheresoever this gospel shall be preached in the whole world, there shall also this, that this woman hath done, be told for a memorial of her.

Why did Mary anoint Jesus' body for burial? Because, although He had told His disciples repeatedly that He had come to Jerusalem to die, I suggest Mary was the only one who really understood this. You see, in Jesus' time, bodies were anointed after burial in order to reduce the stench of putrefaction. Yet Mary anointed His body *before* He died. Why? Because, just as David prophesied, I suggest it was because she knew He would not see corruption, or literally, putrefaction (Psalm 49:9). She knew He would rise again. How did she know this? Revelation and adoration are intricately linked together. When you're at the feet of Jesus in worship, you see things others don't. It's amazing what you'll see when, like Mary, you take the time to sit at His feet.

Matthew 26:14 (a)
Then one of the twelve, called Judas Iscariot . . .

"Judas" means "praise." It's a beautiful name, but Judas wasted it and ruined it for future generations. How many parents name their kids Judas today? "Isacariot" most likely means he was from the town of Carioth. Judas of Carioth was the only one of all the disciples from the southern region of Israel—the educated, wealthy region of the country. So impressive was Judas that the disciples appointed him treasurer.

Matthew 26:14 (b), 15
. . . went unto the chief priests, and said unto them, What will ye give me, and I will deliver him unto you? And they covenanted with him for thirty pieces of silver.

I believe it was his disappointment with Jesus that prompted Judas to entertain a betrayal mentality. I believe that when Judas initially followed Jesus, he was excited about the prospect of a kingdom being set up on earth. But when Jesus began leaving the area every time the multitude wanted to make Him king, perhaps Judas felt his heart sink. So, too, I see a tendency in people today to sell out when they get disappointed in Jesus. "I thought Jesus would bless my business if I became a Christian," they say. "But what happened? I went bankrupt." If we're not careful, a Judas mentality will creep in and we'll sell out.

Matthew 26:16–19
And from that time he sought opportunity to betray him. Now the first day of the feast of unleavened bread the disciples came to Jesus, saying unto him, Where wilt thou that we prepare for thee to eat the passover? And he said, Go into the city to such a man, and say unto him, The Master saith, My time is at hand; I will keep the passover at thy house with my disciples. And the disciples did as Jesus had appointed them; and they made ready the passover.

The other Gospels tell us that the man the disciples were to look for would be carrying a water jug. In those days, men didn't carry water jugs. That was "woman's work." Thus, a man carrying a water jug would have stood out. Evidently, the owner of this house was an unnamed friend of Jesus. He was one who worked behind the scenes, making the necessary preparations so Jesus could celebrate Passover with His disciples. I believe there is a special place in heaven for the unnamed servant.

You might be one of those people no one applauds

or even acknowledges. You simply serve behind the scenes, making things right for Jesus and His people. God bless you! I'm convinced that a whole bunch of us who are seen and applauded are getting our reward now. But those who are serving secretly, those who are unnamed and unknown will be rewarded openly by our Father who sees in secret (Matthew 6:6).

Matthew 26:20–22
Now when the even was come, he sat down with the twelve. And as they did eat, he said, Verily I say unto you, that one of you shall betray me. And they were exceeding sorrowful, and began every one of them to say unto him, Lord, is it I?

When told one of their number would betray Jesus, did the disciples say, "It's the one with the black cape—it's Judas"? No. Everyone said, "Lord, is it *I?*"

Matthew 26:23 (a)
And he answered and said, He that dippeth his hand with me in the dish . . .

One element of the Passover meal was a pastelike dip made of ground dates, figs, and nuts that was eaten with bread. It was a reminder of the mud the Israelites used in Egypt to bake bricks before God sent Moses to deliver them.

Matthew 26:23 (b)–25
. . . the same shall betray me. The Son of man goeth as it is written of him: but woe unto that man by whom the Son of man is betrayed! it had been good for that man if he had not been born. Then Judas, which betrayed him, answered and said, Master, is it I? He said unto him, Thou hast said.

At the very moment Jesus said, "He who dips His hand with Me into the dish . . ." Judas had his hand right there. This is intriguing to me because in Jesus' day, the master of the home would sit in the center of a U-shaped table with the guest of honor to his left. We know from John's Gospel that John was seated to Jesus' right at this meal. Therefore, if Jesus and Judas were sharing the same bowl, Judas must have been seated to Jesus' left—at the place of honor. Thus, even at this point, we see Jesus affirming Judas, saying, "Son of perdition, I'm seating you in the place of honor because I still love you."

Matthew 26:26–29
And as they were eating, Jesus took bread, and blessed it, and brake it, and gave it to the disciples, and said, Take, eat; this is my body. And he took the cup, and gave thanks, and gave it to them, saying, Drink ye all of it; for this is my blood of the new testament, which is shed for many for the remission of sins. But I say unto you, I will not drink henceforth of this fruit of the vine, until that day when I drink it new with you in my Father's kingdom.

The Passover became a new celebration—the Lord's Supper, the Eucharist, Communion. Now, if I were setting up the Lord's Supper, I would have reversed the order. I would have served the cup first. I would have said, "Before the Body of Christ can enter into us, the blood must first cleanse us." But Jesus didn't follow that pattern. He gave the bread first and followed it with the cup. And in so doing, He essentially said, "I will come into you just as you are. And then I will cleanse you with My blood."

Most people have the mistaken idea that they must clean up their act and get it together before they ask Jesus into their heart. But just the opposite is true. The bread is first. He comes in and *He* cleans us up. It's not perspiration—our trying harder. It's impartation—Jesus in us, the hope of glory.

Matthew 26:30
And when they had sung an hymn, they went out into the mount of Olives.

Notice that the worship service Jesus led after the Passover meal consisted of a single hymn. Don't fall into the trap of thinking, "If I'm really going to worship, I've got to worship to the point of exhaustion." The strength of worship is not necessarily related to the length of worship.

Matthew 26:31
Then saith Jesus unto them, All ye shall be offended because of me this night: for it is written, I will smite the shepherd, and the sheep of the flock shall be scattered abroad.

Jesus quoted a prophecy from Zechariah that referred to Him personally (Zechariah 13:7).

Matthew 26:32
But after I am risen again, I will go before you into Galilee.

"Even though you will be offended in Me, even though you will scatter from Me, I will rise again," Jesus said. "And when I do, I will go before you into Galilee and meet with you there." I love Jesus Christ for this aspect of His character. You see, even when we are flaky, even when we flee, even when we are fickle, Jesus the Good

Shepherd never leaves or forsakes us. Instead, He says, "I will search you out. When I rise again, I will see you and go before you into Galilee."

Matthew 26:33–35
Peter answered and said unto him, Though all men shall be offended because of thee, yet will I never be offended. Jesus said unto him, Verily I say unto thee, That this night, before the cock crow, thou shalt deny me thrice. Peter said unto him, Though I should die with thee, yet will I not deny thee. Likewise also said all the disciples.

On the night of the Last Supper, Jesus said, "When I am betrayed and apprehended, you'll all scatter."

"Not me," said Peter. "You can count on me, Lord. I'm solid as a rock."

Matthew 26:36 (a)
Then cometh Jesus with them unto a place called Gethsemane . . .

The word "gethsemane" means "oil press." In an oil press, olives were crushed, broken, and ground up so that oil might be produced. Scripturally, oil is symbolic of the Holy Spirit. The picture is clear: before the Holy Spirit could be given, Someone had to be crushed and broken. And that Someone was Jesus Christ. It is not coincidental that it was in the Garden of Gethsemane where He felt the crushing, the heaviness, and the burden of what was about to happen when He who knew no sin would become sin for us (2 Corinthians 5:21).

- *In the Garden of Eden, man's relationship with the Father was broken because of rebellion.*
  In the Garden of Gethsemane, man's relationship with the Father was restored through submission.
- *In the Garden of Eden, the first Adam tried to hide from God.*
  In the Garden of Gethsemane, the last Adam bared His soul to God.
- *In the Garden of Eden, a sword was unsheathed and man was driven out.*
  In the Garden of Gethsemane, a sword was put away and a man was healed.

Matthew 26:36 (b)–38
. . . and saith unto the disciples, Sit ye here, while I go and pray yonder. And he took with him Peter and the two sons of Zebedee, and began to be sorrowful and very heavy. Then saith he unto them, My soul is exceed-ing sorrowful, even unto death: tarry ye here, and watch with me.

Jesus began to feel sorrowful and very heavy. Why? Because He knew what lay ahead. Should He go through with this plan to pay for our sins, He would not only feel the wrath of God poured upon Him as He died in our place, but His suffering would go much farther and longer than what we could possibly imagine. Jesus didn't suffer for just a few hours on a Friday afternoon. Revelation 13:8 speaks of the Lamb slain even before the foundation of the world. In the Garden of Eden a decision was made that resulted in damnation. In the Garden of Gethsemane a decision was made that resulted in salvation. But the price was incredible.

Matthew 26:39 (a)
And he went a little further . . .

That's Jesus—always going a little further. He didn't stop at Gethsemane. He went all the way to Calvary for you and for me.

Matthew 26:39 (b)
. . . and fell on his face, and prayed, saying, O my Father, if it be possible, let this cup pass from me . . .

"Is there any other way people can be saved, Father? Can they join a church? Can they give canned goods at Christmas time? Can they treat their pets nice?" People think that if they're just a "good person" or a "nice guy" they'll be saved. In reality, it took nothing less than the death of Jesus Christ to save anyone from any one sin.

Matthew 26:39 (c)
. . . nevertheless not as I will, but as thou wilt.

You who are interested in prayer and faith, take note: The key to prayer is not so much "name it and claim it." Rather, the key to prayer is "request and rest." That's the way Jesus prayed. "Father, if it be possible let this cup pass from Me. That's My request. Nevertheless, not My will, but Thy will be done. That's where I will rest."

Matthew 26:40–42
And he cometh unto the disciples, and findeth them asleep, and saith unto Peter, What, could ye not watch with me one hour? Watch and pray, that ye enter not into temptation: the spirit indeed is willing, but the flesh is weak. He went away again the second time, and prayed, saying, O my Father,

if this cup may not pass away from me, except I drink it, thy will be done.

Even while in prayer, Jesus began to understand and receive confirmation that it was the
will of His Father that He be slaughtered as the
Lamb of God for the sins of the world.

Matthew 26:43
And he came and found them asleep again:
for their eyes were heavy.

I can relate to this. I can read *TIME* Magazine
and be fine. But when I open the Bible or start to
pray, my eyes get heavy. Why? Because Satan
knows there is power in prayer and profit in
Bible study. He doesn't care if you're reading the
newspaper. But read the Word or pray, and you
can count on your eyes getting heavy, the telephone ringing, the baby crying, and your stomach rumbling. When I kneel by the couch in
prayer and find myself "resting in the Lord" a little too literally, I go for a walk and pray along the
way. It's much tougher to fall asleep when you're
walking!

Matthew 26:44, 45 (a)
And he left them, and went away again, and
prayed the third time, saying the same
words. Then cometh he to his disciples, and
saith unto them, Sleep on now, and take
your rest . . .

Understanding their humanity and frailty,
Jesus looked at His disciples and said, "Sleep
on." But while His disciples were sleeping, His
enemies were plotting. You can always be sure of
that. There are meetings in hell to cause havoc in
your family, your ministry, your occupation, and
your marriage. Keep that in mind next time you
opt for sleep over prayer. It's not that the Lord
condemns you for lack of prayer. It's that the Enemy will exploit the situation. You see, prayer is
not only for petition. It's also for protection.
When you pray, there is a wall of protection
round about you, your family, your ministry, and
your marriage that is absent when you fail to
pray. Jesus didn't collapse in this moment of
temptation. The disciples did. He was praying.
They were sleeping.

Matthew 26:45 (b), 46 (a)
. . . behold, the hour is at hand, and the Son
of man is betrayed into the hands of sinners.
Rise . . .

Jesus could rise because He had been kneeling. He could stand before His enemies because
He had been kneeling before His Father.

Matthew 26:46 (b)
. . . let us be going . . .

"Let *us* be going," Jesus said. If I were Jesus, I
would have said, "You guys are a bunch of losers.
You're not coming with Me." Not Jesus. Even after His disciples failed Him, He still included
them.

Matthew 26:46 (c), 47 (a)
. . . behold, he is at hand that doth betray
me. And while he yet spake, lo, Judas, one
of the twelve, came, and with him a great
multitude . . .

John tells us this "great multitude" was a "cohort," or literally six hundred Roman soldiers.
Six hundred Roman soldiers came to apprehend
the meekest Man on the face of the earth and a
handful of sleepy disciples.

Matthew 26:47 (b)–49
. . . with swords and staves, from the chief
priests and elders of the people. Now he that
betrayed him gave them a sign, saying, Whom-
soever I shall kiss, that same is he: hold him
fast. And forthwith he came to Jesus, and
said, Hail, master; and kissed him.

The Greek language indicates that Judas
kissed Jesus repeatedly. Why? First, it was as a
sign of identification. Jesus' appearance was so
ordinary that neither the soldiers nor the company of religious leaders could pick Him out of
the small crowd of twelve men. We tend to think
of Jesus as glowing, huge in stature, or somehow
standing out. Not so. Judas said, "He's so ordinary I'll have to identify Him with a kiss." Second, perhaps Judas continued to kiss Jesus not
only to identify Him, but to occupy Him, hoping
that Jesus wouldn't pull a fast one and do a miracle or call down some angels.

Matthew 26:50
And Jesus said unto him, Friend, wherefore
art thou come? Then came they, and laid
hands on Jesus, and took him.

Jesus called Judas "Friend" even at the moment of betrayal. Even here, Jesus gave Judas
the opportunity to turn away and to change his
mind. First Corinthians 10:13 makes it clear that
in every temptation there's always a way out provided by God Himself. Here, Jesus is giving Judas a way out as He asks, "Friend, why are you
here?" In other words, Jesus was giving Judas
one last chance to change his mind.

Matthew 26:51, 52 (a)
And, behold, one of them which were with
Jesus stretched out his hand, and drew his
sword, and struck a servant of the high
priest's, and smote off his ear. Then said
Jesus unto him, Put up again thy sword into
his place . . .

John tells us the one who drew his sword was
Peter. In an attempt to protect Jesus, Peter—a
better fisherman than a swordsman—lopped off
the ear of Malchus, a servant of the high priest.
Luke writes that following Peter's show of force,
Jesus touched Malchus' ear and healed him. I
think that's perhaps the miracle Jesus does most:
healing people who have been needlessly
wounded by His followers who have used the
sword of Scripture foolishly. How often we hurt
one another in our attempts to protect Jesus.
Ears fly everywhere, and the body of Christ is
maimed because well-meaning Christians like
Peter unsheathe their Bibles and start chopping
away at each other. Listen to the words of Jesus.
If you are using the Sword of the Spirit to slice
other people up and put other people down, put it
away.

Matthew 26:52 (b)
. . . for all they that take the sword shall
perish with the sword.

You might want to remember this verse next
time you feel inclined to chop up some believer.
Jesus said, "Blessed are the merciful, for they
shall receive mercy. But those who are unsheathing the sword indiscriminately and causing in-
jury needlessly will die by the sword eventually."

Matthew 26:53
Thinkest thou that I cannot now pray to my
Father, and he shall presently give me more
than twelve legions of angels?

A legion being six thousand, Jesus was talking
about seventy-two thousand angels at His disposal—quite a force, considering it took only one
to wipe out 185,000 Babylonians (2 Kings 19:35).
What a glorious day it is when you learn you don't
have to defend Jesus Christ, when you realize
that He is perfectly capable of defending Himself. Our job is not to protect, defend, or avenge.
Jesus calls us to do one thing: to love.

Matthew 26:54–56 (a)
But how then shall the scriptures be ful-
filled, that thus it must be? In that same
hour said Jesus to the multitudes, Are ye
come out as against a thief with swords and
staves for to take me? I sat daily with you

teaching in the temple, and ye laid no hold
on me. But all this was done, that the scriptures of the prophets might be fulfilled.

Jesus made it clear that He didn't need Peter's
protection and that what was happening was in
accordance with prophecy in Scripture as well as
with the heart of His Father.

Matthew 26:56 (b), 57
Then all the disciples forsook him, and fled.
And they that had laid hold on Jesus led him
away to Caiaphas the high priest, where the
scribes and the elders were assembled.

The disciples split and Jesus was led alone
from the Garden of Gethsemane to stand before
Caiaphas. Jesus was not dragged before Caiaphas unwillingly. Rather, He was "brought as a
lamb to the slaughter," just as Isaiah had prophesied (53:7).

Matthew 26:58
But Peter followed him afar off unto the
high priest's palace, and went in, and sat
with the servants, to see the end.

You're always headed for trouble when you
start following Jesus afar off. Peter followed
Jesus afar off right into the high priest's palace,
where Luke tells us he warmed himself by the
enemy's fire.

Matthew 26:59–60 (a)
Now the chief priests, and elders, and all the
council, sought false witness against Jesus,
to put him to death; But found none . . .

A meeting of the Sanhedrin was immediately
called. The Sanhedrin was the seventy-one-
member Jewish Supreme Court. From the very
outset, however, the trial was illegal, since Jewish
Law forbade evening meetings of the Sanhedrin.

Matthew 26:60 (b), 61
. . . yea, though many false witnesses came,
yet found they none. At the last came two
false witnesses, and said, This fellow said, I
am able to destroy the temple of God, and
to build it in three days.

The Ninth Commandment forbids bearing
false witness. We have the mistaken idea that
"bearing false witness" means telling big lies.
But this account makes it clear that bearing false
witness consists of giving the right information
with the wrong implication. A false witness is not
one who makes up a big fib. A false witness is
simply one who is tricky with the truth. A false

witness gives the right information, knowing the wrong implication will be drawn. Jesus did indeed say, "Destroy this temple and in three days I will raise it up" (see John 2:19). But He was speaking of the temple of His own body.

Matthew 26:62–66

And the high priest arose, and said unto him, Answerest thou nothing? what is it which these witness against thee? But Jesus held his peace. And the high priest answered and said unto him, I adjure thee by the living God, that thou tell us whether thou be the Christ, the Son of God. Jesus saith unto him, Thou hast said: nevertheless I say unto you, Hereafter shall ye see the Son of man sitting on the right hand of power, and coming in the clouds of heaven. Then the high priest rent his clothes, saying, He hath spoken blasphemy; what further need have we of witnesses? behold, now ye have heard his blasphemy. What think ye? They answered and said, He is guilty of death.

When Jesus said, "Thou hast said . . ." He was saying, "I *am* the Son of God." Then He went on to say, "And you will see Me in the place of exaltation." Hearing this, the high priest did what was customary at that time when one experienced great grief or pain. Even as Jacob rent his clothes when he heard Joseph was dead and David rent his clothes when he heard Saul had died in battle, if one was really grieved, he would tear his robe from the bottom up. What's happening here is tremendously symbolic. Unbeknownst to him, as Caiaphas rent his priestly garments with his own hands, he was in fact symbolizing the end of the old Levitical priesthood. A new priesthood is about to be established—the priesthood of Melchizedek.

First mentioned in Genesis 14, "Melchizedek" means "prince of righteousness." He was called the Prince of Salem, or, "Prince of Peace." He came to Abraham with bread and wine. He had no beginning and no end. Who was Melchizedek? The Book of Hebrews tells us he was a picture of Jesus Christ (Hebrews 7).

Matthew 26:67, 68

Then did they spit in his face, and buffeted him; and others smote him with the palms of their hands, saying, Prophesy unto us, thou Christ, Who is he that smote thee?

So brutal was the beating Jesus endured, Isaiah prophesied He would be more disfigured than any man who ever lived (Isaiah 53:2). His beard was plucked; His face was swollen. The spit of His accusers ran down His cheeks. He could have

called ten thousand times ten thousand angels. But He didn't.

This really happened. We're not talking about a fairy tale. We're not talking about poetic mythology or esoteric theology. We're talking about a real Man who absorbed the blows, who felt the pain, who endured the spit, the insult, and the agony because He was thinking about you.

"Oh, Jon, you're being dramatic," you say. "He wasn't thinking about me. How could He be? We're only talking about a few hours of suffering and dying. There wasn't enough time to think about everyone individually."

Not true. You see, we're talking about an event that took place before the foundation of the world and that continues on into eternity. The biggest problem we who are familiar with the Gospel story face is thinking of Jesus dying generically for the whole world. We need to understand that He died for each of us individually and for each of our sins specifically.

How do I know this? Because in the Old Testament, every single sin had to be atoned for specifically (Leviticus 1:4). Forgiveness had to be meted out individually. Spend some time contemplating that. Listen to Jesus praying, "Father, if it's possible that people can be saved any other way, let this cup pass from Me. Nevertheless, Thy will be done." See Him with blood-soaked face leaving the Garden of Gethsemane, His disciples fleeing in fear. Watch as He is led blindfolded before Caiaphas, lied about by false witnesses, beaten up, battered, and humiliated—for you.

Matthew 26:69–73

Now Peter sat without in the palace: and a damsel came unto him, saying, Thou also wast with Jesus of Galilee. But he denied before them all, saying, I know not what thou sayest. And when he was gone out into the porch, another maid saw him, and said unto them that were there, This fellow was also with Jesus of Nazareth. And again he denied with an oath, I do not know the man. And after a while came unto him they that stood by, and said to Peter, Surely thou also art one of them; for thy speech betrayeth thee.

Once you become a believer, if you go back to the fires of the world, you won't fit in. Your speech will betray you. You can try and tell dirty jokes again or try and be suggestive with your innuendoes, but people will say, "It doesn't ring true. Your speech betrays you." If you've really been born again, you can't go back to the old fires. It doesn't work."

Matthew 26:74 (a)
Then began he to curse and to swear, saying,
I know not the man.

"My speech betrays me? I'll show you some speech," said Peter as he began to curse and swear. At that time, fishermen had the roughest language of anyone. Why? Perhaps because as their nets became entangled in the bottom of the Sea of Galilee, they had ample reason to swear. At any rate, all tangled up himself, Peter began to curse and swear once again.

Matthew 26:74 (b)
And immediately the cock crew.

Because the priests felt that birds would make a mess and defile the holy city, according to city ordinances, no roosters or hens were allowed in Jerusalem. Therefore, when Peter heard the sound of a rooster crowing, it would not only remind him of Jesus' words to him previously, but

of his own sin. For just as a rooster had no place in the holy city, Peter must have known immediately that his denial of Jesus had defiled and polluted his relationship with Him.

Matthew 26:75
And Peter remembered the word of Jesus, which said unto him, Before the cock crow, thou shalt deny me thrice. And he went out, and wept bitterly.

Luke tells us that at this moment, as Jesus was led out of the house of Caiaphas, He "turned and looked on Peter" (see Luke 22:61) with a look that must have said, "Peter I told you this would happen. I told you that you would deny Me three times. But, Peter, I'm not through with you. I love you."

For topical study of Matthew 26:75, see "The Pathway to Pain" below.

THE PATHWAY TO PAIN
A Topical Study of
Matthew 26:75

Maybe you've said or heard the phrase, "I fell into sin." In reality, there is no such thing. A person never "falls" into sin but rather walks into sin one step at a time. In chapter 26, we see five steps Peter took that led to his sin and sorrow.

Step One—Overconfidence in the Flesh

Peter answered and said unto him, Though all men shall be offended because of thee, yet will I never be offended.   Matthew 26:33

"I won't leave You, Lord," Peter boldly declared. "Others might be offended in You. Others might turn their backs on You. But not me."

Two ducks and a frog hung out at the pond in Farmer Brown's field. One summer, however, a drought caused the pond to dry up. For the ducks, able to fly elsewhere, this was no problem. But the frog, knowing he would literally croak if he didn't find water soon, said to the ducks, "I'm in trouble here. But I've got a plan. You guys hold a stick in your bills, and I'll jump up and grab it with my mouth. Then you start flying. I'll hang on. And we'll keep going until we find another pond."

The ducks said, "Sure. Sounds good." So they put a stick between their bills. The frog jumped up and grabbed it tightly in his mouth. The ducks began to flap their wings, and suddenly the trio was airborne.

Taking in the whole scene, Farmer Brown watched in amazement below. "What a brilliant idea," he said. "I wonder who thought of it?"—to which the frog opened his mouth wide and proudly answered, "I di—."

Pride says, "Look what I did!" It's an "I" problem.

"Lord, I will never deny You," said Peter. But, like the frog, even as he opened his mouth, he started going down.

Step Two—Sleeping Instead of Praying

And he cometh unto the disciples, and findeth them asleep, and saith unto Peter, What, could ye not watch with me one hour?   Matthew 26:40

Once I am full of pride and feel like *I* can make things happen, I see no reason to pray. Thus, pride and prayerlessness go hand in hand. We must never forget that prayer is not only for petition, but for protection. Prayer not only gives us what we want but also protects us from what we don't want. I have seen things enter into my own life that otherwise wouldn't have whenever I have stopped praying and started sleeping. And that's what Peter discovered.

Step Three—Replacing Devotion with Action

And, behold, one of them which were with Jesus stretched out his hand, and drew his sword, and struck a servant of the high priest's, and smote off his ear.   Matthew 27:51

Catch the scene: Judas comes into the Garden of Gethsemane with a cohort of Roman soldiers behind him. Peter wakes up, sees a need, and grabs his sword. A better fisherman than a swordsman, Peter manages only to lop off the ear of the high priest's servant. Jesus healed the severed ear as much for Peter as for Malchus, for if Jesus hadn't healed Malchus, there would have been four crosses on Calvary the next day instead of three as Peter would have been crucified for attempted murder. But just as the Lord does with us, He healed Peter's mistake, making it impossible for Malchus to press charges.

The same thing happens in the heavenly courtroom. But Jesus has forgiven the very sins of which Satan accuses us. Therefore, there is no record of them because His blood has cleansed us from all sin (1 John 1:7).

Step Four—Following Afar Off

But Peter followed him afar off unto the high priest's palace . . .
                                                        Matthew 26:58 (a)

I have known so many people who have slowly but surely drifted away because they began to follow Jesus from afar. At one time, the desire of their heart was to know the Lord and to walk with Him. But then something happened. That is why Hebrews says: Therefore we ought to give the more earnest heed to the things which we have heard, lest at any time we should let them slip" (see Hebrews 2:1).

The word "slip" means "drift." As we sail along spiritually, the danger is not that a bomb will sink us, but that we will slowly drift away. How does that happen? It happens when we fail to "give heed to the things which we have heard." In other words, we drift when we fail to read the compass of God's Word. There was a time, perhaps, when you needed, desired, and enjoyed getting your bearings by reading the Scriptures. But eventually you began following Jesus afar off, and the Word was no longer important.

When that happens to me, I find myself drifting slowly and imperceptibly until suddenly I wonder, *Where am I? How in the world did I get* here? My faith didn't sink. I just started drifting away. You and I need to set our anchor deeply in the "things which we have heard"—the truths, doctrines, and principles of Scripture. Otherwise we too will be vulnerable to drifting away and following Jesus afar off.

Step Five—Getting Warm by the Enemy's Fire

. . . and went in, and sat with the servants, to see the end . . . and when they had kindled a fire in the midst of the hall, and were set down together, Peter sat down among them.   Matthew 26:58 (b), Luke 22:55

After following Jesus afar off, perhaps Peter thought, *Maybe my old life wasn't so bad after all. I'll go back to the old places, the old ways, the old things and maybe I could even be a witness there.*

The Christian trying to warm himself by the fires of the enemy will always find misery in the world because, although he may have too much of the world to enjoy the Lord, he also has too much of the Lord to enjoy the world. Feeling estranged from the Lord, yet a stranger to the world, Peter began to swear and curse vehemently—until he heard the cock crow. Then he wept bitterly. The Greek phrase, "wept bitterly," speaks of an emotion stemming from the intestines. In other words, it refers to a deep, gut-wrenching weeping.

What caused Peter to weep so bitterly? According to Luke's Gospel, at the moment Peter said, "Blankety blank, I don't know the man," the doors of Caiaphas' house suddenly swung open and Jesus was led out to the courtyard where He saw Peter sitting by the fire. "And the Lord turned, and looked upon Peter," writes Luke (see Luke 22:61). Jesus looked on Peter and Peter was broken. The look was not one of anger, but of understanding; not one of condemnation but one of sympathy. It was a look that touched Peter's heart deeply.

Jesus knew Peter would go through this, for He had told him only hours earlier,

"Simon, Simon, Satan has desired to have you and sift you like wheat, but I have prayed for you and when you are converted (not "*if* you are converted" but "*when*"), strengthen the brethren" (Luke 22:32).

Three days later, when Jesus rose from the dead, the angel in the tomb told Mary Magdalene, "Go tell His disciples *and Peter*" (Mark 16:7, emphasis mine). In 1 Corinthians 15, Paul tells us that when Jesus rose from the dead, before He appeared to the other disciples, He sought out Peter. In John 21, Jesus ministered to Peter specifically when He gave him the opportunity to say, "I love You, Lord," three times—just as Peter had denied Him three times.

Maybe you've been weeping bitterly today. Maybe you've ignored the Word, drifted away, and like Peter, walked into sin. Know this, precious friend: Jesus comes by you at your lowest point, and He looks upon you not in anger but in understanding. "I have prayed for you," He says, "and when you're converted—when you get through this time of pain and sorrow—strengthen your brethren as I anoint you and continue to use you."

Return to Jesus, and watch what our loving Lord will do with the mess you've made. He'll turn it around for His glory.

You watch. You'll see.

27 Chapter 26 came to a close as Jesus was led out of the palace of Caiaphas after an illegal midnight meeting of the Sanhedrin, the Jewish Supreme Court.

Matthew 27:1, 2
When the morning was come, all the chief priests and elders of the people took counsel against Jesus to put him to death: And when they had bound him, they led him away, and delivered him to Pontius Pilate the governor.

It was now five o'clock in the morning. After a night of agony in the Garden of Gethsemane followed by a beating at the hands of the palace guards, Jesus was led before Pontius Pilate. Why? To fulfill prophecy. You see, when the Jews put a man to death, they stoned him. Old Testament prophecies, however, all depict the Son of God being crucified. "Cursed," the Old Testament Law declares, "is everyone that hangs on a tree" (see Deuteronomy 21:23). Thus it was in fulfillment of prophecy that Jesus was brought before a Roman governor in order that He might die a Roman death. Keep in mind, however, that Roman soldiers were drafted from all countries throughout the empire. So, although it was the Jews who sentenced Jesus to die, and although it was the Romans who devised His method of exe-

cution, He who died for the sins of the whole world did, in fact, die by the hands of the whole world.

Matthew 27:3, 4
Then Judas, which had betrayed him, when he saw that he was condemned, repented himself, and brought again the thirty pieces of silver to the chief priests and elders, saying, I have sinned in that I have betrayed the innocent blood. And they said, What is that to us? see thou to that.

If Judas had seen any fault, any inconsistency, any hypocrisy, or any sin in Jesus, he could have justified the betrayal in his own mind. He could have said, "He makes Himself out to be the Son of God, but I've seen Him lose His temper," or "I remember the time He stretched the truth," or "I heard Him gossip." Instead, Judas realized Jesus was exactly who He declared Himself to be—the Lamb of God, the Sinless One.

Matthew 27:5
And he cast down the pieces of silver in the temple, and departed, and went and hanged himself.

It intrigues me that Judas hung himself on a tree. Deuteronomy 19:16–19 says that if a man bears false witness and someone suffers because of the lie, the false witness must share the same fate as the one about whom he lied. Do you see what's happening? As Judas realized Jesus would soon be crucified on a tree, it's as if he got as close as he possibly could to sharing the same fate as the One about whom he lied. This is further proof that Judas realized perhaps more clearly than any other man that Jesus was completely flawless and totally innocent.

Matthew 27:6–10
And the chief priests took the silver pieces, and said, It is not lawful for to put them into the treasury, because it is the price of blood. And they took counsel, and bought with them the potter's field, to bury strangers in. Wherefore that field was called, The field of blood, unto this day. Then was fulfilled that which was spoken by Jeremy the prophet, saying, and they took the thirty pieces of silver, the price of him that was valued, whom they of the children of Israel did value; and gave them for the potter's field, as the Lord appointed me.

What was a potter's field? In Bible times, if a potter discovered cracks or chips in something he had made, he would throw the marred vessel outside of his shop. Over time this area would become full of broken pottery. Because nothing would be able to grow in this portion of land, it was good for nothing except to use as a cemetery for strangers and travelers who had no other place to be buried. Now, think with me for a moment. The blood money of Jesus Christ was used to buy the place where broken pottery and dead bodies were. That's us. Without Jesus we were shattered, dead, and good for nothing.

What hope is there for broken pottery? Only this: If it is reheated and placed in water once again, it will become pliable and able to be reshaped and restored. So, too, if we as broken pieces of pottery become heated by the trials our Master Potter allows in our lives, if we're warmed by the love He has for us and washed by the water of the Word He gives to us, we can be reshaped and used for His glory.

Matthew 27:11 (a)
And Jesus stood before the governor: and the governor asked him, saying, Art thou the King of the Jews?

Jesus stood before Pilate who was at this point in big trouble politically. Pilate had already made three big blunders and had been warned by Tiberius Caesar that if he made one more, he would be removed from his post.

Pilate made his first mistake when he initially came into Jerusalem. As his soldiers carried their standards topped with eagles of gold and silver into the temple area, the Jews saw the eagles as idols and became so infuriated that they rioted on the temple mount. Wanting to quell the rebellion immediately, Pilate ordered the riotous Jews held in an amphitheatre outside Jerusalem where they would be slaughtered unless they repented. These courageous Jews laid their heads down on the ground and said, "Chop off our heads, but there will be ten thousand others to take our places if your images ever come on temple property again." Foreseeing a bloody rebellion and a political strike against him, Pilate backed off. But word got back to Rome that Pontius Pilate had been beaten by some obstinate Jews.

A short time later, Pilate wanted to make up for his bad start with the Jews by bringing in a fresh supply of water. So he built an aqueduct that would carry water from the north down to Jerusalem. It was a great engineering feat. But he financed the undertaking with money from the temple treasury. This infuriated the Jews and blood was shed as Pilate put down the ensuing rebellion.

When Pilate ordered new armor for his soldiers, the new shields bearing the image of Emperor Tiberius Caesar incensed the Jews. Considering them to be a form of idolatry, the Jews rebelled yet again. And when Tiberius heard of it, he was incensed and sent the message to Pilate that if there was one more rebellion, he'd be out of a job.

Matthew 27:11 (b)–14
And Jesus said unto him, Thou sayest. And when he was accused of the chief priests and elders, he answered nothing. Then said Pilate unto him, Hearest thou not how many things they witness against thee? And he answered him to never a word; insomuch that the governor marvelled greatly.

The accusations were being hurled against Jesus, but He answered not a word—just as Isaiah had prophesied seven hundred fifty years earlier (Isaiah 53:7). Jesus could have blown His accusers away. He could have given brilliant legal defense. But He said nothing. Maybe this week you've been defending yourself against accusations or slander. I am learning that the problem with defending yourself is that you'll never be able to stop. Start defending yourself, and that's all you'll do all day long. David found a better solution: Let the Lord be your Defender, your Rock, your Shield, your Fortress, and your high Tower (Psalm 18:2). He who chose not to defend Himself lives to defend you (Hebrews 7:25).

Matthew 27:15–18
Now at that feast the governor was wont to release unto the people a prisoner, whom they would. And they had then a notable prisoner, called Barabbas. Therefore when they were gathered together, Pilate said unto them, Whom will ye that I release unto you? Barabbas, or Jesus which is called Christ? For he knew that for envy they had delivered him.

The name "Barabbas" or "Bar Abba" means "son of the father." From other Gospel accounts, we know Barabbas was an insurrectionist and a murderer. He was despicable, brutal, and hated by the people. As Pilate brought out Barabbas, he must have been certain that the crowd wouldn't want a man like him back on the streets. Pilate must have thought that surely the Jews would want Jesus instead—the true Son of the Father.

Matthew 27:19
When he was set down on the judgment seat, his wife sent unto him, saying, Have thou nothing to do with that just man: for I have suffered many things this day in a dream because of him.

Claudia Procula, the daughter of Augustus, had married Pontius Pilate. History not only tells us she had converted to Judaism, but also that, following this event, she became a convert to Jesus Christ.

Matthew 27:20–22 (a)
But the chief priests and elders persuaded the multitude that they should ask Barabbas, and destroy Jesus. The governor answered and said unto them, Whether of the twain will ye that I release unto you? They said, Barabbas. Pilate saith unto them, What shall I do then with Jesus which is called Christ?

"What shall I do with Jesus?" That's the key question for every person throughout history. Pilate had a choice to make right then. He could either stand up for what he knew was right, or he could follow the crowd and save his political skin. So, too, there are those who truly know in the bottom of their hearts that Jesus Christ is the only Way, even though the crowd all around them says, "Don't be so restrictive. Don't be so narrow. You don't want to be a *fundamentalist* do you?"

Matthew 27:22 (b), 23 (a)
They all say unto him, Let him be crucified. And the governor said, Why, what evil hath he done?

Listen carefully and you'll hear the torment in the voice of Pontius Pilate, who examined Jesus and said, "I find no fault with Him."

Matthew 27:23 (b), 24
But they cried out the more, saying, Let him be crucified. When Pilate saw that he could prevail nothing, but that rather a tumult was made, he took water, and washed his hands before the multitude, saying, I am innocent of the blood of this just person: see ye to it.

This Roman governor who was constantly at odds with the Jews now followed a Jewish practice taken from Deuteronomy 21 that stated that if a man was murdered outside a city and no one knew who the murderer was, the elders were to wash their hands as an illustration of their innocence in the matter.

Matthew 27:25
Then answered all the people, and said, His blood be on us, and on our children.

They got their way. But the Jews—a beautiful, blessed people—would feel the effects of this statement for centuries.

Matthew 27:26
Then released he Barabbas unto them: and when he had scourged Jesus, he delivered him to be crucified.

We know from the other Gospels that the scourging Pilate ordered was his attempt to incite some kind of compassion for Jesus in the hearts of the Jews. Scourging was brutal. It was done with a Roman instrument of torture called a "flagellum"—a whip made of twelve or thirteen leather thongs. Lead balls were attached to the ends of these thongs, and pieces of glass and metal were embedded between the lead balls and the handle. The accused would be tied by his wrists and dangled about a foot off the ground, rendering him helpless to protect himself in any way. Then the beating would begin—usually thirty-nine lashes. The first blows would cause welts to form on his shoulders and back. By the seventh or eighth blow, the glass would begin to cut open these large welts, not only reducing the back to the consistency of hamburger, but also exposing the internal organs. At the end of the beating, the accused would be cut down and he would fall to the ground where he would lay in a pool of his own blood.

Most men died under the beating of the flagellum. But Jesus, of course, did not die here. Soldiers stood Him up, brought Him out, and presented Him to the crowd. "Behold the Man," Pilate said (see John 19:5) as if to say, "Look at this Man. Isn't this enough?"

Matthew 27:27–30
Then the soldiers of the governor took Jesus into the common hall, and gathered unto him the whole band of soldiers. And they stripped him, and put on him a scarlet robe. And when they had platted a crown of thorns, they put it upon his head, and a reed in his right hand: and they bowed the knee before him, and mocked him, saying, Hail, King of the Jews! And they spit upon him, and took the reed, and smote him on the head.

Taking the mock scepter out of Jesus' hand, the soldiers beat the crown of thorns into His skull. With a single word, Jesus could have wiped out these soldiers and ascended into heaven, saying, "If this is the verdict of Israel, if this is the cruelty of the Gentiles, you're on your own." But He didn't.

We're not talking about a myth or a story, a novel or a movie. This *really* happened. And in the process of His scourging and beatings and ultimately His crucifixion, Jesus was thinking of and absorbing it all for you and me.

Matthew 27:31, 32
And after that they had mocked him, they took the robe off from him, and put his own raiment on him, and led him away to crucify him. And as they came out, they found a man of Cyrene, Simon by name: him they compelled to bear his cross.

Because he carried the Cross *of* Christ, Simon of Cyrene became a convert *to* Christ (Mark 15:21; Romans 16:13).

For topical study of Matthew 27:31–32 entitled "The Government upon His Shoulders," turn to page 206.

Matthew 27:33, 34 (a)
And when they were come unto a place called Golgotha, that is to say, a place of a skull, they gave him vinegar to drink mingled with gall ...

In the Greek language, "gall" and "myrrh" are the same word. Since myrrh was used as a narcotic to deaden pain, were the soldiers showing mercy to Jesus by offering Him myrrh? Probably not. More likely, it was because they didn't want Him to die too quickly. They wanted to lengthen His suffering.

Myrrh was a costly substance. Exodus 30 says it was used to anoint prophets, priests, and kings. Psalm 45 refers to it as a perfume. John 19 tells us it was used for embalming. At His birth, Jesus was given myrrh (Matthew 2:11). Why? Because He is the Anointed One, because His Name is as ointment poured forth (Song of Solomon 1:3), because He came to die.

Matthew 27:34 (b)
... and when he had tasted thereof, he would not drink.

Perhaps it was because He knew it was a drug to deaden the pain, Jesus refused to take it.

Matthew 27:35
And they crucified him, and parted his garments, casting lots: that it might be fulfilled which was spoken by the prophet, they parted my garments among them, and upon my vesture did they cast lots.

Each Jewish male wore five articles of clothing: a headband, sandals, an inner cloak sort of like a nightshirt, a belt, and an outer tunic, or robe. The soldiers divided Jesus' clothing among themselves. But when it came to the outer tunic, they threw dice to see who would get it. Why? Because "without seam" (see John 19:23), it was a beautifully constructed garment. As God Himself in the Person of Jesus Christ died for their sins, the soldiers played games on Golgotha.

Matthew 27:36–38
And sitting down they watched him there; And set up over his head his accusation written, THIS IS JESUS THE KING OF THE JEWS. Then were there two thieves crucified with him, one on the right hand, and another on the left.

The pain from the nails piercing Jesus' hands would cause His pectoralis major muscles to go into spasms and His lungs to no longer operate properly. The only way one being crucified could breathe would be to straighten his legs, place his full weight on the nail driven through his feet, and stand straight, thereby forcing air into his lungs. To exhale, he would bend his knees, causing the full weight of his body to hang on the nails in his hands. That is why when they wanted to finally kill a man being crucified, the Romans would break his legs. It was the most cruel, torturous death ever devised by man. Cicero said it was not fit for even the most common criminal.

Matthew 27:39–42 (a)
And they that passed by reviled him, wagging their heads, and saying, Thou that destroyest the temple, and buildest it in three days, save thyself. If thou be the Son of God, come down from the cross. Likewise also the chief priests mocking him, with the scribes and elders, said, He saved others . . .

"He saved others," said the chief priests, scribes, and elders. They had denied this previously, saying that if Jesus had helped anyone, it had been only through the power of the devil (Matthew 12:24). Now comes the moment of truth. When they think they've got Him, they admit He saved others. How could they do otherwise? The lepers were healed. The dead were raised. The blind saw. The deaf heard.

Matthew 27:42 (b)
. . . himself he cannot save.

Jesus could have come down from the Cross and saved Himself. But had He saved Himself, He could not have saved you.

Matthew 27:42 (c)
If he be the King of Israel, let him now come down from the cross, and we will believe him.

This is what the world still wants. The world wants Christ—but not crucified. The world wants a Jesus figure, a Christ-consciousness, a cosmic spirituality, a harmonic convergence, teachings on love, truth, and global unity. The world still says, "Give us Christ—but not on the Cross." Why? Because Christ crucified means we have to acknowledge the part we played in His horrific death. We have to acknowledge that we are murderous sinners in need of a Savior. And the world doesn't want to do that. They want Jesus as a Hero, but not as a Lamb slain for their sin.

Matthew 27:43
He trusted in God; let him deliver him now, if he will have him: for he said, I am the Son of God.

"What's wrong, Jesus?" the crowd heckled. "You trusted in God—now look at You." You'll hear the same thing today. People will say to you—or perhaps you'll hear the enemy whisper in your ear—"I thought you trusted in God. How come you're in this mess?"

But, as the old sermon says, "This is Friday. But Sunday's a-comin'."

Matthew 27:44, 45
The thieves also, which were crucified with him, cast the same in his teeth. Now from the sixth hour there was darkness over all the land unto the ninth hour.

The Greek word translated "land" is *ge*, from which we get our word "geography." It means "earth." In other words, the whole world was blanketed with darkness. As you study literature and mythology, you find that a three-hour darkness is referred to in virtually every culture. At Jesus' birth, a star shone over the manger and light flooded the sky. At His death, darkness covers the earth because when man rejects the Light of the world, darkness covers his world.

Matthew 27:46
And about the ninth hour Jesus cried with a loud voice, saying, Eli, Eli, lama sabachthani? that is to say, My God, my God, why hast thou forsaken me?

Every other time Jesus addressed God, it was always as "Abba." But here He speaks from a distance to His Father as He says, "My God, My God." Why? Of God, Habakkuk declared, "Thou art of purer eyes than to behold evil, and canst not look on iniquity" (Habakkuk 1:13). Yet Paul writes that Jesus not only bore our sin, but actually *became* sin for us (2 Corinthians 5:21). Therefore, unable to behold evil or look on iniquity, the Father had no other choice but to turn His back on His Son—and Jesus felt the agony of that isolation.

Hear not only the agony of isolation, but a word of information. Those who taunted Him as He paid for their sin should have known Jesus was quoting Psalm 22, the classic psalm that described crucifixion. Thus, even as He was dying, Jesus was clueing people in. As they mocked Him, He was saying, "Psalm 22 is being fulfilled in your very presence." But they didn't understand. They were in the dark not only physically but spiritually because they chose not to see the Light.

Matthew 27:47–50
Some of them that stood there, when they heard that, said, This man calleth for Elias. And straightway one of them ran, and took a spunge, and filled it with vinegar, and put it on a reed, and gave him to drink. The rest said, Let be, let us see whether Elias will come to save him. Jesus, when he had cried again with a loud voice, yielded up the ghost.

Jesus didn't die—He dismissed His Spirit. His life wasn't taken away—He gave it away. And at last, the price was paid.

Matthew 27:51 (a)
And, behold, the veil of the temple was rent in twain from the top to the bottom . . .

As the veil in the temple was rent in two, the Holy of Holies became open for anyone to come into the presence of God at any time concerning any matter.

For topical study of Matthew 27:50–51 entitled "Open House," turn to page 209.

Matthew 27:51 (b)
. . . and the earth did quake . . .

When God gave the law to Moses on Mount Sinai, the earth shook (Exodus 19:18) because the Law was meant to shake people up. "You think you're righteous?" the law asked. "You think you're okay? Try this on for size and see how you match up." Paul wrote in Galatians that the law was given as a schoolmaster to make us see that we're sinners in need of a Savior (Galatians 3:24). Here, the earth is shaking again—this time not to shake man up, but to shake him loose. We're free! It is finished. The veil is rent. The price is paid.

Matthew 27:51 (c), 52
. . . and the rocks rent; And the graves were opened; and many bodies of the saints which slept arose.

The word "arose" literally means "appeared." I believe what happened here is this: The earthquake caused the stones that covered the tombs to roll away. The bodies within those tombs then became exposed and visible.

Matt 27:53 (a)
And came out of the graves after his resurrection . . .

Although the stones shook loose, exposing the bodies at the time of the crucifixion, they could not come out of the graves until *after* Jesus' Resurrection. Why? Because Paul says in 1 Corinthians 15 that Jesus is the Firstfruit. Jesus rose first.

Matthew 27:53 (b)
. . . and went into the holy city, and appeared unto many.

These chosen saints who were resurrected after Jesus arose on Easter Sunday began to walk around the Holy City. What a trip it would have been to see people who were dead for ten years cruising around Jerusalem!

Matthew 27:54
Now when the centurion, and they that were with him, watching Jesus, saw the earthquake, and those things that were done, they feared greatly, saying, Truly this was the Son of God.

Centurions were in command of one hundred men. Centurions were tough men—fighters and warriors—chosen for their bravery. This centurion saw the darkened sky, felt the earth quaking, listened as Jesus said, "Father, forgive them; for they know not what they do," and heard Him cry, "It is finished." And the only conclusion he could make was, "Truly this was the Son of God."

Matthew 27:55, 56 (a)
And many women were there beholding afar off, which followed Jesus from Galilee, ministering unto him: Among which was Mary Magdalene . . .

Mary Magdalene was the woman from whom Jesus cast seven demons (Luke 8:2).

Matthew 27:56 (b)
. . . and Mary the mother of James and Joses and the mother of Zebedee's children.

In Matthew 20, James and John's mother had come to Jesus saying, "I have a favor to ask. Could one of my boys be on Your right hand and one on Your left hand in the kingdom?"
"You don't know what you ask," He had answered.
As she looked at Jesus now—with a man hanging on His right and another on His left—I wonder if her heart stopped as she realized how little she had understood.

Matthew 27:57–60
When the even was come, there came a rich man of Arimathaea, named Joseph, who also himself was Jesus' disciple: He went to Pilate, and begged the body of Jesus. Then Pilate commanded the body to be delivered. And when Joseph had taken the body, he wrapped it in a clean linen cloth, and laid it in his own new tomb, which he had hewn out in the rock: and he rolled a great stone to the door of the sepulchre, and departed.

John tells us Nicodemus accompanied Joseph of Arimathaea. Both Nicodemus and Joseph were secret disciples of Jesus. What were they risking by burying the body of Jesus? Everything. They could potentially have been sentenced to death for siding with this One who was crucified. They could have lost their prominent positions in the temple and in society if they were discovered to be sympathizers of this itinerant Rabbi from Nazareth. At the very least, they were risking ritual defilement, which meant they couldn't celebrate Passover after touching the dead body of Jesus.

We often hear Nicodemus and Joseph of Arimathaea criticized for being secret disciples. But where were the prominent disciples? Where were Peter, James, and John? They were hiding. It was the heretofore secret disciples—Nicodemus and Joseph—who were at the Cross, ministering to the body of their Lord.

Perhaps you feel like you don't do much. You don't walk on water very often. You haven't healed a whole lot of lepers lately. You're not real vocal on the job about your belief in Christ. Listen—like Joseph and Nicodemus, you'll have your opportunity. Quite frankly, I think sometimes the secret disciples are the ones who really shine when the way gets dark. The quiet ones, the unknown ones, are often the strongest. So it was with Joseph and Nicodemus. Their moment had arrived.

Matthew 27:61–64
And there was Mary Magdalene, and the other Mary, sitting over against the sepulchre. Now the next day, that followed the day of the preparation, the chief priests and Pharisees came together unto Pilate, saying, Sir, we remember that that deceiver said, while he was yet alive, After three days I will rise again. Command therefore that the sepulchre be made sure until the third day, lest his disciples come by night, and steal him away, and say unto the people, He is risen from the dead: so the last error shall be worse than the first.

These skeptics remembered what Jesus said. With Jesus' words about rising again in three days ringing in their memories, Jesus' enemies were worried about what might happen. The believers? They were skeptics. Had they really believed Jesus would rise, they would have been camped out around the tomb to see it happen.

Have you found that sometimes the unbeliever believes more than we do? The unbeliever often has more of an understanding of the power and reality of God than do we who have "theologized" or "dispensationalized" Him away with our doctrinal systems. Clarification would help.

Matthew 27:65
Pilate said unto them, Ye have a watch: go your way, make it as sure as ye can.

It's almost as if Pilate is saying, "You have a watch—fifty soldiers—at your command. Make it as sure as you can, but good luck." What happened to Pilate? Tradition has it that a year after this event, upset emotionally and in trouble politically, he resigned his position and went to Gaul (Germany), where he committed suicide.

Matthew 27:66
So they went, and made the sepulchre sure, sealing the stone, and setting a watch.

The seal of the imperial sign of Rome was embedded in wax upon the rope in front of the stone. Anyone who tampered with the rope or touched the stone would be executed. The stone was sealed. The watch was set. Chapter 27 ends on Friday.

But Sunday's "a-comin'."

THE GOVERNMENT UPON HIS SHOULDERS

A Topical Study of
Matthew 27:31–32

Approximately seven hundred fifty years before Jesus was born as the Babe of Bethlehem, the prophet Isaiah wrote these words, "For unto us a child is born, unto us a son is given: and the government shall be upon his shoulder: and his name shall be called Wonderful, Counselor, The Mighty God, The Everlasting Father, The Prince of Peace" (Isaiah 9:6).

Shortly after Isaiah gave this prophecy, the Assyrians, a bloodthirsty people, swooped into Israel and conquered the ten northern tribes. As they carried their captives back to Assyria, they did so with extreme cruelty, leading the Jews across the desert with fishhooks in their mouths. Along the way, the Assyrians would skin many of the Jews alive. They would cut off the heads of those who complained and stack the heads in large pyramids to be left in the desert as a warning to any would-be rebels.

"When would the One come of whom Isaiah wrote?" Israel must have wondered as she longed for release from her torment. But the time was not yet.

About one hundred years after the Assyrian aggression, another invasion was launched against Israel. This time it was the Babylonians. Beginning in 605 B.C., the Babylonians launched a series of attacks against the southern part of the country. These attacks climaxed in the year 586 B.C., when the soldiers of Nebuchadnezzar, led by Sennacherib, marched into the Holy City of Jerusalem, raped the women, tortured the children, and destroyed the temple.

The people were terrified. Their hearts cried for the day when He might come of whom Isaiah spoke: the Wonderful Counselor, the Mighty God, the Everlasting Father, the Prince of Peace who would carry the government on His shoulders. But the time was not yet.

The Babylonians were followed by the Greeks. On his deathbed, Alexander the Great turned over control of Israel to the Seleucid family. From that dynasty came a man named Antiochus Epiphanes, a picture of the coming anti-Christ. His hatred for the Jews was so great that one day he went into the temple, sacrificed a pig on the altar, made the priests drink the blood, and smeared the remainder on the temple walls.

How the people longed for the day when Messiah would come and the government would be borne upon His shoulders. But the time was not yet.

The Greeks were followed by the Romans. When the Romans descended upon that region of the world and beat it into bloody submission, the people of Israel must surely have wondered if Messiah would ever come. Then news began a to circulate throughout the country about an itinerant Rabbi from Nazareth whose words were so gracious that the common people hear Him gladly (Mark 12:37). "Truly, He must be the Wonderful Counselor," some might have said.

Others might have said, "Did you hear what He did? He spoke a word and the storm ceased. He calls the dead from their graves. He heals those afflicted with leprosy. Truly, He's the Mighty God."

Others might have said, "Did you see the way He took the little children on His lap, laid His hands on them, and pronounced blessing upon them? Truly, He must be the Everlasting Father."

Others might have said, "Did you hear that when His disciples were out at sea, struggling against the storm, He was asleep in the hold of the boat? Such peace we've never seen, never heard of, never known. Truly, He must be the Prince of Peace."

"Could *He* be the fulfillment of Isaiah's prophecy?"

After He fed five thousand men with just a few loaves and fishes, the people gathered around Him to make Him King. No wonder! Just think—a King who could not only free them from Rome's tyranny, but could feed them as well! "We place the government upon Your shoulders," they cried. "Be our King!" But when He heard that, John tells us Jesus departed from the crowd and went up into a mountain alone (John 6:15).

Time went on and people still wondered. Then, after three years of working miracles, giving wonderful counsel, and radiating peace, Jesus rode into Jerusalem. He was greeted by the cries of hundreds of thousands of people gathered in the city to celebrate Passover. They waved palm branches and cried, "Hosanna. Save Now. Blessed is He who comes in the name of the Lord. This is the time! Take the government upon Your shoulders!"

But as the week went on and as the people realized that Jesus was not going to take control politically, their hearts began to turn. By the end of the week, their cry was, "We will not have this Man rule over us. We will not allow the government to rest upon His shoulders. Crucify Him."

They didn't know that on that very day, the government would indeed be placed upon His shoulders. What was upon His shoulders? What is His government? The Cross. The Cross was His symbol, His proof, His method, His government. Putting the Gospel accounts together, we get the scene in totality . . .

As thousands lined the Via Dolorosa, Jesus was preceded by a man carrying a sign reading "King of the Jews" and by two soldiers in full armor. Two additional soldiers followed Him. Along the way, He collapsed. Not wanting Jesus to die on the street, wanting to see Him make it to Calvary where He could be crucified and tortured further, one of the soldiers stopped and rested the point of his spear upon the shoulder of a man named Simon. Simon was now compelled by Roman law to carry the Cross the rest of the way to Calvary.

Simon was from Cyrene—or present-day Libya. We know he was a proselyte, one who had converted to Judaism. Simon of Cyrene, desiring as all Jews did, to celebrate at least one of the feasts in the Holy City, saved all of his money and made all of the necessary plans and preparations. At last the day arrived when he crossed the Mediterranean to celebrate Passover in Jerusalem! But when he arrived, he realized it was an unusual festival. Controversy abounded. At the beginning, people cried, "Hosanna." At the end, they cried, "Crucify." And Simon didn't know what to make of it.

Lined up along the street with hundreds of thousands of others, Simon watched a Man carrying a Cross to Calvary. On the way, the Man stumbled right in front of him. Simon then felt the unmistakable sensation of iron pressed upon his shoulder—the spear of a Roman soldier—and probably wondered, *Why me? Of all the hundreds of thousands of people here, why do I have to carry this criminal's cross up the hill?* But he had no choice. So he put the Cross on his shoulder. The procession continued on to Calvary and Jesus was crucified—with Simon probably watching and wondering.

What happened to Simon? He became a believer. How do I know? Mark writes, "And they compel one Simon a Cyrenian, who passed by, coming out of the country, the father of Alexander and Rufus, to bear his cross" (Mark 15:21).

Mark, writing his Gospel from the city of Rome identified Simon as the father of Rufus and Alexander—the implication being that Rufus and Alexander were well known in the Christian community in Rome. Forty or fifty years later, in Romans 16:13, Rufus' name again is mentioned when Paul, writing to the church in Rome, salutes Rufus and his mother.

The implication of this is very meaningful to me. Simon of Cyrene, who carried the Cross—the government *of* Christ—became governed *by* Christ. Jesus said, "All who are weary, come to Me and I will give you rest. Take My yoke upon you and learn of Me and you'll find rest in your souls" (Matthew 11:28, 29). What is the yoke Jesus places upon our shoulders? Surprise. It's the Cross.

"Wait a minute," you say. "That's contradictory. How could a cross be easy? How could a cross give rest to my soul?"

Jesus knew and demonstrated as no one else could that the key to life truly lies in death. The key to life lies in taking up the cross and dying to self. Even as Jesus died for our sin, so we too are to die to self. Live for yourself and you'll end up dying. Life will be a drag. You'll be unhappy, cynical, bitter, and mean. But die to self and you'll find His burden easy and His load light. The cross is a sweet yoke. Ask Simon.

This week, I encourage you to say, "Lord, I'm going to take up the cross. I'm going to quit worrying about why I am misunderstood or why no one is helping me. I'm going to die to myself, reach out to others, and reach up to You." If you do, you will have a fabulous week, for whoever loses his life will find it. That's the beautiful mystery of Christianity.

"Oh, Jon, you're manipulating me," you say. "You're trying to motivate me and I resent it."

That's okay. Simon probably resented the touch of the spear upon his shoulder, too. But the spear compelled him to carry the Cross.

And the Cross drew him to Christ.

OPEN HOUSE!
A Topical Study of
Matthew 27:50–51

Sometimes we have a "boys will be boys" attitude toward sin. Human nature being what it is, we wonder what the big deal is about messing up. So what if we miss the mark? We're just human aren't we? What's the problem?

The problem is, being a personal God and loving Father, God is grieved by the sin we commit so easily and nonchalantly. Why? Is it because He's hypersensitive? No. Is He upset that we're not behaving like "good little boys and girls"? No. The Father hates sin because He sees the devastating effects it brings about. He sees the sorrow and the suffering, the problems and the pain that sin leaves in its wake. Thus, contrary to popular opinion, sin is not bad because it's forbidden. Sin is forbidden because it's bad. Sin is serious—deadly serious. In Leviticus 17, God declared there can be no remission of sin, no forgiveness of sin, without the shedding of blood. You see, it's not a matter of "boys will be boys" or "accidents happen." Sin is a deadly matter, and God is deadly serious about it. That's why there can be no forgiveness without bloodshed.

The nation of Israel could experience forgiveness of sin on only one day each year: Yom Kippur, the Day of Atonement. On that day, the high priest would go through a great ceremonial cleansing before robing himself in his priestly garments. He would then take the blood of the bulls and goats and lambs that had been sacrificed on the altar in the courtyard and would walk into the Holy Place, the area of the temple where all priests were allowed.

Beyond the Holy Place was a veil separating it from the Holy of Holies. This veil was massive: sixty feet high, thirty feet wide, and ten inches thick. It was made of seventy-two braids, each consisting of twenty-four cords. The veil was so heavy that it took three hundred priests to hang it. Beyond the veil was the Holy of Holies—a small room only the high priest could enter only on the Day of Atonement. The Holy of Holies contained the Ark of the Covenant. Covering the Ark was the mercy seat, and filling the Holy of Holies was the shekinah glory of God—the visible, tangible presence of the Lord. On one day each year, the high priest went from the altar in the courtyard, into the Holy Place and then through the veil into the Holy of Holies, where he sprinkled the blood and interceded on behalf of the people. If, however, the high priest was not properly cleansed—if he was not right with God—he would die in the Holy of Holies. In Exodus we read that hanging from the hem of the high priest's robes were hung bells and pomegranates, signifying the gifts and the fruit of the Spirit. As long as the priests in the Holy Place could hear the bells on the high priest's robes ringing behind the veil, they knew everything was all right. But if the bells stopped ringing, they knew there was trouble. In later years, a rope was tied around the ankle of the high priest so that if he dropped dead, he could be pulled out of the Holy of Holies without placing anyone else's life in jeopardy.

It was a powerful, awesome, and, in a very real sense, terrifying moment when the high priest entered the Holy of Holies to intercede for the people. With this in mind, can you imagine how the priests in the Holy Place must have felt on the day Jesus died?

First, there was darkness. Then the massive veil was ripped from top to bottom as if it were a piece of paper. Suddenly, these priests who would never have been allowed into the Holy of Holies could look right in. The way was now open.

> *For the law having a shadow of good things to come, and not the very image of the things, can never with those sacrifices which they offered year by year continually make the comers thereunto perfect. For then would they not have ceased to be offered? because that the worshipers once purged should have had no more conscience of sins. But in those sacrifices there is a remembrance again made of sins every year. For it is not possible that the blood of bulls and of goats should take away sins.*   Hebrews 10:1–4

The shedding of blood and the application of the blood in the Holy of Holies could not really make one right with God. If it could, there would have been no need to do it year after year. But the continued sacrifices were a constant reminder that the blood of bulls and goats and lambs was simply a shadow, a picture that pointed to One who was to come—the Lamb of God who would take away the sin of the world forever.

> *By the which will we are sanctified through the offering of the body of Jesus Christ once for all. And their sins and iniquities will I remember no more. Now where remission of these is, there is no more offering for sin. Having therefore, brethren, boldness to enter into the holiest by the blood of Jesus, by a new and living way, which he hath consecrated for us, through the veil, that is to say, his flesh; and having an high priest over the house of God; let us draw near with a true heart in full assurance of faith, having our hearts sprinkled from an evil conscience, and our bodies washed with pure water.*
>   Hebrews 10:10, 17–22

Even as the veil in the temple was ripped from top to bottom, so the body of the Lamb of God was ripped for us. He paid the price for all of my sin, rebellion, and foolishness. "It is finished," He cried. The work is complete. Therefore, Hebrews says, come boldly into the presence of God. You have been cleansed by the blood. The veil is rent. No longer is the Holy of Holies for the high priest only. Every person who simply believes Jesus Christ died for his or her sin can come boldly into the presence of God. That's revolutionary! Not only the high priest, not only the pastor, not only a certain Bible study teacher or prayer warrior or singer can come. "*Everyone* come," God is saying. "The price has been paid by one offering. So come—not hesitantly, fearfully, or reluctantly. Come boldly. It's Open House!"

During the Gulf of Tonkin crisis, Henry Kissinger asked one of his eager young assistants at the State Department to research the area. The assistant labored round the clock for six days to prepare what he felt was a thorough and profound paper. Proudly, he put it on Kissinger's desk. It came back fifteen minutes later with this note scribbled at the top: Please redo. HK.

I've got to do it over? the assistant thought. *I gave it my all.* But he worked doubly hard on the rewrite. He placed the second paper on Kissinger's desk. Fifteen minutes later, it was again returned with these words at the bottom: Please redo. HK.

The weary assistant took his paper and spent yet a third week working feverishly to get it done. Again it went to Kissinger's desk. Again it came back with the same note. Finally, the young man stormed into Henry Kissinger's office and declared, "Mr. Kissinger, I've barely slept in three weeks. This is the very best I can do."

"Well, in that case, I'll read it now," replied Kissinger.

Sometimes I think we picture our Father like that, saying to us, "Pray harder. Study longer. Sacrifice deeper. Give more. And if you continue to give, pray, sacrifice, and give—maybe I'll read your paper. Maybe I'll listen to your prayer. Maybe I'll respond to your question." But, gang, the issue is not trying harder. The issue is realizing Jesus *completed* the work once and for all.

The Father says to us, "Come boldly into My presence. Whether you have devotions or not is immaterial. Whether you study My Word or not is irrelevant. My Son opened the way for you. His body was torn. He was the ripped veil."

Yet what do we do? We get out our little scissors and say, "I realize there's a big opening in the veil, but I'm going to try to cut my own way through with my works of righteousness—my devotion, my prayer, my witnessing."

Listen, precious people, the work is done. The price is paid. The way into God's presence is open to everyone who believes. It is open to any person at any time at any place. Thus, any time and any place, every time and every place can be holy. Changing a diaper can be just as much an act of devotion and worship as reading your Bible if you do it to the glory of God, celebrating the fact that you can come into His presence anywhere. That's what the Samaritan woman heard from Jesus when, in answer to her question concerning the proper place to worship, He said, "The Father is seeking those who will worship Him in spirit and in truth" (John 4:24). In other words, it's not where your body is that matters. It's where your heart is that counts.

Working out at the YMCA can be an act of worship if you say, "Lord, I thank You for the fact that I can exercise. Help me to somehow reflect something of You as I'm doing this. May this be a time, Lord, when I can encourage someone and really be thankful to You for what You've given me today." You are in the Holy of Holies at that time, even though there's not a pew in sight. Does this mean you should never read your Bible, never pray, never tithe, or never come to church? Of course not. It means, however, that your motivation for doing those things changes. Instead of feeling responsible to demonstrate your spirituality, you realize the work has already been done, the price paid, the veil rent. And your motivation to worship, tithe, pray, and study the Word changes from one of responsibility to one of response.

When my wife gives me a Valentine, I don't say, "I better read this. In fact, I'll have to discipline myself to do it. I'll carve out time tomorrow morning. Hope I can stay awake. Hope she's impressed that I read it." That's crazy! And yet we take the Valentine of God's Word—His love letter to us—and say, "Well, I better discipline myself. Hope I can stay awake. Where should I start?" When you're in love with someone, you *want* to know what she's saying, what he's thinking, what they're feeling. You *want* to know her mind; you want to hear his heart. Why do I study the Bible? Because I am so impressed with my Father that I want to know more about Him.

He has torn the veil from top to bottom. And we can enter into His presence—anyone, any place, any time. Glory be to God! The price was paid. The veil was rent. The way is open. Come on in!

28 Matthew is the gospel of the King—the King revealed in chapters 1 through 10; the King resisted in chapters 11 through 13; the King retreating in chapters 14 through 20; the King rejected in chapters 21 through 27; and here in chapters 28—the King resurrected!

morning star, Christ Jesus (Revelation 22:16). You see, everything I believe and everything I do must be measured by who He is. If we're going to be stabilized in an ever-quaking, shifting world, we must fix our eyes upon the fixed One, Jesus Christ—the same yesterday, today, and forever (Hebrews 13:8).

Matthew 28:1
In the end of the sabbath, as it began to dawn toward the first day of the week, came Mary Magdalene and the other Mary to see the sepulchre.

Mary Magdalene and Mary, the mother of James the Less, are not coming in a spirit of expectancy or faith. Rather, they are coming to anoint the dead body of Jesus. Doctrinally, they had missed the point entirely by assuming He would still be in the tomb. But devotionally, they were right on the mark in wanting to minister to Him.

Matthew 28:2 (a)
And, behold, there was a great earthquake ...

I read about a man who was caught in a severe earthquake. "No matter where I looked," he said, "everything was in motion. Then I looked up through the hole in my roof and saw the stars. They became my fixed points of reference."

How true! This world is constantly quaking, trembling, and shaking. We need a fixed reference point—and we have one in the bright and

Matthew 28:2 (b)
... for the angel of the Lord descended from heaven, and came and rolled back the stone from the door, and sat upon it.

Sometimes movies depict the angel moving the stone so Jesus could come out. Believe me, folks, Jesus did not need the help of an angel to get out of the tomb. He's the same One who, a few hours later, would walk through walls. No, the stone was rolled away not to let Jesus out of the tomb, but to let the disciples look in and see that it was empty.

When General Gordon, a godly man, discovered this tomb in 1885, he did a very wise thing. He took a jar of soil gathered from the floor of the tomb to some chemists and asked if there was any trace of decomposition in the soil. The analysis found that there was no trace of decay in the tomb. Indeed, there never was.

Matthew 28:3, 4
His countenance was like lightning, and his raiment white as snow: And for fear of him

the keepers did shake, and became as dead men.

Members of the finest fighting force in the known world were wiped out. Why? Because they saw the angel of the Lord draw a flaming sword? No. Because the angel spoke a word and they fell down? No. I suggest to you it was the awesome power of purity that caused these Roman soldiers to become as dead men.

Gang, do you know where power truly lies? Do you know from whence effectiveness really comes? It doesn't come from being strong and assertive, proving your point, or standing up for your rights. That's not what Jesus taught. He said, "Blessed are the meek. The whole world will be theirs" (see Matthew 5:5). Meekness, holiness, and purity are what cause the Roman soldiers of this world to collapse. When Jesus taught us to turn the other cheek, it was not so we would become lifeless doormats. No, whether it concerns your husband, your wife, your children, your employer, your relatives, or your neighbors, change comes not through asserting yourself. It comes through the power of purity.

Matthew 28:5 (a)
And the angel answered and said unto the women, Fear not ye . . .

"Fear not" was the angelic injunction to the shepherds on the hillside at His birth, to the women at the tomb at His death, and to us today.

For topical study of Matthew 28:5–6 entitled "Freedom from Fear," turn to page 216.

Matthew 28:5 (b), 6 (a)
. . . for I know that ye seek Jesus, which was crucified. He is not here: for he is risen, as he said.

"As he said." I like that phrase. It is a subtle reminder, a gentle rebuke. In other words it's as if the angel said, "You should have known He wouldn't be here. Didn't He tell you He would rise?"

Matthew 28:6 (b)–8
Come, see the place where the Lord lay. And go quickly, and tell his disciples that he is risen from the dead; and, behold, he goeth before you into Galilee; there shall ye see him: lo, I have told you. And they departed quickly from the sepulchre with fear and great joy; and did run to bring his disciples word.

Notice the wording. First: "Come and see." Then: "Go and tell." Sincere in their desire to see missionary work accomplished or evangelism explode, many say, "We're going to win the world for Christ." But it won't happen until they first "come and see." Not until we get a clear vision of the "place where He lay"—of His work on the Cross and His resurrection from the grave—do we have a message to "go and tell."

"Come and see. Then go and tell." That is the message of the angel to these women who were first entrusted with the biggest news story in history. . . .

For topical study of Matthew 28:8 entitled "Being Used by Being There," turn to page 219.

Matthew 28:9
And as they went to tell his disciples, behold, Jesus met them, saying, All hail.

"All hail" was a very common expression. Slang of that day, it meant, "Howdy." I like that! When the women came to the tomb, their doctrine was wrong. They thought Jesus was dead. But He Himself came to them because although they were doctrinally wrong, they were devotionally right. I'm convinced a lot of us take pride in our doctrine when what the Lord desires is our affection. We are committed to precepts about Christ, but are we committed to the Person of Christ? Many believers are doctrinally right, but they're dead right because their doctrine lacks devotion. On the other hand, your knowledge may be limited and your doctrine not perfectly accurate, but if your affection for Him is real, Jesus will appear to you time and time again, saying, "All hail! Howdy!"

Matthew 28:9, 10
And they came and held him by the feet, and worshiped him. Then said Jesus unto them, Be not afraid: go tell my brethren that they go into Galilee, and there shall they see me.

When Jesus was arrested in the Garden of Gethsemane, His disciples split the scene. When He was being tried, Peter was cursing and denying he even knew Him. If you were in Jesus' sandals, would you have said, "Go tell my brothers I'm going to meet them in Galilee"—or would you have said, "Go tell those losers I'm back and they're in hot water"?

After He died, Jesus descended into hell. Then He ascended on high and gave gifts to men (Ephesians 4:8, 9). If *I* went to hell for people who forsook and denied me, I would go to heaven and say, "Father, let's deal with them. They've got some lessons to learn. Didn't You say in Your Word that whom You love You chasten? Well, this is the time to chasten."

We have such a tendency to want to teach people lessons, straighten them out, shake them up, and set them right. But that's not the heart of our Lord, our Hero, Jesus Christ. When He ascended He didn't say, "Father, let's punish these guys." He said, "Father let's give gifts to them."

Matthew 28:11
Now when they were going, behold, some of the watch came into the city, and shewed unto the chief priests all the things that were done.

The Roman soldiers who had stood watch at the tomb came into Jerusalem saying to the priests, "You won't believe what happened. The earth shook. We saw an angel. The stone is gone. Things are happening!" And what did these "holy" men do?

Matthew 28:12–14
And when they were assembled with the elders, and had taken counsel, they gave large money unto the soldiers, saying, Say ye, His disciples came by night, and stole him away while we slept. And if this come to the governor's ears, we will persuade him, and secure you.

After employing deceitfulness, treachery, and mob psychology to bring about the death of Jesus, the chief priests and elders finally resorted to bribery to cover up His resurrection. "Here's some money," they said to the Roman soldiers. "We want you to say that while you slept, the disciples came and stole Jesus' body." This was a ridiculous lie for two reasons. First, if the soldiers were sleeping, how could they have known who took the body? Second, if these soldiers had indeed fallen asleep, they would have been executed according to Roman military law for their failure to keep watch. Far from dying, however, these guys showed up the next day driving BMWs.

Matthew 28:15
So they took the money, and did as they were taught: and this saying is commonly reported among the Jews until this day.

On college campuses today, some so-called intellectuals still parrot this two thousand-year-old lie. Jesus' disciples took His body? That's pretty

hard to swallow when you realize James was sawn in half embracing the Resurrection; Thomas had his brains beaten out with a club; Peter was crucified upside down; and John was placed in a cauldron of boiling oil. To a man, the disciples died violent deaths. Many of them saw their families tortured and killed because they continued to preach the Resurrection. I don't have enough faith to believe that eleven men suffered brutally, watched the annihilation of their families, and died violently for a lie. Certainly one of them would have cracked.

If you do not believe Jesus resurrected, I challenge you to explain to me where His body went. If the Romans had stolen it, why didn't they produce it? Christianity was ultimately the force that led to the destruction of the entire Roman Empire. If His disciples were merely hiding Jesus' body, why did they give their lives believing He had ascended?

You see, I would be a Christian even if I had no emotional feelings about it. Intellectually, when I look at all the evidence, I have no other choice. The body is not there. The Resurrection is the most analyzed event in history. I also believe it is the most provable. That's why Jesus said, "One sign I'll give you. Destroy this body and in three days I will rise again." Truly, the Resurrection verifies that Jesus is exactly who He claimed to be.

Matthew 28:16
Then the eleven disciples went away into Galilee, into a mountain where Jesus had appointed them.

According to 1 Corinthians 15:6, it would seem this was also the time when Jesus appeared to the five hundred.

Matthew 28:17
And when they saw him, they worshiped him: but some doubted.

On any given Sunday, we sense the Lord's presence and we worship Him. But some doubt. Even then, some doubted.

Matthew 28:18, 19 (a)
And Jesus came and spake unto them, saying, All power is given unto me in heaven and in earth. Go ye therefore, and teach all nations. . . .

In this verse, the word "go" is a participle and literally means "as you are going." In other words, "As you are going to the grocery store, as you are going to school, as you are going to Mexico—wherever you're going—share the gospel." In this light, the Great Commission takes on a much broader perspective. We're to be sharing and teaching wherever we're going, whatever we're doing.

Matthew 28:19 (b), 20 (a)
. . . baptizing them in the name of the Father, and of the Son, and of the Holy Ghost: Teaching them to observe all things whatsoever I have commanded you . . .

Jesus didn't say, "Baptizing them in the *names* of the Father, Son, and Holy Ghost." He said, "Baptizing them in the *name* of the Father, Son, and Holy Ghost." Thus, here is another picture of the reality of the great mystery called the Trinity.

Matthew 28:20 (b)
. . . and, lo, I am with you always, even unto the end of the world. Amen.

"As you're going, as you're baptizing, as you're teaching, as you're traveling together as disciples of Me, know that I am with you always even unto the end of the world." That is what Jesus says to you today. That is why the Resurrection is so important. He's *with* us!

I am crucified with Christ: nevertheless I live; yet not I, but Christ liveth in me: and the life which I now live in the flesh I live by the faith of the Son of God, who loved me, and gave himself for me.   Galatians 2:20

"Christ liveth in *me*." That's the beauty of the Resurrection and the genius of Christianity.

FREEDOM FROM FEAR
A Topical Study of
Matthew 28:5–6

June 18, 1815 was one of the decisive days in world history. Napoleon had just left the island of Elba, where he had been rebuilding his army in exile. Sailing back to the mainland of Europe with him were seventy-five thousand soldiers, including the Old Guard—perhaps the finest fighting men in the world. Although the Duke of Wellington, Commander -in Chief of the British forces, offered to do his best to stop Napoleon, it seemed like a futile assignment. At Waterloo, with only sixty-seven thousand allied troops, Wellington engaged Napoleon in battle. If Napoleon was indeed victorious, there would have been no stopping him in his drive to reclaim all of Europe. The people in England waited for hours as the battle raged. Eager for news, they positioned a ship in the Channel that would signal the outcome of the contest to watchmen stationed in towers along the shores of Dover.

Finally, before it became enshrouded in fog, the signal ship signaled this message to the towers: Wellington defeated. Although the hearts of the watchmen sank, they relayed the word quickly to the waiting messengers. And word spread like wildfire throughout England that Wellington had been defeated.

Hopelessness and despair set in as the British knew it would only be a matter of time before Napoleon would sail across the Channel and lay claim to their country. However, when the fog lifted, the ship fired a cannon to get the attention of those in the tower and the third and final word of the message was relayed. The word was "Napoleon." What a difference the third word made, for the completed message read: Wellington defeated Napoleon. Suddenly, the hearts of the British people rejoiced. Napoleon had been stopped. They would remain a free people. The third word filled their hearts with great joy.

But the followers of Jesus experienced far greater joy and liberty on the third day when the rest of His message came through. On the third day, the fog lifted and the third word came forth: He is risen!

In Hebrews 2 we see a passage that will hopefully give you new insight into the glory of the Resurrection.

> *Forasmuch then as the children are partakers of flesh and blood, he also himself likewise took part of the same; that through death he might destroy him that had the power of death, that is, the devil.*   Hebrews 2:14

God Himself became a Man in the Person of Jesus Christ. He became *like* us that He might die *for* us and give hope *to* us.

> *And deliver them who through fear of death were all their lifetime subject to bondage.*   Hebrews 2:15

Why did God become flesh and blood? To deliver us from the fear of death. You see, the Bible says that, although man might deny it on the surface, he is in bondage to the fear of death deep within. We don't like to talk about death, but we know it's inevitable. After all, the statistics on death are pretty conclusive: ten out of ten people die.

Fear of Physical Death

The Bible says the fear of death is bondage. Regardless of what the commercial says, we're not getting better. We're getting older. We can fight it with surgery. We can eat health foods all day. But the fact is, we're not going to win. We're dying. If you're a believer, you've probably already settled the issue of physical death. Because of what Christ did for you on the Cross, you know you're going to heaven. But maybe you're afraid of another kind of death. I suggest this text paints a much broader picture than simply the fear of physical death . . .

Fear of Financial Death

- "Will I have enough money to live comfortably after I retire?"
- "If inflation hits double digits again, what will happen to me?"
- "What if Alzheimer's strikes me?"
- "How will I afford medical costs?"

- "Will Social Security be enough?"
- "Will Social Security be there at all?"

Fear of Relational Death

- "What if he tells me he's seeing someone else?"
- "What if she says she just wants to be friends?"
- "What if the relationship crumbles?"

Fear of Vocational Death

- "What if I get fired?"
- "What if there's a lay-off?"
- "What if there's a cut-back?"
- "What if I can't make the grade?"

Jesus, who became like us, died for us. But it seemed like everything was hopeless and lost. Then suddenly, He came back to life. And because He conquered death, the ultimate enemy, *nothing* can stand in His way—not physical infirmities, not finances, not relationships, not vocations. How we need to hear the message of the Resurrection. Jesus Christ has risen from the dead. Therefore *nothing* can conquer Him. And guess where He is. The One who conquered death now lives in my heart by His Holy Spirit. The resurrected One now indwells *me*.

Physically, if I get sick, the One who lives in me will see me through. He's going to see me through. Either I'll get well and live a few more years or I'll go to heaven—where I long to be.

Financially, He has promised to see us through. He has promised to supply all of our needs (Philippians 4:19) and that no good thing would He withhold from those who walk with Him (Psalm 84:11).

Relationally, maybe your friends have left you or your marriage has collapsed. Know this, dear friend: Jesus is in you. He is the Resurrection. And He has promised in His Word to restore unto you the years the locust has eaten (Joel 2:25). As Jonah discovered, He is the God of the second chance. He is the One who works all things together for good (Romans 8:28). Thus, we have nothing to fear.

"If Christ Jesus be not raised from the dead," Paul said, "then we are of all men most miserable" (1 Corinthians 15:19). But if Christ is raised from the dead, we are free from the fear of death. How does this work practically?

You might be saying, "I believe Jesus died for my sins. I believe He rose again and lives in me. But I am still afraid of this, that, or the other. I'm in bondage to the fear of death. What can I do?" Do what Mary Magdalene and the other Mary did. The next verse in Matthew tells us that they came to the place where Christ lay. They came to where they thought He was. They came to the tomb. Even though they thought He was dead, they longed to be with Him.

So, too, if you find yourself in bondage to the fear of death, go to the place where you last saw Him—even if you're not sure He's still there. And like the women at the tomb, perhaps when you least expect it, you'll feel His touch upon your shoulder and you'll hear Him say, "You came seeking Me. Thank you. Now what can I do for you?"

I'm so thankful for Jesus Christ because, like you, I have experiences of wondering. "Is this going to die? Is that going to die? What's going to happen over here?" But then I go to the place where I last saw Him, and sure enough, I hear His voice again.

And I'm free.

BEING USED BY BEING THERE
A Topical Study of
Matthew 28:8

The greatest news story in the history of humanity broke on a spring morning in A.D. 32. The news? Jesus of Nazareth, an itinerant Preacher, had risen from the dead just as He had predicted. An angel told the story and entrusted it not to an investigative journalist from *60 Minutes*, not to a network anchorman, not to an editor of *TIME* or even *Christianity Today*, not to a theologian, not to one of the remaining disciples. No, the ones who were entrusted with the most profound and incredible story in all history were two women. Why? Here are some possible reasons. . . .

Because God Loves to Use the Weak to Confound the Strong

Peter tells us in his first epistle that the woman is the weaker vessel (1 Peter 3:7). Biblically, the concept of the "weaker vessel" speaks not of inferiority but of sensitivity. Innately, a woman has greater sensitivity than a man. Instead of using Peter, James, John, or any of the boys who hung out with Him, roughing it and sleeping on the hillsides of Galilee, God initially used two women to spread the gospel, seemingly delighting in using the weaker vessel to confound the strong.

Because They Were the Last Ones at the Cross

In Matthew 27:55, we read that a number of women were at the Cross beholding Jesus afar off. The two Marys, mentioned at the end of chapter 27 are the same two Marys who are named at the beginning of chapter 28. It remains true, precious people, that those who go through the deepest sorrow will often be those who experience the greatest joy.

Because Thousands of Years Earlier, Death Had Come by a Woman

Seduced by the serpent to eat of the forbidden fruit, Eve shared with Adam in the fall of humanity. It was in a Garden that death came *by* a woman. Here, it is at a garden tomb that life is announced *to* a woman. That's so often the way of the Lord. He takes those of us who have missed the mark or messed up in a certain area and delights in using us to minister to others at a later time. He heals the hurts. He restores, rebuilds, renews, and revives. And then He releases powerful ministry in the very area where we blew it previously. That's Good News. That's the gospel.

Because the Greatest Love Brings the Greatest Privilege

We know from John's Gospel that when Mary Magdalene came to the tomb and found it empty, she initially thought someone had moved Jesus' body to another sepulcher. Seeing a Man she supposed to be the gardener, she asked, "Where have they laid my Lord? If you have moved Him, tell me where you have laid Him and I will take Him away," (see John 20:15). How did Mary think she could move the body of Jesus all by herself? I suggest the answer is that when you love someone, you don't weigh the heaviness of the difficulties or the obstacles. When you love someone, you just find a way. And Mary loved Jesus deeply.

Women are special to God's heart and indispensable to His church. I believe that the Lord entrusted women first with the gospel message because He delights to use the weak to confound the strong; because they suffered the deepest sorrow at the Cross and would therefore experience the greatest joy at the tomb; because death came by a woman and life was announced through women; because their great love brought great privilege.

But I think there is one more reason . . .

Because *They Were There*

Who came to the tomb? A couple of women. So God said, "I'll use them. They will be the first messengers of the gospel." I believe God uses people who are there. The people who are used are the ones who gather around the body of Christ and desire to minister to the body of Christ even as these women did. Start saying, "I don't need to pray any more with believers. I don't have time for fellowship. I'm doing fine by myself,"—and you will increasingly miss the opportunity to move in the power of ministry and the effectiveness of revelation. If you start to pull away or kick back—watch out. Revelation will pass you by. Oh, God's love for you will still be the same. His grace will be upon you just as much as ever. Your place in heaven will remain secure. But your usefulness will be diminished proportionately to your moving away from the body.

"But the body's dead," you say. That's what the two Marys thought. When they came to the tomb to wrap Jesus' body in spices, they had no idea He would be resurrected. They were coming to minister to His *dead* body. That is why I don't believe it is ever excusable for a person to say, "I'm not going to minister at that place or to those people because they're spiritually dead." No, if you really want to be a servant, like the women at the tomb, you'll minister faithfully regardless of what *seems* to be.

Maybe you're thinking, *Let someone else have the revelation. Let someone else carry the news. I don't care.* But look at how the women left the tomb. Matthew says they left with great joy. How did the disciples, who were hiding out on their own, feel at this point? Discouraged and defeated.

So you have a choice. You can live like the disciples or like the women at the tomb. If you choose to live like the disciples—on your own and hidden away—your life will abound with discouragement and defeat.

But if you say, "I want to be where Jesus is, I want to be with His Body even if it seems dead. I want to be there listening and learning, serving and giving. I want to pray and worship. I want to be *there*"—you will have a life full of great, great joy.

NOTES

[1] C. S. Lewis, *Mere Christianity* (San Francisco, CA: HarperCollins, 2002), p. 201.
[2] Paraphrased from *Messages from The Wild: An Almanac of Suburban Natural and Unnatural History* by Frederick R. Gehlbach, Copyright © 2002. Courtesy of the University of Texas Press.
[3] Jay Rogers, *The Downfall of Communism*, March 1990.
[4] Jerry Moffit, *The Skeptical Review, Volume One, Number One*, 1990.

MARK

Background to Mark

The shortest of the four gospels, Mark's is only sixteen chapters. It's a fast-moving presentation of the life of Christ. And that's appropriate, for Mark's primary audience was the Romans, a fast-moving people. This explains why there are only two Old Testament references in his entire Gospel. Contrast this with Matthew's account—written primarily to the Jews—in which we find numerous Old Testament references. Luke's Gospel was written for the Greek mind-set. John's was written for the world in totality. But because Mark writes to the Romans, we don't see an abundance of sermons and discourses in his Gospel. Instead, the emphasis is upon the works rather than the words of Jesus.

Mark's full name was John Mark (John his Hebrew name, and Mark his Roman name). John Mark was specifically suited to write this Gospel because of his background. We know from Acts 12 that he was the son of a wealthy woman in whose house the early church met. And from Peter's reference to him as his son in the faith (1 Peter 5), it would seem as though Peter was influential in John Mark's conversion. If this be so, it would make Mark's Gospel actually Peter's Gospel—for it would have been Peter who informed Mark of the events contained therein. Thus, scholars believe they are hearing the words and feeling the heart of Peter as they study the Gospel of Mark.

Matthew presents Jesus as the King. Luke presents Him as the Perfect Man. And John presents Him as the Son of God. But in the Gospel before us, Mark presents Jesus as a Servant. Chapters 1—10 portray the Servant living His life in service; chapters 11—16 portray Him giving His life in sacrifice.

In Acts 13:5, Mark himself was called a servant as he accompanied his uncle Barnabas and the apostle Paul on their first missionary journey into Asia Minor, or present-day Turkey. Although translated "minister," the Greek word *huperetes* literally means "under-rower." Picture a Roman galley. On the top deck, all of the passengers are enjoying the cruise through the Mediterranean. But down below, away from the passengers on the upper deck, are the *huperetes*, the under-rowers. No one sees them as they toil hour after hour, day after day, week after week; stroking,

stroking, stroking. Sixty, eighty, one hundred twenty in number, the *huperetes* would be underneath rowing, toiling, sweating, working in order that the ship might move.

What does it mean to be a servant? It doesn't mean to overlord, barking commands from the upper deck. No, to be a servant, to be a minister, means to be one who undergirds, who works behind the scenes, who toils steadily and faithfully—even though he might never be recognized or acknowledged. Too often, our idea of "minister" is wrong. If one wants to be a true minister, a servant, a *huperetes,* he will labor in obscurity if necessary, rowing, undergirding. In Mark's Gospel we see Jesus moving away from the crowd, working in quietness, ministering in relative obscurity.

As Mark accompanied Paul and Barnabas, something happened. The Scriptures don't say why, but simply that John Mark turned back from Barnabas and Paul and went home (Acts 13:13). Consequently, when Paul and Barnabas were preparing to embark on their second missionary venture and Barnabas said he would get John Mark, Paul said, "Not so fast. He turned back last time. We can't be slowed down by one who is so unfaithful." Barnabas, whose name means, "Son of Consolation," insisted, however, that John Mark come along. As a result, Scripture records that "the contention was sharp between them" (see Acts 15:39).

Instead, Barnabas took John Mark, while Paul teamed with Silas and twice headed in different directions. Who was right? I believe Paul was justified in his position because he had in view the ministry in totality. I also believe Barnabas did well in caring about John Mark because later on we see John Mark laboring with Paul (Philemon 24), recommended by Paul to the church at Colosse (Colossians 4:10), and requested by Paul (2 Timothy 4:11). In other words, so good a job did Barnabas in restoring and renewing John Mark that his young nephew went on to have a vital ministry—even to Paul in the apostle's last days.

This gives me great hope. Maybe, like me, you can think of times in your life when you dropped the ball, turned away, fell down. Following such times, the tendency is to think, *It's over. I'll never be used.* But I would encourage you to remember John Mark who, although he chickened out on his first journey, went on to minister effectively—not only to Paul, but also to us through the Gospel before us. . . .

MARK

1 Mark 1:1
The beginning of the gospel of Jesus Christ, the Son of God.

The gospel is neither a discussion nor a debate. It's not good views, but Good News. And Mark wastes no time in getting to its heart.

Mark 1:2, 3
As it is written in the prophets, Behold, I send my messenger before thy face, which shall prepare thy way before thee. The voice of one crying in the wilderness, Prepare ye the way of the Lord, make his paths straight.

Mark quotes only two prophecies in his entire Gospel: this one, from Malachi 3:1; and Isaiah 40:3, which refers, of course, to John the Baptist.

Mark 1:4
John did baptize in the wilderness, and preach the baptism of repentance for the remission of sins.

The baptism of John—this one who came to prepare the way for Jesus Christ—was not for salvation, but for preparation. It was for the one who knew he had missed the mark, the one who knew he was a sinner, the one who knew he needed a Redeemer. Thus, John's baptism was preparatory, but not complete, for Jesus had not yet died for their sins.

Mark 1:5–9
And there went out unto him all the land of Judaea, and they of Jerusalem, and were all baptized of him in the river of Jordan, confessing their sins. And John was clothed with camel's hair, and with a girdle of a skin about his loins; and he did eat locusts and wild honey; and preached, saying, There cometh one mightier than I after me, the latchet of whose shoes I am not worthy to stoop down and unloose. I indeed have baptized you with water: but he shall baptize you with the Holy Ghost. And it came to pass in those days, that Jesus came from Nazareth of Galilee, and was baptized of John in Jordan.

As John called people to repent, suddenly Jesus showed up, requesting to be baptized. Jesus had no sin. What did He need to confess? Why would He ask to be baptized by John? I suggest two reasons . . .

Although baptism is indeed a symbol of death, burial, and resurrection (Romans 6), the word *baptizo* was initially used with regard to dyeing cloth. Material "baptized" in colored dye would assume the color of the dye. Therefore, baptism is not only a symbol of dying, but of dyeing. What is Jesus doing here? He's identifying with us. Dipped in the same water we are, not ashamed of us, but identifying with us, He meets us. We take on the same color in the water of baptism. Regardless of the fact that two thousand years separate us from this event chronologically and six thousand miles geographically, we identify with Jesus and He with us through baptism.

Not only does Jesus' baptism illustrate His identification with us, it shows His submission to the Father, for through baptism, Jesus said, "I have come to die." Every other teacher, philosopher, or guru came to live—and yet, their so-called "ministries" were interrupted by their deaths. Not so with Jesus. He came to die. Death didn't interrupt His ministry. It fulfilled it.

Mark 1:10
And straightway coming up out of the water, he saw the heavens opened, and the Spirit like a dove descending upon him.

Conceived as He was by the Spirit in the womb of Mary, the Spirit was already *in* Jesus. But here we see the Spirit coming *upon* Him at the beginning of His ministry, empowering Him for service.

Mark 1:11
And there came a voice from heaven, saying, Thou art my beloved Son, in whom I am well pleased.

Although it seems too good to be true, if you're a believer, this word of the Father applies to you as well, for, according to 2 Corinthians 5:21, you are in Christ. I can go through the day praising the Lord, casting my burdens upon Him—not because of who I am, but because of where I am, not because of what I've done or haven't done—but because I'm in Christ.

Mark 1:12 (a)
And immediately . . .

Mark's use of the words "immediately" and "straightway" eight times in his first chapter alone illustrate the speed with which he moves through his account.

Mark 1:12 (b)
. . . the Spirit driveth him into the wilderness.

Directly following the glorious experience of hearing the voice of His Father, the Spirit led Jesus into the wilderness. Why? Not to do Him in, but to show Him off. . . .

Suppose you go to the local Jeep dealer and say, "I'm thinking about buying a Jeep." After opening the door of his latest model, a salesman would say, "Hop in"—and proceed to drive you to some rough terrain, where he would shift into four-wheel drive and take you off-road—flying over hills, splashing through rivers. Why? Not to damage the car, but to show you what it can do.

So, too, in driving Jesus to the wilderness, the Father was saying, "Watch My Son. No matter what Satan throws at Him, He will come through beautifully." And the same thing is true of you and me. You see, only what the Father allows can come into our lives. Therefore, when temptations, trials, difficulties, wilderness experiences, hard times come our way, it is because the Father has allowed them in order to silence Satan's accusation that you only serve God in easy times, and to show you off to a doubting world.

Mark 1:13 (a)
And he was there in the wilderness forty days, tempted of Satan . . .

Forty days puts us in mind of the forty years God's people wandered in the wilderness. Because the law will never lead a man into the Land of Promise, Moses, who speaks of the law, was unable to lead the people into the land. No, it was Joshua, whose name is the Hebrew form of "Jesus," who brought the people into the land flowing with milk and honey.

Mark 1:13 (b)
. . . and was with the wild beasts; and the angels ministered unto him.

Because of his sin, the first Adam lost the dominion over nature given to him (Genesis 1:28). Contrast this with the Last Adam, Jesus Christ, to whom dominion is returned as evidenced by the wild beasts that surrounded Him in the wilderness—a sneak preview of the coming kingdom wherein the wolf shall lie down by the lamb (Isaiah 11:6). Where Adam failed in the garden, Jesus came through in the desert.

Mark 1:14–20 (a)
Now after that John was put in prison, Jesus came into Galilee, preaching the gospel of the kingdom of God, and saying, The time is fulfilled, and the kingdom of God is at hand: repent ye, and believe the gospel. Now as he walked by the sea of Galilee, he saw Simon and Andrew his brother casting a net into the sea: for they were fishers. And Jesus said unto them, Come ye after me, and I will make you to become fishers of men. And straightway they forsook their nets, and followed him. And when he had gone a little further thence, he saw James the son of Zebedee, and John his brother, who also were in the ship mending their nets. And straightway he called them . . .

Of the twelve men Jesus called, at least seven were fishermen. To be a fisherman, one must possess patience and perseverance—qualities as valuable in fishing for men as in fishing for fish. I find it interesting that Peter and Andrew were casting their nets into the sea when Jesus called them. On the other hand, James and John were mending nets. The ministry of Peter and Andrew was evangelism, as evidenced by Andrew repeatedly bringing people to Christ, and Peter preaching the sermon on the Day of Pentecost that "caught" three thousand people in the net of the gospel. The ministry of John and James, by contrast, was that of mending people through their emphasis on both the heartfelt and practical nature of love. Whatever your temperament personally, watch the Lord use it in your own ministry.

Mark 1:20 (b)
. . . and they left their father Zebedee in the ship with the hired servants, and went after him.

The fact that Zebedee had servants meant that he had money. Therefore, when James and John left their father and the nets, they were leaving a bright future vocationally and financially. Yet they could do no other, for they found a higher calling than simply money. Filet of sole failed in comparison to saving souls. They were "hooked" and their "net" worth skyrocketed when they chose to follow the One who would impact eternity through their lives.

Mark 1:21
And they went into Capernaum; and straightway on the sabbath day he entered into the synagogue, and taught.

The synagogue is not the temple. The temple—where sacrifices were made, where the priesthood served—was in Jerusalem. Synagogues, on the other hand, dotted the countryside of Israel, having come into being during the Babylonian captivity when Jews were unable to worship at the temple in Jerusalem. Usually small in structure, synagogues were established wherever ten or more Jewish males lived, and were not places of sacrifice, but of study, worship, and prayer. They were overseen not by the traditional priesthood, but by laymen through a council of elders—one of whom was appointed ruler. When a rabbi would come into the area, the ruler of the synagogue would invite him to come and speak on the Sabbath day. As we see in the Book of Acts, Paul took advantage of this, going from synagogue to synagogue preaching Jesus.

Mark 1:22
And they were astonished at his doctrine: for he taught them as one that had authority, and not as the scribes.

The scribes would speak *from* authorities, quoting rabbis in their teachings. Jesus, however, spoke *with* authority. "Ye have heard it said . . . but I say unto you . . . ." He declared (Matthew 5—6).

Mark 1:23, 24
And there was in their synagogue a man with an unclean spirit; and he cried out, saying, Let us alone; what have we to do with thee, thou Jesus of Nazareth? art thou come to destroy us? I know thee who thou art, the Holy One of God.

Although this man may have sat undetected in the synagogue week after month after year, it wasn't until Jesus showed up that all hell broke loose quite literally. This should not be surprising. Whenever the Son of God shows up, the forces of hell respond.

Mark 1:25–28
And Jesus rebuked him, saying, Hold thy peace, and come out of him. And when the unclean spirit had torn him, and cried with a loud voice, he came out of him. And they were all amazed, insomuch that they questioned among themselves, saying, What thing is this? what new doctrine is this? for with authority commandeth he even the unclean spirits, and they do obey him. And immediately his fame spread abroad throughout all the region round about Galilee.

The demon left, but not before he tore up this individual. So, too, when we rid evil from our lives—when we say, "Yes, Lord, have Your way," as old habits, relationships, patterns are forsaken—there may be some tearing initially, but we will also experience freedom and blessing eventually.

Mark 1:29
And forthwith, when they were come out of the synagogue, they entered into the house of Simon and Andrew, with James and John.

Peter took Jesus home with him after church— always a good thing to do. I hope we'll increasingly get to the place where, when we leave Bible studies and services, we won't be those who quickly move into the next activity, but will learn to bring the Lord home.

Mark 1:30
But Simon's wife's mother lay sick of a fever, and anon they tell him of her.

You who spend time in worship and Bible study, beware. Satan will attempt to discourage you by causing fever in your home, heat in your house. But bring Jesus home with you and watch a miracle happen.

Mark 1:31
And he came and took her by the hand, and lifted her up; and immediately the fever left her, and she ministered unto them.

Throughout his Gospel, Mark emphasizes the touch of Jesus. Jesus heals not only through the word He speaks, but through the touch He shares—not only telling us what to do, but touching us and encouraging us as well.

Mark 1:32–35
And at even, when the sun did set, they brought unto him all that were diseased, and them that were possessed with devils. And all the city was gathered together at the door. And he healed many that were sick of divers diseases, and cast out many devils; and suffered not the devils to speak, because they knew him. And in the morning, rising up a great while before day, he went out, and departed into a solitary place, and there prayed.

Jesus had been serving, touching, giving, teaching, praying, healing. And yet, as was His practice morning by morning, He woke early to receive instruction concerning the day before Him.

Mark 1:36, 37
And Simon and they that were with him followed after him. And when they had found him, they said unto him, All men seek for thee.

"This is great!" said the disciples. "All men seek You! Everyone wants You!" You will find yourself frazzled and fried if you listen to such voices. Your priorities will get mixed up; you'll feel wiped out; your ministry will be done in; your heart will be weighed down.

Mark 1:38
And he said unto them, Let us go into the next towns, that I may preach there also: for therefore came I forth.

It was having "come forth" from the place of prayer that Jesus could say with confidence, "Let's split. My Father has other plans for Me today."

For topical study of Mark 1:32–38 entitled "The Key to Keeping Focused," turn to page 227.

Mark 1:39–41 (a)
And he preached in their synagogues throughout all Galilee, and cast out devils. And there came a leper to him, beseeching him, and kneeling down to him, and saying unto him, If thou wilt, thou canst make me clean. And Jesus, moved with compassion, put forth his hand, and touched him . . .

Jesus did the unthinkable when He reached out to touch the leper.

Mark 1:41 (b)–44
. . . and saith unto him, I will; be thou clean. And as soon as he had spoken, immediately the leprosy departed from him, and he was cleansed. And he straitly charged him, and forthwith sent him away; and saith unto him, See thou say nothing to any man: but go thy way, shew thyself to the priest, and offer for thy cleansing those things which Moses commanded, for a testimony unto them.

By going to the priest, the leper would be able to confirm his healing, and Jesus would be insulated from the circus mentality that all too often typifies today's healing ministries.

Mark 1:45
But he went out, and began to publish it much, and to blaze abroad the matter, insomuch that Jesus could no more openly enter into the city, but was without in desert places: and they came to him from every quarter.

Over and over again in the Gospel accounts, we hear Jesus say, "Don't tell anyone." And yet, as did the leper, we see people spreading the word radically. Then, after His death and resurrection, we hear Jesus say, "*Now* go into all the world." And what do we do? We "say nothing to any man." We have it all backward.

Because the healed leper spoke too soon, Jesus was hindered from going into the city. But how many times do we speak too late and hinder someone from coming to Him? Whether we be over-eager ex-lepers, or staid and shy churchgoers, what we must do is God's will—nothing more, nothing less, nothing else.

THE KEY TO KEEPING FOCUSED
A Topical Study of
Mark 1:32–38

They accused Him of being a glutton and a winebibber, of being born illegitimately and casting out demons by the power of Satan. But no one ever accused Jesus of being busy or unapproachable, uptight or upset. Our culture values busyness. In our society, the busier one is, the more important he is. But in reality, deep within our hearts, we know that barely making it here, narrowly making it there is not the way life was meant to be. Jesus moved in serenity and tranquility—opposite of what we value in our society, but what we desire innately.

How did He do this? As I read Mark's Gospel, I am increasingly convinced that Jesus' life focused on three things . . .

The Father's Will

In talking about His relationship with His heavenly Father, Jesus said, "Truly I say unto you, The Son can do nothing of himself, but what he seeth the Father do: for what things soever he doeth, these also doeth the Son likewise" (see John 5:19). "I'm not doing My own thing," Jesus said. "I'm not pursuing My own pleasure, toying with My own hobbies. My life is about one thing: What I see and hear the Father doing and speaking. My own will? I have none."

This was seen nowhere more clearly than in the Garden of Gethsemane, when Jesus prayed, "Father, if it be possible, let this cup of My suffering pass from Me. Nevertheless, not My will, but Thy will be done" (see Mark 14:36).

The Father's Heart

Regarding His earthly ministry, Jesus was able to say, "I always do those things which please the Father" (see John 8:29)—not simply keeping His commandments and following His instructions, but *pleasing* Him.

It's one thing if my kids obey me. But it's something altogether different if they hear my heart and want to please me. That's the way Jesus was. He heard His Father's heartbeat.

The Father's Time

"Son, they're out of wine," Mary said, implying He do something.

"Mine hour is not yet come," Jesus answered. "This isn't the right time" (John 2:4).

"Lord, come quickly," Mary and Martha said. "The one you love is sick" (see John 11:3). Yet Jesus wouldn't go until the time was right. He waited for His Father's timing before moving in any direction.

What did this do?

It freed Him completely from every other demand.

We feel frazzled because we're always trying to figure out, "Should I do this? Should I go there?" We see opportunities open before us, and we think that because we're busy, we're accomplishing a lot. But so does the chicken running in circles whose head has been cut off. People who don't know any better might look at him and say, "Wow! Look at all he's doing. He's really living." In reality, however, he's in the process of dying because he's disconnected from his head. So, too, when you and I lose contact with our Head, Christ Jesus, watch what happens. We'll run here and sprint there; do this and attempt that—but although the world may applaud us, in our hearts, we'll know something is inherently wrong.

Jesus didn't do this. There was a sense of tranquility and serenity about Him because He was focused intently on one thing singularly: pleasing His Father.

When I wake up every morning, I don't have to go through mental gymnastics or philosophical acrobatics concerning the question of whether or not I should brush my teeth. No, as did most of us, I decided a long time ago that I'd brush my teeth every morning. And because of that, I don't spend my day thinking about the question of doing so. The same should be true of spiritual disciplines. Many people think the practices of Christianity are legalistic and confining. Not true. They're freeing and liberating, for we are free from wondering whether or not whatever we consider a non-negotiable priority in our lives will fit into our schedules.

The recent winner of the all-city handball championship in Portland was unusual because, at thirty-seven years of age, he was relatively old for a handball champion. It was also unusual because he didn't start playing the game until he was thirty-five. But more unusual than his age or his newness to the sport was the fact that, having lost his right arm as a Vietnam War veteran, he played handball with only one hand. When asked how he had won, he pared his answer down to one word: decisions. "Every time the ball comes toward my opponents," he said, "they must decide right hand or left hand. I, however, am absolutely sure which hand I'm going to use. There's no debate."

I like that! When you simplify your life concerning certain nonnegotiable issues, you no longer ask, "Should I pray this morning? Should I go to Bible Study on Wednesday?" Should I be in church Sunday night?"—for the decision has already been made. The question then arises, "How do we discern the will, time, and heart of God?" Watch what Jesus does in our text . . .

After teaching the multitude in Capernaum, after healing the sick, and casting out demons, Jesus rose early the following morning to pray. Meanwhile, His disciples realized that everyone was looking for Him. In my imagination, I hear them saying, "Wow! Good job, Jesus! You came through perfectly! Everybody wants You now. Now You can establish Your kingdom—in a beach town no less!"

But Jesus said something remarkable when He said, "Let us go into the next towns." The word translated "town" is an interesting Greek word used only once in all of the New Testament. It refers to an un-walled town, a town with no protection, no identity, but rather just a place on the map. Thus, Jesus was saying, "Let's leave Surf City and go to Cow Town."

This amazes me. I mean, if, as an athlete with aspirations to make the pros, you heard that the 49ers and the Seahawks, the Giants and the Royals all wanted you, would you say, "What an answer to prayer!" or would you say, "Let's get out of here"? If, as a businessman, you realized every corporation in the career of your choice was on the phone saying, "Please come and work for us. We need you. Name your salary," would you disregard their calls?

Didn't Jesus come to reach people? Didn't He come to establish the kingdom? Wouldn't it be wise for Him to take advantage of the publicity and the opportunity in Capernaum? Wouldn't this be a great moment for "Christianity"? Why would Jesus leave Capernaum? The answer lies in the second half of verse 38: "for therefore came I forth." The place from which Jesus came was the solitary place of prayer (verse 35). As He talked to His Father, Jesus was given direction for the day. Thus, even when demands were placed upon Him or seemingly good opportunities opened before Him, He wasn't swayed. How often you and I get detoured and distracted by hearing, "All men seek for you." We spend time talking about a "great opportunity" and pursue it—only to find we're tired. Not so with Jesus. The will of the Father, the timing of the Father, the heart of the Father directed Him to go to the un-walled cities that day. And that's what He did.

The Lord GOD hath given me the tongue of the learned, that I should know how to speak a word in season to him that is weary: he wakeneth morning by morning, he wakeneth mine ear to hear as the learned.   Isaiah 50:4

Morning by morning, Jesus was awakened to hear the directions of His Father that He might know how to speak during the day. If Jesus needed to pray —day by day by day— to hear a word, to gain direction so that He might move in priority and peace and serenity, how much more do we?

Not only is prayer communion with God, but it is also a commandment from God. At least two hundred times in the Scriptures the command to pray is given. Thus, prayer is not a suggestion. It's a command. Why? I suggest two reasons . . .

Preparation

Because life is oh-so-short, our Father has a very big job to do in the seventy, eighty, or ninety years we're here in order to teach us the language we'll be speaking for eternity—the language of prayer.

Is it because doctors were mean and brutal that they used to spank babies upon birth? No. Babies come out of a closed environment into a whole new world in which they must breathe immediately. Time is limited. So doctors used to spank them—causing them to cry out and breathe in. Mission accomplished.

So, too, our Father must get us breathing and communicating. So He spanks us. "Why are You doing this, God?" we sob. Then we inhale. And the process begins in which we are being prepared for the environment of eternity in which prayer is the language spoken. Because our ability to serve in the next billion years depends upon how we communicate with the Father now, He says, "I'm going to have to send you through some difficulty from time to time in order that you will cry out to Me and learn about prayer—for that is the only way you will be prepared for the ages to come."

Participation

And he did not many mighty works there because of their unbelief.
Matthew 13:58

The Lord not only prepares us for eternity *through* prayer, but He partners with us *in* prayer. This means that the relationships we're developing, the kids we're parenting, the places where we work will not be blessed without our partnering with the Lord. He has chosen to use you as a partner in what He desires to do.

I once read an article about a couple in South Africa who saved a seven-day-old puppy from the belly of a python after they heard the puppy yelping inside of the snake. The wife held the snake by the tail while the husband shook the snake's head and rubbed its bulging stomach until the snake's jaws opened and the puppy was forced out. After massaging the puppy's chest, the puppy started to breathe again.

I don't mean to be cute, but in this, I see a real parallel with what we're called to do. I hear the faint yelp of people in our communities, people who are trapped by the devourer, the serpent, the devil. They're caught up in all kinds of stuff, deceived by what the world has to offer. And here's our Hero, Jesus Christ, who will take the head of that serpent and begin to shake it even as Genesis foretold He would (Genesis 3:15). Our job, then, as His bride, is to join hand in hand with Him, binding the work of the Enemy, allowing our families and our communities to be free.

Do you hear the faint cry of people caught in the grasp of the Enemy? Will you say, "Yes, Lord, I will partner with You through prayer, through intercession, with a focus in my life and a determination in my heart to obey You."? If that be our heart, if that be our prayer, our lives will begin to take on the peace and purpose, the stability and tranquility, the flavor and focus of Jesus.

2 After seeing Jesus' work begun in chapter 1, here in chapter 2, we will see it belittled by the religious establishment that was jealous of the attention given to the radical Rabbi from Galilee.

Mark 2:1
And again he entered into Capernaum, after some days; and it was noised that he was in the house.

". . . And it was noised that he was in the house." I love this phrase. If people were to summarize the sounds they hear coming from your home, would they say, "Oh yes, Jesus is there. No doubt about it"?

The only thing that will alter the family is a return to the family altar—when fathers and mothers take the time to gather their families around the Word to worship the Lord. I know it's not always easy to find the time, but regardless of how young or old our kids might be, such a time is essential if our homes are to be known as those in which it is "noised" that Jesus is inside.

Mark 2:2
And straightway many were gathered together, insomuch that there was no room to receive them, no, not so much as about the door: and he preached the word unto them.

Hearing that Jesus did miracles—the sick were healed, the demonized liberated, blind eyes opened, lepers cleansed—no doubt people came to be touched by Him. Therefore, I suspect some were initially disappointed when He began preaching. Yet the ministry of Jesus Christ centered around the teaching and preaching of the Word because faith comes by hearing and hearing by the Word of God (Romans 10:17).

Mark 2:3–5 (a)
And they come unto him, bringing one sick of the palsy, which was borne of four. And when they could not come nigh unto him for the press, they uncovered the roof where he was: and when they had broken it up, they let down the bed wherein the sick of the palsy lay. When Jesus saw their faith . . .

In this story, we first see Jesus looking up. As He's preaching the Word, He hears commotion overhead and sees the faith of four men finding a way to bring their friend to Him.

Mark 2:5 (b)
. . . he said unto the sick of the palsy, Son, thy sins be forgiven thee.

After looking up, Jesus looked down at the man before him and said, "Son, your sins are forgiven."

I wonder if the four friends were initially disappointed. *He's not here for forgiveness,* they could have thought. *He's here for healing.* But Jesus was dealing with the root problem, the most important issue. Church historians suggest this man was paralyzed as a result of an immoral lifestyle. If this be so, forgiveness would be the gnawing need of his heart. Jesus always deals with the root. And the root issue is always sin. So although they might have frustrated the four friends on the roof, I believe Jesus' words were what the paralyzed man longed to hear more than anything else.

Mark 2:6, 7
But there were certain of the scribes sitting there, and reasoning in their hearts, Why doth this man thus speak blasphemies? who can forgive sins but God only?

Next we see Jesus looking around at the scribes, who judged Him with envy (Mark 15:10).

Mark 2:8–12
And immediately when Jesus perceived in his spirit that they so reasoned within themselves, he said unto them, Why reason ye these things in your hearts? Whether is it easier to say to the sick of the palsy, Thy sins be forgiven thee; or to say, Arise, and take up thy bed, and walk? But that ye may know that the Son of man hath power on earth to forgive sins, (he saith to the sick of the palsy,) I say unto thee, Arise, and take up thy bed, and go thy way into thine house. And immediately he arose, took up the bed, and went forth before them all; insomuch that they were all amazed, and glorified God, saying, We never saw it on this fashion.

Finally, we see Jesus looking within, at the hearts of the scribes who were so eager to ensnare Him. "You will see that I have power to meet this man's greatest need now and eternally—the forgiveness of His sins—by My healing of His paralysis," Jesus declared.

Mark 2:13, 14
And he went forth again by the sea side; and all the multitude resorted unto him, and he taught them. And as he passed by, he saw Levi the son of Alphaeus sitting at the receipt of custom, and said unto him, Follow me. And he arose and followed him.

Levi, also known as Matthew, was a tax collector—despised by his countrymen due to the fact that he collected money for their dreaded oppressors, the Romans. But Matthew's occupation didn't prevent Jesus from calling him, because Jesus specializes in using the despised and rejected—people just like us!

Mark 2:15–17
And it came to pass, that, as Jesus sat at meat in his house, many publicans and sinners sat also together with Jesus and his disciples: for there were many, and they followed him. And when the scribes and Pharisees saw him eat with publicans and sinners, they said unto his disciples, How is it that he eateth and drinketh with publicans and sinners? When Jesus heard it, he saith unto them, They that are whole have no need of the physician, but they that are sick: I came not to call the righteous, but sinners to repentance.

The Good News for any of us who feel off the wall, out to lunch, or incapacitated is that Jesus,

the Great Physician, came especially to help people like us.

Mark 2:18, 19
And the disciples of John and of the Pharisees used to fast: and they come and say unto him, Why do the disciples of John and of the Pharisees fast, but thy disciples fast not? And Jesus said unto them, Can the children of the bridechamber fast, while the bridegroom is with them? as long as they have the bridegroom with them, they cannot fast.

According to the Talmud, there is one time a man is absolved of duty, even prayer: at a wedding ceremony. The only duty a man had at a wedding ceremony was to rejoice. Thus, Jesus is saying, "This is not the time to be fasting." And He says the same thing today. I don't know when Christianity began being associated with grumpiness, for ours is not a call to religion, but to relationship, not to sadness, but to gladness, not to a funeral, but to a wedding.

Mark 2:20
But the days will come, when the bridegroom shall be taken away from them, and then shall they fast in those days.

If a church does not have the presence of Jesus, if the joy of the Lord is not there, services will be like funerals. But if the Lord is there, it's time to rejoice and celebrate the gospel and our great salvation. We're forgiven. We're on our way to heaven. The Lord is risen. *Happy* is the people whose God is the Lord! (Psalm 144:15).

Mark 2:21, 22
No man also seweth a piece of new cloth on an old garment: else the new piece that filled it up taketh away from the old, and the rent is made worse. And no man putteth new wine into old bottles: else the new wine doth burst the bottles, and the wine is spilled, and the bottles will be marred: but new wine must be put into new bottles.

There are those who suggest that Jesus came to reform Judaism. Jesus, however, says "I'm not talking about patching up the old system or refilling old wineskins. Something new is happening." The question then arises: What did He mean when He declared in Matthew 5 that He came not to destroy the old, but to fulfill it? Perhaps the answer is best illustrated with an acorn. If I set an acorn on the ground and hit it repeatedly with a hammer, it would soon be destroyed. If, on the other hand, I bury it in the ground, it would likewise be destroyed. But in the second case, its destruction would bring about fulfillment, for it would bring forth a whole new tree.

When Jesus said, "I have come to fulfill the Law," it was in the sense of the buried acorn. That is, once the law shows us we're sinners in need of a Savior, its work is complete—fulfilled in the Person of our Savior, Jesus Christ.

Mark 2:23, 24
And it came to pass, that he went through the corn fields on the sabbath day; and his disciples began, as they went, to pluck the ears of corn. And the Pharisees said unto him, Behold, why do they on the sabbath day that which is not lawful?

Although it was against Pharisaical tradition to pick grain, it was not against Old Testament Law, for Deuteronomy 23:25 allowed those who were hungry to pick grain no matter the day.

Mark 2:25, 26
And he said unto them, Have ye never read what David did, when he had need, and was an hungred, he, and they that were with him? How he went into the house of God in the days of Abiathar the high priest, and did eat the shewbread, which is not lawful to eat but for the priests, and gave also to them which were with him?

In appealing to the fact that, while fleeing from Saul, David ate the showbread from the tabernacle, Jesus is declaring that human need always has priority over religious ritual, that the law is fulfilled in love (Matthew 22:37–40).

Mark 2:27, 28
And he said unto them, The sabbath was made for man, and not man for the sabbath: Therefore the Son of man is Lord also of the sabbath.

The Old Testament regulations were not meant to be burdens, but to be blessings—given not for punishment, but for protection. When reading Old Testament Scriptures in this light, the law provides beautiful principles to free us to live life the way it was meant to be, the Sabbath—a day when man stops his work in order to reflect and relax—being a perfect example.

3 Before we will see Jesus' work blessed in verses 4–7, as chapter 3 opens, we see a continuation of His work belittled.

Mark 3:1, 2
And he entered again into the synagogue; and there was a man there which had a withered hand. And they watched him, whether he would heal him on the sabbath day; that they might accuse him.

Knowing it was Jesus' manner to seek out those in need, the Pharisees kept a close eye on the man with the paralyzed hand for the sole purpose of seeing if Jesus would break their law by healing him on the Sabbath.

Mark 3:3, 4 (a)
And he saith unto the man which had the withered hand, Stand forth. And he saith unto them, Is it lawful to do good on the sabbath days, or to do evil? to save life, or to kill?

"People die every day. Therefore, if evil and death don't take a rest, why should goodness and life cease on the Sabbath day? Your rules and regulations don't make sense," Jesus said to the Pharisees.

Mark 3:4 (b)
But they held their peace.

The Pharisees were learning not to argue with Jesus.

Mark 3:5
And when he had looked round about on them with anger, being grieved for the hardness of their hearts, he saith unto the man, Stretch forth thine hand. And he stretched it out: and his hand was restored whole as the other.

As the man with the paralyzed hand stretched it forth, he was able to do what the Lord had commanded him to do because God's commandments are always God's enablements.

For topical study of Mark 3:5 entitled "The Withered Hand," turn to page 236.

Mark 3:6
And the Pharisees went forth, and straightway took counsel with the Herodians against him, how they might destroy him.

The Pharisees and Herodians had been enemies for years. But now the Pharisees, a religious group, and the Herodians, a political party, found themselves united in their opposition to Jesus. This was as unlikely as seeing the Pro-Choice and Pro-Life movements saying, "Let's join forces."

Yet even though Jesus' work was being belittled by the Pharisees, the Herodians, the scribes, and others, His work is about to be blessed by the Father . . .

Mark 3:7–12
But Jesus withdrew himself with his disciples to the sea: and a great multitude from Galilee followed him, and from Judaea, and from Jerusalem, and from Idumaea, and from beyond Jordan; and they about Tyre and Sidon, a great multitude, when they had heard what great things he did, came unto him. And he spake to his disciples, that a small ship should wait on him because of the multitude, lest they should throng him. For he had healed many; insomuch that they pressed upon him for to touch him, as many as had plagues. And unclean spirits, when they saw him, fell down before him, and cried, saying, Thou art the Son of God. And he straitly charged them that they should not make him known.

Why would Jesus forbid the "free advertising" of the unclean spirits? I believe part of the answer lies in the fact that demonic spirits are not only called unclean spirits, but lying spirits (1 Kings 22:22; 2 Chronicles 18:21). And of what use is the word of a liar?

Mark 3:13
And he goeth up into a mountain, and calleth unto him whom he would: and they came unto him.

The crowd was surrounding Him. Healing was flowing from Him. People were being touched and blessed by Him. And yet Jesus withdrew, no doubt following the directive of His Father.

Mark 3:14, 15
And he ordained twelve, that they should be with him, and that he might send them forth to preach, and to have power to heal sicknesses, and to cast out devils.

Matthew tells us Jesus spent the night in prayer before choosing His disciples. I used to think He did this to receive direction and confirmation from His Father in order that He might choose twelve men who would impact and influence the world most radically. But now I suspect He was praying, "Father, keep Me from choosing those who seem successful outwardly" because look who He chose:

Mark 3:16
And Simon he surnamed Peter.

Simon, whose name means "Shifting Sand," was given a new name, which means "Rock." If you could choose anyone in all of humanity to be your disciples, would you have chosen Peter—a man who would deny he even knew you?

Mark 3:17
And James the son of Zebedee, and John the brother of James; and he surnamed them Boanerges, which is, The sons of thunder.

Jesus called James and John sons of thunder no doubt because of their violent tempers. "Let's call down fire and destroy this city," they said (see Luke 9:54). "Those guys aren't part of our group, Lord, but they're preaching in Your name. Let's forbid them" (see Mark 9:38). Would you have chosen a couple of guys who wanted to blow people away and burn people up if your message was peace, grace, and love?

Mark 3:18 (a)
And Andrew, and Philip, and Bartholomew, and Matthew . . .

How about Matthew? Would you have wanted to spend three years with an IRS agent?

Mark 3:18 (b)
. . . and Thomas . . .

Would you have included a man who would doubt you were even alive?

Mark 3:18 (c)
. . . and James the son of Alphaeus . . .

James the son of Alphaeus is also called James the Less—not a very impressive description.

Mark 3:18 (d)
. . . and Thaddaeus, and Simon the Canaanite.

Simon is also called the Zealot (Acts 1:13). The zealots were those who wanted to violently overthrow the Roman government. If your message was that your kingdom was not of this world, would you choose a political radical like Simon?

Mark 3:19
And Judas Iscariot, which also betrayed him: and they went into an house.

Would you have chosen Judas? More importantly, would you have called him "Friend" even as he betrayed you? (see Matthew 26:50).

Yet with the exception of Judas, Jesus' disciples became men who did indeed turn the world upside down because of His Spirit within them. This means that when Jesus chose you and me, He knew we would also be changed and eventually would be those who impact the world now and eternally. He chose us not because of who we are, but because of who He sees we can be.

When I make choices, sometimes they're good; sometimes they're bad. Why? Because my knowledge is limited. God, however, has no limitations on what He knows. If my knowledge was limitless like God's, I would buy a lottery ticket. Because I would know exactly which numbers to choose, it wouldn't be gambling, but a wise investment. So, too, God picks winners.

You might feel like a loser. Those around you might even call you a loser. But the fact that you were chosen by God, who sees the big picture, means you are a winner. We need to realize that everyone who names the Name of Jesus—regardless of her personality, or of the doctrines he may embrace—is a winner because they have been chosen by Him. And we need to treat each other accordingly.

Mark 3:20, 21
And the multitude cometh together again, so that they could not so much as eat bread. And when his friends heard of it, they went out to lay hold on him: for they said, He is beside himself.

After seeing Jesus' work blessed, now we see it blasphemed. "He's out of His mind," said His friends. "He's so busy preaching and teaching and healing that He's not even eating."

But Jesus would say, "Doing My Father's will is that which sustains and refreshes Me" (see John 4:32–34). So, too, haven't you found that praying for someone, sharing with someone, doing something practical for the kingdom is that which energizes you?

Mark 3:22–26
And the scribes which came down from Jerusalem said, He hath Beelzebub, and by the prince of the devils casteth he out devils. And he called them unto him, and said unto them in parables, How can Satan cast out Satan? And if a kingdom be divided against itself, that kingdom cannot stand. And if a house be divided against itself, that house cannot stand. And if Satan rise up against himself, and be divided, he cannot stand, but hath an end.

"To say I'm casting out demons by the power of demons is illogical," said Jesus. "Why would Satan want to defeat himself?"

Mark 3:27
No man can enter into a strong man's house, and spoil his goods, except he will first bind the strong man; and then he will spoil his house.

In this one-verse parable, Jesus likens Satan to a strong man who, if allowed, seeks to control our families, friends, neighbors, joy, health, and blessings. What must we do? Before we can wrest goods from Satan's control, free people from his grasp, release resources from his restriction, we must first bind the strong man.

The binding of the strong man is done in prayer. Too often we rush in to rescue or reclaim without first binding Satan through prayer. We can do more than pray, but we can't do anything until we pray. To think you don't have time to pray is as foolish as thinking that, because you have places to go, things to do, people to see, you don't have time to stop for gas for your car—even though the needle on the gauge is to the left of "Empty." If you're witnessing or serving without praying, you're fighting a battle you're sure to lose. The strong man must be bound. Prayer must be given priority.

Mark 3:28–30
Verily I say unto you, All sins shall be forgiven unto the sons of men, and blasphemies wherewith soever they shall blaspheme: But he that shall blaspheme against the Holy Ghost hath never forgiveness, but is in danger of eternal damnation: Because they said, He hath an unclean spirit.

According to 1 John 2:2, Jesus died not only for our sins, but for the sins of the whole world. "All manner of sin shall be forgiven all men," He said (see Matthew 12:31). Every sin committed by any man or woman has already been paid for and forgiven because of Calvary. When Jesus said, "It is finished," the price was paid for *all* humanity.

But there is one sin that will lead to eternal damnation: failure to believe in Jesus Christ, the Provision for sin. The blasphemy of the Spirit is saying, "I don't need Jesus." That's the one and only sin that will damn a person. You'll never be held accountable for the candy bar you pocketed twenty years ago. You'll never be held accountable for the lustful thought you had five weeks ago. You'll never be held accountable for the lie you told ten minutes ago. But you *will* be held accountable if you blaspheme the Spirit.

I find it interesting that Jesus addresses the subject of the blasphemy of the Spirit in conjunction with the accusations that He had an unclean spirit. Like the scribes in Jesus' day, unable to deny the things he sees the Lord doing in the lives of others, he who refuses to receive Christ will eventually have no other choice but to attribute them to insanity or fanaticism. And it is then that he moves perilously close to eternal damnation.

Mark 3:31–35
There came then his brethren and his mother, and, standing without, sent unto him, calling him. And the multitude sat about him, and they said unto him, Behold, thy mother and thy brethren without seek for thee. And he answered them, saying, Who is my mother, or my brethren? And he looked round about on them which sat about him, and said, Behold my mother and my brethren! For whosoever shall do the will of God, the same is my brother, and my sister, and mother.

Chapter 3 has presented a new nation, no longer based upon the twelve tribes of Israel, but upon the twelve apostles; a new family; no longer comprised of Jesus' biological mother and brothers, but of anyone who does the will of God. And in establishing a new nation, and a new family, Jesus opens the door to a whole new understanding of true religion.

THE WITHERED HAND
A Topical Study of
Mark 3:5

Focus with me on four elements of this timeless account . . .

The Withered Hand

The historian Jerome tells us there is strong traditional evidence that the man with the paralyzed hand was a stonemason. If so, his paralysis would have very definitely affected his income, and, consequently, the well-being of his entire family. In addition, medicine being in the state that it was, there would have been no painkillers to help alleviate the pain he undoubtedly felt in his arm and through his chest.

Although our medicine and workmen's compensation are more sophisticated than in Jesus' day, our society is filled with people who feel as though they're paralyzed relationally, wounded financially, or withered emotionally. Thus, this account is as impacting today as it was then.

The Wicked Plan

Hearing stories about the Man from Galilee who worked wonders and miracles, the Sanhedrin in Jerusalem grew concerned, for it seemed as though He was getting far too much attention. So they sent a delegation composed of scribes and Pharisees—those devoted to interpreting the law and to keeping its most minute detail—to Capernaum in order to check out the situation. How did they know where to find Jesus? Could it be that, knowing this man with the paralyzed arm would be in that particular synagogue on the Sabbath, they figured Jesus would be there as well? The scribes and Pharisees did not come to worship. They came to watch. They did not come to commune with the Lord, but to confront the Lord. They did not come to find fruit, but to find fault. And they sat there waiting, knowing Jesus, moved with compassion, would surely do something that would violate their Sabbath rules.

The Wonderful Man

Jesus always shows up where people are hurting and needy. Such is the heart of our Lord. He desires to heal the hurts, to bind the wounds, to restore strength, to straighten out situations. The Lord is always present in the place of hurting, and He'll always move toward the one who is hurting the most. If you're hurting today, the Lord will find His way to where you're sitting and come alongside of you especially, singularly, particularly. Jesus likened Himself to the shepherd who leaves ninety-nine of his flock in order to find the one that's lost (Luke 15:3–7). That's our Lord.

Jesus told us that wherever two or three are gathered in His Name, He's in their midst (Matthew 18:20). And yet why is it in the Christian community that, although we believe this theoretically, we refer people away from the church consistently? If a person battles alcohol, we refer him to AA. If a marriage is in danger, we refer the couple to a seminar. If parents are having troubles with their teenagers, we refer them to counseling. I am not against AA or marriage seminars or counseling. However, I suggest that they have become substitutes because people no longer believe they can come into church with their withered hand and that Jesus will meet them there and touch them miraculously. Instead, they believe they must go through hours and hours of dialogue and deep inner searching before they can find an answer. I suggest to you that just as Jesus was in the synagogue dealing with the man with the withered hand, He is in this place, dealing with any of us who acknowledge our weakness, our paralysis.

The Powerful Command

"Stand forth," Jesus said to the man with the paralyzed hand, perhaps hoping to stir up some sense of compassion with the hard hearts of the Pharisees as they viewed a man whose right arm dangled helplessly at his side. And then He said something so essential when He said, "Stretch forth thine hand."

"Wait a minute," the man could have said. "That's easy for *You* to say. My hand is paralyzed. How can I stretch it forth?" The man could have argued with Jesus. After all, he didn't know who Jesus was. Instead, however, he simply obeyed. He didn't argue. He didn't debate. He simply said, "Okay," and as he stretched out his hand, the Lord met him in that place because in the Lord's declaration there is dynamic. When God speaks, power is released. In God's commandments are God's "enablements." If you can grab that simple concept, the Word will become extremely exciting to you.

To you who are saying, "I'm so depressed. I've had demons cast out. I've gone for inner healing. I've had counseling. I've read every self-help book, and followed every technique—all to no avail," this wonderful Man comes and says, "Rejoice evermore. This is the will of God" (see 1 Thessalonians 5:16–18).

You can either argue with Him, or you can say, "If the Word tells me to rejoice evermore, I will now start rejoicing." And in the very act of beginning to rejoice, you'll find reason to continue to rejoice.

The Word says, "Husbands, love your wives . . . ." (see Ephesians 5:25).

"Oh, but you don't know my wife. You don't know what we've been through," you might say. You can argue and debate and go to seminars and read books until you're blue in the face—or you can say, "The apostle Paul, inspired by the Spirit of God, simply tells me to love my wife. So I will love my wife." And because you're doing it, God will give you the power to carry it out.

"Wives, submit to your husbands . . . ." (see Ephesians 5:22).

You can argue and say why this is impossible. Or you can say, "Lord, in Your commandment is Your enablement. I will do it today." And you will receive power.

If you're struggling with drugs, alcohol, pornography, the Lord would say to you today, "Reckon yourself dead unto sin, but alive to Jesus Christ" (see Romans 6:11).

Therefore, if you go home, throw it away, and say, "I'm going to obey the command of Christ," you'll find power and victory.

Maybe you have a problem exaggerating or lying. The Word says, "Wherefore putting away lying, speak every man truth with his neighbor . . . ." (Ephesians 4:25). Simply do it today.

Dear, precious people: Every one of us is withered in some area of our lives. We know that. But the solution does not lie in seminars or books. The solution is simply to obey the command of Christ. And as you do, He'll meet you at that point and give you the power to carry it out. Once I quit saying why I can't; once I quit arguing with the Word and saying, "It's not that easy"; once I quit saying, "I'm an exception to the rule," and instead say, "Lord, if You say it, I'll do it. Period,"—He meets me there and a miracle takes place.

The choice is yours. Stand forth. Stretch out your hand. And be made whole.

4 In Mark's portrayal of Jesus as Servant, in chapters 1—3, we saw the Servant's works. Here in chapters 4 and 5, we'll see the Servant's words. Although our Western belief is that "talk is cheap," Hebrew writers and thinkers viewed words as being arrows that, when shot, would carry packets of energy that would leave a lasting impression upon the hearers. This being the case, in the first part of chapter 4, we see insight from Jesus' words; and at the end of chapter 4 and into chapter 5, we see the impact of His words.

Mark 4:1
And he began again to teach by the sea side: and there was gathered unto him a great multitude, so that he entered into a ship, and sat

in the sea; and the whole multitude was by the sea on the land.

Taking advantage of the natural acoustical properties of water, Jesus spoke from a boat offshore to the group of perhaps thousands who listened to Him on the beach.

Mark 4:2–11 (a)
And he taught them many things by parables, and said unto them in his doctrine, Hearken; Behold, there went out a sower to sow: And it came to pass, as he sowed, some fell by the way side, and the fowls of the air came and devoured it up. And some fell on stony ground, where it had not much earth; and immediately it sprang up, because it had no depth of earth: But when the sun was up, it was scorched; and because it had no root, it withered away. And some fell among thorns, and the thorns grew up, and choked it, and it yielded no fruit. And other fell on good ground, and did yield fruit that sprang up and increased; and brought forth, some thirty, and some sixty, and some an hundred. And he said unto them, He that hath ears to hear, let him hear. And when he was alone, they that were about him with the twelve asked of him the parable. And he said unto them, Unto you it is given to know the mystery of the kingdom of God . . .

Before explaining the meaning of the parable to His disciples, Jesus told them they were those to whom the mystery of the kingdom of God would be revealed. In the Bible, the Greek word *musterion*, or "mystery," refers to a truth previously hidden but now revealed. There are a number of mysteries of which the New Testament speaks, among them the mystery of iniquity, revealed through an understanding of spiritual warfare (2 Thessalonians 2:7), and the mystery of godliness, revealed in the Person of Jesus Christ (1 Timothy 3:16).

Here, Jesus is about to reveal to the disciples the mystery of the kingdom of God. . . .

Mark 4:11 (b), 12
. . . but unto them that are without, all these things are done in parables: That seeing they may see, and not perceive; and hearing they may hear, and not understand; lest at any time they should be converted, and their sins should be forgiven them.

Why would Jesus want to keep anyone from being converted? The answer lies in the fact that because He could have spoken so powerfully that people would have been forced to concede to the logic of His argument and converted against their will, Jesus chose to speak in a way that would not manipulate people or force them into a decision. Because He will not force His will upon anyone intellectually, emotionally, or spiritually, Jesus spoke in parables in order that only those who wanted to hear would hear, in order that only those who wanted to see would see.

Mark 4:13
And he said unto them, Know ye not this parable? and how then will ye know all parables?

This parable is a key to understanding them all.

Mark 4:14
The sower soweth the word.

The sower here is one who is scattering seed—which speaks of the Scriptures. "You're born again not of corruptible seed, but of incorruptible, that is, the Word of God," said Peter (see 1 Peter 1:23). The soil upon which the seed is sown speaks of the condition of men's hearts—not only of the hearts of four different individuals, but of the condition of our own hearts at any given time. When you read this parable, don't think you're automatically always the one who has the good soil and the abundant fruit. On any given day, in any given week, this can change. We don't remain in the same spot. This parable speaks to all of us, depending upon the current condition of our hearts.

Mark 4:15
And these are they by the way side, where the word is sown; but when they have heard, Satan cometh immediately, and taketh away the word that was sown in their hearts.

The first soil described here speaks of people who are hard-hearted. They hear the Word, and it doesn't penetrate at all. "That's for the birds," they say. And the birds come and pluck it away.

Mark 4:16, 17
And these are they likewise which are sown on stony ground; who, when they have heard the word, immediately receive it with gladness; and have no root in themselves, and so endure but for a time: afterward, when affliction or persecution ariseth for the word's sake, immediately they are offended.

This speaks not of hard hearts, but of shallow hearts. "Jesus is great!" say those with shallow commitments as they put bumper stickers on their cars. They spring up quickly—but their roots aren't very deep. And when the sun comes out, when persecution starts coming their way, when people start making fun of them, they begin to wither because their roots are shallow.

Mark 4:18, 19
And these are they which are sown among thorns; such as hear the word, and the cares of this world, and the deceitfulness of riches, and the lusts of other things entering in, choke the word, and it becometh unfruitful.

This speaks not of a hard heart, nor a shallow heart, but of a crowded heart. The cares of the world speak primarily to the person who is poor financially, and thus, always worried about how he'll make ends meet. The deceitfulness of riches, on the other hand, speaks of the wealthy man who mistakenly thinks his new ski boat will make him genuinely happy.

If God blesses you financially, you have every right to freely receive and enjoy the blessings He's brought to you. But don't get caught up in thinking that if you just had one more thing, you'd really be happy. It's simply not true.

Mark 4:20
And these are they which are sown on good ground; such as hear the word, and receive it, and bring forth fruit, some thirtyfold, some sixty, and some an hundred.

Normally, a crop brings forth eight times the seed sown. So even thirty –to one is an incredible ration. Sixty –to one is astronomical. One hundred –to one is miraculous. Where are you? The fact that you have made a decision to receive the Word and allow it to penetrate the soil of your spirit even as you study right now is indicative of the potential for miraculous fruit in your life.

Mark 4:21–23
And he said unto them, Is a candle brought to be put under a bushel, or under a bed? and not to be set on a candlestick? For there is nothing hid, which shall not be manifested; neither was any thing kept secret, but that it should come abroad. If any man have ears to hear, let him hear.

People often use this verse to say everything you've done wrong, said wrong, thought wrong is going to be exposed. That's not what's being said here. Rather, the Lord is saying, "I don't want people to be in the dark concerning My ways or My heart."

Mark 4:24, 25
And he said unto them, Take heed what ye hear: with what measure ye mete, it shall be measured to you: and unto you that hear shall more be given. For he that hath, to him shall be given: and he that hath not, from him shall be taken even that which he hath.

Jesus isn't saying, "Take heed what you hear." He says, rather, "Take heed *how* you hear, the way you hear." In other words, when you receive truth, if you release it to others, more will be given. If, on the other hand, you simply take in truth without allowing it to flow through you to others, you'll begin to lose what was given to you previously, and find fresh revelation or insight no longer being given to you.

Mark 4:26–29
And he said, So is the kingdom of God, as if a man should cast seed into the ground; and should sleep, and rise night and day, and the seed should spring and grow up, he knoweth not how. For the earth bringeth forth fruit of herself; first the blade, then the ear, after that the full corn in the ear. But when the fruit is brought forth, immediately he putteth in the sickle, because the harvest is come.

As he sows seed, a farmer doesn't understand exactly how the seed grows. Yet one day he looks out the window and sees a crop. Keep in mind, Jesus is talking about the mystery of the effect of the Word. And, like the seed sown by the farmer, it's inexplicable how studying the Scriptures causes the kingdom to be established within us and among us. People who are not believers think we're crazy to come week by week to study a page or two from a book thousands of years old. Yet when we study the Word corporately and have devotions personally, something happens miraculously. We begin to look at life differently, and good fruit begins to grow. Oh, we're not perfect. We have a long way to go. But the process has begun.

Mark 4:30–32
And he said, Whereunto shall we liken the kingdom of God? or with what comparison shall we compare it? It is like a grain of mustard seed, which, when it is sown in the earth, is less than all the seeds that be in the earth: But when it is sown, it groweth up, and becometh greater than all herbs, and shooteth out great branches; so that the fowls of the air may lodge under the shadow of it.

After teaching encouragingly about the kingdom, Jesus ends with a warning that the kingdom is like a mustard seed that grows to the point that birds lodge within its branches. Due to the fact that nowhere in the world now or historically has a mustard seed ever grown into a tree big enough to support birds and their nests, I believe Jesus is saying that as the kingdom grows, it will expand unnaturally in its organization and structure; that it will become bigger than it was ever intended to be, that birds—the Biblical symbol of evil—will lodge therein. We see this in so many systems throughout church history, as complexity replaced simplicity and hierarchy swallowed liberty.

Mark 4:33-35
And with many such parables spake he the word unto them, as they were able to hear it. But without a parable spake he not unto them: and when they were alone, he expounded all things to his disciples. And the same day, when the even was come, he saith unto them, Let us pass over unto the other side.

After teaching about the Word, Jesus now gives His word to the disciples that they would indeed pass over to the other side of the Sea of Galilee—a word Satan would soon test.

Mark 4:36
And when they had sent away the multitude, they took him even as he was in the ship. And there were also with him other little ships.

We have the tendency to think that no one faces the same temptations, challenges, or storms we do. Paul, however, tells us no temptation comes to us except that which is common to man (1 Corinthians 10:13). That is why there were with the disciples "other little ships" out on the Sea of Galilee.

Mark 4:37
And there arose a great storm of wind, and the waves beat into the ship, so that it was now full.

Jesus had taught about His Word, and had given His word that the disciples would make it to the other side. But whether regarding a promise Jesus gave to His disciples, or one He gives to you, after teaching comes testing. Always.

Mark 4:38
And he was in the hinder part of the ship, asleep on a pillow: and they awake him, and say unto him, Master, carest thou not that we perish?

If Jesus is in your boat, it can't sink. If He's in your life, you won't go down. He has promised to

perfect that which concerns you (Psalm 138:8). And though the storm might rage, causing you to say, "Master, don't You care that I'm perishing?" He's not worried. He's sleeping—not in apathy, but with great security.

"The Lord thy God in the midst of thee is mighty . . . ." Zephaniah tells us, ". . . He will rest in His love . . ." (Zephaniah 3:17). Thus, concerning the storm you may be going through even now or perhaps will face tomorrow, the Lord is not wondering if you're going to make it. He's resting in His love. He knows He's going to see you through.

Mark 4:39 (a)
And he arose, and rebuked the wind, and said unto the sea, Peace, be still.

The Greek word translated "be still" literally means "be muzzled." This is the same command Jesus issued when He addressed demons, which implies that this storm was actually stirred by Satan.

Mark 4:39 (b)
And the wind ceased, and there was a great calm.

When Jesus thwarted Satan's plan and calmed the storm, not only were the disciples at peace, but all of the "other little ships" were spared as well. So, too, when Jesus makes His power known by the storms He calms for us, those around us benefit as they see His faithfulness to us.

Mark 4:40
And he said unto them, Why are ye so fearful? how is it that ye have no faith?

The One who calmed the storm was the One who had allowed the storm in order to teach the disciples to believe His Word.

Mark 4:41
And they feared exceedingly, and said one to another, What manner of man is this, that even the wind and the sea obey him?

It is not the outward circumstances we have to fear, but the inward waves of fear and faithlessness that well up within us. The Lord has given us His Word that He will never leave us or forsake us (Hebrews 13:5). Therefore, no matter how strong the storm might seem, no matter the force of the waves that beat upon our boat, if we love God and are called according to His purpose, all things will work together for good (Romans

8:28); He will complete that which He began in us (Philippians 1:6)—and we can be at peace.

5 Mark 5:1 (a)
And they came over unto the other side of the sea . . .

"Let us pass over unto the other side," Jesus had said in chapter 4. And here in chapter 5, we see the disciples doing just that, for His Word always comes to pass.

Mark 5:1 (b)
. . . into the country of the Gadarenes.

Leaving Capernaum on the north shore of the Sea of Galilee, it was a five-mile journey by water to Gadara, located on the eastern shore.

Mark 5:2
And when he was come out of the ship, immediately there met him out of the tombs a man with an unclean spirit.

Unlike God, Satan is not omnipresent; he can't be everywhere at once. So he carries out his work through demonic, or unclean, spirits—the angels who fell with him when he rebelled against God (2 Peter 2:4). And in this man of Gadara, we see the results of the demonization of an individual . . .

Mark 5:3 (a)
Who had his dwelling among the tombs . . .

He was robbed of his family and friends. Dwelling among the tombs, infatuated with death and darkness, he was as good as dead.

Mark 5:3 (b)
. . . and no man could bind him, no, not with chains.

Secondly, he was robbed of sanity and self-control, hell-bent on his own destruction.

Mark 5:4
Because that he had been often bound with fetters and chains, and the chains had been plucked asunder by him, and the fetters broken in pieces: neither could any man tame him.

Notice what society did with this man. First, they sought to bind him with chains. We do the same. Statistics show, however, that 72 percent of those released from prison return for similar or worse crimes.

Mark 5:5
And always, night and day, he was in the mountains, and in the tombs, crying, and cutting himself with stones.

Second, society sought to isolate him. Luke tells us a guard actually stayed with him. But even he couldn't stop the man's propensity for annihilation.

Mark 5:6
But when he saw Jesus afar off, he ran and worshipped him.

It is neither society's isolation nor its attempts at rehabilitation that will make a genuine, lasting difference in the lives of men—but only the hope of regeneration through this One who crossed through a storm to reach this man.

Mark 5:7, 8
And cried with a loud voice, and said, What have I to do with thee, Jesus, thou Son of the most high God? I adjure thee by God, that thou torment me not. For he said unto him, Come out of the man, thou unclean spirit.

James says the devils believe—and tremble (2:19). Demons know who Jesus is. And they quake in their boots when they are aware of His presence.

Mark 5:9, 10
And he asked him, What is thy name? And he answered, saying, My name is Legion: for we are many. And he besought him much that he would not send them away out of the country.

A legion is a Roman military term used to denote a unit of six thousand soldiers, so it is possible that there were thousands of demons within this man.

Mark 5:11–13 (a)
Now there was there nigh unto the mountains a great herd of swine feeding. And all the devils besought him, saying, Send us into the swine, that we may enter into them. And forthwith Jesus gave them leave.

Jesus did not command the demons to go into the pigs. Rather, the demons requested it, and Jesus simply allowed it. It makes no difference to demons whether they inhabit people or pigs because they can make people into pigs by getting them to trade their God-given natures for animal behavior.

Mark 5:13 (b)
And the unclean spirits went out, and entered into the swine: and the herd ran violently down a steep place into the sea, (they were about two thousand;) and were choked in the sea.

In light of the current epidemic of teen suicide, I find it more than coincidental that the demons caused the pigs to prefer suicide to life.

Mark 5:14, 15
And they that fed the swine fled, and told it in the city, and in the country. And they went out to see what it was that was done. And they come to Jesus, and see him that was possessed with the devil, and had the legion, sitting, and clothed, and in his right mind: and they were afraid.

Evidently, the fact that this man was torturing himself to death was less frightening to these people than the fact that he was now clothed and in his right mind.

Mark 5:16, 17
And they that saw it told them how it befell to him that was possessed with the devil, and also concerning the swine. And they began to pray him to depart out of their coasts.

Pigs were more important to these people than a man's soul. The fact that they prioritized pigs above people should not shock us, however, when we see people petition and protest today on behalf of the spotted owl or snowy plover while they allow babies to be aborted by the hundreds of thousands.

Mark 5:18
And when he was come into the ship, he that had been possessed with the devil prayed him that he might be with him.

How was this man delivered so completely that he wanted to stay with Jesus continually? By His Word. So, too, the weapons of our war are not carnal, but the Sword of the Spirit, which is the Word of God (2 Corinthians 10:4; Hebrews 4:12).

Mark 5:19
Howbeit Jesus suffered him not, but saith unto him, Go home to thy friends, and tell them how great things the Lord hath done for thee, and hath had compassion on thee.

"You are the one who can witness most effectively to the people who knew you previously," Jesus said to the man delivered from demons. "I want you to go home to those who knew you before and let them see the reality of My touch upon your life."

Remember once again that we are called not to be defense lawyers, prosecuting attorneys, judges, or juries. We're called to be witnesses (Acts 1:8). What does a witness do? He doesn't argue the case. He doesn't try to persuade or judge. He simply reports what he has seen. All too often, I believe, we've been intimidated by thinking we have to defend the veracity of the Bible, prove the fallacy of evolution, or justify church history. No, we're simply called to be witnesses—to share what the Lord has done in and for us.

Mark 5:20
And he departed, and began to publish in Decapolis how great things Jesus had done for him: and all men did marvel.

There are three prayers offered in this story . . .

- "Let us go into the pigs,' the demons cried. *And Jesus said, "Go."*
- "Leave our region," said the Gadarenes. *And Jesus left.*
- "I want to follow You," said the previously demonized man. *And Jesus said, "No."*

When you and I wage war spiritually, when you and I petition and pray perhaps reverently, we must remember, even as this story illustrates so dramatically, that Jesus can say, "No," and "No" is just as much an answer as "Yes." In fact, "No" is sometimes what God reserves especially for those He loves.

Why?

In the case before us, Jesus answered the prayers of the demons and of an unbelieving, cynical, hostile society according to their request. But He answered the prayer of a believer in a way that changed his course rather than affirmed his request. No doubt, this once-demonized man was disappointed initially, but he realized he must keep the directive of his Deliverer and thus returned to speak to his community—his obedience brought to fruition in church history, which records the group of believers that began to surface in the region. The church had a powerful expression in the area—most likely birthed by the man Jesus sent home.

Take hope, dear friend. Your prayers not being answered in the way you desire are not indicative of God not hearing or not caring—for He only said, "No," to the one who loved Him.

Mark 5:21
**And when Jesus was passed over again by
ship unto the other side, much people gathered unto him: and he was nigh unto the
sea.**

One crowd sighed with relief when Jesus left.
On the other side of the lake, however, another
crowd was set to receive.

Mark 5:22–26
**And, behold, there cometh one of the rulers
of the synagogue, Jairus by name; and when
he saw him, he fell at his feet, And besought
him greatly, saying, My little daughter lieth
at the point of death: I pray thee, come and
lay thy hands on her, that she may be healed;
and she shall live. And Jesus went with
him; and much people followed him, and
thronged him. And a certain woman, which
had an issue of blood twelve years, and had
suffered many things of many physicians,
and had spent all that she had, and was
nothing bettered, but rather grew worse.**

Of the crowd set to receive Jesus, Mark draws
attention to two individuals . . .

- The most visible member of the community,
  Jairus was famous.
  The woman was anonymous.
- Jairus was wealthy.
  The woman lived in poverty.
- Jairus was the leader of the synagogue.
  *Because of her physical condition, the
  woman was forbidden from entering the
  synagogue.*
- For twelve years, as his daughter grew, the
  house of Jairus was filled with laughter and
  joy.
  *For twelve years, the house of the woman
  was filled with misery and despair.*

And so these two people—at opposite ends of
the spectrum—waited for Jesus.
Like Jairus, you might be riding high. Your
business might be booming. Your marriage might
be blessed. Your family might be growing. Your
body might be healthy. But you don't know what
the next moment holds. Before the clock strikes
midnight tonight, you might find yourself totally,
unexpectedly in the middle of a major tragedy.
You and I do not know what the next moment
holds. You who are Jairuses right now, realize
this: Like this man, the next moment might bring
tragedy into your world.
Conversely, if, like the woman, you have either
been going through an endless stream of setbacks or one persistent problem, you don't know
what the next hour holds. The next moment

might bring you a miracle of astounding proportion. Pondering this keeps me from complacency
when I feel like I'm in Jairus' sandals, and from
despairing when it seems like I'm standing in the
woman's shoes. Both of their stories remind me
that the Lord is my Shield and my Protector. And
if He allows difficulty, setback, or tragedy to
come into my life, He will also be my Glory and
the Lifter of my head (Psalm 3:3).

Mark 5:27–29
**When she had heard of Jesus, came in the
press behind, and touched his garment. For
she said, If I may touch but his clothes, I
shall be whole. And straightway the fountain of her blood was dried up; and she felt
in her body that she was healed of that
plague.**

As the woman broke through the crowd of people, she didn't come to Jesus with great oration to
impress Him. She simply reached out behind
Him and touched the hem of His garment. But
that was all it took. Why is it we think to receive
from the Lord we have to impress Him with long
prayers, lengthy fasts, or great discipline? If I
can break through the crowd of my unbelief, apathy, and despair, and touch even the hem of His
garment, I know I'll be helped in my difficulty.

Mark 5:30–33
**And Jesus, immediately knowing in himself
that virtue had gone out of him, turned him
about in the press, and said, Who touched
my clothes? And his disciples said unto him,
Thou seest the multitude thronging thee,
and sayest thou, Who touched me? And he
looked round about to see her that had done
this thing. But the woman fearing and trembling, knowing what was done in her, came
and fell down before him, and told him all
the truth.**

Did Jesus ask who touched Him because He
wanted to embarrass the woman? No. I believe it
was because He wanted to encourage Jairus. . . .

Mark 5:34, 35
**And he said unto her, Daughter, thy faith hath
made thee whole; go in peace, and be whole
of thy plague. While he yet spake, there came
from the ruler of the synagogue's house certain which said, Thy daughter is dead: why
troublest thou the Master any further?**

*Come on, Jesus. Let's get going. My daughter's
dying,* Jairus could have thought, not realizing
that it was, in fact, the woman's testimony that
would be used to buoy his own faith. You see, the

fact that he had seen a miracle in her would allow him to believe Jesus could also help him, even though his situation looked hopeless. So, too, when I wonder if the Lord can help me with any given problem, when I hear what the Lord is doing in your life, my own faith begins to grow.

Mark 5:36
As soon as Jesus heard the word that was spoken, he saith unto the ruler of the synagogue, Be not afraid, only believe.

"Only believe," or, literally, "Keep on believing"—even though everything looks impossible.

Mark 5:37, 38
And he suffered no man to follow him, save Peter, and James, and John the brother of James. And he cometh to the house of the ruler of the synagogue, and seeth the tumult, and them that wept and wailed greatly.

The presence of professional mourners would indicate that Jairus was a man of means.

Mark 5:39
And when he was come in, he saith unto them, Why make ye this ado, and weep? the damsel is not dead, but sleepeth.

The word "sleep" is the exact word Paul uses in 1 Corinthians 15 referring to the death of believers. Perhaps Jesus would whisper in our hearts concerning those who have gone on to be with the Lord or concerning those who are in the process of doing so, "Why make ye this ado and weep?" It's not death the way the world thinks. "Today you shall be with Me in paradise," Jesus said to the thief on the Cross. At the moment of death for a believer, the body sleeps, but the spirit celebrates in the presence of the Lord.

Mark 5:40
And they laughed him to scorn. But when he had put them all out, he taketh the father and the mother of the damsel, and them that were with him, and entereth in where the damsel was lying.

Like Jairus, when I'm seeking the Lord for help, when I'm in need of a miracle, I come to Him. I pour out my heart before Him. My faith might falter—until I hear a testimony. Then it soars—until reports come in even more brutal than previous reports, my faith turns to fear. Then I hear Jesus saying, "*Keep* believing." And I do. But then in my own heart, a laughing, a scorning, a mocking begins.

Before Jesus could enter Jairus' house and do a miracle, the mockers had to be put out. Why? Not only because without faith, it is impossible to please Him (Hebrews 11:6), but because the Holy One of Israel is limited by unbelief (Psalm 78:41). Therefore, when the mockers start knocking, let faith answer the door. Don't allow them to set up shop in your heart, to chuckle knowingly, to question cynically. Instead, listen to the Lord saying, "I desire to do exceedingly abundantly above all that you can ask or think"—and put the mockers out.

Mark 5:41
And he took the damsel by the hand, and said unto her, Talitha cumi; which is, being interpreted, Damsel, I say unto thee, arise.

Although I've seen self-proclaimed faith healers use this phrase, there's nothing magical about it. It's not what was said which brought Jairus' daughter back to life. It was *who* said it.

Mark 5:42–43
And straightway the damsel arose, and walked; for she was of the age of twelve years. And they were astonished with a great astonishment. And he charged them straitly that no man should know it; and commanded that something should be given her to eat.

Divine miracles never replace common-sense care. A miracle was done, but then Jesus said, "Make sure she gets some chicken soup." I like that!

The Word of the Servant brought victory over danger in the storm, over demons at Gadara, over disease in a woman, and even over death in a little girl.

May we continue to believe in, embrace, speak out, and stand upon this glorious Word. For through it, like the disciples, we will indeed "pass over" no matter the storm.

6 As we come to Mark 6, we see the unfolding of unbelief: in Jesus' acquaintances (verses 1–6); in His adversaries (verses 14–28); and even in His own disciples (verses 35–37).

Mark 6:1–3 (a)
And he went out from thence, and came into his own country; and his disciples follow him. And when the sabbath day was come, he began to teach in the synagogue: and many hearing him were astonished, saying, From whence hath this man these things?

and what wisdom is this which is given unto him, that even such mighty works are wrought by his hands? Is not this the carpenter, the son of Mary . . .

This is not an insight acknowledging Jesus' unique birth. Rather, it is an insult, for in that culture one was always identified as the son of his father, whether his father was living or dead. In this case, even if Joseph were indeed dead, as most Biblical scholars believe, Jesus would nonetheless be identified as being his son. But by calling Him the son of Mary, Jesus' countrymen were saying, "We do not even know who his father is," thereby accusing Him of being illegitimate.

It was imperative that Jesus be born of a virgin. At the moment of conception, although a baby draws nutrients and liquids from the mother, it draws blood from its own blood supply, which is determined by the father. Therefore, the fact that Jesus, being conceived supernaturally without a human father, and developing in the womb without drawing blood from His mother meant that His blood, unlike any other blood in human history, was free from human pollution of any kind—and was, therefore able to cleanse our sin.

Mark 6:3 (b)–4
. . . the brother of James, and Joses, and of Juda, and Simon? and are not his sisters here with us? And they were offended at him. But Jesus said unto them, A prophet is not without honour, but in his own country, and among his own kin, and in his own house.

After viewing the art in a renowned art museum, a man said to the guard, "I don't see any great value in this artwork."

"Sir," the guard answered, "the paintings are not what's on trial here. The visitors are."

That's true. If you look at a Rembrandt or a Monet, you're saying, "I don't see anything good about that," simply shows your ignorance concerning art.

So, too, these people saying, "We don't see anything so special about Jesus. He's just the carpenter, and we know his mother, brothers, and sisters," showed their ignorance concerning Him.

We are in danger of making the same mistake if we take for granted His proximity to us. Yes, He lives inside us. Yes, He will never leave nor forsake us. Yes, He is always available to us—but He is God nonetheless. And, as God, He has the right to our time, money, abilities, energy, life, and heart. As God, Jesus has the right to all we are.

When Peter at last realized that Jesus was Master of creation, he fell on his face before Him, saying, "Depart from me. I am a sinful man" (see

Luke 5:8). So, too, as we cultivate a friendship with Jesus, let us never forget that because He is God, He deserves our utmost respect and devotion, submission and reverence.

Mark 6:5
And he could there do no mighty work, save that he laid his hands upon a few sick folk, and healed them.

Mark doesn't say Jesus *should* do no mighty work, but that He *could* do no mighty work because of their unbelief. Why? Because the Lord has placed Himself in a partnering position with us in order to prepare us for the next billion years when we will rule and reign with Him.

Mark 6:6
And he marvelled because of their unbelief. And he went round about the villages, teaching.

Scriptures record Jesus marveling on only two occasions. One is here—when He marveled at the unbelief of the Jews. The other is in Luke 7 and Matthew 9, when He marveled at the belief of a Gentile. I wonder what Jesus thinks about us. Does He marvel at our unbelief, saying, "Oh, there is so much more I could do if you would just believe and partner with Me in faith"?

Mark 6:7 (a)
And he called unto him the twelve, and began to send them forth by two and two . . .

Why did Jesus send His disciples out two by two? Perhaps it's because, as we've experienced, faith becomes bolder when ministering with someone else. But more likely, it's because one of the principles of the law was that in the mouth of *two* witnesses, every word would be established (Deuteronomy 19:15).

Mark 6:7 (b), 8 (a)
. . . and gave them power over unclean spirits; And commanded them that they should take nothing for their journey, save a staff only . . .

The connection between power and simplicity is undeniable. Jesus gave His disciples power as He sent them out in simplicity.

Mark 6:8 (b)
. . . no scrip . . .

"Scrip" refers to a beggar's bag. In other words, Jesus said, "Don't beg in ministry." This should be "scrip"-ted into all televangelism programming.

Mark 6:8 (c), 9
... no bread, no money in their purse: But be shod with sandals; and not put on two coats.

"Travel light," Jesus said because the urgency and nature of what His disciples were to do required that they move about freely and simply.

Mark 6:10
And he said unto them, In what place soever ye enter into an house, there abide till ye depart from that place.

In other words, "When you go into a house, stay there until you leave the town. Don't look around for better accommodations."

Mark 6:11
And whosoever shall not receive you, nor hear you, when ye depart thence, shake off the dust under your feet for a testimony against them. Verily I say unto you, It shall be more tolerable for Sodom and Gomorrha in the day of judgment, than for that city.

"Their sin shall remain upon those who don't receive you," Jesus said, "upon those who fail to respond to your message of repentance."

Mark 6:12, 13
And they went out, and preached that men should repent. And they cast out many devils, and anointed with oil many that were sick, and healed them.

This is the only reference in the Gospels to the practice of anointing with oil, which James will later talk about in his epistle. Throughout the Bible, oil is an emblem of the Holy Spirit, so when one is anointed with oil, it symbolizes his placing himself in submission to the work of the Spirit in his life.

Mark 6:14 (a)
And king Herod heard of him; (for his name was spread abroad:) ...

Notice it was Jesus' name that was spread abroad—not the names of the disciples. This means that just as when Jesus ministered, all glory went to the Father, when the disciples ministered all of the attention went to Jesus.

Mark 6:14 (b), 15
... and he said, That John the Baptist was risen from the dead, and therefore mighty works do shew forth themselves in him. Others said, That it is Elias. And others said, That it is a prophet, or as one of the prophets.

Why would Herod think that Jesus was John the Baptist? Josephus tells us that, being second cousins, Jesus and John the Baptist had a remarkable physical resemblance. But more likely, it was because Herod's conscience was haunting him.

Mark 6:16, 17
But when Herod heard thereof, he said, It is John, whom I beheaded: he is risen from the dead. For Herod himself had sent forth and laid hold upon John, and bound him in prison for Herodias' sake, his brother Philip's wife: for he had married her.

Herod Antipas was one of the three sons of Herod the Great—the Herod who, following Jesus' birth, had ordered the deaths of all males less than two years of age. Herod Antipas took his brother Philip's wife—a union that John the Baptist had denounced as immoral.

Why didn't Herod call for this One he thought was John in order the he could investigate for himself? Perhaps it was because he thought John, Jesus, or whoever this was would be out to get him. People make this same mistake today. They look at Jesus as One who is sure to point His finger at them. But such is not the case, for Jesus is the One who dialogued freely with sinners (Matthew 11:19), who ate alongside sinners (Matthew 9:10), who stood up for sinners (John 8:7), who gave great hope to sinners. Jesus' rebukes, in fact, were reserved for the religious people—those who were pious and proud that they "weren't like other men" (see Luke 18:11). I believe had Herod called for Jesus at this time, he would have found Jesus to be exactly who He is to this day: meek and lowly in heart (Matthew 11:29), the Friend of Sinners.

Mark 6:18–20
For John had said unto Herod, It is not lawful for thee to have thy brother's wife. Therefore Herodias had a quarrel against him, and would have killed him; but she could not: For Herod feared John, knowing that he was a just man and an holy, and observed him; and when he heard him, he did many things, and heard him gladly.

Realizing John was a man unlike himself—a man of integrity—Herod respected John the Baptist. Yet his wife, Herodias, was incensed by

His insistence that Herod's marriage to her was unlawful.

Mark 6:21–29
And when a convenient day was come, that Herod on his birthday made a supper to his lords, high captains, and chief estates of Galilee; and when the daughter of the said Herodias came in, and danced, and pleased Herod and them that sat with him, the king said unto the damsel, Ask of me whatsoever thou wilt, and I will give it thee. And he sware unto her, Whatsoever thou shalt ask of me, I will give it thee, unto the half of my kingdom. And she went forth, and said unto her mother, What shall I ask? And she said, The head of John the Baptist. And she came in straightway with haste unto the king, and asked, saying, I will that thou give me by and by in a charger the head of John the Baptist. And the king was exceeding sorry; yet for his oath's sake, and for their sakes which sat with him, he would not reject her. And immediately the king sent an executioner, and commanded his head to be brought: and he went and beheaded him in the prison, and brought his head in a charger, and gave it to the damsel: and the damsel gave it to her mother. And when his disciples heard of it, they came and took up his corpse, and laid it in a tomb.

Herod was "exceeding sorry" to have to kill John the Baptist. Yet kill him he did because he was put on the spot at a party where wine and oaths flowed freely. Stay away from such places, dear people. You'll regret it if you don't because there's always a price to pay. Demands will be made. Peer pressure will mount. Things will happen you'll wish hadn't. Ask Herod. Historians tell us he was haunted all the days of his life by what he had done to John the Baptist.

Mark 6:30, 31
And the apostles gathered themselves together unto Jesus, and told him all things, both what they had done, and what they had taught. And he said unto them, Come ye yourselves apart into a desert place, and rest a while: for there were many coming and going, and they had no leisure so much as to eat.

Jesus models something that a lot us are discovering. That is, if we don't come apart, we'll fall apart. There's an ebb and flow in ministry in which times of service alternate with times of quietness and solitude, prayer, and contemplation. We need to come apart daily and have a quiet, quality time with the Lord. We need to come apart weekly for a Sabbath rest in Him.

Mark 6:32–34
And they departed into a desert place by ship privately. And the people saw them departing, and many knew him, and ran afoot thither out of all cities, and outwent them, and came together unto him. And Jesus, when he came out, saw much people, and was moved with compassion toward them, because they were as sheep not having a shepherd: and he began to teach them many things.

As the true Shepherd, Jesus felt compassion for the sheep who were wandering and hurting; those in need of a Word from Him to set their lives and hearts in order.

Mark 6:35, 36 (a)
And when the day was now far spent, his disciples came unto him, and said, This is a desert place, and now the time is far passed: Send them away. . . .

- The disciples' heart was, "Send them away. We're weary."
- Jesus' heart is, "Come unto Me, all ye who are weary."

I relate to the disciples—but I long to be more like Jesus.

Mark 6:36 (b), 37 (a)
. . . that they may go into the country round about, and into the villages, and buy themselves bread: for they have nothing to eat. He answered and said unto them, Give ye them to eat.

"You saw the need. You meet the need," Jesus said, wanting to partner with them in faith.

Mark 6:37 (b), 38 (a)
And they say unto him, Shall we go and buy two hundred pennyworth of bread, and give them to eat? He saith unto them, How many loaves have ye? go and see.

"I can't do that," we say. "I don't have those kinds of gifts or money." We have all the reasons why nothing can be done. Jesus, however, takes no regard for what we lack. Rather He asks what we *have*.

Mark 6:38 (b)–41 (a)
And when they knew, they say, Five, and two fishes. And he commanded them to make all sit down by companies upon the green grass.

And they sat down in ranks, by hundreds, and by fifties. And when he had taken the five loaves and the two fishes, he looked up to heaven, and blessed, and brake the loaves, and gave them to his disciples to set before them . . .

Blessing and breaking always precede true feeding. The Father must allow our lives to be blessed and broken, blessed and broken, blessed and broken before he can use us to nourish anyone else.

Mark 6:41 (b)–44

. . . and the two fishes divided he among them all. And they did all eat, and were filled. And they took up twelve baskets full of the fragments, and of the fishes. And they that did eat of the loaves were about five thousand men.

So much food did Jesus provide that the Greek word translated "filled" literally means "glutted." John gives us further insight when he says that, following the feeding of the five thousand, some of the men tried to take Jesus by force to make Him king (John 6:15). But their priority was wrong. They saw Jesus as being the king of the material in a physical kingdom. Jesus, however, departed from them because His kingdom is spiritual and eternal.

How easily we make this same mistake. Being so caught up in what is happening presently rather than seeing the big picture eternally, we want the Lord to comfort us now, to provide for us now, to heal us now. While the Lord is indeed a Comforter, a Provider, a Healer, those are not His highest priorities. The priority of God is not our present comfort, but our eternal state. Therefore, He will allow us to suffer presently—be it physically, emotionally, or financially—if that is what it takes to enrich us eternally.

Mark 6:45–48

And straightway he constrained his disciples to get into the ship, and to go to the other side before unto Bethsaida, while he sent away the people. And when he had sent them away, he departed into a mountain to pray. And when even was come, the ship was in the midst of the sea, and he alone on the land. And he saw them toiling in rowing; for the wind was contrary unto them: and about the fourth watch of the night he cometh unto them, walking upon the sea, and would have passed by them.

Jesus sent His disciples into the sea, where He knew a storm would be brewing. And such is the way He works with us today. He blesses us and then allows us to go into the midst of a storm. Why? Because He knows that storms will inevitably come into each of our lives without exception. And were we not seasoned veterans of the storm, we would be blown away.

Even as five thousand men were fed on the hillside of Galilee, five thousand would be saved in the city of Jerusalem (Acts 3—4). But what happened immediately after the five thousand were saved? A storm of fierce persecution arose. Knowing this, Jesus sent them into the storm in Mark 6 in order to develop the faith necessary to keep them from being blown away in Acts 5.

Mark 6:49, 50

But when they saw him walking upon the sea, they supposed it had been a spirit, and cried out: For they all saw him, and were troubled.

We know from the other Gospel accounts that Peter said, "Lord, if it's You, bid me come"—to which Jesus did indeed bid Peter to come to Him, and Peter walked on water. Why isn't that incident mentioned in this account? Because if Mark's Gospel is indeed comprised of Peter's account given to John Mark, perhaps Peter didn't want to draw unnecessary attention to himself.

Mark 6:50

And immediately he talked with them, and saith unto them, Be of good cheer: it is I; be not afraid.

Notice the order. Before Jesus identified Himself, He said, "Be of good cheer." That's always the way it is.

- We say, "Lord, if I can see You, I'll be of good cheer."
- Jesus, however, says, "In faith, be of good cheer first—and then you'll see Me."

Mark 6:51–56

And he went up unto them into the ship; and the wind ceased: and they were sore amazed in themselves beyond measure, and wondered. For they considered not the miracle of the loaves: for their heart was hardened. And when they had passed over, they came into the land of Gennesaret, and drew to the shore. And when they were come out of the ship, straightway they knew him, and ran through that whole region round about, and began to carry about in beds those that were sick, where they heard he was. And whithersoever he entered, into villages, or cities, or country, they laid the sick in the streets, and besought him that they might touch if it were but the border of his garment: and as many as touched him were made whole.

In simple faith and in need of a miracle, the needy ones simply touched Jesus. And as a result, they were made whole physically, spiritually eternally.

Mark 7:1, 2
Then came together unto him the Pharisees, and certain of the scribes, which came from Jerusalem. And when they saw some of his disciples eat bread with defiled, that is to say, with unwashen, hands, they found fault.

Although people were being healed and helped, delivered and fed, the scribes and Pharisees found fault with Jesus' disciples because they didn't wash their hands ceremonially as prescribed by sixty-five pages of the Mishnah, the written version of the traditional oral Jewish Law.

The sect of the Pharisees came into being during the period between the Old and New Testaments. Realizing there was a danger of Judaism becoming polluted and paganized, the Pharisees, whose name means "separated ones," were devoted to keeping the most minute detail of the law and the traditions of the elders. The problem is, the tradition of the elders became more important than the law itself. Ceremonial cleansing was a case in point. As seen in the Old Testament, God had given His people principles of hygiene that precluded the discovery of germs and infection. But as the years went by, a group of people called the scribes began to interpret the law and make application concerning, for example, the procedure for washing one's hands. Their findings were known as the tradition of the elders—a body of work so important to the scribes and Pharisees that one rabbi said, "He who expounds the Scripture in opposition to the tradition of the elders will have no part in the world to come."

Mark 7:3, 4
For the Pharisees, and all the Jews, except they wash their hands oft, eat not, holding the tradition of the elders. And when they come from the market, except they wash, they eat not. And many other things there be, which they have received to hold, as the washing of cups, and pots, brasen vessels, and of tables.

The scribes and Pharisees not only washed their hands ceremonially, but they also washed their cups and plates between the courses of a single meal.

Mark 7:5–8
Then the Pharisees and scribes asked him, Why walk not thy disciples according to the tradition of the elders, but eat bread with unwashen hands? He answered and said unto them, Well hath Esaias prophesied of you hypocrites, as it is written, This people honoureth me with their lips, but their heart is far from me. Howbeit in vain do they worship me, teaching for doctrines the commandments of men. For laying aside the commandment of God, ye hold the tradition of men, as the washing of pots and cups: and many other such like things ye do.

"You're involved in religious traditions that have nothing to do with what God desires," Jesus said. "With your lips you worship God, but your heart is a million miles away." And lest we be too quick to point fingers at the Pharisees, we would do well to search our own hearts during such times as we sing praise songs to the Lord with our lips while our minds are focused on the list of things we have to accomplish that day.

Mark 7:9–13
And he said unto them, Full well ye reject the commandment of God, that ye may keep your own tradition. For Moses said, Honour thy father and thy mother; and, Whoso curseth father or mother, let him die the death: But ye say, If a man shall say to his father or mother, It is Corban, that is to say, a gift, by whatsoever thou mightest be profited by me; he shall be free. And ye suffer him no more to do ought for his father or his mother; making the word of God of none effect through your tradition, which ye have delivered: and many such like things do ye.

The Pharisees had a tradition whereby whatever they declared to be "corban," or "dedicated," belonged to God. While this practice may have sounded pious, in actuality it provided a way for them to circumvent all charitable giving— even to their own parents, who they were commanded by God to honor (Exodus 20:12).

Again, while it is easy for us to point out the fallacies in the rituals of the Pharisees, I often wonder what Jesus would say concerning the traditions of our modern American Christianity. The test for any church practice—from baptism to Communion, from tithing to missions is three-fold: Is it exhibited in the life of Christ? Does it extend into the Book of Acts? Is it expounded in the epistles?

I encourage you to ask yourself, "Is what I'm doing seen in Jesus' life, in Acts, in the Epistles?" If it isn't, you shouldn't be dogmatic about it or insistent that others practice it.

Mark 7:14–23
And when he had called all the people unto him, he said unto them, Hearken unto me every one of you, and understand: There is nothing from without a man, that entering into him can defile him: but the things which come out of him, those are they that defile the man. If any man have ears to hear, let him hear. And when he was entered into the house from the people, his disciples asked him concerning the parable. And he saith unto them, Are ye so without understanding also? Do ye not perceive, that whatsoever thing from without entereth into the man, it cannot defile him; because it entereth not into his heart, but into the belly, and goeth out into the draught, purging all meats? And he said, That which cometh out of the man, that defileth the man. For from within, out of the heart of men, proceed evil thoughts, adulteries, fornications, murders, thefts, covetousness, wickedness, deceit, lasciviousness, an evil eye, blasphemy, pride, foolishness: All these evil things come from within, and defile the man.

Although the scribes and Pharisees were oh-so-careful to follow all of their rituals and practices, Jesus made it clear that the real issue is not external, but internal. In other words, it's not the washing of hands, but the purity of the heart that matters.

Mark 7:24
And from thence he arose, and went into the borders of Tyre and Sidon, and entered into an house, and would have no man know it: but he could not be hid.

I like that phrase. You can't hide Jesus if He's in your house, if He's in your life.

Mark 7:25–29
For a certain woman, whose young daughter had an unclean spirit, heard of him, and came and fell at his feet: The woman was a Greek, a Syrophenician by nation; and she besought him that he would cast forth the devil out of her daughter. But Jesus said unto her, Let the children first be filled: for it is not meet to take the children's bread,

and to cast it unto the dogs. And she answered and said unto him, Yes, Lord: yet the dogs under the table eat of the children's crumbs. And he said unto her, For this saying go thy way; the devil is gone out of thy daughter.

Was Jesus being difficult with this broken-hearted mother? No. He was drawing from her an expression of faith in order that not only would her daughter be healed, but that she herself would develop a relationship with Him. So, too, you might wonder if the Lord is being difficult with you. Why isn't He answering your prayers immediately? Why isn't He helping you presently? It could be that He's doing something much deeper. It could be that He is allowing you to discover true faith, perseverance, and prevailing prayer—invaluable understandings that will help you not only in your present situation, but also in the next billion years to come.

Mark 7:30–32 (a)
And when she was come to her house, she found the devil gone out, and her daughter laid upon the bed. And again, departing from the coasts of Tyre and Sidon, he came unto the sea of Galilee, through the midst of the coasts of Decapolis. And they bring unto him one that was deaf, and had an impediment in his speech. . . .

There is a linkage not only physically but spiritually between hearing and speaking. If I'm not hearing from the Lord on any given day, I'll not be able to speak clearly to the people who come my way. How can you help those who are hurting? It all begins with listening.

Mark 7:32 (b)–35
. . . and they beseech him to put his hand upon him. And he took him aside from the multitude, and put his fingers into his ears, and he spit, and touched his tongue; and looking up to heaven, he sighed, and saith unto him, Ephphatha, that is, Be opened. And straightway his ears were opened, and the string of his tongue was loosed, and he spake plain.

This seemingly small incident tells me a great deal about how I should minister to people if I want to minister the way Jesus did . . .

First, Jesus gave the deaf man *individual attention* as He took him aside from the multitude. Second, there was *close association* as Jesus put His fingers into the deaf man's ears.

Third, there was *open utilization* as Jesus used spit, which, in that day, was thought to contain medicinal value. In so doing, Jesus gave us justification to use the scientific knowledge He so graciously gave mankind to develop medicines and procedures. Fourth, we see *heavenly glorification* as Jesus looked up to heaven—thereby indicating to whom all glory is to go.

Fifth, Jesus demonstrated *heartfelt compassion* in His sigh. How will we feel this kind of compassion? I know of only one way: by going through difficulties ourselves. "Blessed be God who comforts us in our troubles that we may be able to comfort others with the comfort we ourselves have received," Paul would declare (see 2 Corinthians 1:3–4). Why does the Lord allow us to have migraine headaches or to be smitten with cancer, to lose a loved one or see a business fail? Did you ever pray, "Lord, use me"? Did you ever ask the Lord to make your life count, to keep it from becoming mundane and irrelevant? If so, part of His answer means having to go through difficulties in order that you might sigh *for* people, hurt *with* them, feel your heart go out *to* them. There's just no other way.

Finally, there was *articulated expectation* as Jesus said, "Be opened." I might feel *for* people, desire to minister *to* them, relate *with* them—but am I willing to go on record and speak the word of faith on behalf *of* them, to say, "In Jesus' Name, may the depression flee, may He be your health, may He see you through"?

If you follow this pattern when you pray for people—even if circumstances don't unfold the way they wished it would or you thought they should—a person will never resent the fact that you expended the energy in prayer to push through spiritual barricades, to ignore the lies of the Enemy, saying that prayer accomplishes nothing, to speak out a word of faith and expectancy, to wage a spiritual battle on their behalf.

Mark 7:36
And he charged them that they should tell no man: but the more he charged them, so much the more a great deal they published it.

Not only did Jesus most likely want to avoid the circus atmosphere that can so easily accompany miracles of healing, but knowing it wouldn't be long before He would be on a Cross and that those who spread the word about Him would be candidates for the persecution to follow, perhaps Jesus was sparing them from coming oppression.

Mark 7:37
And were beyond measure astonished, saying, He hath done all things well: he maketh both the deaf to hear, and the dumb to speak.

He does all things well indeed—and because He does, whatever we do should be done to the best of the ability He gives us if we are to reflect Him (1 Corinthians 10:31).

8 **Mark 8:1–3**
In those days the multitude being very great, and having nothing to eat, Jesus called his disciples unto him, and saith unto them, I have compassion on the multitude, because they have now been with me three days, and have nothing to eat: And if I send them away fasting to their own houses, they will faint by the way: for divers of them came from far.

For three days, the multitude had hung on His every word. They had stayed at His side, taking in His teaching, receiving His ministry. And because they had done so, Jesus wanted to feed them lest, without nourishment, they be unable to return to their homes.

It is my opinion that this understanding has been somewhat lost. All too often, it seems, the church feels a responsibility to feed people physically before she can impact them spiritually. Scripture, however, gives us no such precedent. Jesus always fed those who were already being taught and instructed. And Paul says, "Do good to all men—but especially, particularly to those of the household of faith" (see Galatians 6:10).

"Silver and gold have I none," said Peter to the beggar asking for alms (see Acts 3:6). Yet because just a few verses earlier, we read that everyone in the early church sold all of their goods and laid the money at the apostles' feet, it is highly likely that Peter and John had access to a great deal of money. Why, then, would Peter say, "Silver and gold have I none"? It is my belief that he was saying to the beggar, "For you, we have neither silver nor gold. Your need is not silver and gold. Your need is to stand up and walk." And a great miracle followed.

So, too, sometimes we feel the need, or others ask us to pray on their behalf for a physical solution to a physical need. But what will it profit us if we gain the whole world but lose our soul (Matthew 16:26)? Because the fundamental issue is to be able to stand strong in the Lord and walk with Him, any other answer to prayer pales in comparison.

Mark 8:4–8
And his disciples answered him, From whence can a man satisfy these men with bread here in the wilderness? And he asked them, How many loaves have ye? And they said, Seven.

And he commanded the people to sit down on the ground: and he took the seven loaves, and gave thanks, and brake, and gave to his disciples to set before them; and they did set them before the people. And they had a few small fishes: and he blessed, and commanded to set them also before them. So they did eat, and were filled: and they took up of the broken meat that was left seven baskets.

There's a remarkable similarity between this story and the one that took place in chapter 6, where we read that Jesus had miraculously fed five thousand people with five loaves and two fish. Yet here we see the disciples say to Jesus, "How are You going to satisfy these men?" Were the disciples that forgetful? I believe the answer lies in the term "these men"—the men of Decapolis. Decapolis was comprised of ten cities on the east side of the Sea of Galilee. The people of Decapolis had their own government, had adopted Greek culture, and willingly lived under Roman authority. This would mean that this crowd of four thousand—unlike the previous crowd of five thousand—was primarily Gentiles. And perhaps this explains the disciples' question when they said to Jesus, "How will You feed these men? We can see You doing a miracle for our people, the Jews, but not these guys!"

The Lord has a wonderful way of working through, working with, working on all kinds of people. Jesus, the Bread of Life, was given to the five thousand, to the Jews first, just as the promises were given to them when the covenant was established in the days of Abraham. But then, beginning with the Incarnation and into the birth of the church, the Bread of Life was made available to the four thousand, to the Gentiles, to us.

Mark 8:9
And they that had eaten were about four thousand: and he sent them away.

Four being the number of the earth, this speaks further of the Gentiles.

Mark 8:10–12 (a)
And straightway he entered into a ship with his disciples, and came into the parts of Dalmanutha. And the Pharisees came forth, and began to question with him, seeking of him a sign from heaven, tempting him. And he sighed deeply in his spirit . . .

Jesus had just fed four thousand men. Before that, he had opened blind eyes, healed lepers, worked powerfully. Yet the Pharisees had the audacity to say, "Show us a sign to establish Your validity." No wonder He sighed deeply.

Mark 8:12 (b)
. . . and saith, Why doth this generation seek after a sign? verily I say unto you, There shall no sign be given unto this generation.

Signs do not produce faith. They only produce a craving for more signs. Faith comes by hearing, and hearing by the Word of God (Romans 10:17). How does your faith grow? Not by seeing miracles, but by studying the Word.

Mark 8:13–15
And he left them, and entering into the ship again departed to the other side. Now the disciples had forgotten to take bread, neither had they in the ship with them more than one loaf. And he charged them, saying, Take heed, beware of the leaven of the Pharisees, and of the leaven of Herod.

The leaven of the Pharisees speaks of legalism. The leaven of Herod refers to the Herodians who were trying to bring about righteousness through political rule. Jesus would also speak of the leaven of the Sadducees, which is liberal theology. Legalism, politics, liberal theology—like leaven, each of these tendencies can start small and innocently, but grow to impact the entire Body.

Mark 8:16
And they reasoned among themselves, saying, It is because we have no bread.

"If any of you lack wisdom, let him ask of God," James tells us (see 1:5). Instead, these disciples reasoned among themselves, and came up with the wrong answer.

Mark 8:17–21
And when Jesus knew it, he saith unto them, Why reason ye, because ye have no bread? perceive ye not yet, neither understand? have ye your heart yet hardened? Having eyes, see ye not? and having ears, hear ye not? and do ye not remember? When I brake the five loaves among five thousand, how many baskets full of fragments took ye up? They say unto him, Twelve. And when the seven among four thousand, how many baskets full of fragments took ye up? And they said, Seven. And he said unto them, How is it that ye do not understand?

Jesus makes it clear that there is a direct correlation between a hardening of heart and a failing of memory. When does my heart become hardened toward the Lord? When does my heart begin to lack the fire of faith? When I forget the bread the Lord provides for me every day.

My faith is strengthened and my heart softened not only through an awareness of the daily bread He provides for me but also through the broken bread of His Body. "Do this in remembrance of Me," Jesus said (see Luke 22:19). Consequently, whenever I partake of the broken body, the bread of the Eucharist, the table of Communion, I am reminded once again of the Lord's provision for the greatest need I will ever have—the need of salvation.

Mark 8:22
And he cometh to Bethsaida; and they bring a blind man unto him, and besought him to touch him.

Like this man, we were once blind spiritually. Blinded by Satan, the god of this age, we could not see. Church seemed weird to us, the Bible incomprehensible, Christians bizarre. But then someone extended an invitation to us to come to Jesus—and a miracle was set in motion.

Mark 8:23 (a)
And he took the blind man by the hand, and led him out of the town . . .

As noted previously, I believe one of the main reasons Jesus led the man out of town was to avoid the frenzied atmosphere often associated with healing ministries.

Mark 8:23 (b)
. . . and when he had spit on his eyes, and put his hands upon him, he asked him if he saw ought.

In the Hebrew culture and much of the ancient world at this time, spit was thought to contain medicinal value. Therefore, in applying spit to this man's eyes, Jesus seems to be putting His seal of approval on the use of the medical technology of any given day.

Sometimes when I cut my finger and watch the blood coagulate, I marvel at the ability of my body to seemingly heal itself. Other times, when I have a pounding headache and down a couple of aspirin, I marvel at modern medicine. Still other times, when I'm hurting physically, a couple of brothers will lay hands on me and pray—and I marvel at the power of prayer. But it is not prayer that heals. It is not medicine that heals. It is not our own body processes that heal. It is God who heals. And as God, He can utilize prayer, medicine, and our natural body processes—or any combination of the three.

Mark 8:24
And he looked up, and said, I see men as trees, walking.

I love this man's honesty with Jesus. He saw the Lord, but he didn't yet have an ability to see people properly. And therein is a lesson. When you and I were touched by the Lord and saved, our eyes were now able to see Him. And yet even though we were now able to see Him, our healing was not complete until we could also see people clearly, for if we love God but hate our brother, we miss the mark entirely (1 John 4:20).

Many of us have no problem loving God. But there are some people who seem like trees to us. They "stump" us. We wish they would "leave." We try to cut them down. It might be a father who ignored you. It might be a husband who divorced you. It might be a boss who fired you. It might be a friend who deserted you.

"What is the greatest commandment?" they asked Jesus.

"Thou shalt love the Lord thy God with all your heart, mind, soul, and strength," He answered. "And the second is like unto it," or literally, "There's a second part to it: Thou shalt love thy neighbor as thyself" (see Matthew 22:35–40). Loving God and loving our neighbor are inextricably linked. But how are we to love those we see only as trees? Read on.

Mark 8:25 (a)
After that he put his hands again upon his eyes . . .

The fact that this man needed to be touched twice encourages me in my own areas of need. Be it with regard to physical healing, spiritual help, material provision—sometimes we need to pray for a second touch, a third touch, a tenth touch. Sometimes we must keep coming back to the Lord over and over and over again. You might have been doing well physically as a result of the Lord's help and healing touch. But then the difficulty returned. Seek Him again and continue on until you're totally healed—even if that total healing won't take place until you get to heaven.

Mark 8:25 (b)
. . . and made him look up . . .

When did the man see not only Jesus but also every man clearly? When Jesus lifted his head toward heaven in the posture of prayer. That's the key. Jesus told us to pray for our enemies—the people who bug us, bother us, or hurt us—to pray for those who despitefully use us (Matthew 5:44). I have found that when I pray for people, something begins to happen miraculously. My feelings towards them change. No longer can I hold a grudge against them. No longer can I get upset with them. When I'm lifting my head toward the heavens and communing with the Father, it's impossible for me to be bitter. Pray for the people who bug you. While they might not change, you definitely will!

Mark 8:25 (c), 26
... and he was restored, and saw every man clearly. And he sent him away to his house, saying, Neither go into the town, nor tell it to any in the town.

Will we be able to love people perfectly? No, for although we are to *look* up in prayer, it is not until we are *called* up to heaven at the moment of the Rapture that we will see perfectly the things that presently confuse and perplex us (1 Corinthians 13:12). What a day that will be!

Mark 8:27–29
And Jesus went out, and his disciples, into the towns of Caesarea Philippi: and by the way he asked his disciples, saying unto them, Whom do men say that I am? And they answered, John the Baptist: but some say, Elias; and others, One of the prophets. And he saith unto them, But whom say ye that I am? And Peter answereth and saith unto him, Thou art the Christ.

"Christ" is the Greek word; "Messiah," the Hebrew word. They both mean "Anointed One."

Mark 8:30
And he charged them that they should tell no man of him.

Matthew tells us that Jesus said, "Blessed are you, Simon bar Jonah. Flesh and blood have not revealed this unto you, but My Father which is in heaven. And upon the rock of your confession— the revelation that I am Messiah—I will build My church" (see Matthew 16:17–18).

Mark 8:31
And he began to teach them, that the Son of man must suffer many things, and be rejected of the elders, and of the chief priests, and scribes, and be killed, and after three days rise again.

Jesus didn't begin to teach His disciples about rejection, suffering, or the Cross until it was first revealed to them that He is the Christ. So, too, in my opinion, it is a mistake to try to explain the necessity of the Cross to those who don't first un-

derstand that Jesus is the Christ. Our first objective in sharing with people must be that they understand who Jesus is.

Mark 8:32
And he spake that saying openly. And Peter took him, and began to rebuke him.

The original language makes it clear that Peter continually rebuked Him. "Come on, Lord," Peter could have said, "cut out this talk about crucifixion and rejection, suffering and pain. You're the Christ. Let's talk about health and wealth, prosperity and the kingdom!" But there is no crown without the Cross. Jesus knew the Cross was part of the plan from the beginning of the world to provide for our redemption. Jesus always sees the big picture.

Mark 8:33
But when he had turned about and looked on his disciples, he rebuked Peter, saying, Get thee behind me, Satan: for thou savourest not the things that be of God, but the things that be of men.

"You've got it all wrong, Peter . . .

- Men are concerned about the material. *God is concerned about the eternal.*
- Men are concerned about prosperity. *God is concerned about sanctity.*
- Men are concerned about power. *God is concerned about purity."*

Only moments earlier, Peter had been a heavyweight prophet, having been given revelation so substantial that the entire church would be built upon it. But here, he's totally off the wall. This encourages me greatly because sometimes I share things I believe are truly the heart of the Lord—only to turn around and say something else that makes me wonder why I even said it. Do you think the Father said, "Oh no! If I had known Peter would say *that,* I would have given revelation to James or John!"? No, He knew Peter. But because God the Father wasn't taken aback by Peter's mistake, I understand He makes room for our humanity. Peter would still go on. God was far from finished with him.

Mark 8:34
And when he had called the people unto him with his disciples also, he said unto them, Whosoever will come after me, let him deny himself, and take up his cross, and follow me.

Jesus spoke not of self-denial, but of denying oneself. And between the two lies a monumental difference.

For topical study of Mark 8:34–35, see "Self Denial or Denying Self?" below.

Mark 8:35

For whosoever will save his life shall lose it; but whosoever shall lose his life for my sake and the gospel's, the same shall save it.

The more you live for yourself, the more miserable you'll be. We have all found this to be true to one degree or another. If you want to feel miserable, start thinking about yourself. Wonder how you're coming across, how you're doing, how you're feeling. When we take the temperature of how we're doing, what we're feeling, what we're thinking, we lose the very essence of what it means to truly live. It's in saving others that we so often save ourselves. It's in helping others that we help ourselves. It's in giving to others that we get ourselves. It's when we die to self that we find life.

Mark 8:36

For what shall it profit a man, if he shall gain the whole world, and lose his own soul? Or what shall a man give in exchange for his soul? Whosoever therefore shall be ashamed of me and of my words in this adulterous and sinful generation; of him also shall the Son of man be ashamed, when he cometh in the glory of his Father with the holy angels.

We wouldn't sell our soul to Satan for a billion dollars. And yet in actuality, we often give it away whenever we allow some cheap trinket, momentary pleasure, or earthly relationship to come between the Lord and us.

Mark 8:37, 38

Whosoever therefore shall be ashamed of me and of my words in this adulterous and sinful generation; of him also shall the Son of man be ashamed, when he cometh in the glory of his Father with the holy angels.

There is no such thing as closet Christians, secret saints, disguised disciples. It's always been this way . . .

- "Where are you?" God called to Adam—not because He couldn't find Adam, but because He wanted Adam to come forward to admit his sin and his need to get right (see Genesis 3:9).
- "Who is on the Lord's side?" Moses asked the Israelites. The sons of Levi stood with Moses publicly, even though to do so was out of sync with the rest of the tribes (see Exodus 32:26).
- "Who is on the Lord's side?" asked Joshua as the people were challenged publicly to make a stand (see Joshua 24:15).
- "How long will you halt between two opinions?" asked Elijah. "If Baal be god, serve him. But if Jehovah be God, serve ye Him," calling people to make a public decision (see 1 Kings 18:21).

Every man Jesus called, He called publicly. And He does the same today.

SELF-DENIAL OR DENYING SELF?

A Topical Study of
Mark 8:34–35

Jesus would have been a political campaign manager's nightmare. After all, because the common people heard Him gladly (Mark 12:37), thousands thronged around Him; thousands listened to Him; thousands loved to be with Him.

- Yet when told all men were seeking Him, what did Jesus say?
  "Let's depart" (see Mark 1:38).

- When told the masses wanted to make Him king, what did He say?
  "Unless you eat of My body and drink of My blood, you can have no part with Me" (see John 6:53).
- When it was revealed to Peter that He was indeed Messiah, what did Jesus say?
  "The Son of man must suffer many things and be killed" (see Matthew 16:21).
- *When the multitude gathered around Him, what did Jesus propose?*
  "If any of you intend to come after Me, you must deny yourself, take up your Cross, and follow Me" (see Matthew 16:24).

So it is that we see an apparent contradiction, a seeming tendency in Jesus to draw people to Himself and then repel them from Himself. This is why Jesus would drive the advisors crazy. He wasn't a politician.

There's a difference between a politician and a statesman. A politician looks toward the next election. A statesman looks toward the next generation. The latter is what Jesus does. He doesn't seize the moment politically. He doesn't use Peter's revelation as a new campaign slogan. Instead, He looks down the road at you and me and says, "Let the chips fall where they may. This is truth. The Son of man came not to set up a material, political kingdom, but to suffer and die in order to provide mankind with salvation. "Whoever will come after Me," He continued, "let him deny himself, take up his Cross and follow Me."

We have sanitized the Cross. We imprint it on our Bibles, wear it on gold chains around our necks, and stamp it on our bulletins. The Cross is a very important and beautiful emblem to us now. But it wasn't in Jesus' day.

Jesus' declaration concerning the Cross would be equivalent in our day to someone standing up in a political rally and saying, "If anyone wants to vote for me, grab your hypodermic needle with a lethal injection and follow me," or, "Put a noose around your neck and follow me," or, "Bring your gas chamber and follow me."

"Whosoever will come after Me, let him deny himself, take up his Cross, and follow Me." You may have heard numerous sermons on this well-known, powerful proclamation of Christ. But all too often they are preached from a perspective of self-denial: Do this and don't do that. Give up this and forsake that.

However, I don't believe that is what Jesus is teaching. His call is not to self-denial. It's to deny self. Our Lord never asks, expects, or desires us to do anything He hasn't done first. Therefore, when He asks us to take up our cross, it means He took up the Cross as well—which He did. But how did He take it up?

As He bore the Cross on His bruised, lacerated, beaten shoulders, the burden caused Him to fall on His face. A Roman soldier leading the procession stopped, placed the flat part of his spearhead on the shoulders of a man named Simon, and ordered him to carry the Cross.

Thus, because Jesus could not carry His own Cross, He would never tell me to carry mine. As Jesus bore His Cross, it brought Him to the place of collapse where He could no longer make it in His own strength. And such is the meaning of denying self. It means coming to the place where we say, "I can't make it, Lord. The loneliness I'm feeling, the misunderstanding hurled in my direction, the pain of separation, the tension I'm experiencing is more than I can bear."

It's my love for Jesus that drives me to my knees—but it's the cross I bear that brings me to my face.

No matter how smart, clever, or capable I think I might be, the burdens, anxieties, worries, and fears I bear show me I'm not any of those things. The temptation, however, is for us to stand up and keep going. But that's not denying ourselves. That's glorifying ourselves and our ability to keep pressing on. It's when we say, "Lord, I want to follow You—but I can't," that we are denying any ability in ourselves to bring this to pass.

When Jesus collapsed under the weight of the Cross He carried, there was someone there for Him. The Father had already orchestrated that Simon be there. We don't have a Simon. We have Someone infinitely better. We have a Savior.

"Two are better than one," Solomon writes, "because they have a good reward for their labour. For if they fall, the one will lift up his fellow: but woe to him that is alone when he falleth; for he hath not another to help him up" (see Ecclesiastes 4:9, 10).

Our "Other" is Christ Jesus.

If you want to have life—real life, abundant life, eternal life the way it was meant to be lived—deny yourself as you take up your cross and follow Jesus. And when the Cross brings you, as it did our Savior, to your face, you will see standing next to you, standing available to you, standing ready to help you Jesus Christ Himself.

9 **Mark 9:1**
And he said unto them, Verily I say unto you, That there be some of them that stand here, which shall not taste of death, till they have seen the kingdom of God come with power.

I believe Jesus was speaking not of the Rapture or His Second Coming, but of the event that would take place six days later when Peter, James, and John would witness His Transfiguration.

Mark 9:2, 3
And after six days Jesus taketh with him Peter, and James, and John, and leadeth them up into an high mountain apart by themselves: and he was transfigured before them. And his raiment became shining, exceeding

white as snow; so as no fuller on earth can white them.

His Transfiguration being a confirmation that He had led a sinless life, I believe that had He so chosen, Jesus could have gone directly to heaven at this point—leaving us with no explanation or justification for our sin before the Father. Instead, Jesus came down from Mount Hermon, the Mount of Transfiguration, to climb Mount Calvary, the Mount of Redemption.

Mark 9:4
And there appeared unto them Elias with Moses: and they were talking with Jesus.

Elijah representing the prophets, and Moses representing the Law, the Law and the Prophets were, in effect, conversing with Jesus.

Mark 9:5, 6
And Peter answered and said to Jesus, Master, it is good for us to be here: and let us make three tabernacles; one for thee, and one for Moses, and one for Elias. For he wist not what to say; for they were sore afraid.

Not knowing quite what to say, Peter blurted out, "Let's build three monuments—one for Moses, one for Elijah and one for You"—thereby putting Jesus on the same plane as the law and the prophets. The law, however, was given to drive people *to* Jesus. And the prophets gave predictions *about* Jesus. Therefore, Jesus is far above the law and the prophets.

Mark 9:7
And there was a cloud that overshadowed them: and a voice came out of the cloud, saying, This is my beloved Son: hear him.

Fortunately for Peter, the Father interrupted him, keeping him from making further mistakes.

Mark 9:8
And suddenly, when they had looked round about, they saw no man any more, save Jesus only with themselves.

This happens to us as well. There comes a time when, after looking around, you realize there is no one save Jesus who is worthy of your attention, your affection, your adulation. In all that He is, in all that He says, in all that He's done, He's perfect. So we come together not to celebrate our righteousness or to congratulate ourselves on our morality, activism or accomplishments, but because we have discovered there is none worthy of praise save Jesus only.

Mark 9:9–11
And as they came down from the mountain, he charged them that they should tell no man what things they had seen, till the Son of man were risen from the dead. And they kept that saying with themselves, questioning one with another what the rising from the dead should mean. And they asked him, saying, Why say the scribes that Elias must first come?

The scribes quoted Malachi, who predicted Elijah would come before the Messiah set up His kingdom (Malachi 4:5).

Mark 9:12, 13
And he answered and told them, Elias verily cometh first, and restoreth all things; and how it is written of the Son of man, that he

must suffer many things, and be set at nought. But I say unto you, That Elias is indeed come, and they have done unto him whatsoever they listed, as it is written of him.

Caught up in a fiery chariot because his ministry was not yet over, Elijah didn't die. He is to come before the Second Coming of Christ and proclaim throughout the nation of Israel the truth concerning Christ Jesus. And yet, Jesus says, he is already come. In Matthew 11 we see Jesus saying that John the Baptist had come in the same spirit as Elijah. Yet when asked if he was Elijah, John the Baptist said, "No" (John 1:21). John the Baptist, the forerunner of Christ at His first coming, came in the same spirit of Elijah. But Elijah himself will prepare the way for Christ's Second Coming.

Mark 9:14
And when he came to his disciples, he saw a great multitude about them, and the scribes questioning with them.

In the account that follows, we first see the disputing scribes. According to this account as recorded in Matthew 17, we know the scribes were arguing and debating with the disciples concerning the reality of demons. So here are the religious scholars debating theology even as a boy was suffering tragically. How true this is of our society today. People debate, argue, and question while all around us people are dying.

Mark 9:15–17
And straightway all the people, when they beheld him, were greatly amazed, and running to him saluted him. And he asked the scribes, What question ye with them? And one of the multitude answered and said, Master, I have brought unto thee my son, which hath a dumb spirit.

Second, we see the despairing father. Luke gives further insight when he tells us this son was the only son of this father (Luke 9:38). Catch the contrast: Up on the mountain, the heavenly Father said, "This is My beloved Son." Here in the valley, a heartbroken father says," Please help my bedeviled son."

Mark 9:18
And wheresoever he taketh him, he teareth him: and he foameth, and gnasheth with his teeth, and pineth away: and I spake to thy disciples that they should cast him out; and they could not.

Third, we see the demonized son. When Jesus called Satan a murderer and a liar (John 8:44), He was not only identifying Satan's personality, but His job description as well. Murder and lying are all he does.

Mark 9:19
He answereth him, and saith, O faithless generation, how long shall I be with you? how long shall I suffer you? bring him unto me.

Fourth, we see our dynamic Lord. First, He issues a compassionate invitation when He says, "Bring the child to Me." The father had come seeking help from the disciples, but the disciples were unable to help. So, too, perhaps you have brought a child, a friend, a co-worker to church or Sunday School, but they were not helped. That's okay, for if you bring anyone to where the disciples of Jesus are, guess who will show up sooner or later. Jesus Himself. Through a testimony shared, a study given, a story told, a song sung—something will happen. Jesus will come.

"Bring your child to Me," Jesus said. How? Morning by morning in intercession, teaching him what you're learning from the Word as you do errands together, making sure he's growing through fellowship with other believers. The cause of destruction is Satan. The cure is Jesus. The question is: Will you bring your friends and family to Him?

Mark 9:20–22
And they brought him unto him: and when he saw him, straightway the spirit tare him; and he fell on the ground, and wallowed foaming. And he asked his father, How long is it ago since this came unto him? And he said, Of a child. And ofttimes it hath cast him into the fire, and into the waters, to destroy him: but if thou canst do any thing, have compassion on us, and help us.

Notice Jesus' command of the situation. As this one is frothing at the mouth, Jesus calmly asks, "How long ago was it when this began?" Jesus was not sweating, shaking, or working Himself into a Pentecostal fervor. Rather, He was simply carrying on a very normal conversation.

Mark 9:23–27
Jesus said unto him, If thou canst believe, all things are possible to him that believeth. And straightway the father of the child cried out, and said with tears, Lord, I believe; help thou mine unbelief. When Jesus saw that the people came running together, he rebuked the foul spirit, saying unto him, Thou dumb and deaf spirit, I charge thee, come out of

him, and enter no more into him. And the spirit cried, and rent him sore, and came out of him: and he was as one dead; insomuch that many said, He is dead. But Jesus took him by the hand, and lifted him up; and he arose.

Notice Jesus' convicting exhortation. "You're asking Me if I can do anything," He says. "But let Me ask you, Can you do this one thing? Can you believe?" The Bible says without faith it is impossible to please God (Hebrews 11:6). Therefore, concerning the son who's not saved, the daughter you're wondering about, the parents you know are far from God, this is what Jesus asks you: "Can you believe? *Will* you believe?" Faith the size of the mustard seed can move mountains that seem insurmountable. But even though a mustard seed is small, it is also alive. Thus, the faith that moves mountains is not a remnant of leftover faith. It is a growing faith. The question is, Are you willing to plant it in the soil of hope, water it with the Word, and see it take root to move the mountain?

Mark 9:28, 29
And when he was come into the house, his disciples asked him privately, Why could not we cast him out? And he said unto them, This kind can come forth by nothing, but by prayer and fasting.

Finally, we see the disturbed disciples. "This kind of problem will not be solved by sharing pearls of wisdom, trying to be a better dad, or following some family program," Jesus told them. "This kind of spiritual warfare is won only through fasting and prayer."

How did we have time to fast and pray? the disciples must have wondered. After all, they certainly didn't know this problem would be laid at their feet that day. But that's the point. We never know when the moment for miraculous ministry will come our way or be needed in our families. Therefore, we must maintain a life of prayer and fasting because when the demonized boy is before you, it's too late to start.

Why were the disciples not maintaining a habit of prayer and fasting? I wonder if it wasn't due in part to the fact that they might have been feeling sorry for themselves. *Thanks a lot, Lord,* they could have thought. *You take Peter, James, and John—your favorites—up on the mountain. They see You shine. They hear the voice from heaven. They get to see Elijah and Moses. Us? We're down here at the bottom, forsaken and forgotten.* If so, how like us they would have been.

So often we think, *I never get called to sing or*

to teach Bible studies. So why should I fast or pray? And because we feel we're not important or useful, we give up. But once a year, once every five years, once in a lifetime an opportunity comes our way that is essential, important—an opportunity to move in the miraculous, to see salvation. Something exceedingly important could take place, but we're impotent and powerless because we haven't been praying, fasting, reading the Word, or seeking the Lord.

As a father, I have no other recourse than to maintain a life of prayer and fasting because I never know when the Enemy will strike one of my kids. He has; he does; he will. And as a believer, I have no other recourse than to maintain a close walk with God because I never know the next conversation that will open up before me at the grocery story or in the park with a neighbor that will impact them for eternity.

"But I've never been used," you say. Ah, but you might have the greatest opportunity for earth-shaking, life-changing ministry in the next moment or the next day. Therefore be ready.

Mark 9:30
And they departed thence, and passed through Galilee; and he would not that any man should know it.

On His way to Jerusalem, His face set like a flint (Isaiah 50:7), Jesus didn't want to be slowed down nor derailed.

Mark 9:31–33
For he taught his disciples, and said unto them, The Son of man is delivered into the hands of men, and they shall kill him; and after that he is killed, he shall rise the third day. But they understood not that saying, and were afraid to ask him. And he came to Capernaum: and being in the house he asked them, What was it that ye disputed among yourselves by the way?

As Jesus was headed to Jerusalem to die, His disciples were arguing along the way.

Mark 9:34
But they held their peace: for by the way they had disputed among themselves, who should be the greatest.

No doubt the disciples were embarrassed to admit the subject of their discussion. But if I were Jesus, I would have rebuked them radically. Instead, rather than coming down on them for wanting to be the greatest, He gives them five foundational principles of true greatness . . .

Mark 9:35–37
And he sat down, and called the twelve, and saith unto them, If any man desire to be first, the same shall be last of all, and servant of all. And he took a child, and set him in the midst of them: and when he had taken him in his arms, he said unto them, Whosoever shall receive one of such children in my name, receiveth me: and whosoever shall receive me, receiveth not me, but him that sent me.

The first principle of greatness Jesus shares with His disciples is to treat all men equally. And to illustrate this, Jesus took a child in his arms. If you want to get ahead in life in the world's eyes, you don't take time to hang out with children. They can't do anything for your career. All they do is take from you and depend on you. I believe this refers to anyone who's little, anyone who's "less"—be it chronologically or economically, socially or mentally. The truly great person embraces them all in the name of Jesus.

Mark 9:38–41
And John answered him, saying, Master, we saw one casting out devils in thy name, and he followeth not us: and we forbad him, because he followeth not us. But Jesus said, Forbid him not: for there is no man which shall do a miracle in my name, that can lightly speak evil of me. For he that is not against us is on our part. For whosoever shall give you a cup of water to drink in my name, because ye belong to Christ, verily I say unto you, he shall not lose his reward.

Second, to be truly great, we are not only to treat everyone equally but also to be as magnanimous as we possibly can be—even toward those who are not traveling with us denominationally or theologically.

There are very few things we should take seriously in this life. And yet sometimes we want to fight and take issue over anything and everything. "Those guys are casting out demons and they're not with us," John said.

"Relax," Jesus said. "Anyone who even gives a cup of cold water in My name will be blessed."

Mark 9:42
And whosoever shall offend one of these little ones that believe in me, it is better for him that a millstone were hanged about his neck, and he were cast into the sea.

Third, the truly great person handles others with sensitivity. Paul says the same thing when he says, "Don't eat meat offered to idols if it will cause those weaker in their faith to stumble" (1 Corinthians 8:13). I have observed that truly great people are always aware of those weaker in faith around them and therefore won't flaunt their liberty if it will trip up someone else in his walk with Jesus.

Mark 9:43–48
And if thy hand offend thee, cut it off: it is better for thee to enter into life maimed, than having two hands to go into hell, into the fire that never shall be quenched: Where their worm dieth not, and the fire is not quenched. And if thy foot offend thee, cut it off: it is better for thee to enter halt into life, than having two feet to be cast into hell, into the fire that never shall be quenched: Where their worm dieth not, and the fire is not quenched. And if thine eye offend thee, pluck it out: it is better for thee to enter into the kingdom of God with one eye, than having two eyes to be cast into hell fire: Where their worm dieth not, and the fire is not quenched.

Fourth, the truly great person deals with himself radically—for although he is to be magnanimous and sensitive toward others, he is to be radical and ruthless concerning the sin in his own life. The world tells us to stand up for our rights and that we deserve a break—in other words, to be harsh with others, but to go easy on ourselves. The key to greatness, however, is to reverse the order.

Jesus says, "Deal radically with whatever it is in your life that's hindering you." And you and I know exactly what those things are. It doesn't take morbid introspection or hours of analysis to figure them out. No, you and I know at this moment what thing or things there might be in our lives that cause offense in us. And if we want to be great, we'll cut them out.

Mark 9:49, 50
For every one shall be salted with fire, and every sacrifice shall be salted with salt. Salt is good: but if the salt have lost his saltness, wherewith will ye season it? Have salt in yourselves, and have peace one with another.

The fifth and final secret to greatness is to live with all men peaceably. In the Middle East during Bible times—and even to a certain degree today—when a peace treaty is made, it's salted. That is, bread was salted, broken, and shared between the two parties. Theirs being a hot, desert climate, salt was invaluable in stemming the effects of dehydration.

Leviticus 2 dictates that the sacrifices offered to the Lord were to be salted as opposed to sweetened with honey. Why was honey not used? Isn't our fellowship with the Lord to be sweet? Honey was forbidden because in high temperatures it breaks down. So, too, my attempt to be "sweet" doesn't hold up in heat. The only way to have peace is to have Jesus Christ, the hope of glory within me.

Treat all men equally. Be as magnanimous as you possibly can be. Handle others with sensitivity. Deal with yourself radically. Live with all men peaceably. These are not prerequisites for us to be saved. If they were, we'd never make it. No, through the Spirit living within us, these are not requirements for salvation—but for greatness.

10 As a Master Teacher, our Lord Jesus employed many techniques by which He communicated truth. Sometimes He spoke in parables and proverbs. Sometimes He used miracles. Other times, He gave lengthy exhortation and instruction. In the chapter before us, we see Jesus employing a method of teaching called the paradox, a statement that turns conventional thinking on its head.

Perhaps the best example of a paradox is the hypothetical story of the father and son who were in a tragic car accident in which the father was killed. The son, critically injured, was rushed to the hospital, where it was determined that surgery would be required. But upon seeing the patient, the surgeon said, "I can't operate on this boy. He's my son." How could this be if the boy's father was killed in the accident? The answer is that the surgeon was the boy's mother.

We will see in the chapter before us five such paradoxes—statements that appear to be impossible initially, but which change our thinking eventually.

Mark 10:1
And he arose from thence, and cometh into the coasts of Judaea by the farther side of Jordan: and the people resort unto him again; and, as he was wont, he taught them again.

Jesus never tired of teaching. When people came to Him or gathered around Him, He taught them. I hope we never tire of studying Scripture. It's the bread that sustains us, the fuel for our faith.

Mark 10:2
And the Pharisees came to him, and asked him, Is it lawful for a man to put away his wife? tempting him.

These Pharisees came trying to trip up Jesus with the most theologically controversial question of the day, an issue that remains controversial to this day: the issue of divorce.

Mark 10:3, 4
And he answered and said unto them, What did Moses command you? And they said, Moses suffered to write a bill of divorcement, and to put her away.

In Jesus' day, divorce was so common that in order to keep the rabbinical courts from being clogged with divorce proceedings, if a man simply said to his wife, "I divorce you," three times, she would be given a bill of divorcement.

Mark 10:5
And Jesus answered and said unto them, For the hardness of your heart he wrote you this precept.

The Greek word translated "hardness" is *skleros*—from which we get "sclerosis," a word most often used in conjunction with a hardening of the arteries. Whenever a divorce occurs, the reason is never what people say it is. The reason is always hardness of heart.

Mark 10:6
But from the beginning of the creation God made them male and female.

"Let's go back to the beginning," Jesus says.

Mark 10:7–9
For this cause shall a man leave his father and mother, and cleave to his wife; And they twain shall be one flesh: so then they are no more twain, but one flesh. What therefore God hath joined together, let not man put asunder.

The first paradox is that two become one. In the marriage ceremony, when a man and woman stand before the Father, when prayer is offered for their relationship and blessing pronounced upon their marriage, the two of them become one in the eyes of the Father.

Mark 10:10–12 (a)
And in the house his disciples asked him again of the same matter. And he saith unto them, Whosoever shall put away his wife,

and marry another, committeth adultery against her. And if a woman shall put away her husband . . .

This would have been a radical statement in the ears of the disciples. You see, nowhere in Levitical law or rabbinical thought could a woman divorce her husband. Thus, Jesus is placing woman on a level she had never before known— not only in the history of Israel, but in the history of the Roman and Grecian empires as well. Paul would go on to say that in Christ there is neither male nor female (Galatians 3:28). We have different functions and responsibilities, to be sure— but there is a wonderful equality in Christ.

Mark 10:12 (b)
. . . and be married to another, she committeth adultery.

This doesn't say the person who remarries after divorce will live in adultery, but that theirs is an act of adultery, the missing of God's best. After a failed marriage, there can be a second opportunity—but it must be approached with great sobriety. No matter how innocent they think they might be, both parties must accept responsibility for their part in the failure. For where sin abounds, grace abounds more.

Mark 10:13
And they brought young children to him, that he should touch them: and his disciples rebuked those that brought them.

The word "they," being masculine in Greek, it was the fathers who brought their children to Jesus.

Mark 10:14–16
But when Jesus saw it, he was much displeased, and said unto them, Suffer the little children to come unto me, and forbid them not: for of such is the kingdom of God. Verily I say unto you, Whosoever shall not receive the kingdom of God as a little child, he shall not enter therein. And he took them up in his arms, put his hands upon them, and blessed them.

The second paradox is that adults must become as children to enter the kingdom. This doesn't mean we are to be childish. It means we must be childlike. One of the most obvious characteristics of children is their trust. My kids never ask me if there will be food in the refrigerator next week. They have absolute confidence that when it's dinnertime, they'll be able to eat. Secondly, although children can't explain a lot, they sure enjoy a lot. As adults, on the other hand, we want to explain everything, but enjoy very little, if anything. The way of the kingdom is not explaining. The way of the kingdom is enjoying—just trusting that our Father will see us through, that He'll provide for us and never give up on us.

Mark 10:17
And when he was gone forth into the way, there came one running, and kneeled to him, and asked him, Good Master, what shall I do that I may inherit eternal life?

This is the only instance in the Bible where a man comes and kneels before Jesus and leaves worse off than when he came. Matthew 19 tells us this man was young. Luke 18 tells us he was a ruler. Mark tells us he was rich. But he comes running to Jesus because he's aware there's something wrong inside. He's everything our society values. He's rich, he's young, he's a ruler—but he's empty.

Mark 10:18
And Jesus said unto him, Why callest thou me good? there is none good but one, that is, God.

"If you're calling Me good," Jesus says, "is it because you understand that I must indeed be God?"

Mark 10:19–21 (a)
Thou knowest the commandments, Do not commit adultery, Do not kill, Do not steal, Do not bear false witness, Defraud not, Honour thy father and mother. And he answered and said unto him, Master, all these have I observed from my youth. Then Jesus beholding him loved him . . .

This man was not only rich, young, and a ruler—but he was also religious. His morals were impeccable. He was a man of integrity. And when he said, "I've done these things from my youth," Jesus didn't disagree.

Mark 10:21 (b)
. . . and said unto him, One thing thou lackest: go thy way, sell whatsoever thou hast, and give to the poor, and thou shalt have treasure in heaven: and come, take up the cross, and follow me.

The third paradox is that the poor will be rich. "You may have kept certain commandments," Jesus said to the rich young ruler, "but the problem is that you are controlled and dominated by

money. Be free. Get rid of it." I don't believe the point was for this man to divest himself of all of his money, but rather to recognize his wrong priority.

Throughout Scripture, there are four hundred ninety verses that deal directly with faith, five hundred or more that deal with prayer, and two thousand that deal with money. Two hundred eighty-eight verses in the Gospels alone—one in every ten—concern money. The Bible contains more verses dealing with our use and handling of money than it does concerning prayer and faith combined.

Mark 10:22–24
And he was sad at that saying, and went away grieved: for he had great possessions. And Jesus looked round about, and saith unto his disciples, How hardly shall they that have riches enter into the kingdom of God! And the disciples were astonished at his words.

Because at this time it was believed that a man who walked with God would be blessed by God financially, it is no wonder the disciples were astonished.

Mark 10:24–27
But Jesus answereth again, and saith unto them, Children, how hard is it for them that trust in riches to enter into the kingdom of God! It is easier for a camel to go through the eye of a needle, than for a rich man to enter into the kingdom of God. And they were astonished out of measure, saying among themselves, Who then can be saved? And Jesus looking upon them saith, With men it is impossible, but not with God: for with God all things are possible.

It's impossible for a rich man to be saved. It's impossible for a poor man to be saved. It takes a miracle for *any* man to be saved.

Mark 10:28–30
Then Peter began to say unto him, Lo, we have left all, and have followed thee. And Jesus answered and said, Verily I say unto you, There is no man that hath left house, or brethren, or sisters, or father, or mother, or wife, or children, or lands, for my sake, and the gospel's, but he shall receive an hundredfold now in this time, houses, and brethren, and sisters, and mothers, and children, and lands, with persecutions; and in the world to come eternal life.

If my house burned down tonight, I know there are believers who would take my family and me in. If I walked out into the church parking lot and discovered my car wouldn't start, I know someone would take me home. Thus, I have hundreds of houses and cars and family members. So do you. The more we give, the more we enjoy the benefits of the entire kingdom—the hospitality, love, support, networking, strength, and community of our brothers and sisters in Christ. Yes, there is sometimes persecution. But the extent to which we give is the extent to which our needs will be met in this life, and to which heaven will be enjoyed.

Mark 10:31
But many that are first shall be last; and the last first.

The fourth paradox is that the last shall be first. This statement runs cross current to that which our culture propagates. Our society is becoming increasingly competitive in its orientation. And yet those who win society's competition seem to be increasingly disillusioned with the prize. This explains why top athletes, for example, often find themselves being sucked into the drug scene. They got the prize—but the prize was too small. Jesus comes on the scene and calls us away from competition. How does this work out practically? In your mind's eye, travel back two thousand years ago to a place called Bethesda . . .

There you see hundreds of people with all sorts of physical ailments positioned around a pool of water. Why are they there? The understanding of the day was that the first one in the water after an angel supposedly stirred it would be healed. Consequently, these blind, lame, hurting people jockeyed for position in order that they might be first in the pool. But what does Jesus do when He arrives at Bethesda? He finds a lame man seemingly at the back of the pack and says, "Do you want to be made whole?"

"I have no man to help me into the water," the man answers. "I don't have a network. I don't have the skills. My college education is outdated. I don't have connections. How can I compete in this culture? I have no one to help me."

This man had no stock options. He wasn't a member of the health club, nor on the city softball team. He wasn't competitive. Yet it was he and he alone who captured Jesus' attention that day.

"Arise," Jesus said. "Take up your bed. I'm

freeing you from this pool of competition." And the man was healed (John 5:9).

I believe Jesus says the same thing to us today. Maybe we've been jockeying, struggling, planning, conniving, attempting to get the edge, to make it happen, to get ahead—be it financially or relationally, in ministry or in spirituality. But Jesus would remind us that the paradox of the kingdom is that the first shall be last and the last first.

Mark 10:32–40
And they were in the way going up to Jerusalem; and Jesus went before them: and they were amazed; and as they followed, they were afraid. And he took again the twelve, and began to tell them what things should happen unto him, saying, Behold, we go up to Jerusalem; and the Son of man shall be delivered unto the chief priests, and unto the scribes; and they shall condemn him to death, and shall deliver him to the Gentiles: And they shall mock him, and shall scourge him, and shall spit upon him, and shall kill him: and the third day he shall rise again. And James and John, the sons of Zebedee, come unto him, saying, Master, we would that thou shouldest do for us whatsoever we shall desire. And he said unto them, What would ye that I should do for you? They said unto him, Grant unto us that we may sit, one on thy right hand, and the other on thy left hand, in thy glory. But Jesus said unto them, Ye know not what ye ask: can ye drink of the cup that I drink of? and be baptized with the baptism that I am baptized with? And they said unto him, We can. And Jesus said unto them, Ye shall indeed drink of the cup that I drink of; and with the baptism that I am baptized withal shall ye be baptized: But to sit on my right hand and on my left hand is not mine to give; but it shall be given to them for whom it is prepared.

James was martyred. John was placed in a cauldron of boiling oil and then exiled on the island of Patmos. They did indeed drink of Jesus' cup of suffering and were baptized into His baptism.

Mark 10:41–43
And when the ten heard it, they began to be much displeased with James and John. But Jesus called them to him, and saith unto them, Ye know that they which are accounted to rule over the Gentiles exercise lordship over them; and their great ones exercise authority upon them. But so shall it

not be among you: but whosoever will be great among you, shall be your minister:

"Unlike Gentile rulers who dominate, manipulate, and control, the great among you shall be your minister," or, literally, "your waiter," said Jesus.

Mark 10:44–45
And whosoever of you will be the chiefest, shall be servant of all. For even the Son of man came not to be ministered unto, but to minister, and to give his life a ransom for many.

The fifth paradox is that the servant shall rule. The easiest way to know if you're a servant is by how you react when people treat you like one. All too often, I'm afraid, my heart is, "Yes, Lord, I want to be a servant as long as people realize I'm serving. I want to be a slave as long as I become Slave of the Year." If you're gladly slaving in the nursery, in the kitchen, or in the Sunday-school class without being noticed, appreciated, or thanked—yours is the heart of a true servant.

Does the Lord want us to be slaves because He likes to see us grovel? No, it's because He's preparing us for the kingdom—for the next billion years—and He knows that the best exercise for strengthening your heart is stooping down to pick up someone else. Others might not acknowledge you. You might not be rewarded presently. But when you move into the kingdom, and the Lord says, "Well done, good and faithful servant. Enter into the joy of the Father," you'll do so with a large heart and a huge capacity to enjoy eternity.

When we get to heaven, gang, not one of us will regret the times we weren't applauded by people for serving the Lord. Instead, we'll say, "Thank You, Father, for sparing me from getting my reward on earth where it passes away so quickly." If you want to rule, become a slave. It's a paradox indeed. But it's true.

Mark 10:46 (a)
And they came to Jericho . . .

Historians tell us that at this time Jericho was the most trafficked intersection in the world due to the fact that all commerce, travel, and movement of troops between Europe to the north and Africa to the south passed through Jericho.

Mark 10:46 (b)
. . . and as he went out of Jericho with his disciples and a great number of people, blind Bartimaeus, the son of Timaeus, sat by the highway side begging.

It has been said that there are three basic categories of people: those who make things happen, those who watch things happen, and those who wonder what happened. Bartimaeus, I believe, would fit into the third category. No doubt he would hear the creaking of the wagon wheels being pulled by snorting oxen. He would hear the shuffle of sandals on rocky roads, the sounds of camels, the conversations of people—everyone moving, while he sat still. Maybe you can identify. Maybe you feel like all around you things are happening, people are moving, times are changing. But you? You're just sitting, wondering, begging.

Bartimaeus sat by the side of the road because he was blind. Perhaps he was blind due to vitamin deficiencies common in that day. But it is more likely that his blindness was the result of heredity. You see, "Bartimaeus" literally means "son of the unclean one." Thus, it is very possible that Bartimaeus was so named because his mother or father passed on a disease that produced blindness in their son.

Mark 10:47, 48
And when he heard that it was Jesus of Nazareth, he began to cry out, and say, Jesus, thou Son of David, have mercy on me. And many charged him that he should hold his peace: but he cried the more a great deal, Thou Son of David, have mercy on me.

Bartimaeus heard that Jesus had come to Jericho. The name "Jesus" is the Greek transliteration of the Jewish name "Joshua," so it was actually "Joshua" who came to Jericho that day.

Thousands of years previously, another Joshua had come into the city of Jericho—not for salvation, but for destruction—for it was his job to bring the people of God into the Promised Land. And here, standing before Bartimaeus, was "Joshua," whose job it was to bring the people of God into the Land of Promise not physically, but eternally—to bring mankind to heaven.

As the feet of the priests and Levites touched the water, the Jordan River parted, and Joshua entered into the Promised Land to begin his ministry. Jesus also began His ministry in the Jordan River when He was baptized at the age of thirty. The water didn't part. Instead, the heavens opened, a dove descended, and the Father declared, "This is My beloved Son in whom I am well pleased."

Joshua's ministry was preceded by Moses, who prepared the people *in* the wilderness as he gave them the law. Jesus' ministry was preceded by a prophet *of* the wilderness named John the Baptist who preached repentance (Mark 1:15).

After circling the city, Joshua told the people to shout. And the walls came down. When Jesus came into the city, Bartimaeus was told not to shout, but to keep quiet. But he would soon stand up.

Mark 10:49 (a)
And Jesus stood still, and commanded him to be called.

Joshua's greatest victory took place on the day he commanded the sun to stand still (Joshua 10:12). So, too, Bartimaeus' life would miraculously change the day the Son stood still.

You who are sitting by the highway of life, saying, "I'm blind. I don't get it. I'm not seeing properly. I'm not going anywhere. Does Jesus care about me, or is He just passing by quickly?" take hope. Bartimaeus cried out—and the Son stood still. Why? I suggest three reasons . . .

Bartimaeus cried out in humility. All too often, we say, "Poor me. Life isn't fair. Why do bad things always happen to me?" Humility, on the other hand says, "I'm a sinner. I deserve judgment. But, Lord, I thank You for Your *mercy.*" And such is the voice the Lord hears most clearly.

Bartimaeus cried out tenaciously. "Keep quiet!" the crowd said to Bartimaeus. It's amazing to me how often perhaps well-meaning people try to get us to quiet down. "Don't keep bothering the Lord," they say. "Just accept your blindness. Accept your confusion. Accept the fact that you don't know what's happening." Bartimaeus, however, kept crying—with humility, yes—but also with tenacity.

Mark 10:49 (b), 50
And they call the blind man, saying unto him, Be of good comfort, rise; he calleth thee. And he, casting away his garment, rose, and came to Jesus.

Bartimaeus cried out expectantly, for when Jesus called him, he left his garment behind. The garment beggars wore was specially striped in order that people would know the wearer was legitimately begging, that he had no other means of financial support. Therefore, in throwing his garment down, Bartimaeus was saying, "I know Jesus will heal me." Truly, without faith it is impossible to please God (Hebrews 11:6)—for it is faith that sees the invisible, believes the impossible, and receives the incredible.

Mark 10:51, 52
And Jesus answered and said unto him, What wilt thou that I should do unto thee? The blind man said unto him, Lord, that I

might receive my sight. And Jesus said unto him, Go thy way; thy faith hath made thee whole. And immediately he received his sight, and followed Jesus in the way.

Bartimaeus was "changed in the twinkling of an eye"—just as we all will be one day. It is no wonder he followed the One who had opened His eyes and given him life.

May today be the day you do what Bartimaeus did: May today be the day you receive the direction, instruction, revelation you need. May you cry out until Jesus stops in front of you. May you cry out until the Son stands still.

And may you join Bartimaeus in following Him anew.

❧

11 Having seen Jesus as the Servant living His life in service in chapters 1—10, chapter 11 marks the beginning of the second section of Mark's Gospel, wherein we see the Servant giving His life in sacrifice. In so doing, Jesus will make a presentation of Himself as King in verses 1–11, followed by provocation as He drives the moneychangers from the temple in verses 15–18, and finally by examination as the political and religious leaders question Him in verses 27 to 12:37.

Mark 11:1 (a)
And when they came nigh to Jerusalem . . .

The population of the city of Jerusalem would have been three times its normal number due to the influx of people who had come to celebrate Passover. In addition, Josephus tells us there were ten times the normal amount of Roman soldiers in the city, guarding against any potential uprising from the zealots—the group of radicals determined to overthrow Roman rule in Israel. Consequently, it was with soldiers watching, people bustling, and the city almost bursting at the seams that Jesus made His way toward Jerusalem.

Mark 11:1 (b)
. . . unto Bethphage and Bethany . . .

"Bethphage" means "House of Figs." "Bethany" means "House of Dates." Bethany is located two and a half miles outside of Jerusalem; Jesus passed through these two small towns on His way there.

Mark 11:1 (c)
. . . at the mount of Olives . . .

Two thousand six hundred feet in elevation, the Mount of Olives offered a commanding view of the city of Jerusalem below.

Mark 11:1 (d)–3 (a)
. . . he sendeth forth two of his disciples, and saith unto them, Go your way into the village over against you: and as soon as ye be entered into it, ye shall find a colt tied, whereon never man sat; loose him, and bring him. And if any man say unto you, Why do ye this? say ye that the Lord hath need of him . . .

The Lord hath need? Why would the Creator of all things have need of anything? The reason He borrowed a manger, a boat, a donkey, an upper room, and a tomb is because He who was rich for our sakes became poor (2 Corinthians 8:9). Why? He chose to place Himself in a position where He would need to partner with us in order to see His will worked out through us.

This is incredible to me. God didn't have to go that route. But He's chosen to place Himself in a position where He will not do what He desires to do in our families, communities, workplaces, marriages, or schools without our partnering with Him. Why? He's getting us ready for the next billion years when we will be ruling and reigning with Him.

"Why should I bother to pray or to study the Word, to worship or to fellowship with other believers?" you might ask. "It doesn't really matter." Oh, but it does. Somehow in God's economy, His blessing and moving in this world are dependent upon our participation. I wonder if one of the mind-blowing moments in heaven might not be when we see what could have happened in the lives of our relatives, friends, and communities had we taken seriously the possibility of partnering with God instead of acting as if the Lord didn't need us.

Mark 11:3 (b)
. . . and straightway he will send him hither.

As the margin of your Bible may render it, this phrase is more properly translated, "He will send him back." That's always the way of the Lord. Anything we give Him—be it our energy or money, our time or abilities—He returns it to us with interest.

Mark 11:4–7
And they went their way, and found the colt tied by the door without in a place where two

ways met; and they loose him. And certain of them that stood there said unto them, What do ye, loosing the colt? And they said unto them even as Jesus had commanded: and they let them go. And they brought the colt to Jesus, and cast their garments on him; and he sat upon him.

When a Roman general was victorious over an army of five thousand or more, he made a triumphal entry upon his return in which he rode a golden chariot pulled by white stallions. Behind him would be the conquered general or king of the nation, followed by the conquered soldiers in chains. At the end of the procession would be the Roman soldiers marching in pomp and pageantry.

Their numbers swollen in order to keep watch on the crowded city, the Roman soldiers in Jerusalem must have chuckled to see Jesus enter the city riding on a donkey, followed by twelve ragtag disciples, the majority of whom smelled like fish. And yet even by Rome's own standards, He warranted a triumphal entry indeed, for the number of those who would believe in Him after His resurrection would be five thousand (Acts 4:4)—conquered not by force or shame, but by love.

Mark 11:8, 9
And many spread their garments in the way: and others cut down branches off the trees, and strawed them in the way. And they that went before, and they that followed, cried, saying, Hosanna; Blessed is he that cometh in the name of the Lord.

Quoting Psalm 118, the crowd cried, "Hosanna!" or, "Save Now!"

Mark 11:10
Blessed be the kingdom of our father David, that cometh in the name of the Lord: Hosanna in the highest.

When the crowd cried, "Save Now!" they weren't speaking of their personal salvation. They were looking for a Messiah who would free them politically, who would lead a revolution militarily to overthrow the rule of Rome. But Jesus was coming with an entirely different kingdom in mind.

Mark 11:11 (a)
And Jesus entered into Jerusalem, and into the temple: and when he had looked round about upon all things. . . .

Jesus was not impressed by the crowd because, knowing the fickleness of humanity, He knew that the cry of the crowd would change from "Hosanna" to "Crucify Him" in a few short days.

Why, then, did He who usually said, "Tell no man" (Matthew 16:20) orchestrate His entry into Jerusalem in a way that was sure to draw attention? In addition to fulfilling prophecy (Zechariah 9:9), I believe it was because had He not done so, people could have said, "If we had known You had come into our city, we would never have turned against You. We would have responded to You." So He came into the city in a way in which no one could have the excuse of not knowing He was there. Riding a donkey in accordance with prophecy, He was proclaiming to be the One sent from God, the Son of David, the Messiah.

Mark 11:11 (b)
. . . and now the eventide was come, he went out unto Bethany with the twelve.

In the temple, Jesus would have observed moneychangers charging exorbitant rates to exchange the currency of those who had traveled great distances to pay their temple tax and to give offerings at Passover. He also would have seen worshipers bullied into buying temple-approved animals to sacrifice at high prices because the priests had declared theirs to be substandard. But what does Jesus do? Does He drive out the moneychangers and chase out the livestock? No. He goes back to Bethany and reflects on what He had seen.

Is something bothering you today? I encourage you to follow the example of Jesus. Before you spout off, take some time and go back to Bethany—the place of quietness and communion—to get instruction from the Father.

Mark 11:12, 13 (a)
And on the morrow, when they were come from Bethany, he was hungry: And seeing a fig tree afar off . . .

As seen in Jeremiah 8, Nahum 3, and Hosea 9, the fig tree is a symbol of Israel. In the account that follows, in speaking of the fig tree, Jesus will be speaking of the fruitlessness of Israel—and of our fruitlessness as well.

Mark 11:13 (b)
. . . having leaves, he came, if haply he might find any thing thereon . . .

Although it was early in the season, because the leaves of a fig tree appear simultaneously with the fruit, seeing leaves on this fig tree, Jesus assumed it would have figs as well.

Mark 11:13 (c)
. . . and when he came to it, he found nothing but leaves; for the time of figs was not yet.

I wonder if Jesus comes by our lives in the morning hours desiring fruit. Outwardly, because of our abundance of leaves—our activities and words—we might look like we've got it together. But upon closer inspection, it is obvious to Him that we lack true fruit—

- the fruit of love (Galatians 5:22, 23),
- the fruit of the conversion of souls (John 4:36),
- the fruit of works of righteousness (Philippians 1:22),
- the fruit of financial giving (Romans 15:28),
- the fruit of praise (Hebrews 13:15).

Why didn't this tree have fruit? Matthew's original text makes it clear that this particular fig tree was a lone fig tree (21:19). Because fig trees require cross-pollenization, a lone fig tree cannot produce fruit. And the same is true with believers. "I don't need to go to church," some say. "I can worship the Lord on my own." Not true.

"Do not forsake the assembling of yourselves," says the writer to the Hebrews (Hebrews 10:25). We need one another in order to bear fruit.

Mark 11:14
And Jesus answered and said unto it, No man eat fruit of thee hereafter for ever. And his disciples heard it.

All of His life, Jesus went about doing good. He healed the sick. He fed the hungry. He raised the dead. But here He performs a miracle that is seemingly destructive—the only time in all of Scripture we see Him doing so. Was this act out of sync with the rest of His life and teaching? Did Jesus curse this tree in a fit of hungry rage?

No. On the contrary, Jesus' seemingly destructive cursing of the fig tree was an act of great mercy—for in so doing, He speaks of the absolute necessity of redemptive faith. We know from Colossians 1 that all things were not only made by Him, but for Him. Therefore, providing fruit for Jesus would have been the fig tree's highest calling. But because it was not able to do this, Jesus showed that in reality, it would not be able to provide fruit for anyone else. The same holds true for us. If we don't satisfy Jesus, other people will not be nourished by us, enriched by us, or blessed by us.

Mom and Dad, your kids won't gain spiritual nutrition and strength from you if you are not pleasing Jesus personally, privately, and devotionally. Bible study teacher, your students won't grow in their walk with the Lord through you un-less you are growing in your walk with Him. There is no shortage of those who say, "I want to serve people. I want to see our country changed, our community cleaned up, people helped." But they will only be going through the motions if they're not first pleasing Jesus.

Mark 11:15, 16
And they come to Jerusalem: and Jesus went into the temple, and began to cast out them that sold and bought in the temple, and overthrew the tables of the moneychangers, and the seats of them that sold doves; and would not suffer that any man should carry any vessel through the temple.

Forbidding people from carrying any vessel through the temple meant, essentially, that all sacrifices came to a halt. How could Jesus have done this? Evidently there was something in His eyes, something in His face, something in His countenance that kept all men from challenging Him as He drove out the cattle, overturned the tables, rebuked the men, and kept the entire temple sacrificial system from taking place. The fig tree represents the nation of Israel nationally; the cleansing of the temple speaks of the nation spiritually. Nationally, Israel was fruitless. Spiritually, she was bankrupt. What about us?

Mark 11:17, 18
And he taught, saying unto them, Is it not written, My house shall be called of all nations the house of prayer? but ye have made it a den of thieves. And the scribes and chief priests heard it, and sought how they might destroy him: for they feared him, because all the people was astonished at his doctrine.

What is a den of thieves? It's where the thieves feel protected and safe. The temple was to be a place of prayer, but instead it became a place where thieving priests preyed upon rather than prayed for God's people.

Mark 11:19, 20
And when even was come, he went out of the city. And in the morning, as they passed by, they saw the fig tree dried up from the roots.

Roots are the secret part of the tree that no one sees. When you feel dry, it's most likely be-cause there's a problem with the root system. Morning devotions are skipped. Evening prayer is no longer a priority. Outwardly, the part of your life that people see might be going along just fine. But the root system, the secret part is dried up.

Mark 11:21, 22
And Peter calling to remembrance saith unto him, Master, behold, the fig tree which thou cursedst is withered away. And Jesus answering saith unto them, Have faith in God.

How do we satisfy the hunger of our Lord? How do we keep the hidden part of our life from becoming dry? The root of the answer is faith. In this passage, we see four aspects of the faith that will keep us from fruitlessness . . .

The Object of Faith

"Have faith in God," Jesus said. Unlike an un-fortunate amount of teaching today that seems to encourage believers to have faith in faith, the ob-ject of our faith is God. And because He is good (Psalm 73:1), I can bring my requests to Him, share my concerns with Him, and cast my care upon Him, realizing that He is God and I am not; that He is a Father and I am but a child; that He is a Shepherd and I a straying sheep. In this way, my faith is not in my faith, but in my Father.

Mark 11:23
For verily I say unto you, That whosoever shall say unto this mountain, Be thou re-moved, and be thou cast into the sea; and shall not doubt in his heart, but shall believe that those things which he saith shall come to pass; he shall have whatsoever he saith.

The Outworking of Faith

Did Jesus tell us to pray that the problem, ob-stacle, or mountain that looms menacingly before us might be removed? No. Did He tell us to study the Word that it might be removed? No. He said, "Say to the mountain Be thou removed, and it will be cast into the sea."

We often hear that prayer changes things. But that's not entirely true. Prayer changes us. Faith changes things. Jesus didn't say, "If you encoun-ter a mountain, pray that it might be gone." No, He said, "Have faith in God and then verbally, au-dibly tell the mountain to be removed. Speak faith."

Why is saying, speaking, verbalizing so impor-tant? Why did Jesus tell us to speak aloud to the mountain? Why does Paul tell us to confess with our mouth that Jesus is Lord (Romans 10:9, 10)? Why does the writer of Hebrews tell us that when a promise is given to us we are to boldly speak it out (Hebrews 13:5, 6)? Because that's when faith kicks in. It's easy for me to think quietly or pray inwardly for the mountain to be moved because then if it doesn't move, no one will know I prayed otherwise. There's no step of faith, no risk involved if I don't speak.

What mountain intimidates you? Is it fear concerning an unsaved child, or depression over a business about to go under? Jesus tells you and me to go on record in the ears of our kids, our parents, our peers, our co-workers and to say, "Be gone." After all, it was what Jesus did Himself in the ears of His disciples, which set the stage for them to believe (Mark 11:14). Maybe you're praying intensely and hoping passionately that a certain problem or a certain situation will somehow be solved. But the fact is, Jesus said it's not enough to simply hope or even to pray. Rather, you must say in faith verbally, "Be gone. Be removed. Be cast into the sea."

Mark 11:24
Therefore I say unto you, What things soever ye desire, when ye pray, believe that ye receive them, and ye shall have them.

The Obtaining of Faith

Maybe you're in a place where you lack the faith to tell the mountain to be removed. The solution? Ask the Father to give you the faith you need, and He'll give it to you in order that you might speak to the mountain directly.

This is where the "Positive Confession, Name It and Claim It" teachers miss the point. Jesus taught on faith not to obtain a mountain. Rather, it was to curse a fruitless situation and to remove an obstacle. Concerning faith, Jesus didn't tell His disciples how to get a Cadillac, a bigger house, a boyfriend, or a higher-paying job. He didn't tell His disciples how to get more of anything. Rather, He told them how to get rid of the carnal tendencies, addictions, habits, or propensities that made them fruitless. Contrary to what the "Name It and Claim It" mentality propagates, cross-current to what the Positive Confession school maintains, Jesus was not talking about accumulating worldly goods, but about obliterating worldly gods. He wasn't telling His disciples to claim in faith that they would be given a vacation cabin on a mountain. He was telling them to get rid of the mountain altogether.

I want the San Francisco Giants to win the pennant. I really do. But when I'm in my times of prayer, guess what. That doesn't surface in my conversation with God. It's in the time of prayer when suddenly the things the Lord wants to do in and through my life are birthed within me. That's why in the original text, the comma does not appear after the word "desire." As we pray, our desires will change. That which is not important will fade away. That which God does not desire to do in your life will dissipate. And you will be set free

to be more like Jesus. To the mountain looming over you today, go on record and say, "Be gone" so clearly that your voice can be heard in hell, in heaven, and in your own heart.

Mark 11:25, 26
And when ye stand praying, forgive, if ye have ought against any: that your Father also which is in heaven may forgive you your trespasses. But if ye do not forgive, neither will your Father which is in heaven forgive your trespasses.

The Obstacle to Faith

Because Jesus clearly links faith to forgiveness, if we're not forgiving, the power of faith is short-circuited. Why? Because a person who does not love or will not forgive cannot be entrusted with that kind of power. He'll misappropriate it. She'll hurt herself and others with it. That is why Paul makes it clear that faith works by love (Galatians 5:6).

Mark 11:27 (a)
And they come again to Jerusalem . . .

As Jesus reenters Jerusalem, He will face a series of questions concerning His authority, integrity, theology, and priorities. Yet unbeknownst to His interrogators, even their questions perfectly fulfill Biblical prophecy and typology. You see, when the Passover was instituted, the lamb that was to be slain for the family was to be set apart and observed, scrutinized, examined for four days before it was slain lest any fault or spot or blemish be found upon it that would disqualify it from being the Passover lamb. So, too, the events before us taking place four days before Passover, it is only fitting that Jesus, the Passover Lamb, would be carefully scrutinized as well.

Mark 11:27 (b)
. . . and as he was walking in the temple . . .

The outer courtyard of the temple was a place where teaching went on continually. The eastern courtyard, known as Solomon's porch, contained sixty large columns that supported a roof, forming an arcade. The courtyard on the south side of the temple was known as the royal porch and, with one hundred sixty-two columns thirty-five feet high and six feet in diameter, was considerably larger than Solomon's porch. It was in these covered courtyards that skeptics wanting to find fault with Him would find Jesus.

Mark 11:27 (c)–28
. . . there come to him the chief priests, and the scribes, and the elders, and say unto him,

By what authority doest thou these things? and who gave thee this authority to do these things?

The first group to question Jesus was comprised of chief priests, scribes and elders, questioning His authority. "By what authority do You come in here turning over tables, driving out cattle, and interrupting the sacrificial system?" they asked Jesus. They said this to place Him upon the horns of a dilemma, for if Jesus answered, "By My own authority," they would have labeled Him a lunatic. But if He said, "By God's authority," they would accuse Him of blasphemy.

Mark 11:29–33
And Jesus answered and said unto them, I will also ask of you one question, and answer me, and I will tell you by what authority I do these things. The baptism of John, was it from heaven, or of men? answer me. And they reasoned with themselves, saying, If we shall say, From heaven; he will say, Why then did ye not believe him? But if we shall say, Of men; they feared the people: for all men counted John, that he was a prophet indeed. And they answered and said unto Jesus, We cannot tell. And Jesus answering saith unto them, Neither do I tell you by what authority I do these things.

Why did Jesus raise this particular question concerning the baptism of John? Because this was the point where the priests, scribes, and elders first took a wrong turn. They rejected the truth John shared about the One who would follow him. Thus, their rejection of John set the stage for their final rejection of Jesus.

It has been rightly said that obedience is the conduit through which fresh understanding flows unhindered. That is, if I am obeying the Lord, I will get more understanding from the Lord. But at the point I stop obeying, oftentimes He will stop revealing. If you're wondering why you haven't heard anything from the Lord this week or this month, this year or this decade, it could very well be that there was a point where you knowingly, willingly, stubbornly disobeyed and refused to respond. I'm not talking about morbid introspection. I'm talking about an obvious point you know very readily where the Lord gave instruction to you, but you said, "No. I will not go there. I will not give that up. I will not do what You say." The cure is simply to repent, to say, "Lord, forgive me. As You did with Jonah, give me another opportunity."

This was a route those who were questioning Jesus chose not to take. As a result, caught by the very trap they thought they had set for Him, they were rendered speechless.

12
Jesus follows His answer to the question concerning His authority posed to Him by the priests, scribes, and elders with a parable . . .

Mark 12:1
And he began to speak unto them by parables. A certain man planted a vineyard, and set an hedge about it, and digged a place for the winefat, and built a tower, and let it out to husbandmen, and went into a far country.

The parable concerns an absentee landlord—a common figure in those days.

Mark 12:2–12
And at the season he sent to the husbandmen a servant, that he might receive from the husbandmen of the fruit of the vineyard. And they caught him, and beat him, and sent him away empty. And again he sent unto them another servant; and at him they cast stones, and wounded him in the head, and sent him away shamefully handled. And again he sent another; and him they killed, and many others; beating some, and killing some. Having yet therefore one son, his well-beloved, he sent him also last unto them, saying, They will reverence my son. But those husbandmen said among themselves, This is the heir; come, let us kill him, and the inheritance shall be ours. And they took him, and killed him, and cast him out of the vineyard. What shall therefore the lord of the vineyard do? he will come and destroy the husbandmen, and will give the vineyard unto others. And have ye not read this scripture; The stone which the builders rejected is become the head of the corner: This was the Lord's doing, and it is marvellous in our eyes? And they sought to lay hold on him, but feared the people: for they knew that he had spoken the parable against them: and they left him, and went their way.

Servants sent to collect rent were either beaten or killed by the servants of the tenant farmer. Finally, certain they would honor him, the owner sent his own son. But the son was killed just as readily as the others.

In a similar parable, Isaiah identified the vineyard as Israel (Isaiah 5:7). Thus, it was a loving God who sent prophet after prophet to Israel, only to see each one beaten or killed. And it was a God of incomparable love who sent His own Son to die for the very ones who nailed Him to a Cross.

This not only speaks volumes concerning the patience of the Father in sending servant after servant and warning after warning, but also concerning the stupidity of man who thinks that because God must be off in some corner of the cosmos, he need not listen to His servants; he need not reverence His Son; he can do whatever he wants. Mankind mistakes the patience of God for impotence. But when He comes, judgment will fall upon those who have not reverenced His Son. So clearly did the priests, scribes, and elders get the point of Jesus' parable that they knew He had to be done away with.

Mark 12:13
And they send unto him certain of the Pharisees and of the Herodians, to catch him in his words.

Unable to trap Jesus with their question concerning authority, the priests, scribes, and elders made way for the Pharisees and Herodians to question Him concerning His integrity. The Herodians supported Herod, who was a puppet of Rome, and the Pharisees wanted no part of Rome, so these two groups would normally be as close as cats and dogs. But because they realized Jesus was a threat to both of their empires, the Herodians and Pharisees came together in a shared hatred of Him.

Mark 12:14, 15 (a)
And when they were come, they say unto him, Master, we know that thou art true, and carest for no man: for thou regardest not the person of men, but teachest the way of God in truth: Is it lawful to give tribute to Caesar, or not? Shall we give, or shall we not give?

"Master," said the Herodians and Pharisees, "You're a great teacher, One who can't be manipulated. Therefore, we have a question to ask You: Should we pay taxes or not?"

If Jesus said, "Yes, pay taxes," the people of Israel—who hated paying taxes to the despised Romans—would have turned against Him. If, however, He said, "Don't pay taxes," He would have been arrested for insurrection. Either way, the Herodians and Pharisees thought they had Him.

Mark 12:15 (b)
But he, knowing their hypocrisy, said unto them, Why tempt ye me? bring me a penny, that I may see it.

"Health, Wealth, and Prosperity" teachers would call Jesus a dismal failure. Foxes have holes, the birds have nests, but the Son of man had nowhere to lay His head (Luke 9:58). He didn't even have a penny to use as an illustration.

Mark 12:16
And they brought it. And he saith unto them, Whose is this image and superscription? And they said unto him, Caesar's.

In Jesus' day, the first thing a ruler did after conquering new territory would be to mint new coinage containing his image as a continual reminder to the conquered people that he was indeed their leader and that his authority extended as wide as his coins were circulated.

Mark 12:17 (a)
And Jesus answering said unto them, Render to Caesar the things that are Caesar's . . .

Although the people in the realm were able to use his coins as currency, the person whose image appeared on the coin actually owned the coin. In this case, it would have been the image and coin of Caesar Tiberius.

Mark 12:17 (b)
. . . and to God the things that are God's.

If the coin with the image of Caesar belonged to Caesar, Jesus reasoned, the person made in the image of God belongs to God.

Mark 12:17 (c)
And they marvelled at him.

Just as the priests, scribes, and elders had failed to trap Jesus concerning His authority, the Herodians and Pharisees were also unable to do so concerning His integrity.

Mark 12:18 (a)
Then come unto him the Sadducees, which say there is no resurrection . . .

Believing only in the five books of Moses, the Sadducees didn't believe in miracles, angels, or resurrection because they saw none of those elements in the Pentateuch. They were smaller in number than the Pharisees or Herodians, but, being the wealthier businessmen, they were the elite of the day.

Mark 12:18 (b)–23
. . . and they asked him, saying, Master, Moses wrote unto us, If a man's brother die, and leave his wife behind him, and leave no

children, that his brother should take his wife, and raise up seed unto his brother. Now there were seven brethren: and the first took a wife, and dying left no seed. And the second took her, and died, neither left he any seed: and the third likewise. And the seven had her, and left no seed: last of all the woman died also. In the resurrection therefore, when they shall rise, whose wife shall she be of them? for the seven had her to wife.

According to Deuteronomy 25, if a man died childless, it was the obligation of his next younger brother to marry his widow and bear a child to be his heir, to carry on his name. In order to examine Jesus' theology, the Sadducees pose this question concerning a hypothetical woman who had been widowed seven times over.

Mark 12:24–27
And Jesus answering said unto them, Do ye not therefore err, because ye know not the scriptures, neither the power of God? For when they shall rise from the dead, they neither marry, nor are given in marriage; but are as the angels which are in heaven. And as touching the dead, that they rise: have ye not read in the book of Moses, how in the bush God spake unto him, saying, I am the God of Abraham, and the God of Isaac, and the God of Jacob? He is not the God of the dead, but the God of the living: ye therefore do greatly err.

Ignoring altogether the absurd hypothetical situation of the widow and speaking to them from the Pentateuch itself, Jesus reminded the Sadducees that five hundred years after Abraham, Isaac, and Jacob had passed from the scene, God identified Himself to Moses as the God of Abraham, Isaac, and Jacob. And by using the present tense to do so, the implication was obvious that Abraham, Isaac, and Jacob were still alive—verifying the reality of resurrection.

Mark 12:28
And one of the scribes came, and having heard them reasoning together, and perceiving that he had answered them well, asked him, Which is the first commandment of all?

In asking which is the greatest commandment of all, the last question addressed to Jesus dealt with priority.

Mark 12:29, 30
And Jesus answered him, The first of all the commandments is, Hear, O Israel; The Lord our God is one Lord: And thou shalt love the Lord thy God with all thy heart, and with all thy soul, and with all thy mind, and with all thy strength: this is the first commandment.

Jesus answered with the Shema, Deuteronomy 6:4, the verse the orthodox Jew quotes many times each day and wears inside the phylactery on his forehead and wrist.

Mark 12:31
And the second is like, namely this, Thou shalt love thy neighbour as thyself. There is none other commandment greater than these.

The Jews had six hundred thirteen commandments from the Old Testament law. Three hundred sixty-five were negative commandments—one for each day of the year, and two hundred forty-eight positive commandments—one for each of the two hundred forty-eight generations from Adam to their day. In Psalm 15, however, David reduced this number to eleven; and in the sixth chapter of his book, Micah reduced it to three (6:8). Here, Jesus reduces it to two; and in Galatians 5:14, Paul would reduce it to one: love.

Mark 12:32, 33
And the scribe said unto him, Well, Master, thou hast said the truth: for there is one God; and there is none other but he: And to love him with all the heart, and with all the understanding, and with all the soul, and with all the strength, and to love his neighbour as himself, is more than all whole burnt offerings and sacrifices.

Realizing that relationship far surpassed religion, the scribes could do nothing but agree with the beauty, simplicity, and logic of Jesus' answer.

Mark 12:34
And when Jesus saw that he answered discreetly, he said unto him, Thou art not far from the kingdom of God. And no man after that durst ask him any question.

After answering their questions regarding authority and integrity, theology and priority, it is now Jesus' turn to ask a question . . .

Mark 12:35–37
And Jesus answered and said, while he taught in the temple, How say the scribes that Christ is the Son of David? For David himself said by the Holy Ghost, The Lord said to my Lord, Sit thou on my right hand, till I make thine enemies thy footstool. Da-

vid therefore himself calleth him Lord; and whence is he then his son? And the common people heard him gladly.

Quoting Psalm 110, which the Jews knew to be a prophecy concerning Messiah, Jesus asked how David could call his son his lord. The only way a son could be greater than his father was if he was more than simply the son of the father. In other words, the Messiah for whom the Jews waited was more than a political leader or religious instructor, more than mere man. He was God.

Mark 12:38–40
And he said unto them in his doctrine, Beware of the scribes, which love to go in long clothing, and love salutations in the marketplaces, and the chief seats in the synagogues, and the uppermost rooms at feasts: Which devour widows' houses, and for a pretence make long prayers: these shall receive greater damnation.

Addressing those who weren't trying to trick Him, those who heard Him gladly, the common people, Jesus said, "Watch out for scribes who make a great show of religion, but are first on the scene to swindle widows."

Mark 12:41 (a)
And Jesus sat over against the treasury, and beheld how the people cast money into the treasury . . .

It was most likely between the columns on Solomon's porch that thirteen chests called "trumpets" were located in which people placed money to help the poor. Jesus was not as interested in what people gave as He was in *how* they gave.

Mark 12:41 (b)–44
. . . and many that were rich cast in much. And there came a certain poor widow, and she threw in two mites, which make a farthing. And he called unto him his disciples, and saith unto them, Verily I say unto you, That this poor widow hath cast more in, than all they which have cast into the treasury: For all they did cast in of their abundance; but she of her want did cast in all that she had, even all her living.

After dealing with the questions of His foes, Jesus finds a friend. The foes of Jesus will always raise questions. And the "foe" within me does so as well whenever I am cynical or critical. How I long for the day when that part of my nature is removed completely.

Jesus' friend, however, is presented in com-

plete contrast to the religious bigwigs of the day who chose to criticize and question rather than to give. May God help us to be like this faithful woman, and to show Him our love as we give of our money, energy, time, and heart in His Name.

13

Mark 13:1
And as he went out of the temple, one of his disciples saith unto him, Master, see what manner of stones and what buildings are here!

Having turned over tables and driven the moneychangers from the temple, perhaps it was because Jesus' disciples thought He had acted somewhat harshly that they drew His attention to the magnificence of the temple itself.

Valued at over one trillion dollars by today's standards, the temple was without a doubt the greatest single building ever constructed. With brass gates one hundred thirty feet high, stones forty feet long and twenty feet thick cut so perfectly that not even a knife blade could fit between them, the temple was nothing less than magnificent indeed.

Mark 13:2
And Jesus answering said unto him, Seest thou these great buildings? there shall not be left one stone upon another, that shall not be thrown down.

The size of the temple is beyond our imagining. Even the Wailing Wall, which was simply the foundation stones of the temple, dwarfs all who stand near it. Yet Jesus said it would come crashing down. And indeed it did. Within forty years of this statement, Roman troops, led by General Titus, would not only destroy Jerusalem, but, against Titus' orders, would throw a torch inside the temple, causing a fire so intense that the gold melted within. Thus, it was to get to the gold that trickled down its walls that the Romans razed the temple, leaving not one stone standing on another.

Mark 13:3, 4
And as he sat upon the mount of Olives over against the temple, Peter and James and John and Andrew asked him privately, Tell us, when shall these things be? and what shall be the sign when all these things shall be fulfilled?

Here we arrive at the Olivet Discourse—paralleled in Matthew 24 and Luke 21—where the longest answer Jesus would ever give deals with end times and future events. Concerning the Olivet Discourse, so named because Jesus gave it as He sat upon the Mount of Olives, I believe it is important to study it four ways . . .

First, it must be studied contextually. That is, it's important to bear in mind that it was four Jewish men asking their Jewish Rabbi when all things would be fulfilled or finalized.

Second, it must be studied comparatively. That is, it must be seen in light of prophecy given previously. It's always dangerous to isolate any passage of Scripture from other passages that give additional information regarding the same topic.

Third, it must be studied practically. Four times in this passage, Jesus says, "Take heed." Therefore, the purpose was not to stimulate controversy or to titillate curiosity. The purpose was to awaken the disciples—and those who would follow.

Finally, it must be studied eschatologically. That is, it must be seen in light of future events.

The Olivet Discourse deals with the Tribulation—the seven-year period following the Rapture of the church when God will pour out His wrath upon a Christ-rejecting sinful world. Verses 5–13 deal with the beginning of the Tribulation, 14–18 with the middle, and 19–27 with the end.

Mark 13:5, 6
And Jesus answering them began to say, Take heed lest any man deceive you: For many shall come in my name, saying, I am Christ; and shall deceive many.

History shows that in the first one hundred years after Jesus spoke these words, no less than sixty-four men came on the scene claiming to be Messiah. And we see a continuance of this today by those who propagate the age-old New Age lie that we all have a "God-consciousness" within us and are all, therefore, deity.

Mark 13:7
And when ye shall hear of wars and rumours of wars, be ye not troubled: for such things must needs be; but the end shall not be yet.

A government study was conducted by fifteen experts representing a wide range of disciplines, including a historian, political theorist, sociologist, economist, professor of international law, biochemist, cultural anthropologist, and industrialist. The group was told to waste no time agonizing over cultural and religious values. It was to give the same kind of treatment to the hypothetical problem of peace should peace break out as has been given to the hypothetical problems of war. The conclusion of this blue-ribbon panel was that wars would cease if the will to make them cease was there. But since war itself is at the very root of mankind's social system, it is not likely that peace will ever be a serious goal because no substitute is known that can better stabilize and control national economies than war. History has shown war to be the foundation of every stable government—that every governing body that has failed to sustain the continuing threat of an external war has lost control of its constituency. Even the world realizes war is a necessary evil. Therefore, although generation after generation cries for peace, there cannot be true peace until the Prince of Peace, Jesus Christ, returns.

Mark 13:8 (a)
For nation shall rise against nation, and kingdom against kingdom . . .

Linguistically, this could speak just as accurately of a nation at war with itself internally as of two separate nations at war. Could "kingdom" speak of a return to monarchies? Very possibly.

Mark 13:8 (b)
. . . and there shall be earthquakes in divers places, and there shall be famines . . .

Studies have shown that, although agricultural scientists are able to develop super strains of wheat and grains, the high price of oil necessary to produce the petroleum-based fertilizers required to make them grow rule them out as viable alternatives to famine.

Mark 13:8 (c)
. . . and troubles . . .

Matthew refers to "troubles" as "pestilences" (Matthew 24:7). We call them plagues.

Mark 13:8 (d)
. . . these are the beginnings of sorrows.

- These are the beginning of sorrows, or "labor pains."
- "But there have always been earthquakes," you say. And there have.
- "There has always been famine," you say. There has.
- "There have always been war and rumors of war." There have.

But what Jesus is saying is that, like birth pains, these things will increase in frequency and intensity as the Tribulation period draws nearer.

Mark 13:9, 10
But take heed to yourselves: for they shall deliver you up to councils; and in the synagogues ye shall be beaten: and ye shall be brought before rulers and kings for my sake, for a testimony against them. And the gospel must first be published among all nations.

Keep in mind that Jesus is speaking to Jews—as evidenced by His reference to synagogues. This distinction is important because the Rapture of the church does not need to wait until Christians are "delivered to councils," or "brought before rulers." Neither is it dependent upon the gospel being published among all nations. Oh, the gospel will indeed be published. But it will be by the 144,000 witnesses, by Elijah and Moses, by angels flying across the sky during the Tribulation. Referred to as *Jacob's* trouble in Jeremiah 30, the Tribulation does not concern the church, but Israel.

Mark 13:11, 12
But when they shall lead you, and deliver you up, take no thought beforehand what ye shall speak, neither do ye premeditate: but whatsoever shall be given you in that hour, that speak ye: for it is not ye that speak, but the Holy Ghost. Now the brother shall betray the brother to death, and the father the son; and children shall rise up against their parents, and shall cause them to be put to death.

During the Tribulation, Antichrist's rule will be so pervasive that there will actually be children betraying their parents who follow Jesus Christ and refuse the mark of the beast.

Mark 13:13
And ye shall be hated of all men for my name's sake: but he that shall endure unto the end, the same shall be saved.

Spoken to those who become believers during the Tribulation, Jesus says, "There's hope. Don't give up in the times of tribulation. If you endure to the end, you'll be saved."

Mark 13:14–19
But when ye shall see the abomination of desolation, spoken of by Daniel the prophet, standing where it ought not, (let him that readeth understand,) then let them that be in Judaea flee to the mountains: And let him that is on the housetop not go down into the **house, neither enter therein, to take any thing out of his house: And let him that is in the field not turn back again for to take up his garment. But woe to them that are with child, and to them that give suck in those days! And pray ye that your flight be not in the winter. For in those days shall be affliction, such as was not from the beginning of the creation which God created unto this time, neither shall be.**

In this section dealing with the middle of the seven-year Tribulation period, referring to the point when Antichrist will set up his image in the rebuilt temple, Jesus says, "Split for the wilderness"—specifically, I believe, to the rock city of Petra, a place the Lord has provided to save His people in the time of this outpouring of Antichrist's wrath. In addition to praying that this won't occur in winter, Matthew adds that the Jews are to pray it won't be on the Sabbath (24:20). To this day, all transportation comes to a halt on the Sabbath day in Israel. Thus, only to a Jew would the Sabbath pose a problem with regard to fleeing to the wilderness.

Mark 13:20
And except that the Lord had shortened those days, no flesh should be saved: but for the elect's sake, whom he hath chosen, he hath shortened the days.

He who uses this verse to say that Christians will be present during the Tribulation fails to understand that "the elect" is a term ascribed to three groups of people: Israel (Isaiah 65:9), believers (1 Peter 1:2), and Tribulation saints (Matthew 24:22).

Mark 13:21–23
And then if any man shall say to you, Lo, here is Christ; or, lo, he is there; believe him not: For false Christs and false prophets shall rise, and shall shew signs and wonders, to seduce, if it were possible, even the elect. But take ye heed: behold, I have foretold you all things.

In an attempt to trick the Tribulation saints, some will claim to be, or to have seen, Christ Himself. Even in these last days before the Tribulation, the cults are growing exponentially, saying, "Lo, here is Christ; or, lo He is there." The basic premise of the Jehovah Witness theology is that Jesus already came back in 1898 (later revised to 1914) to the Watchtower Society in Brooklyn, where He shared truth, understanding, and esoteric insights. Their entire theology is based upon a secret return of Jesus.

The Mormons also believe that Jesus came back already. Where did He go? They claim He came to America and gave fuller teaching to the American Indians.

"But the Mormons are good people," you say.

Indeed, ads on TV and in magazines proclaim the goodness of the Mormons, as if to say, "For the Mormons, home and family come first. Theirs will be a family likely to be admired by neighbors for its quiet confidence and self-assurance, and generally envied for its closeness and good-natured round of family activities. Clean, bright, outgoing, Mormons practice what they preach, setting aside each Monday for Family Home Evening. Stressing family, emphasizing their care for one another, talking about temperance—they don't drink even Coke, coffee, or tea—and an absolute abhorrence of narcotics, they present a goodness, a quality of life attractive to many."

I am troubled when I realize that this sounds a lot like the claims we evangelicals make. We talk about ourselves as those with better than average marriages, good families, and high moral standards. I came across this statement written by a skeptic named Walker Percy: "I'm surrounded by Christians. They are, generally speaking, a pleasant and agreeable lot, not no-ticeably different from other people. But if they have the Truth, why is it the case that they are repellently and precisely a turn-off to the degree that they embrace and advertise their truth? One might even become a Christian if there were a few Christians around. But have you ever lived in the middle of fifteen million Southern Baptists? If the Good News is true, why is one not pleased to hear it?"

Our message has been repellent, unaccepted because we, like the Mormons, like the Jehovah Witnesses, have all too often exalted our good-ness, holding up our standard of living that, at best, becomes pharisaic when we look down on others, and, at worst, hypocritical when we don't live up to our own image. We must not boast of our morality, but of God's mercy. We should not advertise our flawlessness, but God's faithful-ness. It would do us well to remember Luke 18—the parable of the religious man saying, "I thank You, God, that I am not like other men," and the sinner who smote his breast saying, "God have mercy upon me." Jesus said it was the latter—the one who realized his sinfulness but also be-lieved in God's graciousness—who went his way justified.

Let us be those who, rather than saying, "Look how religious we are, how together our families

are, how clean our life is," say, "It is the mercy and grace and goodness of God alone of which we boast. We are not the Moral Majority. We are the Forgiven Few."

Mark 13:24–27
But in those days, after that tribulation, the sun shall be darkened, and the moon shall not give her light, and the stars of heaven shall fall, and the powers that are in heaven shall be shaken. And then shall they see the Son of man coming in the clouds with great power and glory. And then shall he send his angels, and shall gather together his elect from the four winds, from the uttermost part of the earth to the uttermost part of heaven.

I believe the elect spoken of here refers to Is-rael. All Jews will be gathered up and brought home as the Tribulation comes to a close and the kingdom is established at last.

Mark 13:28 (a)
Now . . .

Having talked about the beginning, the middle, and the end of the Tribulation, Jesus changes the subject somewhat . . .

Mark 13:28 (b)–29
. . . learn a parable of the fig tree; When her branch is yet tender, and putteth forth leaves, ye know that summer is near: So ye in like manner, when ye shall see these things come to pass, know that it is nigh, even at the doors.

As seen in the books of Jeremiah, Nahum, Isa-iah, and Hosea, the fig tree is the national symbol of Israel. Therefore, it is my strong conviction that Jesus is talking about the re-blossoming of the nation of Israel that took place in May, 1948, when the Jews returned to their land—the only time in history when a nation came back from the dead—exactly as prophesied by Isaiah, Ezekiel, and Zechariah. We cannot know the day of Jesus' return—but as seen in the fig tree, we surely know the season (1 Thessalonians 5:1).

Mark 13:30–37
Verily I say unto you, that this generation shall not pass, till all these things be done. Heaven and earth shall pass away: but my words shall not pass away. But of that day and that hour knoweth no man, no, not the angels which are in heaven, neither the Son, but the Father. Take ye heed, watch and pray: for ye know not when the time is. For

the Son of man is as a man taking a far journey, who left his house, and gave authority to his servants, and to every man his work, and commanded the porter to watch. Watch ye therefore: for ye know not when the master of the house cometh, at even, or at midnight, or at the cockcrowing, or in the morning: Lest coming suddenly he find you sleeping. And what I say unto you I say unto all, Watch.

If you are watching for Antichrist, you're watching for the wrong person. Those who embrace a post-Tribulation position—saying the church will go through the Tribulation period—are not watching for Jesus. They're watching for Antichrist. As believers, Jesus never taught us to prepare for the Tribulation. He taught us to watch for His appearance.

Today could be the day, and "whoever has this hope purifies himself" (1 John 3:3). Believing Jesus' coming is imminent will have a tremendous effect on the way we live each day. Don't let anyone tell you Jesus can't come back for us until after the Tribulation. He could come back today. And if He does, it's fine by me!

❦

14 We have now come to the longest chapter in Mark's Gospel. To set the stage for this drama, it should be noted that Jesus is not so much the main Actor as He is the One being acted upon; not so much the Deliverer, as He is the One delivered into the hands of men, for in the chapter before us, we will see Mary anointing Him, Judas betraying Him, the religious leaders arresting Him, and finally Peter denying Him.

Mark 14:1–3 (a)
After two days was the feast of the passover, and of unleavened bread: and the chief priests and the scribes sought how they might take him by craft, and put him to death. But they said, Not on the feast day, lest there be an uproar of the people. And being in Bethany in the house of Simon the leper, as he sat at meat, there came a woman . . .

We know from John 11:2 that this woman was Mary, the sister of Martha and Lazarus. It is not surprising that Mary would be here. After all, it is at the feet of Jesus that we most often see her. . . .

While her sister stewed in the kitchen, Mary sat at the feet of her Savior (Luke 10:39).
In grief over her brother's death, Mary poured out her heart at the feet of her Master (John 11:32).
Here, in the house of Simon, we will see her worship her Redeemer.

Whether in the hour of happiness when He was teaching, in the season of sadness when her brother had died, or in this time of questioning as she tries to make sense of Jesus coming to Jerusalem to go to the Cross, Mary positioned herself at His feet.

Mark 14:3 (b)
. . . having an alabaster box of ointment of spikenard very precious; and she brake the box, and poured it on his head.

To keep their money secure, people in Jesus' day often invested it in costly perfumes or ointments that would be hidden in a house or buried in a field. In this case, the spikenard, which was from India, would be worth a year's salary. This spikenard was very possibly Mary's dowry—that which she would have presented to her husband at the time of her marriage. If indeed this was the case, in pouring it out upon Jesus, she was signifying that she was ready to give up everything, even marriage, in order to devote herself completely, tenderly, wholeheartedly to Him.

Mark 14:4, 5 (a)
And there were some that had indignation within themselves, and said, Why was this waste of the ointment made? For it might have been sold for more than three hundred pence, and have been given to the poor.

John tells us it was the treasurer of the apostolic band—Judas Iscariot—who said this. "This money could have been used for the poor," he protested. Yet he said this not because he cared for the poor, but because he held the bag and was a thief (John 12:4–6). The Greek word translated "waste," describing Judas's estimation of Mary's act, literally means "perdition"—the same word Jesus would use to describe Judas himself (John 17:12).

Mark 14:5 (b)
And they murmured against her.

Although Judas cared nothing for the poor but simply wanted to steal the money, the others evidently believed his argument. Whenever there is group activity, look for the real agenda of those spearheading the group. Others might be sincere, but oftentimes, the one making the most noise has another agenda entirely.

Mark 14:6, 7
And Jesus said, Let her alone; why trouble
ye her? she hath wrought a good work on
me. For ye have the poor with you always,
and whensoever ye will ye may do them
good: but me ye have not always.

Poverty will never be solved by political re-
alignment or economic adjustment because, be it
the result of slothfulness or greed, poverty is a
matter of the spirit. Until Jesus comes back and
makes things right, the poor will indeed always
be among us. Therefore, the answer to poverty is
not economics or politics, but a change in the
heart of man.

Mark 14:8 (a)
She hath done what she could . . .

Mary wouldn't be able to keep the priests from
falsely accusing Jesus, the crowds from mocking
Him, the soldiers from crucifying Him—but she
could pour oil upon Him in an act of worshipful
acknowledgment that He had come to die. And in
so doing, Mary did what she could.

You might not be able to speak to large groups
of people. You might be unable to preach, lead
worship, or sing. But can you bake some bread
for someone in need? Can you make a hospital
visit? Can you mow a lawn? Too often I focus on
what I can't do instead of seeing what I can do.
Mary did what she could. And Jesus commends
her.

Mark 14:8 (b)
. . . she is come aforehand to anoint my body
to the burying.

Jesus told His disciples directly that He was
going to die, be buried, and resurrect from the
dead. But they didn't understand. Yet because
she sat at Jesus' feet, Mary was able to understand that which the disciples missed.

Mark 14:9
Verily I say unto you, Wheresoever this gos-
pel shall be preached throughout the whole
world, this also that she hath done shall be
spoken of for a memorial of her.

John tells us that after pouring ointment upon
Jesus' head, Mary wiped His feet with her hair
(12:3). As a result, her hair took on the same fragrance as His feet. She smelled just like Jesus.
That's what worship does. Are you tired of being
a stinky person? One of the surest ways to
change your fragrance is to be a worshiper. Pour
out your love for the Lord in your morning devotions, in worship corporately, in worship daily—

and you will find your entire attitude beginning
to change.

Furthermore, not only did Mary's fragrance
begin to change, but the house began to take on
the fragrance of Christ as well. Is there a stench
in your house? Are tempers flaring? Are cross
words being spoken? How long has it been since
you've had family devotions—where you've sat
down with your kids or as a couple to spend time
worshiping the Lord? When you pour out your
praise, when you worship the Lord, His fragrance fills the house.

Finally, Mary's act of worship affected the entire community. Throughout history, Bethany is a
place of which people who know the Word and
love the Lord have been very aware. Why? Because one woman poured out worship. The early
church referred to this event often in its preaching and teaching. So does the church today—as
all around the world Mary's singular act of worship is spoken of constantly.

Mark 14:10, 11
And Judas Iscariot, one of the twelve, went
unto the chief priests, to betray him unto
them. And when they heard it, they were
glad, and promised to give him money. And
he sought how he might conveniently betray
him.

It would seem that it was Jesus' commendation
of Mary's worship that moved Judas to betray
Him.

Mark 14:12–14
And the first day of unleavened bread, when
they killed the passover, his disciples said
unto him, Where wilt thou that we go and
prepare that thou mayest eat the passover?
And he sendeth forth two of his disciples,
and saith unto them, Go ye into the city,
and there shall meet you a man bearing a
pitcher of water: follow him. And whereso-
ever he shall go in, say ye to the goodman
of the house, The Master saith, Where is the
guestchamber, where I shall eat the pass-
over with my disciples?

Carrying water was the job of women, so a
man carrying a jar of water would have stood out
even in a crowd.

Mark 14:15
And he will shew you a large upper room
furnished and prepared: there make ready
for us.

Many Bible scholars believe this Upper Room
was owned by the mother of John Mark, the au-

thor of this Gospel. Most likely, it was the same room wherein the disciples met on the Day of Pentecost.

Mark 14:16–19
And his disciples went forth, and came into the city, and found as he had said unto them: and they made ready the passover. And in the evening he cometh with the twelve. And as they sat and did eat, Jesus said, Verily I say unto you, One of you which eateth with me shall betray me. And they began to be sorrowful, and to say unto him one by one, Is it I? and another said, Is it I?

Only a few days previously, the disciples had argued over who was the greatest (Mark 9:34). At that time Jesus was not in their midst. Whenever Jesus is not in our midst, we start arguing over our position, our importance, our greatness. But now, in the presence of Jesus, their attitudes change radically. They're not asking "Who's the greatest?" They're asking, "Will I be the one to deny You?"

True humility is always the result of true intimacy with Jesus Christ. If I am close to the Lord at any given moment, rather than boasting of my greatness, I'll be aware of my weakness and His graciousness.

"Woe unto you," said Isaiah the prophet to all of the nations round about Israel in chapters 1—5 of the book that bears his name. But when he saw the Lord high and lifted up, he said, "Woe is me" (Isaiah 6:5).

If we are those who are either overtly or secretly saying, "Woe to you; woe to you; woe to you," it's probably because we haven't seen the Lord as clearly as we should, for once we see Him, we see how sinful and unworthy we are ourselves and find ourselves joining the disciples in asking, "Is it I, Lord? Could I be the one who sells You out? Could I be the one who turns my back? Could I be the one who walks away?"

Mark 14:20, 21 (a)
And he answered and said unto them, It is one of the twelve, that dippeth with me in the dish. The Son of man indeed goeth, as it is written of him: but woe to that man by whom the Son of man is betrayed!

Don't think of the Last Supper as being served on a long maple table with everyone seated in New England ladder-back chairs on the same side of the table to pose for the picture. That's not the way it was. In those days, meals were served on a u-shaped table that was low to the ground.

To eat, one would recline around the table, leaning on his right arm and using his left to dip bread into a common dish. From John's Gospel we know that John was on Jesus' right side (13:23). This means the one who dipped his hand into the dish with the Lord must have been on his left side—which was always the place of honor. In other words, Jesus gave Judas the place of honor the very night he betrayed Him. And when Judas would come a few hours later with the soldiers who would arrest Him, Jesus would say to Judas, "Friend, wherefore art thou come?" (Matthew 26:50). Until the end, Jesus gave Judas an opportunity to repent.

This blesses me greatly because if Jesus placed Judas in a place of honor, and to the very end called him friend, He is a Friend closer than a brother indeed (Proverbs 18:24).

Mark 14:21 (b)
Good were it for that man if he had never been born.

Jesus wasn't saying He wished Judas had never been born. Rather, brokenheartedly, He was saying it would have been better for Judas had he never been born. The same still holds true for any man. He who is not born again soon will wish he had never been born at all because hell is a real place wherein the fire is never quenched and the worm dies not (Mark 9:43, 44).

Mark 14:22–25
And as they did eat, Jesus took bread, and blessed, and brake it, and gave to them, and said, Take, eat: this is my body. And he took the cup, and when he had given thanks, he gave it to them: and they all drank of it. And he said unto them, This is my blood of the new testament, which is shed for many. Verily I say unto you, I will drink no more of the fruit of the vine, until that day that I drink it new in the kingdom of God.

After eating the bread, the cup would be passed seven times. Evidently, on the seventh time, Jesus refused to drink from the cup, but said He would wait until He could drink it with us in the kingdom.

Mark 14:26
And when they had sung an hymn, they went out into the mount of Olives.

Crossing the Kidron Valley, Jesus and His disciples made their way up the side of the Mount of Olives.

Mark 14:27–29
And Jesus saith unto them, All ye shall be offended because of me this night: for it is written, I will smite the shepherd, and the sheep shall be scattered. But after that I am risen, I will go before you into Galilee. But Peter said unto him, Although all shall be offended, yet will not I.

"Lord, I'll never leave You," Peter insisted, cock-sure of his loyalty.

Mark 14:30
And Jesus saith unto him, Verily I say unto thee, That this day, even in this night, before the cock crow twice, thou shalt deny me thrice.

"You're crowing about how great you are, Peter, but you'll soon discover otherwise," said Jesus.

Mark 14:31–33
But he spake the more vehemently, If I should die with thee, I will not deny thee in any wise. Likewise also said they all. And they came to a place which was named Gethsemane: and he saith to his disciples, Sit ye here, while I shall pray. And he taketh with him Peter and James and John, and began to be sore amazed, and to be very heavy.

Facing spiritual and physical suffering more intense than anything we can imagine, Jesus went to the garden to pray—and asked Peter, James, and John to accompany Him. He didn't ask them to pray with Him—simply to be with Him. I find it interesting that during the most intense time of His whole life, Jesus would want human companionship. There is no shortage of people who will say, "Lord, I'll work for You." But I wonder how many say, "Lord, I'm taking some time just to be with You."

Mark 14:34–36
And saith unto them, My soul is exceeding sorrowful unto death: tarry ye here, and watch. And he went forward a little, and fell on the ground, and prayed that, if it were possible, the hour might pass from him. And he said, Abba, Father, all things are possible unto thee; take away this cup from me: nevertheless not what I will, but what thou wilt.

Why could Jesus submit to God's will? Because He understood God's nature. Jesus saw God not as a Cosmic Killjoy or an angry cop, but as a Father, a Papa, an Abba.

The greatest prayer of faith we make is when we say, "Lord, here's my perspective, my intention—but it is Your will that must be done because You see things I don't; You know things I can't." When you are truly secure in who the Father is, you'll find yourself praying His will to be done rather than demanding that your own plan be enacted.

Mark 14:37
And he cometh, and findeth them sleeping, and saith unto Peter, Simon, sleepest thou? couldest not thou watch one hour?

Jesus had changed Peter's name from Simon, or "Shifting Sand," to Peter, or "Rock" (Matthew 16:18). Here, finding him sleeping, Jesus calls him Simon once again.

Mark 14:38
Watch ye and pray, lest ye enter into temptation. The spirit truly is ready, but the flesh is weak.

True prayer is as much protection as it is petition. Things happen to me that wouldn't have happened had I prayed. And the same is true for you.

Mark 14:39–41
And again he went away, and prayed, and spake the same words. And when he returned, he found them asleep again, (for their eyes were heavy,) neither wist they what to answer him. And he cometh the third time, and saith unto them, Sleep on now, and take your rest: it is enough, the hour is come; behold, the Son of man is betrayed into the hands of sinners.

With a time gap of unknown duration between verse 41 and 42, Jesus told His disciples to give in to the sleep that continued to overtake them.

Mark 14:42
Rise up, let us go; lo, he that betrayeth me is at hand.

Jesus could rise up because He had already knelt down. He could stand up because He already had bowed down. Jesus found strength for this moment because of the time He had spent in prayer.

Mark 14:43–47 (a)
And immediately, while he yet spake, cometh Judas, one of the twelve, and with him a great multitude with swords and staves, from the chief priests and the scribes and the elders. And he that betrayed him had given them a token, saying, Whomsoever I shall kiss, that same is he; take him, and

lead him away safely. And as soon as he was come, he goeth straightway to him, and saith, Master, master; and kissed him. And they laid their hands on him, and took him. And one of them that stood by drew a sword . . .

We know from John 18:10 that the one who smote the servant of the high priest was Peter. Perhaps the reason he's not identified here by name is because Mark's Gospel is his story, maybe he wanted to distance himself from this incident.

Mark 14:47 (b)
. . . and smote a servant of the high priest, and cut off his ear.

Peter used the wrong weapon at the wrong time for the wrong purpose with the wrong motive. So, too, any time I use the Sword of the Spirit—the Word—to chop someone else down, I will only leave ears in my wake. "Put away your sword," Jesus said to Peter (Matthew 26:52). And I wonder if He doesn't whisper the same thing to some of us from time to time. Regardless of how many Bible verses we know, if we're chopping off ears and people are bleeding because we're trying to prove our own spirituality, we're in error.

Luke tells us the Lord stooped down, picked up Malchus' ear and reattached it (22:51). Likewise, He restores the ears I've chopped off and corrects the mistakes I've made. After the Lord corrected him, Peter quit swinging and put down his sword. And so must we.

Mark 14:48, 49
And Jesus answered and said unto them, Are ye come out, as against a thief, with swords and with staves to take me? I was daily with you in the temple teaching, and ye took me not: but the scriptures must be fulfilled.

Jesus' teaching was available to anyone and everyone. He didn't have an esoteric secret agenda to share with a few chosen ones. Rather, He gave His teaching publicly, openly to everyone, to anyone who wanted to listen.

Mark 14:50
And they all forsook him, and fled.

"Let him who thinks he stand take heed lest he fall," Paul warns us (1 Corinthians 10:12). The same one who just a few hours previously had declared, "Lord, I will never forsake You," now fled.

Mark 14:51, 52
And there followed him a certain young man, having a linen cloth cast about his naked body; and the young men laid hold on him: And he left the linen cloth, and fled from them naked.

Most commentators agree that this young man was John Mark. Most likely a teenager at this time, awakened by the sound of the commotion outside, he probably quickly wrapped himself in a sheet and followed the soldiers to the Garden of Gethsemane—fleeing the scene when things looked dangerous.

Mark 14:53, 54
And they led Jesus away to the high priest: and with him were assembled all the chief priests and the elders and the scribes. And Peter followed him afar off, even into the palace of the high priest: and he sat with the servants, and warmed himself at the fire.

Peter was cold not only physically but spiritually—which would lead to his denial of Christ altogether. Was there a time when you were following the Lord with a "front-row" mentality before your schedule filled with hobbies and activities to the point that now you're following Him "afar off"? Peter became so cold that he sought to warm himself by the enemy's fire. So, too, your desire to warm yourself by the fires of the old gang or your old haunts will be proportionate to the distance you have allowed between yourself and the Lord.

Mark 14:55–59
And the chief priests and all the council sought for witness against Jesus to put him to death; and found none. For many bare false witness against him, but their witness agreed not together. And there arose certain, and bare false witness against him, saying, We heard him say, I will destroy this temple that is made with hands, and within three days I will build another made without hands. But neither so did their witness agree together.

As we see in the next chapter, the reason the priests and leaders were determined to see Jesus killed was simply envy. Realizing there was something about Him that attracted people to Him, they sought to do away with Him. And wanting to give their actions the appearance of legality, they called men who would bear false witness against Him. What is false witness? It's not always an outright whopper of a lie. As in this case, it's simply the right information but with the wrong implication. Jesus did indeed say He would destroy the temple—but He was talking about His own body (John 2:19–21).

Mark 14:60–62 (a)
And the high priest stood up in the midst, and asked Jesus, saying, Answerest thou nothing? what is it which these witness against thee? But he held his peace, and answered nothing. Again the high priest asked him, and said unto him, Art thou the Christ, the Son of the Blessed? And Jesus said, I am . . .

- "Who shall I say sent me?" Moses asked.
- "I am that I am," God answered (Exodus 3:14).

And here, Jesus uses the same name.

Mark 14:62 (b)
. . . and ye shall see the Son of man sitting on the right hand of power, and coming in the clouds of heaven.

After speaking of His deity, Jesus immediately refers to His humanity, using a phrase from Daniel 7:13, which speaks of Messiah's humanity.

Mark 14:63, 64
Then the high priest rent his clothes, and saith, What need we any further witnesses? Ye have heard the blasphemy: what think ye? And they all condemned him to be guilty of death.

Even as Caiaphas ripped his clothes, the validity would be ripped from the priesthood of Aaron, and the veil in the temple would be ripped in two, signifying that the entire temple system would no longer be necessary.

Mark 14:65
And some began to spit on him, and to cover his face, and to buffet him, and to say unto him, Prophesy: and the servants did strike him with the palms of their hands.

"When someone smites you, turn the other cheek," Jesus had taught (Luke 6:29). Did He do this? There being no inconsistency whatsoever between what He said and what He did, Jesus not only turned His cheek, but He also gave His entire body to die for the very men who beat Him.

Mark 14:66–70
And as Peter was beneath in the palace, there cometh one of the maids of the high priest: And when she saw Peter warming himself, she looked upon him, and said, And thou also wast with Jesus of Nazareth. But he denied, saying, I know not, neither understand I what thou sayest. And he went out into the porch; and the cock crew. And a maid saw him again, and began to say to them that stood by, This is one of them. And he denied it again. And a little after, they that stood by said again to Peter, Surely thou art one of them: for thou art a Galilaean, and thy speech agreeth thereto.

As Peter discovered, our attempts to warm ourselves by the world's fires always backfire. As believers, our accent betrays us. We don't laugh as hard as we once did; we don't enter in as freely as we used to because although we have too much of the world to enjoy the Lord, we also have too much of the Lord to enjoy the world.

Mark 14:71
But he began to curse and to swear, saying, I know not this man of whom ye speak.

When their nets became tangled on the bottom of the sea, fishermen resorted to using the most vulgar oaths and cursing. Having hit bottom himself, Peter is tangled up in his own pride and sin, and therefore does what came naturally to the fisherman he had been.

Mark 14:72 (a)
And the second time the cock crew. And Peter called to mind the word that Jesus said unto him, Before the cock crow twice, thou shalt deny me thrice.

Due to the mess they made, roosters were not allowed in the city of Jerusalem. Therefore, a rooster's crow would have been a strange sound. But, in this case, it was an appropriate one because Peter surely had made a mess of things.

Mark 14:72 (b)
And when he thought thereon, he wept.

Translated "wept," the Greek word doesn't mean to shed a silent tear. Rather, it means to convulse in sorrow. At this point, as far as Peter knew, his relationship with Jesus was permanently and totally severed. As far as he knew, his sin was unpardonable.

No wonder he wept.

15

Mark 15:1 (a)
And straightway in the morning the chief priests held a consultation with the elders and scribes and the whole council, and bound Jesus, and carried him away . . .

Jesus was bound not by puny ropes, but by cords of love. As Creator of the ropes, He could have burst them easily. As the Lamb of God, He chose to be bound by them willingly.

Mark 15:1 (b)–2
. . . and delivered him to Pilate. And Pilate asked him, Art thou the King of the Jews? And he answering said unto him, Thou say-est it.

Pilate, the sixth Roman governor in this region, was in political trouble. He had already made the mistake of allowing a picture of Caesar to be placed on the temple mount, causing the Jews to riot. His second mistake was financing an aqueduct with funds from the temple treasury, again resulting in a riot. Thus, after two riots in which a number of people had been killed, Pilate was warned by Rome that one more strike and he'd be out.

Jesus went through two trials—one before Caiaphas and a second before Pilate and Herod. Due to His claim of deity, the Jews accused Him of being too heavenly, while Herod, thinking He wanted to lead a coup politically, accused Him of being too earthly.

Throughout history, the church has gone through this same two-fold trial—and so will you. People will accuse you of being too heavenly, while, at the same time, another group will accuse you of being too worldly. "You're all pie in the sky," some will say, while others will tell you you're backsliding because they saw you going thirty-six in a thirty-five mph zone. You'll get hit both ways—and when you do, realize Jesus did as well.

Mark 15:3
And the chief priests accused him of many things: but he answered nothing.

Jesus is an oasis of tranquility in a sea of controversy. To any who truly wanted information, Jesus would answer willingly (Mark 14:62). But to those who hurled accusation, He answered not a word. And therein lies a good principle. If someone wants information, we should share freely and openly. But if they only want to accuse us, we need not defend ourselves.

Mark 15:4–7
And Pilate asked him again, saying, An-swerest thou nothing? behold how many things they witness against thee. But Jesus yet answered nothing; so that Pilate mar-velled. Now at that feast he released unto them one prisoner, whomsoever they de-sired. And there was one named Barabbas,
which lay bound with them that had made insurrection with him, who had committed murder in the insurrection.

"Barabbas" means "son of Abba," or an Israelite. The parallel is obvious. Barabbas, a son of Abba, had taken a life, while Jesus, the only be-gotten Son of Abba had come to give His life.

Mark 15:8–10
And the multitude crying aloud began to desire him to do as he had ever done unto them. But Pilate answered them, saying, Will ye that I release unto you the King of the Jews? For he knew that the chief priests had delivered him for envy.

Any crusade to crucify usually has its roots in envy or jealousy. Even Pilate knew this.

Mark 15:11–15
But the chief priests moved the people, that he should rather release Barabbas unto them. And Pilate answered and said again unto them, What will ye then that I shall do unto him whom ye call the King of the Jews? And they cried out again, Crucify him. Then Pilate said unto them, Why, what evil hath he done? And they cried out the more exceedingly, Crucify him. And so Pilate, willing to content the people, released Bar-abbas unto them, and delivered Jesus, when he had scourged him, to be crucified.

Jesus was scourged not because the Father in heaven was allowing sadistic pain to be placed upon His beloved Son, but because, as Isaiah tells us, although it is by the Cross we are saved, it is by His stripes that we are healed (Isaiah 53:5).

Mark 15:16–20
And the soldiers led him away into the hall, called Praetorium; and they call together the whole band. And they clothed him with purple, and platted a crown of thorns, and put it about his head, and began to salute him, Hail, King of the Jews! And they smote him on the head with a reed, and did spit upon him, and bowing their knees wor-shipped him. And when they had mocked him, they took off the purple from him, and put his own clothes on him, and led him out to crucify him.

Jesus was led out of the city because the scape-goat—the one who bore the sins of the people in Old Testament typology—was always led out of the city (Leviticus 16:10).

Mark 15:21 (a)
And they compel one Simon a Cyrenian,
who passed by, coming out of the country . . .

Simon had traveled to Jerusalem to celebrate
Passover, and as he approached the procession
toward Golgotha, he was tapped on the shoulder
with the flat side of the spear of a Roman soldier
and ordered to take up the Cross of the One before him who was no longer able to bear its
weight on His lacerated and bruised shoulders.
Jesus does not bear the Cross for two reasons . . .

It was not His Cross. It was mine. I am the
one who deserves to go to hell.
    Secondly, He's showing us that taking up
our cross doesn't mean gritting our teeth and
being miserable. It means letting the Cross do
to us exactly what it did to Him when it caused
Him to fall on His knees and allow another to
bear it.

Mark 15:21 (b)
. . . the father of Alexander and Rufus, to
bear his cross.

Simon is identified as the father of Alexander
and Rufus because they would have been known
as key members of the early church—which
means that at some point after bearing Jesus'
Cross, Simon got saved.

Mark 15:22–24
And they bring him unto the place Golgo-
tha, which is, being interpreted, The place
of a skull. And they gave him to drink wine
mingled with myrrh: but he received it not.
And when they had crucified him, they
parted his garments, casting lots upon
them, what every man should take.

Because clothing identifies one's culture perhaps more readily than any other single feature,
in being stripped of every article of clothing,
pinned to the wooden Cross of Calvary in naked
humanity, Jesus shed every identifying mark of
any single culture, thereby becoming the Savior
for *all* the world.

For topical study of Mark 15:24 entitled "Christ
for All Nations," turn to page 288.

Mark 15:25–30
And it was the third hour, and they crucified
him. And the superscription of his accusa-
tion was written over, THE KING OF THE
JEWS. And with him they crucify two thieves;
the one on his right hand, and the other
on his left. And the scripture was fulfilled,
which saith, And he was numbered with the
transgressors. And they that passed by railed
on him, wagging their heads, and saying,
Ah, thou that destroyest the temple, and buildest it in three days, Save thyself, and come
down from the cross.

"Come down from the Cross" is still being heard
today as the world continues to clamor for a
Cross-less Christ. "Jesus is cool," they say. "He
was a good teacher, a good example, a good moral
leader. But don't talk to me about the Cross. It's
too bloody."

Mark 15:31
Likewise also the chief priests mocking said
among themselves with the scribes, He
saved others; himself he cannot save.

The fact that Jesus had indeed saved others
was undeniable—for in their midst were lepers
who had been cleansed, blind men who could now
see, lame men who were now walking. The chief
priests were right when they said He saved
others. And they were equally right when they
said, "Himself He cannot save"—for if He had
come down off the Cross, He could not have
saved me.

Mark 15:32 (a)
Let Christ the King of Israel descend now
from the cross, that we may see and believe.

"If I can see it, I'll believe it," said the skeptics.
But the way of the Lord is always if you believe
it, *then* you'll be able to see it.

Mark 15:32 (b), 33
And they that were crucified with him re-
viled him. And when the sixth hour was
come, there was darkness over the whole
land until the ninth hour.

For three hours, there was complete, total
darkness. Why? Think back to Exodus. What
happened before the Passover lamb was killed?
The entire land was covered with darkness for
three days (Exodus 10:21, 22), symbolizing the
darkness that would descend as the Lamb of God
was slain. Because they had no desire to see spiritually, men became unable to see physically what
was really taking place on the Cross of Calvary.

Mark 15:34
And at the ninth hour Jesus cried with a
loud voice, saying, Eloi, Eloi, lama sabach-
thani? which is, being interpreted, My God,
my God, why hast thou forsaken me?

I believe Jesus' cry is kept in the original Aramaic, His native tongue on earth, in order to show the intensity of His cry. Leprosy didn't intimidate Him; storms didn't frighten Him; armies didn't faze Him. The only thing that terrified our Lord was being out of fellowship with His Father. And when He who knew no sin became sin for us, that is exactly what happened. Because we have grown accustomed to being out of touch with God, the things that terrify us are bounced checks, not getting the promotion, or a boyfriend or girlfriend breaking up with us. Jesus, on the other hand, had faith concerning that that frightens us, yet was terrorized by that which we barely notice.

Mark 15:35
And some of them that stood by, when they heard it, said, Behold, he calleth Elias.

Had those at the Cross been perceptive, they would have recognized Jesus' words as the beginning of Psalm 22, a Messianic Psalm describing crucifixion in great detail centuries before it was ever conceived as capital punishment. Instead, some in the crowd thought He was calling for Elijah.

Mark 15:36
And one ran and filled a spunge full of vinegar, and put it on a reed, and gave him to drink, saying, Let alone; let us see whether Elias will come to take him down.

Because vinegar was used as a drug to numb some of the pain, was this done out of compassion? No. It was done out of curiosity—to sustain Jesus' life long enough to see if Elijah would indeed come.

Mark 15:37 (a)
And Jesus cried with a loud voice . . .

Jesus' cry was comprised of the three greatest words spoken in the history of humanity: "It Is Finished." From the day of His birth until the day He died, the Enemy came against Jesus relentlessly, trying to derail Him, to destroy Him, to keep Him from providing salvation. But the Enemy failed when Jesus finished the work of redemption on Calvary. Thus, His was a cry not of agony, but of victory.

Mark 15:37 (b)
. . . and gave up the ghost.

Why isn't there a description of the actual act of crucifixion? I believe it's because, rather than arousing our feelings, the Father wants to affirm

our faith; that His desire is not to move us emotionally, but that we understand rationally that Jesus finished the work.

Mark 15:38
And the veil of the temple was rent in twain from the top to the bottom.

In rending the massive veil in the temple that kept everyone but the high priest from going into the Holy of Holies where the shekinah—the visible presence of God—dwelt, the Father declared, "Open House! You can come boldly into My presence anytime you want because the price has been paid once and for all."

This grace is free—but it's not cheap because it cost Jesus everything to open the way to the Father. Therefore, don't sew the veil back up, gang, with legalism, rules, regulations, or expectations. Don't feel as though you must prove something to God before you can come into His presence to present your petitions or to enjoy His fellowship. Believers do this in subtle ways, like saying, "Before we can enter into the glory of God, we must spend time praising Him." Not true. The way is open. Nothing else remains to be done. Am I discounting the importance of praise? Of course not. Praise allows us to be refreshed in our knowledge of who the Lord is and what He's done. But it is not a prerequisite to fellowship. Neither is confession. As valid as both of these elements are, we can come boldly into the presence of God not because of our ability to articulate confession or express praise, but solely because of what Jesus did on Calvary.

Mark 15:39
And when the centurion, which stood over against him, saw that he so cried out, and gave up the ghost, he said, Truly this man was the Son of God.

It was in the Lord's death that the centurion found life. It was in the time of darkness that he saw the light. "Lord," we cry, "if you loved Me enough to die for me, if the veil was rent to open the way for me, then why am I going through this difficulty, this tragedy?"

"Because there are centurions watching," He declares. "And they will see My light in your dark days."

Dear saint, if you want to be used by God, there is no other way than to go through disappointment, difficulty, and pain in order that people might relate to you, observe you, and see by the reality of Jesus in your life that He truly is the Son of God. People are not convinced of the reality of His reality when they see us sailing through easy times and prosperous days. Such times cause only envy and cynicism. When people are truly touched is when they see us navigating adversity and difficulty all the while trusting the Lord (2 Corinthians 1:4). This centurion was won, saved, converted not because he was one of the five thousand eating bread and fish in the sunlight, but because he saw Jesus in the darkness.

Mark 15:40, 41
There were also women looking on afar off: among whom was Mary Magdalene, and Mary the mother of James the less and of Joses, and Salome; (Who also, when he was in Galilee, followed him, and ministered unto him;) and many other women which came up with him unto Jerusalem.

In all of the Gospel stories, you will never find a woman opposing or resisting the ministry of Jesus Christ. Where were the disciples at this point? Men's love being primarily based on logic, it was no longer logical for them to be at the Cross. After all, what could they do? They couldn't mount a military defense. Peter tried that and failed miserably. So they simply scattered. Women's love being not so much logical as it is emotional and mystical, however, the women remained at the Cross.

Mark 15:42, 43
And now when the even was come, because it was the preparation, that is, the day before the sabbath, Joseph of Arimathaea, an honourable counseller, which also waited for the kingdom of God, came, and went in boldly unto Pilate, and craved the body of Jesus.

Joseph of Arimathaea was a secret disciple. After all, had he identified with Jesus openly, he would have lost his coveted position in the Sanhedrin, the Jewish Supreme Court. But seeing Jesus on the Cross caused such courage and passion to flood his heart that he asked for His body—fully knowing that touching it would defile him and prevent him from celebrating Passover, fully knowing he would be in danger from Roman and Jew alike, fully knowing that he would be ostracized financially and socially.

That is the way it always is. When you really see the Cross, you have no choice but to "crave" the Lord. You have no choice but to openly share the gospel. That's why Jesus said, "Do this in remembrance of Me" (Luke 22:19)—for when I remember what the Lord did for me as I eat of His body and drink of His blood, much of what was important to me only a few hours previously isn't important any longer. As it did for Joseph of Arimathaea, the Cross has an incredible way of changing one's priorities.

Mark 15:44–47
And Pilate marvelled if he were already dead: and calling unto him the centurion, he asked him whether he had been any while dead. And when he knew it of the centurion, he gave the body to Joseph. And he bought fine linen, and took him down, and wrapped him in the linen, and laid him in a sepulchre which was hewn out of a rock, and rolled a stone unto the door of the sepulchre. And Mary Magdalene and Mary the mother of Joses beheld where he was laid.

"Joseph" literally means "addition." And that is exactly what will happen when, in addition to Jesus bursting forth from the grave, believers throughout history will one day burst forth to live eternally.

Maybe you're a Joseph—one who is quieter in personality. Although you may not be one who preaches or distributes tracts to everyone you see, I have found that when the going really gets tough, when push comes to shove, a lot of time it's the Josephs who emerge as heroes, solid and steadfast. In the moment of greatest danger, when the hour of challenge has come, it is the Josephs who are often those who are most solid in time of crisis.

May this be true to an ever greater degree of us.

CHRIST FOR ALL NATIONS
A Topical Study of
Mark 15:24

A number of years ago, I felt as though I was called on the carpet by the Holy Spirit in conjunction with the war that ensued when, in their determination to silence the PLO shelling of the Sea of Galilee region, Israel invaded Lebanon. The Syrians in their Soviet MIG 23s and the Israelis in their modified American F16s engaged in brutal aerial warfare. But the Israelis won decisively. And when I heard that one hundred three Syrian jets went down to only one of the Israeli jets, I cheered loudly—until the Holy Spirit began to speak to my heart very strongly, saying, "I love the Syrians just as much as I love the Israelis, just as much as I love the Americans. I designed each one of those men. I died for each one of those men. And now you're rejoicing and applauding because one hundred three were shot down from the sky? Is that like Me?"

After that, I went through a real time of repenting before the Lord, saying, "Forgive me, Father, for being so prejudiced in a pseudo-spiritual kind of way against people who are not on my side. Forgive even my understanding of prophecy to manifest itself in a heart that is not like Yours."

> *The Lord is not slack concerning his promise, as some men count slackness; but is longsuffering to us-ward, not willing that any should perish, but that all should come to repentance.*   2 Peter 3:9

Peter didn't say that God is not willing that any Americans should perish, that any Israelis should perish, or that any of the Western allies should perish. Peter says God is not willing that *any* should perish.

Cultural Application

I believe the text before us speaks to this issue very clearly. You see, before Jesus was nailed to the Cross, He was stripped of His clothes. Although we know this was done partially to fulfill some of the three hundred-plus prophecies given concerning the birth, life, and death of the coming Messiah, I believe the reason for it is broader than that.

Prophecies were given not only to be fulfilled, but also to help us understand who Jesus is and what He does. And because clothing identifies one's culture perhaps more readily than any other single feature, in being stripped of every article of clothing, pinned to the wooden Cross of Calvary in naked humanity, Jesus shed every identifying mark of any single culture, thereby becoming the Savior for *all* the world.

This, however, does not discount the fact that the Lord uses nations to bring about righteousness and judgment. . . .

> *O Assyrian, the rod of mine anger, and the staff in their hand is mine indignation. I will send him against an hypocritical nation, and against the people of my wrath will I give him a charge, to take the spoil, and to take the prey, and to tread them down like the mire of the streets.*   Isaiah 10:5–6

After the people of Israel had fallen into all kinds of idolatry, ignored the Sabbath, and turned their hearts from Him, the Lord stirred the hearts of the Babylonians—today's Iraq—to come down and discipline His people.

Then the angel of the LORD answered and said, O LORD of hosts, how long wilt thou not have mercy on Jerusalem and on the cities of Judah, against which thou hast had indignation these threescore and ten years? And the LORD answered the angel that talked with me with good words and comfortable words. So the angel that communed with me said unto me, Cry thou, saying, Thus saith the LORD of hosts; I am jealous for Jerusalem and for Zion with a great jealousy. And I am very sore displeased with the heathen that are at ease: for I was but a little displeased, and they helped forward the affliction.   Zechariah 1:12–15

Here, the Lord says, "I am displeased with the Babylonians because they went beyond what I intended for them to do when they began to beat My people, destroy the city, and tear down the temple."

I am not suggesting what American policy should be concerning the Middle East or any other nation. But I know what our attitude and heart must be as believers. If the Lord should choose to use our nation to bring about order in the world, so be it. But let us not "forward the affliction." Let us not rejoice at dead Iraqis. Let us not applaud bombs that hit targets effectively.

The flag with which we must closely identify must not be the one sewn with stars and stripes, but the one stained with blood on wood—the Cross of Christ. May our goal not be nationalism or patriotism—but compassion and intercession.

Personal Application

Not only does the Lord love the Iraqi, Iranian, American, and Indian equally—but He loves us personally as much as He loves Billy Graham. He isn't saying, "I'm really into Montreat where Billy and Ruth are gathering to worship Me. But how I dread going to Calvary Chapel to be with Jon and his wife, Tammy." No! The Lord doesn't see it that way! He is not a respecter of persons (Acts 10:34). He has no favorites.

"What about Abraham?" you ask. "Isn't he specifically referred to as the friend of God?"

Yes (James 2:23). And it is no wonder, for it was Abraham who planted an orchard as a creative, spontaneous act of worship (Genesis 21:33).

But wait.

Centuries later, there was another man whom God called "friend" . . .

There in the town of Bethany in the house where a small group gathered around Jesus only days before He would be pinned to the Cross of Calvary,

Mary broke open a box of costly ointment and poured it upon the Lord as an act of worship and love for Him.

"What a waste," Judas scoffed. "That money could have been used to help the poor" (Matthew 26:9).

How different Judas is from Abraham. Abraham planted a tree in worship, while Judas called worship a waste. And yet, incredibly enough, both were called the friend of God—for there in the garden, even as he was in the very act of betrayal, Jesus called Judas, "Friend" (Matthew 26:50).

Such impartial, unconditional love I don't understand—but I sure do enjoy it. For whether I'm being an Abraham or a Judas, my Lord calls me His friend. And the same is true of you. No matter where you're at, He loves you because His friendship with you is not based upon how you're doing, but upon what He did on Calvary's Cross when He paid the price for every sin you've ever done, are doing, or will ever do.

He loves the person sitting next to you that way as well. And He loves the neighbor who plays his stereo too loudly. He loves the boss who didn't give you the promotion you know you deserve, and the coach who keeps you on the bench so his son can play. He loves the Iraqi, the Egyptian, the Communist, the Jew, Nelson Mandela, Fidel Castro, Jimmy Carter, and George Bush. He's not a respecter of persons, of races, of cultures, of countries.

Oh, that His heart of love for a lost world would beat in me.

16

Mark 16:1
And when the sabbath was past, Mary Magdalene, and Mary the mother of James, and Salome, had bought sweet spices, that they might come and anoint him.

For Mary Magdalene, Mary the mother of James, and Salome, it was a sad Sabbath day indeed. The One in whom they believed, the One to whom they had clung, their Hero, their Leader, their Friend was no longer with them. It wasn't a matter of theology, or His redemptive work on the Cross of Calvary. They loved Jesus personally. They enjoyed being with this One who was so gracious, who forgave so freely, who spoke so truthfully. It wasn't a matter of their Messianic hopes being dashed. It was simply a matter of missing Him.

Mark 16:2
And very early in the morning the first day of the week, they came unto the sepulchre at the rising of the sun.

"I love them that love Me," the Lord says, "and those that seek Me early shall find Me" (Proverbs 8:17). Expecting to see nothing more than Jesus' dead body, in their time of depression, discouragement, defeat, sadness, and confusion these women rose early. How much more, then, should we be willing to get up early to seek the living Lord? This isn't an obligation—it's an opportunity available to each of us on any given day. If you feel as though you're in the dark now, be like these women. Rise early and seek the risen Lord—for these who sought Him early would be the first ones to understand and experience Resurrection Sunday.

Mark 16:3–5
And they said among themselves, Who shall roll us away the stone from the door of the sepulchre? And when they looked, they saw that the stone was rolled away: for it was very great. And entering into the sepulchre, they saw a young man sitting on the right side, clothed in a long white garment; and they were affrighted.

The stone was rolled away not to let Jesus out. After all, He could walk through walls (Luke 24:36). Rather, the stone was rolled away to let these women—and others who would follow—in. Why? To see the reality of the Resurrection.

The Resurrection proves the validity of Jesus' sacrifice because without it, we would never know if His work on our behalf was accepted. Then it would be a toss-up between believing Jesus, Buddha, Mohammad, or any other self-proclaimed prophet or guru. The Resurrection places Jesus in a different category than any other so-called holy man.

Secondly, the Resurrection not only proves the validity of His sacrifice, but it provides the ability for us to live in Christ. The Christian life is not a matter of trying to be a "good" Christian or even of imitating Jesus. It is not imitation, but rather impartation. That is, Jesus is alive. He rose again. And He sends His Spirit to come and dwell in me, to tell me what I should do and then to give me the power to be able to do it. That's why the Resurrection is essential.

Mark 16:6, 7 (a)
And he saith unto them, Be not affrighted: Ye seek Jesus of Nazareth, which was crucified: he is risen; he is not here: behold the place where they laid him. But go your way, tell his disciples and Peter that he goeth before you into Galilee . . .

This was at a time when, having denied the Lord and having walked away from the Lord, Peter would certainly feel excluded from any Good News, from any hope of being used. If you feel the same way tonight, this verse is for you. To you who feel like you've denied the Lord or ignored the Lord, the angel says, "Tell His disciples and Peter—especially Peter, particularly Peter—that the Lord goes before you into Galilee and you will see Him. All you have to do is show up."

Mark 16:7 (b)–8
. . . there shall ye see him, as he said unto you. And they went out quickly, and fled from the sepulchre; for they trembled and were amazed: neither said they any thing to any man; for they were afraid.

The word translated "afraid" doesn't mean terrified. It means "ecstatic." For these women who were so despairing only minutes ago, confused about life, depressed by life, without hope for life—everything had changed simply because they rose up early and sought Him, even though they did not believe they would even find Him alive.

We must not talk about our obstacles, our schedules, our busyness, our activities, or our demands without taking into consideration the two-thousand-pound stone that stood between these women and the Lord they thought was dead. Because the stone didn't stop them, now they're ecstatic.

Mark 16:9–11
Now when Jesus was risen early the first day of the week, he appeared first to Mary Magdalene, out of whom he had cast seven devils. And she went and told them that had been with him, as they mourned and wept. And they, when they had heard that he was alive, and had been seen of her, believed not.

According to the original language, so deeply had they loved Jesus, that after three days, these rugged fishermen were still weeping with convulsive sobs. But when Mary Magdalene reported that He was alive, what did they do? They went right back to weeping and hurting. Why? Because of the thief of unbelief.

Maybe you're weeping tonight because your body is hurting, your business is collapsing, or your relationships are eroding. In reality, however, none of those are the source of your tears. Because the living Lord has said to you everything is working together for good, because He has said we are to give thanks in all things, because He has given us promise after promise that He is with us and will never forsake us, it is neither your job, marriage, family, finances, or health that cause your tears. It is unbelief. Period.

It has been rightly said that a little faith will get you to heaven, but a larger faith will bring heaven to you. Indeed, I will experience heaven in my heart to the degree that I have faith that the Lord is alive, that He's faithful, and that everything is working out exactly as He promised.

If the disciples had believed at that moment, like Mary, they would have moved into ecstasy. But they chose not to believe and remained in their sorrow longer than necessary.

Mark 16:12, 13
After that he appeared in another form unto two of them, as they walked, and went into the country. And they went and told it unto the residue: neither believed they them.

- "We saw Him!" the ecstatic pair on the road to Emmaus exclaimed (Luke 24:35).
  "No you didn't," said the downcast disciples.
- "We talked to Him!" said the travelers.
  "You couldn't have," said His followers.

Hour after hour, day after day the disciples remained in a needless state of depression and despondency simply and solely because of unbelief.

Mark 16:14
Afterward he appeared unto the eleven as they sat at meat, and upbraided them with their unbelief and hardness of heart, because they believed not them which had seen him after he was risen.

Jesus didn't upbraid the disciples for their denying, for their running, for their fear. He upbraided them for one thing only: their unbelief. But then, as only our Lord, does, He quickly moved on.

Mark 16:15
And he said unto them, Go ye into all the world, and preach the gospel to every creature.

It was as if Jesus said, "I've corrected you. I am going to use you. Now get going! There's work to do!"

Although you've probably heard dozens of messages on this text with regard to foreign missions, quite literally what is being said here is not, "Go into all the world," but, "*As* you are going throughout the world, preach the gospel to every creature." In other words, the focus is not on where we are to go, but on what we are to do. Whether it be across the ocean or across the street, around the world or around the neighborhood, on foreign soil or on the camps—whatever we're doing, we're to share the gospel.

I'm convinced most of us really want to do this, but we fail to not so much because of intimidation, but because of articulation. That is, we are not really sure what it means to preach the gospel. Does sharing the gospel mean we're to talk about the creation account of Genesis, about the end times of Revelation, about the praise and worship of the Psalms, about the working of the Spirit in Acts? What does it actually mean to share the gospel?

Paul answers this question masterfully when he reminds the Corinthian believers of the gospel he had shared with them. . . .

For I delivered unto you first of all that which I also received, how that Christ died for our sins according to the scriptures; and that he was buried, and that he rose again the third day according to the scriptures. . . .
1 Corinthians 15:3, 4

The gospel is comprised of three simple but powerful components. . . .

The first component of the gospel is that Jesus Christ died for our sins. You have the opportunity to tell people their sins are forgiven regardless of what they've done, are doing, or ever will do because Jesus Christ was nailed to the wooden beam of the Cross of Calvary, where He bled profusely to pay the price for every sin. You don't need to convince people they're sinners. They already know it . . .

According to scientists, male moths flutter around candles because they think hot wax smells like female moths—a confusion that is usually fatal! That's what we do! We flutter around things that look hot, that smell good—only to get burned time and time again.

So I get to pick up hitchhikers and say, "You look like you feel pretty guilty. But guess what. You're forgiven! A couple thousand years ago, God sent His Son to become a Man and die in your place. You're free! Only one sin is unforgivable: your failure to accept what He did for you. But every other sin is already forgiven." *That's* Good News!

The second component of the gospel is that Jesus was buried and rose again the third day according to the Scriptures. Peter tells us that during the time Jesus was buried He went to hell and preached to the worst of the demons, telling them they no longer had authority over man because their toe-hold of sin had been obliterated by His blood (1 Peter 3:18–20). Therefore, although Satan and his demons can try to intimidate us verbally, they are powerless in reality.

The third and final component of the gospel is that Jesus rose again—something no other guru, holy man, exalted teacher, or revered leader ever did before or has ever done since—thereby substantiating and validating His work on the Cross.

In chapter 1, after Jesus healed a man of leprosy, He said, "Tell no man." But what did the leper do? He "published it much" (Mark 1:45)—he told everyone! Here, at the end of Mark's Gospel, Jesus says, "Go into all the world and preach the gospel to everyone." But what do we do? We don't tell anyone. Why? I believe it's because we forget the beauty, the simplicity, the wonder of the gospel.

Mark 16:16
He that believeth and is baptized shall be saved; but he that believeth not shall be damned.

The Greek word translated "saved" is *sozo,* and while it indeed speaks of the miracle of being born again, it also speaks of experiencing the full orb of God's blessing. We see the same word used in the Gospels and in the Book of Acts with reference to those who were healed from physical disease or delivered from the influence of demons. Thus, the healing and deliverance Jesus ministered were both physical and eternal.

When asked if one has to be baptized to be saved, my answer is "Yes and no." A person doesn't have to be baptized to be born again. A person can go to heaven without being baptized, as evidenced by the thief who was saved even as he hung on a cross (Luke 23:43). But he would not experience the full orb of that which God intends a person to enjoy in liberty, maturity, and ministry.

Following are *six* aspects of the simple yet potent picture of baptism . . .

Baptism is *illustration*. As spoken of in Romans 6, baptism illustrates the death, burial, and resurrection of Jesus. This is why I believe the accurate mode of baptism is immersion. After all, we don't bury heads. We bury entire bodies.

Baptism is *proclamation*. Even if we appear to be "all wet," it is in the act of baptism that we go public with our belief that Jesus died, was buried, and resurrected.

Baptism is *identification*. The Greek word translated "baptize" is *baptizo*, which speaks of immersing cloth into a dye. Jesus did countless things we can't do. But baptism is something He did that we can do as we are immersed in the same way He was, taking upon ourselves the blood-red dye of His death for us.

Baptism is *association*. In being baptized, I am not only identifying with Jesus, but with those all over the world presently and down through the ages of history who, regardless of doctrinal or denominational distinctives, are baptized in the name of the Father, Son, and Holy Ghost. We might not agree on the timing of the Rapture, the meaning of Communion, or the use of tongues. But we are all wonderfully, powerfully associated in the waters of baptism (Ephesians 4:5).

Baptism is *liberation*. Peter tells us that baptism has the same effect today that the Flood did in Noah's day. . . .

Due to its pollution of sin encasing the world, God sent a flood to drown out the corruption. And the same water that cleansed the world lifted up the ark to plant Noah and his family safely on dry ground. So, too, when a person is baptized, the power of the world's evil system is diminished and drowned out. This doesn't mean he will no longer sin. It means the power has been broken, that he no longer *has* to sin, that he's delivered to the firm ground of a walk with the Lord.

Baptism is *impartation*. When Jesus was baptized and emerged out of the waters of the Jordan, the Holy Spirit came upon Him in the form of a dove, empowering Him to minister, to preach, to work miracles. So, too, I believe that the time of baptism is the ideal time to receive by faith the empowering work of the Holy Spirit. "Repent and be baptized," Peter declared, "and you shall receive the gift of the Holy Spirit" (Acts 2:38). Thus, embracing by faith the filling of the Spirit as one emerges from the waters of baptism is what is seen in the baptism of Jesus and the teaching of Peter.

Mark 16:17, 18
And these signs shall follow them that believe; In my name shall they cast out devils; they shall speak with new tongues; they shall take up serpents; and if they drink any deadly thing, it shall not hurt them; they shall lay hands on the sick, and they shall recover.

Notice Jesus did not say those who believe shall follow signs. He said signs would follow those who believe. In other words, as they went into all the world, if they were bitten by a snake or unknowingly partook of something poisonous, the Lord would protect them, and people would see His reality through them. It was as they went into all the world that signs and wonders would accompany them—not as they charged people for seminars or remained within the safety of the church.

Mark 16:19
So then after the Lord had spoken unto them, he was received up into heaven, and sat on the right hand of God.

Jesus left earth and went to heaven to be our Advocate, our Defense Attorney, to intercede for you and me (Hebrews 7:25).

Mark 16:20
And they went forth, and preached everywhere, the Lord working with them, and confirming the word with signs following. Amen.

Even as we see today, the Lord is *indeed* living and working.

Amen!

LUKE

Background to Luke

A companion of Paul on his missionary journeys as well as being referred to as the beloved physician (Colossians 4:14), Luke could be considered the prototype of today's missionary doctors. Some commentators believe that Paul and Luke were classmates at the University of Tarsus. Be that as it may, we do know Luke was a scholar, for he employed the most exacting Greek of any of the Gospel writers. In addition to his education, Luke's command of the Greek language is primarily explained by the fact that he himself was Greek.

Matthew, a Jew, wrote primarily to the Jews, presenting Jesus Christ as King of the Jews. Mark, a Jew, presented Jesus as a Servant, and wrote to the Romans. John, a Jew, presents Jesus as the Son of God, and writes to all men. Luke, a Greek, writes primarily to the Greeks. And because the Greeks were fascinated with Aristotle's ideal republic and Plato's ideal man, Luke writes of Jesus as the Son of Man, the perfect Man.

LUKE

1 Luke 1:1–4
Forasmuch as many have taken in hand to set forth in order a declaration of those things which are most surely believed among us, even as they delivered them unto us, which from the beginning were eyewitnesses, and ministers of the word; it seemed good to me also, having had perfect understanding of all things from the very first, to write unto thee in order, most excellent Theophilus, that thou mightest know the certainty of those things, wherein thou hast been instructed.

After interviewing eyewitnesses, Luke wrote a carefully constructed report for Theophilus concerning the things he had been hearing. Some suggest Theophilus was Luke's previous owner.

You see, although the practice of medicine was a noble calling, there wasn't a lot of money in it. Consequently, men of means had their own slave doctors. Therefore, it is thought that Theophilus was a wealthy man who had Luke as his slave/doctor, got converted, and released Luke to pursue missionary journeys with Paul. This could well be. Others suggest Theophilus, or "Lover of God," was merely an alias for someone who was being protected from possible persecution. Still others suggest that Theophilus was not an individual at all, but a code name for a group of people meeting in the name of Christ. Be Theophilus a real person, an alias for an individual, or a group of people, Luke's intent was to provide a carefully documented account.

Luke 1:5 (a)
There was in the days of Herod, the king of Judaea . . .

These were desperate, dark days for the nation of Israel. Not only had there been a famine of manifestations or words from the Lord for four hundred years, but Herod the Great was on the throne—a ruler who killed his wives and offspring so readily that a popular saying of the day was that it was safer to be Herod's pig than his son.

Luke 1:5 (b)
. . . a certain priest named Zacharias, of the course of Abia: and his wife was of the daughters of Aaron, and her name was Elisabeth.

The priesthood was split into twenty-four courses, or groups, of priests who would take one week off twice a year from farming their land or tending their shops to serve in the temple. During the major festivals or feasts, however, all of the priests would gather in Jerusalem to share the temple duties.

Luke 1:6, 7
And they were both righteous before God, walking in all the commandments and ordinances of the Lord blameless. And they had no child, because that Elisabeth was barren, and they both were now well stricken in years.

In this culture at this time, barrenness was considered a curse from God, indicative that the childless couple must be, or had been doing something very wrong. And yet here we are told that although Elisabeth was barren, she and Zacharias were blameless before the Lord. This is a reminder to me not to judge things too quickly. Yes, Zacharias and Elisabeth are childless presently, but the Lord is setting the stage for something amazing to happen through the child they are about to bear.

Luke 1:8–10
And it came to pass, that while he executed the priest's office before God in the order of his course, According to the custom of the priest's office, his lot was to burn incense when he went into the temple of the Lord. And the whole multitude of the people were praying without at the time of incense.

The altar of incense represents prayer. Every morning and evening, the priests would pour incense upon the altar in the Holy Place, and when it hit the hot coals, the scent would rise up into heaven, creating a sweet-smelling savor before God.

Luke 1:11–13 (a)
And there appeared unto him an angel of the Lord standing on the right side of the altar of incense. And when Zacharias saw him, he was troubled, and fear fell upon him. But the angel said unto him, Fear not, Zacharias: for thy prayer is heard . . .

And another angel came and stood at the altar, having a golden censer; and there was given unto him much incense, that he should offer it with the prayers of all saints upon the golden altar which was before the throne.

Revelation 8:3

I suggest to you the meaning of the passages before us is very practical for you and me—for if indeed prayers are being stored in heaven, it could be that your bowl of prayers concerning any given person, need, or situation is almost full and ready to be released on your behalf. I don't know how many prayers it takes to fill a bowl. Sometimes, but not usually, I pray once, and things happen. More often, however, it takes a continual asking, seeking, and knocking (Matthew 7:7).

Could it be that some of us are just about ready to give up praying for that situation or need, desire or person? Could it be that the Father is saying, "Don't give up now—just a couple more prayers will tip the bowl. Just a couple more prayers will release the blessing"? When we get to heaven, I wonder if we'll see all sorts of bowls poised to be poured had we not given up, had we not stopped seeking, had we not quit praying.

Luke 1:13 (b)
. . . and thy wife Elisabeth shall bear thee a son, and thou shalt call his name John.

"John" means "God is Gracious."

Luke 1:14–18
And thou shalt have joy and gladness; and many shall rejoice at his birth. For he shall be great in the sight of the Lord, and shall drink neither wine nor strong drink; and he shall be filled with the Holy Ghost, even from his mother's womb. And many of the children of Israel shall he turn to the Lord their God. And he shall go before him in the spirit and power of Elias, to turn the hearts of the fathers to the children, and the disobedient to the wisdom of the just; to make ready a people prepared for the Lord. And Zacharias said unto the angel, Whereby shall I know this? for I am an old man, and my wife well stricken in years.

Zacharias could have rejoiced. Instead, he questioned. That's what the thief of unbelief does. At a time when you and I could be celebrating and rejoicing, with folded arms and cynical hearts, we're robbed.

Luke 1:19, 20
And the angel answering said unto him, I am Gabriel, that stand in the presence of God; and am sent to speak unto thee, and to shew thee these glad tidings. And, behold, thou shalt be dumb, and not able to speak, until the day that these things shall be performed, because thou believest not my words, which shall be fulfilled in their season.

"I believe, therefore I have spoken," declared Paul (see 2 Corinthians 4:13). Zacharias didn't believe. Therefore, he will not be able to speak. If you allow the thief of unbelief to rob you of joy, you'll neither witness to others nor praise the Father. Your lips will be sealed if your heart is cynical. But if you are one who embraces with childlike simplicity the promises the Father has given you in His Word, you will speak and rejoice.

Luke 1:21
And the people waited for Zacharias, and marvelled that he tarried so long in the temple.

After the priest burned the incense, he would come out and bless the people. Thus, the people were waiting for the blessing from Zacharias.

Luke 1:22, 23
And when he came out, he could not speak unto them: and they perceived that he had seen a vision in the temple: for he beckoned unto them, and remained speechless. And it came to pass, that, as soon as the days of his ministration were accomplished, he departed to his own house.

Following his week of service in the temple, Zacharias and Elisabeth returned home.

Luke 1:24, 25
And after those days his wife Elisabeth conceived, and hid herself five months, saying, Thus hath the Lord dealt with me in the days wherein he looked on me, to take away my reproach among men.

Although Zacharias' unbelief rendered him speechless, it did not thwart God's purposes.

Luke 1:26, 27
And in the sixth month the angel Gabriel was sent from God unto a city of Galilee, named Nazareth, to a virgin espoused to a man whose name was Joseph, of the house of David; and the virgin's name was Mary.

According to Jewish custom, based upon the arrangement made between their parents, a couple could become engaged even as young children. Then, a year before their marriage, they would become espoused, which meant that although they would not consummate their relationship, they would be considered husband and wife in a legal binding so strong, it required a divorce to break the relationship.

Luke 1:28 (a)
And the angel came in unto her, and said, Hail, thou that art highly favoured. . . .

The Greek word translated "highly favored" is *charitoo*, and means "highly blessed" or "much graced." It is used only one other time in the Bible, not concerning Mary, but concerning you (Ephesians 1:6). We are highly favored not because of who we are, but because of where we are. Where are we? We are in Christ (2 Corinthians 5:17).

Luke 1:28 (b)
. . . the Lord is with thee: blessed art thou among women.

Most scholars believe Mary at this point was about fifteen or sixteen years old, the usual age of espousal in that day. What a wonderful young woman she must have been—a woman selected of all the women of history to be the one to bear God's Son. Later on in the chapter, as we come to the Magnificat, it becomes obvious that she had a heart for God and insight into the Word. And yet I ask you to note that the text reads that she was blessed *among* women, not *above* women. There is no scriptural example to suggest that Mary be worshiped or prayed to. Not a single word. She is indeed the most blessed among women, but she is only a woman.

Luke 1:29–31
And when she saw him, she was troubled at his saying, and cast in her mind what manner of salutation this should be. And the angel said unto her, Fear not, Mary: for thou hast found favour with God. And, behold, thou shalt conceive in thy womb, and bring forth a son, and shalt call his name JESUS.

"Jesus" is the Greek form of the Hebrew "Joshua," which means "Jehovah is Salvation."

Luke 1:32, 33
He shall be great, and shall be called the Son of the Highest: and the Lord God shall give unto him the throne of his father David: And he shall reign over the house of Jacob for ever; and of his kingdom there shall be no end.

The government of the kingdom of God is upon the shoulder of Jesus Christ (Isaiah 9:6). What government did He bear upon His shoulder? The Cross. The Cross identified Him uniquely as a King who would die for His subjects, a King who would become poor so that we might become rich, a King who would go to hell that we might live in heaven, a King who came preaching Good News and great joy for all men.

Luke 1:34 (a)
Then said Mary unto the angel, How shall this be . . .

Unlike Zacharias, Mary didn't question Gabriel's statement. She simply questioned the methodology.

Luke 1:34 (b)
. . . seeing I know not a man?

"I know not a man," said Mary.
"I have no man to help me," said the lame man (see John 5:7).
Could this be the same thing we so often say when we ask, "What man, what leader, what pastor, what author is going to help me?" But watch Gabriel's answer . . .

Luke 1:35
And the angel answered and said unto her, The Holy Ghost shall come upon thee, and the power of the Highest shall overshadow thee: therefore also that holy thing which shall be born of thee shall be called the Son of God.

It's not a man who will bring fruitfulness to our lives. It's the Holy Spirit.

Luke 1:36
And, behold, thy cousin Elisabeth, she hath also conceived a son in her old age: and this is the sixth month with her, who was called barren.

Elisabeth was six months ahead of Mary in the process of the miraculous. So, too, some of you

are six months ahead of me. I can see what the Lord has done in your life. I can see how He's touched you, used you, and helped you. That encourages me. That's what the body of Christ is all about. Find someone who's a little bit ahead of you in the area about which you're wondering or with which you're struggling, and hang out with him or her just as Mary will do with Elisabeth (Luke 1:39).

Luke 1:37, 38
For with God nothing shall be impossible. And Mary said, Behold the handmaid of the Lord; be it unto me according to thy word. And the angel departed from her.

The 1901 American Standard Version (ASV) of the Bible translates verse 37 as: "For no word from God shall be void of power." I like that. Jesus will be birthed in the area of your life that was previously dark and unproductive if, like Mary, you simply embrace the Word He gives you.

Luke 1:39–44
And Mary arose in those days, and went into the hill country with haste, into a city of Juda; and entered into the house of Zacharias, and saluted Elisabeth. And it came to pass, that, when Elisabeth heard the salutation of Mary, the babe leaped in her womb; and Elisabeth was filled with the Holy Ghost: And she spake out with a loud voice, and said, Blessed art thou among women, and blessed is the fruit of thy womb. And whence is this to me, that the mother of my Lord should come to me? For, lo, as soon as the voice of thy salutation sounded in mine ears, the babe leaped in my womb for joy.

Not yet born, John is already worshiping. I've seen that happen, not physically, but spiritually. Sunday after Sunday when I was pastor of Applegate Christian Fellowship, people came with no intention of getting saved, much less baptized. But as they started perceiving the presence of the Lord, even though they were not yet born again, something stirred within them. And before they knew it, they were coming forward for salvation and baptism.

Luke 1:45
And blessed is she that believed: for there shall be a performance of those things which were told her from the Lord.

The literal idea is that because this young, uneducated girl in the backcountry of Israel believed, that which was promised would now be performed.

Luke 1:46–47
And Mary said, My soul doth magnify the Lord, and my spirit hath rejoiced in God my Saviour.

The soul refers to one's mind and emotions. The spirit speaks of one's essence—that which will live forever. The soul relates primarily to people; the spirit relates to God. Thus, Mary says, "My soul—my mind and emotions—magnify the Lord because my spirit— the deepest part of me—has rejoiced in God my Savior. In other words, because God has already elected me, I now choose for my soul to magnify the Lord presently."

Sometimes people say, "I don't worship because I don't feel like it." Mary says just the opposite when she says, "Worship has nothing to do with how I feel emotionally. It's all about what God has already done for me."

Luke 1:48–55
For he hath regarded the low estate of his handmaiden: for, behold, from henceforth all generations shall call me blessed. For he that is mighty hath done to me great things; and holy is his name. And his mercy is on them that fear him from generation to generation. He hath shewed strength with his arm; he hath scattered the proud in the imagination of their hearts. He hath put down the mighty from their seats, and exalted them of low degree. He hath filled the hungry with good things; and the rich he hath sent empty away. He hath holpen his servant Israel, in remembrance of his mercy; as he spake to our fathers, to Abraham, and to his seed for ever.

Herein we see the beautiful theology and the depth of intimacy that was Mary's as she expresses with spontaneity her love for the Lord. No wonder it's called the Magnificat. It's magnificent indeed.

Luke 1:56–59
And Mary abode with her about three months, and returned to her own house. Now Elisabeth's full time came that she should be delivered; and she brought forth a son. And her neighbours and her cousins heard how the Lord had shewed great mercy upon her; and they rejoiced with her. And it came to pass, that on the eighth day they came to circumcise the child; and they called him Zacharias, after the name of his father.

Custom dictated that the firstborn son be named after his father.

Luke 1:60
And his mother answered and said, Not so; but he shall be called John.

Elisabeth reiterated what Zacharias had been told in verse 13.

Luke 1:61, 62
And they said unto her, There is none of thy kindred that is called by this name. And they made signs to his father, how he would have him called.

This means not only was Zacharias unable to speak, but that he was also unable to hear. So, too, if I don't believe, I won't speak. And if I don't speak, I will no longer be able to hear the voice of my Father. It's when I'm speaking, sharing, and ministering that I am in the position to hear my Father more clearly. If you've ever thought you don't want to hear another Bible study, read another chapter, look at another commentary, I suggest it is indicative that you're not sharing with others—because when you're giving out, you'll be hungry to take more in.

Luke 1:63, 64
And he asked for a writing table, and wrote, saying, His name is John. And they marvelled all. And his mouth was opened immediately, and his tongue loosed, and he spake, and praised God.

In naming his son John, Zacharias goes on record that he embraces what God said and what God did. I see in Zacharias a preview of what will come in Acts 2, when on the Day of Pentecost, the tongues of the disciples were also loosed to praise God in languages they did not know. People often say, "If God wants me to speak in tongues, He can move my tongue or make it happen." But Zacharias' tongue being loosed was predicated on the decision he had already made to believe God. Paul echoed this when he said, "I will pray in the Spirit and with understanding also" (see 1 Corinthians 14:15). In other words, it was a choice he made.

Speaking in tongues is not something that happens to a person mystically. Rather, it's the expression of one who says, "Lord, I don't understand how to pray about this situation properly, or how to worship You powerfully. So I will allow my spirit to pray." If you choose to move in this arena, your prayer might consist of a simple word or two or four—but you will find yourself by faith beginning to worship the Lord in a way your intellect is no longer struggling or straining to do. And you'll find your inner person being built up (see 1 Corinthians 14:4).

Luke 1:65–67
And fear came on all that dwelt round about them: and all these sayings were noised abroad throughout all the hill country of Judaea. And all they that heard them laid them up in their hearts, saying, What manner of child shall this be! And the hand of the Lord was with him. And his father Zacharias was filled with the Holy Ghost, and prophesied, saying,

After Zacharias's tongue was loosed, he began to prophesy.

Luke 1:68–75
Blessed be the Lord God of Israel; for he hath visited and redeemed his people, and hath raised up an horn of salvation for us in the house of his servant David; as he spake by the mouth of his holy prophets, which have been since the world began: That we should be saved from our enemies, and from the hand of all that hate us; to perform the mercy promised to our fathers, and to remember his holy covenant; the oath which he sware to our father Abraham, that he would grant unto us, that we being delivered out of the hand of our enemies might serve him without fear, In holiness and righteousness before him, all the days of our life.

Moving in the power of the Spirit, Zacharias began praising God, then prophesying, then pronouncing blessing.

Luke 1:76
And thou, child, shalt be called the prophet of the Highest: for thou shalt go before the face of the Lord to prepare his ways.

People were prepared for the first coming of Jesus through the ministry of John. So, too, I suggest that people will be prepared for the Lord's Second Coming through the ministry of the church. Thus, we have the same three mandates given to John. . . .

Luke 1:77, 78
To give knowledge of salvation unto his people by the remission of their sins, Through the tender mercy of our God; whereby the dayspring from on high hath visited us.

Our first mandate is to give information. What are we to be about this week? We get to tell people the Good News of the gospel—that, except for their rejection of the free gift of salvation, every sin they've ever done, will do, or are presently doing is forgiven because of the tender mercy of God poured out upon them through the Cross of Calvary.

Luke 1:79 (a)
To give light to them that sit in darkness and in the shadow of death . . .

Our second mandate is to provide illumination. How are we to illuminate people's thinking? Because the Word is a lamp unto our feet and a light unto our path, we get to be those who share with people not our philosophies, not our ideas, not our agendas, but the light of the Word.

Luke 1:79 (b)
. . . to guide our feet into the way of peace.

Our third mandate is to share direction. The question I am asked most frequently is, "How can I receive God's guidance?" The answer is to walk the way of peace. The Greek word translated "rule" literally means "umpire," so Paul told the Colossian believers to let the peace of Christ rule in their hearts (Colossians 3:15). How are we to know what to do? We are simply to walk with the Lord, enjoy our relationship with Him, and follow the peace in our heart, which will tell us whether any given direction is "Safe!" or "Out!"

Luke 1:80
And the child grew, and waxed strong in spirit, and was in the deserts till the day of his shewing unto Israel.

We leave a camel-skin-wearing, grasshopper-eating John in the desert, poised to give information, illumination, and direction regarding his Messiah and our Lord.

⁂

2 **Luke 2:1 (a)**
And it came to pass . . .

One of my favorite phrases in all of Scriptures is this one. Whatever you may be facing presently *will* pass.

Luke 2:1 (b)
. . . in those days, that there went out a decree from Caesar Augustus . . .

Known as Gaius Octavius, he was a seemingly successful and powerful ruler. After all, the Gates of Janus—opened only in time of war—had been closed for years due to the Pax Romana—a forced peace brought about after the Roman army bludgeoned her enemies into bloody submission. In light of his position in the known world, Octavius decided he needed a new title—something more elevated than even king or dictator—a name that implied divinity, a name like Caesar Augustus—Caesar the August One.

Luke 2:1 (c)
. . . that all the world should be taxed.

Caesar, "the August One," decreed that everyone return to their homeland to be taxed, little realizing he was simply fulfilling the prophecy of Micah 5:2, which declared that Messiah would be born in Bethlehem. Where else would the Son of David be born but in Bethlehem, the city of David? Where else would the Bread of Life be born but in Bethlehem, the House of Bread? Yes, Caesar made the proclamation, but God ordained the plan.

Luke 2:2
(And this taxing was first made when Cyrenius was governor of Syria.)

On the basis of this parenthetical note, history validates the time and place of Jesus' birth.

Luke 2:3–8
And all went to be taxed, every one into his own city. And Joseph also went up from Galilee, out of the city of Nazareth, into Judaea, unto the city of David, which is called Bethlehem; (because he was of the house and lineage of David:) to be taxed with Mary his espoused wife, being great with child. And so it was, that, while they were there, the days were accomplished that she should be delivered. And she brought forth her firstborn son, and wrapped him in swaddling clothes, and laid him in a manger; because there was no room for them in the inn. And there were in the same country shepherds abiding in the field, keeping watch over their flock by night.

These sheep outside of Bethlehem were most likely the sheep owned by the priests and used for sacrifices in the temple ministry. Because the shepherds who kept watch over them would not have been able to enter into the temple to receive cleansing, they would have been considered unclean. But who are the first to hear of Jesus' birth? The unclean ones, the outcasts, us.

Luke 2:9, 10
And, lo, the angel of the Lord came upon them, and the glory of the Lord shone round about them: and they were sore afraid. And the angel said unto them, Fear not: for, behold, I bring you good tidings of great joy, which shall be to all people.

The angel brought good tidings of great joy not only for Israel, not only for evangelicals, not only for Republicans, but for all people collectively, for each one individually.

Luke 2:11, 12
For unto you is born this day in the city of David a Saviour, which is Christ the Lord. And this shall be a sign unto you; ye shall find the babe wrapped in swaddling clothes, lying in a manger.

Swaddling clothes were strips of cloth similar to those used in the embalming process. In other words, swaddling clothes were essentially grave clothes. This was fitting because Jesus came to die. Although death interrupted the ministry and teaching of Socrates, Plato, Buddha, and every philosopher and thinker throughout history, it did not interrupt the ministry of Jesus Christ. Rather, death fulfilled Jesus' ministry because Jesus alone came to die.

Luke 2:13, 14
And suddenly there was with the angel a multitude of the heavenly host praising God, and saying, Glory to God in the highest, and on earth peace, good will toward men.

Linguistically, the meaning of this first Christmas carol is, "Peace on earth towards men of good will," toward men who are in God's will.

"This is the will of God," Jesus said, "that you believe on Him whom the Father hath sent" (see John 6:29). If you believe on Him whom the Father hath sent, you will indeed be one who, regardless of what's happening around you externally, will experience a peace in your heart internally. Don't let anyone take that peace from you by implying that you should be doing more or trying harder. Instead, say, "Thank You, Lord, for the Good News of great joy that unto me is born a Savior. I embrace this, and I thank You for the peace I experience not because of what I've done, but because of what You did in coming to earth to die for me."

I never tire of talking about the simplicity of the gospel because I have discovered that it is constantly being challenged. Perhaps even subconsciously, we find ourselves saying, "It can't be that simple. Surely I am supposed to do something, to earn something, to prove something." But such is not the case.

"It is *finished*," Jesus declared on the Cross (John 19:30). Therefore, all that remains for us to do is to love Him with all our heart, soul, mind, and strength in response to the goodness, grace, and lovingkindness He pours out upon us.

Luke 2:15–17
And it came to pass, as the angels were gone away from them into heaven, the shepherds said one to another, Let us now go even unto Bethlehem, and see this thing which is come to pass, which the Lord hath made known unto us. And they came with haste, and found Mary, and Joseph, and the babe lying in a manger. And when they had seen it, they made known abroad the saying which was told them concerning this child.

Once you see Emmanuel, God with Us, wrapped in swaddling clothes as the One who came to die for you, you can't help but do what the shepherds did. You can't help but spread the word.

Luke 2:18–23
And all they that heard it wondered at those things which were told them by the shepherds. But Mary kept all these things, and pondered them in her heart. And the shepherds returned, glorifying and praising God for all the things that they had heard and seen, as it was told unto them. And when eight days were accomplished for the circumcising of the child, his name was called JESUS, which was so named of the angel before he was conceived in the womb. And when the days of her purification according to the law of Moses were accomplished, they brought him to Jerusalem, to present him to the Lord; (As it is written in the law of the Lord, Every male that openeth the womb shall be called holy to the Lord;)

According to Leviticus 12, forty days after birth, the firstborn male was to be dedicated totally and completely to the purposes and service of the Lord.

Luke 2:24
And to offer a sacrifice according to that which is said in the law of the Lord, a pair of turtledoves, or two young pigeons.

Leviticus 12:6 states specifically that a lamb was to be brought as a sacrifice of purification, unless one was very poor. In that case, two turtle-doves would be sacrificed. Mary and Joseph brought turtledoves not because they didn't love God, but because they were poor. Although according to prosperity teaching, based upon their financial standing, Mary and Joseph must have had a substandard walk with God because they were poor people. Yet Scripture knows nothing of that kind of theology.

Luke 2:25 (a)
And, behold, there was a man in Jerusalem, whose name was Simeon . . .

Tradition says Simeon was one hundred thirteen years old. Certainly, there is reason to believe that he was well over one hundred years old.

Luke 2:25 (b)
. . . and the same man was just and devout . . .

The word "just" means "dependable." The word "devout" means "devotional." What a combination. Wouldn't it be wonderful if it could be said of us that we are dependable with people and devotional toward God? Such was the case with our brother Simeon.

Luke 2:25 (c)–27 (a)
. . . waiting for the consolation of Israel: and the Holy Ghost was upon him. And it was revealed unto him by the Holy Ghost, that he should not see death, before he had seen the Lord's Christ. And he came by the Spirit into the temple . . .

When you look at Simeon carefully, you see a man of sensitivity. Simeon believed the whisper of the Holy Ghost in his heart that said he would not die until he saw his Messiah.

Luke 2:27 (b)–32
. . . and when the parents brought in the child Jesus, to do for him after the custom of the law, then took he him up in his arms, and blessed God, and said, Lord, now lettest thou thy servant depart in peace, according to thy word: For mine eyes have seen thy salvation, which thou hast prepared before the face of all people; a light to lighten the Gentiles, and the glory of thy people Israel.

Not only was Simeon a man of sensitivity, but he was also a man of flexibility. When told he would see the Messiah, images of pomp and splendor must have filled his imagination as he thought of One who was sure to throw off the yoke of Roman oppression as He entered the city of Jerusalem astride a powerful white stallion. But when Simeon followed the tugging of the

3 Luke 3:1, 2
Now in the fifteenth year of the reign of Tiberius Caesar, Pontius Pilate being governor of Judaea, and Herod being tetrarch of Galilee, and his brother Philip tetrarch of Ituraea and of the region of Trachonitis, and Lysanias the tetrarch of Abilene, Annas and Caiaphas being the high priests, the word of God came unto John the son of Zacharias in the wilderness.

In the eyes of the world, the one emperor, one governor, three tetrarchs, and two high priests were important indeed. But the Word of the Lord did not come to the emperor, to the tetrarchs, or even to the high priests. It did not come to Rome or Jerusalem. It came to a camel-skin-clad man in the wilderness. Therefore, I encourage you who are going through dry times and desert experiences to take hope and listen for the Word of the Lord coming to you.

Luke 3:3–6
And he came into all the country about Jordan, preaching the baptism of repentance for the remission of sins; as it is written in the book of the words of Esaias the prophet, saying, The voice of one crying in the wilderness, Prepare ye the way of the Lord, make his paths straight. Every valley shall be filled, and every mountain and hill shall be brought low; and the crooked shall be made straight, and the rough ways shall be made smooth; and all flesh shall see the salvation of God.

Fulfilling the prophecy of Isaiah, John the Baptist, the forerunner of Jesus, was baptizing in preparation for the Messiah. This blew the Jews away because the idea of baptism of anyone other than Gentiles who wanted to convert to Judaism was foreign to them. Here John was calling the Jews—the very sons and daughters of Abraham—to acknowledge they were sinners in need of a Savior. John's baptism was in preparation for Jesus. Ours is a proclamation that Jesus did indeed come to die for our sins.

Luke 3:7, 8
Then said he to the multitude that came forth to be baptized of him, O generation of vipers, who hath warned you to flee from the wrath to come? Bring forth therefore fruits worthy of repentance, and begin not to say within yourselves, We have Abraham to our father: for I say unto you, That God is able of these stones to raise up children unto Abraham.

"Let's get to the root of the problem," declares John. "You're sinners in need of a Savior. You can't hide in your religiosity, in your denomination, or in your heritage."

Luke 3:9–11
And now also the axe is laid unto the root of the trees: every tree therefore which bringeth not forth good fruit is hewn down, and cast into the fire. And the people asked him, saying, What shall we do then? He answereth and saith unto them, He that hath two coats, let him impart to him that hath none; and he that hath meat, let him do likewise.

"In preparation for the coming of Messiah, start showing your sincerity. Give away your excess. Help others in need."

Luke 3:12, 13
Then came also publicans to be baptized, and said unto him, Master, what shall we do? And he said unto them, Exact no more than that which is appointed you.

Because tax collectors of the day had a certain amount of money they were required to raise— an amount not published among the people—and because they could keep whatever money they raised above this, they were notorious for ripping off the people.

Luke 3:14, 15
And the soldiers likewise demanded of him, saying, And what shall we do? And he said unto them, Do violence to no man, neither accuse any falsely; and be content with your wages. And as the people were in expectation, and all men mused in their hearts of John, whether he were the Christ, or not.

In the margin of your Bible, "do violence to no man" might be more correctly rendered, "Put no man in fear." Maybe the Lord has blessed you with a high degree of intelligence. Or maybe He has blessed you with physical strength or financial means. Don't intimidate people with those "weapons." Don't take pride if people quake in their boots when you come near. That's not the way of the Lord. Jesus spoke the world into existence. Talk about power and authority! Yet people marveled not at His strength, but at His grace (Luke 4:22).

Luke 3:16–20

John answered, saying unto them all, I indeed baptize you with water; but one mightier than I cometh, the latchet of whose shoes I am not worthy to unloose: he shall baptize you with the Holy Ghost and with fire: Whose fan is in his hand, and he will thoroughly purge his floor, and will gather the wheat into his garner; but the chaff he will burn with fire unquenchable. And many other things in his exhortation preached he unto the people. But Herod the tetrarch, being reproved by him for Herodias his brother Philip's wife, and for all the evils which Herod had done, Added yet this above all, that he shut up John in prison.

John preached a message of severity in order that Jesus might come and present a message of serenity. John called for holiness in order that Jesus could give a message of hopefulness. John shone a convicting light in order that Jesus might share comforting love. In other words, John embodied the purpose of the law by showing people they were sinners in need of a Savior.

Luke 3:21

Now when all the people were baptized, it came to pass, that Jesus also being baptized, and praying, the heaven was opened.

Of the Gospel writers, only Luke tells us that heaven opened when Jesus prayed.

"I'm not hearing from God," you might be saying. "I have no feeling of God. I have no sense of His will." Are you praying? Luke makes it clear that Jesus communed with His Father through the same channel available to us: prayer.

Luke 3:22

And the Holy Ghost descended in a bodily shape like a dove upon him, and a voice came from heaven, which said, Thou art my beloved Son; in thee I am well pleased.

Those who deny the Trinity have a tough time with this passage, for here we clearly see the Son being baptized, the Spirit descending in the form of a dove, and the Father speaking from heaven.

Luke 3:23 (a)

And Jesus himself began to be about thirty years of age . . .

The Book of Numbers tells us that thirty years of age was the time the priests began their ministry. It was also the age at which David became king of Israel.

Luke 3:23 (b)–38

. . . being (as was supposed) the son of Joseph, which was the son of Heli, which was the son of Matthat, which was the son of Levi, which was the son of Melchi, which was the son of Janna, which was the son of Joseph, which was the son of Mattathias, which was the son of Amos, which was the son of Naum, which was the son of Esli, which was the son of Nagge, which was the son of Maath, which was the son of Mattathias, which was the son of Semei, which was the son of Joseph, which was the son of Juda, which was the son of Joanna, which was the son of Rhesa, which was the son of Zorobabel, which was the son of Salathiel, which was the son of Neri, which was the son of Melchi, which was the son of Addi, which was the son of Cosam, which was the son of Elmodam, which was the son of Er, which was the son of Jose, which was the son of Eliezer, which was the son of Jorim, which was the son of Matthat, which was the son of Levi, which was the son of Simeon, which was the son of Juda, which was the son of Joseph, which was the son of Jonan, which was the son of Eliakim, which was the son of Melea, which was the son of Menan, which was the son of Mattatha, which was the son of Nathan, which was the son of David, which was the son of Jesse, which was the son of Obed, which was the son of Booz, which was the son of Salmon, which was the son of Naasson, which was the son of Aminadab, which was the son of Aram, which was the son of Esrom, which was the son of Phares, which was the son of Juda, which was the son of Jacob, which was the son of Isaac, which was the son of Abraham, which was the son of Thara, which was the son of Nachor, which was the son of Saruch, which was the son of Ragau, which was the son of Phalec, which was the son of Heber, which was the son of Sala, which was the son of Cainan, which was the son of Arphaxad, which was the son of Sem, which was the son of Noe, which was the son of Lamech, which was the son of Mathusala, which was the son of Enoch, which was the son of Jared, which was the son of Maleleel, which was the son of Cainan, which was the son of Enos, which was the son of Seth, which was the son of Adam, which was the son of God.

Only two of the Gospels contain genealogies. Matthew has a genealogy because he presents Jesus Christ as King—and a king must have the proper pedigree to claim the throne. Mark presents Jesus as a Servant—and no one cares about the genealogy of a servant. Luke presents Jesus as the Son of Man—and it is helpful to know from whence a man comes. And John presents Jesus as the Son of God—rendering a genealogy impossible.

Verses 31–38 of Luke's account are the same as Matthew's account because Mary and Joseph were both descendants of David. But Luke's account from verses 23–31 differs from Matthew's because Matthew traces the line through David's son, Solomon, to Coniah, or Jeconiah—a man upon whom God pronounced a curse (Jeremiah 22:28–30). Therefore, although Joseph was technically in line to take the throne if indeed there was a throne being given, spiritually he couldn't do so because his line had been cursed.

So what happens? The term "son of" can either mean "son of" or "son-in-law of." Therefore, Luke's account is actually Mary's genealogy. And, as seen in verse 31 before us, Mary's genealogy is traced not from David through Solomon, but through Solomon's brother, Nathan—an un-cursed line.

This means that he who traced the royal line legally, ignoring the curses of the Old Testament, would have to conclude that Jesus had a right to the throne because He was supposedly the son of Joseph. But he who believed the curses of the Old Testament could find that in Luke's account, Mary's genealogy bypassed the curse altogether. Therefore, whether legally or spiritually, both genealogies lead to Jesus of Nazareth—the only Person in all of history who could possibly fulfill both lines.

In addition to this, within forty years after Jesus' crucifixion, when the temple was burned in A.D. 70, all records of Jewish genealogies were destroyed—rendering all Jews unable to trace their genealogies. Thus, no one—including the upcoming Antichrist—can claim with integrity to have a genealogical right to the kingdom.

Jesus is Lord uniquely, exclusively, absolutely—of this we can be sure completely.

In Luke 3, we saw Jesus baptized in the Jordan River by John the Baptist. When He came out of the water, the heavens were opened, and the Spirit descended upon Him in the form of a dove. Then He heard a voice saying, "This is My beloved Son in whom I am well pleased." Talk about a radical baptism! But be aware of this fact: After a high time often comes a hard time; on the heels of a triumph, trouble often follows. Consequently, here in chapter 4, we see Jesus, having been baptized, having heard

the voice of the Father, facing a difficult time indeed . . .

Luke 4:1, 2
And Jesus being full of the Holy Ghost returned from Jordan, and was led by the Spirit into the wilderness, Being forty days tempted of the devil.

Notice that Jesus was led—or literally driven—by the Spirit into the wilderness, where Satan would tempt Him. Why? Was the Spirit trying to do Him in? Not at all. The Spirit led Him into the place of temptation not to do Him in, but to show Him off. Think of it this way: If you were to show some interest in a Jeep, the salesman would tell you to take it for a drive in the mountains or the dunes in order to show you its power and durability. So, too, the Spirit was able to show off the power and the ability, the holiness and tenacity of Jesus. The same is true for you. Why does the Lord allow hardship in your life? He's out to show His strength in your life that the devil might be defeated once again.

Luke 4:2, 3 (a)
And in those days he did eat nothing: and when they were ended, he afterward hungered. And the devil said unto him . . .

The three temptations that correlate with what John delineates in his first Epistle constitute Satan's entire game plan. . . .

For all that is in the world, the lust of the flesh, and the lust of the eyes, and the pride of life, is not of the Father, but is of the world.
1 John 2:16

Satan has only three temptations, three plays in his playbook: the lust of the flesh, the lust of the eyes, and the pride of life. And he runs them over and over again . . .

Luke 4:3 (b)
. . . if thou be the Son of God, command this stone that it be made bread.

"And when the woman saw that the tree was good for food . . ." (Genesis 3:6). The first temptation Satan used in the Garden of Eden is the same one He used first in the wilderness: the lust of the flesh. And it's the same temptation he sets before you whenever he whispers, "Don't you deserve a moment of satisfaction, a moment of pleasure? Why should everyone else have all the fun? Aren't you a child of God? Don't you think He wants you to experience life and be fulfilled?"

The author of the letter to the Hebrews was

absolutely right when he said there is pleasure in sin for a season (Hebrews 11:25). If you give in to the lust of the flesh, you will indeed have pleasure for a season—for a moment—but you'll experience pain for the rest of your life. If, on the other hand, you deny your flesh, you might experience pain for a moment, but you'll have pleasure for the rest of your life. The choice is yours.

Luke 4:4
And Jesus answered him, saying, It is written, That man shall not live by bread alone, but by every word of God.

In answer to Satan's temptation, Jesus did what you and I are to do. Submitted to the Word, He quoted the Word (Deuteronomy 8:3). Such was the Sword He used to beat back the seduction of Satan.

Luke 4:5–7
And the devil, taking him up into an high mountain, shewed unto him all the kingdoms of the world in a moment of time. And the devil said unto him, All this power will I give thee, and the glory of them: for that is delivered unto me; and to whomsoever I will I give it. If thou therefore wilt worship me, all shall be thine.

"And that it was pleasant to the eyes" (Genesis 3:6b). After the lust of the flesh came the lust of the eyes. Satan had the right to offer the kingdoms of the world to Jesus, for Paul declares him as the god of this world (2 Corinthians 4:4). You see, when Adam and Eve chose to listen to Satan rather than God, they, in effect, handed him the title deed of the planet. That is the reason for the pain and the problems that beset our world daily, our lives individually.

The lust of the eyes doesn't refer only to looking at something that would tempt or stimulate you to do wrong. The lust of the eyes is seeing any other way than God's to accomplish His purpose. "Why go through the agony and the suffering of Calvary?" Satan asked Jesus. "Just bow down and worship me, and the kingdoms of the world will be yours."

When Satan, one of the highest of all the created angelic beings, was in heaven, his desire to be worshiped was what got him cast out of heaven in the first place. And yet he still desires to be worshiped. "Worship me," he says to Jesus, "and I'll show You a shortcut to saving the world so You won't have to die on the Cross or plunge into hell."

Luke 4:8
And Jesus answered and said unto him, Get thee behind me, Satan: for it is written, Thou shalt worship the Lord thy God, and him only shalt thou serve.

Again, submitted to the Word, Jesus quoted the Word (Deuteronomy 6:13), and therein found victory.

Luke 4:9–11
And he brought him to Jerusalem, and set him on a pinnacle of the temple, and said unto him, If thou be the Son of God, cast thyself down from hence: For it is written, He shall give his angels charge over thee, to keep thee: And in their hands they shall bear thee up, lest at any time thou dash thy foot against a stone.

"And a tree to be desired to make one wise, she took of the fruit thereof" (Genesis 3:6c). After the lust of the eyes came the pride of life, as Satan set Jesus on a pinnacle of the temple and said, "Multitudes will come to hear You preach if You jump from the temple and let angels catch You. Show them who You are."

I find it more than coincidental that this temptation took place at the highest point of the holiest place—the temple. Haven't you discovered that it is when you are at church that you are presented with strong temptations of pride or cynicism, envy or apathy? I believe that one of the places the demons are most active is the place where the body meets together corporately.

Luke 4:12, 13
And Jesus answering said unto him, It is said, Thou shalt not tempt the Lord thy God. And when the devil had ended all the temptation, he departed from him for a season.

Satan quoted Scripture, and Jesus came back with another. That's why we are to be students of the Word (2 Timothy 2:15). Any cult, demon, or false religious teacher can build a case from one isolated text, but be completely in error if he doesn't take into account all of the counsel of God (Acts 20:27). Scripture balances Scripture.

I believe the three temptations Jesus faced at the outset of His public ministry are the same three temptations that will come to anyone involved in any aspect of ministry—be it to family or to the body. . . .

The temptation of materialism. "You should be living in a nicer house," Satan will whisper. "You're the King's kid, aren't you? Don't you think He wants you to drive a Mercedes? Aren't you hungry?"

The temptation of pragmatism. "Look at all those nations," Satan says. "Shouldn't they be saved? So you have to bow down to me for just a moment, and look at what you'll get."

The temptation of sensationalism. "Come and see the power of God as we jump from the temple," the evangelist beckons. "Angels will surround us. The glory of God shall move among us. Healings and wonder and glory will flow through us."

Materialism, pragmatism, and sensationalism—three ways Satan will try to infect a ministry. Watch out. Be as wise as serpents in these last days in which we live.

Luke 4:14–16 (a)
And Jesus returned in the power of the Spirit into Galilee: and there went out a fame of him through all the region round about. And he taught in their synagogues, being glorified of all. And he came to Nazareth, where he had been brought up: and, as his custom was, he went into the synagogue on the sabbath day . . .

If it was Jesus' custom to be in the synagogue, how much more so should it be ours. "I can worship God on the golf course," some say. Or "Our church is so dead. I get more inspired when I'm surfing." Do you think the synagogues Jesus attended were places of "Holy Ghost Happenings"? Do you think they were vibrant and moving? I don't. Do you think Jesus actually learned from the teachings of the rabbis? I don't. Yet it was His custom to attend anyway. Why? Simply to be in the midst of the church (Hebrews 2:12). And His presence in our midst is much more than enough of a reason to come together corporately, to meet together consistently.

Luke 4:16 (b)–17 (a)
. . . and stood up for to read. And there was delivered unto him the book of the prophet Esaias.

As was the tradition in those days, Jesus, a visiting Rabbi, was afforded the opportunity to read and comment briefly on Scripture. And the text for that given day being Isaiah 61—a prophecy concerning the coming Messiah—Jesus' first sermon would be about Himself.

Luke 4:17 (b)–18 (a)
And when he had opened the book, he found the place where it was written, The Spirit of the Lord is upon me, because he hath anointed me . . .

We often hear people say, "I feel the Lord's anointing upon my life." But watch what Jesus says His anointing consisted of. . . .

Luke 4:18 (b)
. . . to preach the gospel to the poor . . .

The poor, the downtrodden, the outcast, the unattractive, and the forgotten people—these are the people to whom we are to reach out, especially if we are to be like Jesus.

Luke 4:18 (c)
. . . he hath sent me to heal the brokenhearted . . .

Brokenhearted people are not easy to minister to because it's not easy to walk with someone who's hurting, to listen to their repetitive rambling, to dry their seemingly endless tears. And yet these are they to whom Jesus came lovingly, tenderly, and specifically.

Luke 4:18 (d)
. . . to preach deliverance to the captives . . .

Jesus was anointed to preach to the very people to whom we all too often impatiently say, "I've told you what to do once; I've told you how to be free twice; why are you *still* in bondage to that habit, that person, that substance?"

Luke 4:18 (e)
. . . and recovering of sight to the blind . . .

Of the spiritually blind, we are tempted to say in frustration, "Why can't they see it? How could spiritual truth be any clearer?" Yet they are precisely for whom Jesus came.

Luke 4:18 (f)
. . . to set at liberty them that are bruised,

Afraid of getting hurt, bruised people hold back. They're defensive, timid, and fearful. Yet because He is anointed to free them, Jesus finds a way to reach them.

Luke 4:19
To preach the acceptable year of the Lord.

For topical study of Luke 4:18–19 entitled "A Most Magnificent Mission," turn to page 312.

I am so impressed with Jesus. He is the One who is patient with those who are bruised, who listens to those who are blubbering, who continues to take time with those who just can't see, who works with the one who is in bondage. Lord, move me in this direction. Make me more like You.

Luke 4:20–22 (a)

And he closed the book, and he gave it again to the minister, and sat down. And the eyes of all them that were in the synagogue were fastened on him. And he began to say unto them, This day is this scripture fulfilled in your ears. And all bare him witness, and wondered at the gracious words which proceeded out of his mouth.

Here an itinerant Rabbi had opened the Scriptures and shared with the people in such a way that they marveled at the gracious words He spoke. He hadn't come down on them. He hadn't preached at them. Rather, He shared with them in a way they had never heard before.

Luke 4:22 (b)

And they said, Is not this Joseph's son?

All too often, I think I've got a teacher, a brother, a co-worker pegged—only to discover later that, because my information is limited, because my ability to understand is not as great as I think it is, my conclusion is completely amiss. As I read a book or listen to a sermon, if I'm not careful, I can find myself doing just what the Galileans did—first marveling at the message, taking in the teaching, receiving the word coming to me—but then missing out on the miracle because I erroneously analyze the messenger.

Luke 4:23

And he said unto them, Ye will surely say unto me this proverb, Physician, heal thyself: whatsoever we have heard done in Capernaum, do also here in thy country.

Jesus knew the people would ask Him to validate His ministry and substantiate His authority by doing a miracle among them even as He had done in Capernaum.

Luke 4:24–27

And he said, Verily I say unto you, No prophet is accepted in his own country. But I tell you of a truth, many widows were in Israel in the days of Elias, when the heaven was shut up three years and six months, when great famine was throughout all the land; but unto none of them was Elias sent, save unto Sarepta, a city of Sidon, unto a woman that was a widow. And many lepers were in Israel in the time of Eliseus the prophet; and none of them was cleansed, saving Naaman the Syrian.

Jesus' word to the Jews was, "When Elijah and Elisha were not received in their own land, they were sent to the Gentiles to do significant miracles. So watch out because if you're not careful, once again, you will miss the opportunity to receive miraculous ministry."

Luke 4:28

And all they in the synagogue, when they heard these things, were filled with wrath.

Because the Jews believed that Gentiles were good for nothing but to keep the fires of hell hot, Jesus' implication that Gentiles would be the recipients of anything other than the disdain of God filled them with wrath.

Luke 4:29

And rose up, and thrust him out of the city, and led him unto the brow of the hill whereon their city was built, that they might cast him down headlong.

So incensed were the Jews that they mobbed Jesus with the intent of killing Him by throwing Him over a cliff.

Luke 4:30, 31 (a)

But he passing through the midst of them went his way, and came down to Capernaum . . .

Why was this mob able to drive Jesus out of the city and all the way to the edge of the precipice, but unable to push Him over? What happened to the crowd that made them part? I don't know. Perhaps it was something in Jesus' eyes, or a look of determination upon His face that allowed Him to walk through them like a hot knife through butter.

Luke 4:31 (b), 32

. . . a city of Galilee, and taught them on the sabbath days. And they were astonished at his doctrine: for his word was with power.

It amazes me that people today don't want to study the Scriptures. They want to go to power seminars and have power meetings wearing power ties at power breakfasts. Everything is power in this decade in which we live. But true power is in the Word—taking in the Word, contemplating the Word, giving priority to the Word. The powerful working of God in our lives is directly connected to our receiving His Word.

Luke 4:33–37

And in the synagogue there was a man, which had a spirit of an unclean devil, and cried out with a loud voice, Saying, Let us alone; what have we to do with thee, thou Jesus of Nazareth? art thou come to destroy us? I know thee who thou art; the Holy One of God. And Jesus rebuked him, saying, Hold thy peace, and come out of him. And when the devil had thrown him in the midst, he came out of him, and hurt him not. And they were all amazed, and spake among themselves, saying, What a word is this! for with authority and power he commandeth the unclean spirits, and they come out. And the fame of him went out into every place of the country round about.

Jesus never went looking for demons. He never held deliverance meetings. He never taught deliverance seminars. But where Jesus is, the demons suddenly get restless, and they expose themselves.

Nowhere in Scripture are believers told to search for the devil and pray against the devil. If you and I are doing our job in just teaching the Word, sharing the Word, and sharing the Lord, demons will surface from time to time and make themselves known—not necessarily physically or tangibly, but we'll sense their activity. Our emphasis, however, must remain on the person and work and nature of Jesus. Demon possession is a real phenomenon of our day. But I also believe the church can suffer from demon obsession—centering on, talking about, dealing with the devil and demons more than walking in the light. If you walk into a dark room, you don't speak against the darkness, have a rally against the darkness, or give seminars on the darkness. You simply turn on the light. And I think that's the best way, the right way, the scriptural way to deal with spiritual darkness as well. Keep your ministry, your focus, your priority on Jesus—and Satan will run for cover.

Luke 4:38, 39

And he arose out of the synagogue, and entered into Simon's house. And Simon's wife's mother was taken with a great fever; and they besought him for her. And he stood over her, and rebuked the fever; and it left her: and immediately she arose and ministered unto them.

Coming home from the synagogue, Peter walks in to find his mother-in-law sick with a fever. How often that happens to us. We leave the refreshment and restoration we find in church only to find feverish activity and fiery trials awaiting us at home. But Peter models the solution because guess who he brought with him! Take Jesus home with you. Then, whatever feverish trials await you, the Lord is there with you. Talk about Him on the way home. Talk with Him when you get home, and you will thwart any attempt of the enemy to undo what you have received.

Luke 4:40, 41

Now when the sun was setting, all they that had any sick with divers diseases brought them unto him; and he laid his hands on every one of them, and healed them. And devils also came out of many, crying out, and saying, Thou art Christ the Son of God. And he rebuking them suffered them not to speak: for they knew that he was Christ.

One of the most effective tactics of the Enemy is to get people who don't know the Lord or care about the Lord to be in positions where they're talking about things of the Lord, even though their lives are a mess and their motives are amiss. In this way, the church, the body of Christ is discredited.

Luke 4:42–44

And when it was day, he departed and went into a desert place: and the people sought him, and came unto him, and stayed him, that he should not depart from them. And he said unto them, I must preach the kingdom of God to other cities also: for therefore am I sent. And he preached in the synagogues of Galilee.

Jesus was accused by His enemies of many things, but one thing He was never accused of was being too busy. He grew tired physically from the demands placed upon Him, but He was never uptight or stressed out. Rather, He moved with a tranquility and a serenity that are sadly lacking in our society.

For topical study of Luke 4:42 entitled "Solitude and Silence," turn to page 317.

A MOST MAGNIFICENT MISSION
A Topical Study of
Luke 4:18, 19

If you have read leadership or management journals, you know that a real trend has been for every organization—whether business or ministry—to issue a Mission Statement, a succinct description of its vision or mission. We find Jesus' Mission Statement in the first message He preached in Nazareth when He said:

> *The Spirit of the Lord GOD is upon me; because the LORD hath anointed me to preach good tidings unto the meek; he hath sent me to bind up the broken-hearted, to proclaim liberty to the captives, and the opening of the prison to them that are bound; to proclaim the acceptable year of the LORD. . . .*
> Isaiah 61:1, 2

Some commentators have suggested that the year Jesus began His public ministry was the Year of Jubilee—a year of celebration and liberation when all debts were canceled and all slaves set free. If this be the case, Jesus' message would be especially fitting, for He was about to set people free from religious domination as well.

In Jesus' day, the rabbis taught that there were 613 commands in the law. Consequently people struggled under a heavy burden of what they were told constituted true religion and holiness. No wonder, then, that they would marvel at the gracious words Jesus spoke to them (Luke 4:22).

But as He continued speaking to them of their need for Him, their marvel turned to wrath. "How dare He give a word of correction to us?" they asked. "We know Him. He grew up here. This is just Joseph's boy." Jesus caught these people off guard because quite possibly there were boys in the town who were much better candidates to be Messiah than He. After all, the other boys wore phylacteries—boxes worn on the forehead or around their wrists which contained Deuteronomy 6:4. Jesus, evidently, never did (Matthew 23:5).

Because I like to take my Bible with me wherever I go, phylacteries seem like a good idea. Obviously, the scrolls were too big and bulky to carry about, so phylacteries would seem to be a wonderful way to express the importance of the Word of God. I'm sure I would have spotted the guys wearing their phylacteries faithfully and said, "There are our leaders, right there." But that's because I'm a closet Pharisee. I'm impressed with signs of spirituality—phylacteries, prayer shawls, broad borders, and all the rest. Jesus, however, models something entirely different. As they watched Him grow up, the people in His hometown didn't say of Him, "Now *there's* a spiritual young man." No, they wanted to kill Him (Luke 4:29). You wouldn't want to kill a man you thought was qualified to be Messiah.

Not only did Jesus not carry a Bible, He evidently never gave a formal Bible study to His disciples. I look for every opportunity to hold a formal or an informal Bible study. That's what the Pharisees did too. Endlessly. They unrolled the scrolls. They had discussions. They prodded and pontificated. But although Jesus knew the Word better than all of them by the age of twelve (Luke 2:47), His approach to spiritual life and Bible study was entirely different. And because Jesus was able to move about without a big Bible in hand, impressing people with His knowledge, He was able to do incarnational ministry that was completely nonintimidating as when He would derive a succinct lesson on spiritual life simply from seeing a man casting seed into a field (Luke 8:5).

I am anything but succinct. I don't make my points quickly. I love to go on and on. Jesus did just the opposite. When Thomas doubted, Jesus didn't say, "Let Me give you five reasons why the Resurrection is true, fifteen Old Testament prophecies that shed light on what is happening before you." No, He simply said, "Touch My wounds" (see John 20:27).

It's not that He didn't know the prophecies. It's not that He didn't have a grasp on Scripture. But it's as though He had distilled them to the point where the people He cared about could be effectively reached without being intimidated by His knowledge. His was an incarnational ministry that amazes me. Nonetheless, I find myself asking, "Couldn't You have given some Bible studies to Your disciples and recorded them in the Word, which we could use as a model for how Scripture is to be taught?" Oh, Jesus did this on one occasion—on the road to Emmaus. But, being that this is the only time such teaching is recorded, it was the singular exception rather than the rule—and even then, it was given to two individuals who were outside of His inner circle of twelve.

Not only do we find an absence of recorded Bible study in the Word, but there is not one recorded instance in the New Testament where Jesus prayed with His disciples. There is not one recorded instance when He gathered His boys around a fire and said, "Let's spend some time in prayer," not one time where He said to His disciples, "It's a great night. Look at the stars above. Let's talk to the Father together."

Finally, after a year and a half, His disciples said, "Lord, teach us to pray. John does. The Pharisees do." Indeed, the Pharisees did pray: in the parking lot, on the street corner, in the marketplace, they loved to give long prayers. I like that. *That's* spirituality. *That's* holiness. If I were Jesus, I would have taught on prayer, given seminars on prayer, called special meetings for prayer. But what did Jesus do? In response to His disciples' request to teach them to pray, He not only repeated the simple prayer He had taught them a year and a half earlier in the Sermon on the Mount, but He shortened it by five words.

Jesus' disciples knew prayer was the foundation of His ministry. Seeing Him slip away before the break of day morning by morning (Isaiah 50:4), they knew He was a man of passionate prayer. And yet He didn't necessarily pray with them. Even in the Garden of Gethsemane, He said, "You stay here while I go and pray" (see Matthew 26:36).

Why? I suggest it was because, although prayer is a glorious privilege, it can also be very intimidating to people. Whenever I tell a congregation to break into groups for conversational prayer, I can feel the tension that fills the room. Evidently, Jesus was so kind, so gracious, so loving that He would not put that kind of trip on anyone. I like to pray with people—but when was the last time I spent all night alone in prayer? Jesus reversed the entire order. He talked about a prayer closet, about praying in secret, as if to say, "Forget the outward expression because it intimidates people. They're burdened by your seeming spirituality, but I came to set them free."

As a result, common people heard Him gladly (Mark 12:37). They were drawn to Him like moths to a flame not because He was well groomed or well attired (Isaiah 53:2), but because there was evidently something in His eyes that welcomed them, something in His voice that warmed them. I'm sad to admit that I look for guys who are sharp in appearance as leadership material. The Pharisees did too. The best-dressed men of their day, they came across as very polished and sophisticated. But they also came across as stern and unapproachable. Not Jesus.

So easy was He to be with that for His inaugural miracle, He made wine for a wedding party. History tells us that in Jesus' day, when a baby girl was born into the family, her father would annually make a batch of wine for himself and one for his daughter's marriage celebration. Therefore, if the bride at Cana was fifteen or sixteen, there would have been presented to the happy couple sixteen years' worth of wine. But after drinking all sixteen years' worth, the wedding party in Cana ran out of wine. So what did Jesus do? Did He give them a lecture on the danger of overindulgence? Did He make a bottle or two? No, He made one hundred eighty gallons (John 2:6).

If I were Jesus, I would have kicked off my public ministry with a nice healing miracle or by bringing someone back from the dead. Instead, Jesus said, "Here's a little bride and groom who are embarrassed. I want to help them." He gave no teaching; He got no glory. He simply provided wine with no strings attached. In fact, in studying His miracles, very rarely do we see Jesus make application to the people He touched, healed, or helped. With the exception of a couple occasions, no tracts were given out, no teaching was given.

"Sell your goods and follow Me," He said to the rich young ruler (see Matthew 19:21). But when he couldn't do this, Jesus didn't say, "Let's get together for coffee and rethink your decision. I want to take you through Ecclesiastes and explain to you the emptiness of riches." No, He simply let His invitation stand.

Reformers intrigue me. Reformers are intense, single-minded, committed. Yet the fire in their eyes and the determination on their faces can cause people to be intimidated, to back away, to feel bad. Reformers can be uptight. Not Jesus. Why? He trusted the Father that in due time the rich young ruler would see the truth of His words and the depth of His love and come back.

Even when He cleansed the temple, John makes it clear the scourge Jesus made was a *small* scourge and that He took care to protect the doves (John 2:15, 16). There's never any panic or frenzy seen in Jesus. Rather, He moved with serenity, certainty, and tranquility. As a result, although He was referred to as a glutton, a winebibber, and the friend of sinners, no one ever accused Him of being too busy.

> "Master, all men seek for You in Capernaum. That's the hot spot of the northern region, the epicenter of the area outside of Jerusalem. What an invitation!"
> But what did Jesus say?
> "For this reason came I forth,"—not from heaven, but from His morning prayer time—"to go to a little un-walled village to talk to the villagers there. And that will about do it for today" (see Mark 1:38).

Jesus cared about one thing: His Father's will. That's all. That is how He was able to move around with serenity, focus, and a complete lack of busyness. "My burden is easy and My load is light," He said (see Matthew 11:30). And He lived this out in such a way that no one ever once suggested or implied He was busy.

Jesus truly breaks the mold of what we perceive holiness and spirituality to be. Although we think this is seen in the fact that He hung around publicans and sinners, I believe it is seen more clearly in the fact that He dined with Pharisees. To be sure, He spoke harshly to the Pharisees because He knew that's what it would take to get through to those about whom He genuinely cared. But when they invited Him to their gatherings, He went.

You see, at the home of Simon, Jesus ministered to the Pharisee and prostitute alike (Luke 7:36–39). We understand so little of this. How easy it is for church congregations to say, "We want more young people. What can we do to be more youthful and vibrant?" Or, "We need some tithers. How can we appeal to the older set?" Or "We want hippies. We want to do the 'Jesus Movement' thing." Or "We want to reach yuppies. That's what is current." Or "We want to be interracial. We want our Fellowship to be one about which visitors say, 'Wow, the people in your church are varied and cool.'" Jesus was completely not interested in this. Pharisee, prostitute, woman, man, young, and old—He loved anyone and everyone the Father sent His way.

"Master, we saw Your disciples picking wheat on the Sabbath day. This ought not be" (see Matthew 12:2–4).

"Have you not read of David stealing the showbread from the temple in order to feed his men?" Jesus asked, as if to say, "There are laws, and there is love. But when love and the law collide, love always has precedence."

> A mother was called to the nursery to take care of her baby. But because she forgot to take her nursery identification with her, the nursery staff understandably wouldn't let her have her baby.
>
> "I'll get my card," she said. But when she returned to the amphitheatre at Applegate Christian Fellowship to get it, she was stopped by deacons who were doing their job, trying to keep disturbances at a minimum. So she was stuck. Everyone was doing his job. Everyone was following the rules, but a woman was crushed in the process.

I like rules, parameters. I like everything in place. But Jesus said, "There's something a whole bunch more important than rules. It's people."

Jesus dealt with the woman at the well without ever dealing directly with the issue of her living with a man who was not her husband. If I were Jesus, I would have made sure she understood the importance of getting out of that relationship, of making things right. But in recording the story, the Holy Spirit seems to say to any who question this, "That's none of your business. You don't need to know whether Jesus dealt directly with that issue or not."

Could this be because, knowing this woman had had five husbands and was living with a man to whom she was not married, she would have obviously been branded as an immoral woman whose only option to survive financially was through prostitution? Could it be that Jesus was saying, "What the religious are concerned about, I'm not all that concerned about. And what the religious aren't concerned about, namely love, concerns me to the utmost"?

"I am anointed to preach the gospel to the poor, to heal the brokenhearted, to preach deliverance to the captives, to give sight to the blind, and to set at liberty those who are bruised," Jesus said in the most magnificent Mission Statement ever conceived. And He fulfilled it perfectly, exquisitely, and completely.

Jesus blows apart every idea I have about spirituality and ministry. And in so doing He sets us all free from the burdens and baggage of grumpiness and condemnation, of fear and intimidation. Revisit Jesus—this laid-back Lover of people whose intensity was private and personal, who didn't put pressure on people. Reacquaint yourself with the Friend of sinners, the Man who spoke gracious words continually, who healed unconditionally, who loved sacrificially—for although He is unrecognized by most religious people, He alone defines true holiness.

SOLITUDE AND SILENCE
A Topical Study of
Luke 4:42

I *f a man wants to be used by God, he cannot spend all of his time with people.*
A. W. Tozer

Jesus was One who, better than any other, knew the importance of solitude. That is why we see Him repeatedly going off into a desert place, alone. Following are four results of time spent in such solitude. . . .

Realization of Self

When you're in a quiet place away from other people, suddenly you can't blame your schedule, your peers, or your family for your frustration or failure. That's why people avoid being alone. That is why they keep the TV on, the radio loud, people around. They don't want to come face-to-face with themselves.

Compassion for Others

After receiving revelation of myself, I am no longer as hard on you. The reason people come down on others, judge others, find fault with others is because they have spent little time alone in the presence of the Lord—for if they did, like Isaiah, who spent the first five chapters of the book that bears his name saying, "Woe unto you"; "Woe unto you"; "Woe unto you";—after seeing the Lord high and lifted up, like Isaiah they would say, "Woe is *me. I* am a man of unclean lips," (Isaiah 6:5). That is why sometimes one of the best things we can do for people is to absent ourselves from them. When we're constantly with people, we have a tendency to find fault. But when we spend a season in solitude, after truly seeing ourselves, we emerge with greater compassion for others.

Transformation of Society

Society is not transformed by people picketing, marching, or even voting. I suggest that when you study history—particularly European history—you cannot help but notice that monarchs, potentates, and powers were moved by monks—men who chose lives of solitude. Withdrawing from society, they changed the face of Europe politically.

Regarding society as a shipwreck from which each individual must swim for his life, the desert fathers knew they were helpless to do any good for others as long as they themselves floundered about in the wreckage. These were men who believed that to allow oneself to drift along passively accepting the tenets and values of society was to court disaster. But once they got a foothold on solid ground, they discovered they had not only the power, but also the obligation to pull their entire culture to safety as well. Consequently, as decades passed, philosophers and thinkers, rulers and politicians journeyed to the desert in order to hear from them and be instructed by them. Thus, Europe was transformed by men who realized the best way to stand on solid ground was to spend moments, years, and decades seeking God and living a solitary life.

Preparation for Ministry

- When did the Word of God come to John?
  When he was in the wilderness.
- When was Moses called to lead the people of Israel?
  After spending forty years in the desert.
- When did Jesus begin His public ministry?
  After spending forty days in solitude.

There is something about solitude that is absolutely essential in the lives of spiritual men and women, for because the Lord has chosen to speak in a still, small voice that is all too often drowned out in everyday activity, it is in solitude that His voice is heard most clearly.

That's all well and good, you may be thinking, *but withdrawing to the desert is simply not practical for me.*

That being the case for most of us, there *is* a way in which every one of us can practice a life of daily solitude. That way is silence. Silence can be the private desert you carry with you wherever you go. But it's not easy. Besides speaking an average of forty to sixty thousand words a day, the average person will receive approximately fifteen messages every day from Madison Avenue, saying, "Buy me; taste me; drive me." Whether generated by Coca-Cola or Cadillac, a constant barrage of noise is hurled at us over billboard, radio, and television.

As a result, the value of words is diminished in our society. But this problem is not ours alone. Concerning much talk, an early church Father wrote the following: "When the door of a steam bath is left open, the heat escapes. Likewise, even though everything it says may indeed be good, the soul's cognizance of God is dissipated through the door of speech. Without the Holy Spirit to keep its understanding free of fantasy, the intellect pours out a welter of confused thoughts. Ideas of value always shun verbosity. Being foreign to confusion and fantasy, timely silence is precious, for it is nothing less than the mother of the wisest of our thoughts."

"That which was from the beginning, which we have heard, which we have seen with our eyes, which we have looked upon, and our hands have handled . . . That which we have seen and heard declare we unto you," said John, "that ye also may have fellowship with us: and truly our fellowship is with the Father, and with his Son Jesus Christ" (see 1 John 1:1–3). John shared freely, but he did not share that which he had not touched.

Could it be that the reason our sharing is sometimes not received or effective is due to the fact that we are speaking that which we ourselves have not touched, heard, or seen? Could it be that the reason we have not touched, heard, or seen is because we have not been in solitude? And could it be that we have not been in solitude because we have not desired to pay the price of silence?

"Learn to be quiet," said Paul (see 1 Thessalonians 4:11).

"Let every man be quick to hear and slow to speak," James echoes (see 1:19).

In Luke's Gospel, as I see the blossoming of John's ministry, and—to an infinitely greater degree—the ministry of Jesus, I realize that both ministries were birthed in times of silence. May the Lord call us into a greater understanding of solitude and silence that we might speak all the more effectively and live in true intimacy with the Father.

Luke 5:1
And it came to pass, that, as the people pressed upon him to hear the word of God, he stood by the lake of Gennesaret.

Over and over, Luke reiterates that the priority of Jesus' ministry was sharing the heart of the Father and the message of the kingdom.

Luke 5:2
And saw two ships standing by the lake: but the fishermen were gone out of them, and were washing their nets.

As we will see, one of these fishermen was Peter. If I were Peter, I would have been tempted not to wash my nets, but to sell them if, after spending an entire night fishing, I had caught nothing. But Peter is an example for me that just because, like him, I may come up empty in ministry, empty in what I put my hand to do, I'm not to sell my nets, I'm not to turn back, I'm not to give up because, like Peter, I don't know what will happen right around the corner.

Peter was washing his nets because if a net wasn't washed and then stretched, it would rot. Every time it was used, a net would have to be washed with fresh water and stretched if it was to remain useful. So, too, as fishers of men, we are nets that must be continually washed with the water of the Word and stretched by the Spirit if we are to remain useful.

You may be thinking, *Why should I get washed and stretched? The Lord isn't using me. Why bother?* But like Peter, you don't know what's going to happen tomorrow. When the Lord wants to use someone, He doesn't find the one who's rotten and brittle. No, He touches the one who's been washed in the water of the Word, who's been stretched and disciplined.

Luke 5:3
And he entered into one of the ships, which was Simon's, and prayed him that he would thrust out a little from the land. And he sat down, and taught the people out of the ship.

Using the water as a natural amplifier to preach to the crowds on the shore, Jesus asked Peter to take Him out in the boat. Why would He need Peter to take Him out? For the same reason He has you teaching Sunday school, parking cars, or working in the sound booth. I'm convinced part of the reason the Lord wants us active in service is because He knows if we're not, we won't be where we can hear the Word. Does the Lord need to use us? No. But we need to be used by Him in order that we might be in a position to hear from and grow in Him.

Luke 5:4
Now when he had left speaking, he said unto Simon, Launch out into the deep, and let down your nets for a draught.

It wasn't until Jesus had told Peter to "thrust out a little" (verse 3) that He told him to launch out into the deep. My problem is, I often say, "Launch me out into the deep, Lord," without first being willing to thrust out a little.

"Use me, Lord, to heal the blind, to raise the dead. But I don't want to teach first graders," we say. Yet Zechariah declared we are not to despise the days of small things (Zechariah 4:10). If you wonder why you aren't in the deeper waters of ministry, maybe it's because you haven't been obedient in launching out in the little things, the simple callings, the unnoticed tasks.

Luke 5:5 (a)
And Simon answering said unto him, Master, we have toiled all the night, and have taken nothing . . .

The Greek word translated "Master" literally means "Rabbi." Peter doesn't refer to Jesus as "Creator of all things," or "God of the Universe." Rather, He addresses Him as "Rabbi," as if to say, "Bible Teacher, we're the fishermen. We'll listen to what You have to say regarding spirituality, but fishing is our territory. And everyone knows that here in Galilee, we only fish at night."

Luke 5:5 (b)
. . . nevertheless at thy word I will let down the net.

"Lord, this doesn't make sense to me," Peter said. "Experience doesn't validate it practically. It's not the way we were taught to do it in fishing school. But Lord, at Your Word, I will do as You say."

Luke 5:6
And when they had this done, they enclosed a great multitude of fishes: and their net brake.

The Greek word translated "brake" speaks only of the beginning of the breaking process. In other words, the net was beginning to show signs of strain. Therefore, had it not been washed and stretched previously, it would have broken completely, and the catch would have been lost.

Luke 5:7
And they beckoned unto their partners, which were in the other ship, that they should come and help them. And they came, and filled both the ships, so that they began to sink.

The Lord spoke this verse to my heart when we at Applegate Christian Fellowship started our first outreach church and sent away a good chunk of our congregation. On the Sunday that was to happen, I had doubts because I really loved those people. Yet the Lord brought this little story to mind as if to say, "If you don't call for help, if you try and take in the haul all by yourself, your boat will sink, and everyone will lose." The Lord does not call us to be reservoirs or containers of His blessings. He calls us to be channels through which blessings, resources, and ministries can flow to others.

Luke 5:8
When Simon Peter saw it, he fell down at Jesus' knees, saying, Depart from me; for I am a sinful man, O Lord.

Peter's confession is what ministry is all about. Here's how to take in a haul in your own spiritual life: Don't try to earn it. Peter didn't say, "Ah yes. This makes perfect sense to me. I was faithful in launching out in little things. Then I was sitting in the boat taking in Your words eagerly. No wonder I am used in such a mighty way. No wonder I am a recipient of this great haul." No, He simply fell at Jesus' knees in utter humility.

I am convinced that the Lord is looking for people, organizations, and churches He can bless who will, like Peter, say, "We don't deserve this." Grace is the key to ministry, the key to prosperity, the key to victory in this body corporately and in our lives personally. The highest form of worship is when we're just amazed by how good God is to sinners like us.

Luke 5:9–11
For he was astonished, and all that were with him, at the draught of the fishes which they had taken: And so was also James, and John, the sons of Zebedee, which were partners with Simon. And Jesus said unto Simon, Fear not; from henceforth thou shalt catch men. And when they had brought their ships to land, they forsook all, and followed him.

My tendency would be to say, "Wow! Look what the Lord has given us. What a haul! How can we keep this flow going? The business will expand. We'll add more boats. We'll get a big warehouse. We'll increase our distribution throughout Galilee. This is terrific!" But that's not what these guys said. In leaving the fish, they said, in effect, "Forget the fish, the industry, even the ministry. Lord, it's You personally that we want." Jesus didn't ask them to leave the fish. They did so on their own, realizing that what they had striven for no longer mattered. That's why Peter will be used so effectively—because he left everything to pursue Jesus passionately.

Luke 5:12
And it came to pass, when he was in a certain city, behold a man full of leprosy: who seeing Jesus fell on his face, and besought him, saying, Lord, if thou wilt, thou canst make me clean.

A terrible, dreadful disease, leprosy is a picture of sin, for like sin, leprosy begins below the surface and then begins to spread and destroy. Like sin, leprosy is contagious, affecting not only the one who commits the sin, but those around him. So desperately did this man plagued with leprosy want to be changed that when he heard Jesus was coming into the area, he broke the rules forbidding lepers from entering any area where uncontaminated people were in order to meet Jesus.

The same is true for you and me. When we feel as though there is something eating at us, causing us to lose our sensitivity, the key is simply to go to Jesus.

"*Today* is the day of salvation," declared Paul. "*Now* is the time" (see 2 Corinthians 6:2). And the leper knew this.

Luke 5:13 (a)
And he put forth his hand, and touched him, saying, I will: be thou clean. And immediately the leprosy departed from him.

Jesus did not say, "Go to a seminar on overcoming leprosy." He said, "You need to be clean. You want to be clean. Therefore you will be clean right now."

Maybe that's a word for some who are feeling tainted, polluted, affected by some habit, some sin, something that has a grasp on you. At the moment you say from your heart, "I want to be clean," the Lord will say, "Be thou clean." Jesus not only spoke a word, but He touched this one who perhaps had not been touched in years due to his disease. So, too, the Lord doesn't hold His nose and look away from us in disgust. Others might be put off by your sin or irritated with your flaws, but not Jesus. He embraces us.

Luke 5:13 (b)–15
And he charged him to tell no man: but go, and shew thyself to the priest, and offer for thy cleansing, according as Moses commanded, for a testimony unto them. But so much the more went there a fame abroad of him: and great multitudes came together to hear, and to be healed by him of their infirmities.

Because He primarily came to save sinners rather than to work wonders, Jesus constantly sought to steer clear of theatrics in His ministry. Likewise, in our lives and ministries, the main thing is to keep the main thing the main thing. And the main thing is Jesus. "I came to you preaching nothing but Jesus Christ and Him crucified," Paul declared (see 1 Corinthians 2:2). Make Jesus the center of your ministry, and you'll be in harmony with what Paul did.

Luke 5:16, 17
And he withdrew himself into the wilderness, and prayed. And it came to pass on a certain day, as he was teaching, that there were Pharisees and doctors of the law sitting by, which were come out of every town of Galilee, and Judaea, and Jerusalem: and the power of the Lord was present to heal them.

According to 1 Corinthians 12:9, there are gifts of healing. This means that at a given time, the Lord releases certain gifts to give out to people who are hurting according to His sovereign will, according to His perfect plan. But I believe it is a misunderstanding for someone to say they have *the* gift of healing because there might be three gifts of healings or eight gifts to be distributed at that meeting or during that time. Why aren't we seeing more times when the power of the Lord to heal is present? Perhaps it's because we haven't followed the model of verse 16, where we read that Jesus was in the place of prayer. Prayer preceded power. There is an intricate connection between the two.

Luke 5:18, 19
And, behold, men brought in a bed a man which was taken with a palsy: and they sought means to bring him in, and to lay him before him. And when they could not find by what way they might bring him in because of the multitude, they went upon the housetop, and let him down through the tiling with his couch into the midst before Jesus.

In Jesus' day, roofs were constructed with dirt packed between beams. So it was that these men climbed up on the flat roof—where people would often either sit or where they would actually have gardens—and began to dig. This was not necessarily that unusual, for Josephus makes mention of the fact that coffins were sometimes lowered through the roofs of larger houses should someone die within.

Luke 5:20
And when he saw their faith, he said unto him, Man, thy sins are forgiven thee.

Tradition tells us this man was paralyzed because of a sexually transmitted disease. If this be true, the greatest need of this man would have been to know his sin had been forgiven. Such is the great need of any man or woman. People today cannot walk through life successfully or joyfully because they are haunted by sins committed previously. Thus, they're as paralyzed spiritually, emotionally, and relationally as this man was physically. Yet Jesus said, "Your sins are forgiven."

Perhaps the men who lowered their friend down were disappointed. After all, they had brought their friend to Jesus not to be forgiven, but to be healed. Yet Jesus knew that the deepest needs people have are not physical and material, but spiritual and eternal. Therefore, although those on the roof may have felt cheated, I suggest that the paralyzed man was elated.

Luke 5:21–25
And the scribes and the Pharisees began to reason, saying, Who is this which speaketh blasphemies? Who can forgive sins, but God alone? But when Jesus perceived their thoughts, he answering said unto them, What reason ye in your hearts? Whether is easier, to say, Thy sins be forgiven thee; or to say, Rise up and walk? But that ye may know that the Son of man hath power upon earth to forgive sins, (he said unto the sick of the palsy,) I say unto thee, Arise, and take up thy couch, and go into thine house. And immediately he rose up before them, and took up that whereon he lay, and departed to his own house, glorifying God.

How do we know sins are forgiven? How do we know the gospel is true? When people who were paralyzed and lame begin to walk and leap and praise God. When people who were paralyzed by sinfulness and foolishness embrace the Good News of forgiveness, the reality of a person's conversion is manifested in his walk. If there's no walk, it's just talk.

Luke 5:26
And they were all amazed, and they glorified God, and were filled with fear, saying, We have seen strange things to day.

Strange things indeed! The roof falling, a bed descending, Jesus forgiving, and a paralyzed man walking.

Luke 5:27, 28
And after these things he went forth, and saw a publican, named Levi, sitting at the receipt of custom: and he said unto him, Follow me. And he left all, rose up, and followed him.

Note the order: First, Matthew left all. Then he rose up. Oftentimes, I want to rise up before I leave all. But when you read the Gospels, it's an interesting study to see all of the things left behind by people who rose up to follow Jesus . . .

- Fishermen left their fish.
- The woman at the well left her waterpot.
- The widow of Nain left her son's casket.
- Lazarus left his grave clothes.
- Mary left the pieces of her alabaster box.
- Bartimaeus left his beggar's clothes.

The people who soar the highest in the Lord presently and who will be rewarded in the kingdom eternally are those who have left things behind. I've seen my own life limited in ministry when I was not willing to do so. Satan wants to weigh us down with the stuff of this world. Jesus wants to set us free.

Luke 5:29–32
And Levi made him a great feast in his own house: and there was a great company of publicans and of others that sat down with them. But their scribes and Pharisees murmured against his disciples, saying, Why do ye eat and drink with publicans and sinners? And Jesus answering said unto them, They that are whole need not a physician; but they that are sick. I came not to call the righteous, but sinners to repentance.

There were three places Jesus consistently frequented: open places, where He preached to the masses; quiet places, where He prayed to His Father; and festive places, where He would celebrate with the people. When you read the Gospels, you cannot help but see that Jesus loved to go to parties. Whether it was in the home of a religious leader like Simon the Pharisee or in that of Matthew, a tax collector with the riffraff of society, Jesus was often in attendance at feasts or festivals. This shouldn't surprise us, considering that the first public miracle He ever did was turning water into wine—not for the purpose of serving Communion, but simply in order that a wedding celebration could continue. Jesus had the ability to attract people to Himself constantly and to enjoy being with others immensely.

Luke 5:33
And they said unto him, Why do the disciples of John fast often, and make prayers, and likewise the disciples of the Pharisees; but thine eat and drink?

Indeed, the Pharisees did fast every Monday and Thursday and make prayers at noon, 3:00 P.M., and 6:00 P.M. daily. "Why don't Your disciples do the same?" they asked Jesus. In his first letter to Timothy, Paul said that there was coming a day when men would refuse marriage ceremonies (1 Timothy 4:3). Cyprian, the third-century Catholic Church leader was one such man. Marriage celebrations are too frivolous, he said. Parties and Christianity must be separated absolutely. Thus, the misconception began to grow, which is still with us today, that true spirituality and misery go hand in hand.

Luke 5:34, 35
And he said unto them, Can ye make the children of the bridechamber fast, while the bridegroom is with them? But the days will come, when the bridegroom shall be taken away from them, and then shall they fast in those days.

I suggest Jesus' answer speaks not only of His crucifixion prophetically, but of His place in our lives presently. A person who truly senses the presence of Jesus in his life will celebrate life as Jesus did. What about us? Have we lost sight of the fact that Jesus Christ came to bring us life and life abundantly, to let us experience real celebration? Would we be invited to a neighborhood function readily? Do our co-workers include us when they get together, or is there something about us so Pharisaical that they conveniently forget to invite us? Jesus was included in all kinds of parties. The common people embraced Him easily and loved to be around Him constantly. Why? Because He brought a higher degree of joy wherever He went.

I pray not only that we might be able to penetrate the parties of our society, that people would feel free to include us in their celebrations, but that we might do what Jesus did—for although He came to people as they were, He left them different than He found them. If you find the party or the people affecting you rather than you affecting them, watch out. But if, like Jesus, you can go into a place and make a difference by your joy and the unmistakable reality of God's work in your life, then go with God's blessing. Acts 8 tells us that the early church was so full of joy that they caused the entire city of Samaria to be full of joy as well. Celebrate your salvation, gang, as you infiltrate your situation. Realize that Jesus can handle your humanity, that He would rather see you a friend of sinners than a self-righteous Pharisee. Then go on to make a difference in your community

Luke 5:36
And he spake also a parable unto them; No man putteth a piece of a new garment upon an old; if otherwise, then both the new maketh a rent, and the piece that was taken out of the new agreeth not with the old.

Jesus is saying, "I didn't come to patch up the old religious system. I came to do something entirely new."

Luke 5:37, 38
And no man putteth new wine into old bottles; else the new wine will burst the bottles, and be spilled, and the bottles shall perish. But new wine must be put into new bottles; and both are preserved.

You can't put new wine in hardened old wineskins because when the new wine begins to ferment, the old hardened structure can't flex with it, causing the wineskin to burst and the new wine to be lost. When people try to put something of a new moving of the Lord into an old structure, they end up not only quenching the wine of the Spirit, but blowing apart the structure in the process.

This applies to people individually as well as to churches corporately, for here's what happens: When people are touched by the Lord and filled with the Spirit, the new wine of joy and vitality begins to bubble within them. But they will often discover that, as happened with Jesus following His own baptism, they will be driven into the wilderness, into a battle, into hard times. And it is at this point that, unwilling to face the difficulty or challenge, the temptation or trial, they burst, give up, and go back to the predictability of their previous ways where they can go to church occasionally, put a dollar in the offering, and play the game.

Does this mean we are doomed to become hardened old wineskins that cannot contain the new work of the Lord at any given time? I don't think so. You see, the Greek word translated "new" in relation to wine is *neos*" But the word translated "new" in relation to wineskins is *kainos* and literally means "renewed." In Bible days, wineskins were relatively expensive, so when they began to get hard, he who didn't have money for a new one would soak the old one in water until the elasticity and the flexibility returned. I find the analogy interesting because the Scriptures are likened unto water (John 15:3; Ephesians 5:26).

How do we stay flexible, usable, and contemporary in whatever the Lord might be doing both corporately and personally? We soak ourselves not in traditionalism or denominationalism, but in the Word. If we make the Word the priority of our life, the emphasis of our ministry, it will have a softening, renewing effect on us. But when the Bible no longer has predominance or priority in the life of a church or an individual and is instead replaced by programs, traditions, or denominational expectations, rigidity is sure to follow.

The entire Bible can be read aloud in seventy-one hours—or twelve minutes a day for a year. Most of us spend more time than that simply brushing our teeth or combing our hair. The question is not whether we have time to read the Word. The question is, do we choose to do it? There is only one place a believer cannot stay. He cannot stay put. That is, he is either growing and expanding in his walk, or he is shrinking and weakening in his walk. Your faith is either more radical today than it was last year, or it is less so. If we are determined together to soak in the Word, we will experience a continuing renewing—new discoveries, new understanding, constant softening. And the Lord will be able to pour new wine into our vessels.

Luke 5:39
No man also having drunk old wine straightway desireth new: for he saith, The old is better.

In a past election, after all the talk of throwing the incumbents out, 94 percent were voted back into office. Why? Because, although we complain about government and say we need new government, the fact is, we're comfortable with the familiar.

I don't need to soak in the Word any longer, you may be thinking. *I've got my knowledge of the Scriptures and my theology in place.* But because it's too late to soften the wineskin when new wine is poured, if you're not soaking in the Scriptures, you'll be left out. I'm not talking about losing your salvation, but about missing out on being on the cutting edge of what the Lord is and will be doing in these last days.

May He give us His wisdom.

6 Chapter 5 ended with Jesus talking about new wine and old wineskins, placing Himself and the Pharisees on a collision course that would center around their most important tradition: the Sabbath . . .

Luke 6:1, 2
And it came to pass on the second sabbath after the first, that he went through the corn fields; and his disciples plucked the ears of corn, and did eat, rubbing them in their hands. And certain of the Pharisees said unto them, Why do ye that which is not lawful to do on the sabbath days?

According to Levitical law, it was perfectly legal for travelers to pluck corn or grain from the fields they passed in order to sustain them on their journey (Deuteronomy 23:24, 25). Thus, the Pharisees had no problem with *what* Jesus and His disciples did. Rather, their accusation concerned *when* they did it. The Jews at this time—and many Orthodox Jews to this day—believe that Messiah will not come until the Sabbath is perfectly kept by the people of Israel. This is why the Pharisees were so intent on keeping Sabbath regulations. Yet in Acts 20, we see the church meeting not on the Sabbath, but on the first day of the week. Why? Under the Old Covenant, man had to work for six days before he could rest. Under the New Covenant, because of the work Jesus did on Calvary, man rests first. We see God's original intent concerning the Sabbath day in the fact that man was created on the sixth day, making his first full day one of rest.

Luke 6:3 (a)
And Jesus answering them said, Have ye not read . . .

I love this! Jesus doesn't begin to argue with them philosophically. Instead, He opens the Scriptures to them clearly. "My Word shall not return void," God declared, "but shall accomplish the purpose for which it was sent out" (see Isaiah 55:11). You might not see the effects right away, but like a time bomb, the Scripture you share will make its way into people's hearts and will eventually be brought powerfully and persuasively to their minds.

Luke 6:3 (b)
. . . so much as this, what David did . . .

"Have you not read what David did?" Jesus asked. So well did the Pharisees know the Scriptures that they could tell you how many letters were in the Old Testament, how many of each letter was in the Old Testament, and where the middle letter in the Old Testament was located. They were thoroughly immersed in the Scriptures. Of course they had read what David did—but that's the point, for although they had read it repeatedly, they had missed the meaning totally. So, too, like the Pharisees, we can be guilty of reading the Word over and over again, thinking we know what it's saying, but missing the very essence of its meaning. The Lord always wants to show us more in His Word than what we presently know, but it takes an open mind and a tender heart to receive it.

I think of Samuel. When he heard his name being called, Eli told him to say, "Speak, LORD, for thy servant heareth" (1 Samuel 3:9). Too often, we say just the opposite: "Listen, Lord, while Your servant speaks," as we approach the Word with our presuppositions or legalistic traditions. In Ezra 7:10, we read that Ezra prepared his own heart to seek the Lord and His law before he taught it to others. May that be true of us as well.

Luke 6:3 (c), 4
. . . when himself was an hungred, and they which were with him; how he went into the house of God, and did take and eat the shewbread, and gave also to them that were with him; which it is not lawful to eat but for the priests alone?

The holy bread was that which was placed in the tabernacle on the Sabbath day. Hungry, David and his men went into the place where only priests were allowed and ate of the bread therein (1 Samuel 21:6). In drawing attention to this account, Jesus gets to the heart of the issue—that human need must always have priority over religious traditions and regulations. Love is the key.

Luke 6:5
And he said unto them, That the Son of man is Lord also of the sabbath.

David was justified in eating the showbread, the Pharisees must have reasoned, because he was an anointed king and prophet. But they failed to realize that so too was the One who stood before them.

Luke 6:6, 7
And it came to pass also on another sabbath, that he entered into the synagogue and taught: and there was a man whose right hand was withered. And the scribes and Pharisees watched him, whether he would heal on the sabbath day; that they might find an accusation against him.

You who feel withered, paralyzed, struggling, know this: When Jesus comes into the meeting place, He is always drawn toward the one who is hurting the most. That is so unlike us. We tend to seek out those who are doing the best, the happiest, the spiritual ones. Not Jesus. He found the one who was experiencing paralysis because He's always drawn to the one with the greatest need.

Luke 6:8, 9
But he knew their thoughts, and said to the man which had the withered hand, Rise up, and stand forth in the midst. And he arose and stood forth. Then said Jesus unto them, I will ask you one thing; Is it lawful on the sabbath days to do good, or to do evil? to save life, or to destroy it?

In effect, Jesus was asking the Pharisees, "Who is in violation of the Sabbath?" "Me for healing, or you for plotting to take My life? Both are work."

Luke 6:10
And looking round about upon them all, he said unto the man, Stretch forth thy hand. And he did so: and his hand was restored whole as the other.

When told to stretch forth his hand, this man could have said, "I can't. I'm paralyzed." But because God's commandments are His "enablements," the moment he decided to obey, he was able to obey.

"Husbands, love your wives," the Word says (Ephesians 5:25).

"But I can't," we say. "You don't know my wife. You don't know my situation. I can't. I'm paralyzed." We can either make our lists of why we can't obey, or we can say, "Lord, You say to love my wife, and I will, knowing that as I do, You will enable me to do that which You've asked of me."

Luke 6:11
And they were filled with madness; and communed one with another what they might do to Jesus.

A paralyzed arm suddenly works. Yet the Pharisees are furious because it does so on the Sabbath.

Luke 6:12, 13
And it came to pass in those days, that he went out into a mountain to pray, and continued all night in prayer to God. And when it was day, he called unto him his disciples: and of them he chose twelve, whom also he named apostles.

From the group of disciples, or "disciplined ones"—those who were disciplined in learning and committed to studying—Jesus chose twelve apostles, or "sent out ones" as ambassadors to represent Him.

Luke 6:14–16
Simon, (whom he also named Peter,) and Andrew his brother, James and John, Philip and Bartholomew, Matthew and Thomas, James the son of Alphaeus, and Simon called Zelotes, and Judas the brother of James, and Judas Iscariot, which also was the traitor.

After establishing a new Sabbath, Jesus establishes a new nation. Twelve being the number of government, twelve being the number of tribes in Old Testament Israel, in choosing twelve apostles, Jesus establishes the new government of the kingdom.

For topical study of Luke 6:15 entitled "Real Zeal," turn to page 327.

Luke 6:17–20 (a)
And he came down with them, and stood in the plain, and the company of his disciples, and a great multitude of people out of all Judaea and Jerusalem, and from the sea coast of Tyre and Sidon, which came to hear him, and to be healed of their diseases; and they that were vexed with unclean spirits: and they were healed. And the whole multitude sought to touch him: for there went virtue out of him, and healed them all. And he lifted up his eyes on his disciples, and said . . .

The following teaching is often called the Sermon on the Mount. But I believe this is a misnomer, for Luke 6:17 tells us Jesus delivered it as He stood in the plain. Thus, I am personally convinced that, although it is an almost exact repetition of Jesus' sermon recorded in Matthew 5–7, it is, in fact, a separate sermon. I point this out because if indeed this was a sermon Jesus gave on more than one occasion, this tells me something. "I will not be negligent to put you in remembrance of these things though you know them until you be established in them," Peter said (see 2 Peter 1:12). Repetition is the mother of learning. Therefore, as a preacher, teacher, or Bible study leader, don't let the Enemy whisper in your ear, "You can't share that. That's too elementary. They've already heard that." And as a student, never think you know enough about any portion of the Word to never need to study it again. The question is not how *much* you know, but how *well* you know it.

The message Jesus had previously given on the mount and now gives on the plain is the message of the King. It was a message meant to drive people to the realization that they couldn't keep it, a message meant to drive people to the place of brokenness, a message meant to drive people to the Cross. Therefore, the only conclusion that can be drawn from the Sermon on the Mount, the Message on the Plain is not, "These are good words to live by," but, "This standard is impossible."

Thus, the one who grasps its meaning doesn't say, "I'm pretty good, but I'll try harder." No, he says, "I'm a sinner in desperate need of a Savior." Then, once he realizes he can't keep this standard on his own, once he is saved, the message becomes helpful to him as it delineates the ways in which the Spirit desires to work in him.

Jesus felt this sermon so significant that He repeated it almost verbatim. It is indeed the greatest sermon ever preached in the history of humanity. So simply read it and let the message of the kingdom impact you afresh . . .

Luke 6:20 (b)–49
. . . Blessed be ye poor: for yours is the kingdom of God. Blessed are ye that hunger now: for ye shall be filled. Blessed are ye that weep now: for ye shall laugh. Blessed are ye, when men shall hate you, and when they shall separate you from their company, and shall reproach you, and cast out your name as evil, for the Son of man's sake. Rejoice ye in that day, and leap for joy: for, behold, your reward is great in heaven: for in the like manner did their fathers unto the prophets.

But woe unto you that are rich! for ye have received your consolation. Woe unto you that are full! for ye shall hunger. Woe unto you that laugh now! for ye shall mourn and weep. Woe unto you, when all men shall speak well of you! for so did their fathers to the false prophets. But I say unto you which hear, Love your enemies, do good to them which hate you, Bless them that curse you, and pray for them which despitefully use you. And unto him that smiteth thee on the one cheek offer also the other; and him that taketh away thy cloke forbid not to take thy coat also. Give to every man that asketh of thee; and of him that taketh away thy goods ask them not again. And as ye would that men should do to you, do ye also to them likewise.

For if ye love them which love you, what thank have ye? for sinners also love those

that love them. And if ye do good to them which do good to you, what thank have ye? for sinners also do even the same. And if ye lend to them of whom ye hope to receive, what thank have ye? for sinners also lend to sinners, to receive as much again. But love ye your enemies, and do good, and lend, hoping for nothing again; and your reward shall be great, and ye shall be the children of the Highest: for he is kind unto the unthankful and to the evil. Be ye therefore merciful, as your Father also is merciful.

Judge not, and ye shall not be judged: condemn not, and ye shall not be condemned: forgive, and ye shall be forgiven: Give, and it shall be given unto you; good measure, pressed down, and shaken together, and running over, shall men give into your bosom. For with the same measure that ye mete withal it shall be measured to you again.

And he spake a parable unto them, Can the blind lead the blind? shall they not both fall into the ditch? The disciple is not above his master: but every one that is perfect shall be as his master. And why beholdest thou the mote that is in thy brother''s eye, but perceivest not the beam that is in thine own eye? Either how canst thou say to thy brother, Brother, let me pull out the mote that is in thine eye, when thou thyself beholdest not the beam that is in thine own eye? Thou hypocrite, cast out first the beam out of thine own eye, and then shalt thou see clearly to pull out the mote that is in thy brother's eye.

For a good tree bringeth not forth corrupt fruit; neither doth a corrupt tree bring forth good fruit. For every tree is known by his own fruit. For of thorns men do not gather figs, nor of a bramble bush gather they grapes. A good man out of the good treasure of his heart bringeth forth that which is good; and an evil man out of the evil treasure of his heart bringeth forth that which

is evil: for of the abundance of the heart his mouth speaketh.

And why call ye me, Lord, Lord, and do not the things which I say? Whosoever cometh to me, and heareth my sayings, and doeth them, I will shew you to whom he is like: He is like a man which built an house, and digged deep, and laid the foundation on a rock: and when the flood arose, the stream beat vehemently upon that house, and could not shake it: for it was founded upon a rock. But he that heareth, and doeth not, is like a man that without a foundation built an house upon the earth; against which the stream did beat vehemently, and immediately it fell; and the ruin of that house was great.

Let's pray. . . .

"The standards, Lord, of Your kingdom—of giving, blessing, forgiving—are qualities I lack in and of myself. Therefore, I need forgiveness, and I embrace You tonight as my Saviour. I bask, Lord, in Your grace. I plead Your blood. I invite You to come into my heart again, Lord. And in so doing, to allow my life to more completely display these qualities. Strip from me, Lord, hypocrisy. Take from me, Lord, attitudes of judgment or condemnation. Keep me, Lord, from being one who hears the Word, but doesn't build my life thereon. I pray that my life might truly be built upon the Rock, that as the storms come, I might stand in that day. So by the Spirit, in the Spirit, I absorb these teachings, this message, and pray that I might do unto others as I would that they would do unto me. Make me like You, Jesus. Allow me to be one who is more concerned about compassion than tradition. Allow me to be one who responds to Your commandments rather than argue why they can't be done. I pause in Your presence, asking You to do Your work in my life. Set me free, Lord, to be a liberator and lover of others as I look to and love You."

REAL ZEAL
A Topical Study of
Luke 6:15

Scanning His group of "disciplined ones," one of the men Jesus chose was Simon Zelotes, or Simon the Zealot—a radical choice, considering that the Zealots were a political party single-minded in their agenda to overthrow the Romans using whatever means necessary. Determined to undermine the Romans at any cost, Zealots were known for carrying large, hooked knives under their garments to use on unsuspecting Romans every chance they had. When Jesus called him, perhaps Simon thought, *Good move. Jesus can use a guy like me. I mean, if we're going to see His new kingdom established, we've got to get rid of the Romans. And I'm the guy to do it. I'll fit into His strategy perfectly.*

But when Jesus went on to choose Matthew, a tax collector who worked for the dreaded Romans, Simon had to rely on Jesus—the only One who could bring two people of such diverse political philosophies together in unity. I believe Jesus still chooses people like Simon—people who will pay the price and expend the energy, people who will move with enthusiasm, people who are zealous. The Word addresses the subject of zeal very directly. Look with me at four examples of misdirected zeal seen in Scripture.

Business

Looking around our culture, we see people consumed with getting their business set up or their finances in order. But at a period when the Jewish people were building bigger houses and driving faster chariots, at a point in their history when they were attempting to make great strides financially, the Lord sent Haggai to talk to Jewish business people who were caught up in developing their companies. "You've sown much," he said. "You've worked hard, but you've reaped little. You drink much and you eat much, but you are not filled. And when you earn your wages, you put them into a pocket which has holes in it" (see 1:6).

Do you relate to this? You're working hard, but you're not reaping what you hoped you would? You're eating more, but you're not as satisfied as you thought you'd be? Haggai said the reason for this was because, although the people were building their houses and businesses zealously, the temple of the Lord lay in ruins needlessly. He went on to say that if they would seek first the kingdom, if they would get involved in the temple construction, the Lord would bless them abundantly. Jesus said the same thing when He said, "Seek first the Kingdom and His righteousness and everything else will fall into place" (see Matthew 6:33).

Politics

We not only see people in our society zealous about business, but those who are zealous about politics. In the Old Testament, we find the story of another who was zealous politically . . .

After three years of famine in the land of Israel, David inquired of the Lord the reason. And the Lord said, "It is for Saul and for his bloody house because he slew the Gibeonites" (see 2 Samuel 21:1). Catch the scene: Shortly after Joshua came into the Promised Land, he was duped into making a peace treaty with the Gibeonites (Joshua 9). But when Saul became king, he thought it politically wise to rid his kingdom of the Gibeonites. And now, years later, God explained to David that there was a dryness in the land because in his political zeal, Saul destroyed an entire group of people with whom he should have kept the treaty made by Joshua.

I still hear the voice of Saul being sounded throughout our land by those who say, "We shouldn't have to worry about homeless people," or "Let the illegal aliens go back to their own countries. We shouldn't have to take care of them." Sometimes zealous people can lack the compassion and tenderness of the Lord in such a way that it brings grief to the Father. Am I arguing for a politically liberal philosophy? No, I am simply saying that in their zeal over political causes, people can cause great hurt to others and deep grief to the heart of God.

Fitness

In this coming year, as a nation, we will spend a collective $2.5 billion on health club fees alone. Yet studies show that even if every disease were wiped out in our society, if heart problems were no longer an issue, and if there were no more pollutants in our air, the human body is so designed that the average person cannot live past eighty-five years of age. Therefore fitness is a losing battle! Paul the apostle specifically declared that bodily exercise profits but a little (1 Timothy 4:8). Does this mean physical exercise is wrong? Of course not. We have a responsibility to make sure our bodies, the temples of the Spirit, can function. But if you are known as a fitness fanatic, if physical exercise is what you think about and live for, your zeal is misdirected.

Business, politics, and fitness—these are all avenues of misguided zeal that abound in our culture. But add to this list religious zeal, for such zeal is misdirected in the following ways . . .

Partial

Woe unto you, scribes and Pharisees, hypocrites! for ye pay tithe of mint and anise and cummin, and have omitted the weightier matters of the law, judgment, mercy, and faith: these ought ye to have done, and not to leave the other undone. Ye blind guides, which strain at a gnat, and swallow a camel.   Matthew 23:23, 24

Numbering six thousand, the Pharisees were so zealous in trying to keep even the most minute details and regulations of the law that they even tithed their grains of spices, all the while ignoring the weightier matters of righteousness, mercy, and love. And in so doing, they were in effect straining gnats out of their soup while swallowing camels.

Boastful

And he said, Come with me, and see my zeal for the LORD. So they made him ride in his chariot.   2 Kings 10:16

As evidenced in 2 Kings 9–10, Jehu was not a godly king. Yet when asked if his heart was right, he didn't hesitate to say, "Come and see my zeal for the Lord."

Hurtful

Concerning zeal, persecuting the church; touching the righteousness which is in the law, blameless.   Philippians 3:6

Paul was absolutely convinced he was right in persecuting Christians—until one day, headed toward Damascus, a bright light knocked him to the ground, and he realized that, although his religious zeal was sincere, he was sincerely wrong. So, too, regarding my political, sociological, or philosophical opinions, I might find down the road, like Paul, that although I was sincere, I was sincerely wrong in beating people up verbally or cornering them intellectually.

You will always know that zeal is a false religious zeal if it is partial, if it is boastful, or if it is hurtful. The only zeal God can use is the zeal seen in Jesus—not religious zeal, but righteous zeal. Seeing those who charged exorbitant rates to exchange currency or for the purchase of animals to sacrifice, Jesus drove them from the temple. And His disciples remembered that it was written, "The zeal of thine house hath eaten me up" (John 2:17). Jesus was consumed with zeal, enthusiasm, energy for His Father's house, His Father's work, for the things of the kingdom. If there's no other reason why you and I should be zealous, let this be the first and foremost: The model and example of Jesus. Scripture tells us that the zeal modeled perfectly by Jesus consists of four elements . . .

Repentance

I know thy works, that thou art neither cold nor hot: I would thou wert cold or hot . . . be zealous therefore, and repent.   Revelation 3:15, 19

Jesus indicts the church at Laodicea for their lack of zeal. If they were hot, He could use them. If they were cold, He could convict them. But being lukewarm, they could be neither used nor convicted. The solution? They were to repent.

For godly sorrow worketh repentance to salvation not to be repented of: but the sorrow of the world worketh death.   2 Corinthians 7:10

The word "repent" means "to change direction one hundred eighty degrees." True, godly sorrow manifests itself in turning one's back on that which is wrong and moving in a brand new direction.

Prayer

> *Epaphras, who is one of you, a servant of Christ, saluteth you, always labouring fervently for you in prayers, that ye may stand perfect and complete in all the will of God.*
>
> Colossians 4:12

Epaphras was one who prayed not half-heartedly but zealously that people would do well in their walk with the Lord. In this, I am reminded of an Old Testament account. . . .

Facing war against the Syrians, Joash, king of Judah, went to visit a feeble and dying Elisha, who told him to open the window and shoot an arrow toward Syria. After Joash did this, Elisha told him to smite his remaining arrows on the ground. So Joash tapped them on the ground three times. Scripture records that at this point, Elisha was "wroth" with Joash, saying, "Thou shouldest have smitten five or six times; then hadst thou smitten Syria till thou hadst consumed it; whereas now thou shalt smite Syria but thrice" (2 Kings 13:19).

Because Joash lacked zeal, his victory would not be complete. And the same is true for us. I wonder how often we miss out on that which the Lord would do for us, in us, and through us because, like Joash, we "tap the arrows" a few times rather than energetically, zealously, and expectantly praying with great fervency.

Why must we pray zealously? Why must we keep asking, keep seeking, and keep knocking (Matthew 7:7)? Why does the Lord want us to come to Him continually? After all, He knows what our need is. Does He want us to grovel and beg? No. The reason He asks us to keep coming, to keep seeking, and to keep beating the arrows is simply because He enjoys our company. He enjoys hearing from us. He enjoys spending time with us.

Righteous Works

> *And, behold, one of the children of Israel came and brought unto his brethren a Midianitish woman in the sight of Moses, and in the sight of all the congregation of the children of Israel, who were weeping before the door of the tabernacle of the congregation. And when Phinehas, the son of Eleazar, the son of Aaron the priest, saw it, he rose up from among the congregation, and took a javelin in his hand. . . .*
>
> Numbers 25:6, 7

Because of their blatant, intentional immorality, the Lord sent a plague upon the people of Israel to correct them, to adjust them, and to keep them from continuing in their iniquity. But during this time of repentance, when Phinehas saw an Israelite walking flagrantly with a Moabite woman on his arm, he followed them into their tent and stuck a javelin through them both. And in so doing, he went on record by zealously taking a stand for God's righteousness.

We always need to pray. But there are times to grab the javelin as well, to deal with issues zealously for the sake of God's name. We must deal a deathblow to those areas in our lives that are Moabitish in nature by driving the spear of the Word right through them and allowing them no more place in our lives. Saying, "Maybe someday I won't commit that sin anymore," is not the Lord's way. Rather, His way is to be zealous for righteousness as was Phinehas.

Service

For I know the forwardness of your mind, for which I boast of you to them of Macedonia, that Achaia was ready a year ago; and your zeal hath provoked very many.
                                                                2 Corinthians 9:2

The Corinthians collected money a year in advance to give generously to those in need. Paul would go on to say that the Lord loves a cheerful giver (2 Corinthians 9:7). Therefore, if you're giving begrudgingly, or out of expectation, don't give. But if you can give, saying, "I can't wait for the offering basket to come my way so I can give away part of my selfishness, my self-centeredness and become more like Jesus,"—give zealously and joyously.

A key concept biblically is to live zealously. How? The only way I know to get hot and to stay hot is to live near the Son. Therefore, if you stay close to Jesus, if you purpose in your heart that He will have priority in your day, you will find the zeal of Jesus reflected toward you and radiating from you. May this be true of each of us.

In Jesus' Name.

7 After the disciples had opportunity to hear instruction from Jesus' lips in chapter 7, they have opportunity to hear His heart in chapter 8. One of the many beautiful things about Jesus is that, not only is He the Instructor par excellence who gives insightful, impacting teachings to us, but He is also the Shepherd who goes before us. The four vignettes that follow deal with a saddened centurion, a weeping widow, a perplexed prophet, and a heartbroken harlot. In each case, Jesus shows His heart of compassion toward them, which blesses me greatly because I know He cares about me in the same way.

Luke 7:1, 2
Now when he had ended all his sayings in the audience of the people, he entered into Capernaum. And a certain centurion's servant, who was dear unto him, was sick, and ready to die.

Centurions are mentioned four times in the New Testament . . .

- As we will see, this centurion is a man of humility and faith.
- It was a centurion on the hill of Calvary who said to Jesus, "Truly this was the Son of God" (Matthew 27:54).
- A centurion named Cornelius was the first Gentile to be converted and baptized in the Spirit (Acts 10).
- A centurion named Julius befriended Paul and assisted him on his journey toward Rome (Acts 27).

The Jews didn't like the Romans in general and centurions in particular. Yet the New Testament paints each of these centurions in a positive light.

Luke 7:3
And when he heard of Jesus, he sent unto him the elders of the Jews, beseeching him that he would come and heal his servant.

Many people are waiting for their ship to come in. The problem is, they never sent one out. Not so with this centurion. He expended the energy and made the effort to send a deputation of Jewish elders to approach the Rabbi of whom he had heard marvelous things.

Luke 7:4–7 (a)
And when they came to Jesus, they besought him instantly, saying, That he was worthy for whom he should do this: For he loveth our nation, and he hath built us a synagogue. Then Jesus went with them. And when he was now not far from the house, the centurion sent friends to him, saying unto him, Lord, trouble not thyself: for I am not worthy that thou shouldest enter under my roof: Wherefore neither thought I myself worthy to come unto thee . . .

His care for his servant and his commitment to the Jews marked this Gentile centurion as a unique individual. No wonder he was highly esteemed by the Jewish elders, who said to Jesus, "He is worthy of Your help."

"No, I'm not," said the humble centurion. Indeed, the greater a person is, the more humble he will be. The smarter a person is, the more he will realize how little he knows.

Luke 7:7 (b), 8
. . . but say in a word, and my servant shall be healed. For I also am a man set under authority, having under me soldiers, and I say unto one, Go, and he goeth; and to another, Come, and he cometh; and to my servant, Do this, and he doeth it.

One who was accustomed to having his commands obeyed without question, the centurion would have understood the power of the spoken word.

Luke 7:9, 10
When Jesus heard these things, he marvelled at him, and turned him about, and said unto the people that followed him, I say unto you, I have not found so great faith, no, not in Israel. And they that were sent, returning to the house, found the servant whole that had been sick.

This centurion was one of two people in the entire New Testament of whom Jesus marveled concerning their faith. The other was a Syro-Phoenician woman. These two Gentiles lacked the stories, the oracles, the heritage, and the history of the Jews. Instead, they simply had faith to believe Jesus' authority. One of the ways to kill faith is to hang around religious people. Religious people will explain to you why your prayers aren't answered, why your faith just won't work. Sometimes it's the Gentiles—those who take the Word at face value—whom the Lord loves to honor. The Jews had their theology refined, but it was the Gentiles who had faith who caused Jesus to marvel.

Luke 7:11, 12
And it came to pass the day after, that he went into a city called Nain; and many of his disciples went with him, and much people. Now when he came nigh to the gate of the city, behold, there was a dead man carried out, the only son of his mother, and she was a widow: and much people of the city was with her.

Jesus went twenty-five miles out of His way to Nain and therein found a miracle waiting to happen.

Luke 7:13
And when the Lord saw her, he had compassion on her, and said unto her, Weep not.

Compassion is your pain in my heart. It's a quality sadly lacking in our society, but one Jesus exemplified constantly. He is called the Man of Sorrows because He took the pain of people into His own heart. And yet the irony is that Hebrews 1:9 tells us He was anointed with the oil of gladness above His fellows. How could He be the Man of Sorrows and yet anointed with the oil of gladness above any other human being who has ever lived—radiating such joy that multitudes would be drawn to Him? These are two qualities that seem contradictory—until we remember the words He taught us when He said, "Blessed, or happy, are they who mourn, for they shall be comforted" (see Matthew 5:4). One of the keys of happiness is to allow sorrow to penetrate your heart.

Eastern mysticism totally rejects this viewpoint. A foundational principle of Buddha's teaching was to avoid pain and sorrow, for if mankind would enter into the state of detached feeling, of nirvana, there would be no more jealousy or envy, no more wars and fighting. This thinking has affected us more than we know. Having permeated the '60s culture, it was Eastern thought that caused us to say, "I am a rock. I am an island," as we sang along with Simon and Garfunkel.

Jesus, however, came on the scene and annihilated that mentality by saying, "Happy is the man not who detaches himself, but who mourns, who is heartbroken, for he is the one who will be comforted."

"Comfort" is an old English word containing the same root as that of the word "fortify." In other words, Jesus said that the one who is mourning will also be the one who is fortified.

In the Garden of Gethsemane, so deeply was Jesus mourning that blood burst from His forehead. And yet Luke tells us that even as He was agonizing in prayer, an angel came and comforted, sustained, and fortified Him (Luke 22:43, 44).

When is the last time I have been at the place of being pained in prayer for someone else's problem, someone else's sin? Could it be that I am not comforted by the Comforter or the angelic presence because I am not doing what Jesus did? Blessed are they who mourn, who plunge into life and feel the pain of life. They shall be comforted.

Are you unhappy? Do you feel comfortless? Take seriously what Jesus said. It's an irony. It's a mystery. It runs crosscurrent to the thinking of our society. And yet the key to happiness is to mourn for others, to carry someone else's pain in your heart.

Luke 7:14–17

And he came and touched the bier: and they that bare him stood still. And he said, Young man, I say unto thee, Arise. And he that was dead sat up, and began to speak. And he delivered him to his mother. And there came a fear on all: and they glorified God, saying, That a great prophet is risen up among us; and, That God hath visited his people. And this rumour of him went forth throughout all Judaea, and throughout all the region round about.

In this account of Jesus' compassion, we see two groups of individuals—two only sons, two hurting people—and one amazing miracle.

For topical study of Luke 7:11–17 entitled "Freedom from Death's Fear," turn to page 337.

Luke 7:18, 19

And the disciples of John shewed him of all these things. And John calling unto him two of his disciples sent them to Jesus, saying, Art thou he that should come? or look we for another?

Of Messiah, not only did Isaiah prophesy that the sick would be healed and the dead resurrected, but that prison doors would open. Yet, here's John the Baptist, the herald of the King, in prison. "Everyone else is feeling the Lord's compassion, but what about me?" he must have wondered.

Luke 7:20–23

When the men were come unto him, they said, John Baptist hath sent us unto thee, saying, Art thou he that should come? or look we for another? And in that same hour he cured many of their infirmities and plagues, and of evil spirits; and unto many that were blind he gave sight. Then Jesus answering said unto them, Go your way, and tell John what things ye have seen and heard; how that the blind see, the lame walk, the lepers are cleansed, the deaf hear, the dead are raised, to the poor the gospel is preached. And blessed is he, whosoever shall not be offended in me.

Concerning whether or not He was the Messiah, Jesus' answer to John's disciples was for them to tell John the things they had seen Him do. But because, according to verse 18, they had already told John these things, it was as if Jesus' message to John was: "You've been hearing about the things that are happening, and yet you're only concerned about what is not happening." And the same is true of us. . . .

For topical study of Luke 7:22 entitled "Dealing with Doubt," turn to page 340.

Luke 7:24–28 (a)

And when the messengers of John were departed, he began to speak unto the people concerning John, What went ye out into the wilderness for to see? A reed shaken with the wind? But what went ye out for to see? A man clothed in soft raiment? Behold, they which are gorgeously apparelled, and live delicately, are in kings' courts. But what went ye out for to see? A prophet? Yea, I say unto you, and much more than a prophet. This is he, of whom it is written, Behold, I send my messenger before thy face, which shall prepare thy way before thee. For I say unto you, Among those that are born of women there is not a greater prophet than John the Baptist . . .

It wasn't until after John's disciples had left that Jesus honored John. So, too, you might feel like a failure, that you haven't done this or accomplished that, that you're in error here or unproductive there. But if you hang in there with the Lord and continue to walk with Him by faith, when you get to heaven, you will hear the words, "Well done, good and faithful servant." In allowing you to struggle presently, the Lord wants you to wrestle through and keep going. But there will come a time when we will truly know how He sees and evaluates us. And I think we will be exceedingly surprised at even the simple things we did that He noticed (Matthew 10:42).

Luke 7:28 (b)
. . . but he that is least in the kingdom of God is greater than he.

John was the greatest of all prophets. And yet guess who is greater than John? You are. Everyone who is a born-again believer, who is part of the kingdom, is greater than John. Why?

- John was part of the Old Testament economy.
  You are a New Testament believer.
- John was a herald of the King.
  You are a friend of the King.
- John was a friend of the Bridegroom.
  You are the Bride of the Bridegroom.

As a person, you are not greater than this bold and fearless prophet. But because of your position in Christ, you are not only greater, you're perfect (Colossians 1:28). If you have no other reason to be elated today, let that alone suffice.

Luke 7:29–35
And all the people that heard him, and the publicans, justified God, being baptized with the baptism of John. But the Pharisees and lawyers rejected the counsel of God against themselves, being not baptized of him. And the Lord said, Whereunto then shall I liken the men of this generation? and to what are they like? They are like unto children sitting in the marketplace, and calling one to another, and saying, We have piped unto you, and ye have not danced; we have mourned to you, and ye have not wept. For John the Baptist came neither eating bread nor drinking wine; and ye say, He hath a devil. The Son of man is come eating and drinking; and ye say, Behold a gluttonous man, and a winebibber, a friend of publicans and sinners! But wisdom is justified of all her children.

The wisdom of the Lord's way is not seen intellectually nor argued logically, but it is seen in the transformation of people practically. Look at the children of the Lord, born-again believers, and you see people who were once strung out on drugs, hooked on pornography, or held captive by materialism; people with messed-up marriages, hurting families, and broken lives who are now in the process of being perfected. God's wisdom is justified in changed lives. Let the Pharisees argue all they want. The irrefutable fact is that lives are changed.

Luke 7:36–38 (a)
And one of the Pharisees desired him that he would eat with him. And he went into the Pharisee's house, and sat down to meat. And, behold, a woman in the city, which was a sinner, when she knew that Jesus sat at meat in the Pharisee's house, brought an alabaster box of ointment, and stood at his feet behind him weeping, and began to wash his feet with tears. . . .

This woman was not, as is often suggested, Mary Magdalene from whom Jesus cast seven demons (Luke 8:2). Nor is she Mary, the sister of Martha and Lazarus, who anointed Jesus' head with ointment and who wiped His feet with her hair in the house of Simon the leper (John 12). This Mary, in the house of Simon the Pharisee, did not feel the openness to presume to anoint Jesus' head as did Mary of Bethany, but rather in brokenness and humility anointed His feet.

I believe this differentiation is an important one. In my opinion, pastors and worship leaders err when they try to get people to be more intimate in expression than their level of commitment warrants. If worship is hard or unnatural for you, perhaps it is because your knowledge of Jesus is shallow. Therefore, the problem lies not in your manner of worship, but in your distance from Him. Get to know Him better, and you will find worship flowing more freely. Mary anointed Jesus' head because she knew Him well.

Luke 7:38 (b)
. . . and did wipe them with the hairs of her head, and kissed his feet, and anointed them with the ointment.

Mary used her hair—one of the "tools of her trade" with which she previously had seduced men—to minister to Jesus.

Luke 7:39
Now when the Pharisee which had bidden him saw it, he spake within himself, saying, This man, if he were a prophet, would have

known who and what manner of woman this is that toucheth him: for she is a sinner.

Like Simon, I can spot certain sins in people miles away. Why? Because they're the same sins that reside in me. Therefore, if you are one who is cynical, if you are one who constantly finds fault with this person or that group, more than likely you're the one with the problem.

Luke 7:40–42
And Jesus answering said unto him, Simon, I have somewhat to say unto thee. And he saith, Master, say on. There was a certain creditor which had two debtors: the one owed five hundred pence, and the other fifty. And when they had nothing to pay, he frankly forgave them both. Tell me therefore, which of them will love him most?

"Simon," Jesus said, "the woman's sins are of the flesh; yours are of the spirit. Her sins are observable; yours are more subtle—but also more damnable."

Luke 7:43
Simon answered and said, I suppose that he, to whom he forgave most. And he said unto him, Thou hast rightly judged.

Fellow Pharisee, take hope. Jesus knew Simon had problems. But He still accepted his invitation to dinner. We know the Lord accepts the invitation of the repentant sinner, but sometimes we forget that He not only accepts the invitation of the self-righteous Pharisee, but also finds something to commend in him.

Luke 7:44–48
And he turned to the woman, and said unto Simon, Seest thou this woman? I entered into thine house, thou gavest me no water for my feet: but she hath washed my feet with tears, and wiped them with the hairs of her head. Thou gavest me no kiss: but this woman since the time I came in hath not ceased to kiss my feet. My head with oil thou didst not anoint: but this woman hath anointed my feet with ointment. Wherefore I say unto thee, Her sins, which are many, are forgiven; for she loved much: but to whom little is forgiven, the same loveth little. And he said unto her, Thy sins are forgiven.

There's not a person who isn't as great a sinner

as this one who was known throughout the city as a prostitute. Oh, perhaps we're not guilty of the obvious sin because ours is a sin of attitude, thought, or corruption within. Yet the one who is truly aware of his sin will, like this woman, be heartbroken and repentant.

Luke 7:49
And they that sat at meat with him began to say within themselves, Who is this that forgiveth sins also?

"Who is this One who can say another's sins are forgiven?" the Pharisees scoffed. The reason Jesus could say such a thing to the woman who kissed His feet, wiped them with her hair, and anointed them is because He will be kissed again by Judas, washed and anointed again by the woman who prepared His body for burial. Therefore, because of His death and resurrection, His is very definitely and uniquely the power to forgive sin.

Luke 7:50 (a)
And he said to the woman, Thy faith hath saved thee . . .

Although she was commended for a tremendous demonstration of love in washing Jesus' feet and drying them with her hair, it was not this woman's love that saved her. It was her faith. Yes, true faith will always manifest itself in love (Galatians 5:6). But it is faith that sees the invisible, hears the inaudible, believes the incredible, and does the impossible. It is faith that makes things happen (Matthew 17:20). It is faith that pleases God (Hebrews 11:6).

Luke 7:50 (b)
. . . go in peace.

In previous generations, Christians would go to the altar, confess their sins, weep before the Lord, and go their way with peace in their hearts. Now they seem to prefer a counselor's office. But it is those who are broken before the Lord who find healing from the Lord. The key is to be broken like Mary rather than self-sufficient like Simon. Our sins are many; our failures are great. But we don't need to mask them, hide them, deny them, or defend them. All we need to do is confess them in brokenness as, like Mary, we spend time at His feet.

FREEDOM FROM DEATH'S FEAR
A Topical Study of
Luke 7:11–17

He was a professional thief. His name stirred fear in the hearts of even the most rugged frontiersman as sure as the desert wind stirred the tumbleweeds. From 1875 to 1883, he successfully held up twenty-seven Wells Fargo stagecoaches. And as amazing as this is, he did so without firing a single shot. His weapons? Fear and intimidation. When a stagecoach driver looked down and saw a man riding alongside whose face was entirely covered with a black hood, he knew he was about to be held up by Black Bart and that he was foolish to fight him. In newspapers and journals from San Francisco to New York City, he was known as one of the most notorious bandits of all time.

Black Bart reminds me of another who haunts all of humanity, one who Jesus called a thief and a robber, a liar and a murderer (John 8:44). His weapons, like Black Bart's, consist of intimidation and fear—especially the fear of death . . .

Forasmuch then as the children are partakers of flesh and blood, he also himself likewise took part of the same; that through death he might destroy him that had the power of death, that is, the devil; and deliver them who through fear of death were all their lifetime subject to bondage.

Hebrews 2:14, 15

Although death is something we don't like to think about or talk about, it is something we deal with constantly. Oh, it might not be the fear of physical death that haunts us. It might be the death of a relationship, a marriage, a business. This spiritual Black Bart, identified in Scripture as Satan, intimidates people constantly with the fear of death and holds them in this bondage all of their lives. But Jesus came not only to meet death head-on, but to conquer it completely in order that we might be set free.

In our text, we see Jesus and death meeting face-to-face in an encounter that is not accidental, but oh, so intentional as Jesus goes twenty-five miles out of His way to the little town of Nain . . .

Two Crowds

In Nain we see two groups of people: one going into the city rejoicing, the other leaving the city weeping. The group going into the city was rejoicing because they were traveling with Jesus. The group leaving the city was weeping, knowing nothing about Jesus.

I suggest every single one of us is in one of these two crowds right now. Either we are traveling with Jesus to the city, or we are traveling without Him to the cemetery. If we're traveling with Him, to what city are we headed? To the same one for which Abraham looked: the city which is solid and real, satisfying and eternal, the city that has foundations, whose builder and maker is God (Hebrews 11:10). Abraham knew such a city would not be found in Mesopotamia, Babylon, New York, or Oregon. He knew the city for which he longed would only be found in eternity. And thus he could head toward it rejoicing.

> Suppose you are an ice skater, and right before you're ready to take to the ice in the final phase of the competition, your coach tells you your preliminary scores are so far ahead of everyone else's that even if you get "0" in the final phase, you'll win. This information would enable you to be as daring and creative as you would want because you'd have nothing to lose.

So, too, life becomes joyful and daring to the one who is not living for this world. Because the pressure is off, because he realizes the gold medal of heaven is already his, he can be carefree and creative (John 14:2). Not so the crowd traveling to the cemetery. Regardless of how popular or powerful they are on earth, they are in bondage to the fear of the death awaiting them.

Two Sons

Not only were there two crowds, but two only sons. The son who had once lived was now dead. The Son who was now living was destined to die.

In the days before Social Security or Welfare, having lost her husband and now her only son, this widow would have no one to look out for her socially or financially. That is why God's only Son, the Son destined to die, was moved with compassion. Jesus uniquely knew His mission was death. In a very real sense, as the Lamb slain before the foundation of the world, He was dead before He lived (Revelation 13:8). Slain in eternity past, He entered the time/space continuum wrapped in swaddling clothes, assuming the appearance of a mummy. And so it was that the Father's only Son, destined to die, encountered the woman's only son, destined to live.

Two Sufferers

In addition to two crowds and two sons, we see two sufferers.

Jesus exuded such abundance of life that people loved to be with Him. Thus, He was called a winebibber and a glutton by His enemies (Luke 7:34). At the same time, He is and always will be the Man of Sorrows (Isaiah 53:3). He was not the Man of Sorrows because He was depressed about His own situation, but because He had such great compassion. That is, He carried the pain of others in His heart.

"Weep not," Jesus said to the woman.
"Arise," He said to the young man.
"Come up," He will say to us as He calls us to meet Him in the air.

He who lives in this hope will be free from the fear of death that keeps people in bondage all of their days. Like birth, the process of death is painful. Nonetheless, who of us would say to the unborn baby, "Don't come out. Stay in there. Your skull will be contracted. Your shoulders will be squeezed. Your body will be covered with fluid. Your best bet is to stay in the womb forever"? Not one of us would tell a baby this because not one of us remembers the pain we went through when we were born. Yes, the process was painful, but there was a whole new life awaiting us—including waves to surf, mountains to ski, people to meet, things to learn—a dimension infinitely greater than the dark confines of the womb.

So, too, death was never meant to hurt. When, after He had lived thirty-three years, Jesus was transfigured on Mount Hermon, He began to glow. So, too, I believe God's intention was that after man had lived sinlessly on earth, he would be transfigured and ushered into heaven. But man sinned. Therefore, part of the repercussion of sin is that now, our moving into eternity, like being born, is painful. We watch someone dying and our heart breaks. But the people in heaven are not saying, "Stay on earth" any more than we would tell the unborn baby to stay in the womb. They're saying, "Get out of there! Come up here! There's a new dimension up here more radical in comparison to earth than the difference between the world and the womb. In heaven, there is joy unspeakable and full of glory, for eyes have not seen nor ears heard the wonderful things God has prepared for those who love Him" (see 1 Corinthians 2:9).

Yes, moving into eternity can be painful because of sin. But just as we have forgotten the pain of our own birthing process, so, too, in heaven, the pain of our death will not even be a distant memory.

Even if the Lord never answers another of my prayers; even if I never sense another feeling of fellowship with Him; even if I never gain another insight from His Word, I'm going to heaven, and that alone is enough. We are a saved people, gang, freed from the fear of what is beyond.

After eight years, Black Bart was finally apprehended. At his arrest, one of the U.S. marshals pulled the black hood from his head to discover not the desperado from Death Valley as legend held him, but rather a squeaky-voiced, mild-mannered druggist from Decatur, Illinois. The reason Black Bart never fired a shot is because he never had a bullet. His only weapons were fear and intimidation.

So, too, because Satan was defeated and death destroyed on the Cross of Calvary, we can join Paul in proclaiming, "O death, where is thy sting? O grave, where is thy victory?" (1 Corinthians 15:55).

We're free. So rejoice, precious people, and celebrate your salvation.

DEALING WITH DOUBT
A Topical Study of
Luke 7:22

In his book *Disappointment With God,* Philip Yancey tells the story of a woman watching her daughter in her early twenties die a painful death due to cystic fibrosis. Both were believers. "I was sitting beside her bed a few days before her death when suddenly she began screaming," recounts the mother. "I will never forget those shrill, piercing, primal screams . . . ."

Yancey continued, "It's against this background of human beings falling apart . . . that God, who could have helped, looked down on a young woman devoted to Him, quite willing to die for Him to give Him glory, and decided to sit on His hands and let her death top the horror charts for cystic fibrosis deaths."[1] Maybe you are in a situation where you are wondering, *Why is God silent? He could have spoken a word and solved my problem. He could have done something to see me through. Why has He chosen to sit on His hands?* Such is the situation in the text before us. . . .

John the Baptist was in Herod's dungeon because he dared to call the king on the carpet. You see, while visiting his brother, Herod lusted after his brother's wife so greatly that he forced his brother to divorce her so that he himself could marry her. Although the gossip columnists of the day were fascinated, John was infuriated. A prophet of righteousness, John came down on Herod like a scorpion in the desert. Stung by his indictments, Herod ordered John imprisoned.

I'm sure when he was first imprisoned, John thought the One who calmed the storm, who brought the dead back to life, who cleansed the temple would surely spring him. But it didn't work out that way. Days passed. Weeks went by. And John was left wondering. "Go ask Jesus if He really is the One," he said to his disciples, "or are we to look for another?"

So the disciples asked Jesus directly, "Are You the One? Or should we look for someone else? It's not working out the way we thought."

This is exactly what happens to us. As has been rightly said, when the warm moist air of our expectations collides with the icy cold of God's silence, inevitably clouds of doubt begin to form.

No Rebuke

In answering these messengers, Jesus didn't say, "How dare he doubt. What's wrong with him? Why would he have questions?" This shouldn't surprise us, for God never rebukes any who come to Him with sincere questions or honest doubts. Be it Job, Abraham, Moses, or Thomas, as you go through your Bible, you'll never see a questioner rebuked if their questions are sincere. And John's was.

Jesus didn't rebuke John. Instead, He told John's disciples to tell him what they were seeing—hurting people helped, dead people raised, and poor people treasured.

No Release

Jesus didn't rebuke John—but neither did He release him. John's presuppositions of what the kingdom would be like were so set in his mind that when it proved to be something different, he couldn't see it. So, too, I suggest that much of the confusion we are feeling in our own lives personally is not so much due to God being silent as it is due to our failure to recognize the answer He has already given.

John wasn't asking too much. The fact is, he was expecting too little. John was expecting a political kingdom, a material kingdom. But Jesus had something altogether different in mind. John was anticipating a political, material, or military kingdom. Jesus' focus was on eternity. John never got out of prison in the way he had hoped. Instead, his release, brought about by his beheading at the request of Herodius, was infinitely better, as it ushered him into an eternity He would spend with the prophets who went before him, and with Jesus, who would soon join him.

No Regret

Do you think that today John the Baptist is mad at not having been released from prison so he could establish a political party? Do you think he's disappointed he didn't see something happen militarily, materially, or monetarily? Or do you think he's saying, "Excellent! Wonderful! Things didn't work out the way I thought they would, but You were so good, Lord, to leave me in the dungeon because I had the opportunity to join the great prophets who went before me and rejoice eternally."

> Blessed are ye, when men shall revile you, and persecute you, and shall say all manner of evil against you falsely, for my sake. Rejoice, and be exceeding glad: for great is your reward in heaven: for so persecuted they the prophets which were before you.
> Matthew 5:11, 12

So, too, let us rejoice in the fact that even if things don't work out the way we think they should, God is choosing to wait for the best.

If you are going through tough times, hard questions, or real persecution, rejoice. For you will have great reward in heaven. And when you get there, your tears will be wiped away by the very One we think sits on His hands (Revelation 7:17). Then, upon closer inspection, you'll discover His hands were never sat upon. They were nailed. And all of your questions and confusion will vaporize in a new understanding of the depth of His love for you.

Are we ready for heaven? Or are we, like John, asking all the wrong questions and looking for all the wrong answers, all the while wondering why God isn't working?

May we who are in doubt or confusion presently set our questions against the backdrop of eternity. And may we ever look to the One whose hands, for us, were nailed to the Cross of Calvary.

8 The last phrase of chapter 7 was, "Thy faith hath saved thee." And chapter 8 picks up where this statement leaves off, as it addresses the topic of faith almost entirely. In verses 5–21, we see teachings about faith. In verses 22–56, we see the testing of faith. Verses 5–21 deal with hearing the Word. Verses 22–56 deal with heeding the Word. . . .

Luke 8:1 (a)
And it came to pass afterward, that he went throughout every city and village, preaching and shewing the glad tidings of the kingdom of God . . .

The glad tidings are these: All manner of sin except one shall be forgiven all men. That one is the blasphemy of the Spirit—rejecting the free gift of salvation (Matthew 12:31). Rejecting the work of Christ is the singular sin that will send a man or a woman to hell—a concept understood even in our own judicial system. . . .

Convicted of mail fraud in 1830, George Wilson was sentenced to death. But since Wilson's brother had done Andrew Jackson a great personal service, President Jackson wrote George Wilson a pardon. When the pardon was delivered to his cell, however, Wilson refused to take it. The man sentenced to die refused to receive the pardon. What to do? When the case went before the Supreme Court, Chief Justice John Marshall wrote this decision: A pardon is a slip of paper the value of which is determined by the acceptance of the person to be pardoned. If it is refused, it is no pardon at all, simply a piece of paper. Thus, George Wilson must be hanged.

So, too, "You're forgiven," Jesus says, "if you'll take the pardon I offer. If you don't, you render it meaningless, and you will be sentenced to death eternally."

Luke 8:1 (b)–3
. . . and the twelve were with him, And certain women, which had been healed of evil spirits and infirmities, Mary called Magdalene, out of whom went seven devils, And Joanna the wife of Chuza Herod's steward, and Susanna, and many others, which ministered unto him of their substance.

As Jesus preached and taught the Good Tidings, an entourage of women traveled alongside the apostolic company, ministering to them from their substance. And in this, we see women of high society and women like Mary Magdalene brought together because of Jesus. I admire Jesus here immensely because, although it is more blessed to give than to receive, it takes more grace to receive than to give. That Jesus would receive from these women is amazing. But that He would receive worship or praise from me is even more incredible.

Luke 8:4
And when much people were gathered together, and were come to him out of every city, he spake by a parable.

Here, Jesus begins His teaching about faith . . .

Luke 8:5–10
A sower went out to sow his seed: and as he sowed, some fell by the way side; and it was trodden down, and the fowls of the air devoured it. And some fell upon a rock; and as soon as it was sprung up, it withered away,

because it lacked moisture. And some fell among thorns; and the thorns sprang up with it, and choked it. And other fell on good ground, and sprang up, and bare fruit an hundredfold. And when he had said these things, he cried, He that hath ears to hear, let him hear. And his disciples asked him, saying, What might this parable be? And he said, Unto you it is given to know the mysteries of the kingdom of God: but to others in parables; that seeing they might not see, and hearing they might not understand.

Why would Jesus teach in such a way that truth would be concealed? Simply because He will honor the wishes of every person. Therefore, if a person does not want to see, the Lord won't force His way upon him. You see, Jesus could have spoken so persuasively and argued so powerfully that people who didn't want to be converted would be converted even against their own will. But Jesus is not after conversion by force. Because He honors man's free choice, He says, "If you don't want to know the truth, I will conceal truth from you. If you don't want to know Me, I won't force Myself upon you." Teaching through parables provided a way that those who wanted to know truth could receive it, while those who didn't want to know would be unable to receive it.

At whatever point you say, "My mind is made up. I don't want to know what the Word says or how the Lord might feel about any given situation," you will be cut off from revelation. It is a dangerous place to be. But eventually, you'll get so banged up trying to blindly walk in your own darkness that you'll finally say, "I'm tired of arguing my case or trying to prove my point. Show me Your heart, Lord." And He will—when you're ready.

Luke 8:11
Now the parable is this: The seed is the word of God.

We are born again not of corruptible seed, Peter declared, but of incorruptible— the Word of God (1 Peter 1:23). Do you want to be more like the Lord, to experience blessing and joy, to radiate love and peace? The way to do so is not by mustering your efforts to be more Christlike. The seed is the Word. You will be more Christlike if you allow the Word of God to continually and consistently penetrate your inner person. That is how you were born again initially. And that is how more of Jesus will be birthed through you contin-

ually. There's just no other way. The seed is the Word of God.

Luke 8:12
Those by the way side are they that hear; then cometh the devil, and taketh away the word out of their hearts, lest they should believe and be saved.

The first group is comprised of people who hear preaching or teaching, but don't respond. Their hearts are hardened; and they are lost in their sin.

Luke 8:13
They on the rock are they, which, when they hear, receive the word with joy; and these have no root, which for a while believe, and in time of temptation fall away.

The second group is comprised of those who say, "Amen" to the Word—but when the hour of temptation comes, or, as Matthew's Gospel says, "the sun begins to shine," they wither (see Matthew 13:6). The problem with the plant withering under the heat of the sun is not the sun, for the same sun could make the plant healthy and prolific. No, the problem is the shallowness of the root system. All too often, we try to shield people from the sun, insulate people from the heat, shelter people from problems. That's all wrong. The sun, the heat, the trial, the difficulty will make them grow. That's why James says we are to count it all *joy* when we fall into various trials (James 1:2), and why Peter said we are not to think it strange concerning the fiery trials that come our way to purify our faith (1 Peter 4:12).

If you desire to truly help people, the key is not to try to shield them, but rather to say, "This trial is causing you to cave in and give up because your roots are too shallow to draw from the water of the Word. You're sporadic in your study. You're inconsistent in your worship. Your prayer is hit and miss. Tend to your root system and you'll overcome." We spend most of our time trying to figure out how to give people sunscreen for their noses when we should be dealing with the root systems of their hearts.

Luke 8:14
And that which fell among thorns are they, which, when they have heard, go forth, and are choked with cares and riches and pleasures of this life, and bring no fruit to perfection.

Cares affect those who live in poverty. Riches affect those who live in prosperity. Pleasure affects everyone. When you find yourself no longer studying the Scripture, the reason can be found in one of these three areas.

Luke 8:15
But that on the good ground are they, which in an honest and good heart, having heard the word, keep it, and bring forth fruit with patience.

The fourth group is comprised of people who have the seed of the Word embedded within them. But notice they bring forth fruit with patience. When planting a garden, one plants the seed, then waters it, then waits, then waters it, then waits before there's even the slightest breakthrough. We understand this about gardens, but we don't understand the same thing is true spiritually. "I've gone to church five times in a row," we say, "but nothing's happening." Or, "I've had morning devotions for two weeks straight, yet I'm not seeing any fruit, or my situation is not changing, or I still don't have peace. I'll give it one more week, and then it's back to sleeping in." We sow the seed, but we don't allow it time to take root and bear fruit. The one who bears fruit is the one who receives the Word with patience.

Luke 8:16–18
No man, when he hath lighted a candle, covereth it with a vessel, or putteth it under a bed; but setteth it on a candlestick, that they which enter in may see the light. For nothing is secret, that shall not be made manifest; neither any thing hid, that shall not be known and come abroad. Take heed therefore how ye hear: for whosoever hath, to him shall be given; and whosoever hath not, from him shall be taken even that which he seemeth to have.

Faith comes by hearing and hearing by the Word of God (Romans 10:17). Take heed what you're hearing, in order that the seed which is the Word might fall upon good soil and bring forth fruit, that you might experience an even greater degree of faith.

Luke 8:19–21
Then came to him his mother and his brethren, and could not come at him for the press. And it was told him by certain which said, Thy mother and thy brethren stand without, desiring to see thee. And he answered and said unto them, My mother and my brethren are these which hear the word of God, and do it.

Thinking He was so involved in ministry that He was losing His mental stability, Jesus' family came to check on Him (Mark 3:21). Upon hearing this, Jesus identified His family as anyone who hears the Word of God and does it. And the three events that follow will give His disciples the opportunity to do just that as they discover that the key to calming storms is faith; the dynamic to defeat the devil is faith; the prescription for painful problems is faith . . .

Luke 8:22–25
Now it came to pass on a certain day, that he went into a ship with his disciples: and he said unto them, Let us go over unto the other side of the lake. And they launched forth. But as they sailed he fell asleep: and there came down a storm of wind on the lake; and they were filled with water, and were in jeopardy. And they came to him, and awoke him, saying, Master, master, we perish. Then he arose, and rebuked the wind and the raging of the water: and they ceased, and there was a calm. And he said unto them, Where is your faith? And they being afraid wondered, saying one to another, What manner of man is this! for he commandeth even the winds and water, and they obey him.

After hearing Jesus teach about faith, the disciples are in a storm where they need to apply faith. I suggest this storm was actually stirred up in hell because when Jesus rebuked it, He used the same phraseology as when He addressed demons (Luke 4:35). Yet even though Satan may have stirred up the storm in an effort to drown Jesus' ministry, the storm didn't bother Him. Neither did the devil. The only thing that bothered Him was the lack of faith in the hearts of His disciples. After all, He had told them they would go over to the other side of the lake. And when Jesus says a person is going over, he'll not go under.

To us who cry, "It's not going to work," the Lord lovingly says, "Where is your faith? Haven't I promised you that everything is working together for good to those who love Me (Romans 8:28)? Haven't I promised you that I will bring you to a glorious end (Jeremiah 29:11)? Haven't I promised you that I will complete that which I've begun in you (Philippians 1:6)? Haven't I promised you that I will restore to you the years the locust has eaten (Joel 2:25)? Haven't I promised you that no weapon formed against you shall prosper (Isaiah 54:17)? Haven't I promised to supply all your need (Philippians 4:19), that if you seek Me first, everything will be added unto you (Matthew 6:33)?"

It wasn't the storm that troubled the Lord. Nor was it Satan. It was the stumbling of faith in the hearts of those He had just finished teaching. Faith and fear will both sail into the harbor of your heart. Don't let fear anchor there. How? Feed your faith and your fear will starve. Stay in the Word. Give your heart to the Word. Fill your mind with the Word and you will overcome the fears that attack you incessantly.

Luke 8:26 (a)
And they arrived . . .

"Let's go over," Jesus had said. And, just as He had promised, that's exactly what they did.

Luke 8:26 (b), 27
. . . at the country of the Gadarenes, which is over against Galilee. And when he went forth to land, there met him out of the city a certain man, which had devils long time, and ware no clothes, neither abode in any house, but in the tombs.

This demonized individual was wearing no clothes and was obsessed with death—not unlike what we see happening in our own day. Nudity and obsession with death are the direct insignias of Satanic and demonic activity.

Luke 8:28, 29
When he saw Jesus, he cried out, and fell down before him, and with a loud voice said, What have I to do with thee, Jesus, thou Son of God most high? I beseech thee, torment me not. (For he had commanded the unclean spirit to come out of the man. For oftentimes it had caught him: and he was kept bound with chains and in fetters; and he brake the bands, and was driven of the devil into the wilderness.)

Who else was driven into the wilderness? Jesus—not by the devil, but by the Spirit to overcome the devil. The Spirit drove Jesus into the wilderness for His development. The devil drove these men into the wilderness for their destruction. If you find yourself in a hot, dry, wilderness situation, the devil means to destroy you—but the Spirit will use it to develop you. If you say, "I'm going to sit in front of TV and be mad at life," you'll be dominated by the forces of darkness. If, on the other hand, you say, "Lord, I know You brought me here. It's hot and barren and dry, but I will look to You in order that this desert experience might do in me what it did in Your Son— that it might give me victory for greater ministry," you'll be blessed indeed. Whichever you

choose, you'll be in the same desert. But, oh how different will be the result.

Luke 8:30
And Jesus asked him, saying, What is thy name? And he said, Legion: because many devils were entered into him.

A legion consisted of six thousand men.

Luke 8:31, 32
And they besought him that he would not command them to go out into the deep. And there was there an herd of many swine feeding on the mountain: and they besought him that he would suffer them to enter into them. And he suffered them.

The *abusso*—the place where demons who were particularly evil were incarcerated—would appear to be somewhere beneath the sea.

Luke 8:33–35 (a)
Then went the devils out of the man, and entered into the swine: and the herd ran violently down a steep place into the lake, and were choked. When they that fed them saw what was done, they fled, and went and told it in the city and in the country. Then they went out to see what was done; and came to Jesus, and found the man, out of whom the devils were departed, sitting at the feet of Jesus, clothed, and in his right mind . . .

You know someone has been freed of demons when he is sitting clothed and in his right mind at the feet of Jesus.

Luke 8:35 (b)–37 (a)
. . . and they were afraid. They also which saw it told them by what means he that was possessed of the devils was healed. Then the whole multitude of the country of the Gadarenes round about besought him to depart from them . . .

The townspeople were more afraid of a man sitting at the feet of Jesus than they were of a man possessed by demons.

Luke 8:37 (b)-39
. . . for they were taken with great fear: and he went up into the ship, and returned back again. Now the man out of whom the devils were departed besought him that he might be with him: but Jesus sent him away, saying, Return to thine own house, and shew how great things God hath done unto thee. And he went his way, and published

throughout the whole city how great things Jesus had done unto him.

Hopefully, we too will find ourselves sharing with people the great things God has done for us. The storms are stilled by faith. The devil is defeated through faith. Faith is the key.

Luke 8:40, 41 (a)
And it came to pass, that, when Jesus was returned, the people gladly received him: for they were all waiting for him. And, behold, there came a man named Jairus, and he was a ruler of the synagogue . . .

A ruler in the religious system, Jairus was a prominent man. Yet he was willing to abandon his pride in order to come to this itinerant, radical Rabbi from Galilee who had no credentials, no authority from the Sanhedrin.

Luke 8:41 (b)–42
. . . and he fell down at Jesus' feet, and besought him that he would come into his house: For he had one only daughter, about twelve years of age, and she lay a dying. But as he went the people thronged him.

For twelve years, Jairus' home had been filled with the joy and laughter that only a child can bring. Then tragedy struck. A painful problem was now before him.

Luke 8:43
And a woman having an issue of blood twelve years, which had spent all her living upon physicians, neither could be healed of any.

During the same twelve years the home of Jairus had been filled with joy and laughter, the home of this woman was filled with despair and suffering. The rabbis having taught that her hemorrhaging was the result of immorality, this woman would have been excommunicated from the synagogue, divorced from her husband, and ostracized by the community. For twelve years, her life was a miserable tragedy.

I find this contrast very interesting because some of you have spent the last twelve years in joy and delight. But difficulty and tragedy will strike every one of us at some point because it rains on the just and the unjust (Matthew 5:45), because no temptation comes to us but that which is common to all men (1 Corinthians 10:13), because in this world we are promised to have tribulation (John 16:33). If you're in a good season, rejoice—but prepare. Now is the time more than ever to be in the Word, to be worshiping the Lord,

to be growing in faith because tomorrow when tragedy strikes, it will be too late. You will not have the resources necessary to see you through the time of difficulty if you don't prepare in the day of prosperity.

Conversely, for those of you who have been miserable in the last twelve years or months or weeks, good news—you don't know what tomorrow holds. You don't know what miracle is about to happen. I promise you, the Lord will enter your situation in a way that will blow your mind if, like this woman, you seize the opportunity to draw near to Him. We need to be in the place where we know the Lord is traveling. Where is that? He promises to be in the midst of His people (Hebrews 2:12). He promises to be heard in the Word (Hebrews 10:7). He promises to be responsive to prayer (Jeremiah 33:3). This woman heard where He was and said, "I've got to get to the place where Jesus is moving and see what will happen." As a result, she will be healed miraculously and studied throughout history because she had the wisdom to expend the energy and break through the crowds to touch Him even in her weakened state.

Luke 8:44, 45
Came behind him, and touched the border of his garment: and immediately her issue of blood stanched. And Jesus said, Who touched me? When all denied, Peter and they that were with him said, Master, the multitude throng thee and press thee, and sayest thou, Who touched me?

The disciples were impressed by the masses surrounding them. Jesus was intrigued by the one who touched Him. All too often, we evaluate ministry by the masses around Jesus. Jesus, however, is interested in the one who touches Him.

Luke 8:46, 47
And Jesus said, Somebody hath touched me: for I perceive that virtue is gone out of me. And when the woman saw that she was not hid, she came trembling, and falling down before him, she declared unto him before all the people for what cause she had touched him and how she was healed immediately.

What Jesus did privately, He now tells this woman to declare publicly. Was this to embarrass her? No, I believe Jesus wanted her to testify publicly in order that Jairus might be able to handle what he was about to hear. Likewise, there are people around you who are hurting and need to hear what the Lord has done for you in order that their own faith might be strengthened.

Luke 8:48 (a)
And he said unto her, Daughter . . .

Terrified that He might come down on her, how the single word "daughter" must have calmed this woman.

Luke 8:48 (b)
. . . be of good comfort: thy faith hath made thee whole; go in peace.

Some go to church determined to hear from the Lord—and they will leave having heard from the Lord. Others go out of obligation or habit, not expecting to hear from the Lord—and they will leave without hearing from the Lord. Jesus smiles on this lady who was one among the multitude and says, "Daughter, be of good cheer. In faith, you broke through the crowd, and received from Me the help you needed."

Luke 8:49–56
While he yet spake, there cometh one from the ruler of the synagogue's house, saying to him, Thy daughter is dead; trouble not the Master. But when Jesus heard it, he answered him, saying, Fear not: believe only, and she shall be made whole. And when he came into the house, he suffered no man to go in, save Peter, and James, and John, and the father and the mother of the maiden. And all wept, and bewailed her: but he said, Weep not; she is not dead, but sleepeth. And they laughed him to scorn, knowing that she was dead. And he put them all out, and took her by the hand, and called, saying, Maid, arise. And her spirit came again, and she arose straightway: and he commanded to give her meat. And her parents were astonished: but he charged them that they should tell no man what was done.

"Only speak the word and my servant will be healed," the centurion said to Jesus in the previous chapter. Jairus did not have this kind of faith. This helps me understand that although faith is the currency of eternity, all it takes is faith the size of a grain of mustard seed—half the size of a grain of sand—to make things happen. Expect the Lord to work as you take even a baby step of faith, and, as He did with Jairus, He will meet you there.

❧

9 **Luke 9:1–6**
Then he called his twelve disciples together, and gave them power and authority over all devils, and to cure diseases. And he sent them to preach the kingdom of God,

and to heal the sick. And he said unto them, Take nothing for your journey, neither staves, nor scrip, neither bread, neither money; neither have two coats apiece. And whatsoever house ye enter into, there abide, and thence depart. And whosoever will not receive you, when ye go out of that city, shake off the very dust from your feet for a testimony against them. And they departed, and went through the towns, preaching the gospel, and healing every where.**

After giving them both ability and authority, Jesus commissioned the twelve to go out in simplicity and do what they had seen Him do previously.

Luke 9:7–9
Now Herod the tetrarch heard of all that was done by him: and he was perplexed, because that it was said of some, that John was risen from the dead; and of some, that Elias had appeared; and of others, that one of the old prophets was risen again. And Herod said, John have I beheaded: but who is this, of whom I hear such things? And he desired to see him.

Herod was haunted by the similarity between this One of whom he was hearing and the one whom he had beheaded.

Luke 9:10
And the apostles, when they were returned, told him all that they had done. And he took them, and went aside privately into a desert place belonging to the city called Bethsaida.

Knowing power had been drawn from Him, Jesus asked, "Who touched My clothes?" (Mark 5:30). So, too, knowing His disciples had need of replenishment and refreshment following their season of ministry, He took them to Bethsaida, or, "the House of Provision." Whether your ministry be to a congregation, Sunday-school class, family, or your friends at school, it is extremely important to allow the Lord to escort you into quiet times and solitary places in order to recharge the batteries of your faith.

Luke 9:11
And the people, when they knew it, followed him: and he received them, and spake unto them of the kingdom of God, and healed them that had need of healing.

Here we see the wonderful flexibility of Jesus—for although He was in a place of solitude and intimacy with His twelve, He was still available to those in need.

Luke 9:12–17 (a)

And when the day began to wear away, then came the twelve, and said unto him, Send the multitude away, that they may go into the towns and country round about, and lodge, and get victuals: for we are here in a desert place. But he said unto them, Give ye them to eat. And they said, We have no more but five loaves and two fishes; except we should go and buy meat for all this people. or they were about five thousand men. And he said to his disciples, Make them sit down by fifties in a company. And they did so, and made them all sit down. Then he took the five loaves and the two fishes, and looking up to heaven, he blessed them, and brake, and gave to the disciples to set before the multitude. And they did eat, and were all filled . . .

The disciples saw the need of the hungry people, and what did they say? "Tell them to go get a burger, to go find a hotel."

When people come to you asking for help with a hard situation or an answer to a troubling question, do you send them away, saying, "Call the church office. See if you can talk to one of the pastors because I can't help you"? The problem is, you and I don't think we have very much. "What good will my few sardines and couple of wheat thins be," we ask, "in light of this huge need?"

But, as He did to His disciples, Jesus would say to you, "*You* feed them. Even though your understanding may be limited and your resources seem scant, put them in My hands and watch Me multiply them miraculously to touch someone else deeply."

Luke 9:17 (b)

. . . and there was taken up of fragments that remained to them twelve baskets.

Twelve baskets of food remained: one for each disciple. When will you be most blessed? When you watch how the Lord uses your crackers and fish to minister His love to someone else. You may think you're over your head. You may think you have nothing to say. You may think you can't handle it. But when you see what the Lord does because you simply took time to pray or share the Word with someone, you'll get back a whole basket yourself. Truly, whatever measure you give out will be given back to you (Luke 6:38). Therefore, take seriously every opportunity to help the people who cross your path—and watch and see what God will do both for them and for you.

Luke 9:18–22

And it came to pass, as he was alone praying, his disciples were with him: and he asked them, saying, Whom say the people that I am? They answering said, John the Baptist; but some say, Elias; and others say, that one of the old prophets is risen again. He said unto them, But whom say ye that I am? Peter answering said, The Christ of God. And he straitly charged them, and commanded them to tell no man that thing; Saying, The Son of man must suffer many things, and be rejected of the elders and chief priests and scribes, and be slain, and be raised the third day.

The first time Jesus mentioned the fact that He would be crucified came only after there was inspiration and revelation that He was the Christ. Inspiration and revelation always precede understanding about tribulation. Therefore, I think believers err when they talk about the cost of being a Christian before talking about the beauty of Jesus.

Luke 9:23–25

And he said to them all, If any man will come after me, let him deny himself, and take up his cross daily, and follow me. For whosoever will save his life shall lose it: but whosoever will lose his life for my sake, the same shall save it. or what is a man advantaged, if he gain the whole world, and lose himself, or be cast away?

Jesus burst on the scene with a revolutionary concept never before heard in any spiritual teaching or philosophy when He said, "If you want life, lose it. The more you let go of yourself, the happier you'll be. The more you give yourself away, the richer you'll be. The key is to deny yourself, to take up your cross and follow Me." He said this not to torture or torment us. He said this to liberate and bless us. And whoever lives for others and takes his eyes off himself will discover the truth of Jesus' words.

Luke 9:26

For whosoever shall be ashamed of me and of my words, of him shall the Son of man be ashamed, when he shall come in his own glory, and in his Father's, and of the holy angels.

He who doesn't take seriously Jesus' call to the cross will not hear Him say, "Well done, good and faithful servant. Enter into the joy of the Lord" (Matthew 25:21). I believe Jesus said this knowing His words in verses 24, 25 would have

sounded so impossible to His disciples that they
would have thought He couldn't have meant what
He said.

Luke 9:27
**But I tell you of a truth, there be some
standing here, which shall not taste of
death, till they see the kingdom of God.**

"Some who are hearing these words of Mine
will see the reality of the kingdom before they
taste of death physically," Jesus said. And indeed
this came to pass eight days later . . .

Luke 9:28, 29
**And it came to pass about an eight days
after these sayings, he took Peter and John
and James, and went up into a mountain to
pray. And as he prayed, the fashion of his
countenance was altered, and his raiment
was white and glistering.**

I believe this transfiguration, this glowing, was
the original intent of the Father for each of us.
That is, I believe that had man lived perfectly
without sinning in the Garden of Eden, we too
would have been transfigured at some point and
taken directly to heaven. But that's not what happened to Adam and Eve. And that's not what happens to you and me. We sin, so we die. We don't
glow; we rot. We don't shine awesomely; we start
to fall apart physically because the wages of sin
is death (Romans 6:23). At this point, Jesus could
have launched straight into heaven. But He
didn't. He would go down the Mount of Transfiguration in order that He might climb the Mount
of Calvary in order to die for you and me.

Luke 9:30–31
**And, behold, there talked with him two men,
which were Moses and Elias: Who appeared
in glory, and spake of his decease which he
should accomplish at Jerusalem.**

The Greek word for "decease" is *exodos*. I like
that word as a description of death. And who better than Moses to talk about an exodus?!

Luke 9:32, 33 (a)
**But Peter and they that were with him were
heavy with sleep: and when they were
awake, they saw his glory, and the two men
that stood with him. And it came to pass,
as they departed from him, Peter said unto
Jesus, Master, it is good for us to be here . . .**

Peter, James, and John came to realize that
even in talking about death, it was good to be with
Jesus.

Luke 9:33 (b)-35
**. . . and let us make three tabernacles; one
for thee, and one for Moses, and one for
Elias: not knowing what he said. While he
thus spake, there came a cloud, and overshadowed them: and they feared as they entered into the cloud. And there came a voice
out of the cloud, saying, This is my beloved
Son: hear him.**

"This is My beloved Son: hear *Him*," God said
to Peter. In other words, Jesus is infinitely superior to Moses and Elijah, to the law and the
prophets.

Luke 9:36–39
**And when the voice was past, Jesus was
found alone. And they kept it close, and told
no man in those days any of those things
which they had seen. And it came to pass,
that on the next day, when they were come
down from the hill, much people met him.
And, behold, a man of the company cried
out, saying, Master, I beseech thee, look
upon my son: for he is mine only child. And,
lo, a spirit taketh him, and he suddenly
crieth out; and it teareth him that he
foameth again, and bruising him hardly de-
parteth from him.**

The Greek phrase translated "for he is mine
only child" is literally "for he is my only begotten
son." Thus, the only begotten Son of God is coming down the mountain to deal with the only begotten son of this father; the beloved Son is about
to free a bedeviled son.

Luke 9:40–43 (a)
**And I besought thy disciples to cast him out;
and they could not. And Jesus answering
said, O faithless and perverse generation,
how long shall I be with you, and suffer
you? Bring thy son hither. And as he was
yet a coming, the devil threw him down, and
tare him. And Jesus rebuked the unclean
spirit, and healed the child, and delivered
him again to his father. And they were all
amazed at the mighty power of God.**

Jesus had given His disciples authority and
power over demons in verse 1. Yet here was a demon they couldn't cast out. Was this because
their power had "run out"? No, for the gifts and
callings of God are without repentance (Romans
11:29). That is, He never takes them back. But
even though the gifts of God remain in place,
their effectiveness is not automatic. This is where
people so easily err. God uses them in a counseling, teaching, evangelistic or hospitality ministry,

and they think, *That's my gift.* And it is. But when it starts losing its effectiveness, they wonder why.

"This kind does not go out except by prayer and fasting," Jesus said. In other words, "The authority is given, the power is present, but it won't operate without your participating in prayer and fasting." Therefore, although you might have been one of the most gifted witnesses in the whole country, you're ineffective today if you have not been maintaining that gift by prayer and fasting, by spending time in the presence of God.

Luke 9:43 (b)–45
But while they wondered every one at all things which Jesus did, he said unto his disciples, Let these sayings sink down into your ears: for the Son of man shall be delivered into the hands of men. But they understood not this saying, and it was hid from them, that they perceived it not: and they feared to ask him of that saying.

Why did Jesus speak of His crucifixion directly after He cast out this demon? I believe the answer is found in Colossians 2, where Paul declared that Jesus was nailed to the Cross, blotting out the handwriting of ordinances against us and spoiling the principalities and powers that would come against us. Where were Satan and his demonic henchmen totally defeated? At the Cross. The Cross is the key to seeing people released from the power of the demonic because Satan gains entry at the point a person commits a sin habitually. And nothing short of the blood of Jesus can cause Satan to lose his grip.

Luke 9:46–48
Then there arose a reasoning among them, which of them should be greatest. And Jesus, perceiving the thought of their heart, took a child, and set him by him, and said unto them, Whosoever shall receive this child in my name receiveth me: and whosoever shall receive me receiveth him that sent me: for he that is least among you all, the same shall be great.

When did the disciples start arguing about their greatness? When, even though they had been given the power to cast out demons, they failed in their attempt to do so. Such is human nature. You can always tell when a person is aware of his shortcomings by his telling you how great he is. Conversely, a person who is truly great never has to talk about it or prove it.

Luke 9:49, 50
And John answered and said, Master, we saw one casting out devils in thy name; and we forbad him, because he followeth not with us. And Jesus said unto him, Forbid him not: for he that is not against us is for us.

Evidently, the disciples forbade this man not because of his theology, but because of their own jealousy. And Jesus' word to them is equally applicable to me.

Luke 9:51–54
And it came to pass, when the time was come that he should be received up, he stedfastly set his face to go to Jerusalem, and sent messengers before his face: and they went, and entered into a village of the Samaritans, to make ready for him. And they did not receive him, because his face was as though he would go to Jerusalem. And when his disciples James and John saw this, they said, Lord, wilt thou that we command fire to come down from heaven, and consume them, even as Elias did?

On the heels of the previous incident, wherein John and James were quick to castigate anyone outside of their circle, this incident casts further light on the tendency of these "sons of thunder" to prove how fired-up they were by blasting others.

A ministry of fault-finding requires no skill because if I say, "You're not praying enough," who will disagree? If I say, "You're not worshiping enough," who will argue? I could rail on people for any number of things, and the response would always be, "Preach it, brother!" because we are all aware of our shortcomings in every area of our walk. It is so easy to blast and call down fire upon people. But all you do is burn them in the process. Of Jesus, Isaiah prophesied, "He shall not strive in the streets, break the bruised reed, or quench the smoking flax" (Isaiah 42:2, 3). In other words, to the flax barely smoldering, Jesus doesn't say, "Only smoldering, huh?" before drowning it with a bucket of water. To the broken reed, He doesn't say, "Broken, eh?" before crushing it with a heavy foot. That's not His ministry, mentality, or personality. He's a compassionate High Priest who understands our frailty (Hebrews 4:15).

Luke 9:55, 56
But he turned, and rebuked them, and said, Ye know not what manner of spirit ye are of. For the Son of man is not come to destroy men's lives, but to save them. And they went to another village.

John, the son of thunder, was transformed into the Apostle of Love. How? By hanging around Jesus. You might feel like you're harsh or insensitive, that you lack tenderness or compassion. The good news is this: Those characteristics will be changed as you continue to spend time with the Lord. You see, the "nature vs. nurture" debate over whether a personality is shaped by one's environment or whether it is determined by one's heredity takes a backseat to the question of with whom one associates. If you spend time with Jesus, you will become like Him. Oh, it may not happen quickly, but it will happen with certainty.

Luke 9:57, 58
And it came to pass, that, as they went in the way, a certain man said unto him, Lord, I will follow thee whithersoever thou goest. And Jesus said unto him, Foxes have holes, and birds of the air have nests; but the Son of man hath not where to lay his head.

Material obstacles kept this man from following Jesus.

Luke 9:59, 60
And he said unto another, Follow me. But he said, Lord, suffer me first to go and bury my father. Jesus said unto him, Let the dead bury their dead: but go thou and preach the kingdom of God.

Parental obligations stood in the way of this man following Jesus. "I hear Your call upon my life," he said, "but first let me wait until my parents are no longer alive—then my obligation to them will be fulfilled."

Luke 9:61, 62
And another also said, Lord, I will follow thee; but let me first go bid them farewell, which are at home at my house. And Jesus said unto him, No man, having put his hand to the plough, and looking back, is fit for the kingdom of God.

"I'll follow You, Lord," said the third man, "but let me talk it over with my family. Let me see what they say about following You so radically."

There are always reasons not to follow Jesus. No wonder He could use a man like Paul, who said, "This one thing I do, forgetting the things which lie behind, I press on. I don't dwell on the past or look back. I simply press on" (Philippians 3:13).

10

Luke 10:1 (a)
After these things . . .

After spending time with His disciples, Jesus will now commission them for service. And as He does, we find in this chapter three clear priorities for life: We are to be ambassadors *for* Christ, neighbors *like* Christ, and lovers *of* Christ.

Luke 10:1 (b)
. . . the Lord appointed other seventy also . . .

I find the number seventy interesting, for, based on Genesis 10, the Jews held that all of the nations of the world were seventy in number. Thus, in appointing seventy disciples, it was as if Jesus was saying, "Go into all the world—into every nation, region, country, and culture—and preach the Gospel."

Luke 10:1 (c)
. . . and sent them two and two before his face into every city and place, whither he himself would come.

As those who went before Him, the seventy were ambassadors of Christ—as was Paul (Ephesians 6:20), and as are we (2 Corinthians 5:20). The seventy were to declare Jesus' first coming. We are to declare His soon return. Our call to be ambassadors is not only a high and privileged calling, but one with prophetic ramifications as well, for when war breaks out between nations, ambassadors are always called home. So, too, I am convinced that before God declares war on the world that rejected His Son, He will call us, His ambassadors, home.

Luke 10:2 (a)
Therefore said he unto them, The harvest truly is great . . .

Jesus sent the seventy not to sow seed, but to bring in the harvest. I have found that people are ripe for the picking a lot more often than we think. We have been given the opportunity and mandate to say to our family, friends, and neighbors, "Why don't you open your heart to the Lord? You've got nothing to lose but hell. Could I lead you in prayer right now?" I think we have been intimidated by a lie from the Enemy, who whispers in our ear that people don't want to get saved. Not true! The harvest is *great*.

Luke 10:2 (b), 3 (a)
. . . but the labourers are few: pray ye there-
fore the Lord of the harvest, that he would
send forth labourers into his harvest. Go
your ways . . .

Ours is not only a privileged work, but it is a
problematic work due, first of all, to the immensity of the task. Yes, the harvest is great, but so,
too, the laborers are few. In this, Jesus paints a
picture of massive fields ripe for plucking, but
with only a few workers laboring. So what are we
to do? We're to pray that the Lord of the harvest
would send forth laborers into the field. And after following the injunction of verse 2 to pray,
don't be surprised if you are then called to obey
verse 3—to go! Pray for the Lord to harvest souls
in your neighborhood, and guess who He's going
to call on to do it. Pray seriously for the area of
the world to which your heart is drawn, and guess
who He will send!

Luke 10:3 (b)
. . . behold, I send you forth as lambs among
wolves.

Not only do we see the intensity of the task,
but also the inevitability of the attack. When Satan sees you are serious about harvesting—
whether it's where you work, on your street, or
across the sea—you can be sure he will launch an
attack against you. "I'm sending you as lambs,"
Jesus said. Lambs are even more vulnerable than
sheep. He didn't say, "I'm sending you forth as
hunters against the wolves," or even, "I want you
to be super-sheep marching militantly or organizing politically." No, He simply said we are to
be lambs walking in humility because in so doing,
the reflection of Jesus can be seen most clearly.

Luke 10:4–9
Carry neither purse, nor scrip, nor shoes:
and salute no man by the way. And into
whatsoever house ye enter, first say, Peace
be to this house. And if the son of peace be
there, your peace shall rest upon it: if not,
it shall turn to you again. And in the same
house remain, eating and drinking such
things as they give: for the labourer is wor-
thy of his hire. Go not from house to house.
And into whatsoever city ye enter, and they
receive you, eat such things as are set before
you: And heal the sick that are therein, and
say unto them, The kingdom of God is come
nigh unto you.

Lastly, we see the immediacy of the call. "Don't
carry purse or money or shoes," Jesus said.
"Don't stop and dialogue with people. Just get

going. I will provide for you through people who
open their doors to you." We who are called to be
ambassadors will never feel adequately prepared. But if you wait until you're ready financially, educationally, or relationally, you'll be
sitting here ten years from now, for there will always be something saying, "Not now, not yet, not
you."

Luke 10:10–12
But into whatsoever city ye enter, and they
receive you not, go your ways out into the
streets of the same, and say, Even the very
dust of your city, which cleaveth on us, we
do wipe off against you: notwithstanding be
ye sure of this, that the kingdom of God is
come nigh unto you. But I say unto you,
that it shall be more tolerable in that day
for Sodom, than for that city.

It's not our responsibility to be successful. Our
responsibility is simply to be faithful.

Luke 10:13–16
Woe unto thee, Chorazin! woe unto thee,
Bethsaida! for if the mighty works had been
done in Tyre and Sidon, which have been
done in you, they had a great while ago re-
pented, sitting in sackcloth and ashes. But
it shall be more tolerable for Tyre and Sidon
at the judgment, than for you. And thou,
Capernaum, which art exalted to heaven,
shalt be thrust down to hell. He that heareth
you heareth me; and he that despiseth you
despiseth me; and he that despiseth me de-
spiseth him that sent me.

What miracles did Jesus do in Chorazin and
Bethsaida? We don't know. There is no record of
Jesus doing wonders or miracles in those cities—
which validates what John said when he said the
world itself couldn't contain a record of all that
Jesus did (John 21:25).

Luke 10:17 (a)
And the seventy returned again with joy . . .

Whether you're witnessing where you work,
ministering at the convalescent hospital down the
street, faithfully discipling your children, going
across the ocean—whatever it might mean in
your context, when you are doing what the Lord
is calling you to do, although initially you went
out with fear and worry, you'll always return with
joy.

Luke 10:17 (b)–19
. . . saying, Lord, even the devils are subject
unto us through thy name. And he said unto

them, I beheld Satan as lightning fall from heaven. Behold, I give unto you power to tread on serpents and scorpions, and over all the power of the enemy: and nothing shall by any means hurt you.

"I saw Satan fall like lightning." What does this mean? It could be that Jesus was giving a word of witness. That is, it could be that He was telling His disciples that, as they were ministering and sharing, the kingdom of darkness was being beaten back, light was breaking forth, and Satan was falling down. More than a cliché, the primary meaning of binding Satan is not something we say verbally, but work we do practically. When we pronounce peace and heal the sick, when we share the gospel, help the hurting, and witness to those who are lost—that is when the Enemy is truly bound.

Secondly, it could be that Jesus was giving His disciples a word of warning. That is, He could have been reminding them that it was when Lucifer was the worship leader of heaven, the anointed cherub, the most powerful of all created beings that he fell. It could be that Jesus was saying, "Be careful that pride doesn't fill your heart, that ministry doesn't become more important to you than I am."

Luke 10:20
Notwithstanding in this rejoice not, that the spirits are subject unto you; but rather rejoice, because your names are written in heaven.

"Don't rejoice about what you're doing," Jesus said to His disciples—and to us. "Rather, rejoice in what I've done on your behalf: that you're saved, that I died for you, that I chose you as My bride." It's exciting to hear what miracles the Lord does in people's lives, but the fact that Jesus chose to write *our* names in the book of life should in itself make us an ecstatic people.

Luke 10:21–24
In that hour Jesus rejoiced in spirit, and said, I thank thee, O Father, Lord of heaven and earth, that thou hast hid these things from the wise and prudent, and hast revealed them unto babes: even so, Father; for so it seemed good in thy sight. All things are delivered to me of my Father: and no man knoweth who the Son is, but the Father; and who the Father is, but the Son, and he to whom the Son will reveal him. And he turned him unto his disciples, and said privately, Blessed are the eyes which see the things that ye see: For I tell you, that many prophets and kings have desired

to see those things which ye see, and have not seen them; and to hear those things which ye hear, and have not heard them.

Have you ever wished you lived in the days of Moses—when you could see the Red Sea parting, the Egyptians drowning, the shekinah glory glowing? Have you ever wished you could live in the days of Elijah when fire came down from the sky and he rode a chariot into heaven? Jesus says, in effect, they wish they were us because we understand what they could only wonder about. They could only guess at the meaning of what they wrote, but we see the full picture because we see Jesus, and in Him everything comes together, everything makes sense.

Luke 10:25
And, behold, a certain lawyer stood up, and tempted him, saying, Master, what shall I do to inherit eternal life?

Lawyers being scholars of the Old Testament law, seeing Jesus as a threat to the rules and regulations of Judaism, this lawyer wanted to trap Him.

Luke 10:26
He said unto him, What is written in the law? how readest thou?

To this one who was a scholar of the law, who lived under the law, who walked in the law, Jesus answered according to the Law.

Luke 10:27, 28 (a)
And he answering said, Thou shalt love the Lord thy God with all thy heart, and with all thy soul, and with all thy strength, and with all thy mind; and thy neighbour as thyself. And he said unto him, Thou hast answered right . . .

In response, the lawyer quoted the Shemah of Deuteronomy 6.
"Good answer," Jesus said.

Luke 10:27 (b)
. . . this do, and thou shalt live.

This do, and thou shalt live. Such is the basis of the law. The problem is, we can't. So we're dead. Grace, on the other hand, says, "Live—be born again—then you'll be able to do."

Luke 10:29 (a)
But he, willing to justify himself . . .

People who are under the law invariably seek to justify themselves by comparing themselves with others.

Two campers got out of their tent and began to pour their morning coffee, when suddenly one of them saw a huge black grizzly bear running their way.

"Look at the grizzly!" he said.

The other guy immediately dropped his cup and began to put on his tennis shoes.

"If you think you can outrun a grizzly, you're crazy," said his friend.

"I don't have to," the smarter of the two called out over his shoulder as he sprinted away. "All I have to do is outrun you!"

That's the way of the law. Religion says, "God will accept me into heaven if I'm just better than the next guy." But that's not what the law declares, for it says that whoever violates even one point breaks the whole law and is doomed and damned unless he receives the free gift of salvation from the One who paid for his sins completely on the Cross of Calvary.

Luke 10:29 (b)
. . . said unto Jesus, And who is my neighbour?

Religionists call for a definition of terms in their attempt to muddy the clarity and simplicity of the gospel.

Luke 10:30 (a)
And Jesus answering said . . .

Not only are we ambassadors *for* Christ, but we are to be neighbors *like* Christ. And in the account that follows, Jesus defines this further. . . .

Luke 10:30 (b)
. . . A certain man went down from Jerusalem to Jericho, and fell among thieves, which stripped him of his raiment, and wounded him, and departed . . .

Twenty miles long, dropping thirty-six hundred feet in elevation, the road from Jerusalem to Jericho was widely known as "the Bloody Way" due to the great number of thieves who lay in wait thereupon to ambush unsuspecting travelers. This being the case, why was this man traveling that road alone? He was dumb, and thus a picture of us. We do dumb things; we go down dumb roads. And waiting to ambush us in our

foolishness is the murderer Jesus identified as Satan (John 8:44).

Luke 10:30 (c)
. . . leaving him half dead.

When we go our own way and fall into sin, although we remain alive physically, we're actually half dead because we're dead spiritually.

Luke 10:31
And by chance there came down a certain priest that way: and when he saw him, he passed by on the other side.

As those who called the shots and controlled the people, the priests were the politicians of the day. And perhaps this priest looked at the man by the side of the road and thought, *That lazy welfare dependant has no one to blame but himself for being there in the gutter. Why doesn't he pull himself up by his own bootstraps like I did?* Is that how I feel? Do I see people lying on the street who have been beat up by the Enemy and think, *Serves them right?*

Numbers 19 tells us that if a priest touched a dead man he would be unclean for seven days. So perhaps this priest was saying, "I've got ministry to tend, things to do. I can't afford seven days off. My schedule is too full, my demands too many." Either way, the priest's heart was as far from the heart of the Father's as it could be.

Luke 10:32
And likewise a Levite, when he was at the place, came and looked on him, and passed by on the other side.

Even though the Levites would have been akin to the social workers of our day, after a closer look, this Levite passed by as well—perhaps worried that had he done otherwise, he would have been vulnerable to being attacked himself if the man who was beat up was simply a decoy to lure travelers into a place where they could be easily robbed.

Luke 10:33
But a certain Samaritan, as he journeyed, came where he was: and when he saw him, he had compassion on him.

Although they were avowed enemies, the Samaritan had compassion on the Jew. Someone wisely said that if we could read the secret history of our enemies, we would find in each enough sorrow and suffering to disarm all of our hostility. I like that. Who is the Samaritan? It is the One who knew no sin, but who became sin. It is Jesus. He came to you and me who have been beaten up because of our sin and stupidity and had compassion on us. Each of us thinks his own sins are understandable but that the sins of others are preposterous. Not so with Jesus. He has compassion on us *all.*

Luke 10:34 (a)
And went to him, and bound up his wounds, pouring in oil and wine . . .

Jesus comes to me and gives me oil and wine. Oil is a symbol of the Spirit, wine a symbol of blood. The Spirit provides power for success; the blood, provision for failure.

Luke 10:34 (b)
. . . and set him on his own beast . . .

The Samaritan elevated the traveler to the position he had enjoyed previously—just as Jesus became a Son of Man that we might become sons of God.

Luke 10:34 (c)
. . . and brought him to an inn, and took care of him.

Guess where Jesus takes people who have been beat up. He deposits them in *our* care as believers individually and as fellowships corporately.

Luke 10:35
And on the morrow when he departed, he took out two pence, and gave them to the host, and said unto him, Take care of him; and whatsoever thou spendest more, when I come again, I will repay thee.

After carrying him into the inn, the Samaritan said to the innkeeper, "Here's money to take care of this man. If you need more, I'll pay you back when I return." This puts the innkeeper in an interesting place. Two pieces of silver were a significant amount of money in that day. If the innkeeper figured the Samaritan was not likely to return, he could dump the traveler on the street and use the silver to remodel his inn. That's what a lot of us do. We've been blessed by the Lord with money, jobs, resources, abilities, and talents. And what do we do with them? Use them for our own gain.

Or the innkeeper could have said, "I'll take care of him until the two pence run out. Then, whether he's healed or not, he's out of here."

A lot of us do this as well. "We'll use what You give us, Lord," we say, "but don't ask us to extend ourselves in faith. We're not going to take on any

new challenge or step into any new opportunity. We'll give what You require, but once that's given, that's it because we're not completely sure You're coming back or that we'll be repaid."

I have news for you: Jesus *is* coming back. And, based upon the Word of God, I promise you that anything you have spent above and beyond the two pence you have been given will be rewarded *greatly.* Not once in the next billion years to come will you regret that which you did not do for yourself because you cared for someone who was beat up, someone who was in need, someone who needed to grow in the ways of the Lord. What we will regret is that which we did not spend because we weren't living as though the Samaritan was really coming back.

The Lord has entrusted to us more than enough to take care of the half-dead people who come our way. The question is, will we release what He's given us? Provision has already been made for every area. Will we let it go? Will we make the time? Will we expend the energy? Fellow innkeepers, I trust we will say to our Good Samaritan, "You've already given me the gifts and the goods to care for whoever You send my way. Therefore, I will do whatever it takes, knowing You are repaying even now."

Luke 10:36, 37
Which now of these three, thinkest thou, was neighbour unto him that fell among the thieves? And he said, He that shewed mercy on him. Then said Jesus unto him, Go, and do thou likewise.

The thief on the Bloody Way saw the traveler as a numbskull to attack. The priest and Levite saw him as a nuisance to avoid. The Samaritan saw him as a neighbor to love. How do you see people? This story challenges me, blesses me, and convicts me all at the same time.

Luke 10:38, 39
Now it came to pass, as they went, that he entered into a certain village: and a certain woman named Martha received him into her house. And she had a sister called Mary, which also sat at Jesus' feet, and heard his word.

Ambassadors for Christ, neighbors like Christ, in Mary we see what it means to be a lover of Christ, for Mary is seen three times in the Gospels—each time at the feet of Jesus.

Luke 10:40
But Martha was cumbered about much serving, and came to him, and said, Lord, dost thou not care that my sister hath left me to

serve alone? bid her therefore that she help me.

Martha is busy but not blessed. She's busy and she's bitter. I've been there. Maybe you have too.

Luke 10:41 (a)
And Jesus answered and said unto her, Martha, Martha . . .

When you hear your name spoken twice, take double heed!

Luke 10:41 (b), 42 (a)
. . . thou art careful and troubled about many things: But one thing is needful . . .

It's as if Jesus was saying, "Martha, you're fixing all kinds of courses. You're preparing a big meal. But don't you understand, I only want one thing—a simple meal?" When I began to think on this, it caused me to wonder how often I give people what I want to give rather than what they really want. For example, if you know guests are coming to your house, do you find yourself busy, busy, busy—only to be exhausted when they arrive? People don't care whether your windows are spotless or your floors waxed. What they care about is substance, peace, love. And those qualities can't be nurtured if we're spending all of our time frantically making sure there are no leaves on our lawn.

Luke 10:42 (b)
. . . and Mary hath chosen that good part, which shall not be taken away from her.

What we do *with* Christ is infinitely more important than what we do *for* Him. You might be performing this duty, caring for that obligation, or involved in other numerous ministries. But in this passage, Jesus shows us that what we do with Him as a Friend is far more important than anything we could ever do for Him in service.

Yes, we are ambassadors for Him.

Yes, we are to look for opportunities to be a neighbor like Him.

But our greatest call and highest privilege is to be a lover of Him.

11
Luke 11:1 (a)
And it came to pass, that, as he was praying in a certain place, when he ceased, one of his disciples said unto him, Lord, teach us to pray . . .

As far as we know, the disciples never said, "Lord, teach us to preach," or, "Teach us to do miracles." I believe this is because, hanging out with the Lord, they understood that His teaching, His witnessing, His miraculous power—that indeed all He was and all He did was linked to, and a result of, His devoted prayer life.

Notice that the disciples didn't say, "Teach us *how* to pray," but rather, simply, "Teach us *to* pray." Every one of us who is a believer knows that the posture of prayer is the place of power. So why don't we pray? I believe one reason is that we have greatly complicated prayer. We have made it something it was never intended to be because we have believed the lie of the Enemy that prayer is difficult, time-consuming, heavy.

Luke 11:1 (b)
. . . as John also taught his disciples.

When I think of John the Baptist, I think of a rugged individual boldly proclaiming the need for repentance. But evidently, John was known as one who prayed and one who taught others to pray.

Luke 11:2–4
And he said unto them, When ye pray, say, Our Father which art in heaven, Hallowed be thy name. Thy kingdom come. Thy will be done, as in heaven, so in earth. Give us day by day our daily bread. And forgive us our sins; for we also forgive every one that is indebted to us. And lead us not into temptation; but deliver us from evil.

In His answer to His disciples' request, we first see Jesus give a pattern for prayer. Teaching them a prayer only sixty-two words long, it was as if Jesus was saying, "Keep it simple." In fact, when Jesus gave this same prayer as a model two years previously in the Sermon on the Mount, it was a sentence longer (Matthew 6:13). I think our Lord is the only One who gets simpler the longer one walks with Him. We have a tendency to become more complicated. Not so the Lord. He gives a short prayer to begin with, then, after a couple of years, He says, "I'll make it even easier for you."

Luke 11:5–10
And he said unto them, Which of you shall have a friend, and shall go unto him at midnight, and say unto him, Friend, lend me three loaves; For a friend of mine in his journey is come to me, and I have nothing to set before him? And he from within shall answer and say, Trouble me not: the door is now shut, and my children are with me in

bed; I cannot rise and give thee. I say unto you, Though he will not rise and give him, because he is his friend, yet because of his importunity he will rise and give him as many as he needeth. And I say unto you, Ask, and it shall be given you; seek, and ye shall find; knock, and it shall be opened unto you. For every one that asketh receiveth; and he that seeketh findeth; and to him that knocketh it shall be opened.

Secondly, we see the necessity for persistence in prayer. In Jesus' day, the middle- and lower-class houses consisted of a single room in which one-third of the floor was elevated about eight inches above the rest and contained a small fire ring around which the family would sleep. The remaining two-thirds of the room housed the animals. Thus, it is easy to see why this man was reluctant to crawl over the kids and stumble over the animals to answer his door. Yet he did so nonetheless. Jesus uses this analogy to say that because our Father never sleeps (Psalm 121:3), because our Father never says, "Don't bother Me," how much more would He be willing to respond to the one who keeps asking, keeps seeking, keeps knocking.

Many people have a huge problem at this point. *Why must I* keep *asking,* keep *seeking,* keep *knocking?* they wonder. There's a reason. God is not trying to play hard to get. Nor is He treating us like puppies, trying to teach us to beg—and if we stand up on our hind legs and yap loud enough, He'll drop a biscuit in our mouth. No, no, no. We need to persist in prayer because it helps us determine that which is important to us.

The closer Christmas got, the more Benjamin and Mary, who were toddlers at the time, changed their minds about what they really wanted—until finally a pattern began to develop, based upon a few things to which they kept returning. The same is true of you and me. We're like kids. We want this to happen, or that to work out. And then three days later, we want something else entirely. Consequently, I believe the Lord teaches us to persist in prayer to help us sort through what really is important to us. But even more fundamentally, I think we are to persist in prayer simply because the Father enjoys being with us. And if He gave us what we asked for the first time every time, He knows us well enough to know we would just grab the goods and run. The fact that we must come to Him repeatedly helps us see that, in the end, it was His fellowship we craved all along.

Luke 11:11–13
If a son shall ask bread of any of you that is a father, will he give him a stone? or if he ask a fish, will he for a fish give him a serpent? Or if he shall ask an egg, will he offer him a scorpion? If ye then, being evil, know how to give good gifts unto your children: how much more shall your heavenly Father give the Holy Spirit to them that ask him?

In addition to a pattern for prayer and the importance of persistence in prayer, Jesus gives the principle of prayer. No good thing will the Lord withhold from them that love Him (Psalm 84:11). Therefore, if that which I want or have prayed does not come my way, I must conclude it is not good for me—at least not at this time—because my Father will do what's best. He will not give me what He knows is a scorpion, even though I think it's a fish. Nor will He give me a rock when what I need is a piece of bread.

Luke 11:14
And he was casting out a devil, and it was dumb. And it came to pass, when the devil was gone out, the dumb spake; and the people wondered.

That last phrase is my life verse. The dumb spake and the people wondered.

Luke 11:15–19
But some of them said, He casteth out devils through Beelzebub the chief of the devils. And others, tempting him, sought of him a sign from heaven. But he, knowing their thoughts, said unto them, Every kingdom divided against itself is brought to desolation; and a house divided against a house falleth. If Satan also be divided against himself, how shall his kingdom stand? because ye say that I cast out devils through Beelzebub. And if I by Beelzebub cast out devils, by whom do your sons cast them out? therefore shall they be your judges.

"If indeed I cast out demons by the power of Satan, why would Satan cast out Satan?" Jesus asks. "That makes no sense because a divided kingdom can't stand."

Luke 11:20
But if I with the finger of God cast out devils, no doubt the kingdom of God is come upon you.

Notice Jesus doesn't cast out devils with the arm of God or even the hand of God. He does so with merely the finger of God. We often think

Satan and God are involved in a struggle that goes back and forth, which ebbs and flows. Not true. Because Satan is incomparable to the Person and power of God, He is no match for God. Satan being nothing more than a fallen angel, his counterpart is neither God nor Jesus, but an archangel like Michael. And even they are victorious over him (Daniel 10:13; Jude 9).

Luke 11:21, 22
When a strong man armed keepeth his palace, his goods are in peace: him all his armour wherein he trusted, and divideth his spoils.

The fact that Jesus cast out demons was undeniable. And since it was ludicrous of the Pharisees to think that He cast them out by the power of Satan, the only logical conclusion was that He was indeed the One stronger than Satan, the One who, on the Cross would "disarm principalities and powers, making a public spectacle of them, triumphing over them in it" (Colossians 2:15).

Luke 11:23
He that is not with me is against me: and he that gathereth not with me scattereth.

No one can be neutral in the area of spiritual warfare. We either embrace Jesus or we are His enemy.

Luke 11:24–26
When the unclean spirit is gone out of a man, he walketh through dry places, seeking rest; and finding none, he saith, I will return unto my house whence I came out. And when he cometh, he findeth it swept and garnished. Then goeth he, and taketh to him seven other spirits more wicked than himself; and they enter in, and dwell there: and the last state of that man is worse than the first.

Continuing His discourse on spiritual warfare, Jesus makes it clear that if someone is freed from the grasp of a demon but doesn't embrace the Lord, demons will return to that individual seven times worse than before. This explains why, although psychology and psychiatry might help someone for a short time, he will end up worse than before if the Lord isn't at the core of the healing process because reformation apart from regeneration only leads to greater frustration. This applies sociologically, culturally, individually.

"We'll march in the streets to ban abortion," we say. "We'll pass laws against it. We'll elect candidates to outlaw it. We'll turn the moral tide of this country against it by reformation and legis-

lation." The result? Seven times the evil has come in the form of RU-486, a pill that causes abortion chemically and quietly. Reformation without regeneration just makes things darker. The real issue is that people must be born again. They must be open to the Word of God to guide them. Therefore, it is not our job as ministers and ambassadors to get people to clean up their acts. Our call is to introduce them to the Person of Jesus in order that they might be born again.

Luke 11:27, 28
And it came to pass, as he spake these things, a certain woman of the company lifted up her voice, and said unto him, Blessed is the womb that bare thee, and the paps which thou hast sucked. But he said, Yea rather, blessed are they that hear the word of God, and keep it.

Although this woman draws attention to His mother—a position that could be claimed by only one, Jesus redirects her attention to His family—a position available to all (John 1:12).

Luke 11:29–32
And when the people were gathered thick together, he began to say, This is an evil generation: they seek a sign; and there shall no sign be given it, but the sign of Jonas the prophet. For as Jonas was a sign unto the Ninevites, so shall also the Son of man be to this generation. The queen of the south shall rise up in the judgment with the men of this generation, and condemn them: for she came from the utmost parts of the earth to hear the wisdom of Solomon; and, behold, a greater than Solomon is here. The men of Nineve shall rise up in the judgment with this generation, and shall condemn it: for they repented at the preaching of Jonas; and, behold, a greater than Jonas is here.

The one sign Jesus would give to this and every generation was His Resurrection. Therefore, whenever you talk to unbelievers, the issue should always center on the Resurrection. The proof of the authority of Jesus Christ over every other so-called religious leader is singular. It is always the Resurrection.

Luke 11:33
No man, when he hath lighted a candle, putteth it in a secret place, neither under a bushel, but on a candlestick, that they which come in may see the light.

The reason light shines is in order that people might see. Therefore, if Jesus is the Light of the world (John 8:12), why don't people see the truth about Him? Read on.

Luke 11:34–36
The light of the body is the eye: therefore when thine eye is single, thy whole body also is full of light; but when thine eye is evil, thy body also is full of darkness. Take heed therefore that the light which is in thee be not darkness. If thy whole body therefore be full of light, having no part dark, the whole shall be full of light, as when the bright shining of a candle doth give thee light.

Even the brightest sun can't make a blind man see. This explains why even though Jesus is the Light of the world, people don't see properly because their eyes are darkened according to their own choice.

Luke 11:37
And as he spake, a certain Pharisee besought him to dine with him: and he went in, and sat down to meat.

Jesus never refused an opportunity to have a meal with someone—be it an invitation from a friend or from a Pharisee.

Luke 11:38
And when the Pharisee saw it, he marvelled that he had not first washed before dinner.

Washing speaks not of hygiene but of ritual. The Book of Leviticus makes it clear that ceremonial cleansing was intended only for the priests. But over the years, the priests required it of the people. I can see this same tendency in my own life. Perhaps you can in yours as well. Sometimes the Lord might speak to us individually about specific things we are or are not to do. But the temptation and tendency is for us to make what the Lord tells us personally a rule for everyone around us corporately. And such is the basis of legalism.

Luke 11:39–41
And the Lord said unto him, Now do ye Pharisees make clean the outside of the cup and the platter; but your inward part is full of ravening and wickedness. Ye fools, did not he that made that which is without make that which is within also? But rather give alms of such things as ye have; and, behold, all things are clean unto you.

True piety is not seen in religiosity, but through generosity. "Forget religion," Jesus says. "Give alms instead. Help people in need."

Luke 11:42, 43
But woe unto you, Pharisees! for ye tithe mint and rue and all manner of herbs, and pass over judgment and the love of God: these ought ye to have done, and not to leave the other undone. Woe unto you, Pharisees! for ye love the uppermost seats in the synagogues, and greetings in the markets.

Jesus indicted the Pharisees for the very thing they were good at: majoring on the minors, concentrating on external details while ignoring that which was essential and eternal. It was not their tithing that was wrong, but their failure to love. If one truly loves, tithing will follow, for while it is possible to give without loving, it is not possible to truly love without giving.

Luke 11:44
Woe unto you, scribes and Pharisees, hypocrites! for ye are as graves which appear not, and the men that walk over them are not aware of them.

According to the law, walking over a grave caused a person to be defiled. Thus, Jesus said to the Pharisees, "When people come into contact with you, they don't know you're dead, but you defile them nonetheless."

Luke 11:45, 46
Then answered one of the lawyers, and said unto him, Master, thus saying thou reproachest us also. And he said, Woe unto you also, ye lawyers! for ye lade men with burdens grievous to be borne, and ye yourselves touch not the burdens with one of your fingers.

"Come unto Me all ye that are weary and heavy-laden," Jesus said, "and I will give you rest" (Matthew 11:28). Jesus is the burden-Bearer.

The more I get to know people, the more I find myself praying, "Lord, don't allow me to burden anyone this day more heavily than they're already burdened." You see, although our tendency is to think we're the only ones going through hard times, everyone we meet, everyone we talk to is fighting a tough battle in some area of their lives. No wonder we are to be kind.

Luke 11:47, 48
Woe unto you! for ye build the sepulchres of the prophets, and your fathers killed them. Truly ye bear witness that ye allow the deeds of your fathers: for they indeed killed them, and ye build their sepulchres.

The religious leaders built impressive monuments for the prophets their own number had killed. Here, the greatest Prophet of all stood before them, and they would kill Him as well.

Luke 11:49–51
Therefore also said the wisdom of God, I will send them prophets and apostles, and some of them they shall slay and persecute: That the blood of all the prophets, which was shed from the foundation of the world, may be required of this generation; From the blood of Abel unto the blood of Zacharias, which perished between the altar and the temple: verily I say unto you, It shall be required of this generation.

From A to Z—the blood of Abel to Zacharias would be required at the hand of the religious establishment.

Luke 11:52
Woe unto you, lawyers! for ye have taken away the key of knowledge: ye entered not in yourselves, and them that were entering in ye hindered.

In the Middle Ages, the Bible was chained to the pulpit, for church leaders believed only a priest could rightly understand its contents. Although we no longer chain the Bible, I wonder sometimes when we say a clear understanding of the Word cannot be had without a knowledge of Greek, Hebrew, and the intricacies of theology if we're not, in effect, doing the same thing. While there is indeed a place in exposition for reaching back to the richness of the original language and culture, it must never be implied that one cannot, by himself, understand the Bible. Surely, the Lord will teach and instruct *anyone* who reads the Word, regardless of his educational or cultural background.

Luke 11:53, 54
And as he said these things unto them, the scribes and the Pharisees began to urge him vehemently, and to provoke him to speak of many things: Laying wait for him, and seeking to catch something out of his mouth, that they might accuse him.

The scribes and Pharisees tried to get Jesus to talk—not to gain understanding from Him, but in an effort to verbally trap Him.

———————————— ✥ ————————————

12

Luke 12:1 (a)
In the mean time, when there were gathered together an innumerable multitude of people, insomuch that they trode one upon another, he began to say unto his disciples . . .

Even as the Pharisees and lawyers, scribes and religious leaders tried to trip up Jesus, the common people flocked around Him. So it was at this point that He gave them two warnings about the perils of popularity. . . .

Luke 12:1 (b)
. . . first of all, Beware ye of the leaven of the Pharisees, which is hypocrisy.

The first danger to watch out for when things seem to be going well in your life, your business, your family, or your ministry is hypocrisy. The word "hypocrisy" comes from the Greek word *hupokrisis* and refers to the actors in Greek theatre who wore masks to identify their characters. Jesus likens this mask-wearing mentality to leaven because, although it may seem insignificant initially, it becomes puffed-up eventually.

Luke 12:2, 3
For there is nothing covered, that shall not be revealed; neither hid, that shall not be known. Therefore whatsoever ye have spoken in darkness shall be heard in the light; and that which ye have spoken in the ear in closets shall be proclaimed upon the housetops.

After identifying the danger of hypocrisy, Jesus goes on to speak of the irrationality of hypocrisy. Hypocrisy is foolish because the truth eventually comes out. "Be sure your sin will find you out," the Word declares (Numbers 32:23)—not because God will track us down, but because our sin itself will.

The same is true with righteousness. Jesus shone on the Mount of Transfiguration because He was light. Thus, the real miracle of the Transfiguration is not that Jesus was shining. The real miracle is that His humanity was able to conceal His divinity for so long. Indeed, that which is inside a man comes out eventually.

Luke 12:4–7
And I say unto you my friends, Be not afraid of them that kill the body, and after that have no more that they can do. But I will forewarn you whom ye shall fear: Fear him, which after he hath killed hath power to cast into hell; yea, I say unto you, Fear him. Are not five sparrows sold for two farthings, and not one of them is forgotten before God? But even the very hairs of your head are all

numbered. **Fear not therefore: ye are of more value than many sparrows.**

Continuing, Jesus speaks of the cause of hypocrisy, which is fear. Although we most often think of hypocrisy in terms of people who pretend to be Christians when they're not, I think an even more subtle form of hypocrisy is seen in Christians who think they'd better "tone down" their witness for fear of being thought of as too spiritual. "Don't worry about people," Jesus says. "Instead, fear the One whose eye is on you constantly." The realization that God is with you is the cure for hypocrisy.

Luke 12:8–12
Also I say unto you, Whosoever shall confess me before men, him shall the Son of man also confess before the angels of God: But he that denieth me before men shall be denied before the angels of God. And whosoever shall speak a word against the Son of man, it shall be forgiven him: but unto him that blasphemeth against the Holy Ghost it shall not be forgiven. And when they bring you unto the synagogues, and unto magistrates, and powers, take ye no thought how or what thing ye shall answer, or what ye shall say: For the Holy Ghost shall teach you in the same hour what ye ought to say.

The second element in the cure for hypocrisy is confession. When you begin a new job, move to a new neighborhood, or enroll in a new school, go on record from day one and let people know you're a believer. Confess Jesus before men, and the Holy Spirit will be right there, telling you what you should say.

Luke 12:13, 14
And one of the company said unto him, Master, speak to my brother, that he divide the inheritance with me. And he said unto him, Man, who made me a judge or a divider over you?

Although ministry can all too often become mired in an attempt to right perceived wrongs, Jesus wisely said, "This is not My area of concern," for His purpose was not to make bad men good or good men better. His purpose was to make dead men live, to see people born again and brought into the kingdom.

Luke 12:15 (a)
And he said unto them, Take heed, and beware of covetousness . . .

In addition to hypocrisy, the second danger of which to beware in the day of prosperity is covetousness. "I have heard the confession of every conceivable sin among men," one priest said, "except the sin of covetousness." People feel bad about immorality, lying, swearing—but when was the last time they cried over the sin of covetousness? Yet in Romans 7, Paul says covetousness is the very sin that plagued him. What is covetousness? Simply wanting more of that which we already have enough. And Jesus said it is a sin of which we must be so careful.

Luke 12:15 (b)
. . . for a man's life consisteth not in the abundance of the things which he possesseth.

Possessions are dangerous because they can possess us. Did you get a new car—or did it get you? You used to be free on Saturdays to toss a ball with your kids. But now you have to wax your car, tune it up, keep it running. Small men seek to get. Great men seek to *be*.

Luke 12:16–20
And he spake a parable unto them, saying, The ground of a certain rich man brought forth plentifully: And he thought within himself, saying, What shall I do, because I have no room where to bestow my fruits? And he said, This will I do: I will pull down my barns, and build greater; and there will I bestow all my fruits and my goods. And I will say to my soul, Soul, thou hast much goods laid up for many years; take thine ease, eat, drink, and be merry. But God said unto him, Thou fool, this night thy soul shall be required of thee: then whose shall those things be, which thou hast provided?

The tragedy of this parable lies not in what the rich man left behind, but in the judgment that awaited him, for he would enter heaven without any evidence of wise stewardship on earth.

Luke 12:21–24
So is he that layeth up treasure for himself, and is not rich toward God. And he said unto his disciples, Therefore I say unto you, Take no thought for your life, what ye shall eat; neither for the body, what ye shall put on. The life is more than meat, and the body is more than raiment. Consider the ravens: for they neither sow nor reap; which neither have storehouse nor barn; and God feedeth them: how much more are ye better than the fowls?

God has given us all things not to possess, but to enjoy. The birds sing because they don't have to pay taxes, work on their wardrobes, or paint their houses. They simply enjoy what God gives. Do we do the same?

Luke 12:25–32

And which of you with taking thought can add to his stature one cubit? If ye then be not able to do that thing which is least, why take ye thought for the rest? Consider the lilies how they grow: they toil not, they spin not; and yet I say unto you, that Solomon in all his glory was not arrayed like one of these. If then God so clothe the grass, which is to day in the field, and to morrow is cast into the oven; how much more will he clothe you, O ye of little faith? And seek not ye what ye shall eat, or what ye shall drink, neither be ye of doubtful mind. For all these things do the nations of the world seek after: and your Father knoweth that ye have need of these things. But rather seek ye the kingdom of God; and all these things shall be added unto you. Fear not, little flock; for it is your Father's good pleasure to give you the kingdom.

Don't worry about what you eat, drink, or wear. God knows you have need of these things. He's not out to restrict you. His purpose is to liberate you now and eternally.

Luke 12:33, 34

Sell that ye have, and give alms; provide yourselves bags which wax not old, a treasure in the heavens that faileth not, where no thief approacheth, neither moth corrupteth. For where your treasure is, there will your heart be also.

In the world's stock market, the word is "Buy." In God's, it's "Sell." This doesn't mean you shouldn't have a home or a boat or a car. But if anything begins to possess you, leaving you less time and energy for the things of the Lord, sell it and invest in people, in heaven, in the kingdom.

Luke 12:35–37 (a)

Let your loins be girded about, and your lights burning; and ye yourselves like unto men that wait for their lord, when he will return from the wedding; that when he cometh and knocketh, they may open unto him immediately. Blessed are those servants, whom the lord when he cometh shall find watching . . .

This text encourages my heart because Jesus doesn't say, "Blessed are those servants who,

when the Lord comes, He shall find working, witnessing, praying, preaching, studying or serving." No. Jesus says, "Blessed, or happy, is the one who the Lord finds simply watching"—the one who realizes this life is not where it's at, that life is empty apart from Him. If you are reeling from a relationship that is not working out, finances that are not coming in, or physical pain that is eating you up, blessed are you, for you are acutely aware of the emptiness of this world—and you look forward to heaven all the more.

Luke 12:37 (b)

. . . verily I say unto you, that he shall gird himself . . .

I am reminded of another time the Lord girded Himself when, a few weeks after this, as His disciples sat around the table in the Upper Room arguing who was the greatest, He washed their dirty, stinky feet (John 13:4, 5).

Luke 12:37 (c)

. . . and make them to sit down to meat . . .

Why would the Lord have to make us sit down to eat? Because the tendency of our flesh is to pop up, run around, and say, "Okay, Lord, I want to serve You." We are quick to jump up, but sometimes the Lord would have us sit down.

Luke 12:37 (d)

. . . and will come forth and serve them.

The one watching for the Lord's coming will be blessed because Jesus will gird Himself with a towel and will serve him, take care of him, bless him. It was to a cold, weary Peter that Jesus served a hot, hearty breakfast. Thus, even at a time of disobedience in his own life—even when Peter was fishing when he was supposed to be in Jerusalem waiting, he found in the hand of the Lord the very thing he had been searching for all night long (John 21:9).

Luke 12:38

And if he shall come in the second watch, or come in the third watch, and find them so, blessed are those servants.

Why, in John 13, did Jesus wash feet and serve His disciples? Why, in John 21, did He cook fish and feed them? Why does Jesus bless those who are simply looking for His coming? Because those whom the Lord serves realize grace has nothing to do with who they are and everything to do with who He is. Those whom the Lord serves understand it's no longer due to their greatness, but solely to His graciousness that they are blessed; that it's not based upon anything they have or haven't done, but completely upon what He did on the Cross when He died for their sins.

Henceforth there is laid up for me a crown of righteousness, which the Lord, the righteous judge, shall give me at that day: and not to me only, but unto all them also that love his appearing.   2 Timothy 4:8

The crown of righteousness is given not to those who fight the good fight or run the race successfully. It's given to those who love His appearing. It's given to those who say, "Lord, I realize that this world is not really where it's at. There's got to be more. Therefore, I'm looking for Your coming."

Luke 12:39, 40
And this know, that if the goodman of the house had known what hour the thief would come, he would have watched, and not have suffered his house to be broken through. Be ye therefore ready also: for the Son of man cometh at an hour when ye think not.

There are those who say that Jesus cannot come back this hour because the church hasn't yet gone through the Tribulation as described in Revelation 6—19. But I challenge this because Jesus in this passage was telling His disciples to watch, to be constantly alert for the possibility of His coming at a time they didn't expect it. If, on the other hand, the church were indeed to go through the Tribulation, we would know precisely the hour of His coming: exactly 1,260 days after the day Antichrist goes into the rebuilt Jewish temple and demands to be worshiped (Daniel 12; Revelation 12—13). Thus, His coming would not be "at an hour we think not." I believe one of the keys to overcoming hypocrisy and covetousness is to live in constant anticipation that *today* could be the day Jesus comes back.

Luke 12:41
Then Peter said unto him, Lord, speakest thou this parable unto us, or even to all?

Jesus will talk to both: to the disciples in verses 42–53, and then to the crowd in verses 54 to 59. . . .

Luke 12:42, 43
And the Lord said, Who then is that faithful and wise steward, whom his lord shall make ruler over his household, to give them their portion of meat in due season? Blessed is

that servant, whom his lord when he cometh shall find so doing.

Blessed, happy is the one living in the expectation that the Son of Man might come even this hour.

Luke 12:44
Of a truth I say unto you, that he will make him ruler over all that he hath.

Here, Jesus hints at the fact that those who are watching for His coming presently will, in the ages to come, hold positions of authority. In other words, what we do now affects what we'll do in heaven. Maybe there are interests or desires God has placed on your heart that have yet to be worked out or realized. It is very likely that when you get to heaven, those will be the very areas that will come into fullness and fruition in your life.

Luke 12:45
But and if that servant say in his heart, My lord delayeth his coming; and shall begin to beat the menservants and maidens, and to eat and drink, and to be drunken.

The result of saying the Lord can't come today will be a two-fold tendency: brutality and carnality. How would we treat one another if we truly believed Jesus would return in the next twenty-four hours? I only lash out at people or beat up on people if I forget Jesus could very well come today. An awareness of the Rapture is not escapism. Quite the opposite. Jesus said a realization of return leads one to living rightly and rewards eternally.

Luke 12:46–48
The lord of that servant will come in a day when he looketh not for him, and at an hour when he is not aware, and will cut him in sunder, and will appoint him his portion with the unbelievers. And that servant, which knew his Lord's will, and prepared not himself, neither did according to his will, shall be beaten with many stripes. But he that knew not, and did commit things worthy of stripes, shall be beaten with few stripes. For unto whomsoever much is given, of him shall be much required: and to whom men have committed much, of him they will ask the more.

I don't believe the evil servant here is doomed to hell. Rather, I believe the implication is that he simply loses out on what he could have enjoyed eternally had he lived his life looking for his Lord's return.

Luke 12:49
I am come to send fire on the earth; and what will I if it be already kindled?

I believe Jesus is speaking of the fire of Pentecost, perhaps as if to say, "I wish I had already gone through the process of the Cross."

Luke 12:50
But I have a baptism to be baptized with; and how am I straitened till it be accomplished!

Speaking of the baptism of His crucifixion, Jesus reaffirms His commitment to go to the Cross, to finish the Work of our salvation, to save our souls.

Luke 12:51–53
Suppose ye that I am come to give peace on earth? I tell you, Nay; but rather division: For from henceforth there shall be five in one house divided, three against two, and two against three. The father shall be divided against the son, and the son against the father; the mother against the daughter, and the daughter against the mother; the mother-in-law against her daughter-in-law, and the daughter-in-law against her mother-in-law.

In the context of this teaching, Jesus' words serve as a warning that His coming will cause division. Perhaps there are some in your family who say, "Do you really believe Jesus is going to come again, that you're going to be raptured up to heaven? You're crazy!" Take heart, Jesus told us this would happen.

Luke 12:54–57
And he said also to the people, When ye see a cloud rise out of the west, straightway ye say, There cometh a shower; and so it is. And when ye see the south wind blow, ye say, There will be heat; and it cometh to pass. Ye hypocrites, ye can discern the face of the sky and of the earth; but how is it that ye do not discern this time? Yea, and why even of yourselves judge ye not what is right?

We can put a man on the moon, but we don't know what in the world is going on. Scientists can tell us how to get to the stars, but not how to get to heaven. So, while our understanding is expanding technologically, we are left in the dark spiritually.

Although the scientists of Jesus' day weren't able to send men to the moon, they did indeed study the skies. And in so doing, they became adept at predicting the weather, but inept at understanding the climate of their times. You see, they should have known their Messiah was among them, for Micah 5:2 declared He would be born in Bethlehem—and hadn't a so-called King been born in Bethlehem thirty-three years earlier, so intimidating to Herod that he ordered the annihilation of all boys two years of age and under? They should have known their Messiah was among them when people began to imply that the Rabbi from Galilee was conceived illegitimately, for didn't Isaiah declare centuries earlier that when this One came the sign given would be that a virgin would conceive and bring forth a son (Isaiah 7:14)? They should have known their Messiah was among them, for the people of Israel had been enslaved in Egypt for four hundred years before a deliverer was raised up to lead them into the Land of Promise. And now, after four hundred years of silence following the Book of Malachi, hadn't a herald in the form of a locust-eating Baptist come on the scene pointing to the One who would lead them not into the Promised Land, but all the way to heaven? No wonder that before He rode into the city to present Himself as King, Jesus looked down on Jerusalem and wept, "O, Jerusalem, Jerusalem, if thou wouldest have known this is thy day"—the day prophesied by Daniel.

Know therefore and understand, that from the going forth of the commandment to restore and to build Jerusalem unto the Messiah the Prince shall be seven weeks, and threescore and two weeks . . .   Daniel 9:25 (a)

A *heptad,* or "week," being seven years, sixty-nine *heptads* would be four hundred eighty-three years. It was on March 14, 445 B.C. that Artaxerxes gave the order to restore and rebuild Jerusalem. And exactly 173,880 days—483 years—later, on April 6, A.D. 32, Jesus rode into Jerusalem. No wonder He said, "You should have known this is your day."

Luke 12:58
When thou goest with thine adversary to the magistrate, as thou art in the way, give diligence that thou mayest be delivered from him; lest he hale thee to the judge, and the judge deliver thee to the officer, and the officer cast thee into prison.

When you have a legal matter, you try to work it out without going to court—especially if you know you're the one in error. Therefore, wouldn't it be logical to prepare for the Day of Judgment?

Luke 12:59
I tell thee, thou shalt not depart thence, till thou hast paid the very last mite.

Just as it is impossible for one to work off his debt once he's put in prison, those who are without Christ on the Day of Judgment will be cast into hell with no way to work their way out. Oh, to be watching and wise concerning the day of His appearing.

13 **Luke 13:1–5**
There were present at that season some that told him of the Galilaeans, whose blood Pilate had mingled with their sacrifices. And Jesus answering said unto them, Suppose ye that these Galilaeans were sinners above all the Galilaeans, because they suffered such things? I tell you, Nay: but, except ye repent, ye shall all likewise perish. Or those eighteen, upon whom the tower in Siloam fell, and slew them, think ye that they were sinners above all men that dwelt in Jerusalem? I tell you, Nay: but, except ye repent, ye shall all likewise perish.

After listening to Him talk about preparing for eternity, those listening to Jesus asked, "What about the tragedy we're seeing presently?"

"I want you to understand something about tragedy," Jesus answered. "Those Galileans were not sinners above others. Nor were those who died in Siloam. And unless you repent, you will perish as well."

This concept is so important. Whether you observe tragedy in the lives of others, or experience it yourself, the question is not, "Why did it happen?" Rather, the question is why it doesn't happen more often. Because of our sin and continual rebellion, we deserve to be wiped out totally. It's only because of the Lord's mercies that we are not consumed entirely (Lamentations 3:22). There's far too much muttering about that which didn't work out in our lives when there should be a whole lot more marveling about how good God has been to sinners like us.

Luke 13:6 (a)
He spake also this parable; a certain man had a fig tree planted in his vineyard . . .

The fig tree was a symbol representing the nation of Israel, so Jesus uses it in a parable to remind the Jews that they are no better than the Galileans or those living in Siloam.

Luke 13:6 (b), 7
. . . and he came and sought fruit thereon, and found none. Then said he unto the dresser of his vineyard, Behold, these three years I come seeking fruit on this fig tree, and find none: cut it down; why cumbereth it the ground?

Even as Jesus ministered publicly for three years to a people who, by and large, would not respond or receive Him, so, too, regarding the fig tree in this parable, after finding no fruit upon it for three years, the owner says, "Cut it down. It's doing nothing more than soaking up nutrients from the soil and taking up room in the garden."

Luke 13:8
And he answering said unto him, Lord, let it alone this year also, till I shall dig about it, and dung it.

Within the year, the vinedresser would do two things: First, he would dig around the roots. The Father, our Vinedresser (John 15:1), does the same with us as He gets to the root issues in our lives by exposing sin. Second, he would "dung"— or fertilize—it. After giving a list of his qualifications and accomplishments, Paul refers to them as dung, an appropriate name for the best the flesh is able to produce (Philippians 3:8).

Luke 13:9
And if it bear fruit, well: and if not, then after that thou shalt cut it down.

After being cultivated for a year, did the fig tree go on to bear fruit? Jesus doesn't say. Because the parable is open ended, because it must be applied personally, that question must be answered individually. What is fruit? Among other things, the Bible defines it as giving thanks to His name (Hebrews 13:15), giving monetary gifts (Philippians 4:17), loving people (Galatians 5:22, 23), winning souls (Romans 1:13), doing works of righteousness (James 3:18). We exist for one reason: That the Lord might be satiated and satisfied by the fruit in our lives (Colossians 1:16). Does the Lord find fruit on the tree of your life— or does He walk away empty-handed each time He passes by?

The way to bear fruit for the Lord's pleasure is to allow Him to "dig and dung," to expose sin and dispel self. How does this happen practically? By beginning each day and every project saying, "Lord, I need You. I can't do this. My own ability, my own personality is dung. My heart is riddled with sin. Oh, I can produce leaves to impress people—but not fruit to satisfy You. It is only by Your mercy and grace that I will have anything of substance or pleasure to offer You."

Luke 13:10, 11
And he was teaching in one of the synagogues on the sabbath. And, behold, there was a woman which had a spirit of infirmity eighteen years, and was bowed together, and could in no wise lift up herself.

This is a mystery to me because Jesus' referring to her as a daughter of Abraham (verse 16) means this woman was a woman of faith. And yet for eighteen years, the work of the Enemy bound her physically. Nonetheless, here she was in the synagogue. She would have missed the moment of the miraculous had she stayed home the day Jesus "just happened" to walk in.

I can recall specific times in my own pilgrimage when I didn't want to go to a Bible study or a church service but went anyway—to experience Jesus ministering to me in a way I'm convinced He wouldn't have otherwise. Therefore, I have learned this secret: The more I don't feel like meeting with the congregation, the more I need to be there. I am convinced that people walk around needlessly crippled because they're not in the company of believers, not in the place where Jesus is (Hebrews 2:12).

Luke 13:12 (a)
And when Jesus saw her, he called her to him . . .

Upon entering a situation, some have an eye to see what's wrong. Others have an eye to see what's right. Jesus has an eye to see who's in need. I like that.

Luke 13:12 (b), 13
. . . and said unto her, Woman, thou art loosed from thine infirmity. And he laid his hands on her: and immediately she was made straight, and glorified God.

When Jesus touches someone addicted to drugs, alcohol, sexual perversion, or any other sin, there comes a moment when he is made straight. Immediately. For some that might sound simplistic. I've seen it happen enough, however, to know that when Jesus touches people through the Word and through the body, they are made straight immediately.

"But I've been coming to church for eighteen months, and I'm still caught up in this addiction or bowed down by that activity," you say. Keep coming. Keep believing. Keep worshiping—for,

because Jesus is the same yesterday, today, and forever, there will come a time when, like the daughter of Abraham, you will hear in your heart, "Thou art loosed." And, like her, you'll be able to stand up straight.

Luke 13:14
And the ruler of the synagogue answered with indignation, because that Jesus had healed on the sabbath day, and said unto the people, There are six days in which men ought to work: in them therefore come and be healed, and not on the sabbath day.

The healing of a godly woman caused the ruler of the synagogue to become indignant. Amazing.

Luke 13:15, 16
The Lord then answered him, and said, Thou hypocrite, doth not each one of you on the sabbath loose his ox or his ass from the stall, and lead him away to watering? And ought not this woman, being a daughter of Abraham, whom Satan hath bound, lo, these eighteen years, be loosed from this bond on the sabbath day?

On the Sabbath, Jesus loosed the woman who had been bound physically. But because of their rules and regulations regarding the Sabbath, this religious leader would remain bound in false piety and hypocrisy.

Luke 13:17
And when he had said these things, all his adversaries were ashamed: and all the people rejoiced for all the glorious things that were done by him.

We follow a radical Leader, gang—One who is liberating, One who is unique, One who is wonderful.

Luke 13:18, 19
Then said he, Unto what is the kingdom of God like? and whereunto shall I resemble it? It is like a grain of mustard seed, which a man took, and cast into his garden; and it grew, and waxed a great tree; and the fowls of the air lodged in the branches of it.

Because mustard seeds don't grow into trees large enough to support birds, and because flocks of birds in Scripture are often symbols of evil (e.g., Genesis 40:19; Matthew 13:4), in this parable, through this analogy, Jesus is saying that the kingdom of God will grow in an unnatural way that will allow strange people to hide out therein. All you have to do is watch religious TV to see that this is so, for there are indeed some strange birds roosting in the name of the kingdom of God.

Luke 13:20, 21
And again he said, Whereunto shall I liken the kingdom of God? It is like leaven, which a woman took and hid in three measures of meal, till the whole was leavened.

Leaven appears ninety-eight times in the Scriptures—and in every instance it speaks of evil. So when people point accusingly to evil even within church history, I don't have to rationalize or defend it because Jesus said this would happen.

Luke 13:22, 23 (a)
And he went through the cities and villages, teaching, and journeying toward Jerusalem. Then said one unto him, Lord, are there few that be saved?

As Jesus journeyed toward Jerusalem, a man asked Him, "Lord, are just a few going to be saved?"—a controversial question even to this day. Many people question the exclusivity of God, wondering how He could exclude people from living eternally.

Luke 13:23 (b), 24
And he said unto them, Strive to enter in at the strait gate: for many, I say unto you, will seek to enter in, and shall not be able.

Hearing this question, Jesus did what He so often did—rather than answering it directly, He dealt with the one who asked it personally. Skirting the hypothetical, He got right to the practical because His concern was not theoretical; it was personal. We are told that the Lord elected us, chose us, predestined us before the foundation of the world (Ephesians 1:4). That is why Jesus told His disciples that it was He who chose them—not vice versa (John 15:16).

Luke 13:25
When once the master of the house is risen up, and hath shut to the door, and ye begin to stand without, and to knock at the door, saying, Lord, Lord, open unto us; and he shall answer and say unto you, I know you not whence ye are.

To those who don't want to open their lives to Him now, Jesus will not open His kingdom then. I can't help but think of Noah. For one hundred years, he told the people they had better turn around and change directions because a flood was coming. But they thought he was all wet— until the rain began to fall. Then they wanted in. But because it was the Lord who shut the door, Noah couldn't open it to let a few more people inside. And in this, the Lord shows us that there comes a day when the door is shut and one's decision is sealed eternally.

Luke 13:26–30
Then shall ye begin to say, We have eaten and drunk in thy presence, and thou hast taught in our streets. But he shall say, I tell you, I know you not whence ye are; depart from me, all ye workers of iniquity. There shall be weeping and gnashing of teeth, when ye shall see Abraham, and Isaac, and Jacob, and all the prophets, in the kingdom of God, and you yourselves thrust out. And they shall come from the east, and from the west, and from the north, and from the south, and shall sit down in the kingdom of God. And, behold, there are last which shall be first, and there are first which shall be last.

"But, Lord," people will protest, "we ate with You. We listened to You. We were at church regularly. We went to the singles' potlucks every Friday."

And the Lord will say, "I don't know you," because the issue is not association. It's regeneration.

That is why Jesus says, "Strive to enter in," (verse 24). The Greek word translated "strive" is *agonizomai,* from which we get our word "agonize." It is the word used to describe what Jesus did in the Garden of Gethsemane, where He agonized about the Father's will with such intensity that He actually sweat blood (Luke 22:44). Although Scripture tells us over and over again not to strive (Proverbs 3:30; 2 Timothy 2:14; 2 Timothy 2:24), there is one question over which we should indeed strive: Am I saved? Whether He comes for us tomorrow, or whether we live thirty more years, how can we know we're going to spend eternity with the Lord? Three ways . . .

The Scripture before us . . .

These things have I written unto you that believe on the name of the Son of God; that ye may know that ye have eternal life, and that ye may believe on the name of the Son of God.
1 John 5:13

The Greek word translated "believe" is *pisteuo.* Used in reference to the way one places his weight on a crutch, *pisteuo* doesn't mean to merely agree with intellectually, but to lean on, or trust in. Yet even though we believe the Word, the fact remains that people can challenge us concerning it. So there is a second place wherein we find assurance of our salvation. . . .

The saints around us . . .

We know that we have passed from death unto life, because we love the brethren. He that loveth not his brother abideth in death.

1 John 3:14

You know you're born again when you start loving Christians—people you couldn't stand before you got saved. You know you're saved when you find yourself feeling comfortable with the Christian community. But lest we doubt our salvation when we don't love the saints as consistently as we should, there is a third assurance. . . .

The Spirit within us . . .

For as many as are led by the Spirit of God, they are the sons of God.   Romans 8:14

The work of the Holy Ghost is to give you a witness in your heart in order that you might know that you know that you know you're saved. Martin Luther and John Calvin called this passage the *Testimonium Spiritus Internus Sanctium*—or the Internal Testimony of the Spirit. If you haven't received the witness of the Spirit in your heart, you must agonize until you know with absolute certainty that you truly are born again, that you can go to the Father freely and say, "Abba, I come to You not because of my spirituality, but because You have cleansed me by the blood of Calvary."

Luke 13:31
The same day there came certain of the Pharisees, saying unto him, Get thee out, and depart hence: for Herod will kill thee.

The Pharisees said this not because they cared about Jesus, but to get Him to leave their region.

Luke 13:32
And he said unto them, Go ye, and tell that fox, Behold, I cast out devils, and I do cures to day and to morrow, and the third day I shall be perfected.

A three-day journey away from Jerusalem, Jesus said, "I'm going to continue dealing with the devil and healing people on My way to Jerusalem." Once there, He would deal a deathblow to Satan and purchase eternal healing and salvation for mankind as He hung on the Cross of Calvary.

Luke 13:33
Nevertheless I must walk to day, and to morrow, and the day following: for it cannot be that a prophet perish out of Jerusalem.

"I don't have to worry about Herod's threats," said Jesus, "because I know I'll make it to Jerusalem, for that's where I must die."

Luke 13:34
O Jerusalem, Jerusalem, which killest the prophets, and stonest them that are sent unto thee; how often would I have gathered thy children together, as a hen doth gather her brood under her wings, and ye would not!

Knowing Socrates was innocent of the charge of corrupting the youth of Athens, it is said that his executioner wept as he handed him the hemlock. Here, however, the executioner doesn't weep for the Condemned, the Condemned weeps for the executioners (John 11:35). Truly, the world has never seen such love. What a picture! Jesus cries not because Jerusalem would reject Him, but because they wouldn't allow Him to protect them. How about you? Have you allowed the Lord to do what He desires to do—to place His arm around you, to protect and comfort you? It is not our shortcomings or our failings that cause the Lord to weep. Rather, it is our failure to allow Him to love us that causes His tears to flow.

Jesus called Herod a fox—devious, sly, destructive (Luke 13:32). Yet He likened Himself to a hen—comforting, nurturing, protective. How about us? Has today been a day of devouring others, or has it been a day of defending others? I'm so deeply impressed with Jesus Christ because of His incredible mercy and largeness of heart. How I long to be less like a fox and more like a hen.

Luke 13:35
Behold, your house is left unto you desolate: and verily I say unto you, Ye shall not see me, until the time come when ye shall say, Blessed is he that cometh in the name of the Lord.

"You won't see Me," said Jesus, "until you are finally ready to acknowledge Me as Lord." That's what the Tribulation is all about—to bring Israel to the point where she is awakened to the fact that Jesus is indeed Messiah (Zechariah 12, 14; Psalm 118).

14

Luke 14:1
And it came to pass, as he went into the house of one of the chief Pharisees to eat bread on the sabbath day, that they watched him.

Whether issued by Pharisee or publican, friend or foe, Jesus never turned down an invitation. At this particular meal, He will speak very pointedly to five groups of people. And what He will say will be shockingly honest. In verses 2–6, He will speak to the Pharisees about their pseudo-spirituality. In verses 7–11, He will talk to the guests surrounding Him about their miserable manners and methodology. In verses 12–14, He will correct the host who invited Him concerning his wrong motives for hospitality. In verses 15–24, He will reply to the man who interrupted Him regarding his mistaken assumption of his destiny. In verses 25–34, He will address the crowd about their need to think carefully.

Whether in relation to parenting, vocation, or ministry, every one of us comes to a certain point when we have the opportunity to choose to do what Jesus did so naturally and so beautifully—to care more about others doing well than about what they think of us. All too often, we shy away from speaking truth because we want others to like us. Not so Jesus, for in the chapter before us, He'll say things that, although hard to hear, were needful not only for His listeners, but for us. . . .

Luke 14:2
And, behold, there was a certain man before him which had the dropsy.

Knowing Jesus had already healed on the Sabbath six times previously, the Pharisees were waiting to accuse Him of breaking the Sabbath law should he do so again.

Luke 14:3, 4
And Jesus answering spake unto the lawyers and Pharisees, saying, Is it lawful to heal on the sabbath day? And they held their peace. And he took him, and healed him, and let him go.

Knowing exactly what the Pharisees were thinking, Jesus tossed the ball back into their court—silencing them in the process.

Luke 14:5
And answered them, saying, Which of you shall have an ass or an ox fallen into a pit,

and will not straightway pull him out on the sabbath day?

The same traditions that stated that a man couldn't be healed on the Sabbath also said that an animal that had fallen into a pit on the Sabbath could be rescued. The same thing happens today. Legislation passed recently declares that he who removes an egg from a spotted owl's nest can be punished five years in the state penitentiary. But a doctor can abort as many babies as he wants without anyone saying a word.

Luke 14:6
And they could not answer him again to these things.

It is not our rules, regulations, or pseudo-spirituality that will impact people. It is our love, our compassion, our desire to help those in need that causes even the Pharisees to wonder.

Luke 14:7–11
And he put forth a parable to those which were bidden, when he marked how they chose out the chief rooms; saying unto them, When thou art bidden of any man to a wedding, sit not down in the highest room; lest a more honourable man than thou be bidden of him; and he that bade thee and him come and say to thee, Give this man place; and thou begin with shame to take the lowest room. But when thou art bidden, go and sit down in the lowest room; that when he that bade thee cometh, he may say unto thee, Friend, go up higher: then shalt thou have worship in the presence of them that sit at meat with thee. For whosoever exalteth himself shall be abased; and he that humbleth himself shall be exalted.

Shifting His attention from the Pharisees to the other guests, Jesus speaks to those who were jockeying for the best spots at the table, who were more concerned about sitting in the right place than about being the right person.

Luke 14:12–14
Then said he also to him that bade him, When thou makest a dinner or a supper, call not thy friends, nor thy brethren, neither thy kinsmen, nor thy rich neighbours; lest they also bid thee again, and a recompence be made thee. But when thou makest a feast, call the poor, the maimed, the lame, the blind: And thou shalt be blessed; for they cannot recompense thee: for thou shalt be recompensed at the resurrection of the just.

Addressing the host of the event, Jesus said, "Don't only invite people who can do something for you—who can pay you back, include you in their circle, or return your invitation. When you give a dinner party, invite the nobodies."

Luke 14:15
And when one of them that sat at meat with him heard these things, he said unto him, Blessed is he that shall eat bread in the kingdom of God.

At this point, the dinner must have been getting a bit tense. After all, the Pharisees and lawyers, guests and host had all been corrected and rebuked. So perhaps it was to change the subject that this man said, "We're all Jews. Let's talk about something we can agree upon. Let's talk about the Resurrection."

Luke 14:16, 17
Then said he unto him, A certain man made a great supper, and bade many: And sent his servant at supper time to say to them that were bidden, Come; for all things are now ready.

Sitting at this dinner party, Jesus speaks of an even greater feast. . . .

Luke 14:18–20
And they all with one consent began to make excuse. The first said unto him, I have bought a piece of ground, and I must needs go and see it: I pray thee have me excused. And another said, I have bought five yoke of oxen, and I go to prove them: I pray thee have me excused. And another said, I have married a wife, and therefore I cannot come.

Aren't these the same excuses men use to this day?

- "I can't accept Your invitation, Lord. I've got to take care of my possessions," or —
- "My job just won't allow me to seek God at this time in my life," or —
- "I'm married. My first priority is my spouse."

Jesus is speaking of heaven, of salvation, of eternity—of matters of the greatest possible significance. Yet people say, "Sorry, I just don't have time."

Luke 14:21 (a)
So that servant came, and shewed his lord these things. Then the master of the house being angry said to his servant . . .

The master of the house was angry. He had given such great opportunity to people. Yet all they gave him in return were weak excuses.

Luke 14:21 (b)
. . . Go out quickly into the streets and lanes of the city, and bring in hither the poor, and the maimed, and the halt, and the blind.

Why would the master of the house invite those who were poor, maimed, and blind? Because poor people wouldn't be distracted by material possessions; maimed people wouldn't be harnessing oxen; and blind people weren't likely to be married. In other words, the servants were to invite those who were not distracted by possessions, vocation, or affections. They were to invite those who wouldn't make ludicrous excuses, who wouldn't be sidetracked by things of the world, who would have a heart for heaven and sensitivity toward the things of the kingdom. That is why Paul would later say to the early church, "Look around. You don't see many rich, many noble, many wise among you,"—and why we find the same to be true two thousand years later (1 Corinthians 1:26).

Luke 14:22–24
And the servant said, Lord, it is done as thou hast commanded, and yet there is room. And the lord said unto the servant, Go out into the highways and hedges, and compel them to come in, that my house may be filled. For I say unto you, That none of those men which were bidden shall taste of my supper.

Because the Jews—those who had been invited initially, those who had the prophets and the Pentateuch, those who had Jesus living among them presently—had excuses, the Gentiles were invited. And, poor, maimed, and blind as we are, we accepted the invitation gladly!

Luke 14:25
And there went great multitudes with him: and he turned, and said unto them,

That the feast at which Jesus was a guest took place in an open courtyard, a crowd would have heard His words to the Pharisees, the host, and the invited guests. And now Jesus has a word for them as well. . . .

Luke 14:26
If any man come to me, and hate not his father, and mother, and wife, and children, and brethren, and sisters, yea, and his own life also, he cannot be my disciple.

It's as if Jesus said to the crowd, "Before you cheer Me on because of what I've said to others, you yourselves need to think more carefully about what it means to be My disciple."

Having been notified that one of his students had done something foolish, the wise professor answered, "That person may have attended my lectures, but he is not one of my students." So, too, just as there is a difference between attending lectures and being a student, there is a difference between being a Christian and being a disciple. "Disciple" means "disciplined one"—one who is committed to the cause of the kingdom. Thus, Jesus is saying, "You can't be My disciple if other affections have priority in your life."

Luke 14:27
And whosoever doth not bear his cross, and come after me, cannot be my disciple.

There is a great deal of misunderstanding concerning what it means to bear one's cross. A noisy neighbor is not a cross. Arthritis is not a cross. Financial pressure is not a cross. Neighbors, illness, finances are just the stuff of life, common to Christian and heathen alike. Jesus showed us what the cross is when He laid down His life in order that we could be lifted up. The cross is the way by which we die to self in order that others can be saved, helped, redeemed, restored. And Jesus says we can't be disciples unless we are willing to lay aside our rights and preferences in order to see others do well.

Luke 14:28–33
For which of you, intending to build a tower, sitteth not down first, and counteth the cost, whether he have sufficient to finish it? Lest haply, after he hath laid the foundation, and is not able to finish it, all that behold it begin to mock him, Saying, This man began to build, and was not able to finish. Or what king, going to make war against another king, sitteth not down first, and consulteth whether he be able with ten thousand to meet him that cometh against him with twenty thousand? Or else, while the other is yet a great way off, he sendeth an ambassage, and desireth conditions of peace. So likewise, whosoever he be of you that forsaketh not all that he hath, he cannot be my disciple.

Whether building or battling—and the Christian life consists of both—a disciple must count the cost carefully and pay the price sacrificially.

Luke 14:34, 35 (a)
Salt is good: but if the salt have lost his savour, wherewith shall it be seasoned? It is neither fit for the land, nor yet for the dunghill; but men cast it out.

"You must hate your family, count the cost carefully, bear the cross daily or risk becoming useless." It was because Jesus loved these people deeply that He spoke to them so honestly.

Luke 14:35 (b)
He that hath ears to hear, let him hear.

The very ideas Jesus conveyed at the table here in chapter 14 are the same ones He speaks to my heart at the table of Communion . . .

As He did with the Pharisees, Jesus deals with my pseudo-spirituality. When I take the bread and drink the cup, all the dials get set back to zero, and my faith becomes miraculously and mystically simple. The Pharisee within me dissipates when I'm at the Lord's table. . . .

As He did with the guests, Jesus reminds me that I put Him on the Cross; I broke His body; He died for me. Therefore, when I'm at the Lord's table, I have no desire to be in a position of honor or prominence. Instead, I want to lose my identity and blend into a oneness with the body of Christ, a oneness with Jesus.

As He did with the host, Jesus zeroes in on my motives. People who want to grow intellectually or who want to be noticed in ministry oftentimes will ignore the Lord's table because they think it doesn't benefit them. Not so the early church. They saw Communion as essential, for it is through Communion that they remembered Jesus.

As He did with the man who brought up the subject of the kingdom, Jesus reminds me of my destiny—that because His body was broken and His blood shed, I'm going to heaven.

And as He did with the crowd, Jesus causes me to think clearly regarding the price He paid for my sin, and the cost of discipleship.

Simple theology, heartfelt humility, motivational purity, a reminder of destiny, and a call to think clearly are found at His table—be it in the home of a Pharisee or at Communion presently.
Come and dine!

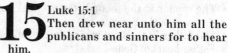

15
Luke 15:1
Then drew near unto him all the publicans and sinners for to hear him.

"Those who have ears to hear, listen up," Jesus said—and the publicans and sinners did just that. The Pharisees and the guests of honor didn't gather quite as closely. It was the sinners who responded to Him.

Luke 15:2 (a)
And the Pharisees and scribes murmured, saying, This man receiveth sinners . . .

Even though they didn't know what they were saying, the enemies of Jesus often shared profound insights about Him. . . .

"He saved others, but Himself He cannot save," they said as Jesus hung on the Cross (Matthew 27:42). How true. If He had saved Himself, He could not have saved me.

"It is expedient that one man die for the nation" (John 18:14). Although Caiaphas meant it was better that a "rabble-rouser" die than that the whole nation be bludgeoned into submission by the Romans, he unknowingly spoke prophetically—for Jesus did indeed die not for a nation, but for the whole world.

"He receives sinners," scoffed the scribes and Pharisees in an attempt to put Jesus down. But what a marvelous truth. He does indeed receive sinners. The religious community might reject me, high society might refuse me—but Jesus Christ will always receive me.

Luke 15:2 (b)
. . . and eateth with them.

In Eastern culture, it was believed that a mystical union took place between those who broke bread or shared a meal together. Seen in this light, Communion takes on an entirely new significance.

Luke 15:3
And he spake this parable unto them, saying,

It is in response to the charge that He received sinners that Jesus gives the following parable. Oftentimes, we view this parable as being three—the first dealing with a lost sheep, the second with a lost coin, and the third with a lost son. But notice that the word "parable" is singular. It is one parable with three aspects, one symphony with three movements, one song with three stanzas. . . .

- The shepherd of the first stanza speaks of the Son.
- The woman in the second stanza speaks of the work of the Spirit.
- The father in the final stanza speaks of the Father heart of God.

Perhaps no debate has been more central to our faith than that of divine sovereignty vs. human responsibility. In the mid 1500s, John Calvin came on the scene as a strong proponent of the exclusive role of divine sovereignty in salvation. That is, that man is depraved and hopelessly lost. Therefore, the Lord chooses him apart from anything he can do. Jacobus Arminius disagreed. A contemporary of Calvin, he believed man's responsibility was definitely a factor in his salvation. After all, hadn't Jesus said, "Come unto Me"? Therefore, Arminius maintained, each person must make his own decision whether to be part of the kingdom.

An extreme Calvinist would never feel a need to witness. An extreme Armenian would be vulnerable to pride. So what is the answer? In this single parable, both positions are taught. Hopelessly and helplessly lost, the sheep and the coin are sought by the shepherd and the woman. But in the story of the prodigal, it is the son who decides to turn toward his father.

Consequently, when people ask where I stand on the issue of God's sovereignty versus man's responsibility, I usually say, "Where do *you* stand?" And when they tell me, I say, "I'm with you, brother." You see, because there are convincing scriptural arguments for both sides, I spent a lot of time trying to reconcile these two positions. But then the Lord reminded me that, because He's bigger than me, He never asks me to reconcile seemingly contradictory positions. He never asks me to figure them out. He just asks me to take them in—to marvel that He chose me as well as to be eternally grateful that He provided a way for me to choose Him.

Luke 15:4
What man of you, having an hundred sheep, if he lose one of them, doth not leave the ninety and nine in the wilderness, and go after that which is lost, until he find it?

The shepherd didn't leave the ninety-nine sheep helpless and defenseless, for in those days, when night fell, shepherds would bring their flocks together into one area wherein all of the shepherds would watch the combined flock. The next day, they would take their individual flocks into separate feeding areas. How did they separate the sheep? Each had a different song, chant, or call that their own sheep recognized—even as Jesus alluded in John 10:4.

Luke 15:5
And when he hath found it, he layeth it on his shoulders, rejoicing.

What was on the shoulders of our Shepherd? A wooden Cross—for not only did He go out and find us, but He Himself became a Lamb to be sacrificed *for* us.

Luke 15:6
And when he cometh home, he calleth together his friends and neighbours, saying unto them, Rejoice with me; for I have found my sheep which was lost.

"Celebrate with me," says the shepherd. "I've found the sheep which was lost." Sheep are so dumb they can't even find their own food or get to water nearby. They wander aimlessly and get mixed up so easily. How right the Lord was in likening us to them (Matthew 9:36).

Luke 15:7
I say unto you, that likewise joy shall be in heaven over one sinner that repenteth, more than over ninety and nine just persons, which need no repentance.

When someone gets saved, there is great celebration. If that be the case, you may wonder, *Why not give more reason to celebrate by wandering off every so often?* To answer this, consider the prayer of another shepherd: "Make me to hear joy and gladness that the bones which thou hast broken may rejoice" (Psalm 51:8). You see, if a lamb wandered away habitually into areas that could be potentially destructive, the shepherd would break its legs. Then, after carefully setting the bones, he would carry the lamb on his shoulders while the bones mended. When the lamb was healed, so close did it grow toward the shepherd that from that time on, it would never leave his side. And therein lies the reason for not wandering away. Every time you think a particular sin isn't so bad, think "crack, snap, pop" because that's what will happen—not because the Lord is vindictive or angry, but because He wants to save us from danger and damnation. If, like me, you've had a few broken bones on your journey, you too are learning to say, "Lord, I want to stay right next to You every step of the way."

Luke 15:8–10
Either what woman having ten pieces of silver, if she lose one piece, doth not light a candle, and sweep the house, and seek diligently till she find it? And when she hath found it, she calleth her friends and her neighbours together, saying, Rejoice with me; for I have found the piece which I had lost. Likewise, I say unto you, there is joy in the presence of the angels of God over one sinner that repenteth.

To explain the seeming panic over the loss of a single coin, it must be understood that in Hebrew households of the time, when a woman was first married, she would string ten coins together and wear them across her forehead as a public announcement of her marriage. Because it sometimes took years to save these coins, losing one would be similar to losing the diamond out of one's wedding ring—a loss not only because of the monetary value, but because of the sentimental value.

A lost coin is worthless. It's only in someone's hand that it becomes valuable. The same is true of people.

"Give Me a coin," Jesus said when asked about taxes. "Whose image is on this coin?"
"Caesar's," came back the reply.
"Then give it to Caesar," Jesus said. "Whose image are you made in?"

Obviously, the answer is God's. But if a person is lost, if they're not saved, if they don't know the Lord, although they still have value—gifts, personality, all kinds of possibilities—they are worthless outside of His hand. Therefore, the work of the Spirit is to sweep frantically in search of them. How? First by lighting the light of the Word (Psalm 119:105). Then by searching through inward conviction. And when the coin is found, great is the rejoicing indeed.

Luke 15:11, 12 (a)
And he said, A certain man had two sons: And the younger of them said to his father, Father, give me the portion of goods that falleth to me.

The word "prodigal" meaning "wasteful," it is a prodigal son indeed who says to his father, "I want goods *from* you but not a relationship *with* you." And such were we before we opened our hearts to the Lord.

Luke 15:12 (b)–16
And he divided unto them his living. And not many days after the younger son gathered all together, and took his journey into a far country, and there wasted his substance with riotous living. And when he had spent all, there arose a mighty famine in that land; and he began to be in want. And he went and joined himself to a citizen of that country; and he sent him into his fields to feed swine. And he would fain have filled his belly with the husks that the swine did eat: and no man gave unto him.

Pig slop never satisfies. Be it through career, money, goods, toys, or trinkets, you're trying to find fulfillment or satisfaction, you'll thirst again. The Lord is the only One who will truly satisfy you deeply (John 6:35).

Luke 15:17–20 (a)

And when he came to himself, he said, How many hired servants of my father's have bread enough and to spare, and I perish with hunger! I will arise and go to my father, and will say unto him, Father, I have sinned against heaven, and before thee, and am no more worthy to be called thy son: make me as one of thy hired servants. And he arose, and came to his father.

"I have sinned." This phrase appears eight times in Scripture . . .

- "I have sinned," said Pharaoh (Exodus 9:27).
- "I have sinned," said Balaam (Numbers 22:34).
- "I have sinned," said Saul (1 Samuel 15:24).
- "I have sinned," said Judas (Matthew 27:4).

Each of these men acknowledged their sin, but none repented from it. But there are four more. . . .

- "I have sinned," said Job (Job 7:20).
- "I have sinned," said Achan (Joshua 7:20).
- "I have sinned," said David (2 Samuel 12:13).
- "I have sinned," said the prodigal.

And each repented. It's not enough just to say, "I have sinned." True repentance takes place at the point the sinner, like the prodigal, changes direction and heads toward the Father.

Luke 15:20 (b)–24

But when he was yet a great way off, his father saw him, and had compassion, and ran, and fell on his neck, and kissed him. And the son said unto him, Father, I have sinned against heaven, and in thy sight, and am no more worthy to be called thy son. But the father said to his servants, Bring forth the best robe, and put it on him; and put a ring on his hand, and shoes on his feet: And bring hither the fatted calf, and kill it; and let us eat, and be merry: For this my son was dead, and is alive again; he was lost, and is found. And they began to be merry.

I'm sure as the prodigal headed home, he thought, *I've sowed my wild oats and now my father is going to bring out the threshing machine.* But what did the father do? He gave his son a robe for his back, a ring for his hand, shoes for his feet, and a meal for his growling stomach. Even to this day in Semitic cultures, a "sacrifice of the threshold" is made whenever someone returns from a journey—to atone for the sins he committed while he was away. So, too, the Lamb of God, Jesus Christ, was slain for our sin in order that we can be welcomed home again.

Luke 15:25–32

Now his elder son was in the field: and as he came and drew nigh to the house, he heard musick and dancing. And he called one of the servants, and asked what these things meant. And he said unto him, Thy brother is come; and thy father hath killed the fatted calf, because he hath received him safe and sound. And he was angry, and would not go in: therefore came his father out, and intreated him. And he answering said to his father, Lo, these many years do I serve thee, neither transgressed I at any time thy commandment: and yet thou never gavest me a kid, that I might make merry with my friends: But as soon as this thy son was come, which hath devoured thy living with harlots, thou hast killed for him the fatted calf. And he said unto him, Son, thou art ever with me, and all that I have is thine. It was meet that we should make merry, and be glad: for this thy brother was dead, and is alive again; and was lost, and is found.

Imagine what would have happened had the prodigal been welcomed by his self-righteous elder brother rather than by his merciful father. Because a lot of prodigal people are greeted by elder brothers, by self-righteous Christians, they think they cannot go home to the Father, that forgiveness and mercy is too much to hope for, that their only choice is to return to the pig slop of the far country. What a tragedy. We are *all* prodigals—elder brother and younger brother alike.

Each of the three portions of the parable presented here in Luke 15 speaks of a different aspect of sin: The sheep was lost due to foolishness. The coin was lost due to the carelessness of another. The son was lost due to rebelliousness. I have observed that virtually any sin can be categorized by one of those three characteristics: Sometimes we make foolish mistakes. Other times, as in the case of child abuse, the sins of others leave their marks upon us. And oftentimes we are intentionally, willfully rebellious.

I have also observed that most people can be very understanding toward any two of those three reasons for sin, but become an elder brother regarding a third. And it's a different third for each person. Some people see a brother caught in a foolish sin, and their heart goes out to him. Or they'll see someone hurt by an unloving spouse and will offer help and healing to them. But when it comes to rebelliousness, all they can say is, "You should have known better."

Others say, "I can relate to the rebel. I know what it feels like to hear the call of the far country. And I can relate to the one who makes foolish mistakes. But why can't those who are abused just get over it and move on?"

Still others can relate to the one who's lost because of another's carelessness or to the one who stubbornly chooses to walk in rebelliousness. But they can't figure out how someone could be so dumb as to wander off in foolishness.

But here's the Good News: The Father feels compassion for all three. Our God does not say to the foolish, "You idiot," to the one who is abused, "Grow up," or to the rebellious, "You're getting what you deserve." No, He runs to meet all three equally the moment they turn toward Him. That's the kind of God we serve.

For topical study of Luke 15:11–32, see "My Three Sons" below.

MY THREE SONS
A Topical Study of
Luke 15:11–32

S everal years ago a survey was taken of literary scholars to determine the greatest short story every written. When the results of the survey came in, 70 percent said the single greatest short story ever recorded is the story of the Prodigal Son—for to qualify as "great," a story must be able to be read time and time again, each time making an impact, leaving an impression. And the story of the Prodigal Son met those requirements perfectly. I have found this to be true personally, for each time I read the story before us, I see something new in it.

The Prodigal Son

The first time I studied this story, I related to the younger son because he showed an immaturity and an impetuousness I see so often in myself.

"Give me the goods," he said to his father.

And the father—so generous, so gracious, so wise—allowed his son his desire. So off the son went to a far country. He had lots of friends initially, but when his money was gone, so were his friends because the old adage is true: A friend cannot be known in prosperity, and an enemy will not be hid in adversity.

When he tired of eating pig slop, Scripture says the prodigal "came to himself" (verse 17). Paul said essentially the same thing when he said it was the sin within him that caused him to do that which he didn't want to do (Romans 7:16, 17). Truly, we all have experienced this, for when we are caught up in sin, we find ourselves doing and saying things we never thought we would do or say. But eventually, like the prodigal, we "come to ourselves" and we say, "This isn't me," as we head home to the Father.

The father knew this would happen. That is why he didn't send a check in a letter to his son, saying, "I know you're hurting. Here's fifty bucks to see you through a week or two." No, the father let his son hit bottom, knowing this was necessary to draw his son back to the place of blessing and protection.

Although this brings me great comfort, it also carries a real warning, for Jesus told us that we are in the Father's hand—never to be let go (John 10:27–29). Now, if the Lord will never let us go, why did the Prodigal Son's father—a picture of the heavenly Father—let the prodigal—a picture of us—travel to the far country? I believe it was to illustrate "bungee theology." That is, I believe there is a bungee cord wrapped around us, the end of which our Father holds in His hand. We can indeed walk away from Him—all the way to the far country. The problem, however, is that when the bungee cord is stretched as far as it can go, it will snap back—carrying us with it. The question is not whether or not we will come back. The question is, how hard will we hit when we do? Maybe like me, you're learning to say, "Lord, don't let me stretch the bungee cord. I'm tired of getting banged up." The prodigal son hit hard. We don't know what the repercussions were due to his journey into the far country. We don't know what diseases and scars and pains he might have picked up. But at a certain point, he realized he had to go home. And as he did, he began rehearsing what he would say to his father.

"Give me the goods," he demanded before leaving home.
"Make me a servant," he cried upon his return.

What is *your* prayer? "Give me the goods"—or "Make me a servant"?

At first sight of him, the father did something Aristotle declared no man of dignity would ever do publicly: He ran. It's the only time in the entire Bible where God the Father is seen as being in a hurry.

And when his son drew near, the father smothered him with hugs and kisses—not only out of affection, but for protection. You see, Deuteronomy 21 makes it clear that if a son was stubborn and rebellious, a glutton and a drunkard—as was the prodigal—he was to be stoned (Deuteronomy 21:18–21). Thus, I suggest that in hugging his son, the father was essentially saying, "No one is going to lay a hand on him."

"Put the best robe on him," the father said. Whose would the best robe be? The father's. That is how Isaiah could say we are robed in the righteousness of God (61:10) and how Paul could declare that we are the righteousness of God because we are robed in Christ Jesus (2 Corinthians 5:21).

"Put a ring on his finger," the father said—which speaks of authority. "Put shoes on his feet," said the father. Servants never wore shoes. But this prodigal was more than a servant. He was a son. On his way home, the Prodigal Son no doubt thought he would get what he deserved: a beating. Instead, he got what he never dreamed possible: blessing.

The Plodding Son

The first time I read this story, I was amazed by the kindness of the Father to the prodigal. But then my attention shifted to the one plodding away in the field—the elder son. "What is the noise I hear coming from the house?" he asked.

"Your dad is throwing a party because your brother is back," answered one of the servants.

"What?!" said the elder son. "I have been working faithfully and diligently, but a fatted calf was never killed for me, a party never thrown for me." And he was angry.

"All that I have is yours," the father said to him. In other words, "You've been so busy trying to earn favor and merit blessing that you never had time to party. It was here for you all the while, but you were too busy working to enjoy it. Yes, your brother was caught up in looseness. But you've been caught up in legalism—and it's robbed you of your joy."

Gang, if you are working to receive blessing, the Father will meet you in that place and give you what you deserve—which won't be much. But what the younger son experienced and what the older son had to learn was that the Father's righteousness and blessing, His merriment and parties, are given not according to works or energy, but simply because of His grace and mercy.

This is a hard concept for us to understand because from very early on, the fact that "there's no free lunch" is ingrained into each of us. The fact that if we want to get ahead, we must pull ourselves up by our own boot straps is very much a part of who we are culturally. Spiritually, however, nothing could be further from the truth. "By *grace* are ye saved, *not* of works lest any man should boast," Paul declared (Ephesians 2:8, 9).

That is why the Father is looking for people the world calls wasted and foolish upon whom He can pour out blessing and receive all of the glory.

You'll know you're an elder brother if you find yourself angry when people are blessed whom you don't think deserve to be. When I find myself feeling this way, I hear the Father whisper to me, "You're relating to Me on the basis of your works, and you'll never enjoy the party until you realize it's all based on grace."

Who do you think became the better worker—the elder son who was resentful and bitter, or the younger son who marveled at the goodness of his father? I suggest that the son who realizes how good the Father has been to him is the son who will begin to be a servant diligently and joyfully, all the while experiencing God's blessings on the merit of grace exclusively.

The Perfect Son

Are you an elder son, still trying to work to prove that God should bless your marriage or your job, your children or your ministry? Are you a prodigal son still in the pigpen? Both of their stories challenge and convict me. But this week in reading the story one more time, I saw a third Son—the One telling the story. . . .

"This is My beloved Son in whom I am well pleased," the Father declared at the outset of His earthly ministry (Matthew 3:17). Why was the Father well-pleased in His Son? Because His Son never sinned. He was tempted indeed (Matthew 4). But He never once sinned. Unlike the younger son, He never wandered off into the pigpen.

Yet He was also unlike the older brother, for the second time He heard His Father say, "This is My beloved Son," was on the Mount of Transfiguration at the end of His earthly ministry (Matthew 17:5). At that point, having demonstrated that it was possible to live a sinless life, I believe Jesus could have launched into heaven, saying, "I worked hard. I made it through. Tough luck for you prodigals." But he didn't. He descended from the Mount of Transfiguration to climb the Mount of Calvary to die for you and me that we might be forgiven of our sin and carnality.

Take heart, fellow prodigal; Good News, fellow plodder: Positionally, you are *in* Christ (2 Corinthians 5:17) and prophetically, you will one day be *like* Christ (1 John 3:2). Therefore, if you're a prodigal son, return; and if you're a plodding son, rejoice for the Perfect Son has made a way for you to run into the embrace of your Father.

---

16 Surprising as it may be, Jesus said more about money than about any other single subject. Fully one-sixth of the Gospels of Matthew, Mark, and Luke deal with money—as do twelve of the thirty-eight parables. Why? A study several years ago revealed that the average American adult male spends 50 percent of his time dealing with money-related matters—how to make more, how to spend less, what to do with what he has. No wonder, then, that Jesus had so much to say about money. The longest chapter in the Bible, Psalm 119, deals with the Word. But the second longest, Numbers 7, is all about the giving of money. I find this to be significant. Here in our text, Jesus weighs in on the matter. . . .

Luke 16:1, 2
And he said also unto his disciples, There was a certain rich man, which had a steward; and the same was accused unto him that he had wasted his goods. And he called him, and said unto him, How is it that I hear this of thee? give an account of thy stewardship; for thou mayest be no longer steward.

There was an interesting story in the news concerning a mysterious shooting spree in downtown Los Angeles, wherein a large number of windows in commercial buildings were blown out by a muted shotgun. There were no injuries or robberies—just a lot of broken glass. For a few weeks detectives were at a loss to explain the motive until the perpetrator was apprehended—the owner of a plate glass company.

Jesus tells of an incident not unlike this concerning a steward who was trying to beat the system. Stewards were business managers for wealthy households. This particular steward was accused of cheating his employer.

Luke 16:3-7
Then the steward said within himself, What shall I do? for my lord taketh away from me the stewardship: I cannot dig; to beg I am

ashamed. I am resolved what to do, that, when I am put out of the stewardship, they may receive me into their houses. So he called every one of his Lord's debtors unto him, and said unto the first, How much owest thou unto my lord? And he said, An hundred measures of oil. And he said unto him, Take thy bill, and sit down quickly, and write fifty. Then said he to another, And how much owest thou? And he said, An hundred measures of wheat. And he said unto him, Take thy bill, and write fourscore.

Realizing his days of employment were numbered, the steward devised a plan whereby he cut in half the debts of those who owed his employer money, knowing they would return the favor by taking care of him when he was out of work.

Luke 16:8 (a)
And the lord commended the unjust steward, because he had done wisely . . .

When the master discovered what his steward had done, far from chastising him for his dishonesty, he commended him for his ingenuity.

Luke 16:8 (b)
. . . for the children of this world are in their generation wiser than the children of light.

How true. The people in the world are on the phone talking to their investment counselors, checking figures on their calculators, shrewdly and carefully planning for their future. Not so the children of light. We are not as aggressive or as wise in preparing for our eternal future as our worldly colleagues are in preparing for their temporal future. This ought not be. After using the incident of the shrewd unjust servant as an example of one who is preparing and planning for the future, Jesus plunges into a discourse about the believer and money in which He will identify four benefits of giving. . . .

Luke 16:9
And I say unto you, Make to yourselves friends of the mammon of unrighteousness; that, when ye fail, they may receive you into everlasting habitations.

Giving rewards us in eternity. Asked how much money his father left when he died, Andrew Carnegie's son gave a classic answer when he shrugged his shoulders and simply said, "Everything." How true. The old adage is correct: You can't take it with you. But equally true is the fact that you *can* send it ahead. The money you give to the Lord is sent ahead, waiting for you in heaven.

I may not know exactly what Jesus meant when he said the money we send ahead to heaven will be waiting with a habitation for me to dwell in. But this I do know: When we get to heaven, not one person will say, "Is this all there is? I wish I had spent the money I gave to the Lord on a new VCR or blender." No! We're going to say, "Wow! What a deal! I traded in that junk for this glory!"

In the early 1800s, Prussia's King Friedrich Wilhelm III was involved in battles against other European countries that bled his bank account. In desperate need of funds to keep his war machine going, he asked the women of his empire to donate their gold jewelry to the war effort. In exchange, they were given chunks of iron fashioned into crosses and were made members of the Order of the Iron Cross—an Order that would go on to impact history. Unlike King Friedrich Wilhelm III, our King isn't bankrupt. On the contrary, He says, "Give Me your chunks of iron, and I'll give you gold and silver in return. Trade in the stuff you're wasting, and see what I will bless you with in the kingdom to come."

Luke 16:10, 11
He that is faithful in that which is least is faithful also in much: and he that is unjust in the least is unjust also in much. If therefore ye have not been faithful in the unrighteous mammon, who will commit to your trust the true riches?

Giving releases us in ministry. I might not be able to sing; you might not be able to preach. But one thing is common to everyone in this room: money. Therefore, the Lord uses money as the ultimate test to see if He can entrust to us even greater ministry. This is why D. L. Moody said, "I can see more about the spirituality of a man by reading through his checkbook than I can by reading through his prayer book." Anyone can write flowery phrases, but giving is the true barometer of where one is at spiritually.

"I don't make hardly any money," you say. Oh, but if you make even fifteen thousand dollars a year between the ages of twenty and sixty, you will have been entrusted with more than half a million dollars in your lifetime.

"What are you going to do with it?" asks Jesus.

"If I can trust you with the least, with unrighteous mammon, I can open up doors of other ministry for you proportionately. But if you are unfaithful with money, I cannot commit to you the true riches of a fuller, more impacting ministry."

Luke 16:12
And if ye have not been faithful in that which is another man's, who shall give you that which is your own?

Giving replenishes us financially. We have been entrusted with that which is Another's. That is, specifically, though not exclusively, the Lord has given to us the first-fruits that are His (Leviticus 23:10). What are first-fruits? First-fruits are the tithe. The word "tithe" simply means "tenth." Therefore, the first tenth of everything we make is the Lord's. When the offering plate is passed in front of us, I'm sure none of us is tempted to reach in and take a handful of money to keep for ourselves. Yet when I don't tithe I am doing just that. I am robbing God of what is His (Malachi 3:8).

To those who protest that the concept of tithing being prescribed in the law is no longer relevant to those who live under grace, I point out the following: Tithing is seen prior to the law when Abraham tithed to Melchizedek (Genesis 14:20). Tithing was commended by Jesus when He told the Pharisees that, although they should remember justice and mercy, they should not cease to tithe (Luke 11:42). Tithing was taught by the apostle Paul when he told the Corinthians to give according to how God had prospered them (1 Corinthians 16:2)—which the early church took to mean tithing, as seen in the writings of Jerome and Chrysostom. Tithing precedes the law, is spoken of by the Lord, and is seen in the Epistles. Therefore, to say tithing is not applicable in this dispensation is, I believe, a failure to understand the full counsel of Scripture and church history. And what is the result of this failure?

Ye are cursed with a curse: for ye have robbed me, even this whole nation. Malachi 3:9

We're cursed with a curse. What curse?

Ye looked for much, and, lo, it came to little; and when ye brought it home, I did blow upon it. Why? saith the LORD of hosts. Because of mine house that is waste, and ye run every man unto his own house. Haggai 1:9

You bring home your paycheck, but where does it go? The Lord says, "I blew on it and it scattered. It's cursed because you've robbed Me.

What could have been, what should have been, what would have been can't be because the blessing is removed."

Bring ye all the tithes into the storehouse, that there may be meat in mine house, and prove me now herewith, saith the LORD of hosts, if I will not open you the windows of heaven, and pour you out a blessing, that there shall not be room enough to receive it. Malachi 3:10

This is the only place in all of Scripture where God says, "Prove Me." And if we do, we'll see three things happen . . .
Reward. The Lord will open the windows of heaven and bless us in ways we can't possibly imagine.

And I will rebuke the devourer for your sakes, and he shall not destroy the fruits of your ground; neither shall your vine cast her fruit before the time in the field, saith the LORD of hosts. Malachi 3:11

Rebuke. Satan is a destroyer, a murderer, a devourer. If you can recall times when you've robbed God and things started happening—refrigerators burned out, cars broke down—and you wondered what was going on, it could be that you removed yourself from the promise of covering; that you made yourself vulnerable to the devouring of the Enemy.

And all nations shall call you blessed: for ye shall be a delightsome land, saith the LORD of hosts. Malachi 3:12

Revival. When we tithe, fruitfulness will reign in our lives once again to such a degree that even those around us will notice it.

Luke 16:13
No servant can serve two masters: for either he will hate the one, and love the other; or else he will hold to the one, and despise the other. Ye cannot serve God and mammon.

"The love of money is the root of all evil," Paul declared (see 1 Timothy 6:10). How can mere paper or copper or silver be the root of all evil? Just as the simple clay idols of Baal, Ashteroth, Moloch, and other Old Testament entities had spirits behind them, mammon is a powerful spiritual force behind the money in our pockets that seeks to dominate, defile, and destroy us. Thus, either the spirit of mammon and Madison Avenue will control us, or the Spirit of God will. But we can't serve both.

Abraham, the friend of God, had just rescued

his nephew, Lot, from captivity. On his way home, he was met by Melchizedek, the king of Salem, who was, I believe, a preincarnate appearance of Jesus. After being presented with bread and wine, Abraham fell down and worshiped Melchizedek, giving tithes to him of all he had taken.

In the next verse, guess who came slithering up to Abraham? The king of Sodom. "Thanks, Abraham, for what you've done," he said. "You can keep all the goods that you took."

But Abraham looked at the king of Sodom, the prince of perversity, and said, "I will not take one shoelace from you," refusing to take from Sodom the goods of the world (Genesis 14).

What gave Abraham power over the pull of the world? Giving tithes to the Prince of Peace. That's what tithing does. The world tempts me; advertisers scream at me, people tell me, "You need this. You must have that. Why not buy the other?" I'm vulnerable—and so are you. The king of Sodom has our number. He knows exactly what bauble, what trinket to wave in front of us to get us caught up in the foolish and vain pursuit of the latest fad. How can we overcome him? Tithe.

Every time I tithe, even as Abraham did, I give away part of my greediness, my covetousness, my selfishness. Tithing changes my personality because I'm not a giver by nature. I'm a hoarder, a collector, a keeper. Not so my Father. God is a Giver (John 3:16; James 1:17). And He wants me to be like Him. In putting money in the basket, you give away part of your carnality. That is why our Father lovingly says, "Give to Me—not because I need the money, but because you need to be set free."

Luke 16:14
And the Pharisees also, who were covetous, heard all these things: and they derided him.

Covetousness is simply wanting more of anything of which one already has enough.

Luke 16:15
And he said unto them, Ye are they which justify yourselves before men; but God knoweth your hearts: for that which is highly esteemed among men is abomination in the sight of God.

The Pharisees taught that the more godly one was, the more money he would have. The original practitioners of Prosperity Theology, they pointed to their riches as a mark of their spirituality. Those who have money are esteemed highly presently. But God says such standards are an abomination to Him. Therefore, when we get to

heaven, there will be some big surprises when things are turned inside out, when the people who are looked down upon as being poor or ugly or social misfits will, because they love the Lord, be those who are wealthy and highly esteemed in eternity. For seventy or eighty years people look on the outside and analyze one another by how they dress, what car they drive, or how big their house is. But for the next zillion years, those things will not matter one whit. That's why Paul pleads with us to run so as to win a prize that is not material, not monetary but spiritual (1 Corinthians 9:24).

To make sure the Pharisees didn't think He was calling the law an abomination, Jesus goes on to clarify His statement . . .

Luke 16:16, 17
The law and the prophets were until John: since that time the kingdom of God is preached, and every man presseth into it. And it is easier for heaven and earth to pass, than one tittle of the law to fail.

Paul tells us the purpose of the law was to be a schoolmaster to point out our sin and drive us to Jesus Christ as our Savior. Therefore, in context of the entire chapter, Jesus is saying, "I'm not talking about the law. I'm talking about your covetousness, your misuse of money." And just to show them He's not trying to undermine the law, He refers to the then-controversial principle of divorce. . . .

Luke 16:18
Whosoever putteth away his wife, and marrieth another, committeth adultery: and whosoever marrieth her that is put away from her husband committeth adultery.

I find it interesting that in talking about money and the law, Jesus used divorce as an illustration because divorce and money often go hand in hand. Divorce is costly not just emotionally or relationally but financially. No wonder the Lord hates divorce (Malachi 2:16). He doesn't hate the people going through the tragedy, but He hates the concept of divorce because it bankrupts people emotionally and financially.

Luke 16:19–21
There was a certain rich man, which was clothed in purple and fine linen, and fared sumptuously every day: And there was a certain beggar named Lazarus, which was laid at his gate, full of sores, and desiring to be fed with the crumbs which fell from the rich man's table: moreover the dogs came and licked his sores.

The rich man would have been on the cover of *People* magazine. Lazarus? No one would have even known his name. But in the economy of eternity, it is Lazarus who we know and the rich man who is nameless.

Luke 16:22
And it came to pass, that the beggar died, and was carried by the angels into Abraham's bosom: the rich man also died, and was buried.

In Proverbs 22:2 it says the rich and the poor meet together before the Lord for He hath created them both. In death, these two men from the opposite ends of the social spectrum meet.

Luke 16:23
And in hell he lift up his eyes, being in torments, and seeth Abraham afar off, and Lazarus in his bosom.

In hell the rich man finally saw "afar off." Presently, the world says, "Eat, drink, and be merry, for tomorrow we die," because they only see what is in front of them. In hell they'll finally see afar off; they'll finally see the big picture of eternity. But it will be too late . . .

Luke 16:24, 25
And he cried and said, Father Abraham, have mercy on me, and send Lazarus, that he may dip the tip of his finger in water, and cool my tongue; for I am tormented in this flame. But Abraham said, Son, remember that thou in thy lifetime receivedst thy good things, and likewise Lazarus evil things: but now he is comforted, and thou art tormented.

Although people mistakenly believe that, at best, when they die they will cease to exist, the fact is that not only will they continue to exist—but they will be able to remember the good things they received on earth—the blessings God poured out upon them, the patience God showed to them, the manifold opportunities He gave them to turn to Him. Therefore, I suggest that one of the most horrendous aspects of hell is the memory people will have of the times they could have received the free gift of salvation, but chose to harden their hearts instead.

Luke 16:26
And beside all this, between us and you there is a great gulf fixed: so that they which would pass from hence to you cannot; neither can they pass to us, that would come from thence.

The Hebrew word translated "hell" is *sheol*, which simply means "the place of the grave." Everyone who died before Jesus was crucified to pay for the sins of mankind went to sheol, which was divided into two compartments, separated by a great divide. One side was filled with fire and torment. The other side was a place called "Abraham's bosom" or "paradise." Those who loved God would go to the paradise, or Abraham's bosom side of sheol. The reason they couldn't go directly to heaven is because the blood of Christ had not yet been shed. So paradise was simply a waiting room. And Abraham, the Father of Faith, the Friend of God, would greet them there. Those who did not believe in God went to the torment side of sheol. And although there was a great gulf between the two, as seen in this passage, those on both sides could call out to one another—which would make the flaming side even more hellish.

Ephesians 4:8–9 tells us that before Jesus ascended into heaven, He first descended into the lower parts of the earth and led those in Abraham's bosom up to heaven. That is why Abraham's bosom no longer exists today. Hell is not the final destiny of the unbeliever, but rather only a temporary holding tank until after the Great White Throne Judgment when he will be cast into Gehenna, or outer darkness (Revelation 20). Contrary to popular belief, hell is not going to be one big New Year's Eve party. Gehenna is a place of heat without light, of eternal isolation, of interminable torment.

In the context of this chapter, the rich man's sin was not that he hated Lazarus, but simply that he neglected him. The Bible says there are sins of commission—things we do that are wrong—and sins of omission—failing to do that which is right (James 4:17). There was a person in need at the rich man's gate, but he didn't offer to help. And that was his sin—indicative that because he cared not about the man at his gate, he had not the love of God in his heart (1 John 3:17).

Luke 16:27, 28
Then he said, I pray thee therefore, father, that thou wouldest send him to my father's house: For I have five brethren; that he may testify unto them, lest they also come into this place of torment.

"If Lazarus can't come over here, send him back from the dead to tell my family that this place exists," begged the rich man. I find it interesting that the rich man realized the power of a testimony. He didn't say, "Send a theologian, a Bible teacher, or a commentary." He said, "Send the one who, although he was poor and covered with sores, believed in God and is now in His presence—that he may share his testimony."

If you haven't already, you will hear Satan whisper in your ear, "You can't witness because you don't know enough about the Bible; you're not that solid in your own walk; your understanding of theology is too elementary." Not true! The most powerful thing you can share is your own testimony.

After he was cornered by the Pharisees, the once-blind man simply said, "I can't answer all of your questions concerning the nature and Person of Jesus. But this I do know: Once I was blind, but now I see." And none could deny it (John 9:25). So, too, the most powerful thing you can tell your unsaved parents or a lost neighbor is simply what the Lord has done for you.

Luke 16:29, 30
Abraham saith unto him, They have Moses and the prophets; let them hear them. And he said, Nay, father Abraham: but if one went unto them from the dead, they will repent.

"Even though they're not listening to the Word, if someone comes back from the dead, surely they will listen and repent," reasoned the rich man. In hell people finally realize the need to repent—not to believe in theology, but to repent from iniquity. Tragically, there will be those who believe in the existence of Jesus and in the inspiration of Scripture who will be lost eternally because of their refusal to repent, to change direction, to follow Jesus. The devils and demons believe, James tells us (2:19), but they're not saved because their belief is based on intellectual acknowledgment rather than humble, personal repentance.

Luke 16:31
And he said unto him, If they hear not Moses and the prophets, neither will they be persuaded, though one rose from the dead.

When Lazarus did indeed come back from the dead, were the religious leaders persuaded to listen and repent? On the contrary, they were determined to put him to death (John 12:10).

Living sumptuously with no compassion for people and no thought of eternity caused the rich man to end up in a real place called hell. On the basis of Job 3:17, the Jehovah's Witnesses falsely propagate that when they die, wicked people simply cease to exist, that hell is nothing more than a scare tactic of Fundamentalist preachers. Turn them to Job 38, where God asks Job if he knows

what lies beyond—the answer being "No" (verse 17).

The Christian Scientist takes it a step further when he says not only is there no hell, but there is no pain at all. Not so. Jesus said hell is real indeed. Because God desires none should perish (2 Peter 3:9), He will not send anyone to hell. "In fact," Jesus says, "if you insist upon going there, you will have to do so over My dead body."

In considering this passage, may we be renewed in our compassion for the lost and our commitment to share what the Lord has given us; may we be reminded of the big picture of eternity and the power of a testimony. In other words, in considering hell, may we become more mindful of heaven.

17

Luke 17:1, 2
Then said he unto the disciples, It is impossible but that offences will come: but woe unto him, through whom they come! It were better for him that a millstone were hanged about his neck, and he cast into the sea, than that he should offend one of these little ones.

Jesus' reference to a millstone—a one-ton stone with a hole in the middle—hung around the neck of anyone who attempted to undermine the childlike faith of His children was in response to the Pharisees who had derided Him in the previous chapter (verse 14). If this doesn't sound like Gentle Jesus "meek and mild," it's because Jesus is also the Good Shepherd who will fight ferociously to protect His lambs from wolves who would come in and seek to destroy their faith.

Luke 17:3 (a)
Take heed to yourselves . . .

Lest we cheer too loudly over His harsh words to the Pharisees, Jesus came back and said, "Take heed to *yourselves* . . ."

Luke 17:3 (b)
. . . If thy brother trespass against thee, rebuke him . . .

Because we are connected as a body, if one of us is hurting due to the offense of another, it affects all of us. Therefore, we have a responsibility to speak the truth to one another because sometimes connection calls for correction.

Luke 17:3 (c), 4
. . . and if he repent, forgive him. And if he trespass against thee seven times in a day,

and seven times in a day turn again to thee, saying, I repent; thou shalt forgive him.

The rabbis of Jesus' day taught that a perfect man would forgive an individual three times for the same sin. Jesus, however, doubles that number and adds one for good measure, as if to say we are to forgive without limit.

Luke 17:5
And the apostles said unto the Lord, Increase our faith.

To truly forgive someone over and over again requires faith that God will correct the offender and protect the one offended. Thus, the only way we can be a forgiving people is if our faith is increased. In this regard, we need not pray for greater love, but for greater faith.

Luke 17:6
And the Lord said, If ye had faith as a grain of mustard seed, ye might say unto this sycamine tree, Be thou plucked up by the root, and be thou planted in the sea; and it should obey you.

The disciples said, "Increase our faith."
Jesus said, "Unleash your faith."
The disciples said, "Expand our faith."
Jesus said, "Express your faith. Say to those about whom you feel a root of bitterness, a tree of unforgiveness, a hedge of hostility, I forgive you. I no longer hold a grudge against you."
Jesus said the same thing regarding any obstacle before us. He didn't say, "Pray that the mountain might be removed. He said, "Speak to the mountain itself," (Mark 11:23). Why were the disciples told to speak? Because while faith is implanted by the Word, it is unleashed through the lips. . . .

But what saith it? The word is nigh thee, even in thy mouth, and in thy heart: that is, the word of faith, which we preach; that if thou shalt confess with thy mouth the Lord Jesus, and shalt believe in thine heart that God hath raised him from the dead, thou shalt be saved.
Romans 10:8, 9

The word translated "saved" is *sozo*, which refers not only to being born again, but to the full orb of God's blessing—to delivering, healing, saving, freeing.

By the word of the LORD were the heavens made; and all the host of them by the breath of his mouth. For he spake, and it was done; he commanded, and it stood fast.
Psalm 33:6, 9

How did God make the world? He spoke it into existence. So, too, Jesus altered the course of the world and eternity when He spoke . . .

"Waves, be still" (Mark 4:39).
"Lazarus, come forth" (John 11:43).
"It is Finished" (John 19:30).

Made in the image of God, we also speak our individual worlds into existence and alter their course with our words.

This book of the law shall not depart out of thy mouth; but thou shalt meditate therein day and night, that thou mayest observe to do according to all that is written therein: for then thou shalt make thy way prosperous, and then thou shalt have good success.   Joshua 1:8

The Hebrew word translated "meditate" means "to mutter over and over again." If you want to be prosperous and successful in that which the Lord has laid before you to do, mutter the Word day and night. The promises of God will be of no effect if they're simply written in your journal or underlined in your Bible. They only take effect when they're in your mouth.
With his back to the Red Sea and the armies of Egypt barreling down upon him, Moses cried to the Lord.

"Why speakest thou to Me? Speak to the children that they are to go forward," the Lord answered (Exodus 14:15).

You might be a great student of Scripture. You might even be a prayer warrior. But if you wonder why the Sea isn't parting, could it be that the Lord is whispering to you, "Why are you asking Me? Speak to the mountain that looms large before you"? Examples abound in the Word of men who understood the absolutely essential principle that the Word in them had to be spoken by them if they were to see results around them. . . .

It was when Joshua spoke to the sun that it stood still, giving him time to accomplish a great victory (Joshua 10:12).

It was when Elisha spoke to king Ahab on the basis of Deuteronomy 11:16–17 that there was no rain (1 Kings 17:1).

It was when Zerubbabel spoke to the cornerstone of the temple that the Lord began moving and the project came to completion (Zechariah 4:7).

So too . . .

Tomorrow morning when the alarm goes off, you will either say, "Oh no, it's Monday morning." Or you will say, "This is the day that the Lord has made. I will rejoice and be glad in it" (see Psalm 118:24)—and the choice you make will alter the course of your day. And when you get to work and discover your co-worker presented one of your ideas as his own, you will either say, "I can't forgive him," or you will say, "I can do all things through Christ who strengthens me," (Philippians 4:13). As the day progresses, you will either say, "I'm grumpy because I'm sick and tired and weak," or you will say, "I am strong in the strength of the Lord," (Joel 3:10). As you walk in your front door and are met by your family's problems, you will either say, "Everything is falling apart," or you will say, "The Word of God declares that all things are working together for good," (Romans 8:28). And as you sort out your finances late at night as your family sleeps, you will either say, "We're not going to make it," or you will say, "The Word declares that our God will supply all our needs according to His riches in glory (Philippians 4:19).

Of God, the writer of the letter to the Hebrews says, "For he hath said, I will never leave thee, nor forsake thee. So that we may boldly say, 'The Lord is my helper, and I will not fear what man shall do unto me,' " (see Hebrews 13:5, 6). God hath said that we may say—not that we may know, not that we may write, not even that we may pray—but that we may *say.*

- Happy is the people whose God is the Lord (Psalm 144:15).
- The Lord is the strength of my life; of whom shall I be afraid? (Psalm 27:1).
- The Lord is my shepherd. I shall not want (Psalm 23:1).
- The Lord is good unto them that wait for Him (Lamentations 3:25).

I challenge you to write down four or five such promises from the Word on three-by-five cards, put them on your dashboard or on your windowsill, and mutter them over and over again. Frame your world and your day with the Word as you speak it forth—and watch what happens.

Luke 17:7–10
But which of you, having a servant plowing or feeding cattle, will say unto him by and by, when he is come from the field, Go and sit down to meat? And will not rather say unto him, Make ready wherewith I may sup,

and gird thyself, and serve me, till I have eaten and drunken; and afterward thou shalt eat and drink? Doth he thank that servant because he did the things that were commanded him? I trow not. So likewise ye, when ye shall have done all those things which are commanded you, say, We are unprofitable servants: we have done that which was our duty to do.

After encouraging His disciples to speak words of faith, Jesus comes right back and reminds them that they are servants. I believe this is precisely where the radical "Name It/Claim It Confession" Movement greatly misses the mark. They've lost the understanding that, while there is power in the spoken word, it is always connected with servanthood. So much of the "Name It/Claim It" teaching is based upon a "Give me the goods" mentality, whereas a correct appropriation of faith and authority is only embedded in a "make me a servant" mind-set. The uprooted tree and moved mountain are always in the context of my serving the King and seeing His will done—not in my personal luxury or prosperity. If you miss this point, you will find yourself erring in your understanding of what faith is all about. Jesus gave His teaching on faith not in the context of getting a bigger house but in that of forgiving others.

Luke 17:11, 12
And it came to pass, as he went to Jerusalem, that he passed through the midst of Samaria and Galilee. And as he entered into a certain village, there met him ten men that were lepers, which stood afar off:

At least one of these ten men was a Samaritan (verse 16), so this group was comprised of two groups who were normally enemies. But they were brought together through the tragedy of leprosy because calamity often brings unity. Our tendency is to avoid hardships, calamities, difficulty, tragedy—but in reality, oftentimes they are the catalysts for a miraculous work of unity.

Luke 17:13
And they lifted up their voices, and said, Jesus, Master, have mercy on us.

No doubt, because of what had happened in Matthew 8 when a leper cried out for mercy, word spread through the leper colonies that Jesus was able to cleanse leprosy.

Luke 17:14
And when he saw them, he said unto them, Go shew yourselves unto the priests.

In Matthew 8, Jesus touched a leper and he was healed immediately. Here, however, he sends lepers on a journey, and they're healed eventually. Sometimes He spat in men's eyes, and they could see instantly (John 9:6–7). Another time, a second touch was required for a blind man to see clearly (Mark 8:25). The same is true today. Sometimes we pray for sick people and hear reports of wonderful healing. Other times, there is no sight of healing. In fact, sometimes things seem to get *worse* after we pray. Sometimes people who are faltering in their walk with the Lord are healed, while those who have a profound walk with God remain in a state of illness. As illustrated by the variety of ways Jesus healed the hurting during His earthly ministry, God will not be boxed in by any preacher or program, by any man or method. Therefore, the manner and time-table of healing remain a mystery. Of, this, however, we can be sure: By His stripes we are healed indeed (Isaiah 53:5)—whether that be on earth presently or in heaven ultimately.

Luke 17:14
And it came to pass, that, as they went, they were cleansed.

At what point the lepers were healed we don't know. But it wasn't until after they began to walk toward Jerusalem—a long journey. So often we have a tendency to say, "Lord, if You heal me, I'll start walking."

The Lord, however, says, "Start walking and then along the way, you'll see I'm working."

Luke 17:15, 16
And one of them, when he saw that he was healed, turned back, and with a loud voice glorified God, and fell down on his face at his feet, giving him thanks: and he was a Samaritan.

Nine lepers went *to* the priest. One came back *as* a priest, offering the sacrifice of thanksgiving to the Lord (Amos 4:5).

Luke 17:17–19
And Jesus answering said, Were there not ten cleansed? but where are the nine? There are not found that returned to give glory to God, save this stranger. And he said unto him, Arise, go thy way: thy faith hath made thee whole.

All ten lepers were healed—but only the one who gave thanks was made whole. That is, he was saved spiritually as well as healed physically. Jesus notices those who come back to say, "Thank you." In fact, according to Malachi 3:16,

the things we say concerning what the Lord has done for us, how He has blessed us, His faithfulness to us are written in a book of remembrance. I think of the baby books parents keep in which to record their children's first words, first steps, and growth. So, too, the Lord keeps such books recording the words, walk, and growth of His children. The question is, how big is yours? I suggest the Lord needs many volumes to contain the thanksgiving of some of His kids. For others, a single pamphlet will do.

When a prostitute began to wash Jesus' feet with her tears and dry them with her hair, Jesus said to his host, "When I came into your home, you didn't greet Me with a kiss or wash My feet"—which means that Jesus not only notices what people do, but what they fail to do for Him (Luke 7:44–46). How many blessings has the Lord given me today without my even pausing to say "Thank You"?

Luke 17:20, 21
And when he was demanded of the Pharisees, when the kingdom of God should come, he answered them and said, The kingdom of God cometh not with observation: Neither shall they say, Lo here! or, lo there! for, behold, the kingdom of God is within you.

The Greek word *entos*, translated "within," is more correctly rendered "among." The kingdom of God was indeed among them because Jesus is the King, and where the King is, there is the kingdom. "You're looking for a material, political, physical kingdom," Jesus said, "all the while missing the true kingdom: Me."

Luke 17:22, 23
And he said unto the disciples, The days will come, when ye shall desire to see one of the days of the Son of man, and ye shall not see it. And they shall say to you, See here; or, see there: go not after them, nor follow them.

Jesus warns His disciples of the days that would come wherein people would falsely say, "The Lord is in Brooklyn, or Utah, or India."

Luke 17:24
For as the lightning, that lighteneth out of the one part under heaven, shineth unto the other part under heaven; so shall also the Son of man be in his day.

"My coming will not be an esoteric mystery perceived by only an enlightened few," Jesus says, "but will be as obvious as lightning in the sky—visible to everyone."

Luke 17:25–30
But first must he suffer many things, and be rejected of this generation. And as it was in the days of Noe, so shall it be also in the days of the Son of man. They did eat, they drank, they married wives, they were given in marriage, until the day that Noe entered into the ark, and the flood came, and destroyed them all. Likewise also as it was in the days of Lot; they did eat, they drank, they bought, they sold, they planted, they builded; but the same day that Lot went out of Sodom it rained fire and brimstone from heaven, and destroyed them all. Even thus shall it be in the day when the Son of man is revealed.

In the days of both Noah and Lot, people ignored the spiritual climate of their day and carried on with their lives as they always did. So, too, people now go about business as usual, even though the storm clouds are gathering again.

Luke 17:31–33
In that day, he which shall be upon the housetop, and his stuff in the house, let him not come down to take it away: and he that is in the field, let him likewise not return back. Remember Lot's wife. Whosoever shall seek to save his life shall lose it; and whosoever shall lose his life shall preserve it.

What did Lot's wife do? She made the mistake of looking back. Linguistic evidence makes it clear that hers was not a quick glance but a longing gaze. It's impossible to make any progress physically without getting bruised ourselves or crashing into others while looking back. And the same is true spiritually (Luke 9:62).

Luke 17:34–37 (a)
I tell you, in that night there shall be two men in one bed; the one shall be taken, and the other shall be left. Two women shall be grinding together; the one shall be taken, and the other left. Two men shall be in the field; the one shall be taken, and the other left. And they answered and said unto him, Where, Lord?

Continuing His discourse on the end times, Jesus speaks of the Rapture.

Luke 17:37 (b)
And he said unto them, Wheresoever the body is, thither will the eagles be gathered together.

Although this is a difficult Scripture, the word "eagles" being better translated "vultures," I be-

lieve the implication is that if dead bodies and vultures are linked together, how much more will the living body of Christ and Jesus Himself be linked together at the time of the Tribulation. But even before then, the degree to which we are linked to the Lord presently is the degree to which heaven will be experienced by us most perceptibly.

18
Luke 18:1, 2
And he spake a parable unto them to this end, that men ought always to pray, and not to faint; saying, There was in a city a judge, which feared not God, neither regarded man.

I find it interesting that, although our own judicial system has increasingly moved to restrict prayer, Jesus uses a parable set in a courtroom to teach us about prayer.

Luke 18:3
And there was a widow in that city; and she came unto him, saying, Avenge me of mine adversary.

In Jesus' time, there was no such thing as a city courthouse. Rather, a judge would travel from town to town, pitching his tent in a given location for three to five days at a time. When the judge was in their town, those with legal issues would begin to make their way toward his tent. Often, however, the needs were so great that the docket would be filled. Then, the only way a person could have his case heard would be to bribe the judge's assistants.

Luke 18:4 (a)
And he would not for a while . . .

This woman's chances at being heard didn't look very promising for three reasons. First, she was a woman in a culture where women were second-class citizens at best. Second, she was a widow—without a husband to stand with her or open the way for her. Third, being a widow, she would have been poor.

Luke 18:4 (b)–5
. . . but afterward he said within himself, Though I fear not God, nor regard man; yet because this widow troubleth me, I will avenge her, lest by her continual coming she weary me.

With three strikes against her, it looked like this widow didn't have a chance to be heard. But that didn't stop her. She came day and night before the judge, pleading and begging that her case be heard, until finally he said, "To get this lady off my back, I'll do what she wants."

Luke 18:6–8 (a)
And the Lord said, Hear what the unjust judge saith. And shall not God avenge his own elect, which cry day and night unto him, though he bear long with them? I tell you that he will avenge them speedily.

Jesus uses the account of the widow to teach what our attitude should be in prayer. But notice, He gave this parable not so much as a parallel, but as a contrast—for our situation is entirely different.

First of all, we appear not before an unjust judge, but before a loving Father. When Jesus taught His disciples to pray, "Our Father which art in heaven," the concept of God as a Father was foreign to the Jews. Paul would go on to address God as "Abba" or "Papa" (Romans 8:15). Thus, far from being our judge, God is our loving Father, our Abba, our Papa.

Second, we appear before God not as strangers, but as His children.

A photographer captured on film Supreme Court Justice Anton Scalia in his chambers at his massive desk when one of his grandchildren came bursting into the room. The photograph shows Scalia looking up and smiling from ear to ear.

It's amazing the access a person has with his parents. No matter how important a man might be, his son or daughter can burst into his presence anytime. That is the privilege we have as children of the God of the universe.

Third, this woman was a widow. We are a bride (Revelation 21:2). Big difference. A widow feels all alone, not so a bride.

Fourth, the widow went alone, but we have an Advocate with the Father (1 John 2:1). Jesus stands right beside us.

Lastly, to get help the widow went to a court of law. We come to a throne of grace (Hebrews 4:16).

Luke 18:8 (b)
Nevertheless when the Son of man cometh, shall he find faith on the earth?

Even though the widow's situation was more difficult than those we usually face, she never gave up asking. What about us? If we know that God is a Father who loves us, that Jesus is an Advocate standing beside us, and that we are a bride

invited to come to a throne of grace, why don't we pray? Why is it that Jesus must ask, "Will I find praying faith when I come again?"

People stop praying whenever they go to the Lord with a problem or a need and He doesn't answer them speedily. "I've come to You, Lord, for weeks and months about this problem, and there seems to be no solution," they say. "I've come for years, but there seems to be no provision. Why pray?" they finally say. They stop praying altogether, failing to understand that, because they are created in the image of God, they are composed of three parts—body, soul, and spirit—and it is the spirit that is most powerfully impacted by prayer.

You see, the body is that which relates to the physical world through the senses of sight and smell, touch, taste, and hearing. The soul, comprised of mind and emotions, is that which relates to people through one's personality. But because it is the spirit—the deepest part of man—that relates to God and will live forever with Him, it is most often through the spirit that prayers are answered. The problem is that we limit our prayers to the realms of only the body or soul. We either want a physical, tangible answer to our prayers, or we want to feel better after we pray. But God knows that what we are truly craving can only be fulfilled in the realm of the spirit.

"Father," we say, "my finances are low. I need bread." And although He is a Father who will indeed provide our daily bread, He also knows bread will not satisfy us ultimately. So He sent His Son to be Bread for us (John 6:35).

"I need direction," we pray.
"I am the Way," Jesus says (John 14:6).

"I need peace," we cry.
"You'll find peace in Me," Jesus answers (John 16:33).

What we think we need is rarely that for which we pray. What we need is the Lord Himself.

Prayer is not to get the goods.
It is to enjoy the One who is good.

Prayer is not to get the gifts.
It is to have fellowship with the Giver of all gifts.

Prayer is not to claim the promises.
It is to embrace the Person.

Everything you crave is found in the Person of Jesus Christ—and you will discover that to be true if you pray and don't faint.

Luke 18:9, 10
And he spake this parable unto certain which trusted in themselves that they were righteous, and despised others: Two men went up into the temple to pray; the one a Pharisee, and the other a publican.

Jewish tradition dictated that prayer be made in the temple at nine o'clock in the morning, twelve noon, and three o'clock in the afternoon.

Luke 18:11
The Pharisee stood and prayed thus with himself, God, I thank thee, that I am not as other men are, extortioners, unjust, adulterers, or even as this publican.

This Pharisee wasn't really seeking God as evidenced by the fact that he "prayed thus with *himself.*"

Luke 18:12
I fast twice in the week, I give tithes of all that I possess.

Not only would a traditional Jew pray three times a day, but he would fast twice a week on Mondays and Thursdays. Not accidentally, Monday and Thursday were market days in Jerusalem, which meant that everyone could see the piety of those who came with the mussed hair and wrinkled clothes of those who fasted. With long faces they made their way into the temple to pray so everyone could see their spirituality.

Luke 18:13
And the publican, standing afar off, would not lift up so much as his eyes unto heaven, but smote upon his breast, saying, God be merciful to me a sinner.

"God be merciful to me a sinner," prayed the publican. With the article "a" better translated as "the," the publican was actually saying, "Lord be merciful to me, the ultimate sinner." And that was all he said. We have a tendency to think our prayers are answered in direct proportion to how many times we've been in church, how many times we've had devotions, how many times we've given offering. But nothing is further from the truth. Prayer is not based upon merit. It's based upon mercy. That's what this sinner discovered— and once you learn this lesson, prayer will become a joy to you as well.

Notice that the publican made no excuses for his sin. He came in total humility and simply said, "Have mercy upon me, the ultimate sinner." He

didn't defend himself, explain his sin, justify his rebellion, or vow to do better in the future.

All too often, we come before the Lord and not only say, "Forgive me," but "I promise I'll never do that again." When I make those kinds of promises, I am expressing a confidence in my flesh that will prove to be an embarrassment to me down the road. I can't promise not to sin again. Like the publican, I must simply ask the Father to have mercy upon me.

Luke 18:14
I tell you, this man went down to his house justified rather than the other: for every one that exalteth himself shall be abased; and he that humbleth himself shall be exalted.

Once you understand that it is based solely upon mercy, prayer becomes a total pleasure. And when the answers come and the blessings are released and things begin to happen, guess who gets the glory. You can't take credit because of your spirituality or discipline. You simply glorify God with humility and great appreciation as you stand in awe of His answer to your prayer and His work in your life.

Luke 18:15–17
And they brought unto him also infants, that he would touch them: but when his disciples saw it, they rebuked them. But Jesus called them unto him, and said, Suffer little children to come unto me, and forbid them not: for of such is the kingdom of God. Verily I say unto you, Whosoever shall not receive the kingdom of God as a little child shall in no wise enter therein.

After teaching on prayer, Jesus prays blessing on the children brought to Him. The Greek pronoun translated "they" is masculine, so it was the fathers who brought their children to Jesus. Dads, it is both your privilege and responsibility to bring your kids to the Lord that they might be blessed by Him. How does this happen? I believe we see the answer in Job. . . .

Knowing his kids were vulnerable to sin perhaps due to his wealth and their youth, Job sacrificed a bull on their behalf lest they forget the Lord and sin in their hearts (Job 1:5). I believe this practice is recorded in the Word as an example for you and me. I have the opportunity in the morning hour to intercede on my kids' behalf—to ask that the Lord would bless them and use them. Conversely, my failure to do so leaves them vulnerable to the attacks of the Enemy. Expend the energy, Dad. Bring your children to the Lord in prayer. It's so important.

Luke 18:18, 19
And a certain ruler asked him, saying, Good Master, what shall I do to inherit eternal life? And Jesus said unto him, Why callest thou me good? none is good, save one, that is, God.

Jesus' statement completely undermines the New Age mentality that says Jesus was a good Teacher, but not God. Jesus is either God, or He's not good. Period.

Luke 18:20, 21
Thou knowest the commandments, Do not commit adultery, Do not kill, Do not steal, Do not bear false witness, Honour thy father and thy mother. And he said, All these have I kept from my youth up.

Jesus gave the rich young ruler a list of commandments, but purposely did not include the last one: Thou shalt not covet.

Luke 18:22
Now when Jesus heard these things, he said unto him, Yet lackest thou one thing: sell all that thou hast, and distribute unto the poor, and thou shalt have treasure in heaven: and come, follow me.

I suggest it was because Jesus knew that coveting—wanting more of that which he already had enough—was this man's weakness and that He was giving him the opportunity to recognize it as well.

Luke 18:23
And when he heard this, he was very sorrowful: for he was very rich.

The problem wasn't that this man possessed riches, but that riches possessed him. Thus, Jesus wasn't trying to make him miserable. He was trying to set him free.

Luke 18:24, 25
And when Jesus saw that he was very sorrowful, he said, How hardly shall they that have riches enter into the kingdom of God! For it is easier for a camel to go through a needle's eye, than for a rich man to enter into the kingdom of God.

Riches have a tendency to control and distract. Therefore, Jesus said, "It's difficult for a wealthy man to enter into the kingdom because all too often, his toys and his bank account blind him to his need."

Luke 18:26, 27
And they that heard it said, Who then can be saved? And he said, The things which are impossible with men are possible with God.

The salvation of rich, poor, or middle-class is impossible in our own energy or efforts. Salvation for anyone and everyone requires a work of God's supernatural grace and miraculous power.

Luke 18:28–30
Then Peter said, Lo, we have left all, and followed thee. And he said unto them, Verily I say unto you, There is no man that hath left house, or parents, or brethren, or wife, or children, for the kingdom of God's sake, Who shall not receive manifold more in this present time, and in the world to come life everlasting.

We who are saved are part of a big family, indeed, who will care for us and stand by us. Not only that, but the riches awaiting those who invest in heaven and serve the Lord sacrificially will make them richly blessed in eternity.

Luke 18:31–34
Then he took unto him the twelve, and said unto them, Behold, we go up to Jerusalem, and all things that are written by the prophets concerning the Son of man shall be accomplished. For he shall be delivered unto the Gentiles, and shall be mocked, and spitefully entreated, and spitted on: And they shall scourge him, and put him to death: and the third day he shall rise again. And they understood none of these things: and this saying was hid from them, neither knew they the things which were spoken.

Drawing closer to the city of Jerusalem, Jesus speaks straightforwardly to His twelve disciples.

As Christopher Columbus sailed west, he actually kept two logbooks. One contained false information that showed them closer to land than they actually were. This was the book made available to the crew in hopes that they wouldn't lose hope in ever seeing land again. The other book, showing their true location, was the one Columbus used.

Columbus evidently decided the morale of the crew was more important than the integrity of the captain. Not so Jesus. He says to His disciples, "When we get to Jerusalem, people will reject Me and crucify Me." But He gave hope to them as well when He said He would rise again.

Luke 18:35
And it came to pass, that as he was come nigh unto Jericho, a certain blind man sat by the way side begging.

In contrast to the rich young ruler who left the Lord in sadness, we're introduced to a blind man who will follow the Lord in gladness. Notice three characteristics of this man—whom Mark identifies as Bartimaeus—that are applicable to you and me. . . .

Luke 18:36–38
And hearing the multitude pass by, he asked what it meant. And they told him, that Jesus of Nazareth passeth by. And he cried, saying, Jesus, thou Son of David, have mercy on me.

Bartimaeus was a man of humility. If you were in Bartimaeus' sandals and knew Jesus was passing by, would you say, "Have mercy on me,"—or would you say, "How come of all the people in Jericho, *I* was the one afflicted with blindness? I deserve better than this." Isn't the latter all too often our tendency? It is only because of the Lord's mercies that we are not consumed (Lamentations 3:22). Therefore, may God give us the wisdom of Bartimaeus to approach Him with humility.

Luke 18:39
And they which went before rebuked him, that he should hold his peace: but he cried so much the more, Thou Son of David, have mercy on me.

Bartimaeus was a man of tenacity. "Pipe down," the multitude told him. But he yelled all the louder. A living example of the parable of the woman and the unjust judge, Bartimaeus simply kept coming all the more. In prayer, in ministry, and in our walk with the Lord, this really is essential. One of the most famous pieces of music in history, "Braham's Lullaby," took over seven years to compose. We let go too quickly. We give up too easily. It was after Abraham *patiently endured* that He received the promise (Hebrews 6:15). The same was true of Bartimaeus.

Luke 18:40–43
And Jesus stood, and commanded him to be brought unto him: and when he was come near, he asked him, Saying, What wilt thou

that I shall do unto thee? And he said, Lord, that I may receive my sight. And Jesus said unto him, Receive thy sight: thy faith hath saved thee. And immediately he received his sight, and followed him, glorifying God: and all the people, when they saw it, gave praise unto God.**

Bartimaeus was a man of expectancy. Mark tells us that when Jesus called him, Bartimaeus left his garment—a garment beggars wore to identify them as those in need of alms. In other words, once he heard Jesus' voice, he said in faith, "I don't need this anymore. I'm expecting the Lord to do a work in me based upon His mercy." You and I will either follow in the footsteps of the rich young ruler or in the footsteps of Bartimaeus. Choose those of Bartimaeus. Call out to the Lord in humility with tenacity and expectancy, knowing that to any who call upon Him, the Lord shows matchless mercy.

---

19 As we come to chapter 19, we are geographically fifteen miles northeast of Jerusalem as Jesus travels toward the Holy City. Chronologically, we are at the final week of our Lord's time on earth.

Luke 19:1, 2
And Jesus entered and passed through Jericho. And, behold, there was a man named Zacchaeus, which was the chief among the publicans, and he was rich.

"Publican" is the name for a tax collector. Tax collectors were not intended to be rich men, but their position allowed them to become exceedingly wealthy if they overcharged the people. Therefore, the fact that Zacchaeus was rich indicates he was probably dishonest.

Luke 19:3, 4
And he sought to see Jesus who he was; and could not for the press, because he was little of stature. And he ran before, and climbed up into a sycamore tree to see him: for he was to pass that way.

What a scene: Zacchaeus, a wealthy Roman official, first ran—something dignified men never did—then scrambled up a tree in order to catch a glimpse of this One passing by. John Calvin said the foundation of faith is childlike curiosity and simplicity. Jesus said that we must enter the kingdom as a little child (Luke 18:17), as one who doesn't have all the answers but simply believes. Zacchaeus models this beautifully.

Luke 19:5 (a)
And when Jesus came to the place, he looked up, and saw him . . .

Although Zacchaeus may have thought he was seeking Jesus, in reality it was Jesus who found him. The same is true of us (Romans 3:11).

Luke 19:5 (b)
. . . and said unto him, Zacchaeus, make haste, and come down; for to day I must abide at thy house.

The word translated "abide" is the same word Paul uses in Ephesians when, praying for the believers, he says, "for this cause I bow my knees unto the Father of our Lord Jesus Christ to *dwell* in your hearts by faith" (see Ephesians 3:17). The word literally means "to be comfortable." I like that! Some people have a very tense or uptight relationship with Jesus, as evidenced by either the formality or excessive emotion of their prayers. What a beautiful thing it is, however, to hear people pray who simply enjoy the Lord and are comfortable with Him.

Luke 19:6–10
And he made haste, and came down, and received him joyfully. And when they saw it, they all murmured, saying, That he was gone to be guest with a man that is a sinner. And Zacchaeus stood, and said unto the Lord; Behold, Lord, the half of my goods I give to the poor; and if I have taken any thing from any man by false accusation, I restore him fourfold. And Jesus said unto him, This day is salvation come to this house, forsomuch as he also is a son of Abraham. For the Son of man is come to seek and to save that which was lost.

Although Abraham is indeed the Father of Faith, James points to him as an example that faith without works is dead. After all, Abraham was ready to sacrifice Isaac as a proof of his faith (James 2:21). Paul, on the other hand, points to Abraham as proof that justification is *apart* from works (Romans 4:13). Interestingly, in the story of Zacchaeus we see the perfect blending of Romans 4 and James 2—for just as Abraham believed God, so did Zacchaeus; and just as Abraham willingly offered to sacrifice his son, so Zacchaeus willingly offered the sacrifice of his goods.

Luke 19:11
And as they heard these things, he added and spake a parable, because he was nigh to Jerusalem, and because they thought that the kingdom of God should immediately appear.

On the heels of Zacchaeus' practical demonstration of his true conversion, Jesus begins to teach on practical stewardship in the parable of the pounds. . . .

Luke 19:12, 13
He said therefore, A certain nobleman went into a far country to receive for himself a kingdom, and to return. And he called his ten servants, and delivered them ten pounds, and said unto them, Occupy till I come.

This parable is different than the parable of the talents (Matthew 25). The parable of the talents—in which men were given one, five, and ten talents—speaks of a variety of gifts and ministries given to believers. On the other hand, the parable of the pounds—in which everyone is given the same amount—speaks of equality of opportunity. . . .

Because of what they accomplish, it seems some people are given more time each day. The fact is, however, that we are all given the same twenty-four hours every day.

Although the amount may differ radically, we have all been given the same opportunity to invest one-tenth of our income in the kingdom.

Although we may be inclined to think that we can't witness because the message we have been given to share is a lot harder than the message others are given, we have all been given precisely the same gospel.

Luke 19:14
But his citizens hated him, and sent a message after him, saying, We will not have this man to reign over us.

"We don't want this man to rule over us," said the citizenry. This was the very thing they would say a few days later of the Lord Himself (John 19:15).

Luke 19:15
And it came to pass, that when he was returned, having received the kingdom, then he commanded these servants to be called unto him, to whom he had given the money, that he might know how much every man had gained by trading.

Even though they were in a setting hostile to the nobleman, his servants still had responsibility to carry out his command.

Luke 19:16–26
Then came the first, saying, Lord, thy pound hath gained ten pounds. And he said unto him, Well, thou good servant: because thou hast been faithful in a very little, have thou authority over ten cities. And the second came, saying, Lord, thy pound hath gained five pounds. And he said likewise to him, Be thou also over five cities. And another came, saying, Lord, behold, here is thy pound, which I have kept laid up in a napkin: For I feared thee, because thou art an austere man: thou takest up that thou layedst not down, and reapest that thou didst not sow. And he saith unto him, Out of thine own mouth will I judge thee, thou wicked servant. Thou knewest that I was an austere man, taking up that I laid not down, and reaping that I did not sow: Wherefore then gavest not thou my money into the bank, that at my coming I might have required mine own with usury? And he said unto them that stood by, Take from him the pound, and give it to him that hath ten pounds. (And they said unto him, Lord, he hath ten pounds.) For I say unto you, That unto every one which hath shall be given; and from him that hath not, even that he hath shall be taken away from him.

The one who is faithful in investing the pound—be it time, tithe, or gospel—will be given ten cities to rule. The one who is semi-faithful will be given five cities. The one who is faithless will lose the opportunity of service altogether. In other words, Jesus is telling us that the reward for good work is more work.

"If the reward for work is more work, why work?" you might ask. Although everyone will be elated in heaven, those who are presently faithful will be challenged and excited. They will grow and develop. On the other hand, those who didn't invest their time, talents, or finances in heaven will walk the streets of gold wishing they had been given responsibility in the kingdom.

Luke 19:27–30
But those mine enemies, which would not that I should reign over them, bring hither, and slay them before me. And when he had thus spoken, he went before, ascending up to Jerusalem. And it came to pass, when he was come nigh to Bethphage and Bethany, at the mount called the mount of Olives, he

sent two of his disciples, saying, Go ye into the village over against you; in the which at your entering ye shall find a colt tied, whereon yet never man sat: loose him, and bring him hither.

Preparing to come down the hillside called the Mount of Olives into the city of Jerusalem, Jesus sends His disciples to get a donkey, fulfilling the prophecy of Zechariah 9.

Luke 19:31
And if any man ask you, Why do ye loose him? thus shall ye say unto him, Because the Lord hath need of him.

"Because the Lord hath need of him." What an irony it is that the Lord would have need of anything. But He does. He needed a boat from which to preach (Luke 5:3–6). He needed some loaves and fishes with which to feed the crowd (Matthew 14:16–18). He needed a coin through which to make a point (Matthew 22:19). He needed a room in which to share the Last Supper with His disciples (Matthew 26:18). He needed a tomb from which to rise from the dead (Matthew 27:60). Our Lord has chosen to place Himself in a position of need. Paul said He who was rich became poor for our sake (2 Corinthians 8:9). Why? I believe one of the reasons was in order that we might partner with Him in what He wants to do on the earth. Whether it's preaching the Word or feeding the multitude, the Lord has chosen to say, "I need you."

Luke 19:32–34
And they that were sent went their way, and found even as he had said unto them. And as they were loosing the colt, the owners thereof said unto them, Why loose ye the colt? And they said, The Lord hath need of him.

Before the donkey could be used by the Lord, it first had to be loosed. That's exactly what we're to do. Even though we are born again, like Lazarus coming forth from the grave, oftentimes, we're still bound (John 11:44). But as we come and hear the Word, as we stand hand in hand with our brothers and sisters in prayer, we find ourselves loosed, released from that which so easily binds us.

Luke 19:35–37
And they brought him to Jesus: and they cast their garments upon the colt, and they set Jesus thereon. And as he went, they spread their clothes in the way. And when he was come nigh, even now at the descent

of the mount of Olives, the whole multitude of the disciples began to rejoice and praise God with a loud voice for all the mighty works that they had seen;

Jesus' usual mode was to shun publicity. However, He knew that once the multitude cried out to Him and once He received their praise, His enemies had to either coronate Him King or crucify Him as a criminal. Thus, He's forcing their hand.

Luke 19:38
Saying, Blessed be the King that cometh in the name of the Lord: peace in heaven, and glory in the highest.

Luke's Gospel began with the angels saying, "Glory to God in the highest and peace on earth" (see Luke 2:14). Here, toward the end of his Gospel, because man will reject the Prince of Peace, there will still be glory to God in the highest—but no peace on earth.

Luke 19:39, 40
And some of the Pharisees from among the multitude said unto him, Master, rebuke thy disciples. And he answered and said unto them, I tell you that, if these should hold their peace, the stones would immediately cry out.

"He came unto His own, and His own received Him not," writes John of Jesus (John 1:11). The first word translated "own" refers to creation; the second to humanity. In other words, as evidenced by the water that supported Him (Matthew 14:25), the storm that stopped for Him (Mark 4:39), the rocks that were ready to praise Him had He not quieted them, nature indeed received Him. It is only humanity that fails to do so.

Put the skeptic in Candlestick Park or the Super Bowl, and he will become a radical worshiper. Watch the hands of those who wouldn't be caught dead lifting their hands in worship to the Lord shoot into the air the minute Jerry Rice scores a touchdown. Listen to the sound of applause from those who wouldn't ever clap in worship to the Lord the moment Roger Craig makes a ten-yard gain. Because man is innately a worshiper, he does indeed worship. But it's misdirected toward movie stars or athletes rather than to the only One to whom worship is truly due.

Luke 19:41–44
And when he was come near, he beheld the city, and wept over it, saying, If thou hadst known, even thou, at least in this thy day, the things which belong unto thy peace! but

now they are hid from thine eyes. For the days shall come upon thee, that thine enemies shall cast a trench about thee, and compass thee round, and keep thee in on every side, and shall lay thee even with the ground, and thy children within thee; and they shall not leave in thee one stone upon another; because thou knewest not the time of thy visitation.

As the crowd rejoiced, our Lord wept. His heart was broken by what He saw everywhere He looked. . . .

As He looked on the city of Jerusalem, He knew she had missed her day. Had the people been studying prophecy, they would have known that this was the exact day of His arrival.

As He looked within, He saw hearts filled with hypocrisy and iniquity.

As He looked ahead, He saw that the city would be surrounded by her enemies, the people slaughtered mercilessly. Indeed, before forty years would pass, the Romans would besiege Jerusalem and in the ensuing one hundred forty-three days, between six hundred thousand and over one million Jews would be killed.

This man's Man who would drive out the moneychangers from the temple with no one daring to stop Him was nonetheless brought to tears as He saw what was happening and where it was leading. Truly there is no one like Jesus, for no one else would weep compassionately for a people He knew would not only reject Him but also crucify Him. I love the Lord because He didn't give up on Jerusalem; He doesn't give up on me; and He won't give up on you.

Luke 19:45, 46
And he went into the temple, and began to cast out them that sold therein, and them that bought; saying unto them, It is written, My house is the house of prayer: but ye have made it a den of thieves.

The priests who were supposed to be praying for the people were instead those who preyed on the people. They charged exorbitant rates of exchange for the foreign currency worshipers brought for offering and inflated prices for temple-approved animals to sacrifice.

Luke 19:47
And he taught daily in the temple. But the

chief priests and the scribes and the chief of the people sought to destroy him.

In a few days, Jesus knew Annas and the chief priests would get revenge. Until then, He would keep teaching.

Luke 19:48
And could not find what they might do: for all the people were very attentive to hear him.

As your margin may render this passage, the people hung on every word Jesus spoke. I find the choice of words interesting, for as they hung on His words, He was about to hang on the Cross for them.

For topical study of Luke 19:47–48, see "Hanging on His Words" below.

HANGING ON HIS WORDS
A Topical Study of
Luke 19:47, 48

As He taught in the temple, people hung on every word Jesus spoke. This is not unusual, for over and over in the Gospel accounts, we come across similar phrases . . .

The common people heard Him gladly (Mark 12:37).
They wondered at the gracious words He spoke (Luke 4:22).
They were astonished at His doctrine (Mark 1:22).

Jesus communicated in a way that captivated people because He not only preached with clarity but practiced what He preached perfectly. I suggest His Word will captivate you as well to the degree that you study it in the following ways. . . .

Conversationally

"You search the Scriptures for in them you think you have eternal life, but these are they which speak of *Me*," Jesus declared (John 5:39). Therefore, whether in your devotions morning by morning or joining with fellow believers on a Wednesday evening, the key to Bible study is to realize the purpose is to touch Jesus intimately.

How does this happen? I believe it takes place most effectively through conversation. When I'm out of town, I always look forward to calling my wife. When I call her, I don't say, "Tammy, this is Jon. Listen carefully . . ." and then proceed to talk nonstop for fifteen minutes before telling her it's her turn to talk, after which time I hang up. No, true communication consists of give-and-take, an ebb and flow.

Yet when it comes to conversing with our Lord, our tendency is to say, "Okay, Lord, You can talk to me for fifteen minutes through Your Word, and then I'll talk to You for fifteen minutes through prayer." I'm not saying you can't communicate that way. But I am saying it lacks intimacy. Therefore, I suggest that you talk to the

Lord even as you're reading the Word. When you come across a phrase that convicts you, pray about it. Say, "Oh, Lord, forgive me. I've missed the mark so badly." And then go back to the Word and take in some more. When you come to a verse that comforts you, pray about it. Say, "Thank You, Lord for this reminder of Your goodness to me." Dialoguing with the Lord back and forth makes such a difference.

The same is true congregationally. Many of you have learned the secret of how to pray even as you're listening to a sermon. When a point is made that comforts you, you pray, "Lord, thank You for that." When a point is made that challenges you, you've learned to pray, "Lord, help me to do that." Thus, Bible study is never boring because you're touching Jesus through the Word even while teaching is taking place. You can experience intimacy with the Lord even as you're listening to the Word if you pray in what you're being taught from the Scriptures.

In the past twenty years, there has been a tremendous renewal of Bible study—and that's terrific. But there's also been a diminished appreciation for prayer, and that is tragic. Bible study will motivate your Christian life, but it is only prayer that activates Christian life. You can hear a wonderful Bible study, but your life will remain unchanged until it is activated by prayer. It's as if Bible study builds the car, but prayer is the key that turns on the ignition. Consequently, we have lots of really nice shiny cars in the parking lot of Christendom today—but hardly any of them go anywhere. There's an abundance of knowledge and insights, but not a whole lot of moving because there's not a whole lot of praying. Wise and blessed is the brother or sister who learns to study the Word conversationally as they pray into their lives the points that penetrate their hearts.

Expectantly

"But let him ask in faith, nothing wavering. For he that wavereth is like a wave of the sea driven with the wind and tossed. Let not that man expect to receive anything," James warns (1:6, 7). If I come to the Lord in the morning or to church in the evening without expecting to receive anything, I probably won't.

> Wrestling with some issues in his own life, Habakkuk was wondering what he should do. "I will go to the tower," he said, "and I will wait and see what the Lord shall say to me." In other words, Habakkuk *expected* to hear from God.

> God honored Habakkuk's expectancy and said, "I'm going to give you a vision, Habakkuk. Get out your pencil and write it down" (Habakkuk 2:2).

When I approach morning devotions with my pencil sharp and journal open, God speaks. When I come yawning and drowsy, He doesn't. It's just that simple. If you are expecting to receive from the Lord, you will always walk away a richer man or woman because you will indeed hear from Him. On the other hand, if you come with lethargy, sleepiness, and apathy, you'll leave lethargic, sleepy, and apathetic.

Even if you don't refer to your notes again, write down truth. Why? Because the very act of writing affords one the ability to better retain information. That is why when Old Testament kings first ascended the throne, they were to copy the Law of Moses into a book in order that it might be lodged in their hearts and minds (Deuteronomy 17:18). Try it. Try having morning devotions this week with pencil and paper before you. Come to Bible study expecting the Lord to speak to you. Then watch and see what happens. I think you'll find a radical difference in your ability to hang on His words.

Obediently

The reason some say, "I'm not receiving anything from the Word I'm reading or the teachings I'm hearing," could very well be that, because they are not obeying that which they've already heard, they will not receive more. This is not because they are being punished, but because our loving Father will not give us more than we can handle (Hebrews 5:12–14).

That's why Jesus told us that the one who has shall be given more, but the one who doesn't have—the one who is not obeying—will actually go backward in his knowledge of the Word and in his understanding of God (Mark 4:24, 25). Either I am doing what God says and finding more meat every time I open the Word, or I will lose even the understanding I had previously. Therefore, I must listen obediently. I must say, "Lord, I'm not here simply to satisfy my curiosity or stimulate my intellect. I'm here to do Your will. I am determined to work out in my life practically the things You're telling me through this study. By Your grace, I will do what You say." Then more meat will be sent your way—more understanding, more insight, more revelation, more opportunity.

Consistently

Read the Word consistently and don't give up—even if you don't understand what you're reading. All too often we become so concerned about what we don't understand in the Bible that we only read it sporadically at best. But I guarantee you that, because the Holy Spirit lives within you, even though you might not understand the majority of a given chapter, there will be a verse or a phrase that will impact your heart. Focus on what you *do* understand. Even that which you don't understand will nonetheless strengthen your inner man.

I can't tell you how the chicken dinner I had last night nourishes me. I don't know how amino acids and protein molecules work chemically or nutritionally. I just dig in and let them sustain me and give weight to me. The same is true of the Word. You might not understand intellectually every nuance or doctrine, but it will still energize and edify your inner person. It will still do its work. It will still give you spiritual weight and stamina (Isaiah 55:11).

If you are faithful to study consistently, even though it might seem dry to you initially, there will come a time when water will fill those dry ditches you dig faithfully.

With a drought in the land, things looked grim. "Dig ditches in the sand," Elisha said to the king."But it's bone dry," Jehoshaphat protested.

"Do it anyway," Elisha insisted.

No doubt the diggers were sweating and complaining, but dig they did. The next day, they woke to see the ditches full of water (2 Kings 3:20).

A lot of things we study seem dry to us initially. But if we don't give up, we'll find those very ditches full of water. Every Scripture is pregnant with meaning. Every text abounds with insight—but it takes a lifetime to discover and appreciate them. If we don't give up, that which we once thought was bone dry becomes refreshing and wonderful. We start seeing that every Old Testament story is given as a picture of a New Testament principle, that all of the stories are powerful illustrations of practical and applicable truth. And as you begin to make the correlations, Bible study becomes an adventure.

Luke 20:1
And it came to pass, that on one of those days, as he taught the people in the temple, and preached the gospel, the chief priests and the scribes came upon him with the elders,

On Sunday, as Jesus rode into Jerusalem, He was hailed as King. On Monday, as He cleansed the temple, He acted as the Great High Priest. Here, on Tuesday, as He answers with tremendous skill and wisdom every question hurled at Him, He will show Himself to be a Prophet like no other. Prophet, Priest, and King are the three offices only Jesus can and does hold simultaneously.

Luke 20:2
And spake unto him, saying, Tell us, by what authority doest thou these things? or who is he that gave thee this authority?

The day the chief priests and scribes decided to question Jesus was the tenth day of Nissan, four days before the slaying of the Passover lambs. This perfectly fulfilled the prophetic picture portrayed in Exodus where we read that Passover lambs were to be scrutinized and inspected for four days to ensure they were without blemish (Exodus 12:3–6). Jesus Christ, our Passover Lamb, would also be examined and scrutinized, and would be found faultless.

Luke 20:3–8
And he answered and said unto them, I will also ask you one thing; and answer me: The baptism of John, was it from heaven, or of men? And they reasoned with themselves, saying, If we shall say, From heaven; he will say, Why then believed ye him not? But and if we say, Of men; all the people will stone us: for they be persuaded that John was a prophet. And they answered, that they could not tell whence it was. And Jesus said unto them, Neither tell I you by what authority I do these things.

In response, Jesus asked the chief priests and scribes a question of His own. Through it, He implied that, because they hadn't responded to John's identification of Him as the Lamb of God, it was pointless to provide them with further identification.

Luke 20:9
Then began he to speak to the people this parable; A certain man planted a vineyard, and let it forth to husbandmen, and went into a far country for a long time.

Isaiah also used a vineyard to portray Israel's relationship with God (Isaiah 5:7). Therefore, Jesus' audience would have recognized the vineyard as a picture of themselves and the vineyard owner as God.

Luke 20:10–15 (a)

And at the season he sent a servant to the husbandmen, that they should give him of the fruit of the vineyard: but the husbandmen beat him, and sent him away empty. And again he sent another servant: and they beat him also, and entreated him shamefully, and sent him away empty. And again he sent a third: and they wounded him also, and cast him out. Then said the lord of the vineyard, What shall I do? I will send my beloved son: it may be they will reverence him when they see him. But when the husbandmen saw him, they reasoned among themselves, saying, This is the heir: come, let us kill him, that the inheritance may be ours. So they cast him out of the vineyard, and killed him.

Jesus likened the prophets to a series of servants sent to collect fruit from the vineyard. Each was either beaten or killed. In this, Jesus was saying, "I know your plan. I know your intention. I know what's going on in your hearts." I believe He didn't say this to indict them, but to plead with them, "Is there any of you who want to change your mind, to change your direction, to repent?"

That's exactly what the Lord does with us. None of us falls into sin, but rather we walk into sin one step at a time. Yet, as He sent His servants in the parable and His prophets in the Old Testament, the Lord is faithful to send messengers and warnings to us. All too often, however, we continue on a path of progressive destruction.

In the parable before us, the first messenger was beaten. The second messenger was not only beaten but also treated shamefully. The third messenger was permanently wounded. The fourth messenger was killed. The same progression is seen in the actions of the Jewish leaders: They allowed John the Baptist to be killed. They demanded Jesus be killed. They themselves killed Stephen.

That's the way sin is. It progresses. At first we might be passively allowing it to take place around us. Next, we're requesting that it happen. Finally, we're participating and making it happen. Yet all the while, the Lord faithfully gives opportunities to change direction. We go to a Bible study and get convicted. We turn on the radio and hear words of warning. A concerned brother or sister says, "What are you doing?" Each one is a messenger sent to save us.

Luke 20:15 (b), 16

What therefore shall the lord of the vineyard do unto them? He shall come and destroy these husbandmen, and shall give the vineyard to others. And when they heard it, they said, God forbid.

In giving the Jewish leaders yet another opportunity to repent, Jesus wasn't trying to protect His own life. He knew He would die on the Cross to pay for their sins. Rather, He was pleading with them to save their own lives. What was their answer? A tragically defensive, "God forbid."

Luke 20:17

And he beheld them, and said, What is this then that is written, The stone which the builders rejected, the same is become the head of the corner?

The verse Jesus quotes—Psalm 118:22—is the most oft-quoted Old Testament verse in the New Testament. It refers to the construction of the temple under Solomon's reign when the massive stones were chiseled miles away from the building site in order that no sound be heard upon the temple mount. When the stones arrived, one stone didn't fit and was thrown down the hill into the Kidron Valley. When it became evident that the cornerstone was missing, the stone that had been rejected turned out to be the one that fit perfectly. Jesus applies this to Himself. "You're trying to build your religion apart from Me," He says, "but you're going to see that I am the Cornerstone. Without Me, nothing stands."

Luke 20:18

Whosoever shall fall upon that stone shall be broken; but on whomsoever it shall fall, it will grind him to powder.

The one who falls upon Jesus, the Cornerstone, will indeed be broken, for it's only in admitting our sin and our need that we can be saved. You see, those who aren't broken before Him will one day be broken by Him. *Every* knee shall bow and every tongue will confess that Jesus is Lord (Philippians 2:10). The only question is when will this happen? Will you do it now in brokenness before Him and be saved? Or will you wait too long and be broken by Him?

Luke 20:19–21

And the chief priests and the scribes the same hour sought to lay hands on him; and they feared the people: for they perceived that he had spoken this parable against them. And they watched him, and sent forth spies, which should feign themselves just men, that they might take hold of his words, that so they might deliver him unto the power and authority of the governor. And they asked him, saying, Master, we know that thou sayest and teachest rightly, neither acceptest thou the person of any, but teachest the way of God truly:

After inspecting His authority, the Jews will now question Jesus' integrity.

Luke 20:22
Is it lawful for us to give tribute unto Caesar, or no?

In Jesus' day, paying taxes to Caesar was tantamount to supporting a man who claimed to be God. Therefore, if Jesus said, "Pay taxes to Caesar," the Jewish leaders could accuse Him of supporting idolatry. If, however, He said, "Don't pay taxes," they could have Him arrested for anarchy.

Luke 20:23–25
But he perceived their craftiness, and said unto them, Why tempt ye me? Shew me a penny. Whose image and superscription hath it? They answered and said, Caesar's. And he said unto them, Render therefore unto Caesar the things which be Caesar's, and unto God the things which be God's.

Jesus answered ingeniously when He said, "Give to Caesar that which is made in his image—money—and give to God that which is made in His image—yourselves."

Luke 20:26
And they could not take hold of his words before the people: and they marvelled at his answer, and held their peace.

With two strikes against them, the Jewish leaders move on to question Jesus' theology.

Luke 20:27–33
Then came to him certain of the Sadducees, which deny that there is any resurrection; and they asked him, saying, Master, Moses wrote unto us, If any man's brother die, having a wife, and he die without children, that his brother should take his wife, and raise up seed unto his brother. There were therefore seven brethren: and the first took a wife, and died without children. And the second took her to wife, and he died childless. And the third took her; and in like manner the seven also: and they left no children, and died. Last of all the woman died also. Therefore in the resurrection whose wife of them is she? for seven had her to wife.

The basis for this question is the Old Testament law that when a man died, his younger brother was to marry his widow, and the first child conceived would be the legal descendant of the deceased brother.

Luke 20:34–38
And Jesus answering said unto them, The children of this world marry, and are given in marriage: But they which shall be accounted worthy to obtain that world, and the resurrection from the dead, neither marry, nor are given in marriage: Neither can they die any more: for they are equal unto the angels; and are the children of God, being the children of the resurrection. Now that the dead are raised, even Moses shewed at the bush, when he calleth the Lord the God of Abraham, and the God of Isaac, and the God of Jacob. For he is not a God of the dead, but of the living: for all live unto him.

Jesus draws the Sadducees' attention to Exodus 3, where, in revealing Himself to Moses, God said, "I am the God of Abraham, Isaac and Jacob." In other words, to these men who, under the guise of a question about marriage, were actually questioning the reality of resurrection, Jesus said the fact that God refers to Himself presently as the God of Abraham, Isaac, and Jacob means that they're still alive.

Luke 20:39
Then certain of the scribes answering said, Master, thou hast well said.

Look at me and you'll find fault easily. Look at the person sitting next to you long enough and close enough, and you will find fault with him or her as well. But look at Jesus and you will find no fault whatsoever. No matter how carefully you scrutinize His teachings or study His actions, He will never disappoint or disillusion you. Not once.

Luke 20:40
And after that they durst not ask him any question at all.

Lest we are too quick to judge the Jewish leaders for their audacity in questioning Jesus, we would do well to listen to ourselves. Do we put Him on trial every time we wonder why we haven't got the raise we deserve, why our marriage didn't work out as we thought it would, why Mr. Right hasn't yet come along, why we aren't healed of our diseases? And when we don't get the answers we think we are due, do we shake our fist at Him, apathetically shrug our shoulders to-

ward Him, or almost imperceptibly walk away *from* Him?

The scribes and Pharisees did not dare question Jesus anymore. Why? The words He spoke and the logic He displayed silenced their cynicism. You and I have an even greater proof before us than the words He spoke, for, unlike the scribes and Pharisees, we can look at the Cross.

You who shrug your shoulders in apathy, look at His shoulder and see it ripped apart by the flagellum and bearing a Cross that should have been yours.

You who shake your fist because things aren't happening in the way you think they should, see His hand not clenched but open, pierced by a nail.

You who have walked away from the Lord in anger or drifted away in busyness, look at His feet and see them pinned to a beam of wood, bleeding for you.

The word "crux" meaning "cross," the crux of every matter is indeed the Cross. Does God love me even when the job doesn't work out as I thought it would, even when people don't treat me the way I think they should, even if I'm not healed in the way I hoped I would be, even if I'm not understanding what's happening presently? It is in Cross-examining that which is happening in my life; it is in looking at everything through the lens of Calvary, that I have absolute assurance that, although I may not understand it, everything taking place in my life is for my good. If Jesus loved me enough to die for me, surely He will do what's best concerning me.

Dietrich Bonhoeffer, perhaps the greatest of the modern German theologians, said, "The words why, when, where, and how are all words of the faithless. The only word spoken by a man or woman of faith is 'who.' And 'who' will lead you to *Him*."

What gave Bonhoeffer the authority to say this? Living in Germany in the 1940s, he began to publicly call for the overthrow of Hitler. As a result, in 1943, SS officers broke into the church where he was preaching and hauled him off to a concentration camp. Upon his arrival, the commandant said, "Dietrich Bonhoeffer, the famous preacher and writer, come up here and address the assembly. I will give you two minutes."

"I don't need two minutes," Bonhoeffer said, "just two words: Watch me."

Although the Nazis beat him mercilessly,

every time they lifted a hand or used a club, Bonhoeffer would smile, lift his eyes toward heaven, and say, "Father, forgive them. They know not what they do." He shared a portion of every meal with either a fellow prisoner or one of the Nazi guards. He was constantly smiling, constantly praying, constantly loving—to the point that revival began to break out in the concentration camp. It wasn't because of a word he said, but because of what he did. Dietrich Bonhoeffer was killed April 9, 1945. He could have asked, "Why," but instead He asked, "who"— and was satisfied.

If I had the power, I would change the punctuation for the language of the believer. I would eradicate the question mark and replace it with the mark of the Cross. Whenever people ask questions, put the mark of the Cross at the end, and you'll have the ultimate answer. If you have been wondering what's happening, consider once more what the Lamb of God did for you—and you will find every question answered conclusively.

Luke 20:41 (a)
And he said unto them . . .

After being questioned concerning His authority, integrity, and theology, Jesus now has a question for His questioners.

Luke 20:41 (b)–44
. . . How say they that Christ is David's son? And David himself saith in the book of Psalms, The LORD said unto my Lord, Sit thou on my right hand, Till I make thine enemies thy footstool. David therefore calleth him Lord, how is he then his son?

Because the Jewish leaders did not want to acknowledge His deity, they tried in vain to trip up Jesus intellectually, philosophically, and theologically. But Jesus silenced them the same way He silenced Satan in the wilderness and the same way we silence Satan as well: through the Word.

Luke 20:45–47
Then in the audience of all the people he said unto his disciples, Beware of the scribes, which desire to walk in long robes, and love greetings in the markets, and the highest seats in the synagogues, and the chief rooms at feasts; which devour widows' houses, and for a shew make long prayers: the same shall receive greater damnation.

Although He denounces the scribes for their self-serving religiosity, because God always has a remnant of faithful ones (1 Kings 19:18), Jesus is about to draw the attention of His disciples to a widow exhibiting sacrificial generosity.

∽◯∽

21

Luke 21:1
And he looked up, and saw the rich men casting their gifts into the treasury.

Mark tells us Jesus watched *how* people gave (12:41). Paul tells us He loves those who give cheerfully, or, literally, hilariously (2 Corinthians 9:7).

Luke 21:2
And he saw also a certain poor widow casting in thither two mites.

Even as the scribes and Pharisees argued, discussed, and debated with Jesus, a woman was making her way to the temple and into the gospel record with two mites—an eighth of a cent—to give joyfully and radically to the Lord.

Luke 21:3, 4
And he said, Of a truth I say unto you, that this poor widow hath cast in more than they all: For all these have of their abundance cast in unto the offerings of God: but she of her penury hath cast in all the living that she had.

In our giving, the issue is not the amount but the cost. For some people, to put one hundred dollars in the offering is very easy. For others, to put in even one dollar is costly.

After a plague had passed through Israel, leaving an incredible death toll in its wake, David was instructed by the Lord to build an altar and sacrifice to Him. To do so, David sought to purchase a piece of property from a man named Araunah. Hearing the reason for his purchase, Araunah offered to donate the land. David, however, insisting to pay the full price said, "I will not sacrifice to the Lord of that which costs me nothing" (2 Samuel 24:24).

A man after God's own heart, David reveals the Father's heart toward giving. God neither needs nor desires our "tips." This woman gave only two mites, but it cost her everything.

Luke 21:5 (a)
And as some spake of the temple, how it was adorned with goodly stones . . .

Forty-eight feet long, eighteen feet thick, and eight to ten feet high, the stones of the temple were massive indeed. Even though it was corrupt internally, the disciples attempted to draw Jesus' attention to the temple's external beauty.

Luke 21:5 (b), 6
. . . and gifts, he said, As for these things which ye behold, the days will come, in the which there shall not be left one stone upon another, that shall not be thrown down.

As impossible as it must have seemed to those hearing Jesus' statement, a mere forty years later, the Roman siege of Jerusalem resulted in the burning of the temple. This, in turn, caused all of the gold inside to melt into the cracks of the huge stones. After it had cooled, the soldiers pulled down every single stone to get the hardened gold—just as Jesus had prophesied.

Luke 21:7
And they asked him, saying, Master, but when shall these things be? and what sign will there be when these things shall come to pass?

Because it was the Jews who required a sign (1 Corinthians 1:22), Jesus' ensuing answer, known as the Olivet Discourse, relates specifically to the Jews.

Luke 21:8
And he said, Take heed that ye be not deceived: for many shall come in my name, saying, I am Christ; and the time draweth near: go ye not therefore after them.

The word "Christ" is in italics. Therefore, the actual statement is, "Many will come saying, I Am—Ego Eimi"—a name of deity. For years, people wondered who would have the audacity to claim deity. But in our day of New Age thinking, it is common for people to walk along the beach with outstretched arms saying, "I am God."

Luke 21:9
But when ye shall hear of wars and commotions, be not terrified: for these things must first come to pass; but the end is not by and by.

In the last days, wars will rage.

Luke 21:10, 11 (a)
Then said he unto them, Nation shall rise against nation, and kingdom against kingdom: And great earthquakes shall be in divers places, and famines, and pestilences . . .

The word "pestilence" refers to incurable disease. Certainly the AIDS crisis would qualify.

Luke 21:11 (b)–13
... and fearful sights and great signs shall there be from heaven. But before all these, they shall lay their hands on you, and persecute you, delivering you up to the synagogues, and into prisons, being brought before kings and rulers for my name's sake. And it shall turn to you for a testimony.

Brought before Felix and Festus, Agrippa and Caesar Nero, Paul would be one to use every opportunity to preach the gospel.

Luke 21:14, 15
Settle it therefore in your hearts, not to meditate before what ye shall answer: For I will give you a mouth and wisdom, which all your adversaries shall not be able to gainsay nor resist.

Would you be able to do what Paul did? Yes. The Lord doesn't give "dying grace" until one is dying. The same is true concerning any difficult situation. It's not until you're in that place that the Lord gives you the corresponding grace.

Luke 21:16, 17
And ye shall be betrayed both by parents, and brethren, and kinsfolks, and friends; and some of you shall they cause to be put to death. And ye shall be hated of all men for my name's sake.

In the first two hundred fifty years of the church—beginning with Caesar Nero and extending through the ten waves of persecution that followed—a minimum of six million Christians were killed for their belief in Jesus Christ.

Luke 21:18
But there shall not an hair of your head perish.

"You will be betrayed and killed—but not a hair of your head shall perish." Isn't that a contradiction? No. Jesus is saying, "Not a hair of your head shall perish" in the sense that we say, "That's no skin off my back." In other words, "They might kill your body, but you will be escorted into eternity. The moment you are there, you won't care about what you lost on earth."

Concerning anything you give up for the Lord—be it a boyfriend you let go because he doesn't want to walk with God, a job you've been fired from because you're not willing to compromise in the area of integrity, or even your life it-self—I promise you when you get to heaven, you're not going to say, "Phooey, I wish I would have kept that."

Luke 21:19–24 (a)
In your patience possess ye your souls. And when ye shall see Jerusalem compassed with armies, then know that the desolation thereof is nigh. Then let them which are in Judaea flee to the mountains; and let them which are in the midst of it depart out; and let not them that are in the countries enter thereinto. For these be the days of vengeance, that all things which are written may be fulfilled. But woe unto them that are with child, and to them that give suck, in those days! for there shall be great distress in the land, and wrath upon this people. And they shall fall by the edge of the sword, and shall be led away captive into all nations ...

Not only was the temple burned in A.D. 70, but also, by the end of the 143-day siege, over one million Jews were killed. Of those who survived, many were taken prisoner, leaving the rest to scatter throughout the world. They wandered as a people without a homeland until May 14, 1948, when Israel became a nation once again.

Luke 21:24 (b)
... and Jerusalem shall be trodden down of the Gentiles, until the times of the Gentiles be fulfilled.

It was in 1967 that the Jews reclaimed Jerusalem. Therefore, since then, we have simply been living in prophetic overtime. If you think it's been a long time, you must realize that twenty-five years is miniscule in comparison to all eternity. Besides, a thousand years to the Lord is as a day (2 Peter 3:8). Therefore, He's only a minute or two overdue.

Luke 21:25 (a)
And there shall be signs in the sun, and in the moon, and in the stars ...

I read recently about the discovery of a black hole one hundred billion times the mass of the sun, a discovery some astronomers call "puzzling."

Luke 21:25 (b)
... and upon the earth distress of nations, with perplexity ...

The Greek meaning of this phrase refers to the quagmires and quicksand that must be navigated to assist nations in political turmoil. There simply are no easy answers.

Luke 21:25 (c), 26 (a)
. . . the sea and the waves roaring; men's hearts failing them for fear . . .

Jesus said the perplexity and complexity of society will cause hearts to fail. We're seeing that happen. Relatively unknown in the time of Jesus, linked to stress, heart disease is now a common cause of death in our culture.

Luke 21:26 (b)–28
. . . and for looking after those things which are coming on the earth: for the powers of heaven shall be shaken. And then shall they see the Son of man coming in a cloud with power and great glory. And when these things begin to come to pass, then look up, and lift up your heads; for your redemption draweth nigh.

When we see these things happen, we shouldn't be upset—we should look up.

Luke 21:29 (a)
And he spake to them a parable; behold the fig tree . . .

The fig tree in Scripture is the symbol of the nation Israel.

Luke 21:29 (b)–31
. . . and all the trees; When they now shoot forth, ye see and know of your own selves that summer is now nigh at hand. So likewise ye, when ye see these things come to pass, know ye that the kingdom of God is nigh at hand.

Israel's blossoming as a nation is one of the key signs that the Lord's coming is drawing near. So is the blossoming of "all the trees"—seen in the resurgence of nationalism in countries like Yugoslavia, the Balkans, and African nations.

Luke 21:32–34
Verily I say unto you, This generation shall not pass away, till all be fulfilled. Heaven and earth shall pass away: but my words shall not pass away. And take heed to yourselves, lest at any time your hearts be overcharged with surfeiting, and drunkenness, and cares of this life, and so that day come upon you unawares.

Gideon's three hundred mighty men were chosen because, rather than putting their faces in the river, they drank from their hands. This way,

they could remain alert (Judges 7:6). In other words, God uses men who don't take unnecessary time doing necessary tasks. Yes, we have to live. Certainly, we must care for our families. But there can come a point when we take too much time doing necessary things. And that is the point we are disqualified from being used by God in these last days.

Luke 21:35, 36
For as a snare shall it come on all them that dwell on the face of the whole earth. Watch ye therefore, and pray always, that ye may be accounted worthy to escape all these things that shall come to pass, and to stand before the Son of man.

What are the Jews to pray to escape? The events of the Tribulation.

How will they be counted worthy to escape? By acknowledging the Son of Man, Jesus Christ, as the only worthy One.

Luke 21:37, 38
And in the day time he was teaching in the temple; and at night he went out, and abode in the mount that is called the mount of Olives. And all the people came early in the morning to him in the temple, for to hear him.

I can so easily be sucked into the cares of this life and bogged down by the things of this world. But when I study the words of Jesus, I am reminded of the big picture all over again. I am reminded that I'm only here for a short time. I am reminded of eternity.

Every single believer who is hurting physically or emotionally, every single saint who is struggling financially will indeed be healed and freed incredibly. It might be tonight. It might be this week. It might be this year. It might be in heaven. But God's promises to you will be kept perfectly if you don't lose sight of the big picture. Spend consistent time with Jesus. Be like those in our text. Come *early* to hear Him—and be reminded of heaven all over again.

❧

22
Luke 22:1, 2
Now the feast of unleavened bread drew nigh, which is called the Passover. And the chief priests and scribes sought how they might kill him; for they feared the people.

The chief priests and scribes wanted to get rid of Jesus, but they had to be careful lest they inadvertently incite the people to rally against them.

Luke 22:3–6
Then entered Satan into Judas surnamed Iscariot, being of the number of the twelve. And he went his way, and communed with the chief priests and captains, how he might betray him unto them. And they were glad, and covenanted to give him money. And he promised, and sought opportunity to betray him unto them in the absence of the multitude.

Matthew tells us the chief priests gave Judas thirty pieces of silver, the Old Testament price of a slave. This was a fitting amount, for Jesus came as the Servant of all. Where did the thirty pieces of silver come from? During Passover, the priests carried small bags of money tied to their belts in order to purchase lambs to be used as sacrifices. Therefore, it is highly likely that the chief priests used money committed to their care for the purchase of sacrificial lambs to "purchase" Jesus, the ultimate sacrificial Lamb.

Luke 22:7
Then came the day of unleavened bread, when the passover must be killed.

Based on the number of lambs slaughtered, there were approximately 2.6 million people packed into Jerusalem to celebrate Passover.

Luke 22:8
And he sent Peter and John, saying, Go and prepare us the passover, that we may eat.

Passover was to be celebrated by families. Therefore, in celebrating Passover with His disciples, Jesus looked at His disciples as His family. I like that because at this point, these men weren't very spiritual. Judas would betray Him. Peter would deny Him. Thomas would doubt Him. Yet Jesus treated them as family. And if He did that with them, He'll do it with us as well.

Luke 22:9, 10
And they said unto him, Where wilt thou that we prepare? And he said unto them, Behold, when ye are entered into the city, there shall a man meet you, bearing a pitcher of water; follow him into the house where he entereth in.

Carrying water was women's work. Therefore, it would have been unusual to see a man doing so.

Luke 22:11–13 (a)
And ye shall say unto the goodman of the house, The Master saith unto thee, Where is the guestchamber, where I shall eat the passover with my disciples? And he shall shew you a large upper room furnished: there make ready. And they went, and found as he had said unto them:

"And they went and found as He had said unto them . . . ." That's not true only for the disciples in their day, but for us as well. Whatever Jesus says, you'll find it to be true. There are no exceptions. When Jesus says something you can be sure it's true.

Luke 22:13 (b)–20
. . . and they made ready the passover. And when the hour was come, he sat down, and the twelve apostles with him. And he said unto them, With desire I have desired to eat this passover with you before I suffer: For I say unto you, I will not any more eat thereof, until it be fulfilled in the kingdom of God. And he took the cup, and gave thanks, and said, Take this, and divide it among yourselves: For I say unto you, I will not drink of the fruit of the vine, until the kingdom of God shall come. And he took bread, and gave thanks, and brake it, and gave unto them, saying, This is my body which is given for you: this do in remembrance of me. Likewise also the cup after supper, saying, This cup is the new testament in my blood, which is shed for you.

Here Jesus institutes the ordinance of Communion, saying, "Do this in remembrance of Me." In Luke's Gospel, this is His last commandment, if you would, His "deathbed wish" for you. I think it's a tragedy when people start diminishing the importance of Communion, for the Lord's Supper is much more than just a little cracker and cup of grape juice. It is much more than something we do out of obligation or tradition. Rather, at the Lord's table, something miraculous happens.

Is it that incredible that a miracle happens through Communion? After all, every time we eat bread or drink juice, a miracle takes place as they literally become part of our blood and body. I have found that stripping the ordinances of their mystery produces sterility in one's walk. Therefore, I am simple enough to believe that if we partake of the Lord's table in faith, saying, "Lord, I'm expecting that You truly are filling me and that Your blood is once again washing me," we participate in a miracle and mystery.

Incidentally, due to the fact that leaven and fermentation both pictured corruption, both were forbidden in the Passover ordinance. Therefore, I believe the wine was not fermented.

Furthermore, I cannot believe Jesus would have equated His blood with a rotting substance.

I love the fact that Jesus chose to use the most common foods possible. Bread and wine have been the most available elements to nourish mankind in virtually every culture and every society on every continent throughout history.

What is bread? Grain that has been ground up and baked in the oven. Jesus, the Bread of Life, was ground up by the religious system and the sin of humanity. He was baked in the oven of adversity and absorbed the very fire of hell for you and me. What is wine? Grapes that have been crushed. When the soldier thrust the spear into Jesus' side, the blood and water that flowed indicate that when Jesus died on the Cross, physiologically, He died from a burst, or broken, heart.

Love desires unity—as seen in the substances Jesus chose to commemorate His death. After being ground, individual grains of wheat are brought together into a single loaf. After they are crushed, individual grapes lose their identity and become one. So, too, when I partake of Communion, I not only intimately and mysteriously become one with my Lord, but I become one with my brothers and sisters as we eat of the same loaf and drink of the same cup.

Communion actually has a three-fold aspect: It looks back in faith as it remembers the Cross. It looks ahead in hope as it waits for the day we will eat with the Lord in the kingdom. It looks ahead in love as we see Christians all around the globe and down the tunnel of history eating of the same loaf and drinking of the same cup. We may never agree on end times, the work of the Spirit, or all points of doctrine. But we will find unity at the Lord's table, at the foot of the Cross.

Of Communion, Jesus didn't say, "Teach it." He didn't say, "Think about it." He didn't say, "Try to fit it in." He said, "*Do* this."

Luke 22:21–24
But, behold, the hand of him that betrayeth me is with me on the table. And truly the Son of man goeth, as it was determined: but woe unto that man by whom he is betrayed! And they began to inquire among themselves, which of them it was that should do this thing. And there was also a strife among them, which of them should be accounted the greatest.

Although one moment the disciples were saying, "Am I the betrayer?" the next they were saying, "Aren't I something?" This is what happens to anyone trying to live a performance-oriented faith. If you live by rules and regulations—trying to impress God with your devotion, your ministry,

your piety—like the disciples, you will vacillate between feeling like a betrayer who can't keep your own standards and a superstar when you do keep them for a day or two. If your walk has been up and down, it is probably because you are clinging to a performance-based Christianity. Instead, realize that, because, on the Cross, Jesus declared, "It is finished," there is nothing else that can or must be done.

Luke 22:25–27
And he said unto them, The kings of the Gentiles exercise lordship over them; and they that exercise authority upon them are called benefactors. But ye shall not be so: but he that is greatest among you, let him be as the younger; and he that is chief, as he that doth serve. For whether is greater, he that sitteth at meat, or he that serveth? is not he that sitteth at meat? but I am among you as he that serveth.

The world says, "Sit at the table and be served."

Jesus says, "I look for every opportunity to serve."

Luke 22:28–32
Ye are they which have continued with me in my temptations. And I appoint unto you a kingdom, as my Father hath appointed unto me; that ye may eat and drink at my table in my kingdom, and sit on thrones judging the twelve tribes of Israel. And the Lord said, Simon, Simon, behold, Satan hath desired to have you, that he may sift you as wheat: But I have prayed for thee, that thy faith fail not: and when thou art converted, strengthen thy brethren.

Did Peter's faith fail? No. He believed in the Lord, even though he ended up denying the Lord. Nor did his love fail. What failed? His hope. When he saw Jesus being led away in ropes, being brought to Caiaphas, his hope was lost. Maybe you're in Peter's sandals. You believe in the Lord. You have a definite love for the Lord. But your hope has been diminished because you can't figure out how what's happening to you could possibly work for good.

A number of years ago, a study was done on Norwegian wharf rats. After being thrown in the open water, one group paddled for about three and a half minutes before drowning. A second group was thrown in, but plucked out right before they drowned. The next day, when the rats were thrown back into the water, scientists were astounded to find them able to tread water for forty-five minutes or more—evidently because they were hoping they would be rescued as they were the previous day.

The same is true with us. If we don't have hope that we'll be rescued, we sink. But if we have hope that a rescue is coming, we can tread water through the hard times.

I don't think it is at all coincidental that the doctrine of the Rapture is called the blessed hope (Titus 2:13) because, although sometimes we feel we're in a rat race and going under quickly, we know today could be the glorious day of the Lord's return.

Luke 22:33
And he said unto him, Lord, I am ready to go with thee, both into prison, and to death.

Cock-sure of himself, Peter was crowing about how reliable he was.

Luke 22:34
And he said, I tell thee, Peter, the cock shall not crow this day, before that thou shalt thrice deny that thou knowest me.

Due to their propensity to be noisy and messy, roosters were not allowed in Jerusalem during the Passover. Thus, when this rooster starts making noise, Peter will no doubt be thinking about the mess he made.

Luke 22:35–38
And he said unto them, When I sent you without purse, and scrip, and shoes, lacked ye any thing? And they said, Nothing. Then said he unto them, But now, he that hath a purse, let him take it, and likewise his scrip: and he that hath no sword, let him sell his garment, and buy one. For I say unto you, that this that is written must yet be accomplished in me, And he was reckoned among the transgressors: for the things concerning me have an end. And they said, Lord, behold, here are two swords. And he said unto them, It is enough.

When Jesus told the disciples to buy a sword, He was using an idiom similar to our saying, "Keep your powder dry." In other words, He was telling them the climate was changing from the days previously when they were embraced and provided for in ministry (Matthew 10).

Luke 22:39
And he came out, and went, as he was wont, to the mount of Olives; and his disciples also followed him.

After celebrating the Passover, after speaking very pointedly to Peter, after warning His disciples that the times would be changing, Jesus leaves the city and crosses the little creek bed of the Kidron. The word "Kidron" means "dark" or "murky" because the blood of the sacrifices would drain out of the temple and into the brook below. Therefore, only hours before His death, Jesus would be stepping over a brook that ran blood red.

Luke 22:40
And when he was at the place, he said unto them, Pray that ye enter not into temptation.

Prayer is not only for procurement, but for protection. In other words, prayer is not simply to ask for things you need or want—but also to protect you from things you *don't* need or want. Stop praying, and you will be tempted unnecessarily. Stop praying, and your kids will be vulnerable to attacks of the Enemy. Stop praying, and your marriage will be attacked constantly. Jesus said one of the keys to protection from temptation or trouble is prayer. We'll never know until we get to heaven just how important our prayers are.

Luke 22:41, 42
And he was withdrawn from them about a stone's cast, and kneeled down, and prayed, saying, Father, if thou be willing, remove this cup from me: nevertheless not my will, but thine, be done.

Gethsemane was an appropriate place for Jesus to pray so passionately, for "Gethsemane" means "olive press," the place where olives were crushed to release their oil. The crushing, the pressing Jesus endured in Gethsemane as He was about to feel the wrath of His Father for the sin of all humanity, so far exceeds anything we can even begin to comprehend that it is rendered incomprehensible.

Luke 22:43
And there appeared an angel unto him from heaven, strengthening him.

Every life has a Garden of Gethsemane. But every Gethsemane has an angel. The Lord will always send an angel into your Gethsemane—an unexpected person, a Bible study, a radio teaching, a book—to strengthen you in your time of need.

Luke 22:44
And being in an agony he prayed more earnestly: and his sweat was as it were great drops of blood falling down to the ground.

- In the Garden of Eden, the first Adam stood in rebellion against God.
- In Gethsemane, the Last Adam knelt in submission to God (1 Corinthians 15:45).
- In the Garden of Eden, the first Adam was sentenced to work by the sweat of his brow.
- In the Garden of Gethsemane, the Last Adam agonized so deeply that blood flowed from His brow.

I say this because perhaps you might be saying, "Life is hard. My job is not going right. My marriage is falling apart. My kids are acting up. Why should I press on in the faith? I'm tired of living by the sweat of my brow. I'm tired of dealing with rebellious kids. I'm tired of trying to make ends meet. I'm just plain tired." When you feel tired because you're sweating as part of fallen humanity, consider Jesus. You might be sweating it out, but have you strived so hard that you've actually bled from your forehead? Jesus did.

Life *is* hard. It's part of the curse humanity brought down on itself. We have all sinned, and the way of the transgressor is hard (Proverbs 13:15). But understand that although it's hard being a Christian, it's a lot harder *not* being a Christian. If we didn't know Jesus, we would still have the same problems, but we'd have no access to the One who solves them.

Luke 22:45–47
And when he rose up from prayer, and was come to his disciples, he found them sleeping for sorrow, and said unto them, Why sleep ye? rise and pray, lest ye enter into temptation. And while he yet spake, behold a multitude, and he that was called Judas, one of the twelve, went before them, and drew near unto Jesus to kiss him.

It was common for a student to kiss his rabbi as a sign of submission and affection. Therefore, Judas' kiss would not have seemed unusual. However, the language implies much more than a simple kiss. It implies that Judas was smothering Jesus' cheeks with kisses, as if to make sure that the soldiers were able to identify the One they were to arrest.

Luke 22:48–51
But Jesus said unto him, Judas, betrayest thou the Son of man with a kiss? When they which were about him saw what would follow, they said unto him, Lord, shall we smite with the sword? And one of them smote the servant of the high priest, and cut off his right ear. And Jesus answered and said, Suffer ye thus far. And he touched his ear, and healed him.

Jesus' final healing miracle was one of healing a hurt unnecessarily inflicted by an overzealous disciple. I think the miracle Jesus does most often is to heal the wounds inflicted by overzealous Christians who, thinking they are standing up for truth and defending the Lord by unsheathing the two-edged sword of the Word, chop off the ears of those round about them. While I do admire Peter's courage in being willing to be outnumbered six thousand to one, his zeal was misdirected.

For topical study of Luke 22:35–51 entitled "Putting Away Your Sword," turn to page 410.

Luke 22:52, 53
Then Jesus said unto the chief priests, and captains of the temple, and the elders, which were come to him, Be ye come out, as against a thief, with swords and staves? When I was daily with you in the temple, ye stretched forth no hands against me: but this is your hour, and the power of darkness.

"Why do you come at Me with this army?" Jesus asks. "I was with you in the temple daily, but I realize this is your hour"—and it's a dark hour indeed.

Luke 22:54
Then took they him, and led him, and brought him into the high priest's house. And Peter followed afar off.

Following Jesus afar off is always a dangerous place to be.

Luke 22:55
And when they had kindled a fire in the midst of the hall, and were set down together, Peter sat down among them.

Praying in the garden, Jesus was sweating. Sleeping in the garden, Peter was cold. The difference between being hot and cold is simply prayer. To warm himself, Peter sat down at the enemy's fire. So, too, if you're following Jesus from a distance, you'll feel a chill inside, and you'll go back to the old places, the old ways to get warm. The problem is, when you warm yourself at the enemy's fire, like Peter, you'll get burned.

Luke 22:56–58
But a certain maid beheld him as he sat by the fire, and earnestly looked upon him, and said, This man was also with him. And he denied him, saying, Woman, I know him not. And after a little while another saw him, and said, Thou art also of them. And Peter said, "Man, I am not."

Peter was identified as a disciple of Jesus on two counts. The maiden recognized him as a disciple because he was with Jesus. The man recognized him as a disciple because he was with the other disciples. Therein are the two characteristics of a disciple. You can hang out in church all the time, but if you don't spend personal and private time with the Lord, you're not really a disciple. On the other hand, you can enjoy spending time with the Lord, but if you don't want to worship with other believers, you're not a disciple either. You will be identified as a disciple—even by the enemies of the Lord—if you spend time with Him personally and with fellow believers corporately.

Luke 22:59
And about the space of one hour after another confidently affirmed, saying, Of a truth this fellow also was with him: for he is a Galilaean.

Peter's accent gave him away. So, too, believers are identified by their speech. They have an accent of another kingdom. They don't use the same expressions, tone, or vocabulary as the world (Colossians 3:8).

Luke 22:60
And Peter said, Man, I know not what thou sayest. And immediately, while he yet spake, the cock crew.

As a result of the rooster crowing, no longer would Peter ever be so cocky. Writing his Epistles, he will identify himself as Simon Peter, a servant of Jesus Christ. Simon was his name before he became a disciple. It means "shifting sand" or "unstable one." The Lord changed Simon's name to Peter, or "Rock." But after this event, it was as if he said, "Yes, I'm Peter in the Lord by His grace. But I'm still also Simon because I know my tendency to fail."

I think there's something else here. I believe in

using a rooster, the Lord was telling Peter that even though he messed up, even though he committed a singularly hideous sin in denying Jesus even as Jesus was about to die for him, there would be a new day dawning—a new day of humility, of brokenness, of forgiveness after which He would use Peter mightily. The same is true of you. You will find the Lord will do a mighty work in and through you if, at the point of failure, you turn to Him.

Luke 22:61, 62
And the Lord turned, and looked upon Peter. And Peter remembered the word of the Lord, how he had said unto him, Before the cock crow, thou shalt deny me thrice. And Peter went out, and wept bitterly.

The look with which Jesus looked upon Peter was not one of condemnation, but of compassion. It was a look not of fury, but of forgiveness. And it broke Peter's heart.

Luke 22:63–65
And the men that held Jesus mocked him, and smote him. And when they had blindfolded him, they struck him on the face, and asked him, saying, Prophesy, who is it that smote thee? And many other things blasphemously spake they against him.

According to Isaiah, the beating Jesus endured was more brutal than that experienced by any other man. Erase the mental image of Jesus with a single trickle of blood down His face. That's not what happened.

Luke 22:66–71
And as soon as it was day, the elders of the people and the chief priests and the scribes came together, and led him into their council, saying, Art thou the Christ? tell us. And he said unto them, If I tell you, ye will not believe: And if I also ask you, ye will not answer me, nor let me go. Hereafter shall the Son of man sit on the right hand of the power of God. Then said they all, Art thou then the Son of God? And he said unto them, Ye say that I am. And they said, What need we any further witness? for we ourselves have heard of his own mouth.

Every cult diminishes the deity of Jesus Christ, saying Jesus never claimed to be God. Yet the chief priests and scribes began to carry out His crucifixion for the single reason that, by the way He answered them, they understood He claimed to be God.

The issue of Jesus' deity is foundational and essential to our faith. Why couldn't He be simply the "First Created One," as the Mormons claim? Why could He be a good teacher, but not really God? Simply because if Jesus Christ was not God, then God did not die for me. And suddenly the gospel loses its potency.

God didn't simply create a sacrificial Son to take care of the sin of mankind." No, God Himself died for me. That Jesus is God in the flesh moves me, breaks me, and touches me in a way nothing else possibly could. "*Great* is the mystery of godliness," Timothy writes—that God became a Man (1 Timothy 3:16).

PUTTING AWAY YOUR SWORD
A Topical Study of
Luke 22:35–51

At the end of World War II, when the Americans moved on Berlin, a couple of German soldiers failed to respond to the instructions given them in German. Upon closer inspection, it was discovered they were not German at all, but were from Tibet. When an interpreter was found, they told how, completely unaware of the war going on, they simply wanted to take a journey and crossed the border into Russia. There, they were picked up by Russian military men and immediately conscripted into the Russian Army. A short time later, scared and confused, they were captured by the Nazis and taken to a German POW camp—until, in desperate need of manpower, they were sent to work on the supply lines, where they were eventually captured by American forces.

"Amazing," said the interpreter after hearing their story. "Do you have any questions?"

"Just one," they said. "What's everyone fighting about?"

Sometimes I think the Lord would ask the same thing of us. Like Peter, we are so apt to unsheathe our swords and start flailing away. Consider with me the ways in which Peter's zeal was misdirected . . .

Peter Fought the Wrong Enemy

Not knowing what to expect, the soldiers marching behind Judas were armed and ready for war if necessary. But when Peter drew his sword, he didn't take on any of the six hundred armed soldiers. No, he went for one of the servants who was, most likely, unarmed and defenseless. In his zeal to protect the Lord, Peter went after perhaps the weakest person in the place.

You and I often do the same thing: We fight the wrong enemy. Because Ephesians tells us we wrestle not against flesh and blood, but against principalities and powers and spiritual wickedness in high places (Ephesians 6:12). Therefore, any time I am wrestling or fighting a person, I am fighting the wrong enemy just as surely as was Peter. I am to wage war, to unsheathe my sword, to release my faith, to express my heart not against people but against the entities that victimize people.

If you're fighting your husband, boss, teacher, or neighbor, you're fighting the wrong battle. Longfellow was right when he said, "If we could read the secret history of our enemies, we would find sorrow and suffering enough to disarm all hostility." Our attack is to be leveled not against people, but against Satan and his demons through prayer, for therein lies the true battle.

Peter Used the Wrong Weapon

Peter used a literal sword—but it is only a spiritual weapon that can pull down the high towers the Enemy has erected in people.

The sword we are to use is not a sword that cuts physically. Rather, it is the Sword of the Spirit, which is the Word of God. But because the Word is powerful, sharper than any two-edged sword, we must be careful not to use it carelessly or incorrectly. All too often, Christians unsheathe their Bibles and start chopping on people mercilessly by using a Scripture or a principle—usually out of context—to leave people bloodied, battered, and beaten. Just because a person is quoting Scripture does not mean it is applicable in every situation. If someone is giving you a misguided earful, it's no different than what Peter did when he sliced off Malchus' ear.

James gives us a very simple test to know whether any given word is really from the Lord. . . .

> But the wisdom that is from above is first pure, then peaceable, gentle, and easy to be intreated, full of mercy and good fruits, without partiality, and without hypocrisy. James 3:17

Is what's being shared with you pure, peaceable, and without hassle and hypocrisy? Or does it cause confusion, strife, and tension? Before you unsheathe your sword or allow another to unsheathe his, be sure it's done with this text in mind.

Peter Harbored the Wrong Attitude

After agonizing in the Garden of Gethsemane, Jesus chose to submit to the will of His Father. This meant that, at this point, He had already decided to allow His enemies to arrest Him, to try Him, to crucify Him. Yet even as Jesus was submitting, Peter was fighting—completely out of harmony with the mind and will of Christ. Many times, we have a tendency to want to fight back when in reality, Jesus would have us mellow out. I think of David fleeing from his son, Absalom, who had launched a rebellion against him. . . .

On his way out of Jerusalem, a pipsqueak named Shimei, an enemy of David, threw rocks and dirt at him, saying, "You're a bloody man, David. That's why you're being sent away from Jerusalem. That's why you've lost your kingdom."

Hearing this, Abishai, one of David's men said, "Let me lop off that dead dog's head."

But David would not allow it. "The Lord has allowed him to say these words to me," David said. David recognized Shimei was part of the process through which the Lord was doing a deep work of humility within him (2 Samuel 16).

"Put away your sword, Peter," our Greater than David said. "Your attitude is all wrong. Something rich is being worked out." Jesus would emerge from this situation rich indeed—for, having purchased our salvation, we would be His treasure (Matthew 13:44–46).

Peter Fought At the Wrong Time

Yes, Jesus' arrest was unjust. Certainly, His trial was unfair. But there is coming a time when Peter can indeed unsheathe his sword and address these miscarriages of justice. It will be in the Second Coming, under the direct leadership of Jesus.

"This person must be corrected," we say, or, "This person must be straightened out." Perhaps—but there will come a time when that will happen righteously, perfectly, and completely. Until then, keep your sword at bay.

Peter Fought for the Wrong Reason

The reason Peter drew his sword was to protect the Lord from the six hundred soldiers standing before Him. Do you think the Lord needs protecting? Has He called you to protect Him? Has He called you to straighten out a wrong situation in your own energy?

"What she did is wrong," we fume. "Therefore, I must stand up for the Lord." Maybe—but make sure *He* is directing you.

Perhaps Peter was trying to demonstrate his sincerity, his willingness to take a stand for Jesus. Maybe he was thinking, *You told me I would deny You, Lord. Well, watch this. . . .* So, too, sometimes we want to show how spiritual we are by nailing this person or that situation. Yet one of the most glorious things about being a Christian is the fact that the Lord will judge, leaving us the opportunity to simply love. We are to love, forgive, and encourage people. Yes, there are times of correction—but only if surrounded by love. If the Lord chooses to use you as an instrument of intervention or correction, it won't be as a sword flying indiscriminately, but as a skillful surgeon working exactingly and lovingly.

Like Peter, I have been all wrong. But as I come to Him humbly, the Lord begins to heal the people I have wounded, as well as myself. Like me, you might have been all wrong. But Jesus is all right.

23

Luke 23:1
And the whole multitude of them arose, and led him unto Pilate.

Under Roman rule, the Jews did not technically have the authority to mete out capital punishment. Therefore, Jesus had to be brought before Pilate. However, in Acts 7, we see the Jews themselves stoning Stephen. The question, then, is, if they killed Stephen, why didn't the Jewish leaders kill Jesus for His perceived blasphemy?

I believe it was because it was God's intent that it would not be only the Jews who would kill His Son, but that all of humanity would be involved—not only Romans and Jews, but those who had traveled from all over the known world to Jerusalem for Passover and would join in the demand to crucify Jesus.

Luke 23:2
And they began to accuse him, saying, We found this fellow perverting the nation, and forbidding to give tribute to Caesar, saying that he himself is Christ a King.

Pilate wouldn't sentence a man to death merely on the basis of a theological issue, so the Jews had to furnish trumped-up charges to present to him. Had Jesus forbidden His followers to pay taxes? No. He did just the opposite (Matthew 22:21).

Luke 23:3-7
And Pilate asked him, saying, Art thou the King of the Jews? And he answered him and said, Thou sayest it. Then said Pilate to the chief priests and to the people, I find no fault in this man. And they were the more fierce, saying, He stirreth up the people, teaching throughout all Jewry, beginning from Galilee to this place. When Pilate heard of Galilee, he asked whether the man were a Galilaean. And as soon as he knew that he belonged unto Herod's jurisdiction, he sent him to Herod, who himself also was at Jerusalem at that time.

Pilate already had two strikes against him due to the riots that erupted when he ordered his soldiers bearing insignias—which the Jews perceived as idols—on to the temple mount, and when he paid for the construction of an aqueduct with money from the temple treasury. Therefore, in political hot water, Pilate was no doubt relieved to send Jesus to Herod.

Luke 23:8, 9
And when Herod saw Jesus, he was exceeding glad: for he was desirous to see him of a long season, because he had heard many things of him; and he hoped to have seen some miracle done by him. Then he questioned with him in many words; but he answered him nothing.

Upon His arrival, Herod asked Jesus for a miracle. Even though Jesus' entire earthly ministry had been filled with miracles, Herod is only the first who will ask Jesus for yet another.

"Prophesy who hit You," the soldiers will taunt.
"Come down off the Cross," the crowd will jeer.

Sadly enough, we do the same thing. "Why doesn't God answer my prayer?" we cry. "Why doesn't He open the job? Why doesn't He bless the relationship? Why isn't He providing for our need? Why doesn't He show me a miracle? I would believe if I could just see Him do something."

Miracles do not produce faith. All they produce is an addiction to more miracles. Read the Book of Exodus, and you will see the Red Sea parting, manna falling, water flowing. Yet so faithless were the children of Israel—even after seeing miracle upon miracle—they didn't want to talk to God (Exodus 20:19). Signs and wonders and miracles do not produce faith because they invariably leave people confused about the miracles that didn't transpire. People might see ten events take place that are answers to prayer, but the *one* prayer that doesn't get answered the way they want is the one that hangs them up. That is why miracles are never enough.

Does this mean the Father won't do miracles? Of course He will. But the miracles of God are never about power. They're about people. Whenever the Lord is working in the area of healing, it's with individual people, not massive demonstrations of His power in order to persuade cynics—which is why seven times in Mark's Gospel, concerning His healings, Jesus said, "Don't tell anyone."

Jesus cares about people, not about power. The most powerful miracle of all was His Resurrection from the dead. And yet following this glorious event, how many times did Jesus appear to unbelievers? Not once. He never appeared to Pilate, to Herod, or to the religious leaders, saying, "I'm back." No, only those who already believed in Him saw the resurrected Lord. Who is the one who sees the miracles and the blessings? I believe it is the person who is not seeking them, but who simply loves Jesus.

Luke 23:10, 11
And the chief priests and scribes stood and vehemently accused him. And Herod with his men of war set him at nought, and mocked him, and arrayed him in a gorgeous robe, and sent him again to Pilate.

Herod was angry that Jesus wouldn't perform during his command performance.

Luke 23:12
And the same day Pilate and Herod were made friends together: for before they were at enmity between themselves.

In their hatred of Jesus, Herod and Pilate become friends. But it will backfire, for history tells us Pilate would become insane, and Herod would be of no help to him.

Luke 23:13–16
And Pilate, when he had called together the chief priests and the rulers and the people, Said unto them, Ye have brought this man unto me, as one that perverteth the people: and, behold, I, having examined him before you, have found no fault in this man touching those things whereof ye accuse him: No, nor yet Herod: for I sent you to him; and, lo, nothing worthy of death is done unto him. I will therefore chastise him, and release him.

Regardless of the fact that neither he nor Herod could find any fault with Jesus, Pilate ordered Jesus scourged. Hoping to appease everyone, he would satisfy no one.

Luke 23:17–19
(For of necessity he must release one unto them at the feast.) And they cried out all at once, saying, Away with this man, and release unto us Barabbas: (Who for a certain sedition made in the city, and for murder, was cast into prison.)

The crowd was to choose between Barabbas, who had been indicted for insurrection, and Jesus, whose ministry would be based upon resurrection.

To this day, there are those who want to bring in the kingdom violently, politically, or legislatively. But the Lord's kingdom is not of this world. Barabbas thought he could bring in the kingdom with a revolution. Only Jesus can bring in the true kingdom through regeneration.

The crowd wanted activity, not spirituality. They wanted insurrection, not resurrection. They wanted to do something, not be something. They wanted Barabbas.

Luke 23:20–25
Pilate therefore, willing to release Jesus, spake again to them. But they cried, saying, Crucify him, crucify him. And he said unto them the third time, Why, what evil hath he done? I have found no cause of death in him: I will therefore chastise him, and let him go. And they were instant with loud voices, requiring that he might be crucified. And the voices of them and of the chief priests prevailed. And Pilate gave sentence that it should be as they required. And he released unto them him that for sedition and murder was cast into prison, whom they had desired; but he delivered Jesus to their will.

Pilate heard two voices very clearly: the voice of his conscience and the voice of the crowd. He succumbed to the former. Historians tell us that, shortly after this event, Pilate went into isolation on the island of Sicily. Approached years later by a disciple of Jesus, he was asked if he remembered Jesus of Nazareth. A blank look came over his face as he said, "Jesus? Of Nazareth? I don't remember a thing about Him." Yet so haunted was Pilate that shortly thereafter, he hung himself. How tragic it is when any of us give in to the loud voice of the crowd instead of submitting to the still small voice of the Spirit within us.

Luke 23:26
And as they led him away, they laid hold upon one Simon, a Cyrenian, coming out of the country, and on him they laid the cross, that he might bear it after Jesus.

Cyrene was located in Tripoli, or present-day Libya. Simon had probably been saving all of his adult life to make the eight hundred-mile journey to Jerusalem to celebrate Passover. As he felt the cold metal of a Roman spear upon his shoulder and heard the command to take up the Cross of the Galilean who had already been beaten beyond recognition, Simon must have wondered, *Why me?*

Mark tells us Simon was the father of Rufus and Alexander (15:21). The fact that Paul sends greetings to Rufus and Alexander means they were well-known Christians (Romans 16:13).

Therefore, the implication is that Simon got saved—perhaps the very day he carried the Cross. This shouldn't be surprising, for those who carry the Cross of Christ will always fall in love with Him. Initially, we say, "Oh no. I don't want to go through that. I don't want to do that. It's too heavy. It's too burdensome. Why me?" But eventually we come to understand the incredible insight Jesus shared with us when He said it is the person who carries his cross daily who finds true life (Matthew 10:39).

Luke 23:27
And there followed him a great company of people, and of women, which also bewailed and lamented him.

In the gospel record, not one woman is ever seen as skeptical, cynical, or an enemy of Jesus. Yes, the disciples were all men. But one of them was Judas. Yes, men play the central parts—but included in their company were Pilate, Herod, Annas, Caiphas, the rulers of the synagogue, and the temple guard. Women in the Gospels have no such mixed multitude—for every one of them was either sympathetic to Jesus or a follower of His.

Luke 23:28–31
But Jesus turning unto them said, Daughters of Jerusalem, weep not for me, but weep for yourselves, and for your children. For, behold, the days are coming, in the which they shall say, Blessed are the barren, and the wombs that never bare, and the paps which never gave suck. Then shall they begin to say to the mountains, Fall on us; and to the hills, Cover us. For if they do these things in a green tree, what shall be done in the dry?

"Don't feel sorry for Me," Jesus is saying. "My agony is about to end—even this day. But you in Jerusalem will go through incredibly difficult times. If they've done this in the time of spring to a green tree—wait until the Romans show their real vehemence toward this city in the season to come."

Luke 23:32, 33
And there were also two other, malefactors, led with him to be put to death. And when they were come to the place, which is called Calvary, there they crucified him, and the malefactors, one on the right hand, and the other on the left.

Although this was deliberately designed to bring humiliation to Jesus, it was also designed by God as an illustration. Here we see two men equally close to Jesus, each having the same perspective of Jesus, and yet each making an entirely different decision about Him. One would be ushered into the kingdom. The other would be lost to eternal damnation.

Luke 23:34 (a)
Then said Jesus, Father, forgive them; for they know not what they do.

One's ignorance that what he's doing is wrong doesn't negate his responsibility to pay a price. Forgiveness, intercession, and provision are required even for a person who is sinning ignorantly or unaware that what he's doing, thinking, or saying is a sin. This is why the longer you walk with the Lord, the more you'll understand both the necessity and the depth of God's forgiveness

Luke 23:34 (b), 35 (a)
And they parted his raiment, and cast lots. And the people stood beholding. And the rulers also with them derided him, saying, He saved others . . .

The crowd who had once called Jesus Beelzebub, the same folks who had said He was a carpenter's son, actually uttered truth about Him when they said, "He saved others." Indeed He had!

Luke 23:35 (b)
. . . let him save himself, if he be Christ, the chosen of God.

The problem, of course, is if Jesus saved Himself, He couldn't save us.

Luke 23:36, 37
And the soldiers also mocked him, coming to him, and offering him vinegar, and saying, If thou be the king of the Jews, save thyself.

A king is known by his ability to assert himself. Jesus, however, is more than a King. He's a Shepherd dying on behalf of His sheep. "Stand up for your rights," the world says. "Intimidate. Dominate." They don't understand that in the kingdom of God, the way to authority is neither through intimidation nor domination, but through sacrifice.

Therefore, the husband who says, "I'm in charge here. Ephesians 5 says so. Submit to me, Wife," has missed the point completely.

Luke 23:38
And a superscription also was written over him in letters of Greek, and Latin, and Hebrew, THIS IS THE KING OF THE JEWS.

Greek was the language of intellect; Latin, the language of government; and Hebrew the language of religion. Philosophically, politically, and religiously, Jesus is indeed King of the Jews.

Luke 23:39–42
And one of the malefactors which were hanged railed on him, saying, If thou be Christ, save thyself and us. But the other answering rebuked him, saying, Dost not thou fear God, seeing thou art in the same condemnation? And we indeed justly; for we receive the due reward of our deeds: but this man hath done nothing amiss. And he said unto Jesus, Lord, remember me when thou comest into thy kingdom.

One thief said, "Get me down."
The other said, "Lord, take me up."

What is your prayer? Is it, "Take me down. Get me out of this mess"—or is it, "Lord, take me up into a higher understanding of You"?

For topical study of Luke 23:32–43 entitled "Faith Alone: Nailing it Down," turn to page 417.

Luke 23:43–45 (a)
And Jesus said unto him, Verily I say unto thee, To day shalt thou be with me in paradise. And it was about the sixth hour, and there was a darkness over all the earth until the ninth hour. And the sun was darkened . . .

Those who said, "We will not have the Light of the world rule over us," would now walk in darkness. So, too, the extent to which you and I reject His light is the extent to which our lives will be filled with a terrifying darkness.

Luke 23:45 (b)
. . . and the veil of the temple was rent in the midst.

The Holy of Holies was now accessible for the first time in centuries. In this, God declared, "Open House! No more ceremonial sacrifices or religious rituals. The Work is done. As believers, come into My presence any time you want."
Don't sew up the veil, gang. Don't get out your needle and thread and say, "You can't come into the presence of God until you sing six worship

songs." Or, "You can't come into the presence of God until you have devotions for three days." Or, "You can't come into the presence of God until you give up that sin." Don't fall prey to the formulas and principles that, stitch by stitch, sew up the veil. Instead, move into God's presence freely.

Luke 23:46
And when Jesus had cried with a loud voice, he said, Father, into thy hands I commend my spirit: and having said thus, he gave up the ghost.

After six days of creation, the Father looked over what He had made and said, "It is very good." Then He rested. So, too, after being on the Cross six hours, the Son said, "It is finished"— and He rested.

Luke 23:47
Now when the centurion saw what was done, he glorified God, saying, Certainly this was a righteous man.

Matthew tells us this centurion would go on to say, "Truly this was the Son of God" (Matthew 27:54). What convinced him? It was the way Jesus handled rejection and pain, suffering and death. Why do we as believers insist on never going through suffering, when it is actually the method the Lord uses to bring about the conversion of many a centurion?

In Exodus 14, God had His people camp between Pihahiroth and Migdol with their backs to the Red Sea and Pharaoh's army headed right towards them. Why? So He would be glorified among the Egyptians when they saw how He delivered His people (verse 4).

Oftentimes, we go to great lengths to avoid being boxed in, to dodge hard times, to escape physical pain. Yet those are the very things that convince the Egyptians, the centurions, and our neighbors of the faithfulness of God as He sees us through.
Yes, we should pray. Yes, we should make our requests and petitions known to our Father. Yes, we should persevere in prayer. But we must also let God be God. We must also allow Him the freedom to do what He wants in our lives no matter how painful it might seem. It was for the joy set before Him that Jesus, our Model, our Lord *endured* the Cross (Hebrews 12:2).

Luke 23:48
And all the people that came together to that sight, beholding the things which were done, smote their breasts, and returned.

The crowd knew they had done wrong, that a travesty of justice had occurred.

Luke 23:49–51 (a)
And all his acquaintance, and the women that followed him from Galilee, stood afar off, beholding these things. And, behold, there was a man named Joseph, a counseller; and he was a good man, and a just: (The same had not consented to the counsel and deed of them;) . . .

Although a member of the Sanhedrin, Joseph had not consented to the crucifixion of Christ.

Luke 23:51 (b)–53 (a)
. . . he was of Arimathaea, a city of the Jews: who also himself waited for the kingdom of God. This man went unto Pilate, and begged the body of Jesus. And he took it down, and wrapped it in linen . . .

Jesus' body was wrapped in linen—the very material the high priests would wear during Yom Kippur, the Day of Atonement.

Luke 23:53 (b), 54
. . . and laid it in a sepulchre that was hewn in stone, wherein never man before was laid. And that day was the preparation, and the sabbath drew on.

History tells us that in A.D. 61, Philip sent Joseph of Arimathea to England. Tradition goes on to say that he took with him the chalice used by the Lord at the Last Supper. Be that as it may, it is highly possible that this one who gave up his position on the Sanhedrin and his standing in the community in order to bury Jesus did indeed take the gospel message to England.

Luke 23:55, 56
And the women also, which came with him from Galilee, followed after, and beheld the sepulchre, and how his body was laid. And they returned, and prepared spices and ointments; and rested the sabbath day according to the commandment.

It's a good thing these women rested on the Sabbath, for they're about to do quite a bit of running on the joyous day to follow.

FAITH ALONE: NAILING IT DOWN
A Topical Study of
Luke 23:32–43

. . . and he was numbered with the transgressors; and he bare the sin of many, and made intercession for the transgressors.　　　　　Isaiah 53:12 (b)

Seven hundred years before Jesus was crucified between two thieves, Isaiah prophesied that He would be numbered among the transgressors and that He would die in the midst of sinners. This was the plan of the Father. Why? Consider the following . . .

To Show the Depth of His Compassion

When Jesus came to dwell among men, there was no room for Him in the inn. So He was born in a stable, placed in a manger, surrounded by animals. Not only was He to be born among animals, but He was to die among criminals. In so doing, He demonstrates the depth of His love for us.

The Fact That God Is Sovereign

Two men guilty of the same crime, cursing the same Lord, were dying the same death. They were equally close to the Lord in proximity, both close enough to talk to Him even amidst the shouts and jeers of the crowd. They were equal in every way except one: One would be lost, the other saved. Herein is a great mystery. How did the man on the right recognize who Jesus was? How did He catch what the apostles missed? How did He see what His disciples didn't? How did he understand that the Lord's kingdom was eternal? How did He get saved? The only answer is the sovereignty of the Father.

To illustrate this principle, Paul goes back through the tunnel of time and points to Jacob and Esau. Before they were even born, God declared that the elder would serve the younger because "Jacob have I loved and Esau have I hated" (Romans 9:13). People have real difficulty with this, wondering how God could say He hated Esau before Esau was even born. I have a problem with it too—not with the fact that God hated Esau, but that He loved Jacob, that He could save anyone, that He would choose *me*. The longer I walk with the Lord, the more I realize how far I am from His standard of holiness. Therefore, the mystery to me is not that God hated Esau, but that He loved Jacob. The mystery to me is not that some are not chosen, but that I was.

Was God right in His choice? Read the story of Jacob and Esau, and you see that Esau was a man who cared nothing about spiritual life. Jacob, on the other hand, although he had all kinds of problems, desired to be blessed by the Lord to the point that he wrestled all night with the angel of the Lord in order to obtain His blessing. So when I read Genesis, I realize God made the right choice—this shouldn't surprise me. Righteous and true are His judgments (Revelation 16:7). He always makes the right choice.

"I protest," you might say. "Because I'm not elected does that mean I have no hope, no possibility of getting into the kingdom?"

How do you know you're not elected?

"Because I'm not saved."

Well, get saved today, and you'll find you *are* one of the elect! After all, who put you in this sanctuary today? It is God who works all things to accomplish His purpose for you in time, in space, in history—even as He put that common criminal right next to Jesus on the mount of Calvary.

A Final Witness to the Innocence of His Son

As people were cursing and spitting, as Jesus was in physical and spiritual torment beyond description, the thief to His right said, "He has done no wrong."

The one who betrayed Him said the same thing. Tossing the thirty pieces of silver on the floor of the temple, Judas said, "I've lived with Him. I've walked beside Him. For three years, I've observed Him—and I have betrayed innocent blood."

Even Pontius Pilate, who six times went out to the crowd and back in to talk to Jesus, concluded unequivocally, "I find no fault in Him." The witness of Judas, the witness of Pilate, and the witness of the criminal combine as a final witness to the world of the innocence of the Son.

To Cushion the Blow

As Jesus was dying, as Satan was snarling, as the demons were cheering, as the crowd was jeering, even as the Father was turning His back on the Son, there, on His right hand, was the first who would follow, the first one who would say, "Lord, remember me." I believe this was a sneak preview of coming attractions, for Jesus could look at that man in his desperation, that man who was previously headed for eternal damnation, and say, "Today you will be with Me in paradise." Suddenly, no doubt, how His heart must have leapt, even though His body was in pain as He saw the very beginning of what would be coming, the first of multiplied millions who would follow.

Life is full of sneak previews of coming attractions even in the midst of the Cross. We see some glorious healings. We see some marvelous victories. Some days are so special, so beautiful, in which things become so clear. All of those are simply sneak previews of what will happen when we move into the kingdom. Each is a "down payment" of what's ahead (2 Corinthians 5:5).

To Nail Down Truth

While all of the above sheds light on the reason Jesus hung between two thieves, I believe the most practical reason is to nail down a truth with absolute certainty and finality. That is, it is faith alone that saves. The man who heard the words, "Today you will be with Me in paradise," simply looked on the Lord and talked to the Lord. That was it. He did nothing more. He could do nothing more. He was pinned to a cross.

Therefore, when anyone says to you,

"Believe in Jesus and get baptized in this manner. . . ." or,
"Believe in Jesus and sell 'Watchtower' . . ." or,
"Believe in Jesus and wear holy underwear . . ."

walk away, change the channel, write them off. "Believe in the Lord Jesus Christ," Paul declared, "and thou shalt be saved." Period (Acts 16:31).

The gospel is so simple. I simply come pinned in helplessness like the thief on the cross and say, "Lord, remember me. Have mercy upon me." That's why Paul refers to the "offence of the Cross" (Galatians 5:11). It's so simple it offends people because it strips them of their pride and power. The Cross affords no possibility of pride in earning salvation, and no potential for power in manipulating one's way into the kingdom.

I'm so thankful for this story—for it nails down with finality the fact that the gospel is profoundly simple and simply profound. This man couldn't get baptized, couldn't sell magazines, couldn't meet in a deep study group. All He could do was call out to the Lord.

And that was all it took.

❧

24

Luke 24:1, 2
Now upon the first day of the week, very early in the morning, they came unto the sepulchre, bringing the spices which they had prepared, and certain others with them. And they found the stone rolled away from the sepulchre.

The last ones at the Cross are now the first ones at the tomb. When Joseph of Arimathea placed the body of Jesus in his tomb, there would not have been time for a complete embalming because Passover would begin at sunset. Consequently, these women were now coming to complete the task. All of the gospel writers tell us that they came early—always a good time to come to the Lord.

"They that seek Me early shall find Me," the Lord declares (Proverbs 8:17). Truly, those who seek the Lord early—early in life, early in a situation, early every day—will uniquely find Him. These precious women would prove to be no exception.

After a grandfather lost his treasured watch during a family gathering, he called his grandchildren together and told them he'd pay twenty-five dollars to the one who found it. This sent the kids on a mad scramble—running and screaming and turning over every rock. But the youngest grandson just sat and watched his brothers, sisters, and cousins all come back empty-handed. The next morning at breakfast he handed his grandfather the watch.

"How did you find it?" asked the puzzled old man.

"I just got up real early and listened for the ticking," replied his clever grandson.

There's some timely advice in that little story. Oftentimes, there's so much noise and commotion going on all around us that it's hard to hear the Lord in the middle of the day. The time to hear Him is early in the morning—just as these women did.

Luke 24:3, 4
And they entered in, and found not the body of the Lord Jesus. And it came to pass, as they were much perplexed thereabout, be-

hold, two men stood by them in shining garments:

Because the other Gospel writers tell us these men were angels, Luke's account implies that angels actually appear to men as men. These women saw two men. Yes, they were shining—but they appeared as men nonetheless. Therefore, when we get to heaven, I think we will be amazed by how much contact we had with angelic beings without even realizing it. "Be not forgetful to entertain strangers," the writer of Hebrews reminds us, "for thereby some have entertained angels unawares" (Hebrews 13:2).

Luke 24:5
And as they were afraid, and bowed down their faces to the earth, they said unto them, Why seek ye the living among the dead?

"Why do you seek the living among the dead?" People still seek Jesus among the dead. "He was a great Example," they say, "a powerful Role Model. Study His life and see how He handled this situation, or what He had to say about that matter." They study Him philosophically. They study Him theologically. But they treat Him as though He's dead. We as believers can fall into that error as well.

As we gather together to worship Him, Jesus is here. He truly is. We're not talking about the thoughts of Jesus or the memory of Jesus. "Whenever two or three are gathered in My Name, I will be in the midst of them," He said (Matthew 18:20). When we begin to grasp this, the way we worship, study, and pray is affected.

Luke 24:6–8
He is not here, but is risen: remember how he spake unto you when he was yet in Galilee, saying, The Son of man must be delivered into the hands of sinful men, and be crucified, and the third day rise again. And they remembered his words,

The fact that the angels said, "Don't you remember how Jesus told you He would be crucified and rise again the third day?" indicates that the angels were listening when Jesus said these words to His disciples. Peter tells us that the angels long to look into the things taught and spoken of concerning Jesus Christ (1 Peter 1:12). Why? Because they are not saved like we are. They're not sinners, rescued by the blood of the Lamb. Therefore, the way they understand that their King and Master is a God of incredible mercy and incalculable love is by watching you and me. "Wow, how could our God love *her?* How could our God be so patient with a guy like *that?*" they say. And it makes them worship Him all the more.

Luke 24:9, 10 (a)
And returned from the sepulchre, and told all these things unto the eleven, and to all the rest. It was Mary Magdalene . . .

I think Augustine was right when he called Mary Magdalene "the apostles' apostle." She, indeed, was the first one to share the gospel with the disciples.

Luke 24:10 (b), 11
. . . and Joanna, and Mary the mother of James, and other women that were with them, which told these things unto the apostles. And their words seemed to them as idle tales, and they believed them not.

Although these women were speaking the absolute truth, because it seemed impossible to believe, the disciples dismissed their report as idle tales—or, literally, "babbling that comes from a fevered and insane mind." As a result, they spent longer in the darkness of despair than was necessary. Wise is the man who takes serious the "babblings" of the woman in his life—for therein often lies great truth that will shine light in his darkness.

Luke 24:12 (a)
Then arose Peter, and ran unto the sepulcher . . .

After initially thinking the women had lost their minds, John 20:3 tells us Peter and John ran to the tomb to check out their story. Peter had sinned incredibly against Christ—yet John keeps his arm around Peter and stays close to him. That's the kind of biblical Christianity we need today—people who will say even to the one who has erred greatly, "I'm still with you. I'm still for you. I'm not going to walk away from you or turn my back on you." Oh, how the church needs more Johns.

Luke 24:12 (b)
. . . and stooping down, he beheld the linen clothes laid by themselves, and departed, wondering in himself at that which was come to pass.

Notice the word "clothes" is plural. The implication from the Greek text is that there was more than just one piece of cloth used to encase the body of Christ. This makes me suspect the authenticity of the Shroud of Turin. I doubt its authenticity not simply on the basis of this text, but also due to the way the Lord works.

Although the brass serpent Moses had been instructed to make was to be an illustration of Jesus on the Cross, the people had begun to worship the serpent itself. So when revival came to Israel during the reign of Hezekiah, it is no wonder he broke the brass serpent into pieces, calling it "Nehushtan," or "thing of brass" (2 Kings 18:4).

Because man has a craving for something tangible and touchable, his tendency is to venerate and idolize relics. But because the Father's purpose is to move us into the realm of the spiritual and eternal, He wants us to walk by faith not by sight.

Luke 24:13–15
And, behold, two of them went that same day to a village called Emmaus, which was from Jerusalem about threescore furlongs. And they talked together of all these things which had happened. And it came to pass, that, while they communed together and reasoned, Jesus himself drew near, and went with them.

I love this! As these two travelers are talking about Jesus, guess who shows up right in their midst. Don't you love talking with brothers or sisters about the Lord? Something more than just an intellectual exchange transpires. These two didn't have answers or insights. They were just talking about Jesus—and He joined them.

Luke 24:16–18
But their eyes were holden that they should not know him. And he said unto them, What manner of communications are these that ye have one to another, as ye walk, and are sad? And the one of them, whose name was Cleopas, answering said unto him, Art thou only a stranger in Jerusalem, and hast not known the things which are come to pass there in these days?

"Are You from out of town?" they asked. "Don't You know what's been going on the last few days?" I love how Jesus answered. . . .

Luke 24:19 (a)
And he said unto them, What things?

Did Jesus not know? Of course He knew. Sometimes we think, *The Lord already knows what's going on. Why pray?* But every parent knows the answer. When your child has something to share with you, even though you already know the story or the facts, you love to hear it from him. So, too, Jesus would say to you today, "Talk to Me—about that trouble at work, about that feeling in your heart. I already know all about it, but I want to hear it from you."

In talking over the events that had transpired in Jerusalem, the two on the road to Emmaus will find themselves convicted by their own words. As they start talking to the Lord, they will inadvertently give all sorts of reasons for why they shouldn't have been sad, shouldn't have been weak in faith. This is the beauty of prayer. Read the Psalms, and you'll find the psalmist often pouring out complaints to the Lord. But by the time he works through it, about ten verses later—he ends by giving praise to the Lord. When I talk things over with the Lord and recount the situation to Him, suddenly I begin to see I'm wrong. Here I thought I had this case or this reason to be upset; yet as I begin to recount the tale to the Lord, my own words convict me.

Luke 24:19 (b)–26
And they said unto him, Concerning Jesus of Nazareth, which was a prophet mighty in deed and word before God and all the people: And how the chief priests and our rulers delivered him to be condemned to death, and have crucified him. But we trusted that it had been he which should have redeemed Israel: and beside all this, to day is the third day since these things were done. Yea, and certain women also of our company made us astonished, which were early at the sepulchre; and when they found not his body, they came, saying, that they had also seen a vision of angels, which said that he was alive. And certain of them which were with us went to the sepulchre, and found it even so as the women had said: but him they saw not. Then he said unto them, O fools, and slow of heart to believe all that the prophets have spoken: Ought not Christ to have suffered these things, and to enter into his glory?

"Don't you see it, guys? The apostles went to the tomb and it was empty. The women had a message from the angels. All of these things are happening. You should be excited and full of expectation. Instead, you're sad, depressed, and

slow of heart. The word from the angel, the witness of the apostle, the emptiness of the tomb should stimulate in you hope and interest. Instead, you're just trudging to Emmaus, sharing your sadness." No wonder Jesus lovingly but pointedly called them fools.

Luke 24:27
And beginning at Moses and all the prophets, he expounded unto them in all the scriptures the things concerning himself.

Whether you're a Sunday-school teacher, a youth worker, or a Bible study leader, your job is to look for Jesus in every part of the Word. Focus on *Him,* look for *Him,* speak of *Him* every time you teach.

Do you think Jesus was carrying scrolls of Moses, the prophets, and the Psalms under His arm? I don't. Thoroughly immersed in the Word, I suggest He was quoting Scripture from memory and from His heart. Sometimes you might think, *I don't need to study the Word because I've already studied it. I already know it.* Do you? Can you walk along the road and discuss Genesis 37—50, Ezekiel 44, Luke 21—24, Romans 5—8? Until you're at that place, you need to be where the Bible is taught consistently.

Luke 24:28
And they drew nigh unto the village, whither they went: and he made as though he would have gone further.

Always the perfect Gentleman, Jesus does not impose Himself, but would have kept going. Jesus will never burst in to your situation. He'll walk with you, but won't force Himself on you. He'll stay with you as long as you want Him to, He'll go with you as far as you want Him to— but He won't break in and make you listen to Him, learn of Him, or be with Him.

Luke 24:29–32
But they constrained him, saying, Abide with us: for it is toward evening, and the day is far spent. And he went in to tarry with them. And it came to pass, as he sat at meat with them, he took bread, and blessed it, and brake, and gave to them. And their eyes were opened, and they knew him; and he vanished out of their sight. And they said one to another, Did not our heart burn within us, while he talked with us by the way, and while he opened to us the scriptures?

The travelers were won by the Word. No longer slow of heart, they are on fire in their hearts simply through hearing the Scripture. I cannot emphasize enough the importance of hearing and studying and reading the Scriptures. Not only were the travelers won, but they were one. "Did not our *heart* burn within us?" they exclaimed. So, too, we have one heart because we're in the Word together, listening to the Lord together. Being with the Lord together, we are one.

Luke 24:33, 34
And they rose up the same hour, and returned to Jerusalem, and found the eleven gathered together, and them that were with them, Saying, The Lord is risen indeed, and hath appeared to Simon.

In 1 Corinthians 15:5, Paul mentions the fact that before the Lord appeared to the others, He appeared first to Peter. Where, when, and how we don't know. It was a personal meeting, a private meeting in which Jesus had a special session with Peter to affirm His love. If you feel like you've blown it completely, the Lord will seek you out first and foremost and meet you uniquely. That's not a sentimental thought. That's a fact based upon the ministry of the Resurrected Lord.

Luke 24:35–40
And they told what things were done in the way, and how he was known of them in breaking of bread. And as they thus spake, Jesus himself stood in the midst of them, and saith unto them, Peace be unto you. But they were terrified and affrighted, and supposed that they had seen a spirit. And he said unto them, Why are ye troubled? and why do thoughts arise in your hearts? Behold my hands and my feet, that it is I myself: handle me, and see; for a spirit hath not flesh and bones, as ye see me have. And when he had thus spoken, he shewed them his hands and his feet.

The only thing man-made in heaven are the nail prints in the hands and feet of Jesus Christ. Why do they remain? I suggest two reasons. . . .
First, to identify Himself. It was the nail prints that showed an unbelieving Thomas not only the reality of His Resurrection, but the depth of His love.
Second, to identify with us. Life is painful. Hurts, pains, and problems abound. So often, we find ourselves tempted to think we can't stand it any longer or handle it anymore. But then we hear Jesus say, "When you think you can't handle it, look at My hands and be reminded that I know the pain you're feeling, the pressure you're facing. When you think you can't stand anymore, look at My feet and be reminded that I understand."

This is the point the writer of Hebrews makes when he writes, "For in that he himself hath suffered being tempted, he is able to succour them that are tempted" (Hebrews 2:18).

If Jesus loves me enough to die in my place and bear nail prints for eternity, why am I going through what I'm going through right now? you might be wondering. *If I'm really in His hand, if I'm really on His heart, why is my business collapsing or my body decaying? Why aren't things working out the way I thought they would at this point in my life? If he really loves me, why am I being scarred?*

Again, I suggest two reasons. . . .
First, that we might identify with Him. Paul said, "That I may know Him and the power of His resurrection . . ." and Christians say, "Amen! I want to know You, Lord, and the power of Your resurrection." But then Paul went on to add, ". . . and the fellowship of suffering" (see Philippians 3:10) A unique intimacy is the result of suffering with someone. The people with whom you are closest are not those with whom you laugh, but those with whom you cry. Therefore, the Father says, "If you want to really know Me, it requires the fellowship of suffering."
Second, we suffer not only that we might identify with Him, but in order to identify with others. The teaching of present-day American Christianity that says that God wants His children to be healthy and wealthy, that those who walk in faith should never have problems flies in the face of the early church and the teachings of the apostles. It flies in the face of the martyrs of every continent of every age who knew nothing of such a so-called gospel.

Shipwrecked on the island of Malta, Paul gathered sticks to build a fire to warm the drenched soldiers and prisoners. When a poisonous snake fastened itself to Paul's hand, the villagers thought Paul must have been a murderer to deserve such a fate. So they watched him and waited for him to swell up and die. But Scripture records that, although he was smitten by the same serpent that had killed others on the island, Paul shook it off. And then they thought he was a god (Acts 28).

When will people listen to what you have to say about Christ Jesus? When, although you've been smitten by the same serpents that smite them, you shake it off and go on. When your business goes bankrupt, when your health fails, when problems mount, unbelievers expect you to swell up or fall down, to no longer love God or walk with the Lord. But when, like Paul, you shake off the snake and keep praising God, the islanders take notice.

The cynics and skeptics who live on your street and work in your office are not waiting to see how rich you can get. What they are waiting to see is what you do when the serpent strikes, when pain comes, when things get tough. Will you swell up and fall down, or will you keep on?

Such are the results of suffering.

Luke 24:41
And while they yet believed not for joy, and wondered, he said unto them, Have ye here any meat?

"I want to share a meal with you," Jesus said. And He still does. "I stand at the door of your heart and knock," He says. "If any man open the door, I'll come in and enjoy a meal with him. I'll have fellowship with him" (Revelation 3:20).

Luke 24:42–45
And they gave him a piece of a broiled fish, and of an honeycomb. And he took it, and did eat before them. And he said unto them, These are the words which I spake unto you, while I was yet with you, that all things must be fulfilled, which were written in the law of Moses, and in the prophets, and in the psalms, concerning me. Then opened he their understanding, that they might understand the scriptures.

Verse 45 is clearly marked in my Bible. Oh, Lord, open my understanding, that I might indeed understand the Word.

Luke 24:46–48
And said unto them, Thus it is written, and thus it behoved Christ to suffer, and to rise from the dead the third day: And that repentance and remission of sins should be preached in his name among all nations, beginning at Jerusalem. And ye are witnesses of these things.

Notice Jesus doesn't call His disciples defense attorneys or judges, lawyers or juries. He calls them witnesses. We often think we have to argue with people, debate against people, present persuasive cases to people. But the Lord doesn't call us to any of that. He simply says, "Share with people what you've seen. Share with people what you've found. Share with people what I have done in and for you."

Witnessing is a total joy when you simply share with people that which blesses you. If you

have an answer to prayer or an insight into the Word, share it with those around you as if they're already saved. That way there will be a lot less arguing and a lot more sharing. Share with those around you whatever you're learning, whatever you're experiencing. Be faithful in being a witness, and leave the rest to the Lord.

Luke 24:49
And, behold, I send the promise of my Father upon you: but tarry ye in the city of Jerusalem, until ye be endued with power from on high.

What is the promise of the Father? It is the Person and power of the Holy Ghost.

But the Comforter, which is the Holy Ghost, whom the Father will send in my name, he shall teach you all things, and bring all things to your remembrance, whatsoever I have said unto you.   John 14:26

Jesus came to implement something brand new—the New Covenant—based upon a promise given centuries previously. . . .

Behold, the days come, saith the LORD, that I will make a new covenant with the house of Israel, and with the house of Judah: Not according to the covenant that I made with their fathers in the day that I took them by the hand to bring them out of the land of Egypt; which my covenant they brake, although I was an husband unto them, saith the LORD: But this shall be the covenant that I will make with the house of Israel; After those days, saith the LORD, I will put my law in their inward parts, and write it in their hearts; and will be their God, and they shall be my people.
                    Jeremiah 31:33

A new heart also will I give you, and a new spirit will I put within you: and I will take away the stony heart out of your flesh, and I will give you an heart of flesh. And I will put my spirit within you, and cause you to walk in my statutes, and ye shall keep my judgments, and do them.   Ezekiel 36:26, 27

In Hebrews 8, we see the New Covenant further articulated. I find the comparison and contrast between Moses, the mediator of the Old Covenant, and our Resurrected Lord, mediator of the New Covenant, intriguing. . . .

Moses went to the top of Mount Sinai to get the law.
Jesus went to the top of the Mount of Olives in order to send us the Spirit.

Mount Sinai was in the wilderness.
The Mount of Olives was in the center of the Promised Land.

On Mount Sinai, Moses ate nothing for forty days.
With His disciples for forty days, one of the first things Jesus said was, "Have ye anything to eat?"

Moses was isolated from the people of God.
Jesus was in the midst of the people of God.

Moses lifted up his hands to smash the law and blast the people.
Jesus lifted His hands because He fulfilled the law and could therefore bless the people.

The law was written on tables of stone.
The New Covenant is written on hearts of flesh.

The law says, "Do."
The New Covenant says, "Done!"

Life is confusing. Therefore, oftentimes the tendency for people is to want a prescribed program of rules and regulations: Ten Steps to Better Parenting, Fifteen Keys to Prayer, Seven Ways to Witness. But we err greatly whenever we look for programs, plans, and pointers instead of to the Person of the Holy Ghost in our lives to guide us moment by moment.

The most radical group of believers in the history of the world was the group of Christians who, having received the promise of the Father, turned the world upside down without a single book of the New Testament (Acts 17:6). They didn't have Romans, Hebrews, or the Epistles of John. They didn't have the Gospels, Galatians, or the Book of Revelation. What they did have, and the reason they were so powerful, is an understanding that Jesus truly was writing His will on the tables of their hearts, whispering, "Go here," "Do that," "Stay away from this," "Avoid that."

Decades later, the Lord saw fit to inspire writers to record New Testament teaching—not to become the law, but rather so that when believers read Paul's writings or Peter's exhortations, they could say, "Right on. That's what we've been doing for years. John tells us to love each other. Of course! That's what the Lord's been showing us all along. Brother Paul tells us to flee youthful lusts. That's exactly what the Lord has been telling us."

Two thousand years later, what do we do? We so often have the tendency to come to church and say, "Give us some rules, programs, regulations, laws—and then we'll go our way." That's why so much of present-day Christianity is so dead. We've made the New Testament the New Law—rules, regulations, and external expectations—instead of expecting the Lord to guide us hour by hour, step by step.

So many Christians wonder why their church is so dead or why their own walk is so dry. The reason is that, although they study the Bible, although they believe the Bible, although they're submitted to the Bible—they've lost the essential message in the Bible, which is that the Old Covenant, the old law is over. It was only the schoolmaster to bring us to Christ who, day by day writes His will upon our hearts. . . .

You're relaxing at home when suddenly you find yourself inspired to call your sister. As you do, you discover she needed the encouragement you alone could give her.

You're at the office, and suddenly the Spirit prompts you to have lunch with your co-worker in the next office. As you do, you find it was ordained of God.

Your Christian walk only becomes vibrant and real to the degree that you're living it hour by hour, moment by moment according to the New Covenant working within you.

The Lord is alive, gang. Moment by moment, not only will He put on your heart the things He wants you to do and say and be, but He'll give you the power to carry them out perfectly (Philippians 2:13). When He says, "Write the letter," write the letter. When He says, "Take a break and worship Me for five minutes," do it. When He says to go into your son's room, lay your hands on him while he sleeps, and bind the work of the Enemy on his life," do just that. When He says, "Bring your wife red roses," don't bring her marigolds. The key to parenting, to the Christian walk, to marriage, and to life is to realize that Jesus is alive in you and will direct you moment by moment. Don't let church become ritual. Don't let Christianity become a series of responsibilities. Don't make the New Testament the Old Covenant. Respond to the Spirit's leading moment by moment and your walk will be transformed.

Luke 24:50–52 (a)
And he led them out as far as to Bethany, and he lifted up his hands, and blessed them. And it came to pass, while he blessed them, he was parted from them, and carried up into heaven. And they worshipped him . . .

The last act of Jesus after His resurrection was to bless. The first act of the believers after

His ascension was to worship. People often think worship is the means of getting blessed. True worship, however, is simply responding to what God has *already* done for us.

Luke 24:52 (b), 53
. . . and returned to Jerusalem with great joy: And were continually in the temple, praising and blessing God. Amen.

The Gospel of Luke began in the temple with Zacharias unable to say a word because he didn't believe what he was told. It ends in the temple with people believing, rejoicing, singing, and worshiping.

We are the temple. Part of our numbers are like Zacharias—not saying a word because they don't believe that the Lord really is with them right now and desires to bless them just as they are. So they leave in silence.

Others, however, do believe. Because of His Word, they believe that the Lord loves them and lives inside of them. They believe the Lord has forgiven them and will walk beside them. As a result, they go their way rejoicing, worshiping, and praising Him. In every session, the choice is ours whether to slink out silently or to leave rejoicing; whether to be slow of heart, or to listen to the One traveling alongside us. May God give us the grace tonight to believe that Jesus is alive, is with us, and is truly *for* us.

THE NARROW WAY
A Brief Look at
The Synoptic Gospels

"**B**road is the way that leads to destruction," Jesus declared. "Narrow is the way that leads to life" (Matthew 7:13, 14). In fact, so narrow is the way that it is only as wide as one Person—the Person of Jesus Christ. Because Jesus is the only One who has done the things He taught us to do, the Christian walk is not about trying to be Jesus. It's about being impressed with Jesus. It's about falling in love *with* Him, being amazed *by* Him, and drawing near *to* Him.

With this in mind, reconsider with me some of the passages we have seen in Luke's Gospel . . .

The Roman Centurion

Directly following the account of Jesus' Sermon on the Mount in Luke 6, we come to the story of the Roman centurion who sent word to Jesus that his servant was sick. When Jesus neared his house, the centurion again sent word, this time that he was not worthy that Jesus should come to his house, but that simply a word from Him would heal the servant (Luke 7:7).

Here, Jesus had just finished giving a sermon in which He had said in effect, "If you think you can get to heaven simply by not killing your brother or committing adultery, I have news for you. You can't even be angry with your brother or look lustfully at another woman. You have to be *more* righteous than those among you who follow the most detailed letter of the law. In short, you must be perfect."

On the heels of this sermon, Jesus hears from a centurion who doesn't say, "I'm okay," or, "I'll try harder," or, "I'll do better," but simply says, "I'm not worthy."

Bingo. No wonder Jesus commended him (Luke 7:9).

There are two ways to heaven: either by keeping the law perfectly or by realizing we need a Savior desperately. And because it is impossible for us to do the former, our only hope is the latter. Therefore, the purpose of the law from before eternity began was to be a schoolmaster, a tutor to show us that it's impossible to think we can enter the presence of God through the law, through our own works, or through our own energy (Galatians 3:24).

A lifeguard's abilities are never seen until someone is drowning. So, too, we never see the magnitude of Jesus' work on our behalf until, like the centurion, we realize we are sinking in our own sin and selfishness. To showcase the glory of His Son, God sent Him to a drowning world to rescue all of humanity, leaving mankind no other option but to say, "*Thou* art worthy, O Lord." His greatness and beauty, His kindness and glory would never be known apart from our collective sinking into the sea of our own iniquity.

You see, it's not as though God said, "Here's Plan A: The law. That didn't work? Okay, let's go with Plan B: the Cross." No, the law was given from the outset to bring people into an awareness of their sinking condition in order that the Son's glory, greatness, and mercy could be seen very clearly by all of humanity.

The Good Samaritan

"What must I do to inherit eternal life?" the lawyer asked Jesus.

"How do you read the law?" Jesus asked in response.

"You shall love the Lord and love your neighbor," the lawyer answered.

"This do and you shall live," Jesus said.

"But just who is my neighbor," the lawyer asked, looking for a loophole.

In answering with the parable of the Good Samaritan, Jesus essentially said, "Your neighbor is anyone at any time in any situation who is in need for any reason."

Who of us is able to say, "I help every person I ever see in need"—be it the person whose car is broken down by the side of the road or the homeless man begging for money in front of the grocery store? Only Jesus has, does, or ever will do this.

The Prodigal Son

When the Pharisees and scribes murmured, saying, "This man receives sinners and eats with them," Jesus gave three parables about lost things. The last parable concerned a lost son and his seemingly righteous older brother. In this parable, when the lost son returned, the older brother was trying to prove his worth by working in the field, even though all that the father had was already his (Luke 15:31).

We often think that the Lord is looking for some good men who will hold the course, steady their hand on the plow, and labor in the field of ministry.

But maybe He's not. Maybe there are times He wants us to come to the party with those who were lost—yet we can't because we're busy trying to prove how spiritual we are. And, like the older brother, we miss out. Even as he was claiming he never disobeyed his father, the older brother was indeed in a place of disobedience because he was working instead of rejoicing.

The Rich Young Ruler

"Good master, what must I do to inherit eternal life?" asked the rich, young ruler.

"Sell all you have, give the money to the poor, and follow Me," Jesus answered (Luke 18:22). But of the rich young ruler, this was, evidently, too much to ask.

The story following that of the rich young ruler is that of Zacchaeus, whom Jesus declared to be saved after he simply said he would give away half of all he owned (Luke 19:8, 9). Why did Zacchaeus get saved after giving only half of all he owned, when the rich, young ruler was told to give *all* he owned? Because Zacchaeus admitted he had cheated people. The rich young ruler claimed to be righteous. Zacchaeus, on the other hand, recognized his need for Jesus.

All of Jesus' stories and parables are for the purpose of bringing people into an awareness that, without Him, we fail completely. We're either prodigals in the pigpen living in sin, or we're older brothers in the field trying to be righteous. Either way, we're guilty. Either way, we're lost.

Jesus took everything the law said and made it tougher. Everything He does in Matthew, Mark, and Luke—until the time of the Cross—says, "You are in a heap of trouble. You're in hot water, and it's going to get hotter."

It's shocking for those who think they are religious to realize that they're not okay. It took three Gospels—Matthew, Mark, and Luke—to say this. Thus, these Synoptic Gospels are, to a certain degree, more closely related to the Old Testament than to the New Covenant.

I suggest this is the reason that, in the thirteen letters he penned, Paul quotes Jesus only once (1 Corinthians 11:23–25). One would think that Paul would quote Jesus constantly. After all, we do. But Paul didn't. He talked about the work of Jesus continually, but not the words of Jesus directly because, I believe, the message of Jesus was intended for the Jew, for the religious person who thinks he's righteous. But Paul was called to the Gentiles.

"Hear O Israel: The Lord our God is one Lord: And thou shalt love the Lord thy God with all thine heart, and with all thy soul, and with all thy might" (Deuteronomy 6:4, 5). How often is this—the great Shema, the most foundational, fundamental tenet of Judaism quoted in the epistles? Not once. We preach sermons on it, but the apostle Paul never mentions it. Neither does James. Neither does Peter. Why? Because it is impossible. Who of us could say, "I love the Lord with *all* my heart, soul, and strength"? There is only *One* who always did the things which pleased His Father (John 8:29). It's all about Jesus.

Jesus would take three years to explain to the people of Israel, to the Jew, to the religious mind-set, the hopelessness of their condition. This is the purpose of the synoptic Gospels. The law had to be established by no less than three witnesses (Deuteronomy 19:15), so Matthew, Mark, and Luke were the three witnesses the Holy Spirit chose to record not only the beauty of the Savior but the helplessness of the sinner.

Therefore, as you journey through the synoptic Gospels, so named because they present similar views of the life and teachings of Jesus, I encourage you to look at them not as a presentation of rules for us to live by, but as the portrait of a Redeemer who came to rescue.

The Gospel of John and the Book of Revelation were the last of the canon to be written. Eusebius tells us that the apostle John had the synoptic Gospels—Matthew, Mark, and Luke—before him and was able to draw from them as he defined, commented upon, and explained them in his Gospel.

John, therefore, wrote not only to the Jew, but also to the Roman centurion, to the prodigal son, to Zacchaeus. He wrote to any and all who believe in the One who made room for us on the narrow way that leads to life by stretching out His arms as wide as they would reach and allowing them to be nailed to a Cross (John 20:31).

NOTES

[1]Philip Yancey. *Disappointment With God.* Zondervan, Grand Rapids, Michigan, 1988, p. 178.

JOHN

Background to John

In 2 Corinthians 3, the apostle Paul gives us a most important understanding when he writes: "But we all, with open face beholding as in a glass the glory of the Lord, are changed into the same image from glory to glory, even as by the Spirit of the Lord" (3:18). In other words, Paul contends we become like Jesus when we spend time looking at Jesus. Similarly, the words of the apostle John from his first epistle, "when he shall appear, we shall be like him; for we shall see him as he is" (3:2), have application not only eternally but presently—for when we truly see the Lord, we cannot help but become like Him.

As David hung out in the hills, fleeing the wrath of Saul, six hundred men gathered around him—men who were in debt, distressed, discontent (1 Samuel 22:2). And as this ragtag group of renegades spent time with David, they became more and more like him—so much so that, as the years passed, these six hundred rebels were transformed into one of the finest fighting units of history. So, too, we are a ragtag group of renegades who are likewise in debt, distressed, and discontent. But as we hang out with our greater-than-David—the Son of David, Jesus Christ—we will begin to find ourselves experiencing and exhibiting *His* characteristics, *His* flavor, *His* fragrance. We will find ourselves changed from glory to even greater glory as we behold *Him*. That's why the Gospels are so important. They let us see Jesus. And as we look upon Him, we become more and more like Him. I believe there are four in number because it's almost as if the Father is saying,

"When you open your New Testament, the first thing you'll see is the story of My Son. But if you sleep through Matthew, there's Mark. And if you skip Mark, there's Luke. And if you overlook Luke, you'll see Him in John. I don't want you to miss My Son. I want you to behold Him, for when you see Him, you'll be like Him."

The writer of the Gospel before us went through an incredible transformation himself. You see, John is known as the "apostle of love" because more than anyone else in Scripture, John both preaches and personifies love. This can be seen even in his initial call. . . .

> *And Jesus, walking by the sea of Galilee, saw two brethren, Simon called Peter, and Andrew his brother, casting a net into the sea: for they were fishers. And he saith unto them, Follow me, and I will make you fishers of men. And they straightway left their nets, and followed him. And going on from thence, he saw other two brethren, James the son of Zebedee, and John his brother, in a ship with Zebedee their father, mending their nets; and he called them.*
>
> Matthew 4:18–21

When called by Jesus, Peter was casting his net, for he would become an evangelist who would bring so many people into the kingdom that three thousand-plus were saved the first time he preached (Acts 2:41). John, however, was mending his net when called by Jesus, for his ministry would be one of restoring relationships and knitting people together in love.

> *Again, a new commandment I write unto you, which thing is true in him and in you: because the darkness is past, and the true light now shineth. He that saith he is in the light, and hateth his brother, is in darkness even until now. He that loveth his brother abideth in the light, and there is none occasion of stumbling in him. We know that we have passed from death unto life, because we love the brethren. He that loveth not his brother abideth in death.*
>
> 1 John 2:8–10; 3:14

This was the message of the one who was mending nets, the one who was trying to keep believers from fragmenting and splitting. John was a man whose message was love. But it is important to understand that John did not speak from a lofty, theological perch far removed from real life. You see, all of Jesus' original disciples died violent, brutal deaths except for John. But it was not for lack of trying. The Roman emperor, Domitian, ordered John put into a cauldron of boiling oil. But when that failed to kill him, he was exiled to a rocky, seemingly God-forsaken island called Patmos, where he received the Book of Revelation.

> Following his release from exile on Patmos, probably nearing one hundred years of age, John returned to Asia Minor, where he went from church to church, sometimes carried on a stretcher. The historian Eusebius tells us that when John would come into the meeting places, people would break out in applause for this one who knew Jesus, this one who had leaned on His breast.
> "Give us the word, John," they would say. "Tell us something heavy."
> But all John would deliver was a single-sentence sermon: "Children, love one another." From church to church, John traveled with his single message: "Children, love one another."

"Why don't you say something a little more weighty, a little more meaningful?" asked an elder.

Eusebius says John looked the elder in the eye and said, "The sole commandment of Christ is to love, for he that loves has no need of anything else."

Folks, this is so freeing. I used to think I had to figure things out and analyze situations. But recently the Lord has impressed on me that all of that is *His* business. My calling is simply to love the brothers—every brother, any brother. John knew this. He taught it. He exemplified it. But here's the interesting thing: the "apostle of love," the one who penned the Gospel that has been called "the love letter to the world," was not always this way. Quite the contrary, John was initially a walking powder keg whom Jesus called a "son of thunder" (Mark 3:17). Take a look at Luke 9 to see "Stormy" in action. . . .

And John answered and said, Master, we saw one casting out devils in thy name; and we forbad him, because he followeth not with us. And Jesus said unto him, Forbid him not: for he that is not against us is for us.

Luke 9:49, 50

John was upset because someone outside the circle of disciples was using the name of Jesus to see people released from demons. "We told him to stop because he's not part of our denomination," he said. "He doesn't share our doctrinal understandings. He's not one of us." We do this as well. People can be saved, blessed, helped, and strengthened—but because we might not have doctrinal agreement, we put them down. Because they might worship differently from us, we find fault. Such is not the way of love. One would think this "son of thunder" would have learned. But the text goes on to tell us differently. . . .

And it came to pass, when the time was come that he should be received up, he stedfastly set his face to go to Jerusalem, and sent messengers before his face: and they went, and entered into a village of the Samaritans, to make ready for him. And they did not receive him, because his face was as though he would go to Jerusalem. And when his disciples James and John saw this, they said, Lord, wilt thou that we command fire to come down from heaven, and consume them, even as Elias did? But he turned, and rebuked them, and said, Ye know not what manner of spirit ye are of.   Luke 9:51–55

Here's John, saying, "Come on, Lord. Let's me and You cast down fire. Let's blow these guys away."

"Oh, John," answered Jesus, "don't you understand? I didn't come to hurt; I came to heal. I didn't come to blast people; I came to bless them." Saints, hear the word of our Lord. He's not out to find fault; He's not out to put down; He's not out to critique. He came to save. John heard this word—yet continued to exhibit "thunderous" tendencies. . . .

> *And Jesus going up to Jerusalem took the twelve disciples apart in the way,*
> *and said unto them, Behold, we go up to Jerusalem; and the Son of man shall*
> *be betrayed unto the chief priests and unto the scribes, and they shall condemn*
> *him to death, and shall deliver him to the Gentiles to mock, and to scourge,*
> *and to crucify him: and the third day he shall rise again. Then came to him*
> *the mother of Zebedee's children with her sons, worshiping him, and desiring*
> *a certain thing of him. And he said unto her, What wilt thou? She saith unto*
> *him, Grant that these my two sons may sit, the one on thy right hand, and*
> *the other on the left, in thy kingdom.* Matthew 20:17–21

I find this incredible. No sooner had Jesus told His disciples He was about to be crucified than we read that John was worried about where he would sit in the kingdom. Jesus was right when He called John "Stormy," for that was his nature—finding fault with other ministers, wanting to cast down fire on unbelievers, concerned about his own position in the kingdom.

Yet along with his faults, John did possess one sterling quality. For of the thousands who came to see Jesus heal lepers, open blind eyes, and raise the dead, only hundreds came to hear Him teach. And of the hundreds who heard Him teach, only seventy would actually follow Him (Luke 10:1). Of the seventy who followed Him, only twelve left everything. Of the twelve who left everything, only three went with Him to the Mount of Transfiguration and prayed with Him in Gethsemane. And of these three, only one was at the Cross. John lacked love, but he had loyalty. Perhaps that's why, from the Cross, Jesus looked down at this loyal one and commended His mother into John's care (John 19:26).

When did John become the "apostle of love"? I believe it was at the Cross. I believe it was when John finally realized how much Jesus loved him. And I believe this is the reason that, throughout his Gospel, he refers to himself not as "the disciple who loved Jesus" but as "the disciple whom Jesus loved." John knew he was a "son of thunder." Therefore, it was no surprise that he loved Jesus. After all, who wouldn't love One so gracious and merciful, so powerful and kind? It was no surprise that John loved Jesus. The surprise was that Jesus loved him. That is why we will spend time in the Gospel of John just looking at Jesus—for, like John, as we see Jesus, we will slowly change from thunder to love.

As we study this book together, I would like us to keep in mind three unique characteristics inherent in John's Gospel. . . .

Authenticity

The apostle John knew Jesus long before he became His follower. John's mother was a woman named Salome. Most commentators agree that Salome was the sister of Mary, the mother of Jesus. This would have made John and Jesus cousins. Like any other Jewish family in that day, John and Jesus probably spent much time together at family reunions, special celebrations, and above all, traveling together to Jerusalem for the celebration of feast days. Most likely, they talked, laughed, and played games together on those long trips from Galilee to Jerusalem. But one day, John became convinced that this cousin of his, this boyhood pal and companion, was God—which gives great authenticity to his Gospel. After all, how many of us would leave all to follow our cousin? Or who of us would say as John did in the first verse of his book, "My cousin is God"?

Selectivity

John closes his Gospel stating that the world could not contain the books that could have been written about Jesus' life and works. Because of this, John was very selective in what he chose to record. He based his entire account upon only eight signs or miracles. Thus, there are no boyhood incidents recorded. Jesus' baptism is not mentioned. There is neither a record of the temptation of Jesus nor one of His Gethsemane agony. There are no publicans and no demoniacs. John chose not to write about much of what the synoptic writers—Matthew, Mark, and Luke—spent a great deal of time recording. Instead, John chose to write about the eight signs Jesus used to illustrate His great "Ego Eimi"—"I Am"—statements.

"What is Your name?" Moses asked God (Exodus 3:13).

"I AM THAT I AM," answered the Lord.

Moses must have scratched his head and thought, *You are . . . what?*

Jesus came on the scene, echoing that same declaration of deity, and in John's Gospel says,

- "I AM the Bread of Life.
- I AM the Good Shepherd.
- I AM the Way, the Truth, and the Life.
- I AM the Resurrection.
- I AM the Vine.
- I AM the Door."

In essence, Jesus filled in the blank left by His Father when God declared His name to be I AM.

Practicality

The reason John wrote this book is given in verse 31 of chapter 20. "But these are written, that ye might believe that Jesus is the Christ, the Son of God; and that believing ye might have life through his name." That is why I love this Gospel. When someone says he doesn't know if he believes Jesus is really God, I can say, "Invest two hours of your life reading the Gospel of John straight through. Ask the Lord to show you if He's real. And, believe me, He will!" Because John was written so people might believe that Jesus is God, I think it is the most powerful tract you can share with anyone. I suggest you have on hand many copies of John's Gospel in order to share with people who are skeptical or questioning.

The second reason John wrote his Gospel was, "that believing ye might have life through his name." He wrote it for those of us who already believe. The Greek word translated "believing" speaks of a continual action. Therefore, John is saying the more we believe, the more life we will experience. Thus, John wrote to convince the skeptic, but also to provoke the believer toward a continual, growing belief in the Savior.

"By your love shall all men know you are My disciples," said Jesus (John 13:35). As we study this Gospel of love, my prayer is that, like its author, we will be transformed and changed from glory to greater glory as we fall in love with Jesus all over again.

JOHN

1

John 1:1 (a)
In the beginning . . .

John marks the beginning of Jesus' life as an event that took place before the beginning of eternity. "In the beginning was the Word"—not "*at* the beginning," not "*from* the beginning," but "*in* the beginning," Jesus was already there.

John 1:1 (b)
. . . was the Word . . .

John's use of the Greek word *logos* is important. The Greeks had developed a philosophy articulated by Plato and others that was built upon the assumption that the logos, the word, was the foundation of everything on earth. The earth, Plato said, was simply a shadow of the reality of the logos that existed somewhere in the heavens. The Jews took the Greek concept of the logos one step further. Whereas Plato said behind everything there's a perfect thought (logos), the Jews said that behind the thought there must be a thinker.

"We don't see perfection (logos) here on earth, but it must exist somewhere," said the Greek.
"Yes. And if there is a true, perfect thought (logos), there must be a true, perfect thinker," added the Hebrew.

John bursts into the middle of this discussion, saying, "In the beginning was the *Logos*, the

Word, God—not just a philosophy but a Personality. In the beginning was the *Logos*—the perfection *and* the Thinker."

John 1:1 (c)
. . . and the Word was with God, and the Word was God.

The Hebrew word for God in Genesis 1:1 is *Elohim,* a word that speaks of three or more. The use of *Elohim* way back in Genesis hints at the mystery of the Trinity. Its use by John reiterates the reality of the Trinity.

For topical study of John 1:1 entitled "Jesus is God," turn to page 443.

John 1:2
The same was in the beginning with God.

Contrary to the teaching of most cults, Jesus was not the first Created Being. He was already present in the beginning. He has always existed.

John 1:3
All things were made by him; and without him was not any thing made that was made.

Everything was made by Jesus Christ—even this day.

Our sun is big—so big that 1,300,000 of our earths could fit inside. It is small, however, compared to Anteres, a star in our galaxy.

Anteres is so big that 64 of our suns could fit inside of it. But Anteres is a relatively dinky star. Hercules is a big star. 110,000,000 Anteres could fit inside Hercules. So, 110 million Anteres, each big enough to hold 64 of our suns, which are big enough to hold 1,300,000 of our earths could fit into Hercules.

When we realize this, it is clear that on this planet, we are nothing more than specks on a speck in a speck. And yet most of the time we think we're pretty "speck-tacular," don't we? Now, put down your telescope, pick up your microscope, and consider a drop of water, which is equally amazing.

If you think back to junior-high science class, you'll recall that each molecule of water is composed of two atoms of hydrogen and one atom of oxygen. If you were able to enlarge each of the atoms in only a single drop of water to the size of a grain of sand, you would have enough sand to make a slab of concrete one foot thick and one half-mile high, stretching from San Francisco to New York City.

Of Jesus, Paul said, "All things were created *by* Him" (see Colossians 1:16). Scientists call the atomic force that holds together the nucleus of the atom "atomic glue." The Bible, however, identifies this mysterious atomic glue as Jesus Christ, for "by *Him*" all things consist, or hold together" (Colossians 1:17). There is coming a day when Jesus will let go of His hold on the atom. And the result will be chaos and utter devastation (2 Peter 3:10, 11). But in this day of grace, He continues to hold the galaxies, the atoms, and our lives together. Why do you exist today? You were made *by* Him. You were made *for* Him. And if you don't give your life *to* Him, like errant atoms you'll fall apart. Life won't make sense. You'll wonder what you're doing, where you're going, and why you're living. The secret of life is found here in the prologue of John. All things were made by Him.

John 1:4, 5
In him was life; and the life was the light of men. And the light shineth in darkness; and the darkness comprehended it not.

The Greek word translated "comprehend" can mean either "extinguish" or "understand." Both meanings are applicable in this verse, for the darkness could neither understand nor extinguish Jesus. For three hours, the earth was darkened when it seemed the Light of the World was extinguished (Matthew 27:45). But three days later, He was back—to shine in our hearts as the

Bright and Morning Star (Revelation 22:16), the Dayspring From on High (Luke 1:78).

John 1:6
There was a man sent from God, whose name was John.

Here, John the apostle introduces us to John the Baptist. As a prophet, John the Baptist spoke to people on behalf of God. As a priest (Luke 1:5), he spoke to God on behalf of the people. That's what ministry is all about. Ministry is both prophetic and priestly—talking to people about God and talking to God about people.

John 1:7 (a)
The same came for a witness, to bear witness of the Light . . .

We are not called to be attorneys. We are not called to debate, argue, convince. We are called to be witnesses—to share the truth, the whole truth, and nothing but the truth concerning what the Lord is doing in our lives.

"I see you got a new car," someone says to you. "Wow. You sure are lucky."
If you're a faithful witness, you'll tell the truth and say, "I'm not lucky. I'm blessed. The Lord provided this car for me."

Or —

"I see your new car was towed away," someone says to you. "You must be angry."
If you are a faithful witness, you'll tell the truth and say, "I know God will work this out for good. He always does."

Too often people think witnessing is confrontational and argumentative. It doesn't need to be that at all. I have found great freedom in simply sharing with people what the Lord is showing me. I feel no pressure to convert or convince anyone. Rather, I find great pleasure in simply sharing what the Lord has done, is doing, and will continue to do in my life.

John 1:7 (b)
. . . that all men through him might believe.

God is not willing that any should perish, but that all should come to repentance (2 Peter 3:9). The desire of God's heart is that not one person should die without knowing Him. Think of the person who bugs and irritates you the most. Did you know that our Lord is madly in love with him, and desires that he be saved? I personally reject the ultra-Calvinistic teaching that says God has already determined that some are born to be damned. The Scripture says John was sent for a witness that *all* through him might believe. The word "all" in Greek is an interesting one. It means "*all*"!

John 1:8
He was not that Light, but was sent to bear witness of that Light.

At the time John wrote his Gospel, in A.D. 75 or so, people were already beginning to worship John the Baptist. We see the same thing happening today with the Baha'i mentality that teaches there are many men of equal greatness. Jesus is good, it says. So is John the Baptist, Moses, Buddha, and Mohammed. The apostle John wanted to nip this idea in the bud. Thus, at the very outset of his Gospel, he makes it crystal clear that John the Baptist was not Jesus' equal.

John 1:9
That was the true Light, which lighteth every man that cometh into the world.

At the end of time, no one will be able to say that he didn't have an opportunity to know that there is a God. The Light has come, and it lights *every* man who comes into the world. Romans 1 tells us that creation around us is a testimony to God's reality and that our conscience within us verifies His truth. Psalm 19 states that the heavens declare the glory of God, and that there is no place on earth where their voice is not heard. Thus, whether a man looks up to the sky, around at creation, or within his own heart, he is left without excuse regarding the existence of his Creator. Every man knows innately, intuitively that there is a God. I firmly believe that if there is someone in the most remote corner of the earth who is hungering and thirsting after a saving knowledge of God, God will do whatever it takes to contact that one. He may choose to speak to him through an angel, a miracle, or through . . . you. If you're concerned about lost people and God's ability to reach them, don't stay here and discuss the ramifications of predestination. Go tell them Jesus died for them! You may be the very messenger the Lord uses to reach one who is waiting to hear the gospel.

John 1:10, 11
He was in the world, and the world was made by him, and the world knew him not. He came unto his own, and his own received him not.

The first time the Greek word translated "his own" is used in this verse, it is in a neuter form, referring to creation. The second time, it is masculine, referring to humanity. In other words, Jesus came into this world, and all of creation acknowledged Him. The winds obeyed Him. The water supported Him. The rocks were ready to cry out to Him. But there was one segment of creation that received Him not: man. Human nature is the only part of nature that refuses to worship God.

When the Bulls and the Blazers play basketball, people in the stands go crazy. They lift their hands in the air victoriously, clap exuberantly, and cheer wildly. They stand, yell, and stomp their feet. And they won't care who sees them. The same thing happens at rock concerts and hockey games, beauty pageants and rodeos. Humanity creatively and radically worships with abandon. But when it comes to worshiping Jesus, arms fold, voices hush, and sitting becomes the position of choice. Our culture finds it very easy to worship sports, movie, or rock stars—but has great difficulty worshiping Jesus.

John 1:12 (a)
But . . .

Praise God for the word "but." How many great truths swing on this small hinge!

John 1:12 (b)
. . . as many as received him, to them gave he power to become the sons of God, even to them that believe on his name.

"Thou shalt call his name Jesus," the angel said to Mary (Luke 1:31). The name "Jesus" means "Jehovah is salvation." You will receive power to become a son of God when you believe that Jesus is not merely *a* Savior, or even *the* Savior, but that He is *your* Savior.

John 1:13 (a)
Which were born, not of blood . . .

Your grandfather may have been an awesome Christian, and you may have fourteen preachers in your family tree. But according to this verse, none of that makes a bit of difference because birth into God's family is not passed on genetically. It has nothing to do with blood, which speaks of descent.

John 1:13 (b)
. . . nor of the will of the flesh . . .

Nor does birth into God's family have anything to do with desire. Paul tells us there is none that seeks after God, not one who really desires Him (Romans 3:11).

John 1:13 (c)
. . . nor of the will of man . . .

Nor does birth into God's family have anything to do with determination. Man can't will himself into a relationship with God.

John 1:13 (d)
. . . but of God.

God does it all. It is His sovereign work in the hearts of men that draws them to Himself. "Wait a minute," you say. "Didn't verse 9 say that His desire is that not one should perish? Why, then, doesn't He do His sovereign work in the heart of every man and draw everyone to Himself?" I don't know. I do know we serve an enormous God. He has given *every* man the opportunity to choose Him and yet has retained His right to choose whom He will. How can these two principles be compatible? I don't know. I do know that, according to Romans 8:29, God's foreknowledge is a big factor. But did God choose us because He knew we'd choose Him—or did we choose God because He had already chosen us? I don't know. I do know that if you think very long about this, your brain will short-circuit. You'll get so frustrated that you'll beat your fist against the wall and finally concur with J. B. Phillips, who said, "If God was small enough to figure out, He wouldn't be big enough to worship." Then you'll fall on your face and worship Him, saying, "Lord, I don't understand it all, but I thank You for choosing me."

John 1:14 (a)
And the Word was made flesh, and dwelt among us . . .

The Greek word translated "dwelt" literally means "tabernacled" or "encamped." The Word, the Logos, the Creator, Sustainer, and Reason for All Things became flesh and tabernacled among us. The tabernacle, covered with badger skins, was plain on the outside. But the interior was adorned with gold, silver, fine embroidery, and precious stones, for the *chabod*—the presence, the substance, the glory of God—was to be found inside. The same is true of Jesus. So ordinary looking was He externally that Judas had to identify Him to the Roman soldiers with a kiss. But the presence, the substance, the glory of God dwelt within Him to such a degree that some of it "leaked out" on the Mount of Transfiguration (Matthew 17:2).

Internal and external evidence indicate that Jesus was probably not born on December 25, the Festival of Saturnalia. Based on the fact that the shepherds were grazing their flocks on the night of His birth, He was probably born sometime in the fall. Some scholars suggest He was born on the fifteenth of Tishri, the beginning of the Feast of Tabernacles—the week-long celebration wherein the Jews came together, lived in pup-tent-like booths, and celebrated how God had seen their forefathers through their pilgrimage from Egypt to the Promised Land. To the Jews, the Feast of Tabernacles was the most joyous time of year. And the fact that Jesus "tabernacles" with us and walks with us through our earthly pilgrimage should produce abundant joy in our hearts as well.

John 1:14 (b)
. . . (and we beheld his glory, the glory as of the only begotten of the Father,) . . .

Just as the *chabod*, the glory of God, was seen in the tabernacle (Exodus 40:34), it was also seen in His Son. In Old Testament times, only the high priest on the Day of Atonement dared enter the Holy of Holies to behold the glory of God. But now, because of His atoning work on the Cross as Jesus rent the veil of the Holy of Holies (Matthew 27:51), we can behold His glory daily, freely, intimately.

John 1:14 (c)
. . . full of grace and truth.

The longer I walk with Him and the more I learn about Him, the more I am impressed with Jesus because He is the perfect blending of grace and truth. Some people are very truthful but show little grace. They're hard to be around because they have a tendency to make you feel guilty. Other people are gracious but not very truthful. They're fun to be with for a time, but they have a tendency to be a little flaky. Jesus was neither hard nor flaky. He spoke the truth with great candor and honesty. Yet His grace caused people to marvel (Luke 4:22).

John 1:15
John bare witness of him, and cried, saying, This was he of whom I spake, He that cometh after me is preferred before me: for he was before me.

Chronologically, John was six months older than Jesus. Yet Jesus said, "Before Abraham was, I AM," (John 8:58). Thus, John's reference was not to the chronological age, but to the eternal nature of his younger Cousin.

John 1:16
And of his fulness have all we received, and grace for grace.

The phrase "grace for grace" literally means "grace upon grace"—continual grace, inexhaustible grace. Even where sin abounds, grace abounds *more* (Romans 5:20). You cannot exhaust the grace of God if you embrace the Person of Jesus Christ.

John 1:17
For the law was given by Moses, but grace and truth came by Jesus Christ.

The law was given on a quaking mountain. Grace and truth were born in a quiet manger. The law was written on tables of stone. Grace and truth were wrought in a heart of love. When the law came down, three thousand people died (Exodus 32:28). When the Spirit came down, three thousand were saved (Acts 2:41). The law kills. Jesus gives life.

John 1:18
No man hath seen God at any time; the only begotten Son, which is in the bosom of the Father, he hath declared him.

The Greek word translated "declared" is *exegeomai,* from which we get our word "exegesis," meaning "to expound." Jesus expounded on the Father because Jesus had seen the Father. We are to expound on Jesus because we have seen Jesus. Therefore, the key to all of Bible interpretation, the key to hermeneutics is really *"Him*aneutics." Whether you're teaching a Sunday-school class, preaching to thousands, or serving on the mission field, expound upon Jesus. Look for Him in every passage and on every page of Scripture. Focus on Jesus and you'll behold the Father as well.

John 1:19 (a)
And this is the record of John . . .

With both of his parents from the house of Levi, John could have followed in his father's footsteps and served comfortably as a priest.

John 1:19 (b)
. . . when the Jews . . .

When John uses the term, "the Jews" (seventy times throughout his Gospel), he is not making a racial or a religious distinction, for virtually all of the people in the Gospels are Jews. No, when he speaks of "the Jews," he is referring to the Sanhedrin—the equivalent of our Supreme Court—comprised of the religious leaders of Jerusalem.

John 1:19 (c)
. . . sent priests and Levites from Jerusalem to ask him, Who art thou?

"Who am I?" John could have answered, "I'll tell you who I am. I am a priest. I am a prophet. I am the miraculously born son of Elizabeth and Zacharias. I am called of God and chosen by God. I am the one prophesied in Isaiah and Malachi. I am the forerunner of the Messiah—that's who I am." But he didn't. . . .

John 1:20
And he confessed, and denied not; but confessed, I am not the Christ.

We will find our true identities when, like John the Baptist, we realize we are not the Christ. "Oh, I already know I'm not the Christ!" you say. Do you? If you go to your job thinking you can pull it off through your own ability; if you work on your marriage thinking you can make it because of your own insight; if you raise your kids thinking you can draw on your own experience—no matter what your mouth may say, your life says, "I am the Christ." If, however, you truly realize you are not the Christ, you will be a man or woman who spends significant time in prayer today, because you will know that without Him, you can do nothing (John 15:5). Life starts when you put away your "Can Do" mentality and realize you can't do anything without Jesus.

John 1:21 (a)
And they asked him, What then? Art thou Elias? And he saith, I am not.

Still needing a label for this paradoxical prophet and peculiar priest, the delegates pressed further. "Are you Elijah?" they asked. "No," answered John.

John 1:21 (b)
Art thou that prophet? And he answered, No.

The term "that prophet" refers to the one prophesied in Deuteronomy 18 who would come to the nation of Israel and fully explain the way of God.

John 1:22, 23
Then said they unto him, Who art thou? that we may give an answer to them that sent us. What sayest thou of thyself? He said, I am the voice of one crying in the wilderness, Make straight the way of the Lord, as said the prophet Esaias.

Folks, you will never lack identity if you learn the secret of John the Baptist: that you're simply a voice to talk to people about Jesus Christ. So many people go through midlife crises because they don't realize their stability can't be found in the right situation vocationally or the right location geographically. Consequently, they're always wondering, *Should I work somewhere else? Should I live somewhere else? Should I do something else?*

Gang, follow the example of the Baptist and say, "No matter where I am, I realize I'm not the Christ; I'm not the prophet; I'm not Elijah. I'm simply a voice to talk to whoever comes my way on any given day about the Person, nature, and return of Jesus Christ.

John 1:24, 25
And they which were sent were of the Pharisees. And they asked him, and said unto him, Why baptizest thou then, if thou be not that Christ, nor Elias, neither that prophet?

Baptism was singularly reserved for Gentile converts to Judaism as a sign of renunciation of their past life. Thus, when John burst on the scene baptizing Jews, he caused a ripple that could be felt all the way to the Sanhedrin.

John 1:26, 27
John answered them, saying, I baptize with water: but there standeth one among you, whom ye know not; He it is, who coming after me is preferred before me, whose shoe's latchet I am not worthy to unloose.

"The One standing in your midst is my motivation for doing what I do," said John. So, too, the person who perceives the presence of the Lord at the office, in the shop, at school, or in the home cannot help but speak about Him. Why was Jesus in the desert with John? Was it because He wanted to talk about politics, sports, or financial strategy? No. Jesus was standing in the midst of that group because He knew John the Baptist would be talking about Him. Talk about Jesus in your home this afternoon, and that's when you will sense His presence. Talk about Jesus in the office tomorrow morning, and that's when you will have an awareness of His nearness. Whenever someone talks about Jesus, He'll be there.

John 1:28
These things were done in Bethabara beyond Jordan, where John was baptizing.

Bethabara was located in the rough, rocky region surrounding the Dead Sea. Sometimes, like John, that's where we are called to witness as

well. Never think you must wait until your life is perfect, your walk pure, or your circumstances plush before you can talk about Jesus. Sometimes we witness most effectively when we share from our desert experiences.

John 1:29
The next day John seeth Jesus coming unto him, and saith, Behold the Lamb of God, which taketh away the sin of the world.

As Abraham climbed Mount Moriah to offer his son as a sacrifice in obedience to God's command, Isaac said, "Behold the fire and the wood: but where is the lamb for a burnt offering?" (see Genesis 22:7). Where is the lamb? That is the question that rings throughout the Old Testament. Here in the New Testament, we hear John the Baptist's answer as he points to Jesus and announces, "Behold the Lamb!" In Revelation 5, we hear ten thousand angels join him, declaring "Worthy is the Lamb!"

- "Where is the Lamb?"—the cry of the Old Testament.
- "Behold the Lamb"—the hope of the New Testament.
- "Worthy is the Lamb!"—the summation of eternity.

The message of the Lamb of God grows wider and becomes more encompassing as you travel through Scripture. In Genesis, as Abel brought a lamb for sacrifice we see a lamb offered for an individual. In Exodus, as each household sacrificed a lamb during Passover, we see a lamb offered for a family. In Leviticus, when the people of Israel were instructed to sacrifice a lamb, we see a lamb offered for a nation. In John, as the Baptist identifies Jesus as the Lamb who takes away the sin of the world, we see a Lamb who would be offered for the world.

John 1:30
This is he of whom I said, After me cometh a man which is preferred before me: for he was before me.

Reiterating his statement of verse 15, John refers to the eternal nature of Jesus.

John 1:31
And I knew him not: but that he should be made manifest to Israel, therefore am I come baptizing with water.

In the Old Testament, a priest was washed with water when he began his role of priest (Leviticus 8:6). Thus, in a sense, as John stood in the water baptizing people, like priests of the Old Testament, he was washed with water. Through His baptism, Jesus Christ was washed with water as well—not because he needed cleansing from sin, but in order that He might identify with sinners.

John 1:32–34
And John bare record, saying, I saw the Spirit descending from heaven like a dove, and it abode upon him. And I knew him not: but he that sent me to baptize with water, the same said unto me, Upon whom thou shalt see the Spirit descending, and remaining on him, the same is he which baptizeth with the Holy Ghost. And I saw, and bare record that this is the Son of God.

Up until this point, apart from His birth, there is no record of the miraculous in the life of Jesus Christ, for it was not until the Spirit descended upon Him that He was miraculously empowered for ministry. You see, Jesus didn't perform miracles simply because He was God. No, He laid aside that power when He became the Babe of Bethlehem and assumed humanity (Philippians 2:7). Every miracle Jesus did was based upon His dependency on the Spirit in obedience to the Father.

For the longest time, I didn't understand this. I would read about Jesus' miracles and think, "That's not such a big deal. Of course He could walk on water, heal the sick, feed the multitude. He's *Jesus.*" But when I began to understand Philippians 2, when I began to see that Jesus emptied Himself of His prerogatives and powers, when I begin to grasp the fact that He was truly just like me yet without sin, His life took on an entirely different dimension to me. He became an example for me, a model of One who worked the miraculous because He walked in the power of the Spirit. At last I realized that the same power upon which Jesus relied was available to me.

Have you been baptized in the Spirit? Oh, I know the Holy Ghost is in you. That happens at salvation. But has He come *upon* you, as He did the disciples at Pentecost, to empower you for greater service? I believe every believer needs his own personal Pentecost—when he knows he has been empowered with the Spirit upon his life. How does this happen? Simply by asking. Jesus said, "If you being evil, know how to give good gifts to your children, how much more will the Father give the Holy Ghost to them that ask?" (see Matthew 7:11). Ask for the Holy Spirit. Ask with the realization that His purpose is not to give you a "Holy Ghost high" or "Holy Ghost goose bumps" but that you might be a witness like John, that you might be a voice in the wilderness drawing people to Jesus.

John 1:35–37
Again the next day after John stood, and two of his disciples; and looking upon Jesus as he walked, he saith, Behold the Lamb of God! And the two disciples heard him speak, and they followed Jesus.

As the disciples of John shift their allegiance to Jesus Christ, we see that the purpose of his preaching was not to draw people to himself, but to push people to Jesus. Such needs to be the purpose of your service as well. As you talk with people, your focus should not be on denominations or personalities. Your intent should always be to nudge people closer to Jesus.

John 1:38 (a)
Then Jesus turned, and saw them following, and saith unto them, What seek ye?

The first words Jesus uttered in public ministry were, "What seek ye?"

John 1:38 (b)
They said unto him, Rabbi, (which is to say, being interpreted, Master,) where dwellest thou?

Perhaps not knowing how to answer Jesus' question, the disciples pose one of their own. Jesus asked them what they were seeking. And in essence, maybe even unbeknownst to them at this point, their answer was, "It's You."

What are *you* seeking? A wife, a husband, a better job? Help with raising your kids or getting them through college? More friends, a better personality, a way out of debt? In 2 Corinthians 1:20 Paul declares, "For all the promises of God in him are yea, and in him Amen . . ." In other words, all the promises of God are wrapped up in a Person—the Person of Jesus Christ. We think we're after a change in our situation, or help with a difficulty. But, like these early disciples, what we're really craving is the Lord Himself, for in Him all God's promises are fulfilled.

John 1:39 (a)
He saith unto them, Come and see.

I love this! Jesus didn't say, "Go down the bank about three hundred yards, turn left, and look for a little house with roses and a white picket fence in front. . . ." No, He said, "Come with Me."

John 1:39 (b)
They came and saw where he dwelt, and abode with him that day: for it was about the tenth hour.

The disciples came and never left. So radically did their lives change when they accepted Jesus' invitation to come that they even remembered the very hour their pilgrimage with Him began.

John 1:40–42 (a)
One of the two which heard John speak, and followed him, was Andrew, Simon Peter's brother. He first findeth his own brother Simon, and saith unto him, We have found the Messias, which is, being interpreted, the Christ. And he brought him to Jesus.

Throughout Scripture, Andrew is referred to as "Simon Peter's brother." If I were in Andrew's sandals, I think at this point, I might have been tempted to say, "At last! I'm out of his shadow! I've found the Messiah, and I'm not breathing a word about it to Peter. This is *my* moment to shine." But that's not what Andrew did because he was one who couldn't help but bring others to Jesus. It was Andrew who introduced his brother, Peter, to Jesus. Jesus would later use Peter to bring three thousand to Himself (Acts 2:41). It was Andrew who brought the little boy to Jesus whose lunch He would multiply to feed five thousand (John 6:8, 9). And when a contingent of Greeks came to Jerusalem, saying, "We would see Jesus," it was Andrew who brought them to the Master (John 12:20–22).

John 1:42 (b)
And when Jesus beheld him, he said, Thou art Simon the son of Jona: thou shalt be called Cephas, which is by interpretation, A stone.

In changing Peter's name, it was as if Jesus said, "Simon, you're about as stable as the sand on the seashore. But I see your potential; I see what you will become. That's why I'm changing your name to Cephas, or Rock. Stick with Me, Peter, and you will see incredible changes take place in your person."

John 1:43–45
The day following Jesus would go forth into Galilee, and findeth Philip, and saith unto him, Follow me. Now Philip was of Bethsaida, the city of Andrew and Peter. Philip findeth Nathanael, and saith unto him, We have found him, of whom Moses in the law, and the prophets, did write, Jesus of Nazareth, the son of Joseph.

This cracks me up! In verse 43, Jesus finds Phillip and says, "Follow Me," but in verse 45, Philip says, "*We* have found *Him*." According to Romans 3:11, we don't find God. *He* finds *us*.

John 1:46 (a)
And Nathanael said unto him, Can there any good thing come out of Nazareth?

Off the beaten path, Nazareth was forgotten and forsaken economically, unimportant militarily, and insignificant politically. Nathanael, however, was referring to more than merely the isolation of Nazareth. A student of Scripture, he knew the promise of Micah 5:2, which stated that the Messiah would come not from Nazareth but from Bethlehem.

John 1:46 (b)
Philip saith unto him, Come and see.

Although Nathanael raised a legitimate question, Philip wasn't thrown off course. Why? One reason: Philip had tasted and seen that the Lord is good and, although at this point he couldn't defend Jesus of Nazareth theologically or intellectually, Philip knew experientially that He was real. So, too, there will come those who will try to confuse you theologically. They'll hand you a green Greek New Testament called The New World Translation, and say, "What John 1:1 *really* says is, In the beginning was the Word and the Word was with God and the Word was *a* god." Or they'll hand you a black Book of Mormon and say, "The Bible is great, but you also need to read this."

At this point in my walk, I'm not thrown off course very easily theologically or intellectually. Because our faith is a rational faith, it can withstand any argument in every situation. There are times, however, when someone like Nathanael, with more clever arguments or keener intellect than I, has challenged me. But, like Nathanael, all of these people have been wrong. You see, what neither Nathanael nor Philip knew was that Jesus was not born in Nazareth but in Bethlehem. We know the story but they didn't. In challenging situations, the best thing to do is follow Philip's lead. Look those who question your faith in the eye, and say, "I can't answer your question right now, but come and see. Come to church with me on Sunday and just watch what the Lord is doing. Come and see for yourself."

John 1:47 (a)
Jesus saw Nathanael coming to him . . .

Good for Nathanael! Even though he had questions spiritually and reservations intellectually, he accepted Philip's invitation to "come and see."

John 1:47 (b)
. . . and saith of him, Behold an Israelite indeed, in whom is no guile!

The word translated "guile" is "Jacob" in the Septuagint. Jacob was tricky. He tricked his brother Esau out of his blessing and birthright and tricked his uncle Laban out of the better part of his goods. But after wrestling one night with the Lord, Jacob realized that what he wanted all along was not Esau's birthright nor Laban's riches but the Lord's blessing (Genesis 32:26). And at that point, the Lord changed his name from "Jacob" to "Israel," from "Heel Snatcher," "Guile," and "Tricky One" to "Governed by God."

John 1:48
Nathanael saith unto him, Whence knowest thou me? Jesus answered and said unto him, Before that Philip called thee, when thou wast under the fig tree, I saw thee.

In Jesus' day, students traditionally studied under fig trees. The fig tree being the national symbol of Israel, I believe it was under a fig tree that Nathanael was very likely studying Genesis 28—the story of Jacob in the wilderness. . . .

Although it has been said that the softest pillow is a good conscience, fearing for his life because of his treachery and deceit, Jacob used a rock. As he slept, he saw a ladder extending from the heavens to the earth, with angels ascending and descending upon it. "Truly God is in this place and I knew it not," Jacob declared.

That is why, in the midst of his study of Genesis 28, Jesus approached Nathanael, calling him an Israelite in whom there is no guile, or no "Jacob."

John 1:49
Nathanael answered and saith unto him, Rabbi, thou art the Son of God; thou art the King of Israel.

Suddenly, Nathanael dropped his theological disputation and said to Jesus, "You're making reference to the very passage I was reading. How can this be? Surely, You are the Son of God, the King of Israel."

John 1:50
Jesus answered and said unto him, Because I said unto thee, I saw thee under the fig tree, believest thou? thou shalt see greater things than these.

"Do you believe simply because I made reference to the passage you were reading?" asked Jesus. "Stick around, Nathanael. You're going to see a lot more than that!"

John 1:51
And he saith unto him, Verily, verily, I say unto you, Hereafter ye shall see heaven open, and the angels of God ascending and descending upon the Son of man.

"Think back to your story, Nathanael," said Jesus. "The ladder you were reading about is Me. I am the stairway between heaven and earth. I am the Way to eternity. Upon Me the angels ascend and descend."

Notice Jesus said "ascending and descending." Most people think angels live in heaven, come down to earth occasionally, fly around a bit, and then head back up to heaven. Not true. Angels are ministering spirits assigned to specific saints, churches, and regions of the world (Acts 12; Revelation 2:1; Daniel 10). Although they can go up into the heavens, their primary place of residence is with us, with this church, and with various nations. Thus, the word order here is significant. Yes, angels ascend into the heavens, but they always descend back to earth.

"I am the ladder," Jesus said to Nathanael.

And from that moment on, Nathanael followed Him.

JESUS IS GOD
A Topical Study of
John 1:1

W hen John wrote his Gospel, heresy was already present within the church. Maintaining that the body is evil and only the spirit is good, Gnostics insisted that if Jesus was God, He couldn't have had a body. According to the Gnostics, when

Jesus walked, He left no footprints; when He ate, He didn't really swallow His food. He appeared as a Person, but He actually had no physical body.

What does John say to this? "We have heard Him with our ears; we have seen Him with our eyes; we have touched Him with our hands."

"Jesus had a body," said John. "He is God. He became Man" (see 1 John 1:1).

"If Jesus did indeed have a body," argued the Gnostics, "He is not God but rather an emanation from God, an extension of God."

"Wait a minute," countered John in the first verse of his Gospel. "There are three proofs that Jesus Himself is God. . . ."

Jesus is eternally God.
In the beginning was the Word . . .

Whenever the beginning was, wherever it was, whatever it might have been, Jesus—the Word—was already there. He had no beginning and He has no end. He is eternally God.

Jesus is equally God.
. . . and the Word was with God . . .

Jesus, the Word, was with God—equal to the Father and the Spirit.

"I thought there was only one God," you say.

There is. "Hear O Israel, the Lord our God is one Lord," Deuteronomy 6:4 declares. But the word "one" is *echad*, which refers to a compound unity, like *one* people, or *one* cluster of grapes. Thus, God is a compound unity, a "tri-unity." One plus one plus one does not equal one. But one times one times one equals one. And that is the mystery of the Trinity.

Jesus is essentially God.
. . . and the Word was God.

In His very essence, Jesus is God. The gnostics denied this, and their heresy is still alive and well today. Every cult stems from Gnosticism for every cult denies that Jesus Christ is God. The Mormons deny it. They say the Son of God is not equal with God. Rather, they maintain He is merely the offspring of God. The Jehovah's Witnesses declare Jesus is *a* God. And the Way International has decided that, although Jesus is the Son of God, He is not equal to God.

What do you say to these present-day gnostics? Turn them to Revelation 21:6: "I am Alpha and Omega, the beginning and the end. I will give unto him that is athirst of the fountain of the water of life freely." Ask a Mormon or a Jehovah's Witness, "Who is the One who gives of the water of the fountain of life? Who is the Alpha and Omega, the beginning and the end?" He will say, "It's God."

Then, have him turn the page to Revelation 22:12–13: "And, behold, I come quickly, and my reward is with me, to give every man according as his work shall be. I am Alpha and Omega, the beginning and the end, the first and the last." Ask him, "Who is going to return?" He will say Jesus. But he will now have a problem, because if he says Jesus is not God, he has two Alphas and two Omegas—two firsts and two lasts. Truly, the only logical conclusion is that Jesus is God. The doctrine of the deity of Jesus Christ is essential and nonnegotiable. Yet there are two verses attacked constantly by those seeking to undermine it. . . .

The Humanist and Genesis 1:1

The humanist—the unbeliever—refuses to believe God created the heavens and the earth. Why? Romans 1 says it's because if he acknowledges that he is created by God, he will then be responsible and accountable to God. Therefore, because man wants to act and live independently from God, he rids himself of his Creator and says, "Because I came from the ooze, I can live in the slime and do whatever I want."

In the 1940s, the seven leading problems in public schools were talking, chewing gum, making noise, running in the hallways, getting out of place in line, wearing improper clothing, and not putting paper in wastebaskets. Fifty years later, the seven leading problems became drug abuse, alcohol abuse, pregnancy, suicide, rape, assault/burglary, and arson/bombing. We've gone from talking and gum chewing to rape and school bombing. Something's going on. But what do we expect when we teach our kids they came from animals? Told they're animals, they act like animals. To counter this, we then spend millions of tax dollars on self-esteem courses to teach high-school kids that they're important.

The problem, however, is that before they ever get to sixth period self-esteem psychology class, they have to go to fourth period biology and hear they came from slime. It just doesn't make sense. We've got to get back to the foundational presupposition that in the beginning, God created the heavens and the earth—that He made us, has a plan for us, and wants to work in us. Without that, the entire fabric of culture begins to unravel in our homes, our schools, and our lives.

The Cultist and John 1:1

The second most commonly attacked Scripture is John 1:1. It also deals with the beginning, and is attacked not by the humanist, but by the cultist. The cultist says, "I've got a new truth to share. Jesus is not God. He's the Son of God, the emanation of God; He's a Prophet who speaks on behalf of God, but Jesus is not God." And on this single premise, heresy is born and cults are founded. You can recognize a cult by three characteristics. . . .

Exclusivity

"Of all of the people living presently and throughout history who have named the name of Christ, only our little group of fifty, or five hundred, or fifty thousand is right," declares the cultist. Listen, gang—if it's new, it's not true. And if it's true, it's not new. This is an absolute fact.

Authority

"Submit to me," says the cult leader. "I will tell you what to read, where to go, and who to marry." Whenever someone tries to put this trip on you—run! Paul said, "We do not seek to have authority over you, but are helpers of your joy" (see 2 Corinthians 1:24). Cult leaders are out to dominate, whereas true ministers of the gospel desire only to serve.

Deity

Every single cult denies the deity of Christ. Why is this so important? Because if you begin to say Jesus is simply a created extension of God, you open the door to every other heresy. But even more important than opening the door to other aberrations, if you deny Jesus is God, you minimize the work God did on your behalf when He became a Man.

Suppose you accidentally get caught in a meat grinder, and I come to your rescue, put my arms around you, and allow my flesh to become hamburger in the process. You leave in shock, but unharmed. And then someone tells you Jon Courson destroyed his own arms to save you. Suppose, hearing this, you said, "No, he didn't. That was someone who looks like Jon. That was an emanation from Jon. That was the son of Jon, Peter-John. But it wasn't Jon." If you didn't acknowledge what I had done on your behalf, it would be an arrogant, ignorant insult.

Yet that is exactly what gnostics propound when they insist God Himself didn't really become a Man. The message given to Abraham in Genesis 22 was that God will provide Himself a lamb—not *for* Himself a lamb, but that He Himself would *be* the Lamb. God became a Lamb. To diminish this is blasphemy. It is the one nonnegotiable heresy. In order for a person to be saved, he must confess that Jesus is Lord (Romans 10:9). What does it mean to confess Jesus is Lord? It does not mean that He is Lord of every area of your life, for who here or down the tunnel of history can truly say that Jesus Christ is Lord of every single area of his life? I suggest none. Consequently, none would be saved.

No, to confess Jesus as Lord means to realize that Jesus is God—that He is your Creator, Redeemer, and King; your Lover, your Friend, your everything. To confess Jesus as Lord means to recognize He is God in the flesh—eternally God, equally God, essentially God. If you deny that, you are a heretic. The Way International is heretical. Jehovah's Witnesses are heretics. Mormons are heretics. What are we to do with heretics? According to Titus 3:10, after a first or second warning, we are to have nothing to do with them.

"For one who constantly preaches grace and love, that sounds kind of tough," you protest. If a brother doesn't understand a doctrine, has erred in sin, or is stumbling in his walk, embrace him. Stand with him. Hang in there beside him. But you must differentiate between a stumbling saint and a devouring wolf, because sheep don't hang around wolves, hoping to convert them. When a wolf is around, sheep split.

A wolf in sheep's clothing might look like a sheep, talk like a sheep, smell like a sheep, even walk like a sheep. How, then, can you tell if he is a sheep? You don't have to be an expert in theology. You don't have to know Greek perfectly. Just watch what he eats. If he eats sheep, he's a wolf. Jehovah's Witnesses, followers of the Way International, Mormons, and other cultists approach people who name the Name of Jesus and begin to cause confusion and doubt. They get people off the mark of simply loving the Lord and loving one another. We under-shepherds hate wolves because we see what they do to the flock as they shift people's focus from the Shepherd to side issues and insignificant matters in order to devour believers for their own purposes and egos.

Keep centered, gang. How? By keeping focused on the Word and on Jesus Christ. Truly, Jesus is God. Love Him. Learn about Him. Talk to Him. Walk with Him. And you'll do well.

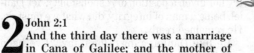

2 **John 2:1**
And the third day there was a marriage in Cana of Galilee; and the mother of Jesus was there.

In Jesus' day, Jewish wedding celebrations lasted for one week, during which time relatives and friends would stay in the home of the bride and groom—sort of a honeymoon/family reunion/bachelor party/wedding shower all rolled into one! During this seven-day celebration, the bride would be tucked away in a secluded part of the house and would not be seen by anyone but her groom. At the end of the week, she would emerge with great fanfare and celebration. This is fascinating as it relates to the Marriage Feast of the Lamb. You see, when the Rapture takes place, we—the bride of Christ—will be carried away into heaven for seven years. Just as the Jewish bride was in seclusion with her groom for seven days, we will be tucked away in intimacy with our Lord Jesus Christ, away from the Tribulation that will be unleashed upon the earth.

John 2:2
And both Jesus was called, and his disciples, to the marriage.

Jesus' presence at this particular wedding signals His stamp of approval upon all aspects of the institution of marriage—civil, legal, and religious. A wedding ceremony itself has an effect that is not often understood. Couples find a commitment made to each other in a public ceremony harder to break when the going gets tough. Perhaps that is why statistics show that those who live together before marriage have a substantially higher divorce rate than those who don't. I continue to be amazed at the large number of couples who say, "What does a piece of paper matter? Why can't we just make a private commitment to God and to each other without all of the legal and religious procedures?" Here in John 2, at the very outset of His public ministry, Jesus honored and elevated the institution of marriage.

John 2:3
And when they wanted wine, the mother of Jesus saith unto him, They have no wine.

Some have suggested Mary's concern over the shortage of wine indicates she may have been a hostess at this wedding. Since the role of hostess at a Jewish wedding was usually filled by an aunt of the groom, this marriage celebration could very well have been that of Mary's nephew, John. Mary turned to her Son for help. However, based on Jesus' following response, it is my personal conviction that Mary was interested in more than simply the provision of wine. Might she have been seeking a restoration of her reputation? You see, as a young woman of perhaps fourteen or fifteen years of age, Mary had become miraculously pregnant by the Spirit of God. Yes, she was highly favored by God and blessed among women. But she also must have become the subject of speculation and slander, raised eyebrows and wagging tongues. Defending their own righteousness, the Pharisees smugly declared to Jesus, "We be not born of fornication" (John 8:41), their implication being that He had been.

For thirty years, Mary had lived with the knowledge that her character had been unjustly maligned. Is it not possible that at this point, she looked to her Son not only for wine but for vindication, thinking that if people could only see who He really was, perhaps they would at last see the truth about her as well?

John 2:4 (a)
Jesus saith unto her, Woman, what have I to do with thee?

Gune is the Greek word translated "woman." It is a term of respect but not of warmth. Thus, Jesus responds to Mary with a gentle rebuke. This sounds like a cold response on Jesus' part to His longsuffering and gentle mother. Yet, as is seen in the remainder of the verse, it was as much for His mother's good as for His Father's glory.

John 2:4 (b)
. . . mine hour is not yet come.

"Mine hour" is a term used in John's Gospel seven times. To what hour is Jesus referring? In John 17:1, He prayed, "Father the hour is come; glorify thy Son that thy Son also may glorify thee."

- "The hour" is the time of Jesus' crucifixion, resurrection, and ascension.
- "The hour" is the time of the irrefutable declaration of who He was, of the undeniable proof of His deity.
- "The hour" is when His earthly ministry would be finished, His appointed mission completed, His Father fully glorified.

"Woman . . . Mary . . . Mother . . ." said Jesus, "I better than anyone know you have been waiting patiently. I know better than anyone how you have been hurt. I understand better than anyone

your situation. But it is not time to rectify everything . . . not quite yet."

What does this say to us? Oftentimes, I think we ask the Lord to do something that will get us off the hook or make us look a little better. We ask Him to do something that will smooth our road or lighten our load. Like Mary's, our requests might sound very noble, very generous, very altruistic—but in reality, they're self-centered. And in such instances, Jesus might whisper in our hearts, as He did to Mary, "What have I to do with thee? This is not the hour. This is not the time. This is not the place. The problem will be solved. Your reputation will be salvaged. The provision will be made. The healing will be enjoyed. But not yet. Mine hour is not yet come."

Daniel was in a place of prominence and tremendous authority in Nebuchadnezzar's kingdom. Then, when he was about sixty-five years old, Nabonidus came into power, and Daniel was removed from office. For twenty years, Daniel is not seen in the narrative given to us in the book that bears his name. But then the day dawned that Belshazzar called for him to interpret the mysterious writing on the wall (Daniel 5:13). When Darius the Mede seized control of the kingdom shortly thereafter, Daniel was placed in a position of prominence once again. Thus, for twenty years, Daniel was neither used in ministry nor given a position of responsibility. Yet Daniel, being a man of integrity, did what we must do: He remained ready.

Be like Daniel, gang. Don't say, "I've been walking with the Lord for five years, and nothing's happening, so I think I'll just go to the movies, join the city softball league, or take up bird-watching." Folks, it is your job and my job to be ready—to walk with the Lord, to spend time in the presence of the Lord, and to learn about the Lord so that when Belshazzar says, "What does this mean?" like Daniel, we can say, "I can tell you because for twenty years I've been in touch with God. For twenty years, I've been in the place of prayer. For twenty years, I've been close to the Lord."

Are you in prayer? Are you studying the Word? Are you loving the Lord? Are you ready? In a certain moment, your hour will come. Your time will arrive. A significant task, a life-changing opportunity will arise, and then it will be too late to prepare.

As Jesus descended the Mount of Transfiguration, He was met by a man who said, "Master, I brought my epileptic son to Your disciples but they couldn't help him." Jesus then cast out the demon within the boy.

"Why couldn't we do that?" asked His disciples.

"This kind does not go out except by prayer and fasting," answered Jesus (Matthew 17:21).

If it takes prayer and fasting to cast out a demon of that nature, how were we to know we would have that kind of encounter? *the disciples must have wondered. But I believe Jesus was implying that, because they wouldn't know when opportunities to minister would come their way, they should have been living a life of continual prayer and fasting.*

Why weren't the disciples praying? I suggest it was because Jesus was on the mountain with Peter, James, and John. I suggest it was because the nine disciples down below were saying, "It's always Peter, James, and John. They get to go up the mountain. They're always in the inner circle. But what about us? We never get to do anything." And because that was their mentality, they weren't interceding. They weren't praying. They weren't ready.

So, too, there are those today who say, "The Lord never uses me. The church never calls on me." But when the opportunity arises before them, they are either unable to meet it or are completely unaware of it. Saint, your responsibility in ministry is to be ready and then to rest. Study the Scripture in the place of intimacy and prayer. Worship the Lord. Get to know Him all the more. Then just rest, saying, "Lord, when the hour comes in which You want to use me to do something for Your glory, I'm ready."

Radical transformation will occur in your walk with the Lord when you realize *He's* the Master and you're not. *He's* the King, and you're the subject. *He's* the Boss, and you're the servant. Your job is not to order Him or even to make suggestions to Him. Your place is to be ready *for* Him, and to rest *in* Him.

John 2:5
His mother saith unto the servants, Whatsoever he saith unto you, do it.

I find it theologically significant that in these, her last recorded words in Scripture, we see Mary directing the servants to her Son rather than acting as a mediator or liaison for Him. Those who believe they need to go through Mary to have their prayers heard or to gain influence in heaven have not studied carefully the relationship between Jesus and His mother. She didn't carry a whole lot of weight with Him. Oh, He loved her and cared for her even when He was on the Cross. But He was neither influenced by her nor did He take orders from her.

When it was told Him that His mother wanted to see Him, Jesus said, "Who is my mother? Who are my brothers? They who hear and heed the Word of God are My mother and My brothers" (see Luke 8:21). Later, in Acts 1, we see Mary with the other disciples praying in the Upper Room. She's not leading the meeting. She's not in a place of honor or prominence. She's just one of them. There is *one* Mediator between God and man—not Mary, but "the Man, Christ Jesus" (see 1 Timothy 2:5).

John 2:6–8
And there were set there six waterpots of stone, after the manner of the purifying of the Jews, containing two or three firkins apiece [about 20 gallons]. Jesus saith unto them, Fill the waterpots with water. And they filled them up to the brim. And he saith unto them, Draw out now, and bear unto the governor of the feast. And they bare it.

For you who seek to serve Jesus to a greater degree, there are three important characteristics of the servants to note in this story....

The first is obedience. The servants didn't argue with Jesus, or ask questions of Him. They simply did what He asked them to do.

The second is exuberance. The servants filled huge twenty-gallon vessels to the brim, even though they had no idea what would happen next. There was nothing halfhearted about these guys!

The third is patience. Jesus didn't say, "Okay, servants, huddle up. Here's the plan. See those big water pots over there? I want you guys to fill them with water. Then, as you begin to pour them out and serve them to the governor, a miracle will take place and the water will turn into wine. John will write about it in the second chapter of his Gospel, and you guys will be famous!" No, Jesus told the servants what to do only one step at a time. First, they were to fill the water pots. After they had done that, He instructed them to draw the water out and take it to the governor. The miracle occurred only as they faithfully followed each step. Too often, I want to know what steps two through five are going to be before I follow step one. "Let me know where this is all going, Lord. Let me know where I will be next month, next year, and three years from now. Lay it out clearly, Lord, and then I'll go for it." The Lord doesn't work that way. He unfolds His plan for us the same way He did for the servants at the wedding: one step at a time. And the point where we stop obeying is the point where that stops happening.

John 2:9 (a)
When the ruler of the feast had tasted the water that was made wine, and knew not whence it was: (but the servants which drew the water knew;) . . .

So well known is this story, it can be recounted today by believer and non-believer alike. At the time, however, the only ones who knew what had transpired were the lowliest people in attendance at the wedding: the servants. No one else knew from whence the wine came. There were no "oohs" and "aahs" as the wine was poured. There were no glances of recognition toward the thirty-year-old Carpenter. There was not a sudden rush of people to Jesus' side. There were only some dropped jaws and wide eyes on the faces of some tired servants. This first public miracle of Jesus was similar to His first appearance on earth, for then only a few shepherds were aware of what had happened. There would be times later in His ministry when He would demonstrate His deity with bold and awesome authority. But on this particular day in Cana, He chose to reveal Himself only to some humble, obedient servants.

John 2:9 (b), 10
. . . the governor of the feast called the bridegroom, and saith unto him, Every man at the beginning doth set forth good wine; and when men have well drunk, then that which is worse: but thou hast kept the good wine until now.

Throughout history, there have been those who use this story as justification for drinking alcohol. "Jesus made wine. Jesus drank wine. So don't talk to me about not drinking," they insist.

"If your argument is sincerely based upon the example of Jesus, you will never drink again," I answer. "Look at Luke 22:18 where Jesus says He will not drink of the fruit of the vine until the kingdom of God shall come. Even if Jesus was drinking fermented wine—a viewpoint to which I don't personally subscribe—since He as your role model will not drink again until the kingdom comes, neither should you."

As a pastor, I'm tired of seeing the damage alcohol inflicts upon our children, our families, and our society as a whole. Everyone who has ever begun to drink has done so thinking they would be careful, that they would remain in control. But the fact that eighteen million Americans are known alcoholics proves otherwise. Solomon declares, "It is not for kings to drink wine, nor for princes strong drink, lest they drink, and forget the law, and pervert the judgment of any of the afflicted. Give strong drink unto him that is ready

to perish, and wine unto those that are of heavy hearts. Let him drink, and forget his poverty, and remember his misery no more" (Proverbs 31:4–7). If you're perishing, which literally means "damned," or if you're depressed to the point where you cannot bear life, you have Solomon's permission to partake of alcohol.

But if you want to be a leader, he warns you to stay away from it lest you short-circuit your thinking process. Solomon was right, for science has since proven that every ounce of alcohol consumed permanently destroys ten thousand dendrites, or filaments, in the nerve cells of the brain. While it is true that each of us has millions of dendrites, I think it is fair to say that none of us has any to spare. If you're like me, you need all the dendrites you can get! Be wise, precious people, and consider very seriously the effects of alcohol upon your spiritual and physical well-being, your family stability, and the health of our society.

John 2:11 (a)
This beginning of miracles did Jesus . . .

Compare this first public miracle of Jesus, the "grace-bringer," with the first miracle of Moses, the lawgiver. Moses turned the water of the Nile into blood, which speaks of judgment. Jesus turned the water at the wedding into wine, which speaks of joy. So, too, if you approach the Word legalistically, it will become like the Nile. You'll bloody yourself and everyone around you. But if you look for Jesus in the water of the Word, you will find the wine of joy producing such hilarity within you that people for miles around will be drawn to you.

John 2:11 (b)
. . . in Cana of Galilee, and manifested forth his glory; and his disciples believed on him.

Our Lord's first public miracle took place at a marriage ceremony. I believe that is because daily miracles are essential to our marriages. In the brief account of the miracle at Cana, a beautiful picture develops that illustrates how the Lord can take a marriage that seems washed-up or watered-down, and turn it into something sparkly, bubbly, and joyful. Marriage should not be simply workable, like water. It should be wonderful, like wine.

As quoted in the *San Francisco Chronicle*, ninety-nine-year-old Abel Kibiak, America's oldest living Olympian, winner of the silver medal in the fifteen hundred-meter race in 1912, said he is looking for a woman to "take up with."

"She doesn't have to have teeth," he said, "just a driver's license."

I think too often we have an "Abel Kibiak" mentality concerning marriage. We settle for so little when the Lord wants to bless us with so much. You see, God has chosen marriage to be the singular illustration by which an unbelieving world might see that Jesus is alive.

How does this happen? Look at the story, and you'll find the procedure to be so simple. Stone vessels were filled to the brim with water, servants drew out the water, and the water became wine. Paul declares we are earthen vessels (2 Corinthians 4:7). Therefore, I am to allow the Word of God to fill me to the brim. Then I am to make the effort and take the time to draw from what has filled me in order to serve my wife, Tammy. She, on the other hand, is to allow the Word of God to fill her to the brim in order that she might serve me. And as we do this, we find ourselves in Cana, where the water of the Word is transformed into the wine of joy. I'm not talking about discussing theological complexities or an exegesis of the Pentateuch. I'm talking about just sharing whatever it is that stimulates, convicts, or interests you on your journey through the Word.

John 2:12 (a)
After this he went down to Capernaum, he, and his mother . . .

Here is Mary still at her Son's side. The rebuke earlier in the chapter did not deter her from following Him. Perhaps it brought them even closer. Do not despise the rebuke of the Lord, gang, for it is meant to draw you nearer to His side.

John 2:12 (b), 13 (a)
. . . And his brethren, and his disciples: and they continued there not many days. And the Jews' passover was at hand . . .

Passover was linked with another feast that took place seven days later—the Feast of Unleavened Bread. During the Feast of Unleavened Bread, the Jews had to make sure that absolutely no leaven was present in their homes. They searched every corner, every cupboard, and every cooking utensil to rid their homes of every trace of leaven, the symbol of sin. In the following account, we will see Jesus bring to life this Old Testament picture as He cleanses His own Father's House from the evil and sin within it.

John 2:13 (b)–14
. . . and Jesus went up to Jerusalem, And found in the temple those that sold oxen and sheep and doves, and the changers of money sitting.

In front of the temple were four courtyards separated by four doors leading from one to the other. The first courtyard, the court of the Gentiles, was accessible to everyone. Men and women, Jews and Gentiles could all enter the court of the Gentiles. Beyond the court of the Gentiles was the court of the Israelites. Gentiles were barred from this court upon penalty of death. The third courtyard was the court of men. Jewish males were the only ones allowed access to this court. Finally, adjoining the temple itself was the court of priests, where only priests were allowed admittance.

In the court of Gentiles, oxen, sheep, and doves were sold. Why? Because the priests were filled with greed and covetousness. Coveting being simply wanting more of that which one already has enough, these Jewish pseudo-religious leaders wanted more money to increase their own coffers. Thus, the oxen, sheep, or doves brought by the people to sacrifice at the temple were, upon inspection by the priests, usually declared unfit for sacrifice due to some microscopic flaw or blemish. Worshipers were then instructed to purchase "preapproved" animals from the stalls in the courtyard. The prices for the "pure" animals were exorbitant, so the priests made a killing off the unsuspecting supplicants.

The moneychangers employed a similar tactic. When foreigners came to the temple to pay their temple tax and to make offering, their money was declared unfit due to the image of Caesar or other foreign deity inscribed upon it. The moneychangers would then exchange foreign currency for shekels at a cost of up to ten times the normal exchange rate. Jesus entered this scene and saw immediately that His people were being robbed and ripped off. In the court of the Gentiles—the very place where the world should have been introduced to the True and Living God—the priests were fleecing His flock instead of feeding them.

John 2:15
And when he had made a scourge of small cords, he drove them all out of the temple, and the sheep, and the oxen; and poured out the changers' money, and overthrew the tables.

Here, the story is quite a contrast to what had happened earlier in the chapter . . .

At the wedding, Jesus sat at the table.
Here, he's throwing tables.
In Cana, He worked quietly and privately.
Here, He's reacting conspicuously and pub-
*   licly.*
At the wedding feast, the emphasis was on joy.
Here, the end result is judgment.

And yet I think there is a very interesting link between these two accounts. Both deal with tables. Both deal with Jesus desiring to bring joy. Our bodies being the temple of the Holy Spirit (1 Corinthians 6:19), there are things in our lives, in our temples, that are ripping us off just as surely as the priests and moneychangers ripped people off in Jesus' day. Consequently, there is a direct connection between the joy produced at the wedding table and the judgment that took place at the temple table, for if I am a going to have joy, the Lord wants to drive out the sin that is ripping me off. Joy and judgment walk hand in hand, for without joy, judgment would be unbearable; but without judgment, sin would run rampant. Yes, there is pleasure in sin for a season, but it is followed by destruction (Hebrews 11:25). Therefore, the Lord lovingly says to you and me, "I want to go through your life, overturn the tables, and drive out the cattle so you won't be ripped off from what I want to do in and through you." How does this happen practically? I believe it takes place at a third table—not the table of the wedding feast or the table in the temple, but at the table of Communion.

Communion produces rich and satisfying joy coupled with deep and purifying judgment, for it's when you hold the elements of Communion in your hand as you're on your knees before the Lord that you can hear His voice of compassion and correction in a uniquely powerful way.

For topical study of John 2:13–15 entitled "Turning over Tables," turn to page 454.

John 2:16 (a)
And said unto them that sold doves, Take these things hence . . .

This short phrase indicates that, even in His righteous anger, Jesus was totally in control. He was not running wildly through the temple courtyard, driving out oxen and throwing over tables in a blind rage. If that were the case, He would have knocked the cages of doves to the ground. No, knowing the doves would die if they fell to the ground locked in their cages, Jesus said, "Would

you guys please take these out?" as He continued to crack the scourge and overturn tables.

"Be angry and sin not," said Paul (Ephesians 4:26). Jesus provides the perfect example of what this means. Although He acted with great strength and firmness, He was never out of control. A spoken word was given to those who sold doves. A show of force was given to the moneychangers. Jesus communicates differently to each of us. Sometimes He comes with His Word. Sometimes He comes with His might. But always He comes in righteousness.

John 2:16 (b)
. . . make not my Father's house an house of merchandise.

Here, Jesus referred to the temple as "my Father's house." At the end of His earthly ministry three years later, because they refused to acknowledge Him as their Messiah, He will tell the Jews the temple was *their* house (Matthew 23:38).

John 2:17 (a)
And his disciples remembered that it was written . . .

John records three times when Jesus' disciples remembered either something in Scripture or something Jesus said (2:17; 2:22; 12:16). Thus, uneducated though they might have been by the world's standards, it was obvious they had the Word hidden in their hearts (Psalm 119:11).

John 2:17 (b)
. . . the zeal of thine house hath eaten me up.

As Psalm 69:9 was brought to their remembrance, the disciples suddenly realized Jesus' passion for the physical temple. So, too, Jesus is zealous and passionate about His spiritual temple—us. We are His temple not only individually (1 Corinthians 6:19) but corporately (1 Peter 2:5). And as His corporate temple, we as a church exist for three reasons . . .

The first reason the church exists is for exaltation—for worshiping, exalting, and extolling the Lord. Why? Because all things were made by Him and for Him (Colossians 1:16)—including the church. Therefore, the church exists for the Lord's pleasure (Revelation 4:11).

The second reason the church exists is for edification. The church exists to edify the saints—to build them up, to bring them into maturity into the "measure of the stature of the fullness of Christ" (see Ephesians 4:12, 13). How? By seeing

Jesus through the study of the Scriptures. I am convinced that the greatest single need in the church of Jesus Christ today both nationally and internationally is the straightforward study of His Word.

The third reason the church exists is for evangelization. The inevitable result of exaltation and edification will be evangelization. Why? Because healthy sheep just naturally reproduce. If sheep are properly fed and tended, the shepherd had better make room because baby lambs can't be far behind. Acts 6:7 declares that when the Word increased, the number of disciples multiplied. That is why the reason we meet together is not primarily for evangelism. Evangelism is the effect. Exaltation and edification are the cause.

There was a man at Applegate Christian Fellowship who had been coming to the Fellowship for about a year. He was studying, digesting, meditating, and taking in the Scriptures. As a result, in the past eleven months, he led eight of his co-workers to Jesus Christ and all eight became a part of the body. Truly, evangelism is the result of edification.

People often said, "You're baptizing fifty or sixty new believers every week. How can this be?" The answer was simple: Healthy sheep reproduce.

I recently talked to a lady at my son Peter-John's baseball game who said, "When I first came to the Fellowship, I remember thinking that people were crazy to travel such a long distance. But as I began to worship with you, take in the Scriptures, and see what the Lord was doing, I found myself saying, 'You know, it's not such a long drive. . . .'"

Folks, if you're not into the church, if you're down on the church, if you don't have time for the church, you're out of sync with the heart of the Lord because He's zealous for and radically in love with His church.

John 2:18
Then answered the Jews and said unto him, What sign shewest thou unto us, seeing that thou doest these things?

Notice they didn't say, "*Why* are You doing this?" Every single person there knew the temple needed cleansing because its practices were corrupt. Thus, no one asked Jesus why He did what He did. Rather, they asked who had given Him the authority to do it.

John 2:19
Jesus answered and said unto them, Destroy this temple, and in three days I will raise it up.

The Greek word translated "temple" is *naos,* which was also used in reference to the Holy of Holies. Perhaps Jesus physically pointed to Himself when He made this declaration. At the very least, He alluded to Himself when He made it. "Destroy this temple—Me," He said, "and in three days I will raise it up"—which is precisely what happened at Calvary.

John 2:20, 21
Then said the Jews, Forty and six years was this temple in building, and wilt thou rear it up in three days? But he spake of the temple of his body.

Herod had begun renovation of the temple in the year 20 B.C. The account before us took place in A.D. 26–28. Thus, the temple had been under construction for forty-six years at this point and would remain under construction until A.D. 64. As impressive as it was massive, Josephus records that eighteen thousand men were employed on the project over the course of its renovation. With this in mind, it is easy to see why the Jews thought the Galilean Carpenter crazy with His claim to rebuild the whole thing in only three days.

John 2:22
When therefore he was risen from the dead, his disciples remembered that he had said this unto them; and they believed the scripture, and the word which Jesus had said.

This is the third recorded instance in this chapter where the disciples "remembered" or "believed." In verse 11, the water changed to wine caused them to believe. In verse 17, the cleansing of the temple caused them to remember. But here in verse 22, the Resurrection caused them to both remember *and* believe.

John 2:23
Now when he was in Jerusalem at the passover, in the feast day, many believed in his name, when they saw the miracles which he did.

There are those who seek miraculous proof that Jesus is real and that He loves them. They search for physical, material, or financial verification of His reality. But theirs is a flimsy, faulty faith built upon a sandbar foundation because, as we will see, Jesus is not committed to those who demand a sign. You see, the problem with signs is that they're never enough. If you base your faith upon signs, you'll always be upset by the one that didn't happen—the prayer that wasn't answered, the healing that didn't come, the payment that didn't arrive. That is why our faith must be built and based not upon what Jesus does, but upon who He is. Who He is as revealed in the Word. That is why Paul says faith comes by hearing and hearing by the Word of God (Romans 10:17). It's the Word pointing to the Person of Jesus Christ that produces genuine faith.

John 2:24, 25
But Jesus did not commit himself unto them, because he knew all men, and needed not that any should testify of man: for he knew what was in man.

The word translated "commit" in verse 24 is the same word translated "believe" in verse 23. In other words, many believed in Jesus when they saw the miracles, but He did not believe in them because He knew their hearts. Stay tuned, folks. In John 3, we'll be introduced to one who, unlike these people, sought Jesus for who He was rather than merely for what He could do.

TURNING OVER TABLES
A Topical Study of
John 2:13–15

I am constantly amazed by how the Lord works in the most predictably unpredictable places and through the most unusual and interesting people. One of the things I love about walking with Him is that I never know what the next step will be—which is exactly how Jesus' disciples must have felt in John 2. Up to this point, they probably thought they had Jesus pretty well figured out. After all, their introduction to Him was as the Lamb of God—He was gentle. Their invitation from Him was, "Come and see"—He was approachable. Their impression of Him was as the miraculous Winemaker—He was wonderful!

But in verse 13 of chapter 2, everything changed. The gentle, approachable Lamb of God becomes the Roaring Lion of Judah. With eyes flashing and scourge flying, muscles bulging and tables soaring, Jesus took on a seemingly new persona. Certainly the disciples must have thought, *Who is this One we thought we knew so well?"*

In verse 7, Jesus quietly met a need.
In verse 14, He conspicuously caused a scene.

In verse 2, Jesus sat at the marriage table.
In verse 15, He overturned temple tables.

At Cana, Jesus created the wine of joy.
In the temple, He initiated the work of judgment.

But Jesus was not schizophrenic. There is a direct connection between the joy He produced at the wedding table and the judgment He pronounced at the moneychanger's table. Joy and judgment are two sides of the same coin. They go hand in hand. And nowhere do they blend more perfectly and more powerfully than in the Person of Jesus Christ. Scripture records four occasions when Jesus exhibited righteous anger. . . .

In Matthew 18:6, Jesus used strong language to describe the punishment of anyone who caused a child to stumble. In Mark 10:14, Jesus was "much displeased" when His disciples hindered little children from coming to Him. In Mark 3:5, Jesus looked with anger on the Pharisees who were eager to prosecute Him for healing on the Sabbath. And here in John 2, Jesus' anger is seen in the cleansing of the temple.

Please note that in all four of these situations, Jesus' anger is directed toward those who put up barriers to prevent others from coming to Him. We often think the Lord is angry with our watching TV or with our imperfections and inconsistency. We think He's angry with us for not reading the Word or for not praying. But in reality, what angers the heart of Jesus are those things that keep others from experiencing and enjoying the presence of God—traditions that say, "You can't be healed on the Sabbath," or inspections that say, "Your sacrifice is unacceptable."

When individually or corporately we erect walls or barriers that discourage people from coming to the Lord, Jesus is angered. That is why, with scourge in hand, He overturned the tables of the moneychangers in the temple. And that is why He scourges us as well. You see, if there are barriers, barricades, people or problems in your life that prevent you or others from enjoying Him, He will scourge you (Hebrews 12:6).

"Well, there are all kinds of barriers in my life, but I'm not being scourged," you boast. Listen—if you are building barriers and are not being dealt with, if you are sinning and not being scourged, according to Hebrews 12:8, you are not truly a son or daughter of God. Even though you're at church every Sunday and Wednesday, if there is no table-turning in your life, if there is no removal of the barriers that so easily erect themselves between you and the Lord, you're not part of the family. The author of Hebrews says to rejoice if you are being scourged because through it, the Lord is removing blockades that would keep you from the joy He wants to produce in your life. How does He scourge us? Often, it's with a scourge made from "small cords" (verse 15) . . .

A number of years ago, I was making a shelf for Peter-John's toy trucks. Due to my lack of carpentry skills, tools, and materials, what should have been a ten-minute project turned into a five-hour ordeal. At long last, after the single shelf was in place, I went into the kitchen to pour myself a well-deserved cup of herb tea. No sooner had I sat down, however, than I heard an excruciatingly loud crash. Running into Peter's room, I found the shelf on the floor, surrounded by trucks and a huge piece of drywall. Sitting on top of the shelf was my then one-and-a-half-year-old daughter, Jessie.

"How could you do this, Jessie?" I said as tears began to roll down her chubby little cheeks. "I spent my whole day putting up this shelf, and now look at it!"

Peter-John was standing in the doorway, hands on his hips. I looked at him, and he looked at me, shook his head, and said, "Daddy, Jesus is going to have to spank you!"

Ouch! A small cord, scourging my heart!

Folks, it might be a son or daughter, a sermon, a letter, or a traffic ticket. It might be a rebuke from a neighbor, sickness, or a setback. But if you're smart, you'll recognize even seemingly minor incidents as small cords in the hand of the Lord and say, "Oh, Lord, teach me. Change me. Remake me. I receive this right now as correction from You."

What gives Jesus the right to do this? Not the scourge in His hand, but the scourge upon His back. You see, in John 19:1, we read of Pilate scourging Jesus—not with a scourge made of small cords, but with a flagellum, commonly called a "cat of nine tails."

The flagellum consisted of a wooden handle about twelve inches in length from which extended thirty strips of leather. On the end of these leather thongs were round iron balls the size of fishing weights. Pieces of glass and iron were embedded between the iron balls and the handle of the flagellum. When Jesus was scourged, the large metal balls caused welts to rise. After about the sixth blow, the pieces of glass and metal tore into those large welts, reducing His back, shoulders, and legs to the consistency of hamburger. Most often, a man would die from such a scourging. Jesus, however, absorbed the full thirty-nine blows.

Jesus took the beating in order to pay the price for my sin. "I did it," He says, "because I want the best for you and because I'm in love with you. Now allow Me to take small cords—irritations, rebukes, hard times—and use them to overturn anything in your temple that is ripping you off, anything that is placing a barricade between you and Me."

And when I submit to His scourging, what happens? Joy returns. Worship flows. Intimacy is restored. Don't despise His scourging, saint. Embrace it, and say, "Lord, as painful as this might be presently, I know You're doing a work in me to bring joy eventually."

When we get to heaven, we will finally see that all of the work the Lord did in us was necessary for us to enjoy eternity. Therefore, let us decide today, dear brothers and sisters, that not only personally, but as a church corporately, we will not allow barriers or barricades of any kind to prevent people from coming into the presence of God.

We must refuse to allow vain traditions, political persuasion, or cultural expectations to become barriers. We must guard against anything that would keep people from worshiping with us. We must keep the way clear for the Lion of Judah to come in regularly to drive out the moneychangers, overturn the tables, and keep this temple free.

3 Chapter 2 ended with belief based on miracles. Chapter 3 begins with a miracle based on belief as we see Jesus' encounter with Nicodemus, a man who sought Him for all the right reasons. As the story unfolds, we will observe Nicodemus and Jesus as they meet face-to-face, in verses 1–3, mind to mind, in verses 4–8, and heart to heart in verses 9–21.

John 3:1
There was a man of the Pharisees, named Nicodemus, a ruler of the Jews.

Three words come to mind in describing Nicodemus: religious, rich, and ruler. As a Pharisee, Nicodemus was extremely religious. We know this because the entire Pharisaical brotherhood, numbering six thousand, was dedicated to keeping the most minute regulations of the Old Testament law, as delineated by their fellow brotherhood, the scribes. It was the scribes' job to interpret the law and the Pharisees' job to implement it.

As for riches, we know Nicodemus was wealthy because in John 19, we read it was he who brought costly myrrh and aloes to the tomb of Jesus. Thus, it is not surprising to read that Jewish tradition names him as one of the three wealthiest men in the nation of Israel. Furthermore, the fact that Nicodemus is identified as a "ruler of the Jews" means he was a member of the elite seventy-member Jewish Supreme Court, the Sanhedrin—a position that would have guaranteed him the highest regard and respect.

John 3:2 (a)
The same came to Jesus by night . . .

It has been suggested that the reason Nicodemus came to Jesus at night was because he was afraid to be seen with Jesus in the light. I disagree with this assumption. You see, in those pre-air-conditioned days, the most enjoyable part of the day was the evening. For this reason, each home had a flat roof, easily accessible by a narrow, outside stairway along the side of the house. Rooftop conversations in the cool of the evening were common.

In addition to cooler temperatures, the evening hours provided a calm not found in the heat of the day. Keep in mind that this encounter took place during the Passover season. As a Pharisee and a member of the Sanhedrin, Nicodemus would have been teaching during this time, and Jesus would have been pressed by crowds familiar with His miracles. Thus, with the days during Passover particularly busy for both men, perhaps evening was the only time Nicodemus could make private contact with Jesus.

David meditated on the Lord in the night watches (Psalm 63:6). I like that, because sometimes, like Nicodemus, I feel pressed by the busyness of the day. In the "night watches," however, my mind is free for concentration and meditation. Just as a radio picks up dozens of extra stations at night, so my heart is sometimes extra-sensitive to Him when the sky is black, the air still, and the house quiet at last. I'm so glad Jesus is One who welcomes late-night company.

John 3:2 (b)
. . . and said unto him, Rabbi, we know that thou art a teacher come from God: for no man can do these miracles that thou doest, except God be with him.

Put yourself in Nicodemus' sandals. He didn't know he was talking with the Son of God. He had simply heard that the thirty-year-old Carpenter who had raised a ruckus in the temple was now performing miracles the like of which he had never seen. Nicodemus felt he had to meet this Man.

John 3:3
Jesus answered and said unto him, Verily, verily, I say unto thee, Except a man be born again, he cannot see the kingdom of God.

Jesus could have answered Nicodemus by saying, "Oh, you're aware of My miracles! Pretty powerful, huh? Quite incredible, eh?" But instead, Jesus cut through the flattery and immediately drew Nicodemus' attention to the kingdom of God. The kingdom of God has past, present, and future application. If you don't understand this, your interpretation of Scripture will be muddled and your understanding unclear.

The past application of the kingdom of God is based upon the realization that when Jesus walked on earth as a Man, the kingdom was present on earth (Luke 10:9). The miracles and signs He ministered on this planet were but sneak previews of what the kingdom will be in its future state. The present application of the kingdom of God is based upon the understanding that it is presently not external but internal (John 17:21). The future application of the kingdom of God is based upon the belief that when Jesus Christ returns, we will see not only the internal manifestations of the kingdom, but the external aspects as well (Isaiah 11:6).

Thus, in essence, Jesus said to Nicodemus, "You'll not see the kingdom presently unless you realize who I am. You'll not experience it internally unless you open your heart. You'll not be there eternally unless you're born again."

John 3:4
Nicodemus saith unto him, How can a man be born when he is old? can he enter the second time into his mother's womb, and be born?

Notice Nicodemus did not ask, "*Why* should a man be born again?" He asked, "*How* can a man be born again?" No doubt, Nicodemus knew something no one else knew. That is, although others looked at him as a respected ruler, he saw in himself frailty and failure. Although others looked to him as someone spiritual, he looked at himself and saw a sinner. I wonder how many nights Nicodemus had fallen asleep with the unspoken desire in his heart to begin life all over again; to do things differently—to love God more fervently, to serve his family more humbly, to treat people more gently. Oh, for a fresh start! And here was this Rabbi, offering him just that chance. Truly, I believe his inquiry was not the challenge of a hardened skeptic, but the question of a wide-eyed seeker.

John 3:5–7
Jesus answered, Verily, verily, I say unto thee, Except a man be born of water and of the Spirit, he cannot enter into the kingdom of God. That which is born of the flesh is flesh; and that which is born of the Spirit is spirit. Marvel not that I said unto thee, Ye must be born again.

To understand the meaning of "water and Spirit," travel back with me to the Book of beginnings, the Book of Genesis. I, along with many others, believe that between Genesis 1:1 and 1:2, Lucifer was thrown out of heaven and cast down to earth, causing a tilting of the axis and cataclysmic changes upon our planet. These changes resulted in darkness, formlessness, and emptiness. Genesis 1:2, therefore, begins an account not of

the creation, but the *re*-creation, the rebirth of planet Earth. How did God re-create the earth? The Spirit of God moved upon the face of the waters (Genesis 1:2). What does water refer to in Scripture? The Word of God (John 15:3; Ephesians 5:26).

God re-created the earth by the Spirit and His Word. How does He re-create us? The same way. When the Word of God, energized and empowered by the Spirit of God, speaks to our dark, formless, empty lives—a new birth, a re-creation takes place. When the Word and Spirit work in tandem to draw us to the Father by way of His Son, we are reborn.

John 3:8
The wind bloweth where it listeth, and thou hearest the sound thereof, but canst not tell whence it cometh, and whither it goeth: so is every one that is born of the Spirit.

Perhaps at this point in their conversation, a cool breeze arose. "The Spirit is like the wind," Jesus said. "You can't predict it. You can't understand it. But you can take advantage of it." It's as if Jesus said, "Put up your sail of faith, Nicodemus, and let the wind of the Spirit carry you into the kingdom."

John 3:9, 10
Nicodemus answered and said unto him, How can these things be? Jesus answered and said unto him, Art thou a master of Israel, and knowest not these things?

The original language intimates that Nicodemus was not only "*a* master of Israel," but "*the* master of Israel"—which is why Jesus was amazed that Nicodemus, the primary spiritual teacher of Israel, would have such a difficult time understanding Him. You see, Jesus' reference to the wind should have drawn Nicodemus' mind to a passage well-known by every Jewish scholar: Ezekiel 37. . . .

After showing him a valley of dry bones, the Lord asked Ezekiel, "How can these bones live again?"

"I don't know," answered Ezekiel.

The Lord then instructed him to prophesy to the bones. Ezekiel did so and the bones connected together to form lifeless human bodies. Then, the Lord told him to prophesy to the wind, or ruwach in Hebrew. Ruwach is also translated "spirit." Ezekiel did so and the dead bones came to life. They were, in essence, reborn.

Prior to this account in Ezekiel, God promised His people a new heart and a new spirit (Ezekiel 18:31). Known as the New Covenant, it was the promise with which Old Testament scholars like Nicodemus were most familiar. It was the hope for which they longed. And in a rooftop conversation that took place during this breezy Jerusalem evening, the Son of God began to explain to Nicodemus how all of the pieces fit together: the Spirit and water; dry bones and a desert wind; the New Covenant and a new life.

John 3:11, 12
Verily, verily, I say unto thee, We speak that we do know, and testify that we have seen; and ye receive not our witness. If I have told you earthly things, and ye believe not, how shall ye believe, if I tell you of heavenly things?

Perhaps it was with a heavy heart that Jesus said, "Nicodemus, you don't understand because you haven't been listening. John the Baptist came as a voice crying in the wilderness to prepare hearts for My coming. The law and the prophets all pointed to Me."

John 3:13–15
And no man hath ascended up to heaven, but he that came down from heaven, even the Son of man which is in heaven. And as Moses lifted up the serpent in the wilderness, even so must the Son of man be lifted up: That whosoever believeth in him should not perish, but have eternal life.

Brass is the metal of judgment. Jesus, the Lamb of God, became like the brass snake of Numbers 21 when He was lifted up on the Cross to absorb the judgment that should have been ours. Here, He says to Nicodemus. "Look to Me and you will be born again. It's so simple."

John 3:16
For God so loved the world, that he gave his only begotten Son, that whosoever believeth in him should not perish, but have everlasting life.

"In twenty-five words or less, tell us why your mother should be Mother of the Year," reads the contest rules. "In twenty-five words or less, explain the importance of the French Revolution upon the economic and social structures of the thirteen colonies," reads the test question. Now, although I probably wouldn't have much trouble with the second question, the first one would be extremely difficult for me because the more we know about any given subject, the harder it is to

communicate our thoughts succinctly. Not so with Jesus. John 3:16 is exactly twenty-five words long, and in these twenty-five words, Jesus communicates the Father's heart, the Father's plan, and the Father's will. . . .

• His heart: He loved the world.
• His plan: He gave His only begotten Son.
• His will: Whosoever believes in Him should not perish, but have everlasting life.

Although I know it is somewhat coincidental, I find it interesting that in our English translation of this verse, the middle word is Son. It is no coincidence, however, that those who have experienced God's presence most powerfully are those who have made the Son the center of their lives. Just as Jesus is the center of the greatest verse in all Scripture, He must be central in our hearts and lives if they are to have meaning, purpose, and impact (Ephesians 1:10). This means that any person, pursuit, or passion in my life that cannot be centered on Jesus Christ has no place in my life.

Surrounding the word "Son" in this verse, there are nine other key words: God, loved, world, gave, whosoever, believeth, perish, have, and life. If you want to be really blessed, meditate on John 3:16 every day for ten days, giving emphasis to a different word each day . . .

• For *God* so loved the world . . .
• For God so *loved* the world . . .
• For God so loved the *world* . . .

Perhaps you memorized this verse when you were three years old. But I believe it will come alive for you in new ways as you contemplate the enormity of its simplicity.

John 3:17
For God sent not his Son into the world to condemn the world; but that the world through him might be saved.

Jesus came to this world not to come down on people, but to reach out to people. God sent His Son into the world not to point His finger at the world, but to embrace the world and draw it to Himself.

An old legend tells of a traveler attempting to circle the globe who found himself trapped in quicksand. As he slowly sank, Confucius came by and said, "Confucius say, it is evident man should avoid such situations." And he went on his way.

Mohammed came by and said, "Alas, it is the will of Allah." And he went on his way.

Buddha came by, and said, "Let this man's dilemma be an illustration for many." And he went on his way.

Krishna came by and said, "Better luck next time." And he went on his way.

Jesus Christ came by, reached out to the man, and pulled him out.

You see, the unique thing about our Lord is that, while all others tell us what we must do to reach up to heaven, He alone reaches down from heaven and pulls us out of the quicksand of sin. God sent not His Son into the world to condemn the world, to give us some cute spiritual sayings, or to make us feel bad because of our spiritual inadequacy. No, the purpose of God in sending His Son was singular: to save us.

John 3:18–21

He that believeth on him is not condemned: but he that believeth not is condemned already, because he hath not believed in the name of the only begotten Son of God. And this is the condemnation, that light is come into the world, and men loved darkness rather than light, because their deeds were evil. For every one that doeth evil hateth the light, neither cometh to the light, lest his deeds should be reproved. But he that doeth truth cometh to the light, that his deeds may be made manifest, that they are wrought in God.

Why don't people come to the light? It is not because they don't believe the gospel intellectually or because they struggle with it philosophically. Please remember this the next time you're involved in a discussion with those who attempt to undermine your faith. The issue is never evolution, Cain's wife, or the Immaculate Conception. According to Jesus, the one and only reason people don't come to the Light is because they prefer darkness.

John 3:22–24

After these things came Jesus and his disciples into the land of Judaea; and there he tarried with them, and baptized. And John also was baptizing in Aenon near to Salim, because there was much water there: and they came, and were baptized. For John was not yet cast into prison.

Why did John baptize in Aenon? Was it because he had received heavenly instructions to minister there? No. Was it because he was fulfilling Old Testament prophecy? No. John baptized in Aenon "because there was much water there."

Too often, we make finding the will of God very difficult. I believe we would do well to demystify the process of discovering what God wants us to do. John simply went where the water was. His location was perfectly suited to what God had instructed him to do. I am reminded of Chuck Smith's account of how he determined it was God's will he go to Costa Mesa . . .

In the early 1970s, Calvary Chapel was located in the middle of nowhere—smack in the center of a huge bean field. In the ensuing twenty years, not only did the church explode numerically, but the Costa Mesa area grew to the point that Calvary Chapel is now sitting on some very valuable real estate. Chuck has often been asked if he had received a vision, a word of prophecy, or a special sign to pastor the little church in the sticks. And he just laughs as he replies, "I took the church in Costa Mesa because I like to surf and it was the closest available church to the beach!"

Augustine said it best when he essentially said, "Love God with all of your heart and do whatever you please." If you truly love God with all of your heart, your desires will be in harmony with His will. Therefore, I encourage you to trust the Lord to use your desires, interests, and abilities in His naturally supernatural way to bring joy to your heart and glory to Himself. Whether it's for baptizing or for surfing, go where the water is!

John 3:25, 26

Then there arose a question between some of John's disciples and the Jews about purifying. And they came unto John, and said unto him, Rabbi, he that was with thee beyond Jordan, to whom thou barest witness, behold, the same baptizeth, and all men come to him.

At this point, John was presented with news from his disciples that multitudes were coming to Jesus for baptism. But John's disciples missed the point. What they perceived as competition to John's mission, John saw as completion of his ministry.

John 3:27

John answered and said, A man can receive nothing, except it be given him from heaven.

John knew he had nothing apart from God. Any abilities, gifts, or ministry he possessed came directly as a gift from his heavenly Father.

So, too, if there is any area in which you excel, it is solely because God sovereignly and graciously gave you the necessary desires, abilities, and provisions. Truly, God uses and blesses us not *because* of who we are but *in spite* of who we are!

John 3:28, 29
Ye yourselves bear me witness, that I said, I am not the Christ, but that I am sent before him. He that hath the bride is the bridegroom: but the friend of the bridegroom, which standeth and heareth him, rejoiceth greatly because of the bridegroom's voice: this my joy therefore is fulfilled.

When John first "met" Jesus, both were in their mother's wombs. John leapt for joy when Mary, pregnant with Jesus, entered the room (Luke 1:41). Here in our text, we see that, at the zenith of his ministry, John still finds his joy in the sound of Jesus' voice. To explain the reason for his ministry and the basis for his joy, John used an analogy very familiar to his disciples. You see, wedding custom in John's day dictated it was the best man, the "friend of the bridegroom," who invited the guests to the wedding, made preparations for the wedding, and finally, upon completion of the wedding, escorted the bride and groom into the bridal chamber. Thus, it was the voice of the bridegroom signaling to him that everything was okay within the chamber that brought joy to the heart of the best man.

Do you know when joy is fulfilled? It is not when we get something *from* the Lord, or do something *for* the Lord, but when we hear the voice *of* the Lord. If you are expecting your joy to be fulfilled through a nicer husband, faster car, or better job, you are headed for disaster. If you are caught up in thinking, *If I can move to this place, teach that Bible study, or sing with the other worship team; if I can just be effective here, or used there,* then *I will be joyful*—you are headed for disappointment and despair. But if you spend time with the Lord, reading His Word, and simply listening for His voice, your joy will be fulfilled. If you are a baby Christian like John in the womb, you will leap for joy at the sound of His voice. And if you are a seasoned saint like John in the desert, your joy will be full when you realize that what you longed for all along is found in Him.

John 3:30
He must increase, but I must decrease.

He must increase, but I must decrease: seven words which capture the essence of true ministry.

For topical study of John 3:30 entitled "Three Major Musts," turn to page 462.

John 3:31, 32 (a)
He that cometh from above is above all: he that is of the earth is earthly, and speaketh of the earth: he that cometh from heaven is above all. And what he hath seen and heard, that he testifieth . . .

Jesus didn't speak theoretically. He spoke experientially. When Moses lifted up the brass snake, Jesus was there. When Ezekiel prophesied to the wind, Jesus was there. Thus, Jesus doesn't teach from secondhand information. His is a firsthand, eyewitness account.

John 3:32 (b)
. . . and no man receiveth his testimony.

God says, "Rejoice evermore. In everything give thanks. Be ye holy, for I am holy." But mankind refuses to receive His testimony, saying, "I can't rejoice evermore because I'm emotionally starved. I can't give thanks because I came from a dysfunctional family. I can't be holy because I'm co-dependent."

John 3:33
He that hath received his testimony hath set to his seal that God is true.

The one who does receive His testimony will proclaim loudly with John, "God is true!" for the one who believes God's commandments are His "enablements" will find God true every time. The one who refuses to excuse sin with psychological jargon and instead steps out in faith to "flee youthful lusts," to "reckon the old man dead unto sin," to "judge not" will experience God's faithfulness at every step.

John 3:34
For he whom God hath sent speaketh the words of God: for God giveth not the Spirit by measure unto him.

In the Old Testament, it was with limitation that the Spirit of God was given to men. Such was not the case with Jesus. He was totally and completely Spirit-filled.

John 3:35, 36 (a)
The Father loveth the Son, and hath given all things into his hand. He that believeth on the Son hath everlasting life . . .

The Son being central to the Father's heart, plan, and will (Ephesians 1:10), it is on the basis of belief in Jesus that we are given not only eternal life but *everlasting* life—life that begins the moment we believe on Him.

John 3:36 (b)
. . . and he that believeth not the Son shall not see life; but the wrath of God abideth on him.

Why does the wrath of God abide on the one who does not believe on His Son? Because he who does not believe is trampling on the sacrificial blood of His only begotten Son. This world is sinking fast in the quicksand of sin. God does not condemn us for being in that place—only for refusing to reach out to the nail-pierced hand offering to pull us out.

THREE MAJOR MUSTS
A Topical Study of
John 3:7, 14, 30

Those who study such things tell us that the average person makes three thousand decisions a day. The majority of these decisions are admittedly inconsequential. But in our text, we are presented with three decisions that are eternally essential. They're not maybes. They're *musts*. . . .

The Must of the Sinner

Marvel not that I said unto thee, Ye must be born again.   John 3:7

George Whitefield, mighty preacher of the Colonial Era, was asked why he always preached that man must be born again. "Why do I preach you must be born again?" said Whitefield? "Because you must be born again!"

Gang, the message of Jesus Christ is not about giving us maxims on how to be better people. It's about seeing the Spirit of God birth something new in our lives. It's not about reformation. It's about regeneration.

Two courtiers argued incessantly over whether a man could be made a gentleman, or whether he had to be born one. Finally, in frustration, the king gave each of them some money and sent them out to settle their dispute. The courtier who held the viewpoint that a man could be made a gentleman walked into an inn, where he ordered a cup of hot chocolate. After a few minutes, in walked a cat, dressed like a waiter, carrying a cup of hot chocolate between his front paws.

"Oho!" said the courtier to the innkeeper. "Here's my answer, for if a common cat can be trained to be a waiter, certainly a man can be trained to be a gentleman. Sir, I want to buy your cat."

"That will be one thousand pounds," said the innkeeper.

"No problem," said the courtier as he paid the innkeeper and went on his way.

As the excited courtier traveled toward the palace, his opponent got word of the cat. "Oh no" he said, "how can I argue my point against a cat who can serve hot chocolate?" But as he headed dejectedly toward the palace, his eye caught something in a shop window that pleased him greatly.

"Could I buy what's in the window?" he said.

"Gladly!" answered the shopkeeper as he put the courtier's purchase in a box.

So it was that both courtiers arrived at the palace within moments of each other. "Do you have your answer?" asked the king.

"Yes," said the fellow with the cat. "Here is proof that a man can be made into a gentleman," he said as the cat walked in, bringing the king a cup of hot chocolate. At this point, the other courtier opened his box and released twelve mice. As the mice scampered across the floor, the cat dropped the cup and saucer, and took off after them—providing conclusive proof that one cannot be made a gentleman because he will eventually return to his baser instincts.

It's true, folks. You can wear a tie, go to church, and learn how to be a Christian. You can sing in the choir and take Communion. You can go through the motions, but sooner or later, a mouse will run across your path and your real nature will suddenly dominate you unless you're born again. That's why Jesus wasn't talking about reformation. He was talking about regeneration when He said, "You *must* be born again."

The Must of the Savior

And as Moses lifted up the serpent in the wilderness, even so must the Son of man be lifted up.   John 3:14

As the children of Israel wandered in the wilderness, they grew tired of the manna God had provided for them. No doubt, they prepared it every way possible: bamanna splits, bamanna bread, manna-cotti—but finally said, "Manna-live! We're tired of this!" Poisonous snakes began to smite them as they complained and grumbled and murmured, and they began to die by the thousands.

Seeking the Lord for a remedy, Moses was instructed to make a brass snake on a brass pole and erect it in the center of the camp. Whoever looked upon the brass snake would not die. When Moses told this to the people, some must have said, "What kind of a cure can there be in a brass snake on a brass pole?" But those who simply looked in faith upon the snake were spared (Numbers 21).

Jesus Christ was made a snake when He was made sin for you and me. Not only have we been bitten by the snake of sin—we are ourselves the snakes. We have hurt other people. We have wounded them, lied to them, and cheated them. But here is the Good News: Jesus said, "Because you've been bitten by the snake of sin and because you are also the snakes through which sin is unleashed, I will become like you, yet without venom. I will go to the Cross in order that you who have been bitten will be healed, in order that you who are biting will be forgiven. If you will just look on Me and believe in Me, you will be saved. I must be lifted up. There is no other way."

The Must of the Servant

He must increase, but I must decrease.   John 3:30

Like John, we must get out of the way and talk to people about Jesus, focus our attention on Him, and live for the purpose of sharing Him. In other words, we must decrease.

If I don't pull in a big salary, so be it. If I don't play for the Forty-Niners, so be it. If I don't have a nice house, I don't care. I must decrease so that I can be about the business of sharing *Him.*

Jesus said, "If you die to self, you'll find life" (see Matthew 10:39). Therefore, the more we spend on our hobbies, pursuits, and pleasures, the more miserable we'll be. But the more we say, "I must decrease and *He* must increase," the more clearly we'll hear His voice and the greater our joy will be.

John 4:1, 2
When therefore the Lord knew how the Pharisees had heard that Jesus made and baptized more disciples than John, (Though Jesus himself baptized not, but his disciples,)

Since the word "but" can also be translated "except," the idea here could be that, although Jesus did not baptize the masses, He did baptize His disciples. Or it could mean His disciples were doing the baptizing. Either way, people were responding to Jesus' ministry.

John 4:3
He left Judaea, and departed again into Galilee.

As the number of Jesus' followers multiplied, the Pharisees realized that their enemy was no longer John the Baptist, but an itinerant Preacher from Galilee. At this point, not wanting to get involved in confrontation with the Pharisees, Jesus decided to go north to Galilee.

John 4:4
And he must needs go through Samaria.

Israel is divided into three regions: Judea in the south, Galilee in the north, and Samaria in the middle. When a Jew wanted to go from Judea to Galilee, the most direct route led through Samaria. But good Jews would never go that way. They would go through Perea on the other side of the Jordan River. Why? Because there was such tension between the Samaritans and the Jews, that Jews uttered the word "Samaritan" only as a curse word. Why were the Samaritans so despised? In the year 722 B.C., the Assyrians invaded Israel from the north and carried the majority of the people from the ten northern tribes into captivity. The Assyrians then sent some of their people to Israel, where they intermarried with the Jews not taken into captivity. The marriages that took place between the Assyrians and the Jews produced the Samaritans— half-breeds in the eyes of the Jews. Barred from the temple, the Samaritans built their own temple on Mount Gerizim. Although they still believed in the Pentateuch—the first five books of Moses—they changed the stories. The Garden of Eden was on Mount Gerizim. Noah's ark landed on Mount Gerizim. And Abraham offered Isaac—you guessed it—on Mount Gerizim.

As Jesus headed north to Galilee, He said, "I'm going straight through Samaria." Why? Because there was a divine appointment awaiting Him there. The following story is another classic illustration of how to witness and share our faith. Contrast this fourth chapter of John with John 3. In John 3, Jesus talks to a religious man named Nicodemus. In John 4, He talks to an immoral woman whose name is not given. In John 3, Nicodemus is a calm contemplator. In John 4, the woman is a fiery debater. In John 3, Jesus speaks with Nicodemus in the cool of the night. In John 4, Jesus speaks with the woman in the heat of the day. In John 3, Nicodemus initiates the conversation. In John 4, Jesus begins the dialogue. For you who are interested in personal evangelism, there is much to chew on as you see the different methods our Lord employs to draw people to Himself.

John 4:5, 6
Then cometh he to a city of Samaria, which is called Sychar, near to the parcel of ground that Jacob gave to his son Joseph. Now Jacob's well was there.

Jacob's well still stands. One hundred fifty feet deep, it's one of few verifiably authentic biblical sites. But if you get the opportunity to visit Jacob's well, take your helmet, as it's located in the war-torn West Bank.

John 4:6 (a)
Jesus therefore, being wearied with his journey . . .

Hebrews 2:11 says Jesus was made like unto his brethren—like you. He knows how it feels to be bone-tired. I'm glad about that because I feel that way not infrequently. The battles rage. The problems mount. The struggles continue. And I just feel weary. Yet it is often at the point when we are weary or feeling weak that we will be used to the greatest degree (2 Corinthians 12:10).

John 4:6 (b)
. . . sat thus on the well: and it was about the sixth hour.

Women typically drew water in the morning or in the evening. But this woman, for reasons we shall see, wanted to avoid the other women of the community. Consequently, she would wait until the hot, noontime hour—when everyone else would be resting or eating—to make her journey to the well.

John 4:7, 8
There cometh a woman of Samaria to draw water: Jesus saith unto her, Give me to drink. (For his disciples were gone away unto the city to buy meat.)

Jesus—the One who fed five thousand on the hillside by the Sea of Galilee with a few loaves and fishes, the One who fed four thousand shortly thereafter, the One who is the Provider of all good gifts—is hungry. And what does He do? He sends His disciples into town to pick up some food. You'll never once see Jesus perform a miracle solely to satisfy His own need, desire, or hunger. "Turn these stones into bread," Satan taunted after Jesus had fasted forty days in the wilderness (see Matthew 4:3). But Jesus' refusal to do so causes me to analyze my own prayers and consider how often I make requests of the Lord for my own satisfaction versus how often I pray for the needs of others and the glory of the kingdom.

John 4:9 (a)
Then saith the woman of Samaria unto him, How is it that thou, being a Jew, askest drink of me . . .

Why isn't Jesus a gentleman here? Why doesn't He say, "Let *Me* draw water for you?" It seems that would be the right thing to do. In actuality, however, Jesus is demonstrating a very important principle. "Give to Me," He says to the woman—not because He wants the water, but because He wants her heart. He wants to see her saved.

As believers, oftentimes we err on this point. We think, *What can I do for other people to find a way of entry into witnessing or sharing?* While there certainly is a place for that, often letting people do something for you—humbling yourself and allowing them to make an investment in or give assistance to you—is the most effective way to reach them. Jesus knew that wherever a person's treasure is, there will his heart be also (Matthew 6:21). If someone shares with you something of his "treasure," something of his heart will be sure to follow—affording you the opportunity of reaching it with the gospel. Our tendency is to want to be helpers rather than "help-ees." We want to be the givers because it's truly more blessed to give than to receive. But, as Jesus shows us, sometimes it's imperative to receive in order that another might come into the kingdom.

The classic biblical example of this principle is found in Numbers 10. As Moses prepares to lead the people of Israel on their journey toward the Promised Land, he invites his Gentile brother-in-law to join them. "Hobab, come with us. It's a good land to which we are going, and good things will happen to you if you travel in our company."

"Sorry," said Hobab. "I'm going back to my own people."

It was then that Moses changed his tactic. "Hobab," he said, "we need you. You understand the wilderness. You can be our eyes. Would you help us?"

Hobab agreed and ended up in the Promised Land with the people of Israel (Judges 4:11).

How important it is that we don't come across simply as those who say, "We're going to heaven. We're great. Join us." Rather, sometimes we need to say, "We need you. The talents you have and the abilities you've been given would be such an asset to us."

John 4:9 (b)
. . . which am a woman of Samaria? for the Jews have no dealings with the Samaritans.

This woman had two strikes against her: She was a Samaritan and she was a woman. In Jesus' day, rabbis refrained from talking to women in public to such an extent that even if one saw his own wife on the street, he would not acknowledge her. That is why this Samaritan woman was so shocked by Jesus' request.

John 4:10
Jesus answered and said unto her, If thou knewest the gift of God, and who it is that saith to thee, Give me to drink; thou wouldest have asked of him, and he would have given thee living water.

Jesus had a way of masterfully reaching the people with whom He shared. To the woman at the well, He spoke of living water. To aging Nicodemus, He talked about being born again. To the blind man, He identified Himself as the Light of the world (John 9:5). To sisters grieving the death of their brother, He was the Resurrection and the Life (John 11:25). To fishermen, He issued an invitation to become fishers of men (Matthew 4:19).

John 4:11 (a)
The woman saith unto him, Sir . . .

I like this! The disdain the Jews had for the Samaritans being mutual, in verse 9, the woman

called Jesus a Jew. Here, however, she elevates Him to "Sir."

John 4:11 (b)–14
. . . thou hast nothing to draw with, and the well is deep: from whence then hast thou that living water? Art thou greater than our father Jacob, which gave us the well, and drank thereof himself, and his children, and his cattle? Jesus answered and said unto her, Whosoever drinketh of this water shall thirst again: But whosoever drinketh of the water that I shall give him shall never thirst; but the water that I shall give him shall be in him a well of water springing up into everlasting life.

The woman was thinking in terms of material, physical water, when Jesus was, in fact, speaking of the eternal, spiritual realm. How often we make the same mistake today. "The kingdom is about prosperity, Cadillacs, and third homes," thunder so many preachers. But Jesus said whoever drinks of this water shall thirst again—because nothing material will ever satiate or satisfy the thirst of the soul. When believers get thirsty, sometimes it's because they have drifted back to the old watering holes. They've pulled away from the Word, from ministry, from the things of the kingdom—and they end up dry as bones, as miserable as fish out of water.

John 4:15, 16
The woman saith unto him, Sir, give me this water, that I thirst not, neither come hither to draw. Jesus saith unto her, Go, call thy husband, and come hither.

Why did Jesus ask her to call her husband? Because there is no true conversion without conviction.

John 4:17, 18
The woman answered and said, I have no husband. Jesus said unto her, Thou hast well said, I have no husband: For thou hast had five husbands; and he whom thou now hast is not thy husband: in that saidst thou truly.

Notice the skill with which the Physician of our soul handles the scalpel of conviction. "You said well," He said. He found something to approve. Jesus shows grace and truth. I love Him for that because that's the way He works with me. Jesus didn't come to condemn the world but to save the world. That's grace. Yet, because there can be no salvation without conviction, He always speaks the truth.

Notice also Jesus didn't say, "You've had five

husbands. Let's talk about Husband number one: Sam. Then, we'll talk about why you left George in session two. Come next week, and in the third session, we'll talk about Pete. In session four, we'll discuss Harry." No, it didn't take Jesus five sessions to discuss the five husbands. He didn't delve into codependency or into the woman's past iniquities. Yes, Jesus revealed her sin—but He didn't revel in it. Big difference. I think it is dangerous for people who mean well to start reveling in the past sin of another—talking about it, exploring it, pursuing it. Jesus does not model this for any minister of the gospel or for any servant of the kingdom. He simply says, "I know you're a sinner. You know you're a sinner. Now, let's go on from there."

John 4:19
The woman saith unto him, Sir, I perceive that thou art a prophet.

Now the woman refers to Jesus as a prophet. As her knowledge of Him expands, her esteem for Him grows.

John 4:20 (a)
Our fathers worshipped in this mountain . . .

The woman is about to ask a hot theological question of her day. And the same thing will happen to you when you share with someone who feels the gentle hand of conviction upon him. You'll hear questions like, "Did Adam have a belly button? Where did Cain get his wife? How could all of the animals fit on the ark?"

To which mountain is the Samaritan woman referring? To Mount Gerizim—where the Samaritan temple was built.

John 4:20 (b), 21
. . . and ye say, that in Jerusalem is the place where men ought to worship. Jesus saith unto her, Woman, believe me, the hour cometh, when ye shall neither in this mountain, nor yet at Jerusalem, worship the Father.

The woman talked about "our fathers." Jesus talked about *the* Father.

John 4:22
Ye worship ye know not what: we know what we worship: for salvation is of the Jews.

Why is salvation of—or through—the Jews? Because Jesus was a Jew, and salvation is through Him.

John 4:23 (a)
But the hour cometh, and now is, when the true worshipers shall worship the Father in spirit and in truth . . .

Could it be that the woman was not simply raising a theological question? Could it be she was also revealing a subconscious desire within? Could it be that her question was not meant to sidestep the issue of her five husbands, but that she was saying, "I want to worship—but where? And how? What does it mean to really worship?"

When I was growing up, people basically had to choose between worshiping the Lord in spirit, and worshiping the Lord in truth. If they wanted to worship the Lord in spirit, they would go to churches where they would hear statements like, "Wow! Wasn't that a great service? The Spirit was moving so powerfully, the preacher didn't even have time to give a message!" If they wanted to worship the Lord in truth, they would go to churches that seemed to believe that the Trinity consisted of God the Father, God the Son, and God the Holy Bible—churches where there was no room for the Spirit to work spontaneously or for the gifts to be exercised congregationally. That's what's neat about the time in which we live. There is an understanding that God must be worshiped in Spirit *and* truth. They flow together. It's not either/or. "The *words* which I speak are *spirit* and life," Jesus said (see John 6:63). It's true—as we take in the *Word*, we grow in the *Spirit*.

John 4:23 (b)
. . . for the Father seeketh such to worship him.

The Father *seeks* worshipers. If this verse isn't underlined in your Bible, underline it now. Whenever you feel far from God, don't try to find Him. Let Him find you. He can find you a lot easier than you can find Him, so just start worshiping. With bended knee, lifted hand, and open heart, embrace Him through your praise. This is a real key for your Christian walk. When you feel God's a million miles away, worship. If it's in your car during lunch hour, if it's locked in your bathroom when everyone else is still asleep, if it's walking down the street—whatever it might take, get away and start worshiping. Start acknowledging the greatness and goodness of God. The Father is seeking those who do.

John 4:24
God is a Spirit: and they that worship him must worship him in spirit and in truth.

The combination is unbeatable. Worship Him in spirit *and* in truth.

John 4:25, 26
The woman saith unto him, I know that Messias cometh, which is called Christ: when he is come, he will tell us all things. Jesus saith unto her, I that speak unto thee am he.

The first of Jesus' Ego Eimi (I AM) statements, the word "he" in verse 26 is absent in the original text. Some folks have the audacity to say Jesus never claimed to be Messiah. Turn them to this verse. Watch our Master as He witnesses. First, He establishes contact with the Samaritan. Then He stimulates curiosity by saying, "You've come to draw water; you're thirsty; let Me tell you about the living water available to you." Finally, He keeps focused. She wants to get off into a theological discussion. But He brings the conversation right back around again, saying that Jerusalem and Gerizim are not the issue, that her fathers are not the point. He brings the conversation back to Himself.

John 4:27
And upon this came his disciples, and marvelled that he talked with the woman: yet no man said, What seekest thou? or, Why talkest thou with her?

The disciples marveled but said nothing because, after spending time with Jesus, they had come to expect the unexpected.

John 4:28 (a)
The woman then left her waterpot . . .

Why did she leave her water pot? I suggest two possible reasons. The first is that it was an illustration. That which was previously important to her no longer mattered. Second, perhaps she left her water pot out of appreciation. "You have told me about my sin and my need," said the woman. "You have told me about true worship. You want a cup of water? Take the whole pot. Take everything I have. It's Yours." When people truly get saved, they quit asking, "What can I get *from* God?" and ask instead, "What can I give *to* God?"

John 4:28 (b)
. . . and went her way into the city, and saith to the men,

You'll always know when someone's truly born again because, like a newborn baby, he'll start crying—proclaiming the Good News of the gospel to all who will listen. Why did the woman talk

only to the men? Most likely it was because the other women would have nothing to do with her.

John 4:29
Come, see a man, which told me all things that ever I did: is not this the Christ?

From "Jew" to "Sir" to "Prophet" to "Christ," we see the woman's understanding of Jesus expanding after spending only a few moments with Him.

John 4:30
Then they went out of the city, and came unto him.

This woman, whose morality was suspect at best, said, "There's a Man who told me everything I've ever done." Thus, it was, no doubt, with a certain degree of apprehension they wanted to find out just how much He knew about them as well.

John 4:31–33
In the mean while his disciples prayed him, saying, Master, eat. But he said unto them, I have meat to eat that ye know not of. Therefore said the disciples one to another, Hath any man brought him ought to eat?

When the disciples arrived with food, Jesus was no longer hungry because He had experienced revival, refreshment, and renewal as a result of reaching out.

John 4:34
Jesus saith unto them, My meat is to do the will of him that sent me, and to finish his work.

"My meat," said Jesus—"that which sustains, refreshes, and nourishes Me—is to do My Father's will and to finish His work."

John 4:35
Say not ye, There are yet four months, and then cometh harvest? behold, I say unto you, Lift up your eyes, and look on the fields; for they are white already to harvest.

See with me in your mind's eye the Samaritan men to whom the women had witnessed coming toward Jesus, dressed in turbans and robes of white. What harvest was white and ready to reap? To which harvest was Jesus referring? The field of the Samaritans. The same is true today. The people in our culture who are ignored and forgotten, those no one else wants to be around, those others we pass by are the ones who are ripe for the picking. We say, "How can we win the quarterback of the high-school football team or the president of the company for Christ?" But the real action lies with the Samaritans—the people others aren't interested in, the people who won't help our business or gain us a reputation in ministry. I am not negating the importance of sharing with those whom the world esteems highly. Yet here we see our Lord's wisdom in gleaning from a field that was already ripe.

John 4:36–38
And he that reapeth receiveth wages, and gathereth fruit unto life eternal: that both he that soweth and he that reapeth may rejoice together. And herein is that saying true, One soweth, and another reapeth. I sent you to reap that whereon ye bestowed no labour: other men laboured, and ye are entered into their labours.

Because the Samaritans were a broken people, despicable in the eyes of the Jews, barred from the temple—the soil for their salvation had already been tilled and cultivated. Truly, they were ready for harvest. The same is still true today. The harvest is ready. Go out and pick it.

"He that winneth souls is wise," Solomon declared (Proverbs 11:30). Daniel said the one who turns many to righteousness shall shine as the stars forever (Daniel 12:3). Jesus says he who reaps presently shall receive wages eternally.

"I don't care about that," you say. "Heaven is too far away. I've got enough problems now. I have to mow my lawn, clean my house, buy a car." If those are your priorities, if that's what you're living for, if that's where your energy is going, you will become exhausted. Those pursuits will not fulfill you here on earth—and when you get to heaven, you'll be bankrupt.

"But it's so tough to witness," you say.

Find the Samaritans. Reach out to the unlovely, to the unlovable, to the ignored person where you work. Reach out and you'll see they're prime for harvest.

John 4:39
And many of the Samaritans of that city believed on him for the saying of the woman, which testified, He told me all that ever I did.

Previously, Jesus used masterful metaphors, perfect parallels in His gentle yet convicting presentation of the gospel. But the woman? She was simple and untrained—just like me. While I long to be more like Jesus as a masterful witness, I also realize that even in very simple, straight-

forward testimony, there will be fruit. I don't need to be intimidated when I can't answer questions or come up with the right illustrations. I can join the Samaritan woman and say, "Come and see," for Scripture records that *many* believed because of her simple testimony.

John 4:40, 41
So when the Samaritans were come unto him, they besought him that he would tarry with them: and he abode there two days. And many more believed because of his own word.

Many believed because of the simple testimony of the woman and many *more* believed when Jesus Himself began to share more fully the Scriptures and the truths of the kingdom.

John 4:42
And said unto the woman, Now we believe, not because of thy saying: for we have heard him ourselves, and know that this is indeed the Christ, the Saviour of the world.

"Jew," "Sir," "Prophet," "Christ," and finally "Savior of the world." The Samaritans understood Jesus was not only the Messiah for the Jews, but a Savior for all of humanity—even for them.

John 4:43, 44
Now after two days he departed thence, and went into Galilee. For Jesus himself testified, that a prophet hath no honour in his own country.

It must have been hard for Jesus to leave the revival in Samaria—where people were responding and folks were getting saved—to return to Galilee, where He knew He would not be received in the same way. Why, then, did He go to Galilee? Matthew 4:12–16 gives us a clue. You see, the prophet Isaiah predicted Messiah would go into the dark region called "Galilee of the nations." Truly, it was an area of darkness and death, for not only was Galilee far removed from Jerusalem, the center of worship, it was also constantly attacked and overrun by Gentiles. Yet Isaiah prophesied that when Messiah came, He would go to this very place and shine brightly (Isaiah 9:1, 2).

Therefore, I believe Jesus returned to Galilee because He understood what the Word said about His ministry. Think through this with me. The Scriptures to Jesus were not only predictive, but directive. That is, when Jesus read the Scriptures, He found not only predictions *about* His ministry, but direction *for* His ministry. As He matured in His understanding, He realized increasingly that the prophecies written *about* Him must be fulfilled *by* Him. Thus, Jesus was not just a hearer of the Word, He was the quintessential Doer of the Word. The great need for the church corporately as well as for you and me personally is not just to be hearers of the Scriptures but to *do* them. Jesus would later say, "Happy are ye if ye do these things" (John 13:17). Happiness does not come from hearing Scripture or agreeing with theology. Happiness comes when we get it in gear and carry out the things the Word directs us to do.

John 4:45
Then when he was come into Galilee, the Galilaeans received him, having seen all the things that he did at Jerusalem at the feast: for they also went unto the feast.

The Galileans received Jesus as a curious miracle-worker—but not as their Savior. They were not interested in who He was, but only in what He could do.

John 4:46
So Jesus came again into Cana of Galilee, where he made the water wine. And there was a certain nobleman, whose son was sick at Capernaum.

This nobleman was popular, prominent, and powerful—a courtier in Herod's court. Yet the saying of Jesus' day is still true today: "The black camel of grief kneels at every man's gate." It doesn't matter how rich, powerful, or successful one might be. Sooner or later, we all experience sorrow and tragedy.

John 4:47
When he heard that Jesus was come out of Judaea into Galilee, he went unto him, and besought him that he would come down, and heal his son: for he was at the point of death.

The nobleman besought Jesus. The idea in the Greek is that he begged Jesus to come and heal his son.

John 4:48
Then said Jesus unto him, Except ye see signs and wonders, ye will not believe.

While the Samaritans simply heard His word and believed (verse 42), the Galilaeans needed miracles, signs, and wonders to believe.

John 4:49, 50 (a)
The nobleman saith unto him, Sir, come down ere my child die. Jesus saith unto him, Go thy way; thy son liveth.

In Matthew 8, another Gentile nobleman—a Roman centurion—faced sickness in his house. He too was a man of prominence and political power. He too lived in the region of Capernaum. He too came to Jesus. But there the similarities end. "My son is dying," said the Roman centurion.

"I'll come to your house and heal him," said Jesus.

"Oh, I'm not worthy to have you come into my house," protested the centurion. "Just speak the word."

And Jesus marveled at the centurion's faith. Contrast this with the account here in John 4, wherein the nobleman directed Jesus to go to his house. Although Jesus did indeed heal his son, He didn't comply with the nobleman's order to go to his house. I wonder how often we are guilty of the nobleman's error—of giving directions to Jesus.

"Okay, Lord, there are the bills, here is the need, and this is what You need to do to make it happen."

"There he is. I'm single and so is he. Let's get this relationship going, Lord."

"Lord, this is a great business opportunity. So bless it by next Monday."

We have a tendency to give instructions and directions. But that is not the finest and highest way to approach our Lord. The centurion in Matthew 8 was a much wiser, deeper man. He simply said, "Lord, here's the situation." Period. No directions. No instructions. No advice.

And Jesus said, "I'll respond to that."

John 4:50 (b)
And the man believed the word that Jesus had spoken unto him, and he went his way.

In fairness to our brother, the nobleman, when the Lord said, "Go your way," he went his way. His wasn't the same quality of faith as the centurion's, but it was a high degree of faith nonetheless.

John 4:51, 52
And as he was now going down, his servants met him, and told him, saying, Thy son liveth. Then inquired he of them the hour when he began to amend. And they said unto him, Yesterday at the seventh hour the fever left him.

The implication here is fascinating because the distance from Cana to Capernaum being only a four-hour walk means that when the nobleman heard Jesus say his son would be well, he didn't go straight home. My tendency would have been to jog home, to rush home, to run home and see. But to this man's credit, he heard the word and didn't show up until the next day—which means he believed the Word he heard. How stress-free and happy you and I could be if we too would just read the Word and believe it.

John 4:53
So the father knew that it was at the same hour, in the which Jesus said unto him, Thy son liveth: and himself believed, and his whole house.

I like this because, although his faith was rather feeble initially, once he heard the Word of Jesus, the nobleman embraced it wholeheartedly. As I have observed families, I have found that when Dad becomes a believer, almost without exception, the whole household will come into real faith. "As for me and my house," said Joshua, "we will serve the Lord" (see Joshua 24:15). How I encourage and bless you men who are taking that kind of stand. You watch. Your family will follow. That's what happened here.

John 4:54
This is again the second miracle that Jesus did, when he was come out of Judaea into Galilee.

The first miracle performed in Cana when Jesus turned water into wine was at a time of family celebration. Here, His second miracle was performed at a time of family devastation. Whether you are experiencing times of gladness or times of sadness, Jesus is the Man for the moment. Whether celebration or devastation, a wedding party or a funeral gathering, Jesus is the One you can count on, look to, and receive from miraculously.

5 Before looking at the following story with regard to its practical application, I would like us to consider its theological implications, for in it we find a clear picture of the impotency of tradition and organized religion. . . .

John 5:1 (a)
After this there was a feast of the Jews . . .

The feast referred to is most likely the Feast of Pentecost—the celebration of the giving of the law.

John 5:1 (b)
. . . and Jesus went up to Jerusalem.

No matter from which direction or elevation one traveled, it was always "up" to Jerusalem because Jerusalem was where the temple was, where worship took place, where the Word was taught.

John 5:2 (a)
Now there is at Jerusalem by the sheep market . . .

The very location speaks of Judaism, of the law, of men's traditions—for it was through the sheep gate that sacrifices were brought into the city of Jerusalem.

John 5:2 (b)
. . . a pool, which is called in the Hebrew tongue Bethesda . . .

Although for years critics doubted its existence, the site of the pool of Bethesda, which means "House of Mercy," has been confirmed archaeologically and is today a must-see site of the Holy Land.

John 5:2 (c)
. . . having five porches.

The pool had five porches—a covered "deck" on each side and one across the middle. Five speaks of the Pentateuch—the first five books of the law: Genesis, Exodus, Leviticus, Numbers, and Deuteronomy. With one of the covered porches extending across the pool, the pool itself created a physical likeness to the stone tablets Moses brought down from Sinai. Thus, the pool portrays a perfect picture of the law.

John 5:3 (a)
In these lay a great multitude of impotent folk . . .

Bible teacher J. Vernon McGee visited a sanitarium many years ago, where, during the Sunday morning devotional service, one of the residents read this passage as, "There lay a great multitude of important folk." McGee was about to correct him, when he realized the man was right. The people at the pool of Bethesda *were* important folk.

John 5:3 (b)
. . . of blind, halt, withered, waiting for the moving of the water.

When people are spiritually blind, they are also "halt." That is, no matter what rules and regulations, ordinances and laws are placed upon them, they cannot walk in righteousness or freedom. And because they are "halt," they are also "withered"—unable to reach out practically, unable to give lasting and beneficial assistance to those who are hurting. Blind, halt, and withered is a description of the condition of every culture globally and of you and me personally without Jesus. If we are not reborn, if the Spirit of Christ does not dwell in us, we will not see; we will not walk uprightly; we will not reach out with impact. Many lay by the pool, sheltered and covered, but not healed. So, too, although religion can shelter people with good values and disciplines, it cannot save them.

John 5:4 (a)
For an angel went down at a certain season into the pool, and troubled the water . . .

Kolumbethra, the Greek word translated "pool," is a very precise term that means "a deep pool from underneath that comes bubbling." Thus, it would seem that the stirring of the water was due to the occasional eruption of an underground spring. "But doesn't the text say an angel came down?" you ask. Yes, but I believe that is a quote. You see, Greek text has no quotation marks. If it did, I believe this phrase would be enclosed in them as reference to the conventional wisdom of the day.

John 5:4 (b)
. . . whosoever then first after the troubling of the water stepped in was made whole of whatsoever disease he had.

Tradition said the first one in the pool after the water stirred would be healed. That's what the law, religion, and man's regulations always say. "Be the first. Be the best. Try harder. Fight your way to the top. God helps those who help themselves."

John 5:5 (a)
And a certain man was there . . .

Jesus singled out one man, just as Israel—one of many nations—was singled out by God to be His people.

John 5:5 (b)
. . . which had an infirmity thirty and eight years.

This man was lame for thirty-eight years, just as Israel wandered in the wilderness for thirty-eight years (Deuteronomy 2:14).

John 5:6, 7 (a)
When Jesus saw him lie, and knew that he had been now a long time in that case, he saith unto him, Wilt thou be made whole? The impotent man answered him, Sir, I have no man, when the water is troubled, to put me into the pool . . .

To whom did Jesus come? Not to those closest to the edge of the pool, but to the one who was clear at the back, farthest out of the way. He came not to the aggressor, the initiator, the leader—but to the one who was the least competitive of them all.

John 5:7 (b)
. . . but while I am coming, another steppeth down before me.

"Every time I try to get up, someone else gets there first." Maybe you can relate. You're just about to get a break in business or in a relationship, but someone comes along and beats you to it. You who, like me, have a tendency to be competitive, please note the fact that Jesus was not interested in helping the lame man be the first one into the pool. His purpose was to take him out of the competition altogether.

John 5:8, 9
Jesus saith unto him, Rise, take up thy bed, and walk. And immediately the man was made whole, and took up his bed, and walked: and on the same day was the sabbath.

The picture is perfect. Jesus comes and delivers a man in the place of competition and tradition, rules and regulations. Jesus delivered the one who was lame, withered, and unable to get the help he so desperately needed. The lame man was delivered not by "a man to help him," but by the Son of Man who saved him.

For topical study of John 5:8 entitled "Read Your Bible," turn to page 477.

John 5:10
The Jews therefore said unto him that was cured, It is the sabbath day: it is not lawful for thee to carry thy bed.

Rather than rejoicing that a man was healed, the Jews were upset that he was carrying his bed. You see, Jewish law said a man could bear no burden on the Sabbath. This meant he could not wear a wooden leg or even his false teeth. Thus, you can imagine the outrage of the Jews at seeing a man flaunting his disobedience by carrying his bed.

John 5:11, 12
He answered them, He that made me whole, the same said unto me, Take up thy bed, and walk. Then asked they him, What man is that which said unto thee, Take up thy bed, and walk?

Isn't this amazing? I mean, here's a guy, lame for thirty-eight years, suddenly walking around—and the clergy is uptight and upset. In all fairness, however, although the violation of tradition might not be a point of contention for you and me, we get just as upset when Jesus violates our expectations—when He doesn't work the way we are claiming, believing, praying, or demanding. We have our own arena of anger. It's not tradition. It's expectation. "Now, Lord," we say, "we fasted. We spoke the Word. We believed. But You didn't come through—and we're ticked off." Oh, we might not say it that straightforwardly, but when Jesus blows apart our expectations—just as He blew apart Jewish tradition—we can get angry.

John 5:13 (a)
And he that was healed wist not who it was: for Jesus had conveyed himself away . . .

Why didn't the lame man know who healed him? Was it because Jesus was busy posing for publicity pictures? No. Was it because He was talking to His agents about appearing on the cover of *Judaism Today?* No. Was it because He was giving an interview on Christian radio? No. The man didn't know who healed him because Jesus had simply left the scene. I really like this. After enabling a man to do the impossible, Jesus splits.

John 5:13 (b)
. . . a multitude being in that place.

If indeed this event took place during the Feast of Pentecost, all of Jerusalem would have been packed with people.

John 5:14 (a)
Afterward Jesus findeth him in the temple . . .

To this man's credit, he wasn't on the testimony circuit, saying, "I was lying there when suddenly I perceived a Power on the deck with me, and with great faith, I embraced His word." No, he humbly went to the temple to worship God. And Jesus met him there. So, too, you will discover that the Lord meets you in the place of praise. You will often find the Lord has just the word you need to hear or just the touch you need to feel when you come to the house of prayer. Quite frankly, it's hard for me as a pastor to hear people say, "I just don't sense the Lord. I just don't feel Him," when I know they haven't been to Bible study for months or at the Lord's table for weeks. I *know* the Lord will find them if, like this man, they'll just go to the temple—to the house of prayer, to the place of praise.

John 5:14 (b)
. . . and said unto him, Behold, thou art made whole: sin no more, lest a worse thing come unto thee.

Many scholars believe this man's lameness was caused by a sexually transmitted disease. Whether or not this was the case, Jesus' warning was very pointed and practical. He didn't say, "Behold, you're made whole. Now call My secretary for therapy." No, He said, "You've been made whole. Now don't sin anymore. Walk in a new way."

John 5:15, 16 (a)
The man departed, and told the Jews that it was Jesus, which had made him whole. And therefore did the Jews persecute Jesus, and sought to slay him . . .

The war is escalating. Tensions are mounting. And because Jesus violated their traditions, the Jews are seeking to destroy Him. So, too, some, even in our midst, have turned their back on Jesus because He violated their expectations. These things are written as a warning to me. Because He is Lord, and I am not, He can sovereignly touch whoever He wants on the deck of lameness and say, "Rise. Take up your bed. Walk." Therefore, if I try to instruct him, or order Him, like the nobleman in the preceding chapter, I will hear Him say, "No. You've got it wrong, Jon. I'm the Lord. You're the servant. I want you to share your heart with Me, and cast all your burdens upon Me. But be careful you don't start advising, demanding from, or directing Me."

Allow the Lord to be the Lord, gang. Be like the centurion in Matthew 8. Say, "Lord, here's the situation. Now just speak the Word, and what You want will happen."

John 5:16 (b)
... because he had done these things on the
sabbath day.

The Jews sought to slay Jesus for desecrating the Sabbath, when, in actuality, they themselves were guilty of distorting the Sabbath. You see, the true Sabbath is not based upon inaction, but upon satisfaction; not upon simply refraining from work, but upon rejoicing in work well done. When God the Father took a Sabbath break after six days of activity, He looked at all He had made and saw it was very good (Genesis 1:31). Thus, because He was satisfied with His work, He rested from His work. This allowed us the glorious freedom to follow His lead and say, "Lord, through Your grace, You've blessed. And now I am going to rest."

John 5:17 (a)
But Jesus answered them ...

At this point, as tension is heightened and the war is at hand, Jesus gives an incredible, insightful, and important defense of why He could blow apart Jewish traditions, of why He was not bound by religious systems, of why He did what He did. Jesus lived the most attractive, powerful, beautiful, joyful, wonderful life ever lived. There was a quality about Him, a joy emanating from Him, a peace within Him, a love flowing through Him that attracted the common people to Him like moths to a flame (Mark 12:37). When He said He had come that they might have life abundantly (John 10:10), no one challenged him, saying, "Why don't we see abundant life in You?" No, so abundant was Jesus' life that people left everything to be near Him.

Hebrews goes on to say Jesus was anointed with the oil of gladness "more than any of His fellows" (1:9). That is, He had a gladness about Him unparalleled in any other person. Truly, whoever looks at the Lord cannot help but be impressed with Him. One would think the secret to such attractiveness, effectiveness, and joy would be very complex. One would think that Jesus must have understood esoteric mysteries and implemented difficult methodology. But such is not the case, for in the remainder of the chapter, we see the simplicity of the secret Jesus understood that produced in Him the life that was so successful and so beautiful. What was this secret? In the following defense, we see not only why Jesus healed on the Sabbath, but the very foundational principle that governed His entire life: His relationship with His Father.

If I were to question you about the defining principle of your life, you might say, "It's my ministry," or "It's my family," or, "It's this vision," or, "It's this attempt to see the kingdom grow." But as valid as those things might be, they are insignificant in comparison to your relationship with the Father. That's all there is—no other agenda, no other ministry, no other vision, no other priority. Jesus was so focused on His relationship with His Father that nothing else mattered. As a result, everything else fell into place beautifully. His life was fruitful. His relationships were special. His ministry was bountiful. In the following passage, we see eight statements Jesus makes about His relationship with His Father. ...

John 5:17 (b)
... My Father worketh hitherto, and I work.

1. *Reflection of the Father.* Truly, the Father works on the Sabbath. The sun rises; rain falls; crops grow; life is sustained. Furthermore, God's Sabbath was "broken" in Genesis 3:8 when He went on a rescue mission to track down Adam and Eve after they had eaten the forbidden fruit. In order to help them, the Father broke the Sabbath He Himself had established. With that in mind, here Jesus is saying, "The reason I do what I do is not based on doctrine, philosophy, or tradition. The issue is singular: My Father works on the Sabbath and I simply reflect Him."

John 5:18
Therefore the Jews sought the more to kill
him, because he not only had broken the
sabbath, but said also that God was his Fa-
ther, making himself equal with God.

The phrase "making himself equal with God" employs a present perfect tense verb, which means Jesus was continually making Himself equal with God. Regardless of what the Mormons, Jehovah Witnesses, or the Way International declare, the fact is, those who heard Jesus knew He was claiming deity. That's why they were out to kill Him.

John 5:19 (a)
Then answered Jesus and said unto them,
Verily, verily, I say unto you, The Son can
do nothing of himself, but what he seeth the
Father do ...

2. *Contact with the Father.* The psalmist picks up this theme, when, in six occasions, he talks specifically about the "blotting out of the names of those who are against God." Why could "the Son do nothing of Himself"? Because in Philippians 2, Paul declares Jesus emptied Himself of all powers, privileges, and abilities He had enjoyed pre-

viously in order to become a Man just like you and me, yet without sin.

"Well, what about all of those miracles He did?" you ask.

Jesus performed miracles only because He was in contact with His Father and empowered by the Spirit in the exact same way we can be. You see, in the Garden of Eden, the forbidden fruit came from the tree of the knowledge of good and evil. And once man ate of the knowledge of good and evil, he said, "I know what's good and what's evil, what's right and what's wrong. I can intellectually figure it out." In so doing, he became independent of the simple childlike relationship that asks, "Father, what about this? Father, should I do that?"

How do you know from which tree you're eating? It's so simple! Do you pray? That's the whole issue. If I pray, I'm saying, "Father, I'm not sure what's right here, and I just pray Your will be done, that You will nudge me in the right direction, that You will inspire my thoughts, that You will guard my heart." If you're praying today—just today—then you're on the right course. But if you haven't prayed today, it's indicative of pride because you think you can pull it off by yourself. Have you eaten of the forbidden fruit today? There's no condemnation, but how I pray you might move into maturation and say, "Lord, I'm tired of thinking I know what to do." The solution is simply prayer.

John 5:19 (b), 20
. . .For what things soever he doeth, these also doeth the Son likewise. For the Father loveth the Son, and sheweth him all things that himself doeth: and he will shew him greater works than these, that ye may marvel.

3. *Security in the Father.* What a day you will have if, like Jesus, you'll simply say, "The Father loves me and shows me everything necessary for me to navigate through this day successfully. And I know He's going to show me greater things down the road." How simple your life will be if you find your security not in what your spouse, the crowds, or society thinks of you, but in what the Father thinks of you. How does the Father feel about you? When you were your most rotten and vile, God said, "I'm so in love with you that I am going to send My Son to die for you (Romans 5:8). Why did the Father send the Son? Why didn't He die for us Himself? He did. He was in Christ, reconciling the world unto Himself (2 Corinthians 5:19). When the Son, pinned to the Cross, cried out, "My God, My God, Why hast thou forsaken Me?" the Father felt the pain, the

Father felt the agony, and something in the Father was dying at the same time, for God was *in* Christ, reconciling the world to Himself. How dare you or I say, "I'm not sure God loves me." God demonstrated His love for us conclusively in that while we were dirty, rotten, foul sinners, He died for each of us personally.

John 5:21–26
For as the Father raiseth up the dead, and quickeneth them; even so the Son quickeneth whom he will. For the Father judgeth no man, but hath committed all judgment unto the Son: That all men should honour the Son, even as they honour the Father. He that honoureth not the Son honoureth not the Father which hath sent him. Verily, verily, I say unto you, He that heareth my word, and believeth on him that sent me, hath everlasting life, and shall not come into condemnation; but is passed from death unto life. Verily, verily, I say unto you, The hour is coming, and now is, when the dead shall hear the voice of the Son of God: and they that hear shall live. For as the Father hath life in himself; so hath he given to the Son to have life in himself.

4. *Harmony with the Father.* "The Father raises the dead, so I too raise the dead," declared Jesus. This would be a mindblower to the Jews who taught that God alone is the keeper of three keys: the key to the heavens, which He uses when rain falls (Deuteronomy 28:12); the key to the womb, which He uses when a couple conceives (Genesis 30:2); and the key to the grave, which He used when the dry bones came to life (Ezekiel 37). But here comes Jesus, saying, "I have the same key. Just as the Father opens the grave and gives life, so do I. Just as the Father receives honor, so must I. If you don't honor Me with the same honor you give Him, then you're not honoring Him at all." This is a good passage to use when talking to the cultist because all cults diminish Jesus. All cults make Him a created being, less than the Father.

John 5:27–29
And hath given him authority to execute judgment also, because he is the Son of man. Marvel not at this: for the hour is coming, in the which all that are in the graves shall hear his voice, and shall come forth; they that have done good, unto the resurrection of life; and they that have done evil, unto the resurrection of damnation.

Why does the Father let Jesus do the judging? Because Jesus walked in the same places we walk. He was tempted in all points like you and me (Hebrews 4:15). "I'm in harmony with the Father," said Jesus. "I do the same things the Father does—including judging."

John 5:30
I can of mine own self do nothing: as I hear, I judge: and my judgment is just; because I seek not mine own will, but the will of the Father which hath sent me.

5. *Submission to the Father.* Jesus had no program, no agenda, no vision other than the Father's will. I challenge us to live each day saying, "My only desire is simply to do the will of the Father—not to make it easier on myself or better for my family; not to find more fulfillment in what I do personally or to establish myself financially. I just want to do the Father's will by the power of the Spirit within Me."

John 5:31–36
If I bear witness of myself, my witness is not true. There is another that beareth witness of me; and I know that the witness which he witnesseth of me is true. Ye sent unto John, and he bare witness unto the truth. But I receive not testimony from man: but these things I say, that ye might be saved. He was a burning and a shining light: and ye were willing for a season to rejoice in his light. But I have greater witness than that of John: for the works which the Father hath given me to finish, the same works that I do, bear witness of me, that the Father hath sent me.

6. *Validation from the Father.* "My validation comes not from Myself. John the Baptist told you I am the Lamb of God who takes away the sin of the world (see John 1:29). If that's not good enough for you, look at the works I'm doing, the miracles happening. Yet even they aren't the issue, for ultimately the validation for what I do comes from the Father Himself."

John 5:37, 38
And the Father himself, which hath sent me, hath borne witness of me. Ye have neither heard his voice at any time, nor seen his shape. And ye have not his word abiding in you: for whom he hath sent, him ye believe not.

The Father validated the Son when He said, "This is My beloved Son in Whom I am well pleased," (Matthew 3:17). And that's the key. Jesus' validation came not from John the Baptist, nor even from His own works. It came directly from the Father. Is your validation coming from

your own accomplishments, or from others patting you on the back? It'll never be enough. You'll always be one pat shy of satisfaction. Validation for your life will not come from someone pointing out how good you are. Nor will it come from your own achievements. True validation comes when you hear the voice of the Father in your heart, saying, "Well done, good and faithful servant." That's the only validation that brings security, satisfaction, and stability. That's the only validation that will make your life attractive, fruitful, and effective.

John 5:39
Search the scriptures; for in them ye think ye have eternal life: and they are they which testify of me.

The Greek word translated "search" is *ereunao*, which means "to track the scent"—like a lion, or a bloodhound. That's the way to study Scripture: Follow the scent of the blood. Sniff out the scarlet thread of the Cross. Look for Jesus.

John 5:40–43 (a)
And ye will not come to me, that ye might have life. I receive not honour from men. But I know you, that ye have not the love of God in you. I am come in my Father's name, and ye receive me not . . .

"You study the Scripture doctrinally," Jesus said, "but you've missed the point entirely because you've missed Me."

John 5:43 (b)
. . . if another shall come in his own name, him ye will receive.

Here Jesus is referring to the peacemaker, the Middle East problem-solver, the anti-Christ who will come in his own name and who will be embraced by the world.

John 5:44
How can ye believe, which receive honour one of another, and seek not the honour that cometh from God only?

7. *Concern about the Father.* Jesus cared only about the honor that came from the Father—not the honor that came from men. That's why He was free to fulfill the Father's will. Solomon was right when he said that the fear of man will trip you up, but the fear of God is the beginning of wisdom (Proverbs 29:25; 9:10). Jesus could say, "Father, I've finished the work You gave Me to do, and I've glorified You" (John 17:4) because He sought honor from God rather than man.

John 5:45, 46

Do not think that I will accuse you to the Father: there is one that accuseth you, even Moses, in whom ye trust. For had ye believed Moses, ye would have believed me: for he wrote of me.

8. *Silence before the Father.* To those who were out to kill Him, Jesus said, "All of the sacrifices and prophecies Moses wrote of in the Pentateuch were about Me. Therefore, I don't need to accuse you before the Father. There is no need for Me to tattle or whine. The Word has condemned you already. Moses nailed you totally."

John 5:47

But if ye believe not his writings, how shall ye believe my words?

Here's a simple experiment: Go through the next twenty-four hours saying, "I want to be a reflection *of* the Father in every conversation, in every encounter. I'm going to depend *on* the Father, making no decisions without prayer. My security is *in* the Father. I'm going to believe He loves me because He proved it on Calvary. I'm going to be in harmony *with* the Father, just doing what I see Him do. I will be submitted *to* the Father, doing nothing on the basis of my own will. My validation will come only *from* the Father. I won't be fishing for compliments, or looking for approval from men. My only concern will be *about* the Father—not what the world says about me, not what my friends think of me, but only how the Father sees me. I will be silent *before* the Father, resting in the sufficiency and potency of His Word."

Fellow adventurers on this spiritual pilgrimage, if you try this tomorrow, you will find tomorrow to be the most successful, wonderful, powerful, fruitful day of your life. My prayer is that some of us might make such a discovery and be set free from agendas, vision, and even ministry—to live for the Father and for Him only.

READ YOUR BIBLE
A Topical Study of
John 5:8

Sitting on a park bench, looking rather glum, Linus said to Charlie Brown, "Sometimes it seems like life has passed me by. Do you ever feel that way?"

Charlie looked at Linus and said, "No. Life has knocked me down, and keeps walking all over me."

As we look at Jesus' words, I think you'll find them intriguing as they relate to you personally in areas where, like Charlie Brown or the lame man in our text, you feel walked on, hurt, or defeated.

Rise

Jesus came to the lame man and said, "I'm going to ask you to do the impossible. Stand up." You see, Christ's words work His will. Truly, God's commandments are God's "enablements." The very word "rise" would enable the lame man to do the impossible. Just because Jesus said it, there would be the power to do it.

Take Up Your Bed

Make no provision for failure. Don't say, "I'll leave my bed here to save my place on the deck in case it doesn't work out." If you have been in bondage to anything that seems to have a grip on your life, the word of Christ comes to you today, and says, "Take up your bed. Make no provision for failure. Don't keep a video stored in your bottom drawer just in case you get a craving again. Don't keep a six-pack tucked away in the back of the pantry in case you might want a sip or two or three. Don't keep his phone number just in case no one else calls you for the next three weeks. Make no provision for failure."

Walk

No one will carry you. When will Christians learn this lesson? Like the lame man, we think we need help from man—from a counselor, a psychologist, or a Christian therapist. "Where is someone to disciple me, pray for me, study with me?" we cry. The lame man had a choice to make. He could either obey the word of Christ, or argue that it wouldn't work for him. So can we. But when we finally realize no man is going to carry us, we will find Jesus is all we needed all along. Corrie Ten Boom was right: You will never discover Christ is all you need until Christ is all you have.

"Well," you say, "if Jesus was here in the flesh as He was with the lame man, I too would walk. But He's no longer in the midst of us. We can no longer hear from Him directly."

Really? Jesus says, "Lo I come in the volume of the book" (see Hebrews 10:7). He is here, gang—not only through His Spirit residing in you, but in the Bible open before you. Read your Bible—and you will hear words that will speak to you personally and specifically.

People are no longer reading the Scriptures. They're too busy saying, "What man is going to help me? What clinic is going to assist me? What pastor is going to solve the problem for me?"

Read your Bible. Peter says, "Whereby are given unto us exceeding great and precious promises, that by these you might be partakers of the divine nature, escaping the corruption that is in this world through lust" (see 2 Peter 1:4). Everything we need to escape the sickness and sadness of this world is found in the exceedingly great and precious promises of the Bible. Yet people don't read their Bibles. They'll drive fifty minutes to go to a thirty-minute counseling appointment but won't spend fifteen minutes in the Word. It's a tragedy. God has clearly said that the one who is meditating in the Word will bring forth fruit, will never shrivel up, and will prosper in all he does (Psalm 1). Yet the top-rated religious broadcasters are no longer Bible teachers. They're psychologists. People flock to the seminars, videos, and books of those who say, "The key is psychology and human understanding. Yes, we're Christians. But Scripture is not totally sufficient. We need to talk to you about how to raise your kids, how to communicate, how to be successful based upon psychology."

Can those things be helpful? Perhaps. Are they necessary? No. The Scriptures are all-sufficient, for they speak of Christ, point to Christ, and bring us to Christ. *Stay* in the Scriptures, gang. Read your Bible! Check out Psalm 19:7–9, and you will see six descriptions and six effects of the Word of God in one's life. . . .

1. *The Law of the Lord is perfect, converting—or restoring—the soul* (verse 7). The law speaks of the totality of the Word. From where does emotional or mental restoration come? Not from delving into or digging up our past. It comes from taking in the Word.

2. *The testimony of the Lord is sure, making wise the simple* (verse 7). The word "sure" means "solid." The word "simple" means "open-minded." Thus, the Word of God gives solid footing to those who would otherwise sink in the sands of open-minded naiveté. How solid is the Word? Peter declares it is even more sure, more solid than the voice of God he himself heard on the Mount of Transfiguration (2 Peter 1:18, 19).

3. *The statutes of the Lord are right, rejoicing the heart* (verse 8). Studying the Word of God will make your heart happy. Jeremiah—who was cast into a pit, and whose ministry was seemingly unsuccessful—said, "Thy Word was found and I did eat it. And thy Word was unto me the joy and rejoicing of my heart" (see 15:16). Jeremiah, the weeping prophet, said, "You know where I find joy? In the Word of God."

4. *The commandment of the Lord is pure, enlightening the eyes* (verse 8). The commandments are pure—without flaw. They are workable, understandable, and powerful. How does one see clearly? Through the Word.

5. *The fear of the Lord is clean, enduring forever* (verse 9). The Word of God is not based upon a passing fad, pop culture, or humanistic understanding. It's clean—pure, straightforward, easy to grasp—and it lasts forever.

6. *The judgments of the Lord are true and righteous altogether* (verse 9). We know in our heart of hearts that the Word is true. Our spirit confirms its veracity.

How can you be healed emotionally? How can you live in stability? How can you have joy experientially? How can you see clearly? How can you be guided continually? How can you find truth in totality? Through the Word, the Word, the Word. Period.

"I've tried that," you say. "But the Word has failed me."

Wrong. The Word hasn't failed. You have. You stopped reading your Bible. You stopped meditating on the Word of God. Movies and television, hobbies and other pursuits became more important than seeking God. The Scriptures have never failed a single person. People have failed the Scriptures. They've turned their back on the Word. They've diminished its priority. They've lost their passion. And they wonder why they're not enlightened, rejoicing, or enduring.

Whatever you do, precious people, don't fall into the trap of seeking a man to help you. Get back in the Word and seek the Lord. In Jeremiah 2:13, God indicts His people for committing two evils: "They have forsaken me, the fountain of living waters, and hewed out cisterns, broken cisterns, that can hold no water." Christians all over the country are carving out cisterns that don't hold water. "Now you are clean through the Word which I have spoken unto you," Jesus said (see John 15:3). "The words which I speak are spirit and life" (see John 6:63). We are cleansed by the washing of the water, which is the Word of God (Ephesians 5:26). It's the Word, the Word, the Word.

I realize I may have lost some people and made some enemies with this particular study. But I am more committed to speaking the truth, as difficult as it might be for some to receive, than I am to keeping the peace because I believe the church is being seduced by humanistic psychology. Such was not the case in previous generations.

Growing up in Depression-era Southern California, my mom cannot recall a single Christian counseling clinic. The term itself would have been oxymoronic. You see, in my mom's day, the Word of God was taught, altar calls were given, and people were convicted. They would kneel at the altar, weep before the Lord, repent from their sin, and go their way rejoicing. Today, people hear Bible studies, then go home, fire up the barbecue, watch the baseball game on TV, and remain troubled inside. Four days later, they call a counselor—then wonder why they're not really helped.

I say this to pastors, elders, psychologists, social workers, and psychiatrists—to all who are involved with people: The key is to point people back to the Person of Jesus Christ. Tell them to get in the Word and do what it says. If that means turning off the TV or shutting down the barbecue to spend time seeking God, tell them to do it. Tell them to spend whatever time it takes to get to the point where rationalization and justification end and where true confession begins.

"Do you want to be made whole?" Why would Jesus ask this of a man who had been lame for thirty-eight years? Because some people want to stay lame. They're comfortable on the deck at Bethesda with their sunglasses, tanning oil, and Walkman. They don't have to take care of their families; they have no responsibilities; they cannot work because they're lame. So others take care of them and put up with them while they ignore the true healing available to them.

You might be living with marital strife, addiction to alcohol, or a fascination with pornography. You might have a tendency to lie, to gossip, or to lose your temper. Will you be made whole? Listen to the words of Jesus: Do the impossible. Make no provision for failure. And don't expect anyone to carry you.

6 In contrast to chapter 5 where we saw Jesus seeking an individual, as chapter 6 opens, we see a multitude seeking Jesus. . . .

John 6:1
After these things Jesus went over the sea of Galilee, which is the sea of Tiberias.

From Mark 6:31, we know that as the crowds began to gather around Him, Jesus didn't have time for leisure or even to eat. That is why He said to His disciples, "Come with Me and rest awhile." It's an invitation still needful today—for if we don't come apart with the Savior, we'll fall apart at the seams.

John 6:2–4
And a great multitude followed him, because they saw his miracles which he did on them that were diseased. And Jesus went up into a mountain, and there he sat with his disciples. And the passover, a feast of the Jews, was nigh.

Although the disciples and Jesus ascended a mountain, the crowd tracked Him down—not so much because they wanted to be with Him, but because they were curious about Him. Having seen His miracles, they no doubt looked at Jesus either as a magician to entertain them or as a physician to assist them. The crowd followed Jesus for the wrong reasons. And it still does. The crowd mentality is still to manipulate the Lord for a personal, private agenda—to get something from Him rather than simply to be with Him.

John 6:5
When Jesus then lifted up his eyes, and saw a great company come unto him, he saith unto Philip, Whence shall we buy bread, that these may eat?

I love this about our Lord! Even though the crowd followed Him for the wrong reason and would, in the space of the chapter, turn away from Him completely, Jesus still has compassion on them, for, as Mark's Gospel tells us, He looked on them as sheep without a shepherd (6:34). If you're a mom or dad, you know how this works. You know when your kids are coming to you for the wrong reasons—when their priorities are amiss or their motives are not right. But you also know you still love them and are there to tend them. So, too, every pastor, elder, or spiritual leader must realize that no matter how wrong people might be, it is never right to beat up on them, to come down on them, or to point a finger at them. When those in ministry say, "If it wasn't for these immature believers, things would really be happening at my church," it only shows that the speaker is not really a shepherd. A true shepherd will never beat the sheep, for he knows he is there to feed the flock. And anyone who tries to beat up on you will feel the wrath of this under-shepherd. I will not stand for it.

John 6:6
And this he said to prove him: for he himself knew what he would do.

"Where shall we buy bread?" It's the only time Jesus appeared to ask for advice. Why did He ask Philip? In order to test him. So, too, Jesus puts us in situations where we feel there's no solution in order to show us our progress in the arena of faith.

John 6:7
Philip answered him, Two hundred pennyworth of bread is not sufficient for them, that every one of them may take a little.

Like a New Deal Democrat, Philip's first thought was that money would solve the problem. But after a quick survey of the situation, he knew the disciples didn't have enough money in their treasury to buy enough to even give folks a crumb.

Our country is $3.5 trillion in debt because we have the "Philip mentality" that money is the key. But there will always be a deficit because he who looks to mammon instead of to the Master will always come up short.

John 6:8, 9 (a)
One of his disciples, Andrew, Simon Peter's brother, saith unto him, There is a lad here, which hath five barley loaves, and two small fishes . . .

Good job, Andrew! Andrew's a people person—always bringing folks to the Lord.

John 6:9 (b)
. . . but what are they among so many?

Andrew almost has it. "There's a boy here with some loaves and fishes, *but . . .*" How easily the word "but" creeps into our thinking. We are aware of the provision, but we start raising an objection when we look at the situation practically. I wonder how many times the Lord has brought us five barley loaves and two small fishes, but we failed to use them because we thought they were too small.

God used a small stone in a small sling to slay a huge giant (1 Samuel 17:50). He used a little maiden girl to lead a mighty Syrian general to the prophet Elijah (2 Kings 5). He used a little child to teach His disciples (Matthew 18:2). The Lord seems to delight in using a little to do a lot. If you're feeling the need for a miracle—for something to break loose or something to take place—perhaps it's already in your hand. Perhaps it's already been entrusted to you. Yet, like Andrew, perhaps you are saying, "Let's be practical. How's this really going to work?"

John 6:10 (a)
And Jesus said, Make the men sit down.

Jesus didn't say to His disciples, "You bozos. Get out of the way and let Me do a miracle." No, He met them where they were and said, "Even though you don't have the faith to see what I can do with the little given to Me, I'll use you anyway. Could you make the people sit down? Could I use you in that way?" Luke's Gospel tells us the people sat down in groups of fifty (9:14). When the Good Shepherd feeds His sheep, He does so decently and in order (1 Corinthians 14:40).

Not only does Jesus feed His flock decently and orderly, but He feeds His flock carefully. Too often we have a "drive-thru" perspective of devotions. "Okay, Lord, I've got six minutes before I have to be out the door," we say as we flip open the Scriptures and expect to be fed. It doesn't happen that way. Not usually. As He did here, the Lord would have us not only sit down, but slow down.

John 6:10 (b), 11
Now there was much grass in the place. So the men sat down, in number about five thousand. And Jesus took the loaves; and when he had given thanks, he distributed to the disciples, and the disciples to them that were set down; and likewise of the fishes as much as they would.

The bread kept coming and coming. And the disciples kept serving and serving. It's astounding to me how many commentators try to nullify this miracle with ridiculous explanations. Some suggest it wasn't a genuine feeding of five thousand, but rather a kind of Communion service, where everyone was given a tiny piece of bread and a tiny piece of fish. Others say that, because in Jesus' day men had long, billowing sleeves wherein they would carry their lunches, when they knew Jesus was looking for some food to share, they tightened their sleeves. Then, when they became convicted by the willingness of a little boy who shared his lunch, everyone opened his sleeves and shared in a big potluck. Nonsense!

For topical study of John 6:5–11 entitled "Facing Frustration," turn to page 488.

John 6:12 (a)
When they were filled . . .

The Greek word translated "filled" means "glutted." What Jesus did wasn't a trick, a gimmick, or a potluck. It was a miracle.

John 6:12 (b), 13
. . . he said unto his disciples, Gather up the fragments that remain, that nothing be lost. Therefore they gathered them together, and filled twelve baskets with the fragments of the five barley loaves, which remained over and above unto them that had eaten.

I like this because it is true that even when our faith is faltering or lacking, if we will simply obediently do what the Lord tells us to do, even our small and insignificant actions will be multiplied and blessed. In obedience to the Lord's command, the disciples simply made the multitude sit down and then distributed the food. The result? Not only were the disciples fed along with the multitude, but there were twelve baskets left over—one for each of them. That's why we're always encouraging each other to get involved in serving, in sharing, in ministry. It's when you do what the Lord sets before you—no matter how mundane it might appear—that, along with those you serve, you receive a full basket as well.

John 6:14
Then those men, when they had seen the miracle that Jesus did, said, This is of a truth that prophet that should come into the world.

In Deuteronomy 18, Moses prophesied that a prophet would come who was like, but greater than, himself. Those who witnessed the miracle that had just taken place thought surely Jesus must be the prophet of whom Moses spoke.

John 6:15
When Jesus therefore perceived that they would come and take him by force, to make him a king, he departed again into a mountain himself alone.

Although the crowd referred to Jesus as a prophet in verse 14 and they desired to make Him a king in verse 15, what they failed to acknowledge was that their real need was for a priest. Jesus, the Christos, the Christ, the Anointed One would not only be the promised Prophet and the King of kings. He would also have to be the great High Priest who would lay down His own life as a sacrifice for the sin of mankind. Thus, perceiving the crowd's misconception as to who He was and what He was about, Jesus withdrew.

John 6:16, 17 (a)
And when even was now come, his disciples went down unto the sea, and entered into a ship, and went over the sea toward Capernaum.

Perhaps it was to turn the focus of His disciples to a spiritual rather than an earthly kingdom that Jesus distanced His disciples from the crowd by sending them to Capernaum.

John 6:17 (b)
And it was now dark, and Jesus was not come to them.

Maybe, like the disciples, you're at a point in your life where it's dark and you don't sense the presence of the Lord at all. Know this: Omnipotence can afford to wait.

John 6:18
And the sea arose by reason of a great wind that blew.

Jesus is not only the Savior *in* the storm but also the sender *of* the storm. And, just as He did with His disciples, He will send you into a storm knowingly and lovingly if He sees you're about to get pulled into the mentality of the crowd.

John 6:19, 20
So when they had rowed about five and twenty or thirty furlongs, they see Jesus walking on the sea, and drawing nigh unto

the ship: and they were afraid. But he saith unto them, It is I; be not afraid.

In the midst of your own struggling and toiling, Jesus knows the perfect time to come to you and whisper in your ear, "It is I. Be not afraid." But it won't be a minute too early, and it won't be a moment too late.

John 6:21 (a)
Then they willingly received him into the ship . . .

Jesus didn't jump into the disciples' boat. He didn't force Himself on board. The disciples received Him willingly. So, too, I can either say, "Nice to see You, Lord, but I'm going to bring this thing to shore myself," or, like the disciples, I can willingly and wisely welcome Him into my boat.

John 6:21 (b)
. . . and immediately the ship was at the land whither they went.

If the Lord has sent you into a storm and then seen you through that storm, don't go back to the same stuff that caused the storm to be sent in the first place. Turn away. Say, "Lord, that storm almost sunk me. My marriage almost dissolved. My business almost went under. My kids were almost wiped out. It seemed so dark and impossible. But You came my way and told me to be of good cheer. You said You were still there, and You saw me through. Lord, I acknowledge that it's You who sent the storm, and it's You who stilled the storm. Therefore, I will not continue on that course one more day."

For topical study of John 6:15–21 entitled "Sender of the Storm," turn to page 490.

John 6:22–24
The day following, when the people which stood on the other side of the sea saw that there was none other boat there, save that one whereinto his disciples were entered, and that Jesus went not with his disciples into the boat, but that his disciples were gone away alone; (Howbeit there came other boats from Tiberias nigh unto the place where they did eat bread, after that the Lord had given thanks:) When the people therefore saw that Jesus was not there, neither his disciples, they also took shipping, and came to Capernaum, seeking for Jesus.

Realizing Jesus was no longer among them, the day after the feeding of the five thousand, the multitude began to look for Jesus in Capernaum—not to simply be with Him, but, as we will see, to get something from Him.

John 6:25, 26
And when they had found him on the other side of the sea, they said unto him, Rabbi, when camest thou hither? Jesus answered them and said, Verily, verily, I say unto you, Ye seek me, not because ye saw the miracles, but because ye did eat of the loaves, and were filled.

The multitude asked Jesus when He had come. Rather than answering them directly, Jesus dealt with the issue of why *they* had come, as if to say, "You came here not because you saw the meaning of the miracle, but because you wanted another free lunch."

John 6:27 (a)
Labour not for the meat which perisheth, but for that meat which endureth unto everlasting life, which the Son of man shall give unto you . . .

All of us realize material things are going to perish eventually, but Jesus says they're perishing even presently. If you're laboring for something in this world—be it anything from a reputation to some kind of physical satisfaction—it will never work. It's cotton candy. You bite into it but there's no substance. Whatever it is you're striving for won't fill you up because everything this side of heaven lacks solidity.

Ninety-six percent of your body is nothing, zip, zero. It's true. Your body is made up of atoms, which, in turn, are made up of protons, neutrons, and electrons. Considering that the distance between the protons and neutrons of the nucleus, and the electrons outside the nucleus is proportionally greater than the distance from the sun to the farthest planet, Pluto, we're talking a lot of empty space!

Our bodies are space. Yet we pamper them, all the while wondering why we're so spaced-out and discontent. The materialistic person doesn't understand that reality lies in the spirit. He doesn't understand that if, instead of looking to the physical, he would labor for true spiritual food, he would be satisfied presently and rewarded eternally. Next time you feel a craving for something earthly, let me suggest something infinitely better: Get in touch with reality. Spend time seeking that which is everlasting. Come into the presence of the Lord with praise and worship. You're not truly craving the video or the hot fudge sundae. You're not craving the sporting event or the bigger car. What you're really craving is the everlasting food found only in the pursuit and enjoyment of God.

The Lord isn't sternly pointing His finger, saying, "Labor not for the meat that perishes." He's saying, "To live life fully, don't get caught up in laboring for things—physical things, relational things, material things. Instead, put your energy and focus on that which leads to life everlasting."

John 6:27 (b)
. . . for him hath God the Father sealed.

In Jesus' day, a baker would put his seal on the loaves of bread he baked. Thus, in using this terminology, Jesus is saying, "I bear the imprint of God the Father."

John 6:28, 29
Then said they unto him, What shall we do, that we might work the works of God? Jesus answered and said unto them, This is the work of God, that ye believe on him whom he hath sent.

"What must we do to do the *works* of God?" the crowd asked.

"The *work* of God is singular," Jesus answered. "It is that you believe on Me."

John 6:30
They said therefore unto him, What sign shewest thou then, that we may see, and believe thee? what dost thou work?

"What sign can You give us to prove You indeed are the One whom the Father has sent?" asked the crowd. Only the day before, Jesus had miraculously fed five thousand. But the crowd asked for another sign because miracles never produce lasting faith.

John 6:31
Our fathers did eat manna in the desert; as it is written, He gave them bread from heaven to eat.

Could it be that, as their stomachs were growling after their journey to Capernaum, the crowd is saying, "We're hungry. Give us something to eat—as Moses did"?

John 6:32
Then Jesus said unto them, Verily, verily, I say unto you, Moses gave you not that bread

from heaven; but my Father giveth you the true bread from heaven.

"Moses didn't provide the manna in the wilderness. It came from My Father," said Jesus.

John 6:33
For the bread of God is he which cometh down from heaven, and giveth life unto the world.

Jesus was speaking of something infinitely greater than manna. He was speaking of Himself.

John 6:34
Then said they unto him, Lord, evermore give us this bread.

Like the woman in John 4 who asked for living water in order that she would no longer have to draw from the well, the crowd failed to understand that Jesus was not speaking in terms of the physical, but of the spiritual; not of the temporal, but of the eternal.

John 6:35–40
And Jesus said unto them, I am the bread of life: he that cometh to me shall never hunger; and he that believeth on me shall never thirst. But I said unto you, That ye also have seen me, and believe not. All that the Father giveth me shall come to me; and him that cometh to me I will in no wise cast out. For I came down from heaven, not to do mine own will, but the will of him that sent me. And this is the Father's will which hath sent me, that of all which he hath given me I should lose nothing, but should raise it up again at the last day. And this is the will of him that sent me, that every one which seeth the Son, and believeth on him, may have everlasting life: and I will raise him up at the last day.

"I understand who Jesus is," you say, "and I understand what's being said. But I'm one who has been laboring for meat that perishes."
I have good news for you! Jesus says, "Of all which has been given to Me, I will lose *nothing.*" Check out verse 12. Jesus said, "Gather up the fragments—the crumbs." That's me. You might feel "crumb-y," insignificant, or fragmented. But Jesus says, "The called will understand My message, and *none* shall be lost."
You gotta love the Lord for speaking the truth in not only telling us how to live, but also saying, "Even when you fail, I've still got you and I'm going to see you through."

For topical study of John 6:35 entitled "Jesus: the I AM," turn to page 493.

John 6:41
The Jews then murmured at him, because he said, I am the bread which came down from heaven.

When the manna was given in the wilderness, what did the people do? They murmured (Exodus 17:3). And now they're murmuring once more in response to Jesus' statement that He is the "bread sent from heaven."

John 6:42 (a)
And they said, Is not this Jesus, the son of Joseph, whose father and mother we know?

The crowd was, of course, wrong. Jesus wasn't Joseph's son. He's God's Son.

John 6:42 (b), 43
... how is it then that he saith, I came down from heaven? Jesus therefore answered and said unto them, Murmur not among yourselves.

"Murmur not," Jesus said. We have a saying that the squeaky wheel gets the grease. Consequently, murmuring and complaining are sort of acceptable to us. First Corinthians 10:10, however, teaches otherwise—for sometimes rather than getting the grease, the squeaky wheel gets replaced.

John 6:44–48
No man can come to me, except the Father which hath sent me draw him: and I will raise him up at the last day. It is written in the prophets, And they shall be all taught of God. Every man therefore that hath heard, and hath learned of the Father, cometh unto me. Not that any man hath seen the Father, save he which is of God, he hath seen the Father. Verily, verily, I say unto you, He that believeth on me hath everlasting life. I am that bread of life.

When the crowd said, "We know Him. He's the son of Joseph," Jesus didn't correct them because the real issue was that they simply believe that He is the "bread sent from heaven"—an impossible feat for them unless the Father drew them.

John 6:49–51
Your fathers did eat manna in the wilderness, and are dead. This is the bread which cometh down from heaven, that a man may eat thereof, and not die. I am the living bread which came down from heaven: if any man eat of this bread, he shall live for ever: and the bread that I will give is my flesh, which I will give for the life of the world.

The human being can survive longer on bread than on any other substance. Although it is baked in different ways and fixed in different forms, bread is truly cross-cultural. It's also extremely palatable, for most of us eat some sort of bread every day. But the most intriguing aspect about Jesus' identification with bread is the process by which bread is made. That is, a seed of grain is planted in the ground. After some weeks, it springs up and grows into maturity. Then it is cut down, ground up, and placed in the fire. After it is thoroughly baked, it is enjoyed by humanity.

That's exactly what happened to Jesus. A seed was planted in the womb of Mary miraculously. God Incarnate came forth and grew to maturity. He was cut down as He was pinned to the Cross; ground up as He was cursed and spat upon; and placed in the fire of God's wrath as He absorbed all of our sin. And because He had been planted, cut down, ground up, and burned in the very fire of God's wrath, you and I have the opportunity to eat of Him daily—never tiring of Him, always receiving strength and sustenance for the challenges of any given day. Truly, Jesus is the Bread of Life. The analogy is perfect.

John 6:52–58
The Jews therefore strove among themselves, saying, How can this man give us his flesh to eat? Then Jesus said unto them, Verily, verily, I say unto you, Except ye eat the flesh of the Son of man, and drink his blood, ye have no life in you. Whoso eateth my flesh, and drinketh my blood, hath eternal life; and I will raise him up at the last day. For my flesh is meat indeed, and my blood is drink indeed. He that eateth my flesh, and drinketh my blood, dwelleth in me, and I in him. As the living Father hath sent me, and I live by the Father: so he that eateth me, even he shall live by me. This is that bread which came down from heaven: not as your fathers did eat manna, and are dead: he that eateth of this bread shall live for ever.

As the Jews wondered what He meant, Jesus began to explain the absolute necessity of their taking this teaching and applying it personally. In other words, they would have to eat of His body or they would not live.

Biblically, we can understand what it means to eat of Jesus when we understand what happened to Adam and Eve when they ate of the tree of the knowledge of good and evil. It was after they ate the forbidden fruit that they fell because they no longer were completely and constantly dependent on the Father. You see, prior to the Fall, whenever they had questions, whenever they had problems, whenever there might be confusion, they said, "Father, what should we do?" But once they ate of the forbidden fruit, they became independent. They no longer talked to their Abba, their Papa, their Father. They said instead, "We know what's good. We know what's evil. We know how to handle this or accomplish that."

Here, Jesus says, "You've eaten of the tree of the knowledge of good and evil, and it led to your fall. Now eat of Me, the Tree of Life. Internalize Me. Allow Me to come into the deepest recess of your being. Allow Me to take control of your life.

Practically, we can understand what it means to eat of Jesus, when we realize that, although we can get by without exercise, excitement, or education, we can't get by without eating. We may not do a lot of things we think we should do. But there is one thing we make sure we do: We eat. And here the Lord, in using this analogy, gets very practical when He says, "I want to be the priority of your life. Make it a necessity to eat of Me daily and consistently.

Mystically, we can understand what it means to eat of Jesus when we come to Communion. Paul wrote that many in the church at Corinth were weak, sick, and had even died unnecessarily because they had not given worth to the Lord's table (1 Corinthians 11:30). The same, in a sense, is still true. I believe the reason so much of Protestant Christianity is sterile, boring, and impotent is because a lot of Protestants, in overreaction to Catholicism, have reduced the importance and necessity of the Eucharist. There is a tremendous power in the Lord's Supper. While I do not believe that the elements are literally transformed into the Lord's body and blood, neither do I believe they are nothing more than symbols, for I have experienced grace and power at the Communion table that I have found nowhere else. Perhaps that is why Satan seems to try to keep people away from Communion even more than from Bible study.

John 6:59, 60
These things said he in the synagogue, as he taught in Capernaum. Many therefore of

his disciples, when they had heard this, said, This is an hard saying; who can hear it?

The Greek text makes it clear that the disciples found Jesus' saying hard not because they couldn't understand it, but because it was offensive.

John 6:61, 62
When Jesus knew in himself that his disciples murmured at it, he said unto them, Doth this offend you? What and if ye shall see the Son of man ascend up where he was before?

"If this offends you," said Jesus, "how will you feel when you see Me ascend to heaven by way of a Cross?"

John 6:63
It is the spirit that quickeneth; the flesh profiteth nothing: the words that I speak unto you, they are spirit, and they are life.

We're not able to comprehend intellectually the mystery of the Lord's table or what it means to eat of Him personally. It is only by the Spirit that we can receive revelation.

John 6:64–66
But there are some of you that believe not. For Jesus knew from the beginning who they were that believed not, and who should betray him. And he said, Therefore said I unto you, that no man can come unto me, except it were given unto him of my Father. From that time many of his disciples went back, and walked no more with him.

Jesus didn't plead with those who left. He didn't say, "Let Me explain further." He neither ran after them nor reasoned with them because He knew they could not understand unless the Father had drawn them. Sometimes we spend hours talking and days dialoguing when we should be following the example of Jesus—realizing that unless the Father is drawing, no one can come. I sense such a "relaxed-ness" in the ministry of Jesus Christ. Not striving, not struggling, not straining to persuade, He simply shared the truth, knowing the Spirit would give application in the hearts of those the Father had drawn.

John 6:67, 68
Then said Jesus unto the twelve, Will ye also go away? Then Simon Peter answered him, Lord, to whom shall we go?

"Where else can we go?" asked Peter. Too often, our answer is, "Cinema 5, Blockbuster Video, Red Lion." We could fill in the blank all too easily, I'm afraid. But Peter had already done all the world's stuff. He knew it was bankrupt.

John 6:68
Thou hast the words of eternal life.

Although they were no doubt excited and inspired by Jesus' works, Peter and the boys were converted and committed by Jesus' *words.* May this be a place corporately, and may we be people individually who understand that conversion and commitment are based not upon signs or miracles, entertainment, hype, or hoopla, but upon the Word of God. I've heard people say, "We don't want to study the Bible. We just want to move in the Spirit." Yet I don't know how much more Spirit-filled a meeting can be than one in which the words of Jesus Christ are proclaimed, for the words He speaks are Spirit and life (verse 63).

John 6:69
And we believe and are sure that thou art that Christ, the Son of the living God.

Note the order: We believe and are sure. People often say, "I would believe if I could be sure." But the way of the Lord is always believe first and then you will be sure, for it is only through faith that we can understand (Hebrews 11:3).

John 6:70 (a)
Jesus answered them, Have not I chosen you twelve . . .

After seeing the crowds walk away from Him, I'm sure there was a momentary smile on Jesus' face as He looked at the twelve who stood beside Him.

John 6:70 (b), 71
. . . and one of you is a devil? He spake of Judas Iscariot the son of Simon: for he it was that should betray him, being one of the twelve.

As He corrected Peter's misconception that all twelve "believed and were sure," the smile must have slowly faded from Jesus' face.

For topical study of John 6:70–71 entitled "Why Jesus Chose Judas," turn to page 495.

FACING FRUSTRATION
A Topical Study of
John 6:5–11

Because there's a good chance you're feeling frustrated about something even now, I want us to look at a man who faced frustration in his own life. The situation is this: The disciples had just returned from a mission in which they had seen blind eyes opened, the sick healed, the oppressed liberated (Matthew 10). Wisely realizing they needed time to unwind, time to be rebuilt, and time to be renewed, Jesus took them across the Sea of Galilee (Mark 6:30–32). Arriving in Bethsaida, however, they discovered that a crowd had figured out where they were headed and had gone around the lake to meet them. Seeing the multitude, and knowing their need, Jesus turned to Philip and said, "Philip, we're in your town. A lot of these people are your friends, your relatives. What are we going to do?" (see John 6:5).

"I don't know," answered Philip. "We don't have enough money to even begin to feed this crowd."

Maybe today you feel that same frustration. Maybe bills are piling up on your desk. Maybe the job you hold is not generating the necessary income to keep your books balanced. Maybe a relationship seems to be lacking the love you desire. Maybe you find yourself frustrated—like Philip.

The Frustration of Philip

Philip was frustrated by the situation he was in. I can relate to that. I face frustrations that are very great, very deep, and weigh heavily upon me. You do too. *Lord, why are You picking on me?* Philip must have wondered. *Why don't You ask Peter what to do? Or James? Why single* me *out, Lord?*

Do you ever feel that way? Amidst times of challenge and periods of frustration in each of our lives, there is a tendency to want to pass the buck. "Why, Lord, are You asking *me* what to do with these five thousand people? Why not ask someone else?"

Philip was frustrated not only by the situation he was in, but by the figures he had. "Lord, as I add up our account, I realize we have enough money to feed about thirteen people." He was frustrated by the figures he had because, dear friend, he was looking to his own resources rather than to the Source. How easily I fall into that same trap. I find myself looking at figures, statistics, and facts—and coming up short. Yet even though Philip failed to see with the eyes of faith, his failure didn't frustrate God's work. I like that! Even though Philip was frustrated, God's work still went on.

Folks, the Lord's work *will* go on. And even if we go through seasons of failure and lapses of faith, I am so thankful He's bigger than our failure and greater than our lack of faith. He's building His church, establishing His kingdom, pouring out

His Spirit, and proclaiming the gospel to the entire world in these last days. Philip's failure had no effect upon the work of the Lord. Neither did it disqualify Philip from the work of the Lord. Although Philip didn't see what could have taken place had he been a man of faith, Jesus still said to Philip, "Can you get everyone to sit down in groups of fifty and pass out the food?" (John 6:10, 11).

This is what is so neat about Jesus. Even though Philip wasn't able to see the miracle come through him, the Lord didn't say, "You turkey, Philip. You lacked faith. I'm not going to use you in any way in any time. Hit the showers. You're through." No, He gave Philip something else to do. Philip didn't see miraculous power flow through him in the way he could have, yet Jesus used him anyway.

The Confidence of Christ

While Philip was sweating it out, Jesus was cool as a cucumber. He knew what He was going to do all along. Why, then, did He ask Philip's advice? In order to give Philip the opportunity to stretch and to grow. The same is true in your situation. Whatever is frustrating you today—whatever fears you face, whatever tensions you feel, whatever burdens you're bearing—Jesus already knows what He's going to do concerning them. We don't, but He does. And He wants us to walk by faith, to trust Him.

Not only did Jesus know what He was going to do, but He also knew *how* He was going to do it. Before the miracle ever took place, He lifted up His eyes and gave thanks to His Father (John 6:11). So, too, regarding your dilemma, your frustration, your fear—do what Jesus did. Lift up your eyes and say, "Thank You, Father, that You're going to take care of this situation. I know You will. You are faithful. You have never let me down but have done exceedingly abundantly above all I could ask or think. When I thought I couldn't make it, You pulled me through. When I thought I was going under, You pulled me up. When I thought I was out of it, You pulled me back. You've been so good. Thus, I give you thanks right now in this moment of frustration."

In *everything* give thanks, for this is the will of God in Christ Jesus concerning you (1 Thessalonians 5:18). There is power in praise, gang. The Lord is pleased with people who are thankful as opposed to those who complain, murmur, and worry as they utter words that are depressing, defeating, and discouraging. The Lord blesses those who take what they have—as insufficient as it might seem—place it in His hands, and say, "Thank You, Lord. I believe in You."

Philip and Jesus were two men standing in the same place. One was frustrated, the other at rest. One was hot and bothered, the other cool and confident. The difference? Philip looked at the figures. Jesus looked to the Father.

We have a choice to make, both as a church and as individuals: We can follow the example of Philip and say, "Why are You picking on me, Lord? My resources are so limited. My situation is impossible." Or we can be like Jesus and lift our eyes to heaven, give thanks to the Father, and watch Him multiply and bless.

I'm asking you today to follow in the footsteps of Jesus Christ. In everything give thanks. Give Him what you have and expect Him to multiply it. You do not have to be frustrated today. You can be free right now if you'll fix your eyes on heaven, have faith in the Father, and in *everything* give thanks.

SENDER OF THE STORM
A Topical Study of
John 6:15–21

The teacher walked into the third- and fourth-grade Sunday-school class just in time to hear one of the students pray. "Dear God," said the nine-year-old, "bless our mothers and our fathers, and our sisters and brothers. And bless the teachers. And oh, by the way, God, take care of Yourself because if anything happens to You, we're all sunk."

The text before us makes it clear to us that Jesus is unsinkable. Truly, our Lord and Friend is our Savior in the storm who will come when the hour is darkest, when the danger is greatest. But I want you to see something else here. That is, Jesus Christ is not only the Savior in the storm but also the Sender of the storm, for in Matthew's account of this same story, Jesus commanded the disciples to cross the Sea of Galilee, even though a storm would be coming (14:22). Why would Jesus be the Sender of the very storm you're going through presently? Why would He allow the wind to rise, and the waves to beat on your little boat? I submit four reasons why Jesus Christ, our Captain, our Savior in the storm, is also the Sender of the storm.

He Sends Storms to Give Us New Direction

They that go down to the sea in ships, that do business in great waters; these see the works of the LORD, and his wonders in the deep. For he commandeth, and raiseth the stormy wind, which lifteth up the waves thereof. They mount up to the heaven, they go down again to the depths: their soul is melted because of trouble. They reel to and fro, and stagger like a drunken man, and are at their wits" end. Then they cry unto the LORD in their trouble, and he bringeth them out of their distresses.   Psalm 107:23–28

The Lord creates storms to cause sailors to come to their wits' end. You see, in times of pride and pomposity we think, *I'm captain of my ship and master of my fate*—until a storm suddenly and savagely comes into our life. Then we find ourselves calling out to the One for whom we had no time previously, or didn't think we had need of personally. Paul says it's the goodness of God that leads men to repentance (Romans 2:4). That's the ideal—but not always how it works practically. With those who don't respond to His goodness, God must deal radically in order to get their attention.

"What does it profit a man," Jesus asked, "if he gain the whole world, but lose his soul?" (Mark 8:36). Sometimes the Lord may have to put us in a difficult situation to get our attention because He's more concerned about our eternal state than He is about our present comfort. Truly, He sends storms to bring us to our wits' end in order that we might call upon Him and change direction.

He Sends Storms to Give Us Necessary Correction

And said, I cried by reason of mine affliction unto the LORD, and he heard me; out of the belly of hell cried I, and thou heardest my voice. For thou hadst cast me into the deep, in the midst of the seas; and the floods compassed me about: all thy billows and thy waves passed over me.   Jonah 2:2, 3

God wanted to use Jonah greatly in Nineveh. But Jonah found a ship going in the opposite direction. It's interesting how that works. Whenever you want to backslide, turn away, or sail in the opposite direction, guess who is in port with a ship all ready to go? Satan never says, "You want to backslide? Great! Where's a ship? Somebody get me a ship!" Nope. He's already got the ship in port, engines revved, sails set. Right now, Satan has a ship waiting for you if you want to jump on it. But the problem is, like Jonah, you pay for it (Jonah 1:3).

A man was telling me about his diet. "It seemed like the Lord spoke to my heart about cutting down," he said. "But one day, I thought it might be His will that I have a donut. So I asked Him to give me a parking place right in front of the donut shop if it was His will. And sure enough—after only the third time around the block, there one was!"

Maybe some of you are circling around the block right now, saying, "Well, Lord, if You want me to get involved with him . . ." or "If you want me to go there . . ." It'll probably happen because Satan always has a ship ready. But know this: If you're running from God or trying to rationalize what you know is not His best for you, a storm is sure to follow.

He Sends Storms to Give Us Needed Protection

And they that had eaten were about five thousand men, beside women and children. And straightway Jesus constrained his disciples to get into a ship, and to go before him unto the other side, while he sent the multitudes away.
                                                                                    Matthew 14:21, 22

The people had been fed miraculously, and now they wanted Jesus to rule them politically. Knowing this would sound like the moment His disciples had been waiting for and realizing it would seem like the fulfillment of their dreams, Jesus sent them away for their own protection.

A fire department received a shipment of high-tech helmets. Brightly colored, scuff-resistant, adjustable-strapped, they were incredible works of art, complete with five-hundred-dollar price tags. There was only one problem: They melted when they got near heat. Likewise, the Lord has to say to you and me, "You're getting your house together, and your car all shiny. You're involved with this gadget and that gizmo, this hobby and the other activity. But they're not going to take the heat." When our lives are tested with fire at the judgment seat of Christ, that which is wood, hay, and stubble will burn. Only that which is gold, silver, and precious stones will remain (1 Corinthians 3:12–15). So what does the Lord do? He says, "To get your mind off the material world, I'm sending you into a storm where you will wrestle with issues and struggle with difficulties. I'm watching over you, praying for you, and living right inside of you. But it's a struggle you'll have to go through in order that your focus can be shifted from the temporal to the eternal."

He Sends Storms to Nurture Perfection

And as they spake unto the people, the priests, and the captain of the temple, and the Sadducees, came upon them, being grieved that they taught the people, and preached through Jesus the resurrection from the dead. And they laid hands on them, and put them in hold unto the next day: for it was now eventide. Howbeit many of them which heard the word believed; and the number of the men was about five thousand.   Acts 4:1–4

After feeding five thousand people, Jesus sent His disciples into a storm while He ascended to a mountain (Matthew 14:23). I believe He did this to prepare them for the time He would ascend not to a mountain, but all the way to heaven. You see, in Acts 4, another crowd of five thousand appears—not being fed but being saved. And immediately after the five thousand were saved, a storm of persecution broke out so brutal that the disciples were cast into prison. Thus, I believe the storm they went through in John for a couple of hours on the Sea of Galilee was simply preparatory for what would happen in the storm of persecution that would follow in Acts.

Our Captain sees what tomorrow holds. That's why He says, "As difficult as this might seem, it's absolutely necessary to prepare you and perfect you for what is coming." Suffice it to say, there were storms I went through previously that were absolutely necessary for the storms that would follow a decade later. Gang, the storms you and I are going through presently are necessary to enable us to navigate what lies ahead.

So what should we do? Should we freak out, give up, turn back? Should we take a ship in the opposite direction? No. We should follow the example of the disciples, embrace the storm, and stay the course, knowing Jesus will appear to us at exactly the right moment, saying, "It is I; be not afraid."

Fellow sailors, be of good cheer, and rejoice that the Sender of the storm is also our Savior in the storm—for without Him, we'd all be sunk!

JESUS: THE I AM
A Topical Study of
John 6:35,48

As we tucked three-year-old Benjamin in bed every night, his request was always the same: Sing "Allelu, Allelu, we have come into His presence, Allelu."

This is great! we thought. *We're raising a spiritual giant!*

After a few weeks, however, Benny asked, "When do we get His presents?" And suddenly it dawned on us that while we were singing, "We have come into His presence," Ben was singing, "We have come into His *presents*"—as in birthday and Christmas!

That's where the crowd was in Jesus' day. They were thinking temporal and touchable, when Jesus was speaking to them of the spiritual and eternal. "Give us bread—as Moses did," they demanded of Jesus.

Truly, the manna that sustained the people of Israel as they wandered through the wilderness for forty years was an interesting substance. It was small, round, and white. It tasted like honey and came from heaven. Its size speaks of humility. So, too, Jesus left His throne of glory to live among us (Philippians 2:7). Its color speaks of purity. So, too, our Lord has no sin, no spot whatsoever (1 Peter 1:19). Its shape speaks of eternity. So, too, Jesus has neither beginning nor end (Revelation 1:8). Its taste speaks of ecstasy. So, too, Jesus satisfies our deepest longing (Psalm 34:8). Its origin speaks of deity. So, too, Jesus is one with the Father (John 10:30).

Because the Jews failed to realize the manna Moses gave the children of Israel was nothing less than a picture of Him, however, Jesus uttered two words that should have taken the crowd all the way back to Exodus 3 when He said, "I AM." You see, when Moses received God's call to lead His people out of Egypt, he debated with God as to whether he would be able to do it. "Who should I say sent me to lead them into the Land of Promise?" Moses asked. "Who are You? What is Your name?"

"My name is I AM," answered the Lord (Exodus 3:14).

At this point, Moses must have scratched his head and thought, *You are . . . what?*—not realizing that what God really is would only be fully and completely revealed when Jesus Christ came on the scene.

At the end of His ministry, Jesus could say, "I have manifested Thy name unto the men which Thou hast given Me (John 17:6) because He filled in the blank completely and perfectly.

Are you hungry today? Is there something gnawing in your soul? Are you dissatisfied? Are you empty? Jesus would say to you, "I am the Bread." Are you in the dark today? Do you feel like you don't know which way to turn? Jesus would say to you, "I am the Light." Are you vulnerable, unsure, or fearful? Jesus would say to you, "I am the Door. I will protect you and keep out anything that would harm you." Do you feel cut off and isolated? Jesus would say to you, "I am the Vine. Abide in Me. Cling to Me. Find your security in Me." Gang, whatever you have need of, Jesus will be. "I am what?" He asks. "I'm everything."

The problem is that all too often we look for something *from* Jesus, instead of simply clinging *to* Him, moment by moment.

If Benjamin had come to me as a toddler, saying he wanted to go home because he didn't feel well, I could say, "Well, Ben, walk through the amphitheatre, take a left down the gravel path, turn right in the parking lot, go up the hill, stick your thumb out, and hitchhike on Highway 238 for eleven miles until you get to the bottom of Jacksonville Hill. Then take a left at Van Wey's Market, turn right on G street, turn left on Huener Lane, go three houses down, and you'll be there."

Or, I could have said, "Come here, Benny." And I could have held him in my arms, walked out to the parking lot, and driven him home. *That's* what Jesus does. He doesn't tell us the way. He *is* the Way.

"Whom seek ye?" He asked of the soldiers who had come to arrest Him.

"Jesus of Nazareth," they answered.

"Ego Eimi," said Jesus. "I AM."

And the soldiers—most likely several hundred in number—fell over backward (John 18:4–6), knocked down not by anything Jesus did, but by the sheer power of who He *is*.

So, too, once you grab this, once you see it's not something Jesus gives *to* you, but who He is *for* you, you'll be bowled over. You'll say, "Lord, I've been asking for this continually and looking for that fervently. But in reality it's all wrapped up in You personally. And if I rest in Your arms, I'll end up at the right spot. If I stay close to You, I'll be protected. If I cling to You, I'll feel whole. If I allow You into my life, I'll feel satisfied at last?"

"That's right," Jesus answers. "I am the Way. I am the Door. I am the Vine. I am the Bread."

When the manna fell from heaven, the children of Israel could have done any one of four things . . .

They could have picked it up. They could eat it morning by morning and receive strength for the day's journey—just as spending time with Jesus, the Bread of life, gives us strength for the challenges of each new day.

They could have trampled on it. Those today who are unwilling to expend the energy or make the effort to partake of the Lord are essentially saying, "I don't need the Lord. I can journey on without Him." Desiring that none should perish, God laid down His life for us (2 Peter 3:9). If, however, we reject Him, He'll allow us to go to hell. But we'll have to trample on Him to get there.

They could have ignored it. So, too, you might not think you're trampling on the Lord—but, you see, if the manna wasn't gathered, it melted (Exodus 16:21). Many times, people say, "I just don't feel the Lord, or sense His strength." And I always have to ask them, "Did you take time this morning to feed on Him and look to Him—or were you simply too busy?" Oftentimes, it's because I have neglected the Lord in the cool of the morning that He can't be found in the heat of the day. Oh, He's still there, for He never leaves us nor forsakes us. But I don't perceive His presence.

They could have stored it. Some said, "Hey this is too hard to do daily. Let's gather a bunch of manna to tide us over for several days." But you know what happened? It bred worms and stank (Exodus 16:20). So, too, there are those who say, "I've had enough Bible study. I don't need to go to church on Wednesday night. I don't need to go to home fellowship. I've been doing this for some time. I've got enough stored up."

Usually, in about the third-to-fifth year of his walk, a believer finds himself vulnerable to saying, "I know it. I've got it down. I don't need to hear the Gospel of John again. I don't need to get up early and seek the Lord." That's why Jesus taught us to pray, "Give us this day our *daily* bread" (Matthew 6:11). Day by day, He wants to be your I AM.

Jesus is everything you have need of personally. The question is, are you going to slow down, stoop down, and pick up the Bread of Life? "I listen to tapes on my way to work," you say. That's fine. But the Lord isn't in the fast-food business, gang. He prepares for us a table (Psalm 23:5). He invites us to come and dine (John 21:12). He feeds us as we sit in His presence (John 6:10).

Each day, may God grace you with the simple reminder that He is the Bread, the Manna sent from heaven. Take the time to feed on Him, and you'll find He will satisfy you now and forevermore.

WHY JESUS CHOSE JUDAS
A Topical Study of
John 6:70–71

As the crowd turned away and as the twelve chose to stay, Jesus said there was one in their midst who would betray Him. Why did Jesus choose Judas? Yes, Jesus had to die on the Cross for the sin of humanity. Yes, Judas was part of that plan. But why did it have to be one of His inner circle who betrayed Him? Why couldn't it have been a Roman soldier, a Pharisee, or a government leader? Why did it have to be one of His own, one whom He had chosen? I'd like to suggest several reasons. . . .

Jesus Chose Judas in Order to Fulfill Bible Prophecy

The Old Testament contains over three hundred exacting prophecies concerning Messiah, including where He would be born, how He would be born, where He would live, how He would be betrayed, and how He would die. Psalm 41:9 is one of those three hundred: "Yea, mine own familiar friend, in whom I trusted, which did eat of my bread, hath lifted up his heel against me." By the time Jesus was twelve years old, His knowledge of the Word was so incredible that He blew the minds of the religious scholars in Jerusalem (Luke 2:46, 47). Jesus knew the Word. Therefore, I wonder what His morning devotions were like as He read prophecy after prophecy that spoke of His own suffering and death.

If you really want to mature in your Christian walk, I suggest you go through your Bibles regularly and claim the promises you have *not* underlined—those that you have sought to avoid. I've never found "Yea all those who live godly in Christ Jesus shall suffer persecution," (see 2 Timothy 3:12) in a "Coffee With Christ" promise box. I've yet to read, "Blessed are you when men shall revile you and persecute you and say all manner of evil against you falsely for my sake" (see Matthew 5:11) in a "Minute with the Master" devotional. There's a big difference between the promises we underline and the full counsel of God. Many brothers and sisters err, I believe, by failing to recognize and claim the promises that are a little bit tougher. Jesus chose Judas because He knew the Scriptures and, as difficult as it was, He knew it was part of the plan of the Father for Him according to the Word.

Jesus Chose Judas in Order to Relate to You Personally

Maybe you have been hurt by someone who has betrayed your trust, broken your heart, misunderstood your motive, and "lifted his heel against you" to kick you in the teeth. Jesus Christ knows exactly how you feel. He was tempted in *all* points like as we are (Hebrews 4:15). There's not a single temptation or hurt you'll ever face that Jesus didn't feel. No matter what your pain is, no matter what your vulnerability might be, Jesus can sympathize because He's gone through the very same trials.

Jesus Chose Judas as an Impartial Witness
of His Moral Excellency

After Judas betrayed Jesus, he threw his reward away, saying, "I have betrayed innocent blood" (Matthew 27:4). This one who was out to destroy Jesus, this one who had lived daily with Jesus concluded he never saw Jesus do a single thing wrong. When you apply for a job and are asked for references, do you list the person who hates you, the person who has a grudge against you, the person who is mad at you? That's what Jesus did. His character reference is the one who was determined to destroy Him, the one who was disappointed in Him, the one who betrayed Him. It's a testimony to the moral excellence of our Lord that even the one who hated Him the most had to admit He never did anything amiss.

Jesus Chose Judas in Order to Enlighten Us about Hypocrisy

"The church is full of hypocrites," grumbles the non-believer—as if this is a new revelation. Listen, if there was a hypocrite even in Jesus' inner circle, there are sure to be hypocrites in the church today. Jesus warned that, along with the wheat, tares were sure to grow (Matthew 13:24–30). And His own disciples were no exception.

Jesus Chose Judas in Order to Warn Us Powerfully

When Jesus sat at the table and said one would betray Him, no one pointed a finger and said, "It's the guy down there with the black cape, the black hat, the beady eyes, and the handlebar mustache. It's Judas." No, no one suspected Judas. No one even suggested Judas. On the contrary, each of the men around the table suspected only himself (Matthew 26:22).

Why did Jesus reveal Judas as being the betrayer at this point in John 6? Because this was the moment when something must have clicked within Judas, when something dark began to happen, when Judas became disappointed in the Lord. *Jesus*, Judas must have thought, *You missed Your chance. A crowd of people wants You to be their king—but You turn them away by telling them to eat of Your body and drink of Your blood? It's political stupidity. It doesn't pay off financially. It's crazy.*

So, too, there are hundreds of people in the Rogue Valley in Oregon who, although they were once on fire for Jesus Christ, turned their backs on Him when He failed to bless their little kingdoms. If things aren't going the way you think they should at work, at home, financially, professionally, or relationally—watch out. At that point, if you're not careful, you will become disappointed because the Lord is not doing what you think He should, and you will be vulnerable to turning your back on Him.

Jesus Chose Judas in Order to Show His Beauty

"Friend, wherefore art thou come?" Jesus asked Judas (Matthew 26:50). Jesus called Judas His friend even as Judas was in the very act of betraying Him. Maybe you can relate to Judas. Maybe you've been demanding your own way. Maybe you've become vulnerable to bitterness. Maybe you're disappointed in the Lord.

I have good news for you: Not a single person sitting here is in a worse place than was Judas at this point. And Jesus called Judas "*Friend.*"

"Wherefore art thou come?" Jesus asked Judas. Certainly He knew why Judas was there. But I believe He was giving Judas one more opportunity to rethink what he was doing, to turn, to repent, to get right.

So, too, the Lord could be saying to you today, "Wherefore art thou come? I'm giving you one more opportunity to come to Me."

The invitation is yours. You can take advantage of the beauty of Jesus right now. You can say, "I surrender, Lord. I'm no longer demanding my will or fighting for my way. Today I give myself totally, wholeheartedly to You."

And such is my prayer for each of us.

John 7:1 (a)
After these things Jesus walked in Galilee . . .

The Greek word translated "walked" is in the perfect tense, denoting continual action. Thus, although the people had walked away from Him, Jesus continued to walk in their region. So, too, when you talk with people who don't respond to the gospel, there comes a point when you have to let them go, even as Jesus did. But, like Jesus, continue to walk in their region. Be available to them should they have a change of heart, should the Spirit work within them to draw them to the kingdom.

John 7:1 (b)
. . . for he would not walk in Jewry, because the Jews sought to kill him.

Because Jesus had healed a man on the Sabbath, thereby claiming equality with the Father (John 5:18), the Jewish leaders made plans to kill Him. Consequently, we see Jesus walking prudently by staying out of Jerusalem altogether.

John 7:2
Now the Jews' feast of tabernacles was at hand.

As they camped out in tabernacles—little lean-tos—the Jews commemorated God's provision for and protection of His people through their wilderness wandering. It was, in effect, the Jewish equivalent to Family Camp.

John 7:3, 4
His brethren therefore said unto him, Depart hence, and go into Judaea, that thy disciples also may see the works that thou doest. For there is no man that doeth any thing in secret, and he himself seeketh to be known openly. If thou do these things, shew thyself to the world.

It's as if Jesus' brothers challenged Him, saying, "Go show the people in Jerusalem what you can do. We dare You." Brothers do things like that.

John 7:5
For neither did his brethren believe in him.

Can you imagine growing up with a Brother who never did anything wrong, who never called you a name, never teased you, or never made fun of you? Jesus was the nicest brother who ever lived. Yet His brothers didn't believe in Him. We know, however, that later on, Jesus' half–brother, Jude, came to such a saving knowledge of Jesus that a Book in the Bible bears his name. And His half brother, James, so strong in the faith that he was the leader of the early church, penned the Book of James. But neither James nor Jude became believers until Jesus was crucified on a Cross and resurrected from the dead.

A lot of times we think, *If I'm a nice person, my neighbor is going to get saved. I'll mow his lawn; I'll bake him cookies; I'll smile when he drives by. I'll be a lovely person—and that will convert him.* Gang, there was no lovelier person than Jesus Christ. Yet His brothers did not believe in Him until after the Resurrection.

Therefore, I think some of us need a greater aggressiveness in preaching Jesus Christ and Him crucified. You can wave to your neighbor for twenty years and wave him right into hell. Or you can take the time at some point to say, "You know what? Jesus Christ died for your sins and rose again from the dead—and you must believe on Him." May we be wisely, but aggressively and radically, bold in sharing the full story of the gospel.

John 7:6–10
Then Jesus said unto them, My time is not yet come: but your time is always ready. The world cannot hate you; but me it hateth, because I testify of it, that the works thereof are evil. Go ye up unto this feast: I go not up yet unto this feast; for my time is not yet full come. When he had said these words unto them, he abode still in Galilee. But when his brethren were gone up, then went he also up unto the feast, not openly, but as it were in secret.

"You can go to Jerusalem anytime you want," Jesus said to His brothers. "You can fit in. You have no reason to fear. But because they hate Me, I must walk wisely." Jesus did, however, end up going to Jerusalem. Why did He go if the Jews were out to kill Him? Why did He go if He couldn't fit into that scene? Because in Deuteronomy 16:16, God commanded Him to go. Therefore, even though it may not have been prudent for Jesus to go, prudence bowed to obedience as He submitted to His Father.

What does this mean for me? It means that, while I am to walk wisely and circumspectly—not looking for confrontation, not endangering myself or others, not moving in the world's scene, or going where it's dark—the Word of God has priority over my own understanding. How I thank the Lord that His Word doesn't change from day to day, month to month, year to year; that it is immutable, timeless, and practical; that it needs no addenda, updates, or changes. I think sometimes we who come week after month after year to study God's Word begin to perhaps take for granted the profundity of the truth that has been given to us therein. Jesus knew the Word completely. Thus, fulfilling the law perfectly, He went to Jerusalem secretly.

John 7:11–13
Then the Jews sought him at the feast, and said, Where is he? And there was much murmuring among the people concerning him: for some said, He is a good man: others said, Nay; but he deceiveth the people. Howbeit no man spake openly of him for fear of the Jews.

As in verse 40, we will see people divided time and time again because of Jesus.

John 7:14
Now about the midst of the feast Jesus went up into the temple, and taught.

The first time Jesus went to Jerusalem, He cleansed the temple (John 2:13–16). This time, He's teaching in the temple. And that's always the way it is: Before Jesus can impart His Word effectively *to* me, there must first be a cleansing *within* me. The moneychangers must be driven out, the cattle chased away. That is why as you study the Word with us corporately and in your devotions personally, it's always good to say, "Lord, before I even begin reading, search my heart. Show me that which needs to be confessed."

"If I regard iniquity in my heart, the Lord will not hear me," declared the psalmist (Psalm 66:18). Why? Because our Father won't allow us to live in sin that will hurt both us and those around us. Consequently, He says, "I'm going to break communication with you not because I'm angry with you or because I'm giving up on you, but because something's amiss within you that will bring pain into your life and problems into the lives of those around you. So when your prayers aren't being answered or when the Word doesn't seem to speak to you, call upon Me. Let Me come in and cleanse your temple. And *then* I will teach. *Then* you will hear My voice. *Then* you will see My face." I think too many of us minimize the importance of quietly waiting on the Lord and asking Him to search our hearts. Before teaching, there must be cleansing.

John 7:15
And the Jews marvelled, saying, How knoweth this man letters, having never learned?

At the time Jesus was ministering, there were at least thirty seminaries in and around Jerusalem. Jesus had a degree from none of them. Consequently, when the Jewish leaders heard Him speak, they wondered where He had garnered such insight. The same thing would later be said of His followers, for when Peter and John spoke in Acts 4, the Jews marveled at their boldness. Then they realized they had been with Jesus. That's the key. You see, it's not what you know; it's who you know that counts. And if you've been hanging out with Jesus, if you've logged in some morning time with Him, some afternoon breaks in His Word, or some evening sessions of contemplation, even if you're unlearned and ignorant according to the world's scholastic system, people will marvel at you.

John 7:16–19 (a)
Jesus answered them, and said, My doctrine is not mine, but his that sent me. If any man will do his will, he shall know of the doctrine, whether it be of God, or whether I speak of myself. He that speaketh of himself seeketh his own glory: but he that seeketh his glory that sent him, the same is true, and no unrighteousness is in him. Did not Moses give you the law, and yet none of you keepeth the law?

Notice Jesus said if any man *do* His will, he shall know of the doctrine. Revelation is directly linked to application. If you do what you've already been told, more will be revealed to you concerning His doctrine. The problem with us so frequently is that we don't do what we already know to do—and then wonder why we don't learn more. Truly, obedience is the door through which revelation enters.

John 7:19 (b)–24
Why go ye about to kill me? The people answered and said, Thou hast a devil: who goeth about to kill thee? Jesus answered and said unto them, I have done one work, and ye all marvel. Moses therefore gave unto you circumcision; (not because it is of Moses, but of the fathers;) and ye on the sabbath day circumcise a man. If a man on the sabbath day receive circumcision, that the law of Moses should not be broken; are ye angry at me, because I have made a man every whit whole on the sabbath day? Judge not according to the appearance, but judge righteous judgment.

"Why are you angry with Me? Why are you out to kill Me?" asked Jesus. "Because I healed a man on the Sabbath day. Yet you allow circumcision on the Sabbath." Indeed they did—and still do. You see, according to Genesis 17, eight days after birth, Jewish boys were to be marked through the cutting away of the flesh as those who had a covenant relationship with God. Jesus' argument here is brilliant. He says, "You're not upset when someone causes pain on the Sabbath, when something is taken away on the Sabbath, when there is a cry of anguish on the Sabbath. Yet because I healed on the Sabbath, because I restored health on the Sabbath, because there was a cry of joy on the Sabbath, you're upset."

Isn't that typical of religion? Religion says,

"You better not be happy. If you're spiritual, you should be miserable. If any of you are having a good time on Sunday, shame on you." That's religiosity, the way of the law—painful, heavy, and miserable.

But here's Jesus, our wonderful, radical Savior, saying, "Does it really make sense that you circumcise on the Sabbath but won't let Me heal on the Sabbath?"

John 7:25–27
Then said some of them of Jerusalem, Is not this he, whom they seek to kill? But, lo, he speaketh boldly, and they say nothing unto him. Do the rulers know indeed that this is the very Christ? Howbeit we know this man whence he is: but when Christ cometh, no man knoweth whence he is.

The reference here is to Isaiah 53—the classic prophecy concerning Messiah. In this passage, the Jews understood Isaiah to say no one would know from whence Messiah came. Therefore, because they knew Jesus' parents (or thought they did), they argued Jesus couldn't be the Messiah.

John 7:28–30
Then cried Jesus in the temple as he taught, saying, Ye both know me, and ye know whence I am: and I am not come of myself, but he that sent me is true, whom ye know not. But I know him: for I am from him, and he hath sent me. Then they sought to take him: but no man laid hands on him, because his hour was not yet come.

Unable to argue with Jesus, the Jewish leaders resorted to violence against Him.

John 7:31–34
And many of the people believed on him, and said, When Christ cometh, will he do more miracles than these which this man hath done? The Pharisees heard that the people murmured such things concerning him; and the Pharisees and the chief priests sent officers to take him. Then said Jesus unto them, Yet a little while am I with you, and then I go unto him that sent me. Ye shall seek me, and shall not find me: and where I am, thither ye cannot come.

Jesus could deal candidly and boldly, straightforwardly yet lovingly with people because He did not live in the fear of men, trying to fashion a reputation or build a ministry. His sights were set on heaven. He knew He would be there soon, and the implication of His statement is that the Pharisees and chief priests wouldn't be joining Him.

John 7:35, 36
Then said the Jews among themselves,
Whither will he go, that we shall not find
him? will he go unto the dispersed among
the Gentiles, and teach the Gentiles? What
manner of saying is this that he said, Ye
shall seek me, and shall not find me: and
where I am, thither ye cannot come?

The Jews wondered what Jesus meant. "Is He
going to be some kind of missionary?" they
asked.

John 7:37–39
In the last day, that great day of the feast,
Jesus stood and cried, saying, If any man
thirst, let him come unto me, and drink. He
that believeth on me, as the scripture hath
said, out of his belly shall flow rivers of liv-
ing water. (But this spake he of the Spirit,
which they that believe on him should re-
ceive: for the Holy Ghost was not yet given;
because that Jesus was not yet glorified.)

On the great day, the last day of the feast, the
priests provided a powerful picture of Israel's
longing for her Messiah. You see, whereas in the
previous seven days, the priests had drawn water
from the pool of Siloam and poured it out in the
temple courtyard as an illustration of God's provision for the thirst of their bodies, on the last day
of the feast, the priests returned from the pool of
Siloam with empty pitchers as an illustration of
their need for One to satisfy the thirst of their
hearts. Thus, it was at the very moment when the
priests held empty pitchers in their hands that
Jesus cried out, "If any man thirst, let him come
to Me and drink." Certainly the crowd must have
wondered about this itinerant Rabbi, this Carpenter from Galilee who had the audacity to cry
out in the midst of the congregation. Yet no one
called for the ushers or deacons to escort Him out
because something about Him rang true. Perhaps something in His eyes, perhaps something
in His voice caused people to listen when He
spoke.

For topical study of John 7:37–39 entitled "Liv-
ing in the Living Water," turn to page 502.

John 7:40–43
Many of the people therefore, when they
heard this saying, said, Of a truth this is the
Prophet. Others said, This is the Christ. But
some said, Shall Christ come out of Galilee?
Hath not the scripture said, That Christ
cometh of the seed of David, and out of the

town of Bethlehem, where David was? So
there was a division among the people be-
cause of him.

There was a division among the people because
of Him. Haven't you found that to be true in your
family, at your job, or in your school? Jesus said,
"Think not that I am come to send peace on
earth: I came not to send peace, but a sword"
(Matthew 10:34). Therefore, don't be surprised;
don't be shocked when you sense divisions due to
your stand as a believer in Jesus Christ. It's inevitable. It happened here, and it will happen in our
lives as well.

John 7:44–46
And some of them would have taken him;
but no man laid hands on him. Then came
the officers to the chief priests and Phari-
sees; and they said unto them, Why have
ye not brought him? The officers answered,
Never man spake like this man.

"We went to arrest Him," said the officers sent
by the Pharisees and chief priests, "but we ended
up arrested by Him, for we never heard anyone
talk like He talks—with such generosity, such
clarity and such authority."

John 7:47–49
Then answered them the Pharisees, Are ye
also deceived? Have any of the rulers or of
the Pharisees believed on him? But this peo-
ple who knoweth not the law are cursed.

"Don't be duped by this Galilean," said the
Pharisees. "*We're* the ones with the education
and degrees."

John 7:50, 51
Nicodemus saith unto them, (he that came
to Jesus by night, being one of them,) Doth
our law judge any man, before it hear him,
and know what he doeth?

In John 3, as Nicodemus first came to Jesus, he
was in the midnight hour of his soul. Here in John
7, not yet sure who Jesus is, he is in the twilight
of transition as he pleads for fairness on the part
of his fellow Pharisees. In John 19, we'll see Nicodemus in the daylight of salvation. When did the
sun finally rise on Nicodemus' understanding? At
the Cross (John 19:39).
Folks, as you talk with people about the Lord,
don't get tangled up in evolution, philosophy, or
existential mind games. Keep focused on what
Jesus Christ did on the Cross and how He rose
from the dead. *That's* where people see the
Light. Turn every conversation, every debate,

and every discussion back to the Cross. "Jesus died, rose again, and wants to be your Savior, King, and Friend. What are you going to do with Him?"

John 7:52
They answered and said unto him, Art thou also of Galilee? Search, and look: for out of Galilee ariseth no prophet.

Thinking Nicodemus a fool, his fellow Pharisees asked him if he too was an unschooled Galilean. I am amazed that these guys who prided themselves on their knowledge of Scripture didn't know that, according to 2 Kings 14:25, there was indeed a prophet from Galilee. His name? Jonah.

John 7:53
And every man went unto his own house.

The great day of the feast over, the little booths knocked down, the sleeping bags rolled up, everyone headed to his own house. Not Jesus. Having no house, He headed home—into the company of His Father, as we'll see in the opening verse of chapter 8.

LIVING IN THE LIVING WATER
A Topical Study of
John 7:37–39

It is the last day of the Feast of Tabernacles. Within six months, Jesus would be pinned to a Cross as payment for our sin and rebellion. If I were Jesus, I think my tendency would have been to say, "I'm about to be betrayed, tortured, and slaughtered as I personally take upon Myself the wrath that should be vented upon a sinful world. Therefore, I am going to withdraw from people until that time." But that's not what Jesus does. Instead of holing up in isolation, Jesus heads to Jerusalem for an important convocation. There, standing in the midst of a huge congregation, He gives a great invitation, saying, "If any man thirst, let him come unto Me and drink."

One of three major festivals celebrated in Jerusalem each year, the Feast of Tabernacles was the happiest and most joyful. Camped out in little lean-tos similar to pup tents, parents would tell their children how God miraculously provided for their fathers for forty years in the wilderness. They would tell of a pillar of fire by night and a cloud by day; of bread from the sky and water from a rock.

To commemorate the miraculous provision of water, a procession of priests would draw water from the pool of Siloam and pour it out on the floor of the temple courtyard during each day of the feast. On the eighth day, the last day, the great day of the feast, however, the priests would return from the pool of Siloam with empty vessels, signifying that when the Israelites entered the Promised Land, water from the rock was no longer needed. The Feast of Tabernacles not only commemorated the past—it anticipated the future. As the priests symbolically poured out their empty vessels on the last day, the high priest would read Isaiah 44:3: "For I will pour water upon him that is thirsty, and floods upon the dry ground: I will pour my spirit upon thy seed, and my blessing upon thine offspring."

The picture was unmistakably clear. You see, "Siloam," the name of the pool from which the priests drew the water, means "Sent One"—just as Messiah would be the Sent One who would pour out His Spirit upon a thirsty people. It was at this climactic moment of the week-long celebration that a thirty-three-year-old Carpenter from Galilee stood up and broke the silence as He cried, "If any man thirst, let him come to Me. And out of his innermost being shall gush forth torrents of living water."

The long-awaited Messiah had come to the people of Israel. And here, in their midst, He invited them to come to Him. If they had, they would have received rivers of water—not only water within, but flowing forth from them in order that others might be served and refreshed. It is what is called the filling of the Spirit, the overflow of the Spirit, the coming upon of the Spirit, the baptism in the Spirit. The same is true today. If you're a believer, you have the Holy Spirit *in* you. But has the Holy Spirit come *upon* you? Is He overflowing *from* you?

After Jesus died and rose from the dead, He said to His disciples, "Receive ye the Holy Ghost." He breathed on them, and they did indeed receive the Holy Ghost *within* them (John 20:22). But were they empowered? Were they like rivers of water? No. They were hiding in an upper room. Yes, they were Christians. Yes, they were born again. But they were still timid and unsure of what they should do. Then, forty days later, the Spirit came *upon* them on the Day of Pentecost, and three thousand were saved (Acts 2).

Gang, there's a difference between the Spirit being *in* you, and the Spirit coming *upon* you, flowing *from* you. People say, "I received the Holy Spirit when I was saved."

"Amen," I say. "You did. Like the disciples in John 20, when you opened your heart to Jesus Christ, the Holy Spirit took up residence within you. You have the Holy Spirit. My question is: Does the Holy Spirit have you?"

"Go and wait in Jerusalem until the Holy Ghost comes *upon* you," Jesus said to His disciples (see Luke 24:49). "Then you shall receive power." The Greek word translated "power" is *dunamis,* from which we get the word "dynamite." Jesus promised dynamic power to enable them to be His witnesses as His Spirit not only satisfied them but also overflowed from them.

In a vision of the millennial kingdom, Ezekiel saw a river flowing from the temple (Ezekiel 47). "Walk with me," a man said to him. And they walked fifteen hundred feet. "Step in," the man said. And Ezekiel stepped into the river up to his ankles. "Walk with me," the man said again. And they walked fifteen hundred feet further. Again, Ezekiel was instructed to step into the river. This time, the water came up to his knees. A third time, they walked together; and a third time Ezekiel stepped into the river, which came up to his waist. Finally, after walking further, Ezekiel stepped into the river once again—but this time, he could not stand. The water being over his head, Ezekiel was enveloped in the flow of the river.

It's a perfect illustration of life in the Spirit. That is, you get saved. You step in. And you're up to your ankles, standing on the promises of Jesus Christ. As you head down the road toward heaven, you go a little deeper in your walk, and you become aware of impotence in your life. So you call upon the Lord, and you're up to your knees in prayer. A little further on in your pilgrimage, you want to see others saved. You start witnessing and ministering, and you're up to your waist—a picture of the reproductive life of the Spirit. Finally, you get to the place where you say, "I just want to be over my head in You, Lord, immersed in Your Spirit. I no longer want to control my ministry or my destiny. Take me, Lord. Sweep me off my feet. Baptize me in Your power. Do with me as You wish."

That's being filled with the Spirit. "But how does that happen practically?" you ask. "How can I live in the Spirit? How can I be like Ezekiel—over my head, immersed in His power?" I would like to suggest three steps for your consideration. . . .

Come to the Rock

Moses struck the rock in Exodus 17, and it poured out water for a thirsty people. Paul tells us that Rock was Christ (1 Corinthians 10:4). You see, when Jesus Christ, the Rock of our salvation, was smitten on the Cross, blood and water flowed from His side (John 19:34). While the blood speaks of the cleansing of sin, the water speaks of the Spirit. The blood must be shed before the Spirit can flow (1 John 5:6). Therefore, because the Holy Spirit cannot dwell in you or come upon you until your sin is dealt with, the first step to being filled with the Spirit is simply to get saved. Come to the Rock. And, like the woman at the well, you will find your thirst quenched forevermore.

Speak to the Rock

In Numbers 20, the Israelites were thirsty once again. Moses cried to the Lord, and the Lord said, "Speak to the rock and it shall give forth water."

But Moses, weary of the whining of his congregation of three million, said, "You rebels, must we fetch water for you?" as he struck the rock twice. And, although water came out graciously, Moses was punished for his misrepresentation of God to the people. "I'm not mad at My people," God said to Moses. "I'm not disappointed in them. I'm not through with them. Therefore, because you called them rebels and smote the rock when I told you to speak to it, you'll not enter into the Land of Promise."

Folks, because the Rock of Ages, Jesus Christ, was smitten when He died for our sins, when you are thirsty, when you are aware you need empowering—you don't need to work something up emotionally or expend a lot of energy physically. You don't need to lash out in frustration as Moses did. All you need to do is *speak* to the Rock. Say, "Lord, I'm thirsty. My life is not flowing. Nothing's happening. Have mercy."

Jesus said, "If you, being evil, know how to give good gifts to your children, how much more will the heavenly Father give the Holy Spirit to them that *ask* Him?" (Luke 11:13). Why do we think we have to position ourselves in a certain way physically, shout emotionally, or dance heatedly in order to receive the water of the Spirit—when all we need to do is speak to the Rock? All we need to do is *ask.*

Sing to the Rock

In Numbers 21, the Israelites thirsted once again. This time, however, they simply sang a song (verses 17, 18), and water sprang from the well they dug. You see, the rock didn't actually literally, physically follow them in their wilderness wanderings. Rather, most commentators agree that a subterranean river flowed from the rock, providing a perpetual flow of water under their feet. Consequently, all the Israelites had to do to be refreshed at any given moment was realize that even if they couldn't see it, the current was moving below them. All they had to do was sing out in faith, and water would bubble to the surface. So, too, if you're saved, the Spirit is in you and with you wherever you go. But He will come upon you and overflow from you if you will simply sing out in faith. "Be filled with the Spirit," Paul said, "speaking to yourselves in psalms and hymns and spiritual songs, singing and making melody in your heart to the Lord" (Ephesians 5:18, 19).

Why do we gather together on Sundays? Because something happens when people come together to sing praise and to speak to each other in psalms, hymns, and spiritual songs. Something happens at the Lord's table when we realize the Rock has already been smitten. Something happens in the place of prayer when we simply talk to the Rock. Something happens when we begin to sing. Something begins to bubble up and overflow. How do you get filled with the Holy Ghost? How do you experience the coming upon of the Spirit? Not by incantations, gyrations, or manipulation, but simply by coming to the Rock given to us, speaking to the Rock smitten for us, and singing to the Rock present within us. Come to the Rock. Speak to the Rock. And sing out—believing that the Rock has already provided a flow underneath the surface. It's there presently, so sing out expectantly. Receive it by faith today. And may the Lord cause you to be over your head in Him, carried along in the refreshment, joy, and power of the Holy Ghost.

John 8:1
Jesus went unto the mount of Olives.

In the last verse of chapter 7, we read that, following the Feast of Tabernacles, every man went unto his own house. Not having a house, Jesus went to the Garden of Gethsemane, nestled on the slope of the Mount of Olives, in order to commune with His Father. So frequently did Jesus do this, Judas would later know right where to find Him at the time of his betrayal.

John 8:2
And early in the morning he came again into the temple, and all the people came unto him; and he sat down, and taught them.

The morning after the conclusion of the Feast of Tabernacles, Jesus was in the temple, ready to meet with any who might seek Him. "I love them that love Me," declares the Lord, "and those that seek Me early shall find Me" (Proverbs 8:17).

John 8:3, 4
And the scribes and Pharisees brought unto him a woman taken in adultery; and when they had set her in the midst, They say unto him, Master, this woman was taken in adultery, in the very act.

Caught in the act of adultery, the woman was brought, perhaps naked, to the Rabbi from Galilee.

John 8:5 (a)
Now Moses in the law commanded us, that such should be stoned . . .

While Leviticus 20 and Deuteronomy 22 both declare adultery to be a capital offense punishable by death, due to the severity of the sentence, there were safeguards to protect the innocent. That is, there could be no doubt about any of the details. The evidence had to be conclusive and unmistakable. In fact, there had to be a number of witnesses to the actual act of immorality. And their stories had to collaborate perfectly. History tells us that one couple was set free simply because the witnesses who observed their adulterous act couldn't name the tree under which it took place. Consequently, the Jewish historian Josephus tells us adultery would be punished on the average of only once every seven years.

John 8:5 (b)
. . . but what sayest thou?

If Jesus said, "Stone her," He would jeopardize His position as Friend of Sinners. Prostitutes and publicans, tax collectors and street people would no longer feel comfortable around Him, knowing He had sentenced one of their own to death. If, on the other hand, He said, "Let her go," He would be dishonoring the very Word of God He had come to fulfill (Matthew 5:17).

John 8:6 (a)
This they said, tempting him, that they might have to accuse him.

Had these scribes and Pharisees been truly interested in justice, why didn't they bring the man along with the woman? Most scholars believe it was because it was a setup to entrap Jesus and that the man himself was in collusion with them.

John 8:6 (b)
But Jesus stooped down, and with his finger wrote on the ground, as though he heard them not.

It was the finger of God that wrote, "Thou shalt not commit adultery" in tablets of stone (see Exodus 31:18). Two thousand years later, we see the finger of God once more—this time on the hand of Jesus Christ, writing in the dust of the earth.

John 8:7 (a)
So when they continued asking him, he lifted up himself . . .

In defense of the woman, the Rock of Ages stood up to the men who held rocks in their hands.

John 8:7 (b)
. . . and said unto them, He that is without sin among you, let him first cast a stone at her.

Commentator J. Allen Blair properly translates Jesus' statement as: "Let he who is without *the same* sin cast the first stone."

John 8:8, 9 (a)
And again he stooped down, and wrote on the ground. And they which heard it, being convicted by their own conscience, went out one by one, beginning at the eldest, even unto the last . . .

What did Jesus write that would cause the men to become so heavily convicted? I suggest what He wrote was in fulfillment of Jeremiah 17:13, where Jeremiah prophesied that the names of all who forsook the Lord would be written in the earth. I suggest He wrote the names of those who held rocks in their hands—and by each one a female name, a date, a place, or some other reminder of something in their past that they themselves may have long ago forgotten. Am I suggesting that all of the scribes and Pharisees present had committed adultery or that they were all involved in immorality? All I know is this: Jesus said if a man looked on a woman with lust in his heart, he was guilty (Matthew 5:28). Therefore, the words Jesus wrote on the ground were, very possibly, reminders that, because none of them was without sin, none of them was qualified to cast a stone.

John 8:9 (b), 10
. . . and Jesus was left alone, and the woman standing in the midst. When Jesus had lifted up himself, and saw none but the woman, he said unto her, Woman, where are those thine accusers? hath no man condemned thee?

Finally, when all her accusers were gone, Jesus lifted up His eyes and spoke to the woman. Notice He didn't call her, "harlot" or "sinner". He called her *gune*, or "woman"—the same title with which He had addressed His mother (John 2:4).

John 8:11 (a)
She said, No man, Lord.

The scribes and Pharisees called Jesus "Master" or "Rabbi." The woman called Him "Lord."

John 8:11 (b)
And Jesus said unto her, Neither do I condemn thee . . .

In the strictest sense of the word, Jesus couldn't have condemned her because the Law of Moses specifically states that it took a minimum of two witnesses to condemn someone (Deuteronomy 19:15). Therefore, in dismissing the scribes and Pharisees who had witnessed her sin, Jesus relinquished His opportunity to condemn her.

John 8:11 (c)
. . . go, and sin no more.

Jesus didn't say, "I won't condemn you this time, but if it happens once more, you're toast." No, He said, "Go your way, free to sin no more."

John 8:12 (a)
Then spake Jesus again unto them . . .

How I love the serenity and tranquility of our Lord. He never was and never is uptight. He had every reason to object to the rude intrusion of the keyhole-peeping, sin-sniffing, self-righteous Pharisees (verse 1). But He didn't. He simply used their interruption as an illustration. And just as a jeweler most effectively displays the radiance of his gems against a background of black, so the next statement Jesus would make would be seen all the more vividly when placed against the backdrop of the blackness and darkness of what had preceded it.

John 8:12 (b)
. . . saying, I am the light of the world: he that followeth me shall not walk in darkness, but shall have the light of life.

During the years of the wilderness wanderings, the tabernacle was lit by the shekinah glory of God (Exodus 40:34). Later, the temple was also filled with the glory of God (2 Chronicles 7:1). But because the people chose to live in darkness, there came a point when the tangible, visible presence of the light of God departed (Ezekiel 10:18). Consequently, the people of God had to light candles and trim lamps in the temple because the shekinah, the true light, had long since departed. Now, here stands Jesus, perhaps right in front of one of the candlesticks in the temple, saying, "I am the Light of life—the shekinah, the glory. I'm back." And I suggest He made this declaration with a smile on His face and His arms outstretched as He offered Himself to them.

John 8:13
The Pharisees therefore said unto him, Thou bearest record of thyself; thy record is not true.

After one thousand years, the glory returned in the Person of Jesus Christ. Yet what did the Pharisees do? They questioned Him, rejected Him, and, finally, extinguished Him.

John 8:14–19
Jesus answered and said unto them, Though I bear record of myself, yet my record is true: for I know whence I came, and whither I go; but ye cannot tell whence I come, and whither I go. Ye judge after the flesh; I judge no man. And yet if I judge, my judgment is true: for I am not alone, but I and the Father that sent me. It is also written in your law, that the testimony of two men is true. I am one that bear witness of myself, and the Father that sent me beareth witness of me. Then said they unto him, Where is thy Father? Jesus answered, Ye neither know me, nor my Father: if ye had known me, ye should have known my Father also.

Jesus said this not to defend Himself but to condemn those who declared His words invalid on the grounds that He lacked a second witness (Deuteronomy 19:15). Jesus' second witness was His Father, who validated Jesus' mission and position when He said, "This is My beloved Son in whom I am well pleased," on the day of His baptism (Matthew 3:17).

John 8:20–24
These words spake Jesus in the treasury, as he taught in the temple: and no man laid hands on him; for his hour was not yet come. Then said Jesus again unto them, I go my way, and ye shall seek me, and shall die in your sins: whither I go, ye cannot come. Then said the Jews, Will he kill himself? because he saith, Whither I go, ye cannot come. And he said unto them, Ye are from beneath; I am from above: ye are of this world; I am not of this world. I said therefore unto you, that ye shall die in your sins:

for if ye believe not that I am he, ye shall die in your sins.

The word "he" is italicized in your Bible because the original manuscript reads "for if ye believe not that I am, ye shall die in your sins." The singular issue of salvation is one of believing that Jesus is I AM, that Jesus is God. It's not enough to believe Jesus is a good guy, a great guru, or even the Son of God. The Mormons and Jehovah's Witnesses, the Moonies and cults down the line are all damned in their teachings because they deny this most essential, basic truth of salvation in denying that Jesus is God.

"Here's the fire, and here's the wood, but where's the sacrifice?" Isaac asked Abraham on Mount Moriah, which today is known as Calvary.

"God shall provide Himself a lamb," Abraham answered prophetically (see Genesis 22:8).

Abraham didn't say, "God shall provide *for* Himself a lamb." He said, "God will Himself *be* the Lamb." Therefore, if I say God did not Himself become a Lamb, if God Himself did not take on my sin but instead created a Son to die, I diminish what God did for me. And this is the great hinge of salvation that separates us from the cults. Every single cult robs Jesus Christ of deity. Some will say He's God's Son. Some will say He died for the sins of the world. Some will even say He rose again. But look a cultist in the eye and ask him if Jesus Christ is God, and he'll say, "He's God's Son," at best. And in so doing, he destroys what God did redemptively on his behalf.

John 8:25, 26
Then said they unto him, Who art thou? And Jesus saith unto them, Even the same that I said unto you from the beginning. I have many things to say and to judge of you: but he that sent me is true; and I speak to the world those things which I have heard of him.

It has been rightly said that the art of eloquence is knowing when not to speak. This is nowhere demonstrated more beautifully than in Jesus. As the Jews continue to badger Him, Jesus says, "There is so much I could say. But I only speak those things the Father instructs Me to say."

John 8:27, 28 (a)
They understood not that he spake to them of the Father. Then said Jesus unto them,

When ye have lifted up the Son of man, then shall ye know that I am he . . .

The lifting up of the Son of Man speaks of the Cross. "When you see Me on the Cross, you're going to know I AM," declares Jesus. "When the sky is dark and the earth shakes; when the graves open and the veil is rent, you will at last understand that I AM."

John 8:28 (b)–30
. . . and that I do nothing of myself; but as my Father hath taught me, I speak these things. And he that sent me is with me: the Father hath not left me alone; for I do always those things that please him. As he spake these words, many believed on him.

It's proof of His purity that not one of Jesus' contemporaries raised an objection to this statement, that not one ever saw Him do anything that would not please God. On the contrary, even as He made this claim, many believed on Him.

John 8:31, 32
Then said Jesus to those Jews which believed on him, If ye continue in my word, then are ye my disciples indeed; and ye shall know the truth, and the truth shall make you free.

The word "disciple" means "disciplined one." Who are Jesus' disciples, His disciplined ones? Those who continue in, take heed to, and make a high priority of His Word. And it is as they comprehend the truth of the Word that they are free—really, truly free.

For topical study of John 8:32 entitled "Really Set Free," turn to page 511.

John 8:33
They answered him, We be Abraham's seed, and were never in bondage to any man: how sayest thou, Ye shall be made free?

"What do you mean be made free?" protested the Jews. "We're the people of Israel. We've never been in bondage to any man."

Really? What about when they were in bondage to Pharaoh for four hundred years, baking bricks in the brutal, burning Egyptian sun century after century? What about the three-hundred-five-year period chronicled in the Book of Judges when they were in bondage to seven different nations? What about the year 722 B.C. when the Assyrians—a people so cruel that merely upon hearing they were coming, many nations would commit mass suicide—used fishhooks in the mouths of the Jews to lead them captive to Assyria? What about the Babylonians who, in 586 B.C., destroyed not only the temple, but the entire city of Jerusalem? What about the fact that even as they spoke these words, the Jews were in submission to Rome? Truly, their rejection of Jesus rendered these scribes and Pharisees incapable both of viewing their history correctly and discerning their situation presently.

John 8:34
Jesus answered them, Verily, verily, I say unto you, Whosoever committeth sin is the servant of sin.

The one who practices sin becomes enslaved to that sin. Nowhere is this truth more plainly illustrated than in the life of Samson. Samson took a Nazarite vow that forbade three things: touching dead bodies, drinking wine, and cutting his hair. Yet he touched dead carcasses (Judges 14:8, 9), and no doubt drank wine at the Philistine parties he attended. Therefore, when Delilah cut his hair, I'm convinced he thought nothing would happen because nothing had happened when he touched the carcass and drank the wine. But when Delilah said, "Samson, the Philistines are upon thee," the third time, Samson was bound and taken captive to grind like an ox in prison because no one beats the rap. No one gets away indefinitely with sin and compromise.

John 8:35 (a)
And the servant abideth not in the house for ever . . .

The one who continually sins becomes enslaved to sin. And sin is a cruel master indeed. By offering pleasure for a season (Hebrews 11:25), it is initially comfortable to serve in the household of sin. But sooner than later, sin eventually throws everyone out on the street.

John 8:35 (b)–41 (a)
. . . but the Son abideth ever. If the Son therefore shall make you free, ye shall be free indeed. I know that ye are Abraham's seed; but ye seek to kill me, because my word hath no place in you. I speak that which I have seen with my Father: and ye do that which ye have seen with your father. They answered and said unto him, Abraham is our father. Jesus saith unto them, If ye were Abraham's children, ye would do the works of Abraham. But now ye seek to kill me, a man that hath told you the truth, which I have heard of God: this did not Abraham. Ye do the deeds of your father.

"I know you are Abraham's seed," Jesus says in verse 37. "You are not Abraham's children," He says in verse 39. Is this a contradiction? No. Abraham's seed and Abraham's children are two separate entities—an important distinction to make in understanding prophecy.

The term "Abraham's seed" refers to the physical offspring of Abraham—the people of Israel. "Abraham's children" refers to all who believe God (Romans 4:1). If you don't understand this point, you'll be confused when people say, "The church is equivalent to Israel. Therefore the promises of the Old Testament do not speak to a literal, physical restoration of Israel, but to the church," as they misinterpret prophecy to conform to this foundational error.

"I know you're Israelites. I know you're Jews physically and racially," Jesus said. "But you're not Abraham's children because you don't believe in Me."

John 8:41 (b)
Then said they to him, We be not born of fornication . . .

The Pharisees respond by striking at Mary, raising the question of the legitimacy of Jesus' birth.

John 8:41 (c)–42
. . . we have one Father, even God. Jesus said unto them, If God were your Father, ye would love me: for I proceeded forth and came from God; neither came I of myself, but he sent me.

Anyone who says, "We love Jehovah. We love the God of the Bible. We love the God of Israel. But we don't love Jesus Christ as God"—doesn't really love God.

John 8:43
Why do ye not understand my speech? even because ye cannot hear my word.

"You can't understand what I'm saying because we're speaking two different languages," said Jesus. "You're talking about worldly stuff, and I'm speaking of the eternal."

John 8:44
Ye are of your father the devil, and the lusts of your father ye will do. He was a murderer from the beginning, and abode not in the truth, because there is no truth in him. When he speaketh a lie, he speaketh of his own: for he is a liar, and the father of it.

Scripture declares the wounds of a friend to be faithful (Proverbs 27:6) because only a friend cares enough to tell the truth. Jesus is not being vindictive here. On the contrary, His words prove His faithfulness. He's using strong language because nothing less would get through to these men.

John 8:45, 46 (a)
And because I tell you the truth, ye believe me not. Which of you convinceth me of sin?

"Why don't you believe Me? What wrong have I done in your sight?" Jesus asks.

John 8:46 (b)–48
And if I say the truth, why do ye not believe me? He that is of God heareth God's words: ye therefore hear them not, because ye are not of God. Then answered the Jews, and said unto him, Say we not well that thou art a Samaritan, and hast a devil?

Jesus' point is so well taken, His logic so irrefutable, that the Pharisees' only recourse is to resort to name-calling.

John 8:49–51
Jesus answered, I have not a devil; but I honour my Father, and ye do dishonour me. And I seek not mine own glory: there is one that seeketh and judgeth. Verily, verily, I say unto you, If a man keep my saying, he shall never see death.

Pleading with the Pharisees, Jesus says, "If you'll simply receive and embrace what I'm saying, you'll never see death." The same is true for us. You see, for those who know Jesus, death is neither annihilation nor termination. Death is transformation because the moment we close our eyes in the final minute of this life, we'll see Jesus (2 Corinthians 5:8). And in seeing Him, we'll become like Him (1 John 3:2).

John 8:52–56
Then said the Jews unto him, Now we know that thou hast a devil. Abraham is dead, and the prophets; and thou sayest, If a man keep my saying, he shall never taste of death. Art thou greater than our father Abraham, which is dead? and the prophets are dead: whom makest thou thyself? Jesus answered, If I honour myself, my honour is nothing: it is my Father that honoureth me; of whom ye say, that he is your God: Yet ye have not known him; but I know him: and if I should say, I know him not, I shall be a liar like unto you: but I know him, and keep his saying. Your father Abraham rejoiced to see my day: and he saw it, and was glad.

When did Abraham see Jesus? I believe this reference is to the story in Genesis 14 when, after rescuing his nephew, Abraham was greeted by a man named Melchizedek. "Melchizedek" means "King of Righteousness." Melchizedek was from Salem. Salem means "Peace." Melchizedek had no mother or father, no beginning or end (Hebrews 7:3). He offered bread and wine to Abraham and accepted a tithe from him—all of which point to the distinct possibility that Melchizedek was a Christophany, an earthly appearance of Jesus before He came as the Babe of Bethlehem.

John 8:57
Then said the Jews unto him, Thou art not yet fifty years old, and hast thou seen Abraham?

This interests me because, at this point, Jesus was only in His early thirties. Yet the Pharisees used fifty years as a reference to His age. Perhaps as the Man of Sorrows who carried the burden of a sinful world, He looked older than His age.

John 8:58, 59 (a)
Jesus said unto them, Verily, verily, I say unto you, Before Abraham was, I am. Then took they up stones to cast at him . . .

So clear was Jesus' claim to deity that those who heard these words were ready to stone Him on the spot.

John 8:59 (b)
. . . but Jesus hid himself, and went out of the temple, going through the midst of them . . .

After being absent one thousand years, the shekinah glory reappeared in the Person of Jesus Christ. But because the people rejected Him, the Light departed once again from the temple.

John 8:59 (c)
. . . and so passed by.

Where did Jesus go? In the next chapter, we'll see exactly where He went: He found a blind man. He found me.

REALLY SET FREE
A Topical Study of
John 8:32

After committing adultery with Bathsheba and then murdering her husband, David was sitting in his palace when Nathan the prophet came to him, saying, "There's a poor man who lives next door to a wealthy man. The wealthy man threw a party and needed a lamb to serve his guests. Instead of taking one from his own flock, however, the wealthy man went to his neighbor's house and took his only sheep—the family pet."

"What?!" said an enraged David. "That man shall surely die" (see 2 Samuel 12:5).

That's always the way it is when we sin. You see, Old Testament law prescribed restoration and restitution for such an offense—not the death penalty. But indignation and harsh judgment are always the result of the failure of sinners to see their own sin.

How Sinners Treat Sinners

Speak unto the children of Israel, and say unto them, If any man's wife go aside, and commit a trespass against him, and a man lie with her carnally, and it be hid from the eyes of her husband . . . and the spirit of jealousy [suspicion] come upon him . . . then shall the man bring his wife unto the priest . . . and the priest shall bring her near, and set her before the LORD: And the priest shall take holy water in an earthen vessel; and of the dust that is in the floor of the tabernacle the priest shall take, and put it into the water: And the priest shall charge her by an oath, and say unto the woman, If no man have lain with thee, and if thou hast not gone aside to uncleanness with another instead of thy husband, be thou free from this bitter water that causeth the curse: But if thou hast gone aside to another instead of thy husband, and if thou be defiled, and some man have lain with thee beside thine husband . . . the LORD make thee a curse and an oath among thy people, when the LORD doth make thy thigh to rot, and thy belly to swell; and this water that causeth the curse shall go into thy bowels, to make thy belly to swell, and thy thigh to rot: And the woman shall say, Amen, amen. And when he hath made her to drink the water, then it shall come to pass, that, if she be defiled . . . the water that causeth the curse shall enter into her, and become bitter, and her belly shall swell, and her thigh shall rot: and the woman shall be a curse among her people.   Numbers 5:12–27

If you, as an Old Testament husband, suspected your wife was unfaithful, you would take her to the tabernacle or temple, where the priest would pour holy water into an earthen vessel, add dust from the floor, and give it to your wife to drink. If she was guilty, her belly would swell, her legs would tremble—and she would be a curse among her people. Although they didn't know it, this is exactly what was taking place as the scribes and Pharisees brought the woman taken in adultery to Jesus. You see, Israel being the wife of Jehovah (Ezekiel 16; Hosea 2), it was not the woman taken in adultery, but the nation of Israel who was already on trial.

Think with me. Just as the Old Testament priest was to pour holy water into an earthen vessel, the water of the Word (Ephesians 5) was spoken through an earthen vessel—Jesus Christ. Just as the Old Testament priest was to add dust from the floor of the temple, so Jesus wrote in the dust of the floor of the temple. They thought they were bringing a woman caught in adultery, but in reality, the Jews themselves were on trial in the temple before the great High Priest, Jesus Christ. But they didn't see it. They couldn't understand it. They missed the point because that's what sin does. When you are caught up in sin, when you are enslaved by sin, you will not see the need you have personally. You'll say, "I'm free. I'm okay. It's them; it's him; it's her who's in sin," as you point your finger, find fault with, put blame on everyone else. Sinners treat sinners brutally. It's true. I will lash out at you most strongly for that sin that is most tempting to me.

If you're trying to prove you're more deserving of blessing because you're more righteous than the person sitting next to you, like the Pharisees, you'll be a rock-thrower. Sin-sniffing, fault-finding, and keyhole-peeping always take place in the lives of those who do not understand the grace or goodness of Jesus. But if you realize you're a sinner saved only by grace, you'll see how far you are from what you could and should be in the Lord. And you'll lose your interest in throwing rocks.

How the Law Treats Sinners

If there ever was a standard that would bring salvation, it would be the Old Testament law. It's perfect (Psalm 19:7). The problem is, we can't live up to it. That is why I believe that in the midst of the accusations by the self-righteous Pharisees concerning the woman taken in adultery, Jesus wrote on the ground twice (John 8:8).

You see, after Moses had received the law on Mount Sinai, he returned to the people only to find them worshiping the golden calf. In anger, he threw the tablets to the ground, where they shattered—a picture physically of what the people had already done to the law spiritually (Exodus 32:19). Moses returned to the Lord and was given a second copy of the law. This time, the tablets were not smashed, but carefully placed inside the ark of the covenant, covered by the mercy seat upon which blood was sprinkled—which speaks of the only way the law can be kept.

The ark speaks of Jesus Christ. He kept the law perfectly—and guess where you are. If you're a Christian, you are in Christ (2 Corinthians 5:17) just as surely as the law was in the ark. Therefore, when the Father looks on you, He doesn't see your sins and mistakes, your rebellion and iniquity. He sees His Son. Positionally, you are perfect because you are in Him.

In Romans 7, Paul declares that we who are believers are dead to the law. This is the glory of biblical Christianity—for although the rules and regulations are still in effect, they no longer have jurisdiction over us because no court of law tries dead men.

How the Savior Treats Sinners

Having captured the ark of the covenant, the Philistines placed it in the temple of their fish god, Dagon (1 Samuel 5:2). The next morning, they entered the temple to find Dagon facedown before the ark of the covenant. The Philistines helped their god up—only to return the next day to find him prostrate before the ark once more—this time with head and hands cut off. "Something's gotta go," said the Philistines, so they sent the ark back to the Jews.

The ark is a picture of Jesus Christ. What was in the ark? The tablets of stone, the Word of God. You might have some Dagon in your life right now—some addiction, some habit, some problem you've been trying to get rid of, to push over. But the harder you try, the more frustrated you become. The key, gang, is not to deal with Dagon. The key is to bring in the ark. Bring in the Word. Stay in the Word. Study the Word. Obey the Word. And watch Dagon fall. "How shall a young man cleanse his way?" asked the psalmist. "By taking heed according to thy Word," was his answer (see Psalm 119:9).

"Go your way and sin no more," Jesus said to the woman taken in adultery. And by virtue of the very fact that the Lord said this, she would be free to sin no more. She didn't need a syllabus. She didn't need ten steps. She didn't need a counseling appointment or a discussion group. She needed only the Truth to set her free.

Precious people, God's commandments are God's "enablements." Therefore, when He tells you to rejoice evermore (1 Thessalonians 5:16), don't say, "I can't because I'm hurting." When He tells you to love one another (John 15:12), don't say, "Impossible. You don't know my husband." No, when the Lord speaks, there is power in the very commandment He gives. It's so simple. If you just do what He says, you will find Him meeting you at that point, empowering you to keep His command. Nowhere in the New Testament will you find any other model than that of a simple command given, with the choice being either to reject it and walk away, or to believe it and obey.

If you simply say, "Thank You, Lord. I choose this day to receive Your grace and obey Your command," you will find you will be free. And he whom the Son sets free is free *indeed*.

9

John 9:1
And as Jesus passed by, he saw a man which was blind from his birth.

Incensed by His claim to deity, the Jews took up stones to throw at Jesus (John 8:59). But not more than a stone's throw away sat a man whose life was about to change radically and eternally.

John 9:2
And his disciples asked him, saying, Master, who did sin, this man, or his parents, that he was born blind?

The disciples voice the foundational question of all suffering: "Why?"—and then proceed to give Jesus two possible answers. The blindness is either the result of the blind man's sin, they reason, or it is the result of his parents' sin. If his blindness was a result of his own sin, when did he sin? He was, after all, *born* blind. Based on the story of Jacob and Esau in Genesis 25, the rabbis taught man could sin in the womb. That's the way they explained birth defects. If his blindness was the result of his parents' sin, however, on the basis of Exodus 20:5, the rabbis taught that his mother's, father's grandparent's or great-grandparent's sin could have repercussions in him.

Is this what God means when He says He is a jealous God, visiting the iniquity of the fathers upon the children to the third and fourth generation? No—that's the godfather, not Father God. Exodus 20:5 simply means that God doesn't change the rules. He continues to visit, deal with, convict, and judge generation after generation. Regardless of what society says; the fact remains that sin is always sin because God is consistent in His heart and in His ways.

John 9:3 (a)
Jesus answered, Neither hath this man sinned, nor his parents . . .

It is true that all sadness and sorrow are the indirect result of sin. But Jesus says no one can point a finger at another as the culprit. I talk to many people who say the reason they are vulnerable to the occult or pornography is because the vulnerability has been passed from generation to generation in their family. Scripture, however, teaches exactly the opposite. In the days of Ezekiel, people would justify their own sin with a proverb that said, "The fathers have eaten sour grapes and the children's teeth are set on edge." God, however, said, "As I live, ye shall not have

occasion any more to use this proverb in Israel. Behold all souls are mine," (see Ezekiel 18:2–4). In other words, "Every single soul is created by Me, belongs to Me, and is individually responsible to Me."

John 9:3 (b)–5
. . . but that the works of God should be made manifest in him. I must work the works of him that sent me, while it is day: the night cometh, when no man can work. As long as I am in the world, I am the light of the world.

"The issue is not sin," said Jesus. "Rather, this man's misery gives Me opportunity for ministry. I am the Light of the world, and I have only so many hours in which I can work before night falls on the day of My public ministry."
Misery always opens the door for ministry.

As a junior in high school, I had the opportunity to represent our district at the Athletes in Action National Conference. Although the conference began Monday morning, the featured speaker failed to show up for Monday's, Tuesday's and Wednesday's meetings. He was on campus, but the pain he lived with continually prevented him from joining us.

Maybe you've heard his story: During the '68–'69 season, Brian Sternberg was at the West Coast Relays in Fresno, California, pumped, primed, and poised to break the world record in the pole-vault. The day before the meet, he was doing what pole-vaulters often do—working out on the trampoline. But following one particular double flip, he hit the metal railing and broke his neck. It was a tragedy and a shock to the track and field world when Sternberg was told not only that he would never vault again, but that he would be a quadriplegic for the rest of his life.

Other speakers and athletes filled in for Brian at the AIA Conference. Then came Thursday night. After Brian was wheeled out, he began to share with this group of young athletes how he had been a nominal, lukewarm Christian for a number of years. Then came the tragedy. And he said, "As I was in the hospital flat on my back, hearing I would never run, never walk, never even lift my hands again, God started to do a work in my life and gave me a peace I cannot explain. Jesus became so incredibly real to me at that time and has been real to me since then in a way I could never comprehend or explain." Then, with tears rolling down his cheeks, this world-class athlete said, "If that was the only way I could have what I have right now in my heart, I would take that jump all over again."

When he extended an invitation to make a real commitment to Jesus Christ, virtually the entire audience came forward. We saw revival happen unlike anything I've ever seen before or since. But it came through a man who was broken and in pain.

You who are going through difficulties, you who are experiencing tragedy, sickness, or hard times—watch out that you don't become introspective and wonder what you've done wrong. Jesus would say to you today, "Sin is not the issue. The question is not, "Who caused the misery?" The question is, "Will you allow Me to use it?" The Greek language has no punctuation, so I believe a better rendering of this passage would be: "But that the works of God should be made manifest in him, I must work the works of him that sent me while it is day." In other words, "It's not a time to speculate philosophically. It's a time to reach out compassionately."

Not only does this passage provide an explanation of suffering, but it also provides an illustration of salvation. Did the blind man see Jesus pass by and say, "I want to follow Him"? No. He didn't have a clue as to what was happening. The same is true of you and me. You and I are the blind man. Before we were saved, we stumbled in the dark (Ephesians 4:18).

"I'm kind of a spiritual guy," you might be saying. "I've been pursuing the cosmic reason for being. And in my pursuit, I came across Christianity." Wrong. You and I were blind as bats as we sat begging for a tidbit of pleasure, a crumb of happiness, a scrap of satisfaction from materialism, relationships, or anything else that passed our way. But even though we couldn't see Jesus, He saw us. And as He passed by, He said, "I'm going to stop and do a work in them. I'm going to save them from their own misery and poverty."

John 9:6
When he had thus spoken, he spat on the ground, and made clay of the spittle, and he anointed the eyes of the blind man with the clay.

The man was now doubly blinded: not only blind from birth, but blind from the clay—which speaks of humanity, of depravity. "In sin did my mother conceive me," wrote the sweet psalmist of Israel (Psalm 51:5). So, too, we were born in sin. We live in sin. We're sinners in desperate need of a Savior.

John 9:7 (a)
And said unto him, Go, wash . . .

Feeling the irritation of the mud in his eyes, the blind man was no doubt ready to follow instructions. How often it is the way of the Lord to cause irritations in us in order to drive us to the place of healing and redemption.

For topical study of John 9:1–7 entitled "Here's Mud in Your Eye," turn to page 518.

John 9:7 (b)
. . . in the pool of Siloam, (which is by interpretation, Sent.)

Jesus was *sent* to be the Light of the world. He in turn *sent* this man to the pool of Siloam in order to receive his sight.

John 9:7 (c)
He went his way therefore, and washed . . .

The Puritan writers say this man blindly obeyed the Lord's command. I like that!

John 9:7 (d)
. . . and came seeing.

Not only does this miracle give insight into the nature of suffering, but it gives encouragement regarding the need for service. You see, in their theologizing and philosophizing, the disciples were attempting to be teachers when in reality Jesus had called them to be "touchers." It's easy to discuss situations and solutions. But when we get to heaven, the Lord is not going to say, "Well said, good and faithful servant." No, He's waiting to say, "Well *done.*"

In addition to being an encouragement to the disciples, I suggest this miracle was an encouragement to Jesus. For as the Jews picked up stones to throw at Him in John 8, just outside the temple sat a man who would receive not only his sight, but his salvation. So, too, perhaps you feel rejected and misunderstood. But it could very well be that a mere stone's throw away from where you are right now sits someone who needs love. If you will reach out to him, listen to him, and pray for him, you will find great encouragement and your own depression will lift. Follow Jesus' example: Take your eyes off yourself and let the Father use you to bring sight to someone else.

John 9:8–10
The neighbours therefore, and they which before had seen him that he was blind, said,

Is not this he that sat and begged? Some said, This is he: others said, He is like him: but he said, I am he. Therefore said they unto him, How were thine eyes opened?

The disciples asked *why* the man was blind. His neighbors asked *how* his eyes were opened. But both groups missed the most important question, which was, "*Who* performed the miracle?"

John 9:11
He answered and said, A man that is called Jesus made clay, and anointed mine eyes, and said unto me, Go to the pool of Siloam, and wash: and I went and washed, and I received sight.

This man omitted part of the story. He said Jesus made clay but failed to say how He did it. Why? Because, blind when Jesus spat in the ground, he didn't see it. In other words, he didn't see exactly how the miracle took place. He just knew it did. So, too, we have felt the Lord's touch on our lives. Exactly how it happened, we are at a loss to explain. We only know that, after walking in darkness from birth, like the blind man, we received sight.

John 9:12
Then said they unto him, Where is he? He said, I know not.

This breaks my heart. After receiving the gift of vision, the blind man lost sight of the Giver.

John 9:13–16 (a)
They brought to the Pharisees him that aforetime was blind. And it was the sabbath day when Jesus made the clay, and opened his eyes. Then again the Pharisees also asked him how he had received his sight. He said unto them, He put clay upon mine eyes, and I washed, and do see. Therefore said some of the Pharisees, This man is not of God, because he keepeth not the sabbath day.

Here, a man born blind now sees. Yet the Pharisees say, "Wait a minute. That violates Statue 2482.6, which forbids making clay on the Sabbath."

John 9:16 (b), 17
Others said, How can a man that is a sinner do such miracles? And there was a division among them. They say unto the blind man again, What sayest thou of him, that he hath opened thine eyes? He said, He is a prophet.

In verse 11, the blind man called Jesus a man. But now, about five minutes old in his knowledge of Jesus, he realizes He is more than a man—He's a Prophet.

John 9:18–20
But the Jews did not believe concerning him, that he had been blind, and received his sight, until they called the parents of him that had received his sight. And they asked them, saying, Is this your son, who ye say was born blind? how then doth he now see? His parents answered them and said, We know that this is our son, and that he was born blind.

As parents, we know our kids were born blind spiritually. After all, how many of us have said, "Okay, sweetheart, you're three months old. I'm now going to teach you how to cry your head off until you get your way. And when you turn two, we'll start working on lying. At four, we'll move on to stealing"? Having watched the demise of Communism, understand that the flaw of Marxism is the completely erroneous presupposition that man is basically good. "From each according to his ability, to each according to his need," said Karl Marx. In reality, however, because all men are born blind, the question we ask is not, "What is your need?" but "What's in it for me?" Thus, Marxism was doomed from its very inception.

John 9:21–23
But by what means he now seeth, we know not; or who hath opened his eyes, we know not: he is of age; ask him: he shall speak for himself. These words spake his parents, because they feared the Jews: for the Jews had agreed already, that if any man did confess that he was Christ, he should be put out of the synagogue. Therefore said his parents, He is of age; ask him.

Being put out of the synagogue meant one lost his ability to pray to God or to be blessed by God. It meant that his family was to treat him as though he were dead and that his business would be absolutely off-limits to all Jews. Thus, to be put out of the synagogue was a serious matter.

John 9:24, 25
Then again called they the man that was blind, and said unto him, Give God the praise: we know that this man is a sinner. He answered and said, Whether he be a sinner or no, I know not: one thing I know, that, whereas I was blind, now I see.

I like this! The blind man said, "You may be able to trip me up intellectually and outmaneuver me logically, but all I know is this: Once I was a miserable, blind, wretched sinner like you—and now I see!"

John 9:26, 27
Then said they to him again, What did he to thee? how opened he thine eyes? He answered them, I have told you already, and ye did not hear: wherefore would ye hear it again? will ye also be his disciples?

"Do you want me to tell you again so you can be converted too?" asked the once-blind man.

John 9:28–33
Then they reviled him, and said, Thou art his disciple; but we are Moses' disciples. We know that God spake unto Moses: as for this fellow, we know not from whence he is. The man answered and said unto them, Why herein is a marvellous thing, that ye know not from whence he is, and yet he hath opened mine eyes. Now we know that God heareth not sinners: but if any man be a worshipper of God, and doeth his will, him he heareth. Since the world began was it not heard that any man opened the eyes of one that was born blind. If this man were not of God, he could do nothing.

Isaiah prophesied three times that when Messiah came, He would open blind eyes (29:18; 35:5; 42:7). Here, the blind man, now six minutes old in his faith, says, "The One who opened my eyes is of God. How else do you explain what happened to me? It's never happened in all of history. You're professing to be authorities, yet you can't answer this simple question?"

The story is told of a teacher who was as wise as this blind man. Four of her seniors came cruising into class one day, saying, "Sorry we're late again, but we had a flat tire on the way to school."

"Oh?" she said, "Okay. You sit here in this corner, Bill, and you in that one, Steve. Jim, you take a seat in the third corner; and, Joe, you're in the fourth. Now take out a piece of paper, and tell me which tire was flat."

This newly sighted man is doing the same thing. He's deflating the puffed-up egos of his accusers.

John 9:34
They answered and said unto him, Thou wast altogether born in sins, and dost thou teach us? And they cast him out.

It's interesting how the Pharisees resort to name-calling whenever they're backed into a corner. When you're sharing your faith, and people start calling you names, when they get uptight, when they get angry—rejoice because when you throw a rock into a pack of dogs, the one that barks the loudest is the one that got hit. I'd far rather someone react in this way than to hear him say, "You found your way. I found my way. And we'll all end up in bliss together." No, I like it when someone's angry because it means he's convicted.

John 9:35, 36
Jesus heard that they had cast him out; and when he had found him, he said unto him, Dost thou believe on the Son of God? He answered and said, Who is he, Lord, that I might believe on him?

At last we hear the pivotal question as the blind man asks, "Who is He?"

John 9:37, 38 (a)
And Jesus said unto him, Thou hast both seen him, and it is he that talketh with thee. And he said, Lord, I believe.

The blind man went from calling Jesus a man to a prophet of God to Lord.

John 9:38 (b)
And he worshipped him.

By receiving worship, Jesus once again assumes deity.

John 9:39
And Jesus said, For judgment I am come into this world, that they which see not might see; and that they which see might be made blind.

Although judgment is not the reason for Jesus' coming (John 3:17), it is the result.

John 9:40, 41
And some of the Pharisees which were with him heard these words, and said unto him, Are we blind also? Jesus said unto them, If ye were blind, ye should have no sin: but now ye say, We see; therefore your sin remaineth.

"If you truly didn't understand," said Jesus to the Pharisees, "you wouldn't be held responsible." But such was not the case with the Pharisees, for, had they desired, they could have understood. However, preferring the darkness of their pride, they rejected the Light of the World.

HERE'S MUD IN YOUR EYE
A Topical Study of
John 9:1–7

In chapter 8, Jesus said, "I am the Light of the World." And His dealing with the woman taken in adultery verifies His declaration, for in it He revealed the blindness of the scribes and Pharisees. In chapter 9, Jesus again says, "I am the light of the world." This time, however, the account that follows does not show Him *revealing* blindness, but *healing* blindness.

I've read about the amazing benefits of laser surgery. A shaft of light when used carefully and exactingly on the eyeball can correct not only nearsightedness, but in some cases, even blindness. People who were once in darkness are given their sight through a beam of light. But let me tell you—the technology of laser surgery can't hold a candle to the methodology of Jesus in John 9 because what does Jesus do? He uses something more amazing than a laser. He packs the blind man's eyes with mud. Why does He do this? I suggest several possible reasons. . . .

Medicinally

Both Tacitus and Pliny, ancient writers of this era, tell us that in Jesus' day, people believed spit had curative powers. Thus, in using spit and clay perhaps Jesus was, in a sense, blessing and approving the medical knowledge of the day.

Some people say, "Because God is the God who heals (Exodus 15:26), there is no need for medicine." But while God does indeed heal through prayer, through the laying on of hands, through the anointing of oil, through the gift of healing—He also heals through medicine. Even my own body has an incredible ability to heal itself. When I cut my finger, it's amazing what happens as coagulation begins right before my eyes. The bleeding stops. A scab forms and then falls off. And the skin is restored like new.

Listen, gang, it is not my own body system in and of itself that heals. It is not prayer in and of itself that heals. It is not gifts of healing in and of themselves that heal. It is not medicine in and of itself that heals. It is *God* who heals. And He can use medicine. He can use prayer. He can use the anointing of oil. He can use the gifts of the Holy Spirit. He can use my own body. Or He can use any combination. But it's all God.

Symbolically

The healing of the man born blind was a creative not a restorative miracle. Sight had to be created. So what did Jesus do? He used clay. When Adam was formed in the Garden of Eden, the entire process began with clay. Thus, I suggest that by using clay once again, Jesus shows He is our Creator—and that He knows the stuff of which we are made (Psalm 103:14). Truly, we're nothing but dust. And yet so often we deny our earthiness. We spray-paint our dustiness, add some chrome, and put expectations on ourselves that God never intended. Being dust, it's ludicrous for us to walk around cloaked in pseudo-spirituality or to burden others with heavy expectations. We need not be uptight with ourselves or condemned by others. God knows exactly what we are. And yet He's put His Treasure—His Son— within our dusty, earthen vessels (2 Corinthians 4:7).

Practically

The healing of the blind being the miracle most often recorded in the Gospel accounts, we see it happen in various ways: In one case, Jesus spoke to a man (Mark 10:46–52). In another, He touched the man's eyes with His hands (Matthew 20:30– 34). In a third, He touched the man's eyes twice (Mark 8:22–25). Here, He uses mud. Jesus works creatively, individually, uniquely. Yet we have a tendency to want to box Him in according to how He works in our own lives.

If this miracle had happened today, I'm convinced the man who was healed by simply hearing the Word and believing would say, "I'm going to start a denomination of healing. I'll call it the Word of Faith Ministry. Just hear the Word, and if you believe you'll be given sight. You'll experience a miracle."

The next man would say, "No, no, no. That's not the way God works. He works through the laying on of hands. I'm going to write a book and begin a movement called Healing Hands Ministries. The power is in the touch."

The third man would say, "No. It takes more than one encounter with the Lord to really be healed. I'm going to offer a course in Second Touch ministry. It will be a two-step program because everyone knows true healing can't happen all at once."

And this man in John would say, "No, that's not it at all. Mud is what's important. Mud In Your Eye Ministries. That's the key. That's where the blessing lies."

We err greatly whenever we think that because the Lord worked one way in our lives, He must work the same way in everyone's life. You can't box the Lord in. The last people who tried put Him in a tomb—and He refused to stay there.

Personally

When Jesus put mud in the blind man's eyes, the man could have said, "Wait a minute. You're putting mud in my eye. You're not making things better—You're making them worse."

Gang, many, many times the way of the Lord is to make things seem worse than they were before in order to get you to the place you really want to be: healed and seeing clearly. When the Lord muddies the waters, we usually don't know what

He's doing. "I've been praying; I've been believing, but things are only getting darker and dimmer," we say. "What are You doing, Lord?"

But you know what mud does in one's eye? As a veteran of more mud fights than I care to remember, I know it causes pain. So when Jesus said, "Go to the pool and wash," this guy didn't have to be asked twice. I don't believe his obedience was so much a statement of his great faith as it was a simple desire to get the mud out of his eye!

Maybe this week Jesus has allowed an irritation to come into your life that is causing you pain. Maybe a situation at work or a problem with a relationship is causing you to say, "Lord, I'm talking to You. I'm looking to You. I'm calling on You—but all I'm getting is mud in my eye." Here's what to do: Run quickly to the pool of Siloam, and you will receive your sight more clearly than if the mud—the irritation—had never been there in the first place.

Where is the pool of Siloam? Jesus said, "You are clean through the Word which I have spoken unto you" (see John 15:3). Ephesians 5 says we are washed by the water of the Word. It's oftentimes when we are most irritated and most frustrated that we finally turn back to the Word. And when we do, we see things clearly in the way the Lord always intended us to see. Consequently, I am learning that when irritations come, it's not for me to despise them or to wonder what's going on, but rather to embrace them and to stumble, if need be, to the pool of Siloam—to the Word of God—where I can have my eyes opened once again.

10 Chapter 9 ended with a once-blind man's excommunication from the Jewish religious system. Here in chapter 10, Jesus addresses this issue by speaking of a new order, a new fold, a new flock of which the once-blind man would be a part. Bear in mind that although sheep and shepherds might sound a bit foreign to us, the role sheep played in Jewish history rendered this analogy tailor-made for Jesus' audience.

In what is most likely the oldest book of the Bible, we are told Job had fourteen thousand sheep (Job 42:12). On the day the temple was dedicated, Solomon offered one hundred twenty thousand of his sheep as a sacrifice to God (1 Kings 8:63). David and Moses, the two great leaders of Old Testament Israel, were both shepherds. Isaiah, Jeremiah, Amos, and Zechariah all drew analogies from sheep and shepherds. Therefore, talking to Jews about shepherds would be similar to talking to West Virginians about coal miners, to Texans about cowboys, to Californians about surfers, or to Oregonians about loggers. It was an analogy to which they could easily relate.

A shepherd of Jesus' day would wear a cotton tunic held together by a leather cord belt, upon which hung a leather pouch to carry dried fruit or small stones for the sling that also hung upon his belt. The sling was used not only to ward off predators but also to herd wandering sheep, for an experienced shepherd would have such precise aim that he would be able to drop a stone right in front of the nose of a straying sheep, thereby drawing it back to the flock. Another item attached to the belt of the shepherd was a horn of oil. Oil was used to anoint the heads of the sheep in the flock—not only as an insect repellent but also to reduce the friction that occurred when they butted each other. Fourthly, attached to the shepherd's belt was a small clublike instrument called a rod that was used to fight predators in close "hand-to-hand combat" situations. The rod was also used as an instrument of correction, for if a lamb continually, persistently wandered away from the flock, the shepherd would use the rod to break its legs. Then he would put the lamb on his shoulders and carry it until its legs healed. When at last the lamb was again able to walk on its own, because of the bonding that took place during the time the shepherd carried the lamb on his shoulders, it never again wandered. Finally, in his hand the shepherd held a staff—a large stick seven or eight feet long with a crook at one end with which the shepherd would hook lambs or sheep headed in the wrong direction. With this picture of a Middle-Eastern shepherd in mind, Jesus begins His discourse . . .

John 10:1
Verily, verily, I say unto you, He that entereth not by the door into the sheepfold, but climbeth up some other way, the same is a thief and a robber.

During certain times of the year, shepherds would lead their flocks away from the village to greener pastures. During such times, the sheep slept in temporary sheepfolds made of brush. When the sheep remained in the village, however, all of the shepherds of the community brought their sheep nightly into a common sheepfold that had stone walls six or seven feet high. Theft from these communal sheepfolds was common. A two-man operation, a thief would stand upon the shoulders of a partner and climb into the sheepfold. Then, with great stealth, he would slit the throats of four or five sheep and toss them over the wall to his buddy.

John 10:2, 3 (a)
But he that entereth in by the door is the shepherd of the sheep. To him the porter openeth; and the sheep hear his voice . . .

While the sheep stayed in the communal sheepfold, all of the shepherds would return home each night except the one who would act as a porter, or watchman. In the morning, the shepherds would return for their flocks. How did they know whose sheep was whose if they were all mixed together in the sheepfold? Each shepherd had a distinctive call, or song, to which only his own sheep responded.

John 10:3 (b)
. . . and he calleth his own sheep by name . . .

In Revelation 2:17, we are told that our Great Shepherd, Jesus Christ, will give us new names that will fit us perfectly and that we'll possess for eternity.

John 10:3 (c)
. . . and leadeth them out.

Shepherds never drove the sheep, never beat the sheep, never pushed the sheep. They led the sheep. Go to Israel today, and you'll see shepherds just walking along with a stream of sheep following right behind them. Americans tend to drive themselves and others. Not so a Middle-Eastern shepherd. So, too, Jesus, the Good Shepherd, doesn't drive me. He *leads* me. In other words, He goes first through the valley of the shadow of death before He ever asks me to go through it. Scripture declares that Jesus, our Shepherd, our Leader, was tempted in all points like as we are, yet without sin (Hebrews 4:15). Consequently, there is nothing you will ever face He hasn't felt or isn't feeling presently. Gang, Jesus doesn't send you into battle or drive you into any given trial. He doesn't pontificate or preach. He *leads*.

John 10:4, 5
And when he putteth forth his own sheep, he goeth before them, and the sheep follow him: for they know his voice. And a stranger will they not follow, but will flee from him: for they know not the voice of strangers.

You can always tell when a stranger creeps into the flock. He will cause division. Knowing something's not quite right, the sheep will scatter.

John 10:6, 7 (a)
This parable spake Jesus unto them: but they understood not what things they were which he spake unto them. Then said Jesus unto them again . . .

I have the word "again" circled in my Bible. Jesus didn't say, "You dumb sheep. How can you miss this obvious picture? I'm going to write you off." No, He came to them *again*. And haven't you found that the Lord keeps coming to you time and time and time again, saying the same thing until it finally sinks in? Have you ever resisted something the Lord has told you, only to hear a teaching over the radio on the same subject or a scripture from a friend along the same line? The Lord is faithful to keep coming time and time again, dealing with you and me concerning those issues that need to be addressed in our lives.

John 10:7 (b)
. . . Verily, verily, I say unto you, I am the door of the sheep.

"Wait a minute," you say. "Is Jesus mixing metaphors? I thought He was the Shepherd. But here He's talking about being the Door. Is He drawing another analogy?" No. Jesus' audience would have understood this perfectly. You see, neither the sheepfolds made of brush in the high country nor the sheepfolds made of stone in the community had need of doors, for once the sheep came in to the fold, the shepherd would lie down across the opening and would literally become the door. That way, no sheep could leave, and no man could enter without stepping on the shepherd and waking him up. Thus, in referring to Himself as the Door, Jesus was saying, "I'm the Shepherd on duty. I'm the One whose job it is to guard the flock."

John 10:8
All that ever came before me are thieves and robbers: but the sheep did not hear them.

"I am the Door—not a door, not one of the doors. I am *the* Door. And everyone else is a thief." Jesus alone makes this claim. Whether you read the writings of Krishna or Buddha, Confucius or Zoroaster, you'll find that every one claimed to be *one* of the ways in which the God-consciousness was manifested. Jesus uniquely says, "I am the Door and everyone else is a rip-off." How do we know Jesus is truly who He says He is? It gets back to the foundational issue of the Resurrection. Buddha kicked the bucket—and he's still down. You don't see Confucius walking around. These guys gave their rap until death came and terminated their so-called ministries. Only Jesus fulfilled His ministry by dying for our sins and rising again to verify, to validate, to substantiate His claim to be the Door.

John 10:9, 10 (a)
I am the door: by me if any man enter in, he shall be saved, and shall go in and out, and find pasture. The thief cometh not, but for to steal, and to kill, and to destroy.

It would do us well if we really grasped the fact that Satan only wants to rip us off. He tantalizes us with a variety of fancy lures, but ultimately all he wants to do is destroy us. In my reading this week, I came across an interesting little nugget in the Book of 1 Chronicles. Tucked away in the fourth chapter is the prayer of a man named Jabez, who prayed, "Lord, that You would keep me from evil so that it won't grieve me" (see 4:10). So often we think of sin only in terms of its grieving God—which indeed it does. Jabez, however, shows great insight in saying, "Keep me from evil, Lord, so it doesn't grieve *me*." There's a misconception in our society today that sin brings pleasure, that sin is fun, that there's happiness in a little escapade here and a little carnality there. Jabez, this man of God, knew better. He knew sin would grieve *him*.

John 10:10 (b)
I am come that they might have life, and that they might have it more abundantly.

I love John 10:10, but increasingly as I hear testimonies and preaching, it comes across this way: "Come to Jesus, and you will have abundant life. Get saved, and you'll have peace, joy, and love you've never known." While that is all true, if people respond to the gospel based solely upon John 10:10, when they get fired from their job or dumped by their girlfriend, they say, "Wait a minute. Jesus said I would have life abundantly—but look at me." And they become disillusioned and disoriented in their faith. John 10:10 is the result of the gospel but not the essence. The essence of the gospel is found in the next verse. . . .

John 10:11
I am the good shepherd: the good shepherd giveth his life for the sheep.

The essence of the gospel is not what Jesus will do for you—it's what He *already* did for you when He died for your sin. Because Jesus bore the wrath of God we deserved, our sins past, present, and future are forgiven in totality. Thus, the gospel means we need to be about the business not of saying, "Get saved so you can buy a new car," or, "Get saved so you won't have any more problems," but, "Get saved because Jesus Christ died for your sins."

John 10:12, 13
But he that is an hireling, and not the shepherd, whose own the sheep are not, seeth the wolf coming, and leaveth the sheep, and fleeth: and the wolf catcheth them, and scattereth the sheep. The hireling fleeth, because he is an hireling, and careth not for the sheep.

Usually, the shepherd was either the owner of the sheep or a son of the owner. In some cases, however, a man would have to hire help. Hirelings had the tendency to split the scene when danger came. That's why, according to Amos 3:12, if a flock was harmed while under the care of a hireling, the hireling would have to produce the ears or the legs of the lambs that were carried off as proof that he did everything in his power to fend off the attack. The Good Shepherd tenaciously cares for His flock because He's not a hireling. He's the Son.

John 10:14–16 (a)
I am the good shepherd, and know my sheep, and am known of mine. As the Father know-

eth me, even so know I the Father: and I lay down my life for the sheep. And other sheep I have, which are not of this fold: them also I must bring, and they shall hear my voice ...

I don't think we have any idea how big our Shepherd is. That's why we must watch out for sectarianism—for thinking people are suspect concerning their place in the kingdom if they don't believe exactly as we do on nonessential issues. "I have sheep you don't even know about," Jesus says.

John 10:16 (b)
. . . and there shall be one fold, and one shepherd.

One fold, one Shepherd. Unity in the body of Christ is not our responsibility—it's reality. When I was pastor of Applegate Christian Fellowship, people would often ask what we were doing to unify the believers in the Rogue Valley in Oregon. My answer was, "We're already unified." "But the believers don't get along," they would protest. "They squabble."

"Well, so do my kids," I would say, "but we don't have big rallies to remind ourselves that we're all Coursons."

So, too, did I worry that some folks only worshiped with us for three months and then worshiped somewhere else?

No. Did I chase them down when they weren't around any longer?

No. I didn't chase them in. Why would I chase them down?

The Lord is alive. *He's* the Good Shepherd, and His is a big fold. He'll lead people to that corner of His pasture for however long they're supposed to be there.

John 10:17, 18 (a)
Therefore doth my Father love me, because I lay down my life, that I might take it again. No man taketh it from me, but I lay it down of myself.

In New York City on February 24, 1925, Dr. Evans Keith, a surgeon who had practiced medicine for thirty-seven years, took part in an operation he had performed dozens of times previously. The only solution for the patient complaining of severe intestinal pain was an appendectomy—a rather common operation. This particular appendectomy, however, was unusual for two reasons. One was that it was the first time in medical history that a local anesthetic was used. Dr. Keith had been arguing for a number of years that the use of local

anesthesia was a safer, less complicated procedure. Yet although other doctors agreed in theory, none would endorse the practice until it was actually performed successfully. And therein lay the problem, for no one was brave enough to volunteer for the procedure. Consequently, this day in February was unusual not only because of the medical procedure, but because of the patient, for, you see, the patient was Dr. Keith. The doctor became the patient in order that patients might trust their doctors.

Jesus did something infinitely more remarkable than that. He willingly laid down His life that we might find life. The Shepherd became a Sheep that we sheep might know our Shepherd.

As an Old Testament believer, if you wanted to be touched by God, you would bring a lamb to the temple. There, the priests would carefully inspect and scrutinize it for any spot or blemish. It was not the worshiper who was judged. It was the lamb. In this lies a fabulous truth. You see, I can be guided by the Father tonight and led by the Father tomorrow. I can expect to receive abundant life. I can look forward to His blessing upon me and upon my family. I can trust He will anoint my head with oil and that He will take care of the predators who are coming out to get me. I can expect that He will lead me through the valley of darkness. I can expect all of this not because I'm spotless, but because the Lamb has been inspected and found perfect. Worthy is the *Lamb*. I can receive blessing not because I've gone to church, not because I've read fifteen chapters in my Bible, not because I didn't watch television. I enjoy the blessing of God upon my life solely because of the Lamb.

"I lay down My life," Jesus said. He didn't say, "You'd better lay down your life if you expect to be blessed." While it is true that He would call us in discipleship to take up our cross daily and follow Him, my entry into the presence of the Father is not based upon who I am, what I do, or what I don't do. It is based upon who *He* is, and what He did on the Cross. The Shepherd became a Lamb that we dumb sheep might know the Shepherd.

John 10:18 (b)
I have power to lay it down, and I have power to take it again.

In laying down His life, Jesus became the Door through which we enter His fold. In taking it up again by rising again, Jesus remains our Good Shepherd, guiding us, watching over us, tending us, His flock.

John 10:18 (c)–21
This commandment have I received of my Father. There was a division therefore again among the Jews for these sayings. And many of them said, He hath a devil, and is mad; why hear ye him? Others said, These are not the words of him that hath a devil. Can a devil open the eyes of the blind?

The Puritans rightly said that not all unity is holy, and not all division is from hell. Over and over again in John's Gospel, we see people divided because of Jesus.

John 10:22
And it was at Jerusalem the feast of the dedication, and it was winter.

The Feast of Dedication, which took place on December twenty-fifth, commemorated the overthrow of the terrible Syrian General, Antiochus Ephiphanes, by Judas Maccabee and his band of brave guerrillas. To this day, the Jews still celebrate the Feast of Dedication, also known as the Feast of Lights, or Hanukkah.

John 10:23, 24 (a)
And Jesus walked in the temple in Solomon's porch. Then came the Jews round about him . . .

The Greek meaning of the Greek text is, "They boxed Him in, hemmed Him in, surrounded Him."

John 10:24 (b)–29
. . . and said unto him, How long dost thou make us to doubt? If thou be the Christ, tell us plainly. Jesus answered them, I told you, and ye believed not: the works that I do in my Father's name, they bear witness of me. But ye believe not, because ye are not of my sheep, as I said unto you. My sheep hear my voice, and I know them, and they follow me: And I give unto them eternal life; and they shall never perish, neither shall any man pluck them out of my hand. My Father, which gave them me, is greater than all; and no man is able to pluck them out of my Father's hand.

Like a little child crossing the street, holding Mommy and Daddy's hands—on one hand, we have the Father, on the other we have our Lord Jesus Christ. We are eternally secure because we are secure in the Eternal One.

For topical study of John 10:27–30 entitled "You're in Good Hands," turn to page 525.

John 10:30
I and my Father are one.

In verse 24, the Jews said to Jesus, "If thou be the Christ, tell us plainly." Here, Jesus gives His answer.

John 10:31
Then the Jews took up stones again to stone him.

Sometimes people ask questions not because they want to know the answer, but because they want to argue. Such was the case here. The Jews didn't want to know the answer. They just wanted to hear Jesus give it again in order that they might have reason to stone Him.

John 10:32, 33
Jesus answered them, Many good works have I shewed you from my Father; for which of those works do ye stone me? The Jews answered him, saying, For a good work we stone thee not; but for blasphemy; and because that thou, being a man, makest thyself God.

The fact that the Jews picked up stones to throw at Jesus proved they understood His claim to deity. The fact that they were unable to throw them shows they experienced the proof of His deity.

John 10:34–36
Jesus answered them, Is it not written in your law, I said, Ye are gods? If he called them gods, unto whom the word of God came, and the scripture cannot be broken; Say ye of him, whom the Father hath sanctified, and sent into the world, Thou blasphemest; because I said, I am the Son of God?

Quoting Psalm 82:6, Jesus refers to the Old Testament, wherein judges were called gods because they held the power of life and death in their hands. "Doesn't Scripture say you are gods?" asked Jesus. "Why, then, are you so upset when I say I am the Son of God?" He throws them a curve ball—and they have a tough time hitting it.

John 10:37–42

If I do not the works of my Father, believe me not. But if I do, though ye believe not me, believe the works: that ye may know, and believe, that the Father is in me, and I in him. Therefore they sought again to take him: but he escaped out of their hand, and went away again beyond Jordan into the place where John at first baptized; and there he abode. And many resorted unto him, and said, John did no miracle: but all things that John spake of this man were true. And many believed on him there.

When I went through a time of questioning and wondering why I wasn't perceiving the power of the Holy Spirit moving through my life in the way I desired, I began to become somewhat disori-ented in my walk—until the Lord laid this passage on me. Jesus said the greatest prophet born in the history of the world was a man who did no miracle. None. At that point, I realized that if I were never to see any miracle through my life, if I were never to see the power of the Spirit in a tangible way, it would be fine with me if it could be said of me what was said of John: that all things I spoke of Jesus were true.

What's the priority of ministry? Doing exactly what John did: talking about Jesus, pointing people to Jesus, exalting Jesus. No wonder John was the greatest prophet of all (Matthew 11:11).

For topical study of John 10:39–42 entitled "Resorting Unto Jesus," turn to page 529.

YOU'RE IN GOOD HANDS
A Topical Study of
John 10:27–30

S tatistics show the average adult American is exposed to between two hundred fifty and three hundred commercials every day. But of those two hundred fifty-plus commercials, only a few have what is referred to in the industry as "sticking power." That is, very few are remembered for any length of time. The ad campaign with perhaps the greatest sticking power in advertising history was launched when the Allstate Indemnity Company declared, "You're in good hands with Allstate."

But the temporal life insurance policy you can buy from Allstate does not compare to the eternal life assurance you can get free from God Almighty, for while the Allstate salesman tells you you're in good hands, the Son of Man says, "You're in God's hands."

Strong Hands

> *And Jesus went into the temple of God, and cast out all them that sold and*
> *bought in the temple, and overthrew the tables of the moneychangers, and the*
> *seats of them that sold doves. . . .*   Matthew 21:12

A carpenter in the days before Black and Decker, Jesus felled His own trees and made His own lumber. Thus, I see callused hands holding a scourge, overturning tables, driving moneychangers from the temple, exuding such strength that none dared challenge Him. I see the strong hand of Jesus reaching into the raging waves to pull Peter out of the Sea of Galilee (Matthew 14:31). Considering that the church fathers referred to Peter as "the Giant," I picture Jesus pulling this big fisherman—doubly heavy with the weight of his waterlogged clothing—out of the water with an incredible one-armed curl.

Tender Hands

> But Jesus said, Suffer little children, and forbid them not, to come unto me: for of such is the kingdom of heaven. And he laid his hands on them, and departed thence.   Matthew 19:14, 15

When children were brought to Him, Jesus laid His hands upon them and blessed them. As Christmas draws nearer, the line to see Santa gets longer. Watch the kids, and, as they get closer to Santa, you'll see terror fill their eyes. After all, they have to sit on the lap of a fat man with a big beard, dressed in a red suit, saying, "Ho, ho, ho." If it weren't for the elves blocking the exits, none of them would probably stay long enough to even have their picture taken! Not so with Jesus. Something in His touch and in His countenance caused little children to feel comfortable around Him. They came to Him willingly and were touched by Him tenderly.

Wonder-Working Hands

> From whence hath this man these things? and what wisdom is this which is given unto him, that even such mighty works are wrought by his hands?
>   Mark 6:2

"What wonders hath His hands wrought," the people said as Jesus multiplied a few loaves of bread to feed five thousand men and as He touched the skin of the lepers and made them whole. A grotesque, disfiguring, highly contagious disease, leprosy was most likely more dreaded in Jesus' time than AIDS is today. Old Testament regulations dictated a distance of one hundred yards be kept between lepers and the general populace. But what did Jesus do? While He could have healed them with a simple command, He chose instead to risk contamination and *touch* them. If you had the ability to simply say, "Be healed," would you put your fingers in the ears of the deaf or on the eyelids of the blind? Jesus did. Knowing that the greatest need people have is to feel loved, Jesus touched them compassionately.

Inclusive Hands

> And he stretched forth his hand toward his disciples, and said, Behold my mother and my brethren!   Matthew 12:49

While it has been said that you can choose your friends but not your family, such is not the case with Jesus. He chooses His friends to *be* His family. He stretches out His strong yet tender hands and says to you and me, "You who hear My Word and receive it in your heart are My mother, My brothers, My family." As I consider the strong, tender, compassionate, wonder-working, inclusive hands of Jesus Christ, I know I'm in a good place if I'm in His hands. But Jesus declares to us in our text that, not only are we in His hand, but we're in the Father's hand as well—which causes me to consider the Father's hand. . . .

The Hand That Spans the Cosmos

Who hath measured the waters in the hollow of his hand, and meted out heaven with the span? . . .   Isaiah 40:12

With the naked eye, man can see 1,029 stars on a clear night. With his first telescope, Galileo counted 3,336 stars. Now we know there are more than 100 billion stars in our galaxy, more than 100 billion galaxies in our universe, each having at least 100 billion stars. That's a lot of stars—and the Lord knows each of them by name (Isaiah 40:26). Can you imagine remembering the names of 100 billion stars times 100 billion more?

Right now, the earth is spinning 1,000 miles per hour on its axis. At the same time, it's traveling around the sun at 67,000 miles per hour. While that's happening, the sun is moving across the Milky Way with her planets at 64,000 miles per hour. And the galaxy as a whole is moving across the universe at 483,000 miles per hour. Added together, we are moving at a speed of 1,350,000 miles per hour. No wonder we feel spun out and dizzy! In actuality, however, we are one of the slowest-moving galaxies in the universe. We're lumbering along at 400,000 miles per hour, while most galaxies move at 10,000 miles per second. What keeps it all together? What keeps everything from colliding and exploding? Who's the cosmic traffic cop? Who's in charge of the whole show? The Lord—"for he is strong in power. Not one faileth" (see Isaiah 40:26). Nothing can compare to the big Hand of the Father. The entire universe and whatever is beyond is spanned in His hand.

The Hand That Holds the Worm

For I the LORD thy God will hold thy right hand, saying unto thee, Fear not; I will help thee. Fear not, thou worm Jacob, and ye men of Israel; I will help thee, saith the LORD, and thy redeemer, the Holy One of Israel. Behold, I will make thee a new sharp threshing instrument having teeth: thou shalt thresh the mountains, and beat them small, and shalt make the hills as chaff.
                                                                                    Isaiah 41:13–15

The same Hand that spans the cosmos holds *you*. The Lord says to His people, "I'm going to keep you in the right hand of My righteousness. I'm going to make you into a threshing instrument with teeth—to eat up the mountains of difficulty that threaten you, to chew up the challenges which lie before you."

"But He's speaking to Israel, to His people," you say, "and I feel so far from what or where I should be. He must get tired of keeping His hand on me. I'm just a worm."

Good News! Look at verse 14. God says, "I'll make even you worm, Jacob, into a lean, mean threshing machine."

That's why, in talking about His eternal life assurance policy, Jesus calls us sheep (John 10:27). He doesn't say, "My lions hear My voice," or "My tigers and bulls know Me." No, He says, "My sheep—creatures known for their stupidity, for their tendency to stray, for their helplessness and vulnerability—hear My voice."

You might be as stupid as a sheep or feel as low as a worm. That's okay. You are eternally secure in the Father's hand. Am I saying you can never lose your salvation? Worms can't and sheep can't—but I'll tell you who can: the dog who returns to his own vomit (2 Peter 2:22). In speaking of those who relish returning to their own sin time and time again, Peter says they were never sheep and not even worms. They are dogs who love to eat their vomit, pigs who long to return to the pen.

The prodigal wandered away, erred greatly, and ended up in the pigpen. But he came to his senses and said, "I don't belong here. I'm going home" (see Luke 15:18). The difference between a pig and a prodigal is that, although you can scrub a pig, shampoo his hair, and put a bow on his tail—he'll dive into mud the first chance he gets. Perhaps there are those here who can't wait for this service to end so they can dive back into the mud. Be careful. That could identify you as a pig and not a prodigal. Others of you, however, know you're splattered with mud. But, like the prodigal, you say, "I don't want to be in the pigpen. I want to be in my Father's house."

The Hand That Bears Your Name

Behold, I have graven thee upon the palms of my hands; thy walls are continually before me.   Isaiah 49:16

"Behold My hands," said Jesus to Thomas (John 20:27), for in those hands, love was engraved. When Jesus was pinned to the Cross for you and me, He nailed down our eternal state. The price was paid for any sin and every sin—whatever it was, is, or will be. That's why He was able to say, "Your name is permanently engraved in the palms of My hands, and no man shall pluck you out." That's eternal life assurance, gang.

Don't let the Enemy tell you you're not saved or that you've blown it once too often. Don't let the Enemy say your salvation is in jeopardy. Don't let him produce in you a feeling of insecurity. Instead, marvel at what Jesus said when He declared, "You're in the Father's hand and you're in My hand. Therefore, you're not only in good hands—You're in the best hands."

RESORTING UNTO JESUS
A Topical Study of
John 10:39–42

Chronologically, at this point in our study, we are approximately three and a half months away from Jesus' crucifixion. In our text, we see Him leave Jerusalem, not to return until His final week. When John declares in verse 22 that it was winter, I don't think he was simply giving us information seasonally, but rather providing us insight into the climate of the city spiritually. You see, when Jesus walked throughout Jerusalem, it was summer. The people had opportunity to see His works, to hear His words, to be gathered into His kingdom. But, because they rejected Him, as He left Jerusalem, Jeremiah 8:20 was indeed fulfilled. The harvest was past. The summer had ended. But the people were not saved.

Crossing the Jordan River, Jesus went to Bethabara—the place where His public ministry had begun three years previously. He went there not because He was running from the people, but rather that He might be readied for the battle He knew lay ahead. He went to Bethabara not out of fear of the future but to retreat into the presence of the Father. And, as Jesus spent three and a half months at Bethabara, seeking His Father and preparing for what He knew would be the culmination of His earthly ministry, John writes that many resorted unto Him there. They left the cold city where it was winter—where people were rejecting Him—and went out to the desert, where they found refreshment and rest.

So, too, I believe every one of us needs to withdraw from the city, to withdraw from the cold climate and hectic pace of our usual activities, to withdraw even from ministry occasionally in order to resort unto Jesus at Bethabara. Why Bethabara? Because that is where we will call to mind John's words that rang out in that region when he said, "Behold the Lamb of God which taketh away the sin of the world!" (John 1:29).

The Man Became a Lamb

Great is the mystery, Paul declared, that God left heaven and became a Man (1 Timothy 3:16). But God didn't stop there. He went lower still. He became a Lamb.

If you were to transport yourself through the tunnel of time back to the days of the tabernacle or the temple, your entry into those places of worship would depend not upon whether you were worthy, but upon the purity of the lamb you brought with you. If, upon inspection, the lamb was found pure, you were free to enter into the tabernacle or the temple. So, too, I come to Bethabara today—I resort unto Jesus and enter into God's presence—not on the basis of my perfection, my good deeds, or my activity. I enter only through the worthiness of Jesus, the Lamb of God.

"I find no fault in Him," declared Pontius Pilate, the very one who ultimately sentenced Jesus to death (Luke 23:4). Even Judas, the one who betrayed Him, said, "I have betrayed innocent blood," (see Matthew 27:4). Worthy is the blood of the Lamb.

In speaking of the Lamb of God, David prophesied not a bone would be broken (Psalm 34:20)—unusual because after a period of time, the guards usually broke the legs of those crucified in order to hasten death. In addition to a prophecy to be fulfilled, however, Psalm 34:20 is a reminder that the blood of Jesus Christ is *continually* available to cleanse me from all sin past, present, and future. Why? Because where is blood produced? In the marrow of the bone. No wonder, then, that the Father dictated none of Jesus' bones be broken, for in so doing, He says the blood supply will never be diminished. That is why Paul could declare that where sin abounds, grace abounds yet more (Romans 5:20). Worthy is the Lamb!

The Lamb Became a Worm

Not only did God become a Man, and the Man became a Lamb, but Psalm 22:6 tells us that the Lamb became a worm. Why? The Hebrew word for worm, *tolàath*, is translated two ways in the Old Testament: either as scarlet or as worm. To obtain the color specified for the garments of the priests and the curtains of the tabernacle throughout the Book of Exodus, *tolàaths*, or worms, were ground up, thereby producing a scarlet dye in which cloth would be dipped. When bearing its young, the female *tolàath* would climb a tree and fasten herself to a branch, where, in the process of giving birth, she would explode, leaving a spot of blood on the tree. Truly, Jesus was right when He declared, I am a *tolàath*, for as our High Priest, He is clothed in the dye of His own blood; the spots of blood left on the tree of Calvary being the only way we could be born again. No wonder Isaiah declares, Though your sins be as scarlet (*tolàath*), they shall be white as snow (1:18). *Great* is the mystery. God became a Man, became a Lamb, and became a worm. Would you have done that?

Suppose you die today and go to heaven. There, the Father takes you on the tour of the cosmos, where you see places to surf that have never been discovered. You're ready to ski down Mount Zion. You're blown away by the beauty and glory of heaven. Then He takes you beyond the farthest star and shows you a tiny planet, isolated in a far corner of the universe. As you look closely, you see it is inhabited by dogs. "Little dogs on a planet—how cute," you say.

"Look a little more closely," says the Lord. And as you do, you see the dogs are not so cute after all. With teeth bared and foam dripping from their mouths, they're biting and devouring one another.

"This is sick," you say. "Those dogs are all rabid. Destroy them, Lord."

"No," He answers. "I love them. I want to tell them I have a plan to heal them, but they don't listen to Me because I'm too big for them to relate to. That's why I brought you here today. I want you to go down there and tell them I have an antidote for their rabid sickness."

"Okay," you say.

"But wait. There's more," says the Lord. "If they're going to listen to you, you must become like them: a dog."

"Let me get this straight," you say. "You want me to become a dog and tell them You have a plan for them, an antidote to heal them?"

"Yes," answers the Lord. "But there's something else: They're not going to listen to your message. On the contrary, they'll turn upon you, rip you to shreds, and kill you. I will resurrect you with great glory and honor—but from that point on, you'll be a dog forever."

If God asked that of me, I would say, "No, Lord." But you know something? Jesus Christ becoming a man is a far greater step down than you becoming a dog. His descent was a lower step than we will ever comprehend this side of eternity. Granted, He is resurrected. Granted, He is glorified. But He remains in His humanity in order that He might pray for us as a compassionate Priest and feel the hurts we're going through right now. He remains a Man to this day. Great is the mystery. Incomprehensible is the love. No wonder many resorted unto Him at Bethabara, where they remembered the words of John the Baptist. No wonder we join them and say, "John, you were right. He *is* the Lamb who takes away the sin of the world."

We are free to enter into the presence of the Father and receive blessing today solely because of the worthiness of the Lamb, the sufficiency of the blood, the bones never broken. Dear brother, precious sister—if it is winter in your soul today, make your way to the desert. Resort to Jesus at Bethabara and behold the Lamb once again.

11 Living together in a house presumably given them by their parents, two sisters and a brother became friends with a radical Rabbi, a controversial Figure, a miracle Worker named Jesus of Nazareth. And as they opened up their hearts to Him, they also opened up their home for Him. Yet although no doubt Jesus greatly appreciated their hospitality and loved the friendship they offered Him so freely, their linkage with Him and their relationship to Him did not insulate them from difficulty nor immunize them from tragedy. Thus, as chapter 11 opens, we see ominous storm clouds hovering over this little home in Bethany. So, too, I think most of us who love the Love have opened the home of our hearts to Him and who want to be linked with Him have discovered that these sentiments do not insulate or protect us from dark days. Let's take a look and see how this family navigated the waters of difficulty. . . .

John 11:1–3
Now a certain man was sick, named Lazarus, of Bethany, the town of Mary and her sister Martha. (It was that Mary which anointed the Lord with ointment, and wiped his feet with her hair, whose brother Lazarus was sick.) Therefore his sisters sent unto him, saying, Lord, behold, he whom thou lovest is sick.

Mary and Martha sent word to Jesus, about twenty miles away in Bethabara, that the one He loved was sick. I like that! They didn't say, "The one that loves You is sick," but rather, "The one You love is sick." Like Martha and Mary, I don't approach the Lord on the basis of my love for Him. You know why? Because my love for the Lord is fickle and feeble. But His love for me, however, is fixed and firm. He's never surprised by what I say, never taken aback by what I do. Therefore, wise is the man or woman who approaches the Lord based on *His* love.

Interestingly, the Greek word translated "lovest" is not *agapao*—the perfect love that gives simply for the sake of giving—but *phileo*, which refers to affection or friendship. Maybe you think the Lord loves you because He is love and, therefore, has to love you. Not true. Jesus said, "I have not called you servants but friends" (see John 15:15). He doesn't love you simply because He's stuck with you. No, He *chose* to love you (John 15:16). He loves you as you would love a friend.

Notice that Mary and Martha didn't instruct the Lord concerning what He should do. Oh, how often I make that mistake. I become aware of some problem or need and immediately start instructing the Lord about how He can solve the situation. "Who hath given the Lord counsel?" asked the prophet rhetorically. (Isaiah 40:13). A lot of us try. We would be far wiser to follow the example of Martha and Mary. "Lord, the one who You have affection for is sick," they said. They weren't commanding. They were communing.

John 11:4, 5
When Jesus heard that, he said, This sickness is not unto death, but for the glory of God, that the Son of God might be glorified thereby. Now Jesus loved Martha, and her sister, and Lazarus.

Precious Mary—songwriters sing of her; poets write about her; artists draw pictures of her. Mary is always elevated. But did you catch what the Holy Spirit inspired John to write? "Now Jesus loved *Martha* and her sister." You who are Marthas, be encouraged. You who say, "I'm not one who easily sits at Jesus' feet and contemplates His character. I'm the one who's washing dishes after the potluck is over, the one who's changing diapers in the nursery"—take hope. Scripture says Jesus loved Martha.

John 11:6-7
When he had heard therefore that he was sick, he abode two days still in the same place where he was. Then after that saith he to his disciples, Let us go into Judaea again.

As the messenger returned with Jesus' message that Lazarus' sickness was not unto death, no doubt relief flooded the hearts of Mary and Martha. Yet as time passed, Lazarus became weaker by the hour. Meanwhile, Jesus remained in Bethabara for two more days, letting events play out before He said, "Let's go to Judaea."

John 11:8
His disciples say unto him, Master, the Jews of late sought to stone thee; and goest thou thither again?

"You're going back toward Jerusalem? Lord," warned His disciples, "they're out to get You there."

John 11:9, 10
Jesus answered, Are there not twelve hours in the day? If any man walk in the day, he stumbleth not, because he seeth the light of this world. But if a man walk in the night, he stumbleth, because there is no light in him.

"Don't worry," answered Jesus. "It's still daylight. There are still things for me to do before the night falls." Oh, night would come soon enough when He would be crucified on a Cross, when His work on earth would cease. But not yet. Consequently, Jesus was implying that He was indestructible. So are you. The Bible says man is appointed unto death (Hebrews 9:27). No matter how many airbags you have in your car, no matter how many injections of vitamin C you take, once your appointed hour comes, that's it. But until that time, you're basically indestructible. Does that mean you can skydive without a parachute? No, for the moment you do will then become your appointed hour. When Satan told Jesus to jump off the temple in order to prove who He was, Jesus said, "It is written thou shalt not tempt the Lord thy God" (see Matthew 4:7). Don't be foolish—but realize there is a period of time in which you can work without being destroyed.

John 11:11-14
These things said he: and after that he saith unto them, Our friend Lazarus sleepeth; but I go, that I may awake him out of sleep. Then said his disciples, Lord, if he sleep, he shall do well. Howbeit Jesus spake of his death: but they thought that he had spoken of taking of rest in sleep. Then said Jesus unto them plainly, Lazarus is dead.

In my mind's eye, I see Martha getting ready for the funeral, taking care of the arrangements perhaps, or cooking a meal for the family, guests, and mourners who would be coming. I see Mary, with her beautiful contemplative spirit, quietly ministering to people or perhaps pondering the events that had transpired.

John 11:15
And I am glad for your sakes that I was not there, to the intent ye may believe; nevertheless let us go unto him.

There was sadness in the home, but gladness in the heart of Jesus Christ. Why? Because He saw the big picture. He knew the end of the story. He knew that this event that began with grief would end in belief.

John 11:16 (a)
Then said Thomas, which is called Didymus . . .

I've always liked Thomas. I think he gets a bad rap. He should be remembered not only as the doubting one, but also as the devoted one because watch what he says. . . .

John 11:16 (b)
. . . unto his fellow disciples, Let us also go, that we may die with him.

When the other disciples were saying, "Don't go near Jerusalem," Thomas said, "Let's go and die too." I think this shows real devotion and true courage. When Jesus appeared to the disciples in the Upper Room after His Resurrection, Thomas wasn't there (John 20:24). Why? I suggest that while the other guys were hiding in the Upper Room, Thomas was the only one who had the guts to be out on the streets. A lot of times, I think we read things into the lives of Bible characters that aren't totally fair. I think Thomas, for example, is one who deserves a little more credit.

John 11:17–20 (a)
Then when Jesus came, he found that he had lain in the grave four days already. Now Bethany was nigh unto Jerusalem, about fifteen furlongs off: And many of the Jews came to Martha and Mary, to comfort them concerning their brother. Then Martha, as soon as she heard that Jesus was coming, went and met him . . .

In running out to meet Jesus, Martha broke Oriental custom and tradition. Thus, I see Martha as being very much like Peter (John 21:7).

John 11:20 (b)
. . . but Mary sat still in the house.

I think Mary and John are also similar. Mary is a contemplator and John a mystic who received Revelation from Jesus.

John 11:21
Then said Martha unto Jesus, Lord, if thou hadst been here, my brother had not died.

I think remorse rather than rebuke was the incentive for Martha to say, "Lord, if You had been here, I know Lazarus would still be with us."

John 11:22
But I know, that even now, whatsoever thou wilt ask of God, God will give it thee.

Here we see a spark of faith ignite in Martha's heart.

John 11:23
Jesus saith unto her, Thy brother shall rise again.

Responding to Martha's faith, Jesus gives a promise.

John 11:24
Martha saith unto him, I know that he shall rise again in the resurrection at the last day.

Jesus gives a promise to Martha. But rather than embracing it joyfully and expectantly, Martha looks at it as a theological principle. Do you ever do that? The Lord opens a promise to you in the Word about a situation, a relationship, or a financial struggle and you think, *Well, this probably doesn't apply to this dispensation. This can't really be true for me today. Come on, the Lord isn't really going to bless, heal, restore, or help. There must be some other meaning theologically. It's just too good to be true.* But in so doing, you share the mind-set of Martha.

John 11:25, 26
Jesus said unto her, I am the resurrection, and the life: he that believeth in me, though he were dead, yet shall he live: And whosoever liveth and believeth in me shall never die. Believest thou this?

"You're talking theologically, Martha," says Jesus. "But I'm relating to you personally. *I* am the resurrection. *I* am what you need right now."

John 11:27
She saith unto him, Yea, Lord: I believe that thou art the Christ, the Son of God, which should come into the world.

There's not a believer in this room tonight who doubts the Lord's ability to do a miracle. What we struggle with is the same thing with which Martha struggled. That is, we don't question His ability. But we do question His willingness. Like Martha, we say, "I believe You're Someone special, unique, powerful, the Son of God, Messiah. But I can't believe You would be willing to do something for *me*."

John 11:28 (a)
And when she had so said, she went her way . . .

Although there was a spark of faith initially within Martha, we'll see her get sidetracked theologically, wondering whether Jesus would do a work for her personally.

John 11:28 (b)–30
. . . and called Mary her sister secretly, saying, The Master is come, and calleth for thee. As soon as she heard that, she arose quickly, and came unto him. Now Jesus was not yet come into the town, but was in that place where Martha met him.

In waiting for Jesus to call her, Mary held to Eastern tradition.

John 11:31, 32 (a)
The Jews then which were with her in the house, and comforted her, when they saw Mary, that she rose up hastily and went out, followed her, saying, She goeth unto the grave to weep there. Then when Mary was come where Jesus was, and saw him, she fell down at his feet . . .

How special Mary is. In Luke 10, we see her at the feet of the Lord in a happy time. Here, we see her at His feet during a hard time. Mary is one who both in days of delight and difficulty positioned herself at the feet of Jesus Christ.

I have found that some are inclined to spend time with the Lord in easy times. "Oh, Lord," they say, "You're so good to me. I'll sing Your praises. I'll be at church on Sunday." But when the hard times come, they pull away. In anger and frustration and confusion, they say, "Why expend the energy? Why pay the gas money? I'll just stay home and watch TV." Others run to church in hard times. This is seen, for example, in times of war. In hard times, many seek the Lord and sit

at His feet. But when things are back to normal, they disappear.

Many of you, however, are like Mary, who, regardless of the circumstances, find themselves *always* at Jesus' feet. People often wonder how they can experience intimacy with the Lord to the degree Mary did. The answer is simple: Spend time at His feet.

John 11:32 (b)
. . . saying unto him, Lord, if thou hadst been here, my brother had not died.

Mary repeats verbatim what Martha had said previously. This tells me something about human nature. That is, we begin to talk like the people with whom we spend time. Watching their brother grow paler and weaker, no doubt Martha and Mary said, "Where's the Lord? Didn't He get our message? Doesn't He care?" And they spoke the same words.

I have chosen, as much as possible, to establish relationships with people who speak words of faith, who rejoice in the Lord, who give thanks in everything because that's the language I want to speak. I don't want to be one who is cynical, one who doubts, one who complains, murmurs, or is grumpy. This doesn't mean we shouldn't minister to those people and bear their burdens. But in establishing long-lasting relationships, I encourage you to be with those who speak faith, who love God, who trust the Lord. Spend time with people who will take you a notch higher, because if you don't—if your closest friends are those who are always questioning and doubting and grumbling—their language will sooner or later flow from your lips as well.

John 11:33–35
When Jesus therefore saw her weeping, and the Jews also weeping which came with her, he groaned in the spirit, and was troubled, and said, Where have ye laid him? They said unto him, Lord, come and see. Jesus wept.

As the mourners wail, as Mary weeps, as Jesus is at the scene, He finds Himself also crying, which intrigues me because He knew what would be happening. Why, then, does He weep?

Perhaps Jesus wept because He was reminded that sin destroys, sin kills, sin stinks. Aren't you finding this to be so? Aren't you seeing heartache and sadness all around because of sin? Doesn't it make you heavy of heart sometimes when you realize that precious people are hurting because of sin?

Perhaps Jesus wept because of the unbelief that surrounded Him. He had given a promise that Lazarus would rise, but no one embraced or believed it. On the contrary, they were all mourning. Jesus said, "It's going to be all right." But they said, "No, it's not." So, too, when He says all things are working together for good (Romans 8:28), and we say, "No they're not," our unbelief must break His heart as well.

Perhaps Jesus wept because He knew He was going to pull Lazarus out of Paradise and bring him back to this planet. Poor Lazarus!

Perhaps Jesus wept because, although He knew everything would turn out well eventually, those around Him were hurting presently. We are told in the Book of Hebrews that Jesus is a High Priest who sympathizes with us, feels for us, and prays on behalf of us. Therefore, even though I should be stronger in faith, when I'm hurting, Jesus hurts too.

So it is that the shortest verse in Scripture becomes the most powerful when seen in light of both the deity and humanity of our Lord.

John 11:36, 37
Then said the Jews, Behold how he loved him! And some of them said, Could not this man, which opened the eyes of the blind, have caused that even this man should not have died?

Couldn't Jesus have done something? Yes and no. Yes, He had the power. But no, it wasn't His plan—not until a few moments later . . .

John 11:38, 39
Jesus therefore again groaning in himself cometh to the grave. It was a cave, and a stone lay upon it. Jesus said, Take ye away the stone. Martha, the sister of him that was dead, saith unto him, Lord, by this time he stinketh: for he hath been dead four days.

No doubt in that hot climate, the body of Lazarus took on a distinct odor. That is why Martha said, "Lord, just let it be. Don't ask me to roll away the stone. It stinks." The same is true of you and me. The Lord wants to do something in our lives. But before He does, oftentimes He'll say, "Roll away the stone. Expose the problem. Let Me have total access to the situation."

"Oh, Lord, not that," we say. "Do we have to deal with *that?* I'm embarrassed about it. I'm ashamed of it. It stinks."

The Lord said, "I gave you a promise, Martha. But here's the prerequisite: Roll away the stone." Do you think Jesus could have rolled away the stone Himself? Later on, He did—His own stone. But here He says to Martha, just as He says to me, "The promise is given, but here's the prereq-

uisite: Roll away the stone. Even though what's inside stinks, let Me deal with it."

John 11:40–42
Jesus saith unto her, Said I not unto thee, that, if thou wouldest believe, thou shouldest see the glory of God? Then they took away the stone from the place where the dead was laid. And Jesus lifted up his eyes, and said, Father, I thank thee that thou hast heard me. And I knew that thou hearest me always: but because of the people which stand by I said it, that they may believe that thou hast sent me.

Jesus didn't pray in public very frequently. His communion with His Father was not like that of the Pharisees who loved to be seen on the street corners praying at great length. No, Jesus communed privately with His Father moment by moment. Here, however, He prays audibly, saying, "Father, I'm praying aloud in order that they who are watching might know what's happening."

John 11:43
And when he thus had spoken, he cried with a loud voice, Lazarus, come forth.

Jesus had to address Lazarus by name lest everyone in the cemetery came forth.

John 11:44
And he that was dead came forth, bound hand and foot with graveclothes: and his face was bound about with a napkin. Jesus saith unto them, Loose him, and let him go.

Turning to His disciples, to His followers, to the family, Jesus said, "I resurrected Lazarus. But I'm giving you the privilege and responsibility of loosening him." That's what happens Sunday after Sunday in the amphitheatre at Applegate Christian Fellowship? People are born again by the score. And the Lord says to you who know them, "I resurrected them. Now you loose them by praying for them, sharing with them, and standing by them."

John 11:45
Then many of the Jews which came to Mary, and had seen the things which Jesus did, believed on him.

In light of this fabulous miracle—the last miracle John records before Jesus Christ is crucified—I call your attention to two principles to jot down, think through, and pray in. . . .

The first is that delays are determined by the Lord for His glory. "Where are You, Lord?" we cry. "I sent a message to You in prayer. I've cried out to You in sincerity. But You're not working. You're not coming. Where are You?

"Lord, come and heal," cry Mary and Martha.

"I'm going to do something a whole lot more impacting than that," answers Jesus. "I'm going to resurrect Him. But that means He has to die first."

I have found that the longer the Lord waits to do His work in my life, the longer He waits to come on the scene, oftentimes the greater blessing it is for His glory and my good. You more mature believers have sung, "Lord, use my life." But what if that means tragedy? What if it means cancer, bankruptcy, death, setback, or pain? What if God can get the maximum amount of glory when a world who doesn't believe watches you go through terrible times and sees His strength see you through? Samson's greatest victory did not take place until he stood as a blind man in the temple of Dagon and brought the roof down upon himself (Judges 16:30).

"Use my life, Lord," I pray. "I'm ready for the Jon Courson Evangelistic Association, or the 'Jon Courson's Greatest Hits' album."

But the Lord says, "Okay. I'll use you. I'll show My goodness and reality as you go through horrendous difficulty—for when the roof caves in and the house comes down, the demons will flee; the Philistines will fall; and I will be glorified."

If you really want your life to be used, precious people, let the Lord do what He knows will bring Him the greatest glory. Baby Christians don't understand this. Like all babies, all they care about is themselves. They want their stomachs full and their diapers changed. They want to be satisfied. While there's nothing wrong with younger believers wanting to be pampered and fed, there comes a time to put away childish things (1 Corinthians 13:11). There comes a point when a believer grows up and says, "To God be the glory—whatever that may mean in my life."

Second, not only are delays determined by the Lord for His glory, but the solution to your frustration is not something. It's Someone. "*I* am the resurrection," Jesus says. "It's *Me*. I am what you're looking for." Dear brother, precious sister, the solution to your frustration is the Person of Jesus. You don't need more money necessarily, for Jesus says, "I am the Bread." You don't need some kind of mystical experience to guide you directionally, for Jesus says, "I am the Way." It's *Him*. If you realize He is the I AM, you'll make it through—and you will find yourself actually embracing the difficult day rather than resenting it.

Shadrach, Meshach, and Abed-Nego left their fiery furnace only when commanded to do so by Nebuchadnezzar. Why? Because it was in the fire

that they found Jesus (Daniel 3:25). So, too, if you allow the Lord to do His work, you will perceive the presence of Jesus Christ so clearly that you will say, "Lord, keep me in the fire all of the time if that's the only way we can see You."

"I'm going through tough times," you say, "but I'm not finding the Lord in the fire."

Easter Sunday, Mary was at the tomb. Seeing who she thought was the gardener, she said, "Where's the body of my Lord"—not realizing the One standing right before her was the very One she was looking for. Why didn't Mary recognize Jesus? Perhaps it was because there were tears in her eyes and she wasn't seeing clearly. So, too, sometimes our own fears and tears blind us to Jesus' nearness. He's here, saint. He promised to be. He's been there for you previously. He's been there for me personally. And sometimes to experience His presence, all we have to do is quit blubbering, dry our eyes, and say, "Lord, I believe You will see me through."

John 11:46
But some of them went their ways to the Pharisees, and told them what things Jesus had done.

Lazarus comes out of the grave and what happens? Some believe—but others say, "Let's go tattle to the Pharisees about what Jesus is doing now."

John 11:47, 48
Then gathered the chief priests and the Pharisees a council, and said, What do we? for this man doeth many miracles. If we let him thus alone, all men will believe on him: and the Romans shall come and take away both our place and nation.

"What are we going to do about Jesus?" the Jews ask each other. "If we don't stop Him, the Romans will come down to quell a potential insurrection and we'll lose our place." You see, for the Pharisees, the ministry was simply a platform for personal prestige and power. Thus, they weren't concerned about God being in His rightful place. They were only concerned about losing their place.

John 11:49–52
And one of them, named Caiaphas, being the high priest that same year, said unto them, Ye know nothing at all, Nor consider that it is expedient for us, that one man should die for the people, and that the whole nation perish not. And this spake he not of himself: but being high priest that year, he prophesied that Jesus should die for

that nation; and not for that nation only, but that also he should gather together in one the children of God that were scattered abroad.

So wealthy did Annas, the high priest, become from the money-making schemes that surrounded the temple, to avoid a conflict of interest, he appointed his son-in-law, Caiaphas, to serve as high priest. From his office of high priest, Caiaphas spoke more profoundly than he could possibly have known when he said, "It's prudent that one man dies in order that the whole nation might live."

Little did Caiaphas know that what he said was inspired by the Spirit. This shows me something about our Lord. God can use anyone to speak His heart, to reveal His truth. Caiaphas was a loser, a charlatan, a fleecer. Yet the Spirit still inspired him at this moment to speak truth. Just as Caiaphas prophesied, one Man did indeed die—not only for the nation, but for the sins of all men. God can use a Caiaphas; God can use a donkey (Numbers 22), a neighbor, a professor, or any other voice He chooses to speak truth. Be wary of the mind-set that thinks if a person isn't born-again, he cannot speak truth. God can use *anyone*.

John 11:53–57
Then from that day forth they took counsel together for to put him to death. Jesus therefore walked no more openly among the Jews; but went thence unto a country near to the wilderness, into a city called Ephraim, and there continued with his disciples. And the Jews' passover was nigh at hand: and many went out of the country up to Jerusalem before the passover, to purify themselves. Then sought they for Jesus, and spake among themselves, as they stood in the temple, What think ye, that he will not come to the feast? Now both the chief priests and the Pharisees had given a commandment, that, if any man knew where he were, he should shew it, that they might take him.

Now we are coming to the very end—the last week in the life of our wonderful Lord, the last week before He would be crucified on the Cross. At this time, many are going to Jerusalem to celebrate the Passover. How many? Josephus tells us temple records indicate that at least 250,000 sheep were slaughtered in the temple during this particular Passover. Since one lamb was sacrificed for a household, and since each household averaged ten people, including extended family, there would have been 2.5 million people flooding into Jerusalem. In your mind's eye, catch the

scene: 2.5 million people jammed into a city only a few miles square, standing room only, sheep everywhere. And in the midst of those crowded people and bleating sheep walks the Lamb of God—coming to die for the sin of the world.

12

John 12:1
Then Jesus six days before the passover came to Bethany, where Lazarus was which had been dead, whom he raised from the dead.

In the final week before He would be pinned to the Cross, Jesus went to Bethany, about two miles outside the city of Jerusalem, to the house of His friends.

John 12:2, 3
There they made him a supper; and Martha served: but Lazarus was one of them that sat at the table with him. Then took Mary a pound of ointment of spikenard, very costly, and anointed the feet of Jesus, and wiped his feet with her hair: and the house was filled with the odour of the ointment.

Jesus taught us that whenever two or three gather in His name, He would be in the midst of them (Matthew 18:20). And here, in this house in Bethany, we see the components of the church in the three who opened their house to Him as we observe Martha working, Lazarus witnessing, and Mary worshiping.

Martha Working

This is the same Martha who, a few months previously, said, "Lord, tell my sister to get in here in the kitchen and give me a hand."

"Martha, you're troubled by many things," Jesus had said. "*One* thing is needful, but you're striving and stressing and troubled about many things" (see Luke 10:41). The same is true of us. How often we are so busy, but not very blessed. People come to simply spend time with us, but we make fancy desserts, vacuum the carpets, wash the windows, mow the lawn, sweep the walks— and by the time they get there, we have a headache and want them to leave. "One thing I desired, Martha," said Jesus, "sitting at My feet, Mary has chosen better."

Martha evidently learned this lesson, because now, several months later, the scene is repeated again. Martha is still working—only this time it's not for one guest, but for seventeen: Jesus, His disciples, Simon (mentioned in Luke's account), Mary, Martha, and Lazarus. Martha's still in the kitchen—but this time she's not complaining. Good for her.

Certain of you are workers by nature, Martha-like in your mind-set. That's good, as long as you're not complaining and striving, feeling obligated, burned-out, or hassled. If you can work joyfully as unto the Lord, great! The body of Christ desperately needs Marthas. I thank the Lord for the Marthas who serve joyfully, helping people practically. If such is your role, I commend you.

Lazarus Witnessing

Although Lazarus never speaks a word, he's a major witness. Jesus would be doing the teaching, the speaking, and the sharing. But Lazarus was the proof of the pudding (verse 9) because witnessing is not only what you say. More importantly, it's what you are. Jesus didn't commission us to go into all the world and witness. He said, "You shall *be* My witnesses (Acts 1:8). In other words, it's as if Jesus said, "Like Lazarus, you were dead. Your countenance was drab; you reeked of the grave; you were bound up in all sorts of stuff. But I freed you. And now you shall be My witnesses because people will look at the difference in you and be amazed."

I like what Samuel Chadwick, the classic Methodist evangelist and educator of the 1900s, said: "If God is at work week by week raising men from the dead, there will always be people coming to see how it is done. You cannot find an empty church that has conversion as its leading feature. Do you want to know how to fill empty chapels? Here is the answer: Get your Lazarus."

I'm convinced that Applegate Christian Fellowship sees the amphitheatre packed to overflowing because a lot of folks go to see people being baptized Sunday after Sunday. It intrigues, interests, stimulates, and draws. And not only does conversion fill empty churches—it fills empty lives. If you are finding your own joy diminishing, let me ask you this question: How long has it been since you've shared with an unbeliever? You see, saved sinners not only cause joy in heaven (Luke 15:10), but they bring about feasting and merriment in our own hearts as well (Luke 15:23, 24). Living your life before the unbeliever in such a way that he'll be curious about the gospel is the key not only to filling empty churches, but also to filling empty Christians. Find Lazarus. Be Lazarus. Evangelize.

Mary Worshiping

Mary is a symbol of the beauty of worship. Worship is costly. It might cost you a relationship even as it cost Mary when, in pouring the ointment upon the feet of Jesus, she was pouring out her very dowry. If we are true worshipers, people in our lives might shy away from us a bit and call us crazy. "Lifting hands, singing songs, praising, and kneeling are signs of fanaticism. I'm not interested in that or in you if that's what you're going to do," they might say. Worship can be costly. It cost Mary not simply her alabaster box and oil, but she would be analyzed and criticized by Judas. So will we be.

When David danced before the Lord with all his might, stripped down to his undergarments, his wife mocked him (2 Samuel 6:20). David went on to continue worshiping the Lord all the days of his life. But Michal "had no child unto the day of her death" (2 Samuel 6:23). The same is still true. Those who critique or find fault with worship will experience barrenness, dryness, and a lack of productivity. Ask Michal. Ask Judas. Then ask Mary about worshiping. . . .

The ointment she poured out upon Jesus was not used several days earlier on her brother Lazarus possibly because she was saving it for Jesus' burial. Yet she did not use it at His burial either, for it was Mary Magdalene who went to anoint His body with perfume and spice on Easter morning—not Mary of Bethany. Nor was Mary of Bethany at the foot of the Cross. Mary, the mother of Jesus, was there—but not Mary of Bethany. Why did Mary of Bethany seemingly have no part in the death and burial of her Lord? Because Mary evidently understood something no one else comprehended. Although Jesus had spoken directly to His disciples, saying, "I'm going to die, be buried, and rise again after three days," they didn't get it. Mary is the only one who understood what was going to happen. She alone saw the big picture. She alone understood there was no need to save the ointment for Jesus' burial—because He wasn't going to stay buried. There was no need to go with the other Marys to the Cross—because that wouldn't be the end of the story.

How did Mary have such profound insight? I suggest it was because she was at His feet constantly, expressively, and expectantly. Be a worshiper in your morning devotions and in your evening watches. Be a worshiper in church on Sundays and Wednesdays. Be a worshiper and watch and see what will happen, for, like Mary, you'll hear the Lord's heart and know things others don't.

John 12:4, 5
**Then saith one of his disciples, Judas Iscar-
iot, Simon's son, which should betray him,
Why was not this ointment sold for three
hundred pence, and given to the poor?**

I find it interesting that the first recorded utterance of Judas the traitor is, "Why?"

John 12:6, 7
**This he said, not that he cared for the poor;
but because he was a thief, and had the bag,
and bare what was put therein. Then said
Jesus, Let her alone: against the day of my
burying hath she kept this.**

"Leave her alone," said Jesus to Judas. "Mary
saved this ointment for My burial. But she's giving it to Me now."

John 12:8
**For the poor always ye have with you; but
me ye have not always.**

In other words, Jesus says, "You'll always have
opportunity for activity, but don't miss these precious moments of intimacy."

John 12:9–11
**Much people of the Jews therefore knew
that he was there: and they came not for
Jesus' sake only, but that they might see
Lazarus also, whom he had raised from the
dead. But the chief priests consulted that
they might put Lazarus also to death; Because that by reason of him many of the
Jews went away, and believed on Jesus.**

"Not only must we put Jesus to death—but we
also must deal with Lazarus," concluded the
Jewish leaders, "because he's a testimony of
Jesus' power." They would have to keep going,
however, for they would have to not only silence
Jesus, Lazarus, and the disciples—but all of
the believers. In the days of the early church,
six million Christians were killed in an effort to
stamp out Christianity. The more Christians
killed, however, the stronger the church became.

In March 1990, *Christianity Today* reported
that between the years 1900 and 1990, an average of three hundred thousand believers have
been martyred every year. Yet where the
church is persecuted, the church is powerful.
Truly, the blood of the saints is the seed of the
church.

John 12:12 (a)
**On the next day much people that were
come to the feast . . .**

It was Sunday, the tenth day of Nisan—by our
calendar, the sixth day of April—four days before
the Feast of the Passover. According to the Book
of Exodus, it was the day when every family celebrating Passover would choose a lamb to sacrifice. Then priests would watch it closely from the
tenth to the fourteenth day of Nisan in order to
ensure it was in the best of health and was without flaw or blemish. Picture in your mind's eye
tens of thousands of lambs being brought into the
holy city. And in the midst of all the choosing, inspecting, and bleating, the Lamb of God entered
the city of Jerusalem.

The Lamb of God came to Jerusalem on the
tenth day of Nisan—the very day prophesied
hundreds of years previously. "Know this," Daniel was told, "from the going forth of the commandment to restore and rebuild Jerusalem until
Messiah the prince, shall be sixty-nine heptads,
sixty-nine seven-year-units, or four hundred
eighty-three years." Four hundred eighty-three
years from March 14, 445 B.C.—the day Artaxerxes gave the Jews the charge to rebuild Jerusalem—was April 6, A.D. 32. No wonder Jesus
cried, "Oh, Jerusalem, Jerusalem" (Matthew
23:37), for they should have known the day of His
coming.

John 12:12 (b), 13
**. . . when they heard that Jesus was coming
to Jerusalem, they took branches of palm
trees, and went forth to meet him, and cried,
Hosanna: Blessed is the King of Israel that
cometh in the name of the Lord.**

The waving of palm branches and crying of
Hosanna was a tradition that began two hundred
years earlier, following the reign of a bloodthirsty
Syrian king named Antiochus Epiphanes. A man
so blasphemous that he slaughtered a pig in the
Holy of Holies and made the priests drink its
blood, Epiphanes bludgeoned the Jews into submission. After several years of this, however, a
man named Judas Maccabee, whose name meant
"hammer," and his brothers decided to nail Antiochus Epiphanes by launching a guerrilla war
against him. Approximately nine years later,
when Maccabee and his band of renegades miraculously overcame the Assyrian army and drove
Epiphanes from Jerusalem, the people spontaneously celebrated by waving palm branches. And
from that time on, the back of Jewish coinage depicted a palm branch as a symbol of deliverance
from oppression.

Here in John's account, two hundred years after Maccabee, the Jews find themselves oppressed again, not by the Syrians, but by the Romans. Consequently, what the people were essentially saying when they cried Hosanna and waved palm branches as Jesus rode into Jerusalem, was, "Be Judas Maccabee. Deliver us from the Romans." But when they realized Jesus had a different agenda than a political one, a different agenda than a national one, a different agenda than a material one—their cry changed from "Hosanna" to "Crucify him."

The same is still true. Christians individually and churches corporately mobilize politically for this cause or for that personality; to change our government or to change our economy. But very few are interested in a Cross that speaks of dying to self. An arresting picture of Calvary depicts three empty crosses on Golgotha, with a donkey in the background, chewing on a palm frond. You see, it's one thing to shout at a parade, and something else altogether to stand at the foot of the Cross.

John 12:14, 15
And Jesus, when he had found a young ass, sat thereon; as it is written, Fear not, daughter of Sion: behold, thy King cometh, sitting on an ass's colt.

According to rabbinical theory, when Messiah came, He would ride into Jerusalem on a white horse. If, however, Israel was not ready for Messiah, He would ride in on a donkey. And here's Jesus riding on a donkey—not to confirm rabbinical speculation, but to fulfill prophetic indication made hundreds of years earlier when Zechariah said the King would come riding on a donkey (9:9).

John 12:16
These things understood not his disciples at the first: but when Jesus was glorified, then remembered they that these things were written of him, and that they had done these things unto him.

Jesus riding in to Jerusalem on a donkey, the people waving palm branches and shouting Hosanna meant nothing to the disciples until Jesus was glorified. Are the Scriptures confusing to you? Do they make no sense? Keep reading; keep studying—for as Jesus is glorified in your life, you will have a greater and greater understanding of Scripture. The problem is, we want understanding, but we don't want to glorify the Lord by obeying Him.

We want to understand esoteric insights; we want to grasp the meaning of this verse, or that chapter—but it is only when we glorify the Lord in obedience that we will understand what's being said in any given passage. The disciples didn't understand initially. But when Jesus was glorified, they understood eventually.

John 12:17–19
The people therefore that was with him when he called Lazarus out of his grave, and raised him from the dead, bare record. For this cause the people also met him, for that they heard that he had done this miracle. The Pharisees therefore said among themselves, Perceive ye how ye prevail nothing? behold, the world is gone after him.

The Pharisees felt threatened needlessly—for this very crowd that seemed ready to leave everything to follow Jesus would soon desert Him.

John 12:20
And there were certain Greeks among them that came up to worship at the feast.

At Jesus' birth, Gentiles came from the East to worship Jesus (Matthew 2:1, 2). Here, prior to His death, Gentiles came from the West for the same reason.

John 12:21, 22 (a)
The same came therefore to Philip, which was of Bethsaida of Galilee, and desired him, saying, Sir, we would see Jesus. Philip cometh and telleth Andrew . . .

Perhaps it was because he knew Jesus had come to minister to the lost sheep of Israel and was unsure whether He would receive these Gentiles that Philip went to Andrew.

John 12:22 (b)
. . . and again Andrew and Philip tell Jesus.

Andrew, in turn, did what he always did (John 1:41; 6:8, 9). He brought Philip to Jesus.

John 12:23, 24
And Jesus answered them, saying, The hour is come, that the Son of man should be glorified. Verily, verily, I say unto you, Except a corn of wheat fall into the ground and die, it abideth alone: but if it die, it bringeth forth much fruit.

In answering the Greeks, Jesus didn't allude to Old Testament prophecy as He did on other occasions. Instead, He talked about a grain of wheat falling into the ground. Why? Because these

Greeks would be far more familiar with science, nature, and philosophy than with Old Testament prophecy. Therefore, Jesus gave Andrew and Philip an analogy the Greeks would understand readily when He said, "You can't see the potential of a grain of wheat until it dies. So, too, the only way you can see Me is in light of My death, burial, and resurrection."

Gang, unless you see Jesus in light of what He did at Calvary, you'll miss Him. Truly, no matter to whom you're talking or what you're facing, the answer for everyone is always found at the foot of the Cross. I believe that with all of my heart.

"If the Lord loves me, why did my husband leave me?" says the brokenhearted woman. "I don't understand."

I don't either. But this I do know: Jesus' arms are open on the Cross of Calvary, and He's saying to you for all He's worth, "Trust Me. You watch. You wait. You'll see that out of death will come life." It's so great to be a believer, because in every situation, we get to take people to the Cross and say, "Here's your answer. The love that pinned Jesus to the Cross and the power that resurrected Him from the grave are all you need."

John 12:25
He that loveth his life shall lose it; and he that hateth his life in this world shall keep it unto life eternal.

In this chapter, Jesus gives His final public teaching. And in this final public teaching before His crucifixion, He lets everyone in—Jews and Greeks alike—on the secret of life. "Get a life," people say. And Jesus tells us how. "Get a life," He says, "not by asserting yourself, not by pampering yourself, not by changing yourself—but by dying to self."

For topical study of John 12:21–25 entitled "The Only Way to See Our Lord," turn to page 544.

John 12:26
If any man serve me, let him follow me; and where I am, there shall also my servant be: if any man serve me, him will my Father honour.

The story is told of a prince and his servant traveling through a hostile region who were taken captive by the enemy. After being beaten and thrown into a dungeon, the prince developed a terrible fever, and it looked as though his days were numbered. Semiconscious as he was, how-

ever, he didn't miss the opportunity to alert his servant when their guard fell asleep one day.

"Get his keys and get out of here," the prince said. "I'm too weak; I can't make it. But you go. This is your chance."

"My prince," answered the servant, "where you are, there I will be. If need be, we'll both die here together."

Two weeks later, the prince's father launched an invasion and freed his imprisoned son in the process.

"Oh, Father," said the prince immediately upon his return, "even as my servant stayed with me in my danger, suffered with me in my sickness, stood by me in my imprisonment, honor now him." And the servant was honored throughout the kingdom.

The same is true with you. The Lord knows you could opt to escape, that the Cross and obedience are not always easy. The Lord knows many of you are truly paying a price to follow Him. You've been passed by for promotions at work because you've stood for integrity. Or you've stayed in a relationship because you committed yourself in matrimony.

"Forget it," the world says. "Here's a key: Get out. Go on. Be free."

But you've said, "No. My Master, my Prince, my Savior has called me to follow Him. And even when it's not easy, I will stay by Him."

I've got good news for you who have taken this stand by the Father's Son, the Prince of Peace. After the invasion, when He brings you safely home to heaven, you will be honored greatly, for the Father honors those who honor His Son.

John 12:27
Now is my soul troubled; and what shall I say?

Thinking about the implications of the Cross troubled Jesus' soul, but notice what He does in His troubled time: He prays. . . .

John 12:27 (a)
Father, save me from this hour . . .

In complete honesty, Jesus asks, "Can I get out of this, Father? Can You save Me from this hour?"

Did you know you can be totally honest with God? Jesus was.

John 12:27 (b)
. . . but for this cause came I unto this hour.

"Father, can I get out? But wait," says Jesus. "This is why I came." Haven't you found that often it is in your own time of prayer, even as you're expressing your hurt or fear, that you're reminded of your calling. And everything becomes crystal clear once again.

John 12:28 (a)
Father, glorify thy name.

Jesus didn't pray, "Glorify My name," He prayed, "Glorify *Thy* name."

John 12:28 (b)
Then came there a voice from heaven, saying, I have both glorified it, and will glorify it again.

This is the third time the voice of the Father thunders from heaven. The first time was at Jesus' baptism at the beginning of His ministry (Matthew 3:17). The second time was on the Mount of Transfiguration in the middle of His ministry (Matthew 17:5). The third time is here at the end of His ministry as He talks about the Cross. All three of these occasions spoke ultimately of His death. In baptism, Jesus was, in effect, saying, "I submit to the death and burial I know awaits Me." On the Mount of Transfiguration, Luke tells us He talked with Moses and Elijah about His death (9:31). And here, Jesus struggles with the Cross.

"I never hear from God," you say. "He never speaks to me." Here's the question: Where do you stand in relation to the Cross? Are you dying to self, or are you living for self? The one who dies to self is going to hear the heart and voice of the Father as it resonates within his inner man.

John 12:29
The people therefore, that stood by, and heard it, said that it thundered: others said, An angel spake to him.

"That's not really God," said the crowd. "It's just thunder." They didn't understand. Neither will they understand when you say, "You know, the Father's really speaking to me." But just because the crowd mistakes Him for thunder, that won't negate the truth of what He speaks to your heart.

John 12:30, 31 (a)
Jesus answered and said, This voice came not because of me, but for your sakes. Now is the judgment of this world . . .

"That which has damned man, that which has held mankind in bondage—sin—is being judged by My going to the Cross," Jesus declared.

John 12:31 (b)
. . . now shall the prince of this world be cast out.

Because the sin of the world is being judged, the prince of this world is cast out. You see, gang, when you sin, you give Satan a handle to grab. But the good news of the gospel is that the blood of Jesus Christ cleanses you from all sin (1 John 1:7). Therefore, because Satan has no more dominion over you, no more toe hold in your life, no more grip on your heart, he is inevitably cast out.

John 12:32, 33
And I, if I be lifted up from the earth, will draw all men unto me. This he said, signifying what death he should die.

"How come you have so many kids at Applegate Christian Fellowship?" people asked. Or, "How do you reach older folks?" The answer is very simple. The reason there are teenagers, as well as folks in their seventies and eighties, in abundance is because of this verse. Jesus said if the Cross is central, He would draw all men. Truly, the message of the Cross is crossgenerational. We don't have to be hip to reach the kids or conservative to reach the older people because the Cross is the magnet that draws all men to Jesus. Teach the Cross. Share the Cross. Walk in light of the Cross. Revel in its riches and apply it to your life. Share it with your friends however young or old they might be. And watch it draw them to Jesus, just as it drew you.

John 12:34
The people answered him, We have heard out of the law that Christ abideth for ever: and how sayest thou, The Son of man must be lifted up? who is this Son of man?

"What do you mean Messiah is going to die? Our law says He will live forever," said the Jews. The people didn't understand the two comings of Christ—that first He came as a Lamb to die for you and me, but that He's coming again as the Lion of Judah who will rule eternally. Watch, however, what Jesus says in light of their confusion. . . .

John 12:35, 36
Then Jesus said unto them, Yet a little while is the light with you. Walk while ye have the light, lest darkness come upon you: for he that walketh in darkness knoweth not whither he goeth. While ye have light, believe in the light, that ye may be the children of light. These things spake Jesus, and departed, and did hide himself from them.

"What does this mean Messiah must die? How does this jive with His eternal reign?" the people wondered. Jesus doesn't answer their question directly, because you see, He Himself is the Answer.

He answers as if to say, "You guys want to talk about theology, but I want to talk about relationship. While you have Me, link yourselves to Me. Stay close to Me. Enjoy Me."

John 12:37
But though he had done so many miracles before them, yet they believed not on him.

Miracles don't produce faith. Faith comes by hearing and hearing by the Word of God (Romans 10:17). The only path to faith is to be in the Word and to grab hold of the Word.

John 12:38 (a)
That . . .

The word translated "that" would be better translated "consequently."

John 12:38 (b)–40
. . . the saying of Esaias the prophet might be fulfilled, which he spake, Lord, who hath believed our report? and to whom hath the arm of the Lord been revealed? Therefore they could not believe, because that Esaias said again, He hath blinded their eyes, and hardened their heart; that they should not see with their eyes, nor understand with their heart, and be converted, and I should heal them.

Those who *would not* believe in verse 37 *could not* believe in verse 39. Since they didn't want to believe, they weren't able to believe because God hardened their hearts. Why? To ratify their choice. You see, had not God blinded their eyes and hardened their hearts, Jesus' teachings would have been so powerful, so persuasive, and so overwhelming that they would have believed against their will. The same is true today. To those who don't want to believe, to those who continually stand in the posture of unbelief, there will come a time when they *cannot* believe (Matthew 12:31).

John 12:41
These things said Esaias, when he saw his glory, and spake of him.

When was verse 40 given initially? In Isaiah 6:1. Everyone—including Jehovah Witnesses—agrees that Isaiah 6 concerns Jehovah. But John here says Isaiah spoke of *Him*, the subject being

Jesus, making this a good verse to use in discussions concerning the deity of Christ.

John 12:42, 43
Nevertheless among the chief rulers also many believed on him; but because of the Pharisees they did not confess him, lest they should be put out of the synagogue: For they loved the praise of men more than the praise of God.

Fearing excommunication and prioritizing the praise of men above the praise of God, although they believed in their heart, many did not name the name of Jesus openly.

John 12:44–48
Jesus cried and said, He that believeth on me, believeth not on me, but on him that sent me. And he that seeth me seeth him that sent me. I am come a light into the world, that whosoever believeth on me should not abide in darkness. And if any man hear my words, and believe not, I judge him not: for I came not to judge the world, but to save the world. He that rejecteth me, and receiveth not my words, hath one that judgeth him: the word that I have spoken, the same shall judge him in the last day.

"I didn't come to judge," says Jesus. "I came to save. But if you don't believe Me, the Word itself that I have given will condemn and judge you. If you don't accept the free gift of salvation, My words will condemn you on the last day and will haunt you forever."

John 12:49, 50
For I have not spoken of myself; but the Father which sent me, he gave me a commandment, what I should say, and what I should speak. And I know that his commandment is life everlasting: whatsoever I speak therefore, even as the Father said unto me, so I speak.

And so Jesus ends His public ministry with the promise that he who embraces His Word would have life everlasting. Finished talking with the crowd, Jesus now huddles His intimate followers together and in the next three chapters, known as the Upper Room discourse, gives them the ultimate lessons, the heaviest and most meaningful teachings, the chalk talk before the kickoff, the last-minute strategy before the invasion.

THE ONLY WAY
TO SEE OUR LORD
A Topical Study of
John 12:21–25

In the midst of millions of people packed into the city of Jerusalem were certain Greeks who had journeyed hundreds of miles to attend the Passover celebration. Why would these men have left their home country—the fountainhead of philosophy, the matrix of mythology, the cradle of civilized society—to worship Yahweh, the God of Israel? Perhaps they were frustrated with Greek philosophy which said that, because everything is either a reflection or an imperfection of an ideal thought, one could never be sure if what he saw or experienced was a true prototype or rather a misrepresentation of the ideal. Or perhaps they found their own mythology embarrassing— what with their gods so susceptible to fighting, partying, incest, and immorality. Perhaps they found their "civilized society" disillusioning because in reality it was crumbling. Homosexuality was pervasive and justice so perverted that Socrates, tried on nothing more than charges of hearsay, was sentenced to death.

Fatalistic philosophy, foolish mythology, flawed society— the Greeks could have come to Jerusalem for any or all of these reasons. Once there, they heard rumors and stories, thoughts and impressions concerning a Jesus of Nazareth. So they approached Philip, the only one of Jesus' disciples with a Greek name, saying, "We want to see Jesus." Why? Perhaps, as has been suggested by some, it was their intent to save Him from Socrates' fate. Or, more likely, perhaps they were just curious about Him and wanted to converse with Him.

Whatever the reason, these Greeks wanted to see Jesus. Yet, as far as we know, Jesus never gives audience to them. Instead, He says to Andrew and Philip, "No one can see Me except in light of the Cross. No one can understand or comprehend Me except they see Me in light of My death, burial, and resurrection."

Maybe you have the same request. "I don't get what's happening in my life. I don't understand what's coming down. I don't understand what's going on. I need to see Jesus."

And Jesus would say to you precisely what He said to these Greek seekers: "You will only see Me in light of Calvary."

"Why is the Lord doing this? Why isn't He taking care of that? Doesn't He love me?" I can't answer the question of why your loved one died, why your wife left, why your business went bankrupt, why your cancer returned. But I can say that Jesus declares to the seeker, to the Greek, to you and to me, "You will never understand apart from the Cross. For it is there that you will see that I am madly in love with you. I died in your place. My heart was broken over your sin. Everything I have, I gave for you personally. Can't you trust Me? Won't you trust Me?"

Gang, the only answer you'll have this side of eternity is the Cross, for rather than dialogue endlessly about every problem and hurt, Jesus demonstrated His love conclusively by dying in our place. That's why we celebrate Communion. At the Lord's table, I am reminded I can trust My hand to His nail-scarred hand and that I must stand by His sword-pierced side. I may not understand what's going on. I may not be sure which direction to take, but I know that in His hands and by His side I'm exactly where I need to be.

And once you see the Lord on the Cross, you'll want to take up His Cross.

He that loveth his life shall lose it; and he that hateth his life in this world
shall keep it unto life eternal. If any man serve me, let him follow me . . .
John 12:25, 26 (a)

"Tell the Greeks they'll not see Me except in light of the Cross—and if they desire to follow Me, the only way it can happen is if they take up their cross and lose their lives," Jesus told Andrew and Philip.

If you took a single grain of wheat and put it in the ground, it would produce a single stalk. If you took the seeds from the stalk, planted them, and kept repeating the process, within fourteen years, every square inch of the earth would be covered in wheat. Mortification brings multiplication. Death brings life.

The family of a missionary in the Amazon Basin went to visit him. After travel-ing by plane, helicopter, canoe, and foot, they reached him at last.

"Wow, you've really buried yourself down here," they exclaimed.

"Not buried—planted," said the missionary. "Big difference."

Death brings life.
Is it easy?
No.

Now is my soul troubled; and what shall I say? Father, save me from this
hour: but for this cause came I unto this hour.   John 12:27

Reflecting on the Cross, Jesus was in agony as He realized He would take upon Himself the sins of all men, that He would be estranged from His Father, that He would be plunged into hell for my rebellion.

Father, glorify thy name. Then came there a voice from heaven, saying, I have
both glorified it, and will glorify it again.   John 12:28

Jesus ends His prayer, saying, "I'm not in it for Me. I'm in it for Thee. Father, glorify Thy Name—even though that means death." And from that point on, He never looked back.

The same can be true for you today. Maybe you're saying, "I've been living for myself. I've been questioning the Lord. I've been uptight and upset, wondering why I can't see Jesus, and why I don't hear from Him."

Understand today that the only way you'll see Him is at the Cross. Go to Calvary, for it is there you will see Jesus.

---

13 Within a span of five days, the two most important foot washings in the history of the world took place. On the Saturday before Palm Sunday, the Saturday before Jesus rode into Jerusalem to present Himself as King, He went into the house of Mary, who washed His feet with costly perfume (John 12:3). Five days later, this One who had His feet anointed with the spikenard of Mary washes the dirt off the feet of the disciples before sharing with them a powerful, penetrating teaching known as the Upper Room discourse. That's always the way it is with the Lord—before He teaches, He touches.

John 13:1 (a)
Now before the feast of the passover, when Jesus knew that his hour was come that he should depart out of this world unto the Father, having loved his own which were in the world . . .

Regardless of the fact that at this moment, as Luke tells us, His own disciples are bickering and arguing among themselves concerning who is the greatest, Jesus looks at His disciples and calls them His own. So, too, as Jesus' followers, we are His own—His own sheep in John 10, His own brethren in Hebrews 2, His own bride in Ephesians 5, His own Body in 1 Corinthians 12. His ownership was creative in that He made us, elective in that He chose us, redemptive in that He died for us.

John 13:1 (b)
. . . he loved them unto the end.

Jesus looked at this motley crew of ragtag renegades and loved them to the end, or, literally "unto the uttermost." In other words, He loved them with no limit—even though He was aware of their past faltering.

"Let's call down fire from heaven and kill everyone who doesn't respond to You," said James and John heatedly (see Luke 9:54).

"Can any good thing come out of Nazareth?" scoffed Nathanael skeptically (see John 1:46).

He was also aware of their future failings.

"Satan desires to sift you like wheat, Peter," He would say. "But I have prayed for you, and when you come through, strengthen the brothers" (see Luke 22:31, 32).

He was also aware of their present flaws.

As they sat together in the Upper Room, Luke tells us the disciples were not sitting in ladder-backed chairs gazing piously at Jesus. No, they were reclined around a low table, arguing among themselves about who was the greatest (Luke 22:24).

Not only was there arguing around the table, but stinking feet underneath the table. You see, it was customary for a servant to wash the dust off the feet of anyone who entered the home of his master. In this case, however, no one humbled himself to wash feet, so everyone's feet remained dirty.

Past faltering, present failure, future flaws, and stinking feet notwithstanding, Jesus saw His disciples not only in their present vulnerabilities but also in their eventual victory—and loved them to the uttermost.

John 13:2, 3
And supper being ended, the devil having now put into the heart of Judas Iscariot, Simon's son, to betray him; Jesus knowing that the Father had given all things into his hands, and that he was come from God, and went to God.

Jesus looked at His bickering, stinky disciples and loved them because He knew from whence He came and where He was headed. Both are absolute prerequisites for love. You see, only faith concerning the past and hope concerning the future allow one to genuinely love in the present.

John 13:4 (a)
He riseth from supper . . .

Just as Jesus rose from the Last Supper, He rose, in eternity past, from the banquet that He enjoyed with the Father and Spirit continually to willingly take upon Himself the form of a Man. It wasn't that a committee of three—Father, Son, and Holy Ghost—voted who would go, and Jesus lost two to one. No, in the council of eternity past, the Son said, "I choose to leave the intimacy of this heavenly banquet to invade the time/space continuum in order to redeem mankind" (see Philippians 2:7, 8).

John 13:4 (b)
. . . and laid aside his garments . . .

Just as Jesus laid aside His earthly garments, Philippians 2 says He laid aside His garments of glory to come and dwell among us. When you grasp this vital concept, your reading of the Gospels will take on an entirely new dimension, for you will understand that the miracles Jesus did— the walking on water, the multiplying of the loaves and fishes, the quieting of the storm— were all done not because of any innate power, but simply because of His dependence upon the Father.

John 13:4 (c)
. . . and took a towel, and girded himself.

Just as Jesus wrapped Himself in a towel, so He wrapped His divinity in human flesh. He was still God, totally God, always God—yet wrapped in the towel of humanity. One commentator points out that the word "towel" used here refers to a linen towel. Linen speaking of righteousness, the picture is perfect. Jesus wraps Himself in the righteous towel of human flesh, for He was like us—yet without sin (Hebrews 4:15).

John 13:5 (a)
After that he poureth water into a bason . . .

Water speaks of the Word. "You are clean through the Word which I have spoken unto you," said Jesus (see John 15:3). We are washed, says Paul, by the water of the Word (Ephesians 5:26). So, wrapped in the towel of human frailty, Jesus pours out His Word to us. He tells us who God is. He tells us how to live. He becomes flesh and dwells among us.

John 13:5 (b)
. . . and began to wash the disciples' feet . . .

This model is not a picture of salvation, but of sanctification; not of conversion, but of confession (1 John 1:9). As I walk through this world, I get dirty feet. And here's Jesus, who not only pours out the truth of purity, but then makes application for you and me as He washes us continually.

John 13:5 (c)
. . . and to wipe them with the towel wherewith he was girded.

Just as He dried the disciples' feet, what's Jesus doing at this moment? He is interceding for us. And He's going to complete the job. He'll not leave us all wet. He'll dry our feet. He'll see us through (Philippians 1:6).

John 13:6–8
Then cometh he to Simon Peter: and Peter saith unto him, Lord, dost thou wash my feet? Jesus answered and said unto him, What I do thou knowest not now; but thou shalt know hereafter. Peter saith unto him, Thou shalt never wash my feet. Jesus answered him, If I wash thee not, thou hast no part with me.

The washing of feet being the job of a slave, Peter couldn't understand why Jesus would do this. Yet instead of saying, "Peter, this is a beautiful type or model of Philippians 2," Jesus simply said, "Peter, you're not going to understand what I'm doing now—but later you will." Did Peter? Yes, for in 1 Peter 5:5, it's as if he draws upon this very scene as a picture of humility.

Is the Lord speaking to you right now about some area of obedience—some challenge, some adjustment in your life—but you're saying, "I'm not going to do it until I can see how it's going to work out"? Husband, are you saying, "I'm not going to stay with her until I see a change in her attitude"? Wife, are you saying, "I'm not going to submit to him until he proves himself"? Teenager, are you saying, "I'm not going to obey them until they make sense"? That's backward. Revelation *follows* obedience.

John 13:9–11
Simon Peter saith unto him, Lord, not my feet only, but also my hands and my head. Jesus saith to him, He that is washed

needeth not save to wash his feet, but is clean every whit: and ye are clean, but not all. For he knew who should betray him; therefore said he, Ye are not all clean.

"You don't need a bath, Peter. You're already clean. You see, it's just your feet that need washing." This speaks of communion with Jesus on a daily basis. If I walk in pollution and don't allow cleansing to take place in my life, I will experience a separation from Him. "If I regard iniquity in my heart, the Lord will not hear me," declares the psalmist (Psalm 66:18). It's not about losing salvation—it's about losing intimacy. In Exodus 30, we see the Old Testament illustration of this New Testament principle. . . .

When a priest was first called, he was washed from head to toe in a ceremonial bathing equivalent to our baptism. From that point on, although he never again needed a head-to-toe cleansing, before entering the tabernacle, he would wash his hands and feet in the laver that stood in the tabernacle courtyard. Otherwise, although he would still be a priest, although he would still be a son of Aaron, he wouldn't be allowed access to the Tabernacle and would therefore be hindered in his ability to minister and receive blessing.

So, too, as the priests needed a continual cleansing of their hands and feet, we need a continual cleansing of our hearts through confession (1 John 1:9). The word translated "confess" in Scripture is *homologeo*, or, "speak the same." Confession is not promising never to sin again, but rather saying, "Father, Your Word is right. That's sin, and I confess it as such. Have mercy upon me. Lord, deal with me."

Considering the fact that the blood of Jesus has already been shed and that the work of the Cross is fully completed, why is confession so important? I suggest three reasons. . . .

Appreciation of the Cross

Confessing my sin ten, fifteen, or even thirty times a day causes me to appreciate what Jesus did for me all the more. I look at myself as the chief of sinners and say, "Wow, Lord. I've had to confess fifty things today—just today. How I appreciate Your love. How I appreciate the work You did for me in paying the price for each of my sins individually." Gang, true confession and trivial Christianity are mutually exclusive because when we really see our sin, we can't help but marvel at the immensity of God's love.

Realization of Grace

If you're not a confessor, you can start to think, *I can see why I'm being blessed. It makes sense because when the Lord chose me, He made a wise choice.* But when you're in a mode of continual confession, those kinds of thoughts never enter your mind. Instead, you say, "Lord, it's only because of your mercies that I am not consumed" (Lamentations 3:22).

Liberation from the Enemy

Unconfessed sin in any area provides the bricks with which the enemy builds a "stronghold" (2 Corinthians 10:4) from which he manipulates you over and over again in that area until that particular sin becomes an addiction, a habit, a part of your life to be used at will by him. "How did I get *here?*" we ask. "How did I get so entangled? How did I get caught up in this attitude or that sin?" The answer can be found at the point where we began to say, "I don't need to confess"—for it is then that the Enemy starts building his stronghold.

"If you don't let Me wash your feet, I have no part with you," Jesus said. "You don't need to be baptized again. You don't need to be saved again. You don't need a bath, Peter. You just need your feet washed." And so do we.

John 13:12
So after he had washed their feet, and had taken his garments, and was set down again, he said unto them, Know ye what I have done to you?

"Do you understand the example I have set for you?" Jesus asks His disciples—for it would only be in understanding what He had done for them that they would be able to do the same for others.

John 13:13 (a)
Ye call me Master and Lord . . .

In the Gospels, the disciples call Jesus "Lord" and "Master," but never "Jesus." When describing Him, the Gospel writers were inspired by the Holy Spirit to write "Jesus"—but in addressing Him, it is always as "Lord" or "Master." Am I suggesting we should not call the Lord "Jesus"? No, because as in the Book of Acts, these same apostles refer to Him as Jesus because, having been born again after Jesus died for them, rose again, and set His Holy Spirit within them, they are now the bride of Christ. The relationship has changed. Therefore, I personally feel at perfect liberty to call my Lord and Master Jesus because I, too, am His bride.

John 13:13, (b), 14
. . . and ye say well; for so I am. If I then,
your Lord and Master, have washed your
feet; ye also ought to wash one another's
feet.

"Master," or *didaskalos*, refers to a teacher—
a fitting title for the One who is the Truth (John
14:6).

John 13:15, 16
For I have given you an example, that ye
should do as I have done to you. Verily, ver-
ily, I say unto you, The servant is not greater
than his lord; neither he that is sent greater
than he that sent him.

Why humble myself and wash feet? Because
after humiliation comes exaltation (Philippians
2:8, 9). Tired of being in the pits? Want to be lifted
up to a higher plane? Want to experience joy on a
level you've never known before and happiness in
a dimension you've never understood? The key is
humility. Just as the branch that bears the most
fruit bows the lowest, the one who's really fruitful
in the things of Jesus Christ will bow the lowest
to serve others.

John 13:17
If ye know these things, happy are ye if ye
do them.

Either Jesus is telling the truth when He says
we'll be happy if we follow His example and love
as He loved, or He is lying. I have found Jesus to
be true in everything He's ever said—absolutely,
completely, totally true. And here He's saying the
way to happiness lies not in agreeing with what
He's told us to do, not in taking notes on what
He's told us to do, but in *doing* what He's told us
to do. Next time you feel depressed or distressed,
discouraged or despondent; next time you feel
like throwing in the towel, do what Jesus did instead. Grab the towel, find some dirty feet to
wash, and experience the happiness He promised.

For topical study of John 13:1–17 entitled
"Washing Feet," turn to page 551.

For topical study of John 13:1–17 entitled
"Washing Feet," turn to page 551.

John 13:18, 19
I speak not of you all: I know whom I have
chosen: but that the scripture may be ful-
filled, He that eateth bread with me hath
lifted up his heel against me. Now I tell you
before it come, that, when it is come to pass,
ye may believe that I am he.

Explaining that there was one in their midst
who needed more than just his feet washed,
Jesus quotes Psalm 41:9, where the reference is
to David's betrayal by a man named Ahithophel.
You recall the story. When David's son, Absalom,
launched a rebellion against him, Ahithophel, David's key advisor, defected and joined Absalom.
"He who ate bread with me—the guy who sat at
my table, the one who shared with me—has
kicked me," a crushed David lamented. What
happened to David, though, was simply a picture
of what would happen to the Son of David, Jesus
Christ, as Jesus would be betrayed by one who
ate bread with Him, one who traveled alongside
of Him, one who had his feet washed by Him. And
Ahithophel was a picture of what would happen
to Judas, for, like Judas, he too eventually hanged
himself because of guilt (2 Samuel 17:23).

There is another who was guilty of betrayal.
Peter denied Jesus, but he didn't end up hanging
from the limb of a tree because he looked to the
One who hung on the tree of Calvary in his place.
Every one of us has a choice to make, for you and
I are Peter, Judas, and Ahithophel. We have all
sinned. The only question is, are we going to get
hung up and say, "I'm going to end it all"—or are
we going to look to Him who hung on the tree and
say, "Thank You for dying in my place"?

John 13:20
Verily, verily, I say unto you, He that re-
ceiveth whomsoever I send receiveth me;
and he that receiveth me receiveth him that
sent me.

"Don't be blown away by what's about to happen," says Jesus. "I'm sending you out that
others might hear about and receive Me."

John 13:21, 22
When Jesus had thus said, he was troubled
in spirit, and testified, and said, Verily, ver-
ily, I say unto you, that one of you shall
betray me. Then the disciples looked one on
another, doubting of whom he spake.

Each disciple suspected himself before he ever
suspected Judas (Matthew 26:22).

John 13:23 (a)
Now there was leaning on Jesus' bosom one
of his disciples . . .

As was customary, the disciples were reclining
around a U-shaped table, propping themselves
up on one arm while eating with the other.

John 13:23 (b)
. . . whom Jesus loved.

As Karl Barth—the father of neo-Orthodoxy, a prolific writer, a man of great intellect—got older, his faith got simpler, and I believe, deeper. Toward the end of his life, he was asked to state the most profound truth he knew. He replied by repeating the words of a well-known child's song, "Jesus loves me, this I know, for the Bible tells me so." The more I know Jesus, the more I love Him. But the more I know me, the more amazed I am that Jesus loves me. I believe it's in this spirit of amazement that John refers to himself as the disciple Jesus loved.

John 13:24, 25
Simon Peter therefore beckoned to him, that he should ask who it should be of whom he spake. He then lying on Jesus' breast saith unto him, Lord, who is it?

Whatever your question, the best place to get it answered is at the breast of Jesus Christ. "That may sound good poetically," you say, "but how does it translate practically?" I believe you are nearest His heart when you're at His table. That's where John was. I know of no finer place to feel the love of Jesus Christ and to experience oneness with Him than at the table of Communion. I have found I hear the heart of the Lord at His table in a way I do nowhere else.

John 13:26 (a)
Jesus answered, He it is, to whom I shall give a sop, when I have dipped it.

John being seated to the right of Jesus, Judas was seated to His left—the customary place of honor. So amazing is Jesus that even at the very end, He showed His love for Judas by giving him a place of honor at His table, still offering Judas opportunity to come to Him.

John 13:26 (b), 27
And when he had dipped the sop, he gave it to Judas Iscariot, the son of Simon. And after the sop Satan entered into him. Then said Jesus unto him, That thou doest, do quickly.

Even though Jesus identified Judas with the sop—a piece of bread dipped in sauce—the other disciples still didn't realize the one who would betray Him was Judas. Why? Perhaps they didn't hear Jesus speak this word to John. Or perhaps they couldn't put it together, for, evidently, Judas, their treasurer, was the last one they suspected.

John 13:28, 29
Now no man at the table knew for what intent he spake this unto him. For some of them thought, because Judas had the bag, that Jesus had said unto him, Buy those things that we have need of against the feast; or, that he should give something to the poor.

The rest of the disciples thought Jesus was merely sending Judas on an errand.

John 13:30
He then having received the sop went immediately out: and it was night.

It was night when Judas left to betray Jesus. And Judas' soul would itself become increasingly darker.

John 13:31–35
Therefore, when he was gone out, Jesus said, Now is the Son of man glorified, and God is glorified in him. If God be glorified in him, God shall also glorify him in himself, and shall straightway glorify him. Little children, yet a little while I am with you. Ye shall seek me: and as I said unto the Jews, Whither I go, ye cannot come; so now I say to you. A new commandment I give unto you, That ye love one another; as I loved you, that ye also love one another. By this shall all men know that ye are my disciples, if ye have love one to another.

Even though it was dark, Jesus said to His disciples, "This is the hour of glory. I'm going to be leaving, and where I'm going, you can't come now. So in the meantime, I'm giving you a new commandment to love one another." A *new* commandment? Doesn't it say way back in Leviticus that we are to love God and that we are to love our neighbor? Isn't that the message, really, of the Scriptures in their entirety? Hadn't Jesus Himself said that upon these two commandments—to love God and to love people—hang all the law and the prophets? What does He mean a *new* commandment?

Look carefully at what Jesus is saying because it's radical. Yes, the Old Testament is filled with commandments and exhortations to love. But Jesus here makes everything new when He says, "Love one another *as I have loved you.*" How did Jesus love them? How does Jesus love us? *That's* what's new. Paul tells us how He loves us when he writes, "Husbands love your wives even as Christ also loved the church and *gave Himself for it*" (Ephesians 5:25).

The newness, the unfolding, the fullness of this

new commandment is that we are to love in a way that costs us your life—not just loving generally, but loving sacrificially to the place of death. You see, biblically there is never true reconciliation apart from someone or something dying. In the Old Testament, reconciliation was impossible without the sacrifice of an animal. In the New Testament, we see Old Testament typology become reality with the death of the innocent Lamb of God, Jesus Christ. There will never be true reconciliation between you and the person with whom you're angry or from whom you're estranged until you say, "I'm not going to grind my ax any longer. I'm not going to press my point any further. I'm not going to prove I'm right anymore. I'm just going to die." The question is, will you?

"But I'm innocent," you say.

So was Jesus.

"But I'm right."

Wasn't He?

The commandment He gave us is to die—to our pride, our complaints, our position, our proof. "What if I die?" you ask. "Does laying down my life and giving up my rights guarantee reconciliation?"

Was everyone reconciled to Jesus? No. Not everyone is born again. Not everyone says, "Thank You, Lord, for laying down Your life for me." When you love like Jesus, some will respond and there will be reconciliation. Others, however, will continue to spit and curse and mock—even as they did to Jesus as He was in the very act of dying for their sins. But if we are to love as Jesus

loved, like Him, we'll pray, "Father, forgive them. They just don't know what they're doing."

"By this kind of love shall all men know you are My disciples," said Jesus, "—when you love like I do—when you love to the point of death."

John 13:36
Simon Peter said unto him, Lord, whither goest thou? Jesus answered him, Whither I go, thou canst not follow me now; but thou shalt follow me afterwards.

Peter wanted to get back to Jesus' earlier statement in which He said He was going somewhere no one else could come (verse 33).

John 13:37
Peter said unto him, Lord, why cannot I follow thee now? I will lay down my life for thy sake.

"You can count on me, Lord," insisted Peter. "I'll die for You if necessary."

John 13:38
Jesus answered him, Wilt thou lay down thy life for my sake? Verily, verily, I say unto thee, The cock shall not crow, till thou hast denied me thrice.

"Peter I know what you're about to go through," said Jesus. "I know the failure that will haunt you. But read ahead to chapter 14. Let not your heart be troubled, Peter. Why? You're going to heaven!"

WASHING FEET
A Topical Study of
John 13:1–17

"What the world needs now is love, sweet love. It's the only thing that there's just too little of." Written by Burt Bacharach, it was a song destined to become a top-seller because it struck a chord in my generation. "All you need is love," sang the Beatles. And we answered, "Yeah, yeah, yeah." Not only my generation—but in every generation there is a craving for the reality of love. Jesus Christ addressed this issue radically. In John 13–16, He reaffirms to His disciples that the key commodity, the key component of Christianity is love. As He calls His boys together only hours away from the Cross, the commandment He gives them is not a commandment to be more zealous, more dedicated, or more committed. The commandment He stresses so emphatically is that they love one another, for by this, He would say, all men would truly know they were His disciples (John 13:35). Before He gives this teaching *to* them, however, Jesus sets the stage by being an example *for* them as He washes their feet. And in the example He sets for His disciples, I see four key factors I believe will help you and me to carry out the commandment to love one another.

The Freedom to Love

Even as they're arguing, even as Judas is preparing to betray Him, even as the hour is heavy, Jesus has perfect liberty to love. Why? Because He knew He came from God (verse 3). If you are still struggling with mistakes you made last week or last month or last year, you will not be free to love. If you are still working through your past, living in your past, haunted by your past, you will not be able to love in the present because the more you try to love someone, the more Satan will whisper in your ear, "You're a hypocrite." We are told in Revelation 12 that Satan is the accuser of the brethren. How does he accuse us? He accuses us by constantly replaying our past failures and inconsistencies to the point where we feel unqualified to do anything but wallow in defeat.

But the good news is that, if you're a believer, the blood of Jesus has washed away all of your failures and sin. Every sin you've ever committed is not only forgiven, but also forgotten (Hebrews 8:12). I am absolutely at peace with my past not because of my perfection—not by a long shot—but because of my position in Jesus Christ and in what He did for me at Calvary (Romans 5). Not only did Jesus know He came from God, but He also knew He was going to God (verse 3). If you're always concerned about how the stock market's going, or if the relationship will survive—if you're living in the future, you'll miss the opportunity to love in the present.

If my past is taken care of by the blood of Calvary and my future is in heaven, I am free to love in the present. That's why Paul said that of the three great virtues, the greatest is love (1 Corinthians 13:13). It takes faith for the past and hope for the future to allow men to love in the present. Faith makes all things possible. Hope makes all things inevitable. But love makes all things enjoyable. Knowing from whence He came, knowing where He was going, Jesus was free to love.

The Cost of Love

Sitting at dinner, Jesus was suddenly aware that His disciples needed their feet washed. And in choosing to wash them, His meal was interrupted. So, too, if you are going to be one who loves people, count on interruptions. There you'll be with a bag of popcorn in your hand and the 49ers on TV when suddenly there will be a knock on your door or a ring of your phone. If you're going to be one who loves, it means you'll have to be willing to be interrupted. Notice not only interruptions, but also involvement. Jesus didn't stand up and say, "There's a strange odor in here. I now want to tell you guys why you should wash your feet before you eat. Peter, you big heel, don't you see your foot is cruddy? James, your sole is dirty." No, Jesus didn't give a lecture on dirty feet. He simply got down on His hands and knees and washed them.

If you are not willing to wash feet, then keep your mouth closed when you see dirt. When I see dirt, I can either talk about the dirt, which then is called judging— or I can involve myself in that person's life by tending the situation on my knees in humility through intercession. Jesus chose the latter. He didn't simply point out the dirt on the feet of His disciples. He did something about it.

A Model for Love

Jesus' act was unannounced. He didn't stand up and say, "Disciples, you will now see love in action. Watch Me. Take notes. A few photos will be allowed." No, He just quietly got up and washed feet. It was not something He announced. It was not something all of Jerusalem could see. He just quietly took care of the situation.

"Well, that would be easy," you say, "if I had the opportunity to minister to guys like the disciples."

Really? Have you ever been around a political rabble-rouser? That was Simon the Zealot. How about someone so shy that not a single word of his is ever recorded? That was James the Less. How about one who was skeptical of you? That was Nathanael. One who would deny you? That was Peter. How about one who would stab you in the back like Judas? Go from man to man in the group, and you'll see they're people just like the folks around you every single day. Yet Jesus, in a beautiful, humble way, loved these guys who were not very lovable. This gives me great hope because I'm not very lovable either. And it gives me great comfort to realize that the Lord loves me not because I'm lovable, but because He is Love.

The Difficulties with Love

Jesus wants to wash Peter's feet, but what happens? Peter protests, saying, "You're not going to wash any part of me." When Jesus corrected him, he said, "Wash all of me." But that wasn't right either. You see, in addition to the pride of independence, there's a problem of overdependence. Some people essentially say to us, "If you don't help me every day in every way, you're not a good Christian." Such people expect much from us and lay demands on us. They seek to exploit and manipulate us to get more than what they need. Therefore, sometimes the loving thing to do is to say, "I'm not the Lord in your life. I can't be the solution to your problem. I can help you. I can wash your feet. But you don't need a bath."

What's the solution? Simply to say to people, "I'll go with what I believe the

Lord is showing me in my heart. I'll respond according to His leading, but not according to your demanding." Gang, the Lord's burden is easy, and His load light (Matthew 11:30). Therefore, to any who would overload or overburden you, sometimes you gotta learn to say no.

Practically

In our culture, not everyone wears sandals or goes barefoot. And even if they did, the roads aren't dusty or muddy—so this passage might not mean washing feet. You're washing your car in the front yard. Maybe it's old and cruddy and doesn't run very well. Instead of complaining about it—why not extend your hose a bit and wash your neighbor's car? Or maybe it means washing your neighbor's windows while he's on vacation. It might mean washing diapers in the nursery—or washing the dishes without being asked.

"That sounds good," you say, "but I'm going through such hard times right now that I'm not in a position to wash anything."

Really? At any given point, at every single point in our lives, we live by "basin theology." That is, we either call for the basin, like Pontius Pilate did (Matthew 27:24) and wash our hands of everything we know to be true of ministry and service—or we take up the basin and wash someone's feet in humility and love. At the very time Jesus was going through a time of intensity we will never understand this side of eternity, He didn't wash His hands of those who would deny and betray Him. He washed their feet.

Theologically

Positionally, we are the very righteousness of God in Christ Jesus (2 Corinthians 5:21). But as we walk through the world, there is a need for the cleansing of fellowship that takes place in the confession of sin. We're born again. We're believers. We're going to heaven—but we still have failings. We still have shortcomings. And we need to be washed continually. How? 1 John 1:9 says if we confess our sins He is faithful and just to forgive us our sins and to cleanse us from all unrighteousness. We need to live in the place of continual confession in order to appropriate the finished work of Calvary and to eliminate Satan's toehold in our lives.

Mystically

So often, people come to me, saying, "I was baptized six years ago. But since then, I've gone through a period of backsliding. Should I be baptized again?"

"No," I say. "But there is something else available to you . . ."

You see, in my understanding, the washing of feet is a mini-baptism for those who say, "I know I didn't lose my salvation, but I've been walking in pollution and defilement. I just want to do something tangibly and outwardly to express what I'm feeling inwardly—that I'm back in fellowship with the Lord." And as others humble themselves to wash their feet and pray for them, to give a word of prophecy or encouragement to them, there's a unique, undeniable dynamic that takes place.

It's not enough just to hear a Bible study and agree with it intellectually. We must not simply be a community where we affirm our beliefs. We must be a place where we encounter God.

How? We can partake of the body and blood of Jesus Christ in Communion, take a stand in baptism, and make confession through the washing of feet.

***

14 The Texas Chauffeurs and Drivers' Association's "Driver of the Decade" was so excited about her commendation that she invited seventeen of her friends to accompany her to the award banquet. On her way there, however, she flipped the van she was driving, and, although no one was seriously injured, all seventeen of her passengers were hospitalized. Here the Texas "Driver of the Decade" was on her way to pick up her award, and what happened? She crashed.

So, too, every one of us find ourselves going through times when it all comes down, when the roof caves in, when things fall apart. And the disciples were no exception. In the previous chapter, Jesus had told them that one of them would betray Him (13:21), that Peter would deny Him (13:38), and that He would leave them (13:33).

"How can this be?" they must have wondered. They had left all to follow Jesus. But now it seemed as though it was all for nothing. We know the story. We know it has a glorious, happy ending. But if you put yourself in their sandals, you can see it must have been a moment of real intensity not only for the disciples, but for Jesus as well.

Oftentimes we look at these events through the eyes of the disciples. But consider what Jesus was going through, as only hours after this He would be nailed to a Cross to absorb the sin of humanity—and would remain as a Lamb slain into eternity (Revelation 5:6). No wonder He prayed, "Father, if it be possible, remove this cup from Me" with such intensity that He actually sweat blood (see Luke 22:42–44).

Here in John 14, in the midst of His Upper Room discourse, Jesus knew the hour of great difficulty was upon Him. Yet notice how He ministers to those around Him . . .

John 14:1 (a)
Let not your heart be troubled . . .

Even in the hour of His own temptation and struggle, Jesus looked at His disciples with com-

passion. What a model for you and me. What an example for what we deal with daily. What a comfort to know that Jesus looks on me—dirty feet and all—and His heart is full of compassion toward me.

John 14:1 (b)
. . . ye believe in God, believe also in me.

Jesus gives the commandment, "Do not let your heart be troubled." And then He gives the way to obey it when He says, "Believe in God; believe in Me."

Belief being the singular key to a trouble-free heart, Jesus goes on to give the disciples five reasons why they shouldn't be troubled—and why we shouldn't be troubled when things seem to be falling down around us. . . .

John 14:2 (a)
In my Father's house are many mansions:
if it were not so, I would have told you.

The key to keeping your heart from being overwhelmed in sadness and depression is to remember that you have a home in heaven.

John 14:2 (b)
I go to prepare a place . . .

To those who doubt the existence of heaven because no matter how far we travel in space, we have yet to locate it, consider the following: The distance between the electrons and the nucleus of an atom being proportionate to the distance between Pluto and the sun, all matter on this earth is comprised of ninety-five percent space—leaving plenty of room for an unseen dimension to coexist with the material world we presently perceive.

Flanked by enemies, Elisha prayed that the eyes of his servant, Gehazi, would be opened.

When the Lord did so, Gehazi saw a mountain full of angels previously invisible to him (2 Kings 6:17). Could it be that when Paul said we are surrounded by a great cloud of witnesses (Hebrews 12:1), he meant that they are literally surrounding us? Is this what Jesus meant when He said the kingdom of God is within us (Luke 17:21)? Stay tuned for more information. We'll know the answer when we get to heaven.

John 14:2 (c)
. . . for you.

When Jesus says, "I go to prepare a place for you,"—He is not speaking generically, but specifically. Jesus is preparing a place for *you* specifically. Think through this. What do you enjoy? What has God built into your being? Whatever it is, know this: Jesus is preparing a place for you to fulfill the elements He's woven into the fabric of your personality uniquely and specifically.

John 14:3
And if I go and prepare a place for you, I will come again, and receive you unto myself; that where I am, there ye may be also.

Jesus is what makes heaven heaven.

For topical study of John 14:1–3 entitled "Heaven," turn to page 558.

John 14:4–6
And whither I go ye know, and the way ye know. Thomas saith unto him, Lord, we know not whither thou goest; and how can we know the way? Jesus saith unto him, I am the way, the truth, and the life: no man cometh unto the Father, but by me.

If there's ever a bone of contention people want to pick with believers, it's exclusivity. "You're too narrow," they say to us. "I don't mind you believing what you believe, but don't say it's the only way."

We don't say this—it's Jesus who declared it. Call me narrow if you wish, but *Jesus* is the One who said, "Narrow is the way which leads to life eternal, and broad is the path that leads to destruction," (see Matthew 7:13). In His wisdom, the Father kept the way to heaven very exclusive, knowing that if there were ten ways, there would be fifty counterfeits and it would be all the more confusing. "Neither is there salvation in any other," Paul would say, "for there is no other

name under heaven given among men, whereby we must be saved" (see Acts 4:12). Period. Case closed.

Understanding the naiveti of people, God said, "I'm going to keep it real simple. There's only one Way"—making His not an act of exclusivity, but of love.

John 14:7–11
If ye had known me, ye should have known my Father also: and from henceforth ye know him, and have seen him. Philip saith unto him, Lord, shew us the Father, and it sufficeth us. Jesus saith unto him, Have I been so long time with you, and yet hast thou not known me, Philip? he that hath seen me hath seen the Father; and how sayest thou then, Shew us the Father? Believest thou not that I am in the Father, and the Father in me? the words that I speak unto you I speak not of myself: but the Father that dwelleth in me, he doeth the works. Believe me that I am in the Father, and the Father in me: or else believe me for the very works" sake.

Not only do we have the hope of heaven, but we know the nature of the Father. "Show us the Father," Philip said. "That would help."

Is "Where is God?" your cry in troubling times?

Jesus looked at Phillip and said, "You know the Father already because you've been with Me. He that hath seen Me hath seen the Father."

The trend in our generation is to blame our parents for our present perversions, problems, depressions, and difficulties. Such thinking has also infected the Christian community wherein believers are saying, "I can't relate to the Father because my earthly father ignored me, abused me, or abandoned me." I think that's bogus. The issue is not a matter of understanding one's earthly father. The issue is one of understanding Jesus Christ. If you want to know the nature of the Father, study the Son. The character of one's earthly father is immaterial. The sole issue is Jesus, for in seeing Him, we see the Father.

John 14:12–14
Verily, verily, I say unto you, He that believeth on me, the works that I do shall he do also; and greater works than these shall he do; because I go unto my Father. And whatsoever ye shall ask in my name, that will I do, that the Father may be glorified in the Son. If ye shall ask any thing in my name, I will do it.

In addition to the hope of heaven and an understanding of the nature of the Father, we have been given the privilege of prayer. We have the privilege of asking in Jesus' name for anything of which we have need. "I have a hard time with that," you say, "because I've asked for a lot of things in Jesus' name that haven't come my way."

Gang, asking in Jesus' name is not simply attaching the phrase, "In Jesus' name" to our prayers the way a trucker closes his calls with "Ten-four, good buddy." No, asking in Jesus' name means asking in harmony with His character and His personality, for the Name speaks of nature.

"Show me Your glory, Lord," prayed Moses. So after hiding Moses in the cleft of a rock, the Lord passed by and in proclaiming His nature to Moses thereby revealed His glory and proclaimed His name (see Exodus 34:6, 7).

If I'm praying, "Lord, she's been really mean to me. Sic her!" or, "Lord, what I really need is a new Cadillac so I can make everyone jealous," I'm not praying in the name of the Lord no matter how many "In Jesus' name's" I attach. Is what I'm praying for full of mercy and goodness? Is it in line with the personality of Jesus? That's what it means to pray in His name.

John 14:15–25
If ye love me, keep my commandments. And I will pray the Father, and he shall give you another Comforter, that he may abide with you for ever; even the Spirit of truth; whom the world cannot receive, because it seeth him not, neither knoweth him: but ye know him; for he dwelleth with you, and shall be in you. I will not leave you comfortless: I will come to you. Yet a little while, and the world seeth me no more; but ye see me: because I live, ye shall live also. At that day ye shall know that I am in my Father, and ye in me, and I in you. He that hath my commandments, and keepeth them, he it is that loveth me: and he that loveth me shall be loved of my Father, and I will love him, and will manifest myself to him. Judas saith unto him, not Iscariot, Lord, how is it that thou wilt manifest thyself unto us, and not unto the world? Jesus answered and said unto him, If a man love me, he will keep my words: and my Father will love him, and we will come unto him, and make our abode with him. He that loveth me not keepeth not my sayings: and the word which ye hear is not mine, but the Father's which sent me. These things have I spoken unto you, being yet present with you.

We have also been given the comfort of the Spirit. The word translated "Comforter" is *parakletos,* referring to someone "called to one's side." With His disciples, Jesus was limited in that He could only be in one place at one time. That is why He would say, "It is expedient for me to go away that the Comforter might come (John 16:7). The Comforter is One who will heal your hurts, still your storms, and supply your needs."

John 14:26
But the Comforter, which is the Holy Ghost, whom the Father will send in my name, he shall teach you all things, and bring all things to your remembrance, whatsoever I have said unto you.

Although sometimes comforting involves correcting and convicting, the Spirit is not a buzzard who circles over us waiting for us to fail that He might come and pick at us. Nor is He a screeching hawk who makes a lot of noise, striking fear in the hearts of everyone around Him. Neither is He a hummingbird who flaps His wings incessantly, yet makes no progress practically. The Spirit is a dove (Matthew 3:16)—known for His gentleness, beauty, and purity. Truly, He is a *Comforter* in reality.

John 14:27, 28
Peace I leave with you, my peace I give unto you: not as the world giveth, give I unto you. Let not your heart be troubled, neither let it be afraid. Ye have heard how I said unto you, I go away, and come again unto you. If ye loved me, ye would rejoice, because I said, I go unto the Father: for my Father is greater than I.

Finally, we have been given the peace of Jesus Christ. Even though I might not understand what's going on, I have a peace that bypasses my brain and permeates my heart. I might not know why things aren't working out, or why things are coming down. But in the midst of it all, Jesus offers me His peace.

John 14:29, 30
And now I have told you before it come to pass, that, when it is come to pass, ye might believe. Hereafter I will not talk much with you: for the prince of this world cometh, and hath nothing in me.

"Don't let your heart be troubled," Jesus said. "Believe in God. Believe in Me." Therefore, I can either drown in doubt or I can choose to say,

"Thank You, Father, that I'm going to heaven. Thank You that I can know Your nature because I can see it in Your Son. Thank You that I can talk to You freely because of the privilege of prayer. Thank You for the ministry of the Holy Spirit. Thank You for the peace you give to me in Jesus Christ. In obedience to Your command, Lord, I will not let my heart be troubled."

John 14:31
But that the world may know that I love the Father; and as the Father gave me commandment, even so I do. Arise, let us go hence.

To you who are down in the mouth, down in the dumps, and troubled in spirit, Jesus would say, "Don't be! Believe in God. Believe in Me. Arise and let's go out in ministry."

HEAVEN
A Topical Study of
John 14:1–3

No doubt the disciples were deeply distressed, for there in the Upper Room Jesus began to inform them of the troubling news that one would betray Him, that Peter would deny Him, and that He would leave them.

Yet, as the room fills with confusion, Jesus looks at His disciples and says, "Let not your heart be troubled. Heaven is the key."

According to an April 24, 2000, *Washington Post* article, 88 percent of all Americans believe in a literal place called heaven—an important statistic because imagine what our society would be like if we *didn't* believe in heaven. . . .

A society that didn't believe in heaven would be obsessed with youth. It would spend hundreds of thousands of dollars trying to look, stay, and feel young through plastic surgery, diets, and exercise programs. A society that didn't believe in heaven would spend billions of dollars on life support systems to delay facing an unknown future. In a society that didn't believe in heaven, crime would soar without fear of eternal judgment. The theology of a society that didn't believe in heaven would be based upon the here and now—on health and prosperity.

Wait a minute. We *are* that culture, because although our generation gives lip service to the *idea* of heaven, we do not live out the *reality* of heaven.

Why isn't Heaven a reality?

I suggest the following reasons . . .

Ministry

There is tremendous pressure in the ministry presently to "teach to the times," to "scratch where it itches." "No one wants to hear about heaven," we are told. "Preach to people here and now."

Accused of being old-fashioned because he always preached on heaven, a classic English preacher gave this response: "While everyone is preaching to the times, may not this poor soul speak for eternity?"

Such is my feeling. Let others talk about cultural relevancy—I desire to be a voice for eternity. The Bible speaks of heaven 557 times; it's a fundamental, foundational truth.

Society

Ours is the first generation to teach that, materially, one can have heaven on earth.

"Your life will be perfect if you use Arrid Extra Dry," we are told. And, although we fall for this pitch time and time again, each time we do, we rediscover that nothing on this earth is substantial, that nothing this side of eternity can do more than whet our appetite for heaven.

Has your soul ever been stirred simply by watching the water cascade down a waterfall? Has your heart ever been overwhelmed by the beauty of the sun setting into the ocean? Have you ever been moved to tears by the "Hallelujah Chorus"?

I suggest these are feelings common to man. And I suggest that what they rekindle is a vague, foggy, misty memory of a place called Eden—where there was no sin, no sorrow, no disease, and no death; where man walked with God in the cool of the day, and where things were right. When such a memory stirs within me, I feel like a frog that has been cursed. I'm waiting for the prince to come and kiss me before I "croak."

And that's where our society is. We know there has to be something more because our experiences with true beauty and with true reality are always so fleeting.

"What happened to the waterfall experience?" we cry.

"What happened to the sunset?

What happened to the "Hallelujah Chorus"?

Why do they elude me?

Where's my prince?"

Good news! Jesus Christ, the Prince of Peace, is a frog-kisser. How do I know? Because in the moment of confusion, He says to us, as He said to His disciples, "Don't lose sight of the big picture. The solution to your confusion lies in a single word: heaven."

As always, Jesus was right, for whenever we consider the ramifications of heaven, our confusion turns to clarity, our despair to delight, and our fear to faith.

The Perspective of Eternity

Believers are sometimes accused of being so heavenly-minded that they're no earthly good. The Bible, however, teaches just the opposite—that we won't be any earthly good *until* we are heavenly-minded because, as Paul points out, "if in this life only we have hope in Christ, we are of all men most miserable" (see 1 Corinthians 15:19). This one who was shipwrecked, beaten, imprisoned, starved, stoned, and left for dead declared, "If there is no heaven, then life is miserable." Perhaps it was his proximity to death on so many occasions that prompted him to write, "Set your affections on things above" (see Colossians 3:2)—for once Paul experienced even a taste of heaven, nothing else mattered to him except to run the race, to win the prize, and to live with eternity in view.

The Puzzle of Prosperity

Suppose you're waiting to board a flight to Portland, Oregon, and the pilot walks in, saying, "You are going to have the flight of your life. Smooth sailing all the way! I guarantee we won't hit one pocket of turbulence. You will have quadraphonic earphones, an Epicurean experience with a seven-course meal, and your choice of first-run movies. There's only one problem: We haven't figured out how to land. We've tried it a thousand times, and everybody dies—but while you're in the air, I promise your flight will be smooth and your experience fulfilling."

At this point, a second pilot enters the boarding area, saying, "I can't promise smooth sailing. In fact, from here to Portland, you'll no doubt hit some bumps and you might even have the 'urge to re-gurge.' However, we have a perfect landing record, and we will get you to your destination safely. Guaranteed."

Which plane would you board?

To some, the question itself poses a problem, for, like David, they feel envious of the foolish when they see the prosperity of the wicked (Psalm 73:3). What's the answer? It is found in the sanctuary of God—for it is there that David understood that although the wicked were experiencing smooth sailing presently, they were headed for hell eternally (Psalm 73:17–19).

The 1991 Oakland/Berkeley Hills fire consumed million-dollar homes, leaving nothing. "I not only lost my house, I lost everything," an elderly man was quoted as saying. "My life's savings were in cash, which I kept in my home. My wife and I were very careful all of our years to save our money. We were saving for a rainy day, never counting on a fiery night."

Listen, gang, for the unbeliever, life on earth is as good as it gets. But for the believer, life on earth is the worst it gets.

The Promise of Productivity

Most people have the idea that heaven is sort of like a long, Sunday afternoon nap—plucking a few strings on a harp, eating a grape or two now and then, lounging around on a white cloud. Not true, for in heaven you will be able to experience to the fullest extent the desires of your heart.

Maybe you just love music, but you don't really have the gift to do a lot with it. When you get to heaven, you can own a choir! You can sing gloriously to your heart's content. Maybe your love is gardening. In heaven, the grass really is greener. No weeds!

Or maybe you're a people person. The people you know here, you'll know there. Won't our bodies be changed? Yes, but look at Jesus—when He came back from the dead, although He walked through a wall, Thomas still recognized Him immediately (John 20:28). As for those in heaven we haven't yet met, nametags will be unnecessary, as it seems we will instinctively know people there. Why do I think this? Because on the Mount of Transfiguration, Jesus didn't say, "Peter, James, and John, I'd like you to meet Moses and Elijah. Moses and Elijah, say 'Hi' to Peter, James, and John." There were no formal introductions, yet Peter, James, and John knew intuitively that it was Moses and Elijah talking to Jesus (Matthew 17:4).

Productivity like we've never known awaits us in heaven, where we will rule angels, govern cities, and manage the universe (Revelation 22:5).

The Reality of Relativity

The source of the greatest frustration of people presently is the lack of time—which is why we constantly find ourselves saying, "Where did the time go?" or "My kids are growing up too fast," or "There's so much I want to do, but I can't find the time."

Do the birds complain about the air in which they fly? Do the fish complain about the sea? Only man complains about his environment because it is one in which he doesn't belong. Time frustrates him because he is made for a timeless eternity

C. S. Lewis said it best when he wrote, "If I find in myself a desire which no experience in this world can satisfy, the most probable explanation is that I was made for another world."[1]

The fact that, according to Ecclesiastes, there is no past, present, or future in eternity means heaven is a continual "now." How can this be? Ask Albert Einstein. His "theory of relativity" has more to do with eternity than he probably could have guessed, for in propounding that when one travels at the speed of light, time stops, he validated the fact that, because God is Himself light (1 John 1:5), in His presence, time ceases.

Thus, if time—man's biggest frustration on earth—is nonexistent in heaven, we can be sure every lesser frustration will be obliterated as well. Heaven will truly be absolutely, wonderfully, and incredibly perfect.

"How can it be perfect if those I love are still on earth?" some ask.

If you put a glob of peanut butter at one end of a shoebox, ants at the other end, and a maze in between, you would see the ants begin to wind their way through the maze, journeying toward their celestial peanut butter glob city. You would see it all: the beginning, the journey, and the end. But they wouldn't. All they would see is the next wall in front of them. So, too, those in Heaven see the whole thing unfolding simultaneously. Not only are events occurring concurrently, but from their perspective, we are already standing beside them in eternity.

Still others are concerned about the people who won't be in heaven. *How can it be heaven if I know people I care about aren't there?* they wonder.

Concerning the Amalekites who were hassling the people of Israel, the Lord said, "I will destroy them and remove their memory from your minds" (see Deuteronomy 25:19). The psalmist picks up the same theme when, in six occasions, he talks specifically about the "blotting out of the names of those who are against God." Thus, I suggest you will not even remember the people who are not saved.

The Answer to Inequity

Heaven is the place where we will at last have all our questions answered. Why was this person born severely retarded? Why was that person born to starvation? Why wasn't this person healed when we prayed in faith? Why was that baby allowed to be conceived only to be aborted? Why, why, why?

Psalm 139 tells us that all of our days are written in a book. Could it be that the "book" is what science now calls the DNA genetic code—the strand wherein is packed all of one's characteristics, appearance, and entire being? So much information is crammed into the DNA genetic code that it would fill one hundred volumes of an encyclopedia. Consequently, could it be that even if a baby is aborted or born prematurely, his or her genetic code will be fully revealed and realized in heaven?

"Hang on," Jesus said. "It's not over yet. The first will be last; the last will be first; and the score will be settled."

The Response to Opportunity

Maybe you've had opportunity to hear Jesus say, "I am the Way, the Truth, and the Life,"—but you have rejected Him. God will honor your choice. You'll be allowed to go where you want. But know this: Hell is not a party. It's a place of eternal weeping, wailing, and gnashing of teeth (Matthew 8:12).

But for you who have taken Jesus up on His offer as the Way, the Truth, and the Life, congratulations! You're going to heaven! So, let not your heart be troubled.

Get ready. Get packed. Get set. We're going home!

15 In the previous chapter, Jesus had said, "There's hope for you—hope in heaven. See the big picture. Get a handle on your destiny. Let not your heart be troubled." Here, in chapter 15, He puts in the clutch, changes gears a bit, and gives us a message not so much dealing with hope in heaven but rather about help on earth. The last phrase in chapter 14 being, "Arise and let us go hence," Jesus and the disciples left the Upper Room, made their way through the city of Jerusalem, and headed toward the Garden of Gethsemane via the Kidron Valley. Thus, it would seem that John 15 is actually given to the disciples when they are en route from the Upper Room to the Garden of Gethsem-

ane. It being Passover season, they would have been traveling under a full moon and would, very possibly, have seen the magnificent temple structure, with its massive vine-engraved doors, off in the distance. The vine being the historic as well as the religious symbol of Israel (Isaiah 5; Ezekiel 19; Psalm 80), perhaps it was the gold-covered vine reflected in the moonlight that inspired the masterful teaching that follows.

John 15:1 (a)
I am the true vine . . .

In His eighth *"Ego Eimi"* or "I AM" statement, Jesus says, "I am the True Vine." I find this intriguing. Why would He use the word "true" at this time? Perhaps it is because as we go through this chapter into the next, we'll see that Jesus knew His disciples would soon be kicked out of temple worship, barred from the synagogue, ostracized from the glory, tradition, and beauty of Judaism. Thus, I believe it is in this reference that Jesus declared, "I am the *true* Vine," as if to say, "Don't be deceived. It's not Judaism. It's not religion. It's *Me*."

John 15:1 (b), 2 (a)
. . . and my Father is the husbandman. Every branch in me that beareth not fruit he taketh away . . .

If I had a nickel for every message or study I've heard on the pruning procedures of Jesus Christ based upon this passage, I would be a wealthy man. It's a commonly used text for the premise that if you're bearing fruit—if things are going good, watch out because Jesus is on His way, hedge clippers in hand. Hearing such messages, I invariably leave bloodied and bruised, battered and afraid Jesus is going to come with His clippers and prune me. I believe such teaching is a complete misunderstanding of this passage because linguistically, contextually, and logically it doesn't fit. Let me explain. The word translated "takes away" in verse 2 is *airo*—a word in which three of the four definitions deal with lifting up, raising up, or pulling up. Yes, the fourth definition in the Greek lexicon is "take away." But there are three that precede it. *Airo* is used in John 11:41, where Jesus *lifts* up His eyes toward the heavens—and again in Luke 17 when the people *lifted* their voices. Thus, the idea here is not "take away" but "lift up."

John 15:2 (b)
. . . and every branch that beareth fruit, he purgeth it, that it may bring forth more fruit.

The word translated "purge" is *kathairo* from which we get our word "catharsis," referring to a cleansing process. *Kathairo* is used in John 13 when Jesus cleansed the feet of His disciples. In fact, in virtually every case in New Testament language, *kathairo* being translated not "purge" but "cleanse," I believe the use of "purge" here in John 15 is a mistranslation. If you put these thoughts together, you get an understanding of what Jesus is really saying—and it's wonderful. It's not terrorizing; it's terrific. It doesn't cause consternation, but rather comfort, for He says, "Every branch in Me that bears not fruit, I lift up. And every branch that bears fruit, I cleanse that it might bring forth more fruit."

You see, in vineyards, it is not uncommon for branches to become so heavy with fruit that they sag to the ground—leaving them vulnerable to the mud from the rainy season sure to follow. Consequently, the vinedresser, seeing a branch in the mud, lifts it up and braces it. And if there is fruit on it, he washes the mud off the fruit—lovingly, carefully, and tenderly.

Thus, Jesus paints a picture not of the Lord lopping you off, but of Him lifting you up; not of Him cutting you, but of Him cleansing you. How do I know this with certainty? Look at the next verse. . . .

John 15:3
Now ye are clean through the word which I have spoken unto you.

In following this analogy, in keeping with the flow logically, what Jesus is saying is, "I lift the downtrodden branch; I wash the contaminated fruit. How? Through the Word." You're clean through the Word. Gang, how do you bear more fruit? Not by the Lord butchering you or bloodying you, but by being in the Word. How do we get our lives cleaned up? How does more fruit come? Fruit comes by a commitment to the Word, a receptivity to the Word, and by staying in the Word. The psalmist said the same thing in Psalm 119 when he said "How shall a young man cleanse his way? How does a young man walk in a clean way? By taking heed thereto according to thy Word." And Paul picks up the same analogy in Ephesians 5 where, talking about husbands and wives, he says that the bride is washed by the water of the Word.

Jesus gives us an important, absolutely essential exhortation when He says, "I am the True Vine. You're the branches. When you're downcast or dirty, the Father will come and pick you up and wash you off via the Word through your morning devotions, Wednesday evening Bible study, home groups." Being in the place where the Word is taught, where we are basing our beliefs on what Jesus said, has a cleansing effect upon our lives.

John 15:4
Abide in me, and I in you. As the branch cannot bear fruit of itself, except it abide in the vine; no more can ye, except ye abide in me.

"Stay close to Me," Jesus is saying. "Abide in Me. Cling to Me because if you don't, there won't be any fruit coming forth from your life." What is fruit? Fruit is vital to spiritual life presently and will affect you eternally. Romans 1:13 and John 4 identify fruit as winning lost souls. Romans 6:22

defines fruit as holiness. Romans 15:28 names financial giving as fruit. Colossians 1 describes fruit as helping practically. Hebrews 13 tells us that the fruit of our lips—giving praise to His Name—is fruit. And ultimately, most importantly, Galatians 5:22 teaches that the fruit of the Spirit is love. Love is the ultimate fruit. What about joy, peace, and longsuffering; gentleness, goodness, and faith; meekness and self-control? Doesn't Galatians list them as fruit? Yes, but the fruit (not *fruits*) of the Spirit being singular, those are definitions of what love is.

So, when your life is filled with love, when you're giving financially, when you're praising the Lord verbally, when you're doing good things practically, when you're witnessing to the lost boldly, when you're joyful, peaceful, and patient—all of these constitute fruit.

John 15:5 (a)
I am the vine, ye are the branches: He that abideth in me, and I in him, the same bringeth forth much fruit . . .

I like this! In the beginning of verse 2, there was no fruit. In the middle of verse 2, there was fruit. At the end of verse 2 there was more fruit. And here in verse 5, there is *much* fruit! How is "much fruit" produced? By abiding. I have an apple tree in my backyard that bears prolifically. Suppose I brought in a branch from this apple tree and said, "Hey, gang, this tree produces so much fruit that we're going to set this branch right here. In April it'll start blossoming, and a couple months later we'll have all kinds of apples right here in the sanctuary."

"That's crazy," you'd say. "The branch has to be linked to the trunk. Otherwise, there's no way fruit will be produced on that limb."

And that's what Jesus is getting at. We might know how we should behave and what we should do—but if we're cut off from the Lord, if we're distanced from the Lord, there won't be any fruit. We need to be in His presence daily, in His Word continually. If not, we'll cut off the flow of sap that would have produced fruit for His pleasure and rewards in eternity. If there's a lack of fruit in our lives, we mustn't say, "I can't understand why there's not more fruit coming my way"—because an irrefutable fact of spiritual life is that every man, every woman is only as close to the Lord as he or she chooses to be. And if you choose to abide in Him, to intertwine your life with His, to wrap yourself around Him and stay close to Him, you will inevitably bring forth much fruit.

How is fruit produced? By abiding—not struggling, not striving. The apple tree in my backyard is interesting. As I've watched it for many years, I have never once observed it struggling, complaining or groaning to bear apples. I've never in my whole life seen branches struggling or straining to produce fruit. Yet I have seen Christians, myself included, struggling and straining to control temper or change character. But it never works in the long haul because sooner or later (usually sooner), the old character will emerge and dominate once more. The only way you can really bear fruit—which is love defined by joy, peace, longsuffering, gentleness, goodness, and faith; the only way you really bear fruit—which is boldness in witnessing, sincere expression of praise, and generous giving—is just to abide in Christ. What does the apple branch do? It just hangs in there day after week after month after year. And in due season, the blossoms come and the apples appear, and there's fruit—all because it just hangs in there. So, too, you hang in there with the Lord, and as the days turn into weeks, months, and years, you will see fruit and then more fruit and then much fruit.

John 15:5 (b)
. . . for without me ye can do nothing.

If you're not abiding in Christ, whatever you're doing is a huge waste. It's nothing. Zip. Zilch. Zero. It's worth nothing. It will not count. It will not be there in eternity. "Oh, but I'm a Kiwanan, or a Rotarian, or I work for the Red Cross." If it's not done as you're abiding *in* Christ, for the glory *of* Christ, because you were led *by* Christ, it is for nothing. Period.

Why, then, do people donate time to the Red Cross? Why do they join service organizations? Why do they perform good deeds? Perhaps to appease a guilty conscience, to be part of a fraternity, to strike up business deals, for camaraderie—for lots of reasons which have nothing to do with absolute goodness. Only what you do in Christ and for Christ and because of Christ will count in the ages to come. That's why Jesus says, "If I'm not in the center of it, it's worth nothing."

John 15:6
If a man abide not in me, he is cast forth as a branch, and is withered; and men gather them, and cast them into the fire, and they are burned.

Does this mean that if we don't abide in Jesus, we'll be lopped off and cast into the fire? If we don't abide in Him, the fruit-bearing part of our life will indeed burn—but not our position because our salvation was secured by what Jesus did on the Cross. The wood of a vine is so soft it is useless to build with, so here, Jesus is saying, "If your life is not bearing fruit, it's good for nothing but kindling." It's an interesting analogy because that's what life is all about. We're either bearing fruit, or we're just burning up the clock.

John 15:7 (a)
If ye abide in me, and my words abide in you . . .

The word "abide" is really important. It means "be at home in." "Thy Word have I hid in my heart," said the psalmist (see Psalm 119:11)—not in his head, but in his heart. Paul prayed in Ephesians 3 "that Christ may dwell in your *hearts.*" Why does the Lord want His Word to abide in our hearts and not just in our heads? Because affected by data, discussions, and information, the mind is incredibly fickle. I can change my mind one hundred times in a single day concerning a single issue. So can you. But not so the heart. If a girlfriend or boyfriend ever broke up with you, you know how this works. You may have known in your head that you were better off without him or her, but you still cared for that girl or guy. Why? Because the heart doesn't let go that easily. That's why the Lord wants His Word to dwell there. How does this happen? For me the most practical way knowledge moves from the head to the heart is through meditation and contemplation—so that the Word can sink in and permeate my inner man. It must not just be written on paper; it's gotta be written in my heart.

John 15:7 (b)
. . . ye shall ask what ye will, and it shall be done unto you.

"If you're clinging to Me, if your life is intertwined with Mine, you can ask whatever you want, and your prayers will be answered without exception." Notice the qualification: "If you abide in Me and My words abide in you." This is the problem with most of our prayers. James 4:2, 3 says, "You have not because you ask not. But when you ask, you receive not because you ask amiss." In other words, our requests are out of line. Gang, when we're not in the Word, we don't know how to pray. Prayer and the Word go hand in hand. As I'm in the Word, His words abide in me, and it is then that I know how to pray and for what to ask.

If I went to the Father tonight and said, "Oh, Father, we need money for missions or for expanded ministry, so I pray You would help me find a big stash of cocaine to sell,"—would the Lord answer that prayer? No, because it is completely out of line with what His Word says I should be doing. We chuckle at that, but I have a hunch that if we could play back our prayers, we would be both shocked and amused by them. "Oh, how foolish that was," we would say. "How out of line with what I now know is God's heart. No wonder that prayer wasn't answered!"

John 15:8–11
Herein is my Father glorified, that ye bear much fruit; so shall ye be my disciples. As the Father hath loved me, so have I loved you: continue ye in my love. If ye keep my commandments, ye shall abide in my love; even as I have kept my Father's commandments, and abide in his love. These things have I spoken unto you, that my joy might remain in you, and that your joy might be full.

"I'm telling you these things," Jesus says, "so that you might be full of joy."

You're playing on the church softball team. The pitcher hurls one in your direction. You cock your arm, swing mightily, and hear the crack of the bat as it sends the ball deep into left field. You watch the left fielder fade deeper and deeper. His back is against the fence. He leaps into the air. The ball clears his glove. And are you ever happy! It's a four-bagger with bases loaded. You're ready to take your victory trot—when you hear the voice of the umpire yell, "Foul." And suddenly, your happiness dissipates.

Jesus promises not happiness, but a constant sense of joy in your heart regardless of whether you hit a homer or a foul. That doesn't mean your life is going to be trivial, giddy, and trite. It does mean, however, that even when you feel discouraged, underneath it all somehow mystically, miraculously, mysteriously there's still joy. And Jesus said this joy will be in proportion to our abiding in His Word.

John 15:12
This is my commandment, That ye love one another, as I have loved you.

"Speaking of abiding in My Word," Jesus says, "My Word to you is that as I have loved you, so I want you to love one another. It doesn't matter how much theology you know, or how much wisdom you claim to have. If you don't love Me and the person sitting beside you, nothing else matters." Notice it's a commandment—which means love is not a matter of emotion, but of volition. It's a choice. Jesus doesn't ever command us to feel something. He commands us to do something. "Help the world to see I am alive," the Lord says. "They pinned Me to a Cross. They thought they did Me in. But I'm alive. And how will they know I'm alive? By your love one for another."

Again, in the context of Jesus' teaching, love is not so much an emotion as a decision. And the beautiful thing is, oftentimes when you implement the action, the emotion will follow. Guys, maybe you've lost the feeling for your wife. Treat her like a treasure, and your emotions will follow because Jesus taught that where our treasure is, there will our heart be also (Luke 12:34). Our culture has lost the meaning of what real love is. Consequently, husbands and wives are saying, "I don't have feelings for him or her anymore, so I'm leaving." But feelings aren't the issue. Love is not an emotion or a feeling. It's a decision. It's an action. "My commandment," Jesus said, "is that you make the decision to love."

You will come across people tomorrow who might initially seem to be an interruption to your schedule. But if you say, "Wait a minute. Here's an opportunity for me to love," you know what will happen? As you make that decision, there will be a change in your emotions. The Lord will meet you in that place. I guarantee it.

John 15:13
Greater love hath no man than this, that a man lay down his life for his friends.

An entire nation was revived when John Knox prayed, "Lord, give me Scotland, or I die." But what many people don't know is what Knox wrote concerning the answer to that prayer. The Lord responded in his heart, saying, "First die, then I'll give you Scotland."

"Make this relationship work, or I'm going to die," we pray.

"Die first," the Lord says.

Lay down your life for your wife, your neighbor, your friend. That is not only the proof of your love, but the pathway to love, because love is not some feeling you hope returns, not some kind of elusive mystical emotion. It's the decision to die to your dreams, your desires, your needs, and your wants and instead lay down your life for your friend, your husband, your neighbor, or your kids.

John 15:14, 15
Ye are my friends, if ye do whatsoever I command you. Henceforth I call you not servants; for the servant knoweth not what his lord doeth: but I have called you friends; for all things that I have heard of my Father I have made known unto you.

Jesus considers me His friend. That's amazing. I'm flaky, fickle, and foolish. But the Lord looks at us and calls us His friends. This means He doesn't love us because He has to, but because He chooses to. He *likes* us. He gets a kick out of us. We're a delight to His heart. We bring a smile to His face. Amazing! And because we're His friends, He wants us to know what He's doing.

"Shall I hide from Abraham this thing which I do?" asked the Lord in Genesis 18:17. "No," He answered. So God did, indeed, tell the man singularly called the Friend of God (James 2:23) He was about to destroy Sodom and Gomorrah. As He did to Abraham historically, God will whisper in your heart concerning what He's doing presently. You'll know things about which the world is unaware because He calls you His friend.

John 15:16 (a)
Ye have not chosen me, but I have chosen you, and ordained you, that ye should go and bring forth fruit, and that your fruit should remain . . .

"Not only does Jesus tell us what's going on and what's coming down eventually, but He ordains us to be involved in ministry presently. Whether or not you've been credentialed by some ordination council is irrelevant, for on the basis of this passage, you are ordained just as much as Billy Graham. What, then, is the purpose of formal ordination—when we put the title Reverend in front of someone's name? It's simply a legal ratification that confirms a man has, indeed, been keeping the commands of Jesus, thereby allowing him to move through the legal processes of marrying and burying. But there's really not a whole lot to it because nowhere in the Scripture do you see councils and tests and examinations for ministry. Jesus said, "I've ordained you." That's all you need.

The story is told that as Napoleon was talking to a group of his high-ranking officers, his horse, standing nearby, spooked and bolted. A quick-thinking private, observing the scene, pursued the runaway on his own steed, and was able to return Napoleon's horse safely.

"Well done, Captain," said Napoleon upon his return.

The private, with eyes as big as saucers, saluted smartly and said, "Yes, sir."

Then he went immediately to the supply tent, got himself a captain's uniform, and moved into officer's quarters. He never said, "I don't deserve it. I should have worked my way up through the ranks. I need to earn this." No, he just said, "Yes, sir."

Likewise, the Lord calls us "Friend," "Ordained Minister"—and all that's left for us to say is, "Yes, Sir!"

John 15:16 (b)
. . . that whatsoever ye shall ask of the Father in my name, he may give it you.

If you walked into a store, made one hundred thousand dollars worth of purchases, and then pulled out a check upon which was written at the top "Jon Courson," you would be laughed out of the store. But if you walked into that same store with an authorized check from Donald Trump, there would be no problem because the issue isn't how rich you are, but how rich is the person upon whose account you draw. And that's the beautiful thing about prayer. My request isn't based upon how many devotions I've had this week, how many folks I've witnessed to this month, how many hours I've spent in prayer today. No, that's all irrelevant. I draw from the bank of heaven based solely upon the riches of Jesus Christ, who gave me His Name to use. How free your prayer life will be when you understand what it means to use Jesus' name with the Father.

John 15:17
These things I command you, that ye love one another.

"Okay, Lord, we hear You. You want us to love one another by laying down our lives, by making the decision to love based not upon ethereal emotions or fuzzy feelings, but on the basis of Your command. And if we do that, You say we are Your friends—giving us the privilege and power of prayer; the right to be ordained by You in service and ministry. Incredible! That's a wonderful package You've given us. And now we'll just carry it out. We'll make the decision to love." Now, it seems if you, if I, if any of us do this—if we really love people—we would be popular and embraced. After all, everybody loves a lover. But watch what Jesus says. . . .

John 15:18, 19
If the world hate you, ye know that it hated me before it hated you. If ye were of the world, the world would love his own: but because ye are not of the world, but I have chosen you out of the world, therefore the world hateth you.

If the world loves you, watch out—you're in hot water. Paul told his protigi, Timothy, that all who

live godly in Christ Jesus shall suffer persecution (2 Timothy 3:12). That's a fact. If you are living godly, you're not going to make it into the *Who's Who* of the world's system. It just won't work that way.

John 15:20–22
Remember the word that I said unto you, The servant is not greater than his lord. If they have persecuted me, they will also persecute you; if they have kept my saying, they will keep yours also. But all these things will they do unto you for my name's sake, because they know not him that sent me. If I had not come and spoken unto them, they had not had sin: but now they have no cloke for their sin.

The reason the world will hate you is because you're light (1 Thessalonians 5:5). And when light shines, people in the dark get real uneasy. Like bugs under a rock, they start scrambling and fleeing. "If I hadn't come," said Jesus, "men could continue on in their sin, and no one would feel uncomfortable. But because I came, because of how I lived, because of where I stand, men have no cloak for their sin. Consequently, they feel exposed and foolish in their iniquity. And will hate you as a result."

John 15:23
He that hateth me hateth my Father also.

Many people claim to love God, Yahweh, Elohim, or Jehovah. But they hate Jesus Christ. Here Jesus goes on record saying that the one who hates Him hates His Father. Therefore, a person cannot say he loves God but doesn't acknowledge Jesus Christ. The Buddhist in his monastery may be sincere in his desire to attain the state of a snuffed-out candle (the state also known as Nirvana) so that no desires can pollute him, no feelings can cause ill will between him and another. But when you talk to him about Jesus Christ, he doesn't want to listen. The Hindu can claim to love the Brahma; the Jew can claim to love Jehovah. Regardless of how many prayers the Hindu offers, or how many synagogues the Jew attends, however, the fact remains that Jesus Christ made a powerful, nonnegotiable proclamation when He said to all mankind, "If you don't love Me, if you don't acknowledge Me, if you hate Me, you hate My Father also. Period. End of quote."

John 15:24–27
If I had not done among them the works which none other man did, they had not had sin: but now have they both seen and hated

both me and my Father. But this cometh to pass, that the word might be fulfilled that is written in their law, They hated me without a cause. But when the Comforter is come, whom I will send unto you from the Father, even the Spirit of truth, which proceedeth from the Father, he shall testify of me: And ye also shall bear witness, because ye have been with me from the beginning.

Here's our Lord, saying, "They hated Me without a cause." When people hate you or me, they've got cause. Oh, I'm not speaking just about our making them uncomfortable because of our Christian witness or testimony. I'm saying that the hatred of people toward us is justifiable because we deserve it. Yes, there might be persecution, yes there might be lies, yes there might be hurtful words spoken or wrong deeds done against us. But the fact is, every one of us deserves more of that than we get because we're sinners.

Having fallen sick, Benhadad, king of Syria, sent his servant, Hazael, to inquire of Elisha the prophet if he would recover.

"You'll recover from your disease," answered Elisha, before proceeding to weep uncontrollably.

"What's wrong?" asked the servant.

"I see the evil you will do," answered Elisha. "You'll set the cities of the Israelites on fire; you'll kill her young men, dash her children, rip open her pregnant women."

"That's preposterous," said Hazael. "What do you think I am? A dog? I would never do those things."

But the very next day, we see Hazael smothering Benhadad and reigning in his stead, setting into motion the events that would culminate in a fulfillment of Elisha's prophecy (2 Kings 8).

The Word of God tells us we are depraved and sinful. "I would never do *that*," we say. "What do you think I am—a dog?" But yet so sinful is our flesh that even the good things we do are tainted with wrong motives and mistakes. Because we all want to be liked and appreciated, we carefully cultivate an image to impress people. It might be through intellectual ability or appearance, athletic prowess, or through service to humanity. It doesn't work, however, because there is *none* righteous (Romans 3:10). And sooner or later we *all* act like dogs.

But here comes Jesus on the scene with cloth in hand, not to smother our face, but to wash our feet. And it is this One who has chosen us, ordained us, and called us to abide in Him that we might bring forth much fruit for His glory. Truly, they hated Him without a cause. But He is the only One who can say that. We're all dogs. This doesn't depress me about my human nature. It just causes me to be impressed all the more with Jesus' lovingkindness.

———— ✺ ————

16 Hours before His crucifixion, Jesus is in the Upper Room. After investing three years of His life in His disciples, He's sharing final instructions with them when suddenly He says, "Verily, I say unto you, one of you shall betray Me" (John 13:21).

"Ask Him which of us it is," whispered Peter to John.

And Jesus said, "The one to whom I hand this bread is the one who will betray Me." He then handed the bread to Judas Iscariot and said, "What you do, do quickly."

But the disciples didn't get it. They thought Judas was going to buy more food for their celebration. Here Jesus had clearly said the one to whom He gave bread would betray Him—yet no one in the room caught on. Why couldn't they see?

Then Jesus said, "I'm going away and you can't come with Me for a while."

Peter pipes up and says, "What do You mean we can't come with You? I'm going to go wherever You go. I'm going to die if necessary to be with You" (see John 13:37).

"Oh, Peter," Jesus said, "before the rooster crows, you will have denied Me three times. But let not your heart be troubled. In My Father's house are many mansions. I'm going to prepare a place for you."

It was then Thomas's turn to interject, "Lord, we don't know where You're going," (see John 14:5).

Hadn't Jesus just said, "I'm going to My Father's house"?

Jesus went on to say, "If you had known Me, you should have known My Father also."

But in the very next verse, Philip says, "Show us the Father" (see John 14:8).

Jesus had just said, "You're seeing the Father when you see Me."

But Philip still said, "Show us the Father."

I wonder if at this point Jesus was thinking, "What have I gotten Myself into with these numskulls?" Still, He continued on. "When the Spirit comes," He said, "He will abide in you, and the world will know I am living. I will manifest Myself to the world when My Spirit dwells in you."

But Judas (not Iscariot) said, "How are You going to manifest Yourself to us and not to the world?" (see John 14:22).

At this point, if I were in Jesus' sandals, I would have fired them all. I would have said, "This is our final session together, and you guys don't have a clue about anything I'm sharing. How could you be so thick-headed. How could you be so blind?"

And maybe that's the way you feel about your unbelieving wife, your teenage daughter who's straying, your friend who's just not seeing. But watch what Jesus does. As chapter 16 opens, He continues to teach them, confident in due time that the Spirit will put it all together.

John 16:1–6
These things have I spoken unto you, that ye should not be offended. They shall put you out of the synagogues: yea, the time cometh, that whosoever killeth you will think that he doeth God service. And these things will they do unto you, because they have not known the Father, nor me. But these things have I told you, that when the time shall come, ye may remember that I told you of them. And these things I said not unto you at the beginning, because I was with you. But now I go my way to him that sent me; and none of you asketh me, Whither goest thou? But because I have said these things unto you, sorrow hath filled your heart.

Although the disciples were not grasping what Jesus was saying, He knew that, due to the ministry of the Holy Spirit, they would understand eventually. Thus, He could continue to teach His disciples with confidence—not confidence in them, but confidence in the Spirit soon to come.

John 16:7
Nevertheless I tell you the truth; It is expedient for you that I go away: for if I go not away, the Comforter will not come unto you; but if I depart, I will send him unto you.

"It's expedient I go away in order that the Spirit might come to you," Jesus said. How does He work? Read on.

John 16:8
And when he is come, he will reprove the world of sin, and of righteousness, and of judgment.

What does the Spirit do to the blinded eye, to the hardened heart? He convicts it of sin, of righteousness, of judgment.

John 16:9
Of sin, because they believe not on me.

The one and only sin the Holy Spirit will convict an unbeliever of is that of not believing in Jesus. He doesn't convict people of smoking. He doesn't speak to them about their swearing, drinking or partying—only of their unbelief in Jesus. And this is what makes being a believer, a minister, so incredible. We get to share with people the good news that no matter what they've done or where they've been, if they believe in Jesus, they are forgiven of *all* sin (Matthew 12:31).

Doesn't the Holy Spirit convict us of sin once we're Christians? Yes, He does. But the conviction of the Spirit does not drive us away from God. On the contrary, it draws us to God. It's the condemnation of Satan that makes us ashamed to talk to the Father. You can always tell the difference between the Spirit convicting you and Satan condemning you because if it's Satan condemning you, you won't want to pray, and you won't want to spend time in the Word. You'll just hang out in a hole and hide your head. But if it's the Spirit convicting you, you'll hear, "Come unto Me all that are weary and heavy laden and I will give you rest,"—and you'll be drawn back to Jesus.

John 16:10
Of righteousness, because I go to my Father, and ye see me no more.

The Spirit also convicts of righteousness by pointing to the only righteous One. "Because I go to My Father, you see Me no more," said Jesus.

"I'm okay," you say. "I belong to Rotary. I volunteer for the American Cancer Society. I'm pretty righteous." Oh? Righteous enough that death can't hold you? So righteous that when you die you'll rise again? Did Ghandi? Did Mohammed? Did Confucius? Did Buddha? Unlike any other figure in history, Jesus Christ alone rose from the dead and ascended to the Father. Thus, He is the only Righteous One to whom the Spirit points, of whom the Spirit convicts.

John 16:11
Of judgment, because the prince of this world is judged.

When Jesus died on the Cross, the ruler of this world was judged and his power permanently broken. It's not we who were judged. No, the one who held you in his grasp, the one who made you miserable, the one who caused you problems has been judged. That's good news!

John 16:12, 13
I have yet many things to say unto you, but ye cannot bear them now. Howbeit when he, the Spirit of truth, is come, he will guide you into all truth: for he shall not speak of himself; but whatsoever he shall hear, that shall he speak: and he will shew you things to come.

Jesus here is wrapping up His teaching. But is He doing so worried and frustrated that none of His disciples understand what He's saying? No. Look at the next verse. . . .

John 16:14, 15
He shall glorify me: for he shall receive of mine, and shall shew it unto you. All things that the Father hath are mine: therefore said I, that he shall take of mine, and shall shew it unto you.

Jesus is not worried—and neither should you be about your son, daughter, wife, brother, neighbor, friend.
"But they're not seeing it," you protest. "I'm talking to them. I'm sending tapes to them. I'm lining up counseling for them—and they're still not getting it."
Jesus said, "I know you can't understand what I'm saying. But I also know that when the Spirit comes, He will guide you into all truth."
Truly, it's not by excellent argumentation or through a powerful presentation that the light goes on and the heart opens up. It's only by the work of the Spirit that people who are blind begin to see. Jesus knew this. That's why He didn't worry. And neither should you.

John 16:16, 17
A little while, and ye shall not see me: and again, a little while, and ye shall see me, because I go to the Father. Then said some of his disciples among themselves, What is this that he saith unto us, A little while, and ye shall not see me: and again, a little while, and ye shall see me: and, Because I go to the Father?

This, of course, is a reference to the fact that Jesus' disciples would see Him again in heaven. But they didn't understand this. Unable to figure out what Jesus was saying, they discussed it among themselves.

John 16:18
They said therefore, What is this that he saith, A little while? we cannot tell what he saith.

Here the disciples are discussing things about Jesus, while He is in the room with them. They were talking *about* Him when they should have been talking *to* Him. How often that's true of you and me as well. "What's going on?" we say. "What does this mean?" or "Why did that happen?" we one another rather than talking directly to the Lord. I'm always amazed at how ready I am to talk to another person—when it is the Lord alone who knows the solution.

John 16:19–22
Now Jesus knew that they were desirous to ask him, and said unto them, Do ye inquire among yourselves of that I said, A little while, and ye shall not see me: and again, a little while, and ye shall see me? Verily, verily, I say unto you, That ye shall weep and lament, but the world shall rejoice: and ye shall be sorrowful, but your sorrow shall be turned into joy. A woman when she is in travail hath sorrow, because her hour is come: but as soon as she is delivered of the child, she remembereth no more the anguish, for joy that a man is born into the world. And ye now therefore have sorrow: but I will see you again, and your heart shall rejoice, and your joy no man taketh from you.

Keep in mind that the disciples listening to this discourse had left everything to follow Jesus. Friends, family, and business positions—they had left it all to put their stock in Him. They had hitched their wagons to Him and followed after Him for three years. And now, in this Upper Room, He tells them He would no longer be with them. Thus, understanding their confusion, Jesus gives His disciples three elements that would replace their depression with joy. . . .
First, He gives them a principle to hold on to. The principle is simply this: The object of your pain presently will produce great joy eventually. To illustrate, He spoke of a woman going through labor. Yes, there's pain and struggle, perspiration and anguish. But yet it's the very object that produced the pain that provides the joy when the baby is finally born. In other words, Jesus says, "My leaving, My being crucified, My death is going to cause you great joy when you see Me again in heaven, when you finally understand it was necessary for Me to go to Calvary in order that your sins could be forgiven completely."
When you go through pain, the Lord does not take away that which caused the pain and replace it with something else to bring joy. It is not substitution, but *transformation* as He produces joy with the very thing that once caused pain.

Joseph was thrown into a pit by his envious older brothers. But, picked up by some merchants in a passing caravan, he ended up in Egypt. Sold as a slave into the house of Potiphar, he worked his way up in Potiphar's household until suddenly things turned sour when Potiphar's wife wrongly accused him of sexual assault. Cast into prison, Joseph languished there day after month after year until God miraculously worked through a series of incredible events to release him from prison and elevate him to the position of Prime Minister of Egypt. Thus, the very things that produced the pain—rejection by his brothers, the pit, the prison—were transformed not only to work out for his own good, but to save his entire family in the day of famine (Genesis 50:20).

John 16:23–28
And in that day ye shall ask me nothing. Verily, verily, I say unto you, Whatsoever ye shall ask the Father in my name, he will give it you. Hitherto have ye asked nothing in my name: ask, and ye shall receive, that your joy may be full. These things have I spoken unto you in proverbs: but the time cometh, when I shall no more speak unto you in proverbs, but I shall shew you plainly of the Father. At that day ye shall ask in my name: and I say not unto you, that I will pray the Father for you: For the Father himself loveth you, because ye have loved me, and have believed that I came out from God. I came forth from the Father, and am come into the world: again, I leave the world, and go to the Father.

Second, Jesus gives His disciples a power to plug in to. The power to transform that which produces sorrow into that which provides joy is the power of prayer. "You've asked nothing in My name," Jesus says. "Ask and you shall receive that your *joy* might be made full." Notice Jesus says we must ask in His name. What does this mean? Two things: authority and conformity.

Short on cash, I decide to cash a check at Valley Bank in California. As I hand the teller my check, however, she says, "This check is out of state. We can't cash it."

"Look at the name on the top," I say. And as she does, she quickly apologizes and cashes my check immediately. It's great—but it has nothing to do with me. You see, my dad is President of Valley Bank, so I am treated well because of his name. So, too, when I approach the Father in heaven, I don't come saying, "Did You see how long I prayed last week, Father? Fourteen hours logged in, eighteen chapters read, twenty-two

verses memorized. On that basis, I come to You with these requests, and I'm sure You'll give them to me." No, I come simply on the authority of the name I've been given to use: *Jesus'* name.

Third, Jesus gave His disciples a name to conform to. If I went into that same Valley Bank, pulled out a gun, and said to the teller, "I'm Jon Courson. Now, give me all your money, or I'm blasting your brains out," she might perhaps start loading my bag with money—but she would also hit a silent alarm, for although I would be using the name of Courson, I would not be acting in conformity with that name, with the nature of my dad. So, too, when we ask in the name of Jesus, we must do so not only in His authority, but in conformity to His nature. Consequently, if someone cuts me off as I'm driving and I pray, "Father, in Jesus' name, help that guy to drive off the road"—it's not going to happen because that's not in conformity with His nature. Oftentimes, we ask for things that are out of harmony with the nature of our Lord—and we wonder why our prayers aren't answered. That's why, for me, a real secret in prevailing prayer is to be in the Word constantly, studying the life of Christ specifically, so that the things I pray for are in conformity with His character.

John 16:29, 30
His disciples said unto him, Lo, now speakest thou plainly, and speakest no proverb. Now are we sure that thou knowest all things, and needest not that any man should ask thee: by this we believe that thou camest forth from God.

After Jesus gave this word about childbearing, prayer, and joy, the disciples thought, *Okay. We get it now.* But they really didn't. . . .

John 16:31
Jesus answered them, Do ye now believe?

The implication is that they really didn't.

John 16:32
Behold, the hour cometh, yea, is now come, that ye shall be scattered, every man to his own, and shall leave me alone: and yet I am not alone, because the Father is with me.

"You don't get it," Jesus is saying. "In fact, the hour is coming when your unbelief in My words will cause you to scatter from My side."

John 16:33
These things I have spoken unto you, that in me ye might have peace. In the world ye

shall have tribulation: but be of good cheer;
I have overcome the world.

Fourth, Jesus gives His disciples a position to
lay claim to. "I have overcome," Jesus said. "And
you are in Me. So even if you do scatter, even if
you do stumble, even if you do fail—be of good
cheer. I have overcome the world. I lived a life in
which the world did not seduce Me, in which Satan could not conquer Me, in which sin never
tainted Me. I have overcome and you are in Me.
Therefore, you will overcome as well."

With Goliath towering over him, David goes to
the brook and grabs five stones. Why five? Five
is the number of grace. Besides, Goliath had four
brothers, and I believe David was ready to take
on the whole family if necessary. He slings one
stone in the air, and Goliath is down for the count.
And because Goliath was defeated, *all* of the Philistines fled. And the men of Israel who were previously reluctant to take on the giant, now *all*
share in the victory won by a shepherd boy singularly. So, too, our Champion—the Good Shepherd, the Son of David, Jesus Christ—took on the
Goliath of my sin and failure, of Satan and the
world system—and He beat them. And I just enjoy the victory.

The Christian race is the only race in the world
that begins at the finish line. We don't fight *for*
victory. We fight *from* victory. The battle's already won. Jesus has already overcome. No wonder He says, "Be of good cheer."

⸎

17 John Knox, great Scottish reformer of
the sixteenth century, called John
chapter 17 the "Holy of Holies in the
Temple of Scripture." So much did Knox love this
chapter, that as he lay on his deathbed, he had it
read to him over and over again. I believe John
Knox's choice was a good one, for in John 17, we
see Jesus approaching His own death. About to
be crucified, He pauses to talk things over with
His Father, giving a report concerning what He
did in the three years He was here on earth in
public ministry. And in His evaluation, I see eight
areas Jesus identified as the foundations of His
success. The world names money, power, and
prestige as foundational. Jesus shows us an entirely different way of evaluating life and ministry. . . .

John 17:1 (a)
These words spake Jesus, and lifted up his
eyes to heaven, and said, Father . . .

After talking about the Father to His disciples
in the Upper Room, Jesus talks to the Father
about His disciples.

John 17:1 (b)
. . . the hour is come; glorify thy Son, that
thy Son also may glorify thee.

Prayer is not the way to get God to do our will
in heaven. Prayer is the way to get man to do
God's will on earth. Once this is understood, you
will find yourself praying in an entirely different
manner. And that's what Jesus is doing here.
"Glorify Me," He prays, "so that You might be
glorified—even if that means that I will be
pinned to the Cross of Calvary."

"That sounds sadistic," you say. But it isn't because on the other side of the Cross is a crown—
joy unspeakable, full of great glory. We only see
five months or ten years down the road. But God
sees the next ten zillion years. You see, Jesus' allowing the Father to be glorified *through* Him ultimately bought a bride *for* Him for all eternity.

It's so radical when a believer finally gets the
big picture and stops saying, "God do it my way."
God is not Burger King. We can't give orders
about how things should be done, and then complain when we don't get the lettuce and onions we
asked for. God is not Burger King—He's the
King of kings, and He sees what is going to be absolutely best in the long run.

John 17:2–4 (a)
As thou hast given him power over all flesh,
that he should give eternal life to as many
as thou hast given him. And this is life eter-
nal, that they might know thee the only true
God, and Jesus Christ, whom thou hast sent.
I have glorified thee on the earth.

"I have glorified You on the earth." This is the
first point in determining how successful in life
you are. It is said that former Mayor Ed Koch
used to walk the streets of New York City asking everyone—the garbage man, the meter
reader, the businessman—"How am I doing?"
So, too, I think it's sometimes good for us to
say, "How am I doing, Father? Who has received the glory?"

Maybe you're an excellent mother, a gifted musician, a deep Bible teacher, a wonderful neighbor, a hard worker. But who has received the
glory? Jesus had a way of working where, without exception, every time He showed power,
Scripture says the people saw it and glorified God
in heaven.

How about you? Jesus said, "Let your light so

shine among men that they might see your good works and glorify the Father in heaven" (Matthew 5:16). Are you getting the glory, or is God? God chooses to use the foolish things of the world (1 Corinthians 1:27) because then people say, "Wow! God is good to use a foolish weakling like him."

John 17:4 (b)
I have finished the work . . .

Jesus didn't say, "I started the work," or, "I thought about the work," or, "I was going to get to the work." He said, "I have *finished* the work." The roads from Bible studies and Bible conferences are strewn with the broken commitments of men and women who began but never finished what God told them to do. I'm sure glad that after Noah finished the frame on the ark, he didn't say, "Close enough. We don't need a roof." No, he *finished* the work. He *completed* the task. If he hadn't, we would all be sunk. What about you? If you knew you only had a few hours to live, could you say, "Father, I finished the work You gave me to do"? Or would you have to say, "I know you put this on my heart last year and I meant to get to it, but . . ."?

Have you finished the work? Saul didn't. "Let not one Amalekite remain," Samuel told Saul (1 Samuel 15:3). And Saul killed *almost* every one—but he decided to keep Agag, king of the Amalekites as a trophy. Twenty-five years later, wounded in battle, rather than being captured by the enemy, Saul turns to a young man on the field and says, "Kill me." And the young man—an Amalekite—did just that. Where did he come from? Somewhere along the way, Agag fathered a son.

"Don't leave a single Amalekite alive," Samuel said.

"I gave it a pretty good shot," said Saul. "Ninety-nine point nine percent isn't bad."

But the one he didn't finish was the one who did him in.

What has God called you to do? What has He spoken to your heart about? Maybe it's a certain sin that's got to go, and you think, *Well, I've got it pretty much taken care of. I know the Lord's told me not to do this, but I've cut way back.*

"Have you finished it?"

"No, but I've got it under control."

Watch out. Agag is out to get you.

"It is Finished," cried Jesus from the Cross. I'm so glad He didn't say, "I almost did it, but I'm going to come down now"—because if He came down from the Cross, we would go down to hell. He paid the price. He finished the work.

John 17:4 (c)
. . . which thou gavest me to do.

"The whole city wants You," Jesus was told in Mark 1:37. Having spent the morning in prayer, however, He knew that the directive of His Father was for Him to minister in the backwoods region of Galilee. Thus, He went in the opposite direction of the clamor of the crowd. I believe this is why you never see Jesus accused of being busy. His enemies accused Him of being a winebibber, a glutton, demon-possessed, and crazy—but never busy. Jesus moved with a paced peace and an ordered steadiness because He knew the heart of the Father. People's burdens will give you an ulcer. People's expectations will drive you crazy. Whenever the burden's not light, I know I'm not doing the will of the Father. But when He directs me morning by morning, I find His yoke easy (Matthew 11:30).

John 17:5–7
And now, O Father, glorify thou me with thine own self with the glory which I had with thee before the world was. I have manifested thy name unto the men which thou gavest me out of the world: thine they were, and thou gavest them me; and they have kept thy word. Now they have known that all things whatsoever thou hast given me are of thee.

"I have manifested Thy name." The word translated "manifest" is *phaneroo*, which means "to shine forth." It doesn't mean so much declaration as it does illustration. When Jesus said, "I have manifested Your name," He wasn't saying, "I have preached about it verbally," but rather, "I have lived it out observably."

"Great is the mystery," Paul would later say, "that God was *manifest* in the flesh," (see 1 Timothy 3:16). Truly, the Word became flesh and dwelt among us (John 1:14). Jesus said, "This is what I've done Father—I have fleshed out, lived out Your Name and Your Nature before these men You've entrusted to Me. They have seen You by seeing Me."

As the law came down from Mount Sinai, it read, "Thou shalt have no other gods before me. Thou shalt not make unto thee any graven image. Thou shalt not commit adultery. Thou shalt not covet." It was heavy—but the people received it because it was delivered to them by a man whose face glowed (Exodus 34:29). So, too, if you come down on your friends, colleagues, or kids, and you're growling instead of glowing, they'll resent you and reject the law you bring. Your kids will rebel; your friends will leave; your employees will quit because they'll resent what you share. But if, like Moses and like Jesus, you're spending time with the Father, you will be able to correctly manifest *Him.*

John 17:8 (a)
For I have given unto them the words which thou gavest me . . ."

I have given them thy words." The word translated "words" in this verse is *rhema,* and refers not to the written word, but to the spoken word. *Rhema* is also found in Ephesians 6:17, in conjunction with the sword of the Spirit. In this context, *rhema* refers not to a theological, scriptural, doctrinal statement, but to a particular word for a particular person.

"You have said well you have no husband. You've had five husbands and the man you're living with now is not your husband at all" (see John 4:18) said Jesus, as He tenderly wielded the daggerlike, Spirit-inspired rhema—*the particular word for a particular person.*

Maybe you've been following the story that has been in the news several times lately about a group of kids who preach at the top of their lungs on their way to school, using their Bibles for megaphones. Recently kicked out of school because they refused to quit preaching, they're now being home-schooled. "Obviously what they're doing doesn't seem right," people say. "But they *are* preaching the Word."

Ah, but it's not the *rhema* word. It's not the exact word. It's not the right word at the right time. It's offending, not convicting. When people justify obnoxious behavior under the guise of preaching the Word, we need to say, "Wait a minute, brother. The Word of God is exact—for the right person at the right time in the right way. And what you're doing is not right."

John 17:8 (b)–11
. . . and they have received them, and have known surely that I came out from thee, and they have believed that thou didst send me. I pray for them: I pray not for the world, but for them which thou hast given me; for they are thine. And all mine are thine, and thine are mine; and I am glorified in them. And now I am no more in the world, but these are in the world, and I come to thee. Holy Father, keep through thine own name those whom thou hast given me, that they may be one, as we are.

"I pray not for the world," said Jesus. The term "world" has three references scripturally. First, it speaks of the planet, of the earth (Job 37:12). Second, it speaks of humanity (John 3:16). But the world Jesus is talking about here is neither the planet nor the people, but the system. Consequently, He is praying not to transform the system, not to politically organize to change the system, but rather He is praying for those the Father has called *out* of the world's system.

John 17:12 (a)
While I was with them in the world, I kept them in thy name: those that thou gavest me I have kept . . .

"I have kept them," Jesus said. According to the teaching of Jesus in John 10, we are in the Father's hand and no man can pluck us out. *Nothing* can loosen us from His grip. Therefore, while we must not be ignorant of Satan's devices, the key to overcoming darkness is to walk in the light and to realize that Jesus Christ promises to keep us (Jude 24). Yes, there is a danger in demon possession or demon oppression—but I believe the greatest danger right now is demon obsession. We should be obsessed not with darkness, but with Jesus. *He* should be the subject of your study, the passion of your ministry.

"I have kept them," Jesus said. What about us? In one sense, in order to apply this to our lives, we need to realize we cannot keep our children, grandchildren, or people to whom we're linked in ministry because they're not ours to keep. They're His. You have opportunities one day at a time to be a blessing to your children and others to whom you minister—to serve them, discipline them, and love them. But you can't cling to them because they're not yours (Ezekiel 18:4). I cannot keep people selfishly—but I must keep them in my heart tenderly. This is what Paul speaks of in virtually all of his epistles when he says, "I have you in my heart."

Old Testament priests wore stones representing each tribe both over their hearts on a breastplate and on their shoulders because there's a connection between the burden of intercession and the heart of compassion. When you pray for people, you will find that as you bear them on your shoulders in intercessory ministry, they will become jewels on your heart.

John 17:12 (b)
. . . and none of them is lost, but the son of perdition; that the scripture might be fulfilled.

The word "perdition" means "wasteful." What did Judas say when Mary anointed Jesus with oil? The son of waste himself said, "Is not that wasteful? Couldn't it have been used more practically?" (see John 12:4–5). This son of perdition could not understand the reason one would bestow anything of worth on Jesus.

"Have not I chosen you, yet one of you is a devil?" Jesus said (see John 6:70). Judas was never saved. That is why he was not kept.

John 17:13, 14 (a)
And now come I to thee; and these things I speak in the world, that they might have my joy fulfilled in themselves. I have given them thy word . . .

Unlike in verse 8, the word translated "word" here in verse 13 is *logos*. "I have given them the Scriptures," Jesus says.

John 17:14 (b)–17
. . . and the world hath hated them, because they are not of the world, even as I am not of the world. I pray not that thou shouldest take them out of the world, but that thou shouldest keep them from the evil. They are not of the world, even as I am not of the world. Sanctify them through thy truth: thy word is truth.

"Thy Word is truth." Truth comes in a three-volume set. The first volume is the Scriptures—a Book you can learn from. The second is the Son (John 14:6)—a Person you can love. The third is the Spirit (1 John 5:6)—a Power to live by. If you are learning from the Scriptures, loving the Son, and living in the Spirit, you will be walking in truth.

John 17:18
As thou hast sent me into the world, even so have I also sent them into the world.

"I have sent them." Jesus not only kept those entrusted to Him, but He sent them out. He made opportunities for them. Earlier, He had said, "They are not of the world,"—but yet He sends them into the world. Christian, listen carefully. We are not to be of the world—but we must be in the world. The mistake of the monastery movement lies in isolation from the world. You can get away, yes, but don't stay away. Jesus ripped into that wrong understanding when He told the parable of the Good Samaritan. You can't walk on the other side of the street to avoid the stench and infection of the world. The answer lies not in isolation, but in incarnation—for just as God became Man yet retained His deity, so we

are a people who, although we live among humanity, are linked to eternity. We're here in the flesh, but we are really living in the heavenlies. That's where our hope, our destiny, and our source of strength lie.

In the aftermath of the December seventh bombing of Pearl Harbor, divers were sent to rescue the survivors. In one compartment of the USS *Utah*, however, it was impossible to get to the men trapped inside. The divers could hear men tapping "Is there any hope?" in Morse Code—but rescue was impossible with the technology then available.

We're deep-sea divers, gang—down here on earth, but connected to heaven. We don't fit in here, we don't belong here, and we ain't gonna stay here. But the Lord has allowed us to be here, pumping the oxygen of the Spirit and the Scriptures to us, saying, "There are people to rescue. Do what you can as I guide and lead you."

If you're of the world, you're in big trouble. You're going to try to boogie eighty feet underwater, and it's just not going to work. We've got souls to save, people to reach, things to do. Let's get moving—and let's go home to heaven.

John 17:19, 20
And for their sakes I sanctify myself, that they also might be sanctified through the truth. Neither pray I for these alone, but for them also which shall believe on me through their word.

Jesus prayed not only for those with Him at that time, but for those who would believe later on—for you and me.

John 17:21
That they all may be one; as thou, Father, art in me, and I in thee, that they also may be one in us: that the world may believe that thou hast sent me.

Keep in mind that it was after talking about truth in verse 14 that Jesus prays His people might be one here in verse 21. Ephesians 4:15 says we are to speak the truth in love because love without truth is hypocrisy, while truth without love is brutality. You see, if I speak the truth without love, it's like a fire without warmth. Who wants to be in a room on a cold night with light but no warmth? If I speak love without truth, however, it's like a blaze without light. And who wants to be in the dark? The idea is to have light *and* warmth. Unity is based upon telling the truth in love—not always easy, but absolutely necessary.

Such a powerful evangelist was George Whitefield that thirty thousand people would regularly attend his open-air meetings. So anointed and eloquent was he, history records many orators and actors would come just to watch him. Charles Wesley, a contemporary of Whitefield's, was also preaching to multitudes. Yet so diverse were the views of these two men on certain doctrines, they took out advertisements in the newspapers explaining why they believed what they did—and why the other was amiss. People thought these men hated each other—until one reporter asked Whitefield, "Tell me, Mr. Whitefield, do you expect to see Charles Wesley in heaven?"

"No," answered Whitefield. "He's going to be so close to the throne, and I'm going to be so far back, I'll never see him."

I like that! Here these guys had very different views doctrinally, and very different flavors in ministry, but they had unity through love in their diversity.

John 17:22, 23
And the glory which thou gavest me I have given them; that they may be one, even as we are one: I in them, and thou in me, that they may be made perfect in one; and that the world may know that thou hast sent me, and hast loved them, as thou hast loved me.

"I have given them the glory," Jesus said, speaking of the *chabod*, the substance, the reality of holiness.

Jesus gave the glory to His disciples? To men who would deny Him and abandon Him? Yes. And that same glory has been given to you, for whom He justified, He glorified (Romans 8:30). Listen carefully, saint: The Father looks at you and says, "You are not only elected and predestined, called and justified, but you are already glorified." I'm so glad the Father doesn't see me in my frailty and my flesh, my carnality and stupidity. I'm so thankful He sees me glorified in His Son.

Wouldn't it be radical if you looked at your sons and daughters, husband or wife in their glorified state? Think about the person who bugs you the most. Now, ask the Lord to show you how He views him. You see, it's not that love is blind. It's that love sees *more*. And because love sees more, it is willing to see less. Filled with glory, the eyes

of love don't have room for shortcomings and failure.

For topical study of John 17:20–23 entitled "Unity in the Family," turn to page 577.

John 17:24, 25
Father, I will that they also, whom thou hast given me, be with me where I am; that they may behold my glory, which thou hast given me: for thou lovedst me before the foundation of the world. O righteous Father, the world hath not known thee: but I have known thee, and these have known that thou hast sent me.

I know for a fact we're going to heaven because of the promise Jesus made in John 14:1, the prayer He prayed here in John 17:24, and the price He paid (1 Thessalonians 5:10).

John 17:26
And I have declared unto them thy name, and will declare it: that the love wherewith thou hast loved me may be in them, and I in them.

"I have declared thy Name," said Jesus. Unlike manifesting God's Name, which involves living it out (verse 6), declaring His Name refers to speaking it out. "I AM the Bread of life," Jesus declared. "I AM the Door. I AM the Way. I AM the Vine. I AM the Truth. I AM the Light. I not only showed people illustratively, but I declared Your Name verbally."

Gang, as we treat people as though they are already glorified, as we speak the truth in love that we might be unified, as we keep those the Lord has given to us on our hearts through intercession, as we manifest as well as declare the nature of the Father, as we give people the exact word, and share with them the Scriptures, as we finish the work He gives us to do, we will be doing the very things Jesus said our lives should be about.

But as you who are students of management know, this measurement of success is radically contrary to what is propagated in our American culture. It doesn't chart well in popularity polls, on financial fact sheets, or resumes. It won't produce trophies in your case or plaques on your wall—only a voice in your ear, saying, "Well done, good and faithful servant."

UNITY IN THE FAMILY
A Topical Study of
John 17:20–23

W e are part of a family, a big family—the family of God. And according to the Scriptures, our Father is proud of us. Are we perfect? Well, it depends on how you look at it. Oh, I know we still have flaws and faults and shortcomings. No doubt about it. But Hebrews 10:14 says that by one offering, God has perfected forever those who are sanctified. So, by the offering of Jesus Christ on the Cross of Calvary, we have been perfected positionally. We are family—and as family, it is the intention of our Father that we dwell together in unity. Why is the Lord so concerned about unity? I suggest a couple of reasons....

Pleasure in Unity

Behold, how good and how pleasant it is for brethren to dwell together in unity!
                                                            Psalm 133:1

Parents are blessed by seeing their kids playing together, sharing toys, and being kind to one another. Conversely, they're grieved when they see their kids fighting and bopping one another. The same is true of the Heavenly Father. Seeing His kids together, with all of their various personalities and characteristics, yet dwelling together in unity, causes Him to say, "Behold, how good and how pleasant it is for brethren to dwell together in unity!"

Power in Unity

The locusts have no king, yet go they forth all of them by bands.
                                                            Proverbs 30:27

If a single cricket or grasshopper lands in your garden, you simply brush him off. Locusts, however, have a secret: They move together in vast numbers. They don't have a king, but instinctively they travel across a country into a community and are able devour everything in sight simply by their unity. So, too, the world says to us as individual believers, "Quit bugging me, you little cricket," as they brush us off and put us down. But when God's people, under the direction of the Holy Spirit, move in unity—without king, pope, or denominational headquarters—we can storm the very gates of hell and make a lasting, permanent impact.

The Christian community is splintering and that is why, more than ever, we need to hear the heart of the Lord in this area—that we might be one as a family in our homes, as a congregation, as a body. Now, if the prayer of Jesus is for unity and cohesion, what is the program of Satan? Division. What does Satan intend to do to disrupt the unity in your family, in your church locally, or among the church universally? Lacking creativity or innovation, he seeks to divide and conquer the same ways he has since the beginning . . .

Competition

> *And in process of time it came to pass, that Cain brought of the fruit of the ground an offering unto the LORD. And Abel, he also brought of the firstlings of his flock and of the fat thereof. And the LORD had respect unto Abel and to his offering: But unto Cain and to his offering he had not respect. And Cain was very wroth, and his countenance fell.*   Genesis 4:3–5

Here we see the first tactic of the Enemy: getting brothers to compete against each other. Although the world exalts competition as a key component of its system, such is not the way of the kingdom. We're one body, one family, (1 Corinthians 12). Therefore, when one part of the body is blessed, the whole body should rejoice. If good things are happening to a brother or sister, don't be intimidated, but rejoice because you're being blessed as well.

Jesus showed us what He thought of competition at the pool of Bethesda. The conventional wisdom of the day was that whenever the water stirred, the first one in would get healed. When Jesus came on the scene, He went to a guy at the very back—the one who was not fighting to get ahead, the one forgotten by everyone else and said, "Rise, take up your bed. Let's get out of this place of competition," (see John 5). And I suggest to you that's still the heart of Jesus.

Exposure

> *And Noah began to be an husbandman, and he planted a vineyard: And he drank of the wine, and was drunken; and he was uncovered within his tent. And Ham, the father of Canaan, saw the nakedness of his father, and told his two brethren without.*   Genesis 9:20–22

The Flood over, Noah became a vinedresser. It is possible Noah didn't know that, due to the collapse of the water canopy that had surrounded the earth before the Flood, fermentation would occur under the damaging rays of the sun. But as he drank the grape juice that perhaps had been sitting out for a few months, maybe he did indeed know exactly what he was doing. Either way, drunk and naked in his tent, he was exposed by his son.

Why do we expose the nakedness of others? I suggest it's for the sense of camaraderie that follows. You see, if Rick says to Roger, "I can't believe what Peter did last week," initially there's something in human nature that produces a bond between Rick and Roger as they talk about Peter. They might sound very spiritual, as in, "Did you hear what happened to Peter? I know you'll pray about it, so I want to share with you what he did . . ." but cut through all the piety, and gossip is at the root.

A day or two later, however, when Rick sees Roger talking with Peter, he thinks, *Uh, oh. I bet they're talking about me.* And paranoia creeps in.

Thus, exposure produces a false fellowship because you can be sure that if someone has listened to you gossip about another, they will also be involved in gossip about you. "Oh, but I didn't say anything. I was just listening." According to Proverbs 17:4, even if you listen, you are a partner in that sin. Proverbs goes on to say, "Where there is no wood, there can be no fire" (see 26:20), because if you refuse to listen, guess what. The gossip stops.

Proverbs goes even further in saying, "He that covers a transgression seeks love" (see 17:9). And that's what is seen in Genesis 9. Ham exposed his father's sin—but his brothers covered it. Shem and Japheth walked in backward with a blanket between their shoulders lest anyone walking outside look in and see Noah's nakedness. It's tragic when Christians talk about the dirty laundry that's in the tent and expose the nakedness of their brothers and sisters, because those outside the tent—the ones who aren't saved—say, "I don't want to go in there." Instead of talking and gossiping, Shem and Japheth covered the iniquity carefully and completely. And they were blessed as a result (Genesis 9:26–27).

Legalism

And the child grew, and was weaned: and Abraham made a great feast the same day that Isaac was weaned. And Sarah saw the son of Hagar the Egyptian, which she had born unto Abraham, mocking. Genesis 21:8, 9

Galatians 4 gives us the interpretation of this event: Ishmael represents the law, the Old Covenant. Isaac represents grace, the New Covenant. The law always mocks grace. The law will always come down on grace, find fault with grace, belittle grace. Watch out for this third attack of the Enemy—where we come down on others, make fun of others, separate ourselves from others when they don't keep our prescribed rules. Beware of legalism. Don't let cultural traditions or personal convictions cause division between you and any other believer.

Favoritism

And the boys grew: and Esau was a cunning hunter, a man of the field; and Jacob was a plain man, dwelling in tents. And Isaac loved Esau, because he did eat of his venison: but Rebekah loved Jacob. Genesis 25:27, 28

Isaac grew up, married Rebekah, and fathered twin sons—Jacob and Esau. As Esau grew up, Isaac said, "I like this kid—All-State in hunting." But Rebekah loved Jacob. Thus, because of favoritism, seeds of division were planted, which caused life-long tension between these two brothers. In 1 Corinthians 3, Paul warns of the same danger. "You're carnal," he said to the Corinthians believers, "not because of some gross and obvious sin, but because you each have your favorite teacher. Some follow me; others follow Apollos; others Peter. This ought not be."

Jealousy

> *And when his brethren saw that their father loved him more than all his brethren, they hated him, and could not speak peaceably unto him. And Joseph dreamed a dream, and he told it his brethren: and they hated him yet the more.*
> Genesis 37:4, 5

Whenever we look at someone else's power, position, or possessions and think, *That would make me happy,* jealousy is the inevitable result. Such was the case with Joseph and his brothers. After Joseph was bestowed with a coat, signifying a position of prominence, and after he prophesied that they would one day bow to him, so angry did his brothers become that they tossed him into a pit to die. Then, seeing a band of slave traders traveling through the region, his brothers picked him up and sold him as a slave in Egypt, where he was eventually thrown into a dungeon before finally rising to the position of prime minister. Keep Joseph in mind when you see someone who seems to have more prowess spiritually, more power vocationally, more possessions materially than you. As was Joseph's, the path of their prominence is often strewn with pits and prisons about which you know nothing. So be thankful where you are. Like Paul, learn to be content wherever the Lord has planted you (Philippians 4:11).

Competition, exposure, legalism, favoritism, jealousy all constitute the plan of the Enemy to cause division. What, then, is the pathway to unity?

It's not crusades. It's not saying, "Let's get all of the churches together and have a unity rally." Neither is it causes. It's not saying, "We'll all stand together for a certain cause politically or morally—and that will unify the body of Christ." I don't see any hints in Scripture that indicate crusades or causes unify the body. I only see one force that does: the Cross of Christ.

Revelation of the Cross

Some believers sense the presence of God through high liturgy. That is, when they hear the swishing of robes and the chanting of choirs, when they smell the burning of incense, and see the flickering of candles, they think, *Wow. I'm with God. I feel His presence.*

Other churches employ what is called a "low" liturgical order. "Forget formality," they say, for unless there's prophecy, tongues, an interpretation, some healings, and some spontaneous sharing—they don't sense the Spirit moving.

Others say, "It's not high or low liturgy that matters. Rather, the church should be caring for the poor, feeding the hungry, housing the homeless." We might put them on the left side of the spectrum. They're social activists, caring about people practically.

Fundamentalists, who tend to congregate on the right side of the spectrum, say, "We're going to ground our people in the Word, in the importance of doctrine."

Put all these flavors together—the height, the depth, the left, the right—and they form a cross. And that's where fellowship is found. Not in doctrine, not in activism, not in causes, not in crusades. True fellowship is found when we finally say, "The Lord is bigger than I thought." You see, gang, the Lord looks at those in high liturgical churches as a reflection of His holiness; at those who worship sans liturgy as a reflection of His power; at "left wing" activists as a reflection of His compassion; at "right-wing" fundamentalists as a reflection of His righteousness.

There's room for *all* who truly name the Name of Jesus. Catholics, Lutherans, Pentecostals, Episcopalians, even renegades like us—there's room for everyone at the Cross. God made all kinds of different people. He loves them all and He's provided churches to minister to the way He made them. It's not a matter of better or worse, right or wrong. It's not a matter of finding oneness doctrinally or trying to get together politically. It's a matter of joining together at the Cross of Calvary.

Appropriation of the Cross

How do we come to the Cross practically?

At Communion.

Just as my family gathers around our table, so, too, the family of Christ gathers around His table. No matter where we've come from, or what our flavor might be, we all eat of the same Bread, we all drink of the same Blood. Communion, how important it is because it is there we find all the dials set back to zero, all of the divisions melted away as we are reminded that His Body and Blood are our common ground.

Application of the Cross

With every church, with every brother or sister who names the name of Jesus, we must come to the realization that we are all sinners saved by grace. Therefore, our prayer must be, "Lord, remind me of what I am, and of where I've been in order that I might look lovingly and mercifully on *every* sister, on *every* brother, on *every* church who is preaching Your name and has received You as their Savior."

May we truly, practically, daily walk in unity. We'll do it to the extent that we live in the shadow of Calvary.

---

18 John 18:1 (a)
When Jesus had spoken these words, he went forth with his disciples over the brook Cedron . . .

Leaving the area of the temple, where, following the Upper Room discourse of John 13–14, He very likely prayed His High Priestly prayer of John 17, Jesus and His disciples made their way down the side of the small valley wherein flowed a small river called the Kidron. Crossing the Kidron, I wonder if Jesus wasn't deeply moved by what He saw at His feet.

When David numbered the people to ascertain the strength of the nation, the result was great punishment because their strength was to be in God alone. (2 Samuel 24). Therefore, when the Romans wanted to know how many people were in Jerusalem during Passover, they could only do it by counting the sheep offered as sacrifices. Josephus tells us that during this particular Passover, 256,000 sheep were counted. The Kidron, meaning, "Murky" River, the river flowing at the foot of the temple mount, would be flowing blood-red from the blood of a quarter-million sheep.

I wonder if Jesus' mind went back to how David, centuries before, crossed the very same brook when there was a rebellion launched against him by his own son, Absalom (2 Samuel 15)—for even as David was rejected by the people of Jerusalem, so the Son of David would be rejected as well.

John 18:1 (b)
. . . where was a garden, into the which he entered, and his disciples.

On the side of the Mount of Olives were many private enclosed gardens, where the well-to-do people of Jerusalem would go to escape the heat of the city. Jesus had access to one such garden. Named, "Gethsemane," or "Oil Press," it was a site where olives grew and were crushed by a press in order to produce oil. In Gethsemane, the place of the Oil Press, Jesus would Himself be crushed as, submitting to the will of the Father, He sweat great drops of blood (Luke 22:44).

In another Garden, called Eden, the first Adam rebelled against the Father's will. In the Garden of Gethsemane, Jesus—the Last Adam (1 Corinthians 15)—submitted to the Father's will. In the Garden of Eden, Adam hid from God. In the Garden of Gethsemane, Jesus is transparent before God. In the Garden of Eden, man was driven out because of his sin. In the Garden of Gethsemane, Jesus prepares to die for sin. In the Garden of Eden, a sword was unsheathed (Genesis 3:24). In the Garden of Gethsemane, a sword is put away (John 18:11). That which was lost in the Garden of Eden will be reclaimed in the Garden of Paradise—all because of the Garden of Gethsemane.

John 18:2
And Judas also, which betrayed him, knew the place: for Jesus ofttimes resorted thither with his disciples.

About to betray Jesus, Judas knew right where to find Him in time of trouble. He knew Jesus would be found in the place of prayer. Do people know where you would be in troublesome times or difficult days? Would they look for you at church, studying the Scriptures, in the place of prayer—or would they look somewhere else first?

John 18:3 (a)
Judas then, having received a band of men and officers from the chief priests and Pharisees . . .

"A band of men" speaks of a cohort, which was one-tenth of a legion, or six thousand soldiers. Think about this. Here comes Judas with six hundred soldiers—not including the contingent of chief priests and Pharisees—all to confront the Lamb of God.

John 18:3 (b)
. . . cometh thither with lanterns and torches and weapons.

Passover took place under a full moon, so what would be the need for torches and lanterns? No doubt, the thinking was that Jesus would be hiding and His disciples positioned for an ambush.

John 18:4
Jesus therefore, knowing all things that should come upon him, went forth, and said unto them, Whom seek ye?

Jesus disarms the mob by coming out to meet them, saying, "Who are you looking for?" You see, Jesus is not caught off guard, surprised by what is happening. No, He's in complete control of the entire situation.

John 18:5
They answered him, Jesus of Nazareth. Jesus saith unto them, I am he. And Judas also, which betrayed him, stood with them.

The word "he," in italics, Jesus is actually saying, "I AM," "*Ego Eimi*"—a declaration of deity.

John 18:6
As soon then as he had said unto them, I am he, they went backward, and fell to the ground.

With torches flying, armor clanking, and swords falling, these guys go down under the sheer power of Jesus' proclamation.

John 18:7 (a)
Then asked he them again, Whom seek ye?

With His captors sprawled on the ground, Jesus could have walked away. Instead, He waited until they came to, and repeated His question.

John 18:7 (b)
And they said, Jesus of Nazareth.

I bet this time, the mob answered a whole lot more cautiously—and braced themselves for His answer.

John 18:8, 9
Jesus answered, I have told you that I am he: if therefore ye seek me, let these go their way: That the saying might be fulfilled, which he spake, Of them which thou gavest me have I lost none.

"If you want Me, here I am. But let My disciples go," Jesus said. Indeed, the disciples scattered at that point—all except for Peter and John.

John 18:10 (a)
Then Simon Peter having a sword drew it . . .

Why did Peter have a sword? Because Jesus had previously said, "Times are changing. Be prepared for hostility. Buy a sword" (see Luke 22:36). Perhaps Jesus spoke figuratively, but Peter must have taken Him literally.

John 18:10 (b)
. . . and smote the high priest's servant, and cut off his right ear.

It was Thomas who had said, to Jesus, "We'll die with You if necessary" (see John 11:16)—but it's Peter, here, who was ready to do just that. While commendable, Peter's zeal was misdirected because it was not based on knowledge. Why didn't Peter understand what was happening? Why didn't he see clearly that everything was transpiring according to pattern? Because instead of praying, Peter had been sleeping (Matthew 26:40). Consequently, Peter wakes up groggy, sees a battle, whips out his sword, and swings it wildly.

So, too, many times we as disciples hurt people unnecessarily as we whip out the Scriptures and let them fly, all the while thinking, *Others may be carnal and weak, but not me, Lord. You can count on me. I'll stand up for You.* Like Peter, we cause pain and hurt whenever our zeal is not based on the knowledge that can only come from spending time in prayer.

John 18:10 (c)
The servant's name was Malchus.

Luke tells us at this point, Jesus reached down, picked up Malchus' ear, and placed it back on his head (22:51). Had Jesus not done so, there would

have been four crosses on Calvary a few hours later because Peter would have been crucified for such an offense. The last recorded miracle of our Lord was to heal a wound inflicted by one of His right hand men who was flailing the sword indiscriminately and inappropriately.

John 18:11
Then said Jesus unto Peter, Put up thy sword into the sheath: the cup which my Father hath given me, shall I not drink it?

"Do this in remembrance of Me," Jesus said (see Luke 22:19). If we would take more often the cup, we would lay down more easily the sword. What's in your hand? A sword causing pain or the cup of suffering that brings about humility and unity in the body of Christ?

John 18:12
Then the band and the captain and officers of the Jews took Jesus, and bound him.

It was not the chains, the ropes, or the soldiers that bound Jesus. It was love.

John 18:13
And led him away to Annas first; for he was father in law to Caiaphas, which was the high priest that same year.

High Priest from A.D. 5 to A.D. 16, Annas turned his position over to his son-in-law, Caiaphas, in favor of the temple concessions that needed his full attention and were making him a wealthy man. So here is Jesus, standing before the one whose livelihood He had dared to threaten when He overthrew the tables of the moneychangers and drove the oxen out of His Father's house (John 2).

John 18:14
Now Caiaphas was he, which gave counsel to the Jews, that it was expedient that one man should die for the people.

Although Caiaphas didn't realize it, he spoke profound truth—for one Man must indeed die for the salvation of mankind.

John 18:15 (a)
And Simon Peter followed Jesus . . .

Matthew tells us Peter followed from afar (Matthew 26:58). I like Peter because, although all but John had scattered, he continued to follow Jesus. But at the same time, I learn from Peter that if I follow Jesus from a distance, I'm going to get in trouble.

John 18:15 (b)
. . . and so did another disciple: that disciple was known unto the high priest, and went in with Jesus into the palace of the high priest.

The disciple spoken of here is John. There is a spot in Jerusalem traditionally and historically identified as Zebedee's fish stand. With boats and servants, Zebedee was a successful entrepreneur. According to history and tradition, it would seem as though this is how John knew the high priest, for, you see, Zebedee and his boys would sell the fish they caught in the Sea of Galilee to the wealthy folks in Jerusalem—salted fish from the north was considered a delicacy in the days before refrigeration. With the revenue from their thriving temple concessions, the priestly family could afford to eat at Zebedee's fish shop, where, according to tradition, John worked as a young boy or teenager.

John 18:16–18
But Peter stood at the door without. Then went out that other disciple, which was known unto the high priest, and spake unto her that kept the door, and brought in Peter. Then saith the damsel that kept the door unto Peter, Art not thou also one of this man's disciples? He saith, I am not. And the servants and officers stood there, who had made a fire of coals; for it was cold: and they warmed themselves: and Peter stood with them, and warmed himself.

Uh-oh, Peter, not only are you following Jesus from afar, but now you're warming yourself at the fires of His enemies.

When you feel cold, where do you go to get warm? If you go to the fires of the world when you're confused, hurting, or lonely, you're sure to get burned. Ask Peter.

John 18:19
The high priest then asked Jesus of his disciples, and of his doctrine.

The high priest is completely out of line here in asking Jesus of His doctrine. You see, Jewish law had a stipulation, much like our Fifth Amendment, in which it was considered illegal to ask the accused anything that might implicate him. Thus, at the very outset, the illegality of the trial of Jesus is evident.

John 18:20, 21
Jesus answered him, I spake openly to the world; I ever taught in the synagogue, and in the temple, whither the Jews always re-

sort; and in secret have I said nothing. Why askest thou me? ask them which heard me, what I have said unto them: behold, they know what I said.

"Ask some witnesses," said Jesus. And in so saying, He was reminding the high priest of the illegality of the proceedings.

John 18:22
And when he had thus spoken, one of the officers which stood by struck Jesus with the palm of his hand, saying, Answerest thou the high priest so?

Understanding Jesus' implication that the high priest was in violation of the law, the officer struck Jesus.

John 18:23, 24
Jesus answered him, If I have spoken evil, bear witness of the evil: but if well, why smitest thou me? Now Annas had sent him bound unto Caiaphas the high priest.

It was during His religious trial that the intense suffering of Jesus began. You see, it was in the courtyard of the high priest where, with a bag over His head, Jesus was punched in the face by the religious guards and challenged to prophesy who it was that hit Him. Think about this. When someone is about to strike you, you usually see it coming out of the corner of your eye. And even though you might take the blow, you're able to instinctively move in its direction. But when you're blindsided, the result is excruciating pain. No wonder He became marred beyond recognition—more than any other man (Isaiah 52:14).

John 18:25–27
And Simon Peter stood and warmed himself. They said therefore unto him, Art not thou also one of his disciples? He denied it, and said, I am not. One of the servants of the high priest, being his kinsman whose ear Peter cut off, saith, Did not I see thee in the garden with him? Peter then denied again: and immediately the cock crew.

The crowing of the rooster would have been a very penetrating sound, for, due to the mess they made, roosters were outlawed in the city of Jerusalem during the holy festivals. Thus, it was appropriate that Jesus would say, "You'll hear the cock crow, Peter, because you're going to mess up." But I suggest to you there's a bright side as well—for the crow of a rooster also signifies the dawn of a new day. Thus, it's as if Jesus said, "Yes, Peter, you've blown it. Yes, you've cursed and sworn and denied Me not once but thrice. But a new day is dawning. I'm not through with you—not by a long shot." Following His Resurrection, Jesus sought out Peter individually and specifically. He dealt with Peter in chapter 21 and commissioned him back into ministry. On the Day of Pentecost, it was Peter who stood up and preached the Word and three thousand were saved. Peter became the most prominent apostle in Jerusalem.

I tell you this because wherever Peter went, there were those who followed him around, crowing like roosters as a reminder of his failure. But they didn't stop Peter. He kept preaching. "Brethren," Paul would later write, "if any of you be overtaken in a fault, you who are spiritual restore such a one" (Galatians 6:1). Notice Paul didn't say, "remind," "rebuke," or "reveal." He said, "*restore*." We ought to always be looking for opportunities to see men and women continue on, to be restored, to not be held back because of a failure. Aren't you glad our God is the God of the second chance—and the tenth chance, and the eight hundred eightieth chance? I am.

John 18:28
Then led they Jesus from Caiaphas unto the hall of judgment: and it was early; and they themselves went not into the judgment hall, lest they should be defiled; but that they might eat the passover.

Here they are, about to kill the Son of God, yet worrying about defiling themselves by stepping on Gentile territory. Jesus said it's crazy how people will strain at gnats but swallow camels (Matthew 23:24). And yet we do the same thing in religious circles. We are so careful about certain issues, but we risk missing the big picture altogether.

John 18:29
Pilate then went out unto them, and said, What accusation bring ye against this man?

When Herod the Great died, his three sons became Tetrarchs, ruling over Israel. So lousy a ruler was Herod Archelaus, however, that the Jews appealed to Rome to send someone else to reign in his place. Rome answered with Pontius Pilate—a former slave who, through marriage and political maneuvering, became a Procurator, or overseer. The first time he came to Jerusalem, Pilate made a big mistake by bringing with him soldiers carrying busts of the emperor. As they approached the temple area with what the Jews considered to be idols, a riot broke out, and blood was shed. Rome sent a warning to Pilate, saying,

"Get it together. We don't want this kind of ruckus." Thinking he could appease the people by building them an aqueduct, Pilate diverted funds from the temple treasury to finance the project. The Jews were infuriated. Rome heard about it and issued yet another warning: "You have two strikes against you, Pontius. One more and you're out." So Pilate, already on the political hot seat, goes out to survey the situation.

John 18:30, 31 (a)
They answered and said unto him, If he were not a malefactor, we would not have delivered him up unto thee. Then said Pilate unto them, Take ye him, and judge him according to your law.

Hoping to ward off yet another outburst, Pilate puts the ball back in the court of the religious leaders.

John 18:31 (b)
The Jews therefore said unto him, It is not lawful for us to put any man to death.

In the year A.D. 30—two years prior to these events—the Romans took away the Jewish right of capital punishment. In response, the rabbis ripped their clothes, donned sackcloth, threw dirt on their heads, and said, "God has failed us. God has failed us," as they marched through the streets of Jerusalem. Why did they cry, "God has failed us"? Because in the Book of Genesis, the promise was given that the scepter would not depart from Judah until Messiah came (49:10). But the basic foundation of government was the ability to deal with lawbreakers, so the scepter had, indeed, departed—with Messiah seemingly nowhere in sight. Oh, but Messiah *was* there—right in their midst. They just didn't recognize Him.

John 18:32–34
That the saying of Jesus might be fulfilled, which he spake, signifying what death he should die. Then Pilate entered into the judgment hall again, and called Jesus, and said unto him, Art thou the King of the Jews? Jesus answered him, Sayest thou this thing of thyself, or did others tell it thee of me?

"Do you really want to know?" asked Jesus. As we have all discovered, a lot of times people ask questions without really wanting to know the answer. They just want to argue. You would be wise to learn whether people are asking for answers or asking to argue. If they're asking to argue, don't cast your pearls before swine. That way, you'll avoid endless hours of argumentation that will get you nowhere.

John 18:35–37 (a)
Pilate answered, Am I a Jew? Thine own nation and the chief priests have delivered thee unto me: what hast thou done? Jesus answered, My kingdom is not of this world: if my kingdom were of this world, then would my servants fight, that I should not be delivered to the Jews: but now is my kingdom not from hence. Pilate therefore said unto him, Art thou a king then? Jesus answered, Thou sayest that I am a king.

In other words, Jesus said, "You're right, Pilate."

John 18:37 (b)
To this end was I born, and for this cause came I into the world, that I should bear witness unto the truth. Every one that is of the truth heareth my voice.

No matter where they live, no matter when they live, every person who wants to know the truth will hear God's voice. "God's not fair in choosing some and not choosing others," some protest. Not true. Jesus said *every* one who wants to know the truth will hear His voice.

John 18:38 (a)
Pilate saith unto him, What is truth? And when he had said this, he went out again unto the Jews . . .Notice that Pilate asks, "What is truth?"—but doesn't even stick around to hear the answer. How many of our prayers are like that?

John 18:38 (b)
. . . and saith unto them, I find in him no fault at all.

Finding Jesus faultless, Pilate yet hopes to appease the crowd . . .

John 18:39, 40
But ye have a custom, that I should release unto you one at the passover: will ye therefore that I release unto you the King of the Jews? Then cried they all again, saying, Not this man, but Barabbas. Now Barabbas was a robber.

"Barabbas" means "son of the father." History tells us that his first name was Jesus. "Who do you want released," asked Pilate, "Jesus Bar-Abbas—Jesus, son of the father—or Jesus the Christ?" Barabbas will be set free because Jesus would go to the Cross in his place. And Jesus went to the Cross in my place as well.

We're all a bunch of sinners, gang. But the good news is that Jesus Christ truly went through all of this in our place. Therefore, there is no condemnation, no record kept of our sins or failures (Romans 8:1). This leaves us free to bask in God's grace and express our appreciation to the One who was bound with cords of love.

19 It has been rightly said that people are a lot like teabags—you never really know what their true flavor is until they get in hot water. In a political boiling pot, Pontius Pilate was determined to keep the peace at any price—even if it meant ignoring his own conscience. With the cries of, "Crucify Him! Crucify Him!" ringing in his ears, Pilate buckles under the pressure of the crowd, hoping that by subjecting Jesus to thirty-nine lashes with the flagellum—an ordeal in itself that killed many men—perhaps the crowd would be satisfied.

John 19:1–3
Then Pilate therefore took Jesus, and scourged him. And the soldiers platted a crown of thorns, and put it on his head, and they put on him a purple robe, And said, Hail, King of the Jews! and they smote him with their hands.

The scourging that took place was painful beyond our understanding. Prophesied by Isaiah in chapter 53, to the thinking student of Scripture, the question becomes, "If the crucifixion of Christ provided for our redemption and salvation, what was the purpose of the scourging?" Peter tells us in his epistle that by His stripes we are healed (1 Peter 2:24). Thus, while the Crucifixion provides for our redemption presently and eternally—it is the stripes Jesus bore and absorbed that actually release the grace of healing for our bodies physically.

John 19:4, 5
Pilate therefore went forth again, and saith unto them, Behold, I bring him forth to you, that ye may know that I find no fault in him. Then came Jesus forth, wearing the crown of thorns, and the purple robe. And Pilate saith unto them, Behold the man!

"Behold the man," or literally, "Here is a man." After having endured the bursting of blood vessels as He prayed in the Garden of Gethsemane, the beating in the courtyards of the high priest and Pontius Pilate, and the brutal blows of the flagellum, Jesus, as Isaiah prophesied, was marred beyond recognition (52:14).

We have heard this account so often, and we know it so well that it loses its punch oftentimes. We know Jesus was beaten. We know He was marred more than any man and eventually nailed to a tree. But I think it would do us well sometimes to take a long walk in the evening or get up early in the morning to consider what Jesus willingly went through with you on His mind and in His heart. We were on His mind. We were on His heart when He took those blows, felt that pain, and endured unspeakable suffering. It was all for me. It was all for you.

John 19:6
When the chief priests therefore and officers saw him, they cried out, saying, Crucify him, crucify him. Pilate saith unto them, Take ye him, and crucify him: for I find no fault in him.

The uniqueness of Jesus is verified by the fact that Pilate went on record, saying, "I find no fault in Him"—a finding that has never been disputed by historian or cynic. According to many historical records, Pilate himself committed suicide not long after this.

John 19:7
The Jews answered him, We have a law, and by our law he ought to die, because he made himself the Son of God.

"Jesus never claimed deity," the cultist insists. Take him to this passage and say, "The Jewish leaders understood very clearly His claim to deity. That is why they killed Him."

John 19:8–11
When Pilate therefore heard that saying, he was the more afraid; and went again into the judgment hall, and saith unto Jesus, Whence art thou? But Jesus gave him no answer. Then saith Pilate unto him, Speakest thou not unto me? knowest thou not that I have power to crucify thee, and have power to release thee? Jesus answered, Thou couldest have no power at all against me, except it were given thee from above: therefore he that delivered me unto thee hath the greater sin.

Pilate thought he was in a position of power, when in reality he was simply a pawn. God is always on the throne. Everything goes according to *His* plan.

John 19:12, 13
And from thenceforth Pilate sought to release him: but the Jews cried out, saying, If thou let this man go, thou art not Caesar's

friend: whosoever maketh himself a king speaketh against Caesar. When Pilate therefore heard that saying, he brought Jesus forth, and sat down in the judgment seat in a place that is called the Pavement, but in the Hebrew, Gabbatha.

As Pilate sits down in his judgment seat to make a decision, the irony is that he himself is being judged on the basis of his response to Jesus Christ. So, too, some of you will sit back and say, "I'm going to analyze, scrutinize, and evaluate Jesus Christ." In reality, however, you're not judging Him, but your reaction to Him is judging you because He is the King of kings regardless of what you decide. He's going to have His way whether you choose to get on board or not. Thus, the judgment seat you're occupying right now is that of your own judgment. And how you respond to Him will determine whether you go to heaven or spend eternity in hell.

John 19:14, 15
And it was the preparation of the passover, and about the sixth hour: and he saith unto the Jews, Behold your King! But they cried out, Away with him, away with him, crucify him. Pilate saith unto them, Shall I crucify your King? The chief priest answered, We have no king but Caesar.

Throughout history, the nation of Israel has undergone unparalleled pain and problems. Why? In 1 Samuel 8, we see the Jews rejecting the Father as they begged Samuel for a king to rule over them. Here in John 19, we see them refusing the Son as they cry, "We have no king but Caesar." Finally, in Acts 7, we see them resisting the Spirit, and stoning Stephen as a result. Rejecting the Father in the Old Testament, refusing the Son in the Gospels, and resisting the Spirit in the Book of Acts caused the collapse of the people of Israel. But God is faithful. The message of Romans 9–11 is that even though Israel has refused the Son, rejected the Father, and resisted the Spirit—God will keep His promises to her. And all of Israel shall be saved.

John 19:16, 17
Then delivered he him therefore unto them to be crucified. And they took Jesus, and led him away. And he bearing his cross went forth into a place called the place of a skull, which is called in the Hebrew Golgotha.

In Latin, "Golgotha" is "Calvary," or "The place of the skull."

John 19:18
**Where they crucified him, and two other with
him, on either side one, and Jesus in the
midst.**

Between two thieves is a fitting place for our
Lord to be positioned because He is the Ultimate
Thief. He's stolen my heart and wants to steal
yours.

John 19:19, 20
**And Pilate wrote a title, and put it on the
cross. And the writing was, JESUS OF NAZ-
ARETH THE KING OF THE JEWS. This
title then read many of the Jews: for the
place where Jesus was crucified was nigh to
the city: and it was written in Hebrew, and
Greek, and Latin.**

Hebrew was the theological language; Greek,
the intellectual language; and Latin, the political
language. Let those who view things theologically; let those who view things intellectually; let
those who view things politically know this: Jesus
is King.

John 19:21, 22
**Then said the chief priests of the Jews to
Pilate, Write not, The King of the Jews; but
that he said, I am King of the Jews. Pilate
answered, What I have written I have
written.**

Pilate at last shows a little courage when he
says, "What I've written stays."

John 19:23, 24
**Then the soldiers, when they had crucified
Jesus, took his garments, and made four
parts, to every soldier a part; and also his
coat: now the coat was without seam, woven
from the top throughout. They said therefore among themselves, Let us not rend it,
but cast lots for it, whose it shall be: that
the scripture might be fulfilled, which saith,
They parted my raiment among them, and
for my vesture they did cast lots. These
things therefore the soldiers did.**

According to Exodus 28, the high priest's robe
was to be made of one piece of material. Jesus being the great High Priest, His robe was seamless
as well. So here are the soldiers—playing games
on Golgotha, even as Jesus was dying for their
sins. Are we doing that? I wonder. Those in the
"Name It and Claim It" camp say, "I'll get some
nice clothes, a faster car, a bigger house on the
basis of the finished work of the Cross." This
ought not to be.

John 19:25, 26 (a)
**Now there stood by the cross of Jesus his
mother, and his mother's sister, Mary the
wife of Cleophas, and Mary Magdalene.
When Jesus therefore saw his mother, and
the disciple standing by, whom he loved . . .**

When Jesus was healing the sick, and feeding
the multitudes, He captivated people's attention.
Like metal filings to a magnet, the masses were
drawn to Him. But as His ministry progressed,
when His teaching became a little more intense,
the number of those who followed Him was reduced from thousands to seemingly hundreds.
Only seventy shared the gospel of the kingdom
(Luke 10:1). Only twelve left everything to follow
Him. And of the twelve only three would be with
Him on the Mount of Transfiguration, where He
spoke of His death and in the Garden of Gethsemane, where He prayed with such intensity.
And of the three, only one would be at the foot of
the Cross.

But there were four women there—although it
was not easy for them. It was not easy for Mary
to watch her Son convulsing in pain, or for her
sister to hear the curses hurled at Him. It was
not easy for the wife of Cleophas to see the spit
of the crowd running down His face, or for Mary
Magdalene to see His blood flowing from His
wounds. But these four women, lovers of the
Lord and followers of Him, were there at the foot
of the Cross, no matter how great the price, no
matter how deep the pain.

John 19:26 (b)
. . . he saith unto his mother, Woman . . .

Why would Jesus use the word *gune,* or "woman"—a term of great respect but not particularly affectionate? Perhaps because His use of
this term would cause Mary's mind to race back
to a point three years previously when, at the
very outset of His public ministry, He had used
this same term. "They have no wine," she had
said—perhaps hoping that her own reputation
would be salvaged when a thirsty wedding party
saw that her Son was who she had always said He
was.

"Woman, what have I to do with thee? My hour
is not yet come," Jesus had answered her (John
2:4). Jesus did, indeed, provide wine for the wedding. But no one knew about it except some lowly
slaves.

Yet here on the Cross, Mary's request is finally
answered, for it was at the Cross where even the
most cynical Roman centurion would look at Him
and say, "Truly, this must be the Son of God" (see
Matthew 27:54).

John 19:26 (c), 27 (a)
. . . behold thy son! Then saith he to the
disciple, Behold thy mother!

I find this fascinating in light of the fact that, as we know from Matthew 13:55, 56, Jesus had four half brothers and a bunch of sisters. Yet He bypassed the earthly bloodline and established a new family. And in so doing fulfilled the prophecy of Psalm 69:8: "I am become a stranger unto my brethren and an alien unto my mother's children." You see, at this point, Jesus' brothers didn't believe in Him. So He turned to one who did. Why John? No doubt it was partly because John was there—the only male disciple willing to jeopardize his life by taking a stand at the foot of the Cross. Yet perhaps it was only fitting that Jesus entrust the one whose breast had cradled Him to the one who had himself reclined on His own breast (John 13:25).

John 19:27 (b)
And from that hour that disciple took her
unto his own home.

A family is formed at the Cross because that's where true families are forged and held together.

For topical study of John 19:25–27 entitled "The Family Tree," turn to page 590.

John 19:28, 29
After this, Jesus knowing that all things were now accomplished, that the scripture might be fulfilled, saith, I thirst. Now there was set a vessel full of vinegar: and they filled a spunge with vinegar, and put it upon hyssop, and put it to his mouth.

"My God, My God, why hast thou forsaken Me?" cried Jesus—signifying to all in attendance that He was the fulfillment of Psalm 22. "Today you will be with Me in paradise," He said to the thief—setting the precedent for salvation by faith alone. "Behold thy mother," He said to John, thereby establishing a new order of family. Redemption and sanctification, justification and propitiation—questions of eternal import were being settled on the Cross. And yet Jesus also declared, "I thirst"—reminding us of the personal agony He endured through it all.

John 19:30
When Jesus therefore had received the vinegar, he said, It is finished: and he bowed his head, and gave up the ghost.

Mom and Dad, when your kids have questions—be it concerning resentment toward some other kid at school, bitterness about someone who hurt them, or rivalry in the family—the crux of the matter is always discerned at the foot of the Cross. No wonder that the Latin word *crux* means "cross."

"It is finished." This Greek phrase denotes such power that if Jesus' hands hadn't been nailed down, it would have been uttered with a clenched fist raised in the air. It was the phrase an artist would use when he put the last stroke on his paper; a writer when he put the last period in his book. It was the statement a businessman would make when a transaction was final; the pronouncement given concerning a lamb that passed inspection.

Every other religion and cult bases its teaching on what one must do. Only true New Testament Christianity bases a belief system not on what remains to be done, but on what He's already done. We can't do anything to get right with God or closer to God except to realize that it's all been done. And as we continue in our walk, we continue to say, "I'm coming to You, Father, expecting Your blessing and confident of Your grace not because of who I am, but because of what Your Son accomplished when He cried, "It is Finished."

John 19:31
The Jews therefore, because it was the preparation, that the bodies should not remain upon the cross on the sabbath day, (for that sabbath day was an high day,) besought Pilate that their legs might be broken, and that they might be taken away.

The next day was Passover, so the Jews didn't want the bodies left on the crosses. "Let us break their legs," the Jews said to Pilate, "and speed up death so we can move on with our holy convocation."

John 19:32–34
Then came the soldiers, and brake the legs of the first, and of the other which was crucified with him. But when they came to Jesus, and saw that he was dead already, they brake not his legs: But one of the soldiers with a spear pierced his side, and forthwith came there out blood and water.

Medical experts tell us that the outpouring of blood and water indicates that Jesus died literally of a ruptured heart, a broken heart. Blood and water are also the fluids of birth—for just as a bride was birthed from the side of the first Adam, so the church was birthed through the blood and water from the side of the last Adam.

John 19:35–37
And he that saw it bare record, and his record is true: and he knoweth that he saith true, that ye might believe. For these things were done, that the scripture should be fulfilled, A bone of him shall not be broken. And again another scripture saith, They shall look on him whom they pierced.

If you look at prophecies given and fulfilled in Jesus simply to prove that He is the fulfillment of those prophecies, you're missing a great deal. In this case, John takes four or five verses to make it clear that, just as prophesied, not a bone of Jesus was broken. Why is this so important? Because where is blood continually produced in the body? It's produced in the bone. Therefore, God mandated not a bone of His would be broken, ensuring a perpetual and inexhaustible supply of blood. That's why Paul could later declare, "Where sin abounds, grace abounds yet more," (Romans 5:20). Truly, the blood of Jesus Christ is sufficient to cleanse you from every sin you have ever committed or will commit because not a bone of His was broken.

John 19:38, 39
And after this Joseph of Arimathaea, being a disciple of Jesus, but secretly for fear of the Jews, besought Pilate that he might take away the body of Jesus: and Pilate gave him leave. He came therefore, and took the body of Jesus. And there came also Nicodemus, which at the first came to Jesus by night, and brought a mixture of myrrh and aloes, about an hundred pound weight.

Suddenly, Nicodemus and Joseph of Arimathaea, men who were once hesitant to be seen with Jesus, asked permission to take His body. Because the bodies of crucified victims were destined for a garbage heap, this request would ruin Joseph's business and jeopardize Nicodemus' religious standing. The way to motivate people to serve Christ is not to make them feel guilty, not to put pressure on them, not to try to manipulate their emotions—but simply to allow them, like Nicodemus and Joseph, to see what He did for them on the Cross.

John 19:40–42
Then took they the body of Jesus, and wound it in linen clothes with the spices, as the manner of the Jews is to bury. Now in the place where he was crucified there was a garden; and in the garden a new sepulchre, wherein was never man yet laid. There laid they Jesus therefore because of the Jews' preparation day; for the sepulchre was nigh at hand.

Joseph takes the body, wraps it in linen, and places it in a stone tomb with myrrh and spices—just as another Joseph, thirty-three years earlier, had taken the same body, wrapped Him in swaddling linen cloth, placed Him in a stone manger, and watched as He was presented with myrrh.

In Leviticus 16, it is prescribed that on one day each year—Yom Kippur, the Day of Atonement—the high priest was to trade his beautiful priestly robes for the simple linen robes worn by his fellow priests. And what did the high priest do on the Day of Atonement? He went through the veil into the Holy of Holies to sprinkle blood on the lid, or mercy seat, of the ark of the covenant—the two-foot-by-three foot box that held the Ten Commandments. If he were defiled, he would stay in that place as a dead man and would later have to be pulled out with a rope. But if he wasn't defiled, he would walk out into the courtyard of the temple to the jubilant cries of the people who knew they were forgiven for another year.

Here, our great High Priest, Jesus Christ, is inside the tomb. Would He emerge? Did the sacrifice work? Are we free? Only if He came out among the people as He had prophesied could there truly be celebration and could we know our sins are forgiven—not just for one year, but forever.

THE FAMILY TREE
A Topical Study of
John 19:25–27

Crucifixion was developed by the Persians, today called the Iranians, around the year 1000 B.C. Designed to be excruciatingly painful, its purpose was to bring a man such agony that not only would his body convulse physiologically, but he would be tormented psychologically to such an extent that he would blaspheme and curse the very life he lived. But because the Persians considered the ground of their country to be holy, they mandated that a crucified victim be elevated lest his cursing defile it. That is why when a man was crucified he was raised up usually three to four feet off the ground. When the Greeks took over the Persian Empire, they adopted crucifixion. And when the Romans came on the scene, they borrowed it from the Greeks.

Here in John 19, the Romans are ruling the world. And on a hill outside Jerusalem, we see Jesus being crucified on a tree. Yet even as His body was writhing in pain beyond anything we could possibly even begin to imagine, even as His body was bleeding, even as His muscles were twitching, Jesus our Lord had such clarity of thought and such a heart of love that in the midst of His misery, He was able to look down from the Cross and care for His mother.

"Woman," He said, "behold thy son." Then, looking at John, He said, "Behold thy mother,"—and in that single moment a family was birthed. Perhaps John took Mary into his house that very hour, sparing her from having to witness the most painful part of her Son's crucifixion.

As reported in newspapers and magazines, unmarried couples living together is growing in acceptability in our country even as divorce rates soar and the family unit breaks down. At the same time, surveys indicate that the divorce rate in the church is only about five percentage points behind the soaring divorce rate of the world. Whereas divorce in the church was virtually unheard of thirty years ago, it is now taking place at a dizzying rate. What's going on? I believe the vignette before us powerfully underscores the fact that Jesus did more to solve the problems of marriage and the family in two sentences than Christian books have done in two hundred thousand volumes, for it is here we see the true family tree: the Cross of Calvary.

Family Forms Around the Cross

When the soldier thrust his spear in Jesus' side, out came a mixture of blood and water. Every woman who has given birth knows blood and water are the fluids of birthing. The blood and water that flowed from the side of Jesus resulted in the birth of a bonding between John and Mary that was absolutely unbreakable until death separated them.

Why is it that you and I will do just about anything to keep our families together—from taking a family vacation to Hawaii, to playing Monopoly on Tuesdays or soccer together on Saturdays—yet when it comes to telling a father or mother, a husband or wife that bonding and binding take place only at the foot of the Cross, our response is usually, "But I was looking for something a little more practical"?

I'm a fool if I take my kids to basketball games, go on family vacations, and read every parenting book available, but don't take them to the one place where bonding and binding truly take place. Satan will let you do all kinds of good things if he can keep you away from the Cross of Calvary—for it is there alone, through prayer and humility, through remembering what Jesus did on our behalf, that true bonding begins.

Forgiveness Flows from the Cross

Think back to the soldier with the spear. As he withdrew the spear that had cut Jesus deeply, that had been thrust into His side callously, on the tip of the spear was the blood of the Lamb—a reminder that no matter how deep the wound, how callous the cut, the blood of the Lamb cleanses and covers. It's at Calvary—when a husband and wife drink of the cup and eat of the body together—that they can no longer foster petty bickering and unforgiving attitudes toward each other. It's at Calvary where cruelty between brothers and sisters ends, where wounds inflicted upon us by our own family are healed, where forgiveness flows freely.

If your home is a battlefield, you can watch Christian TV and listen to Christian radio by the hour—or you can choose to go to Calvary together and say, "Let's remember what He's done for us," as we eat together of His body. Many of you will choose to take the other route. You'll keep searching and struggling, trying this, that, and the other as you wonder what's wrong. But until you go to the Cross and pray together, you're fighting a losing battle. It's only at Calvary that forgiveness flows freely.

Fickleness Flees at the Cross

Jesus didn't say, "Woman, if you're into this, would you consider opening your heart to John and maybe begin a relationship and see if it works out? And if it does, John, would you consider perhaps trying to communicate your heart and talk with Mary?" No, with blood flowing freely, Jesus said, "This is the way it is. Woman, that's your son. John, there's your mother." Period. No discussion. No debate. No argument. It's a done deal.

What does the Lord say to you? He says the same thing. "Husband, wife, you're married. That's it. Divorce is not an option. Trial separations are not an option. Period." You will see your fickleness flee when you say, "Divorce is not a word that shall be uttered from my lips. It will not be spoken in this house. It is not an option." Precious people, there are only a few things in Scripture that God says He hates. And one of them is divorce. I don't care how tough it might be living with her because she's so cold to you, or how much you might want to split because he doesn't say nice things. If you really understood how God feels about divorce, you would *make* your marriage work.

I know there are many in this room who have been divorced, who have been deserted. Your husband or wife just walked out. Divorce was the last thing you desired. The Lord looks on you and at you with love. And if you continue to trust in Him, He will restore to you the years the locust has eaten (Joel 2:25). But if you willingly and rebelliously walk out on your family, the repercussions and scars will follow you all the days of your life. That's why a loving Father says, "I hate divorce" (see Malachi 2:16).

Any man who stands at the foot of the Cross, any woman who bows in front of the Tree, will find fickleness replaced with fortitude, and capriciousness with commitment as they are reminded of the One who gave His life for them.

Fuzziness Fades at the Cross

Not only were Salome's two sons in the apostolic band, but she herself was part of a group of women who followed the Lord and ministered to the practical needs of Jesus and His disciples. At one point, we see Salome begin to worship Jesus. But Scripture says she also "desired of Him" (see Matthew 20:20)—meaning she had a request for Him. How often that's a mistake I make. "I love You, Lord. Oh, and by the way, I have this request. . . ." How easily we fall into the subtle error of worshiping the Lord that we might "soften Him up" and then slip in our petition.

How much better it is to be like the wise men. They traveled a great distance, bringing gold, frankincense, and myrrh to a toddler, who, at that point, could do nothing for them. They didn't come for manipulation; they came for adoration. They didn't come to get something from Him; they came to give something to Him. They didn't come for what He could do; they came because of who He was.

Not so Salome. She worshiped Him and then asked, "Lord, could one of my sons be at Your right, the other at Your left when You come into Your kingdom?"

Perhaps gently shaking His head, Jesus answered, "You know not what you ask." At the time, Salome didn't understand His answer. But at the foot of the Cross, as she saw one man being crucified on Jesus' left, one man on His right, it must have all become so clear.

So, too, when, like Salome, you really see Jesus on the Cross, dying for you, you'll say, "If You loved me enough to die for me, I know I can trust You with my life completely. And if You say I don't know what I'm asking, I'm just going to leave it there and trust You."

Gang, the Lord always does what's best. Even if you don't see it immediately, you'll look back and see it eventually. But don't take my word for it. As Salome did, climb the hill to Calvary and see Jesus on the Cross. And as you look at the One dying for you, the fuzziness of your faith, the double-mindedness of your worship, God's Provision in the past and promise for the future will all come sharply into focus.

If He died for you then, don't you know He loves you now? If He paid that price for you then, can't you trust Him today? You know He's going to only do what's best for you and for your family. The Cross of Calvary proves it and experience will verify it.

20 John 20:1 (a)
The first day of the week cometh Mary Magdalene early, when it was yet dark, unto the sepulcher . . .

Mary Magdalene—the woman who was last at the Cross because she loved the Lord deeply—had been possessed by seven demons previously. But the Lord freed her, and from that time on, she followed Him with all of her heart. "I love them that love Me, and they that seek Me early shall find Me," declares the Lord (see Proverbs 8:17). How are your morning devotions? Mary Magdalene is going to be the first one to see the Resurrected Jesus simply because she was at the tomb early in the morning.

John 20:1 (b)–3
. . . and seeth the stone taken away from the sepulchre. Then she runneth, and cometh to Simon Peter, and to the other disciple, whom Jesus loved, and saith unto them, They have taken away the Lord out of the sepulchre, and we know not where they have laid him. Peter therefore went forth, and that other disciple, and came to the sepulchre.

Peter the Activist, John the Mystic; Peter Impulsive, John Contemplative travel together in the Book of Acts. Others, no doubt hearing of Peter's denial, looked down on Peter and distanced themselves from him. Not John. The "apostle of love" takes Peter into his home and into his heart—not knowing exactly how events would unfold. Praise the Lord for people like John, who, when folks flounder and falter, will take them in even before they know how the story's going to conclude.

John 20:4
So they ran both together: and the other disciple did outrun Peter, and came first to the sepulchre.

Nicknamed "The Giant" in church history, Peter was obviously a big man—and perhaps that's why John outran him. John was also younger. Called by Jesus when he was perhaps only seventeen years old, at this point, John was possibly only twenty.

John 20:5
And he stooping down, and looking in, saw the linen clothes lying; yet went he not in.

John looks into the tomb but doesn't rush in. Contemplators don't.

John 20:6, 7 (a)
Then cometh Simon Peter following him, and went into the sepulchre, and seeth the linen clothes lie, and the napkin, that was about his head, not lying with the linen clothes . . .

This proves to me conclusively the Shroud of Turin is not authentic. Think of the pictures you've seen of the shroud. They always show the imprint of the crucified victim from head to toe. Here, the Scripture record says there was a napkin—a separate piece of cloth around the head. Thus, the shroud does not meet this particular criterion.

John 20:7 (b)
. . . but wrapped together in a place by itself.

As is His custom—never in a hurry, never frustrated, but always moving at the right pace—the Prince of Peace folds the napkin carefully.

John 20:8
Then went in also that other disciple, which came first to the sepulchre, and he saw, and believed.

In verses 5, 6, and 8, the word "saw" or "see" is used. First, John came to the tomb and saw the linen clothes lying. The word translated "saw" is *blepo*, meaning, "to look at, to see visibly." In verse 6, Peter saw the linen clothes lie, and the word used is *theoreo*, meaning, "to study more carefully," and from which we get our word "theory." Finally, in verse 8, the word translated "saw" is *eido*, from which we get the word "idea"—or "I get it."

I find it interesting that most of the time our faith progresses according to this pattern. First you're exposed to some piece of information. You hear what the teacher is saying. Then you give it some more thought down the road. And finally comes that moment when you really get it. It's not just a concept theologically—but it becomes part of your life personally. But if you never hear the information, you'll never be able to embrace it. And that is why you'll never see the process unfold if you don't come to the place where you can investigate the claims of Christ. So keep in the Word, gang.

"But I'm not getting much out of it," you say.

You wait. Eventually, it will begin to stir something in your thinking, and finally it will become part of your being. Read your Bible. Stay in the Scriptures and see the process unfold for you even as it did for Peter and John.

John 20:9, 10
For as yet they knew not the scripture, that he must rise again from the dead. Then the disciples went away again unto their own home.

They went their way wondering. Oh, they were believers—but their belief is not yet full-blossomed or fully comprehended.

John 20:11, 12
But Mary stood without at the sepulchre weeping: and as she wept, she stooped down, and looked into the sepulchre, and seeth two angels in white sitting, the one at the head, and the other at the feet, where the body of Jesus had lain.

The two angels, the blood-spattered mercy seat, the linen garments—of course the picture is of the ark of the covenant.

John 20:13 (a)
And they say unto her, Woman, why weepest thou?

Mary didn't write a book entitled *I Saw Angels*—because when your passion is for the Person of Jesus Christ, you're not caught up in other things, no matter how spectacular or supernatural.

John 20:13 (b)
She saith unto them, Because they have taken away my Lord, and I know not where they have laid him.

I have the word "my" circled. "He's *my* Lord," Mary said. "He is all that matters to me."

John 20:14 (a)
And when she had thus said, she turned herself back . . .

Mary turned away from the angels. You and I would have stared at the angels, taken pictures of them, been all caught up in dialoguing with them. Not Mary. She was more concerned about what she thought was the dead corpse of Christ than the living presence of angels.

John 20:14 (b), 15 (a)
. . . and saw Jesus standing, and knew not that it was Jesus. Jesus saith unto her, Woman, why weepest thou? whom seekest

thou? She, supposing him to be the gardener . . .

Jesus comes through the unexpected person at the unexpected time in the unexpected place. The Lord will come to you through a brother or sister, through a family member or friend. But so often, like Mary's, our eyes are so filled with tears that we don't even recognize it's the Lord speaking to us.

John 20:15 (b)
. . . saith unto him, Sir, if thou have borne him hence, tell me where thou hast laid him, and I will take him away.

"I will carry Him back," said Mary because love bears all things (see 1 Corinthians 13:7).

John 20:16 (a)
Jesus saith unto her, Mary.

Something in the way Jesus said her name caused Mary to recognize His voice (John 10:4).

John 20:16 (b), 17 (a)
She turned herself, and saith unto him, Rabboni; which is to say, Master. Jesus saith unto her, Touch me not; for I am not yet ascended to my Father . . .

"Don't cling to Me in the way you knew Me previously as a Teacher, a Rabbi, or a miracle Worker. I came to restore you to the Father eternally. And I am working on that restoration presently."

For topical study of John 20:17 entitled "Finding Fulfillment in the Father," turn to page 597.

John 20:17 (b)
. . . but go to my brethren . . .

Earlier, Jesus said to His disciples, "I call you not servants, but friends" (John 15:15). Here, He takes it a step further. He calls them brothers. The Book of Hebrews says He is not ashamed to call *us* brothers as well (2:11). Amazing.

John 20:17 (c)
. . . and say unto them, I ascend unto my Father, and your Father; and to my God, and your God.

"It is better that the words of the law be burned than to be entrusted to a woman," taught the Rabbis. So what does Jesus do? He gives the gospel to a woman. Mary's love for the Lord qualified her to be the first missionary with the full story.

John 20:18, 19
Mary Magdalene came and told the disciples that she had seen the Lord, and that he had spoken these things unto her. Then the same day at evening, being the first day of the week, when the doors were shut where the disciples were assembled for fear of the Jews, came Jesus and stood in the midst, and saith unto them, Peace be unto you.

Here are the disciples, with questions mounting and confusion rising like waves on the sea—when suddenly, just as before, Jesus comes to them and stills their storm with one word: Shalom. His first word is, "Peace." He doesn't say, "You guys are busted. Where have you been? I'm on the Cross and you're running around, pretending like you don't even know Me. What's the big idea?" No, that's not what Jesus does. He comes to them and says, "Peace." And that's what He says to you (Romans 5:1).

John 20:20
And when he had so said, he shewed unto them his hands and his side. Then were the disciples glad, when they saw the Lord.

No wonder the disciples were glad when they saw the Lord. If someone died, Jesus could bring him back to life with a simple word. Hungry? A few loaves could feed thousands. His provision was abundant; His presence, a delight.

John 20:21, 22
Then said Jesus to them again, Peace be unto you: as my Father hath sent me, even so send I you. And when he had said this, he breathed on them, and saith unto them, Receive ye the Holy Ghost.

At this point, the disciples are born again. Although they were already following Jesus, they were not yet regenerated because He had not yet died for their sins. But here Jesus breathes on them—reminiscent of Genesis 2:7, when God breathed life into Adam's nostrils and he became a living soul.

John 20:23
Whose soever sins ye remit, they are remitted unto them; and whose soever sins ye retain, they are retained.

In Mark 2, when Jesus pronounced forgiveness to a paralyzed man, the Pharisees were aghast. "Only God has the right to forgive sin," they said (see verse 7). And they were right. What, then, does this verse mean? It means we as His ambassadors don't provide forgiveness, but we do proclaim it. Therefore, to the one who says, "I don't feel forgiven," it is our responsibility to say, "According to the Word of God, if you open your heart to Jesus Christ and believe in His work on the Cross, your sin is gone." Conversely, to the one who says, "I don't need Jesus Christ. I'm into meditation,"—it is our responsibility to say, "Your sin remains because only the blood of Jesus can wash it away."

John 20:24
But Thomas, one of the twelve, called Didymus, was not with them when Jesus came.

I suppose one of the saddest things I see as a pastor are disciples who miss the meeting. They're out there struggling, while at a Sunday evening service, for example, at some point Jesus begins to appear through the Word or in worship, through prophecy or the washing of feet. "I can worship at home," they say. But Jesus didn't go to Thomas's house. He went where the saints were meeting together. "Don't forsake assembling together," Paul would say (see Hebrews 10:25)—because Jesus shows up in the midst of the congregation.

Thomas missed the meeting. Why? He's been called Doubting Thomas throughout history—but keep in mind the kind of guy he was. When Jesus announced He was going to Jerusalem, Thomas said, "Let's go and die with Him" (see John 11:16). Thomas was a guy who went for it. And so now, while the other disciples huddled together behind closed doors, where was Thomas? I suggest he was out on the street saying, "I'm not hiding. I'm out here in public. Anybody want to take me on?"

After catching a cargo ship to India to preach Jesus Christ, Thomas was warned to be quiet. When he kept preaching, his opponents ran a spear through his back. But the church he started in India still flourishes today.

John 20:25 (a)
The other disciples therefore said unto him, We have seen the Lord.

Galatians 6:1 tells those who are spiritual to restore those who are overtaken in faults. That's what's happening here. These guys are reaching out to their brother Thomas.

John 20:25 (b)
But he said unto them, Except I shall see in his hands the print of the nails, and put my finger into the print of the nails, and thrust my hand into his side, I will not believe.

Thomas was loyal but he lacked imagination. That is, he didn't know that Jesus specializes in taking that which was dead and bringing it to life. Maybe you've had shattered expectations in marriage, business, or family, and, like Thomas, you're not going to dream anymore. Don't give up, for Jesus "is able to do exceeding abundantly above all you can ask or even think" (see Ephesians 3:20).

John 20:26 (a)
And after eight days again his disciples were within, and Thomas with them . . .

I suggest the disciples said, "Thomas, we're meeting again next week, and you'd better be there. In fact, we're bringing you with us."

John 20:26 (b), 27
. . . then came Jesus, the doors being shut, and stood in the midst, and said, Peace be unto you. Then saith he to Thomas, Reach hither thy finger, and behold my hands; and reach hither thy hand, and thrust it into my side: and be not faithless, but believing.

Here Jesus is teaching a lesson of great import, for in repeating Thomas's ultimatum, it's as if He's saying, "Boys, even though you don't see Me, I'm with you always."

John 20:28
And Thomas answered and said unto him, My Lord and my God.

When Peter went into the house of Cornelius, Cornelius fell at his feet. "Stand up," said Peter. "I'm a man also" (see Acts 10:26). When the people of Lystra started worshiping Paul and Barnabas, Paul and Barnabas ripped their clothes and said, "Stop. We are men of like passions" (see Acts 14:15). When John fell down before an angel, the angel said, "Don't do that" (see Revelation 22:9). Paul, Peter, and the angel all refused to be worshiped. Regardless of what the cults say, Jesus accepted this proclamation of deity for one reason: He is God.

John 20:29
Jesus saith unto him, Thomas, because thou hast seen me, thou hast believed: blessed are they that have not seen, and yet have believed.

"Thomas, you believe because you've seen," said Jesus. "But blessed, happy are those with an imagination, with vision, with faith to see what is not physically visible." Faith sees what the man who lacks faith never does. It's a whole different dimension and an entirely different perspective.

John 20:30, 31
And many other signs truly did Jesus in the presence of his disciples, which are not written in this book: But these are written, that ye might believe that Jesus is the Christ, the Son of God; and that believing ye might have life through his name.

Other signs were done, but they were done to help people rather than to produce belief. What we have before us are the stories, the miracles, the work Jesus did, recorded for you and me that we might truly believe and go on believing in Him.

FINDING FULFILLMENT IN THE FATHER

A Topical Study of
John 20:17

No doubt her eyes would often flame like fire—not unlike the look in the eyes of Charles Manson when he was apprehended. Other times, her eyes must have been dark, dull, and dead. You see, according to Dr. Luke, Mary Magdalene had previously been possessed by seven devils (8:2). But when she encountered

Jesus, she was freed from the demons that had dominated her. No wonder that from that point on, she loved Him deeply and followed Him radically. Tradition says Mary is the woman spoken of not only in Luke 8, but also in Luke 7. You know the story. A Pharisee named Simon invited Jesus to his house for dinner. And as he sat at the head of the table with the other Pharisees listening to Jesus, skeptical about Jesus, a woman burst into the room and wept. The tears streaming down her face hit Jesus' feet. And with her hair previously used to entice men, she wiped the feet of the Son of Man. Observing the scene, Simon thought, *If this man were truly a prophet, He would have known what kind of woman this is.*

Knowing Simon's thoughts, Jesus said, "Simon, there were two men in debt to a creditor. One man owed five thousand dollars, the other owed five hundred dollars. But out of the goodness of his heart, the creditor said to both men, "Your debt is forgiven." Which of these two debtors would love the creditor more?"

"The one who was forgiven the larger amount," answered Simon.

"You have said well, Simon," was Jesus' gracious reply, "for the one who is forgiven much loves much. Notice, Simon," He continued, "I came into your house, and you didn't greet Me with a kiss; you didn't anoint My feet with oil; you didn't welcome Me lovingly. But this woman has not stopped kissing My feet, washing them with her tears, and wiping them with her hair."

You see, Jesus knew what kind of woman Mary was all along. Love is not blind—it just sees more. And because love sees more, it chooses to see less. Maybe you feel like a terrible sinner today. The good news is that you have the potential, the possibility of loving God greatly. If you don't feel like you're a sinner today, you can join Simon the Pharisee and love a little bit. But if you are aware of your sin, your failures, and your shortcomings, you have the potential to be a lover of God and a lover of people in the biggest sense of the word. The one who is forgiven little—the one who is unaware of his sins—loves little. That's why many church people are not lovers of God. They fail to see their need for forgiveness. But people like you and me *know* God's great grace and mercy because we experience it daily.

And now Mary is at the tomb. The last one at the Cross was the first one at the tomb. That's what love does. It stays the longest. It bears all things and believes all things. It endures all things and hopes all things. It's the last one at the Cross and the first one at the tomb. And when she gets there, her eyes swollen from crying, she stoops down to look inside. But when she sees the body is gone, her tears begin again. "Woman, why are you weeping?" asked the angels in attendance.

"Because they've taken away my Lord," Mary answered. And turning away from the angels, she saw Jesus. But she didn't know it was Him. Why? I suspect it was because her eyes were full of tears. Supposing Him to be the gardener, she said, "If you've moved the body for some reason, let me know where you've moved Him, and I will return Him to the tomb."

Think about this. As a woman, Mary would have been significantly smaller than Jesus. Yet Mary doesn't say, "You bring Him back," nor even, "Help me carry Him back." She just says, "*I'll* carry Him"—because love doesn't take into account the heaviness of its object. It pays the price. It expends the energy. It finds a way. At that point, Jesus uttered her name, and recognizing His voice, Mary fell at His feet. The picture is wonderful, for if she was indeed the same woman of Luke 7, even as she fell at His feet previously—washing His feet with her tears and drying them with her hair—she falls at His feet again as she clings to Him.

"Don't cling to Me, Mary," was Jesus' response, "because I have not yet ascended." At first reading, this sounds harsh. Yet there's an important lesson here, for Jesus is saying, "Mary, My mission was to come to earth to die for your sins. The purpose of My coming was to provide reconciliation so that you and all who believe could be reconciled to the Father and have relationship with *Him.* Don't cling to Me."

Ours is a generation of "cling-ons." Books, seminars, retreats about this subject abound. A wife will cling to her husband, hoping she might find fulfillment in him. And the tighter she clings to him, the more he backs away. So she clings harder—and he backs away further. Or the husband clings to his wife, hoping to find satisfaction in her. But feeling used and smothered, she backs away. Husbands and wives say, "If you're not going to fulfill me, I'll find someone who will; if you're not going to satisfy me, I'll find someone who can." It happens over and over again. We cling—but never find what we want. Inevitably, the results are divorce, depression, and destruction. Not even children are exempt. "If you don't meet the needs of your daughter," say the best-selling books, "she'll try to fill them in someone else." And so we think we've got to make sure our kids cling to us and receive from us—otherwise who knows what will happen to them.

But Jesus comes in an entirely different manner to this sister of His, saying, "Don't cling to Me. You've got to see the big picture. It's called reconciliation between you and the Father. That's why I came—to die for your sins, to pay the price for your iniquity, so that you won't have to cling to your husband or wife, your pastor or the church."

Who clings to the pastor, the boss, or a so-called lover on the side? People who are insecure. And the reason they are insecure is because they don't understand that what they really need is, like Adam and Eve, to walk with God in the cool of the day. You see, any of you who say, "This afternoon I'm going to put down the paper. I'm going to turn off the TV. I'm not going to cling to my husband or wife. I'm going to go for a walk. I'm going to talk to my Father; I'm going to tell Him the things that are troubling me, laugh with Him about a sight we might see, look at the sky in its beauty"—will come back with a sparkle in your eye, and a peace in your heart. You won't cling to the first person you see, suffocate those around you, or be disappointed in those you love.

The most secure Being in the entire universe is God. God doesn't need you. He loves you, but He doesn't need you. He likes you, but He doesn't need you. God got by for billions and trillions and zillions of years without us—totally content because the Father, Son, and Spirit fulfilled one another and loved one another. But part of God's plan was to show another side of His character—grace and mercy—to the entire universe. To do that required sinners like you and me.

There are those who teach God needs you. No, He doesn't. I'll find in God strength, joy, and love—but He doesn't smother me. And He won't smother you.

The real issue, gang, is a lack of spending time with the Father, because a person who spends time with the Father will not have dependent characteristics and fifteen steps to work through to begin recovery. When you get rid of the clinging, relationships take on maturity, depth, and solidity. But it doesn't happen by psychology or twelve-stepping your way out. It comes by doing one thing: walking with the Father. That's where you find security.

We need to care and to share. We need to interact with one another. But we mustn't cling because the sad thing about clinging is that it drives people away. And the more they back away, the more we want to cling. It's a cycle that can only be broken by spending time with the Father. But you can't talk to the Father, walk with the Father, or receive security from the Father until you realize what Jesus Christ did for you on the Cross.

And all things are of God, who hath reconciled us to himself by Jesus Christ . . .
2 Corinthians 5:18 (a)

God is holy and beautiful. But because of our sin, we couldn't relate to Him or be one with Him. So Jesus Christ came to bridge the gap, to die for our sin that we might be forgiven and fellowship with the Father anytime we want.

. . . and hath given to us the ministry of reconciliation.   2 Corinthians 5:18 (b)

Not only can we come freely to the Father because we have been reconciled to Him through Jesus Christ, but we are to reconcile others to the Father as well. Mom and Dad, your ministry is not to reconcile your kids to you—to get them to depend on you or to look to you. Your ministry ultimately is to reconcile your kids to the Father. If you say, "I'm going to meet their needs. I'm always going to be there for them," they'll rebel because you'll eventually let them down. But if you are a minister of reconciliation, you'll say, "I want my kids to grow up knowing God. I know I have failings and shortcomings as a dad, but the heavenly Father will never let them down. Never. Therefore, I don't care what they think about me as much as I care about them being one with God."

When my daughter says, "Dad, I need thirty bucks," sometimes I give it to her. But other times I say, "Would you pray about it? Would you see what doors God opens for you?" It is far easier for me to open my checkbook. But it's infinitely more important for my kids to learn not to cling to me because I won't always be there for them. Therefore, I want them to learn to pray, to walk with God, to know the Lord.

I have been given the ministry of reconciliation—and so have you. "Don't cling to Me," Jesus lovingly says to Mary. "I go to the Father." May God give us this understanding as well.

---

21 We come to the epilogue of John's Gospel, the final chapter in this glorious study presenting Jesus Christ as the Son of God. To many people, the epilogue seems as though it's been tacked on—for in chapter 20, concluding with the Resurrection of Jesus Christ, John signs off by saying, "These things were written that you might believe that Jesus is the Christ, the Son of God, and believing you might have life through His name"—a seemingly logical conclusion to his Gospel presentation. Yet John goes on to tell one more story. Why? A couple of possible reasons . . .

John 21 provides validation of ministry. You see, although Peter and John would go on to travel together in ministry, there would be those who would question Peter's ministry due to his denial of the Lord previously. John seems to write this epilogue, including this final story, to let us know that our God being the God of the second chance, Peter's ministry was particularly and singularly commissioned by the Lord. Secondly, John 21 provides a correction of a misunderstanding. That is, word had gone out through the early church that John wouldn't die before the Lord's return. We'll see John address this issue toward the end of the chapter.

John 21:1
After these things Jesus shewed himself again to the disciples at the sea of Tiberias; and on this wise shewed he himself.

Jesus showed Himself again. I really like that because my desire is that Jesus would show Himself again to me, to you, and to the church. Robert W. Gale, a famous Congregational minister with numerous degrees, was preparing an Easter message. Hundreds of people would hear this particular address, thus he worked very hard on polishing it. He had a historical faith, but he later said that on that night before Easter Sunday, his historical faith became "hysterical faith" as he realized the Lord is

truly alive. I hope you have hysterical faith. Historical faith says, "Christ lives." But hysterical, radical faith says, "Christ lives *in me*" (see Galatians 2:20).

John 21:2 (a)
There were together Simon Peter, and Thomas called Didymus, and Nathanael of Cana in Galilee, and the sons of Zebedee . . .

Seven of the twelve disciples were fishermen. I find it interesting that Jesus seemed to be inclined toward choosing fishermen to be His disciples. Fishermen by nature must know how to persevere through both calm seas and stormy weather. The same is true of ministry. If you want to serve the Lord, you must learn to serve Him, as Paul would tell Timothy, "in season and out of season" (2 Timothy 4:2). Whether the sun is shining or the trials abounding, we must be like fishermen, who, regardless of the weather, make their way to the sea. Working in teams, fishermen were those who could take commands. One would tell the other where to cast the net and when to draw it in. Certainly those of us who want to be used by the Lord must be those who work as a team and take commands easily. Perhaps more than any other occupation, any other endeavor, fishing requires patience. So, too, those who minister for the Lord must be those who are exceedingly patient as they wait for the haul to come in.

John 21:2 (b)
. . . and two other of his disciples.

Two of the disciples in the boat are unnamed. Why? I suggest it allows you and me to take our place with these disobedient renegades, for we too have found ourselves going fishing when we should have been on the mountain. You see, in Matthew 28, we read that the Lord specifically told His disciples to meet Him in Galilee at a mountain He had appointed. But where did these disciples go? To the beach. Thus, maybe your name fits as one of these unnamed disciples. Mine certainly does as the other.

John 21:3
Simon Peter saith unto them, I go a fishing. They say unto him, We also go with thee.

The problem with going off on our own excursions is that others are affected by our little detours, our disobedient side trips. Jesus warned us about setting our hand to the plow and looking back (Luke 9:62). "Forgetting that which lies behind, I press on," declared Paul (see Philippians 3:13). But Peter here is looking back—and looking back will paralyze. Ask Lot's wife.

John 21:3 (b)
They went forth, and entered into a ship immediately; and that night . . .

It's not surprising that the disciples entered the ship at night because it's always dark when you say, "I wonder if I should go back to the old gang, to the old ways, to the old spots." Truly, whenever you go back, it's *always* dark.

John 21:3 (c)
. . . they caught nothing.

Isn't this what we've found when we've gone back? When you go back, it's just not there. It just doesn't work any longer. You come up empty.

John 21:4 (a)
But when the morning was now come, Jesus stood on the shore . . .

Daylight was breaking for the Dayspring was observing (Luke 1:78).

John 21:4 (b), 5 (a)
. . . but the disciples knew not that it was Jesus. Then Jesus saith unto them, Children, have ye any meat?

"Backsliders!" Nope. "Rebels!" Nope. "Ex-Apostles! Former Disciples!" Nope. Jesus calls these disobedient disciples His kids.

John 21:5 (b)
They answered him, No.

Here is where a true miracle takes place. When asked if they had caught anything, these fishermen answer, "No." Fishermen always say, "The nibbles have been fabulous," or "You should have seen the one that got away." But there comes a point in life when you go back and realize it stinks, that there's nothing there. It sounded so good as you reminisced about the wind blowing your hair and the smell of fish in the air; the rocking of the boat and being with the boys. It sounded so good when you thought about it, but when you actually got there, it wasn't the way you thought it would be. Satan has the ability to remind us of the kicks of the old ways. But what he fails to bring to mind are the kickbacks that inevitably follow.

John 21:6 (a)
And he said unto them, Cast the net on the right side of the ship, and ye shall find.

Why the right side? Because whatever Jesus says is always right.

John 21:6 (b)
They cast therefore, and now they were not able to draw it for the multitude of fishes.

Think about this, you who have been toiling, working, wondering when it's going to happen. Success for these disciples was only a boat's width away. Three, perhaps four, feet from one side of the boat to the other—that's how close they were to success in this fishing endeavor. And you might be just three or four feet away from seeing success happen in your life, in your ministry, in your occupation. How do you move the three or four feet that make all the difference?

"Mr. Getty," asked an eager young man, "what's the secret of success?"
"It's very simple," answered the billionaire. "Rise early, work late . . . and strike oil."
How do you strike oil?

How do you find success? You do what Jesus says. Listen to what He's telling you in your heart. Perhaps He's been dealing with you, speaking to you about a certain issue, but you've thought His direction doesn't relate to the challenge you face or the endeavor you've undertaken. The disciples could have said, "We've been fishing all night. We're experts. What do three feet have to do with anything?" But when they did what He said, they were immediately on the right side.

So, too, you might be very close to success in the best sense of the word. All you have to do is decide to obey what Jesus has told you in your heart. It's not mystical. It's not difficult. It's just a matter of saying, "You've been telling me in my heart that I am to do a certain thing, Lord. And I now purpose to do it."

John 21:7 (a)
Therefore that disciple whom Jesus loved saith unto Peter, It is the Lord.

There's the contemplator, the mystic, John.

John 21:7 (b)
Now when Simon Peter heard that it was the Lord, he girt his fisher's coat unto him, (for he was naked,) and did cast himself into the sea.

Literally "stripped for work" to his undergarments, Peter grabs his coat and dives in. That's the doer, the activist, Peter.

John 21:8, 9
And the other disciples came in a little ship; (for they were not far from land, but as it were two hundred cubits,) dragging the net with fishes. As soon then as they were come to land, they saw a fire of coals there, and fish laid thereon, and bread.

All night long the disciples had been looking for fish—when all the while, Jesus had it right at hand, freshly grilled, ready to eat. Haven't you discovered this to be so? Haven't you discovered over and over again when you go off on your little excursions, that when you come back to the Lord you find in Him what you longed for all along?

John 21:10, 11 (a)
Jesus saith unto them, Bring of the fish which ye have now caught. Simon Peter went up, and drew the net to land full of great fishes . . .

In verse 6, the disciples were not able to lift the net. Yet the same word is used here in verse 11 to say that Peter himself was able to draw it. In other words, in drawing the net, Peter did single-handedly what the group could not do collectively. How? There is only one explanation: because the command of the Lord was given. Thus, what the disciples couldn't do in their own strength, Peter could do by himself simply because the Lord had said, "Bring the fish." The Word God speaks is the very source of power to do what He asks.

John 21:11 (b)
. . . and hundred and fifty and three: and for all there were so many, yet was not the net broken.

Why do you suppose the number of fish is recorded? And why are we told the net was not broken? Earlier, in a similar miracle, Luke says when they took in a miraculous haul, the net broke (5:6). This speaks of evangelism. In the amphitheatre at Applegate Christian Fellowship or in crusades, the gospel is preached and a haul is taken in, but not all who respond will continue on. In the parable of the soils, only one in four goes on to bear abundant fruit (Matthew 13). Consequently, when sixty or eighty people are baptized on a Sunday morning at Applegate, not every one is going to go on and bring forth fruit abundantly. But of those who are truly in the kingdom, of those who are brought to shore, not one will be lost. Each one will be accounted for exactly. Thus, as this scenario unfolds, Jesus shows Peter and John that they are not only fishers of men, but tenders of sheep.

In the arena of evangelism, we cannot deal with statistics because we can't see men's hearts. But in the shepherding ministry—in pastoring, discipling, or parenting—we must account for every sheep. We must be aware of the brother or sister in need of tending, of touch, of care. Whose job is this? Each of ours. Those of us who love the Lord have the joint responsibility of saying, "Where is #151? I gotta go find him." And here Jesus makes a transfer in Peter's thinking, showing him he is to be not only a fisher of men evangelistically, but a tender of sheep pastorally.

John 21:12 (a)
Jesus saith unto them, Come and dine.

"Come and see," Jesus said in John 1.
"Come and drink," He said in John 7.
"Come and dine," He says in John 21.

John 21:12 (b), 13
And none of the disciples durst ask him, Who art thou? knowing that it was the Lord. Jesus then cometh, and taketh bread, and giveth them, and fish likewise.

A meal of fish and loaves—does that ring a bell? (Matthew 15:36).

John 21:14, 15 (a)
This is now the third time that Jesus shewed himself to his disciples, after that he was risen from the dead. So when they had dined . . .

It wasn't until after Peter was fed that Jesus talked to him about feeding others. Gang, if you're not being fed, don't attempt to feed others, because what you give out will not be nutritious. It'll be junk food, hollow calories. If, however, you are being fed, make sure you feed others—because if you just keep getting fed and don't feed others, you'll become spiritually bloated and lethargic.

John 21:15 (b)
. . . Jesus saith to Simon Peter, Simon, son of Jonas, lovest thou me more than these?

To what does the word "these" refer? Perhaps Jesus was pointing to the disciples. "Lord, if they all fail you, I never will," Peter had said earlier. Perhaps Jesus was pointing to the one hundred fifty -three fish, thereby saying, "Do you love Me more than fishing, Peter?" Perhaps it was in reference to the boats. "Do you love Me more than your occupation—or is work your highest priority?"

"Do you love Me more than these disciples, more than those fish, more than that boat? Do you *love* Me, Peter?" The word Jesus uses is *agapao*—the highest kind of love. "I've fed you; I've shown grace to you; I'm reaching out toward you," said Jesus. "Do you love Me with a perfect kind of love?"

John 21:15 (c)
He saith unto him, Yea, Lord; thou knowest that I love thee.

There are four words in Greek for love. *Storge* is the affection one feels for a puppy. *Eros* is a sexual kind of love. *Phileo* is brotherly love. *Agape* love gives for the sake of giving, never expecting anything in return. Here, Peter uses *phileo*.

John 21:15 (d)
He saith unto him, Feed my lambs.

"A good place for you to start, Peter, in this restorative process is to feed lambs." Want to be a good minister, a good teacher, a good communicator? The best training you'll ever get is with children because they won't snow you. If you're boring, they won't look at you and nod politely. If you're not communicating, if you're not connecting, you'll know it. Children force you to define your terms. They don't let you hide behind big words. Maybe you feel like you've been on a fishing excursion. Get involved in kids' ministries. Feed the lambs. It's a privilege and the finest preparation you'll ever have.

John 21:16
He saith to him again the second time, Simon, son of Jonas, lovest thou me? He saith unto him, Yea, Lord; thou knowest that I love thee. He saith unto him, Feed my sheep.

The Greek word translated "feed" is *poimaino*, which means "to tend, or to shepherd." "Feed my lambs, Peter, but also care for them," Jesus instructed.

John 21:17 (a)
He saith unto him the third time, Simon, son of Jonas, lovest thou me?

This time Jesus uses the word *phileo*.

John 21:17 (b)
Peter was grieved because he said unto him the third time, Lovest thou me? And he said unto him, Lord, thou knowest all things; thou knowest that I love thee. Jesus saith unto him, Feed my sheep.

Peter *would* not say, "I love You unconditionally" because He *could* not say it. You see, Jesus had earlier said that the one who loves Him is the one who keeps His commandments (John 14:21). He had commanded His disciples to meet Him on the mountain (Matthew 28:16)—which is why Peter here says, "You know all things, Lord. You know I'm in the wrong place even now. That's why I can't say I love You the way You taught us to love You. But I do like You."

"Great," answered Jesus. "I'll meet you there. Feed My sheep. Get involved in service. Let Me use you."

The Lord will meet us wherever we're at—and He'll go with us as far as we want to go. You can go on in ministry, in knowing the Lord intimately, in worship, in praise, and in prayer. You can go on as far as you want, and He'll go with you.

John 21:18, 19
Verily, verily, I say unto thee, When thou wast young, thou girdedst thyself, and walkedst whither thou wouldest: but when thou shalt be old, thou shalt stretch forth thy hands, and another shall gird thee, and carry thee whither thou wouldest not. This spake he, signifying by what death he should glorify God. And when he had spoken this, he saith unto him, Follow me.

"Peter, when you were young, you wanted to give your life for Me. But you didn't. You backed down. Guess what. You're going to make it when you're old. Yes, they'll carry you off—but it's ultimately what you aspired to in your younger days."

John 21:20–22
Then Peter, turning about, seeth the disciple whom Jesus loved following; which also leaned on his breast at supper, and said,

Lord, which is he that betrayeth thee? Peter seeing him saith to Jesus, Lord, and what shall this man do? Jesus saith unto him, If I will that he tarry till I come, what is that to thee? follow thou me.

What about John? John would be poisoned, boiled, and exiled before he finally died. But Jesus doesn't tell Peter this.

For topical study of John 21:18–22, see "What is That to Thee" below.

John 21:23
Then went this saying abroad among the brethren, that that disciple should not die: yet Jesus said not unto him, He shall not die; but, If I will that he tarry till I come, what is that to thee?

Jesus didn't say John would live until He returned. He simply said John's days were in His hand.

John 21:24, 25
This is the disciple which testifieth of these things, and wrote these things: and we know that his testimony is true. And there are also many other things which Jesus did, the which, if they should be written every one, I suppose that even the world itself could not contain the books that should be written. Amen.

The world could not even hold all that should be written of Jesus. But Ephesians 2 indicates that in the ages to come, we will at last be able to explore more fully His grace and mercy.

John tells us in Revelation that there are four creatures in heaven who praise the Lord ceaselessly, perpetually, and eternally. This goes on day and night because they're continually seeing different facets, different sides, different aspects of the Person of Jesus (4:8).

And the same thing will happen eternally with you. Jesus will so captivate your heart and expand your mind that, as you explore and experience the exceeding riches of His grace and goodness, you will praise Him throughout eternity.

WHAT IS THAT TO THEE?
A Topical Study of
John 21:18–22

Some folks seem to be not accident-prone but incident-prone. That is, they always seem to be doing or saying the wrong thing at the wrong time in the wrong place. Such a man was the apostle Peter. He had a tendency to be involved in incidents where he said and did the wrong thing. And here in our text, he's at it once again. You see, Jesus, who had been resurrected from the dead at this point, told the disciples to meet Him at the appointed mountain in Galilee (Matthew 28:16). But on their way to Galilee, Peter had said, "I'm going fishing," the language indicating more than a one-time excursion. In other words, "I'm going back to fishing—back to what I used to do, back to my old way of living."

Here's Peter on the beach, when he should have been on the mountain, hearing Jesus say, "When you're old, you're going to be carried where you don't want to go"—speaking of the death Peter would die by crucifixion. "You can count on me," Peter had said earlier. "If everyone else forsakes You, Lord, I never will." And there in Gethsemane, Peter took out his sword and started swinging. Peter wasn't dumb. He was serious about going to the end with the Lord. Yet a few hours later, feeling threatened by a servant girl, he denied the Lord three times. So here's Jesus, saying, "Peter, we're at another fire now. Remember the other fire—where you caved in, where you turned back, where you denied Me? I'm telling you before this fire on the beach that you're going to burn brightly, that you're going to make it, that you're going to die for Me." But Peter didn't hear the blessing. Instead, he took his eyes off Jesus, pointed to John, and said, "What about him?"

Remember what happened in Matthew 14? The wind was blowing; the waves were rolling. Suddenly, the terrified disciples see a figure walking toward them. "Lord, if that's You," Peter said, "then bid me come." The Lord did, and Peter actually walked on water—until, looking at the waves, he started to sink. The same thing happens to you and me. We start looking at the storm, fretting over circumstances, wondering about people—and we start to sink. "It's none of your business what happens to John," Jesus told Peter as they stood by the fire. "*You* follow Me." And Peter did.

I find four aspects of this vignette tremendously helpful. . . .

It Encourages Me

Like Peter, I'm a bumbler and a stumbler. Perhaps you are too. Yet Jesus, in His grace and mercy says, "You're going to make it." Truly, the Lord will see us through, gang. Maybe you're straining and striving to hold on to the Lord, fearing that if you let go, you'll be lost. Relax. The truth is, He's got you in the right hand of His righteousness (Isaiah 41:10). If you've opened your heart to the Lord, I can assure you that you are going to make it because He completes that which He has begun (Philippians 1:6). "Now unto Him," Paul says, "who is able to *keep* that which is committed unto Him . . ." (see 2 Timothy 1:12) Jesus told Peter He would keep him all the way to death. So I know He'll do the same for us.

It Enables Me

It seems like he's got it made in the shade, this one who leaned on Your breast at the table, this one who's so close to Your heart, Peter must have thought concerning John.

Do you ever look at a person, a couple, a family, and say, "They've got it made. It's not fair"? Let me tell you what happened to John. We know, because Iranius, a disciple of Polycarp, who was a disciple of John himself, wrote an exhaustive history of John. According to Iranius, John ministered in Jerusalem for a season, then found himself in Rome, capital city of the empire. There, he experienced such difficulty and persecution that the enemies of the gospel poisoned his drink in an attempt to kill him. That is why in early church records, John's symbol is a chalice with a snake emerging from within. Although John drank it, he miraculously did not die from it. Still determined to destroy him, Caesar Nero ordered John to be placed in a cauldron of boiling oil. But although his skin was burned, John did not die. So he was sentenced to exile on the island of Patmos, where the most perverted people, the most incorrigible prisoners were sent. A rocky, barren island, it was the most hell-like place the Roman Empire knew about. Yet it was on Patmos that John was given the Book of Revelation.

Now this enlightens me because Jesus didn't say to Peter, "You're asking about John? Let me tell you about him. Yes, Peter, you're going to be crucified, but then you'll go straight to heaven. John, on the other hand, is going to be poisoned; he's going to be put in a cauldron of boiling oil; he's going to be exiled. He's going to live a very painful and difficult life." No, Jesus simply said, "If I will that John lives until I come back, what does it matter to you? You, Peter, follow Me. Period."

You will have a temptation at some time or another to look at someone else and say, "Poor me. I'm being crucified while he's cruising," because you won't understand what battles the person you envy is presently fighting or will be facing. The Bible says no temptation comes to any of us except that which is common to *all* people (1 Corinthians 10:13). Every person goes through equal difficulty. We just don't see it. When we get to heaven, not one of us will say, "Well, I really had it rough. Lord, You picked on me." On the contrary, we will fall before the throne and say, "Lord, You were fair and equitable in everything You did," (see Revelation 16:7). So next time you are tempted to have a personal pity party, remember that Jesus doesn't explain. He simply says, "You follow Me."

It Enlarges Me

John and Peter had very different temperaments, very different personalities. John was a thinker, a contemplator, a mystic. Peter was an activist, a go-getter. In fact, when Jesus called them, what were these two men doing? Peter was casting his net into the sea (Matthew 4:18). "Follow Me and I'll make you a fisher of men," Jesus said. And indeed Peter became an evangelist who would bring many people into the kingdom—three thousand saved during his first sermon alone. John, on the other hand, wasn't casting his net. He was mending nets (Matthew 4:21). And John would go on to mend people, as he taught, preached, and practiced love. These two were very different in ministry, in mentality, in temperament, in personality. But you know what? God used them both. Peter's wondering about John, when in reality, the Lord would use them equally.

I think of two other men used powerfully by the Lord . . .

Leading a contingent of people from Babylon to Jerusalem to rebuild the temple, Ezra realized he was short of provision and lacking protection. So what did he do? Not wanting the king to doubt the Lord's provision, he instructed the people to fast and pray. And indeed the Lord came through (Ezra 8). Seventy years later, Nehemiah led another group back to Jerusalem from Babylon to rebuild the walls around the city. Whereas Ezra had said, "I'm not going to ask the king for anything because the hand of God is upon us," Nehemiah said, "Because the hand of God is upon us, O king, we want provision and protection" (see Nehemiah 2).

Who was right? They both were. Arriving in Jerusalem, Ezra was dismayed to find the Jews had intermarried with Gentiles. So what does he do? He pulls out his beard in remorse, and the people repent (Ezra 9). Seventy years later, Nehemiah reacts to the same situation not by plucking his hair, but by plucking the hair of the people—and the people repent (Nehemiah 13). Who was right? The Lord used *both* Ezra and Nehemiah. God can work through an Ezra, a mystic, a John. And He can work through a Nehemiah, a beard-plucker, a Peter. When I understand this, I can accept ministry from different kinds of people and of different types of flavors.

It Instructs Me

"Follow Me," Jesus says.

"Why should I," you might say, "if it means being crucified upside down, if it means being placed in a cauldron of boiling oil? Thanks, but no thanks. I'll chart my own course. I'll live my own life." And you can. Our loving God gives you and me that option—because if you follow Him, you'll have to deny yourself and take up His Cross. Why should you do that? I suggest two reasons. . . .

First, follow Jesus for abundant life. Jesus said He came that we might have life and life abundantly (John 10:10). The reality of the world never lives up to its hype. Not so with the Lord. "Whoever believes in Me shall never thirst," He said (see John 6:35). And it's true. We've found that to be so. We have fished all night in the world, only to come up empty. But when we come back to the Lord, we find the substance, the solidity, and the reality of what we were looking for all along.

Second, follow Jesus for eternal life. If you want to go to hell, to live in outer darkness where there's weeping and wailing and gnashing of teeth, where you won't see another individual for age to age and eternity-to-eternity, where your body will convulse, where your conscience will haunt you, where your sin will be ever before you, then don't follow Him.

But if, like the disciples, you say, "Lord, You alone have the words of eternal life," you'll follow Him and you'll end up in heaven. It's such a good deal—abundant life now and eternal life in the ages to come. Who *wouldn't* want to follow Him?

"Follow thou Me," Jesus says.

Accept His invitation today. And continue to do so all the days of your life.

NOTES

[1] C .S. Lewis. *Mere Christianity.* Harper Collins, 2001, pp. 136, 137.

ACTS

1

Acts 1:1 (a)
The former treatise have I made . . .

The Book of Acts was written by Luke. The "former treatise" referred to is the Gospel that bears his name. From his exacting use of the Greek language, we know Luke was an intelligent man. We also know from Colossians 4:14 that he was a doctor. Many Bible scholars and historians further believe that, since the slaves of wealthy men usually held the position of physician, Luke was a slave.

Acts 1:1 (b)
. . . O Theophilus . . .

Scholars and historians believe Theophilus was Luke's owner who, following his own conversion to Jesus Christ, freed Luke to travel with the apostle Paul. I am intrigued as I stop to consider the incredible energy and effort Luke expended to communicate the gospel to his former owner. After all, Luke didn't say, "Today I am writing the Bible. I had better keep my wits sharp because people will be studying these words for many centuries." No, for all Luke knew, he was simply writing to one man, which is the same mentality our Lord had.

Jesus was the Good Shepherd who left the ninety and nine to find one who was lost (Matthew 18:12). He was the Great Communicator who conversed with one woman at a well (John 4:7). He was the gifted Teacher who sought out one man in a tree (Luke 19:5).

Acts 1:1 (c)
. . . of all that Jesus began . . .

In his Gospel, Luke had written of the life, death, and Resurrection of Jesus, but that was only the beginning. The Book of Acts is the continuation of the gospel story. And the story goes on. Africa and South America are experiencing great revival. And only now are we beginning to discover the depth and breadth of the church in communist China. Jesus is still working, folks. That's what makes being a Christian so exciting!

Acts 1:1 (d)
. . . both to do and teach,

That's always the divine order—doing first, then teaching. If you want to impact your children, if you want to have power in ministry, follow this simple principle: Do it before you teach it. Our Lord moved with incredible authority, and those who heard Him were "astonished at his doctrine" (Matthew 7:28) because He didn't only teach the Word theoretically, He lived it out before them.

Acts 1:2, 3 (a)
. . . Until the day in which he was taken up, after that he through the Holy Ghost had given commandments unto the apostles whom he had chosen: To whom also he shewed himself alive after his passion by many infallible proofs . . .

After His Resurrection, Jesus "dropped in" on His disciples over a period of forty days, causing them to understand that even though they would no longer see Him visibly, He would be in their midst in reality.

"I'm not going to believe this resurrection stuff unless I can put my hand into the wound in His side and the nail prints in His hands," said Thomas (see John 20:25). The following week, when Jesus said to him, "Put your hand in My side. Touch My wounds," Thomas's eyes were opened, and he realized that, even though he hadn't seen Jesus, Jesus had seen him.

My prayer is that, like Thomas, we would grasp the fact that, even though we may not see Him or feel Him, Jesus truly is with us.

Acts 1:3 (b)
. . . being seen of them forty days . . .

The Greek word for "seen" is *optanomai,* from which we get our word ophthalmologist, or eye doctor. It literally means Jesus was being "eye-balled" by them, "stared at," or "scrutinized." The disciples didn't gaze at Jesus with wispy, dreamy looks. No, they stared at Him. Wouldn't you? If your leader had been crucified, but came back on the scene from time to time, wouldn't you eyeball him? Not only did His disciples see Him, but according to 1 Corinthians 15:6, there were five hundred eyewitnesses to whom Jesus appeared following His Resurrection.

Acts 1:3 (c)
. . . and speaking of the things pertaining to the kingdom of God.

We might not hear Jesus audibly or see Him visibly as the disciples did, but He continues to speak to us "of the things pertaining to the kingdom of God." How? Through pains and problems. If you had a hard day today or a hard week, a hard year, or a hard life, understand this: It's the Lord speaking to you concerning His kingdom, saying, "Child, this is not your home. I don't want you to sink your roots here too deeply because all of this is going to pass away quickly. I know that if I don't allow dark days to poke you and prod you to look heavenward, you'll put your time and energy into things that are destined to burn, and you'll be disappointed for the next billion years to come."

So don't be upset and bitter when times are tough. Realize they are God's reminder to seek first the kingdom (Matthew 6:33).

Acts 1:4, 5
And, being assembled together with them, commanded them that they should not depart from Jerusalem, but wait for the promise of the Father, which, saith he, ye have heard of me. For John truly baptized with water; but ye shall be baptized with the Holy Ghost not many days hence.

There is so much confusion today about the baptism in the Spirit. People get hung up and miss out because they don't understand there are three relationships Jesus talked about that a person can and should have with the Holy Ghost.

- He is *with* us when we are convicted of our need to be born again (John 14:17);
- He comes *in* us the moment we open our heart to the Savior (John 20:22); and
- He comes *upon* us when He empowers us for service (Acts 1:5).

For topical study of Acts 1:4–5 entitled "The Gift of the Spirit," turn to page 614.

Acts 1:6
When they therefore were come together, they asked of him, saying, Lord, wilt thou at this time restore again the kingdom to Israel?

"Are You finally going to establish Your kingdom?" the disciples asked Jesus.

Acts 1:7
And he said unto them, It is not for you to know the times or the seasons, which the Father hath put in his own power.

"It is not for you to know," answered Jesus. I have this phrase underlined in my Bible. What makes me think I need to know everything? Certain things are just not for me to know.

Acts 1:8 (a)
But ye shall receive power, after that the Holy Ghost is come upon you . . .

The steam in a locomotive does not exist to toot the whistle. Its purpose is to power the engine and move the train. So, too, the empowering of the Spirit is not given for people to feel "Holy Ghost goose bumps," emotional highs, or warm fuzzy feelings. The Spirit comes upon people in order that the message of the gospel might be moved throughout the world.

Acts 1:8 (b)
. . . and ye shall be witnesses unto me . . .

Jesus didn't say, "You will witness." He said, "You'll *be* witnesses. Things will happen in a naturally supernatural way in and through you that will witness My reality."

Acts 1:8 (c)
. . . both in Jerusalem, and in all Judaea, and in Samaria, and unto the uttermost part of the earth.

Billy Sunday used to say, "The Lord has anointed me to preach to the *guttermost* parts of the earth." What made Billy Sunday tick? What drove D. L. Moody, R. A. Torrey, or Charles Finney? Read their biographies, and you will see that, without exception, each of these men had an undeniable encounter with the Spirit.

Acts 1:9
And when he had spoken these things, while they beheld, he was taken up; and a cloud received him out of their sight.

When the temple was dedicated, Scripture records the cloud of glory filling it (1 Kings 8:10). Here in Acts, I believe Luke is speaking of this same cloud of glory—the shekinah glory of the Father.

Acts 1:10, 11 (a)
And while they looked stedfastly toward heaven as he went up, behold, two men stood by them in white apparel; which also said, Ye men of Galilee, why stand ye gazing up into heaven?

Some have suggested that the two men in white apparel were Moses and Elijah, which would correspond with their appearance during the Transfiguration in Matthew 17.

Acts 1:11 (b), 12
This same Jesus, which is taken up from you into heaven, shall so come in like manner as ye have seen him go into heaven. Then returned they unto Jerusalem from the mount called Olivet, which is from Jerusalem a sabbath day's journey.

On the Mount of Olives, there is a church called the Church of the Ascension. If you go there today, guides will show you a footprint that is supposedly the place from which Jesus took off when He ascended to heaven. Yet Luke 24 says that Jesus traveled with His disciples *past* the Mount of Olives to Bethany before He ascended (Luke 24:50). When people don't read the Word, they are vulnerable to traditions and myths that have no biblical base at all.

Acts 1:13, 14 (a)
And when they were come in, they went up into an upper room, where abode both Peter, and James, and John, and Andrew, Philip, and Thomas, Bartholomew, and Matthew, James the son of Alphaeus, and Simon Zelotes, and Judas the brother of James. These all continued with one accord in prayer and supplication, with the women . . .

Prayer produces unity, and unity empowers prayer. When you pray with people, you experience a glorious unity that allows a greater release of blessing. That is why Jesus said, "If two or three of you agree in prayer, there's a dynamic released, and things will happen" (see Matthew 18:20). As a result of this prayer meeting, the church would soon no longer consist of one hundred twenty believers hiding away in an upper room, but would, in a single day, explode to number over three thousand (Acts 2:41).

Acts 1:14 (b)
. . . and Mary the mother of Jesus . . .

Renewal and revival continue to take place in the Catholic Church today as many are opening up to the power and the Person of the Spirit of God. I say to those who are considering such things, "Look at Mary. There she was in the Upper Room when the Spirit came down—the first charismatic Catholic!" This is the first and last time Mary is seen in the Book of Acts. In some quarters of the Catholic Church, there is a skewed theology concerning Mary. They do not see her as simply an especially blessed woman, but as a co-redemptress.

In Jerusalem today, there is a Catholic Church called the Church of Mary. Located on Mount Zion, for many centuries it was thought to be the spot where Mary was buried. However, when the Catholics changed their theology and decided that Mary never died, but instead ascended into heaven, they permanently shut the doors of the Church of Mary.

In Rome, a Catholic Church next to the railroad depot is also called the Church of Mary. In this church, a two-sided crucifix depicting Jesus on one side of the Cross, and Mary on the other is prominently displayed.

Dear friend, Mary did not supernaturally ascend into heaven. She did not die on the Cross. She cannot gain favors for those who pray to her.

When Jesus was told His mother and brothers wanted to speak with Him, He answered, "Who is my mother? and who are my brethren? Whosoever shall do the will of my Father which is in heaven, the same is my brother, and sister, and mother" (see Mark 3:33–35).

In John 2:5, we find the last recorded words of Mary when she said to the servants at the marriage feast, "Whatever He [Jesus] saith unto you, do it." She didn't say, "Tell me your problem, and I'll take care of it." She said, "Whatever He saith unto you, that's what you need to do."

Mary is seen here in the midst of the disciples, but not in a place of prominence. She is the most blessed of all women—uniquely and singularly chosen by God to bring forth His Son. She is honored, indeed, but she does not have special pull or power with God.

Acts 1:14 (c)
. . . and with his brethren.

James and Jude—sons of Joseph and Mary and half brothers of Jesus—were in the Upper Room. This is interesting, because the Gospels make it clear that they had previously been cynical, skeptical unbelievers. What changed their minds about their Brother? His Resurrection. When James and Jude saw Jesus resurrected from the dead, they became believers in Him. James went on to write the Epistle of James; Jude, the Epistle of Jude. If anyone could have questioned the deity of Jesus Christ, it would have been His own brothers, yet here are James and Jude, numbered among the believers.

Acts 1:15, 16 (a)
And in those days Peter stood up in the midst of the disciples, and said, (the number of names together were about an hundred and twenty,) Men and brethren, this scripture must needs have been fulfilled . . .

Notice that Peter was a student of prophecy. He said, "This Scripture *must* be fulfilled." He was absolutely certain that prophecy would come to pass. So am I.

Acts 1:16 (b)
. . . which the Holy Ghost by the mouth of David spake before concerning Judas, which was guide to them that took Jesus.

Not only was Peter a student of prophecy, but he believed in the divine inspiration of Scripture, saying it was the Holy Spirit who spoke through David.

All Scripture is inspired (2 Timothy 3:16). It's God-breathed, gang. And if you ever get involved in a church or become part of a Bible study group where the teacher says, "Well now, we can't be sure if this verse or this section is inspired," I would encourage you to immediately stand up, walk out, and never go back. Why? Because once you start to say, "I'll decide which part of the Bible is inspired and which part isn't," you suddenly become the judge of the Bible rather than allowing the Bible to judge you. And it's amazing what verses we will cross out given the opportunity! I've often encouraged people to go through their Bibles and meditate on all the verses they *don't* have underlined. We have all the promises starred and all the blessings highlighted, while verses like, "Yea, and all that will live godly in

Christ Jesus shall suffer persecution" (2 Timothy 3:12) are strangely unmarked!

Acts 1:17, 18 (a)
For he was numbered with us, and had obtained part of this ministry. Now this man purchased a field with the reward of iniquity . . .

We know from Matthew 27:10 and Zechariah 11:13 that this field was originally a potter's field—the field outside the house of every potter wherein he would throw any of his marred creations that, because they had become hardened, could not be reshaped. Over the years, due to the accumulation of broken pottery, the potter's field would thus be useless for anything but a burial ground.

What happened to the money for which Jesus was betrayed? It was used to purchase a potter's field—a useless field full of broken pots and dead bodies. The picture to me is powerful: The blood money of Jesus—His work on the Cross—was spent to redeem useless vessels and lifeless bodies—us.

Acts 1:18 (b)
. . . and falling headlong, he burst asunder in the midst, and all his bowels gushed out.

"Contradiction!" cry the skeptics. "Doesn't Matthew 27:5 say Judas hanged himself?" Judas *did* hang himself, then the rope broke, and he was disemboweled as he fell to the ground. Thus, rather than contradicting Matthew's account, Luke confirms it.

Acts 1:19
And it was known unto all the dwellers at Jerusalem; insomuch as that field is called in their proper tongue, Aceldama, that is to say, The field of blood.

The next time you feel like a cracked pot, the next time you feel useless, the next time you feel there's no hope for you, remember Aceldama—the field of blood—for even the place where the traitor died was purchased with the blood of Jesus Christ.

Acts 1:20
For it is written in the book of Psalms, Let his habitation be desolate, and let no man dwell therein: and his bishoprick let another take.

Making application to Judas, Peter quoted from Psalm 69:25 and Psalm 109:8. This tells me Peter was no ignorant fisherman. He knew the

Scriptures. And I strongly suspect Peter's knowledge of the written Word came from hanging out with the Living Word, Jesus Christ.

Acts 1:21, 22
Wherefore of these men which have companied with us all the time that the Lord Jesus went in and out among us, Beginning from the baptism of John, unto that same day that he was taken up from us, must one be ordained to be a witness with us of his resurrection.

The one who took Judas' office was to have been a witness of the Resurrection. Paul will use this same argument concerning his own claim to be an apostle. When did Paul see the resurrected Lord? Some commentators believe, as do I, that Paul, following his conversion, was discipled personally by Jesus in the Arabian desert (Galatians 1:17, 18).

Acts 1:23–25
And they appointed two, Joseph called Barsabas, who was surnamed Justus, and Matthias. And they prayed, and said, Thou, Lord, which knowest the hearts of all men, shew whether of these two thou hast chosen, That he may take part of this ministry and apostleship, from which Judas by transgression fell, that he might go to his own place.

The casting of lots was a common practice in Old Testament times. If a person wanted to know God's will, he would go to the high priest who had the Urim and the Thummim in his breastplate. The Urim and the Thummim were possibly two stones, one black and one white. When asked a question, the high priest would offer a prayer and then pull out a stone, perhaps black meaning "No" and white meaning "Go."

A specific example of an Old Testament character involved in the casting of lots is found in the Book of Jonah. Sailors on the boat cast lots to determine whose fault the storm was before they tossed him overboard (Jonah 1:7).

People today still think that casting lots is a nifty idea. Borrowing an idiom from the account of Gideon in Judges 6, they call it "setting out a fleece" (see Judges 6:36–40). But that's not the way of the New Testament. When Paul and Barnabas were commissioned for ministry in Acts 13, it was not through the casting of lots, but through the voice of the Spirit. How did He speak? I suggest it was through the gift of prophecy (Acts 13:2).

Next time you have a decision to make, or a struggle within, I would highly encourage you to get together with other brothers and sisters and say, "Would you pray with me about this?" While you may not get immediate vision or direction, God will indeed honor such prayer and will fulfill His promise to "write His will upon the table of your heart" (see Hebrews 8:10). It amazes me how reluctant we are to do that. We'll talk to our spouses, we'll wrestle with ourselves, but we will rarely ask someone else to seek the Lord with us. The one who does, however, will hear His voice in wonderful ways.

Acts 1:26
And they gave forth their lots; and the lot fell upon Matthias; and he was numbered with the eleven apostles.

Although Peter knew the Word and was right in discerning that Judas needed to be replaced, I believe he and the other disciples erred when they chose two men and said, "Now, Lord, which of these two do You want?"

I believe God's choice was neither man. Revelation 21:14 tells us that the names of the apostles are written on the twelve foundations in heaven. My personal conviction is that we won't see Matthias' name on any of those foundations. We'll see Paul's name. I believe Paul was the one who should have filled Judas' office.

I believe the disciples got ahead of the Lord by trying to make something happen before the power of the Spirit came upon them on the Day of Pentecost. That's a mistake I make frequently. I'll see a principle in the Word and say, "Okay, now how can I make this happen?" instead of saying, "I see the principle, Lord. Now I'm going to wait on You for the power of Your Spirit to bring it about."

Maybe you're wrestling with a decision right now, saying, "Which one is it, Lord? This or that? Here or there? What do You want, Lord? Here are Your choices."

In Numbers 11, we see something so typical of what we do.

The Israelites were murmuring, saying, "We're sick and tired of this manna."

Hearing their complaints, Moses said to the Lord, "What am I supposed to do? You told me You would give them meat. Do You want me to kill the flocks and the herds we're bringing into the Promised Land? Or do You want us to fish all the fish out of the Red Sea? Which is it, Lord?"

But the Lord said, "Trust Me, Moses, and you'll see that I have more choices than just those two. I have options you would never think about, even in your wildest dreams." And suddenly quail by the thousands flew into the camp two feet off the ground—right in the strike zone. The Israelites grabbed sticks and batted them down. I know that's what happened because verse 32 says, "He that gathered least gathered ten homers."

Be careful about saying, "Okay Lord, is it this, or is it that?" because the Lord has options we've never even heard of. Wait on Him and listen for His answer. Like the children of Israel, you'll hit one out of the park every time!

THE GIFT OF THE SPIRIT
A Topical Study of
Acts 1:4, 5

Vance Havner was right on the money when he said, "We will move this world not by criticism *of* it, nor conformity *to* it—but by combustion *within* it of lives ignited by the Spirit of God."

The early believers found this to be true, for even their enemies referred to them as those who "turned the world upside down" (see Acts 17:6). They did it without a single media consultant, church growth seminar, management strategy, or slick presentation. They impacted the Roman Empire and the entire known world without buildings, busses, or budgets. They turned the world upside down through one thing: the power of the Holy Spirit.

In verse 8, Jesus promised that after the Holy Spirit came upon them, they would be witnesses—not that they would witness, but that they would *be* witnesses. Truly, the early believers had such joy in their hearts and such love in their lives that it was undeniable something radical had happened and that Jesus must be real.

Gang, it's not "witnessing" that will turn your world upside down. It's *being* a witness, an example of what the Lord can do in a marriage and in a family, at your job and at your school. How exciting it is to see our world impacted by the power of the Spirit upon our lives. What a joy it has been to see Applegate Christian Fellowship grow—without strategies or demographic studies, slick programming or hype—by watching the Holy Spirit do His beautiful work in a very simple way.

I once received a book in the mail entitled *Marketing the Church*. After thumbing through it, I was greatly grieved by it, as I was reminded once again that the present trend to get the church to be culturally relevant is the way of the world, not the way of the Lord. The Lord has a better way: not by might, nor by power, but by His Spirit (Zechariah 4:6), igniting individuals who will be witnesses of His reality and who, in turn, will draw people to Him like moths to a flame. That's the way it worked in the Book of Acts. The early church never heard of "marketing the church." They were simply in love with Jesus Christ and were experiencing the power of the Holy Ghost. As a result, the world was permanently altered.

Many years ago, before the first Sunday service at Applegate Christian Fellowship, one of the brothers shared this word of prophecy to a group of us who had gathered in a living room to pray and seek the Lord: "The Lord has given me a vision. He showed me a map in which our valley was ignited by a fire, which in turn generated sparks that ignited other fires all around it." He continued, "I believe this means that the Lord will ignite our fellowship, and from it will come many other fellowships."

As a twenty-three-year-old, I wrote that prophecy in my journal, filed it away, and thought, *We'll see.* For at that point, it was my prayer that if God's grace were upon us, Applegate Christian Fellowship might blossom to a group of one hundred people. Then the Lord began to move in ways that were completely unpredictable and totally unplanned. The fellowship began to grow and grow, not because of our strategy or slickness, but in spite of us! And as we grew, we began to establish other fellowships round about us—in Grants Pass, Medford, and other communities in this area; then north into Roseburg, Eugene, and Washington; and south to California, Mexico, Honduras, and Jamaica.

Reading this journal entry some time ago, I thought, *Lord, You did it just like You said You would—not by might, nor by power, but by the simple, significant work of Your Spirit. Our hearts have been touched, our lives are being changed, and people are seeing not our strategy, but Your reality.*

I remember our first Sunday together. We met in a place called Grange Hall past Little Applegate Road. At that time, Oregon and California were in the midst of a significant drought. But as I was teaching, rain began beating down on the tin roof. The congregation started laughing, which made me kind of nervous, but I went on anyway. After the service, I walked outside, grabbed Tom Patrick, and said, "Tom, what was all the laughing about?"

Tom answered, "Before you moved here, a prophecy was given to us that God would rain upon us and pour out His Spirit upon this ministry—and that it would happen simultaneously with rain falling physically. So, when it started pouring while you were preaching, we started rejoicing!"

I could go on about how, in the earliest days of this ministry, prophecies were given and visions shared that have come to pass, each one by the power of the Spirit of God. "Not by might, nor by power, but by my spirit, saith the LORD of hosts" (Zechariah 4:6). We shall see, as we study Acts together, that the early church impacted the world in a greater way than any other group in history because they were ignited by the power of the Spirit. That was their simple key.

Maybe your world—your kids, your marriage, your business, or your school— is "wrong-side up." How will it be impacted? How will it be turned upside down and therefore made right? The same way the world has been impacted globally: by the power of the Holy Ghost upon your life. What's needed is not more programming, not more fleshly striving, not more clever organizing. It is the power of the Spirit that will make things start happening. The power of the Spirit will change you, your marriage, your family, your business, and your service for Jesus Christ. It will change every aspect of your life.

Keep in mind that the disciples in Acts 1 were already born again and had already received the indwelling of the Spirit. How do we know this? Because following His crucifixion, as the disciples met behind locked doors in the Upper Room, worried that someone would discover them, Jesus appeared to them, breathed on them, and said, "Receive ye the Holy Ghost" (see John 20:19–22). But, as they were about to discover, the indwelling of the Spirit is only one of three relationships available to a believer.

The Holy Spirit *with You*

In John 14:17, Jesus said to His disciples, "The Holy Spirit is with you, but He shall be in you." Those prepositions are important. The Holy Spirit is *with* a person when He begins to talk to that person about becoming a believer.

You never would have been born again unless the Holy Spirit had been *with* you, whispering, "God loves you. You're a sinner, but Jesus died in your place." Whether it was through a meeting at church, or at a Billy Graham crusade, whether it was over the radio, or through a friend, it was the Holy Spirit *with* you who began to tug on the strings of your heart, drawing you to salvation. If the Holy Spirit had not been with you, you could not have been born again.

"There is none that seeketh after God," wrote Paul (Romans 3:11). "We are born again not of the will of man, but of God" (see John 1:13). A person can't, on his own, say, "Hmm. I think I'll be born again." The only way someone can be born again is for God to sovereignly choose to send His Holy Spirit to work *with* him.

The Holy Spirit *in* You

When you opened your heart to Jesus, the Holy Spirit came *into* you. He indwelled you. You were born again. You were regenerated.

In John 20, the disciples had the Spirit *in* them, just as He is *in* every one of you who has been born again (John 20:22). You have the Holy Ghost. The question is: Does the Holy Ghost have you?

You see, Jesus not only breathed on His disciples, He also instructed them to go to Jerusalem and wait for the promise of the Father (Luke 24:49). What is the promise of the Father? It is the third relationship Jesus spoke of concerning the Spirit.

The Holy Spirit *upon* You

The Spirit of God is available not only to work with you to become a Christian, or to come into your life once you open your heart to Him, but He is now available to come upon your life and to empower you to see your own world turned upside down and made right-side up.

In the Old Testament, when the Holy Ghost came upon men like Moses and David, Gideon and Ezekiel, Samson and Bezaleel, it was to empower them for service.

So, too, Jesus said to His disciples, "The Spirit is in you, but when the Spirit comes upon you, you will be empowered for unique ministry and service, and then you will be My witnesses" (see Acts 1:4–8).

So it was that these born-again disciples, one hundred twenty in number, huddled together in the Upper Room for ten days, waiting and praying with one accord. Suddenly, on the Day of Pentecost, they heard the sound of a mighty rushing wind. Why wind? *Pnoe* means "wind" in Greek. It also means "breath" and "spirit." *Ruwach* means "wind" in Hebrew. It also means "breath" and "spirit."

Since both Hebrew and Greek have one word for wind, breath, and spirit, the *breath* of Jesus upon His disciples in John 20 and the mighty rushing *wind* in Acts 2 are unmistakable illustrations of the *Spirit.* The mighty rushing wind filled the room, tongues of fire sat upon each of the disciples, they were all filled with the Holy Ghost, and the world hasn't been the same since (Acts 2:1–5).

The same is true today. The Spirit of God is made available not only to work *with* you to become a Christian, and to come *into* you once you open your heart to Him, but to come *upon* your life and to empower you in your service for Him. We no longer have to wait for the Spirit as the disciples did. On the Day of Pentecost, GOD made the power of the Spirit available to the church corporately and to all believers individually. The power of the Spirit is a gift that has already been given and that is available to you even today.

What do you have to do to receive or appropriate that gift? The same thing you did to become a Christian. . . .

The Power of the Spirit Is Appropriated by Believing

For GOD so loved the world, that he gave his only begotten Son . . . John 3:16

If ye then, being evil, know how to give good gifts unto your children: how much more shall your heavenly Father give the Holy Spirit to them that ask him?   Luke 11:13

But as many as received him, to them gave he power to become the sons of GOD, even to them that believe on his name.   John 1:12

Just as God *gave* His Son, He *gives* the Holy Spirit. How did you receive the Son? By faith. How do you receive the power of the Spirit? The same way.

For some, when you asked Jesus into your heart, tears rolled down your cheeks, you felt a weight lifted from your shoulders, and you felt warm inside. For others, it was not an emotional experience at all. You simply said, "Okay, I've prayed the prayer. Now what?" So, too, when some receive the power of the Spirit, they speak in tongues, prophesy, or see visions. But others receive it and say, "Now what?" As with the salvation experience, some have an emotional response, while others don't. But as with the salvation experience, *all* who receive the gift of the power of the Spirit look back and see their lives radically altered from that moment on.

While I was a student at Biola University, the Spirit came upon my own life, but I didn't have a tremendous emotional experience. The Lord touched me, and I knew He impacted me at that moment, but it wasn't until later that I began to see some significant changes: My faith wasn't dry, as it had been previously. Bible study was no longer merely a discipline or a drudge. Sharing the Word was no longer an obligation. You see, although I had the Holy Spirit for many years, it wasn't until He had me and flowed from me that Bible study became my passion and sharing the Word my joy.

Suppose someone came forward today to receive Christ, saying, "I want Jesus in my life," and he prayed the sinner's prayer. Then the next day he came back, saying, "I *really* want the Lord in my life," and he prayed the sinner's prayer again. And the third day, and the fifth day, and the eighteenth day, he came again and again and again, saying, *"Please,* I want the Lord in my life." What would you tell that person?

Hopefully you would say, "By grace are you saved through *faith.* It's the gift of God (see Ephesians 2:8). You don't need to keep begging or pleading or crying. Just embrace what He has *already* given you!"

Why then do we have an entirely different mind-set when it comes to the power of the Spirit? We go to meetings. We pray with intensity. People lay hands on us and say, "Come on, brother. Hold on. Pray through." Then someone else comes along and says, "Let go, brother. Let go." So we hold on. We let go. And finally we give up because much of classic Pentecostalism has subtly transmitted the message that we have to prove ourselves worthy by our intensity or purity to receive the power of the Spirit. But that's not what Scripture teaches.

In Acts 8, after Peter and John laid hands upon them, believers in Samaria were empowered with the Holy Spirit. Simon, the resident magician, observed the scene and said, "Wow! That's neat. Hey, Peter, I'll buy that trick from you" (see Acts 8:14–19).

Peter looked at Simon and said, "Your money perish with you. The gift of the Holy Ghost cannot be purchased" (see Acts 8:20).

The gift of the Spirit cannot be purchased—not with money, intensity, purity, or anything else. It is a gift to be received by faith. At this moment, you can be a recipient of the power of the Holy Ghost upon your life if by faith you simply say, "Thank You, Father, for the promise. Jesus, do the work You said You would. Baptize me with Your Spirit."

"Wait a minute," you say. "My Baptist background doesn't confirm this. First Corinthians 12:13 says: For by one Spirit we have all been baptized into one body. So what's this about a second "coming upon" of the Spirit?"

The moment you opened your heart to Jesus Christ, the Spirit baptized you, immersed you, and plunged you into the body of Christ. First Corinthians 12:13 speaks of the baptism into the body. But that's an entirely different baptism than that of Jesus baptizing you into the Spirit.

Check your concordance, and you will see a number of baptisms mentioned in the Word. There's the baptism of John (Acts 1:22), the baptism of repentance (Acts 13:24), the baptism of suffering (Matthew 20:22), and the baptism into Moses (1 Corinthians 10:2). In fact, there are at least seven different baptisms in Scripture.

"But doesn't Ephesians 4:5 say there is *one* Lord and one baptism and one faith?" Yes. But, again, that speaks of the unity of the body. Study carefully before you build any theology upon an isolated verse.

The Preparation of the Spirit Comes Through Waiting

"Wait a minute," you say. "Didn't you just say we no longer have to wait for the Spirit?" Yes. We don't need to wait *for* the Spirit. But we need to wait *on* the Spirit.

That is why Jesus didn't say to the early believers, "Receive the power of the Spirit right now." He could have done it that way, but instead He said, "For ten days, lock yourselves in a room and wait on Me that I might pour out the Spirit of promise upon you."

Now, if the power of the Spirit is available right now—and it is—then what's the purpose of waiting on Him?

There are several reasons . . .

Transition

After a psalmist came to a profound point, he would often say, "Selah" or, "Stop and think about it." So, too, concerning the dynamic of the Spirit—the new song of the Holy Ghost. I suggest for some, "selah" means not merely taking someone else's word for it, but thinking it through themselves as they wait on the Lord and study His Word. Many of us came out of a dispensational background and were taught that there is no second blessing; that there is no baptism with the Spirit; that the gifts of prophecy, healing, tongues, and visions were for an earlier dispensation and are no longer available for us today.

Personally, I had to go through a couple of years of transition—of rethinking and reevaluating—before I received the empowering of the Spirit by the laying on of hands.

Protection

The danger facing the early believers was not in failing to do something, but in *trying* to do something. Look what happened. . . .

As they were praying in the Upper Room, Peter said, "The Scriptures declare that someone should take the place of Judas. So let's draw straws here between these two guys to see which one of them God wants to use" (see Acts 1:15–26). A man named Matthias drew the long straw and was chosen, but he's never again mentioned in the Book of Acts.

I believe Peter's plan was a big mistake. Why? Because Peter spoke *before* the empowering of the Spirit. Using his own logic and analysis, he said, "We've got to replace this guy, and here's how we'll do it." Shortly thereafter, however, Paul the apostle came on the scene, and I believe Paul was the one intended to fill the office of Judas Iscariot.

Did God throw up His hands and say, "Oh no! I wanted to use Paul. But I'm stuck with Matthias. Now what am I going to do?" Of course not. God used Paul mightily, regardless of what seems to be Peter's mistake.

Vision

It was in the dungeon that the Lord said to Jeremiah, "Call on Me, and I'll show you things you never would have imagined" (see Jeremiah 33:3).

It was when Abraham was well-advanced in years that God said, "Look now toward heaven, and count the stars if you are able to number them. So shall your descendants be" (see Genesis 15:5).

As we wait on the Lord, He directs our vision beyond even prison walls and physical limitations in order to give us His vision of what He wants to do in our lives.

Evaluation

After the Spirit of the Lord carried the prophet Ezekiel to a valley full of dry bones, He told Ezekiel to preach to the bones (Ezekiel 37:4). When Ezekiel preached, there was a great noise as the bones started to connect. But Ezekiel realized that although his preaching had produced commotion, there was no creation—the bones were still dead. God then told him to prophesy to the wind, the *ruwach*, the Spirit. Ezekiel was no longer to prophesy to the people, but to intercede in the Spirit on behalf of the people. What happened? The bones came to life. The rattling bones became a mighty army when creation replaced commotion (Ezekiel 37:1–10).

The same thing happened in the Book of Acts. One hundred twenty believers in an upper room were wondering what to do and where to go. When the mighty rushing wind filled the room, however, the dry bones became living witnesses who turned the world upside down. And the world has marveled ever since.

2 Acts 2:1
And when the day of Pentecost was fully come, they were all with one accord in one place.

Pentecost was a celebration. Taking place in the early spring, fifty days after Passover, it celebrated the completion of the winter harvest.

Pentecost was a commemoration. As outlined in Leviticus 23, the Jews were to bring two loaves of bread as an offering representing the two stone tablets on which the Law was written.

Pentecost was an illustration. Three thousand people died the day the law was given (Exodus 32:28). But on the day the Spirit was given, three thousand were saved (Acts 2:41). Thus, the two loaves commemorating the tablets of stone came to illustrate Jew and Gentile coming together in one new organization called the church. Unlike most other sacrifices, these loaves had leaven in them, a picture of the sin that would exist in a church made up of sinners saved by grace.

Acts 2:2
And suddenly there came a sound from heaven as of a rushing mighty wind, and it filled all the house where they were sitting.

The disciples were seated. They weren't rolling around, lying on the floor, or even kneeling in prayer. Sixty-dollar seminars teaching people how to hold their hands in order to experience the power of God, thereby merchandising the gospel. This ought not be! Are you waiting on the Lord? Are you hungering and thirsting for Him? You don't have to do something weird to get His attention, just be open to Him.

Acts 2:3
And there appeared unto them cloven tongues like as of fire, and it sat upon each of them.

The audio came before the visual, the sound of the wind before the sight of the fire because the Word of the Lord always precedes the work of the Lord.

Man says, "If I can see it, I'll believe it."
God says, "Believe it, and then you'll see it."

Acts 2:4
And they were all filled with the Holy Ghost, and began to speak with other tongues, as the Spirit gave them utterance.

While the wind and the fire are never seen again in the New Testament, speaking in tongues is seen repeatedly.

- In 1 Corinthians 14:18, Paul wrote, "I speak in tongues more than you all."
- In Acts 10, when Peter was in the house of Cornelius preaching the Word, he didn't even finish his message before the Holy Spirit came upon the believers and they started speaking in tongues (Acts 10:44).
- In Acts 19, Paul led the Ephesians into a knowledge of Jesus Christ, laid hands on them for the power of the Spirit, and they spoke in tongues (Acts 19:1–6).

Although the word "tongues" conjures up wild images of a big tongue flapping up and down, all it means is "languages" or "dialects." The direction of tongues is to God (1 Corinthians 14:2). The purpose of tongues is to strengthen the inner man (1 Corinthians 14:4). The effect of tongues is to build our faith (Jude 20).

Praying in the Spirit is an invaluable weapon in the spiritual arsenal God has given us. However, I'll tell you the truth: Almost everyone I've ever talked with has discovered that when they began to pray in the Spirit with words they had never learned and sounds they had never uttered, they were immediately challenged by Satan's voice in their ears, saying, "That's bogus. That's gibberish. That's dumb." But this should not be surprising, for in every area of spiritual life, God declares, Satan denies, and we decide.

- God declared to Adam and Eve, "Eat of the fruit and you will die" (see Genesis 2:16, 17).
- "Did God *really* say that?" the serpent asked (see Genesis 3:1).
- And Eve decided to listen to Satan rather than to believe God.

I came to a point in my early twenties when I said, "I see in the Word, Lord, that You encourage the private devotional use of praying in the Spirit for faith to be edified. It's a tool available for me, and, Lord, I choose right now to move into that." Satan immediately challenged my decision, yet thirty years later, praying in the Spirit is still a wonderful part of my spiritual life. Is it the key? No. Am I on a tongues kick? Absolutely not.

"Let all things be done decently and in order," Paul wrote in 1 Corinthians 14:40. The Pentecostal churches have the first part of that verse down pat: Let all things be done! The Baptist churches are experts on the second part: Decently and in order. I believe that the Lord wants us to experience *both* portions. Let all things be done, yes, but decently and in order.

Acts 2:5–7
And there were dwelling at Jerusalem Jews, devout men, out of every nation under heaven. Now when this was noised abroad, the multitude came together, and were confounded, because that every man heard them speak in his own language. And they were all amazed and marvelled, saying one to another, Behold, are not all these which speak Galilaeans?

Dispersed Jews from all nations had gathered together in the Holy City for the Feast of Pentecost. When they heard about what was happening in the Upper Room, they gathered together to see for themselves what was going on. As they heard praise, adoration, and worship in their native tongues, they were amazed.

Acts 2:8–11
And how hear we every man in our own tongue, wherein we were born? Parthians, and Medes, and Elamites, and the dwellers in Mesopotamia, and in Judaea, and Cappadocia, in Pontus, and Asia, Phrygia, and Pamphylia, in Egypt, and in the parts of Libya about Cyrene, and strangers of Rome, Jews and proselytes, Cretes and Arabians, we do hear them speak in our tongues the wonderful works of God.

Are tongues always in a known language? In 1 Corinthians 13:1, Paul refers to the tongues of men and of angels. Because 1 Corinthians 12—14 deals specifically with the manifestations of the Spirit, I believe the implication is clear: When people praise and worship the Lord in tongues, it may very well be in a language unknown on earth but known in heaven, the dialect of angels. Thus, tongues can be known, or unknown; the language of men, or the language of angels.

I'll never forget a meeting I attended at the Lake Arrowhead Hilton in California where about one hundred believers had gathered together for a time of waiting upon the Lord. Since hotel rules dictated that the bar remain open whenever the conference room was in use, the bartender stood in the back of the room polishing glasses while we studied, worshiped, and prayed. Toward the end of the meeting, a fellow stood up and gave a beautiful utterance in tongues. Because there was no interpretation, the brother overseeing the meeting wisely said, "We thank the Lord for that utterance, but since there is not interpretation flowing here tonight, that will be our only public utterance of tongues."

When the meeting concluded, the bartender approached us, and with tears running down his cheeks, said, "I must talk to that man who stood up and prayed. How does he know my tongue? I'm Iranian, and he worshiped the True and Living God in perfect Farsi." Needless to say, the bartender got saved that night.

Acts 2:12, 13
And they were all amazed, and were in doubt, saying one to another, What meaneth this? Others mocking said, These men are full of new wine.

Whenever people start experiencing the dynamic of the Holy Spirit, there are those who say, "What meaneth this?" Others mockingly say, "They're full of new wine."

While David worshiped the Lord and danced before God with all his might in his underwear, his wife, Michal, watched from her window. When David walked in, she sarcastically said, "Didn't you look wonderful out there? That was real kingly."

"What I have done I have done as unto the Lord," David replied. "But, Michal, because you have mocked this, you will be barren all the days of your life" (see 2 Samuel 6:20–23).

So, too, the Michal in you and me will forever mock. "You're lifting your hands, isn't that great? You're praying in gibberish. Isn't that wonderful? Come on, now. Get real." There are born-again believers with the mentality of Michal who mock the things of the Spirit and call them demonic. I'm not saying they don't love the Lord. I'm not saying they're not born again. I am saying there's a "barren-ness" about them.

Acts 2:14 (a)
But Peter, standing up with the eleven, lifted up his voice . . .

Peter, the giant of a fisherman who had cowered before a servant girl, now towers above the crowd. Why? One reason: He was empowered with the Spirit.

Acts 2:14(b), 15
. . . and said unto them, Ye men of Judaea,
and all ye that dwell at Jerusalem, be this
known unto you, and hearken to my words:
For these are not drunken, as ye suppose,
seeing it is but the third hour of the day.

"These are not drunk as you suppose," can have a couple of implications. It can mean, "These men are not drunk, as you're suggesting." Or it can mean, "These men are not drunk in the way that you think. They're drunk with a different wine, the new wine of the Holy Ghost, not distilled spirits, but the dynamic Spirit."

Acts 2:16 (a)
But this is that which was spoken . . .

When people have questions about things they see happening in ministry, in the Spirit, or in worship, like Peter, we should be able to answer, "This is that which is spoken of scripturally." I believe this is where many in the Pentecostal movement have greatly erred. When I ask about the scriptural basis for some of the things they do, I hear answers like this one given by a Pentecostal "superstar": "You have to realize more can be cooked up in the kitchen than appears on the menu. God is bigger than the Bible."

Not so. What makes for solid doctrine and good church practice are those occurrences or precedents we see in the Gospels which continue in Acts and are taught in the Epistles. Anything else throws the door wide open to New Age author and actress Shirley MacLaine and anyone else who claims to have had his or her own special encounter with God.

Acts 2:16 (b)
. . . by the prophet Joel.

Peter was an incredible expositor, quoting from the Psalms in Acts 1 and from Joel in Acts 2. The fisherman became a scholar by hanging out with Jesus. If you want to be one whom the Lord uses, be like Peter. Hang out with Jesus, and inevitably, you will get a firm grasp of the Word.

Acts 2:17
And it shall come to pass in the last days,
saith God, I will pour out of my Spirit upon
all flesh: and your sons and your daughters
shall prophesy, and your young men shall
see visions, and your old men shall dream
dreams.

Joel prophesied that in the Last Days the Spirit would be poured out upon the young men

and the old men, the young men seeing visions, the old men dreaming dreams (Joel 2:28).

Acts 2:18
And on my servants and on my handmaidens
I will pour out in those days of my Spirit;
and they shall prophesy.

Who will prophesy? Servants and handmaidens. I have found that women often possess an especially blessed ministry of prophecy because of their sensitivity to the still, small voice of the Spirit.

Acts 2:19, 20
And I will shew wonders in heaven above,
and signs in the earth beneath; blood, and
fire, and vapour of smoke: The sun shall
be turned into darkness, and the moon into
blood, before that great and notable day of
the Lord come.

Joel 2 speaks about the Day of the Lord, the day when the church is raptured and judgment comes down. Pentecost was not the fulfillment of Joel 2, but only a sneak preview of coming attractions. In many ways, what happened at Pentecost is being experienced to a much greater degree today in countries other than America. Why? Because who needs the gift of healing when we have Blue Cross and Excedrin PM? Who needs a word of wisdom or a word of knowledge when we have computers? I believe many of the blessings our society enjoys medicinally and technologically have shut us off from what the Lord does elsewhere miraculously as a picture of what's to come prophetically.

Acts 2:21
And it shall come to pass, that whosoever
shall call on the name of the Lord shall be
saved.

People are being exposed today to the name of the Lord in more ways than ever before—through billboards, T-shirts, books, bumper stickers, and Christian music. I believe this is because the Lord is already preparing the hearts of a whole bunch of our friends, relatives, and neighbors who, although they are presently closed to the gospel, will open their hearts in the incredible revival that will take place during the Tribulation period.

Acts 2:22 (a)
Ye men of Israel, hear these words . . .

Following Peter's quotation of Scripture, he explains Scripture.

Acts 2:22 (b)–24 (a)

Jesus of Nazareth, a man approved of God among you by miracles and wonders and signs, which God did by him in the midst of you, as ye yourselves also know: Him, being delivered by the determinate counsel and foreknowledge of God, ye have taken, and by wicked hands have crucified and slain: Whom God hath raised up, having loosed the pains of death. . . .

In verse 22, Peter summed up the life of Jesus. In verse 23, he talked about the death of Jesus. In verse 24, he spoke of the Resurrection of Jesus. Thus, in less than thirty seconds, Peter encompassed Jesus' life, death, and Resurrection. That's good preaching!

In verse 23, we see the tension between the sovereignty of God and the responsibility of man when Peter said, "You crucified Him. But it was by the determinate counsel and foreknowledge of God."

"Wait a minute," you say. "If it was by the determinate counsel and foreknowledge of God, it was God's will that it happened. How then could the Jews be indicted for the death of Jesus?" It beats me. It's an endless argument we pea brains cannot figure out. All I know is this: God is sovereign, yet man is responsible. God's will is worked out, yet man is held accountable. In the words of J. B. Phillips: If God was small enough for us to figure out, He wouldn't be big enough for us to worship.

Acts 2:24 (b)

. . . because it was not possible that he should be holden of it.

Romans 3:23 says the wages of sin is death. Since Jesus never sinned, death could not hold Him. He died in place of you and me, He died for us personally, but death could not hold Him permanently. He rose again.

Acts 2:25 (a)

For David speaketh concerning him . . .

Here, Peter quotes yet another psalm, as he says, "David speaks concerning Him," or "in place of Him" (see Psalm 16:8–11).

Acts 2:25 (b)–28

. . . I foresaw the Lord always before my face, for he is on my right hand, that I should not be moved: Therefore did my heart rejoice, and my tongue was glad; moreover also my flesh shall rest in hope: Because thou wilt not leave my soul in hell,
neither wilt thou suffer thine Holy One to see corruption. Thou hast made known to me the ways of life; thou shalt make me full of joy with thy countenance.

Put quotation marks around these verses, because although David is speaking prophetically, it's actually Jesus speaking personally, who, following His crucifixion, descended into hell (Ephesians 4:9, 10).

Acts 2:29, 30 (a)

Men and brethren, let me freely speak unto you of the patriarch David, that he is both dead and buried, and his sepulchre is with us unto this day. Therefore being a prophet . . .

Although we always think of David as a king, he was also a prophet.

Acts 2:30 (b)–32

. . . and knowing that God had sworn with an oath to him, that of the fruit of his loins, according to the flesh, he would raise up Christ to sit on his throne; he seeing this before spake of the resurrection of Christ, that his soul was not left in hell, neither his flesh did see corruption. This Jesus hath God raised up, whereof we all are witnesses.

Since David's body did indeed see corruption when it became dust, he couldn't have been speaking about himself, but about the One who would succeed him—the Anointed One, the Messiah, the Christ.

Acts 2:33–35

Therefore being by the right hand of God exalted, and having received of the Father the promise of the Holy Ghost, he hath shed forth this, which ye now see and hear. For David is not ascended into the heavens: but he saith himself, The Lord said unto my Lord, Sit thou on my right hand, until I make thy foes thy footstool.

David called his descendant his Lord. In Jewish culture, one would never call his offspring "Lord." "What is Peter implying?" his audience must have wondered. Peter's implication was simply this: Jesus, the Son of David, is more than merely a descendant of David. He is the Son of God.

Acts 2:36, 37 (a)

Therefore let all the house of Israel know assuredly, that God hath made that same Jesus, whom ye have crucified, both Lord and Christ. Now when they heard this, they were pricked in their heart . . .

The Jews had heard amazing things through the utterance of tongues. They had seen Peter stand up boldly to preach powerfully and persuasively. They heard him use Scripture accurately and irrefutably. As a result, they were pricked in their hearts.

Acts 2:37 (b)
. . . and said unto Peter and to the rest of the apostles, Men and brethren, what shall we do?

"What shall we do?" they asked. The same question had been asked of John in Luke 3, to which the Baptist had replied, "If you have two coats, give one away. If you collect taxes, do not collect more than his due. If you're a soldier, do no man unnecessary violence."

"Do, do, do" was John's message of preparation—but it's not the message of salvation. The message of salvation is not: "Do." It's: *"Done!"*

Acts 2:38
Then Peter said unto them, Repent, and be baptized every one of you in the name of Jesus Christ for the remission of sins, and ye shall receive the gift of the Holy Ghost.

To repent simply means to change direction. "You once thought Jesus was a blasphemer, a heretic, a dangerous individual," said Peter. "Change your mind about who He is." Gang, the gospel is not based upon people cleaning up their lives or getting their acts together. The gospel is simply based upon a change of mind concerning Jesus Christ.

For many of you, Jesus was no more than a curse word. To others, He was a political revolutionary, a good teacher, or a wise man. But then you heard the Word, you saw the power, and you were pricked in your heart. You had no other recourse but to repent, no other choice but to admit He is the Christ, and you were saved.

Acts 2:39
For the promise is unto you, and to your children, and to all that are afar off, even as many as the Lord our God shall call.

There are those today who say the gift of the Holy Ghost is no longer available. I disagree. The promise of the Father is to you, your children, and to those who are afar off in coming generations and in other regions. Precious people, don't let anyone deny you the gift and empowering of the Holy Ghost. Don't let them say it's no longer applicable or no longer available. The promise of the Father experienced on the Day of Pentecost is available to you, to your children, and to those who are afar off, regardless of how far spiritually or geographically we might be.

Acts 2:40, 41 (a)
And with many other words did he testify and exhort, saying, Save yourselves from this untoward generation. Then they that gladly received his word were baptized . . .

I like that word "gladly." On one of my walks, I was reading the Scriptures and found myself placing a kiss upon my Bible as I felt my heart overflow with the goodness, the truth, the practicality, the encouragement, and the reality of the Word.

Acts 2:41 (b)
. . . and the same day there were added unto them about three thousand souls.

When the law came down, three thousand men died (Exodus 32:28). When the Spirit came down, three thousand souls were saved. The law kills. Move into a legalistic Christianity, and you will reek of death. But allow the Spirit to come upon you, and life will flow from you.

Acts 2:42
And they continued stedfastly in the apostles' doctrine and fellowship, and in breaking of bread, and in prayers.

The early church taught the Word, shared in fellowship, broke bread in Communion, and prayed.

For topical study of Acts 2:42 entitled "The Church: Keeping it Simple," turn to page 626.

Acts 2:43–45
And fear came upon every soul: and many wonders and signs were done by the apostles. And all that believed were together, and had all things common; and sold their possessions and goods, and parted them to all men, as every man had need.

College professors in the '60s and '70s who used this verse to say that the early church was Communist missed the "Marx" completely. The early believers were not Communists. They were "commonists." And there's a big difference. Communism says: What's yours is mine. "Commonism" says: What's mine is yours.

The story is told that a number of years ago in London's Hyde Park, where free speech is the order of the day, a Communist took the podium, pointed to an impoverished elderly gentleman in the crowd, and said, "When the Communists are in charge, they will put a new suit on that old man!"

A pastor in the audience responded, "When Christ is in charge, He'll put a new man in that old suit."

Political systems claim to have the ability to put a new suit on an old man. But Jesus Christ truly puts a new man in the old suit by changing people from the inside out.

If you were around in the '60s and '70s, you might remember the many communal-type ministries that sprang up on the West Coast. Where are they now? Why didn't they work? I suggest they failed in their attempt to duplicate what happened in Acts 2 because there was no inherent reason for them to do so. On the Day of Pentecost, three thousand folks were saved in one day—three thousand people who had come from all over the world to celebrate Pentecost. Following their conversion, they sensed the need to remain in Jerusalem in order that they might be grounded in their newfound faith. But what were they to do? Jump on a 747, fly home, get their stuff, and come back?

You see, the early church didn't arbitrarily say,

"Wow! Here's a groovy idea: Let's live communally!" No, the believers in Jerusalem pooled whatever resources they had for the express purpose of allowing the new believers to remain in Jerusalem rather than having to return to the lands from which they came.

I suggest to you that we may very well see Christians living communally again, but it won't happen because someone says, "Here's a neat idea . . . ." If persecution were to fall upon this country, which it may; if the economy were to collapse, which it might; if things really get tough, which they could, you'll be amazed how quickly and how beautifully the church will come together communally. But until then, it's artificial.

Acts 2:46
And they, continuing daily with one accord in the temple, and breaking bread from house to house, did eat their meat with gladness and singleness of heart,

They met together daily in the temple and spontaneously in one another's homes.

Acts 2:47
Praising God, and having favour with all the people. And the Lord added to the church daily such as should be saved.

Programs and evangelistic techniques didn't add to the church. The *Lord* added to the church.

THE CHURCH: KEEPING IT SIMPLE
A Topical Study of
Acts 2:42

Some things are hard for me to understand—like the recent case of a mugger who won a court settlement of nearly twenty-five thousand dollars for injuries suffered when a cab driver chased him down and pinned him against a wall until police arrived. The criminal took the hero to court, and the criminal won. Fifty years ago, such a judgment would never have been rendered. As a society, we seem to have set aside our moral compass, if we have not put it away all together.

Consequently, many people long for simpler days and simpler ways, not only judicially, but technologically. If you were in high school or college during the '70s, you may remember reading Alvin Toffler's book, *Future Shock*, which predicted that by the early '90s, technology would be so advanced that the average American would work less than twenty hours per week, yet make twice as much as he did in the '70s. Toffler was wrong, for the truth is, although we are more technologically advanced than ever, we are also more frazzled and frayed.

Economically, things don't look much better. As of September 25, 2002, our country was over $6.2 trillion in debt.[1] "That may be so," you say, "but I'm doing okay. I'm living as well as my parents did when I grew up." If you're living as well as your parents did, it's probably because both you and your wife work. And, should the Lord tarry, by the time our fourteen-year-olds reach twenty-one, it will take five incomes to live as well as you do now.

No wonder we long for simpler days and simpler ways judicially, technologically, economically, and even ecclesiastically. Acts tells us that the early church turned the world upside down (Acts 17:6). Our text tells us they did so by steadfastly continuing in four simple pursuits. . . .

1. The Apostles' Doctrine

The early church didn't just dabble in the Word, folks. They devoured it. Joshua 1:8 says, "This book of the law shall not depart out of thy mouth; but thou shalt meditate therein day and night, that thou mayest observe to do according to all that is written therein: for then thou shalt make thy way prosperous, and then thou shalt have good success."

How can you be successful and prosperous? By being steadfastly committed to the Word of God. A Bible that's falling apart usually belongs to a person who isn't. If you're wearing out your Bible because you're continuing steadfastly in the apostles' doctrine, you will be prosperous and successful. That's a promise.

2. Fellowship

The Greek word for "fellowship" is *koinonia*, which means "communion," or "communication." *Koinonia* is people sharing with one another the things of the kingdom and the things of God. Unfortunately, the richness of *koinonia* has been reduced to a lightweight frivolity in so many churches today, where a time of fellowship is usually synonymous with nothing more than a time of cookies and punch.

"I don't need *koinonia*," you say. "I've been a Christian for fourteen years. I'm as strong and tall as a redwood tree." Really? Think about the redwood tree: Redwood trees appear invincible, but in reality, a relatively mild wind can topple one. You see, above the surface, redwoods seem strong, but their root systems are very, very shallow. That is why they always grow in groves. Their strength comes from interlocking their roots with other redwoods.

Exodus 36 paints a wonderful picture of this principle. As the tabernacle, which speaks of the body of Christ, was being constructed, God gave these instructions: The length of a board was to be ten cubits, and the breadth of a board one cubit and a half (Exodus 36:21). Now, if you study Biblical numerology, you know that one and a half is an imbalanced number. Only when the boards were joined *together* would they form the perfect number of balance and stability, the number of the Trinity—the number three. Thus, through the picture of the tabernacle, the Lord declared, "There needs to be a linkage, a bonding within My people, without which they will be imbalanced."

The picture continues: "And he made bars of shittim wood; five for the boards of the one side of the tabernacle, and five bars for the boards of the other side . . ." (Exodus 36:31, 32). Individual boards were paired together. The pairs were then held in congruency and kept straight by five bars. What are the five bars? I believe Ephesians 4:11 tells us: "And he gave some, apostles; and some, prophets; and some, evangelists; and some, pastors and teachers." You see, it's not enough for you and me to be linked individually. We need the following "five bars" to bind us together in congruency and harmony.

A. Apostles—Apostles have a governing ministry. As seen in Romans 16:7, the Holy Spirit appoints apostles, "sent out ones," to establish and oversee ministry within the Church.

B. Prophets—Prophets have a guiding ministry. They speak the heart of God and reveal the mind of God. We see them throughout the Book of Acts, as they guide the church, saying, "You need to move in this direction," or "Watch out as you head off in that direction."

C. Evangelists—Evangelists have a gathering ministry as they invite people to follow Jesus. I'll never forget the first time I heard one of my colleagues preach. As I listened to him, I thought, *Oh, no! He's butchering the text.* But it was when he gave an invitation and over three hundred college students came forward that I understood the gift of evangelism.

D. Pastors—Pastors have a guarding ministry. Although some pastors are teachers, a pastor isn't by definition a teacher. A pastor is one who cares for people, watches out for people, and prays on behalf of people.

E. Teachers—Teachers have a grounding ministry. They love to explain the Scriptures and set folks on a firm foundation in the Word of God. We need the entire church, saints. It's not enough to have a special brother or an intimate little group, for it is through apostles governing, prophets guiding, evangelists gathering, pastors guarding, and teachers grounding that there is stability in the church.

3. Breaking of Bread

The breaking of bread speaks of Communion. Communion is vital to the health of the church corporately and to believers individually. Paul wrote to the church at Corinth that, because they took Communion lightly, many of them were weak, sick, and even dying unnecessarily (1 Corinthians 11:30). Whenever we fail to give worth to the Lord's table, I believe we jeopardize not only our spiritual life, but our physical, marital, and emotional life as well (see 1 Corinthians 11:29, 30 notes for further commentary).

4. Prayer

"Prayer?" you say. "I don't need to go to church to pray. I can pray by myself." Yes, you can pray by yourself. In fact, Scripture commands us to do so (Matthew 6:6). However, Jesus also spoke of a dynamic that takes place uniquely when we pray corporately (Matthew 18:19, 20).

Years ago, my four-year-old son, Benjamin, came to me, saying, "Daddy, can you please take me to the park?"

"I'd like to, son," I said, "but I'm kind of busy."

Two minutes later, Mary, then five years old, appeared on the scene. "Daddy, *please* can we go to the park?"

There we were: Mary was batting her eyes, Benny was hopping up and down, the two were in agreement—and my resistance was breaking down rapidly when Tammy, my bride, walked in, saying, "Let's go to the park, honey."

We went to the park.

So, too, when we as God's children come to Him together, saying, "Father, this is our desire, this is our prayer," He delights in our request. I'm not suggesting that we can manipulate or pressure God by "ganging up" on Him. I am saying that He enjoys and responds to our corporate requests in a unique way.

The early church devoted themselves to teaching, fellowship, Communion, and prayer. And they did so *steadfastly*. Unfortunately, steadfastness is not characteristic of much of the church today. Many believers reflect the attitude of the following letter, purportedly written by a faithful church member. . . .

Dear Pastor,

You often stress the importance of attendance at worship. But I think a person has a right to miss now and then. I think every person ought to be excused for the following reasons and the number of times indicated: Christmas (1) Death in the family (3) Anniversary (1) New Years (1) Easter (1) Last day of school (1) July 4th (1) Labor Day (1) First day of school (1) Sleeping late (4) Memorial Day (1) Family reunions (2) Anniversary (1) Sickness (5) Vacation (3) Business trips (3) Unexpected company (4) Bad weather (6) Time changes (2) TV specials (3) Ball games (5). But you can count on us to be in church on the fourth Sunday of February and the third Sunday in August—unless it's Leap Year, or we're otherwise providentially hindered.

Why should we steadfastly continue in the Word, Communion, fellowship, and prayer? Look at three other places Luke uses the word "steadfastly."

1. Steadfast Because of the *People* We're With

In Acts 6, Stephen was about to be stoned. After the elders had challenged him and were ready to sentence him to death, "All that sat in the council, looking stedfastly on him, saw his face as it had been the face of an angel" (Acts 6:15).

How can you, like Stephen, have the face of an angel? Ask Moses. . . .

Moses was in the presence of God for forty days on the mountain. So blessed was he, so full and satisfied, he forgot to eat (Exodus 34:28). And when he came down, his face glowed. Steadfastly spend time with God, and like Moses and Stephen, your face will glow with the peace and joy of His presence.

2. Steadfast Because of the *Place* We're Going

In Acts 7, we read that before Stephen died, "He, being full of the Holy Ghost, looked up stedfastly into heaven, and saw the glory of God, and Jesus standing on the right hand of God" (Acts 7:55). Stephen saw heaven, and that was all that mattered.

Gang, in heaven it won't matter how shiny my car was or how many hobbies I had. The only thing that will matter will be what I did for Christ. Therefore, I am a fool of immense proportion if I prioritize anything but the kingdom.

3. Steadfast Because of the *Price* that Was Paid

"And it came to pass, when the time was come that he should be received up, he stedfastly set his face to go to Jerusalem" (Luke 9:51). Jesus set His face steadfastly to die with *me* on His mind.

What if Jesus had done what I so often do? If He had said, "I *think* I'm going to Jerusalem," or "I'd *like* to go to Jerusalem," or "I *hope* to go to Jerusalem," I would fry in hell.

Instead, Jesus said, "I have a job to do, and nothing is going to stop Me. I *steadfastly* set My face to Jerusalem"—and our salvation was the result. May the Lord keep our ministry simple as we *steadfastly* continue in the Word, Communion, fellowship, and prayer.

"But what about our singles?" you ask. "We have to have ice cream socials and singles' activities."

Do we?

"Yeah. How else will they meet one another?"

Listen gang, the church was never intended to figure out peoples' social activities. Ask Isaac. . . .

And Isaac went out to meditate in the field at the eventide: and he lifted up his eyes, and saw, and, behold, the camels were coming. And Rebekah lifted up her eyes, and when she saw Isaac, she lighted off the camel.   Genesis 24:63

Did Isaac meet Rebekah through a Christian dating service? No. Through an ice cream social? No. Isaac was simply meditating in his field—enjoying God, thinking about the Word, walking with the Lord—when at the perfect moment, he saw camels in the distance.

"Well, what about our youth? We have to have something for our high-schoolers." Do we? If we try to entertain our kids into Christianity, we're missing New Testament church life. The world can out-fun us, out-entertain us, and out-slick us every time because whenever Christians try to copy what the world does, they never do it as well.

But I'll tell you what we can do with our kids: We can love them and give them truth like the world never can. And so we have two hundred high-schoolers gathering together at the youth center to study the Scriptures, sing praise, offer prayer, and share in *koinonia*.

It's so simple. Precious people, we must continue steadfastly to keep a simple perspective, because the tendency of ministry, just like government, is to get bigger and more complicated. And it ought never to be.

May our churches be oases where we come together to continue steadfastly in the power and simplicity of the Word, Communion, fellowship, and prayer.

In Jesus' Name.

Acts 3:1
Now Peter and John went up together into the temple at the hour of prayer, being the ninth hour.

Peter and John were men of consistency. Like all devout Jews, according to the Jewish custom of the day, every day at 9:00 A.M., noon, and 3:00 P.M., they stopped what they were doing and headed to the temple, where they spent an hour in prayer. This time consisted of fifteen minutes of silent meditation, thirty minutes of petition, and fifteen minutes of adoration—which, by the way, I think is a neat pattern for prayer. Meditate on the greatness and goodness of God, and you will be confident in bringing your requests *to* Him. When you realize that even your biggest concerns are no problem *for* Him, your heart will overflow in worship *toward* Him.

Acts 3:2–4 (a)
And a certain man lame from his mother's womb was carried, whom they laid daily at the gate of the temple which is called Beautiful, to ask alms of them that entered into the temple; who seeing Peter and John about
to go into the temple asked an alms. And Peter, fastening his eyes upon him with John . . .

Peter and John were men of sensitivity. As the lame man called out to them, they found their eyes "fastened" on him. *We've passed this guy hundreds of times before,* they must have thought, *but at this moment something unique is happening.*

Acts 3:4 (b)
. . . said, Look on us.

Peter and John were men of flexibility. When they saw this man, they could have said, "We don't have time for him. We have to start the temple prayer meeting in just a few minutes." But they realized what we all must learn: Interruption is often divine inspiration. For some of us, life is one bother after another. I have found that when I start a day, saying, "Nobody better bother me," I find myself getting bothered at every turn. But if I expect to be bothered and remain flexible, I allow the Lord room to work in moments of the miraculous.

Acts 3:5
And he gave heed unto them, expecting to receive something of them.

It's interesting to me that even unbelievers understand that because Jesus Christ cared about hurting sinners, so should His body. Like the lame man, the hurting people in our culture know intuitively that the one group of people most likely to help them is the Christian community. Unfortunately, many times the world understands this better than even the Church does.

Acts 3:6 (a)
Then Peter said, Silver and gold have I none . . .

"Silver and gold have I none." That's a far cry from the "Name It And Claim It /Prosperity/ Seed Faith" mentality of today.

The story is told that the pope was counting the silver and gold coins in his coffers one day when Thomas Aquinas walked in. "Greetings, Thomas," he said as he gleefully held up some coins for Thomas to see. "We can no longer say, silver and gold have we none, now can we?"
  Thomas looked at the pope and said, "And neither can we say, "In the Name of Jesus Christ of Nazareth, rise up and walk."

Throughout history, whenever the church has traded purity for prosperity, she has lost power.

Acts 3:6 (b)
. . . but such as I have give I thee: In the name of Jesus Christ of Nazareth rise up and walk.

Peter and John were men of authority. Having the power of the Spirit upon their lives, they were given the green light by the Spirit to proceed in the arena of the miraculous.

Acts 3:7
And he took him by the right hand, and lifted him up: and immediately his feet and ankle bones received strength.

The original Greek text seems to indicate that this man's ankles were congenitally and permanently dislocated.

Acts 3:8–11
And he leaping up stood, and walked, and entered with them into the temple, walking, and leaping, and praising God. And all the people saw him walking and praising God: And they knew that it was he which sat for alms at the Beautiful gate of the temple: and they were filled with wonder and amazement at that which had happened unto him. And as the lame man which was

healed held Peter and John, all the people ran together unto them in the porch that is called Solomon's, greatly wondering.

Peter and John were men of humility. I believe the moment of greatest potential peril for Peter was when he took the lame man by the hand and lifted him to his feet. How easy it would have been for Peter to say, "Hey, look what just happened! I had this surge of faith and power and I grabbed this man, and he's now walking and leaping. This calls for the birth of a new ministry: THE APOSTLE PETER HEALING MINISTRIES INTERNATIONAL. I hope we got a picture of this. I can put it on my prayer calendar. I can take this guy on tour!" In the next verse, however, we see Peter do exactly the opposite.

For topical study of Acts 3:1–11 entitled "Helping the Hurting," turn to page 635.

Acts 3:12
And when Peter saw it, he answered unto the people, Ye men of Israel, why marvel ye at this? or why look ye so earnestly on us, as though by our own power or holiness we had made this man to walk?

At this very crucial moment when Peter could have been shelved from ministry, what did he do? He said, "Men of Israel, why do you marvel at this? You know your history, how God parted the Red Sea, provided manna from heaven, used a slingshot to kill a giant. Our God is the God of the miraculous. Why, then, are you surprised that He healed a lame man?"
  Whenever God uses people in any way, there will be those who will look to them and say, "You're special. You're anointed. My goodness, you're spiritual." Watch out! Be careful. It is the base part of our nature that wants people to assume we're deeper than we really are, think we're special, and know our name.
  Go into a crowded room where nine or ten conversations are taking place simultaneously, and no matter whom you're talking with, if someone speaks your name, you'll pick it up because each person's ears are tuned to the sound of his own name. Salesmen know this. That's why the first thing they do is ask your name. Industry understands this. That's why they monogram shirts, imprint pencils, and personalize coffee mugs. People are stuck on themselves! They want to see their name in print or hear their name on people's lips.
  But what does God say?

633   ACTS 3

I am the LORD: that is my name: and my glory will I not give to another, neither my praise to graven images.   Isaiah 42:8

If you're a musician or a Sunday-school teacher, a writer or a singer, a pastor or a worship leader, know this: The quickest way to be taken out of ministry is to say, "I want my name exalted." I know a number of men and women who were at one time greatly used by the Lord but are now on the shelf gathering dust because they wanted the glory—or even just a portion of it.

Acts 3:13 (a)
The God of Abraham, and of Isaac, and of Jacob, the God of our fathers, hath glorified his Son Jesus . . .

Peter wisely and immediately took the spotlight off himself and pointed it at Jesus, for it is at His Name that every knee shall bow and every tongue confess (Philippians 2:10). Before leaving this vignette, I would like to consider one other aspect: Not only do Peter and John provide principles *for* us, but the lame man is a picture *of* us.

You see, like the crippled man, we too were lame from birth. Adam, our father in the flesh, fell. And so great was his fall that all of his descendants were born lame. Unable to walk with God, or after the things of God, we sat outside the temple—alienated from God because of our sin—and begged enough silver or gold to get us by for one more day. Maybe we weren't bitter about life, but every one of us realized our handicap to some extent.

And then something happened.

Through a brother or sister, a church or a fellowship, perhaps when we least expected it, Jesus grabbed us by the hand and said, "Stand up and walk. I'm calling you into the kingdom. I'm taking you to heaven." Thus, it is no wonder that like the crippled man, we not only walk, but we leap and praise God for His goodness and grace to us lamebrains.

Acts 3:13 (b)–15
. . . whom ye delivered up, and denied him in the presence of Pilate, when he was determined to let him go. But ye denied the Holy One and the Just, and desired a murderer to be granted unto you; and killed the Prince of life, whom God hath raised from the dead; whereof we are witnesses.

"You killed the Prince of Life," Peter declared. "You murdered the One who came to *give* life to you and *be* life for you."

Acts 3:16
And his name through faith in his name hath made this man strong, whom ye see and know: yea, the faith which is by him hath given him this perfect soundness in the presence of you all.

"The faith which is by him hath given him this perfect soundness." Not only did the healing itself come from God, but even the faith to believe came from Him—which is why I thoroughly reject the implication that people are sick because they don't have enough faith to be made well. I would say to the preachers and faith healers who propound such an idea, "Why isn't *your* faith kicking in?" In this example it wasn't the lame man's faith that figured into the equation at all; he was just begging for bucks. It was the faith given by God to Peter and John that healed him.

Acts 3:17
And now, brethren, I wot that through ignorance ye did it, as did also your rulers.

I like Peter's tact here. He said, "What you did, you did through ignorance." He left the door open for his audience to repent. Sometimes I think we press our point so hard that we win the argument, but lose the soul.

Acts 3:18
But those things, which God before had shewed by the mouth of all his prophets, that Christ should suffer, he hath so fulfilled.

Even though Peter allowed that they acted ignorantly, he also insisted that Christ's death was not accidental. It wasn't a massive mistake. It was part of a prophetic plan.

Acts 3:19 (a)
Repent ye therefore, and be converted, that your sins may be blotted out . . .

"Repent," said Peter. "You looked at Jesus as One worthy of death. Change your mind concerning Him and see He is the Prince of Life. Your ignorance nailed Him to the tree. Now repent and bow your knee."

Peter is not saying, "Get your life together." He's saying, "Change your mind."

At one time, you may have said, "Christianity is a crutch for weak people." Then you changed your mind and realized Christianity is a crutch, but it is also a wheelchair, a hospital bed, a surgical team, and an ambulance! It's everything we need because we have been run over and wiped out by the dump truck of sin.

"I'm a sinner," you said, "and He died for me.

I'm sick, and He came to heal me. I'm weak, and He wants to be strong through me." It's no longer: I'm okay, you're okay. It's: He's okay, and I'm a mess.

Acts 3:19 (b)
. . . when the times of refreshing shall come from the presence of the Lord.

"The times of refreshing" have a prophetic meaning spoken of in Deuteronomy 30, Joel 2, and Zechariah 12, as they speak of the time when Jesus returns. But they also speak to you and me personally.

We can be refreshed presently whenever we repent of how we used to think and turn toward Him.

For topical study of Acts 3:19 entitled "Our Relationship with His Spirit," turn to page 639.

Acts 3:20, 21
And he shall send Jesus Christ, which before was preached unto you: Whom the heaven must receive until the times of restitution of all things, which God hath spoken by the mouth of all his holy prophets since the world began.

There are those who say "the restitution of all things" spoken of here means that every person will one day be saved—including demons and even Satan. The problem with that interpretation is that Jesus didn't teach it. In Matthew 25:41, He spoke clearly of sending some into everlasting fire. The word "everlasting" is the Greek word *aionios,* which is the same word used in John 3:16. Therefore, whoever says that the fire in Matthew 25 is not really everlasting—that people will only burn for a while until they're purged (i.e., purgatory), or until the restitution of all things—must also say that the everlasting life God promised in John 3:16 is equally transitory.

"The restitution of all things" refers not to the condition of the soul, but to the people of Israel. Israel shall be restored (see Romans 9—11). She will one day acknowledge Jesus as Lord because the promises and covenants of the Old Testament toward the Jewish people are unconditional. They will be fulfilled.

Perhaps because Karl Marx was himself a Jew, many Jewish young people and intellectuals have been fascinated by and drawn toward Marxism since the founding of the modern state of Israel in 1948. Consequently, the kibbutzim were perhaps the purest form of true Marxism on the face of the earth. But since the collapse of Communism in the Soviet Union, thousands of Russian Jews have returned to Israel, bringing with them stories about where Communism actually leads. Because of this, the kibbutzim have experienced a whole-scale turning from Communism and a turning toward traditional Judaism. As a result, there is now a massive move by many of the kibbutzniks to explore traditional Judaism once again. In many kibbutzim, the Sabbath and traditional hours of prayer are kept, the Shema is recited, and the Torah is studied. To those who understand Israeli society, this movement is just as remarkable and impacting as the demise of Communism in Russia, or the dismantling of the Berlin Wall in Germany.

I personally think this sudden interest in Judaism is preparatory for the Jews to at last recognize their Messiah (Zechariah 13:9). God is not through with Israel, folks—not by a long shot.

Acts 3:22–26
For Moses truly said unto the fathers, A prophet shall the Lord your God raise up unto you of your brethren, like unto me; him shall ye hear in all things whatsoever he shall say unto you. And it shall come to pass, that every soul, which will not hear that prophet, shall be destroyed from among the people. Yea, and all the prophets from Samuel and those that follow after, as many as have spoken, have likewise foretold of these days. Ye are the children of the prophets, and of the covenant which God made with our fathers, saying unto Abraham, And in thy seed shall all the kindreds of the earth be blessed. Unto you first God, having raised up his Son Jesus, sent him to bless you, in turning away every one of you from his iniquities.

A street preacher with an incredible handle on the Word, Peter quotes here from Genesis, Deuteronomy, and 1 Samuel to those who had gathered on the porch of the temple. If you want to be used by the Lord, learn the Word. The study of Scripture is a lifelong discipline and an eternal delight. It's pleasurable. It's fascinating. It's stimulating. Take notes. Write in the margins of your Bible. Do whatever it takes to help you remember and become thoroughly familiar with the Scriptures. If you do, not only will your heart be filled and your mind enlightened, but like Peter, you will be used by the Lord time after time.

HELPING THE HURTING
A Topical Study of
Acts 3:1–11

Y ou've seen homeless people on the freeway exits and entrances holding card-
board signs, asking for work or food. You've seen them pushing their shopping
carts downtown.

> You've seen them, and perhaps your heart has gone out to them, to those who
> are homeless and hurting, to those who beg for change and cry for help.
>   You've seen them, and perhaps your heart has been angry with them.
> Those lame people. Didn't they see the "Help Wanted" sign at Burger King?
> Why don't they get a job?
>   You've seen them, and perhaps your heart goes out to them one moment,
> and is angry with them the next.

I believe this passage in Acts sheds light on how we are to respond to the hurting people around us.

During World War II, a church in France was bombed by the Luftwaffe. When the
war concluded, the people in the community cleared away the rubble and found a
statue of Jesus, the base of which was inscribed with these words: Come unto Me,
all ye that are weary. It was remarkably preserved except for both hands, which
had been destroyed. Hearing of this, the sculptor whose work it was immediately
offered to replace the hands. But the pastor wisely declined. And so it was that
the statue was returned to its original position in front of the church, but with a
new inscription that read: He has no hands on earth but ours, for we are His body.

It's true; we are the body of Christ. If Jesus is going to reach out and touch a
lame person—a beggar, a hurting individual—it will be through our hands. He will
use us. In our text, I see three key components that will help us deal with the hurting folks around us.

Sensitive Hearts

No doubt Peter and John had glanced at the lame man many times, but this
particular day something took place deep within their hearts that drew them to him.
It was a moment of the miraculous. It was a time for ministry.

The same is true for you and me. When you drive by the fellow who is asking for help, and you know it is not merely general cultural guilt being imposed upon you, but a spiritual dynamic taking place deep within you, you have a choice to make. You can say, "Wait a minute. The Lord is doing something here." Or you can look away, adjust your radio, and drive on.

Now, understand this: As the lame man sat in the Gate Beautiful, Jesus Himself probably walked past him a number of times. This tells me that Jesus didn't minister according to need, but according to obedience. We see an example of this in John 5. . . .

A whole lot of hurting people were lying by the Pool of Bethesda, each one hoping to be the first in the pool when the water stirred, for the first one in would be healed. Jesus went in the back way, found the man farthest from the edge of the pool, and healed him (John 5:2–9).

If I had been Jesus, I would not have come in the back door and talked to one man at the rear. I would have gone to the front, looked at everyone, and said, "Everyone stand up! You're *all* healed!" Why didn't Jesus do that?

I suggest it is because He didn't minister according to the needs He saw, but according to the directive of His Father, who said, "There's one person I want You to touch at the Pool of Bethesda today." I believe that's why Jesus was so at peace in Himself and why tranquility radiated from Him. Although Jesus was accused of being a glutton, a winebibber, and a friend of sinners, He was never accused of being busy or frazzled. He didn't act according to the needs He saw. He acted in obedience to what His Father said.

So, too, when we do what He tells us to do, we won't be weighed down or stressed out because His burden is easy and His load is light (Matthew 11:28–30). He won't overwhelm us with the needs we see; rather He'll direct us specifically.

> "You have a ten-dollar bill in your pocket; give it to that person," or "Give some of your time to that man who needs to hear about Me."

Listen to the voice of the Spirit, and like Jesus, you will respond not out of compulsion, but out of compassion.

Discerning Minds

"Give me some money," the lame man said.

"Silver and gold have we none," answered Peter and John.

Really? Hadn't at least three thousand believers sold their goods and pooled their money? Peter and John must have had access to a lot of money. Were they lying? No. I believe this is what Peter and John were saying when they said they had neither silver nor gold: "For *you*, sir, silver and gold have we none because your need is not for a coin or two, or ten, or twenty. Your need is more profound. You need to be healed."

Impacting Words

As Peter grabbed the lame man by the hand, saying, "In the Name of Jesus, stand up and walk," I wonder if at that moment he thought, *What if nothing happens? Here I am, the leader of the Church. What if I say, "In the Name of Jesus, walk"—and he falls down? It's not going to look good on my application for pope.*

But Peter's words were impacting. He told the lame man to walk, and the lame man did just that. Why? I suggest three reasons. . . .

Peter and John Were Men of Preparation

Where were Peter and John when this event took place? They were on their way to the temple for prayer, as was their custom.

Often we're confronted with an opportunity to touch someone in order that he might take steps physically or spiritually, but because we have not built up a history of prayer, we are impotent and miss the moment of the miraculous. In Matthew 17, we see the disciples in this position. . . .

> The disciples asked Jesus why they were powerless to cast a demon out of a boy brought to them for healing. Jesus answered, "This kind does not go out except by prayer and fasting."
>
> The disciples probably scratched their heads and thought, "How were *we* to know that a demonized boy would be brought into our presence? We didn't have *time* to fast."
>
> And perhaps with a smile on His face, Jesus may have said, "That's the point. You can't wait to begin fasting until it's time to minister. You need to live a *life* of prayer and fasting."

You see, when the moment of the miraculous opens before you, it's too late to say, "Boy, I had better get my faith together." Unless there has been a backlog of prayer and the Word, of fasting and seeking, it will be too late. Perhaps you've seen a lame man. Your eyes became fastened to him, and you knew it was an opportunity to share, but you felt impotent and powerless. Was it because you were not a person of preparation?

Precious people, be in a place where you are constantly being prepared, because you don't know what's coming an hour, a week, a month, or a year down the road.

> You don't know when your colleagues at work are going to say, "I need something from you," even as this lame man did.
>
> You don't know when your neighbors are going to come to you crying and brokenhearted.
>
> You don't know when your kids are going to need you to minister powerfully in the Spirit.

I don't know when those moments will be, but I do know this: Like the disciples, we're powerless unless we've been prepared.

Peter and John Were Men of Impartation

Peter and John had been filled with the Holy Spirit.

You can look at the lame people with whom you work, the homeless who come your way, the hurting folks who surround you every day; but unless you are filled with the Spirit, you will have neither impacting words nor a healing touch. Jesus said to His disciples, "Go to Jerusalem. Wait for the promise of the Father for you shall receive power when the Holy Ghost comes upon you. And *then* you will be My witnesses" (see Acts 1:8). How thankful I am to be linked to a body of believers—where so many hunger and thirst for more of the Lord, for more of His Spirit.

Peter and John Were Men of Authorization

In addition to the power of the Spirit upon our lives, we need authority—the okay, the green light—for a miracle to happen.

You might drive a Corvette with a four-hundred-cubic-foot engine under the hood. When you drive, the ground shakes, people stare, and men drool. You've got power. But when you come to a red light, it doesn't matter how big your engine is or how much power you have—you've got to stop. So, too, many of you have been empowered by the Spirit. The ground may shake and rattle all about you, and that's terrific. But until the Lord turns the light green, until He says, "Now is the time to deal with that man, or give to that person," you can rev your engine all you want, but you won't make any progress.

On the other hand, you might drive a car like my Volkswagen Beetle: Even though the light may be green, there's no power when you hit the accelerator. You see, to cross the intersection of the supernatural, we need power *and* authority; and when those two points come together at a given moment, the result is a miracle.

In the tiny compartment of a passenger train sat a young lieutenant in uniform. Next to him sat his commanding officer, a crusty old general. Across from him sat a beautiful young lady. Next to her was her grandmother. As the hours passed, an attraction developed between the young lieutenant and the young lady. They were laughing and talking and enjoying the trip when suddenly the train went through a long dark tunnel. Midway through the darkness, the sound of a kiss was followed by the smack of a slap.

As the train emerged from the tunnel, the four travelers looked at one another with a variety of expressions. The young lady was delighted that the lieutenant would kiss her at that moment, but puzzled as to why her grandmother would slap him. The grandmother was angry that the lieutenant had the audacity to kiss her granddaughter, but grateful to the general who slapped the young man in line.

The general was proud of his lieutenant for kissing the young lady, but confused and smarting from the slap of the young girl. The lieutenant was hardly able to contain the laughter within him, as he alone knew what had actually transpired in the tunnel. Under the cover of darkness, he had seized the moment to kiss the girl and smack the general.

Seize the moment, folks! Watch for the moment of the miraculous when the Lord will use you in this dark tunnel of time to slap the Enemy in the face, as you heal a hurting world.

OUR RELATIONSHIP WITH HIS SPIRIT

A Topical Study of
Acts 3:19

All Jerusalem was abuzz. Tens of thousands of Jews from all over the world had congregated in the Holy City to celebrate the Feast of Pentecost, just as they had done annually for centuries.

But this Pentecost was different.

There were rumors that there was a group of Christians, followers of the radical Rabbi from Galilee, huddled together in an upper room, praising and worshiping God in different languages. The Jews on the street below, recognizing the various mother tongues of their homelands, were amazed. Some said, "What does this mean?" Others mockingly said, "These guys are drunk."

Hearing their accusations, Peter declared, "These men are not drunk as you suggest. This is the fulfillment of Joel 2, which speaks of an outpouring of the Spirit." Many, hearing the preaching of Peter, responded to what he shared and to what they saw—and three thousand were saved that day.

Acts 2 goes on to say that the new believers lived together in great hilarity, with gladness of heart, sharing all of their possessions communally. They were immersed in the teaching of the Word, they loved each other intensely, and the whole city looked upon them and found favor with them.

Then in chapter 3, after Peter and John were used by God to heal the lame man, the people began to congregate on Solomon's porch to see for themselves the man who walked and leapt and praised God. Peter realized he had an opportunity to preach again—so he did. The thesis of his message is found in our text: "Repent and be converted, that your sins might be blotted out when the times of refreshing shall come."

"The times of refreshing" spoke to Israel nationally. For centuries, the prophets had spoken of a time of refreshing when the kingdom would be established in Israel—a time when the wolf would lie down with the lamb, when there would be prosperity, and when men would study war no more. "The kingdom is coming," Peter said to the Jewish people nationally. "Repent. You rejected the Messiah. You crucified Jesus Christ, but He is the King. You nailed Him, but He is Messiah. Now repent, turn around, and you will see the times of refreshing which are to come."

I suggest that the times of refreshing spoke not only to Peter's audience nationally, but to each one of them individually. "If you will individually give your heart to this One, Jesus Christ," Peter said, "you will have a time of refreshing, knowing that your sin is forgiven."

Not only nationally and individually, I suggest to you "the times of refreshing" speak to you and to me personally. You might be saying, "I read about the power of the Holy Spirit and the love of the saints. I see the miracles happening and the boldness emanating from the disciples. Wow! How wonderful. But even though I read about the power of the Spirit on the pages of the Bible, I'm dry as a bone. I read about it. I believe in it. But I am not personally experiencing the times of refreshing."

I've got news for you, dear saint: The Holy Spirit is the agent of the times of refreshing. Water is a symbol, or type, of the Spirit throughout the Scriptures. "The times of refreshing," "the latter rain," "the overflow" all relate to the dynamic work of the Holy Spirit—not just for Israel eschatologically, not just for Peter's audience historically, but for you and me presently. If you're dry, listen carefully: "Times of refreshing" are what the Lord desires for you today. This is the day of refreshment.

Jesus said, "If any man thirst, let Him come unto Me and drink. And out of his innermost being shall gush forth torrents of living water. This spake He of the Holy Ghost" (see John 7:37–39). Now, as we have seen and experienced, Scripture clearly presents three relationships a person can have with the Holy Ghost.

The Spirit *with* You

In John 14:17, Jesus said, "The Spirit is with you, but he shall be in you." The first relationship you can have with the Holy Spirit is when He is with you. The Spirit was with you before you became a Christian, telling you to get saved.

Blaspheming the Spirit

There is a negative counterpart to this first relationship.

In Genesis 6:3, God says, "My spirit shall not always strive with man."
In Acts 7:51, Stephen, talking to people who were not responding to the

Word, said, "You stiffnecked and uncircumcised in heart and in ears, ye do always resist the Holy Ghost: as your fathers did, so do ye."

Jesus said, "All manner of sin and blasphemy shall be forgiven unto men: but the blasphemy against the Holy Ghost shall not be forgiven unto men" (Matthew 12:31).

In other words, the Spirit is with you, but He won't always be there. If you continually say, "I'm not interested in becoming a believer," there will come a point when the Spirit is blasphemed. He will no longer be with you. You see, the Holy Spirit is a perfect gentleman. He will woo you. He will invite you. He will draw you. But He will not force Himself on you.

The Spirit *in* You

You can have a second relationship with the Spirit. Jesus said, "The Spirit is with you, but he shall be in you" (see John 14:17).

When does the Spirit come in you? When you open your heart and say, "Jesus, be my Lord," you are sealed with the Spirit (Ephesians 1:13). He comes into your life.

When did this happen to the disciples? It couldn't have happened in John 14 because Jesus had not yet died for their sins. But in John 20, after Jesus had died and risen from the dead, He met again with His disciples and breathed on them, saying, "Receive ye the Holy Ghost." At that point the Holy Spirit was in them. They were born again.

Grieving the Spirit

Just as there is a negative response to the "with" ministry of the Spirit, there is a negative response to the "in" ministry of the Spirit. Paul writes: "Grieve not the holy Spirit whereby ye are sealed unto the day of redemption" (Ephesians 4:30).

You can grieve the Spirit. He is not a force. He is not a power. He's a Person. Once He has come into your heart, He will never leave you, but He can be grieved greatly. How? Ephesians 4 tells us we are to put away lying, that we are to steal no more, that we are not to let corrupt communication come out of our mouths, that we are not to be bitter or full of wrath or anger or evil speaking. Those things will grieve the Spirit (Ephesians 4:25–31).

What happens when the Spirit is grieved? Ask David . . .

David, who should have been fighting with his army against the enemies of Israel, one day found himself relaxing on the rooftop of his house. Looking down, he saw a woman taking a bath, whose name, appropriately, was Bathsheba. Feeling attracted to her, David called for her. Adultery was committed, and Bathsheba conceived. To cover his tracks, David ordered her husband back from battle, saying, "Hey, Uriah, spend some time with your wife. You've been fighting hard, you've earned some time off." But Uriah didn't go to his house. How could he be with his wife when his brothers were dying in battle? He slept on the steps of the palace.

David knew he was in trouble; his plan wasn't working. Then he had another idea. "I'll send a message to my general Joab. All the forces will rush against the enemy, and on a certain signal they'll all retreat, all except Uriah." Thus, Uriah died in battle, murdered by the diabolical plan of David (2 Samuel 11).

I got away with it! thought David. But something happened inside him because the Spirit was grieved, as seen in the psalm he wrote in the course of the following year.

> *O Lord, rebuke me not in thy wrath: neither chasten me in thy hot displeasure. For thine arrows stick fast in me, and thy hand presseth me sore. There is no soundness in my flesh because of thine anger; neither is there any rest in my bones because of my sin. For mine iniquities are gone over mine head: as an heavy burden they are too heavy for me.* Psalm 38:1–4

"I'm a mess," David said. "My skin shows it. My bones ache. I'm over my head in sin."

> *My wounds stink and are corrupt because of my foolishness. I am troubled; I am bowed down greatly; I go mourning all the day long. For my loins are filled with a loathsome disease: and there is no soundness in my flesh.* Psalm 38:5–7

"I stink. There's an odor that emanates from me." Perhaps David was speaking spiritually. But perhaps he was speaking physically, for you see, most Bible scholars believe that the "loathsome disease in his loins" speaks of a sexually transmitted disease that resulted from his affair with Bathsheba.

> *My heart panteth, my strength faileth me: as for the light of mine eyes, it also is gone from me. . . . For I am ready to halt, and my sorrow is continually before me.* Psalm 38:10, 17

"I am feeble; I'm broken. The sparkle is gone from my eye; the spring is no longer in my step; I'm ready to give up."

For a year, David went through an unbelievably dry time. He had grieved the Spirit, and the result took its toll physically and emotionally, as well as spiritually. And I would bet there are people who have, for the past year or longer, been going through a very dry season as well. The times of refreshment, the latter rain, the torrents of living water are not happening in your life as they once were. There is no longer the outpouring, the bubbling of the Holy Ghost within your heart.

It could very well be because you have grieved the Spirit. You haven't dealt with the sin you know the Lord has put His finger on. You find yourself getting dry—desert dry. Your bones are aching, your walk faltering, and your eyes dulling.

The Spirit *upon* You

After Jesus breathed on His disciples and said, "Receive ye the Spirit," He said, "Go to Jerusalem, and wait until the Spirit comes upon you" (see Luke 24:49). As the Spirit came upon Samson, upon Moses, upon David, and upon Gideon in Old Testament times, so, too, Jesus said the Spirit would come upon His disciples, and they would be His witnesses (Acts 1:8). The "coming upon," "the baptism," "the overflow" of the Spirit, whatever term you want to use, is an empowering for service.

Quenching the Spirit

The negative response to the "coming upon" ministry of the Spirit is quenching Him. "Quench not the Spirit," wrote Paul (1 Thessalonians 5:19). How is the Spirit quenched? First Thessalonians 5:20 says, "Despise not prophesyings." People quench the Spirit whenever they say, "The gifts of prophecy, tongues, healing, word of knowledge, and discernment of spirits are all irrelevant."

"Well," you protest, "I don't really despise those things. I'm open. And if the Lord wants to bring a prophecy to me or through me, I'll be happy to accept that gift."

That's not what Noah said . . .

A dove was released, and it circled the earth, which was covered with water. As it looked for a place to land, the Bible says it found no place for the sole of its foot. Throughout Scripture, the dove is the symbol of the Holy Spirit. And I believe the Holy Spirit is still circling—looking for churches, looking for people whom He can come upon, those who will not quench Him. Has He found a place to land in your church? Has He found a place to land in your life?

Genesis 8 goes on to say that Noah stretched forth his hand and grabbed the dove, bringing it unto himself. C. H. Spurgeon nailed it when he said this is an illustration of the active pursuit of the Spirit in a man's life. You see, Noah didn't say, "Well, dove, you know where I am. If you want to land on me, that's fine." No, Noah reached out his hand in faith and brought the dove in.

The person who moves in the overflow of the Spirit is not one who sits passively with arms folded. Rather, he is one who hungers and thirsts after rightness; he is one who says,

> "I deeply desire the power of the Spirit upon my life. I'm going to reach out in faith and pursue all that God has for me. I'll not be satisfied with a theology of the Spirit. I want the power of the Spirit upon my life and the gifts to flow through my life. I will not despise prophesying. I will not quench the Spirit."

Now, even if you have already received the "coming upon" of the Spirit, if you are presently not pursuing Him in the way you once did, He'll be quenched, you'll be dry, and the times of refreshing will just be a nice historical event to read about in Acts 3. What's the solution? In all three cases—whether we're resisting the Spirit, grieving the Spirit, or quenching the Spirit—the cure is repentance.

"Repent ye therefore," Peter preached, "and be converted, that your sins may be blotted out, when the times of refreshing shall come from the presence of the Lord" (Acts 3:19). He didn't say, "Get your life together, and be converted." He said, "Repent and be converted."

> Remorse says, "I feel bad about what I did, but that's my weakness, so I'll probably do it again." Repentance is not remorse.
>
> Regret says, "I feel bad about what I did because I got caught." Repentance is not regret.
>
> Resolve says, "I feel bad about what I did, but I'll try harder next time." Repentance is not resolve.

Repentance says, "I change my mind about who Jesus is." Repentance is a return to the Lord, a change of thinking, and a change of direction, which results in a change of heart.

> If you have been resisting the Spirit's tug at your heart, change your mind about who you think Jesus Christ is, and give your life to Him.
>
> If you have been grieving the Spirit, change direction and deal directly with the sin you know He is speaking to you about.
>
> If you have been quenching the Spirit, change direction and pursue Him instead of being apathetic toward Him.

And guess what? You will experience times of refreshing upon your life.

That's what happened to David when he finally dealt with the issue of his sin, for you see, David, the broken man who wrote Psalm 38, also wrote Psalm 51.

Nathan the prophet came to David and said, "David, we have a problem. Within your kingdom, there's a rich man who owns many sheep. Wanting to give a visitor leg of lamb, he went to his next-door neighbor's house. Now, his neighbor was so poor that he had only one little lamb that he treated as a pet. But the rich man took the poor man's single lamb and fed it to his guest."

"What?" thundered David. "The rich man ripped off the poor man? He shall surely die!" (see 2 Samuel 12).

You'll always know you're in sin when you're harsh with other people. Stealing a lamb was not a capital offense, yet David was treating it as such. Whenever a person is in sin, his tendency is to start nailing everyone else because finding fault with others makes us feel a little better about our own sin.

Nathan then said, "David, thou art the man. It's you. The story relates to *your* sin." And David repented. After a year of bones aching and skin stinking, after a year of failing to deal with the issue, he changed the direction of his life, and he cried out to God, "Against thee, thee only, have I sinned . . ." (Psalm 51:4).

Wait a minute. Didn't David sin against Bathsheba, against Uriah, and against Ahithophel, Bathsheba's grandfather, who was one of David's own advisors? What about them?

The psalmist rightly declared that he had sinned against God. Sin is always only against God because no matter what we do to someone else, and no matter what someone else does to us, it's less than what we or they deserve. We're all sinners and we all deserve to be wiped out, destroyed, and consumed. But God? He is perfect and holy, loving and gracious, patient and kind. He is the only One unfairly hurt by the consequences of our sin.

David went on to say, "Restore unto me the joy of thy salvation. Then will I teach transgressors thy way (see Psalm 51:12, 13). I've learned my lesson, Father. Restore me." And God did. Oh, there were still repercussions of his sin, but there was also the restoration of joy. David became a psalm-writer once again, and he experienced the time of refreshing upon his life. So will you, and so will I if today we choose to repent.

As we study the Holy Spirit in the Book of Acts, perhaps you are saying, "I just can't seem to get filled. I've been praying. I've been asking. But I can't get filled." Perhaps it is because you don't need to be filled as much as you need to be emptied—of carnality and sin, of rebellion and unbelief. How? By saying, "No more excuses, no more justifying, no more whitewashing, I repent."

Repent, precious people, and you will experience times of refreshing in beauty and in reality.

4 **Acts 4:1–3**
And as they spake unto the people, the priests, and the captain of the temple, and the Sadducees, came upon them, being grieved that they taught the people, and preached through Jesus the resurrection from the dead. And they laid hands on them, and put them in hold unto the next day: for it was now eventide.

In the Gospels, the Pharisees were the primary opponents of Jesus. Radical fundamentalists, they claimed Jesus and His disciples violated their rituals and traditions. Here in Acts, however, the Sadducees are the primary opponents of the church. Materialists through and through, they were upset with the church because of the stories of miracles and resurrections, angels and healings that circulated throughout Jerusalem.

Acts 4:4
Howbeit many of them which heard the word believed; and the number of the men was about five thousand.

Share the Word with the guys at work, the kids at home, your neighbors who are unbelievers, your mother-in-law, and your grandfather. Share the Word—it's powerful!

Acts 4:5–7
And it came to pass on the morrow, that their rulers, and elders, and scribes, and Annas the high priest, and Caiaphas, and John, and Alexander, and as many as were of the kindred of the high priest, were gathered together at Jerusalem. And when they had set them in the midst, they asked, By what power, or by what name, have ye done this?

Old Testament Scriptures declare he who did a miracle in the name of any other besides Jehovah was to be stoned (Deuteronomy 13). Here, Caiaphas, Annas, and the boys—perhaps with rocks in hand—were hoping Peter would say, "We did it in the Name of Jesus."

Acts 4:8
Then Peter, filled with the Holy Ghost, said unto them, Ye rulers of the people, and elders of Israel.

Only two months previously, Peter stood by a fire and denied Jesus Christ (Luke 22:55–57). But now, this same Peter, having been touched by a tongue of fire in Acts 2, is a different person. By the enemy's fire, Peter was burned. Touched with fire, he's hot. Under fire, he stands.

Acts 4:9, 10 (a)
If we this day be examined of the good deed done to the impotent man, by what means he is made whole; be it known unto you all, and to all the people of Israel, that by the name of Jesus Christ of Nazareth, whom ye crucified, whom God raised from the dead . . .

Look at Peter's boldness. He's saying, "We did this in the Name of Jesus Christ, whom you crucified."

Acts 4:10 (b)–12
. . . even by him doth this man stand here before you whole. This is the stone which was set at nought of you builders, which is become the head of the corner. Neither is there salvation in any other: for there is none other name under heaven given among men, whereby we must be saved.

Quoting Psalm 118:22, Peter referenced the construction of the temple. He would later write that *we* as living stones are part of a spiritual house (1 Peter 2:5). Sometimes we rub each other the wrong way. That's what living stones are supposed to do. That guy you married, the one you thought would be such a rock, turned out to be a blockhead. Why did you get stuck with him? Because that blockhead is the living stone who will knock the rough edges off you and prepare you for heaven.

Tradition has it that in the days of the construction of Solomon's temple, although the engineers at the temple mount searched and searched, they couldn't find the cornerstone. A message was sent to the quarry: "Where is the cornerstone?"

Word came back to the mount: "We sent it to you months ago."

Then someone remembered: "Oh, maybe it was that stone we didn't know what to do with. It didn't fit anywhere, so we rolled it down the hill into the Valley of Gehenna."

The Valley of Gehenna was the place of burning, the place of rubbish, the place where babies were sacrificed in the days of Ahaz, the place of weeping and sorrow, refuse and stench. And the rejected stone was indeed found in the Valley of Gehenna.

Thus, Peter makes application, saying, "The Chief Cornerstone is Jesus Christ. This One rejected by you, this One who went to hell for you is the Rock of Deuteronomy 32 (verse 4), the Cornerstone of Psalm 118 (verse 22), the Smiting Stone of Daniel 2 (verse 35), the Rock of our salvation."

Acts 4:13 (a)
Now when they saw the boldness of Peter and John, and perceived that they were unlearned and ignorant men, they marveled . . .

"Who are these unlearned and ignorant men?" asked the Jewish leaders. "They didn't study with our scholars. How is it they understand the Scriptures?"

Acts 4:13 (b)
. . . and they took knowledge of them, that they had been with Jesus.

How could Peter and John, uneducated men, get away with saying, "We did this in the Name of Jesus of Nazareth whom you crucified" (see Acts 4:10)? Because those who heard them perceived that they had been with Jesus.

After spending forty days in the presence of the Lord, Moses' face shone (Exodus 34:29). And the glow of his face prepared the people for the law he held in his hand.

Mom and Dad, how do you get Junior to listen when you need to lay down the law in your house? Spend time with Jesus and replace a glowering face with a glowing face. I'm in the process of learning that before I come down with the law, I better make sure I have spent time with the Lord. I better make sure my face is glowing.

Acts 4:14
And beholding the man which was healed standing with them, they could say nothing against it.

Please note that the lame man not only stood with Peter and John in the temple (Acts 3:11), but he stood with them in their trouble. Peter and John were in hot water here, and this guy could have said, "Hey, this is a little heavy. Thanks for healing me, but I gotta go." But he didn't. He stood by Peter and John, even though he could have been executed with them.

You see, it's easy to be friends in the temple. But you can only find out who your true friends are when you're in trouble. So, too, you will be able to evaluate the depth of your friendship with Jesus by how willing you are to stand with Him in times of testing and difficulty. Stand with the Lord, fellow lamebrains, for He stood for you and stood by you.

And stand by your brothers and sisters even

when they're blowing it, even when they're in hot water, even when they're in difficulty, even when they're in trouble.

Acts 4:15, 16
But when they had commanded them to go aside out of the council, they conferred among themselves, saying, What shall we do to these men? for that indeed a notable miracle hath been done by them is manifest to all them that dwell in Jerusalem; and we cannot deny it.

The man who was lame previously had been healed—and all Jerusalem knew it.

Acts 4:17, 18
But that it spread no further among the people, let us straitly threaten them, that they speak henceforth to no man in this name. And they called them, and commanded them not to speak at all nor teach in the name of Jesus.

You may not be able to grab the hand of a lame man and say to him, "In the Name of Jesus, stand up and walk," but there are other things you can do.

- In Mark 9:41, Jesus said we can give a cup of cold water in His Name. Every one of us can go to someone who is thirsty, someone who needs a simple act of kindness shown to them, and say, "I'm doing this in the Name of Jesus because He's blessed me."
- He said we could receive a little child in His Name (Matthew 18:5). When you go to the nursery and change a diaper or two, you can do it in the Name of Jesus.
- We are to baptize in His Name (Matthew 28:19).
- We can pronounce the remission of sins in His Name (Luke 24:47). You can be a champion of the gospel, a carrier of the Good News to the person who is despairing and feeling he has failed miserably. You can say, "In the Name of Jesus, I want to tell you that your sin is truly forgiven and forgotten."

Acts 4:19, 20
But Peter and John answered and said unto them, Whether it be right in the sight of God to hearken unto you more than unto God, judge ye. For we cannot but speak the things which we have seen and heard.

Peter and John said, "We can't help but speak that which we've seen and heard."

Do you have a hard time speaking about the

Lord? Perhaps it's because you haven't seen or heard much from Him lately. I find that my witness is proportional to what I am presently seeing and hearing from the Lord in my own life. If I am not seeing or hearing from Him, I find I don't speak as boldly, as quickly, or as readily as during those times when I am hearing His Word and seeing His work.

Acts 4:21
So when they had further threatened them, they let them go, finding nothing how they might punish them, because of the people: for all men glorified God for that which was done.

The people who saw a lame man leap for joy glorified not Peter, but God. I encourage you to keep your antennae up and your eyes open concerning ministries that are built upon men, around men, and for men. The response to the healing of the lame man is how it should always be: people glorifying God. Jesus said, "Let your light so shine before men, that they might see your good works, and glorify your Father which is in heaven" (Matthew 5:16).

Acts 4:22
For the man was above forty years old, on whom this miracle of healing was shewed.

This man had been lame for forty years, but his healing came at the exact moment that would maximize glory to God and confirm the fact that although Jesus was no longer seen physically, He was still working through His church. So often we wonder, *Lord, why aren't You working? I've been praying. I've been believing. Where are You, Lord?* It's been forty minutes, forty days, or perhaps even forty years. Take hold, dear saint. Don't give up. At the right time, the Lord will work to His glory. You watch. You wait. You'll see.

Acts 4:23
And being let go, they went to their own company, and reported all that the chief priests and elders had said unto them.

"They went to their own company." When pressure mounts, when things come down, you'll always go to your own company. When you face intimidation, problems, and potential difficulty, where do you go? Do you polish your gold chain and hang out with the lounge lizards? Or do you find yourself heading toward fellowship? Where do you go—to the lounge, or to the Lord?

Acts 4:24
And when they heard that, they lifted up their voice to God with one accord, and said, Lord, thou art God, which hast made heaven, and earth, and the sea, and all that in them is.

Please note with me three elements of this prayer.

Who He Is

When you're feeling pressured, when you're being threatened, it's always a good idea to start prayer by remembering to whom you're talking. Sometimes my problems seem so big and insurmountable until I start to worship and remember who He is—the Creator of all things.

What if I told you no one made this watch on my wrist. That's right; an incredible, fortuitous occurrence of accidental circumstances took place in which there was some crystallization under intense heat on the beach of Malibu, where the positioning of the sand crystals was such that a glass face formed. And then, amazing as this sounds, there was an explosion in a print shop down the street from Malibu out of which came a round circular object with numbers miraculously printed on it. Then, there was a turbulent storm at sea that washed some gold out of the Mariana Trench and onto the glass face. Next, a cow, walking down the beach died, and part of his skin joined to the gold that had formed around the glass face. Finally, some gears and springs joined together, and lo and behold, the watch started ticking.

You would say, "Who are you trying to fool?" Yet consider the wrist underneath the watch. With its nervous system, muscle structure, sensors, the ability to heal itself, it is a million times more complicated than the watch on the wrist. Yet people actually believe not only their wrists, but their arms, heart, brain, and eyes are all the result of an amazing, unplanned, uncreated event that "just happened."

Why has our culture been so deceived, duped into believing that the human body with all of its intricacies and capabilities "just happened"? Ask people if this watch could form by itself, and they'll say, "No." But ask them if the human body could form by itself and they'll say, "Yes." It doesn't make sense!

We need to start our prayers by remembering, "Father, You're the Creator of all things. There is nothing too hard for You" (see Jeremiah 32:17).

Acts 4:25–28
Who by the mouth of thy servant David hast said, Why did the heathen rage, and the people imagine vain things? The kings of the earth stood up, and the rulers were gathered together against the Lord, and against his Christ. For of a truth against thy holy child Jesus, whom thou hast anointed, both Herod, and Pontius Pilate, with the Gentiles, and the people of Israel, were gathered together, for to do whatsoever thy hand and thy counsel determined before to be done.

What Is Happening

"In Psalm 2, Father," the believers prayed, "You told us that the heathen would try to come against You and Your people—just as we're seeing here. We acknowledge that this is all in accordance with Your will."

David wrote that the heathen seem to prosper while the godly suffer (Psalm 73). Peter would later write, "Think it not strange when fiery trials come upon you" (see 1 Peter 4:12).

When persecution comes, it is in accordance with the Word and the will of the Father.

Acts 4:29, 30
And now, Lord, behold their threatenings: and grant unto thy servants, that with all boldness they may speak thy word, by stretching forth thine hand to heal; and that signs and wonders may be done by the name of thy holy child Jesus.

Why We Come

The early church didn't pray that they might have a break from persecution, but that they might have boldness in persecution. And that kind of prayer prevails!

Acts 4:31 (a)
And when they had prayed, the place was shaken where they were assembled together . . .

We often pray when we are shaken up. These guys prayed so they could *be* shaken up!

Acts 4:31 (b)
. . . and they were all filled with the Holy Ghost, and they spake the word of God with boldness.

They were all filled with the Holy Ghost, and they spoke—not in tongues—but the Word of God. Never forget that the purpose of the empowering of the Spirit is not that we might speak in tongues. The purpose of the power of the Spirit is that we might be bold witnesses (Acts 1:8).

Acts 4:32, 33
And the multitude of them that believed were of one heart and of one soul: neither said any of them that ought of the things which he possessed was his own; but they had all things common. And with great power gave the apostles witness of the resurrection of the Lord Jesus: and great grace was upon them all.

They had great power and experienced great grace. I like that!

Acts 4:34–37
Neither was there any among them that lacked: for as many as were possessors of lands or houses sold them, and brought the prices of the things that were sold, and laid them down at the apostles' feet: and distribution was made unto every man according as he had need. And Joses, who by the apostles was surnamed Barnabas, (which is, being interpreted, The son of consolation,) a Levite, and of the country of Cyprus, having land, sold it, and brought the money, and laid it at the apostles' feet.

They shared together not out of compulsion, but out of compassion; not out of obligation, but out of love.

5 **Acts 5:1–2**
But a certain man named Ananias, with Sapphira his wife, sold a possession, And kept back part of the price, his wife also being privy to it, and brought a certain part, and laid it at the apostles' feet.

George MacDonald rightly said, "Half the misery in the world is caused by people trying to look rather than trying to be."

Such was the case with Ananias, whose name means "God is gracious," and his wife Sapphira, whose name means "Beautiful." Wanting to fit in with the believers who sold their goods and shared their resources with the new believers who were in Jerusalem for Pentecost (Acts 4:32–37), Ananias and Sapphira sold a piece of land and brought a portion of the proceeds to the apostles. The problem was not that Ananias held back some money for himself, but that he was trying to appear more religious than he really was. The issue was not selfishness. The issue was hypocrisy.

Acts 5:3
But Peter said, Ananias, why hath Satan filled thine heart to lie to the Holy Ghost, and to keep back part of the price of the land?

Oliver Wendell Holmes said, "Sin has many tools, but a lie is the handle which fits them all."[2] As with Ananias, no matter what the area of sin, a lie can always be found at the root.

Acts 5:4 (a)
Whiles it remained, was it not thine own? and after it was sold, was it not in thine own power?

"We didn't ask you to sell the property," Peter said to Ananias. "But when you did, you could have done with the money whatever you wished."

Acts 5:4 (b)
Why hast thou conceived this thing in thine heart? thou hast not lied unto men, but unto God.

In verse 3 Peter said, "Why have you lied to the Holy Ghost?" In verse 4 he said, "You have not lied to men, but to God." Thus, this is an important proof text for the doctrine of the Trinity.

Acts 5:5–7
And Ananias hearing these words fell down, and gave up the ghost: and great fear came on all them that heard these things. And the young men arose, wound him up, and carried him out, and buried him. And it was about the space of three hours after, when his wife, not knowing what was done, came in.

Sapphira had no idea about what had happened to Ananias. Why? Because Satan always keeps his victims in the dark. Perhaps there was a time when you were involved in an area of sin, and although others prayed for you, talked to you, and were concerned about you, you remained in the dark until everything came down on top of you.

Satan always operates that way. Like Sapphira, his victims are always the last to know of the destruction he has planned for them. We are so easily blinded, and that is why we need one another. How I thank the Lord for the brother or sister who will come to me and say, "Be careful. Beware."

Acts 5:8–11
And Peter answered unto her, Tell me whether ye sold the land for so much? And she said, Yea, for so much. Then Peter said unto her, How is it that ye have agreed together to tempt the Spirit of the Lord? behold, the feet of them which have buried thy husband are at the door, and shall carry thee out. Then fell she down straightway at his feet, and yielded up the ghost: and the young men came in, and found her dead, and, carrying her forth, buried her by her husband. And great fear came upon all the church, and upon as many as heard these things.

The church went from "great grace and great power" in Acts 4:33 to "great fear" in Acts 5:11.

For topical study of Acts 5:1–11 entitled "Hypocrisy Kills," turn to page 654.

Acts 5:12–13
And by the hands of the apostles were many signs and wonders wrought among the people; (and they were all with one accord in Solomon's porch. And of the rest durst no man join himself to them: but the people magnified them.

People held the early church in high esteem, but they didn't rush to join. After hearing about the penalty for Ananias' lie, can you blame them?

Acts 5:14
And believers were the more added to the Lord, multitudes both of men and women.)

Although the church was no longer the "in" place to hang out for anyone and everyone, those who had truly been touched by the Lord said, "This is where I need to be: in the place of power and purity. Even if it's painful, even if I'm smitten, and even if I'm uncomfortable from time to time, this is where I'll stay." The Book of Acts illustrates how intimately purity and power are linked together. Many times, we sing, "More love, more power . . ." when in reality our need is less sin and less carnality. A wise and loving Father, knowing the results of the misuse of power, will not give it to those who are not pure.

Acts 5:15, 16
Insomuch that they brought forth the sick into the streets, and laid them on beds and couches, that at the least the shadow of

Peter passing by might overshadow some of them. There came also a multitude out of the cities round about unto Jerusalem, bringing sick folks, and them which were vexed with unclean spirits: and they were healed every one.

Peter's shadow was not powerful in and of itself. It was simply a point of contact and a place of release for people who were prepared to receive healing.

As a child, I suffered from intense asthma. My mom told me that many nights, after I stopped breathing and started turning blue, she would rush me into the bathroom and turn on the hot water so the steam could open my breathing passages. She also told me recently that during those long nights, she would listen to the radio, while a certain preacher would often instruct people to pray for healing by placing their hands on their radios.

Many were the nights, Mom said, she would hold me on her lap, lay her hand on the radio, and pray for my healing. Now, there was nothing magical or mystical about the radio, but like Peter's shadow, like anointing with oil, like the laying on of hands, like agreeing together with a verbal amen, it was simply a contact point for the release of faith, blessing, and eventual healing.

Acts 5:17
Then the high priest rose up, and all they that were with him, (which is the sect of the Sadducees,) and were filled with indignation.

Vehemently opposed to anything having to do with the supernatural, it is no wonder that, after observing the multitude of healings, the Sadducees were filled with indignation.

Acts 5:18
And laid their hands on the apostles, and put them in the common prison.

Although the Sadducees were a numerical minority, they were the ones who held the purse strings as well as the political power.

Acts 5:19, 20
But the angel of the Lord by night opened the prison doors, and brought them forth, and said, Go, stand and speak in the temple to the people all the words of this life.

"All the words of this life"—I like that phrase! You see, we're not just talking about future life, afterlife, or eternal life. Jesus said, "I have come

that you might have life now and have it more abundantly" (see John 10:10).

Life is what the Bible is all about. I don't understand those who say, "Well, the Bible's great and it's a good starting point, but we have more to add. We have some innovative techniques, some educational tools, and some resources that were unavailable to those who penned the Bible that can help heal people psychologically and emotionally." Peter would later write that God has given us everything that pertains to life and godliness (2 Peter 1:3). It's all in the Word.

Acts 5:21
And when they heard that, they entered into the temple early in the morning, and taught.

"They entered into the temple early in the morning." I like that! It doesn't say, "They went into the temple the first chance they had," or "They waited until noon." No, following their release from prison the night before, the apostles headed straight for the temple early the next morning. The largest nation in the world today is procrasti-nation. No doubt about it! Our tendency is to say,

"Thank You, Lord. You freed me from prison. You freed me from eternal damnation, from meaningless existence, and from emotional depression. You opened the door for Me, Lord, and I'm going to share Your gospel with others real soon—maybe at noon, maybe tomorrow night. I know You told me to go and share the Word with everyone. And I'll get right on it, Lord—pretty soon."

Procrastination is a real problem in spiritual life and spiritual discipline. When the Lord speaks to your heart, be it in Bible study, in devotions, through a book you read, or through a sister or brother, learn to respond immediately.

I read of one very wealthy inventor who said, "Without exception, after I have invented something and patented it, at least ten men come to me and say, "I thought of that a long time ago." But the difference between their poverty and my wealth is that they thought about it, and I *did* it."

The same thing is true spiritually. There are those who think, *You know, I really should share my faith,* or *I really should intercede,* or *I really should get involved.* They think and they think and they think, while they remain poor spiritually. The ones who are used by the Lord are those who hear and *do.*

Acts 5:21–24

But the high priest came, and they that were with him, and called the council together, and all the senate of the children of Israel, and sent to the prison to have them brought. But when the officers came, and found them not in the prison, they returned, and told, saying, The prison truly found we shut with all safety, and the keepers standing without before the doors: but when we had opened, we found no man within. Now when the high priest and the captain of the temple and the chief priests heard these things, they doubted of them whereunto this would grow.

These officials were greatly disturbed. "What next?" they wondered. "Where's this thing going to go? Where's it going to stop?" Good question!

Acts 5:25–28 (a)

Then came one and told them, saying, Behold, the men whom ye put in prison are standing in the temple, and teaching the people. Then went the captain with the officers, and brought them without violence: for they feared the people, lest they should have been stoned. And when they had brought them, they set them before the council: and the high priest asked them, Saying, Did not we straitly command you that ye should not teach in this name? and, behold, ye have filled Jerusalem with your doctrine . . .

"Ye have filled Jerusalem with your doctrine." What a wonderful indictment! The first time my life was threatened in ministry was when a fellow knocked on my door, looked me in the eye, and said, "You have ruined Applegate Valley. I suggest you leave, or I can't guarantee you'll be alive a year from now."

He went on to explain that before Applegate Christian Fellowship started, there were some wonderful parties in the area. But when some of the best party-ers got saved, the party was over.

Acts 5:28 (b)

. . . and intend to bring this man's blood upon us.

Hadn't the crowd said to Pontius Pilate, "Let His blood be upon us and our children" (see Matthew 27:25)? Yet here they are complaining because they're being made to feel guilty and responsible for the death of Jesus.

Acts 5:29

Then Peter and the other apostles answered and said, We ought to obey God rather than men.

"We must obey God," declared Peter. "Even though you have legislative and political authority, the fact remains that there is a higher authority than you: God. He has told us to go into all the world and preach the gospel to every creature. We have no other recourse than to obey Him."

God has set men in positions of authority in order to maintain peace (Romans 13). But if the authorities the Lord has ordained act contrary to Him, we must submit to Him rather than them. Consequently, should there come a time when those in authority say, "We're not going to allow witnessing on the streets or in public places because it violates the separation of Church and State," we must not submit to that kind of law. We answer to a higher Authority who has commanded us to share the Word wherever we go (Matthew 28:19).

Civil disobedience is not uncommon in the Scriptures.

- The midwives in Egypt were told to destroy all of the Jewish male children. They refused, and God honored them (Exodus 1:17, 21).
- Rahab the harlot hid the spies who were sent in to scope out the Land, and she withstood the questioning of civil authorities. God blessed her and put her in the line of Messiah (Joshua 2:4; Matthew 1:5).
- Against the king's command, Shadrach, Meshach, and Abed-nego did not bow their knees to the image of Nebuchadnezzar. God blessed them and stood with them in the fiery furnace (Daniel 3:18, 25).
- Daniel refused to cease from praying three times a day, even though doing so was in direct violation of the law. God honored him and saved him in the lions' den (Daniel 6:10, 21, 22).

However, regarding biblical civil disobedience, there are two important requirements to keep in mind.

Civil Disobedience Must Be Carried Out with Scriptural Authority

The angel of the Lord said to the apostles, "Go speak in the temple" (see Acts 5:20). In addition, Jesus had already commissioned them, saying, "Go into all the world and preach the gospel" (see Matthew 28:19). Thus, the disciples weren't following a nebulous feeling; they were following the Word of God. You see, one cannot simply say, "God told me I can go seventy-five miles per hour in this thirty-five-mile-per-hour zone," or "I'm not going to obey my parents because I just don't feel right about what they're saying."

If you are going to disobey your parents, oppose the leading of your husband, or contradict the laws of the land, it must be by the authority of Scripture.

Civil Disobedience Must Be Carried Out with Humility

Peter and the apostles willingly took their lumps. In every case throughout Scripture, those who said, "We can't do this because we have a higher authority," did so without hostility, bitterness, or violence.

Acts 5:30–32
The God of our fathers raised up Jesus, whom ye slew and hanged on a tree. Him hath God exalted with his right hand to be a Prince and a Saviour, for to give repentance to Israel, and forgiveness of sins. And we are his witnesses of these things; and so is also the Holy Ghost, whom God hath given to them that obey him.

"You allowed Jesus Christ to be crucified and hung on a tree, but God has exalted Him," declared Peter. "We're not going to back down from this message."

Acts 5:33–34
When they heard that, they were cut to the heart, and took counsel to slay them. Then stood there up one in the council, a Pharisee, named Gamaliel, a doctor of the law, had in reputation among all the people, and commanded to put the apostles forth a little space.

Due to his knowledge of the law and because he walked with great integrity in his attempt to keep the law, Gamaliel was called "The Beauty of the Law" by his contemporaries. A brilliant thinker and one of the most influential teachers in all of Jewish history, Gamaliel was Paul's teacher. Jewish historians tell us that Gamaliel's one criticism of Paul was that it was impossible to find enough reading material for him. This is not surprising, since those who study Greek tell us that Paul's vocabulary and sentence structure is the most sophisticated of any Greek writer. The guy was brilliant.

Acts 5:35–39
And said unto them, Ye men of Israel, take heed to yourselves what ye intend to do as touching these men. For before these days rose up Theudas, boasting himself to be somebody; to whom a number of men, about four hundred, joined themselves: who was slain; and all, as many as obeyed him, were

scattered, and brought to nought. After this man rose up Judas of Galilee in the days of the taxing, and drew away much people after him: he also perished; and all, even as many as obeyed him, were dispersed. And now I say unto you, Refrain from these men, and let them alone: for if this counsel or this work be of men, it will come to nought: But if it be of God, ye cannot overthrow it; lest haply ye be found even to fight against God.

Gamaliel wisely said, "If what these guys are doing is through human energy, it will come to nothing. But if what they're doing is of God, you'll be fighting against God, and you won't have a prayer. So back off. Let them go. Don't forget what happened to Theudas," continued Gamaliel. "Men gathered around him, and when they were slaughtered, the movement died as well. And what about Judas of Galilee? When he launched an insurrection, his followers also perished in the process."

Theudas came on the scene claiming to possess deep spirituality. He claimed to be a Messiah who would lead Israel into spiritual illumination. Judas of Galilee launched a political reformation based upon less taxation. He claimed to be a Messiah who would free Israel from Roman bondage. Both were phonies. It's easy for you and me to spot a false Messiah, a false teacher, or a false leader. He will do the same two things that Gamaliel said Theudas and Judas of Galilee did: Like Theudas, he will "boast himself to be somebody," claiming to have supernatural or special powers. Or like Judas, he will "draw away much people after him," saying, "Follow me, and I'll set you free."

Acts 5:40–42
And to him they agreed: and when they had called the apostles, and beaten them, they commanded that they should not speak in the name of Jesus, and let them go. And they departed from the presence of the council, rejoicing that they were counted worthy to suffer shame for his name. And daily in the temple, and in every house, they ceased not to teach and preach Jesus Christ.

Winston Churchill once defined a fanatic as someone who can't change his mind and won't change the subject. That's what these guys did. They wouldn't change their minds, and they didn't change the subject. Knowing Jesus is Lord, they kept talking about Him wherever they went.

HYPOCRISY KILLS
A Topical Study of
Acts 5:1–11

Things are not always what they appear to be, particularly in the realm of spirituality.

Some years ago, a painting was auctioned for many thousands of dollars. It portrayed a monk sitting at a table with a prayer book before him, his hands folded in the posture of prayer. Upon closer inspection, however, the buyer discovered that the prayer book on the table was not a prayer book at all, but a shallow pan. And the hands folded together seemingly in prayer actually held a lemon. Thus, the picture portrayed not a monk praying, but a man squeezing lemons.

So, too, oftentimes, we think, *My, that person is spiritual.* But upon closer examination, it proves to be a bitter, sour story when we see the real picture. This is precisely what happened in our text concerning the story of Ananias and Sapphira.

At this point, the church was experiencing great grace (Acts 4:33). Jews had come from all over the world to celebrate the Jewish festival of Pentecost. During the Feast of Pentecost, thousands were converted to Christ. Apparently not wanting their new brothers and sisters to return to their homes without being instructed and grounded in the Word, the Jerusalem believers pooled their resources and shared with one another in order that the new believers could remain in Jerusalem where they could grow together.

Ananias and Sapphira, apparently wanting to fit in and seem spiritual, sold their property but secretly kept a chunk for themselves. As they brought their money to the apostles, Peter asked, "Is this the total amount of the land?"

"Certainly," replied Ananias. And he fell down dead.

Three hours later, his wife Sapphira came in. "Tell me, Sapphira," said Peter, "when you and your husband sold your property, did you bring all the money?"

"Yes," she answered. And like her husband, Sapphira was history.

"I don't understand," you say. "The Christians were flourishing, and a couple brought some money to the apostles to share with their brothers and sisters. Wasn't it a little severe to strike them dead because they didn't give it all? Wasn't death a rather extreme penalty for fibbing?"

The answer to that question lies in the principle of precedence that says:

God will make a strong statement at *one* point in time to be remembered and applied to *all* points in time.

An example of this is seen in Joshua 6.

After wandering in the wilderness for forty years, the children of Israel were at last ready to enter the Promised Land. With great rejoicing and anticipation, they crossed the Jordan River only to find the powerful and seemingly impenetrable city of Jericho looming large before them. But the Lord miraculously delivered the city of Jericho into their hands as the walls came tumbling down. Then He said, "Don't take anything from Jericho. Other cities you can spoil, but let this city be a sacrifice to Me" (see Joshua 6:18, 19).

All except one of the Israelites obeyed the Lord's command. His name was Achan. Seeing the glimmer of gold, the shining of silver, and some Babylonian garments that were the hot threads of the day, Achan thought, *What would it matter if I borrowed a bit of gold, took a sliver of silver, and lifted a garment or two?* So, he grabbed the goods and hid them under the floor of his tent.

The next battle found the Israelites at war with a little town called Ai. It should have been an easy fight, but they got whipped. "What's going on, Lord?" Joshua cried. "We conquered Jericho in Your Name, but at Ai, we were soundly defeated. Why?" God informed Joshua that sin in the camp had defeated the country—and the one who sinned was to be put to death (Joshua 7:15).

"Isn't that a bit severe?" you ask.

No, because in this new country, the Lord wanted to reveal from the very outset how deadly serious He was about sin. Why? Because sin would kill them. Not just Achan, the one who committed the sin, but his whole family as well.

Precious people, when you and I sin, other people are bruised and beaten and end up in the pit along with us. That's why, among other reasons, sin stinks. God made that point very clear in those first days in the new land. "Listen," He said. "Sin brings pain. It'll hurt you. It'll affect your family and others who are linked to you. You'll end up in the pit."

Now we're in another new country here in Acts—not a new country physically, but a new country spiritually. The church has been formed as an entirely new entity. And just as sin had to be dealt with severely and pointedly in the Old Testament, so, too, a powerful point is being made in the New Testament. I'm so glad we can study this chapter and see what God thinks and how He feels about sin, because if we were dealt with in the same way that Ananias and Sapphira were, our church would be very small. Certainly, you wouldn't have a pastor—at least not this one!

Think about it: What if, like Ananias and Sapphira, we were struck down for the same sin for which they were struck down—the sin of hypocrisy? Whenever we stood up and sang, "All to Jesus, I surrender; all to Him I freely give . . . I surrender all, I sur . . ." Boom! Down we'd go! If we were treated in the same manner as Ananias and Sapphira were, the church would be thinned out real fast! And so God is saying, "I'm going to make a severe point at this point in time in order that you might get the point for all time. Learn the lesson: Hypocrisy kills."

Hypocrisy was the one sin that riled our Lord Jesus. He loved to eat with the sinners. He hung out with the publicans. The tax collectors and prostitutes felt comfortable with Him. But when He said, "Woe unto you . . ." it was always directed at those who wanted to be thought of as more spiritual than they really were.

The word "hypocrite" comes from the Greek word *hupokrites,* which means "one who is wearing a mask." It refers to actors who wore large masks on stage in order to be seen by those in the back row. *Hupokrites,* then, were those who had two faces: one for the stage and one for the street.

I am told there is a restaurant in New York City whose business is thriving because of hypocrisy . . .

> A couple is seated, and the maitre d' hands them menus. Both contain the same items, but because the prices listed on the woman's menu are three times higher than the prices on the man's menu, when the man says, "Order whatever you want," the woman is highly impressed.

Hypocrisy may be good for the restaurant business, but it is grievous to the heart of God. Psalm 103:14 says the Father knows our frames, He remembers we are but dust. Paul writes in 2 Corinthians 4:7 that we have this treasure, Christ Jesus, in *earthen* vessels. In other words, God knows we have frailties and earthiness, but it doesn't bother Him. Jesus loved to be around real people. It was the *hupokrites*—the religious folks and the play-actors—who were a problem to Him because hypocrisy truly kills.

What does it kill?

Hypocrisy Kills Your Witness.

How many people say, "I'm not going to go to church. I took my car to a mechanic who had a fish in the yellow pages. And man, I got ripped off. He charged high prices and did lousy work, and yet he has a Bible on his desk and his radio tuned to the Christian station"? Or how many make a business deal with one who claims to be a believer and they find out later they were charged exorbitant prices?

If you say, "I'm not going to become a believer because of hypocrites," you will spend eternity in hell with the very hypocrites you hate. So if you don't like them, get saved, get to church, and get right. Otherwise, you'll be with them forever. Whenever people say to me, "There are hypocrites in church," I say, "You're right. That's why you will fit right in! We freely acknowledge that we are not even close to perfection."

When people say, "I'm not going to go to church or get saved because of hypocrites," they're wrong. Nonetheless, the fact remains that people use that excuse more than any other for not going to church or seeking the Lord. Hypocrisy kills your witness.

Hypocrisy Kills Your Joy.

Just as Ananias and Sapphira were struck down, so, too, is your joy whenever you're hypocritical. You become sour. You become analytical. In order to justify your own hypocrisy, you begin to analyze others and see how hypocritical they are that you might feel better about your own hypocrisy. You become a sour, dour believer, soaking in the lemon juice of bitterness. You lose the joy of just being real before the Lord.

Hypocrisy Kills Your Peace.

Living in hypocrisy, one must always keep his mask on and his guard up. Fearing that someday someone will see the real him, he becomes tense, uptight, and unstable. Therefore, as it did with the early church, great fear should come upon us—the fear of hypocrisy. While such fear could potentially freak us out, in reality it should free us up. You see, when we finally get the picture of Acts 5, we understand that the Lord is asking us just to be who we are. Paul put it this way: "By the grace of God I am what I am . . ." (1 Corinthians 15:10)

Hypocrisy works from the outside in and says, "I'm going to try to be this way, and maybe it'll sink in a bit." It's imitation.

Christianity works from the inside out as Jesus says, "I'm going to work within you to do and to will of My good pleasure" (see Philippians 2:13). It's impartation.

How I need to understand that the Lord delights in me just the way I am. Those areas that need to be changed, He will change—not by my imitation of spiritual people, but rather by His impartation of the Holy Spirit. I don't have to play a game. I don't have to learn the phrases. I don't have to wear a tie. I can just be who I am, because the Lord looks at me and says, "I know what you are, and I love you. I'll work within you regarding the areas of your life that need changing. Don't try to pretend to be something you're not. Don't put on airs. Don't be a church person—learning the phrases and going through the motions."

When this begins to sink in, am I ever free!

"You mean, Lord, You love me just as I am, and You want me to be just the way I am, with my humor or lack thereof, with my style or lack thereof? You just love me? You want me to be how You made me? This earthen vessel?"

"Yes," answers the Lord. "I not only love you, I enjoy you—except when you put on an act, pretend to be something you're not, or try to impress people with a spirituality that isn't really there."

Hypocrisy will kill your witness as others see the masks you wear and the act you put on. Hypocrisy will kill your joy as you analyze and criticize others in order to justify your own deceit. Hypocrisy will kill your peace as you live in fear that someone will someday see the real you.

Put it away. Give it up. Be free!

In Jesus' Name.

6

Acts 6:1 (a)
And in those days, when the number of the disciples was multiplied . . .

Notice the mathematics in the Book of Acts. In chapter 2, the Lord added to the church daily such as should be saved (Acts 2:47). Here in chapter 6, the number of the disciples was multiplied. But between the addition to the church and the multiplication of the church, there was subtraction from the church when the Lord removed Ananias and Sapphira in chapter 5.

Sometimes that happens to us as well. That is, things are moving along. We're growing. We're being added to—then suddenly we're hit with a painful period of subtraction. If you're in that place today, take hope. It means good things are coming. As He did in Acts, the Lord often subtracts right before He multiplies.

Acts 6:1 (b)
. . . there arose a murmuring of the Grecians against the Hebrews, because their widows were neglected in the daily ministration.

Three potential problems began to appear in the church at this point: the surfacing of discrimination, the temptation of professionalism, and the challenge of prioritization.

The Surfacing of Discrimination

During the days of Alexander the Great, Greek culture, style of dress, and philosophy of life permeated the then-known world. As a result, many Jews, known as Grecians or Hellenists, adopted Grecian ways. Other Jews, referred to as Hebrews, remained true to the old ways and traditions of Judaism. The Hebrew believers looked down on the Grecian believers as compromising, "second-class" Jews. Thus, with the Grecians claiming that their widows were being neglected in the daily serving of food, discrimination set in. Consequently, there was a potential division in the baby church based upon who was supposedly "more spiritual"—a problem that can surface whenever a church grows. . . .

"Can you believe it? He actually wore a business suit. Who let *him* in?"

"Hey, those bikers can't come dressed like that."

Discrimination can take place in all kinds of subtle ways, and the early church was no exception. Here in Acts 6, as the church was multiplying, storm clouds were forming that could have blown the whole thing apart.

Acts 6:2
Then the twelve called the multitude of the disciples unto them, and said, It is not reason that we should leave the word of God, and serve tables.

The Temptation of Professionalism

Oftentimes people have said to me, "What are you going to do about this situation, Jon? You're the pastor. Murmur, murmur, murmur."

More often than not, I have replied, "What are *you* going to do about it? That's the issue. Don't look to the professionals. If you're aware of the problem, it could be that you've been called to be part of the solution. The reason you feel the burden, the reason you're aware of the situation is because God is calling *you*."

Acts 6:3–5 (a)
Wherefore, brethren, look ye out among you seven men of honest report, full of the Holy Ghost and wisdom, whom we may appoint over this business. But we will give ourselves continually to prayer, and to the ministry of the word. And the saying pleased the whole multitude . . .

The Challenge of Prioritization

The apostles said, "The widows are in need—Hebrews and Hellenists, traditionalists and Grecians alike. But our calling is not the distribution of food. Our calling is the distribution of the Word. Therefore, choose people whom you know to be good men, godly men, gifted men—and let them take care of this matter."

Acts 6:5 (b)
. . . and they chose Stephen, a man full of faith and of the Holy Ghost. . . .

Stephen would become the first martyr. He was a powerful Bible expositor, as we will see in chapter 7.

Acts 6:5 (c)
... and Philip ...

Philip went on to become an evangelist. The father of four daughters who became prophetesses, he was a godly man who increased the boundaries of ministry.

Acts 6:5 (d)
... and Prochorus ...

Church history tells us that Prochorus would later become the secretary, or the assistant, to the apostle John. Following John's death, Prochorus became the bishop of Nicodema—a large and growing church—before being martyred himself.

Acts 6:5 (e)
... and Nicanor, and Timon, and Parmenas, and Nicolas a proselyte of Antioch.

Many Bible scholars believe that, after serving faithfully for a season as a deacon, Nicolas started a sect known as the Nicolaitans, mentioned in Revelation 2 and 3. Although we might be mistaken and will find Nicolas to be a good brother when we see him in heaven, the weight of evidence seems to indicate that he was one who veered into heresy.

For topical study of Acts 6:1–5 entitled "The Church: A Place for Programs?" turn to page 660.

Acts 6:6
Whom they set before the apostles: and when they had prayed, they laid their hands on them.

We usually lay hands on someone and *then* pray. These guys went about it differently. They prayed before the laying on of hands. Perhaps this is what Paul meant when he told Timothy to "Lay hands on no man suddenly" (see 1 Timothy 5:22). Over the years, I have ordained people and ratified ministry far too quickly. Thus, I am slowly learning the importance of praying *before* the laying on of hands in order that I might hear the heart of the Lord and the witness of the Spirit before setting someone apart for ministry.

Acts 6:7 (a)
And the word of God increased; and the number of the disciples multiplied in Jerusalem greatly ...

This verse should be starred, circled, underlined, and highlighted by everyone involved in ministry. The secret to church growth and ministry expansion is simply to feed the flock. Healthy sheep reproduce. It's inevitable.

Acts 6:7 (b)
... and a great company of the priests were obedient to the faith.

For topical study of Acts 6:7 entitled "Finding and Focusing Your Gifts," turn to page 666.

Any priest walking into the temple on the first Good Friday, seeing the veil rent from top to bottom, would have known something miraculous had taken place. After all, it would have been unthinkable for any man to tear the veil. Everyone knew the penalty for entering the Holy of Holies unworthily was death. It also would have been impossible for any man to tear the veil. Sixty feet wide, thirty feet high, and ten inches thick, the veil was so massive it required a company of priests to hang it. No wonder a great number of priests—some seeing the torn veil, others hearing about it and watching what was happening in Jerusalem—were converted.

Acts 6:8
And Stephen, full of faith and power, did great wonders and miracles among the people.

In Matthew 25:21, Jesus taught that those who are faithful in little things will be made rulers over greater things. If we desire to be used by the Lord, we must be faithful in whatever God gives us to do in the beginning days of our ministry. Although Scripture tells us not to despise the days of small things (Zechariah 4:10), yet many people find themselves reluctant to do the seemingly insignificant tasks. Desirous of something grander, they feel menial service is beneath them. But the way of the Lord is that we first prove ourselves in smaller things and, as we are faithful in them, He will give us greater responsibility.

The reward for faithfulness in service is greater service. Jesus came on the scene and said something radical when He said, "Happiness is found in losing your life, in giving yourself away.

Happiness is found in serving, not in being served; in giving, not in getting" (see Matthew 10:39). Today if you're feeling somewhat blue, perhaps it's because you're not engaging yourself in serving others. When you feel like throwing in the towel, take up the towel instead. Wash someone's feet and suddenly you'll be refreshed.

Stephen modeled this beautifully. He began by serving tables, helping feed widows—not necessarily a glorious position, not an exalted ministry. But because he was faithful, he was then elected to the office of deacon (Acts 6:5)—one of seven men chosen by the early church as being a man full of the Holy Ghost, full of wisdom, and full of good works. Here, two verses later, we see him doing "great wonders and miracles among the people." Stephen went from being a table server to a deacon to a miracle-worker because he was faithful at each step.

Acts 6:9–11
Then there arose certain of the synagogue, which is called the synagogue of the Libertines, and Cyrenians, and Alexandrians, and of them of Cilicia and of Asia, disputing with Stephen. And they were not able to resist the wisdom and the spirit by which he spake. Then they suborned men, which said, We have heard him speak blasphemous words against Moses, and against God.

These who came against Stephen and argued with Stephen were outgunned by Stephen. They couldn't beat his logic. They couldn't resist his reasoning. They couldn't withstand his persuasive speech. So what did they do? They hired liars who said, "We've heard him speak blasphemous words against Moses and against God."

Acts 6:12–15
And they stirred up the people, and the elders, and the scribes, and came upon him, and caught him, and brought him to the council, And set up false witnesses, which said, This man ceaseth not to speak blasphemous words against this holy place, and the law: For we have heard him say, that this Jesus of Nazareth shall destroy this place, and shall change the customs which Moses delivered us. And all that sat in the council, looking stedfastly on him, saw his face as it had been the face of an angel.

Addressing his students concerning ministry, C. H. Spurgeon said, "Men, when you teach on heaven, let there always be a glow on your face, a gleam in your eye, and a smile on your lips. When you teach on hell, your normal face will do fine."

As false accusations, lies, and anger preceded the rocks that would soon follow, Stephen's face reflected neither hatred nor horror, but heaven.

THE CHURCH: A PLACE FOR PROGRAMS?
A Topical Study of
Acts 6:3, 4

A nother parable put he forth unto them, saying, The kingdom of heaven is like to a grain of mustard seed, which a man took, and sowed in his field: Which indeed is the least of all seeds: but when it is grown, it is the greatest among herbs, and becometh a tree, so that the birds of the air come and lodge in the branches thereof.   Matthew 13:31, 32

As Jesus taught about His kingdom, He used an analogy that, at first reading, is rather puzzling and perplexing, for nowhere in the world has there ever been a mustard seed known to grow into a tree big enough to support birds. Was Jesus mistaken in His botany? Was He sloppy with His analogy? Was He confused factually?

No, what Jesus said, while at first puzzling and perplexing, was actually profound and prophetic, as it relates to His kingdom, the church. For, like the mustard seed, the church would begin in simplicity, but would grow into something abnormal and complex. And whenever the church loses her simplicity, birds—a scriptural symbol for evil—have roosted in her branches.

At the outset, the early church was about only four things (Acts 2:42): the apostles' doctrine, fellowship, the breaking of bread, and prayer. But here in the sixth chapter of Acts, her simplicity was challenged as the temptation arose to pull the apostles away from the ministry of the Word into the organization of a food distribution program.

Is there any place for programs in the church?

To answer that question, whatever we want to know concerning the body of Christ is not found in ministry magazines or theological manuals. Rather, everything we need to know concerning any point of theological understanding can be found in Jesus. Hebrews 12:2 tells us that it is Jesus who is the author and finisher of our faith. Therefore, when I want to know what the body should be like, I needn't turn to a manual, but to the Master. I should look at Jesus. How? The Gospels reveal certain aspects of His physical body that tell us what His spiritual body—the church—should be like.

His Body Was Conceived Miraculously.

Jesus' physical body was conceived when the Holy Spirit came upon the virgin Mary. His body was conceived miraculously and supernaturally (Luke 1:35). The same is true of the body of Christ in any given location. It must not be born through demographic strategy or statistical studies. It must not be born from clever organizing or careful analysis. I believe that when the Lord chooses to birth His body, He sovereignly moves upon virgin territory—a new area, a new place, a new work He desires to do. And by His grace, something is miraculously conceived.

I think about the body at Applegate Christian Fellowship and how the Lord miraculously, sovereignly, graciously did something there that none of us expected. It wasn't the result of studies or strategy. It wasn't carefully worked through or thought out. It was just the Lord moving in a new place. Before that Fellowship was birthed twenty-five years ago, I am told there was a group of elderly ladies who, for ten years, met every week to pray that the Lord would do something special in that region. Only heaven will reward and reveal fully what took place in the Spirit as a result of those ladies praying, tilling the soil, and readying this place for the seed that would be planted when the Word was opened.

His Members Functioned Harmoniously.

Jesus wasn't paralyzed in His right hand, or lame in His left foot. No, all of the members of His earthly body functioned harmoniously. So, too, every member is to function in the body of His church. In Romans 12 we are told that we are His body, and each member is to function accordingly.

He Was Coordinated Physically.

Jesus' body was not spastic. Parts of His body were not going off in one direction or lurching off in another. So, too, the body of His church is meant to move in coordination. How? The same way our physical bodies are coordinated—by the body responding to impulses sent from the brain through the nervous system. Jesus is the Head (Ephesians 1:22). The impulses that will guide us and direct us as a church will come from Him through the "nervous system" of the Holy Spirit. When we, the body, respond to Jesus through the leading of the Spirit, we will move in coordination and harmony.

Upon Birth, His Body Was Attacked Ruthlessly.

Following the birth of Jesus, Herod ordered the annihilation of all male children two years of age and younger (Matthew 2:16). In the attack launched against this newborn baby, His physical body was immediately threatened. So, too, I recall as the Applegate Body was formed twenty-five years ago, we were attacked sometimes ignorantly, other times intentionally. In those early years, as we met at Cantrell Buckley Park, baptizing people in the river and playing guitars on the hillside, the attacks and vicious rumors were very real. So, too, any body—any expression of Jesus—will be attacked initially.

He Grew in Wisdom and Stature Favorably.

Luke 2:52 tells us that as Jesus grew in wisdom and stature, He found favor with God and man. Jesus did not remain the babe of Bethlehem. He was not a two-foot-high midget walking around preaching the gospel. He grew into a Man. He matured. He developed. So, too, a church that is truly of the Lord and from the Lord will grow. It's inevitable. And like Jesus, she will find favor with God and man. I have letters from the Sheriff's Department, the Mayor's Office, and from different people in prominent positions who wrote expressing their appreciation for Applegate Christian Fellowship—not necessarily because we taught and preached Jesus Christ—but because we impacted the drug scene. God was so gracious in allowing us to find favor in His eyes and in the eyes of man.

But notice that even though Jesus grew, even though He found favor in the eyes of God and man—following His sermon at Nazareth in Luke 4, the people drove Him out of the city and took Him to a cliff over which they wanted to throw Him. At the edge of the cliff, He stopped and looked at the crowd, as only He could, and, like the Red Sea, it suddenly parted. Why? Because the body of Christ cannot be destroyed. There are times in this body—and in any true expression of Jesus—when it seems as though we're going down. But then Jesus somehow miraculously makes a way because He gave us His promise that the gates of hell could not prevail against the body of His church (Matthew 16:18).

He Was Baptized in Water and in the Spirit Simultaneously.

The Spirit came upon Jesus at the time of His baptism, empowering Him for His public ministry. As He emerged from the water, He looked up, and the Spirit of God came upon Him in the form of a dove (Matthew 3:16). It was then that He was sent out into public ministry.

"Wait a minute," some might say, "this idea of being baptized in the Spirit, this idea of a second blessing, is not needed. When a person becomes a Christian, he has all of the Spirit he'll ever need."

Really? Before the Spirit came upon Jesus—was He a believer? Yes. Even at the age of twelve, He confounded the Pharisees with His knowledge of the Word and with His heart for the Father (Luke 2:47). Yet, as He entered the dimension of public ministry, He was empowered by the Spirit. Therefore, I suggest that if Jesus needed the baptism of the Spirit and was receptive to it, how much more do you and I? If the body of His church is to be like His physical body on earth, we need the Spirit to come upon us as well.

He Ministered Powerfully.

All five ministerial offices were seen in the life of Jesus: apostle, prophet, evangelist, pastor, and teacher. The word "apostle" means "sent one." Jesus was the Apostle sent from heaven (John 20:21). He was the Prophet who spoke God's heart with perfect accuracy (Matthew 21:11). He was the Evangelist who spoke to the multitudes and brought them into the kingdom (Matthew 5:1, 2). He was the Pastor who looked at the people with compassion, as sheep having been scattered without a shepherd (Matthew 9:36). He was the Teacher the common people heard gladly because of the gracious words He spoke (Mark 12:37; Luke 4:22).

The five-fold ministry was seen in Jesus' body when He was on earth, and it must be seen in the body of His church if we are to be like Him. Not only did the offices function within Him, but the gifts flowed through Him. The gifts listed in Romans 12 all flowed through Jesus Christ. The manifestations found in 1 Corinthians were all seen clearly in His life.

"Wait a minute," you say. "What about tongues?"

There is no record of Jesus speaking in tongues. It is the one manifestation not recorded. Why? I suggest to you the reason might be very simple. How could Jesus speak in an unknown tongue? Although as a Man, Jesus spoke Aramaic, as

God, He knows all the tongues of men and of angels. He knows every dialect of heaven, every language on earth. There is no tongue unknown to Him.

His Body Was Broken Finally.

Jesus' body was broken on the Cross for you and me. So, too, if the body of His church is to be like Him, there will come times of breaking. Why? Because revelation comes through breaking. On the road to Emmaus, the followers of Jesus didn't recognize Jesus initially. It wasn't until He broke bread with them that their eyes were opened (Luke 24:30, 31). So, too, it is often in time of trouble—in the day of difficulty, in the process of breaking—that others can see the reality of the resurrected Jesus in the midst of His church.

The eight similarities between the physical body of Christ and the body of his church are more than merely interesting theologically. They have much to say to us personally. You see, even though Acts makes it very clear that the church was to function in the simplicity of teaching, fellowship, the breaking of bread and prayer—in Acts 6, a program surfaced.

Thus, I can see that programs are not necessarily wrong. In fact, they're part of the life of the body. But notice we're not talking about bureaucracy. We're not talking about fleshly energy. In the program seen in our text, believers had been feeding the widows—tending them, caring for them, ministering to them. And when cultural tensions arose, the apostles gave instruction. I believe this is the pattern for the way the church is to be involved with programs. The apostles didn't sit in their office and say, "Hmmm. What we need is a widow-feeding program, so let's get an architectural rendering; let's print up brochures; let's make a presentation; and let's recruit." No, the apostles simply recognized what the Lord was already doing in their midst.

Many times, churches become vulnerable when they initiate programs because then they have to crack the whip to get people involved. That is the reason why so many folks are burned-out on church. They're exhausted by the programs and the pressure. That's not the way it should be.

Applegate Christian Fellowship currently sends thousands of teaching tapes all over the world. But it began twenty-five years ago, with an elderly gentleman who brought his $39.95 K-Mart tape recorder to church, sat in the front row, and recorded our studies in the Gospel of Mark. In the middle of the message, he would bend down to the condenser mike and whisper, "This is the end of side 1. Please turn tape over for Side 2." Following the service, he'd take his recorder back to his trailer, where, using another $39 recorder, he'd copy the tapes one at a time. Today, Tree of Life has a lot of sophisticated machinery and staff and all kinds of stuff. But it all began with one man having a tape ministry on his heart.

A few years later, someone else came along who said, "We've been listening to your tapes. They would be great to put on the radio. It's real workable. And here's what we have on our heart. . . ." So some guys who were trained in media began to invest some time and energy and thought. One of them, who worked at a TV station, took it up a notch higher, developed it further, and we saw the birth of Searchlight—a radio program that produces real fruit as it airs across the nation.

Twenty-two years ago, some women approached us and said, "We have a desire to help unwed mothers. We don't want them to feel condemned or to succumb to the temptation of abortion. We want to provide an alternative for them." As I listened to them, I said, "Go for it." And from their burden, Living Alternatives—Applegate's outreach to unwed mothers—was born.

A number of years ago, a man named Ross Meador and some of his buddies came to me and said, "We know how we can practically teach our high-school kids the truths of God's Word: We'll take them on week-long trips. Day one, they'll climb sheer rocks outside of Bend, Oregon. Day two, we'll race bicycles down Mount Bachelor. Day three, we'll kayak in white water. Day four, we'll hang-glide. When we teach on faith and prayer before those events take place, those kids will listen!" And Maranatha Mountain Ministries was born.

Years ago, a man named Jeff Bates came up with an idea for a rock band. "We can reach kids for Jesus this way," he said. So the band Zion went out, touched lives, and introduced kids to the Savior.

Another man from the body had a heart to start a small orphanage in Mexico. It did so well, he found himself up to his ears and asked us to step in and help. That was the beginning of the Mission in Carmen Serdan.

Then, a lady contacted my brother, saying, "My husband and I had a mission school here in Honduras. But there have been some problems, and I've been wondering what to do. I heard of your fellowship and want to turn this mission base over to you." That was the origin of Applegate's mission station in Honduras.

Gang, this is why it was such a joy for me to pastor there. I didn't have to initiate, program, or strategize. I just stuck to the simplicity of teaching, fellowship, communion, and prayer. Out of that came "Acts 6 people" with a heart to take on new challenges. When they came our way, as a body, we said to them, "Go for it! If it works, if God's in it, we'll join you and give you the resources or advice needed. And if it doesn't work, you will come out wiser, deeper, and more knowledgeable than if you hadn't tried."

I can vividly recall my own introduction to ministry. As a sophomore in high school, working at a camp for junior-high kids, I planned an activity in which I put fourteen junior-high boys in a large circle and gave them raw eggs to attach to their foreheads by placing nylon stockings over their heads. I tied blindfolds over their eyes and put a junior-high girl on top of their shoulders. The game was simple: The girls were to take fresh flounders that I had bought at the fish market and smash as many of the eggs on the guys around them as possible while trying to protect the egg of the guy beneath them.

The one thing I wasn't expecting was the exuberance of those junior-high girls! With one hand on their nose and the other hand holding the raw flounder, they went for it! They started slapping those boys with those flounders so hard that by the fifth or sixth hit—not only were eggs breaking, but the flounders started breaking apart as well. Fish guts were everywhere!

I obviously didn't know what I was doing! And yet, even though I hadn't chosen the best way to reach kids, the fact is that the Lord saw my heart and said, "I'm going to use you anyway. I'm going to take you on down the road in ministry for Me."

You might "flounder" about a bit. You might think you're making a mess of things. But keep going—and the Lord will bless you for it.

I think of David. At thirty years of age he became king over all of Israel. He saw the city of Jerusalem in the distance, which was held by the Jebusites—enemies of Israel. "I want that city as my capital," David said to his army. "The first man to find a way into the city and open the gates will be my general, my chief of staff." Joab—not a man of the highest integrity or the deepest spirituality—found a way to get in by shinnying up a seventy-foot water shaft. He opened the gates, David's soldiers rushed in, and the city was conquered (1 Chronicles 11: 6).

I suggest to you, fellow soldier, that the Son of David—the King of kings, Jesus Christ—says to us, "There's a city I want to take. There are people I want to touch. There's a project that will manifest My nature. Who will find a way in? Who will go for it?"

Don't expect something to happen from the top, gang. Just do what the Lord directs. If you hit a snag or a problem—as they did in Acts 6— hopefully those in authority over you will be available to provide some counsel, and to help facilitate what the Lord is already doing. And pray that the Lord will keep them on track. Please pray that He will place on your heart the things you should do and how you should function in His body for His glory.

FINDING AND FOCUSING YOUR GIFTS

A Topical Study of
Acts 6:7

I am convinced that people who are productive in their lives are people who have priorities for their lives. That is, I believe that productivity and proper priority go hand in hand. In Acts 6 we see this principle wonderfully modeled and beautifully illustrated. When the administrative problem concerning food distribution to the widows arose, the apostles could very easily have been sucked into the struggle. Instead, they kept their focus fixed and their priority in place. As a result, the Word of God increased and the number of disciples multiplied greatly.

I firmly believe that, in these last days, the Lord is not looking for machine gunners who spray spiritual bullets everywhere hoping to hit something. I believe He's looking for sharpshooters—people who will focus on a singular target and be effective in a singular ministry.

- David said, "*One* thing have I desired of the Lord, and that will I seek after" (see Psalm 27:4).
- Paul said, "This *one* thing I do" (see Philippians 3:13).
- Jesus said to Martha, "*One* thing is needful for you" (see Luke 10:42).

The Lord wants every one of us to know the one thing we are to do for the kingdom—and to do it wholeheartedly. Perhaps you say, "I've been a Christian for some time, but I don't know what the one thing is that I should do. How can I know what God's will is?"

> *I beseech you therefore, brethren, by the mercies of God, that ye present your bodies a living sacrifice, holy, acceptable unto God, which is your reasonable service.*   Romans 12:1

The first step is to present your body to the Lord. Give your life to Him wholly and completely. It's the reasonable thing to do. Why is it reasonable to give your whole life to the Lord sacrificially? Here are three reasons. . . .

Because of What Jesus Did on Calvary

Jesus died for my sins and paid the price for my rebellion. Jesus loves me and gave everything for me. Therefore, it's only reasonable that I should say, "Lord, I'm Yours because of what You've done for me."

Because of Where We Will Spend Eternity

We're racing toward eternity, and what we do here will affect the rewards we receive there. Maybe you're saying, "Frankly, Jon, I don't care about rewards in heaven."

Listen, you might not care now—but I guarantee you will then.

Because of What It Does for Us Presently

Jesus taught us that we will receive to the degree that we give (Luke 6:38). If you want to be miserable, unhappy, and depressed—just live in a little tiny world where you're only concerned with your trinkets, your feelings, and your hobbies. If, however, you want a life that is full, rich, and expansive, get involved in ministry. I have discovered when I pray for people who are sick, *I* feel better! When I share the gospel with people who are lost, *I* get born again, again! When I share the Scripture, *I'm* the one who gets fed and blessed! Jesus was right. To the extent I give out, I get back.

"Sounds good," you say, "but how do I know what I should do?"

Read down five verses to Romans 12:6 where Paul gives the list of the seven motivational gifts.

"Wait a minute," you protest. "I heard there were *nineteen* or more spiritual gifts. Aren't there gifts listed in Corinthians and Ephesians that are different from these?"

Students, tune in here: Romans 12 is the only place where the term "spiritual gift" is used. In 1 Corinthians 12, we see the difference. . . .

Now concerning spiritual gifts, brethren, I would not have you ignorant.
                                                              1 Corinthians 12:1

In your Bible, the word "gifts" is in italics, which means it was added by the translators. The Greek word translated "spiritual" here is *pneumatikos,* or, "spirituals." The word gift is not there. And this is what has caused so much confusion. First Corinthians 12 deals with *spirituals*—operations and manifestations, while Romans 12 deals with *gifts.* Paul makes the distinction clear in the verses that follow.

- In verse 4 of 1 Corinthians 12, he writes of "diversities of gifts."
- In verse 5, he writes of "differences of administrations."
- In verse 6, he writes of "diversities of operations."

- In verse 4, he writes of the Spirit.
- In verse 5, he writes of the Son.
- In verse 6, he writes of the Father.

- Romans 12:6–8 deals with the gifts of the Spirit.
- Ephesians 4:11 relates to the ministries linked with Jesus.
- Corinthians 12:8–10 speaks of operations—or manifestations appointed by God.

I firmly believe there is a differentiation between the gifts of the Spirit, (Romans 12), the operation or manifestation of the *pneumatikos* (1 Corinthians 12), and ministries (Ephesians 4).

Not everyone will function in these 1 Corinthians 12 manifestations because many people say, "These are not for today. There are no more miracles possible.

They are for a different age." That may be their position, and that's fine. God's not going to force those operations on anyone.

But *every* person has a Romans 12 gift embedded within him or her. I believe that as you exercise your Romans 12 gift and if you're open to the powerful operation of God in the *pneumatikos* of 1 Corinthians 12, you will simply move in an extra dimension through which God can, if He so chooses, open an Ephesians 4 ministry for you.

Everyone has one of the motivational gifts found in Romans 12. How can you know which is yours? Whenever you want to understand anything about how the body of Christ is to function, study the earthly ministry of Jesus, for, although you have one primary motivational gift and may experience others from time to time, all of these gifts existed simultaneously in Him. And, because Jesus declared, "I am the Way, the Truth and the Life" (John 14:6), I believe each of these seven gifts can be linked to the Truth as seen in and through Him:

Prophecy—Declaring Truth

In John 4, Jesus declared truth both by forth-telling and by foretelling. "Woman, go call your husband," He said to the woman at the well.

"I don't have a husband," she countered.

"You've said well that you have no husband," Jesus replied. "You have five husbands, and the man you're living with now is not your husband at all."

"I perceive you're a prophet," she answered.

Bingo.

Then Jesus said, "The time is coming and now is when worship will not be based in Jerusalem or Mount Gerazim, but the Father is seeking those who will worship Him in spirit and in truth."

As Jesus demonstrated through his conversation with the woman at the well, prophecy is declaring truth through a powerful, pointed proclamation. It is often spontaneous and invariably moves people a notch higher in their perception of Jesus and their understanding of Him. Maybe you have the ability to speak powerfully and pointedly as you proclaim truth and take people forward in their knowledge of Jesus. If so, yours is the gift of prophecy—an important function in the body.

Ministry—Illustrating Truth

Ministry simply means service. It's one thing to talk about love, but what did Jesus do? He illustrated it practically when, after seeing hungry people and hearing their stomachs growling, He said, "Let's feed them," (Matthew 14:16) Ministry means caring for people practically—not just talking about it, but actually doing it.

In Acts 9, there was a death in the early church. Everyone said, "Quick, call for Peter! We've got to pray for a miracle, a resurrection!" Who died? John the apostle? No. James? He was already dead. Some heavy-hitter? Not in the way you might suspect. The person the entire church was so upset about losing was not an anointed apostle or a dedicated deacon, but a woman named Dorcas. Why was the whole church so upset about losing her? Was she a prophet? No. Was she a teacher? No. She sewed clothes—and in so doing, she demonstrated the practicality of love. People who say, "I can sew your shirt. I can tune up your car. I can bake you a cake," more than likely have the gift of ministry.

Teaching—Clarifying Truth

In Matthew 5, Jesus said, "You've heard it said of old that you're not to commit murder. But let Me clarify that point. Let Me tell you the real issue: If you hate your brother, you're guilty of murder. Why? Because you will kill his reputation, destroy his character, and rip him apart bit by bit with your gossip, hatred, and bitterness."

What did the people say to this? "No man speaks like this man. He speaks with authority," (Matthew 7:29). If you are one who has the ability to clarify truth—to make things clear to people's minds and applicable to their lives—your gift is probably that of teaching.

Giving—Furthering Truth

Jesus exemplified the gift of giving when He shed His blood for you and laid down His life on Calvary for me. He died in the place of despicable sinners like us. Thus, His was the ultimate gift of giving.

There are those who figure out their tithe with computers and calculators, saying, "Okay. I made $331 this week. Ten percent of that is $33.10 cents. We'll round it down to $33." And that's okay. It's certainly better than not tithing at all! But the person with the gift of giving has an entirely different mind-set.

Around the turn of the century, a man who owned a fledgling business had the gift of giving. "Lord," he said, "I know it's important to tithe. But as far as the profits of my little business go, I'm not going to give you ten percent. I'll keep ten percent. From this day on, as long as I live, You, Lord, will get ninety percent of the profits of this company." He became a multimillionaire on ten percent. You see, he founded the Quaker Oats Company. The person with the gift of giving gives with abandon and hilarity.

Ruling—Administrating Truth

What did Jesus say when He fed the five thousand? "Make these men sit in groups of fifty (Luke 9:14). Let's do everything decently and in order. Let's do things carefully, not haphazardly. Let's make sure things are done with integrity." There are those who look for ways of doing things decently and orderly. And theirs is the gift of ruling.

Mercy—Radiating Truth

Jesus wept at the tomb of Lazarus, even though He knew that in a moment or two He would say, "Lazarus, come forth," and Lazarus would indeed come out (John 11:35). The Greek word John used for "wept" speaks of great intensity. Jesus felt the hurt of those around Him. Perhaps you are one who hurts for people and with people, one who feels the pain of others as if it were your own. You may be one who empathizes with the poor in spirit and who feels drawn toward the lowly of heart. If so, you have the much-needed gift of mercy—a gift that radiates the reality of the love of Jesus.

Exhortation—Recalling Truth

The storm was raging and the disciples were struggling. They shouldn't have been, for hadn't Jesus directed them to go to the other side? Wasn't His command also His promise that He would bring it to pass? Yet they were afraid. So He walked out on the water toward them and exhorted them. "Be of good cheer," He said. "It is I. Be not afraid" (see Matthew 14:27).

The Greek word translated "exhortation" is *paraklesis,* the root of *parakletos*—a word that refers to the "coming alongside" of the Spirit. If you have the ability to come alongside someone who is either going through a storm or sitting in the doldrums and get them going again in the right direction, yours is the gift of exhortation.

Of the seven motivational gifts, how can you know which is your primary gift? Here's one way to find out: If the pastor of your church fell down dead today and the elders said to you, "Please, be the pastor"—what would be the first thing you would do?

Those with the gift of prophecy would say, "This Fellowship is wonderfully loving and glorying in grace, but we need a new call for righteousness and holiness. If I were pastor, I would proclaim truth boldly and seek to take our people a notch higher spiritually."

Those with the gift of ministry would say, "If I were pastor, I would make sure folks are being helped practically. Are we helping people make sense of their finances? Are the new mothers being cared for?"

Those with the gift of teaching would say, "We need a deeper understanding of hermeneutics, homiletics, and eschatology. We need to be more serious in our study and application of the Word."

Those with the gift of giving would say, "If I were pastor, I would raise money in order to see ministries continue and missionaries go out. We need to further the truth of the gospel in these last days."

Those with the gift of ruling would say, "The great need is for better organization—that we may do all things decently and orderly."

Those with the gift of mercy would say, "Hospital care, concern for those who are homeless and hungry, compassion for those who are hurting, help for the orphans and widows—that's what we need."

Those with the gift of exhortation would say, "If I were pastor, I would concentrate on personal counseling for those who are going through storms or are stuck in depression. We need more one-on-one interaction."

What would you do if *you* were pastor?

The problem is, we have a tendency toward "gift projection"—of seeing everything in terms of our own individual motivational gift. Oftentimes, we'll wonder why everyone doesn't see the same needs we see and feel the same way we feel. Instead of using our gifts to complement one another and to build up the body, we grow frustrated when that which we view as crucial is not top priority for everyone else.

Let me put it this way: Suppose my four-year-old son, Benjamin, left Sunday school and came in to the sanctuary to bring me a glass of water. Suppose as he made his way toward the platform, he stumbled and fell—spilling the water and shattering the glass. How would you respond? I suggest the way you would respond will further identify your motivational Romans 12 gift.

The one with the gift of prophecy would say, "Benjamin, listen carefully. The world is full of pitfalls. Be careful how you walk. Walk straightly. Walk carefully."

The one with the gift of ministry would say, "Where's the mop? Where's the broom? I'll clean this up."

The one with the gift of teaching would say, "Ben, listen. When you carry a glass of water, make sure that you wipe away all the condensation from the outside of the glass. Then, apply equal pressure with both hands, grip tightly, and walk slowly."

The one with the gift of giving would pull out his wallet and say, "How much does that cost? Let me take care of it."

The one with the gift of ruling would say, "Hmm. Who put those stairs there? That was poor planning. We should have had a ramp."

The one with the gift of mercy would blubber, "Come here, big guy. I know just how you feel. I used to spill things too. Don't worry."

The one with the gift of exhortation would say, "Come on, Benny. Let's go get another glass of water. Be a little more careful and try again. I know you can do it!"

That's the body acting in unity. Everyone looks at the same event and sees it through his own motivational ministry perspective. It doesn't mean anyone's right or wrong, better or worse. It just means we're differently gifted. How do you view an event? Don't come down on others for not seeing it the way you do. Wisdom says, "This is the way I see this situation, so it must mean that this is my place in the body. My job is not to change *them*, but to do what *I'm* supposed to do."

My strong encouragement to you today is to present yourself a living sacrifice to God. Find out what your gift is. Keep focused on it. And be a sharpshooter in the Name of Jesus for the benefit of His Body.

7 Here in chapter 7, Stephen gives a defense that is absolutely brilliant. A masterpiece of logic and theological understanding, it is one of the most profound and powerful arguments in all of Scripture.

Serving faithfully first as a waiter, then as a deacon, then as a miracle-worker, we now see Stephen as a theologian par excellence. This is precisely what Paul said would happen when he wrote that those who use the office of deacon well purchase for themselves a great degree of boldness (1 Timothy 3:13). But as Stephen boldly proclaimed and declared the truth of the gospel, it caused great consternation among the enemies of the church. Unable to refute his wisdom and his logic, their only recourse was to hire false witnesses to lie about him and indict him on trumped-up charges. What were the charges? Stephen was accused of speaking blasphemy concerning the temple and the law, which was tantamount to charging him with undermining the entire Jewish faith.

Acts 7:1, 2
Then said the high priest, Are these things so? And he said, Men, brethren, and fathers, hearken; The God of glory appeared unto our father Abraham, when he was in Mesopotamia, before he dwelt in Charran.

Stephen began his defense by reminding his accusers that God appeared to their father, Abraham, not in the Holy City of Jerusalem, but in the pagan city of Mesopotamia, where worship centered around a moon goddess.

Acts 7:3
And said unto him, Get thee out of thy country, and from thy kindred, and come into the land which I shall shew thee.

Abraham became a pilgrim because spirituality is not static—it's dynamic. We keep flowing. We keep growing. We keep expanding our understanding if we remain open to the moving of God.

Acts 7:4
Then came he out of the land of the Chaldaeans, and dwelt in Charran: and from thence, when his father was dead, he removed him into this land, wherein ye now dwell.

Abraham left Mesopotamia and stopped in Haran, evidently at the suggestion of his father, Terah. The years in Haran were lost until Terah

passed away and Abraham got moving again. The point for you and me is simply this: Whenever we stop and park, we're missing it. There must be continual movement and growth in spirituality. It's a pilgrimage we're on—not a place we arrive.

Acts 7:5
And he gave him none inheritance in it, no, not so much as to set his foot on: yet he promised that he would give it to him for a possession, and to his seed after him, when as yet he had no child.

Abraham owned no land—only a promise. Even at the end of his life, the only portion of the land he actually possessed was the cave he purchased in which to bury his wife (Genesis 23:9).

Acts 7:6, 7
And God spake on this wise, That his seed should sojourn in a strange land; and that they should bring them into bondage, and entreat them evil four hundred years. And the nation to whom they shall be in bondage will I judge, said God: and after that shall they come forth, and serve me in this place.

What happened while Abraham's descendants were in Egypt—away from the Promised Land? They grew and multiplied. In recounting Jewish history, Stephen is reiterating the fact that "place" is not important. The Jews grew and multiplied not in the Promised Land, but in Egypt.

Acts 7:8 (a)
And he gave him the covenant of circumcision: and so Abraham begat Isaac, and circumcised him the eighth day . . .

God said, "Abraham, I want you to circumcise your son. Deal with the area that speaks of reproductive energy in the flesh." And Abraham did it. Without a temple, Abraham obeyed God.

Acts 7:8 (b)–10
. . . and Isaac begat Jacob; and Jacob begat the twelve patriarchs. And the patriarchs, moved with envy, sold Joseph into Egypt: but God was with him, and delivered him out of all his afflictions, and gave him favour and wisdom in the sight of Pharaoh king of Egypt; and he made him governor over Egypt and all his house.

When was God with Joseph? Not when he was in Israel, but when he was in Egypt. Joseph is a perfect picture of Jesus Christ. . . .

- Joseph's brothers were "moved with envy." Pilate "knew that for envy" they delivered Jesus unto him (see Matthew 27:18).
- Joseph was sold for twenty pieces of silver. Jesus was sold for thirty pieces of silver.
- Joseph was punished for sins he did not commit.
Jesus, the sinless One, was punished for our sins.
- Joseph was cast into prison.
Jesus descended into the "prison" of the earth (see Ephesians 4:9).
- Joseph became ruler of the prison.
Jesus preached in hell and led captivity captive (Ephesians 4:8).
- Joseph miraculously was freed from prison.
Jesus miraculously arose from the grave.

The picture is perfect.

Acts 7:11
Now there came a dearth over all the land of Egypt and Chanaan, and great affliction: and our fathers found no sustenance.

When his brothers rejected Joseph, what happened? Famine came. The same was true in Stephen's day. When the Jews rejected Jesus Christ, a spiritual famine descended upon the land.

Acts 7:12–16
But when Jacob heard that there was corn in Egypt, he sent out our fathers first. And at the second time Joseph was made known to his brethren; and Joseph's kindred was made known unto Pharaoh. Then sent Joseph, and called his father Jacob to him, and all his kindred, threescore and fifteen souls. So Jacob went down into Egypt, and died, he, and our fathers, and were carried over into Sychem, and laid in the sepulchre that Abraham bought for a sum of money of the sons of Emmor the father of Sychem.

During a time of famine, Joseph's brothers went to Egypt for help. They stood before the Prime Minister of Egypt, not recognizing him to be their own brother. As Joseph began to question them when they appeared before him a second time, they admitted that they had sinned greatly against their brother. Then, in that powerful emotional scene, Joseph said, "I am Joseph" (Genesis 45:4). It wasn't until the second time they saw him that Joseph's brothers realized who he was. So, too, after going through a time of famine, drought, and tribulation, Israel will finally recognize Jesus in His Second Coming (Romans 11:26).

Acts 7:17–19
But when the time of the promise drew nigh, which God had sworn to Abraham, the people grew and multiplied in Egypt, till another king arose, which knew not Joseph. The same dealt subtilly with our kindred, and evil entreated our fathers, so that they cast out their young children, to the end they might not live.

Stephen continued his history lesson. As the nation of Israel multiplied and grew—not in Israel, but in Egypt—Pharaoh saw their number grow from seventy-five to two million. Fearing a rebellion, he sought to reduce their population by ordering the destruction of all Jewish baby boys.

Acts 7:20 (a)
In which time Moses was born . . .

Stephen shifts gears here. He had spoken of Abraham in relation to "the place"—the land of Israel—as he proved that the land was not really the issue, since Abraham had an encounter with God in Babylon, and since God's people had prospered and multiplied even in Egypt. God is not confined to a piece of property, argued Stephen, but to a Person—Jesus Christ. And now he develops his argument further as he speaks of Moses in relation to a procedure, proving that God is not confined to the law.

Acts 7:20 (b), 21
. . . and was exceeding fair, and nourished up in his father's house three months: And when he was cast out, Pharoah's daughter took him up, and nourished him for her own son.

Where did Moses' mother get the idea of putting him in a boat? I suggest that, being a godly woman, she had pondered the Scriptures and was reminded of another family in danger during dark times—Noah's. I point this out not merely for the sake of speculation—but for application. Reading the Bible is a wonderful thing to do. It will help you out in very practical ways and in all areas of life. Ask Jochabed!

Acts 7:22, 23
And Moses was learned in all the wisdom of the Egyptians, and was mighty in words and in deeds. And when he was full forty years old, it came into his heart to visit his brethren the children of Israel.

Moses returned to his brethren not out of curiosity, but out of kinship. Raised in the house of Pharaoh, he left the palace to serve his brothers.

my throne, and earth is my footstool: what house will ye build me? saith the Lord: or what is the place of my rest? Hath not my hand made all these things?

Keep the context in mind. To these people who were so concerned about the temple, Stephen quotes the prophet, saying, "God never even asked for a temple. It's foolish to think you can box the almighty God into a little temple."

By this time, I bet the blood of Stephen's audience was beginning to boil. After all, they couldn't have liked being reminded of their own history, of their own tendencies, of what God had spoken so pointedly. They couldn't have liked being reminded that God never asked for a temple in the first place. They couldn't have liked being reminded that they had a tendency to reject every prophet God had sent their way.

Acts 7:51
Ye stiffnecked and uncircumcised in heart and ears, ye do always resist the Holy Ghost: as your fathers did, so do ye.

"The issue," Stephen declared, "is not reviling the holy temple. The issue is resisting the Holy Spirit."

Acts 7:52 (a)
Which of the prophets have not your fathers persecuted?

The Jews were brutal to the prophets. They tried to stone Moses. They put Isaiah into a dead tree trunk and sawed it in half. They threw Jeremiah into dungeons several times before they finally stoned him to death. They killed Zechariah in the temple.

Acts 7:52 (b)
And they have slain them which shewed before of the coming of the Just One; of whom ye have been now the betrayers and murderers.

"You accuse me of slighting Moses," Stephen argued. "But you have slain the prophets and even Messiah Himself."

Acts 7:53
Who have received the law by the disposition of angels, and have not kept it.

"The issue is not my blaspheming the law," declared Stephen. "The issue is your breaking the law."

Acts 7:54–55 (a)
When they heard these things, they were cut to the heart, and they gnashed on him with their teeth. But he, being full of the Holy Ghost, looked up stedfastly into heaven, and saw the glory of God . . .

Stephen began his sermon by talking about the God of glory (7:2). At the end of his sermon, he saw the glory of God. That's the way it always is. Whenever you start talking to people about some quality of the Lord, by the time you've finished the conversation, you find yourself enjoying and seeing that very quality in your own heart. It's incredible how that works. Start telling someone how wonderful Jesus is, and by the time you conclude, you'll be totally in wonder of Jesus. Begin sharing about the God of grace, and you'll find yourself receiving the grace of God. That is why I encourage you to share your faith—not because it is a job to do—but because it is a joy to experience.

- "I'm so dry," you say.
  When was the last time you talked to someone about Jesus?
- "It's just not very real to me."
  When was the last time you got into an interesting full-on dialogue with someone about what you believe?
- "I'm just not experiencing joy."
  When was the last time you ministered to someone who was depressed?
- "I just don't know if I really have faith."
  When was the last time you shared what faith you do have with someone who had less than you?

Acts 7:55 (b)
. . . and Jesus standing on the right hand of God.

Many times in Scripture, we read of Jesus sitting at the right hand of God. Here, however, we see Him standing—not in anxiety, but to welcome Stephen into glory.

Acts 7:56–58 (a)
And said, Behold, I see the heavens opened, and the Son of man standing on the right hand of God. Then they cried out with a loud voice, and stopped their ears, and ran upon him with one accord, and cast him out of the city, and stoned him . . .

The contrast is great between the uptightness, anger, and bitterness of the crowd and the peace and tranquility of Stephen, who had the "face of an angel" (see 6:15). While these men were frenzied, Stephen was totally at peace. Why? Because while the crowd looked down on Stephen, Stephen looked up to heaven.

Acts 7:58 (b)
. . . and the witnesses laid down their clothes at a young man's feet, whose name was Saul.

This is Paul, who would later become the great apostle.

Acts 7:59–60
And they stoned Stephen, calling upon God, and saying, Lord Jesus, receive my spirit. And he kneeled down, and cried with a loud voice, Lord, lay not this sin to their charge. And when he had said this, he fell asleep.

How could Stephen be so peaceful—dying, without fighting back or lashing out, crying, "O, Lord, don't hold this against these guys"? He looked into heaven and saw Jesus. You see, Revelation 5:6 tells us that when we see Him, we will see Him as a Lamb having been slain. Therefore, if I'm looking up to heaven and seeing the Lord, inevitably I will understand that the scars He still bears were caused by me. My sin, my rebellion, my carnality, my depravity caused Him to be slaughtered on Calvary. And as I look into heaven and see what my sin did, what my sin wrought, I have no other alternative but to say even of those who are gnashing their teeth and throwing stones at me, "Lord Jesus, forgive them. Don't hold this against them."

When I truly see Jesus, I have no other choice but to be amazed at His grace and to be at peace with others. It's only when I lower my sight and begin to look at people horizontally that I want to say, "Who do you think you are to say that about me?" It's only when I take my eyes off Jesus that I become defensive and antagonistic, uptight and combative, abrasive, callous, and critical.

What about you? Are you tense? Nervous? Uptight? Losing sleep, hair or teeth unnecessarily? The solution is so simple: Don't look down on people. Look up into heaven and see the Lord. See how He has forgiven you. See the grace He has shown to you. See His mercies extended in your direction.

In 2 Kings, we read the account of a battle between Israel and Moab. Losing the battle, and realizing his number was up, the king of Moab in desperation sacrificed his eldest son on the wall of his city. When the people of Israel saw the sacrifice of the king's own son, they departed from him and returned to their own land (2 Kings 3:27). They lost the will to fight when they saw the sacrifice the king made.

So, too, when we see the sacrifice of our King's Son, when we see clearly the price that was paid, we lose the will to fight. And, like Stephen, we're at peace even when the enemy throws stones.

---

8 Chapter 7 recounted the defense and death of Stephen, the dynamic deacon who boldly declared that the Lord was not interested in religion, but in relationship. And chapter 8 picks up the story. . . .

Acts 8:1 (a)
And Saul was consenting . . .

This Saul, of course, would later be known as the apostle Paul. The word "consenting" actually means "voting," implying that Saul was a voting member of the Sanhedrin, the Jewish Supreme Court. This interests me because marriage was one of the requirements for a position on the Sanhedrin—and yet Paul wrote to the church at Corinth that it was good for the unmarried and the widows to remain in a single state even as he was (1 Corinthians 7:8). If Paul was married in Acts and single in 1 Corinthians, what happened to his wife?

Some suggest she died, that he was a widower who chose to remain single in order to give himself more fully to ministry. Much more probable, however, based upon the writings of early church history, is that Paul's wife left him when he was converted. Either way, it's interesting that Paul doesn't tell the story. Truly, he practiced what he preached when he wrote, "Forgetting those things which are behind, and reaching forth unto those things which are before, I press toward the mark for the prize of the high calling of God in Christ Jesus" (Philippians 3:13, 14).

If you've experienced pain or a problem in the past, perhaps Paul can be an example to you today. I know it's not easy, but Paul shows the possibility of forgetting the past, pressing on, and seeing how the Lord can do something unique and special in your situation presently.

Acts 8:1 (b)
. . . unto his death.

Was Paul actually a thrower of stones?
No.
We read in Acts 7:58 that the witnesses laid their clothes at the feet of a young man named Saul. This brilliant young theologian would vote for Stephen's death, but he was above bloodying his own hands to bring it about. And yet something happens as we read the story, for later in the Book of Acts, we'll see Paul use his own hands

to drag men and women out of their homes in order to imprison and persecute them. This would haunt him all of his days—so much so that he would write about it to his young protigie, Timothy, calling himself a blasphemer, a persecutor, and an injurious person (1 Timothy 1:13). In Romans 15, Paul wrote that wherever he went he raised money for the poor saints in Jerusalem. No doubt, whenever he walked through the streets of Jerusalem and saw a wife sitting without her husband, or a man without his wife—he would be reminded of the results of his radical and relentless persecution.

I find this to be a word of warning to us personally. We can think we're doing the Lord a big favor by coming down on people, beating up on people, or pointing our finger at people—all in the name of "purifying the church" or "taking a stand for righteousness." But what a shock it must have been for Paul on the road to Damascus when he finally realized that all of the time he thought he was doing God a favor, he was actually persecuting His Son. Be careful. Remember Paul when you feel like going from house to house pointing out sinners or finding fault with preachers. Like Paul, we can be radical—but we can be radically wrong.

Acts 8:1 (c)
And at that time there was a great persecution against the church which was at Jerusalem; and they were all scattered abroad throughout the regions of Judaea and Samaria . . .

"You shall receive power when the Holy Ghost comes upon you, and you shall be witnesses in Jerusalem, Judaea, Samaria, and to the uttermost parts of the earth," promised Jesus (see Acts 1:8). In other words, "My work starts here in Jerusalem, but it must move on from here." We all have a tendency to camp out where it's comfortable. So did the early church. Because Jerusalem was the center of spiritual activity, for six years, no one wanted to leave. It took persecution to get the believers moving, to scatter them to Judaea and Samaria. It was the persecution in Acts 8:1 that moved the church to obey the command of Acts 1:8.

Maybe you face a job transfer, a relational change, or something else that makes you unsettled or unsure. Maybe doors are closing and you're wondering why. Although it would be wonderful if we were all so spiritually sensitive that we would feel the prompting of the Lord and respond immediately, most of us don't have that kind of sensitivity. For most of us, it takes a pink slip, a job transfer, a broken romance to get us

moving. Perhaps you'd rather stay where you are, but in reality the Lord sees where He can use you most effectively. Trust Him.

Acts 8:1 (d)
. . . except the apostles.

Why didn't the apostles leave? I believe it was because they had previously fled in fear. You remember the story: The night Jesus was brought to trial in the court of Caiaphas, only a few of His disciples followed Him—and even then from afar. The next day when He was nailed to the Cross, all except John had deserted Him. Now, six years later, perhaps recalling their former fear, they said, "We're staying here in Jerusalem even if it means risking our lives."

Acts 8:2
And devout men carried Stephen to his burial, and made great lamentation over him.

Does this verse imply that we should make "great lamentation" when a believer dies? Notice Luke didn't say, "The *apostles* carried Stephen to his burial," or, "The *disciples* carried Stephen to his burial," but "*Devout men* carried Stephen to his burial." "Devout men" means "God-fearers." Thus, it could be that those who carried Stephen to his burial weren't believers. If, on the other hand, these devout men were indeed Christians, perhaps they didn't understand heaven very clearly. You see, as we read in 1 Thessalonians 4, many in the early church believed they would see the Second Coming of Christ—that any believer who died before His return would miss the rapture and not make it into Heaven. That is why Paul explained to them that, although the dead in Christ would rise first, they wouldn't be left behind (1 Thessalonians 4:16).

Acts 8:3
As for Saul, he made havock of the church, entering into every house, and haling men and women committed them to prison.

The word "havock" comes from a root word used to describe the results of wounding a wild boar. When a boar is wounded, he goes on a rampage and loses all sense of sanity—which is exactly what happened to Paul. This refined, cultured, religious scholar who sat at the feet of Gamaliel—this student par excellence, this man whose command of the Greek language was greater than any other writer—lost all sense of sanity. At first he merely consented to the death of Stephen. But then, like a shark that smells blood, he began going from house to house, hauling out and imprisoning believers, committing them to their deaths.

Acts 8:4
Therefore they that were scattered abroad went every where preaching the word.

Running from Saul and his posse, the early church fled, preaching the Word as they went. So even as Paul tried in vain to stomp out the flames of faith in Jerusalem, sparks were flying and igniting fires everywhere.

Acts 8:5 (a)
Then Philip . . .

Philip was another one of those dynamic deacons we read about in Acts 6. Like Stephen, he is a powerful reminder that if we are faithful in the little things, God will open up more and more for us to do.

Acts 8:5 (b)
. . . went down to the city of Samaria, and preached Christ unto them.

Second Kings 17 gives the account of the Assyrian invasion of Israel in 721 B.C., when the ten northern tribes were carried into captivity before the Assyrians claimed the northern part of Israel. As they moved into the area, the Assyrians married the impoverished Jews who were left behind, and a half-breed race was produced known as the Samaritans. The Jews in the south looked down on the Samaritans, calling them half-breeds and dogs, and went out of their way to avoid any contact with them. That is why it would have been shocking to hear Jesus say, "I must need go through Samaria" (see John 4:4). Seven years after Jesus talked with the Samaritan woman at the well, I wonder if she was there, hearing Philip preach.

Acts 8:6
And the people with one accord gave heed unto those things which Philip spake, hearing and seeing the miracles which he did.

We usually think of miracles in terms of sight, but miracles can be heard as well—through a word of wisdom, a word of knowledge, a word of prophecy, and the teaching of the Word.

Acts 8:7
For unclean spirits, crying with loud voice, came out of many that were possessed with them: and many taken with palsies, and that were lame, were healed.

There are those who read the Gospels and the Book of Acts and say, "It's interesting that Jesus cast out demons and that the early church was involved in deliverance ministry. But we're beyond that today." Are we really? Or have we allowed psychology to simply shift the attention away from demonic activity with terms like "psychosis" and "syndrome," "dysfunction" and "disorder"?

Acts 8:8
And there was great joy in that city.

The word "gospel" means "good news." Wherever the gospel is preached and received, great joy replaces pseudo-spiritual heaviness.

Acts 8:9–11
But there was a certain man, called Simon, which beforetime in the same city used sorcery, and bewitched the people of Samaria, giving out that himself was some great one: To whom they all gave heed, from the least to the greatest, saying, This man is the great power of God. And to him they had regard, because that of long time he had bewitched them with sorceries.

Was Simon simply a clever magician? Or was he a conduit of demonic power? Whether it was magic, trickery, or demonic activity, I don't know. But I do know that Satan used Simon to keep people away from God. That is why we need to keep ourselves and our kids away from crystals, pyramids, hypnosis, and anything else that smacks of the occult. Satan can, indeed, empower individuals to do signs, wonders, and impressive miracles. But he can only make things worse. . . .

In Exodus 7, when Pharaoh demanded a sign from Moses, Aaron cast down his rod, and it became a snake. Pharaoh then called for his magicians, and they duplicated the miracle, as their rods became snakes as well. Moses then touched the Nile River with his rod, and it turned to blood. Pharoah's magicians did the same thing to other sources of water, turning them all to blood. Moses called for a plague of frogs to cover the land. What did Pharoah's magicians do? They conjured up frogs as well. Now, the last thing the Egyptians needed was more snakes, more blood, or more frogs. What they needed was deliverance from those things. But Pharoah's magicians were powerless to help. That's the way it always is. Satan and demons can and do perform miracles and wonders—but only to bring about harm.

Acts 8:12
But when they believed Philip preaching the things concerning the kingdom of God, and the name of Jesus Christ, they were baptized, both men and women.

Philip came and began to preach Jesus Christ and the Good News of the kingdom. Suddenly, people realized there was hope, joy, a reason for living—and they responded to his preaching.

Acts 8:13 (a)
Then Simon himself believed also . . .

Simon believed, but he was not a born-again believer. James 2:19 says that even the devils believe in God and they tremble. But they're not saved. Did you know you can miss heaven by eighteen inches? You can believe in your head intellectually. You can affirm the theology mentally. But if faith is not in your heart, you are in no better shape than the demons in hell. There is not one demon who doubts the reality of hell. That is why James points out the fallacy of intellectual faith. "Your heart must be touched," he says. "Your faith must affect the way you live, for faith without works is dead" (see James 2:17).

"Faith without works?" you say. "I thought salvation was by faith." It is. It's not faith *and* works. It's not faith *or* works. It's faith *that* works.

Acts 8:13 (b)–17
. . . and when he was baptized, he continued with Philip, and wondered, beholding the miracles and signs which were done. Now when the apostles which were at Jerusalem heard that Samaria had received the word of God, they sent unto them Peter and John: Who, when they were come down, prayed for them, that they might receive the Holy Ghost: (For as yet he was fallen upon none of them: only they were baptized in the name of the Lord Jesus.) Then laid they their hands on them, and they received the Holy Ghost.

Notice that, although the people in Samaria were born again and baptized, they were not yet empowered with the coming-upon of the Spirit. So Peter and John came down from Jerusalem and laid hands on them. Why didn't Philip do it? Since Philip was the one who led the city into a knowledge of Christ Jesus; since Philip was the one who baptized and taught and shared the Good News of the kingdom—why didn't Philip lay his hands on the Samaritans to receive the power of the Spirit?

I suggest two possible reasons. In sending for Peter and John, the "Big Guns in Jerusalem," Philip was linking the Samaritan Christians to the Jewish Christians in Jerusalem. He was not starting a separate movement in Samaria nor a distinct denomination of believers. They were all one body. Sending for Peter and John verified the linkage and support between the believers in Jerusalem and those in Samaria.

But a second and more important reason may have been that perhaps Philip wasn't gifted in that way. Although he was gifted in preaching and in evangelism, it is possible he was not gifted in the laying on of hands for the empowering of people. Wise enough to realize that a couple of his brothers had that anointing, that gifting, that calling—he sent for them.

Again we see the importance of the body working together. No one person can do it all. No one person should do it all. Every part of the body has a specific role to play. It's so relaxing when you finally realize you don't have to do it all. People around you might expect you to be everything for them, but you know you're not and can't be. So what should you do? Do what you're called to do and let a brother or a sister do those things you haven't been gifted or called to do. The Lord's burden is not heavy. His yoke fits perfectly (Matthew 11:29).

Acts 8:18, 19
And when Simon saw that through laying on of the apostles' hands the Holy Ghost was given, he offered them money, saying, Give me also this power, that on whomsoever I lay hands, he may receive the Holy Ghost.

"Wow!" Simon said. "That's a neat trick. Let me buy it from you." To this day, magicians buy tricks from each other, which is why I believe Simon was operating through magic and not necessarily through demonic power.

Acts 8:20–24
But Peter said unto him, Thy money perish with thee, because thou hast thought that the gift of God may be purchased with money. Thou hast neither part nor lot in this matter: for thy heart is not right in the sight of God. Repent therefore of this thy wickedness, and pray God, if perhaps the thought of thine heart may be forgiven thee. For I perceive that thou art in the gall of bitterness, and in the bond of iniquity. Then answered Simon, and said, Pray ye to the Lord for me, that none of these things which ye have spoken come upon me.

When Simon was called on the carpet, he didn't say, "Pray that my heart will be changed." He said, "Pray that these things won't happen to me." He wasn't interested in having his life corrected. He just wanted to be protected from the consequences of his sin.

Acts 8:25
And they, when they had testified and preached the word of the Lord, returned to Jerusalem, and preached the gospel in many villages of the Samaritans.

What happened to Simon? Tradition says he went insane and buried himself alive—but not before he introduced the heresy of Gnosticism, which, among other things, stated that, matter being evil and spirit good, God could not have created the world out of matter, nor could Jesus have become Man and died for our sin. John wrote his first epistle, in part, to counter the threat of Gnosticism within the early church.

Acts 8:26, 27 (a)
And the angel of the Lord spake unto Philip, saying, Arise, and go toward the south unto the way that goeth down from Jerusalem unto Gaza, which is desert. And he arose and went . . .

Philip, whose ministry had brought about the wonderful work of the Lord in Samaria, was now being called to Gaza. "But, Lord, what about the posters?" he could have protested. "What about the book-signings? Lord, I'm so influential here in Samaria. The entire city is getting turned on to You. Why are You asking me to go to the desert? There's nothing down there."

Please note that the Lord didn't say why He was sending Philip to the desert. He simply said, "Arise and go." And Philip arose and went. If you struggle with finding God's will, know this: God's will is for you to obey what He tells you to do one step at a time. He doesn't give us the full story. He just says, "I want you to go down to the desert. And once you do that, I'll show you the next step." That's why the Christian life is so incredibly exciting. We never know what's ahead.

An experiment was performed in which caterpillars were placed on the rim of a large pot containing dirt and several of their favorite plants. The caterpillars began to move along the rim of the pot—each one following the one in front, every caterpillar thinking the one ahead of him knew where he was going. Around and around and around they went until they all died of starvation. Do you feel like you're drying up and get-

ting dizzy? Could it be because the Lord spoke to you at some point but, because you were so intent on following the caterpillar in front of you, you missed the adventure? The key to the exciting, impacting Christian life is to be like Philip and obey when you hear the Lord's voice or feel His pull—even though you don't know the end of the story at the beginning.

Acts 8:27 (b), 28
. . . and, behold, a man of Ethiopia, an eunuch of great authority under Candace queen of the Ethiopians, who had the charge of all her treasure, and had come to Jerusalem for to worship, was returning, and sitting in his chariot read Esaias the prophet.

The treasurer in the kingdom, this man was perhaps the second most powerful individual in Ethiopia. Evidently, he was a God-fearer who had gone to Jerusalem to worship. Very likely, it was his first pilgrimage to the Holy City. But not finding answers in the law, or in the ritualism of temple worship, he rode home in his chariot with his heart still hungry as he pored over the Scriptures.

Acts 8:29
Then the Spirit said unto Philip, Go near, and join thyself to this chariot.

This proves to me that the Lord will do whatever it takes to reach a person who desires to know Him. On the Day of Judgment, no one will be able to say, "I really wanted to know You, God, but I couldn't figure out how." God will send a Philip to anyone who wants to know Him. And that Philip could be you!

Acts 8:30 (a)
And Philip ran thither to him . . .

I love this phrase! It doesn't say, Philip said, "Okay. I hate the desert, but if I gotta go, I'll go." No. Philip *ran.* How wonderful it is to see someone full of enthusiasm concerning ministry and service. The word "enthusiasm" comes from the Greek words *en* and *theos,* meaning, "full of God." An enthusiastic person is a person who is full of God. And Philip was enthusiasm personified.

Acts 8:30 (b)–34
. . . and heard him read the prophet Esaias, and said, Understandest thou what thou readest? And he said, How can I, except some man should guide me? And he desired Philip that he would come up and sit with

him. The place of the scripture which he read was this, He was led as a sheep to the slaughter; and like a lamb dumb before his shearer, so opened he not his mouth: In his humiliation his judgment was taken away: and who shall declare his generation? for his life is taken from the earth. And the eunuch answered Philip, and said, I pray thee, of whom speaketh the prophet this? of himself, or of some other man?

Already sovereignly drawn by the Spirit, the eunuch was searching and wondering.

Acts 8:35
Then Philip opened his mouth, and began at the same scripture, and preached unto him Jesus.

Philip preached not Judaism, not denominationalism, not water baptism, but Jesus.

Acts 8:36, 37 (a)
And as they went on their way, they came unto a certain water: and the eunuch said, See, here is water; what doth hinder me to be baptized? And Philip said, If thou believest with all thine heart, thou mayest.

The same Peter who saw the deception of Simon the sorcerer would later write, "Brethren, give diligence to make your calling and election sure" (2 Peter 1:10).

For topical study of Acts 8:35–37, see "Avoiding the Unexpected End" below.

Acts 8:37 (b), 38
And he answered and said, I believe that Jesus Christ is the Son of God. And he commanded the chariot to stand still: and they went down both into the water, both Philip and the eunuch; and he baptized him.

The Ethiopian had at last found what he was looking for—not a ritualistic religion, but a dynamic relationship with Jesus Christ.

Acts 8:39
And when they were come up out of the water, the Spirit of the Lord caught away Philip, that the eunuch saw him no more: and he went on his way rejoicing.

The eunuch had come seeking to the Holy City. He had left struggling with the Scriptures. Now he returns rejoicing in his salvation.

Acts 8:40
But Philip was found at Azotus: and passing through he preached in all the cities, till he came to Caesarea.

As a deacon, Philip served tables. In Samaria, he became an evangelist. In Gaza, he was removed from the public arena to minister one on one to the Ethiopian eunuch. In Caesarea, he found himself raising a family of four daughters who became prophetesses (Acts 21:9). Wherever he was, Philip flowed in ministry. I'm sure he was as thrilled serving tables as he was preaching to multitudes and as enthusiastic talking to the Ethiopian as he was raising daughters to be godly women.

In your walk with the Lord and your work for the Lord, like Philip, you will go through different seasons. There will be times when you'll wait tables and minister practically. There will be other times when the Lord might use you to speak to multitudes as you minister publicly. Other times, you will work one on one as you minister personally. Still other times, you'll invest in your kids as you minister to your family. To everything there is a time and a purpose. Trust the Lord. Go with the flow. Walk with Him one step at a time, and He'll lead you in paths you could never imagine. Just ask Philip!

AVOIDING AN UNEXPECTED END
A Topical Study of
Acts 8:35–37

W hen my son Benjamin was four years old, he was completely and wonderfully obsessed with Bible stories and Bible characters. If you came to our house, chances are you would have seen Benjamin wearing what looked suspiciously like a burlap sack. That was his David outfit. He was David for a good part of each day. Then he would become Joshua, marching around and knocking down his building-block walls. He loved Bible stories in a way that blew me away. Once on his "special day," I said, "Benjamin, where do you want to go? Do you want to go to the park? Do you want to go to McDonald Playland?" No, he wanted to go to the Christian bookstore. So that's where we went. We spent two hours there, with Benny sitting on the floor looking at books and playing with puzzles. After watching Ben's enthusiasm, Fred, the owner, offered to hire him!

Thus, it was not surprising that after every service, Benjamin would head for the bookstore at Applegate Christian Fellowship. One week he saw something that had escaped his notice in all of his previous visits. Way up on the top shelf sat a Bible Nintendo game. Intrigued as he studied the pictures of Noah and the ark, Joshua and Jericho, Jonah and the whale on the cover, Benjamin brought it home.

Now, at four years of age, Benny was not very adept at video games—but he patiently and laboriously pushed the buttons and tried to advance to the different levels where he could see Noah's ark sail and Jericho's walls tumble down. After a couple of hours, however, frustration began to cloud his face. Finally, he said to my wife, Tammy, "Mommy, get a piece of paper and write down what I tell you. I want to send a letter to the bookstore." This is what he said:

Dear Bookstore,

I am talking about Nintendo and so please help me to get to Goliath. Please help me to get to the flood of Noah and help the animals to go two by two. I am Benjamin. I am only four. Don't you know that? Bye-bye, bookstore. I love you, bookstore.

Benny

Benjamin was disappointed because the game didn't end the way he thought it would. So, too, many, many people will encounter a far greater tragedy when they find themselves face-to-face with the Lord, believing that they have a right to enter into heaven, but instead hearing Him say, "Depart from Me. I never knew you" (see Matthew 7:23).

Here in Acts 8, knowing we need stories and illustrations to understand truth, the Lord ingeniously placed the stories of two conversions back to back—those of Simon the sorcerer and the Ethiopian eunuch. These two men appear side by side in Scripture, I believe, so that you and I can verify the reality of our salvation and thereby avoid an unexpected and tragic end.

Look first at Simon's conversion and note four characteristics that prove it was not real.

Simon Had a Wrong View of Self

> *But there was a certain man, called Simon, which beforetime in the same city used sorcery, and bewitched the people of Samaria, giving out that himself was some great one. . . .*   Acts 8:9

You'll always know someone's off the wall if he tries to pretend he's someone great. That's what Simon was doing—making himself out to be someone special. Although it is true that "pride is a weed that grows in the garden of every man," in Simon's case, his weed of pride was a tree, for as the story unfolds, we will see Simon seeking to be a superstar above all rather than a servant of all.

Simon Had a Wrong View of Supernatural Power

> *And when Simon saw that through laying on of the apostles' hands the Holy Ghost was given, he offered them money, Saying, Give me also this power, that on whomsoever I lay hands, he may receive the Holy Ghost.*   Acts 8:18, 19

Simon wanted to buy the gift of the Holy Ghost—not to change his character, but to fulfill his ambition. So, too, before leaving home, the prodigal said, "Father give me the goods" (see Luke 15:12). But when he returned—humbled and broken—he said, "Father, make me a servant" (see Luke 15:19). True conversion never says, "Give me the goods." It says, "Make me a servant."

Simon Had a Wrong View of the Spirit

> *But Peter said unto him, Thy money perish with thee, because thou hast thought that the gift of God may be purchased with money.*   Acts 8:20

This is where we get the term "simony"—the practice of buying a position in church hierarchy. During the Middle Ages, many of the popes actually bought their way into the office. To this day, in many churches, positions on boards or ministry teams can still be bought. Even though that is not the case here, there is a "Simon mentality" that can creep into our lives whenever we subconsciously think we can purchase the gift of God through our devotional life, our piety, our fasting, or our spirituality. The Holy Spirit is a *gift* (Luke 11:13). He cannot be purchased with money or energy. Jesus said, "If you, then being evil, know how to give good gifts to your children, how much more will the heavenly Father *give* the Holy Spirit to them that ask?"

Simon Had a Wrong View of Sin

> *Then answered Simon, and said, Pray ye to the Lord for me, that none of these things which ye have spoken come upon me.*   Acts 8:24

Simon didn't want the sin rooted out of his life; he only wanted protection from its repercussions. The Lord declared that unless the days were shortened, no man would survive (Matthew 24:22). Like Simon, however, our society is concerned only with the repercussions of our sin rather than regeneration and deliverance from sin.

Now contrast Simon with the Ethiopian eunuch as you note four aspects of his conversion that prove it was real. . . .

The Sovereign Work of the Spirit

And the angel of the Lord spake unto Philip, saying, Arise, and go toward the south unto the way that goeth down from Jerusalem unto Gaza, which is desert.   Acts 8:26

True conversion is always the result of God's stirring and moving rather than of some plan or plot someone hatches to get ahead. True conversion takes place when the Lord stirs and brings a Philip—a radio broadcast, a tract, a New Testament, a neighbor, a church, or a crusade—to someone who, like the eunuch, is simply riding along in the chariot of life, pondering and curious.

The Searching Heart of a Sinner

And Philip ran thither to him, and heard him read the prophet Esaias, and said, Understandest thou what thou readest? And he said, How can I, except some man should guide me? And he desired Philip that he would come up and sit with him.   Acts 8:30, 31

Already sovereignly drawn by the Spirit, the eunuch was searching and wondering. "You shall seek me and find me when you search for me with all your heart," the Lord declared in Jeremiah 29:13. God tugs on our hearts sovereignly, but it's up to us to respond personally.

The Scriptural Base for Salvation

Then Philip opened his mouth, and began at the same scripture, and preached unto him Jesus.   Acts 8:35

Simon's so-called conversion was based on seeing wonders. The eunuch's conversion was based upon seeing Jesus in the Word. True conversion always comes not by seeing wonders, but by hearing the Word (Romans 10:17). Build your faith upon the Word of God. Become students of the Scriptures. Stay in the Scriptures. Submit to the Scriptures. And you will experience true conversion.

The Sincere Expression of a Servant

And as they went on their way, they came unto a certain water: and the eunuch said, See, here is water; what doth hinder me to be baptized? And Philip said, If thou believest with all thine heart, thou mayest. And he answered and said, I believe that Jesus Christ is the Son of God. Acts 8:36, 37

Simon the magician asked for power to promote himself. The Ethiopian eunuch asked for baptism to die to self. "Bury me in the waters of baptism," he said. "I want to serve God. I want to submit to His authority. I want to submerge myself in His will."

The same Peter who saw the deception of Simon the sorcerer would later write, "Brethren give diligence to make your calling and election sure" (2 Peter 1:10). There's nothing more important for you to consider than if you are truly saved! You may have been sitting in a pew for years—but are you truly saved? You may have been baptized—but are you truly saved?" You might be active in church—but are you *sure* you're saved?

Romans 8:16 declares His Spirit bears witness with our spirit that we are the sons of God. Do you have that witness? Does His Spirit affirm and resonate in your heart, "Yes, you are My child"—or is it still a little fuzzy? If you're not sure, take time today to let the Holy Spirit minister to you and give you His witness that you are born again.

Dear people, make your calling and election *sure*.

9 Acts 9:1, 2
And Saul, yet breathing out threatenings and slaughter against the disciples of the Lord, went unto the high priest, and desired of him letters to Damascus to the synagogues, that if he found any of this way, whether they were men or women, he might bring them bound unto Jerusalem.

Saul of Tarsus was religious. Trained by Gamaliel, the "teacher's teacher" of that day, Saul knew the Scriptures well. Saul was respected. He was a member of the Sanhedrin—the Jewish Supreme Court. Saul was refined. We read in chapter 7 that when Stephen was being stoned, Saul gave consent to the execution, but he was above picking up a rock himself. And now we see Saul as relentless, traveling throughout Judea, Samaria, and northern Israel—even across the border into Damascus, one hundred forty miles from Jerusalem—to hunt believers down and bring them back bound.

Why did this religious, respected, refined man become relentless in his pursuit of those who named the name of Jesus? I believe that when Saul saw Stephen's face glow like an angel's and heard the words, "Lord, lay not this sin to their charge," from his lips, something snapped within Saul. Witnessing not only Stephen's death, but the reality of his faith, Saul was shaken. And, in his insecurity, he became a crazed reactionary. But even as his anger ignited and his rage rose, something else happened within Saul as he watched the stoning of Stephen, for years later (Acts 17), Saul would make reference to the very message Stephen preached moments before his execution.

This encourages me because it proves that, although people might seem to be turning a deaf ear to what we're saying—or worse, picking up stones to put us down or shut us up—the Word of God does not return void (Isaiah 55:11). Scripture is like a time bomb, gang. Share the Word. Even though the person you're talking to might look at you as if you're crazy, you're planting little time bombs in his inner man. Share the Word with your kids, your co-workers, your friends—

and wait for the "bombs" to go off, just as they did in the heart of Saul.

Acts 9:3
And as he journeyed, he came near Damascus: and suddenly there shined round about him a light from heaven.

While walking down the road, a light shone on Saul. Do you know people who seem absolutely hardened to the gospel? Maybe you work with one. Maybe you're married to one. The Lord has ways of breaking through to them and shining His light on them unpredictably and unexpectedly—even as He did with Saul.

Acts 9:4
And he fell to the earth, and heard a voice saying unto him, Saul, Saul, why persecutest thou me?

"Why persecutest thou me?" This is not the voice of protestation; it's the voice of consideration, as if to say, "Saul, stop and think about what you're doing, for in persecuting those people, you're persecuting Me." We are the bride of Christ. He's jealous for us and in love with us. Thus, when we find fault with one another—even if there's reason—He takes it personally, as any husband would. Next time you want to come down on one who is in love with Jesus Christ, be careful, for in attacking His bride, we attack Him.

Acts 9:5
And he said, Who art thou, Lord? And the Lord said, I am Jesus whom thou persecutest: it is hard for thee to kick against the pricks.

"It's hard to do what you're doing, isn't it, Saul, when in your heart you know what you're doing isn't right?"

Acts 9:6 (a)
And he trembling and astonished said, Lord, what wilt thou have me to do?

Underline this verse, because it is the essence of what conversion is all about. You'll always know when a person is truly born-again, for when he's had an encounter with the Lord, he will invariably ask, "Lord, what do You want me to do?"

A man in a restaurant, choking on a chicken bone, grabbed his throat and fell to the floor. From five tables over a doctor stood up, ran to the scene, and quickly dislodged the bone. "Doctor, what do I owe you?" asked the man.

"Whatever you thought it was worth when you were choking," replied the doctor.

So, too, what the Lord asks us to do is not a pressure upon us, but a privilege for us when we realize the price He paid to save us when we were choking on sin and headed for eternal damnation.

Acts 9:6 (b)
And the Lord said unto him, Arise, and go into the city, and it shall be told thee what thou must do.

The Lord always directs one step at a time. How often I want to see the big picture, but the Lord doesn't work that way. Be obedient to what you know you should do, and, as you do it, more will be revealed to you.

Acts 9:7–9
And the men which journeyed with him stood speechless, hearing a voice, but seeing no man. And Saul arose from the earth; and when his eyes were opened, he saw no man: but they led him by the hand, and brought him into Damascus. And he was three days without sight, and neither did eat nor drink.

What happened to Saul is a perfect picture of what happens in photography: Film, coated with light-sensitive salts and chemicals, is kept in darkness. When the shutter opens, light pours in, and whatever is seen in the light at that second is printed on the film. Then it's quickly returned to darkness, lest it be overexposed. Finally, it is taken into a darkroom, where it is placed in a chemical solution and fully developed.

When Saul was persecuting Christians, he was in spiritual darkness. Suddenly, on the road to Damascus, the shutter release was pushed, and he saw the Light. Then he was returned to darkness through physical blindness in order for the image of Jesus alone to be permanently imprinted upon his heart and developed within his life.

Acts 9:10, 11 (a)
And there was a certain disciple at Damascus, named Ananias; and to him said the Lord in a vision, Ananias. And he said, Behold, I am here, Lord. And the Lord said unto him, Arise, and go into the street which is called Straight . . .

Straight Street is still in Damascus. It's the main road that runs east to west through the downtown section of this, the oldest city in the world.

Acts 9:11 (b)
. . . and inquire in the house of Judas for one called Saul, of Tarsus: for, behold, he prayeth.

How do you know when a person is converted? First, he says to the Lord, "What do You want me to do?" Secondly, he continues talking to the Lord. He prays.

Acts 9:12–14
And hath seen in a vision a man named Ananias coming in, and putting his hand on him, that he might receive his sight. Then Ananias answered, Lord, I have heard by many of this man, how much evil he hath done to thy saints at Jerusalem: And here he hath authority from the chief priests to bind all that call on thy name.

It's interesting that the Lord used a man named Ananias to be the instrument of Saul's recovery and that Ananias was to go to the house of Judas. Ananias and Judas are two names that are infamous in the New Testament. Judas was the betrayer of Jesus. Ananias was the liar of the early church (Acts 5). And certainly the name Saul doesn't exactly conjure up images of spiritual perfection! The Lord is doing something neat here, I think: He's redeeming names even as He continues His redemptive work in people.

Acts 9:15, 16
But the Lord said unto him, Go thy way: for he is a chosen vessel unto me, to bear my name before the Gentiles, and kings, and the children of Israel: For I will shew him how great things he must suffer for my name's sake.

God told Ananias that Paul's ministry was to be to the Gentiles first and foremost, secondly to kings, and lastly to the people of Israel. Initially, however, Paul would keep trying to minister to the Jews and find himself frustrated in the process. So, too, sometimes the reason we get upset in serving the Lord is because we don't understand or aren't obedient to His plan for our individual ministry.

Acts 9:17 (a)
And Ananias went his way, and entered into the house; and putting his hands on him said, Brother Saul . . .

Not "Brutal Saul" or "Bruiser Saul," Ananias called him "Brother Saul" because Ananias immediately accepted the fact that Saul was a brother regardless of his previous spiritual blindness, regardless of his present physical blindness.

Acts 9:17 (b), 18
. . . the Lord, even Jesus, that appeared unto thee in the way as thou camest, hath sent me, that thou mightest receive thy sight, and be filled with the Holy Ghost. And immediately there fell from his eyes as it had been scales: and he received sight forthwith, and arose, and was baptized.

Notice that although Saul was a brother, he was not yet empowered with the Spirit. Although some argue this point, I believe the Book of Acts clearly depicts an empowering subsequent to salvation.

Acts 9:19, 20
And when he had received meat, he was strengthened. Then was Saul certain days with the disciples which were at Damascus. And straightway he preached Christ in the synagogues, that he is the Son of God.

Thinking he was custom-made to be a witness to the Jews—educated by Gamaliel, and a member of the Sanhedrin—Paul headed for the synagogues. In Romans 9 he would write, "I would be accursed if it would lead to the salvation of my brethren" (see Romans 9:3).

Acts 9:21
But all that heard him were amazed, and said; Is not this he that destroyed them which called on this name in Jerusalem, and came hither for that intent, that he might bring them bound unto the chief priests?

The Jews in Damascus were amazed—but they weren't converted. They were confounded, but not persuaded. At this point, realizing the Jews were not receiving his testimony, Paul took off for the desert, where he would spend three years in Arabia (Galatians 1:17). What did he do there? Saul, the Old Testament scholar par excellence, enrolled in a three-year course taught by the Holy Spirit on how every symbol, every sacrifice, every picture in the Old Testament related to the Person of Jesus Christ. Seminarians today graduate with a DD, a Doctorate of Divinity. Saul graduated with a much more powerful DD, a Doctorate of the Desert.

Acts 9:22
But Saul increased the more in strength, and confounded the Jews which dwelt at Damascus, proving that this is very Christ.

Three years later, Paul came back and said, "Wait until you hear what I've got to share," as he talked to the Jews once more.

Acts 9:23–25
And after that many days were fulfilled, the Jews took counsel to kill him: But their laying await was known of Saul. And they watched the gates day and night to kill him. Then the disciples took him by night, and let him down by the wall in a basket.

Paul won the debate, but he didn't win their hearts. Although it seemed like he was the perfect one to carry out ministry to the Jews—that was not the plan of the Lord. In fact, his ministry to the Jews was met with such animosity that he had to be let down in a basket under cover of night to save his life.

Acts 9:26 (a)
And when Saul was come to Jerusalem . . .

Now does Paul go to the Gentiles? Not yet. He goes to Jerusalem, the capital of Judaism.

Acts 9:26 (b), 27
. . . he assayed to join himself to the disciples: but they were all afraid of him, and believed not that he was a disciple. But Barnabas took him, and brought him to the apostles, and declared unto them how he had seen the Lord in the way, and that he had spoken him, and how he had preached boldly at Damascus in the name of Jesus.

The disciples didn't buy Paul's conversion story. Only Barnabas, whose name means "son of consolation," said, "Hey, boys, give Saul a break. He really has had an experience with the Lord. I saw him in Damascus preaching Jesus Christ."

Acts 9:28–30
And he was with them coming in and going out at Jerusalem. And he spake boldly in the name of the Lord Jesus, and disputed against the Grecians: but they went about to slay him. Which when the brethren knew, they brought him down to Caesarea, and sent him forth to Tarsus.

Finally, the brothers sent Saul to Gentile territory, saying, "It's just not working here, Paul. Go back to Tarsus."

Acts 9:31
Then had the churches rest throughout all Judaea and Galilee and Samaria, and were edified; and walking in the fear of the Lord, and in the comfort of the Holy Ghost, were multiplied.

The churches were edified and multiplied—when? When they got rid of Paul. Paul, who had such a heart for the people of Israel, was finally sent out of Israel, into Gentile territory, where he would spend the next seven to ten years living in obscurity in Tarsus.

Maybe you can relate. Maybe you were saved ten years ago, and you had such vision, such desire to be used in ministry or service. You thought, *I'm tailor-made to do this,* or, *I've got a call upon my life for this.* And you tried. But it just didn't work out. Maybe for the past ten years, you've been waiting, wondering, *Is the Lord ever going to use me?*

Be of good cheer! The man who would turn the world upside down—the most important preacher of all time, the most powerful person who has ever lived except for the Lord Jesus Christ—had to first experience shut doors, shut doors, shut doors, and ten years of sitting in Tarsus while the Lord reworked and rewired him. If the Lord is doing that in your life, don't be discouraged. Don't throw in the towel. Don't walk away. Let Him do His work and have His way. Go with the flow. Put away your agenda. Get back to basics and say, "Lord, what wilt Thou have me to do?"

For topical study of Acts 9:25–31 entitled "Let Down? Look Up!" turn to page 692.

Acts 9:32 (a)
And it came to pass, as Peter . . .

With Paul tucked away in Tarsus, the focus returns to Peter.

Acts 9:32 (b)
. . . passed throughout all quarters . . .

"Peter passed through all quarters." I feel this is a key component in this vignette. Peter was on the move, a man of motion, a man looking for opportunities. So, too, today—when the Lord wants to use a man or a woman, He'll use someone who, like Peter, is on the move, looking for ways to serve Him.

Acts 9:32 (c), 33
. . . he came down also to the saints which dwelt at Lydda. And there he found a certain man named Aeneas, which had kept his bed eight years, and was sick of the palsy.

I'm so blessed and challenged and intrigued by my brother Peter. Even though he was the "Big Gun in Jerusalem," here we see him ministering to people one at a time.

Acts 9:34, 35

And Peter said unto him, Aeneas, Jesus Christ maketh thee whole: arise, and make thy bed. And he arose immediately. And all that dwelt at Lydda and Saron saw him, and turned to the Lord.

Notice not only Peter's motion, but notice his motivation when he said, *"Jesus Christ* maketh thee whole."

Acts 9:36–38

Now there was at Joppa a certain disciple named Tabitha, which by interpretation is called Dorcas: this woman was full of good works and almsdeeds which she did. And it came to pass in those days, that she was sick, and died: whom when they had washed, they laid her in an upper chamber. And forasmuch as Lydda was nigh to Joppa, and the disciples had heard that Peter was there, they sent unto him two men, desiring him that he would not delay to come to them.

"Quick! Call for Peter. Dorcas is dead." Following the demise of no other apostle or spiritual leader did the early church ever call in the apostles. "The apostles, the prophets, the spiritual superstars, they're dead? Well, let's move on. But Dorcas? We *need* her." Why? Because Dorcas was one who ministered practically. She did good things for people. She sewed clothing. She cared for them in a very tangible way. She was down to earth. She was real. When your car isn't working, you don't want a prophet or an apostle or a preacher—you want a mechanic. Give us more mechanics! Give us more seamstresses! Give us more cooks! God, give us more practical, loving people like Dorcas.

Acts 9:39 (a)

Then Peter arose and went with them.

Peter was available. That is the most important requirement for personal ministry. He didn't say, "I'm too big to minister to one dead woman. Do you think that's a good use of my time?" No, Peter responded to the need at hand. Maybe there's a dead person in your life—not physically but spiritually—whom the Lord wants to revive through you, as He taps on your shoulder and says, "Come quickly."

Acts 9:39, (b), 40 (a)

When he was come, they brought him into the upper chamber: and all the widows stood by him weeping, and shewing the coats and garments which Dorcas made, while she was with them. But Peter put them all forth, and kneeled down, and prayed . . .

Peter was prayerful. I suggest to you the reason Peter knelt down was because he realized that not only was he inadequate for this ministry, but if anyone happened to look into his room while he was praying, they would see him calling upon the Lord.

Acts 9:40 (b)–42

. . . and turning him to the body said, Tabitha, arise. And she opened her eyes: and when she saw Peter, she sat up. And he gave her his hand, and lifted her up, and when he had called the saints and widows, presented her alive. And it was known throughout all Joppa; and many believed in the Lord.

Peter was fruitful. His ministry to one dead woman caused an entire city to be exposed to the gospel.

By many peoples' evaluation, Mordecai Ham was one of the least effective preachers of his day. But a young man named William heard his message, responded, and got saved. This makes Mordecai Ham's entire ministry valid, for William Franklin Graham, better known as Billy, would, in turn, reach millions.

When you reach one third-grader in Sunday school, you don't know if that third-grader might not be the next Billy Graham. Like Peter, you never know the fruit that will come from working with one "dead" person.

For topical study of Acts 9:32–42 entitled "What Would Jesus Do?" turn to page 695.

Acts 9:43

And it came to pass, that he tarried many days in Joppa with one Simon a tanner.

Peter was flexible. Where did he lodge? With a tanner. Because they dealt with dead animals, so unclean did the Jews esteem tanners that the Mishnah—Jewish regulation—stated that the wife of a tanner had the right to divorce him.

Thus, the Lord's work with Peter concerning the issue of legalism began in the house of a fellow whom Peter previously would have avoided completely. If we're going to be used individually and corporately, like Peter, we need to show flexibility within the parameters of Scripture—not bound by traditions or preconceived opinions—even if it means hanging out with tanners.

Be like Peter. Be available. Be prayerful. Be flexible—and watch the Lord make you fruitful.

LET DOWN? LOOK UP!
A Topical Study of
Acts 9:25–31

Years ago, a book appeared on the *New York Times* bestseller list that dealt with statistics and probabilities. It was an intriguing volume, wherein the author, a statistician, presents nuggets of information like these:

> One in one thousand Americans will have murdered someone in his lifetime.
> (Next time you're at a baseball park or a football stadium with forty thousand
> other folks, keep in mind that statistically there are forty murderers in the
> stadium with you.)
> One in two hundred Americans will spend time in prison.
> Seven in ten who start a company will see it go bankrupt.
> Nine in ten who lose weight on a diet will gain back every single pound.
> (If you start a business, the odds are 70 percent it will go belly-up. And if
> you go on a diet, the odds are 90 percent it will be belly out!)
> The chance of being hit by lightning is one in nine thousand.
> The chance of winning the lottery is one in four million.

But the chance of being let down by someone or something is one in one—which brings us to our text—where we see the apostle Paul, still called Saul at this point, let down from the city wall in a basket. Initially, it must have been disconcerting, disappointing, and disillusioning to him. But Paul would later write that this time of being let down—in more ways than one—would be the second greatest event in his life.

> *If I must needs glory, I will glory of the things which concern mine infirmities.*
> *The God and Father of our Lord Jesus Christ, which is blessed for evermore,*
> *knoweth that I lie not. In Damascus the governor under Aretas the king kept*
> *the city of the Damascenes with a garrison, desirous to apprehend me: And*
> *through a window in a basket was I let down by the wall, and escaped his*
> *hands.*   2 Corinthians 11:30–33

Paul says, "If I'm going to glory, this is what I will glory in: my difficulty."
Listen to this paraphrase of 2 Corinthians 11: "The greatest event in my life was

when they took me at night and let me down over the wall of Damascus in a basket. That was the most meaningful experience I have ever had since the day I met Christ."

Far from feeling let down by this event, Paul actually gloried in it. But it took time. You see, following his conversion, Paul's singular passion was to preach Christ to the Jews. In Romans 9:3 he says he would literally go to hell if doing so would bring about their salvation. Would you do that? Would you spend eternity in hell if your brother would be saved? I know nothing of that kind of love.

Paul cared so deeply for Israel that he said he would be accursed for his brethren. Trained as a Jewish scholar and theologian, it would seem as though Paul was tailor-made to be a minister unto the Jews. But in Acts 9:15, God had told Ananias that Paul's ministry would be first to the Gentiles, second to kings, and lastly to Jews. So what did Paul do? Acts 9:20 tells us he headed straight for the synagogues—to preach to the Jews. So poorly was he received, however, that his audience wanted to kill him, necessitating his escape by night in a basket. What did he do then? He headed for Jerusalem—the very capital of Judaism!

We pick up the story as Paul shares his testimony in Acts 22. . . .

> *And it came to pass, that, when I was come again to Jerusalem, even while I prayed in the temple, I was in a trance; and saw him saying unto me, Make haste, and get thee quickly out of Jerusalem: for they will not receive thy testimony concerning me. And I said, Lord, they know that I imprisoned and beat in every synagogue them that believed on thee: And when the blood of thy martyr Stephen was shed, I also was standing by, and consenting unto his death, and kept the raiment of them that slew him. And he said unto me, Depart: for I will send thee far hence unto the Gentiles.* Acts 22:17–21

What's happening here? After spending fifteen days in Jerusalem (Galatians 1:18), Paul went into the temple. Through a trance, the Lord said to him, "I'm sending you to the Gentiles, Paul," to which Paul answered, "But, Lord, You're missing a great opportunity! The Jews here know I was a radical on their behalf, going into the synagogues and the homes where Christians met to drag them out and have them killed. They know I consented to the death of Stephen, the first martyr. Don't you see, Lord, how powerful my testimony could be here in Jerusalem?"

And the Lord responded by saying, "Depart, Paul. I'm sending you to the Gentiles."

So Paul was sent to Tarsus, where he would spend between seven and ten years laboring in obscurity. Maybe you can relate to this. Maybe, like Paul, you have said, "Lord, You're missing a great opportunity. I'm custom-made to reach these people. If You bless my business, my family, this project—Lord, just think how good it would be!"

And the Lord says, "Depart. I'm sending you somewhere else."

In Matthew 11:28, Jesus said, "Come unto Me, all ye that labor and are heavy-laden and I will give you rest." Rest from what? Rest from your works, rest from trying to be spiritual, rest from trying to be religious.

Jesus said,

Take my yoke upon you, and learn of me; for I am meek and lowly in heart: and ye shall find rest unto your souls.   Matthew 11:29

When you come to Jesus initially, you find rest from your works. But it's only when you are yoked to Jesus that you find rest in your heart. Perhaps today you might have rest from your works—you've been born again; you're a believer—but you don't have rest in your heart. You're troubled about many things: family, finances, ministry, health, and relationships. Do you know why that is? We are troubled in our hearts when we fail to take His yoke upon us; when *we* try to call the shots and direct what *we* think should happen. Our ideas could be good, our motives noble. But they're worthless if they're not what God intends.

If you're troubled today because someone let you down, some project didn't open up, some relationship didn't work out, you can become a basket case—let down over the side of the wall in bitterness and defeat. Or, like Paul, you can learn to trust the Lord and see a bigger picture by saying, "*Your* way, Lord, not mine. I give up. I let go. What do *You* want to do? I yoke myself with You."

What is a yoke? A device that connects a weaker, dumber ox to a stronger, wiser ox. Guess which ox you are. "Take My yoke upon you and learn of Me," Jesus says to us. "Link to Me and learn of Me. Let Me lead you."

"But, Lord," we say, "we can bless those folks. We can see things happen! Come on, Lord." And we try to pull God in our direction.

I believe that's what Paul was trying to do. And it took seven to ten years before he finally gave up. Paul, the great apostle to the Gentiles, changed the world when he accepted the yoke the Lord placed upon him and said, "Okay, we'll go in *Your* direction." And that is why he looked back on the day he was let down in a basket as the most important day in his life, second only to the day he met Christ (2 Corinthians 11:30–33). What if Paul hadn't learned that lesson? What if he kept storming into synagogues, trying to make a way into Jerusalem? He would have either died at a very young age or he would have had a very ineffective ministry.

Don't try to persuade the Lord to go your way. When you're let down, don't give up. Instead, say, "Okay, Lord, what do You want to do now?" His plan for you might be very different from your own. His vision of you might be different from the way you see yourself because those whose ministry is based upon their own abilities, skills, and talents are those who have a tendency to take the glory for themselves.

"To the Gentiles, Paul. I want to do an entirely different thing through you," said the Lord.

"But my heart—" protested Paul.

"To the Gentiles, Paul," answered the Lord.

"But my background—"

"To the Gentiles, Paul."

"But my training—"

"To the Gentiles, Paul."

"But, Lord—"

"To the Gentiles, Paul."

"But—"

"To the Gentiles, Paul."

"Okay, Lord."

Some of you will make that decision today. You'll finally choose to say, "Okay, Lord." And when you do, you will find rest in your soul.

WHAT WOULD JESUS DO?
A Topical Study of
Acts 9:32–41

Five hundred million dollars up in smoke; forty-one lives senselessly snuffed out; a city smoldering; a nation questioning. The images we saw on television eleven years ago of the Los Angeles riots have been indelibly imprinted on our collective memory.

We'll never forget the shopkeeper shaking his head in disbelief as gang members broke into his shop and carried out his life's work while police stood by watching. We'll never forget the woman cradling her fifteen-year-old daughter in her arms after she had been struck down by a stray bullet on Crenshaw Boulevard. We'll never forget the drugstore manager with tears in his eyes, telling his employees they no longer had a job. We'll never forget the truck driver being pulled from his cab by six young men who proceeded to grind his face into the pavement.

It's been a dark week. I'm so glad that on this Sunday we can come to God's house and look into His Word—because, for any dark time, His Word is a lamp unto our feet and a light unto our path. How are we to deal with the sickness and the sadness we see all around us? I believe our text gives us the answer. . . .

And it came to pass, as Peter passed throughout all quarters, he came down also to the saints which dwelt at Lydda. And there he found a certain man named Aeneas, which had kept his bed eight years, and was sick of the palsy. And Peter said unto him, Aeneas, Jesus Christ maketh thee whole: arise, and make thy bed. And he arose immediately. And all that dwelt at Lydda and Saron saw him, and turned to the Lord.   Acts 9:32–35

What intrigues me about this passage is that the story is incredibly similar to what had transpired a few years previously when Jesus was at a pool called Bethesda. Lame people were lying all around the pool, waiting for the stirring of the water, after which the first one to take the plunge would be healed of his infirmity. It was there that Jesus approached a man who had been lame for thirty-eight years and said, "Rise and take up your bed" (see John 5:8). And here a few years later, Peter used virtually the same phraseology when he said to the lame man at Lydda, "Rise, make up your bed."

"Rise"—a command.

"Take up your bed"—an exhortation.

So, too, the Lord comes to you and me and says, "Rise. I'm giving you victory today. I'm healing you of that lame sin with which you've been involved. Now take up your bed and don't expect or provide for any relapse whatsoever."

"Rise, take up your bed," said Jesus.

"Rise, make up your bed," echoed Peter.

And miracles happened.

After finding sickness in Lydda, Peter found sadness in Joppa . . .

Now there was at Joppa a certain disciple named Tabitha, which by interpretation is called Dorcas: this woman was full of good works and almsdeeds which she did. And it came to pass in those days, that she was sick, and died: whom when they had washed, they laid her in an upper chamber. And forasmuch as Lydda was nigh to Joppa, and the disciples had heard that Peter was there, they sent unto him two men, desiring him that he would not delay to come to them. Then Peter arose and went with them. When he was come, they brought him into the upper chamber: and all the widows stood by him weeping, and shewing the coats and garments which Dorcas made, while she was with them. But Peter put them all forth, and kneeled down, and prayed; and turning him to the body said, Tabitha, arise. And she opened her eyes: and when she saw Peter, she sat up. And he gave her his hand, and lifted her up, and when he had called the saints and widows, presented her alive. Acts 9:36–41

Tabitha was dead, and there was great sadness in the city. The disciples called for Peter, and when he arrived, he immediately put out the mourners. Why? Some say it was because he needed the room. Others say it was because if he prayed and nothing happened he wouldn't be embarrassed. But I say it was because that's what he had seen Jesus do.

You recall the story. Jesus was asked to come to the house of Jairus to heal his daughter. But before He arrived, she died. When Jesus said, "She's not dead. She's just sleeping," the mourners who were gathered around the house, mocked Him to scorn. Luke wrote that Jesus sent all of the mockers out (Luke 8:53, 54). Then He went into the room of Jairus' daughter, took her by the hand, and said, "Talitha cumi," or "Little lamb, arise."

"Talitha cumi," said Jesus.

"Tabitha cumi," echoed Peter.

And miracles happened.

What does this have to do with the LA riots of eleven years ago? Plenty. No doubt at the time you engaged in discussions about the events that took place—the sickness and sadness, the death and darkness, the destruction and despair. And no doubt the discussions centered around these questions. . . .

Why Did This Happen?

Why was there looting and robbing and killing and rabble-rousing? There are those who say, "It's indicative of the end times. Doesn't the Bible say that in the last days perilous times will come when men will be lovers of themselves, boasters, disobedient, unthankful, unholy, unloving, without self-control, despisers of good" (2 Timothy 3:1–3)?

Others say, "I'm not sure it's end-time prophecy. Rather, I suggest it's Old Testament prophecy. Haven't you read Isaiah, Micah, or Amos? Don't you recall what the prophets of God said in days of old—that if the poor were forgotten and there was a lack of compassion, there would be judgment throughout the land?"

So goes the debate among believers.

Who Was to Blame?

Some say it was a jury in Simi Valley.

Others say, "It's youth. The verdict in Simi Valley was merely their excuse to practice anarchy. Didn't you see the picture of the man breaking out of the store carrying a TV and declaring, "Forget Rodney King. I'm king today"?

Others say, "It's not the jury in Simi Valley, and it's not the kids roving about in anarchy. It's the fault of our prosperous white society. The comfortably wealthy have seen the plight of the poor on their TV screens and heard about it on their radios. But, like Cain, they have chosen to shrug it off, asking, "Am I my brother's keeper?"

But I suggest we're asking the wrong questions. We who name the name of Jesus should not have been asking, "Why?" or, "Who?" but "What?"

"*What* would Jesus have done if He were there in the flesh that day?" You see, when there is sadness or sickness in our society, in our families, or in our lives personally, I suggest to you the issue is not "Who is to blame?" or, "Why did this happen?" but . . .

What Would Jesus Do?

What *would* He have done? Would He have called Rush Limbaugh? Would He have politicized the event? Would He have analyzed the outcome?

"How can we know what He would do?" you ask. "He never saw a city like LA."

Oh, really?

As He came down the mount called Olivet and rode toward the city of Jerusalem, Jesus heard the people crying, "Hosanna!" But He knew that within a few hours their cry would change. Anarchy would sweep through the city, and a bloodthirsty mob would unjustly and unlawfully cry out, "We will not have this man rule over us. Crucify Him!" So Jesus stopped, and what did He do? He cried not for Himself, but for the people. "O Jerusalem, Jerusalem, how often would I have gathered thy children together, as a hen doth gather her brood under her wings" (see Luke 13:34).

And if you think this is stretching the point because the crowds weren't rioting or violent, consider the soldiers who plucked Jesus' beard and spat in His face. Consider the soldiers who rolled dice for His garments even as He hung on the Cross to pay the price for their sins. Did Jesus give a discourse on the ills of society? No. He said, "Father forgive them. They don't know what they're doing."

What about us? We usually make our case, give our opinion, and justify our position. When I get to heaven, I know I'm going to be absolutely stunned by the prejudiced and flawed opinions I held that I was sure were so right. No wonder Paul writes, "For now we see through a glass, darkly; but then face to face: now I know in part: but then shall I know even as I am known" (1 Corinthians 13:12).

So what are we to do in the meantime? Philosophize? No. Analyze? No. In dealing with your boss, your spouse, your neighbor, or your children, the question is not: "Who is to blame?" or "Why is this happening?" The question always is: "What would Jesus do?"

"How do *I* know what Jesus would do?" you ask.

The answer is very simple: Read your Bible.

Put down the paper, turn off your TV, and open Matthew, Mark, Luke, and John—four accounts of the actions, thoughts, and heart of Jesus. Found in the very beginning of the New Testament, the Gospels are the Father saying, "Here is the life of My Son. I'm repeating it four times so you won't miss it."

What do the Gospels tell us Jesus did in dark days? According to Matthew, Mark, Luke, and John, as He overlooked Jerusalem, and as He hung on the Cross surrounded by people acting like animals, Jesus did a singular thing: He prayed. Compassionately and forgivingly, He prayed. That is what you and I are called to do in dark days like these: Pray.

"I'd rather discuss. I'd rather debate. I'd rather write a letter to the editor," you say. Pray. That's what Jesus did. He didn't discuss the situation philosophically. He didn't debate it politically. He saw a city headed for anarchy. He hung on the Cross and was tortured brutally. Yet He did one thing singularly: He prayed.

If my people, which are called by my name, shall humble themselves, and pray,
and seek my face, and turn from their wicked ways; then will I hear from heaven,
and will forgive their sin, and will heal their land.   2 Chronicles 7:14

"If My people who are called by My name"—
> That's us

"Will humble themselves"—
> Will quit theorizing, analyzing, and philosophizing

"And pray and seek My face and confess their sin"—
> Will pray not about the wicked ways of those in LA or anywhere else, but about the sin within themselves

"*Then* will I hear from heaven and forgive their sin and heal their land."

The promise of God practiced in the life of Jesus is so incredibly simple. For whatever problem you face, whatever sickness or sadness, darkness or death in your life—ask yourself a very simple question:

What Would *Jesus* Do?

I pray that, like Peter, we'll be imitators of Jesus—knowing His ways, hearing His heart, and praying as He prayed.

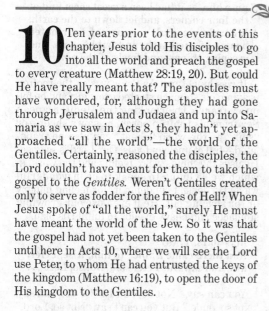

10 Ten years prior to the events of this chapter, Jesus told His disciples to go into all the world and preach the gospel to every creature (Matthew 28:19, 20). But could He have really meant that? The apostles must have wondered, for, although they had gone through Jerusalem and Judaea and up into Samaria as we saw in Acts 8, they hadn't yet approached "all the world"—the world of the Gentiles. Certainly, reasoned the disciples, the Lord couldn't have meant for them to take the gospel to the *Gentiles*. Weren't Gentiles created only to serve as fodder for the fires of Hell? When Jesus spoke of "all the world," surely He must have meant the world of the Jew. So it was that the gospel had not yet been taken to the Gentiles until here in Acts 10, where we will see the Lord use Peter, to whom He had entrusted the keys of the kingdom (Matthew 16:19), to open the door of His kingdom to the Gentiles.

Acts 10:1
There was a certain man in Caesarea called Cornelius, a centurion of the band called the Italian band.

The Italian band wasn't the entertainment at Luigi's on Saturday night, but a band of soldiers. The Roman army was divided into legions of six thousand men. The legions were divided into cohorts of six hundred men. The cohorts were divided into six groups of one hundred men—each overseen by a centurion. Centurions were the "master sergeants" of the Roman army. They were brave of heart, sound of mind, and strong in discipline. Interestingly, every time a centurion is mentioned in the New Testament, he is always spoken of in a favorable light. . . .

It was a centurion in Luke 7 who caused Jesus to marvel when he said, "I am not worthy for You to come under my roof. Just speak the word and my servant will be healed" (see Luke 7:6, 7). It was a centurion in Matthew 27, who, upon witnessing the crucifixion of Jesus and the events that followed said, "Truly this was the Son of God" (Matthew 27:54). And here is Cornelius— yet another centurion whom God will use.

Acts 10:2 (a)
A devout man, and one that feared God . . .

The Holy Spirit calls our attention to three important qualities in the life of Cornelius. Here we see the faith of Cornelius. Cornelius feared God. Yet, although he was a very religious man, he was a very lost man. Although he was a man of prayer and of almsgiving, he was not saved.

Acts 10:2 (b)
. . . with all his house . . .

Secondly, we see the family of Cornelius. After seeing the vanity and fallacy of the gods of Rome, Cornelius wanted his family to know the True and Living God. This is amazing to me. His family had seen Rome—the Hollywood or New York of that day—and yet somehow Cornelius was able to inspire in them a fear of God.

Acts 10:2 (c)
... which gave much alms to the people, and prayed to God alway.

Thirdly, we see the fervency of Cornelius as he went about doing good and praying always. There are those who say, "Even though a person doesn't know Jesus Christ, as long as he loves God and does good to his fellow man, he'll be okay." But this account tells me they are wrong, for if all it took for a man to get into heaven was that he loved God and his fellow man, God would have said, "There's Cornelius down there. He's a pray-er. He's a God-fearer. He's a giver. I'll let him be."

That's not what God said. Instead, Acts 10 is the story of a seeking Savior searching out a seeking sinner. This comforts me because whether a person lives in America, Israel, or a country dominated by Islam; in the subtropical jungle of South America, or the outback of Australia—this story tells me that God will do whatever it takes to get *anyone* who is truly seeking Him pointed in the right direction.

Acts 10:3-8
He saw in a vision evidently about the ninth hour of the day an angel of God coming in to him, and saying unto him, Cornelius. And when he looked on him, he was afraid, and said, What is it, Lord? And he said unto him, Thy prayers and thine alms are come up for a memorial before God. And now send men to Joppa, and call for one Simon, whose surname is Peter: He lodgeth with one Simon a tanner, whose house is by the sea side: he shall tell thee what thou oughtest to do. And when the angel which spake unto Cornelius was departed, he called two of his household servants, and a devout soldier of them that waited on him continually; and when he had declared all these things unto them, he sent them to Joppa.

Why did the Lord send an angel to tell Cornelius to find Peter? Why didn't the angel himself share the gospel with Cornelius? Because it is not the job of angels to share the gospel. It's ours. God could thunder the gospel from heaven if He so desired. But He's chosen to use you and me as instruments to tell people His good news. Gang, if we ever get it through our heads that the gospel really is good news, we wouldn't need classes or motivational seminars on witnessing. Telling people that the Lord loves them—that every sin

they've ever committed, are committing, or will commit is forgiven because of Jesus' death on the Cross—is not a burden. It's a privilege! Talking about religion is a pain. But sharing the gospel is pure joy.

Daniel 12:3 says those who turn many to righteousness shall shine as the stars forever. If you're a soul-winner, a Good News-sharer, you're going to shine—not only in heaven, but here on earth as well. How long has it been since you looked someone in the eye and said, "I've got Good News for you! Jesus loves you and died for your sin"? A week? A month? If you feel kind of dull and burned-out, share the gospel and shine once again!

Acts 10:9-12
On the morrow, as they went on their journey, and drew nigh unto the city, Peter went up upon the housetop to pray about the sixth hour: And he became very hungry, and would have eaten: but while they made ready, he fell into a trance, and saw heaven opened, and a certain vessel descending unto him, as it had been a great sheet knit at the four corners, and let down to the earth: Wherein were all manner of fourfooted beasts of the earth, and wild beasts, and creeping things, and fowls of the air.

It was lunchtime. As Peter was on the rooftop praying, his stomach started growling, and he fell into a trance. Overlooking the Mediterranean Sea from his rooftop perch, he saw a sheet—or "sail," as the word "sheet" can also be translated—full of unclean foods. Our Lord is so good! He uses the things we're feeling and the world in which we're living to speak to us in wonderful ways. He doesn't condemn us for feeling hungry or for spacing out. He'll even use our growling stomachs and heavy eyelids to fulfill His plan.

Acts 10:13, 14 (a)
And there came a voice to him, Rise, Peter; kill, and eat. But Peter said, Not so, Lord ...

You can say, "Not so, buddy." Or you can say, "Not so, dude." But you can't say, "Not so, Lord." If Jesus is truly Lord, you can't say, "Not so" to Him.

Acts 10:14 (b)
... for I have never eaten any thing that is common or unclean.

That's the language of legalism, the pride of the Pharisee. Legalism says, "I have never done this." Liberty says, "I have never done this *before.*"

Acts 10:15, 16
And the voice spake unto him again the second time, What God hath cleansed, that call not thou common. This was done thrice: and the vessel was received up again into heaven.

What God has cleansed, don't call common. God has cleansed you. He's washed you in the blood of His only begotten Son. Don't call yourself common. Most of us have the tendency to say, "God couldn't use me. I'm no good. I don't pray like I should. I say things I regret. I struggle with things. I'm just common. I'm just dirt. I'm nothing."

But God says to us, "Don't call common or unclean what I have cleansed. I've cleansed you. I chose you by name before the foundation of the world" (see Ephesians 1:4).

Acts 10:17–21 (a)
Now while Peter doubted in himself what this vision which he had seen should mean, behold, the men which were sent from Cornelius had made inquiry for Simon's house, and stood before the gate, and called, and asked whether Simon, which was surnamed Peter, were lodged there. While Peter thought on the vision, the Spirit said unto him, Behold, three men seek thee. Arise therefore, and get thee down, and go with them, doubting nothing: for I have sent them. Then Peter went down to the men which were sent unto him from Cornelius . . .

Notice that God works on both sides. He spoke to Cornelius through an angel and to Peter through a vision. When these three men showed up at Peter's gate, it was confirmation that both Cornelius and Peter had heard God correctly. Sometimes well-meaning brothers and sisters come to you and say, "The Lord told me to tell you . . ."

When this happens, your answer should be, "If that's so, He'll tell me, too."

So much is said in the name of the Lord that is not from the Lord or of the Lord. We need to be careful. Well-meaning people are sometimes convinced they've had a vision or a prophecy, and they'll share it freely—even though it may never come to pass. Acts 10 shows us the model of how the Lord works. He works on *both* ends.

For topical study of Acts 10:9–20 entitled "Vision," turn to page 703.

Acts 10:21 (b)–23 (a)
. . . and said, Behold, I am he whom ye seek: what is the cause wherefore ye are come? And they said, Cornelius the centurion, a just man, and one that feareth God, and of good report among all the nation of the Jews, was warned from God by an holy angel to send for thee into his house, and to hear words of thee. Then called he them in, and lodged them.

According to the law, a Jew could not allow Gentiles into his house for any reason. But Peter, realizing the Lord was breaking down the wall between clean and unclean, said, "Come on in, boys." And they came in.

Acts 10:23 (b)
And on the morrow Peter went away with them, and certain brethren from Joppa accompanied him.

Peter took an entourage of six disciples with him. He was stepping out in faith, but perhaps it was because he was worried he could get in big trouble that he took six witnesses along.

Acts 10:24–26
And the morrow after they entered into Caesarea. And Cornelius waited for them, and had called together his kinsmen and near friends. And as Peter was coming in, Cornelius met him, and fell down at his feet, and worshipped him. But Peter took him up, saying, Stand up; I myself also am a man.

Cornelius fell at Peter's feet and worshiped him. Do you know people still do that in Rome today? In St. Peter's Basilica, they line up in front of Michelangelo's statue to kiss the feet of Peter. Over the centuries, the statue has been kissed so many times that the big toe on Peter's right foot is missing. It's wrong. It's not healthy. People can get "toe-maine" poisoning! Then they have to call a "toe" truck! Why is it we worship people? We elevate and idolize people and it ought not be. Peter instinctively knew this. He knew his frailties, he knew his weaknesses, and he knew only One is worthy of worship—his Lord and Savior, Jesus Christ.

Acts 10:27
And as he talked with him, he went in, and found many that were come together.

I like this! It's a home Bible study!

Acts 10:28
And he said unto them, Ye know how that it is an unlawful thing for a man that is a

Jew to keep company, or come unto one of another nation; but God hath shewed me that I should not call any man common or unclean.

Although Peter didn't understand the vision immediately, as events began to unfold, walking from Joppa to Caesarea, he got the picture.

Acts 10:29–31
Therefore came I unto you without gainsaying, as soon as I was sent for: I ask therefore for what intent ye have sent for me? And Cornelius said, Four days ago I was fasting until this hour; and at the ninth hour I prayed in my house, and, behold, a man stood before me in bright clothing, and said, Cornelius, thy prayer is heard, and thine alms are had in remembrance in the sight of God.

Have you ever heard people say God doesn't hear the prayers of unbelievers? This passage says otherwise, for although Cornelius was not yet a believer, an angel appeared to him saying God had heard his prayers.

Acts 10:32, 33
Send therefore to Joppa, and call hither Simon, whose surname is Peter; he is lodged in the house of one Simon a tanner by the sea side: who, when he cometh, shall speak unto thee. Immediately therefore I sent to thee; and thou hast well done that thou art come. Now therefore are we all here present before God, to hear all things that are commanded thee of God.

What a great congregation! Peter walked in and Cornelius said, "We're all ears." When asked what makes a great preacher, Charles Spurgeon is said to have answered quickly: "A great congregation." Where people want to hear the Word, there will always be good teaching and preaching. I'm convinced it's not a good preacher that produces a great congregation, but a great congregation that produces a good preacher.

Acts 10:34
Then Peter opened his mouth, and said, Of a truth I perceive that God is no respecter of persons.

God is not a respecter of persons. He doesn't care if you are intellectually brilliant or if you flunked kindergarten four times, if you spend eight hours in prayer or if you haven't prayed in

eight months. God is not a respecter of people. He's a lover of people.

Acts 10:35–37
But in every nation he that feareth him, and worketh righteousness, is accepted with him. The word which God sent unto the children of Israel, preaching peace by Jesus Christ: (he is Lord of all:) That word, I say, ye know, which was published throughout all Judaea, and began from Galilee, after the baptism which John preached.

"The word which was published" was the Word become flesh—Jesus Christ.

Acts 10:38, 39
How God anointed Jesus of Nazareth with the Holy Ghost and with power: who went about doing good, and healing all that were oppressed of the devil; for God was with him. And we are witnesses of all things which he did both in the land of the Jews, and in Jerusalem; whom they slew and hanged on a tree.

Why did Peter use the phrase, "Hanged on a tree"? Why didn't he just say, "Whom they slew"? The Jewish method of execution was by stoning. It was the Romans—the Gentiles—who utilized crucifixion. Thus, by using this phrase, Peter was saying, "There's no room for anti-Semitism. All men are guilty—Jew and Gentile alike."

Acts 10:40–43
Him God raised up the third day, and shewed him openly; Not to all the people, but unto witnesses chosen before of God, even to us, who did eat and drink with him after he rose from the dead. And he commanded us to preach unto the people, and to testify that it is he which was ordained of God to be the Judge of quick and dead. To him give all the prophets witness, that through his name whosoever believeth in him shall receive remission of sins.

Whoever believes in Jesus will enjoy and receive the forgiveness of sin.

Acts 10:44 (a)
While Peter yet spake these words . . .

Peter was a man who was frequently interrupted. He was interrupted by the Father in Matthew 17 when, on the Mount of Transfiguration, God said, "This is my beloved Son, in whom I am well pleased; hear ye him" (Matthew 17:5).

He was interrupted by the Son when Jesus said, "What thinkest thou, Simon? Do the children of the king pay taxes to the king?" (see Matthew 17:25). And here in Acts 10, he was interrupted by the Spirit. Like Peter, I need to be interrupted by the Father, by the Son, and by the Spirit. I hope you're not upset when your plans are interrupted or when your program is altered, for truly the Lord is the Great Interrupter.

Acts 10:44 (b)–45
. . . the Holy Ghost fell on all them which heard the word. And they of the circumcision which believed were astonished, as many as came with Peter, because that on the Gentiles also was poured out the gift of the Holy Ghost.

When did the Spirit move? When Peter spoke the Word. There was no mumbo-jumbo. There was no seminar entitled, "How to Speak in Tongues." It was simply when Peter taught the Word that the Spirit began to move. People often say, "Your church spends too much time teaching and not enough time moving in the Spirit." My answer to them is that the biblical pattern is that of the Spirit moving *through* the teaching of the Word.

Colossians 3 says, "Let the word of Christ dwell in you richly, speaking to yourselves in psalms and hymns and spiritual songs, singing and making melody in your heart to the Lord. Wives submit to your husbands. Husbands love your wives. Children obey your parents. Employees obey your employers." Ephesians 5 says, "Be not drunk with wine but be filled with the Spirit,

speaking to each other with psalms and hymns and spiritual songs, singing and making melody in your heart to the Lord. In everything give thanks. Wives submit to your husbands. Husbands love your wives. Children obey your parents. Employees obey your employers."

The results of "letting the Word of Christ dwell in you richly" (see Colossians 3) are exactly the same as being "filled with the Spirit" (see Ephesians 5). Therefore, it follows that the Word and the Spirit are intimately linked together. If you want to live in the Spirit, keep in the Word. Become totally saturated with the Scriptures, and you'll find yourself overflowing with the Spirit.

Acts 10:46 (a)
For they heard them speak with tongues, and magnify God.

Without exception, in every biblical reference, tongues are directed to God to give praise and adoration and exaltation to Him. They are never directed to man, never a message for man. Tongues are always used to praise God.

Acts 10:46 (b)–48
Then answered Peter, Can any man forbid water, that these should not be baptized, which have received the Holy Ghost as well as we? And he commanded them to be baptized in the name of the Lord. Then prayed they him to tarry certain days.

Reminiscent of the Ethiopian eunuch in chapter 8, these believers were eager to be baptized, eager to demonstrate their acceptance of God's amazing grace that was vast enough to embrace even Gentiles.

VISION

A Topical Study of
Acts 10:9–20

Saul DeVries was a billionaire who made his fortune during the Great Depression. Born of immigrant parents, he grew up in poverty. But as a young adult he had an idea, a vision of how he might become a rich man. Realizing that in the Depression years, people were unable to buy new appliances or to remodel their kitchens and bathrooms, DeVries decided what was needed was a single product that would clean appliances and keep things sparkling. So he invented an all-purpose cleaner, the first of its kind, called Spic and Span®. It sold well throughout the years of the Depression and continues to do so today. Saul DeVries made billions from his vision and literally cleaned up!

So, too, in our text, Peter had a vision dealing with cleanliness. Unlike Saul DeVries, Peter would not become a rich man materially. He would, however, become wealthy spiritually. And the entire Gentile world would become the beneficiary.

Whenever God wants to do something new, something special, something wonderful, He will usually motivate a man or a woman through a vision. . . .

When God wanted to deliver the children of Israel from Egypt, He called Moses by causing a bush to burn in the desert that caught Moses' attention. Wondering why the bush burned without becoming consumed, Moses approached it, and it was then that God called him to go to Egypt to free His people from bondage (Exodus 3:3).

When God wanted to open Europe to the gospel, He called Paul through a vision in which he heard a man from Macedonia saying, "Come over and help us" (see Acts 16:9). Until that time, it had never entered Paul's mind to cross the Mediterranean sea with the gospel.

And here in Acts 10, God is again about to do something new, something special, something wonderful as He is about to fling wide open the door of the church to the Gentiles.

The *Gentiles?*

How shocking this would have been to the apostles and to the leaders of the early church, for as Jews, they had been taught throughout their history that Gentiles were unclean. The Mishnah itself stated that Gentiles existed for one primary purpose: to fuel the fires of hell. Thus, Jews had nothing to do with Gentiles. If a Jew even accidentally brushed against a Gentile, he would immediately go home, burn the clothes he was wearing, and take a ceremonial bath. Jews did not talk to Gentiles. They did not care about Gentiles. They had no hope for Gentiles.

This was not the original plan of God. The prophets—particularly Isaiah—proclaimed very clearly that Israel was to be a light to the Gentiles and that God would bless the people of Israel in order that Gentiles might see the benefits of walking with Him (Isaiah 42:6; 49:6). But the Jews lost that understanding. They turned inward and thought Gentiles were good for nothing but to keep hell hot.

Here in Acts 10, God is about to use Peter to bring salvation to the Gentiles. First, however, He must give Peter a new understanding. He must prepare Peter's heart. So what does He do? He gives Peter a vision.

Whether you're Saul DeVries marketing Spic and Span®, or an apostle with a much more significant calling—you need to have vision. Solomon said, "Where there is no vision, the people perish" (Proverbs 29:18). Thus, God desires to give us vision for our lives, our families, our ministries, and our country. How?

In this passage, I see three steps God uses to give vision. . . .

Preparation *for* Vision

> *On the morrow, as they went on their journey, and drew nigh unto the city,*
> *Peter went up upon the housetop to pray about the sixth hour.*   Acts 10:9

In Bible times, housetops were flat and accessed by a stairway that ran up the outside of the wall. They were used as places of quiet retreat away from the crowd and clamor of the cities. So it was that Peter went to the housetop to pray. Vision always begins away from the crowd, away from the busyness—in a quiet place, through a quiet time, with a quiet heart.

In Isaiah 30, the people of Israel were panicking because they were surrounded by their enemies, the Assyrians. Afraid of the Assyrian threat, the Jews sent ambassadors to Egypt seeking safety through an alliance with them. However, Isaiah came on the scene saying, "Woe to the rebellious children, saith the Lord, that take counsel, but not of me. . . . For thus saith the Lord God, the Holy One of Israel; In returning and rest shall ye be saved; in quietness and in confidence shall be your strength: and ye would not" (Isaiah 30:1, 15).

How often we seek advice and help from other people, and yet fail on a daily basis to get away to a "rooftop" and seek the Lord. We make our plans, form our alliances, and get counsel—all dependent upon other people. But the Lord says to us, as He did to the children of Israel, "It's not going to work. The Egyptians are unable to help you. Return to *Me* and rest, for in *My* quietness and confidence shall be your strength."

Illumination *in* Vision

> *And he became very hungry, and would have eaten: but while they made ready,*
> *he fell into a trance, and saw heaven opened, and a certain vessel descending*
> *unto him, as it had been a great sheet knit at the four corners, and let down*
> *to the earth: Wherein were all manner of fourfooted beasts of the earth, and*
> *wild beasts, and creeping things, and fowls of the air. And there came a voice*
> *to him, Rise, Peter; kill, and eat.*   Acts 10:10–13

In Leviticus 11, the Jews were given very specific instructions concerning what foods they could and couldn't eat. Here in Peter's vision, he sees clean and unclean, kosher and un-kosher foods all together upon a sheet. I find it fascinating that in this illumination in vision, the Lord used food. This is great! I love Peter because, just like me, he sometimes had a hard time being spiritual. In the Garden of Gethsemane when the Lord asked him to pray with Him for an hour, what did Peter do? He fell asleep (Matthew 26:40). He wanted to pray. His spirit was willing. But he fell asleep because his flesh was weak.

Here, Peter wanted to pray again. He went up to the rooftop, but he was hungry. And in his hunger he sort of spaced out. Did the Lord come down on Peter and say, "What's wrong with you? You should be spiritual. You should be able to miss a meal or two"? No, He said, "You're hungry, Peter? Okay. I'll use your hunger to show you something new. Watch out. Here comes some food!" This story helps me a whole lot because through it I understand that the Lord uses common, everyday things to teach us lessons and to give us vision. Don't think the Lord only gives vision at church or in a Bible study. Yes, He uses His Body and His Word powerfully, but not exclusively. If He has already prepared your heart to receive it, He can give you vision anytime, any place—even when, like Peter, you're in line waiting for a Quarter Pounder®!

Confirmation *of* Vision

> *While Peter thought on the vision, the Spirit said unto him, Behold, three men seek thee.*   Acts 10:19

God spoke to Cornelius through an angel and to Peter through a vision. When three men showed up at Peter's gate, it was confirmation that both Cornelius and Peter had heard God correctly. Whenever God gives a vision in your heart, it will be confirmed by a knocking on your door. The voice of the Lord will always be confirmed. That's always the way of God throughout Scripture.

> *And Jeremiah said, The word of the LORD came unto me, saying, Behold, Hanameel the son of Shallum thine uncle shall come unto thee, saying, Buy thee my field that is in Anathoth: for the right of redemption is thine to buy it. So Hanameel mine uncle's son came to me in the court of the prison according to the word of the LORD, and said unto me, Buy my field, I pray thee, that is in Anathoth, which is in the country of Benjamin: for the right of inheritance is thine, and the redemption is thine; buy it for thyself. Then I knew that this was the word of the LORD.*   Jeremiah 32:6–8

Sometimes we say, "Wow! It's the Lord," when in reality, it could just be Satan bugging us.

> When my son Benjamin was a toddler, he spent some time with his uncle Jimmy and aunt Julie. Julie later told us that Ben was saying, "Wow," as he moved his head in circles. "Do you hear that buzzing?"
> "What buzzing?" she asked him.
> "*That* buzzing. Don't you hear that buzzing?"
> Finally, looking a little closer, Julie discovered a ladybug in Benny's ear.

Benjamin believed there was a buzzing in the room—but actually, it was all in his head. That's why confirmation is essential. Make sure you're hearing the *Lord's* voice.

Wait for His confirmation. God is faithful. It will come. And when it does, like Jeremiah, you can say, "Then *I knew* it was the Word of the Lord." And you can press ahead.

My prayer is that we will not wander around aimlessly year after year, wondering what our life is about—but that we will be men and women of vision. For without vision, we'll wander indefinitely and perish eventually.

Saul DeVries became a billionaire because he had a vision about people in depression needing to clean up. When he died, as was instructed in his will, his body was cremated and his ashes were poured into his kitchen sink. You see, although Saul DeVries was a billionaire, because he didn't know the Lord, his life went down the drain literally. He is said to have died a miserable man.

You might have vision today to build a big business, to have a glorious ministry, to accomplish something athletically or academically. But Jesus said, "What does it profit a man if he gains the whole world, but loses his soul?" (see Mark 8:36).

The reason you're studying the Word is because God is giving you a new vision even now—an invitation to be a part of His kingdom. It is confirmed by the knocking of opportunity as Jesus says to you, "Behold, I stand at the door and knock. And if any man hears My voice and opens the door, I will come in to him and sup with him and he with Me" (see Revelation 3:20).

Today, wherever you've been, I invite you to be born again—to confess you are a sinner, to call Jesus your Lord—and to emerge truly Spic and Span®!

11

Acts 11:1
And the apostles and brethren that were in Judaea heard that the Gentiles had also received the word of God.

To the Jews living in biblical times, world population was divided into two groups: Jews and Gentiles. In God's economy, the Jews were to be a testimony to the Gentiles of how to live and in whom to believe (Isaiah 42:6). But something happened over the years. Instead of seeing themselves as a light unto the Gentiles, the Jews saw Gentiles as despicable, grotesque, and to be avoided at all costs. With this in mind, imagine what a shock it must have been to Jewish Christians when they heard that Peter had the audacity to go into the house of Cornelius—a *Gentile*—and actually share a meal with him.

Acts 11:2–4 (a)
And when Peter was come up to Jerusalem, they that were of the circumcision contended with him, saying, Thou wentest in to men uncircumcised, and didst eat with them. But Peter rehearsed the matter from

the beginning, and expounded it by order unto them . . .

In response to the accusations of his Jewish Christian brothers, Peter repeated the vision he was given in chapter 10. This intrigues me. Luke was not writing in a book, but on a scroll. The largest scrolls were thirty-five feet in length. Longer than that, they would have been too big to handle. Thus, with only a limited amount of space, literature in biblical times had to be concise and succinct. Why, then, would the Holy Spirit inspire Luke to take valuable space to repeat the story of chapter 10 almost verbatim in chapter 11? I suggest it's because it's real important—as though the Holy Spirit is saying, "Don't miss this. I want you to grab hold of, and never forget that what the Father calls clean, you are not to call common."

Acts 11:4 (b)–10
. . . saying, I was in the city of Joppa praying: and in a trance I saw a vision, A certain vessel descend, as it had been a great sheet, let down from heaven by four corners; and

it came even to me: Upon the which when I had fastened mine eyes, I considered, and saw fourfooted beasts of the earth, and wild beasts, and creeping things, and fowls of the air. And I heard a voice saying unto me, Arise, Peter; slay and eat. But I said, Not so, Lord: for nothing common or unclean hath at any time entered into my mouth. But the voice answered me again from heaven, What God hath cleansed, that call not thou common. And this was done three times: and all were drawn up again into heaven.

Isaiah wrote, "I will greatly rejoice in the Lord, my soul shall be joyful in my God; for he hath clothed me with the garments of salvation, he hath covered me with the robe of righteousness, as a bridegroom decketh himself with ornaments, and as a bride adorneth herself with her jewels" (61:10).

What a fabulous day it is when we say, "I'm righteous because I'm in Christ Jesus and because of what He has done for me on the Cross of Calvary. I'm His bride. I am aware of my uncleanness, my "four-footed beastliness," and my "fowl" mentality—but God has cleansed me eternally."

Why is it that we beat ourselves when, in so doing, we only cast aspersions on the work Jesus did on Calvary? Salvation is so wonderful! What the Lord has done for us is incredible! But it's so hard for us to receive grace graciously because there's something in us that says, "I don't deserve that kind of unconditional, unmerited love. I've got to earn it. I've got to prove myself worthy of it." Whenever you talk to the Lord freely and cast your care upon Him joyfully, expect Satan to whisper in your ear, "You're a creep, a four-footed beast, foul and unclean. You don't deserve to even enter God's presence, much less stay there!"

May your answer always be, "What He has cleansed, don't call common. And He has cleansed me."

Acts 11:11, 12 (a)
And, behold, immediately there were three men already come unto the house where I was, sent from Caesarea unto me. And the spirit bade me go with them, nothing doubting. Moreover these six brethren accompanied me . . .

Peter was smart. Called to the house of a Gentile, he took six men with him to witness what would transpire.

Acts 11:12 (b)–17
. . . and we entered into the man's house: And he shewed us how he had seen an angel

in his house, which stood and said unto him, Send men to Joppa, and call for Simon, whose surname is Peter; who shall tell thee words, whereby thou and all thy house shall be saved. And as I began to speak, the Holy Ghost fell on them, as on us at the beginning. Then remembered I the word of the Lord, how that he said, John indeed baptized with water; but ye shall be baptized with the Holy Ghost. Forasmuch then as God gave them the like gift as he did unto us, who believed on the Lord Jesus Christ; what was I, that I could withstand God?

"Don't blame me," Peter said. " I didn't make this happen. I was just waiting for lunch when I saw a vision wherein the Spirit told me three men would come and escort me. When they showed up at my gate, I went with them and heard about the angelic preparation in Cornelius' heart and life. Then I started teaching the Word, and the Holy Ghost fell upon them, and they began to speak in tongues. This wasn't *my* idea!"

Acts 11:18
When they heard these things, they held their peace, and glorified God, saying, Then hath God also to the Gentiles granted repentance unto life.

"Oy vey!" At last the light began to dawn on the Jewish Christian mentality that the barriers were broken down between clean and unclean, between Jew and Gentile. Finally, they began to realize that the Gospel was indeed to be preached to the entire world.

Acts 11:19 (a)
Now they which were scattered abroad upon the persecution that arose about Stephen . . .

Following the stoning of Stephen, a wave of persecution scattered the church.

Acts 11:19 (b)
. . . travelled as far as Phenice . . .

Phenice was located in the southern part of present-day Israel, on the coast of the Mediterranean Sea.

Acts 11:19 (c)
. . . and Cyprus . . .

Cyprus was an island off the coast of present-day Syria.

Acts 11:19 (d)
. . . and Antioch, preaching the word to none
but unto the Jews only.

The Christians scattered—but still spoke of salvation only to Jews. In Antioch, that would all change, for it was in Antioch that a base was established for missionary work in Gentile territory. Antioch, the third largest city in the Roman Empire, was dedicated to the Greek goddess, Daphne, who had been seduced by the Greek god, Apollo. With the possible exception of Corinth, immorality abounded in the city of Antioch more so than in any other city of the empire.

Acts 11:20–22
And some of them were men of Cyprus and
Cyrene, which, when they were come to Antioch, spake unto the Grecians, preaching
the Lord Jesus. And the hand of the Lord
was with them: and a great number believed,
and turned unto the Lord. Then tidings of
these things came unto the ears of the
church which was in Jerusalem: and they
sent forth Barnabas, that he should go as
far as Antioch.

When the believers in Jerusalem heard folks were being saved in Antioch, they sent Barnabas to check it out.

Acts 11:23 (a)
Who, when he came, and had seen the grace
of God, was glad . . .

I love this phrase! People say, "Why are you Christians so glad?"

"Because of the unmerited, undeserved, unearned grace of God," I answer. "You see, legalism makes people sour, but grace always produces great gladness."

Acts 11:23 (b)
. . . and exhorted them all, that with purpose
of heart they would cleave unto the Lord.

Barnabas didn't exhort the Antioch believers to cleave unto the law, but to cleave unto the *Lord!* He didn't lay down rules and trips on them. He said, "Cleave to the Lord Jesus. Enjoy Him, hang on to Him, abide in Him, with purpose of heart."

It's the heart that's important, folks—not the mind. "For with the heart man believeth unto righteousness," (Romans 10:10). Why is the Lord so interested in the heart? Because the mind can change very quickly and very easily. I can change my mind about something a hundred times in a given day. I can go back and forth and back and

forth, depending on what I hear, the conclusions I make, the information I have. But the heart does not change easily. Think of that time, guys, when the girl of your dreams told you to pack sand—or girls, when your boyfriend walked out of your life. Your mind may have accepted it—but your heart was broken. It didn't let go that easily.

The Lord is not after an intellectual assertion. He desires heartfelt unification. That's why He says, "Open your *heart* to Me—not your brain, but your heart." You see, the Lord knows that if my faith is intellectual only, academic arguments about evolution or existentialism will cause me to get confused and to vacillate. But if my heart is His, even though I may not be able to counter intellectual assaults, my relationship with Him will remain secure.

Acts 11:24, 25 (a)
For he was a good man, and full of the Holy
Ghost and of faith: and much people was
added unto the Lord. Then departed Barnabas to Tarsus. . . .

Barnabas looked around and said, "Wow, here are all of these Hellenists, Grecians, and pagans being added to the church. Who can really speak to them effectively? I know! The guy I left at Tarsus seven or eight years ago—Saul!"

Acts 11:25 (b)
. . . for to seek Saul.

The word translated "to seek" is *anazeteo,* which means "to search up and down, or high and low." It's used only one other time by Luke—in Luke 2 where he wrote that Mary and Joseph searched diligently for Jesus after Passover. The idea of *anazeteo* is that of a parent frantically, desperately, energetically searching for a lost child. And that's exactly what Barnabas, the "son of consolation," the quintessential discipler, the ultimate encourager, did. He searched high and low for Saul, who had been in Tarsus for seven to ten years, living in obscurity.

I know some of you have been gifted and graced by the Lord to be Barnabases. Blessings on you—what a wonderful calling! You're encouragers, "sons and daughters of consolation." You're one-on-one kind of people. You have no need to be the big gun or the head hog at the trough. Like Barnabas, you're "good men and women—full of the Holy Ghost and of faith." I encourage you to search high and low for that one who, like Paul, is stuck off in obscurity—loving the Lord and committed to the Word, but in need of someone to throw an arm around him and strengthen him in the Lord.

Acts 11:26 (a)
**And when he had found him, he brought
him unto Antioch. And it came to pass, that
a whole year they assembled themselves
with the church, and taught much people.**

In verse 20, men from Cypress "preached the
Lord Jesus." In verse 23, Barnabas "exhorted
them." In verse 26, Paul "taught much people."
That's generally the order of effective ministry:
First, there is preaching as we present the gospel
evangelistically. Then comes encouragement as
we say, "I rejoice with you. Cleave to the Lord."
Finally, there is teaching in order that believers
may mature in their faith. Preaching, encouraging, and teaching—all three are important and
essential for a healthy ministry.

Acts 11:26 (b)
**And the disciples were called Christians
first in Antioch.**

What does the word "Christian" mean? It
means "Little Christ." Wouldn't it be great if
someone called you "Little Jesus" because you
had so much of Him in you?

Acts 11:27, 28
**And in these days came prophets from Jeru-
salem unto Antioch. And there stood up one
of them named Agabus, and signified by the
spirit that there should be great dearth
throughout all the world: which came to
pass in the days of Claudius Caesar.**

Into this atmosphere of teaching, exhortation,
and preaching came a prophet named Agabus
who, given opportunity to declare a prophetic
word, said drought would fall upon Jerusalem.
This is exciting for me, as it relates to our own
Christian community. How important it is that we
as a body have opportunity to hear the heart of
the Lord through prophecy.

I was once asked by a pastor, "How do you
maintain a sense of excitement in your fellowship? I know you stress teaching, but so often in
my situation, teaching becomes dry and the people lose interest." My answer? Teaching does indeed become dry when there is not opportunity
to hear what the Spirit desires to say personally
and directly to the body. So much of what I personally have enjoyed in my walk with the Lord
over many years has been the result of hearing
something from the heart of the Lord when He
speaks to the body through the body as He did
here in Acts.

Acts 11:29
**Then the disciples, every man according to
his ability, determined to send relief unto
the brethren which dwelt in Judaea.**

It has been wisely said that we make a living by
what we get. But we make a life by what we give.
There was life in the early church because they
gave. After hearing the word of prophecy, they
didn't say, "Wow, there's going to be a drought,
huh? We better store our beans, buy guns, get
gold, and build shelters." No, they said, "There's
a drought? Let's take an offering. Tough times?
How can we help?"

I personally have a hard time with the prophecy mentality in our day that says, "Hard times
are coming, so get your gold and get your guns,
and if anybody tries to get your food, let them
have it with both barrels." I reject that. I don't
think it's the heart of the Lord.

Acts 11:30
**Which also they did, and sent it to the elders
by the hands of Barnabas and Saul.**

So it was that Barnabas and Saul left Antioch
to travel three hundred miles south to share with
the body in Jerusalem.

---

12 Acts 12:1
Now about that time Herod the king
stretched forth his hands to vex certain of the church.

Whenever Herod's name appears in Scripture,
it's easy to get confused. "Wasn't Herod the one
who killed the infants when Jesus was born?
Didn't he die in Matthew 2? What's he doing
here?" The answer to those questions lies in the
fact that "Herod" is a family name. Herod the
Great—the one who slaughtered the infants at
Jesus' birth—was an Idumean—a descendant of
Esau, who married Mariamne—a descendant of
the Maccabeans. Mariamne was one of Herod's
eight wives, and one of at least six he killed. But
before she died, Mariamne gave Herod a son
named Aristobulus. Aristobulus was one of at
least fifteen sons Herod killed. But before he
died, Aristobulus fathered a son named Herod
Agrippa. Realizing it was dangerous living in Jerusalem with people getting butchered right and
left, Aristobulus' mother shipped her son to
Rome—where he became friends with a man
named Caligula. You might remember Caligula
from your history lessons. He was a terribly depraved man, who, when he came into power, said,
"I'm going to put my buddy Herod Agrippa on

the throne in Jerusalem." Thus, it is Herod Agrippa of whom we read here in Acts 12.

Acts 12:2, 3
And he killed James the brother of John with the sword. And because he saw it pleased the Jews, he proceeded further to take Peter also. (Then were the days of unleavened bread.)

Herod Agrippa, Idumean on his father's side, Jewish on his mother's, was very interested in Jewish culture and deeply desirous of Jewish acceptance. But, although he was circumcised and followed Jewish customs and rituals, the Jews never embraced him as one of their own because they considered him a half-breed at best. Here in Acts 12, Herod Agrippa finally—although perhaps quite accidentally—gained the approval of the Jews by ordering James sawn in half lengthwise. *At last I've found a way to get the Jews to like me,* he must have thought and decided to go after Peter next.

Acts 12:4 (a)
And when he had apprehended him, he put him in prison, and delivered him to four quaternions of soldiers to keep him . . .

Four quaternions is literally four soldiers. The worst criminal would have had two soldiers—one chained to each arm. But Herod ordered four soldiers chained to Peter to make sure he wouldn't escape.

Acts 12:4 (b)
. . . intending after Easter to bring him forth to the people.

"After Easter" should have been translated "after Passover." Knowing it was against Jewish law to kill a man during Passover, Herod Agrippa intended to wait until after Passover to execute Peter.

Acts 12:5
Peter therefore was kept in prison: but prayer was made without ceasing of the church unto God for him.

Prayer was made on Peter's behalf, and what a difference it would make! What would have happened had the believers prayed when James was in prison? I wonder. Why didn't the church pray for James? Perhaps they thought, *Why pray? God's will is going to be done anyway.* The Bible says we have not because we ask not (James 4:2). Why are we so dumb? Why do we have to learn the hard way? Why does there have to be diffi-

culty, sadness, and tragedy before we say, "You know what? I better pray"?

What difference does it make if you pray? All I know is this: The church didn't pray for James, and he was sawn in half. They prayed for Peter, and he is about to be spared. You see, the Lord has sovereignly chosen to work through the avenue of prayer in order to teach us how to talk to Him, and depend on Him, so that in the ages to come when we rule on behalf of Him, and we will already have established communication with Him.

Acts 12:6
And when Herod would have brought him forth, the same night Peter was sleeping between two soldiers, bound with two chains: and the keepers before the door kept the prison.

This cracks me up! Here's Peter—sleeping again! Luke tells us that while Jesus talked with Moses and Elijah on the Mount of Transfiguration, Peter slept (Luke 9:32). Matthew writes that while Jesus prayed in the Garden of Gethsemane, Peter slept (Matthew 26:40). And here in Acts 12, we see Peter asleep on the night before his execution. But this time it's different. On the Mount of Transfiguration, Peter slept because he didn't expect anything to happen. In the Garden of Gethsemane, he slept in disobedience to the Lord's command to pray with Him. In prison, he slept because he was totally at peace.

Put yourself in Peter's chains. If you were bound to two soldiers and knew you were going to be killed the next morning, what would you do? I know what Peter did: Blanketed with the "peace that passeth understanding" (see Philippians 4:7), he slept.

Acts 12:7
And, behold, the angel of the Lord came upon him, and a light shined in the prison: and he smote Peter on the side, and raised him up, saying, Arise up quickly. And his chains fell off from his hands.

Throughout Scripture, angels are almost always pictured as being in a hurry. Conversely, God is seen hurrying only once—in the person of the father who ran down the road to welcome home his prodigal son (Luke 15:20). Why do angels always seem to be rushing around? Perhaps it's because angels understand human nature so well that they just want to come on the scene, do their work, and get out before men get caught up in worshiping them.

Acts 12:8, 9
And the angel said unto him, Gird thyself,
and bind on thy sandals. And so he did. And
he saith unto him, Cast thy garment about
thee, and follow me. And he went out, and
followed him; and wist not that it was true
which was done by the angel; but thought
he saw a vision.

I'm dreaming, thought Peter. *What a trip!*

Acts 12:10, 11
When they were past the first and the sec-
ond ward, they came unto the iron gate that
leadeth unto the city; which opened to them
of his own accord: and they went out, and
passed on through one street; and forthwith
the angel departed from him. And when Pe-
ter was come to himself, he said, Now I
know of a surety, that the Lord hath sent
his angel, and hath delivered me out of the
hand of Herod, and from all the expectation
of the people of the Jews.

What if Peter, sitting in prison, had said, "Wow,
what a dream," and then continued sitting there?
He would have been dead before his time. You
see, even though Peter wasn't sure what he was
seeing was reality, he acted on it as if it were. I
wonder how many of us remain imprisoned because, although we hear teachings and exhortations, prophecies and illuminations—although we
take notes and nod our heads in agreement, we
just sit in our cells thinking they must be dreams.
Our culture says, "Take it easy." Christianity
says, "Take a chance." We'll never experience
what God intends us to enjoy until we follow what
He lays on our hearts by stepping out in faith.

Now, sometimes when we step out, we find it
was only a vision after all. That's okay. Proverbs
says an empty stable stays clean, but an empty
stable brings no profits (Proverbs 14:4). Some
people say, "I've never messed up. I've never
made the mistake of following a vision. Look how
clean my barn is. The floor is spotless." But the
farmer who has some meadow muffins on the
floor and a few flies swarming around is the one
who is productive. Follow the Lord's leading even
if it seems like only a vision. The worst that could
happen is that a pasture patty or two could appear in your barn. But the best that could happen
is, like Peter, you could be set free!

Acts 12:12 (a)
And when he had considered the thing, he
came to the house of Mary the mother of
John, whose surname was Mark . . .

This was probably the same upper room used
for the Last Supper and on the Day of Pentecost.

Acts 12:12 (b), 13
. . . where many were gathered together
praying. And as Peter knocked at the door of
the gate, a damsel came to hearken, named
Rhoda.

"Rhoda" means "Rose."

Acts 12:14, 15 (a)
And when she knew Peter's voice, she
opened not the gate for gladness, but ran in,
and told how Peter stood before the gate.
And they said unto her, Thou art mad.

Oh, Rose. You're a blooming idiot, the believers must have thought. *That can't be Peter. Don't
you know he's in prison?* Then they returned to
their praying: "Lord, free Peter in Jesus' Name.
Oh, Lord, we look to You to free Peter." Isn't this
a great story? Aren't these early believers just
like you and me? I mean, here they are, praying
fervently for Peter's release, while he's standing
right outside their door!

Acts 12:15 (b)
But she constantly affirmed that it was even
so. Then said they, It is his angel.

This intrigues me because evidently these
early believers were so accustomed to seeing angels, they didn't even bother to get up to see this
one. It seems the early church had the awareness
that angels were always around. We've lost that
awareness. Our eyes have become dull. As a result, I think we're missing something because we
don't really believe angels are here right now.

Acts 12:16, 17 (a)
But Peter continued knocking: and when
they had opened the door, and saw him, they
were astonished. But he, beckoning unto
them with the hand to hold their peace, de-
clared unto them how the Lord had brought
him out of the prison. And he said, Go shew
these things unto James. . . .

This is James, the half brother of Jesus, author
of the Book of James, leader of the church in Jerusalem.

Acts 12:17 (b)
. . . and to the brethren. And he departed,
and went into another place.

This story encourages me a whole bunch because it shows that the Lord responds to prayer

even when it's not accompanied by a great deal of faith. These believers were praying fervently and intensely, but you cannot say they were praying the prayer of faith, since they didn't even have enough faith to believe Peter was free when he was knocking at their gate! I like this story because I find myself praying a whole lot like them. I pray fervently, even intensely—but a lot of times I'm not sure anything's going to happen. This story tells me that's okay. God can still work through a tiny smattering of faith. Jesus said faith the size of a mustard seed—just a tiny bit of faith—can move mountains (Matthew 17:20). If you have faith enough just to pray, things can happen. Doors can open. Ask Peter!

You who feel imprisoned, boxed in, and as though nothing's happening, in your job, in your family, in your ministry—take heart and take hope and pray anyway. Sometimes it takes only enough faith to pray for a miracle to happen.

Peter would later write these words:

For the eyes of the Lord are over the righteous, and his ears are open unto their prayers: but the face of the Lord is against them that do evil.   1 Peter 3:12

The eyes of the Lord are over the righteous—that's why Peter had peace. The ears of the Lord are open to prayer—that's why the church could pray. But the face of the Lord is against evil—that's why Herod was about to perish.

Acts 12:18, 19
Now as soon as it was day, there was no small stir among the soldiers, what was become of Peter. And when Herod had sought for him, and found him not, he examined the keepers, and commanded that they should be put to death. And he went down from Judaea to Caesarea, and there abode.

Infuriated by the news of Peter's escape, Herod left Jerusalem for the seacoast city of Caesarea, the resort town of the day. A beautiful city built by the Romans on the beach of the Mediterranean Sea, Caesarea was opulent and luxurious.

Acts 12:20 (a)
And Herod was highly displeased with them of Tyre and Sidon . . .

Tyre and Sidon were two cities located in present-day Lebanon. We do not know why Herod was displeased with them, but we do know his displeasure would have been bad news for them, since non-agrarian communities such as theirs were totally dependent upon Herod for food.

Acts 12:20 (b)
. . . but they came with one accord to him, and, having made Blastus the king's chamberlain their friend, desired peace; because their country was nourished by the king's country.

When the delegation from Tyre and Sidon arrived in Caesarea, they somehow persuaded Blastus, Herod's chief of staff, to make an appointment for them with his boss.

Acts 12:21 (a)
And upon a set day Herod, arrayed in royal apparel . . .

Jewish historian Josephus tells us Herod's royal robes were actually made of pure silver threads—a gown that would have made even Elton John envious!

Acts 12:21 (b), 22
. . . sat upon his throne, and made an oration unto them. And the people gave a shout, saying, It is the voice of a god, and not of a man.

In need of Herod's bread, what did the delegation from Tyre and Sidon do? They buttered him up. "You're a god! You're a god," they shouted. Folks, flattery is like bubble gum—you can enjoy it for a moment, but don't swallow it. More often than not, when someone flatters you, he is attempting to get something from you—which is exactly what was happening here.

Acts 12:23
And immediately the angel of the Lord smote him, because he gave not God the glory: and he was eaten of worms, and gave up the ghost.

Here, Herod—arrayed in silver splendor, glistening in the Mediterranean sun, drinking in the praise of the people—was suddenly eaten by worms. Now whether worms actually began to eat his flesh—or whether, as Josephus suggests, Herod, struck with severe intestinal pains, died five days later, and, during the autopsy, his insides were found to be full of worms—we can't be sure. Whether the worms ate him from inside out, or from outside in—either way, it was gross! But the Lord doesn't tell us this to gross us out. He tells us this to fill us in, for I believe the purpose of this account is to teach us the absolute necessity of giving God glory.

For topical study of Acts 12:20–23, see "What's Eating You?" below.

Acts 12:24
But the word of God grew and multiplied.

Herod was struck down—but the Word of God grew and multiplied. I like that!

Acts 12:25
And Barnabas and Saul returned from Jerusalem, when they had fulfilled their minis- try, and took with them John, whose surname was Mark.

After delivering the offering of the believers in Antioch to the believers in Jerusalem, Barnabas and Saul returned to Antioch, bringing John Mark with them. John Mark, the nephew of Barnabas and the son of the woman whose upper room was used by the disciples for the Last Supper and on the Day of Pentecost, was a young man who had a rich Christian heritage. He also had a lot to learn, as we will see in chapter 13.

WHAT'S EATING YOU?
A Topical Study of
Acts 12:20–23

When we talk about giving God glory, people get very confused. Why are we to give God glory? Is He insecure? Does He have a poor self-image? Does He need us to gather together and tell Him how wonderful He is so He'll feel better about Himself? No. God doesn't need us—but He does love us. And He knows that, although He doesn't need our praise, we need to praise. He knows it is in thanksgiving and in glorifying Him that we are de-wormed. He knows that, like Herod, if we do not honor Him, worms will destroy us.

Following are three worms that will torment us, gnaw on us, and ultimately devour us if we do not give God glory and thanksgiving continually.

The Worm of Anxiety

Paul wrote that in everything we are to give thanks to the Lord (Ephesians 5:20). Why? Because, as James wrote, every good and perfect gift comes from above (1:17).

If I think the job I have, the house in which I live, the family I enjoy are mine because I have worked hard and have been clever and diligent, I will eventually be eaten up by the worm of anxiety because I will either be worried about maintaining what I have or attaining what I don't. If I say, "I have health because of my commitment to physical fitness, success because of my business acumen, and a place on the baseball team because of my athletic prowess," I will be consumed by worry because if I strived to attain these things, I'll have to strive to maintain them.

If you believe you are where you are today because of your diligence, your ability, your personality, or your creativity—you will be eaten up with anxiety. On the other hand, if you believe every good gift comes from *above*, you realize you neither earned nor deserve the blessings in your life. And since you didn't work for them, since they are yours by God's grace, you can trust in Him and give thanks to Him for where you are today.

Then, if the job doesn't work out, if the relationship goes kaput, if you get cut from the team, you can say, "Lord, You gave it to me in the first place. And if You're taking it away from me now, then I know it's ultimately for my good and Your glory." And when you thank the Lord for whatever situation you're in and give Him glory for everything you've enjoyed, you'll be at peace—wonderful peace that passes understanding (Philippians 4:7).

Miriam led the children of Israel in praise and worship as they danced and celebrated after God miraculously parted the Red Sea (Exodus 15:20). But do you recall what the children of Israel were doing *before* the Lord parted the Sea? They were complaining and murmuring (Exodus 14:11, 12). They were stressed out. They were uptight. They were eaten up. How much better it would have been for the people to dance before the Lord and give glory to Him *before* the Red Sea parted—while they were trapped and boxed in by the Sea in front of them and the Egyptians behind them.

It's relatively easy to give thanks after the answer has come. But how much better for your health, your faith, your witness, if you'll take up the tambourine in faith before you see the Red Sea part—and watch the worm of anxiety drown in the waters of praise!

The Worm of Perversity

Romans 1 gives us the pathway to perversion . . .

For the wrath of God is revealed from heaven against all ungodliness and unrighteousness of men, who hold the truth in unrighteousness; because that which may be known of God is manifest in them; for God hath shewed it unto them. For the invisible things of him from the creation of the world are clearly seen, being understood by the things that are made, even his eternal power and Godhead; so that they are without excuse: Because that, when they knew God, they glorified him not as God, neither were thankful; but became vain in their imaginations, and their foolish heart was darkened.

Professing themselves to be wise, they became fools, and changed the glory of the uncorruptible God into an image made like to corruptible man, and to birds, and fourfooted beasts, and creeping things. Wherefore God also gave them up to uncleanness through the lusts of their own hearts, to dishonour their own bodies between themselves: Who changed the truth of God into a lie, and worshipped and served the creature more than the Creator, who is blessed for ever. Amen.

For this cause God gave them up unto vile affections: for even their

women did change the natural use into that which is against nature: and
likewise also the men, leaving the natural use of the woman, burned in their
lust one toward another; men with men working that which is unseemly, and
receiving in themselves that recompence of their error which was meet.

Romans 1:18–27

When a man, a woman, or a society stops glorifying God and giving Him thanks, perversion is the ultimate result. Oh, we might not make idols of men and birds of wood and stone as they did in Paul's day—but we fashion rock idols, Hollywood idols, and political idols. We might not worship creeping things and four-footed animals anymore—but we teach our kids that they came from primordial slime and evolved into monkeys.

We are surrounded in this country by perversity that leads to homosexuality and God's judgment inevitably. And, according to Romans 1:21, it all began when we stopped giving God thanks. I'm so sorry about our culture. I take responsibility for it and repent to the Lord concerning it. Like Herod, our society is being devoured by the worm of perversity because, as a nation, we refuse to glorify God.

The Worm of Negativity

A man or woman who does not continually give thanks in everything becomes vulnerable to the worm of negativity. He or she will become grumpy, grouchy, and cynical. The way to escape from the worm of negativity is to give thanks to God continually.

In the late 1800s, when cotton was undisputed king of the South, every cotton plantation in Coffee County, Alabama, was wiped out by the boll weevil. The economic fallout was disastrous, causing the Christians in the little town of Enterprise to meet together and pray, "We thank You, Lord, that You have blessed us for so many years with cotton. Now it's gone, but we know You work all things together for good. So we trust You."

Following their prayer meeting, the town of Enterprise decided to change crops from cotton to peanuts. Now, although peanuts at that time were virtually unknown, there was a man of exceptional intelligence—one of the greatest thinkers in our country's history—who in the same year the folks of Enterprise felt the Lord nudging them to plant peanuts, was also talking to the Lord. A wonderful believer, with a deep interest in astronomy, he prayed, "Father, teach me the secrets of the universe." Then he hung his head and said, "Lord, I know that's too presumptuous to ask. Just teach me about the peanut."

The man's name, of course, was George Washington Carver—and how the Lord answered his prayer! Beginning in 1895, Carver developed over three hundred products from the lowly peanut—of which the primary discovery, as far as

I'm concerned, was peanut butter! As a result of George Washington Carver's discoveries, suddenly there was an unexpected, unprecedented demand for peanuts. And Coffee County began to prosper beyond belief. What had been a disaster became a blessing. What had been adversity became prosperity—all because instead of being eaten up by the worm of negativity, the people of Enterprise glorified God.

If you go to Enterprise today, you will see a monument in the town square with a boll weevil on top and this inscription underneath:

> In profound appreciation for the boll weevil and what he has done as the herald of prosperity, this monument is erected by the grateful citizens of Coffee County, Alabama. All things work together for good (see Romans 8:28).

Gang, you and I can be de-wormed by giving God glory. May He give us wisdom and application. And may this be the most un-wormy congregation in the whole country!

13 In Acts 1:8, Jesus told His disciples they would be His witnesses in Jerusalem, Judaea, Samaria, and to the uttermost parts of the earth. That's what He said—and that's exactly what happened. First, the early believers were accused of filling all Jerusalem with their doctrine (Acts 5:28). Then, persecution scattered the church throughout Judaea (Acts 8:1). Later, revival broke out in Samaria after Philip preached Christ unto them (Acts 8:8). And here in Acts 13, we see the final phase of Jesus' commission coming to pass, as Paul is about to launch out on his first missionary journey to the uttermost parts of the earth.

I say this not only to give you a basic feeling for the Book of Acts, but for a very practical reason as well. You see, throughout Scripture, the commands of the Lord are not heavy exhortations—they're glorious expectations. Therefore, instead of reading Acts 1:8 like this: "You shall be *witnesses* unto Me, so get out there and pass out tracts. Be My witnesses. That is My command"—it should be read like this: "You *shall* be witnesses unto Me. It *will* happen!"

So often people say the commands of Jesus are heavy. But Jesus said His burden is easy and His load light (Matthew 11:28). So, when the Lord says, "You shall be holy for I the Lord your God am holy" (Leviticus 19:2), He's not saying, "You'd *better* be holy like Me," but—"You *will* be holy

like Me. The holiness inherent in Me will be enjoyed by you. You watch. You'll see!"

It's like me saying to Benjamin, "Son, you shall have a big nose, for I, your father, have a big nose. It *will* happen!" As we learn the Scriptures, my prayer is that we catch the inflection of the Father's voice so we can more clearly hear His heart.

Acts 13:1 (a)
Now there were in the church that was at Antioch certain prophets and teachers . . .

"There were certain prophets and teachers." Notice the distinction: Prophets are those who, under the inspiration of the Spirit, guide the church as they speak the heart of God through edification, exhortation, and comfort. Teachers are those who ground the church as they point out the ways and mind of God revealed through the Word. There are those in certain denominations who say that prophets and teachers are one and the same in the New Testament. Not so. Here in Acts 13, there's a clear-cut distinction.

Acts 13:1 (b)
. . . as Barnabas . . .

Remember Barnabas, the "son of consolation"? He was the one who took Paul under his wing before anyone else in Jerusalem believed Paul was born again. Later on, we'll see Barnabas take John Mark under his wing and walk with him through a season of failure.

Acts 13:1 (c)
. . . and Simeon that was called Niger . . .

Simon was from present-day Nigeria. This is probably Simon the Cyrene, the one who carried the Cross to Golgotha after Jesus sank beneath its weight (Luke 23:26).

Acts 13:1 (d)
. . . and Lucius of Cyrene . . .

How did Lucius get saved? I suggest Simon the Cross-bearer went back to Cyrene, talked to his buddy Lucius, and together they started walking with the Lord, eventually becoming significant figures in ministry.

Acts 13:1 (e)
. . . and Manaen, which had been brought up with Herod the tetrarch. . . .

Manaen was a foster-brother of Herod Antipas—the Herod who cut off John the Baptist's head. Talk about the grace and sovereignty of God! Manaen grew up in Herod's vile, polluted family—yet the Lord rescued him and saved him for ministry.

Acts 13:1 (f)
. . . and Saul.

We'll see Saul's name change later in this chapter. The word "Saul" means "requested one"— even as King Saul was requested by the people (1 Samuel 8:6). What does "Paul" mean? "Little." You see, something happened in Paul's life when he was converted to Christ. No longer did he identify himself as Saul, the "requested one," the "man in demand." No, he said, "Call me little."

In the early part of his ministry, Paul said, "I am the least of the apostles" (see 1 Corinthians 15:9). In the middle of his ministry, he said, "I am less than the least of all saints" (see Ephesians 3:8). At the end of his life, he said, "I am the chief of sinners" (see 1 Timothy 1:15). I find it interesting that the longer Paul walked with the Lord, the more he realized how far he was from Him. That's always the way it is. The Pharisee, praying on the street corner said, "God, I thank thee, I am not as other men," while the true convert beat his breast and said, "God be merciful to me a sinner" (see Luke 18:11–13).

Acts 13:2 (a)
As they ministered to the Lord, and fasted . . .

Luke doesn't say they ministered *for* the Lord. He says they ministered *to* the Lord. Lots of people desire to minister for the Lord, but there are few who desire to minister to the Lord.

In Ezekiel 44:11 and 15, the Lord said, "The Levites that are gone away far from me, when Israel went astray, which went astray away from me after their idols; they shall even bear their iniquity. Yet they shall be ministers in my sanctuary, having charge at the gates of the house, and ministering to the house: they shall slay the burnt offering and the sacrifice for the people, and they shall stand before them to minister unto them. But the priests the Levites, the sons of Zadok, that kept the charge of my sanctuary when the children of Israel went astray from me, they shall come near to me to minister unto me."

It was the faithful sons of Zadok whom God reserved for ministry to Himself. This shows me that in the eyes of the Lord, the most important ministry is not ministering *for* Him, but ministering *to* Him in worship and praise, in prayer and adoration.

Acts 13:2 (b)
. . . the Holy Ghost said, Separate me Barnabas and Saul for the work whereunto I have called them.

The Holy Ghost said, "Separate me Barnabas and Saul." How did the Holy Ghost say this? I suggest it was through the prophets mentioned in verse 1. Later on, Paul would write, "Neglect not the gift that is in thee, which was given thee by prophecy, with the laying on of the hands of the presbytery" (1 Timothy 4:14). In other words, "Timothy, don't neglect the gift you received when prophecy was uttered over you and hands laid upon you."

Twenty-five years ago when I was part of a ministry in San Jose, California, a word of prophecy was given by a very quiet businessman during a time when about thirty of us were worshiping and waiting on the Lord. He said, "Jon, I think the Lord is giving me a word for you to consider: He wants to move you to a higher mountain." Now, unbeknownst to him, that very day I had been wrestling with whether I should move from San Jose to Applegate. "Applegate?" I thought. Who's ever heard of Applegate? To me, the area was as rugged and mountainous as the Yukon Territory! So, that particular prophecy was very important for me to hear. It edified me. It exhorted me. It comforted me greatly. Looking back through my journal I find many such accounts of a prophetic word for me personally or for the body corporately. Prophecy is vital.

Acts 13:3
And when they had fasted and prayed, and laid their hands on them, they sent them away.

Notice they were *sent* away. In the area of missions, we need more people to be *sent*. A lot of people are hyped into going on a missionary venture or journey. But throughout Scripture, I never see people capriciously going because of some presentation. As is the case here, I see a deep work of the Spirit saying, "Separate *these* guys. *They're* to go and minister."

Now, I'm not discounting taking a couple of weeks and going on a missionary journey or a short-term ministry. That's fine. But before you sell your house and quit your job—make sure you're not being pulled or manipulated by some kind of presentation that moves you emotionally. Pray. Wait on the Lord. Minister to Him. And then go not as one who went, but as one who is *sent*.

Acts 13:4 (a)
So they, being sent forth by the Holy Ghost, departed . . .

Here is an important truth for you who are trying to discern God's will for your life. Look carefully. The text says, "they, being sent forth by the Holy Ghost, departed." The Holy Ghost pushed them out, but *they* departed. The Holy Ghost gave direction, but it was up to *them* to begin the journey. There comes a point when the Lord, having made His will for you clear to you, expects you to depart—to take the first step on whatever path He has directed you to walk.

Acts 13:4 (b)
. . . unto Seleucia; and from thence they sailed to Cyprus.

Why Cyprus? I suggest it was because Cypress was the homeland of Barnabas. You see, the Lord gave the inspiration, but the practical application was worked through Saul and Barnabas as they simply began to move out in a supernaturally natural way. It was natural for Barnabas to want to go to Cyprus. Cyprus was home. "The Lord's calling us. Where should we go, Paul?"

"What do *you* think, Barney?"

"Well, there's great surf in Cyprus and good fishing. It's my home country, and I care about those people there. Besides, there's great need in Cyprus." And indeed there was. The worship of Venus, also known as Aphrodite, the love goddess, was centered in Cyprus. Every woman on Cyprus was required to serve as a temple prostitute at least once in her life. And as you read the history of Cyprus, you read of disease, debauchery, and tragedy. Even the appearance of the women as recorded by historians was unbelievably sad. It was a sick island. Sin always takes a toll. Some years ago, I was talking to a promiscuous young lady. "If you keep living this way," I said, "by the time you're thirty, you're going to look like forty and feel like fifty." The wages of sin is death (Romans 3:23). And sin kills emotionally as well as physically.

Acts 13:5
And when they were at Salamis, they preached the word of God in the synagogues of the Jews: and they had also John to their minister.

John Mark, first mentioned in verse 25 of chapter 12, was the nephew of Barnabas. According to 1 Peter 5:13, it seems he was converted by Peter and later discipled under the tutelage of his uncle Barnabas.

Acts 13:6
And when they had gone through the isle unto Paphos, they found a certain sorcerer, a false prophet, a Jew, whose name was Bar-jesus.

Traveling through the depraved island of Cyprus, Barnabas and Saul encountered Bar-jesus, literally "Son of Jesus"—a false prophet, a sorcerer, a wizard.

Acts 13:7
Which was with the deputy of the country, Sergius Paulus, a prudent man; who called for Barnabas and Saul, and desired to hear the word of God.

Sergius Paulus, the Roman-appointed governor of the island, hearing of two men traveling through his island who were sharing the truth of God's love and grace, said, "I want to hear more."

Acts 13:8
But Elymas the sorcerer (for so is his name by interpretation) withstood them, seeking to turn away the deputy from the faith.

Bar-jesus, also called Elymas, or "Enlightened One," was jealous and worried. After all, if Sergius Paulus, the Roman governor, got saved, where would that leave him? So Elymas started speaking against Barnabas and Paul to Sergius Paulus.

Acts 13:9 (a)
Then Saul, (who also is called Paul,) . . .

This is where Saul's name changed to Paul—from "requested one" to "little."

Acts 13:9 (b), 10
. . . filled with the Holy Ghost, set his eyes on him, and said, O full of all subtilty and all mischief, thou child of the devil, thou enemy of all righteousness, wilt thou not cease to pervert the right ways of the Lord?

What a look this must have been! With eyes of discernment, Paul saw this man was no good. So, too, today, people might say, "I'm a follower of Jesus. I'm close to Jesus. I speak for Jesus"—but you'll know in your heart if something's amiss.

Acts 13:11
And now, behold, the hand of the Lord is upon thee, and thou shalt be blind, not seeing the sun for a season. And immediately there fell on him a mist and a darkness; and he went about seeking some to lead him by the hand.

Paul was not a wimpy Christian, but his heart was always for restoration—even with a guy like Elymas. How do I know? Consider what happened to Paul before he was converted: Like Elymas, he was blinded (Acts 9:9). It wasn't until Paul was blinded physically that he could see spiritually. And I suggest that although Paul was not mincing words with Elymas, his prayer was not, "Sic him, Lord." It was "Save him."

Acts 13:12
Then the deputy, when he saw what was done, believed, being astonished at the doctrine of the Lord.

It interests me that Luke didn't say Sergius Paulus was astonished at the miracle that took place. No, Luke said he was astonished at the doctrine of the Lord. "You mean God loves *me?*" Sergius Paulus must have wondered in amazement. "You mean He became a Man and died in *my* place? You mean *I* can be forgiven and saved—made right and redeemed?" May we never become so accustomed to hearing the story of the Cross that we become hardened. The won-

der of it all! *Amazing* grace! O, Lord, keep us astonished.

Acts 13:13 (a)
Now when Paul and his company . . .

Wait a minute. Before, it had been, "Barnabas and Saul" (13:2). Now it's "Paul and his company." This means that, although Paul was originally following Barnabas, at this point Paul was thrust into the forefront.

Acts 13:13 (b)
. . . loosed from Paphos, they came to Perga in Pamphylia . . .

Visualize a map of the Middle East. Paul and Barnabas left Palestine, traveled to Cyprus, and headed north to Turkey.

Acts 13:13 (c)
. . . and John departing from them returned to Jerusalem.

John Mark split. He turned back and ran home to Jerusalem. Why? Perhaps the most logical reason is found at the beginning of this verse. When Paul took the helm, Uncle Barnabas was demoted to second in command at best. Can't you hear John Mark saying, "Well, if *he's* going to be in charge, I'm going home. I like you, Uncle Barnabas. You're always so encouraging. But Paul is mean. I'm not going to serve with *him!*"

David said it is the *Lord* who sets up one and puts down another (Psalm 75:7). I believe John Mark forgot this. My prayer is that we might be those who learn to say, "Lord, righteous and true are Your judgments and decisions. You're on the throne. You're in control. Regardless of whether my uncle is in charge or not, Lord, I'm traveling with You and in the company to which You've called me."

Acts 13:14 (a)
But when they departed from Perga, they came to Antioch in Pisidia. . . .

This was not the same Antioch from which Paul and Barnabas sailed. There were seven cities named Antioch in this region during this time. The Antioch in this verse was located northeast of Perga, the city in present-day Turkey from which John Mark left.

Acts 13:14 (b)
. . . and went into the synagogue on the sabbath day, and sat down.

Paul always followed the same mode of operation. That is, upon arrival in a new city, he would head into the synagogue on the Sabbath day and share with the Jews who were studying there. In Romans 1:16, he said, "For I am not ashamed of the gospel of Christ: for it is the power of God unto salvation to everyone that believeth; to the Jew first, and also to the Greek." Paul always shared the gospel with the Jews before he shared with the Gentiles. It was not a matter of preference, however. It was a matter of precedence.

The Jews had precedence for two reasons. First, they were a people who had preparation. For two thousand years, they had been given Old Testament prophecies, types, and stories—all pointing to the coming Messiah, Jesus Christ. Thus, converted Jews made radical Christians due to their thorough understanding of Old Testament Scripture. Second, the Jews were a people who had a promise. From their midst arose One who would come to be a deliverer for them, a King over them, a comfort to them.

Acts 13:15
And after the reading of the law and the prophets the rulers of the synagogue sent unto them, saying, Ye men and brethren, if ye have any word of exhortation for the people, say on.

Seeing Paul and Barnabas were well-educated, well-traveled, well-informed visitors, the rulers of the synagogue invited them to address the synagogue.

Acts 13:16
Then Paul stood up, and beckoning with his hand said, Men of Israel, and ye that fear God, give audience.

Here is Paul's first recorded sermon—remarkable in its similarity to Stephen's sermon in Acts 7. As Stephen was going down, had he glanced in the direction of Paul, who was holding the garments of those throwing stones, no doubt he would have thought, *I failed. These people aren't receiving or responding to my message.* But because the Word of God will not return void (Isaiah 55:11), Stephen's words rattled around inside Paul, and fourteen years later, out of Paul's mouth came a replay of Stephen's sermon. This gives me great hope because, although sometimes when I share with people and feel that no one is listening, that none are responding, the Word of God is living and powerful, sharper than any two-edged sword (Hebrews 4:12).

Acts 13:17
The God of this people of Israel chose our fathers, and exalted the people when they dwelt as strangers in the land of Egypt, and with an high arm brought he them out of it.

Paul began his sermon by reminding the Jews of their history—reminding them of their ancestors who were held captive in Egypt, baking bricks under the burning sun. How many bricks did they bake? Using only the bricks from the pyramids, sphinxes, and monuments that remain today, a person could build a wall ten feet thick and fifteen feet high that would stretch from Medford, Oregon, to Brooklyn, New York. That's a lot of bricks!

Acts 13:18
And about the time of forty years suffered he their manners in the wilderness.

The phrase "suffered their manners" is a unique Hebrew idiom that can either mean "to feed" or "to put up with." So which is it? When Scripture says God "suffered their manners," was He putting up with the Israelites, or feeding them? He was doing both. God both hung in there with the children of Israel and provided for them for forty years.

Acts 13:19, 20
And when he had destroyed seven nations in the land of Chanaan, he divided their land to them by lot. And after that he gave unto them judges about the space of four hundred and fifty years, until Samuel the prophet.

Paul singled out Samuel because Samuel was preparatory to David; just as John the Baptist, to whom Paul will make later reference, was preparatory to the Son of David, Jesus Christ.

Acts 13:21
And afterward they desired a king: and God gave unto them Saul the son of Cis, a man of the tribe of Benjamin, by the space of forty years.

Israel wanted a king. They got one in Saul—a man who stood head and shoulders above the rest; a man who was initially humble and who moved in the power of the Spirit; a charismatic man who was able to galvanize the nation around him.

Acts 13:22 (a)
And when he had removed him . . .

God removed Saul from the throne. Why? First Samuel 15 tells the story. God spoke to Saul through Samuel the prophet, saying, "Destroy the Amalekites—the people who snuck up behind you and attacked your weakest and most feeble when you were wandering in the wilderness (see Deuteronomy 25:18). Make sure you destroy every man, woman, child, and beast. Leave nothing behind."

So Saul gathered two hundred thousand footmen from Israel and ten thousand footmen from Judah, marched on the Amalekites and utterly destroyed them—all except for one. He kept Agag, king of the Amalekites, along with some sheep. As Saul returned victorious to Israel, he saw Samuel in the distance. "Blessed be the name of the Lord!" Saul said. "I have obeyed all of His commandments!"

"Really?" said Samuel. "Then what's that bleating I hear?"

"Well, we saved the best of the sheep and the oxen to bring back as a sacrifice to Jehovah!" declared Saul.

Samuel looked at Saul and said, "To obey is better than sacrifice and to hearken more than the fat of rams. Rebellion is as witchcraft and stubbornness is as idolatry. Who's he?" asked Samuel, catching a glimpse of Agag.

"This is Agag, king of the Amalekites. I brought him back as a trophy," answered Saul.

Samuel grabbed a sword and hacked Agag into pieces right there on the spot, threw down the sword in utter disgust, and said, "Saul, you have disobeyed. No longer will you be king—neither you, nor your descendants. The kingdom is taken from you." And indeed his kingdom was taken away.

"That seems pretty harsh," you say. "I mean what's wrong with bringing home some sheep to sacrifice and Agag as a trophy to march in the victory parade?" Read on. At the very end of 1 Samuel and in the first chapter of 2 Samuel, we see Saul twenty years later on Mount Gilboa, fighting the Philistines. Wounded in battle, he heard the voice of his attacker behind him.

"Who are you?" Saul cried out.

"I am an Amalekite," came the answer.

You see, the period between the time Saul brought Agag back until the time he talked to Samuel was probably less than a week, but in that time, Agag must have escaped and fathered a son.

We think we have sin under control, but whenever we keep a little trophy hanging around to show how powerful we are, we're playing with fire. Ask Saul. "MTV used to be a problem," you boast, "but I've got it under control now. No need to block out that channel. I can turn it off whenever I want." Watch out. The son of Agag is out to get you.

That's why a Father who loves you says, "Destroy completely every Amalekite. If something is wrong, if something is tempting, if something is pulling on you carnally, if something is attacking you from behind annihilate it. Don't play around with the Amalekites because if you leave even one, he'll come back and get you."

Acts 13:22 (b)
. . . he raised up unto them David to be their king; to whom also he gave testimony, and said, I have found David the son of Jesse, a man after mine own heart, which shall fulfil all my will.

Like Saul, David was a sinner. The difference was that David wasn't playing games with God. He had weaknesses, problems, and failures to be sure. But his heart was right in the sight of the Lord.

Acts 13:23
Of this man's seed hath God according to his promise raised unto Israel a Saviour, Jesus.

Paul now turns the attention of his audience to Jesus.

Acts 13:24–27
When John had first preached before his coming the baptism of repentance to all the people of Israel. And as John fulfilled his course, he said, Whom think ye that I am? I am not he. But, behold, there cometh one after me, whose shoes of his feet I am not worthy to loose. Men and brethren, children of the stock of Abraham, and whosoever among you feareth God, to you is the word of this salvation sent. For they that dwell at Jerusalem, and their rulers, because they knew him not, nor yet the voices of the prophets which are read every sabbath day, they have fulfilled them in condemning him.

"Don't you get it?" asked Paul. "All of history led to the moment when the Son of David—the Promised Seed, Messiah—came on the scene. The fact that you neither recognized nor received Him fulfills the very prophecies that were written about Him."

Acts 13:28
And though they found no cause of death in him, yet desired they Pilate that he should be slain.

Why did the Jews demand of Pilate that Jesus be slain? They themselves stoned Stephen in Acts 7. They'll stone Paul in Acts 14. Why didn't they stone Jesus? Because the prophecies of the Old Testament all pointed toward crucifixion. The serpent on the pole in Numbers 21, the law that declared "Cursed is every one who hangs on a tree" (see Deuteronomy 21:23), and Psalm 22 all portray crucifixion. Therefore, moved by forces they didn't even understand, the Jewish leaders appealed to a Roman Pilate so that Christ would die a Roman death—exactly as prophesied.

Acts 13:29
And when they had fulfilled all that was written of him, they took him down from the tree, and laid him in a sepulchre.

Put yourself in these guys' sandals. You're sitting in the synagogue on the Sabbath day when a visiting rabbi stands up and begins to recount Jewish history, ending with the statement, "And it all came to a crescendo in the One who was crucified on a tree and resurrected from the dead."

How would that hit you if you had never heard it before? You would probably say, "Okay, who let him in? Come on, get real. What are you saying? I mean, we enjoy your history lesson. But your conclusion is preposterous." And then Paul threw in the clincher.

Acts 13:30, 31
But God raised him from the dead: And he was seen many days of them which came up with him from Galilee to Jerusalem, who are his witnesses unto the people.

Paul said, "Don't take my word for it. A whole bunch of guys saw Him." Later on in 1 Corinthians, he'll say "Five hundred men saw Him, talked to Him, and give witness that He rose from the dead." Five hundred witnesses is a formidable group.

Suppose there was a holdup at a 7–11 store near your house. Curious about it, you sit in the courtroom observing the trial, listening carefully as the first witness takes the stand and says, "I was in 7–11 on June 24, getting a Big Gulp, and this guy with black hair, a handlebar mustache, and a scar down his left cheek walked in, pulled out a pistol, and said, "Hit the ground! This is a stickup!" So I hit the ground along with everyone else. He took

the money, fired a shot, ran out the door, and jumped in his car, a blue Corvair." And then a second witness took the stand, saying, "On June 24, I was in 7–11 buying a Slurpee. A guy came in with a scar down his left cheek and a black handlebar mustache. He pulled out a pistol and told us to hit the ground. Then he took the money, fired a shot, and took off in a blue Corvair." And a third witness said, "I was in 7–11 buying a Reese's Peanut Butter Cup and this guy—I'll never forget him as long as I live—with a scar and a handlebar mustache came in holding a gun and told us to hit the deck. He fired a shot and drove away in a blue Corvair." And as you listened, a fourth witness, a fifth, an eighth, a tenth, a two hundreth, a three hundred eightieth, a four hundred fortieth, a four hundred ninety-eighth—five hundred witnesses come in and told the very same story. Since our system of jurisprudence is based upon eyewitness evidence, the accused would be convicted of robbery if five hundred witnesses gave corroborating evidence.

Paul appealed to this reasoning when he said, "Five hundred men saw Him." It is interesting to me that Paul's contemporaries, who were trying to disprove the Resurrection, gave all sorts of explanations—ranging from mass hypnosis to mass delusion—in an attempt to nullify the eyewitness accounts of those who saw the resurrected Jesus. But none of them—not one of the unbelieving historians of that day—said, "There are no eyewitnesses. Paul's making that up." The fact that there were eyewitnesses was as irrefutable as the empty tomb.

If I weren't a believer simply because of what Jesus has done for me personally, I would be a believer because of the overwhelming proof intellectually. Anyone who looks at the evidence historically must factor in the eyewitnesses—men who chose to die brutal and violent deaths rather than deny they had seen the resurrected Christ.

Acts 13:32, 33
And we declare unto you glad tidings, how that the promise which was made unto the fathers, God hath fulfilled the same unto us their children, in that he hath raised up Jesus again; as it is also written in the second psalm, Thou art my Son, this day have I begotten thee.

The cults use this phrase, "This day have I begotten thee," to say, "Jesus was the first created Being. He's important, He's wonderful," a Jehovah's witness or a Mormon will say, "but He's not

God. He was created." Wait a minute. They're missing the point. "This day have I begotten thee." What day? The day of His Resurrection.

Psalm 2, as quoted here by Paul, is not talking about the Incarnation, but about the Resurrection. Jesus is unique among all men by virtue of the fact that He rose again from the dead. It's not the womb David is speaking of—it's the tomb. This is a key understanding when you talk with people who try to sell you *Watchtower Magazine*, or the Mormon rap. Look at the context. Paul is talking about Jesus being raised from the dead.

Acts 13:34 (a)
And as concerning that he raised him up from the dead, now no more to return to corruption . . .

The corruption spoken of here is in regard to the decomposition of a dead body.

Acts 13:34 (b), 35
. . . he said on this wise, I will give you the sure mercies of David. Wherefore he saith also in another psalm, Thou shalt not suffer thine Holy One to see corruption.

This promise, although given to David, does not apply to him, for he would indeed see corruption as his body decayed in the coffin. To whom, then, does the promise apply? It applies to the *Son* of David—Jesus Christ.

Acts 13:36–38
For David, after he had served his own generation by the will of God, fell on sleep, and was laid unto his fathers, and saw corruption: But he, whom God raised again, saw no corruption. Be it known unto you therefore, men and brethren, that through this man is preached unto you the forgiveness of sins.

Man's greatest need is God's greatest deed. The greatest need for your sixteen-year-old son at home, or your thirty-eight-year-old husband sitting beside you, the greatest need for *every* person is the same: forgiveness. And we have the privilege of telling people, even as Paul told his audience, "Through this Man is the forgiveness of sin."

Acts 13:39
And by him all that believe are justified from all things, from which ye could not be justified by the law of Moses.

You are justified from all things. The word "all" in Greek means "*all*"!
One Sunday, before I baptized a young man, I told him, "Your being here testifies to everyone that you're serious about Jesus Christ. And because of that, any compromise that you're involved in, any sin or stuff that's going on in your life that's not right—" At this point, the guy started weeping, no doubt thinking that the sin in his life presently would disqualify him from salvation. I said, "You're here because you're serious about the Lord, and I want you to know any sin you're now committing is forgiven." With a look of amazement on his face, he looked up at me and said, "Really? You mean I'm forgiven of the sin I'm *presently* involved in?"

"Yep," I said.

We don't get it. We know our old sins are forgiven, but we think, *Now I've got to toe the line and make sure I don't mess up from here on out.* That's not salvation. That's not justification. *Every* sin you've ever committed, or are presently committing, or ever will commit in the future is forgiven and forgotten because where sin abounded, grace did much more abound (Romans 5:20). The price has been paid.

Acts 13:40, 41
Beware therefore, lest that come upon you, which is spoken of in the prophets; Behold, ye despisers, and wonder, and perish: for I work a work in your days, a work which ye shall in no wise believe, though a man declare it unto you.

There are people even now, saying, "I don't believe I am justified. I've got to prove my morality, prove my righteousness, prove my spirituality." Habakkuk 1, quoted here in verse 41, says the work of salvation is so wonderful that there will be those who will not believe it. They'll just say, "It's too good to be true." The fact is, it's so good it has to be true! Only an omnipotent God *could* provide total justification and complete forgiveness of sin. Only a loving God *would*.

Acts 13:42
And when the Jews were gone out of the synagogue, the Gentiles besought that these words might be preached to them the next sabbath.

"Hey, Paul! Come and tell us more about this justification," said the Gentiles. "Maybe the Jews don't get it, but this is terrific news to *us!*"

Acts 13:43
Now when the congregation was broken up, many of the Jews and religious proselytes followed Paul and Barnabas: who, speaking to them, persuaded them to continue in the grace of God.

To his followers, Paul said, "Continue in grace. Continue in grace. Continue in grace." Did they? No. This same group had to be addressed later in the Book of Galatians because they believed the rap of those who came to them, saying, "It's nice that you're believers in Jesus and that you think you're forgiven. But if you really want to be spiritual, you must be circumcised because spirituality and misery go hand in hand." The same thing happens today in Christian experience:

- "Why is she wearing that?"
- "Why is he raising his hands like that?"
- "Why is that guitar so loud?"

I have heard all of these critiques from people who want to dispense their miserable attitude to people who are excited about justification and salvation. But we must continue in the grace of God. And we must not, by God's grace and with His help, become sin-sniffing circumcisers or legalistic analyzers, judging the flesh of others by whatever miserable standards we ourselves are unable to keep.

Set up standards of legalism, and you'll keep your little rules and regulations for a month or two or three. You'll walk around with your nose in the air and your heart bitter and hardened, saying, "Who can I rebuke? Who can I correct?" Then, because no one can keep the law, you'll eventually break your own rules and say, "Woe is me. I'm such a miserable failure. I'm such a loser. I'm not going to church anymore. I don't belong there. I don't belong anywhere. Nobody likes me." That's what legalism does. Up and down, up and down, up and down we go until the day comes when at last we understand what justification is all about—that our Lord, our Love, Jesus Christ fully paid the price when He said, "It is *finished*" (John 19:30).

Acts 13:44–47
And the next sabbath day came almost the whole city together to hear the word of God. But when the Jews saw the multitudes, they were filled with envy, and spake against those things which were spoken by Paul, contradicting and blaspheming. Then Paul and Barnabas waxed bold, and said, It was necessary that the word of God should first have been spoken to you: but seeing ye put it from you, and judge yourselves unworthy of everlasting life, lo, we turn to the Gentiles. For so hath the Lord commanded us, saying, I have set thee to be a light of the Gentiles, that thou shouldest be for salvation unto the ends of the earth.

"Okay, if you Jews are not receiving this, we'll do what Isaiah 49 prophesied," said Paul and Barnabas. "We'll be a light to the Gentiles."

Acts 13:48
And when the Gentiles heard this, they were glad, and glorified the word of the Lord: and as many as were ordained to eternal life believed.

Who believed? Those who were ordained to believe.

"You have not chosen Me, but I have chosen you," Jesus said (see John 15:16). A man doesn't decide to be saved. A man must be ordained, chosen, predestined, elected to be saved.

"That's not fair," you say. "What if I'm not ordained to be saved?"

Well, get saved and you'll find that you too were ordained and elected to receive Jesus Christ!

Acts 13:49–52
And the word of the Lord was published throughout all the region. But the Jews stirred up the devout and honourable women, and the chief men of the city, and raised persecution against Paul and Barnabas, and expelled them out of their coasts. But they shook off the dust of their feet against them, and came unto Iconium. And the disciples were filled with joy, and with the Holy Ghost.

In ministry and in life, we will either "shake it off" or get shaken up. Those who shake the dust off their feet when an attack comes or when rejection hits will go on. Those who get shaken up will quit. I pray you and I will be those who, like Paul and Barnabas, shake off the dust and keep going in order that those around us might be "filled with joy and with the Holy Ghost."

❧

14 Traveling through present-day Turkey, Paul and Barnabas pressed on to the city of Iconium after being expelled from Antioch.

Acts 14:1 (a)
And it came to pass in Iconium, that they went both together into the synagogue of the Jews . . .

As was their usual practice, Paul and Barnabas went first to the synagogue.

Acts 14:1 (b), 2
... and so spake, that a great multitude both
of the Jews and also of the Greeks believed.
But the unbelieving Jews stirred up the
Gentiles, and made their minds evil affected
against the brethren.

Although many believed, those who didn't believe sought to sabotage the ministry of Paul and Barnabas by speaking evil against them, gossiping about them, and starting rumors concerning them.

During a freak electrical storm, a couple was
gossiping on the telephone. The storm caused
a scramble in the electrical signals and sent
their conversation from the phone line to a
cable TV line through which close to one mil-
lion people heard their conversation.

Would we say the things we do if we thought our conversation would be transmitted through the TV set? Is our conversation honoring to the Lord? Or does it grieve Him as it short-circuits ministry and hinders His work?

Acts 14:3
Long time therefore abode they speaking
boldly in the Lord, which gave testimony
unto the word of his grace, and granted
signs and wonders to be done by their hands.

The Lord confirmed the Word of His grace with signs and wonders—even as He promised He would in Mark 16:17, 18.

Acts 14:4 (a)
But the multitude of the city was divided ...

Due to the whispering campaign led by unbelieving Jews, Iconium was divided.

Acts 14:4 (b)
... and part held with the Jews, and part
with the apostles.

Bible students, take note that Barnabas is referred to here as an apostle. God appointed one Apostle: Jesus Christ. Jesus appointed twelve apostles: His disciples. The Holy Spirit continues to appoint numerous apostles: church-planters, founders, and spiritual statesmen like Barnabas.

Acts 14:5, 6 (a)
And when there was an assault made both
of the Gentiles, and also of the Jews with
their rulers, to use them despitefully, and to
stone them, they were ware of it, and fled ...

The gossip campaign became so intense that Paul and Barnabas had to flee for their lives. The good work begun in Iconium was short-circuited by jealousy, unbelief, and innuendo. That is why I pray our churches would make covenants saying, "Accusations, insinuations, and allegations will find no place here. They will not have an audience. Period."

Acts 14:6 (b), 7
... unto Lystra and Derbe, cities of Lycao-
nia, and unto the region that lieth round
about: And there they preached the gospel.

Notice that Paul and Barnabas didn't go to the synagogue when they arrived at Lystra and Derbe. Because every town with at least ten Jewish males had a synagogue, we can assume that there were not even ten Jews in Lystra or Derbe. Legend had it that many years earlier, Jupiter and Mercury came to Lystra and walked among the people. Because no one but a man named Philemon and his wife, Baicus, realized they were gods, Jupiter and Mercury killed everyone in the city—except for Philemon and Baicus, whom they turned into trees to stand in front of the temple of Jupiter.

Acts 14:8–10
And there sat a certain man at Lystra, impo-
tent in his feet, being a cripple from his
mother's womb, who never had walked: The
same heard Paul speak: who stedfastly be-
holding him, and perceiving that he had
faith to be healed, said with a loud voice,
Stand upright on thy feet. And he leaped
and walked.

As Paul preached, he saw a lame man in the crowd who seemed to have a measure of faith. "Stand upright," Paul said. And the man not only stood, but leaped and walked.

Acts 14:11–13
And when the people saw what Paul had
done, they lifted up their voices, saying in
the speech of Lycaonia, The gods are come
down to us in the likeness of men. And they
called Barnabas, Jupiter; and Paul, Mercur-
ius, because he was the chief speaker. Then
the priest of Jupiter, which was before their
city, brought oxen and garlands unto the
gates, and would have done sacrifice with
the people.

Thinking Mercury and Jupiter had returned in the form of Paul and Barnabas, the people of Lystra rushed to worship them. I personally believe this was the most dangerous point in Paul's entire ministry—more dangerous than any snakebite, shipwreck, or stoning he would ever face. You see, when the entire town offered them garlands and called them gods, I wonder if the thought didn't cross Paul's mind that he could use their adulation as a platform for ministry; that he could accept their adoration as a way to be relatable.

When Captain James Cook, discoverer of the Hawaiian Islands, first dropped anchor in Hanauma Bay, he was greeted with great ceremony. Realizing the islanders thought he was their god, Lono, Cook thought, *Oh, well. Why not?* Consequently, he and his men were treated to everything the island had to offer—until one evening, when, Cook, about to take advantage of yet another woman, was clubbed in the back of the head by her husband, who, in his anger, forgot that Captain Cook was Lono. Bleeding and groaning, the Captain went down. By the time he regained consciousness, he found himself looking into the eyes of his aggressor, who said, "Gods don't bleed. Nor do they groan." And Cook was killed on the spot.

Acts 14:14, 15 (a)
Which when the apostles, Barnabas and Paul, heard of, they rent their clothes, and ran in among the people, crying out, And saying, Sirs, why do ye these things? We also are men of like passions with you . . .

Paul and Barnabas were as wise as they were humble. They didn't flirt with, joke about, or take lightly the worship of the people of Lystra. Instead, they rent their clothes in an outward demonstration of deep inner grief. No wonder God could use them so powerfully.

Acts 14:15 (b)
. . . and preach unto you that ye should turn from these vanities unto the living God . . .

"Vanities" means "idols." Paul said, "Turn from Jupiter, Mercury, and all the other vain idols you worship—and turn instead to the living God."

Several years ago in India, ten people drowned when a mammoth stone statue of Buddha slid off a barge in the city of Hyderabad. Fifty people were aboard the barge at the time of the accident, but only forty were able to swim to safety. As tragic as this is, we must not be too quick to judge any other country for their idols when, in our own culture, we idolize men who

can hit a leather ball with a wooden bat. Psalm 115:8 says we become like whatever we idolize—which is why worship is so important. When we worship the Lord, we become like Him.

Acts 14:15 (c)
. . . which made heaven . . .

"The heavens declare the glory of God," wrote the psalmist (Psalm 19:1). And indeed they do! The vastness of space is truly incredible. If the distance between here and the sun (ninety-three million miles) was represented by the thickness of a single sheet of notebook paper, it would take a stack of paper seventy-one feet high to represent the distance between us and the nearest star; thirty-one miles high to represent the distance between us and the edge of the Milky Way, and three hundred ten thousand miles high to represent the distance between us and the edge of the known universe. It's *big* out there, folks!

Acts 14:15 (d)
. . . and earth, and the sea, and all things that are therein.

Scientists have recently discovered worms ten feet long living a mile below the surface of the earth. The blue whale, a gigantic creature with a tongue equivalent to the weight of thirty-six full-grown men, survives on microscopic plankton. The Creator of whom Paul spoke filled His creation with incredible wonders.

Acts 14:16
Who in times past suffered all nations to walk in their own ways.

God could have forced His ways upon this world. Instead, He chose to allow people and nations to "walk in their own ways." What happens when nations choose their own way rather than God's? When people ignore the Word, the results are tragic. If I were God, I would have judged this world, this country, this society long ago. I would have devastated this planet. But what does God do? Read on.

Acts 14:17
Nevertheless he left not himself without witness, in that he did good, and gave us rain from heaven, and fruitful seasons, filling our hearts with food and gladness.

Although society rejects Him and nations turn from Him, God still does good. He allows rain to fall upon the just and the unjust. He allows food to be produced. He allows our hearts to be filled with gladness. He allows people to have life, to experience the joy of a sunrise, to surf, to hold a baby—all because of His goodness.

Acts 14:18
And with these sayings scarce restrained they the people, that they had not done sacrifice unto them.

After Paul finished this simple yet powerful sermon, the people decided not to offer sacrifices to him. It was a close call. But watch what happens next.

Acts 14:19 (a)
And there came thither certain Jews from Antioch and Iconium . . .

Those who had expelled Paul from Antioch and those who had sought to stone him in Iconium joined forces and followed him to Lystra.

Acts 14:19 (b)
. . . who persuaded the people . . .

One minute the people of Lystra cried, "They're gods!" The next, "Kill them!" We do the very same thing whenever we idolize an author, a speaker, or a teacher one day but criticize him the moment we see something in him of which we disapprove. The way to break free from the "Lystra syndrome" is not through adoration, nor annihilation—but through appreciation. The Lord instructed His people not to lay an axe to a fruit-bearing tree (Deuteronomy 20:19), for their own hunger would be the result. That's what happened to the people of Lystra—and it happens to us whenever we pick on groups, ministries, churches, or authors instead of picking from them. It's the treasure, folks, not the earthen vessel that is important (2 Corinthians 4:7). I can be enriched, fed, and blessed by the Word others share, even though I may see some earthiness in their vessels. On the other hand, God also instructed His people to chop down any trees that did not bear fruit (Deuteronomy 20:20). There is no place for ministries or cults that undermine our faith, deny the Word, or cast aspersions on the finished work of Christ.

Acts 14:19 (c)
. . . and, having stoned Paul, drew him out of the city . . .

The men of Lystra backed down. They heard the Word—but then turned away. Why? Why were the men of Lystra so fickle and so easily ma-

nipulated by those who wanted to see Paul dead? I believe Jeremiah 26 gives the answer . . .

Thus saith the LORD; Stand in the court of the LORD's house, and speak unto all the cities of Judah, which come to worship in the LORD's house, all the words that I command thee to speak unto them; diminish not a word: If so be they will hearken, and turn every man from his evil way, that I may repent me of the evil, which I purpose to do unto them because of the evil of their doings.   Jeremiah 26:2, 3

In obedience to the Lord's command, Jeremiah stood in the temple courtyard and preached powerfully, telling the people to repent of their evil ways so that the Lord could bless instead of chastise them.

Now it came to pass, when Jeremiah had made an end of speaking all that the LORD had commanded him to speak unto all the people, that the priests and the prophets and all the people took him, saying, Thou shalt surely die.
                                                    Jeremiah 26:8

"We don't like what you're saying, Jeremiah. We're going to kill you," the people said.

Then spake Jeremiah unto all the princes and to all the people, saying, The LORD sent me to prophesy against this house and against this city all the words that ye have heard. As for me, behold, I am in your hand: do with me as seemeth good and meet unto you. But know ye for certain, that if ye put me to death, ye shall surely bring innocent blood upon yourselves, and upon this city, and upon the inhabitants thereof: for of a truth the LORD hath sent me unto you to speak all these words in your ears.
                                          Jeremiah 26:12; 14, 15

"Do with me as you want," said Jeremiah. "But if you kill me, you will only compound your problems and bring innocent blood upon your own head."

Then said the princes and all the people unto the priests and to the prophets; This man is not worthy to die: for he hath spoken to us in the name of the LORD our God.
                                                    Jeremiah 26:16

Jeremiah took a stand. He refused to back down, and his life was spared.

And there was also a man that prophesied in the name of the LORD, Urijah the son of Shemaiah of Kirjath-jearim, who prophesied against this city and against this land according to all the words of Jeremiah . . .

Jeremiah 26:20

"Jeremiah, what you're saying makes sense," said Urijah. "So I'm going to prophesy just like you. The very words you say, I'll say."

And when Jehoiakim the king, with all his mighty men, and all the princes, heard his words, the king sought to put him to death: but when Urijah heard it, he was afraid, and fled, and went into Egypt . . . Jeremiah 26:21

When Urijah heard his life was at stake, he backed down, ran away, and fled to Egypt.

And Jehoiakim the king sent men into Egypt, namely, Elnathan the son of Achbor, and certain men with him into Egypt. And they fetched forth Urijah out of Egypt, and brought him unto Jehoiakim the king; who slew him with the sword, and cast his dead body into the graves of the common people.

Jeremiah 26:22, 23

Let me tell you one simple way to get wiped out: Run. Back away from the things you know are true and say, "I need a fix from the world. I think I'll go to Egypt." Whenever you take a vacation from the Lord or from the Word, like Urijah—you'll get chopped up.

Why did Urijah back down? Because, while Jeremiah was hearing and receiving directly from the Lord, Urijah was merely mimicking Jeremiah. He agreed with Jeremiah's message mentally, but it wasn't in his heart personally.

Mom and Dad, pray for your kids fervently that they'll have more than a head knowledge of the Lord based upon what they hear from you. Pray that, like Jeremiah, they'll own the truth in their hearts based upon their own fellowship with Him. How does truth move from one's head to one's heart? Through prayer.

Following the church service on Sunday, your devotions tomorrow, or the radio message you will hear next week—if your response is merely, "That's interesting," the Word of the Lord will never penetrate your heart. And when tough times come, you will join Urijah in Egypt. On the other hand, if you leave church, your morning devotions, or the radio message, saying, "Lord, what do You have in this for me today?"—you will be able to stand strong like Jeremiah. You see, it's not enough to mimic what we hear. Urijah did that and died. We, like Jeremiah, must internalize what we hear because it's not enough to hear the Lord's voice through an interpreter—be it an

author, a pastor, or a speaker. We must hear His voice *ourselves*.

Nevertheless the hand of Ahikam the son of Shaphan was with Jeremiah, that they should not give him into the hand of the people to put him to death.

Jeremiah 26:24

Jeremiah stood his ground and thereby saved his life. Had the men of Lystra done the same, their city would have been blessed.

Acts 14:19 (d)
. . . supposing he had been dead.

I personally believe that Paul was indeed dead. He will later refer to this event in 2 Corinthians 12 and write, "I know a man in Christ who, fourteen years ago, (whether alive or dead, I really don't know), was caught up in the third heaven, where he saw things unlawful to speak about."

When people write books saying, "I died on the operating table, went to heaven, and here's what I saw. . . ." I get very suspicious because when Paul went to heaven, he was forbidden to talk about what he witnessed.

Paul went on in 2 Corinthians 12 to say that at that time he was given a thorn in the flesh to keep him from becoming too proud about what he had seen in the heavenlies (2 Corinthians 12:7). The word "thorn" doesn't mean a thorn like you would find on a rosebush. It means "tent stake." Thus, Paul's thorn in the flesh wasn't some inconvenience he had to put up with now and then. It was painful and very possibly, according to many Bible scholars, the result of permanent injuries he received from this stoning. Yes, he went to heaven. Yes, his spirit was changed. But his body was permanently weakened as a result.

Acts 14:20 (a)
Howbeit, as the disciples stood round about him, he rose up . . .

These disciples were risking their own lives by standing around Paul's body. What were they doing? Were they praying? Was Luke trying to revive him? Were they crying? Were they having a memorial service? The Bible doesn't say. It just says they were there.

My mom, who lives in Southern California after being a widow for about a month, told me her days were very, very challenging. During that time, following an earthquake, she told me she felt helpless as the house and pool were rocking and rolling. When it was over, she went outside and started walking around her neighborhood, looking for someone to talk to. Since no one was outside, she went back to her house, only to feel a second quake. Just then, she said, the phone rang and on the other end was a sister from Applegate Christian Fellowship saying, "Mary, I know you know God's promises, so you don't need a sermon. I just want to talk with you. No sermon, no promises—just talk." My mom was deeply touched and greatly encouraged.

We all have experienced times when we have felt wiped out, finished, dead. And then some precious people gathered around us and we felt our hearts resurrected, our spirits revived. There are those whom the Lord will lead you to stand by, hang out with, and be there for—be it in person, over the phone, or through a letter. Be sensitive to His leading—and watch for revival.

Acts 14:20 (b)
. . . and came into the city . . .

After he was stoned, what did Paul do? He went right back into the city. How do you stop a guy like that?

Acts 14:20 (c), 21
. . . and the next day he departed with Barnabas to Derbe. And when they had preached the gospel to that city, and had taught many, they returned again to Lystra, and to Iconium, and Antioch.

Wrapping up their year-long tour that began in Acts 13, Paul and Barnabas doubled back on their return trip. In 2 Timothy 3:11, Paul made mention of Lystra, Iconium, and Antioch when he wrote of the persecutions and afflictions he suffered there. In Antioch, he was expelled. In Iconium, he narrowly escaped. In Lystra, he was stoned.

The Lord delivered Paul out of all of these dangerous traps. But in each case it was in an entirely different way. In Antioch, he was kicked out. In Iconium, he caught wind of a plot. In Lystra, he was left for dead. I point this out because our tendency is to say, "If I'm going to get out of my dilemma, it must be in this way, or according to these ten steps." But God will not be boxed in by any program, agenda, or formula. He has promised to deliver us (2 Corinthians 1:10), but He has not predicted how He'll do it.

Acts 14:22
Confirming the souls of the disciples, and exhorting them to continue in the faith, and that we must through much tribulation enter into the kingdom of God.

How do we enter into the kingdom? Through much tribulation. Shadrach, Meshach, and Abednego knew this. They were in a fiery trial, indeed, yet they didn't come out until they were ordered out (Daniel 3:26) because they preferred walking in the fire with the Lord to sitting in the shade without Him.

What happened to the fourth Man in the furnace (Daniel 3:25)? He remained in the fire. Where is Jesus—the fourth Man—today? In the fire. We have a tendency to try to avoid the fire whenever possible—and it's a great mistake. I'm not saying we should be masochists. I am saying it's in the fire, when times are tough, when your heart is breaking that Jesus is most visible, most real, and most precious.

Acts 14:23
And when they had ordained them elders in every church, and had prayed with fasting, they commended them to the Lord, on whom they believed.

These elders were probably only a few months old in the faith. Yet, with prayer and fasting, Paul and Barnabas commended them to the Lord.

Acts 14:24–28
And after they had passed throughout Pisidia, they came to Pamphylia. And when they had preached the word in Perga, they went down into Attalia: And thence sailed to Antioch, from whence they had been recommended to the grace of God for the work which they fulfilled. And when they were come, and had gathered the church together, they rehearsed all that God had done with them, and how he had opened the door of faith unto the Gentiles. And there they abode long time with the disciples.

Did Paul and Barnabas live happily ever after? Not by a long shot. Stay tuned. In chapter 15, we'll find out what happens next.

---

15 The story is told that, on a snowy January day at the turn of the century, a crowded passenger train steamed its way from Chicago to St. Louis. At one of many stops along the way, one of the travelers observed a young mother board the train with two small children in tow. "Please, sir, I need to get off at the city of Beaumont," he heard her say to the conductor.

The passenger, taking note of the overworked conductor, approached the young woman and said, "The conductor is busy. No doubt he'll forget you want to get off at Beaumont. I've been on this train a hundred times. I'll make sure you get off at the right place." Several hours later, as the train decelerated, the man made his way to the young mother and said, "This is the spot. Here's where you want to get off." Thanking him, she gathered her children and went out into the blizzard.

Half an hour passed before the conductor called out, "Where is the woman who wants to get off at Beaumont? It's coming up in five minutes."

Horrified at what he heard, the man said, "What do you mean? Beaumont was the last stop we made."

"No, sir," replied the conductor. "The last stop we made was to pick up water at a tank in the middle of nowhere." And both men instantly realized that the woman and children had been sent off the train to their deaths.

"Let not many of you desire to be teachers," James wrote, "because if you seek to give instruction and direction, there is an inherent possibility that you will lead someone astray" (see James 3:1). And that is precisely what happened in Acts 15. Those who desired to be teachers in the radical missionary church at Antioch came from Jerusalem to give teaching to the new Gentile converts. But, as we will see, their teaching led to a blizzard of confusion and a storm of controversy.

Acts 15:1 (a)
And certain men which came down from Judaea taught the brethren . . .

These teachers carried weight because they were from Jerusalem—Headquarters, the Mother Church. Galatians 2 tells us they were associated with James himself. Even Peter was on the scene at this time, at least for a short season, for in Galatians we read that when Paul showed up, not only did he dispute the legalizing teachers, but he withstood Peter himself (Galatians 2:11).

Acts 15:1 (b)
. . . and said, Except ye be circumcised after the manner of Moses, ye cannot be saved.

Perhaps these men were sincere. Nonetheless, they were sincerely wrong in insisting that the new Gentile believers be circumcised before they could be saved. In other words, they were wrong to insist that to become a Christian, one had to first become a Jew.

Acts 15:2
When therefore Paul and Barnabas had no small dissension and disputation with them, they determined that Paul and Barnabas, and certain other of them, should go up to Jerusalem unto the apostles and elders about this question.

I wonder if Paul didn't say, "You want us to go to *Jerusalem?* The headquarters of Judaism? Can we get a fair trial there? Will I have the opportunity to speak? Will the Lord be able to work in the city where Judaism is so deeply entrenched?"

Acts 15:3
And being brought on their way by the church, they passed through Phenice and Samaria, declaring the conversion of the Gentiles: and they caused great joy unto all the brethren.

When the legalizers came into town there was heaviness, but when Paul and Barnabas passed through, there was great joy. I like that! Some people bring joy wherever they go. Others bring joy *when*ever they go. We can bring joy wherever we go because the gospel is such good news. We have the privilege of telling people, "Your sins are forgiven. You don't have to be better or try harder. The price has been paid. The work is complete!"

Acts 15:4, 5
And when they were come to Jerusalem, they were received of the church, and of the apostles and elders, and they declared all things that God had done with them. But there rose up certain of the sect of the Pharisees which believed, saying, That it was needful to circumcise them, and to command them to keep the law of Moses.

Unlike the Sadducees, Pharisees embraced the miraculous—especially the possibility of resurrection. So, when Jesus rose from the dead, many Pharisees became believers. Here, they are arguing that Christianity should become a denomination within Judaism. Within the broad context of the Jewish religion, there are all sorts of flavors: Orthodox, Ultra-Orthodox, Reformed, Ultra-Reformed. Thus, if these Pharisees had their way, we would be just another flavor—following Rabbi Jesus.

Acts 15:6, 7 (a)
And the apostles and elders came together for to consider of this matter. And when there had been much disputing, Peter rose up . . .

As Peter took the stand, I wonder if Paul's heart sank. After all, there had been obvious and unmistakable tension between them. You see, these early believers were anything but "cookie cutter" Christians. Read the writings of Paul and contrast them with James and Jude. Read 1 and 2 Peter, contrast them with Galatians, and you'll sense wonderful individualism and a very healthy tension.

Acts 15:7 (b), 8
. . . and said unto them, Men and brethren, ye know how that a good while ago God made choice among us, that the Gentiles by my mouth should hear the word of the gospel, and believe. And God, which knoweth the hearts, bare them witness, giving them the Holy Ghost, even as he did unto us.

Peter is alluding to the events of Acts 10, wherein he shared the gospel with the household of Cornelius.

Acts 15:9
And put no difference between us and them, purifying their hearts by faith.

They were purified *because* of their belief, not *before* their belief. Although we're to be fishers of men (Matthew 4:19), the problem with so many Christians today is that they are trying to clean the fish before they catch them. In reality, it is not until *after* men are hooked on Christ and brought into the boat of salvation that their hearts will change. Therefore, the great need of our world, our communities, and our families is not reformation but regeneration.

Acts 15:10
Now therefore why tempt ye God, to put a yoke upon the neck of the disciples, which neither our fathers nor we were able to bear?

"Neither we nor our fathers could ever do enough to justify ourselves, to cleanse our sin, to earn God's favor," argued Peter.

When asked the reason for his wealth, a multi-millionaire is reported to have said, "As a young man, when I was first married I was dirt poor. Those were tough times, but being energetic, I took my last nickel and bought an apple. I spent the night polishing it until it became so shiny that it was indeed a thing of beauty. The next day, I sold it on the street corner for a dime. I took the dime and bought two apples, which I again laboriously polished. The next day, I sold those two apples for twenty cents. I took the twenty cents and bought four apples, which I polished and sold for forty cents. I took the forty cents, bought eight apples, and went on this way until I reached $1.60. Then, my wife's dad died—and left us a million dollars."

That's just like us! We try to say, "I am rich in the things of God because of my fasting and prayer, my devotion, sacrifice, and apple polishing"—when in reality we are rich only because Jesus died and opened the floodgates of God's grace upon us.

For topical study of Acts 15:10 entitled "Is the Yoke on You?" turn to page 736.

Acts 15:11
But we believe that through the grace of the Lord Jesus Christ we shall be saved, even as they.

I love this! Peter didn't say, "*They* shall be saved even as *we*," but "*we* shall be saved, even as *they*." In other words, "We believe that through the grace of the Lord Jesus Christ, we Jews, who are so entangled in legalism, can be free to enjoy salvation by grace—even as Gentiles do."
This sounds dangerous to me, you might be thinking. *After all, if we don't keep a yoke on young Christians, they'll run wild.* Not so. The law leads to rebellion. Love leads to relationship.

Growing up, every Saturday I had the job of washing our family car, a 1966 green Buick Skylark. The "law" demanded it—so I did it. I squirted it down, threw a towel across it, and called, "It's done, Pops," even though there were spots on the windows and soap suds on the roof. But when I was sixteen, I got my license and fell in love (I thought) with a girl named Stephanie. From that point on, before every date, I could be found in the driveway washing, drying, waxing, and polishing my 1960 turquoise Falcon. And when I finished there wasn't a spot to be seen, not a soap sud in sight. What was the difference? Love.

Dear brothers and sisters, love is the ultimate source of spirituality. Don't put yokes on people. Instead, let them see how much Jesus really

loves them, and watch their relationship with
Him soar (Romans 2:4).

Acts 15:12, 13 (a)
**Then all the multitude kept silence, and
gave audience to Barnabas and Paul, declaring what miracles and wonders God had
wrought among the Gentiles by them. And
after they had held their peace, James answered . . .**

Called "James the Just" because he was so
righteous and "James the Camel-Kneed" because
he spent so much time in prayer, this was the half
brother of Jesus and the leader of the church at
Jerusalem.

Acts 15:13 (b), 14
**. . . saying, Men and brethren, hearken unto
me: Simeon hath declared how God at the
first did visit the Gentiles, to take out of
them a people for his name.**

James wisely used Peter's Hebrew name because the debate centered on Jewish issues.

Acts 15:15, 16
**And to this agree the words of the prophets;
as it is written, After this I will return, and
will build again the tabernacle of David,
which is fallen down; and I will build again
the ruins thereof, and I will set it up.**

Many Bible scholars believe Amos 9, quoted
here in Acts 15, alludes to the fact that before the
temple is rebuilt, a tabernacle will be pitched in
Jerusalem as a temporary temple. Be that as it
may, Romans 11:25–26 declares that when the
time of the Gentiles is over, the Lord is going to
turn again to the nation of Israel and all of Israel
shall be saved. But notice it is *after* the time of
the Gentiles.

At the end of the Gentile Age, the Rapture of
the church will take place. Because Jesus said Jerusalem would be trodden down by the Gentiles
until the times of the Gentiles be fulfilled (Luke
21:24), and because under Israeli rule, the city of
Jerusalem has not been trodden down by the
Gentiles for the last twenty-five years, does that
mean the Rapture is twenty-five years late? No,
it means we're in overtime. The Age of the Gentiles is complete. The Rapture is imminent. But
the Lord has chosen to extend His grace before
ushering in the Tribulation.

Acts 15:17
**That the residue of men might seek after
the Lord, and all the Gentiles, upon whom**

**my name is called, saith the Lord, who doeth
all these things.**

"The residue of men" refers to those who will
survive the Tribulation.

Acts 15:18
**Known unto God are all his works from the
beginning of the world.**

A group of theologians recently introduced the
theory that God doesn't really know exactly
who's going to be saved or what's going to happen—that He's kind of playing everything by
ear as He goes along. Not true! When you get
to heaven, God's not going to say, "Oh, I'm glad
you made it! I wasn't sure you would." No,
James says God has known everything from
the beginning of the world.

Acts 15:19, 20
**Wherefore my sentence is, that we trouble
not them, which from among the Gentiles
are turned to God: But that we write unto
them, that they abstain from pollutions of
idols, and from fornication, and from things
strangled, and from blood.**

"In light of the Gentile Age," concluded James,
"there are four things from which we should
tell new believers to abstain"—one of which
dealt with morality, the remaining three with
sensitivity. The moral issue was fornication. I
read in the paper recently that, according to
one survey, couples who live together before
marriage are fifty percent more likely to divorce during the first eight years of marriage
than those who don't. The Word is right again.

The remaining three issues dealt with sensitivity because Jews were very sensitive about
the issues of blood, strangulation, and meat offered to idols. You see, the best meat in those
days was offered as a sacrifice in pagan temples before it was sold in the market at cheap
prices. That is why in 1 Corinthians 10, Paul
said, "It doesn't matter whether meat is offered to idols or not. For yourself, don't ask
where it came from—just enjoy it. But if your
eating it will cause a weaker brother to stumble—stay away from it."

The same is true today. Every one of us is either a stepping-stone or a stumbling stone, as we
either allow people to get closer to God or cause
them to stumble unnecessarily. In our freedom,
we also need sensitivity.

Acts 15:21
For Moses of old time hath in every city them that preach him, being read in the synagogues every sabbath day.

Moses was unable to lead the people of God into the Promised Land because the law never leads to the land of milk and honey. It was Joshua who led the people into the Promised Land. What is the Greek name for the Hebrew name Joshua? Jesus. Jesus leads us into the Land of Promise because the law never can.

Acts 15:22
Then pleased it the apostles and elders, with the whole church, to send chosen men of their own company to Antioch with Paul and Barnabas; namely, Judas surnamed Barsabas, and Silas, chief men among the brethren.

One of the men who was sent to Antioch was named Barsabas, which means literally "son of the Sabbath." I like that! Son of the Sabbath was sent to tell the Gentile believers they were free to rest in the finished work of Christ.

Acts 15:23–25 (a)
And they wrote letters by them after this manner; The apostles and elders and brethren send greeting unto the brethren which are of the Gentiles in Antioch and Syria and Cilicia: Forasmuch as we have heard, that certain which went out from us have troubled you with words, subverting your souls, saying, Ye must be circumcised, and keep the law: to whom we gave no such commandment: It seemed good unto us, being assembled with one accord. . . .

The question I am asked more than any other is: "How can I know God's will for my life?" Following are six ways I believe we can know the will of God as we see the hand of God guiding His people.

God guides through church unanimity.

The letter written to the church at Antioch stated that the believers in Jerusalem were in one accord. That's so important. Whether you're wrestling with an issue of lifestyle or doctrine, find out what the church says about it. Throughout church history, what has been the stance of the church regarding the subject with which you're struggling? Beware of those who say, "You don't need the church. It's outdated and old-fashioned." Proverbs 22:28 says, "Remove not the ancient landmark, which thy fathers have set." It is through the wisdom of church unanim-

ity presently and historically that God has guided His people very significantly.

Acts 15:25 (b)–27
. . . to send chosen men unto you with our beloved Barnabas and Paul, Men that have hazarded their lives for the name of our Lord Jesus Christ. We have sent therefore Judas and Silas, who shall also tell you the same things by mouth.

God Guides Through Gifted Men and Women in the Body

God gave to the church prophets, pastors, evangelists, and teachers for the perfecting of the saints and the work of the ministry (Ephesians 4:11, 12). How can you know God's will? Be around whenever prophets, pastors, evangelists, or teachers expound the Word. It's the wise woman, the mature man who approaches every Bible study, every time of fellowship expecting the Lord to speak through His body.

Acts 15:28, 29
For it seemed good to the Holy Ghost, and to us, to lay upon you no greater burden than these necessary things; that ye abstain from meats offered to idols, and from blood, and from things strangled, and from fornication: from which if ye keep yourselves, ye shall do well. Fare ye well.

God Guides Through the Gifts of the Spirit

Earlier in this chapter, there was much debate and discussion. Suddenly, James the Camelkneed stood up, and as he spoke, an interesting thing happened. Everyone in the room melted into unity and agreement. The same is true for us. There are times when, during an endless dialogue or discussion, someone suddenly says something that settles not only in your brain or your mind, but deep within your heart—and you know it's the Lord, speaking through a word of wisdom. I hope when you're struggling with finding God's will for your life, you avail yourself of settings where words of wisdom, knowledge, and prophecy are being exercised. Frequently, that's how the Lord speaks most clearly.

Acts 15:30, 31
So when they were dismissed, they came to Antioch: and when they had gathered the multitude together, they delivered the epistle: Which when they had read, they rejoiced for the consolation.

"Wonderful!" these Gentile men would have cheered in unison. "We don't have to be circumcised. We don't have to carry the heavy burden of legalism!"

It amazes me how many people feel they haven't been to church unless they walk out emotionally bloodied and battered. "I'm such a wretch," they say. "Beat me, Pastor. Beat me. That was great. I can't wait until next Sunday." I believe this is due to a failure to understand the finished work of the Cross. We are truly forgiven—not just theologically, but in reality.

Acts 15:32–34
And Judas and Silas, being prophets also themselves, exhorted the brethren with many words, and confirmed them. And after they had tarried there a space, they were let go in peace from the brethren unto the apostles. Notwithstanding it pleased Silas to abide there still.

God Guides Through Desires We May Have Personally

As the delegation headed back to Jerusalem, Silas said, "I like it here in Antioch. I think I'll stick around." We'll see how the Lord will use Silas' personal desire as the book unfolds. The reason I teach the Word is because I love to teach. I'm doing exactly what I want to do. Those who imply that ministry is supposed to be a drudgery are lying. That's bad theology and a blasphemy to the nature and character of our Father.

In the highlands of Papua New Guinea, there is an area where it rains 362 days a year and the frogs spit poison. As of yet, Wycliffe Bible Translators has not found anyone to go into that region to translate the Word for the few folks who live there. But somewhere the Lord is preparing someone who will have a fascination with spitting frogs and rainy weather. That's the way the Lord works. How do I know? Because Psalm 37:4 declares, "Delight yourself in the Lord and He will give you the desires of your heart."

Acts 15:35, 36
Paul also and Barnabas continued in Antioch, teaching and preaching the word of the Lord, with many others also. And some days after Paul said unto Barnabas, Let us go again and visit our brethren in every city where we have preached the word of the Lord, and see how they do.

God Guides Through Concerns We Feel Internally

Paul said, "I'm curious about how the believers we saw five years ago are doing." The same thing happens today. Suddenly, a situation, a need, or an opportunity will tug on your heart. The person next to you might not feel a thing—not because he's insensitive or unspiritual, but because meeting that particular need is not his calling. The way of the Lord is to guide us individually through concerns we feel internally.

Acts 15:37–39 (a)
And Barnabas determined to take with them John, whose surname was Mark. But Paul thought not good to take him with them, who departed from them from Pamphylia, and went not with them to the work. And the contention was so sharp between them, that they departed asunder one from the other . . .

God Guides Through Interpersonal Difficulty

"Let's take John Mark with us," said Barnabas. "I know he backed out last time, but I see potential in him."

"We can't afford to bring someone we can't count on," insisted Paul. "Let's leave him here."

Paul said, "What can he do for God's work?"

Barnabas said, "What can God's work do for him?"

Who was right?

They both were.

When Paul was in prison awaiting his death, who did he send for to comfort him? John Mark (2 Timothy 4:11). The consoling ministry of Barnabas paid off. Who crisscrossed the known world with the gospel? Paul. The compelling ministry of Paul paid off.

God often guides through interpersonal difficulty. Is it the best way? I don't think so. I think it's much better to hear a word of wisdom, to learn from a teaching, to receive counsel and understanding from a gifted brother or sister. But a lot of times I'm just too dull of hearing and hard of heart to receive a word of wisdom or to make personal application from a Bible study. I have to bump heads with someone for God to get me going in the right direction. I wish I could say, "My spiritual sensitivity is at such a level that I never have conflict with anyone at any time. I hear the voice of the Lord whispering in my ear in every situation. Consequently, I never have to go through contention or difficulty"—but I'm not there, folks. I find great comfort, however, knowing that even Paul the apostle, at the high point of his ministry, was directed through interpersonal difficulty.

Acts 15:39 (b)–41

. . . and so Barnabas took Mark, and sailed unto Cyprus; and Paul chose Silas, and departed, being recommended by the brethren unto the grace of God. And he went through Syria and Cilicia, confirming the churches.

The Lord used interpersonal difficulty to send two teams out instead of one. As a result, twice as many believers were encouraged, and twice as much ministry ensued.

Six ways in which God guides His people are: through Church unanimity, through gifted men and women in the body, through the gifts of the Spirit charismatically, through the desires we have personally, through concerns we feel internally, and through interpersonal difficulty. Travel with us, and we'll see three more in chapter 16.

IS THE YOKE ON YOU?
A Topical Study of
Acts 15:10

Now therefore why tempt ye God, to put a yoke upon the neck of the disciples, which neither our fathers nor we were able to bear?

Acts 15:10

Peter's question is pointed directly at me: "Jon, why do you attempt to correct God by laying burdens upon people?" In thinking through my answer, I believe there are five explanations for the propensity within each of us to put expectations, stipulations, obligations, and regulations upon our kids and our wives, our husbands and our friends as we burden them with yokes they are unable to bear.

We put yokes on people because we sincerely care about them.

"Because I really care about you," we say, "I must tell you this Christianity thing is not as simple as you might think. You see, there are a few rules and regulations you need to know in order to be successful. Otherwise, you'll go hog-wild and do things you shouldn't." And then we proceed to furnish people with our personal list of do's and don'ts.

Such has always been the tendency of people involved in religion. For example, God said, "Honor the Sabbath day." Judaism said, "It's not that simple." That's why the Talmud contains seven volumes concerning the do's and don'ts of keeping the Sabbath. But the problem with rules and regulations is, there's always a way to get around them. For example, although the Talmud forbade travel of more than one thousand paces on the Sabbath, if a Pharisee had to travel farther than that, he would stretch a rope from his house one thousand paces and call it an extended hallway. From the end of his new "hallway," he would stretch another rope one thousand paces and continue doing so until he finally reached his destination.

There's a better way than the law—it's love.

As a father read to his three-year-old one night, his son interrupted him and
said, "Daddy I love you."
    "That's great," the father said and kept reading.
    Two minutes later, the toddler interrupted again, "Daddy, I love you."
    "That's great, son. I love you, too."
    Finally, the little boy stood up on his dad's lap, hugged him around the
neck, smothered his face in his chest and said, "Daddy, I love you so much I
just gotta do something about it."

Human nature will always find a way around the law. Love, however causes us
do more than the law ever could.

We put yokes on people because we secretly desire control over them.

When Rehoboam, Solomon's son, ascended the throne, he called the older men
of the kingdom together and said, "Give me some advice."
    "Your dad worked us hard and taxed us heavily," they said. "Free us from the
yoke he put upon us, and we'll serve you to the end."
    Then he called the younger men together and said, "What do you guys think
I should do?"
    "Put a *heavier* yoke upon the people," they answered (see 1 Kings 12:10–12).
    Rehoboam followed the advice of the younger men. Under his rule, the people
labored continuously, were taxed outrageously—and finally rebelled completely.
The country split in two because yokes always lead to division and rebellion.
    Watch out, parents. Compassion for people will produce what control over
them never can. The heavy yokes you think will control your kids may do just the
opposite and cause them to rebel, dividing your entire household in the process.

We put yokes on people because we selfishly need to be esteemed by them.

Because the Pharisees wanted to be thought of as more spiritual than they really were, they strutted through town with their phylacteries, praying long prayers
on the street corners.

After being instructed by God to dig through a wall in the temple, Ezekiel
discovered a door through which he saw "every form of creeping things, abominable beasts and all the idols of the house of Israel" being worshiped by the
elders of Israel (Ezekiel 8:10, 11).
    "This is what is happening in the chambers of imagination of the elders
of Israel," said the Lord. "Outwardly, they walk around piously in their flowing
robes and phylacteries—but inwardly they're carnal and full of iniquity."

God never intended us to walk in false piety or phony spirituality—which is why Jesus said, "Blessed are the pure in heart and the poor in spirit" (see Matthew 5).

We put yokes on people because we simplistically
think we know what's best for them.

Because each of us is so different, God wants to work with us individually and in our hearts personally. Philippians 2:12 tells us to work out our own salvation with fear and trembling, for it is God who works within us to will and to do of His good pleasure. The principle of the New Covenant, as seen in Jeremiah 31, says the Lord will write His plan for *each* of us on the tables of our hearts. Thus, there is no need for us to tell others what they can and can't do.

Many years ago, I observed my kids as they watched a thunderstorm. Seeing the lightning, Benjamin, who was four at the time, immediately said, "I want to play Noah!" while Mary Elizabeth, who was five, started waving. One saw a flood; the other saw flashbulbs.

As parents, we know how different our kids are. So, too, we must give that same space to our heavenly Father to deal with each of His children uniquely.

We put yokes on people because we sadistically
want to share our misery with them.

The circumcisers said, "Because we endured pain, you have to endure pain as well." And there are those today who, because of their misery and lack of joy, make everyone around them equally miserable by placing yokes of rules and regulations upon them. This ought not be. God's desire is that we walk in joyfulness and with gladness of heart (Deuteronomy 28:47), which is why Jesus was accused of being a glutton, winebibber, and a friend of sinners. "Surely *He* cannot be the Son of God," the Pharisees said. "He's too happy."

Jesus said, "Take *My* yoke upon you—not the yoke of religion, legalism, manipulation or expectation. My burden is easy. My load is light. Under My yoke, you will find rest for your souls." (see Matthew 11:28–30)

Paul said,

Finally, my brethren, rejoice in the Lord. To write the same things to you, to me indeed is not grievous, but for you it is safe. Beware of dogs, beware of evil workers, beware of the concision. For we are the circumcision, which worship God in the spirit, and rejoice in Christ Jesus, and have no confidence in the flesh.   Philippians 3:1–3

Who is the true circumcision? Who are the true God-lovers? Not those who point to themselves, puff up themselves, or depend upon themselves; but those who worship God in the Spirit, rejoice in Christ, and have no confidence in the flesh. Gang, I want you to be the most free people in all the earth—free to walk in the glorious liberty to which you've been called, and free to allow others to do the same.

—————————— ✺ ——————————

16 Perhaps you recall the story. A man bought a painting at a Philadelphia flea market for eighteen dollars. The painting was rather plain, but the frame was of interest to him. After returning home, he set to work to remove the canvas, when a piece of paper tucked inside caught his eye. As he carefully extracted the document, he was amazed to find one of only four original copies of the Declaration of Independence, which he in turn sold for over four million dollars.

This incident interested me because often when I look at a passage of Scripture, I see it framed and painted, only to find that behind the scenes there can be a wealth of information waiting to be discovered. Such is the case in Acts 15 and 16, where, not only does Paul deal with the issue of legalism but also with the ways God makes His will known to us.

Acts 16:1, 2
Then came he to Derbe and Lystra: and, behold, a certain disciple was there, named Timotheus, the son of a certain woman, which was a Jewess, and believed; but his father was a Greek: Which was well reported of by the brethren that were at Lystra and Iconium.

Five years have passed. Upon his return to the people who had stoned him, Paul discovered that his ministry "took" in a young man of real promise named Timothy.

One Wednesday night, I was blessed by a lady who said, "You probably don't remember me, but when you were a sophomore in college, you spoke to our youth camp at Big Bear and I got saved." And now almost twenty years later, here she was, still walking with the Lord and growing in grace. The proof of faith is not initial excitement. It's long-term commitment. Jesus said, "I have chosen you and ordained you that you should go and bring forth fruit and that your fruit should remain" (see John 15:16).

Acts 16:3 (a)
Him would Paul have to go forth with him . . .

It seems as though Paul was always looking for young men to bring alongside him. Six times, in six different epistles, Paul referred to Timothy and called him "my son in the faith." If you're older in the faith, one of the greatest joys you'll ever have is that of investing yourself in a younger person.

Acts 16:3 (b), 4
. . . and took and circumcised him because of the Jews which were in those quarters: for they knew all that his father was a Greek. And as they went through the cities, they delivered them the decrees for to keep, that were ordained of the apostles and elders which were at Jerusalem.

Paul had Timothy—with whom he would deliver decrees of liberty to new believers—circumcised. Why would Paul, the champion of liberty and grace, place Timothy under this ritualistic burden? Understand that Paul was not compromising his theology. No, he was conforming to the higher priority of love. You see, although Timothy's father was Greek, his mother was a Jew—making Timothy a Jew as well. Therefore, Paul didn't want Timothy to be a stumbling block to the very people he sought to win. On the other hand, in Galatians 2, when the Judaizers wanted to circumcise Titus, Paul absolutely forbade it. Why? Because Titus was a Gentile.

Paul would later write,

For though I be free from all men, yet have I made myself servant unto all, that I might gain the more. And unto the Jews I became as a Jew, that I might gain the Jews; to them that are under the law, as under the law, that I might gain them that are under the law; to them that are without law, as without law, (being not without law to God, but under the law to Christ,) that I might gain them that are without law. To the weak became I as weak, that I might gain the weak: I am made all things to all men, that I might by all means save some.   1 Corinthians 9:19–22

Are we willing to give up our rights so that we won't unnecessarily cause someone else to stumble? Are we, like Timothy, willing to give up our liberty for the sake of love and effective ministry?

Acts 16:5
And so were the churches established in the faith, and increased in number daily.

They were established not in programs, not in hype, but in faith. Later on, Paul would say to these very people, "O foolish Galatians . . . having begun in the Spirit, are ye now made perfect by the flesh?" (Galatians 3:1, 3). 1 think if Paul were writing to the church in America, he would say the same thing. "O foolish American Christians, having begun in the Spirit are you now made perfect by programs?"

Acts 16:6, 7
Now when they had gone throughout Phrygia and the region of Galatia, and were forbidden of the Holy Ghost to preach the word in Asia, after they were come to Mysia, they assayed to go into Bithynia: but the Spirit suffered them not.

Here is the seventh time in Acts 15 and 16 we see the Lord directing His people. This time it is through physical infirmity. Paul, wanting to go into Asia (present-day Turkey), was forbidden by the Holy Ghost. But Paul was one who didn't take "no" easily. He was stoned in Lystra—but returned to the city the very next day (Acts 14:20). In Acts 21, the Spirit said, "Don't go to Jerusalem." But Paul went anyway.

Once Paul decided to do something, nothing would deter him. So how did the Spirit stop Paul from going into Turkey? Most Bible scholars believe Paul was struck at this time with a brutal infirmity, a sickness, an Asian fever so severe that his eyesight would be permanently damaged (Galatians 4:13–15). I also personally believe this is what happened because in verse 10, we see the pronouns "we" and "us" replacing "they" and "them" as Luke joined the journey very possibly to attend to the medical needs of Paul.

Sometimes, to those of us who are stubborn and thick-headed like Paul, the Lord gives guidance through infirmities. I am not saying every illness is a word from the Lord. However, sometimes the Lord does, indeed, work though infirmities.

As a freshman in high school, I wanted to be a distance runner like my big brother, Dave. The only problem was, where Dave was lean and lanky—I was husky and stocky. But with only five other guys trying out for six spots, I earned a place on the distance team and found myself participating every day after school in what were, to me, grueling workouts. Every day after practice, I hit the locker room sicker than a dog until the week before my first meet,

when I landed in the hospital with double pneumonia. Tom McKee, my youth pastor, came in and prayed for me, and I was confident I would be healed in time for the first meet. But it didn't happen quite that way. Upon reexamination of my lungs, my doctor said, "Jon, you're not running this week, next week, or for a couple of years. Your lungs are too scarred."

When I was finally well enough to go back to school, I wandered rather forlornly out to the track and to the upper field where the discus throwers tossed frisbeelike objects into the air. They wore sunglasses. They listened to the radio. They laughed and joked with each other between throws. Suddenly, it dawned on me that this was the sport for me! In my sophomore year, I set the league record in discus, and by the time I threw for the last time, I had set some central California records, gone to college on a scholarship, and traveled across the country and into Africa—all by throwing a flat plate!

I'm so thankful I got pneumonia! I would have been a very poor runner, hating every step. The Lord had another plan for me. But He made it clear to me only after I was knocked flat on my back.

Acts 16:8, 9 (a)
And they passing by Mysia came down to Troas. And a vision appeared to Paul in the night.

At Troas, with his back against the Mediterranean Sea, forbidden to go into Turkey, Paul returned to the coast, where the environment was much healthier. Once there, he must have wondered, *Where do I go? What do I do now? Here I launched out enthusiastically to serve the Lord—but nothing's going right.* Ever feel that way? You're probably in just the right spot for a vision.

Acts 16:9 (b)
There stood a man of Macedonia, and prayed him, saying, Come over into Macedonia, and help us.

Here is the eighth time in Acts 15 and 16 we see God guiding His people, as He directs through vision supernaturally. While I have had dreams that have ministered to my heart, I have never had a vision that directed me—which is okay because I am reminded in Jeremiah 23:28 that dreams are as chaff compared to the wheat of the Word. As a pastor, I sometimes get frustrated with people who want to know God's will but won't come to Bible study. If I had to choose between the Word and a vision, I'd take the Word every time.

Acts 16:10–13

And after he had seen the vision, immediately we endeavored to go into Macedonia, assuredly gathering that the Lord had called us for to preach the gospel unto them. Therefore loosing from Troas, we came with a straight course to Samothracia, and the next day to Neapolis; and from thence to Philippi, which is the chief city of that part of Macedonia, and a colony: and we were in that city abiding certain days. And on the sabbath we went out of the city by a river side, where prayer was wont to be made; and we sat down, and spake unto the women which resorted thither.

Upon entering the city of Philippi, Paul and his company must have looked for a synagogue, as was their custom. Finding none, they instead found women gathered on the bank of a river for their own Sabbath meeting. It is interesting to me that, although Paul heard the voice of a Macedonian male in verse 9, when he arrived he found only women in verse 13. So, too, sometimes I feel the Lord directing and guiding—but when I reach my destination I find it a whole lot different than I expected.

Acts 16:14, 15

And a certain woman named Lydia, a seller of purple, of the city of Thyatira, which worshipped God, heard us: whose heart the Lord opened, that she attended unto the things which were spoken of Paul. And when she was baptized, and her household, she besought us, saying, If ye have judged me to be faithful to the Lord, come into my house, and abide there. And she constrained us.

"If you have found us to be faithful, come to our house," said Lydia. What could Paul say? No wonder Lydia was a successful saleswoman!

Acts 16:16

And it came to pass, as we went to prayer, a certain damsel possessed with a spirit of divination met us, which brought her masters much gain by soothsaying.

Here, a demon-possessed girl was exploited by greedy men in the dark world of the fortune-telling trade.

Acts 16:17, 18

The same followed Paul and us, and cried, saying, These men are the servants of the most high God, which shew unto us the way of salvation. And this did she many days. But Paul, being grieved, turned and said to the spirit, I command thee in the name of Jesus Christ to come out of her. And he came out the same hour.

Why did Paul want this girl to stop? Because, although her message was true, the medium was all wrong. I have been asked hypothetically, if I had the chance to give my testimony in *Playboy* magazine, would I do it? My answer is no, because I don't need nor want this ministry to be advertised by that which is contrary to the message of Jesus Christ. The Christian community is becoming increasingly weakened, I believe, because we have too often said, "We'll use this worldly source to communicate the gospel." Why, then, did Paul allow this girl to cry out for many days before commanding the spirit to come out of her? I believe he was waiting for the green light, the authority of the Holy Spirit before stepping out in the power of the Spirit.

Acts 16:19–25

And when her masters saw that the hope of their gains was gone, they caught Paul and Silas, and drew them into the marketplace unto the rulers, and brought them to the magistrates, saying, These men, being Jews, do exceedingly trouble our city, and teach customs, which are not lawful for us to receive, neither to observe, being Romans. And the multitude rose up together against them: and the magistrates rent off their clothes, and commanded to beat them. And when they had laid many stripes upon them, they cast them into prison, charging the jailor to keep them safely: Who, having received such a charge, thrust them into the inner prison, and made their feet fast in the stocks. And at midnight Paul and Silas prayed, and sang praises unto God: and the prisoners heard them.

The final way we see God guiding His people throughout the past two chapters is through the giving of thanks continually. As He did with Paul and Silas, God directs our lives when we're in the posture of prayer and praise. "I'm in the midnight hour," you say. "It's so dark. I'm trapped, locked in, with no way out. I don't know what to do." Quit griping and start singing. Then, like Paul and Silas, you will see things happen to you, around you, and through you.

For topical study of 16:19–25 entitled "Being Beaten," turn to page 743.

Acts 16:26, 27
And suddenly there was a great earthquake, so that the foundations of the prison were shaken: and immediately all the doors were opened, and every one's bands were loosed. And the keeper of the prison awaking out of his sleep, and seeing the prison doors open, he drew out his sword, and would have killed himself, supposing that the prisoners had been fled.

Knowing heads would roll when news of the escape reached his superiors, the jailer said, "I'll just kill myself now and get it over with."

Acts 16:28–30
But Paul cried with a loud voice, saying, Do thyself no harm: for we are all here. Then he called for a light, and sprang in, and came trembling, and fell down before Paul and Silas, and brought them out, and said, Sirs, what must I do to be saved?

"Not only have I been shaken up by the earthquake under me, but I am shaken up by the fact that you guys didn't split when you had the chance," said the jailer.

Why are you in prison? Why are things not happening? Why aren't things opening up as quickly as you hoped they would? Could it be because there are prisoners and jailers watching, who are about to see what happens in your life when things are shaken up? Could it be because there are people who need to see what's going to happen to you in the midnight hour? For the most part, prosperity only creates jealousy. But when those around you hear you singing in the day of adversity, like the jailer they will say, "What must *I* do to be saved?"

Acts 16:31
And they said, Believe on the Lord Jesus Christ, and thou shalt be saved, and thy house.

This does not mean, as has been suggested, "If you believe, your whole house will be saved." No, it means, "You believe and you'll be saved. And when your family believes, they'll be saved as well."

Acts 16:32, 33 (a)
And they spake unto him the word of the Lord, and to all that were in his house. And he took them the same hour of the night, and washed their stripes . . .

You know a person is truly saved when he wants to wash feet and cleanse wounds.

Acts 16:33 (b)–36
. . . and was baptized, he and all his, straightway. And when he had brought them into his house, he set meat before them, and rejoiced, believing in God with all his house. And when it was day, the magistrates sent the serjeants, saying, Let those men go. And the keeper of the prison told this saying to Paul, The magistrates have sent to let you go: now therefore depart, and go in peace.

After the jailer had held Paul and Silas under "house arrest," word came to let them go.

Acts 16:37 (a)
But Paul said unto them, They have beaten us openly uncondemned, being Romans . . .

Thinking Paul and Silas were merely Jews, the magistrates felt completely justified in beating them without a trial. But to have done so to a Roman citizen was a great and grave offense.

Acts 16:37 (b), 38
. . . and have cast us into prison; and now do they thrust us out privily? nay verily; but let them come themselves and fetch us out. And the sergeants told these words unto the magistrates: and they feared, when they heard that they were Romans.

Why didn't Paul say, "Wait a minute. I'm a Roman citizen," *before* the flagellum was unleashed, *before* his back was beaten, *before* he was cast into the dungeon, *before* he was locked in stocks? Why didn't Paul claim his Roman citizenship earlier? And why did he claim it when he did? I believe the answer lies in verse 40. . . .

Acts 16:39, 40
And they came and besought them, and brought them out, and desired them to depart out of the city. And they went out of the prison, and entered into the house of Lydia and when they had seen the brethren, they comforted them, and departed.

Notice that Paul and Silas comforted the *brethren*. This poses an interesting question: Up until the time Paul and Silas landed in prison, all they had seen were women. Who, then, were these brethren? I suggest they were the prisoners who, in the dungeon with Paul, were converted when they heard his songs of praise. Paul's mind-set concerning himself was, "Go ahead. Beat me. Throw me in prison. I've been looking for some men to work with—now I can begin a jail minis- try!" But his mind-set concerning others was, "I am a Roman citizen and I'll be watching you, so you had better watch your step with my brothers."

When you and I come to the point where we can say, "I don't care what happens to me—but when it comes to my brothers and sisters, I'll go to the wall for them and do whatever I can to cover and protect them," *that's* maturity. Most of us protect ourselves and figure whatever happens to others is God's will. Paul did just the opposite. No wonder the Lord could use him.

BEING BEATEN
A Topical Study of
Acts 16:19–25

None of us likes to get beat up.

I think back a number of years ago to the day when my oldest son came home from kindergarten with tousled hair, torn shirt, and tearstained cheeks.

"What happened, Peter-John?" I asked.

With quivering chin he said, "The biggest kid in my class beat me up."

I gave Peter a hug and we talked for a while.

The next morning Peter-John was up bright and early getting ready for school. As he walked out the door, I couldn't help but notice the baseball bat he carried over his shoulder. "Where are you going with that bat, Peter?" I asked.

With eyes of steel, he said, "Daddy, today is "show and share" day. I'm taking my bat to show and share."

Knowing exactly to whom and on whom he wanted to show and share his bat, I insisted he choose something else.

In our text, we see Paul and Silas beaten, bruised, and bloodied—but instead of grabbing their bats and swinging, they glorified God by singing. I suggest three reasons Paul and Silas could sing in such a dark hour.

Paul and Silas' beating showed the desperation of the enemy.

When you find yourself beaten up, it means Satan considers you a threat to his dominion of death and darkness. I can recall one such incident that stands out vividly in my memory. It blew my mind when a man I had never met, but who was obviously demonized, looked me in the eye and said in a voice not completely his own, "Jon Courson, I know you, and I hate you." Although it freaked me out initially, I rejoiced later on because whenever Satan and his demons have our number, it means they're threatened.

Paul's and Silas' beating was a validation of their ministry.

In Colossians 1:23, 24, Paul would later write, "I Paul am made a minister; who now rejoice in my sufferings for you, and fill up that which is behind of the afflictions of Christ in my flesh for his body's sake, which is the church." In other words, part of Paul's job as a minister was to fill up—or complete—the sufferings of Jesus.

"Wait a minute," you say. "Are you saying that the suffering of Christ on the Cross was not sufficient?"

No. His work on the Cross was completely sufficient—validated by His resurrection. The idea here in Colossians relates to the church.

You see, even as Jesus today has thornprints on His brow, nail holes in His hands and feet, lash marks on His back, a spear wound in His side—so, too, His church must bear the marks of suffering. If His body is to fully conform to and correctly reflect Him, some, like Paul and Silas, will have to suffer brutally.

Paul's and Silas' beating was an indication of their maturity.

You'll never know how far along you are in the maturation process until you get beaten up. Trials neither make nor break us. They reveal what is going on inside of us. Thus, when you're beaten up verbally, emotionally, or perhaps even physically—you have an opportunity to see how much the Lord has accomplished in your life. Christians are like tea bags, folks. We'll never know what our flavor is until we're in hot water.

After teaching at a retreat in Palm Springs, I decided to go for a walk. It was about nine-thirty at night and about ninety-five degrees outside. Walking briskly down Palm Canyon Drive, I was reading the Word and thinking about this text when, failing to see a puddle in the middle of the pavement, I lost my footing and fell flat on my back. My glasses flew off, my Bible landed in the middle of the street, and I lay there in the mud and blood, rejoicing and thinking what a great illustration it would be for this study. Feeling pretty good as I picked up my Bible and glasses, I continued on. After about three miles of walking and reading, my foot hit a crack in the cement, causing me to lunge forward and break my sandal in the process. Knowing I had to walk back barefoot for five miles on hot cement, I wasn't rejoicing. Thinking one trial per walk should be sufficient, when the second one came my way, I was far from singing. By the time I got back to the hotel, it was 11:30. My feet were cut. I was upset—and then the Lord whispered in my ear, "You see, Jon, it's not the expected trial that reveals where you're at. It's the one that sneaks up behind you that shows what's really going on inside."

We all know of potential trials that will come our way next week—but it's the ones we don't expect that will reveal what's going on internally. You who are beaten up today by persecution on the job, ridicule on the campus, or ostracism from your family—Isaiah 54 is for you.

No weapon that is formed against thee shall prosper; and every tongue that shall rise against thee in judgment thou shalt condemn. This is the heritage of the servants of the LORD, and their righteousness is of me, saith the LORD.
Isaiah 54:17

Know this, you who are beaten up: no weapon that comes against you will prosper. You can be sure of that. Ask Paul and Silas. Yes, they were beaten up—but they went out victoriously into deeper ministry and fuller glory.

Perhaps you're saying, "It's fine for you spiritual giants to talk about being beaten up for your spirituality. Good for you. But that's not where I'm at. I'm not being beaten up—I'm being beaten down by my family, my marriage, my job."

You, too, can have hope today because, although Paul and Silas were beaten up, the jailer was beaten down—just like you! Roman law decreed that prison guards were to serve the sentence of any prisoner who escaped while in their charge. No doubt in that Philippian dungeon there were those who had committed capital offenses and were about to be executed. Consequently, this jailer said, "My head's going to roll tomorrow, so hand me a sword and I'll take my life right now."

Just as he was about to do himself in, Paul said, "Don't do that! We're all still here." So it was that the jailer, beaten down by circumstances beyond his control, was saved in the very dungeon in which he sought to take his own life.

If you're beaten down, know this: God is going to do something wonderful even in the situation that is presently depressing or distressing. If you're beaten up, like Paul and Silas, God will work through you to bring others to Himself. If you're beaten down, like the Philippian jailer, God will work for you to bring you to Himself.

Whether you're beaten up or beaten down, you can rejoice. Why? Because Satan has been beaten back.

Surely he hath borne our griefs, and carried our sorrows: yet we did esteem him stricken, smitten of God, and afflicted. But he was wounded for our transgressions, he was bruised for our iniquities: the chastisement of our peace was upon him; and with his stripes we are healed. All we like sheep have gone astray; we have turned every one to his own way; and the LORD hath laid on him the iniquity of us all.   Isaiah 53:4–6

Satan has been beaten back because the back of Jesus was beaten. By whom? By the Father (Isaiah 53:6). The Father beat the Son. Why? One reason: to purchase a bride for Him.

The Father said, "I love My Son so much I'm going to smite Him, beat Him, and lay upon Him the judgment, wrath, and damnation that should have fallen on Jon—because forgiven, pure, and robed in righteousness, Jon will make a perfect bride for Him."

Now, if this be so—if God the Father paid that kind of price for me to be the bride of His Son, if He beat His Son in order that I might be healed—then He is equally committed to continue to do good things through me and good things for me.

You who are beaten down today by a relationship that isn't working out, money that isn't coming in, a job that isn't opening up—Isaiah 54 is for you.

Sing, O barren, thou that didst not bear; break forth into singing, and cry aloud, thou that didst not travail with child: for more are the children of the desolate than the children of the married wife, saith the LORD.   Isaiah 54:1

Sing! Shout for joy, you who are barren and dry, you who are beaten down by the circumstances of life, because you will be more fruitful, more prosperous, more blessed than the one who seems to be doing so well in the world right now.

Enlarge the place of thy tent, and let them stretch forth the curtains of thine habitations: spare not, lengthen thy cords, and strengthen thy stakes; for thou shalt break forth on the right hand and on the left; and thy seed shall inherit the Gentiles, and make the desolate cities to be inhabited.   Isaiah 54:2, 3

What are you to do, you who are beaten down? Because His back was beaten, know this: He's going to do good things for you. Don't kill yourself. Don't curse. Don't mourn. Don't moan. Don't gripe. Don't despair. Rather sing out today and say, "Lord, if You loved me enough to smite Your Son for me, I trust You. And even though I feel barren, dry, and desolate, I'm going to enlarge my tent and prepare for Your blessing."

Beaten up or beaten down—either way rejoice because Satan has been beaten back through the beaten back of the Son.

17

Acts 17:1 (a)
Now when they had passed through
Amphipolis and Apollonia . . .

On his second missionary journey, Paul left Philippi and headed toward Thessalonica, approximately two hundred miles away. On his way there, he traveled through two cities. Evidently, Paul passed through these two cities quickly, for they were small, and his strategy was to impact the major population centers so that in due time they could send out their own missionaries into the more remote areas.

Historically, such was the pattern of Christian missionary service. But when news of David Livingstone's work in the jungles of Africa reached the church, mission strategy began to take a new course as missionaries left the urban centers and headed into the bush. While I praise the Lord that missionaries are going to primitive areas, I pray that the Christian com-

munity will not neglect the metropolitan areas of the world, for if major population centers can be reached with the gospel, I believe we will see a renewing of Paul's missionary strategy as national believers in turn effectively minister to the more isolated areas in their own countries.

Acts 17:1 (b), 2 (a)
. . . they came to Thessalonica, where was
a synagogue of the Jews: And Paul, as his
manner was, went in unto them . . .

Whenever Paul went into an urban area, the first thing he did was head for the synagogue. To those with an understanding of the Old Testament and somewhat instructed in the ways of God, he would explain the plan of salvation. If Paul were to go into a city of Europe today, he would probably make his way toward the Catholic church in order to minister to those who, because of their affiliation with the church, have already shown an interest or an inclination toward God. If he were in Egypt, on the other hand, he would head probably for the Coptic Church and talk with those whose association with that church expresses an interest in the Lord, even though they may not yet have a personal relationship with Him.

Acts 17:2 (b)
. . . and three sabbath days reasoned with them . . .

When Paul walked into a synagogue, it was obvious by the way he carried himself and by his style of speech that he was a learned scholar, a rabbi. As was the custom in those days, the ruler of the synagogue would turn part of the meeting over to a visiting rabbi of Paul's stature.

Acts 17:2 (c)
. . . out of the scriptures,

Parents, how we need to reason with our kids out of the Scriptures—not merely telling our kids what to do, but telling them why. Truly the Word is reasonable. It's logical. It makes sense.

Acts 17:3
Opening and alleging, that Christ must needs have suffered, and risen again from the dead; and that this Jesus, whom I preach unto you, is Christ.

This presented a thorny problem to the Jewish theologian who knew passages like Isaiah 53, which spoke of a suffering Messiah, but also Psalm 2, which spoke of a ruling Messiah. The only way to reconcile a Messiah who reigned with authority, with a Messiah who suffered brutally, was to have two Messiahs. Thus, the Jews called the reigning Messiah "Messiah Ben David," after Israel's mightiest king. They called the suffering Messiah "Messiah Ben Joseph," after the Old Testament hero who suffered unjustly at the hands of his brethren. In the synagogue, Paul opened the Scriptures and explained how both sets of prophecies were fulfilled in one Person, how Jesus—son of Joseph—was the suffering Messiah who was crucified on the Cross, but after three days, He—Son of David—rose from the dead to rule and reign forever.

As seen so beautifully in the ministry of Paul, the key to opening the Scriptures is always to look for, talk about, and focus on the Person of Jesus Christ. Whether sharing with children, talking to a neighbor, or teaching a Bible study— the key to opening men's hearts is to look not for principles of parenting or methods of marital communication, but for Jesus Christ. Our faith is not in a philosophy, not in principles, but in a Person. You will be a wonderful Bible student and an excellent Bible teacher if you learn this simple lesson: talk about *Jesus.* Look for *Jesus. He* is the key to opening Scripture.

Acts 17:4
And some of them believed, and consorted with Paul and Silas; and of the devout Greeks a great multitude, and of the chief women not a few.

The Word, the Word, the Word—that's what impacted the Jews in the synagogue. It wasn't Paul's excellence of speech, but his exposition of the Scriptures that caused them to believe.

Acts 17:5 (a)
But the Jews which believed not, moved with envy . . .

The unbelieving Jews, envious of the ministry of Paul and Silas, decided to take action against them. When people bring accusations, almost invariably it is due to a deeper reason than that which appears on the surface. Therefore, if you're working with people, it's wise not to listen to the charge itself, but to seek the Lord concerning the underlying problem.

Acts 17:5 (b)
. . . took unto them certain lewd fellows of the baser sort, and gathered a company, and set all the city on an uproar, and assaulted the house of Jason, and sought to bring them out to the people.

Envious Jews gathered some rabble-rousers to start a riot and assault the house of Jason, wherein Paul and Silas were staying.

Acts 17:6, 7 (a)
And when they found them not, they drew Jason and certain brethren unto the rulers of the city, crying, These that have turned the world upside down are come hither also; whom Jason hath received . . .

"Those who have turned the world upside down are come hither also." When man rebelled against God in the Garden of Eden, he caused this world to be plunged into rebellion. The world, therefore, is not what it was supposed to be, nor what it was intended to be. It's upside down. Thus, by turning an upside-down world upside down, Paul and Silas actually turned it right-side up!

Acts 17:7 (b), 8
. . . and these all do contrary to the decrees
of Caesar, saying that there is another king,
one Jesus. And they troubled the people and
the rulers of the city, when they heard these
things.

The charge against Paul and Silas was treason.
Church historians record six million Christians
were killed in the first two and a half centuries
for refusing to say, "Caesar is Lord."

Acts 17:9
And when they had taken security of Jason,
and of the other, they let them go.

Evidently, the Jews made a deal with Jason,
saying, "If Paul and Silas get out of here and
don't come back, we won't press charges. Send
them out, Jason, and give us money as security."
Jason complied in order that Paul and Silas could
go free. I'm not sure if this was wise of Jason, but
I understand his heart. Perhaps it wasn't the
highest road, but it was certainly understandable. He didn't want Paul and Silas harmed.

Acts 17:10
And the brethren immediately sent away
Paul and Silas by night unto Berea: who
coming thither went into the synagogue of
the Jews.

You gotta like these guys! I think I would have
been burnt out by repeatedly being beaten and/
or imprisoned every time I entered a new city—
but not Paul and Silas. They just kept going for
it.

Acts 17:11
These were more noble than those in Thes-
salonica, in that they received the word with
all readiness of mind, and searched the
scriptures daily, whether those things were
so.

The Bereans listened to Paul as he taught in
the synagogue. Every day, they searched the
Scriptures, saying, "Let's check out the teaching
Paul's giving. Let's consider what he's saying as
it relates to the Scriptures." And because the Bereans searched the Scriptures daily, they have
been noted throughout the ages as being noble.

Acts 17:12
Therefore many of them believed; also of
honourable women which were Greeks, and
of men, not a few.

Folks, the power is in the Word—it's not "What
do you think?" or "What do I think?" but "What
does *God* say?" How many problems would be
solved, how many questions would be answered if
people would only take the time to study the
Scriptures daily. Faith comes not by encounter
sessions or group therapy, but by hearing the
Word of God (Romans 10:17). Faith comes to
those who are in the Word, for only the Word can
affect lives, change hearts, strengthen faith, and
renew minds.

Acts 17:13, 14
But when the Jews of Thessalonica had
knowledge that the word of God was
preached of Paul at Berea, they came
thither also, and stirred up the people. And
then immediately the brethren sent away
Paul to go as it were to the sea: but Silas
and Timotheus abode there still.

"Time to go, Paul," said the Bereans. "We've
heard the Word and understand it. Now, since the
Jews are out to get you again, you'd better keep
moving."

Acts 17:15
And they that conducted Paul brought him
unto Athens: and receiving a commandment
unto Silas and Timotheus for to come to
him with all speed, they departed.

Paul left Berea and headed for the next city, the
city of Athens—the intellectual capital of all of
history, the city of Aristotle, of Plato, of Socrates. The Athenian architecture alone was overwhelming. To this day, the Parthenon is
considered the most architecturally sophisticated building in history. To allow for optical il-
lusion, it was constructed in such a way that the
roof lines are concave and the columns lean inward so that the structure looks perfectly
straight when viewed from any direction at any
distance.

Acts 17:16
Now while Paul waited for them at Athens,
his spirit was stirred in him, when he saw
the city wholly given to idolatry.

While Paul waited for Timothy and Silas to join
him, his spirit stirred within him, for here, in the
intellectual center of the world, were over three
thousand altars and temples built to different deities. The temple dedicated to Aphrodite, with
temple prostitutes abounding, was man's attempt to justify sexual promiscuity. The Temple
of Zeus was for those with a "Clint Eastwood
Make My Day Mentality" who were into sav-

agery. The Temple of Bacchus was for those who enjoyed alcohol. Paul's heart was stirred within him. But notice that he neither mobilized people politically to campaign against idolatry nor gathered a group of people to take a stand culturally. What did he do? Read on.

Acts 17:17
Therefore disputed he in the synagogue with the Jews, and with the devout persons, and in the market daily with them that met with him.

What did Paul do about the idolatry that broke his heart? He talked. In the church and on the street, Paul dialogued daily concerning the idolatry that gripped the city. I am discovering that it's my job as both a pastor and as a father to dispute, to dialogue, and to discuss in depth.

Mom and Dad, we have the responsibility and the privilege to talk to our kids constantly, to share with our kids consistently, to invest in our kids wisely—not so much telling them what to do, but teaching them how to think so that, slowly but surely, they will make the right decisions.

How do we teach our kids how to think? Through the Scriptures. How long has it been since, like Paul, you've talked with your kids in depth concerning issues as they relate to the Word?

In 2 Kings 4, we read that the responsibility of one of the young men who studied under Elisha was to prepare breakfast. But when the other students dove into the meal, they spit it out, saying, "This stuff is terrible. There's poison in the pot." Spitting and sputtering, they were about to dump out the whole thing, when Elisha said, "Hold on. Don't dump it out. Take the meal—the good stuff—and pour it into the bad stuff." They did, and a miracle transpired, for when the good was poured in, the poison dissipated.

That's the key, Mom and Dad: We are not to pick the poison out of our kids' lives, for that will only lead to legalism and result in resentment and rebellion. Instead, we're to pour in the meal of the Word when our kids are poisoned by the pottage of the world, for greater is He that is in us than he that is in the world (1 John 4:4).

Not only are we to pour in the meal, but we are to let the dirt go, for in 2 Kings 5, we see another relevant example in the life of Elisha. . . .

Naaman, a Syrian who had leprosy, was told by Elisha to dip in the Jordan River seven times. When Naaman obeyed, he was healed immediately. He then said to Elisha, "I must go back to Syria, but I want to take some soil from Israel

with me so I can worship Jehovah at home." You see, in this region of the world, the prevailing point of view was that gods were local and could only be worshiped on the soil of the country of their origin. That is why Naaman wanted to take dirt from Israel back to Syria. Elisha's response? "Go in peace. Do it."

"Elisha, what are you doing?" I protest. "You know that the God of Israel is not a local deity to be worshiped superstitiously. Why didn't you correct Naaman?" But upon further reflection, I believe there's a wise reason Elisha let Naaman return to Syria with dirt from Israel. That is, Elisha knew Naaman's understanding of God was very limited. Naaman had been touched by God, had received healing from God, but he was not yet very deep in his knowledge of God. Did Elisha give him a lecture on theology? No. Elisha simply let him go his way, knowing that as a brand-new baby believer, he would, in time, discover he didn't need the dirt at all.

So, too, Mom and Dad, if we fight every side issue our kids struggle with, when they face the crucial issues—the ones dealing with sin and black-and-white matters—we will not have their attention. We see a lot of Christian young people whose circuits are blown because a well-meaning parent pushed too hard on nonessential matters and fought the wrong battles. Consequently, as a father I have to pray, "Heavenly Father, help me to know what issues are essential for my kids. Help me see which questions need to be addressed, and help me, Lord, to let the bags of dirt go."

Folks, our Father delights in dilemmas without easy answers because they make us go to Him. A lot of us would rather talk to a pastor, read a book, or seek counsel from a friend—but in so doing, we are robbed of the opportunity of cultivating a deep, intimate, eternal relationship with a Father who says, "See Me for specific instructions. Search the Scriptures daily, and I'll guide you and show you what battles need to be fought, for I alone know the hearts of your children."

Acts 17:18 (a)
Then certain philosophers of the Epicureans, and of the Stoicks, encountered him.

The Epicureans and Stoics now get involved in the fray. Epicureans were the philosophers who said, "Eat, drink, and be merry. Tomorrow we die, so satisfy yourself sensually. Live the good life. Relax. Take it easy." Epicureans were couch potatoes. The Stoics, on the other hand, were aerobics instructors. "Be disciplined," they said. "Free yourself from anything that is emotional,

Acts 17:22
Then Paul stood in the midst of Mars' hill, and said, Ye men of Athens, I perceive that in all things ye are too superstitious.

"I can see, as I look around, that you are very religious." So Paul began what is unquestionably his most polished presentation—complete with good introduction, applicable illustrations, and sequential order of thought. In verse 24, he spoke of the greatness of God. In verse 25, he spoke of the goodness of God. In verses 26, 27, he spoke of the government of God. In verses 28, 29, he spoke of the glory of God. In verses 30–34, he spoke of the grace of God. Yet I personally believe, as we will see, that this was one of the most ineffective messages of Paul's ministry. While it was his most polished, it was his least powerful. While it had great finesse, it bore little fruit.

Acts 17:23
For as I passed by, and beheld your devotions, I found an altar with this inscription, TO THE UNKNOWN GOD. Whom therefore ye ignorantly worship, him declare I unto you.

Although the Athenians had three thousand altars and temples in their city, worried that they might have missed or forgotten someone, they dedicated a huge altar to the Unknown God.

Acts 17:24
God that made the world and all things therein, seeing that he is Lord of heaven and earth, dwelleth not in temples made with hands.

God is our Creator. "The Unknown God is the God who made everything," Paul declared. "He's too big for any singular temple or any carved altar no matter how beautiful or impressive it might appear."
In Exodus 20, the Lord said, "An altar of earth thou shalt make unto Me . . . And if thou make an altar of stone, thou shalt not build it of hewn stone, for if thou lift up thy tool upon it, thou hast polluted it" (Exodus 20:24, 25). In other words, the Lord said, "If you build Me an altar, make it very simple—preferably of dirt. If you use rock, don't carve or polish it. Keep it simple so that the attention of the people will remain focused upon Me instead of on the altar." This gives me great hope because, although I want my life to be used by the Lord, I am increasingly aware of my plainness, my earthiness. I'm not very polished. I don't know if I'm "cut out" to do great things for God. Yet, according to Exodus 20, these very doubts make me eminently qualified! Paul said,

sensual, or material." The Epicurean said, "Enjoy life." The Stoic said, "Endure life." Neither considered eternal life.

Acts 17:18 (b)
And some said, What will this babbler say? other some, He seemeth to be a setter forth of strange gods: because he preached unto them Jesus, and the resurrection.

Neither Stoic nor Epicurean believed in eternal life. Therefore, Paul's talk about the resurrection captured the attention of both.

Acts 17:19, 20
And they took him, and brought him unto Areopagus, saying, May we know what this new doctrine, whereof thou speakest, is? For thou bringest certain strange things to our ears: we would know therefore what these things mean.

The Areopagus—Mars Hill—was three hundred and thirty-seven feet in elevation and located in the center of Athens. It was the place where philosophers hung out and where the council of education and religion met daily. Whenever a new religious thought was propounded, it had to clear the council of education and religion. I find it fascinating that the Athenians—the smartest men in history from the world's perspective—said, "Religion and education are inseparable." How far we have come from that today.

Acts 17:21
(For all the Athenians and strangers which were there spent their time in nothing else, but either to tell, or to hear some new thing.)

The Athenians endlessly analyzed and continually discussed new things. But, folks, if it's true it's not new. And if it's new, it's not true. What the Athenians needed, what saints today need, is not some novel truth or new understanding. We need a return to the old truths that have been with us from the beginning. If you're searching for some new book, tape, or teaching that will suddenly unlock the mystery of spirituality, you'll be on a wild goose chase. Paul warned that in the last days people will not endure sound doctrine, but will heap up unto themselves teachers who will tickle their ears with some strange doctrine (2 Timothy 4:3). How I thank the Lord for every church family that has over the months and years determined to know the Word and the sound doctrine of this timeless Book.

"We have this treasure [Jesus Christ] in *earthen* vessels" (2 Corinthians 4:7). We're not fancy vases. We're just plain canning jars, boasting not of our exterior—but of whom we have within. If you don't feel capable to share, witness, teach, or minister, you are an ideal candidate because God will get the glory, not you.

Acts 17:25

Neither is worshipped with men's hands, as though he needed any thing, seeing he giveth to all life, and breath, and all things.

God is our Provider—we are not His provider. Any implication that God needs our money to keep from going under financially is completely amiss. God needs nothing. I, however, need to tithe, for if I don't give the way the Word instructs me to, I will become a restricted person—selfish, materialistic, and very unlike my Father. The Father is a giver. He loves us so much He gave the ultimate gift when He gave His Son (John 3:16).

Acts 17:26, 27

And hath made of one blood all nations of men for to dwell on all the face of the earth, and hath determined the times before appointed, and the bounds of their habitation; that they should seek the Lord, if haply they might feel after him, and find him, though he be not far from every one of us.

God is Creator, Provider—and Ruler. He has established the boundaries of all men, the boundaries of all nations. This means that the boundaries of the nations are governed by God. There is a lot of talk today, even in Christian literature, about getting rid of nationalism. "If there were no separate nations," proponents say, "the world could just be one big village, one Spaceship Earth." In reality, however, the Bible teaches it was God who established nations. In Genesis 10, it is clearly seen that after the Flood, boundaries were established in which men would dwell nationally. This is part of God's plan for the world in its fallen state. Study history, and you will see the wisdom of His plan, for invariably, whenever a nation has overstepped its boundaries in an effort to swallow another country or culture, oppression, racial prejudice, bitterness, and death have been the result. Therefore, while there is indeed a unity of humanity in which God has made of one blood all nations, there is also a diversity of nationality in which He has established boundaries for our protection until the time Jesus Christ returns to rule and reign with righteousness.

Acts 17:28, 29

For in him we live, and move, and have our being; as certain also of your own poets have said, For we are also his offspring. Forasmuch then as we are the offspring of God, we ought not to think that the Godhead is like unto gold, or silver, or stone, graven by art and man's device.

Creator, Provider, Ruler, God is also our Father. I'm so thankful that our God is also our Father.

Near the turn of the century, a little boy, walking along the Mississippi River, saw an old man on the bank and began to chat with him. Suddenly, the little boy saw the majestic riverboat, the *River Queen,* making her way down the river. As the boat drew closer, the little boy stood up and began to shout at the top of his lungs, "Let me ride! Let me ride!"

The old man looked at him, smiled and said, "Sit down, sonny. That riverboat's not going to stop for you." Then, to the old man's amazement, the mighty *River Queen* did indeed slow down and pull up to the bank. And as the little boy ran up the gangplank into the arms of the awaiting captain, the old man heard him utter two words that explained it all: "Hi, Dad!"

That's the way it is with us. "God's not going to answer you," say the old men in our lives. "He's too busy. He's got elections to oversee and famines to figure out." Not true. Any of us who have little children know that the cry of our children has precedence over anything else we do. And the same is true of God.

Acts 17:30

And the times of this ignorance God winked at; but now commandeth all men every where to repent.

Creator, Provider, Ruler, Father—finally, God is our Savior. "Previously, in His grace," said Paul, "He overlooked your ignorance. He winked at your idolatry." Here is where many people make a grave mistake. Because God is not judging them or chastening them, they think they're getting away with the sin in which they're involved. What they fail to factor in, however, is the longsuffering of God. Folks, we make a critical error whenever we mistake the patience of God for apathy or impotence. As Paul said, "God has been gracious. But now is the time to repent—to change your mind, to change your direction."

Acts 17:31
Because he hath appointed a day, in the which he will judge the world in righteousness by that man whom he hath ordained; whereof he hath given assurance unto all men, in that he hath raised him from the dead.

In John's Gospel, Jesus said the Father had committed to Him all judgment (John 5:22). Therefore, Jesus is "that man" to whom Paul referred. I'm so grateful Jesus is my Judge because, having been "in all points tempted like as we are" (see Hebrews 4:15), He understands what I'm going through and the battles I wage.

Before he began his ministry, Ezekiel was caught up by the hand of the Lord and brought to the river Chebar, where the people of Judah were held captive (Ezekiel 3:15). Before Ezekiel delivered His heavy message of judgment, God first had him sit with the captives. So, too, Jesus looked on the multitude with compassion (Matthew 9:36). He didn't come down on the sheep—He felt for them. Why? Because He sat where they sat. He walked where they walked. Our Leader, Jesus Christ, has gone through everything we're going through or will ever face. He understands it. Others might say, "What's wrong with you?" Not our Lord. He says, "I understand. I was tempted in the same way. I know exactly what you're struggling with."

Before I can be effective in ministry, I must first sit where others have sat. It's easy to come down on people, easy to find fault with people, easy to be critical of people. But when you sit where they've sat, you have a ministry based on compassion and mercy, forgiveness and love. I believe the Lord allows us to go through hurts, pains, and struggles physically, emotionally, and spiritually because they are what give us hearts of compassion.

For topical study of Acts 17:30–31 entitled "Here Comes the Judge," turn to page 753.

Acts 17:32 (a)
And when they heard of the resurrection of the dead, some mocked . . .

Some will always mock. They mocked Noah for one hundred years. "You're all wet, Noah," they said. But when judgment came, they missed the boat.

Acts 17:32 (b)
. . . and others said, We will hear thee again of this matter.

"We want to think about it," some said. "Come back tomorrow."

Folks, tell your children, your friends, your relatives—anyone you care about—that, regarding their eternal state, it's a very dangerous thing to say "tomorrow." The Bible warns about a hardening of the heart that takes place in people who say, "Later." If you are a believer—if you have already responded to the Lord regarding your salvation—when you hear His voice calling you to do certain things or change certain attitudes, respond immediately. It's a dangerous thing to say, "I'll think about it."

Acts 17:33, 34
So Paul departed from among them. Howbeit certain men clave unto him, and believed: among the which was Dionysius the Areopagite, and a woman named Damaris, and others with them.

Paul left Athens. And I personally believe that the message he gave there is recorded not as a model to copy, but as an example of failure. Why? In most of the other cities Paul visited, a church was born as a result of his ministry. Not so in Athens. Even though Paul gave an incredibly polished sermon, only a couple of folks believed. Why? I believe it is because in Acts 17, Paul never mentioned the crucifixion of Christ, nor even the name of Jesus. Why? Could it be that, knowing he was in the company of brilliant men, Paul thought the coarseness of the crucifixion was not culturally correct?

In church leadership journals and seminars today, the overriding message is that we must be culturally relevant. That is why we see ministries, churches, Bible studies, and witnesses trying to be careful that they are relatable philosophically and relevant culturally. But, as a result, very few believe. From Athens, Paul went to Corinth, and in his letter to the Corinthians, he explains how he came to them.

For Christ sent me not to baptize, but to preach the gospel: not with wisdom of words, lest the cross of Christ should be made of none effect. For the preaching of the cross is to them that perish foolishness; but unto us which are saved it is the power of God. For the Jews require a sign, and the Greeks seek after wisdom: But we preach Christ crucified, unto the Jews a stumblingblock, and unto the Greeks foolishness; but unto them which are called, both Jews and Greeks, Christ the power of God, and the wisdom of God.

And I, brethren, when I came to you, came not with excellency of speech or of wisdom, declaring unto you the testimony of God. For I determined not to know any thing among you, save Jesus Christ, and him crucified. And I was with you in weakness, and in fear, and in much trembling. And my speech and my preaching was not with enticing words of man's wisdom, but in demonstration of the Spirit and of power: That your faith should not stand in the wisdom of men, but in the power of God.

1 Corinthians 1:17, 18, 22–24; 2:1–5

A great church was born in Corinth, and a powerful, impacting work of God took place there because Paul said, "After Athens, I came to you in weakness, fear, and trembling, preaching nothing but Jesus and Him crucified." Gang, it doesn't matter whether you're preaching in South America, South Central Los Angeles, or South Medford, Oregon—wherever you go, whomever you're with, whether it be college grads or high-school dropouts, liberals or conservatives, teen-agers or golden-agers—the key to relating to anyone and everyone is to preach the Cross of Jesus Christ. That's where the power is; that is how we will truly be "Cross-cultural."

I have found that every single question and problem in life and ministry is always answered at the foot of the Cross and in the Person of Christ Jesus. Jesus said, "If *I* be lifted up, I will draw all men to Myself" (see John 12:32). Preach Jesus Christ and the power of the Cross, saints. Learn the lesson of Paul. Keep your ministry focused. Keep your message simple. Point people to the Cross. And they'll find Jesus.

HERE COMES THE JUDGE
A Topical Study of
Acts 17:30–31

How will God judge the aborigine in Australia who never knew the gospel?

How will He judge the woman in New Guinea who never heard of Jesus?

How can He judge the man in central Africa who was never exposed to the plan of salvation?

I don't know.

But I do know that our text tells us He will judge righteously, fairly, and perfectly. On the day of judgment, no one will say, "Unfair!" On the contrary, all will bow and say, "Righteous and true are Your judgments, O, Lord" (see Revelation 16:7).

The Bible teaches that the Day of Judgment is comprised of two parts: judgment of believers and judgment of unbelievers.

Judgment of Believers

The next event on God's timeline is the Rapture of the Church—when the Lord will come for we who believe and escort us to heaven, where we will spend a seven-year honeymoon with Him. During that time, we will stand before Jesus at the judgment seat of Christ (2 Corinthians 5:10). Please understand that the judgment seat of Christ is not a place where we will be judged for our sins—for every flaw and failure, every sin and shortcoming was paid for on Calvary.

"I, even I, am he that blotteth out thy transgressions for mine own sake, and will not remember thy sins" declares the Lord (Isaiah 43:25).

"As far as the east is from the west, so far hath he removed our transgressions from us" (Psalm 103:12).

I'm so glad God said, "as far as the east is from the west." If He had said, "as far as the north is from the south," we'd be in trouble, since there are places where north is only one step away from south. Consider the North Pole, for example. If I were to go as far north as possible—to the North Pole—with the next step I took, I would be going south. Not so with east and west. Although I circle the globe, going east indefinitely, I will never arrive at "west."

The judgment seat of Christ is not a place where we will be judged for our sins, but where we will be rewarded for the things we've done in the name of God. It is the place where all of our works will pass through a purifying fire. The things we did with the right motives—not to glorify self, but because we loved the Lord and wanted to serve Him—will, like gold, silver, and precious stones, be purified by the fire. But those things that were done for other motives will, like wood, hay, and stubble dissipate totally. That which makes it through the fire—the gold, silver, and precious stones—will determine the crowns we receive. The Bible names five such crowns: those of righteousness, witnessing, serving, overcoming adversity, and resisting temptation.

"Why would I want a crown?" you say. "Who cares about walking around heaven with a crown on my head? I'm not into crowns. They're not my style."

Folks, these crowns are not mere ornaments in which to parade around. No, they are what will determine our capacity to enjoy heaven. You see, just as the stars in the sky have different intensities, so, too, our capacity to enjoy heaven will vary greatly (1 Corinthians 15:41).

"But I thought everyone will be completely happy in heaven," you say.

They will, but the potential for happiness will differ. A thimble and a barrel, when filled to the brim, are both considered completely full. However, the difference in their capacities determines the difference in their volumes.

When my daughter Christy was a baby, she loved to pull pots and pans from the cupboards and use them for drums. One day I decided to join her. But although Christy was intrigued and fascinated by the clanging of kettles, it did nothing for me because my capacity to enjoy and understand life was greater than hers.

Paul understood that the crowns he would receive would be significant in relation to the next zillion years. Consequently, he said, "I'm running the race. I'm stripping myself of anything that would entangle me, slow me down, or otherwise keep me from winning the prize of the high calling of God" (see 1 Corinthians 9:24–27 and Philippians 3:14).

Judgment of Unbelievers

Following the seven-year-period we as believers will share with the Lord, we will return to earth, where we will rule and reign with Him for one thousand years. At the end of that thousand-year period, there will be another judgment, called the Great White Throne Judgment, where unbelievers will come before the Lord. Many at the Great White Throne Judgment will probably say, "Okay, so I didn't believe in Jesus. I was a lot better than most Christians I knew. I was a member of Rotary and the United Way. I gave blood faithfully and was a good person morally."

Then, the books will be opened—and suddenly all of the deeds, motives, and hidden aspects of their lives will be revealed. Every thought they've ever had, every deed they've ever done, things they've long ago forgotten, stuff they were never even aware of will be brought to light. You see, if you're not a believer in Jesus Christ and you stand at the Great White Throne, saying, "I'm a pretty good person," the Father will simply say, "Let's open the books." And the Judge, Jesus Christ, will look upon you and wait to hear from you as you attempt to defend yourself.

But no excuse will come to your mind; no defense will come to your lips because you will finally understand the extent of your sin. You will at last realize that you're *not* a good person, for although you may have polished up the outside pretty well, and learned how to behave externally in a way that impresses people around you, at the Great White Throne, your *heart* will be exposed.

It is the end of time. Billions of people are gathered in small clusters on a large plain. A low rumble from the sound of their conversations floats across the air. Suddenly, a woman stands up, rolls up her sleeve, and shouts, "God, how can You judge me? Look at this." And on her arm is the tattoo of a swastika with seven numbers underneath. "I died at Auschwitz for nothing more than my ethnic background and my religious belief. How can You judge *me?*"

Then the voice of a man rings out. "And what about this?" he asks, unbuttoning the collar of his shirt to reveal rope marks around his neck. "I was hung for no other reason than the color of my skin. How can You judge *me?*"

Next, a Japanese woman comes forward, saying, "And what about me, God? I was only a young girl when my life was destroyed in Hiroshima. How can You judge *me?*"

Hearing these arguments, the entire crowd begins to shout its assent, until finally, these three people, along with everyone else who had gone through very painful experiences, join together and approach God, saying, "Before You can judge any of us, You must first be sentenced to life on earth as a man so that You can see and understand what we have gone through. And to ensure that You don't make it too easy on Yourself, You must be born in such a way that the legitimacy of Your birth will be questioned."

"Yes!" agrees the crowd.

"Second, You must be born to a racially persecuted and oppressed people."

"Yes!" from the crowd.

"Third, You must grow up in a working class and denied a formal education."

"That's right!" the crowd concurs.

"Fourth, You will have to champion a cause so just and so radical that every religious organization and political body will be against You.

And finally, You must be betrayed by one of Your closest friends, sold out for an insignificant amount of money, brought before a cowardly judge on false charges, indicted by a prejudiced jury, and sentenced to die the most excruciatingly painful death ever devised by man."

The crowd goes wild—until suddenly on that plain covered by billions of people it becomes so quiet one could hear a nail drop as all of humanity at last realizes that God had already served His sentence.

God became a Man. He walked where we walk. He sat where we sit. He went through all the hurts and pains we do. That's why His judgment will be absolutely righteous, perfect, and fair.

Come to Jesus today, precious people. He uniquely understands where you've been. He alone identifies with where you are.

---

18 Here in chapter 18, Paul arrives in Corinth, where a great work will begin as he gets back to basics—preaching Jesus Christ and Him crucified.

Acts 18:1
After these things Paul departed from Athens, and came to Corinth.

Corinth was an exceedingly wicked city. In the center was a temple dedicated to Aphrodite, from which one thousand prostitutes would emerge each evening to offer themselves to men as an act of worship to the goddess of sensuality. So sinful was Corinth, calling someone a Corinthian was synonymous with calling him a "party animal" or a "lounge lizard." It is therefore not surprising that Paul wrote the first chapter of the Book of Romans—the passage that traces the devolution of man—while in Corinth.

Acts 18:2
And found a certain Jew named Aquila, born in Pontus, lately come from Italy, with his wife Priscilla; (because that Claudius had commanded all Jews to depart from Rome:) and came unto them.

After Emperor Claudius, an anti-Semite, drove the Jews from Rome, Aquila and Priscilla fled to Corinth, where they would eventually come into contact with Paul.

Acts 18:3
And because he was of the same craft, he abode with them, and wrought: for by their occupation they were tentmakers.

Like all Jewish rabbis, Paul had a trade. To this day, the rabbis teach that every man—be they rabbis, teachers, or business executives—have a trade to fall back on should something unforeseen happen in their professions. Paul was a tentmaker, but as he sewed tents, he was primarily sowing seeds as he shared the truth of the gospel with Aquila and Priscilla.

Acts 18:4
And he reasoned in the synagogue every sabbath, and persuaded the Jews and the Greeks.

As was his custom, Paul went into the synagogue on the Sabbath.

Acts 18:5
And when Silas and Timotheus were come from Macedonia, Paul was pressed in the spirit, and testified to the Jews that Jesus was Christ.

It interests me that although Paul went into the synagogue and shared prophecy and theology, he never specifically said, "Jesus is Messiah" until Timothy and Silas arrived on the scene. Why did he wait to make this declaration? I believe there are two reasons. First, he was emboldened by the presence of his friends. Don't you find yourself becoming a whole lot bolder when standing by a fellow believer? That's why Jesus sent His disciples out two by two (Luke 10:1). It's wonderful to minister with another brother or sister. Second, he was emboldened by the pressure in his heart. He knew he had held back long enough, and that he had to share Jesus or, like a volcano, erupt!

Acts 18:6 (a)
And when they opposed themselves, and blasphemed . . .

When the Jews heard Paul say, "Jesus is Messiah," they were blasphemously angry because they were looking for a politically powerful personality who would free them from the oppression of Rome—not Someone who talked about being poor in spirit, turning the other cheek, and setting one's heart on things above.

Acts 18:6 (b)
. . . he shook his raiment, and said unto them, Your blood be upon your own heads; I am clean . . .

The Lord said to Ezekiel, "If you don't tell people the truth, their blood will be upon your hands" (see Ezekiel 3:17-21). So, too, if we're not faithful to communicate to the people the Lord has called us to share, their blood will be on our hands, so to speak. There's a difference, however, between blood on the hands and blood on the head.

In Joshua 2, prior to the fall of Jericho, the spies told Rahab that whoever remained in her house would be spared when destruction came upon the city. Blood would be upon the head, however, of anyone who ventured outside her house. Blood on the head means, "I've brought judgment on myself." Blood on the hands means, "I have failed to reach out to others." Therefore, because Paul was faithful in sharing the gospel with the Jews at Corinth, their blood would not be upon his hands, but upon their own heads if they rejected his message.

Acts 18:6 (c)
. . . from henceforth I will go unto the Gentiles.

This statement would have pierced the heart of the Jews. "What? You, Paul—a Jewish rabbi— are going to the *Gentiles?*" Paul would later write that this was all part of God's plan to provoke the Jews to jealousy (Romans 11:11).

Acts 18:7
And he departed thence, and entered into a certain man's house, named Justus, one that worshipped God, whose house joined hard to the synagogue.

"I'm going to the Gentiles," said Paul. Where did he go? Next door. Talk about provoking the Jews to jealousy! With Paul right next door, these Jews couldn't help but see miracles happening, joy abounding, the church growing.

Acts 18:8
And Crispus, the chief ruler of the synagogue, believed on the Lord with all his house; and many of the Corinthians hearing believed, and were baptized.

What was happening next door to the synagogue was so irresistible and undeniable that even the ruler of the synagogue believed.

Acts 18:9
Then spake the Lord to Paul in the night by a vision, Be not afraid, but speak, and hold not thy peace.

If the Lord came to Paul at night, saying, "Don't be afraid," the implication is that Paul must have, indeed, been afraid. As he saw revival happening, he must have been reminded of the stoning he endured in Antioch and of the beating he received at Philippi. Paul was beginning to realize that wherever he saw external gain, it was followed by personal pain. Thus, as he rejoiced in his heart over what was happening in Corinth, no doubt he was concerned in his mind about what was to come. So the Lord appeared to Paul and gave him the same two gifts He gives to us in the dark seasons of our lives: His promise and His presence.

Acts 18:10 (a)
For I am with thee, and no man shall set on thee to hurt thee . . .

"Paul," said the Lord, "I'm giving you this promise: I am with thee, and no man shall set on thee to hurt thee." So, too, the Lord has given over three thousand promises to you and me in His Word. He has already given them. All that remains to be done is for us to believe them. Consequently, we have a choice to make: to freak out in the night, or, like Paul, to continue in the city. You see, contrary to Paul's typical pattern of making short stops in the cities to which he ministered, Paul stayed in Corinth a year and a half. Why? I suggest he was established because of the Lord's promise. Gang, we don't need to be on an emotional roller coaster—rejoicing one moment and fearful the next. Like Paul, we can say, "The Lord gave a promise to me. Therefore I will continue on steadfastly."

In Isaiah 7, we see another man who also received a promise from the Lord. Rezin, king of Syria, and Pekah, king of the ten northern tribes of Israel, formed an alliance and planned an attack against Judah, the two southern tribes. The Lord told Isaiah to speak to Ahaz, king of Judah, who was fearful and upset about the upcoming battle. "Your response to the promise of God will have no effect on the outcome of the battle," Isaiah told Ahaz, "for God has already determined that Israel and Syria will be unsuccessful. *However,* your response to God's promise will have great effect upon you, for if you don't believe God, you won't be established. You'll be unstable. You'll be emotional. You'll cave in unnecessarily."

The same is true with us. The Lord says to you and me, "In my Father's house are many mansions: if it were not so, I would have told you. I go to prepare a place for you. And if I go and prepare a place for you, I will come again, and receive you unto myself, that where I am, there ye may be also" (see John 14:2, 3).

Like Paul, we can be established and strengthened in such promises, or, like Ahaz, we can fret and fear needlessly. Whether we choose to claim them or ignore them, God will keep His Word. He will prepare a place for us as believers and return for us whether we consciously and consistently ascribe to this or not. But if we don't take Him at His Word, we will live a life of instability, inconsistency, and anxiety—totally needlessly.

"But what if I'm misunderstanding the promises?" you ask. "What if I'm misreading the Bible? What if I'm misinterpreting the context? So often I come across a promise and I believe it's for me—but what if it's not?"

Consider Isaiah's words to Ahaz: "Therefore the Lord himself shall give you a sign: Behold a virgin shall conceive, and bear a son, and shall call his name Immanuel" (Isaiah 7:14). The word "you" in this verse is plural—which means the sign was not only for Ahaz but for everyone. "Ahaz," the Lord declared, "a sign will be given to you—and not to you only, but to all people. A virgin shall conceive, and a Son shall be born whose name will be Immanuel, or God with us."

God still says to the Ahaz in you and me, "I am Immanuel. I am the ultimate source of stability." You see, I might question if I understand the Scriptures properly. I might wonder if what I'm reading is applicable to me personally. I might doubt whether I interpret the theology correctly. But the Lord says to me, "Even if you're not sure if the promises apply to you, I, Immanuel, am with you."

On a trip to Los Angeles years ago, my daughter Mary Elizabeth rode in the front seat between my wife, Tammy, and me. Fascinated by a map of California, she kept busy trying to figure out where we were and where we were going. At five years of age, Mary could barely read. So, even if she was confused about where we were in relationship to her map, or if we were going the right way according to her interpretation of the map, it didn't matter at all because she wasn't driving. I, her father, was in the driver's seat. She could have been reading the map backward and upside down, and it would have had no affect whatsoever on my ability to get her to Los Angeles.

So, too, even if we're not reading the map of God's Word correctly—even if sometimes we feel like we're holding it upside down and backward—the fact remains that Immanuel is with us, and He's in the driver's seat. The only thing that could have gone wrong on our trip to L.A. would have been if Mary suddenly lurched out of her seat and grabbed the wheel, saying, "Let me steer. Let me steer." You see, gang, anytime we grab the wheel of our lives and say, "Let me steer; I gotta figure this out; I have to make this happen," our lives begin to careen and swerve—and we end up wondering why we crash. Read the Word, saints. Saturate yourselves in Scripture, and look for His promises as you rest in His presence.

Acts 18:10 (b)
. . . for I have much people in this city.

"I am with you, Paul," promised the Lord. But where was He when Paul was left for dead at Lystra and thrown in prison at Philippi? As He did with Paul in Corinth, sometimes the Lord keeps us from trouble. Other times, however, the Lord is with us in trouble, as He was with Paul in Lystra and Philippi.

For topical study of Acts 18:10 entitled "Seeing Our City," turn to page 762.

Acts 18:11
And he continued there a year and six months, teaching the word of God among them.

The fact remains that the great need in the church and in our homes today is not "encounter sessions" or pie-eating contests, but the teaching of the Scriptures.

Acts 18:12 (a)
And when Gallio was the deputy of Achaia . . .

Gallio was the brother of Seneca, a philosopher in Rome and the tutor of Caesar Nero. When he was appointed governor, the Jews thought, *Aha! A change of leadership! Here's our chance to get rid of Paul.*

Acts 18:12 (b)–14 (a)
. . . the Jews made insurrection with one accord against Paul, and brought him to the judgment seat, saying, This fellow persuadeth men to worship God contrary to the law. And when Paul was now about to open his mouth . . .

In his own defense, Paul would have said, "I object! I'm not teaching men to worship contrary to the law. I am preaching the fulfillment of the law in the Person of Jesus Christ." Paul didn't get the chance to defend himself, however, because Gallio spoke instead.

Acts 18:14 (b)–16
. . . Gallio said unto the Jews, If it were a matter of wrong or wicked lewdness, O ye Jews, reason would that I should bear with you: But if it be a question of words and names, and of your law, look ye to it; for I will be no judge of such matters. And he drave them from the judgment seat.

"This is not a question of civil judgment," Gallio said. "It's a religious matter for you Jews to figure out among yourselves."

Acts 18:17 (a)
Then all the Greeks took Sosthenes, the chief ruler of the synagogue . . .

Newer translations say it was the Jews who "took Sosthenes," the man who replaced Crispus as chief ruler of the synagogue after Crispus got saved.

Acts 18:17 (b)
. . . and beat him before the judgment seat. And Gallio cared for none of those things.

Whether it was the Jews who took Sosthenes because he didn't argue their case persuasively— or whether the Greeks took him because he was bugging them about things that didn't concern them—Sosthenes was beaten. Later on, in 1 Corinthians 1:1, Paul greets Sosthenes. Therefore, guess who got converted!

Like Sosthenes, people are often brought to salvation when they get beat up. If someone you care about is in the process of being beaten, don't try to protect him or her because oftentimes it is through that very process that people finally see their need of the Lord. If you are being beaten up presently, take heart. Blessing will follow, if, like Sosthenes, you allow the beating to draw you closer to Jesus.

Acts 18:18 (a)
And Paul after this tarried there yet a good while, and then took his leave of the brethren, and sailed thence into Syria, and with him Priscilla and Aquila . . .

Paul worked *for* Aquila and Priscilla when he sewed tents. He worked *on* Aquila and Priscilla by giving them the gospel. He worked *with* Aquila and Priscilla as they headed for Ephesus together.

Acts 18:18 (b)
. . . having shorn his head in Cenchrea: for he had a vow.

When he left Corinth on his way to Jerusalem, Paul got a haircut. Why? He had taken a Nazarite vow to touch no grapes, drink no wine, touch no dead body, and to allow his hair to grow before cutting it off as a sign of purification (Numbers 6).

"Wait a minute," you say. "Why would Paul, the champion of grace, put himself under such bondage?"

Consider the mentality of Paul, this one who said, "I am made all things to all men, that I might by all means save some" (see 1 Corinthians 9:22). Heading toward Jerusalem, the capital of Judaism, Paul was willing to go with the flow and to fit in with the Jews not because he was under the law, but because he was filled with love for his people.

Acts 18:19, 20 (a)
And he came to Ephesus, and left them there: but he himself entered into the synagogue, and reasoned with the Jews. When they desired him to tarry longer time with them . . .

The Ephesians wanted Paul to stick around. Because he was a treasure chest of truth and a storehouse of spiritual knowledge, people always wanted Paul to stay a little longer. Folks enjoyed his company not because of an endearing personality, vivaciousness, or friendliness—but because he shared with them concerning the kingdom. And I'm convinced the same is still true today. How I love to be around those who are rich in the things of God. Take in the Word, dear people. Give out the Word, and you too will find that others will want you to stick around.

Acts 18:20 (b), 21 (a)
. . . he consented not; But bade them farewell, saying, I must by all means keep this feast that cometh in Jerusalem . . .

With a directive in his heart and determination on his face, Paul was headed for Jerusalem.

Acts 18:21 (b)
. . . but I will return again unto you, if God will.

"I will return, if God wills," said Paul. James echoed this when he wrote, "Be careful that you don't say I'm going to do this thing on such and such a day." Instead, say, "If God wills, I am going to do this thing" (see James 4:13–15). There is only One who didn't have to say, "If God will," and that One is our Hero, Jesus Christ. He said, "I *will* come again" (John 14:3). Period.

Acts 18:21 (c), 22
And he sailed from Ephesus. And when he had landed at Caesarea, and gone up, and saluted the church, he went down to Antioch.

Although he was determined to go *to* Jerusalem, and although he had taken a vow in order to fit in *at* Jerusalem, Paul didn't stay *in* Jerusalem. You see, Paul was not always real popular in Jerusalem. The Jerusalem boys—Peter, James, and John—had a different flavor than the Antioch boys—Paul and Barnabas, Timothy and Silas.
James would stress that faith without works is dead (James 2:20). John would say, "Children,

keep yourself from idols" (1 John 5:21). Peter would write, "Be sober, be vigilant because your adversary the devil, as a roaring lion, walketh about, seeking whom he may devour" (1 Peter 5:8). But Paul just went on chapter after chapter celebrating the finished work of the Cross of Calvary.
As you read the New Testament, you can feel the healthy tension between the brothers in Antioch and the brothers in Jerusalem. I share this with you not simply as a historical note, but to realize that even today different people will have different flavors within the body of Christ. There will be Pauls and Barnabases who will comfort you by reminding you that you're perfect in Christ, that the veil is rent, that the work is done. And just when you begin to settle in maybe a bit too much, a James or a Peter will remind you that faith without works is dead, that you must be sober and vigilant. Like the tension on a trampoline, this balance is healthy and important, for without it, we would hit bottom in one extreme or the other.

Acts 18:23, 24
And after he had spent some time there, he departed, and went over all the country of Galatia and Phrygia in order, strengthening all the disciples. And a certain Jew named Apollos, born at Alexandria, an eloquent man, and mighty in the scriptures, came to Ephesus.

Alexandria was the second largest city in the Roman Empire. One-third of the city was Jewish. It was a city of such intellectual wealth that recent excavations have uncovered an Alexandrian library of seven hundred thousand volumes. Apollos, a man mighty in the Scriptures and eloquent in speech, hailed from the learned city of Alexandria.

Acts 18:25 (a)
This man was instructed in the way of the Lord; and being fervent in the spirit . . .

Apollos was not only brilliant intellectually, but he was fervent of heart spiritually. So charismatic a figure was he that Paul would later chide the Corinthians for priding themselves in being his followers (1 Corinthians 3:4).

Acts 18:25 (b)
. . . he spake and taught diligently the things of the Lord, knowing only the baptism of John.

Apollos had never heard about the death of Jesus Christ nor of His Resurrection from the dead. All he knew at this point was what John the Baptist preached. That is, "Repent, Messiah is coming." This encourages me greatly because, although there was a huge gap in his understanding, Apollos was commended for sharing what little he did know.

Acts 18:26 (a)
And he began to speak boldly in the synagogue: whom when Aquila and Priscilla had heard . . .

Who was in the synagogue listening to Apollos? Aquila and Priscilla. Aquila and Priscilla could have said, "We're beyond this synagogue stuff. We're more advanced than this," but they didn't. You see, even though Aquila and Priscilla were Christians, they went back into the synagogue to see what the Lord would have them do there—not to be ministered unto, but to minister to others.

Acts 18:26 (b)
. . . they took him unto them, and expounded unto him the way of God more perfectly.

Realizing Apollos didn't have the full story, Aquila and Priscilla took him aside. They didn't interrupt the service, but they privately shared with him the message of the gospel. I love Aquila and Priscilla for being there with hearts to serve in humility. And I love Apollos for being teachable. After all, he could have said, "Who are you, you tentmakers? I am a man mighty in the Scriptures, eloquent of speech, fervent of spirit. Read Acts 18 if you don't believe me." But that wasn't his heart. Apollos shared what he had, and the Lord sent Aquila and Priscilla to give him more.

How can you know more about the way and heart of the Lord? Share what you already know. I read about an army paratrooper who had completed his twenty-thousandth jump. Asked by one of his students why he got into parachuting, he answered, "I was an infantryman fifteen thousand feet in the air when the third engine on our plane went out. I jumped because I had no other choice." When do you become a teacher, a Bible student, an evangelist? When you take the jump, knowing you are the person on your street, in your office, or at your school who knows more about the kingdom than does the person next to you.

God will give you opportunity to minister tomorrow if you choose to take it because I guarantee you will find yourself next to someone who is dumber than you concerning the things of the Lord. And when He does, you can either say, "I'm not a pastor. I don't have a lot of knowledge theologically. I don't know that much about the Bible, so I won't say anything,"—or you can be a Priscilla or an Aquila and say, "I may not be a pastor or a theologian, but I know more than this guy next to me, so I'm going to jump in because his plane is going down."

Acts 18:27, 28
And when he was disposed to pass into Achaia, the brethren wrote, exhorting the disciples to receive him: who, when he was come, helped them much which had believed through grace: For he mightily convinced the Jews, and that publicly, shewing by the scriptures that Jesus was Christ.

Apollos went on to use his newfound knowledge of the gospel to prove Jesus was the Christ, the Messiah, the Anointed One. Isaiah, referring to the Syrian rule of the people of Israel, prophesied this concerning the anointing upon Jesus Christ: "And it shall come to pass in that day, that his burden shall be taken away from off thy shoulder, and his yoke from off thy neck and the yoke shall be destroyed because of the anointing" (Isaiah 10:27).

Gang, the bondage that people are in, the yoke that people are under, is broken not through our understanding of behavior or through counseling, but through the work of the Anointed One. I received this letter one day:

Dear Jon,

I smoked for thirty-four years and enjoyed every cigarette. I wanted to stop, but the thought of quitting ran chills down my spine. A year ago, I heard your message taken from John 5:8, "Take up your bed and walk." I had no idea how powerful that message was, or how it would change my life. I left the service that Sunday morning, and the Lord took my cigarettes from me that day. I did not need "the patch" or anything else. The Lord is my "patch" and my light.

This person understood the reality of Jesus Christ—that when He says, "Go your way and sin no more," it is not a word of warning, but a word of liberation. Folks, the answer to every burden lies not in techniques or counseling, behavior modification or clinical psychology. The Answer is Jesus. Jesus is the Christ. He is the Anointed One. And the yoke of bondage shall be broken because of Him.

SEEING OUR CITY
A Topical Study of
Acts 18:10

It has rightly been said that Europe is looked over by millions of travelers and overlooked by millions of believers. Such was not the case with Paul, who, on his third missionary journey, went to Europe not as a sightseer, but as a soul-winner. Here in chapter 18, however, after meeting opposition in Corinth, Paul was ready to throw in the towel and move out of the region before the Lord spoke to him, saying, "Fear not, Paul. Speak boldly. Don't hold back, for in this place of moral decay and depravity, I have many people."

It is important to keep in mind that the people of whom the Lord was speaking were not yet Christians. You see, at this point, "His people" were still wandering the streets, frequenting the temples of prostitution, partying, struggling, and straying. Yet in the Lord's perspective, they were His people nonetheless. There-fore, I can't help but wonder what He would say about Grants Pass, Medford, Ash-land, or Jacksonville, Oregon; about the cities in which we live, the schools we attend, the places we work. For although we might be disgusted by them and grieved by what goes on within them, surely the Lord would say to you and to me as He did to Paul, "Don't pull away. Don't hold back. I have many people in your city, in your school, in your neighborhood. They're just not saved yet."

Therefore, I believe the Lord wants us as a Christian community to be city-takers for Him. How? Three ways.

Envisioning

Acts 18:9 tells us that Paul had a vision from the Lord in the night—in a time of darkness. So, too, when you go downtown to the dark areas of Medford and you cruise by the Sunrise Hotel, what's your attitude toward the men and women there who will become part of the millions of people this year who will contract a sexually transmitted disease? Some of those very people are the Lord's people—they're just not saved yet.

What about the high-school kids who smoke during lunch hour? How does the Lord view them? I believe He would say to you and to me, "Don't pull back. Don't pull away. I have many people in that orchard. They're Mine. Many of them think they're seeking some sort of family and some kind of acceptance, but in reality, they're seeking Me. I'm going to work on them and reach out to them, and I want to use you in the process of praying for them and sharing the truth with them."

What about the guys who sit on the hoods of their cars, waiting for a drug deal to take place? We say, "Let's clean up those areas. Let's call in the law." But the Lord says, "I have many people there—people who are doing these things because they're craving Me. I know them; I want to reach out to them. And I want to use you in the process."

Gang, I'm praying that every time you go into a "dark" place—into an area that tends to turn you off, that your eyes are opened and your heart is deeply touched by the Lord's perspective of the people there.

Invading

In Acts 5, we read that the apostles were accused of "filling Jerusalem with their doctrine" (see Acts 5:28). How did they do it?

I believe the answer lies in the fact that one of the Greek words for "preaching" means "conversing." You see, "preaching" is not limited to speaking behind a pulpit or into a microphone. Preaching can also mean conversing, talking with people, and filling the city with the doctrine of Jesus Christ. I have found that one of the keys to talking about Jesus is to share with people as if they are already believers. That's what Jesus did. He treated folks as if they were already part of His kingdom as He spoke to them of heaven. He didn't come down on them. He didn't preach at them. He simply shared with them.

Be bold, saints, as you invade your home, your school, your neighborhood for the Lord. And listen for His voice as He says to you, "Fear not. Speak out—for I am with you and I have many people on your street or in your community who are waiting to hear about Me."

Enjoying

In Acts 8, we read that after Philip shared the gospel with the people of Samaria, there was great joy in the city, for not only did the people of Samaria see miracles, but they heard them as well (Acts 8:6). So, too, in a world that is drifting aimlessly and confused incredibly, when you or I speak truth clearly, saying, "This is the fact about that matter," or "Here's the big picture," miracles will follow because people will see changed lives and hear a new perspective.

Imagine what would happen if five people in your office, in your neighborhood, or on your campus got saved next week, next month, or next year. You would see parents start parenting again, husbands and wives working out their difficulties, people who were once disenfranchised and disoriented made whole again. As a result, not only would they be filled with joy, but joy would fill your heart as well.

"Behold, I bring you good tidings of great joy," proclaimed the angel the night of Jesus' birth (Luke 2:10). And we can bear the same message of joy today to the people in our schools, our offices, our communities. How I pray that the Lord will change us to a greater degree—that the people we once looked down upon or were disgusted with might become part of a tremendous harvest of souls for His kingdom.

I pray that we might envision—that we may see people the way the Lord sees them. I pray that we might invade—filling our city with His Good News. I pray that we might enjoy what the Lord is doing as He drives out demons, heals souls, and works wonders in our community.

Perhaps you're saying, "That all sounds great, but how does it happen practically?" There's only one way I know in which our perspective on our cities, our communities, our schools, or our neighborhoods can be changed. It's found in Mark 8. . . .

After He touched the eyes of a blind man, Jesus asked if he could see.

"I see men as trees," the blind man answered. And Jesus touched his eyes again and *made him look up.*

"Now I see all men clearly," declared the once-blind man (see Mark 8:22–25).

Maybe, like the blind man, you see the people at work, next door, or in the questionable areas of town as trees. They "stump" you. You want to "cut them down." You wish they would "leave." Maybe you say, "The people in my city bug me. I want to move away from them to a place where I can find peace and quiet, to a place where I won't have to deal with depravity, to a place where I can get away from it all." But I believe, just as He did with the blind man, the Lord desires to make us look up to another tree—the tree of Calvary.

You see, Jesus was pinned to a tree, saying, "Jon, I'm in love with the person for whom you have no time and in whom you have no interest. And I care deeply about the person you want to chop down."

Gang, Jesus loves the girlfriend who dumped you, the husband who deserted you, and the boss who fired you. He cares about the kids on skateboards who cuss and swear and wear blasphemous T-shirts. He died for the prostitutes and for the drug dealers. But we'll never come to that realization until we look up and see Jesus on the tree of Calvary.

Join in Communion. Eat of His body. Drink of His blood. And be reminded all over again that Jesus *loves* people. If your perspective on people is a little fuzzy, go to the Lord's table in brokenness and openness. See Jesus on the Cross of Calvary, and you'll see people more clearly. Then you will be able to envision what He wants to do. Then you will be able to invade the area in which you live as you share the Good News of His gospel. Then you will be able to enjoy watching Him work in and through you as He takes your city for His glory.

19 Acts 19:1 (a)
And it came to pass, that, while
Apollos was at Corinth, Paul having
passed through the upper coasts came to
Ephesus . . .

On his third missionary journey, en route to Jerusalem, Paul traveled through present-day Turkey and came to one of the major cities in the
region—the city of Ephesus.

Acts 19:1 (b), 2 (a)
. . . and finding certain disciples, He said
unto them, Have ye received the Holy Ghost
since ye believed?

In Ephesus, Paul found a group of believers
who prompted an important question from him,
one I strongly believe is a valid question for every
believer to consider: "Have you received the
Holy Spirit since you believed?" Keep in mind
that these Ephesian believers were disciples—or
"disciplined ones." So, too, maybe the people you
work with, or those in your Bible study group,
are devoted to the Lord and disciplined in their
walk—but there's no light in their lives, no sparkle in their eyes. Worship is a drudge and witnessing a chore. There is about them a lack of
boldness, a dearth of excitement, an absence of
enthusiasm. To them, Paul would probably echo
the same question he asked of the Ephesian believers: "Have you guys received the Spirit since
you believed?"

Acts 19:2 (b)
And they said unto him, We have not so
much as heard whether there be any Holy
Ghost.

"What Holy Ghost?" they asked.

Acts 19:3 (a)
And he said unto them, Unto what then were
ye baptized?

Their answer was a mystery to Paul, who, on
the basis of the life of Christ and the birth of the
church, believed that water baptism and baptism
in the Spirit were intimately and intricately
linked (Matthew 3:16; Acts 2:38).

Acts 19:3 (b)–7
And they said, Unto John's baptism. Then
said Paul, John verily baptized with the baptism of repentance, saying unto the people,
that they should believe on him which
should come after him, that is, on Christ

Jesus. When they heard this, they were baptized in the name of the Lord Jesus. And
when Paul had laid his hands upon them,
the Holy Ghost came on them; and they
spake with tongues, and prophesied. And all
the men were about twelve.

These Ephesians were disciples of John the
Baptist because they had not yet heard the story
of Jesus.
John's baptism was in preparation for the Messiah. Jesus' baptism was in celebration of the
Messiah. John's baptism was a sign of repentance. Jesus' baptism was a sign of regeneration.

*For topical study of Acts 19:1–7 entitled "Have
Ye Received the Spirit?" turn to page 768.*

Acts 19:8, 9 (a)
And he went into the synagogue, and spake
boldly for the space of three months, disputing and persuading the things concerning
the kingdom of God. But when divers were
hardened, and believed not, but spake evil of
that way before the multitude, he departed
from them . . .

Paul taught in the synagogue until the Jews rejected his ministry and his message.

Acts 19:9 (b)
. . . And separated the disciples, disputing
daily in the school of one Tyrannus.

History tells us that the pattern of a workday
in Ephesus was as follows: People worked from
seven to eleven o'clock in the morning, took a
break during the heat of the day from eleven to
four o'clock in the afternoon, and went back to
work from four to nine o'clock at night. Taking
advantage of this schedule, Paul held classes
during the afternoon, when the building used
by Tyrannus, the philosopher, was vacant. I'm
so impressed with the servant's heart and mentality of Paul. Not only did he support himself
in ministry by making tents, he used his time
off to teach about the things of the kingdom.

Acts 19:10–12
And this continued by the space of two
years; so that all they which dwelt in Asia
heard the word of the Lord Jesus, both Jews
and Greeks. And God wrought special miracles by the hands of Paul: So that from his

body were brought unto the sick handkerchiefs or aprons, and the diseases departed from them, and the evil spirits went out of them.

The handkerchiefs spoken of here were actually the sweatbands Paul wore around his forehead when he labored as a tentmaker. The aprons were not the kind June Cleaver wore in the kitchen. They were the leather aprons of a blacksmith. Why were Paul's sweatbands and aprons used for healing? Certainly it was not because they had any magical power in and of themselves. Rather, they were powerful because of what they represented. I suggest to you that, as proofs of Paul's love for the people to whom he ministered, his sweatbands and aprons provided a point of contact and triggered within the Ephesians faith to be healed and set free.

For topical study of Acts 19:10–12 entitled "The Sweetness of Sweat," turn to page 772.

Acts 19:13
Then certain of the vagabond Jews, exorcists, took upon them to call over them which had evil spirits the name of the Lord Jesus, saying, We adjure you by Jesus whom Paul preacheth.

These Jews weren't believers. They were using the name of Jesus merely as a formula to exorcise demons.

Acts 19:14
And there were seven sons of one Sceva, a Jew, and chief of the priests, which did so.

The seven sons of the chief priest, Sceva, were among those who used the name of Jesus to exorcise demons. Why? Since in those days, exorcists collected a fee whether or not they were successful, perhaps they did it for the money. Or perhaps they were sincere in their efforts to alleviate misery. Whatever their motive, their method was to copy Paul.

Acts 19:15
And the evil spirit answered and said, Jesus I know, and Paul I know; but who are ye?

The Word very clearly warns against using someone else's formula to try to accomplish spiritual victory. In Exodus 30, for example, the law states specifically that if anyone duplicated the compound of the holy anointing oil, he would be cut off from the people (Exodus 30:33). There-

fore, if you want to see your ministry, your effectiveness, or your witness curtailed, be like the sons of Sceva and say, "I think I'll copy that person. I'll wear the same clothes he wears, speak the same words he says, do the same things he does. He's successful in ministry, and I will be too." As seen in verse 16, it won't work.

Acts 19:16
And the man in whom the evil spirit was leaped on them, and overcame them, and prevailed against them, so that they fled out of that house naked and wounded.

I have been here. I have felt naked when, in my own energy, I have tried to imitate someone else. Folks, if you want to be fruitful and effective in your service for Jesus Christ, don't try to copy another's anointing. Instead, seek the Lord. Spend time with Him. Log in some history with Him. And He will work in and through you effectively, uniquely, powerfully.

Before leaving this passage, I want to commend these seven sons of Sceva for believing enough to confront demonized people in the name of Jesus. In our culture—even in the Christian community—the possessed man would not be called demonized. He would be labeled depressed, distressed, or manic depressive; psychotic, neurotic, or schizophrenic. We have diluted our effectiveness by referring to spiritual battles as "disorders." Therefore, before I come down too hard on the sons of Sceva, I must ask myself when the last time was I had enough faith to look someone in the eye and say, "In the name of Jesus Christ, be healed."

The story is told that, years ago, a man came into a small town in the Bible belt and wanted to open the first tavern. Upset by this, the local Christians called a prayer meeting. "Lord," they begged, "don't let this happen." The man built his tavern anyway, but the Christians kept praying. The tavern was demolished by lightning the first week it was open. The owner, knowing the Christians had been praying, hired a lawyer and sued them for destroying his business. The Christians, in turn, hired a lawyer, saying, "We had nothing to do with the lightning that struck your tavern." Now, isn't that curious? The tavern owner had more faith in the power of prayer than did the believers.

That's often the way it is. Like the sons of Sceva, people who have no relationship with Jesus Christ often believe in the potency and power of His name more than we who do.

Acts 19:17–19

And this was known to all the Jews and Greeks also dwelling at Ephesus; and fear fell on them all, and the name of the Lord Jesus was magnified. And many that believed came, and confessed, and shewed their deeds. Many of them also which used curious arts brought their books together, and burned them before all men: and they counted the price of them, and found it fifty thousand pieces of silver.

Even though fifty thousand pieces of silver would have been equivalent to the yearly wage of one hundred fifty men, these new believers didn't hold a garage sale or give their stuff away. They burned it. Folks, don't sell stuff you know is harmful. Be like these guys, and trash it. Pour it down the drain. Destroy it.

Acts 19:20

So mightily grew the word of God and prevailed.

When did the Word of God grow and prevail? When the believers burned their junk. If you're burned-out with Bible study, prayer, or meditation—chances are it's because you need to burn something up. When my appetite is dull, when I'm not interested in spiritual things the way I once was, when I find worship a drudge or a discipline—inevitably I say, "Father, search me and show me the junk in my life that has caused my appetite for You to be diminished." And you know what? He does.

I've been there a thousand times. Whenever my appetite for the meat of the Word diminishes, invariably it's because I'm filling up on the junk food of the world. I'm not talking about blatant sin, but rather empty calories for my mind, Twinkies for my spirit. But when I finally say, "Enough of that," my appetite for the Word returns.

Acts 19:21

After these things were ended, Paul purposed in the spirit, when he had passed through Macedonia and Achaia, to go to Jerusalem, saying, After I have been there, I must also see Rome.

Paul wasn't talking about sight-seeing, but about soul-winning. He wanted to go to Rome not to take in the Coliseum or catch a chariot race, but to share the gospel and touch people. Indeed, he did go to Rome as we will see—although not in the way he expected. He went as a prisoner.

Acts 19:22–27

So he sent into Macedonia two of them that ministered unto him, Timotheus and Erastus; but he himself stayed in Asia for a season. And the same time there arose no small stir about that way. For a certain man named Demetrius, a silversmith, which made silver shrines for Diana, brought no small gain unto the craftsmen; whom he called together with the workmen of like occupation, and said, Sirs, ye know that by this craft we have our wealth. Moreover ye see and hear, that not alone at Ephesus, but almost throughout all Asia, this Paul hath persuaded and turned away much people, saying that they be no gods, which are made with hands: So that not only this our craft is in danger to be set at nought; but also that the temple of the great goddess Diana should be despised, and her magnificence should be destroyed, whom all Asia and the world worshippeth.

The idol of the goddess Diana was unbelievably ugly. Fashioned from a chunk of black rock believed to have been sent from Jupiter, she was a grotesque-looking multibreasted female. Yet people came from all over Asia to worship at the shrine of Diana, the goddess of fertility. Consequently, enterprising businessmen like Demetrius decided to go into the souvenir business, making miniature shrines, which they sold for big bucks—until Paul came to town.

In the Welsh Revival of 1901, under the anointed ministry of Robert Murray McCheyne, so great was the revival that every tavern and pub in Wales went broke. How many anti-alcohol sermons did McCheyne deliver? None. How many tirades against taverns? Zero. People simply lost all interest in alcohol when they got touched by the Lord and filled with the Spirit. The same thing happened in Ephesus. When people got saved, the idol business dried up.

Acts 19:28–30

And when they heard these sayings, they were full of wrath, and cried out, saying, Great is Diana of the Ephesians. And the whole city was filled with confusion: and having caught Gaius and Aristarchus, men of Macedonia, Paul's companions in travel, they rushed with one accord into the theatre. And when Paul would have entered in unto the people, the disciples suffered him not.

Although the disciples saw danger, Paul saw an opportunity to preach.

Acts 19:31–32
And certain of the chief of Asia, which were his friends, sent unto him, desiring him that he would not adventure himself into the theatre. Some therefore cried one thing, and some another: for the assembly was confused; and the more part knew not wherefore they were come together.

Have you ever seen a fight on the beach? It always amazes me how a crowd starts to gather, growing so large so quickly that those on the perimeter don't even know why they're there. That's what was happening here.

Acts 19:33
And they drew Alexander out of the multitude, the Jews putting him forward.

As in every community throughout history, the Jews knew they would inevitably be held responsible for any trouble. So they picked their leading spokesman, Alexander, and instructed him to tell the crowd they were not linked to Paul, but were actually in opposition to him.

Acts 19:33, 34
And Alexander beckoned with the hand, and would have made his defence unto the people. But when they knew that he was a Jew, all with one voice about the space of two hours cried out, Great is Diana of the Ephesians.

When I first read this a number of years ago, I wondered, *How could this be? How could people shout for two hours?* But that was before the hostage situation in Iran, when, nightly on the news, we watched Iranians shout outside our embassy by the hour. And what about our own country? When the Houston Oilers made it to the playoffs fifteen years ago, seventy-five thousand people packed the Astrodome—not to watch a game, not to cheer for their team, but to yell "We love you, Big Blue" for hours across an empty field.

Acts 19:35–41
And when the townclerk had appeased the people, he said, Ye men of Ephesus, what man is there that knoweth not how that the city of the Ephesians is a worshipper of the great goddess Diana, and of the image which fell down from Jupiter? Seeing then that these things cannot be spoken against, ye ought to be quiet, and to do nothing rashly. For ye have brought hither these men, which are neither robbers of churches, nor yet blasphemers of your goddess. Wherefore if Demetrius, and the craftsmen which are with him, have a matter against any man, the law is open, and there are deputies: let them implead one another. But if ye inquire any thing concerning other matters, it shall be determined in a lawful assembly. For we are in danger to be called in question for this day's uproar, there being no cause whereby we may give an account of this concourse. And when he had thus spoken, he dismissed the assembly.

This constable knew that if the Romans had to come in to settle the dispute, it would be disastrous for the free citizens of Ephesus. "Calm down," he said. "Don't do anything rash." And the crowd, at last listening to reason, dispersed.

HAVE YE RECEIVED THE SPIRIT?
A Topical Study of
Acts 19:1–7

On his third missionary journey, in the city of Ephesus, Paul found himself face-to-face with a group of believers who seemed dull and dry, listless and lifeless. I wonder if, at this time, Paul was not reminded of another man who ministered in a very dry and dull arena. The man's name? Ezekiel.

In Ezekiel 37, we read how he was caught up in the Spirit of the Lord and taken to a valley. As he looked across the plain, he saw only dead, dry bones. The Lord said to him, "Son of man, can these bones live again?"

"I don't know," Ezekiel answered.

"Speak to the bones," the Lord commanded.

So Ezekiel preached to the bones. And as he did, something incredible happened. With a great noise, the bones began to miraculously link themselves together into skeletons. Yet, although skin appeared on them, they remained lifeless. And Ezekiel realized that commotion is not equivalent to creation.

If you watched the political conventions before the last presidential elections, like Ezekiel, you saw a great deal of commotion—lots of noise and shaking, rhetoric and oration, banners waving and people applauding. What happens at political conventions can also happen in churches. There can be all kinds of noise, shaking, and commotion—but that doesn't mean creation is taking place.

So the Lord said to Ezekiel, "Prophesy to the wind." The Hebrew word for wind is , which also means "breath" or "spirit." The same word in Greek, *pneuma*, means "wind," "breath," or "spirit" as well. As Ezekiel prophesied to the wind, life entered the lifeless bodies, and they became a living army. It was not when Ezekiel preached *at* them, but when he interceded *for* them—when he preached to the wind on behalf *of* them—that they became an effective, vibrant, living army.

"Not by might, nor by power but by My Spirit, saith the Lord," (Zechariah 4:6). And in Acts 19, as Paul talked to the disciples in Ephesus, he realized that even though they were disciplined, even though they were students, there was a dullness in them, a dryness about them that could only be cured by the ruach, the pneuma, the Spirit within them. That is why he was pressed to ask if they had received the Spirit since they believed.

I must ask the same question to myself and to this congregation. I know you're believers, but have you received the Holy Ghost since the time you opened your heart to Jesus Christ?

"Wait a minute," you protest. "I thought when I opened my heart to Him, I automatically became a recipient of His Spirit."

You did. Paul declared that any man who does not have the Spirit is none of His (Romans 8:9). In other words, if you don't have the Holy Spirit, you're not a Christian. When you opened your heart to Jesus Christ, the Holy Spirit took up residence with you. You have the Holy Spirit. But the question for you, your children, and the people you care about is this: Does the Holy Spirit have you? That's the issue. You see, there are different relationships you can have with the Spirit.

In John 14, addressing His disciples, Jesus said, "The Spirit is *with* you, but He shall be *in* you" (see John 14:17). When did the Holy Ghost come in them? In John 20, when, following His Resurrection, Jesus breathed on them and said, "Receive ye the Holy Ghost." Then He said, "Now that the Holy Spirit is in you, go to Jerusalem and wait for the Holy Ghost to come *upon* you, for that is when you shall receive power" (see Acts 1:8). The word Luke used for "power" was *dunamis* from which we get our word "dynamite." The disciples went to Jerusalem and waited for ten days until the Day of Pentecost. When a mighty wind blew through the Upper Room, the Spirit came upon them and they emerged as mighty dynamos.

The question still must be asked today: Have you received the Spirit since you believed? I know the Spirit is in you, but have you allowed the Spirit to come upon you, to empower you? Or are you still in the Upper Room, hiding out, cloistered away, with a lack of boldness, a lack of living water flowing from you, and lots of dryness within you? Have you, or the ones you care about, received the Holy Ghost since you believed? That's what Paul asked the men here in Acts 19.

"What Holy Ghost?" they said. "We never heard about this."

"You've never heard about the Holy Spirit?" Paul asked. "Then how were you baptized?" You see, to Paul, baptism in water and baptism in the Spirit were intimately and intricately linked. In Acts 2:38, we read that Peter emerged from the Upper Room and declared to the crowd gathered outside, "Repent and be baptized. And you will receive the gift of the Holy Ghost." Peter linked water baptism with baptism in the Spirit. In Matthew 3, we read it was when Jesus was baptized in water that the heavens opened and the Spirit descended upon Him in the form of a dove.

I find it extremely significant that throughout Scripture, the Holy Spirit is typified by a dove. The Spirit came in the form of a dove—not a hawk.

When my son Peter-John was about two years old, we were driving into town, and I said, "Peter, do you know what Daddy does every day?"

He said, "Yeah. You're a creature."

"No, Peter," I answered, "I'm not a creature."

"Oh. You're a screecher."

"No, Peter, I'm a preacher."

Due to the misconception that those who really have the anointing of the Spirit will shout and screech, a lot of preachers are screechers. But the Spirit came not in the form of a screeching, shrieking hawk. Nor did He come in the form of a duck. He's not a "quack." Maybe you've followed the sad story of Ivan Popov, the evangelist who, claiming to have the power of the Holy Ghost, called people out of the crowd and "miraculously" told them where they were from. As it turned out, Popov was getting his information through the wireless microphones of his assistants planted in the audience.

Neither is the Holy Spirit pictured as a peacock, for He is not proud. In John 16, Jesus said the Spirit does not speak of Himself. Therefore, any church or person who is truly Spirit-filled will be one who draws attention not to the Holy Ghost—but to Jesus Christ.

Nor is the Holy Spirit symbolized by an ostrich—with His head in the sand, oblivious to the sin in our lives. The Spirit does indeed convict, for part of His ministry is to keep us from sin. Listen for His voice within you as He speaks to you, saying, "Be careful. This is the way, walk ye in it," (see Isaiah 30:21).

The Holy Spirit is not likened to a vulture, for He doesn't swoop down to pick on you, to pick at you, or to pick from you. There have been people with a "vulture mentality" who have said to me, "The Holy Spirit is moving me to prophesy doom and gloom against you, or against Applegate Christian Fellowship." But because the Spirit is not like a vulture, I know it is not Him speaking.

The Spirit is like a dove—gentle and pure, acceptable and pleasing, beautiful and loyal. One of the few species of animals that mate for life, if a dove loses its mate, it will spend the rest of its days mourning. So, too, the Holy Spirit is loyal and unwavering in His desire to come upon you and to empower you in order that you might walk in a way that is sweet in the sight of the Father and successful in ministry.

Simultaneous with the baptism of Jesus, the Holy Spirit came upon Him in the form of a dove. I suggest to you that's the ideal. There should not be confusion about baptism in the Spirit. We should tell people, "Even as you come to the waters for baptism, expect by faith to receive the coming upon of the Holy Spirit at that time."

There has been unneeded division between pentecostal and dispensational theology over the issue of the baptism of the Spirit. By and large, pentecostal theology declares the baptism of the Spirit is subsequent to water baptism. On the other hand, dispensational theology generally teaches the baptism of the Spirit is inherent in water baptism. I believe that the baptism of the Spirit, ideally, is simultaneous with water baptism.

As seen in Jesus' baptism, when a believer comes out of the waters of baptism, that is the ideal time to expect the baptism of the Spirit as well. Now, it doesn't always happen that way because many people aren't aware of the possibility of being baptized in the Spirit at the time of water baptism. Consequently, it can be months, years, or even decades before they understand that the lifelessness and listlessness, the dullness and dryness of their spiritual lives is the result of an absence of the "coming upon" ministry of the Spirit.

If, like the Ephesian disciples, you have been baptized, but would have a hard time answering Paul's question as to whether you had received the Spirit, the way to do so is so simple. You see, the baptism of the Spirit is truly within your reach even now.

I am reminded of another baptism—that of a man named Noah. According to Peter, the drowning of the polluted and corrupted world of Noah's day was an illustration of what happens when we symbolically say goodbye to the corruption and pollution of our sin nature in the waters of baptism (1 Peter 3:20, 21). Following his "baptism" in the Flood, Noah released a dove, which circled the skies as it searched for a place upon which to set the sole of its foot. So, too, I believe the Spirit of the Lord is circling our world and our lives, saying, Is there room for Me to come upon you?"

This is the point where many believers miss out. "I'm open," they say. "If the Lord wants to empower me, baptize me, or come upon me in a fresh way through His Spirit, He knows where to find me." Noah could have stood on the deck of the ark saying the same thing. "If the dove wants to land on me, he sees where I am." But that's not what Noah did. We read that Noah "put forth his hand, and took her, and pulled her in unto him into the ark" (Genesis 8:9).

Ezekiel 22 teaches the same lesson. "I looked for a man to stand in the gap, but I couldn't find one," said the Lord (see 22:30). Saints, the economy of God is such that He partners with us. He doesn't work apart from us. He waits for an intercessor. If there's trouble in your family, if there's sin in our country, the problem is not with God—it's with us. Where are we? Why aren't we partnering with God? He's waiting to bless. He desires to move. He wants to touch your kids. He wants to save your parents. He wants to work in the situation you see as so tragic. But He's waiting for you to partner with Him. Does He need to? No. But He's chosen to.

It has been wisely said that without God, I can't. But without me, He won't. He's waiting to partner with us. Why? Because He's preparing us for the next billion, zillion, quadrillion years, when we will partner with Him for eternity. Therefore, you can either say, "I'm open," and wait for something to happen for the next forty years, or, like Noah, you can say, "I see the dove circling above. Oh, Lord, I need Your empowering. With the hand of faith, I now receive the dynamic of Your Spirit upon my life."

Precious people, the Spirit is even now within reach. Grasp Him by faith. Draw Him to you. And if you do, your walk will never be the same.

THE SWEETNESS OF SWEAT
A Topical Study of
Acts 19:10–12

Did you hear the news? A cosmetic company has collected the sweat of various movie stars, analyzed it, and reproduced the contents so it can be marketed throughout the country as "Scent From the Stars." Personally, I think the idea "stinks"—yet in our text, we see the people of Ephesus seemingly likewise interested in Paul's sweat as they collected his sweatbands and aprons. Were these people "spiritual groupies"—precursors of the modern-day "roadies" who follow rock stars around?

Greg Eckler, a drummer at Applegate Christian Fellowship, was at the Monterey Pop Festival when Hendrix smashed his guitar over a loud speaker, lit it on fire, and threw it into the audience. Greg, who happened to catch a piece of the guitar as it flew over his head, sold it for thousands of dollars at an auction in New York City.

Is that the type of thing that was happening here in Acts 19? No, the Ephesians were not spiritual groupies—nor were they spiritual quacks. You might hear TV evangelists or radio preachers, who on the basis of this passage, say, "Send us an offering today, and we'll send you a prayer cloth." While I believe some of these men are sincere, most are spiritual quacks who, on the Day of Judgment, will find themselves dead ducks.

If the Ephesians were not spiritual groupies, nor spiritual quacks, then what *was* happening? I believe there are three lessons to be learned from this brief passage that can have eternal impact upon you and me.

The Element of Mystery

There are many passages in the Bible I can't figure out—like the one in 2 Kings 13. Following the death of Elisha, some Moabites were marauding the country of Israel when one of them died suddenly. Wanting to dispose of the body of their comrade as quickly as possible, the Moabites threw his body into Elisha's tomb. But when the corpse touched Elisha's remains, the Moabite sprang back to life (2 Kings 13:21).

Incredible! Amazing! The Lord is too big to be boxed in by the theology or intellectual capacity of finite man. Thus, there is an underlying element of mystery about Him and about His dealings that we cannot begin to grasp or comprehend until we see Him face-to-face.

The Illustration of Ministry

Although there is an element of mystery inherent in the passage before us, there is also an illustration of ministry that is important for us personally. You see, oftentimes, we know the Lord *can* work, but we have trouble believing He will. That is why we find our faith wavering. We don't question His ability, but we do wonder about His willingness to work in the situations that confront us personally.

Consequently, God has given us certain physical expressions to help trigger our faltering faith. This is what I believe the laying on of hands, for example, is all about. When we lay hands on people to pray for them to be filled with the Spirit, or to ordain them for ministry, there's nothing magical, mystical, or miraculous about the act in and of itself. Rather, the laying on of hands simply provides a point of contact for the person who needs to be filled or who desires to be used, as it triggers his faith and unlocks his ability to believe.

That's what happened with the woman who was hemorrhaging. For twelve years to no avail, she sought a doctor who could help—but only lost all of her money in the process. When she heard Jesus was coming to her region, she said to herself, "If I could just touch the hem of His garment, I know I would be healed." So when

Jesus came through the city, although a great crowd of people lined the street, this woman fought her way through the crowd and touched Him. Jesus stopped instantly. Now, although there was nothing magical about the hem of His garment, it provided a point of contact for the woman. And as the faith bottled up within her was released, she received healing that very day (Luke 8:43–48).

The anointing of oil, spoken of in James 5, is another example of something material being used spiritually. As with the laying on of hands, there is nothing supernatural or particularly special about oil. But as a picture of the Spirit, it is a physical illustration the Lord has graciously given to us as a point of contact to release faith. There are those who are so skeptical, so uptight, and so rigid that they say, "No one's going to lay hands on me. No one's going to put oil on my forehead. No one's going to dunk me in water." But others, who understand that faith can be triggered and released through physical points of contact, are blessed and healed as a result of these external expressions.

The Alleviation of Misery

All around us we see people who are miserable—depressed, discouraged and defeated; hurting, helpless, and hopeless—like the people in Ephesus who were diseased in body and demonized in spirit.

I believe the reason sweatbands and aprons are particularly mentioned by the Spirit and recorded for us to study is that they were proofs of Paul's love for the people to whom he ministered. You see, six days a week, Paul sewed tents from seven to eleven o'clock in the morning, taught the Word from eleven to four o'clock in the afternoon and sewed tents again from four to nine o'clock in the evening. It was an exhausting schedule, yet Paul did this for over two years in Ephesus in order to support himself in ministry. Thus, his aprons and sweatbands were saturated not only with the sweat of his brow, but with his love for the people.

So, too, the people in our homes, in our church families, and in our communities who are distressed, discouraged, and defeated are greatly helped and their misery alleviated to a tremendous degree whenever we are willing to love them practically. For Paul, that meant sewing tents and teaching in the afternoon. For you, it might mean making a pie, making a phone call, or mowing a lawn; taking someone out to lunch, fixing a washing machine, or chopping a cord of wood. In the past week, what have you done to help someone else? What have you done to practically say, "You're loved" to someone who's discouraged, defeated, or depressed?

Do you know people who are miserable and lost because there are no sweatbands for them to see—no aprons for them to touch? Miracles will happen, and misery will be alleviated if you will practically love someone through the sweat of your brow. You can be used just as Paul was if you're willing to take your eyes off yourself and your problems, your struggles, and your needs, and instead say, "Who can I love today?"

"How can I love someone else?" you ask. "No one has ever loved me."
Really?

Go to the Garden of Gethsemane, and there you will see One who loved you so intensely that Luke tells us He actually sweat blood (Luke 22:44). Why did He sweat blood? Because He was about to absorb your weaknesses, your failings, your shortcomings. He was about to pay the price for every sin I have done, am doing, or ever will do. It is, therefore, nothing less than audacity, nothing short of insanity, for us to say, "Nobody cares about me."

Go to the Garden of Gethsemane and see His sweat of blood. Go to Calvary and see His sweatband of thorns. In Genesis 3, because Adam sinned, God said, "Cursed is the ground for thy sake; in sorrow shalt thou eat of it all the days of thy life; thorns also and thistles shall it bring forth to thee," (Genesis 3:17, 18). In the Person of Jesus Christ, this prophecy is seen in an entirely different dimension. You see, as the thorns and thistles—the very curse of the earth—were embedded in His brow for me, He carried upon Himself the curse of Genesis 3. Thus, because of the sweat and the thorns upon His brow, the way is opened for me to live eternally in the new heaven and the new earth, where there will be no more sweat, no more pain, no more thorns.

Know today, precious people, that there is One who sweat blood for you. Once you truly see how much He loves you, you'll find yourself reaching out to touch the crown of thorns that circled His head. And once you touch it, once you grasp it, once you understand it, His love will trigger in you such faith that demons of depression and discouragement, defeat and despair will flee. Like the Ephesians, you will be healed. And then you will say, "Who can I love practically? What can I do to encourage someone else so that my apron or sweatband might become a point of contact for his or her faith to be released?"

Saints, I pray that, because you've been touched by the blood-stained sweat of Jesus, you'll find you have no other choice than to touch someone else for His sake.

20

The apostle Paul is on his third missionary journey and headed toward Jerusalem, where it is his desire and intention to celebrate Passover.

Acts 20:1
And after the uproar was ceased, Paul called unto him the disciples, and embraced them, and departed for to go into Macedonia.

Realizing it was time to get moving, Paul embraced his Ephesian brothers and headed north to Macedonia in northern Greece, where he would gather money from the Macedonian believers to share with the famine-stricken church in Jerusalem.

Acts 20:2, 3 (a)
And when he had gone over those parts, and had given them much exhortation, he came into Greece, and there abode three months.

During these three months in Corinth, Paul penned the Epistle to the Romans. Corinth was a very sinful city, and Paul found himself inspired by the Spirit to talk about the depraved, sinful nature inherent in man.

Acts 20:3 (b)
And when the Jews laid wait for him, as he was about to sail into Syria, he purposed to return through Macedonia.

As he was ready to board the ship to cross the Mediterranean Sea, Paul caught wind of the plot of certain unbelieving Jews who intended to toss him into the ocean once his ship set sail. Consequently, he returned to Macedonia, to eventually go south to Jerusalem.

Acts 20:4, 5
And there accompanied him into Asia Sopater of Berea; and of the Thessalonians, Aristarchus and Secundus; and Gaius of Derbe, and Timotheus; and of Asia, Tychicus and Trophimus. These going before tarried for us at Troas.

As Paul returned to Macedonia, he gathered an entourage to accompany him. Very likely, each one of these men was carrying money raised from his own fellowship. Thus, for the purpose of safety as well as of accountability and unanimity, they made the journey together.

Acts 20:6
And we sailed away from Philippi after the days of unleavened bread, and came unto them to Troas in five days; where we abode seven days.

As the entourage headed for Jerusalem, they sailed from Philippi to Troas in five days. This intrigues me, because in Acts 16:11 we read they made the same journey going the other direction in only one day. So, too, sometimes, in our journeying, we experience seasons of smooth sailing. Other times, it's tough going. Some of you may be in rough waters right now. Take heart: It doesn't mean you're out of the Lord's will. Be like Paul, and keep sailing.

Acts 20:7 (a)
And upon the first day of the week, when the disciples came together to break bread, Paul preached unto them, ready to depart on the morrow . . .

The early church met many times during the week, but the first day of the week, the Lord's Day, seemed to be a special time of Communion and fellowship. I point this out because there are those who say we shouldn't worship on "Sunday" because we're worshiping the sun.

I respond, "Well, if you worship on "Saturday," you're worshiping Saturn."
Others say, "Sunday was not when the early church met because it was not until Constantine came into power in A.D. 313 that the Lord's Day was paganized."
"Wrong," I protest. "Tertullian, the early

church father who preceded Constantine argued that Sunday, the first day of the week, was the only day in which Christians should celebrate Communion."

Such arguments aside, I believe Paul gave the best answer when he said we are not to be those who judge the personal convictions of others, since each of us will give an account to our Master individually (Romans 14:4, 5).

Acts 20:7 (b)–12
. . . and continued his speech until midnight. And there were many lights in the upper chamber, where they were gathered together. And there sat in a window a certain young man named Eutychus, being fallen into a deep sleep: and as Paul was long preaching, he sunk down with sleep, and fell down from the third loft, and was taken up dead. And Paul went down, and fell on him, and embracing him said, Trouble not yourselves; for his life is in him. When he therefore was come up again, and had broken bread, and eaten, and talked a long while, even till break of day, so he departed. And they brought the young man alive, and were not a little comforted.

The story of Eutychus, whose name means "fortunate," is one that contains practical application for each of us who desires a keen spirit and focused attention.

For topical study of Acts 20:7–12 entitled "The Danger of Drowsiness," turn to page 785.

Acts 20:13
And we went before to ship, and sailed unto Assos, there intending to take in Paul: for so had he appointed, minding himself to go afoot.

Paul let the team sail while he made the twenty-five-mile journey on foot. Headed toward Jerusalem where he knew he would encounter great difficulty, Paul had many things to think through, sort out, and pray about. Perhaps that's why he said, "Boys, you sail. I'm walking. Pick me up on the other side."
I can't tell you how wonderful it is, and how important for me it has become, to walk. Oftentimes, when I kneel and pray, I find myself "resting in the Lord" a little too literally. Jesus told us to watch and pray (Mark 13:33)—and I find praying while walking brings that about in a very practical way.

Acts 20:14–16
And when he met with us at Assos, we took him in, and came to Mitylene. And we sailed thence, and came the next day over against Chios; and the next day we arrived at Samos, and tarried at Trogyllium; and the next day we came to Miletus. For Paul had determined to sail by Ephesus, because he would not spend the time in Asia: for he hasted, if it were possible for him, to be at Jerusalem the day of Pentecost.

Although Paul had planned to be in Jerusalem for Passover, when it didn't work out that way, rather than getting upset or uptight, he simply said, "I'll try to make it for Pentecost." Blessed are the flexible, for they shall not break! That was Paul's mentality. You don't sense a tension in his personality. Rather, he seemed to be wonderfully flexible as he trusted the Lord to work all things out perfectly.

Acts 20:17
And from Miletus he sent to Ephesus, and called the elders of the church.

In His grace, the Lord has allowed me to be involved in ministering to pastors. Many are the times I've heard people say, "Jon, can I go with you to a pastors' conference? I'd love to hear from the various brothers who will be teaching and speaking." To them I say, "Here's your chance!" I want to invite you all to what I think is the richest pastors' conference ever convened—when here on the island of Miletus, Paul called for the pastors and elders from Ephesus. Knowing he was headed for imprisonment, and, ultimately, eternity, Paul called the elders together to give them final instruction and exhortation about ministry and service. Thus, besides the teachings of our Lord Jesus in the Upper Room the night before His crucifixion, this is perhaps the richest text dealing with ministry in the entire New Testament.

When you're reading through the New Testament, keep in mind that "elder," "pastor," and "bishop" are all interchangeable terms describing the same position. The Greek word translated "elder" doesn't speak of chronological years, but of spiritual maturity. Thus, "elder" describes the man. The Greek word translated "bishop" means "overseer." Thus "bishop" describes the ministry. The Greek word translated "pastor" means "feeder" or "shepherd." Thus, "pastor" describes the method. Although certain denominations teach that elders are subordinate to pastors, who are subordinate to bishops, in New Testament terminology, there's no hint of such a hierarchy.

Acts 20:18 (a)
And when they were come to him . . .

It has been rightly said that one of the greatest abilities in the kingdom of God is availability. The elders had jobs. They had family obligations. They had responsibilities. But when Paul called, they came. And by making the journey from Ephesus to Miletus, these elders demonstrated that the kingdom of God had priority in their lives.

Deuteronomy 20 gives a powerful illustration of the importance and necessity of being available if you're going to be used in service to any degree. In this chapter concerning warfare, the priest was instructed to say to the people of Israel, "When you see the enemy more numerous than you—with horses and chariots and armor—be not afraid because the Lord is with you and He will bring you victory." Right after that word was spoken, however, the captains were instructed to go to the same group of people and say, "Whoever among you has a new house and has not yet dedicated it, a vineyard and has not yet eaten of it, a new wife, or fear in your heart—go home lest you die in battle."

In other words, if you say, "What if I get wounded and can't hold a hammer or power saw any longer? How will I finish my house?" or, "I'd like to teach Sunday school or go overseas, but I'm climbing the corporate ladder and my job won't allow for it," or, "I'd like to serve more, but my wife really needs me, and she doesn't like me to be away at night or on Saturdays," or simply, "I'm afraid," you won't make it on the front line. These areas of concern referred to in Deuteronomy 20 are actually concentric circles. For most of us, our material possessions don't have priority. Our jobs? That's a little closer to home. Our wives? That's getting real close. Our own hearts? Bull's-eye.

If you want to be used in ministry, these four areas must be committed to the Lord. When you can say, "My material possessions, my vocation, my family, and even my own fears and insecurities do not have priority and will not dominate me," you will see the Lord minister through you powerfully. Please understand, this is not a word of condemnation—it's a word of honest evaluation. Many men and women have entered positions of ministry only to find once they're in, they're not ready for them.

The key to ministry is availability. The elders came. It wasn't easy. There was no workmens' comp, no paid vacations. To come when Paul called required sacrifice, and it was difficult indeed. But when Paul said, "Brothers, we need to get together. We need to be instructed, exhorted, and encouraged"—they showed up.

Acts 20:18 (b)
. . . he said unto them, Ye know, from the first day that I came into Asia, after what manner I have been with you . . .

Paul said, "From the day I arrived in your city, you knew what kind of man I was."

In talking to a couple moving to a different part of the country, I said, "You're going fifteen hundred miles away from here. No one will know you. You don't have to live down, worry about, or explain any mistakes and misunderstandings of the past. So from day one, identify yourself as a radical Jesus person. If you carry your Bible to your new job or school the first day, people are not going to say to you, "Hey, want to party?" because they'll know from the very beginning that you're a follower of the Lord.

Parents, help your kids: When they graduate from elementary school and go to junior high, say, "You have a new start. Be radical for the Lord." And when they get through junior high, say, "You're going off to high school. Here's another chance for a first impression. Be extreme for Jesus." At each stage of life, encourage your kids or your grandkids to go for it from the first day. I don't know where we get this idea that we should "fit in" and "relate," because if people don't know where we stand, there will be temptations coming our direction that wouldn't have been there had we taken a stand the first day.

Acts 20:18 (c)
. . . at all seasons.

In ministry and in service, you will inevitably go through various seasons. There is the excitement of spring when you get new understandings from the Word and fresh insights into the Lord. Things blossom and bud; new growth abounds. Spring leads to the fruitfulness of summer, when you start to see ministry opportunities open. The Lord uses your life and you say, "Wow! Fruit!" Then comes fall when the Lord says, "There are some dead leaves that need to be knocked off." The winds blow, trials come, and you wonder what's going on. Fall is followed by winter—long periods where you feel nothing and hear very little.

Early in my walk, not understanding the necessity of seasons, I used to get discouraged when winter came. Oh, my, I thought, I must

be backsliding. I must be doing something terrible because I don't feel the Lord's presence. *In reality, however, it was in the wintertime that the Lord was giving me the opportunity to walk by faith and not by feeling. What are we to do during the winter times in our lives? Worship. Praise. Sing. Why? Because in the wintertime, we have unique opportunities to worship the Lord without immediately receiving more than we give.*

As I sat in the sanctuary at Applegate Christian Fellowship in early morning worship, I saw a brother in the winter season of his life come toward the Communion table and go to his knees in prayer while lifting his hands in praise. A few hours earlier this man's wife had been taken home to heaven, yet he didn't call for counseling. He didn't ask for pity. He came to worship.

How contemporary Christianity needs this kind of maturity.

Acts 20:19 (a)
Serving the Lord . . .

How was Paul able to continue in ministry even when people threw rocks at him? By serving the Lord rather than serving people. If you're in ministry to serve people, you might last for a year, or ten, or fifteen—but you'll burn out eventually because oftentimes, like Paul, all you'll receive from those you serve will be stones and beatings. If, however, you are in ministry not to serve people or to satisfy some innate need within you, but to serve the Lord because of what He did for you—you will endure through good times and bad times, through the spring, summer, fall, and winter seasons of your life.

Acts 20:19 (b)
. . . with all humility of mind . . .

Paul's gifts were great. His abilities were mind-boggling. Intellectually, theologically, oratorically, the guy was incredible. Yet he said, "I served you with humility of mind," because he knew each of his abilities was a gift from God. Humility of mind means truly esteeming others better than oneself (Philippians 2:3). Humility of mind means not finding fault with a brother or sister, but finding fruit—approving those things that are excellent within them. Humility of mind means realizing it's the grace of God, not our own merit, that allows us to know Him and walk with Him.

I recall driving Highway 42 from San Bernardino, California, to Twin Peaks Conference Center, where I was to address a group of spiri-

tual leaders. As I wound my way up the road, I found myself praying, "Lord, I want to be like You when I talk to my brothers at the conference."

I thought it was a pretty good prayer—until the Lord spoke to my heart so clearly that I literally had to pull of the road.

"You want to be like Me?" He asked.

"Yes," I answered.

"Why do you want to be like Me, Jon?"

"Well, Lord, because You're so awesome."

"Did you ask to be like Me when you were with your kids two mornings ago?"

"No."

"But you're asking to be like Me now—when you're about to talk to a group of pastors?"

I was busted. I had prayed that prayer hundreds, if not thousands, of times before. It was a noble request. But my motivation was amiss. I didn't necessarily want to be like Him so I could serve my kids humbly. No, I wanted to be like Him so I could minister powerfully.

Be like Paul. Serve the Lord with humility of mind, and watch out for those times when you think you are being spiritual lest an entirely different form of pride surfaces.

Acts 20:19 (c)
. . . and with many tears, and temptations, which befell me by the lying in wait of the Jews.

Those who were out to get Paul were on a righteous crusade, sure that they were keeping Judaism free from heresy. Paul himself was absolutely convinced he was doing the right thing when he went from house to house dragging Christians out to have them imprisoned and executed (Acts 9:2). This sobers me greatly and causes me to say, "Lord, before I crusade against this person, or come down on that person, am I, like Paul, thinking I am sincerely right, but in reality imprisoning people and hurting them unjustly? Will I see the light a year or five from now and realize what I did was unfair, unnecessary, or unkind?"

Acts 20:20 (a)
And how I kept back nothing that was profitable unto you, but have shewed you, and have taught you publickly . . .

"I gave you everything I had," Paul declared. "I shared with you everything I knew; I held back nothing that would be profitable for you."

Acts 20:20 (b)
. . . and from house to house.

Milk trucks used to come through neighborhoods and deliver milk house to house. Paul was like that. He delivered the milk of the Word one house at a time to the newborn believers. Jesus did the same thing. He talked to Nicodemus on the rooftop (John 3), to a woman at a well (John 4), to a demoniac in a cemetery (Mark 5), and to a woman in the middle of a crowd (Luke 8). I appreciate Jesus so much for His individual nurturing.

Acts 20:21
Testifying both to the Jews, and also to the Greeks, repentance toward God, and faith toward our Lord Jesus Christ.

What was Paul's message? "Turn toward God and have faith in our Lord Jesus Christ." The city of Ephesus was filled with idolatry and brimming with immorality. The culture was decayed. The problems were great. Yet Paul didn't preach against sin—he preached repentance toward God. So often, we try to get people to turn from sin. But that was not the methodology of Paul nor of Jesus, for they knew that when people turn toward the Lord and see His goodness, they will automatically turn from sin.

When Billy Graham was in Portland, Oregon, for a Crusade, reporters tried to get him to comment on Proposition 9, the Oregon anti-homosexual bill. I think Billy hit a home run when he responded, "I didn't come to Oregon to talk about politics. I came to talk about Jesus Christ."

Never forget, precious people and fellow servants, it is the *goodness* of God that leads men to repentance (Romans 2:4).

Acts 20:22–24 (a)
And now, behold, I go bound in the spirit unto Jerusalem, not knowing the things that shall befall me there: Save that the Holy Ghost witnesseth in every city, saying that bonds and afflictions abide me. But none of these things move me, neither count I my life dear unto myself . . .

In every city Paul visited, the Holy Spirit warned him he would face tremendous difficulty in Jerusalem. Paul responded by saying, "I don't care." Why could Paul say this? Because he didn't count his life dear.

"Deny yourself," Jesus said, "and take up the

Cross" (see Matthew 16:24). And what Jesus taught, Paul caught.

Such is the great need of the baby-boomers, self-centered generation that we are, miserable lot that we have become. In the fifties, one of the most popular magazines was *LIFE*. In the sixties, it was *PEOPLE*. In the seventies, it was *US*. In the eighties, it was *SELF*. If you want to make millions in the new millennium, publish a magazine called *ME*. Shame on our generation! We're so caught up in ourselves. Paul genuinely didn't care about himself in light of the gospel. That is why the danger awaiting him had no hold over him.

Acts 20:24 (b)
. . . so that I might finish my course with joy, and the ministry, which I have received of the Lord Jesus, to testify the gospel of the grace of God.

The word "joy" means "exceedingly happy." The way to happiness is to testify of the grace of God. Many people grew up in an atmosphere or in a church that said, "It's your responsibility to pray, to study, to serve." And they became burdened by a weight of responsibilities they could never fulfill. Then, at some point in their walk, they understood that, on the basis of the finished work of Jesus Christ, they didn't *have* to study, pray, or worship.

"You mean, Lord, my sin is forgiven?" they said. "I'm robed in Your righteousness? I don't have to work to try to attain Your favor or merit Your blessing?"

"Yes," answered God. "It's all grace."

"You mean You love me as much when I'm not doing so well as when I'm studying Leviticus and Deuteronomy?"

"Yes."

"Wouldn't You love me more if I was studying Leviticus and Deuteronomy?"

"No, I can't love you any more than I love you right now."

And what does that do? "Wow," we say, "I wonder what Leviticus says. Where is Deuteronomy, anyway?" We find ourselves *wanting* to study. We find ourselves *enjoying* worship. We find ourselves freely talking to the Lord. Our Christian walk changes from responsibility to response— and that's when it becomes a whole lot of fun.

If you want an explosion of joy in your heart tomorrow, go to the person you work with and say, "Every sin you committed last weekend is forgiven. Every sin you're thinking about today is paid for. You're free because when Jesus died on the Cross, He died for every sin every man has

ever done. There's only one unpardonable sin, and that is refusing to receive His forgiveness."

I guarantee if you're grumpy, critical, or weary in your walk, it's because you have not been "testifying the gospel of the grace of God." A funny thing happens to a person who's sharing his faith: He becomes a channel through which the joy and power of the Lord flow. For just as electricity will not enter an object unless there's an outflow from that object, the power of the Lord will not enter a church or an individual in whom there is no conduit for evangelism. When people say, "The electricity is gone from our church corporately or from my life personally," invariably it's because there's no outflow.

Paul was one who was charged-up and red-hot because he was one who continually testified of the gospel. He never stopped sharing his faith in Christ Jesus—with Jews and Gentiles, "publicly and from house to house."

Acts 20:25
And now, behold, I know that ye all, among whom I have gone preaching the kingdom of God, shall see my face no more.

"Boys," said Paul, "this is it. I know this is the last time we will share together on this earth. You won't see my face anymore." And indeed, they wouldn't.

Acts 20:26, 27
Wherefore I take you to record this day, that I am pure from the blood of all men. For I have not shunned to declare unto you all the counsel of God.

"I'm free from the blood of all men," said Paul. This refers to Ezekiel 3:18, wherein the Lord said, "Ezekiel, I've given you the message to tell My people to believe in Me and walk with Me. If you don't tell them, Ezekiel, their blood will be upon you." Paul echoed this principle when he said, "I have not shunned any part of the counsel of God. I have delivered His entire message to you."

The temptation for teachers, parents, and Christian workers is to share only certain topics or subjects. I understand that. Certainly, there are parts of the Bible I would rather not teach and issues with which I would rather not deal. But we need to have the full counsel of God. That is why I believe it is necessary for Christians to know the Bible from cover to cover, and for churches to go through the Bible from Genesis to Revelation—not skipping over any part, but dealing with every book, studying every chapter. I don't want to leave anything out. Like Paul, I want to be able to say, "To the best of my ability, by Your grace, Lord, I've declared Your full counsel—even those things I would rather not have preached or talked about. If it was in Your Word, Lord—we dealt with it." Because the Bible is written in such a way that it contains the perfect proportion of encouragement and exhortation, I encourage you to get involved in a church or a Bible study that studies the entire Word systematically. I'm convinced the way to spiritual maturity and health is to study the Bible book by book, chapter by chapter.

Acts 20:28 (a)
Take heed therefore unto yourselves . . .

Notice the order. Take heed to yourself first. Make sure you're cultivating a personal devotional life—that you're a man or a woman of prayer. Make sure you're one who is engaged in consistent communion with the Lord personally. Take heed to yourself.

Here is a great danger: When you get involved in Christian service, you can find yourself serving the Lord and doing the work of the Lord at the expense of your own personal walk with the Lord. True ministry is the overflow of what is taking place in your life personally, secretly, intimately. So take heed to yourself. Make sure you are personally cultivating a walk with the Lord.

Abraham was a lover of God. On his way to the Promised Land, wherever he went, he built an altar. As he traveled, because the Lord prospered him more and more, his flocks began to increase. So he dug wells to ensure that his flocks were sufficiently watered. When Abraham's son, Isaac, came on the scene, seeing his father's expansive flocks, he decided the key to his father's success was digging wells. So Isaac dug many wells—but he built only one altar. Consequently, his wells were named Sitnah and Esek, or "Strife" and "Contention." When Isaac's son, Jacob—the third generation from Abraham—appeared, he built no altars and dug no wells. Instead, he said, "The key to seeing the flock grow is ingenuity, creativity, and genetic engineering" (see Genesis 30).

That's what often happens. A man or woman loves God, and from that love, there's an overflow whereby the flock grows. Then the second generation says, "I, too, want to be in ministry and see a flock grow"—so they copy the outward activity of the generation before them—but it only produces tension, strife, and agony. Why? Because they're not altar-builders. Finally, the third generation comes along and says, "Programs—that's

the key. We'll have excellent entertainment. We'll have relevant, current messages that, although they aren't necessarily biblical, speak to the needs of the people." And it's exciting for a while, but it's not sustaining. They have to try harder and harder in their Jacob mentality to keep everything going with creativity and ingenuity.

Folks, true ministry starts with an altar-building man or woman loving God and enjoying the Lord. All too often, however, the lover of God is followed by a well-digger—one who wants to see the flock watered, but who has lost the understanding of the altar and a personal, private passion for the Lord. The third generation, the program people, the Jacobs, then come on the scene and say, "We're going to really wow the world with our creativity."

I see this happening not only in churches, but in my own life as well. Quite frankly, I can go through all three generations in one day. I can begin the day as an altar-builder, a lover of God. Then, sometime around noon, I can become a well-digger, saying, "Lord, I don't have time to talk to You. I've got to water these sheep." As a result, in the evening, I find myself thinking, *Oh no. My ministry's slipping. I better do something creative and ingenious.*

What happened to Jacob? Finally, this clever heel-snatcher came to the end of his rope when he heard his estranged brother, Esau, was coming with four hundred men to meet him. After Jacob crossed a little creek called Jabok, he wrestled the angel of the Lord and said, "I'm not going to let You go until You bless me" (see Genesis 32:26). Talk about close contact and a restoration of intimacy! Jacob was no longer striping stakes. He was wrestling with God all night long.

In the morning, the Lord said, "Jacob you have prevailed. No longer will you be called Jacob, or, 'Clever One.' You'll now be called Israel, which means 'Governed by God,' because at last you understand it's staying close to Me; it's wrestling with Me; it's depending on Me that matters."

I've seen churches finally get to the place of being exhausted from "Jacob-ing" it. They get back to the altar, back to saying, "Lord, we just want to know You." Churches like that are used by the Lord time after time because they touch people from the overflow of an "altar-ed" life.

Acts 20:28 (b)
. . . and to all the flock . . .

Take heed to yourself first and then to the flock because if you're in right relationship with the

Lord, blessings will flow through you to the flock of your family, to the Sunday-school kids you teach, to the people to whom you witness.

Toward the end of his life, David was surrounded by a group of men who are recorded as being men who killed giants (2 Samuel 21:15–22). Saul, on the other hand, who had been afraid of Goliath, was surrounded by men who never engaged in battle against a giant. Therein lies an extremely important principle as it relates to ministry: If I want those around me to be giant-killers, I must kill giants myself. I often tell pastors that if they're not worshiping or witnessing, chances are, their congregations won't worship or witness, because, as seen in the lives of David and Saul, what we are is what those around us will become. I cannot stress too heavily the importance of a secret, personal devotional life. "Take heed to yourself and to the flock," wrote Paul—not because the priority is to be on self, but because a preparation of self will allow you to see those around you kill giants.

Acts 20:28 (c)
. . . over the which the Holy Ghost hath made you overseers . . .

People often ask, "How does one become an elder?" In the Scriptures, it is very clear that elders were never elected. In America we're into democracy, but since (and this may be news for some) God is not an American, the church is not a democracy. Nor is the church a dictatorship. It's an oligarchy—a small group of men ruling together, who oversee—not overbear, or overlord—but *oversee* the work.

How, then, does one become part of this oligarchy? I see in New Testament teaching four ways in which a man is appointed to eldership:

First, a man points to himself. As Paul wrote to Timothy, "If any man desires the office of a bishop, he desires a good work" (see 1 Timothy 3:1).

Second, the Holy Ghost points to him. I believe the Holy Spirit points to a man through the fruit of the Spirit, which is love (Galatians 5:22). To be effective in ministry, a man must be a lover of God and a lover of people. I talked to a pastor a number of years ago who, with great anguish, told me, "I love the ministry. I just don't like people."

"The fact is, you're not called to ministry if you love ministry but not people," I replied. "What was Moses doing when he was called to pastor his congregation of three million? He was on the backside of the desert watching his father-in-law's sheep (Exodus 3:1). Where was David when Samuel was looking for the next king of Israel? He was watching his father's flock (1 Samuel 16:

11). You'll always find a true shepherd amongst the sheep."

Third, the sheep point to him. Jesus said the sheep recognize the voice of their shepherd (John 10:27). A man will know he's being raised up by the Lord for the office of elder when his peers respond and receive from him.

Finally, the present leadership points to him. Paul told Timothy and Titus to ordain elders in every city (Titus 1:5).

When these four areas point to any one person—when he wants to serve in ministry; when the Spirit points to him with the overflow of love; when the sheep receive from him; when the present leadership recognizes God's anointing upon him—you can be sure he is being raised up to serve in the office of elder.

Acts 20:28 (d)
. . . to feed the church of God . . .

The only way the flock will grow, the only way the church will expand, is if we, as sheep, are being fed consistently and faithfully—for when sheep are fed properly, they will reproduce very naturally. Thus, the great need today is for people to be fed. In many places, believers gather together, but are never really taught the Word. Consequently, the flock is anemic and not reproducing numerically. The pastors or boards of such churches will often implement programs or techniques to bring about growth—door-to-door evangelism, contests, and all sorts of tricky activities to try to motivate people to share their faith. But they don't work. So then the pastor does something oh, so dumb: Instead of feeding the flock, he begins to beat the flock, saying, "Why aren't you evangelizing more? Why aren't you working harder? Why aren't you engaged in this ministry, or joining that committee, or involved in the other activity?"

After shepherding sheep on the backside of the desert, the Lord called Moses to shepherd three million people through the wilderness. On their way to the Promised Land, Moses' authority was questioned repeatedly. In Numbers 16, we read that Dathan, Abiram, and Korah brought two hundred fifty leaders of the nation of Israel to Moses, saying, "Who gave you your authority? Who do you think you are?" In response to their question, the Lord instructed Aaron to have one leader from each tribe place a rod in the tabernacle along with his. They did so, and the next morning, the rods looked just as they had left them—all except for Aaron's, which had blossomed.

From whence comes authority in ministry or in your family? From the blossom of fruitfulness. What is fruit? Galatians 5:22 defines it as love—love that is joy, love that is peace, love that is longsuffering, love that is gentle, good, faithful, meek, and temperate. If we truly love people, we will have authority to give direction to them because they will see the fruitfulness of the Lord's love blossoming in us.

The story of Moses continues. The years passed and the people began complaining once again saying, "We're out of water, Moses. You've brought us out here to die." In response to their complaint, the Lord instructed Moses to speak to the rock from which water would flow (see Numbers 20:8). Instead of speaking to the rock, however, Moses struck it with the rod, while saying to the people, "You rebels. Must we fetch water for you?" What happened to the rod as he smote the rock? No doubt, the blossoms fell off. Most likely, the fragrance was diminished. Surely, the fruitfulness was lost.

Whenever I beat one of God's people verbally or in my heart, I'm smiting Christ, the Rock of my salvation, and destroying the fruit of His Spirit in the process. Therefore it is not my job to beat the flock—to analyze, scrutinize, or criticize. It is my job to feed the flock—to encourage, nourish, and love. Certainly feeding includes warning and exhorting. But it does not include beating, bruising, or wounding. "Feed the flock," said Paul. He didn't say, "Beat the flock," because there has already been One who was bloodied, bruised, and beaten on our behalf. They beat His face. They beat a crown of thorns into His scalp. They beat Him with rods. They beat Him with fists. They beat Him with words. Therefore, because He was beaten in our place, I must not beat myself or beat others.

Acts 20:28 (e)
. . . which he hath purchased with his own blood.

Use this verse with your Jehovah's Witness friends who doubt the divinity of Jesus Christ. It is irrefutable that if God purchased the church with His own blood, then Jesus—the One who gave His blood—must be God.

For topical study of Acts 20:28 entitled "Shed Blood . . . Shared Blood," turn to page 789.

Acts 20:29
For I know this, that after my departing shall grievous wolves enter in among you, not sparing the flock.

"After I leave," said Paul, "wolves will move in." You can always recognize wolves because, rather than feed the flock, they'll fleece the flock. A wolf in sheep's clothing looks like a sheep, smells like a sheep, and may even bleat like a sheep. The only difference between a sheep and a wolf in sheep's clothing is their diet. Wolves eat sheep. And you can always identify a wolf because inevitably there will be sheep carcasses in his wake.

Acts 20:30
Also of your own selves shall men arise, speaking perverse things, to draw away disciples after them.

While David was in the palace conducting the affairs of state, his son, Absalom, sat outside the gate saying to passersby, "David doesn't have time for you, does he? If I were on the throne, it would be different. Your needs would be met. Your voice would be heard." Ultimately, Absalom launched a full-scale rebellion against his father and drove him from the palace (see 2 Samuel 14—15).

"Not only will wolves from the outside sneak in," warned Paul, "but perverse men will stir things up from within."

Acts 20:31
Therefore watch, and remember, that by the space of three years I ceased not to warn every one night and day with tears.

Paul not only fed the flock—he warned them night and day. So, too, in our own families or ministries: If we feed but don't warn, we're just fattening up the flock for the kill.

Years ago, an eight-and-a-half-foot Burmese python escaped in Medford, Oregon. When hungry, he was capable of eating small animals or even babies. Now, suppose I said, "Folks, there's an eight-and-a-half-foot python slithering around and I know where he is. But I don't want to offend or frighten anyone unnecessarily, so I won't be too specific in telling you his location." You'd think I was crazy! Why, then, is the tendency in ministry to say, "There are some general things we should watch out for, but I don't want to name names or be too specific lest people say I'm not very loving"?

Folks, under the inspiration of the Holy Ghost, Paul named those who were poisoning the people of God (1 Timothy 1:20). So, too, although we must not be judgmental for condemnation, we must be analytical for the purpose of protection and correction in order that those new in the faith won't get swallowed by the Enemy.

Acts 20:32 (a)
And now, brethren, I commend you to God . . .

Knowing he would never again see these men this side of heaven, Paul said, "I commend you to God." The same is true of our kids and the people we serve. We feed, warn, and love them. But ultimately, we must say, "God, they're Yours."

Acts 20:32 (b)
. . . and to the word of his grace, which is able to build you up . . .

Grace is what will build you up. So often in ministry or service, parenting or discipling, we tend to emphasize what man should do rather than what God has done. In Ephesians 4—6, Paul stressed the behavior of the believer—but not until after he had spent chapters 1—3 telling us we're blessed with all spiritual blessings in heavenly places, that we're in Christ, that we have been adopted and sanctified. Paul spoke of what God had done before he spoke of what man should do.

I can say to my kids or to the people to whom I'm ministering, "Read your Bible. Worship. Pray. And they'll do it out of obligation for a day or two. But once they begin to understand that they are loved unconditionally, that they are in Christ, that their sin, past, present, and future, is washed away—they will worship and pray, witness and serve not because they *have* to but because they *get* to.

Acts 20:32 (c)
. . . and to give you an inheritance among all them which are sanctified.

The inheritance waiting for you is incredibly wonderful. Don't allow anything to obscure that fact. Paul said to these men whom he knew would go through difficulties, troubles, and challenges, "Remember the inheritance that is yours. Keep focused. Keep centered on the eternal."

Acts 20:33
I have coveted no man's silver, or gold, or apparel.

At one point, Paul did covet (Romans 7:7). At this point, however, he says, "I have coveted after no man's gold, silver, or apparel." It has been rightly said that the happiest person is not the one who has the most, but the one who needs the least.

The young bride flashed her diamond ring at the party. It was the biggest rock anyone in attendance had seen. "Wow," they said. "Where did you get that diamond?"

"This is the famous Rabinowitz diamond, the second largest diamond in the world," she said. "But it comes with a curse."

"A curse?" asked her friends.

"Yes," she answered. "It comes with Mr. Rabinowitz."

Aren't we discovering that things that are flashy and shiny come with a curse? Once you get them, you've got to maintain them, worry about them, and keep track of them. Paul was free from the curse that accompanies material possessions because they were no longer important to him.

Acts 20:34
Yea, ye yourselves know, that these hands have ministered unto my necessities, and to them that were with me.

Paul didn't want gifts for himself. He wanted fruit for the believers. You see, whenever you give to a ministry—whether in service, finances, or prayer—whatever the Lord does through that ministry goes to your account eternally. That's why giving is such a good deal!

Acts 20:35
I have shewed you all things, how that so labouring ye ought to support the weak, and to remember the words of the Lord Jesus, how he said, It is more blessed to give than to receive.

I have heard preachers use this text to say, "Since it is more blessed to give than to receive, give to my ministry and you'll be blessed." But, folks, keep the context of this verse in mind. Paul was giving *of* himself, not asking *for* himself. To the rich young ruler, Jesus said, "You're in bondage to material things. Go sell all your goods and give to the poor." He didn't say, "Give to Me." He said, "Give to the poor" (see Matthew 19:21).

Does that mean you should give your tithe to the poor? No, because the tithe is not yours to give—it's God's. When people say, "I'm not going to bring my tithe to church. I have a Jesus Fund and I'll just give wherever I want," I say, "Hold on. The tithe isn't something for you to figure out what to do with or how to spend—it's God's. Now, if you want to give to the poor above and beyond your tithe, terrific! You'll be blessed indeed. Just make sure it's your money, however—not God's."

Studies have shown that if Christians would tithe, within two years, every church facility in the world would be paid for, every ministry would be functional and out of debt, every Christian University, Bible school, and training center would be funded, and every hungry person would be fed. People wonder why ministries struggle or why people starve—but if Christians would be obedient to God's principle of the tithe, incredible power would be released through the church. In verse 33, Paul said, "I have not coveted." In verse 35, he said, "It is more blessed to give than to receive." I believe the proximity of these two statements is more than coincidental because the divine prescription for the disease of coveting is giving.

Look at Abraham. After he rescued Lot and Lot's servants, the king of Sodom offered him anything he wanted. Abraham looked him in the eye and said, "I won't take even a shoelace from you" (Genesis 14:23). Why was Abraham not enticed by the offer of the king of Sodom? Because he had met the King of Salem. You see, before the king of Sodom came to Abraham, another King appeared to him—Melchizedek, the King of Salem, whose name means "King of Righteousness." Melchizedek was a Christophany—an Old Testament appearance of Jesus Christ. And Abraham fell before Him and paid tithes to Him (Genesis 14:20).

The principle is practical and powerful. That is, because Abraham paid his tithes to the Lord, he could look the world in the eye and say, "I'm not interested in what you have to offer." How do you defeat greediness in your own life? Give to the Lord, and, like Abraham and Paul, you will covet no more.

Acts 20:36–38
And when he had thus spoken, he kneeled down, and prayed with them all. And they all wept sore, and fell on Paul's neck, and kissed him, Sorrowing most of all for the words which he spake, that they should see his face no more. And they accompanied him unto the ship.

Paul finished his message, and with tears and prayer, he went on his way.

THE DANGER OF DROWSINESS
A Topical Study of
Acts 20:7–12

After reading this text, I wonder if it would be wise to print this label on the bottom of our bulletin: "Warning! The Supreme Surgeon General has declared sleeping in church to be hazardous to your health." I think our brother, Eutychus, would wholeheartedly agree!

I really feel for Eutychus. His story in the original Greek indicates that, although he fought sleep, sleep won—which is understandable, considering that Sunday being a workday like any other, Eutychus had very likely put in a full day of work before coming to church.

A precious brother who works unbelievably long hours once told me that, because he came during his breaks or at the end of a shift, sometimes, like Eutychus, he found himself nodding off during Bible study at Applegate Christian Fellowship.

"What you do is amazing," I said. "Not many men would make the effort you do. Therefore, know that even though sometimes you might doze a bit, the Lord sees your heart. Remember Samuel? He fell asleep in the temple and the Lord spoke to him three times—even as he slept!" (see 1 Samuel 3).

And I believe the Lord can speak to each of us as well—whether we're wide-awake, or dozing off—through the story of Eutychus. Following are three lessons we can learn from him, as his situation relates to the very real danger of our own spiritual drowsiness.

The Reason for Drowsiness

And upon the first day of the week, when the disciples came together to break bread, Paul preached unto them, ready to depart on the morrow; and continued his speech until midnight. And there were many lights in the upper chamber, where they were gathered together.   Acts 20:7, 8

The reason there were many lights in the room where Paul was preaching was because of the rumors circulating throughout the community concerning the early church. Christians were accused of sexual promiscuity because they always talked about agape love. They were accused of cannibalism because they talked about eating the body of Jesus and drinking His blood in Communion. Consequently, when the early church met together, they lit their meeting halls very brightly in order that anyone walking by could clearly see what was going on.

Inherent within people is the tendency to think the worst. . . .

The hostess of a party called the liquor store. "My name is Susie Smith," she said. "Please send me a case of vodka as soon as possible."

Unbeknownst to her, however, she had mistakenly dialed not the liquor store, but her minister.

"This is Reverend Jones," said the voice on the other end.

"Reverend Jones!" she said incredulously. "What are *you* doing at the liquor store?"

So often we impose whatever sin or temptation we struggle with upon others. To the pure, all things are pure, but to the depraved, suspicion and rumors abound (Titus 1:15). So the Christians lit lamps. And because Eutychus was in this room with warm lights and a bunch of bodies—this room wherein the oxygen supply decreased as the temperature rose—it is no wonder his eyelids began to feel heavy.

So, too, if the only time we're letting our light shine, if the only time we're singing forth praise or speaking out testimony, is in a place where there's lots of light and a whole bunch of Christians, we will become spiritually drowsy. If church is the only place you vocally express your belief in Jesus Christ, the only place wherein you seriously think about the Word, you will begin to doze in your pew. On the other hand, if you really believe you will be called upon to practice what you hear preached, you will remain wide-eyed and on the edge of your seat.

If you knew today you would be expected tomorrow to share this passage with some guys at work, your family, some kids on your campus, or some cultists at your door—you would have pencil and paper in hand, an alert mind, and an eager heart. You would say, "If I'm going to give this out, I better get it down."

But so often, we say instead, "Ho, hum. There are lots of Christians here. I'll just sit on this ledge here in the back row . . . ZZZ." It's no wonder we feel lethargic at that point, because spiritual drowsiness is exactly proportionate to our failure to give out what we take in.

In Israel, there are two major bodies of water, both fed by the Jordan River: the Sea of Galilee and the Dead Sea. While the Sea of Galilee teems with life, not even single-celled beings can survive in the Dead Sea. Why? Because, although the Jordan River flows into both, it only flows out of the Sea of Galilee. Thus, the Dead Sea is devoid of life because there's input but no outflow.

You and I will either be like the Sea of Galilee, giving out the Word, and teeming with life as a result—or we will be like the Dead Sea, taking in but, because we don't give out, dozing in the back row.

The Result of Drowsiness

And there sat in a window a certain young man named Eutychus, being fallen into a deep sleep: and as Paul was long preaching, he sunk down with sleep, and fell down from the third loft, and was taken up dead.   Acts 20:9

Now, while it is possible that a drowsy Eutychus may have moved to the back row and sat near the window in order to stay awake, over the years, I've seen many people who, although at one time, were in the front row and excited about Bible study, start moving toward the back and gradually lose all interest in the things of the Lord.

Believers are like automobiles, folks. When we start to miss, we eventually stop running altogether. When people start pulling away from Bible study, from prayer, from Communion, from corporate expression, they weaken their walk without exception.

"Do not forsake the assembling of yourselves together," said the writer to the Hebrews (see Hebrews 10:25). Those who do so are in danger of experiencing what happened to Eutychus: moving toward the back, then falling out altogether.

The Recovery from Drowsiness

And Paul went down, and fell on him, and embracing him said, Trouble not yourselves; for his life is in him. When he therefore was come up again, and had broken bread, and eaten, and talked a long while, even till break of day, so he departed. And they brought the young man alive, and were not a little comforted.   Acts 20:10–12

Perhaps you are working with someone like Eutychus who is spiritually drowsy, or even dead. It might be your husband or your brother, your high-school son or your next-door neighbor. This person, who was once on fire, is now like Eutychus. He moved to the back, fell off the ledge, and now he's dead.

How are you to minister to him? Our text gives the answer. We read that Paul didn't *come* down on Eutychus, but *went* down to Eutychus. I believe the account in 2 Kings chapter 4 sheds light on the reason Paul did this. . . .

Because Elisha the prophet had been lovingly tended by a Shunammite woman who had prepared a room in her house for him to stay whenever he passed through the area, Elisha promised her that, although she was barren and her husband was old, she would bear a son. Sure enough, she conceived and gave birth to a son. A few years later, while working with his dad in the field, the child fell down, crying, "My head, my head." The father ordered servants to take the boy to his mother, but, although she put his head on her lap and comforted him, he died. The Shunammite woman then took her son's body into a room to prepare him not for burial, but for a miracle. "Saddle up the donkey," she ordered her servants. "We're going to get Elisha." Finding the prophet at Mount Carmel, she grabbed him by the feet and said, "You deceived me, Elisha. You allowed this son to come into our family, and now he's dead."

Elisha responded by ordering his servant, Gehazi, to take his staff and lay it upon the boy. But that wasn't enough for the wise and wonderful Shunammite woman. "I'm not going back, Elisha," she said, "until you come with me." So while Gehazi took the staff and went quickly, Elisha and the Shunammite woman followed a little more slowly. When Gehazi reached the woman's home, he laid the staff on the boy, but nothing happened. When Elisha arrived, however, he himself lay on the boy—mouth to mouth, eye to eye, hand to hand. And as he did so, Elisha felt warmth in the boy's body.

Mom, Dad, fellow brother, minister, sister—when someone has fallen off the third story because of his own spiritual lethargy or apathy, the tendency is for you and me to say, "Let's call the church and get the staff on the job," or, "Let's send the rod of rigidity. Let's preach at him." But, as Gehazi found, neither will bring life.

The key is for us to be like Elisha—to go hand to hand, mouth to mouth, eye to eye—to do what Paul did: to embrace the person and say, "I love you unconditionally. I care about you. I'm here for you. I will stand by you."

It's *love*, gang, not delegation or doctrine, that will bring about resurrection. We need to go hand to hand, mouth to mouth, eye to eye with folks who have fallen. And what will happen? Like Elisha, we'll feel some warmth, sense a stirring, hear some sneezing (a clearing of the system), see an opening of the eye—and finally they will sit up.

You might be saying, "That *sounds* great, but you don't understand my situation. No one has ever even sent his staff to me, much less pressed in to me personally. How can I do for someone else that which has never been done for me?"

"Oh, but there *is* One," I answer, "who came and pressed in to you in a way we cannot even begin to understand. God Himself came down not on you, but came down to you in the Person of Jesus Christ. His hands were pressed to the Cross for you and me. His mouth cried, "Father forgive them." His blood, sweat, and tear-filled eyes said, "I love you." Therefore, it is *His* love that motivates us to love others (2 Corinthians 5:14). In *His* love may you find the Eutychuses—those who were once doing well, but who moved to the back and fell off the ledge—and come down not *on* them, but *to* them.

May God grant us the grace to be ministers of resurrection. May He give us opportunity to touch lives this week. May He use us greatly.

SHED BLOOD . . . SHARED BLOOD
A Topical Study of
Acts 20:28

W e who teach the Bible are often accused of preaching a bloody religion. To such a charge, I proudly plead guilty. Hebrews 4:12 declares that the Word of God is living. Therefore, we should not be surprised that blood pulsates through its pages and courses through its chapters. Truly, there is a scarlet thread connecting every verse, every chapter, every book in the Bible. That thread is the blood of the Lamb. Five times more often than he talked about the death of Christ, Paul talked about the blood of Christ. Three times more often than he spoke of the Cross of Christ, he spoke of the blood of Christ.

There are those who say the emphasis Paul placed on the blood is a throwback to ancient mythology or to present-day superstition. They cite Homer, the Greek poet, who wrote of ghosts drinking the blood of men in order to regain their lives. They point to the practice that took place in the days of the Roman gladiators wherein those who were diseased—particularly with epilepsy—would be brought down to the floor of the Coliseum to lap up the blood that was shed because it was believed to have healing powers. They refer to the tribes in Africa who established peace treaties through the drinking of the blood of cows or goats.

Those who criticize you and me as Bible-believers say, "The emphasis on the blood is nothing more than a throwback to mythology or superstition. It has no more validity than the antiquated belief that the fourth finger of the left hand is the apex of the circulatory system—which is why we wear our wedding ring on that finger to this day."

"No way," I reply. "The emphasis on the blood is not a remnant of ancient mythology. It is relevant in light of modern biology." Four thousand years ago, God said that the life is in the blood (Leviticus 17:11). And what Moses declared under inspiration four millennia ago, science confirms today, for truly the life is in the blood. If you're an average person, five quarts of blood are presently coursing through your body. For what reason? There are three reasons—all of which apply to you not only physiologically, but also spiritually and eternally.

Your blood provides nourishment to sustain you.

The five quarts of blood within you nourish every one of the one hundred trillion cells in your body. How? In every microliter of blood, there are five million red blood cells that function as tiny supply rafts. They load up oxygen, potassium, calcium, and amino acids before beginning a journey in which they travel sixty thousand miles of veins, arteries, and capillaries every twenty-three seconds.

Your blood produces cleansing that invigorates you.

Not only do the red blood cells deliver nourishment, but they also pick up waste material. As they give out the goodies, they also pick up the garbage—never confusing the two. Surely the psalmist was right when he said we are fearfully and wonderfully made (Psalm 139:14).

What would happen if the red blood cells shut down—if there was a garbage strike in your body? To find out, put a tourniquet around your arm, and watch what happens when the toxins begin to build up: First, your arm will get a tingly feeling. Then it will turn blue. Remove the tourniquet. Blood will rush in; the toxins will be carried out. And you will have use of your arm again—all because of the cleansing power of your blood.

Your blood prevents infection from destroying you.

In every micro-liter of blood not only are there five million red blood cells— there are also three hundred thousand platelets. What do the platelets do? When your body gets cut, the platelets rush into the injured area and melt into a weblike substance called fibrinogen. When the red blood cells come cruising by, they crash into the fibrinogen, causing a traffic jam, which we call coagulation. The amazing thing is that the platelets must act with perfect precision because if too many gathered together and caused too major a traffic jam, your arteries would become completely clogged, and you would die immediately.

Not only are there three hundred thousand platelets in every micro-liter of blood, but there are seven thousand white blood cells. What do the white blood cells do? The white blood cells make up an army numbering twenty-five billion—with twenty-five billion reserves—which gathers around any virus, germ, or invader that threatens you. White blood cells actually die in battle—which is what constitutes pus. The white blood cell cannot do battle, however, against a virus or germ until the spikes, the strange protrusions that are on every virus, are first covered and softened.

What does this? Antibodies. Before the white cells begin their attack, an antibody specifically designed to fit the spikes of the invading virus covers the virus and blunts its spikes, thereby allowing the white blood cells to do their work. Consequently, you are vulnerable to whatever disease for which you don't have antibodies—which is the problem with the AIDS virus. The AIDS virus actually mutates—changes its spikes—making it very difficult if not impossible for scientists to come up with an antibody. As you study history, you realize that the greatest devastation to mankind has come not through famine or even war—but through disease. Because it takes the human body at least eight hours to diagnose infection and manufacture antibodies, before the discovery of vaccines, a single disease had the potential to destroy entire civilizations.

Edward Jenner and Louis Pasteur did work of great significance when they injected the antibody-laden pus of an infected person—or, in the case of smallpox, a cow—into a person who was not yet infected. In 1802, smallpox threatened to virtually wipe out the entire population of Columbia. With Jenner's work fairly accepted throughout Europe, it was decided that smallpox vaccine should be sent from Spain to Columbia. However, there was a problem: Because the vaccine lasted only a few days, it would die during the journey across the Atlantic. The solution? The Spaniards chose twenty boys who would sail to Columbia and who would be infected one at a time with smallpox, thereby keeping the vaccine alive with their own bodies. The plan worked. The ship carrying the boys arrived in Columbia just as the twentieth boy was showing symptoms of the dreaded disease. King Carlos called the boys "Overcomers" because they were the means by which the entire civilization of Columbia was spared the deadly scourge of smallpox.

"That's great," you say. "But what does any of this have to do with me?" If you're a believer, it has everything to do with you. God told us that the life is in the blood. Following are three things His blood will do in your life.

His blood provides nourishment to sustain you.

Jesus said, "He who does not eat My flesh and drink My blood has no part with me, no life from Me" (see John 6:53). It is no wonder that Scripture goes on to say that, because of this, many were offended in Him and followed Him no more (John 6:66). After all, although the Jews were accustomed to eating the meat of the sacrifices they brought to the temple, they were forbidden to eat the blood (Leviticus 17: 10). Thus, it must have been highly offensive to hear this Rabbi from Galilee say, "Drink My blood."

Yet, although it remains offensive to many people today, partaking of His blood in Communion is powerful and essential. For even as the blood in my body consistently circulates to nourish each part of my body, so, too, at His table, the blood that He shed for me can be shared by me to provide nourishment to me. You see, whenever I want, I can say, "I need to be nourished by You right now, Lord. I'm tired. I'm weary. I'm weak. Infuse Your life in me through Your blood." And in so doing, I am, in a sense, born again—again.

Cut yourself off from the life flow of His blood, and you will become weak and sick and dead spiritually just as surely as you would if you were to cut off your blood supply physiologically. I'm not talking about death as it relates to your eternal state. I'm talking about the death of your present joy. On the other hand, when you eat of His body and drink of His blood, when you say, "Lord, infuse me again with Your life," you will be nourished greatly and revived continually.

His blood produces cleansing that invigorates you.

I'm so thankful for the cleansing work of His blood because it only takes about twenty-three seconds for me to get full of sin and carnality. Even as my blood continually cleanses me physically, so, too, the blood of Jesus cleanses me spiritually.

The error that many people have concerning Communion is thinking they need to repent and to be cleansed before they can partake. Not true. Repentance is not doing something so you can come to the Lord. Repentance is coming to the Lord just as you are! The table is available to anyone who has been polluted, wiped-out, infected by sin and carnality. That's why it's more than a table of commemoration— it's a table of celebration, where we can say, "Oh, Lord, thank You that You invited me to come and dine. Thank You that I can come right now just as I am to not only be sustained in my spiritual life, but also to receive cleansing through Your blood."

His blood prevents infections from destroying you.

In life there are temptations that number in the millions. These temptations bombard us constantly, just as germs and viruses do physiologically. How are we protected from so vast a number of temptations? How are we to overcome the attacks planned in hell that threaten to destroy us? Through the spiritual antibodies contained in the blood of the Lamb (Revelation 12:11).

There is only One Man who has been tempted in every point of sin possible and was an overcomer: Jesus Christ. That's what is so great about His blood. He was tempted in every single sin—not just pride or lying or gossip—but the grossest kind of sin you can imagine, the kind of sin that turns your stomach, the kind of sin you could never even fathom. He was tempted in every possible sin known to humanity or to the demons in hell—and He overcame (Hebrews 4:15). Therefore, His blood is overcoming blood.

The smallpox-infected boys who sailed from Spain to Columbia produced antibodies that sustained an entire culture. So, too, the blood of Jesus Christ is laden with antibodies capable of overcoming every infection Satan throws my way and every sin to which I am so vulnerable—past, present, and future.

Now, when those early scientists and physicians began to understand that truly life was in the blood, they decided to infuse healthy blood into people who were sick and weak and dying. Sometimes, as a result of such a transfusion, their patients would spring back to life. Other times, however, their patients would die. This puzzled physicians for many years—until the discovery of blood types.

It is now known that we can only take blood from those whose blood type is the same as ours. Otherwise, the nourishing, cleansing, and protection hoped for in a blood transfusion would instead be detrimental and deadly. The Bible says that we are all of one blood (Acts 17:26). It's true. We all have one blood: polluted blood, Adam's blood. When he fell in the Garden of Eden, we all fell with him (1 Corinthians 15:22). And the fallout from Adam's bomb infects our blood to this day. So what must happen? Pure, healthy, untainted blood must be transfused into us. Who can give us untainted, uninfected, pure blood that will match our individual blood types? One who has blood untainted by Adam.

Although a fetus gets its nutrients from, and grows in the placenta of its mother, it never takes a single drop of the mother's blood because at the moment of conception it begins the process of producing its own blood supply, which is genetically influenced by the blood of the father. Therefore, only One born of a virgin would have blood untainted by humanity. There is only One Man who has been born of a virgin: Jesus Christ. And His Blood can be transfused into you today.

Four-year-old Billy was informed that his three-year-old sister had a very serious disease that required a draining of her infected blood and a transfusion of healthy blood. "Billy, would you be willing to share your blood with your little sister?" asked the doctor.

Billy looked at the doctor. His chin began to quiver. A tear rolled down his chubby little cheek, and he said, "Okay, Doctor." The nurse came in, stuck a needle in Billy's arm, and began to draw blood from him. After a few minutes, she removed the needle from his vein and said, "Okay, Billy. You're all done," to which Billy replied, "Well, when do I die?"

You see, Billy thought when the doctor asked him to give his blood, it meant he would give his life for his little sister.

Seeker, skeptic, non-believer—there is One who did, indeed, give His life by giving His blood. Jesus Christ so loved you that He poured out His blood in order that it might be transfused into you. He drained Himself that He might give you life. You who have never believed, you who have never opened up your heart to Him—you are dying. The toxins of your past and the sin of your present struggle are making you sicker and weaker by the day. Jesus said, "Unless you drink of My blood, open your heart and receive My life, you'll die in your sin." God loved you so much, precious friend, that He became a Man in Christ Jesus, born of a virgin, so that His blood—pure and untainted—could cleanse, nourish, and strengthen you today.

And you who know the Lord—what if we were really convinced His blood would provide nutrition that would sustain us eternally? What if we knew beyond any doubt that the blood of Jesus Christ would produce in us cleansing that would invigorate us completely? What if we truly believed that by taking in His blood, we would be protected from infections that would otherwise destroy us spiritually?

I hope you will place a high priority on the Lord's table, for in so doing, you will begin to experience the wonder-working power of His blood in your life. May you be renewed by and committed to His shed blood, His shared blood in a fresh way today.

21

From the earliest days of his conversion, Paul had a deep desire to minister effectively to his own people—the Jews. In Romans 9, he declared he was willing to be accursed, or damned, if it would mean their salvation. In Romans 10, he said it was his heart's prayer and desire that Israel might be saved. Yet although he desperately wanted to minister to his countrymen, it was made very clear to him from the outset of his salvation that his ministry was to be primarily to Gentiles, secondarily to kings, and lastly to the children of Israel (Acts 9:15). His was to be a ministry to Gentiles—yet Paul struggled with this.

Following his conversion, Paul spent three years being discipled by the Lord in the Arabian Desert. When he returned to Damascus, he headed straight for the synagogue, thinking that the Jews there would surely receive his ministry once he explained to them how their Old Testament Scriptures pointed to Jesus prophetically. Far from receiving Paul, however, the Jews wanted to kill him. So the brothers put him in a basket and lowered him over the wall to safety (Acts 9:25).

Where did Paul go next? To Jerusalem—the capital of Judaism. When he got there, I'm sure he was still thinking, *Come on, guys. You've got to admit what I'm saying has validity. I'm one of you. I was a Pharisee of Pharisees, schooled at the feet of Gamaliel.* But they, too, were out to kill him. So off he went to Tarsus, where he hung out for about thirteen years. Finally, Paul got to the place where he was at peace with the calling the Lord had given him—ministering to the Gentiles.

Here in chapter 21, after Paul had been working effectively for years in the Gentile countries of Asia Minor and Macedonia, the desire to minister to his people surfaced in his heart once again. It was a passion he just couldn't seem to get out of his system. So here he is, headed once more toward Jerusalem—this time knowing that bonds and afflictions await him there.

Acts 21:1–3 (a)

And it came to pass, that after we were gotten from them, and had launched, we came with a straight course unto Coos, and the day following unto Rhodes, and from thence unto Patara: And finding a ship sailing over unto Phenicia, we went aboard, and set forth. Now when we had discovered Cyprus, we left it on the left hand, and sailed into Syria . . .

Paul is sailing south from Asia Minor toward the coast of Israel to eventually dock at the seacoast city of Caesarea.

Acts 21:3 (b)

. . . and landed at Tyre: for there the ship was to unlade her burden.

When Paul arrived in Tyre, the boat stopped for seven days to load and unload cargo. You see, Paul was traveling on a cargo carrier, not a cruise ship. In Tyre on this seven-day break, it certainly would seem justifiable for Paul to have said, "I deserve a break. I'm going to retire and be tired here in Tyre." But, as we'll see, that's not what he said.

Acts 21:4 (a)

And finding disciples, we tarried there seven days . . .

The Greek word translated "finding" is a powerful one that means Paul was "diligently searching out, and looking for" disciples. During this unexpected break, others might have said, "What a great opportunity for a vacation."

Not Paul.

He said, "I want to be with the brothers. I desire fellowship."

There's a misconception among believers that, when they're out of town on vacation or business, it's a good time to take a break from church. But then they wonder why they end up fighting on their vacation, why they're angry with their family, why things don't work out right. When you are traveling or vacationing, find a fellowship to attend. God will honor you, and you'll be amazed to find special brothers and sisters wherever you go.

Acts 21:41 (b)

. . . who said to Paul through the Spirit, that he should not go up to Jerusalem.

The brothers whom Paul sought out said, "Don't go to Jerusalem, Paul." So what did Paul do? He went to Jerusalem.

Acts 21:5 (a)

And when we had accomplished those days, we departed and went our way; and they all brought us on our way . . .

This group of believers, like another group we'll see further on in the chapter, traveled with and stood by Paul—even though they didn't agree with the direction in which he was going. Why? Because they loved and respected him in the Lord. So, too, it would be radical if we would put away the need to be heard and simply say, "Here's my opinion. Here's my perspective. But I respect you in the Lord, regardless of your decision."

Acts 21:5 (b)

. . . with wives and children, till we were out of the city . . .

The disciples took their families with them on this journey to be with Paul, to listen to Paul, and to pray for Paul. Sometimes I hear people say, "We don't go to church on Wednesday night because it's family night"; or "We don't make it to church Sunday evening because it's family time"—as if coming to church as a family, hearing the Word of God, driving home discussing what was said, and praying together doesn't qualify as "family time." I strongly believe it's a fallacy in this age of emphasis upon the family to say that "family time" and church attendance are mutually exclusive. As one who grew up in the church and in a strong family, I believe there's nothing you can do that will be more beneficial to your family than to come to church.

Acts 21:5 (c)

. . . and we kneeled down on the shore, and prayed.

What a witness it must have been to the fishermen and surfers there at Tyre to see the believers bowing in prayer together on the sand. One of the things I so enjoy about the amphitheatre at Applegate Christian Fellowship is the opportunity to witness to the unbelievers in the service through baptism. Even more so, at baptisms in the Applegate River on a summer Sunday afternoon, the people out there chugging beer and throwing frisbees are certainly stimulated by the witness. So, too, it's a witness whenever you pray before your meal at Denny's® or McDonald's®. Don't be ashamed. Like the believers in the early church, you can witness even through prayer.

Acts 21:6
And when we had taken our leave one of another, we took ship; and they returned home again.

As they went home, do you think any of these men, women, or children said, "Boy, walking all this way to pray for Paul was really a waste of time. We should have had family hour back home"? I don't think so. I don't think one person regretted the energy expended or the time it took to pray for Paul and to be a witness on the beach at Tyre.

Acts 21:7–8
And when we had finished our course from Tyre, we came to Ptolemais, and saluted the brethren, and abode with them one day. And the next day we that were of Paul's company departed, and came unto Caesarea: and we entered into the house of Philip the evangelist, which was one of the seven; and abode with him.

I would love to have been a mouse in the house of Philip. You see, twenty years earlier, Philip's colleague, Stephen—another one of the original seven deacons—was martyred, his death unleashing great persecution in the church. Who was the one behind the stoning of Stephen? Who was the one who voted for it in the Sanhedrin? Who was the one who held the coats of those who threw the rocks? Paul. Paul was the one who, in a very real sense, brought about the death of Stephen. Paul was the one who caused the persecution of the church, which drove Philip to Caesarea. And Paul was the one who was knocking on Philip's door. Thus, I wonder what Paul and Philip said when they first encountered each other face-to-face. I imagine they embraced each other, realizing that which was behind them was buried beneath the blood of Calvary.

Acts 21:9
And the same man had four daughters, virgins, which did prophesy.

Philip was a dedicated worker in the church (Acts 6), a dynamic preacher in the world (Acts 8), and now a devoted father in the home.

For topical study of Acts 21:8–9 entitled "A Focused Family," turn to page 799.

Acts 21:10
And as we tarried there many days, there came down from Judaea a certain prophet, named Agabus.

Prominent in the early church, Agabus was the one who correctly prophesied there would be a famine in Jerusalem (Acts 11:28).

Acts 21:11
And when he was come unto us, he took Paul's girdle, and bound his own hands and feet, and said, Thus saith the Holy Ghost, So shall the Jews at Jerusalem bind the man that owneth this girdle, and shall deliver him into the hands of the Gentiles.

Rough and rugged individuals, prophets like Agabus tended to do amazing things that jarred people into attentiveness. Ezekiel lay on his side for days in order to deliver a message to God's people (Ezekiel 4:4–9). Many days after the Lord told Jeremiah to put his underwear under a rock on the Euphrates River, He told him to dig it up, put it on, and walk through the city, saying, "You people are like this underwear" (see Jeremiah 13:1–11). And here, Agabus used Paul's belt to deliver an illustrated sermon.

Acts 21:12, 13
And when we heard these things, both we, and they of that place, besought him not to go up to Jerusalem. Then Paul answered, What mean ye to weep and to break mine heart? for I am ready not to be bound only, but also to die at Jerusalem for the name of the Lord Jesus.

"I know there's trouble awaiting me in Jerusalem," said Paul, "but I'm going anyway. And if I die there, so be it."

For topical study of Acts 21:11–13 entitled "Burning Out or Burning Bright?" turn to page 804.

Acts 21:14, 15
And when he would not be persuaded, we ceased, saying, The will of the Lord be done. And after those days we took up our carriages, and went up to Jerusalem.

"We've shared our hearts," said the brothers. "And now the will of the Lord be done," they said as they ceased arguing and started traveling.

For topical study of Acts 21:14–15 entitled "Go with the Flow," turn to page 809.

Acts 21:16
There went with us also certain of the disciples of Caesarea, and brought with them one Mnason of Cyprus, an old disciple, with whom we should lodge.

We know nothing of Mnason's history. Perhaps his name, which means "solicitor" or "pleader," reflects the kind of man he was—one given to hospitality.

Acts 21:17
And when we were come to Jerusalem, the brethren received us gladly.

When Paul arrived in Jerusalem with the offering he had gathered on this, his third missionary journey, the brothers received him gladly. Rather than thank Paul for the gift, however, they started telling Paul he needed to do more.

Acts 21:18–23 (a)
And the day following Paul went in with us unto James; and all the elders were present. And when he had saluted them, he declared particularly what things God had wrought among the Gentiles by his ministry. And when they heard it, they glorified the Lord, and said unto him, Thou seest, brother, how many thousands of Jews there are which believe; and they are all zealous of the law: And they are informed of thee, that thou teachest all the Jews which are among the Gentiles to forsake Moses, saying that they ought not to circumcise their children, neither to walk after the customs. What is it therefore? the multitude must needs come together: for they will hear that thou art come. Do therefore this that we say to thee.

Although the Christians in Jerusalem were believers in Jesus, they still adhered to the rituals and ceremonies of Judaism. Thus, the leaders of the church said to Paul, "Because the Christians in this community have heard you tell people they don't have to circumcise their children, observe the rituals, or attend the festivals, they will be offended when they see you. To show them you can be trusted, here's what you need to do. . . ."

Acts 21:23 (b)
We have four men which have a vow on them.

Four men had taken a Nazarite vow. That is, they had let their hair grow long; they drank no wine; they ate no grapes or raisins; they didn't touch anything dead; and they devoted themselves for a period of time to singular dedication to God. At the end of their vow, they would go into the temple, spend seven days worshiping God, cut off their hair, burn it, and give offerings and sacrifices to God. It was all part of the prescribed process of purification following a time of separation (Numbers 6).

Acts 21:24, 25
Them take, and purify thyself with them, and be at charges with them, that they may shave their heads: and all may know that those things, whereof they were informed concerning thee, are nothing; but that thou thyself also walkest orderly, and keepest the law. As touching the Gentiles which believe, we have written and concluded that they observe no such thing, save only that they keep themselves from things offered to idols, and from blood, and from strangled, and from fornication.

Because those who took a Nazarite vow had to take time off work to carry out the procedures at the conclusion and because the sacrifices required were costly, it was customary for wealthy men to sponsor them. And because Paul had in his possession the offering for the church in Jerusalem, the brothers in Jerusalem asked him to foot the bill for the four men. "We're not putting this trip on Gentiles, Paul. But supporting these men in their vow would be a wonderful way for you to relate to the Jewish believers here in Jerusalem who still subscribe to the rituals of Judaism."

Acts 21:26 (a)
Then Paul took the men, and the next day purifying himself with them entered into the temple, to signify the accomplishment of the days of purification . . .

Paul, wanting so desperately to be effective in Jerusalem, perhaps said, "If this is a way to make them listen, I'll do it. I'll cut my hair. I'll purify myself. I'll go through the sacrificial rituals even though I know they've already been fulfilled in Christ." Exhibiting a great deal of grace and flexibility, Paul would later write, "To the Jew I became a Jew that I might win some" (see 1 Corinthians 9:20); and, "If it be possible, as much as lieth in you, live peaceably with all men" (Romans 12:18). So here, even though he was not a believer in rituals and regulations, Paul said, "Okay, if that's what you guys want, I'll do it."

Acts 21:26 (b)
. . . until that an offering should be offered for every one of them.

I'm sure Paul did not offer a sin offering, for he would later point out very clearly that Jesus

Christ is the ultimate offering for sin. But he did probably offer one of the other offerings that spoke not of atonement but of fellowship. While I commend Paul's flexibility, I am grieved by the church's frailty. The Jerusalem church was not as powerful as the church in other regions during this period because they were still caught up in traditionalism and compromise.

The Book of Hebrews, probably written by Paul, was written to the Hebrews to tell the Hebrews to quit being Hebrews. "Give it up," the Book of Hebrews says, "you can't go back to the old sacrificial system and traditionalism because all of those things are only pictures pointing to Jesus Christ. Why are you still caught up in the pictures when the Reality is here, the Fulfillment has come, the Work is complete?"

When my daughter Jessie and I were at Van Wey's Market years ago, a little girl was out in front of the store giving away puppies. I had no desire or intention of getting a puppy, but Jessie made an airtight case about how all of her life all we've ever had have been "used" dogs, stray dogs, or old dogs. "Dad," she said, "do you really think I should go through all of my growing-up years never having had a puppy? Here I am, a freshman in high school, and this could have a deep psychological effect on my life." So we got a puppy and named him Zeke. Now, Jessie, who was active in school and church groups was gone most of the time. One afternoon, however, she happened to be home when there was a knock on the door by Ed, the man who was pouring cement in our driveway. Zeke had gotten loose yet again, and Ed was returning him to us. But Jessie couldn't be bothered to answer the door. Why? She was watching a video on "How To Train Your Dog." You see, Jessie had no time to get her dog or be with her dog because she was too busy watching a video about her dog!

Such was the problem with the Hebrews. Jesus was among them. Jesus had died for them. But they weren't focusing on Him because they were still caught up in the rituals pointing to Him. They were watching the video, but missing the Reality.

Acts 21:27–29
And when the seven days were almost ended, the Jews which were of Asia, when they saw him in the temple, stirred up all the people, and laid hands on him, Crying out, Men of Israel, help: This is the man, that teacheth all men every where against the people, and the law, and this place: and further brought Greeks also into the temple, and hath polluted this holy place. (For they had seen be-
fore with him in the city Trophimus an Ephesian, whom they supposed that Paul had brought into the temple.)

Although anyone could go into the outer courtyard of the temple, beyond that, there was a sign reading: "Any Gentile entering in will be put to death." It was absolutely forbidden for Gentiles to go past the outer court. Paul had come into the city with some Gentile believers, and the Jews erroneously assumed they were the men who were in the temple with him.

Acts 21:30 (a)
And all the city was moved, and the people ran together: and they took Paul, and drew him out of the temple . . .

Wherever Paul went, one of two things happened: either a revival or a riot. This time it was a riot.

Acts 21:30 (b)
. . . and forthwith the doors were shut.

Oh, Paul, the doors were shut long ago—you just didn't see it, dear brother. I am sorry to say there have been times more than once when, like Paul, I have been determined to enter closed doors. You know what happened? I got a smashed nose and a headache from running into them.

"Oh, I just want to do this so badly. I'm called to it. I feel good about it. It's on my heart," we say. But is the Lord opening the door? Are we flowing—or are we striving? Perhaps this incident was the reason Paul would later write to Timothy, "The servant of the Lord must not strive" (2 Timothy 2:24).

Acts 21:31, 32 (a)
And as they went about to kill him, tidings came unto the chief captain of the band, that all Jerusalem was in an uproar. Who immediately took soldiers and centurions, and ran down unto them . . .

On the northwest corner of the temple mount sat the Fortress Antonia from which Roman soldiers could look down upon the temple to make sure nothing was out of order. When they saw the entire city running toward the temple, they headed there as well.

Acts 21:32 (b)
. . . and when they saw the chief captain and the soldiers, they left beating of Paul.

Here's the question: Where were the Jerusalem believers? Paul had come bringing an offering for them. He had shown flexibility in doing what they asked of him, even though it wasn't his conviction—and now he was getting beat up as a result. Where was the church when Paul was in trouble? Nowhere to be found.

That's what happens whenever legalism and compromise begin to set into a church or an individual. Energy and commitment are replaced by traditionalism and ritualism. And the church becomes the "frozen chosen." How I pray we will continually be adjusted as a church and as individuals. "Lord, don't let us care more about external regulations and forms than we do about love, commitment, and standing by one another when someone's getting beaten up." It's a tragic commentary that in Jerusalem, it was the Romans rather than the Christians who rescued Paul.

Acts 21:33, 34
Then the chief captain came near, and took him, and commanded him to be bound with two chains; and demanded who he was, and what he had done. And some cried one thing, some another, among the multitude: and when he could not know the certainty for the tumult, he commanded him to be carried into the castle.

Paul was carried into the Fortress Antonia.

Acts 21:35, 36
And when he came upon the stairs, so it was, that he was borne of the soldiers for the violence of the people. For the multitude of the people followed after, crying, Away with him.

About whom else did the crowd say, "Away with Him"? About another Radical who said, "It's not outward religion that matters—it's inward righteousness"; about One who reduced everything to great simplicity when He said, "Love God with all your heart and soul and mind and strength,

and love your neighbor as yourself" (see Matthew 22:37–39).

"Away with Him," they said concerning Jesus. And, "Away with him," they're saying concerning Paul, champion of His grace.

Acts 21:37, 38
And as Paul was to be led into the castle, he said unto the chief captain, May I speak unto thee? Who said, Canst thou speak Greek? Art not thou that Egyptian, which before these days madest an uproar, and leddest out into the wilderness four thousand men that were murderers?

In the year A.D. 54, an Egyptian, whose name meant "dagger-bearer," led men to the wilderness to launch a revolt against Rome. Here in Acts, the captain, thinking Paul was this same Egyptian terrorist, was taken aback when Paul started speaking Greek. "You speak Greek?" he said. "I thought you were an Egyptian."

Acts 21:39
But Paul said, I am a man which am a Jew of Tarsus, a city in Cilicia, a citizen of no mean city: and, I beseech thee, suffer me to speak unto the people.

Paul was a gutsy guy. Here, the Jews were out to kill him—yet he still wanted to speak to them.

Acts 21:40
And when he had given him licence, Paul stood on the stairs, and beckoned with the hand unto the people. And when there was made a great silence, he spake unto them in the Hebrew tongue, saying . . .

Paul must have thought, *This is my opportunity! Virtually the entire city is here. This is the moment I've been waiting for twenty years!* I'm convinced Paul was sure there would be a great revival among his brothers. Suffice it to say, however, his sermon was not the best-received sermon ever preached, as we'll see in chapter 22.

A FOCUSED FAMILY
A Topical Study of
Acts 21:8, 9

I n election seasons, we hear a lot about family values. But I would like us to look instead at a valued family, for in the family of Philip, we see a family that was focused, a family that was valuable for the kingdom, a family that provides a wonderful example for you and me.

At this time, Philip was living in the seacoast city of Caesarea—an incredibly beautiful spot on the Mediterranean coast of northern Israel. Philip's wife is not mentioned in this passage perhaps because she was quietly behind the scenes. It is also very possible that at this point she had died. Others suggest that Philip was deserted by his wife—something that happened not infrequently in the days of the early church, when rabbis encouraged the spouses of those converted to Jesus Christ to divorce their mates.

Heading south from Turkey on their way to Jerusalem, Paul and his entourage stopped at Caesarea to hang out with Philip and his family. This doesn't surprise me, for, according to our text, Philip's was a house of hospitality and spirituality. Even though there were four daughters and perhaps cramped quarters, Paul and his company enjoyed being there. It was a good place to be—not the circus many families can tend to be.

P. T. Barnum, the man who said there's a sucker born every minute, promoted one of his circus acts as a unique family situation: a lion, a tiger, a bear, and a lamb all living together under one roof. Taking Barnum aside, a reporter said, "Mr. Barnum, seriously, how long has this family been together?

"Eight months," answered Barnum.

"You mean they've all been in that cage for eight months?" pressed the reporter.

"Well, the lion, tiger, and bear—yes. We do change the lamb regularly," the showman said.

So, too, many homes are places where people get chewed up and torn apart—but not Philip's. His was a family that Paul and his company sought out and stayed with many days.

The Hospitality of Philip's Family

Romans 12 teaches that one of the components in the life of the believer is hospitality. We are to be men and women of hospitality—not out of obligation, but out of opportunity. Why? Because the writer to the Hebrews would later tell us to let brotherly love continue and be not forgetful to entertain strangers, for thereby some have entertained angels unaware (Hebrews 13:2).

Open your home. Open your heart. Be hospitable. Why? Not only because the Word demands it, but because there's a blessing in it: You will entertain angels unaware. What does that mean? Ask Abraham. In Genesis 18, we see him sitting in front of his tent. Seeing three men in the distance walking toward him, Abraham went out to greet them, saying, "Let me fix a meal for you and give refreshment to you," little realizing that the group of strangers was actually two angels and Jesus Himself in a Christophany—an appearance of Christ before He came to earth as the Babe of Bethlehem.

Jesus would later say, "When you take care of someone who's naked and poor, someone who's hurting and troubled, someone who's in jail, someone who's not doing well—when you do that to the least of My brethren, you're doing it to Me. When you reach out in hospitality and open your heart and your home to people who are hurting, you're doing it to Me." (see Matthew 25:40).

The word "angel," or *aggelos* in Greek, means "messenger." You'll be surprised, amazed, and blown away by the messages the Lord will give you when you open the doors of your home and heart, and show hospitality to people. Conversely, when folks say, "I'm not hearing anything from the Lord," sometimes I wonder when the last time was they opened their home to a stranger.

The word "hospitality" has embedded within its meaning the word we use for hospital—that is, a place to bind up, patch up, lift up folks who are hurting, bruised, or wounded. Hospitality includes not only the people we might like to be around, or the people we enjoy being with—but also those who are "strangers" to us.

You might be saying, "I don't have a home of my own. I'm a teenager," or "I'm homeless." Check out what Peter said in 1 Peter 4:9, when he exhorted believers who had been scattered throughout all of the world—homeless quite literally because of persecution—to show hospitality. You see, you don't need a house to show hospitality. You can show hospitality at school by sitting with the person who sits alone in the cafeteria, by reaching out to the person who's hurting at work, by spending a moment or two with the person who's discouraged in the supermarket. And if you do, because you'll be entertaining angels unaware, you'll be surprised at how the Lord will bless you, the things He'll show you, the honors He'll give you—just as He did to Abraham.

The Spirituality in Philip's Family

Notice first the purity of Philip's daughters. Dominated by Gentiles, Caesarea was a wicked, hedonistic beach town. Yet Philip's daughters were singled out as being pure—as being virgins. How vital it is in these days that we stress within our families the importance and the blessing of purity.

Our kids are being taught that freedom of choice is the key as it relates to the abortion dilemma. I, too, believe in the freedom of choice: the choice whether or not to come together sexually outside of marriage. Once that choice is made, there are no other choices—not logically, not ethically, not biblically.

The final score of a women's basketball game was 175–42. In a post-game interview, the losing coach said, "The entire game hinged on one call."

"Incredible," said the sportswriter. "What call was it?"

"The call I made a few months ago to schedule this game," answered the weary coach.

So, too, regarding the issue of abortion, the entire game hinges on one call: the call to enter into a sexual relationship in the first place. Philip was a man who, living in a very sinful city, raised his daughters in such a way that they were pure. He must have taught them, as Proverbs 6:32 declares, that he who commits sexual immorality destroys his own soul.

Sex within marriage can be illustrated by taking a glass of red-colored water and mixing it with a glass of blue-colored water. The result? A glass of purple-colored water. That's what sex is: two individual souls being unified into one. On the other hand, sex outside of marriage can be illustrated by taking a glass of red-colored water, a glass of blue-colored water, and slowly emptying each one down the drain.

Referring to sex, the world says, "I got a piece of her," or "I got a piece of him." That's exactly true. Outside of marriage, a piece of one's soul is removed with each intimate encounter. It's like an onion—if you keep peeling off layers, pretty soon there's nothing left. And there are kids and adults who, not understanding the nature of sexuality, are being peeled away layer by layer until there's nothing left.

Mom and Dad, I'm convinced that in the days in which we live, we must make sure our kids thoroughly and completely understand that the issue is not contraception, safe sex, or abortion. The issue is that of the soul being eroded and destroyed.

Kids often say, "If sex is so dangerous, why didn't the Lord just give us a switch that couldn't be turned on until we're married? Why do we have to wrestle with this issue from the time we're teenagers all the way until we get married?" In Revelation 14, we read of 144,000 who do not take the mark of the Beast during the Tribulation period. Instead, they take a stand for the Lord, walk with the Lord, and are used by the Lord. Revelation 14:4 says, "These are they which are not defiled with women; for they are virgins. These are they which follow the Lamb whithersoever He goeth."

Teenager, single brother, single sister—you might be saying, "Yeah, if I was part of the 144,000, I'd make a stand, too."

Well, here's your chance! Every one of you who is single has the unique opportunity to follow the Lamb in the tribulation you're in right now—with society flashing messages of compromise to you and with kids who are flaunting the fact they're no longer virgins all around you. You can say, "I will follow the Lamb. Like Shadrach, Meshach and Abed-nego, I will not bow to the passions that burn within me. I will stand tough. I will stand strong."

Then, your single state becomes not a curse, but rather an opportunity for you to demonstrate your love for, and your commitment to, the Lord. Follow the Lamb, and I guarantee you will not say, "I wish I would have messed around. I wish I had picked up some sexually transmitted disease. I wish I had had an abortion or two. I wish I would have given myself to this guy and lost part of my soul to that one." I have yet to talk to one person who has said, "I really regret being a virgin when I got married." But I have talked to hundreds of couples who have said, "I regret compromising my virginity—because even in my marriage, I'm suffering the effects."

Mom and Dad, it's not enough to tell our kids to "Just Say No." We've got to tell them *why*. We must remind them that sin is not bad because it's forbidden—but that sin is forbidden because it's bad. Sin hurts, maims, and destroys. Sin will strip and rob us of what could have been and of what God wants us to be. Truly, Philip is to be commended. In a seacoast city and in a carnal culture, he was able to teach his daughters the importance of being pure.

Notice not only the purity of Philip's daughters, but also the piety of his daughters. Paul makes it clear in 1 Corinthians 7:34 that the word "virgin" not only meant sexual purity but spiritual piety. You see, the married woman must constantly factor the care of her husband and family into her life. But the virgin can live a life of unparalleled piety, caring only about the things of the Lord. Philip's daughters were not self-righteous prudes, but young women who were singularly devoted to God.

Notice, finally, the power of Philip's daughters. "I will pour out my spirit upon all flesh; and your sons and your daughters shall prophesy . . ." said the Lord (Joel 2:28). First Corinthians 14 tells us that prophecy consists of words of edification to build up, words of exhortation to stir up, and words of comfort to cheer up. Philip's daughters were women who were not gossiping, arguing, and fighting—but building up, stirring up, and cheering up.

"Good for Philip," you say. "But how does his story help me in my situation with my family?"

There's a connection between the hospitality of Philip's house and the spirituality in Philip's house that I don't want you to miss. Keep in mind, this isn't the first time we hear of Philip in the Book of Acts. In chapter 6, he was a dedicated worker in the church. In chapter 8, he was a dynamic preacher in the world. Here in chapter 21, he is a devoted father in the home—not by focusing on his family, but by seeking first the kingdom.

"We can't be hospitable," some might say, "because we're focusing on our family. We can't come to Wednesday night Bible study because of our family problems and needs. And we can't come to pray on Sunday nights because it cuts into family time." As a result, the church is becoming less and less spiritual, less and less hospitable—all in the name of "family time" and "family values." Consequently, we are seeing kids grow up who are drifting because parents are not seeking first the kingdom of God and His righteousness (Matthew 6:33).

I heard a story on the news one night concerning what happened to a couple who really wanted to create a safe and secure environment for their kids. They moved to the outskirts of San Francisco—three weeks before the San Francisco earthquake hit the Bay Area. After part of their house actually collapsed, they said, "We can't live here. Our family's in danger." So they moved away from the earthquakes to Florida—five weeks before Hurricane Andrew flattened their home. Distraught and upset, they took their family on vacation to Hawaii—two days before Hurricane Iniki wiped out their hotel.

When I heard this, I thought, *That's just like me—trying to plot and figure out what is best and safest for my family, when in reality it's not up to me to protect them or our time together—but to seek first the Kingdom.*

Mom and Dad, seek first the kingdom. Make spiritual life priority. Establish family devotions. Get your kids plugged into church and a youth group. Open your own heart and home to those in need of hospitality.

Seek first the kingdom of your family, and like the family on the news, you'll be shaken-up, wiped-out, and blown-away. But seek first the kingdom of God, and, like Philip, you'll see your family walk in purity, piety, and power.

BURNING OUT OR BURNING BRIGHT?
A Topical Study of
Acts 21:11–13

I can recall many times as a young boy, when Gertie came to visit. What a character! Whenever she returned from town or came back from church, the first thing she would say when she walked into the house was, "I can't wait to take my girdle off—it's killing me!" In fact, so often did Gertie say this, for years I thought her name was "Girdie"—short for the girdle she always talked about.

In our text, the girdle Paul wore was used by a prophet named Agabus to vividly communicate to him that his life would be in jeopardy. You see, Agabus took Paul's girdle—a leather belt—and bound his hands and feet with it, saying, "The owner of this girdle will be bound in Jerusalem and delivered into the hands of the Gentiles." The message was unmistakable: "Your life will be in danger, Paul. Don't go."

What was Paul's response? He said, "I am ready not to be bound only, but also to die at Jerusalem if necessary for the name of the Lord Jesus."

It is important to understand that Paul was not simply stating a silly sentiment—like the guy who wrote to his girlfriend, "I love you so much, I would be willing to climb the highest mountain to be with you, to swim the widest river to see you, to cross the hottest desert to be near you. P.S. If it's not raining tonight, I'll be over at eight."

Nor was Paul mouthing empty words—as we do so often when we sing, "I have decided to follow Jesus." "The world behind me, the Cross before me," we sing— until someone challenges us and we change our tune.

No, Paul meant what he said. Truly he was ready to die in Jerusalem. After all, according to 2 Corinthians 11, Paul was the one who had been given thirty-nine lashes with the flagellum five times, stoned, beaten, left for dead, shipwrecked, imprisoned—all while carrying the burdens of those to whom he ministered upon his heart. Thus, when Paul told Agabus he was ready to suffer persecution in Jerusalem, he knew what he was talking about.

I marveled when I received an issue of *Ministry Today* magazine. The cover story, entitled "Burnout in the Ministry," talked about how the average pastor in America stays with a congregation only two and one third years before leaving— burned-out by his congregants, his board, or the stress of daily life.

"That's the professional clergy's problem," you say. "It doesn't relate to me." Oh, but the article went on, describing how laypeople are leaving churches as well— taking back-row seats, no longer engaged in service, no longer involved in teaching. In other words, the article concluded that everyone's getting burned-out on ministry.

Why didn't Paul burn out? What kept him going strong through shipwrecks and beatings, stonings and imprisonment? In the Book of Leviticus, we find a classic passage on burn-out and what I believe was the reason for Paul's endurance. . . . The children of Israel had just finished construction of the tabernacle.

And Aaron lifted up his hand toward the people, and blessed them, and came down from offering of the sin offering, and the burnt offering, and peace offerings. And Moses and Aaron went into the tabernacle of the congregation, and came out, and blessed the people: and the glory of the LORD appeared unto all the people. And there came a fire out from before the LORD, and consumed upon the altar the burnt offering and the fat: which when all the people saw, they shouted, and fell on their faces.   Leviticus 9:22–24

With fire coming down from heaven, the burnt offering igniting, people shouting and falling on their faces in worship, it was certainly a Grand Opening!

And Nadab and Abihu, the sons of Aaron, took either of them his censer, and put fire therein, and put incense thereon, and offered strange fire before the LORD, which he commanded them not.   Leviticus 10:1

Nadab and Abihu, sons of Aaron and next in line to be high priest, took their censers, the instrument in which incense was burned, and lit them with "strange fire."

And there went out fire from the Lord, and devoured them, and they died before the Lord.   Leviticus 10:2

Why were Nadab and Abihu destroyed? Following are three reasons I would like you to consider . . .

Presentation of Ministry

Then Moses said unto Aaron, This is it that the Lord spake, saying, I will be sanctified in them that come nigh me, and before all the people I will be glorified. And Aaron held his peace.   Leviticus 10:3

"*I* will be sanctified. *I* will be glorified," said the Lord—implying that Nadab and Abihu were drawing glory and attention to themselves.

Look how spiritual we are, they must have thought. *Look how devoted, how anointed, how special we are.*

Contrast Nadab and Abihu with our Great High Priest, Jesus Christ. Every time He did a miracle—without exception—Scripture records that people glorified God. He was able to do His work in such a way that people didn't glorify Him but gave glory to His Father.

In anything we do—whether it's offering worship in solitude, talking with one individual, singing before fifty, or preaching to ten thousand—it's only by God's grace that He uses any of us to any degree at all. After all, He could bypass us so easily.

"Quiet your disciples," the Pharisees demanded.

"If they quieted down, the stones would take their place," Jesus answered (see Luke 19:40).

That means all Jesus needs to replace us are a few rocks.

"*I* will be glorified," saith the Lord. And if you or I start to think we're kind of hot, like Nadab and Abihu, we'll burn out in ministry.

Tribulation in Ministry

And Moses said unto Aaron, and unto Eleazar and unto Ithamar, his sons, Uncover not your heads, neither rend your clothes; lest ye die, and lest wrath come upon all the people: but let your brethren, the whole house of Israel, bewail the burning which the Lord hath kindled.   Leviticus 10:6

There are times in each of our lives when we will go through personal trage-dies and difficulties. It might be that of a loved one taken from you, a girlfriend walking out on you, a bankruptcy in your business, or an affliction in your body. But here's the key. The Lord says to us, "Didn't you sing,

Refiner's Fire, my heart's one desire is to be holy . . .
I will serve You because I love You . . .
Have Thine own way, Lord, have Thine own way . . .?
Why, then, are you surprised that I have allowed tribulation to come into your
    life?"

A. W. Tozer was right when he said, "Before God can use a man greatly, He must allow him to be hurt deeply." When we are comforted in times of trouble, it's not to make us comfortable, but to make us comforters (2 Corinthians 1:4) because it's only when we have gone through tribulation personally that we can say to others, "I *know* God will see you through. He's done it for me."

Motivation for Ministry

And he shall take a censer full of burning coals of fire from off the altar before the Lord.   Leviticus 16:12

The only fire from which the priests were to ignite their censers was the fire on the altar. What did Nadab and Abihu do? They lit their own fire. As fire came down from heaven, as people were worshiping, Nadab and Abihu must have said, "Wow—what a holy happening! Let's join in—let's get involved in the ministry."

Often, we enter into ministry—be it youth work, on a worship team, or teach-ing a Bible study—because we look around and say, "Wow, look at the people getting saved. Look at the folks loving the Lord. I want to be a part of that too." And in our enthusiasm, in our desire to participate in some sort of revival, we light our own fire.

Sometimes people start a Bible study but find little or no response. They be-come burned-out on people and ministry if their motivation was to see souls saved and lives changed.

Jeremiah preached forty years, and guess how many people responded to his message. Zero. Finally, he found himself in a dungeon, saying, "This just isn't work-ing. I'm not going to speak anymore." But because people were not Jeremiah's mo-tivation for ministry, Scripture says the Word of the Lord was like fire in his bones

(Jeremiah 20:9). You see, although Jeremiah was burned-out temporarily, he was fired up eventually—and he began to prophesy again.

Perhaps your motivation is not to see others' lives changed, but to see your own life used. Understand this, precious people: You will join the ranks of the burned-out ministers and congregants if your motivation for ministry is to find some inner fulfillment because something else will come along that will pull those same strings within you and you'll be distracted. It might be some hobby, sport, or activity; it might be vegetarianism, political activism, or intellectual philosophy. But sooner or later, it will tug on your heart, and you'll lose interest in ministry.

Only one thing will keep you from burning out regardless of what troubles come into your life or what testings you go through. There is only one thing that will keep you going year after year like Paul the apostle, who said, "I've been beaten, I've been stoned, I've been imprisoned—but I don't care."

What is that one thing?

Fire from the brass altar where sacrifices were slain.

Of what does the brass altar speak?

Calvary.

In 2 Corinthians 5:14, Paul declared it was the love of Christ that motivated him. He kept going not because he wanted to be a part of the happening, not because he wanted some inner fulfillment, not even because he wanted to see people changed. He kept going because of what Jesus did on the Cross at Calvary.

So, too, the fire that will keep you fired up, the fire that will never burn you out, comes from seeing that Jesus Christ, the Son of God, died for you personally and for each of your sins individually. Then, ministry will no longer be

"How can I be part of the happening?"

"How can I change lives?"

"How can I find fulfillment?"

It will be,

"Jesus, You did so much for me on the Cross. I have no other choice but to serve You."

We've seen people burn out. We've watched people who were once engaged in ministry and used effectively fade away. And, although they might blame people or situations, it's always for one simple reason: Strange fire has crept in. They've lost the vision of the Cross.

The hunter took his new bird dog out on the first trip of the season. Hiding in his blind, he stood up, pulled the trigger of his shotgun, and a duck fell into the water. To the hunter's amazement, his dog walked out on the water and retrieved the duck. The incredulous hunter scratched his head, rubbed his eyes, and thought he was seeing things. Fifteen minutes later, he popped out of his blind once again, pulled the trigger, and down went another duck. Again, the dog walked on water to retrieve it. This happened a third and a fourth time. Finally, seeing another hunter approaching, he said, "Watch this"—as he hit his target once again. Sure enough, the dog walked on water to retrieve the duck.

"Did you see anything unusual about my bird dog?" he asked.

"Yep," answered the other hunter. "Your dog can't swim."

Some people, like the second hunter, are oblivious to the miraculous. They either can't or won't see what Jesus Christ did for them personally. They can only say, "I'm burned-out on serving. I'm disappointed in people. I'm giving up on ministry."

And maybe you feel like that today.

The cure? Go back to the altar and see what Jesus did for you. And like Paul, you will say, "What people do is irrelevant. My personal fulfillment is not the issue. My fire comes from the altar, the Cross of Calvary."

In the Name of Jesus Christ, may you who have been burned-out be restored currently. May the Spirit give you revelation in your inner man to see the Cross clearly once again. May it be like fire in your bones and may you go forth again in ministry—not burned-out, but burning bright.

GO WITH THE FLOW
A Topical Study of
Acts 21:14–15

When Peter-John, my oldest son, got his driver's license, this produced a certain amount of parental anxiety within me. In reality, however, it was ridiculous for me to worry about Peter-John driving his 1982 Subaru Galaxy—considering the unbelievable rate of speed at which we are all moving constantly.

The earth is spinning on its axis 1,000 miles per hour. It is also traveling 67,000 miles per hour around the sun. The sun is moving in an orbit within our galaxy at 385,000 mph. And our galaxy (one of the slowest-moving galaxies known to man) is moving across the universe at 1,350,000, miles per hour.

So, if you feel a bit dizzy this morning, you have good reason!

Now, when you think about the incredible speed with which everything is moving—it would seem like a galactic collision is inevitable. And yet, I bet not one person got up this morning and said, "My goodness. The galaxy is moving at 1,350,000 miles per hour through the universe. With millions of galaxies moving at least that speed, what's to keep us all from colliding in a gigantic Cosmic Destruction Derby?"

No, we don't give a thought about the galaxy moving at 1.3 million miles per hour. Yet I got uptight about Peter-John going forty miles per hour. Why?

I have discovered something about my fallen nature: I don't worry about the planet *on* which I live, but I am constantly vulnerable to worrying about the world *in* which I live. I have opinions about the way my family should behave, the way my country should be run, the way my church should respond. And in my flesh, I worry that if my opinions are not heard and heeded, chaos, confusion, and collision are inevitable. Therefore, within the little world in which I live, my flesh dictates I must make sure I am heard and heeded. Otherwise, my tendency is to get hurt, back off, and pull away.

In our text, the men who were traveling with Paul had reason, in their flesh, to be hurt and to pull away. Why? Because they felt they were headed for chaos and collision. You see, Paul deeply desired to go to Jerusalem. But on the way, he was warned repeatedly that problems and persecution awaited him there. Hearing of trouble in Jerusalem in every city they visited, Paul's companions began to beg him not to go. But Paul responded, "Why are you breaking my heart? I don't care if I'm bound, or even killed in Jerusalem—I'm going anyway."

Was Paul being stubborn and sinful? Commentators are divided. Some say Paul erred in ignoring the warnings and going to Jerusalem. Others, with whom I'm inclined to agree, say Paul was right in going to Jerusalem because it was made clear to him from the first days of his salvation that he would suffer great things and be brought before kings (Acts 9:15, 16). "If in Acts 9 the Spirit told Paul he would suffer great things," you ask, "why were all the warnings given here in Acts 21?"

Perhaps because the Spirit was simply saying, "Paul, the end is near. You can back out if you want to."

Here's the question: If you were in Paul's entourage and you plead with him not to go to Jerusalem, but he continued on anyway, what would you have done? Hurt and angry, would you have pulled away? These men didn't. They simply said, "The will of the Lord be done," and not only went with him, but they carried the baggage that went along with his decision.

Were these men blindly following Paul?

No, they were not blindly following their friend. They were fully trusting their Father. You see, they knew Paul had been wrong before. Do you recall the story? He thought he was protecting God's honor as he went throughout an entire region tracking down heretics who called themselves Christians, pulling them out of their homes, putting them in chains, and carrying them off to be imprisoned, tortured, and killed. As he traveled down the road to Damascus on one such mission, the Lord intervened and straightened him out. Thus, knowing God knocked Paul off his feet once (Acts 9:4), Paul's friends knew He could do it again if He so chose. That's why they could "cease, saying, The will of the Lord be done."

What a difference a comma makes.

It was not until after he had sent his wife on a buying spree to Europe that the financial empire of millionaire John Astor began to crumble. Unaware of her husband's financial crisis, Lady Astor tracked down one of the most expensive pieces of jewelry in the world and sent a wire to her husband telling him what a treasure it would be to own. When he saw that the price was $250,000, Astor wired back immediately: "No, price too high!" Unfortunately, the cable operator forgot the comma. So when Lady Astor got the cable, she read: "No price too high!"—and happily purchased the diamond.

So, too, when your wife doesn't see it your way, or when your employee, boss, teacher, or coach doesn't take your advice, perhaps your tendency is to remove the comma and change verse 14 from "We ceased, saying, The will of the Lord be done" to "We ceased saying, The will of the Lord be done."

Paul's friends didn't forget the comma. They ceased arguing and started traveling, knowing the will of the Lord would be done. As a result, the Lord blessed them greatly and used them mightily.

What the Lord Did *for* Paul's Friends

Please note three blessings the Lord bestowed upon those who stood by and with Paul:

Protection. Throughout the Book of Acts, Paul's friends went through storms at sea, riots in cities, and all kinds of challenges. But they were protected in them all.

Provision. Paul's great passion was to go to Rome. These men went with him, although not exactly as they planned. He went as a prisoner. Nonetheless, the journey was all-expenses-paid!

Promotion. What would have happened if Luke, who was in this group, had said, "Paul, you're stubborn. You're bullheaded. You're not listening to our advice. Go ahead and go to Jerusalem—but count me out. I'll just hang out here at the beach and date one of Philip's daughters"? He would not have become the author of the Book of Acts. Unlike these friends who traveled with Paul, after a dispute with him over John Mark, Barnabas parted company with Paul (Acts 15:39). While

Barnabas is a great man and a wonderful example in so many ways, following his split with Paul, he is never again seen in Scripture.

I suggest Barnabas lost something by demanding his own way. And I wonder how many brothers and sisters miss out on what God could have done in and through their lives had they not bailed out and said, "If my advice isn't being heeded, if I don't get my way, I'm pulling back; I'm getting out."

Wives, you may not like the decision your husband is making. He's not hearing what you're saying. He's not following your suggestions. And perhaps you're tempted to say, "I've had it. See you later."

Before you do, consider Sarah.

"When Abimelech sees you," her husband, Abraham—the man of faith, the friend of God—said, "he's going to want you in his harem—and he'll kill me to get to you. Protect me, Sarah. Tell him I'm your brother" (see Genesis 20).

Abraham made a decision; Sarah carried the baggage of his decision—and what happened? Like Paul's friends, Sarah was given protection when the Lord spoke to Abimelech, saying, "You touch her, you're dead" (see Genesis 20:3); provision when Abimelech offered Abraham great riches for her sake (see Genesis 21:16); and promotion when she was singled out in the New Testament as the quintessential example of a good wife (1 Peter 3:6).

What the Lord Did *in* Paul's Friends

The Lord replaced their arguing with His peace. They never again brought up the issue. When storms came down, when persecution rose up, they didn't say, "See, Paul—we told you not to go to Jerusalem." No, they had peace in their hearts because they had faith in their God.

Faith and worry are mutually exclusive. Thus, at any given moment you will either be in a state of tranquility, saying, "The will of the Lord be done,"—or you will worry, get uptight, and develop an ulcer.

The mature man or the wise woman is the one who says, "The will of the Lord be done. Where are your bags? I'm going with you."

Keep in mind that this debate between Paul and his friends did not deal with rebellion against the Lord, but rather the direction of the Lord. Paul wasn't saying, "I want to go sell drugs," or, "I think I'll dabble in pornography." No, this argument did not concern a violation of the Scriptures, but an interpretation of the Spirit.

If someone says to you, "Let's do this"—and you know it's sin, you are not to say, "The will of the Lord be done. Let's go do it." That was not the issue here. This was an honest debate about a decision dealing with the will of the Lord and the direction of the Spirit.

These guys didn't agree with Paul's interpretation of the Spirit—but they had trust in the Father, saying, "Father, You stopped him before on the road to Damascus. If necessary, You can do it again."

What will happen when that becomes your mind-set? What will happen if, like these men, you say, "Here's my opinion—but the will of the Lord be done"?

You will experience what Paul's friends did. You will experience protection—even if it's a wrong decision. You'll experience provision—God will bless you. And you'll experience promotion—you will be honored for your willingness to trust in the sovereignty of God.

You will not be a worrier. You will not be hurt or tempted to pull back. All of the stuff that eats at a person will not be eating at you. With a smile on your face, a sparkle in your eye, and a spring in your step you can say, "I've shared my thoughts. Now the will of the Lord be done. I trust Him. Surely, the One who spans the universe in His hand can control the little universe in which I live."

What the Lord Did Previously

I've made the wrong decision time and time again. In outright rebellion, I have turned my back on what I knew was right and have hardened my heart against the Lord. Yet not once has He ever said to me, "Jon, you're not heeding My advice. That's it. You're toast." No, time and time again He has said, "Jon, you're not listening. You're not heeding. Okay. I'll carry your baggage."

What baggage?

The baggage the Lord carried for me was not a nice leather suitcase. It was a rough wooden Cross. He carried it to pay for my stupidity, my rebellion, my iniquity. Therefore, in light of what the Lord has done for me, it is absurd for me to think I have the right to get mad at, hurt by, or upset with anyone who doesn't take my advice.

Truly, it is the wise man or woman who says, "The will of the Lord be done because of what He will do for me, because of what He'll do in me, and because of what He did in my place when He carried my baggage."

---

22 Working through this section of Scripture, some days I think Paul must have known something no one else knew. He must have been completely convinced that no matter what everyone else told him, no matter what persecution he would face—it was the Lord's will he go to Jerusalem.

Others days I think he was just stubborn. He had a heart for the Lord, and yet, on this issue, he thought he knew better than the Lord. The Book of Isaiah asks, "Who has been the Lord's counselor?" (see Isaiah 40:13). The answer? I have. And most of you have as well. We've counseled the Lord, saying, "Now, Lord, this is the way it should work out. Here's who needs to do this, and here's how we need to do that." And I'm wondering if Paul, this great man, this giant of the faith, wasn't showing his humanness by insisting that he could be effective in Jerusalem.

It's an open question to which I don't know the answer.

But I do know that when Paul arrived in Jerusalem, trouble was there to greet him, for no sooner had he entered the temple than the entire city was filled with the rumor that he had taken Gentiles in with him. A riot erupted, which would have ended in his demise had not Roman soldiers rushed in and rescued him from his own people.

Taken into protective custody, on his way into the Fortress Antonia, Paul stopped long enough to ask Claudius Lysias permission to speak to the crowd that wanted to kill him. Surely his heart must have been pounding as he anticipated the opportunity to address the city. *At last the Lord will see how powerful I can be,* he might have thought.

We pick up the story on the steps of the Fortress as Paul addresses virtually the entire city of Jerusalem.

Acts 22:1 (a)
Men, brethren, and fathers, hear ye my defence . . .

The Greek word translated "defence" is *apologia*, from which we get our word "apologetics." Theologically, "apologetics" means defending the faith—giving reason and rationale for the things we believe.

Acts 22:1 (b), 2 (a)
. . . which I make now unto you. (And when they heard that he spake in the Hebrew tongue to them, they kept the more silence . . .

Paul spoke to the centurion in Greek, but he addressed his countrymen in Hebrew. Why? Because although the Jews understood Greek, Hebrew was the language they learned from birth. Therefore, Paul used their mother tongue to speak to their hearts.

Acts 22:2 (b), 3 (a)
. . . and he saith,) I am verily a man which am a Jew . . .

Paul's message was neither a teaching on Old Testament prophecy nor an exposition of temple typology. No, Paul's "apology" was his own testimony. And this encourages me greatly—because even I can give my own testimony.

"Who is this Jesus?" asked the Pharisees of the blind man whom Jesus had healed.
"All I know is this," he answered. "Once I was blind and now I see" (see John 9:25).

The most powerful defense you have is your own testimony. People can argue with anything you say theologically or philosophically. But they cannot argue with what the Lord has done for you personally.

Acts 22:3 (b)
. . . born in Tarsus, a city in Cilicia . . .

Tarsus being a city in Asia Minor (present-day Turkey), Paul would have been a Hellenist—a Jew with a Greek background.

Acts 22:3 (c)
. . . yet brought up in this city . . .

"I was born in Tarsus, yet I was brought up in Jerusalem,"said Paul. This meant he could relate not only to the Hellenists but also to the Hebrews.

Acts 22:3 (d)
. . . at the feet of Gamaliel . . .

One of the greatest rabbis in Hebrew history, Gamaliel was respected by all Jews—Hebrews and Hellenists alike.

Acts 22:3 (e), 4 (a)
. . . and taught according to the perfect manner of the law of the fathers, and was zealous toward God as ye all are this day. And I persecuted this way unto the death . . .

"The Way" was a phrase that referred to believers.

Acts 22:4 (b)–6 (a)
. . . binding and delivering into prisons both men and women. As also the high priest doth bear me witness, and all the estate of the elders: from whom also I received letters unto the brethren, and went to Damascus, to bring them which were there bound unto Jerusalem, for to be punished. And it came to pass, that, as I made my journey . . .

With letters from the high priest in hand, prior to his conversion, Paul headed toward Damascus on a mission to bring the Christians from that region to trial in Jerusalem.

Acts 22:6 (b)–9
. . . and was come nigh unto Damascus about noon, suddenly there shone from heaven a great light round about me. And I fell unto the ground, and heard a voice saying unto me, Saul, Saul, why persecutest thou me? And I answered, Who art thou, Lord? And he said unto me, I am Jesus of Nazareth, whom thou persecutest. And they that were with me saw indeed the light, and were afraid; but they heard not the voice of him that spake to me.

In Acts 9:7, we read, "And the men which journeyed with him stood speechless, hearing a voice, but seeing no man." Here in his testimony, however, Paul said, "They heard not the voice of him that spake to me." Is this a contradiction? No.

The Greek usage in 9:7 indicates the men with Paul heard a noise. But here in 22:9, Paul used the Greek word *phonea* to indicate that the men with him heard no words.

Acts 22:10 (a)
And I said, What shall I do, Lord?

You'll always know when someone's truly saved because, like Paul, he'll say, "Lord, what do You want me to do? What do You want *from* me? What do You want *for* me? What do You want to do *in* and *through* me?"

Acts 22:10 (b)
And the Lord said unto me, Arise, and go into Damascus; and there it shall be told thee of all things which are appointed for thee to do.

"Go into the city, Paul. And when you get there, further instructions will be given." The way of the Lord is always one step at a time. He gives His people one instruction and waits until they obey it before more information is given.

In the midst of a great revival taking place through Philip's ministry in Samaria, the Lord told him to go to Gaza. Philip obeyed, and the Ethiopian eunuch was saved (Acts 8).

While Peter was praying on his rooftop, the Lord instructed him to follow three men who would knock on his door. Peter obeyed and the house of Cornelius was converted (Acts 10).

The Lord called Abraham from Ur and told him to follow Him one step at a time. Abraham obeyed and a nation was born (Hebrews 11:8).

Every time the Lord calls a man or a woman, every time He wants to bless someone, He does it by encouraging them to take a step of faith. Many times a lot of us miss out on years, or even a lifetime, of being in God's will because we don't act on the singular instruction He gives us. Precious people, we must obey the one thing the Lord has made known to us either through His Word, times of prayer, or the desires He has placed within our hearts.

- If we knew how it was going to work—it wouldn't be faith.
- If we knew where the supplies would come from—it wouldn't be faith.
- If we had it all mapped out—it wouldn't be faith.

Faith says, "Okay, Lord. Like Abraham, I don't know exactly how it's all going to work out—but here we go!"

In 1 Samuel 14, the Israelites were at a stand-off in a battle against the Philistines. Perhaps looking up at the stars one night, Jonathan was reminded that the Creator who made such beauty and displayed such glory was with him constantly. Perhaps pondering God's promise that one could chase one thousand and two could put ten thousand to flight if they were in God's will (Deuteronomy 32:30), he poked his armor-bearer and said, "Let's sneak over to the Philistine camp and see what the Lord might want to do."

So while the other guys snoozed, Jonathan and his armor-bearer made their way to the camp of the Philistines. As they approached the Philistine garrison, Jonathan said to his armor-bearer, "Now wait a minute. We want to be men of faith, but we don't want to be fools. I'll yell to the Philistines, and if they say, "Stay there, you guys. We see you, and we're coming to get you,"—we'll split and make our way back to camp as fast as we can. But, if they say, "Come up here, you guys. We'll take you on"—we'll take that as a word from the Lord, and we'll go get them."

That's the way I believe the Christian life should be lived: by taking steps of faith without being foolish. We should put on our armor, get ready for battle, go out to the edge, and say, "Here we are, Lord. What do You want to do?"

Jonathan called out. The Philistines answered, "Hey, come up here, and we'll teach you guys a lesson,"—and Jonathan said to his armor-bearer, "God is with us. Let's go get 'em." God was indeed with them. And a great, miraculous victory took place that day as two guys took on an entire army—and won.

Stepping out in faith and yet always being willing to pull back if God isn't in it—that's the key. Step out in faith—but if you sense the Lord's not in it, regroup, and see what else He might want to do. Be a Jonathan. Take a step of faith. You'll never regret it.

Acts 22:11 (a)
And when I could not see for the glory of that light . . .

Paul could have sat by the roadside, saying, "I can't go to Damascus, Lord, because I can't see."

But although he was blinded physically, he had 20/20 vision spiritually because he knew he must go in accordance with the divine directive he had been given.

Acts 22:11 (b)–13
... being led by the hand of them that were with me, I came into Damascus. And one Ananias, a devout man according to the law, having a good report of all the Jews which dwelt there, came unto me, and stood, and said unto me, Brother Saul, receive thy sight.

Speaking to a Jewish audience, Paul pointed out that Ananias was a devout man according to the law, a good man in the sight of all Jews. Conveniently, however, Paul didn't bother to mention that Ananias also happened to be a Christian.

Acts 22:13
And the same hour I looked up upon him.

The last thing Paul saw before he was blinded was the Person of Christ. The first thing he saw when he received his sight was a disciple of Christ. He saw the Head first—and then the body. So, too, although I've seen the Lord through a glass darkly, I've seen His body very clearly. I see the reality of Jesus in you, His body.

Act 22:14
And he said, The God of our fathers hath chosen thee, that thou shouldest know his will, and see that Just One, and shouldest hear the voice of his mouth.

This was my prayer for each of you—that you might know His will, see His face, and hear His voice.

Acts 22:15–17 (a)
For thou shalt be his witness unto all men of what thou hast seen and heard. And now why tarriest thou? arise, and be baptized, and wash away thy sins, calling on the name of the Lord. And it came to pass, that, when I was come again to Jerusalem ...

Continuing his testimony, Paul said, "After I left Damascus by way of a basket, I went to Jerusalem."

Acts 22:17 (b)–21 (a)
...even while I prayed in the temple, I was in a trance; and saw him saying unto me, Make haste, and get thee quickly out of Jerusalem: for they will not receive thy testimony concerning me. And I said, Lord, they know that I imprisoned and beat in every synagogue them that believed on thee: And when the blood of thy martyr Stephen was shed, I also was standing by, and consenting unto his death, and kept the raiment of them that slew him. And he said unto me, Depart ...

"Get out of Jerusalem," the Lord said.
What did Paul say?
"But, Lord, my background and my talents, my training and my gifts fit perfectly with these people."
And what did the Lord say?
"Split, Paul. This isn't what I want for you."

Acts 22:21 (b), 22 (a)
... for I will send thee far hence unto the Gentiles. And they gave him audience unto this word ...

The Jews listened to Paul—until he said the word "Gentile."

Acts 22:22 (b)
...and then lifted up their voices, and said, Away with such a fellow from the earth: for it is not fit that he should live.

"Blasphemy!" cried the Jews. "How dare Paul say that God sent him to the *Gentiles.* Everyone knows Gentiles are good for nothing but to keep hell hot."

Acts 22:23
And as they cried out, and cast off their clothes, and threw dust into the air.

It was fortunate there were no rocks on the temple mount, for had there been, Paul would most likely have been stoned on the spot.

Acts 22:24
The chief captain commanded him to be brought into the castle, and bade that he should be examined by scourging; that he might know wherefore they cried so against him.

Examination by scourging was a tortuous, cruel method used to extract information. The accused would be bound and beaten with the flagellum until he either confessed or died.

Acts 22:25
And as they bound him with thongs, Paul said unto the centurion that stood by, Is it

lawful for you to scourge a man that is a
Roman, and uncondemned?

It was a jailable offense to even bind a Roman
citizen without following proper legal procedures
and a capital offense to scourge him without doing so. Why did Paul wait until he was bound to
declare his Roman citizenship? Because in so doing, he had Claudius Lysias right where he
wanted him.

Sometimes people ask, "Should a Christian
stand up for his civil rights?" When dealing with
believers, we are told very clearly that we are not
to take them to trial (Matthew 18:15). But Paul's
example tells me that when dealing with the
world, sometimes it's appropriate and very necessary to do so. Surely in the litigation-mad
world in which we live, this has been taken to an
extreme. But I believe there are times when it is
valid.

Acts 22:26–28 (a)
**When the centurion heard that, he went and
told the chief captain, saying, Take heed
what thou doest: for this man is a Roman.
Then the chief captain came, and said unto
him, Tell me, art thou a Roman? He said,
Yea. And the chief captain answered, With
a great sum obtained I this freedom.**

The wife of Emperor Claudius encouraged him
to raise money for their personal treasury by
selling Roman citizenships. Claudius Lysias was
one who took advantage of that practice.

Acts 22:28 (b)
And Paul said, But I was free born.

Most historians believe Paul's father was a Jew
who had been granted Roman citizenship because of some service he had given to the empire.

Acts 22:29
**Then straightway they departed from him
which should have examined him: and the
chief captain also was afraid, after he knew
that he was a Roman, and because he had
bound him.**

Claudius Lysias knew he was on thin ice.

Acts 22:30
**On the morrow, because he would have
known the certainty wherefore he was accused of the Jews, he loosed him from his
bands, and commanded the chief priests and
all their council to appear, and brought Paul
down, and set him before them.**

Unable to examine Paul by scourging, yet still
wanting to get to the bottom of the issue, Claudius Lysias decided to bring Paul before the Jewish Supreme Court—the Sanhedrin.

23 At last, Paul had returned to Jerusalem, where, following two riots and
one near scourging, he found himself
standing before the Sanhedrin—the Jewish Supreme Court.

Acts 23:1 (a)
**And Paul, earnestly beholding the council,
said, Men and brethren . . .**

Customarily, members of the Sanhedrin were
addressed as "fathers." Referring to them as
"brethren" implies that before his conversion,
Paul had himself been a member of this auspi-
cious body.

Acts 23:1 (b)
**. . . I have lived in all good conscience before
God until this day.**

It has been said the only way to have a good conscience is to have a bad memory. Paul was an exception. He was an incredible individual who, before
his conversion, could truly say, "According to my
conscience, I was blameless." The only indication
Paul ever gave of violating any part of the Law was
in Romans 7, when he said, "I violated the commandment not to covet," (see Romans 7:7).

What did Paul covet? Probably not material
possessions or sensual pleasures—but prestige
and power in the religious system of which he
was a part.

From the outside, Paul looked impeccable—
radical for righteousness, a Pharisee of Pharisees—which proves to me conclusively that, although a conscience can be a good goad, it's a
lousy guide. Paul's conscience goaded him into
enslaving, incarcerating, and ultimately execut-
ing Christians, but it was unable to guide him to
the truth.

Acts 23:2
**And the high priest Ananias commanded
them that stood by him to smite him on the
mouth.**

A multimillionaire by today's standards, Ananias was one of the worst high priests in the history of Israel. He had worked out a deal with the
priests so that animals brought to the temple for

sacrifice would conveniently be found flawed upon inspection.

"Can't use this one," the priest would say. "This sheep is blemished. But this is your lucky day. We just happen to have some sheep over here you could purchase."

"Really?" the relieved supplicant would say. "How much?"

"Well, they're a little pricy—but they're worth it," the priest would answer. "They've already been preapproved."

Through such deals, Ananias gouged the people and pocketed huge amounts of money. No wonder that, after serving twelve years as high priest, he was assassinated by his own countrymen.

Acts 23:3 (a)
Then said Paul unto him, God shall smite thee, thou whited wall . . .

If you were in Israel at this time, making your way to Jerusalem to celebrate Passover, for example, it would have been very important that on your way you didn't accidentally become ceremonially unclean by stepping on or brushing against a grave or sepulchre. Consequently, graves and sepulchres were painted white to warn people of the dead bones within. Thus, in calling Ananias a "whited wall," Paul was actually calling him a bag of bones.

This passage is often cited by people who say there are times when it's right to respond vehemently. "Because Paul raised his voice and called Ananias a bag of bones," they say, "it's okay for me to speak my mind just as pointedly."

I suggest to you, however, that although Paul does do that here—there is a higher example of Another who was struck in the mouth in the presence of a high priest. Like Paul, Jesus was struck by one who stood by the high priest. But instead of heatedly raising His voice, He humbly raised a question when He said, "If I said something wrong, correct Me. But if what I have said is true, then why are you doing this?" (see John 18:23).

As excellent a model as Paul might be for us, we must always make sure our model for behavior is the Person of Jesus Christ, for He set a higher standard than any other.

Acts 23:3 (b)
. . . for sittest thou to judge me after the law, and commandest me to be smitten contrary to the law?

"How dare you judge me," said Paul to Ananias, "when you're violating the law yourself."

You see, according to Deuteronomy 25, it was absolutely forbidden for a man to be smitten without due process of law. And if smitten, he was to be smitten on the back, not on the mouth.

Acts 23:4
And they that stood by said, Revilest thou God's high priest?

Those who stood by Ananias were aghast. "Do you *dare* to revile God's high priest?" they asked Paul.

Acts 23:5
Then said Paul, I wist not, brethren, that he was the high priest: for it is written, Thou shalt not speak evil of the ruler of thy people.

Why didn't Paul know Ananias was the high priest?

It could have been an oversight. Ananias may not have been wearing his high priestly regalia.

It could have been because Paul was out of sight. That is, because he had been away from Jerusalem for many years ministering in Asia Minor, Paul may not have been aware that Ananias had ascended to the office of high priest.

It could have been due to bad eyesight. Many scholars believe Paul's vision was extremely impaired (Galatians 4:15; 6:11).

"Well, then," you say, "since Paul didn't know who Ananias was, it is excusable that he lashed out at him." But isn't that the point? We never know people like we think we do.

I love the story of the German schoolteacher who clicked his heels together and bowed before each of his second- and third-grade students as they entered his classroom every morning. When asked why he did this, he said, "I don't know which of these students might one day be a king or a chancellor. I want to respect them now because I don't know what they'll become."

The reason this story is known is because it was told by one of his more famous students—a man named Albert Einstein. Truly, before I call someone a bag of bones, I better realize I may not know as much about him as I think I do.

For topical study of Acts 23:5 entitled "Speak no Evil," turn to page 821.

Acts 23:6–8

But when Paul perceived that the one part were Sadducees, and the other Pharisees, he cried out in the council, Men and brethren, I am a Pharisee, the son of a Pharisee: of the hope and resurrection of the dead I am called in question. And when he had so said, there arose a dissension between the Pharisees and the Sadducees: and the multitude was divided. For the Sadducees say that there is no resurrection, neither angel, nor spirit: but the Pharisees confess both.

Looking at the crowd, Paul saw two parties in the room: the Pharisees, who believed in the supernatural—and the Sadducees, who didn't. Paul exploited this division when, referring to the Resurrection of Jesus Christ, he said, "Resurrection is the reason for the controversy that surrounds me."

Acts 23:9

And there arose a great cry: and the scribes that were of the Pharisees' part arose, and strove, saying, We find no evil in this man: but if a spirit or an angel hath spoken to him, let us not fight against God.

When Paul said the word "resurrection," the Sanhedrin was immediately split in two. "If he saw someone resurrected or an angel—we have no problem with that," said the Pharisees. But, of course, the Resurrection presented a major problem for the Sadducees.

Acts 23:10

And when there arose a great dissension, the chief captain, fearing lest Paul should have been pulled in pieces of them, commanded the soldiers to go down, and to take him by force from among them, and to bring him into the castle.

Here's Claudius Lysias again—rescuing Paul from riot number three.

Acts 23:11

And the night following the Lord stood by him, and said, Be of good cheer, Paul: for as thou hast testified of me in Jerusalem, so must thou bear witness also at Rome.

As Paul reflected on the events that led to his being held in protective custody, he must have thought, "I went into the temple to try to appease James and the other brothers—and a riot broke out. I shared my testimony on the steps of the Fortress—and people wanted to kill me. I came into the Sanhedrin—and created tumult and turmoil. I failed. There's no fruit, no headway whatsoever."

But that's precisely when the Lord came to him, saying, "I have seen you witness for Me. Be of good cheer, Paul. You're doing more than you think."

For topical study of Acts 23:11 entitled "Be of Good Cheer," turn to page 824.

Acts 23:12–16

And when it was day, certain of the Jews banded together, and bound themselves under a curse, saying that they would neither eat nor drink till they had killed Paul. And they were more than forty which had made this conspiracy. And they came to the chief priests and elders, and said, We have bound ourselves under a great curse, that we will eat nothing until we have slain Paul. Now therefore ye with the council signify to the chief captain that he bring him down unto you tomorrow, as though ye would enquire something more perfectly concerning him: and we, or ever he come near, are ready to kill him. And when Paul's sister's son heard of their lying in wait, he went and entered into the castle and told Paul.

Forty men took an oath not to eat until Paul was dead. Their plan was to tell Claudius Lysias that the Sanhedrin wanted to question Paul the next day, but when he was brought to the council, they would spring out and kill him. However, it "just so happened" that Paul's nephew heard the entire conversation.

Acts 23:17–21

Then Paul called one of the centurions unto him, and said, Bring this young man unto the chief captain: for he hath a certain thing to tell him. So he took him, and brought him to the chief captain, and said, Paul the prisoner called me unto him, and prayed me to bring this young man unto thee, who hath something to say unto thee. Then the chief captain took him by the hand, and went with him aside privately, and asked him, What is that thou hast to tell me? And he said, The Jews have agreed to desire thee that thou wouldest bring down Paul to morrow into the council, as though they would inquire somewhat of him more perfectly. But do not

thou yield unto them: for there lie in wait for him of them more than forty men, which have bound themselves with an oath, that they will neither eat nor drink till they have killed him: and now are they ready, looking for a promise from thee.

It was neither coincidence nor accident that Paul's nephew was in earshot of the plan to kill Paul; it was part of God's program for Paul.

At some point in their walk, most believers ask, "How can I know what God wants me to do?" And, like Elijah in 1 Kings 19, they sit in a cave, wondering. Like Elijah, they feel the earth shaking—but the Lord is not in the earthquake. They see the fire glowing—but the Lord is not in the fire. They watch the wind blowing—but the Lord is not in the wind. Many people are still looking for an earth-shaking confirmation, a fiery illumination, or a wind to blow them in divine direction.

But it's much simpler than that: As Elijah discovered, God's is a still, small voice (1 Kings 19:12). The Lord whispers in your heart, writes desires upon your heart, and then gives confirmation to your heart through situations and people around you. Accuse me of being simplistic, but I find it so wonderful to say, "Father, this is the desire of my heart. I'm going to pursue this course, knowing You will close and open doors—as You lead me in a supernaturally natural way."

For whatever question you face presently, just make sure your heart is open to the Lord—and He'll have a nephew in the right place at the right time who will overhear a conversation, go to the Roman captain, and set events in motion, which the world will call luck, but in which you'll see the hand of God.

Acts 23:22–24 (a)
So the chief captain then let the young man depart, and charged him, See thou tell no man that thou hast shewed these things to me. And he called unto him two centurions, saying, Make ready two hundred soldiers to go to Caesarea, and horsemen threescore and ten, and spearmen two hundred, at the third hour of the night; and provide them beasts, that they may set Paul on. . . .

What a trip! Paul is about to be escorted by two hundred infantrymen, seventy horsemen, and two hundred spearmen to the seaport city of Caesarea in the middle of the night. Imagine the reaction of the forty men who took the oath to kill Paul. Can you hear their stomachs growling?

Acts 23:24 (b)
. . . and bring him safe unto Felix the governor.

The only slave in Roman history to become a governor, Felix was a cruel character who received his appointment because his brother, Pallos, was a friend of Caesar Nero. Of Felix, the brilliant Roman historian, Tacitus, said, "He executes the prerogatives of a king with the spirit of a slave," for although he was in power as governor, Felix retained a slave's mentality of getting back at the world for all the abuses it had heaped upon him.

Acts 23:25–27
And he wrote a letter after this manner: Claudius Lysias unto the most excellent governor Felix sendeth greeting. This man was taken of the Jews, and should have been killed of them: then came I with an army, and rescued him, having understood that he was a Roman.

It's funny how Claudius Lysias conveniently forgot to mention he had Paul bound and was ready to beat him.

Acts 23:28–30
And when I would have known the cause wherefore they accused him, I brought him forth into their council: Whom I perceived to be accused of questions of their law, but to have nothing laid to his charge worthy of death or of bonds. And when it was told me how that the Jews laid wait for the man, I sent straightway to thee, and gave commandment to his accusers also to say before thee what they had against him. Farewell.

"I'm sending Paul to you, Felix," wrote Claudius Lysias. "Let his accusers come and present their case to you. You're the governor. Now Paul's your problem."

Acts 23:31–35
Then the soldiers, as it was commanded them, took Paul, and brought him by night to Antipatris. On the morrow they left the horsemen to go with him, and returned to the castle: Who, when they came to Caesarea, and delivered the epistle to the governor, presented Paul also before him. And when the governor had read the letter, he asked of what province he was. And when he understood that he was of Cilicia; I will hear thee, said he, when thine accusers are also come. And he commanded him to be kept in Herod's judgment hall.

Herod's judgment hall was neither a dungeon

nor a prison, but rather a palace on the shore of the Mediterranean. Thus, as we'll see in chapter 24, Paul would spend two years in protective custody on the beach.

SPEAK NO EVIL
A Topical Study of
Acts 23:5

I feel this is an important verse in light of the political climate. It's so easy to feel emotions rising and passions stirring—and to find ourselves saying things that are not right in the sight of the Lord, for truly, "we are not to speak evil of the ruler of the people."

"But politicians are so undeserving of respect," you say. "They're all a bunch of con artists."

"Read the eye chart," the draft board physician said.

"What eye chart?" asked the draft dodger.

"Son, you better sit in that chair while I check your records," the concerned doctor said.

"What chair?"

Convinced the would-be soldier had terrible eyesight, the doctor wrote him a deferment. Greatly relieved, the young man walked into a darkened theatre and sat down with a bag of popcorn to celebrate. He had a great time—until the lights came on and he realized he was sitting next to the eye doctor.

Thinking fast, the young man turned to him, and said, "Is this the bus to Detroit?"

Sometimes, as we see politicians change their stories and position themselves quite cleverly, we find ourselves becoming cynical and bitter toward our leaders. "I'm so upset with those guys and how they behave. I'm perfectly justified in berating them verbally and criticizing them caustically," we say.

Really? That's not what Paul said. When he realized Ananias was the high priest, he said he would not have called him a bag of bones because the position is to be honored even if the person holding it is dishonorable.

Let every soul be subject unto the higher powers. For there is no power but of God: the powers that be are ordained of God. Whosoever therefore resisteth the power, resisteth the ordinance of God . . .   Romans 13:1, 2 (a)

To whom then will ye liken God? or what likeness will ye compare unto him? It is he that sitteth upon the circle of the earth, and the inhabitants thereof

are as grasshoppers; that stretcheth out the heavens as a curtain, and spreadeth
them out as a tent to dwell in: That bringeth the princes to nothing; he maketh
the judges of the earth as vanity.   Isaiah 40:18; 22, 23

In the day Isaiah wrote these words, every culture and every society had determined that the world was flat.

- Those living in India thought a huge elephant held the flat world on its back.
- The Egyptians thought the flat world rested on the back of a large tortoise.
- Greeks were convinced it was held up by the strong arms of Atlas.

Although Isaiah declared that God sits upon the circle of the earth, and that Job said He hung the earth upon nothing (Job 26:7), it would not be until centuries later that scientists would make the "profound discovery" that the earth is round and suspended in mid-air.

Truly God sits upon the circle of the earth. He's on the throne. He is the One who makes princes, presidents, and Supreme Court justices come and go as He wishes. Therefore, it is up to us not to criticize and complain, but to take heed to Peter's words.

Honour all men. Love the brotherhood. Fear God. Honour the king.
                                                    1 Peter 2:17

"That was easy for Peter," you say. "In his day, those in positions of authority had character."

Really?

When Peter wrote these words, Caesar Nero was on the throne. Caesar Nero was the man who rode naked in his chariot, shrieking at the top of his lungs in demonic laughter while he watched over one thousand Christians who had been dipped in wax, ignited as human candles to light his garden. What did Peter say to do about Nero? He didn't say to impeach him, sign petitions about him, or rebel against him. He said to honor him.

Am I suggesting we shouldn't be engaged politically?

No.

I'm suggesting we do what God's people were to do in Jeremiah's day. The Babylonians had carried the Israelites into what would turn out to be a seventy-year captivity in Babylon. "Since we're only going to be here for a little while," said the Israelites, "let's not get too settled."

But the Lord said otherwise:

Build ye houses, and dwell in them; and plant gardens, and eat the fruit of
them; take ye wives, and beget sons and daughters; and take wives for your

sons, and give your daughters to husbands, that they may bear sons and daughters; that ye may be increased there, and not diminished. And seek the peace of the city whither I have caused you to be carried away captives, and pray unto the Lord for it: for in the peace thereof shall ye have peace.

Jeremiah 29:5–7

Some Christians say, "We're only here on earth for seventy years. Since our real home is in heaven, we're not going to get involved with what's going on down here."

But the Lord says we are to be like the children of Israel. We're to leave this place better than we found it. Therefore, even though Babylon is not our home, even though we're only here for a relatively short season, we are to build houses, plant gardens, seek peace, and pray for our cities. And as we pray, we can trust our Lord, knowing He is sovereign and He sees what needs to happen presently based upon what will happen prophetically.

This applies not only politically, but parentally. Kids, you are told to honor your parents (Exodus 20:12). "Oh, but they're such idiots," you say. "My dad's a bag of bones, and my mom's out of it. They don't relate to me, and I can't understand them." Listen, if you are living at home, the word to you is to *honor* your parents. Why? Because of all the billions of parents throughout history who have peopled this planet, God chose *your* mom and dad as the ones to work on your life in a unique way.

The same is true in marriage. Ephesians 5 says wives are to reverence their husbands (Ephesians 5:33). "You don't know my husband," you say. "Everything he does rubs me the wrong way."

Oh, but that's the way it's *supposed* to be.

The massive stones used in the construction of Solomon's temple were actually shaped and chiseled to perfection a great distance from the temple mount. Why? So that on the temple mount the sound of a hammer or chisel would not be heard (1 Kings 6:7).

So, too, Peter says we are living stones, being fit together for eternity (1 Peter 2:5). This earth is the rock quarry wherein we are being shaped, chipped, and chiseled. As living stones, we are constantly moving, each of us knocking rough edges off, smoothing, shaping one another. Why? So that when we reach heaven, the ultimate temple, the sound of a hammer or chisel will not be heard.

We must realize the Lord has allowed us to be in the situation we're in—be it politically, parentally, or maritally—for our good and His glory. Therefore, we are not to revile. We are not to reject. We are to realize He is sovereign and in control. Then we can say,

"Lord, if You're allowing this politician to be elected to fulfill Your purpose nationally and prophetically—so be it."

"If You're allowing these people to parent me, even though I may not understand them presently—I will honor them."

"If You're allowing my husband or wife to shape me for eternity—Thy will be done."

My prayer for you, precious people, is that during these days you will not be uptight or stressed-out, cynical or caustic—but that in the midst of political, parental, or marital turmoil, you will remember that the God who sits on the circle of the earth is still in complete control.

BE OF GOOD CHEER
A Topical Study of
Acts 23:11

Training to be a paratrooper, an army private was instructed to jump out of the airplane, count to ten, and pull his ripcord. If his primary parachute didn't open, he was to pull the ripcord on his front pack, which would open his auxiliary chute, whereby he would float to safety, after which time a truck would pick him up and take him back to the base. The private did exactly as he was told: On command, he jumped out of the airplane, counted to ten, pulled his ripcord—but nothing happened. He then pulled the ripcord on his front pack, but, again—nothing happened.

"Great," he said. "My parachute didn't open. My backup didn't open. The truck probably won't be there to pick me up, either."

Paul must have felt the same way. After twenty years of ministering to the Gentiles, he had finally returned to Jerusalem. When he arrived in the Holy City, he must have expected something wonderful to happen. Instead, it seemed as though everything came crashing down around him, when, after causing three riots, nothing less than the Roman army was needed to save his life.

Maybe you can relate to Paul. Maybe you've longed to do something for the Lord and have stepped out in faith to serve Him. But you feel like nothing's happening except a mess. I have good news! Our text is for *you*.

The Lord Appearing *to* Paul

And the night following . . .   Acts 23:11 (a)

When did the Lord appear to Paul? In the darkest hour of Paul's darkest day. When does the Lord appear to you and me? Frequently, He becomes most real to us when we're in the midst of darkness—when we're discouraged and defeated, when things appear hopeless.

Why?

Didn't Jesus say He was the Light of the World (John 8:12)? If I strike a match in a well-lit room, it won't be noticed at all. But if I strike a match in a pitch-black room, it will be seen very readily. The same is true of the Lord. I have found He is seen most clearly by me when things are pretty dark. When things go fine, I get caught up in everything around me, and I'm not always tuned in to the Lord. It's in the night, when I'm wondering, *Lord, am I doing anything right at all? Why am I so stubborn? Why am I so hard of heart?* that I see the Lord most clearly, for, as the Light of the World, the darker the situation, the brighter He shines.

The Lord Standing *by* Paul

. . . the Lord stood by him . . .   Acts 23:11 (b)

The Lord didn't say, "Forget it, Paul. You're so stubborn coming here to Jerusalem. I'm not standing by you." No, the Lord stood by Paul because, when we are faithless, He is faithful still, for He cannot deny Himself (2 Timothy 2:13).

Even if I am fickle, faithless, and foolish, the Lord is faithful. He can't be anything other than that, for His faithfulness is not a decision He makes—it's who He is.

> *And he shewed me Joshua the high priest standing before the angel of the Lord, and Satan standing at his right hand to resist him. And the Lord said unto Satan, The Lord rebuke thee, O Satan; even the Lord that hath chosen Jerusalem rebuke thee: is not this a brand plucked out of the fire? Now Joshua was clothed with filthy garments, and stood before the angel. And he answered and spake unto those that stood before him, saying, Take away the filthy garments from him. And unto him he said, Behold, I have caused thine iniquity to pass from thee, and I will clothe thee with change of raiment.*
>
> Zechariah 3:1–4

There is a courtroom drama constantly taking place in heaven wherein Satan accuses me day and night. But Jesus is my Advocate, my defense lawyer, who says, "Father, Jon is spotless because My blood has cleansed him totally" (see 1 John 2:1).

The Father then hits the gavel, if you would, and says, "Case dismissed for complete lack of evidence."

Satan, however, comes back again and again, bringing up case after case before becoming so frustrated by his inability to win his case in heaven that he chooses a different tactic: He perches on my shoulder and whispers in my ear, "You've really blown it. Your motives are mixed. You're lacking in prayer. Your ministry is empty. Your service is nothing."

It's then that, like Paul, I can begin to think, *Maybe I'm not doing anything at all. Maybe I'm out of God's will. Maybe He's no longer interested in me.*

It was when Paul was in a dark hour that the Lord said, "Be of good cheer. I'm standing by you. Why? Because, Paul, even if you have failed, the work of the Cross covers and cleanses totally."

Moses had taken Aaron and Hur up on the mountain at Rephidim, where he instructed his protigie, Joshua, to lead the Israelite troops into battle against the Amalekites. Joshua obeyed, while Moses stayed upon the mountain with the rod of God in his hands. As long as Moses held up the rod, the Israelites were victorious. But whenever his arms got heavy and began to fall, the Amalekites took control. Finally, Aaron stood on one side of him, and Hur stood on the other, and together they propped up Moses' arms, and Israel won the battle (Exodus 17).

While this story has wonderful application concerning the importance of prevailing prayer, there's something else I want you to see here. That is, every time Joshua looked back and could see three men on the hill—one in the middle holding up the rod with outstretched hands—he knew he would be victorious in battle.

So, too, on another hill, called Calvary, another Man's hands were outstretched between two men (Matthew 27:38). And, like Joshua, as long as I see His hands on the Cross and understand that even if my motives are mixed, even if my vision is fuzzy, even if I'm not exactly where I should be—I can engage in battle, I can keep going, I can be of good cheer, knowing He has provided His blood to cleanse me.

I can look to the mountain and see One who does not fail, One whose hands have never fallen, One who paid the price completely. And as long as I see Him, even when I do fail, and even if I am failing, Satan has no case against me."

The Lord's Evaluation *of* Paul

> . . . *For as thou has testified of me in Jerusalem, so must thou bear witness also at Rome.*   Acts 23:11 (c)

"You testified of Me here," said Jesus.

"Really, Lord?" Paul must have said. "I thought I only caused problems."

In Matthew 10:42, Jesus said, "If you offer a cup of cold water to a little one in My Name, you'll have reward." When you gave a cup of cold water to a kid; when you helped your neighbor get his trash out to the street; when you wrote a letter of encouragement—the Lord took note. "For God is not unrighteous to forget your work and labour of love" (Hebrews 6:10).

You see, although we have a tendency to think we're never doing enough, and that the little we are doing is probably flawed—in reality, the Lord keeps record of all the good stuff we do—even the things we think are insignificant.

In Matthew 25 Jesus told the story of a man who went to a far country. Before he left, he gave talents to his servants, a talent being one year's salary. To one servant he gave one talent, to another, five talents, to another, ten. When he came back, he found the man who had ten talents had doubled the money by investing it wisely. The same was true of the man with five talents. But the man with one talent said, "Master, I know you're a harsh man, that you reap where you have not sown, and gather where you have not strawed. So I buried my talent."

"It is true I reap where I have not sown and gather where I have not strawed," said the master. "But you are a fool because you could at least have put the money in the bank and drawn interest. I'm going to give your talent to the one who has ten; and you will be cast into outer darkness."

Now, a lot of us hear that story and say, "That's me. I'm the foolish servant. I have buried my talent. I'm not doing enough. And I know when the Lord returns, I'll just hand Him my one muddy talent, and He'll send me to outer darkness.

No, no, no! The man who was cast into outer darkness didn't even know the Lord. He wasn't a believer. That's why he said, "You are a harsh man" (see verse 24). The world always views the Lord as a "harsh man." Yet, although the master in the parable repeated the servant's claim that he reaped where he had not sown, and gathered where he had not strawed—he did not repeat the claim that he was a harsh man (verse 26)—because he wasn't.

"I am meek and lowly in heart," Jesus said in the only autobiographical statement He ever made (Matthew 11:29). "Give a glass of cold water to someone and I'll reward you. I'll take notice of even the simplest expression of My love. Even if you're making a mess of things in Jerusalem, Paul, I can find something good in what you've done. You did testify of Me. And because of that, I'm sending you somewhere you've always wanted to go: on an all-expenses-paid trip to Rome."

Folks, in the times you thought you messed up and were disobedient, the Lord says, "Even though you think you've made a mess of the situation, I acknowledge the good you have done."

If you don't believe me, let's look at Hebrews 11.

As you read the list in God's "Hall of Faith," you come across Rahab the harlot.

"But she lied," you say.

"She also hid My people," counters the Lord.

Next is Gideon. The Lord said, "I'm going to use you, Gideon."

"Give me a sign," said Gideon. "I'll put a fleece out, and if it is wet in the morning, I'll believe You."

Sure enough, the fleece was wet, and the ground was dry.

"Hmm. I still don't believe You," said Gideon. "This time make the ground wet and the fleece dry."

The next day Gideon rowed his boat out to the fleece, and it was totally dry. Yet the Lord lists Gideon as a hero of *faith?*

Next is Samson.
Would you put *Samson* in your "Hall of Faith"?

After Samson is Barak, who was told by the prophetess Deborah that he would experience victory as he led the Israelites against Sisera to battle. What did Barak say to Deborah? "I'm not going unless you go with me." Yet Barak, hiding behind Deborah's skirts, makes it into Hebrews 11 as a hero of *faith.*

I'm perplexed by this until I understand the nature of my Father, the character of my Lord, the heart of my Savior. He's incredibly kind, and if there's any good thing He can find, He will. You see, gang, in the New Testament, there is *no* mention of *any* sin of an Old Testament saint.

"Well, Barak, at least you went."
"Gideon, you finally did get out there."
"Samson, you did some good things (we won't mention Delilah)."
"Rahab, despite your lie, you saved the spies," says the Lord.

So, too, here's Paul sitting in prison. The Lord stood by him, threw an arm around him, and said to him, "Be of good cheer, Paul. You have been a witness for Me here. Now I'm sending you on to further ministry."

Dear brother, precious sister—don't listen to the condemning accusation of the Enemy saying, "You're not doing enough—and what you are doing is tainted by false motives." Instead, look behind you to the three men on the hill. See the Man in the middle with outstretched hands, and understand the price He paid. Jesus Christ has cleansed you from all sin. And even when you are faithless, He is faithful to come to you time and time again, saying, "Be of *good* cheer."

24 Here is Paul, standing before Felix—a man who, according to biblical scholar and secular historian alike, had no business being in a position of power.

Acts 24:1
And after five days Ananias the high priest descended with the elders, and with a certain orator named Tertullus, who informed the governor against Paul.

Paul had been in Caesarea for five days, when one of the most famous lawyers of his time, an eloquent speaker named Tertullus, arrived from Jerusalem to argue against him. It is interesting to me that Ananias made the journey along with Tertullus. At this point, Ananias was eighty years old, and the trip from Jerusalem to Caesarea was an arduous sixty-mile journey. For Ananias to make such a difficult trip at his age to see Paul go on trial before Felix speaks to me of the great degree of animosity he felt in his heart toward Paul.

Acts 24:2 (a)
And when he was called forth, Tertullus began to accuse him saying, Seeing that by thee we enjoy great quietness . . .

Quietness? There were riots breaking out constantly.

Acts 24:2 (b)
... and that very worthy deeds are done unto this nation by thy providence.

Worthy deeds? Felix had robbed the people blind and had appointed corrupt leaders.

Acts 24:3, 4
We accept it always, and in all places, most noble Felix, with all thankfulness. Notwithstanding, that I be not further tedious unto thee, I pray thee that thou wouldest hear us of thy clemency a few words.

Everyone in the country knew Felix was a rat, yet Tertullus came on with flowery language and flattery, knowing his case would be strengthened as Felix drank it all in.

Acts 24:5 (a)
For we have found this man a pestilent fellow, and a mover of sedition among all the Jews throughout the world ...

"Paul's a pest," charged Tertullus. "Wherever he goes, he causes riots and problems."

Acts 24:5 (b)
... and a ringleader of the sect of the Nazarenes ...

The enemies of the early church called the believers either Christians or Nazarenes. "Christian" or "little Christ" was meant to mock the Lord, and "Nazarene" called attention to the fact that He was from Nazareth—the hick-town about which Nathanael asked, "Can any good thing come out of Nazareth?" (see John 1:46).

Acts 24:6 (a)
... who also hath gone about to profane the temple ...

Rumor had it that Paul had taken Gentiles into the temple. Although that was not true, Tertullus didn't care about the truth. He simply wanted to make his point and win the case.

Acts 24:6 (b), 7
... whom we took, and would have judged according to our law. But the chief captain Lysias came upon us, and with great violence took him away out of our hands.

Contrary to the testimony of Tertullus, the Jews were not about to judge Paul according to their law, but rather to tear him limb from limb (Acts 23:10). It was only through the intervention

of Lysias and the Roman army that Paul's life was spared.

Acts 24:8
Commanding his accusers to come unto thee: by examining of whom thyself mayest take knowledge of all these things, whereof we accuse him.

After rescuing Paul from three riots and one death threat, Claudius Lysias decided he had done his part and turned Paul over to Felix.

Acts 24:9
And the Jews also assented, saying that these thing were so.

Those who went with Tertullus and Ananias from Jerusalem to Caesarea were all in one accord—united in their stand against Paul.

Acts 24:10 (a)
Then Paul, after that the governor had beckoned unto him to speak, answered ...

Paul acted as his own defense lawyer.

Acts 24:10 (b)
... forasmuch as I know that thou hast been of many years a judge unto this nation, I do the more cheerfully answer for myself.

Paul addressed Felix with the only truthful thing he could say about him: "Felix, it's true you've been here many years."

Acts 24:11–13
Because that thou mayest understand, that there are yet but twelve days since I went up to Jerusalem for to worship. And they neither found me in the temple disputing with any man, neither raising up the people, neither in the synagogues, nor in the city: Neither can they prove the things whereof they now accuse me.

"These men speak lies, rumors, and innuendoes. They cannot present any proof whatsoever," insisted Paul.

Acts 24:14, 15
But this I confess unto thee, that after the way which they call heresy, so worship I the God of my fathers, believing all things which are written in the law and in the prophets: And have hope toward God, which they themselves also allow, that there shall be a resurrection of the dead, both of the just and unjust.

"These are the things of which I am guilty," said Paul. "I'm a follower of the Way. I'm a believer in the Scriptures. I'm waiting for the Resurrection."

For topical study of Acts 24:14–15 entitled "Paul: Guilty or not Guilty?" turn to page 832.

Acts 24:16
And herein do I exercise myself, to have always a conscience void of offence toward God, and toward men.

"I have a clean conscience toward God and men," said Paul.

Acts 24:17–20
Now after many years I came to bring alms to my nation, and offerings. Whereupon certain Jews from Asia found me purified in the temple, neither with multitude, nor with tumult. Who ought to have been here before thee, and object, if they had ought against me. Or else let these same here say, if they have found any evil doing in me, while I stood before the council,

Here's the question: since the law required every accusation to be verified by at least two witnesses (Deuteronomy 19:15), where were the witnesses? I have another question: Not only where were the witnesses, but where were James and the leaders of the church in Jerusalem who gave Paul the counsel to go into the temple in the first place? Tertullus, Ananias, and the elders made the journey to accuse Paul. Why did no one make the same journey to defend him?

Acts 24:21
Except it be for this one voice, that I cried standing among them, Touching the resurrection of the dead I am called in question by you this day.

When Paul went into the Sanhedrin and said he believed in the resurrection, he caused a riot to break out. "I am guilty of that," he said.

Acts 24:22 (a)
And when Felix heard these things, having more perfect knowledge of that way, he deferred them . . .

How did Felix get his knowledge of the Way—of Christianity? We don't know for sure, but there are references in ancient literature to Felix spending a great deal of time with Simon the Sor-cerer. After Simon's conversion was called into question (Acts 8:20), he disappeared from the scene scripturally. But history records much about Simon the Sorcerer, including his becoming a friend of Felix.

Acts 24:22 (b)
. . . and said, When Lysias the chief captain shall come down, I will know the uttermost of your matter.

Felix said, "I'll send for Lysias and see what he has to say about this matter." Why? Because Felix must have begun to suspect that Paul had committed no crime—that this was a religious rather than a civil issue.

Acts 24:23
And he commanded a centurion to keep Paul, and to let him have liberty, and that he should forbid none of his acquaintance to minister or come unto him.

"Keep him in protective custody," said Felix, "but allow him liberty and visitors." Paul had the opportunity to have his friends come—but as far as we know, none came.

Acts 24:24 (a)
And after certain days, when Felix came with his wife Drusilla, which was a Jewess . . .

Daughter of Herod Agrippa (whom worms ate in the amphitheatre at Caesarea), great-granddaughter of Herod the Great (who ordered the slaughter of the infants when Jesus was born), and great niece of the Herod who beheaded John the Baptist—Drusilla didn't have the greatest heritage, and hers is a tragic story. Tradition has it that she was married to a Syrian prince when a magician, secretly in the employ of Felix, told her she should marry Felix. Enamored with the occult, Drusilla, at the age of nineteen, left her husband to become Felix's third wife.

Acts 24:24 (b)
. . . he sent for Paul, and heard him concerning the faith in Christ.

Paul now stands before Felix and Drusilla.

Acts 24:25 (a)
And as he reasoned . . .

Paul, an intellectual giant of theology, a lover of God, and a lover of people, begins to reason with

Felix and Drusilla. Our faith is exceedingly reasonable. The longer I walk with the Lord, and the more I learn about the Word, the more I welcome opportunities to go into high-school classes or college seminars to discuss the faith with any who question it.

Our faith is reasonable in every way—logically, philosophically, and scientifically.

The cover story in *TIME* magazine recently was about a six-thousand-year-old frozen corpse discovered in the crevice of a glacier in the Alps one summer. I chuckled my way through this very interesting article as I read that the scientific world was shocked to find out that the "Ice Man" wasn't bowed over with sloping forehead and thick jaw, as had been hypothesized and accepted as fact for decades—but that he looked just like us. He had lined shoes, sewn clothes, and sophisticated tools centuries before he was "supposed" to have been able to do any of those things.

Prior to this discovery, ancient man was regarded as little more than a glorified ape at best. But the discovery of Ice Man calls all previous suppositions into question. If only these scientists had read their Bibles—they wouldn't have been surprised. Truly the Word is reasonable!

Acts 24:25 (b)
. . . of righteousness . . .

Paul reasoned with Felix and Drusilla concerning the nature of righteousness. Felix and Drusilla were not righteous. Their life was filthy, their history diabolical. They were not liked by the people they ruled and were not trusted by even their own household of slaves, servants, and companions. But Paul must have told them that if any man be in Christ he is a new creature. Old things pass away; all things become new (2 Corinthians 5:17). "Felix, Drusilla, you can have a new beginning. You can become righteous in Christ Jesus," Paul must have said.

When I was saved, not only did Jesus come into me, but, just as wonderful, just as fabulous is the fact that I was hidden in Him (Colossians 3:3). Therefore, when the Father looks at me, He doesn't see my sin. He sees Jesus. When a believer finally understands this concept, how his walk will change. No longer will he think, *God won't listen to me because I'm such an idiot.* No, he'll say, "When God looks at me He doesn't see my sin. He sees His Son."

Acts 24:25 (c)
. . . temperance . . .

Paul reasoned with Felix and Drusilla concerning the need for temperance. We live in a world that knows very little of temperance, self-control, or moderation. That is why our world is emotionally bruised, physically wiped-out, and spiritually dead. Temperance is so good and so necessary. "Let your moderation be known unto all men," wrote Paul (Philippians 4:5). Lead tempered lives and you'll be blessed.

Acts 24:25 (d)
. . . and judgment to come . . .

Finally, Paul reasoned with Felix and Drusilla concerning the nearness of judgment.

While he was President, Harry Truman was awakened at three-thirty one morning by an energetic young aide. "Mr. President, I'm sorry to wake you," he said, "but I had to inform you that the Commissioner of Highways just died, and I was wondering if you would be open to my taking his place."

Disgusted by such self-serving audacity, Truman is said to have replied, "Son, it's okay by me if it's okay with the undertaker."

The statistics on death are conclusive: Ten out of ten people die. Yet most people refuse to spend any significant time contemplating the fact that they're dying. Paul reasoned with Felix and Drusilla—reminding them of the nearness of judgment and the reality of eternity.

Acts 24:25 (e)
. . . Felix trembled . . .

The Greek word for "trembled" is the same word used to describe an earthquake. In other words, Felix was literally shaking.

Acts 24:25 (f)
. . . and answered, Go thy way for this time; when I have a convenient season, I will call for thee.

The tactic of the Enemy is always to whisper in the ear of a man or woman who is convicted, "You don't have to decide right now. Think about it a little longer." You'll always know it's the voice of Satan when you hear, "Take your time. There's no hurry. Ssssleep on it."

Acts 24:26
He hoped also that money should have been given him of Paul, that he might loose him: wherefore he sent for him the oftener, and communed with him.

"You have friends in Jerusalem, Paul," said Felix. "In fact, you have friends all over the world. If they care about you, they'll pay for your release." You see, Felix sent for Paul for one reason: not to engage in spiritual discussion, but to attempt financial manipulation.

Acts 24:27
But after two years, Porcius Festus came into Felix' room: and Felix, willing to shew the Jews a pleasure, left Paul bound.

Felix was kicked out of power, called back to Rome, and replaced by Porcius Festus. Why? A riot broke out in Caesarea between the Greeks and the Jews. When the Greeks emerged victorious, Felix vented his frustration with the Jews by ordering the Greeks to go throughout the city bludgeoning Jewish men, raping Jewish women, and plundering Jewish possessions. When Caesar heard about this, he immediately sent for Felix. Thus, Felix lived out the rest of his life in disgrace in Rome.

What happened to Drusilla? Two years after this event, in Europe on a shopping spree when Mount Vesuvius exploded, she was caught in the lava of the volcano and died at the age of twenty-one. Felix and Drusilla both had an opportunity to hear the gospel, but they put off making a decision.

Eighty-two percent of all Christians are saved at the age of nineteen or younger. The lower the age, the higher the percentage of those who make a commitment to Jesus Christ. Why? Because a person who puts off a decision, saying, "I'll think about it; I'll wait until later; I want more information," will find himself falling into a pattern that becomes more and more difficult to break.

He trembles when He says no to the Holy Spirit the first time.
The next time he hears the gospel and says no, he trembles less.
The third time, it's pretty easy to say no.
The fourth time it's a piece of cake.

This happens not only when the Spirit is convicting unbelievers, but also when He convicts Christians. The first time we are tempted to do wrong, we tremble. The second time the temptation comes our way, it still kind of bothers us, but not as much as it did the first time. The third time bothers us a little less. And the fourth time, giving in to temptation doesn't bother us at all.

The conscience must be guarded very carefully because it can become seared very easily (1 Timothy 4:2).

In fact, not only will our conscience become seared, or desensitized, it will become evil (Hebrews 10:22), justifying wrong and whispering to us, "Don't worry about what you're doing, or the show you're watching. That's simply the way society is. There's nothing wrong with it. It's just life."

Felix and Drusilla went from having a tender conscience—shaken when they felt the convicting work of the Spirit, to having a seared conscience—when they didn't tremble quite so easily, to having an evil conscience—where they were only interested in making a deal monetarily. The result? Their lives were destroyed and they were damned eternally.

You might be saying, "What if I'm doing stuff that used to bother me, but doesn't anymore? What if I have a seared or an evil conscience? Is there any hope for me?"

Yes. The Lord is so faithful. He comes to us over and over again, giving us opportunity to get right with Him. But in Genesis 6:3, God said, "My spirit shall not always strive with man. I'll come to you. I'll speak to you. But I'm not always going to wrestle with you."

PAUL: GUILTY OR NOT GUILTY?
A Topical Study of
Acts 24:14, 15

The apostle Paul was just too hot to handle. Following the swirl of controversy that surrounded him in Jerusalem, Paul was called to defend himself before

Felix, the governor. Denying he was guilty of pestilence and sedition, as he was accused (24:5), Paul admitted being guilty of the following three charges:

I am a follower of the Way.

But this I confess unto thee, that after the way which they call heresy, so worship I the God of my fathers.   Acts 24:14 (a)

Six times in the Book of Acts, believers are referred to as "the Way." Only three times in the New Testament are they called Christians because "Christian" was a term of degradation—like "Jesus Freak" or "Holy Joe." I'm sad that in our day "The Way International" cult has clouded this term, because I think "the Way" is an excellent name. What Jesus taught and the model He gave is "the Way" to go indeed! Only the Way of the Lord leads to our own well-being and welfare, for truly, the Way of the Lord is right.

Early Christians were called the Way not simply because Jesus points out the Way, but because He *is* the Way (John 14:6). That makes Christianity unique. Unlike Alcoholics Anonymous and other twelve-step programs, Christianity does not say, "Go through therapy. Follow these principles. Work hard—and you'll be a better person." No, Christianity is resurrection—not resuscitation. It's not twelve steps—it's one step: Allow Jesus Christ to live His resurrected life in and through you because it is only the living Lord in your heart who can change you powerfully and permanently from within.

I am a believer in the Scriptures.

. . . Believing all things which are written in the law and in the prophets. . . .
                                                                  Acts 24:14 (b)

I bet Paul emphasized the word "all." You see, he believed every picture painted in the law, and every illustration given by the prophets because they all pointed to Jesus Christ. Not so the Jews.

Paul's Jewish audience would have been unable to explain Isaiah 53, where the prophet declared, "He was wounded for our transgressions, he was bruised for our iniquities: the chastisement of our peace was upon him; and with his stripes we are healed" (Isaiah 53:5). Nor would they have been able to explain Psalm 22, where the psalmist accurately depicted God's Son crucified on a Cross hundreds of years before crucifixion was even known in the Middle East.

Like Paul, we believe *all* Scripture. The pseudo-intellectual false pastors and teachers who contend that certain passages imply cultural understanding that is no longer relevant today are wrong. God hasn't changed His mind just because we've "progressed" culturally.

Here's the problem, gang. If I adopt the pseudo-intellectual posture that says, "I will decide which parts of the Bible are relevant to my culture and meaningful to my society, which words are inspired and which are no longer applicable," I place myself in a very precarious position because I then become the judge of the Bible rather than allowing the Bible to judge me.

I say to you with absolute certainty and with intellectual integrity that *all* Scripture is inspired. How do I know? One way: Jesus quoted the most controversial Scriptures as being absolutely factual. He talked about Adam and Eve literally. He talked about Sodom and Gomorrah geographically. He talked about Lot's wife turning into a pillar of salt physically. He talked about Jonah being swallowed by a great fish in reality.

You see, the question of inspiration does not center around culture or geography, linguistics or history. When you talk to your professor, your neighbor, or your co-worker, the question is singular: Who do you believe Jesus is? He's either Lord, a lunatic who only *thought* He was God, or a liar who knowingly deceived people.

How do we know He's God? "One proof I'll give you," He said. "Destroy this temple and in three days I'll raise it up" (see John 2:19). And just as He said, three days after He was crucified, He rose again.

In the debate over inspiration, you can go in circles endlessly unless you keep returning the dialogue to the subject of Jesus Christ. Move the question from inspiration to the Resurrection. It's a powerful, irrefutable argument.

I am looking for the Resurrection.

And have hope toward God, which they themselves also allow, that there shall be a resurrection of the dead, both of the just and unjust.   Acts 24:15

In actuality, there are two resurrections. When Jesus comes back, the world will experience one thousand years of unparalleled peace and prosperity. At the end of that time, the unbeliever will be resurrected and will stand before the Great White Throne.

And I saw a great white throne, and with him that sat on it, from whose face the earth and the heaven fled away; and there was found no place for them. And I saw the dead, small and great, stand before God: and the books were opened: and another book was opened, which is the book of life: and the dead were judged out of those things which were written in the books, according to their works.   Revelation 20:11, 12

There will be those who will say, "I'm okay. You're okay. Why should I go to hell?"—until the books are opened wherein is recorded every deed, every thought, every lie, every attitude. You see, for our own sanity, God has made us in such a way that we don't remember how rotten we've been throughout our lifetime. Oh, we remember the big things—but the day-to-day junk conveniently fades from our conscience over time. When the books are open, however, when people see their lives as they really were, when people are reminded of their sin, they will, for all intents and purposes, condemn themselves to hell.

> A preacher vehemently pounded his pulpit, saying, "Every member of this congregation is going to stand before the Lord. Every member of this congregation will have to give account of what he's done. Every member of this congregation will be judged. There will be no exceptions."
>
> A man in the front row began to laugh, and the preacher said, "What are you laughing at?"
>
> "I'm not a member of this congregation," the man said.

So, too, you might think, *This doesn't apply to me. I don't believe this stuff.* But that doesn't matter. As a member of the congregation of humanity, you will stand before the Lord, where you will either hear Him say "Depart from Me, I never knew you" (see Matthew 7:23), or "Well done, good and faithful servant. Enter into the joy of the Lord" (see Matthew 25:21). The choice is yours.

The second resurrection—the one in which the unbeliever stands before the Lord at the Great White Throne—takes place at the end of the millennium. When does the first resurrection—the resurrection of the believer—take place?

Based on 2 Corinthians 5, I believe the first resurrection takes place over a period of time.

> *For we know that if our earthly house of this tabernacle were dissolved, we have a building of God, an house not made with hands, eternal in the heavens. For in this we groan, earnestly desiring to be clothed upon with our house which is from heaven: If so be that being clothed we shall not be found naked. For we that are in this tabernacle do groan, being burdened: not for that we would be unclothed, but clothed upon, that mortality might be swallowed up of life.*
>
> 2 Corinthians 5:1–4

"The body I'm in presently," said Paul, "is nothing more than a tabernacle, a tent."

How much time do I spend on the tent in which we camp every summer? Not very much. There are some stakes missing. There's some mildew in the creases. There are some holes in the sides. It's adequate lodging for a week or two—but I don't live there permanently. It's portable. It's temporary. It's flimsy.

So, too, the body you're in is just a tent—and a lot of us are becoming a little mildewy and are missing a few stakes. But when we die, when our tent is dissolved, buried, returned to dust—Paul said we have a building—literally a mansion—waiting to take its place. This, I believe, is the commentary on what Jesus said in John 14.

In my Father's house are many mansions: if it were not so, I would have told you. I go to prepare a place for you.   John 14:2

Although when most people think of a mansion, they think of white columns in the front, lots of rooms inside, and a pool in the back—I don't think that's what Jesus was talking about. I believe the mansion He spoke of was a new body.

You see, designed to take only fourteen pounds of pressure per square inch, dependent upon a mixture of seventy-nine percent nitrogen and twenty percent oxygen, my body is extremely limited. But there is a body waiting for me designed for total joy and exploration of all the cosmos—no longer limited by the restrictions and flimsiness of this present "tent."

"Wait a minute," you say. "Doesn't 1 Thessalonians 4:16, 17 say that we will all be resurrected at the same time? How, then, can you speak of a resurrection that takes place over a period of time?"

> I believe Einstein shed light on this through his "theory of relativity," which essentially says, "When an object travels at the speed of light, time ceases to be." Since God is light (1 John 1:5), there is no time in heaven—no past, no future, just an "eternal now."

Therefore, at the moment a person dies, he or she moves into the "eternal now." From his perspective, the Rapture has already occurred. Thus, no one in heaven is saying, "I miss my mom," or, "I can't wait until my husband gets here." While it might be poetic to talk about being greeted by those who have gone before, in actuality, from the heavenly perspective, it's all simultaneous.

From eternity's viewpoint, the first resurrection has already taken place.

If you read in the obituary column tomorrow that Jon Courson died—call the paper and correct that error. I didn't die. I simply moved out of this musty, crusty tent into a much better place. Like Paul, therefore, I stand accused of following the Way, believing in the Scriptures, and looking for the resurrection.

And, like Paul, I gladly plead guilty.

25

"Count it all joy when you enter into various trials," wrote James in the second verse of the first chapter of his Epistle. Truly, Paul was one who had entered "various trials"! His legal ordeal, which had begun on the steps of the Fortress Antonia in Jerusalem, took him to the Sanhedrin and on to Caesarea, where he stood before the Roman Governor, Festus.

Acts 25:1 (a)
Now when Festus was come into the province . . .

When Festus took over from Felix, he was about seventy years of age. History tells us he would rule in this province for two years before dying in office.

Acts 25:1 (b)
. . . after three days he ascended from Caesarea to Jerusalem.

Leaving the seacoast city of Caesarea, Festus went to the capital city of Israel to check on the situation and to introduce himself to the citizenry.

Acts 25:2, 3
Then the high priest and the chief of the Jews informed him against Paul, and besought him, and desired favour against him, that he would send for him to Jerusalem, laying wait in the way to kill him.

The root of bitterness within Paul's enemies seems to have grown deeper and deeper in the soil of their spirits during his two-year absence. "Nice to meet you, Festus. Glad you're here," they said. "Now do us a favor: bring Paul back here to Jerusalem." Of course, their plan was not for justice. Their plan was to ambush and kill Paul.

Acts 25:4 (a)
But Festus answered, that Paul should be kept at Caesarea . . .

Perhaps sensing this request was not sincere, Festus smelled trouble.

Acts 25:4 (b), 5
. . . and that he himself would depart shortly thither. Let them therefore, said he, which among you are able, go down with me, and accuse this man, if there be any wickedness in him.

"I'm going back to Caesarea," said Festus. "If you have that much against Paul, come with me, and I'll hear your accusations there."

Acts 25:6, 7
And when he had tarried among them more than ten days, he went down unto Caesarea; and the next day sitting on the judgment seat commanded Paul to be brought. And when he was come, the Jews which came down from Jerusalem stood round about, and laid many and grievous complaints against Paul, which they could not prove.

Paul's enemies traveled sixty miles to argue their case against Paul. But they still couldn't prove their charges.

Acts 25:8 (a)
While he answered for himself . . .

Once again, Paul acted as his own defense.

Acts 25:8 (b), 9
. . . Neither against the law of the Jews, neither against the temple, nor yet against Caesar, have I offended any thing at all. But

Festus, willing to do the Jews a pleasure, answered Paul, and said, Wilt thou go up to Jerusalem, and there be judged of these things before me?

Pressured by the Jews to try Paul in Jerusalem, Festus gave in and asked Paul for a change of venue.

Acts 25:10, 11 (a)
Then said Paul, I stand at Caesar's judgment seat, where I ought to be judged: to the Jews have I done no wrong, as thou very well knowest. For if I be an offender, or have committed any thing worthy of death, I refuse not to die: but if there be none of these things whereof these accuse me, no man may deliver me unto them.

Disgusted with the legal maneuvering and political manipulation of the entire judicial system, Paul was tired of being a political pawn. "I'm not going back to Jerusalem," he said. "Enough is enough. I have done no wrong."

Acts 25:11 (b)
I appeal unto Caesar.

It was the right of any Roman citizen who felt he was getting an unfair deal judicially to appear before Caesar.

Acts 25:12
Then Festus, when he had conferred with the council, answered, Hast thou appealed unto Caesar? unto Caesar shalt thou go.

"You want to go to Caesar?" said Festus. "Okay. To Caesar you'll go."

Acts 25:13
And after certain days king Agrippa and Bernice came unto Caesarea to salute Festus.

The new governor is now being paid a courtesy call by King Agrippa and Bernice. This is Agrippa II, son of Agrippa I, great-grandson of Herod, the one who tried desperately to destroy Jesus at the time of His birth. His great-uncle was the one who beheaded John the Baptist. His sister was Felix's wife, Drusilla. And his father, Agrippa I, was the one who ordered the execution of James and imprisoned Peter, hoping to execute him—until the Lord miraculously released him from prison (Acts 12).

Agrippa II was the last of the Herods. With his

power greatly diminished, his rule was limited to the northern area of Israel, near the Sea of Galilee. More a figurehead than a potent political player, Agrippa called on Festus in order to strengthen his weakened political ties. Agrippa came with Bernice. Described in literature as being a ravishing beauty, Bernice was Drusilla's sister—making her the half sister of Agrippa. Because of this, Agrippa and Bernice were never married, but they lived together.

History tells us Bernice would eventually leave Agrippa for Titus, a Roman general who would later lead his armies to destroy Jerusalem and burn the temple. Following a short stay in Rome, however, Bernice would go back to Agrippa II. Bernice was a shady lady and Agrippa was no angel. Thus, many historians say they deserved each other.

Acts 25:14–18
And when they had been there many days, Festus declared Paul's cause unto the king, saying, There is a certain man left in bonds by Felix: About whom, when I was at Jerusalem, the chief priests and the elders of the Jews informed me, desiring to have judgment against him. To whom I answered, It is not the manner of the Romans to deliver any man to die, before that he which is accused have the accusers face to face, and have licence to answer for himself concerning the crime laid against him. Therefore, when they were come hither, without any delay on the morrow I sat on the judgment seat, and commanded the man to be brought forth. Against whom when the accusers stood up, they brought none accusation of such things as I supposed.

Festus complained to Agrippa that, after hearing Paul's case in order to appease the Jews, he could find nothing wrong with Paul.

Acts 25:19–21
But had certain questions against him of their own superstition, and of one Jesus, which was dead, whom Paul affirmed to be alive. And because I doubted of such manner of questions, I asked him whether he would go to Jerusalem, and there be judged of these matters. But when Paul had appealed to be reserved unto the hearing of Augustus, I commanded him to be kept till I might send him to Caesar.

The reason Festus shared this information with Agrippa was because Festus was in a real jam. Festus knew Caesar would think him incompetent for sending Paul to Rome without valid accusation.

Acts 25:22
Then Agrippa said unto Festus, I would also hear the man myself. Tomorrow, said he, thou shalt hear him.

"Let me hear him," said Agrippa. "I'll find a charge you can write on your report to Caesar."

Acts 25:23
And on the morrow, when Agrippa was come, and Bernice, with great pomp, and was entered into the place of hearing, with the chief captains, and principal men of the city, at Festus' commandment Paul was brought forth.

The "place of hearing" was the amphitheatre on the beach at Caesarea. It would have been packed. People would have been dressed up. Soldiers would have been standing guard. Dignitaries would have been in attendance. You see, it was a real "happening" whenever there was an official hearing in this beautiful amphitheatre overlooking the Mediterranean.

And here was Paul. In 2 Corinthians 10, Paul described his own appearance as being physically weak. Historians verify that he was a short man with bowed legs, a long hooked nose, little hair, and runny eyes. And yet, here this "little man" commanded the attention of the entire Roman provincial capital of Caesarea.

It's amazing what the Lord can do with a little of anything. Consider Bethlehem: a tiny, insignificant town, but the most well-known village in all of history because Jesus was in it. And where Jesus is, things happen in a big way.

Acts 25:24, 25
And Festus said, King Agrippa, and all men which are here present with us, ye see this man, about whom all the multitude of the Jews have dealt with me, both at Jerusalem, and also here, crying that he ought not to live any longer. But when I found that he had committed nothing worthy of death, and that he himself hath appealed to Augustus, I have determined to send him.

"I find this man has done nothing worthy of death," said Festus, "but since he has appealed to

Augustus, I am required to send him." Octavius, who preceded Julius Caesar, was the first Roman ruler to use the name "Caesar Augustus," or "august one." "Augustus" was a title of strength and authority, so every Caesar who followed Octavius chose to use the title "Augustus." The Augustus spoken of here was Caesar Nero.

Acts 25:26 (a)
Of whom I have no certain thing to write unto my lord.

"My lord" is not a title of honor—but of deity. This is the first time in Scripture we see Caesar deified. Caesar Nero was the first Caesar who claimed to be God.

Acts 25:26 (b), 27
Wherefore I have brought him forth before you, and specially before thee, O king Agrippa, that, after examination had, I might have somewhat to write. For it seemeth to me unreasonable to send a prisoner, and not withal to signify the crimes laid against him.

"Help me to find something to write. Help me get 'A-grippa' this situation," pleaded Festus.

———— ❧ ————

26
Acts 26:1 (a)
Then Agrippa said unto Paul, Thou art permitted to speak for thyself.

Wanting to help Festus find some charge to send to Caesar concerning Paul, Agrippa must have been eager to hear Paul's defense.

Acts 26:1 (b)
Then Paul stretched forth the hand . . .

This was a salute, a sign of respect. Paul had the wonderful ability to respect the position of authority, even if the person holding it was unworthy.

Acts 26:1 (c)—3(a)
. . . and answered for himself: I think myself happy, king Agrippa, because I shall answer for myself this day before thee touching all the things whereof I am accused of the Jews: Especially because I know thee to be expert in all customs and questions which are among the Jews . . .

Being half Jew and half Edomite, the Herods had a tremendous fascination with all things Jew-

ish. They studied Judaism. They read Jewish history. They were intrigued by Jewish culture. Paul knew this. "I'm happy to talk to you, King Agrippa," he said, "because I know you understand our culture, our traditions, and our religion." Agrippa did—but when push came to shove, this same Agrippa would, in A.D. 70, join Titus in helping to destroy Jerusalem and the temple. Thus, his interest was intellectual rather than heartfelt.

Acts 26:3 (b)
. . . wherefore I beseech thee to hear me patiently.

"This might take a while," said Paul, "but give me some time to explain the situation to you."

Acts 26:4, 5
My manner of life from my youth, which was at the first among mine own nation at Jerusalem, know all the Jews; which knew me from the beginning, if they would testify, that after the most straitest sect of our religion I lived a Pharisee.

"The Jews know where I'm coming from," said Paul. "If they would come and testify, they would tell you, Agrippa, I was a Pharisee. The most orthodox of orthodox Jews, the most traditional, the most religious."

Acts 26:6
And now I stand and am judged for the hope of the promise made of God unto our fathers.

"I stand here because of the hope of the promise made to our fathers," said Paul. Agrippa knew that the promise to which he referred was Messiah. In other words, "The issue is my belief in Jesus as Messiah," contended Paul.

Acts 26:7, 8
Unto which promise our twelve tribes, instantly serving God day and night, hope to come. For which hope's sake, king Agrippa, I am accused of the Jews. Why should it be thought a thing incredible with you, that God should raise the dead?

"Oh, Agrippa, you who know the stories of the Bible, you who are aware of our history, why should it seem like an amazing thing to you that God could raise the dead?" asked Paul, referring to the Resurrection of Jesus Christ.

The same question could be asked today. People have trouble with miracles because they fail to comprehend the power and the reality of God. You see, the difficulty of a task can only be determined when measured against the agent who attempts to accomplish it.

J. B. Phillips was right in his contention that sometimes our God is indeed too small. If we get hung up on the problems and the challenges before us, it's because we fail to realize the size, strength, and heart of our Father.

The God who made billions of stars in the Milky Way Galaxy and millions of galaxies at least the size of the Milky Way spans the entire universe between His thumb and little finger (Isaiah 40:12). Our Father is big, gang!

Yet He is the same God who made the atom—a miniature planetary system so small it takes one million bunched together to equal the thickness of a single strand of human hair.

Now, do you think the God who made the vastness of the universe and the intricacies of the atom can raise the dead? It all depends on your view of God. Most of us do not doubt the power of God, but we doubt His willingness to intervene in our situations personally.

Why should He care about us? The answer lies in the Cross. "If God did not spare His only Son that we might be saved, shall He not freely give us all things pertaining to life?" asked Paul (see Romans 8:32). He will supply everything that's good for me. How do I know? Because He already gave me the very best when He gave me His Son, Christ Jesus.

Acts 26:9, 10 (a)
I verily thought with myself, that I ought to do many things contrary to the name of Jesus of Nazareth. Which thing I also did in Jerusalem: and many of the saints did I shut up in prison . . .

Continuing his testimony, Paul said, "I went around wasting the church, imprisoning believers."

Acts 26:10 (b)
. . . having received authority from the chief priests; and when they were put to death, I gave my voice against them.

In other words, Paul said, "As a member of the Sanhedrin, I voted against these Christians, these heretics."

Acts 26:11 (a)
And I punished them oft in every synagogue, and compelled them to blaspheme . . .

The realization that he forced believers to blaspheme must have haunted Paul all of his days.

Acts 26:11 (b), 12
. . . and being exceedingly mad against them, I persecuted them even unto strange cities. Whereupon as I went to Damascus with authority and commission from the chief priests.

"I was trying to find Christians wherever I could and do them in however I might," continued Paul.

Acts 26:13, 14
At midday, O king, I saw in the way a light from heaven, above the brightness of the sun, shining round about me and them which journeyed with me. And when we were all fallen to the earth, I heard a voice speaking unto me, and saying in the Hebrew tongue, Saul, Saul, why persecutest thou me? it is hard for thee to kick against the goads.

Goads were sticks farmers used to prod their oxen into submission. Therefore, when the Lord said to Paul, "It is hard for you to kick against the goads," He was implying that Paul was a dumb, stubborn ox who could be guided no other way. Stubborn indeed—I'm convinced Paul was under conviction from the time he witnessed the stoning of Stephen, as he saw the vision of an angel on Stephen's face and heard the words, "Father forgive them," from Stephen's lips (see Acts 7).

Acts 26:15–17
And I said, Who art thou, Lord? And he said, I am Jesus whom thou persecutest. But rise, and stand upon thy feet: for I have appeared unto thee for this purpose, to make thee a minister and a witness both of these things which thou hast seen, and of those things in the which I will appear unto thee; delivering thee from the people, and from the Gentiles, unto whom now I send thee.

"I am making you a witness and a minister," the Lord said to Paul.

Acts 26:18, 19
To open their eyes, and to turn them from darkness to light, and from the power of Satan unto God, that they may receive forgiveness of sins, and inheritance among them which are sanctified by faith that is

in me. Whereupon, O king Agrippa, I was not disobedient unto the heavenly vision.

"The vision God gave me was that I was to open men's eyes from darkness to light, and to turn men's lives from Satan to God in order that they might receive forgiveness of sins and the inheritance of faith." And in Paul's vision, we see ours.

For topical study of Acts 26:16–18 "Heavenly Vision," turn to page 843.

Acts 26:20
But shewed first unto them of Damascus, and at Jerusalem, and throughout all the coasts of Judaea, and then to the Gentiles, that they should repent and turn to God, and do works meet for repentance.

Repentance is changing one's mind. Regeneration is changing one's heart. Redemption is changing one's state—trading the kingdom of darkness and death for the kingdom of light and life. "This was my message," said Paul.

Acts 26:21
For these causes the Jews caught me in the temple, and went about to kill me.

Why did the Jews want to kill Paul?
Because he preached repentance.

- Noah didn't stand on the steps of his ark and say, "Something good is about to happen to you."
- Amos was not confronted by priests who threatened to kill him because he was preaching, "I'm okay. You're okay."
- Jeremiah was not cast into the dungeon because he talked about the "power of possibility thinking."
- Daniel was not thrown to the lions for saying, "Smile, God loves you."
- John the Baptist wasn't beheaded for having a "Honk If You Love Jesus" bumper sticker.

The message of Noah and Daniel, Amos and Jeremiah, John the Baptist and Jesus Christ, was singular. The message was: Repent.

The message of repentance is not a popular message because it says people who think they've got it together—don't. People who think they're okay—aren't. People who think they'll make it to heaven on their own—won't.

Acts 26:22
Having therefore obtained help of God, I continue unto this day, witnessing both to small and great, saying none other things than those which the prophets and Moses did say should come.

"Wait a minute," Claudius Lysias could have said. "Help from God? I was the one who was there with my soldiers, risking our necks to save yours, Paul."

"No, it was God," Paul would have insisted because Paul was a man who saw God's hand in everything.

I read about a preacher named Frederic Nolan. Fifty men were chasing him through a hilly area of North Africa. Trapped in a canyon, he saw the mouth of a cave and scooted in. Lying at the back of the shallow cave, the exhausted Nolan knew that within ten minutes he would be discovered and killed. But as he lay there, a spider appeared and began to quickly weave a web over the cave's mouth. Twenty minutes later, when Nolan's persecutors arrived, four or five guys stopped at the opening of the cave, saw the web, and said, "He's not in there."

And Frederic Nolan went on to record something in his journal that I think is wonderful: Where God is, a spider web becomes a wall. But where God isn't, a wall is like a spider web.

Like Nolan, Paul knew it wasn't chance—it was God.

Acts 26:23, 24
That Christ should suffer, and that he should be the first that should rise from the dead, and should shew light unto the people, and to the Gentiles. And as he thus spake for himself, Festus said with a loud voice, Paul, thou art beside thyself; much learning doth make thee mad.

"You're crazy, Paul," shouted Festus. "You're talking about seeing a light, having a change of heart, God rescuing you, opening men's eyes, changing men's lives. This can't be."

And there will be those who look at you and say the same thing. "It's not that simple," they'll say. "Jesus can't change a person—without therapy, seminars, and counseling."

Let the scoffers say what they may. But let us stand by what Paul declared to be the heavenly vision. That is, God is capable and desirous to change men, to take them out of the power of Satan, and to place them into His glorious, gracious kingdom.

Acts 26:25, 26 (a)
But he said, I am not mad, most noble Festus; but speak forth the words of truth and soberness. For the king knoweth of these things . . .

Realizing Festus was not tuned in to what he was saying, Paul returned his attention to Agrippa. With Agrippa's knowledge of Scripture, I'm sure Paul thought he would be converted.

Acts 26:26 (b), 27
. . . before whom also I speak freely: for I am persuaded that none of these things are hidden from him; for this thing was not done in a corner. King Agrippa, believest thou the prophets? I know that thou believest.

"Agrippa, do you believe the prophets? Sure you do," said Paul. What a salesman!

Acts 26:28
Then Agrippa said unto Paul, Almost thou persuadest me to be a Christian.

"Paul, could it be that my life of debauchery and immorality could be turned around like yours was—in an instant? You're almost persuading me to become a Christian," said Agrippa.

Acts 26:29
And Paul said, I would to God, that not only thou, but also all that hear me this day, were both almost, and altogether such as I am, except these bonds.

"I wish you would believe," said Paul, "and not you only, but all who hear me."

Acts 26:30
And when he had thus spoken, the king rose up, and the governor, and Bernice, and they that sat with them.

Agrippa was deeply touched by what he was hearing. It was ringing true in his heart—and yet he bailed out.

A computer whiz, a Boy Scout, and a minister were flying in a three-passenger plane. The pilot said, "It's not looking good, guys. Our engines are cutting out and we're going down. The problem is, we have only three parachutes—and I'm taking one." Realizing one of them would be left behind, the passengers looked at one another. Immediately, the computer whiz grabbed a chute, calling out, "Sorry, guys, but I've got to take this because I'm the

smartest man in the world," as he jumped out the door.

The minister then turned to the Boy Scout and said, "I've had a good life. The Lord is real to me. I know I'm going to heaven. So you go ahead and take the last chute. I'll go down with the plane."

"That won't be necessary," said the Boy Scout. "The smartest man in the world just jumped out with my backpack."

So, too, Agrippa had the opportunity to make it safely into eternity. But he grabbed the wrong bag. He grabbed Bernice. You see, every time Agrippa is mentioned (25:13; 25:23; 26:30), he's always with Bernice. She had a hold on him.

An eagle swooped down and grabbed a rodent in its powerful talons. Pulling it to its chest, he soared higher and higher. Suddenly, however, he no longer looked majestic, but began to flap his wings rapidly before losing altitude and crashing into a rock. Upon investigation, a naturalist observing the scene discovered that the little rodent had its teeth imbedded in the chest of the mighty eagle. Although the eagle thought he was controlling the rodent, all the while the rodent was actually draining the life from him.

That's what happened to Agrippa, and that's what happens in life. People think, *I'm controlling him, or her, or it,* as they tighten their grip. But in reality, the thing they cling to is the very thing that will drain the life from them. Sin does that to you and me. It's a rat. It'll drain you and keep you from being what God knows you could be.

Acts 26:31, 32
And when they were gone aside, they talked between themselves, saying, This man doeth nothing worthy of death or of bonds. Then said Agrippa unto Festus, This man might have been set at liberty, if he had not appealed unto Caesar.

In other words, Agrippa said, "Festus, you blew it. This guy hasn't done anything wrong at all. If he hadn't appealed to Caesar, he'd be set free." Agrippa saw Paul's trial as a mistake. Paul, however, used it as an opportunity to share the gospel.

So, too, in whatever trial you face, may God give you grace to say, "Happily I stand here today, knowing this is an opportunity for me to share something of my faith and something of His life."

HEAVENLY VISION
A Topical Study of
Acts 26:16–18

When Bill Clinton was first elected president, political pundits weighed in with their theories on why President Bush didn't win the election. Essentially, they offered two reasons. One was the lingering recession. But secondly, and perhaps more importantly, they cited the president's failure to articulate vision. In fact, you might remember that President Bush himself told reporters upon taking office, "I have trouble with the vision thing."

In Proverbs 29:18 we are told that without vision, people perish. Literally, "People run wild," or, as seen in some marginal notes, "people run naked." Thus, vision is necessary not only for every President but for every person—for without it, people run wildly, aimlessly, shamefully.

"Write the vision, Habakkuk," said the Lord, "and make it plain so he that runneth by may be able to read it" (see Habakkuk 2:2). In other words, "Write the vision so clearly that even the person who runs rapidly might be able to understand it"—for without vision, people wander in mediocrity and meander in mundanity.

Nowhere is necessity of vision seen more clearly than in the life of the apostle Paul. He had purpose and meaning because he understood from the moment of his conversion the heavenly vision for his life.

Perhaps you're saying, "Good for Paul. I'm glad he had a vision from heaven. But I have neither seen the Lord physically as Paul did nor heard His voice audibly as Paul did. So how am I supposed to get vision like Paul did? If vision is necessary for a productive, successful life, how am I supposed to receive vision personally?"

I have good news for you. Paul the apostle, the one who had heavenly vision, was also the one who said, "Follow me as I follow Christ" (see 1 Corinthians 11:1). In other words, the vision the Lord gave Paul, recorded in our text, is the vision the Lord intends for you and me as well. Paul's vision is to be our vision.

What Paul Was to Be

> *But rise and stand upon thy feet: for I have appeared unto thee for this purpose, to make thee a minister and a witness . . .*   Acts 26:16

When the Lord appeared to Paul on the road to Damascus, He said, "You are to be a minister and a witness." The Greek word for minister means "under-rower."

It's a word that described the guys in the belly of a large ship who, although they were unseen, unnoticed, and unapplauded, rowed steadily and moved the ship to its ultimate destination.

And Paul's commission is for you as well. You see, Jesus said, "You have not chosen Me, but I have chosen you and ordained you that you should bring forth much fruit" (see John 15:16). Whoever you are—man, woman, teenager, young person—if you are a believer in Christ, He has ordained you into ministry.

We are not only to be ministers, but secondly, we are to be witnesses. A witness is one who goes into the courtroom and simply shares what he or she has seen. The Lord did not call you to be an attorney to argue the case, or a judge to hand down a verdict. The Lord simply called you to be a witness to tell people what He has done for you personally.

When I don't live up to that calling, my life becomes dull, incredibly ordinary, and meaningless. But when I minister and witness, a funny thing happens. I get back more than I give—which shouldn't be surprising, considering that Jesus said, "The measure that you give out shall be meted back to you" (see Luke 6:38).

What Paul Was to Do

> *To open their eyes, and to turn them from darkness to light, and from the power of Satan unto God . . .*   Acts 26:18

To Open Men's Eyes

Why do people need their eyes opened? Because they have been blinded by sin.

As Samson laid his head on Delilah's lap, he sinned by sharing with her the secret of his strength. "If you cut my hair," he said, "I'll be like any man." Delilah reached for the scissors and began snipping. When Samson awoke, Scripture says he knew not that the Spirit had departed from him (Judges 16:20). He thought he could take the Philistines on. Instead, they took him down. They placed him in fetters, poked out his eyes, and led him to the granary where, hitched to a grinding stone like a common ox, he went round and round in circles.

That's what sin does. It binds, it blinds, and it makes life a grind. "What's my life about? Why am I here? Why should I get out of bed?" we say as round and round we go.

Sin blinds people. First, it blinds people to their need for Jesus.

"Do you enjoy being a preacher?" asked the cashier.
"Yes," I answered. "As a matter of fact, I love what I do."

"Well, I was raped two years ago," she said as she started to cry, "and people have tried to get me to church, but church is a crutch."

"You're right," I said. "But it's more than a crutch. Church is an ambulance, an emergency room, a hospital, a surgical team. It's for people who realize they're hurt—either by their own sin or the sin of others. It's for people who say, "I need a Helper. I need a Healer. I need a Savior."

I don't know what she did, but I'm so thankful I was able to share with her the reality that Jesus *is* the Answer.

Second, sin blinds people to the nature of Jesus. It's amazing the misconceptions people have about our Lord. They think He is some kind of Cosmic Killjoy who looks down from heaven, worried that someone, somewhere might be having fun. But nothing could be further from the truth, for Jesus said, "I have come that you might have *life* and life *abundantly*" (see John 10:10). Jesus came to set people free—not to put a religious trip on them.

How?

To be free, to get a fresh start, "you must be born again" (see John 3:7).

A lady called her husband and said, "Honey, the car isn't working."

"What's wrong?" he asked.

"There's water in the carburetor," she said.

"Water in the carburetor? That's impossible. The cooling system doesn't touch the carburetor. There can't be water in the carburetor."

"Yes," insisted his wife. "There's definitely water in the carburetor."

"Well, I'll come home and take a look," he said. "Where's the car?"

"At the bottom of the pool," she answered.

You might disagree with the divine diagnosis, but the Bible says that although you have been buried in the pool of iniquity and the sea of sin, it is the desire of the Lord's heart to rescue you, to breathe life into you, and to put you on your feet once again.

To Turn Men's Lives

Not only was Paul to open men's eyes, he was to turn men's lives from darkness to light, from the power of Satan to the power of God. You see, two kingdoms dwell simultaneously on this earth: the kingdom of light and love, which is the kingdom of God—and the kingdom of darkness and death, which is the kingdom of Satan. *Every* man is in one of these two kingdoms. No one is neutral, for Jesus said, "He who is not for Me is against Me" (see Matthew 12:30). Therefore, if you are not in the kingdom of God, if He is not your Lord and King and Leader—then you are in Satan's kingdom of death and darkness.

Satan loves darkness.

Most crimes are committed at night.

The period in history when people didn't worship God is called the *Dark Ages*.

A continent that has not been exposed to the gospel is called a *dark* continent.

Hell is called "outer *darkness*" (see Matthew 8:12).

Some people think hell is a bunch of guys playing poker and telling dirty jokes. Nothing could be further from the truth. Astrologists tell us about the existence of black holes so dense that nothing escapes their gravitational pull—not even light itself.

When the guide turns out the lights in the Oregon Caves, there's an absolute absence of light. So dark you can't see your hand in front of your face, it's a darkness that seems to have a substance of its own, a darkness you can actually feel.

Hell is like that. In hell, no one will see a thing—for a day, a month, a year, a century, a millennium, a billion millenniums. Men who choose to live in darkness on earth will spend eternity surrounded by darkness in hell.

That's why Paul said, "My ministry, my job, my vision is to open men's eyes and to turn men's lives from darkness to light, from the power of Satan to the power of God.

"Wait," you say. "I may not be a follower of God—but neither am I dominated by Satan. I'm master of my own destiny, captain of my own fate." The Bible says otherwise. According to the Word, people who aren't walking with the Lord are actually opposing or hurting themselves through their lifestyles and attitudes, their activities and habits (2 Timothy 2:25). How are men freed from Satan's grasp? "You shall know the truth and the *truth* shall set you free," said Jesus (see John 8:32).

"What is truth?" Pontius Pilate asked (John 18:38).

"I Am," said Jesus (see John 14:6).

Gang, we have the privilege of opening men's eyes to their need for Jesus and to the nature of Jesus. We get to turn men's lives from the power of darkness and the devil to the power of light and the Lord.

How? Through a principle of physics called the expulsive power of the greater force, which says, for example, that if you want to rid a room of darkness, you don't fight against the darkness by trying to karate chop it, rebuke it, or yell at it. You turn on the light, and light—the greater power—will flood the room, expelling the darkness. Jesus said, "I am the Light of the world" (John 8:12). Therefore, when a man or woman opens up his or her heart to Jesus Christ, the light of the Lord naturally drives out the darkness of Satan. It's glorious!

Men's eyes are opened and their lives are turned by the power of the Spirit—not by programs, principles, or procedures. It is the power of the resurrected Lord that works change in a person. It's God's one-step program: Get saved, let the Spirit direct your life—and you will be absolutely free.

Men's eyes are opened and their lives are turned by the prayers of the saints. You can witness to people until you're blue in the face, but if their eyes are blinded, they won't receive what you say. How is the blindfold removed? Ephesians 6 says the weapons of our warfare are not fleshly, but spiritual. Prayer is the number one weapon in our arsenal. We can do more than pray—but we can't do anything *until* we pray.

Men's eyes are opened and their lives turned by proclaiming the Scriptures. If someone is complaining, tell them the Bible says to give thanks in everything (1 Thessalonians 5:18). If someone is upset because his candidate didn't win, say, "The Bible says all things work together for good to them that love God," (see Romans 8:28). Jesus said, "The words which I speak are Spirit and life" (see John 6:63). Share the Word—it's powerful!

> A seminary student asked Charles Spurgeon how to defend Scripture against
> unbelievers, skeptics, and cynics. The three-hundred-pound preacher laughed
> aloud and said, "How do you defend the Scriptures? Son, that's like asking
> how to defend a lion. Just let it out of its cage. It'll defend itself."

How long has it been since you "let the Word out" and shared the Scriptures with an unbeliever? Share the Word—that's where the power is.

Paul's vision was to turn men's eyes and turn men's lives in order that men would experience the forgiveness of sins and the inheritance of faith (Acts 26:18).

Forgiveness of sin is man's greatest need and God's greatest deed. If you've been saved for a while, this concept might have become dulled in your understanding because you live in the realm of forgiveness. But the world doesn't. "Follow me as I follow Christ," Paul says to you today.

Be a minister. Be a sharer. Open men's eyes and turn men's lives in the power of the Spirit, by the praying of the saints, through the proclaiming of the Scriptures.

They will experience forgiveness as they've never known—and you will be fulfilled presently and rewarded eternally.

27

Early in his ministry, the apostle Paul knew that if he could impact Rome with the gospel, it would have ramifications throughout the known world. And at last, here he was—on his way to Rome, traveling all-expenses-paid as a prisoner of the Empire.

Acts 27:1
And when it was determined that we should sail into Italy, they delivered Paul and certain other prisoners unto one named Julius, a centurion of Augustus' band.

In command of the soldiers and the prisoners on the ship was a centurion named Julius.

Acts 27:2, 3 (a)
And entering into a ship of Adramytium, we launched, meaning to sail by the coasts of Asia; one Aristarchus, a Macedonian of Thessalonica, being with us. And the next day we touched at Sidon.

Setting sail from Caesarea, the ship made its way north.

Acts 27:3 (b)
And Julius courteously entreated Paul, and gave him liberty to go unto his friends to refresh himself.

Throughout Scripture, centurions—the backbone of the Roman army—are always seen in a favorable light (Matthew 8; Luke 7; Acts 10). And Julius was no exception. He showed kindness to Paul by granting him liberty for refreshment and fellowship. I find this intriguing, for although Paul could only have known Julius for perhaps a day at the most, there must have been something in Paul's character that gave Julius absolute confidence that he would not try to escape.

Acts 27:4–7
And when we had launched from thence, we sailed under Cyprus, because the winds were contrary. And when we had sailed over the sea of Cilicia and Pamphylia, we came to Myra, a city of Lycia. And there the centurion found a ship of Alexandria sailing into Italy; and he put us therein. And when we had sailed slowly many days, and scarce were come over against Cnidus, the wind not suffering us, we sailed under Crete, over against Salmone.

These are the various stops Paul and his company made as they worked their way up the coast, eventually crossing the Mediterranean Sea, and on to the island of Crete.

Acts 27:8, 9 (a)
And, hardly passing it, came unto a place which is called The fair havens; nigh whereunto was the city of Lasea. Now when much time was spent, and when sailing was now dangerous, because the fast was now already past . . .

"The fast" referred to here was the Day of Atonement, which would have been during the first part of October—a dangerous time to be at sea, with winter storms soon approaching.

Acts 27:9 (b), 10
. . . Paul admonished them, and said unto them, Sirs, I perceive that this voyage will be with hurt and much damage, not only of the lading and ship, but also of our lives.

Paul spoke to the captain, saying, "This is a bad time to be sailing." Now, although Paul was a tentmaker by trade, a rabbi by profession, and a prisoner by decree, the fact that he had been shipwrecked three times and had spent an entire day and night in the open ocean (2 Corinthians 11:25) qualified him to be able to give advice concerning the dangers of the sea.

Acts 27:11
Nevertheless the centurion believed the master and the owner of the ship, more than those things which were spoken by Paul.

The centurion listened first to Paul and then to the owner of the ship, with the rest of the crew no doubt chiming in. "We'll go with the majority," he said. "Let's set sail."

Acts 27:12–14
And because the haven was not commodious to winter in, the more part advised to depart thence also, if by any means they might attain to Phenice, and there to winter; which is an haven of Crete, and lieth toward the south west and north west. And when the south wind blew softly, supposing they had obtained their purpose, loosing thence, they sailed close by Crete. But not long after there arose against it a tempestuous wind, called Euroclydon.

At first the wind blew softly, and in a favorable direction. That's always the way it is. When you don't listen to the Word of the Lord, when you go your own way, when you do your own thing, at first you're just blown along softly. But when the fierce winds come—which they always do—you're blown away totally.

Please note four reasons that make this a perfect example of how *not* to know God's will as you sail through life and journey towards heaven:

- The sailors were impatient. Although it was not the season for sailing, these guys wanted to get on with their journey. The Word says, "He that believeth in the Lord must not make haste" (see Isaiah 28:16). Are you impatient? Slow down. When you don't know what to do—don't do anything. When you're not sure which way to go, stay where you are. Wait on the Lord. It's so hard to do, but so important.
- The sailors took a vote. The centurion said, "Okay Paul, I hear what you're saying, but I also hear the owner, the captain, and the crew," and Paul was outvoted. God is not an American, folks, and if we make decisions relating to the kingdom on a democratic basis, we're in a heap of trouble. Ask Moses. If the Israelites had voted during their journey through the wilderness, he would have been ousted the first week. We need to know what the heart of God is—not what the majority says.
- The sailors tested the winds. "The answer is blowing in the wind," may be true for Bob Dylan, but it's not true for you and me as believers. We're not to say, "The way the wind is blowing and circumstances are pointing will determine my course." No, there needs to be a solid inner conviction, a Holy Spirit direction.
- The sailors sought ease. They wanted to get to Phoenix. Why? Phoenix was where all of the sailors wintered. There were lots of restaurants, movie theatres, golf courses. No doubt these guys thought, *Why should we stay here? We're only sixty-eight miles from Phoenix. That's the place to be—we can even pick up a Suns game.* Sometimes we, like these sailors, ask, "Where is it most comfortable? Where is it easiest?" instead of "What does the Lord know will be best for me?"

Acts 27:15–17 (a)
And when the ship was caught, and could not bear up into the wind, we let her drive. And running under a certain island which is called Clauda, we had much work to come by the boat: Which when they had taken up, they used helps, undergirding the ship . . .

Following the stress and strain of the storm, the crew wrapped the hull of the ship with cables and ropes in an attempt to hold it together.

Acts 27:17 (b)
. . . and, fearing lest they should fall into the quicksands, strake sail, and so were driven.

They took the sail down to avoid being grounded on a sandbar.

Acts 27:18–20
And we being exceedingly tossed with a tempest, the next day they lightened the ship; and the third day we cast out with our own hands the tackling of the ship. And when neither sun nor stars in many days appeared, and no small tempest lay on us, all hope that we should be saved was then taken away.

All hope was lost. These veteran seamen knew they were going down.

Acts 27:21, 22
But after long abstinence Paul stood forth in the midst of them, and said, Sirs, ye should have hearkened unto me, and not have loosed from Crete, and to have gained this harm and loss. And now I exhort you to be of good cheer: for there shall be no loss of any man's life among you, but of the ship.

Notice it wasn't until "after long abstinence" that Paul spoke. He waited to say, "You should have listened to me," until he could also say, "Be of good cheer; we're going to make it."

Mom and Dad, this is a good word for you as well. Hold your tongue until, like Paul, you can give your kids words of encouragement, instruction, and practical application along with your words of correction.

Acts 27:23–25
For there stood by me this night the angel of God, whose I am, and whom I serve, saying, Fear not, Paul; thou must be brought before Caesar: and, lo, God hath given thee all them that sail with thee. Wherefore, sirs, be of good cheer: for I believe God, that it shall be even as it was told me.

The centurion believed the master of the ship (verse 11). Paul believed God—and what a difference it made.

Acts 27:26–28
Howbeit we must be cast upon a certain island. But when the fourteenth night was

come, as we were driven up and down in Adria, [present-day Ionia] about midnight the shipmen deemed that they drew near to some country; and sounded, and found it twenty fathoms: and when they had gone a little further, they sounded again, and found it fifteen fathoms.

Perhaps hearing the crashing of waves in the distance, the sailors took a sounding and discovered the water was getting shallower.

Acts 27:29
Then fearing lest we should have fallen upon rocks, they cast four anchors out of the stern, and wished for the day.

Fearing the ship would be dashed on the rocks, the sailors put the lifeboat over the side, ready to take their chances in a small, more navigable boat.

Acts 27:30–32
And as the shipmen were about to flee out of the ship, when they had let down the boat into the sea, under colour as though they would have cast anchors out of the foreship, Paul said to the centurion and to the soldiers, Except these abide in the ship, ye cannot be saved. Then the soldiers cut off the ropes of the boat, and let her fall off.

Don't jump ship. I know the storms get to be tough, and instincts tell you to bail out, give up, turn back. But Paul's word of admonition to his shipmates is a very important one for you and me as well.

For topical study of Acts 27:31–32 entitled "Don't Jump Ship!" turn to page 851.

Acts 27:33
And while the day was coming on, Paul besought them all to take meat, saying, This day is the fourteenth day that ye have tarried and continued fasting, having taken nothing.

The crew had been fasting for fourteen days—not because they were seeking God, but because they were sick to their stomachs. Filled with fear, they lost their appetites.

Acts 27:34
Wherefore I pray you to take some meat: for this is for your health: for there shall not an hair fall from the head of any of you.

As de facto commander, Paul said, "It's time to eat."

Acts 27:35
And when he had thus spoken, he took bread, and gave thanks to God in presence of them all: and when he had broken it, he began to eat.

Paul had hope in his heart. He believed in God. And he thanked the Lord in the sight of everyone on deck.

Acts 27:36
Then were they all of good cheer, and they also took some meat.

I believe one of the best things we can do when people around us are discouraged is break bread with them in Communion. And just like the crew on this ship, they will experience good cheer.

Acts 27:37–39
And we were in all in the ship two hundred threescore and sixteen souls. And when they had eaten enough, they lightened the ship, and cast out the wheat into the sea. And when it was day, they knew not the land: but they discovered a certain creek with a shore, into the which they were minded, if it were possible, to thrust in the ship.

The two hundred seventy-six men on board didn't know where they were—but they could see a creek running into the ocean, which they thought might be a possible point of entry for them.

Acts 27:40–41
And when they had taken up the anchors, they committed themselves unto the sea, and loosed the rudder bands, and hoisted up the mainsail to the wind, and made toward shore. And falling into a place where two seas met, they ran the ship aground; and the forepart stuck fast, and remained unmovable, but the hinder part was broken with the violence of the waves.

Here they were, close to shore, trying to navigate their ship into the river. But as they did, it fell apart.

Acts 27:42–44
And the soldiers' counsel was to kill the prisoners, lest any of them should swim out, and escape. But the centurion, willing to save Paul, kept them from their purpose; and commanded that they which could swim should cast themselves first into the sea,

and get to land: And the rest, some on boards, and some on broken pieces of the ship. And so it came to pass, that they escaped all safe to land.

Just as the Lord promised, everyone on board survived the storm. Please note four types of storms that blow into our lives:

Storms of correction. Ask brother Jonah about these. When a storm arose and he was tossed overboard and swallowed by a great fish, it was because he was rebelling against the Lord (Jonah 1:10). So, too, sometimes when I'm in a place of disobedience or rebellion, the Lord will allow a storm to get me on track again.

Storms of perfection. After Jesus fed the five thousand, He sent His disciples across the Sea of Galilee (Matthew 14). Midway through their journey, a storm arose around them for their perfection. You see, Jesus knew it wouldn't be too many months before these same disciples would see another multitude of five thousand—not fed, but saved (Acts 4:4)—followed by another storm—not on the sea, but of persecution within the church (Acts 8:1). Thus, Jesus was training His boys to endure the storms of persecution that inevitably follow the seasons of blessing.

Faith is not a pill we take, folks. It's a muscle we work. Therefore, the Lord will send me into a storm from time to time not for correction, but for perfection because the way I react to storms internally will tell me where I'm at spiritually. Storms provide unique opportunity for me to see where I'm at and to grow in my understanding that the Lord will come through at the right time, saying, "Be of good cheer. We're going to make it."

Storms of protection. Because "Noah found grace in the eyes of the Lord" (Genesis 6:8), God sent a storm to drown out all of the carnality, sin, and iniquity that surrounded him. The storm raged for forty days and nights, but Noah and his family were not only protected in the storm—they were protected by the storm. "Oh no!" we cry. "My TV blew up," or, "My stereo doesn't work. What a storm I'm in." But, as in Noah's case, it might be a storm of protection—protecting us from the carnality and iniquity that surround us continually.

Storms of direction. Knowing there was a group of people on the island of Malta in need of ministry, the Lord said, "Before you go to Rome, Paul, I'm going to allow you to be blown off course because there is something I want you to do for Me—something you never would have thought of on your own, something that wasn't part of your agenda. I have some people to whom I want to minister, so I'll allow a storm to arise, which, although it looks like it's blowing you off course, will put you in the very place I want to use you."

"How come I got canned?"

"Why did she dump me?"

"How come it's not working out?" you ask.

Don't be blown away. Realize that the Lord is changing your direction because there's something He wants to do that will ultimately be a blessing.

Storms of correction and perfection, storms of protection and direction—how can you know which one you might be in?

Talk to the Father.

"Why am I in this storm, Lord? Is it correction—or are You perfecting me for what You see is coming my way? Is there a new direction for my life—or are You protecting me from something that would be very damaging?"

How long has it been since you got away to spend time with the Lord? Clear your schedule, seek Him, and you'll be blown away by His goodness rather than by the storm.

DON'T JUMP SHIP!

A Topical Study of
Acts 27:31, 32

After jumping through legal hoops in Caesarea, Paul was finally sailing toward Rome to plead his case before Caesar. On the way, a storm arose that threatened the lives of the two hundred seventy-six soldiers, sailors, and prisoners on board with Paul. After the crew readied a lifeboat to avoid the inevitable dashing of the ship against the rocks, Paul, the little rabbi who was a tentmaker by trade and a prisoner by decree, said, "Except ye abide in the ship, ye cannot be saved."

I believe Paul's words are the heart of the Lord for us today. There are times—maybe you're in one right now—when the wind is howling, the waves are rising, and you find yourself saying, "I'm out of here. I'm jumping ship. I cannot take this marriage one more day," or—"I can't take my parents one more minute. Adios."

Storms come, and the temptation arises within all of us to bail out when we think we've been tricked or cheated. I share with you the story of a man who truly had reason to feel this way. His name was Jacob; and his story begins in Genesis 29.

Jacob was young, single, footloose, and looking for a wife. Arriving in Pandanaram, he found a group of shepherds milling around a well. Industrious by nature, Jacob couldn't understand this—until he saw a beautiful shepherdess approaching, bringing her flock with her. Immediately, Jacob flexed his muscles, single-handedly removed the stone that covered the well, and gallantly said, "Come and water your flock." She did, he kissed her, and then cried aloud, for she had smitten his heart.

When Jacob discovered that this beautiful maiden was the daughter of his uncle, he went to her father and told him he wanted to marry his daughter.

"Okay," said Laban. "Work for me seven years, and I'll give her to you."

Jacob agreed, and the Bible says it seemed to him but a few days because of the great love he had for her.

The big night finally came. Jacob took his beloved bride—veiled from head to toe according to Jewish tradition—back to his tent where they consummated the marriage. The next morning, when Jacob opened his eyes, he couldn't believe what he saw. It wasn't Rachel he had married—it was her older sister, Leah—whose name meant "tender-eyed" or "one who makes your eyes hurt." Jacob stormed out of the tent, found Laban, and said, "You tricked me."

"I'm sorry, Jacob," his uncle said, "but we have a tradition that the older daughter must marry before the younger daughter. Therefore, it was necessary that Leah, Rachel's older sister, marry first. But I'll tell you what I'll do. Work seven more years, and I'll throw in Rachel."

Now, if anyone ever had a right to say, "I got tricked. I want out," it was Jacob. "Listen, Leah," he could have said, "I realize we went through the ceremony, but I was tricked. I didn't know who you were. I'm in love with Rachel. She's the one who captured my heart. So I'm out of here."

But that's not what Jacob said. He agreed to Laban's proposal, and thereby ended up with both Leah and Rachel as his wives. Time passed, and after a while, Leah began to have children. Rachel, who had none, said to Jacob, "Give me children, or I die."

Having had three sons with Leah, Jacob knew it wasn't *his* fault and said to her, "Am I in the place of God? I can't do anything about this situation."

"Then take my servant girl, have relations with her, and the kids will count as ours," said Rachel.

And Jacob did just that.

Not to be outdone, Leah—who had stopped bearing children—said, "Here, Jacob, take my servant girl, and the children she bears will count as ours." The end result from these four women were the twelve sons who became, of course, the twelve tribes of Israel.

Interestingly, Rachel, the one who had said, "Give me children or I'll die," did indeed die when she gave birth to Benjamin. Jacob buried this one, about whom he was so passionate, in Canaan.

Years later, Leah died, and Jacob buried her in the Promised Land, at a place called Machpelah.

When, as an old man in Genesis 49, Jacob himself was about to die, he called his sons together, and, after blessing each one, said, "I am going the way of my fathers. When I die, bury me at—" Now, I would have thought he would have said, "Bury me by the love of my life. Bury me by Rachel." But that's not what he said. He said, "Bury me at Machpelah—by Leah."

Why would he say that? Because at the end of his life, Jacob realized Leah was where the blessing was all along. What he thought was an unfair trick was in reality the biggest blessing in his life because from Leah—not Rachel, not Bilhah, not Zilpah—from Leah came Judah. And from the tribe of Judah came the Messiah, Jesus Christ. Jesus was birthed through Leah, the one Jacob thought he had every right to bail out on. And at the end of his life, Jacob said, "Leah was it all along. I want to be buried by her."

Wife, you might look at the man next to you and say, "I was tricked. He's not the man I thought he would be." Husband, you might look at the woman you married and say, "She's not the passion of my life. I didn't know she would turn out this way." But if you jump ship, know this: You will miss the blessing of the birthing of Jesus in a supernatural, incredible, wonderful way because there are no tricks in the life of a child of God.

Employee, you might look at your boss and say, "When I signed that contract, I didn't know he would be such a jerk. I don't care what I signed. I'm going to find a legal loophole. I'm jumping ship." But when you put pen to paper and signed your name, your Father was there. And to the child of God, there are no tricks.

Teenager, you might look at your parents and say, "I was tricked. I must have been switched at birth. God couldn't have chosen *these* people to raise me." But know this: You are not only their child—you are a child of the King. He, in His wisdom, hand-picked them for you. And He makes no mistakes.

Paul said, "If you jump ship, you'll lose your life." And the centurion, knowing how tempting it would be for the sailors to bail out, to jump ship, to give up, ordered the soldiers to cut the lines so there would be no possibility of escape.

I know there are some who are saying, "I haven't jumped ship. I've only lowered a lifeboat over the side. I'll give it three more months, or two more weeks, or one more year."

But if you keep an escape option open in your mind, I guarantee you will end up using it.

> Think about divorce—and you will end up divorced.
>
> Think about other men or other women you wish you had because you're feeling tricked by the one you're with—and inevitably, you'll bail out.
>
> Think about changing jobs, even though you gave your word—and you'll miss out on what could have been.
>
> Think about leaving home, even though that's where God has you—and you'll never see His reality.

Get rid of the lifeboats.

Cut the lines.

"It's easy for you to pontificate," you say. "You don't know the storm I'm in. You don't know how vehemently the wind is blowing, how violently the waves are pounding. You just don't understand."

You're right. I don't. But there is One who does.

> In 1902 a fire broke out, which flared up rapidly in the home of an elderly woman. Asleep in the upstairs bedroom was her grandson, whom she tried to rescue before she died in the process. Someone outside heard the screams of the five-year-old boy, however, and found a way to climb hand-over-hand up a drainpipe, until he made it to the roof, broke through a window, and pulled the boy out to safety.
>
> This story, which appeared in the St. Louis *Globe Herald,* generated quite a bit of interest in the orphaned boy. During the hearings that followed, a schoolteacher came forward and gave reasons why he felt he should be appointed the boy's guardian. So did a wealthy businessman, a minister, and several other upstanding people in the community. The little boy, however, looked down and never raised his eyes—until a man came through the back doors of the courtroom, walked up to him, and opened his hands. The boy looked at the charred and badly blistered hands of the stranger and jumped into his arms, saying, "This is my dad."
>
> And the judge pounded the gavel and said, "So be it."

So, too, I'm asking you to look at the hands of One who loves you so much He absorbed the heat of hell to pull you out of eternal destruction. I'm asking you to listen to this One who says, "Trust Me. Don't jump ship, or all will be lost."

Precious people, Jesus will come in a way that will blow your mind if you don't jump ship. I don't care what the sailors of society are saying about breaking commitments, bailing out, and giving up.

Cut the ropes. Let the lifeboat crash in the sea below. Stay on board and, like Jacob, you'll look back and say, "Bury me by Leah. That's where the blessing was all along."

28 Paul was a marked man. His name was known in hell. The sizable storm he had endured was no doubt an attempt of Satan to do him in. "But I thought the storm was ordained by the Lord in order for him to bring the gospel to the island of Malta," you say.

It was. You see, in Greek, there is no linguistic differentiation between the words "trial" and "temptation," which is why some versions of James 1:2 read: "Count it all joy when you fall into various trials," while others read: "Count it all joy when you fall into various temptations." Therefore, the temptation instigated by the Enemy to pull me down or do me in is ultimately the trial allowed, even ordained by the Lord to build me up and strengthen my faith.

This is seen in the life of Job. Before Satan could bring any difficulty to him, or to those around him, he first had to ask permission of God (Job 1:9–12). But the ultimate example of this principle is seen at Calvary. Satan attempted to destroy Jesus Christ, only to discover that the Father allowed Judas Iscariot to betray Him and the Roman soldiers to crucify Him in order to bring about our salvation. Thus, it is the mature man, the wise woman who realizes that whatever is coming down in life is allowed by the Father to do something wonderful in, or to, or through them.

Acts 28:1, 2
And when they were escaped, then they knew that the island was called Melita. And the barbarous people shewed us no little kindness: for they kindled a fire, and received us every one, because of the present rain, and because of the cold.

The Greeks called anyone who didn't speak Greek a barbarian because they thought the languages of other people sounded like "bar-bar"—gibberish. Far from being "barbarous" however, the Maltese people showed kindness to the drenched soldiers, sailors, and prisoners who had washed up on their shore.

Acts 28:3 (a)
And when Paul had gathered a bundle of sticks, and laid them on the fire . . .

I like this. Paul could have said, "Hey, I told you a storm would happen. I told you the boat would go down. I told you all would be saved. That makes me the "big kahuna." But that's not what he did. Instead, he saw some guys lighting a fire and said, "I can help warm others," as he started gathering sticks. How do you stop a guy like Paul—always looking for an opportunity to serve, always going for it?

Two frogs fell into a can of cream, or so I
   heard it told.
The sides of the can were shiny and steep.
   The cream was deep and cold.
"Oh, what's the use?" croaked number
   one.
   "'Tis fate no help's around.
Goodbye my friend, goodbye cruel world."
   And weeping still—he drowned.
But frog number two, of sterner stuff,
   dogpaddled in surprise,
The while he wiped his creamy face and
   dried his creamy eyes.
"I'll swim awhile at least," he cried, or so
   I've heard he said,
"It really wouldn't help the world if one
   more frog were dead."
An hour or two he kicked and swam, not
   once he stopped to mutter.
But kicked and kicked and swam and
   kicked—
And hopped out via butter.

Paul was definitely a frog number two kind of individual—always kicking, always finding a way to do something to warm someone else.

Acts 28:3 (b)
. . . there came a viper out of the heat, and fastened on his hand.

Sometimes Satan tries to destroy or discourage us with sizable storms. Other times, he uses sneaky little snakes. While Paul was helping people, the snake struck. And you can be sure that's when the serpent will strike you. When you are helping others, serving others, loving others—from out of the heat of hell, Satan will strike.

Paul, however, would use this opportunity to share the gospel with these people in a uniquely powerful way. You see, the fallacy of the overemphasis of the faith movement—the mentality that says we should never be smitten by snakes—is that it robs us of opportunities to share the gospel. The Maltese people knew about these snakes. They had watched their families and loved ones succumb to their poison. Now they were about to see how Paul would handle the power, the danger, the pain of their venom.

So, too, the Lord will allow you to go through difficulties. The doctor may say, "It's inoperable." And no matter how you name it and claim it, folks, it may be the Lord's plan for you to navigate that pain and venom in such a way that the barbarians around you, who are also losing their loved ones to cancer, will change their minds about who God is as a result.

Jesus didn't say to Thomas, "Watch this miracle or listen to this sermon." He said, "Touch My wounds."

The world is rarely impacted and drawn to Jesus Christ through the sight of Christians prospering. No, it's through seeing believers suffering and not giving up that the barbarians change their minds. Perhaps the most important ministry you'll ever have is when people see how you react to the pain they go through all of the time. Difficulty is the agent that often allows people an opportunity to see the reality of Jesus Christ most clearly.

Acts 28:4
And when the barbarians saw the venomous beast hang on his hand, they said among themselves, No doubt this man is a murderer, whom, though he hath escaped the sea, yet vengeance suffereth not to live.

People are interesting. We always think the worst. When the snake strikes, invariably we start to think, *Oh, my. You must be a bad person or else that snake wouldn't be hanging from your hand.*

Acts 28:5
And he shook off the beast into the fire, and felt no harm.

Paul shook it off. I like that! It reminds me of my high-school football coach, Al Matucci—five feet two inches tall, five feet six inches wide. In

our Thanksgiving Bowl game against Camden High School, Coach Matucci called a sweep around the left end. As right guard, my job was to pull and lead the blocking. Bob Fontaine, our quarterback set us down, gave the count, took the snap, and I pulled. The next thing I remember was Coach Matucci standing over me, saying, "Shake it off, Courson. Shake it off." After he broke smelling salts in my face and I staggered off the field, I discovered that the play Bob called was not a sweep around the left, but a sweep around the right—which explains why Paul Newbauer, our left guard, and I met helmet to helmet right behind center, and were both knocked out. Coach Matucci would have loved Paul! Paul just shook the snake off—right back into the fire.

Acts 28:6
Howbeit they looked when he should have swollen, or fallen down dead suddenly: but after they had looked a great while, and saw no harm come to him, they changed their minds, and said that he was a god.

Isn't this human nature? First, the islanders thought Paul was a murderer. Then, just as quickly, they thought he was a god. If you're seeking the adulation of people—good luck! They'll put you down just as quickly as they'll build you up.

Acts 28:7
In the same quarters were possessions of the chief man of the island, whose name was Publius; who received us, and lodged us three days courteously.

How about this for drop-in guests! For three days, two hundred and seventy-six murderers, thieves, extortionists, kidnappers, soldiers, and sailors lodged with Publius and his family.

Sometimes people show up on your doorstep who might appear to be washed-out. But perhaps the Lord has sent them your way to bless you. If you open your heart, home, and life to people in the name of the Lord, He will reward you for your ministry of hospitality—as Publius was about to discover.

Acts 28:8 (a)
And it came to pass, that the father of Publius lay sick of a fever and of a bloody flux . . .

The word Dr. Luke used for fever is *ducentario*, meaning "many fevers," and from which we get our word "dysentery." Publius' father came down with dysentery, which produced a great fever—a condition still known on the island of Malta today, called, appropriately, Malta Fever.

Acts 28:8 (b)
. . .to whom Paul entered in, and prayed, and laid his hands on him, and healed him.

God will be a debtor to no man. Open your house, open your heart, and the people who come in will either bring a great blessing to you—as Paul did when he healed Publius' father—or He will use someone else to bring a blessing your way.

Acts 28:9 (a)
So when this was done, others also, which had diseases in the island, came, and were healed . . .

It is interesting to me that, although Paul prayed for everyone on the island and they were healed, he himself remained afflicted with a "thorn in the flesh" (2 Corinthians 12:7), which most Bible scholars believe was an eye disease, and from which Paul prayed for deliverance three times (2 Corinthians 12:8). Sometimes the greatest work flows through the very areas of our lives with which we ourselves struggle. For example, even though you might have a difficult marriage situation, you might find yourself with an effective ministry in helping other couples.
Why?
Because the very struggles you go through give you a compassion for and a sensitivity toward others in the same situation. Consequently, I think it's a mistake for us to say, "I'm not going to listen to that sister or receive from that brother because they're struggling with the same issues I do."
Beethoven wrote his greatest symphonies when he couldn't hear a note. And Paul healed multitudes when he was in need of healing himself.

Acts 28:10, 11
. . . Who also honoured us with many honours; and when we departed, they laded us with such things as were necessary. And after three months, we departed in a ship of Alexandria, which had wintered in the isle, whose sign was Castor and Pollux.

With the winter season behind them, the prisoners, sailors, and soldiers departed from the island of Malta on a ship dedicated to Castor and Pollux—twin sons of Zeus, the gods of navigation.

Acts 28:12, 13
And landing at Syracuse, we tarried there three days. And from thence we fetched a compass, and came to Rhegium: and after one day the south wind blew, and we came the next day to Puteoli:

They finally made it to Italy—within one hundred twenty-five miles from Rome.

Act 28:14 (a)
Where we found brethren, and were desired to tarry with them seven days . . .

Evidently, the captain had business in the city and allowed Paul and Luke to hang out with the brothers there.

Acts 28:14 (b), 15
. . .and so we went toward Rome. And from thence, when the brethren heard of us, they came to meet us as far as Appiforum, and The three taverns: whom when Paul saw, he thanked God, and took courage.

Hearing Paul was on his way, the brothers in Rome set out to meet him. The Appiforum being forty-three miles from Rome, The Three Taverns thirty-three—some men traveled farther than others to meet the apostle who had stirred their hearts through his Epistle to the Romans. So, too, people travel different distances in their desire to learn of the Lord. The wise men from the East traveled at least a year and a half to see the Christ child, while the religious leaders in Jerusalem couldn't be bothered to make the five-mile trip to see what was happening in Bethlehem.

Acts 28:16
And when we came to Rome, the centurion delivered the prisoners to the captain of the guard: but Paul was suffered to dwell by himself with a soldier that kept him.

Paul was put under house arrest. Under this provision, the guard was changed every six hours. Paul would later write to the Philippian believers, "All the saints salute you, chiefly they that are of Caesar's household" (Philippians 4:22).
How did men in Caesar's household get saved? By being chained to Paul!

Acts 28:17 (a)
And it came to pass, that after three days Paul called the chief of the Jews together . . .

The Jews in Rome, observing Paul enter the city surrounded by the parade of believers who had met him at the Appiiforum and The Three Taverns, must have wondered, *Who is this guy?*

So, when Paul said, "I want to talk with you"—they came.

Acts 28:17 (b)–20
. . . and when they were come together, he said unto them, Men and brethren, though I have committed nothing against the people, or customs of our fathers, yet was I delivered prisoner from Jerusalem into the hands of the Romans. Who, when they had examined me, would have let me go, because there was no cause of death in me. But when the Jews spake against it, I was constrained to appeal unto Caesar; not that I had ought to accuse my nation of. For this cause therefore have I called for you, to see you, and to speak with you: because that for the hope of Israel I am bound with this chain.

"I am here on a judicial matter," said Paul. "I have come to clear my name, not to condemn Israel."

Acts 28:21
And they said unto him, We neither received letters out of Judaea concerning thee, neither any of the brethren that came shewed or spake any harm of thee.

"Don't worry, Paul," said the Jewish leaders in Rome. "We haven't heard anything negative from Jerusalem about you." This is curious to me. I mean, the Jews in Jerusalem were out to kill Paul. Certainly they must have written a scathing report against him, warning the Jews in Rome about his heresy—perhaps even trying to enlist their aid in finally doing away with him completely. Why is it, then, that the Jews in Rome never heard anything? Could it be because their letter was on the ship that went down at Malta?

I have found that when storms strike—when someone says, "I have cancer," "My marriage is failing," or "My son ran away," the accusations of people who would otherwise be snipping at him or finding fault with him sink to the bottom of the sea of forgetfulness.

Acts 28:22, 23 (a)
But we desire to hear of thee what thou thinkest: for as concerning this sect, we know that every where it is spoken against. And when they had appointed him a day, there came many to him into his lodging; to whom he expounded and testified the kingdom of God, persuading them concerning Jesus . . .

Paul said, "You want to hear about the "sect" of Christianity? Great!" And they set up a meeting wherein, beginning with the law, and going through the prophets, Paul explained the kingdom as it related to Jesus. The Jews were always eager to hear about the kingdom—but Paul's message was singular: He talked about the King.

Acts 28:23 (b)
. . . both out of the law of Moses, and out of the prophets, from morning till evening.

I would love to have a tape of that study.

No doubt Paul would have directed their attention to Genesis 22, wherein Abraham was told to take his only son to Mount Moriah and offer him as a sacrifice unto the Lord. On their way up the mountain, Isaac, who was probably thirty-three years old at the time, said to his father, "Here's the wood and there's the fire—but where is the sacrifice?"

And Abraham spoke prophetically when he answered, "God will provide Himself a Lamb"—not, "God will provide for Himself," but, "God will provide Himself. He will be the Lamb."

Certainly, Paul would have reminded his audience of Exodus 12, wherein each family was instructed to place the blood of a lamb at the top, sides, and threshold of their doors—thereby depicting a cross.

He would have taken them to Leviticus 14, wherein, following the cleansing of leprosy, priests were instructed to take two birds, place one in an earthen vessel, kill it, and sprinkle the blood on the second bird before letting it go free. "Don't you see," Paul must have said, "how this perfectly describes the work of Jesus Christ—how, like the first bird, He came from heaven, was placed in the earthen vessel of a human body, and was killed? Yet, like the second bird, although the bloody marks of death remained upon Him—He rose again."

Paul would have turned their hearts to Psalm 22, where crucifixion was described centuries before it was known in the Middle East and wherein the very words Jesus spoke on the Cross were recorded.

He would have reminded them of Micah 5, which prophesied specifically that Messiah would be born in Bethlehem; and of Daniel 9, which pinpointed the very day of Jesus' entry into Jerusalem,

He would have reviewed Zechariah 11 with them, wherein it was prophesied that Messiah would be betrayed by His friend and sold for thirty pieces of silver, which would be cast on the floor of the temple, scooped up, and used to purchase a potter's field.

From morning until night, Paul showed how the entire Old Testament pictured, pointed to, and prophesied Jesus Christ. What are the chances that the three hundred-plus prophecies given concerning Messiah would be fulfilled by one man? 1 in 100,000,000,000,000,000,000,000. Think of it this way:

> Suppose the entire state of California was covered with acorns three feet deep—one of which was painted green. You and a squirrel go up in an airplane, and, as you fly over California, you open the door and shove the squirrel out. After landing safely, he wanders up and down the state—through San Francisco, San Jose, Fresno, Los Angeles, San Diego, Lake Tahoe, Redding, Yreka until he feels hungry and decides to eat an acorn. The chance of him choosing the green acorn would be 1 in 10 to the twenty-third power— the same chance that all of the prophecies concerning Messiah would be fulfilled in one man.

It doesn't make any sense intellectually for a person to deny the irrefutable facts of the Old Testament prophecies, pictures, and portraits that predicted who Jesus would be, how He would be born, how He would live, and how He would die. It takes more faith *not* to believe Jesus Christ is the Messiah than it takes to believe in Jesus Christ as Messiah.

Acts 28:24
And some believed the things which were spoken, and some believed not.

Some believed and some didn't. That's still the way it is—even among Christians. You see, we know our sins are forgiven. We know Jesus is the Messiah, and that we'll soon be with Him in heaven. Yet in the meantime, we might be in hellish situations of depression, defeat, and despair because of unbelief.

The Word of God says, "In everything give thanks" (see Ephesians 5:20). Why? Because all things are working together for good (Romans 8:28).
"Oh, but you haven't seen the stack of bills on my desk."
Well, the Word says, "My God shall supply all your need according to His riches" (see Philippians 4:19).
"Yeah, but you don't understand the hurt I feel because she dumped me."

Well, the Bible says even if she meant it for evil, God will use it for good (Genesis 50:20).
"But I feel so bad about my son. He's not walking with the Lord."
Well, the Bible says we can be confident that He who began a good work in him will perform it until the day of Christ Jesus—He'll finish what He started (Philippians 1:6).

Some Christians believe what God says and some don't. Those who don't find themselves engulfed in despair, defeat, and discouragement. You see, it's not enough just to know the Scriptures, gang. It's not enough just to hear the Word. It's not enough just to come to Bible study. You and I must *believe.* And "believe" is not a noun—it's a verb.

We can be the happiest, most carefree people in the world if we believe—and act on that belief. You might know the Scriptures backward and forward—but Jesus said, "Happy are you if you *do* them" (see John 13:17).

It's what you *do*—not what you know that matters. And it all begins by saying, "Today I'm going to believe that God is working, and that He is fulfilling what He has promised. You are faithful, Lord; and I will live in that today. I will proclaim Your faithfulness, and I will choose to rejoice in You."

Acts 28:25–27
And when they agreed not among themselves, they departed, after that Paul had spoken one word, Well spake the Holy Ghost by Isaiah the prophet unto our fathers, saying, Go unto this people, and say, Hearing ye shall hear, and shall not understand; and seeing ye shall see, and not perceive: For the heart of this people is waxed gross, and their ears are dull of hearing, and their eyes have they closed; lest they should see with their eyes, and hear with their ears, and understand with their heart, and should be converted, and I should heal them.

"Isaiah spoke rightly of you, gentlemen," said Paul, "when he said seeing, you wouldn't see and hearing, you wouldn't understand." Through this prophecy, also quoted by Jesus to His countrymen (see Matthew 13:13–15), Isaiah said, "God will blind the eyes of the person who does not want to see Him. He will harden the heart of the one who does not want to believe Him."
Why?
Because the Good News of the gospel is so potent and powerful that unless God blinded the eyes and hardened the hearts of those who don't want to believe, they would have no choice but to believe. And since God will not force Himself

upon any man, in this way He bows to the choice of the person who wants nothing to do with Him.

That is why resisting the Lord is a very dangerous thing to do, for there will come a time when He will do what He did to Pharaoh: He will harden the heart (Exodus 9:12). He will do what He did to Israel: He will blind the eyes (John 12:40), lest someone be converted against his will.

Acts 28:28

Be it known therefore unto you, that the salvation of God is sent unto the Gentiles, and that they will hear it.

Following the rejection of his message, Paul said, "I've talked to you from morning until evening. The proof is powerful, but you don't want to see it. Therefore, the message will go to the Gentiles."

Act 28:29–31

And when he had said these words, the Jews departed, and had great reasoning among themselves. And Paul dwelt two whole years in his own hired house, and received all that came in unto him. Preaching the kingdom of God, and teaching those things which concern the Lord Jesus Christ, with all confidence, no man forbidding him.

For two years, chained to a guard, Paul would teach all who came to him. To know what Paul was thinking during this two-year house arrest, hear his heart in the books of Ephesians, Philippians, Colossians, and Philemon—all written during this period of captivity.

Now, although this is where Luke, the author of Acts, put down his pen, Paul's story continued. Released from house arrest to stand before Caesar Nero, Paul witnessed powerfully for the Lord. Nero, however, rejected Paul's message and proceeded instead to go on a rampage against Christians. Historical records verify that he lost his mind at the very time he listened to Paul and rejected the gospel.

Released by Caesar because there was no legal case against him, the Book of Romans and the writings of Eusebius tell us Paul preached the gospel in Spain and Europe before he was brought back to Rome under arrest once more. This time, however, it was no longer house arrest. He was thrown into a dungeon.

Knowing death was imminent, Paul wrote these words to his young protigie, Timothy:

For I am now ready to be offered, and the time of my departure is at hand. I have fought a good fight, I have finished my course, I have kept the faith: Henceforth there is laid up for me a crown of righteousness, which the Lord, the righteous judge, shall give me at that day . . .

"Paul *should* get a crown or righteousness," you say. "He went for it totally. But me? No way." Really? Read on.

. . . And not to me only, but unto all them also that love his appearing.

"Hey! Even *I* qualify for that," you can say. After reading the news, don't you long for His coming?

Do thy diligence to come shortly unto me; for Demas hath forsaken me, having loved this present world, and is departed unto Thessalonica, Crescens to Galatia, Titus unto Dalmatia. Only Luke is with me.

Paul had ministered to thousands, yet Luke was the only one who stood by him in his imprisonment.

Take Mark, and bring him with thee: for he is profitable to me for the ministry. And Tychicus have I sent to Ephesus. The cloke that I left at Troas with Carpus, when thou comest, bring with thee, and the books, but especially the parchments.

What were these parchments? The Old Testament. Here, the man who wrote much of the Bible is saying, "I want to study until the day I die." Paul never stopped learning. Saints, God will use a man or woman who—no matter what dungeon they might be in, no matter what time constraints, physical impairments, or emotional pressure they're under—will say, "I want to know more of the heart of God."

Alexander the coppersmith did me much evil: the Lord reward him according to his works: Of whom be thou ware also; for he hath greatly withstood our words. At my first answer no man stood with me, but all men forsook me: I pray God that it may not be laid to their charge. Notwithstanding the Lord stood with me, and strengthened me; that by me the preaching might be fully known, and that all the Gentiles might hear: and I was delivered out of the mouth of the lion.

Some left Paul and went back to the world. Others were afraid to stand by him. But the Lord stood with him.

And the Lord shall deliver me from every evil work, and will preserve me unto his heavenly kingdom: to whom be glory for ever and ever. Amen. Salute Prisca and Aquila, and the household of Onesiphorus, Erastus abode at Corinth: but Trophimus have I left at Miletum sick. Do thy diligence to come before winter.

"Get here quickly," wrote Paul. "I know I'm about to die."

Eubulus greeteth thee, and Pudens, and Linus, and Claudia, and all the brethren. The Lord Jesus Christ be with thy spirit. Grace be with you. Amen.   2 Timothy 4:6–22

Shortly after Paul penned these words, he died—most likely beheaded at the command of Caesar Nero.

You might feel like you're in a damp, dark dungeon. The people you were counting on aren't there—maybe some are even attacking you. Thus, you can relate to something of what Paul wrote to Timothy. Understand this: If you are suffering without succeeding, someone will succeed after you. Paul died virtually alone, perhaps thinking, *Was my entire ministry a failure? Is it all going to fall apart now that I'm in trouble? What's going on?*

But look what happened: We are indebted to Paul as we are to no other brother besides our Elder Brother, Jesus Christ, for as we read Romans, Corinthians, Galatians, Ephesians, Philippians, Colossians, Timothy, Titus, Philemon, Hebrews—it is Paul who clarifies truth so incredibly, who teaches grace so beautifully.

Paul went through hard times, and his life ended on a seemingly difficult note. That is why if you are suffering without succeeding, I cannot promise you that you will succeed before you die. But I can promise you that if you are suffering for the cause of Christ, someone who comes after you will succeed. Ask Paul. Look at the church today—the result of his suffering.

There may be children or grandchildren, friends or neighbors, who, after your departure, will blossom and bloom because of the example you set, the life you lived, the suffering you endured. If, on the other hand, you are succeeding without suffering, know this: Someone suffered who went before you. Perhaps it was a grandmother or grandfather, a mother or father, a brother, sister, child, or friend who wept and prayed you into the kingdom.

Ultimately, however, the One who suffered for and before you was Jesus Christ. For as Paul—the Pharisee-turned-believer, the tent-making rabbi, the champion of grace, the defender of the Finished Work—would write, "He who was rich, for our sakes became poor, that we might become rich. He who knew no sin was made sin, that we might be righteous in Him."

Amen.

NOTES

[1]U.S. National Debt Clock, September 25, 2002, http://www.brillig.com/debt_clock.
[2]www.bartleby.com, John Bartlett (1820–1905). Familiar Quotations, 10th ed. 1919.

ROMANS

Background to Romans

The Epistle to the Romans has been called "the Fort Knox of Bible doctrine."

- John Chrysostom had it read to him once a week for eighteen years.
- The heart of John Wesley was "strangely warmed" upon hearing it preached.
- Dr. Donald Barnhouse said the Bible of a believer should automatically open to it.
- Seventy-five percent of Bible teachers today said if they could teach from just one book, it would be this one.

All roads lead to Rome. Thus, Paul would no doubt conclude if all roads lead *to* Rome, all roads must also lead *from* Rome. *If I can get to Rome,* he must have thought, *and share the gospel, it will spread rapidly and reach the entire world.* At this point in time, Rome's ship of state was sailing along quite nicely, but belowdeck, having lost her moral bearing, the empire was already beginning to sink. Aware of this, Paul desired to go to the Imperial City not only to launch the gospel from Rome, but to bless the people in Rome. Although his plan was strategically brilliant, he was unable to get there. But instead of feeling defeated by what he couldn't do, Paul grabbed parchment and pen, and did what he could do.

That's what David did. After becoming king of Israel, David said, "Why should I dwell in this palace, while God lives in a tent?" (see 2 Samuel 7:2). "I want to build God a temple."

"All that's in your heart, do," Nathan replied (see 2 Samuel 7:3).

But that night the Lord said to Nathan in a dream, "You spoke too quickly. David can't build Me a temple. He's a man of war, and the temple must be a place of peace" (see 1 Chronicles 22:8).

So what did David do? Did he pout? No. Did he vegetate? No. He drew plans, gathered materials, and lined up laborers so that when his son, Solomon, ascended the throne, everything was ready for him to begin construction

(1 Chronicles 22:1–5). David wasn't hung up by what he couldn't do. Rather he asked, "What *can* I do?"

Unable to go to Rome, Paul instead penned a letter to the Romans and, because he had never been to Rome, he was able to concentrate solely on life-changing, impacting, revolutionary theology. You see, in his other epistles, Paul addressed the problems and personalities unique to the cities to which he wrote. Not so with the Book of Romans.

Paul did what he could do, and I'm so glad, because, just as all roads lead to Rome, truly, the road to revival leads through the Book of Romans.

In the early days of the church, John Chrysostom—so named because "Chrysostom" means "golden throat"—was an incredible orator. His preaching was so powerful that in the middle of his sermons, the congregation would burst out in applause time and time again. Embarrassed by the applause, one day John gave a sermon on why people shouldn't clap in the middle of his sermons. So persuasive and incredible was the sermon, however, that the congregation responded with a resounding ovation! John Chrysostom began his ministry by reading the Book of Romans and went on to read Romans in its entirety once a week for eighteen years.

Chrysostom was followed by a man named Augustine. As a young man, Augustine despaired greatly because his sin weighed on him heavily. One day, with a copy of the New Testament in hand, he sat under a tree and wept over his own immorality. Just then, a group of children walked by, singing a well-known ditty of the day: "Pick it up and read it through; pick it up and read it through." So Augustine did just that. He picked up the New Testament, and, by divine design, it fell open to these words: "Let us walk honestly, as in the day; not in reveling and drunkenness, not in immorality and wantonness, not in strife and envying. But put ye on the Lord Jesus Christ, and make not provision for the flesh, to fulfil its lusts" (Romans 13:13, 14). Augustine was blown away. He went back to Romans 1 and was converted by the time he came to the end of the book.

After Augustine, another intellectual giant arrived on the scene—a Catholic monk named Martin Luther. Sitting at his monastic desk, he was attacked by thoughts so ungodly that he picked up an inkwell and threw it against the wall, aiming at what he believed to be an image of the devil. Luther was a broken man. Then the concept of justification by faith as seen in the book of Romans hit him. At last his eyes were opened. His life was changed—and so was the world, as he ushered in the Great Reformation.

John Wesley left England and sailed across the sea as a missionary to the American Indians. After failing miserably, he returned to England, saying, "I went to save the Indians, but who shall save me?" Wesley stumbled into a little church on Addington Street, where he listened to the minister read from Martin Luther's commentary on Romans. "My heart was strangely warmed," he would later write. And John Wesley was saved as he understood at last that the price for his sin was paid and that the work of salvation was complete.

Truly, the road to revival leads through this book. While Chuck Smith was teaching through Romans in a Foursquare Church, realizing he could throw off the yoke of religion, his life was changed. He went on to pastor a little twenty-five-member church called Calvary Chapel in Costa Mesa, which today numbers in the tens of thousands and is one of the fastest-growing evangelistic movements in the world today. It is not the result of any attempt at organization. It's just revival.

My own life was changed when, as an eighteen-year-old college freshman, I went to Calvary Chapel and heard Chuck teach through Romans. I heard for the first time that I didn't have to pray more, study more, or witness more; that the Lord loved me regardless of what I did because the price was paid completely. The result? I couldn't wait to pray more, study more, and talk to everyone I met about the glorious grace and goodness of God.

The religion of the law thunders, "responsibility!" But relationship with the Lord says, "Just respond. The work is done. The price is paid. And in responding to Me, you'll do more than you would ever do under the pressure of religion."

And this is what we're about to discover once again as we go through this glorious Book together.

ROMANS

1 Romans 1:1 (a)
Paul . . .

Following his conversion, Paul changed his name from Saul to Paul. "Saul" means "requested One"—the man in demand. "Paul," on the other hand, means "little." Commentators are divided as to why Paul changed his name from "requested one" to "little." Some say it was the result of his humility. As Saul, he was a proud Pharisee who looked down on other men. But when he was converted, he was broken. Others say Paul changed his name because of accessibility. About to travel throughout the Roman Empire, Paul jettisoned the Hebrew name of Saul to take on the Roman name of Paul.

Humility or accessibility—which caused Paul to change his name? I suggest it was both. Paul was a great man who lived in humility, which, in turn, gave him accessibility. In this I am re-

minded of perhaps one of the most humble men of our generation: Billy Graham.

Billy Graham is absolutely amazing. There he was at the inauguration of President Clinton, praying so simply and beautifully, "Lord, help us to carry out the challenges we've heard."

Now, if I had been asked to pray at the inauguration, I know I would have given a "sermonette" and caused a riot. But not Billy. On *20/20* a couple of weeks before the inauguration, Diane Sawyer said to him, "Tell me, Dr. Graham. What do you consider to be your greatest failure? Was it your association with Nixon? Your involvement with Russia?"

Billy just looked at her and said, "Well, Diane, I consider my whole life pretty much a failure."

He wasn't giving a clever response, for that is what he genuinely feels. Truly, Billy Graham lives in humility. And because of that he has great accessibility to kings, presidents, and leaders all over the world.

Romans 1:1 (b)
. . . a servant of Jesus Christ . . .

The word "servant" is *doulos,* meaning "bondslave." Exodus 21:2 sheds light on what this means: In Israel, a slave was required to serve only six years before he was set free. If, however, at the end of six years, he said, "I like it here. I want to become a bondslave," the master would drive a nail through his right earlobe and place an earring in it, signifying he was a *doulos,* a slave by choice.

It's a wise decision to give yourself fully to the Lord as His bondslave because He takes excellent care of those committed to Him. Their lives are filled with purpose and focus; their hearts with peace and joy.

Perhaps you're saying, "I'm my own man— captain of my destiny, master of my fate. I don't serve anyone." But reality says otherwise. *Everyone* will serve someone. Bob Dylan was right when he sang, "It may be the devil, or it may be the Lord, but you gotta serve somebody." And Paul chose to serve the Lord in totality.

Romans 1:1 (c)
. . . called to be an apostle . . .

The word "apostle" means "one who is sent out." In the New Testament there are three groups of apostles: God appointed one Apostle— Jesus Christ (Hebrews 3:1). Jesus appointed twelve apostles who traveled with Him. In the Book of Acts, Barnabas, Titus, Andronicus, Junia, and a whole host of others are called apostles appointed by the Holy Spirit.

To this day, the Spirit continues to appoint apostles—missionaries who are "sent out" with the message of the gospel. "What a great calling that is," you say. But you know what? A call to be a carpenter, a science teacher, or a repairman is just as holy and just as important if you're doing what God has opened up for you, and you're doing it for Him. Whether you're a baker, banker, mechanic, or cook, yours is an important calling because of the need for brothers and sisters to serve in all kinds of arenas and locations. Don't think you're missing God's best if you're not a missionary. If the Lord wants you selling insurance or pouring cement, be at peace about it and say, "Lord, if this is what You have for me, I'll do it for Your glory. I'll be salt and light as I labor here for You."

There's a tendency within us to think everyone should have our calling. There's a tendency to think that if I'm called to be a missionary, everyone should be a missionary; that if I'm called to be a teacher, everyone should be a teacher. Not true. That's not the way it works in the body of Christ. The Lord calls each of us uniquely, individually, personally.

How can you know what your calling is? It's very simple. What's flowing from your life presently? What comes easy to you? What's working out supernaturally for you?

Isaac dug a well in order to water his flock. But the inhabitants of the land challenged his right to be there. So he called that well "Esek," or "Contention," moved down the road, dug another well, and struck water once more. A second time, the inhabitants came and said, "This is our territory. Get out of here." So Jacob named the well "Sitnah," or "Hatred," and went down the road a little farther. He dug a third well. This time, no one bothered him—so he called the name of this well "Rehoboth," or "there's room for me" (Genesis 26).

I have found life basically follows this pattern. You dig and strike some water. You find refreshment and good things happen. But strife or hatred follows. So you go down the road and dig a second time. Again there are problems. Eventually, however, if you don't give up, you'll find your Rehoboth.

Isaac had the job of watering sheep. He didn't agonize over it. He didn't complain about it. He just tended to what was at hand—and he ended up at Rehoboth. That's the key. Do what's before you. Say, "Lord, here I am. You've allowed me to do this, and I'm going to do it as unto You. And if there's strife or hatred, I'll just move down the road and dig again until I find Rehoboth." God has a Rehoboth for every one of us. Paul's was apostolic ministry.

Romans 1:1 (d)
. . . separated . . .

When was Paul "separated unto the gospel"? When he was ministering to the Lord—worshiping, praising, and honoring Him in thanksgiving (Acts 13:2). There's a lot of talk about ministering for the Lord, and that's good. But ministering *to* the Lord is even more important.

And the Levites that are gone away far from me, when Israel went astray, which went astray away from me after their idols; they shall even bear their iniquity. And they shall not come near unto me, to do the office of a priest unto me, nor to come near to any of my holy things, in the most holy place: but they shall bear their shame, and their abominations which they have committed. But I will make them keepers of the charge of the house, for all the service thereof, and for all that shall be done therein. But the priests the Levites, the sons of Zadok, that kept the charge of my sanctuary when the children of Israel went astray from me, they shall come near to me to minister unto me, and they shall stand before me to offer unto me the fat and the blood, saith the Lord GOD: They shall enter into my sanctuary, and they shall come near to my table, to minister unto me, and they shall keep my charge.

Ezekiel 44:10, 13–16

This is an extremely important passage that says standing before people, sharing with people, and ministering to people is punishment in comparison to coming before the Lord and ministering to Him. It was as Paul ministered to the *Lord* that he was called to minister to people. But even before the Spirit separated Paul unto the gospel in Acts 13:2, the Son separated him in Acts 9. On his way to Damascus, he was knocked to the ground by a bright light and a voice that said, "Saul, Saul, why do you persecute Me?" But even before the Son separated Paul unto the gospel on the Damascus Road, the Father separated him at the very moment of his birth (Galatians 1:1).

Thus, all the while Paul was persecuting the church, the Father knew what he would be doing eventually. I say this to remind us as parents that our kids have destinies. Therefore, our job is not so much to mold them as it is to unfold them. We have our own expectations, feelings, and desires for our kids. But in reality, wise is the mother or father who says, "Lord, show me this day what *You* want my son or daughter to do or to be. And help me to flow with what *You* want."

Romans 1:1 (e)
. . . unto the gospel of God.

The Greek word translated "gospel" is *euaggelion,* from which we get our word "evangelist." In the Septuagint, this was the word used when the people of Israel were released from their Babylonian captivity. It meant, "You can go home. You're free. Good news!"

Truly, the gospel is Good News—not just good advice. A lot of preachers, authors, and speakers try to make Christianity a bunch of good advice. Most best-selling Christian books today are full of good advice about child-rearing, financial planning, or marriage counseling. But remove the name of Jesus Christ from most of them, and it won't affect the book at all.

We've got something so much better than good advice, folks. And I would encourage you to be on guard against sermons or authors, churches or organizations that give you good advice. If you can take Jesus Christ out of a sermon without affecting it, you're probably wasting your time listening to it. If you can take Jesus Christ out of a book without affecting it, you're probably wasting your time reading it. Paul wasn't separated unto the good advice of Christian living. He was separated to the Good News of God.

Romans 1:2, 3
(Which he had promised afore by his prophets in the holy scriptures,) concerning his Son Jesus Christ our Lord, which was made of the seed of David according to the flesh.

Twenty-five years before Paul penned this Epistle, he became a servant of the Lord Jesus Christ on the road to Damascus when he said, "Lord, what wilt Thou have me to do?" (Acts 9:6). And for twenty-five years he kept at it. Commitment was really a key to Paul's success in ministry. He left everything to focus on one thing singularly: serving Jesus Christ passionately (Philippians 3:7).

Some people today get excited about ministry or about walking with Jesus—but only in spurts. Why was Paul so dedicated, consecrated, and separated in his service? I suggest it was because he had an encounter not with a theological principle or a philosophical ideal, but with a risen Lord. If you're only a student of theology or ecclesiology, you'll miss the heart of ministry entirely. But if we really understand Jesus is risen and dwelling within us—that we can talk with Him, share our concerns with Him, and fellowship with Him—our lives and ministry will be revolutionary.

I talked to a lighting contractor one afternoon who said, "I'm scheduled to light a New Age bookstore. Although there's some money in it, I don't feel good about it. What should I do?"

"Because you're born again," I said, "the Lord promised He would write His will not on tablets of stone, but upon the tender tablets of your heart (see Jeremiah 31:33). Have you talked it over with Him? Does He want you to stay away from that bookstore because it is dark? Or, does He want you to go in and bring light—not just physically, but spiritually?"

"I don't know," he said.

"Well, that's for you to find out," I continued. "You see, I could give you all kinds of reasons why you should avoid that pagan place. Or, I could give you reasons why you should go in, storm the gates of hell, and be

*light in that place. I don't know what God
wants you to do. Talk to Him."*

*Suddenly, his face lit up as he saw that it's
not a matter of principles or theology. It's a
matter of touching "the seed of David," Jesus
Christ personally.*

Romans 1:4
**And declared to be the Son of God with
power, according to the spirit of holiness, by
the resurrection from the dead.**

"I'm separated unto the gospel," Paul declared, "and that gospel concerns Jesus, born of
the seed of David, declared to be the Son of God.
He's one of us—and yet He is much greater than
us. He became a Man, yet remains the Son of
God."

Romans 1:5, 6
**By whom we have received grace and apos-
tleship, for obedience to the faith among all
nations, for his name: Among whom are ye
also the called of Jesus Christ.**

"We have received grace—unmerited blessing.
We have received apostleship—direction for ministry," declared Paul. This was not only theology
for him. It was reality.

Romans 1:7 (a)
**To all that be in Rome, beloved of God,
called to be saints.**

The words "to be" are in italics in the King
James Version because they don't appear in the
original Greek text. Thus, this verse should read,
"You are called saints." Most people have the idea
that saints are special people in religious history.
But the truth is, there are only two categories of
people: saints and pagans. Therefore, if you're a
believer—you're a saint.

A little boy attended a church that had beautiful stained-glass windows depicting St. Paul, St.
Peter, and St. John. One day, when asked in his
Sunday-school class, "What are saints?" he answered, "They're people who the light shines
through." Good answer!

Romans 1:7 (b)
Grace to you and peace . . .

In Paul's day, when Greeks greeted each other,
they would say, "*Charis,*" which means "grace."
When Jews greeted each other, however, they
would say, "*Shalom,*" which means "peace." In
the salutation of each of his epistles, Paul linked
these two words together. He always put them
in the same order because man will never experi-

ence peace until he understands grace. If you're
trying to be holier or more deserving of God's
blessings, your Christian life will not be full of
peace. But if you understand grace—that God
blesses and gives unconditionally—you'll stop
trying to earn His blessings, and you'll have
peace.

Romans 1:7 (c)
**. . . from God our Father, and the Lord Jesus
Christ.**

Peace from God has two components. First of
all, peace from God implies peace *with* God,
which is positional and unconditional because
Jesus Christ took upon Himself all of our shortcomings and sins, problems, weakness, and rebelliousness (Romans 5:1). Most of us believe the
Lord is disappointed in us because we haven't
spent time in the Word, because we don't pray as
we should, because we're not doing very much for
Him. But here, Paul the apostle says, "There is
grace and peace for *all* because Jesus did it all!"

Second, we have the peace *of* God, which is ex-
periential and comes through prayer (Philippians
4:7). Perhaps this is what happened to you today:
The kids didn't behave. The job didn't go well.
Your husband didn't come through, or your
friends let you down. As you felt the burdens begin to come and the tension begin to build, you
thought, *I should pray.* But no sooner did you
think this than the Enemy was there, saying,
"Pray? Now that you have a problem you want to
pray? What about devotions, Mr. Prayer Person?
You didn't have devotions this morning, did you?
And you think you can pray *now?*"

You see, gang, we know we have problems, and
we are all too aware of our failures. But we think
the Father won't hear us if we haven't talked to
Him for a day or three or ten. We think He won't
answer us if we haven't been doing what we
should do, or going where we should go. In reality, nothing is further from the truth. Look at our
Lord, our Friend, Jesus Christ. After He had
prayed in the Garden of Gethsemane so intensely
that He sweat blood, He looked up, and saw a
group of soldiers coming toward Him, led by His
disciple, Judas. Jesus looked at Judas and said,
"Friend, what seekest thou?" And His heart was
revealed in that moment—for Jesus looked at Judas at the moment of betrayal and called Judas
"Friend." Judas was at the lowest ebb possible,
yet Jesus still said, "Friend, what seekest thou?"
(see Matthew 26:50). This One with whom we
walk is so incredibly gracious. He'll respond to
you and work with you anytime you call upon
Him.

Romans 1:8 (a)
First, I thank my God through Jesus Christ . . .

"I thank *my* God," said Paul.

"My Lord and *my* God," said Thomas, upon seeing the Resurrected Lord (John 20:28).

No wonder Martin Luther said, "Christianity is uniquely the religion of the possessive pronoun."

Romans 1:8 (b)
. . . for you all . . .

Paul didn't say, "I thank my God through Jesus Christ for eighty percent of you." He didn't say, "Most of you guys are great, but there's a couple of exceptions." No, under the inspiration of the Spirit, Paul said, "I thank God for you *all.*"

Romans 1:8 (c)
. . . that your faith is spoken of throughout the whole world.

Although Paul had never met these believers, he had already heard about their faith.

Romans 1:9
For God is my witness, whom I serve with my spirit in the gospel of his Son, that without ceasing I make mention of you always in my prayers.

How does one pray without ceasing? The Greek phrase "without ceasing" literally speaks of a tickle in the throat. In other words, to pray without ceasing means to go through the day praying as often and as reflexively as you would cough to suppress a tickle in your throat. As you drive down Main Street and see someone from church, praying without ceasing means you just shoot up a prayer for them. As you see your neighbors or co-workers, you say, "Father, You see what their need is. Be all You want to be for them." Life becomes an adventure when you pray without ceasing.

Romans 1:10
Making request, if by any means now at length I might have a prosperous journey by the will of God to come unto you.

By "making request if by any means I might come to you," Paul was giving God a blank check. He was giving God permission to use any means He chose to get him to Rome. How different that is from the way I often pray. I say, "I'm the quarterback, Lord. You be my offensive Lineman.

Run interference for me, and, together, we'll make this happen."

Are your prayers direct—or are they directive? That is, are you being honest and open before the Lord in humility, or are you telling Him what to do? The best way to pray is to say, "Lord, You know the needs I have. You've asked me to share them with You. This is my desire, my burden, my concern. Now, Lord, Your will be done by any means You see fit."

"But aren't we supposed to name it and claim it?" you ask.

Ask Hezekiah. . . .

"O Lord, let me live," he prayed. "I know Isaiah said I was supposed to die, but, Lord, let me live. I name it and claim it." In Hebrew, the account reads that he turned his face to the wall and chirped like a bird incessantly, demanding his own way until finally the Lord said, "Okay. Live" (see 2 Kings 20:1–6). When messengers from Babylon came to congratulate him on his recovery, Hezekiah responded by taking them on a tour of the treasures of Israel. And it was this report that led Nebuchadnezzar to subsequently invade Israel. Meanwhile, Hezekiah fathered a son named Manasseh, who would become the worst king in Israel's history.

The Lord did indeed answer Hezekiah's prayer by prolonging his life fifteen years. But those fifteen years were disastrous both to Hezekiah personally and to the kingdom nationally. How much better it would have been had Hezekiah simply shared his heart with the Father and said, "Not my will, but Thy will be done."

That's how Jesus prayed in the hour of His greatest need (Luke 22:42). Our faith is not to be in our own plans, but in the goodness and wisdom of our Father.

Romans 1:11, 12
For I long to see you, that I may impart unto you some spiritual gift, to the end ye may be established; that is, that I may be comforted together with you by the mutual faith both of you and me.

"In giving to you, I will benefit as well because our faith will grow mutually," said Paul. That's always the way it is in ministry. Give and you'll get. Share and you'll receive.

Romans 1:13–15
Now I would not have you ignorant, brethren, that oftentimes I purposed to come unto you, (but was let hitherto,) that I might have some fruit among you also, even as among

other Gentiles. I am debtor both to the Greeks, and to the Barbarians; both to the wise, and to the unwise. So, as much as in me is, I am ready to preach the gospel to you that are at Rome also.

"I'm a debtor to everyone," said Paul—"to the Greek and to the barbarian, to the sophisticated and to the simple, to the businessman and to the biker, to the housewife and to the hippie, to the jock and to the jailbird." Why did Paul feel this way? Because he was amazed at the goodness of God that saved him so radically at the very time he was erring so greatly.

Romans 1:16
For I am not ashamed of the gospel of Christ: for it is the power of God unto salvation to every one that believeth; to the Jew first, and also to the Greek.

Paul was not ashamed of the gospel for two reasons. The first is that the gospel revives men's lives. Dead in sin, and without the Lord, men go through the motions of living. But in reality, without any real purpose, they wonder why they exist. Paul was not ashamed of the gospel because it is the power of God unto salvation. It is literally the *dunamis*—from which we get our words "dynamic" and "dynamite"—to totally turn people around and give them reason for being.

For topical study of Romans 1:16 entitled "I Am Not Ashamed of the Gospel," turn to page 872.

Romans 1:17 (a)
For therein is the righteousness of God revealed . . .

The second reason Paul was not ashamed of the gospel is that it reveals God's love. God's love is seen in the fact that He doesn't just wink at sin and say, "Boys will be boys." After all, who would want to live in a community in which righteousness was not enforced, in which police officers simply said, "People will be people. So let's just close our eyes to robberies and murders"? If that was the policy of the community in which you lived, you would move. God neither winks at sin nor wipes us out because of sin. Rather, He washes away our sin by the blood of His Son

Romans 1:17 (b)
. . . from faith to faith: as it is written, The just shall live by faith.

Here's where many of us are vulnerable to error. We know salvation is *from* faith because we begin by simply embracing the Good News of the gospel but then we go from faith to works. We think we have to mobilize, organize, and agonize over our spirituality.

"No, " says Paul. "It's *from* faith *to* faith." The just shall live by faith. Faith is not only the starting point of your salvation—it's the staying power of your Christian walk. "Even as you received Christ," Paul would say to the Colossians, "so walk ye in Him" (see Colossians 2:6). "Oh foolish Galatians," he would write, "are you so foolish? Having begun in the Spirit are you now made perfect by the flesh?" (see Galatians 3:1–3). The just shall live by faith—faith in the finished work of the Cross, faith in the resurrected presence of Jesus Christ.

Romans 1:18 (a)
For the wrath of God is revealed from heaven . . .

Here, Paul puts in the clutch and changes gears as he paints the canvas black in order that the gem of the Gospel might stand out against the dark backdrop of human depravity. God will not allow people to continue in sin any more than a physician would say to a person with cancer, "Well, I don't want to carve into you or cause you any discomfort, so I won't do anything about it." No, just as a doctor knows there must be surgery, so, too, the wrath of God will deal surgically and powerfully with humanity whenever people fail to embrace Jesus Christ and refuse to allow His blood to remove the cancer of their iniquity.

Romans 1:18 (b)
. . . against all ungodliness and unrighteousness of men . . .

Ungodliness is sin against God. Unrighteousness is sin against man. When Moses came down from Sinai, he had two tablets in his hand. I suggest that one tablet contained the first four commandments—all dealing with our relationship to God—and that the second tablet contained the remaining six commandments—all dealing with our relationship to our fellow man.

Romans 1:18 (c)
. . . who hold the truth in unrighteousness.

The word "hold" is very important. Referring to a helmsman steering a boat against the current, it means "to suppress." In other words, the current wants to take the boat a certain way, but, determined to go the opposite way, the helmsman *holds* the rudder in such a way that he might go his way instead of the way of the current. So, too, the wrath of God is revealed against those who are determined to go their own way regardless of what they know is true. For, as we will see, Romans 1 makes it clear that creation around him testifies of the reality of God to every man, while chapter 2 clearly declares that conscience within him tells every man how he ought to live.

Romans 1:19, 20
Because that which may be known of God is manifest in them; for God hath shewed it unto them. For the invisible things of him from the creation of the world are clearly seen, being understood by the things that are made, even his eternal power and Godhead; so that they are without excuse.

Creation all around testifies of God's reality. The grandeur of heaven alone has spoken to every tongue, every culture, and every society throughout history (Psalm 19:1–3). Concerning the acceptance of the "Big Bang Theory" by the scientific community, Robert Jastrow, an astrophysicist and director of NASA's Goodard Institute for Space Studies, wrote:

Now we see how the astronomical evidence supports the biblical view of the origin of the world. The essential elements in the astronomical and biblical accounts of Genesis are now the same. Consider the enormity of the problem. Science has proved that the universe exploded into being at a certain given moment. It asks what cause produced this effect. Who or what put the matter and energy into the universe? And science cannot answer this question. For the scientist who has lived by his faith in the power of his own reason, the story ends now like a bad dream. He has scaled the mountains of ignorance. He is about to conquer the highest peak. He pulls himself over the final rock, and he is greeted by a band of theologians who have been there for centuries.

Walking with a group of admirals one evening who were discussing whether or not God existed, Napoleon is said to have pointed to the heavens and said, "Sirs, if you're going to get rid of God, you must get rid of those." Napoleon was right. The heavens declare the glory, the reality, the substance, the weight of God.

Romans 1:21 (a)
Because that, when they knew God, they glorified him not as God . . .

Every man knows there's a God, but men choose to suppress the truth and deny God exists because they don't want to give glory to Him as God. You see, if there is a God, then I am required to submit to Him. But my flesh doesn't want to do that, so I'll suppress the truth I see all around me. I'll say God doesn't exist—even though the heavens and stars scream at me, "Yes He does!"

We can fall into this same error as believers. Knowing God, we can fail to glorify Him as God. How? By insisting on our own way, by saying, "God, I believe in You, and now I'm telling You what I want You to do. You better solve this situation, take care of this problem, grant this request, or heal this sickness. I'm naming it. I'm claiming it."

He's God. We're not. He knows things we can't know and sees things we can't see. Therefore, for me to rub the lamp of faith and expect God to become my genie is, in a sense, blasphemous. Father knows best. Therefore, my part is to talk things over with Him, cast my cares upon Him, and have faith that He will do what's right—even though I might not initially agree or understand.

Romans 1:21 (b)
. . . neither were thankful . . .

Although we know God, we fail to glorify Him as God whenever we stop being thankful for whatever He sends our way.

Romans 1:21 (c), 22
. . . but became vain in their imaginations, and their foolish heart was darkened. Professing themselves to be wise, they became fools.

Anyone who thinks he knows exactly what should happen in his life and precisely how it should take place is a fool.

Romans 1:23 (a)
And changed the glory of the uncorruptible God into an image made like to corruptible man, and to birds, and fourfooted beasts . . .

What Paul is saying is borne out in anthropology: On every corner of the planet, throughout all of history, every culture has had an innate need to worship. But, suppressing the truth about God, they have substituted gods of their own choosing. The Egyptian said, "If I were God, I would be bright and powerful, causing the crops to grow and blasting people who were out of line." So his god was Ra, the sun god. The Hindu said, "If I were God, I would be gentle and caring." So his god is a cow. The American Indian said, "If I were God, I would soar over the mountains majestically." So his god is an eagle.

Suppression and substitution have been the pattern throughout the history of mankind. And lest you think our society is an exception, what about the Bears and the Seahawks, the Lions and the Falcons? We spray-paint our bodies; we put watermelons on our heads; we stand up and yell; we live and die for our teams. Such is our nature of worship.

Romans 1:23 (b)
. . . and creeping things.

Look at the musicians, the fashion models, the TV shows, movies, and other creeping things our culture elevates, and you will have to conclude that we are as heathen as the pagans to whom Paul was writing.

Romans 1:24
Wherefore God also gave them up to uncleanness through the lusts of their own hearts, to dishonour their own bodies between themselves.

Because the pagans worshiped animals, they became like animals. Truly, we become like that which we worship. That's why we are to fix our eyes on Jesus. Jesus had such a robust quality about Him, such light emanating from Him that the common people heard Him gladly and the masses surrounded Him constantly. They left everything to follow Him wholeheartedly because there was substance and reality within Him. With open face, behold His glory—and you will be changed from glory to greater glory (2 Corinthians 3:18).

Romans 1:25
Who changed the truth of God into a lie, and worshipped and served the creature more than the Creator, who is blessed for ever. Amen.

Herein is the devolution of man. He who suppresses the truth and denies there is a God begins to act like an animal and to worship the creation rather than the Creator. Does that ring a bell in light of what's happening in our culture?

A physician attempting to discover how to heal brains of people who have been traumatized was using anesthetized cats for his research. When the animal rights people heard of this, however, they shut the experiment down. The doctor is frustrated because, although his findings could

have saved thousands of lives in a wartime situation, his work was brought to a premature end because our culture says there is no difference between a cat and a man.

Romans 1:26, 27
For this cause God gave them up unto vile affections: for even their women did change the natural use into that which is against nature: And likewise also the men, leaving the natural use of the woman, burned in their lust one toward another; men with men working that which is unseemly, and receiving in themselves that recompence of their error which was meet.

The pit of perversity is evidenced by a culture accepting and glorying in homosexuality.

For topical study of Romans 1:26–27 entitled "The Problem of Perversity," turn to page 877.

Romans 1:28–32 (a)
And even as they did not like to retain God in their knowledge, God gave them over to a reprobate mind, to do those things which are not convenient; being filled with all unrighteousness, fornication, wickedness, covetousness, maliciousness; full of envy, murder, debate, deceit, malignity; whisperers, backbiters, haters of God, despiteful, proud, boasters, inventors of evil things, disobedient to parents, without understanding, covenantbreakers, without natural affection, implacable, unmerciful: Who knowing the judgment of God, that they which commit such things are worthy of death . . .

After denying God, making their own idols, behaving like animals, and worshiping nature, finally a society is given over to homosexual activity, which is unmistakably the breeding ground for the sins enumerated in this passage.

Romans 1:32 (b)
. . . not only do the same, but have pleasure in them that do them.

"Oh, I would never murder anyone. I would never invent an evil thing," we say. But do we enjoy watching the inventions of evil things and murder in movies? "I would never commit adultery," we say, "but I love to watch the soaps." We're guilty! You see, gang, if you are one who enjoys watching murder after murder after decapitation after adulterous affair because you've allowed your carnal appetite to be developed, you are guilty. And death will come to you. I don't mean necessarily you're going to die physically—but watch what will happen to your marriage. Watch how it will cease to be vital and warm. Watch how your kids will grow up and you'll wonder why there's darkness on their faces and posters of despair in their rooms.

"Be ye holy," the Lord says to us (Leviticus 20:7)—for our choice to live either in holiness or carnality will greatly affect not only us, but also those around us.

I AM NOT ASHAMED OF THE GOSPEL
A Topical Study of
Romans 1:16

H e had to be one of the gutsiest guys in all of history. This bow-legged, poor-sighted, little Jewish rabbi named Paul was ready to preach the gospel in Rome.

Rome was the city wherein anti-Semitism had reared its ugly head, resulting in waves of brutal persecution.

Rome was the home of Caesar Nero, the madman who was determined to exterminate Christianity. Nero, the one who dressed thousands of Christians in the skins of lambs and threw them to wolves and lions as he cried, "Where is your Good Shepherd now, little flock?" Nero was the one who dipped Christians in hot wax and lit them as candles in his garden while he shrieked, "How does it feel to be the light of the world now, Christians?"

Rome was the entertainment capital of the world with a moral standard so low it would make Hollywood blush.

Rome was the military mecca where generals and captains paraded pompously on the backs of black stallions.

Rome was where the accepted greeting of the day was, "Caesar is lord."

For a Jewish Christian who claimed no other Lord than One who commanded no army, One who made His triumphal entry on the back of a donkey, One who was pinned to a Cross by Roman soldiers, to preach a message of repentance in Rome, would take guts indeed.

Why could Paul not only declare that he wasn't ashamed of the gospel, but that He was ready to preach it in Rome"? I suggest five reasons. . . .

The Gospel Is Prophetic

Paul, a servant of Jesus Christ, called to be an apostle, separated unto the gospel of God, (Which he had promised afore by his prophets in the holy scriptures,) . . . .   Romans 1:1, 2

The gospel is not something new and faddish, for it was promised from the very beginning. You see, way back in the Garden of Eden, the gospel was shared. In Genesis 3:15, called the Proto Evangelicum, or "the first sharing of the Good News," the Lord said to the serpent, "There shall be war between you, Satan, and the Seed of woman. You shall bruise His heel, but He shall crush your head." That's the gospel. The singular Seed of woman, virgin-born, is Jesus Christ. On the Cross, He was bruised badly; but on the Cross, He crushed Satan completely.

Truly, the gospel is not new. Look at Genesis 5. . . .

In the first genealogy ever given, we see Adam, whose name means "man." Adam had a son named Seth, whose name means "appointed." Seth had a son named Enosh, whose name means "subject to death." Enosh had a son named Cainan, whose name means "sorrowful." Cainan had a son named Mahalalel, whose name means "from the presence of God." Mahalalel had a son named Jared, whose name means "One comes down." Jared had a son named Enoch, whose name means "dedicated." Enoch had a son named Methuselah, whose name means "dying He shall send," because the year he died was the year of the Flood. Methuselah had a son named Lamech, whose name means "to the poor being destroyed," and Lamech had a son named Noah, whose name means "comfort."

Together, the names read: Man, appointed subject to death, sorrowful. From the presence of God, One comes down dedicated. Dying, He shall send to the poor being destroyed comfort. It's the gospel.

"We are not preaching something new," said Paul. "From the very beginning of time, and down through the centuries, three hundred thirty-two specific prophecies were given concerning the One who would come as a Messiah for you and me."

The Gospel Is Provable

And declared to be the Son of God with power, according to the spirit of holiness, by the resurrection from the dead.

Romans 1:4

"Show us a sign," they said.

"One sign I'll give to you," Jesus answered. "Destroy this body and in three days I will rise again" (see John 2:18, 19).

Bhagwan Shree Rajneesh didn't rise again when he died. Buddha couldn't rise again. Neither could Confucius, Mohammed, or any of the gurus, philosophers, or religious teachers throughout history. Only Jesus rose again. And it's provable. Go to Jerusalem. Check out the tomb.

"Well," you say, "I know you claim the tomb is empty, but how do we know the disciples went to the right tomb on that Easter Sunday morning? Maybe, with clouded minds and tear-filled eyes, unable to see or think straight, they went to the wrong tomb."

Do you really think so? Don't you think those in authority would have checked it out and gone to the tomb themselves?

"It must have been the disciples," you argue. "They must have hidden Jesus' body in order to continue His teachings."

Do you really believe that eleven disciples who were crucified upside down, had their brains beaten out with clubs, were speared in the back, were placed in boiling oil would not only experience persecution themselves, but would stand by while their wives and children were tortured—all for a lie? If you believe that, you have much more faith than I could ever have.

"Well, then," you suggest, "it was the Jews. They took the body and hid it in order to harass the Christians."

Why would they do that? The Jews were trying to disprove Christianity. To do so, they would simply have had to produce Jesus' body.

"It was the Romans," you conclude. "They took the body to tease the Christians."

Really? History shows that Christianity was a major contributor to the fall of the Roman Empire. The body of Jesus would have put an end to Christianity forever. If the Romans had it, surely, they would have made it known.

Determined to disprove the Resurrection, a brilliant lawyer went to Jerusalem. He returned six years later, a radical born-again Christian, with the book entitled *Who Moved The Stone?* The book he wrote in defense of his newfound faith.

It doesn't take six years. Anyone who will spend even six hours checking out historical records and thinking through the Resurrection must, if he's intellectually honest, conclude that there's no logical alternative to the fact that something supernatural happened.

The Gospel Is Personal

By whom we have received grace and apostleship . . .   Romans 1:5 (a)

Not "by *what*" but, "by *Whom* we have received grace and apostleship." "I know whom *I* have believed and am persuaded that He is able to keep that which I have committed unto Him," declared Paul, (see 2 Timothy 1:12). It was Jesus who did a work in Paul—just as it's Jesus who is doing a work in you.

The Gospel Is Powerful

For I am not ashamed of the gospel of Christ: for it is the power of God unto salvation . . .   Romans 1:16 (a)

The gospel doesn't talk about the power of God, gang. It *is* the power of God. The gospel pricks the conscience, grabs the mind, warms the heart, and sanctifies the life. The gospel makes perverted men pure, drunken men sober, crooked men straight. The gospel is powerful because it is not good advice. It's *Good News*.

What is the Good News? That Christ died for our sins, and that He was buried and rose again the third day according to the Scriptures (1 Corinthians 15:3). Jesus is alive, folks. And He will come into your life and do His work through you.

As you witness or share your faith, does the thought ever cross your mind, *What if it doesn't work for this person? What if his life isn't changed?* Listen, precious believer, Jesus proved Himself to you. That's why you're here today. And He will prove Himself to *every* single person who gives Him the opportunity—no matter his addiction, no matter his background.

The gospel alone declares we *were* saved from the penalty of sin (justification), that we *are* saved from the power of sin (sanctification); and that we *will be* saved from the presence of sin (glorification). That's Good News because it's based not upon a program, but upon a Person—the Resurrected Jesus living in my heart, telling me how to live, and giving me the power to do what He tells me to do.

The Gospel Is Preachable

. . . to every one that believeth . . .   Romans 1:16 (b)

To *everyone* who believes. My five-year-old can get it. The college professor can receive it. The man on his deathbed can embrace it.

When I was teaching at the Ashland Christian Fellowship a number of years ago, between the Ashland service and the Applegate service, I had a break, so one Sunday, I stopped in at the Kingdom Hall outside Ashland. Although I sat in the back row and tried to be unobtrusive, I looked suspicious not only because of my long hair, but because I was neither wearing a suit and tie, nor carrying a briefcase and *Watchtower* magazine.

After the service, an elder approached me and said, "You're new here, aren't you?"

"Yes," I said.

"What do you think?" he continued.

"Well," I answered, "If I only have an hour to live, what must I do to make it into heaven?"

At this point, he called over a few more elders, who began talking to me. But there was no hope given because, if I only had an hour to live, I couldn't become one of the 144,000; I couldn't be trained in Watchtower theology; I couldn't make it to heaven. Then I shared the gospel with them—and was asked to leave.

I'm so thankful I'm a minister of the gospel. I'm so thankful I don't have to tell a person to follow this procedure or that program before he can be saved. No, I get to say, "The Work is done! Just believe."

"Paul," you might say, "the more I understand the simplicity and potency of the gospel, the more I can see why you aren't ashamed. But you also said you're ready to go to Rome. Why Rome, Paul? You're a Christian Jew. You're sure to have problems there."

Indeed he would, for although he was mobbed in Jerusalem and mocked in Athens, he was martyred in Rome. Why was he so eager to go there? The answer is found in verse 14, where he writes: "I am debtor both to the Greeks and to the barbarians; both to the wise and to the unwise."

The Syrians had laid siege to the region of Samaria. As a result, the Israelites were starving. The situation became so brutal that dove's dung sold for five pieces of silver, and a donkey's head for eighty pieces—a life's savings. As Jehoram walked on the walls of the city one day, a woman said, "O, King, help us. Yesterday my son died, and my neighbor and I ate him. Today her son died, but she won't let me eat him."

Grieved that the people had resorted to cannibalism, Jehoram ripped his clothes and said, "God do so and more unto me if the head of Elisha the prophet remains on him another day." Calling for a messenger, Jehoram said, "Bring Elisha to me."

The messenger did as he was told. But Elisha's message to the king was, "Tell that son of a murderer that tomorrow everyone will have more than enough to eat."

That night, something happened to the Syrians who were surrounding the city. As they cooked their dinner, they heard a strange, rumbling sound. "We're being attacked," they cried. And Scripture records that they stood up and ran as fast as they could to get out of the country, leaving their food, their gold, and their weapons behind.

Unaware of these happenings, four lepers, who lived outside of the city, decided to pay a call on the Syrian camp, hoping for a few scraps of food. "If they kill us, so what?" they reasoned. "We're starving to death anyway." But as they arrived at the Syrian camp, they couldn't believe what they saw. The camp was empty. The fires were still going, the food still simmering. They went from pot to pot, from tent to tent. They ate the food, put on the clothes of the soldiers, and climbed on the chariots. Then, in the middle of their celebration, one of them said, "We do not well. This is a day of good tidings, and we hold it to ourselves. Let's go back to the city and share the good news" (see 2 Kings 7:9).

And when the people in the city heard there was food available, they stormed the gates and made their way to the camp to find the bounty, just as Elisha had prophesied.

Gang, we are those lepers. Do we go from meeting to meeting, saying, "Whee! We're saved! We're forgiven! We're going to heaven! Isn't this great?" Like the lepers, we do not well this day if we keep the gospel to ourselves, if we go from service to service, from house to house celebrating, but do not share with a city that's starving. Paul knew this. That is why he said, "I'm a debtor to every man. Because of what I've enjoyed—the grace, the mercy, the peace, the forgiveness—I owe everyone. And if you're saved, you have a debt as well—to share what you've discovered in Christ Jesus with a dying society, with a starving community, with a dying society.

How long has it been since you threw your arm around a co-worker, or talked to a neighbor, and said, "You know what? I'm so blessed. The Lord's really been good to me. I'd love to tell you about it"? Could this be the week, could tomorrow be the day in which you, like Paul, say, "I'm not ashamed of the gospel"? If you do, you'll find great joy.

The Lord doesn't need us, gang. He could have communicated through angels. But He chose to use us because He knows there's incredible joy to be had by former starving lepers who point the way to the Bread of Life.

THE PROBLEM OF PERVERSITY
A Topical Study of
Romans 1:26, 27

Ten years ago, our country was caught up in a heated debate concerning homosexuals in the military. But I believe the controversy entails much more than a political, constitutional, or philosophical question. Rather, I believe the outcome revealed that we can only nominally call ourselves a culture built upon a Judeo-Christian foundation. I watched *Nightline* in wonder at the time as I saw Senator Bob Dole of Kansas ponder aloud whether homosexuality isn't a generational value. The strongest conclusion he came to on this particular evening was that allowing homosexuals in the military would raise some problems with regard to privacy. As the interview came to a close, I thought, "Here's a conservative senator, a traditionalist, a war hero who never once thought to bring up the issue of morality." And that made me sad, for if even the traditionalists are not raising the issue of morality, what hope is there for our country?

Are we still indeed a Judeo-Christian culture? What does the God of Old Testament Judaism and New Testament Christianity have to say concerning the issue of homosexuality? Plenty. In the Old Testament He makes it crystal clear that He is deadly serious concerning His ban on homosexuality (Leviticus 20:13). And here in the New Testament, He declares homosexuality to be the lowest point in the pathway to perversion. When a culture embraces homosexuality, that's the end of the line biblically, for, as seen both in Old Testament law and New Testament theology, the Lord absolutely and unmistakably forbids homosexuality.

Why? Like all sin, homosexuality is not bad because it's forbidden. It's forbidden because it's bad. Most people have the mistaken idea that God arbitrarily set up certain standards and parameters and called anything outside of those boundaries sin. Not true. Sin is not bad because it's forbidden—it's forbidden because it's bad. It's forbidden because it will destroy us corporately and individually. ...

Homosexuality Damages Psychologically

Perhaps you followed the reports in which doctors declared that the person who is homosexual has a different chemical component flowing through his brain. While I'm not sure that's not true, it has also been reported that there is a question as to whether such chemical changes are the reason for homosexuality, or whether they're the result of homosexuality.

I believe our text hints at the latter. In verse 27, Paul writes, "they receive in themselves that recompense of their error" (verse 27). It could very well be that "the recompense of their error" manifests itself in a chemical that affects the psychology of a person who practices this kind of perversity.

Homosexuality damages people psychologically. It changes who they are and what they could be. Knowing this, God says, "Stay away from it."

Homosexuality Devastates Physiologically

Sixty-five percent of certain Central African nations are now infected with the HIV virus. The death rate is incredible and appalling because of AIDS. But this is neither new in our day nor confined to our time. Recent research indicates that HIV could have indeed been the plague that wiped out civilizations of antiquity. For four hundred years, the Canaanites, whom the Bible calls Sodomites (1 Kings 14), controlled the Promised Land. God gave them four hundred years to change, but, because they wouldn't, God ordered the Israelites to annihilate them (Joshua 9:24). If indeed, as many are now suggesting, the Canaanite culture was reaping the physical repercussions of sodomy, then the Lord was actually merciful in saying to Joshua, "They're dying a slow, painful death. Destroy them, lest they continue on in misery."

Homosexuality Destroys Societally

I wish in the debate, someone would quote not the Christian writer, but the historian, the scholar who wrote *The Rise and Fall of the Roman Empire*. Gibbons makes the case that in the years before Rome fell, fourteen of the last fifteen emperors were homosexual. Not only were they homosexual, but they appointed homosexual generals and commanders. According to Gibbons, this was a major reason the forces no longer had the will to fight. The army broke down; the Visigoths stormed in; the empire fell. Thus, history verifies that something happens not only physiologically and psychologically, but sociologically to any culture that persists in aberrant behavior.

I'm sure many of you have thought through or read about the above three reasons for why God forbids homosexuality. But there's a fourth reason, which I believe is the most important of all.

Homosexuality Disfigures Theologically

When God created him, Adam was not lacking. But he was lonely. So God put him to sleep, took a rib from his side, and fashioned a woman, a "completer" for him. Although Adam was no longer lonely, he had lost more than his rib in the process. He had lost a certain degree of sensitivity and an orientation toward communication. You can try to get man to be more sensitive and communicative, but good luck. You can take him to seminars or have him read books and cry. But you know what? He's not all there, for there is a certain sensitivity and tenderness absent in man since the Garden of Eden when they were removed from him and given to the woman.

But wait. That was the first Adam. Jesus came on the scene and showed us how it was supposed to be. The perfect blend of the strength of masculinity and the sensitivity of femininity was present in Jesus Christ, the Last Adam (1 Corinthians 15:45).

A carpenter before the days of power tools and Ace Hardware, Jesus exuded such strength that when an angry mob threatened to throw Him over a cliff, it took only a look from Him to part the crowd (Luke 4:29, 30). Yet He exuded such sensitivity that children loved to be around Him (Matthew 19:13–15).

He was masculinity personified as He strode through the temple with eyes flashing and biceps bulging, turning over tables, driving out the money-changers, and the oxen, with no one daring to stop Him. Yet He was tenderness exemplified when, in the midst of His righteous anger, He stopped to make sure the doves would suffer no harm (John 2:16).

He was the picture of strength as He pulled Peter—the one whom history calls "the Giant"—out of the Sea of Galilee with a one-armed curl (Matthew 14:31). Yet He was the picture of sensitivity in His desire to retreat with His disciples (John 18:2).

He was the essence of masculinity as He rode an donkey into Jerusalem, yet a portrait of tenderness as He wept over Jerusalem.

Jesus Christ is the Bullock of Leviticus 1 and the red Heifer of Numbers 19. Masculinity and femininity come together in Him perfectly.

What does this have to do with homosexuality? Everything. Because of what homosexuality does to a person physiologically and psychologically, it diminishes the strength of the male and the sensitivity of the female. Through homosexuality, men become effeminate and women become masculine. Satan knows this and desires to destroy the image of the Last Adam, Jesus Christ, by destroying role models of what the strength of masculinity and the sensitivity of femininity should be. Thus, we can't see as clearly in our culture as we ought what it means to be a man of strength or a woman of tenderness. The roles are compromised. The image is blurred.

Not only does this androgyny, this blurring of the roles, confuse people about the nature of the Person of Jesus Christ, but it also confuses people about His passion. What is His passion? His passion is His Bride, the church (Ephesians 5:25). You see, homosexuality says, "Love your own kind—a reflection of who you are." Thus, love between men does not properly depict Christ's love for the church. And love between women does not reflect the church's love for Christ. It skews it. It perverts it. It clouds it. Yet most churches today preach tolerance and acceptance of homosexuals and lesbians. Some even ordain them in ministry because most churches today have no passion for the Person of Jesus Christ. They're in love with themselves.

Satan is sneaky, folks. He uses homosexuality to blur our perception of the Person and Passion of Jesus Christ. That is why the Father says homosexuality must not be tolerated.

How does homosexuality affect you and me? Consider the following three premises.

Homosexuality Is Inevitable

Speaking of the end times, Jesus said, "As it was in the days of Lot, so shall it be in the day when the Son of Man is revealed" (Luke 17:28–30). What was it like in the days of Lot? When the angels came to visit him, the homosexuals did something that, twenty years ago, I couldn't understand: They marched in the streets (Genesis 19:4). *How could this be?* I thought. But that was before Gay Pride Parades. Jesus said an acceptance and a celebration of homosexuality would be a sign of the very end of this age before His coming.

Does the fact that homosexuality is inevitable mean we are to be passive about it?

No.

When Asa, a man who was righteous in the sight of the Lord, brought about revival in the land, one of the first things he did was destroy the Sodomites (1 King 15). Now, in our New Testament day, we are not called to annihilate homosexuals. But we are called to annihilate in our hearts the thinking that homosexuality is acceptable.

You see, as New Testament believers, our fight is never against people, but against principalities and powers (Ephesians 6:12). Thus, we should be waging war in the Spirit through prayer against this perversion that has blinded so much of our country and our leaders. Like Asa, we must refuse to let the sodomite spirit go unchallenged. And our battle must be waged in prayer.

Homosexuality Is Inexcusable

"But I was made that way," is the argument of those who practice homosexuality.

Wait a minute. Every man, every woman has some tendency of sin that must not be accepted. You might be heterosexual and have a desire to attack people. Does that mean we should say, "Well, that's just the way you are. That's your thing and you have to be who you were made to be"? What about the thief or the pornographer? All people are depraved. And because of that, a loving Father set boundaries to regulate behavior.

Like any sin, homosexuality is inexcusable—but it's also changeable. How do I know? Corinth, was the homosexual capital of the Roman Empire, and Paul said to the church there, "such were some of you" (see 1 Corinthians 6:9–11). They had been sanctified, justified, and changed by the reality of Jesus Christ.

Homosexuality Is Indicative

God says the sin of Sodom started with pride, fullness of bread, idleness of time, and a lack of concern for the poor (Ezekiel 17). Pride, too much to eat, too much leisure time, too little compassion for other people ultimately led to experimentation sexually. In Sodom there was too much time for MTV and HBO, too much time to go to movies and cruise the Internet. And because of their prosperity, the people fell into perversity. Paul echoes the same thought here in Romans when he says perversion begins when people who know God don't glorify Him as God nor give thanks to Him for being God.

I was on an airplane one day. Walking down the aisle during the time lunch was being served, I didn't see one person giving thanks for the food. Granted, it's hard to say thanks for airline food, yet Paul says perversion begins when people who know God don't take time to give thanks to Him, worship Him, or glorify Him because they're too busy with their concerns, their hobbies, their worldly pursuits.

Homosexuality is not generational or unique to us culturally. Rather, it's indicative of where we are spiritually. I say this to you not only that we might have insight, but that we might be warned. Don't stop thanking the Lord, precious people. Don't stop giving Him glory. Continue acknowledging Him as the King of your life and the absolute Authority of your home. If you do, you'll do well—and so will your kids and family.

2 In chapter 1, Paul carefully and concisely made it clear that all men are without excuse in their failure to glorify God. The self-righteous Jews would have been quick to agree, indicting the pagan for the very sin of which they themselves were guilty. That is why, after dealing with the unrighteousness of the heathen in chapter 1, Paul deals with the self-righteousness of the hypocrite in chapter 2.

Romans 2:1
Therefore thou art inexcusable, O man, whosoever thou art that judgest: for wherein thou judgest another, thou condemnest thyself; for thou that judgest doest the same things.

"You who judge the pagan nature and homosexual culture," said Paul, "you who are bitter and angry about someone else's sin are also guilty."

Does this mean my condemnation of another is an indication that I am guilty? Yes. The Greek word *krino*, translated "judge," means to judge to condemnation. In other words, it speaks of judging with a sneer on one's face and a finger angrily pointed at him, or her, or them. That kind of judgment is wrong because, although it might appear in a different form, the same sort of sin is going on within us whenever we judge condemningly.

Now, while we are not to make judgments in condemnation, we are to judge for identification. Jesus said, "By their fruits you'll know them" (see Matthew 7:16), and "Beware of wolves in sheep's clothing" (see Matthew 7:15). For example, if a guy came to take my daughter out and he arrived in a pickup truck with beer cans rolling around in the back, a cigarette dangling from his mouth, and a *Playboy* magazine rolled up in his back pocket, I would be justified to judge for identification and to keep her home. Although there's a fine line between condemnation and identification, we inherently know the difference between identifying something that is wrong and self-righteously condemning someone with hostility.

Romans 2:2
But we are sure that the judgment of God is according to truth against them which commit such things.

"God will judge," said Paul. "And His judgment is according to truth." Folks, we can't know where a man's heart is. Therefore, because all things are naked and open before the Lord (Hebrews 4:13), our job is to love people and to leave the judging to God, who will judge perfectly, according to truth.

Romans 2:3
And thinkest thou this, O man, that judgest them which do such things, and doest the same, that thou shalt escape the judgment of God?

The patience of our Father is incredible, but people mistake His patience for impotence, ignorance, or apathy. "He's unable to do anything," they say. Or, "He's too busy to do anything." Or, "He just doesn't have time."

Romans 2:4
Or despisest thou the riches of his goodness and forbearance and longsuffering; not knowing that the goodness of God leadeth thee to repentance?

"Because you've mistaken His goodness and patience for apathy and impotence," writes Paul, "you've failed to see your need for repentance."

For topical study of Romans 2:4 entitled "The Route to Repentance," turn to page 885.

Romans 2:5
But after thy hardness and impenitent heart treasurest up unto thyself wrath against the day of wrath and revelation of the righteous judgment of God.

If you put a water balloon on a kitchen faucet and turned on the water, the balloon would get bigger and bigger—even though initially it might look like very little was happening. Some people do the same thing with life. They say, "I know I'm pouring sin into my life, but everything's getting bigger and brighter." Then there's a big *Boom!* And everything explodes.

"Be not deceived," Paul would later write. "God is not mocked. Whatever a man sows, that shall he reap" (see Galatians 6:7). "Watch out," he says. "You're in for problems presently and damnation eternally unless you acknowledge your need for a Savior and give your heart and life to Jesus Christ."

Romans 2:6–11
Who will render to every man according to his deeds: To them who by patient continuance in well-doing seek for glory and honour and immortality, eternal life: But unto them that are contentious, and do not obey the truth, but obey unrighteousness, indignation and wrath, tribulation and anguish, upon every soul of man that doeth evil, of the Jew first, and also of the Gentile; but glory, honour, and peace, to every man that worketh good, to the Jew first, and also to the Gentile: For there is no respect of persons with God.

Is Paul saying here that salvation comes by works? Of course not. But he is saying that judgment will be according to works. That is, all unbelievers will one day stand before God at the Great White Throne, where what they have done will be judged. If they have done total good, giving God all glory in everything they've said, done, or thought, they'll make it to heaven. In other words, to the moralist, to the person who is super pious, Paul is saying, "If you are really good, you'll make it in. If all of your days you've glorified God with all of your heart, and have lived honorably in everything you do, say, and think, you'll inherit eternal life." But guess what. Only one Man has ever lived like that—and it was His blood that was shed for the rest of us.

"This picture doesn't do me justice," said the politician to the photographer.

And the photographer replied, "With a face like yours, you shouldn't be asking for justice, but for mercy!"

So, too, we don't need justice. We need mercy. You see, God made our minds in such a manner that we don't remember the sins we committed even an hour ago. If we remembered all of the wrong thoughts, lousy attitudes, critical spirits, lust, and everything else that goes on in our minds—much less the things we say and do out-

wardly—we would lose our sanity. So to the self-righteous moralist who says, "I'm a good person," what a shock it will be when the books are opened and the depth of his sin is brought to light. Presently, we sing in this big choir of humanity. There are almost five billion of us on this planet, so if we're a little out of tune, nobody knows. But there's coming a time when man will sing solo. Then we'll find out how off-key we really were.

Romans 2:12
For as many as have sinned without law shall also perish without law: and as many as have sinned in the law shall be judged by the law.

Not having the law, by what standard will the pagan be judged? Paul will go on to say that his conscience within him and creation around him will indict every man—leaving all men without a case in the courtroom of God's judgment.

Romans 2:13
(For not the hearers of the law are just before God, but the doers of the law shall be justified.

I believe one of the great hazards for those who love to study the Scriptures, and who take seriously the privilege of plowing through God's Word, is that we can begin to think that hearing the Word automatically implies doing the Word. It's a very subtle, but a very real danger.

How do you know if you're obeying the Word? If you're grumpy, you're not obeying the Word because Jesus said, "Happy are you if you do these things" (see John 13:17). The word "happy" in Greek means "happy." It means "elated." It speaks of emotion. You will be happy if you're obeying the Word. But if you're just hearing about it, or being analytical of it, you will not be happy. So Paul would say to the self-righteous, to the Hebrew, to the biblical scholar, "It's not what you hear or know, it's what you *do* that will affect you."

In your morning devotions, during Wednesday night study, in a Sunday morning service, or whenever you're in the Word, ask the Lord to give you one thing to do—not just to journal, or to ponder, but one thing through His Word to do by His Spirit. And happy will you be if you do it.

Romans 2:14 (a)
For when the Gentiles, which have not the law, do by nature the things contained in the law . . .

"The Gentiles don't have the Scripture, but they understand right and wrong intuitively," said Paul.

Romans 2:14 (b), 15
... these, having not the law, are a law unto themselves: Which shew the work of the law written in their hearts, their conscience also bearing witness, and their thoughts the mean while accusing or else excusing one another;).

Men know right from wrong intuitively. In no culture is murder ever allowed. In no culture is adultery ever accepted. "Wait a minute," you protest. "That doesn't square with Anthropology 101. We studied Polynesian cultures where, before the influence of white society, husbands and wives were traded freely, and everyone was happy continually."

Not true. A couple of years ago, the interpreter for Margaret Mead revealed that the famed anthropologist was sold a huge bill of goods—that the Pago Pago people about whom she wrote would tell jokes about her at night, laughing at all the false information they were feeding her.

Men innately know right from wrong and will be judged according to whether or not they live up to that knowledge.

Romans 2:16
In the day when God shall judge the secrets of men by Jesus Christ according to my gospel.

In the Day of Judgment, the heathen will be judged by the conscience he has honored or violated, and the Hebrew will be judged by the Scriptures with which he has been entrusted.

Romans 2:17, 18
Behold, thou art called a Jew, and restest in the law, and makest thy boast of God, And knowest his will, and approvest the things that are more excellent, being instructed out of the law.

"We have the law," boasted the Hebrews, "and we know the things that are excellent."

Romans 2:19, 20
And art confident that thou thyself art a guide of the blind, a light of them which are in darkness, an instructor of the foolish, a teacher of babes, which hast the form of knowledge and of the truth in the law.

"Just because you have information," Paul is saying, "you can't assume you have justification or are qualified to be a guide for others."

Romans 2:21
Thou therefore which teachest another, teachest thou not thyself? thou that preachest a man should not steal, dost thou steal?

"When did we steal?" the Jews asked God in Malachi.
"In not giving the tithe you've robbed Me," He answered (see Malachi 3:8).

Romans 2:22
Thou that sayest a man should not commit adultery, dost thou commit adultery? thou that abhorrest idols, dost thou commit sacrilege?

The Book of Hosea declares that the adultery of the Jews was demonstrated in the way they had distanced themselves from God by following after other lovers, other priorities, and other affections.

Romans 2:23, 24
Thou that makest thy boast of the law, through breaking the law dishonourest thou God? For the name of God is blasphemed among the Gentiles through you, as it is written.

The hypocrisy of the Pharisees gave the Gentiles cause to blaspheme God. That's always the problem with sin: It gives the skeptic, the cynic, the unbeliever a reason not to become a Christian. You and I are to proclaim not our greatness but God's grace. We set ourselves and others up for a huge fall if we start pointing to anything or anyone other than Jesus Christ and Him crucified.

Romans 2:25–27
For circumcision verily profiteth, if thou keep the law: but if thou be a breaker of the law, thy circumcision is made uncircumcision. Therefore if the uncircumcision keep the righteousness of the law, shall not his uncircumcision be counted for circumcision? And shall not uncircumcision which is by nature, if it fulfil the law, judge thee, who by the letter and circumcision dost transgress the law?

Circumcision was (1) an identification of God's covenant people, an outward sign of what was to be an inward reality; and (2) an illustration of God's dealing with the flesh. In the Old Testament,

God defined how the illustration of circumcision was intended to work.

- Exodus 6:12 speaks of the circumcision of the lips.
- Jeremiah 6:10 speaks of the circumcision of the ears.
- Ezekiel 44 speaks of the circumcision of the heart.

God's people were to speak with tenderness, hear with sensitivity, feel with compassion. Circumcision was meant to be a picture externally of the transformation that takes place internally. Yet although the Jews were outwardly circumcised, they were far from where they should have been internally.

As the Israelites were about to enter the Promised Land, the Lord said, "Before you can take on Jericho in victory, before you can enter the Promised Land and enjoy the milk and honey, you must circumcise all those who came out of Egypt" (see Joshua 5). They needed to do away with the flesh before they could have victory in the Spirit. But this principle became lost in the community of the super-religious, for although they boasted of their circumcision physically, their hearts, lips, and ears were hardened to the Lord in reality.

I point this out to you because Paul is making a very important point concerning outward signs and religion. "I've been baptized," people say. "I've gone through Confirmation. I've had Communion." And many people think that, because they've gone through a baptismal ceremony, been christened as an infant, or come to the Lord's table, they will be especially blessed. Not so. Outward expression means nothing if not accompanied by inward experience.

Romans 2:28, 29
For he is not a Jew, which is one outwardly; neither is that circumcision, which is outward in the flesh: But he is a Jew, which is one inwardly; and circumcision is that of the heart, in the spirit, and not in the letter; whose praise is not of men, but of God.

A derivative of the word "Judah," the word "Jew" means "Praise." Who is the true circumcision, the true Jew, the one worthy of praise in the sight of God? Not those who legalistically and self-righteously try to deal with the flesh—but rather those who, in joy and amazement, worship God in the Spirit. The true Jew rejoices in Christ Jesus, has no confidence in his own flesh, and simply says, "Lord, I know that apart from You I can do nothing."

THE ROUTE TO REPENTANCE
A Topical Study of
Romans 2:4

They caught her in the very act of adultery and brought her still naked before the Rabbi of Galilee. "Master," they said, "Moses said she should be stoned. What sayest thou?"

What would the Rabbi say? If He said, "Let her go," they would accuse Him of violating the Law of Moses. But if He said, "Stone her," He would no longer be known as the Friend of Sinners. Surely they had Him cornered.

Jesus stooped down as though He heard them not, and with His finger began to write in the dust something that must have hit them like a bolt of lightning. "Let he who is without sin—literally in Greek, the same sin—cast the first stone," He said. What a scene it must have been as, one by one, each man dropped his stone and went his way (John 8:3–9).

What did Jesus write in the dust that day? The Greek word translated "wrote" in John 8:6 is a word that means "to write against." Therefore, I suggest Jesus wrote the names of the woman's accusers, and beside each one, the name of a woman, a place, or a time that would remind them of something they had done or some fantasy they had entertained. In so doing, Jesus showed us very pointedly that we had better not be too quick to throw a rock at someone, for we are guilty of the same sin. Oh, our sin might not manifest itself in the flesh, but Jesus said, "If you've even looked at a woman with lust in your heart you are guilty of adultery. If you're even angry with your brother, you're guilty of murder" (see Matthew 5:22, 28). In other words, we're *all* guilty.

The self-righteous man is just as guilty, if not more so, than the unrighteous individual. In the story of the prodigal son, who was guiltier? Was it the prodigal who spent time in the pigpen and came back repenting, or the elder son who complained and murmured because his father never killed a fatted calf for him? The heathen and the Hebrew alike are without excuse. One might sin in the flesh, the other in the spirit—but both sin.

Because only God sees what's going on internally, only He can judge righteously.

> A woman ran through the airport. On her way to the gate, she grabbed a magazine and a little package of cookies. Boarding the plane, she sat in an aisle seat, one seat away from a man in the window seat. A few minutes later, hungry from her race to catch her flight, she opened her bag of cookies and took one. To her astonishment, the man in the window seat also reached into the bag, which was setting in the middle seat, and grabbed a cookie. Utterly amazed at his audacity, she stared at him, reached for a second cookie, and ate it. He looked at her and took another cookie as well. That left only one cookie, which the man took and broke in half, before giving half to her. The lady was dumbfounded. The behavior of her seatmate left her puzzled, angry, and hungry throughout the entire flight. But her greatest surprise came when she opened her purse upon landing—and found her bag of cookies inside.

That's the way it always is! We're so sure we're right—when in reality we don't have all of the facts. In the Day of Judgment, we will be shocked at how wrong we were and how little we knew when the handbags are opened and all things will be judged truthfully.

Watch out, self-righteous person. You are he who perhaps is most vulnerable to despising the goodness of God.

How? I suggest three ways. . . .

We Can Despise the Goodness of God When It Is Extolled by Others

As David brought the ark of the covenant back to Jerusalem, he danced before the Lord. Watching him from her window, his wife despised him. "Didn't the king behave himself seemly?" she said mockingly.

"Woman, what I have done, I have done as unto the Lord," David replied. "And I will become even more base in thy sight, for I'll continue to extol Him with all of my might. As for you," he continued, "you will be barren all the days of your life" (see 2 Samuel 6:20–23).

Want to be barren? Want to be spiritually unproductive and impotent? Here's how: Despise the goodness of God when it is extolled by others. Mock it. Make fun of it. Don't participate in it. And I guarantee there will be a barrenness in your soul and a fruitlessness in your life just as there was in Michal's.

We Can Despise the Goodness of God When It Is Extended to Others

This is tricky. This happens very frequently in my own heart. "How can they go on in that sin, Lord?" I ask. "They're not walking with You. They don't even have time for You. They're living contrary to Your plan. Sic 'em, Lord."

David voiced this same sentiment in Psalm 73 when he wrote, "Truly God is good. But as for me, my feet had well nigh slipped when I saw the prosperity of the wicked. Their eyes stand out in fatness. They're not in trouble like other men. They have more than they could wish for. Their mouths are filled to the brim. When I thought upon this it was too painful for me."

It's crazy how indignant I am with the sins of others and how indulgent I am with the sin in my own life. The result? I begin to despise the goodness of God when He shows the same goodness and mercy to others that He shows to me.

We Despise the Goodness of God When It Is Exploited Within Ourselves

God's goodness can be exploited. He's forbearing. He's patient. He's incredibly good—so much so that the Anglo-Saxon word for God is literally "the Good One."

In the days of Genesis, people sinned exceedingly. So God sent Noah to preach to a world that was carnal, sinful, and rebellious. As Noah hammered away on the ark for one hundred twenty years, God waited forbearingly, patiently, all the while providing graciously.

While His people were in Egypt, God gave the Canaanites four hundred years to turn from their sin.

Israel was carried into captivity because of iniquity. But eight hundred years later, God was still working with her, dwelling in her midst in the Person of Jesus Christ.

God is so patient. Yet I despise His goodness whenever I think, *Well, I'm getting away with my sin. Nothing negative is happening to me. So I'll just keep sinning because either God doesn't care about it, or maybe He even approves of it. Maybe I'm an exception.*

Not so. His goodness should lead you not to excuses of rationalization, but to the about-face of repentance.

> In Luke 13, Jesus told a parable so important for us to understand and remember. "Master," the servant said, "the fig tree has not borne fruit for three years. Let's cut it down."
>
> "Don't cut it down," said the master. "Expose the roots, fertilize it, and give it one more year. Yes, it's been absorbing nutrients from the soil and taking space in the garden without producing anything—but I still desire fruit from this tree. Give it one more year."

Some of us are in that place right now. The Lord has been so good to us. He's dug around us. He's fertilized us through His Word. He's tended us in His love. He's provided for us in so many ways—and yet we think, *Sure, I'm out of fellowship, but I'm not getting cut down, so I must not be doing that bad.*

Rather than exploit God's mercy and goodness, we should be amazed by it, for in our text, Paul said that in hardening our hearts, we store up wrath for ourselves.

> The story is told that in the late 1880s, a bank teller stole a silver dollar every day and hid it in his attic. Knowing how to juggle the books and cover his tracks, this went on for days, weeks, months, years—until one day, after eighteen years, he was lying in his bed and judgment came. The rotting attic finally gave way, causing the coins to fall through the ceiling, crush the embezzler in his own bed, and bury him in his iniquity.

The same thing is happening right now with some of us. We think we're cleverly hiding our little secret. Nobody sees it. Nobody knows about it because we have figured out a way to juggle the books. But at a certain point, we'll place our last silver dollar in the attic—and everything will come down on our heads. The goodness of God makes possible indulgence in the hearts of foolish men, but brings about repentance in the hearts of wise men. If you have been despising the riches of His goodness, be wise and repent. Change direction and, by His grace, walk with God today.

3 You may have seen the results of a report by a group of researchers in England who spent thirty-one years and millions of dollars studying the effects of smoking. Their conclusion? Smoking can kill people. The tobacco industry, however, issued a statement that said the study has yet to be substantiated by their own research.

So, too, Paul makes the point that people innately and intuitively know they are sinners. Not the Surgeon General, but the Great Physician tells us that sin pollutes and affects every man. Yet, like the tobacco industry, we put up smokescreens and say, "Wait a minute. I'm not sure I can be held liable for sin. I'm not sure I can be labeled a sinner." The first two chapters of Romans blow those smokescreens away, for in chapter 1,

Paul addresses the unrighteous heathen. In chapter 2, he deals with the self-righteous hypocrite. And here in chapter 3, he'll speak to the super-righteous Hebrew. "Creation around them condemns the unrighteous," Paul declared in chapter 1. "Conscience within them condemns the self-righteous," he proclaimed in chapter 2. And in chapter 3, we will hear him say that the commandments given to them condemn the super-righteous.

Romans 3:1
What advantage then hath the Jew? or what profit is there of circumcision?

"Wait a minute," the Hebrew would protest. "If we're on the same level as the heathen or the hypocrite, then what's the advantage of circumcision?"

Romans 3:2–4 (a)
Much every way: chiefly, because that unto them were committed the oracles of God. For what if some did not believe? shall their unbelief make the faith of God without effect? God forbid.

"Even though you don't understand that the reason the law was given to you was to show you your sin and your need of a Savior," answered Paul, "the fact remains that, because you had the law to guide you, you have been uniquely blessed." In other words, although throughout history the Jews missed the reason for the law, they nonetheless benefited from the results of keeping the law.

When the bubonic plague swept across Europe, killing one of every three people, the Jewish population was left virtually untouched. Why? Because in keeping the law, the Jews were protected from the plague due to the hygienic and dietary regulations contained within the law. So, too, throughout history, the Jews have always done well monetarily. Why? Because the financial principles contained within the law work—regardless of whether those who practice them walk close to the Lord or even believe in Him.

Romans 3:4 (b)
Yea, let God be true, but every man a liar . . .

There are times when people say, "I prayed and nothing happened," or, "I had devotions and it's not working," or, "I go to church and don't re-

ceive anything," or, "I'm doing all the things Scripture tells me to, but it's just not happening."

And I have to respond in love, "You're a liar because God promises that if we draw close to Him, He'll draw close to us, (James 4:8). Therefore, somebody's lying—and it's not God."

Feeling a bit dry in my spirit and a bit distanced from the Lord in my heart, I grabbed my Bible one evening and strolled through Jacksonville, Oregon, reading the books of Amos and Joel as I walked. And you know what happened? Even though Amos and Joel are far from lighthearted reading, I found myself smiling. Why? Because the Lord used His Word to minister to my heart in a beautifully satisfying way. Truly the Lord will meet anyone who will take time to open the Word and seek Him.

We're so fortunate, gang. We don't have to answer everyone's questions or solve their problems. But with great confidence we can just tell them that if they seek Him, the Lord *will* draw near to them.

Romans 3:4 (c)
. . . as it is written, That thou mightest be justified in thy sayings, and mightest overcome when thou art judged.

As open as God's invitation to draw nigh to Him is, He knew all along that not everyone would accept it. Therefore, Paul maintains that the unbelief of the Jews actually verifies what God said would happen.

Romans 3:5
But if our unrighteousness commend the righteousness of God, what shall we say? Is God unrighteous who taketh vengeance? (I speak as a man).

Anticipating the reasoning of his Jewish audience, Paul poses this question: "If our unbelief validates the foreknowledge of God, then why will we be judged for our unbelief?

Romans 3:6–8
God forbid: for then how shall God judge the world? For if the truth of God hath more abounded through my lie unto his glory; why yet am I also judged as a sinner? And not rather, (as we be slanderously reported, and as some affirm that we say,) Let us do evil, that good may come? whose damnation is just.

Some believers think that as long as God is glorified, it doesn't matter how He gets glory. So they'll "stretch the story and give God the glory." Paul, however, stands firm against the thinking that says the end justifies the means. In other words, according to Paul, it's never right to do wrong to do right.

Romans 3:9
What then? are we better than they? No, in no wise: for we have before proved both Jews and Gentiles, that they are all under sin.

Whatever smokescreens have been put up by the heathen or the Hebrew, Romans 1, 2, and 3 blow them away. The heathen are indicted by creation, the hypocrite by conscience, and the Hebrew by the commandments. God has spoken clearly to every generation throughout history—leaving all without excuse.

Romans 3:10–18
As it is written, There is none righteous, no, not one: There is none that understandeth, there is none that seeketh after God. They are all gone out of the way, they are together become unprofitable; there is none that doeth good, no, not one. Their throat is an open sepulchre; with their tongues they have used deceit; the poison of asps is under their lips: Whose mouth is full of cursing and bitterness: Their feet are swift to shed blood: Destruction and misery are in their ways: And the way of peace have they not known: There is no fear of God before their eyes.

The Great Physician's diagnosis of the condition of humanity is bleak: All are sinners without exception. This description is not just of the "bad guys"—but of you and me as well. Now, if I forget this divine diagnosis and start to think, *He's a pretty good person,* I'm setting myself up for disappointment and disillusionment. Therefore, instead of being surprised when someone does something bad, I should be amazed when someone does something good because the divine diagnosis is that we are all depraved.

"But what about the guy in the Philippines," you ask, "who flagellates his body and is hung on a Cross every Easter? Yes, his theology might be askew, but surely he is seeking God."

No, he's not. Paul says none seeks after God.

"What about the Tibetan monks who live their entire lives in simplicity and celibacy? Surely they're seeking after God."

No, they're not. The Bible says none seeks after God.

"Then what's the guy in the Philippines seeking?" you ask.

Perhaps he's seeking alleviation from his guilt, perhaps recognition from his peers, perhaps exaltation of his soul. But he's not seeking God.

"What about the monks in Tibet? What are they seeking?"

Perhaps they're seeking peace, perhaps some kind of transcendent emotional experience, perhaps a higher consciousness—but they're not seeking God.

The Bible says none seeks after God, no not one. Every believer was chosen solely by grace, completely because of God's unmerited, undeserved, unearned favor.

Romans 3:19
Now we know that what things soever the law saith, it saith to them who are under the law: that every mouth may be stopped, and all the world may become guilty before God.

In the Sermon on the Mount, Jesus made it clear that the keeping of the law lies not in external regulations, but in internal attitudes. Thus, we are all murderers, liars, and adulterers because even though we might not exhibit those behaviors externally, they take place in our hearts inwardly.

Romans 3:20
Therefore by the deeds of the law there shall no flesh be justified in his sight: for by the law is the knowledge of sin.

After speaking of our sad situation, Paul introduces the fabulous doctrine of justification. Justification is a legal term that speaks of much more than forgiveness or pardon. Justification means being declared righteous—as though we never sinned at all.

An English gentleman bought a Rolls Royce in England and had it shipped across the English Channel so he could motor through France. In the midst of his tour, however, the Rolls broke down. So the man called the dealer in London and said, "The car I bought is broken."

"We'll take care of it immediately," was the dealer's reply. And, sure enough, within the hour, a team of mechanics flew to France, took the Rolls apart, repaired it, and returned to England.

Following the completion of his tour, the Englishman returned home and waited for what was sure to be a hefty bill for the repair of his car. But it never came. So finally he called the Rolls dealership and said, "I've been back for several months, but I haven't received a bill for your services."

"A bill for what?" asked the voice on the other end.

"A bill for the repairs you did in France on my Rolls."

"Sir," insisted the dealer, "we have no record whatsoever of any repairs being done on any Rolls Royce at any time. Thank you."

That's justification—just as if it never broke down! You see, the Lord doesn't say, "I've been bearing with you and putting up with all of your sin, but I'm such a good God that I'll overlook it." No! Once I have faith in Jesus Christ, God looks at me as being justified—as though I never sinned at all.

Let's suppose my daughter Christy ran up a huge bill at Meier & Frank Department Store and couldn't make the payments. Eventually, Meier & Frank would dispatch a lawyer, who, upon finding Christy, would say, "Miss Courson, pay up immediately, or we'll see you in court."

Now, if Christy responded, "I can't pay. Please forgive me," they would most likely insist that justice be done. Three months later, Christy's court date would arrive. Eager to face their adversary, Meier & Frank's lawyers would arrive at the courthouse early and search for her.

Seeing Christy arrive on the arm of a handsome young man, they would say, "I hope you're ready, Miss Courson. The day of reckoning is here. By the way, who's the man with you?"

"Oh, this is my fiancé, Mr. Meier. His father is the partner of Mr. Frank. You wanted to talk to me about a lawsuit?"

"What lawsuit?" they would say.

You see, suddenly, the situation would change if Christy showed up with Mr. Meier's son. She could never have won the case. Her only way out was to have the case dropped completely. And that's exactly what happens with us. Satan accuses us. Our sin condemns us. The law convicts us—until we enter the courtroom on the arm of our Bridegroom. Then everything changes. Because we are justified, all charges are dropped for lack of evidence. In the following verses, note six characteristics of justification.

Romans 3:21
But now the righteousness of God without the law is manifested, being witnessed by the law and the prophets.

Justification is apart from the law. If you're trying to relate to the Father on the basis of your own goodness or devotion, your consistency or your Bible study, your do's and don'ts—you'll never be justified. The law cannot justify you. It can only bring you to the realization that you are a sinner in need of a Savior.

Romans 3:22 (a)
Even the righteousness of God which is by faith . . .

Justification is by faith in the Lord. Our justification comes from our being linked not to God generally, but to Jesus Christ personally. James says the demons have a belief in God, but they're not saved. They're not justified. They won't be in heaven (James 2:19). It's not enough for a person to say, "I believe in God and go to church." No, he must believe in the Lord Jesus Christ because the source of justification lies embedded in the Person and work of Jesus.

Romans 3:22 (b)
. . . of Jesus Christ unto all and upon all them that believe: for there is no difference.

Justification is for all mankind. Whether Jew or Gentile, yuppie or hippie, heathen or Hebrew—there's only one way to enter into salvation: by faith. It's not in what you've done or who you are, but in Jesus Christ.

Romans 3:23
For all have sinned, and come short of the glory of God.

Everyone sins. Everyone falls short of the glory of God. You might say, "I'm doing pretty well compared to my neighbor." But you're comparing yourself to the wrong person. The comparison is not between you and your neighbor or between you and your pastor. It's between you and God.

Warming up at the Mount Sac Relays during my senior year of college, I remember thinking, I have a chance at doing pretty well in this meet. It was one of those days when everything was "clicking": My form was good; the disc was landing well; and from the looks of my opponents' practice throws, I had every reason to feel confident. Then John Van Rienen emerged from the locker room. John Van Rienen was huge—six feet seven inches tall, three hundred-plus pounds, zero-percent body fat. I watched as this world-class athlete strode across the field, his arms so long (crucial for a discus thrower), his knuckles seemed to almost rub the ground as he walked. In his first warm-up throw, he didn't even take off his sweats, and he didn't even spin. Yet in his standing throw, he popped the disc past the best marks of all of the rest of us. And the pride I had felt only moments before dissipated with each of his successive throws.

So, too, when the Lord comes on the scene, He sets the standard. It's not how you compare with your neighbor, but how you compare with the glory of the Father that counts. And in His light, we all come up short.

Romans 3:24 (a)
Being justified . . .

Justification is by grace exclusively. What is grace? It is unmerited, undeserved, unearned favor. The riches of God climax in justification. And if that isn't enough, the phrase "being justified" is in the aorist tense, which means it is an action that happens continually. Justification didn't only take place the day we were saved or baptized, for even this very moment we are being justified and declared righteous. So often we feel that, because of our sin, we've forfeited the access and the freedom we once had with God. Not true. Justification is a continual action, a continual declaration of righteousness.

Romans 3:24 (b)
. . . freely . . .

In John 15:25, the Greek word here translated "freely" is translated "without a cause." That's how it should have been translated here as well: "being justified without a cause."

Romans 3:24 (c)
. . . by his grace through the redemption that is in Christ Jesus.

If you're as old as I am, you know what redemption is . . .

Each December, my mom would take boxes and bags full of S&H Green Stamps and Blue Chip Stamps from out of the hall closet. We kids would sit around the table, sponges in hand, wetting down the backs of the stamps and pasting them in little paper books made for such a purpose. Then we would take the filled books to their respective redemption centers where we would trade them in for items printed in the S&H and Blue Chip catalogs. In other words, we would use them to redeem lamps or bikes or toys.

To Paul's readers, the concept of redemption was even clearer, for in the center of every Greek city stood the agora—the place of redemption—where buying and selling took place. Specifically, although not exclusively, this was the place were slaves were bought and sold. Thus, the Greek word for the act of redemption is *agorazo*. But *agorazo* is not the word used in this verse.

There's a second word for redemption that the Greek reader of Scripture would readily understand: *exagorazo*, or "the act of purchasing or redeeming never to return." You see, oftentimes, a man would buy a slave, use him for a season of harvesting or cultivating, and then return him to be sold again. *Exagorazo* was the antithesis of this practice, in that it spoke of permanent possession. But *exagorazo* isn't the word used in this verse.

Apolutrosis, the third Greek word for redemption, is the word used in this verse. *Apolutrosis* speaks of a man going into the agora to purchase a slave for the purpose of setting him free totally and completely—never to be a slave again. I love it! Yes, for us redemption is *agorazo*—for we have been purchased by the Lord. Yes, it's *exagorazo*—for we'll never be sold again. But even more than that it's *apolutrosis*—for we were purchased for the purpose of being set free. "I no longer call you servants, but friends," Jesus said (see John 15:15).

Undoubtedly the clearest picture of this glorious concept of redemption is found in the Book of Ruth, where Boaz demonstrates the redemptive work of our greater than Boaz, Jesus Christ.

Romans 3:25
Whom God hath set forth to be a propitiation through faith in his blood, to declare his righteousness for the remission of sins that are past, through the forbearance of God.

Justification comes at an incalculable cost. Jesus Christ left heaven to dwell among us and die for us. "I have tremendous difficulty with that," you say. "How could He pay the price for all of our sins when He was only on the Cross for a few hours?"

He wasn't on the Cross only a few hours. The Bible says He was slain before the foundation of the world (Revelation 13:8). Thus, to a mysterious degree, His punishment for our sin individually, and for the sins of the world collectively, was, and is, eternal.

A doctor was on trial because, although he attempted to abort an eight-and-a-half-month-old baby, the baby survived but lost her arm in the process. Yet, as one journalist pointed out, this is controversial only because the abortion didn't work. Had the doctor been successful, the story never would have surfaced.

Certain things on the news or in our community anger us. But imagine how God feels seeing everything—not only the stories that make the news, but the hidden sins, the tragedies no one cares about. It is impossible for us to begin to comprehend the multiplied millions of sins that have been committed by the people in this sanctuary alone, let alone by the whole world throughout all of history.

What if you were God? What if you saw everything every person is thinking—not just a botched abortion here and there, but everything everyone is thinking and doing? What would you do? Here's what God did: He took the anger He feels and hurled it on His Son, whose blood flowed redemptively in order that we, the hostages of sin, might be set free.

For topical study of Romans 3:23–25 entitled "Propitiation!" turn to page 894.

Romans 3:26
To declare, I say, at this time his righteousness: that he might be just, and the justifier of him which believeth in Jesus.

Justification solves a divine dilemma. In 1 John 4:8, John declares that God is love. But 1 John 1:5 tells us He is also light. Therefore, although God loves us deeply, He also sees our rebellion clearly. And if He said, "I love them so much I'm going to overlook their sin," He would no longer be light.

The eyes of the world were recently drawn to England when two ten-year-old boys were arrested for the death of a two-year-old. Now, if, following their trial, the judge said, "I know these boys beat that toddler to death, but I'm going to let them go because I really love these boys," the world would be justifiably outraged and incensed.

Such is God's dilemma. He's love, but also light. The solution? The only solution is justification through the redeeming work of Jesus Christ.

A seventeen-year-old was arrested for reckless driving in a rural community. As he was brought into court, he was relieved to see that

his father was the presiding judge. An hour later, the judge rendered his decision. "Your reckless driving," he said, "has endangered the people of our community. Consequently, justice must be served. You will either pay one thousand dollars or serve one year in jail."

"Dad," the boy said. "You know I don't have a penny to my name."

"Young man," said his father, "in this court you will address me as Your Honor. I am your judge." And down went the gavel as the boy stood incredulous before the bench.

The bailiff approached. He was ready to take the boy to jail when the judge stood up, took off his robe, and left the bench to stand by his son. "Behind the bench," he said, "I am your judge. But here beside you, I stand as your father." And he took a checkbook from his pocket to pay his son's fine.

That's precisely what the Lord did for us when He left the bench of heaven to come to earth as Jesus of Nazareth—to write the check of redemption, to pay the price of propitiation. It's fabulous. It's perfect. It's beyond comprehension that God would have come up with a plan so beautiful that it confirms both His light and His love without compromising either one.

Now, if the young man in the illustration, following his dad's offer to pay his fine, said, "Get out of here, Dad. Why did you have to pronounce such harsh judgment in the first place? I'd rather take my chances in jail than to accept charity from you," no one would feel sorry for him; no one would shed a tear on his behalf. So, too, no tears will be shed for those who say, "I couldn't care less that God became a Man and was slaughtered on the Cross for my sin. I've got places to go, things to do, a career to pursue," because the price paid on their behalf was offered so lovingly and would have cleansed them so completely.

Romans 3:27
Where is boasting then? It is excluded. By what law? of works? Nay: but by the law of faith.

In heaven no one will say, "Look what we accomplished by our piety and our devotional life, our depth, our study, and our praise." No, boasting is excluded.

Five hundred law school graduates were taking the bar exam, when one of them had a heart attack and dropped to the floor. One of the young men sitting near him rushed to his assistance and administered CPR for thirty minutes. When the paramedics arrived, the young man who had administered the CPR asked for an additional thirty minutes to complete his test. His request denied, he left the room stunned. The media picked up the story and, as a result, the young man went on the talk show circuit, received job offers and congratulations for being the only one in five hundred to come to the aid of a dying man. Thus, the savior was honored.

The same is true in heaven. All attention presently and eternally is focused on Jesus Christ because He's the Savior. We're only the "save-ees."

Romans 3:28–30
Therefore we conclude that a man is justified by faith without the deeds of the law. Is he the God of the Jews only? is he not also of the Gentiles? Yes, of the Gentiles also: Seeing it is one God, which shall justify the circumcision by faith, and uncircumcision through faith.

There are two groups in religion today: those who emphasize behaving and those who emphasize believing. In actuality, James tells us that the emphasis needs to be on believing, since the way we believe will affect the way we behave.

Romans 3:31
Do we then make void the law through faith? God forbid: yea, we establish the law.

Why does Paul say faith in Jesus Christ establishes the law? Because the purpose of the law, according to Galatians 3:24, is to bring us to Christ. Therefore, belief in Christ accomplishes the very purpose for which the law was given.

The management of a lakeside hotel had a problem. Guests would fish off the balconies of their rooms. With the restaurant located on the bottom floor, many times the fisherman would inadvertently crack the restaurant window with their sinkers as they cast their lines into the lake below. The hotel called in a consultant, and he solved the problem immediately.
"The solution is very simple," he said. "Just remove the 'No Fishing Allowed' signs from every balcony." This done, it no longer occurred to anyone to fish.

Truly, whether it be "No Fishing," "Keep Off the Grass," or "Thou Shalt Not Steal"—the law undermines faith and underlines failure by setting a standard we are unable to keep. Does this mean that, because we can't keep the law, we are free to break it? Stick around, and we'll see how Paul answers that very question.

PROPITIATION!
A Topical Study of
Romans 3:23–25

A man in Texas had the urge for a midnight snack. So he rolled out of bed and walked down the hallway toward the kitchen. Passing the nursery, he noticed his three-month-old son's bassinet toppled on the floor. Racing back into the bedroom, he woke his wife to see if she had taken the baby from the bassinet, but his wife was sound asleep and knew nothing of the matter. Panic filled his heart as he ran down the hall, down the stairs, and into the living room, where, much to his horror and shock, he saw his twelve-foot pet python with a large lump in its center. He knew immediately what happened to his baby. In anger and outrage, he went to the back porch, grabbed a splitting maul, chopped up the snake, and ran out of the front door screaming. He was later committed to a mental institution.

This true story haunts me and is helpful to me in understanding a biblical concept often misunderstood by people who wrestle with theology. You see, although people do not have a problem when we talk about the love of God, the wrath and judgment of God are things with which people struggle. Yet if the man in Texas was justified in smashing that snake, how much more is God justified in dealing with snakelike people who have devoured others mindlessly and heartlessly.

> I think of what happened in Somalia. Tens of thousands of babies starved. Why? Because war lords were fighting for territory geographically, jockeying for position politically, and preventing food from reaching kids who were dying needlessly.
> I think of what happened in Bosnia Herzegovina—where women were raped and men slaughtered by the thousands, all in the name of ethnic cleansing.
> I think of Medford, Oregon, where the school board forbids the distribution of Bibles on school campuses as well as the use of any school buildings to be rented to any church group for any reason. I think, wonder, and ponder how it can be that a society that distributes condoms refuses to allow the distribution of Scripture.

Why does God allow this insanity? Why does He, who sees not only the tragedy of Bosnia and Somalia, but the utter depravity of even the most seemingly together person, put up with a world so bent on self-destruction?

The answer is very simple: Because God made man in His image, He gave him the ability to choose. And when man chose to listen to the hissing of Satan rather than to the Word of God, he unknowingly handed dominion of the planet over to Satan. That's why Jesus called Satan the prince of this world (John 14:30) and why Paul called him the god of this world (2 Corinthians 4:4). In the Garden of Eden, man turned this planet over to Satan. That's why there are diseases and rape, war, death, and sadness on our planet. It's not a matter of God allowing these things. It's a matter of man giving Satan the authority to cause them.

Meanwhile, God looks down from heaven, and, as He was in Noah's day, is filled with righteous indignation (Genesis 6:5–7). Yet even in Noah's day, man found grace in the eyes of the Lord (Genesis 6:8). God looked at Noah, had grace on Noah, and did a work through Noah. So, too, He will again pour out His wrath in the period called the Tribulation.

Until then, however, what's the solution for the very genuine wrath God feels concerning snakelike creatures like you and me? The answer is propitiation. Why such a big word? Because no smaller word would suffice. The Greek word translated "propitiation" is *hilasterion,* which means "to appease the wrath of." We often say, "God hates the sin but loves the sinner." While that is true, it is at best a shallow understanding because the distinction between sin and sinner is not so easily made. You see, I am not only the baby devoured by the python. I am the python. I am a victim of sin, yes—but I am also its perpetrator.

Sin hurts people. It destroys mankind. It's cruel, vicious, and wrong. And my own sin is no less devastating. Thus, God is understandably filled with righteous indignation, which can only be appeased through propitiation.

> The people of Israel, having been delivered from Egypt, were on their way to the land promised to them—a land flowing with milk and honey and wonderful blessings. But en route, they started murmuring and complaining (Numbers 21:5). The sin of complaining led to suffering in verse 6 as the people were bitten by poisonous snakes. Suffering led to sorrow in verse 7. Sorrow led to salvation in verses 8, 9, when those who looked upon the brass serpent were healed. Who was the Brass Serpent? Jesus (John 3:14–16).

Propitiation is God wielding a splitting maul upon the snake, the Brass Serpent, Jesus Christ—instead of upon me. Am I calling Jesus Christ the snake? Yes, because He who knew no sin became sin for us (2 Corinthians 5:21) in order that the wrath of the Father over the sin of the world would be appeased. Instead of smashing a world that is snakelike and bestial, He turned to His innocent Son and laid upon Him the iniquity of us all.

Jesus understood this. That's why in the Garden of Gethsemane, He prayed with such intensity, "Father, if possible, don't let Me drink of this cup" (see Matthew 26:39). Socrates took the cup of hemlock and drank it bravely. Was Jesus less than Socrates? No. It wasn't physical death Jesus feared; it was the wrath of His Father that caused Him to break out in a bloody sweat (Luke 22:44). Jesus knew what it meant to be the propitiation, the satisfaction, the appeasement of wrath.

"The Father pouring out His anger upon His innocent Son is a form of child abuse," you say. Wait a minute. What is the name of the Son? Almighty God, Everlasting Father (Isaiah 9:6). You see, God Himself became a Man and absorbed the wrath of His own indignation. The mystery of the Trinity, the mystery of propitiation is that God actually wielded the splitting maul upon Himself.

Hilasterion, or "propitiation"—the word we don't hear much today—is used only five times in the entire New Testament: Romans 3:25; 1 John 2:1–2; 1 John 4:10; and Hebrews 9 are four of them. The Hebrews reference, I believe, is a real key to unlocking this understanding, for in describing the mercy seat, the author of Hebrews uses the word *hilasterion.* The mercy seat, or *hilasterion,* covered the ark of the covenant. The ark of the covenant contained the law. Therefore, through the mercy seat, God says, "I know you've broken the law. I know you deserve to be consumed because of it. But I'm going to put a lid on it through the sacrifice of My Son. *He* is the *helasmos,* the mercy seat, the propitiation. It's not something He gives. It's who He is, for He has come between you and the broken law. The wrath that I should vent on you was instead placed upon My Son, who died in your place."

The fifth use of the word "propitiation" is found in Luke 18. If you feel offended that I would liken you to a baby-eating python, if you are repulsed by a God who would became a Man and slaughter Himself to propitiate His righteous indignation,

Luke 18:10–14 is the passage for you. It is a brief vignette, concerning the prayers of a Pharisee and a tax collector. Look at verse 13: "God, be merciful to me a sinner." It begins with "God" and ends with "sinner." The middle phrase, "be merciful"—the verb form of *hilasterion*—stands between God and sin. Every one of us is in one of two categories. You're either the self-righteous Pharisee, or you're the tax collector, grateful that Jesus is standing between God and your sin.

What does a correct understanding of the concept of propitiation do?

Propitiation blows my mind. Propitiation adds an entirely different dimension to what Paul calls "so great salvation" (Hebrews 2:3). It's not just the Father saying, "I'm going to settle mankind's problem judicially." No, He deals with it personally.

Propitiation warms my heart. That God would love me so much He would actually become the object of His own wrath touches my heart in a profound way.

Propitiation weakens my knees. Considering the righteous wrath of a powerful God makes me realize that sin is serious. The Bible says the beginning of wisdom is to fear God (Proverbs 1:7). And it goes on to say that to fear God is to hate sin (Proverbs 8:13). The concept of propitiation makes me question my own view of sin. How do I react when I see things on the screen or hear unkind words come from my own mouth? If you're knowingly sinning today in what you're doing, or where you're going, I encourage you to think through propitiation.

Propitiation tickles my toes. Jacob was in a place he called Luz, or "separation" After tricking his brother Esau out of his birthright and blessing, he was in the wilderness running for his life. That night, as he laid his head on a rock and tried to sleep, God revealed Himself to him, pouring out a blessing upon him and giving a promise to him. Jacob woke up and said, "Surely I am in the presence of God and I knew it not." And he changed the name of the location from Luz to "Bethel," or "house of God." Then, as we read in Genesis 29:1, Jacob "went on his journey." Translated literally this phrase reads, "Jacob had happy feet."

"I'm a creep. I'm a crook. I'm a criminal," he said, "but the Lord met me, has a plan for me, and is going to travel with me. Now I have happy feet."

So, too, I say, "Oh, Lord, I know I'm a sinner. But because You absorbed the anger that should have been poured out upon me, I leave here today with tickled toes, weakened knees, a warmed heart, and a blown mind!"

May God continue to give us a comprehension of His love through an understanding of propitiation.

In Jesus' Name.

4 In Romans 3, Paul shared something that must have appeared radical, almost heretical to his readers when he said salvation does not come from keeping rules and regulations, from trying to be "good little boys and girls," from trying to be mystical or spiritual—but by faith, apart from the deeds of the law. "For what purpose was the law given?" his readers must have wondered.

A Hindu philosopher came forth after a ten-year silence and declared to his followers at an ashram in India that the whole world runs by the Ten Commandments. Now, if even a Hindu made such an observation, how could Paul say salvation comes not through the law or as a result of the law? He could do so because he contended that the sole reason the law was given was to show people that they are depraved and despicable sinners in desperate need of a Savior (3:31). "We're not voiding the law," Paul insisted. "We're fulfilling the very reason for which it was given—to make you see your need of a Savior and to drive you to grace."

So, after arguing theologically in chapter 3 that justification and salvation come simply by believing, Paul makes his point historically here in chapter 4.

Romans 4:1, 2 (a)
What shall we say then that Abraham our father, as pertaining to the flesh, hath found? For if Abraham were justified by works, he hath whereof to glory . . .

First, Paul appeals to Abraham, father of the Hebrew family racially.

Romans 4:2 (b), 3
. . . but not before God. For what saith the scripture? Abraham believed God, and it was counted unto him for righteousness.

Was it when Abraham left Ur of the Chaldees—a place of real sophistication and wealth—that God declared Abraham righteous? No. Was it when Abraham took his son Isaac to Mount Moriah in order to offer him as a sacrifice that God declared him justified? No. God declared Abraham righteous when Abraham simply believed Him (Genesis 15:6). When is a man saved? Not when he follows God's call obediently or even offers himself sacrificially, but when, like Abraham, he simply says, "Lord, I believe You. I believe what You say is true—that I'm righteous in Christ Jesus, that my sins past, present, and future are all forgiven."

To these Jews who knew Scripture well, Paul said, "Think about it. Abraham was not pronounced righteous when he was doing something spiritual or sacrificial. He was pronounced righteous when he simply believed God."

Romans 4:4
Now to him that worketh is the reward not reckoned of grace, but of debt.

If Abraham had been pronounced righteous because he left Ur, or because he was willing to

sacrifice his son, then he would have been given salvation as a reward. God would have been paying off a debt. But Paul's argument is that it was nothing Abraham did or didn't do—other than believe what God said was true—which justified him. So, too, if you are attempting to work your way into God's favor—either prior or subsequent to your salvation—then He owes justification to you. Whenever we subconsciously think, *Now, Lord, I prayed a whole bunch today, so I know it's going to be a great day,* the implication is, *Lord, You owe me.* And that nullifies grace. God will not be a debtor to any man. He won't owe us anything.

That is why there will be no boasting in heaven—not only with regard to our salvation, but with regard to any of God's blessings. A lot of times we forget that and think it's because of our great faith or our prevailing prayer, our diligent works or our dedicated devotion that God has blessed our life.

It's a hard thing to say, but it's true: Some of the greatest blessings both in my life and flowing through my life have come when I have not been in prayer, when I have not had strong faith, when I've not been what I should or want to be. God's blessings during those times remind me that *everything* that comes my way is because of grace—unmerited, undeserved, unearned favor. This creates in me a heart that wants to love the Lord and worship Him rather than a tendency to say, "If I've accomplished this with three hours of prayer, I wonder what I could do with six!"

Am I saying we should never pray? If you're praying to earn reward, give it up. But if you're praying because you enjoy the Lord, are amazed at His goodness to you, because you want to participate with Him in what He's doing on the earth, because you love to spend time with Him, or because you're thankful for Him and want to be close to Him—then pray! If you get up at three o'clock tomorrow morning to pray in order to fulfill an obligation, God won't be impressed a whit. But if you get up at three o'clock just to enjoy Him, He'll be blessed. The man, woman, or congregation that truly understands that salvation is all about grace will find themselves praying, worshiping, studying, witnessing—not because they're trying to earn God's blessing, but because they're responding to the One who's already been so good to them.

Romans 4:5 (a)
But to him that worketh not, but believeth on him that justifieth the ungodly . . .

Who does the Lord justify? Who gets blessed? Not the Pharisee, but the one who realizes he's worthy of nothing.

Romans 4:5 (b)
. . . his faith is counted for righteousness.

It is not the one who has faith in his faith, but the one who has faith in the goodness, the provision, and the loving-kindness of the Lord who is righteous. Such is the one to whom the Father says, "Because you're not trying to earn My favor or earn My blessing, because you're just believing in who I am as the Justifier of the ungodly, I pronounce you righteous."

Romans 4:6 (a)
Even as David . . .

In addition to Abraham, Paul brings out Big Gun Number Two, saying, "The idea that what matters is not the rules and regulations of the law but rather simply believing in God and having confidence in Him is not new. Look at David, founder of the Hebrew royal family . . ."

Romans 4:6 (b)
. . . also describeth the blessedness of the man, unto whom God imputeth righteousness without works.

The word "blessed" literally means "O how happy." Here in Psalm 32, from which Paul is quoting, David says, "O how happy is the man whom the Lord accounts righteous—apart from works." Happy is the man who sees this. For him, Christianity will not be a burden to carry or a battle to fight in a way that makes him sour, dour, and miserable. No, David says happy is the man who understands that God accounts, imputes, pronounces righteousness apart from works— apart from anything he does or doesn't do.

Romans 4:7
Saying, Blessed are they whose iniquities are forgiven, and whose sins are covered.

Blessed are those whose iniquities are sent away—like the scapegoat on Yom Kippur, which was sprinkled with blood and then sent out of sight (Leviticus 16:22).

For topical study of Romans 4:6–7 entitled "Forgiven!" turn to page 903.

Romans 4:8
Blessed is the man to whom the Lord will not impute sin.

Once we receive the work God did redemptively in order that we might be pronounced righteous, He no longer sees us as sinners. For me to utter this would be presumption. But because David said it, it's inspiration. It's interesting to me that in David's early psalms, he talked about how righteous he was, how there was no vanity in his life, and how there was no iniquity on his hands. But then what happened? David stumbled when he walked into sin with Bathsheba. As a result, he discovered he was not as righteous as he thought he was previously—and his later psalms reflect this discovery.

A young couple moved into an upstairs apartment and bought a waterbed. Forgetting to bring a hose, they bought one at the nearest hardware store and hooked it from their sink to their waterbed before going out for about an hour. The surprised couple returned to find their floor had collapsed and fallen onto the apartment below—not because of the weight of the waterbed, but because they had accidentally purchased a sprinkler hose with holes in it.

That's so much like me! I think I've got my act so together—until I find a few holes I wasn't counting on. Maybe you think you've got it all wired, but you watch. Sooner or later, you'll discover that your floor has collapsed, that you're a sinner. That is why David says, "Happy is the man who's not trying to prove his worth or merit God's blessing. Happy is the one whose sins are forgiven." It doesn't matter how long you've walked with the Lord, or how much you know about the Lord. The fact is, the man or woman who is happy is the one who is not working, but simply believing in the goodness and loving-kindness of the Father revealed through the Son on Calvary's Cross.

Romans 4:9, 10 (a)
Cometh this blessedness then upon the circumcision only, or upon the uncircumcision also? for we say that faith was reckoned to Abraham for righteousness. How was it then reckoned? when he was in circumcision, or in uncircumcision?

Paul held up Abraham and David as examples of men who had been justified apart from works. "But they were Jews. What about Gentiles?" you might ask. Read on. . . .

Romans 4:10 (b)
Not in circumcision, but in uncircumcision.

To the Jew, circumcision was everything. It proved his Jewishness, his worthiness. "Wait a minute," said Paul. "Abraham was pronounced righteous in Genesis 15 *before* he was circumcised."

Romans 4:11
And he received the sign of circumcision, a seal of the righteousness of the faith which he had yet being uncircumcised: that he might be the father of all them that believe, though they be not circumcised; that righteousness might be imputed unto them also.

Paul here is saying Abraham is the father not only of the circumcised Jew, but of the uncircumcised Gentile because Abraham was pronounced righteous before he was circumcised. Circumcision did not confer righteousness. It confirmed righteousness. So, too, you can be baptized a dozen times next summer, but it won't save you if you don't believe in your heart that the work is done, that the price is already paid for your sin. The basis of everything we enjoy is that which God has done for us and on that fact that He views us through the lens of His Son.

So I get baptized because I want to go on record externally, declaring what I know is already true internally. I come to Communion because I want to do outwardly what I'm excited about inwardly. I have devotions not to earn His favor, but because He has already shown me such favor. It's not responsibility, folks. It's *response.* Why is it so hard for us to understand this? Could it be because our culture says, "There's no free lunch," and "God helps those who help themselves"? Could it be because our flesh says, "Set the alarm earlier. Stay up later. Memorize more. Study harder. And maybe, just maybe, you'll be blessed"?

If I could communicate one thing to you precious people it would be this: Quit trying to give God a reason to bless you. It'll never work because God will be a debtor to no man. Just marvel at His goodness. Enjoy an intimate relationship with Him. And watch what He can pour out on you because you won't be taking the credit.

Romans 4:12
And the father of circumcision to them who are not of the circumcision only, but who also walk in the steps of that faith of our father Abraham, which he had being yet uncircumcised.

Whether you're Jew or Gentile, if, like Abraham, you just say, "Thank You, Lord," you are part of the family of faith.

Romans 4:13 (a)
For the promise, that he should be the heir of the world, was not to Abraham, or to his seed, through the law . . .

The promise given to Abraham wasn't given because of the law. It was given before the law.

Romans 4:13 (b)–15
. . . but through the righteousness of faith. For if they which are of the law be heirs, faith is made void, and the promise made of none effect: Because the law worketh wrath: for where no law is, there is no transgression.

Years ago, when the Susan B. Anthony dollar was issued, no one could get rid of them. One bank in Georgia, however, moved record numbers of the coins. When a Washington bureaucrat traveled to Georgia to determine the reason, he discovered their simple secret was a sign on the window that read: Susan B. Anthony Dollars Available. Limit Two Per Customer. "People kept sneaking back," said bank officials, "hoping to get more than their limit." That's what the law does. It not only undermines faith, but it underlines failure because, unable to keep its standard, we have no recourse but to break it.

Romans 4:16 (a)
Therefore it is of faith, that it might be by grace . . .

Salvation must be by faith. If it were by works, we would always wonder if we were really saved. We would feel like we had to come forward every service and get baptized every Sunday. We would walk around feeling beat up, cast down, and done in continually. But when we understand that our relationship with the Lord is not based upon anything we do or don't do other than simply believing, salvation becomes something we are not afraid of losing every week.

Salvation: The Father thought it. The Son bought it. The Spirit taught it. The Bible brought it. Satan fought it. But, praise the Lord, by His grace, we got it!

Romans 4:16 (b)
. . . to the end the promise might be sure . . .

Remember the game Chutes and Ladders, and the frustration you felt when, in the first place, you came to the last chute and down you went? If salvation came by trying, striving, religion, or works, our walk would be a perpetual game of Chutes and Ladders. On Monday, we would have devotions and move two rungs up the ladder. On Tuesday, we would go to morning worship and advance five more steps. On Wednesday, we would come to Bible study and climb three rungs higher. On Thursday, we would seek the Lord in the evening and find ourselves only 3 rungs from the top. On Friday, we would talk with our neighbor about the Lord. But on Saturday, we would get angry and down the chute we would tumble.

Tragically, a lot of people live their spiritual life that way—trying to work their way up the ladder by keeping rules and trying harder, failing to realize that, because it's the result of grace, the promise is sure. The promise is sure to the one who simply believes that God did what He said He did when on the Cross He declared, "It is *finished*" (John 19:30).

Romans 4:16 (c)
... to all the seed ...

"The word "all" in Greek means "all." It means you. It means me. In other words, the Father said, "The only way the promise can be sure for Jon Courson is if it's totally by grace, if all he must do is believe in what I did and that I love him. Otherwise, he's not going to make it. He'll climb the ladder for a day or two, but eventually down the chute he'll go.""

Romans 4:16 (d)
... not to that only which is of the law, but to that also which is of the faith of Abraham; who is the father of us all.

Paul returns to Abraham as an illustration of faith. Romans 4 is such a key chapter in this day in which cults abound and receive so much media attention. Like Paul, we must say, "What we embrace and believe is not some new theological fad, but has its roots clear back in the Book of Genesis as seen in the life of Abraham."

I am reminded of what happened on Mount Carmel, when, in order to get Baal's attention, his prophets hooted, hollered, and slashed their bodies (1 Kings 18:28). But nothing happened. Then it was Elijah's turn. After spending all day in a radical frenzy, the prophets of Baal watched as Elijah, the man of faith, simply said, "Father, show us who You are." Fire came down and consumed not only his sacrifice but also the altar and the water that surrounded it. Incredible! Elijah's faith prevailed because it was based upon something

much deeper, richer, and fuller than man's efforts, energy, or emotion.

"Go to the Old Testament," said Paul. "Study Elijah. Take a look at Abraham. And learn a lesson about the beauty, the simplicity, the power of faith."

Romans 4:17 (a)
(As it is written, I have made thee a father of many nations,) ...

Notice the tense of this verse. God spoke to Abraham in Genesis 17:5, saying, "I *have made* thee"—although in reality it hadn't yet happened. God speaks His promise in the past tense, even though from our perspective it hasn't taken place because so certain is His promise, it's as though it has already happened. I like that!

Romans 4:17 (b)
... before him whom he believed, even God, who quickeneth the dead ...

God "quickens" or "raises" the dead. Was Paul speaking of Abraham's body reproductively, or was he referring to Abraham's belief that God would raise his son Isaac, whom he was willing to sacrifice at Mount Moriah? I don't know. I only know Abraham was a man of faith—whether concerning Isaac's birth, Isaac's resurrection, or both.

Romans 4:17 (c)
... and calleth those things which be not as though they were.

God called Abraham a father even before the birth of Isaac because, from His perspective, Abraham was already a father. Read Ecclesiastes 3:15 for a glimpse into the great mystery of God calling things that are not yet as though they already were. The implications are fabulous.

Romans 8:29, 30 tells us that, on the basis of His foreknowledge, God predestined those who would want to know Him. And because they're predestined, they're called by Him. And when they respond to His call, they're justified—declared righteous—and they're glorified. The implication is staggering. God views us as already glorified. What does this do? It frees me incredibly, knowing the Father sees me not in my cruddy humanity, but in my glorified state. I see myself flailing, faltering, and failing. But the Father sees me as already glorified.

Think of it this way. ...

Picture yourself in New York City, watching the St. Patrick's Day parade. A band marches by, followed by some floats and big balloons. Your buddy, standing a mile down the road has not yet seen the band, the floats, or balloons that pass before you. You're enjoying them presently, and you know he's going to enjoy them eventually when the parade works its way to him.

That's the way the time/space continuum works. But suppose on this St. Patrick's Day, you were invited to sit in the Goodyear blimp. Suddenly you would see the whole parade simultaneously. The people down below would be watching the parade go by. But not you. You would see the whole thing in its entirety. That which is yet to be for your buddy, you'd already see. And that which already was for him, would still be in your sight. From your vantage point, it would all be happening in the present.

That's how it is for the Father. We're marching through the parade of life, trying hard, doing good sometimes, stumbling other times. But He sees our whole life—past, present, future. He sees the whole thing in totality. Thus, He views us as already glorified, as already in the kingdom of heaven. Consequently, we have beautiful freedom today. We can just enjoy the Lord because He has said we are already glorified. We're not a disappointment or an embarrassment to Him. We're already perfect in Him.

Romans 4:18 (a)
Who against hope believed in hope . . .

Even though it looked hopeless physically and logically, Abraham had hope. Biblically, hope is the absolute expectation of coming good. Abraham said, "From God's perspective, His promise has already been fulfilled. So I know with absolute certainty it will happen in me and for me."

Romans 4:18 (b)–22
. . . that he might become the father of many nations; according to that which was spoken, So shall thy seed be. And being not weak in faith, he considered not his own body now dead, when he was about an hundred years old, neither yet the deadness of Sara's womb: He staggered not at the promise of God through unbelief; but was strong in faith, giving glory to God; and being fully persuaded that, what he had promised, he was able also to perform. And therefore it was imputed to him for righteousness.

Abraham was declared righteous not because of something he did for the Lord, or by virtue of

the fact he proved himself to the Lord, but because he simply believed in the Lord.

Romans 4:23, 24
Now it was not written for his sake alone, that it was imputed to him; but for us also, to whom it shall be imputed, if we believe on him that raised up Jesus our Lord from the dead.

On the basis of Romans 4, if you believe Jesus was raised from the dead, you are exercising the same quality of faith as did Abraham—a hero of faith. So, whatever problem or pressure is upon you at this time, it's nothing in comparison to the incredible faith you have already demonstrated. Once a believer grasps the fact that he's already done the hard stuff—that his belief in the Resurrection sets him apart as a hero of faith—then any other pressure or problem is a piece of cake, minute in comparison to the fact that he has already embraced a concept that the world mocks (Acts 17:32).

For topical study of Romans 4:19–24 entitled "Jumbo-sized Faith," turn to page 908.

Romans 4:25
Who was delivered for our offences, and was raised again for our justification.

Not only did Jesus die for our sins to redeem us, but He was raised from the dead to justify us and to be an Advocate for us. As our Advocate, our defense attorney, Jesus lives to make intercession for us continually (Hebrews 7:25). Satan, on the other hand, condemns us not only in our hearts day and night, but before the very throne of God (Revelations 12:10), saying, "Look at those people down there. They're hypocritical, weak, and faltering."

But the moment he hisses these accusations, Jesus is literally there, saying, "Depart, Satan. They're washed in My blood and robed in My righteousness."

And the Father says, "Case dismissed for lack of evidence," as He casts our sins into the depths of the sea (see Micah 7:19).

Why did Micah say God cast our sins into the depths of the sea? Because, as a people, the Jews were terrified of the ocean. Therefore, the Lord put their sins in the last place a Jew would have gone looking for them. To our culture, He would say, "I have cast your sin into the bottom of a toxic waste dump. Your sins are not only forgotten by Me, but I'm putting them in a place where there's no danger of anybody looking at, digging up, or talking about them. On the basis of the finished work of Calvary, every sin you've ever committed, are committing, or will commit is forgiven, forgotten, and out of sight." That's forgiveness. That's justification. That's Good News!

FORGIVEN!
A Topical Study of
Romans 4:6, 7

I was a California boy when we moved to Oregon in 1977, so some things relating to rural culture caught me off guard initially. The first weekend we were there, we spent some time out at a ranch in the Little Applegate Valley. As we walked the grounds, I saw something that puzzled me, for tied around the neck of the family pet, a big German Shepherd, was a dead chicken. Never having seen anything like that, I asked the reason and was given this explanation: "If any of our ranch dogs attack the chickens, we teach it a lesson by tying the dead chicken around its neck and leaving it there for several days. As the chicken decays, the dog learns to stay away from chickens."

Oregon is bizarre! I thought. In reality, however, such a practice is not unique to Oregon. As you study history, you see certain ancient cultures tying the corpse of a victim to its murderer. And should the accused ever sever the rope, he would be executed immediately. That's what happened in antiquity—and Paul made application spiritually when he wrote, "Oh, wretched man that I am! Who shall deliver me from the body of this death?" (Romans 7:24), or more literally, "Who shall deliver me from this dead body?"

"Who will free me from the stench of my past—my failings, my sins, my shortcomings—which follow me wherever I go?" asked Paul. You see, although others would look at Paul and see a Pharisee, a rabbi, a "good person," Paul knew he was a sinner. So, too, maybe to others you appear together and wonderful, but like Paul, you know there's a dead body of past failings or present shortcomings tied to you. Even David, whom Paul quotes in the passage before us, a man after God's own heart, was a man who had a dark side and was tied to a dead body.

In David's day, instead of football, basketball, and baseball season, there were only two seasons: peace season during the fall and winter, and war season in the spring and summer. During one such season of war, after ruling for twenty years, David opted to remain at home rather than join his men in battle. But unbeknownst to him, in so doing he was headed for trouble. That's always the way it is. Whenever we decide to kick back, sit out, or pull away from ministry, from service, from walking with the Lord; whenever we say, "I deserve a break today"—we're headed for disaster.

While his boys waged war, David strolled about his palace. Looking down upon the roofs below, he saw a woman taking a bath. Lusting after her, he sent for her and had relations with her. When she discovered she was pregnant, David knew he was in trouble. After all, what would the people who extolled him so highly and exalted him so readily think of their king if they knew he had taken another man's wife? So David hatched a plan in which he sent Uriah, Bathsheba's husband, into a battle, wherein on a certain signal, all of the soldiers except Uriah were instructed to turn and run.

Thus, David committed first-degree murder when his plan was executed perfectly.

Free to marry Bathsheba, David thought none would be the wiser when the baby was born. From outward appearances, it looked like David would literally get away with murder. But on the inside, something entirely different was taking place within him, as seen by what he wrote in Psalm 32, quoted here by Paul in Romans 4. . . .

Blessed is he whose transgression is forgiven, whose sin is covered. Blessed is the man unto whom the LORD imputeth not iniquity, and in whose spirit there is no guile. When I kept silence, my bones waxed old through my roaring all the day long. Psalm 32:1–3

"When I covered up my adultery and murder, it affected me physically," said David. Do your bones ever ache? Do you feel weary? It could be because of unconfessed sin. We do know in this day that there is a definite connection between one's emotional state and his physical health. Therefore, the physical affliction David experienced was no doubt linked to the emotional turmoil with which he struggled.

For day and night thy hand was heavy upon me . . . Psalm 32:4 (a)

It wasn't for punishment that God's hand pressed upon David. It was for protection. Think about it—if your three-year-old child or grandchild was chasing a ball that rolled into the street, and you saw a car coming, what would you do? You would run after that child, lay your hand on him, and do whatever it took to keep him out of the way of danger. So, too, the Lord sees you and me playing in the street of sin, and His hand comes down on us heavily—not for punishment, but for protection, saying to us as He did to David, "You're going to feel the pressure of My hand until you get out of the path of destruction."

. . . my moisture is turned into the drought of summer. Selah. Psalm 32:4 (b)

Ever feel like there's a drought inside you? Once there was moisture. Once there was a flow of the Spirit; there was living water. But now? There's a drought like the middle of summer. As with David, it may very well be the result of unconfessed sin.

Perhaps eight months passed before Nathan the prophet came to David and said, "Your sin is known" (see 2 Samuel 12:7–9).

Hearing this, David cried to the Lord, "Against thee and thee only have I sinned" (see Psalm 51:4).

"Wait a minute," we say. "What about Uriah? Didn't David sin against him?"

Certainly David sinned in killing Uriah, but his sin against Uriah was infinitesimal in comparison to his sin against God.

You see, contrary to modern psychology, the Bible doesn't give any man or woman a reason to say, "I'm a victim because my mom, dad, or my ex sinned against me." Why not? Because, no matter how bad we have it, every one of us deserves a whole lot more trouble than we get. You're a wretched, rotten, smelly, defiled, iniquitous sinner. So am I. Therefore, we can never say, "We're victims."

Turn away from this pop theology, folks, and listen to what David said under the inspiration of the Spirit: "Father," he said, "the only issue is my rebellion against You. As for Uriah and Bathsheba, You will minister to them directly. But as for me, my sin is against You only."

I acknowledged my sin unto thee, and mine iniquity have I not hid. I said, I
will confess my transgressions unto the LORD . . .   Psalm 32:5 (a)

After aching in his bones, and feeling dry in his spirit, after being pressed by the heavy hand of God's conviction, and being confronted by Nathan, David decided to confess.

. . . and thou forgavest the iniquity of my sin. Selah.   Psalm 32:5 (b)

After a season of conviction, David was forgiven at the moment of confession. The implication of this is incredible, for the minute we get to the place of even preparing for confession, the Father says, "It's done."

The Hebrew word for "forgavest" implies immediacy. In other words, God doesn't say to you or me, "Once you make your confession you're on an eight-month probation, and I'll see how sincere you are."

Man says, "Was she, was he, were they sincere? Are they really repentant?" But the Bible knows nothing of that kind of analysis. The Bible says that the moment you make confession, you are completely and totally forgiven. So it is that we join with David saying, *"Blessed* is he whose transgression is forgiven, whose sin is covered!" The word "blessed" literally means "oh, how happy."

David never said, "Oh, how happy is the one who has power." As king of Israel, David had power not only in his own nation but also in the surrounding nations that were in submission to Israel. But he didn't extol power.

David didn't say, "Oh, how happy is the one who has popularity." When David walked through town, women sang songs about him (1 Samuel 18:6, 7). If Gallup,

Harris, or CNN had taken polls in David's day, his popularity rating would have been off the charts. But he didn't extol popularity.

David didn't say, "Oh how happy is the one who has prowess." Not only could David jump over walls (Psalm 18:29) and wrestle lions and bears (I Samuel 17:34–36)—he also wrote the hit songs of his day. Yet he didn't extol musical ability or athletic prowess.

David didn't say, "Oh, how happy is the one who has prosperity." David had more gold and silver than he could use in his lifetime. Yet those things meant nothing to him because he was haunted by the sin, which, like a dead corpse, was tied about him.

"Oh, how happy," David said, "is he whose transgression is forgiven, whose sin is covered." I used to think David was being a little redundant when he said, "whose transgression is forgiven, whose sin is covered," but upon further study, I found something that intrigues me. The word "forgiven" literally means "to send away." The word "covered" means "to be sprinkled." There was only one day in which these two acts were practiced together. That was the day we call Yom Kippur—the Day of Atonement (Leviticus 16).

On one day each year, around October 10, two goats would be brought before the high priest. Upon one, the scapegoat, the high priest would symbolically lay the sins of the entire nation, then release it into the wilderness. As for the second goat, its throat was slit, and the blood was sprinkled on the mercy seat.

Gang, this has wonderful and practical implications for us even today, for as the scapegoat was sent out of sight into the wilderness, Psalm 103 says our sin is sent away as far as the east is from the west. How far is that? If you took off from Applegate Christian Fellowship in Oregon, you could only go north for thirty-five hundred miles, because once you reached the North Pole, the next step you took, you would be going south. But if you left Applegate and traveled east, you could go east over the Rockies, to the Eastern Seaboard, across the Atlantic Ocean to Britain, into Europe, Eastern Europe, Russia, India, Japan, and back to Oregon—and the compass would still read east. The distance from east to west is infinite. And that's how far your sin—the dead corpse you've been carrying around and dragging behind—is from God.

Not only is our sin out of God's sight, but it's out of His memory (Jeremiah 31:34). Remember—there was a second goat, whose blood, sprinkled on the mercy seat on the Day of Atonement, covered the law that was inside the ark of the covenant. So, too, the blood of Jesus Christ blots out even the memory in God's mind of the law that you've broken. Whether you've been into pornography, adultery, gossiping, lying, or cheating on your taxes, God says once confession is made, your sin is blotted out. He cannot remember it.

"Happy is the man," said David, "who, upon confession of his sin, finds immediate forgiveness and release." But even though there is release from the penalty of sin, there is repercussion from the consequences of sin. As Nathan said to David, "When this gets around, people will make fun of your God" (see 2 Samuel 12:14). Not only that, there would be repercussion within his own family in the form of incest and rebellion (2 Samuel 13–18).

With this in mind, check out Psalm 84.

> *How amiable are thy tabernacles, O LORD of hosts! My soul longeth, yea, even fainteth for the courts of the LORD: my heart and my flesh crieth out for the living God.*   Psalm 84:1, 2

"The only place I really have peace," said David, "is not in my family, not in my country, not in some other nation geographically—but in the sanctuary."

> *Yea, the sparrow hath found an house . . .*   Psalm 84:3 (a)

Sparrows were the most worthless creatures in the land of Israel. The Jews would fry them and eat them as appetizers. Jesus said two sold for a farthing (Matthew 10:29); and, according to Luke, you could get five for two farthings (Luke 12:6). In other words, if you bought four, they'd throw in an extra one for free. "How blessed," David said, "is even the most worthless animal in the whole nation, because even he finds peace in the tabernacle, in the place where the blood covered the mercy seat."

> *. . . and the swallow a nest for herself, where she may lay her young, even thine altars, O LORD of hosts, my King, and my God.*   Psalm 84:3 (b)

Swallows are known for their restlessness. Because their feet are weak, they can't perch. That's why they're always in the air. Yet even the most restless animal in all of Israel could find a home in the sanctuary.

> *Blessed are they that dwell in thy house: they will be still praising thee. Selah.*   Psalm 84:4

Listen to the heart of David: You can be happy. I can be happy when we simply make confession and realize God's provision in Jesus Christ. Practically, however, that happiness may not be realized or enjoyed in any other place than the sanctuary.

One night, as I was on the church grounds, I noticed a fellow sitting on the grass, who later shared with me some difficult struggles he was walking through. Now, while he could have been taking in a movie, playing golf, or hoisting some cold ones at the local bar, he still would have been forgiven—but he wouldn't have found what he was really longing for. That could only be found in the sanctuary, in the place of separation. There's something that happens uniquely in the sanctuary. If you feel worthless as a sparrow or restless as a swallow, go into the sanctuary, for in God's presence, no one throws your sin before you, no one makes fun of you, and no one condemns you.

It's in God's presence alone that you will experience a serenity that will make you, like David, want to "shout for joy" (Psalm 32:11) as you are reminded of the forgiveness of your sin and the goodness of your God.

JUMBO-SIZED FAITH
A Topical Study of
Romans 4:19–24

We seem to have a terrible tendency to overcomplicate spirituality. Knowing this, Jesus shared with us that we must become as little children if we want to enter into the kingdom (Matthew 18:3). This doesn't mean we're to be childish in immaturity, but, instead, childlike in simplicity.

In the Book of Romans, Paul was shockingly simple when he wrote that our salvation is based not upon some esoteric understanding or something we should be doing—but that it is a free gift founded not upon behaving, but upon believing; not upon trying, but upon trusting; not upon doing, but upon what Jesus has already done.

Was this some bizarre, new doctrine Paul was preaching, some New Age revelation, some secret understanding? No. In Romans 4, Paul said, "This is not something new—it's the way it was meant to be from the beginning," as he reached all the way back to Abraham for an example of one who was justified by faith.

Look at Romans 4:19–21, and note four elements of Abraham's faith that are vital for you and me.

Abraham Did Not Look at His Limitations

And being not weak in faith, he considered not his own body now dead, when he was about an hundred years old, neither yet the deadness of Sara's womb.

Romans 4:19

At the age of eighty-six, Abraham received the promise that he and his wife, Sarah, would have a child. Fourteen years later, at the age of one hundred, Abraham still believed God would honor His Word. Reproductively, his body was dead. Physiologically, Sarah had been barren all the days of her life. But Abraham didn't consider the frailties of his flesh. Instead, he counted on the faithfulness of his God.

You who are wondering why God's promise has not been fulfilled in your own life, take hope and know this: There is almost invariably a time gap between the promise of God and the performance of God. Why? So that the Lord can prepare you for what's coming. Therefore, don't look at your limitations because you will be sure to find all kinds of them.

When the spies went in to check out the Promised Land, they discovered a land that flowed with milk and honey, and brought back grapes as big as basketballs. "What a fabulous land it must be!" the people said.

"Yes, it is. But there's a problem," said all but two of the spies. "There are giants in the land. And in comparison to them, we are but grasshoppers" (see Numbers 13:33).

Do you feel as if there's a giant facing you—a financial, vocational, relational problem looming large before you? Take your eyes off your limitations and put them on the One who is limitless, for your problems are but grasshoppers compared to the One who spans the universe between His little finger and His thumb (Isaiah 48:13).

Abraham Did Not Lower His Expectations

He staggered not at the promise of God through unbelief; but was strong in faith.   Romans 4:20 (a)

"Abram," the original name given to Abraham, means "Exalted Father." Thus, for the first one hundred years of his life, Abraham must have had his fill of taunts like, "Hey, Exalted Father, how many kids do you have?" But it got worse when, at one hundred years of age, the Lord told Abram he was to change his name to Abraham, or, "Father of *Many* Nations." Yet he didn't stagger. He didn't say, "I refuse to go by that name. Call me Father Wannabe." No, he said, "Call me Father of Many Nations. It's going to happen."

Abraham Gave God Adulation

. . . giving glory to God . . .   Romans 4:20 (b)

Here's a real key to faith: I find that faith comes and fear flees when I give God glory. I can be struggling when I go into the sanctuary, or when I head up to the mountaintop. But when I start worshiping, my faith begins to grow. That is why worship is so important. Not only does it bless the Father—it feeds our faith.

When Jesus arrived at Jairus' house, mourners met him outside, saying, "Don't bother going in. The girl is dead."

"She's not dead," Jesus said. "She's sleeping"—a reply that caused the mourners to "laugh Him to scorn" (see Luke 8:53). What did Jesus do? Luke 8:54 records that before He healed Jairus' daughter, He dismissed the mockers.

I love this story because it helps me understand a very real principle with regard to faith. You see, whenever the Lord gives you a promise in the Word, there will be those who laugh, saying, "You can't claim that promise. You don't understand it contextually. You don't have the proper background linguistically. You just don't get it theologically." And what are you to do at that point? Do what Jesus did. Get rid of the mockers. How? Do what Abraham did. Start exalting, extolling, and praising the Lord—and the mockers will leave.

Abraham Handed God the Situation

And being fully persuaded that, what he had promised, he was able also to
perform.   Romans 4:21

Abraham knew that if God promised, it was up to Him to fulfill His promise. So often I try to figure out how He's going to do it. "Okay, God, how is it going to happen?" I ask. Not Abraham. He was fully persuaded that what God had promised, He would perform.

"Good for Abraham," you say. "I'm glad Paul used him as an illustration of faith, and that we sing songs in Sunday school about his faith. But I'm not Abraham. I falter frequently, stagger easily, and fail constantly."

Wait a minute. Abraham failed, too. When God gave him the promise initially that he would have a son, Sarah's response was "You've got to be kidding, Abe. I'm seventy-six—and barren on top of that! God must have meant for you to have relations with my handmaiden, Hagar, and call the child from that union ours." Abraham agreed—and the Jews in the Middle East are paying the price of his faltering faith to this day.

Why, then, did Paul commend Abraham's faith? Check this out, Bible students: Although the Old Testament tells it like it is, including flaws and failures, the New Testament never once mentions any shortcoming of any Old Testament saint. Why? Because the blood of the Son causes the heart of the Father to forget the sins of the saints.

Therefore, instead of concentrating on Abraham's failures, Paul commends Abraham's faith.

"But Abraham's faith, flawed as it may have been, is monumental compared to mine," you say.

Wait a minute. On the basis of Romans 4:23–25, if you even believe God raised Jesus from the dead, your faith is every bit as incredible as was Abraham's. You see, the world doesn't believe in the Resurrection. When Paul addressed the thinkers and scholars on Mars Hill, they listened to him—until he brought up the Resurrection, at which point they laughed at him (Acts 17:32).

Now, if you're a believer, your faith and salvation are based upon the Resurrection. You didn't see it visually. You haven't touched Jesus physically. You haven't heard His voice audibly—but somehow you believe. And, even though our culture mocks it, science disputes it, people doubt it—because God has graced you with faith to believe what the world doesn't understand—anything else you're struggling with is a piece of cake. It is nothing to believe in victory over whatever giant is before you, whatever pressure is upon you compared to believing in the Resurrection of Jesus Christ from the dead.

> Jumbo was the biggest elephant in captivity. So powerful was he that he could uproot a full-grown tree. Yet when Jumbo traveled with P. T. Barnum's circus, he was secured with nothing more than a twelve-inch stake. Why? Because when he was first captured as a baby, he was unable to pull free from the twelve-inch stake that held him captive. Thus, he grew up accepting the fact that he would never be able to remove the stake. He bought into the lie that he didn't have the strength to pull out the stake.

The same is true of you and me. Nothing remaining will demand more faith than believing that Jesus is God, that He died for our sins, and that He rose again. We're Jumbo. We've already accomplished the incredible. Yet we remain tied to twelve-inch stakes when we've already shown we are capable of uprooting trees.

"How will I make this payment?" "When will I get my house?" "What will I do if I lose my job?" are all twelve-inch stakes compared to the redwood of unbelief we've already uprooted.

> Suppose you ran the Boston Marathon, and a week later, I asked you to jog out to the mailbox a couple hundred yards away to get the mail, and you said, "I can't. I'd like to—but I can't. I'm so out of shape. I just can't run that far."
>
> I would say, "You ran the Boston Marathon—but you can't jog to the mailbox? What's wrong with you?"

And I think that's what the Lord lovingly says to us. "What's wrong with you? You have exercised faith like Abraham, the father of all faith. You've already exercised faith of astounding proportion because you have believed that I died for your sin and rose again. So how can you be worried about the phone bill?"

Gang, you are men and women of magnificent faith, following in the footsteps of Abraham. Now use the faith that caused you to embrace the Resurrection to also believe God is going to take care of your present situation. Give Him the glory. Leave it in His hands. Be free.

You're Jumbo. Go get 'em!

5 Romans 5:1
Therefore being justified by faith, we have peace with God through our Lord Jesus Christ.

By embracing the simple fact that Jesus died for our sins and rose again, we have peace with God. Why, then, do so many Christians still fight Him?

It was in 1972 that the last Imperial Japanese soldier was discovered on a South Sea island. Because he was living in complete isolation, he hadn't heard the news that World War II was over. So there he was—still building fortifications, ready to hold off the American invasion of his little atoll.

"What a waste," you say. "He could have been enjoying the Japanese economic boom, but instead he was stuck on an island, fighting malaria—all because he didn't hear that a peace treaty had been signed."

Yet, it's amazing how many of us do the same thing. *I hope the Lord doesn't come down on me for this, or get mad at me for that,* we think. *He must be really upset with me. I better hide here in the jungle.* We don't get it! The war is over! We have peace with God. The sin that separated us from God is forgiven and forgotten because of what Jesus Christ did for us.

Gang, whether you've prayed for three hours today, or you haven't prayed in three months, the war is still over. If you are a believer in what God the Father did for you in sending Jesus Christ to die in your place, you are righteous—justified by faith. We have a tendency to fall back into thinking we have to earn something or prove something to the Father. Not so. We can relax in our relationship with Him, talk to Him freely, and fellowship with Him continually because we have peace with Him eternally.

Romans 5:2 (a)
By whom also we have access by faith into this grace wherein we stand . . .

We not only have peace *with* God, but access *to* God. Notice the word "stand." Paul didn't say we have access by faith into this grace wherein we sneak in, or hurriedly race through before we get zapped. No, he said we can stand—we can plant ourselves in the presence of God and enjoy Him as long as we want, anytime we wish.

The story is told that a young boy cried outside Buckingham Palace after a beefeater refused his request to talk to the Queen. Twenty-year-old Prince Charles, observing the scene, approached the boy, took him by the hand, and said, "Come on, son. If you want to talk to the Queen, come with me."

So, too, we can talk to the King continually when we take the hand of the Son.

Romans 5:2 (b)
. . . and rejoice in hope of the glory of God.

I can rejoice in the absolute certainty that the glory of God will be made manifest in me. From God's perspective, I am already glorified. But from my perspective, locked in the time/space continuum as I am, I know He is at work, being confident that He who has begun a good work in me shall complete it (Philippians 1:6).

Romans 5:3 (a)
And not only so, but we glory in tribulations also . . .

"Tribulations," or *thlipsis* in Greek, means "crushings"—a word that describes the process of crushing an olive with heavy rocks in order to extract oil. Paul says we glory not only in what we're going to be, or who we are positionally, but also in the tribulations which happen constantly.

Why should we glory in times of crushing tribulations? Because it is during those times that we realize we can do nothing. You see, concerning a bad situation, as long as I can pull it out, I'll try to. If there's any way I can "finesse" a trial, I'll attempt to. My flesh is so present that if I can work anything out on my own, that's what I'll seek to do. But when trials arise wherein I can't do a thing, when the crushing rock is too great for me to bear, when I can't pull it off or work it out, that's true tribulation.

Nowhere was *thlipsis* more clearly illustrated than at Gethsemane, or literally, "the place of the olive press," where Jesus Christ was pressed so heavily that He sweat great drops of blood. Unable to do anything else, He said, "Father, if it be possible, take this cup from Me, but Your will be done. I submit to You completely" (Matthew 26:39–42).

For topical study of Romans 5:3 entitled "Glorying in Tribulation," turn to page 915.

Romans 5:3 (b)
. . . knowing that tribulation worketh patience.

Why are tribulations good? Because pressing and crushing works patience. They make me say, "Okay, Lord, I've tried to pull it out. I've tried to think it through. I've tried to make it happen—but now I just wait on You."

And what does God say? "Good. I've been waiting for you to get to this point for some time. Now you'll see what I can do."

Romans 5:4 (a)
And patience, experience . . .

What does patience work? Experience. Why? Because when you can't pull something off or bring it about, you're patient before the Lord and you experience His love for you in ways you never would have otherwise.

Romans 5:4 (b)
. . . and experience, hope.

What does experience work? Hope. Why? So that the next time a trial comes my way, I can look back to the previous experience and rejoice, knowing God came through for me before.

Romans 5:5
And hope maketh not ashamed; because the love of God is shed abroad in our hearts by the Holy Ghost which is given unto us.

Hope being the absolute expectation of coming good, the times in my life of which I am most ashamed are the times that, because I have lost hope, I've done or said things I wish I hadn't. I've embarrassed myself so many times because panic and sweat, anxiety and negativity have overcome me whenever I have lost hope that God was at work, that His timing was right, that He was in control. Why did I lose hope? Because I didn't have experience. Why didn't I have experience? Because I hadn't allowed the crushing times of trial and tribulation to produce patience in me.

So now when the crushing times come, my prayer is to see the divine design and to say, "Okay, Lord. I get it: Tribulation works patience, patience gives me experience, experience gives me hope, and hope makes me not ashamed so I won't say and do things I'll later on regret." It's a beautiful pattern.

Romans 5:6–11
For when we were yet without strength, in due time Christ died for the ungodly. For scarcely for a righteous man will one die: yet peradventure for a good man some would even dare
to die. But God commendeth his love toward us, in that, while we were yet sinners, Christ died for us. Much more then, being now justified by his blood, we shall be saved from wrath through him. For if, when we were enemies, we were reconciled to God by the death of his Son, much more, being reconciled, we shall be saved by his life. And not only so, but we also joy in God through our Lord Jesus Christ, by whom we have now received the atonement.

Our atonement is based completely on the work of one Man, at one time, in one event when Jesus Christ died two thousand years ago on Calvary. One Man, at one time in one event paid the price totally. Although we know this theoretically, when it truly clicks, when we really understand it, we can *enjoy* our relationship with the Father and celebrate our salvation.

There are those who, at this point in the discussion, say, "Can a *single* occurrence truly have repercussions two thousand years later for all of humanity? Can one act done by one Man in one place really alter world history?"

In answer to that, I think of another event that altered world history. On August 6, 1945, one man, Harry Truman, ordered the atom bomb dropped over Hiroshima. And the death, the devastation, and the destruction that followed were unparalleled in history. The atom bomb changed the entire course of geo-political events, as every building within 4.7 miles of the epicenter was leveled instantly, as ninety-three thousand people died immediately, as three hundred thousand died eventually from the fall-out.

One event, at one moment, ordered by one man resulted in devastation and destruction beyond comprehension. But that is not the atom bomb Paul was talking about. No, he wrote not of the atom bomb that fell in Hiroshima in 1945, but of the Adam bomb that fell when Adam bombed out in the Garden of Eden at the beginning of history—for when Adam bombed out, the fallout and aftershocks affected all of humanity even to this day.

Romans 5:12 (a)
Wherefore, as by one man sin entered into the world . . .

In the remainder of chapter 5, Paul draws our attention to four consequences of Adam's sin, the first one addressed here in verse 12:

First, because of Adam's failure, sin entered the world. Adam ushered in sin, which brought with it sorrow, suffering, and sickness. "Thanks a lot, Adam," you say. "It's not fair that we should feel the repercussions of your rebellion." But when Adam represented us in the Garden of Eden, he did better than we would have done. He was our champion. Think of it this way. . . .

Suppose we send our country's finest power-lifting team to the World Games. If these guys of immense strength, who have dedicated their lives to lifting weights, go to the Games and get beaten badly by the Russians, which of us would say, "The Russians didn't really win. After all, they didn't beat me"? That would be absurd. If we send our champions and they are defeated, we all lose because they are our best.

So, too, Adam was the best humanity had to offer. But he got beat in the Garden of Eden. He represented us, and we would have done no better. "I don't know about that," you say.

Well, I dare you to go one week without sinning. Go seven days without thinking a bad thought, without having a rotten attitude, without saying an unkind word, without doing anything wrong. And if you can go one week without sinning, come and talk to me. I want to meet you!

Romans 5:12 (b)
. . . and death by sin; and so death passed upon all men, for that all have sinned.

Second, because of Adam's failure, death entered the world. Death came because of Adam's sin—and death is the dictator to which every man must bow. People can say they think Adam is a myth, or that the Bible is full of baloney. But they cannot deny the fact that people die.

"Give me one more hour, and I will give you everything I own," said the atheistic French philosopher Voltaire to his physician. But if you cannot give me one more hour, then go to hell." The reason he wanted one more hour is reportedly because earlier that morning he had seen Hell in a vision and was terrified by what he saw.

Spiritual death, physical death, and eternal death came because of Adam's sin. Paul didn't say, "The wages of *sins* are death." No, he said, "The wages of *sin* is death," referring to Adam's sin (Romans 6:23). The reason we are dying physically and the reason we would have been damned eternally is because Adam failed. And Adam's sin brought death to all.

Romans 5:13, 14
(For until the law sin was in the world: but sin is not imputed when there is no law. Never-

theless death reigned from Adam to Moses, even over them that had not sinned after the similitude of Adam's transgression, who is the figure of him that was to come.

Read Old Testament genealogy, and you'll see that, with the exception of Enoch, every man who came on the scene died. Did they die because of their sin, because they broke the law? No. For many of them, there was no law.

If you took your new BMW for a drive on the interstate, at ninety miles per hour, it wouldn't be long before you'd see flashing lights in your rearview mirror. But if you drove the same car ninety miles per hour on the German Autobahn, it would be perfectly acceptable. Why? Because where there is no law, you can't be arrested.

Thus, Paul said, "Because men died even before the law was given, it had to be Adam's sin that caused death to come for everyone."

Romans 5:15
But not as the offence, so also is the free gift. For if through the offence of one many be dead, much more the grace of God, and the gift by grace, which is by one man, Jesus Christ, hath abounded unto many.

Not only did Jesus Christ come through *for* us, but He came bringing gifts *to* us. It is the wise man, the intelligent woman who understands that, although Adam caused problems and pain, sin and death—Jesus heaps unmerited, undeserved, unearned favor of God upon us. The first Adam let us down, but the Last Adam—our Hero, our Champion, Jesus Christ—rains grace upon us.

Romans 5:16, 17
And not as it was by one that sinned, so is the gift: for the judgment was by one to condemnation, but the free gift is of many offences unto justification. For if by one man's offence death reigned by one; much more they which receive abundance of grace and of the gift of righteousness shall reign in life by one, Jesus Christ.)

Third, because of Adam's failure, condemnation entered the world. Again, you protest that it's illogical that one man's decision should bring this kind of condemnation. But if our president ill-advisedly gave the signal to launch nuclear missiles toward another country, which, in turn, caused their computers to kick into action, sending their missiles toward us—there would be massive destruction, and billions of people would be destroyed because of one man's foolishness— which is exactly what happened when Adam bombed.

Romans 5:18
Therefore as by the offence of one judgment came upon all men to condemnation; even so by the righteousness of one the free gift came upon all men unto justification of life.

Adam polluted us. Jesus purifies us.
Adam washed out. Jesus washes us clean.

Romans 5:19
For as by one man's disobedience many were made sinners, so by the obedience of one shall many be made righteous.

Finally, because of Adam's failure, sin continually enters the world. Like the babies tragically born addicted to crack/cocaine because of the sin of their mothers, we have been condemned because of Adam's sin and continue sinning as a result. "You're being pretty tough on Adam," you say, "by placing the rap for all of the sin in the world, all of the death of mankind, all of the junk in my own life on him." Perhaps—but that's the very point Paul is making. Why? Because if all of this negativity happened because one man bombed out, how much good can happen because of one Man coming through?

Who is that Man?

The Second Man (1 Corinthians 15:47), the Last Adam (1 Corinthians 15:45), Jesus Christ.

Romans 5:20, 21
Moreover the law entered, that the offence might abound. But where sin abounded, grace did much more abound: That as sin hath reigned unto death, even so might grace reign through righteousness unto eternal life by Jesus Christ our Lord.

Everything wrong with the world today, everything wrong with you, your family, and the people you work with is all due to Adam's failure. Knowing this allows me to see people in an entirely different light. I realize that whether a man is a sly entrepreneur who cheats his way into money he shouldn't have by cutting deals he shouldn't make, or whether he's as obvious and gross in his sin as Charles Manson—I am no less a sinner than he. And it's all because of Adam.

No wonder Jesus could look at the multitudes and have compassion on them—not crusade against them, march to get rid of them, or mobilize to neutralize them. He looked at the multitudes and in every instance He had compassion. You see, when it finally sinks in that by one Man righteousness, justification, and grace came—I stop striving and struggling to prove I'm a notch or two above you, and I stop feeling bad if I'm a notch or two below you. I'm not the issue at all. He is. When I understand this, I stop being a worker and become a worshiper.

Do I find myself trying to earn blessings by intensive prayer or Bible study? Do I try to prove I'm saved by street witnessing, or by ministering in Mexico? If I fall into that trap, my Christian experience will always be one of analyzing, scrutinizing, and condemning myself as well as others. Salvation is not based upon my knowledge, my deep study, or my twenty-four-hour prayer chain. It's based upon one thing only: the grace and goodness of God in sending One Man, the Last Adam—Jesus Christ.

GLORYING IN TRIBULATION
A Topical Study of
Romans 5:3

The apostle Paul's middle name could well have been "trouble." Wherever he went, whatever he said caused difficulty and controversy. Think you had a tough time this week? Think about Paul. From the time he became a minister of the gospel, he was: put to hard labor, beaten, imprisoned, given thirty-nine lashes five times, stoned, shipwrecked three times, stranded a day and a night in the open ocean, and left for dead. When Paul talked about difficulties, he knew from whence he spoke. Yet he said we are not only to rejoice in coming glory, but in present tribulations. Why? Because tribulation is the catalyst God uses to bring about patience, experience, and hope.

We see this principle in nature.

> The Seventeen-Mile Drive on the Monterey Peninsula is world famous for, among other things, the beautiful cypress trees that abound in that region. Because of their beauty, these cypress trees are photographed, painted, and sculpted by artists from all over the world. The beauty of the cypress tree is due to the wind that blows them constantly. And the wind that produces their outer beauty also develops their inner strength. You see, the root system of the cypress tree sinks proportionately deeper than that of any other tree in the state. This is especially interesting considering the mighty Redwood also makes California its home.

"Lord, I want to be an object of beauty," we say.

"All right," He says—and proceeds to send winds of adversity, not to blow us out, but to make us beautiful; not to sink us, but to strengthen us. The cold winds of adversity, the hot winds of tribulation cause us to sink our root systems deeper in the soil of Scripture, to ground and root us in faith. That's why Paul says we are to rejoice in tribulation.

Tribulation and testing are what God uses to take the dings and dents out of our body—both corporately and individually. God takes us into His body shop. He starts pounding away, pulling out dents, and doing some grinding. It's not during the party times when strength is developed, when beauty is born. It's when the wind is howling and the sander humming that God is doing His finishing work.

Ask Johann Sebastian Bach. . . .

> This man, who was one of the most prolific composers in history, locked himself in a room day after day, where he put pen to paper and scored the glorious compositions he heard in his mind. Why did he lock himself in the confines of a single room? He had twenty kids. You would lock yourself in a room too if twenty kids were running around your house! Yet from his own times of testing, tribulation, and challenge came beautiful music.

Paul makes the same point, saying, "Don't only rejoice in your peace with God, your access to God, or your hope in God. Rejoice also in your present difficulty because it's working in you something of beauty."

"I know that," you say. "Everyone knows we're to count it all joy when we fall into various trials. I already understand that concept."

Do you? The prophet Jeremiah was a man who knew the Lord, but he struggled with something the Lord had told him prophetically and which he observed personally. That is, the Babylonians would soon march on Jerusalem. When Jeremiah asked why, God told him to do something very interesting. "Arise," He said. "Go down to the potter's house and I will cause you to hear My words" (see Jeremiah 18:2). So Jeremiah went to the potter's house, wherein he observed clay on a potter's wheel.

The most common of all substances, clay typifies you and me. Psalm 103 declares that as a father has compassion on his children, so the Lord has compassion on us. He remembers our frames and knows that we are but dust, earth, and clay. God is not mad *at* us, disappointed *in* us, or tired *of* us. Knowing we're nothing more than lumps of clay, He has chosen to work *on* us. That is why Jeremiah saw not only the clay. He saw the Master Potter as well—pumping the pedal that caused the wheel to turn.

> "The problem with life," said one philosopher, "is that it's so daily." Maybe you can relate to that. If you're in school, it's geometry, history, English, and lunch. Then it's science, study hall, and P.E. You go home, have a Twinkie, watch TV, do homework, go to bed—and get up the next morning to begin the same cycle all over again. If you work, it's the same old people, same old problems, same old struggles every morning. Round and round you go, day after day. That's how the clay felt. And sometimes we become so tired of the routine of our lives that we say, "I'm getting off this wheel."

What, then, does the Master Potter do? Even as Jeremiah observed, he picks us up—lumps of clay that we are—kneads us a bit, and puts us right back on the wheel. All of us are aware of the circuitousness, the sameness of daily life. But it's all part of the plan of the Potter. And if I try to escape, I will only be crushed in the process and end up right back where I started.

> The storm raged. The disciples rowed and complained. Then they saw Jesus walking on the water. "Lord! If that's You, bid me to come," Peter cried— perhaps not so much an act of faith as a plea to get away from the disciples.
> "Okay. Come on, Peter," Jesus said (see Matthew 14:29).
> Peter got out of the boat and started walking to Jesus. But when he took his eyes off the Lord and focused on the storm, what happened to him is the same thing that happens to us: He began to sink. "Save me, Lord!" he cried. So Jesus lifted Peter, the giant fisherman, out of the water with a one-armed curl and put him where? Right back in the boat.

God puts us in fixes to fix us. Therefore, if I try to fix the fix God put me in, He's sure to put me in another fix to fix the fix He wanted to fix in the first place. As a result, slowly but surely, I learn to be content in the boat, to remain on the wheel. Yet no sooner do I accept the confines and routine of my situation than I feel the hand of the Master Potter suddenly and unexpectedly poking me, pinching me, shaping me. And if I'm not careful, I will jump off the wheel once more—this time not because of predictability, but because of pressure. If I do, I'll find myself face-down on the floor before I feel the hand of my Master Potter picking me up and plopping me on the wheel once again.

This process may go on over and over again—until I finally give up and lie still on the wheel. But when I do, if I catch my reflection in the window, I'll see myself taking shape as the Potter forms me into something useful. *Far out!* I think as the wheel comes to a stop. Then I feel the hands of the Potter under me and I think, *This is great! Now He's going to put me on the top shelf, in a place where everyone can see me.* But instead, He walks right by the top shelf and keeps going until I hear the sound of a door opening. It's the kiln. In I go. The door closes behind me. The temperature rises. And I start sweating.

"What now, Lord?" I cry. "Why am I in this place? What in the world is going on?"

And He answers, "It takes not only pressure points but also fiery trials to produce in you a solidity that will keep you from cracking up or flaking out." This process continues until the Potter takes me out and carries me to His shop.

Now, according to Romans 9:21, the Lord makes some vessels to honor and some to dishonor. This means He makes some people beautiful vases to hold flowers. But others He makes spittoons. "Wait a minute!" I protest. "Let me get this straight. I should rejoice in tribulation because tribulation works patience that produces experience, which produces hope, which makes me unashamed. But what if He's making me a spittoon? The daily-ness of my job, the boringness of my career, the sameness of my school, the pressure financially, relationally, emotionally—when all is said and done, am I going to end up a spittoon? Is *that* what it's all about, Lord?"

But wait. Look again at the Master Potter. In the feet pumping the pedal that causes the wheel to turn so routinely, you will see holes where a nail pierced them for the sake of the clay. Look at the hands putting pressure on the clay. See the holes in each palm, and realize the Master Potter is the Wonderful Counselor, the Everlasting Father, the Prince of Peace, your Savior, Jesus Christ. If He loves you so much He was willing to be pinned to the Cross, you can trust that the repetitiveness of your schedule and the pressure in your life are meant to make you into something wonderful.

Not only does He love you that much now—but when you were a sinner, when you were ungodly, when you were an enemy, He was in love with you (Romans 5:8).

Suppose my wife, Tammy, and I go house shopping and find a house for five thousand dollars. The roof is caving in. The wires are hanging out. The floors are sagging. The foundation is gone. But Tammy loves it anyway, so we buy it. Then, unbeknownst to her, I call fifteen master carpenters and craftsmen and pay them five hundred thousand dollars to replace the roof, rewire, and rework the entire house from top to bottom. When I take Tammy back to the house, she's sure to say, "This is fabulous. I loved it when it was a shack, but now look at it!"

So, too, God loved you when you were a shack. He said, "I see there's no foundation under your life, no covering over your life, no wiring in your life. But I love you just the way you are." And because He was in love with you at your worst, you can be assured that for the rest of your life—especially now that you're beginning to be reworked, rewired, and rebuilt—you'll never have to doubt His love, not even for a moment.

Why am I sharing this? Because I know bunches of us understand with our minds the value of tribulation and trials. But even though we embrace the understanding theologically, we struggle with it internally and we start sniveling. "If God loves me," we murmur, "why isn't He doing this or working out the other?"

Something big was about to happen. The mother of James and John could sense the excitement in the air. Indeed, in a few hours, the city would be crying, "Hosanna! Hosanna! Blessed is the King of Israel who cometh in the name of the Lord!" So it was that Salome came to Jesus and worshiped Him right before His triumphal entry (Matthew 20:20).

Fully aware that she was worshipping Him not out of love, but in order to manipulate Him and get what she wanted, Jesus lovingly looked at her and said, "Woman what do you want?"

"Well, now that You ask, Lord," she answered, "when You come into Your kingdom, can my two boys be on your right hand and on your left?"

Jesus looked at her and answered very cryptically when He said, "Are you able to drink from the cup I'm to drink from and be baptized with the baptism with which I'm about to be baptized?"

Salome must have wondered about such a strange answer to such a simple question. And Jesus probably smiled and said no more. He went into Jerusalem, and you know the story. It wasn't too many days later that the same Salome would stand with three other women on a hill right outside the Holy City. Seeing Jesus pinned to a Cross with two other men, one on His right, one on His left, hanging beside Him on the day He entered His kingdom, the foolishness of her request must have hit her like a ton of bricks.

What I am asking of the Lord right now can be just as dumb. "But, Lord," I cry, "this is a great idea. Bless it, Lord."

And He lovingly says to me, "You don't know what you're asking. You don't see the whole story. I loved you enough to die on the Cross. Therefore, if I'm not doing what you're begging me to do, what you're naming and claiming, trust Me. And like Salome, in retrospect, you'll be thankful I didn't respond to your request and do your bidding."

That's the argument Paul makes. Rejoice in tribulation. Because God fell in love with you and proved His love to you even when you were a sinner, you never have to wonder why the wheel is so dizzying, the pressure so painful, and the kiln so hot. And on the basis not of what you feel emotionally, nor of what you ascribe to theologically, but on His love for you unconditionally, you can trust Him to come through totally.

---

6 Here, we come to a new section and break new ground in our study through the Epistle to the Romans. Chapters 1 through 5 dealt with justification. In chapters 6 through 8, the emphasis switches from the positional truth of justification to the practical truth of sanctification. To be sanctified means to be set apart. Because we are justified positionally, we are sanctified practically. That is, we are set apart to be used by the Lord, and to become more like the Lord. Romans 1 through 5 tells us we are dead *in* sin. Chapters 6 through 8 tell us we are dead *to* sin. Chapters 1 through 5 tell us we are free from the penalty of sin. Chapters 6 through 8 tell us we are free from the power of sin.

Thus, we have arrived at one of the most powerful and potent passages ever penned by the apostle Paul. As a lawyer, Paul masterfully and persuasively made his point in the first five chapters that salvation is apart from works. But this causes problems for people who say, "If you preach grace, people will live loosely unless you lay down the law, and tell them what to do and how to think." In chapter 6, Paul will address that issue as he presents his argument to those who insist that grace leads to loose living.

Romans 6:1, 2
What shall we say then? Shall we continue in sin, that grace may abound? God forbid. How shall we, that are dead to sin, live any longer therein?

Paul will make a three-fold argument against grace being a danger. All too often, Christians try to fight sin by preaching, "No, no, no." Paul's method was to teach, "Know, know, know." He said, "Know you have a new identification with Jesus Christ (verses 3–5); know you have liberation through Jesus' Cross (verses 6–15); and know some things about Jesus' cause" (verses 16–23).

Romans 6:3–5
Know ye not, that so many of us as were baptized into Jesus Christ were baptized into his death? Therefore we are buried with him by baptism into death: that like as Christ was raised up from the dead by the glory of the Father, even so we also should walk in newness of life. For if we have been planted together in the likeness of his death, we shall be also in the likeness of his resurrection.

Our identification with Jesus Christ is symbolized by baptism.

An army chaplain reported his amazement at the large number of Desert Storm soldiers who gave their hearts and lives to Jesus Christ, then asked if they could be baptized. To accommodate their requests, a wise pastor used the only "baptismal" available in the middle of the Saudi Arabian desert: a coffin—a potent and perfect symbol of the death, burial, and resurrection of which baptism is a picture.

"Know this," Paul said. "When you were baptized, you received a new identification. Dead to your old life, you became publicly linked to Jesus Christ through baptism." Does one have to be baptized to be saved? Ask the thief on the cross, to whom Jesus said, "*Today* you'll be with Me in paradise" (Luke 23:43).

There are those who say, "Unless you are baptized in a specific manner, your salvation is invalid." Not true. Anyone can be saved without baptism, for salvation is by faith alone in the work of Jesus Christ on the Cross. The role of baptism simply serves as an outward symbol of an inward commitment. On the day Tammy and I were married, I gave her a ring. That ring didn't make us married. But if she had refused it, saying, "No thanks. I'm not into outward symbols of inward commitments," although we would still be married, I would wonder why she didn't want to publicly identify with me.

Chuck Colson tells of an event that took place when Russia was still very much closed to the gospel as a group of Christians meeting secretly in the basement of a home outside Kiev heard a knock on the door. Because they refused to answer the knock, suddenly the door was kicked in, and two armed KGB officers walked into the room. "This meeting is illegal," they thundered. "If anyone wants to deny he's a part of this Christian movement, he can leave right now. If you stay, however, you must be willing to pay the price and suffer the consequences." With terror on their faces, two or three left the meeting, after which time, the KGB officers said, "Anyone else want to join those who left?" No one did. "Keep your hands up," they said to those who remained, "and we'll put our hands up and worship the Lord with you. You see, two weeks ago, we broke into a group like this one and we got saved. But as KGB officers, we know that if people are not fully committed to Christ, we cannot trust them in our company."

Baptism is a marvelous way of getting Christians out of the spiritual closet. And Paul refers to this by saying, "Know this: when you were baptized, you were identified with Jesus Christ and a new way of living."

Romans 6:6 (a)
Knowing this, that our old man is crucified with him . . .

When Jesus died on the Cross two thousand years ago, something incredible happened. My old sin nature was crucified with Him. I'm thankful that my failure to fully understand this concept doesn't prevent me from being forever grateful for it.

Romans 6:6 (b)
. . . that the body of sin might be destroyed, that henceforth we should not serve sin.

Katargeo, the Greek word translated "destroyed" in this verse, means "rendered inactive" or "paralyzed." It doesn't mean "annihilated." Therefore, when your old sin nature screams, "You've got to take that smoke, pour that drink, toy with that fantasy, lose your temper, or gossip"—Paul says that, although he can yell, he is powerless to act, since the Cross paralyzed him from the neck down.

Romans 6:7–9 (a)
For he that is dead is freed from sin. Now if we be dead with Christ, we believe that we shall also live with him: Knowing that Christ being raised from the dead dieth no more . . .

In other words, the work of the Cross was complete.

Romans 6:9 (b)–11
. . . death hath no more dominion over him. For in that he died, he died unto sin once: but in that he liveth, he liveth unto God. Likewise reckon ye also yourselves to be dead indeed unto sin, but alive unto God through Jesus Christ our Lord.

The word *logizomai,* or "reckon," is an accounting term. "Add it up," says Paul, "and the answer you'll arrive at will be that you are dead to sin." Communion has two elements because, in tak-

ing the cup, we celebrate the fact that we are free from the penalty of sin. And in taking the body, we appropriate the fact that we are free from the power of sin. Consequently, when I partake of the body in Communion, sometimes I will chew thirty-nine times—even as Jesus received thirty-nine lashes on His back, because it is by His stripes that we are healed (Isaiah 53:5). You see, the shed blood of Jesus provides forgiveness *of* sin. But the breaking of His body provides victory *over* sin. All of this is ours to chew on and appropriate through the simple act of Communion.

Romans 6:12–14
Let not sin therefore reign in your mortal body, that ye should obey it in the lusts thereof. Neither yield ye your members as instruments of unrighteousness unto sin: but yield yourselves unto God, as those that are alive from the dead, and your members as instruments of righteousness unto God. For sin shall not have dominion over you: for ye are not under the law, but under grace.

Following the radical information that we are free from the power and penalty of sin, and on the heels of Paul's exhortation to simple appropriation of this fact, here is practical application. When you are about to give in to gossip, lose your temper, or fall prey to jealousy, say, "Lord, I understand I no longer have to succumb to this because the old man of sin was crucified. I reckon it to be so and I appropriate it even now."

There you are in the grocery store. A Mounds bar is calling your name. Your old sin nature whispers, "You've got to give in. Dark chocolate, coconut, you've just got to have it. You've got to steal it. Just think how much you'll enjoy it. You have no power over it. It's just too great a temptation."
  But on the basis of Romans 6, before you take the candy bar, you can say, "I yield this hand to You, Lord." And you'll be free.

Gang, if you will pause and, even audibly if necessary, yield to the Lord whatever instrument of your body with which you're struggling, your inclination to sin will decrease dramatically.

There you are, in the car. You're struggling with passion as you take your date home. What do you do? On the basis of Romans 6, say, "Lord, bless these next few moments. Cause us to honor You. We give ourselves totally to You right now." And the mood in the car will change radically.

Precious people, you're free from the power of sin. How? Three ways: through the radical information that the power of sin is broken, through simple appropriation as you reckon this to be true, and through practical application as you give your body to the Lord.

For topical study of Romans 6:1–14, see "The Old Man—Nailed!" below.

Romans 6:15, 16
What then? shall we sin, because we are not under the law, but under grace? God forbid. Know ye not, that to whom ye yield yourselves servants to obey, his servants ye are to whom ye obey; whether of sin unto death, or of obedience unto righteousness?

Why not continue in sin? I'm reminded of the entertainer who, although he was warned that lions could never be completely tamed, treated the lion he used in his act as a pet—until the night the lion jumped on him and killed him. So, too, our adversary goes about as a roaring lion, seeking whom he may devour (1 Peter 5:8). "Oh, but I've got this sin under control," we say. "Nice lion, nice lion. It's part of my act; I need it for my job."

Watch out. Paul says, "Know this: the sin with which you're playing around, the sin you think you've got under control, is going to come back and eat you alive."

- "But I only shoplift occasionally."
- "I only look at pornography sporadically."
- "I lie rarely."

Be careful. Paul doesn't say, "No," he says "know." Your pet sin will get you. It will hurt you. It will kill you.

Romans 6:17–20
But God be thanked, that ye were the servants of sin, but ye have obeyed from the heart that

form of doctrine which was delivered you. Being then made free from sin, ye became the servants of righteousness. I speak after the manner of men because of the infirmity of your flesh: for as ye have yielded your members servants to uncleanness and to iniquity unto iniquity; even so now yield your members servants to righteousness unto holiness. For when ye were the servants of sin, ye were free from righteousness.

"Before you were saved, neither your relationships nor your perspective was right," Paul said. "Therefore, you couldn't enjoy the righteous kind of living God intended for you."

Romans 6:21
What fruit had ye then in those things whereof ye are now ashamed? for the end of those things is death.

At Southern Oregon College, I talked to a student who said, "It's so hard being a Christian."

"If you think it's hard being a Christian, imagine how hard it would be to be an unbeliever without hope eternally or peace presently."

Folks, let's quit saying, "It's so hard to be a believer." We've been saved too long if we've forgotten the sin, the stench, the junk in our lives before we knew Christ.

Romans 6:22, 23
But now being made free from sin, and become servants to God, ye have your fruit unto holiness, and the end everlasting life. For the wages of sin is death; but the gift of God is eternal life through Jesus Christ our Lord.

Sin brings death. But righteousness—the righteousness of the Lord's way—brings life abundantly. I'm so thrilled we're free.

THE OLD MAN—NAILED!
A Topical Study of
Romans 6:1–14

While at Hometown Buffet many years ago, without asking permission or finishing her dinner, Mary, my kindergartener, scooted away from the table and made her way to the ice cream dispenser. When she returned a few moments later, she brought with her a bowl that had ice cream overflowing and cascading down its sides. So even though Mary had failed to get her father's permission, even though she had failed to finish her dinner, she discovered something very important. That is, even though she was a sinner, if she positioned herself under the spout where the blessing comes out, she would be on the receiving end because the dispenser didn't discriminate against her, saying, "Here comes Mary. She didn't ask permission. She didn't finish her dinner. I'm shutting down."

So, too, the sister or brother who realizes that grace is based solely upon the work Jesus did on the Cross will continually be a recipient of good stuff because they realize it's not based upon who they are or anything they've done. And even if, like Mary, they're sinning, as they position themselves under the spout where God's blessing comes out, His grace keeps flowing. For where sin abounds, grace abounds even more (Romans 5:20).

This brings us to Paul's question in Romans 6:1. That is, if grace abounds when we sin, why not keep sinning? Paul answers this question with two words: "God forbid," or "You're nuts," or "That's crazy!" You see, folks, although Mary carried an abundance of ice cream in her bowl, she also wore a look of panic on her face. "Daddy, look," she said as she drew near. And as I did, I was shocked to see vanilla ice cream pouring out of the machine onto the floor below. The handle was stuck.

Yes, you can sneak away from the table and disobey Daddy and pull the lever, and good stuff will still be given to you—but watch out. There are also inevitable repercussions and problems. You get in sticky situations that cause people to slip.

After David confessed to committing murder in order to cover his adulterous relationship with Bathsheba, the prophet Nathan said to him, "Thou shalt not die, David. With your confession comes instantaneous and complete forgiveness. But because by this deed you have given great occasion to the enemies of the Lord to blaspheme His name, the child born unto you shall surely die" (see 2 Samuel 12:13, 14).

In other words, "You're forgiven, David. Your sin is forgotten. But know this: There will be inevitable repercussions of your sin. You planted seeds, and even though you've made confession, even though you are forgiven, the crop will come in. The enemies of the Lord will put your sin on the cover of *TIME* magazine. They will use your sin to blaspheme and make fun of the Lord. People will slip and stumble because of your sin. And your child will die."

"Be not deceived," warned Paul, "whatever a man sows, he'll surely reap" (see Galatians 6:7). And no one beats the rap.

Driving through a rural section of Pennsylvania, a man crossed a wooden bridge, where he saw a boy fishing. "Hey, son," he called out, "are the fish biting?"
"No," answered the boy. "But the worms sure are."
The stranger chuckled and kept on driving. About five miles later, he stopped at a gas station and asked if there were any good fishing spots in the vicinity.

"Sure," answered the attendant. "There's a great one about five miles back at the bridge you just crossed."

"Oh, I know all about that one," answered the traveler. "I saw a kid there and he said the fish weren't biting, but the worms were."

The two men chuckled together—until a look of horror came over the gas station attendant's face. He dropped the hose, ran to his car, and raced down the road toward the bridge. When he got there, he found the little boy on the edge of the riverbank—dead. You see, after his initial chuckle, the attendant suddenly realized that the "worms" the boy was playing with were actually baby rattlesnakes, which are every bit as venomous as their adult counterparts.

So, too, when we see people playing with sins they think are cute or interesting, horror fills our hearts and we say, "They're going to die." Oh, not physically perhaps—but their lives will be filled with sadness and despair. The Bible says there's pleasure in sin for a season, but after that comes destruction (Hebrews 11:25). And that's what Paul's letter to the Romans is all about. Through it, the Father says to you and me, "You're forgiven. I pronounce you just as righteous as My dear Son. But if you fool around with sin, you're going to bring venom and deadly repercussions not only upon yourself, but on those around you."

Therefore, after walking with the Lord for a while, we begin to say, "Father, You're right. Sin stinks. It brings terrible repercussions and I hate it. But what can I do about it? This sin seems to have a grip on me." At that point, there is the temptation to enroll in a twelve-step program in order to get victory over our substance abuse, addiction, or depression. But the Bible knows nothing of a twelve-step program, folks. Romans 6 has a way of cutting through the fuzziness, the dysfunctional excuses, the reasons we cannot have victory. Romans 6 sweeps it all away as God clearly says, "Here is the solution. It's oh, so simple."

Appreciation

Knowing this, that our old man is crucified with him, that the body of sin might be destroyed, that henceforth we should not serve sin. Romans 6:6

The first step is appreciation. When Jesus Christ was crucified on the Cross two thousand years ago, not only was His blood shed for your salvation, but His body was broken for your liberation. Thus, there are two elements in Communion. His blood brings about forgiveness of our sin, while His broken body provides freedom from our sin. Appreciate the fact, saint, that when Jesus Christ was crucified, your sinful nature was crucified with Him in order that the body of sin might be destroyed. When Jesus was pinned to the Cross, my old sinful nature was there with Him. When the body of Christ was being broken physically, your body of sin was being broken on that same tree. How can this be? It beats me. Yet although I don't understand it mentally, I've tied in to its reality and have found that by faith it works tremendously.

Whenever God declares a truth, Satan will deny it, saying, "Get real, how can that be?" At that point, I must decide whether to believe what God declares or believe what Satan denies. It's like three men walking on top of a fence.

The first man is Fact. The second man is Faith. The third man is Feeling. Now, Faith, the man in the middle, will walk straightly and in balance as long as he keeps his eyes on the man in front of him. But if he turns around to check out Feeling, he's going to tumble. Truly, this is where we err so often, for the point we turn around and analyze our emotions or evaluate our experience is the point we start to fall.

Paul says, "Know this: when Jesus was crucified, our old sin nature was crucified with Him that the body of sin might be destroyed." The world translated "destroyed" is *katargeo. Katargeo* does not mean "annihilated." It means "rendered inactive, or paralyzed." Our old sin nature is a quadriplegic. He's paralyzed from the neck down. Thus, all he can do is intimidate us verbally as he whispers, "You have no choice. You gotta give in. You gotta gossip. You gotta overindulge. You gotta take another look. You gotta tell that lie. I've got power over you."

And so we spend years going through psychoanalysis, trying to get victory. But Paul would say, "Victory is not a matter of positive thinking or imaging. Appreciation of what happened on Calvary two thousand years ago is the point where victory begins."

Appropriation

Likewise reckon ye also yourselves to be dead indeed unto sin, but alive unto God through Jesus Christ our Lord.   Romans 6:11

The word "reckon" in this verse doesn't mean what it means today—as in, "Well, ah reckon ah'll mosey on down to the barn." No, the word "reckon" as used here in verse 11 is an accounting term. It means "add up the figures and come to an irrefutable conclusion." The figures add up to this: If indeed it's true that your sin nature was crucified with Christ on the Cross, then you no longer are in bondage to it. "Come to a conclusion based upon this fact," said Paul.

If you were hungry, I might tell you to go to McDonalds. But if you had no money, you'd say, "I can't. I'm bankrupt."

Then I might say, "Yes, you can. I put money in your account. Here is the deposit slip, signed by the teller and stamped with the bank seal.

But if you said, "I don't believe that," your failure to reckon it to be so, to add it up, and to appropriate what I did on your behalf would keep you poor and hungry. But the reason for your poverty and hunger would not be due to my failure to provide for you. It would be due to your failure to believe what I did for you.

The same is true concerning appropriation. Jesus paid the entire penalty for our sin and paralyzed our sin nature. The question is not whether His provision is sufficient. The question is whether or not we reckon it to be true.

Application

Neither yield ye your members as instruments of unrighteousness unto sin: but yield yourselves unto God, as those that are alive from the dead, and your members as instruments of righteousness unto God.   Romans 6:13

After appreciation and appropriation comes application—when I really understand what Jesus did for me as He yielded His body on the Cross. So here I am, walking into the store, and there it is in a shiny wrapper, fifteen percent larger than last year: a Three Musketeers bar—my favorite—with that deep chocolate covering and the light gooey stuff in the center. Immediately, the old man within me says, "You gotta give in. There's fifteen percent more than before. Be reasonable. It's a good buy!"

My stomach begins to growl. My mouth starts to salivate. My old sin nature demands to be satisfied. "You're right," I concede. "I really don't have very much power over this particular temptation." So I buy the candy, take a bite, and am hounded by feelings of guilt. Depression sets in, and I say, "Sign me up for a support group. That's what I need."

Not true! The Word says if we will appreciate, appropriate, and apply, we never have to give in to whatever "Three Musketeers" we're dealing with at any given moment. Never. Folks, it's not a twelve-step program. It's a one step solution called the Cross, for not only did the blood of Jesus cleanse me from the penalty of sin, but His broken body sets me free from the pollution of sin. And when I choose to walk in that fact, I find myself saying, "I will not buy you, Three Musketeers," as I walk down the aisle toward the bananas. Miracle of miracles!

For every New Testament principle, God gives us an Old Testament illustration. And this one is no exception, as seen in the Book of Judges. . . .

The people of Israel were in bondage to the Canaanites. For thirty years, they had been intimidated and dominated, repressed and oppressed. The leader of the Canaanites was a man named Jabin. Jabin turned over control of his empire in that particular region to a man named Sisera. Sisera, then, represents the old man, our old sin nature. Jabin is a picture of Satan—one whose ultimate desire is to oppress, suppress, and depress you and me.

After thirty years of serving Jabin and Sisera, the people of Israel cried to the Lord. The Lord, in turn, raised up a deliverer—a woman named Deborah. When the time came for the Israelites to engage in battle against the Canaanites, Barak, the Israelite general, said to Deborah, "I won't go unless you go with me."

"Okay," said Deborah, "I'll go with you, but you must realize that credit for the upcoming victory will go to a woman."

Engage in battle they did. With nine hundred chariots at his command, Sisera had a huge advantage. The chariot was equivalent to a Phantom Jet, or an Abrams A-1 tank. And the people of Israel had nothing like that. It looked like the Israelites would be slaughtered. But God intervened miraculously and gave Israel victory. Sisera, however, managed to escape.

Running for his life, off in the distance he saw a tent. In front of the tent was a woman Sisera recognized as Jael, the wife of Heber the Kenite. The word *eber*, from which we get the word "Hebrew," means "crossing over." Who were the Kenites? They were part of the Canaanites. This means Heber the Kenite left the old Canaanite stuff and said to his wife, "Honey, we're crossing over to a new land." And they traded their old world for a new country.

That's just what you did when you left the old world system and said, "I want to be a part of Your kingdom, Lord. I've had it with the world's corruption, deception, and pollution. I choose to follow You." You set up camp in the new land—and what happened? Guess who suddenly and unexpectedly showed up on your front doorstep? The guy who used to dominate you, the guy who used to have authority over you, the guy who used to intimidate you: Sisera.

"Come in," said Jael to Sisera. Huffing and puffing, Sisera entered Jael's tent and gasped, "Give me a little water to drink."

Folks, that's what the old sin nature always says. "Give me a little something to satisfy me—just one quick look, just one wrong thought, just one more time. I'm thirsty, and if you satisfy me, I won't bug you anymore." But we've discovered lust is like a fire. The more you feed it, the more it demands and the hotter it gets. Try to appease your lust to satisfy Sisera, and it will never work. He'll demand more and more, and his lusts will burn hotter and hotter within your heart.

Sisera wanted water. What did Jael give him? A bottle of milk. Can you imagine running a great distance on a hot day and being given a bottle of room-temperature, unpasteurized milk? It must have felt like cotton in Sisera's mouth. The Word says, "Like newborn babes, desire the sincere milk of the Word, the profound simplicity of the Scriptures" (see 1 Peter 2:2).

It is the foolish man or woman who says, "I already know that passage or that book, so I don't have to study it or meditate upon it," because Sisera needs to be given a continual dose of the milk of the Word.

After asking for water, Sisera made a second request of Jael. "Lie for me," he said (see verse 20). "Cover me up and don't let anyone know I'm here." And that's what our old sin nature says to you and me: "Hide your sin. Cover it up. Don't let anyone know I'm here." So what did Jael do? No longer afraid of the old general, this great lady of faith threw a rug over Sisera, knowing that having chugged a glass of warm milk after running a semi-marathon, he would be dozing off before long. At this point, with hammer in hand, Jael snuck into the tent, drove a tent stake into Sisera's temple, and pinned his head to the ground. Talk about a splitting headache! With spike and hammer, the old man was reckoned dead.

What does the spike speak of? It speaks of the spikes that pierced the hand and feet of our Savior. It speaks of Calvary, where Sisera, the old man in you who gives orders to you and demands to be covered up by you, was paralyzed on the Cross. The hammer? It speaks of the Word (Jeremiah 23:29). This is the key, folks. We're to say, "Wait a minute, Sisera. Wait a minute, Jabin. Wait a minute fleshly tendency. You who are demanding to be satisfied and covered up, I want you to know something. I do not have to give in to you. Even though I don't fully understand it, I appropriate the finished work of the Cross as I see it in Romans 6." And you nail Sisera to the ground.

Precious people, I don't care what struggle you're going through, or what temptation you're wrestling with. It is powerless in light of the Cross. When you finally have enough of Sisera, when you at last have your fill of the venom that has infected you and those around you, when you finally determine you don't want to be under dominion any longer, you can be free at that moment—no support group needed, no counseling required—if you say, "Lord, You've told me that this old man was paralyzed on the Cross. I believe it. That settles it."

And with the spike of the Cross, and the hammer of the Word, you nail it right there and walk away free.

It's that simple.

As we are discovering, the Book of Romans is radical in concept, rich in content, and readable in construct. Truly, the concepts in Romans are indeed radical. But they're not esoteric. They're not difficult to comprehend or hard to understand because of the logical way in which Romans is laid out. It's laid out perfectly, which is not surprising, considering the Author, who always does everything just right (Mark 7:37).

Romans 1 deals with the perversity of sin; Romans 2—3:18 with the pervasiveness of sin; Romans 3:18—5:21 with the penalty of sin. Romans 6 deals a death blow to the power of sin. And this brings us to chapter 7, wherein Paul will deal with the question of preoccupation with sin.

Romans 7:1 (a)
Know ye not, brethren . . .

The brothers Paul is referring to are his Jewish brothers, the people of Israel.

Romans 7:1 (b), 2 (a)
. . . (for I speak to them that know the law,) how that the law hath dominion over a man as long as he liveth? For the woman which hath an husband is bound by the law to her husband so long as he liveth . . .

According to Old Testament law, a husband could divorce his wife, but a wife could never divorce her husband. Paul uses the analogy to say, "You were married to the law, and there's no way you could get away from it."

Romans 7:2 (b), 3
. . . but if the husband be dead, she is loosed from the law of her husband. So then, if, while her husband liveth, she be married to another man, she shall be called an adulteress: but if her husband be dead, she is free from that law; so that she is no adulteress, though she be married to another man.

If only the law would die, we would be free from its hold on us. But the law is in excellent health (Matthew 5:18). This husband is not about to die.

Romans 7:4 (a)
Wherefore, my brethren, ye also are become dead to the law by the body of Christ . . .

This is so wonderful! You have become dead to the law. That's the key. You'll never see a dead body in a courtroom trial because when a person is dead, he's no longer under the authority of the law. So, too, because you died in Christ (Galatians 2:20), you are free from legalism. Thus, there is no reason to be preoccupied with your failings, your lack of prayer, your lack of love, your lack of anything. There is no reason to try to live up to the rules, regulations, and expectations you've put upon yourself. When you realize that you died with Christ positionally on Calvary, you're free from the demands of the law and free instead to just love the Lord.

Romans 7:4 (b)
. . . that ye should be married to another, even to him who is raised from the dead, that we should bring forth fruit unto God.

Because the Christian who finally throws off the yoke of legalism inevitably becomes fruitful, churches grow whenever believers become excited about their relationship with Jesus.

For topical study of Romans 7:1–4 entitled "Loosed from Legalism," turn to page 931.

Romans 7:5, 6
For when we were in the flesh, the motions of sins, which were by the law, did work in our members to bring forth fruit unto death. But now we are delivered from the law, that being dead wherein we were held; that we should serve in newness of spirit, and not in the oldness of the letter.

"Newness of spirit" speaks of the New Covenant, of an entirely new way of living (Jeremiah 31; Ezekiel 36). "No longer will I give you tables of stone," the Lord declares in the New Covenant, "but I will write My will upon the table of your heart. Every day will be an adventure. Some days I might awaken you at 4:30 A.M. to seek My face and to pray, while other times, I might tell you to sleep in."

That's the way Christianity was meant to be. But what have we done? We have constructed legalistic systems and expectations both personally and corporately.

We were meant to live in a newness of the Spirit, moment by moment obeying, yielding, and asking, "Lord, what next?" Therefore, throw off the yoke of legalism. Walk in the Spirit. Respond to His direction—and I guarantee you will find yourself on the adventure of a lifetime!

Romans 7:7
What shall we say then? Is the law sin? God forbid. Nay, I had not known sin, but by the

law: for I had not known lust, except the law had said, Thou shalt not covet.

What was Paul lusting after? I suggest the object of Paul's desire was not the sensual type of sin we usually associate with lust. No, I believe Paul was lusting after prestige. He wanted to excel as a scholar—which seems a noble goal. Yet as he studied the law, I believe he saw that the underlying reason for his pursuit was a hunger for prominence.

Romans 7:8–10
But sin, taking occasion by the commandment, wrought in me all manner of concupiscence. For without the law sin was dead. For I was alive without the law once: but when the commandment came, sin revived, and I died. And the commandment, which was ordained to life, I found to be unto death.

The more Paul studied the law, the more he realized how far he was from the law.

I can recall a period of time when then four-year-old Peter-John would walk around whistling and snapping his fingers. "What are you doing, Pete?" I asked him one day.
"Practicing my snaps," he said. "I know how to whistle. I'm getting my snaps down. And when I learn how to tie my shoe, all the hard stuff will be done."

As he has since discovered, there's a little more to life than tying shoes and snapping fingers. So, too, Paul thought all he had to do was study the law, but the more he did, the more he realized how far he was from true spirituality.

Romans 7:11–13
For sin, taking occasion by the commandment, deceived me, and by it slew me. Wherefore the law is holy, and the commandment holy, and just, and good. Was then that which is good made death unto me? God forbid. But sin, that it might appear sin, working death in me by that which is good; that sin by the commandment might become exceeding sinful.

Whenever I sense a pharisaical tendency in myself, I know it is indicative that I have not been immersing myself in the Word. You see, if we're truly spending time in the presence of the Lord, we'll find ourselves saying just what Isaiah said. After spending the first five chapters of his book pronouncing woe on peoples and nations, in chapter 6, he saw the Lord and said, "Woe is *me*" for in the presence of the Lord he realized he was no better than those he was indicting.

A life lived in God's presence excludes judgment of others. "I'm lusting; I'm coveting," said Paul. But he didn't realize this until he spent time in the Scriptures and saw that he was a sinner. Now this was all pre-conversion. As evidenced by the use of the past tense, Paul was looking back. But as Chapter 7 unfolds, we see that even after he was saved, he still struggled.

Romans 7:14
For we know that the law is spiritual: but I am carnal, sold under sin.

As outlined in 1 Corinthians 2—3, there are basically three types of people. The natural man is what we all were before we were saved. The spiritual man is the one who is saved and who walks in the Spirit. The carnal man is born again but lives in the energy of his flesh. Therefore, although the carnal man can appear to be saintly and righteous, he is miserable internally because he knows he can't live up to the rules, regulations, and expectations he has placed upon himself. That's where Paul was. Yes, he was converted, but he was miserable in his carnality.

Romans 7:15
For that which I do I allow not: for what I would, that do I not; but what I hate, that do I.

"I want to do what's right," said Paul, "but I end up doing the things I hate." Ever feel that way, dieters?

Romans 7:16, 17
If then I do that which I would not, I consent unto the law that it is good. Now then it is no more I that do it, but sin that dwelleth in me.

"The problem isn't with the law," said Paul. "The problem is with the sin in *me*."

Romans 7:18 (a)
For I know that in me (that is, in my flesh,) dwelleth no good thing . . .

Whenever I'm disappointed in myself, it's because I'm denying what God said when He said, "Jon, in you dwells no good thing." I still struggle with this. I understand the concept theologically and can quote the verse from memory. But sometimes I think, *There's some good in me—isn't there? Am I really this bad, Father?*

Every time I get down on myself, I hear His voice again saying, "Jon, didn't I tell you straight out, didn't I record it in black and white that in your flesh, in you personally, dwells no good thing? Why, then, are you disappointed in yourself?"

Those who have a tendency to despair of life do so because they think there's something good in them that they're failing to utilize. They're not living up to their self-image. Although we want our kids to have high self-esteem, the Scriptures say, "Sorry. In you dwells no good thing." Far from depressing me, I am incredibly free when I finally understand this.

Romans 7:18 (b), 19
. . . for to will is present with me; but how to perform that which is good I find not. For the good that I would I do not: but the evil which I would not, that I do.

"How to perform I find not." Ever feel that way? Can you relate to Paul in his carnal state? I can!

Romans 7:20
Now if I do that I would not, it is no more I that do it, but sin that dwelleth in me.

Here's how to differentiate between a pig and a prodigal, between an unbeliever and a carnal Christian: Take the pig out of the pigpen, wash him in bubble bath, spray him with cologne, put a ribbon in his hair, a bow on his tail, and watch what happens the first time he sees some mud. The pig will wallow in it with joy. The prodigal, on the other hand, although he might foolishly find himself in the mud from time to time will not be comfortable there. Eventually, he'll come to his senses and say, "Get me out of here. I hate this stuff"—which is exactly where Paul was.

Romans 7:21–23 (a)
I find then a law, that, when I would do good, evil is present with me. For I delight in the law of God after the inward man: But I see another law in my members, warring against the law of my mind.

In my mind I want to follow the law of God. I want to walk in His ways and keep His commandments. That's truly my determination and my mind-set. But my body rebels. My eyes are prone toward lusting. My ears strain to hear something juicy. My tongue wags so readily to gossip. There's a war going on. How can I get victory?

Romans 7:23 (b), 24 (a)
. . . and bringing me into captivity to the law of sin which is in my members. O wretched man that I am!

When Paul was a natural man, the law slew him. When he became a believer, he found himself once again under legalism, with a war going on inside of him. The original translation of the last phrase of this verse sums up Paul's state perfectly: "O wretched man—me!"

Romans 7:24 (b)
Who shall deliver me from the body of this death?

In Paul's day, the sentence of a man convicted of first-degree murder could be to be tied to the body of his victim. Often, the stench alone would kill the murderer. It is possibly this Roman practice to which Paul is referring when he cries, "Who will free me from the failures, shortcomings, and sinful tendencies I'm forced to drag behind me wherever I go?"

Paul is now ready to lead us into an explosively liberating truth. In verse 18, he said, "How can I get victory?" After struggling a little longer, he realizes it's not "how." It's "*who.*" And he's only a verse or two away from the most exciting part of Romans because he's no longer looking for how. He realizes it's *Him. Many Christians are concerned with "how." "Please give us procedures, plans, and programs," they say, not realizing those things only produce perpetual struggle. The flesh always cries, "How?" The Bible always answers, "Him!"*

Romans 7:25
I thank God through Jesus Christ our Lord. So then with the mind I myself serve the law of God; but with the flesh the law of sin.

While we may readily agree with Paul that the answer lies not in a program or a procedure—it is harder for us to understand that neither is the answer found in a principle. At this point in my study of Romans, I can say, "Wow! I get it. The penalty for my sin was paid on the Cross. The power of my sin was broken by the Cross. Preoccupation with my sin is eliminated because of the Cross. I'm free! It's a principle I'm going to jot down in my journal, a principle in which I will rejoice."

But wait. Even as I have immersed myself in the Book of Romans, I've been on edge. When my temper has flared, I've been taken aback by the ugliness of my own flesh until the Lord dealt with my heart again, saying, "You *are* free. But you're missing out on what only I can produce as you spend time with Me. Even if you have the principles down and the theology right, without Me, there will be no self-control or peace, love or joy, gentleness or goodness, faith or meekness. Those only come from spending time with *Me."*

One morning, I was kneeling beside my bed in prayer. As I got up to let in some air, my finger got caught between the two windows. Now, although this was just the kind of irritation that had been getting to me, this time I didn't get upset at all. Why? It wasn't because I was reading a book on how not to get mad when your finger gets stuck in the window. No, it's because I was simply enjoying the Lord's presence.

Who shall deliver me? Not "How shall I be delivered theologically"—but "*Who* shall deliver me personally?" Like Paul, I declare to you experientially and emphatically that Jesus Christ is the key!

LOOSED FROM LEGALISM
A Topical Study of
Romans 7:1–4

Philosopher, social critic, and writer for *The London Daily Observer,* G. K. Chesterton was addressed by a woman who wrote a letter asking him to write a series of articles explaining what was wrong with the world. The following day, Chesterton penned this classic reply: "Madam, I will tell you what is wrong with the world in two words: I am."

What's wrong with the world? I am. Not a political problem, or an economic situation, the real reason for the problems of the world is you and me personally.

And what is responsible for the problems within us? Sin. Sin *in* us causes problems to come pouring out *from* us, which affects the world *around* us. Sin is the problem. Sin is the issue.

In our culture, people don't want to talk about sin. When he was nearing the end of his illustrious career, Dr. Karl Meninger, the brilliant psychiatrist and prolific author, wrote one final book in which he appraised the psychiatric health of the nation. In this book, entitled *Whatever Happened To Sin?* he concluded that the problem with our culture is that we have forgotten the word "sin."

We call people "dysfunctional" or "victims," but Meninger maintained the real issue is just plain sin. Some may extol the power of positive thinking, but the apostle Paul declares it to be no match for the destructiveness of sin. Thus, because Paul tackles the root issue head-on, I find those who propose only positive thinking appalling, but the apostle Paul very appealing.

"The power of sin brings destruction," wrote Paul in Romans 6:20, 21. It's true. Everything I'm ashamed of in my life is always directly linked to sin. Yet the preoccupation with sin only brings depression and exhaustion.

> It's like two guys riding a tandem bike uphill. After what seems like an eternity, they finally reach the top and the guy in front says, "Man, I didn't think we would ever make it to the top. I thought we'd end up rolling back down."
>
> "Me too," answers the guy in back. "That's why I kept the brakes on the whole time."

The same thing happens to Christians. "I get it," we say. "I see what Paul is saying. I don't want to fall back down the hill. I don't want to roll back into carnality, so I'll put the brakes on. I'll put rules and regulations around myself in order that I might not sin." But the rules and regulations we think will break our fall into sin only lead us to exhaustion and depression as we discover we are unable to keep them.

In Romans 7, Paul deals with this very issue as he likens the relationship between the law and the believer to the relationship between a husband and wife.

Mr. Perfect

> You wake up. Lying next to you is your husband, Mr. Perfect. His breath is mint-fresh and not a single hair is out of place. His pajamas are pressed, and even the sheet over him is unruffled. He's perfect, and he's your hubby! "Good morning," he says as he gives you a perfect peck on the cheek. Then, with amazing energy, he bounds out of bed with a smile on his face, goes to his closet, and takes out his perfectly tailored suit with his perfectly white starched shirt, and perfectly matched tie. He dresses himself impeccably, puts his belt

around his perfect-sized waist, and goes into the kitchen to make his breakfast. He has no coffee, no sweet rolls, no eggs, and no cholesterol. He has granola with skim milk, and tomato juice to drink. Finished with breakfast, he picks up his bowl, rinses it out, puts it in the dishwasher, and sets the timer. Then he gives you another peck on the cheek, and out the door he goes to work.

He drives perfectly—not one mile over the speed limit, nor one mile under, stopping for pedestrians along the way. At work, he fulfills his tasks to the letter. Then, at 5:00—not 4:59, not 5:01 he finishes cleaning up his spotless desk, walks to his car, and drives home. As you greet him at the door, you're again amazed that you had the good fortune to marry Mr. Perfect. But as he walks into the house, he stops and looks at you rather quizzically. You realize he's looking at your hair because there's a strand out of place. Then he goes into the kitchen, and, being a perfect six feet four inches tall, he notices dust on top of the refrigerator. "How can this be?" he wonders.

Panic begins to fill your heart, and anguish begins to set in until you remember that you fixed a fabulous meal. As he sits down to dinner, you bring out the six-course meal you prepared, the aroma filling the room. But as you uncover the entree, you realize your husband, Mr. Perfect, is staring at the parsley, which, to your dismay, looks a bit wilted. As he reaches for something to drink, your heart sinks as you see a spot on his glass. The evening goes downhill from there, and you go to bed, thinking, *Yes, I'm married to Mr. Perfect—but he's driving me crazy.*

This goes on until you become filled with so much tension and anxiety that you decide it was a mistake to marry Mr. Perfect. "I want a divorce," you say.

"On what grounds?" asks the judge.

"My husband is perfect," you answer.

"Request denied," declares the judge. "Perfection is not grounds for divorce."

You go your way thinking you can't last a moment longer, when suddenly you remember Romans 7:2, 3, which says that the woman is bound to her husband only so long as he is alive. So the next day, as he's reading the paper, you pour a bottle of arsenic into your husband's celery juice. You wait with anticipation as he takes a sip and two and three. Your anticipation turns to amazement as he asks for seconds—until you remember that he's in perfect health. His kidneys filter out the poison totally.

"Oh no," you say. "I can't divorce him because he's perfect. He won't die because he's perfect. I'm stuck in this bondage forever. And in your despair, you slam the door behind you as you walk out into the rain. You return half an hour later sniffling, sneezing, and coughing; and you know you're coming down with pneumonia. Your lungs start to fill with fluid. Your temperature rises. You get sicker and sicker—and you realize you're dying.

As you let go of your life, you say to yourself, "This is the way out. I'm finally free. Mr. Perfect couldn't be divorced. Mr. Perfect wouldn't die. But I'm dying. And that sets me free to marry another one—Mr. Love—Who's waiting for me in heaven."

On the basis of Jesus' words in Matthew 5:18, like Mr. Perfect, the law will never die. Because of this, the law looms over us continually, ever making us aware of our imperfections and inconsistencies. We can't live with it. We can't divorce it. We can't kill it. "There's only one way out," says Paul in Romans. "And when you discover it, you're free!"

You see, folks, the penalty for sin was paid on the Cross (Romans 1—5). The power of sin was broken by the Cross (Romans 6). The preoccupation with sin is solved through the Cross (Romans 7:4–6). You are no longer married to the rules and regulations of the law. Why? Is the law dead? No. You are (Galatians 2:20).

You've died to Mr. Perfection—and you're linked to Mr. Love. Consequently, you're free from roller-coaster spirituality.

Mr. Love

In the years when I thought I was still married to Mr. Law, even though I was a Christian, I set up rules and regulations, disciplines and expectations. When I kept them, I would look down on other Christians who didn't, thinking, *What time did* he *get up for devotions this morning?* And I would walk around like a self-righteous prude inside.

But invariably, I couldn't keep my own rules and regulations. I'd sleep late one morning, or two, or three—and then what happened? I plummeted into depression. "Woe is me," I'd say. "I'm such a wretch. I can't go to church. Why should I even read the Bible? I'll just watch TV all day."

Up and down I went until I understood that Paul said, "The rules and standards you set up to prove you're a good little Christian are all irrelevant."

That is why, when people say Christianity is narrow and restrictive, I respond, "You're not reading your Bible. Jesus represented such radical *freedom* that the only way the religious community could contain Him was to kill Him."

"All things are lawful—but all things are not expedient," wrote Paul (see 1 Corinthians 6:12). In other words, "I'm not going to jeopardize this glorious liberty I have, this wonderful freedom I enjoy by becoming enslaved to any substance, habit, or activity. I'm free not to sin, even though all things are lawful to me." Then he went on to say, "All things are lawful for me—but not all things edify" (see 1 Corinthians 10:23). In other words, "Even though I have liberty to do all things, seeing me do certain things might cause someone else to become entangled. So I choose not to do those things which will cause others to stumble."

Forget your regulations, your rules, your external stipulations, saint. You're free in Christ totally and completely. You're married now to Mr. Love. When we understand this, what happens? We no longer live by rules written down on a list, or by commandments etched in stone, but by the Word written in our hearts (Romans 7:6). If you have rules written down in your journal or Bible, perhaps you're dangerously close to falling into the Old Covenant—into legalism. You may pride yourself when you keep them and turn up your spiritual nose at others who aren't as devoted or as committed as you, but watch out. Exhaustion and depression are inevitable.

"But," you protest, "if we're no longer married to the law, we'll do all kinds of bad stuff."

Not true. Your own experience tells you differently.

As a sixteen-year-old, washing the family car was one of my Saturday chores. The law was laid down, and I followed it: I squirted some water on our green Buick Skylark, flung a towel over it a couple times, and went on my way. But that all changed when I thought I fell in love with a girl named Stephanie. You see, because Dad gave me permission one weekend to use the Skylark to take Stephanie out to dinner, I washed it, dried it, waxed it, buffed it, shined the chrome, polished the hubcaps, vacuumed the interior, and washed the windows. I transformed the Skylark into a thing of beauty. Why? Because of love—for while the law made me wash the car, love made me do the rest.

So, too, when you really grasp what Jesus Christ did for you and how much He cares about you, it's no longer, "I gotta have devotions,"—but, "I get to talk with You today, Lord." And you end up doing much more than you ever did with your rules, regulations, and tradition-based Christianity. You're free because the Lord whispers in your heart, in the newness of the Spirit day by day, moment by moment.

"You don't want to be with those kids. They're walking in a way that will be damaging to you."

"Okay, Lord," you say. "Thanks for the tip."

"You don't want to go into that place. There's a bunch of stuff coming down there that's really ugly."

"Okay, thanks, Lord."

Folks, the law says, "Responsibility!" Love says, "Just respond to Me." It's wonderful. From day to day, I never know what lies ahead as the Lord guides me in the newness of the Spirit rather than the oldness of the letter.

"I'm glad my kids aren't here," you say, "because if Junior hears that all things are lawful, that there are no rules and regulations—I'm in real trouble."

This brings up a valid question. What about kids who are unruly, or criminals in our society? Paul says although the law is not made for a righteous man—for a guy who's in love with the Lord, walking close to the Lord, desiring to please the Lord—it is made for the lawless, the disobedient, the ungodly (1 Timothy 1:8–9). Those who don't care about the Lord need the law laid upon them for their own protection. Thus, the law has a two-fold purpose. It keeps the unrighteous from rampant sin and drives the self-righteous to Jesus Christ.

"If the law's sole purpose in the life of a believer is to drive us to Christ, then why even bother reading the Old Testament with all of its ordinances and regulations?"

Because each ordinance, each statute, each Old Testament picture points to Jesus and gives us a clearer picture of Him (Luke 24:27). Consider, for example, the Sabbath. There are those who say things like, "If you don't worship on Saturday, you're violating the law."

Like Paul, our answer can be, "Sabbaths and all of those regulations are simply a shadow of the reality of the Person of Jesus Christ" (see Colossians 2:16, 17). Folks, there are people in "church-ianity," in legalism, who are caught up in the shadows when the reality is Christ. You see, *He* is our Sabbath. *He* is our Rest. *He* is the Reality.

Not only is Jesus the reality of the law, but there is practicality for us in the law. That is why Jesus said, "The Sabbath was made for man's benefit. It was given to you by the Father in order that you might have a day of rest and relaxation. But you've turned it into a responsibility and an obligation" (Mark 2:27). When you look at the law, listen to the heart of the Father. Don't get caught up in the technicalities. When you read the Old Testament, say, "Lord, show me something about You and something practical for me."

Precious brother, dear sister—my prayer for you today is a very simple one: that God would keep you from the depression and exhaustion that are the result of a preoccupation with rules and regulations, obligations and stipulations—that you might know what it means to be dead to Mr. Perfect and married to Another who loves you unconditionally and will lead you day by day in joy and liberty.

8 If anyone is wrestling with depression, I have good news for you: You're in the right place, for Romans 8 is the true antidote for depression. You see, when a person is going through depression, it is always in one of three areas. He is either haunted by something in his past, anxious about something in his future, or weighed down by something presently.

Romans 8 is the perfect solution for each of these situations. Verse 1 declares there is no condemnation concerning the past. Verses 38, 39 promise there can be no separation from God's love in the future. And verse 28 states that all things are working together for good in the present. Now, if we believe this, there's no room for depression, and if we'll embrace it,

we'll experience an alleviation of the depressed spirit that inflicts us so easily. Perhaps that is why Dr. Donald Barnhouse said that whenever a believer's Bible accidentally falls on the floor, it should automatically open to Romans 8.

Romans 8:1 (a)
There is therefore now no condemnation . . .

To the woman taken in the act of adultery, Jesus said, "Where are thine accusers? Go your way and sin no more" (see John 8:10, 11).

So, too, when, in naked honesty, you say to the Lord, "I know I'm a sinner, but I realize You are my Savior and that what You did on the Cross is sufficient to pay the price for my sin," then you can go your way free.

"Wait a minute," you protest. "Yes, Jesus said,

'Go your way,' but He also said, 'and sin no more.' *That's* the key."

Listen, precious people. I don't believe Jesus' tone with the woman taken in adultery was, "I'll let you off the hook this time, lady. But if it happens again, you'll be in big trouble." No, I believe His tone was, "Go your way a free woman. By the Word I'm sharing with you, and the love I'm showing to you, I'm giving you liberation from your tendency to indulge your flesh, and freeing you to live in an entirely different lifestyle." And I believe there was a smile on His face, not a finger in her face as He said it.

Romans 8:1 (b)
. . . to them which are in Christ Jesus . . .

We're *in* Christ Jesus, folks. That's the key. The Lord said to Noah, "Rooms shalt thou make in the ark and thou shalt pitch it within and without with pitch" (Genesis 6:14). The word "pitch" is the same word used in the Old Testament for "atonement," so the ark is a perfect picture of our salvation, for when the rain began to fall, the Lord shut Noah and his family *in* (Genesis 7:16).

He didn't say, "I'm going to put eight pegs on the outside of the ark, Noah. You and your family are to hang on for dear life, and as long as you hang on, you'll make it through." No, He said, "I'm going to put you *in*." And the same is true of us. It's not a matter of holding on, hoping that if we can keep from sinning, we'll be okay. No, our Ark is Jesus Christ; and we are *in* Him. Therefore, there is no condemnation. No matter how rough the seas might be or how heavy the rain comes down, we're sealed, safe, and secure.

A friend came by one day with a couple boxes of Häagen-Dazs bars—the dark chocolate-covered ones—my favorites. Now, if you've ever read the ingredients on the side panel of a Häagen-Dazs box, you know they're sinful. And yet that sinfully delicious Häagen-Dazs is now hidden and buried in me. You no longer see it.

So, too—you are *in* Christ—with all of your sinful tendencies, calories, and fat grams. Thus, when the Father looks on you, He doesn't see you with all of your failings and shortcomings. No, He sees you robed with the righteousness of Christ Jesus (Isaiah 61:10). He doesn't see you in your sin; He sees you in His Son. Therefore, there's no condemnation whatsoever. Regardless of where you've been or how badly you've failed, regardless of who you are or where you are, there is *no* condemnation.

Romans 8:1 (c)
. . . who walk not after the flesh, but after the Spirit.

After realizing that only Jesus could set him free from the demands and the expectations of the law (Romans 7), Paul explodes with this understanding, as we'll see him mention the Spirit *nineteen* times in chapter 8.

Romans 8:2
For the law of the Spirit of life in Christ Jesus hath made me free from the law of sin and death.

The law of sin and death is comprised of three forces working in conjunction with each other: Satan, the flesh, and the world. Now, in my own energy, I can take on any two. But I'm doomed by the combination of three. You see, if Satan and the world system were alive and well—but if I didn't have a body, sin would have no pull on me. If I had a body and was in the world—but there was no Satan, there would be no problem because, as the prince of this world (John 12:31), it is Satan who activates the world system that plays on my flesh. If I had a body and Satan was present—but there was no world system, Satan could not have access to me, because he would have no way to influence me. It is because I have a body and live in a world controlled by Satan that, without the Lord, I am subject to the law of sin and death.

If you go to the airport, you'll see planes sitting on the runway. They're not going anywhere because the law of gravity is keeping them on the ground. But as soon as their engines are turned on, the law of aerodynamics takes over. Although gravity is still in effect and still pulls on the planes, there's a higher law, a more powerful force at work that allows them to overcome the law of gravity. That's what Paul is saying. We're free from this law of sin and death by possibility thinking? No. By positive mental imaging? No. We're free by the Spirit of Jesus Christ. He lives *in* us, enabling us to fly high and overcome the law of sin and death.

Romans 8:3, 4
For what the law could not do, in that it was weak through the flesh, God sending his own Son in the likeness of sinful flesh, and for sin, condemned sin in the flesh: That the righteousness of the law might be fulfilled in us, who walk not after the flesh, but after the Spirit.

The weakness of the law lies in the fact that we can't keep it. Folks, you can write, "I'm going to pray three hours every morning" in your journal. You can post, "I will read my Bible three hours every night" on your fridge, But sooner or later, you'll find the weakness lies not in those commitments, but in your own flesh. That's why Paul rejoices that God took care of the matter by sending His own Son—that the righteousness of the law might be fulfilled not by us, but in us, as the Spirit guides us spontaneously, leads us daily, corrects us constantly, and frees us practically.

Romans 8:5, 6
For they that are after the flesh do mind the things of the flesh; but they that are after the Spirit the things of the Spirit. For to be carnally minded is death; but to be spiritually minded is life and peace.

The question then becomes, "Paul if this is so, if there's no condemnation, if we're free from rules and regulations, then why shouldn't I just continue in my carnal tendencies and fleshly activities?"

"Because," Paul would say, "to be carnally minded is death."

Want to know how to experience the stench of death in your life? Live carnally. What does it mean to live carnally? Jesus associated it with Gentiles who were concerned with nothing more than what they would eat, what they would wear, and where they would go (Matthew 6:31, 32). A carnal person asks, "Where can we eat now? What new hobby can we enjoy? What vacation can we take?"

You see, we think living in the flesh is synonymous with committing blatant sins. But in reality, to live in the flesh simply means to give priority to the things of the material realm. Why is that death? Because man was created in the image of God. Since God is a Trinity—Father, Son and Spirit—He created man as lesser trinity of spirit, soul, and body. The spirit is the deepest part of you, the "real" you. The soul is your mind and emotions. The body is the thing you live in temporarily. When God created man, there was a beautiful connection between the spirit of man and the Spirit of God as Adam and God walked together in the Garden of Eden in the cool of the day (Genesis 3:8). But when Adam gave in to his flesh and ate the forbidden fruit, he allowed his body—the material aspect of his nature—to assume predominance over his spirit, thereby severing his direct communion with God's Spirit.

Romans 8:7, 8
Because the carnal mind is enmity against God: for it is not subject to the law of God,
neither indeed can be. So then they that are in the flesh cannot please God.

With the soul—the mind—lodged between the spirit and the flesh, the question becomes one of what will control my mind. Will it be the spirit, as my spirit is linked to God's Spirit? As the day unfolds, will I be a spiritual man? Or will I be carnal, wondering, *Where am I going to go? How am I going to be entertained? What am I going to eat?* Truly, if my body controls my thoughts, I am carnally minded and cannot please God.

What's life about? wondered Solomon. *It must be about money.* So he gathered so much gold that even silver had no value in his kingdom. Ever notice how it is the wealthy people in our society who oftentimes end up taking drugs? Why is this? Because the ones who hit the top find out money isn't the answer, whereas the rest of us think that if we could just make more money, work harder, or invest more wisely we would be happy. Solomon knew better. He had more money than he knew what to do with, and still wasn't happy—so he thought happiness must lie in women.

He amassed one thousand wives and concubines, but he found they weren't the answer either. "Happiness must be found in intellectual pursuit," he decided. So he became a botanist, a biologist, an ichthyologist. He became so knowledgeable that he penned books by the hundreds. And he became philosophical to such a degree that people traveled from all over the world to hear him share his proverbs. But, after all of this he concluded that much study wearies the flesh (Ecclesiastes 12:12). The answer must be in partying, he thought. So he imported peacocks and apes from Africa, and made sure wine flowed freely during parties so lavish they would make Hollywood jealous. But it was still empty in his eyes. Deciding the answer to his restlessness must lie in power, he built his empire to be the most powerful empire of his day. Yet he remained empty.

Poor Solomon. Put yourself in his golden sandals. What frustration! All the power he could ever want, more money than he could even count, one thousand of the most beautiful women at his beck and call, endless parties, education, philosophy—he had it all. But here was his dilemma: Nothing satisfied. Whereas the average person thinks, *I'm almost happy. If I can just get a bigger house, or a newer car, I know I'll be happy,* Solomon was stuck. He was at the top. There was no bigger car to buy, no other woman to go after, no higher investment to make. He was at the top and he said, "It's empty."

And here little Paul comes along with his

bowed legs, hooked nose, and bald head, saying, "It's real simple. To be carnally minded is death—but to be spiritually minded is life and peace."

Brother Solomon finally did figure it out. After approximately twelve years of women, money, power, and philosophy, he said, "Let us hear the conclusion of the whole matter: Fear God, and keep his commandments; for this is the whole duty of man" (see Ecclesiastes 12:13). And from that time on, Solomon was known as "the preacher."

I ask you this question: What has been ruling your soul? Has it been your flesh, or has it been God's Spirit? If you're going to pursue the material and live for your flesh, you'll never be satisfied. But if you live for the Spirit, you'll know life and peace eternally and presently.

Romans 8:9 (a)
But ye are not in the flesh, but in the Spirit, if so be that the Spirit of God dwell in you.

The word "dwell" means "to be at home." Is the Spirit of God at home in you? If you're a believer, He's in you—without question. But is He *at home* in your life? Can He just kick back in the easy chair of your heart and say, "I'm so glad to be in your life; I'm so glad you're Mine"? Or do you take Him to activities, listen to conversations, and involve yourself in that which makes Him uneasy?

In writing about a believer who joined himself to a harlot, Paul said he was joining Christ Himself to the harlot (1 Corinthians 6:15). So, too, I suggest to you that, in these immoral days in which we live, Christians all too often force the Lord into activities of which He wants no part. Would you think about this the next time you turn on TV, listen to gossip, or go to a movie? Praise the Lord, there's no condemnation (Romans 8:1)—but there must be a realization of what's going on.

Romans 8:9 (b)
Now if any man have not the Spirit of Christ, he is none of his.

Although the Spirit may not be comfortable in your life, if you are a Christian, He is still in you. However, if Christ is not in you, you're not saved.

Romans 8:10, 11
And if Christ be in you, the body is dead because of sin; but the Spirit is life because of righteousness. But if the Spirit of him that raised up Jesus from the dead dwell in you, he that raised up Christ from the dead shall also quicken your mortal bodies by his Spirit that dwelleth in you.

How are we to deal with these sinful tendencies, these carnal activities, habits and thoughts? Paul gives us the key: The Spirit of Him that raised up Jesus from the dead is in us, and He'll live His life through us.

Romans 8:12, 13
Therefore, brethren, we are debtors, not to the flesh, to live after the flesh. For if ye live after the flesh, ye shall die: but if ye through the Spirit do mortify the deeds of the body, ye shall live.

"I must mortify the deeds of the body," some people say. "I've got to crucify my flesh"—but it's impossible to crucify yourself. If you lie down on a cross and pound a nail through your wrist, even if you somehow endure the pain, you're only half crucified because you can't pound in the other nail. How do you mortify the deeds of the flesh? There's only one way: through the Spirit.

After capturing the ark of the covenant, the Philistines placed it in the temple of their fish god, Dagon. The next morning, the Philistine priests got up to find Dagon had fallen down before the Ark (1 Samuel 5:3). They stood Dagon up and went their way. The next morning, they came in again, and there was Dagon, facedown on the floor, with his head and hands cut off. Now, at this point, you would think the priests would have said, "Something's fishy here. This isn't working." But, instead, they chose to side with Dagon. They stood him up, patched him together, and said, "The ark's gotta go."

Precious people, the way to gain victory over whatever it is you're struggling with is not to try to topple Dagon, but to bring in the ark, for the ark represents the presence of God. Whatever your Dagon might be, bring in the Spirit of the Lord. How? Just love the Lord. Get up tomorrow morning and before your feet hit the ground, drop to your knees, and give your life to Him. When He whispers in your heart during your coffee break, "Pull away and talk with Me," do it. When you're deciding which dial to press on your radio during lunch, just do what the Spirit tells you to do. Allow the Spirit of God to fill your heart, and you know what will happen? You'll lose interest in the stuff that dominated and controlled you—not because you wrestled with Dagon, but because you brought in the ark.

That's why Romans 8 is so thrilling! Too many believers are trying to fight evil habits and tendencies on their own—and it's exhausting. If you walk into a dark room, you don't scream, karate chop, give teachings about, or rebuke the darkness. You turn on the light.

Romans 8:14
For as many as are led by the Spirit of God, they are the sons of God.

Just as the Spirit of God gives you victory over the flesh, the Spirit of God will give you guidance in life. People struggle so hard with finding God's will, yet it's so simple.

When asked how to find the will of God, Augustine simply said, "It's real simple. Love the Lord and do whatever you want." How could he say this? Because if we love the Lord, Psalm 37 says the Spirit will change the desires of our heart to conform to His will.

Romans 8:15, 16
For ye have not received the spirit of bondage again to fear; but ye have received the Spirit of adoption, whereby we cry, Abba, Father. The Spirit itself beareth witness with our spirit, that we are the children of God.

The word "Abba" is Aramaic for "Papa." When my youngest son Benjamin says "Dad, what do you want me to do today?" my answer is not, "I'm not going to tell you." Yet that's the way a lot of people see God. They think He gets a kick out of keeping us in the dark as long as possible.
"No," says Paul. "By the spirit of adoption, God is our papa. Therefore, there's no need to fear."

Romans 8:17, 18
And if children, then heirs; heirs of God, and joint-heirs with Christ; if so be that we suffer with him, that we may be also glorified together. For I reckon that the sufferings of this present time are not worthy to be compared with the glory which shall be revealed in us.

Many years ago, we adopted our cat Gabriel *into* our family. From that point on, he had to be adapted *for* our family. That is, he had to learn not to use Peter's bed for his litter box, not to climb on the curtains, not to claw the couch. So, too, as adopted sons, the suffering we experience presently is for the purpose of adapting us spiritually and will one day disappear totally in light of the glory we will partake of eternally.

Romans 8:19
For the earnest expectation of the creature waiteth for the manifestation of the sons of God.

There are groups who teach that in the end times the "manifested sons of God" will be super-saints who will not have struggles or problems like others, but will exist on a different level than the rest of us. "Join us," say these groups, "and you, too, can be one of the manifested sons of God."

I have a real problem with this interpretation because the Bible never even hints at such heresy. Who, then, are the manifested sons of God? We are (1 John 3:1, 2). The manifestation of the sons of God will take place when Jesus comes back, when we see Him, when we are made like Him, and when, at last we will be the kind of people we've longed to be.

Romans 8:20
For the creature was made subject to vanity, not willingly, but by reason of him who hath subjected the same in hope.

The word "vanity" means "emptiness." Pascal was right when he said there is a God-shaped vacuum in the heart of every man, for here, Paul tells us the creature was made subject to vanity, or emptiness. Man has a hole in his heart—and although we try to fill that hole with materialism, sexual experience, or recreation, nothing can fill the emptiness but God.

I once read a story of a goose who chose a mailbox for a mate after its partner died when it was accidentally run over by a snowmobile. The goose flailed wildly at the letter carrier and nipped at anyone who came to get the mail from the box. It stood by the box night and day. Finally, the goose itself died, standing guard next to its chosen mate—the mailbox.

A lot of people are looking for something to satisfy them, some relationship to fulfill them. But in the end, we all find that anything short of God is a mailbox.

Romans 8:21, 22
Because the creature itself also shall be delivered from the bondage of corruption into the glorious liberty of the children of God. For we know that the whole creation groaneth and travaileth in pain together until now.

Creation is hurting. Julie Andrews notwithstanding, the hills may be alive with the sound of music—but they're singing in a minor key. Why?

Because all creation was cursed when man sinned in the Garden of Eden. Consequently, the more you study nature, along with its beauty, the more you see its cruelty. We enjoy the delicate flower, but shudder at the devastating flood. Earthquakes and tornadoes, thunder and avalanche are as much a part of nature as gentle streams and peaceful meadows. That is why nature groans and waits for the day when the King comes back and for the day when the trees of the field will clap their hands (Isaiah 55:12).

Romans 8:23–25
And not only they, but ourselves also, which have the firstfruits of the Spirit, even we ourselves groan within ourselves, waiting for the adoption, to wit, the redemption of our body. For we are saved by hope: but hope that is seen is not hope: for what a man seeth, why doth he yet hope for? But if we hope for that we see not, then do we with patience wait for it.

Not only does nature groan environmentally, but we groan internally. Do you ever wake up in the morning, look in the mirror, and just groan? Our bodies are wearing out, folks. They're not what they once were—but, praise the Lord, they're not what they one day will be.

Romans 8:26, 27
Likewise the Spirit also helpeth our infirmities: for we know not what we should pray for as we ought: but the Spirit itself maketh intercession for us with groanings which cannot be uttered. And he that searcheth the hearts knoweth what is the mind of the Spirit, because he maketh intercession for the saints according to the will of God.

I spent some time with a man in his early thirties who was on his deathbed. The body of this young man, once a good athlete and a vibrant father, was racked by cancer. His family asked, "Why doesn't the Lord just take him home? Why the suffering? We prayed for his healing and that didn't happen. What's the Father doing?"

I understood the family saying, "Take him home." But what if, in these final days of our brother's difficulty and suffering, the Father is putting on the final touches of the inner person, shaping and molding what he will be for the next billion years in heaven? Is that what's happening? I don't know, for, like Paul, I know not how to pray. The only thing I do know is that I don't know.

Let us ever remember that while prayer is to be directed to God, it is not to be directing God. Most people, at least for part of their pilgrimage,

try to direct the Lord, thinking that's what prayer is about. "Let me explain the situation, Lord. Here's what you need to do," we say with great authority and audacity.

"We know not how to pray," said Paul.

Someone comes to us and says, "Pray I'll get the job." "Pray this project will prosper." Wait a minute. So many things I thought would be wonderful have proven to be detrimental, a distraction, and a curse. Conversely, so many things I thought would be terrible have proven to be a huge blessing.

The same is true nationally. It might be that the Lord wants to close us down. That's a possibility. Maybe the best thing that could happen to our country would be a collapse economically, politically, or militarily—because that's what it might take to heal us spiritually. I don't know. I'm not God. Therefore, I'm not going to give Him direction on what He should or should not do. Instead, I just groan, "Lord, You see what's going on in the nation. You see what's going on with that person. You see what's going on in our congregation. I don't know how to pray. I don't know what Your will is. But I just give it all to You to work out according to Your perfect and beautiful plan."

Now, if we don't know how to pray, then why pray at all? Understand this: Prayer is not getting my will done in heaven. Prayer is getting God's will done on earth. It's not me giving directions to the Father, but rather me saying, "Father, direct me. I open the door for You to work. I hold up this need for You. I place this situation in Your hand." I do this all through prayer because the Word tells us that God has chosen to work through the vehicle of prayer. And if we do not pray we will limit what He would do, what He could do, what He desires to do (James 4:2).

Therefore, if I don't pray, I will never know if God got His way with Peter-John, this congregation, or our nation. But if I do pray and say, "Lord, here's the situation. I'm not directing You, but I'm just looking to You to have Your will done"—then I can be at peace. Whatever happens, I know I played my part; I opened the door, and since the Father knows best, I can rest. The Spirit groans through me, the Son intercedes for me, and the Father will do what's right concerning me. But if I don't pray, I'll always wonder if things would have been different if I had.

Romans 8:28
And we know that all things work together for good to them that love God, to them who are the called according to his purpose.

We usually rewrite Romans 8:28 to read: "*Most* things," or "*some* things work together for good."

Paul says even though there's groaning and suffering as we're being adapted for heaven, know this: It's *all* working for good."

"We *know* all things work together for good," said Paul. You see, it's not something we have to learn—it's something the Spirit witnesses in our hearts. No matter what's coming down, no matter what's going on—we know innately that all things are working together for good."

Jacob declared just the opposite. Famine was in the land. His wife, Rachel, was dead. He thought his beloved son, Joseph, was dead as well. His oldest son, Simeon, was being held hostage in Egypt. And the man in charge was saying, "I will give you no more supplies until you bring your youngest son, Benjamin, to Egypt." It was more than Jacob could bear.

"All things are working against me," he said (see Genesis 42:36). But then what happened?

In the succeeding chapter, he did, indeed, send Benjamin to Egypt. Why? I suggest it was because even though he was murmuring, complaining, and doubting, Jacob knew Benjamin would come back, that things would work out, that everything would be okay. Otherwise, he never would have allowed Benjamin to go.

So, too, in the times we have, like Jacob, said, "Everything's working against me," even then we knew that wasn't true.

That's why Paul said, "We know"—not "I want you to know," not "I'm going to teach you"—but "We already know that all things are working for good." By the Spirit we know this intuitively, and by our experience, we see how God has worked everything together for good previously. Therefore, we can trust Him to keep working for our good—and for His glory.

For topical study of Romans 8:28 entitled "It's All for Good," turn to page 946.

Romans 8:29, 30 (a)
For whom he did foreknow, he also did predestinate to be conformed to the image of his Son, that he might be the firstborn among many brethren. Moreover whom he did predestinate, them he also called . . .

Suppose you had absolute foreknowledge. For you, playing the lottery wouldn't be gambling because you could pick the winning numbers with absolute certainty. The same is true for God. When He predestined you before the world began, He knew you would make it (Philippians 1:6). Folks, God is not in heaven biting His nails saying, "Boy, I hope that gang makes it." No, God foreknows, then He predestines, calls, justifies, and glorifies. It is tremendous news to me that when God looks at me, He sees a winner.

Now, although He has predestined us, concerning His people, God says, "I'm choosing you. I'm going before you. I'm guaranteeing victory to you, but it's not because of your righteousness, for you are a stiffnecked people" (see Deuteronomy 9:6). In other words, the Lord was saying, "I know what you are. So when you come into the Promised Land and experience victories, watch out that you don't think they're because of your righteousness or spirituality. No, you are a stiffnecked, hard-hearted, uncircumcised people. However, knowing you are but dust (and some are a lot dustier than others!)—I have compassion on you" (see Psalm 103:14).

I know God loves me. He's elected me. Therefore, He's going to see me through and usher me into eternity. At the same time, however, I recognize it's not because of my righteousness or anything I am or have done that causes Him to elect me into the kingdom. Quite the contrary. We are all trophies of His grace. Angels will scratch their heads with their wings and marvel perpetually at the grace and goodness God demonstrated in choosing a guy like me. You see, wanting to illustrate His grace to all of creation through all of the ages to come, the Father chose not righteous people, but sinners and rebels and stiffnecked people like you and me.

"I don't get down on myself," said Paul. "I did that in my Romans 7 days when I was under the law—religion, rules, and regulations. But now I realize I am a trophy of His grace, and that He, by His goodness and because of His big-heartedness, chose people like me in order that all of eternity might marvel at His mercy."

"If a person is indeed predestined, what choice does he have?" you ask. "What about free will?"

Picture with me two chess players. One is a master, the world's best. He knows hundreds of opening and closing moves. Having only learned to play a week ago, the other player forgets which way the pawn goes and how the horse hops. These two players are engaged in a match, the master and the novice. Now, the novice has free will. He can move wherever he wants. But, by playing against the master, he's going to find that any move he makes is countered brilliantly. In the end, he will find himself boxed into a corner, surrounded by the master's men. Thus, although the novice is exercising his freedom, he really doesn't have a chance.

The same is true, as it relates to our freewill vs. God's election and predestination. Man has free will—but he's boxed in because the Master will inevitably corner those He chooses and bring them into the kingdom.

"That's great," you say, "if you're part of the chosen. What about the person who's not elected?" Jesus said,

> He that believeth on him is not condemned: but he that believeth not is condemned already, because he hath not believed in the name of the only begotten Son of God. And this is the condemnation, that light is come into the world, and men loved darkness rather than light, because their deeds were evil. For every one that doeth evil hateth the light, neither cometh to the light, lest his deeds should be reproved.
> John 3:18–20

You see, the singular issue concerning predestination is neither intellectual nor theological. It's moral. Through His foreknowledge, God sees the person who wants to continue to walk in darkness—and doesn't choose him. So, too, before the foundation of the world, He saw those who, like you, wanted to walk in light—and chose them.

Romans 8:30 (b)
. . . and whom he called, them he also justified . . .

As we saw in Romans 5, "justified" means "just as if I never sinned."

Romans 8:30 (c)
. . . and whom he justified, them he also glorified.

The word "glorified" is in the aorist tense—meaning it's taking place right now. This is great news! You see, Paul didn't say, "Whom He justified, them He will glorify." No, he said, "Whom He justified, them He is glorifying right now." Why? Because God—who transcends the time/space continuum, God who is light, God who lives in the eternal now—sees our glorified state as if it has already taken place.

What is the implication for us? Suppose you knew the person sitting next to you was about to inherit fifty billion dollars next week. Not only that, but he would have the heart of a philanthropist as well. Wouldn't you be just a tad bit nicer to him? Understand this: The one you're sitting next to is richer than that. He or she is a joint-heir with Christ (Romans 8:17).

From our vantage point, we all have a long way to go. But from God's perspective, our glorification is a done deal. Therefore, before we pick on

one another, it would be wise to stop and look at one another through our Father's eyes.

Romans 8:31 (a)
What shall we then say to these things?

In light of the fact that there's no condemnation to those who are in Christ Jesus, in light of the fact that everything is working out for our good because of Christ, in light of the fact that we are already glorified from God's perspective, Paul finds himself speechless.

When Nathan told David that, although he wouldn't be able to build a temple for the Lord, the Lord wanted to establish His royal line through David, David was amazed. "What can I say?" he said (see 2 Samuel 7:18–20)—which was quite a question for David to ask, considering the psalmist had a way with words, and was perhaps more skilled in expression than anyone else in history. Yet here he was, speechless in response to God's kindness to him.

Do you ever feel that way? The Lord touches you and ministers to you, gives you a verse in your devotional time, or impresses you with a truth as you're driving in your car, or looking at your grandchildren or wife—and you just become overwhelmed at the goodness and mercy of God. I believe praise often reaches its highest point when we're speechless, blown away by His mercy and grace.

Romans 8:31 (b)
If God be for us, who can be against us?

This verse literally reads, "*Since* God is for us, who can be against us?" We have the tendency to think God is disappointed with us. Not true. God is *for* you. And He's for me. God views His people very highly and loves His people very deeply. Why? Because He already sees the end product. We're already glorified in His eyes.

If God be for us, who would dare to be against us? Only one: Satan. But Satan is no problem because Satan is not God's counterpart. He's only a fallen angel whose equivalent is, perhaps, Michael. God is so far above Satan and so much greater than this world system that any power that comes against you or any problem that creeps up within you is no match for the One who says, "I'm *for* you."

God is *for* you. "That sounds nice," you say. "It might even be true theologically. But you don't know where I've been personally. You don't know how weak I am."

About a week ago I was reading through the Gospel of John once more, and I had to stop and chuckle. You see, the problem for a lot of us is, because we are so familiar with the stories in the gospel, they lose their impact. I mean, think with me. . . .

Two stories appear in John 2, both dealing with Jesus and a table. Around the first table, men have been drinking quite heartily—so much so that there was no wine left at the party. Around the second table, men were in the courtyard of the temple, exchanging money into Jewish currency that they might buy doves, lambs, and cattle to offer to Jehovah.

Jesus turned over the table in one of those vignettes. Which one? If you hadn't heard the story, you would say, "It's obvious. He would be ticked off with the party-ers. He would overturn their table. He would drive them out." But that's not what happened, because time and again, Jesus did the opposite of what people expected Him to do. And the only reason His actions don't shock us is because we're so familiar with them. You see, if you didn't know the story, you would say, "He dealt with the party-ers. But in reality, He made them more wine but overturned the tables of the outwardly pious moneychangers.

Jesus is radical, folks. He caused the religious people of His day to be continually shocked and scandalized. They didn't know what to do with Him because He loved to be with real people—people who had struggled with life, people who knew they weren't all that great—people just like us.

Romans 8:32 (a)
He that spared not his own Son . . .

The word "spared" is used only one other place in the Septuagint, the Greek translation of the Old Testament. When Abraham took his son Isaac to Mount Moriah (today called Golgotha, or Calvary), God said, "Abraham, lay not your hand upon the lad. Neither do anything unto him, for now I know that thou fearest God seeing thou hast not withheld thy son, thine only son from Me" (see Genesis 22:12). The word "withheld" is the same word translated "spared" here in Romans.

I suggest to you the reason God could pour out so many blessings on Abraham in so many ways was because Abraham was ready to sacrifice the one thing in his life that mattered most. In so doing, Abraham said, "I'll plunge a knife into my son's chest, even though I don't understand, because I love You, Father, more than I trust my ability to figure out what's going on."

So, too, if the thing that means the most to you—be it your wife, kids, house, car, job, fu-

ture—doesn't matter at all to you in comparison to your relationship with your Father, God can pour out all kinds of blessings on you because they won't be a distraction for you.

Romans 8:32 (b)
. . . but delivered him up for us all . . .

Here, God is saying, "You can be sure that because I gave you My Son, I'll do what's best for you from this point on." When God gave His Son, He proved His magnanimity, His generosity, and His kindness conclusively. So why question what's going on presently? Anything He shares with us or withholds from us cannot begin to compare with what He's *already* given us in Christ.

Romans 8:32 (c)
. . . how shall he not with him also freely give us all things?

Embedded in the phrase "all things" is the idea "all good things." In other words, if it's a good thing, He'll give it to you because He already gave you the best in Christ Jesus.

Romans 8:33
Who shall lay any thing to the charge of God's elect? It is God that justifieth.

There is one who does indeed lay things to the charge of God's elect. Satan, the accuser of the brethren (Revelation 12:10), points his finger at us constantly.

As Joshua, the high priest, stood in the presence of the Lord, his garments became filthy (Zechariah 3:3), because in God's presence, man's spirituality always appears as filthy rags (Isaiah 64:6). Quick to exploit the situation, Satan pointed his finger at Joshua's sin. "Is not this a stick I have plucked out of the fire?" said the Lord as Joshua's garments became dazzling white.

The same is true of us. We were little sticks headed for the fire of damnation. But the Lord plucked us out, robed us in His righteousness, and gave us the garment of praise for the spirit of heaviness (Isaiah 61:3).

"Look at his sin," thunders Satan.

"What sin?" asks God. "All I see is My Son."

There is no condemnation to them who are in Christ Jesus. Then what were we doing on our knees this morning, confessing sin? Confession is the result of conviction, not condemnation. Conviction is the work of the Spirit. When He convicts me of sin, I say, "Oh, Father, I realize this is wrong. I agree with You. And I thank You that

I'm forgiven." Conviction draws me to the Father. Condemnation, on the other hand, drives me from the Father. Condemnation makes me say, "I'm such a wretch. I can't pray and I sure can't go to church."

When Adam sinned in the Garden of Eden, God asked him a simple question. He didn't say, "Where were you? How could you? Why did you?" No, He simply said, "Where are you?" (Genesis 3:9).

And that's still the heart of the Father. His heart is not, "Where have you been?" or "What did you do? but "Where are you right now? Take off those scratchy fig leaves, and let Me clothe you with My righteousness."

Romans 8:34
Who is he that condemneth? It is Christ that died, yea rather, that is risen again, who is even at the right hand of God, who also maketh intercession for us.

In Mark 16, we read that when Jesus ascended into heaven, He sat down at the right hand of the Father (16:19). This interests me because when you look at the temple or the tabernacle, you find no place for the priest to sit. There was a table to eat from, a lamp stand to see by, a laver to wash in, an alter to sacrifice on—but there was no place to sit because the work of the Old Testament priest was never done. It went on and on and on.

But when the Great High Priest Jesus Christ died and said, "It is finished" (John 19:30), He meant it. He went to the right hand of the Father and sat down.

When a person is tense and unsure of the outcome, he stands to his feet and paces. Jesus sits. The only record of Him standing in heaven is when He stood to welcome Stephen, the first martyr, home (Acts 7:56).

Romans 8:35-37
Who shall separate us from the love of Christ? shall tribulation, or distress, or persecution, or famine, or nakedness, or peril, or sword? As it is written, For thy sake we are killed all the day long; we are accounted as sheep for the slaughter. Nay, in all these things we are more than conquerors through him that loved us.

Paul is saying to you and me, "God is for you. He'll never lay any charge against you. He doesn't come down on you. He'll give you every good thing freely because He already gave you the best in Jesus." The question then becomes, "If

this be so, why do we go through tribulation, famine, distress, nakedness, peril, sword?" The answer is because we are like sheep (Psalm 44:11). Sheep are easily picked off, easily put down, easily done in. It seems the Christian community has forgotten that it is comprised of lambs. We gear up, arm ourselves, and come out swinging. But the imagery is all wrong. After all, which NFL football team goes by the Lambs? Which Marine Corps unit would choose the lamb for its mascot?

"If they hated Me, they'll hate you," Jesus said (see John 15:18). But the Good News is that in all these things we are more than conquerors. What does it mean to be more than a conqueror? It means that, instead of flexing our muscles politically or marching in protest socially, we draw people's attention to an entirely different dimension spiritually. We're to influence positively—no question about it. But it's not our passion, our purpose, or our priority to conquer the system.

"Aren't we to be salt and light?" you ask.

"Yes, but salt is meant to be sprinkled. I had some clam chowder last night and asked for some salt. Now, what if the waiter had said, "You want salt? Here you go," and proceeded to unscrew the lid and empty the shaker into my bowl? The chowder would have been ruined. The same is true of light. Do you appreciate it when an oncoming car shines its high-beams in your face? We wonder why the world doesn't listen to us. Could it be because we empty the saltshaker in its soup and shine high beams in its face in our attempt to be salt and light?

We're to be lambs. We're to be salt that's sprinkled to add flavor, create thirst, and bring healing. We're to be light that illuminates, not dominates. And know this: From the world's perspective, we'll never win. If you don't understand this, you'll be frustrated, disillusioned, embittered. We're not conquerors. We're more than conquerors.

Shadrach, Meshach, and Abed-nego were tossed into the fiery furnace. But while they were in it, even Nebuchadnezzar saw Jesus Christ in the fire with them (Daniel 3:25). Do the Nebuchadnezzars of this world look at us and say, "They went into the furnace without a fight, but somehow they're walking around. They're doing fine. We're the ones who are hurting"?

That's what it means to be more than a conqueror.

Romans 8:38, 39
For I am persuaded, that neither death, nor life, nor angels, nor principalities, nor powers, nor things present, nor things to come, nor height, nor depth, nor any other creature, shall be able to separate us from the love of God, which is in Christ Jesus our Lord.

Although we are "accounted as sheep for the slaughter," in the place of slaughter, we see the Savior and He will never leave us. We will never be separated from His love. Paul is elated by this—for if God be for us, who can be against us?

IT'S ALL FOR GOOD
A Topical Study of
Romans 8:28

There are certain things we don't know. For example, we don't know how a honeybee can fly. You see, theoretically, the wings of a honeybee are too short and too light to support him when he is carrying pollen. It's an aerodynamic impossibility for a honeybee to fly when he's loaded with pollen. But guess what. Honeybees fly even when loaded with pollen. Certain things we don't know—things as simple as the flight of a bee.

There are some things we can't know—things like the day or hour of the Rapture (Matthew 25:13), or who will be in heaven (Matthew 13:24–30).

There are several things we *should* know. "Don't be ignorant," admonished Paul, "concerning the second coming (see 1 Thessalonians 4:13), spiritual gifts (see 1 Corinthians 12), and Satan's devices" (see 2 Corinthians 2:11).

And there are some things we truly *do* know . . .

The Promise Given *to* Us

In our text, Paul doesn't say, "You should know that all things work together for good." He doesn't say, "I want you to know all things work together for good." He says, "You already know that all things work together for good to them that love God and are called according to His purpose."

How do we know this?

"Because this verse is in the Word," you answer. "Therefore, it must be true."

All right. But what about those in Rome to whom Paul was writing? They had never heard of Romans 8:28. How, then, could Paul assume they knew its truth?

The Price Paid *for* Us

Look down a few verses to verse 32: "God spared not His own Son but delivered Him up for you and me." If He loved you enough to send His Son to be slaughtered in your stead to pay the price for your sin, don't you know God will do what's good for you continually? When I begin to doubt the love of God, or wonder if things are really working together for good, all I need to do is look to Calvary and see Jesus there dying for me.

The Peace *Within* Us

God's goodness was known and understood by Old Testament saints long before the Cross of Calvary. How? Because, deep within their hearts, in the midst of tragedy, in the face of difficulty, all those who love God know that all things are truly working together for good.

There is a man in the Old Testament who did this very thing. His name is Jacob, and this part of his story is found in Genesis 42. Jacob had twelve sons. Although he loved them all, number eleven was especially dear to him. His name? Joseph. You recall the story. . . .

Jacob gave Joseph a "coat of many colors," or, more accurately, "a coat with big sleeves." You see, in those days, laborers wore vests without sleeves in order that their arms could be unrestricted. But the bosses—the head honchos—wore coats with sleeves, which served as lunchboxes or briefcases because they kept important documents and/or food in them. Joseph's big sleeves made his brothers so jealous that they threw him into a pit, where they were going to leave him to die—until one of the brothers suggested they could make some money if they sold him as a slave. So sell him they did, after which they smeared blood all over his coat and took it to Jacob, saying, "Bad news, Dad. Joseph was eaten by wild animals."

Meanwhile, through an incredible series of events, Joseph became prime minister of Egypt—second in command only to Pharaoh himself. When famine hit Israel, Jacob called his sons together and said, "I've heard there's a man in Egypt who has food. Go ask him if we can buy some grain." So his sons, ten in number, appeared before the prime minister, whom they didn't recognize.

"Why are you here?" asked Joseph.

"We're here to buy grain, Your Highness."

"I think you're lying," said Joseph. "I think you've come to spy out the land."

"No," insisted his brothers. "We're brothers. In fact, there were twelve of us originally—but one of our brothers is dead, and our youngest brother is at home."

"If that's true," countered Joseph, "go bring your youngest brother to me. That will validate your story. Meanwhile you, Simeon, will stay in prison until the youngest one is brought back."

The nine went back home, taking the grain with them that Joseph had given them. The famine grew worse, and soon they were out of food once more. "Go back to Egypt," Jacob said.

"We can't go back unless we take Benjamin," said the brothers.

Watch what Jacob said in verse 36: "Me have ye bereaved of my children; Joseph is not, and Simeon is not, and ye will take Benjamin away: all these things are against me," or literally, "all is working against me."

- What does Romans 8 say?
  "All things work for good."

- What is Jacob declaring?

"Everything is working against me. My son, Simeon, is a hostage. My son Joseph is dead. And my son Benjamin is soon to disappear."

Jacob was completely wrong about what had happened: Joseph wasn't dead. As a matter of fact, he was in perfect health. And Jacob was wrong about what would happen: Benjamin would return, and Simeon would be released.

"Doesn't what Jacob said disprove your premise that everyone who loves God knows innately that everything is working out for good?" you ask.

Even though Jacob said, "Everything is against me," I suggest to you deep down inside, he didn't believe it.

Why?

Read the next chapter. Knowing Jacob, if he really believed Benjamin would die in Egypt, he would not have allowed Benjamin to go. Clever, cunning Jacob would have figured out another way. But his sending Benjamin proves he didn't really believe everything was working out negatively for him.

The story continues. . . .

The brothers return to Egypt and appear before Joseph with Benjamin in tow. "I'm the brother you put in a pit, the one you sold into slavery," announced Joseph. And the brothers fell at his feet in fear. "Don't fear," he said. Although you meant evil against me, God meant it for good" (see Genesis 50:20).

Joseph said, "Everything you did to me was part of a plan, so don't worry." And he spoke kindly to them and showed great love toward them.

Here's the question: How do I react to difficulty? Am I like Jacob, saying, "All things are working against me. How can this be happening to me? What good is going to come out of this tragedy"—even though I know in my heart that such is not the case? Or am I like Joseph, saying, "Man may have meant this for evil, but God meant it for good"?

Unfortunately, all too often I choose the sniveling of Jacob rather than the security of Joseph. Why? To elicit sympathy. My flesh is terribly ugly, and one of the things that makes it that way is my desire for you to feel sorry for me. What is it about our flesh that wants people to think we have it harder than anyone else? While that may seem an insignificant quirk, in reality it borders on blasphemy because in getting you to feel sorry for me, I get you to question God's goodness, provision, and protection in my life. Thus, your pity for me is at God's expense.

Who am I going to be? Am I going to be self-indulgent and allow God to be cast in a bad light—even though I know in my heart the promise given to me, the price paid for me, the peace available for me? Am I going to deny all of that and say, "I want you to feel sorry for me. Listen to my tragedy"? Or am I going to say, "I will not dishonor this good, gracious, loving God who has been so kind to me, who has been so good to me. Therefore, I will not bring shame to His name in eliciting sympathy from anyone"?

That is called the fear of the Lord. It's respect. It's reverence. It's saying, "Father, I care more about Your reputation than I do about getting sympathy from the congregation. I don't want them to think questioningly, negatively, or blasphemously of You."

What is the fear of God? The fear of God means you're so in love with God that you are afraid of doing anything that would hurt Him. Oh, that we would be those who say, "We fear God. We will not snivel. God is good and we know in our hearts deep within us that all things are working together for good"?

Does this mean we're not to sympathize with others when they're going through difficulties?

While the Bible does, indeed, say we are to weep with those who weep (Romans 12:15), what does it actually mean? Whenever you want to know what a verse or concept means, look at Jesus Christ who was the Word made flesh.

"Come quickly, Lord. The one whom thou lovest is sick," pleaded Martha and Mary (John 11:3). Four days later, when Jesus finally arrived, Martha greeted Him, saying, "Where were You?"

Do you ever hear yourself talking like that? Do you ever hear yourself saying, "The bills are stacking up; my marriage is falling apart, my health is breaking down—where's the Lord?"

After Martha came Mary. "Lord," she cried, "if only You had been here, our brother would not have died." Seeing her weep, Jesus wept. Why? Was it because Lazarus died? No. Jesus knew Lazarus would soon be called back from the dead. He wasn't weeping for Lazarus. He was weeping because Mary didn't get it.

In Luke 19, we read of Jesus weeping again—this time over the city of Jerusalem.

As the multitude shouted, "Hosanna! Blessed is He that comes in the name of the Lord," Jesus wept over the city. Why? Because of the people's failure to understand that He came to give them spiritual salvation, not a political solution.

The third time Jesus spoke of weeping was in Luke 23.

His back was beaten, His face swollen, and a crown of thorns was smashed into His skull, as He stumbled down the Via Dolorosa up to a hill called Calvary. To the women weeping along the way He said, "Don't weep for Me. Weep for yourselves because you don't understand what lies ahead for this city" (see verses 28, 29).

When I see Jesus weeping, I am amazed because He never weeps for Himself. He only weeps when other people don't understand. Here, then, is the question: Thinking you're being compassionate, are you one who constantly weeps with others? Perhaps what we need in the Christian community during this time of self-centered Christianity are men and women who say, "I fear God. Dear brother, even if you don't understand—precious sister, even if you think this is cold-hearted or lacking compassion, you know that this difficulty or this tragedy will work for good. Stand on that knowledge. Cling to it. I will weep for you if you don't get it. But I'm not going to weep with you as you question God and snivel. He's too good for that. Righteous and true are His judgments (Psalm 19:9). Whatever He does will prove to be excellent. And I will stand on that."

May God give us wisdom. May God give us peace. May God give us understanding. All things work together for good to them that love God, to them that are called according to His purpose.

I know this to be true. So do you.

9 After his glorious discourse on the building blocks of our salvation in chapters 1—8, why would Paul veer off in chapters 9—11 to talk about the people of Israel? Some have suggested that Paul's giant intellect was blown out at the end of chapter 8, so in chapter 9, he began to meander intellectually and theologically. "It's good stuff," they say, "but it doesn't fit in with the rest of the book." These commentators miss the point entirely. They don't understand that, far from being an interruption, chapters 9—11 are actually a perfect illustration.

Having established the principles of salvation in chapters 1—8, and before he will discuss the practicality of salvation in chapters 12—16, Paul addresses the problem of salvation in chapters 9—11. You see, Paul ended chapter 8 with the victorious declaration that nothing shall separate us from the love of Christ. At this point, the scholar, the Bible student could say, "But what about the Jews? Are they separated from His love? Are they lost? And if so, what hope do *we* have? If they, who were once God's chosen people, are no longer walking with Him, what chance do we Gentiles have?"

Romans 9—11 is essential to the flow of the rest of the Book of Romans because Paul uses the Jew as an illustration of the faithfulness of God.

- In chapter 9, God's past dealings with Israel show His sovereignty.
- In chapter 10, God's present dealings with Israel show His equity.
- In chapter 11, God's promised dealings with Israel show His integrity.

Romans 9:1–3
I say the truth in Christ, I lie not, my conscience also bearing me witness in the Holy Ghost, that I have great heaviness and continual sorrow in my heart. For I could wish that myself were accursed from Christ for my brethren, my kinsmen according to the flesh.

In Exodus 32, Moses said, "Oh, Lord, even though Your people have turned from You, and have fallen into idolatry and immorality, if You don't forgive them, if You don't continue working with them, blot my name out of Your book of life as well" (see verse 32).

Here in verse 3, it's as if Paul says, "The same heart that beat within Moses is in me, for if possible, I would go to hell and suffer eternally if my kinsmen could be saved."

Where did Paul get such passion, such love for people who were out to do him in? It was cultivated in prayer, as seen in chapter 10, where he says, "Brethren my heart's desire and prayer to God for Israel is they might be saved" (see verse 1). Truly, when you pray for people, your heart changes toward them as you become concerned about them and involved with them.

For topical study of Romans 9:1–3 entitled "Loving and Praying," turn to page 954.

Romans 9:4 (a)
Who are Israelites; to whom pertaineth the adoption . . .

After his anguish for the Jewish people seen in verses 1–3, we come to Paul's analysis of the Jewish problem here in verse 4. Consider, first of all, the gifts of God to Israel. They were chosen not because they were more righteous than others, for God called them a stiffnecked and hardhearted people (Deuteronomy 7:6–8). No, He chose them to be trophies of His grace.

We have a tendency to think, *You were wise when You picked me, Lord. You saw my dedication, my determination. Good choice. Truly You're a wise God—proven by the way You chose me and adopted me into Your family.* But that's not what the Bible teaches. It says you were chosen not to the glory of His wisdom, but to the glory of His *grace* in order that throughout the ages, the angels will be perpetually amazed by God's mercy and kindness when they see you in heaven.

Romans 9:4 (b)
. . . and the glory . . .

"Glory" refers to the Hebrew word *chabod*— which means weight, substance, heaviness. The *chabod* was the cloud over the Jews as they traveled through the wilderness by day. The *chabod* was also the pillar of fire that went before them by night. It was the glory that filled the tabernacle as well as the glory that filled the temple. It was the visible, tangible presence of God, the substance people still crave in their hearts. The *chabod* is what every man is looking for when he searches for something weighty, something substantial, something real.

Romans 9:4 (c)
. . . and the covenants, and the giving of the law . . .

The covenants and the law gave the Jews principles that they might do well, excel, and succeed in life.

Romans 9:4 (d)
. . . and the service of God . . .

There's nothing more satisfying than serving God—and Israel was blessed with such a calling.

Romans 9:4 (e), 5 (a)
. . . and the promises; Whose are the fathers . . .

Israel was also blessed with great men—Abraham, Isaac, Jacob, Moses, and David.

Romans 9:5 (b)
. . . and of whom as concerning the flesh Christ came, who is over all, God blessed for ever. Amen.

The best gift of all was that Jesus Christ was born to a Jewish mother, grew up in a Jewish home, went to a Jewish school, sat in a Jewish synagogue, ministered to the Jewish people, and said, "I have come to the lost sheep of the house of Israel" (see Matthew 15:24). What an unspeakable gift was given to the Jews.

Romans 9:6 (a)
Not as though the word of God hath taken none effect.

After considering the gifts of God to Israel, Paul goes on to talk about the grace of God upon Israel. Not all Jews rejected God's grace. Some received His Son as their Messiah—which is why Paul said, "It's not as though the Word of God has taken none effect."

Romans 9:6 (b)–8
For they are not all Israel, which are of Israel: Neither, because they are the seed of Abraham, are they all children: but, In Isaac shall thy seed be called. That is, They which are the children of the flesh, these are not the children of God: but the children of the promise are counted for the seed.

"Not everyone who claims to be a Jew is a Jew," said Paul, and to illustrate his point, he appealed to Abraham. Abraham had two sons: Isaac, the promised son; and Ishmael, the attempt of his flesh to help God get the job done. How did God view Ishmael? "Abraham, take your son, your only son up to the mount," He said (see Genesis 22:2). In other words, God didn't even acknowledge Abraham had another son.

This comforts me greatly. You see, a lot of us have a lot of Ishmaels running around—things we've done in our flesh, trying to help God. But God doesn't even acknowledge them. When God reminded Abraham, however, that He would give him a promised son, what did Abraham say? "Oh that Ishmael might live before Thee" (Genesis 17:18).

Abraham's is my cry far too often. "Lord, bless my fleshly endeavor. I know it was done in my own energy and my stupidity, but bless it anyway, Lord."

But God did not work through Ishmael. So, too, using Abraham as an illustration, Paul says, "Understand that not all who are from Abraham are children of Abraham. Look at Ishmael."

Not all who claim to be Israel are Israel. "Israel" means "governed by God," and not all who claim to be of Israel are governed by God. So, too, not all who claim the name "Christian" are Christians. Go to any college history class, and they'll attack you if you're a believer when they talk about the Crusades, and what "Christians" have done in Northern Ireland and the Middle East. The name is not important. Many name the name, but they're not of the true lineage of Jesus Christ. They're not born again. They're not governed by Him.

So Paul says, "Be careful. Not all who claim to be Israel are of Israel. Those descendants of Abraham through Isaac, and those who descend through the spiritual seed (like you and me) are those who are truly governed by God."

Romans 9:9, 10
For this is the word of promise, At this time will I come, and Sara shall have a son. And not only this; but when Rebecca also had conceived by one, even by our father Isaac.

Not only did Abraham have two sons—Isaac chosen, Ishmael forgotten—but when Isaac had kids, the story continued.

Romans 9:11, 12
(For the children being not yet born, neither having done any good or evil, that the purpose of God according to election might stand, not of works, but of him that calleth;) it was said unto her, The elder shall serve the younger.

Even as God sovereignly chose Isaac and ignored Ishmael, He sovereignly chose Jacob, the younger of Isaac's sons, and rejected Esau. "Don't you see how good God has been to you?" asks Paul. "You are descendants of Abraham through Isaac and through Jacob—simply because of God's sovereignty."

Romans 9:13, 14
As it is written, Jacob have I loved, but Esau have I hated. What shall we say then? Is there unrighteousness with God? God forbid.

A lot of people have a real problem right here. "How could God choose to love Jacob, and choose to hate Esau before they were even born?" they ask. The answer is simple. It is because God is sovereign. The mystery to me is not that God hated Esau. The mystery to me is that God loved Jacob—and that He loves me, a conniver just like Jacob.

Did God choose correctly? Read your Bible and you'll see that Esau wasn't interested in spiritual things, but attracted to carnal things. Yes, God chose correctly—He always does.

Romans 9:15
For he saith to Moses, I will have mercy on whom I will have mercy, and I will have compassion on whom I will have compassion.

When did God say this? After the people of Israel had sinned by dancing around the golden calf, Moses prayed for them, and God said, "I'll pardon them" (see Exodus 33:19). Why? Because of His sovereignty.

Romans 9:16
So then it is not of him that willeth, nor of him that runneth, but of God that sheweth mercy.

The election of God is not something to run for, earn, or win. As Paul continues talking about the nation of Israel, he will contrast the sovereign pardon of God on our behalf with His sovereign punishment of Pharaoh.

Romans 9:17
For the scripture saith unto Pharaoh, Even for this same purpose have I raised thee up, that I might shew my power in thee, and that my name might be declared throughout all the earth.

God has compassion and mercy on Israel, while He has only condemnation and punishment for Pharaoh.

Romans 9:18
Therefore hath he mercy on whom he will have mercy, and whom he will he hardeneth.

In the Exodus account, Scripture records twenty times when Pharaoh's heart was hardened—ten times of which God hardened his heart and ten times of which Pharaoh hardened it himself. Understand, Bible students, that when God hardened Pharaoh's heart, He was only confirming Pharaoh's own decision. So don't feel too bad about Pharaoh, for even though he saw miracles

happening and heard God's Word very powerfully presented, he hardened his own heart.

Romans 9:19
**Thou wilt say then unto me, Why doth he yet
find fault? For who hath resisted his will?**

Paul anticipated the next question: "If He
chooses some and rejects others; if he raises up
Pharaoh only to put him down, what choice does
anyone have?"

Romans 9:20–24
**Nay but, O man, who art thou that repliest
against God? Shall the thing formed say to
him that formed it, Why hast thou made me
thus? Hath not the potter power over the clay,
of the same lump to make one vessel unto
honour, and another unto dishonour? What
if God, willing to shew his wrath, and to make
his power known, endured with much longsuffering the vessels of wrath fitted to destruction: And that he might make known
the riches of his glory on the vessels of mercy,
which he had afore prepared unto glory,
even us, whom he hath called, not of the
Jews only, but also of the Gentiles?**

A popular phrase in the political climate of the
'80s was, "Let Reagan be Reagan." Paul would
say, "Let God be God. Let Him do what He wants.
Who are you to argue against Him? From one
piece of clay, a potter can make a beautiful vase.
From another, he can make a trashcan. So, too,
the Master Potter can do with you whatever He
wants."

Now, I could worry about placing my life in the
hands of One who sovereignly decides whether
I'll be a vase or a spittoon, a thing of beauty or a
trashcan—but only until I see the hands of the
Potter as He shapes the clay. For then I see the
prints where nails scarred those hands, where
He loved me so much He died for me on Calvary.
Surely, if He loved me enough to die for me, I can
trust Him with my life absolutely, and say to Him,
"Do with me whatever You wish."

Romans 9:25, 26
**As he saith also in Hosea, I will call them my
people, which were not my people; and her
beloved, which was not beloved. And it shall
come to pass, that in the place where it was
said unto them, Ye are not my people; there
shall they be called the children of the living
God.**

Here, Paul is referring to Gentiles, to the
church. God sovereignly chooses us, just as He
sovereignly chose Israel in the past.

Romans 9:27
**Isaiah also crieth concerning Israel, Though
the number of the children of Israel be as
the sand of the sea, a remnant shall be saved.**

A small group of the Jews will be saved. They'll
see the light and become part of the church.

Romans 9:28, 29
**For he will finish the work, and cut it short
in righteousness: because a short work will
the Lord make upon the earth. And as Esaias
said before, Except the Lord of Sabaoth had
left us a seed, we had been as Sodoma, and
been made like unto Gomorrha.**

"If God hadn't saved a seed or a remnant, we
would have been wiped out entirely," Paul says
concerning the Jews nationally. "But He saved a
seed, a remnant, a group that has been preserved
both historically and spiritually." Not only that,
He brought this seed into the church, along with
others who were not His people—Gentiles like
you and me.

You see, in God's economy, there are three
groups of people: the Jew, the Gentile, and the
church. The church is made up of Jews and Gentiles chosen by God to make up a brand-new entity. "Something new is happening," said Paul.

God in His sovereignty gave opportunity for
Israel to come to Him. But most of Israel passed
up the invitation. Paul says only a seed, only a
remnant responded to the message of grace.

Romans 9:30
**What shall we say then? That the Gentiles,
which followed not after righteousness,
have attained to righteousness, even the
righteousness which is of faith.**

Realizing he's a sinner unable to earn his way
into the kingdom, the Gentile enters the kingdom
solely by faith.

Romans 9:31–33
**But Israel, which followed after the law of
righteousness, hath not attained to the law
of righteousness. Wherefore? Because they
sought it not by faith, but as it were by the
works of the law. For they stumbled at that
stumblingstone; as it is written, Behold, I
lay in Sion a stumblingstone and rock of
offence: and whosoever believeth on him
shall not be ashamed.**

The Jew, on the other hand, attempted righteousness by the law and failed because the law
cannot save man (Galatians 3:24). The law was

given to show us we're sinners. Yet to this day, Israel is trying to be saved by her good works. Ask a Jew in Israel today how he's going to make it spiritually, and he'll say, "We will make it by our good deeds."

I've talked to sincere Jews about this, and they blush even as they say those words because they understand that without the shedding of blood, there is no remission of sins (Hebrews 9:22). The Jewish people desperately want to rebuild the temple in order that they may offer Old Testament sacrifices again. For until that time, his only option presently is to hope his good works will cover his sins—as he continues to stumble over the very Cornerstone of the temple he is so desperate to build (Ephesians 2:20).

LOVING AND PRAYING
A Topical Study of
Romans 9:1–3

Did I ever blow it! Flying into Pocatello, Idaho, I found the flight a bit bumpy. The plane was bouncing. My stomach was churning. And, once again, I was ready to toss my cookies. We finally landed, however, and I made it safely to the group in Pocatello with whom I was to share. "Coming into Pocatello International, I understand why they call airport lobbies terminals. I felt my condition was just that—terminal," I cracked in my opening remarks. "Especially if you're flying on Horizon Scareways." The crowd laughed. Then we got into the Word and had a fabulous time together.

The next morning, as I stood at the ticket counter in the Pocatello terminal, the lady facing me looked at my ticket and said, "Oh, you're Jon Courson."

"Yes," I said.

"You were speaking here last night?"

"Yes," I said. "We had a great time. Were you there?"

Her wan smile turned into an icy frown. She looked at me with steely eyes and said, "Absolutely not. All I know is, you called our company Horizon Scareways."

At this point, two other agents joined her and said, "How could you call our company Horizon Scareways?"

"Oh, I was just joking," I answered meekly. "I think your airline is wonderful." But then I felt bad for lying! "Could I please have an aisle seat?" I asked, changing the subject.

"No," was her curt reply.

So I got my ticket, found my seat, and strapped myself in, feeling awful. After a few minutes, I thought, *Wait a minute. Why would they say those things to me— a paying customer? Whatever happened to the philosophy that made America great, the understanding that the customer is always right?* And I found myself getting mad at the way I perceived I was being treated at the ticket counter. So I went from feeling bad to feeling mad. And as the plane took off, I went from feeling mad to feeling sad, realizing I was becoming defensive, critical, and small. Thus, as the plane got up in the air, the flight was turbulent—not only because of the weather outside, but because of the storm raging within me.

How very different was my reaction to this situation than was the apostle Paul's. You see, as he traveled throughout Europe, sharing the gospel and communicating grace and love, a group of his countrymen awaited him—men of Israel who arrived in every city in order that they might lie about him and either greet him with stones (Acts 14:19), or arrange to have him thrown in prison (Acts 21:27). So serious were Paul's enemies that they took an oath, saying, "We will not eat another meal until Paul is dead" (see Acts 23:12).

Talk about tough traveling! Here I was complaining because I felt my little comment was taken too seriously. But Paul? People were lying about him, throwing rocks at him, grabbing hold of him, determined to do away with him. Paul really had a tough time at the hands of his countrymen. But what was his reaction concerning those who were out to do him in? It blows my mind!

> *I say the truth in Christ, I lie not, my conscience also bearing me witness in the Holy Ghost, That I have great heaviness and continual sorrow in my heart. For I could wish that myself were accursed from Christ for my brethren, my kinsmen according to the flesh . . .*
> Romans 9:1–3 (a)

The Holy Spirit testifying to the truth of his words, Paul said, "I would go to hell for these guys if only they could be saved." Would you say that concerning the person who's coming down on you, regarding the person who wants to do you in? It might be a teacher, a parent, a neighbor, a co-worker, or an old girlfriend. It might be someone who's done you wrong, lied about you, hurled insulting stones at you, wanted to grab hold of you, and if possible would annihilate and destroy you. Think about the person who is most difficult for you to deal with. How do you honestly feel about him? Would you go to hell eternally if that person could go to heaven?

Paul's words absolutely amaze me. To the Philippian believers, Paul said, "I'm craving heaven, but for your sakes, it's needful for me to stick around here on earth" (see Philippians 1:20–24). Commendable indeed! But to me how much more powerful is his statement to the very ones who were out to get him when he said not only, "I won't go to heaven," but "I would go to hell for you if it were possible."

How did Paul develop such love for people who wanted only to do him in? And how can we develop the same love? How can we overcome our bitterness and disappointment, our anger and hostility toward people who come against us, disappoint us, or hurt us?

Turn the page to Romans 10, for I believe that is where the answer lies.

> *Brethren, my heart's desire and prayer to God for Israel is, that they might be saved.*
> Romans 10:1

The Greek rendering of this verse is: "Brethren, my heart's desire and continual prayer to God for Israel is that they might be saved." In other words, "My heart's desire and continual prayer for Israel—the country that misunderstands me, the people who are out to destroy me, the nation which has totally rejected me—is, Lord, save them."

Paul not only proved his love by praying for his countrymen, but his prayer for his countrymen actually produced that kind of love in Paul. This is why Jesus specifically told us we are to pray for our enemies (Matthew 5:44).

You see, here's what happens: Something begins to take place in me when I pray for people—particularly for my enemies. My heart toward them begins to change.

When he came down from Mount Sinai after meeting with God on behalf of the children of Israel, Moses saw them dancing naked around a golden calf. What was his reaction? He was so mad he threw the tablets he was carrying to the ground. But then he said something hauntingly familiar: "Lord, if You don't forgive these, Your people, blot my name out of Your book" (see Exodus 32:32). In other words, "If You don't forgive these people, I'll go to hell with them."

How could Moses have that kind of love, particularly when earlier in the chapter, the Lord said, "These are a stiffnecked people you're leading, Moses. Let Me wipe them out and make from you a new nation" (see Exodus 32:10)? I suggest to you had Moses not spent forty days with the Lord prior to this occurrence, he would not have had the heart he did.

So, sitting in the airplane, going through this internal turmoil, the Lord reminded me of Moses and Paul. And as I chewed on this text, thinking these things through, I suddenly realized, I had to pray for those Horizon ladies. So I did. I prayed that they would be blessed, that the Lord would place it in their hearts to forgive me, that their day might go well, that they might somehow be touched by God's grace and love.

Then I prayed for the president of Horizon Airlines. And I prayed for Horizon, that they would be prosperous and blessed—and that they would get better planes. I prayed for the steward in the cabin, and the pilot in the cockpit. As I was en route, I prayed for my fellow passengers. As I sat in the lobby in Boise, I prayed for people who walked by.

And, eventually, something began to happen, for as I prayed, I found my heart being filled with love toward anyone and everyone for whom I took the time to pray. Paul said, "I continually pray for my brethren." That's why he had such a deep love for them and was willing to go to hell on their behalf.

I suggest to you two reasons why you need to pray for people with whom you're having a hard time, for people with whom you don't see eye to eye, for people who bug you . . .

Pray for Your Own Sake

A man opened a door for a lady in New York City. She stopped, turned to him, and said, "You don't have to open the door for me just because I'm a lady."

He looked at her and said, "I'm not opening the door for you because you're a lady. I'm opening the door because I'm a gentleman."

Good point! You see, when I pray for people who bug me, I realize my praying will not only affect them, but it will affect my own attitude, my own tendency toward cynicism, my own critical spirit, my own bitterness. In other words, prayer will change *me*.

So why should you pray for the person who's bugging you, who's letting you down or trying to do you in? Because it will make you a better person. It will keep you soft and tender. It will make you a loving man, a loving woman. That's why Jesus said, "Don't preach at, argue with, or analyze your enemies. Just pray and bless them."

And if we'll take Jesus seriously, we will find prayer changing us in the process.

Pray for Christ's Sake

Jesus was done in, beaten up by you and me. Isaiah tells us He was wounded for our transgressions, bruised for our iniquities. The chastisement of our peace was upon Him. By His stripes we are healed (Isaiah 53:5). Therefore, when somebody beats up on me and I think it's unfair, I need to remember that I beat up on Jesus. My sin and stupidity were what caused Him to be pinned to the tree. He was beaten up for me.

And what did He do even as He was being beaten up? He prayed, "Father, forgive them. They don't know what they're doing" (see Luke 23:34).

Not only was He beaten up by me, He continues to be let down constantly, for I am not doing the things I know I could do. I am not the man I know I should be. And yet what does He do? He who was pinned to the tree rose again and went to heaven, where He lives to ever make intercession—to pray for me (Hebrews 7:25). Now if Jesus—beaten up by me, let down because of me—prays for me, I need to do what He says.

"If you love Me," He says, "keep My commandments" (see John 14:15). And what are His commandments? Simply these: to love God with all your heart and soul and mind and strength—and to love the person who's around you, who works beside you, who lives next to you, who bugs you (Matthew 22:37–40).

If we don't have love, we don't have anything (1 Corinthians 13:2). "But, Lord, how can I have love?"

"Very simple," He says. "By spending time with Me and by praying for your enemies."

Pray for others and your own heart will change. You'll find the flight will be a whole lot smoother than if you're justifying your position. Right now the Lord can set you free if you'll just do what Paul did, what Moses did, what Jesus did. Pray. Pray for people continually.

"God forbid," said Samuel, "that I should sin against the Lord in ceasing to pray for you" (1 Samuel 12:23). Prayer is the proof of love. And love is produced by prayer. Pray—both for your sake and for the sake of the One who continually prays for you.

10 After talking about God's sovereignty in His past dealings with Israel, Paul goes on to speak of God's equity in His present dealing with Israel.

Romans 10:1
Brethren, my heart's desire and prayer to God for Israel is, that they might be saved.

Truly, God is an equal opportunity Savior, for He still gives Gentiles an invitation to salvation, while giving the Jews the same opportunity. In this chapter, we will see Christ revealed as Savior to all of Israel (verses 2–4), Christ received as Savior by some of Israel (verses 5–15), and Christ rejected as Savior by most of Israel (verses 16–21).

Romans 10:2 (a)
For I bear them record that they have a zeal of God . . .

To this day, the Jews are zealous for God.

Romans 10:2 (b), 3
. . . but not according to knowledge. For they being ignorant of God's righteousness, and going about to establish their own righteousness, have not submitted themselves unto the righteousness of God.

You can be sincere in your crusading or your critiquing, your sin-sniffing or your fault-finding—but you'll be sincerely wrong. Ask Paul. With great zeal, he persecuted the church, going about to establish his own righteousness (Philippians 3:6). Like the majority of Israel, He was sincere, but he was sincerely wrong.

Romans 10:4
For Christ is the end of the law for righteousness to every one that believeth.

Concerning the law, Jesus said, "Not one jot or tittle shall pass away until all be fulfilled" (see Matthew 5:18). Yet the law ended when Christ came. Why? Because it was fulfilled in Him.

Romans 10:5
For Moses describeth the righteousness which is of the law, That the man which doeth those things shall live by them.

If you want to keep the law, you must live in the law. In other words, you must keep working.

On the day the law came down from Mount Sinai, three thousand died (Exodus 32:28).
On the day the Spirit descended, three thousand were saved (Acts 2:41).

Legalism in your life, in our churches, or in our communities will always lead to death because no one can fulfill its righteousness. The Spirit in your life, in our churches, in our communities, on the other hand, will always lead to life because of the finished work of the Cross.

Romans 10:6, 7
But the righteousness which is of faith speaketh on this wise, Say not in thine heart, Who shall ascend into heaven? (that is, to bring Christ down from above:) Or, Who shall descend into the deep? (that is, to bring up Christ again from the dead.)

There are those who say, "If I go to Mount Shasta and get a solar hut, change my name, and drink herb tree, perhaps I can transcend and go up into the heavens and bring down the Christ consciousness." Others say, "I'll plumb the depths of theology, and if I get deep enough, perhaps I can bring Christ up from the dead and make Him real." Some float on clouds of philosophy, trying to bring Christ down. Others dig in studiously, trying to bring Christ up. But in reality, Paul says neither is necessary.

Romans 10:8, 9
But what saith it? The word is nigh thee, even in thy mouth, and in thy heart: that is, the word of faith, which we preach; that if thou shalt confess with thy mouth the Lord Jesus, and shalt believe in thine heart that God hath raised him from the dead, thou shalt be saved.

Jesus is known not through theology, not through philosophy, but through childlike simplicity. That is, you believe in your heart that He is risen, that He died for your sins and is alive. And you make a simple confession with your mouth: "Jesus is my Lord. I'm going on record verbally. I believe in my heart internally that He died for my sins; He's risen; and He's my Lord." You don't have to float off into space or dig deep into thought. The word is near you—even in your mouth. It's so very simple: Just believe and confess.

Romans 10:10
For with the heart man believeth unto righteousness; and with the mouth confession is made unto salvation.

Why believe in your heart? Why didn't Paul say believe in your mind? I suggest it is because the Lord is after our heart first. "You shall love the Lord with all your heart and mind and strength and soul" (see Mark 12:30). You see, my mind can be swayed very easily. I'm convinced about something—until I get a new set of facts and change my mind. Or I have an opinion one day and then I flip-flop the next.

But if something is in my heart, I don't change my mind about it daily. For example, at one time in your life, a boyfriend or girlfriend may have turned his or her back on you. Yet your heart was still drawn toward him or her because it's difficult to change your heart. Your mind changes easily, constantly, with every new bit of data. But the heart? It doesn't change so easily. It breaks, but it doesn't change. And so the Lord says, "I want you to believe in Me with your heart—not

simply rationally, but emotionally and intimately."

Romans 10:11
For the scripture saith, Whosoever believeth on him shall not be ashamed.

I love preaching, teaching, and sharing the gospel. Why? Because it works. I get to see lives changed, families put back together, and people doing better than they were previously. It *works.* So, too, when you share with people, you never have to think, *I hope it takes. I hope it works for him, her, or them.* It will. Whoever submits to Jesus' lordship will not be ashamed. His Word guarantees it.

Romans 10:12
For there is no difference between the Jew and the Greek: for the same Lord over all is rich unto all that call upon him.

Jesus is Lord *of* all, and He is Lord *for* all. Jew and Gentile can both be rescued, and they can be brought together into His kingdom, the church.

Romans 10:13–15 (a)
For whosoever shall call upon the name of the Lord shall be saved. How then shall they call on him in whom they have not believed? and how shall they believe in him of whom they have not heard? and how shall they hear without a preacher? And how shall they preach, except they be sent?

I like preaching! I get to bring glad tidings of good things. You do too. You get to share with people over coffee, on your job, or at school, the Good News that the penalty for every sin they have ever committed has been paid.

Romans 10:15 (b)
As it is written, How beautiful are the feet of them that preach the gospel of peace, and bring glad tidings of good things!

A lot of people are unnecessarily depressed and discouraged. The reason? They're not sharing the gospel. Thus, they end up self-absorbed and self-focused. Another translation renders this verse, "How lively are the feet of them that preach the gospel of peace." If you want to have beautiful feet, lively feet, happy feet, share the glorious Good News of the gospel.

Romans 10:16
But they have not all obeyed the gospel. For Isaiah saith, Lord, who hath believed our report?

Isaiah correctly prophesied that all those who would hear would not believe (Isaiah 53:1).

Romans 10:17–19 (a)
So then faith cometh by hearing, and hearing by the word of God. But I say, Have they not heard? Yes verily, their sound went into all the earth, and their words unto the ends of the world. But I say, Did not Israel know? First Moses saith, I will provoke you to jealousy by them that are no people . . .

"In the past, I chose you sovereignly," said the Lord to the nation Israel. "Presently, I've made Myself known to you, but you have rejected Me. So I'm going to provoke you by bringing the Gentiles into the family in order that you might see what you missed when you neglected the opportunity to be saved."

Whether you're talking to Jews or Jehovah's Witnesses, provoke them to jealousy by sharing your freedom with them. You see, because the work of the Cross is complete, all that is left for us to do is to respond and enjoy the Lord. So when you talk to the Jehovah's Witness with his black book, knocking on his quota of doors, say, "Hey, I'm just enjoying the Lord today. How about you?" Or say to the Mormon who is pedaling down the street, "I'm so glad we don't have to wear ties or badges and ride bikes." Truly, when you talk about the finished work of the Cross and your liberty in the Lord, it's like putting a glass of cold water before someone who just ran back-to-back marathons.

Romans 10:19 (b)
. . . and by a foolish nation I will anger you.

"A foolish nation"—that's you and me!

Romans 10:20 (a)
But Isaiah is very bold, and saith, I was found of them that sought me not . . .

We weren't walking in the covenants. We weren't studying the Torah. We weren't aware of the adoption. We didn't find God. He found us.

Romans 10:20 (b), 21
. . . I was made manifest unto them that asked not after me. But to Israel he saith, All day long I have stretched forth my hands unto a disobedient and gainsaying people.

"All day long, I have stretched forth My hands," says the Lord to Israel. "I stretched

them out for you on the Cross, and to you even now."

11 As evidenced by the number of lottery tickets sold each day, there's a growing fascination in our culture with gambling. The one thing you do not have to gamble on is God's promise to you. The Lord doesn't say to us, "Take a chance. Come unto Me and maybe you'll hit the jackpot." No, He promises you and me that if we come to Him, we will find rest in our souls, peace in our hearts, and purpose for our lives. That's no gamble. That is certainty. And that is why the apostle Paul wrapped up chapter 8 of Romans with the fabulous promise that all things are working together for good to them that love God. Gang, if you love God at all, everything coming down, everything going on is working together for good. That's not hyperbole. It's reality.

If the situation you're going through, the struggles with which you're wrestling, or the pressure surrounding you seem to indicate otherwise, Romans 9—11 is for you, because in this important insert, Paul uses the nation Israel as an illustration that God is faithful even when His people are fickle. You can go to the bank on that. You can count on Him. No matter what your situation is, no matter what you're going through, God will be faithful to you.

How can I be sure? Look at God's relationship with Israel . . .

In chapter 9, Paul points to God's past dealings with Israel and highlights the sovereignty of God.

In chapter 10, he deals with God's present dealings with Israel, based upon equity. Whether Jew or Gentile, all are invited to be saved.

Here in chapter 11, we come to God's future dealings with Israel, which show His integrity. That is, God made certain promises to the nation of Israel, which He will fulfill. For even though they've blown it badly, God has promised to see Israel through on the basis of His own integrity and faithfulness.

The same is true for us. He who has begun a good work in us shall complete it (Philippians 1:6). That's His promise. And in it I rest.

Romans 11:1 (a)
I say then, Hath God cast away his people? God forbid.

Students of prophecy, this verse should be noted in your Bible, because many people teach that God is finished with Israel. "The church is now the recipient of the blessings that were promised to Israel and forfeited by Israel when she rejected Jesus Christ," they contend.

Why do they teach this? They do so in order to make their case that the church will go through the Tribulation. You see, the post-Tribulation theological viewpoint makes the church synonymous with Israel, since to explain the fact that, although 144,000 Jews are seen in the Tribulation period, the church is never mentioned. Thus, those who embrace a post-Tribulation viewpoint, always teach that God is through with Israel. Yet Romans 11 deals a deathblow to this mentality, as Paul asks, "Has God cast away His people? God forbid. No way." And then he points to Exhibit B: himself.

Romans 11:1 (b)
For I also am an Israelite, of the seed of Abraham, of the tribe of Benjamin.

"God isn't through with the Israelites. Look at me. *I'm* saved," said Paul. The point Paul makes here is not the fact that he's saved, but the *way* he was saved. Persecuting the church, coming against Christianity, in an audible and tangible encounter with Jesus Christ, Paul's eyes were opened (Acts 9). So, too, at a time when persecution will be coming down on Israel, when Jerusalem will be surrounded and about to be annihilated in the Tribulation period, what will happen? Suddenly, the Lord will appear, and, like Paul, Israel will realize they erred greatly and will turn to Him and be saved (Zechariah 13).

You see, Paul was simply a shadow of what will happen to the entire nation prophetically. Paul points to himself and says, "Is God through with Israel? Consider me and my conversion as an illustration of what will happen eventually."

Romans 11:2 (a)
God hath not cast away his people which he foreknew. Wot ye not what the scripture saith of Elijah?

"Look not only at my life personally," said Paul, "but check out history. Remember Elijah?"

After his great victory in taking on four hundred prophets of Baal and calling down fire from heaven, Elijah caved in when Jezebel threatened him. Running for his life, he hid in a cave, depressed. "What are you doing here?" asked God (see 1 Kings 19:13).

By the way, what are you doing in the cave of depression today? "Well, all of the Christians in my community are carnal. All of the Christians at my church are shallow. I alone serve God," we say all too often.

"You think you're so spiritual and everyone else is so carnal? Look down in the valley below you. There are seven thousand who have not bowed the knee to Baal," God said to Elijah (see 1 Kings 19:18).

Paul goes on to use Elijah's story. . . .

Romans 11:2 (b), 3
How he maketh intercession to God against Israel, saying, Lord, they have killed thy prophets, and digged down thine altars; and I am left alone, and they seek my life.

How would you like to have Elijah for a pastor? People say, "Give us a man of passion and power. Give us a man who can pray down fire from heaven. Give us Elijah." But look how Elijah prayed. He made intercession to God *against* Israel. Yet even this man to whom James points as an example of one who prevailed in prayer, an example of one who knew how to pray, didn't influence God in this case at all.

Sometimes you may have someone curse you, pray against you, or come down on you. But their curses and prayers don't move God. If God be for us, who can be against us? (Romans 8:31). Elijah was unable to pray successfully against the people of Israel, for God had made promises to Israel that still needed to be kept. He had a remnant in Israel Elijah didn't know about.

Next time you, like Elijah, pray God will get someone, remember that there are things about him you don't know. There are qualities in her you are just too blind to see. God sees people in a whole different light than we do. Yes, He's aware of their failings and frailties—but He also sees what He's doing, and the work that has already taken place in their lives. We miss it. We judge people by what we think they should be. God looks at them and sees what they would have been without Him.

Romans 11:4, 5
But what saith the answer of God unto him? I have reserved to myself seven thousand men, who have not bowed the knee to the image of Baal. Even so then at this present time also there is a remnant according to the election of grace.

Just as there was a remnant in Elijah's day, so, too, Paul says, there will always be a remnant in Israel. There always has been, presently is, and always will be a believing minority in Israel. And the believing minority in Israel is wonderfully radical for Jesus Christ.

Romans 11:6
And if by grace, then is it no more of works: otherwise grace is no more grace. But if it be of works, then is it no more grace: otherwise work is no more work.

The remnant does not refer to Jewish believers who keep the law. No, the remnant is made up of those who are saved by grace. Now, what's true in Israel is true for you and me as well. If we're saved by grace, let us continue to walk in grace alone. If I start mixing works into the equation, saying, "Lord, I anticipate Your blessing on my life or this church or my family because of how hard I'm working," I will be rewarded on that basis. I am convinced that the Lord is looking for people, families, and churches He can bless who will truly say and believe, "It is only by God's grace that we've been blessed. It is not because of our powerful prayer, our diligent devotions, or our endless energy. It's simply, purely, solely grace."

Romans 11:7
What then? Israel hath not obtained that which he seeketh for; but the election hath obtained it, and the rest were blinded.

Only the elected ones, the believers, have obtained true spirituality. The rest are blinded. Yes, there is a believing minority in Israel today. But there is also a blinded majority. You can show them verses in black and white concerning the prophecies that were fulfilled in Christ. But they'll just look at you and smile pleasantly.

I recall, during our first trips to Israel, thinking, *Our guides are so close to getting saved. Next year, we'll really get them.* But the next year came, and they were still listening and smiling pleasantly. *They're really getting close now,* I thought. *Wait till the next trip.* Then eventually I began to see the truth of the Bible. "You're right, Lord," I concluded at last. "The majority are blind."

Romans 11:8
(According as it is written, God hath given them the spirit of slumber, eyes that they should not see, and ears that they should not hear;) unto this day.

Is it mean-spirited of God to blind people? No, God only blinds those who want to be blind. You see, God's goodness is so completely irresistible

that, were He not to blind their eyes, people who didn't want to know Him or walk with Him would have no other choice. Thus, God would violate man's free will. So, in His love and wisdom, God says to humanity, "If you don't want to see Me, you won't." That is why you can witness until you're blue in the face to someone who's not called—only to realize he just doesn't get it.

"Well, then," you say, "we should only witness to the elect." Right! But who are they? I'm not sure—so I just talk to everyone I possibly can. I am slowly learning, however, that I need to invest my energy and time where the harvest is ripe rather than spin my wheels hour after day after month after year with people who are blinded.

Romans 11:9, 10
And David saith, Let their table be made a snare, and a trap, and a stumbling block, and a recompence unto them: Let their eyes be darkened, that they may not see, and bow down their back alway.

"If you could just see how Jewish people worship on Shabbat—the lighting of the candles, the wearing of the shawls, the ceremonial cleansing—it gives me goose bumps," some say. Perhaps—but it's all a snare because their trust in their tradition and ritual keeps them from coming to Jesus Christ in the only way any man can come: by faith.

Romans 11:11 (a)
I say then, Have they stumbled that they should fall?

After pointing out the lost condition of the blinded majority, Paul asks if they've stumbled in such a way that their fall is permanent. Have they been shoved down never to stand up? Have they been snared by their ritualism, caught up in their traditions and ceremonies in a way that will never allow them to stand as a nation?

Romans 11:11 (b)
God forbid: but rather through their fall salvation is come unto the Gentiles, for to provoke them to jealousy.

"Absolutely not," Paul answers. "Rather, their fall opened the doors for God to work among the Gentiles, which, in turn, makes the Jews jealous of the simplicity of our salvation."

I'll never forget Al Matucci. As a sophomore on the Del Mar High School football team, he was my line coach, the one who put us through the dreaded "meat grinder"—a drill in which you move down a line of eight guys by hitting them with your head. I can recall Russ LeBlanc coming up from the freshman squad to play with us. He went through the meat grinder one day, and you should have heard Matucci. He loved the guy. "Courson," he barked, "look at LeBlanc. Look how he's doing the grinder." Matucci yelled at me, got in my face, put his cleats on my helmet, pushed me into the ground and told me how wonderful Russ was. It made me mad. It provoked me to jealousy so much so that only a couple of days ago, when I met a fellow whose last name was LeBlanc, I could feel the blood rush to my head. Matucci knew what he was doing and got more out of me because he provoked me to jealousy.

And that's what the Lord did. He provoked His people to jealousy by blessing the Gentiles. He hasn't written them off; He hasn't cast them away. Quite the contrary, He said, "What can I do to reach My people? I know. I'll bless the Gentiles."

Romans 11:12
Now if the fall of them be the riches of the world, and the diminishing of them the riches of the Gentiles; how much more their fulness?

If the world's been blessed because of the Jews stumbling, how much more will the world be blessed when they stand in belief and submission to Jesus Christ. This will happen in the kingdom age when Jesus comes back to rescue the people of Israel in the face of destruction at the end of the Tribulation.

Romans 11:13, 14
For I speak to you Gentiles, inasmuch as I am the apostle of the Gentiles, I magnify mine office: If by any means I may provoke to emulation them which are my flesh, and might save some of them.

"I'm talking to you Gentiles," Paul says, "not only to explain God's grace to you, but to exploit God's grace through you—that is, to provoke my countrymen, the Jews, to jealousy."

Romans 11:15
For if the casting away of them be the reconciling of the world, what shall the receiving of them be, but life from the dead?

As seen in the original text, the "casting away" spoken of here is temporary—for when the Jews come into the kingdom, there will be life where there once was death.

Romans 11:16 (a)
For if the firstfruit be holy, the lump is also holy . . .

The reference here is to Numbers 15, where the Israelites were instructed to bring the firstfruit, the first portion of even their dough, and give it to the Lord, thereby sanctifying the remainder.

I suggest this as an irrevocable, valuable principle for you, for me, and congregationally: Give the firstfruit of your dough, and the whole lump will be sanctified. The firstfruit is the Lord's. The first tenth is the Lord's. The tithe is the Lord's. If I don't tithe, it's not that I am not giving, but rather that I am stealing from God (Malachi 3:8). Ever wonder why you bring home wages, yet it seems as though you have holes in your pockets? Ever wonder why you're not being blessed or stabilized? Perhaps it is because you have built your own house, but have neglected God's (Haggai 1:9). And I remind those who cry, "Legalism!" that the tithe was instituted *before* the law (Genesis 14:20).

Romans 11:16 (b)
. . . and if the root be holy, so are the branches.

Because the people of Israel understood that the firstfruit would sanctify the whole lump, Paul used the analogy to refer to the nation itself, saying, that because Israel's "firstfruit"—consisting of Abraham, Isaac, and Jacob—was sanctified, the entire nation would one day be sanctified as well. Does that mean, as some suggest, that every Jew will be saved because they're linked to Abraham, Isaac, and Jacob? No. Every person must stand before the Lord and give an account of what they did personally with Jesus Christ. But as a nation, because the firstfruit was sanctified, then the whole nation will be blessed in totality. The promises will be fulfilled.

Romans 11:17, 18
And if some of the branches be broken off, and thou, being a wild olive tree, wert grafted in among them, and with them partakest of the root and fatness of the olive tree; boast not against the branches. But if

thou boast, thou bearest not the root, but the root thee.

The tree provides three symbols of Israel: (1) The vine speaks of the spiritual privileges of Israel (Isaiah 5; Matthew 21); (2) the fig tree speaks of the national privileges of Israel (Matthew 24); and (3) the olive tree speaks of the religious privileges of Israel (Hosea 14). The vine speaks of Israel up to the time of Jesus Christ. The fig tree speaks of Israel from the crucifixion of Christ to the present. The olive tree speaks of Israel in the millennial period. As Gentiles, we were grafted into the olive tree. But because we "partake of its fatness" solely by God's grace, we have no room to boast, or look down upon the Jew.

Romans 11:19–22
Thou wilt say then, The branches were broken off, that I might be grafted in. Well; because of unbelief they were broken off, and thou standest by faith. Be not highminded, but fear: For if God spared not the natural branches, take heed lest he also spare not thee. Behold therefore the goodness and severity of God: on them which fell, severity; but toward thee, goodness, if thou continue in his goodness: otherwise thou also shalt be cut off.

"Learn a lesson from the Jew," Paul says to the Gentile. "Realize that, although you were grafted in by God's grace, you can be cut off if you refuse to respond to His grace."

In John 15, Jesus said, "If the branch abides not in Me, it is cut off and cast into the fire and burned." It is a strong warning with which I do not wish to tamper. How we need to understand both the goodness and the severity of God.

Romans 11:23
And they also, if they abide not still in unbelief, shall be grafted in: for God is able to graft them in again.

God has a plan for Israel. Although they are "cut off" presently, He is in the grafting mode.

Romans 11:24
For if thou wert cut out of the olive tree which is wild by nature, and wert grafted contrary to nature into a good olive tree: how much more shall these, which be the natural branches, be grafted into their own olive tree?

As Gentiles, we came from a wild tree—yet God put us in the tree of faith. How much more, then, shall the true olive branches be grafted into their own olive tree?

Romans 11:25
For I would not, brethren, that ye should be ignorant of this mystery, lest ye should be wise in your own conceits; that blindness in part is happened to Israel, until the fulness of the Gentiles be come in.

When will the fullness of the Gentiles come? In Luke 21, Jesus said Jerusalem would be trodden down until the "times of the Gentiles" are fulfilled. In 1967 Jerusalem was recaptured by Israel. Thus, I believe the "times of the Gentiles" were fulfilled in 1967. We are simply in overtime right now, due to God's goodness and patience. If you got saved after 1967, aren't you glad He took us into overtime?

The times of the Gentiles (Luke 21) deals with the recovering of Jerusalem. But the fullness of the Gentiles is a different issue. What is the fullness of the Gentiles? It's when the full number of Gentiles are saved. In other words, there is a Gentile somewhere on the earth who is the last one to be saved. When that person acknowledges Jesus Christ as Savior, the fullness of the Gentiles will be complete, and at that moment, we'll be raptured. So if you're not yet saved—get saved. You could do us all a great favor because you might be the last one!

The Lord will wait until all one hundred are in the flock. He'll leave the ninety-nine and search out the one, and when that last one is brought into the fold, the fullness of the Gentiles concludes and up we go. The times of the Gentiles deals with Jerusalem; the fullness of the Gentiles deals with the last individual coming into the fold and accepting Jesus Christ—which will usher in the Rapture and the completion of the Gentile Age.

Romans 11:26–28
And so all Israel shall be saved: as it is written, There shall come out of Sion the Deliverer, and shall turn away ungodliness from Jacob: For this is my covenant unto them, when I shall take away their sins. As concerning the gospel, they are enemies for your sakes: but as touching the election, they are beloved for the fathers' sakes.

Who is "the election"? When people read Matthew 24, they say, "In the Tribulation God calls the elect from every corner of the earth. Therefore, the church must be in the Tribulation." Wrong. Israel is also called the elect (Isaiah 45:4). The election of God deals both with the church and with the nation of Israel. So in Matthew 24, when God says He's going to bring the elect from all corners, it means He's going to gather His people, the Jewish nation together.

Romans 11:29
For the gifts and calling of God are without repentance.

Why will God gather Israel? Because His calling is sure. He didn't change His mind about Israel. Nor does He change His mind about you. Even if we are faithless, He remains faithful because He cannot deny His nature (2 Timothy 2:13).

For topical study of Romans 11:29 entitled "God's Unchanging Call," turn to page 966.

Romans 11:30, 31
For as ye in times past have not believed God, yet have now obtained mercy through their unbelief: Even so have these also now not believed, that through your mercy they also may obtain mercy.

The best thing you can do when you go to Israel is to love Jesus Christ. Worship Him, and let the Jews see your glorious liberty in the way you're free from your sin. Sin is the big problem for the Jews. They light their candles. They keep Shabbat. They cleanse themselves. But they still sin. They know the Bible. They know the Old Testament says that without the shedding of blood, there is no remission of sin (Leviticus 17:11). But there's no shedding of blood in Israel today because there's no temple. Consequently, it causes a great deal of consternation within the Jew. But our celebrating the one sacrifice of Jesus Christ and the mercy of God upon us will perhaps provoke them to be part of the remnant at this time.

Romans 11:32, 33 (a)
For God hath concluded them all in unbelief, that he might have mercy upon all. O the depth of the riches both of the wisdom and knowledge of God!

Here, Paul's theology turns into a doxology, as he just begins to worship. God is so good. Who can figure out His ways? Truly, they are unsearchable.

Romans 11:33 (b), 34 (a)
How unsearchable are his judgments, and his ways past finding out! For who hath known the mind of the Lord?

I like what J. B. Phillips said when he said, "If God was small enough to figure out, He wouldn't be big enough to worship."

When I was a freshman at Biola University, about ten of us guys spent almost all of one night in Phil Bishop's room, pondering the question of whether God can make a rock so big He can't lift it? Back and forth we went, wondering and debating by the hour, our faith growing a little bit weaker with each volley. The next Sunday, I went to Calvary Chapel in Costa Mesa, and Pastor Chuck was talking about unprofitable questions. He stopped and said, "For example, some people ask, "Can God make a rock so big He can't lift it?"

Oh, boy, I thought. Here comes the answer.
But, "That's a stupid question," was Chuck's only reply.

It was. You see, there are things we'll never figure out—election vs. free will, sovereignty vs. responsibility. And although we could spend hours reading and studying, pondering and arguing, some things we'll never reconcile because our brains are too small. Forget trying to figure it all out. Just marvel at the goodness God has shown you!

Romans 11:34 (b)
Or who hath been his counseller?

Who has been His counselor? I have. "Well, Lord," I pray, "don't forget . . ." and, "by the way . . ."—as if I know what's best for this country, or for this church, or for me personally. Sometimes, I'm amazed at the audacity of my prayers. Prayer is coming to God not to get our will done in heaven, but to get heaven's will done on earth. Prayer is saying, "Lord, what do You want to do in my life, in this church, in our family? What do *You* want to do?"

Romans 11:35
Or who hath first given to him, and it shall be recompensed unto him again?

Not only is God greater than our understanding—He's greater than our giving. You can't out-give God in time, money, love, or any other commodity. He'll never "owe you one."

Romans 11:36
For of him, and through him, and to him, are all things: to whom be glory for ever. Amen.

And so we close this section, knowing that God has proven Himself to the Jews. He chose them sovereignly, deals with them equitably, and promises He will not give up on them eternally. Gener-ations before ours studied this section of Romans and thought, *We hear what you say, Paul—but where is Israel today?*

We're so blessed because we don't have to say, "Someday, Israel is going to come together." No, we can say, "We've already seen it happen, Lord. Therefore, we know that things are going to come together for us as well. You've promised they would, and we trust in You."

GOD'S UNCHANGING CALL
A Topical Study of
Romans 11:29

On a fall day in the Sierra Nevada mountain range, a man was on an afternoon hike several miles from where he parked his vehicle. The temperature dropped precipitously as ominous clouds began to form. Realizing a storm was approaching, the man headed back to where he left his car. But on the way, he was caught in a whiteout. The hours passed as he wandered in circles—unable to see even two feet ahead of him. He felt his energy giving out and a deadly lethargy creeping in, yet he knew that if he listened to his body and sat down to rest, he would never get up again. After wandering around a few more minutes, however, he finally gave in and decided to rest, knowing he would soon die. But as he sat down, he felt something next to him. He brushed away the snow and found the body of someone who, like him, had been caught in the storm. He felt for a pulse, and finding there was still life flowing through the body, he stood up, and with super-human strength hoisted the body to his shoulders and began to walk. After a mere one hundred feet, he came face to door with a cabin.

A cabin was only one hundred feet away from where the hiker was ready to give up. He didn't see it because of the blizzard, but once he attempted to save someone else and started moving, the cabin materialized before him. Inside, there was a fire in the fireplace and a man cooking dinner. Both of the travelers were warmed, fed, and saved.

Perhaps you feel like giving up, as though you want to sit down and die. The key for you is to look for someone who is worse off than you in order that you may give out the gifts God has given you.

"I agree," some may say, "but you don't know where I've been. Certainly, the call to share in ministry is no longer on my life. I've sinned so badly that surely any gifts the Lord may have given me have been taken from me."

The Problem of Sinfulness

Are you more iniquitous than Samson? You know the story. He fell in love with a lady who had honey lips and a poison heart. "Oh, please, Sammy," she said, "tell me the secret of your strength."

"Well, babe, I'll tell you," Samson answered, "if you put bowstrings of raw leather around me, I'd be as weak as any other man."

So when Samson fell asleep on her lap, Delilah tied him up with leather strings and called for the Philistines, then yelled, "Samson! Wake up! The Philistines are here!" Samson stood up, snapped the bowstrings off, and did the Philistines in. When the dust settled, Delilah looked at Samson and said, "You lied to me."

"Forgive me," apologized Samson. "I'll tell you what: Put new green ropes around me, and I'll be like any other individual."

When Samson fell asleep again, Delilah did just that. "Sammy! The Philistines are here again," she said. Just as he did before, Samson woke up, popped the ropes off as if they were threads, and took on the Philistines.

"You lied to me," sobbed Delilah.

"Okay, Okay," said Samson, "If you weave my hair, (watch out, Samson, you're getting a little close now), I'll be like any other man." He fell asleep, and you know the story. He woke up and his hair was woven.

"Samson, the Philistines are upon you," said Delilah. He woke up, did them in, and trashed Delilah's loom.

You gotta wonder about Samson. What's the deal? Could anyone be that dense? Could anyone be that dumb? But Delilah continued to cry day after day, until finally he said, "Okay, I'll tell you the secret of my strength. If you cut my hair, I'll be like any other man." He fell asleep once more and she sheared his hair.

"Samson! The Philistines are here," she cried.

And Judges 16:20 tells what happened next in one of the saddest verses in Scripture: "And he awoke out of his sleep, and said, I will go out as at other times, before, and shake myself. And he knew not that the Lord was departed from him." Samson took on the Philistines, but this time they did him in. They blinded him by poking out his eyes, bound him in brass, and made him grind grain round and round like an ox.

The question cannot help but arise: Was Samson really that stupid? I suggest that Samson knew he was going to get a haircut when he told Delilah his secret.

As a Nazarite, Samson was absolutely forbidden to drink wine, touch dead bodies, or cut his hair (Numbers 6). Yet Samson had taken of wine at the Philistine parties and nothing happened (Judges 14:10). He had touched the dead body of a lion in which there was honey, and, again, nothing happened (Judges 14:9). Thus, I suggest to you that what Samson was really thinking was, *Well, I've already drunk wine; I've already touched a dead body. Nothing's going to happen to me if I cut my hair.* Samson thought he was an exception—but he wasn't. And neither are you.

Maybe you haven't yet felt the repercussion of your rebellion, but know this: If you continue down that road, you'll find some real trouble. Today is the day for you to stop trying the mercy and testing the patience of God.

Back to Samson. His hair began to grow (Judges 16:22). And when he was brought into the temple of Dagon, he prayed, "Lord, use me one more time." After requesting his captors to stand him between two supporting pillars, Samson stretched out his arms, pushed, and literally brought the house down—literally. Three thousand people in the balconies crashed to their deaths, and Scripture records he killed more enemies of Israel in his death than he did in his life (Judges 16:30).

Truly, the gifts and callings of God are without repentance. Maybe you feel your experience has been somewhat "hairy." Know this: If, like Samson, you're willing to die to self and say, "Lord, use me. I'm tired of living for myself, focused on myself, concerned about myself. Just use me"—you, too, will bring the house down because the callings and giftings of God are without repentance.

The Problem of Rebelliousness

"I agree that the Lord could use a sinful person like Samson—for then His grace and mercy are seen all the more clearly," you say. "But me? I have already failed in what He has asked of me. How could He ask me again?"

"Go to Nineveh," God said. Instead, Jonah went to Tarshish—the exact opposite direction. En route, a storm arose and, you know the story. He was swallowed by a great fish. Jonah was in a tight spot so dark he couldn't see the hand in front of his face. No doubt entwined with seaweed and sweating from the internal body temperature of the great fish, it is no wonder Jonah felt like he was in hell (Jonah 2).

Maybe you feel that way. Perhaps God called you to do something for Him. He gifted and equipped you to carry out a specific task for the kingdom, but like Jonah, you chose to go in the opposite direction. And now you find yourself saying, "I don't know where I'm going. Nothing's happening. I can't think straight. No wonder the Lord has given up on me."

Listen. The Lord didn't give up on Jonah. All the time Jonah thought he was going nowhere, in the dark, feeling cramped, getting hot—the whale was moving in the right direction. Why? Because the gifts and calling of God are without repentance.

And once Jonah said, "I'm sorry," the whale regurgitated him on to the beach. His hair must have been bleached from the gastric juices. His clothes must have been tattered. He must have looked like an albino. But at last he was in Nineveh—right where God wanted him all along. He walked into the city, smelling like the digestive tract of a whale, saying, "Repent. In forty days judgment will come."

The Ninevites saw him, smelled him, and couldn't believe what they heard about him. Yet, Scripture records that the entire city repented. The greatest revival in world history came by way of a man who previously thought he was going nowhere because of his rebellion. So, too, even though you feel like you don't deserve it—God's not through with you because the calling and gifting of God are without repentance. He doesn't take them back.

The Problem of Cowardice

"I don't know Him," swore Peter. Why?

Because a little girl said to him, "I think I recognize you. Aren't you one of His followers?"(see Matthew 26:71).

"I can't continue on in ministry," Peter said. "I know Jesus is alive—but I've been such a coward. I've failed miserably. I'm going back to fishing" (see John 21:3).

So it was, that after fishing all night with his buddies, he heard a voice calling, "Caught anything, children?"

"Nothing," he yelled back.

It's true. When you feel like you've failed so badly that you just have to go back to fishing—back to the old places, back to the old gang, back to the old stuff—you'll always come up empty-handed.

"Put your net on the right side of the boat," called the voice from the shore. And when Peter and the others did, they pulled in such a haul, it almost sank their boat.

"It's the Lord!" they said at last. And when they reached the shore, what did they find? Fish roasting on the fire. You see, the very thing Peter went to sea to find was in the hand of Jesus all along.

"Do you love Me?" He asked Peter three times (John 21:15–17). He didn't say, "Peter, if you love Me, you're on probation. Prove yourself for three more years—and if you do well, we might allow you to hang out with us again." No, He said, "Peter, if you even like Me, then feed My sheep, and tend my lambs. Go back to where you were before you went on this fishing trip. Get going again."

And that's what the Lord says to you who have felt as though you've chickened out in cowardice, to you who have dabbled in sinfulness, to you who have fled in rebelliousness. "Get going again. Feed My flock. Do what you were doing before your excursion into sin. Get back to it once again."

Gang, only the Lord shows that kind of grace. People don't. Churches often won't. But Jesus does. "Follow Me," He says, "because My gifts and callings are without repentance." Get going and you'll find satisfaction in your heart, fulfillment in your life, and reward for eternity. Don't waste any more time. Your hair is growing. The whale is moving. The fish aren't biting.

So get going!

12 Almost invariably, Paul began his Epistles dealing with the position we have as believers. That is, he addressed doctrine before he dealt with duty. Sad to say, such is not the case all too often in the church today. The result? A legalistic guilt trip that is very foreign to the nature and message of Jesus Christ. When, however, the concepts of doctrine precede the call to duty, we understand that the work is done, that we are righteous in Christ, and that there is nothing more to do to get close to the Lord, or to enjoy the blessing of the Lord. The result? We find ourselves saying, "Far out! Lord, in light of what You did for me, I want to serve You." And that is why, after spending eleven chapters talking about man's ruined condition and God's rich salvation, in chapter 12, Paul begins to encourage us to start serving Him.

Romans 12:1 (a)
I beseech you therefore, brethren . . .

Whenever you come to the word "therefore," stop and ask, what it's there for. It's as if Paul is saying, "In light of the previous eleven chapters, in light of the previous three hundred and fifteen verses, in light of who you are in Christ and what you enjoy because of Christ, I beseech you."

Romans 12:1 (b)
. . . by the mercies of God, that ye present your bodies a living sacrifice, holy, acceptable unto God, which is your reasonable service.

Give yourself to Him completely. Why? Because of what He did for you. Truly, it's reasonable to give yourself to the Lord, to say, "I'm laying my life down for You, Lord, because You gave Yourself for me. You have great things awaiting me. And I don't want to miss any of them now or eternally."

Romans 12:2 (a)
And be not conformed to this world: but be ye transformed . . .

Every one of us is in one of two categories: Either we're conformers or transformers. Right now you're either trying to figure out what she's wearing, what he's driving, or how you can fit in and be cool—or, like J. B. Phillips, you're saying, "I don't care what the world is doing. I'm not going to let it squeeze me into its mold."

Are you a thermometer—adjusting to the temperature of the culture, or are you a thermostat—changing the climate of the culture? If you are a conformer, a thermometer, you're in for perpetual frustration because by the time you take the temperature and figure out what's hot, by the time you change your look, or buy the car, or redo your house—the world will have moved on, leaving you out of style. Truly, this is a great mystery to a lot of Christians. They try to make their ministries relatable by analyzing what the world is doing in order to emulate it. But by the time they figure it out and implement it, the world has moved on. That's why Christians are known for being out of style.

What's the key? Don't be a thermometer. Be a thermostat. Don't be a conformer. Be a transformer. Say, "I'm in a whole different place than you are, world. I'm living for eternity. I'm preparing for heaven."

The word translated "transformed" is the word for "metamorphosis." Interestingly, it is used two other times in the New Testament—one to describe what happened to Jesus Christ on the Mount of Transfiguration when He began to shine (Matthew 17:2); and once to describe what happens to us when we see the Lord (2 Corinthians 3:18).

How are we transformed? How are we metamorphosed?

Read on.

Romans 12:2 (b)
. . . by the renewing of your mind, that ye may prove what is that good, and acceptable, and perfect, will of God.

Just as Jesus was metamorphosed, so, too, you can be changed if you keep your mind on Him. How do we keep our minds on Him? By keeping in the Word. "Lo, I have come in the volume of the book," Scripture declares concerning Jesus (see Psalm 40:7 and Hebrews 10:7).

You see, I can give my body to Him—that's a real key. But it's incomplete in and of itself unless I keep my mind on Him—and that happens through a diligent contemplation of the "volume of the book," the Word. However, you can read your Bible every morning for devotions; you can study it with us every Wednesday night; you can know the Word backward and forward and not go through a metamorphosis. Indeed, Paul would say that, in and of itself, the letter kills (2 Corinthians 3:6). If you read the Scriptures just to get insights into theology, or practical tips about parenting or relationships, metamorphosis will not take place because transformation occurs only when we study the Word not for the sake of the Word, but in order to touch the Lord.

"In the beginning," John wrote, "was the Word . . . And the Word became flesh and dwelt among us" (John 1:1, 14). It's the Incarnation—the Word becoming flesh, becoming personable, touchable, and relatable—that will transform you. If you approach the Word strictly from an intellectual, academic, theological perspective, you might gain a point or two, but you'll not be changed.

At the stereotypical American breakfast table, the husband reads the newspaper. Across from him sits his wife, waiting to talk with him. But the man is interested in the impartation of information, not the intimacy of communication—and I suggest the same thing happens all too often in the devotional life of believers. They read the information in the Word but completely neglect communication with the Word made flesh. I am concerned about the great number of people who have a devotional life that is basically informational. Only in the last couple of generations has this happened, because throughout the vast majority of Christian history, Bible study was neither academic nor theological. It was oral. It was relational as people heard the Word being read. Communication transpired as the Living Word was fleshed out in real life.

Those who say, "Lord, I'm reading Your Word in order to hear Your voice" are those who leave their time of devotion metamorphosed—soaring like a butterflies.

For topical study of Romans 12:1–2 entitled "God's Will: So Simple!" turn to page 975.

Romans 12:3
For I say, through the grace given unto me, to every man that is among you, not to think of himself more highly than he ought to think; but to think soberly, according as God hath dealt to every man the measure of faith.

"Be careful," warns Paul. "As you discover and live in the good, acceptable, and perfect will of God, be sober. Don't think of yourself more highly than you ought."

Fifteen years old, and dressed in suit and tie, I headed for the San Jose Rescue Mission, twelve-page sermon on the eschatological significance of Zacchaeus in the sycamore tree in hand. At about page six, I could hear the shuffling of feet, see the nodding of heads, and feel the rumbling of stomachs, for, as I later discovered, only those who listened to the sermon could partake of the meal. By page seven, I knew I was in trouble. On page eight, as I was perspiring and turning red in embarrassment, one gentleman in the back row called out, "Hey, you overgrown tomato—sit down!" I sat down and lost my place before even making it to page nine.

"Don't think of yourself more highly than you ought," warned Paul. If you do, the Lord has ways of bringing you back down to earth! God can use anyone to do His work. If you don't think so, ask Balaam (Numbers 22:28)!

Romans 12:4, 5
For as we have many members in one body, and all members have not the same office: So we, being many, are one body in Christ, and every one members one of another.

Brother Hammer was appointed to preside over the Master Tool Convention. Brother Screwdriver objected, saying, "Brother Hammer, you're too noisy to preside over this meeting. You're always driving home your point, always nailing people. I call for your resignation immediately."

Brother Hammer responded, "Well, what about you, Brother Screwdriver? All you ever do is spin around in circles."

"That may be true," said Brother Screwdriver, "but at least I'm not like Brother Plane. His work is so surface, so shallow. What right does he have to even be here?"

"If you're going to kick me out," protested Brother Plane, "what about Brother Ruler? He thinks he's always right, measuring everyone else by his standard."

"Well, if you're going to come down on me," argued Brother Ruler, "what about Brother Pliers? He needs to get a grip!"

"At least I don't rub people the wrong way," said Brother Pliers, staring at Brother Sandpaper."

Just then, the Master Craftsman walked in.

And, as He used each tool at the perfect time,
He created an object of great beauty.

A lot of times, we look at the gifts of other people and the way God made them, and we think, *She's shallow,* or, *He rubs me the wrong way,* or, *They're too noisy*—until we finally come to the point where we understand that there are many members in the body—each one with a part to play, a function to fulfill.

Romans 12:6 (a)
Having then gifts differing according to the grace that is given to us . . .

This is the only time in Scripture where spiritual gifts are spoken of directly. "Wait a minute," you say. "What about 1 Corinthians 12 and 14, and Ephesians 4?"

Look at those passages, and you will see that the word "gifts" is in italics, meaning it was not present in the original Greek. You see, the gifts listed here in Romans are the motivational gifts, the manifestations of which are listed in 1 Corinthians 12, and the ministries of which are found in Ephesians 4. That is why you will see that the list of gifts here in Romans 12 contains the motivational gift that God, by His grace, has given every believer. As we become open to the Spirit, He adds the manifestations of the Spirit (1 Corinthians 12), as well as ministry in the Spirit (Ephesians 4).

Romans 12:6 (b)
. . . whether prophecy, let us prophesy according to the proportion of faith.

As Paul lists the motivational gifts—the tools in the box of the Master Carpenter—he divides them into two groups: those that expound the Word (verses 6–8a), and those that expand the work (8b). The first motivational gift Paul discusses is prophecy. Prophecy means more than foretelling. It primarily means "forth-telling"—expounding the Word, declaring truth. The Word burns within the heart of those with the gift of prophecy. They know what should be shared and feel a pressing need to speak out.

Romans 12:7 (a)
Or ministry, let us wait on our ministering . . .

Prophecy declares truth. Ministry depicts truth. Jesus modeled this over and over again when He would first teach and then touch. He would teach truth and then touch people as an illustration of what He taught. Ministering simply means serving. I think of Dorcas in Acts 9. When she died, the early church went into an upheaval. Why was she so loved? Because she was a minister in the truest sense of the word. Others declared truth and warmed people's hearts; Dorcas depicted truth by sewing people's garments and warming their bodies.

Romans 12:7 (b)
. . . or he that teacheth, on teaching.

A teacher defines truth. A prophet might share sporadically; but a teacher shares systematically. "You've heard it said of old, you're not to commit adultery. But let Me define what that means," said Jesus (see Matthew 5:27, 28). And people marveled, for He taught with authority.

Romans 12:8 (a)
Or he that exhorteth, on exhortation . . .

Exhortation develops truth. The one with the gift of exhortation is often one who gives a kick in the proverbial seat of the pants. "O, ye of little faith," Jesus said when His disciples were fearful in the storm" (Matthew 8:26).

How I need brothers and sisters who come by me with a word of exhortation. Yes, sometimes they irritate me—but they're needed very definitely!

Romans 12:8 (b)
. . . he that giveth, let him do it with simplicity . . .

Giving expands the work. Giving with simplicity means giving with no strings attached. "I want to know where this money's going," some demand. "I'll only give if it goes here, or for that, or if you agree to do this." Don't give that way. Rather, give with simplicity.

"Simplicity" can also be translated "liberality." Maybe God has blessed you with the gift of giving. If so, exercise it with generosity!

Romans 12:8 (c)
. . . he that ruleth, with diligence . . .

The winner of the "Best Use of Duct Tape" contest used duct tape to patch the wing of the plane he flew from Guatemala to Honduras. There are people in the body like that. They know how to patch things up. They know how to make things fly. They have a feeling for how things should happen. Theirs is the gift of ruling, of governing, of doing all things decently and in order—exemplified beautifully in the life of Jesus and seen practically when He instructed His disciples to make the multitude sit in groups of fifty in order that He could feed them (Luke 9:14).

Romans 12:8 (d)
. . . he that sheweth mercy, with cheerfulness.

If you're expanding the work by giving, do it generously and with simplicity. If you're expanding the work by ruling, do it diligently. If you're expanding the work by showing mercy, do it cheerfully. Those who care for people in the hospital, those who sympathize with those going through a traumatic relational experience, or those who cry with those experiencing the heartbreak of divorce have the gift of mercy. If you wish to study these things further, look at Jesus. See how He ministered mercy; how He ruled diligently; how He gave sacrificially; how He moved in prophecy. Study Jesus, and you'll find the perfect example of how these gifts are to function in His body of believers.

I believe the Lord is looking for an army of sharpshooters who will zero in on their target and say, "This is where I function," as they make the development and exercise of their spiritual gift their priority and passion. How can you know which gift is yours? I believe the answer is amazingly simple: If you suddenly became pastor of Applegate Christian Fellowship, what changes would you make?

If you would grab the microphone and call the fellowship to activism, if you would try to get folks fired up to share the gospel, if you have a burden to speak forth God's Word to a hurting society, chances are yours is the gift of prophecy.

If, on the other hand, you would divide the fellowship into small groups in order that members of the body might serve one another and meet one another's spiritual needs, yours is most likely the gift of ministry.

If, given the opportunity, you would lead the fellowship in a study of Hebrew, Greek, and Aramaic, of homiletics and hermeneutics, of eschatology and ecclesiology, yours is probably the gift of teaching.

If your primary concern would be funding worthy causes for needy people, if your energy would be spent organizing bake sales and car washes, yours is the gift of giving.

If your heart would go out to hurting people, if your passion lies in hospice ministry, jail evangelism, or crisis hotlines, yours is the gift of mercy.

If, however, the first thing you would do would be to head for the church office and straighten things out in order that the fellowship would operate more smoothly and effectively, yours is the gift of ruling.

What would you change, what would you do if you were in charge? Your answer will give you a good clue as to what your spiritual gift is. The problem is, I have a tendency to analyze others in light of my gift, wondering why they're not functioning as I do. Great is the day and mature will be the church family who will simply say, "She's different," or, "He's different"—and that's as it should be because they're functioning the way God made them." That's the point Paul is making here. Find your gift, develop it, and let others function in theirs.

Romans 12:9 (a)
Let love be without dissimulation.

Find God's will by giving your life to Him and by keeping your mind on Him. Don't think too highly of yourself. Just flow in the gifting God has given you. And above all, and in all, let love be without dissimulation or hypocrisy.

Romans 12:9 (b)
Abhor that which is evil . . .

The Greek rendering of this verse is: Treat evil as you would treat a cow pie. How many of you say, "My kids might get involved with cow pies, so I'm going to keep some cow pies in my room in order that I can study them. It's my calling as a parent"? That's absurd. Yet it's exactly what people are saying when they say, "I gotta know what's happening on the screen or in the magazines. Gotta keep current."

No you don't. Treat evil like a cow pie. It's abhorrent, repulsive, disgusting. Later on, Paul would write, "Concerning evil, you should be simple, or naive" (Romans 16:19).

Romans 12:9 (c)–11
. . . cleave to that which is good. Be kindly affectioned one to another with brotherly love; in honour preferring one another; not slothful in business; fervent in spirit; serving the Lord.

Twenty years ago, a missionary candidate was summoned to appear before a certain examiner. A veteran missionary himself, the examiner instructed the young man to come to his house at 5:00 A.M. the next Monday morning. So the young man got up at 4:00 and was at the examiner's house by 4:55. "Wait for me," the examiner said as he ushered the candidate into his study. Three hours later, the examiner returned and said, "How do you spell baker?"

"B-a-k-e-r," answered the young man.

"How's your math?" asked the examiner. "What's two plus two?"

"Four," answered the young man.

Satisfied, the examiner said, "I'm going to recommend you for service in our mission." And the young candidate left the interview perplexed.

That evening, the examiner met with his mission board and said, "I highly recommend this young man for ministry. I tested him on self-denial. He rolled out of bed and showed up at 4:55 A.M. Patience? I made him wait three hours in my study, and he didn't say a word. Temper? I asked him to spell baker, and he didn't become agitated. Humility? I asked him what two plus two was and he answered readily. This man will make a great missionary."

Folks, you never know what tests the Master Examiner is putting before you. We're interested in credentials, but the Lord is interested in character. "Whatever you do, be fervent," said Paul. Be fervent for the Lord however simple your service might be or how insignificant it might seem—for in so doing, you just may be qualifying yourself for even greater service.

Romans 12:12
Rejoicing in hope; patient in tribulation; continuing instant in prayer.

Verse 12 is a beautiful garden of growth, listing as it does the three sweet peas of praise, patience, and prayer. Plant these seeds in your heart, and you'll do well throughout your walk.

Romans 12:13
Distributing to the necessity of saints; given to hospitality.

What does "hospitality" mean? It means to be a "hospital" for the hurting, lonely people who come your way.

Entertaining says, "I want to impress you with my home, my decorating, my cooking."

Hospitality says, "This house is simply a gift from my Master. I use it however and whenever He desires."

Entertaining needs to impress.

Hospitality aims to serve.

Entertaining puts things before people, saying, "As soon as I get the house clean, I'll start inviting people over."

Hospitality puts people first, saying, "No furniture? No problem. We'll picnic on the floor."

Entertaining subtly declares, "This house is mine—an expression of my personality, and my ingenuity."

Hospitality whispers, "What's mine is yours. Enjoy it anytime."

Truly, hospitality is practical Christianity.

Romans 12:14, 15 (a)
Bless them which persecute you: bless, and curse not. Rejoice with them that do rejoice . . .

Sometimes it's harder to rejoice with those who are rejoicing than it is to weep with those who are weeping. "How come she lucked out? How come they got that? Why does he get the big breaks?" we wonder all too often.

Romans 12:15 (b)
. . . and weep with them that weep.

Paul doesn't say, "Preach to those who are weeping." No, he says, "Weep with those who are weeping." Concerning those who are weeping, we don't have to preach at them or speak something profound to them. We just need to weep with them without questioning God's goodness in the process.

Romans 12:16 (a)
Be of the same mind one toward another. Mind not high things, but condescend to men of low estate.

Don't try to climb any social, intellectual, or spiritual ladders.

Romans 12:16 (b)–18
Be not wise in your own conceits. Recompense to no man evil for evil. Provide things honest in the sight of all men. If it be possible, as much as lieth in you, live peaceably with all men.

Whenever you can, to the degree you possibly can, live peaceably with all men.

Romans 12:19
Dearly beloved, avenge not yourselves, but rather give place unto wrath: for it is written, Vengeance is mine; I will repay, saith the Lord.

Vengeance is the Lord's department. Man's responsibility is to love.

Romans 12:20, 21
Therefore if thine enemy hunger, feed him; if he thirst, give him drink: for in so doing thou shalt heap coals of fire on his head. Be not overcome of evil, but overcome evil with good.

In Paul's day, when a fire went out in a home, it was difficult to reignite it. Therefore, if someone's fire went out, the women would carry live coals in clay jars upon their heads to share with the person who had no fire. Thus, the implication here was not of burning one's enemy, but of warming him in order to ultimately win him to the kingdom.

GOD'S WILL: SO SIMPLE!
A Topical Study of
Romans 12:1, 2

I suppose that, as a pastor, the question asked of me more often than any other is: How do I find God's will for my life? This question is based upon the presupposition that God's will is something hidden, lost, or hard to determine. But, gang, nothing could be further from the truth. God's will is not something that has to be found. It isn't lost. It's not hidden. It shouldn't be tough to discern. In our text today, in only two verses, Paul tells you and me exactly what to do to discover God's plan for our life. It's profoundly simple and incredibly wonderful.

The word translated "prove" in Romans 12:2 is a word not of academics, but of intimacy—as in Genesis 4:1, where Scripture records that Adam "knew" Eve. This doesn't mean Adam knew about Eve intellectually. It means he knew her intimately. And this is what Paul is declaring to us. You can know God's will intimately. You can know it not only intellectually but experientially if you do a couple of things . . .

Give Yourself to the Lord

I beseech you therefore, brethren, by the mercies of God, that ye present your bodies a living sacrifice, holy, acceptable unto God, which is your reasonable service.   Romans 12:1

"Well, that disqualifies me," you say. "My body is anything but holy. Therefore, how can it be acceptable?"

This is where a lot of people get discouraged unnecessarily. They say, "Until my body is holy and acceptable, I really can't offer it as a living sacrifice." But that's because they failed to read the most important word of the verse: "I beseech you, *therefore*, brethren."

In this case, "therefore" is in reference to the first eleven chapters, wherein Paul makes it clear that when you became a Christian, God placed you in His Son, making you at once holy and acceptable in His sight. *Therefore,* the first step to finding God's will is to present your body a living sacrifice to Him.

What does it mean to be a living sacrifice? It means to say, "Lord, I'm Yours. I love You more than anything else I might pursue." The problem, however, with a living sacrifice, unlike a dead one, is that a living sacrifice has a tendency to climb off the altar regularly. I squirm and escape not infrequently. Thus, I need to continually return and say, "Oh, Lord, on this new and beautiful day, I again give You my life. I'm tired of trying to figure out where I should go or what I should be. I've messed up time and time again. I've gone my own way and done my own thing—and it's been disastrous. I give up, Lord. Take my life."

That's the first step to experiencing God's will.

Be Transformed

And be not conformed to this world: but be ye transformed by the renewing of your mind, that ye may prove what is that good, and acceptable, and perfect, will of God.
Romans 12:2

The word translated "transformed" is *metamorphoo,* from which we get our word "metamorphosis." *Metamorphoo* also appears in Matthew 17, when it is used to describe the change that took place in the appearance of Jesus as He began to glow on the Mount of Transfiguration. When was Jesus metamorphosed, or transformed? When He spoke to Moses and Elijah about His death (Luke 9:31), when He spoke about laying down His life sacrificially.

How do you become transformed? Become a living sacrifice to the Lord and keep your mind on the Lord. "Don't be conformed to the world's thinking," warns Paul. "Instead, give your mind to God, and you will know His good, acceptable, and perfect will."

"That sounds good," you say. "But how does it work for me practically, in my situation presently?"

When the disciples were wondering what was going on, what was coming down, what was next, Jesus looked at them and said, "Let not your hearts be troubled. You believe in God, believe also in Me. In my Father's house are many mansions. I'm going to prepare a place for you—that where I am, there you may be also. And if I go and prepare a place for you, I will come and receive you unto Myself. And where I go you know, and the way you know" (John 14:1–4).

Thomas said, "Lord, we don't know where You're going, and we don't know the way" (see John 14:5).

And Jesus said to those confused, distressed, disturbed disciples on the night before His crucifixion "I am the Way. You know the way. It's Me. It's not information I give to you; it's who I'll be for you" (see John 14:6).

If my granddaughter wanted to know the way to her Sunday-school class, I could say, "Listen, go up those stairs; turn left; go down the ramp; turn right; go up the walkway; and after about forty feet, you'll see another set of stairs. Go up the stairs and down the hall to the third door. After you get inside, take a left; go about fifteen more feet—and you're there." Or—I could pick her up, put her on my shoulders and carry her to her class.

What a great day it is when, at last, the light goes on, the bells ring in our spiritual understanding, and we realize that we don't need to get directions or follow instructions from the Lord—we just need to climb on His shoulders and let Him be the Way.

As you let Jesus be the Way, Colossians 3:15 says His peace will rule in your heart. The word translated "rule" is a Greek word that speaks of a sports official, so Christ's peace will act as an umpire in your heart—calling every thought or action "safe" or "out." Not only that, but His will will be written in your heart (Jeremiah 31:33; Hebrews 10:16). No longer will you struggle with or wonder about what you should do. With His will imprinted upon your heart, you can follow your heart's desire and know that it is God's will for you.

- "My heart's desire is to go to Mexico and work in a mission."
  Great! That is God's will for you.
- *"My heart's desire is to go windsurfing."*
  Go for it!
- "My heart's desire is to ask her to marry me."
  Do it!
- *"B-b-but what if it's not God's will?"*
  If it's not God's will, she'll tell you to pack sand, because He said, "I will open doors no man can close, and close doors no man can open (see Revelation 3:7).

"Delight thyself in the Lord, and He will give you the desires of your heart," wrote the psalmist (see Psalm 37:4). To "delight thyself in the Lord" simply means to have a good time with Him. Give your body to Him; keep your mind on Him; climb on His shoulders and enjoy the ride. Suddenly, you'll have desires in your heart that will constitute His will for your life.

You see, I am simple enough to believe that if I just delight in Him, He will change my desires to conform to His perfect plan. I just hang on to Him and let Him work within me the desires He sees would be His best will for my life. Look again at Psalm 37. The first words of verses 1–7 spell it out perfectly: *Fret not* (verse 1), *for* (verse 2), *trust* (verse 3), *delight* (verse 4), *commit* (verse 5), *and* (verse 6) *rest* (verse 7).

Stay on the shoulders of the One who said, "I am the Way. It's not a plan I give to you. It's who I am for you. I am God's will. Cling to Me. Give yourself to Me. Keep your mind on Me—and you'll end up right where you're supposed to be vocationally, relationally, in every way. I am the Way. You'll see."

13

After discussing the believer's function in the body of Christ in chapter 12, Paul opens chapter 13 addressing the believer's function in society. What role do we as believers have in the society in which we live? Chapter 13 is devoted to this question, telling us how we, as believers, are to be engaged in our culture.

Scripturally, we see three divinely ordained institutions: the family (Genesis 2), government (Genesis 9), and the church (Acts 2). Those are the only three divinely inspired institutions. There are no others. And here in chapter 13, Paul speaks with specific regard to the second one—namely, government and authority.

Romans 13:1
Let every soul be subject unto the higher powers. For there is no power but of God: the powers that be are ordained of God.

"Paul can't mean those guys in Washington D.C. Certainly we're not to be subject to them. They're just fiddling around," we complain.

Wait a minute. Who was on the throne when Paul wrote this epistle? The best known "fiddler" of history: Caesar Nero. We are told through church history that, after sentencing the apostle Paul to death, Nero went on a rampage, persecuting Christians, burning them in his garden, feeding them to the lions. Caesar Nero was a diabolic, terrible, brutal, evil individual. Yet here, even while Nero was in power, Paul says believers were to be subject to the higher powers, for there is no person in power but that God has ordained him to be there.

You might not respect the person who is in power, but you must realize the Lord has ordained him or her to be there—even if it's a person as brutal as Caesar Nero—or Adolf Hitler.

"Come on," you protest, "God would never ordain Adolf Hitler to come into power."

Really? What does history tell us? The nation of Israel would never have been born had not world sentiment, for a short period of time, been sympathetic toward the Jew because of Hitler's atrocities. As World War II came to a close, newsreels showed the bodies of Jews being bulldozed into ditches, the mounds of glasses, false teeth, and shoes producing horror in the heart of humanity. And so it was, that, although it went right down to the wire, the League of Nations voted in favor of the establishment of the nation of Israel.

Truly, this verse changes my perspective on everything that happens. "Lord," I can say, "You know where we are on the prophetic calendar. You know exactly what time it is. And You're lining up certain events that will fulfill prophecy, usher in Your coming, and establish Your kingdom. I might not like what's happening, yet I realize ultimately that You are in control and that every power in place has been ordained by You. Therefore, I acknowledge that it's all part of Your plan."

That's why I don't lose sleep over the political situation—for while I pray for those in authority over us, and while I want to see salt and light have an effect in this society, I know God says all power is ordained by Him.

As believers, we know that all of society must fall apart. Jesus said it is inevitable (Matthew 24:37). People call such thinking a cop-out. No, it isn't. If I promised you that tomorrow at this time your house would be caught up in a tornado, carried to the Pacific Ocean, and dumped between here and Hawaii, how many of you would say, "If that's the case, I better go home and start painting" or, "Wow, I better vacuum," or "I better finish weeding"? I don't think any of us would do that. No, we would say, "If that's the case, forget mowing and painting, there's people to get out of the house." And you would have an entirely different set of priorities.

Why, then, is so much energy expended trying to straighten up this country politically if it's going to get blown away? I challenge you to at least consider where in the New Testament you hear an exhortation or see an example of political mobilization in the church.

If political activism is not the ultimate answer, what should we be about? Getting folks engaged in Jesus and excited about the Lord. We're to be ministers of reconciliation rather than ministers of confrontation. I'm not asking you to agree with me. I'm saying search the Scriptures. Study the life of Jesus from beginning to end. At a time when there was corruption governmentally, abortions taking place continually, and degradation morally, what was Jesus about?

Read the Epistles. What did Paul encourage us to do? Study Acts. What was the focus of the early Christians? It was not the goal of Jesus, Paul, or the early church to change their world temporally. No, their focus was on the kingdom eternally.

Romans 13:2
Whosoever therefore resisteth the power, resisteth the ordinance of God: and they that resist shall receive to themselves damnation.

Does this verse mean we're never to disobey those who are in authority over us? No. In Acts 5, the Pharisees forbade Peter to speak any more of Jesus. "We ought to obey God rather than man," Peter replied. But the issue was spiritual—not political.

So, yes, there is a time when we are not to be subject to those in authority. Yes, wives, there is a time when you are not to be submitted to your husband. Yes, children, there is a time to disobey your parents. When? When they tell you to do something that is directly contrary to the written Word of God. But make sure that if you follow such a course, you have Scripture in context and rightly divided—not just a feeling—to back you up.

Romans 13:3, 4 (a)
For rulers are not a terror to good works, but to the evil. Wilt thou then not be afraid of the power? do that which is good, and thou shalt have praise of the same: For he is the minister of God to thee for good.

Just as God established the power, God established the officers who enforce the power. They are ministers of God. Therefore, if you're doing good, you don't need to be afraid.

Driving a tad faster than I should have been, I saw red lights in my rearview mirror. After pulling me over, the officer asked for my license, and said, "Aren't you a minister?"

"Yeah," I said. "And, according to Romans 13, you are too."

So next time you get pulled over, thank that minister—even if, like me, you get a ticket—for, according to Paul, he is truly there for our good.

Romans 13:4 (b)
But if thou do that which is evil, be afraid; for he beareth not the sword in vain: for he is the minister of God, a revenger to execute wrath upon him that doeth evil.

While law enforcement officers are ministers of God for good for the protection of good men,

they are also ministers of God for vengeance against those who do evil. Understand this, folks: The foundation of the institution of government in Genesis 9 is singularly based upon capital punishment.

"That's the law," you might protest. "We're under grace."

Wait a minute. The establishment of government took place *before* the law was given. In Genesis 9:6, God gave one word concerning the way government is to function. That is, it is to function as a deterrent to evil through the implementation of capital punishment. Although that might sound harsh to you, the fact remains that, after watching mankind live through the evil, debauchery, violence, promiscuity, and wickedness of the days before Noah, God said, "From this time on, I'm going to let mankind share the responsibility to police and govern himself."

But man has failed in this because we have not taken seriously the mandate of the Father when He said, "If a man kills, his life is to be taken." This is the singular governmental injunction He gave. He didn't talk about capitalism vs. socialism, about the Parliamentary system vs. Republicanism. He simply said the one thing He wanted us to know was that there must be the taking of life from those who snuff out the life of another. When this is embraced, understood, and carried out, it has an effect on the entire legal and judicial system of a nation. When it breaks down, frustration and anarchy are imminent.

True government exists for the deterrent of evil through the reality of capital punishment. Once a nation or a society begins to chuck capital punishment, the whole system begins to unravel. Case in point? The U.S.A.

If you are following geopolitical trends, you know Islam is sweeping the world. Look at a country like England, and you will see Islam is growing at a phenomenal rate. Analysts say there is one fundamental reason for this: Tired of crime and lawlessness, people know Islam deals with crime swiftly and with finality. Under Islamic justice, if a man is caught raping a woman, he is castrated immediately. If a person is found shoplifting, he loses his hand. Whoever kills a man dies without appeal. Whether you agree with this is not the issue. The fact is, people around the world are turning to a religion that promises order, structure, and protection because government seems increasingly unable to do so.

Romans 13:5
Wherefore ye must needs be subject, not only for wrath, but also for conscience sake.

We are to submit to those in power not only for safety's sake but also for the sake of conscience. It's true: A clean conscience makes a soft pillow.

Romans 13:6 (a)
For this cause pay ye tribute also: for they are God's ministers . . .

It might come as a big surprise to hear that IRS agents are actually ministers of God. "We're not paying our taxes," some say. "We're part of the God, Gun, and Gold movement." Their reason? "Tax money goes to all kinds of ungodly stuff." And money sent to Caesar Nero was going to establish Christian schools and hospitals? Listen, gang, tax money in Paul's day was used for every kind of evil beyond our imagination. Yet Paul said, "Pay your taxes,"—just as Jesus did before him (Matthew 22:21).

Romans 13:6 (b)
. . . attending continually upon this very thing.

And how they do attend continually! The IRS has a conscience fund wherein it receives fifty to one hundred million dollars annually from people who feel bad about cheating on their taxes in years past. One note said, "Dear Sirs, enclosed are one hundred seventy-five dollars that I owed from taxes ten years ago. P.S. If my conscience is still bothering me, I'll send the rest later."

Romans 13:7
Render therefore to all their dues: tribute to whom tribute is due; custom to whom custom; fear to whom fear; honour to whom honour.

"Tribute" speaks of that which was paid annually, comparable to our income tax. "Custom" speaks of that which was paid upon purchases, comparable to a sales tax. Thus, those to whom Paul wrote were perhaps financially stretched in the same way many of us are.

Romans 13:8 (a)
Owe no man any thing . . .

What does it mean to "owe no man anything"? Look at the context. I have a question for those who use this verse to say Christians shouldn't have bank loans. Although I wouldn't argue the point, I do question it because in Matthew 25 and

Luke 19, when Jesus was talking about the talents, He said the man who buried them should have put them in the bank to draw interest.

Thus, rather than condemning the banking system, Jesus was condoning it. And, because the entire banking system is built upon loans, I personally disagree with those who propound you should never have a mortgage, car payment, or loan of any sort. I don't think that's what's being said. I think Paul is specifically talking about paying what you owe the government.

Romans 13:8 (b)
. . . but to love one another: for he that loveth another hath fulfilled the law.

Love must be the key because without it, if I'm saying, "Okay, I gotta obey these laws, pay these taxes, and submit to those in authority," I will find myself becoming small and bitter, cynical and cantankerous, confrontational and argumentative. As interesting and entertaining as commentators like Rush Limbaugh are, if you listen to very much of them, you will find your love diminishing. Be careful.

Romans 13:9
For this, Thou shalt not commit adultery, Thou shalt not kill, Thou shalt not steal, Thou shalt not bear false witness, Thou shalt not covet; and if there be any other commandment, it is briefly comprehended in this saying, namely, Thou shalt love thy neighbour as thyself.

All of the laws God has given—six hundred thirteen according to the Rabbis—are summed up in a singular word: love. "Vengeance is mine," saith the Lord (Romans 12:19). "I know what I'm doing. Therefore, let Me be the Lord while you minister reconciliation, telling people what I've done for them and the glory awaiting them. You love people and leave the judging to Me." In the midst of this dissertation on government, Paul's reminder to love puts everything in perspective.

Romans 13:10, 11 (a)
Love worketh no ill to his neighbour: therefore love is the fulfilling of the law. And that, knowing the time, that now it is high time to awake out of sleep . . .

"If we allow the people in power presently to remain in their positions, if we don't overthrow the government and take matters into our own hands, society is sure to crumble," some might insist.

Paul answers by saying, "Wake up."

Wake up to what? To political mobilization? No. Read on.

Romans 13:11 (b)
. . . for now is our salvation nearer than when we believed.

Wake up to the fact that your salvation is nearer than when you first believed. You who are inclined toward theology, make a note of this verse because through it we understand that salvation unfolds progressively. You see, while it is true that the moment we open our hearts to Jesus Christ, our salvation is complete internally, when Jesus comes back, there will be salvation externally. Equity and justice will reign. Complete salvation—individually and corporately, internally and externally—is drawing near.

Romans 13:12 (a)
The night is far spent, the day is at hand . . .

Indeed, the night is far spent. We live in dark days. But we're headed for sunrise—the coming of the risen Son!

Romans 13:12 (b), 13
. . . let us therefore cast off the works of darkness, and let us put on the armour of light. Let us walk honestly, as in the day; not in rioting and drunkenness, not in chambering and wantonness, not in strife and envying.

In light of the fact that the kingdom is coming, what should we do? First, wake up (verse 11). Second, dress up (verse 12). That is, put on the armor not of condemnation, not of judgment, but of light. Third, clean up (verse 13). That is, put away drunkenness, envy, and everything else that pollutes and defiles.

Romans 13:14
But put ye on the Lord Jesus Christ, and make not provision for the flesh, to fulfil the lusts thereof.

Fourth, in light of the coming kingdom, we should grow up. That is, we are not to make any provision to fulfill the lusts of the flesh. If you struggle with alcohol and say, "I'm not going to drink, I'm just going to take the table closest to the bar"—you're making provision for the flesh. You'll get sucked back in. You'll go down. You're only kidding yourself. Make no provision for the flesh—and take hope. The day of His coming is nearer than when you first believed. Soon we'll be out of here!

14 Here, in the final five chapters of the Book of Romans, Professor Paul takes us to class: Applied Christianity 101. Chapter 12 deals primarily with functioning in the body. Chapter 13 deals with functioning in society. As we are about to see, chapter 14 deals with functioning in controversy, particularly controversies within the church family.

You see, even here in Rome, the early church had already engaged in that most favorite of Christian indoor sports: trying to change one another. Truly, there is something within each of us that wants to change those around us. Why is this so? What is it within me that wants others to see everything the way I do, to conform to my opinions and perspectives? I suggest two possibilities. . . .

The first is depravity. Depravity began the moment Lucifer wanted to be like God (Isaiah 14:14). He passed on this desire to Eve by suggesting that if she ate of the forbidden fruit, her eyes would be opened and she would be like God (Genesis 3:5). There's something diabolically depraved within us that still wants to be godlike, which desires to create people in our own image and get them to see things our way.

The second possibility is misery. I want people to see things my way because a lot of times I'm miserable. And if I'm miserable, I want others to be miserable too. So rather than saying, "Let the Lord guide you. Let Him work in you. Let Him give direction to you," I say, "If I can't do a certain thing, I'm going to make sure you can't either." That is why oftentimes you can tell the difficulties a preacher has personally by what he preaches against most vehemently.

Be it depravity, misery, or some other reason entirely, there is unquestionably a tendency in people to want others to conform to their image. Thus, Christians are forever engaged in controversy—which brings us to Romans 14. . . .

Romans 14:1
Him that is weak in the faith receive ye, but not to doubtful disputations.

The phrase "but not to doubtful disputations" means "without passing judgment on disputable material." In other words, Paul's injunction is to receive those who are weak in the faith. Embrace and enjoy them without passing judgment on the areas in which you don't see eye to eye. Who is the one who is weak in faith? The answer, to me, is shocking. . . .

Romans 14:2, 3 (a)
For one believeth that he may eat all things:
another, who is weak, eateth herbs. Let not
him that eateth despise him that eateth not;
and let not him which eateth not judge him
that eateth.

The weak brother, as we are going to see as the
chapter unfolds, is the one who seems to be the
most morally upright, the one who is most rigid
in discipline, the one who appears to have the
highest standards of conduct.

In Paul's day, the controversy in the church at
Rome centered on meat. Those who didn't eat
meat were uptight and upset with those who did
because the meat had been sacrificed to idols before being sold in open-air markets at a discount.

"How can you eat meat that has been offered
to idols?" asked the vegetarian believers.

"It's a bargain," answered the carnivores.

Perhaps the controversy arose because Jewish
legalists were trying to burden Gentile believers
with Jewish dietary laws. Whatever the reason,
the vegetarians looked down their noses on the
meat-eaters. But in reality, the vegetarians were
the weaker brothers.

Amazing. The more legalistic and uptight a
man is, the weaker he is. It's not those who walk
around as though they've been baptized in lemon
juice, looking down their noses and reciting a list
of do's and don'ts that are the stronger Christians. Quite the opposite. "Receive the weaker
brother," Paul says. "Receive the one who is religious, the one who's uptight, the one who's always looking down on others. Don't engage in
controversy with him—just understand he's a
weaker brother."

Romans 14:3 (b)
. . . for God hath received him.

Do you realize God doesn't care about a lot of
things we get upset about, fight over, and debate?
The Father's agenda is a whole lot different from
ours. Sad to say, the things that shock us most are
insignificant when compared to the bigger issues
of eternity. We become so engaged in miniscule
rules and regulations, political discussions and
theological hairsplitting that we miss the big picture entirely. I'm convinced God doesn't care
about most of the things we discuss endlessly.
He's concerned about people being saved,
brought into the kingdom, walking in the Spirit,
and growing in grace.

Romans 14:4
Who art thou that judgest another man's
servant? to his own master he standeth or

falleth. Yea, he shall be holden up: for God
is able to make him stand.

I like that! God makes to stand the person I
can't understand. The person I want to put down,
God Himself holds up. Others may think, *You're
not going to make it.* But what they fail to factor
in is God's grace and mercy and His faithfulness
to see us through.

*For topical study of Romans 14:4 entitled
"Judge Not, For You Are Not Judged," turn to
page 985.*

Romans 14:5 (a)
One man esteemeth one day above another:
another esteemeth every day alike.

This controversy was not only about diets but
also about days. There were some who suggested
the proper day to worship was on Saturday, the
traditional Sabbath. Others said worship should
take place on the first day of the week—Resurrection day, Sunday. This debate still rages today,
as many Seventh Day Adventists who embrace
the older traditions believe that those who worship on Sunday are in danger of losing their salvation.

Romans 14:5 (b)
Let every man be fully persuaded in his own
mind.

Let every man be persuaded in his own mind.
You might have a conviction or persuasion. Terrific. But you needn't force that conviction on
anyone else. Rather, let us see you live it through
and work it out. Let us observe the benefits and
the fruit. Then we will come and ask you counsel.
Let every man be persuaded in his own mind concerning what he should do without laying a burden on anyone else in controversial matters.

The vast majority of the issues that cause division in the body are those that are not clearly
spelled out in the Word. They're opinions.
They're perspectives. They can be solid and excellent. But we must always be mindful to give
our brothers and sisters great latitude and to allow them the freedom to be persuaded in their
own minds.

Romans 14:6 (a)
He that regardeth the day, regardeth it unto
the Lord; and he that regardeth not the day,
to the Lord he doth not regard it.

When Applegate Christian Fellowship used to meet in the Western Auto building, we held one of our Sunday morning services on Friday nights. We found these times to be productive and fruitful. Yet some people were really uptight. "You can't have a Sunday service on a Friday night," they said.

"Why not?"

"Because Friday is not a holy day."

Attempting to honor their opinion, I said, "You don't have to come on Friday night. You just come Sunday morning if that's your conviction."

We need to exercise great latitude, folks.

Romans 14:6 (b)
He that eateth, eateth to the Lord, for he giveth God thanks . . .

"Oh, Lord, thanks," says the stronger brother as he sits down to the filet mignon he bought in the open-air market and sinks his teeth into the slab of beef.

Romans 14:6 (c)
. . . and he that eateth not, to the Lord he eateth not, and giveth God thanks.

"Thank You, Lord, that I don't have to clog my system with dead cow, that I am not causing the rain forest in Brazil to be depleted, that I have been given the ability to say 'No,'" says the weaker brother as he sits down to a fresh green salad. And Paul says both are right.

Romans 14:7–9
For none of us liveth to himself, and no man dieth to himself. For whether we live, we live unto the Lord; and whether we die, we die unto the Lord: whether we live therefore, or die, we are the Lord's. For to this end Christ both died, and rose, and revived, that he might be Lord both of the dead and living.

This is a key component in the equation of liberty and responsibility. There are those who say, "Jesus was right when He said, 'I have come that you might have life and life abundantly,'" as they eat their beef and live it up in the Lord.

Others say, "Didn't Jesus say if any man come after Him let him deny himself, take up the cross and follow Him?" as they enter a monastery and give everything up for the Lord.

We are so blessed! We can learn from, be enriched by, and rejoice with those who are contemplative in their piety, as well as from those who are carefree in their joviality. What great latitude the Lord has given us and those sitting next to us in our relationship with Him. For whether we live it up *in* the Lord or give it up *for* the Lord, we can glorify Him.

Romans 14:10 (a)
But why dost thou judge thy brother? or why dost thou set at nought thy brother?

In other words, "Why do you write off the brother who doesn't see things the way you do, or who has regulations you don't?"

Romans 14:10 (b), 11
For we shall all stand before the judgment seat of Christ. For it is written, As I live, saith the Lord, every knee shall bow to me, and every tongue shall confess to God.

Every Christian will one day stand before the judgment seat of Christ not to be judged for sin, but to be given awards for that which was done for the Lord's glory in obedience to Him (1 Corinthians 3:13–15). But until that day, we can't know what the motives of men are. That's why Paul says we are not to judge.

Romans 14:12
So then every one of us shall give account of himself to God.

Of whom will you give account? Yourself. That's all. You don't have to give an account for the person in front of you or behind you. Every one of us will give account of ourselves—not of our sins, but of what we did with the possessions the Lord gave us materially, the opportunities He opened for us in ministry, and the gifts He embedded in us spiritually. All of these will pass through the fire—and whatever comes out will be all that matters.

It was after Paul was caught up into heaven (2 Corinthians 12:2) that he said, "From here on out, my one goal is to win the prize" (see Philippians 3:13, 14). Gang, be sure your lives count in light of the big picture eternally, where every one of us will give an account individually.

Romans 14:13
Let us not therefore judge one another any more: but judge this rather, that no man put a stumblingblock or an occasion to fall in his brother's way.

Sprinkled throughout Paul's writings are negative exhortations directly followed by positive applications. . . .

- Let him that stole steal no more: rather let him labour . . . (Ephesians 4:28).

- Let every man put away lying and speak the truth . . . (Ephesians 4:25).
- Flee youthful lusts and follow after righteousness . . . (see 2 Timothy 2:22).
- Be anxious for nothing but in everything give thanks . . . (see Philippians 4:6).

So, too, here Paul says, "Let us not judge any man, but rather judge ourselves." Is your legalism causing others to stumble by making them feel condemned, weighed down, and beaten up? Is your liberty causing others to stumble as they follow you to their own destruction? If we don't judge ourselves, the Lord will judge us—not to condemn us, but to correct us. Yes, He gives us liberty for a while. But He loves us as well as those around us too much to let us travel a dangerous road indefinitely.

Romans 14:14 (a)
I know, and am persuaded by the Lord Jesus, that there is nothing unclean of itself . . .

A Pharisee of Pharisees, Paul had been a legalist in the strictest sense of the word. After spending time with Jesus in the desert (Galatians 1:17), however, he emerged, as seen in this verse, a great champion of liberty.

Romans 14:14 (b)
. . . but to him that esteemeth any thing to be unclean, to him it is unclean.

"Personally, I'm persuaded there is nothing unclean of itself," said Paul. "But for those who esteem something to be unclean, then for them it is unclean."

Due to the presence of bikinis and alcohol at Applegate Lake in Oregon, some people question how Applegate Christian Fellowship can have after-church activities there. To those people, I say, "If you have a problem going to Applegate Lake, then to you it's unclean. Don't go. But don't put that trip on anyone else." So, too, while it is unclean for me to smoke cigarettes, there are those who are Christians, who love the Lord, who are born again, who smoke cigarettes. Traditionally, the church has made smoking an issue of salvation, saying, "You can't be saved if you smoke cigarettes." This is nothing new. . . .

Charles Haddon Spurgeon could not understand how Joseph Parker could go to the theatre and watch plays. Parker, on the other hand, came down on Spurgeon, saying he couldn't understand how Spurgeon could smoke cigars. Both of these men were powerful preachers who were greatly used by the Lord, and yet they had a public fight.

Spurgeon finally gave up smoking in his later years when one day he opened the *London Times* and saw a full-page cigar ad under the headline, "The Cigar that Charles Spurgeon Smokes."

People are often shocked and appalled at how someone else could do something other than what they themselves have liberty to do. Trips are laid on people. Fights start. Churches split. Historically, entire denominations have actually been formed in protest of those who had the audacity to wear buttons on their clothes. Just ask the Hole and Eye Baptists.

"Such ought not be," said Paul.

Romans 14:15
But if thy brother be grieved with thy meat, now walkest thou not charitably. Destroy not him with thy meat, for whom Christ died.

You might have the freedom to chomp down a big piece of meat, but don't do it in a way or at a place where the weaker brother, the legalist, the vegetarian will be offended, turned off, or uptight.

In the early days of World War II, German U-boats attacked Allied ships traveling from the East Coast to Europe. To remedy this, they traveled in large convoys. But the convoys could go only as fast as the slowest boat. So the faster boats slowed down to the speed of the slowest boat in order that they all might be protected from attack.

The same holds true in spiritual life. You might be freer and faster and stronger than your brothers and sisters in Christ—but keep in mind with whom you are traveling. We're linked together. Don't do something that will cause a slower boat to be exposed to the underwater attacks of the Enemy, to be torpedoed by Satan. Slow it down. We're in this together.

Romans 14:16, 17 (a)
Let not then your good be evil spoken of: For the kingdom of God is not meat and drink . . .

There's something about us that wants to be contrary and confrontational. But that's not what the kingdom is about.

Romans 14:17 (b), 18
. . . but righteousness, and peace, and joy in the Holy Ghost. For he that in these things

serveth Christ is acceptable to God, and approved of men.

You will be acceptable to both God and approved in the eyes of men if you focus not on meat or drink, controversies or confrontations, but on the righteousness, peace, and joy imputed to us and bestowed upon us by the grace and goodness of God through Jesus Christ.

Romans 14:19, 20
Let us therefore follow after the things which make for peace, and things wherewith one may edify another. For meat destroy not the work of God. All things indeed are pure; but it is evil for that man who eateth with offence.

Everything is pure, but anything with which you have a personal problem is unclean for you. Therefore, determine where you're at—but don't impose your convictions on others.

Romans 14:21
It is good neither to eat flesh, nor to drink wine, nor any thing whereby thy brother stumbleth, or is offended, or is made weak.

Stay away from anything that would cause someone in the convoy to stumble. Be careful with the liberty you enjoy.

Romans 14:22
Hast thou faith? have it to thyself before God. Happy is he that condemneth not himself in that thing which he alloweth.

You're a happy man if you're not condemning yourself, if you're not bound up with regulations.

Romans 14:23
And he that doubteth is damned if he eat, because he eateth not of faith: for whatsoever is not of faith is sin.

If you engage in an activity only to prove a point to yourself or others, you'll bring damnation upon yourself—not eternal damnation, but present depression and destruction.

"Behold, how good and pleasant it is for brothers to dwell in unity," wrote the psalmist (Psalm 133:1). What does this mean? Augustine summed it up best when he said, "In essentials, there must be unity. In nonessentials, there must be liberty. But in all things, there must be charity."

May God give us wisdom to walk in both liberty and love.

JUDGE NOT—FOR YOU'RE NOT JUDGED
A Topical Study of
Romans 14:4

The story is told of a poor, simple woman who visited an upper class, sophisticated church. . . .

After attending for some time, she applied for church membership. Her application was rejected. She sent a second one a few months later, which was also returned. After a third and a fourth, she went to the chairman of the membership committee and said, "Why are my applications being rejected?"

"You need to go home and pray," answered the chairman. "And I think the Lord will show you what the real issues are."

A few years later, the chairman saw her scrubbing floors in a hotel lobby and said to her, "You haven't made application for membership lately. In fact,

I don't think I've seen you in church at all. Tell me, when I sent you home to pray, did God speak to you?"

"Why, yes," answered the woman, "He did. He told me not to feel bad about being rejected because He tried to join your church for twenty years before He finally gave up."

All too often, there are those in churches who are super-spiritual, who look down their noses on others, who put heavy burdens upon others. They set standards for who will be accepted educationally, financially, or spiritually. And inevitably a sense of exclusivity creeps into the church.

This is nothing new. The same thing was true in Paul's day. You see, when Paul was writing to the brothers and sisters at Rome, there were those who came into the fellowship and who judged others over the issue of diet. They maintained that those who ate certain kinds of meat were not quite up to par spiritually.

Why was the issue of eating meat so controversial? Some suggest it was due to the Essenes in the church at Rome. The Essenes were men who lived in the desert and were very Spartan in their discipline. John the Baptist, many believe, was part of the Essene community before he went into public ministry. Having been converted to Jesus, the Essenes propagated the thinking that people who ate meat weren't spiritually minded.

Others suggest that the issue of meat arose in the church because of Jews converted to Christ in the Church at Rome who were still bound by Levitical traditions of what should and should not be eaten.

I believe, however, the question of meat in the early church was due to the buying and selling of meat in places called "shambles." Shambles were open-air markets that sold the best cuts of meat for the lowest price. The owners of these shambles could keep their prices low because their meat was "second-hand," since it had already been offered to pagan idols. Whatever the reason, Paul was aware of the tendency of some of the brothers and sisters in the Roman church to question the sincerity or spirituality of others within the family.

Perhaps you have gone through a week where you have been judged because of some liberty you have enjoyed. Paul would encourage you who feel judged, you who feel condemned, you who feel looked down on because some seemingly "super-spiritual" saint has come and "tsk-tsk-tsked" in your face or found fault with the liberty you enjoy in Christ. You can have hope, and I can find peace as we listen to what Paul says to those who put down believers who enjoy freedom in Christ.

It's Presumptuous to Judge

Who art thou that judgest another man's servant? to his own master he standeth or falleth.

Romans 14:4 (a)

A conductor on the train from Basil, Switzerland, to Germany looked out
the window and noticed unfamiliar scenery. "Leave immediately!" he said to
everyone in the car. "You are all on the wrong train!" The passengers looked
at one another quizzically and confused. Questioning the conductor, they
learned that it was he who was on the wrong train.

Those who judge others essentially tell everyone else they are on the wrong
train. Paul says, "It's Jesus to whom you must answer. It's Jesus to whom you must
give account"—not to any man or leader, spiritual person or pastor. "We do not seek
to have dominion over you," he said, "but are simply helpers of your joy" (see 2 Corinthians 1:24). You see, if a man is a true spiritual leader, he will not seek to have
dominion over you or to lay burdens upon you. Rather, he will seek to come alongside of you and undergird you in order that your joy might be made full.

A woman was seeing a psychiatrist. After several sessions, sensing parenting
problems were the root of her difficulty, the psychiatrist asked her which of
her three children she loved the most.

"I love them equally," she answered.

"Impossible," said the psychiatrist. "You're deceiving yourself, and it is
this self-deception that is keeping you from experiencing liberty. You must
be honest, or I will have no other choice than to terminate these counseling
sessions. Which of your three kids do you care about the most?"

The woman broke down in tears and said, "You're right. When one of
my kids is sick, I love that one the most. When one of my kids is lost in the
store when we're shopping, that's the one I love the most. When one of my
kids is bad, that's the one I love the most. The one who's hurting the most
at any given point is the one my heart goes out to most fully."

The same is true with our heavenly Father. While others might judge you because you're lost, hurting, or bad—the Father looks upon you compassionately and
says, "Those who are hurting and lost are the ones I particularly care about." Jesus
Himself told us this in the parable of the Good Shepherd. Ninety-nine sheep were
okay. But He left them to go find the one who was lost (Luke 15:3–7). Therefore,
don't let anyone come down on you—for even if you are a bit lost, the Lord loves us
especially when we need Him most.

It's Humorous to Judge

Yea, he shall be holden up: for God is able to make him stand.   Romans 14:4 (b)

The Lord will hold up the one we put down. The Lord will make stand the one
we can't stand.

As freshmen at Biola University, we had brutal dorm wars during spring semester. I recall walking into the quad of Stewart Hall, only to have the trashcan of water that was balanced on top of the door come crashing down on us. This called for retaliation and set off a series of skirmishes during finals week so brutal, that, fearing for our lives, we barricaded ourselves in our rooms every night. We found a way, however, to penetrate the barricades of Stewart Hall—not by knocking down the doors or bashing in the windows (which we tried to no avail).

We went to McDonald's, downed as many milkshakes as we could and brought the empty cups back to the dorm—where we filled them with a mixture of shaving cream and mud. We then pinched the tops closed and quietly slipped the lips of the cups under the doors of those who needed to learn a lesson. After strategically positioning ourselves outside each door, on the count of three, we stomped on the cups, effectively coating the inside of the rooms with shaving cream and mud. It was great!

That same semester, after my roommate broke his arm jumping out our second-story window, the Resident Assistant, a Bible major, came to me and said, "Jon, you're never going to make it in ministry. Neither will your roommate."

My roommate was Rick Booye, pastor of Trail Fellowship. It's humorous to me because the people who thought we would never make it failed to take into account the great grace, goodness, and faithfulness of God. Looking at us, they had every reason—and still do—to be dubious, but only if they forget that it is God who holds us up.

So, too, the very people I have judged negatively, those I thought would never make it, I look at years later and see God's grace on their lives and the way the Lord is using them. I marvel at the goodness and bigness and grace of God—and I have to laugh.

If you feel like you've been judged, the Lord says to you, "I'm with you. I'll never leave you. I'll never forsake you. People might come down on you and find fault with you, but I will see you through."

It's Needless to Judge

But why dost thou judge thy brother? or why dost thou set at nought thy brother? for we shall all stand before the judgment seat of Christ.   Romans 14:10

Every Christian—every brother, every sister, every one of us, those who have been judged, those who are judging—will stand before the judgment seat of Christ where all of our works will be tried by fire (1 Corinthians 3:13). Everything we've done in the name of the Lord will be put through fire. And only that which is gold, silver, and precious stones—only that which was done sincerely—will remain.

This means that there are people who are doing seemingly spiritual things, leading seemingly disciplined lives, doing seemingly wonderful works—but for the wrong reasons. Truly, we do not know what motivates people. Jesus told us some would do their works only to be seen of men (Matthew 6:2). But their true motives will be revealed at the *bema*, or judgment seat of Christ.

Folks, we don't know as much as we think we do. Because the heart is deceitfully and desperately wicked (Jeremiah 17:9), it's hard enough to figure out why I do what I do, much less try to figure out why another does what he does.

> About fifty years ago, a preacher was riding a train, studying for his Sunday sermon. Across the aisle from him, a two-year-old girl was being obnoxiously loud, throwing a temper tantrum, and crying. Finally, in his frustration, the preacher said to the woman with the baby, "Madam, please control your child."
>
> "She's not my child, sir," the woman answered.
>
> "Well, is her mother on board?"
>
> "Yes. She's on board," answered the woman. "She's in the next car, in the cargo department—in a casket."
>
> Feeling totally humiliated, the preacher spent the rest of the journey tending the crying baby as best he could.

So, too, those who judge you don't know the full story. Be patient with them. They don't know what you've gone through. They don't know where you've been. Earthly judgment is based upon limited information, but Paul says the day is coming when judgment will be perfect and righteous.

Past Judgment

As He headed to the Cross, Jesus declared, "Now is the judgment of this world" (John 12:31). In this, He told us something freeing and exciting. That is, all of the sin we have ever done, are doing, or ever will do has been paid fully and completely when He died. The judgment we should have received because of our sin was poured out on Him.

> In the days of the pioneers, brushfires would break out so quickly, that they were impossible to outrun or outride. So the settlers soon learned that the only way they could be protected from such fires was to burn a large circle in their own field upon the first sight of smoke on the horizon. Then they would stand in the burned-out circle so that, having nothing left to burn, the fire would bypass them.

That is exactly where you are today if you know Jesus Christ. You are at the foot of the Cross. You will never be held accountable for any sin you have done or ever will do as long as you embrace the work of the Cross and thank Jesus for doing what He did in your place. The punitive fire of God's wrath and judgment will never touch you. You are absolutely safe in the circle of the Cross of Calvary.

Present Judgment

Having said that, Paul says there is a present judgment that is to be taking place in the heart of every believer (1 Corinthians 11:28). Paul says we ought to judge ourselves. Where? At the Communion table. Why? If you spend time with the Lord confessing your sin, you will save yourself a lot of heartache. What kind of heartache?

If my son Benjamin had a propensity to stick knives into electric sockets when he was a boy, I would have loved him enough to discipline him—not because I would have been coming down on him, not because I would have been mad at him, not because I would have been trying to be cruel to him, but because I care about him.

So, too, if I continue doing things that are dangerous to me spiritually, the Father will judge me—not in order to punish me, but in order to save me from destruction.

You see, I believe in "bungee theology." That is, the Father hooks a bungee cord of love to us and then gives us all kinds of space. Now, although we can stretch this cord by walking contrary to God's will, we must realize that we *will* come back. If you're a believer, the Lord's love is wrapped around you in such a way that He'll let you go your way to a certain degree. But you *will* come back. The only question is: How hard will you hit?

I talk to kids every week who stretch the bungee cord and say, "We're cool. We can do what we want"—until they end up crying in my office.

"Didn't you know you were doing something that wasn't right?" I ask. "Didn't you hear God's voice in your heart? Why, then, did you continue?"

"I don't know."

I have never heard anyone say, "I'm sure glad I got drunk," or, "I'm glad I did drugs," or, "I'm glad I stole." Never.

But I've heard story after story of those who have said, "What was I doing?" "What was I thinking?" "Why did this happen?"

"Judge yourself," said Paul. Come to the Communion table and say, "Lord, search my heart. Show me where my attitudes or activities are amiss," lest you find yourself splatting against the wall of God's love.

Future Judgment

Finally, there will be a future judgment. Paul refers to this here in Romans 14 and talks about it further in the Corinthian Epistles. At the *bema*, or judgment seat of Christ, everything you have done will go through a fire of purification. Whatever gold, silver, and precious stones remain will be your reward.

"Big deal," you say. "I'm not into gold. I could care less about silver. Precious stones? They don't mean much to me."

Listen, those things might not be important now. But they will be, for they will determine your capacity to enjoy eternity. They will determine what you do in the next zillion years. While I know that just being in heaven will be glory beyond words, I also know that when Paul came back from being caught up into heaven, his purpose in life was to win the prize (Philippians 3:13, 14). Having seen the reality of heaven, he knew nothing else mattered. Jesus said the same thing when He said, "Seek first the kingdom" (see Matthew 6:33).

"Take my word for it," Paul would say to you and me today: "Your house, your car, your hobbies, trinkets and toys will all burn. They will not matter ultimately. What does matter is the *bema* seat, the judgment seat—where you will stand before Jesus and be rewarded."

Here's the added bonus, folks: If you live for this life, you'll always be miserable because nothing will ever be quite right. It will always be "one more piece of furniture to buy," "one more flower to plant," "one more promotion to get," "one more person to date"—but it will never be quite enough. If you live for heaven, on the other hand, this world is just a bonus. Therefore, you can relax, knowing you will find joy unspeakable in heaven.

15 The advice is sound. We need to take a whole lot more things a whole lot less seriously. Because there is a tendency for Christians to get uptight and to major on the minors, it is essential to remember that the main thing is to keep the main thing the main thing. And the main thing is Jesus Christ. But somehow, for some reason, we get sidetracked from the main thing. We find our little cause, pet doctrine, or personal perspective on ministry and think we've got to push this on everyone in the body of Christ. And in so doing, we find ourselves getting caught up in peripheral issues that don't really matter.

As evidenced by Paul's discussion on diets and days in chapter 14, it seems the church in Rome had the same tendency. "These hobby horses ought not be," said Paul as he continues his argument in chapter 15.

Romans 15:1
We then that are strong ought to bear the infirmities of the weak, and not to please ourselves.

As we saw in chapter 14, it is the weaker brother who is the legalist. This is shocking to me because my tendency would be to think the stronger Christian is the one who has the most dos and don'ts, and, therefore, the most discipline. Not so. It's the weaker brother who moves and lives in legalism and rigidity, who has rules and regulations surrounding him that are not scriptural commands, but are personal opinions or conclusions. There are those who will look down on you because they think you're too loose or too free. But in reality you're to be patient with them because they're the weaker brothers, the weaker sisters.

Two guys in the woods found themselves eye to eye with a grizzly. Stunned, they sat stock still—until one of them began to slowly put on his tennis shoes.

"What are you doing?" said the other guy. "Don't you know you can't outrun a grizzly bear?"

"Yes," said his friend. "But all I've got to do is outrun you!"

That's the way we sometimes think. "I'm free to run in liberty. If you get eaten up, pulled down, or done in that's your problem." Now, while that kind of thinking might work in the woods—it won't in the body, for when one part is injured, the whole body suffers.

If the folks in my fellowship family are not doing well, it will have a direct influence on how I do. Therefore, I must slow down in my liberty and take into consideration those who are not as strong or as free, those who might stumble over this idea or that practice.

Romans 15:2, 3
Let every one of us please his neighbour for his good to edification. For even Christ pleased not himself; but, as it is written, The reproaches of them that reproached thee fell on me.

While we are to bear the infirmities of the weak, quoting from Psalm 69:9, Paul makes it clear that Jesus did not allow people to remain entrenched in their own legalism.

While Jesus was healing on the Sabbath Day, the Pharisees began to reproach Him. Did He stop? No. He corrected their misunderstanding and then continued healing (Luke 14:1–4).

On the other hand, there were times when Jesus laid aside His liberty.

"Does your Master pay taxes in the temple?" the Pharisees asked Peter.
"Of course," Peter responded.
But when Peter asked this same question of Jesus, Jesus said, "Do kings charge their own kids taxes? Of course not. But, in order that we don't offend, go fishing—and the first fish you catch will have a coin in his mouth to cover the taxes" (see Matthew 17:24–27).

"I'm confused," you say. "Do I bear my neighbor's infirmity—or do I correct him for edification?"

Just do what the Lord tells you to do at any given moment. Sometimes, He will tell you to bear with those who are weak. Other times, He'll tell you to love them enough to give them a word of correction—even if it means you will suffer reproach. Christianity is not rules, principles, or regulations. It's walking with the Lord moment by moment, saying constantly, "Lord, how do I deal with this situation? Is it a time for backing away and bearing weakness—or is it a time for loving exhortation and confrontation? What do I do?"

It's as though the Lord gives us broad principles in the Word and then says, "See Me for further instructions. Talk to Me about specific application." If any man lack wisdom, let him ask of God who giveth to all men generously (James 1:5).

Romans 15:4 (a)
For whatsoever things were written aforetime were written for our learning . . .

The Scripture account is filled with men who laid aside their liberty and rights for the sake of their weaker brothers. Abraham (Genesis 13:8, 9), Jonathan (1 Samuel 19:4), David (1 Samuel 24:10), and Moses (Hebrews 11:24) are all examples of men who willingly let go of their rightful possessions or positions. They didn't demand their own way—and they prospered as a result. "Learn from their example," said Paul.

Romans 15:4 (b)
. . . that we through patience and comfort of the scriptures might have hope.

Underline the word "patience." Yes, the Scriptures comfort us—but we have to be patient. "I've claimed a promise for three weeks. Why hasn't it happened?" we say, forgetting that it was after Abraham patiently endured that he obtained the promise (Hebrews 6:15).

Romans 15:5 (a)
Now the God of patience and consolation . . .

Why should you be patient with God? Because He's patient with you. Do you realize how patient God has been with you? Think about it. If you were God, how long would you put up with you?

Romans 15:5 (b)
. . . grant you to be likeminded one toward another according to Christ Jesus.

Be likeminded in Christ and because of Christ, letting people have space, as you show them lots of grace.

Romans 15:6, 7
That ye may with one mind and one mouth glorify God, even the Father of our Lord Jesus Christ. Wherefore receive ye one another, as Christ also received us to the glory of God.

Something happens when we hear the Scriptures and study the Word together. There's a oneness of mind that takes place—even if we differ on certain interpretations or certain applications. That's why you will notice that when a person stops coming to Bible study and worship, slowly but surely, they no longer have one mind and one heart. It's not that they don't love the Lord. It's not that they're not saved. But, as they become isolated, they become vulnerable. "Don't divide. Don't pull away," said Paul. "Be of one mind."

Romans 15:8
Now I say that Jesus Christ was a minister of the circumcision for the truth of God, to confirm the promises made unto the fathers.

Jesus came as a Minister of the circumcision. He came to the Jew and lived as a Jew in order to share truth with the Jews.

Romans 15:9 (a)
And that the Gentiles might glorify God for his mercy . . .

Jesus came to the Jews but also to the Gentiles. The Jews saw God's truth in Jesus. The Gentiles saw His mercy.

Romans 15:9 (b)
. . . as it is written, For this cause I will confess to thee among the Gentiles, and sing unto thy name.

Jesus is among the Gentiles—you and me. So when we sing, "Father, I adore You," guess who's joining in. Guess who's in the midst of our praise. Jesus is not only the object of our praise—but He's in the midst of our praise, participating with us.

Romans 15:10–12
And again he saith, Rejoice, ye Gentiles, with his people. And again, Praise the Lord, all ye Gentiles; and laud him, all ye people. And again, Esaias saith, There shall be a root of Jesse, and he that shall rise to reign over the Gentiles; in him shall the Gentiles trust.

Paul quoted from the Psalms in verse 9, from Deuteronomy in verse 10, and from Isaiah in verse 12. Thus, the three categories of the Jewish Bible—the Psalms, the law, and the prophets—are all represented in this brief section as Paul continues to drive home the fact that Jesus came for the Gentiles as well as the Jews.

"The Gentiles?" the Jew would say. "They're so trite and shallow. They're unschooled in theology and have such a limited background in biblical history."

"Aha!" Paul would answer. "Guess who's singing in their midst!"

And the Gentile would say, "Those Jews are so bound in legalism and tradition. They're so stuffy."

"Wait a minute," Paul would interject, "Jesus Christ was a Minister of the circumcision."

The implications of this are pretty radical.

There are some churches I walk into and think, This place is dead. The pastor wears robes. The people sit all dressed up like corpses. There's no life whatsoever.

Then I hear the Lord say, "Wait a minute. These people might not be your style, but that doesn't mean they're not My people."

Other places I walk into and say, "Oh, my. These people aren't dead, but they're shallow. Sure, they're exuberant in their praise. But the preaching lacks substance."

Then I hear the Lord say, "Wait a minute. I love these people. I am in the midst of this church."

"You are?" I ask.

"Yes," He answers.

"You mean You're into both the Jews and Gentiles, both this group and that group?"

"Yes. They love Me, so give them space."

The Lord is so big. Yet we can be so provincial and so narrow. "Well, if they worship in this manner or with that intensity, or with that kind of liturgy, they're wrong," we say. Not necessarily. If they love Jesus Christ and desire to walk with Him, give them space. Don't be critical of them or divided from them. Just rejoice with them.

Romans 15:13
Now the God of hope fill you with all joy and peace in believing, that ye may abound in hope, through the power of the Holy Ghost.

What is hope? Hope is the absolute expectation of coming good. Hope is the antidote for divisiveness and defensiveness. And throughout Scripture, hope is most often referred to in conjunction with the coming of Jesus Christ. Therefore, it is pointless for us to argue and debate here on earth, for soon we'll be in heaven with Jesus, where all questions will be answered, all divisions will cease.

After spending the first half of chapter 15 talking about unity in the body, we'll see Paul put in the clutch and shift gears to discuss ministry in the world. Why? Because the two are very closely related. When does unity in the church happen? When people are ministering in the world. Check out a Billy Graham Crusade. It's amazing who's on the platform. Ministers and denominations that normally wouldn't speak to one another are brought together for one purpose: to let folks know that heaven is around the bend and that there's hope in Jesus Christ.

A tourist approached a farmer in Iowa and said, "Don't you think all these fences ruin the beauty of the fields out here?"

"Yep," said the farmer—"until the corn starts growing. When the corn starts growing you don't even see the fences."

When are fences seen in the church? When there's no fruit. That's when the divisions become real and pronounced. But when there's growth and fruit, evangelism and ministry, the fences of factionalism disappear. That is why the more evangelistic a church is, the less divided it becomes.

Romans 15:14, 15
And I myself also am persuaded of you, my brethren, that ye also are full of goodness, filled with all knowledge, able also to admonish one another. Nevertheless, brethren, I have written the more boldly unto you in some sort, as putting you in mind, because of the grace that is given to me of God.

"I know you're filled with knowledge and goodness, and that you're able to admonish one another," said Paul. "However, I've written these things to you in order that you might remember these truths."

Peter said the same thing when he wrote, "I would not be negligent to put you in remembrance of these things though ye know them, and are established in the present truth" (2 Peter 1:12). Haven't you found it incredible that you forget the things you really want to remember, yet remember the things you wish you could forget? It's a mystery to me—and yet partially explained by the fact that Satan reminds us of our failings day and night (Revelation 12:10), while he constantly seeks to pluck away Scripture from our memories (Matthew 13:19).

It's not how much you know, gang. It's how well you know what you know.

Romans 15:16
That I should be the minister of Jesus Christ to the Gentiles, ministering the gospel of God, that the offering up of the Gentiles

might be acceptable, being sanctified by the Holy Ghost.

D. L. Moody, a shoe salesman captured by Christ, who became one of the most effective soul-winners of all time, purposed in his heart as a young man that he would never let a day go by wherein he didn't talk to at least one person about Jesus Christ. One night it was approaching midnight and, because of the events of the day, he had not shared the gospel with an unbeliever that particular day. So he went out onto the streets of Chicago, found a man, and said, "Sir, are you ready for heaven?"

"Mind your own business," said the startled man.

"This *is* my business," Moody answered.

And it is our business as well. Walking the hills of Jacksonville, Oregon, one day, I found myself in the old Jacksonville cemetery. The tombstones of the early settlers provided an ironic backdrop for the women who were picnicking and the children who were playing hide-and-seek. Observing the scene, I was reminded of the simple calling God has given you and me—to minister the gospel of God. For while the world plays games among the tombstones, eternity is only a heartbeat away.

As Paul told his young protégé, Timothy, "Put the brethren in remembrance of these things. In so doing, you will be accounted as being a faithful minister" (see 1 Timothy 4:6).

Romans 15:17, 18 (a)
I have therefore whereof I may glory through Jesus Christ in those things which pertain to God. For I will not dare to speak of any of those things which Christ hath not wrought by me, to make the Gentiles obedient . . .

"I won't speak of anything that hasn't been wrought by me," said Paul. In other words, "I'm only going to tell you what I have seen, of what the Lord has done through me by His grace."

Romans 15:18 (b)
. . . by word . . .

How are we to share the gospel with a world that's playing hide-and-seek in the cemetery? By word—by sharing the Scriptures. You may not understand all of the implications doctrinally. You may have trouble defending the Scriptures intellectually. But, like C. H. Spurgeon said when asked how to defend the Bible, "You defend the Bible as you would a roaring lion. You just open the cage and let it out." The Word is alive and powerful, sharper than any two-edged sword (Hebrews 4:12). Just start sharing the Scriptures and watch and see what the Lion of the Tribe of Judah does with the Word He's given to you.

Romans 15:18 (b)
. . . and deed . . .

Spiritual authority and power come when we share the things we ourselves are living out. That's why I share so much about grace. I need it, I've embraced it, and I'm so thankful to God for it. Grace is not a theological concept to me—it's what I need desperately. You see, those truths of which you are personally in need, for which you are personally thankful, in which you are personally growing are the truths that will come alive in a very powerful and profound way as you share them with others.

Romans 15:19 (a)
Through mighty signs and wonders, by the power of the Spirit of God . . .

Concerning signs and wonders, Jesus said signs shall follow them that believe (Mark 16:17). He said this in the context of evangelism. In other words, "Get going. And as you're going, I'll be flowing through you. I'll be doing signs and wonders before you."

Gang, the Holy Spirit is like steam in a locomotive. He's there to move the engine down the track—not to toot the whistle. Too many people look at the power of the Holy Spirit as a whistle-tooter, as an end in itself—but the Lord says, "You shall receive power when the Holy Ghost comes upon you to be My witnesses" (Acts 1:8). Thus, when people ask why we don't see more signs and wonders today, I say, "Go to Honduras. Go to Mexico. Go to Russia. Start evangelizing and watch and see what the Lord will do in you and the miracles that will flow through you."

But even if you never see an external sign, wonder, or miracle, you're in good company. Jesus said of all of the men who had lived, John the Baptist was the greatest of them all. No man was greater—not Elijah who called down fire from heaven, not Elisha who raised the dead, not Moses who parted the Red Sea. Jesus said, "Among them that are born of women there hath not risen a greater than John the Baptist" (Matthew 11:11). And yet John did no miracle (John 10:41). So if you've never performed a miracle or

even seen a miracle, take heart. You're in good company.

John did no miracle but "all things John spoke of this Man were true" (see John 10:41). What Man? Jesus Christ. Talking about Jesus is something I can do—and so can you. Yes, I would love to have the powerful, miraculous ministry of Paul. But in the meantime, I'll try to walk in the footsteps of John the Baptist, pointing others to the Lamb of God.

Romans 15:19 (b)
. . . so that from Jerusalem, and round about unto Illyricum, I have fully preached the gospel of Christ.

In his fourteen-hundred-mile parish, Paul preached the gospel. Truly, the simplicity of the gospel is powerful. Don't be embarrassed about it. Don't back away from it. Don't feel like you need to be deeper than Paul was. Paul said, "I travel everywhere, simply preaching the Good News of Jesus Christ."

Romans 15:20
Yea, so have I strived to preach the gospel, not where Christ was named, lest I should build upon another man's foundation.

"I'm not going to build upon another man's foundation," said Paul. "I'm not going to dip into aquariums—I'm going to be a fisher of men." To do this, Paul walked fourteen hundred miles.

So, too, we must find areas where no one is meeting a specific need, no one is touching certain folks, no one is reaching a particular group, and ask the Lord if, by His grace, you can reach this group, touch those folks, or meet that need.

Romans 15:21
But as it is written, To whom he was not spoken of, they shall see: and they that have not heard shall understand.

Paul quotes Isaiah 52:15 as his confirmation of Scripture for going to those who have not seen and who have not heard in order that they might see and hear and understand.

Romans 15:22
For which cause also I have been much hindered from coming to you.

Keep in mind when Paul wrote this, he was in Corinth, wanting desperately to go to Rome.

Romans 15:23–29
But now having no more place in these parts, and having a great desire these many

years to come unto you; whensoever I take my journey into Spain, I will come to you: for I trust to see you in my journey, and to be brought on my way thitherward by you, if first I be somewhat filled with your company. But now I go unto Jerusalem to minister unto the saints. For it hath pleased them of Macedonia and Achaia to make a certain contribution for the poor saints which are at Jerusalem. It hath pleased them verily; and their debtors they are. For if the Gentiles have been made partakers of their spiritual things, their duty is also to minister unto them in carnal things. When therefore I have performed this, and have sealed to them this fruit, I will come by you into Spain. And I am sure that, when I come unto you, I shall come in the fulness of the blessing of the gospel of Christ.

Perhaps due to persecution or drought, the saints in Jerusalem were undergoing a season of poverty. Gentile believers, realizing their indebtedness to the Jerusalem church for evangelizing their region, collected an offering for the church in Jerusalem. After delivering their gift, Paul planned to go to Spain (verse 24). Did he ever make it? We don't know. Church tradition indicates he did, indeed, go to Spain and then on up into England. But this can't be emphatically verified. I personally believe he did go to Spain. Why? Because right before his death, he wrote, "I have finished my course" (2 Timothy 4:7).

Now, whether or not Paul's plan unfolded the way he hoped, the fact remains that he had a plan. A lot of people go through seasons where they're not doing anything. "What's your plan?" I ask.

"I don't have one," they answer.

"What's your intention?"

"I don't know."

"What do you hope to accomplish in the remaining years of your life?"

"Beats me."

Paul was a man with a plan. I would encourage all of us to seek the Lord and say, "Show me Your plan, Lord, as it relates to my kids, my wife, my employment, my ministry. Lord, I really want to hear from You." Without vision, people perish (Proverbs 29:18). Why is there such a lack of vision today? I believe television is a big part of it. Next time you feel a lack of vision, turn off your television, go for a walk, and ask the Lord for His plan for your life.

Romans 15:30
Now I beseech you, brethren, for the Lord Jesus Christ's sake, and for the love of the Spirit, that ye strive together with me in your prayers to God for me.

The word translated "strive" is *sunagonizo-mai*, from which we get our word "agonize." In other words, Paul was asking for passionate, fervent prayer because he knew danger awaited him in Jerusalem. How did he know this? Because people in every city on his journey warned him, "You're headed for real problems in Jerusalem" (see Acts 20:23; 21:4; 11).

Paul's parish was the Gentile world (verse 18). His power came from the Spirit of God (verse 19). His priority was the gospel (verse 19). His policy was to build on no man's foundation (verse 20). His plan was to go to Rome (verses 22, 23). One thing was left. He needed prayer.

Romans 15:31 (a)
That I may be delivered from them that do not believe in Judaea . . .

Paul requested prayer in three specific areas. The first is seen here—that he might be protected from the unbelievers in Jerusalem who were out to do him in.

Romans 15:31 (b)
. . . and that my service which I have for Jerusalem may be accepted of the saints.

Second, Paul requested prayer that the believers in Jerusalem might accept him.

Romans 15:32, 33
That I may come unto you with joy by the will of God, and may with you be refreshed. Now the God of peace be with you all. Amen.

Third, Paul requested prayer that he might come with joy to Rome. "Agonize with me in prayer," he said, "that I might be protected from the unbelievers who are out to get me, that I might be accepted by the believers who are there waiting for me, and that I might come to you with joy and be refreshed mutually."

Was Paul protected? So severe was the stoning he received at the hands of unbelieving Jews that his life was spared only when he was taken into protective custody by Lycinius, a Roman centurion (Acts 21).

Was he accepted by the believers? The believers themselves were the underlying reason for the stoning he received. Furthermore, they never thanked him for the offering he risked his life to deliver to them, nor does Scripture record any of them speaking with him or caring for him during the two years he was in protective custody.

Did he come to Rome with joy? He traveled to Rome as a prisoner of the Roman Empire.

And so we wonder. It looks like the prayers of the Romans weren't answered—or were they?

Was he protected? Yes. He didn't die. Bloodied? You bet—but he didn't die.

Was he accepted by the believers? Oh, not initially—but eventually, for Peter himself instructed the believers to listen to what Paul had to say (2 Peter 3:15).

Did he make it to Rome? While he didn't travel in the way he intended, at least his trip was all-expenses paid!

Gang, like Paul, sometimes we say, "Pray for me. I'm going through this struggle, and here are three things I need to see happen . . . ." And although we pray with fervency, sometimes initially it seems like just the opposite of what we hoped for happens. But wait. I have discovered that usually when I think prayers are not being answered, it's simply because I have not seen the unique and beautiful way God is working.

I once read an article in the paper about a woman in Alaska who tried to call her sister in Idaho, but she mistakenly dialed a house in Vermont because she dialed Vermont's 802 area code rather than Idaho's 208 area code. The woman in Vermont who answered the call was, at that moment, suffering a severe heart attack. As a result, the woman in Alaska heard only a gasping voice on the other end of the line, saying, "Help me. Help me. Please, God, help me." The woman in Alaska was able to work with telephone operators and emergency personnel to save the Vermont woman's life.

Sometimes, when I pray, I think all I get are busy signals or wrong numbers. But God is working in ways that, if I'll just hang in there, I'll see His hand—as evidenced in this familiar prayer by a Confederate soldier:

I asked God for strength, that I might
*   achieve,*
I was made weak, that I might learn
*   humbly to obey.*
I asked for health, that I might do greater
*   things,*
I was given infirmity, that I might do
*   better things.*
I asked for riches, that I might be happy,
I was given poverty, that I might be wise.
I asked for power, that I might have the
*   praise of men,*
I was given weakness, that I might feel
*   the need of God.*

I asked for all things, that I might enjoy
*   life,*
I was given life, that I might enjoy all
*   things.*
I got nothing that I asked for,
But everything I had hoped for.
Almost despite myself,
My unspoken prayers were answered.
I am among all men, most richly blessed.

That's the way of the Lord. In the middle of our own civil wars, we may not see God's hand. But on the other side, we'll say, "Lord, I got nothing I asked for—but everything I really wanted." The purpose and the power of prayer are not to get your way for your life, but to get the Lord's blessing on your life. The prayers Paul requested were truly answered in the best possible way, for lives were touched, folks were saved, and we're encouraged here today because people prayed.

16 Paul was not only a soul-winner, but he was a friend-maker as well. And here in chapter 16, we see ample evidence of that fact. The chapter contains a list of thirty-three people to whom Paul is sending his greetings. The first list (verses 1–16) is comprised of those who Paul is greeting. The second list (verses 21–23) is comprised of those who are with Paul in Corinth.

Romans 16:1 (a)
I commend unto you Phebe our sister . . .

Having known her in the city of Corinth, Paul says to those in Rome, "I commend Phebe to you." "Phebe" is another name for "Diana." Evidently, Phebe was named after the goddess Diana—Corinth's most famous deity. If that be so, Phebe was not Jewish but was most likely a heathen Gentile who had been converted to Christ.

Romans 16:1 (b)
. . . which is a servant of the church which is at Cenchrea:

The word translated "servant" is literally *diakonos,* or "deaconess", which indicates that women were in positions of ministry in the early church. According to the writings of the church fathers, deaconesses visited the sick, helped young women grow in the Lord, and tended the poor. How we need those who have a heart to be servants like Phebe—those who say, "Our call is to tend those who are sick, poor, and young in the Lord."

Romans 16:2 (a)
That ye receive her in the Lord, as becometh saints, and that ye assist her in whatsoever business she hath need of you . . .

"Receive her and assist her," said Paul. "She's coming to you as one who has proven her ministry."

Romans 16:2 (b)
. . . for she hath been a succourer of many, and of myself also.

The word "succourer," or "strengthener," linguistically speaks of what a mother does as she tenderly nourishes her baby through breastfeeding.

Romans 16:3
Greet Priscilla and Aquila my helpers in Christ Jesus.

When Paul first came to Corinth, he was introduced to Aquila and his wife, Priscilla—tentmakers, like himself. Evidently, Paul led them to a saving knowledge of Jesus Christ, for when Paul left Corinth for Ephesus, Aquila and Priscilla accompanied him as his companions and co-workers. As Paul made his way yet farther north, Aquila and Priscilla remained in Ephesus, where they were influential in the salvation of Apollos, one of the most powerful preachers of the early church (Acts 18:26). As evidenced by this verse, Priscilla and Aquila ended up in Rome. Some have even suggested Paul sent them ahead to set the stage and do some groundwork for his own journey to Rome.

It's interesting to me that in the six times this couple is mentioned, Priscilla's name is seen first four times. Why is this significant? Because in those days, the man's name was always mentioned first. Thus, it is agreed by virtually all commentators that Priscilla seems to be the one who had the more dynamic and powerful ministry. Yes, they traveled together—but it seems as though Aquila, realizing his wife had special and beautiful gifts, facilitated them and was not threatened by them.

Romans 16:4
Who have for my life laid down their own necks: unto whom not only I give thanks, but also all the churches of the Gentiles.

To what this refers, we don't know—but Paul makes it clear Aquila and Priscilla put their lives on the line for him.

Romans 16:5 (a)
Likewise greet the church that is in their house.

As you travel with Priscilla and Aquila, you see a pattern begin to unfold in their lives. That is, wherever they went, they started a fellowship group in their house. I like that. They not only worked together by day making tents, but they also opened their home at night.

I hope that's true of you and me. I hope the church is meeting in our homes. How? Jesus said, "Wherever two or three are gathered together, I am in their midst" (see Matthew 18:20). Therefore, if you want your families altered, develop what the previous generation called "family altar"—times when your family gets together for a season of worship, prayer, and Bible study.

Be warned, however. Nothing will be more difficult than having family altar. You can go on vacation, go bowling, have pizza, or watch baseball on TV without a hitch. But say the words, "It's time for family devotions"—and you'll be amazed by what happens. Dad will get a headache. Mom will suddenly remember the quiche bubbling over in the oven. Junior will get a phone call. Sis will have to leave. Baby will start crying. The dog will start barking. And the doorbell will ring. The Enemy will do everything possible to keep you as parents from getting your kids together and praying with them.

I know the struggle. I know the battle. I know how difficult it is. But I would suggest to you who desire your family to be strengthened, that, more than "focusing on the family," working legislatively, or sharing in groups about child-rearing, nothing in my opinion is more powerful or more effective than pulling your kids together for family altar. The church can be in your house. It doesn't take a lot of time. You don't have to teach fifteen chapters of Leviticus. Just share a simple story, make a simple application, and pray together.

Romans 16:5 (b)
Salute my wellbeloved Epaenetus, who is the firstfruits of Achaia unto Christ.

Epaenetus was Paul's first convert. I've discovered that folks never forget the name of the first person they lead to the Lord because nothing is more exciting than praying with someone, talking to someone, having the opportunity to see someone you care about come to know Jesus.

Romans 16:6
Greet Mary, who bestowed much labour on us.

The word "labour" is interesting. The same word is used in Luke 5:5 in reference to the fishermen who toiled all night. It embodies the idea of sweating. Thus, Mary bestowed much "sweat" upon them, if you would. That is, she gave of herself in a laboring type of ministry.

This intrigues me because six Marys are mentioned in the New Testament. When you think of Mary, you either think of Mary the mother of Jesus, or Mary of Bethany, who sat at the feet of Jesus while her sister Martha toiled in the kitchen (Luke 10:42). This Mary, however, is a worker. I wonder if this Mary ever thought, *My name is Mary, and all these Marys before me were sensitive, "sitting at the feet" kind of ladies. But I'm a labourer. That's just the way I am.*

I find it's truly a red-letter day in the walk of a believer when he sheds the self-imposed pressures or expectations of what he thinks he should be. Oftentimes, because we admire someone else and want to be like him or her, we put pressure on ourselves to be what we're not. Great is the day when you realize, "Even though my name is Mary, I'm one who likes to roll up my sleeves. So I'm just going to be who I am."

Mary's name is recorded throughout history as one who was noteworthy because she did what she was made to do, regardless of what the other Marys before her did. And her example is a good one.

Romans 16:7
Salute Andronicus and Junia, my kinsmen, and my fellowprisoners, who are of note among the apostles, who also were in Christ before me.

Bible students, this is an important verse because it is a key to understanding the apostolic ministry. There are those who say there are only eleven apostles—twelve if Paul is included in the position vacated by Judas—and that there are no apostles in the church today.

On one hand, I agree with them. On the other hand, I disagree. That is, if they're speaking of apostles that were appointed by Jesus Christ, I agree that there were only twelve, for such apostles had to have seen Jesus visibly. They had to have a firsthand knowledge of His ministry; and their ministries had to be confirmed with observable signs and wonders that validated their apostolic ministry.

But there are two other categories of apostles, each linked with the other two Persons of the Trinity. The Father sent out one Apostle: Jesus Christ (Hebrews 3:1). The Spirit sent out many apostles—Andronicus, Junia, Titus, Timothy, Barnabas, and a host of others called apostles in

Scripture (Acts 13:2). Therefore, in my opinion, the apostolic ministry continues today in those who are sent out by the Spirit, those who feel called in their hearts to go forth. Missionaries could be more accurately called apostles. The problem with the term "apostle" arises only from a misunderstanding of the word.

Romans 16:8–10 (a)
Greet Amplias my beloved in the Lord. Salute Urbane, our helper in Christ, and Stachys my beloved. Salute Apelles approved in Christ.

How can we be approved in Christ? You're doing it! By studying the Scriptures, you are showing yourself as being approved of God (2 Timothy 2:15).

Romans 16:10 (b)
Salute them which are of Aristobulus' household.

Historians tell us Aristobulus was the grandson of Herod the Great—the one who tried to annihilate Jesus by slaughtering all Jewish males under two years of age. Herod was the one who killed his sons and murdered his wife, butchering anyone who was a threat to his power. Yet here was his grandson, numbered among the household of faith.

Romans 16:11 (a)
Salute Herodion my kinsman.

Following verse 10 as it does, and "Herodion" being a derivative of "Herod," this verse could indicate that Paul himself was related to Herod. If this is true, the implications are intriguing. You who are students of Paul know he was a driven man. Before his conversion, he said, "I was a Pharisee of Pharisees. Concerning the law, I was blameless" (see Philippians 3:6). Vehement in his zeal to stand up for the laws of Judaism, he became enraged when he felt Judaism was threatened by a new group called Christians.

What made him so zealous for righteousness? Could it be that he was embarrassed to be linked to this butcher, this half-Jew/half-Idumean named Herod—the despised, despicable despot who left a bad taste in the mouth of every Jew in Israel? I think it's a very real possibility. And if that be so, I think Paul models for us the way we're to react or respond to family members.

You see, Paul didn't say, "I'm dysfunctional." He didn't say, "I need to join Herodions Anonymous." He didn't say, "I need therapy because I'm related to Herod." No, he took off in the opposite direction, saying, "Herod was a murderer, a blasphemer, a loser. I am going to strive to keep the law and live for God." And even though Paul was initially misdirected in his zeal, God saw his heart and corrected him on the road to Damascus.

I believe in this time in which we live—when everyone is claiming they have problems because of ancestors—we see in Paul a refreshingly wonderful, practical model. "This one thing I do," he said, "forgetting the things which lie behind, I press on toward the high mark of the calling of Christ" (see Philippians 3:13). Everyone has pain in their past. The key is to move on.

Romans 16:11 (b), 12 (a)
Greet them that be of the household of Narcissus, which are in the Lord. Salute Tryphena and Tryphosa, who labour in the Lord.

Tryphena and Tryphosa are sisters whose names mean "Dainty" and "Delicate." Notice, however, like Mary in verse 6, they laboured in the Lord. Thus, even Dainty and Delicate rolled up their sleeves for the kingdom.

Romans 16:12 (b)
Salute the beloved Persis, which laboured much in the Lord.

Persis being a feminine name, Paul is speaking of yet another woman who put her all into serving the Lord. Compare his use of "the beloved" here in verse 12 with his use of "my beloved" in verses 8 and 9. Stachys and Amplias, the subjects of verses 8 and 9, were males. I believe Paul's use of the possessive pronoun only with men models an important principle of ministry. That is, he was very careful to relate to his brothers in a different way than he did to his sisters. Some might call this legalism or chauvinism. I call it wisdom.

Romans 16:13
Salute Rufus chosen in the Lord, and his mother and mine.

Rufus, it seems, is the same Rufus spoken of in Mark 15:21. Rufus' father was Simon of Cyrene—the one who came up from Africa to Jerusalem to celebrate and observe the Passover proceedings. When he lined up along the Via Dolorosa, the crowd gathered on that Good Friday, he watched the proceedings, no doubt straining his neck and squinting his eyes, trying to get a perspective of what was happening. Suddenly, a Man collapsed before him under the weight of a cross. Instead of forcing Him to carry the burden

any further, a soldier on the scene placed the flat head of his spear upon the shoulder of Simon the Cyrene, saying, "You take the Cross."

Simon must have thought, *Oh no. What a catastrophe. I came to celebrate the Passover, and now I'm going to be defiled by associating with this criminal.* But he discovered that the catastrophe was, in fact, a great opportunity because something happened to Simon when he took up the Cross. Could it be that he understood the prophecy of Isaiah 9:6, which says, "The government shall be upon His shoulder"? The government of what? The government of the Cross. As Simon carried the Cross of Christ, he was, in a sense, governed in a way he never would have anticipated or wanted. Yet carry the Cross he did, eventually becoming converted to the One whose Cross he carried. And not only did Simon get saved, but, as can be inferred from this verse, his wife and his sons did as well.

What's the point for you and me? Jesus said, "If any man come after Me, let him deny himself and take up his cross" (see Matthew 16:24). He didn't say this because He wants us to be miserable or burdened. He didn't say this because He wants to see us squirm or suffer. No, He said it because He came to teach us the very important truth that the way to really have happiness and fulfillment in life is to die to self. The more you live for yourself, the more you focus on yourself, the more you are concerned about yourself, the more discouraged and defeated you'll be. "I came that you might have life and life abundantly," Jesus said (John 10:10) "And the way to have abundant life is to take up your cross."

Romans 16:14
Salute Asyncritus, Phlegon, Hermas, Patrobas, Hermes, and the brethren which are with them.

These are all Greek names, and, because they're lumped together along with "the brethren with them," it is likely these guys lived together in a commune.

Romans 16:15 (a)
Salute Philologus . . .

What a great name! It comes from "Philos Logos" or "Lover of the Word."

Romans 16:15 (b)–17 (a)
. . . and Julia, Nereus, and his sister, and Olympas, and all the saints which are with them. Salute one another with an holy kiss. The churches of Christ salute you. Now . . .

After giving a greeting to his friends, Paul gives a warning of foes to avoid.

Romans 16:17 (b), 18 (a)
. . . I beseech you, brethren, mark them which cause divisions and offences contrary to the doctrine which ye have learned; and avoid them. For they that are such serve not our Lord Jesus Christ . . .

Many "Lord Jesus Christs" are being taught— the Lord Jesus of the Mormons, of the Jehovah's Witness, of the Modernist, of the New Ager. But they're not our Lord Jesus.

For topical study of Romans 16:17–18 entitled "Another Jesus?" turn to page 1003.

Romans 16:18 (b)
. . . but their own belly; and by good words and fair speeches deceive the hearts of the simple.

The word "simple" does not mean "dumb." It means "sincere." What's being said here is that there are sincere people who are being deceived by those who preach another Jesus Christ. Therefore, in your sincerity to want to learn more about the Lord or to be students of the Word, don't allow those who teach a different Jesus to come into your home. Don't engage in discussions with them. Don't spend time arguing with them. Mark them and avoid them. Why? I offer two reasons. . . .

One reason is *protection.* Satan is clever. And many a believer who thought he was strong in theology has succumbed to those who are inspired satanically. The second reason is *prioritization.* Invest your energy in the fields that are already white and ready for harvest (John 4:35), in the lives of those who are already open to the gospel.

Romans 16:19
For your obedience is come abroad unto all men. I am glad therefore on your behalf: but yet I would have you wise unto that which is good, and simple concerning evil.

"Be wise about spiritual matters but simple, or naive, concerning evil," warned Paul. I believe the trend in ministry today to keep culturally current and socially relevant is contrary to this word of warning.

"But I won't be effective," we say.

That's what Moses thought. . . .

At forty years of age, Moses had enough of Egypt. "I'd rather suffer with God's people who are laboring out in the sun baking bricks than to be in the palaces of Pharaoh enjoying sin, which brings pleasure only for a short season," he said (Hebrews 11:25). *So he left the palace, saw a Jew being hassled by an Egyptian taskmaster, and did what he was trained to do in Egypt: He flexed his muscle, clenched his fist, and dealt a deathblow to the taskmaster.*

The next day, when he came to hang out with the Jews, they said, "Get out of here. Are you going to kill us too?" (Exodus 2:14). And Moses fled to the desert, where, for the next forty years he unlearned Egypt.

Forty years later, God called him back to Egypt. "They won't believe me," he cried (Exodus 4:1). "Look at me. I don't dress like an Egyptian pharaoh anymore. I don't know the latest songs. I can't tell you the top ten shows. I don't get People *magazine anymore. How am I going to relate to them? They won't listen to me."*

"Oh, yes they will," God answered. "You left Egypt overnight. But it's taken me forty years to get Egypt out of you. Now I can use you." And how He did!

I want our kids to see the vanity of Egypt, to leave it behind, forget it, and not feel they have to know what's going on. To do so, they have to see that in you, Mom and Dad. They have to see you as those who live with an entirely different mindset than that of the world.

For topical study of Romans 16:19 entitled "Be Simple Concerning Evil," turn to page 1007.

Romans 16:20
And the God of peace shall bruise Satan under your feet shortly.

Remain naive concerning evil and watch how God will stomp Satan under you through the peace you have in your heart, the peace that flows from your lips, the peace seen on your face.

Romans 16:20–22
The grace of our Lord Jesus Christ be with you. Amen. Timotheus my workfellow, and Lucius, and Jason, and Sosipater, my kinsmen, salute you. I Tertius, who wrote this epistle, salute you in the Lord.

Tertius was Paul's secretary, to whom Paul dictated this Epistle. His name means "Third." The last name in verse 23 is Quartus, whose name means "Fourth." These guys were slaves. In those days, slaves were referred to only by number. Consequently, it's interesting that these two, who were considered unworthy of names, became historically and eternally significant because they were brought into the kingdom.

So, too, you might feel like a number, like no one cares about you, like no one takes notice of you. But the Lord has a plan for you. He's got your number. And as you give yourself to Him and walk with Him, you'll find significance. Ask Tertius and Quartus!

Romans 16:23
Gaius mine host, and of the whole church, saluteth you. Erastus the chamberlain of the city saluteth you, and Quartus a brother.

Those who were with Paul in Corinth send their greetings to those in Rome.

Romans 16:24
The grace of our Lord Jesus Christ be with you all. Amen.

Paul gives his usual closing as he writes, "The grace of the Lord be with you." But wait. There are three more verses. What's going on? At this point, Paul does what he frequently was inclined to do. He grabbed the pen himself and "autographed" this letter with the final three verses.

Romans 16:25 (a)
Now . . .

Here Paul takes the pen and writes himself. He makes mention of this practice in 2 Thessalonians 3:17. We see it was Paul's custom, after closing his dictation, to grab the pen and add a final thought or two before signing the letter. . . .

Romans 16:25 (b)
. . . to him that is of power to stablish you . . .

Not infrequently I have been asked about Applegate Christian Fellowship's follow-up program for the numbers of folks who are saved and baptized each week. "We don't have a follow-up program," I would say. "We have a follow up Person—the One who is able to stabilize, establish, and steady us."

Romans 16:25 (c)
. . . according to my gospel . . .

On the basis of this verse, some say Paul had a unique gospel, different from the one Peter or John preached. But such is not the case.

In John 20, Mary said, "They've taken away my Lord, and I don't know where they've laid Him."

Also in John 20, Thomas said, "My Lord and my God."

So, too, Paul says, "*my* gospel" because the gospel had not only impacted him theologically— he claimed it personally.

Romans 16:25 (d)–27
. . . and the preaching of Jesus Christ, according to the revelation of the mystery, which was kept secret since the world began, but now is made manifest, and by the scriptures of the prophets, according to the commandment of the everlasting God, made known to all nations for the obedience of faith: To God only wise, be glory through Jesus Christ for ever. Amen.

The word translated, "mystery" is the Greek word *musterion.* It doesn't mean that which can't be figured out, but rather that which was previously hidden.

Musterion is like the car commercials in which the new model is covered with a sheet or canvas. You can see the shape of it, but not the details. The engineer knows what's underneath the canvas. The designer already knows the shape of the car. But the car remains hidden to the rest of us. So, too, the mystery of which Paul spoke was hidden until the right moment. What is the mystery? It begins to unfold in Romans 11:25, where Paul uses the word *musterion* for the first time in regard to the mystery that Gentiles would be brought into the kingdom. "Gentiles in the kingdom?" the Jew would say. "That's a mystery!"

But the mystery continues, for in Ephesians 3:2–6, *musterion* appears again. Not only would the Gentile be brought into the kingdom, but Gentiles would be incorporated into a brand-new entity called the church, the body of Christ. No more would there be a differentiation between Jews and Gentiles, men and women, slaves and freemen (1 Corinthians 12:13). This was revolutionary.

But it is the third appearance of the word *musterion* that touches the heart of the mystery, for it is there Paul writes of the mystery of "Christ in you—the hope of glory" (Colossians 1:25–27). It's not a program given to us, not rules and regulations laid on us, not expectations placed before us, but rather Christ *in* us, the hope of glory.

Folks, it's not religions, not programs, not twelve-stepping, not trying harder, not getting it together, not follow-up materials that are needed. What's needed is Christ living in us. A lot of people think Christianity involves some rules, some regulations, a standard, a code to live by, and some activities to take part in. Nothing could be further from the truth because Jesus did not come to make bad people good, nor to make good people better. He came to make dead men alive by living in them.

The last time *musterion* is found is in 1 Timothy 3:16, where Paul says,

- God was manifest in the flesh when Jesus came as the Babe of Bethlehem;
- He was justified in the Spirit when the Spirit came upon Him at His baptism;
- He was seen of angels when they ministered to Him in the wilderness after He had been tempted for forty days;
- He was preached unto the nations when He healed and ministered not to the Jews only, but to the Gentiles;
- He was believed on in the world when multitudes gathered around Him;
- And He was received unto glory when He rose from the dead.

"Great is this mystery," said Paul, "that Jesus, who was victorious over the Enemy, who never succumbed to any temptation personally, who was justified by the Father as the voice from heaven rang out audibly, and yet is One who can relate to you and me personally. This same Jesus was received up into glory and returned to us through His Spirit."

This means that when my kids are tempted to do something they ought not do, or when I plunge into something I shouldn't, even at the very time of the temptation, sin, or difficulty, we will be exceedingly uncomfortable because Jesus is in us.

Gang, He is faithful to establish you, your kids, your friends, your neighbors, those who have been baptized Sunday after Sunday—anyone who comes to Him. *Great* is the mystery!

Without the mystery of godliness, man is sentenced either to despair as he worries about whether his friends and loved ones will live right—or to legalized religion as he sets up rules and regulations to ensure the people he loves won't stray.

But if we understand the mystery of Christ dying for us, living within us, relating to us, we can be sure we'll make it. So will our children, our neighbors, and all who are recipients of the mystery.

"This is the mystery," said Paul. "Jesus will establish you because He lives in you."

What wonderful comfort.

ANOTHER JESUS?
A Topical Study of
Romans 16:17, 18

The sixteenth chapter of the Book of Romans makes obvious the fact that, although Paul had never been to Rome, there were at least thirty-five people there he knew by name.

But there is something else in this chapter that intrigues me. That is, in the middle of his list of friends to greet, Paul inserts a list of foes to avoid. "Mark those who cause division by teaching what is contrary to the doctrine I have shared with you," he said. Notice he doesn't say, "Debate them," "Study them," or even, "Have compassion on them." He says, "Mark and avoid them. For they that are such serve not our Lord Jesus Christ."

I was surprised by the results of a poll that showed over 80 percent of the people in our country claim to believe in Jesus Christ? Do 80 percent of Americans really have a saving faith in Jesus Christ? Are 80 percent of your neighbors, co-workers, or acquaintances headed for heaven? I doubt it. You see, even though many talk about Jesus Christ and claim to be interested in Jesus Christ, or they do not serve our Lord Jesus Christ because there are many "Lord Jesus Christs" being talked about today.

There is the Lord Jesus Christ of the modernist. "Jesus was not really born of a virgin," the modernist says. "That's just a piece of Hebrew mythology. He didn't perform miracles, either."

> Consider the feeding of the five thousand. According to the modernist, what really happened was quite simple to explain. That is, as was the custom of the day, people had their lunches in the sleeves of their robes. And when one little boy stepped forward and said, "I'll share," everyone followed his example. Thus, everyone was fed.

Preposterous! Our Lord Jesus Christ is not the Jesus Christ of the modernist.

Nor is He the Jesus Christ of the Jehovah's Witness. The Jesus Christ of the Jehovah's Witness is actually Michael, the archangel. According to Witness theology, Michael came to this earth and became Jesus Christ. His death on the Cross does not apply to the common person, and His resurrection is denied altogether. Thus, the Lord Jesus Christ of the Jehovah's Witness is not our Lord Jesus Christ.

Nor is He the Jesus Christ of the Christian Scientist, who simply holds Him up as a Divine Ideal. The Christian Scientist denies anything negative or evil—including hell. The Scientist holds Jesus as a Master whose primary purpose was to teach us a positive way to think and live. But He's not our Lord Jesus Christ.

Nor is our Lord Jesus Christ the Jesus Christ of the Mormon, who teaches that Jesus Christ was the offspring of Adam, God, and Mary—and that when Jesus appeared in the flesh, He was a polygamist, secretly married to several of the Marys of the Bible, as well as to Martha. The more you study the teachings of Mormonism, the more you realize their Jesus Christ is not our Jesus Christ.

Nor is our Lord Jesus Christ the Jesus Christ of the New Ager, who says, "Christ is everywhere. He's in you; He's in me. He's the Divine Spark who simply needs to be fanned through contemplation and meditation." The Jesus Christ of the New Ager is a crystal Christ. Our Jesus Christ is the Rock of Ages.

Now, while we are to avoid any who teach contrary to our Lord Jesus Christ, we are also to be ready to give an answer to any man who asks the reason for the hope within us (1 Peter 3:15). We should know the Scriptures and be able to give an answer to the New Ager and the Modernist, the Jehovah's Witness, Mormon, and Scientist—but giving an answer doesn't mean endless dialogue and debate.

Too many people, in attempting to straighten out those who teach another Jesus Christ, have found themselves shipwrecked in their own faith. Heed the simple word the Scriptures share concerning those who teach another Jesus Christ: Mark them and avoid them.

If our Lord Jesus Christ is not the Jesus Christ of the New Ager, the modernist, the Jehovah's Witness, the Mormon, or the Christian Scientist, who is He?

Turn back to Romans 1, and see what Paul has to say about who our Lord Jesus Christ is.

The Revealed One

(Which he had promised afore by his prophets in the holy scriptures,) concerning his Son Jesus Christ our Lord . . . Romans 1:2, 3 (a)

Jesus is not some weird guru who showed up on the scene, claiming to have some fresh new revelation. Rather, centuries before He appeared, promises were given concerning Him that we might know for certain that He is the Chosen One, the Messiah, the Savior for all humanity.

- Micah tells us where He would be born (chapter 5).
- Isaiah tells us the way in which He would be born (chapter 7).
- Daniel tells us the very day He would enter the Holy City and present Himself as King (chapter 9).
- Zechariah not only tells us He would be betrayed by a friend and sold for silver, but also that the silver would be cast on the floor of the temple and used to buy a potter's field (chapter 11).
- David tells us the kind of death He would die (Psalm 22).

What is the statistical possibility that these eight prophecies could be fulfilled by any one person? In his excellent work, *Science Speaks,* author Peter Stoner says the probability is $1:10^{27}$.

But, folks, there were not only eight prophecies given concerning Jesus Christ. There are over *three hundred*—all fulfilled perfectly. Truly, He is the Revealed One.

The Reigning One

. . . which was made of the seed of David according to the flesh . . . Romans 1:3 (a)

Our Lord Jesus Christ is not only revealed in prophecies of old, but reigns as King of kings, sitting on the throne of David. He is not some wispy consciousness, not some floating spirit. He is 100 percent human.

What does this mean for us practically? It means that, because He was tempted in all points as we are (Hebrews 4:15), He felt every single temptation.

If you put a great big rutabaga in front of me, I would not be tempted at all. But put a hot fudge sundae in front of me—*that's* temptation!

What does it mean that Jesus was "tempted in all points like as we are"? It means that every temptation mankind experiences was to Him not a rutabaga, but a hot fudge sundae because temptation is not temptation unless it's tempting. This means Jesus can reign over my life as my King because He was tempted by the same sins that tempt me. Whatever sin tempts you, precious people, He understands because it tempted Him too.

Jesus doesn't look down on you. He's not disgusted with you. He's not confused by you. He understands you because this "Seed of David according to the flesh" has been tempted by the same things that tempt you.

The Resurrected One

And declared to be the Son of God with power, according to the spirit of holiness, by the resurrection from the dead. Romans 1:4

Our Lord Jesus Christ is not only 100 percent man, but He's one hundred percent God as well. "Give us a sign," they said. "Do something to prove Your claim" (see John 2:18).

"One sign I'll give," Jesus replied. "Destroy this body and in three days I'll rise again from the dead" (see John 2:19).

Our Lord Jesus did something that neither Mary Baker Eddy, Joseph Smith, Mohammed, Bhagwan Shree Rajneesh, or any other so-called spiritual leader has ever done. He rose from the dead. Jesus is alive, gang. He doesn't just tell you how to live or what you should do. He is the Resurrected One. He is God. And He lives inside you. Therefore, because our Lord Jesus is uniquely the Revealed One, the Reigning One, and the Resurrected One, we are to mark those who teach otherwise.

What does it mean to be marked? The Old Testament picture of this New Testament principle is found in Ezekiel 9. . . .

Caught up by the Lord and taken to Jerusalem, Ezekiel was instructed to go throughout the city and mark those who were crying over the sins and abominations of Jerusalem. They were to be marked with the final letter of the Hebrew alphabet—"taw"—which was an X, a cross. "Mark the heads of those who are sighing and weeping over sin, who are saddened by the carnality, rebellion and iniquity in this city," said God, "for those not marked with a cross are to be wiped out and destroyed" (see Ezekiel 9:4–6). And where was the marking to begin? In the sanctuary, in the house of God (Ezekiel 9:6).

The same is true today. I know those who are truly of our Lord Jesus Christ because they carry on them the mark of the Cross. They realize the seriousness of sin and that Jesus paid its price by dying for them. Not only that, they realize He asks them to bear the Cross as well (Matthew 16:24).

Precious people, there are two marks. . . .

The mark of the Cross is upon those who realize the seriousness and repercussion of sin, upon those who embrace Jesus Christ and take up their Cross daily to follow Him.

The mark of apostasy and heresy is upon those who teach another Christ, an Easy Jesus, a Nice Guy, an Interesting Teacher.

Are you marked with the Cross—or are you a believer in another Jesus Christ, a Cross-less Christ? If you're a believer in another Jesus Christ, you're marked for destruction. But if you're a believer in the Revealed, Reigning, Resurrected One, and an embracer of His Cross, you're marked for heaven.

BE SIMPLE CONCERNING EVIL
A Topical Study of
Romans 16:19

As Paul the apostle closes this Epistle, he shares with the Romans a very powerful, practical principle. That is, he would have them be wise to that which is good and ignorant concerning evil. You see, Rome, being the capital city of the empire, was the place to be for anyone who was moving up in society. It was the power point politically, the hot spot culturally. Rome was where the movie stars hung out and the musicians lived. It was the happening place—which is why Paul was concerned that the believers there remain naive concerning evil, that they be ignorant concerning what was happening around them culturally.

"Hey," they could have argued, "We've got to keep up with the latest trends and fads."

"No, you don't," Paul would counter. "I want you to be wise and knowledgeable about things that are good. But when it comes to what is evil, you should be the most naive of all people."

In America, where many of the trends of the world are set, I believe we have become very knowledgeable about evil. And I think that's dangerous.

"Oh, but I'm just keeping current," we say. "I'm just monitoring the trends by reading those books, watching those shows, going to those movies."

"I'm concerned about you," said Paul. "Yes, your faith is spoken of throughout the world. But are you naive concerning evil?"

Why shouldn't we follow cultural trends? Why shouldn't we be those who monitor activities, music, or movies so that we might know what's happening?

Take careful note: In the very beginning God warned His people that they were in danger of becoming ensnared by the same gods and influences that damned the Canaanites before them. How? By inquiring after their gods, saying, "How did these nations worship? What were they doing? What was their mind-set and perspective? I need to be informed about it. I need to keep up with it. I need to be tuned in to it" (Deuteronomy 12:29, 30).

"Even though you are in the land," God said to His people, "even though the Canaanites are wiped out, don't research their idolatry, for it will ensnare you. You'll become interested in it. You'll become intrigued by it. Even though your motives might have been okay initially—watch out. There are powerful forces at work, demonic entities behind those idols, videos, movies, magazines, and books. Stay away."

In other words, the Word of God in Deuteronomy is the same as it is in Romans: "Be naive concerning evil." In trying to keep current, too many people in the church have been caught up in the current of carnality, carried down the river and wiped out. Why? Because they failed to heed the warnings so clearly given in the Word.

"The idols of the nations are silver and gold," the psalmist declared (Psalm 135:15). So, too, in order to sell their CD, movie, or book, the idols on MTV and in Hollywood today will be seductive, immoral, or outrageous. They'll do whatever it takes to get silver and gold.

The tragedy is that the one who makes the idol becomes like the idol (Psalm 135:18). Truly, what we fix our eyes on is what we become. Fix your eyes on the culture and you will mirror the culture.

The Life of the Holy

David understood this. This man who killed giants, bears, and lions, this one who was a musician, a poet, and the most popular man in the kingdom said, "I will set nothing wicked before my eyes" (see Psalm 101:3). This verse should be attached to every TV in every home of every Christian.

"Oh, but I gotta check it out. I gotta see what's hot."

No, you don't. Evil is a snare. It will erode your soul, zap your spiritual energy, and diminish your hunger for the Word. And slowly, but surely, you'll become like what you are beholding.

Joseph was another who understood the seductiveness of sin. When Potiphar's wife grabbed him and said, "Lie with me," Joseph replied by splitting the scene (Genesis 39:12). What happened to Joseph? He became second only to Pharaoh in the kingdom of Egypt. He ascended to power and prominence because he lived a life of purity.

The same was true of Daniel. "I'll not eat the king's meat and drink," he said.

"Pass the broccoli" (Daniel 1:12). What happened to Daniel? He was promoted to the position of satrap—one of the most successful men in all of Babylon.

Knowing the day in which he lived was exceedingly wicked, Job said, "I made a covenant with my eyes. Why then should I think upon a maid?" (Job 31:1)—the inference being, "I'll not look on that which would stimulate lust. I make a covenant right now not to look on the screen, to read the book, or listen to the music that flirts with evil or toys with wickedness."

You can either engage in demonic activities and darkness that will pull you down and do you in—or you can be like David or Daniel, like Joseph or Job, and say, "I will be naive when it comes to things that are dark and evil," and in so doing find the blessing of God upon your life.

Job and David, Joseph and Daniel were men who were blessed, prosperous, and successful because they stood for purity. Sure, they had failings and shortcomings—but their hearts and lives were geared toward integrity.

Contrast these men with another, one who thought he needed to be in the middle of the scene: Herod.

The Life of Herod

Mark 6 tells us Herod was one who lived in luxury, was a lousy leader politically, and was caught up in lascivious activity. He took his brother's wife as his mistress, threw wild parties, and kept up with all that was the latest in Rome. He knew what was happening culturally—but he also knew inside he was wrong. He knew that flirting with the world made him a debauched, depraved loser—despised by the very people he ruled.

John the Baptist came on the scene, wearing camel skin and chewing on grasshoppers, saying, "What you're doing, Herod, is not right" (see Mark 6:18). Although Scripture records that Herod "heard him gladly" (see Mark 6:20), his mistress knew John was a problem, so she demanded he be thrown in prison.

Soon afterward, at one of Herod's notorious parties, the teen-aged daughter of Herod's wife danced before Herod and his guests. Knowing such dancing would cause Herod to crumble, her mother instructed her to ask for the head of John the Baptist in return. Sure enough, following her dance, Herod told the girl that anything up to half of the kingdom could be hers. And, as instructed by her mother, the girl asked for the head of John the Baptist. Although Herod knew John was a good man, he was trapped. Afraid of backing down under the pressure of his peers, Herod gave in.

Not long after John was beheaded, Herod began to hear rumors of a Man teaching and healing in the area. Haunted by his sin, Herod cried, "It's John the Baptist back from the dead." But two years later, as recorded in the twenty-third chapter of Luke, the One who Herod thought was John the Baptist was brought before him to judge. "I've been wanting to see You," said Herod (see Luke 23:8). "Do some miracle for me."

But Jesus answered him not a word—which infuriated Herod. Consequently, Herod began to mock and taunt Jesus, while ordering his men to beat Him. Jesus was crucified, but He rose again. Herod, on the other hand, lived—only to go insane and, as some historians believe, take his own life. Today, Herod is studied as the quintessential picture of a total loser—for although he lived in the holy city of Jerusalem, he got caught up in the Roman scene, in Greek culture, in the latest happening, and drowned in the cesspool of sin.

Precious people, there's a better route for us. It's called purity. "Oh, but we can't be ostriches with our heads in the sand," you might protest. First of all, not one ostrich has ever been known to stick his head in the sand. Secondly, it's not a matter of sticking your head in the sand. It's a matter of keeping your head out of the sewer!

As a young Man, Jesus found favor with God and man (Luke 2:52). Kids, if you want favor in the eyes of men, here's what to do: Live righteously. But if you want to be a dead fish that goes with the flow, just keep up with the latest thing on MTV. Stay tuned. Be cool—and you'll become a nothing. Ask Herod.

The choice is yours and mine today. We can either be like Herod, the quintessential loser, the party-er, the drinker, the movie expert—or we can be like Jesus, who became strong in spirit, filled with wisdom, upon whom was the grace of God (Luke 2:40). May God give us modern-day Romans wisdom. I know you have faith in the gospel—and I commend you for that. But, as Paul would say, this one thing I would have of you: Be ignorant concerning evil and wise concerning good.

And so, as we come to the end of Paul's letter to the Romans, my prayer is that the Lord will give you a continual hunger and appetite to devour the meat of His Word.

May He give you the energy to mine its riches.

May He make you strong in theology—not that you might be puffed up with pride, but that, understanding your liberty, you might perpetually praise Him.

May you be free from religion and legalism.

May He bless you immensely.

1 CORINTHIANS

Background to 1 Corinthians

If churches were graded, the church at Corinth would be given a D for divided, defiled, and defamed. But the letter written by Paul to address these problems rates an A+.

Paul's first Epistle to the Corinthians can be divided into two parts. Chapters 1—6 deal with concerns Paul had *about* them. Chapters 7—16 deal with answers Paul had *for* them. In these concerns and answers, Paul instructed the Corinthian church—and every subsequent church—regarding effective ministry, true unity, Christian charity, spiritual maturity, and the meaning of liberty. He instructed them regarding Church conduct, spiritual gifts, and the resurrection of the dead. He wrote to them regarding the problem of division and the definition of love.

Although best known for its thirteenth chapter, the whole of Paul's first letter to the Corinthians is a glorious Epistle—one I believe you'll find to be exceedingly practical and uniquely helpful.

---

1 CORINTHIANS

1 Corinthians 1:1 (a)
Paul, called to be an apostle of Jesus Christ through the will of God . . .

The words "to be" appear in italics. As is usually the case, when the translators added them to clarify the sentence, they actually clouded it. This verse should actually read: "Paul, called an apostle of Jesus Christ." Apostleship was not an office he was trying to achieve, but rather a definition of who he was—one who was sent out by Jesus Christ.

1 Corinthians 1:1 (b)
. . . and Sosthenes our brother.

As Paul wrote this Epistle, a man named Sosthenes was beside him. Perhaps that name rings a bell.

When Paul was in Corinth the first time, he preached the gospel in the synagogues. But when he proclaimed that Jesus is Messiah, the Jews protested so vehemently that Paul shook off his raiment and said, "Your blood be upon your own heads. I'm going to the Gentiles" (see Acts 18:6). When he went to the Gentiles, where did Paul go? Right next door to the house of Justus, also called Gaius. When he started teaching there, many were converted—including Crispus, the leader of the synagogue. As a result, the Jews were "provoked to jealousy" (see Romans 1).

When Gallio, a new deputy, was assigned to the region, the Jews wasted no time presenting their accusations against Paul. Led by a man named Sosthenes, they stormed into Gallio's office, saying, "A man next door to our synagogue is teaching things contrary to the law."

Yet even before Paul could open his mouth in his own defense, Gallio said, "I don't have *time to settle religious disputes." And he drove them out. Angry with the one who pled their case, the Jews beat Sosthenes. Evidently, it was at this point that something happened within him—for shortly thereafter, Sosthenes was converted.*

I remind you of this story for a reason. That is, although it was Sosthenes who led the protest against Paul, in our text we see Sosthenes laboring with Paul. The same is still true. People who are most violently opposed to you and your faith are often the very ones who are most convicted by the Spirit, the very ones who are closest to conversion. Just let them take a few more hits from their friends in the world, and, like Sosthenes, they'll come around.

When I share the gospel, the response I least want to hear is, "I'm glad that works for you." On the other hand, when someone responds vehemently or angrily, I know I've got a candidate because he or she is provoked.

1 Corinthians 1:2 (a)
Unto the church of God which is at Corinth . . .

Paul doesn't say, "Unto the church of Corinth." He says, "Unto the church of God which is at Corinth." There is not a church of Corinth. There is not a Church of England. There is only one church: the church of God.

This church of God located at Corinth was in an interesting place. Corinth was a city in south central Greece that was prosperous economically due to its location geographically. You see, Corinth was only four miles from the Aegean Sea, so to avoid sailing around the southern tip of Greece where waters were rough and treacherous, sailors would sail through the channel to Corinth, unload their ships, put them on rollers, and roll them four miles to the Aegean. As a result, Corinth became a very prosperous port. And it was as wicked as it was prosperous. Every night, one thousand temple prostitutes left the temple of Aphrodite, the love goddess, and went through the city recruiting business in the name of worship. As a result, the coffers of the temple were filled.

In addition, Corinth was a philosophical center. Along with Athens, Corinth was a favorite of philosophers. This made for an interesting mix in Corinth—a city engaged in lofty discourse by day and depravity and debauchery by night. Thus, it is no surprise that it was from Corinth that Paul penned his Epistle to the Romans, wherein he traced the devolution of man (Romans 1).

1 Corinthians 1:2 (b)
. . . to them that are sanctified in Christ Jesus . . .

The word "sanctified" literally means "set apart." The Greek word has its roots in the idea of marriage, wherein one is set apart *to* someone and *for* someone. The Hebrew concept of sanctification is seen in the instruments used in the tabernacle and temple that were used exclusively for the offering of sacrifices. Thus, from the very get-go, Paul comes in with a powerful word to the Corinthians as he says to them, "I know the reputation Corinthians have, but you Christians are different. You're set apart for God's service exclusively."

1 Corinthians 1:2 (c)
. . . called to be saints . . .

The words "to be" are in italics. Therefore, for a more correct rendering of this phrase, delete the words "to be." We don't work to be saints. It's not an honor given to a holy few. No, every one of us is who is born again is a saint.

1 Corinthians 1:2 (d)
. . . with all that in every place call upon the name of Jesus Christ our Lord, both theirs and ours.

These truths apply not only to those in Corinth but also to everyone who calls on the name of the Lord.

1 Corinthians 1:3
Grace be unto you, and peace, from God our Father, and from the Lord Jesus Christ.

"Charis," or "Grace," was the typical Greek greeting. "Shalom," or "Peace," was its Hebrew counterpart. Here and in his other epistles, Paul marries these two ideas—always putting grace first because a person cannot have true and lasting peace unless he first understands God's matchless grace.

1 Corinthians 1:4
I thank my God always on your behalf, for the grace of God which is given you by Jesus Christ.

Paul couldn't say, "I thank my God for your righteousness," because the Corinthians weren't very righteous. He couldn't say, "I thank my God for your faith," because they weren't very faithful. Paul could, however, say, "I thank my God for His grace given on your behalf"—because they needed it! Although he realized the seriousness of the situation, I, nonetheless, picture Paul with a smile on his face as he wrote, "When I think about you, I thank God for grace."

1 Corinthians 1:5
That in every thing ye are enriched by him, in all utterance, and in all knowledge.

"Utterance and knowledge" is a reference to the *charisma*—the gifts of the Spirit.

1 Corinthians 1:6, 7
Even as the testimony of Christ was confirmed in you: So that ye come behind in no gift; waiting for the coming of our Lord Jesus Christ:

The grace of God was shown to the church in Corinth in that they lacked no spiritual gift. This tells me something very important: The flow of spiritual gifts either in a man individually or in a congregation corporately is not an indication of spirituality. It's an indication of grace. When someone has a gift of healing, a word of prophecy, or otherwise moves in the miraculous, our tendency is to assume he must be very holy. The gifts of the Spirit, however, are not dependent upon our attaining a certain level of spirituality. They're simply a matter of our being recipients of grace. This means ministry and spiritual gifts are not based upon how we're doing at all—but solely upon what God wants to do in and through us.

1 Corinthian 1:8
Who shall also confirm you unto the end, that ye may be blameless in the day of our Lord Jesus Christ.

"God's been good to you Corinthian Christians," says Paul. "He'll see you through." Why? Read on.

1 Corinthians 1:9
God is faithful, by whom ye were called unto the fellowship of his Son Jesus Christ our Lord.

We're going to make it. Why? Not because of anything within ourselves—but because God is faithful. That's why the psalmist says that we are held by His right hand (Psalm 73:23).

When my son, Benjamin, was five years old, if he and I were crossing a busy street on a cold, rainy day, I would say, "Hold my hand, Benjamin. He would put his hand in mine, and we would start across the street. But if he slipped and let go of my hand, would it be

curtains for him? No, because, although I said, "Hold my hand, Ben," in reality, I would be holding his. So if he slipped, it would be no problem because no matter what, I would never let go.

So, too, even to these Corinthian Christians who were entangled in a whole host of problems, Paul says, "You're going to make it. Why? Because God is faithful."

1 Corinthians 1:10, 11
Now I beseech you, brethren, by the name of our Lord Jesus Christ, that ye all speak the same thing, and that there be no divisions among you; but that ye be perfectly joined together in the same mind and in the same judgment. For it hath been declared unto me of you, my brethren, by them which are of the house of Chloe, that there are contentions among you.

When Paul was in Rome, he heard from members of Chloe's house that the church in Corinth was splintering into factions and deep divisions—something he knew he needed to address.

1 Corinthians 1:12
Now this I say, that every one of you saith, I am of Paul; and I of Apollos; and I of Cephas; and I of Christ.

The church at Corinth was divided into four groups:

- Some said, "We follow Paul, the founder of this fellowship."
- Others said, "Paul's not impressive. We follow Apollos. He is an eloquent orator, a powerful personality, a true intellectual."
- A third group said, "Apollos may be a skilled speaker, but we can't figure out what he says. We follow Peter, the great big fisherman. He speaks practically and simply."
- A fourth group said, "We don't follow any man. We follow Christ."

These same four groups can still be seen today . . .

- "We're going to stay with the pastor who founded this church," some say.
- Others say, "We want someone more eloquent."
- "We want someone more practical," says a third faction.
- "We only need Jesus," says a fourth.

Perhaps it is the last group that is the most proud because their mentality would be that of a private in the U.S. Army who, when asked what division he is with, would answer, "I'm not into companies or divisions. I'm a freelancer. I fight where I want; I come and go as I please. I'm a soldier, but I'm not into the structure of command. It's too restrictive. I only answer to my Commander in Chief, the President of the United States."

There are those who say, "I'm not responsible, accountable, linked to any elder, pastor, or group of brothers. I answer only to Jesus." Although Jesus is indeed our Commander in Chief, and we do answer to Him, He has chosen to work through the structure of the body of Christ.

1 Corinthians 1:13
Is Christ divided? was Paul crucified for you? or were ye baptized in the name of Paul?

When the body of Christ is divided, who bleeds?
Jesus.

1 Corinthians 1:14
I thank God that I baptized none of you, but Crispus and Gaius.

The leader of the synagogue, Crispus, got saved when Paul first went to Corinth (Acts 18:8). Gaius was Paul's host in Rome (Romans 16:23).

1 Corinthians 1:15, 16
Lest any should say that I had baptized in mine own name. And I baptized also the household of Stephanas: besides, I know not whether I baptized any other.

"I didn't baptize any of you except for Crispus, Gaius, and the household of Stephanas because I wasn't trying to draw people to myself," said Paul.

1 Corinthians 1:17
For Christ sent me not to baptize, but to preach the gospel: not with wisdom of words, lest the cross of Christ should be made of none effect.

Can we say the same thing concerning our family, our community, or our church corporately? What are we to be about? So often we who are teaching or preaching are inundated with the latest trend or the newest doctrine. But attempting to keep up with these fads only causes fatigue in the pastor and frustration in the congregation. Paul never burned out because his goal was simple and singular, never changing, never wavering. "I came to you," he said, "preaching nothing but Jesus Christ and Him crucified."

"Come on, be practical," people say. "We need more than just hearing about Jesus Christ crucified. We have problems in our marriage. We have problems with addictions. We have problems with our children. We have problems with guilt. We have problems with doubt." But I suggest that throughout the Epistle, we'll see that the solution to every problem that plagues every person is the same: Jesus Christ and Him crucified.

1 Corinthians 1:18 (a)
For the preaching of the cross is to them that perish foolishness . . .

The literal translation would more correctly render this verse: "For the preaching of the Cross is to them that *are perishing* foolishness." When we tell people that Jesus loves them, died in place of them, and offers a new life to them, those who are perishing just don't get it because to deny one's self and take up the Cross seems foolish to them.

1 Corinthians 1:18 (b)
. . . but unto us which are saved it is the power of God.

Again, a more literal rendering of this verse would be ". . . but unto us which are *being saved*, it is the power of God." Salvation is, in a sense, progressive. When you opened your heart to Jesus Christ, you were saved from the penalty of sin. Day by day, we're saved from the power of sin. And when Jesus comes to take us to heaven, we'll be saved from the presence of sin. The message of the Cross gives hope when I have failed because Jesus' blood cleanses me from all sin. It also gives direction to the way I live, for it is only when I deny myself and take up the Cross that I find life (Matthew 10:38, 39).

1 Corinthians 1:19, 20
For it is written, I will destroy the wisdom of the wise, and will bring to nothing the understanding of the prudent. Where is the wise? where is the scribe? where is the disputer of this world? hath not God made foolish the wisdom of this world?

"Where are the debaters, scribes, and thinkers? Where are the psychiatrists and psychologists?" asks Paul. "What have they done for your culture? Hasn't God made foolish the wisdom of the world?"

We can either become depressed over the foolish political and judicial decisions of our leaders—or we can realize they are exactly what God planned to do all along. We won't be upset if we realize that even the foolishness of the world is part of God's plan.

1 Corinthians 1:21
For after that in the wisdom of God the world by wisdom knew not God, it pleased God by the foolishness of preaching to save them that believe.

People have their hope restored in the big picture of eternity through that which the world deems foolish: the preaching of the Word. Paul doesn't say that people are saved by the preaching of foolishness. You'll know the difference between the preaching that is the power of God and the preaching of foolishness by one simple rule of thumb: Does what is being said match up with the Scriptures? Is it seen specifically in the life of Jesus? Is it practiced throughout the Book of Acts? Is it taught by Paul in the Epistles? In other words, is it consistent with the entire New Testament?

Every true teaching, doctrine, and practice is seen in the life of Jesus, practiced in the Book of Acts, and taught by Paul in the Epistles. Therefore, if a teacher of preacher suggests something that doesn't match up in all those areas, reject it. Because there is enough in the Word to keep us busy for every day of our lives, there is no need to supplement it with deviant doctrine or bizarre practices.

1 Corinthians 1:22, 23 (a)
For the Jews require a sign, and the Greeks seek after wisdom: But we preach Christ crucified . . .

Whether relating to marriage or government, depression or addiction, parenting, finances, or doubt, the Cross is indeed the crux of every matter.

1 Corinthians 1:23 (b)–25
. . . unto the Jews a stumblingblock, and unto the Greeks foolishness; but unto them which are called, both Jews and Greeks, Christ the power of God, and the wisdom of God. Because the foolishness of God is wiser than men; and the weakness of God is stronger than men.

The Jews stumble at the crucified Christ. Why? They were looking for a Messiah to lead them militarily and provide for them economically. Therefore, when Jesus came on the scene and was nailed to a Cross, they discounted Him immediately. Today we see crosses around necks, on bookmarks, or above churches. In Jesus' day, however, this would have been equivalent to

wearing a little gold electric chair around one's neck, attaching a mini gas chamber to a bookmark, or hanging a noose atop a church.

The Greeks didn't find the Cross to be humiliating. They found it to be too simple. And the Greek mind-set is still present today in those who think the preaching of the Cross is too simple, that it doesn't deal with the dysfunctional families, drug addictions, and cultural differences of our complex culture. We who have personally experienced its power know otherwise.

1 Corinthians 1:26
For ye see your calling, brethren, how that not many wise men after the flesh, not many mighty, not many noble, are called.

The same is still true. Look around. How many of you are listed in *Who's Who in America?* The only place most of us would find our names would be in *Who's He?*!

1 Corinthians 1:27, 28
But God hath chosen the foolish things of the world to confound the wise; and God hath chosen the weak things of the world to confound the things which are mighty; and base things of the world, and things which are despised, hath God chosen, yea, and things which are not, to bring to nought things that are:

God uses weak and foolish things. Why? Read on.

1 Corinthians 1:29
That no flesh should glory in his presence.

The Lord uses weak things in order that only He gets credit. Why? Is He on some huge ego trip? Is He saying, "I don't want anyone else to get any glory because I need to be affirmed?" Obviously not! God uses weak things not because of a lack in His nature, but due to a lack in ours. You see, God knows when He uses someone who is impressive in the eyes of the world, people set themselves up for a huge fall because they look to him rather than to God. Therefore, He says, "I don't want any flesh to glory because all flesh will fail ultimately."

It was not until Uzziah died that Isaiah saw the Lord high and lifted up (Isaiah 6:1). Who was Uzziah? One of the most powerful, successful, gifted kings in the history of Judah and Israel, Uzziah increased the boundaries of the nation, ushered in economic prosperity, and invented war machinery. Yet although his name was on the lips of all people (2 Chronicles 26:8), it wasn't until he died that Isaiah saw the Lord.

The Lord still allows people to die—not physically—but in the estimation of others in order that our focus can more clearly be upon Him. Therefore, wise is the man and mature the church that realizes that Uzziah's death is not a reason to quit. Instead, it's a reason to say, "Once again, Lord, I see that You are the only One upon whom I can truly and totally rely."

1 Corinthians 1:30, 31
But of him are ye in Christ Jesus, who of God is made unto us wisdom, and righteousness, and sanctification, and redemption: That, according as it is written, He that glorieth, let him glory in the Lord.

Wisdom doesn't come *from* the Lord. Wisdom is *in* the Lord. All the promises of God are *in* Him yea and Amen (2 Corinthians 1:20). Wisdom and righteousness, sanctification and redemption, all that we could ever need or want both now and eternally are wrapped up in Jesus.

2 **1 Corinthians 2:1, 2**
And I, brethren, when I came to you, came not with excellency of speech or of wisdom, declaring unto you the testimony of God. For I determined not to know any thing among you, save Jesus Christ, and him crucified.

Paul came to Corinth following what I consider to be a disastrous session in Athens. In Acts 17, we see him going to Mars Hill in the city of Athens—the place where the intelligentsia of the day dialogued with one another in the city known for an on-going stream of philosophical interaction. Referring to the one thousand altars throughout Athens dedicated to various deities, Paul opened his message, saying, "The unknown god to whom you have dedicated an altar is the God of whom I want to speak." And as he delivered a dissertation to the Athenians explaining the true and living God, Paul quoted from their poets, discussed their philosophy, and alluded to their culture. But the success of his sermon was very minimal. Most of those who heard him mocked him. Others said, "Come back later, and we'll hear more." Only a handful believed.

Why? I suggest that a careful reading of Acts 17 shows he never mentioned Jesus Christ crucified. Although he alluded to the Resurrection, he never stated straightforwardly and with simplic-

ity that Jesus had died for their sins and had risen from the dead. Instead, he tried to be philosophical. He tried to be professional. He tried to be relatable. As a result, no church was established in Athens.

So at the next stop—Corinth—Paul changed his mode of operation radically. He forsook flowery speech and talked about Jesus Christ and Him crucified. Many responded and a church was founded. Oh, it's true that the church at Corinth would have problems and need correction—but the fact remains that a great church was started when, in contrast to what he did at Athens, Paul simply preached Jesus and the Cross.

For topical study of 1 Corinthians 2:2 entitled "Nothing but the Cross," turn to page 1018.

1 Corinthians 2:3–8
And I was with you in weakness, and in fear, and in much trembling. And my speech and my preaching was not with enticing words of man's wisdom, but in demonstration of the Spirit and of power: That your faith should not stand in the wisdom of men, but in the power of God. Howbeit we speak wisdom among them that are perfect: yet not the wisdom of this world, nor of the princes of this world, that come to nought: But we speak the wisdom of God in a mystery, even the hidden wisdom, which God ordained before the world unto our glory: Which none of the princes of this world knew: for had they known it, they would not have crucified the Lord of glory.

Paul maintained that, had the princes of this world understood the Cross and the Resurrection, they wouldn't have crucified Christ. Does this mean that had Pontius Pilate or Herod, the Pharisees or the Sadducees, the scribes or the lawyers known who Jesus was, they wouldn't have gone through with their plan to destroy Him? No, for many of them did know who He was. After all, they saw the miracles; they heard the Word. They understood that He was innocent and that they were involved in treachery. They didn't really believe He was a threat to that which was good and righteous—but only to their own little empire, their own power structure.

Who are the princes to whom Paul refers? Because Jesus referred to Satan as the prince of this world (John 12:31), and because Paul would say that we wrestle not against flesh and blood, but against the principalities of spiritual wickedness in high places (Ephesians 6:12), I believe the princes of the world refer to Satan and his demons. I believe Paul is saying that had Satan and his demons known what would happen when Jesus was crucified, they wouldn't have gone that route.

Why? They thought that by crucifying Christ, they would get rid of Him. Therefore, what a shock it must have been when they realized it was His plan all along to pay for man's sins and break the power of sin.

I camp here for a moment to remind you that Satan's plans always backfire.

"We'll kill Him," Satan hissed.

"We'll crucify Him," his demons echoed—only to find out that there was now salvation for people who could never have been saved otherwise, that the doors of heaven were now open to sinners like me.

"We'll stop the Second Coming of Christ," they said. "We'll inspire a German wallpaper hanger to go crazy, rally an entire nation around him, and destroy the Jews in totality"—which he would have done had World War II lasted another six months. But even this plan backfired because Hitler's madness created such sympathy in the world community for the Jews that they were given their own country.

"We'll kill babies one by one," Satan and his demons declare as hundreds of thousands of babies are slaughtered through abortion. But even this plan is backfiring because Scripture tells us clearly that those who die before the age of accountability—before they can mentally make a decision concerning their own destiny—are taken up into heaven (2 Samuel 12:23; 1 Corinthians 7:14). Thus, multiplied thousands of children who statistically would not have opened their heart to Jesus are being short-circuited into heaven to live eternally.

Am I suggesting we should be pro-abortion? Of course not! I am saying that although Satan is a murderer and a destroyer, that although he never has a good day, that although he never says, "I'll back off and be nice"—his plans ultimately blow up in his face, and that God's purposes—whether in your life personally or throughout history—come to pass perfectly.

1 Corinthians 2:9, 10 (a)
But as it is written, Eye hath not seen, nor ear heard, neither have entered into the heart of man, the things which God hath prepared for them that love him. But God hath revealed them unto us by his Spirit . . .

In addition to this being a reference to heaven, I believe Paul is saying even this side of heaven, we as believers see things others don't and know things others can't because the Spirit reveals to us the big picture eternally.

1 Corinthians 2:10 (b), 11
. . . for the Spirit searcheth all things, yea, the deep things of God. For what man knoweth the things of a man, save the spirit of man which is in him? even so the things of God knoweth no man, but the Spirit of God.

Who knows what God is doing? Only the Spirit of God—the same Spirit given to us (John 14:16). The Spirit of God reveals to His people that which human eyes can't see, that which human ears don't hear.

1 Corinthians 2:12, 13
Now we have received, not the spirit of the world, but the spirit which is of God; that we might know the things that are freely given to us of God. Which things also we speak, not in the words which man's wisdom teacheth, but which the Holy Ghost teacheth; comparing spiritual things with spiritual.

We see things others don't. We hear things others can't because the Holy Spirit ministers to our spirits concerning spiritual truth. As a result, we look at the world around us entirely differently. For example, the spiritual man says, "No matter what the forecasters are predicting economically, the Scriptures tell me God shall supply all my need, according to His riches" (see Philippians 4:19). So, too, when the news anchors tell us the Middle East is heating up and that conflict is about to erupt once more, I already know what the political pundits can only guess at—that the armies of the world will indeed converge upon the Middle East and that there will be a battle ultimately.

1 Corinthians 2:14
But the natural man receiveth not the things of the Spirit of God: for they are foolishness unto him: neither can he know them, because they are spiritually discerned.

The natural man goes to Food 4 Less and buys all-natural salad dressing and naturally grown tomatoes. When a lady pushes her way in front of him in the checkout line, it's only natural that he gets upset. After ringing up his groceries, the checker accidentally gives him too much change. He keeps it, naturally.

Then he comes home and does what comes naturally: He eats, drinks, and is somewhat merry—until the emptiness in his soul drives him to look for something else. So he comes to a Bible study. He hears the Word being taught, the Scriptures being discussed, but they are foolishness to him because, as a natural man, he is spiritually blind.

The idea that man is a free moral agent is somewhat of a misconception. Paul told Timothy that men are taken captive by the Enemy against their wills, as they are blinded and bound by Satan (2 Timothy 2:26). That is why when the natural man hears the Word, it's foolishness to him.

Much of our witnessing is ineffective because we fail to pray, "Lord, please remove the blindfold Satan has put on this person's eyes. Otherwise, he won't see the real issues. Please open his ears. Otherwise, He won't hear Your voice."

1 Corinthians 2:15
But he that is spiritual judgeth all things, yet he himself is judged of no man.

Although the spiritual man is able to put everything in perspective, the worldling can't figure him out. The world can't understand why you go to Bible study, why you have devotions, why you spend time in worship. You're a puzzle, an enigma, a dilemma to the unbeliever.

1 Corinthians 2:16
For who hath known the mind of the Lord, that he may instruct him? But we have the mind of Christ.

How do we have the mind of Christ? He lives *in* us by His Spirit. He's given His Word *to* us in the Scriptures.

NOTHING BUT THE CROSS
A Topical Study of
1 Corinthians 2:2

"Y ou have not chosen Me," Jesus said, "but I have chosen you and ordained you that you should go forth and bear much fruit" (see John 15:16). That makes you an ordained minister every bit as much as I am. Following are eighteen questions you, as a minister, have been or will be asked. I suggest that the answer to each of them is the same. If you try to be philosophical or psychological, clever or creative, you'll get tripped up. But, if like Paul, you determine to talk about nothing but Jesus Christ and Him crucified, you'll do well.

How Do I Know God Loves Me?

But God commendeth his love toward us, in that, while we were yet sinners, Christ died for us.   Romans 5:8

If someone doubts God's love, should he reexamine his childhood hurts to determine if he was rejected by his father and therefore unable to receive God's love? No. The answer is much simpler. When someone says, "I'm not sure God loves me," say, "God proved His love for you in that while you were sinning, rebelling, and couldn't care less about knowing Him, He became a Man, was pinned to a Cross, and died for you specifically. He proved His love for you not when you were going to church, trying hard, being good—but when you were terrible. So don't you know that now that you're starting to get it together a bit, now that you want to be washed by the water of the Word, now that you're wanting to know Him, He loves you all the more?"

The water and blood that flowed when a spear was thrust into Jesus' side as He hung on the Cross was indicative of a broken heart. Thus, He cares about you so dearly and loves you so deeply that even when you were sinning and rebelling, His heart burst for you.

How Do I Know God Will Provide for Me?

He that spared not his own Son, but delivered him up for us all, how shall he not with him also freely give us all things?   Romans 8:32

Years ago, my son Peter-John's grandpa gave him a Datsun pickup truck. If Peter-John had discovered that the jack handle was missing, he would have said, "Thanks so much for the truck. It's perfect. But the jack handle isn't there."

The question is, would his grandpa have said, "I can't believe this. I've given you the truck. I've given you the jack. But now you want the jack handle, too? You're asking too much!"? Of course not! If Peter-John's grandpa gave him the truck and the jack, giving him the jack handle would have been no problem.

That's what Paul is saying. If God gave us His Son—the greatest gift He could have given to you and me—then surely He won't withhold any good thing we ask of Him (Psalm 84:11).

According to the Old Testament sacrificial system, each of our sins must be atoned for individually. Therefore, the suffering of Jesus far transcends what took place one Friday afternoon. That is why when we see Him, we shall see Him as a Lamb having just been slain (Revelation 5:6). If He loved you that much, don't you know He's going to help you with the electric bill, the doctor bill, the grocery bill? Those things are mere jack handles in comparison to what He already gave us when He gave us His Son.

Why Aren't Things Working Out for Me?

Then came to him the mother of Zebedee's children with her sons, worshipping him, and desiring a certain thing of him.   Matthew 20:20

Jesus must have chuckled when He saw the worship she was lavishing upon Him, knowing that she was coming not only to worship Him but also to get something from Him.

"What do you want?" He asked her.

"Well, since You're asking," Salome answered, "when You come into Your kingdom, could my two boys be on Your right hand and on Your left?"

"You don't know what you're asking," Jesus replied. "Are you able to drink of the cup that I shall drink, and to be baptized with the baptism with which I am baptized?"

No doubt Salome went her way, confused by Jesus' cryptic answer. But a few days later, when she saw Jesus flanked on the Cross by a thief on His left and on His right, her request must have thundered in her memory.

Take those who wonder why things aren't working for them to the Cross. Remind them what happened to Salome when she gave advice to the Lord concerning what He should do. Let them see that the decisions the Lord makes ultimately prove to be the right ones.

How Do I Know God Will Forgive Me?

But when they came to Jesus, and saw that he was dead already, they brake not his legs. . . .   John 19:33

The greatest three words ever spoken in history are not, "It's a boy," or, "Hot and sunny," or even, "I love you," but, "It is finished." On the Cross of Calvary, all sin was paid for completely. So what do we do with people who feel guilty? We take Communion with them and remind them that there is no limitation to the blood of Jesus. "Where sin abounds, grace abounds yet more," declared Paul (Romans 5:20). That is why, when Jesus was nailed to the Cross as the Lamb who came to take away the sin of the world, not a bone of His was broken. In addition to fulfilling prophecy regarding the Passover lamb of Exodus 12, this speaks of forgiveness. You see, because blood is produced in the marrow of the bone, the fact that not a bone of Jesus was broken tells us the supply of blood to wash away sin is endless. No matter how much sin you might have been caught up in, no matter how heavy it was or how recent it has been, because of Calvary, there is no limit to the forgiveness available to you.

How Do I Overcome Addiction?

Knowing this, that our old man is crucified with him, that the body of sin might be destroyed, that henceforth we should not serve sin.   Romans 6:6

In the early Colonial days and into the 1800s, East Coast fisherman found their nets filled with starfish that were a nuisance to them. They took out their frustration by hacking the starfish up and throwing them back into the ocean—little knowing that each piece would grow into a new starfish.

Such is the case with addictions. "I'm going to do this," we declare. "I'm going to hack this up. I'm going to resolve the other." In reality, however, the more we try to deal directly with any given sin, the more we become obsessed by that sin. So what is the solution? Not a twelve-step program, but a one-step program: the Cross.

When Jesus was crucified, not only did His blood cleanse us from our sin, but our old man, our old nature was crucified with Him. Mystically and miraculously—yet very powerfully and practically—our old sinful tendencies were crucified with Christ and destroyed. The original text says they were rendered *katargao*, or paralyzed.

This means that, although our old sinful nature can still say to us, "You must give in. The craving is too strong," it now has neither power nor authority. As decisively as Jael drove the spike through the temple of Sisera (Judges 4:21), we can pound the stake of the Cross through the temple of our sinful nature with the hammer of the Word (Jeremiah 23:29). In so doing, we silence every fleshly taunt and each sinful suggestion the Enemy whispers to us.

How Do I Overcome Depression?

And he said to them all, If any man will come after me, let him deny himself, and take up his cross daily, and follow me.   Luke 9:23

The key to overcoming depression is not to pop pills, but to carry the Cross. What is the Cross? Some people say it refers to the allergies they suffer, or to the husband who left them. As hard as those situations might be, they do not fall under the biblical definition of the Cross. The Cross is not something we don't want, don't like, or can't understand. The Cross is something we bear willingly to help someone else redemptively. The Cross is something by which we die to our wishes, our pleasure, our time schedule in order that we might lay down our lives for others.

If we try to protect our life, we lose it. When we let go of our life, we find it (Luke 9:24). Those who take up the Cross by saying, "Who can I help today? With whom can I pray or share? What can I do to get my eyes off myself and die to my situation?" live lives free of depression.

How Do I Overcome Bitterness?

And he cried unto the LORD; and the LORD shewed him a tree, which when he had cast into the waters, the waters were made sweet . . .   Exodus 15:25

As the sun beat down on the people of Israel, their mouths were dry, their lips were parched, their skin was peeling. They hadn't had water for three days when someone cried out, "Water ahead!" Three million thirsty people ran for the pool and drank deeply—only to spit it out immediately, for the water was poisonous. "What have you done?" they cried to Moses. "You've lead us to a pool we thought would be refreshing, but instead it's bitter." And they called the name of that place "Marah," or "Bitter."

So what did Moses do? He called upon the Lord, and the Lord showed him a book on psychology. No. He called upon the Lord, and the Lord told the people to sit down before an empty chair and talk to those toward whom they were bitter. No. He called upon the Lord, and the Lord told the people to write a letter and express their anger. No. Those are all man's methods. Endless counseling sessions, play-acting, and talking to empty chairs are fine for the world, for they know no other way. But what does the Bible say? Moses called to the Lord, and Scripture says the Lord showed him a tree—a tree that had been there all along—and said, "Cast it into the water." When Moses did, the water became sweet.

So, too, when you feel bitter toward the boyfriend who dumped you, the wife who left you, the boss who fired you, or the business partner who cheated you, the solution is the tree of Calvary. "Look to the Cross," Jesus says. "I died for the very sin about which you're so upset. Are you saying that My atonement is insufficient, that My blood is not enough?" It's impossible to be bitter if you see the Cross, if you understand the price that was paid for the very sin that bothers you so much.

How Can I Love People?

After that he put his hands again upon his eyes, and made him look up: and
he was restored, and saw every man clearly.   Mark 8:25

When Jesus touched the eyes of the blind man at Bethsaida, the man opened his eyes and saw Jesus. But when he looked around, he said, "I see men, but they're like trees walking." That's what happened when Jesus encountered each of us who were born, blinded by sin. He touched us and we saw Him. We were converted, born again. But then what happens? Oftentimes, although I see Jesus clearly, the people around look like trees to me. They "stump" me. I want to "cut them down." I want them to "leave." So I subtly start cutting them down through humor, gossip, or in-nuendo.

What's the solution? The solution is to do what Jesus did to the blind man. It's to lift my eyes higher. It's to look to the Cross—for it is in the light of Calvary that I will see people clearly.

How Can I Have a Better Marriage?

Husbands, love your wives, even as Christ also loved the church, and gave
himself for it. . . .   Ephesians 5:25 (a)

The key to a good marriage is not seminars. The key is Calvary. It's dying, husband, to your dreams, your desires, your wishes—and instead taking into consideration your wife's welfare and well-being. The woman being the glory, or liter-ally the "outshining" of the man, means that she is the reflection of her husband (1 Corinthians 11:7). Therefore, if you're having a hard time with your wife, hus-band, the problem is yours. Give yourself totally, wholeheartedly, and sacrificially to your wife as Christ did—and watch what happens in your marriage. Serve your wife for a week or a month redemptively, and watch what takes place in your own heart.

How Can I Be a Better Parent?

When Jesus therefore saw his mother, and the disciple standing by, whom he loved, he saith unto his mother, Woman, behold thy son! Then saith he to the disciple, Behold thy mother! And from that hour that disciple took her unto his own home.   John 19:26, 27

The one instance we see family bonding take place in Scripture wasn't in a therapist's office. It was at the foot of the Cross, where Jesus said of John to His mother, "Behold thy son," and where Jesus said to John of Mary, "Behold thy mother." And from that point on, John adopted Mary as his mother, caring for her until she died.

Mom, Dad, foster parent, step parent, grandparent—how long has it been since you had Communion with your kids or grandchildren, since you knelt beside them with the Lord's blood and body in hand? More impacting than any vacation, more important than any talk session will be the times you gather your kids around Calvary. There, a bonding and binding will take place unlike any other the world can even begin to offer.

How Can I Motivate People to Discipleship?

And as they came out, they found a man of Cyrene, Simon by name: him they compelled to bear his cross.   Matthew 27:32

Crowds mocked and taunted Jesus as He made His way through the city. But because of the beating He had already endured and the loss of blood He had already experienced, His body collapsed under the weight of the Cross beam He carried. At that point, a Roman soldier tapped the shoulder of an African man who had come to Jerusalem to celebrate Passover. Feeling the cold steel of the spear upon his shoulder, Simon no doubt thought, *Oh no. I came here for a vacation. I came here to celebrate Passover. Now I'm going to carry the cross for a criminal—with all of these people jeering and shouting? I don't want to get involved in this. I'm just a tourist.* But he had no choice. So Simon stepped out, took up the Cross, and carried it to Calvary.

But here's the interesting thing: He who no doubt was reluctant to carry the Cross not only became a believer, but the father of two prominent figures in the structure of the early church (Mark 15:21). This tells me that a person who sees the Cross and carries the Cross will become a disciple of Jesus Christ. There's no other option. Once a thirteen-year-old, an eighteen-year-old, or a forty-two-year-old carries the Cross, he, too, will become a disciple. It's inevitable. Therefore, it's our responsibility to tell people, to share with people, to keep pointing people to the Cross, saying, "Look what Jesus did on your behalf."

No one would have thought of Nicodemus and Joseph of Arimathea as radical disciples. But something happened to Nicodemus—the one who came to Jesus by night because he didn't want to be openly associated with Him. Something happened to Joseph of Arimathea, who was probably a member of the Sanhedrin: When they saw Jesus crucified on the Cross, their hearts were changed radically—so much so that, following His crucifixion, they boldly went to Pontius Pilate and asked for the body of Jesus (John 19:38, 39).

This meant they would be ceremonially defiled for Passover. It meant Joseph would lose his standing in the Sanhedrin. It meant Nicodemus would no longer be the master teacher of Israel. But they didn't care. They gave it all up. Why? Because when these fringe disciples, these secret followers, saw the Cross, they had no choice but to become radical in their service for Jesus.

Between two thieves was an appropriate place for Jesus to be crucified. He is, after all, the ultimate thief. He'll steal the heart of anyone who understands what He did on the Cross of Calvary.

How Can I Encourage People to Continue in Discipleship?

Ye shall offer no strange incense thereon, nor burnt sacrifice, nor meat offering; neither shall ye pour drink offering thereon.   Exodus 30:9

It was an amazing scene when, following the completion of the tabernacle, the glory of the Lord descended in a bolt of fire from heaven, when the sacrifice on the newly erected altar was consumed in flame, when the people shouted for joy and bowed down in a holy hush. "We want to be part of the action," said Aaron's sons, Nadab and Abihu. So they lit their censers and began to burn incense—until a second fire bolt came down from heaven and struck them dead. Why were Nadab and Abihu killed? Because the fire the priests were to use was to come only from the altar—which was a picture of the Cross of Calvary, where Jesus would become the burnt Offering, the sacrificial Lamb for you and me.

Like Nadab and Abihu, 80 percent of those in ministry today claim to be affected by "burnout." This ought not be. If I am feeling burned out in serving the Lord, in ministering to the Lord, or in ministering for the Lord, it is because I have lost the vision of Jesus Christ and Him crucified.

Whether they're discipling adults or teaching Sunday school, whether they're pastoring, evangelizing, or leading worship, those who say, "I want to be a part of what's happening there, or I want to be involved in this because it sounds like a hot place to be or a good thing to do," will burn out when people don't appreciate them in the way they had hoped, when those who once applauded them begin to find fault with them, when people they share the gospel with turn away. The only legitimate reason for serving, the only way to continue on without burning out is to be fired up from the altar, to be ignited by the Cross. Trying to be part of a "happening scene" or trying to reach lost people, trying to make others feel better or trying to find personal fulfillment just won't work because all of that is "strange fire" (Leviticus 10:1). There is only one source of ministry, and that is the Cross of Calvary.

How Can I Be Effective in Evangelism?

And I, if I be lifted up from the earth, will draw all men unto me.

John 12:32

As I spoke to three hundred junior-highers at a retreat, one of the boys let out a burp, which, of course, caused the rest of the kids to start giggling. My realization that I didn't have a chance to regain their attention was confirmed when a bat flew in and began to swoop around the kids' heads, causing every girl in attendance to scream. After the big burp and the flying bat, I knew I was in trouble!

But it was at that point that the Lord whispered in my heart, "Jesus Christ and Him crucified." So at that moment, once the bat had lodged in the rafters, I changed subjects and segued into talking about the Cross of Christ, the sufferings of Jesus, the price He paid for the sins of everyone in that room. And as I did, the kids dialed in so closely that I can remember to this day the fifty-five kids who responded to the invitation to receive Christ. They came forward not because I was clever or relatable, not because I was socially relevant or culturally correct. They came forward because I preached Jesus Christ. He always draws people to Himself.

"If I am lifted up on the Cross, I will draw *all* men," Jesus declared—be they junior-highers or senior citizens. Regardless of how old a person is, how young he is, from what culture he comes, or where he lives geographically, he doesn't need to be an expert in culture or generational understandings to share the gospel. He simply needs to do one thing. He simply needs to point to Jesus Christ and the Cross, for that is the key to evangelism.

How Can We Find Unity?

There is one body, and one Spirit, even as ye are called in one hope of your calling; One Lord, one faith, one baptism, One God and Father of all, who is above all, and through all, and in you all.   Ephesians 4:4–6

Whether within one given fellowship or between fellowships, unity is found only at the foot of the Cross. True and lasting unity is never found in eschatological agreement, in one's position concerning speaking in tongues, or in dispensational agreement. Whether one is "high church"—formal and liturgical—or "low church" like us; whether one is conservative and fundamental on the right, or more socially active on the left, the picture formed is that of the Cross. Thus, it's no surprise that doctrinal differences dissipate when believers come together to celebrate the Lord's Supper. Church unity is found at Calvary, so go there frequently. Hang out at the foot of the Cross, and you'll find people coming together miraculously.

How Can I Study the Bible Effectively?

Jesus said unto him, Thou shalt love the Lord thy God with all thy heart, and with all thy soul, and with all thy mind. This is the first and great commandment. And the second is like unto it, Thou shalt love thy neighbour as thyself. On these two commandments hang all the law and the prophets.

Matthew 22:37–40

"Love God and love your neighbor," Jesus said, "for on these two commandments *hang* all the law and the prophets." Then He showed us how this works as He *hung* on the Cross for our sins. Loving God, He prayed, "Father not My will but Thine be done" (see Luke 22:42). Loving man, He prayed, "Father, forgive them for they know not what they do" (Luke 23:34).

We are to love God with all our heart, soul, and mind. We are also to love our neighbor as we love ourselves. If we do this, Jesus said we understand the Scripture in its entirety. If I'm loving God and loving people, I've got the whole message down. Look for Jesus Christ and Him crucified throughout the Word, and you will be a Bible student par excellence, for on Him hang *all* the law and the prophets.

How Can I Be an Effective Leader?

For unto us a child is born, unto us a son is given: and the government shall be upon his shoulder: and his name shall be called Wonderful, Counsellor, The mighty God, The everlasting Father, The Prince of Peace.   Isaiah 9:6

What government did the Almighty God, the Everlasting Father, the Prince of Peace bear on His shoulder? The Cross. How should you govern or lead, teach or coach? You have one model: the Cross. The style of government upon Jesus' shoulders was not seeking His own way or manipulating the situation, but rather dying to self to redeem others.

How Can I Get People to Worship with More Intensity?

And they sung a new song, saying, Thou art worthy to take the book, and to open the seals thereof: for thou wast slain, and hast redeemed us to God by thy blood out of every kindred, and tongue, and people, and nation . . .

Revelation 5:9

How do we get folks to love the Lord and express their heart with a new song? I do not believe it comes through manipulation by worship leaders. Revelation 5 tells us it comes from beholding the slain Lamb of Calvary. The key to seeing a sister or brother, a church or denomination worship with intensity and sincerity is not to teach on worship or exhort to worship, but to let people see Jesus Christ and what He did for them—for then they will have no other recourse but to worship Him in spirit and truth.

How Can I Get People to See the Seriousness of Sin?

For the wages of sin is death; but the gift of God is eternal life through Jesus
Christ our Lord.   Romans 6:23

We who have walked with the Lord for some time know that sin will find us out and do us in, but how do we help others who haven't yet come to that understanding? Take them to the Cross and say, "Look and see what sin does. It was my sin that caused the humiliation, the pain, the bleeding, the broken heart, the spectacle. See what sin did to Jesus on the Cross. And it will do the same to you. Oh, you may chuckle or wink at it now, but sin will eventually break your heart and wipe you out."

The best way for people to learn to hate sin is to go to the Cross and see what their sin did to Jesus.

Whether concerning ministry, theology, or problems practically, I hope you have begun to see that your message, like Paul's, must be singular. You will give right answers and wise counsel; you will see deliverance and freedom and health if, like Paul, you keep your message profoundly simple, focused on Jesus Christ and the Cross of Calvary.

3 **1 Corinthians 3:1 (a)**
And I, brethren, could not speak unto you
as unto spiritual, but as unto carnal . . .

"I was hoping I could address you as men and women who are spiritual," Paul said to those at Corinth—"but I can't because you're carnal." The Greek word translated "carnal" is *sarkinos* and means "fleshly." Thus, a carnal person is one who is dominated by the inclinations of his flesh.

1 Corinthians 3:1 (b)
. . . even as unto babes . . .

This doesn't mean those at Corinth were new believers, but that they were retarded in their spiritual growth. I love babies. I love their cooing, gurgling, and especially hearing them say, "Da-Da," for the first time. Babies are wonderful! But if I go home today and my teenager is gurgling in a playpen, even if he stands up and says, "Da-Da," when I walk in, I would know there was a problem. So, too, Paul is talking not to newborn

believers, but to those who should have been moving on in maturity and engaged in ministry.

1 Corinthians 3:1 (c)
. . . in Christ.

The fact that Paul refers to the Corinthians as being "in Christ" shows they're saved. But instead of moving on to maturity, they remained spiritually stunted. Why? Because they were mixing the world and the Word. They came to church on Sunday and took in the studies. They clapped their hands in worship and even put money in the offering. But on Monday they were out in the world again. Consequently, they were neither fish nor fowl, miserable because they had too much of the world in them to really enjoy the Lord, yet too much of the Lord in them to really enjoy the world.

1 Corinthians 3:2 (a)
I have fed you with milk, and not with
meat . . .

The carnal man can only receive milk. Like a baby, someone has to pamper him and burp him, counsel him and constantly explain things to him. The carnal man does not know what it means to open up the Word, seek the Lord, and walk day by day with Him.

1 Corinthians 3:2 (b)
. . . for hitherto ye were not able to bear it, neither yet now are ye able.

Here's a very simple way to evaluate whether you are carnal or not: How is your appetite? Do you crave the meat of the Word, or are you still only able to digest milk? According to Hebrews 5:10–14, the milk of the Word deals with what Jesus did for us. The meat deals with what Jesus is now doing on behalf of us in heaven presently and the big plan that will unfold eschatologically. The baby Christian only knows, "Jesus loves me, this I know." But as great a truth as that is, he has not gone on to see who Jesus is presently and what's ahead prophetically.

Do you know more about what Jesus is doing today in heaven and on earth through His church than you did last year? If you do, you're progressing and growing. Good for you! But if you don't, then perhaps you might fall into the category of the carnal believer who still has to be fed with milk, who can't get the meat on his own. Is there any hope for you? Of course there is! The Lord would have you simply confess your carnality. And the good news is that, following confession *to* the Lord, there is liberation *from* the Lord. He sets you free. How? Not by positive thinking, not by determining to try harder or do better, but by His Spirit within you.

Although a pair of shoes used in the movie *The Wizard of Oz* cost only nine dollars to make, they were auctioned for over twelve thousand dollars. Why? Because Judy Garland wore them.

So, too, it's the One who brings value and freedom to us as He works in us both to will and to do His good pleasure (Philippians 2:13).

You're driving home from church, and the Lord says, "Share with Junior something you learned this morning." At this point, you have a choice. You can either say, "I'm tired. I just want to get home." Or you can say that magical three-letter word that leads to the Spirit-filled life: "Yes."

You get home and settle in with the Sunday paper, when you feel an impression, a stirring in your heart saying, "Why don't you pick up

the Bible and get a start in 1 Corinthians? Just ten verses."

You can either say, "No, I just got home." Or you can say, "Snoopy, you'll have to wait for a few minutes. It's time to get into the meat of the Word."

You see, spiritual life consists not of your regulations, your rules, or your effort. It simply consists of doing what the Lord tells you to do at any given moment. All you have to do is say, "Yes." It's so incredibly freeing.

Greek poet, Homer, tells the story of the sailors who were drawn to the island in the Aegean Sea called the Island of Enchantment. Mythical female creatures, called sirens, would sing so beautifully that sailors would be drawn to the rocky island only to smash against the rocks and drown.

Although everyone in Greece knew the danger of the sirens, everyone thought he would be the exception. But no one was—until Jason came up with a plan. After commissioning a ship to take him to the Island of Enchantment, Ulysses ordered the sailors to put wax in their ears so as not to hear a thing. Then he chained himself to the mast of the ship so he would not have the ability to dive in when he heard the sound of the sirens' song. As the ship neared the Island, hearing the sirens' song, Ulysses tried to break out of the chains, but he couldn't. Thus, the boat sailed by. Bruised, battered, and exhausted by his struggle against the chains, Ulysses returned to Greece.

There was another fellow named Odysseus. He also was sailing through the Aegean Sea by way of the Island of Enchantment, but he had a better plan. He took Pan with him as his guest on the ship, a man who played the flute. When they neared the Island of Enchantment, Odysseus ordered Pan to start playing—and so beautifully did Pan play that the sailors didn't even care about the song of the sirens.

Those who bind themselves with the rules and regulations of legalism in order to protect themselves from the sirens' song of the world will have a faith that is bruised and battered, sour and cynical. There's a better way, for the spiritual man hears a different song altogether. Walk in the Spirit and you will not fulfill the lust of the flesh (Galatians 5:16). Say "yes" to whatever He tells you to do—even as insignificant as it might appear—and you'll find you're on an adventure that will keep you away from the destructive Island of

Enchantment, sailing joyously all the way to Heaven.

1 Corinthians 3:3
For ye are yet carnal: for whereas there is among you envying, and strife, and divisions, are ye not carnal, and walk as men?

In addition to an inability to take in the meat of the Word, carnality manifests itself in envy, strife, and division. Envy always wants something else, which leads to strife—always finding something wrong, which leads to division—always looking for something new. This is what was happening in the church at Corinth as carnal believers fought with and split from one another.

1 Corinthians 3:4, 5
For while one saith, I am of Paul; and another, I am of Apollos; are ye not carnal? Who then is Paul, and who is Apollos, but ministers by whom ye believed, even as the Lord gave to every man?

You'll know you're in a carnal church when there's factions and fighting within the congregation.

1 Corinthians 3:6–8
I have planted, Apollos watered; but God gave the increase. So then neither is he that planteth any thing, neither he that watereth; but God that giveth the increase. Now he that planteth and he that watereth are one: and every man shall receive his own reward according to his own labour.

"Why are you splintering?" Paul would ask the Corinthian Christians. "Apollos and I are in this together. We both have a part to play. We simply plant and water. It's God who works the miracle of germination."

1 Corinthians 3:9 (a)
For we are labourers together with God . . .

If you don't think the Lord uses different kinds of people to do His work, ask Ezra or Nehemiah.

Ezra had brought a group of Jewish men out of captivity in Babylon in order to establish a priesthood in Jerusalem. Brokenhearted to discover that they had married heathen women, he plucked out his own beard in sorrow (Ezra 9:3).

Years later, Nehemiah also came upon Jews who had married heathen women. But what did Nehemiah do? He pulled out not his own hair—but the hair of the men (Nehemiah 13:25).

Who was right—Ezra, who in his brokenhearted tenderness and sensitivity plucked out his own beard—or Nehemiah, who plucked out the hair of others? The answer is both were right. God used both, for in both cases the people repented.

Some people are sensitive and tender, and pluck out their own beards. Others are strong and expressive and pluck the beards of others. And because the Lord uses all kinds of different people to accomplish His purposes, I can be who I am and appreciate the brothers or churches that may be a different flavor than I am as we both labor together with God.

1 Corinthians 3:9 (b)
. . . ye are God's husbandry . . .

Perhaps your margin correctly renders the word "husbandry" as "tillage" or "field." Feel like you've been tilled a bit this week? Don't be surprised. You're God's field. The good news is that when fields get plowed, it means something excellent is about to be planted.

Although we read in Genesis 1:1 that God created the heavens and the earth, in Genesis 1:2, we read that the earth was "without form and void." What happened? Many Bible scholars, with whom I'm inclined to agree, believe that it was between Genesis 1:1 and 1:2 that, after launching a rebellion in heaven, Lucifer was cast to earth. The result was that our planet became "without form and void." In Genesis 1:3, we see God re-creating earth as the Spirit moved upon the face of the waters.

So, too, I suggest if you wonder why your life has been overturned and plowed, if you feel that suddenly your world is without form and void—take hope! If He's turned the topsoil of your life, God is getting ready to plant something wonderful. He's in the process of re-creating that which will supersede all that you enjoyed previously.

1 Corinthians 3:9 (c)
. . . ye are God's building.

Here, Paul shifts analogies from agriculture to architecture.

1 Corinthians 3:10, 11
According to the grace of God which is given unto me, as a wise masterbuilder, I have laid the foundation, and another buildeth thereon. But let every man take heed how he buildeth thereupon. For other foundation can no man lay than that is laid, which is Jesus Christ.

The foundation upon which Paul built was not principles, but a Person—Jesus Christ. "Upon this rock will I build My Church," Jesus said. What rock? The rock of Peter's confession that Jesus is the Christ (see Matthew 16:18).

When Peter said, "You are the Christ, the Son of the Living God. You're the Hope, the Promise, the One," Jesus had a foundation upon which to build His church.

The true church of Jesus Christ is not built upon, "Let's get together and make something happen politically," or, "Let's launch a moral crusade," or, "Let's be socially responsible." It's based upon Jesus Christ—our Hero, our Savior, our Friend, our coming King.

1 Corinthians 3:12, 13 (a)
Now if any man build upon this foundation gold, silver, precious stones, wood, hay, stubble; every man's work shall be made manifest . . .

Once one realizes that Jesus is the Christ, everything he does from that point on builds upon that foundation. And the material is either wood, hay, and stubble—or gold, silver, and precious stones.

1 Corinthians 3:13 (b), 14
. . . for the day shall declare it, because it shall be revealed by fire; and the fire shall try every man's work of what sort it is. If any man's work abide which he hath built thereupon, he shall receive a reward.

Every day I live, I build upon the foundational principle that Jesus is the Christ, that He is my Lord. The question is, do I build with gold, silver, and precious stones—or with wood, stubble, and hay? What is the telling difference between these materials? Gold, silver, and precious stones don't burn.

I used to picture the fire of which Paul speaks as a big oven into which are shoved all the prayers we've prayed, Bible studies we've attended, and witnessing we've ever done. But because John speaks of Jesus' eyes as a flame of fire (Revelation 1:14), when we see Him, the look He will give us will warm us as it melts all the junk in our lives that drew attention to ourselves or was done to impress others—leaving only the gold, silver, and precious stones of what we did only in and for *Him.*

1 Corinthians 3:15
If any man's work shall be burned, he shall suffer loss: but he himself shall be saved; yet so as by fire.

Everyone who understands that Jesus is the Foundation of life will be saved. But some shall be saved as by fire. They'll make it into heaven. They'll be warmed when they see Jesus' face, but they'll look around and say, "Oh no, everything on earth I did vaporized before His eyes, and now I have no crown to cast at His feet."

Because God shall wipe away every tear (Revelation 7:17), there will be tears in heaven. For what will they be shed? Not for the bigger house we wish we had built, not for the newer car we wish we had purchased, not for the nicer clothes we wish we had worn—but for the opportunities we missed to lay up treasure there.

"Dress me up in my best suit," said the man who knew he was about to die.
His wife complied.
"Now fill my pockets with gold," he said, "and sew them closed."
When he died shortly thereafter, he went to heaven, and was pleased to feel the bulges in his pockets.
"I made it! I did it!" he exclaimed. "Who said you can't take it with you?! Look at this!" he said to Peter, opening his pockets.
And Peter said, "Why did you bring asphalt up here?"

That which we are so interested in, fighting for, and worried about here on earth is mere asphalt in heaven.

Although the primary reference of verses 13–15 is to the *bema* seat, where we will be rewarded for that which we've done on earth, I believe a secondary reference is to the fires the Lord allows to sweep through our lives presently.

"You're fired," your boss says to you. And now you get a chance to see how much of your character is gold, silver, and precious stones, and how much is wood, hay, and stubble. In ministry, in relationships, and on the job, fires will break out around you that you might think you have to put out immediately. But I have found that when you sense a wildfire starting, it's a good idea to be careful before you grab your bucket and shovel and try to put it out in your own energy and by your own wisdom. If you have good people skills, you can meet with people, try to reason with them, and maybe control the fire for a year or two. But more often than not, it will explode eventually with a flame more devastating than the original.

Thus, when fires come, I am slowly but surely learning to let them burn. I don't defend myself. I don't defend my church. I don't try to soothe feelings or calm tension. I let the fire burn. And when the fire is over, I poke around and see if any gold, silver, or precious stones are left with which to rebuild.

To you who are involved with people in your family or in ministry, I suggest letting any given fire burn. And when you see what's left, you'll either know you were building with gold, silver, and precious stones—or with the wood, hay, and stubble of your own self-importance.

1 Corinthians 3:16
Know ye not that ye are the temple of God, and that the Spirit of God dwelleth in you?

The Greek word translated "temple" is not the usual word *hieron*, which refers to the whole temple, but rather *naos*, which speaks of the Holy of Holies—the part of the temple wherein dwelt the *shekinah*, the *chabod*, the visible perception of the presence of God.

Because the word "ye" is plural, Paul is saying, "Don't you know that together you are the holy of holies, where the glory, the weight, and the reality of God are enjoyed and perceived?"

Paul develops this analogy further when he tells the Ephesians they "*grow* unto an holy temple in the Lord" (see Ephesians 2:21). The church grows because we are *living* stones—and this presents some interesting challenges. Dead stones fit together nicely. Living, squirming stones, however, tend to rub one another the wrong way. Yet in this we can rejoice, for the Lord knows there are rough edges that need to be knocked off us blockheads.

That is why it is the mature believer who says, "Okay, Lord, I'm not going to try to change my location or situation. Instead, I'm going to stay right here and allow You to do Your work through people who might irritate me in order that I might be more like You."

1 Corinthians 3:17 (a)
If any man defile the temple of God, him shall God destroy . . .

The Greek word translated "destroy" doesn't mean "damned." It means "diminished." Taken in context, Paul is saying he who defiles the church by either overtly or subtly causing division within the church, by coming down on the church, or by pulling away from the church will himself be diminished. His ability to know the Lord, walk with the Lord, and be used by the Lord will decrease perceptibly. Why? Because the Lord is very protective of His church. He is madly, outrageously, head-over-heels in love with His bride.

1 Corinthians 3:17 (b)
. . . for the temple of God is holy, which temple ye are.

What does it mean to be holy? When Moses realized he was in the presence of the Lord, he was told to take off his shoes because the ground he was on was holy ground (Exodus 3:5). As he overlooked the city of Jericho, Joshua had an encounter with the Lord and was also told to take off his shoes (Joshua 5:15). Therefore, since the church is holy, it would seem fitting that we take off our shoes as well.

How?

After walking through mud on their way home from school, our kids take off their shoes before walking into the house so they don't bring the mud in with them. So, too, when we come together as a body, we are to leave the mud of the world at the door. We're to leave behind grudges and pride, attitudes that are amiss, and hearts that are quick to judge.

But there's another reason to remove our shoes. Even if my shoes are clean, I take them off at home because I'm comfortable there. So, too, when we fellowship with the body, we don't have to keep our guard up or our best foot forward. We can relax in God's amazing love for us and for one another.

Concerning His priests, God said,

> And it shall come to pass, that when they enter in at the gates of the inner court, they shall be clothed with linen garments; and no wool shall come upon them, whiles they minister in the gates of the inner court, and within. They shall have linen bonnets upon their heads, and shall have linen breeches upon their loins; they shall not gird themselves with any thing that causeth sweat.   Ezekiel 44:17, 18

God's desire is that, rather than causing us to be uptight, upset, or hot under the collar, our service for Him and fellowship with Him cause us to be relaxed, refreshed, and renewed.

1 Corinthians 3:18 (a)
Let no man deceive himself.

With regard to the Corinthian problem of division within the body, Paul will give three strong exhortations. . . .

1 Corinthians 3:18(b)–20
If any man among you seemeth to be wise in this world, let him become a fool, that he

may be wise. For the wisdom of this world is foolishness with God. For it is written, He taketh the wise in their own craftiness. And again, The Lord knoweth the thoughts of the wise, that they are vain.

First, the Corinthians were to stop extolling themselves, thinking they alone had been given insights into deeper spirituality.

When the first three letters blew off of the sign on a Jesus Only church—a denomination which, among other things, holds to the erroneous belief that baptism is not to be in the name of the Father, Son, and Holy Spirit, but in the name of Jesus only—its true nature came to light when its name inadvertently became "Us Only."

1 Corinthians 3:21, 22 (a)
Therefore let no man glory in men. For all things are yours; whether Paul, or Apollos, or Cephas, or the world, or life, or death, or things present, or things to come . . .

Second, the Corinthians believers were to stop exalting others.

"Wilt thou be made whole?" Jesus asked the lame man.
"I have no man to help me," he answered" (see John 5:7).

How long will we remain in a lame condition spiritually because we are depending on or exalting men in a way that ought not be?

1 Corinthians 3:22 (b), 23
. . . all are yours; and ye are Christ's; and Christ is God's.

Third, the Corinthians were to stop excluding their brothers.

Before entering the Promised Land, the Lord instructed His people to be careful that they didn't let their axes fly indiscriminately in the heat of battle, cutting down trees that could later provide fruit for them (Deuteronomy 20:19).

The same is true spiritually. If we're not careful, we will find ourselves chopping down trees that, although they may not be our flavor, are fruitful nonetheless. "Don't pick *at* them;" the Lord would say to us. "Pick *from* them, Become enriched as you listen to them. You're one body, one temple, one church."

4 **1 Corinthians 4:1 (a)**
Let a man so account of us, as of the ministers of Christ . . .

The literal meaning of the Greek word *huperetes,* translated "minister," is "under-oarsman." An under-oarsman was a slave on the lowest deck of the ship who simply followed the cadence of the drummer. What does it mean to be a minister? It doesn't mean to set the course or determine direction, but rather to simply do what the Captain of the ship, Jesus Christ, tells us to do, knowing that *He* will bring us to the right destination.

1 Corinthians 4:1 (b)
. . . and stewards . . .

The word "steward" refers to the slave who knew the location of his master's wealth. As seen in Genesis 39, Joseph was this type of a slave to Potiphar.

1 Corinthians 4:1 (c)
. . . of the mysteries of God.

As faithful stewards in ministry, we're to be able to know the location of the riches of Scripture.

Then said he unto them, Therefore every scribe which is instructed unto the kingdom of heaven is like unto a man that is an householder, which bringeth forth out of his treasure things new and old.   Matthew 13:52

Jesus is talking about the ability to relocate the illustrations, types, and stories of the Old Testament to His own life—and later to the entire New Testament.

Read your Bible, dear brother. Don't give up, precious sister.
But I'm reading through Leviticus right now, and I don't understand a thing, you might be thinking.

That's okay. Keep reading because you're feeding your inner man, and in due season, you will understand even the Book of Leviticus to a much greater degree than you do now.

With drought ravaging the land, Jehoram, king of Israel, called for Elisha the prophet.
"Here's what you are to do," said Elisha.
"Dig ditches here in the dry sand."
The people did, and the next day, the ditches were filled with water (2 Kings 3).

So, too, water being a type of the Word (Psalm 119:9; John 15:3; Ephesians 5:26), we're to keep digging ditches—even if it's dry. And eventually, the refreshing springs of Scripture will flow into our hearts.

Why did the Lord write the Bible the way He did? Why didn't He simply write Section I: Marriage. Section II: The Doctrine of the Holy Spirit. Section III: Bible Prophecy. That's the way I would have written it. But the Lord in His infinite wisdom says, "Analogies and stories, pictures and genealogies will be mysteries to the carnal mind. On the other hand, they will be exciting, applicable, and wonderful to any man of any age in any culture who plugs away studying them day after week after month after year after decade."

1 Corinthians 4:2
Moreover it is required in stewards, that a man be found faithful.

I'm not required to be successful—only faithful. The most successful minister in the Old Testament was a prophet who caused people to get saved everywhere he went. Not only did the entire crew of the boat in which he traveled get saved, but the entire population of Nineveh—perhaps numbering two million—got saved as well (Jonah 3:5).

Contrast Jonah with another prophet who preached for thirty years without seeing a single conversion. If Jonah were alive today, books would be written about him. Conferences would feature him. Videos would be made of him. Jeremiah? He'd be sitting in the back row of one of Jonah's seminars. But in God's economy, so impacting was Jeremiah that when Jesus came on the scene, no one ever mistook Him for Jonah. They thought He was Jeremiah (Matthew 16:14).

Be faithful, gang. You might not be noticed, applauded, or patted on the back. That's okay. Neither was Jeremiah.

1 Corinthians 4:3, 4
But with me it is a very small thing that I should be judged of you, or of man's judgment: yea, I judge not mine own self. For I know nothing by myself; yet am I not hereby justified: but he that judgeth me is the Lord.

"I'm not worried about your judging me," said Paul to the Corinthians. "In fact, I don't even put much stock in my own assessment of myself." Some people are constantly down on themselves—but the Lord isn't. Others have a perfectly clear conscience—when, in reality, all they have is a bad memory. Because the heart is de-

ceitfully and desperately wicked (Jeremiah 17:9), Paul was exceedingly wise to leave judgment to the Lord.

1 Corinthians 4:5 (a)
Therefore judge nothing before the time, until the Lord come . . .

The only judgment that matters will be at the *bema* seat of Christ, where all of our works will be tried by fire. Therefore, it is neither our place nor our calling to judge others or ourselves.

1 Corinthians 4:5 (b)
. . . who both will bring to light the hidden things of darkness, and will make manifest the counsels of the hearts: and then shall every man have praise of God.

This doesn't mean that when the Lord comes back, all the dark stuff we did will be brought to light. No, the blood of Jesus Christ has cleansed us so completely that God will "remember no more" our sins and iniquities (Hebrews 10:17). Paul is referring to the things we can only see through a glass darkly (1 Corinthians 13:12)— why the Lord is doing certain things and why He isn't doing other things; why some people suffer and others don't; why God answers some requests but denies others. When He comes back, everything that now seems dark to us—seeming contradictions of His character, seeming violations of His nature—will be seen in the light of His unspeakable glory. The result? Everyone will praise God for His wisdom and righteousness in all things (Revelation 19:2).

1 Corinthians 4:6
And these things, brethren, I have in a figure transferred to myself and to Apollos for your sakes; that ye might learn in us not to think of men above that which is written, that no one of you be puffed up for one against another.

"I've used Apollos and myself as illustrations of those who work together, who labor in the same field, members of the same holy temple, the same building," says Paul. "We're both yours. Don't divide yourselves over us or become puffed up concerning us."

1 Corinthians 4:7
For who maketh thee to differ from another? and what hast thou that thou didst not receive? now if thou didst receive it, why dost thou glory, as if thou hadst not received it?

Paul, the theologian par excellence, had a mind sharper and keener than any other. Apollos, polished orator, impressed people with his rhetoric and powerful personality. God made them both. Who makes us different from one another? God. Who gifts us differently and individually? God. So why do we glory in ourselves or in any other person when it's God who made every one of us the way we are? To Him be all glory—for His creativity and sense of humor in making and using people like us!

1 Corinthians 4:8–13

Now ye are full, now ye are rich, ye have reigned as kings without us: and I would to God ye did reign, that we also might reign with you. For I think that God hath set forth us the apostles last, as it were appointed to death: for we are made a spectacle unto the world, and to angels, and to men. We are fools for Christ's sake, but ye are wise in Christ; we are weak, but ye are strong; ye are honourable, but we are despised. Even unto this present hour we both hunger, and thirst, and are naked, and are buffeted, and have no certain dwellingplace; and labour, working with our own hands: being reviled, we bless; being persecuted, we suffer it: Being defamed, we intreat: we are made as the filth of the world, and are the offscouring of all things unto this day.

Lest the Corinthians thought Paul lucky to be so gifted, he said, "You have it easy compared to what we go through daily. We're beaten and defamed. We don't even have a place to hang our hats. We're put down, mocked, and persecuted."

Paul makes a very important point about ministry when he says, "Be careful that you don't think everyone is lucky, gifted, blessed but you." I can't begin to imagine what our brother, Billy Graham, goes through—the temptations, pressures, and subtle maneuvering of the Enemy directed at him. So be content where the Lord has you planted and serve Him boldly in that place.

1 Corinthians 4:14, 15

I write not these things to shame you, but as my beloved sons I warn you. For though ye have ten thousand instructors in Christ, yet have ye not many fathers: for in Christ Jesus I have begotten you through the gospel.

What does it mean to be a spiritual father? In the lives of those you lead to the Lord or nurture in the Lord, you will see the process unfold whereby they will look to you for a number of years and think you can do no wrong. Then, as they go through spiritual adolescence, they will think you can do no right. And finally, they will come into maturity when they will say, "Right or wrong, you are my spiritual father, and I appreciate you."

1 Corinthians 4:16

Wherefore I beseech you, be ye followers of me.

Spiritual fathers—both men and women—how I pray we can say what Paul said when he said, "Follow me. Do what I do."

1 Corinthians 4:17–21

For this cause have I sent unto you Timotheus, who is my beloved son, and faithful in the Lord, who shall bring you into remembrance of my ways which be in Christ, as I teach every where in every church. Now some are puffed up, as though I would not come to you. But I will come to you shortly, if the Lord will, and will know, not the speech of them which are puffed up, but the power. For the kingdom of God is not in word, but in power. What will ye? shall I come unto you with a rod, or in love, and in the spirit of meekness?

"I'm coming shortly," Paul says. "Will that day be a festival of love, or a day of discipline?"

So, too, Jesus said, "Surely I come quickly" (Revelation 22:20). And when He does, will we hear Him say, "Depart from Me" or, "Well done, good and faithful servant"?

5 In chapter 1, we saw that the Corinthian believers were divided when they should have been united. Here in chapter 5, we'll see them united when they should have been divided.

1 Corinthians 5:1

It is reported commonly that there is fornication among you, and such fornication as is not so much as named among the Gentiles, that one should have his father's wife.

Even as carnal as the culture of Corinth was, the entire city was abuzz about the member of the Corinthian church who was living in immorality with his stepmother.

The world still loves to see Christians involved in immorality because it eases their conscience and justifies their own loose lifestyle. Knowing this, one of Satan's favorite tactics is to get Christians involved in immorality. He runs the same play over and over again. It's very easy for Satan to bring Christians into temptation in the area of morals by simply nudging agape—the caring, sharing, tenderness, concern, and compassion in which believers are called to walk—into the area of *eros*, or sensual love.

I believe the simple solution of Scripture to this subtle strategy of Satan is for men to disciple, encourage, and pray with other men, and for women to do the same with other women.

"I'm too old to be vulnerable," you say. "After all, I'm fifty. So I can counsel women or hang around the ladies and share with them my pearls of wisdom." Really? How old was David—a man after God's own heart, a man who loved the Lord deeply and was honored by the Lord singularly—when he fell into sin with Bathsheba? Fifty. Let he who thinks he stands take heed lest he fall (1 Corinthians 10:12).

1 Corinthians 5:2
And ye are puffed up, and have not rather mourned, that he that hath done this deed might be taken away from among you.

Rather than being grieved, the Corinthian believers were proud of their open-mindedness, their tolerance, their political correctness in allowing the offending brother to remain in their midst.

1 Corinthians 5:3–5
For I verily, as absent in body, but present in spirit, have judged already, as though I were present, concerning him that hath so done this deed, In the name of our Lord Jesus Christ, when ye are gathered together, and my spirit, with the power of our Lord Jesus Christ, to deliver such an one unto Satan for the destruction of the flesh, that the spirit may be saved in the day of the Lord Jesus.

Paul's instruction to the Corinthians was that they were to deliver this man into the hand of Satan—not for damnation, but for restoration, in order that his flesh would be destroyed and his spirit saved. "This is where you should be divided congregationally," Paul said. "Stay away from this man and let him live his life of immorality away from the joy, peace, and covering of the body. And hopefully, he will become so sick of his sin that he'll long for the days when he was in fellowship with you—where there was worship ascending and true love abounding."

As we will see in his second letter to them, the church at Corinth did, indeed, take Paul's advice, and it worked to such a degree that Paul was later able to instruct them to welcome their brother back into their company.

This is an important word for congregations and for parents. We do not serve each other or our children well by allowing them to live in sin. There comes a point when a person needs to be turned over to Satan in order to reap the repercussions of his sin. But lest anyone become too eager to arbitrarily turn others over to Satan in the name of Jesus, Paul gives three specific qualifications for doing so.

First, it's to be done in the name of our Lord Jesus Christ. The name of Jesus is not some mystical incantation. No, praying, ministering, meeting in the name of Jesus simply means doing so in the nature or character of our Lord.

I can't ask for a new car in Jesus' name because I'm not convinced that's what He would ask for in my situation. But I can pray with all confidence, "Father, make me a loving parent in Jesus' name." I can't ask for a multimillion dollar house in Jesus' name because I don't think He would. But, because such is the nature of Jesus, I can ask for compassion and wisdom in His name with absolute assurance that I'll receive an answer.

Second, turning someone over to Satan can only be done by the instruction of Paul. That is, one must understand the writings of the Word and base his action on nothing short of scriptural, biblical, apostolic authority.

Third, turning someone over to Satan must be done with the power of Jesus. Because any one person or small group of people is vulnerable to seeing things through the lens of bitterness, it must be done in the power of Jesus as seen in the confirmation of the congregation.

1 Corinthians 5:6
Your glorying is not good. Know ye not that a little leaven leaveneth the whole lump?

Leavening is not easily seen initially, but it becomes very obvious eventually, making it the perfect symbol of evil throughout Scripture.

1 Corinthians 5:7, 8
Purge out therefore the old leaven, that ye may be a new lump, as ye are unleavened. For even Christ our passover is sacrificed for us: Therefore let us keep the feast, not with old leaven, neither with the leaven of malice and wickedness; but with the unleavened bread of sincerity and truth.

The day before Passover was called the Day of Preparation, in which the Jews would rid their homes of every trace of leaven in preparation for Passover and the six-day Feast of Unleavened

Bread. Paul draws on this well-known understanding as a call for a recommitment to holiness and purity on the part of the Corinthian body.

The picture for us is that we have left Egypt—the world—through the blood our Passover Lamb shed for us on the Cross. Therefore, let us continue on from that point without leaven—without the secret sins that puff up and spread throughout our fellowships so easily.

1 Corinthians 5:9–11

I wrote unto you in an epistle not to company with fornicators: Yet not altogether with the fornicators of this world, or with the covetous, or extortioners, or with idolaters; for then must ye needs go out of the world. But now I have written unto you not to keep company, if any man that is called a brother be a fornicator, or covetous, or an idolater, or a railer, or a drunkard, or an extortioner; with such an one no not to eat.

The Greek tense of this passage makes it clear that we are to cut off from our company not the one who has fallen into or struggles with these sins—but the one who knowingly, obstinately, perpetually practices them. Why?

I believe the first reason is to correct the offender. If a tumor is growing in my body, no competent doctor would say, "I'm not going to operate on you because I don't want to be too harsh with you." And yet that is exactly what we say to believers who are mired in sin when we fail to take the sword of the Spirit and show them where they are wrong. If I really care about someone, I'll say, "I'm not going to fellowship with you—not because I'm mad at you or don't love you. On the contrary, I care about you so much that I cannot allow you to go on as though there's nothing amiss in your life because sooner or later the tumor of sin within you will take a terrible toll on you."

Secondly, we are not to fellowship with insistent, persistent sinners in order to protect the body.

When Jesus arrived in Bethany, Martha ran out to Him, saying, "Oh, Lord, if You had been here, our brother would not have died."

A few minutes later, Mary uttered the same phrase to Him word for word (John 11:21, 32).

We begin to think like and talk like those with whom we spend time. We assume the flavor of those around us. Therefore, Paul says we are not to hang around those who are consistently, persistently covetous, drunkards, idolaters, or fornicators.

1 Corinthians 5:12, 13

For what have I to do to judge them also that are without? do not ye judge them that are within? But them that are without God judgeth. Therefore put away from among yourselves that wicked person.

What about the woman, the stepmother? Why didn't Paul deal with her? Evidently, she wasn't a believer. "We don't judge unbelievers," says Paul. "God will take care of them." I find this interesting because there is a tendency on the part of Christians today to want to judge the world, to change the culture. All too often, we're activists against the world's wickedness, but we fail to judge our own congregation. We march, petition, crusade, vote, and talk about the world's sin as we turn a blind eye to our own. We've got it exactly backward. We're to deal with the Christian community and let God take care of the world's iniquity.

6 Not only did the Corinthian believers have a problem with moral looseness, but they were filing meaningless lawsuits.

1 Corinthians 6:1–4

Dare any of you, having a matter against another, go to law before the unjust, and not before the saints? Do ye not know that the saints shall judge the world? and if the world shall be judged by you, are ye unworthy to judge the smallest matters? Know ye not that we shall judge angels? how much more things that pertain to this life? If then ye have judgments of things pertaining to this life, set them to judge who are least esteemed in the church.

According to Revelation 20 and other passages, as we reign and rule with Christ in the millennial kingdom, part of our job will be to govern and judge those who get saved during the Tribulation. You see, although we'll be in a glorified state, Tribulation believers will still have fleshly inclinations. Therefore, we will be involved in the process of enforcing righteousness.

Not only that, but according to the text before us, we will also judge angels. How? It is my personal opinion that we'll say to the angels that rebelled with Lucifer, "How could you have rebelled against the Lord when you were in His presence daily? We were on earth. We didn't see Him visibly. We couldn't touch the things of heaven tangibly—yet we believed. Why didn't you?"

In light of this, Paul says to the church at Corinth, "You who will one day judge the world, you who will one day judge angels, how is it that you rely on the legal system of the world to judge yourselves? Even the person least esteemed in the church has more wisdom than the most highly esteemed of the world.

1 Corinthians 6:5–7
I speak to your shame. Is it so, that there is not a wise man among you? no, not one that shall be able to judge between his brethren? But brother goeth to law with brother, and that before the unbelievers. Now therefore there is utterly a fault among you, because ye go to law one with another. Why do ye not rather take wrong?

In addition to judging themselves, the Corinthian believers were to absorb the wrongs done to them, to turn the other cheek, to give up the cloak, to go the extra mile (Matthew 5:39–41).

1 Corinthians 6:7, 8
Why do ye not rather suffer yourselves to be defrauded? Nay, ye do wrong, and defraud, and that your brethren.

Paul told the Corinthians that, rather than going through all the legal hassles to defend themselves judicially, the better way was to trust the Lord to solve the problem.

1 Corinthians 6:9 (a)
Know ye not that the unrighteous shall not inherit the kingdom of God? Be not deceived: neither fornicators, nor idolaters, nor adulterers . . .

In verse 18, Paul will tell the Corinthian believers to flee fornication. Here, he gives them the first reason they should do so: Fornication jeopardizes one's eternal state.

Does this mean anyone who's fallen into fornication or committed adultery is not going to make it into heaven?

No, for the tense used in the original language would have made it clear to anyone reading this letter that Paul was speaking not of those who struggled with, or even failed in these areas, but of those who flagrantly and blatantly continued in them. On the basis of 1 John, some suggest that it's not that those who continue in these sins lose their salvation, but that they were never truly born again in the first place.

All I know is this: Whether a person loses his salvation or was never really saved, either way, he ends up in the same place. I wouldn't want to be in his shoes when he stands before the Lord— for no matter how often he came to church, or

how big the Bible he carried, I can't guarantee he will enter into heaven. The Bible makes it painfully clear that those who continue in these sins will not inherit the kingdom.

1 Corinthians 6:9 (b)
. . . nor effeminate, nor abusers of themselves with mankind.

The Greek word translated "effeminate" speaks of a passive role in homosexual behavior. The term "abusers of themselves with mankind" speaks of an active role. Either role places one's eternal state in jeopardy.

1 Corinthians 6:10, 11
Nor thieves, nor covetous, nor drunkards, nor revilers, nor extortioners, shall inherit the kingdom of God. And such were some of you: but ye are washed, but ye are sanctified, but ye are justified in the name of the Lord Jesus, and by the Spirit of our God.

Again, the tense in the original language indicates that Paul is saying that those who *habitually* practice these behaviors either were never saved or have greatly jeopardized their salvation.

1 Corinthians 6:12
All things are lawful unto me, but all things are not expedient: all things are lawful for me, but I will not be brought under the power of any.

Because he addresses the numerous problems of morality in the Corinthian congregation, one might think Paul led a restricted life. Nothing could be further from the truth. Here, we see that, because he was not bound by rules and regulations of any kind, he was, in fact, the freest person on the face of the earth. It was for this reason that he refused to be in bondage to any person, activity, or substance that would compromise his liberty.

The ethic we enjoy as believers is the largest ethic in the world today, for *all* things are lawful to you and me. Why would we want to do anything to compromise our glorious freedom?

1 Corinthians 6:13
Meats for the belly, and the belly for meats: but God shall destroy both it and them. Now the body is not for fornication, but for the Lord; and the Lord for the body.

The Corinthian culture held the position that the act of physical intimacy was nothing more than the satisfying of one's physical appetite—no different than the need for food. Not so, said

Paul. Physical intimacy involves the coming together not only of two bodies, but of two souls—the very essence of one's person, that which belongs to God.

1 Corinthians 6:14–17
And God hath both raised up the Lord, and will also raise up us by his own power. Know ye not that your bodies are the members of Christ? shall I then take the members of Christ, and make them the members of an harlot? God forbid. What? know ye not that he which is joined to an harlot is one body? for two, saith he, shall be one flesh. But he that is joined unto the Lord is one spirit.

Secondly, fornication not only jeopardizes one's eternal state, but it agonizes our holy King. Paul says, "Don't you understand that you're bringing Jesus into that situation?" The concept is so shocking that Paul doesn't even get into it very much except to say that if you're in an immoral situation, you place Christ in that situation. God forbid.

1 Corinthians 6:18
Flee fornication. Every sin that a man doeth is without the body; but he that committeth fornication sinneth against his own body.

Thirdly, fornication compromises one's very being. Although the repercussions of every sin are serious, sexual sin is unique in that it's the only sin against oneself. Solomon shed further light on this when he said, "But whoso committeth adultery with a woman lacketh understanding: he that doeth it destroyeth his own soul" (Proverbs 6:32).

Because we are made in the image of a triune God, we are comprised of three parts as well: body, soul, and spirit. The body relates to the physical world. The soul is one's essence, one's personality, and relates to people. The spirit relates to God and will live eternally. Thus, each time one engages in immoral activity, a part of his soul is permanently and irreplaceably forfeited. The tragedy, then, is that the one who continues to live in promiscuity becomes less and less of a person as a piece of his soul is stripped away with each encounter.

1 Corinthians 6:19, 20
What? know ye not that your body is the temple of the Holy Ghost which is in you, which ye have of God, and ye are not your own? For ye are bought with a price: therefore glorify God in your body, and in your spirit, which are God's.

Whether it was Nebuchadnezzar in 586 B.C. or Roman General Titus in A.D. 70, to destroy the effectiveness of Israel, her enemies burned the temple.

So, too, what does the Enemy do to you? He comes time and time again to burn the temple of your body with lust in order that you might be burned-out and decommissioned from effective service.

> And they sung as it were a new song before the throne, and before the four beasts, and the elders: and no man could learn that song but the hundred and forty and four thousand, which were redeemed from the earth. These are they which were not defiled with women; for they are virgins. These are they which follow the Lamb whithersoever he goeth. These were redeemed from among men, being the firstfruits unto God and to the Lamb.
> Revelation 14:3, 4

Used by the Lord, rewarded in eternity, the 144,000 evangelists in the Tribulation say, "We will follow the Lamb wherever He goes." So, too, if you follow Jesus in a life of purity, God will bless you presently. He'll reward you eternally. And you will never, ever regret fleeing fornication.

I have yet to talk to one person who was glad he committed adultery, was happy he was into pornography, was proud that he was caught up with homosexuality. Never. And yet I have talked with a bunch of folks who said, "I would give anything if I could go back and live differently. I would flee that situation. I would resist that inclination. I would choose to follow the leading of the Lamb, for doing otherwise has destroyed, deceived, and undone me."

The Bible is profoundly simple when it says, "Flee fornication." If you do, the Lord will be there to see you through.

> There hath no temptation taken you but such as is common to man: but God is faithful, who will not suffer you to be tempted above that ye are able; but will with the temptation also make a way to escape, that ye may be able to bear it.   1 Corinthians 10:13

"Lie with me," she said as she grabbed him by the coat. Who would ever know if he did? After all, having been mistreated by his family, he was far from his home country.

But Joseph looked at Potiphar's wife and said, "How can I sin against the Lord and do this thing?" as he slipped out of his coat and ran for his life (see Genesis 39:7–12).

"Flee fornication," Paul says to the Corinthians. "Flee youthful lusts," he says to Timothy, "and run to those who call on the Lord, seek after the Lord, walk with the Lord" (see 2 Timothy 2:22). In other words, run from sin to the saints—and you'll do well.

7 After addressing his concerns for them, here we come to the second section of Paul's letter to the church at Corinth, wherein he will give answers to them regarding six specific questions they had asked of him. Chapter 7 deals with marriage; chapters 8—10 with Christian liberty; chapter 11 with church conduct; chapters 12—14 with spiritual gifts; chapter 15 with the resurrection of the dead; and chapter 16 with giving and offering.

The first question the Corinthian church asked Paul concerned marriage and intimacy in marriage. Why? Due to the prevalent heresy of Gnosticism that propounded that anything physical was inherently evil, whatever one did with one's body became either evil or immaterial. This resulted in two extreme reactions. One group said, "Since purity in the material realm is impossible, we can do whatever we want with our bodies." The other group beat and abused their bodies in an attempt to rid themselves of the evil within.

Thus, it is no wonder that, because of cultural confusion, the church had some questions for Paul concerning marriage.

1 Corinthians 7:1, 2
Now concerning the things whereof ye wrote unto me: It is good for a man not to touch a woman. Nevertheless, to avoid fornication, let every man have his own wife, and let every woman have her own husband.

Paul will later explain that certain people have a gift whereby they don't have the inclination or need for intimacy. However, Paul says for everyone else, marriage is the way to avoid the entire realm of immorality.

1 Corinthians 7:3, 4
Let the husband render unto the wife due benevolence: and likewise also the wife unto the husband. The wife hath not power of her own body, but the husband: and likewise also the husband hath not power of his own body, but the wife.

Due to the fact that when two people get married their bodies are no longer their own, the hus-

band is to give his wife the intimacy she desires, and likewise the wife to the husband.

1 Corinthians 7:5
Defraud ye not one the other, except it be with consent for a time, that ye may give yourselves to fasting and prayer; and come together again, that Satan tempt you not for your incontinency.

Contrary to the wisdom of the world, which prescribes separation for ailing marriages, the principle of the Word is that, rather than moving out to find oneself, to discover what one wants, or to determine what's wrong, husbands and wives are to give themselves to each other because intimacy binds people uniquely.

1 Corinthians 7:6
But I speak this by permission, and not of commandment.

Chapter 7 is a most interesting chapter for many reasons—not the least of which is that throughout his discussion on marriage, we'll see Paul offering his personal opinion quite freely. Paul's example shows us there's a place for us to share our opinions—as long as people understand the difference between our personal persuasion and the Word of God.

1 Corinthians 7:7 (a)
For I would that all men were even as I myself.

Although he was single at this point, there are two strong indications that Paul had been married previously.

As they do to this day, the rabbis taught that God's edict to be fruitful and multiply (Genesis 1:28) was a commandment given to all holy or godly men. Therefore, they said whoever didn't marry and have children violated the commandment. And, concerning the law, Paul was blameless (Philippians 3:6).

Secondly, Paul was most likely a member of the Sanhedrin—the Jewish Supreme Court. To be a member of this seventy-member body, one had to be married because the Jews believed that he who was married was more prone to mercy.

What happened to Paul's wife? Some suggest she died. History, however, weighs in on the side of the premise that his wife left him when he converted to Christianity.

1 Corinthians 7:7 (b)
But every man hath his proper gift of God, one after this manner, and another after that.

Jesus referred to the gift of which Paul speaks when He said,

But he said unto them, All men cannot receive this saying, save they to whom it is given. For there are some eunuchs, which were so born from their mother's womb: and there are some eunuchs, which were made eunuchs of men: and there be eunuchs, which have made themselves eunuchs for the kingdom of heaven's sake. He that is able to receive it, let him receive it.   Matthew 19:11, 12

Jesus said some are born without a need or desire to be married. Others—for example those who were in charge of a king's harem—were involuntarily made that way. I suspect that Jesus was speaking of those who made themselves eunuchs in the sense that they said, "I am not going to become involved with women in order that I might focus on the kingdom."

1 Corinthians 7:8
I say therefore to the unmarried and widows, It is good for them if they abide even as I.

If you are at a place where you can live by yourself, Paul says, "Good for you. I wish all men were like that—living in single-mindedness and in freedom."

1 Corinthians 7:9
But if they cannot contain, let them marry: for it is better to marry than to burn.

Although Paul enjoyed his single state, he knew it was better for someone to get married than to burn with passion. And such would be the normal pattern for the vast majority.

1 Corinthians 7:10
And unto the married I command, yet not I, but the Lord, Let not the wife depart from her husband.

Wives, do not leave your husbands. Period. Marriage is like a violin—it doesn't work without strings. But even when the music stops, the strings are still attached.

1 Corinthians 7:11 (a)
But and if she depart . . .

After saying under no circumstance should a wife leave her husband, why does Paul give instruction to the wife who leaves? Because he's realistic. Although leaving is against the heart of the Lord and the command of God, Paul knew the frailty of the flesh.

1 Corinthians 7:11 (b)
. . . let her remain unmarried, or be reconciled to her husband: and let not the husband put away his wife.

According to this passage, the wife who leaves her husband has only two options: to remain unmarried or to return to her husband.

1 Corinthians 7:12, 13
But to the rest speak I, not the Lord: If any brother hath a wife that believeth not, and she be pleased to dwell with him, let him not put her away. And the woman which hath an husband that believeth not, and if he be pleased to dwell with her, let her not leave him.

Again, giving his opinion, Paul says a person who gets saved is not to divorce or drive away his unbelieving spouse.

1 Corinthians 7:14
For the unbelieving husband is sanctified by the wife, and the unbelieving wife is sanctified by the husband: else were your children unclean; but now are they holy.

The unbelieving husband or wife is sanctified by the believing spouse. This doesn't mean the unbeliever is saved, but rather that he or she is sanctified, set apart, blessed simply because they're linked to a believer.
Of his firstborn child with Bathsheba who died as a result of his sin, David said, "He cannot be with me, but I will be with him" (see 2 Samuel 12:23)—which tells me the baby was taken into heaven.

1 Corinthians 7:15
But if the unbelieving depart, let him depart. A brother or a sister is not under bondage in such cases: but God hath called us to peace.

Because God has called us to peace, if a man is blatantly mistreating his wife, I don't tell her to tough it out. No, I say, "God has called you to get out."

Having said that, however, we are not to use the argument of peace as an excuse to walk out of a marriage we feel is less than perfect. This is a loophole Christians use all too readily, one that ought to be closed tightly. Short of physical abuse or abject negligence, even if your marriage is tough and full of heartache, my word to you is to stay. If you travel to enough counselors, you'll find one who tells you to leave—but be careful. Far too many marriages break up due to a failure to take into account the *full* counsel of God.

1 Corinthians 7:16, 17

For what knowest thou, O wife, whether thou shalt save thy husband? or how knowest thou, O man, whether thou shalt save thy wife? But as God hath distributed to every man, as the Lord hath called every one, so let him walk. And so ordain I in all churches.

You never know what the next year, month, or day holds. Stick with the calling of God for your life, whatever that may be.

1 Corinthians 7:18–20

Is any man called being circumcised? let him not become uncircumcised. Is any called in uncircumcision? let him not be circumcised. Circumcision is nothing, and uncircumcision is nothing, but the keeping of the commandments of God. Let every man abide in the same calling wherein he was called.

Not only as it relates to your marriage situation, but in every area—be who you are. Paul says, "If you're called as a Jew, then be a believing Jew. If you're called as a Gentile, be a believing Gentile."

1 Corinthians 7:21

Art thou called being a servant? care not for it: but if thou mayest be made free, use it rather.

"If you're a slave, don't try to escape. But if you're set free, go for it," says Paul. Again, he's saying, "Just be yourself, doing all things for God's glory in a spirit of contentment."

1 Corinthians 7:22

For he that is called in the Lord, being a servant, is the Lord's freeman: likewise also he that is called, being free, is Christ's servant.

The dynamic of Christianity is that the slave is free in Christ, while the free man is a slave to Him (Romans 1:1).

1 Corinthians 7:23, 24

Ye are bought with a price; be not ye the servants of men. Brethren, let every man, wherein he is called, therein abide with God.

After paying forty-one million dollars for Barry Bonds to play a few seasons for them, you can be sure that the San Francisco Giants will take very good care of him. They made sure he had the finest trainers, dietician, and health care available. They made sure he had everything he needed to stay healthy and happy. Why? Because their investment is was significant. But guess what. Forty-one million dollars is nothing compared to the blood of Christ paid for you. Therefore, He's going to see to it that you are tended well, that whatever comes into your life or goes on in your life is according to His plan and for your good.

1 Corinthians 7:25, 26

Now concerning virgins I have no commandment of the Lord: yet I give my judgment, as one that hath obtained mercy of the Lord to be faithful. I suppose therefore that this is good for the present distress, I say, that it is good for a man so to be.

Again offering his opinion, Paul reiterates that the single state allows one to be singularly committed to the kingdom.

1 Corinthians 7:27

Art thou bound unto a wife? seek not to be loosed. Art thou loosed from a wife? seek not a wife.

If you're married, stay married, says Paul. If you're single, don't strive to find a wife.

For topical study of 1 Corinthians 7:27 entitled "The Right Mate: Finding and Being," turn to page 1044.

1 Corinthians 7:28

But and if thou marry, thou hast not sinned; and if a virgin marry, she hath not sinned. Nevertheless such shall have trouble in the flesh: but I spare you.

Because they consist of two imperfect people, every marriage has days of struggle and difficulty. Therefore, if yours does, don't think you're alone, off the wall, or out to lunch. Paul says matrimony inevitably brings its own challenges.

1 Corinthians 7:29 (a)
But this I say, brethren, the time is short . . .

"Time is short," Paul says.
"Life is a vapor," James echoes (see James 4:14).
Whether the Lord comes back for us today—or whether we live out full lives, time is rapidly coming to a close because we're getting older and the Lord's coming is nearer. In light of this, Paul identifies three obstacles that could keep us from investing in the things of eternity. . . .

1 Corinthians 7:29 (b)
. . . it remaineth, that both they that have wives be as though they had none.

The first potential pitfall is in the area of relationships. There are people who miss out on being engaged in the kingdom because they're caught up in family relationships. There are people called into ministry, missions, or other opportunities to serve the Lord who say, "We can't do it now because we're getting married. But after we're settled, we're going to really go for it for the Lord." So I talk to them a year later, only to hear them say, "We're really excited about serving the Lord, but we have to get our baby out of diapers. Then we're really going for it." But then Junior is in elementary school and they say, "We can't pull him out of school, Boy Scouts, and sports." And what happens? All too often those who focus completely on the family find problems abounding within the family because they weren't true to the calling God placed upon their lives in the first place.
Get outside of yourselves, married couple. Say, "We're engaged in something bigger than ourselves—it's called eternity." Seek first the kingdom, Mom and Dad—and watch everything else fall into place (Matthew 6:33).

1 Corinthians 7:30 (a)
And they that weep, as though they wept not; and they that rejoice, as though they rejoiced not . . .

The second obstacle to keeping eternity's values in view is in the area of emotions. The most widespread disease today is "I" disease—people focused on themselves, analyzing why they're depressed or why they're discouraged. But the more they analyze themselves, the more depressed they become. Paul's remedy is simple:

Weep with those who weep and rejoice with those who rejoice (Romans 12:15). In other words, get involved with how others are doing. It's amazing what will happen. The Lord will use you, and you'll be set free if you get your eyes off yourself.

1 Corinthians 7:30 (b), 31
. . . and they that buy, as though they possessed not; and they that use this world, as not abusing it: for the fashion of this world passeth away.

Finally, Paul names possessions as the third obstacle to seeing the big picture of the kingdom. He who is caught up in his investment portfolio or in the fashion of this world will be too busy, too preoccupied to engage in ministry. Yes, we should be wise stewards—but our possessions should not preoccupy us. Tithing is so important and giving so freeing because every time you put money in the offering, you're giving away a part of your stinginess, shortsightedness, and selfishness.
The Lord isn't saying, "Don't focus on your relationships, your emotions, or your possessions because I want you to be miserable." Quite the opposite. His intention is for you to be free. And the way to freedom is to forget about yourself and seek first the kingdom. This applies to marriage, to emotions, to possessions. When you seek first the kingdom, everything else is added to you—and you're blessed beyond belief. Time is short, gang. Be about the work of eternity. Maintain a walk with the Lord personally. Serve Him however He leads you enthusiastically. And you'll be blessed abundantly.

1 Corinthians 7:32, 33
But I would have you without carefulness. He that is unmarried careth for the things that belong to the Lord, how he may please the Lord: But he that is married careth for the things that are of the world, how he may please his wife.

If you are married, you will inevitably find yourself caring for your spouse—and that's the way it should be. But it will distract you nonetheless from the freedom you would have enjoyed had you remained in a single state.

1 Corinthians 7:34
There is difference also between a wife and a virgin. The unmarried woman careth for the things of the Lord, that she may be holy both in body and in spirit: but she that is married careth for the things of the world, how she may please her husband.

The woman who is married has an obligation to please her husband. The single sister, on the other hand, has the opportunity to be about pleasing the Lord singularly.

1 Corinthians 7:35
And this I speak for your own profit; not that I may cast a snare upon you, but for that which is comely, and that ye may attend upon the Lord without distraction.

There is a woman in Scripture who models this very effectively. Her name is Anna. . . .

And she was a widow of about fourscore and four years, which departed not from the temple, but served God with fastings and prayers night and day. And she coming in that instant gave thanks likewise unto the Lord, and spake of him to all them that looked for redemption in Jerusalem.   Luke 2:37, 38

Anna didn't panic about her single state. She didn't lament her situation. Rather, she realized she had an opportunity to serve the Lord without distraction. And what happened? She was given special revelation, for she recognized that which only one other man—a man named Simeon— knew. She knew the Babe in the arms of Mary and Joseph was not an ordinary Child.

How I encourage you who have been widowed or divorced to follow the example of Anna: Look for the Lord. Pray to the Lord. Walk with the Lord. Anna didn't hang out in the temple with God's people because she was miserable there. Rather, I suggest she stayed there year after year because she found in the Lord exactly what her soul was craving. So will you.

1 Corinthians 7:36
But if any man think that he behaveth himself uncomely toward his virgin, if she pass the flower of her age, and need so require, let him do what he will, he sinneth not: let them marry.

After talking about the freedom found in the single state, in his day of arranged marriages, Paul goes on to talk to fathers about their unmarried daughters, saying that if their daughters desired to marry, that was acceptable.

1 Corinthians 7:37, 38
Nevertheless he that standeth stedfast in his heart, having no necessity, but hath power over his own will, and hath so decreed in his heart that he will keep his virgin, doeth

well. So then he that giveth her in marriage doeth well; but he that giveth her not in marriage doeth better.

On the other hand, Paul says that the father who can guide his daughter into living as a single woman, devoting herself to the Lord, does a good thing.

1 Corinthians 7:39, 40
The wife is bound by the law as long as her husband liveth; but if her husband be dead, she is at liberty to be married to whom she will; only in the Lord. But she is happier if she so abide, after my judgment: and I think also that I have the Spirit of God.

Clarifying the questions presented to him, Paul tells the Corinthian believers that a wife is bound to her husband until death separates them. After that, she is at liberty to marry anyone she wishes as long as he's a believer and the Lord so directs.

Throughout the centuries, people have read 1 Corinthians 7 and come to the conclusion that, because he speaks so highly of the single state, Paul has a problem with marriage. But that is because they fail to take into account Paul's full counsel—for in his letter to the church at Ephesus, Paul elevates marriage to a place of utmost glory when he uses it as an illustration for no less a relationship than that of Christ and His church.

Husbands, love your wives, even as Christ also loved the church, and gave himself for it; that he might sanctify and cleanse it with the washing of water by the word, that he might present it to himself a glorious church, not having spot, or wrinkle, or any such thing; but that it should be holy and without blemish.
                          Ephesians 5:25–27

The way a husband lays down his life for his wife, and the way a wife submits to her husband is a powerful illustration seen on every street in every neighborhood. Bunches of people aren't into going to church. So the Lord brings the church to them through the illustration of marriage wherein people see how much He loves the church and how the church submits to Him. It's an awesome responsibility for all who are married. Unbelievers don't need to see perfection in our marriages—just something remarkably different from what they see in society.

And yet, as seen here in 1 Corinthians 7, Paul says singleness has its own unique beauty, its own important role to play in the body. The single state is not to be looked down upon, dreaded, or merely endured. Those who are called to a single life or who find themselves in a single state fulfill a very real function: to serve the Lord with spontaneity and without distraction. Marriage is a picture, but, in a sense, singleness can be the reality—for it is the single person uniquely who can say, "I am married to You, Lord. You are my Husband, my Love, my best Friend. And I will be devoted to you single-heartedly for as long as You have me in this state."

Whether single or married, widowed or divorced—be content wherever God has you. And whatever your position, make Jesus your passion.

THE RIGHT MATE: FINDING AND BEING
A Topical Study of
1 Corinthians 7:27

S*o God created man in his own image, in the image of God created he him; male and female created he them. And God blessed them, and God said unto them, Be fruitful, and multiply, and replenish the earth . . .*

Genesis 1:27, 28

Whoso findeth a wife findeth a good thing, and obtaineth favour of the LORD.

Proverbs 18:22

The church in Corinth was, no doubt, familiar with these Scriptures. And yet they saw their spiritual father, their church founder, the apostle Paul living a life of single devotion to the Lord. And so they asked him, "Should we get married as the Scriptures declare? Or should we follow in your footsteps and serve the Lord in a single state?"

Paul sums up his answer to them by saying,

Art thou bound unto a wife? seek not to be loosed. Art thou loosed from a wife? seek not a wife.   1 Corinthians 7:27

The full understanding of his answers lies in the understanding of the word "seek." The Greek word implies a frantic, obsessive searching—an activity that dominates one's thoughts and fills one's days. With regard to finding a mate, the way of the Lord is very much different than this—seen perhaps most powerfully and practically in His provision of a wife for Adam.

God Saw Adam's Need

Of each thing He created, God said, "It is good"—until He created Adam. Of Adam exclusively, He said, "It is *not* good that man should be alone. He needs help" (see Genesis 2:18). Thus, before Adam even had a clue that he was alone, God saw his need.

God Made Adam Aware of His Need

Recognizing Adam's need, God did something most intriguing. He told Adam to name the animals in the Garden of Eden. So, as they perhaps paraded before him two by two, Adam said, "There's Mr. and Mrs. Rhino, Mr. and Mrs. Giraffe, Mr. and Mrs. Hippo, Mr. and Mrs. Anteater." And somewhere in the process, it must have dawned on him that, while there were two of every animal, there was only one of him.

Maybe, like Adam, you feel like you're missing something. Maybe the desire to be married is increasingly tugging at your heart. The Lord is not surprised. He knew you would have this need before you did.

God Provided for Adam's Need

After the Lord made Adam aware of his need, He didn't say, "Adam, cruise through the jungle and try your luck. There's a singles' bar over there, and a meeting on the other side where singles mingle. Climb the trees, beat the bushes, and see what you can come up with." If that had been God's plan, Adam would most likely have ended up with a gorilla, an ape, or an orangutan—something that vaguely resembled him, but was far from a match for him.

Too many people say, "I want to be married, so I'll climb this tree. I'll beat that bush. I'll find somebody"—and they end up with someone who's somewhat compatible, kind of close, but hardly a perfect match. That's why God didn't tell Adam to beat the bushes—but to take a nap. And that's what He says to you who are single when He says, "Rest in Me." When Adam did this, he woke to find a being so compatible to him, so perfect for him that he described her as "bone of my bone, flesh of my flesh" (Genesis 2:23).

Single brother or sister—how will you recognize the perfect match God has for you? I believe within Adam's description of Eve lies the answer. You see, God is a triune Being: Father, Son, and Spirit. Being made in His image, we are, in a sense, a trinity as well—consisting of body, soul, and spirit (1 Thessalonians 5:23). The body is our material nature that relates to the physical world around us. The soul consists of our mind, emotions, and will—our personality, that which relates to people. The spirit is our true nature—that part of us which relates to God and will live eternally.

When, as a single man or woman, you meet the counterpart for your body, soul and spirit, you'll know he or she is God's choice for you. Physically, there will be a romantic spark, a physical attraction between the two of you. In the area of the soul, you will appreciate the uniqueness of each other's personality. In spirit, you will be moving in the same direction with the same intensity concerning the things of the kingdom.

Too often, however, people settle for a match in only one or two of these three areas . . .

"We're so attracted to each other physically," says the starry-eyed young man. "And spiritually, we both go to church, pray, and study the Scriptures together. But our personalities are quite different. I love hunting and fishing. She loves the mall. I love football. She can't stand sports. She listens to Bach and Beethoven. I like the Beach Boys and the Beatles. She talks by the hour. I hardly talk at all."

Watch out. While there's romantic and spiritual unity, in the area of the soul, you're on different wave-lengths—and there will be problems. Am I saying that two people must have identical interests in order for their marriage to work? No, for there is truth in the old adage that opposites attract. But there must be genuine appreciation rather than mere toleration of the other's interests.

"We're best friends," boasts the young lady. "We talk by the hour and love hanging out with each other. We also go to church and pray together. But physically? I don't really like him to touch me."

Watch out. You're going to have problems because sooner or later, someone will come into your life who will cause a romantic spark within you. And then there will be trouble.

Others say, "We see fireworks romantically. We have the same flavor in personality. But spiritually? I want to serve the Lord radically, but she only goes to church sporadically."

Watch out. Even though you are both believers, if you're not united in the spiritual realm, you're headed for hard times.

I believe you will recognize your perfect match when, regarding body, soul, and spirit, you can say, "We're romantically attracted, personally connected, and spiritually united in our priorities, zeal, and intensity." If you desire to be married, don't settle for a match in one or even two of these three areas. Instead, go to sleep. Wait on the Lord. And in due season—at just the right time—He'll bring you someone who matches you beautifully on all three levels.

"Great," you say. "Where was this teaching ten years ago? I thought I was supposed to go out and find someone on my own. So I did—and now I'm stuck. What do I do now?"

Understand this: Even if the person you married was #886 on the Lord's list of ideal mates for you—the moment you said, "I do," #886 became #1. You see, even if there was a mistake made initially, no one on the face of the earth will be better for you than the person you're sitting with right now. Once you get married, your spouse automatically becomes your Adam or your Eve, God's perfect match for you.

"But our marriage is so flat," you say. "The sparkle is no longer there."

I have good news for you! The first public miracle Jesus ever did was that of putting the sparkle back into a watered-down, washed-up marriage ceremony. "Servants," He said, "fill those earthen jars to the brim with water, pour it out, and watch what happens" (see John 2:7, 8). They did, and that which was once water became the wine of joy.

Husband and wife, listen carefully. Paul says that we have the treasure of Christ in earthen vessels (2 Corinthians 4:7). Thus, the Lord will miraculously fill your relationship with joy if you will fill your earthen vessel with the Water of the Word and pour it out to your spouse as you share with him or her the things of the Lord; as you study the Scriptures, pray, serve, rejoice, and worship together.

Jesus said, "If you, being evil, know how to give good gifts to your children, how much more will the heavenly Father give good gifts to His" (see Matthew 7:11). Whether that be providing the single brother or sister with the mate He has for them, or infusing a lifeless marriage with His wine of joy, He will be faithful.

Rest in Him, gang. Spend time waiting on Him. And watch and see what our faithful, creative, matchless God will do.

8 In chapters 8—10, Paul uses a question the Corinthians had asked him about meat to address the larger issue of Christian liberty. Within the city of Corinth were numerous temples dedicated to various idols wherein animals would be sacrificed. A portion of the meat would be consumed on the altar. Another portion would be given to the priest. The remainder of the sacrifice would be sold in markets, called shambles, at reduced rates. It was concerning the meat sold in shambles that the Corinthians questioned Paul.

1 Corinthians 8:1
Now as touching things offered unto idols, we know that we all have knowledge. Knowledge puffeth up, but charity edifieth.

Before answering the Corinthians' question concerning meat, Paul begins by addressing the foundational issue. At the very outset of his discussion of liberty, Paul makes it clear that knowledge puffs up, but love builds up.

1 Corinthians 8:2
And if any man think that he knoweth anything, he knoweth nothing yet as he ought to know.

"You don't know as much as you think you do," says Paul. I find it interesting that after he will say that idols are nothing here in chapter 8,

he'll say there are demons behind them in chapter 10 (10:20).

1 Corinthians 8:3
But if any man love God, the same is known of him.

On one hand, Paul will say, "Because idols are nothing, go ahead and eat meat offered to them." But on the other hand, he'll say, "There are indeed demonic forces behind idols." So what were the Corinthians to do?

I believe the answer is found in Genesis 2. . . .

What was the one tree of which Adam and Eve were forbidden to eat? The tree of the knowledge of good and evil. Yet once they disobeyed God and ate of this tree, they immediately thought they knew good from evil, right from wrong without having to depend on the Father as they had done before. Suddenly, knowing they were naked, they hid from God. The result? Intimacy with the Father was broken.

So, too, if I'm not oh, so careful, even biblical knowledge and theological understanding will make me less of a prayer, less of a lover, less inclined to depend wholly on the Father because I will mistakenly think I can handle any given situation on the basis of my own knowledge or understanding.

Thus saith the LORD, Let not the wise man glory in his wisdom, neither let the mighty man glory in his might, let not the rich man glory in his riches: But let him that glorieth glory in this, that he understandeth and knoweth me, that I am the LORD which exercise lovingkindness, judgment, and righteousness, in the earth: for in these things I delight, saith the LORD.   Jeremiah 9:23, 24

The word "know" speaks of intimacy, as a man knows his wife. There are many people who know about the Lord—but they don't know Him intimately. "Lord, Lord," they will say, "didn't we prophesy in Your name and do signs and wonders for Your kingdom?"

"Depart from Me," He will say. "I never knew you. Yes, you worked for Me. Yes, you knew about Me. But we had no relationship intimately" (see Matthew 7:21–23).

Saints, be students of the Word. Grow in the knowledge of the Lord. Become solid in theology—but as you do, make sure that love has the priority. Make sure your love for God is preeminent. The Word will confirm God's leading and correct your misunderstanding. But it must not be a substitute for walking with Him day by day, or for talking with Him about every situation. It must never take the place of your walking with Him in intimacy and dependency lest it become as the fruit of the tree of knowledge.

1 Corinthians 8:4–6
As concerning therefore the eating of those things that are offered in sacrifice unto idols, we know that an idol is nothing in the world, and that there is none other God but one. For though there be that are called gods, whether in heaven or in earth, (as there be gods many, and lords many,) but to us there is but one God, the Father, of whom are all things, and we in him; and one Lord Jesus Christ, by whom are all things, and we by him.

"It's no big deal," Paul says, "to eat meat sacrificed to idols, for we know there is only one true God—our Father. We know there is only one true Lord—our Savior, Jesus Christ."

1 Corinthians 8:7 (a)
Howbeit . . .

Although eating meat offered to idols is not a threat to the true God, and although eating meat offered to idols won't affect me personally, I need to be aware that it may indeed affect those around me.

1 Corinthians 8:7 (b)
. . . there is not in every man that knowledge: for some with conscience of the idol unto this hour eat it as a thing offered unto an idol; and their conscience being weak is defiled.

Our natural tendency is to think that the brother or sister who would be righteously indignant over the eating of meat offered to idols would be the spiritual giant, the one most sensitive to the heart of God. But Paul calls such a one "weak." Paul says, in effect, the person who is bound by rules and regulations isn't mature, but weak—for the more spiritually mature one is, the more free he or she will be.

1 Corinthians 8:8, 9
But meat commendeth us not to God: for neither, if we eat, are we the better; neither, if we eat not, are we the worse. But take heed lest by any means this liberty of yours become a stumblingblock to them that are weak.

"We know that the eating of meat makes us neither better nor worse in God's sight," says Paul. "However, our knowledge must be tempered by a higher principle—that of love. We must be aware that there are people who might struggle with seeing us scarf down a top sirloin that was previously offered to a pagan idol. We must be mindful of those who are weak."

Why are people weak or immature in their faith?

I suggest three reasons. . . .

First, some people are immature because they're new Christians who haven't had time to grow in the knowledge of grace or the finished work of Christ. In our culture, we are steeped in thinking that there's no free lunch, that we must work our way up in life, that we must pick ourselves up by our own bootstraps. Therefore, it takes time for those who are new in the faith to grow in the understanding that the way of the kingdom is totally different than the world's system. Because of the Cross, the Christian race starts at the finish line. We don't fight *for* victory; we fight *from* victory. This is so foreign to the world's thinking that many new Christians are hypersensitive about issues of conscience and the possibility of failing.

A second reason for immaturity is not because someone is a spiritual baby, but because he is a spoiled brat. It is to such a one the author of the Book of Hebrews says, "At a time you should be eating meat, when you should be teaching others, you're still in need of milk, learning simple things (Hebrews 5:12). Some people refuse to grow. They will not come to Bible study; they will not take time to worship the Lord corporately; they will not fellowship with other believers regularly. As a result, they are locked in to a permanent state of immaturity.

A third reason for immaturity is that some people are scared children. Scared children won't go outside because they're afraid they'll get kidnapped, that a bee will sting them, or that a bird will carry them away. So, too, in the spiritual realm, there are those who say, "I can't go there; I can't do that because I'll get wiped out." And their whole life is characterized by the fear that something bad will happen to them. Consequently, they stay locked up in their house of legalism.

Perhaps you see these tendencies in your own life or in the lives of those you're discipling—the baby who hasn't had time to grow, the spoiled brat who refuses to grow, the scared child who is afraid to grow. It is only when a man becomes mature spiritually that he finds himself at liberty.

1 Corinthians 8:10, 11
For if any man see thee which hast knowledge sit at meat in the idol's temple, shall not the conscience of him which is weak be emboldened to eat those things which are offered to idols; and through thy knowledge shall the weak brother perish, for whom Christ died?

More important than the knowledge that I am free to have a burger is the realization that my liberty could adversely affect my weaker brother. You see, I might be able to talk him into participating in an activity that is fine for me. But if he does, he may later feel that his walk has been compromised, or that his prayers won't be heard. That is why I never talk anyone out of a personal conviction he has—even if his conviction seems legalistic to me. Oh, I'll discuss it with him if he asks my opinion, but I won't encourage him to abandon his convictions simply on the basis of my own freedom.

1 Corinthians 8:12
But when ye sin so against the brethren, and wound their weak conscience, ye sin against Christ.

Not only can a weak conscience become defiled, but it can become wounded. That is, a weaker brother can be shocked or saddened by observing my liberty. And when we so wound a weaker brother, we sin against Christ. Why? Because Jesus cares about even His weakest children. Yes, they might be spiritual babies, spoiled brats, scared children—but they're all His, nonetheless. And He cares about them so much that He died for them. Therefore, before I say, "I'll do what I want, go where I want, eat what I want," I must realize that if, flaunting my liberty and boasting of my maturity, I knowingly cause my weaker brother to stumble, I sin not only against him but against Christ.

1 Corinthians 8:13
Wherefore, if meat make my brother to offend, I will eat no flesh while the world standeth, lest I make my brother to offend.

"Here's the bottom line," says Paul. "If meat offends my weaker brother, I will eat no meat. Period."

Is it any wonder the Lord so powerfully used him?

9 After exhorting the Corinthian believers to lay down their liberty in order that others wouldn't stumble, here in chapter 9, Paul uses himself as an example of what it means to do this. . . .

1 Corinthians 9:1–3
Am I not an apostle? am I not free? have I not seen Jesus Christ our Lord? are not ye my work in the Lord? If I be not an apostle unto others, yet doubtless I am to you: for the seal of mine apostleship are ye in the Lord. Mine answer to them that do examine me is this.

An apostle is one who was sent out as a spiritual statesman. Paul had been sent to the Corinthians to bring them to a saving knowledge of Jesus Christ and to disciple and develop them as he labored among them.

1 Corinthians 9:4–6
Have we not power to eat and to drink? Have we not power to lead about a sister, a wife, as well as other apostles, and as the brethren of the Lord, and Cephas? Or I only and Barnabas, have not we power to forbear working?

In these first six verses, Paul says, "Because we are apostles, we have the right to be supported financially as are James, Jude, Peter, and the other apostles."

1 Corinthians 9:7 (a)
Who goeth a warfare any time at his own charges?

"In addition to our apostleship, human logic dictates that we be supported, says Paul. "After all, who goes to war and pays for his own equipment?" Paul is right. Those who enlist in the navy don't have to provide their own ships. Those who join the air force don't have to bring their own planes. No, if you serve in the army or navy, your needs are covered.

1 Corinthians 9:7 (b)
... who planteth a vineyard, and eateth not of the fruit thereof? or who feedeth a flock, and eateth not of the milk of the flock?

Not only are military personnel provided for, but the farmer and the shepherd are allowed to eat of the fruit of their own labor.

1 Corinthians 9:8
Say I these things as a man? or saith not the law the same also?

Paul appeals to the law itself as substantiation for his right to financial support.

1 Corinthians 9:9
For it is written in the law of Moses, Thou shalt not muzzle the mouth of the ox that treadeth out the corn.

In other words, "The ox who grinds the corn should be able to eat of the corn." Paul will use this Old Testament reference (Deuteronomy 25:4) again in 1 Timothy 5:17 when he tells his young protégé that elders should be counted worthy of double honor.

1 Corinthians 9:9, 10 (a)
Doth God take care for oxen? Or saith he it altogether for our sakes? For our sakes, no doubt, this is written ...

This law is not only for the benefit of oxen. It's an illustration for people.

1 Corinthians 9:10 (b)
... that he that ploweth should plow in hope ...

Hope being the absolute expectation of coming good, the one who plows away in ministry should expect good things to come his way.

1 Corinthians 9:10 (c), 11
... and that he that thresheth in hope should be partaker of his hope. If we have sown unto you spiritual things, is it a great thing if we shall reap your carnal things?

"Carnal things" referring to finances, Paul goes on to give a fourth reason why he had a right to be supported in ministry. . . .

1 Corinthians 9:12
If others be partakers of this power over you, are not we rather? Nevertheless we have not used this power; but suffer all things, lest we should hinder the gospel of Christ.

"It's already your custom to support other ministers," says Paul. "So why would it be unusual to support us?"

1 Corinthians 9:13
Do ye not know that they which minister about holy things live of the things of the temple? and they which wait at the altar are partakers with the altar?

Paul not only referred to Old Testament law, but to the practices of the Old Testament community as he reminds the Corinthian believers that priests partook of a portion of the sacrifices brought to the altar.

1 Corinthians 9:14
Even so hath the Lord ordained that they which preach the gospel should live of the gospel.

"Provide neither gold, nor silver, nor brass in your purses, nor scrip for your journey, neither two coats, neither shoes, nor yet staves," Jesus said when He sent His disciples out, "for the workman is worthy of his meat" (Matthew 10:9–10). It is to this command Paul refers.

1 Corinthians 9:15
But I have used none of these things: neither have I written these things, that it should be so done unto me: for it were better for me to die, than that any man should make my glorying void.

On the basis of apostolic authority, human logic, Old Testament law, present custom, Old Testament community, and Jesus' command, Paul makes a persuasive and powerful case that he had the right to be supported in ministry. But then he says he would rather die than cause the Corinthian believers to stumble in this area. You see, in Corinth at this time there were a number of teachers—both Christian and pagan—who were ripping people off financially. Therefore, Paul laid aside his right to be supported in ministry so as not to wound the weak conscience of the Corinthian church.

There are those who use this passage to say that's the way every ministry should be—that pastors or ministers have no right to be supported. But those who do fail to figure 2 Corinthians 11:8 into the equation, wherein Paul says he was able to forfeit his right to be supported by the Corinthian church only because he was receiving support from other churches. In addition, we know from Acts 18:3 that Paul worked with his own hands making tents so as not to be a burden to the believers.

1 Corinthians 9:16
For though I preach the gospel, I have nothing to glory of: for necessity is laid upon me; yea, woe is unto me, if I preach not the gospel!

"I don't glory in the fact that I let go of my right to be supported in order that I might preach to you," says Paul, "for I have no other choice but to preach."

"I'm tired of speaking in the name of the Lord," cried Jeremiah from his dungeon cell. "No one is listening to me. People are mad at me. Some are even trying to kill me. I'm going to speak no more," he said—until he realized that the Word of God was like fire in his bones and he could not keep quiet (Jeremiah 20:9).

That's what happens in ministry, doesn't it? You just can't keep God's Word to yourself!

1 Corinthians 9:17
For if I do this thing willingly, I have a reward: but if against my will, a dispensation of the gospel is committed unto me.

"Woe is me if I don't preach," says Paul. "If I do it willingly, I'll have a reward. But even if I do it because I have no other choice, the gospel has been entrusted to me."

1 Corinthians 9:18
What is my reward then? Verily that, when I preach the gospel, I may make the gospel of Christ without charge, that I abuse not my power in the gospel.

"I'm not going to charge for the gospel," Paul declares. "I'm not going to lay a burden on people, play games with people, or present fundraising gimmicks to people."

1 Corinthians 9:19 (a)
For though I be free from all men . . .

"Because I laid down my rights in order that you wouldn't stumble, I'm free," declares Paul.

1 Corinthians 9:19 (b), 20
. . . yet have I made myself servant unto all, that I might gain the more. And unto the Jews I became as a Jew, that I might gain the Jews; to them that are under the law, as under the law, that I might gain them that are under the law.

"To the Jews, I don't flaunt my liberty. Instead, I become like them," said Paul. And indeed he did. It was for this reason he circumcised Timothy (Acts 16:3).

1 Corinthians 9:21, 22
To them that are without law, as without law, (being not without law to God, but under the law to Christ,) that I might gain them that are without law. To the weak became I as weak, that I might gain the weak: I am made all things to all men, that I might by all means save some.

Even as he didn't flaunt his liberty before the Jews, Paul didn't force the law upon the Gentiles. Without compromising his morals or violating his principles, he fit in with the folks to whom he was called to minister—that he might win them to Christ.

1 Corinthians 9:23
And this I do for the gospel's sake, that I might be partaker thereof with you.

Paul gave up his rights in ministry. He blended in with Jews and Gentiles in humility because, rather than be an obstacle that caused people to stumble, Paul chose to be a stone upon which they could step.

1 Corinthians 9:24 (a)
Know ye not that they which run in a race run all, but one receiveth the prize?

"Here's why I let go of my liberty," declares Paul. "I understand the big picture of eternity." Paul knew heaven was real. Left for dead outside the city of Lystra (Acts 14:19), Paul was caught up into the third heaven. "Whether or not I was in the Spirit or actually transported physically, I don't really know," he said, "but somehow I was there. And what I saw was so amazing that I can't even describe it to you" (see 2 Corinthians 12:2–4). Because he had a "sneak preview of coming attractions," Paul set his sight on winning the prize.

1 Corinthians 9:24 (b)
So run, that ye may obtain.

Lest you think there's no use running a race in which spiritual giants like Paul are sure to lap you time and time again, understand this: We're not competing against any other brother or sister. We're competing against ourselves. In His teaching on the talents and pounds (Matthew 25; Luke 19), Jesus makes this very clear. Is what the Lord entrusted uniquely to you being developed for His glory? Are you laying down your rights and privileges to see others brought into the kingdom? Such is the nature of the race we run.

1 Corinthians 9:25
And every man that striveth for the mastery is temperate in all things. Now they do it to obtain a corruptible crown; but we an incorruptible.

Still speaking of sports, Paul changes his metaphor to that of a wrestling match. The reason Paul alludes to sports in this way is because the Isthmus Games—the second most important athletic games in the region—took place in Corinth. Consequently, they knew about running races and wrestling matches. They watched the athletes arrive a year before the games took place to train single-mindedly in order to win the prize— a little laurel wreath to put on one's head.

"Look at what these athletes do to win a simple crown of leaves," Paul says. "The crown for which you race is incorruptible. It will last forever."

"So what?" you say. "If you looked in my closet, you wouldn't find a single crown because I'm not into them."

Really?

Of the five crowns identified in Scripture, the crown to which Paul refers here, is linked to the declaration in Proverbs 11:30 that "he who wins souls is wise"—and to that of Daniel, that "they that turn many to righteousness shall shine as the stars for ever and ever" (see 12:3). To you who are more concerned about seeing people saved than about your own pleasure, ease, or liberty a crown will be given—not merely to wear on your head, but, in light of 1 Corinthians 15:41, 42, that will determine your function and capacity to enjoy eternity.

You see, while everyone in heaven will be completely happy and totally joyful (Psalm 16:11), the crowns we win on earth will have a direct link to our function and our capacity to enjoy eternity.

Benjamin was thrilled. Mrs. Williams, his kindergarten teacher, appointed him Chair Monitor. As Chair Monitor, he got to make sure all the chairs were slid under the desks when the bell rang. He couldn't have been happier. Now, if I were appointed Chair Monitor, I wouldn't jump up and down and say, "I can't wait to tell my wife, Tammy!" For me, the position of Chair Monitor no longer has an impact because at this point, my capacity, understanding, and involvement with life is bigger than that.

So, too, Jesus told us that in heaven, some will rule over ten cities, others five cities, others one—and some will be Chair Monitors. Understanding this, Paul knew that a crown is not a fashion statement, but rather an indication of what we will be doing for the next zillion years.

What if we, like Paul, really believed this? I guarantee every one of us would be looking for opportunities to be stepped on if it meant that the person for whom we laid down our rights would see something of Jesus or come into a saving knowledge of Him. What you do with your life is so important, gang. Don't bury your talents. Don't waste your time. Don't fritter away your resources and money foolishly. Run to win the prize.

1 Corinthians 9:26, 27 (a)
I therefore so run, not as uncertainly; so fight I, not as one that beateth the air: But I keep under my body . . .

This last phrase would be more correctly translated, "I keep my body under." Before you were saved, your body was not "under." Your body was on top. That is, your flesh governed your soul—your mind and emotions. It also governed your spirit—the real you that lives forever. To see how true this is, all you have to do is listen to the conversations that take place at work or on the campus, wherein you'll hear the average person talk only about his body—about his financial concerns and recreational pursuits, his occupational goals and physical needs. But when the natural man gets saved, suddenly everything is different. The flesh no longer dominates him. The spirit is now on top, and suddenly there's peace in his heart and life makes sense.

Because the flesh hates the basement, however, as time goes on, it demands to be on top again. And when it is, the new believer's life is a mess, for to be carnally minded is death (Romans 8:6). So eventually, he gets to the place where he says, "Lord, forgive me. I've given in to the flesh again." He confesses his sin, turns his life back over to God, and his body is "under" once more.

Does this war have to go on daily, hourly, constantly? Paul says here's the key: "I *keep* my body under. I will not allow my body to determine what I watch, read, listen to, or think about. I will keep my body in the basement."

How can this be accomplished?

Let me suggest to you one very practical way: How long has it been since you've said, "No," to your stomach? How long has it been since you've said, "I'm going to use the hour I would have spent feeding my growling, demanding stomach in order to pull away and pray for my family, for the community, and for myself."

I find it interesting that Jesus didn't say, "*If* you fast, . . ." but, "*When* you fast . . ." (Matthew 6:16). In other words, the assumption is that we will fast. When you regularly say, "No," to your stomach, you'll be amazed how much easier it will be to say, "No," to the other temptations that plague you.

Fasting from food is only one of the many disciplines the Bible teaches. Another is saying, "No," when your body says, "Hit the snooze bar." It's saying, "See, body, you're under. You're not ruling me. I'm out of bed. I'm on my knees. I'm in the Word." It's following the example of Jesus, who rose up a great while before morning to seek His Father.

"I keep my body under," Paul says. "I'm tired of my body ruling me, and the death it brings inevitably. Therefore, my spirit, ruled by God's Spirit, will be that which controls my soul—my will, my personality, my emotions."

1 Corinthians 9:27 (b)
. . . and bring it into subjection: lest that by any means, when I have preached to others, I myself should be a castaway.

Newer translations correctly render the word "castaway" as "disqualified." Thus, Paul is saying, "I let go of my liberty in order that I might win people to Jesus. Why? Because I'm in a race for a prize that will affect who I am and what I do in the ages to come. Therefore, even though I am free to do all things, I can be disqualified if I don't keep my flesh under control, if I cause another to stumble."

You'll never regret knocking fleshly pursuits out of your life, gang. I promise you, you'll never regret the things you let go of that would have tripped others and disqualified you; those things that would have wiped out your spiritual stamina and affected your endurance. Are you as disciplined in your spiritual life today as you were a year ago? Or has your appreciation for the finished work of the Cross and your understanding that your salvation is secure apart from anything you do or don't do skewed your thinking? Yes, you're free, but have you used that liberty in a way that's tripping others and disqualifying yourself?

Use your liberty wisely, precious people. Keep your body under, for to be carnally minded is death, but to be spiritually minded brings abundant life and perfect peace.

10 After using himself as an example of what it means to lay down one's liberty sacrificially, here in chapter 10, Paul will use the nation of Israel as an example of those who lost their liberty needlessly.

1 Corinthians 10:1, 2
Moreover, brethren, I would not that ye should be ignorant, how that all our fathers were under the cloud, and all passed through the sea; and were all baptized unto Moses in the cloud and in the sea;

After being released from bondage, God's people were led through the wilderness by a cloud. Why a cloud? With the desert temperature rising, the Lord said, "I'm going to guide you by providing a covering from the sun for you. When the cloud moves, simply move with it."

I love this because as we journey with the Lord, we've got it made in the shade. That's the way He moves, the way He guides. People sweat and struggle and strive to determine the will of God. "Where should I go? What should I do?" they ask—when in reality, their question simply should be, "Where is the shade?"

Oh, the goodness of the Lord. "Keep cool," He says. "Where the cloud goes is where I want you."

1 Corinthians 10:3, 4
And did all eat the same spiritual meat; and did all drink the same spiritual drink: for they drank of that spiritual Rock that followed them: and that Rock was Christ.

Baptized in the Red Sea, led by the Lord as they stayed in the shade, fed with manna every morning, the nation of Israel drank water from a Rock—Jesus Christ—the perpetual source of refreshment (John 7:37).

1 Corinthians 10:5
But with many of them God was not well pleased: for they were overthrown in the wilderness.

"With many of them God was not well pleased" is an understatement of mammoth proportion, for of the three million Jews who left Egypt and were provided for supernaturally, only two entered the Promised Land.

1 Corinthians 10:6
Now these things were our examples, to the intent we should not lust after evil things, as they also lusted.

The wandering in the wilderness and warfare in the Promised Land are not simply historical incidents, but they're to be practical illustrations for our personal application. We're to learn lessons from them—one of which is that, even though we are set free, even though we are at liberty, lust will trip us up. The reference is to Numbers 11, where we read that, tiring of manna, the Israelites lusted after meat. Isn't that what lust really is—not being satisfied with what God has given us, wanting something or someone different?

"Oh, sure, manna is supernatural. Sure, it's miraculous—but we want meat to eat," they said.

So God said to Moses, "Give them meat."

"How are we going to do that?" asked Moses. "Do You want me to kill the cattle that we are bringing into the Promised Land—or do You want me to fish the Red Sea?"

Moses made a mistake I often make. He looked at his options and said, "Okay, Lord, which of these two do You want?" He failed to understand that the Lord had an alternative he could never have imagined. God sent so many quail their way that His people ate until they could eat no more. The psalmist sheds further light on this when he says, "God gave them their request, but He sent leanness to their soul" (see Psalm 106:14, 15). That's the way lust is. Never satisfied, it brings leanness to the soul, weakness to the body, emptiness to the spirit.

1 Corinthians 10:7
Neither be ye idolaters, as were some of them; as it is written, The people sat down to eat and drink, and rose up to play.

The reference here is to Exodus 32. Tired of waiting for Moses to return from Mount Sinai, the people pressed Aaron to fashion a golden calf from their jewelry—not to compete against Jehovah, but to be a visible, tangible representation of Him. Many cultures at that time considered the cow to be representative of deity.

Why? The cow is a gentle yet powerful animal that provides milk for its young. But here's the problem with idolatry: If I allow anything or anyone to represent God to me, it will, at best, be only a partial representation of the full nature and character of the Father. You see, if I look at God as only being a cow in the sense of gently providing for His young, I need not fear if I act immorally in His sight.

Yes, God is gentle. Yes He provides graciously—but He is also lionlike in His holiness and purity. Therefore, I err greatly when I ignore this aspect of His nature.

You may not have a Buddha on your mantel or a shrine in your home—but watch out that you don't allow a person, author, ministry, or book to represent God to you. That's idolatry.

1 Corinthians 10:8
Neither let us commit fornication, as some of them committed, and fell in one day three and twenty thousand.

Referring to the Numbers 25 account wherein, after committing fornication with the women of Moab, twenty-three thousand died in one day and one thousand more shortly thereafter, Paul says, "In the glorious life of liberty which you enjoy, make sure your freedom doesn't lead to immorality."

"I can watch that. I can go there," we say of the questionable movie or activity—unaware that immorality kills. It kills our marriages and our families, our witness and our joy.

1 Corinthians 10:9
Neither let us tempt Christ, as some of them also tempted, and were destroyed of serpents.

"Why did you bring us out here in the wilderness to die?" the Israelites cried to Moses. "We had it made back in Egypt—where there were onions and melons and leeks."

Even if they did have onions and melons and leeks—an assumption many historians question in light of the fact that such crops were cultivated only in Israel and unknown in Egypt at that time—the cry of the children of Israel is so much like ours when we long for the old gang, the wild parties, the fun times, and fail to remember the loneliness, the emptiness, the guilt; when we long for the melons, onions, and leeks, but fail to remember the laboring, the beatings, the slavery of Egypt.

Don't tempt Christ by saying, "I miss the old days. My job is a drag. Why am I stuck with him?"—for when I complain about my situation, I am directly complaining about Christ, the One who allowed me to be in the situation in the first place.

1 Corinthians 10:10
Neither murmur ye, as some of them also murmured, and were destroyed of the destroyer.

After being covered by the cloud and provided for by the goodness and graciousness of the Father, as the Israelites were poised to enter the Land of Promise, Moses sent twelve spies to check out the land. And although they returned with reports of its beauty, although they returned with fruit as proof of its productivity, they also returned with reports of Anakim—giants they believed were sure to squish them like bugs should they dare to enter (Numbers 13:26–33).

But there were two spies who had a different perspective. "Don't rebel against the Lord," said Joshua and Caleb. "Don't fear the people of the land, for they are our bread" (see Numbers 14:9). I love that! Caleb said, "These giants are bread for us. We'll eat them up. And as a result, we'll actually be stronger for battle."

Forty years later, it was to an eighty-five-year-old Caleb that Joshua said, "We made it, Caleb. Out of the original three million, it's just you and me. Take any territory you want. It's time to retire." But what does Caleb say?

> Now therefore give me this mountain, whereof the LORD spake in that day; for thou heardest in that day how the Anakims were there, and that the cities were great and fenced: if so be the LORD will be with me, then I shall be able to drive them out, as the LORD said.
> Joshua 14:12

"Don't give me a beach cabin, give me the mountain where giants live," said Caleb. "Why? Because I'm hungry for some bread."

When you pray the Lord's prayer, "Give us this day our daily bread," think Anakim. You see, we complain and murmur, "Why is this trial happening? Why that? Why not the other?" when in reality, the very situations or people about which we murmur are those through which God wants to strengthen us. That which seems so big and so intimidating are Anakim—and it is the wise man or woman who, like Caleb, says "You've let them cross my path, Lord, therefore they must be there to make me stronger."

Can you imagine how different our homes would be if we really believed that the trials that come our way and the giants that loom before us are actually beneficial to us if we would eat them up in faith? "More bills?" we'd say, "Great! Keep them coming. Another rejection notice? All right!"

Most will die murmuring in the wilderness. "If God loves me, why doesn't He . . . ?" or "How come this giant is marching toward me?" But there will be those—and I pray I might be one and you might be the other—who will say, "Giants? I smell bread. Pass the butter!"

1 Corinthians 10:11
Now all these things happened unto them for ensamples: and they are written for our admonition, upon whom the ends of the world are come.

When you pore over the Scriptures, realize the Father provided powerful, pointed, and sometimes even shocking examples to teach us important lessons. "Don't miss them," says Paul. Read your Bible looking for the lessons, for the examples that you might be made wiser. The old adage is true indeed: Experience is the best teacher. It doesn't, however, have to be our experience. Do you realize how good the Lord is to let His people learn those lessons so *we* could gain understanding?

"But what about them?" you ask. "Is it right that they had to suffer and even die so we could be made the wiser?" God is fair. Being an example to us may have been the fulfillment of their highest ministry. And it is possible that they will be hugely important in eternity because they fulfilled their appointed purpose in providing lessons for believers like us to study for centuries.

1 Corinthians 10:12
Wherefore let him that thinketh he standeth take heed lest he fall.

After miraculously delivering them from bondage in Egypt, God's intent was to lead His people directly to the Promised Land. According to verses 6–12, however, lust, idolatry, immorality, and murmuring kept all but Joshua and Caleb from ever reaching the land He had for them.

So, too, the Lord has graciously delivered us from the bondage of sin. It is His intent that we live a Spirit-filled, fruitful life here on earth. But the same sins that barred the Israelites from the

Promised Land will prevent us from living the abundant life He has for us.

1 Corinthians 10:13
There hath no temptation taken you but such as is common to man: but God is faithful, who will not suffer you to be tempted above that ye are able; but will with the temptation also make a way to escape, that ye may be able to bear it.

After twelve verses of caution, Paul gives this glorious word of comfort.

For topical study of I Corinthians 10:13 entitled "Temptation," turn to page 1058.

1 Corinthians 10:14
Wherefore, my dearly beloved, flee from idolatry.

Flee from any person, any activity, any hobby, or idea that gets in the way of your relationship with the Lord.

1 Corinthians 10:15
I speak as to wise men; judge ye what I say.

Paul's argument is not one of legalism, but of wisdom.

1 Corinthians 10:16
The cup of blessing which we bless, is it not the communion of the blood of Christ? The bread which we break, is it not the communion of the body of Christ?

Following his answer regarding sacrifices to idols, Paul changes the subject from physical meat to spiritual meat—the Lord's Supper. The Greek word translated "communion" is *koinonia,* or "oneness."

1 Corinthians 10:17
For we being many are one bread, and one body: for we are all partakers of that one bread.

The culture to which Paul was speaking understood something we don't. That is, they looked at sharing a meal as being one of the most intimate expressions possible between two people or a group of people. Why? Before the days of silverware, people would eat reclined around a low table, sharing pieces of bread from a common loaf they dipped into a common dish filled with a stewlike sauce. Therefore, because they were

eating of the same bread and meat, they believed they were uniquely bonded through the common nutrients they were sharing.

As Christians, when we come to the Lord's table to eat of the same loaf and drink of the same vine, there's a oneness, a *koinonia* between us as well as a oneness between us and Jesus.

1 Corinthians 10:18
Behold Israel after the flesh: are not they which eat of the sacrifices partakers of the altar?

Israel understood the *koinonia* of Communion, for when the Jews offered their peace offerings to the Lord in the tabernacle, and later in the temple, part of the meat sacrificed would rise to the Lord in smoke. They were able to eat of the remainder. Thus, through the peace offering, they were able to commune with God as they shared meat together.

1 Corinthians 10:19, 20
What say I then? that the idol is any thing, or that which is offered in sacrifice to idols is any thing? But I say, that the things which the Gentiles sacrifice, they sacrifice to devils, and not to God: and I would not that ye should have fellowship with devils.

Deuteronomy 32:17 is one of many Old Testament Scriptures that indicate that when the people of Israel offered sacrifices to idols, they actually offered them to demons. An idol in and of itself is nothing. But demonic entities can, indeed, be connected to idols.

1 Corinthians 10:21
Ye cannot drink the cup of the Lord, and the cup of devils: ye cannot be partakers of the Lord's table, and of the table of devils.

In chapter 8, Paul said it was perfectly acceptable to eat meat that had been offered to idols. Here, he's saying one can't eat at both the Lord's table and the table of the demons. Is he contradicting himself? No. You see, it's not the meat, but the meeting that is the problem, for while it was permissible to buy meat in the shambles, it was not permissible to take part in idol worship in the temples.

What does this mean for us today? It means that, although I have liberty to go into certain bars or social scenes to have a Pepsi, if that place has been dedicated to devilish activity, I shouldn't be there. I can't hang out with the demons on Saturday night and come to church Sunday expecting things to be hunky-dory. It just doesn't work that way.

1 Corinthians 10:22
Do we provoke the Lord to jealousy? are we stronger than he?

If I hang around places where the atmosphere is corrupt, I push the Lord to jealousy. Why is He jealous? When you or I get jealous, it's because we feel threatened. The Lord's jealousy, however, is entirely different. He's not jealous of other gods. He's jealous for you and me.

If you saw someone's face on the screen of America's Most Wanted whom you recognized as someone who had asked one of the women of your fellowship out to dinner, you would say, "I saw this guy on TV. He's a mass murderer. Stay away from him."
If she said, "Oh, you're just jealous," it would be because she failed to understand that you were not jealous of him, but jealous for her.

So, too, the Lord is not jealous of pipsqueak demonic entities. They're not a threat to Him. But He's jealous for us. He doesn't want to see us destroyed. Therefore, He'll do whatever is necessary to bring us back to where we need to be.

1 Corinthians 10:23
All things are lawful for me, but all things are not expedient: all things are lawful for me, but all things edify not.

It's not a matter of, "Can I go there; can I do this?" *Everything* is lawful. The question is: Do you want to be hanging out with demons? Do you want to provoke the Lord to jealousy?

For topical study of 1 Corinthians 10:23 entitled "Give Me Liberty!" turn to page 1061.

1 Corinthians 10:24
Let no man seek his own, but every man another's wealth.

You may have the freedom to go to a certain place or to take part in a given activity. Again, the question is: What will your participation do to your brother? Even if it doesn't affect you, will people who see you be made the poorer for it? Will their faith be compromised if they follow in your footsteps?

1 Corinthians 10:25–28 (a)
Whatsoever is sold in the shambles, that eat, asking no question for conscience sake: For the earth is the Lord's, and the fulness

thereof. **If any of them that believe not bid you to a feast, and ye be disposed to go; whatsoever is set before you, eat, asking no question for conscience sake. But . . .**

"Whether purchased in the shambles or eaten in one's home, meat offered to idols is not a problem because—along with the whole earth—it is the Lord's," Paul declares. However, there is an exception. . . .

1 Corinthians 10:28 (b)
. . . if any man say unto you, This is offered in sacrifice unto idols, eat not for his sake that shewed it, and for conscience sake . . .

If someone makes a point of telling you the meat before you had been sacrificed to idols, he does so for a reason. Therefore, don't partake lest he be made to stumble.

1 Corinthians 10:28 (c)
. . . for the earth is the Lord's, and the fulness thereof.

Some commentators suggest the repetition of verse 26 is a mistake made by those who copied this letter. I don't think so. In light of the passage preceding it, I believe Paul is underscoring this understanding to say, "If eating a steak would make your brother stumble, there's an entire earth full of food you can choose to replace it."

This is an excellent word for our kids. "There's nothing to do but that," they say of questionable activities. "There's nowhere to go but there," they complain.

"Wait a minute," we as parents can say. "The whole earth is the Lord's. Surely there are other things to do and other places to go where you won't have to compromise your walk with Him."

1 Corinthians 10:29, 30
Conscience, I say, not thine own, but of the other: for why is my liberty judged of another man's conscience? For if I by grace be a partaker, why am I evil spoken of for that for which I give thanks?

Paul voices the argument of the person who says, "I can thank the Lord for this piece of meat, so why should I pass it up?" He then answers it in the following verse. . . .

1 Corinthians 10:31–33
Whether therefore ye eat, or drink, or whatsoever ye do, do all to the glory of God. Give none offence, neither to the Jews, nor to the Gentiles, nor to the church of God: Even as I please all men in all things, not seeking

mine own profit, but the profit of many, that they may be saved.

The underlying reason for giving up liberty is an awareness of how it affects the salvation or walk of another. As he brings to a close this important question of Christian liberty, Paul gives three questions to ask ourselves regarding any activity. . . .

- Can I thank the Lord in it? (verse 30)
- Will God be glorified through it? (verse 31)
- Will someone be tripped up by it? (verse 32).

Like a weather vane that changes direction, depending upon which way the wind is blowing, the wise man will adjust his activities to the way the wind of the Spirit is moving.

TEMPTATION
A Topical Study of
1 Corinthians 10:13

“**L**et him who thinks he stands take heed lest he fall,” Paul said to the Corinthian Christians. Then, as he so often does, following this word of caution, Paul issues a word of comfort.

- “Take heed,” he says in verse 12.
- “Take hope,” he says in verse 13 . . .

An Enlightening Premise

There hath no temptation taken you but such as is common to man . . .
1 Corinthians 10:13 (a)

So often, people say, “I'm embarrassed to share that vulnerability, temptation, or problem because no one else goes through that, no one else thinks thoughts like that, no one else struggles with that.” Not so. You'd be shocked if you knew the temptations of the people sitting right next to you.

Temptation in and of itself is not sin. And it's common to *everyone*.

Not only is temptation common to all men, but, more importantly, it is common to the Son of Man, Jesus Christ.

For we have not an high priest which cannot be touched with the feeling of our infirmities; but was in all points tempted like as we are, yet without sin.
Hebrews 4:15

Jesus was tempted in *all* points. No matter what the sin, Jesus does not look with disgust at the person struggling with it and say, “How could you?” He looks at him with compassion and says, “I know what you're going through.”

Wherefore in all things it behoved him to be made like unto his brethren, that he might be a merciful and faithful high priest in things pertaining to God, to make reconciliation for the sins of the people. For in that he himself hath suffered being tempted, he is able to succour them that are tempted.

Hebrews 2:17, 18

An Encouraging Promise

. . . but God is faithful, who will not suffer you to be tempted above that ye are able; but will with the temptation also make a way to escape, that ye may be able to bear it.   1 Corinthians 10:13 (b)

You might be fickle. I know I am frail. But God is faithful, and He will not allow the temptation I face to become too intense, but He will make a way of escape every time. Sometimes I close my eyes and say, "I don't see it,"—but in reality, a way of escape is always there for you and me if we'll choose to see it.

"That's great as far as it relates to theology," you say. "But how does it work out practically? How does it work out in my situation where I'm vulnerable to murmuring about my job, lusting after that Lexus, or prone to immorality?"

Listen, gang, whenever you want to know how some aspect of the Word works out, look to the Word made flesh, Jesus Christ, and you'll see it lived out practically. . . .

As He came out of the waters of baptism, Jesus heard a voice from heaven, saying, "This is My beloved Son in whom I am well pleased" (Matthew 3:17). Immediately after that, Scripture tells us He was driven into the wilderness where He would be tempted by Satan in a profound and significant way.

Those who study such things tell us that the return of the appetite after a fast for a great period of time is the body's way of saying it's on the threshold of death. Therefore, the fact that Jesus was hungry after fasting forty days indicates He was physiologically at the point of death. It was at this point that Satan came to Him, saying, "If thou be the Son of God . . ." In other words, "Didn't Your Father just tell You that You were His beloved Son in whom He was well pleased? If that's so, why are You dying of starvation? Why not command these stones to be made into bread?" he hissed, tempting Jesus to doubt His Father's provision (Matthew 4:3).

Satan will whisper that same temptation into your ear or mine. "Why aren't you satisfied materially, physically, relationally, or vocationally?" he'll say. "I thought you were God's child. I thought you were born again. Why, then, are you still hungry?"

What did Jesus do? Quoting Deuteronomy 8:3, He said, "It is written that man shall not live by bread alone, but by every word that proceeds out of the mouth of God." I believe it was audibly and forcefully that Jesus said, "It is written, Satan, that man is not satiated by material bread, but by the Word of God."

Then the devil took Him into Jerusalem, set Him on the pinnacle of the temple, and tempted Jesus to doubt His Father's protection. "If you are the Son of God," he said, "cast yourself down. After all, Psalm 91 says He shall give His angels charge over thee, and they shall bear thee up lest thou dash thy foot against a stone" (see Matthew 4:6). In other words, Satan said, "Jump. Take a leap of faith. Are You afraid Your Father won't protect You? Jump—and see how the Father comes through for You."

Satan can quote Scripture—but he purposely left out a very important phrase, for Psalm 91:11 actually says, "He shall give His angels charge over thee, *to keep thee in all thy ways*"—not to do our thing, but to walk in God's way.

So, too, Satan will come to you and me, saying, "'Jump! Start the business. Take a leap of faith. Name it and claim it. Doesn't the Father care about you? Surely, He won't let you hit bottom. Just jump into that relationship. He hasn't directed it—but He won't let you crash, will He?"

How did Jesus answer Satan's temptation to doubt the Father's protection? Quoting Deuteronomy 6:16, He said, "Thou shalt not tempt the Lord thy God." Again, I believe it was audibly and forcefully that Jesus said, "I will not test My Father. If He wants Me to jump, He'll set Me up and tell Me when."

Jesus balanced Psalm 91 with Deuteronomy 6, comparing Scripture with Scripture. All too often, people crash in the name of faith because, on the basis of a single verse, they jump off, hit bottom, and wonder why. That is why it is so essential to be a student of the entire Word—chapter by chapter, verse by verse, steadily and consistently receiving the full counsel of God.

Finally, the devil took Jesus to a high mountain, showed Him all the kingdoms of the world, and tempted Him to doubt His Father's promise by saying, "All of this will be Yours if You will fall down and worship me" (see Matthew 4:9).

Truly, the world was Satan's to give. The title deed to planet earth was his. Adam and Eve had handed it to him when they chose to listen to him instead of God in the Garden of Eden.

"It is written," Jesus said, again quoting from Deuteronomy 6:13, "thou shalt fear the Lord thy God and Him only shalt thou serve." And again, I believe it was audibly and forcefully that Jesus said, "I will worship My Father only, singularly, exclusively."

Concerning any temptation we face, what is the way of escape?

First, we are to stay *in* the Word. To overcome temptation, lust, fornication, murmuring—and everything else that can trip you up—stay in the Word. I believe the reason Jesus quoted from Deuteronomy 6—8 is because it was that passage upon which He was meditating at the moment Satan came to tempt Him. Stay in the Word, gang. It is the Sword of the Spirit with which you can do battle with the Enemy most effectively.

Second, we are to speak out the Word. In His wilderness temptation, Jesus spoke audibly. Satan cannot read your mind. He cannot look into your heart. Therefore, he is beat back by what we *say*.

> . . . *for he hath said, I will never leave thee, nor forsake thee. So that we may boldly say, The Lord is my helper, and I will not fear what man shall do unto me.*   Hebrews 13:5 (b), 6

"He hath said . . . that we may say," the writer of Hebrews declared. It's not, "He hath said that we may think," or, "He hath said that we may know," or even, "He hath said that we may pray," but, "He hath said that we may *say.*" Therefore, I suggest that speaking the Word at the moment of temptation changes the entire situation. Since the words "It is written" are like the sound of fingernails on a blackboard to Satan, I challenge you to speak them the next time you're tempted. Whatever the challenge might be, speak the Word audibly and watch how it changes the atmosphere radically.

Finally, we are to submit *to* the Word. Both Satan and Jesus knew the Scriptures. Both spoke the Scriptures. But only Jesus *submitted* to the Scriptures. Big difference. Jesus wasn't using the Word like a magic charm or incantation to cause Satan to flee. Rather, He was committing Himself to obey it completely. Jesus did what the Word said, and *that* is where the power is.

For example, maybe you find yourself wanting to gossip about your boss or murmur against your wife. But, knowing the Word says to bless those who persecute and despitefully use you, you choose instead to pray for them. That is what it means to be submitted to the Word. And that is what renders Satan powerless.

Staying in the Word, speaking out the Word, submitting to the Word—if we do these things as Jesus modeled them for us, there will be a wide-open door through which we can escape temptation very easily. Try it. You'll see.

"GIVE ME LIBERTY!"
A Topical Study of
1 Corinthians 10:23

"I'm not really interested in Christianity," some people tell me. "I'm not interested in being born again."

"Why?" I ask.

"Because I'm not into all of the do's and don'ts, the rules and regulations, the restrictions and the limitations you church people are under. I want my liberty," they'll say.

And that's when I really get excited. "Wonderful!" I say, "because liberty is Jesus' specialty."

The world is mixed up. Our culture is a mess. People are mistaken about life, about liberty, about freedom. They don't understand that we become enslaved by the very sins we commit in the name of freedom. That's why Jesus came—to set us free to live life the way it was meant to be lived.

As believers, we are the freest of all people, for what other religion, philosophy, or ethic dares to say, "All things are lawful"?

"Then what is the law for?" you say. "Why should we even study the Old Testament at all?"

Following are three aspects of the law that I believe will help us walk in liberty. . . .

The Purpose of the Law

Wherefore the law was our schoolmaster to bring us unto Christ, that we might be justified by faith. But after that faith is come, we are no longer under a schoolmaster.   Galatians 3:24, 25

"Here is the purpose of the law," Paul says. "It is to be a schoolmaster to show us we are sinners."

People basically feel they're pretty good. That's why they write books entitled, *I'm OK, You're OK.* It's not until they see God's standards of holiness and righteousness that they change the title from *I'm OK, You're OK* to *God's OK, and We're Not.*

When I play basketball with five-year-old Benjamin, I'm awesome. I get over half the rebounds; I make over half my lay-ups. When I play against seventeen-year-old Peter-John, however, suddenly I'm not quite as good—and getting worse all the time! But if I were to play Michael Jordan, it would be downright ugly.

You see, if my standard is Benny, I'm pretty good. If my standard is Michael, I'm a basketball basket case. That's why the law was given. "I'm pretty good," people say as they compare themselves to the guy next door. But when the Lord shows us *His* standard of holiness and righteousness, we suddenly realize we're in big trouble.

Once we realize this, once we see clearly our need for salvation, we become dead to the very rules and regulations that drove us to Jesus initially. I know this is so because in Romans 6—8—three of the most important chapters in all of Scripture—Paul tells us that when Jesus died on the Cross, we who are believers died with Him positionally.

Wherefore, my brethren, ye also are become dead to the law by the body of Christ; that ye should be married to another, even to him who is raised from the dead, that we should bring forth fruit unto God.   Romans 7:4

Suppose after this service is over, feeling a bit hungry, I go to Ron's Market, stand at the counter with Twinkies in hand, and reach into my pocket, only to find I have no money. So I reach for my pistol, instead, and say, "Give me the Twinkies."

Looking rather shocked, Ron hands me the Twinkies—and I run out of the store, little knowing that Ron has pushed a button under his cash register that calls the County Sheriff. Arriving on the scene, they yell at me to stop. Instead, I fire a shot and hit one in the shoulder. Down he goes. But before I can get another shot off, the Deputy shoots me, and I fall down dead.

Now, even though I broke numerous laws—armed robbery, resisting arrest, assault with a deadly weapon—I wouldn't go to trial. Why? Not because the law changed, but because I'm dead. Dead men don't go to trial.

That's the profound truth of Romans 7. The law is still there, and we've violated every single one of its requirements. But because we died with Christ, we'll never go to trial. Instead, we'll remain at liberty.

The Place for the Law

The purpose of the law is to show us we're sinners. Yet even for unbelievers, the law has a place.

But we know that the law is good, if a man use it lawfully; knowing this, that the law is not made for a righteous man, but for the lawless and disobedient, for the ungodly and for sinners, for unholy and profane, for murderers of fathers and murderers of mothers, for manslayers, for whoremongers, for them that defile themselves with mankind, for menstealers, for liars, for perjured persons, and if there be any other thing that is contrary to sound doctrine . . .
1 Timothy 1:8–10

The Lord created man to live in liberty. Yet due to the sin that permeates our society, the law is necessary to protect mankind from perversion that would otherwise run rampant.

Perspective from the Law

As believers, we are dead to the demands of the law. Yet it is our delight and privilege to discover the principles, the reasons the law was given—for in them we gain perspective regarding the nature of our Father and the way He would have us navigate life successfully.

We must gain perspective from the law because if we violate the principles embedded within it, there will be repercussions. Because of the finished work of Calvary, I am forgiven of past, present, and future sins in their entirety. Therefore, the repercussions don't come from the Father but from my own sin.

Thine own wickedness shall correct thee, and thy backslidings shall reprove thee: know therefore and see that it is an evil thing and bitter, that thou hast forsaken the LORD thy God, and that my fear is not in thee, saith the Lord GOD of hosts.   Jeremiah 2:19

"It's not Me chasing you down," God says. "It is your own sin that reproves you."

Tell this to your sons and daughters. Remind the new believer that God is not saying, "I'm going to track you down and do you in because you've been bad." No, all things are lawful unto you. But because all things are not expedient, or profitable; because not all things edify, or build up, certain attitudes in and of themselves will tear you down, will do you in, will cause pain and sorrow.

And the land be subdued before the LORD: then afterward ye shall return, and be guiltless before the LORD, and before Israel; and this land shall be your possession before the LORD. But if ye will not do so, behold, ye have sinned against the LORD: and be sure your sin will find you out.   Numbers 32:22, 23

It is our sin, not God, that finds us out. It is our sin that tracks us down.

But doesn't the Father chasten His children? Yes. Hebrews 12 says there will indeed be chastening and correction. The parable of Luke 15 gives us insight concerning how this takes place. . . .

"Give me my inheritance, Dad. I want my freedom. I want my liberty. I want to go into the city," said the son.

"Okay," said his father, "if that's what you want."

But as, no doubt, the father knew he would, the son spent his money foolishly. When famine struck, he ended up eating pig slop with the pigs. "What am I doing here?" he finally asked himself. "I'll go back to my father and beg him to allow me to be a slave in his house."

When his father saw him coming from a long way off, he ran out to meet him—not to point a finger at him, but to wrap his arms around him.

That's how the Father chastens.

You see, when God chastens us, He simply allows those things we do that are wrong to bring about their own inevitable repercussions. In the story of the prodigal, the father didn't say, "Uh-oh, my son's headed for problems. I better send him an extra twenty dollars to see him through, or drive to the city and find out what he's up to." No, the father simply sat tight with a loving heart and waited patiently until the backsliding, the stupidity, the stubbornness of the son brought about their own inevitable repercussions.

Yes, all things are lawful for me—but not all things are profitable for me. So what must I do? I must celebrate my liberty. I must study the Word regularly—not as one who is under rules, regulations, and restrictions—but as one who understands that through the Old Testament laws and stories, we learn to navigate life successfully so that we won't have to wander needlessly into the pigpens of the big city.

Precious people, may we be those who understand that because of the Cross of Calvary, we are truly free. And may we be those who immerse ourselves in the Word in order that we might walk wisely in our liberty.

11

1 Corinthians 11:1
Be ye followers of me, even as I also am of Christ.

If chapters 10 and 11 were divided most logically, this verse would be at the end of chapter 10. After ending his discussion of Christian liberty, Paul simply says, "If you want to know what to do—just follow me." Paul's is a statement I pray we can make increasingly our own when our kids are confused, our neighbors are questioning, or newer Christians are wondering about what they should do. I'm so impressed with the work the Lord did in our brother Paul, work that enabled him to say to an entire city, "Do what I do, and you'll do well."

1 Corinthians 11:2 (a)
Now . . .

In chapter 7, Paul answered the Corinthians' questions about marriage. In chapters 8—10, he addressed their questions concerning liberty. Here in chapter 11, he'll discuss church order with regard to women (verses 2–16) and Communion (verses 17–24).

1 Corinthians 11:2 (b)
. . . I praise you, brethren, that ye remember me in all things, and keep the ordinances, as I delivered them to you.

Paul commended the church at Corinth for the fact that they were observing the ordinances he had taught them when he was with them five years earlier.

1 Corinthians 11:3 (a)
But . . .

After commending them, however, Paul goes on to tell the Corinthians that some adjustments were necessary. . . .

1 Corinthians 11:3 (b)
. . . I would have you know, that the head of every man is Christ; and the head of the woman is the man . . .

The place of women in the church is not a question of superiority or inferiority, but is based upon humility and liberty. How do I know? Read on.

1 Corinthians 11:3 (c)
. . . and the head of Christ is God.

Jesus willingly, voluntarily, gladly submitted to the authority of the Father. Does this mean He was inferior to the Father? No. Philippians 2 makes it clear that He *chose* to humble Himself. So, too, the woman who chooses to submit to the authority of her husband does so not out of inferiority, but of humility.

1 Corinthians 11:4
Every man praying or prophesying, having his head covered, dishonoureth his head.

To this day, Jewish rabbis teach that, because Moses covered his face after he met with God on Mount Sinai (Exodus 34:33), the wearing of a hat, yarmulke, or prayer shawl is a sign of humility before the Lord. In 2 Corinthians 3, however, Paul says it was to hide the fact that the reflection of God's glory was fading from his countenance that caused Moses to cover his face.

"You're free from this requirement," said Paul. "So come as you are."

1 Corinthians 11:5, 6
But every woman that prayeth or prophesieth with her head uncovered dishonoureth her head: for that is even all one as if she were shaven. For if the woman be not covered, let her also be shorn: but if it be a shame for a woman to be shorn or shaven, let her be covered.

There are those who say women should never share prophecy or pray in the assembly. Paul would disagree. A woman can pray and prophesy, and is encouraged to do so—but she is to have her head covered. Why? An understanding of the culture is helpful here, for in the Corinthian culture, women wore veils to differentiate themselves from the prostitutes whose heads were shaved as a sign of their service to Aphrodite. Thus, a woman who exercised her liberty in Christ by praying or prophesying with her head uncovered caused confusion in the congregation and dishonor to her husband.

1 Corinthians 11:7
For a man indeed ought not to cover his head, forasmuch as he is the image and glory of God: but the woman is the glory of the man.

The woman is the glory—or literally, the outshining, the reflection—of the man. Husband, if you think your wife is out to lunch or off the wall, if you're disappointed in her, tired of her, down on her, or mad at her—guess what. She is simply reflecting you.

1 Corinthians 11:8, 9
For the man is not of the woman; but the woman of the man. Neither was the man created for the woman; but the woman for the man.

Dear married sister, seeing yourself not as your husband's "compete-r," but as his "completer," is where you will find your greatest fulfillment.

1 Corinthians 11:10
For this cause ought the woman to have power on her head because of the angels.

In newer translations, the word "power" is correctly rendered "covering." In the Corinthian culture, covering one's head spoke of modesty. In addition, Paul says it is for the sake of the angels that women were to cover their heads. Why? Angels are hypersensitive about things being done in order. Why? They saw one-third of their company cast out of heaven after one of them said, "I want to do my own thing. I want to be like God" (see Isaiah 14:14). Therefore, the covering on the head of a woman who is praying or prophesying in the congregation is a sign to the angels that she is not out of order, but that she does so under the authority of her husband.

1 Corinthians 11:11, 12
Nevertheless neither is the man without the woman, neither the woman without the man, in the Lord. For as the woman is of the man, even so is the man also by the woman; but all things of God.

From the side of man, woman was made. From the woman, however, man is born. Both are of God. Both are vital to His body.

1 Corinthians 11:13–15
Judge in yourselves: is it comely that a woman pray unto God uncovered? Doth not even nature itself teach you, that, if a man have long hair, it is a shame unto him? But if a woman have long hair, it is a glory to her: for her hair is given her for a covering.

If a guy combs his hair by the hour, it's not necessarily a sin—it's just dumb. On the other hand, if a woman has long hair, it's a sign of her covering.

1 Corinthians 11:16
But if any man seem to be contentious, we have no such custom, neither the churches of God.

In other words, Paul is saying, "If this discussion concerning head covering causes problems or division, it's not worth becoming legalistic."

The key to good theology is to note how many times a particular subject is dealt with in Scripture. As opposed to subjects like the finished work of the Cross and the importance of love, this is the only time the subject of head covering is seen in all of Scripture, and thus should be given proportionate attention.

1 Corinthians 11:17 (a)
Now . . .

Having concluded his discussion of issues related to women in the church, Paul moves on to talk about Communion in the church.

1 Corinthians 11:17 (b)
. . . in this that I declare unto you I praise you not, that ye come together not for the better, but for the worse.

In verse 2, concerning the ordinances in general, Paul had said, "I praise you, brethren . . . ." Here in verse 17, concerning the Lord's Supper specifically, he says, "I praise you not . . . ."

1 Corinthians 11:18, 19
For first of all, when ye come together in the church, I hear that there be divisions among you; and I partly believe it. For there must be also heresies among you, that they which are approved may be made manifest among you.

The first problem Paul mentions with regard to Communion is the same problem he addressed at the very outset of his letter: division. Even in celebrating the Lord's Supper, the Corinthian church was splintered into factions.

1 Corinthians 11:20–22
When ye come together therefore into one place, this is not to eat the Lord's supper. For in eating every one taketh before other his own supper: and one is hungry, and another is drunken. What? have ye not houses to eat and to drink in? or despise ye the church of God, and shame them that have not? What shall I say to you? shall I praise you in this? I praise you not.

Catch the scene: Paul had spent eighteen months in the Corinthian community, teaching the Corinthian believers daily. But in the course of the five years he had been absent from them, something had happened. The agape feast—which Paul had established as a time when believers would share their meals in a common place and where they would partake of the Lord's Supper together—had become nothing more than a drunken party.

I find Paul's assessment extremely interesting, for in many—if not most—churches today, Communion is a very somber, sad experience. I suggest that the reason for this is due to the emphasis placed upon the process of Jesus' death rather than on the purpose for His death. Is this what Jesus intended?

I suggest Jesus' intent for us is not so much that we remember His pain, but that we are amazed at our gain—that because of the finished work of the Cross, we're miraculously, gloriously totally free from the power and penalty of sin.

1 Corinthians 11:23–26
For I have received of the Lord that which also I delivered unto you, That the Lord Jesus the same night in which he was betrayed took bread: And when he had given thanks, he brake it, and said, Take, eat: this is my body, which is broken for you: this do in remembrance of me. After the same manner also he took the cup, when he had supped, saying, This cup is the new testament in my blood: this do ye, as oft as ye drink it, in remembrance of me. For as often as ye eat this bread, and drink this cup, ye do shew the Lord's death till he come.

In order that we might remember Him, Jesus didn't ask for a monument to be erected or a holiday to be established. He asked that a meal be enjoyed.

- Spotting Zacchaeus in a tree, Jesus said, "Come down. I'm coming over to eat with you" (see Luke 19:5).
- To the disciples out on the Sea of Galilee, He said, "Come and dine" (see John 21:12).
- "He's a glutton," His enemies said of Him (see Matthew 11:19).
- "He eats with sinners," scoffed His critics (see Luke 7:34).

Get the picture? The Lord is into eating! That's why, describing the coming kingdom, He says through the prophet Isaiah, "Let your soul delight itself in fatness!" (Isaiah 55:2). Therefore, it should not be surprising to us that He would say, "To remember Me, break bread, drink the fruit of the vine, and share a meal together."

1 Corinthians 11:27–30
Wherefore whosoever shall eat this bread, and drink this cup of the Lord, unworthily, shall be guilty of the body and blood of the Lord. But let a man examine himself, and so let him eat of that bread, and drink of that cup. For he that eateth and drinketh unworthily, eateth and drinketh damnation to himself, not discerning the Lord's body. For this cause many are weak and sickly among you, and many sleep.

On the basis of this passage, many think they are unworthy to partake of Communion if they are struggling with a certain sin or wrestling with a particular temptation. Yet this reasoning would be equivalent to—

- a doctor saying to a sick person, "Get well, and then come and see me,"
- a loan officer saying to a poor person, "You need a loan? Get some money, and then I can help you"; or,
- a cook saying to someone who is hungry, "Starving? Gain some weight, and I'll give you a meal."

The Lord's table is the very place for the person struggling with sin, wrestling with temptation, or caught up in carnality, for it is there that he can say, "Lord, I desperately need You in my life. I eat of Your body and I drink of Your blood, knowing I am forgiven. Thank You, Lord. I celebrate what You did for me."

"Because you don't value the Lord's Supper," said Paul, "there are people in your midst who are weak, folks who are sick, some who have even died because they haven't understood the potency or the vitality inherent in Communion." Too often, Communion is nothing more than a meaningless tradition or ritual. Thus, many remain in a state of spiritual weakness because they don't give worth to or value the place of Communion.

Ours is the first generation in history that does not emphasize Communion. One cannot read the Book of Acts or church history without a very real awareness that the Lord's Supper was central to the life of the congregation. Today, however, some go months, even years without Communion because it's not important to them. And because of this failure to give it worth, people are dying physically, emotionally, and spiritually in ways they need not be, failing to discern the power of the broken body, the cleansing of the shed blood.

Hippopotami have been known to travel two thousand miles in search of a single meal. Hungry and dry, they have traveled virtually across the continent of Africa in search of food.

We go through dry times spiritually, yet we won't come to church to partake of Communion. We won't take twenty minutes to sit down with our family and say, "We need to eat of the Lord's body and drink of His blood together." We get weaker and skinnier and have less heft spiritually whenever we fail to make Communion an essential part of our spiritual life.

1 Corinthians 11:31–34
For if we would judge ourselves, we should not be judged. But when we are judged, we are chastened of the Lord, that we should not be condemned with the world. Wherefore, my brethren, when ye come together to eat, tarry one for another. And if any man hunger, let him eat at home; that ye come not together unto condemnation. And the rest will I set in order when I come.

Paul strongly admonishes the Corinthian church to approach the Lord's Supper in the manner he had taught them when he was in their midst five years previously—that they would neither feel condemned by it, ignore it, nor treat it so lightly that it became nothing more than a drunken party.

"This is what I want you to do in remembering Me," Jesus said. "This is how you honor Me. You need vitality—and it is at My table that I make it available to you most readily."

12

1 Corinthians 12:1 (a)
Now concerning spiritual gifts . . .

In italics, the word "gifts" does not appear in the original Greek manuscripts. Paul actually said, "Now concerning *pneumatikos*"—or "spirituals"—referring to the entire realm of the manifestations of the Spirit.

1 Corinthians 12:1 (b)
. . . brethren, I would not have you ignorant.

"I would not have you ignorant." Paul voices this same desire concerning Old Testament typology in 1 Corinthians 10, the Rapture in 1 Thessalonians 4, the tactics of Satan in 2 Corinthians 3, and the future of Israel in Romans 11. The areas about which Paul wanted believers to be knowledgeable are the very ones about which believers throughout history have had the most questions. Thus, his concern was inspired indeed.

1 Corinthians 12:2, 3 (a)
Ye know that ye were Gentiles, carried away unto these dumb idols, even as ye were led. Wherefore I give you to understand, that no man speaking by the Spirit of God calleth Jesus accursed . . .

A rumor circulating in Paul's day said, "If you pray in the Spirit, you can actually unknowingly curse Jesus." And such a rumor is heard to this day. Paul, however, makes it clear that it is impossible for a person praying in the Spirit to say Jesus is accursed.

1 Corinthians 12:3 (b)
. . . and that no man can say that Jesus is the Lord, but by the Holy Ghost.

Do you believe that Jesus is Lord, that He died for your sins, that He rose again, that He is God Incarnate? The ability to believe these things comes only one way—through the Holy Ghost who dwells within us. Therefore, if you can truly say Jesus is Lord, you can be assured that the Holy Spirit is residing in you and working through you.

1 Corinthians 12:4
Now there are diversities of gifts, but the same Spirit.

Here is where the word "gifts," or *charisma*, appears in the original text. I find it not coincidental that *charisma* is a form of the word *charis*, or "grace"—that which is undeserved and unearned.

1 Corinthians 12:5
And there are differences of administrations, but the same Lord.

Newer translations correctly render the word "administrations" as "ministries."

1 Corinthians 12:6
And there are diversities of operations, but it is the same God which worketh all in all.

The Greek word translated "operations" is *energema*, from which we get our word "energize."

- In verse 4, we see different gifts, but the same Spirit.
- In verse 5, we see different ministries, but the same Lord Jesus.
- In verse 6, we see different energies, but the same God.

- The gifts are linked to the Spirit.
- The ministries are linked to the Son.
- The operations are linked to the Father.

It is my personal conviction that these three verses unlock the mystery of chapter 12. You see, although the word of wisdom, tongues and interpretation, healings, miracles, and faith are often referred to as the gifts of the Spirit, I believe the gifts of the Spirit are technically found in only one place: Romans 12. That is the only time the word "gifts" is actually used. It is in Romans 12 that we see the gifts of prophecy, ministry, teach-

ing, exhortation, giving, ruling, and mercy. I believe every brother and sister has one of the primarily motivational gifts seen in Romans 12. The Lord then opens up a ministry for this gift.

The word "ministry" is used in Ephesians 4, wherein we see five ministries listed: apostle, prophet, evangelist, pastor, teacher.

"But I'm none of those things," you say.

Think with me. Suppose someone with the motivational gift of mercy says to the brother or sister who's going through all kinds of struggles in balancing their checkbook, paying their bills, and working out a budget, "Let me meet with you one day a month. I want to share with you what I have learned in this area." At that point the person with the gift of mercy would be fulfilling the role of pastor as he shepherds people to financial stability.

You see, the ministries are supernaturally natural. When an older lady helps a younger woman learn how to navigate marriage and childrearing based upon insights she's found in the Word, she is actually functioning as a teacher. And although she's not teaching predestination, pneumatology, or eschatology—she's employing the gift of teaching to the very same degree as one who stands behind a pulpit.

Those who exercise their Romans 12 gift (1 Corinthians 12:4) will find a ministry opened to them (1 Corinthians 12:5) either as an apostle—one sent out into some area or situation to share the reality of Jesus Christ; as a prophet—one who shares words of edification, exhortation, and comfort at precisely the right time in exactly the right way; as an evangelist—one who simply shares the Lord wherever he goes; as a pastor—one who comes alongside people to partner with them in their spiritual growth; or as a teacher—one who shares truth with others.

The ministry of the Spirit is supernaturally natural when we get away from the titles and organizations, and simply respond to the Lord's leading.

Gifts are given by the Spirit (Romans 12). Ministries are opened by the Son (Ephesians 4). Everything is energized by the Father (1 Corinthians 12). In addition to my motivational gift and opportunity for ministry, God wants to energize what I'm doing in a supernaturally natural way. This is what Paul will address in the remainder of the chapter before us.

He will talk about the discerning operations—the power to know—which includes the word of knowledge, the word of wisdom, and the discerning of spirits (verses 8, 9). He will talk about the dynamic operations—the power to do. This includes faith, miracles, and gifts of healing (verses 9, 10). And he will talk about the declaring operations—the power to speak. This includes prophecy, tongues and interpretation (verse 10).

1 Corinthians 12:7
But the manifestation of the Spirit is given to every man to profit withal.

The word "manifestation" means "to make known." The gifts, ministries, and operations are made known through our lives not so we can write them down in our diaries, but so we can bless others.

1 Corinthians 12:8 (a)
For to one is given by the Spirit the word of wisdom . . .

The word of wisdom doesn't come from one's ability to figure out a situation. It is supernaturally given to answer a question or solve a problem.

"Master," they said, bringing with them a woman caught in the act of adultery, "Moses declared she should be stoned. What say Ye?"
If Jesus said, "Stone her," He would no longer be thought of as a Friend of Sinners. On the other hand, if He said, "Let her go," He would be in violation of the very law He came to fulfill. So what did He say?
He spoke a word of wisdom when He said, "Let him who is without sin cast the first stone" (see John 8:7).

Even as it flowed in Jesus Christ, we see the word of wisdom flowing in His body of believers . . .

Should the new Gentile converts be circumcised? Many said, "Yes." But, concerned about this, Paul said, "We're going to Jerusalem and hash this out." And so they went. The early church fathers had a big meeting. They debated back and forth—when suddenly James stood up and shared with them a perspective that settled the dust and answered the question perfectly (Acts 15:13–22).

If you have the gift of ruling, or overseeing, pray that the Lord would give you the operation of the word of wisdom in order that you could express that which is right in the sight of the Lord, and that which others recognize as wisdom.

1 Corinthians 12:8 (b)
. . . to another the word of knowledge by the same Spirit.

Because He laid aside all of His power when He came to earth (Philippians 2:7, 8), Jesus was a Man just like you and me—but without sin. So when He moved in the arena of the miraculous and operated in the realm of the supernatural, it was not because He was Jesus. Rather, it was because He was walking with the Father and was empowered by the Spirit—just as we can be.

"Go call your husband," Jesus said to the woman at the well.
"I don't have a husband," she answered.
And I believe He smiled when He said, "You've said well you have no husband. You've had five husbands, and the one you're living with now is not your husband at all" (see John 4:17, 18).

Was this the result of undercover investigative work? Had the disciples been sent out to get the scoop on this lady? No. At that moment, inspired by the Spirit, Jesus knew what could not have been known apart from revelation. He spoke a word of knowledge. How we need this operation functioning in our homes and in the church today. . . .

"Why have you lied to the Holy Ghost, Ananias? You're deceiving yourself," said Peter (see Acts 5:3, 4).
How did Peter know Ananias was lying?
It was the word of knowledge.

These operations aren't ours to use whenever we wish, but only as the Holy Spirit wills—be that once every ten years, or ten times a day. I believe the word of knowledge most readily manifests itself in the teaching of the Word—whether through those who are teaching third graders in Sunday school or those who are teaching adults in Bible study. When you read through the Word and you hear yourself saying, "I can see how this really works," it's very likely that the word of knowledge is functioning in conjunction with your ministry of teaching.

1 Corinthians 12:9 (a)
To another faith by the same Spirit . . .

"Let no more fruit dwell on thee forever," Jesus said to the fig tree. The next day when His disciples walked by the tree and saw it dried up from the roots, they were amazed.
"Have faith in God," Jesus said (Mark 11:22). Such is the potency of faith.
Every believer has a measure of faith. If he didn't, he wouldn't be saved. There are those, however, who move in the supernatural arena of faith, where, because of an exercise of faith,

things happen that wouldn't happen otherwise. . . .

"In the name of Jesus Christ of Nazareth, rise up and walk," said Peter and John to the lame man. The people who watched this exercise of faith marveled.

"Why do you marvel at this?" Peter asked. "It is faith in His name that has made this man strong; the faith which is by Him hath given him this perfect soundness" (see Acts 3:16).

In other words, Peter said, "It's not our faith, our fasting, our praying, or our holiness. It's by Him. God gave us the faith at this moment to take this man by the hand and tell him in Jesus' name to stand."

The operation of faith is the ability to step out in response to the leading of the Spirit and do something you would never have done otherwise.

1 Corinthians 12:9 (b)
. . . to another the gifts of healing by the same Spirit.

The word "gifts" is plural. I do not believe that anyone has a singular gift of healing whereby he can line people up and heal them all. I do believe, however, that there are individual gifts of healing distributed through a person or through a group of people.

1 Corinthians 12:10 (a)
To another the working of miracles . . .

When Jesus talked about the miraculous—drinking poisons that would not hurt, handling deadly serpents that would not harm, speaking with new tongues, laying hands on the sick and seeing them recover—it's important to see that these wonderful, miraculous operations and expressions were all in connection with the Great Commission (Mark 16:15).

Therefore, I believe one of the best ways to see the miraculous happen to a greater degree is to be involved in radical evangelism. The miracles of Mark 16 are not intended for us to huddle together in the sanctuary so we can see a miracle. No, it's as we're going into the jungles, into the inner city, throughout the community sharing the Lord that He will confirm our message with miracles.

As you study the Book of Acts, you see the operation of miracles most closely linked with the office of evangelism because the operation of miracles is primarily for the unbeliever. Why? Because the believer's faith is not increased by seeing miracles. In fact, it's stunted. The Lord

dedicated an entire segment of history to prove this point. Read Exodus and Numbers, and you will see God continually performing signs and wonders for His people. The Red Sea parted before them. Manna came down from heaven to them. They were directed by a huge cloud each day and a pillar of fire every night. They were bitten by poisonous snakes and miraculously preserved. The earth opened up and swallowed the rebellious among them. They were a people who witnessed miracle after miracle daily. And yet what was the end of the story? They couldn't enter the Promised Land because of unbelief.

People think if they could just see a miracle or two, their faith would soar. Not so. Faith comes by hearing and hearing by the Word of God (Romans 10:17). For the believer, the way to grow in faith is not to see the miraculous, but to take in the Scriptures. It is for the *unbeliever* that God will confirm His Word with signs and wonders. That is why it's as we're involved in missions, in evangelism, in service to the unbeliever and the skeptic that the Lord will most often confirm His Word through the arena of the miraculous.

1 Corinthians 12:10 (b)
. . . to another prophecy . . .

The operation of prophecy is not to foretell the future, but to "forth-tell" God's heart. Prophecy consists of words of edification, exhortation, or comfort spoken at the very time they're most needed. Paul will deal with the operation of prophecy in conjunction with tongues and interpretation in chapter 14.

1 Corinthians 12:10 (c)
. . . to another discerning of spirits . . .

"You are the Christ, the Son of the living God," said Peter.

"Blessed art thou, Simon bar Jonas," Jesus answered. "Flesh and blood has not revealed this to you, but my Father in heaven" (see Matthew 16:17). But then, as recorded only a few verses later, in response to the denial of His Crucifixion, Jesus said to this same Peter, "Get behind me, Satan." At one moment, Jesus discerned the Spirit flowing through Peter. At another moment, He discerned the work of Satan.

Especially as we're involved in pastoring—caring about people, sharing with people, and helping people—we need to discern if what they're saying is coming from the Lord, the influence of demons, or simply the result of their own human wisdom.

"Listen to these men. They're speaking about the most High God," a girl said of Paul and the apostolic band. *Discerning she was under demonic influence, however, Paul demanded the demon leave her (see Acts 16:18).*

Yes, she was saying the right words, but Paul was given the discernment to sense a demonic spirit behind them.

1 Corinthians 12:10 (d)
. . . to another divers kinds of tongues; to another the interpretation of tongues.

Paul will discuss tongues and interpretation of tongues with the third declaring operation—that of prophecy—in chapter 14.

1 Corinthians 12:11
But all these worketh that one and the self-same Spirit, dividing to every man severally as he will.

If we move in the operation of the gifts of healing, if we speak prophetically, or if we see miracles flowing from our ministry, Paul is very careful to say it's because of God's sovereignty rather than according to anything we earn or deserve.

"Your money perish with you," said Peter to Simon the sorcerer when asked if he could purchase the gift of the Holy Spirit (see Acts 8:20).

The ministry and gifts of the Holy Spirit cannot be earned either through spirituality or through money. They're gifts that are given sovereignly.

"You rebels, must we fetch water from the rock?" Moses cried as he smote the rock.
"Wait a minute, Moses," said God as He barred him from the Promised Land. *"It is not you who fetch water, but I who give it" (see Numbers 20:10–12).*

Once we begin to say, "Look what *I'm* doing intellectually, monetarily, musically, or athletically"—once we start taking the credit, we bar ourselves from moving into the Promised Land of blessings the Lord would otherwise have for us.

1 Corinthians 12:12
For as the body is one, and hath many members, and all the members of that one body, being many, are one body: so also is Christ.

In chapter 1, Paul had rebuked the Corinthian believers for their carnal divisions. Here in chapter 12, he touches the same subject once again. Only this time he reminds them of a cardinal doctrine as he teaches them that they are the body of Christ. Although each of them had different ministries, operations, and gifts, they were still one entity, one body.

1 Corinthians 12:13
For by one Spirit are we all baptized into one body, whether we be Jews or Gentiles, whether we be bond or free; and have been all made to drink into one Spirit.

Those who use this verse as proof that all Christians are baptized in the Spirit fail to understand that there are many baptisms seen in Scripture. . . .

- John's baptism is the baptism of repentance (Luke 7:29).
- The baptism of Moses refers to those who followed him through the Red Sea (1 Corinthians 10:2).
- Jesus told His disciples they would be baptized with the Holy Ghost (Acts 1:5).
- Paul speaks of being baptized into Jesus Christ (Romans 6:3).

What baptism is being talked about here? It's the Spirit baptizing us into the body of Christ. Jesus baptizes us into the Holy Spirit (Matthew 3:11). And, as seen here, the Spirit baptizes us into one body.

1 Corinthians 12:14–18
For the body is not one member, but many. If the foot shall say, Because I am not the hand, I am not of the body; is it therefore not of the body? And if the ear shall say, Because I am not the eye, I am not of the body; is it therefore not of the body? If the whole body were an eye, where were the hearing? If the whole were hearing, where were the smelling? But now hath God set the members every one of them in the body, as it hath pleased him.

Because we're all part of the body, everyone has a function and a role to play. Because God has placed us where it pleases Him, it's not up to us to try to change our position, but to rest in the place God has us. . . .

If, growing tired of being at the bottom of the body, in a dark, unseen, smelly shoe, my big toe climbed up and planted himself on my kneecap, not only would I look weird, but it would definitely affect the way I walk.

So. too, although our fleshly tendency is to want to be seen, Paul tells us the Lord has planted each of us where we need to be and where we'll function most effectively.

1 Corinthians 12:19–22
And if they were all one member, where were the body? But now are they many members, yet but one body. And the eye cannot say unto the hand, I have no need of thee: nor again the head to the feet, I have no need of you. Nay, much more those members of the body, which seem to be more feeble, are necessary:

The seemingly feeblest members are indeed sometimes the most necessary members. . . .

An above-ground pool was donated to Applegate Christian Fellowship's mission for handicapped orphans in Mexico. But, because it arrived in what seemed to be a million pieces, try as they might, the Mission staff was unable to assemble it. It wasn't more than a few days later, however, that my brother, Jimmy, who runs the mission got a call from a man at Twin Peaks Bible College.
"I just feel like the Lord would have me come and spend some time at the mission," he said. "I can't do much. I'm not a Bible teacher. I'm not a children's worker. I'm not a cook. I'm not a gardener. But I just feel I should come."
"Come on down," said Jimmy. "By the way, what did you do before you were in Bible school?"
"I spent twenty years installing above-ground pools," he said.
Within four hours of his arrival, the kids were swimming.

Without exception, whatever you do, whatever gifts God has embedded in you, whatever the operations flowing through you, whatever the ministries opened to you—you are needed in the body.

1 Corinthians 12:23, 24
And those members of the body, which we think to be less honourable, upon these we bestow more abundant honour; and our uncomely parts have more abundant comeliness. For our comely parts have no need: but God hath tempered the body together, having given more abundant honour to that part which lacked:

Which parts of your body do you spend extra time concealing and camouflaging? The parts you want to hide. So, too, in the body of Christ, who gets the extra attention, the spotlight? The uncomely parts. We think just the opposite. We think the spiritual superstars are the ones who get the attention. In reality, however, when we get to heaven, there will be some real shocks. The people who were not seen, not known, not up in front; the people who were worshiping and praying, loving and sharing, cutting firewood or visiting rest homes will be honored in heaven. Conversely, those of us who have been "center stage" on earth will be in the back row somewhere in heaven.

1 Corinthians 12:25
That there should be no schism in the body; but that the members should have the same care one for another.

There is no hierarchy in the body of Christ.

1 Corinthians 12:26–28
And whether one member suffer, all the members suffer with it; or one member be honoured, all the members rejoice with it. Now ye are the body of Christ, and members in particular. And God hath set some in the church, first apostles, secondarily prophets, thirdly teachers, after that miracles, then gifts of healings, helps, governments, diversities of tongues.

If you have a headache, do your legs say, "That's tough. We're going hiking anyway"? No. If one part of your body hurts, your whole body rests. If you throw a touchdown pass and win the game, does your left arm get upset because your right arm threw the ball? No, your whole body celebrates. So, too, as believers, we both suffer and celebrate together because we're all members of the same body.

1 Corinthians 12:29, 30
Are all apostles? are all prophets? are all teachers? are all workers of miracles? Have all the gifts of healing? do all speak with tongues? do all interpret?

The answer to all these questions is obviously "No" because there's wonderful, needful diversity in the body.

1 Corinthians 12:31
But covet earnestly the best gifts: and yet shew I unto you a more excellent way.

As important as it is to covet earnestly the best gifts and to be all that we can be in the Lord, something is more essential still, to which Paul will devote the next chapter—perhaps the most beautiful in all of Scripture.

———————— ❧ ————————

13 Suppose, living centuries ago in Israel, you journey to Jerusalem in order to worship in the temple. . . .

Upon your arrival, you ask the whereabouts of the high priest and are told he's ministering in the holy place—the area in the temple containing the golden candlestick, table of showbread, and the ark of the covenant.

"How do you know he's in there?" you ask.

"Listen carefully," you're told.

As you do, you hear the unmistakable sound of bells ringing inside the holy place. The Book of Exodus tells us that golden bells hung from the hem of the high priest's robe. We know from Alfred Edersheim and other Bible scholars that these bells were made in such a way that they rang in harmony.

When we talk about our great High Priest, Jesus Christ, people sometimes ask how we know He's alive, how we know He's truly in heaven interceding on our behalf. We should be able to say to them, "Listen carefully, and you will hear the harmonious ringing of the bells as He works through His body, the church."

The golden bells in biblical typology are a picture of the manifestations, the gifts of the Spirit. As people see the working of the Holy Spirit through words of wisdom, knowledge, and prophecy; through gifts of healing, faith and miracles; through tongues and interpretation—as they begin to see the reality of the Spirit of Jesus sounding forth through His body, they will know that He is indeed alive.

You see, according to Exodus 39:25, between each of the bells on the high priest's robe was a pomegranate—a fruit uniquely related to the Promised Land. . . .

When the spies returned from the Promised Land, they came carrying grapes and pomegranates as a sign of the land's productivity (Numbers 13:23).

In the Song of Solomon, the pomegranate speaks of peace and certainty, beauty and romance (4:3; 6:7).

Joel refers to the pomegranate in connection with joy (Joel 1:12).

The New Testament equivalent is the fruit of the Spirit, which is love—defined as joy, peace, longsuffering, gentleness, goodness, faith, meekness, and self-control.

Without the pomegranate between the bells on the robe of the high priest, there would be nothing but clanging. This was the case in the church at Corinth. Although Paul says they possessed every gift of the Spirit, they lacked the fruit of the Spirit. This led to all kinds of noise, irritation, and confusion.

This is why, between his discussion of the manifestation of the gifts of the Spirit in chapters 12 and 14, here in chapter 13, Paul inserts a pomegranate—the fruit of love. . . .

1 Corinthians 13:1 (a)
Though I speak with the tongues of men and of angels . . .

The word "tongues" may refer to human dialects or to an angelic language not known on earth.

1 Corinthians 13:1 (b)
. . . and have not charity, I am become as sounding brass, or a tinkling cymbal.

Without love, whatever I say is just noise. The word "charity" appears here rather than the word "love" because the Greek word *agape* was translated *charitas* in the Latin Vulgate, the first translation of the original Greek manuscripts. John Wycliffe, the man responsible for translating the Latin Vulgate into English, used a similar-sounding English word for *charitas* when he used "charity"—a word that spoke of giving simply for the sake of giving. Unfortunately, in our day, charity has come to be associated with pity. So modern translators have rightly chosen the word "love" rather than the maligned "charity." Yet, even the word "love" is not without its problems.

I love my wife. I love my kids. I love Big Macs. I love walks in the park on summer evenings. We use the word "love" so freely that we diminish its meaning. The Greeks circumvented this problem by using four words for love. . . .

- *Storgi* means affection. Storgi is the kind of love one feels toward his cat or dog.
- *Eros* refers to sexual, physical love.
- *Phileo*, from which we get the name "Philadelphia," speaks of brotherly love. *Phileo* says, "If you're nice to me, I'll be nice to you."

It wasn't until the New Testament apostles introduced the concept of unconditional love that the Greeks added *agape* to their vocabulary. *Agape* is a love that gives simply for the sake of giving, never expecting anything in return. People who don't know the Lord can experience all of the other kinds of love. But for them, *agape* is impossible because it is found only in God. *Agape* is the love of which Paul speaks when he says, "If I don't have love, I'm just making noise even if I speak in tongues fluently."

In the year 1647, during England's Civil War, a deserter in Cromwell's army was captured and brought before him.

"When the curfew bell sounds tonight, you shall be executed," said the general.

But that night, the curfew bell was not heard. Upon investigation, it was discovered that, receiving news of her fianci's sentence, his betrothed made her way quickly to the camp and hid in the bell tower. As curfew neared, she positioned herself within the bell in such a way that when the rope was pulled, the clapper hit her body rather than the inside of the bell. Seeing the bruised and battered lady standing before him, Cromwell was so deeply touched by her love that the soldier's life was spared.

Jesus Christ climbed not a bell tower, but the hill of Calvary in order that you and I would be spared the execution we so rightfully deserve. Whether the word is charity, love, or *agape*, the love Jesus showed us, the love we are to extend to one another is spelled one way: S-a-c-r-i-f-i-c-e.

1 Corinthians 13:2
And though I have the gift of prophecy, and understand all mysteries, and all knowledge; and though I have all faith, so that I could remove mountains, and have not charity, I am nothing.

Jesus said faith only the size of a mustard seed could move mountains (Matthew 17:20). But Paul says even though one has *all* faith—the fullest possible expression of faith—if it is without love, it doesn't amount to a hill of beans.

Paul would tell the Galatians that faith works by love (Galatians 5:6). God can only entrust true faith to the one able to love, for the power of faith would be dangerous in the hands of one who doesn't love (Luke 9:54).

1 Corinthians 13:3
And though I bestow all my goods to feed the poor, and though I give my body to be burned, and have not charity, it profiteth me nothing.

Even if a person were so zealous that he burned out for Jesus, his zeal would mean nothing without love. Following Paul's admonition to

love in verses 1–3 is a definition of love in verses 4–13. . . .

1 Corinthians 13:4 (a)
Charity suffereth long . . .

"Lord, how often should I forgive someone who offends me? Seven times?" Peter asked, perhaps thinking Jesus would be impressed with his growth.

"You're to forgive seven times seventy," Jesus answered (see Matthew 18:22). In other words, "You're to keep forgiving until you lose track of how many times someone has offended you."

Love never says, "I've had enough." It suffers indefinitely.

1 Corinthians 13:4 (b)
. . . and is kind . . .

Love not only suffers long, but it is kind. I believe we would do well to examine well-meaning activism through the lens of *agape*. Is what we're doing in the name of righteousness kind? Love is long-suffering—yet while it's suffering, it doesn't become cynical or bitter. It remains kind.

1 Corinthians 13:4 (c)
. . . charity envieth not . . .

Love never asks why another is exalted or promoted.

1 Corinthians 13:4 (d)
. . . charity vaunteth not itself, is not puffed up.

Love doesn't try to prove itself. It doesn't say, "Watch how loving I can be." Rather, it works behind the scenes.

For topical study of 1 Corinthians 13:4 entitled "A Deeper Look," turn to page 1078.

1 Corinthians 13:5 (a)
Doth not behave itself unseemly . . .

Some people confuse weirdness with love. Some people say, "I'm going to demonstrate my love for Jesus with a megaphone and a sandwich board. Sure, people might think I'm weird, but it's because I'm so radical in my love for God."

Concerning Jesus, Isaiah prophesied and Matthew confirmed that He did not strive or cry in the streets (Isaiah 42:2; Matthew 12:19). In fact, so unrecognizable was Jesus that He had to be identified to the soldiers who came to arrest Him (Luke 22:48).

Sometimes people put pressure on us to cry in the streets, to take a stand. But I look at Jesus and see that He exuded such love, warmth, and integrity that people flocked to Him. Mark tells us the common people heard Him gladly (12:37). It was the religious folks who had problems with Him. I wonder if that hasn't been reversed far too often in our day—to the point where religious people understand us, but common people want nothing to do with us because they think we're bizarre. Because love doesn't behave unseemly, this ought not be.

1 Corinthians 13:5 (b)
. . . seeketh not her own . . .

Love doesn't demand its own way.

1 Corinthians 13:5 (c)
. . . is not easily provoked . . .

Although it is not italicized, the word "easily" does not appear in any of the Greek manuscripts. Thus, love is simply not provoked. *Phileo, eros, storgi* can become irritated, aggravated, provoked. But not *agape*.

1 Corinthians 13:5 (d)
. . . thinketh no evil.

Newer translations render this "is not suspicious." True love trusts. When I think I can't trust him, or that I've got to keep my eye on her, it's because I no longer believe that God is on the throne, able to deal with the situation. All things are naked and open before Him with whom we deal (Hebrews 4:13). In addition, God chastens and corrects those He loves (Hebrews 12:6). Therefore, *agape* love doesn't think evil of people because it has absolute trust in the faithfulness of the Father.

1 Corinthians 13:6 (a)
Rejoiceth not in iniquity . . .

True love does not rejoice when trouble or problems befall another—even if they're a result of his own stupidity or iniquity.

1 Corinthians 13:6 (b)
. . . but rejoiceth in the truth.

Some translators render "truth" as "good." In other words, love says to another, "You're lifted up? You're being honored? Great! I'm delighted for you!" Love rejoices when the other guy does well, when the other guy is blessed.

1 Corinthians 13:7
Beareth all things, believeth all things, hopeth all things, endureth all things.

If you are one who bears all things, believes all things, hopes all things, and endures all things, people will accuse you of being blind to certain situations. But they will be wrong. *Agape* love is not blind. Quite the opposite. Because love sees *more*, it's willing to see less.

What does love see? It sees the price that was paid on the Cross of Calvary for the person or situation that threatens to make us mad or bitter. The older I get, the more clearly I see the work of the Cross. I see the reality of the Holy Spirit's power to convict people. I see the promise of the Father—that in due season, if they choose not to listen to the Word and respond to the Spirit, their sin will track them down (Numbers 32:23).

Therefore, rather than feeling I have to solve every problem and deal with every situation, I can simply bear with, believe in, and hope the best for people because of the commitment Jesus made to them when He died for them.

How can we exhibit this kind of love? The only way is to let Jesus Christ live it through us, for He is the embodiment of these characteristics. We can't psyche ourselves into this, gang. This kind of love is nothing less than the fruit of the Spirit. But as I walk with the Lord, talk to the Lord, and learn about the Lord, His Spirit produces this character in me ever so slowly, but ever so surely.

"If you abide in Me," Jesus said, "you shall bring forth much fruit" (see John 15:5). What fruit? Love. He told us we're branches, and that He is the Vine. What do branches do? Just hang in there, close to the vine. Therefore, as I stay connected to the Vine by getting to know Him and enjoying Him, the fruit will come of its own.

Fruit comes when you continue doing just what you're doing now—spending time with Him, hanging in there week after week, month after month, year after year. Slowly, but surely, as you stay connected to Jesus, more and more of His *agape* love will seep through you. You watch; you wait; you'll see.

1 Corinthians 13:8
Charity never faileth: but whether there be prophecies, they shall fail; whether there be tongues, they shall cease; whether there be knowledge, it shall vanish away.

Prophecy, tongues, words of knowledge will one day all vanish. Why? In heaven there will be no need for prophecy—words of edification, exhortation, or comfort—because everyone will be perfectly comforted and edified in heaven and will no longer need to be exhorted. Unknown tongues will vanish because everything will be known in heaven. And words of knowledge will be swallowed up in the perfect knowledge we'll have when we see Jesus (verse 12).

1 Corinthians 13:9, 10
For we know in part, and we prophesy in part. But when that which is perfect is come, then that which is in part shall be done away.

Debate continues over the meaning of "that which is perfect." Some say "that which is perfect" refers to the Bible. They say the canonization of the New Testament negated the need for prophecy, words of knowledge, and words of wisdom, since everything man needed to know could be found in Scripture.

Yet, I find it interesting that this interpretation—so common in our time—was not suggested by a single commentator until shortly after 1906—the year of the Azusa Street Revival wherein an outpouring of the Holy Spirit took place that spread across the country and ultimately around the world. Those in the body of Christ who were threatened by this revival used this text to say, "Prophecy, tongues, and knowledge will vanish when that which is perfect is come. The Bible is that which is perfect. Therefore, there is no need for these manifestations anymore."

The problem is, not only is this a relatively new interpretation of this passage, but it violates the context. Paul is not talking about the Bible. He's talking about seeing Jesus face-to-face. It will be when Jesus comes again that there will be no need for prophecy, tongues, or interpretation. So it is my strong opinion that "that which is perfect" refers to the perfect One—Jesus Christ.

1 Corinthians 13:11, 12 (a)
When I was a child, I spake as a child, I understood as a child, I thought as a child: but when I became a man, I put away childish things. For now we see through a glass, darkly . . .

Mirrors as we know them did not exist until the mid-1200s. Prior to that time, polished brass or ordinary glass was used to see one's image—albeit only dimly, or "darkly." Thus, Paul says that although we see things spiritually, we don't see them clearly. We still have lots of questions.

1 Corinthians 13:12 (b)
. . . but then face to face . . .

When we see Jesus, we shall be like Him (1 John 3:2). At that point, we will see clearly at last.

1 Corinthians 13:12 (c)
. . . now I know in part; but then shall I know even as also I am known.

Jesus knows every detail of my life—even to the number of hairs on my head. And when I see Him, I'll know Him in the same way.

1 Corinthians 13:13 (a)
And now abideth faith . . .

Faith looks back. Faith tells me Jesus came. Faith allows me to embrace what Jesus did for me on the Cross. Faith reminds me that my sins are forgiven. Therefore, I don't have to worry about or be haunted by my past.

1 Corinthians 13:13 (b)
. . . hope . . .

Hope looks ahead. Hope tells me Jesus is coming. Hope reminds me I don't have to be upset or uptight about the future.

1 Corinthians 13:13 (c)
. . . charity . . .

Love looks around. Love tells me Jesus is here. Love frees me in the present.
Many believers have a "mattress spirituality." That is, knowing their sins are forgiven, they have no question about their past. Knowing they're going to heaven, they have no question about their future. It's the present that presents problems. Like a mattress, they're firm on both ends, but they sag in the middle.

1 Corinthians 13:13 (d)
. . . these three; but the greatest of these is charity.

As essential as faith and hope are, Paul singles out love as the greatest virtue because it is only through love that we are able to respond to God and to others presently.
You see, the person who lacks faith will not be able to love in the present because he will be paralyzed by the hurts and sins of his past. On the other hand, the person who lacks hope will not be able to love in the present because he will be too worried about his retirement account in the future. Only the person who has put his past

behind him through the power of the Cross, only the person who looks forward to the future through the promise of heaven can truly love in the present.

A DEEPER LOOK
A Topical Study of
1 Corinthians 13:4

The description of *agape* seen in 1 Corinthians 13 is glorious indeed. But, to the believer, this passage can be very frustrating as well. You see, in 1 Corinthians 13, we read that love is longsuffering and kind, that it neither envies nor seeks its own, that it bears all things, believes all things, hopes all things, and endures all things, that it never fails.

"What a beautiful description of love," we say with one breath, but, "too bad I'm so far from it," with the next.

Today, however, I want you to look at the chapter before us from a slightly different perspective. The apostle John tells us that God is love—literally that God is *agape* (1 John 4:16). Paul tells us that this Fountainhead of *agape*, the Essence of love, God Himself demonstrated His love for us in that while we were yet sinners He died in place of us (Romans 5:8). Seen in this light, 1 Corinthians 13 becomes not only an exhortation to love others, but, more importantly, a description of God's love for us. . . .

Love suffereth long . . .   1 Corinthians 13:4 (a)

God suffers long. He suffers long toward me. Think of Jesus on the Cross. As men cursed Him and spit on Him, what did He do? He suffered long. He said, "Father forgive them. They don't know what they're doing" (see Luke 23:34). My tendency is to think I've blown it so badly that surely God has given up on me. But the Cross shows me otherwise.

. . . and is kind . . .   1 Corinthians 13:4 (b)

If you think God is vengeful, angry, and mean-spirited, you have the wrong image of God. So kind, so gentle, so big-hearted is He that He does more for us than we could ever ask or even think (Ephesians 3:20).

The psalmist tells us that the Lord will withhold no good thing from those that love Him (Psalm 84:11). Therefore, if I'm not getting something for which I'm asking, it's because what I'm asking for would not be good for me. If the timing isn't right, if the request is wrong, He'll withhold it not because He's mean, but because He is love.

> . . . *love envieth not* . . .   1 Corinthians 13:4 (c)

Bound together in the Trinity, Father, Son, and Spirit are completely self-sufficient and totally happy. God says, "I want to walk with you; I'll never give up on you; I avail Myself to you—but I'm not dependent on you." God's love is mature.

> . . . *love vaunteth not itself* . . .   1 Corinthians 13:4 (d)

God doesn't have to hype Himself. What He says, He does. Who He claims to be, He really is.

> . . . *is not puffed up.*   1 Corinthians 13:4 (e)

God doesn't say, "I'm God and you're dust." No, He came to dwell among us, to walk with us, to die for us. And He's the same today. He's always available to me, always ready to hear my prayers, always ready to share with me truths from His Word.

When I read 1 Corinthians 13 in this light, what does it do?

The apostle John tells us exactly what it does when he literally says, "We love because He first loved us" (see 1 John 4:19). The person who understands that 1 Corinthians 13 is most fundamentally talking about the nature and character of God's love toward him personally will be one who inevitably overflows with love to the people around him.

We looked at only one verse in Paul's perfectly placed pomegranate of love. As you make your way through the rest of the chapter, you will see God's love for you in every verse. Marvel at it. Bask in it. Then let it overflow from your life to everyone around you.

---

14 After grazing in the peaceful pasture of chapter 13, we come to the potentially thorny territory of chapter 14 wherein Paul picks up his discussion of the manifestations of the Spirit. . . .

1 Corinthians 14:1 (a)
Follow after charity, and desire spiritual gifts . . .

Notwithstanding the fact that they were abusing the manifestations of the Spirit, Paul doesn't tell the church at Corinth to dismiss "spirituals."

Nor does he tell them to deny them. He tells them to desire them.

If, after seeing a man who weighed four hundred pounds lumber down the street, you decided to give up eating altogether, you wouldn't live very long. Yes, the man you saw may have eaten too much—but the answer to abuse is not non-use. It's proper use.

So, too, the church at Corinth had a heavyweight problem. They had abused the manifestations of the Spirit. They had misunderstood the principles of ministry. But the answer was not to deny the work of the Spirit. The answer was to learn how to use the manifestations properly. Much of what we see today in the church is a re-action against those who have misused the gifts or the manifestations of the Spirit. However, the answer to that which is being abused is not to for-sake, but to properly understand. This is what Paul presses for in the chapter at hand.

1 Corinthians 14:1 (b)
. . . but rather that ye may prophesy.

"Desire spiritual manifestations," says Paul—"but especially that you might share the heart of the Lord with the congregation."

1 Corinthians 14:2 (a)
For he that speaketh in an unknown tongue speaketh not unto men, but unto God . . .

Perhaps you've been in church services where someone stands up and gives an utterance in tongues, followed by what is supposed to be the interpretation—a word to the congregation. I do not believe such an occurrence is a proper under-standing of tongues and interpretation. Paul says a true interpretation of tongues will not be ad-dressed to men, but to God. A true interpretation of tongues gives praise and adoration to the Fa-ther—not a message to the congregation. Go through the Book of Acts, and you will see that prophecy consists of words spoken to the congre-gation, while tongues and interpretation consist of praise to God.

1 Corinthians 14:2 (b)
. . . for no man understandeth him; howbeit in the spirit he speaketh mysteries.

In Romans 8, Paul would say there are times that the Spirit prays through us with groanings that cannot be uttered (Romans 8:26). Have you ever been at the place where you simply don't know how to pray and you just start groaning? Many times people will say, "Pray that I'll get this job." Now, I don't know if it is necessarily God's will that they get that particular job. It might be a disaster for them. It might be a dis-traction to them. They might make more money, but lose their passion for the kingdom in the pro-cess. So what do I do? Oftentimes, when I don't know how to pray, I just allow the Spirit to pray through me—sometimes with groanings, some-times in an unknown language—because the Spirit understands perfectly that which is a mys-tery to me. And as I let Him pray through me, I know I'm praying according to God's will.

1 Corinthians 14:3 (a)
But he that prophesieth speaketh unto men . . .

The prayer language or the manifestation of tongues is God-ward. Prophecy is directed to-ward people.

1 Corinthians 14:3 (b)
. . . to edification, and exhortation, and com-fort.

When someone stands up on a Sunday evening and shares a word of prophecy, it will either be for edification—through which the Lord builds us up, for exhortation—through which He gets us going, or for comfort—through which He wraps His loving arm around us.

1 Corinthians 14:4 (a)
He that speaketh in an unknown tongue edi-fieth himself . . .

Our faith is built up when we study the Word (Romans 10:17). Faith is built up through seasons of prayer. Faith is built up through worship and adoration. In Jude 20 and here in 1 Corinthians, we are told faith is built up by praying in tongues. Ever feel torn down, worn out, caving in? Here's a weapon in the arsenal, a tool in the toolbox to pull out at such times. Pray in the Spirit. Utilize your prayer language and watch your faith grow.

1 Corinthians 14:4 (b)
. . . but he that prophesieth edifieth the church.

Although praying in the Spirit builds up my faith, it has no impact on anyone else unless it is accompanied by interpretation. Prophecy, how-ever—speaking forth the heart of the Lord through words of edification, exhortation, or comfort—has a powerful impact on others.

1 Corinthians 14:5 (a)
I would that ye all spake with tongues . . .

"Are all apostles, are all prophets, do all speak with tongues?" asked Paul (see 12:29, 30). The implied answer being no, why, then, would he say here, "I want you all to speak in tongues"?

In chapter 12, Paul is talking about the public expression of tongues, followed by interpreta-tion—and only a few people will move in that par-ticular expression. Here in chapter 14, he's talking about the private, devotional use of tongues, which is available to everyone.

Jesus said one of the signs of those who believe is that they would speak with new tongues (Mark

16:17). He didn't say tongues were a sign of those who are "Pentecostal" or even of those who are baptized in the Spirit, but simply of those who believe.

1 Corinthians 14:5 (b)
... but rather that ye prophesied: for greater is he that prophesieth than he that speaketh with tongues, except he interpret, that the church may receive edifying.

When the manifestation of tongues is followed by interpretation, the entire church can be built up through the praise and prayer that are offered. But without interpretation, prophecy is infinitely more valuable to the congregation.

1 Corinthians 14:6, 7
Now, brethren, if I come unto you speaking with tongues, what shall I profit you, except I shall speak to you either by revelation, or by knowledge, or by prophesying, or by doctrine? And even things without life giving sound, whether pipe or harp, except they give a distinction in the sounds, how shall it be known what is piped or harped?

"It is through words of doctrine or revelation of prophecy that you will grow," says Paul. "If I come speaking words you can't understand, it would be of no more help to you than listening to someone play random notes on a musical instrument."

1 Corinthians 14:8
For if the trumpet give an uncertain sound, who shall prepare himself to the battle?

It's amazing what one can do if he knows how to play the bugle. One set of notes will get the troops out of bed. Another set signals day's end. But if the bugler plays unfamiliar notes, the soldiers won't know whether it's time to have breakfast or to charge into battle.

1 Corinthians 14:9
So likewise ye, except ye utter by the tongue words easy to be understood, how shall it be known what is spoken? for ye shall speak into the air.

Again, referring to the congregational setting, Paul says he who speaks words that have no significance to the listener is simply speaking into the air.

1 Corinthians 14:10, 11
There are, it may be, so many kinds of voices in the world, and none of them is without signification. Therefore if I know not the meaning of the voice, I shall be unto him that speaketh a barbarian, and he that speaketh shall be a barbarian unto me.

When you're in another country, although the words spoken have significance to the people who live there, they mean nothing to you.

1 Corinthians 14:12
Even so ye, forasmuch as ye are zealous of spiritual gifts, seek that ye may excel to the edifying of the church.

"You're zealous for these spiritual expressions or manifestations. Good for you," Paul says. "But seek after the gift of prophecy—speaking to people by the Spirit in a language all can understand—words simple to embrace, words that edify, comfort, or exhort.

1 Corinthians 14:13
Wherefore let him that speaketh in an unknown tongue pray that he may interpret.

If you do speak in an unknown tongue in a group setting, pray that you will also be able to give the interpretation of your praise and adoration.

1 Corinthians 14:14
For if I pray in an unknown tongue, my spirit prayeth, but my understanding is unfruitful.

Although when I pray in the Spirit, I don't understand what I'm praying, my spirit—the deepest part of me, the core of my being—is built up miraculously and beautifully.

1 Corinthians 14:15
What is it, then? I will pray with the spirit, and I will pray with the understanding also: I will sing with the spirit, and I will sing with the understanding also.

"I will," says Paul. This is where many people have a terrible time with the prayer language, or tongues. They say, "If this is for me and if it will edify my spirit, I'm open to speaking in tongues." They might ask for the laying on of hands. They might be in a position where they are sincerely waiting on the Lord. But nothing happens. "I just want to express my love to the Lord in this unique way, but nothing's happening," they say in frustration—as though they believe that somehow they're going to go into a trance, their eyes will become glazed, they'll quiver and shake, and their tongue will begin moving against their will.

Paul simply says, "I *will* pray in the Spirit. It's a choice I make."

When we teach our kids or new believers to pray, we don't say, "Sit there until something happens. If you're really supposed to pray, you'll pray." No, we set an example for them and give a model to them. Many times, I'll have someone repeat after me, "Dear Jesus, come into my heart . . ." as a simple prayer of salvation. Does the fact that they're echoing my words make their prayer ineffective or insincere? No. They're just learning how to pray, and that's where they're at in their development.

So, too, I suggest that praying in the Spirit is a lot simpler than we make it. It's just saying, "I will pray right now with words I don't understand, trusting the Lord is inspiring these words and partnering with me in the process." Praying in the Spirit is not a feeling I feel. It's a decision I make. And once I begin to do this, it's so simple.

I'm not on a tongues-speaking kick by any stretch of the imagination. But it's a beautiful expression for me personally to say, "I don't know how to pray with understanding about this. I'm frazzled and fried mentally. So I'm going to pray in the Spirit." As I do, my spirit is edified. The prayer language is available to anyone, to everyone who simply believes.

1 Corinthians 14:16
Else when thou shalt bless with the spirit, how shall he that occupieth the room of the unlearned say Amen at thy giving of thanks, seeing he understandeth not what thou sayest?

"Amen" is one of two words understood by every believer in every culture—the other is "Alleluia." Paul says, "Unless there is interpretation of tongues, how can the congregation say Amen?"

Why should we say Amen? "Amen" literally means "So be it."

When the word was given to those charging exorbitant rates of interest to quit ripping off their fellow Jews, the people said, "Amen!" (see Nehemiah 5:13)

"Blessing and honor and glory and power be unto Him that sits upon the throne," says every creature.

"Amen!" say the four beasts (see Revelation 5:13, 14).

The Corinthian believers were also those who said, "Amen" when prayer ascended. And that is as it should be. Too many of our prayer meetings are lethargic because while someone is praying,

others are nodding off. How much better it would be if, when there is praise ascending and prayer being offered, we would be like those in Nehemiah's day, those in heaven, those in the early church who say, "Amen," engaging ourselves in the process of prayer.

Jesus taught about the importance of agreeing together in prayer. One of the most practical ways this can happen is when I simply say, "Amen, Lord. So be it," to the prayer of my brother.

1 Corinthians 14:17–19
For thou verily givest thanks well, but the other is not edified. I thank my God, I speak with tongues more than ye all: Yet in the church I had rather speak five words with my understanding, that by my voice I might teach others also, than ten thousand words in an unknown tongue.

Lest any at Corinth thought Paul was quenching the Spirit by putting parameters on the public expression of tongues, he reminds them that he spoke in tongues more than any of them. Even so, in the congregational setting, he preferred speaking that which would be understood by all.

1 Corinthians 14:20
Brethren, be not children in understanding: howbeit in malice be ye children, but in understanding be men.

"Of malice, be ignorant; but in understanding, be wise," says Paul as he goes on to add understanding to the subject of tongues. . . .

1 Corinthians 14:21, 22
In the law it is written, With men of other tongues and other lips will I speak unto this people; and yet for all that will they not hear me, saith the Lord. Wherefore tongues are for a sign, not to them that believe, but to them that believe not: but prophesying serveth not for them that believe not, but for them which believe.

In Deuteronomy 28, the Lord said, "As My people turn their back on Me and become cold toward Me, they will hear the tongues of other nations when foreigners invade their land." We see the fulfillment of this in Isaiah 28, when, because God's people had grown indifferent toward Him, the Assyrians were allowed to occupy their land. Because of this historical reference, when Paul says tongues are for a sign to them that believe not, it is my strong personal opinion that he is speaking not of unbelievers, but to believers who, like those in Isaiah's day, have grown indifferent or callused toward the Lord. In other words, he's speaking to those who don't believe in the present power of the Holy Spirit.

For some reason, the issue of tongues seems to be the line in the sand that separates people who, having grown callused, say, "No. God is not working today. He cannot be moving in this manner. Those miracles and expressions were for a different era, a different day."

1 Corinthians 14:23
If therefore the whole church be come together into one place, and all speak with tongues, and there come in those that are unlearned, or unbelievers, will they not say that ye are mad?

As valid a sign as the proper expression of tongues may be, the improper use of them in a congregational setting is helpful to no one.

1 Corinthians 14:24
But if all prophesy, and there come in one that believeth not, or one unlearned, he is convinced of all, he is judged of all.

Whether prophecy is shared through the teaching of the Word or through individual utterance, even those who have not been exposed to the manifestations of the Spirit gain insight from it.

1 Corinthians 14:25
And thus are the secrets of his heart made manifest; and so falling down on his face he will worship God, and report that God is in you of a truth.

When God's Word is spoken forth through the power of the Spirit—in the sanctuary, in home groups, among believers in all sorts of contexts—it convinces and convicts through a single message miraculously custom-made for each hearer.

1 Corinthians 14:26
How is it then, brethren? when ye come together, everyone of you hath a psalm, hath a doctrine, hath a tongue, hath a revelation, hath an interpretation. Let all things be done unto edifying.

Because Greek manuscripts contain no punctuation, the question is, where does the question mark belong? The context strongly indicates that it actually belongs after the word "interpretation." This would change the meaning of this verse to, "How is it that every one of you is trying to get into the act? When you meet together, there is total confusion."

1 Corinthians 14:27–29
If any man speak in an unknown tongue, let it be by two, or at the most by three, and that by course; and let one interpret. But if there be no interpreter, let him keep silence in the church; and let him speak to himself, and to God. Let the prophets speak two or three, and let the other judge.

Paul's solution to the confusion was to allow only two or three to speak in tongues in the congregational setting—and only if accompanied by interpretation. The rest were to think through what was being shared, determining if what they heard was in harmony with the totality of Scripture.

1 Corinthians 14:30
If any thing be revealed to another that sitteth by, let the first hold his peace.

"As these manifestations of the Spirit are operating in the congregational setting, be careful not to dominate or monopolize the session as you're waiting on the Lord together," says Paul.

1 Corinthians 14:31, 32
For ye may all prophesy one by one, that all may learn, and all may be comforted. And the spirits of the prophets are subject to the prophets.

Sometimes people will justify odd behavior by saying they were overwhelmed by the Spirit. But here Paul says even while ministering in the Spirit, a man is never out of control.

1 Corinthians 14:33
For God is not the author of confusion, but of peace, as in all churches of the saints.

If a teaching is being given, the Lord is not going to interrupt Himself with some kind of prophetic outburst, for He is not the author of confusion.

1 Corinthians 14:34
Let your women keep silence in the churches: for it is not permitted unto them to speak; but they are commanded to be under obedience, as also saith the law.

Following Jewish tradition, when the church at Corinth met together, the men sat on one side, the women on the other. Because *laleo*, the Greek word translated "speak," can mean "chatter" or "interrupt," there are those who say Paul is simply forbidding women from calling out to their husbands on the other side of the church, "Hey,

Joe, what did he mean by that?" It could be that this is, indeed, what Paul is referring to. But I don't think so.

You see, once a person decides a particular text is only relevant to the culture in which it was written, where does he stop? He could just as easily conclude that baptism or Communion—topics discussed in this same Corinthian letter—were culturally related and don't have meaning for modern America.

"For God is not the author of confusion, but of peace, as in *all* churches of the saints," Paul said in verse 33. Therefore, to suggest that verse 34 relates only to the Corinthian congregation creates problems contextually.

The verse before us—a principle for all churches in all cultures—does not mean that women are not to participate in the service, for in chapter 11, Paul said that women who pray and prophesy are free to do so as long as they are under the authority of their husbands.

The best commentary on the Bible is the Bible itself. In 1 Timothy, we find a parallel text to the one before us. . . .

Let the woman learn in silence with all subjection. But I suffer not a woman to teach, nor to usurp authority over the man, but to be in silence.   1 Timothy 2:11, 12

From this passage, we can see that Paul's injunction that women not speak in church means they are not to teach men. Lest we think Paul chauvinistic, he goes on to give his reason. . . .

And Adam was not deceived, but the woman being deceived was in the transgression.
      1 Timothy 2:14

Appealing to a woman's innate desire for deeper spirituality, Satan suggested to Eve that eating the forbidden fruit would make her more godly (Genesis 3:5). Thus, in her desire for a more godly character, Eve was tricked. It is this admirable tendency in women that also makes them more susceptible to deception. Therefore, because of women's vulnerability to error, man is to be the teacher of doctrine.

Notwithstanding she shall be saved in childbearing, if they continue in faith and charity and holiness with sobriety.   1 Timothy 2:15

Women, your call is to pour your lives into your kids and grandchildren. Should the Lord tarry, if women took this charge seriously, we would see a church in the next generation that would change the world.

1 Corinthians 14:35 (a)
And if they will learn any thing, let them ask their husbands at home . . .

If a woman talks to her pastor or an elder about spiritual questions or matters, her husband is inadvertently left farther and farther in the background. On the other hand, if she asks her husband, he will be motivated to dig into Scripture himself. Even if her husband is not a believer, she is to ask him anyway. There are numerous men at Applegate Christian Fellowship as a result of their curiosity concerning their wives' questions.

1 Corinthians 14:35 (b)
. . . for it is a shame for women to speak in the church.

"Barak, if you don't lead your men into battle, the glory of the victory will eventually go to a woman," said Deborah. And indeed it did (Judges 4:9). I believe that when Paul says it's a shame for a woman to speak, it's because her speaking is indicative of a lack of leadership by the men. It's a sad state when, in any group, a woman is the only one who can teach because the men are all too carnal, too weak, or too unwilling. God has and will bless women for filling in—but that is not His ideal.

1 Corinthians 14:36–40
What? came the word of God out from you? or came it unto you only? If any man think himself to be a prophet, or spiritual, let him acknowledge that the things that I write unto you are the commandments of the Lord. But if any man be ignorant, let him be ignorant. Wherefore, brethren, covet to prophesy, and forbid not to speak with tongues. Let all things be done decently and in order.

There are two parts to this last verse: Things must be done decently and in order—but let all things be done. Our Baptist brothers have the first part down perfectly, while our Pentecostal brothers excel at the last. What I believe the Lord has for Baptists, Pentecostals, and everyone in between is to allow prophecy, tongues, interpretation, gifts of healing, and words of knowledge and wisdom to flow—but in a decent, orderly manner.

The same applies to us individually.

According to those who study such things, the vast majority of people who own running shoes don't run. That's a lot like us. We say we believe that praying in the Spirit is meant for today. We believe in the validity of prophecy. We know the Holy Spirit wants to work wonders in and through us congregationally. We've got the running shoes. Let's step out in the Spirit and run.

Like Paul, let's covet the gifts and then use them in a way that is harmonious, beautiful, and acceptable. The Holy Spirit is pictured as a dove for a reason. He's not portrayed as a hawk coming in for the kill, or a vulture circling over the congregation to pick people to death with prophecies and words of knowledge. The dove is a bird of beauty, gentleness, and peace. And when the gifts and manifestations of the Spirit it represents are operating properly, the effect will likewise be beautiful, gentle, and peaceful.

15 So carnal was the city of Corinth that the term "Corinthian" was synonymous with "party animal." This was due in no small part to the fact that Corinth was the center of the Epicurean philosophy, which said that, because there is no eternity, man should eat, drink, and be merry on earth. Part of this Epicurean mentality had filtered into the church. Specifically, there were those in the church who taught there was no resurrection from the dead. "Be a Christian," they said. "Believe in Jesus Christ. Believe that on the Cross He atoned for the sin of mankind. But don't believe He really rose again."

Paul tackles this issue head-on in chapter 15 as he talks about the reality of the Resurrection in order to counteract the philosophy of the Epicurean.

1 Corinthians 15:1–2
Moreover, brethren, I declare unto you the gospel which I preached unto you, which also ye have received, and wherein ye stand; by which also ye are saved, if ye keep in memory what I preached unto you, unless ye have believed in vain.

"If you do not believe in the Resurrection, your faith is in vain, empty, and useless," contends Paul. "It all hinges on the Resurrection."

1 Corinthians 15:3, 4
For I delivered unto you first of all that which I also received, how that Christ died for our sins according to the scriptures; and that he was buried, and that he rose again the third day according to the scriptures.

Here, Paul gives us the two-fold definition of the gospel: that Christ died for our sins, and that He rose again—as was prophesied in Old Testament Scripture.

For topical study of 1 Corinthians 15:2–4 entitled "Really Believing the Gospel," turn to page 1091.

1 Corinthians 15:5, 6
And that he was seen of Cephas, then of the twelve: After that, he was seen of above five hundred brethren at once; of whom the greater part remain unto this present, but some are fallen asleep.

"After Jesus rose again, He appeared to Peter, then to the twelve disciples, then to five hundred others—most of whom are still alive today," Paul said.

1 Corinthians 15:7 (a)
After that, he was seen of James . . .

This refers to the half brother of Jesus who, as seen in Mark 3, initially didn't believe his brother was who He claimed to be. Following Jesus' Resurrection, however, James changed his mind so completely that he went on to become a leader in the early church.

1 Corinthians 15:7 (b), 8
. . . then of all the apostles. And last of all he was seen of me also, as of one born out of due time.

It was in the Arabian desert that Jesus taught Paul how the Old Testament types and pictures all spoke of Him. "Although I came on the scene after the other guys, I saw Jesus, too," said Paul.

1 Corinthians 15:9
For I am the least of the apostles, that am not meet to be called an apostle, because I persecuted the church of God.

"Because I persecuted the church, I'm the least of the apostles," says Paul. Later on, he would say, "I'm less than the least of all the Christians" (see Ephesians 3:8). And finally at the end of his life, he would say, "I'm the chief of sinners" (see 1 Timothy 1:15). The longer Paul lived, the more aware he became of his own sin in light of the beauty and grace of Jesus.

1 Corinthians 15:10 (a)
But by the grace of God I am what I am . . .

"Who shall I say sent me?" Moses asked God when told he was to lead the Israelites out of bondage.

And God said unto Moses, "I AM THAT I AM" (Exodus 3:14).

I suggest that this phrase was ringing in Paul's mind and resonating in his heart when he said, "By the grace of God I am what I am"—for in Exodus 34, God went on to explain just who He is. . . .

And the LORD passed by before him, and proclaimed, The LORD, The LORD God, merciful and gracious, longsuffering, and abundant in goodness and truth, keeping mercy for thousands, forgiving iniquity and transgression and sin, and that will by no means clear the guilty; visiting the iniquity of the fathers upon the children, and upon the children's children, unto the third and to the fourth generation.
Exodus 34:6, 7

Because of the injustice that seems to plague our culture, we could have a tendency to think that if God came on the scene today, surely it would be as a God of Justice. Yet while God is indeed just, He chooses instead to identify Himself as being merciful and gracious. What a relief this should be to us. Justice means getting what we deserve. Mercy, on the other hand, means being spared the judgment we rightfully deserve. Grace goes even further than that, for grace means getting blessings we don't deserve.

Yet God didn't stop there. He went on to say that He is longsuffering. The Hebrew word translated "longsuffering" means l-o-n-g suffering. "Why aren't You doing something, God? How can You put up with him?" or, "Why don't You deal with them?" we cry. God bears with the sin we see in others for the same reason He bears with the sin He sees in us: He is longsuffering. That's His nature.

He's abundant in goodness and truth—lavishing blessings upon us, being completely honest and truthful with us.

God alone is the One who is merciful to thousands, forgiving iniquity, rebellion, and sin. Even if generation after generation continues to turn their back on Him, He visits each one, bringing conviction for the purpose of conversion.

"What gives me the right, the authority to correct you?" Paul could have asked the Corinthians. "There was a time when I thought I had earned that right. After all, I was born into the tribe of Benjamin, circumcised the eighth day, a Pharisee of Pharisees, zealous for the law, righteous in my

behavior. But although I was religious outwardly, I was sinning inwardly. And all of my attempts to earn God's blessing, all of my seeking to manipulate Him to get Him to bless me proved to be a waste (Philippians 3:7). Now I know I'm a sinner. But because God is who He is—because He is merciful and gracious, longsuffering and forgiving—I am who I am: a trophy of His grace."

1 Corinthians 15:10 (b)
. . . and his grace which was bestowed upon me was not in vain; but I laboured more abundantly than they all: yet not I, but the grace of God which was with me.

When we were new in faith, many of us looked at works—Bible study, prayer, service, tithing—as ways to get God to respond to us. But as we grow in faith, we come to understand that works are the inevitable response to the goodness and grace God has *already* lavished upon us. When I consider that I'm going to heaven, that my sins are forgiven, that God has given me His Word, and that the Holy Spirit lives within me, I have no other choice but to serve Him wholeheartedly.

An understanding of the grace of God results in works. But the works are a response to God rather than a means of getting God to respond to us. The fallacy of "seed faith theology"—in which people are told to give money, offer prayers, or engage in service in order to get something back from God—is that all of those activities are an inevitable response for one who understands what God has *already* done on his or her behalf.

"I labor more abundantly than everyone," Paul says. "Because God has been so good to me, I can't help it." So, too, if you are one who truly embraces and enjoys the grace of God, you will be more engaged in His service than you were a year ago. You just won't be able to stop yourself.

1 Corinthians 15:11
Therefore whether it were I or they, so we preach, and so ye believed.

Paul is referring to those who had seen the resurrected Jesus—himself, Peter, the apostles, James, and five hundred others.

1 Corinthians 15:12–18
Now if Christ be preached that he rose from the dead, how say some among you that there is no resurrection of the dead? But if there be no resurrection of the dead, then is Christ not risen: And if Christ be not risen, then is our preaching vain, and your faith is also vain. Yea, and we are found false witnesses of God; because we have testified of God that he raised up Christ: whom

he raised not up, if so be that the dead rise not. For if the dead rise not, then is not Christ raised: And if Christ be not raised, your faith is vain; ye are yet in your sins. Then they also which are fallen asleep in Christ are perished.

"Show us a sign that You are who You claim to be," they said.

"One sign I'll show you. Destroy this temple—this body—and in three days I will raise it up" Jesus answered (see John 2:19).

Houdini claimed that on the fiftieth anniversary of his death, he would come back from the dead. So on that date, a group of his followers gathered around his grave in San Francisco, waiting for him to return. They waited and waited and waited. Then they went home.

Jesus uniquely, singularly rose from the dead. Lots of people make all sorts of claims, but our Hero, our Leader, our Lord Jesus Christ delivered. He came through. And had His offering not been acceptable, our Great High Priest would never have emerged from the tomb on Easter Sunday. . . .

As the high priest, dressed in linen, went into the Holy of Holies on the Day of Atonement to sprinkle blood on the mercy seat, the people would wonder and wait. If the high priest was himself defiled, if the high priest was himself polluted by sin, he would be smitten dead in the Holy of Holies. But if he emerged, his linen garments sprinkled with blood, the people would know the offering "took." They would know their sins were forgiven.

What about our Great High Priest, Jesus Christ? Wrapped in linen, He was placed in the tomb. All of heaven wondered. All of history waited. Did the offering take? Was His blood accepted? Because He emerged from the tomb on that glorious Easter Sunday, we know the offering did, indeed, take. We know His blood was accepted. We know that we are forgiven.

Whether you're talking to the skeptic on the campus, at work, or in your neighborhood, the issue is singular: Did Jesus rise from the dead? If He did, He is unique in history. It validates His claim. And it means our sins are forgiven. The entire argument hinges on the single issue of the Resurrection.

1 Corinthians 15:19
If in this life only we have hope in Christ, we are of all men most miserable.

If in this life only we have hope in Christ, why are we of all men most miserable? Because we have hope that life will get better, that things will be right, that bills will be no more, that tears will cease to flow. On the other hand, if heaven isn't real, the Epicurean is right. There is no tomorrow. There is no hope.

1 Corinthians 15:20
But now is Christ risen from the dead, and become the firstfruits of them that slept.

In the Levitical calendar, the day following Passover was a day of celebration called the Feast of Firstfruits. During this feast, the Jews waved wheat from their crops toward heaven, signifying their gratitude to the Lord for His provision and the promise of more to come.

When did Christ rise? The day following Passover—on the Feast of Firstfruits. Jesus is the Firstfruit because there's more to come. Who? You and me. Jesus was the first One truly resurrected never to die again—but many more will follow.

1 Corinthians 15:21–23
For since by man came death, by man came also the resurrection of the dead. For as in Adam all die, even so in Christ shall all be made alive. But every man in his own order: Christ the firstfruits; afterward they that are Christ's at his coming.

The resurrection spoken of here is a process that began with the Resurrection of Christ and will conclude when those who are martyred during the Tribulation for their faith in Christ are resurrected.

Revelation 20 goes on to talk about a second resurrection that takes place at the end of the Millennium when all of the unbelievers will stand before the Great White Throne. The first resurrection is the resurrection unto life because it is made up only of those who are saved. The second resurrection is the resurrection unto death because it is made up only of unbelievers.

1 Corinthians 15:24–26
Then cometh the end, when he shall have delivered up the kingdom to God, even the Father; when he shall have put down all rule and all authority and power. For he must reign, till he hath put all enemies under his feet. The last enemy that shall be destroyed is death.

When at last the kingdom of death is cast into outer darkness, Christ will rule and reign unchallenged. What a day that will be! The last enemy to be destroyed, nevermore to haunt or burden anyone, will not only be physical death, but the death of marriage, the death of joy, the death of peace, the death of everything that brings about hopelessness, heaviness, and sorrow.

1 Corinthians 15:27
For he hath put all things under his feet. But when he saith, all things are put under him, it is manifest that he is excepted, which did put all things under him.

With the exception of God, all things are under the feet of Jesus Christ. Soon, He will take control of that which is twice His—that which was given to Him by the Father and that which was purchased by His own blood on Calvary.

1 Corinthians 15:28
And when all things shall be subdued unto him, then shall the Son also himself be subject unto him that put all things under him, that God may be all in all.

The Son shall remain in submission to the Father not because He is inferior, but because it was a choice He made (Philippians 2:7, 8), the effects of which remain.

1 Corinthians 15:29
Else what shall they do which are baptized for the dead, if the dead rise not at all? why are they then baptized for the dead?

The Mormons use this verse to teach that a person can be baptized in place of relatives who died generations ago. This is why they place such importance upon genealogies. However, unbeknownst to most people, a dark spiritualism is linked to this aspect of Mormonism. What Paul is talking about is actually quite simple. Baptism is a symbol of death, burial, and resurrection. "If Jesus is not risen," he asks, "why would you be baptized?"

1 Corinthians 15:30, 31
And why stand we in jeopardy every hour? I protest by your rejoicing which I have in Christ Jesus our Lord, I die daily.

"While you are celebrating your Epicurean Christianity, I'm risking my life every day. Why would I do this if there is no resurrection?" asks Paul.

1 Corinthians 15:32
If after the manner of men I have fought with beasts at Ephesus, what advantageth
it me, if the dead rise not? let us eat and drink; for to morrow we die.

Commentators are divided over the identity of the beasts at Ephesus. It could very well be that Paul was cast into the arena at Ephesus where he stood face-to-face with hungry lions, as did countless Christian martyrs. Or, it could be Paul is talking about men who, acting like beasts, wanted to rip into him. Either way, what he endured at Ephesus was all for nothing if, indeed, there was no resurrection.

1 Corinthians 15:33
Be not deceived: evil communications corrupt good manners.

"Your discussions with the Epicureans are making you confused about the simplicity of the gospel," Paul warns the Corinthian believers.

1 Corinthians 15:34, 35
Awake to righteousness, and sin not; for some have not the knowledge of God: I speak this to your shame. But some man will say, How are the dead raised up? and with what body do they come?

This wasn't an honest question, but was instead meant to challenge Paul.

1 Corinthians 15:36–38
Thou fool, that which thou sowest is not quickened, except it die: And that which thou sowest, thou sowest not that body that shall be, but bare grain, it may chance of wheat, or of some other grain: But God giveth it a body as it hath pleased him, and to every seed his own body.

Look at nature. If you put an ugly brown bulb in the ground, what happens? It sends down its roots, cracks in half, and sends up greenery. As the warm sun beats down on the budding plant, a beautiful yellow daffodil appears from what once was an ugly brown bulb. So, too, Paul says the same thing we observe in nature will take place in the resurrection.

1 Corinthians 15:39, 40 (a)
All flesh is not the same flesh: but there is one kind of flesh of men, another flesh of beasts, another of fishes, and another of birds. There are also celestial bodies, and bodies terrestrial . . .

Just as we see different bodies now—those of lions, fish, and beasts; those of sun, moon, and stars—our resurrected bodies will be different from those we have now. Because our present bodies are designed for fourteen pounds of pressure per square inch, we can only travel in the air or underwater in pressurized cabins or suits. And because our present bodies are designed to take in a specific mix of air composed of 78 percent oxygen, 21 percent nitrogen, and 1 percent of assorted gases, we remain essentially earthbound.

But our eternal bodies will require neither space suit nor oxygen tank. We're going to be free to explore, soar, and do all kinds of things we can't even dream about doing today as we cruise the cosmos without limitations or restrictions. Right now, we inhabit ugly brown bulbs. But when we see Him, we shall be like Him. Oh, happy day that will be!

1 Corinthians 15:40 (b)–42 (a)
. . . but the glory of the celestial is one, and the glory of the terrestrial is another. There is one glory of the sun, and another glory of the moon, and another glory of the stars: for one star differeth from another star in glory. So also is the resurrection of the dead.

If you look at the sky tonight, you'll see stars shining with different intensities. Likewise, there will be different intensities in heaven. Daniel 12 tells us that those who win souls shall shine as the stars forever. In other words, those who are serving the Lord now and making their lives count today will shine brightly throughout eternity. On the other hand, although those who give priority to their own bodies, possessions, interests, hobbies, careers, or agendas, will be in heaven if they believe in Jesus Christ, they will not shine with the same intensity. Make the kingdom the priority and passion of your life, and I promise you, you'll not regret it.

1 Corinthians 15:42 (b)–44 (a)
It is sown in corruption; it is raised in incorruption: It is sown in dishonour; it is raised in glory: it is sown in weakness; it is raised in power: It is sown a natural body; it is raised a spiritual body.

The body we put in the ground decays. Paul says that's not the end of the story, for it rises in glory and power.

1 Corinthians 15:44 (b), 45 (a)
There is a natural body, and there is a spiritual body. And so it is written, The first man Adam was made a living soul . . .

"From dust you came and to dust you will return," God told Adam (see Genesis 3:19). Therefore, it is no wonder that the seventeen elements that compose the dirt under your feet are the same elements of which your body is comprised.

1 Corinthians 15:45 (b)
. . . the last Adam was made a quickening spirit.

Adam was made a living soul. The last Adam, Jesus Christ, was made a quickening, or, literally, life-giving spirit. Jesus is the One who gives life.

1 Corinthians 15:46
Howbeit that was not first which is spiritual, but that which is natural; and afterward that which is spiritual.

We begin as natural men. It is not until we're born again by the life-giving Spirit of the last Adam that we become spiritual beings.

1 Corinthians 15:47 (a)
The first man is of the earth, earthy . . .

According to Psalm 103, the Father understands that we are earthy. Therefore, I am personally persuaded that many of us expect more of ourselves than our Father expects of us. We put pressure upon ourselves, set lofty goals, and make endless promises. But in reality, we're just dusty and earthy. "We have this treasure, Jesus Christ, in earthen vessels," Paul will say in his second letter to the Corinthians (4:7). Jesus is the Treasure. We're just the earthen vessel, the clay pot.

From time to time, many of us try to polish and paint our earthen vessels by trying to put on an act of spirituality. In reality, however, all that does is detract from the beauty of the Treasure inside. That is why, in describing how He wanted to be worshiped, the Lord didn't prescribe an altar made of cut stones, polished brass, or beaten gold. It was to be made of earth in order that nothing would detract from the sacrifice laid upon it (Exodus 20:24).

Many people don't witness, teach Sunday school, or serve in other ways because they don't feel polished or articulate enough. Little do they realize that they are the ideal candidates for ministry because people will marvel at the Treasure and not at them. Whether it be congregationally or personally, the key to ministry is to get out of the way and let people see the beauty of Jesus, the Treasure within.

1 Corinthians 15:47 (b)–49
. . . the second man is the Lord from heaven. As is the earthy, such are they also that are earthy: and as is the heavenly, such are they also that are heavenly. And as we have borne the image of the earthy, we shall also bear the image of the heavenly.

Although presently I am free to be who I am—just an earthy, clay pot—I know someday I'll be much more. Someday I'll bear the image of Christ, in a body custom-made for the heavenlies.

1 Corinthians 15:50
Now this I say, brethren, that flesh and blood cannot inherit the kingdom of God; neither doth corruption inherit incorruption.

Our present bodies of flesh and blood cannot move into the kingdom because they're not designed for heaven. That is what death is all about. For the believer, death is simply a way of leaving our earthly tabernacles and moving into our new bodies, exchanging our crusty brown bulbs for creations of beauty.

1 Corinthians 15:51 (a)
Behold, I shew you a mystery.

The Greek word translated "mystery" is *musterion*. Musterion speaks of something that has previously been hidden, but is now known. Following Paul's discussion of the necessity of dying in order that we might move into the eternal realm, he says there is something new to factor in to the equation. . . .

1 Corinthians 15:51 (b)
We shall not all sleep, but we shall all be changed.

Although everyone will be changed—like caterpillars into butterflies—not everyone will die. How can a person be changed if he doesn't die? Read on.

1 Corinthians 15:52, 53
In a moment, in the twinkling of an eye, at the last trump: for the trumpet shall sound, and the dead shall be raised incorruptible, and we shall be changed. For this corruptible must put on incorruption, and this mortal must put on immortality.

Here is the first reference to the hope of the Rapture. Paul tells us that, rather than dying, some will be changed in the twinkling of an eye. When the trumpet sounds, as 1 Thessalon-

ians 4:16, 17 more fully explains, the Lord Himself shall descend from heaven. The dead in Christ shall rise, and then we who are alive and remain shall be caught up to meet with them in the clouds. We'll be changed immediately without going through the death process at all.

1 Corinthians 15:54
So when this corruptible shall have put on incorruption, and this mortal shall have put on immortality, then shall be brought to pass the saying that is written, Death is swallowed up in victory.

Death is swallowed up in victory. Because our hearts tell us this is so, because the Word declares it to be, instead of moaning and mourning over believers who have died, we can truly be happy and elated for them if we understand the big picture of eternity.

1 Corinthians 15:55–57
O death, where is thy sting? O grave, where is thy victory? The sting of death is sin; and the strength of sin is the law. But thanks be to God, which giveth us the victory through our Lord Jesus Christ.

A little girl was having a picnic with her daddy. Deathly allergic to bee stings, she became terrified as a bumblebee buzzed overhead. Seeing the bee, her father caught it and held it in his hand for a few seconds before letting it go. As it buzzed around once more, the little girl cried, "Daddy, Daddy, why did you let the bee go?"

Rather than explain, the father chose to simply open his hand to show his daughter the stinger embedded in his palm.

That's precisely what Jesus did for me when He absorbed the sting of my sin and stupidity.

1 Corinthians 15:58
Therefore, my beloved brethren, be ye stedfast, unmoveable, always abounding in the work of the Lord, forasmuch as ye know that your labour is not in vain in the Lord.

In light of the reality of eternity, in light of the Cross of Calvary, in light of the fact that what we do on this earth will determine our heavenly intensity, Paul says, "Work for the Lord so that your labor will not be in vain." So much of what we do with our time, energy, and money is vain. So much of what we do is going to fall apart, pass away, or break down. But that which we do for the Lord—the worship we give Him, the work we do for Him, the gifts we bring to Him—will not be in vain.

Even if it seems that what you're doing for Him is not making a very big impact, know this: Your labor is not in vain. The Lord does not pay you on commission. He pays you for your labor. He doesn't pay you depending upon how successful you are in service. He pays you by the hour. Just be faithful to do what He has called you to do, and leave the results to Him.

REALLY BELIEVING THE GOSPEL
A Topical Study of
1 Corinthians 15:2–4

"Gospel" is a word we hear frequently. One of the fastest-growing segments of the music market is gospel music. We speak of "old-time" gospel meetings, and of ministers of the gospel. Gospel is a word we use to describe music, meetings, and ministers. But what exactly is the gospel?

The Greek word translated "Gospel" is *euangelion,* and has its origins in the soap merchants of ancient times who would advertise their wares by calling out, "Good news!" upon entering a town. In those days before deodorant or cologne, the arrival of soap was good news indeed!

How fitting, then, that those who went from city to city sharing the Good News that people could be cleansed from the stench of their sin would, like their soap-merchant counterparts, be called evangelists. In the text before us, Paul defines their message: first, that Christ died, and second, that He rose again—both according to Scripture.

. . . how that Christ died for our sins according to the scriptures
1 Corinthians 15:3 (b)

That Christ would die for our sins is seen clearly throughout the Old Testament . . .

- Psalm 22 presents a clear and accurate description of the process of crucifixion centuries before crucifixion was first practiced.
- Psalm 69 speaks of the vinegar Jesus would be offered to drink on the Cross.
- Isaiah 50 foretells that Jesus would be spat upon, that His beard would be plucked, that He would be hit in the face.
- Isaiah 52 and 53 describe how Jesus would be beaten for our sins, bruised for our iniquities.

When Paul said Christ died for our sins according to the Scriptures, no doubt he had these passages in mind.

And that he was buried, and that he rose again the third day according to the scriptures.   1 Corinthians 15:4

Like the Crucifixion, the Resurrection is also seen throughout the Old Testament. . . .

For three days and nights he was in the belly of the great fish. Thinking he had died and was in hell itself, Jonah cried out to the Father, Who "resurrected" him when the whale spit him onto dry land (Jonah 2:10).

In Genesis we find an even more descriptive picture. . . .

"Take thy son, thine only son unto a mountain I shall show thee of and there offer him as a sacrifice unto Me," God said. Abraham carried fire and a knife while Isaac carried the wood. Together, father and son set off toward a mount called Moriah. At the bottom of the mountain, Abraham said to the two servants who accompanied them, "You stay here. My son and I will go up and worship and we will come again unto thee."

When Abraham and Isaac reached the top of the mountain, Isaac said, "Here's the wood. There's the fire. But where's the sacrifice?"

And Abraham looked at his son and said, "God will provide Himself a lamb" (Genesis 22:8). Not, "God will provide for *Himself a lamb," but, "God will provide* Himself *a lamb." He will* be *the Lamb.*

I don't know if Abraham understood the significance of his statement. I'm not sure Isaac got it at all. But as Abraham was ready to plunge a knife through the chest of his only son, God said, "Stop, Abraham. Now I know that you fear God."

The picture is as complete as it can be—for that mountain called Moriah is today called Calvary. The very spot Abraham was ready to offer his son, Isaac, is the spot God did, indeed, offer His only Son, Jesus Christ.

Even as Isaac carried the wood, Jesus carried the Cross. Even as Jesus was crucified between two thieves, Isaac walked with two servants. Even as Abraham was ready to put a knife through his son, a spear pierced the Son of Man. Even as Abraham had fire in his hand, the fiery wrath of God's holy indignation was hurled down upon His Son as He bore my sin and yours.

One of the most powerful portraits of the Resurrection is seen in the law itself. . . .

When a person was cleansed of leprosy, the priest would take two birds, one of which would be killed over running water and placed in an earthen jar. The second bird, along with cedar wood, scarlet, and hyssop, would be dipped into the blood of the first bird and then released (Leviticus 14).

Jesus, the One who left the "nest" of heaven to come and dwell among us, confined Himself in an earthen vessel, His earthly body. The running water speaks of the living water He proclaimed Himself to be (John 4:10), as well as the water that gushed forth when a spear was thrust into His side (John 19:34). The wood speaks of the Cross; scarlet of His blood, hyssop of that which was offered Him to drink. As the living bird, sprinkled with the blood of the sacrificial bird, soared back into the sky, the picture of Resurrection was complete.

As seen in our text, the gospel is two-fold: Jesus died for our sin and rose again. We who name the Name of Jesus believe the gospel—especially the first half. We believe Jesus died for our sin. But do we truly believe the second aspect of the gospel? Do you really believe that Jesus Christ is alive, that right now, by His Spirit, He lives within you, that physically He's in heaven praying for you? If you do, today and every day is Easter Sunday. . . .

Mary was heartbroken. She went to the tomb that Sunday morning but realized Jesus' body wasn't there.

"What are you seeking?" the "gardener" asked her.

"If you have taken the body of my Lord, tell me where you have laid Him and I will take Him away," she said (see John 20:15).

But when she heard this One whom she supposed to be the gardener speak her name, she threw her arms around Him, recognizing Him to be Jesus.

Was Mary excited because of the validation of the atoning work of Christ on the Cross? Was she elated because the Millennial reign could be instituted eventually? I don't think so. I believe that Mary and the others who were caught up in the wonder of Easter were not thinking about the theological or eschatological ramifications of the Resurrection. No, the reason Mary hugged Jesus and wouldn't let Him go is because her Friend was with her again—and that was all that mattered.

What if we believed this? What if we really believed not only that Jesus died for our sins, but that He has risen again and is here with us today, right now? We wouldn't be saying, "Woe is me. What am I going to do about this situation, about those bills, about that obligation?" No, we'd be saying, "Good News! Jesus is alive! He's here!" He who truly believes the gospel cannot help but be hilariously happy.

Terrified by reports that the Assyrians were on the move, the Israelites sent emissaries south to set up an alliance with the Egyptians.

Woe to the rebellious children, saith the LORD, that take counsel, but not of me; and that cover with a covering, but not of my spirit, that they may add

sin to sin: That walk to go down into Egypt, and have not asked at my mouth;
to strengthen themselves in the strength of Pharaoh, and to trust in the shadow
of Egypt! Therefore shall the strength of Pharaoh be your shame, and the trust
in the shadow of Egypt your confusion. For thus saith the Lord GOD, the Holy
One of Israel; In returning and rest shall ye be saved; in quietness and in
confidence shall be your strength: and ye would not.　　　　Isaiah 30:1–3, 15

The Lord says the same thing to us today. "In returning to Me, you'll be saved. In quietness and confidence—literally in lingering with Me—shall be your strength."

If Jesus is not risen, we better get counsel from the Egyptians. We better set up an alliance. We better run here and go there and get all the help we can.

If, on the other hand, we truly believe the Good News that Jesus not only died for our sins, but that He rose again, we can cast our care upon Him, talk to Him, linger with Him, hear from Him. Like Mary, we can wrap our arms around Him and say, "Lord, I'm so glad You're here. What would I do without You? You are the ultimate solution to every problem, the source of strength for every weakness, my King, my Deliverer, my Friend."

Do you believe the gospel? Do you really believe the *full* gospel? To the extent you do, happy you'll be. The Lord is risen. He is risen *indeed!*

❧

16

1 Corinthians 16:1–4
Now concerning the collection for the saints, as I have given order to the churches of Galatia, even so do ye. Upon the first day of the week let every one of you lay by him in store, as God hath prospered him, that there be no gatherings when I come. And when I come, whomsoever ye shall approve by your letters, them will I send to bring your liberality unto Jerusalem. And if it be meet that I go also, they shall go with me.

After encouraging the church at Corinth to labor faithfully, Paul gives them a practical opportunity to do so in giving financially. Specifically, Paul was collecting money to give to the believers in Jerusalem who were feeling the effects of a famine in the region. "In light of this," Paul said to the Corinthians, "when you meet together, bring money proportionate to the Lord's provision for you."

I personally and strongly believe that this proportionate amount is represented by 10 percent—the tithe. The tithe is required throughout Old Testament law. But it also precedes the law, as seen in the account of Abraham giving tithes to Melchizedek—a pre-Incarnate appearance of

Christ (Genesis 14:20). In addition, tithing is seen in the New Testament—for although Jesus indicts the Pharisees for neglecting the weightier matters of justice and mercy, He, nonetheless, says they shouldn't leave tithing undone (Matthew 23:23).

Will a man rob God? Yet ye have robbed me.
But ye say, Wherein have we robbed thee? In
tithes and offerings.　　　　Malachi 3:8

If I don't tithe, I am robbing God. The tithe isn't a gift I give to God. It is simply a return of what's already His.

Bring ye all the tithes into the storehouse, that
there may be meat in mine house, and prove
me now herewith, saith the LORD of hosts, if I
will not open you the windows of heaven, and
pour you out a blessing, that there shall not be
room enough to receive it.　　　　Malachi 3:10

This is the only place in all of Scripture where God says, "Test Me." He says, "See how you'll be blessed when you quit robbing Me. Bring the tithe into the storehouse. Let it go. Give it up. And watch what happens. See if I don't bless you in ways that will be beyond your ability to even contain it. Be it emotionally, financially, or eternally. I'll bless you so much you'll never regret bringing Me the tithe."

And I will rebuke the devourer for your sakes, and he shall not destroy the fruits of your ground; neither shall your vine cast her fruit before the time in the field, saith the Lord of hosts.   Malachi 3:11

Not only will God bless those who tithe, but He will rebuke the devourer—that which eats away at our finances. Do you feel your money gets eaten up? It may be that part of the problem is robbery. That is, your money is being stolen by the devourer.

"I'm not going to pressure you with charts, gimmicks, or fund-raising drives," said Paul. "Just bring your tithe weekly. Then, when I come there will be no need to scramble for your checkbook."

1 Corinthians 16:5–7
Now I will come unto you, when I shall pass through Macedonia: for I do pass through Macedonia. And it may be that I will abide, yea, and winter with you, that ye may bring me on my journey whithersoever I go. For I will not see you now by the way; but I trust to tarry a while with you, if the Lord permit.

Although it was Paul's plan to winter in Corinth before traveling to Jerusalem, he adds a very important phrase when he says, "if the Lord permit."

"Trust in the Lord with all thine heart," Proverbs tells us. "And lean not unto thine own understanding. In all thy ways acknowledge Him and He shall direct thy paths" (3:5, 6). Therefore, wise is the man or woman who says, "This is the way the day is mapped out or the week is supposed to go—but, Lord, You can interrupt it as much as You want whenever You want."

I have found that if I am expecting to be divinely interrupted by this person, that situation, or the unknown event, I go through the day with a smile on my face. But if an unexpected interruption comes on a day when I have written my schedule in stone—watch out! The key? Expect to be bothered, and you'll never be bothered.

1 Corinthians 16:8, 9
But I will tarry at Ephesus until Pentecost. For a great door and effectual is opened unto me, and there are many adversaries.

Paul was neither an optimist nor a pessimist. He was a realist. "I'm going to Ephesus," he said,

"where there is a great door opened before me, but also many adversaries waiting to pounce on me." Paul's realistic appraisal of the situation is a true sign of maturity.

1 Corinthians 16:10, 11
Now if Timotheus come, see that he may be with you without fear: for he worketh the work of the Lord, as I also do. Let no man therefore despise him: but conduct him forth in peace, that he may come unto me: for I look for him with the brethren.

Why would Paul have to tell the Corinthians not to despise Timothy? Because Timothy was weak physically (1 Timothy 5:23) and emotionally (2 Timothy 1:7). Yet Paul saw in him a heart for the kingdom. "Don't let your gifts lie dormant because of your timidity," he said, "but stir up the gifts within you" (see 2 Timothy 1:6). Timothy lived up to the potential Paul saw in him and went on to become a giant in Church history.

1 Corinthians 16:12
As touching our brother Apollos, I greatly desired him to come unto you with the brethren: but his will was not at all to come at this time; but he will come when he shall have convenient time.

Even though Apollos had a fan club in Corinth, Paul was eager for him to come. Paul did not view Apollos as a rival or a competitor—which is further evidence of Paul's maturity.

1 Corinthians 16:13 (a)
Watch ye . . .

What are we to watch for? For the roaring lion (1 Peter 5:8), who seeks to attack the weakest among us—but also for the Promised Lion of the tribe of Judah, who is coming back for us. Our perspective is balanced to the degree that, as we watch what's going on around us, we also watch for Jesus' return for us.

1 Corinthians 16:13 (b)
. . . stand fast in the faith . . .

I look at the massive oak tree and realize it wasn't massive initially. An oak tree is nothing more than just a little nut that refused to give ground. So, too, by God's grace, we don't have to give ground. We can be consistent in our time of worship; we can be committed to the study of the Scripture; we can be faithful in prayer. People who are successful in any endeavor have one thing in common: They're part of the one percent who finish what they begin. Whether regarding career, kids, or the kingdom—most people have great ideas and start well. But they don't finish. They give up. They give ground.

"Father, I have glorified Thee and finished the work Thou gavest me to do," Jesus said (see John 17:4). Finishing the work God gave Him to do wasn't just an idea in His journal or a thought stirring in His mind. It was something Jesus *did*.

Has God called you to teach Sunday school? Do it and stay with it until He leads you in a different direction. Has He called you to have a time of morning worship? Then do so. Has He spoken to you about spending time discipling your kids? Then do it. I believe the Lord wants every one of us to be hugely successful in the things of the kingdom. His burden is easy, His load light. The only question is, will you give ground—or will you stand fast?

1 Corinthians 16:13 (c)
. . . quit you like men . . .

The word "quit" means "act." Linguistically, this is a most powerful exhortation. And Paul was not the first to use it. . . .

Hearing a great shout from the camp of the Israelites, the Philistines knew the ark of the covenant had been brought into the camp of Israel. "Woe unto us," they cried. "Who shall deliver us out of the hand of the mighty God of Israel?"

But when one of them said, "Be strong. Quit yourselves like men and fight," they dried their eyes, engaged in combat, and won the battle (see 1 Samuel 4:5–10).

1 Corinthians 16:13 (d)
. . . be strong.

"Be strong and of good courage," Moses told his protigi, Joshua (see Deuteronomy 31:7; 23).

"All that thou commandest us we will do. Only be strong," the people echoed (see Joshua 1:16, 18).

Our families will follow us, men, if we heed the exhortation of Paul and be strong. Scripture tells us Job made a sacrifice for each of his children daily (Job 1:5). That's strength; that's hard work. I'm not asking you to kill a bull, Dads. But we must sacrifice our energy, our comfort, our ease on behalf of our wives and our children. In the perilous days in which we live, to do anything less is simply not an option.

1 Corinthians 16:14
Let all your things be done with charity.

"Watch out. Stand fast. Grow up. Be strong"— but lest we go out of here chewing nails, Paul comes right back with the most important exhortation of all when he says, "Let everything be done in love." How can we watch out and stand fast and grow up and be strong—and at the same time be loving? We can't. This can only happen as the Son of Man, Jesus Christ, lives His life through us day by day.

1 Corinthians 16:15, 16
I beseech you, brethren, (ye know the house of Stephanas, that it is the firstfruits of Achaia, and that they have addicted themselves to the ministry of the saints,) that ye submit yourselves unto such, and to every one that helpeth with us, and laboureth.

It would seem as though the family of Stephanas was among the first of Paul's converts in that region. Of them, Paul says the whole family was addicted to the ministry of the saints. I like that! Every single person will eventually be drawn to and infatuated with a master passion. For the family of Stephanas, this passion was ministry. They must have seen Mom and Dad committed to the congregation at Corinth. They must have watched Mom and Dad opening up their home and hearts, spending time with the saints. They must have been included in the home meetings, in the congregational setting. Traveling with Mom and Dad, these kids were not left behind spiritually. As a result, they got hooked on ministry.

1 Corinthians 16:17–19
I am glad of the coming of Stephanas and Fortunatus and Achaicus: for that which was lacking on your part they have supplied. For they have refreshed my spirit and yours: therefore acknowledge ye them that are such. The churches of Asia salute you. Aquila and Priscilla salute you much in the Lord, with the church that is in their house.

When Paul first went to Corinth, he lodged with fellow tentmakers, Aquila and his wife, Priscilla. Not only did Aquila and Priscilla become believers, but they became so strong in the faith that when Paul went to Ephesus, he left Aquila and Priscilla in charge of the fellowship (Acts 18:18). After ministering in Ephesus, Aquila and Priscilla joined Paul in Rome, where a church met in their house (Romans 16:5). Then they returned to Ephesus to help Timothy, who would eventually become the pastor at Ephesus. Aquila and Priscilla were a couple who were on the move, flexible, determined to serve the Lord in any way possible—wonderful models for you and me.

1 Corinthians 16:20
All the brethren greet you. Greet ye one another with an holy kiss.

The church neither can nor should compete with the world in areas of technology or entertainment because the world will "out-glitz" and "out-hype" us every time. Rather, it is the responsibility and privilege of the church to offer junior-highers and collegians, high-schoolers and senior citizens something they'll never get anywhere else: love and truth. Only the church can say, "We'll tell you the truth, and we'll speak it in love. Unlike the world, we're not out to make merchandise of you or to exploit you. In Jesus' name, we're here to love you."

The world is in desperate need of love and truth. Paul had told the Corinthians the truth. And yet he had a deep love for them and encouraged them—even through their doctrinal differences—to love one another.

1 Corinthians 16:21
The salutation of me Paul with mine own hand.

Here, Paul takes the pen out of the hand of the secretary to whom, perhaps due to an eye disease, he had been dictating.

1 Corinthians 16:22
If any man love not the Lord Jesus Christ, let him be Anathema Maranatha.

The word *anathema* simply means "accursed." The word *maranatha* means "Lord, come."

"Whoever doesn't love Jesus, let him be accursed." Is this a word of harshness? I don't think so. I think Paul took pen in hand to plead with the Corinthians, saying, "If you don't love the One who is altogether lovely, the One who died for you, the One who cares about you, the One who gave everything that He might be with you in this life and in the ages to come; if you don't love this One who is all-wise and all-knowing yet all-loving and all-forgiving, then you curse yourself. Maranatha. The Lord is coming. You need to make your decision."

1 Corinthians 16:23, 24
The grace of our Lord Jesus Christ be with you. My love be with you all in Christ Jesus. Amen.

There could have been those in Corinth who said, "If you care so much about us, Paul, why did you point out our carnality and rebuke us for our immorality? Why were you so rough on us?"

Yet, under the inspiration of the Spirit, Paul simply says, "I do love you."

Because open rebuke is better than secret love (Proverbs 27:5), the rebukes and exhortations that come our way should be embraced as friends. It's much more comfortable for me to ignore a prickly situation or issue. But that's not love. Love says, "I care more about your well-being than about what you think of me. If you think I'm not a nice guy, that's okay, if what I'm saying will provoke you to love and to good works, to think through what you're doing and perhaps repent from the direction you're heading."

Faithful are the wounds of a friend (Proverbs 27:6). But make sure your correction is done in love. . . .

As the disciples sat at the Last Supper, under the table were twenty-four dirty, stinking feet. To remedy the situation, Jesus didn't give a lecture on foot washing. No, He girded Himself with a towel and washed feet Himself (John 13:4, 5).

I have the right and responsibility to give admonition, exhortation, and correction; to openly rebuke and wound if necessary only if I am willing to wash the feet of the people with whom I deal. If I'm not willing to walk with them through their difficulty, stand by them in their trouble, kneel with them in prayer, it would be wiser for me to keep silent.

Paul was one who had the right to correct, admonish, and rebuke the Corinthian Christians because he worked with his hands, put up with their insults, and risked his life to be with them. Thus, it was truly from his heart that Paul said to the church at Corinth, "My love be with you all in Christ Jesus."

What was their reaction?

While some would receive his words with humility and repentance, others would say, "Who does he think he is?"—prompting Paul to compose a second Epistle—the most personal of any he would write.

2 CORINTHIANS

1 After hearing from Timothy that some of the Corinthian Christians had questioned his authority to write his first letter of correction and exhortation, Paul wrote a second letter to them. This second Epistle would be the most personal of any he would write. Through it, we see the heart of a man committed to the kingdom.

2 Corinthians 1:1
Paul, an apostle of Jesus Christ by the will of God, and Timothy our brother, unto the church of God which is at Corinth, with all the saints which are in all Achaia.

"By the grace of God, I am what I am," Paul had declared in his first letter to the church at Corinth (15:10). Here in his second letter, to those questioning his apostolic authority, he says, "Not only is it by God's grace, but it is by His will that I am an apostle."

2 Corinthians 1:2
Grace be to you and peace from God our Father, and from the Lord Jesus Christ.

Although many in the Corinthian congregation attacked Paul rather mercilessly, he greets them with grace and peace. In so doing, he sets a wonderful example as one who is a peacemaker even in the midst of difficulty.

David modeled this as well, for no matter how many times Saul threw the javelin at him, he didn't fire back (1 Samuel 18, 19). So, too, I have found that those who walk close to the Lord and are used consistently by Him are those who, even when they have the right, do not fire back. I have also found that I can gauge my own spiritual state by the priority I give to defending my position, motives, or reputation; by how quick I am to throw the javelin back at those who threw it at me.

The truly anointed brother, the truly mature sister does not fire back. That is why we will see Paul explaining certain things to the Corinthian congregation, but not brutally firing at them. It is why he is firm with them, but never loses his heart of love for them.

2 Corinthians 1:3–7
Blessed be God, even the Father of our Lord Jesus Christ, the Father of mercies, and the God of all comfort; Who comforteth us in all our tribulation, that we may be able to comfort them which are in any trouble, by the comfort wherewith we ourselves are comforted of God. For as the sufferings of Christ abound in us, so our consolation also aboundeth by Christ. And whether we be afflicted, it is for your consolation and salvation, which is effectual in the enduring of the same sufferings which we also suffer: or whether we be comforted, it is for your consolation and salvation. And our hope of you is stedfast, knowing, that as ye are partakers of the sufferings, so shall ye be also of the consolation.

Paul found genuine comfort in God. You will, too. As you go through difficult times, real storms, immense challenges, you will find, even as Paul found, that God is a God of comfort. You will discover that He is the Father of mercy, who will comfort you in order that you can comfort others.

This is such a key passage because it clearly explains to us that the degree we can comfort others is the degree we have been comforted ourselves. It is only when we have experienced God's faithfulness firsthand that we can assure others that God will be faithful to them.

For topical study of 2 Corinthians 1:4 entitled "Shake It Off!" turn to page 1100.

2 Corinthians 1:8
For we would not, brethren, have you ignorant of our trouble which came to us in Asia, that we were pressed out of measure, above strength, insomuch that we despaired even of life.

Demetrius, a silversmith, was angry with Paul. So many people were getting saved in Ephesus that his business was being affected by loss of revenue from the sale of idols. Following his instigation of a riot, soon the entire city was in an uproar (Acts 19:29).

2 Corinthians 1:9 (a)
But we had the sentence of death in ourselves, that we should not trust in ourselves . . .

The dark days at Ephesus had a purpose: They caused Paul to rely solely on God. Like Paul, the tendency of most of us is to try to solve our problems with our own strength. Therefore, as He did with Paul, the Lord brings us to the end of ourselves from time to time. He brings us to the point where we feel pressed beyond measure, despairing even of life—in order that we will have no other choice but to call upon Him and find in Him greater strength than we could ever find in our own ability.

He was a go-getter from the very beginning. After all, he grabbed his twin brother's heel in a failed attempt to be first-born. Throughout his life, Jacob, or "heel-snatcher," was one who drew from his own cunning and acumen to get ahead. Then, one day, he heard that his brother, from whom he had cheated his birthright and blessing, was headed his way, accompanied by four hundred men.
When an angel appeared to Jacob, he said, "I have no other heel to snatch. I'm at the end of my resources. I won't let you go until you bless me." So they wrestled all night. Jacob ended up with a blessing when his name was changed from Jacob to Israel, from "heel-snatcher" to "governed by God." But he also limped away with a dislocated hip, as though God said, "With every step you take, you will be reminded that when you—who once walked so proudly, who once stood so confidently— came to the end of yourself, it was the best thing that ever happened to you, for in your brokenness and weakness, you'll be stronger and more useful than you could have ever been in your own energy and cleverness."

It's a great day when a man finally comes to the end of himself and realizes, "I don't need to go to another seminar or call another counselor; I don't need to enroll in another program or come up with another creative idea. All I need is You, Lord. I'm going to wrestle with You. I'm going to cling to You. I'm going to depend on You because I need to be governed by You."

2 Corinthians 1:9 (b)
. . . but in God which raiseth the dead.

Maybe your marriage seems dead. Maybe your joy or love or peace or ministry seems dead. Quit trying to figure it out and fight it in your own energy. Instead, seek the Lord. Trust the God who specializes in raising the dead.

2 Corinthians 1:10
Who delivered us from so great a death, and doth deliver: in whom we trust that he will yet deliver us.

I love this. God has delivered us in the past. He does deliver us in the present. He will deliver us in the future. Think about the things that were bothering you a year ago—how you thought, *It's all over. This is never going to work out. I'm toast.* Then look at where you are today. Unless we really stop and search our memories, most of us don't even remember the things we thought were going to do us in and wipe us out even a few months ago. Why? Because the Lord delivered us. He saw us through. He's faithful. I believe one of the biggest obstacles in our spiritual growth is our tendency to forget how the Lord sees us through all the times we think things could never work out.

"Because God *has* delivered us," Paul says, "He *will* deliver us."

2 Corinthians 1:11 (a)
Ye also helping together by prayer for us . . .

"Your prayers are part of the process God used to deliver us," Paul told the Corinthian church. And the same thing still happens. Have you ever wrestled with something or been discouraged by something, when suddenly you felt an infusion of peace and life and joy, and you knew someone was praying for you? Paul says, "When we were despairing even of life itself, you helped us by praying for us."

2 Corinthians 1:11 (b)–13
. . . that for the gift bestowed upon us by the means of many persons thanks may be given by many on our behalf. For our rejoicing is this, the testimony of our conscience, that in simplicity and godly sincerity, not with fleshly wisdom, but by the grace of God, we have had our conversation in the world, and more abundantly to you-ward. For we write none other things unto you, than what ye read or acknowledge; and I trust ye shall acknowledge even to the end;

The word "sincere" comes from a Latin phrase meaning "without wax"—referring to the wax used to hide the cracks in defective pottery or statuary. "We lived a life of godly sincerity before you," Paul says. "We weren't trying to deceive you or hide anything from you."

2 Corinthians 1:14
As also ye have acknowledged us in part, that we are your rejoicing, even as ye also are ours in the day of the Lord Jesus.

Paul had a wonderful ability to "know no man after the flesh" (see 2 Corinthians 5:16). So often, we point out one another's fleshiness. Paul didn't. He saw people positionally in Christ. He saw what they would be by the work of the Holy Ghost. Oh, he was a shepherd who knew there were wolves and false apostles. But when it came to the believers, he had a bigness of heart that allowed him to view them in the best possible light. This is why he could say even to the Corinthians, "You are our rejoicing, a treasure to us."

2 Corinthians 1:15–17
And in this confidence I was minded to come unto you before, that ye might have a second benefit; and to pass by you into Macedonia, and to come again out of Macedonia unto you, and of you to be brought on my way toward Judaea. When I therefore was thus minded, did I use lightness? or the things that I purpose, do I purpose according to the flesh, that with me there should be yea yea, and nay nay?

Although it was Paul's heart and plan to return to Corinth to minister again, he was delayed in his journey—a delay to which his enemies pointed as proof that his word couldn't be trusted.

2 Corinthians 1:18
But as God is true, our word toward you was not yea and nay.

In other words, Paul is saying, "We did not speak to you out of both sides of our mouths."

2 Corinthians 1:19–22
For the Son of God, Jesus Christ, who was preached among you by us, even by me and Silvanus and Timotheus, was not yea and nay, but in him was yea. For all the promises of God in him are yea, and in him Amen, unto the glory of God by us. Now he which stablisheth us with you in Christ, and hath anointed us, is God; Who hath also sealed us, and given the earnest of the Spirit in our hearts.

In the old covenant, we read over and over again, "*If* you do this, *then* you will be blessed." But in Christ Jesus it's not a matter of "if and then" but "Yea and Amen!"

For topical study of 2 Corinthians 1:20 entitled "Yea and Amen!" turn to page 1104.

2 Corinthians 1:23
Moreover I call God for a record upon my soul, that to spare you I came not as yet unto Corinth.

"It was a good thing that the Lord closed the doors and changed my plans," Paul says, "because had I come as soon as I wanted, I probably would have been too harsh with you."

2 Corinthians 1:24
Not for that we have dominion over your faith, but are helpers of your joy: for by faith ye stand.

Contrary to many churches today who set up pastors as those who have dominion over their flock, the true call of ministry is not to dominate others, but to be helpers of other's joy in humility as we point them to Jesus.

SHAKE IT OFF!
A Topical Study of
2 Corinthians 1:4

He was not speaking theologically or theoretically, for Paul was in a pretty tough spot personally. Sailing across the Mediterranean Sea to Rome, a storm began to beat and batter the boat full of prisoners, of which he was one. Finally, after many days, the 270 soldiers, sailors, and prisoners aboard were all cast into the sea. Some grabbed on to the splintered remains of the ship, some started swimming; but miraculously all made it to the shore of Mileta, present-day Malta. The "barbarians" on the beach, showing these waterlogged newcomers "no little kindness" (Acts 28:2), lit fires to warm them. And Paul, ever looking for an opportunity to serve others, joined in as he gathered sticks to fuel the flames. But lurking in one of the bundles was a deadly viper, which leapt out and bit him. When Paul shook off the snake into the fire, the local Miletans, who had initially thought Paul was cursed to suffer such a fate, now thought him a god.

Paul used the opportunity to share the True and Living God with an audience eager to hear from this one who had been bitten by the same type of snake that doubtless had claimed the lives of many of their family members and friends.

"Make my life count," we plead.

"OK," the Lord says as He allows us to be smitten by the snake of sickness and sorrow. "I will allow this to happen because the 'barbarians'—the natives in your community—are watching to see if there are any answers, any solutions, any hope for them.

A. W. Tozer, spiritual giant of the previous generation, was right when he said, "Before God can use a person greatly, He must allow that person to be hurt deeply." Why? Is it because God is cruel? Does He enjoy seeing us in pain? No. The issue is not cruelty. The issue is ministry. There are two essential, nonnegotiable prerequisites for those who desire to be used by God. . . .

Compassion for People

We may have our theology down pat, but if our hearts are not full of compassion for people, what we say will not be fully received. The old adage is true: People don't care how much we know until they know how much we care. How can I have compassion? By absorbing the bite of the same snake that bites others. There is no other way.

Therefore, God puts us in situations and tribulations, hard places and tough times, in order that we might develop compassion for people who are also experiencing difficulties—in order that we might be able to say, "I *know* what you're going through."

Confidence in God

Many Christians have compassion for people, but it is at the expense of God's reputation. "I really feel for you," they say. "I don't know why this is happening"—the implication being, "Where is God?" On the other hand, one who truly ministers will say, "God is *good.* Here's what He did in my life, and here's what He will do for you. Put your confidence in Him."

Quite frankly, gang, I think we should be more concerned about the reputation of our perfect heavenly Father than about our own ability to be relatable. He has promised to never let us be tempted above that which we are able, and that all things are working together for good. He has promised He will never leave us, and He has told us to rejoice in Him always. Paul does that. Because he had endured beatings in prison, storms at sea, and snakebites on the beach, he had compassion for the problems of others. Because he had experienced God's faithfulness through it all, he never compromised his belief that God is good.

Well," you might be thinking, *if the only way to have compassion for people and confidence in God is to be bitten by a snake or two, then count me out. I'll be an every-other-Sunday believer, but don't ask me to get involved in ministry or service.*

You can choose to be left out if you wish—but you must understand that the snake will still bite you.

Why?

It all has to do with the snake in the Garden of Eden. That is why there is starvation and sickness in the Sudan. That is why there was war in Iraq. And that is why there is pain in your world. "What is God doing?" people cry, when, in fact, it is not God's doing at all.

Having just encouraged His followers to develop faith, when the evening was come, Jesus said to His disciples, "Let us go over to the other side" (see Mark 4:35). But when a storm arose on the Sea of Galilee, the terrified disciples woke Jesus, who was asleep in the boat. "Peace, be still," or literally, "be muzzled," He said—the same term He employed when speaking to demons.

Thus, the insurance companies have it all wrong. The flood or earthquake that threatens your house is no more an "act of God" than the storm that bullied the disciples. They're acts of Satan, who was given permission by mankind to wreak havoc upon the earth when Adam rebelled in the Garden of Eden. You see, the disciples weren't the only ones on the Sea of Galilee when the storm arose. They were just the ones who had Jesus on board. Consequently, whether you decide to engage in ministry or not, you will still experience the snakebite of sickness and the storm of sorrow because the whole world has been polluted by the fallout of Adam's bomb. In this life, everyone experiences equal difficulty because everyone has been bitten (1 Corinthians 10:13).

After murmuring yet again, the children of Israel were dying by the thousands from the fiery serpents God sent to bite them. "What do we do now?" cried Moses.

"Make a brass snake on a brass pole," God answered, "and put it in the middle of the camp so that anyone who is bitten can look at the serpent hanging there and be made whole." Many were healed. Others, however, thinking it useless, perished in their stupidity (see Numbers 21).

Centuries passed, and all the while, no doubt, people were wondering what was the deal with the brass serpent. Then came a Rabbi from Galilee who explained it all when He said, "As Moses lifted up the serpent in the wilderness, so must the Son of Man be lifted up" (see John 3:14, 15).

So, too, it might take a year or two, or five or ten—or maybe an eternity—until we understand why we were bitten by the snake of sorrow, smitten with the sting of despair. But when we see Him who was made sin for us, it will all make sense. As in Numbers 21, some will refuse to look upon Him, saying instead, "Look at my snake. Can you believe how bad this is? Help me, help me."

But others will follow the example of Paul and will shake the snake of Satan's sting into the fire of God's promise.

Years ago, my son Peter-John accompanied me to a speaking engagement. Our flight landed in Orlando at 11:30 P.M. Although there was supposed to be a rental car ready for us at the airport, evidently our reservation had been mixed up. So we found ourselves on a bus headed to the "vacation center" where surplus cars were stored. Upon arriving there, it was obvious that "vacation center" was just another name for "one-step-above-junkyard." It was midnight by now, and without having any other recourse, we walked into the office to pick up our car. Behind the counter was a tired-looking man. Perhaps expecting us to complain, his countenance changed as I began joking with him and he with me—especially when he learned that I was in the ministry. "I haven't met any Christians like you," he said.

Half an hour later, nearing 1:00 A.M., he said, "I think I've got a car for you. It's a brand-new, fully loaded, convertible Mustang with no miles on it. You guys want it?"

The next day found Peter-John and me cruising to Pensacola with the top down, hearing people say, "Nice car," all day long.

It was a once-in-a-lifetime experience. If I had walked into the vacation center saying, "What's the deal? Where's my car? You guys really blew it," would we have had that experience? I wonder.

Turn your miseries into Mustangs, saint. Sure, things go wrong, but whether they are little inconveniences or major heartbreaks, trust in the Lord. Realize they are opportunities to learn compassion for people and to gain confidence in God.

Whether it be a big python or a little garden variety, shake off the snake and see God use you in the lives of the amazed barbarians and rental-car attendants who are watching you.

YEA AND AMEN!
A Topical Study of
2 Corinthians 1:20

Of the over three thousand promises given to us in Scripture—promises that deal with health and happiness, peace and prosperity, family and freedom, finances and security—most of the promises people claim for themselves are based upon the Old Testament formula seen in the Book of Deuteronomy. . . .

> *For if ye shall diligently keep all these commandments which I command you, to do them, to love the LORD your God, to walk in all his ways, and to cleave unto him; then will the LORD drive out all these nations from before you, and ye shall possess greater nations and mightier than yourselves.* Deuteronomy 11:22, 23

So many of the promises we embrace follow the formula that says, "If you diligently keep these commandments, then God will drive your problems from you, do wondrous things for you, and take total care of you."

But therein lies the problem.

Oh, I know that *if* I love the Lord with all my heart, walk in all of His ways, and cleave totally to Him, *then* the Lord will indeed do wondrous things for me and through me, in me and to me. The problem is, do I love the Lord with all of my heart? Do I walk in all of His ways? Do I cleave only to Him? The answer, sadly, is no. Therefore, if I'm not doing the "ifs," I can't expect to receive the "thens."

This shouldn't surprise me, for that was the purpose of the law all along. According to Galatians 3:24, 25, the purpose of the law was to show us that we're not righteous, that we can't earn salvation, that we can't possibly keep the standard of righteousness that would be necessary to qualify us to receive the blessings we so desire. The law—including the Old Testament promises—was given to produce in us the realization that although we wish we could receive the blessings, we can't fulfill the obligations.

But here comes Paul, telling us that, because Jesus has fulfilled all the "ifs" in the Old Testament, the promises are all "Yea" and Amen" in Him. Look again at Deuteronomy 11:22 to see how this works. . . .

> For Jesus diligently kept all the commandments that I command you. He loved the Lord His God, He walked in all His ways, He clave unto Him.

Jesus fulfills the "ifs" perfectly.

"I'm thankful that all of the promises were kept by Jesus," you might be saying. "But what about me? Because I've failed so miserably keeping the "ifs," do I have no hope for the "thens"?"

For ye see your calling, brethren, how that not many wise men after the flesh, not many mighty, not many noble, are called: But God hath chosen the foolish things of the world to confound the wise; and God hath chosen the weak things of the world to confound the things which are mighty; and base things of the world, and things which are despised, hath God chosen, yea, and things which are not, to bring to nought things that are: That no flesh should glory in his presence.   1 Corinthians 1:26–29

By His grace and for His glory, when we opened up our hearts to Jesus, God placed us—weak and foolish that we are—in Christ. And because Christ fulfilled the "ifs," we get the "thens," leaving us nothing to do but say, "Yea and Amen!"

If that sounds too good to be true, think of it this way. . . .

Suppose I'm in Switzerland and I begin to crave a hamburger, fries, and a shake. The two dollars I have in my pocket will buy just that at Hot and Now Burgers in Medford, Oregon. Therefore, *if* I can get to Medford, *then* I will have a burger, fries, and a shake. So I call the airport and say, "Can you give me directions to Medford?"

"What is your mode of transportation?" the official asks.

"I'm broke," I say. "So I'm going to walk."

"Do you realize there are mountains to climb, rivers to ford, and a little pond called the Atlantic Ocean to cross?" he asks incredulously.

"Yes," I say, "but *if* I can do it, *then* I can have a burger."

"Go west," he says. "And good luck." But then, after a moment, he says, "I'm interested in your plight. It just so happens that Swiss Air Jumbo Jet 747 flight 203 is leaving for Medford in about an hour. I'll reserve a seat in first class for you."

As I board the jet and find my seat, I'm not concerned about directions because I'm in the jumbo jet, and I know the jumbo jet will make it. As we fly, people on the ground won't even know I was poor and foolish enough to think I could walk all the way to Medford for a hamburger. No, they won't even see my foolishness because all they will see is a fabulous jet flying through the sky headed for Medford.

So, too, when we who were foolish and weak became believers, the Lord said, "I have a seat reserved for you. Come in." And, because we are placed in Christ positionally, we cruise to our destination gloriously—not by walking, climbing, swimming, or hiking, but simply by resting in Him.

You'll know if you are living in the Old Covenant if you hear yourself saying, "I prayed for forty-five minutes last Thursday. I read four chapters in Leviticus two months ago. I tithed three years ago. Why aren't I being blessed?" It is a monumental day in the life of any believer who finally sees that in Jesus it's no longer "if and then" but "Yea and Amen!"

Not only is all that we enjoy *because* of Him, but all that we crave is found *in* Him. You see, although we think we need Jesus to give us bread, He says, "I *am* the Bread" (John 6:35). We think we need Him to give us direction, but He says, "I *am* the Way" (John 14:6). We think we need Him to open up a job or a relationship or a ministry for us, but He says, "I *am* the Door (John 10:7). It's Me you're craving. All the promises of God are not something that come *from* Me, but are found *in* Me."

So there I am on the 747, looking forward to my Hot and Now burger. But then something amazing happens. As I'm sitting quite comfortably in the plane, a steward comes by with a thick, juicy steak, a steaming baked potato, sautied vegetables, crisp salad, flaky croissant, and chocolate mousse. Suddenly, a Hot and Now burger is the furthest thing from my mind. Although I thought the Jumbo Jet was simply a way to get me to Hot and Now, in reality, I'm finding more satisfaction than I ever could have imagined just being on board.

So, too, we say, "Oh, Lord, I need help." But as we talk things over with Him, we find that although we initially thought if He answered our prayer, we'd be happy, we realize it was Him we were craving all along. As a result, little by little, we find ourselves saying, "Whether the relationship develops, the sickness is healed, the job opens—it's all irrelevant compared to what I'm discovering just by spending time with You, Lord."

The price is paid, dear brother, precious sister. You're in the Jet. Jesus perfectly fulfilled the "ifs" so you can fully enjoy the "thens." And, as you do, you'll discover that what you were craving was Him all along.

Yea and Amen!

2 The apostle Paul had no intention of being a burden on the Corinthian congregation. Rather, his desire was to be a blessing to them. That is why chapter 1 ended with him saying, "I don't want to have dominion over you. I seek to be a helper of your joy."

2 Corinthians 2:1, 2
But I determined this with myself, that I would not come again to you in heaviness. For if I make you sorry, who is he then that maketh me glad, but the same which is made sorry by me?

"When you go to Corinth again, make sure you don't go with a heavy heart," Paul said to himself.

I point this out because sometimes spiritual self-talk is absolutely necessary. I believe the psalmist set the example for us when he said, "Bless the Lord, O my soul. And all that is within me, bless His holy name" (Psalm 103). In other words, "Get it in gear, soul. Wake up and start praising."

In 1 Samuel, we read of an ill-fated military endeavor wherein David and his men left their camp in Ziklag only to return to find their city burned down and their wives and children taken into captivity. As a result, David's men were so angry with him that they wanted to kill him. It was at this point that David could have descended into real depression. Instead, we read that he encouraged himself in the Lord (1 Samuel 30:6).

Do you ever do that? Do you say, "I'm not going to become discouraged. I'm going to talk to myself about what God has done for me, how good He has been to me, how He's seen me through so many times previously"? I encourage you to encourage yourself in the Lord. Talk to your soul. Speak out the Scriptures. Memorize them or read them aloud. And as they go from your mouth into your ear, let them bless your heart.

Encourage yourself in the Lord when you're stuck in traffic, when you're walking down the street, when you're feeling kind of blue. David did. And what happened? His countenance changed. He rallied the troops once again. They went after the marauders and captured everything that was lost. I wonder how much is lost and wasted in our own lives because we fail to follow the example of David and Paul, because we don't encourage ourselves in the Lord.

Knowing they misunderstood his intention in the first Epistle, Paul said, "I'm still determined to come to you with happiness rather than heaviness."

2 Corinthians 2:3
And I wrote this same unto you, lest, when I came, I should have sorrow from them of whom I ought to rejoice; having confidence in you all, that my joy is the joy of you all.

"I wrote my first letter to you not to burden you," Paul says, "but to give you the opportunity to work things out, so that we can celebrate together when I come."

The first time my wife, Tammy, went to a pastors wives' conference, I said, "On your flight back home, please call when you get to San Francisco." Although I wanted to hear her voice, I also wanted to know how much time the kids and I had to get the house in order!

This was Paul's intent in writing to the Corinthians.

2 Corinthians 2:4
For out of much affliction and anguish of heart I wrote unto you with many tears; not that ye should be grieved, but that ye might know the love which I have more abundantly unto you.

"It was not with a finger pointing at you, but with tears in my eyes for you that I wrote to you," said Paul. It's so important that as we mature in the Lord we don't err as the Corinthians did. We must not only read the Lord, but listen to the tone in which it was written.

For topical study of 2 Corinthians 2:4 entitled "A Hearing Aid," turn to page 1109.

2 Corinthians 2:5–9
But if any have caused grief, he hath not grieved me, but in part: that I may not over-

charge you all. Sufficient to such a man is this punishment, which was inflicted of many. So that contrariwise ye ought rather to forgive him, and comfort him, lest perhaps such a one should be swallowed up with overmuch sorrow. Wherefore I beseech you that ye would confirm your love toward him. For to this end also did I write, that I might know the proof of you, whether ye be obedient in all things.

Concerning the man in their midst who was living in immorality with his mother-in-law, Paul told the church at Corinth to turn him over to Satan in order that his soul might be saved (1 Corinthians 5:5). The Corinthians heeded Paul's word and banned him from their fellowship. Now the problem was that even though he had turned from his sin, the church wouldn't let him back into their midst. "You took it too far," said Paul. "I told you to deal with the situation, but the prescribed course of action has been overdone."

We must be those who do not flaunt or tolerate immorality. At the same time, we must be those who love and embrace anyone who says, "I want to walk with you and be part of your company."

2 Corinthians 2:10, 11
To whom ye forgive any thing, I forgive also: for if I forgave any thing, to whom I forgave it, for your sakes forgave I it in the person of Christ; lest Satan should get an advantage of us: for we are not ignorant of his devices.

Here, we see Paul's exhortation to be knowledgeable concerning Satan's devices—one of which is not only to get someone to sin, but to make him feel terrible about his sin, and to cause division among believers concerning the issue of his sin. Paul says to the church at Corinth, "Don't let Satan ostracize this one who needs to come back into your midst. And don't let him divide you in the process."

2 Corinthians 2:12, 13
Furthermore, when I came to Troas to preach Christ's gospel, and a door was opened unto me of the Lord, I had no rest in my spirit, because I found not Titus my brother: but taking my leave of them, I went from thence into Macedonia.

An opportunity for great ministry was opened to Paul in Troas. Yet because Titus failed to meet him there with news of how the church at Corinth was doing, Paul left Troas to find Titus. Here, we see an interesting side of Paul not often seen in other places. That is, he left a wide-open door in

Troas because he cared about one man, Titus, who was to inform him about an individual church—the church at Corinth.

2 Corinthians 2:14 (a)
Now thanks be unto God . . .

Why was Paul so easily able to praise God even in hard times? Because trials don't make or break a man~—they simply reveal the contents of his heart.

When someone cuts you off on the freeway, the way you respond is not a result of his action. Rather, it's an indication of what was already in your heart at that moment. This explains why Paul and Silas could sing in prison (Acts 16:25). They weren't praising God in order that He might set them free, for they had no idea their praise would open their prison door. Paul's praise in prison as well as in this Epistle was simply the overflow of the praise already in his heart.

2 Corinthians 2:14 (b)
. . . which always causeth us to triumph in Christ . . .

The Greek word translated "triumph" is linked to the Roman triumphal march. When a Roman general went into battle and killed five thousand or more of the enemy as he secured new territory for Rome, upon his return, he rode in a chariot, followed by his soldiers marching in all of their glory. Behind the soldiers were the men who had been taken captive. Alongside the procession, priests would walk, swinging their incense pots to create a sweet smell of victory as the entire procession made its way through the main thoroughfare to the Circus Maximus, where, for the entertainment of the crowd, the captives would do battle against wild beasts.

So, too, we are in a victory march as well. General Jesus, our Leader, our King left His empire in heaven, "invaded" this planet, and conquered the enemy on a hill called Calvary. However, five thousand didn't die. Instead, five thousand were saved (Acts 4:4). And the Enemy forces—demons—are not headed to the Circus Maximus, but to the lake of fire (Revelation 20:10).

2 Corinthians 2:14 (c), 15
. . . and maketh manifest the savour of his knowledge by us in every place. For we are unto God a sweet savour of Christ, in them that are saved, and in them that perish.

Marching behind our King as a kingdom of priests (Exodus 19:6), the gospel we share and the praise we offer become the incense of victory.

2 Corinthians 2:16 (a)
To the one we are the savour of death unto death; and to the other the savour of life unto life.

To the enemies of the Cross, our praise and testimony stink. But to those who are headed for heaven, the aroma is wonderful. I say this to let you know in advance that when you go to school or work tomorrow, to those who are destined to live eternally, you will be a sweet savor of Christ. But to those who are destined for hell, you'll stink. Don't take it personally. Just realize that it's a revelation of the fact that they are not yet part of the kingdom.

2 Corinthians 2:16 (b)
And who is sufficient for these things?

Who is sufficient to march behind Jesus, to carry the fragrance of Him, to be used by Him? Paul will answer this question in the next chapter when he says our sufficiency is of God (verse 5).

2 Corinthians 2:17 (a)
For we are not as many, which corrupt the word of God: but as of sincerity . . .

This is crucial for every Sunday-school teacher, preacher, Bible study leader, music minister, or anyone else who deals in any way with the Word. We are not to corrupt the Word with our own agenda or axes to grind.

2 Corinthians 2:17 (b)
. . . but as of God, in the sight of God speak we in Christ.

We who teach the Word are to realize that when we speak, we're not speaking theoretically, but that God is very much in attendance (Hebrews 2:12). If we approach family devotions and Bible studies, Sunday-school lessons and sermons as though God is present, our teaching and sharing become acts of worship.

I find that some of my most intense times of worship take place when I'm teaching the Word, for although I'm talking *about* God, in reality, I'm talking *to* Him. I'm saying, "Lord, it's amazing that we can march behind You. It's awesome that You have captured the Enemy by Your authority. It's comforting that You are our victory."

A HEARING AID
A Topical Study of
2 Corinthians 2:4

I have discovered that the more familiar with the Word we become, the more vulnerable we are to being tone-deaf. Oh, we know the Scriptures. We have our theology down pat. We know where to find all the stories, and we can give the references for major points of doctrine. We know the Word—but are we hearing its tone?

This is the question Paul is up against—for although he had written the Corinthians a letter that was admittedly corrective, failing to hear the tone with which he had written it, they felt he was unduly harsh with them. In this, I am reminded of another incident in Scripture in which tone played an important role. . . .

"Father, glorify Thy name," Jesus said only days before His crucifixion.
     Regarding the voice from heaven that answered, "I have both glorified it and will glorify it again," some heard thunder, others the voice of an angel (see John 12:28, 29).

This intrigues me. Within a single group of people on the same spot at the same time hearing the same voice, some thought it thundered menacingly, while others thought it spoke angelically.

So, too, we can give a single sermon or Bible study, and some will hear it as thunder, while others will hear it as a message from heaven. It all depends upon what's happening in the heart.

And they bring unto him one that was deaf, and had an impediment in his speech; and they beseech him to put his hand upon him. And he took him aside from the multitude, and put his fingers into his ears, and he spit, and touched his tongue; and looking up to heaven, he sighed, and saith unto him, Ephphatha, that is, Be opened. And straightway his ears were opened, and the string of his tongue was loosed, and he spake plain.   Mark 7:32–35

A deaf man who could neither hear nor speak was brought to Jesus, the Great Physician, the Ultimate Hearing Specialist. And as soon as this man's ears were opened, he could speak plainly as well—for the way we hear truly affects the way we speak.

So let me ask you, how is your hearing?

A Hearing Test

Realizing they were naked, Adam and Eve hid from God. And as they were hiding, they heard a voice in the garden, calling, "Adam, where art thou?" (Genesis 3:9).

You know the words, but what tone do you hear? Do you hear a Cosmic Cop saying, "Where are you? Wait until I get my hands on you!"? That is the way most people hear Genesis 3:9. But they hear it wrong. This is not the voice of an angry God tracking down a rebellious sinner. Rather, it's the cry of a heartbroken father looking for a lost son. God doesn't say, "Where were you?" or "How could you?" He says, "Where *are* you? Look at your situation. Allow Me to cover you" (see Genesis 3:21).

Shortly thereafter, God said to Adam, "In the sweat of thy face shalt thou eat bread" (Genesis 3:19). If you hear Him saying this in anger or frustration, you're missing the true tone of His voice, for God knew it was work that would keep Adam and the rest of us out of trouble.

The chapter ends with God driving Adam and Eve out of the Garden of Eden lest they eat of the tree of life and live forever in their fallen, sinful state. Yet many people read this story and see an angry God raining punishment on sinful man. They read the words, but they don't hear the tone.

How do you hear John 8?

They caught her in the very act of adultery. With stones in hand, they were ready to execute her as prescribed by the Law of Moses.

Jesus defended her, protected her, and then looked at her and said, "Woman, where are thine accusers? Dost no man condemn thee?"

And she looked at Him and said, "No man condemns me, Lord."

Jesus said, "Neither do I condemn you. Go, and sin no more" (see John 8:11).

How do you hear this story? Most people hear it as, "Woman, I'm letting you off the hook this time. Go your way. But don't let it happen again." But this perception is wrong on at least two counts. . . .

First, *gune*, the word translated "woman," was a term of deepest possible respect toward a woman. It was the same term Jesus used to address His own mother (John 2:4).

Second, "Sin no more," was not said as a stern word of warning, but rather as a loving word of hope. "Go your way free because now you don't have to sin anymore."

My heart melts when I hear the tone of the Lord's voice—not thundering a warning, but rather delivering an angelic message of comfort for you and me.

"It is finished," He cries (see John 19:30). And the world hears it as the cry of a tragic hero, the end of a sad situation. But wait. The Gospel writers tell us He cried with a loud voice—not the whimper of defeat, but the shout of victory.

"It is finished! The price is paid. The work is done. You are free," He said—a declaration that caused the earth to quake, graves to open, and the veil in the temple to split from top to bottom. The magnitude of His statement was such that had His hands not been nailed to the Cross, I'm convinced they would have been raised in the air in victory. Yet we miss this completely if we don't hear the tone.

How is your hearing? What tone do you hear when you read the Word? Do you hear the thunder of condemnation and damnation—or do you hear the heart of a Father who loves you so much that He gave His Son for you?

A Hearing Aid

James gives us a hearing aid to ensure that we hear the heart of the Lord as we read His Word. . . .

> *But if ye have bitter envying and strife in your hearts, glory not, and lie not against the truth. This wisdom descendeth not from above, but is earthly, sensual, devilish. For where envying and strife is, there is confusion and every evil work.*   James 3:14–16

This is the filter through which to view every sermon or Bible study, every commentary or devotional. Whatever causes envy or strife, confusion, bitterness, or anguish is not from heaven.

> *But the wisdom that is from above is first pure, then peaceable, gentle, and easy to be intreated, full of mercy and good fruits, without partiality, and without hypocrisy.*   James 3:17

Conversely, you can be sure that whatever is pure and peaceable, gentle and merciful, whatever is approachable and comforting is from the heart of the Father.

In other words, the characteristics James gave describe perfectly the personality and nature of Jesus Christ. Therefore, when you hear a sermon, read a book, or have morning devotions, all you have to ask yourself is, "Does this sound like Jesus—the One who ate with sinners and prostitutes; the One the common people heard gladly—or is it harsh and heavy, condemning and accusatory?" If it's not like Jesus, then what you're thinking, hearing, reading, or saying is not from above.

Jesus is pure and peaceable. Jesus is gentle. Jesus is easy to be approached. To those who want to know Him, He doesn't say, "Jump higher, run farther, try harder," but rather, "I stand at the door of your heart and knock. If you open the door, I'll gladly come in."

Because the only autobiographical statement Jesus ever made was, "I am meek and lowly of heart; My burden is easy and My load light," whatever is a burden to you or a weight upon you is not from Him.

Read the Word in the light of James 3:17. And as you do, you'll see not only words on the page, but you'll hear the heart of the Father.

※

3 **2 Corinthians 3:1–3**
Do we begin again to commend ourselves? or need we, as some others, epistles of commendation to you, or letters of commendation from you? Ye are our epistle written in our hearts, known and read of all men: Forasmuch as ye are manifestly declared to be the epistle of Christ ministered by us, written not with ink, but with the Spirit of the living God; not in tables of stone, but in fleshy tables of the heart.

"Do we need letters to validate our ministry?" Paul asks. "Do we need credentials to make you understand that the Lord has called us to this work? No. You are our letters. You who have been born again and are now walking with the Lord are the proof of the ministry to which we've been called." In other words, Paul is saying, "The proof is in the pudding—and you are the pudding. Look and see the work that has taken place in your midst. Look at the fruit."

Fruit is always the name of the game. . . .

Following a failed insurrection against Moses in which two hundred fifty lost their lives, the children of Israel continued to question Moses' authority.
"Let every tribe bring a rod to place in the tabernacle," he said.
The next day, although the rest of the rods remained as they were, the rod of Moses had blossomed—the fruit being the validity of his ministry (Numbers 17).

I suggest it was to this account Jesus referred when, concerning true and false teachers, He said, "You will know them by their fruit" (see Matthew 7:20).

2 Corinthians 3:4, 5
And such trust have we through Christ to God-ward: Not that we are sufficient of ourselves to think any thing as of ourselves; but our sufficiency is of God;

"We're not boasting in who we are or what we've done," Paul says. "Our sufficiency comes from God by His grace alone."

2 Corinthians 3:6
Who also hath made us able ministers of the new testament; not of the letter, but of the spirit: for the letter killeth, but the spirit giveth life.

There were those at Corinth who came into the congregation, saying, "Paul is a lightweight. Sure, he talks about grace—but the real issue is the law. If you really want to prove your spirituality, you'll submit to the Jewish rite of circumcision."

Those who are under the law are miserable because of their own legalism. So what do they do? They seek to make others as miserable as they are, believing that the more miserable one is, the more spiritual he is.

2 Corinthians 3:7–11
But if the ministration of death, written and engraven in stones, was glorious, so that the children of Israel could not stedfastly behold the face of Moses for the glory of his countenance; which glory was to be done away: How shall not the ministration of the spirit be rather glorious? For if the ministration of condemnation be glory, much more doth the ministration of righteousness exceed in glory. For even that which was made glorious had no glory in this respect, by reason of the glory that excelleth. For if that which is done away was glorious, much more that which remaineth is glorious.

The law was indeed glorious, as evidenced by the glow on Moses' face when he received it (Exodus 34). "Therefore," asks Paul, "if the law which brings condemnation and death is glorious—how much more glorious will be the ministry of the new covenant, the grace of God?"

2 Corinthians 3:12, 13
Seeing then that we have such hope, we use great plainness of speech: And not as Moses, which put a veil over his face, that the children of Israel could not stedfastly look to the end of that which is abolished.

Here, Paul points out something we would never have known otherwise. You see, we know from Exodus 34 that when Moses came down from the mountain with the law in hand, he covered his glowing face with a veil. One would assume he did this so that people wouldn't be blinded by the brightness of his face. But here Paul says Moses put a veil over his face so that the people of Israel wouldn't see the glow fading.

So, too, we might keep our rules and regulations for a day or two. Yes, we can shine for a while—but the glow fades quickly because we're sinners.

2 Corinthians 3:14–17
But their minds were blinded: for until this day remaineth the same veil untaken away in the reading of the old testament; which veil is done away in Christ. But even unto this day, when Moses is read, the veil is upon their heart. Nevertheless when it shall turn to the Lord, the veil shall be taken away. Now the Lord is that Spirit: and where the Spirit of the Lord is, there is liberty.

The veil over the face of those who live by the Old Covenant blinds their own eyes to the reality and identity of their Messiah, Jesus Christ. That is why you can talk by the hour with Jewish people about the way Jesus perfectly fulfilled Old Testament prophecy—and they still won't see Him as their Messiah. There's a veil over their eyes. And because this veil is done away in Christ, it is only as they turn to Christ that they are able to see clearly.

2 Corinthians 3:18
But we all, with open face beholding as in a glass the glory of the Lord, are changed into the same image from glory to glory, even as by the Spirit of the Lord.

Because there is none righteous, because none seeks after God (Romans 3:11), we are able to see the Lord only by His grace. Because He's lifted the veil from our eyes, we can look into His face. And in so doing, we are changed. We are changed not by a program, a practice, or a procedure. We are changed by a Person. We are changed by looking at Jesus—by spending time with Him, learning about Him, and worshiping Him.

Stay in the Scriptures, gang. Spend time in the Word daily. Come together for Bible study. Sing songs of adoration—for it's in worshiping, in studying, in looking at Him that you'll become like Him.

2 Corinthians 4:1, 2
Therefore seeing we have this ministry, as we have received mercy, we faint not;

but have renounced the hidden things of dishonesty, not walking in craftiness, nor handling the word of God deceitfully; but by manifestation of the truth commending ourselves to every man's conscience in the sight of God.

"By God's mercy, we walk in integrity," says Paul. "We're not using deceitful means to do something in the name of ministry." This is where Saul made such a mistake and where David did so well. Saul used the things of God to glorify himself, while David used his life to glorify God.

2 Corinthians 4:3, 4
But if our gospel be hid, it is hid to them that are lost: In whom the god of this world hath blinded the minds of them which believe not, lest the light of the glorious gospel of Christ, who is the image of God, should shine unto them.

"Those who say the gospel we preach is shallow and unworkable in an attempt to ensnare you in legalism are blinded by Satan," says Paul. So, too, when we tell people the good news that their past, present, and future sins are paid for if they'll embrace the free gift of salvation; that in this life they will have a Friend who sticks closer than a brother, a Warrior-King who will give them victory, a Bridegroom who will truly love them; that when they die they will be ushered into heaven where they will live eternally—we wonder why wouldn't *everyone* become a believer?

Paul answers this question when he says the god of this world blinded the eyes of those who don't believe. This happened when Adam and Eve chose to believe the lies of the Serpent rather than to walk in obedience to the Father (Genesis 3). That is why Paul would tell Timothy that the servant of the Lord must "be gentle to all men, apt to teach and patient, in meekness instructing those who oppose themselves . . . that they may recover themselves out of the snare of the devil who were taken captive by him at his will" (2 Timothy 2:24–26).

What does it mean to "oppose oneself"? It means to do that which is contrary to one's good. Thus, the reason we can witness until we're blue in the face and debate endlessly with a friend, coworker, or neighbor only to have them look at us with a blank stare is because they are held hostage, bound up, and blindfolded by Satan. Thus, they are unable to do that which would be to their eternal benefit.

So what should we do? We find the cure for spiritual blindness in a statement Jesus made after healing one who was physically blind. . . .

Or else how can one enter into a strong man's house, and spoil his goods, except he first bind the strong man? and then he will spoil his house.   Matthew 12:29

The real issue is that Satan must first be bound before those who are held hostage can be set free. How does this happen? A few chapters later, Jesus said that whatever we bind on earth would be bound from heaven, and whatever we loose on earth would be loosed from heaven (Matthew 16:19). Therefore, before my neighbor, my loved one, my friend who's spiritually bound and blinded can ever see clearly enough to make a choice, Satan, the strong man, must be bound and the blindfold lifted.

How does this happen? The Old Testament picture of this New Testament principle is found in 2 Kings . . .

With the enemy soldiers drawing near to capture him, Elisha prayed . . .

And when they came down to him, Elisha prayed unto the LORD, and said, Smite this people, I pray thee, with blindness. And he smote them with blindness according to the word of Elisha.   2 Kings 6:18

Was Elisha being vindictive or hateful? No, as we will see, Elisha's prayer was not for the purpose of retaliation, but for their salvation—similar to Hosea's prayer when he asked the Lord to put a hedge of thorns in front of his wife to keep her from pursuing adulterous relationships (Hosea 2:6).

Like Elisha, like Hosea, we must pray that the Lord would bind the steps of those who don't know Him in order that they wouldn't be able to continue in their path of destruction.

And Elisha said unto them, This is not the way, neither is this the city: follow me, and I will bring you to the man whom ye seek. But he led them to Samaria. And it came to pass, when they were come into Samaria, that Elisha said, LORD, open the eyes of these men, that they may see. And the LORD opened their eyes, and they saw; and, behold, they were in the midst of Samaria.   2 Kings 6:19, 20

After binding the Syrians, Elisha loosed them by asking the Lord to open their eyes in order that they might see that he had led them to the king of Israel—the very one they sought. And that's exactly what we need to do.

First, we need to pray that the work of Satan would be bound. Then we need to pray that God's power would be loosed in order that people might see the One they were seeking all along.

The result?

And he prepared great provision for them: and when they had eaten and drunk, he sent them away, and they went to their master. So the bands of Syria came no more into the land of Israel.   2 Kings 6:23

As changed men, the Syrians no longer attacked the people of God. So, too, the answer concerning the people we care about who don't know Jesus lies in prayer—in binding the work of the Enemy and releasing the power of God; in blinding their eyes to sin, and opening their eyes to the Savior. Without this, we witness in vain. The key is prayer. Oh, we know we should pray. But until we take seriously the necessity of Spirit-filled, intensive, persevering prayer, we'll never be as fruitful in evangelism as we would have had we prayed.

2 Corinthians 4:5
For we preach not ourselves, but Christ Jesus the Lord; and ourselves your servants for Jesus' sake.

The Greek word translated "servants" is actually "slaves." Thus, Paul says to the Corinthians, "We preach not programs, not principles, not procedures, not ten steps or fifteen ideas—but Jesus Christ singularly. And we're simply your slaves to help you in your understanding of Him."

2 Corinthians 4:6
For God, who commanded the light to shine out of darkness, hath shined in our hearts, to give the light of the knowledge of the glory of God in the face of Jesus Christ.

Unlike the light on the face of Moses, the light of the glory of God as seen in the face of Jesus is a light that never fades. How do I know what God is like? How do I know He's not vengeful and vindictive, angry, and upset? After all, I have certainly given Him plenty of reasons to be. But the face of the One who freed the woman taken in adultery and who, despite her reputation, commended the woman who washed His feet with her tears tells me differently.

- "Show us the Father and it will suffice us," Philip said.
- "He who hath seen Me hath seen the Father," Jesus answered (see John 14:9).

Both the face and the grace of God are revealed in the Person of Jesus.

2 Corinthians 4:7 (a)
But we have this treasure in earthen vessels...

In contrast to the beauty and grace of Jesus, Paul was earthy, indeed—as we all are. But this should not be surprising, considering the dust of which we're made (Psalm 103:14).

2 Corinthians 4:7 (b)
... that the excellency of the power may be of God, and not of us.

Our dustiness and earthiness serve to cause people to be just that much more impressed with the treasure of the beauty of Jesus inside of us.

For topical study of 2 Corinthians 4:7 entitled "Cracked Pots," turn to page 1116.

2 Corinthians 4:8–12
We are troubled on every side, yet not distressed; we are perplexed, but not in despair; persecuted, but not forsaken; cast down, but not destroyed; always bearing about in the body the dying of the Lord Jesus, that the life also of Jesus might be made manifest in our body. For we which live are alway delivered unto death for Jesus' sake, that the life also of Jesus might be made manifest in our mortal flesh. So then death worketh in us, but life in you.

It was piano craftsman Theodore Steinway who said that it is the forty thousand pounds of pressure exerted on the two hundred forty-five strings of a piano that creates beautiful harmony. Sometimes, it is only the pressure, the persecution we undergo that causes a song to resonate in the hearts of those with whom we share. Paul knew this. That is why he could say, "Good things are happening even in our tribulation and difficulty, for through our hard times, Jesus shines brighter."

2 Corinthians 4:13–16
We having the same spirit of faith, according as it is written, I believed, and therefore have I spoken; we also believe, and therefore speak; knowing that he which raised up the Lord Jesus shall raise up us also by Jesus, and shall present us with you. For all things are for your sakes, that the abundant grace might through the thanksgiving of many redound to the glory of God. For which cause we faint not; but though our outward man perish, yet the inward man is renewed day by day.

Quoting Psalm 116, Paul says, "I speak that which I believe—that the Lord will raise us up, that all things will work out for His glory." This same concept is present in the Book of Hebrews...

> Let your conversation be without covetousness; and be content with such things as ye have: for he hath said, I will never leave thee, nor forsake thee. So that we may boldly say, The Lord is my helper, and I will not fear what man shall do unto me.   Hebrews 13:5, 6

"He hath said... that we may say..." To speak out words of faith in the time of difficulty is so important in the life of the believer. If all we talk about is our frustration, pain, and sadness, we will faint. But if we speak that which He hath said—that He is with us always (Matthew 28:20), that all things work together for good to those who love God (Romans 8:28), that greater is He that is in us than He that is in the world (1 John 4:4)—we will be renewed day by day.

In Hebrews 11, we read that the worlds were framed—as a carpenter frames a house—by the Word of God. So, too, we frame the world in which we live by the words we speak. Speak words of grumpiness, doubt, fear, cynicism—and that's the world you and your family will inhabit. But speak words of faith, hope, and joy even when you're going through hard times—and such will be the characteristics of your world. Paul could have been murmuring and complaining, doubting, whimpering, and crying. But that's not what he chose to do. "Yes, we're going through tough times," he said, "but we have the spirit of faith."

2 Corinthians 4:17, 18
For our light affliction, which is but for a moment, worketh for us a far more exceeding and eternal weight of glory; while we look not at the things which are seen, but at the things which are not seen: for the things which are seen are temporal; but the things which are not seen are eternal.

Paul refers to his afflictions as light. Light? He was stoned, beaten, shipwrecked, thrown out on the open sea, cast into dungeons. "No problem," he says. "Those light afflictions are doing some heavyweight work in us."

Oh, to have the eyesight of Paul—to see whatever it is that we endure presently as light compared to the weight of God's glory.

CRACKED POTS
A Topical Study of
2 Corinthians 4:7

Having initially been brought to an awareness of Jesus by a light that shone so bright it stopped him in his tracks, Paul shines a light on three important understandings for anyone who desires to shine brightly in the dark days that seem ready to engulf our culture. . . .

Light Reflected *from* Us

Then spake Jesus again unto them, saying, I am the light of the world.

John 8:12

Ye are the light of the world.   Matthew 5:14

"I am the light of the world," Jesus said. Then He said to you and me, "You are the light of the world." Was He confused? Are there two lights? No. Think of it this way: Jesus is the Sun, the source of light. We are like the moon. We live in dark times. Yet, as we walk with Jesus, we reflect His light.

The moon is not visible during a lunar eclipse because the earth comes between the sun and the moon. In other words, when the world gets in the way, the "ministry" of the moon can no longer be seen.

How about you and me? We are to be the light of the world. Yet the degree to which we allow the pleasures, pursuits, and passions of the world to creep into our lives will be the degree to which the Light is eclipsed. On the other hand, if we look at Jesus without allowing the world to creep in, His reflection will be clear in our lives. That is why Paul tells us to behold the Lord with an open face—to remove anything in our life that comes between the Son and us. If we do, we'll shine not with the fading light of legalism, but with the glow of the liberty in the Spirit—which never fades.

Light Imparted *to* Us

For God, who commanded the light to shine out of darkness, hath shined in our hearts, to give the light of the knowledge of the glory of God in the face of Jesus Christ. But we have this treasure in earthen vessels, that the excellency of the power may be of God, and not of us.   2 Corinthians 4:6, 7

By His Spirit, God places the treasure of His Son into the clay pots of our lives. This is like placing the Hope diamond in a Glad trash bag. After all, it's only logical that if one has a thing of beauty and value, he would have a gold-covered box or something exquisite to contain it. Therefore, it's a mystery, indeed, as to why God would place the treasure of His Son in clay pots like us—until we realize that God does this so that the excellency of the treasure would be that much more brilliant.

Light Shining *Through* Us

We are troubled on every side, yet not distressed; we are perplexed, but not in despair; Persecuted, but not forsaken; cast down, but not destroyed; always bearing about in the body the dying of the Lord Jesus, that the life also of Jesus might be made manifest in our body.   2 Corinthians 4:8–10

Finally, Paul says that whenever we go through hard times, there is opportunity for the light to shine forth through the breaking of the vessel. . . .

As they charged oppressive taxes and plundered their cities, the Midianites provoked the children of Israel mercilessly—until God called a reluctant Gideon to deliver His people. When Gideon blew the trumpet and called men to march with him into battle against the Midianites, thirty-two thousand men responded.

"There are 145,000 Midianites, and only 32,000 of us. I don't like the odds," said Gideon.

"Neither do I," said God. "There's too many of you." So He instructed Gideon to tell anyone afraid of the battle to go home.

Twenty-two thousand walked way.

"Ten thousand is still too many," God said, and weeded out an additional ninety-seven hundred men who drank face-first from the river rather than keeping an eye out for the enemy. The three hundred remaining men—those who didn't spend unnecessary time doing necessary tasks, those who realized the seriousness of their call and the reality of the enemy—were the men who accompanied Gideon into battle.

Following the strategy given him by God, Gideon gave each man a trumpet and a torch within an earthen vessel. Then he positioned them on the hills surrounding the valley of Jezreel, where the Midianites lay sleeping. On a given signal, they blew their trumpets, broke the clay pots, and shouted, "The sword of the Lord and of Gideon." Hearing the sound, the men of Midian stumbled out of their tents, saw the lights surrounding them, and no doubt assumed that each torch represented not a single soldier, but an entire division.

"We're surrounded by thousands!" they cried. In their confusion, the Midianites began attacking one another (see Judges 7).

Thus, there was victory in the dark night because the light caused the enemy to be confused and beaten back. But the light could only be seen when the earthen vessels were broken.

This is why Paul could say, "Yes, we are persecuted; yes, we are crushed—but it doesn't bother us because through this, the light of the Lord comes flooding out of us in ways that beat back the darkness and deception of Satan."

As I ponder Paul's words, two things happen.

First, the light goes on within me. I understand that the Lord allows me to go through times of breaking so that those around me might see His reality shining forth from me.

Second, I lighten up as I realize that, because I'm just a clay pot, I don't have to put on an act or come across as a "religious" person. As a result, all glory goes to the power and mercy, the greatness and kindness of God, who placed in me the unspeakable gift, the incredible treasure of His Son.

5 After speaking of his affliction in chapter 4, it is no wonder that Paul's heart turns toward heaven here in chapter 5. . . .

2 Corinthians 5:1 (a)
For we know that if our earthly house of this tabernacle were dissolved . . .

Paul realized that the body he lived in was just a tent. As a tentmaker, Paul must have appreciated the craftsmanship of a well-made tent. Yet he also knew that tents are meant to be temporary. Thus, he says, "Don't take your physical situation too seriously. Your body is fine to camp out in for a while, but before long, the tent will begin to sag; a stake or two will be lost along the way; seams will begin to tear."

Our Father is so good to gently remind us every time we look in the mirror that we're rushing toward eternity. Paul was one who truly understood that his body was only a temporary dwelling.

2 Corinthians 5:1 (b)
. . . we have a building of God, an house not made with hands, eternal in the heavens.

Most people think of heaven as a big Beverly Hills in which everyone has a mansion, and there, on the corner of Glory Lane and Hallelujah Avenue, is theirs. But if the tent, or tabernacle, in the verse before us speaks of our earthly body, the house not made with hands must speak of our resurrected body—a glorious body custom-made for eternity.

2 Corinthians 5:2
For in this we groan, earnestly desiring to be clothed upon with our house which is from heaven.

We groan because our tents are showing signs of use, because our bodies are wearing out.

2 Corinthians 5:3, 4
If so be that being clothed we shall not be found naked. For we that are in this tabernacle do groan, being burdened: not for that we would be unclothed, but clothed upon, that mortality might be swallowed up of life.

"Nakedness" in this context speaks of disembodiment. Paul is setting straight the misunderstanding that when a person dies, he becomes a disembodied spirit—an idea completely contradictory to Scripture. Buddha was wrong. The goal of man is not to reach Nirvana, the "state of the snuffed-out candle." Rather, it is to inhabit the body prepared for us that will make the one we're living in now a tent by comparison.

2 Corinthians 5:5 (a)
Now he that hath wrought us for the selfsame thing is God . . .

Because God "doeth all things well" (see Mark 7:37), I promise you that even though we may have questions now about the nature of our resurrected bodies, when we get to heaven, not one person will say, "Boy, I wish I had my old body back."

2 Corinthians 5:5 (b)
. . . who also hath given unto us the earnest of the Spirit.

The Greek word translated "earnest" is used in reference to an engagement ring. Likewise, we pay "earnest" money toward something we're committed to purchasing. Paul tells us we can be sure that something great is going to happen because God has given us the earnest, the "down payment," the "engagement ring" of His Holy Spirit.

The times you have been overwhelmed by God's artistry as you look at a sunset, when you have been amazed by His grandeur as seen in a starry night, when you have been awed by His power, grace, and goodness as you look at the ocean, your family, or His Word are all "engagement rings"—sneak previews, down payments toward what lies ahead.

2 Corinthians 5:6–8
Therefore we are always confident, knowing that, whilst we are at home in the body, we are absent from the Lord: (For we walk by faith, not by sight:) We are confident, I say, and willing rather to be absent from the body, and to be present with the Lord.

Although we understand that the Lord is all around us and lives inside of us, we, nonetheless, walk by faith rather than sight.

"And why dost thou not pardon my transgression, and take away mine iniquity?" asks Job, "for now shall I sleep in the dust; and thou shalt seek me in the morning, but I shall not be" (Job 7:21). On the basis of this single reference, some teach that when a person dies, his soul sleeps in the grave until the Rapture of the church. Yet, because God called Job's statements "words without knowledge" (Job 38:2), it is faulty theology that is based solely upon Job.

As is seen in the text before us, the moment we are absent from the body, we are present with the Lord. This is an understanding seen most clearly in Jesus' words to the thief on the cross when He said, "*Today* you will be with Me in paradise" (see Luke 23:43).

2 Corinthians 5:9
Wherefore we labour, that, whether present or absent, we may be accepted of him.

"In light of eternity, in light of where we're going, in light of the new body awaiting us, we labor," Paul says. And in the remainder of the chapter, he will go on to give three reasons he endured beatings, shipwrecks, and persecution in addition to the lack of appreciation from the very people for whom he laid down his life.

2 Corinthians 5:10
For we must all appear before the judgment seat of Christ; that every one may receive the things done in his body, according to that he hath done, whether it be good or bad.

The Corinthians would have readily understood Paul's reference to the judgment, or *bema* seat—for that was where athletes were given their rewards. Paul tells us that we all will stand

before the reward stand, the judgment seat of Christ, where everything we've done will be judged. In 1 Corinthians 3, he shed further light on this when he said that all of our works—teaching a Sunday-school class or a Bible study, tithing or witnessing—will be judged by fire.

2 Corinthians 5:11
Knowing therefore the terror of the Lord, we persuade men; but we are made manifest unto God; and I trust also are made manifest in your consciences.

The fear of the Lord motivated Paul in ministry. This was not fear that God would hurt him, but rather that he would hurt God through his sin and stupidity. Having been caught up into the third heaven, Paul knew that one day we will all stand before the Lion of the Tribe of Judah and see Him in His majesty and love. Paul wanted to spare anyone from saying, "Why did I waste my time on that hobby, spend my money on that insignificant trinket, squander my energy so foolishly? Why did I take so lightly that which Jesus did for me on the Cross of Calvary?"

2 Corinthians 5:12, 13
For we commend not ourselves again unto you, but give you occasion to glory on our behalf, that ye may have somewhat to answer them which glory in appearance, and not in heart. For whether we be beside ourselves, it is to God: or whether we be sober, it is for your cause.

Paul is parenthetically saying, "The reason I'm telling you what motivates us in ministry is not to boast, but in order that you might be able to give a defense to those who criticize you for listening to us."

2 Corinthians 5:14, 15
For the love of Christ constraineth us; because we thus judge, that if one died for all, then were all dead: And that he died for all, that they which live should not henceforth live unto themselves, but unto him which died for them, and rose again.

Paul's second motivation was the love of Christ—not his love for Christ, but Christ's for him.

A few years ago, a ministry magazine reported that over 80 percent of those involved in full-time ministry experience "ministerial burn-out," which is causing clergymen to leave the ministry at a higher rate than those who are entering the ministry, and which results in the average pastor staying in the pulpit for less than three years.

"The Lord loves me," Paul said. "He died for me. And He rose again that I might live for Him." Thus, it was the love of Christ that kept Paul from burning out and giving up.

2 Corinthians 5:16
Wherefore henceforth know we no man after the flesh: yea, though we have known Christ after the flesh, yet now henceforth know we him no more.

As a member of the Sanhedrin, it is very likely Paul had heard Jesus speak in Jerusalem. Certainly Paul had heard about Jesus and was determined to put an end to His followers—when suddenly he saw the light on the Damascus Road (Acts 9). From that point on, Paul no longer knew Jesus after the flesh, for he saw Him in a different light. As a result, Paul saw all men differently. He didn't see them in their earthly bodies. He saw who they could become in Christ.

2 Corinthians 5:17
Therefore if any man be in Christ, he is a new creature: old things are passed away; behold, all things are become new.

"I'm a believer, but I don't feel like a new creation," you say. Check out Genesis 1, where we read that in the beginning, God created the heavens and the earth. But the earth became formless and void when Lucifer was cast out of heaven. So God spoke a re-creation into being (Genesis 1:1–3).
The same is true with humanity. God made us in His image, but we became "without form and void"—wiped out when we chose to submit to Satan. So the Spirit of God began to move upon the face of the water—upon the pages of the Word as we heard it opened to us. "Let there be light," He said—and when at last we saw the light, the re-creation process within us was put into motion.

2 Corinthians 5:18–20
And all things are of God, who hath reconciled us to himself by Jesus Christ, and hath given to us the ministry of reconciliation; to wit, that God was in Christ, reconciling the world unto himself, not imputing their trespasses unto them; and hath committed unto us the word of reconciliation. Now then we are ambassadors for Christ, as though God did beseech you by us: we pray you in Christ's stead, be ye reconciled to God.

The third motivating reason for Paul's ministry was the joy of service. "We get to be ambassa-

dors," he says. "We get to share the word of reconciliation, to give out the good news of the gospel." So, too, as ambassadors of the kingdom, we get to tell the girl who works behind the counter at 7–11, the boy who bags our groceries at the grocery store, the guy who picks up our garbage on Wednesday morning, our next-door neighbor, our co-worker, that their sins past, present, and future are truly, totally forgiven.

2 Corinthians 5:21
For he hath made him to be sin for us, who knew no sin; that we might be made the righteousness of God in him.

As Jesus hung on the Cross, a spear was thrust into Him, drawing forth water and blood, and opening His side so that we might, positionally, enter in. Jesus opened the way for us through the rending of His own flesh. That is why we can tell anyone and everyone that they, too, can be tucked away in Christ; that when God looks at them, He will see only the righteousness of His Son; that they can have a fresh start as a new creation. What a fabulous truth!
May the fear of the Lord motivate us. May the love of Christ constrain us. May the joy of service thrill us. May we, like Paul, say, "No matter what problems we face or what challenges come our way, it's an unbelievable privilege to be an ambassador of the King."

6 **2 Corinthians 6:1 (a)**
We then, as workers together with him . . .

As we saw in chapter 5, we are ambassadors for Christ, sharing the Good News of the gospel with everyone we meet. But here's the most delightful part—we are workers not just *for* Him, but *with* Him. He doesn't send us on an assignment, wishing us luck as we leave. No, moment by moment He's with us as we talk to, share with, and love people. And He's with them, too! This gives me a great deal of confidence in ministry.

If you were hungry, I could share with you my favorite lunch—a peanut butter and pickle sandwich. But I would not be certain it would minister to you. Maybe you'd like it, but maybe you wouldn't. Thus, it would be with a certain amount of apprehension that I would offer it to you.

There are a number of things we could offer to people about which we could feel some hesitancy. But when we share Jesus Christ, all hesitancy dissipates—for He is guaranteed. Consequently, to the person who comes to me with a troubled heart, I can say, "Let me pray with you right now because Jesus is truly right here, and He will give you peace. He'll walk with you through this valley. He'll make Himself known to you in the right way at the right time. I *know* this to be so."

I've yet to send a person out to seek the Lord who has come back saying, "It didn't work. I prayed. I read my Bible. I talked to Him. I waited on Him. But it didn't work." That's because the promise of James 4:8 is that if we draw near to Him, He will draw near to us—not that He might draw near—but that He *will.*

2 Corinthians 6:1 (b), 2
. . . beseech you also that ye receive not the grace of God in vain. (For he saith, I have heard thee in a time accepted, and in the day of salvation have I succoured thee: behold, now is the accepted time; behold, now is the day of salvation.)

"As we work with Him," Paul says, "I remind you of the immediacy, the urgency of receiving what the Lord wants to do for you." Truly, now is the time for each of us to be saved—not just born again eternally, but to be saved from that which would hold us back presently.

In Genesis 6:3, God says, "My Spirit will not always strive, or wrestle, with men." Therefore, we know He will not pull on the strings of your heart or whisper in the ear of your spirit indefinitely. If you continually say no to Him, there will come a point when He will let your decision stand—a decision Jesus would later call the blasphemy of the Holy Ghost (Matthew 12:31), the one and only unpardonable sin.

2 Corinthians 6:3
Giving no offence in any thing, that the ministry be not blamed.

Because of the importance and urgency of our calling, we cannot allow anything into our lives or ministry that would give people a reason not to respond.

2 Corinthians 6:4 (a)
But in all things approving ourselves as the ministers of God . . .

People often ask me what school they should attend in order to be approved for ministry. Check out the school in which Paul was enrolled. . . .

2 Corinthians 6:4 (b), 5
. . . in much patience, in afflictions, in necessities, in distresses, in stripes, in imprison-

ments, in tumults, in labours, in watchings, in fastings;

Paul attended a school wherein he was imprisoned, beaten, and starved. He attended the school that required much patience. Who's approved in ministry? The one who goes to the school of patience. So many people launch off in ministry before they're really ready. Their hearts are good, their intentions right—but so were the heart and intentions of Moses. . . .

Second in command in all of Egypt, his heart was moved as he saw the bondage of his Jewish brothers. Wanting to help, when he saw an Egyptian beating a Jewish slave, Moses killed the Egyptian and buried him in the sand. But when he realized word of his deed was spreading, he fled for his life and spent forty years watching his father-in-law's sheep before he was ready to lead God's people.

Paul was one who would have been eager to minister immediately. Instead, he was sent to the Arabian desert for three years. And even after that, he ministered not in Jerusalem, but in relative obscurity in places like Antioch, Corinth, Ephesus, and Philippi.

2 Corinthians 6:6–8 (a)
By pureness, by knowledge, by longsuffering, by kindness, by the Holy Ghost, by love unfeigned, by the word of truth, by the power of God, by the armour of righteousness on the right hand and on the left, by honour and dishonour, by evil report and good report . . .

What courses did Paul take in the school of patience and persecution? Homiletics? No. Systematic theology? No. Hermeneutics? No. Greek? No. Hebrew? No. Church growth? No. He enrolled in pureness, intimacy, kindness, longsuffering, and love unfeigned. Wouldn't those be great course requirements in a seminary?

2 Corinthians 6:8 (b), 9
. . . as deceivers, and yet true; as unknown, and yet well known; as dying, and, behold, we live; as chastened, and not killed;

Did Paul finish his education with a Master of Theology or a Doctor of Divinity degree? No, he finished being thought a deceiver, as unknown—not received by the intellectuals in Jerusalem. Although Paul may have been unknown in Jerusalem, he was well known in hell. . . .

Going about casting out demons, the sons of Sceva said, "We adjure you in the name of Jesus whom Paul preaches, Come out."

"Jesus we know," the demons answered, "and Paul we know. But who are you?" (see Acts 19:15).

The demons understood Paul was a real threat, that he was one who would impact their kingdom of darkness and death and beat it back in the name of Jesus Christ.

2 Corinthians 6:10
As sorrowful, yet alway rejoicing; as poor, yet making many rich; as having nothing, and yet possessing all things.

Although he faced continual persecution, the tears Paul shed were not for himself, but over the state of others (Acts 20:18, 19). What about us? If two vials were placed before you, one labeled "Tears shed for yourself" and the other "Tears shed for others," how would they compare?

2 Corinthians 6:11, 12
O ye Corinthians, our mouth is open unto you, our heart is enlarged. Ye are not straitened in us, but ye are straitened in your own bowels.

In other words, "Our hearts are open to you," said Paul. "Any tension you feel is not the result of anything we feel toward you, but the result of your own emotions." This is an important understanding, for sometimes if I'm with a person I feel is not very open to me, it could be that I'm not open to him.

2 Corinthians 6:13
Now for a recompence in the same, (I speak as unto my children,) be ye also enlarged.

"Because we are approved ministers—through the school we attended, the courses we took, the degree we were given—accept our ministry to you with largeness of heart," says Paul.

2 Corinthians 6:14 (a)
Be ye not unequally yoked together with unbelievers . . .

"I want to be big-hearted and open-minded, so I'm going to marry her or develop a business partnership with him, even though he or she isn't a believer."

"Wait a minute," says Paul. "Don't misunderstand. Be big toward your brothers and sisters in the Lord. But be careful you don't err by being yoked in partnership or relationship with an unbeliever."

Come unto me, all ye that labour and are heavy laden, and I will give you rest. Take my yoke upon you, and learn of me; for I am meek and lowly in heart: and ye shall find rest unto your souls. For my yoke is easy, and my burden is light.   Matthew 11:28–30

The Greek word translated "easy" means "good fit." Because an ill-fitting yoke would cause chafing of the hide or even a dislocation of the animal's shoulder, yokes were custom-designed to ensure a perfect fit. No doubt Jesus knew whereof He spoke in using this analogy, for the Greek word translated "carpenter," used concerning Joseph and, by implication, Jesus, is *tekton,* from which we get our word "technical." The *tekton* was not the framer, but rather the finish carpenter, a master craftsman. Jesus and His father, Joseph, were master craftsmen. Thus, there is historical evidence to support the tradition that the specialty in their carpenter shop was yokes.

"Take My yoke upon you," Jesus says. "It will fit you perfectly, and the load you're pulling will become light as you link with Me." But here's the problem. Many of us are like the Corinthians. We are not yoked to Jesus exclusively. Rather, we find ourselves yoked to unbelievers. "Whether relationally or vocationally, don't yoke with someone who is not linked to Jesus," says Paul. And then he gives four reasons why. . . .

2 Corinthians 6:14 (b), 15
. . . for what fellowship hath righteousness with unrighteousness? and what communion hath light with darkness? And what concord hath Christ with Belial? or what part hath he that believeth with an infidel?

The first reason we are not to be unequally yoked is due to the nature of the believer. "He's so strong in character," she says. "A lot of believers are flaky, but he's so steady and stable. And I know he'll get saved someday. He promised me he would come to church. Sure, he's not a believer yet, but what's the big deal? I see potential. So I'm going to yoke myself with him in marriage."

Thou shalt not sow thy vineyard with divers seeds: lest the fruit of thy seed which thou hast sown, and the fruit of thy vineyard, be defiled. Thou shalt not plow with an ox and an ass together. Thou shalt not wear a garment of divers sorts, as of woollen and linen together.   Deuteronomy 22:9–11

Paul reaches back into the Old Testament, pulls out this Scripture, and says to you and me, "Don't be unequally yoked with unbelievers." It won't work because the nature of the believer and the unbeliever are so different. Oh, you might be able to get along now, but down the road, you'll experience pain and unnecessary heartache.

"We're not really serious," the Christian guy says of his unbelieving girlfriend. Sure, his intention might not be to marry her initially, but something happens unintentionally, which limits his ability to see clearly. I can't count how many people I have counseled who want out of their marriages because of this very issue. How much pain and heartbreak would be avoided if we took to heart this straightforward, simple command.

2 Corinthians 6:16
And what agreement hath the temple of God with idols? for ye are the temple of the living God; as God hath said, I will dwell in them, and walk in them; and I will be their God, and they shall be my people.

The second reason we are not to be unequally yoked is because of the effect it has on others. If there's a rotten beam overhead and the church roof collapses during Sunday service, the whole congregation is affected by the state of a single beam. So, too, because we are the temple of God, because we're linked together as living stones, because we're fit together as a holy habitation, if you're linked with an unbeliever, it will affect the entire body of Christ.

As they entered the Promised Land, the walled city of Jericho loomed large before them. "I will give you this city," God declared. "But when I do, make sure you don't take anything from it. You'll be able to spoil other cities, but not Jericho."

True to His Word, God did, indeed, give them the city. And the people moved on—except for one man. Seeing a Babylonian garment he just had to have, Achan took it, along with some gold and silver, and hid it in his tent. Unaware of Achan's disobedience, the Israelites went on to battle the little city of Ai—where they were whipped soundly.

"How could this be?" Joshua cried to the Lord.

"There is sin in the camp," the Lord answered.

Achan's sin affected the entire nation. And people died in battle because of his sin. (Joshua 7).

When we choose to ignore the way of the Lord, to rebel and disobey, it affects our sons, daughters, the church corporately, and the believing community.

2 Corinthians 6:17
Wherefore come out from among them, and be ye separate, saith the Lord, and touch not the unclean thing; and I will receive you,

The third reason we are not to be unequally yoked is due to the command of the Scriptures.

Depart ye, depart ye, go ye out from thence, touch no unclean thing; go ye out of the midst of her; be ye clean, that bear the vessels of the Lord.   Isaiah 52:11

Does this mean we shouldn't have conversations with sinners? Of course not. Jesus was called a Friend of Sinners (Luke 7:34). But the important thing to note is that wherever Jesus went, He permanently and radically impacted sinners. Therefore, when you walk into places where worldly stuff is going on, if people start turning to God and repenting from their sin, go for it! If you're truly impacting the place you're in—excellent! But if the place is impacting you, causing your own spirit to sag, get out. Pull away. Back off immediately.

"Oh, but I'm mature in the Lord," you say. "So it's okay for me to go into this business venture even though my partners are unbelievers."

Is it really? I refer you to what happened to one of the greatest men of history. . . .

Jehoshaphat was a uniquely blessed man. Revival happened around him; blessings flowed from him; good things came to him. And then, as his life is coming to an end, there's a P.S. in his story. . . .

And after this did Jehoshaphat king of Judah join himself with Ahaziah king of Israel, who did very wickedly: And he joined himself with him to make ships to go to Tarshish. . . .
2 Chronicles 20:35, 36 (a)

A godly Jehoshaphat joined with an ungodly Ahaziah in the shipping business. But the venture sunk.

Don't be like Jehoshaphat, saying, "This might not be God's best for me—but I know my ship will come in eventually." A person might become rich financially by joining with an unbeliever, but what does it profit him if he gain the whole world and lose his soul (Mark 8:36)? What good is it if it causes him to be only a shell of what he once was spiritually?

What's your legacy, Dad? At one time, you were about the things of the kingdom. You were a servant, a leader, a worker. But now you're known as a business whiz. How tragic. Don't be yoked with unbelievers in any endeavor that will cause you to sink spiritually.

2 Corinthians 6:18
And will be a Father unto you, and ye shall be my sons and daughters, saith the Lord Almighty.

The fourth reason we are not to be unequally yoked is because of the desire of the Father. "Separate yourself from the unbeliever, and you will be My sons and daughters," He says. Does this mean that if we are unequally yoked in marriage or business, we are not His children? No. We who have opened our hearts to Jesus Christ are children of the Father regardless. But if we are linked to the world, it limits His ability to be a Father to us. Think of it this way. . . .

If I wanted to take my family out to dinner, but my kids were all muddy from playing outside, I'd say, "I want to take you out to dinner. Go wash up."

Now, if they responded by saying, "We don't want to wash. We like this mud," they'd still be my children, but I couldn't take them out for dinner.

So, too, God says to us, "I will be a Father to you, taking you great places, doing wonderful things for you if you're separate and clean. If you're not separate, you're still My child, but I can't do for you what I would have done in and with and through you had you separated yourself from the world."

Let God be the Father He wants to be to you and your family by separating yourself from unclean partnerships and relationships, activities and priorities. As you do, never lose sight of the yoke He carried, when, in the Person of Jesus Christ, He carried the Cross on which He would shed His blood for you.

7 When Paul wrote this letter, he did not write it in chapters. In fact, there were no chapter divisions whatsoever in the Bible until the late 1300s. At that time, someone added chapter divisions in order to help people locate passages more easily. Then in the 1500s, someone divided the chapters into verses. And for the most part, the job these scholars did is excellent. But every once in a while, one wonders what the reasoning was behind their choices. Second Corinthians 7:1 is one such example . . .

2 Corinthians 7:1 (a)
Having therefore these promises, dearly beloved, let us cleanse ourselves from all filthiness of the flesh . . .

Verse 1 of chapter 7 should really be the last verse of chapter 6 because it's a continuation of the promises to which Paul referred in verses 16–18, wherein God promised He would dwell with

us and be a Father to us. "Having these promises, let us cleanse ourselves," Paul says. What does this mean? The Old Testament picture of this New Testament principle is found in the fifth chapter of 2 Kings. . . .

In the Old Testament, leprosy is a very appropriate picture of sin, for it begins seemingly insignificantly, but spreads insidiously. When Naaman, a prominent Syrian ruler who had contracted this terrible disease, was told by his servant girl that there was a prophet in Israel who could cure him, he sent a message to the king of Israel, who, in turn, sent for Elisha. Expecting Elisha to pronounce some sort of magical incantation over him, Naaman was "wroth" when Elisha told him to wash in the Jordan River seven times. After all, Naaman thought the Jordan nothing more than a muddy creek compared to the rivers of his own country. Thus, Scripture says he "turned and went away in a rage."

But his servants didn't give up so easily. "If Elisha had asked you to do something difficult, you would have done it," they said to Naaman. "Therefore, why not see what happens if you comply with this seemingly simple command?" So Naaman did, indeed, dip himself into the Jordan seven times—the number of completion—and he came out healed and whole.

Likewise, we who are eaten by the leprosy of sin must dip in the water over and over and over again. What water? The psalmist said in Psalm 119 that a young man shall cleanse his way by taking heed according to the Word. Jesus said in John 15 that we are clean through the Word He has spoken unto us. Paul declared in Ephesians 5 that we are washed by the water of the Word of God.

Let the Word of God cleanse you, and an amazing thing will happen. You may never become a scholar of theology, but as you submerge yourself in Scripture, the leprosy that once gnawed on you will begin to be cleansed. To those who are struggling with their flesh and looking for a quick answer, we need to say, "Plunge into Scripture. Plug into Bible study. Keep at it over and over and over again—for it's God's Word that will cleanse you and wash away the sin that hounds you."

2 Corinthians 7:1 (b)
. . . and spirit, perfecting holiness in the fear of God.

We are to cleanse ourselves not only from the filthiness of the flesh, but also of the spirit. As believers, we are very cognizant of the sins of the flesh—those sins that are done outwardly and that seem to permeate our culture increasingly.

Yet how often we fail to even notice the much more dangerous sins of the spirit—like gossiping, fault-finding, laziness, cynicism.

Jesus indicted the Pharisees for being more concerned about their rituals and ceremonial cleansing than about the big issues of justice and mercy (Matthew 23:23). That is why it is imperative that we take to heart what Paul is saying. Our flesh might appear quite presentable, but what about the grudges we keep, the anger that wells up within, the lustful thoughts, and the wrong perspectives we know need to be corrected? Paul says, "Cleanse yourselves from filthiness of both the flesh *and* the spirit. Deal with it *all*."

2 Corinthians 7:2
Receive us; we have wronged no man, we have corrupted no man, we have defrauded no man.

I believe this is where the chapter should more logically begin. "Don't reject us," Paul says. "We have defrauded, cheated, or tricked no one."

2 Corinthians 7:3
I speak not this to condemn you: for I have said before, that ye are in our hearts to die and live with you.

"I'm not down on you," Paul tells the Corinthians. "I don't want to bring condemnation to you. You're in our hearts; we live and die with you."

2 Corinthians 7:4–6 (a)
Great is my boldness of speech toward you, great is my glorying of you: I am filled with comfort, I am exceeding joyful in all our tribulation. For, when we were come into Macedonia, our flesh had no rest, but we were troubled on every side; without were fightings, within were fears. Nevertheless God, that comforteth those that are cast down, comforted us ...

I love this Scripture. If you're going through a hard season in your life, know this: God loves to comfort those who feel cast down. Blessed be the Father of mercy, the God of *all* comfort (2 Corinthians 1:3).

2 Corinthians 7:6 (b)
... by the coming of Titus.

When Paul was going through the wringer internally, externally, emotionally, and physically, how did God comfort him? Through Titus. This amazes me. You see, Titus was one of Paul's students, one of his disciples. After sending him to

Corinth with his first letter, Paul says it was when Titus returned that he was built up.

I'm afraid my reaction would have been, "Oh, it's just Titus. Lord, why didn't You send me someone famous or deep? Billy Graham perhaps. But Titus? He's just one of my boys. How can he help me?"

I think of Jesus in the Garden of Gethsemane. As He sweat great drops of blood while He prayed with intensity, an angel came and strengthened Him (Luke 22:43). Jesus could have said, "I'm way above the angels." Instead, He received the ministry of the angel. So, too, Paul received encouragement from Titus because he recognized an important principle: Often the Lord comes to us in the unexpected person at an unexpected time in an unexpected way....

- "We know Him," they said. "He's the carpenter's son" (see Mark 6:3). But they were wrong. He was the Son of God.
- Mary wept at the tomb, mistaking the Lord for a gardener (John 20:15).
- On the road to Emmaus, the travelers thought Jesus was a stranger (Luke 24:18).
- On the Sea of Galilee, His disciples thought Jesus was a ghost (Matthew 14:26).

Don't miss your Titus, gang. It might be your son or daughter. It might be a neighbor or co-worker. It might be someone you would never think had much to offer, but they'll come to you with words of encouragement—if you're wise enough to listen. Many people miss out, waiting for a pastor or a prophet, because they fail to recognize the Lord in the person sitting right next to them.

2 Corinthians 7:7–9
And not by his coming only, but by the consolation wherewith he was comforted in you, when he told us your earnest desire, your mourning, your fervent mind toward me; so that I rejoiced the more. For though I made you sorry with a letter, I do not repent, though I did repent: for I perceive that the same epistle hath made you sorry, though it were but for a season. Now I rejoice, not that ye were made sorry, but that ye sorrowed to repentance: for ye were made sorry after a godly manner, that ye might receive damage by us in nothing.

"At first, I regretted sending my first letter," Paul says. "But, due to your growth from it, I no longer regret it." Many of us regret things we've said, written, or done. Like Paul's, our heart may have been right, but then we second-guess our actions. The solution? Do your best at any given moment—be it in teaching, witnessing, or sharing.

And then commit it to God and forget about it because God sees your heart.

2 Corinthians 7:10
For godly sorrow worketh repentance to salvation not to be repented of: but the sorrow of the world worketh death.

"Godly sorrow leads to salvation," Paul says.
"But weren't the Corinthian believers already saved?" you ask.
Absolutely.
Then what does this mean?
Soteria, the Greek word translated "salvation," means more than simply being born again. When the Scriptures talk about salvation, they speak of the full orb of God's blessing—not only of being born again eternally, but of being saved from bondage and pain presently.
What brings about this kind of salvation?
Paul says the answer is repentance.

For topical study of 2 Corinthians 7:8–10 entitled "Real Repentance," turn to page 1126.

2 Corinthians 7:11
For behold this selfsame thing, that ye sorrowed after a godly sort, what carefulness it wrought in you, yea, what clearing of yourselves, yea, what indignation, yea, what fear, yea, what vehement desire, yea, what zeal, yea, what revenge! In all things ye have approved yourselves to be clear in this matter.

True repentance doesn't say, "Maybe I'll get to it next year." No, true repentance says, "This is wrong, and I'm going to deal with it now—with finality and certainty, no matter the cost."

2 Corinthians 7:12
Wherefore, though I wrote unto you, I did it not for his cause that had done the wrong, nor for his cause that suffered wrong, but that our care for you in the sight of God might appear unto you.

Any parent knows the easiest thing to do is to ignore the problems he sees in his children. But that's not the right thing. If you love your kids, you deal with issues through dialogue and discipline.
So, too, concerning the issue of immorality in the church, Paul says, "I did this that you might know that we care about you in the sight of God and that we want you to do well."

2 Corinthians 7:13, 14
Therefore we were comforted in your comfort: yea, and exceedingly the more joyed we for the joy of Titus, because his spirit was refreshed by you all. For if I have boasted any thing to him of you, I am not ashamed; but as we spake all things to you in truth, even so our boasting, which I made before Titus, is found a truth.

This interests me because the church at Corinth was far from perfect. Yet Paul finds himself boasting about them. Such was the bigness of his heart, the sureness of his faith.

2 Corinthians 7:15, 16
And his inward affection is more abundant toward you, whilst he remembereth the obedience of you all, how with fear and trembling ye received him. I rejoice therefore that I have confidence in you in all things.

"You received Titus and responded to the Word we shared. Good for you, Corinthians," says Paul to this church so dear to his heart.

REAL REPENTANCE

A Topical Study of
2 Corinthians 7:8–10

From Genesis through Revelation, God's men came on the scene and consistently said, "Here's the key: Repent."

- From the steps of the ark, Noah didn't look out at the crowd and say, "Something good is going to happen to you!" No, he said, "Repent" (Genesis 6).

- It wasn't for saying, "I'm okay, you're okay," that Joel was confronted by the high priest. It was because he said, "Rend your heart. Get right. Repent" (see Joel 2:13).
- Daniel was in the lions' den not because he said, "Inch by inch, anything's a cinch," but because his message was, "You have been weighed in the balance and found lacking" (see Daniel 5:27).
- Jeremiah was in the pit not for preaching, "The me I see is the me I'll be," but for calling a nation to repentance.
- John the Baptist lost his head not because he preached, "Smile, God loves you," but because he told people to turn from wickedness and repent (Matthew 3:2).
- When Jesus Himself came on the scene, the first message He would bring would not be, "God loves you and so do I," but, "Repent, the kingdom of God is among you" (see Mark 1:15).
- In the Book of Revelation, we read that the two witnesses will be killed and left lying in the streets of Jerusalem not because their message is, "God's in His heaven and all's right with the world," but because, dressed in sackcloth, they will call people to repent (Revelation 11).

We need to understand that the key to unlocking the full blessing of salvation is found in repentance.

What is repentance?

It's a word that simply means "to change direction." In other words, if you were going to the left, you go right; if you were going down, you go up. Contrary to popular belief, repentance is not an emotion. It's an action. Most people think repentance means feeling bad. But to repent simply means to change direction—not a quarter turn, but a total about-face.

"Godly sorrow works repentance," Paul says, "but the sorrow of the world leads to death."

If you go to Pelican Bay penitentiary, you'll see people who are really sorry—sorry they robbed that bank, sorry they murdered that man. But have they repented? Not necessarily, for theirs is primarily the sorrow of the world—sorrow about being caught. That is why the lower house of one state legislature passed a bill forbidding weight-lifting in its penitentiaries. Innately realizing the lack of true repentance, legislators concluded that weight-lifting in jail produces nothing more than super criminals. Praise God, in the hearts of many inmates, there is true repentance—but in the majority of instances, such is not the case.

Paul identifies two kinds of sorrow—worldly sorrow that leads one to be hung up with guilt, and godly sorrow that leads to repentance. I believe these two types of sorrow can best be illustrated by looking at the stories of two men remarkably similar in many ways—both having left everything to follow the Rabbi from Galilee, both having walked with Him for three years. After failing on the same exact day, however, one experienced worldly sorrow that led to death; the other godly sorrow that led to repentance and salvation. . . .

Hung Up by Guilt

Determined to betray the One with whom he had walked daily, to whom he had listened closely, Judas cut a deal in the temple and sold his Master for thirty pieces of silver—the price of a slave. But after placing an identifying kiss on Jesus' cheek, sorrow filled the heart of the man from Carioth—not the godly sorrow that leads to repentance, but the sorrow of the world that would culminate in his death.

> Then Judas, which had betrayed him, when he saw that he was condemned, repented himself . . .   Matthew 27:3 (a)

Judas didn't repent to the Lord. He repented in himself, perhaps regretting nothing more than the messiness of the situation. He took the silver to the temple and tried to return it. The priests, however, would have nothing to do with it. So Judas hurled it to the floor of the temple in an act that demanded their participation due to the fact that only the priests were allowed in the temple.

Then, after forcing the priests to deal with the blood money, this one who was hung up by guilt hanged himself on the branch of a tree.

Why?

Old Testament law clearly prescribed that the punishment for one who bore false witness was to be the same punishment unfairly borne by the person about whom he lied (Deuteronomy 19:16–19). Therefore, knowing Jesus was about to be nailed to a tree, Judas, either intentionally or subconsciously, hanged himself on a tree.

Held Up in Glory

At the same time Judas was betraying Jesus, Peter was denying Jesus. In fact, there's a remarkable parallel between Judas and Peter. . . .

- Both were called devils by Jesus.
  Of Judas, Jesus said, "Have not I chosen you twelve and one of you is a devil?" (John 6:70)
  And to Peter, He said, "Get thee behind me, Satan," when Peter insisted Jesus would not die (Matthew 16:23).

- Jesus warned both Judas and Peter they would fail.
  "He who dips his bread with Me will deny Me," He said concerning Judas (see Matthew 26:23).

"Before the cock crows, you'll deny Me thrice," He said to Peter (see Matthew 26:34).

- Both were given opportunity to turn from their sin.
  "Friend, what seekest thou?" Jesus asked Judas in the Garden of Gethsemane, thereby saying that even then He considered Judas a friend (Matthew 26:50).

  And as Peter cursed in the courtyard, Jesus looked at him (Luke 22:61)—not, I believe, with a look of condemnation, but rather with a look that said, "Peter, I know what you're doing. But remember what I told you. I'm not through with you."

- Both repented.
  Judas repented in himself (Matthew 27:3).

  Peter wept bitterly (Matthew 26:75)—*not a tear or two, but a deep, heaving cry.*

Yet one man goes down to the bottom of the heap in the history of humanity, better for him if he hadn't ever been born (Matthew 26:24), while the other is elevated to a position of admiration, a pattern for spiritual leadership, an inspiration to you and me.

What's the difference?

Simply this: Judas' repentance was the sorrow of the world that says, "Look at the mess I'm in." Peter, on the other hand, repented to the Lord and changed direction—although not fully immediately.

On Easter Sunday, there was new hope infused in Peter. But his repentance was still incomplete, for although Peter knew Jesus was risen, due to his failure, he felt he could never again be used in ministry. That is why, in John 21, we see him returning to his old occupation as a fisherman. Others went with him and fished all night. In the morning, they saw a Figure standing on the shore.

"Children," He called to them. I like that! He didn't call them sinners, backsliders, or rebels. He called them children. "Have you caught anything?"

"No," they answered—which is not surprising, since any time we return to the old pastimes, the old habits, the old ways, we always end up with nothing.

"Cast your net on the right side" He said. Why the right side? Because whatever Jesus tells us to do is always right.

Over the right side the net went, returning so full it almost sunk the boat.

At last recognizing the One on the bank as the Lord, John identified Him to Peter, who grabbed his coat and swam to shore.

After breakfasting on roasted fish and bread prepared by His hand, Peter didn't hear Jesus say, "I'm disappointed in you. I can't use you. I'm through with you." No, Peter heard Jesus say, "Do you love Me, Peter? Feed My lambs. Feed My sheep. Tend My flock."

And all the while, what did Peter have in his hand as he stood on the shore talking to Jesus? He had a wet, soggy coat, for Scripture says Peter grabbed his coat before swimming to shore (John 21:7). If you were about to go for a swim, would you grab your coat? This perplexes me—until I see Peter's coat as an emblem of repentance.

You see, when Peter heard Jesus say, "Forget fishing. Get back to shepherding. I'm not sending you to fish in the sea. I'm telling you to feed My lambs," Peter didn't have to say, "Okay, Lord. Just let me get my coat out of the boat." No, Peter had his coat in hand so he would have no reason to ever go back to the boat again.

Godly sorrow works repentance. Repentance means you don't return for your coat. Repentance means you rip her name out of your address book, brother. It means you go to the cupboard and throw away that which you were keeping as a little something to help your next celebration on a special occasion. It means you turn your back on the magazines or movies, people or activities you know compromise your walk.

Godly sorrow works repentance. And repentance brings salvation. Judas went down to hell. Peter went on to greatness. Both repented. One felt bad because of the mess he was in. But the other turned his back on that which held him previously, determined to walk in a totally new direction. Oh, that's not to say Peter's life was easy. In fact, he, too, ended up on a tree—not hung up by guilt, but crucified upside down on a cross for the sake of the One who not only hung on a tree for him, but rose and lived within him, empowering him to live a life of incredible impact and ministry.

Godly sorrow works repentance, which brings salvation never to be regretted. Paul knew this. Peter knew this.

And so can you.

8 I love teaching through the Bible because it forces me to deal with issues I might otherwise conveniently choose to avoid. Chapters 8 and 9 of Paul's second letter to the Corinthians are one such example, for they deal exclusively with the subject of giving. I'm not alone in my tendency to cringe when the subject of giving comes up, for evidently the Corinthian congregation felt the same way. And Paul knew that, although they were excited about spiritual gifts, they needed to be exhorted about the spirit of giving.

You see, on his third missionary journey, as Paul traveled between the churches of Macedonia and Achaia, he took an offering—not for himself, but for the church at Jerusalem, which was going through hard times financially due to a severe famine in the region. Seeing this as an opportunity for a bonding between the Gentile Christians in Greece and the Jewish believers in Jerusalem, Paul was eager to complete the gift. Yet, although the Corinthian congregation had initially welcomed the opportunity to help their brothers in Jerusalem, after a year had passed, they hadn't raised any money in the endeavor. So it is this issue Paul addresses in chapters 8 and 9. . . .

2 Corinthians 8:1
Moreover, brethren, we do you to wit of the grace of God bestowed on the churches of Macedonia;

Macedonia, located in present-day northern Greece, and Corinth, located in the south, Paul wanted to fill Corinth in on what was happening with the believers to the north of them.

2 Corinthians 8:2, 3
How that in a great trial of affliction the abundance of their joy and their deep poverty abounded unto the riches of their liberality. For to their power, I bear record, yea, and beyond their power they were willing of themselves;

The churches to the north of Corinth—Thessalonica, Berea, and particularly Philippi—were going through tough times, too. Yet they shared generously. In this, I am reminded of the account in Mark 12, where, sitting in the courtyard of the temple, Jesus saw a widow drop two mites—equivalent of an eighth of a cent—into the offering. Because Jesus watched *how* the people gave rather than what they gave, He singled out this woman as the one who gave the most. Like this widow, the church at Philippi gave out of their poverty.

George Washington Carver wisely said, "How far you go in life depends on your being tender with the young, compassionate with the aged, sympathetic with the striving, and tolerant of the weak and the strong because someday in life, you will have been all of these." Perhaps that is why poor people generally seem to have a greater ability to identify with those in need, have a greater longing for the coming of the kingdom of God, and, as a result, tend to release their finances more easily. Indeed, statistics bear out the fact that it is the poorer segment of any given congregation that supports the ministry.

Of the church at Philippi, Paul said, "Although they were in great affliction, they shared out of their poverty." The result? Paul's letter to the Philippians is the most joyous of all his letters. How do we keep from becoming small, harsh, and caught up in our own little materialistic worlds? By giving. Giving is a privilege and a joy—a fact proved conclusively by the Philippians.

2 Corinthians 8:4
Praying us with much intreaty that we would receive the gift, and take upon us the fellowship of the ministering to the saints.

Not only did the northern churches give generously, but they also gave consistently. The implication is that, due to their own poverty, Paul was reticent to take their money. But they insisted. Why? Perhaps because of the fellowship that takes place when there is a sharing of finances. "Where your treasure is, there will your heart be also," Jesus said (Matthew 6:21). Therefore, perhaps the Philippians knew that if their treasure

went to their brothers in Jerusalem, their hearts would be united to them as well.

The pathway to fellowship is often through the pocketbook because our money is representative of our time and energy. Therefore, when you give a check to a brother, a sister, or a ministry, you're actually giving a part of your life. Thus, the most practical way of laying down your life is to give financially.

2 Corinthians 8:5 (a)
And this they did, not as we hoped, but first gave their own selves to the Lord . . .

Thirdly, the northern churches gave by priority. "We were hoping they would give generously, but they gave more than we hoped," said Paul. "It wasn't a matter of giving an offering, for they gave themselves first." The pastor of a congregation who gives themselves to the Lord will never have to send fundraising letters or collect second offerings. When people have an open heart, they'll invariably have an open hand. Such was the case in Macedonia.

As the offering was being taken during a revival in Africa, a brand-new Christian told the deacon holding the collection plate to put it lower. "Lower, lower, lower," he said—until the offering plate was on the ground. Then he stood up and stepped in. This man understood. This brand-new believer got the picture. He gave himself.

2 Corinthians 8:5 (b)
. . . and unto us by the will of God.

Finally, the northern churches gave obediently. They did what God told them to do. The tithe is God's, but I wonder how many times He hears someone ask Him what He would like to receive above and beyond the tithe.

2 Corinthians 8:6, 7
Insomuch that we desired Titus, that as he had begun, so he would also finish in you the same grace also. Therefore, as ye abound in every thing, in faith, and utterance, and knowledge, and in all diligence, and in your love to us, see that ye abound in this grace also.

"You're known for all of your charismatic expressions," Paul told the Corinthians. "But don't neglect the grace—or gift—of giving" (see Romans 12:6–8).

"Lord," prayed a young man, "I'm going to start a business and of whatever money it makes, I will keep 10 percent and give You 90 percent." Founder of the Quaker Oats Company, he kept his word and died a wealthy man, even though he gave nine cents of every dime to the Lord.

2 Corinthians 8:8
I speak not by commandment, but by occasion of the forwardness of others, and to prove the sincerity of your love.

"I'm not laying the law down on you," Paul says to the Corinthians, "but here is an opportunity to prove the sincerity of your love for Jesus."

2 Corinthians 8:9
For ye know the grace of our Lord Jesus Christ, that, though he was rich, yet for your sakes he became poor, that ye through his poverty might be rich.

Born in a borrowed cradle, Jesus preached from a borrowed boat, rode into Jerusalem on a borrowed donkey, ate His Last Supper in a borrowed room, and was buried in a borrowed grave. He who made everything laid it all down and entered into total poverty that I might be rich.

"This is the real issue," says Paul. "Not only did the believers in Macedonia give in their poverty, but to an infinitely greater degree, Jesus gave everything to set us free."

To the person not in love with Jesus, giving is a difficult, painful, arduous, burdensome task. He who loves Jesus, on the other hand, welcomes the opportunity to demonstrate his love.

2 Corinthians 8:10
And herein I give my advice: for this is expedient for you, who have begun before, not only to do, but also to be forward a year ago.

"Being forward" means it was partly the Corinthians' idea in the first place that the offering be taken.

2 Corinthians 8:11
Now therefore perform the doing of it; that as there was a readiness to will, so there may be a performance also out of that which ye have.

"You've expressed the desire to give," Paul says. "Now do it." Herein lies a great danger for us, for one of the great hazards of Bible study is thinking that by writing something in our notes, or agreeing with it in our hearts, we're actually doing whatever it is we're writing down or agreeing with. James likens this to one who looks in a mirror and realizes there should be some

changes made, but doesn't do anything about it (James 1:23, 24).

"Happy are ye if ye *do* these things," Jesus said (see John 13:17). If you're basically unhappy, melancholy, depressed, discouraged, or defeated, the reason could very well be that there is something the Lord has told you to do with which you agree theoretically, but which you have failed to work out practically.

Her physical condition rendered her ceremonially unclean for twelve years. As a result, her husband would divorce her; the community would shun her; she would not be allowed to worship in the temple. But then the Rabbi from Galilee walked through her city. Thinking if she could even touch the hem of His garment, she might be healed, she did just that—causing Jesus to call her something He never called any other woman. "Daughter," He said, "your faith has made you whole" (see Matthew 9:22). What faith? Just a simple touch.

Forget the big plans, the high hopes, the visions of grandeur. Just do something now. Open your heart. Share with the person who's struggling financially. Write a letter of encouragement. Pray for the person who's hurting. Do something. Do anything. Just do it. The blessing is not in agreeing—it's in doing.

2 Corinthians 8:12
For if there be first a willing mind, it is accepted according to that a man hath, and not according to that he hath not.

Don't worry about giving what you don't have. Just do what you can.

2 Corinthians 8:13, 14
For I mean not that other men be eased, and ye burdened: But by an equality, that now at this time your abundance may be a supply for their want, that their abundance also may be a supply for your want: that there may be equality:

"I'm not trying to get you to go out on a limb and give more than you have," Paul says. "But even as the northern believers shared generously, so should you because you don't know when the situation will change unexpectedly. You don't know when you will need their help." This is a principle not only of finances but of life. "Give and it shall be given unto you," Jesus said (Luke 6:38). Whether regarding money or mercy, goods or grace—whatever you extend will come back your way.

I wrestle with this in my own life and in the life

of our congregation. We've been given so much. Is there equality? Do we say, "We've been so blessed, and now here's what we can do for others who are less fortunate"? Or are we guilty of heaping things upon ourselves with no thought of equality?

2 Corinthians 8:15
As it is written, He that had gathered much had nothing over; and he that had gathered little had no lack.

The Israelites were to gather just enough manna to last one day. Those who decided to "stock up" found their supply stinky and full of worms. So, too, the longer we walk with the Lord, the more we discover that those things that used to impress us quickly become wormy and stinky to us. Does this mean we're not to have anything? No. Abraham, the father of faith, was a very wealthy man. But he was completely ready to sacrifice Isaac—his only possession that meant anything to him.

When God is your only passion, He can trust you with anything He wants to send your way. That is why Paul could say, "I've learned both to abound and to be abased" (see Philippians 4:12). It's not wrong for us to have things—but it's wrong for things to have us because God wants us to be free. It's an issue of the heart.

2 Corinthians 8:16, 17
But thanks be to God, which put the same earnest care into the heart of Titus for you. For indeed he accepted the exhortation; but being more forward, of his own accord he went unto you.

"You're bogged down, Corinthians," says Paul, "but, just as He has in mine, God has put it in the heart of Titus to care about you, to get you back on the right track."

2 Corinthians 8:18
And we have sent with him the brother, whose praise is in the gospel throughout all the churches.

A brother whose passion for the gospel was known throughout all of the churches accompanied Titus. Some believe this one was Luke. Regardless of who it was, what a wonderful thing to be said about any man.

2 Corinthians 8:19–21
And not that only, but who was also chosen of the churches to travel with us with this grace, which is administered by us to the glory of the same Lord, and declaration of
your ready mind: Avoiding this, that no man should blame us in this abundance which is administered by us: Providing for honest things, not only in the sight of the Lord, but also in the sight of men.

Regarding the collecting of the offering, it was not one person who handled the money—but rather a group of men. This way, there would be accountability and integrity.

2 Corinthians 8:22–24
And we have sent with them our brother, whom we have oftentimes proved diligent in many things, but now much more diligent, upon the great confidence which I have in you. Whether any do inquire of Titus, he is my partner and fellowhelper concerning you: or our brethren be inquired of, they are the messengers of the churches, and the glory of Christ. Wherefore shew ye to them, and before the churches, the proof of your love, and of our boasting on your behalf.

"Receive this team with love," Paul instructed the Corinthians, "for then they will see our pride in you is well-founded."

9 **2 Corinthians 9:1, 2 (a)**
For as touching the ministering to the saints, it is superfluous for me to write to you: For I know the forwardness of your mind . . .

Continuing on with the subject of giving, Paul tactfully says to the Corinthians, "Even though you're not carrying out your commitment, I know your heart is right."

2 Corinthians 9:2 (b)
. . . for which I boast of you to them of Macedonia, that Achaia was ready a year ago; and your zeal hath provoked very many.

Paul reminds the Corinthians that it was their desire to give that inspired the believers in Macedonia to begin giving.

2 Corinthians 9:3, 4
Yet have I sent the brethren, lest our boasting of you should be in vain in this behalf; that, as I said, ye may be ready: Lest haply if they of Macedonia come with me, and find you unprepared, we (that we say not, ye) should be ashamed in this same confident boasting.

Hebrews 10:24 says we are to provoke one another to love and good works. Thus, Paul says, "I provoked the believers in Macedonia by telling them how generous you are. Now follow through—don't let us down."

2 Corinthians 9:5
Therefore I thought it necessary to exhort the brethren, that they would go before unto you, and make up beforehand your bounty, whereof ye had notice before, that the same might be ready, as a matter of bounty, and not as of covetousness.

The word "covetousness" is better translated "pressure," so Paul is saying, "I'm sending Titus and company ahead of me so that I won't have to pressure you to gather that which you promised to give previously."

2 Corinthians 9:6, 7
But this I say, He which soweth sparingly shall reap also sparingly; and he which soweth bountifully shall reap also bountifully. Every man according as he purposeth in his heart, so let him give; not grudgingly, or of necessity: for God loveth a cheerful giver.

Here is the key to the entire discussions. If you miss this point, 2 Corinthians 8 and 9 will not make sense to you the way they could or should. Paul is telling us that just as there are natural laws in the universe—laws of gravity, inertia, and thermodynamics—there are spiritual laws as well. If you give sparingly, you will reap sparingly; if you give bountifully, you will reap bountifully. That's an absolute law of God as certain as is gravity or any other physical law.

I don't know how electricity works—whether the electrical current travels through the wire or spins around the wire. I don't know how light works—whether it's a wave, a particle, something in between, or something altogether different. I don't know how gravity works—but I utilize them all. And even if I ignore them, my ignorance or denial of them does not alter their effect in the least. In other words, if I jump off a tower, my denying the existence of the law of gravity will not slow my descent one iota. So, too, whether I am aware of it or not, the law of sowing and reaping is as certain as the law of gravity. And so insistent is the Lord upon this principle that it is the only one about which God says, "Test Me."

Bring ye all the tithes into the storehouse, that there may be meat in mine house, and prove me now herewith, saith the LORD of hosts, if I will not open you the windows of heaven, and pour you out a blessing, that there shall not be room enough to receive it.   Malachi 3:10

Satan tried to get Jesus to prove God by jumping off the pinnacle of the temple. "It is written, you're not to test the Lord your God," He answered (see Matthew 4:7). Yet with regard to tithing, God makes an exception when He says, "Start tithing and watch and see how I'll bless you in ways that will blow your mind, warm your heart, build your faith, and set you free."

For topical study of 2 Corinthians 9:7 entitled "Giving Gladly: Why Should I?" turn to page 1135.

2 Corinthians 9:8
And God is able to make all grace abound toward you; that ye, always having all sufficiency in all things, may abound to every good work:

If you invest in the kingdom, God is not going to say, "I wish I could return the favor, but I just can't keep up with your generosity." No, He is able to give back infinitely more than we could ever begin to even think about giving.

2 Corinthians 9:9–11
(As it is written, He hath dispersed abroad; he hath given to the poor: his righteousness remaineth for ever. Now he that ministereth seed to the sower both minister bread for your food, and multiply your seed sown, and increase the fruits of your righteousness;) being enriched in every thing to all bountifulness, which causeth through us thanksgiving to God.

Foolish would be the farmer who, given some seed, said, "This seed is too valuable to bury in the soil where I can't see it." Therefore, Paul says, "It's the Lord who gives the seed, who tends the seed, who causes it to spring forth both for nourishment and for a new supply of seed." This is true of every resource entrusted to Him.

2 Corinthians 9:12
For the administration of this service not only supplieth the want of the saints, but is abundant also by many thanksgivings unto God.

"Your giving will not only help the Jerusalem believers practically, but it will help them spiritually. It will cause them to abound in thanksgiving," Paul told the Corinthians.

2 Corinthians 9:13, 14
Whiles by the experiment of this ministration they glorify God for your professed subjection unto the gospel of Christ, and for your liberal distribution unto them, and unto all men; and by their prayer for you, which long after you for the exceeding grace of God in you.

Not only would the Jerusalem believers praise the Lord because of the generosity of the Corinthian believers—but they would pray for the Corinthian believers as well. After all, don't you find yourself automatically praying blessing for those who bless you? Want to get prayed for? Give!

2 Corinthians 9:15
Thanks be unto God for his unspeakable gift.

Due to the immensity of Greek vocabulary and the precision of its tenses, voices, and moods, there has never been a language as exact as Greek. And of all the writers, philosophers, historians, and poets who wrote in koini Greek, none had a command of the language to rival the apostle Paul's. Yet, as he gave the Corinthians the foundational reason why they should be people who give, when this master of language tried to describe God's gift to us, Paul was speechless—for truly Jesus is too wonderful for words.

GIVING GLADLY: WHY SHOULD I?
A Topical Study of
2 Corinthians 9:7

It is true that we make a living by what we get, but it is equally true that we make a life by what we give. Perhaps it was Paul's knowledge of this principle that enabled him to say with certainty, "God loves a cheerful giver." The Greek word translated "cheerful" is *hilaros,* from which we get the word "hilarious." Thus, according to Paul, giving should not be a pain. It should be a party. It should not be heavy, but happy.

Why would giving produce hilarity, happiness, and joy when everything in our flesh says it should produce just the opposite? Paul gives five reasons why giving does indeed produce hilarity. . . .

God's Promise to Us

> But this I say, He which soweth sparingly shall reap also sparingly; and he which soweth bountifully shall reap also bountifully.   2 Corinthians 9:6

After Jesus used Peter's boat to preach from the Sea of Galilee, He said, "Take your boat out, Peter, and throw your nets into the water." Peter did so—and took in a massive haul of fish (see Luke 5:3–6). In other words, because Peter gave Jesus his boat, Jesus returned it full of fish. That's just the way God is. He is a debtor to no man.

> Will a man rob God? Yet ye have robbed me. But ye say, Wherein have we robbed thee? In tithes and offerings. Ye are cursed with a curse: for ye have robbed me, even this whole nation.
>   Malachi 3:8, 9

What is the tithe? The word simply means a tenth. That is, the first 10 percent of anything we earn—be it a dollar a week or a million dollars a day—is God's. And according to Malachi 3, failure to release this tithe to Him constitutes robbery. Because of this failure, Malachi told the Jews they were cursed—not cursed in the sense that God is in heaven stirring a cauldron with a broomstick, pronouncing a curse upon them—but cursed because they limited what God could do for them.

Is it time for you, O ye, to dwell in your cieled houses, and this house lie waste? Now therefore thus saith the LORD of hosts; Consider your ways. Ye have sown much, and bring in little; ye eat, but ye have not enough; ye drink, but ye are not filled with drink; ye clothe you, but there is none warm; and he that earneth wages earneth wages to put it into a bag with holes.

Haggai 1:4–6

"Your wages disappear," says Haggai. Why? Because you have ignored the work of the Lord.

Bring ye all the tithes into the storehouse, that there may be meat in mine house, and prove me now herewith, saith the LORD of hosts, if I will not open you the windows of heaven, and pour you out a blessing, that there shall not be room enough to receive it.   *Malachi 3:10*

Over and over throughout Scripture, we are warned about the folly and presumption of testing God. We're not to test Him—we're to trust Him. Yet here in Malachi we see the single exception when God says, "Test Me. Bring the tithe to My storehouse. Watch and see what I will do."

And I will rebuke the devourer for your sakes, and he shall not destroy the fruits of your ground; neither shall your vine cast her fruit before the time in the field, saith the LORD of hosts.   *Malachi 3:11*

The Lord says, "I will protect you from this one who causes your appliances to break down, your car to stall, your finances to crumble." Am I suggesting that the devil is behind every car problem? No. But I am saying that the Enemy has all kinds of plans to keep us in debt, to keep us perpetually in the hole. That is why the Lord says, "Let Me defend you. Let Me see you through miraculously. Test Me. Trust Me to rebuke the devourer, the one who eats at you personally and financially.

And all nations shall call you blessed: for ye shall be a delightsome land, saith the LORD of hosts.   *Malachi 3:12*

Does this mean if we tithe we'll be rich? No, but we will be blessed. When people look at us, they will sense an absence of tension, a freedom, and a contentment within us due to God's protection of that which He has given us.

Why should we give hilariously? Because of God's promise that He will reward, that He will rebuke, that He will revive.

God's Purpose for Us

For where your treasure is, there will your heart be also.   Matthew 6:21

Secondly, we should be hilarious in giving because of God's purpose for us. What is God's purpose for us? To live in heaven eternally. Therefore, because we so easily get stuck in the world's system, God says, "I have a way to get your heart in heaven: Put your treasure there."

Inevitably, people who invest in heaven become increasingly interested in the coming of Christ and the coming of the kingdom. This should not be surprising. If your treasure is in a retirement fund, your heart will be as well. If your treasure is in some material object—a sports car or vacation home—that's where your heart will be. But if your treasure is regularly invested in heaven, you'll find yourself increasingly kingdom-oriented.

As illustrated by Jesus in the parable of the ten talents (Luke 19), when He returns, we will give an account as to whether we invested what He gave us wisely or buried it foolishly. If we have invested wisely, we will be given significant responsibility. Why does money impact our role in eternity? Because we work forty to fifty hours a week, what we do with our money is a direct reflection upon what we do with our lives. That is why those who say, "Lord, You're not getting a tenth. You're not getting a twentieth. You're getting nothing," are actually saying, "You're not getting me."

And the Lord has no choice but to say, "I can't allow you to rule, to enjoy what you otherwise would have in the kingdom."

Oh, how we need to hear this. Jesus is coming, and it will not matter that we got a new car or a bigger house. At that moment, nothing will matter except that we'll see Him face-to-face. This One who loves us so much will say, "What did you do with My tenth? You bought a new CD player, a new mountain bike? That's what you think of Me? I love you, but I can't allow you to have the responsibility you would have had."

God's Premise About Us

Be ye therefore merciful, as your Father also is merciful. Judge not, and ye shall not be judged: condemn not, and ye shall not be condemned: forgive, and ye shall be forgiven: Give, and it shall be given unto you; good measure, pressed down, and shaken together, and running over, shall men give into your bosom. For with the same measure that ye mete withal it shall be measured to you again.   Luke 6:36–38

Thirdly, we should give hilariously because of God's premise about us. You see, over and over throughout Scripture, God looks at His people and calls them stiff-necked and hard of heart. He doesn't say this hatefully or condemningly, but rather knowingly. "I know what you are," He says. "You're stiff-necked and hard of heart, greedy, and lazy. I want you to be different. I want you to be bigger. I want you to be forgiving, merciful, and compassionate. I want you to relate to people, to care about people, to love people like I do. So give money."

"Wait a minute," you say. "There is no direct correlation between caring about people and giving money."

Really? We might think we're fairly compassionate, sufficiently forgiving, quite merciful. But how do we measure these characteristics? According to Luke 6:35–38, Jesus said we are to measure them by how generous we are financially. Thus, there is, indeed, a direct correlation between what we do with material resources and how we relate to people.

In other words, we will know how we're doing with people by how we handle our money. If we are truly forgiving, merciful, and compassionate, it will show in our checkbook registers. If we claim to love people but are not giving financially, we're fooling ourselves, for Jesus inextricably tied the two together.

Giving is not God's way of raising cash. It's His way of raising kids. Knowing we're stingy and greedy, God wants to free us from these tendencies. Consequently, every time the offering basket comes along, I have the opportunity to give away part of my smallness and greediness. If I pass up this opportunity, I'm in effect saying, "Keep me a small person, Lord."

God's Process in Us

Charge them that are rich in this world, that they be not highminded, nor trust in uncertain riches, but in the living God, who giveth us richly all things to enjoy.   1 Timothy 6:17

God is a giver. And He wants us to be like Him. Why? Because He is hilariously happy. You see, God isn't in heaven, saying, "It's hard being God." No, there is hilarity in heaven day and night. Praise is resounding. Joy is unspeakable. There is a holy happiness unparalleled to anything this world has ever seen. Knowing giving is hard for us, God demands it—not because He's mean, but to help us be like Him.

What will this do? The same thing it did for Abraham. . . .

Following the successful rescue of his nephew Lot, Abraham was met by Melchizedek, the king of Salem, who, with bread and wine in hand, blessed him. Inherently sensing God was in His midst in the person of Melchizedek, Abraham did what any man of God must do—He gave tithes of all he had.

Abraham was also met by the king of Sodom, who said, "Abraham, give me the people you rescued and keep these goods for yourself."

"I will not take even a thread or shoelace from you," Abraham answered, "lest you say you made me rich" (see Genesis 14).

The king of Sodom comes to us constantly through the newspaper, TV, and radio, saying, "You need this. Buy this. Grab this." In essence, the king of Sodom tells us to buy things we don't need with money we don't have to impress people we don't like.

What's the solution? Abraham was able to resist the king of Sodom because he had given to the King of Salem. Had he not given to the King of Salem, I suggest he would have perhaps succumbed to the temptation to take from the king of Sodom.

God's Presence with Us

For ye know the grace of our Lord Jesus Christ, that, though he was rich, yet
for your sakes he became poor, that ye through his poverty might be rich.
2 Corinthians 8:9

The final reason we can give with hilarity is because God gave us Jesus. If this were the only reason to give, it would be more than enough.

When the wise men came to Bethlehem, they brought gold, frankincense, and myrrh, not because Jesus would do a miracle for them, give insight to them, or pronounce blessing upon them. As a two-year-old, He could do none of those things. They gave not to receive, but simply because He is the King.

"Thanks be unto God for His unspeakable gift," Paul declared (2 Corinthians 9:15). After spending two chapters discussing the importance and benefits of giving, for Paul, it all came down to Jesus.

God's promise to us, His purpose for us, His premise about us, His process in us, and His presence with us are each reason enough for us to give with joy. Together, they leave us no other option.

May God give us the grace to be people who give hilariously.

10 In 2 Corinthians chapter 10, we come to the beginning of what many scholars believe is the letter to which Paul referred in 2 Corinthians 2:4 and 7:8. You see, chapters 1—6 of 2 Corinthians constitute Paul's defense of his apostolic authority that had been questioned by some in Corinth. Then, in chapters 7 and 8, he deals with the subject of giving—a section he ended by saying, "Thanks be unto God for His unspeakable gift."

At this point, it seems as though Paul is closing his letter. He's defended his ministry, he's given the Corinthians an exhortation about giving, and he's made a closing statement. So as you follow the flow of this letter, it seems as though this should be the end of the Epistle. But it's not. There are four more chapters. And the interesting thing about these final four chapters is that Paul doesn't pull any punches, but instead comes down on the Corinthians rather aggressively. And this is what perplexes scholars and students. Why would he end the letter this way? After all, any preacher, teacher, or pastor knows the time to get in people's faces is not following an exhortation to give.

The answer could possibly lie in the fact that 2 Corinthians 10—13 actually constitutes a different book altogether—the letter that caused

Paul such sorrow and anguish (2 Corinthians 2:4; 7:8). If this be the case, 2 Corinthians would be comprised of chapters 10—13, and "3 Corinthians" would be comprised of chapters 1—9. The possibility that at some point 2 and "3" Corinthians were inadvertently combined seems to explain both the missing Epistle and the reason for the heaviness of chapters 10—13.

2 Corinthians 10:1 (a)
Now I Paul myself beseech you by the meekness and gentleness of Christ . . .

Meekness does not mean weakness, but rather strength under control. Used to describe a powerful stallion so well trained that it yields to the slightest nudge of the rider, the Greek concept of meekness was exhibited nowhere more perfectly than in Jesus. It is this controlled strength that Paul employs as he deals with the church at Corinth.

2 Corinthians 10:1 (b)
. . . who in presence am base among you, but being absent am bold toward you.

Paul quotes his detractors, who said about him, "Sure, he can write a strong letter, but in person he's not all that impressive," as they resorted to the age-old tactic of criticizing one's opponent physically if unable to counter his argument logically.

2 Corinthians 10:2
But I beseech you, that I may not be bold when I am present with that confidence, wherewith I think to be bold against some, which think of us as if we walked according to the flesh.

"I don't want to be harsh," Paul says, "but they who accuse us of being carnal leave me no other choice."

2 Corinthians 10:3
For though we walk in the flesh, we do not war after the flesh.

"Because we're human, of course we walk in the flesh, but the battle we wage for you is spiritual—not dependent upon oratorical skill or physical stature," Paul argues.

2 Corinthians 10:4, 5
(For the weapons of our warfare are not carnal, but mighty through God to the pulling down of strong holds;) casting down imaginations, and every high thing that exalteth itself against the knowledge of God, and bringing into captivity every thought to the obedience of Christ.

As we pull down the strongholds of the Enemy, the battle we wage is spiritual.

For topical study of 2 Corinthians 10:3–5 entitled "The Real Battle," turn to page 1141.

2 Corinthians 10:6
And having in a readiness to revenge all disobedience, when your obedience is fulfilled.

"We'll keep fighting on your behalf until you Corinthians grow into spiritual maturity, for that's our ministry," declares Paul.

2 Corinthians 10:7
Do ye look on things after the outward appearance? If any man trust to himself that he is Christ's, let him of himself think this again, that, as he is Christ's, even so are we Christ's.

There were those in Corinth who said, "We are Christ's, but Paul is nothing." To them, Paul maintains that he is Christ's as well.

In 1 Corinthians 4:5, Paul had warned about judging people prematurely, before the day when all things will come to light at the *bema* seat, the award stand of Christ. I often think about this. At the judgment seat of Christ, the beauty, power, and importance of the beautiful, powerful, important people will evaporate. On the other hand, those who, like Paul, although they were unimpressive physically, or unknown socially, cultivated a deep and meaningful walk with Jesus will be beautiful throughout eternity. There are people now who physically, mentally, financially seem to be nothing. But in secrecy they have developed an intimacy with the Lord. Right now, they're proverbial ugly ducklings. They don't fit in; they're not acknowledged. But in that day, they will be beautiful swans. What a day it will be when those people who have been plugging away and seeking God rather than getting the breaks in this world will hear Jesus say to them, "Well done, good and faithful servant! Enter in to the joy of the Lord" (see Matthew 25:21).

2 Corinthians 10:8 (a)
For though I should boast somewhat more of our authority . . .

"Although I don't want to, I'll have to boast here a bit," says Paul.

2 Corinthians 10:8 (b)
. . . which the Lord hath given us for edification, and not for your destruction, I should not be ashamed.

"We don't seek to have dominion over you, but are helpers of your joy," Paul had said in chapter 1 (see 1:24). "The authority we claim is not to do anything other than to build you up and be helpers of your joy."

2 Corinthians 10:9
That I may not seem as if I would terrify you by letters.

"I'm going to talk to you firmly and straightforwardly so you won't think I'm bluffing," says Paul.

2 Corinthians 10:10
For his letters, say they, are weighty and powerful; but his bodily presence is weak, and his speech contemptible.

Perhaps the word "contemptible" refers to Paul's high-pitched voice. Or perhaps, like Moses, Paul stuttered. Either way, his enemies made fun of his speaking style.

2 Corinthians 10:11, 12
Let such an one think this, that, such as we are in word by letters when we are absent, such will we be also in deed when we are present. For we dare not make ourselves of the number, or compare ourselves with some that commend themselves: but they measuring themselves by themselves, and comparing themselves among themselves, are not wise.

There were those who, comparing themselves with one another, put themselves in the top ten and Paul at the bottom of the heap. But, under the inspiration of the Spirit, Paul says measuring ourselves against one another is unwise. Why? Measuring yourself against another will do one of two things. It will either puff you up or pull you down. You can always find someone seemingly less spiritual than you. And when you do, you'll be puffed up by pride. You can also find people seemingly more spiritual than you. Yet trying to emulate them leads only to frustration.

2 Corinthians 10:13–16
But we will not boast of things without our measure, but according to the measure of the rule which God hath distributed to us, a measure to reach even unto you. For we stretch not ourselves beyond our measure, as though we reached not unto you: for we are come as far as to you also in preaching the gospel of Christ: Not boasting of things without our measure, that is, of other men's labours; but having hope, when your faith is increased, that we shall be enlarged by you according to our rule abundantly, To preach the gospel in the regions beyond you, and not to boast in another man's line of things made ready to our hand.

"We don't stretch ourselves beyond the parameter that God has placed around us," declared Paul.

As believers, yes, we should be stretched. Yes, we should go for it in faith. But concerning his own ministry, Paul says, "We do not stretch ourselves beyond that which we've been called to do."

Happy is the man and wise the woman who understands what God has given him or her to do and who devotes himself or herself to doing that wholeheartedly without stepping into other areas to which God has not called them. Such was not the case with those who were eager to speak against Paul in Corinth, even as they "piggybacked" on the work he had already done.

2 Corinthians 10:17, 18
But he that glorieth, let him glory in the Lord. For not he that commendeth himself is approved, but whom the Lord commendeth.

"Our glorying lies simply in doing what we're supposed to do," said Paul. "Our glorying is in the Lord. And that is where your glory should be as well."

THE REAL BATTLE

A Topical Study of
2 Corinthians 10:3–5

On June 6, 1944, General Dwight David Eisenhower made a pivotal decision when he said, "Let's go." At 4 A.M., over 155,000 made their way across the English Channel in the greatest single military invasion in world history. Having been told that only one in three would likely return from the morning excursion, they landed on the beaches of France that were code-named Utah and Sword, Juneau and Gold, and, most famously, Omaha.

As they landed on the shores, the enemy, already entrenched, began to fire round after round on those 155,000 brave soldiers. Ten thousand men lost their lives at Omaha Beach on that bloody, brutal day. Yet the Allied soldiers kept coming—wave after wave after wave—until they took the strongholds, the high towers from which the Nazi soldiers fired. Had the Allies failed, Germany would have dominated Europe, indeed the world militarily. But their success ensured eventual victory.

The greatest military invasion in the history of the world took place on D-Day. But an infinitely greater invasion took place the day God invaded this world in the Person of Jesus Christ. Monumental were the repercussions of the sacrifice and bloodshed on the beaches of Normandy. But they were nothing compared to the results of the sacrifice and blood shed at Calvary.

Satan's plan of nailing Jesus to the Cross backfired totally because the only foothold Satan has on humanity is getting people to succumb to sin and thus turn over the authority of their lives to him. Therefore, because the blood of Jesus paid the price for the sin of all men, Satan's foothold is obliterated. Yet even though the victory has been won, the battle goes on because the Enemy will not give up that which we do not take.

When the Allied invasion succeeded, Hitler and the boys in Berlin knew their days were numbered. They knew they didn't have a chance—but they continued fighting to the bitter end. This explains the reason that although the outcome of the war was determined on June 6, more blood was shed in the year following the victory at Normandy than at any other time in history.

So, too, Satan knows he doesn't have a chance. He knows that the one grasp he had on man is gone. He knows his time is running out. Yet so deep is his hatred of God that he continues to hang on to the territory he knows is no longer his. And he fights to the bitter end.

"It is finished," Jesus declared from the Cross (John 19:30). The victory is won. Although the war goes on, we do not fight *for* victory. We fight *from* victory. That is why Paul tells us to pull down, root out, take control of the strongholds our adversary has erected in our minds and hearts. Concerning this Enemy, Paul says we are not to be ignorant of his devices. And we aren't.

We know that when we were saved, Jesus took up residence in our lives. Our sin—past, present, and future—was cleansed completely. We were born again. And yet each time I give in to sin, each time I succumb to an attitude or an activity I know is wrong, a brick is added to the high tower of the Enemy from which he can manipulate my thinking. This explains how I can be driving down the road, enjoying the day, when suddenly a thought will come into my mind, or an attitude into my heart that causes me to say, "Where in the world did *that* come from?" It didn't come from the world. It came from hell.

Ephesians 6 tells us that Satan fires fiery darts—a bit of hell—into our minds. Oh, he can't possess our hearts. But there's still a battle going on for the mind. The spirit is secure, but the soul—the mind, emotions, and will—is still up for grabs. In Ephesians 6, Paul tells us more about the warfare we wage.

> *For we wrestle not against flesh and blood, but against principalities, against powers, against the rulers of the darkness of this world, against spiritual wickedness in high places.*   Ephesians 6:12

Any time we are wrestling against flesh and blood—against family members, bosses, employees, neighbors, or friends—we're fighting the wrong battle. Anytime we're upset with people, we are waging the wrong war. The enemy is not your husband, your teenage daughter, or your boss. The enemy is Satan.

> *Be sober, be vigilant; because your adversary the devil, as a roaring lion, walketh about, seeking whom he may devour.*   1 Peter 5:8

Peter identifies Satan not as *the* adversary, but as *your* adversary. You might think, *I'm not that important. The devil doesn't care about me.* Wrong. "Your adversary" means you have a personal enemy—Satan—who has a specific plan to manipulate you and rob you of joy, power, and your ability to influence others.

Because there is a war going on, it is imperative that we pull down the high tower, the stronghold of the Enemy—the areas Satan controls, even though you're a Christian, even though your sin is forgiven, even though you're on your way to heaven.

How are they pulled down? What does it mean to cast down the imagination?

For every New Testament principle, there's an Old Testament picture. And concerning the pulling down of strongholds, there are two. The first is seen in Joshua 6. . . .

Proclaim Aloud the Victory

Just as we have been delivered from the world, the people of Israel had been freed from the bondage of Egypt. After wandering for forty years in the wilderness, they were now ready to move and possess their possessions, to take the Land of Promise—a picture of the Spirit-filled life. But what happened? When they crossed the Jordan River, there before them stood the walled city of Jericho—a city that seemed absolutely impregnable. God said to Joshua, "I want you to pull down this stronghold in a way that's going to surprise you—not by catapult, not by dynamite, not by atomic power. I want you and the people to march around the city once a day for six days."

So Joshua and the Israelites—perhaps three million in number—marched around the city once a day. And as they did, no doubt they saw just how strong the walls were and how impossible the situation seemed. On the seventh day, they were to march around Jericho seven times, the seventh of which they were to shout audibly. This didn't make a lot of sense logically. But shout they did. And as they did, something amazing happened. The walls of Jericho that so intimidated them came down.

The principle is essential. If we want to see the strongholds that keep us from experiencing God's blessing and promises brought down, the first thing we must understand is that they will be pulled down by audibly proclaiming victory.

God knows the power of the citadel that threatens you. Therefore, He doesn't ask you to deny its reality. Rather, He asks you to proclaim aloud the victory.

Proclaim ye this among the Gentiles; Prepare war, wake up the mighty men, let all the men of war draw near; let them come up: Beat your plowshares into swords, and your pruninghooks into spears: let the weak say, I am strong.

Joel 3:9, 10

Don't talk about your sickness, your weakness, your discouragement, or your despondency. Don't talk about that which perpetuates your problems. Instead, speak out the promises of Scripture. When you were saved, you confessed with your mouth that Jesus is Lord (Romans 10:9). The prerequisite for victory is the same as for salvation. . . .

For this commandment which I command thee this day, it is not hidden from thee, neither is it far off. But the word is very nigh unto thee, in thy mouth, and in thy heart, that thou mayest do it.   Deuteronomy 30:11, 14

This passage speaks not only of salvation, but about liberation and blessing. . . .

That then the LORD thy God will turn thy captivity, and have compassion upon thee, and will return and gather thee from all the nations, whither the LORD thy God hath scattered thee.   Deuteronomy 30:3

Do you feel scattered, unstable, and as though you're spread too thin? The Lord promises to pull in the reins, to bring us into a "togetherness."

And the LORD thy God will bring thee into the land which thy fathers possessed, and thou shalt possess it; and he will do thee good, and multiply thee above thy fathers.   Deuteronomy 30:5

Do you feel disenfranchised, that good is not happening to you? God promises to bring you to the land and do good to you. . . .

And the LORD thy God will make thee plenteous in every work of thine hand, in the fruit of thy body, and in the fruit of thy cattle, and in the fruit of thy land, for good: for the LORD will again rejoice over thee for good, as he rejoiced over thy fathers.
Deuteronomy 30:9

Over and over in this chapter promises are given to help us out, to free us up. The stipulation? Obedience and the proclamation of God's Word.

What has been your conversation the past week, month, or year? Have your words been those of doubt and discouragement, despondency and despair? Have you said, "This is never going to work. That job will never open up. I'll never get well. I'm destined for loneliness and poverty"? As long as that is what is spoken from your lips, Jericho will loom over you menacingly. It's when you finally speak out the promises of Scripture that Jericho will fall before you.

Am I suggesting you "Name It and Claim It"? No. I'm not suggesting we make our own reality. I'm reminding us that if we draw nigh to God through the glorious promises of His Word, He will indeed draw nigh to us (James 4:8).

Plow Away Diligently

Not only are we to proclaim aloud the victory, but we are to plow away diligently.

The Midianites controlled the people of Israel with such a heavy hand that Gideon sifted his wheat in a cave in order to avoid detection. Then God came to him and said, "The Lord is with thee, thou mighty man of valor" (Judges 6:12). I love this! Here's a guy hiding in a cave, worried that someone might see him—and yet the Lord views him not in his present weakness, but in his potential greatness. That's always the way of the Lord.

"If You're real, God, how come Your people are having such problems?" asked Gideon. "Why aren't we seeing miracles happen?"

"Here's the way to victory," God said. "Take your dad's two oxen and pull down the stronghold, the image, the idol that has been erected in your land, which has been worshiped by your family." So Gideon took ten men and did just that (Judges 6:27).

What does this mean for you and me? It means there comes a time when we have to say, "It might take ten men, ten days, ten years—but I'll plow away. I'll come to church on Wednesdays. I'll go to a Bible study on Tuesdays. I'll attend a prayer meeting on Thursdays. Ten being the number of completion, I'm going to keep on plowing away until the image is pulled down." And as you continue to plow through the Scriptures day after day, book by book, chapter by chapter, line upon line, precept upon precept, something happens. As you plow away, the images, the strongholds begin to topple.

People might say, "You've been going to Bible study for fifteen years. Why do you keep going?" But wise is the man or woman who understands that once he gives up, once she quits plowing, the images will return and take control once again.

I believe that anyone who will proclaim aloud the victory and plow away diligently will see once-formidable strongholds fall.

"I've tried that," you say. "I've tried speaking the Word, even shouting it at times. And I've been plowing through the Scriptures consistently—but nothing seems to be working."

Consider the following. . . .

> Sandi Anderson, a lady who runs a relief agency in Zaire grew up a child of missionaries in that region. When she was about eight years old, there was a big celebration in Zaire, commemorating the one hundredth anniversary of the arrival of the Evangelical Christian Missionary Alliance—a ministry God used to save virtually 80 percent of the people in the region.
>
> During the celebration, a very old man stood up and said, "I must speak. I am one hundred three years old. I am the last person who was alive in those days when your missionaries first came to our land. I have knowledge of a situation, the story of which will be lost if I don't share it." Given permission, he continued. "When your missionaries came, they told us how to live. We thought their message was strange. We wanted to know if what they said was true, and we knew the only way to find out was to see how they would die. So we began poisoning them and their children one by one." Indeed, it was true that within the first twelve years, every single one of the original missionaries and their children died mysteriously.
>
> "When the last one died, we held a council meeting and determined that there was something real about your faith, something real about your God—not because the missionaries told us how to live, but because we saw the way they died."

This story is incredible to me—not only because this group of brave missionaries lived out their faith through pain and suffering so powerfully that an entire tribal group was converted—but because of the fact that no one knew about this for one hundred years.

Why is your ordeal continuing? Could it be that people are watching you, that God is allowing you to be an example of a man or woman who keeps plowing away, who keeps proclaiming the victory, even though the situation doesn't change outwardly? Could it be that by your proclaiming and plowing, greater victory than you ever imagined will one day be yours?

I think so.

If you despair, whine, and complain, the Enemy will have a field day with you. But if you say, "Jericho's going down as I proclaim the Word. Baal's going to bail as I plow through the Scriptures day after day," you will see God not only free you, but impact those watching you.

11 "You have ten thousand instructors, but not many fathers," Paul had told the Corinthians (see 1 Corinthians 4:15). In chapter 11, we see the heart of a father in Paul—his jealousy for the Corinthians in verses 1–4, his generosity toward them in verses 5–11, and his anxiety about them in verses 12–28.

2 Corinthians 11:1, 2
Would to God ye could bear with me a little in my folly: and indeed bear with me. For I am jealous over you with godly jealousy: for I have espoused you to one husband, that I may present you as a chaste virgin to Christ.

In Paul's day, it was the responsibility of the father to ensure that his daughter was a virgin on her wedding day. If she wasn't, he would be put to shame. Thus, as the spiritual father of the church at Corinth, it was Paul's responsibility to make sure they retained their purity, that they weren't seduced by those who sought to lure them away from the simplicity of the gospel.

2 Corinthians 11:3
But I fear, lest by any means, as the serpent beguiled Eve through his subtilty, so your minds should be corrupted from the simplicity that is in Christ.

How was Eve seduced? Not by being offered a sip or a peek or a puff, but by the potential to be more spiritual. So, too, false teachers came into the Corinthian congregation, saying that Paul's teaching was too simple, that there was something deeper they needed to explore and experience.

2 Corinthians 11:4
For if he that cometh preacheth another Jesus, whom we have not preached, or if ye receive another spirit, which ye have not received, or another gospel, which ye have not accepted, ye might well bear with him.

Paul picks up the same theme in Galatians 1 when he says, "If an angel comes and preaches another Jesus, another gospel, let him be accursed." If there's a single issue in the New Testament that seems to be fighting ground, it's over the issue of the deity of Jesus.

2 Corinthians 11:5
For I suppose I was not a whit behind the very chiefest apostles.

The false teachers claimed to be "super apostles." Yet, although Paul would claim to be the least of the apostles and the chief of sinners (1 Timothy 1:15), he doesn't say he was less than any of these pseudo-spiritual teachers.

2 Corinthians 11:6
But though I be rude in speech, yet not in knowledge; but we have been throughly made manifest among you in all things.

"My speech might be a little rough," said Paul, "but not my knowledge."

Asked to quote Psalm 23, the famous Shakespearean actor articulated each and every phrase perfectly. Then the host of the party asked his pastor, who was also in attendance, to quote the same psalm. The pastor lacked the rhythmic cadence, the powerful voice, and the smooth speech. All he had was a tear rolling down his cheek.
"I know the psalm," said the actor. "But this man knows the Shepherd."

Paul knew the Shepherd. Paul knew Jesus. "I might not match up to your favorite speakers or profound teachers," he said. "I might not measure up in speech, but in knowledge I do, for I know Him."

2 Corinthians 11:7
Have I committed an offence in abasing myself that ye might be exalted, because I have preached to you the gospel of God freely?

The "super apostles" were exceedingly wealthy from the exorbitant speaking fees they charged. Paul, on the other hand, charged nothing. "Is it because I haven't taken money from you that you esteem me so lightly?" he asks.

2 Corinthians 11:8, 9
I robbed other churches, taking wages of them, to do you service. And when I was present with you, and wanted, I was chargeable to no man: for that which was lacking to me the brethren which came from Macedonia supplied: and in all things I have kept myself from being burdensome unto you, and so will I keep myself.

"Others were supporting me in the ministry in order that I wouldn't have to burden you financially," said Paul.

2 Corinthians 11:10
As the truth of Christ is in me, no man shall stop me of this boasting in the regions of Achaia.

"I'm going to keep reminding you that I have not taken a penny from you," said Paul.

2 Corinthians 11:11
Wherefore? because I love you not? God knoweth.

"If Paul really loved us, he would charge us," some were saying.
"God knows I love you," Paul answered.

2 Corinthians 11:12
But what I do, that I will do, that I may cut off occasion from them which desire occasion; that wherein they glory, they may be found even as we.

"I'm not going to charge you," said Paul. "And I dare these false teachers to follow my lead."
There have been times in this ministry when we didn't have the money to support the ministers, myself included. And it's really interesting what happens. Some keep serving, teaching, working, doing whatever they're called to do. Others fade away. Jesus called them hirelings (John 10:12, 13). I believe God almost inevitably allows men to be tested in this way, to allow them to see whether what they're doing is merely a job or truly a calling on their life—something they would do whether or not they were financially supported.
Although Paul sometimes had support from Macedonia, we know from the Book of Acts that during this time he would support himself by making tents in order that he could teach the Word at nights or in the afternoon. "I know how to abound and how to be abased," he said (see Philippians 4:12). "I'm just going to keep doing what I've been called to do."

2 Corinthians 11:13, 14
For such are false apostles, deceitful workers, transforming themselves into the apostles of Christ. And no marvel; for Satan himself is transformed into an angel of light.

We shouldn't be surprised when false teachers seem to live so righteously, when their standards seem to be so moral, when they stress the importance of family and separation from the defilement of the world. We shouldn't be surprised that their TV commercials sound so right and look so warm and fuzzy, nor that their temple in Salt Lake City glows with light—for Paul says Satan himself transforms into an angel of light.
You see, Satan will go either way with people. If people want to be dark and devilish and heavy, he'll meet them there. But if people want to be exemplary and upstanding, he'll meet them there. As an angel of light, he'll say, "You don't need to admit you're a sinner and need a Savior. Just live morally."
It's interesting to me that so many who talk about near-death experiences report seeing a warm, bright light beckoning them—the implication being that if we are "good people," regardless of the route we choose, we'll all make it to the bright light at the end of the tunnel. But wait. That bright light may not be the Father of Lights. It may be the one who transforms himself to appear as an angel of light. It might be a train barreling down the track in your direction. Because Satan transforms himself into an angel of light, we should be wary about the conclusions of those who write about such experiences.

2 Corinthians 11:15
Therefore it is no great thing if his ministers also be transformed as the ministers of righteousness; whose end shall be according to their works.

"What must we do to do the works of God?" they asked.
And Jesus said, "This is the work of God—one thing—that you believe on Him whom the Father hath sent (see John 6:28, 29).
"What must we do to do the works of God?"
"Join our temple and be baptized," the doorknockers say.
No. The work of God is singular: It's simply to believe. He who adds anything to believing on Him whom the Father hath sent is on dangerous ground and will be judged according to their human effort—by which they will fail miserably.

2 Corinthians 11:16, 17
I say again, Let no man think me a fool; if otherwise, yet as a fool receive me, that I may boast myself a little. That which I speak, I speak it not after the Lord, but as it were foolishly, in this confidence of boasting.

"Because you're questioning my authority as an apostle, I'm going to have to boast," Paul says. "But don't blame the Lord for my boasting." I like that. All too often, the Lord gets blamed for the erratic behavior of those who claim to be controlled by Him. It's an embarrassment to the Christian community when people do bizarre things in the name of the Lord. Here, Paul seems to go out of his way to do otherwise.

2 Corinthians 11:18, 19
Seeing that many glory after the flesh, I will glory also. For ye suffer fools gladly, seeing ye yourselves are wise.

Here, Paul says, "If you who are so wise value fleshly credentials, I'll give you mine. . . ."

2 Corinthians 11:20, 21 (a)
For ye suffer, if a man bring you into bondage, if a man devour you, if a man take of you, if a man exalt himself, if a man smite you on the face. I speak as concerning reproach, as though we had been weak.

According to rabbinical tradition, it was the right of the teacher to strike the student who didn't listen to him or agree with him. Consequently, not only were the false teachers laying spiritual and financial burdens on the Corinthians—they were evidently striking some as well. It's a real mystery to me why Christians feel blessed when someone screams at them, tells them they're doing terribly, or burdens them with expectations and pressure.

Of Jesus, Isaiah prophesied that He would neither break the bruised reed nor quench the smoking flax (42:3). In other words, Jesus is One who uses even the weakest instrument and fans even the faintest flame of any who show an inclination towards Him.

2 Corinthians 11:21 (b), 22 (a)
Howbeit whereinsoever any is bold, (I speak foolishly,) I am bold also. Are they Hebrews? so am I.

Those who were trying to undo Paul's ministry were evidently Jewish teachers who said, "Grace lacks substance. There's more to it than that. You need not only to believe in Jesus, but you must

embrace Judaism, legalism, ritualism, and regulations."

There's a tendency within us to want to live under legalism and ritualism. That's why Jesus was so radical. He lived as a common Man rather than subscribing to the traditional cleansings and rabbinical rituals. "He's a glutton and a winebibber," said His critics. "Look who He hangs out with. Look how He teaches in such simplicity with those little parables." So, too, the believers in Corinth were being told faith is not that simple.

2 Corinthians 11:22 (b), 23 (a)
Are they Israelites? so am I. Are they the seed of Abraham? so am I. Are they ministers of Christ? (I speak as a fool) I am more . . .

"They talk about being servants of Christ with their Jewish credentials, their rules and rituals— but I am more," declared Paul.

2 Corinthians 11:23 (b)
. . . in labours more abundant . . .

"I support myself with the work of my own hands."

2 Corinthians 11:23 (c)
. . . in stripes above measure . . .

This speaks of beating.

2 Corinthians 11:23 (d)
. . . in prisons more frequent, in deaths oft.

"I'm at the point of death constantly," Paul declared.

2 Corinthians 11:24
Of the Jews five times received I forty stripes save one.

A single beating of thirty-nine lashes was often enough to kill a man. Paul endured such a beating five times.

2 Corinthians 11:25
Thrice was I beaten with rods, once was I stoned, thrice I suffered shipwreck, a night and a day I have been in the deep.

Even at this point in his ministry, Paul had been beaten, imprisoned, stoned, shipwrecked. Thus, I am humbled, indeed, when I consider the price our brother Paul paid to be a minister of the gospel.

2 Corinthians 11:26, 27
In journeyings often, in perils of waters, in perils of robbers, in perils by mine own countrymen, in perils by the heathen, in perils in the city, in perils in the wilderness, in perils in the sea, in perils among false brethren; in weariness and painfulness, in watchings often, in hunger and thirst, in fastings often, in cold and nakedness.

"All these things are happening to me," Paul says. "Yet you say I'm weak in comparison to the false teachers in your midst." Then he gives the clincher. . . .

2 Corinthians 11:28
Beside those things that are without, that which cometh upon me daily, the care of all the churches.

"That which happens to me externally—the stonings and the beatings, the shipwrecks and the muggings—are beside the point. So I get beat all the time, so people throw rocks at me, so they're out to kill me constantly, so I'm hungry a lot, cold at night, in jail wherever I go—those things are nothing compared to the concern I have for the churches," Paul says.

This is not the heart of a spiritual guru or a motivational speaker. This is the heart of a father. Dads, you know something of this. As tough as things can be externally, financially, or physically—they're nothing compared to the concern you have that your kids do well.

I raise this question to you as I do to myself: What made Paul tick? Would you take thirty-nine lashes five times for the people sitting three rows in front of you—not for the ones you're married to or related to, but for the body of Christ in general?

I believe Paul gives us three reasons he was the man he was. . . .

First, as we'll see in chapter 12, Paul knew the reality of eternity. Heaven wasn't just some foggy, fuzzy "pie in the sky in the sweet bye and bye" idea for Paul. He had seen it personally. Has the Lord ever made heaven real to your heart? Has He ever made hell real to your heart? Have you ever just stopped and looked at a crowd of people, your family, or your classmates and thought, *My aunt, my neighbor, my friend is going to hell unless they receive the free gift of salvation which God has so generously provided for them?*

Knowing the reality of heaven, Paul said, "Let them beat me; let them stone me; let them imprison me; let them make fun of me. I know the

reality of eternity. So those things don't bother me."

Second, Paul knew the potency of the gospel. "I am not ashamed of the gospel of Christ," he declared in Romans 1. Paul knew that the gospel not only is the power by which people will be ushered into heaven eternally, but through which they will be blessed, helped, and saved presently.

When people come forward for salvation on Sunday mornings, do I have confidence that the profundity of the words I share with them will see them through? No way. At that point, my stomach is rumbling. I can't wait for lunch. I'm second-guessing the sermon I just gave. But this I know: Every person who comes will be met by the Lord not because of who I am, but because He is faithful. I know that as sure as I know my name.

He will in no wise cast out any who come to Him with any degree of sincerity (John 6:37). Such is the potency of the gospel.

Third, Paul knew the mystery of God's mercy. It was the love of Christ that enabled him to absorb the beatings, put up with the prisons, and care about the people (2 Corinthians 5:14). "I was a blasphemer, a persecutor, an enemy of those who named the name of Christ. But the Lord stopped me in my tracks, knocked me to the ground, and called out to me." Paul did what he did because he realized how merciful the Lord had been in saving him, in using him.

So, too, I believe that to the degree to which we understand the reality of eternity, the potency of the gospel, and the mystery of God's mercy is the degree to which, like Paul, we will say, "I'm going for it recklessly, wholeheartedly, whatever the cost might be."

How does one understand these things? I suggest a simple secret—not easy, but simple. That is, compassion is the result of contemplation. It was as Jesus sat on the hillside and looked at the city that He wept with compassion (Luke 19:41). So, too, it is in our own times of contemplation—when we quietly consider the plight of the people in the car next to us as we drive on the freeway, or the destiny of the person ahead of us in line at the supermarket—that the Lord can begin to work within us a heart of compassion. That is why consistent devotional times are so important. They're not to earn brownie points with God. He already loves us completely. But if we fail to stop and sit, to think and pray, to listen and worship, our eyes get dry and our hearts become callused.

2 Corinthians 11:29
Who is weak, and I am not weak? who is offended, and I burn not?

"When you're hurting, I hurt. If someone trips you up in your walk, I'm angry with that person," Paul said with the heart of a father, the heart of a mature believer.

2 Corinthians 11:30 (a)
If I must needs glory . . .

"If you're not satisfied by what I've gone through on your behalf, the generosity I've shown you, the jealousy I have for you—if you're still asking me to prove my authority," Paul says, "I will continue . . . ."

2 Corinthians 11:30 (b)
. . . I will glory of the things which concern mine infirmities.

Paul does not point to a university degree as his authority for ministry. He points to his greatest difficulty, for it proved to be his greatest glory.

2 Corinthians 11:31, 32
The God and Father of our Lord Jesus Christ, which is blessed for evermore, knoweth that I lie not. In Damascus the governor under Aretas the king kept the city of the Damascenes with a garrison, desirous to apprehend me: And through a window in a basket was I let down by the wall, and escaped his hands.

We find the story to which Paul alludes in Acts 9. . . .
As he headed toward Damascus in order to persecute Christians, the Lord confronted Paul, and he was converted immediately. Shortly thereafter, God said of him, "He is a chosen vessel unto me, to bear my name before the Gentiles, and kings, and the children of Israel" (Acts 9:15). In other words, God said, "Paul will talk to kings and impact some Jews. But he'll be a minister to Me among the Gentiles."
Yet such a heart did Paul have for the Jews that he said he would be damned for their sake if it meant they would be saved (Romans 9:3). So he headed straight for the synagogues, as if to say, "I can do You a whole lot of good, Lord. I was trained to be a Pharisee. I know how they think." And it made sense logically. Paul seemed to have the gifts, the background, and the testimony to impact the Jews radically. But they didn't buy what he was saying, so he left Damascus and spent three years in the Arabian wilderness being tutored by Jesus Himself (Galatians 1:17). Then he headed once again to the Jews.

He proved to them biblically and persuasively that Jesus is, indeed, the Christ. The result? They wanted to kill him (Acts 9:23). And his heart must have sunk. He went to Jerusalem next. And when he got there, heartsick, let down, wondering what was happening, he joined himself to the disciples. But even they were afraid of him, so he spoke boldly to the Grecians—those Jews who had adopted Gentile customs—as if to compromise with the Lord. What did they do? They decided to kill him (Acts 9:29).

At this point, the believers sent him out of the country. He went to Tarsus for seven to ten years, where he ministered in obscurity. But the Lord had plans for Paul. Barnabas sought him out, saying, "Let's go minister in the north to the Gentiles."

"Great!" said Paul. When at last he began ministering to those he was supposed to, the world was turned upside down, and the fruit remains to this day.

That is why he said, "I'm going to glory in what was the hardest thing in my life—when I was let down, when things weren't working out, when I was wondering where the Lord was. The greatest glory in my whole life was when the doors I thought would open up were shut tight—because it was then that God had His way."

"Use me, Lord," we cry. "I would make such a great worship leader." Yet as the weeks turn into months and the months into years, we wonder, *What's happening?*

"Don't worry," Paul would say to us. "I look back now and see that the day I was denied the ministry in which I thought I would do so well was the most important turning point in my life outside of my salvation."

If you're let down, understand that time will always prove the Lord to be right. That is why Paul could say, "If I must glory, I glory in the biggest disappointment of my life. Yes, I was heartsick at the time, but now I see the incredible wisdom of God."

12

2 Corinthians 12:1 (a)
It is not expedient for me doubtless to glory.

"I'm embarrassed that I have to glory in anything—even in my difficulties," said Paul.

2 Corinthians 12:1 (b)
I will come to visions and revelations of the Lord.

The false teachers who were undercutting Paul's ministry said, "He's a lightweight. All he does is teach doctrine. We have visions and revelations."

"All right," said Paul. "If you want to talk about visions and revelations. . . ."

2 Corinthians 12:2 (a)
I knew a man in Christ . . .

So reticent to talk about this was Paul that he doesn't even use his own name.

2 Corinthians 12:2 (b), 3
. . . above fourteen years ago, (whether in the body, I cannot tell; or whether out of the body, I cannot tell: God knoweth;) such an one caught up to the third heaven. And I knew such a man, (whether in the body, or out of the body, I cannot tell: God knoweth;)

From the Book of Acts, we know that fourteen years prior to this, Paul had been left for dead after being stoned in the city of Lystra. It seems certain that this is the backdrop for the text before us.

2 Corinthians 12:4 (a)
How that he was caught up into paradise . . .

What is the third heaven? The Bible refers to three heavens: The atmosphere around us is the first. The stars above us constitute the second. And the place where God dwells is the third. This is another proof text that nullifies the theory of "soul sleep"—the theory that says that when a person dies, he remains in a state of nothingness until the resurrection of the dead at the Second Coming of Christ. After being stoned, Paul did not enter a state of nothingness but was taken immediately to paradise—literally "a walled garden"—to heaven.

2 Corinthians 12:4 (b)
. . . and heard unspeakable words, which it is not lawful for a man to utter.

It was literally impossible for Paul to describe what he saw and heard in heaven. But I suggest that whatever it was, it was the reason he wanted to immediately go back into the city and start preaching again. *I've had a sneak preview of coming attractions, and I'm ready to go!* he might have thought. *Maybe they'll kill me once more!*

This verse makes me a bit skeptical of those who write books and embark on speaking tours after "dying" on the operating table. Paul didn't even mention this experience for fourteen years—and only then to say he couldn't describe it.

2 Corinthians 12:5, 6
Of such an one will I glory: yet of myself I will not glory, but in mine infirmities. For though I would desire to glory, I shall not be a fool; for I will say the truth: but now I forbear, lest any man should think of me above that which he seeth me to be, or that he heareth of me.

Do you hear the tension? Do you feel the struggle? "I don't want to talk about some revelation or vision or heavenly experience," says Paul. "Rather, I want you to judge me by the way I lived among you day after day after day."

Human nature says, "Let me share with you my revelation, my vision." Not Paul. He said, "I want you to judge what I'm saying based not on what I experienced mystically, but on how I lived among you practically."

2 Corinthians 12:7
And lest I should be exalted above measure through the abundance of the revelations, there was given to me a thorn in the flesh, the messenger of Satan to buffet me, lest I should be exalted above measure.

Following his heavenly excursion, a messenger of Satan was sent to keep Paul humble. Think about this. What was the singular reason Satan was cast out of heaven? Pride. Yet here God used the very pride of Satan to work humility in Paul.

Directly following a presentation I gave in sixth grade, in which I was able to share the Lord, I got into a fight at lunchtime—the one and only fight of my school career. It wasn't about the gospel. It was over a girl. The guy who drew me into this fight was Doug Gerdwagen. Of all the guys in the school, Doug Gerdwagen was my nemesis. To me, he was an arrogant, cocky bully. But guess who the Lord used to humble me. And guess who the Lord will use in your life—your own Doug Gerdwagen—the very person you think is worse than you.

What was the thorn in the flesh of which Paul speaks? Commentators have suggested it was an eye disease, malaria, an irritating person who followed him around, or physical repercussions of the stoning he endured. We don't know for sure what it was. But this we do know: The word translated "thorn" is the word for "tent stake"— the eighteen-inch-long spikes necessary to anchor Bedouin tents in the fierce desert winds.

Thus, Paul's thorn more closely resembled a sword in his side than it did a sliver under his skin.

2 Corinthians 12:8
For this thing I besought the Lord thrice, that it might depart from me.

Whether it was concerning a pain in his body, eyesight that was failing rapidly, or a person causing great difficulty, three times Paul prayed, "Lord, take it away."

2 Corinthians 12:9 (a)
And he said unto me, My grace is sufficient for thee: for my strength is made perfect in weakness.

Like Paul, we ask for help from the Lord. As far as our Father is concerned, however, the purpose of prayer is not that He might give help to us, but that He might give *Himself* to us.

The Father says, "You want Me to take away the pain, to solve the problem, to get you out of the situation—but that's not what you need. You need Me. And the very problem you're seeking to get away from, the very situation you desire to get out of is the very one that is causing you to talk to Me, spend time with Me, and depend on Me. You'll be stronger when you're weak because you'll have no other choice than to draw strength from Me. You'll do better when you're weak because you'll have to rely on Me."

2 Corinthians 12:9 (b)
Most gladly therefore will I rather glory in my infirmities, that the power of Christ may rest upon me.

It is the wise woman who says, "Okay, Lord. I'm not going to get out of the marriage because he's a thorn in my flesh."

It is the wise man who says, "I'm not going to try to alleviate that problem the way the world suggests, Lord. Instead, I'll just glory in it—for it's the way You get me close to You. And when I'm close to You, Your strength is made known to me."

2 Corinthians 12:10 (a)
Therefore I take pleasure in infirmities . . .

"It's a pleasure, Lord, to have this thorn under my skin that causes me grief," said Paul. What a statement! I want to get there!

2 Corinthians 12:10 (b)
. . . in reproaches, in necessities, in persecutions, in distresses for Christ's sake: for when I am weak, then am I strong.

"What power there is in an accepted sorrow," wrote Madame Guyon four hundred years ago. Understand this, dear saint, it is not wrong to pray to the Father when there's a thorn jabbing at you, or to share with the Father the desires that are mounting within you. You desire a certain thing to open up, to work out, to be taken away. There's no problem with communicating this to the Father. Whether it's a physical thorn in the flesh—sickness, disease, or bodily difficulty—or whether it's an emotional thorn in the flesh, we are to pray not once, not twice, but without ceasing (1 Thessalonians 5:16).

However, life is not a playground. It's a battlefield. And the sooner we understand this, the wiser we'll be. This is not heaven. If you're seeking to have heaven here now—no thorns in your flesh, no problems poking you, no disappointments coming to you—your life will be hellish because this is not heaven. When I finally realize that, like Paul, for me to live is Christ and to die is gain, life becomes extremely meaningful and completely enjoyable. We're here for a short season. There will be thorns in our flesh. There will be things poking us and disappointing us. Oh, what power there is, though, in accepted sorrow.

Pray without ceasing until the Lord either takes away the difficulty, brings about healing, develops the relationship, opens the job—until He either does that which you're asking or lets you know, as He did with Paul, that His grace is sufficient for you to bear the pain or the disappointment. Never forget that God is not as interested in your present comfort as He is in your eternal state. Trust Him when He says, "This thorn is necessary to draw you close to Me, that you might give your all in service to Me, that you might depend wholly upon Me." For it is then you will hear from Him the words your soul longs to hear: "Well done, good and faithful servant. Enter into the *joy* of the Lord" (see Matthew 25:21).

Pray. For as you grab the lever of prayer with the hand of faith, one of two things will happen: Blessings, healing, the working of God will come down upon you—or else the lever will yank you up into heaven, where you'll hear your Father say, "Now that I've got your attention, I don't want you healed because it is in your weakness that My strength will flow through you."

Brothers and sisters, pray three times, thirty

times, three hundred times until you either get the answer you're asking for or you hear the Father say, "No, and here's why..." Don't settle for anything less. If you pray this way, I believe you'll experience successful prayer 100 percent of the time. Talk to the Father about your thorns, your difficulties, and keep praying until the answer comes your way or until, like Paul, you have understanding and revelation and can say, "That's a closed issue. I don't need to talk about that anymore. I get it, Father. Your grace is sufficient for me."

For topical study of 2 Corinthians 12:7–10 entitled "Prickly Problems," turn to page 1155.

2 Corinthians 12:11
I am become a fool in glorying; ye have compelled me: for I ought to have been commended of you: for in nothing am I behind the very chiefest apostles, though I be nothing.

In 1 Corinthians 4:7, Paul had told the Corinthians that whatever a man has is given to him by the Lord. Therefore, Paul was not superior to the self-described "super apostles" because he was anything special, but because the ministry he had was given to him by the Lord.

2 Corinthians 12:12
Truly the signs of an apostle were wrought among you in all patience, in signs, and wonders, and mighty deeds.

The "superstars" stressed the miraculous. Paul, on the other hand, labored daily, teaching the Word. Although miraculous gifts did, indeed, flow through Paul, he didn't boast about them or focus on them the way others did. Why? Because he knew that miracles don't produce faith. Faith comes only by hearing and hearing by the Word of God (Romans 10:17).

2 Corinthians 12:13
For what is it wherein ye were inferior to other churches, except it be that I myself was not burdensome to you? forgive me this wrong.

"The one thing I didn't do to you that I did in other churches is take money from you because I didn't want to be a burden to you," Paul said.

2 Corinthians 12:14
Behold, the third time I am ready to come to you; and I will not be burdensome to you:

for I seek not yours, but you: for the children ought not to lay up for the parents, but the parents for the children.

"I'm going to come and see you, but I'm not going to raise an offering for myself," Paul told the Corinthians. "I'm not interested in your money. I'm interested in you. Why? Because I'm a father to you."

2 Corinthians 12:15
And I will very gladly spend and be spent for you; though the more abundantly I love you, the less I be loved.

"Others come and smite you in the face, take your money, pounce on you—and yet you respect them," says Paul. "I give my all for you, yet the more I give to you, the less I'm loved by you."

Why is it that the more you give to some people, the less they respect and love you? If someone is haughty and arrogant, sometimes people will be in awe of him. But if someone says, "I'm willing to spend all I have on your behalf," people think he must not be very special.

Don't be depressed, surprised, or discouraged when the more you love people, the less they love you—for this provides you a great opportunity to give simply for the sake of giving in true *agape* love. When you give to someone and he gives back to you, when you're nice to someone and she's nice to you—that's wonderful. But the highest form of giving is when you give and nothing is given back. Your reward will be great in heaven, and your personality will be shaped more closely into the image of Jesus Christ.

2 Corinthians 12:16
But be it so, I did not burden you: nevertheless, being crafty, I caught you with guile.

Paul quotes his critics who claimed that even though he was not charging the Corinthians, he had a plan and was simply setting them up for the big take.

2 Corinthians 12:17–19
Did I make a gain of you by any of them whom I sent unto you? I desired Titus, and with him I sent a brother. Did Titus make a gain of you? walked we not in the same spirit? walked we not in the same steps? Again, think ye that we excuse ourselves unto you? we speak before God in Christ: but we do all things, dearly beloved, for your edifying.

"Titus, a third brother I sent, and I are ministering with the same mentality. We're not tricky.

We have no ulterior motive. We just want to be a blessing to you," said Paul.

The world still thinks we as believers have another agenda politically or monetarily. "You claim to just love Jesus," they say, "but what's your real agenda? Is it to take control of the government, or to get rich?" The answer is neither. Like Paul, we just want people to be built up in their faith that they would do well in the Lord.

2 Corinthians 12:20
For I fear, lest, when I come, I shall not find you such as I would, and that I shall be found unto you such as ye would not: lest there be debates, envyings, wraths, strifes, backbitings, whisperings, swellings, tumults:

"I'm worried that when I come, you'll not like what you see in me, and I'll not like what I see in you because of the correction that will need to take place," Paul told the Corinthians.

2 Corinthians 12:21
And lest, when I come again, my God will humble me among you, and that I shall bewail many which have sinned already, and have not repented of the uncleanness and fornication and lasciviousness which they have committed.

What does "bewailing" mean? It speaks of a death moan, of grieving because of death. "Things are so out of order," said Paul, "that when I come I fear there will be some discipline—even the death of some." In this regard, we think of Ananias and Sapphira whom God had to deal with severely (Acts 5:1–11) and of Elymas, the sorcerer who was smitten with blindness that others might see (Acts 13:8–12). Sometimes some dark and heavy correction comes down when things get out of order the way they did at Corinth.

PRICKLY PROBLEMS
A Topical Study of
2 Corinthians 12:7–10

It's a most prickly problem, a truly thorny issue. We hear about it regularly and struggle with it frequently. That is, why does the pain persist? Why does the problem keep poking me? I've prayed about it, claimed victory over it, and want deliverance from it. But it just seems to always be there, causing consternation and agitation within me. Why does the problem remain?

If you have wrestled with such issues, the text before us is just for you. What was the thorn in Paul's flesh? Some think it was a demon hassling him. Some say it was a person who was harassing him. Others believe it was a physical problem hurting him.

Some suggest Paul suffered from the recurring migraines associated with certain types of malaria. Others surmise Paul had an eye disease due to the fact that the Galatians were willing to give him their own eyes, if that were possible (Galatians 4:15). According to a second-century document, Paul squinted constantly and his eyes ran continually. "You see with what large letters I write to you . . ." Paul writes in Galatians 6:11—perhaps implying that he didn't see very well.

Although we don't know for certain what Paul's thorn in the flesh was, this much we do know: It wasn't a sliver because the Greek word used for "thorn" is the same used for "tent stake." The Bedouins are a nomadic people who, with the exception of the TV antennas sticking out of their tents, live today as they have lived for thousands of years. Since their only concession to modern society is color TV, the "thorn" we read of here in 2 Corinthians would be similar to the eighteen-inch spikes used by the Bedouins to pitch their tents today.

Why did God allow this tent stake, this problem, this pain in Paul's life? Our text gives three reasons. . . .

To Produce Protection

In the verses prior to our text, Paul explained to the Corinthian believers how he had been caught up into heaven (2 Corinthians 12:1–4). Therefore, because he had such an incredible, unspeakable experience, the thorn in his flesh kept him from becoming proud.

> One morning, during a particularly successful season, the wife of a college basketball coach knocked on the bathroom door as he was shaving.
>
> "Honey," she said, "someone from *Sports Illustrated* is on the phone."
>
> "*Sports Illustrated!*" he said as, with lather still on his face, he grabbed a towel and ran down the stairs.
>
> "Sports Illustrated?" he said eagerly, adjusting the phone to his ear.
>
> "Yes," said a cheerful voice on the other end. "For seventy-five cents an issue, you can subscribe to *Sports Illustrated* for a full year!"
>
> And his bubble was burst.

Pride goes before destruction and a haughty spirit before a fall (Proverbs 16:18). Therefore, to protect us, the Lord sends pains and problems to hedge us in. Through the harlot Gomer as a picture of Israel, and the prophet Hosea as a picture of the everlasting love of God, He says,

> *Therefore, behold, I will hedge up thy way with thorns, and make a wall, that she shall not find her paths. And she shall follow after her lovers, but she shall not overtake them; and she shall seek them, but shall not find them: then shall she say, I will go and return to my first husband; for then was it better with me than now.*   Hosea 2:6, 7

The Lord knows my vulnerabilities. And He knows your weaknesses. Thus, by His grace, the thorns He allows in us are truly His protection for us.

To Propel Prayer

I have found oftentimes when my prayer life becomes lax or lazy, I find myself estranged from my Father. But prickly problems indeed propel me to pray. So, too, as one who prayed night and day (Romans 1:9; 1 Thessalonians 2:13; 2 Timothy 1:3), Paul prayed three times for the thorn in his flesh to be removed.

When you are dealing with an issue, which returns again and again, what should you do? Pray and pray and pray. Pray until you are either healed, delivered, set free—or until the Lord speaks into your heart the reason why the problem will remain. Pray for either a release from the thorn or a revelation concerning the situation. Such is the model of Paul and of Jesus.

Three times in the Garden of Gethsemane Jesus prayed, "Father if it be possible, let this cup pass from Me" (Matthew 26:39, 42, 44). The thorn of the Cross was not removed, but Jesus received peace when He concluded His prayer, "Thy will be done." Keep praying, saint. The Lord will either remove your thorn, your pain, your struggle—or give you understanding to go along with it.

To Precede Power

It was after Paul prayed three times for deliverance that at last he could say, "Most gladly, therefore will I rather glory in my infirmities, that the power of Christ may rest upon me" (see verse 9).

"Let me mow the lawn," begged Benjamin when he was four.

"Okay," I said. So, grabbing hold of the handle to my push mower, Ben pushed and grunted as the veins stuck out on his four-year-old neck.

"Help me, Daddy!" he called.

"Okay, Ben," I said. And with Ben in my arms, I mowed a few strips of the lawn.

When we decided to take a break, it was an excited and elated Benny who ran in the house yelling, "Mommy! Mommy! I mowed the lawn!"

What does God want to do? He wants to empower your life. But it's not until you come to the end of your rope that you can see your need for His strength. That's why the strongest people you will ever meet are those, who at some point in their lives, have absorbed a "thorn in the flesh" and have come to be at peace with it.

Rapport with Me

Whenever I think I am the only one suffering from a particular thorn in my flesh, the judgment hall of Pilate tells me otherwise. You see, it was there that Jesus absorbed not a single thorn in His flesh, but an entire crown of thorns, pressed into His skull (Mark 15:17). Therefore, He can relate to whatever problem I face; whatever battle I fight; whatever sharp, pointed thorn I endure because He has been there, tempted in all points like me—yet without sin (Hebrews 4:15).

Reminder to Me

My tendency is to say, "Only my thorn is heavy." But the crown of thorns on Jesus' brow reminds me that because of Adam's sin, we're *all* cursed with thorns

(Genesis 3:18). Therefore, God is not picking on me alone. We're all in this together, for every one of us will bear our own thorn.

Revival Within Me

The crown of thorns preceded the Cross of Calvary, which opened the way to heaven for me—where there will be no more tears, no more pain, no more thorns. This produces revival within my heart and renewed love for the One who absorbed more thorns than I could ever imagine.

Precious sisters, dear brother, don't try to remove the thorn the Lord has given you. Embrace it and see it produce protection in your walk, prayer in your heart, and power in your life—all to the glory of the One who endured the thorns; all to the praise of the One who paid the price.

13 **2 Corinthians 13:1, 2**
This is the third time I am coming to you. In the mouth of two or three witnesses shall every word be established. I told you before, and foretell you, as if I were present, the second time; and being absent now I write to them which heretofore have sinned, and to all other, that, if I come again, I will not spare:

"I'm coming to you again. Hopefully, you're getting the message. If you're not, I will have to deal with you severely," said Paul.

2 Corinthians 13:3, 4
Since ye seek a proof of Christ speaking in me, which to you-ward is not weak, but is mighty in you. For though he was crucified through weakness, yet he liveth by the power of God. For we also are weak in him, but we shall live with him by the power of God toward you.

When Jesus was crucified, they thought He was weak, but three days later, He rose again. "So, too," Paul says, "you look at us as weak, but when we come back, you'll see His power flowing through us."
Why is Paul being so stern? Because this is what it took to get these people to understand that they were being duped, sucked in by false teachers.

2 Corinthians 13:5 (a)
Examine yourselves, whether ye be in the faith; prove your own selves.

"You're criticizing us, finding fault with us," Paul says, "but here's what you should do: Exam-

ine yourself. Are you in the faith?" The implication is sobering. There can be those who come to church week after month after year after decade but who are not saved. How do you know if you're in the faith? Read on.

2 Corinthians 13:5 (b)
Know ye not your own selves, how that Jesus Christ is in you, except ye be reprobates?

Is Christ in you? It's not a matter of religion, but of relationship. It's not a question of theology, but of intimacy. It's not knowing about Jesus intellectually, but knowing Him personally.

2 Corinthians 13:6, 7
But I trust that ye shall know that we are not reprobates. Now I pray to God that ye do no evil; not that we should appear approved, but that ye should do that which is honest, though we be as reprobates.

"Look at us and see how Christ lives in us, how He's given guidance to us," says Paul. "And even if you don't buy our ministry, we still hope you'll do what's right."

2 Corinthians 13:8, 9 (a)
For we can do nothing against the truth, but for the truth. For we are glad, when we are weak, and ye are strong . . .

"If we're weak but you're strong, we are glad. If you're doing good, even though we're going through hard times, we rejoice."

2 Corinthians 13:9 (b)
. . . and this also we wish, even your perfection.

The tendency of many of us would be to say, "I hope you get judged." Not Paul. He says, "I hope things will be perfect for you, that you'll walk in maturity, that you'll do excellently." The only way Paul could have had that kind of heart for this kind of people is if he did what he said he did—if he prayed for them continually.

When you want to see someone get wiped out because they've done you wrong, pray God's best blessing upon his life. When you pray for the people who irritate you, your heart changes toward them. Oh, they might be changed in the process as well—but whether or not that happens, you will be changed, for one cannot be angry, hostile, or mad at those for whom he consistently prays. When you pray for people, you find your own heart desiring their perfection. You want their best.

2 Corinthians 13:10
Therefore I write these things being absent, lest being present I should use sharpness, according to the power which the Lord hath given me to edification, and not to destruction.

"I'm writing these things to you that you might make corrections now," said Paul, "so we won't have to come to you and bewail your condition."

2 Corinthians 13:11–14
Finally, brethren, farewell. Be perfect, be of good comfort, be of one mind, live in peace; and the God of love and peace shall be with you. Greet one another with an holy kiss. All the saints salute you. The grace of the Lord Jesus Christ, and the love of God, and the communion of the Holy Ghost, be with you all. Amen.

And so we come to the end of this second Corinthian letter—a beautiful and heartwarming ending to what was sometimes a necessarily brutal and heart-rending Epistle. Paul's closing statement begins with some simple and solid exhortations—"be of good comfort; be of one mind; live in peace."

And then he shares with them the wonderful ramification that if they do these things, the God of love and peace would be with them.

He follows this with an encouragement for warm but godly affection when he tells them to greet one another with a holy kiss, and then gives a message of affirmation to them when he tells

them that, rather than being down on them, all the saints salute them.

Finally, he gives them a beautiful and blessed benediction by saying, "The grace of the Lord Jesus be with you all."

No doubt, the hearts of the Corinthians would be encouraged and inspired by these warm words of Paul. Mine is. But there is one phrase that troubles me greatly. And I bet it troubled the Corinthians as well—for in the midst of Paul's beautiful benediction and heartwarming affirmation are words that cause within me a real consternation: Be perfect. Why couldn't Paul have said, "Be happy," or "Be good," or "Be all that you can be"? Why did he have to say, "Be perfect"?

If you have a newer translation, perhaps your Bible renders this phrase, "Be mature." Other paraphrases read, "Grow up." And while these are both close to the meaning, linguistically, the word Paul uses encompasses more than maturity or growth. It means, literally, "Be perfect." We can seek to sidestep it. We can try to get around it, but it means just what it says.

The implications are amazing, for if the Scriptures tell you and me that we are to be perfect, to do what's right, it must mean that in every situation there is right and there is wrong. This should be obvious to us, but there's a point in the history of Israel when the Lord sent the prophet Isaiah to indict the people concerning this very issue.

> Woe unto them that call evil good, and good evil; that put darkness for light, and light for darkness; that put bitter for sweet, and sweet for bitter!   Isaiah 5:20

At this juncture in their history, the people of Israel were confused in their understanding of right and wrong. They were entirely mixed up in their morality. So the prophet Isaiah thunders, "Woe to those in your society who say that light is dark and dark light, who are all mixed up in their morals and ethics." We see the same thing in our own culture.

Even as people argue for traditional family values, we still miss the mark. Why? Because values are subjective. For example, I value my Volkswagen van. But you and I could argue indefinitely about what the value is because of the subjective nature of values. No, the issue is not values. The issue is perfection.

What is perfect? The law of the Lord is perfect (Psalm 19:7). Given to us by God rather than generated within the mind of man, the law of God is nonnegotiable. The law of the Lord is perfect.

"Be ye perfect," Jesus said, "even as your Father in heaven is perfect" (Matthew 5:48). But He had already defined His terms when He said,

"Unless your righteousness exceeds that of the scribes and Pharisees, you'll not enter into the kingdom of heaven" (Matthew 5:20).

There are two ways to go about trying to be perfect. You can steel yourself morally and ethically by placing rules and regulations around yourself. Then you'll be like a man in a bathysphere—those big balls made out of cast iron with walls six inches thick—exploring the deepest trenches of the Pacific Ocean. Yet as you sit cramped and confined within your bathysphere, what will you see? Little fish with extremely thin skin swimming around totally free. How can these fish survive such depths? The answer is simple: The pressure within them is equal to the pressure outside of them.

There are those on the Religious Right who say, "We're going to construct iron plates of rules and regulations around us." But there's a better

way. Christ *in* us is the hope of glory (Colossians 1:27). It's not the law outside of us, but the Lawgiver, the Lover of our Soul, Christ Jesus *in* us who will whisper to us, "Why are you going in there? Why are you watching that? Why are you thinking those thoughts? Let Me show you a better way of thinking, of speaking, of acting, of living."

"I will write My will in your heart," God declared (Jeremiah 31:33). And He does so through His Spirit who dwells within us.

My bathysphere has sprung a leak or two along the way. So has yours. But when Jesus Christ died for our sin, He paid the price for the leaks we've sprung, for every mistake we've made. Thus, it is through Him and Him alone that we can be perfect by being perfectly forgiven.

Amen!

GALATIANS

Background to Galatians

Most likely, the first epistle penned by the apostle Paul was the one addressed to the Galatians, a people of whom Julius Caesar reportedly said, "They are fickle, fond of change, and not to be trusted." Originally from Gaul, or present-day France, the Galatians migrated south, settling into a region in present-day Turkey. Galatia was not a city, but a region.

Paul experienced firsthand the fickle nature of these people when, after he healed a lame man, the Galatians bowed before him and worshiped him as Jupiter. That was in the morning. In the evening, the same people picked up rocks, threw them at Paul, and left him for dead outside the city in response to a whispering campaign instigated by his enemies (Acts 14).

Too tough to die, however, Paul continued teaching the Good News of the gospel of grace—nowhere more clearly set forth than in this letter to the very people who once tried to kill him.

- In chapters 1 and 2, Paul wrote of his personal experience *with* grace.
- Chapters 3 and 4 address Paul's doctrinal instruction *about* grace.
- Chapters 5 and 6 give practical application *of* grace.

It's a fabulous book—Paul's manifesto on the absolute necessity of standing in liberty and his glorious defense of the gospel of grace.

GALATIANS

1 Galatians 1:1
Paul, an apostle, (not of men, neither by man, but by Jesus Christ, and God the Father, who raised him from the dead;).

Paul always began his Epistles in one of two ways: To the Romans and the Philippians, to Titus and Philemon, he introduced himself as a servant, or prisoner of Christ. To the Corinthians and the Ephesians, to the Colossians and the Galatians, he presented himself as an apostle. Why? Because to those who embraced and welcomed his ministry, he was a servant; but to those who challenged his authority, he was an apostle, a "sent one" of Jesus Christ.

Thus, even the opening verse of this letter underscores the fact that Paul's enemies—those who taught the "three R's of religion": rules, regulations, and rituals—sought to undermine the ministry of grace in the region of Galatia by questioning the authority of Paul.

This still happens today. When someone wants to subvert a ministry, he invariably slanders the minister—especially if he can't argue proficiently against the doctrine. Paul's enemies were no exception. They continually challenged his authority, saying, "He doesn't have the credentials to teach as he does."

So, too, the religionist comes to us, saying, "You believe in Jesus? That's great. So do I. But there's a little more to it than that."

"Really? Then how is man saved?" I ask.

"Well, believe in Jesus Christ and join our church," or, "Believe in Jesus Christ and sell magazines," or, "Believe in Jesus Christ and wear holy underwear."

Whenever you hear the word *and* in conjunction with belief, you know you're talking to a religionist. Jesus said it all boils down to only one thing: Believe on Him whom the Father hath sent (John 5:24). Put your trust in Him. Keep focused on Him. Open your heart to Him, for He alone is the basis of true faith.

The question of authority is most often raised by those who want to keep people under the restraints of religion and legalism. "What authority do you have to do the things you do, to preach the way you preach, or to baptize in the manner you baptize?" they ask.

"Who are you?" the priests and Levites asked John the Baptist. "Are you Elijah?"

"No."

"Are you Messiah?"

"No."

"Well, then, in whose authority do you do these things?" (see John 1:19–25).

After questioning John in chapter 1, the Jews questioned Jesus in chapter 2. Following His cleansing of the temple, they came to Him, saying, "By what authority do You do these things?" (see John 2:18).

The questioning of authority is a strategy often used by religious organizations and ritualistic people. "We alone are the direct descendants of the apostles," they say. "Through the tunnel of history, their apostolic anointing has been passed generation by generation to us."

Not true. Nothing in Scripture indicates that anointing can be passed on by man. Only God can impart authority.

"Then what is the value of being formally ordained?" you ask.

At best, ordination says that the Lord has touched this brother, or that ministry; that His hand is upon it, and His grace flowing through it.

Ordination, therefore, is nothing more than a ratification of what the Lord is already doing. That's why Paul said at the outset of this Epistle, "My authority was not given me by men, but by Jesus Christ."

Galatians 1:2, 3 (a)
And all the brethren which are with me, unto the churches of Galatia: Grace be to you and peace . . .

Why did Paul so often link peace with grace (1 Corinthians 1:3; 2 Corinthians 1:2; Ephesians 1:2; Philippians 1:2; Colossians 1:2; 1 Thessalonians 1:1; 2 Thessalonians 1:2; Philemon 3)? Because man will never know peace until he understands grace.

What is grace? Grace is unmerited, undeserved, unearned favor. The old acrostic still says it best: God's Riches At Christ's Expense—not because of anything you do or have done, but because of who Christ is and what He's done. You don't need to go through rituals. You don't need to live under regulations. You can have peace today if you understand grace because the grace of God brings peace in a profound way.

Galatians 1:3 (b), 4
. . . from God the Father, and from our Lord Jesus Christ, Who gave himself for our sins, that he might deliver us from this present evil world, according to the will of God and our Father.

"Evil world?" you say. "Don't we sing, 'This Is My Father's World'? If it's God's, then why is it evil?"

God the Father placed this world in the custody of Adam and Eve, our representatives in the Garden of Eden. When they fell, they, in turn, transferred ownership of the world to the one to whom they chose to submit—Satan. That is why when Satan offered Jesus all of the kingdoms of the world in return for worship (Matthew 4:8, 9), Jesus didn't dispute his right to make such an offer. Therefore, when people indict God for the corruption and evil of this world, it belies their ignorance of world history. The reason the world is so messed up and perverted is because, in rejecting God, mankind gave Satan dominion of the world system.

While it is true that God has placed perimeters around Satan, as we move toward the end of the ages, things will become more and more bizarre. People will excuse every sort of aberrant behavior by saying, "It's not my fault. I'm made that way." And evil will run rampant.

"As it was in the days of Noah"—punctuated with sexual aberrations; "as it was in the days of Lot"—permeated with homosexual exaltation—"so it will be in the last days," said Jesus (see Luke 17:26–28).

The Good News is that Jesus Christ died for our sins so that He could deliver us from this present evil world. We're going to heaven, folks. And that day is not very far off.

Galatians 1:5
To whom be glory for ever and ever. Amen.

I'm convinced we are on the verge of witnessing the coming of Jesus Christ. We'll be taken to heaven, where things will be right at last. Then we'll come back to earth, where He will rule and reign with righteousness for one thousand years. No wonder Paul says, "To Him be glory forever and ever"—for He has delivered us from this present evil world and into His glorious kingdom.

Galatians 1:6, 7 (a)
I marvel that ye are so soon removed from him that called you into the grace of Christ unto another gospel: Which is not another . . .

So-called "spiritual men" came on the scene in Galatia, saying, "It's great that you're born-again Christians and that you believe in the gospel. But it's not quite that simple. If you *really* want to be spiritual, you must follow the law—particularly the rite of circumcision. You must show you're serious by inflicting pain upon your body."

Paul said, "I marvel that you guys in Galatia have fallen for this."

Galatians 1:7 (b)
. . . but there be some that trouble you, and would pervert the gospel of Christ.

The Greek word translated "trouble" means "seasick." It's the same word used in Matthew 14:26, when, in the midst of a storm, the disciples were troubled when they saw Jesus walking on the water. The word connotes queasiness. This is understandable, since hearing they needed to be circumcised would be troubling news indeed to the Gentile believers.

Galatians 1:8, 9
But though we, or an angel from heaven, preach any other gospel unto you than that which we have preached unto you, let him be accursed. As we said before, so say I now again, If any man preach any other gospel unto you than that ye have received, let him be accursed.

"Anyone—a preacher, prophet, or even an angel from heaven—who preaches another gospel is to be damned," said Paul.

In 1 Kings 13, a young prophet burst onto the scene, found Jeroboam standing before an altar he had built to worship idols, and said, "Thus saith the Lord, Upon this altar shall the bones of your prophets be burned. And this shall be a sign: this altar will split in half." Upon hearing this, Jeroboam stretched out his hand and ordered the prophet seized. But as he did, his arm became paralyzed. At that moment, the altar did indeed crack and Jeroboam was filled with fear.

"I repent," Jeroboam cried. "Please pray for me." The prophet complied, and Jeroboam's hand was immediately restored. "Come to the palace," said a relieved and grateful Jeroboam, "and I will give you food and clothing."

"I can't," the prophet replied. "God told me very plainly that I was only to deliver the Word, and then return to my people."

On his way home, he was met by an older prophet, who, having heard what had transpired said to him, "I heard about what happened with Jeroboam. Come to my house, have dinner with me, and we'll talk about prophet stuff."

"I can't," said the young prophet. "God told me I'm to go back to my own people."

"Well," the old prophet argued, "I've been a prophet longer than you—and an angel came and told me to tell you you're to come to my house."

Finally, the young prophet gave in and accompanied the older prophet to his house. In the middle of the meal, the old prophet began to cry.

"What's wrong?" asked the young prophet.

"You're going to die," said the old prophet.

"Why?"

"You shouldn't have come here. You should have obeyed God. Why did you listen to me? The word of the Lord to you, young man, is that when you leave here, a lion will devour you."

And, sure enough, as the young man hurried home, a lion attacked and killed him.

If you know the Word but listen instead to a seemingly older or wiser so-called apostle or prophet who says something contrary to the Word, like the young prophet, you will be eaten by the roaring lion that goes about seeking whom he may devour (1 Peter 5:8).

I camp on this point because in the days in which we live, there are many who will suggest to you practices, customs, and traditions that seem spiritual but aren't scriptural.

A so-called revival in the Church of England wherein people were laughing like hyenas, roaring like lions, and barking like dogs recently captured the attention of the secular media. My question is: Where is it written in the Word that people are to bark like dogs, roar like lions, or laugh hysterically for hours at a time?

I firmly believe that everything we do in the practice of our faith and in the expression of worship must be seen in the Scriptures.

"Well, that's too restrictive," you say.

No, it isn't. Whenever there is a phenomenon or an expression of the Spirit, if, like Peter on the Day of Pentecost, you can say, "This is that spoken by the Word" (see Acts 2:16), you will have a solid and stable walk. A good rule of thumb concerning any practice or tradition is this: Where do you see it in the life of Jesus? Secondly, does it continue through the Book of Acts? Finally, is it taught by Paul in the Epistles?

There is so much in the life of Jesus, expressed through the Book of Acts, and taught by the apostle Paul that we are not yet experiencing, we have our work cut out for us just doing the things we see in Scripture—let alone exploring avenues that are not there.

"The two sticks in Ezekiel 37 refer to the Gospel and the Book of Mormon," said the angel Moroni. "Put on these glasses, Joseph, and you'll see another gospel, a further revelation."

Not true.

Paul says let the person, prophet, preacher, or angel who says there's another gospel be accursed.

Galatians 1:10
For do I now persuade men, or God? or do I seek to please men? for if I yet pleased men, I should not be the servant of Christ.

"Religious ritualists might come down on me and call me narrow-minded and simple," said Paul. "I don't care. I must please God rather than men. If I was trying to please these heavy-handed leaders, I could not be the servant of Christ."

For topical study of Galatians 1:10 entitled "Fearing God or Fearing Man?" turn to page 1165.

Galatians 1:11, 12
But I certify you, brethren, that the gospel which was preached of me is not after man. For I neither received it of man, neither was I taught it, but by the revelation of Jesus Christ.

In verses 1–11, we saw grace declared in Paul's message. Beginning with verse 12, we see grace depicted in Paul's life as he shares his own story.

Galatians 1:13, 14
For ye have heard of my conversation in time past in the Jews' religion, how that beyond measure I persecuted the church of God, and wasted it: And profited in the Jews' religion above many my equals in mine own nation, being more exceedingly zealous of the traditions of my fathers.

"You know my story," Paul said. "I was into Judaism radically, a Pharisee of Pharisees (Philippians 3:5, 6). In addition, I wasted the church, looking for Christians to bring to trial (Acts 9:1, 2).

Galatians 1:15, 16 (a)
But when it pleased God, who separated me from my mother's womb, and called me by his grace, to reveal his Son in me, that I might preach him among the heathen . . .

"Even though I was a Jew's Jew," Paul argued, "God had something else in mind for me. From my mother's womb, I was called into the ministry of sharing the Good News of the gospel. Sidetracked for a while, I got involved in religion. God, however, knew all along that I would be an apostle of the gospel of grace."

Galatians 1:16 (b), 17 (a)
. . . immediately I conferred not with flesh and blood: Neither went I up to Jerusalem to them which were apostles before me; but I went into Arabia . . .

In religious circles today, it's impressive to have a D.D.—a Doctorate of Divinity. Paul had a D.D.—a Doctorate of the Desert. He was in good company: Moses, John the Baptist, and Jesus all spent time in the desert.

Maybe these are dry, difficult days for you. It could be that God wants to reveal Jesus Christ to you in a fresh way. For that to happen, He may do to you what He did to John the apostle when He sent him to Patmos. . . .

At one hundred years of age, John was exiled to Patmos—a rocky, barren, seemingly God-

forsaken island. It was a tough situation, and, no doubt, John questioned what was going on. "I'm old," he could have said. "I've trusted in the Lord. I'm linked to Him. Why this isolation?"

When he saw Jesus Christ, John started writing. Twenty-two chapters later, the Book of Revelation was complete.

When was revelation given to John? When he was isolated on an island.

Perhaps you're at a point where you're saying, "Who can I talk to?" or, "What counsel can I receive?"—when the Lord may have you on an island of isolation for a season in order to give you a revelation of Jesus Christ. Don't bemoan your condition. Don't bewail your situation. Worship the Lord. Draw close to Him. Be still—and you will see Him in ways you never would have had you been anywhere else.

Galatians 1:17 (b)–19
. . . and returned again unto Damascus. Then after three years I went up to Jerusalem to see Peter, and abode with him fifteen days. But other of the apostles saw I none, save James the Lord's brother.

"After three years, I went to Jerusalem to see Peter," said Paul. "I didn't see any of the other apostles, except James, the Lord's brother. Peter greeted me and welcomed me for fifteen days. James did so briefly. The other apostles wanted nothing to do with me."

This is understandable. Seeing Paul spending time with Christians would have been comparable to seeing Adolf Hitler attending synagogue. Paul, being a persecutor of Christians, and a waster of the church, the church didn't quite know what to make of him.

Galatians 1:20–24
Now the things which I write unto you, behold, before God, I lie not. Afterwards I came into the regions of Syria and Cilicia; and was unknown by face unto the churches of Judaea which were in Christ: But they had heard only, That he which persecuted us in times past now preacheth the faith which once he destroyed. And they glorified God in me.

In some regions, people wondered about Paul. In others, they glorified God in him.

FEARING GOD OR FEARING MAN?
A Topical Study of
Galatians 1:10

"The fear of man is a snare," Solomon declared (see Proverbs 29:25). Paul elaborated on this, saying if we fear men, we cannot be the servants of Christ.

Try to fit in with this group on campus, or that group on the job site, try to speak their lingo, laugh at their jokes, be cool like them—it will end in disaster. Ask David. . . .

The Rear of Man Brings Humiliation

Fleeing from Saul, David went to the Philistine city of Gath (1 Samuel 21). Upon his arrival, the servants of Achish, king of Gath, said, "Is not this David? Did not they sing one to another of him, saying, Saul hath slain his thousands, but David his ten thousands?"

Oh no, thought David. *They know who I am.* So, the Word says, "He changed his behavior before them and feigned himself mad in their hands." He scratched on the doors of the gate and let spittle run down his beard. Poor David. The same guy who killed Goliath, the same one noted for courage and valor is now falling prey to the fear of man, acting like an idiot. It's tragic. Although his plan worked, David was humiliated and embarrassed even to this day. Thousands of years later, we're talking about David playing the fool because of the fear of man.

It's amazing to watch teenagers, adults, and even older people act like fools. It's amazing to see people try to fit in because they're afraid of man. It's amazing to see people, who, like David, love God and have seen victories in the Lord in times past, fearing man, look like idiots with spit running down their beards as they try to fit in and be cool.

Truly, the fear of man brings humiliation, for even the Achishes of this world say, "Get this guy out of here" (see 1 Samuel 21:14, 15).

The Fear of Man Brings Devastation

"Saul, you are to go and do battle against the Amalekites," said Samuel (see 1 Samuel 15). "You are to destroy all of the men, women, sheep, and cattle." Saul engaged the Amalekites in battle and was indeed victorious. Upon his return, he saw Samuel off in the distance. "Praise the Lord," he shouted. "I did what you told me to do."

"Then what's that bleating I hear?" asked Samuel.

The people wanted to bring some of the best sheep back to sacrifice to the Lord," answered Saul.

"What about him?" asked Samuel, pointing to the man hiding behind Saul.

"That's Agag, king of the Amalekites. I brought him back as a trophy," said Saul.

"Didn't I tell you that all of the sheep and people were to be killed?" said Samuel. "The Lord requires obedience, not sacrifice. Because you listened to the people rather than to God, you will lose your authority and your monarchy."

Years later, Saul was wounded in battle. With his last breath, he asked his attacker from whence he came.

"I am an Amalekite" was the reply (2 Samuel 1:8).

Saul not only lost his crown, but he lost his life because of the fear of man.

The Fear of Man Brings Disqualification

Moses came down from the mountaintop to find the people of Israel dancing around a golden calf.

"What's going on?" he asked Aaron, the high priest.

"It's not my fault," Aaron said. "The people brought me their golden earrings. I simply threw them into the fire and out came this golden calf" (see Exodus 32:24).

And so it was that Aaron was removed from the kind of ministry he could have had, for it was at this point that God instituted the Levitical priesthood. You see, it was only the Levites who said, "We fear not man, but will stand with the Lord, no matter what others do" (see Exodus 32:26).

Truly, the fear of man brings humiliation, devastation, and disqualification.

Those things won't happen to me," you say. "I'm a 'No Fear' kind of guy. Look, It even says so on my T-shirt."

Folks, the "No Fear" mentality is a fallacy because at any given moment, we are either living in the fear of man or in the fear of God. The fear of man is a snare (Proverbs 29:25). The fear of the Lord, on the other hand, is the beginning of wisdom (Proverbs 1:7).

What does it mean to fear the Lord?

It doesn't mean being afraid of Him. It means being afraid of doing anything that would disappoint Him.

> The son of a pastor friend of mine was misbehaving in Sunday school. "God's watching you, William," the teacher said. Little William went home that afternoon and asked his dad if it was true that God was always watching him.
>
> Knowing the reason for his son's question, this wise father said, "Yeah, William. It's true—God's always watching you. He loves you so much He just can't take His eyes off you."

The fear of God says, "Thank You, Father, for Your goodness, Your grace, Your kindness. Oh, Father, I don't want to do anything to grieve You." The fear of the Lord is the beginning of wisdom (Proverbs 9:10). The word "beginning" doesn't mean "the starting point." It means "the basis of." In other words, the foundation of wisdom is to fear God, realizing at any moment, in every moment, His eye is upon you.

Not only is the fear of the Lord the beginning of wisdom, but it "prolongeth days" (Proverbs 10:27). When you fear the Lord, your days are long or, literally, "enriched." The fear of the Lord enriches your days and makes prosperous all you do.

The fear of the Lord is to hate evil (Proverbs 8:13). Knowing God's loving gaze is fixed upon you will cause you to steer clear of anything that is corrupt or carnal.

> From the time she was a baby, my daughter Jessie never went anywhere without her blanket. As the day drew near for her to start school, I became increasingly worried. But as we walked out the door together on that first day of kindergarten, I was as shocked as I was relieved to see her without her beloved blanket. "Where's your blanket, Jessie?" I asked somewhat fearfully.
>
> "I'm not going to let the boys see me with a blanket, Daddy," she said. And she never picked up her blanket again.

Truly, when you care about someone, you find yourself behaving differently!

The fear of the Lord is strong confidence and a fountain of life (Proverbs 14:26, 27). If you want to go through life confidently, if you want to experience a continual flow of refreshment, live your life in the fear of the Lord.

Precious people, right now you either fear what family, friends, co-workers, or neighbors think of you—or you are living in the fear of God. If you're living in the fear of man, trying to fit in, like David, people will see you as an idiot. Like Saul, you'll be destroyed. Like Aaron, you'll miss out on what could have been.

But if you're living in the fear of God, your days will be prosperous, your foundation sure, and your life blessed.

May the Lord give us a new desire and a new resolve to say, "We choose today to give no place to the fear of man. We choose, instead, to walk in the fear of God." According to Paul, only then can we be servants of Christ.

2 In chapter 1, we saw grace declared in Paul's message (1:1–18), and depicted in his life (1:19–24). Here in chapter 2, we will see grace defended in his ministry—both before the church collectively and before Peter personally.

Galatians 2:1 (a)
Then fourteen years after . . .

Following Paul's conversion, he spent approximately three years in the Arabian desert, where he was personally tutored by Jesus Christ. Emerging from the desert, he spent fifteen days in Jerusalem primarily with Peter. He then made his way to Syria, Cilicia, and finally back to his hometown of Tarsus—where he remained for eleven years.

During those eleven years, outside the flow of the story transpiring in the Book of Acts, Paul labored quietly making tents—until suddenly people started getting saved in Antioch. Jews by nationality but Grecian in culture and custom, the new believers had a hard time relating to the traditional Jewish believers who had led them to the Lord. Hearing of the outpouring of the Spirit in Antioch, leaders of the church in Jerusalem dispatched Barnabas to see what was happening. After surveying the situation, Barnabas believed the solution lay in his old friend with the keen intellect—Paul. So Barnabas tracked Paul down and brought him back to Antioch, back into ministry (Acts 11:19–26).

Galatians 2:1 (b)
. . . I went up again to Jerusalem with Barnabas, and took Titus with me also.

Paul took Titus, a young Gentile protégé, with him to Jerusalem.

Galatians 2:2
And I went up by revelation, and communicated unto them that gospel which I preach among the Gentiles, but privately to them which were of reputation, lest by any means I should run, or had run, in vain.

Paul, Barnabas, and Titus told Peter, James, John, and the rest of the church in Jerusalem about their ministry among the Gentiles.

Galatians 2:3
But neither Titus, who was with me, being a Greek, was compelled to be circumcised.

The Jerusalem brothers responded, saying, "Titus, because you're Greek, you need to submit to the regulation that speaks of the cutting away of the flesh, and which shows you're serious about your commitment to God. You need to be circumcised." In other words, "Become a Jew, Titus."

Galatians 2:4
And that because of false brethren unawares brought in, who came in privily to spy out our liberty which we have in Christ Jesus, that they might bring us into bondage.

The religionists crept in to observe the liberty of Paul, Titus, and Barnabas—not to celebrate it, but to regulate it.

Galatians 2:5
To whom we gave place by subjection, no,
not for an hour; that the truth of the gospel
might continue with you.

Paul had no time for those whose aim it was to
bring people into bondage. I'm so glad Paul held
his ground, for had he given in to these Judaizers,
how much different Christianity would be today.
Had Paul given in to the religionists, we would be
required to keep all of the rules, ordinances, and
regulations of the Jewish religious system.

Paul understood the vital concept that Jesus
Christ came to do something new. You see, before
Jesus came, the world was divided into only two
groups: Jews and Gentiles. But the blood and water that flowed at Calvary (John 19:34) marked
the birth of a new entity that was neither Jew nor
Gentile. For just as a bride was created for the
first Adam from out of his side (Genesis 2:22), the
church, the bride of Christ, was born when the
sword pierced the side of the Last Adam. As a result, we are neither Jews nor Gentiles. We are the
church.

Galatians 2:6 (a)
But of these who seemed to be somewhat,
(whatsoever they were, it maketh no matter
to me: God accepteth no man's person:) . . .

As a freshman at Biola University, I was about
to give a Bible study before a group of professors.
The night before my presentation, when I finally
fell asleep, I dreamed I saw each of my professors, along with Billy Graham and a whole bunch
of other Christian leaders, standing hand in hand
with me around a huge tree. The interesting
thing was this: Every single guy was exactly the
same height. When I awoke, I knew immediately
that the Lord was reminding me that He truly is
no respecter of persons—even of those who
"seem to be somewhat" (see Acts 10:34).

Galatians 2:6 (b)
. . . for they who seemed to be somewhat in
conference added nothing to me.

"Peter, James, John, and the others didn't tell
me anything I didn't already know," said Paul.
This is understandable, considering Paul had
been tutored personally by Jesus Christ Himself
(see 1:16).

Galatians 2:7–10
But contrariwise, when they saw that the
gospel of the uncircumcision was committed unto me, as the gospel of the circumcision was unto Peter; (For he that wrought
effectually in Peter to the apostleship of the
circumcision, the same was mighty in me
toward the Gentiles:) And when James, Cephas, and John, who seemed to be pillars,
perceived the grace that was given unto me,
they gave to me and Barnabas the right
hands of fellowship; that we should go unto
the heathen, and they unto the circumcision. Only they would that we should remember the poor; the same which I also was
forward to do.

Here is Paul's account of the Acts 15 Jerusalem
Council. After listening to Paul, and seeing what
the Lord was doing through him, Peter, James,
and John said, "We'll continue ministering to the
Jews here in Jerusalem. You minister to the Gentiles. Just don't forget the poor." This is humorous to me because where were the poor to which
Peter, James, and John were referring? In Jerusalem. In other words, they were saying, "Don't
forget us, Paul. Send us some money."

Four men—Peter, Paul, James, and John—
were the main players in the drama of the early
church.

As I look at Peter, I see he is the apostle of order. He was the one who talked about a spiritual
priesthood, offering spiritual sacrifices, and being a spiritual house. He's the one who talked
about Jesus as the Bishop of our soul. Peter had
a distinctly Jewish flavor. Parts of the body
of Christ can really relate to Peter. With their
bishops and spiritual sacrifices, the liturgical
churches come from Peter's line.

Paul, on the other hand, was the apostle of candor. He was an "in-your-face, this-is-the-way-it-
is" renegade kind of guy. Where Peter would be
the apostle of the liturgical church, Paul would be
the apostle of the evangelical church. C. S. Lewis,
G. K. Chesterton, C. H. Spurgeon would all relate
to Paul.

John was the apostle of passion. The one who
leaned on the breast of Christ at the Last Supper,
the one who was caught up into heaven in the
Book of Revelation, John best represents those
who are mystical, Pentecostal, and visionary by
nature. George Fox, Thomas à Kempis, and Madame Guyon would relate most closely to John.

Finally, there was James. "Pure and undefiled
religion is this," the apostle of action said, "visit
the fatherless, take care of the widows, and keep
yourself unspotted from the world (see James
1:27). You can talk about your faith until you're
blue in the face—let me see your works." James
would reflect the ecumenical mentality that says,
"We have a responsibility to feed the poor in
Rwanda. We need to get involved in Habitat for
Humanity. We need to forget our differences,
come together, and do something practical for a

hurting world." While I don't agree with a lot of the theology of the ecumenical movement, I can and do commend them for much of what they do in caring for people's practical needs.

As I look at the churches in our communities, I can see "Peter" kinds of churches, "Paul" types of fellowships, "James" groups of believers, and "John"-flavored bodies. I can embrace them all because I can see the Lord's wisdom in having different kinds of churches for different kinds of people.

Paul would later write, "Work out your own salvation with fear and trembling, for it is God who works in you both to will and to do of His good pleasure" (Philippians 2:12, 13). Both as individuals, and as a corporate church, our salvation is to be worked out, or expressed with a little different flavor than that of other individuals or other churches.

The fact remains, however, that we must not be a "Paul" chapel, a "James" body, a "Peter" fellowship, or a "John" group of believers. We must be a Jesus church. Truly, He must be pre-eminent. No matter how big a church might be numerically, how much incense it might burn sacrificially, how much work it does practically, or how many visions it might see mystically—if it does not lift up Jesus Christ it is a false fellowship.

Galatians 2:11 (a)
But when Peter was come to Antioch . . .

Peter left Jerusalem to travel north to Antioch—Gentile territory.

Galatians 2:11 (b)
. . . I withstood him to the face . . .

Paul didn't go storming down to Jerusalem, saying, "Have a sausage, Peter. I dare you." No, Peter was in Paul's arena, and because Peter was trying to get the people to whom Paul was ministering to go in a different direction, Paul was justified in pointing out Peter's hypocrisy.

There have been occasions when, as a shepherd, I have had to physically remove those who came in, wanting to take this flock in a direction contrary to the gospel of grace. But I will not go into another church and pronounce judgment or give correction. When Paul was in Peter's face, he was on his own turf—in Antioch, not Jerusalem.

Galatians 2:11 (c)
. . . because he was to be blamed.

This phrase indicates very simply and clearly that traditions claiming either that Peter was the first pope, or that popes are infallible in matters of doctrine and church practice, are mistaken. If Peter was the first pope, he was far from infallible here.

Galatians 2:12 (a)
For before that certain came from James, he did eat . . .

The early church had *agape* feasts wherein believers would gather together and share a meal. Many of them being poor, everyone would pool his resources and contribute to a big potluck dinner.

Galatians 2:12 (b)
. . . with the Gentiles . . .

Jewish tradition held that there was a special connection with whomever one shared a meal. The Jews, therefore, were forbidden to eat with Gentiles. Thus, Peter broke tradition not only in eating the food of Gentiles, but in eating with Gentiles.

Galatians 2:12 (c)
. . . but when they were come, he withdrew and separated himself, fearing them which were of the circumcision.

When the men from Jerusalem came, suddenly Peter distanced himself from the Gentile believers.

Galatians 2:13, 14
And the other Jews dissembled likewise with him; insomuch that Barnabas also was carried away with their dissimulation. But when I saw that they walked not uprightly according to the truth of the gospel, I said unto Peter before them all, If thou, being a Jew, livest after the manner of Gentiles, and not as do the Jews, why compellest thou the Gentiles to live as do the Jews?

"You ate right alongside of us, Peter," said Paul. "Therefore, if you, a Jew, are unable to keep the rules and regulations of Judaism, how can you expect Gentiles to keep them? It makes no sense!"

That's what hypocrisy always does: It tries to make other people do what we ourselves can't.

Galatians 2:15, 16
We who are Jews by nature, and not sinners of the Gentiles, knowing that a man is not justified by the works of the law, but by the faith of Jesus Christ, even we have believed in Jesus Christ, that we might be justified by the faith of Christ, and not by the works

of the law: for by the works of the law shall no flesh be justified.

"Peter, why are you advocating the rebirth of religion?" asked Paul. "We Jews couldn't even keep the rules. We know that a man is justified only by faith in Christ—not by works, but simply by believing."

Are you trying to earn God's favor through morning devotions or Wednesday night Bible study attendance, through memorizing verses or witnessing, through not going here or not doing that? It's a big mistake. You are justified by faith and faith alone—not only when you were born again, not only when you were saved ten years ago—but today, right now. God's blessing will be upon the life of any man, woman, teenager, or older person who simply says, "I know I can't earn Your blessing, Lord. However, if You want to bless me by Your grace through my belief in Your Son, I welcome such blessing."

Dear brother, precious sister—the blessings of God are not based upon what you do or don't do. It's not a matter of saying, "Okay, God, I didn't see that movie. Aren't You proud of me? And because I didn't, here's what I'm expecting You to do for me. . . ."

No. The blessings of God are based solely upon grace. We can receive His blessing only because the sin that separated us from the Father has been washed away by the blood of Jesus Christ. Therefore, if I choose to sin, it's not that God will withhold His blessing in order to punish me. No, the blood of Jesus Christ has cleansed me from all sin—past, present, and future (1 John 1:7, 9). If I choose to sin, I destroy myself.

Balak, king of the Moabites, hired Balaam the prophet to curse the people of Israel (Numbers 22). No matter how Balaam tried, however, he could only pronounce blessing upon them. "Let's build another altar, and you can try again," said Balak. So again Balaam opened his mouth—but only blessing came out. After a third altar, a third try, and a third failure, Balak was desperate.

"I can't help it," explained Balaam. "I'm trying to curse them, but they're God's people." Seeing his fee slip through his fingers, however, Balaam came up with a new plan. "I can't curse them," he told Balak, "but they can curse themselves. Here's what you do: Send your women into the Israelite camp and tell them to invite the Israelite men into their tents. Then have them pull out their little idols—their Ashtaroths—and say, "This is the way we worship in this country. Don't you want to worship with us?"

"Good plan," Balak said. So he got his girls

and sent them into the camp of Israel. They enticed the guys into their tents and, just as planned, the Moabite women pulled out their idols. Sure enough, the Israelites took the bait—and ended up cursing themselves, resulting in a plague that wiped out twenty-four thousand of them (Numbers 25:9).

The same is true today. God says, "You're justified by the hearing of faith because you believe in the work of My Son." As far as God is concerned, the sin that would bar me from "the spout where the blessings come out" was taken away by the blood of Jesus Christ. I cannot be cursed. But I can curse myself and so can you.

Watch your step, young person. Listen up, forty-five-year-old. "Oh, it's okay to see that film," you say. "It's only got a few scenes that are slightly compromising," or "It's okay to hear that music. There are only a few questionable words." Watch out. You're cursing yourself. We live in a culture where the advice of Balaam is being worked out unlike any other time in human history. Be very careful. You'll get drawn into tents you never thought you would enter and be wiped out in the process.

Galatians 2:17
But if, while we seek to be justified by Christ, we ourselves also are found sinners, is therefore Christ the minister of sin? God forbid.

"Peter, if we eat with Gentiles, are we then sinners?" asked Paul. "Is Christ a sinner? Of course not! It's not what goes into a man that defiles him, it's what comes out" (see Mark 7:18–23). It's how you live rather than what you eat that matters.

Galatians 2:18
For if I build again the things which I destroyed, I make myself a transgressor.

You who are discipling men, you who are ministering to women, you who are teachers, servants, and mature saints—understand this verse. Do not erect another set of rules and regulations. You were saved by grace when you simply came to God as a sinner. Now, you are to remain in the realization that to come to the Lord, you must come just as you are—not because of what you do, or what you promise to be. Do not erect another set of barriers. The veil was rent when Jesus cried, "It is finished" (Matthew 27:50, 51). Don't sew it up again by saying to those to whom you minister, "You have to attend six meetings a week, listen to Christian radio every afternoon, read eight chapters in the Word every night, vote

Republican, and have three hours of morning devotions every day if you want to grow in Christ."

Are morning devotions wrong? Of course not! You don't *have* to have morning devotions—you *get* to! You *get* to start your day talking to God. That's a tremendous privilege—not an obligation. Anyone who doesn't start his day with the Lord is missing so much. Therefore, we don't do it because we *have* to. We do it because we *get* to.

Galatians 2:19
For I through the law am dead to the law, that I might live unto God.

"The law is no longer a factor in my life," said Paul. "I tried to keep it for years, but finally it just did me in."

Galatians 2:20
I am crucified with Christ: nevertheless I live; yet not I, but Christ liveth in me: and the life which I now live in the flesh I live by the faith of the Son of God, who loved me, and gave himself for me.

"The law served its purpose when it showed me I couldn't keep it," continued Paul. Now I'm dead to the external rules of the law, but alive to the internal rule of Jesus Christ in my heart."

Galatians 2:21
I do not frustrate the grace of God: for if righteousness come by the law, then Christ is dead in vain.

If you tried to rob a bank, but were shot and killed in the attempt, no one would drag your corpse into the courtroom. Even though you broke the law, you wouldn't go to court. So, too, when Christ died, you died with Him (Romans 7:4). Therefore, you are dead to the rules and regulations of the law. But if you choose to live again to the law, then, for you, the death of Christ was in vain.

How I thank the Lord that Paul stood his ground and spoke so boldly to Peter. And how I pray that, where there is a Peter tendency within our own hearts, the Lord might use the words of Paul to speak to us. How I pray that we might not frustrate grace or try to add to the work of the Cross. How I pray that we might love the Father all the more because of the great grace He has shown us in His Son.

GOD'S GRACE: ENJOY!
A Topical Study of
Galatians 2:21

O n our way to Family Camp years ago, Benjamin and Mary were munching their way through their cache of junk food in the backseat of the van while my wife, Tammy, and I tried to talk to them about the benefits of eating nutritiously. When it was time for dinner, they wanted to stop at Taco Bell®. Tammy and I opted instead for that well-known haven of health food: Denny's®.

Once inside, we told the kids they could order whatever they wanted. Mary Elizabeth, who was in first grade, immediately ordered waffles with whipped cream and that fake strawberry stuff on top. Benjamin, a kindergartener at the time, ordered spaghetti and meatballs. When their orders arrived, Mary found herself somewhat sickened by sweetness after a few bites. Benny, on the other hand, scarfed down the spaghetti, gobbled up the meatballs, and with eyes as wide as his voice was loud, said, "Wow! These are the *best* meatballs I've ever had! Can I have more?"

We ordered another plate of spaghetti. By this time, Mary was craving something other than waffles. "Benny," she said sweetly, "may I please have just one of your meatballs?"

Benny frowned. "Just one, Benny," pleaded Mary. "What would *Jesus* do?"

With that, Benjamin looked right at Mary and said, "Mary, Jesus would eat nutritiously."

I think we have a meal before us that is both nutritious *and* delicious. I love Paul's Epistle to the Galatians because it deals with the meatiest of subjects: the grace of God. Throughout this book, Paul pleads passionately with the Galatians that they not get entangled with the works of the law—but that they remain in the simplicity of grace.

What is grace? It's unmerited, undeserved, unearned favor. We get the riches of God and blessings from God because of what Christ did for us on Calvary. You see, the one thing that would keep us from being blessed by God is sin, for sin cuts off the flow of God's blessing upon our lives. But because our sin was washed away by the blood of Jesus Christ on the Cross of Calvary, all barriers have been removed.

In our text, we hear Paul saying, "I do not frustrate the grace of God. If God wants to bless me for no reason, if He wants to pour out His goodness upon me and provide salvation for me, if He wants to do that by grace, because of what Christ did, I will accept it gladly!"

Suppose you want to show someone your appreciation and take him out to dinner. You enjoy your time together immensely. Then the waiter comes with the bill, and your guest grabs it.

"Give me that," you say.

"No," he says. "I'm going to pay."

"No," you insist. "I invited you. I want to do this for you. It's my way of showing appreciation to you."

"No," he says. "I'm paying the bill."

You get into a fight right there. He ends up with the bill and writes a check to pay for it. But when the waiter runs his check through Insta-Check®, the screen flashes "Insufficient Funds." Five minutes later, the cops arrive, slap handcuffs on your friend, and carry him off to prison, where he is later executed for "Insufficient Funds."

You would be frustrated, indeed—not only because your friend was too proud to let you pay the bill, but because he was incapable of paying it in the first place.

That's the message of Galatians 2. God wants to bless you by paying the bill. If you say, "No, I'll pay for it myself," sooner or later, you'll discover that your funds are completely insufficient. By refusing to accept the grace of God, not only will you be poorer presently, but you'll suffer eternally.

The secret I have discovered in the Christian life is the same one Paul will propagate throughout the Book of Galatians. That is, we are to let God bless us without giving Him a reason to do so.

"Well, I've really prayed a lot this week, Lord, so I deserve to be blessed," we say. Or, "I went to church not once but twice this week, Lord, so now I'm expecting You to come through for me."

Listen, if you relate to the Lord in that way—through works, law, rules, and bartering—He will let you. If you say, "Lord, I want what I've earned. Give me what I deserve," He'll give you what you deserve and reward you according to what you've earned—which won't be much.

But if you realize God wants to bless you solely according to His mercy, He will pour out His unmerited, undeserved, unearned favor upon you. Don't frustrate the grace of God. Don't grab the bill. You don't have the funds to cover it anyway. Instead, allow God to bless you, and respond with worship and thanksgiving, affection and appreciation."

In 2 Samuel 9, we find a story that beautifully illustrates this principle . . .

How David Sought Mephibosheth

And David said, Is there yet any that is left of the house of Saul, that I may shew him kindness for Jonathan's sake? And there was of the house of Saul a servant whose name was Ziba. And when they had called him unto David, the king said unto him, Art thou Ziba? And he said, Thy servant is he. And the king said, Is there not yet any of the house of Saul, that I may shew the kindness of God unto him? And Ziba said unto the king, Jonathan hath yet a son, which is lame on his feet. And the king said unto him, Where is he? And Ziba said unto the king, Behold, he is in the house of Machir, the son of Ammiel, in Lo-debar. Then king David sent, and fetched him out of the house of Machir, the son of Ammiel, from Lo-debar.   2 Samuel 9:1–5*

Due to his love for Jonathan, David sent for Jonathan's servant, Ziba, and asked how he might show kindness to Jonathan's family. This was a radical gesture, considering that in David's day, when a king came into power, he would annihilate everyone in the previous ruling family lest the descendants make a move to reclaim the throne.

Jonathan's son, Mephibosheth, or "Living Shame," was hiding in a place called Lodebar, or "Nothingness." Think about that. How would you like to be "Living Shame" dwelling in a place called "Nothingness"?

As if that weren't bad enough, Mephibosheth was lame.

Why?

Chapter 4 tells us that when David was coming into power, Mephibosheth's nanny picked him up and ran in an attempt to hide him from David. While running, she stumbled and fell, dropping Mephibosheth, who became lame because of the fall.

Do you see the analogy? Mephibosheth is a picture of you and me. We are "Living Shame." We fell in Adam and have been lame ever since. Afraid of the King, we fled from Him as best we could and made our home in "Nothingness." But what did our King do? He said, "I want to bless those who are living in nothingness and shame, who can't walk or stand because of the fall." And He sent not a servant, but the Holy Spirit Himself to seek us.

What David Showed Mephibosheth

Now when Mephibosheth, the son of Jonathan, the son of Saul, was come unto David, he fell on his face, and did reverence. And David said, Mephibosheth. And he answered, Behold thy servant! And David said unto him, Fear not: for I will surely shew thee kindness for Jonathan thy father's sake, and will restore thee all the land of Saul thy father; and thou shalt eat bread at my table continually.
                                                                 2 Samuel 9:6, 7

Was kindness shown to Mephibosheth because of his togetherness?
No. He was "Living Shame."
Was it because of his steadfast walk?
No. He was lame.
Was it because he was in a place of significance?
No. He was in Lodebar.
David said, "I'm going to bless you, Mephibosheth, because of my love for Jonathan. I know you're 'Living Shame.' I know you're living in 'Nothingness.' I know you had a great fall. I know you're lame. I know you've been running from me. I know you're afraid of me. But I want to show you kindness—unmerited, undeserved, unearned favor nonetheless."
David showed kindness to Mephibosheth for his father's sake.
The Lord shows kindness to us for the sake of His Son.

Where David Seated Mephibosheth

Then the king called to Ziba, Saul's servant, and said unto him, I have given unto thy master's son all that pertained to Saul and to all his house. Thou therefore, and thy sons, and thy servants, shall till the land for him, and thou shalt bring in the fruits, that thy master's son may have food to eat: but Mephibosheth thy master's son shall eat bread alway at my table. Now Ziba had fifteen sons and twenty servants. Then said Ziba unto the king, According to all that my lord the king hath commanded his servant, so shall thy servant do. As for Mephibosheth, said the king, he shall eat at my table, as one of the king's sons. And Mephibosheth had a young son, whose name was Micha. And all that dwelt in the house of Ziba were servants unto Mephibosheth. So

Mephibosheth dwelt in Jerusalem: for he did eat continually at the king's table; and was lame on both his feet.   2 Samuel 9:9–13

I love that last phrase, for it means Mephibosheth didn't walk proudly to the table—he hobbled there. You may think, *Now that I'm saved, in order to eat at the King's table, in order to be blessed by the Lord, I've got to get my walk together. I've got to stand strong.* Not true! Like Mephibosheth, all you have to do is hobble!

It was after Peter denied Jesus that Jesus said to him, "Come and dine" (see John 21:12). He says the same thing to us who are hobbling today. "Come and dine," He says. "I'm blessing you not because of what you've done or who you are. I'm blessing you because I love My Son, and I want to perfect you as a bride for Him."

Why Mephibosheth Stayed with David

And Mephibosheth the son of Saul came down to meet the king, and had neither dressed his feet, nor trimmed his beard, nor washed his clothes, from the day the king departed until the day he came again in peace.

2 Samuel 19:24

As the story of David unfolds, we see Mephibosheth remaining loyal to David even when others turned away from him. Absalom, one of David's own sons, launched a rebellion against his father, took control of the city of Jerusalem, and drove David out of the city. But Mephibosheth remained loyal to David. Scripture tells us he didn't wash his clothes, he didn't take care of his feet, he didn't trim his beard. So impressed was he with David's kindness, so amazed was he by David's love that, although it placed his life in jeopardy, he refused to acknowledge any other king.

The same is true of us today. We're here because we're so impressed with the goodness of God. Like Mephibosheth, through great times or difficult days, through prosperity or lean seasons, we choose to stay by the One who's been so good to us. Perhaps you're thinking, *Mephibosheth may have hobbled to the king's table—but at least he got to eat of the king's fare. Quite frankly, I don't see anything on my plate at all.* Following are three steps to consider if you find yourself in that spot....

Repent

Are you trying to earn God's favor by your devotion or commitment? Repent. Say, "Father. I've been so foolish. Saved by grace, I've now gone back under the law, with its rules and regulations. I'm through trying to make a deal with You. Instead, I realize every good gift comes from You by grace. So give to me whatever You know is best."

Request

"I'm not trying to earn God's favor," you say, "but still, there are no meatballs on my plate." Well, have you requested? Benjamin got two plates of spaghetti and meatballs because he asked. Have you asked? So many times, we have not simply because we ask not (James 4:2). The Lord doesn't say, "Work, work, work." He says, "Ask. Talk to me. I'm your Abba, your Father. I want to develop communion with you and cultivate a relationship with you. Just talk to Me."

Relax

"I still have a problem," you say. "I have repented and I have asked. But my plate is still empty." Relax. After you repent and request, relax in what the Lord decides to do sovereignly. You see, it just may be you need to go on a diet. Maybe you're asking for root beer floats, cherry pie ' la mode, and chocolate chip cookies—when your loving Father knows you need something entirely different.

"As you come to My table and ask for hot fudge sundaes and chocolate-covered brownies, I know where you're at," He says. "You think they will be so delicious—and they may be for a short season—until you're sitting in the dentist's chair with the drill humming. I see your situation," says a loving Father. "I know you think you know what's best. But trust *Me*. I'm a Father who will give you only what's absolutely best for you. That may mean not having as much as you're asking for financially, or the success you're craving vocationally. You think these are good things, but I know what's ahead. They would wipe out your faith. They would distract you from the kingdom. They would make you poor in heaven. You've asked of Me. Now I'm asking you to trust that what I give you will be the best for you."

Today, we come to the King's table once more. We respond to His blessing with worship, affection, praise, and adoration. We repent from a works mentality. We make our requests. And we relax in whatever our Father sends our way.

Do not frustrate the grace of God, precious people. Don't grab the bill—your funds are insufficient. Just let God bless you for no other reason than because He loves His Son and wants to bless you for His sake.

3 The apostle Paul was deeply concerned about what was happening in the series of towns and cities known as Galatia. You see, after he had shared the Good News of Jesus Christ with the Galatians, men came in who began to complicate the gospel. "Paul's message is cool," they said, "but not complete. In addition to believing on Jesus Christ, you must show you are serious about Him by keeping rules and regulations."

In this third chapter of Paul's letter to the Galatians, he shifts his focus from his personal experience with grace (chapters 1 and 2) to doctrinal instruction about grace (chapters 3 and 4).

Galatians 3:1
O foolish Galatians, who hath bewitched you, that ye should not obey the truth, before whose eyes Jesus Christ hath been evidently set forth, crucified among you?

"Why do you no longer embrace and enjoy the simplicity of Jesus Christ? Who put this spell on you?" Paul asks the Galatians.

Galatians 3:2
This only would I learn of you, Received ye the Spirit by the works of the law, or by the hearing of faith?

"How did you receive the Spirit when you were born again? Was it by the works of the law—doing this or refraining from that? No. You received the Word simply by faith."

This verse speaks not only of being born again, but also of receiving the fullness, baptism, or "coming upon" of the Spirit to empower one's life.

After Jesus was crucified and had risen again, He appeared to the disciples in the Upper Room and said, "Receive ye the Holy Ghost." As He breathed on them, they indeed received the Spirit (John 20:22).

At that point, the disciples were saved. But then Jesus said, "Go to Jerusalem and wait for the promise of the Father" (see Acts 1:4). "You shall receive power when the Holy Ghost comes upon you and you shall then be My witnesses in Jerusalem, Judaea, Samaria, and the uttermost parts of the earth" (see Acts 1:8). So they went to Jerusalem and waited. On the tenth day, as they were in the Upper Room, they heard the sound of a mighty rushing wind, and saw cloven tongues of fire hovering over their heads. The Spirit came upon them. They began to praise the Lord in other tongues. They were energized to boldly proclaim the gospel. And the world has never been the same.

That is what the Lord wants for you and me. When you became a Christian, the Holy Spirit came *in* you. But has the Holy Spirit come *upon* you? I know you have the Holy Spirit—but does the Holy Spirit have you? "Have you received the Holy Spirit since you believed?" Paul asked the people of Ephesus (see Acts 19:2). And I ask you the same question.

In years past, many of us were part of churches or traditions that said, "The way to receive the power of the Spirit is to get rid of all of the sin in your life. Give up your drinking. Sell your TV. Stop smoking. Get it together. Then the Holy Spirit will come upon you to empower and use you." Consequently, many people spent months, years, even decades trying to clean up their acts in order to earn the power of the Holy Spirit.

Others of us waited day after day in what used to be called "tarrying meetings." "We're going to wait for the Holy Spirit to come upon us," we said. "And if we praise loud enough, pray hard

enough, and wait long enough, the Lord will give us the Holy Ghost. Then we'll be changed. Then we'll impact people radically."

Both of these methods would be foreign to Paul. How do you receive the Holy Spirit? Neither the indwelling of the Spirit through salvation nor the empowering of the Spirit through baptism come by works of the law. They come by *faith*—just by hearing the Word.

"That's it?" you ask. "You mean I don't have to clean up my act, get it together, or fast thirty days?"

No. We receive the Spirit not by works, but by the hearing of faith. Therefore, by faith I can take that which was provided for me and say, "Thank You, Lord. Even as I sit in this pew, I ask of You and receive from You the power of the Holy Spirit upon my life right now."

"That's too simple," you say.

Talk to Paul. He said, "Don't let anyone complicate this. You receive the Spirit simply by the hearing of faith."

Galatians 3:3
Are ye so foolish? having begun in the Spirit, are ye now made perfect by the flesh?

"You began in the Spirit," said Paul, "hearing the Word, and receiving it by faith. So don't let people tell you more is required of you. That's foolishness."

Galatians 3:4
Have ye suffered so many things in vain? if it be yet in vain.

"When you began," said Paul, "you were persecuted because of your simple faith in Jesus Christ. People came down on you, laughed at you, and made fun of you. Yet you continued to believe in the simplicity of the gospel. You've gone through the put-downs and persecution. You've already taken some hits and experienced some beatings because of your belief in grace. Don't turn from grace now."

The same is true today. Those who are under bondage to the law and live their lives by trying to earn blessings from God will make fun of those who live by faith and have confidence in grace. They'll mock you. They'll say you're immature. They'll say what you believe is frivolous and trite. Mark it well, saint: If you are an embracer of grace, people will call you shallow.

"Our group is really heavy," they'll say. "We understand what it means to carry the Cross and pay the price. We're the few, the chosen—the spiritual marines." There's an arrogance that permeates those who are trying to earn God's blessings. But when you celebrate what Jesus did on the Cross, you are free from exalting yourself.

Galatians 3:5
He therefore that ministereth to you the Spirit, and worketh miracles among you, doeth he it by the works of the law, or by the hearing of faith?

To whom does "he that ministereth the Spirit and worketh miracles among you" refer? I believe the reference is to Paul himself. When he entered the region of Galatia, seeing a lame man in the city of Lystra, Paul healed him. How did he do it? Was it by fasting and praying? Was it by proving to God that he was worthy to be used in a powerful way?

So many books are written, and so many testimonies are given by people who say, "I really began to move in the power of God when I did this, that, or the other."

"Not true," says Paul. "The one who ministers the Spirit, the one who is used by God is not the one who does works, but the one who simply believes."

This solves a huge problem for me. No doubt you've seen all kinds of people being used by the Lord whose lives are far from perfect. I think of one well-known healing evangelist, and I marvel. This man supposedly heard Jesus tell him that unless he was given money to complete a certain project by a certain date, he would die. It made the news, of course. The world chuckled. Christians hid their faces in embarrassment. The more I read about this particular man and his family, the more I found myself saying, "This is bizarre."

Yet, interestingly enough, when I was a little boy suffering from acute asthma, there were times my mom would rush me into the bathroom, turn on the hot water, and fill the room with steam, just so I could breathe. Concerned about the situation, the doctor gave Mom a little vial of kerosene, with the instruction that, should I come to the place where I would die if I couldn't get another breath, she was to pour a drop down my throat. On a number of occasions, close to the point of having to use the kerosene, Mom would hear the very radio evangelist of whom I'm speaking, say, "Place your hand upon the radio as a point of contact. Expect the Lord to heal you. Something good is going to happen to you." As my mom did this, time after time, the Lord intervened. Thus, this evangelist about whose ministry I wonder, this evangelist whose methods I question, had an undeniable impact upon my life.

If you go back even further, to the days when the healing evangelists criss-crossed the country, drawing huge crowds under big-tops, many thousands of people were truly touched and definitely impacted by one of the biggest faith healers of all: A. A. Allen. A. A. Allen had the biggest meetings and the most powerful impact in the healing arena—until he died in San Francisco in a cheap motel of cirrhosis of the liver. A servant of God an alcoholic? How could this be?

It is because the miracles wrought and the Spirit given are not by the works of the law, but simply by the hearing of faith. A. A. Allen understood that what he did was centered not upon his great faith in God, but upon God's great faithfulness to him. And once you understand that simple truth, it will affect everything you do in ministry.

For years, I was under the impression that the key to ministry, to being used by God, to seeing folks saved or filled with the Spirit, was my faith. Therefore, the greater my faith, the more God would do. Not true. The key was not my faith in God at all—but His faithfulness to people.

Many years ago at Caveman Park in Grants Pass, Oregon, at the end of my teaching, I gave an invitation to the two hundred high-schoolers in attendance. I just expected kids to respond—not because of the persuasiveness of my message, but because I know the goodness of God. He wants to save people. He cares about every single kid there. It wasn't because of my presentation or preparation that I expected them to respond. No, it was because I knew God was eager to respond to any of those kids who wanted to come to Him.

So, when I said, "Who wants to receive the coming upon of the Spirit right now?" most of them raised their hands.

Uh-oh, you may have thought had you witnessed the scene. *What are you going to do now, Jon? What if you pray and nothing happens? What if they don't speak in tongues? Worse yet, what if they do?*

Folks, it's not my job to be concerned about those things. I just have total confidence in the great faithfulness of God to touch anyone, anytime, anywhere who is hungering and thirsting for righteousness. When this is understood, it is so incredibly freeing. But until it's understood, Satan will whisper in your ear, "You don't have the technique down. You don't know enough verses yet. You haven't prayed hard enough. You haven't worshiped long enough."

Precious people, Satan will paralyze you until

you understand that every area of ministry is based not upon your faith, but upon God's faithfulness. If you believe this, you'll find yourself talking to people and expecting them to respond in some way.

If it's dependent upon me, my knees knock, my forehead breaks out in beads of sweat, my mouth gets dry, my lips become sealed. I am paralyzed by fear because I know I haven't done enough. But once I understand that the One who ministers the Spirit, the One who works miracles doesn't do it by the works of the law, I am free!

For topical study of Galatians 3:5 entitled "Ministering the Spirit," turn to page 1185.

Galatians 3:6
Even as Abraham believed God, and it was accounted to him for righteousness.

Abraham wasn't doing something to impress God. He just believed God, and God declared him righteous. Paul pointed to Abraham—the father of the Jewish nation, the one whose heritage the religionists and Judaizers claimed as their own—as an example of the all-sufficiency of faith.

Galatians 3:7
Know ye therefore that they which are of faith, the same are the children of Abraham.

"Whether you're Jew or Gentile," Paul continued, "if you have faith in God, then you are linked to Abraham, the father of faith."

Galatians 3:8
And the scripture, foreseeing that God would justify the heathen through faith, preached before the gospel unto Abraham, saying, In thee shall all nations be blessed.

"Because you believe in Me, Abraham, I can do a mighty work through you," said the Lord.

Galatians 3:9, 10
So then they which be of faith are blessed with faithful Abraham. For as many as are of the works of the law are under the curse: for it is written, Cursed is every one that continueth not in all things which are written in the book of the law to do them.

Why is the law a curse? Because if you're going to try to earn God's favor through keeping rules and regulations, you've got to do it *all.*

Suppose you are one of the thousands of refugees who are presently making their way to America via raft. You carefully construct your little boat, using ten boards to make up the hull. Then you set sail. Thirty miles out to sea, one of the boards comes loose and floats away. The water comes flooding in, and you go down—because in that situation, even 90 percent isn't good enough.

The same is true with regard to the Ten Commandments. If you're going to try to earn God's favor through keeping them, you'll have to keep all ten. or else you're lunch for some hungry shark. Jesus gave us an understanding of what this really means when He said, "You've heard it said of old you're not to commit adultery, but I say unto you if you have lust in your heart you're guilty. You've heard it said of old you're not to commit murder, but I say if you've been angry with someone you're guilty" (see Matthew 5). You're cursed if you try to keep the law because unless you keep all of it perfectly, you're sunk.

Galatians 3:11
But that no man is justified by the law in the sight of God, it is evident: for, The just shall live by faith.

The words "the just shall live by faith" are first seen in Habakkuk 2:4, when, in response to his complaints concerning the prophesied Babylonian invasion, the Lord told Habakkuk to look to Him rather than at the circumstances.

They are seen again in Romans 1:17, where Paul stresses justification; and in Hebrews 11, where the emphasis is on faith. Here in Galatians, the accent is on *live.* Want to be happy, fruitful, excited, and set free in your Christian life? The *just* shall *live*—really live—by *faith.*

Martin Luther beat his body, crawled on his knees, and fasted in order to get close to God. But nothing worked. And then one day he read this verse—and he understood that the Christian experience is not "Do, do, do"—it's "DONE!" Jesus did it *all.* Dear saints, get rid of the burden of trying to be spiritual. Get rid of the notion that since you had morning devotions ten times in a row, God owes you a blessing. It doesn't work that way. You are justified by faith *alone.*

"Then I don't have to have morning devotions?" you ask.

No, you don't.

"I can sleep in?"

Yeah, you can.

"I don't have to pray, or study the Word?"

Nope.

You don't *have* to do any of those things. You *get* to. You *get* to check in with God morning by morning, moment by moment. You *get* to spend time late at night or before the sun rises, seeking the face of the Lord. It's not *got* to, it's *get* to. And that makes all the difference in the world, for once you're free from the "got to's," you invariably do more than you ever did before.

James said, "Faith without works is dead" (James 2:20) because true faith will always bring about lots of works. When you fell in love with your husband or wife, you didn't have to be told to call her; you didn't have to be reminded to hold his hand; you didn't have to be urged to communicate. When you're in love, you long to be in touch—and that's what the Father wants from you and me. "Love Me," He says. And the more I realize that He loves me by His grace and mercy being poured out upon me, the more I have no choice but to love Him in return. So I do more under love than I ever would do under the law.

Think about that first letter your girlfriend wrote you, guys. As you stuck it in your pocket, did you say, "Boy, one of these days I really need to read this letter. I'll set my alarm fifteen minutes earlier tonight and read it first thing in the morning"? And then as you rolled out of bed half an hour after the alarm went off, did you say, "I really want to read this letter, but I don't have time now. Maybe tonight. No, *Home Improvement* is on. Can't miss that. I'll get to it tomorrow"?

No! It doesn't work that way. When you got that letter, you ripped it open, read it, analyzed it, parsed the verbs, researched it, and read between the lines. You couldn't put it down! The same thing happens when you understand grace and mercy. You say, "You bless me, Lord, when I don't pray. You love me when I'm not lovable. You take care of me when I fail to walk with You. You're faithful to me day after week after year. I want to find out more about You." That's what it means for the just to *live* by faith.

Galatians 3:12
And the law is not of faith: but, The man that doeth them shall live in them.

The law says, "You must do it and keep doing it" (see Leviticus 18:5). Faith says, "He did it. It's done" (John 19:30).

Galatians 3:13 (a)
Christ hath redeemed us from the curse of the law, being made a curse for us ...

When man sinned, God said to Adam, "From this point on, you will labor for bread, live by the sweat of your brow, and work through thorns and thistles." Then came Jesus, the Last Adam. In the Upper Room, His broken body became our bread. In the Garden of Gethsemane, His sweat mingled with blood. On Calvary, the thorns of the earth were embedded in His brow.

"I've absorbed it all," Jesus said, as He who knew no sin became sin for us, as He Himself became the curse. This is what Paul is driving home. What Jesus did is so incredible, so wonderful, how could we think that through our own efforts we could add anything to His work on our behalf?

Galatians 3:13 (b)
... for it is written, Cursed is every one that hangeth on a tree.

This verse has obvious application to Jesus Christ as He hung on Calvary's tree. Yet I believe it has application for us as well if we look at it in light of another who hung on a tree....

For topical study of Galatians 3:13 entitled "Hanging on a Tree," turn to page 1189.

Galatians 3:14
That the blessing of Abraham might come on the Gentiles through Jesus Christ; that we might receive the promise of the Spirit through faith.

Jesus paid the price so we could receive the promise of the Spirit—all the power and blessing of the Holy Ghost—not by our works, but by faith in what He accomplished on Calvary.

Galatians 3:15
Brethren, I speak after the manner of men; Though it be but a man's covenant, yet if it be confirmed, no man disannulleth, or addeth thereto.

"Let me use an example you're familiar with," said Paul. "Once two parties sign their names on a contract, neither can add to it nor take away from it."

Galatians 3:16
Now to Abraham and his seed were the promises made. He saith not, And to seeds, as of many; but as of one, And to thy seed, which is Christ.

In the minds of most, "Abraham's seed" is synonymous with "the Jews." Paul contended, however, that the promise was made not to seeds, but to one seed. And that one Seed is Jesus Christ. The promises of God to bless the world come not through the Jewish nation, but through Jesus; not through any national entity, but through Jesus Christ exclusively to all people, in all places.

Galatians 3:17, 18 (a)
And this I say, that the covenant, that was confirmed before of God in Christ, the law, which was four hundred and thirty years after, cannot disannul, that it should make the promise of none effect. For if the inheritance be of the law, it is no more of promise . . .

God made a promise, a covenant, with Abraham that through his Seed, Jesus Christ, everyone who wanted would be blessed. Four hundred and thirty years later, the law was given. But the law could not take away the promise of blessing given to Abraham. In other words, the law does not legally or logically have the power to negate the blessing God gave to Abraham through Christ. And Paul is about to show us that, since we are in Christ, the blessing that comes to us is neither given because we keep the law nor nullified by our failure to keep it. The law is completely irrelevant as it relates to the blessing of God. What a fabulous truth!

Galatians 3:18 (b)
. . . but God gave it to Abraham by promise.

It was when Abraham had no children that God told him his offspring would number as the stars of the sky and as the sand on the seashore. But Scripture records that Abraham believed God anyway. "Okay, Lord," Abraham replied, "I don't know how You're going to do it, but if You want to bless me in that way, it's fine with me."

And God said, "That's the faith that will justify you, Abraham—just believing in Me."

Time passed and again the Lord appeared to Abraham. "I am your shield and your great reward," He said.

"That's great, Lord," answered Abraham, "but I still don't have any kids. The years are going by, and I'm not getting any younger."

"Abraham," said the Lord, "let's cut a covenant."

In Abraham's day, when two parties wanted to seal an agreement, they would cut an animal in half and meet each other in the middle, thereby saying, "We're dead serious about this." So Abraham got a bullock, cut it in half, laid it out, and sat there waiting for God to show up. He waited and

waited, wondering where God was. When birds started swarming around the carcass, Abraham shooed them away. Time passed. Abraham's eyes grew heavy. His head started bobbing, then slumping. Finally, he was sound asleep. Sometime later, he awoke, looked at the bullock, and saw it had been barbecued. God had come when Abraham was asleep and had moved all the way through the carcass (Genesis 15:17).

God didn't meet Abraham halfway. He did the whole thing, saying, "Abraham, this promise I'm giving you is not based upon your agreeing with Me and doing your part. No, I'm going to do it *all*. I'll even do it while you're asleep." God still does it all, precious people. Your salvation, the blessings that are poured upon you, the work of the Spirit flowing through you in ministry—it's *all* God.

"Don't I have any part to play?" you ask. Yes. Your part is to shoo away the birds of unbelief that will invariably come and pick at the promises of God's Word. Whatever God said He will do is an accomplished fact. Yet vultures of doubt and buzzards of cynicism will come and say, "God's not going to use you. He's not going to bless you. You haven't been praying enough." Peck, peck, peck.

Your part is to chase away those birds by saying, "Lord, You told me You would supply all my needs according to Your riches. You told me You would never leave me. You told me You're preparing a place in heaven for me. You told me You would give the Holy Ghost to me. Thank You, Lord."

Galatians 3:19 (a)
Wherefore then serveth the law?

If our walk is to be based simply upon believing what God said, receiving His promise, and resting in what He's done, then why was the law given at all?

Galatians 3:19 (b)
It was added because of transgressions, till the seed should come to whom the promise was made . . .

Because of sin, the law was given until Jesus Christ—the Lamb of God who would take away the sin of the world—came on the scene.

Galatians 3:19 (c), 20
. . . and it was ordained by angels in the hand of a mediator. Now a mediator is not a mediator of one, but God is one.

On Mount Sinai, the law was given to angels.
Angels gave it to Moses; Moses brought it down
to the people. In other words, the law was not directly communicated. The promise, on the other
hand, was given without mediators or middle-
men. It was given to Abraham directly and intimately.

Galatians 3:21
**Is the law then against the promises of God?
God forbid: for if there had been a law given
which could have given life, verily righteousness should have been by the law.**

Does the law given to Moses contradict the
promise given to Abraham? No. The law doesn't
contradict the promise. It simply gives an alternative to the promise. The law offers man a
choice. You see, we can either receive a righteous
standing before God by simply believing what
God says—or we can keep every point of the law.
If any legal system could bring a person salvation, it would be the Ten Commandments. The
law is absolutely perfect. The only problem with
it is this: It can't be kept.

*"You've heard it said you're to love your neigh-
bor, but I say, you're to love your enemy,"
Jesus said in Matthew 5. "Therefore, if you've
ever been angry at an enemy, you're guilty.
You've heard it said you're not to swear falsely,
that you're to commit your oaths to the Lord.
But I say unto you, anything more than a
simple yes or no is from the evil one."*

If you've ever failed to love your enemy or
made a promise and backed it up with anything
more than a simple yes or no, you're guilty.

Galatians 3:22
**But the scripture hath concluded all under
sin, that the promise by faith of Jesus Christ
might be given to them that believe.**

No one can be justified by keeping the law. All
the law does is tell us that we're sinners in need
of a Savior. That is why it was given. You see, the
promise given to Abraham preceded by centuries
the law given to Moses. Grace came first.

But man began to think, *I don't need to be a recipient of grace because I'm pretty good. I don't
need to embrace this promised Seed, because I'm
doing okay.* So they began to write books like,
I'm OK, You're OK and *Esteeming Yourself
Highly.* The Word, however, says there is none
righteous, no not one. There is none that seeketh
after God (Romans 3:10, 11). There is not one
person who can say, "Because of the sincerity of
my search and the integrity of my pursuit of

truth, I discovered God." No, the Bible says none
seeks after God. Zip. Zilch. Zero.

God sought *you.* But in order for you to realize
that you needed to be sought, the law was given
to all mankind as a mirror, saying, "Take a look.
You're a mess. Here's the standard of righteousness. It's beautiful. It's workable. It's profoundly
simple—but you can't keep it."

The law serves an incredibly important purpose.

*Suppose I said to my friend John, "John,
someone from Applegate Christian Fellowship
just went to the Jackson County Courthouse
and paid twenty-five thousand dollars on your
behalf for a violation."*

*"What are you talking about?" he would
say. "What kind of violation?"*

"A traffic violation."

*"That's ridiculous," he would say. And he
wouldn't appreciate the gift given on his behalf, the price paid for his mistake.*

*On the other hand, if I said, "John, didn't
you know there is a new law that protects
snails as an endangered species? When you
drove through town the other day, you
smashed dozens of them and received a fine of
twenty-five thousand dollars. But a man in
the Fellowship paid your fine,"—John's response would be entirely different. He
wouldn't haughtily say, "A twenty-five thousand dollar fine? That's ridiculous." No, in
humility and brokenness, he would say, "Who
paid for me? Certainly, I am deeply indebted
to him.*

"The law of the Lord is perfect, converting the
soul" wrote the psalmist (Psalm 19:7). Who is
converted? The person who hears and understands the law—for without hearing and compre-
hending the law, people will not appreciate or
receive the Good News.

I believe this is a fundamental mistake we often make in modern-day evangelism. We present
the gospel, the Good News that Jesus loves us,
died for us, and wants to take us to heaven to be
with Him forever—but we don't talk about the
law. We talk about the concepts of salvation without saying anything about the consequences of
sin.

*You're in a 747 jumbo jet headed to Honolulu.
Two hours into the flight, the pilot calls for the
senior flight attendant and says, "There's a
leak in our gas tank. We're not going to make
it to Hawaii."*

*The flight attendant, wiping the sweat off
her brow, dabbing the tears from her eyes,
smiles as she returns to the cabin, saying,*

"Greetings, passengers. Could I interest any of you in a parachute? It will make your flight more enjoyable, and in it, I think you'll discover a new measure of peace, joy, and love. Who would like a parachute?" Maybe three or four people raise their hands.

If you are among the three or four taking one, you see the other passengers snickering and pointing at you. Before long, you discover your parachute is tight and uncomfortable. You begin to think, This isn't giving me any joy at all. This is ridiculous. And after twenty minutes or so, you take it off and say to the stewardess, "You lied to me. You promised I would be comfortable, full of joy, and warmed by love. But all I got were snickers, jeers, and a rash."

Such is what we see happen all too often in present-day evangelism. "I was promised love and joy," new converts complain, "but my friends made fun of me, and I felt restricted." That's why many people who come to Jesus turn away from Him.

Another stewardess in the same situation hears the message from the captain. She enters the cabin, saying, "Stop what you're doing. Put down your reading material. I want your full, undivided attention. The captain has informed me that this plane is losing fuel fast. We're going down. Who wants a parachute?"

Suddenly, people are fighting for parachutes. No one cares if the flight for those remaining minutes is smooth, or if they have enough mobility to play video games. No, everyone is clinging to his parachute, making sure it's secure because everyone knows the plane is going down.

I suggest that oftentimes the reason we are ineffective in long-term evangelism is because we have not been honest enough with people to say, "You are a damned, doomed sinner. You have a hole in your tank. You have broken the law. You're headed for destruction. I could sit here, hold your hand, and talk about warm, fuzzy thoughts—but I love you too much. You need to know the truth, and the truth is this: "The soul that sinneth shall surely die, for the wages of sin is death" (see Ezekiel 18:20; Romans 6:23).

"Wait a minute," you protest. "I thought it was the goodness of God that leads men to repentance" (Romans 2:4).

It is.

"But it sounds to me like you're talking about the severity of God."

I am.

They're both valid. To the broken of heart, share grace. But to the hard of heart, share the law, for the law of the Lord is perfect, converting the soul. Those who understand they're damned and weep because of their sin don't throw off their salvation when people snicker at them or when something more exciting is presented to them.

I ask this very pertinent question: Have you shared the reality of the law with the unsaved people you care about? Perhaps you've shared your testimony with them—and that's great. But if their heart was hard, they probably said, "I'm glad you've found happiness. I'm glad it works for you. I'm proud of you, honey. It's so good to see your life on a good, solid, moral footing. I'm happy for you, but I don't need that."

Such arrogance can only be penetrated with the presentation of the law. That's why the law was given—to show people the plane they're on is going down and that they're doomed unless they take the gift of salvation, the Promise, the Seed of Abraham—Jesus Christ.

Galatians 3:23
But before faith came, we were kept under the law, shut up unto the faith which should afterwards be revealed.

We were in trouble because we were supposed to keep the commands of the law, but we couldn't do it. We were cut off from the faith that would later be revealed.

Galatians 3:24 (a)
Wherefore the law was our schoolmaster to bring us unto Christ . . .

If your Bible is a King James Version, you'll see that the words "to bring us" are in italics. Therefore, since italicized words are not present in the original language, verse 24 should read: "Wherefore the law was our schoolmaster until Christ."

Galatians 3:24 (b)
. . . that we might be justified by faith.

Suppose there was conclusive evidence that O. J. Simpson was guilty. If Judge Ito had said, "I forgive you, you're free," O. J. could have gone his way, and I'm sure he would have been happy. But that's not what justification is. Justification would mean all the evidence against O. J. would be obliterated, that his record would be totally clean. Like O. J., we're all sinners. God, however, looks at believers not as being forgiven—but as though they had never sinned at all. Why? Because God is a Good Guy who says, "Kids will be kids"? No. Because the blood shed on Calvary's Cross was so powerful it blotted out every violation written against us (Colossians 2:14).

Galatians 3:25
But after that faith is come, we are no longer under a schoolmaster.

The law was a schoolmaster with red pencil in hand, circling our mistakes. But once Christ came into our lives, the law is no longer to be a part of our lives. This is such a radical statement that if God didn't say it, I would be afraid to share it.

Galatians 3:26, 27
For ye are all the children of God by faith in Christ Jesus. For as many of you as have been baptized into Christ have put on Christ.

When you became a believer, you put on Christ. You were placed in Christ. If any man be in Christ, he is a new creature. Old things are passed away (2 Corinthians 5:17). Therefore, when the Father looks at you, He doesn't see you in all of your sin. He sees you in Christ Jesus, robed with His righteousness. That's Good News! So why would you return to rules to try to

clean up your act or prove your worthiness? It makes no sense.

Galatians 3:28
There is neither Jew nor Greek, there is neither bond nor free, there is neither male nor female: for ye are all one in Christ Jesus.

Each morning, a Jewish man would pray, "I thank You, God, that I was not born a Gentile, a slave, or a woman." Referring to this same Jewish prayer, Paul says, "In Christ, there is neither Jew nor Gentile, neither bond nor free, neither male nor female. All those barriers are broken down. You're all one in Christ." You see, the law sets up walls and separates those who do from those who don't, those who are keeping their rules from those who have failed in their attempts. But once you put on Christ, all those walls crumble. We're all sinners saved by grace. God doesn't hear men more than women, those who are free more than those who are oppressed, Jews more than Gentiles.

Galatians 3:29
And if ye be Christ's, then are ye Abraham's seed, and heirs according to the promise.

If we are in Christ, we are not of Moses, not of the law, not of performance. We are of Abraham, of faith, of promise.

MINISTERING THE SPIRIT
A Topical Study of
Galatians 3:5

The Galatian believers were bewitched—but not in the way you might think. It wasn't Samantha Stevens wiggling her nose, but a group of men pointing their fingers. "It's nice that you believe in Jesus Christ," they said, "but it's not that simple. In order to be used by the Lord, or to go deeper in the Lord, you need to keep certain rules and regulations. You need to deal with your flesh. You need to be circumcised."

"Who has bewitched you?" cried Paul. "You began in the Spirit. You were saved simply by believing in the Lord, trusting in Him, enjoying what He's done. Why do you now think you're going to be made perfect by the energy of the flesh?"

I ask that same question today. When you were saved—the day you opened your heart to Jesus—you didn't come to Him in the energy of your flesh, making promises to Him, pledging to clean up your life, or vowing to get your act together.

No, you came as a sinner, saying, "I have nothing to offer, Lord, but if You want to save me, if You want to do a work in Me, I gladly accept it." Why, then, do we think we will be perfected by striving to keep our own rules and regulations?

"He, therefore, that ministereth to you the Spirit, and worketh miracles among you, doeth he it by the works of the law, or by the hearing of faith?" Paul asks.

"I would love to minister the Spirit," you might be thinking, "but I'm so afraid I'm not capable of being effective in service. What if someone told me he wanted to know the Lord, or to be empowered by the Spirit? What would I do? What if I laid hands on him, prayed that the power of the Holy Ghost would come upon him, and nothing happened? What if I tried to teach a Bible study, and no one came? What if I witness, yet people just walk away?"

You who long to be used, but are afraid you can't be, understand this point: The one who ministers the Spirit and works miracles is not the one who says, "God can really use me because I've taken care of this sin; I've overcome that problem; I've mastered theology." No, the one who ministers the Spirit and works miracles is one who simply hears in faith. Hears what? The Word.

- "Go and teach all nations, and lo, I am with you always" (see Matthew 28:19, 20).
- "Ye shall be witnesses unto Me" (Acts 1: 8).
- "If you, being evil, know how to give good gifts to your children, how much more will the Father give the Holy Ghost to them that ask" (see Matthew 7:11).

We have a tendency to say, "I can't teach. I can't witness. I can't pray for the empowering of the Spirit because I don't have the technique down yet. I don't have the necessary insights and the understanding." But in so doing, we're saying, "The ministry of the Spirit, the ministry of miracles, being used by God, and seeing the power of God is dependent upon my knowledge, my togetherness, and my worthiness."

No. No. No. You were saved by faith. You will be used in the same manner—just believing not in who you are and what you know, but in who God is and in what He has promised to do. Therefore, our ministry, our service, our walk with the Lord is not based upon works of great faith, but simply upon our faith in a great God.

When Bartimaeus asked to receive his sight (Mark 10:46–52), Jesus didn't say, "Why do you want to see? Is it so you can behold My beauty? Is it so you can study the Torah? Is it so you can do the work of God? Get your act together, Bartimaeus, and when you have your motives purified, then I'll deal with you." No, He simply said, "Be healed"—no questions asked.

We think we need to analyze our reasons for wanting to be used by the Lord. "I better go through a year of heavy introspection," we say, "before I dare ask the

Lord to use me in ministry. I better make sure my motives are pure and my methods are proper before I can help someone else." Not true. If you want to be used by
the Lord, just go to Him and say, "Father, use me." Then, when someone comes to
you, struggling with a marital problem, physical disease, or emotional depression,"
you can simply say, "Let me pray for you."

You don't need to put people on a program or teach them a procedure. Simply
take them to a Person. Take them to the One who said, "He that comes to Me, I will
in no wise cast out" (see John 6:37). Jesus didn't say, "I'm not interested in those
who don't have their theology down, their lives together, or their motives pure." No.
He said, "I will not cast out *anyone* who comes to Me." And that's what makes service such a joy. That's what makes walking with the Lord so delightful.

Precious people, the hearing of faith says, "Lord, You said, 'Come to Me,' so
here I am."

"I have a problem with that," you say. "You see, I've come to Him concerning
my daughter's situation. I've come to Him about a physical infirmity. I've come to
Him about a broken relationship. But nothing happened."

That's because all too often we come to the Lord and give Him instructions or
directions instead of just saying, "Lord, here's my situation. You see what's best for
me."

I am so thankful that the Lord in His goodness did not answer thousands of
my prayers. I was convinced I knew what I needed. I thought I knew what was right
for this person or that situation. I was so sure I knew what was best for Applegate
Christian Fellowship. I can recall walking around the Grange Hall on Upper Applegate Road, saying, "You told Joshua that the land whereupon he set the sole of
his foot would be given him. So, Lord, I'm claiming this building. It's perfect for us.
Why, it seats *sixty* easily!" But because the Lord had something entirely different
in mind, the deal we were pursuing with the Grange Hall didn't work out. And I'm
so glad.

You see, the key in praying for your own situation or for the people with whom
you're sharing or ministering is not to give God direction, but simply to say, "Lord,
here's the situation. You do what's right."

As I left Germany one day, the plane was packed. It was stuffy and noisy, and
all I wanted to do was get home. I sat down next to a guy who, although he was from
a Mediterranean country, spoke English. *I need to share with him,* I thought. But,
having arrived in Frankfurt only three days earlier, serious jet lag was beginning
to set in, and I was not in a real pleasant mood. So when he put his earphones on
and tuned in the music, I was thrilled.

"No open door here," I said to myself, relieved. "The guy doesn't have ears to
hear, so what's the point in talking?" Consequently, on the entire twelve-hour flight

to Chicago, I didn't speak a word to him. He had his earphones on the entire time—and that was fine by me.

But as we landed, I felt in my heart that an opportunity had been missed. So when I got on the plane that would take me from Chicago to San Francisco, I bowed and prayed, "Lord, I feel like I missed an opportunity on the previous flight. Use me on this one in some way." No sooner had I prayed that prayer than one of the stewards came on board, saying, "The thermostat on this aircraft is not functioning properly. You'll have to de-plane and wait for another flight."

When it was time to board again, I said to the steward, "Sir, I've got to preach in Medford, Oregon, tomorrow morning. Will this flight be able to make the connection?"

"No way," he said. "We'll have to find something else for you."

As a result, I found myself all alone in first class. *This is amazing,* I thought. *Here I prayed to be used on the flight headed for San Francisco. And what did He do? He kicked me off the plane and put me here, all by myself.*

Shortly into the four-hour flight, a steward named Ricardo, who had heard of my plight, approached me and said, "So you're going to preach?"

"Yep," I answered. "I'm going to preach tomorrow morning in a place called Applegate."

"What's Applegate?" he asked.

That was the only opening I needed to start sharing with him about what the Lord was doing there by His grace. "It's the greatest thing," I said. "There's a group of people who just love Jesus and who celebrate what He's done."

Then a stewardess, a Jewish lady named Ellie, joined us. So here I was, talking about grace to a Jewish stewardess and a Catholic steward. Before long, the other steward and stewardess assigned to first class joined our group. I'm not exaggerating when I say that from the moment we took off until the time we touched down in Portland, we talked nonstop about the gospel, end times, the finished work of the Cross, evolution, and creation. Did they fully understand and embrace what I shared with them? I don't know. But each of them asked me to take his or her phone number and address, and to be put on our mailing list.

I share that with you to say this: I prayed specifically to be used on the flight to San Francisco. I felt it was a very noble prayer, a very spiritual thing to do. But I got kicked off the plane and was put in a cabin all by myself. Why? The Lord saw what was ahead in ways I could never have figured out. That's why He says, "Come to Me. And as you talk things over with Me, trust that I'll do things in the right way, at the right time—not because you're naming it and claiming it, not because you're instructing Me as to what you think should happen, but because you're just trusting Me."

So I say to any who are wrestling with troubled marriages, to any who are struggling with physical problems, to any who are emotionally depressed or financially stressed, to any who are worried about a father or mother who's not saved, or a son or daughter who's falling away: The Holy Spirit is given and miracles happen not by the works of the law, but by the hearing of faith—simply by believing that the Lord cares about you and that He'll do the best for you.

Rejoice. You were saved in a simple way, embracing a simple message. You began in the Spirit. Now walk in the Spirit. Depend on the Lord. Have confidence in Him. Come to Him, all you that are heavy-laden. He will energize and empower. He will save and work—not because of who you are, but simply because of your faith in who He is. Your motives may not be pure. He doesn't ask for that. Your methods may not be perfect. That's irrelevant. Just come to Him, and you'll see miracles happen. You'll be escorted to first class, and you'll fly high—marveling at what He does.

HANGING ON A TREE
A Topical Study of
Galatians 3:13

A sixteen-year-old boy was recently sentenced to thirty years in prison for the stabbing death of a fifteen-year-old girl who shunned him at a party. "From everything this court has seen of you," said the judge, "the bottom line is, you don't have a conscience. Certainly no culture tolerates the kind of behavior in which you have engaged."

Contrary to the judge's statement however, so common is such behavior that stories like this don't even make the front page of the newspaper. After serving only a fraction of their sentences, most criminals repeat their offenses again and again because legislation doesn't deal with the real issue.

What is the real issue?

Old Testament Israel had no penitentiaries, no prisons, no penal system. Why? Because in that culture, crime was dealt with swiftly and severely. Stoning was the most common form of punishment for capital offenses that included cursing or disrespecting one's parents, adultery, fornication, homosexuality, and murder. This was not cruelty on God's part. People knew that breaking God's law resulted in immediate consequences. Therefore, it kept people free from the junk that permeates and pollutes our culture presently.

If a particular sin was committed, the perpetrator wouldn't be stoned. He would be hung on a tree. "My goodness," you say. "If murder merited stoning, what would possibly cause one to be hung on a tree? Child abuse? Mass murder?"

I think you'll find the answer shocking as we look at a story in the Old Testament that shows us from God's perspective what merited death by hanging. . . .

He seemed to have everything going for him. He was the most handsome man in the country, and the Word of God declares that from the crown of his head to the sole of his feet, there was not a single blemish upon him. We are told that when the barbers cut his hair, the weight of it was two hundred shekels' worth, or five times the weight of the hair of any other man.

Not only was he unbelievably good-looking, but he had a winning personality. Scripture records that, with the men wanting to be like him, and the women swooning over him, he actually stole the hearts of the nation of Israel. In addition, he had prestige. His mom was a princess, and his dad was the king of the most powerful empire of the day. So with his handsome countenance, his engaging personality, his prestige and power, his name seemed to summarize what people thought of him: "The father of peace"—Absalom.

But this one who had everything going for him, this one whose name was synonymous with peace was a man greatly troubled within. You see, Absalom had a sister named Tamar who also possessed unsurpassed beauty—so much so that Scripture tells us her half brother, Amnon became sick with lust toward her.

Cousin Jonadab, noticing Amnon's deteriorating condition, said, "Hey, Amnon, you don't look so well. What's wrong?"

"I'm in love," answered Amnon. I can't eat. I can't sleep. Tamar has captured my heart."

"You're the heir apparent," said Jonadab. "If you want Tamar, just pretend you're seriously ill. Send word to your father saying that you want Tamar to come in and feed you. Then, when she's in your room, have your way with her."

"Sounds great," said Amnon.

Why? Because when lust is ruling someone, he doesn't think straight. Amnon called for Tamar, and, as planned, he pulled her to himself.

"Don't do this," pleaded Tamar. "You'll shame yourself. You'll shame me. You'll bring disaster upon us all."

Amnon was deaf to her cries, however, because lust demands satisfaction. Scripture records that the hatred Amnon felt toward Tamar was exceedingly greater than the love he had for her before he raped her (2 Samuel 13:15).

Girls, here's how to lose your boyfriend: Give in. Once he's through with you, the guy who once said, "I love you," will hate you. That's what makes lust so tragic: Once it gets its way, it turns to hatred. How many people become involved in a relationship based on lust only to discover that there's no communication, no relationship, only bitterness. How right our Father is to tell us not to give in to the lusts of the flesh (1 Peter 2:11).

So it was that with ashes in her hair and garments shred in mourning, Tamar went to her father.

"What?" the king cried, "Your brother raped you?"

But although he was angry, he did nothing to discipline Amnon. Why? It could be that, as a poet, he lacked the strength to deal with his son. Or, perhaps, like many of us, rather than seeing his children walk in righteousness, he desired to be liked by them. Most likely, however, the king didn't discipline his son because the king's name was David—and he was guilty of satisfying his own lusts with a woman named Bathsheba.

Mom and Dad, when we sin, we lose a great deal of authority. We can't talk to our kids about the dangers of alcohol if we're sipping wine with dinner. We can't deal with the drug problem if we ourselves are dependent upon certain questionable habits or medications. In forfeiting our authority, we lose our credibility.

"My son has blown it," lamented David. "But what can I do? I'm guilty of worse sins than his." So David did nothing. For two years, anger seethed inside Tamar's brother, Absalom, causing him to hate not only his brother Amnon, but his father as well.

Want your kids to hate you, Dad? Here's how: Don't be strong in the family. Don't bring about correction in the home. It interests me that the kids who dislike their moms and dads the most are most often the ones who are the most undisciplined. The parents who try the hardest to be a buddy are often the ones who end up mocked and despised. Be warned, Dad. When you see things wrong in your family and you fail to deal with them, like Amnon, your son will one day despise and mock you in his heart.

After two years, Absalom decided to deal with the situation himself. "Father," he said. "My servants have just finished shearing the sheep at Baal Hezor. We're going to celebrate. Come and join us."

"Oh, Absalom," David said. "I can't get away right now."

"Well, can my brothers—especially Amnon—come?"

Although David should have been somewhat suspicious, he gave his permission, thereby unwittingly enabling Absalom to put his plan into action.

"Bring out the wine," Absalom said as the celebration began.

When everyone was drunk, Absalom raised his hand and gave the sign for his servants to thrust their swords into Amnon, while the rest of David's sons immediately awoke from their stupor and stumbled out to their donkeys to ride for their lives. With word on its way to his father, Absalom knew he needed to flee for his life as well. So he mounted his mule and headed for his mother's hometown of Geshur.

Although David could have easily sent an army to pursue Absalom, he continued to do nothing. For three long years, Absalom remained in Geshur while David's heart pined for his Absalom. Seeing the king eaten up with grief, David's right-hand man, Joab, enlisted the help of a woman who said to David, "I am a widow and I had two grown sons who took care of me—until the day they got in a fight and one killed the other. Now the people in my community are demanding that my living son be put to death. But if that happens, I will have no one to care for me. What should I do?"

"Woman," David said, "truly I say to you that not one hair on his head shall be hurt."

"What about you?" the woman said. "Don't you know that our days are short, and, like water spilt upon the ground, cannot be gathered up again? God is not a respecter of persons." In other words, "Time is short. God forgave you. Forgive your son. Bring him back" (see 2 Samuel 14:13, 14).

Unable to deny the wisdom of her words, David sent Joab to track down Absalom and bring him home. But when Absalom entered the city of Jerusalem, David refused to see him. For two years, Absalom had no communication with his dad whatsoever. Finally, not knowing how else to get his father's attention, Absalom lit the fields of Joab on fire.

Parenthetically, I cannot help but wonder what fires our own kids have to light in order to get our attention.

"Send him in," commanded David at last. And Scripture records that when David saw his son, he kissed him (2 Samuel 14:33). But the plot thickens. After Absalom received the kiss of his father, he left the palace and got a new chariot with fifty men to run before him, announcing his arrival. With his hair blowing in the breeze, and the bass thumping on his stereo, Absalom's daily rides through Jerusalem were impressive, indeed. Thus, it is no wonder that when he parked his chariot at the gates of the palace, those who were waiting to get an audience with David would bow before him.

"Don't bow to me," Absalom would say. "You're my buddies."

"Us?" they said. "We're nobodies."

No," said Absalom, throwing his arms around as many as he could. "You're my buddies. If I were king, I would take care of whatever it is that's troubling you."

That is how this good-looking, prestigious, rich, seemingly together individual who was a mess inside, stole their hearts. And one by one, the men of Jerusalem began to say, "Absalom, you're our man."

When Absalom felt he had enough support, he went to his father and said, "While I was in exile, I made a vow to God that I would offer Him a sacrifice in Hebron. I need to fulfill that vow." So Absalom headed for Hebron—not to worship the Lord, but to wrest the throne from his father. When the trumpets sounded in Hebron, the prearranged signal was translated throughout Jerusalem: Absalom is taking over.

Upon hearing the news, David prepared to leave Jerusalem. "We'll grab the ark and go with you," said the priests Abiathar and Zadok.

"No," insisted David. "The ark must not leave Jerusalem. God is not on the run. The fault is mine for not dealing with my sons. Stay here in Jerusalem, and be my eyes and ears."

Taking a few of his men with him, David left his ten wives to keep house in the palace as a sign he would be back. Upon his departure, Ittai, the Hittite, said, "Six hundred of our men are traveling with you."

"You're Philistines," said David. "You don't have to come."

"But we do," said Ittai. "Although you were once our conqueror, we now count you our friend. Where you go, we'll go. If you die, we'll die beside you."

"Okay," said David. "Let's go" (see 2 Samuel 15:22). At this point, Hushai, one of David's advisors, approached him and asked to be included in the entourage. But David refused his request on the grounds that he was too old and too valuable. "Stay here, Hushai," David said. "Pretend you're on Absalom's side, and give him bad advice."

As Absalom assumed power, Ahithophel, David's former top advisor, told him to consolidate his power at once. "Take David's ten wives upon the palace roof where the whole nation can see," he said, "and have relations with them. Meanwhile, I'll take twelve thousand men, track David down, and do him in."

The question arises: Why did Ahithophel defect to Absalom after being loyal to David for so many years? One possible reason was that his granddaughter was a beautiful woman named Bathsheba. His resentment over David's affair with her, along with the subsequent murder of her husband, could have turned to revenge as soon as Absalom came into power.

But Ahithophel's sin had a far worse outcome than did David's. Thousands would be killed in the war that would result from his encouragement of Absalom's rebellion. Watch out, gang—the sin you resent in others may be far less dangerous than the sin of resentment in your own heart.

"Wait," said Hushai, "David's sly. You'll need more than twelve thousand men to get him. Gather an army of hundreds of thousands. Then make your move."

"No, no, no," argued Ahithophel. "Give your dad time, and he'll regroup. You must strike now."

Absalom listened to both advisors. In the end, he sided with Hushai. Hushai's plan worked. David now had time to regroup. He crossed the Jordan River and received word that Absalom would be commanding a massive army from his chariot. David decided to set up his ambush in Ephraim, where Absalom's chariots would have trouble navigating the woods.

With his men in position, David sounded the trumpets, and the battle began. But as Absalom entered the fray, he found himself in unfamiliar territory. Too busy cultivating his image, he had never fought a day in his life. When David's men began springing out from all sides, unable to control his chariot, Absalom abandoned it for a mule. But even the mule was unprepared for battle. As it ran wildly through the woods of Ephraim, Absalom's long, flowing hair became entangled in the branches of a tree.

Absalom's hair got caught; the mule kept going; and Absalom was left hanging by his hair. This is intriguing to me. After all, if you were in battle and your hair got caught, wouldn't you take your sword or knife, cut your hair, and set yourself free? Not Absalom. Either he was so inexperienced in warfare that he didn't even have a weapon with him, or, he said, "I would rather die than lose my hair." Either way, it's amazing.

Upon hearing of Absalom's predicament, David's general, Joab, found him still hanging by his hair. Straightway, Joab fired three darts into Absalom's chest, putting an end to Absalom's life as well as his attempted coup.

"That's an interesting story," you say. "But what does this have to do with Galatians?"

Everything.

"Cursed is everyone who hangs on a tree," wrote Paul.

Who hung on a tree? A mass murderer?

No.

A crazed rapist?

No.

It was a man who was proud, manipulative, and ambitious. That is the man whom God says is especially cursed. That's you. That's me. But wait.

"O, Absalom. O, Absalom, I would die if you could live," cried David.

"O, Jerusalem, Jerusalem, I will hang on the tree in your place," cried the Son of David, Jesus Christ.

- Absalom rebelled against his father.
  Jesus said, "I do the will of My Father."
- Absalom had beauty.
  Jesus had "no form or comeliness."
- Absalom sounded the trumpet.
  Jesus walked in humility.

They're opposite in every way. Yet they both hung on a tree—Absalom because of his sin, Jesus for mine. The biggest difference between Absalom and Jesus Christ is that only One burst forth from the stone that covered His grave. Only One rose from the dead. Only One says, "Because I hung on the tree, you are forgiven."

Cursed is everyone that hangs on a tree. It should have been you. It should have been me. But He who knew no sin was made sin for us that we might be forgiven. Consequently, we're saved. We're forgiven. We've been brought back from exile."

I'm Absalom. But because Jesus hung in there on the tree for me, I'm free. And I want you to be, too."

4 Look at a young man in love. No one tells him to write love letters, pick flowers, or go for a walk in the park with his sweetheart. These things just happen when we're in love. That's what the Lord wants for you and me. He wants to set us free and wants us to respond to that freedom in love. Legalism, however, will drain us of our passion for Jesus Christ.

If you are feeling dry or dragged down in your spiritual life, it could well be because you have fallen back into a pattern of legalism. Perhaps you have imposed rules upon your spiritual life—structure, commitments, and vows. Because you can't keep them, however, you inevitably find yourself feeling dragged down, dried up, and wiped out. Such is what was happening to the believers in Galatia. Judaizers came on the scene, saying, "You need to follow rules and regulations. You need to become circumcised. You need to adhere to the Jewish traditions."

Responding with holy indignation, Paul said, "No. Don't let anyone burden you with rules, rituals, or expectations. Stand fast in your liberty. You'll end up serving the Lord more energetically, talking to the Lord more frequently, studying His Word more joyfully, and giving more generously than when you had rules and legalistic trips that you couldn't keep and that only drained you of joy."

The question then becomes, "Why was the law given?" At the end of chapter 3, we saw the law was given to show us that we don't measure up, that we're sinners in need of a Savior. The law is a schoolmaster, said Paul, to bring us to Christ. But after faith is come, we no longer need the schoolmaster, as we exchange a relationship based on the law for a relationship based on love.

Galatians 4:1, 2
Now I say, That the heir, as long as he is a child, differeth nothing from a servant, though he be lord of all; but is under tutors and governors until the time appointed of the father.

Donald and Marla Trump had a baby. As heir to the Trump fortune, this little Trumpette will one day inherit multiplied millions of dollars. Does this mean when she was five years old she could write checks, use credit cards, and make investments? No. Even though she was an heir, being a child, she was under the restrictions of her parents, nannies, and teachers.

The same is true of God's people. Before they were brought into adult sonship through Jesus Christ, they were kept under a tutor, a school-

master—the law. God knew all along He would send His Son to die for His people. He knew they would eventually be brought into a right standing with Him through the blood of Jesus Christ. Thus, the law was only a temporary tutor.

Galatians 4:3
Even so we, when we were children, were in bondage under the elements of the world.

The "elements of the world" refer to the law. Why is the law referred to in this way? Because the basic building block of society must be the law. Any society that ignores the foundational principles of the law will crumble, dissipate, and be destroyed from within. The problem is, the law tells us what to do, but it fails to give us the power to do it.

Galatians 4:4, 5 (a)
But when the fulness of the time was come, God sent forth his Son, made of a woman, made under the law, to redeem them that were under the law . . .

In the fullness of time—at just the right time—Jesus Christ came to purchase we who were under the law, we who were trying hard to obey it, but powerless to do so.

Galatians 4:5 (b)
. . . that we might receive the adoption of sons.

The Greek word translated "adoption" is *huiothesia. Huios* meaning "son," and *thesis* meaning "position," *huiothesia* means "taking the position of a son." The Son of God took our position on the Cross of Calvary in order that we might in turn take the position as sons of God.

Adoption is not the means of entry into God's family. As Jesus told Nicodemus in John 3, we enter into God's family only by being born again. Rather, adoption speaks of our privilege and standing *within* God's family. The moment we were born again, we were placed in an adopted state as heirs, as sons of God.

We think of adoption in terms of adopting a little baby. But that's not the biblical concept of adoption. Biblical adoption refers to a full-grown adult. It would be like, before retiring from Ford Motor Company, having no sons, but wanting his name to continue, Henry Ford approached a twenty-four-year-old Harvard graduate and said, "Would you let me adopt you? If you will, you'll have a place on the Board of Directors, a salary of three million dollars a year, a summer house in Hawaii, a winter house in Tahiti, a private jet, and your own yacht."

The moment you were born again, you assumed the position of an adopted son—heir to the riches of the Father. Too often people say, "I really can't be used by the Lord because I've only walked with Him five years," or, "I can't get involved in intercessory prayer because I'm just a new Christian." Wrong. Concerning the privileges and responsibilities of the kingdom, you were adopted as a mature son with as much right to be blessed and used by the Lord as is Billy Graham.

This does not mean, however, that we are equal to Jesus Christ. We are adopted sons, but God so loved the world that He gave His *only begotten* Son. There's a lot of misunderstanding concerning this point within the "faith movement." There are those who say, "Jesus is the Son of God, and you're a son of God. Jesus created all things by His Word, therefore you can create all things by your word. Speak the word of faith. Name it and claim it. Blab it and grab it."

Wrong. The word of faith teachings are totally in error when they say that because God said let there be light, whatever we say will come to pass. It's not that God *said, "Let there be light," but that God* said, "Let there be light," which caused the light to shine.

If you remember that you are an *adopted* son, you'll be free of heresy and misunderstanding.

Galatians 4:6
And because ye are sons, God hath sent forth the Spirit of his Son into your hearts, crying, Abba, Father.

Because we're adopted sons, we have the Spirit of the only begotten Son, Jesus Christ, in our hearts. Therefore, we can call God "Abba," the Hebrew word that means "papa," or "daddy"—and He will respond.

Galatians 4:7
Wherefore thou art no more a servant, but a son; and if a son, then an heir of God through Christ.

Although we're no longer servants but sons, we need to understand that the privilege of prayer, wherein we cry, "Abba, Father," is not given to enable us to give God orders, to say, "Bless this, do that, provide the other." Such is not prayer at all. Prayer is the Spirit of Jesus Christ working in and through us in order to bring us into harmony with the perfect purposes of the Father. Prayer is the Spirit of Jesus in me crying, "Abba"—not for manipulation, but for unification—to become one with His perfect purpose and plan.

Galatians 4:8
Howbeit then, when ye knew not God, ye did service unto them which by nature are no gods.

"Before you were saved," Paul said, "you served those which were not gods." The same is true today. People who are into the worship of idols wear robes and put on masks. They sprinkle water, burn incense, spin prayer wheels, and light candles—all in an effort to manipulate their gods.

Galatians 4:9–11
But now, after that ye have known God, or rather are known of God, how turn ye again to the weak and beggarly elements, whereunto ye desire again to be in bondage? Ye observe days, and months, and times, and years. I am afraid of you, lest I have bestowed upon you labour in vain.

"What are you doing?" asked Paul. "You're burning incense. You're sprinkling holy water, lighting candles, fingering beads, and repeating prayers over and over again. You've gone right back into pagan ritualism, but you've been set free from all that stuff."

There's something within us that gravitates towards the law and rituals, legalism, paganism, and all the stuff from which Jesus Christ came to set us free. "Well, I just feel more holy if I can hear the chants or the swishing of robes," you say. That's okay—but you don't need those things. There's a better way: Be totally free in your love relationship with God. Just enjoy the Lord!

Galatians 4:12 (a)
Brethren, I beseech you, be as I am; for I am as ye are . . .

"I'm not keeping 'kosher' rules. I'm not under Judaistic traditions," said Paul. "You're Gentiles. I live like you do."

Galatians 4:12 (b)–14
. . . ye have not injured me at all. Ye know how through infirmity of the flesh I preached the gospel unto you at the first. And my temptation which was in my flesh ye despised not, nor rejected; but received me as an angel of God, even as Christ Jesus.

"When I first came to you," said Paul, "you received me and the message which I brought, even though I was suffering from a physical infirmity."

Galatians 4:15
Where is then the blessedness ye spake of? for I bear you record, that, if it had been possible, ye would have plucked out your own eyes, and have given them to me.

Here, many commentators believe we are given a clue as to what Paul's infirmity was—perhaps an eye disease that caused his eyes to ooze and always appear runny, similar to perpetual pinkeye. Not only would such an infection be painful for Paul, but it would be painful for others to look at as well. Yet Paul says his infirmity didn't prevent the Galatians from receiving him with such a measure of devotion that they would have given him their own eyes if possible.

Galatians 4:16
Am I therefore become your enemy, because I tell you the truth?

"Are you turning away from me now because I am speaking truthfully by telling you that you're missing the mark by getting involved in legalism again?" asked Paul.

Galatians 4:17 (a)
They zealously affect you, but not well . . .

Legalists appeal to the macho mentality within each of us. "Come join us," they say. "We're really radical. We pay the price. We bear the Cross. We deal with stuff that only a few can deal with."
And we are prone to say, "I want to be one of the few, one of the chosen, one of the elite group that God will use in these last days. So I'll submit to stipulations and regulations in order that I can be among the few, the chosen—the spiritual marines!"

Galatians 4:17 (b)
. . . yea, they would exclude you, that ye might affect them.

"Legalizers have their own agenda," said Paul. "They want to exclude you from grace in order that by your own works, you can support them."

Galatians 4:18–20
But it is good to be zealously affected always in a good thing, and not only when I am present with you. My little children, of whom I travail in birth again until Christ be formed in you, I desire to be present with

you now, and to change my voice; for I stand in doubt of you.

"I travail in birth for you," said Paul. To another group of believers, he said, "You have ten thousand instructors, but not many fathers" (see 1 Corinthians 4:15). Paul's goal was not merely to dispense theological information, but to see the reality of regeneration. He wanted to see people born again, to see them grow in grace, to see them mature in liberty.

Galatians 4:21–23
Tell me, ye that desire to be under the law, do ye not hear the law? For it is written, that Abraham had two sons, the one by a bondmaid, the other by a freewoman. But he who was of the bondwoman was born after the flesh; but he of the freewoman was by promise.

To validate his argument, Paul appealed to Abraham, father of the Jewish race. God said to Abraham, "I'm going to bring you into a new land. I'm going to give you a new name. I'm going to make you great. And from you will come forth a people as innumerable as the stars in the heavens or the sand on the seashore."
Abraham believed God. But when he was eighty-six years old, with the promise yet to be fulfilled, his wife said, "Honey, I realize God spoke to you, but let's be practical. You're eighty-six. I'm seventy-six. This promise isn't going to come to pass the way we thought it would. Therefore, take my slave girl, Hagar, have relations with her, and the child you produce will be the promised seed from which will come the nation God promised you."
When God gives a promise, there is almost invariably a gap of time between the giving of the promise and the fulfillment of the promise. And it is in that gap of time that we get impatient. "Time is running out," we say. "I've got to make something happen."
Abraham agreed to Sarah's plan. The result was the conception and birth of a baby boy named Ishmael. Thirteen years went by. Then God spoke to Abraham again, saying, "I'm still going to give you a child."
"Let Ishmael live," said Abraham. "He'll do."
"No," said God. "Ishmael is not the fulfillment of My promise. He's only your fleshly attempt to help Me."
As I look back over my life, I see that every time I got impatient and tried to help God, the result has always been trouble—Ishmael. Because God is so good, the promise still comes because He's faithful to His Word. But the problem is, I

have a bunch of Ishmaels to deal with. You see, to this day, blood is shed daily in the ongoing struggle between the children of Ishmael and the children of Israel. So, too, in my own life, whenever Ishmael is born as a result of my own fleshly efforts, strife, anxiety, and tension are also birthed in my life.

Push God, rush God, help God out—and you'll have an Ishmael on your hands. Abraham was a great man. Yet this friend of God, this father of faith, this incredible saint had a problem that God recorded as a lesson for each of us today: He was impatient.

"Impatient?" you say. "He waited how many years for God to keep His promise?"

It was at least twelve years between the time Abraham was given the promise and the time he went in to Hagar. But it could have been as many as eighteen years. Some of us think, *I've been waiting eighteen days, eighteen weeks, eighteen months. When is God going to fulfill His promise to me?* Abraham waited eighteen *years* before he said, "I better help God." But it was a disaster, nonetheless.

Galatians 4:24
Which things are an allegory: for these are the two covenants; the one from the mount Sinai, which gendereth to bondage, which is Agar.

Evidently, Hagar was born in Sinai, a significant site indeed, as it also speaks of the place where the Law was given.

Galatians 4:25, 26
For this Agar is mount Sinai in Arabia, and answereth to Jerusalem which now is, and is in bondage with her children. But Jerusalem which is above is free, which is the mother of us all.

"Hagar illustrates Jerusalem—or Judaism," said Paul. "But the Jerusalem which is above— the heavenly Jerusalem—is free."

Galatians 4:27
For it is written, Rejoice, thou barren that bearest not; break forth and cry, thou that travailest not: for the desolate hath many more children than she which hath an husband.

Paul reminded the Galatians that, according to Isaiah 54:1, the barren one—the Gentiles— would produce more children than the people of promise—the Jews.

Galatians 4:28
Now we, brethren, as Isaac was, are the children of promise.

We're Isaac, the children of promise. It's a miracle we're here. Ten years ago, would you have thought you would be sitting in church—called out of the kingdom of darkness, into the kingdom of God's glorious light?

Galatians 4:29
But as then he that was born after the flesh persecuted him that was born after the Spirit, even so it is now.

The custom in Abraham's day was to throw a party to celebrate the day one's son was weaned. Thus, it was at Isaac's "weaning party" that Ishmael, his half brother, began to taunt and tease him. That is what the law does to this day: It causes those who live by it to taunt and tease those who don't. "You're shallow. You're carnal. You're weak. You're immature. I'm disciplined. I'm chosen. I'm a spiritual marine," says the legalist to the child of promise.

Galatians 4:30, 31
Nevertheless what saith the scripture? Cast out the bondwoman and her son: for the son of the bondwoman shall not be heir with the son of the freewoman. So then, brethren, we are not children of the bondwoman, but of the free.

The cure for the mocking and taunting of the legalizers is to get rid of the law. Cast it out. We are to preach the law to those who are hard of heart. Once a man opens his heart, however, the law has done its job.

The Law Is a Mirror to Show Us Our Sin

A necessity for those who don't know the Lord because it places restrictions on an exceedingly sinful world (1 Timothy 1:8), the law can be a monitor, but it cannot be a mother. It cannot produce the promise.

The Law Is Not to Be Married Again

Just as Hagar never married again after she was cast out, once we open our hearts to Jesus, the law has accomplished its purpose and is never to be embraced again. We are not to say, "I've been living in grace for ten years now. I'm going to do a little bit of law from here on out." No, that which was begun in the Spirit cannot be finished by the flesh (Galatians 3:3).

The Law Was Made Manifest *After* Grace

Sarah was the wife of Abraham before Hagar ever came into the picture. God's intention from the beginning was grace. But man said, "I don't need God's grace. I'm doing okay by myself. I can handle everything by my own ability." The law was given to show man his need. Don't be confused by those who say the law existed for several thousand years before God got tired of it and switched to grace. No, the promise was given to Abraham long before the law was given to Moses.

The Law Materialized in the World

Where did Abraham get Hagar? In Egypt. You recall the story: When there was famine in Canaan, Abraham and Sarah went to Egypt for food. While there, Abraham got entangled in lies and deception. Pharaoh sent him away with riches and servants—one of whom was Hagar.

Whenever someone is legalistic, judgmental,

and uptight, I know he got those attitudes not from the Word, but from the world. You see, the more sin we're exposed to, the more sin we're involved in, the more cynical we become. Had Abraham never gone into Egypt, he never would have had Hagar.

If someone is pompous, pious, and full of pride; if someone is legalistic, fault-finding, and sin-sniffing, I know he or she is one who has spent quite a bit of time in Egypt. Conversely, if someone is loving and kind, forgiving and gentle, he or she is one who has spent time in the Promised Land, enjoying the grace and goodness of God.

Legalism doesn't protect us from carnality, folks. It is the result of carnality. To the pure, all things are pure (Titus 1:15). People who are legalistic are those who have been peeking at *Playboy*, going to R-rated movies, or otherwise engaged in Egypt in one way or another. Angry at themselves, they're out to persecute others.

May God give you wisdom as you think and pray through this powerful picture.

LEGALISM: IT'S GOTTA GO!

A Topical Study of
Galatians 4:21–31

It could and should have been the most glorious, the grandest, the happiest day of Abraham's life. His son was finally weaned—an event that called for a huge celebration. In that day, there were two milestones in the life of every child. . . .

The first took place eight days after his birth when his parents performed the rite of circumcision. Although this was painful for the parents as well as for the child, because it was part of God's plan for His people at that time, they obeyed out of dedication to Him.

The second milestone was marked not out of dedication, but with delight as the parents gave a feast at the time their child was weaned.

On the day Isaac was weaned, his old man was no doubt proud as punch.

"Aren't you being a bit disrespectful, referring to Isaac's father as his 'old man'?" you ask.

No. It's not a question of respect, but of reality. You see, when we first met Isaac's dad, he was already seventy-five years old. Living in the Mesopotamian town of Ur—the upscale town wherein bathtubs were invented, Abram was most likely very prosperous. Although he was a worshiper of the moon goddess commonly worshiped in that region (Joshua 24:2), God spoke to him, saying, "Get thee out of thy land, and away from thy kindred unto a land that I will show thee. And I will make of thee a great nation. And I will bless thee. And I will make thy name great. And I will bless them that bless thee, and curse them that curse thee. And in thee shall all the families of the earth be blessed" (see Genesis 12:1–3).

If you're a senior citizen or retired, don't think God is through with you. He's not. You never know when He will whisper in your ear something of new instruction, or of greater ministry—just as He did to Abram.

Abram did, indeed, leave Ur. He traveled northwest to the little town of Haran, where he stayed until his father died. Then he journeyed southwest to the land to which God was leading him—to Canaan. When he arrived, he looked around, pitched his tent, and built an altar to worship the Lord.

But then something interesting happened. Famine came, and things got tough. "We have to leave this land," Abram said to his wife. "There's plenty to eat in Egypt." So they left the Promised Land and journeyed south to Egypt. Upon their arrival, Abram came to the conclusion that, because of his wife's great beauty, Pharaoh would order him killed in order to add her to his harem. Tell everyone you're my sister," Abram told her. And this beautiful woman submitted to the foolishness of her husband.

Just as Abram feared, Pharaoh's scouts spotted Sarah and notified him she was wanted in Pharaoh's harem. "Fine," said the father of faith. "She's my sister." In return, Abram was given menservants and maidservants, camels, and all kinds of riches. That night, God plagued Pharaoh and his household so intensely that Pharaoh recognized the hand of God. Knowing Abram had tricked him, the next morning, Pharaoh rebuked Abram and sent him and Sarai back to Bethel.

I find it interesting that there is no record of God talking to Abram while he was in Egypt. "Why doesn't God talk to me?" you may be saying today. It could be because you're in Egypt. You're not where you are supposed to be, doing what you were called to do, or being what you were called to be. Don't expect the Lord to speak to you in Egypt. He loves you too much. If He spoke to you while you were in Egypt, you would probably settle down there, and it would be disastrous for you. God shouts loudly through His silence whenever we're in Egypt until we finally say, "Let's go back to Bethel, back to the place of God."

The Lord spoke to Abram a second time, saying, "I am your exceeding great reward and shield" (see Genesis 15:1).

"Lord, You might be my reward, but I still don't have any children," Abram replied.

God said, "Look up at the stars, Abram. So shall your seed be." And, because Abram believed God, God declared him righteous (Galatians 3:6).

The years went on. Finally, at seventy-six years of age, Sarai said to her eighty-six-year-old husband, "I know God said you would be a great nation. I know He showed you the stars in the heavens. But the time has come to get your head out of the clouds and your feet on the ground, Abram. Have relations with my hand-maiden, Hagar. The child will count as ours." Scripture says Abram "hearkened unto the voice of his wife," and the child born was named Ishmael.

Thirteen years later, the Lord came to Abram again, saying, "You're no longer going to be called Abram, or "Exalted Father." From this time on, your name will be Abraham, or "Father of Multitudes."

Great, Abraham must have thought. *I only have one child. It was bad enough being called Exalted Father. But the Father of Multitudes?*

Why did God change Abram's name? Because "h" was the fifth letter in the Hebrew alphabet. Five being the number of grace, in changing Abram's name to Abraham, it was as if God inserted grace into Abraham's life. So, too, when God changed Sarai's name to Sarah, it was as if He bestowed grace upon her. At the age of ninety, she gave birth to a son.

Elated to be parents at last, Abraham and Sarah named their baby Isaac, or, "Laughter." The celebration commemorating his weaning must have been a joyous occasion, indeed—until Ishmael, a teenager at this point, began teasing his little brother.

Observing Ishmael's taunts and jeers, Sarah implored Abraham to cast out Hagar and Ishmael. And Abraham again "hearkened unto the voice of his wife," this time being instructed by God to do so (Genesis 21:12). Scripture records that the thought of casting out his son was "very grievous in his sight." Abraham is the greatest example of faith in the Old Testament simply because he did what God said—even when he didn't understand or couldn't agree.

With a broken heart, Abraham filled water skins for Hagar and Ishmael and sent them to the desert—which brings us, at last, to our text. You see, every New Testament principle has an Old Testament picture. Justification by faith, as outlined here in Galatians, is no exception.

Consider the picture-perfect allegory: Hagar represents the law. Ishmael—Abraham's attempt to "help God out"—represents the flesh. Sarah represents grace.

Legalism will always persecute the person who is living in grace and enjoying the free gift of salvation. Just as Ishmael taunted Isaac, those who are trying to be religious mock those who celebrate liberty in Jesus, calling them shallow, immature, and undisciplined.

You will find this to be true. Not only will those around you mock you, but a voice will well up within you, saying, "Look what you're doing. Real Christians don't do that. You must not be a Christian." In addition to the voices around and within you, Satan himself will condemn you day and night (Revelation 12:10).

Contrary to our natural inclination, the solution to all of these accusations is not to get more religious, try harder, vow more earnestly or work more diligently. No, the solution is to cast out the bondwoman. The solution is to say, "Away, rules and regulations, religion, and tradition. I'm not going to try to deal with or compromise with the bondwoman. I'm going to cast her out."

My mind rebels against that. My heart wonders about that. I am tempted to think, *The best way to help the people I'm shepherding is to set up rules and restrictions, to set up certain standards of spirituality, to draw up pledges for them to sign, commitments for them to make, promises for them to keep.*

But the Book of Galatians says just the opposite. It tells us to get rid of the promises, the pledges, the commitments, and the rules. They're all Ishmaels. They will come back and persecute us because, inevitably and invariably, we'll hedge on our commitments, break our promises, and be unable to keep our rules. Then we'll be down on ourselves, depressed about ourselves, disgusted with ourselves until at last we'll say, "Forget it. Why even bother walking with God? I just can't do it."

Cast out Hagar and Ishmael, on the other hand, and what will happen? You'll cleave only to Sarah—to grace. And when you realize that the work is done, and that the price has been fully paid, you'll exchange the legalistic relationship you once had with God for a loving relationship with Him. If we truly love God, we won't be attracted to the places or activities of those who don't care about Him. You see, the reason I don't go to bars, for example, is not because God says, "Thou Shalt Not Go to Bars." It's because I can't think of anything worse than sitting in a dark room by the hour when I could be tossing the football or riding bikes with my son Ben. Thus, I abstain from bar hopping not because I've promised to—but because I want to.

If you're sitting here today, skeptically saying, "Just as I suspected. Sinners talking about cheap grace," remember that Hagar represents legalism. Where did Abraham get Hagar? In Egypt, in the world. The extent to which we look down on and find fault with others is indicative of our own Egyptian wanderings. To the pure, all things are pure (Titus 1:5), but the one who is in sin will spot sin in everyone else because Hagar is traveling with him. Therefore, the degree to which I place bonds on others is indicative of my own Egyptian wanderings.

Consequently, when I begin to find fault with everyone else, it would behoove me to say, "Uh-oh, Lord, have I been cruising in Egypt? Have I picked up this legalistic tendency because of my excursion into the world? Has my joy been robbed because I've brought Hagar back with me?"

If that is the case, what must I do? Again, the answer lies in casting out the bondwoman. I must say, "Away, legalism; away cynicism; away, works of the flesh. I choose to cleave to Sarah. I will celebrate grace."

Folks, because legalism and love cannot dwell together in the same tent any more than could Hagar and Sarah, you will either become more rigid and ritualistic, or you'll become more liberated and loving. The two cannot dwell together. One has got to go. Let me recommend that you cast out Hagar, and that you cleave to Sarah—that you let go of legalism, and grab hold of grace.

5 We come to the third and final section of this glorious Epistle written to the Galatians. In chapters 1 and 2, Paul outlined his personal experience with grace. In chapters 3 and 4, he gave doctrinal instruction about grace. And now in chapters 5 and 6, he will demonstrate the practical application of grace.

Galatians 5:1
Stand fast therefore in the liberty wherewith Christ hath made us free, and be not entangled again with the yoke of bondage.

Paul borrowed the term "yoke of bondage" from Peter, who, in Acts 15, used it in reference to the rules and regulations of Judaism. You see, years previously, Paul was involved in this same basic controversy. Accused of preaching "cheap grace," he and Barnabas were summoned to appear before the church leaders in Jerusalem. "Believing in Jesus is terrific," they said, "but it's not enough. To be a good Christian, one must also be a good Jew."

"Wait a minute," protested Peter, "neither our fathers nor we were able to bear the yoke of Judaism. Why should we expect the Gentiles to be able to bear it?"

"Don't let anyone put a yoke of bondage on you," echoed Paul. The yoke Jesus bore on His shoulders as He carried the Cross to Calvary is all-sufficient.

Galatians 5:2
Behold, I Paul say unto you, that if ye be circumcised, Christ shall profit you nothing.

"If you add anything to the Cross in an attempt to obtain a right standing with God, you're not saved. That's how strongly the Father feels about the sufficiency of the finished work of His Son," said Paul.

I know the Mormons are sincere. I see the zeal of the Jehovah's Witnesses. But their doctrines very clearly state that, although the Cross is a good starting point, it is not enough in and of it-self to save a man. Therefore, they're lost. The Word says if any man adds anything to the Cross, Christ profits him nothing.

Galatians 5:3, 4
For I testify again to every man that is circumcised, that he is a debtor to do the whole law. Christ is become of no effect unto you, whosoever of you are justified by the law; ye are fallen from grace.

Suppose, while driving through town, you saw a flashing red light in your rearview mirror. You pulled over, and the policeman said, "You were driving fifty-five miles an hour. You broke the law."

If you said, "Oh, come on now, Officer. Lighten up. I never robbed a bank. I never shot a person. I never was involved in drugs. So don't give me this ticket," he would say, "I don't care how many other laws you *haven't* broken, you *did* break this one. You're guilty."

The same is true of the law. If you're seeking justification by keeping the law rather than by accepting grace, breaking the law in even one point means you're guilty—regardless of how many "good things" you've done in other areas.

Galatians 5:5, 6 (a)
For we through the Spirit wait for the hope of righteousness by faith. For in Jesus Christ neither circumcision availeth anything, nor uncircumcision . . .

It doesn't matter whether you're circumcised or uncircumcised, whether you worship on Saturday or on Sunday, whether you eat meat or live on birdseed. As far as your relationship with the Father goes, this stuff is irrelevant.

Galatians 5:6 (b)
. . . but faith which worketh by love.

Grace does not produce lazy, hazy Christianity. On the contrary, as James would write, true faith works (James 2:17). Why? Not because it's got to, but because it gets to.

I asked one of the brothers at Applegate Christian Fellowship what he was going to do on his day off. "Oh, I can't wait," he said. "I'm going to my fiancie's house, and I'm going to paint her living room, fix the plumbing in her bathroom, and then do some yard work."

"That's your day *off?*" I said. "Plumbing, painting, and yard work? It's amazing what love does!" Truly, when you're in love with someone, it's not "got to's"—it's "get to's."

We *get* to worship the Lord as a congregation. We *get* to start our day with morning devotions. We *get* to tithe and be free from our own greediness. We *get* to lift our hands. We *get* to share our faith. We don't have to do those things. We *get* to. The reason faith works is not to fulfill a requirement of the law. It was in response to an incredible love.

Galatians 5:7
Ye did run well; who did hinder you that ye should not obey the truth?

Perhaps the reference in your margin says, "Who cut in front of you?" The idea is exactly as it sounds: Paul is referring to an Olympic race, saying, "You were running well, but someone cut into your lane and caused you to stumble."

One of the major showdowns in Olympic history was in the 1500 meters, as Mary Decker Slaney took on archrival Zola Budd from South Africa. Although Slaney held every record on the books, she had not yet won Olympic gold. In the middle of the race, Budd crossed into Slaney's lane, sending Slaney sprawling. The image of the American Olympian watching the rest of the pack run by is etched on our collective memory.

So, too, allowing legalists to cut in front of them and obstruct their freedom in Christ, the Galatians had set themselves up for a fall.

Galatians 5:8
This persuasion cometh not of him that calleth you.

When cultists knock on your door, try to sell you their magazine, or lay their esoteric trip on you, on the basis of this verse, say, "Where did you get that idea? You didn't get it from the Bible, did you?"

"Well, not really," they'll say. "It's from *The Pearl of Great Price*," or, "from our magazine," or, "from a pamphlet."

We who are believers in Jesus Christ, on the other hand, can truly say, "Just read your Bible. It's all you need. You don't need special literature. You don't need something some man has written to reveal the keys of spirituality to you. If you really want to know the truth, just read the Word."

I'm constantly encouraging people to read their Bibles because I know that if they do, they'll be on solid, secure footing. They won't fall prey to some new idea or philosophy.

Galatians 5:9
A little leaven leaveneth the whole lump.

Shifting his analogy from sports to cooking, Paul relates leaven, the symbol for evil throughout Scripture, to legalism. "Be careful," he said. "Just as leaven hidden in a portion of dough causes all of the dough to rise, if you open the door to even a little legalism, it will surely spread."

The tricky thing about legalism is that it begins with the right motives. Because we care so much about our congregations or our kids, we put legalistic perimeters around them. Although the motive is sincere, it ends in disaster because rules and regulations produce only one of two things: self-glorification, or self-condemnation.

"The secret to God's blessing lies in getting up at four o'clock every morning," you might say. Consequently, for two years you roll out of bed every morning at four o'clock on the dot, thinking, Look at me. I've got it all together. One morning, however, you ignore the alarm. Self-glorification turns to self-condemnation, as you cry, "Alas. The Lord will not hear my prayer today. For that matter, He probably won't hear any more of my prayers ever."

You then find yourself on a spiritual roller coaster—up when you succeed and down when you fail.

Suppose you're sitting on a 747 Honolulu-bound jumbo jet. Just before takeoff you hear the voice of the captain over the loudspeaker, saying, "We have a small problem here today. Our navigational instrument is one degree off. But what's one degree? Sit back and relax, and we'll be taking off shortly."

If I were on that plane, I would say, "Open the door. I'm out of here." One degree might not make a very big difference from Medford, Oregon, to Ashland, but it would cause the plane to miss Hawaii by three hundred miles. We'd all be shark bait!

Legalism might not make any noticeable difference at first, but over the long haul it will be disastrous.

Galatians 5:10 (a)
I have confidence in you through the Lord, that ye will be none otherwise minded . . .

In other words, "I'm confident you're getting my point," said Paul.

Galatians 5:10 (b)
. . . but he that troubleth you shall bear his judgment, whosoever he be.

Let every Sunday-school worker, every Bible study teacher, and every family devotion leader hear Paul's heart as he says to the Galatians, "Those who are causing you to get entangled in legalism will bear the responsibility for what they're doing." James would echo the same warning. "Let not many of you desire to be teachers," he said, "knowing that you shall receive the greater condemnation" (see James 3:1). Each of us involved in teaching needs to approach our calling soberly and prayerfully. Like Timothy, we need to "study to show ourselves approved unto God, workmen that needeth not to be ashamed, rightly dividing the word of truth" (2 Timothy 2:15).

Galatians 5:11
And I, brethren, if I yet preach circumcision, why do I yet suffer persecution? then is the offence of the cross ceased.

Accused of preaching circumcision, Paul said, "If I am, indeed, preaching circumcision, why is it the legalizers who persecute me? It's not circumcision, but the Cross that offends them."

The same is true today. When we tell people that the work is done and the price paid, it was all taken care of on the Cross," they most likely say, "It's not that simple. You're being naive. There's a lot more to it than that."

The Cross is offensive to the religious person because he wants to get in on the action and contribute to his own salvation or blessing. However, the finished work of Jesus Christ doesn't allow for that.

Galatians 5:12, 13 (a)
I would they were even cut off which trouble you. For, brethren, ye have been called unto liberty; only use not liberty for an occasion to the flesh . . .

Before we were saved, we were in bondage to our own lusts. There was no alternative. We thought the coolest thing was to find the darkest place and go party. But it wasn't too long before we found out that sin stinks. Sin ruins relationships. Sin kills joy. Sin wipes people out. It destroys families, messes up kids, and results in mental fuzziness and physical illness. Praise God! We're free from that stuff. Therefore, the liberty to which we're called is not liberty *to* sin, but liberty *from* sin.

Galatians 5:13 (b)
. . . but by love serve one another.

"If I'm not going to party anymore," you say, "what *am* I going to do?" Serve one another! "But I'm so bored." Serve one another! Pour yourself into people. Get involved in talking to others who are doomed and damned and struggling. You'll find that talking to them about eternal issues will be more exciting and thrilling than anything you've ever done. Get involved in the things of the kingdom, and you won't miss the old stuff at all.

Galatians 5:14 (a)
For all the law is fulfilled in one word . . .

Get ready. You are about to become an Old Testament scholar, knowing the one word that sums up the entire law. . . .

Galatians 5:14 (b)
. . . even in this; Thou shalt love thy neighbour as thyself.

Love is the one word that encapsulates the entire law. Not legalism—love.

Galatians 5:15
But if ye bite and devour one another, take heed that ye be not consumed one of another.

What if we really believed that every time we put someone down, made a snide remark, or rolled our eyes in response to someone else, sooner or later we would be hurt to the same degree? Scripture says flat out, straight on, and with great clarity that if you bite and devour, take heed—you will be consumed by another. Others will talk about you to the degree you talk about others.

On the other hand, the more grace-oriented you are, the more loving you'll be.

Galatians 5:16
This I say then, Walk in the Spirit, and ye shall not fulfil the lust of the flesh.

In the arena of liberty, the key is not to suppress the flesh. The key is to surrender to the Spirit. Legalism says, "Deal with the flesh through ritual, pain, and agony."

Paul says, "There's a much better way. The solution is not to worry about the flesh, but to walk in the Spirit."

Walking in the Spirit is so exciting. The way the Lord will lead you on any given day, the opportunities that will open before you to do something significant, the insights He'll give to you as you're reading the Scriptures, the joy of just looking at a sunset and realizing you know the Creator of such beauty—will be overwhelming to you. Too many believers miss all of that because, caught up in wrestling with sin, they live in a perpetual "sin-drome."

If I said to you tonight, "Thou shalt not think of a purple elephant,"—suddenly, you would be able to think of nothing else. But, if I then set before you a huge hot fudge sundae— creamy vanilla ice cream, laced with deep dark fudge, topped with mounds of whipped cream, lightly toasted almonds, and a juicy red cherry—the purple elephant wouldn't enter your mind because you'd be captivated by something much better right before your eyes.

So, too, to overcome preoccupation with sin, walk in the Spirit. Enjoy the Lord. Do what He tells you to do in any given moment, and you'll forget sin. I see this in Moses' life. On two occasions, while in the presence of the Lord on Mount Sinai, we are told he did not eat or drink for forty days and nights (Deuteronomy 9:9; 10:10). What was the reason for his fast? Was he trying to impress God? No. He was just so entranced and enthralled in the presence of God, that he forgot to eat.

How do people overcome the lusts of the flesh? The simplest, most effective way is to walk in the Spirit. Just be enraptured with the goodness of the Lord. Do what He's telling you in your heart—whether it be some practical expression of love, a moment of intercession for someone, an encouraging word to share, or a merciful act to do.

Galatians 5:17
For the flesh lusteth against the Spirit, and the Spirit against the flesh: and these are contrary the one to the other: so that ye cannot do the things that ye would.

If you're trying to overcome the flesh in your own energy, you'll struggle perpetually, regardless of how many resolutions you make on De-

cember thirty-first, or how many slogans you paste on your refrigerator. The fact is that you'll never overcome the pull of the flesh on your own. Even though the spirit may indeed be willing, the flesh is too weak (Matthew 26:41). "Down with purple elephants!" you may write upon your mirror. But in reality, whatever your elephant is, whatever your heavyweight fleshly tendency might be, it will never be overcome by your own resolve or religion.

Galatians 5:18
But if ye be led of the Spirit, ye are not under the law.

I love this word "but." Gaining victory over the flesh by keeping the law is futile in our own ability, *but* if we're led of the Spirit, we're not under the law theologically or practically. We're free!

Galatians 5:19 (a)
Now the works of the flesh are manifest, which are these; adultery, fornication, uncleanness . . .

Uncleanness speaks of impurity of thought or life.

Galatians 5:19 (b)
. . . lasciviousness . . .

Lasciviousness speaks of licentiousness—or, literally, doing things without a license. "Who needs a marriage license if we love each other?" people say.

Galatians 5:20 (a)
Idolatry . . .

Although I'm an athlete, I think one of the biggest idols in our culture is sports. I'm convinced that if we're not careful, we actually teach our kids the idolatry of athletics whenever we say, "You don't have to go to church today. You have a game." Too many believers don't have time to study the Bible or fellowship with other believers due either to their own athletic pursuits or those of their kids. While I encourage you to keep in shape and to cheer for your kids, if you forsake ministry, worship, or the study of the Word to do so, you are guilty of idolatry.

Galatians 5:20 (b)
. . . witchcraft . . .

The Greek word translated "witchcraft" is *pharmakeia. Pharmakeia* refers to drugs. In Paul's day, those who were involved in witchcraft would brew potions that were, in reality, hallucinogens. Thus, it is no surprise that the drug culture and the world of the occult remain linked together to this day.

Galatians 5:20 (c)
. . . hatred, variance, emulations, wrath . . .

A teenage golfer was killed when he whacked a bench in frustration with his club after a bad shot. The broken shaft pierced his pulmonary vein, and he bled to death.

Don't lose your temper. It will break your heart in one way or another! Most of us can literally feel our blood boil, the hair on the back of our neck begin to stand up, or our veins bulge as wrath manifests itself in our flesh quite literally. When you begin to feel wrath welling up within you, don't smash a club or lash out at someone else. Instead, walk away from the confrontation. It may save your life.

Galatians 5:20 (d)
. . . strife . . .

Closely related to wrath, strife means "being antagonistic."

Galatians 5:20 (e)
. . . seditions, heresies . . .

Why would heresy be a manifestation of the flesh? Because people who propagate heresy do so for one reason: to glorify their flesh. "Look what I have discovered," they say. "I have been studying the Dead Sea Scrolls, and now I alone have insight into the true Jesus." Heresies always arise from someone wanting attention, wanting to build a movement around his flesh.

Galatians 5:21 (a)
Envyings, murders, drunkenness, revellings . . .

"Revelling" means partying.

Galatians 5:21 (b)
. . . and such like . . .

This list is not exhaustive. Paul says, "Here is only a sample of what the flesh is like."

Galatians 5:21 (c)
. . . of the which I tell you before, as I have also told you in time past, that they which do such things shall not inherit the kingdom of God.

"I'm telling you again," Paul says, "that those who are involved in heresy, adultery, strife, envy-

ing, drunkenness, and reveling shall not inherit the kingdom." When did Paul say this before? In I Corinthians 6:9; Ephesians 5:5; and Colossians 3:6.

"That's legalism!" you protest.

No. It's not legalism—it's revelation. The works of the flesh in one's life reveal an absence of relationship with the Lord. You see, Paul is not speaking of the person who struggles with these things, or has fallen into these things. He's speaking of the one who perpetually, habitually practices these things arrogantly, stubbornly, and with no desire to be set free from them. People who have a mind-set or a heart attitude that says, "Once saved, always saved. I'm doing this stuff, like it or not," will not inherit the kingdom of God.

Therefore, wise is the man or woman who takes Paul's words at face value and says, "Lord, forgive me and help me. Cause me to be full of Your Spirit lest I miss out on heaven."

Galatians 5:22, 23
But the fruit of the Spirit is love, joy, peace, longsuffering, gentleness, goodness, faith, meekness, temperance: against such there is no law.

The fruit (not fruits) of the Spirit is love—as defined by joy, peace, longsuffering, gentleness, goodness, faith, meekness, and self-control.

For topical study of Galatians 5:22–23 entitled "The Fruit of the Spirit," turn to page 1208.

Galatians 5:24
And they that are Christ's have crucified the flesh with the affections and lusts.

There are many ways to execute yourself. You can hang yourself, shoot yourself, poison yourself, or jump from the top floor of a ten-story building. But there's one form of execution you cannot do by yourself: crucifixion. If you pounded a nail in one of your hands, how could you do it to the other hand?

What does this mean? Go back to Romans 6, and see what Paul said so powerfully and beautifully when he wrote, "Knowing this, that our old man is crucified with him, that the body of sin might be destroyed, that henceforth we should not serve sin. Likewise, reckon ye also yourselves to be dead indeed unto sin, but alive unto God through Jesus Christ, our Lord" (see Romans 6:6, 11). We don't have to crucify ourselves. Our sin nature already died on the Cross with

Jesus. Therefore, the bottle, pills, anger, gossip, or temptation that used to dominate us no longer has control over us if we simply acknowledge that we've already been crucified with Christ. We who are in Christ have already been crucified, said Paul—not "should be," not "better be," but *"have been."* The work is done!

Galatians 5:25
If we live in the Spirit, let us also walk in the Spirit.

Walking in the Spirit simply means doing what the Lord tells you to do moment by moment—whether it's making a phone call to someone in need of encouragement, getting away for five minutes to pray, or chopping wood for someone in need. It is also the most impacting, exciting, unpredictable life there is.

For topical study of Galatians 5:25 entitled "Walking in the Spirit," turn to page 1212.

Galatians 5:26
Let us not be desirous of vain glory, provoking one another, envying one another.

Those who live in legalism desire vainglory. "Look how many people I witnessed to. Look how many hours I prayed. Look what I don't do," we say whenever legalism creeps into our lives. But the problem with vainglory is this: It's never enough.

Don't get caught up in the cycle of legalism, saint. Don't be one who competes with people. Instead, be one who completes people.

THE FRUIT OF THE SPIRIT
A Topical Study of
Galatians 5:22, 23

The beloved Rabbi was on his deathbed. His students had one last question to ask of him: "What is the secret of life?"

Looking into the eyes of the earnest young men, the Rabbi said, "Life is like a river." Then he drifted into a coma that lasted for several months. Through the duration of the Rabbi's silence, his disciples discussed and pondered the puzzling analogy.

Life is like a river? What does that mean? they wondered. A few months later, the Rabbi awoke from his coma. The young men quickly gathered around him once again and said, "Rabbi, we've been considering the last word you gave us. What did you mean when you said life is like a river?"

With furrowed brow, the Rabbi said, "Maybe life is not like a river"—and he died.

What *is* the secret of life? Although we might look to gurus or rabbis, pastors or philosophers, thinkers or movie stars for the answer, the only One who truly explains life *to* us is the One who came to be Life *for* us. . . .

The Secret of Life

Ye have not chosen me, but I have chosen you, and ordained you, that ye should go and bring forth fruit, and that your fruit should remain: that whatsoever ye shall ask of the Father in my name, he may give it you.   John 15:16

What is the secret of life?

Bearing fruit.

What is fruit?

Galatians 5 describes it in its simplest form. The fruit of the Spirit is love.

"What about joy and peace, longsuffering and gentleness, goodness, meekness, and self control?" you ask.

When Paul said that the fruit of the Spirit is love, the implication is that joy, peace, longsuffering, gentleness, goodness, faith, meekness, and self-control all describe what love is.

Fruit doesn't exist for itself. It exists for others. Too often, we want the fruit of the Spirit in our lives so *we* can be satisfied, so *we* can be happy, so *we* can be fulfilled. But that's not the purpose of fruit.

So fruitful was Joseph that his branches hung down into the neighbor's yard (Genesis 49:22)—ready to be picked and stripped.

"Picked and stripped?" you say warily. "I don't know if I like that."

Really? In Song of Solomon 4:16, we read: "Awake, O north wind; and come, thou south; blow upon my garden, that the spices thereof may flow out. Let my beloved come into his garden, and eat his pleasant fruits."

"That's more like it!" you say. "The desire of my heart is to be a garden for my King—just Jesus and me in silence and solitude."

Wait a minute. Read on. What does Jesus do? He brings His friends with Him into our garden (Song of Solomon 5:1). They trample on us and pick from us, until we protest, "Who invited *them?*"

"I did," answers the Lord. "I've produced this fruit in you, not for you, and not even primarily for Me—but for My friends."

Truly, the secret of life is fruit-bearing—not for our own satisfaction, but in order that others might be nourished from the fruit produced in, through, and often, in spite of us! Focus on yourself, and you'll be miserable. Be a lover of God and of people. Get your eyes off your problems and pains, your tears and fears. Look for ways to refresh, satisfy, and bless others—and you'll find the secret of life itself.

The Secret of Fruit-bearing

Abide in me, and I in you. As the branch cannot bear fruit of itself, except it abide in the vine; no more can ye, except ye abide in me.   John 15:4

What is the secret of fruit-bearing?

Abiding.

What is abiding?

Abiding simply means "hanging in there."

Suppose I said, "My family loves apples. So to make their favorite fruit a little more accessible I'm going to cut a branch from the apple tree in the backyard, put it in the kitchen, and when spring comes, it will blossom right here—where the apples will be easy to pick."

That would be ridiculous—which is precisely why Jesus said, "Here's the key to bearing fruit: Stay close to Me. If you cut yourself off from Me in any way, at any time, you won't bring forth fruit. If you abide in Me, fruit will come supernaturally, naturally."

Looking at my apple tree, I notice that when the branches abide, when they simply cling to the trunk, blossoms come forth, and fruit is produced. I never see the apple tree struggling, sweating, or red in the face. Yet I do see Christians straining and striving, grunting and groaning because they fail to understand that the secret of fruit-bearing is not to try to figure out how to make fruit. The secret of fruit-bearing is abiding, just hanging in there with the Lord.

Our text gives three identifying marks of one who is abiding:

First, there is production of fruit. "I am the vine, ye are the branches: He that abideth in me, and I in him, the same bringeth forth much fruit: for without me ye can do nothing" (John 15:5).

Second, there is correction from the Father. "Every branch in me that beareth not fruit he taketh away: and every branch that beareth fruit, he purgeth it, that it may bring forth more fruit (John 15:2).

Some say the purging spoken of here means pruning. Others say "to purge" means "to clean" (John 15:3). You see, when a vine was prolific, the branches would become weighed down with an abundance of fruit. Add a rainy season to the picture, and the result would be muddy grapes. Thus, the vinedresser would wash the branches periodically in order that the fruit would remain pure.

What does it mean to be purged? Does it mean to be pruned—or does it mean to be washed? I think it means both. You see, the Lord will cleanse you as you study the Word corporately on Sundays and Wednesdays, intimately in your quiet times with Him, and practically through small-group study with other believers. And He will prune you through trials and difficulties, dark days and hard times.

God is so in love with you, He is committed to teaching you—one way or the other. Let me suggest that you choose to be washed by the water of the Word rather than trimmed by the trials of the world!

Finally, the third mark of an abiding believer is fruition in prayer. "If ye abide in me, and my words abide in you, ye shall ask what ye will, and it shall be done unto you" (John 15:7). Answered prayers are indicative of an abiding heart. If your prayers are not being answered, it means you're not in harmony with the heart of God.

You'll understand the heart, nature, and character of Jesus if you're abiding in Him. Consequently, your prayers will be in line with His desires.

The Secret of Abiding

If ye keep my commandments, ye shall abide in my love; even as I have kept my Father's commandments, and abide in his love.   John 15:10

What is the secret of abiding?

Obeying—simply doing what the Lord is telling you to do at any given moment.

"I did all that God told me to do. I wiped out the Amalekites," boasted Saul (see 1 Samuel 15:13).

"Then, who's that guy standing with you?" asked Samuel.

"Him? Oh, he's their king. I brought him back as a trophy, along with a few sheep we're going to sacrifice," Saul answered.

"Oh, Saul," said Samuel. "Don't you know that to obey is better than sacrifice, that disobedience is as the sin of witchcraft?" (see 1 Samuel 15:22, 23).

Gang, whatever we don't deal with in obedience will return to destroy us. Years later, as Saul lay dying in battle on Mount Gilboa, perhaps the last words he heard were those of his attacker saying, "I am an Amalekite" (2 Samuel 1:8).

Obedience is the key to abiding. If we don't obey, an Amalekite will be produced within us that will eventually rise up and destroy us.

The Secret of Obeying

Jesus answered and said unto him, If a man love me, he will keep my words: and my Father will love him, and we will come unto him, and make our abode with him.   John 14:23

What is the secret of obeying?

Love.

Jesus didn't say, "If a man love me, he *should* keep my words," or, "he had *better* keep my words." He said, "If a man love Me, He *will* keep My words." It's true. Obedience is no problem if you love someone. Saul had no love for God. That's why obedience was so difficult for him.

The Secret of Loving

Henceforth I call you not servants; for the servant knoweth not what his lord doeth: but I have called you friends; for all things that I have heard of my Father I have made known unto you.   John 15:15

What is the secret of loving?

Knowing.

"I've let you know all that I know," Jesus said. "What I have heard from My Father, I've shared with you."

The old adage "familiarity breeds contempt" is only true regarding contemptible objects. The longer we know people, the greater the chance we'll be disappointed with them. Not so with the Lord. The longer we know Him, the more impressed we are with Him.

The Secret of Knowing

"If the key to loving is knowing, how do I know Him?" You already know the answer. Knowing Him means taking in the Word—just as you're doing right now. I know it would be easier for you to be at the lake, or watching the 49'ers. But the fact that you're studying the Word proves that you already know what it takes to know the Lord.

Walking by a once-productive vineyard that had become covered with thorns, Solomon stopped to see what had brought about its decline. His conclusion? "A little sleep, a little slumber, a little folding of the hands" (see Proverbs 24:30–34).

The same is true for the believer. The longer we walk with the Lord, the greater the temptation to say, "We've been to plenty of church meetings (yawn). Morning devotions? I've done them long enough (zzz). I don't need fellowship anymore" (hands folded in repose).

Then what happens? The walls break down; the thorns creep in; the fruit dries up.

Don't let that happen, saint. The secret of life is to bear fruit. The secret of bearing fruit is to abide in Him. The secret of abiding is obedience. The secret of obedience is love. The secret of love is knowledge. The secret of knowledge is to do just what you're doing right now—studying the Word.

Stay the course, pilgrim. Continue on, branch. You'll see fruit produced in you in a way that will not only bless others, but that will bring great satisfaction to you.

WALKING IN THE SPIRIT
A Topical Study of
Galatians 5:25

It has been rightly said that the problem with life is, it's so daily. A lot of people find their life to be rather mundane, unexciting, predictable. One writer declared that in his situation, life was like a merry-go-round without the merry.

That's not the way life for the believer is meant to be lived. As Paul said, "If— or as is more properly rendered, "*Since* you live in the Spirit, walk in the Spirit."

What does it mean to walk in the Spirit?

Walking in the Spirit is the most exciting, interesting, wonderful way to live. It is the direct opposite of routine, drudgery, and predictability. As proof, consider the lives of three men who did indeed walk in the Spirit. . . .

Paul

In Acts 16, setting out on his second missionary journey, Paul, Silas, and Timothy headed for Asia in order to check on the churches planted there during Paul's first missionary journey. In verse 6, however, the Spirit suddenly closed the door, preventing them from accomplishing what they had set out to do. Changing their plans, they headed for Bithynia—but were again forbidden by the Spirit to proceed. So it was that Paul found himself in the seacoast town of Troas (Acts 16:8).

In my mind's eye, I can visualize Paul walking up and down the beach questioning, wrestling, wondering, "What are You doing, Lord?" Suddenly, a vision of a man from Macedonia, saying, "Come and help us," appeared to him. Consequently, although the thought of taking the gospel to Europe had never before occurred to him, Paul and company set sail across the Aegean for Greece.

Upon their arrival, they met with a group of women (verse 13), for there was evidently not a male believer to be found. Paul was expecting to find a Macedonian man. Instead, he found a group of women. That's the way it is when we walk in the Spirit. Doors close unexpectedly. Others open miraculously. But when we go through them, things are rarely how we thought they would be initially.

While the Macedonian man does, indeed, appear as the chapter unfolds, he could hardly have been who Paul thought he would be. Who was the Macedonian man? I believe he was the jailer, who put Paul in stocks before coming to a saving knowledge of Jesus (Acts 16:30–34).

Prison doors opening, churches starting, miracles abounding—that's what it means to walk in the Spirit. Walking in the Spirit means letting the Holy Ghost close doors, open others, and surprise us at every turn.

Peter

In Acts 10, we find Peter waiting for lunch on Simon the tanner's rooftop. Looking out over the Mediterranean Sea, Peter saw a vision of a sheet carrying all sorts of unclean animals previously forbidden for the Jews to eat. In this, the Lord said, "The law, given to drive you to Christ, has done its job. You're free, Peter."

Taken aback by this, Peter went downstairs to find three men at the door—just as the Spirit had promised (Acts 10:19). Accompanying them to the house of Cornelius, Peter preached the Word—and the entire household of Cornelius was radically converted.

Now, I am certain that when Peter first arrived at Simon the tanner's house, the last thing he dreamed he would do was preach to a family of Gentiles. But, like Paul, as Peter walked in the Spirit, he was led to people and places beyond his wildest expectations.

Philip

In Acts 8, we see the entire city of Samaria responding to the ministry of Philip. Demons fled. Souls were saved. Joy filled the entire community. Suddenly, however, the Lord said to Philip, "Leave this revival and go to the desert" (see Acts 8: 26).

And, because he walked in the Spirit, Philip went—most likely not understanding why.

When he reached Gaza, the Spirit prompted him to talk to a certain political leader from Ethiopia. Returning from Jerusalem, he was sitting in his chariot, reading the Book of Isaiah. What did Philip do? Scripture says Philip ran to him (Acts 8:30). After receiving the gospel from Philip, the Ethiopian asked to be baptized immediately—a request to which Philip complied eagerly.

How I want to be more like Philip. When the Lord places an impression on my heart, or puts a thought in my mind, how I want to respond not begrudgingly or reluctantly, but to run!

"Go to the desert," the Spirit said. Philip went, not knowing why—and the single conversation that took place still has ramifications two thousand years later, as the light of the Good News of salvation continues to shine in Africa.

Look at Paul called to Macedonia, Peter going into the house of Cornelius, Philip called to the desert—and you will see that each man walked in the Spirit.

Perhaps you're saying, "I'd like to walk in the Spirit, but I don't have visions of men from Macedonia; I don't see sheets dropping down from heaven. I don't hear a voice telling me to go to Gaza. I agree in theory that life should be exciting and meaningful, impacting and Spirit-led—but how does that happen practically?"

I suggest three ways. . . .

Request

Jesus gave us the first key to walking in the Spirit when He said, "Ask and it shall be given you; seek and ye shall find; knock and it shall be opened unto you" (see Luke 11:9). It's interesting to me that the Greek verbs translated "ask," "seek," and "knock" are in the perfect tense. This means they speak of a continual asking, a continual seeking, a continual knocking. It's not something we do once a week at church, or once a year on a retreat. It's what we do every day, as we say, "Lord, I need Your help. I want to be used by You. Give me sensitivity to Your Spirit."

Relax

If the first step to walking in the Spirit is to request, the second step is to relax. In 1 Samuel 9, we see Saul looking for his father's donkeys. Unable to find the lost livestock, Saul was about to return to his father empty-handed—when he heard about a man of God who could help him. Making his way to the prophet Samuel's house, Saul inquired of him concerning the lost herd. "Set not your mind on the donkeys," said Samuel. "Come to my table. There's a far bigger issue at hand: You are about to be made king of Israel" (see 1 Samuel 9:19, 20).

We're Saul, folks. Bunches of us are searching high and low for our lost donkeys. Desiring to come to our Father with something of substance in our lives, we, nonetheless, wander aimlessly and return empty-handed. We struggle with a job, a house, a career, a relationship. Yet as important as those things might be, they're only donkeys in comparison to the bigger issue, in comparison to the kingdom.

The Lord calls us to significant service, to touch people's lives, to impact our world. He says to us, "Set not your mind on the donkeys. I know right where they are. Instead, come to My table, and fellowship with Me."

Receive

What happened when Saul went to Samuel's table? First, Samuel said, "Stand thou still awhile that I may shew thee the Word of God." Then he anointed Saul king (see 10:1). Lastly, he told Saul where his father's donkeys could be found (10:2).

Do you want to walk in the Spirit? Do what Saul did: Forget the donkeys; set aside your own agenda, and commune with the Lord at His table. Chew on His Word. Stand still in His presence. Receive His anointing.

Then, like Saul, you will be told where to find your lost donkeys. Jesus said, "Seek *first* the kingdom, and all these things shall be added unto you" (see Matthew 6:33). It's just that simple. In the morning hours, during the day, Wednesday night, Sunday evening, Sunday morning—seek first the kingdom of God.

Not only will you be anointed by the Spirit with significant opportunities opening before you, but, like Saul, you'll find what you were looking for all along.

6 Galatians 6:1 (a)
Brethren, if a man be overtaken in a fault, ye which are spiritual, restore such an one in the spirit of meekness . . .

Continuing his exposition on the practical application of grace, Paul says, "If you're spiritual, when someone fails, don't rejoice—restore."

Noah lay in his tent, naked. Ham couldn't wait to share this news with his brothers. Shem and Japheth, on the other hand, walked backward into their father's tent, a blanket stretched between them, to cover his nakedness (Genesis 9:21–23).

Scripture declares that love covers a multitude of sins (1 Peter 4:8). Love doesn't talk about sin, doesn't draw attention to sin, and doesn't call a prayer meeting to discuss sin. Love walks in backward and covers sin.

Galatians 6:1 (b)
. . . considering thyself, lest thou also be tempted.

How much of our day is spent analyzing the faults and shortcomings of others? The answer is a good barometer of where we stand spiritually.

The carnal man wants to reveal. The spiritual man wants to restore. Why? Because, while the carnal man is puffed up with a false sense of pride and security, the spiritual man knows how close he himself is to succumbing to temptation.

For topical study of Galatians 6:1 entitled "Caring for Casualties," turn to page 1217.

Galatians 6:2
Bear ye one another's burdens, and so fulfil the law of Christ.

What is the law of Christ? To love God with all your heart, and to love your neighbor as yourself (Matthew 22:36–40).

Galatians 6:3
For if a man think himself to be something, when he is nothing, he deceiveth himself.

"I'm too important to bear someone else's burdens," some say.

It has been wisely said that to determine how important you are, stick your finger into a bucket of water, pull it out, and see how long it takes to fill the hole. We all have a tendency to think we're irreplaceable—but we're not. Paul doesn't say we deceive ourselves *if* we are nothing. He says we deceive ourselves *because* we are nothing.

Galatians 6:4
But let every man prove his own work, and then shall he have rejoicing in himself alone, and not in another.

In other words, "Don't try to impress others with your importance. Just do the things God has called you to do regardless of whether anyone notices or appreciates you."

Galatians 6:5
For every man shall bear his own burden.

"Wait a minute," you say. "Doesn't this contradict verse 2?" No. The Word translated "burden" here in verse 5 speaks of a soldier's pack, while the word "burden" in verse 2 refers to taking a hit in the chest. You see, in this battle we're in, we're each supposed to bear our own pack. But when someone has been walloped by the Enemy, we're supposed to carry his load with him. Consequently, we should not be people who are always trying to get someone else to carry our pack. At the same time, there are moments, events, and days that wallop us. During those times we need brothers and sisters to stand with us.

May God give us wisdom concerning when to buck up and bear our burden, and when to open up and share our burden.

Galatians 6:6
Let him that is taught in the word communicate unto him that teacheth in all good things.

The Greek word translated "communicate" refers to a physical sharing. In other words, we need to give materially to those who teach us spiritually. How I thank the Lord for this congregation that says, "Because this is the place where our needs are met and where we're being blessed, we're going to share in order that the ministry can continue."

I believe a lot of people are missing out on so much in so many ways because they fail to "communicate unto him that teacheth." The only time in all of Scripture God tells us to test Him is in regard to giving. "Bring all the tithes into the storehouse, that there may be food in mine house, and test me now herewith, saith the Lord of hosts, if I will not open for you the windows of heaven, and pour out for you a blessing, that there shall not be room enough to receive it" (see Malachi 3:10).

Galatians 6:7
Be not deceived; God is not mocked: for whatsoever a man soweth, that shall he also reap.

If you're sowing stingily, you'll reap sparingly. If you're sowing generously, you'll reap abundantly.

Galatians 6:8
For he that soweth to his flesh shall of the flesh reap corruption; but he that soweth to the Spirit shall of the Spirit reap life everlasting.

The law of the harvest is irrevocable and incontestable. If I say, "Lord, forgive me. I shouldn't have gone there, said that, or done the other," He does (see 1 John 1:9)—but the seed I planted in sin will still come to fruition.

"What about grace?" you say.

Grace still abounds. Ask Samson. After being where he shouldn't have been and getting a haircut in the process, as he ground at the wheel, his hair began to grow. When he at last stood in the temple of Dagon and pulled down the supporting pillars, Scripture records that Samson conquered more Philistines in that one moment than he had in his entire lifetime (Judges 16:30). Samson sowed to his flesh and lost everything as a result, for such is the law of the harvest. Yet his hair grew back and his strength was restored for a final pivotal moment of ministry, for such is the grace of God.

Galatians 6:9
And let us not be weary in well doing: for in due season we shall reap, if we faint not.

"I've been sowing good seed, but I'm not seeing much return," you might say. Hang in there, saint. You will reap in due season if you don't give up.

Galatians 6:10
As we have therefore opportunity, let us do good unto all men, especially unto them who are of the household of faith.

Do good to everyone—but especially to your brothers and sisters in God's family.

Galatians 6:11
Ye see how large a letter I have written unto you with mine own hand.

"I'm underlining this," said Paul.

Galatians 6:12 (a)
As many as desire to make a fair shew in the flesh, they constrain you to be circumcised . . .

The Greek word translated "constrain" is a term used in sales. Paul said, "Like salesmen, the legalizers put the hard sell on you to be circumcised."

Galatians 6:12 (b)
. . . only lest they should suffer persecution for the cross of Christ.

"The legalizers sell circumcision because they don't want to suffer persecution," said Paul. The legalists who are trying to put you under rules and regulations are doing so to protect themselves because in so doing, they can look their fellow legalists in the eye and say, "We got those Galatian believers straightened out."

Galatians 6:13
For neither they themselves who are circumcised keep the law; but desire to have you circumcised, that they may glory in your flesh.

"You'll be notches on their belts," Paul said. "They'll get credit for what they got you to do."

Galatians 6:14
But God forbid that I should glory, save in the cross of our Lord Jesus Christ, by whom the world is crucified unto me, and I unto the world.

"I'm not interested in notches on my belt," said Paul. "The only thing I glory in is Jesus Christ, and His work on the Cross.

Galatians 6:15, 16
For in Christ Jesus neither circumcision availeth anything, nor uncircumcision, but a new creature. And as many as walk according to this rule, peace be on them, and mercy, and upon the Israel of God.

Paul speaks of a new creature in verse 15 and of a new nation in verse 16—"the Israel of God"—a spiritual Israel of which every believer is a citizen.

Galatians 6:17
From henceforth let no man trouble me: for I bear in my body the marks of the Lord Jesus.

"Those who boast of marking their bodies by circumcision and of convincing others to do the same have nothing on me," said Paul. "The marks of circumcision are nothing compared to the marks I bear from stonings, beatings, imprisonment, and shipwreck—all for the cause of Christ."

Galatians 6:18
Brethren, the grace of our Lord Jesus Christ be with your spirit. Amen.

Following a stern word of final warning to the Judaizers who sought to compromise the work of the Cross, Paul ends his letter as he began it—drawing the attention of the Galatians to the glorious grace of God.

CARING FOR CASUALTIES
A Topical Study of
Galatians 6:1

Indicative of the perilous times in which we live, some stores now carry bulletproof vests—in the School Supplies section. Not only are these perilous days for our world—but for believers as well, for Jesus said, "And because in those days iniquity shall abound, the love of many shall wax cold" (see Matthew 24:12). Therefore, when you see people who were once on fire, once being used in ministry, once plugged in to fellowship, but no longer are—don't be surprised. Scripture declares that such would happen in the last days (2 Timothy 3). Rather than being surprised by the large number of casualties, we should prepare for them.

How?

By realizing that a war is going on, that casualties are inevitable, and that the church is to be a place of refuge. Folks, we must never lose sight of the fact that we are to be a refuge for hurting people—and not only a refuge, but a school as well. "Study to shew yourselves approved unto God," wrote Paul (see 2 Timothy 2:15), "a workman that needeth not to be ashamed, rightly dividing the word of truth."

Not only are we a refuge, and a school—we're also a gym, for we are told to work out our salvation, to exercise it with fear and trembling (Philippians 2:12). A refuge, a school, a gym—we're also a restaurant, serving the milk and meat of the Word (Hebrews 5:12–14), and a temple, wherein we "offer the sacrifice of praise, giving thanks to His name" (see Hebrews 13:15). One of the most important roles of the church is that of travel agency—making sure that people understand the price that has been paid for their ticket to heaven.

Finally, the church of Jesus Christ is a hospital—which is why I believe it is wrong for people to say, "I can't believe I saw him, or her, or them at church on Sunday. They're really sick." If someone's sick—a hospital is exactly where he *should* be!

Imagine a hospital administrator saying, "Check out our hospital. There are no bad odors in our halls, no stains on our linen, not a bedpan on the premises."

"Wow! This place is immaculate," you'd say. "How do you keep it this way?"

"It's simple," the administrator would answer. "We don't admit anyone who's sick. We want only a sterile environment."

That is a ridiculous scenario, yet exactly the way some would like to see the church. However, if we are to be what the Lord wants us to be, we should rejoice when He sends sick people in our direction.

Imagine, on the other hand, a hospital wherein bedpans are overflowing, dirty needles are stacked up, and all of the bandages and blankets are drenched in blood. "What's going on?" you would say.

If the administrator said, "We're not into cleanliness. We're just into helping people," you would most likely say,

"If you allow dirty needles to be used, and bedpans to overflow; if you never mop the floor or wash the linens, you will actually be doing more harm than good because infection will spread and problems will compound."

So, too, on one hand we need to be cognizant of our calling to welcome all into our midst. On the other hand, we are to make sure we are not being infected by allowing disease to spread throughout our congregation.

I camp on this medical analogy for a reason. Paul uses the same kind of imagery in our text as he writes, "Brethren, if a man be overtaken in a fault, ye which are spiritual, restore such an one in the spirit of meekness; considering thyself, lest thou also be tempted" (Galatians 6:1).

The Greek word translated "restore" is a medical term meaning to mend or set a broken bone, so we are to be those who keep our eyes and our hearts open to people who are struggling, to the one who, because of a "broken bone," is unable to walk spiritually.

Who is this one?

In the text before us, he is the blundering believer. . . .

The Blundering Believer

Paraptoma, the Greek word translated "fault" in our text, means "to blunder." *Prolambano*, the Greek word translated "overtaken," is a word used to describe how an animal corners his prey. Thus, the picture is that of a brother who has been crippled by his own mistake and is being chased down by the Enemy.

What are we to do with such a one?

According to Galatians 6:1, if we're spiritual, if we're walking with the Lord, if we want to be used by the Lord, we are to reach out to him and restore him, or literally to "set his broken bone" in a spirit of meekness, realizing we could just as easily have been in his situation.

There are those in our churches who have blundered. Perhaps due to their own stupidity or ignorance, they've broken a bone, and now the Enemy has overtaken them. I'm not speaking of one who has plunged wildly into sin—but of one who has been ensnared. Our responsibility to such a person is to come alongside him and walk with him through his difficulty.

Many years ago, there was a man at Applegate Christian Fellowship who was overtaken in a blunder. Over his head in debt, he was hounded by his creditors. One of his creditors, a member of our church family, said, "I see that you're overtaken, crippled, paralyzed by your financial situation. Therefore, I'm going to meet with you twice a week, and we're going to go through the Scriptures and see everything God's Word has to say about properly managing money— from the procedures given in the law, to the practices Solomon speaks of in Proverbs, to the principles Jesus taught in the gospels. And as we do that, I'm going to help you draw up a budget." Less than a year later, the fellow was virtually out of debt.

That is the kind of thing we need to be about. Our job is not to say, "How could you? Why did you? Why can't you?" Our job is to say, "It's my responsibility and my privilege to walk with you, to restore you, to set the bone once again."

That's what Jesus did. As the disciples sat around the table the night before He would be crucified, arguing about which of them was the greatest, Jesus got up quietly, girded Himself with a towel, and began to wash their feet (John 13). In so doing, Jesus was saying that it's not enough to point out the dirt on someone else's feet. The key is to kneel down and wash them.

It's wrong for me to say, "What she did is unbelievable," or "What he said is out of line," or "What they did is out to lunch," unless I'm willing to do what Jesus did—unless I'm ready to get down on my knees with the water of the Word and wash feet.

While we are to walk with the blundering believer—to wash his feet, and bear his burden until there is healing and restoration—there is another person in our midst who needs to be dealt with in an entirely different manner. . . .

The Bragging Backslider

The man described in 1 Corinthians 5:1–6 was not a blundering believer. He was a bragging backslider who boasted about living in immorality. To the church at Corinth, Paul said, "Although you think you're showing grace to this man by tolerating his behavior and allowing him to continue to fellowship with you, like leaven, his sin will spread through your congregation and bring about terrible repercussions. Therefore, not only for the protection of the body corporately, but for the sinner's restoration personally, you're to turn him over to Satan for the destruction of the flesh," Paul wrote emphatically.

"Excommunicate him. Send him away in order that, after Satan destroys his flesh, his spirit might be saved. Don't allow him to experience the joy and peace of the congregation, the richness of studying the Scriptures, the beauty and holiness of praise. Rather, confine him to the world until, having had his fill of his own sin, he'll see the stupidity of worldly living, and want to come back."

Sadly, there are times when we have to turn a bragging, boasting backslider over to Satan, saying, "We love you. We've talked with you. We've offered ourselves to you. However, because you continue to arrogantly persist in sin that will destroy you and pollute others, you are no longer welcome here."

Jesus taught the same thing in the story of the prodigal son. When the son wanted to go into the world and recklessly spend his father's money, his father let him go. Yet even when famine hit the city, the father didn't wire his son money, or send care packages. Rather, he simply waited for his son to become sick of the world and long for home.

So, too, there are times when the best thing we can do for someone is to let him go, praying that, like the prodigal, he'll eventually "come to himself" (see Luke 15:17), and return home with a different heart. Evidently, that's exactly what happened in the case of the Corinthian man, for in 2 Corinthians 2:6–8, Paul told the church to receive him again.

Turning someone over to Satan is not to be done lightly. Please note three prerequisites outlined in 1 Corinthians 5:4 for this procedure. . . .

It must be done in the name of our Lord Jesus Christ. In other words, it must be done according to the heart and nature of Jesus Christ. We must ask ourselves, "Is this what Jesus would do in this situation?"

It must be done "when ye are gathered together" as a church—not by a single individual. In Matthew 18, Jesus said if we have a problem with someone we're to go to him personally and see if we can work it out. If the situation can't be resolved in that way, we're to take a brother with us and try again. And if that doesn't work, it is up to the church to deal with it corporately.

It must be done "in my [Paul's] spirit." In other words, we need to ask ourselves, "Is turning this individual over to Satan in accordance with what Paul revealed in Scripture? For only a clear and direct violation of Scripture warrants such a drastic procedure.

Finally, there's a third person who comes into our fellowships in need of help and healing.

The Beguiled Brother

Described in James 5:19, 20, the beguiled brother is one who has "erred" or literally "wandered from the truth." Beguiled by some cult or heresy, he is no longer on solid ground biblically. "He who restores such a one," says James, "saves him from death"—either the death of his spiritual life, or physical death that could take him home prematurely.

Jesus talked to a beguiled brother in John 3. Nicodemus, being a "master" or spiritual leader of Israel, should have understood that when Jesus spoke to him of new birth, He was alluding to the passage in Ezekiel 37, wherein dry bones were brought to life again through the power of the wind, the *ruach*, the Spirit. Yet because he had erred in his understanding of spiritual things, Nicodemus missed the allusion, prompting Jesus to say, "Art thou a master of Israel, and knowest not these things?" (John 3:10). But Jesus didn't give up on Nicodemus. He talked with him further. And Nicodemus eventually became one of Jesus' most faithful followers (John 19:39).

What are we to do with the beguiled brother? Just as Jesus did with Nicodemus, we're to talk with him. We're to share with him the Scriptures and the principles of the Word. Because the Word of God is quick and powerful, sharper than any two-edged sword, it will not return void, but will accomplish the purpose for which it was sent (Hebrews 4:12; Isaiah 55:11). It might take a year or two, five or ten—but the Word *will* work in his heart.

Saints, casualties of the war that is escalating in these last days will come into our midst and travel with us. We need wisdom to determine whether they are backsliding believers with whom we should walk, bragging backsliders from whom we should turn, or beguiled brothers to whom we should talk.

May the Father help us to make the right diagnosis and to use the right prescription in each situation in order that people might be healed and helped, strengthened and set free, for the furtherance of the kingdom, and the glory of the Son.

EPHESIANS

Background to Ephesians

The Book of Ephesians has been commonly, and I believe, correctly called "the Alps of the New Testament," for the reader ascends into the heavenlies in this glorious Epistle—and the view is breathtaking indeed.

The flow of Ephesians follows an order similar to each of Paul's Epistles. It is this order, I believe, that is the solution to the works-oriented, legalistic ministry mentality seen in the lives of believers and churches who emphasize duty prior to an understanding of doctrine. You see, if we simply think through, bask in, and meditate on the doctrine of what Christ has done for us, we find ourselves saying, "I *want* to serve Him." Duty then becomes not a demand but a delight.

For example, Paul's injunction for wives to submit to their husbands is not a problem if husbands and wives understand they're both already seated in heavenly places. But if a woman doesn't understand Ephesians 1—3, she'll chafe under Ephesians 5. Likewise, kids will rebel when Paul tells them to obey their parents because it will sound like a burdensome obligation—unless they grasp where they already are in Christ.

Over the years, I have observed that people read through the first half of Ephesians very quickly in order to get to the practical stuff about husbands and wives, employees and employers, children and parents. But sooner than later, they find chapters 4, 5, and 6 burdensome and legalistic because they haven't spent time in chapters 1, 2, and 3.

To remedy this, we will take our time scaling the mountain of this Epistle and seeing who we are in Christ.

After buying fanny packs (the kind with a water bottle and a place to put granola bars), walking sticks, and bandanas, my wife, Tammy, and I were ready for our big hike. I drove her up to Mount McLoughlin, just a few miles from Applegate Christian Fellowship, parked in the paved parking lot at the base of the mountain, said, "Come on, hon'"—and we started walking.

If you haven't climbed Mount McLoughlin, it's a great experience. The trail winds up the side of the mountain and is relatively easy. The view at the top is exhilarating and inspiring, so I couldn't wait to show it to Tammy. So we walked and we walked and we walked. And we walked. And finally, I thought, *You know, we've been walking for almost an hour and a half and we still haven't ascended very high.*

"Are you sure we're going up?" she asked.

"Yeah," I said confidently.

A few minutes later, I stopped and said, "You know, we really aren't gaining much altitude"—only to turn around and see the mountain *behind* us. For an hour and a half, I thought I was climbing a mountain, when in reality I was walking away from it!

So we sat down, ate our granola bars, and went home.

A lot of people set off on similar journeys, saying, "Okay. I'm going to get my family together. My wife is going to submit to me, and I'm going to love her. Our kids are going to be obedient. We're going to be good bosses, or good employees. We're going to nail Ephesians 4, 5, and 6. But they walk and walk and walk—never gaining much elevation because they're going in the wrong direction.

The divine design of Ephesians is first to sit with Christ in the heavenlies (2:6), then to walk worthy of the vocation to which we're called (4:1), and finally to stand fast (6:13). All too often, we reverse the order. We think if we stand fast and hold our ground, then we can start walking, and maybe one day we'll sit in the heavenlies.

In grace-oriented theology, the order is to first sit with Christ in the heavenlies, then to walk with Him responsively, and finally to stand fast in Him securely.

That's why I'm looking forward to this study immensely. . . .

EPHESIANS

1 Ephesians 1:1 (a)
Paul, an apostle of Jesus Christ by the will of God . . .

"Make your calling and election sure," Peter declared (2 Peter 1:10). Paul was one who knew his calling. He was called by the will of God to be an apostle, prepared from the earliest days of his life. Growing up the son of a rabbi, seated at the feet of Gamaliel—the foremost rabbinical scholar of the day—Paul eventually became a member of the Sanhedrin, the Jewish Supreme Court. And all of his studying, all of his efforts to be righteous in his own energy, all of his attempts to keep the law blamelessly would be preparatory to make him the minister of the gospel of grace. Not only did Paul know his calling—he also knew the Bible. With this knowledge came the absolute frustration of trying to live under the law.

All of Paul's experiences prepared him to be an apostle of Jesus Christ. The same is true for you. God wants to place each one of us in the spot for which He has prepared us from the beginning. God's will is not heavy or difficult. His will fits perfectly with the personality and the experiences He's given you.

God sees where He wants you to serve Him—whether on a construction site, a classroom, or a courtroom; as a butcher, baker, or banker. We often make a mistake in thinking that what we're doing is second best, that if we were really serious about our faith, we'd be in "full-time ministry." Wrong. The Lord stations His men and women ingeniously where He sees they can minister most effectively and where people around them will be impacted eternally.

What has God prepared and trained *you* for? Be content to do what God has called you to do—to serve where He has placed you—for yours is just as holy and high a calling as that of any preacher or apostle.

Ephesians 1:1 (b)
. . . to the saints which are at Ephesus, and
to the faithful in Christ Jesus.

Paul writes to the saints at Ephesus and to the
faithful in Christ Jesus. "That's not me," you say.
"I'm no saint."

Yes, you are. We often think of saints in the
terms of canonization—the procedure where a
group of cardinals or bishops analyze a person's
life to determine if it meets the requirement for
beatification, or sainthood. But that's not what
the word "saint" means. "Saint" simply means
"set apart." Thus, because Paul writes to the
"set-apart ones," the saved ones—if you're a
Christian, this letter is to you.

Ephesians 1:2 (a)
Grace be to you, and peace . . .

Paul's salutation is common throughout his
Epistles as he links grace to peace. He always
places them in this order because one will never
have true peace until he really gets a handle on
grace. When it finally sinks in that we are blessed
not because of our devotions, not because of our
prayer, not because of our studying, but solely
because of what Christ did for us, entirely because of grace—then we have peace. Then we can
talk to our Father. Then we receive blessing.

Ephesians 1:2 (b)
. . . from God our Father, and from the Lord
Jesus Christ.

Not only do Paul's letters begin with grace and
peace, but they also begin and end with "God our
Father and our Lord Jesus Christ."

The question arises: Why is there no mention
of the Holy Spirit? Didn't Paul believe in the Trinity? Of course he did. But in John 16:13, Jesus
said when the Holy Spirit came, He wouldn't
speak of Himself. Thus, I suggest to you that, as
He inspired Paul to write this letter, the Holy
Spirit purposely left His name out.

Ephesians 1:3 (a)
Blessed be the God and Father of our Lord
Jesus Christ . . .

Here begins the longest sentence in the Bible,
the beginning of the first stanza of the sweet,
sweet song of salvation.

- The first stanza, verses 3–6, declares the
  work of the Father in the past.
- The second stanza, verses 7–12, celebrates
  the work of the Son in the present.

- The third stanza, verses 13–14, trumpets the
  work of the Spirit in the future.

Each stanza ends with the refrain: "to the
praise of His glory."

Ephesians 1:3 (b)
. . . who hath blessed us with all spiritual
blessings in heavenly places . . .

"I am so blessed," Paul says from inside a Roman prison. "Oh, maybe not physically, maybe
not materially—but spiritually, because the
blessings found in Jesus Christ are spiritual
blessings." How the church in America needs to
understand this. Many church meetings today
sound like Amway conventions, with teachings
based on Deuteronomy 28 about how to structure
finances and how to manipulate the system spiritually in order to be blessed materially.

But those who teach such things fail to understand that all of the Old Testament truths dealing
with physical, financial, or military blessings depict New Testament truths that are spiritual,
eternal, and heavenly. For example, David desired to break the bones and kick in the teeth of
his enemies (Psalm 58:6) and wished that the
heads of the Babylonians would be bashed with
rocks (Psalm 137:9). Does this mean we're to find
our enemies, break their bones, and smash their
skulls? No. Paul says all of these things are examples or types, for we'll see in chapter 6 that our
wrestling is not with flesh and blood, but with
principalities and powers. It's spiritual wrestling.

All of the Old Testament stories—from Ehud
sticking a sword into Eglon in Judges 3, to Jonathan and his armor bearer destroying an entire
army in 1 Samuel 14—help us understand how
we gain spiritual victory. The Bible will be nothing but confusion and disillusionment for you if
you don't understand that all of the Old Testament pictures, stories, and precepts point to the
eternal, spiritual life we have in Christ Jesus.

Just as you don't bring bulls and oxen to
slaughter, just as you realize the sacrificial system was to paint a picture of the Lamb of God
who took away our sin—understand that the
same principle carries through the entire Old
Testament. We're rich in *heavenly* places. We're
blessed with all *spiritual* blessings.

Ephesians 1:3 (c)
. . . in Christ:

"We're blessed with all spiritual blessings in
heavenly places," Paul writes jubilantly from his
prison cell, "and they're all in Christ"—not from
Christ, but *in* Christ.

- "Oh, Lord," we say, "I need some bread."
  "I am the Bread," Jesus answers (John 6:35)
- "Show me the way," we cry.
  "I am the Way," Jesus declares (John 14:6).
- "Tell me the truth," we pray.
  "I am the Truth," Jesus proclaims (John 14:6).

We think we need help in this area, or deliverance from that thing. We think we need satisfaction in a profession, or blessing in a relationship—little knowing that our heart's desire will only be truly fulfilled in Jesus. "Yea, all the promises of God are in Him yea and amen" (see 2 Corinthians 1:20). All the promises of God are fulfilled in *Him,* in Jesus.

One night, with Tammy away at a pastors' wives conference, and the kids tucked in, I grabbed my Bible and had the best time reading Isaiah 54 while walking the streets of Jacksonville. God spoke to me through each phrase as I stopped under the streetlights to read another verse and marvel how it related to me. I returned home awed at how the Lord walked with me in the evening hour.

Do I tell you this to impress you? No. I say it because you can find the same thing tonight. Turn off the TV. Put down the *Time* magazine. Grab your Bible, go for a walk, and I promise you God will meet you.

"Draw near to Me," He says, "and I will draw near to you" (see James 4:8). Does this apply only to people who seem to have everything together? No. God says, "Draw near to Me—no matter who you are—and I will meet you wherever you are," even, as Paul discovered, in jail.

Ephesians 1:4 (a)
According as he hath chosen us in him . . .

Here, we arrive at the interesting discussion of election. Try to figure out the doctrine of election—that we were chosen in Him, yet we also have a choice—and you may lose your mind. But try to explain away the doctrine of election, and you will surely lose your heart—for as confusing as election may appear to be, the fact that God actually chose us warms and strengthens our hearts.

Ephesians 1:4 (b)
. . . before the foundation of the world . . .

God chose us. When? Before the foundation of the world. D. L. Moody made a statement with which I concur heartily when he said, "I'm so glad God chose me before I was born, because I don't think He would have chosen me after I've lived!"

Ephesians 1:4 (c)
. . . that we should be holy and without blame before him in love:

Leviticus 19:2, where we are told that we shall be holy, is made possible by Ephesians 1:4, where we are told we are chosen. You see, wanting a holy people for Himself, God knew He would have to choose them Himself because, as Romans 3:11 declares, there is none that seeks God.

"Didn't Joshua say, 'Choose you this day whom ye will serve'" (Joshua 24:15)?

Yes.

"But I thought Paul says God chose us."

He does.

How can God choose us but still give us the free will to choose Him? It's as if, when a person decides to choose the Lord, he walks through a door over which is written the words, "Whosoever will, let him come" (see Revelation 22:17). Yet the moment he walks through the door, he looks back and sees the words, "Ye have not chosen me, but I have chosen you" (John 15:16).

Ephesians 1:5 (a)
Having predestinated us . . .

There is a predetermination concerning salvation. But guess what. God is never seen anywhere at any time in the Bible predestining someone to go to hell. He only predestines people to go to heaven.

He that overcometh, the same shall be clothed in white raiment; and I will not blot out his name out of the book of life, but I will confess his name before my Father, and before his angels.
                                    Revelation 3:5

The implication of this passage is enormous, for it seems to suggest that every man's name is written in the Book of Life—until he makes it clear that he has no interest *in* the Lord, that he doesn't want to walk *with* the Lord, and that he wants to turn his back *on* the Lord. Only then is his name blotted out.

Thus, when the Book of Life is opened at the Great White Throne judgment, when all of the unbelievers are brought before God and discover their names absent from its pages, it's not that their names were never in the book. It's that their names were blotted out because they chose not to accept God's plan of salvation for their lives.

For whom he did foreknow, he also did predestinate to be conformed to the image of his Son, that he might be the firstborn among many brethren.
                                    Romans 8:29

Before the world was even spoken into existence, God saw the people who would respond to His love. Whom He foreknew, He predestined. He said, "I can see that Mitch is going to respond when I make Myself known to him, when the gospel is shared with him. Therefore, I predestine Mitch to be part of My eternal kingdom."

"Well," you say, "then why was someone who God knew wouldn't respond to Him allowed to live in the first place?"

The answer is that if a person was not allowed to play his life out to the fullest extent, he could protest at the Great White Throne."

"I got rid of you early because I could see that you weren't going to respond to Me," God would say.

"Oh, but I would have," the unbeliever would protest.

"No, you wouldn't," God would say.

"Yes, I would have," the unbeliever would insist.

And there would be a perpetual argument. So even though it is His desire that none should perish, but that all should come to repentance (2 Peter 3:9), God lets Joe Schmo live his seventy years to prove that righteous and true are His judgments (Revelation 16:7).

Then why does hell exist?

Jesus gave us the reason. Hell exists for Satan and his demons (Matthew 25:41). It was never God's intent to allow anyone on earth to spend eternity in hell. In fact, the only way anyone can get there is over the dead body of His Son.

Ephesians 1:5 (b)
. . . unto the adoption of children by Jesus Christ to himself . . .

Huiothesia, the Greek word translated "adoption," means "taking the place of an adult son." Therefore, the Ephesians would think of adoption not in terms of bringing a baby into a family, but in terms of a slave becoming a joint heir in his master's business. New Testament adoption speaks of a mature cooperation. As we saw in Galatians, spiritual adoption speaks not so much of our entry into the family of God, for we enter into His family by regeneration when we are born again. Spiritual adoption speaks not of how we enter into the family, but of our involvement with the family.

If you're a new Christian, you might be "young" in terms of regeneration. But when you were born again, you were simultaneously adopted (Romans 8:14–17)—making you a mature member of God's family. Therefore, don't let the Enemy whisper in your ear, "You can't do this or go there or be that because you're too young in the faith." No, when you were saved, you also were adopted and made a joint heir with Christ. You're treated as an adult as you partner with the Lord and become involved in significant things for His kingdom.

Ephesians 1:5 (c)–6 (a)
. . . according to the good pleasure of his will, to the praise of the glory of his grace . . .

Here's why God adopted you. Here's why He predestined you. Here's why He chose you. Here's why He's blessed you in Christ in heavenly places: Because it's His good pleasure to the praise of the glory of His grace. Period. Knowing that we are elected, predestined, and adopted, we can have the tendency to think we're pretty special—that God knew what He was doing when He chose us. In reality, however, just as He did with another group of people, God chose us not because of who we are, but *in spite* of who we are. . . .

The LORD did not set his love upon you, nor choose you, because ye were more in number than any people; for ye were the fewest of all people: Speak not thou in thine heart, after that the LORD thy God hath cast them out from before thee, saying, For my righteousness the LORD hath brought me in to possess this land: but for the wickedness of these nations the LORD doth drive them out from before thee. Understand therefore, that the LORD thy God giveth thee not this good land to possess it for thy righteousness; for thou art a stiffnecked people.   Deuteronomy 7:7; 9:4, 6

Here, God says to the people of Israel, "The blessings you enjoy, the victories you'll see are not because you're a mighty people, for you're small and weak. Nor is it because you're righteous in heart, for you're stiff-necked and stubborn. But I must drive the Canaanites from the land in order that they won't infect others with their sin—and I'm going to use you to do it."

Like Israel, we are called a chosen people. Why are we chosen? According to the verse before us, we are chosen to the praise of the glory of His grace. That is, we are chosen to showcase God's grace. This means that in the ages to come, millions of angels, living creatures, and all of creation will look at you and me who have been chosen, who have been adopted, who have been elevated to be with Christ in heavenly places—and they will say, "Look at the people God chose to be joint heir with His Son. They're just a bunch of ragtag renegades. Truly His grace is unbelievable, unfathomable, incomparable!"

That's why Paul said, "Look around you. There are not many wise, many strong, many noble among you" (see 1 Corinthians 1:26).

When I was in high school, I thought the key to an effective ministry was to get the quarterback and the cheerleader saved, to go for the head honchos, the big guns, the beautiful people. But that's not what Jesus did. He turned the world upside down with the street people, the outcasts, the forgotten folks. In other words, He used people just like us.

Ephesians 1:6 (b)
. . . wherein he hath made us accepted . . .

The literal idea of the word "accepted" is "embraced." I like that! We're caught up in God's embrace. Why? Read on.

Ephesians 1:6 (c)
. . . in the beloved.

We are accepted because we're in the beloved—we're in Christ. It doesn't matter how you feel about yourself. You don't have to take your spiritual temperature hour by hour. You don't have to wonder, *Am I hot? Am I cold? How am I doing?* You won't have to go through the kind of introspection that will inevitably set you up for spiritual depression if you understand the simple principle that you are embraced not because of who you are, but because of where you are. You're in Christ. And once you accept this truth, you will enjoy your relationship with the Father in a new way. You'll throw away your spiritual thermometer; you'll quit analyzing how you're doing; and you'll rejoice that you are simply, totally, wonderfully in Christ.

Ephesians 1:7
In whom we have redemption through his blood, the forgiveness of sins, according to the riches of his grace.

Here we come to another high point, another peak in this mountain range of spiritual truth—the glorious doctrine of redemption. Jesus told us that he who commits sin is a slave to sin (John 8:34). Therefore, He came on the scene to buy us, to deliver us, to *redeem* us from the slave market of sin.

Ephesians 1:8, 9
Wherein he hath abounded toward us in all wisdom and prudence; having made known unto us the mystery of his will, according

to his good pleasure which he hath purposed in himself.

The Greek word translated "mystery" is *musterion,* or, "that which was previously hidden or obscured." God has forgiven us, chosen us, predestined us, and elevated us—but He's also made known to us, by His grace, the mystery of life. What is this mystery? Read on.

Ephesians 1:10
That in the dispensation of the fulness of times he might gather together in one all things in Christ, both which are in heaven, and which are on earth; even in him.

What is the big picture? What is the mystery? It is that in due time, *everything* in heaven and earth will be gathered together in Christ, around Christ, and for Christ.

When my son Benjamin was seven years old, we went to Pappy's for a pepperoni pizza. "This is the kind of pizza the Ninja Turtles™ eat," Ben declared. "They like it so much, they even steal it."

"They do?" I said. "Well, that reminds me of a story. . . ."

And I proceeded to tell Ben the sad story of how Achan stole from Jericho (Joshua 7). When I finished, Benny understood that stealing leads to problems and pain. And suddenly, sitting down over a pizza at Pappy's had meaning, substance, and depth in a way it wouldn't have had the moment not been brought together in Christ as we talked about the things of the Lord.

You've found this to be true. Whether it's talking to your kids or planting flowers in your garden, listening to a co-worker or practicing with a teammate—whenever you're focused on Christ and bringing the moment under the authority of Christ, you're right in the middle of the flow of what God says life is all about.

Isn't God gracious to make His will known to us? After all, He could have said, "There's a mystery to life. Figure it out. Good luck." But He didn't. I'm so thankful I can live wisely and prudently because He's made known to me the mystery that everything is in Christ and for Christ.

Are you full of joy tonight? Are you at peace? Are you content? Do you have rest? If so, you understand the mystery of His will. Are you bitter, angry, frustrated, or upset? Then you don't. On any given day, the extent to which you understand the mystery of His will, that will be the extent to which peace reigns in your heart.

Ephesians 1:11 (a)
In whom also we have obtained an inheritance . . .

We've obtained an inheritance not *from* Christ, but *in* Him.

When Tammy became my wife, she received an inheritance—all that I owned—which was basically a house with a mortgage and a 1972 Volkswagen. But she didn't marry me, as far as I know, for my house and Volkswagen. Those were just added benefits.

So, too, when we get to heaven, yes, we will have all sorts of wonderful experiences and marvelous things that eyes haven't seen and ears haven't heard (1 Corinthians 2:9). But those things will pale in comparison to the inheritance we have in Jesus. When we walk down the aisle, so to speak, in that heavenly marriage scene to stand at the side of our Bridegroom, we will at last experience what it means to be absolutely, incredibly, wonderfully fulfilled because *He* is our inheritance. If you're in a less than satisfactory marriage situation, hang in there because what you're really craving is the Ultimate Bridegroom. . . .

As Nabal sheared his vast flocks in Carmel, David and his band of four hundred men protected him from the bandits to the south. David sent ten of these men to Carmel in order to replenish their provisions. But when the ten men found Nabal and asked for payment for their protection, his response was, "Who is David?"

Upon hearing this, David said to his men, "Strap on your swords, guys. We're going to show Nabal who I am." However, as David and his men were en route to do Nabal in, they were intercepted by Nabal's wife, Abigail, a woman of beautiful countenance and good understanding (1 Samuel 25:3).

"Listen, you guys," she said. "My husband is just living up to his name, which means "fool." He's one brick short of a full load. He's just not all there. You don't want to lower yourself to his level. You don't want his blood on your hands. You're bigger than that. I've been baking all day. Take this bread and wine and have a feast. But don't touch my husband."

"You've spoken wisely," David said. So he and his men ate the bread, drank the wine, and rode back. Time passed—and when Nabal heard that David and his men had almost killed him, he fell over backward, broke his neck, and died (1 Samuel 25:38).

Husbands and wives, maybe if you were in Abigail's sandals, and you heard that David was going to kill your spouse, you would have said, "Oh, well. God's will be done. Who am I to stop David and four hundred men?" But you know what? Had Abigail let events run their course, she would have missed out on being married to David (1 Samuel 25:42).

Let me tell you how to miss out on what you could enjoy in the ages to come in the palace of the Son of David, your Bridegroom, Jesus Christ: Bail out.

"But I don't love him anymore."

"I can't love her anymore."

On your wedding day did you say, "I'll stay with you as long as I love you"? Marriage isn't based primarily on love. It's based on commitment. You said, "For better or for worse, for richer or poorer, in sickness or in health, until death separates us." End of discussion.

Anyone can find reason to walk out. You're an only child. You're afraid of heights. You're allergic to seafood. If you go to enough counselors and read enough books, you'll find a reason you can say, "In my case, I'm justified in walking away from my marriage." But if you do, you're going to miss out. Am I saying you won't go to heaven? No. I am saying, however, that there is an inheritance, a special reward, a crown of life awaiting those who walk in obedience (Revelation 2:10).

The Son of David, Jesus Christ, is impressed by you, who, like Abigail, choose to simply hang in there, knowing that better days are coming. He finds you, like Abigail, to be a person of beautiful countenance and good understanding because you understand the shortness of life and the vastness of eternity.

Ephesians 1:11 (b)
. . . being predestinated according to the purpose of him who worketh all things after the counsel of his own will:

"Who hath counseled the Lord?" asked Isaiah (Isaiah 40:13).

The answer? Most of us.

"Now, Lord," we say, "I don't know if You're seeing this right. I don't know if You understand the severity of my situation. Lord. Did You see what he just did? Did You hear what she just said?"—as if we expect the Lord to say, "No. Thanks for filling Me in! What should I do about it?"

God works everything after the counsel of His *own* will. And although we might be tempted to ask what right the Lord has to do this, Paul asks the much more logical question when he says, "Who are you—a lump of clay—to question the plan of the Father?" (see Romans 9:20)

I'm sure Jeremiah was confused when, after preaching forty years to the people of Judah, no one responded. So it was that at a certain point in his ministry, the Lord said to him, "Jeremiah, take a break. Go to the house of the potter and there you will learn a lesson." When Jeremiah did, indeed, go to the house of the potter, he watched him place a lump of clay upon the wheel and position his foot upon the pedal. As the wheel began to spin round and round, the potter began to put pressure on the clay, skillfully shaping and molding it into something of beauty (Jeremiah 18).

There are times when I feel as though I'm spinning my wheels, going in circles, feeling pressured. "Where are You, Father?" I cry. "Don't You care about me? How could You allow this to happen in my life?" But then the Lord brings me back to the very simple realization that the hands that put pressure on my life, and the foot that spins the wheel have holes in them where nails pierced them as the Master Potter hung on the Cross to die in my place.

That's why Communion is so very important in the life of the believer. All of the questions and confusion I feel as I analyze my situation and question my circumstances are solved immediately when I remember Jesus' unbelievable, undeniable love for me.

Ephesians 1:12
That we should be to the praise of his glory, who first trusted in Christ.

When we Abigails are by the side of our Greater than David, not only will we glory in Him, but He will be glorified throughout the ages to come because of His work in us.

Ephesians 1:13
In whom ye also trusted, after that ye heard the word of truth, the gospel of your salvation: in whom also after that ye believed, ye were sealed with that holy Spirit of promise.

"Sealing" speaks of ownership and would have been a term very familiar to Paul's readers. It was at Ephesus that crates were sealed with the imprint of merchants' rings before being shipped across the Aegean. "Sealing" speaks of commercial ownership. But "sealing" also speaks of commitment because the modern Greek translation of Paul's *koine* Greek for the word "sealed" conveys the idea of an engagement ring.

The picture is perfect. When you were saved, the Lord put the seal of His Holy Spirit on you, signifying that He would see you through not only your voyage across the Aegean but also your voyage across the storm-tossed ocean of life to bring you safely to His side as His bride.

Ephesians 1:14
Which is the earnest of our inheritance until the redemption of the purchased possession, unto the praise of his glory.

If you wanted to buy my VW, I'd hold it for you—if you put down some "earnest" money to show you were serious about it. That's what the Holy Spirit is—a "down payment" to show God will finish that which He has begun in us (Philippians 1:6). Think of the times when you have been most profoundly touched or impacted by the Lord—the times when the Holy Spirit welled up within you, or when you felt enveloped by His presence. Those are simply earnest money, a down payment, "sneak previews of coming attractions."

Ephesians 1:15 (a)
Wherefore . . .

Whether you're sharing with a neighbor, working with your kids, or dealing with your spouse, I think a real key that is often neglected and overlooked is that which Paul models for us here in Ephesians 1. After talking to the Ephesians about the Lord, he talks to the Lord about the Ephesians. He prays for them. And what a difference that makes. After talking with someone who may be facing a difficulty or a challenge, I have found over and over again that if I don't talk *to* the Lord concerning those to whom I've talked *about* Him, the loop never quite closes and frustration sets in. Even in my own home, after saying a word or two in a difficult circumstance, if I simply slip away and pray—a peace enters the situation that is not the result of my exhortation, but simply because the Lord moved in through a simple prayer of intercession.

Mom and Dad, husband, wife, roommate, or co-worker—would you try this? When you feel tensions rise, slip away, step outside, and don't just count to five. Pray. Because we wrestle against principalities and powers, there are forces at work seeking to cause tension in our homes, in our marriages, at school, or on the job site—and we need to wrestle against them.

Paul lives this. Throughout his ministry, we see him sharing *about* the Lord and then following it up by talking *to* the Lord.

Ephesians 1:15 (b)
. . . I also, after I heard of your faith in the
Lord Jesus, and love unto all the saints,

Here, we come to one of two prayers in this
Epistle. Two aspects of these inspired prayers of
Paul surprise me. First, I am surprised for whom
Paul prays. He says, "Because you guys at Ephe-
sus are saints, because you understand the big
picture, because I have heard of your faith in the
Lord and your love for God's people, I am moti-
vated to pray for you."

Who do you pray for? I have a tendency to pray
for those who are hurting, for those who are going through tragedies and difficulties, for those
who are backsliding and failing—and that's fine.
But here Paul is saying something very different
when he says, "When I heard how *well* you're doing, I was moved to pray for you."

I think a lot of times we have it a bit backward.
We follow the American health program mentality when we should be copying that of the ancient Chinese. That is, in our culture, we don't
go to the doctor until we're sick. But in ancient
China, people paid a doctor an annual stipend
to keep them *well.*

I think we need to learn from Paul and pray for
people who are doing well because Satan doesn't
use his heavy artillery on the guy who's getting
drunk and indulging his flesh. He saves it for
those who are walking with the Lord, loving the
saints, and believing in Jesus. Many times, we
see strong people fall hard. Could it be that perhaps we could have propped them up, been a
shield around them, a blessing for them if we had
followed the example of Paul and prayed for them
while they were doing well?

Ephesians 1:16
Cease not to give thanks for you, making
mention of you in my prayers.

Second, notice not only for whom Paul prays,
but notice *when* he prays. The Greek idea of
"cease not" is the same as "a tickle in the throat."
In other words, Paul would be praying throughout the day as naturally and as spontaneously as
if he were clearing a tickle in his throat.

Ephesians 1:17
That the God of our Lord Jesus Christ, the
Father of glory, may give unto you the spirit
of wisdom and revelation in the knowledge
of him.

All of us crave wisdom and revelation. Each of
us longs for instruction and insight in knowing
how we should walk, what we should do, and
where we should go. But notice what Paul tells us.
It is profoundly simple and simply profound, for
he says that the wisdom and revelation you and I
so desperately desire is found solely in the knowledge of *Him.* Peter and John found this to be
true. The singular explanation for their ability to
boldly and intelligently address the multitude
was the acknowledgment that they had been with
Jesus (Acts 4:13).

When people ask, "What should I do? What is
God's will in this situation?" the answer is very
simple. The wisdom you need, the revelation you
seek is found in knowing Jesus. How do we know
Jesus? By spending time in the Gospels. You may
be working your way through Ezekiel, or chewing on Romans. Make sure, however, that you
daily take in something from Matthew, Mark,
Luke, or John. I believe a real key to understanding God's will for your life is to continually focus
on Jesus. There's only one Isaiah, only one Hebrews—but there are four Gospels. Could it be
that, in this, God is saying, "I don't want you to
miss this. Whatever else you're learning, the key
to it all is My Son"?

Just as Jesus said on the Emmaus Road, all
Scripture points to Him (Luke 24:27). If you're
spending time with Him in the Gospels, the rest
of the Word will become clear.

Ephesians 1:18 (a)
The eyes of your understanding being en-
lightened . . .

Finally, notice *how* Paul prays. We so often
pray about the fruit of issues. Paul prays for their
root. We pray, "Lord, get Billy off drugs." Paul
would pray, "Lord, give Billy wisdom. Let him
know You."

So often we want to change behavior patterns
through pressure, counseling, or by reasoning.
The change, however, doesn't come until a person
has revelation, until his eyes are opened. How are
a person's eyes opened? Through prayer. Be like
Paul. Pray without ceasing for your kids, for your
family, and for your friends. Pray that they'll see
Jesus.

Ephesians 1:18 (b)
. . . that ye may know what is the hope of
his calling . . .

Throughout Scripture, the word "hope" always
refers to that which is coming, to that which is
ahead. I'm convinced the single greatest problem
carnal Christians have is that they don't know

the hope of His calling. They don't know the reality of heaven. Consequently, they constantly strive for material things and are continually caught up in carnal pursuits. They're depressed and discouraged because they don't see the big picture of eternity.

If you're not happy, neither will you be with a change of location, salary, or ministry. You'll not be happy until you know the hope of His calling. That's why Jesus said, "Let not your hearts be troubled . . . I go to prepare a place for you" (see John 14:1, 2). The key to overcoming a troubled, perplexed, stressed heart is to focus on the hope of His calling, on what's ahead, on heaven.

"But heaven seems so far away," you say. "For years, I've been hearing Jesus could come at any time. But where is He?"

"Beloved," Peter said, "be not ignorant of this one thing: One day is with the Lord as a thousand years, and a thousand years as one day" (2 Peter 3:8).

A day is as a thousand years. Maybe you're saying, "Is that ever true! Will this day *ever* end?" If you are in a strained marriage, a single person aware of your loneliness, or if you're physically afflicted, a day can, indeed, seem like a thousand years. "Lord, where are You?" you cry. "I've been talking to You. I have total trust in You. But where *are* You?"

This day is as a thousand years because in your day of difficulty and dilemma, pressure and pain, sadness and sorrow, you have the unique opportunity to share the fellowship of the Lord's suffering, and to pray for others in a way you never would have been able to otherwise. We want to get out of the trial, solve the problem, move on. The Lord, however, says, "Not so fast." I want this day to be as a thousand years for you. The discoveries you'll make, the understanding you will glean, the gifts of praise, and the expression of even frustrated prayer will affect you for the next zillion years. Because My coming is near, and your heavenly account is small, I'm giving you an opportunity to make some huge investments in the few days that remain before you go to heaven."

You for whom this day has seemed as a thousand years—rejoice. Savor each moment. Extract each minute. Take every opportunity in this long, long day you're in to thank the Father for the opportunity to store up treasure that will make you rich for eternity.

Ephesians 1:18 (c)
. . . and what the riches of the glory of his inheritance in the saints.

As saints, we're God's inheritance, His treasure, His prize.

In Jesus' day, men would bury their treasure in a field for safekeeping. But if a man died before he could tell someone where his treasure was buried, it would be left in the field until someone stumbled upon it. Such is the case in Matthew 13. . . .

One day a man is walking through a field. He trips over something, brushes the dirt from it, and discovers it's a treasure. So what does he do? He does everything he can to buy the field in which the treasure is buried. Because he wants the field? No, because he's after the treasure.

Jesus said that's the way the kingdom is. The field is the world. God the Father gave the world to Adam. But when Adam sinned, he inadvertently handed it over to Satan. That's why there is rape, famine, pollution, corruption, and death on our planet. Jesus came to buy the world back. Why? Because He wants to hang out on the Columbia River? No. He's not interested in the world. He bought the world to get the treasure. He bought the world to get *you.*

Ephesians 1:19, 20
And what is the exceeding greatness of his power to usward who believe, according to the working of his mighty power, which he wrought in Christ, when he raised him from the dead, and set him at his own right hand in the heavenly places.

"I just don't know if I can get over my smoking habit," we sigh.

"My temper just seems to control me," we say.

"These lustful thoughts will always be with me," we decide.

In response, Paul wouldn't pray, "Lord, give them power over their sin." He'd pray, "Lord, help them see the power they already have." The dominating power of the resurrected Christ is *already* in us.

Ephesians 1:21
Far above all principality, and power, and might, and dominion, and every name that is named, not only in this world, but also in that which is to come.

Principality, power, might, and dominion are all words that describe various categories of demonic entities and angelic beings. Jesus has power over them all, and the same power that caused Him to be resurrected is in you. Whatever you're struggling with, whatever I'm wrestling through is infinitesimal compared to the power it took to raise Christ into heaven and give him dominion over all. Therefore, if I'm in bondage, it's not because I need more power, but because I've failed to utilize that power that is already in me.

- We say, "I'm addicted."
  God says, "You're free."
- We say, "I'm wounded."
  God says, "You're as whole as you need to be."
- We say, "I need counseling. I need drugs. I need a program."
  God says, "You have Me."

"That's nice-sounding theology," you say. "But how does it work out practically?"

Read on.

Ephesians 1:22 (a)
And hath put all things under his feet . . .

All things are under His feet. What things? Dominions, powers, addictions, problems, pornography, profanity, gossip, depression, meanness, temper, sadness, laziness—whatever it is you can't get over.

"But my problem is so overwhelming," you say.

It couldn't be any more overwhelming than the waves threatening to drown the disciples. Yet even the waves that rolled over their heads were under Jesus' feet, the very waves He walked upon to go to His disciples (Matthew 14:25).

Nothing is over His head. All things are under His feet. Jesus is in absolute control of every situation, be it financial, physical, relational, vocational, or parental. Whatever might seem to be rolling your way, ready to sink your boat and wipe you out is already under His feet—and might be the very path He chooses upon which to walk to you.

Ephesians 1:22 (b), 23
. . . and gave him to be the head over all things to the church, which is his body, the fulness of him that filleth all in all.

The name of the game is community. We need another. We need to be with brothers and sisters who pray with us and care about us because the more closely we're linked to the body, the more clearly we'll experience the authority of Jesus' headship. That's just the way it works.

The church is the "fulness of Him which filleth all in all." How can we be full of the Lord? The church is where the headship of Jesus will be enjoyed. You can say, "I can study the Bible on my own." But that's not the heart of the Father any more than if I went home and said, "Okay, kids, grab your plates, and each of you go into your room to have Sunday dinner by yourself." If I did, they would still be getting nutrition. They would survive. But the heart of a true father is to see his kids *together*—interacting, loving, sharing, growing.

Many a time, when I go to church for a meeting, a study, a prayer time, I find I am attached to the body once again. In a very real and practical way, I hear the voice of the Lord anew. I am reminded that the storm that threatens to intimidate me is underneath the feet of the One who is the Head of the body.

2 In the second chapter of Ephesians, the theme is God's work—God's work *for* us in verses 4–7, God's work *in* us in verses 8–9, God's work *through* us in verse 10, and God's work *among* us in verses 11–22.

Ephesians 2:1
And you hath he quickened, who were dead in trespasses and sins.

God's work in us is crucial because of the sin that worked against us. The words "hath he quickened" are in italics because they aren't in the original text. Therefore, Ephesians 2:1 originally read, "And you were dead in trespasses and sins."

Death is separation in three ways—the first is physical death, when the spirit is separated from the body. Although the medical community debates endlessly about what actually constitutes death, the Bible makes it very clear that death occurs the moment the spirit departs.

Second, there is spiritual death—that which is spoken of here in Ephesians 2:1. Maybe you've seen *National Geographic* specials on zombies in Haiti and other islands of the Caribbean. Zombies are people who walk around in an almost corpselike stupor due to voodoo, demons, and drug-induced states. Spiritually, we were like zombies—alive physically, but because we had no sensitivity toward the Lord, we were dead spiritually.

Third, there is eternal death, spoken of in 2 Thessalonians 1:9, referring to those who refuse the life-giving gift of salvation and are cast into outer darkness.

Ephesians 2:2 (a)
Wherein in time past ye walked . . .

The word translated "walked" speaks of meandering, or walking without direction or goal.

Ephesians 2:2 (b)
. . . according to the course of this world . . .

The Greek phrase translated "course of this world" refers to wind. Therefore, the implication is that whichever way the wind was blowing was the way we were going.

Ephesians 2:2 (c)
. . . according to the prince of the power of the air, the spirit that now worketh in the children of disobedience.

Who was doing the blowing? Satan. He was the one dictating the styles, trends, and interests that so captivated you and me before we were saved, when we were still dead in our sin.

Ephesians 2:3 (a)
Among whom also we all had our conversation in times past in the lusts of our flesh, fulfilling the desires of the flesh and of the mind . . .

Completely caught up in our own fleshly inclinations, we were enslaved in a futile attempt to satisfy our flesh.

Ephesians 2:3 (b)
. . . and were by nature the children of wrath, even as others.

Finally, not only were we dead because of sin, drugged by our sin, and depraved in our sin—as children of wrath, we were doomed by our sin. Why were we children of wrath? Because the wrath of God abides on those who do not receive the gift of salvation (Ephesians 5:6).

Ephesians 2:4 (a)
But God . . .

I find these two words to be perhaps the most important in all of Scripture, for although we were doomed by sin, God broke through anyway.

For topical study of Ephesians 2:4 entitled "But God . . ." turn to page 1236.

Ephesians 2:4 (b), 5
. . . who is rich in mercy, for his great love wherewith he loved us, even when we were dead in sins, hath quickened us together with Christ, (by grace ye are saved;).

When God broke through, what did He do? First of all, He loved us. God doesn't only love you when you go to church, read your Bible, or try to be spiritual. He loved you at your stinkiest. He loved you when you were dead.

Ephesians 2:6
And hath raised us up together, and made us sit together in heavenly places in Christ Jesus.

Not only were we loved by the Lord, but we were lifted by Him when He raised us up together and made us sit with Him in heavenly places. In John 11, we see Lazarus raised from the dead. In John 12, we see him seated with Christ around the table. The same is true of you and me. We are not only made alive in Christ, but now we can come to His table. We can fellowship with Him, talk to Him, and learn from Him. Soon, we'll be in heaven, sitting at the ultimate banqueting table at the marriage feast of the Lamb. What a day that will be!

Ephesians 2:7
That in the ages to come he might shew the exceeding riches of his grace in his kindness toward us through Christ Jesus.

God raised us to sit with Him in heavenly places in order that we might be trophies of His grace, in order that people will look at you and me in the ages to come and say, "The grace of God is unbelievable! Look at how God loves them! Look at what He's done with them! *Amazing!*"

Ephesians 2:8, 9
For by grace are ye saved through faith; and that not of yourselves: it is the gift of God: Not of works, lest any man should boast.

In verses 4–7, we saw God's work *for* us as He brought us back from the dead and raised us to sit with Him in heavenly places. Here in verses 8, 9, we see His work *in* us.

"It might be God's work," you say, "but it's *my* faith."

No. Here, Paul says specifically that even the faith it took to be saved is not of ourselves. Why? Because dead men don't have faith. That is why Paul declares that there is none that seeks after God, no not one (Romans 3:11).

"Then what part did I have in salvation?" you ask.

None. You were elected before the foundation of the world, and the faith you finally exercised to receive Jesus Christ was faith that God Himself put in your heart. That is why Jesus declared,

"No man can come unto Me except the Father draws Him" (John 6:44).

The entire orb of salvation is totally due to God's grace. We become worshipers now and eternally because His work in us and for us is truly amazing.

Ephesians 2:10
For we are his workmanship, created in Christ Jesus unto good works, which God hath before ordained that we should walk in them.

In verse 10, we see God's work through us. . . .
The Greek word translated "workmanship" is *poiema*—from which we get our word "poem." Thus, we are God's poetry.

On my way out to Chiloquin, Oregon, a number of years ago, I stopped by the side of the road at a little craft area where woodcarvings of bears, eagles, and Indians were for sale. I thought they were pretty good—until I learned they were carved without hand tools of any sort, but only with chainsaws. Then I thought they were incredible!

The same is true of you and me. You might think you're not very impressive—but look in the mirror and consider what God had to work with!

There is no shortage of those who say, "You Christians aren't all that great. I see all kinds of inconsistency, hypocrisy, and problems."

Whenever I hear that, I don't defend myself, nor do I defend you. I simply say, "You're right! But you wouldn't believe how bad we used to be! If you knew how we used to be, you would realize that compared to our former state, we're *poetry!*"

Ephesians 2:11, 12
Wherefore remember, that ye being in time past Gentiles in the flesh, who are called Uncircumcision by that which is called the Circumcision in the flesh made by hands; that at that time ye were without Christ, being aliens from the commonwealth of Israel, and strangers from the covenants of promise, having no hope, and without God in the world.

Here we see God's work *among* us. "Remember what you used to be," Paul says to the Gentile Christians. "You were at one time without Christ, without hope, without God. You were in trouble. You had no hope for a Messiah. You had no knowledge of God. You had no future."

Ephesians 2:13, 14
But now in Christ Jesus ye who sometimes were far off are made nigh by the blood of Christ. For he is our peace, who hath made both one, and hath broken down the middle wall of partition between us.

"Although at one time, you Gentiles had no God, no Christ, no hope," Paul continues, "He's made you one with the Jews who believe in Him."

Ephesians 2:15–18
Having abolished in his flesh the enmity, even the law of commandments contained in ordinances; for to make in himself of twain one new man, so making peace; and that he might reconcile both unto God in one body by the cross, having slain the enmity thereby: And came and preached peace to you which were afar off, and to them that were nigh. For through him we both have access by one Spirit unto the Father.

What is God doing among us? Two things: He has created a new man (verse 15), and a new body (verse 16). Jews and Gentiles used to feel such animosity toward one another that if a Jew even accidentally brushed against a Gentile in the crowded marketplace, he would have to immediately ceremonially cleanse himself. The Gentile community responded by saying the Jews were the devil incarnate. But what did the Lord do? He took those two groups, Jew and Gentile, and brought them together into a new man, a new body—the church.

Ephesians 2:19–22
Now therefore ye are no more strangers and foreigners, but fellowcitizens with the saints, and of the household of God; and are built upon the foundation of the apostles and prophets, Jesus Christ himself being the chief corner stone; in whom all the building fitly framed together groweth unto an holy temple in the Lord: In whom ye also are builded together for an habitation of God through the Spirit.

Not only did God create a new body—He is creating a new building, built upon the foundation of the message of the apostles and prophets. That message is Jesus Christ. He is the Chief Cornerstone. But the building is not done. He *has* created a new man. But He *is* creating a new building. Why? Because it's growing.

Peter tells us we are living stones being fit together to build a holy priesthood (1 Peter 2:5). And as living stones, we are growing ourselves as we expand in our own understanding of God's ways. Inevitably, then, there will be friction between us. Sometimes I can resent that. But I am learning that the Lord puts me with people He specifically has ordained to knock the rough edges off of me.

In 1 Kings 6, we read that as the temple was being constructed, all of the cutting took place away from the temple mount. Consequently, when the rocks arrived on site, there was not the sound of a hammer or a chisel heard.

So, too, there is coming a time when there will not be the sound of a hammer or chisel in our lives. We're going to heaven, where all of the stones—Jew, Gentile, male, female, brother, sister—will fit together perfectly, the chiseling and shaping having been done here in this quarry called earth. So let the hammering take place, dear brother. Don't try to short-circuit the process, precious sister. You're being fit together as living stones for a holy habitation in which God can dwell forever.

BUT GOD . . .
A Topical Study of
Ephesians 2:4

Asked what I enjoy most about the ministry, I was surprised by my own answer. "What I enjoy most about the ministry are the messes," I said—"just seeing the wonderful things the Lord creates from the muddle and mayhem in which we continually find ourselves."

It's been this way from the very beginning. You see, Genesis 1:1 says that in the beginning God created the heavens and the earth. In Hebrew, verse 2 goes on to say the earth was "*tohuw va bohuw,*" or, "without form and void." We see this phrase again in Isaiah 45:18, where we read that God created the heaven and earth *not* in vain—*not* "*tohuw va bohuw.*" Now, if Isaiah says God did *not* create the earth "*tohuw va bohuw,*" but Genesis 1 says the earth *was* "*tohuw va bohuw,*" what's going on?

Along with many Bible scholars, I believe an event took place between Genesis 1:1 and 1:2, described in Isaiah 14 and Ezekiel 28, wherein an archangel named Lucifer launched a rebellion against God and was kicked out of heaven. Along with one-third of the angels who followed him in his rebellion, he came to earth, where he would become "the god of this world" (2 Corinthians 4:4). So great was the impact when, in a sense, hell hit earth, that Bible scholars believe it caused the earth to tilt on its axis and ushered in the Ice Age.

So it is, that even from the very beginning of time, we see a dismal, dark mess. But Scripture goes on to say that when God said, "Let there be light," what was once without form and void began to become something incredibly wonderful: the amazing earth upon which we live.

Not only does God re-create the world around us but also the world within us.

You see, according to Ephesians 2:1, we were all "without form and void," dead. But according to verse 4, just as He did at creation, God moved in and revived us.

Perhaps you feel that the axis of your world has tilted, that you're living in the cold blast of a perpetual Ice Age, or that darkness surrounds and abounds. "Yes, you're a mess," Paul would say to you. Then he would add the two words that made all the difference at the creation of the physical world, and which will make all the difference in your world as well: *But God.*

Abraham and his wife, Sarah, were traveling, and Abraham was fearful. Why? Sarah was so beautiful, Abraham knew that Abimelech, the king of the region through which they passed, would want to kill him in order to add Sarah to his harem. "Tell him you're my sister," Abraham said. "He'll take you away—but at least I won't die." Sure enough, Abimelech, sent for Sarah (Genesis 20:2).

"*But God* came to Abimelech in a dream by night and said to him, Behold thou art a dead man, for the woman whom thou hast taken; for she is a man's wife" (Genesis 20:3).

Abraham messed up royally. His marriage to Sarah teetered on disaster. *But God* moved in unexpectedly, unpredictably, miraculously, and rescued them both.

People say to me, "My wife just doesn't understand." "My husband is an idiot." "My marriage is a mess." "What do I do?"

I listen to their stories, shrug my shoulders, and say, "I don't have a clue. *But God*—somehow God is going to come through for you. I don't know how. I don't know when. But I know Him. God will break through somehow."

"Your dad ripped me off," Jacob said to his wives, Leah and Rachel, after being shortchanged by Laban one too many times. "*But God* suffered him not to hurt me" (Genesis 31:7).

"No wonder in-law problems rank third in the struggles of married couples," says the weary couple. "We can't seem to please either of ours. What should we do?"

"I have no idea," I say. "*But God* used Jacob's ordeal with Laban to eventually change Jacob from "Heel Snatcher" to Israel, the one "governed by God."

On his deathbed, Jacob was no doubt reminded of his own deceit repeated in the lives of his sons gathered around him. Perhaps realizing that his time to impact them positively was growing short, it was with an air of resignation that he said, "Behold I die." Yet as he uttered the last word of that sentiment, hope reclaimed his heart, for he added, "*but God* shall be with you and bring you again to the land of your fathers" (Genesis 48:21).

"What can I do about my son?" cries the broken-hearted father. "It's as if I don't even exist in his life. Yes, I made mistakes raising him, but what can I do now?"

"I don't know," I say. "*But God* will be with him just as He was with Jacob's sons, to bring him to the land of his fathers—to somehow, some way, bring him back home."

> After being thrown in a pit by his own brothers, he was sold into slavery. Joseph was forsaken by his family and without hope completely. *But God* moved in miraculously and elevated him to the position of prime minister in one of the greatest empires in human history (Genesis 50:20).

"Everyone is against me—even my own family," cries the heartbroken young man. "What do I do?"

I listen to his story and say, "I don't know. *But God* was with Joseph, and God will be with you."

> After killing one thousand Philistines with the jawbone of an ass, Samson was so thirsty he thought he would die. "But God clave an hollow place that was in the jaw, and there came water out of it; and when he had drunk, his spirit came again, and he revived" (see Judges 15:19).

"I'm so dry spiritually," she says. "I come to church and I'm dry. I pray and I'm dry. I study the Word and I'm dry. What am I doing wrong?"

"I don't know," I say. "*But God* hears your prayer and will revive you, perhaps, as He did with Samson, in a way you least expect it."

> Although Saul was king of Israel, he knew it was actually David who had the anointing of God. Consequently, Saul sought to take David's life. "*But God* delivered him not into his hand" (1 Samuel 23:14).

What temptation, what sin, what Saul is trying to track you down and do you in? You'll never be able to elude it on your own, *but God* can establish and strengthen you. He can give you victory (1 Peter 5:10).

"Oh, but you don't know the Saul that's chasing me," you say. "It's a very real temptation, an incredibly powerful problem."

Perhaps. "*But God* will not allow you to be tempted beyond what you're able and will provide a way of escape every single time you're tempted" (see 1 Corinthians 10:13).

Precious brother, dear sister, God, who is rich in mercy and full of love, will break through your situation if you'll allow Him. The mess you're in may be real. The struggle ahead may be exhausting, the trial you face may be overwhelming— but the message is yet more powerful: But God, but God, but *God*. . . .

3 Ephesians 3:1
For this cause I Paul, the prisoner of
Jesus Christ for you Gentiles.

Paul penned this Epistle seemingly as a prisoner of Rome. Yet he gives us a different perspective of his situation when he writes, "Indeed, I'm
a prisoner. But I'm a prisoner for a cause." What
cause? The incredible revelation, as seen in chapter 2, that Jews and Gentiles are brought together in Jesus Christ into a new entity. "We're
in this thing together," said Paul.

Not only was Paul a prisoner for a cause, He
was a prisoner of the Christ. "I'm not a prisoner
of Nero," he declared. "I'm not a prisoner of the
Roman Empire. I'm a prisoner of Jesus Christ.
And He has brought me to this place."

I hate to say it, but I'm glad Paul was in
prison—because our Bible is a whole lot richer
and the body much more complete as a result.
You see, while he was in prison, Paul wrote the
letters we value so greatly. In addition, the
guards to whom he was chained as a prisoner began getting saved one by one before returning to
Caesar's palace as born-again believers. That is
why in his letter to the Philippians, Paul says,
"The saints in Caesar's palace, your new
brothers in Christ, greet you" (see Philippians
4:22).

Happy will be the one who realizes that wherever he is has been ordained by the Lord to bring
about good things if he will have eyes to see and
patience to wait. Whenever I complain about my
circumstances or situation, I am really complaining about my Father, for it is He who sets our
course and determines our days.

Paul never lost this perspective. That is why
He could say, "I'm a prisoner of Jesus Christ, for
it is He who has captivated my heart and brought
me to this place."

Ephesians 3:2–6
If ye have heard of the dispensation of the
grace of God which is given me to youward:
How that by revelation he made known unto
me the mystery; (as I wrote afore in few
words, whereby, when ye read, ye may understand my knowledge in the mystery of
Christ) which in other ages was not made
known unto the sons of men, as it is now
revealed unto his holy apostles and prophets
by the Spirit; that the Gentiles should be
fellowheirs, and of the same body, and partakers of his promise in Christ by the gospel.

In Scripture, the word "mystery" refers to
something that was previously unknown or hid-

den but is now revealed because the timing is
right. The mystery of how Jews and Gentiles are
heirs together is based on the dispensation of
grace.

As you read through the Bible from Genesis to
Revelation, it will help you greatly, it will clear a
lot of fog and remove a lot of confusion if you understand that basically God is taking mankind on
a march through eight primary dispensations or
ways in which He has related to us.

*There are those who say, "We don't need God.
We just need to get the right man in the White
House. We don't need a spiritual revival. We
just need a political revolution."*

*Others say, "If we could just get rid of all of
the toxic waste and pollutants, if we could
make our environment better, we would surely
live in peace and harmony."*

*Others say, "If only my parents weren't so
weird, I would be happy."*

*Others say, "The problem is faith. We're
asked to believe something we can't see, can't
hear, and can't touch. If we could just see and
touch and hear, then we would believe whatever it is we're supposed to believe."*

So what does God do? He says, "Okay, human
race, have it your way. I'm going to march you
right through these different theories, these
different ideas that you think will bring about
happiness." And He began with the first dispensation. . . .

The Dispensation of Innocence

The "Dispensation of Innocence" began with
the creation of man, lasted until the Fall, and
completely obliterates the "Mommie Dearest"
syndrome. Adam and Eve were perfectly healthy
and had neither human parents nor a dysfunctional family. But what happened? They chose to
rebel against God. Thus, the "Dispensation of Innocence" shows mankind that even if he had a
perfect family situation, he's still a sinner who
will rebel against God and wander away into his
own error. How our generation and culture need
to understand that the "Dispensation of Innocence" nullifies the argument that the reason
we're so messed up is because of our parents.

The Dispensation of Conscience

The "Dispensation of Conscience" lasted approximately 1,650 years—from the fall of man to
the Flood. "If we could just follow our own conscience and let everyone do his own thing, we
could all live in harmony," people say. But look

what happened. In the dispensation wherein God said, "Follow your conscience," the world was filled with such violence and sexual aberration that giants were produced on the earth. So perverted was the planet that only one man had an interest in walking righteously and responding to God (Genesis 6:8).

The Dispensation of Government

The "Dispensation of Government" lasted approximately 425 years—from the Flood to the Tower of Babel. During this time, God established the first governmental order, based upon capital punishment (Exodus 21:23, 24). Man decided to add to God's order by undertaking the first governmental building project: the Tower of Babel. Genesis 11 tells us it was constructed with bricks and slime—a fitting description for the venture that ended in disaster.

The Dispensation of Promise

The "Dispensation of Promise" lasted approximately 430 years—from Abraham to the Exodus. "If I just had a promise, I know my life would be successful," man says. "I don't need God—I just need a vision." Abraham received just such a promise, for God told him that his posterity would number as the sand on the seashore and the stars in the heavens, and that he would live in a new land. But what happened? His descendants ended up in Egypt, baking bricks in the blistering desert sun.

The Dispensation of the Law

The "Dispensation of the Law" lasted approximately fifteen hundred years—from the Exodus to the Cross of Calvary. There are those who think if man just had some rules and regulations, he'd be okay. So God gave man the law. There are still those who think that if they could just find the right how-to book, life would make sense. But the law was wonderfully sensible and beautifully practical. The only problem with it is that man can't keep it.

The Dispensation of Grace

The "Dispensation of Grace" is the dispensation in which we live, and of which Paul writes. The "Dispensation of Grace" brings us to the place where we realize neither innocence nor conscience, government nor promise, vision nor rules and regulations will save us. The "Dispensation of Grace" is God saying to us, "I love you. I died for your sin. I rose again. If you confess your

need for Me with your mouth and believe on Me in your heart, you'll be saved" (see Romans 10:9).

The Dispensation of the Tribulation

The "Dispensation of the Tribulation," spoken of in Revelation 6–19, is a seven-year period of unbelievable difficulty. People complain about believing in something they can't see or hear. So God says, "Okay. You want to see something? You want to hear something? Here it comes. . . ." Angels will fly across the skies. Hailstones will pelt the planet. Seas will turn to blood. Mountains will disappear. Continents will break apart. The result? The majority of those who experience these cataclysmic changes will cry not to the Rock of Ages to save them, but to the rocks to fall upon them (Revelation 6:16).

The Dispensation of Righteousness

Following the seven-year period of the Tribulation, the Lord comes back to earth, where He will rule and reign in Jerusalem for one thousand years. The lion will lie down by the lamb. There will be no more war. Disease will no longer plague the planet. The environment will be perfect. "If we just didn't have pollution, disease, and crime, we would be happy and content," people say. But what happens at the end of the millennial kingdom? There will be a rebellion against God—which totally disproves B. F. Skinner's theories that a good environment makes good people. For one thousand years, man will live in a perfect environment—yet some will still rebel against God.

An understanding of the dispensations will keep you from being confused by the way God deals differently throughout Scripture—for in the unfolding story of His progressive revelation, God shows that man has no idea how to find success or satisfaction apart from Him.

Ephesians 3:7
Whereof I was made a minister, according to the gift of the grace of God given unto me by the effectual working of his power.

Paul was a minister not because of his piety, his spirituality, or his ability. The means of Paul's ministry was singular. It was grace.

Ephesians 3:8 (a)
Unto me, who am less than the least of all saints, is this grace given . . .

Paul was aware of the fact that he was ministering not because he deserved to serve, but solely by grace. The closer we get to the Lord, the more we are aware of the sin in our lives that was previously unnoticeable to us. The closer Paul walked to the Lord, the more amazed he was by a God who would use him—the least of the apostles (1 Corinthians 15:9), the least of all saints (Ephesians 3:8), the chief of sinners (1 Timothy 1:15)—to minister the unsearchable riches of His grace.

Ephesians 3:8 (b)
. . . that I should preach among the Gentiles the unsearchable riches of Christ.

Paul didn't talk about philosophy, psychology, or theology. The message of Paul's ministry was Jesus exclusively.

Ephesians 3:9
And to make all men see what is the fellowship of the mystery, which from the beginning of the world hath been hid in God, who created all things by Jesus Christ.

The method of Paul's ministry was not simply to allow all men to hear about the mystery of the indwelling Christ—but to make them *see* it through the working of God in his own life.

Ephesians 3:10, 11
To the intent that now unto the principalities and powers in heavenly places might be known by the church the manifold wisdom of God, according to the eternal purpose which he purposed in Christ Jesus our Lord.

Paul is a minister of the gospel of grace not only that all men might see the mystery of Christ—but that the angels might see as well. According to 1 Peter 1:12, the angels are studying us, intrigued that God would reside in people like *us*.

Ephesians 3:12
In whom we have boldness and access with confidence by the faith of him.

The angels in heaven must be saying, "This motley crew can come marching into Your throne room anytime they want, Father, cast their cares upon You, and get help from You?" The answer is a resounding "Yes!" Because of what Christ did for us on Calvary.

When my daughter Mary Elizabeth was in second grade, she had a best friend named Rachel. One day, I was in my study, and about every five minutes, Rachel would come in and

say, "Mary wants to know if we can go to the store."

"Not right now," I'd answer.

"Mary wants to know if we can go to the school," she'd ask, only to receive the same response.

After about the tenth such request, I finally said, "Rachel, if Mary wants to know, have Mary come and ask me."

You see, Mary thought, I'll send Rachel in. That way, if Dad gets mad, it will be at Rachel, and not at me!

Such was the mind-set with the children of Israel. "Moses, you go get the Word from God. Then come down and tell us," they said, afraid of God.

But in this dispensation, in this glorious "Age of Grace," God says, "Come boldly unto Me. I want to hear from you because I care about you and want to do good things for you" (see Hebrews 4:16).

Ephesians 3:13
Wherefore I desire that ye faint not at my tribulations for you, which is your glory.

"Don't lose heart over my troubles," says Paul. "They're for *you*."

How could that be?

In his tribulation, in his confinement, Paul was a living demonstration of what it means to have Christ living in him, the hope of glory.

A. W. Tozer was right when he said that before God can use a man greatly, He must allow him to be hurt deeply. Why? Because the old adage is true: People don't care how much we know until they know how much we care. And what makes us care in our service to people, our interactions with people? Paul gives the answer in 2 Corinthians 1 when he writes:

Blessed be God, even the Father of our Lord Jesus Christ, the Father of mercies, and the God of all comfort; Who comforteth us in all our tribulation, that we may be able to comfort them which are in any trouble, by the comfort wherewith we ourselves are comforted of God. For as the sufferings of Christ abound in us, so our consolation also aboundeth by Christ.

2 Corinthians 1:3–5

In other words, the degree of the crushing, the tribulation, the difficulty in which you find yourself will be the degree of consolation you will receive. And consolation comes to us in order that we may in turn comfort others with the comfort we have found in Him.

This passage is so important, gang. God allows us to go through crushing trials even as Paul did in order that we can explore and experience His presence and His comfort—and then share it with others. In our darkest times, we only truly receive from those who have gone through similar difficulties. When the one who has walked the same path we're walking says, "I found consolation in Christ," his words are like water to the desert of our soul because he's not simply telling us a theory—he's telling us what he has experienced personally and practically.

That's why, in talking about his own ministry here in Ephesians 3, Paul says, "Don't faint. Don't lose heart because of our tribulation. It's for you. God meets us and comforts us in the dungeon of difficulty, in the prison of tribulation so that we can comfort *you.*"

Not only does God use tribulation to comfort the saints—He uses it to convince the sinner.

How?

Many unbelievers have been witnessed to hundreds of times by sincere Christians. Yet they remain unmoved because they are unknowingly waiting to see the mystery of Christ in the life of a believer. How will this happen? Here in Ephesians 3, Paul links the answer to his own difficulty.

Innumerable as grasshoppers, the Midianites were an intimidating enemy, indeed. Nevertheless, God instructed Gideon to take only three hundred men to do battle against them. After choosing his men, Gideon gave each one a trumpet, a jar, and a torch—and led them up into the hills surrounding the valley wherein the Midianites slept. Then, following his lead, Gideon's men blew their trumpets and broke their earthen vessels—each of which contained a lit torch. Hearing the commotion, the Midianites woke up and, seeing the torches—each of which they assumed represented at least a division of soldiers—they grabbed their swords and in their confusion began swinging wildly, destroying one another in the process. Thus, Gideon's men experienced firsthand what happens when light comes pouring forth from a broken vessel (Judges 7).

We have this treasure—the Light of the World, Jesus Christ—in earthen vessels, declares Paul (2 Corinthians 4:7). But how is He seen by the world below? Not when things are comfy and cushy and easy. Not when things are hunky dory. The world is not impressed with that. The Enemy

is not beaten back by that. The world wants to see the mystery of Christ in us—not just hear about it. How do they see it? They only see it when the vessel is broken.

They see it, wife, when your husband walks out on you unexpectedly—and yet you keep worshiping the Lord faithfully. They see it, Dad, when the doctor says, "It's malignant"—and yet you remain strong in your faith. When the business goes belly-up, when your teenager breaks your heart, when you get cut from the team, when you don't make the squad people get to see the light in the earthen vessel as the vessel is broken. They get to see Christ in you, the hope of glory. And in seeing this mystery, they are drawn to the Master.

Ephesians 3:14–16
For this cause I bow my knees unto the Father of our Lord Jesus Christ, of whom the whole family in heaven and earth is named, that he would grant you, according to the riches of his glory, to be strengthened with might by his Spirit in the inner man;

"While I'm in prison, I'm praying for you that the Holy Spirit might strengthen you in the inner man," says Paul.

- Do you care about your kids, Mom and Dad? Pray for them.
- Do you care about your church, saint? Pray for us.
- Do you care about your community? Pray that the Holy Spirit will work in the inner man.

So many have knowledge in their heads, but it hasn't dropped eighteen inches into their hearts.

How does that happen?

Through prayer.

Paul says, "I bow my knee—I assume the posture of intensity—and I pray. My prayer is that the knowledge of theology will make its way from your head to your heart."

Ephesians 3:17 (a)
That Christ may dwell in your hearts by faith . . .

The Greek word translated "dwell" literally means "settle down and be at home." Is Christ at home in your heart? Paul says, "My prayer is that Christ would be comfortable in you. And where He's comfortable, where He's at home, you will be happy and blessed."

For topical study of Ephesians 3:14–17, see "Jesus: At Home in Your Heart," below.

Ephesians 3:17 (b)–19
. . . that ye, being rooted and grounded in love, May be able to comprehend with all saints what is the breadth, and length, and depth, and height; and to know the love of Christ, which passeth knowledge, that ye might be filled with all the fulness of God.

How can you know something that passes knowledge? How can you be filled with the fullness of God when God cannot even be contained in the universe? I suggest to you the answer lies in this phrase "being rooted and grounded in love." What is rooted? What is grounded? What is love? The tree of Calvary was rooted. The Cross was grounded. Therefore, the only way I can truly know the love that passes knowledge is by focusing my eyes upon the Cross of Calvary and seeing what is the breadth and the length, the depth and the height of the love of God. . . .

I see the breadth of His love as Jesus stretched out His hand on the Cross.

To what lengths did He go? Because He was slain before the foundation of the world (Revelation 13:8), His sufferings are elongated beyond anything we can comprehend.

How deep did Jesus go? Listen as He cried out on the Cross, "My God, My God Why hast Thou forsaken Me?" He cries out, in the depths of despair, from the depth of hell, paying for our sin.

What is the height of His love? Look up

and see Him on the Cross, praying, "Father, forgive them, for they know not what they do."

The only way I can truly know that which passes knowledge is to consider the height, depth, length, and breadth of the Cross—that which was rooted and grounded on a hill called Calvary. I am reminded of this each time I partake of the Lord's table. Do not forsake the Lord's table, dear saint, for it is there you will know that which cannot be known. It is there you will be filled with the fullness of God. It is there you will be rooted and grounded in the mystery of God's love as you consider the Cross.

Ephesians 3:20, 21
Now unto him that is able to do exceeding abundantly above all that we ask or think, according to the power that worketh in us, unto him be glory in the church by Christ Jesus throughout all ages, world without end. Amen.

"Unto Him be glory in the Church and throughout all the ages." In other words, what begins here will continue on to a greater degree—for heaven will not be that much different than when we experience His glory here on earth in times of adoration, in times of Communion, in times of meaningful interaction, in times of heartfelt intercession.

I suggest that when a person is truly walking in the Spirit, it may take a little while for him to realize he's in heaven when he finally gets there because he'll just continue worshiping and rejoicing and experiencing the Lord as he did on earth—minus the constraints of time, limited energy, and ever-present flesh. Oh, happy day that will be!

JESUS: AT HOME IN YOUR HEART
A Topical Study of
Ephesians 3:14–17

Confusion must have filled their hearts. Questions must have flooded their minds, for hadn't Jesus said, "In My Father's house are many mansions. I go to prepare a place for you" (see John 14:2)? Why, then, a few moments later did He say, "If a man love Me, He will keep My words. My Father will love him and We will come unto him and make our abode with him" (see John 14:23)?

"I'm going to prepare a place for you," Jesus said—"and yet I will come and live in you." We see Paul the apostle using the same imagery in our text when he says his prayer is that Christ will dwell in our hearts by faith. The Greek word translated "dwell" is *katoikeo*. *Oikeo* means "to dwell in a house." *Kat* means "down." Therefore, *katoikeo* means "down home."

The idea is that Jesus would be completely at home in our hearts.

"Behold, I stand at the door of your heart and knock," Jesus said. "If any man hear my voice and open the door, I will come in to him and will sup with him and he with Me" (Revelation 3:20).

Holman Hunt's famous painting, depicting Jesus standing at the door of what appears to be an English cottage, hangs in St. Paul's Cathedral in London.

"There's a problem with your painting, Mr. Hunt," a critic is reported to have said upon first viewing his work. "There's no doorknob on the door."

"Ah," Mr. Hunt is said to have replied, "the door handle is only on the inside, for it's up to the one within to respond to the knock of Jesus."

Jesus will not force His way into a heart. He won't barge in where He's not welcome. He's a perfect gentleman who knocks and says, "If you'll respond to Me, I'll come in and dine with you. But the choice is up to you."

Most of us have made that choice. We heard His knock and said, "Come in, Lord. Come into the home of my heart." And He did.

The Living Room

The first room He saw in the home of my heart was the living room. "Nice room," He said.

"Thanks, Lord. It's one of my favorite spots because it's relatively quiet and secluded."

"I'll meet you here every morning of every day," He said. "Before the day gets going, I'll meet you here in the early morning, and we'll talk about what's ahead. When I walked in Israel, I needed instruction and help daily from My Father. So morning by morning, the Father spoke into My ear, giving me the tongue of the learned that I should know how to speak a word in season to him that is weary (Isaiah 50:4). And now I'll do the same for you."

What followed was great. I would come into the living room, a fire would be crackling in the fireplace, and Jesus would be there, ready to talk with me and listen to me. It was a great way to start the day. As time went on, however, things got busy, or so I thought. Rushing out the door to a meeting, I caught a glimpse of Him, sitting. And I realized I hadn't met with Him for a number of mornings. I stopped in my tracks and walked sheepishly over to where He was sitting, thinking He would lecture me. But He didn't. There was a smile on His face and a sparkle in His eye as He said, "As I was saying . . ." continuing the conversation we had shared the last time we were together. And I understood then, truly, that there is no condemnation to those who are in Christ Jesus (Romans 8:1). He just continues to make Himself available morning by morning to help me speak wisely and to navigate life successfully.

The Study

As the morning drew to a close, Jesus said, "What is that room over there?"

"Oh, that's my study. Come on in." He followed me in, and I noticed He was looking rather intently at the books on the shelves.

"Look, Lord," I said proudly, "I've got all the latest bestsellers: *Winning Through Intimidation, Watch Out for Number One, I'm OK You're OK, Dressed for Success,* and *Awakening the Giant Within.*

"Do these books work?" He asked.

"Not really," I answered. "That's why I keep collecting more."

"How about a book trade?" He asked.

"Sure, Lord. What do You have in mind?"

You give Me your books, and I'll give you sixty-six books bound in a single volume—one that will make you unashamed as you study to show yourself approved unto Me (2 Timothy 2:15), one that comes with an incredible guarantee that if you meditate upon it day and night, you will navigate life prosperously and successfully" (Joshua 1:8).

He took my books. I took His. And suddenly my study was filled with a Book that would intrigue me for the rest of my life.

The Family Room

"What's that I hear down the hall?" Jesus asked.

"That's my family room," I said, opening the door. My kids stopped their playing and rushed toward Him.

"Back off, you guys," I said, laughing.

"I think I've heard that before," He said, "when some other disciples tried to keep their kids away from Me (see Matthew 19:13). Allow them to come."

So they tackled Him, and He wrestled with my kids on the floor. They had the time of their lives. Then He calmed them down a bit and began telling them stories. I could see my oldest son nod his head in agreement, and a smile on the face of my youngest daughter. Suddenly, a peace enveloped the room that was usually so rambunctious, so disorderly, so chaotic.

"This is amazing, Lord," I said. "You've altered this room radically."

"That's why I asked you, as head of the house, to let me into the family room," He said. "I'll alter your kids, your marriage, your home, if you will build a family altar to Me. You see, more than any other group of people—more than your congregation or your elders or your friends—your wife and your kids are your primary disciples. So bring your family together, and learn of Me. There's nothing more important you can do."

The Recreation Room

Hearing a knock on the door, I opened it to find my buddies. We walked down the hall into the recreation room. "Lord, You wouldn't like it in here," I said. "This group is real rowdy. So I'll meet you in the living room in an hour or so."

The boys and I grabbed our pool cues, turned on the radio, and began doing what we did every Tuesday. But this time, it didn't work. The jokes just weren't as funny, and the conversation suddenly seemed shallow and empty. Even the lyrics of the music bothered me. After half an hour or so, I heard a knock on the door. It was Jesus.

He began to talk with my buddies, and I was absolutely amazed because they all loved Him. Oh, a couple of guys got upset and stormed out. But I learned later they weren't my friends after all. They just wanted to use my pool table.

I learned that Jesus is the Life of the party in the truest sense of the word. I also learned that I'm free to do anything as long as I have Him with me because He changes the atmosphere. Now, if I go into a party and the party changes me, then I must leave. But if the party changes and people start thinking about Jesus as a result of my being there, I am free. And I discovered that Jesus Christ had spoiled me—for I had too much of Him to enjoy the old spots. So I've learned to bring the Lord with me to all of my recreational pursuits, and to watch how He infuses them with His life.

The Dining Room

After working up quite an appetite, I said, "Lord, let's go get something to eat." We went into the dining room and sat down to my usual meal.

"This is what you eat?" the Lord asked.

"Every day," I answered.

"Really? This is the way you satisfy your appetite?" He asked incredulously as He looked at the large glob of cotton candy on my plate.

"This is the way I try to satisfy my cravings," I said. "I must admit, however, that although it looks good, when I take a bite, there's just nothing there. That's why I follow it with a hot fudge sundae. I eat the ice cream and the hot fudge and the whipped cream, and there's something there, all right—but every time I'm done, I feel sick. So I decide never to have another one. Then about five hours later, I think another hot fudge sundae would taste pretty good, so I dish one up again. But although I feel full—I never feel satisfied.

After hearing this, He went into the kitchen and came back a few minutes later with a most interesting meal for me: a little cup full of juice and a little piece of unleavened bread. "This is My body, eat of Me. This is my blood. Drink deeply," He said.

Something happened at my table that evening. It became the Lord's table. And it became incredibly satisfying to commune with Jesus. Feeling satisfied in a way I never had before, I suddenly understood what He meant when He said, "Whoever drinks of the water I shall give shall never thirst again" (see John 4:14).

Brother or sister—if you're thirsting today, it's because you've gone back to the old watering holes. If you're feeling empty and troubled, it's because you've gone back to the old ways. Whoever drinks of the water of the world will thirst over and over again, for it will never be enough. But whoever drinks of the water Jesus gives, will be satiated at last.

The Workshop

"What's behind that door?" the Lord asked.

"That's my workshop. I don't go out there much anymore," I said, opening the door, to find some unfinished wooden planes and cars on the worktable. "I've lost interest in these things," I said, "Besides, I'm not that good at woodworking"

"I'm a Master Carpenter," He said. "I can give you some help on these projects." So He gave me some advice on putting them together.

Then He said, "Now take those toys—the hobby you've been pursuing—and give them away."

So I grabbed my little toys, found some kids at the park, and said, "You guys want some planes and cars?" Their eyes lit up. And suddenly my hobby made sense.

"So *that's* what You meant, Lord, when You told us that in the measure we give out, it will be given back," I said (see Luke 6:38).

People garden, paint, remodel, bowl, and collect things only to get bored and go on to the next hobby. If hobbies, however, were used for someone else, what a difference it would make. You who like to garden—mow someone's lawn for free next Saturday and leave a note on the door saying, "God bless you." You who like to bake—make some cookies and give them to someone in need in Jesus' name. You who like to ride bikes—how about taking a kid who doesn't have a dad on a ride around the lake? In this way, biking, gardening, and baking have meaning because you're in the workshop using the talents and interests God gave you to share with others. Use those talents only for yourself, and you'll be boring and shallow. But give them away, and you'll be blown away with blessing.

What a difference the Lord has made in my heart. The workshop has meaning again. The family room is not so chaotic. The dining room satisfies the appetites and cravings of my heart. The study is rich with wisdom and insight.

But one day, the Lord said to me, "From the day I came in here, I've smelled something foul. It's making Me ill—not because of how it affects Me—but because I know it is poisonous to you and your family. There's a toxic dump somewhere in this house, and I've determined it's behind that door right down the hall."

"Oh, Lord," I said, "that's just an old closet. I'm going to take care of it some-time. I know it stinks, but You'll grow accustomed to it. Trust me, I've had it for a number of years, and I don't even notice anymore."

"Can I have a look?" He asked.

"No, Lord," I said. "I've given You entry into every room in the house of my heart. But that one closet is mine. I know it stinks, but it's mine. You're welcome to go where You want and do what You wish in every other room—but that closet be-longs to me."

With that, He slipped away into the farthest corner of the home. And suddenly, the family room lost its life. The study became tedious. The old songs began to be played in the recreation room. And the dining room table held only cotton candy and hot fudge sundaes. After several days, I said, "Lord, I don't want You stuck off in a corner of the house. I want You to move around freely. I need You in my family room. I need You in my study. I need You in the living room. But I can't deal with that closet, Lord. I don't know what to do."

"All I'm asking," He replied, "is that you agree with Me that it stinks and that it's got to go. I'll do the rest—but you must give me your permission." That's what confession is. Confession simply means to agree. That's why the apostle John says if we confess our sin, He will be faithful and just to forgive our sin and to cleanse us from all unrighteousness (1 John 1:9).

I had forgotten how good a house could smell. I was reminded of the home of Mary, Martha, and Lazarus. Mary poured ointment on Jesus, and John records that the fragrance filled the whole house (John 12:3). In other words, the whole house smelled like Jesus.

"Lord, You have been such a wonderful influence in the house of my heart," I said. "From now on, it's Your house. I'll be the guest. You be the owner.

Smiling, He said, "I have a better idea. Now that you've given Me your house, let's go to My house. I've been working on it for two thousand years. I can't wait to show you what I've prepared for you."

Once I gave Him control of my home, His work was done. Now He could take me to His home. And that's a whole new story. I can't tell it to you because eyes have not seen and ears have not heard the things God has prepared for those who love Him (1 Corinthians 2:9). It's a story beyond description.

That's where we're going, gang. You who, by faith, have allowed Christ to dwell in your hearts, to be at home in your hearts, will soon find yourself at home in the place He's preparing for you. In the meantime, while we await that day, we can experience a bit of heaven in our lives presently as we allow Him to be at home in every room of our hearts. May the Lord help us to give Him the keys to every closet, the title deed to the home in its entirety. May we be those who say, "Come on in, Lord. It's all Yours."

Ephesians 4:1 (a)
I therefore, the prisoner of the Lord, beseech you . . .

The word "therefore" is such a pivotal word in Scripture that whenever you come across it in the Word, it's good to stop and ask what it is there for. In this case, as Paul begins the second half of his letter, launching into the practical aspects of our life in Christ, he refers to the doctrinal foundation he laid in chapters 1—3. In other words, before telling us how we are to walk, he reminds us we must first understand where we sit.

In chapters 1—3, Paul told us we were adopted into God's family, elected before the foundation of the world, redeemed by the blood of the Lamb, and sealed with the Holy Spirit—all while we were dead in our sin. This is where so many Christians stumble. They try to walk before they sit. Sermons are preached; seminars are given; books are published on how husbands should love their wives and the way wives should submit to their husbands; or the way we should live in purity; or what we should do as a church body—all without acknowledging what God has already done for us, all without factoring in the fact that there's nothing we can do to make God love us any more than He loves us right now.

I have found that most Christians believe they are the initiators in spiritual life, feeling that if they can just pray enough, do enough, and be enough, God will love them and bless them. So they try to walk worthy—but sooner or later, they fail and throw in the towel.

Our Christian walk is not something we do to try to earn God's favor or merit His love. Rather, it is a response to how He loves us, what He's done for us, and how good He's already been to us. We love Him, the apostle John said, because He first loved us (1 John 4:19). He is the Initiator, we the responders. We don't love Him *so* He'll love us. We love Him *because* He first loved us.

Any parent who would try to teach his child to walk before the child learned to sit would be headed for frustration. So, too, if you try to get your kids to walk spiritually before they understand where they are seated in Christ, they'll rebel. But if you remind your kids over and over again what the Lord has done for them and how

He loves them—that they are seated with Him in heavenly places, and that there's nothing they can do to make Him love them less—watch and see how they will begin to walk with Him.

Without chapters 1—3, chapters 4—6 lead only to frustration, legalism, and rebellion. That's why Paul uses the word *therefore*. "In light of all you have, in light of all that's been done, in light of all you are in Christ Jesus," he says, "Walk worthy." How? Read on.

Ephesians 4:1 (b)
. . . that ye walk worthy of the vocation wherewith ye are called.

In the second half of the letter to the Ephesians, the emphasis is on walking. In addition to its appearance here, the apostle Paul uses the word "walk" four times . . .

- First, he tells us to walk in unity (4:1–16).
- Next, he tells us to walk in purity (4:17—5:18).
- Third, he tells us to walk in harmony (5:19—6:9).
- And finally, he tells us to walk in victory (6:10–24).

Ephesians 4:2 (a)
With all lowliness and meekness . . .

He who is finally free from a works-oriented Christianity will walk with lowliness and meekness. No longer will he think God blesses him because of his dedication, diligence, and devotion; his piety, purity, or prayer. Instead, he'll realize everything he has is because of God's lovingkindness, because of *His* generosity, *His* mercy, *His* goodness.

Ephesians 4:2 (b)
. . . with longsuffering . . .

"Longsuffering" means "exceeding patience." How much more patient we would be if we really understood how incredibly patient God has been with us. After all, would you have put up with yourself if you were God? I, for one, wouldn't be here right now because I would have blasted myself a long time ago! Therefore, in light of what

He's done for us, in light of how long He continues to put up with us, we must be those who are patient with others. We must be those who extend mercy lavishly and bestow grace freely.

Ephesians 4:2 (c)–6
... forbearing one another in love; endeavouring to keep the unity of the Spirit in the bond of peace. There is one body, and one Spirit, even as ye are called in one hope of your calling; one Lord, one faith, one baptism, one God and Father of all, who is above all, and through all, and in you all.

Because we're all in this together and are all recipients of our Father's grace and kindness, there's no room to say, "We're better than they are," or, "I'm more holy than he is." Rather, there's one body, one Spirit, one hope, one Lord, one faith, one baptism. There's no room for dividing, for splintering, for saying, "We're more spiritual than you." No, we're to walk in unity.

Ephesians 4:7
But unto every one of us is given grace according to the measure of the gift of Christ.

Although there is unity within the body of Christ, there is also diversity. We are all united in Christ and because of Christ, but there are differences among us due to the different gifts we've been given. In our physical bodies, our hands function differently than our eyes, which function differently than our toes. So, too, in the body of Christ, each part functions in a unique way according to the gift each has been given.

Ephesians 4:8–10
Wherefore he saith, When he ascended up on high, he led captivity captive, and gave gifts unto men. (Now that he ascended, what is it but that he also descended first into the lower parts of the earth? He that descended is the same also that ascended up far above all heavens, that he might fill all things.)

When were these gifts given? Quoting Psalm 68:18, Paul gives the answer. After Christ was crucified, before He ascended into heaven, He first descended to the lower parts of the earth, into Hades, or "the place of the dead." In this, He fulfilled the prophecy of Matthew (16:4), wherein He said, "A wicked and adulterous generation seeks a sign, but one sign I will give you. Even as Jonah was in the belly of the whale three days and three nights, so shall the Son of Man be three days and three nights in the center of the earth." In other words, during the three days His body

lay in the tomb, before He ascended to heaven, Jesus descended into hell.

According to Jesus' parable in Luke 16, "Abraham's bosom," or "paradise," was where the Old Testament believers—those who were believers in God and who looked forward to the coming Messiah—went after they died. Unable to go directly to heaven because Jesus had not yet died for their sins, they went to Abraham's bosom, paradise, the "good" side of hell (Luke 16:22–31). After Jesus died, He went to Abraham's bosom and led the Old Testament believers into heaven, where they are today.

Not only that, but, according to our text, He gave gifts to men. This is amazing. Three days after He was crucified by us—for we *all* turned our backs on Him, we *all* like sheep have gone astray—our Lord is so magnanimous, so generous, merciful, and kind that He heaped us not with grief nor with guilt, but with gifts.

What gifts? Read on.

Ephesians 4:11 (a)
And he gave some, apostles ...

The apostolic ministry is a governing ministry and refers to those who are sent out as spiritual statesmen to establish ministries. There are three kinds of apostles: God the Father appointed one Apostle—His Sent One, Jesus Christ. Jesus, in turn, appointed twelve apostles. Thirdly, the Holy Spirit appointed apostles—Andronicus and Junia, Timothy and Titus, Barnabas and Paul, and a host of others. This third type is the type of apostles who are still being appointed to this day.

Ephesians 4:11 (b)
... and some, prophets ...

The prophetic ministry is a guiding ministry and refers to those who speak the Word of the Lord in the Spirit.

Ephesians 4:11 (c)
... and some, evangelists ...

The evangelistic ministry is a gathering ministry and refers to those who bring people to the kingdom.

Ephesians 4:11 (d)
... and some, pastors ...

The pastoral ministry is a guarding ministry and refers to those who protect the flock from the wolves who seek to destroy them.

Ephesians 4:11 (e)
. . . and teachers.

The teaching ministry is a grounding ministry and refers to those who ground God's people in the truths of His Word.

Ephesians 4:12
For the perfecting of the saints, for the work of the ministry, for the edifying of the body of Christ.

The church of Jesus Christ exists for three reasons:

- To exalt God—which is why we sing praises and offer prayer
- To edify His people—which is why we study the Word
- To evangelize the unsaved—which is why we preach salvation

Contrary to what many think, the church does not exist primarily to evangelize. It exists to build the saints so that they, in turn, will do the work of the ministry. If you come from a church background, the tendency is to think that Christian service happens primarily at church. In reality, however, the most effective ministry happens when you're on the job site, at school, with your buddies, working out, or eating a burger. In the Book of Acts, we see the early church hearing the apostles teach, breaking bread together—and then going out to turn the world upside down.

Ephesians 4:13
Till we all come in the unity of the faith, and of the knowledge of the Son of God, unto a perfect man, unto the measure of the stature of the fulness of Christ.

Our goal is to be like Jesus—and Jesus did not spend His life hanging out in the temple. He was out among people, impacting the world.

Ephesians 4:14
That we henceforth be no more children, tossed to and fro, and carried about with every wind of doctrine, by the sleight of men, and cunning craftiness, whereby they lie in wait to deceive.

The goal of the church is one of maturity—to conform to the Person of Jesus Christ. To this end, I challenge anyone talking about any new doctrine or experience to find it in the gospels, the Book of Acts, and the Epistles. Otherwise, it's just a passing breeze that will toss you to and fro in your walk.

Ephesians 4:15
But speaking the truth in love, may grow up into him in all things, which is the head, even Christ.

We are drawn to a crackling fire in a fireplace on a cold winter night because it provides both light and warmth. And such is the perfect combination of truth and love. Truth without love is like the light of a fire without warmth. Love without truth is like the heat of a fire without light. Truth without love makes people cold in the light. Love without truth makes people stumble in the dark. Thus, we need both.

Ephesians 4:16
From whom the whole body fitly joined together and compacted by that which every joint supplieth, according to the effectual working in the measure of every part, maketh increase of the body unto the edifying of itself in love.

Each of us has a role to play—for just as the joints of our physical bodies are fashioned in such a way that if we didn't have ligaments and tendons, our movement would be spastic and painful at best—the same is true spiritually. We need one another, gang. The Lord has brought us all together in order that together we may conform to Him.

Ephesians 4:17
This I say therefore, and testify in the Lord, that ye henceforth walk not as other Gentiles walk, in the vanity of their mind.

Not only are we to walk in unity, but Paul goes on to say we are to put away vanity, or "empty-headedness," and walk in purity. "Create in me a clean heart," David prayed because he couldn't create a clean heart in himself. We don't have the power to change our hearts. But we do have the power to change our minds. If I stop justifying that activity or that habit—if I change my mind, God will change my heart. But He won't change my heart until I change my mind.

Ephesians 4:18
Having the understanding darkened, being alienated from the life of God through the ignorance that is in them, because of the blindness of their heart.

Why are people around us so blind? Romans 1 says it's because, instead of worshiping God, they profess to be wise in themselves (1:22).

Ephesians 4:19
Who being past feeling have given themselves over unto lasciviousness, to work all uncleanness with greediness.

After Dr. Donald Barnhouse, the classic preacher from a generation ago, shared a message about the repercussions of sin, a young man approached him and said, "I sin, but it doesn't seem to matter at all. I'm not haunted by it. I don't get depressed about it. It doesn't bother me a bit."

Dr. Barnhouse looked at him and said, "Tell me, son, what would happen if I dropped an eight-hundred-pound weight on the body of a dead man? Would he feel it? Would he be in pain? Would it bother him?"

"Of course not," said the young man.

"That's the point," said Dr. Barnhouse. "If you don't feel the weight of sin, if it's not heavy upon you, if it's not having an impact on you, it's because you're spiritually dead."

Ephesians 4:20, 21
But ye have not so learned Christ; If so be that ye have heard him, and have been taught by him, as the truth is in Jesus.

The world embraces greediness, uncleanness, and empty-headedness. "But you," said Paul, "have not learned Christ that way." Notice Paul doesn't say, "You haven't learned *about* Christ that way." He says, "You haven't learned Christ that way."

I can learn about Abraham Lincoln. I can read books about him. I can go to Disneyland and "Meet Mr. Lincoln" fifteen times in a row. That's the way some people learn about Jesus. They read Matthew, Mark, Luke, and John fifteen times in a row and think they know Him. But in reality, they only know *about* Him.

To learn Christ implies communion and intimacy with Him. How does this happen practically? As you spend time studying John's Gospel, for example, read a verse or two, then say to the Lord, "That convicts me," or, "That confuses me," or, "That reminds me," or, "That blesses me." In so doing, you will be communing *with* Him personally rather than merely learning *about* Him academically. So whether you go for a walk, lock yourself in your bathroom, or drive to a secluded spot—find a place you can talk to the Lord as you read about Him. It will make all the difference in the world, for then you will truly learn Christ.

Ephesians 4:22 (a)
That ye put off concerning the former conversation the old man . . .

As you learn Christ, you'll find yourself changing your mind about everything. You will be "transformed by the renewing of your mind, that you may know what is the good, and perfect, and acceptable will of God" (see Romans 12:2).

Ephesians 4:22 (b), 23
. . . which is corrupt according to the deceitful lusts; and be renewed in the spirit of your mind.

I like the phrase "deceitful lusts" because there is no greater deceit than lust. There is no greater deceit than the desire of the flesh to have something or someone. "If I could just indulge myself, I would be so happy," lust says. "If I could just indulge myself, I would be so satisfied." Wrong. You'll be destroyed.

"Oh, but I just want to pray with her and have fellowship in the Lord with her," he says. "I just want to help her through her problems, or be with her in her time of difficulty." But he knows there's another agenda lurking inside of him. He prays with her, and then finds himself involved with her. It's a deceitful lust, even though it's couched in spirituality, or clothed in ministry.

The old adage is so true. Lust is like a fire. The more you feed it, the more it demands. The hotter it gets, the hotter it burns. "Put it off," Paul says. "Instead, be renewed in the spirit of your mind."

Ephesians 4:24
And that ye put on the new man, which after God is created in righteousness and true holiness.

Notice the order here. First you put off the old. Then you're renewed in your mind. In other words, you decide you're no longer going to walk like those who are involved in sin. And as you begin to put on a whole new way of talking, living, and behaving, your new lifestyle eventually becomes who you are. It's not deception. It's a decision. People who are like Christ have made a conscious decision to put on the new man, to put on Christ. As a result, they become what they have chosen to put on.

If I merely sit here and wait for something to happen—for my personality to change, for my heart to feel loving, for my soul to feel kind—I'll wait forever. I've got to make a choice. I must choose to be compassionate. I must choose to love. And as I do, I become compassionate; I become loving.

Ephesians 4:25 (a)
Wherefore putting away lying . . .

"Put on righteousness and put away lying," says Paul. He doesn't say to go to counseling to overcome the dysfunctional tendency of exaggeration or miscommunication. He simply says, "Stop lying. Now."

Ephesians 4:25 (b)
. . . speak every man truth with his neighbour: for we are members one of another.

If I place my hand on a hot burner, but my nerves lie to my brain, saying, "It's not hot," I will get burned. So, too, if one part of the body of Christ lies to another, everyone gets hurt.

Ephesians 4:26 (a)
Be ye angry, and sin not . . .

How does one be angry without sinning? As always, Jesus shows the way. When He overturned tables in the temple, He was not angry because His feelings were hurt, or because He felt ignored. He was angry because people were being hindered from worshiping the Father freely.

Ephesians 4:26 (b)
. . . let not the sun go down upon your wrath.

If you go to bed angry, you're in danger. Why? Read on.

Ephesians 4:27
Neither give place to the devil.

Satan can work even while you sleep. If you're angry with your husband or your neighbor when you go to sleep, you give the Enemy the opportunity to plant a root of bitterness within you, and you'll wake up the next day feeling angry (Hebrews 12:15). While there's a place for righteous indignation that leads us to pray about an unfair situation or an injustice, and to seek the Lord for its resolution—there is simply no place for the devil in our lives.

Ephesians 4:28
Let him that stole steal no more: but rather let him labour, working with his hands the thing which is good, that he may have to give to him that needeth.

Stealing from the tree of the knowledge of good and evil, the first Adam was a thief and was kicked *out* of paradise. To a thief on a cross, the Last Adam—Jesus Christ—said, "Today you will be with Me *in* paradise" (see Luke 23:43). Jesus makes everything different. Thus, the Lord would say to those who have a tendency to steal—be it time from their employers or money from the government as they pay their taxes—"Start working. Start giving."

Ephesians 4:29
Let no corrupt communication proceed out of your mouth, but that which is good to the use of edifying, that it may minister grace unto the hearers.

Warming himself by the fire outside the house of Caiaphas, Peter denied ever knowing Jesus. But a servant girl knew otherwise because his accent gave him away (Mark 14:70).

You can always tell which kingdom a person is from by his speech. The language of the kingdom of darkness and death is that of complaining and murmuring, fault-finding and cynicism, cursing and corrupt communication. A person living in the kingdom of light and life, on the other hand, speaks graciously and kindly, using words of hope and thanksgiving.

Ephesians 4:30, 31
And grieve not the holy Spirit of God, whereby ye are sealed unto the day of redemption. Let all bitterness, and wrath, and anger, and clamour, and evil speaking, be put away from you, with all malice.

My bitterness, my anger, my speaking evil of someone or losing my temper with someone grieves the Spirit. Why? It's not that God says, "Anger and evil speaking cause My ears to burn," or, "Bitterness and wrath are offensive to Me." That's not the idea. There's not a curse word God hasn't heard. There is nothing that shocks Him. God is not grieved by how our speech, anger, or malice affects Him, but by how it affects us. He's grieved not because He can't handle our sin, but because it hinders Him from doing His work in, through, and for us.

Ephesians 4:32
And be ye kind one to another, tenderhearted, forgiving one another, even as God for Christ's sake hath forgiven you.

In sharp contrast to bitterness and malice, kindness and forgiveness delight the heart of our heavenly Father. Kindness and forgiveness delight the hearts of earthly fathers as well. That's why this is one of the first verses I taught my kids!

Forgiveness is not a burden God places upon us, but rather a safeguard for our mental health and emotional stability.

After teaching His disciples to pray, Jesus went on to underscore only one point: Forgiveness (Matthew 6:14, 15). Why? Was He trying to make it rough on them? On the contrary, He was saying, "I want you to be free from the burden of holding a grudge. If you don't choose to forgive, you won't enjoy the intimacy and closeness with the Father you would have otherwise. It's all based on forgiveness."

If there's someone toward whom you're bitter, do yourself a huge favor and forgive him—even as God has forgiven you.

---

5 In chapter 5, Paul continues his exhortation to walk in purity.

Ephesians 5:1
Be ye therefore followers of God, as dear children.

Again, we see the word "therefore." And what is it there for? It refers to the last verse in the previous chapter, where we are told to forgive one another because God has forgiven us for Christ's sake. In other words, Paul is saying, "It only makes sense to follow the One who has forgiven you."

Ephesians 5:2
And walk in love, as Christ also hath loved us, and hath given himself for us an offering and a sacrifice to God for a sweetsmelling savour.

A "sweet-smelling savour" refers to Leviticus 1—5, wherein we see the burnt offering, meal offering, and the peace offering—all called sweet-smelling offerings because their aroma was sweet to the Father. So, too, when you choose to follow Jesus' example by sacrificing your rights, by walking in love, the scent is sweet to the Father.

Ephesians 5:3
But fornication, and all uncleanness, or covetousness, let it not be once named among you, as becometh saints.

According to Proverbs 6:32, he who is involved in fornication or adultery destroys his soul, his inner person. The world doesn't understand this. The world thinks fornication is nothing more than two bodies coming together in a moment of ecstasy. But the Bible says it's actually two souls being joined as one. Thus, a person who engages in fornication or lives in adultery will become only a shell of a person, as layer after layer of his inner person is stripped off with each different encounter. That's the tragedy of sexual sin. The issue is not AIDS, sexually transmitted disease, or unwanted pregnancy. The issue is that of losing part of one's soul.

Ephesians 5:4 (a)
Neither filthiness, nor foolish talking, nor jesting, which are not convenient . . .

The filthiness, foolish talking, and jesting here in verse 4 are related to the fornication, uncleanness, and coveting of verse 3. Anyone watching culture knows that what once caused people to blush is now nothing but a joke because our culture has become totally desensitized.

Ephesians 5:4 (b)
. . . but rather giving of thanks.

Instead of talking like the world, just start praising the Lord. Whenever the conversation takes a sinful or suggestive turn, alter its course by bringing the Lord into it, by saying, "Isn't God good? Let me tell you what He did for me today. . . ."

Ephesians 5:5
For this ye know, that no whoremonger, nor unclean person, nor covetous man, who is an idolater, hath any inheritance in the kingdom of Christ and of God.

The Greek word translated "whoremonger" is *pornos,* from which we get our word "pornography." Whore-mongering is embracing a prostituted life. And that can happen on the "900" telephones lines, on the Internet, in the things you read, and in the movies you see.

Paul says your heart tells you and your spirit confirms that if you are a whoremonger—if you are delighted by and caught up in pornography—you are not part of the kingdom. You can come to church every time we meet; you can show up every time the doors are open. But if you are involved in this stuff—if this is your idol, if this is what you're living for—you're not saved.

"You *know* this," says Paul. You don't need a preacher to tell you, or a friend to remind you. In your heart, you already know that if you're a whoremonger, an unclean person, making sexual fulfillment your idol—you do not have an inheritance in the kingdom of God."

Ephesians 5:6
Let no man deceive you with vain words: for because of these things cometh the wrath of God upon the children of disobedience.

Concerning uncleanness and pornography, people use vain words when they say to us, "Hey, don't be so uptight." The Gnostics, or, literally, "those with special knowledge" did the same thing in Paul's day. Believing themselves to be especially knowledgeable, the gnostics essentially said, "Matter is evil and only the spirit is pure. Therefore, it doesn't matter what one does with his body. Man can indulge his flesh because it's only his spirit that matters."

The heresy of Gnosticism rears its ugly head in our day in those who say, "God knows you're a sexual creature and that you need to indulge your flesh. So go ahead."

Don't be deceived. If you've been walking with the Lord, but still succumb to fleshly indulgences, you're on shaky ground. I'm not talking about the struggle a person has with his flesh. I'm talking about a lifestyle of embracing one's flesh. If you cater to your flesh day after week after month after year after decade, you need to take a careful look at your spiritual standing.

Ephesians 5:7–10
Be not ye therefore partakers with them. For ye were sometimes darkness, but now are ye light in the Lord: walk as children of light: (For the fruit of the Spirit is in all goodness and righteousness and truth;) Proving what is acceptable unto the Lord.

"You used to walk in darkness. But now you're proving, or literally learning, what is really acceptable in the sight of the Lord," says Paul.

Gang, if I sit in the theater and watch people indulging their fleshly lusts on the screen, I am a partaker of their activity. I support it financially when I buy the ticket. And I vote for our culture to keep making this kind of movie whenever I fill a seat to watch it. There's a better way. We can pray, "You know I struggle with my flesh, Lord. You know I'm tempted by it. But, Lord, I want nothing to do with it. I've learned through Your Word and by experience that sin stinks. I'm not going to justify it any longer. I'm not going to excuse it anymore. Instead, I choose to walk in the light."

Ephesians 5:11, 12
And have no fellowship with the unfruitful works of darkness, but rather reprove them. For it is a shame even to speak of those things which are done of them in secret.

To "reprove" means "to rebuke." In other words, when a dirty joke or an unclean phrase is spoken, I am not simply to hold my tongue, but I am to rebuke, correct, and deal with the situa-tion. I am to say, "I know you're my office-mate, my boss, or my teammate, but I have to share this with you because I want to see you do better. Here's why this kind of talk is not wise. . . ."

Ephesians 5:13
But all things that are reproved are made manifest by the light: for whatsoever doth make manifest is light.

Some of the merchandise on the crowded streets of old Jerusalem looks pretty good while in the windowless shops. But I have learned not to buy anything until I first take it outside, until I first examine it in the light because it's amazing how even junky stuff looks okay in the dim light of those shops. So, too, only the light of the Word and the light of fellowship makes known that which is acceptable, that which is truly good.

Ephesians 5:14
Wherefore he saith, Awake thou that sleepest, and arise from the dead, and Christ shall give thee light.

"Wake up!" says Paul. "Look what's happening in your lives."

I know of young men who could have turned this world upside down for the Lord. I know of young guys who could have really made a mark for the kingdom. But because they weren't awake to what the Word of God says concerning filthiness, coarse jesting, uncleanness, fornication, and pornography, they're ineffective to this day.

Ephesians 5:15
See then that ye walk circumspectly, not as fools, but as wise.

The word "circumspectly" suggests the idea of a circle. "See that you look around," Paul says. "See that you're vigilant, not being blindsided, not being tricked."

Ephesians 5:16
Redeeming the time, because the days are evil.

We live in an evil day, a dark time. Redeem it by integrating the Lord into whatever you do. For example, when you jog, don't just think about your aches and pains. Instead, start praying for people who are worse off than you. Thank the Lord for things you see. Pray about things that come to mind. Redeem the time by bringing the Lord into all you do. Anything we do that doesn't have a spiritual texture to it is a waste of time.

Ephesians 5:17
Wherefore be ye not unwise, but understanding what the will of the Lord is.

What is God's will? That we would walk in purity. How does that work out practically? Read on.

Ephesians 5:18
And be not drunk with wine, wherein is excess; but be filled with the Spirit.

Forget the distilled spirits. Drink deeply of the dynamic Spirit of the Holy Ghost.

Ephesians 5:19 (a)
Speaking to yourselves . . .

Talk to yourself. David did. "Bless the Lord, O my soul," he said (Psalm 103). "Come on, soul, start blessing the Lord. Why art thou disquieted? Why are you depressed? Hope thou in God" (see Psalm 43:5).

Ephesians 5:19 (b), 20
. . . in psalms and hymns and spiritual songs, singing and making melody in your heart to the Lord; giving thanks always for all things unto God and the Father in the name of our Lord Jesus Christ.

When I feel things aren't going very well, I'm tempted to lose heart. When this happens, the only thing to do is to speak to myself in psalms, hymns, and spiritual songs.

No wonder David was discouraged. He and his men returned from fighting the Amalekites only to discover not only that their town had been burned by their enemies, but that their wives and kids had been taken hostage.
"This is your fault, David," said his men. "You took us away from here." And so angry were they that they wanted to kill him.
What did David do? He encouraged himself in the Lord (1 Samuel 30:6). He sang songs. He wrote psalms. He began to praise and worship. As a result, he rallied his men once again and they recovered all that was lost.

Had David remained in his depressed state, not only would he have been rendered ineffective, but the women and children would have remained captive. And so will you until you begin to worship. God's will is that you be free—and nothing will free you from the tyranny of your own situation like worship. You will be profoundly blessed and amazingly productive whenever you

give thanks to God for *all* things in the name of our Lord Jesus Christ.

Ephesians 5:21
Submitting yourselves one to another in the fear of God.

Walking in harmony in our marriages is based upon the key component of submission. Scripture talks about marriage in such a profoundly simple and simply profound way. You don't need countless books, seminars, or videos dealing with marriage. The Word spells out simply and succinctly how it is to work.

Ephesians 5:22
Wives, submit yourselves unto your own husbands, as unto the Lord.

Great is the day, wife, when you realize that ever since the Garden of Eden, males have been missing something. You see, when Adam went to sleep in the Garden, God took a rib from his side, and from it fashioned the woman, the "completer" of the man. Why doesn't your husband communicate more freely? Why doesn't he feel things more deeply? I believe it all stems from the fact that he's missing a rib; he's missing the part that was given to you.

"Well, if he's missing something, yet I still want to communicate, what do I do?" you ask.

In the Garden of Eden, the first Adam lost something. But there's another Adam—the Last Adam, Jesus Christ. So complete is the Last Adam that He is not only portrayed in Scripture as a male bullock (Numbers 15), but as a red heifer, a female cow (Numbers 19). Not only is He the epitome of strength; He is also the very essence of tenderness.

Dear sister, as long as you look to your husband to meet your deepest needs, you'll be frustrated perpetually. You'll put pressure on him to be what he can't be because he's missing something. It is only in Jesus Christ that you will find true fulfillment. In talking to Him, in learning of Him, in walking with Him, you will find the satisfaction your heart is craving. Drink deeply of the Last Adam—the Perfect One, Jesus Christ—for when you tap in to Him and maintain a vital, personal daily devotional life, you won't push your husband to be something he cannot be.

Wives, continue to love the Lord with all your heart and soul, with all your mind and strength—just as you did before you were married. For it is only in Him that you will find the answer to the cry of your heart.

Ephesians 5:23, 24
For the husband is the head of the wife, even as Christ is the head of the church: and he is the saviour of the body. Therefore as the church is subject unto Christ, so let the wives be to their own husbands in every thing.

If you are a Christian wife, you are to submit to your husband even as you would submit to the Lord. Let society say what it may. God's Word has stood the test of time, for whenever a wife chooses to be submitted to her husband, her marriage is on the way to becoming a blessed union, indeed.

Husbands, in turn, must never forget that, as commanded in verse 21, they are to submit to their wives. How does this work out practically? I believe the best way to understand this is to look at the example of the marriage held up in the New Testament as a model marriage—the marriage of Sarah and Abraham.

At seventy-six years of age, having received a promise from the Lord that they would have a child, Sarah said, "Listen, Abraham, we're not getting any younger. So let's help the Lord out a bit. Have relations with my handmaid, Hagar, and the child produced will count as ours."

Abraham "hearkened unto the voice of his wife" (see Genesis 16:2), and a child named Ishmael was born.

Thirteen years later, after the promised child had indeed come and was weaned, Sarah said to Abraham, "Hagar's son and my son cannot live in the same tent. Ishmael must go."

"No way," said Abraham.

"Hearken unto the voice of your wife," said God (see Genesis 21:12).

Interestingly, when Sarah told him to have relations with Hagar, Abraham submitted to his wife. But when she told him to deal with Ishmael, he said, "No." In so doing, Abraham hearkened to his wife in something contrary to God's ways, but ignored the voice of his wife when it was actually right in the sight of the Lord.

This means that while I as a husband am held responsible for the direction of my family, I must not be dictatorial in my behavior toward them. There are times when I need to listen to my wife. There are times when I must choose to submit to what she's saying, realizing the Lord can speak through her. Therefore, it is the wise husband who says to his wife, "I want to hear your heart and mind on this matter and match it against the Word of God because I know I am the one who will ultimately be held responsible." And sud-

denly, rather than being a justification for me to be dictatorial over my wife, Ephesians 5:22 humbles me before the Lord, realizing *I* am held accountable for the direction of my family.

Ephesians 5:25 (a)
Husbands, love your wives . . .

Again, God's instructions are so clear. Inspired by God's Spirit, Paul simply says, "Husbands, love your wives." How? Read on.

Ephesians 5:25 (b)
. . . even as Christ also loved the church, and gave himself for it.

How should you love your wife?
Just as Jesus loves you, just as Jesus loves the Church.
First of all, He loves us sacrificially.

- In the Garden of Eden, the first Adam parted with a bone.
  On the hill of Calvary, the Last Adam poured out His blood.
- At creation, the First Adam gave something of himself.
  On the Cross, the Last Adam gave all of Himself.

This means that if I am to love my wife as Christ loved the Church, I'll love her to the point where I die to my own dreams, my own desires, and my own wishes. In other words, I'll love her to death.

Second, Jesus loves the church unconditionally. Jesus doesn't love us only if we're "good boys and girls," only if we have morning devotions, only if we tithe. He loves us period. And I am to love my wife in the same manner. I'm not to love her only if she makes good meals, laughs at my jokes, or if she pleases me. I'm to love her period. And there isn't a woman on the face of the earth who will have difficulty submitting to a man who loves her in that way. Submission is never a problem when a man loves his wife as Christ loves the church.

Ephesians 5:26, 27
That he might sanctify and cleanse it with the washing of water by the word, That he might present it to himself a glorious church, not having spot, or wrinkle, or any such thing; but that it should be holy and without blemish.

As the bride of Christ, what does Jesus do to us? He washes us with the water of the Word. He irons out the wrinkles. He takes away the blemishes. In so doing, Jesus says, "I know My bride isn't perfect. But I'm going to work on her and in her that she might be sanctified, made beautiful, washed by the water of My Word."

If you don't like your wife, brother, it's because you've been a miserable husband. First Corinthians 11:7 tells us the woman is the glory of the man. The word "glory" literally means "reflection." If I look at my wife and don't like what I see, it's because I'm seeing a reflection of my own failure. You who say, "I just don't like my wife"— when was the last time you washed her with the water of the Word? When was the last time you opened the Bible with her? When was the last time you humbled yourself before the Lord and prayed with her?

If I don't like my wife's appearance or attitude or actions, the tendency could be for me to say, "I'll just find someone else." But that won't work either because my next wife, also being a reflection of my own shortcomings, will inevitably seem just as flawed to me.

The first miracle Jesus ever did was at a marriage ceremony. That's where miracles need to happen most often. The wine having run out, Jesus called the servants apart and said, "Take those stone pots. Fill them to the brim with water. Then serve the water to the guests." Sure enough, as the servants began to pour, the water was changed to wine of the highest quality (John 2:10).

So, too, husband, just as Jesus came as the servant of all, you're to be a servant to your wife. If the wine of romance, the wine of happiness, the wine of joy is gone from your marriage, first fill up your own earthen vessel with the water of the Word. Get back into the Word. Reestablish a devotional time. Study the Scriptures. Join a men's fellowship group. Do whatever it takes to fill up your life with the Word. And once you're filled, take what you're learning and serve your wife the water of the Word. Then watch it be transformed into the wine of joy.

Ephesians 5:28
So ought men to love their wives as their own bodies. He that loveth his wife loveth himself.

According to Paul, the best thing you can do for yourself, husband, is to love your wife. Loving your wife is actually better for you than playing racquetball, lifting weights, playing golf, or jogging. Love is a verb. It's an action, not a feeling. It's something you *choose* to do.

Ephesians 5:29, 30
For no man ever yet hated his own flesh; but nourisheth and cherisheth it, even as the Lord the church: For we are members of his body, of his flesh, and of his bones.

Contrary to what society says, the Bible declares we don't have to be taught to love ourselves. We already do.

Ephesians 5:31
For this cause shall a man leave his father and mother, and shall be joined unto his wife, and they two shall be one flesh.

For a marriage to be successful, a man must leave those who were closest to him and cleave to his wife. If there's another female he's sharing with, talking with, or ministering to—he's headed for disaster. "Oh, but she's just a co-worker. She's just telling me her problems, and I'm winning her to the Lord," he says. No. Jesus said wherever a man's treasure is, there will his heart be also (Matthew 6:21). Therefore, if he puts his treasure in her, if he shares his heart or Scripture or insights with her, his heart will follow inevitably. Then, because no man can serve two masters without hating one (Matthew 6:24), he'll end up hating his wife.

I firmly believe this is one of the biggest dangers to marriages in the church today. It's not the seductress who's a problem. It's the person with whom you're casually sharing and giving counsel. Therefore, if you're a wise man, you'll choose not to talk with women in a deep way about your frustrations or your fears, your doubts or your dreams. You'll cleave only to your wife. And as you do, you'll find romance and love being rekindled again and again. The world says, "If I loved her, I would cleave to her." The Bible says, "Cleave to her, and then you'll love her."

Ephesians 5:32
This is a great mystery: but I speak concerning Christ and the church.

Paul spoke of a mystery far bigger than the mere mechanics of marriage. . . .

It shouldn't be surprising that the place of His first miracle was at a marriage ceremony, for Jesus' entire mission was to proclaim and preach a message of love. Yet because Israel was so steeped in the law—in religion, rules, and regulations—they didn't understand it. Consequently, this Messenger of love received spikes in His hands, a nail in His feet, and was raised up on a Cross to die. When a Roman soldier thrust a spear into His side, blood and water came forth, reminiscent of the water turned into blood-red wine at Cana.

Even as the first Adam was asleep in a garden when his side was opened and his bride was brought forth, so, too, the Last Adam was in a garden tomb "asleep." When He arose, who was the first one He talked to? A woman, Mary. Mary was the beginning of a bride for Jesus. Although she was once a demon-possessed sinner, she was one who loved Jesus to such a degree that she was ready to carry His body alone (John 20:15). So deeply did she love Him that she couldn't let Him go (John 20:17).

How easy it is for me to miss what is our true purpose this week, this day this moment. The Lord is not asking for our sacrifice, our service, our study. Hear, O Christian, the Lord your God is one Lord. And thou shalt *love* the Lord thy God with all thy heart and soul and might (Deuteronomy 6:4, 5). Love is what He asks for. Love is what we're created for.

We are Eve—fallen like Eve, indeed; seduced like Eve, yes; flawed like Eve, absolutely. But Jesus Christ loves us. And even as Adam knowingly ate of the forbidden fruit in order that he might be with Eve, so the Last Adam knowingly took upon Himself the sin of the world that He might spend eternity with us.

The mystery of marriage is that Jesus wants to be one with you. He wants to communicate with you. He wants to walk in the rain with you. He wants to go to the lake with you. He loves you and wants you to love Him. How? Marriage will teach you, for it's an illustration of what you should be doing with the Lord, and for the Lord, in the Spirit. Don't get sidetracked, gang. Don't fall prey to religion and rules, sacrifice and service. You are the Lord's love. *That's* the mystery of marriage.

Ephesians 5:33
Nevertheless let every one of you in particular so love his wife even as himself; and the wife see that she reverence her husband.

After celebrating her seventy-fifth wedding anniversary, a lady was asked the secret of her marriage. "On my wedding day, I intended to write a list of ten things for which I would forgive my husband," she said. "But I never got around to writing it down. So over the years, whenever he would make me hopping mad, I would just tell myself it was a good thing for him that what he did was on my list!"

Honor your husbands, women. Love your wives, guys. That's the way it works.

6 Continuing his call for harmony in the home, Paul addresses the children in the Ephesian congregation, knowing they would be in attendance when his Epistle arrived. In other words, Paul didn't see church attendance as an activity only for Mom or Dad. He simply assumed the children would be in church. . . .

Ephesians 6:1 (a)
Children . . .

Teknon, the Greek word translated "children," refers to anyone of any age living under his parent's roof. One could be nineteen, twenty-three, or thirty-two years of age and still fall under the category of *teknon*. Thus, as long as you choose to live with your parents, this is the Word of the Lord for you.

Ephesians 6:1 (b)
. . . obey your parents . . .

The Greek word translated obey is *hupakouo*, which speaks of a soldier about to engage into battle, listening carefully for the orders and instructions of his commanding officer. If he didn't listen carefully, he could be in the wrong place at the wrong time, costing him his life. The scriptural command to obey one's parents doesn't call for a "yeah, yeah, yeah" kind of response. No, it calls for one to obey them as if his life depended on it.

In the fourth quarter, twenty yards from the end zone, six points down, every person in the huddle listens intently to the quarterback, knowing they have to hear the play and get the count lest they cost their team the victory. That is the degree of intensity wrapped up in *hupakouo*.

Ephesians 6:1 (c)
. . . in the Lord: for this is right.

Although children are to listen to their parents as if their life depended on it, they need only embrace what their parents say if it's "in the Lord." That is, if a parent tells a child to do something contrary to the heart and will of God, he is under no obligation to obey. However, if a child forgoes obeying his parents on the grounds that what they ask of him is contrary to the will of God, he better have chapter and verse and theology down pat. Otherwise, the person under the roof of his parents is to submit to them enthusiastically. It's just that simple.

Ephesians 6:2, 3
Honour thy father and mother; (which is the first commandment with promise;) that

it may be well with thee, and thou mayest live long on the earth.

Why is it right to obey Mom and Dad? Because there's a promise connected with that premise: He that does so will live long on the earth (Exodus 20:12). What does this mean? The rabbis say it means that the days of the one who obeys his parents will be rich—not necessarily long in quantity, but long on quality. This could very well be true, for some of the finest saints in church history died at relatively young ages. Jim Elliot, for example, was perhaps the most impacting missionary of the last fifty years—even though he died at age twenty-three. His days weren't long, but they were rich, indeed.

What if you feel you know more than your parents concerning a certain issue? I am reminded of another who could have felt this way. . . .

Having lost track of Him, Joseph and Mary returned to the temple to find Jesus. "Where have You been?" they asked Him.

"Don't you understand?" He answered. "I must be about My Father's business" (Luke 2:49).

At that point, obviously knowing more than His earthly parents, Jesus could have remained in the temple. Instead, Scripture records that He returned to Nazareth and was subject to His parents. The result? He increased in wisdom and stature and in favor with God and with man (Luke 2:52).

Jesus submitted to His parents even though He knew more than they did. And because He submitted to them, we read that He grew in favor with God and man. In other words, there was something about Him that attracted people to Him to such a degree that a few years later, fishermen would drop their nets, a tax collector would abandon his table, and multitudes would leave their homes to follow Him.

Ephesians 6:4 (a)
And, ye fathers . . .

Paul doesn't say anything to mothers as it relates to raising children. Why? Because it's natural for a mother to care about her kids, to do whatever she can for her kids. Dads, however, are sometimes a different story. . . .

Ephesians 6:4 (b)
. . . provoke not your children to wrath . . .

What does it mean to provoke your children to wrath? Colossians 3:21 gives the amplification when it says, "Fathers provoke not your children to

anger, lest they be discouraged." To provoke your kids to wrath means to make them discouraged. How? By loading them down with expectations.

Because men have a dangerous tendency to want to relive their glory days through their kids, they often say, "I played ball, so you'll play ball," or, "I was good at math, so you'll be good at math," or, "I'm gregarious and outgoing, so you'll be gregarious and outgoing." Don't do it, Dad. Wise is the father who understands that his children are not to be molded, but to be unfolded. In other words, you have the privilege, Dad, of observing your child carefully, seeing how God made him—and then unfolding what God has built into him from the moment of conception, all for His glory.

Ephesians 6:4 (c)
. . . but bring them up . . .

The tendency for men is to say, "Earning a living is my job. Raising the kids is my wife's job." Scripture says otherwise. The Word of God says dads are to bring up their children. How? First of all, by being there. . . .

During "Show and Tell," elementary kids were telling what their dads did for a living. "My daddy is the president of his company," one said. "He travels all over the world."

"Well, my daddy is really rich," said another. "We have nice cars and a pool and even an airplane."

"My daddy," said a little boy, "is a professional baseball player."

Kids and teacher alike were impressed with the stories—until a little girl in the back of the room cautiously said, "My daddy is . . . here."

Are you there, Dad? Although we hear lots of talk about "quality time," in many cases, I think it's nothing more than an excuse for not spending enough time with our kids.

Ephesians 6:4 (d)
. . . in the nurture . . .

We see the same word translated "nurture" here in Ephesians in Hebrews 12:6 when the writer says, "Whom the Father loves, He *chastens*—or nurtures, or disciplines." Even as you help your children walk in the path God has laid out for them uniquely, it is your responsibility, Dad, to deal with the sin within them innately.

"In sin did my mother conceive me," the psalmist declared (Psalm 51:5). This means David was born a sinner. The depravity of man is a doctrine that today's educators deny, but which God's Word underscores from cover to cover. Kids are born sinners. Oh, they're talented. After all, they're made in the image of God. There is all kinds of potential packed into their little bodies. But there's also sin, anger, rage, and hostility within them.

> One study of juvenile delinquency came to this conclusion: Every baby starts life as a little savage. He is completely selfish and totally self-centered. He wants what he wants when he wants it: his bottle, his mother's attention, his playmate's toys, his uncle's watch. Deny him these things and he seethes with a rage and aggressiveness that would be murderous were he not so helpless. He's dirty. He has no morals, no knowledge, no developed skills. This means that all children, not just certain children, are born delinquent. If permitted to continue on in their self-centered world of infancy, every child would grow to be a criminal, a thief, a rapist, a killer.

> He that spareth his rod hateth his son: but he that loveth him chasteneth him betimes.
> Proverbs 13:24

Empty threats produce unresolved guilt without healing or restoration. On the other hand, when I spanked my children, they were dealt with quickly, emotionally, and in a way they understood completely. They cried; I hugged them; they hugged me—and the issue was put behind us totally.

Ephesians 6:4 (e)
. . . and admonition of the Lord.

"Admonition of the Lord" means you talk to your son and daughter constantly about the things of God.

> And thou shalt teach them diligently unto thy children, and shalt talk of them when thou sittest in thine house, and when thou walkest by the way, and when thou liest down, and when thou risest up.   Deuteronomy 6:7

Dad, you are to talk to your kids all the time about the Word of God.
"But they won't like me," you say.
You're not parenting to be liked by your children. You're parenting to train them how to live on earth successfully and in heaven eternally.
"But they'll think I'm preaching at them."
You don't have to give your kids a ten-point outline of Leviticus 23. You simply need to use opportunities that arise naturally to help them to grow spiritually.
"But my kids won't let me. They don't open up conversationally."

Then you have the privilege of doing what the most righteous man on the face of the earth did. Scripture says Job got up every morning and offered sacrifice on behalf of his kids. He bloodied his hands; he sweat; he expended energy in prayer for his children "lest today be the day they forget God or curse Him" (see Job 1:5).
Even if he doesn't have access to his children because of physical or emotional barriers, there's not a dad who can't say, "Even though it's bloody, even though it makes me sweat, I'm going to pray for my kids with intensity and consistency." If your children are still under your roof, even if they don't talk to you, you can slip into their rooms at night while they sleep, kneel at the foot of their beds, lay your hand gently upon them and pray,

> "Father, please bless what goes on in my son's heart or in my daughter's mind even as they sleep. I pray Your Spirit to come upon them. I pray for wisdom to be understood and embraced by them. I pray that their lives would be pleasing to You. I pray that, even now, Your blood would cover them and that Your angels would stand by them so that the evil one would not be allowed to penetrate, seduce or destroy them."

No matter what else you may or may not do, Dad—you can and must pray.

Ephesians 6:5
Servants, be obedient to them that are your masters according to the flesh, with fear and trembling, in singleness of your heart, as unto Christ.

When Paul penned these words, there were over six million slaves in the Roman Empire. Because they were viewed as less than human, they were treated brutally in most cases. Thus, Paul's words are shocking when he says, "Servants—or slaves—you are not to rebel against your masters, run away from your masters or be angry with your masters. You're to obey your masters."

> David had a brutal boss. While he played his harp, King Saul tried to pin him to the wall with a spear—not once or twice, but three times. Realizing his services were not wanted, David headed to the caves at En-Gedi. Saul, in turn, gathered an army of three thousand to chase him down. When Saul inadvertently took a nap in the very cave in which David was hiding, David's men were overjoyed.
> "God has delivered Saul into your hand!" they said. "Now you can chop off his head!"

Instead, David did nothing more than cut off a piece of Saul's garment.

But even then, Scripture says David's heart "smote him" (1 Samuel 24:5).

David shows us that he saw Saul as God's instrument in his life to produce patience, maturity, compassion, and a greater dependence upon God within him.

Here's the question: Have you clipped the garment of your boss? Of your teacher? Of your parents? They are God's instruments, anointed ones in your life to develop depth, character, and maturity in you. Lop off their heads by launching a rebellion or losing your temper, finding fault with, or gossiping about them—and you will forfeit what God wants to do for you and through you.

You might not respect the person in authority over you, but you must respect his position because God has put him in your life. Lop off the skirts of the people in authority over you, and you will stunt, retard, and cripple that which God wants to do for you. But be like David and say, "Forgive me. I will never do that again"—and God will honor you.

Ephesians 6:6, 7
Not with eyeservice, as menpleasers; but as the servants of Christ, doing the will of God from the heart; with good will doing service, as to the Lord, and not to men.

We are to enthusiastically do what's asked of us. The word "enthusiasm" comes from the Greek phrase *en theos,* or "full of God."

Eugene Ormandy, a conductor of the Philadelphia Philharmonic, dislocated his right shoulder because he conducted with such enthusiasm. We know so little of this kind of service. We don't separate our shoulders. We barely wrinkle our ties. That's why we don't ascend to the level God would have us enjoy in so many arenas.

David was a man who went above and beyond the call of duty, bounding over walls expending great energy (Psalm 18:29). The men around him developed that same mentality. Hiding out in the cave at Adullam one day, David said, "I would give anything for a drink of water from the well at Bethlehem."

Hours later, as the sun began to set, three of his men—Adino, Eleazar, and Shammah—approached him. Their clothes were tattered, their flesh bruised and bleeding.

"Where did you guys go?" David must have asked.

And in my mind's eye, I can see a tear

running down his dusty cheek as they handed him a skin of water, drawn from the well of Bethlehem (2 Samuel 23).

The most precious gift David ever received was from three of his "employees" who had risked their lives to please him. No wonder it was Adino, Eleazar, and Shammah who remained chiefs of his mighty men once he became king.

Who becomes a mighty man on the job, in the church, for the kingdom? The one who hears the heart of his employer. The world says, "Skate by. Leave early. Cover up." God, however, says, "I'm looking for men and women who, with good cheer, enthusiasm, and singleness of heart, respect those in positions over them."

Ephesians 6:8
Knowing that whatsoever good thing any man doeth, the same shall he receive of the Lord, whether he be bond or free.

The enthusiastic work you do for your boss is not primarily for him—it's for the Lord. And what will be your reward?

First, you'll receive rewards in eternity (Matthew 25:23). Even if your boss, coach, or supervisor never notices what you're doing, God does. If you haven't "despised the days of small things" but have been faithful in your present situation—you will be given responsibility, blessing, and reward eternally (Zechariah 4:10).

A missionary was sailing home after spending forty years in Africa. On the ship with him was President Teddy Roosevelt, returning from a safari. As the ocean liner pulled into the docks of New York City, thousands of people were on the wharf cheering. Bands were playing. Reporters were waiting. And everyone was saying, "Wow! Teddy Roosevelt killed a rhinoceros and an elephant!"

The missionary turned to his wife and said, "You know, I'm a little bit bitter. After two weeks of big game hunting, Teddy Roosevelt receives a hero's welcome because he killed a rhino and an elephant. Yet we spent forty years in the jungle, laying down our lives to help people, and no one's here to welcome us home."

That night, the Lord spoke to the missionary's heart and simply said, "You're not home yet."

Even if you arrive early, stay late, and work hard at your job as unto the Lord—you still might not climb very high on the corporate ladder because you're not home yet. That day is yet to come.

Second, if you work enthusiastically and wholeheartedly, you will receive benefits presently. If you're thinking about serving the Lord in full-time ministry, it would be wise to remember that throughout Scripture, it was those who were already hard at work whom God called to serve Him.

Moses was shepherding his father-in-law's sheep when God called him (Exodus 3:1).

When the mantle was passed from Elijah to Elisha, Elisha was plowing a field (1 Kings 19:19).

Peter was fishing when Jesus called him (Matthew 4:18).

Even Paul was wholeheartedly persecuting Christians when God called him! (Acts 9:1, 2).

If you're thinking about the ministry eventually, work hard as unto the Lord in whatever He has set before you presently. Too many young men and women who want to enter the ministry or missionary service sit and wait for something to happen. Certainly that could not be said of Paul. . . .

While in Ephesus, Paul taught during the afternoon break from two o'clock to four-thirty every afternoon. The remainder of the time, he worked by the sweat of his brow, making tents. He didn't have to do this. He could have said, "If you guys can't support me, I'm gone." But he didn't. And what happened? His sweatbands—the tangible evidence of Paul's commitment to and love for the people of Ephesus—were used as agents of healing (Acts 19:12).

Whether you're a banker or carpenter, an electrician or a businessman, when you're working hard, giving your all, going above and beyond the call of duty, your boss will say, "What makes you work so well for me? I pay you minimum wage, yet you're putting forth maximum effort." The name of Jesus will be exalted by even the most hard-hearted employer if you demonstrate the love in your heart through the sweat of your brow.

Not only is there power, but there is also protection in perspiration. . . .

It was after the Fall that Adam was told to work by the sweat of his brow—perhaps as a way to keep from further trouble (Genesis 3:19).

"You don't understand how boring my job is," you say. "How can I possibly wash dishes at Denny's wholeheartedly?"

One of the greatest men who ever lived washed pots and pans for a living and went on to write the classic, *Practicing the Presence of God.* As Brother Lawrence washed pots and pans day after day, he worshiped, prayed, and shared truth. Over time, people began to hear about the dish washer who loved God and who glowed with God's glory—and they traveled to see him for themselves.

It is possible that at your job or in your school there is one person who will be impacted by watching you—one co-worker or colleague who will see in you something special, something different. Such was the case with Philip.

Called away from a city-wide revival in Samaria, God told him to go to the desert. There, he found one man—a leader in the Ethiopian government—reading the scroll of Isaiah.

"Do you understand what you're reading?" asked Philip. "Let me explain it to you" (Acts 8:30).

The Ethiopian was saved and baptized. He returned to Africa and ushered in a revival, the effects of which can be seen to this day.

So, too, there might be only one guy who works with you, only one person you will influence. But great will be your reward in heaven if you do it faithfully, enthusiastically, and with single-hearted energy.

Ephesians 6:9
And, ye masters, do the same things unto them, forbearing threatening: knowing that your Master also is in heaven; neither is there respect of persons with him.

Employers, just as your employees are to serve you, you are to serve them, for God is not a respecter of persons. He's not impressed by titles or positions.

Ephesians 6:10
Finally, my brethren, be strong in the Lord, and in the power of his might.

Paul begins this last section with a wonderful exhortation: Be strong in the Lord. This is a particularly good word for us today, for I believe we live in the generation of the "sissification" of the saints—due at least in part, I believe, to the idea that we should be vulnerable, sensitive, transparent, and all of those other '80s and '90s buzz words. A lot of Christians are moaning and groaning about their situation because their lives are centered on—how *they* are doing, how *they* are feeling, how *they* are treated.

Moses had died. The people were now ready to move into the Land of Promise where there was great fruit, into the land that flowed with milk and honey. At that time, however, there were giants in the land. Consequently, there were very real battles ahead of them. So three times in the first chapter of the book which bears his name, Joshua heard God say, "Be strong and of good courage. You're up to bat, Joshua. You cannot afford to become introspective or self-centered because there are three million people looking to you" (see Joshua 1:6, 7, 9). Not only did God exhort Joshua to be strong—but the people did as well. "We will follow you in the way you lead us," they said, "only be strong" (see Joshua 1:18).

So, too, I encourage you to be strong in the Lord because we are being inundated with Christian radio programs and books telling us to be introspective and to seek counseling. I believe this kind of thinking flies directly in the face of Scripture, for the exhortation of the Word is to be strong. God will never ask me to do what He does not enable me to do if I choose to believe Him for it and obey Him in it. How are we to be strong? Read on.

Ephesians 6:11
Put on the whole armour of God, that ye may be able to stand against the wiles of the devil.

The first step to being strong is to realize that life is not an encounter group. Life is not a bonding meeting. Life is not a playground. Life is a battleground. The reason so many in the church are weak is because they're not armed for battle.

If the men who stormed the beaches of Normandy on D-Day did so dressed in their jammies, something would have been terribly wrong. Yet I believe we live in a day of "jammy Christianity." "Let's put on our jammies and talk about how we feel," we say. "Let's have a slumber party, and we'll all bond." No. Paul tells us to put on our armor, to take advantage of the equipment God has given us to navigate life and negotiate the war that surrounds us. Dear saint, you can stand against the wiles of the devil—the cunning, clever attacks of Satan—only to the degree that you're protected with the whole armor of God.

Ephesians 6:12 (a)
For we wrestle not against flesh and blood, but against principalities . . .

Any time I am wrestling against flesh and blood, anytime I'm striving against people, I'm fighting the wrong battle. If you're fighting with your boss or your employees, if you're fighting your parents or your teenagers, you are fighting the wrong battle.

In the way with Israel and Judah, the king of Syria called his captains together and said, "Do not fight against any man great or small, but only against the king" (see 1 Kings 22:31). In other words, "Don't get sidetracked with any of the little guys. Stay focused on your main target and victory will follow."

The same is true with us. We are not to get sidetracked fighting against mere flesh and blood. We're to battle the spiritual entities that cause tension in our marriages, problems with our children, struggles with our parents. These entities are organized into principalities.

For twenty-one days, Daniel fasted and prayed as he set his face to seek God. At the end of that time, an angel appeared to him, saying, "Your prayers have been heard. I'm here to help you and to give you understanding. I would have been here sooner, but I got hung up between here and heaven. The demonic entity overseeing the region of Persia intercepted me, and a battle followed that was so intense that Michael the archangel had to come to set me free (Daniel 10:13).

According to this vignette, we understand that there are principalities—demonic entities over given regions of the world. Certain civilizations and cultures both historically and presently seem to be more oppressive and darker than others because, evidently, the demonic forces overseeing them are particularly potent.

Ephesians 6:12 (b)
. . . against powers . . .

Whereas "principalities" speak of territories or regions, "powers" speak of the demonic forces that keep people in bondage.

For eighteen years, she was unable to lift herself up. But when Jesus called her to Him and said, "Woman, thou art loosed of this infirmity," He laid His hands on her, and immediately she straightened up (see Luke 13:11).

If we fail to see that there are powers that cause people to be doubled over or bowed down in bondage, we're going to fight the wrong battle. We can take people through hundreds of hours of counseling—but if we don't deal with the real issue of principalities and powers, they'll never be truly set free.

Ephesians 6:12 (c)
... against the rulers of the darkness of this world ...

This speaks of the demonic forces that oversee the leaders in any given society—and provides the only explanation for the darkness that seems to increasingly permeate the world.

Ephesians 6:12 (d)
... against spiritual wickedness in high places.

Newer translations render this verse correctly as "against spiritual wickedness in *heavenly* places"—which speaks of the arena of mysticism. People can seem so heavenly as they look into a candle and proclaim they are light. But the New Age rap is nothing other than the age-old lie from the Garden of Eden. "Eat this fruit, Eve," Satan said. "Your eyes will be opened. (You'll experience enlightenment). You'll be like God. (You'll assume divinity). You'll never die." (You'll be reincarnated). Sound familiar? (see Genesis 3:4, 5)

Ephesians 6:13 (a)
Wherefore ...

While we need to be sober, we need not be scared because look what we've been given to combat Satan's attacks.

Ephesians 6:13 (b)
... take unto you the whole armour of God, that ye may be able to withstand in the evil day, and having done all, to stand.

Regardless of where you live, what school you attend, or who occupies the White House, you can stand. You can be strong because you've been given the perfect defense. Rather than feeling sorry for himself, Paul must have looked carefully at the guard to whom he was chained, using his armor as a vivid analogy.

Ephesians 6:14 (a)
Stand therefore, having your loins girt about with truth ...

Loins speak of the personal area of one's life. The private life of a spiritual man is surrounded by truth. He will do well who determines to put away lying.

In the day he should have been in battle, David took off his armor, got involved with Bathsheba, killed her husband, and tried to cover it up. "Blessed is he whose transgression is forgiven," he wrote a year later, "whose sin is covered. For when I kept silent, my bones waxed old. Day and night Thy hand was heavy upon me. My moisture was turned to the drought of summer. Then I acknowledged my sin unto Thee. Mine iniquity I hid not" (see Psalm 32).

In the Christian walk, the safest place to be is on the front lines of the battle. At age fifty, David thought he deserved some rest and relaxation. Big mistake. He left the front lines, got tangled up in sin, and lived a lie. The only way to stand is to have your loins—the secret part of you—supported by and bound up in truth.

Ephesians 6:14 (b)
... and having on the breastplate of righteousness.

Righteousness means doing what's right. A lot of people have sad hearts, hard hearts, broken hearts because they have failed to put on the breastplate of righteousness. There's such a wonderful freedom and liberty that comes from knowing you're not intentionally doing things that aren't right, and that your heart is protected by righteousness.

Does this mean your heart will never feel convicted?

No.

But it does mean your heart will never feel condemned. Our own hearts can condemn us (1 John 3:20). Satan can condemn us (Revelation 12:10). We can, however, recognize the difference between conviction and condemnation because condemnation causes us to run away from God, while conviction draws us toward God. Condemnation says, "What's the use?" and causes us to stop praying, to stop going to church, to stop reading the Word. Conviction, on the other hand, says "You can be forgiven," and draws us back to the Word, back into fellowship, back to the Lord.

Ephesians 6:15
And your feet shod with the preparation of the gospel of peace.

Having my feet shod with the gospel of peace means I don't walk *on* people, but I get to share *with* people. The word "gospel" means "good news." Therefore, as I walk through my day, it is my privilege say to those in my path, "Good news! The Lord loves you. He knows what you're going through. He can set you free."

Ephesians 6:16 (a)
Above all . . .

"Above all" does not mean "most importantly." It literally means "covering all."

Ephesians 6:16 (b)
. . . taking the shield of faith, wherewith ye shall be able to quench all the fiery darts of the wicked.

"Where in the world did that terrible, ugly thought come from?" we sometimes ask ourselves. It didn't come from the world. It's a fiery dart launched from hell. You might be in church, in prayer, or doing something very noble, when—boom—a fiery dart aflame with lust or gossip, cynicism or anger enters your mind. The only protection for this kind of assault is the shield of faith. . . .

When Roman soldiers went into battle, their enemies would not only shoot fiery arrows directly at them, but would launch them into the air above them. So what did the Romans do? The front row would hold their four-foot-by-two-foot shields in front of them side by side to form a protective wall. The remaining soldiers held their shields over their heads—"above all"—forming a roof of protection.

What are you to do when you're being barraged with the fiery darts of lust, cynicism, envy, anger, or gossip? Do what Paul told his young protigie Timothy to do: "Run from them, and follow after faith, righteousness, charity, and peace with them that call on the Lord out of a pure heart" (see 2 Timothy 2:22). In other words, run from sin and take cover under the shield of faith with your brothers.

Come into the congregation. Come to prayer meeting. Come to Bible study. Corporate worship, study, and prayer form a covering that is not found individually. Many a person has fled a particular lust only to encounter a worse one because he didn't run to the congregation of them who follow after faith and righteousness, love, peace, and purity. When you're hit with fiery darts, gang, get to church. Run as fast as you can to those who will provide a shield of covering for you.

Ephesians 6:17 (a)
And take the helmet of salvation . . .

Paul defines the helmet of salvation as the hope of the coming of the Lord (1 Thessalonians 5:8). I'll become greatly distressed as I see the world and culture collapsing around me unless the blessed hope of the coming of Jesus Christ is con-

stantly on my mind. I am thoroughly convinced His coming is very close. So was C. H. Spurgeon. So was Martin Luther. So was Augustine. So was Paul. So was Peter. All were great men who lived their lives anticipating and looking for the coming of Jesus Christ. Put me in their company any day! The great saints of history all lived in the anticipation that Jesus would come shortly. I will live until the day I die looking for and believing in the hope, the blessed hope of Jesus appearing and calling me home. That's the helmet of my salvation.

Ephesians 6:17 (b)
. . . and the sword of the Spirit, which is the word of God.

Machaira, the Greek word translated "sword," refers not to a big battle sword, but to a small dagger for use in hand-to-hand combat. *Rhema*, the Greek word translated "word," refers not to the Bible, but to an exact spoken word. Therefore, the idea here is that you'll have just the right word for the right person at the right time. As you study and meditate upon the full counsel of the written Word of God—the *rhema* word—the precise word—will come to you the moment you need to do exacting "surgery" regarding any specific situation.

Ephesians 6:18
Praying always with all prayer and supplication in the Spirit, and watching thereunto with all perseverance and supplication for all saints.

If you can't engage in hand-to-hand combat, if you can't give an exacting word because your kids have moved away or your neighbor is no longer speaking to you, you can still go to them in prayer. One of the neat things about prayer is that I can visit missionaries all over the world. I can pray blessing upon them in the Spirit. I can join with what they're doing. I can stand by them by using the long-range artillery of prayer. So, too, even if you're separated by physical or emotional distance, you can speak exacting words to the Lord through prayer on behalf of your family, friends, neighbors, co-workers, and fellow students.

For topical study of Ephesians 6:18 entitled "Praying in the Spirit," turn to page 1267.

Ephesians 6:19
And for me, that utterance may be given unto me, that I may open my mouth boldly, to make known the mystery of the gospel.

If I were Paul, I'm afraid I would have said, "As for me, pray that the doors of this prison might open so that I could get out of here. I'm tired of the dungeon. I'm tired of being chained to the soldier. I'm tired of my pain." But Paul didn't say that. He simply said, "Pray that I might be bold in sharing the gospel."

Ephesians 6:20
For which I am an ambassador in bonds: that therein I may speak boldly, as I ought to speak.

"I'm right where I should be, here in the dungeon," said Paul. "I'm thrilled to be here. After all, I've got a captive audience!" That's what it means to be strong in the Lord.

Ephesians 6:21, 22
But that ye also may know my affairs, and how I do, Tychicus, a beloved brother and faithful minister in the Lord, shall make known to you all things: Whom I have sent unto you for the same purpose, that ye might know our affairs, and that he might comfort your hearts.

"Don't feel sorry for me," said Paul. "My friend Tychicus will tell you I'm doing well."

Ephesians 6:23, 24
Peace be to the brethren, and love with faith, from God the Father and the Lord Jesus Christ. Grace be with all them that love our Lord Jesus Christ in sincerity. Amen.

The way to be strong is to wear the armor. I know some who almost physically put on the armor of God every morning. "I'm going to be conscious of truth in my inner life today," they say. "And I'm going to make sure my heart is right. I'm going to tell everyone I meet today something of the Good News of the gospel. And should I be barraged with fiery darts, I'll run to the protection of the congregation. I'll be consciously looking for the Lord's return today. And I'll carry my Bible with me in order that I might meditate upon it in order to have an exacting word for someone in need."

While all of that is wonderful for some, I have found that the majority of us are more like my son Benjamin. . . .

When Benjamin was in first grade, he was in such a hurry to get out the door and off to school in the morning, he thought he couldn't be bothered with getting dressed. His solution—until we told him otherwise—was to go to bed wearing the clothes he would wear the next day.

Maybe, like me, you find it overwhelming to go through the practice of putting on your armor a piece at a time. I suggest you do something a whole lot simpler: Just put on Jesus.

- He is the Truth (John 14:6).
- He is our Breastplate of Righteousness (Romans 13:14).
- He guides our feet in peace (Luke 1:79).
- He is our Shield of Faith (Hebrews 12:2).
- He is the Captain of our Salvation (Hebrews 2:10).
- He is the Word Made Flesh (John 1:14).

It's all wrapped up in Him.

PRAYING IN THE SPIRIT

A Topical Study of
Ephesians 6:18

The fact that the disciples said, "Lord, teach us to pray," intrigues me—for there is no record of them ever saying, "Lord, teach us to preach," or, "Teach us to cast out demons," or, "Lord, teach us to work miracles," or, "Teach us to heal people."

Why would they only ask Jesus to teach them to pray? I believe it's because, after observing Him, following Him, and living with Him, they understood that the power behind His preaching, behind His ability to overcome demonic entities, behind the miracles He worked so beautifully, indeed behind everything that happened through Him lay singularly in His prayer life.

They observed Him slip away to pray before the break of day. They knew that whether they were struggling on the Sea of Galilee or sleeping in the Garden of Gethsemane, Jesus was praying with intensity and consistency. Therefore, I suggest His disciples figured out early on that the key to everything Jesus did could be traced to the way He prayed. That is why they came to Him that day, saying, "Lord, teach us to pray."

Most of us understand the principle of the primacy of prayer—that prayer is to be a priority in our lives, and that it is vital to our walk. Yet, for many of us, prayer is little more than an obligation and all too often a burden. We know we should pray. We agree that there's power in prayer. But for many of us, prayer is a chore.

That's not the way prayer was meant to be. I suggest that the reason prayer has become no more than a duty is because we fail to comprehend three words in the text before us: "Praying always with all prayer and supplication *in the Spirit. . . .*"

Following are three applications connected to these all-important words.

A Theological Application

How can we who are sinful approach a holy God? Only through the Son. You see, if, as an Old Testament believer, you wanted to approach Jehovah, you would bring a lamb to the tabernacle, where it would be thoroughly and carefully inspected. Only if the priest found the lamb to be spotless and without blemish could you go into the tabernacle and commune with God.

So, too, we approach the Father not through a little lamb, but through the spotless Lamb of God. I come boldly before the Father, talk things over with the Father, receive help from the Father not because I am flawless, not because I am faultless, but because the Lamb is spotless, because Jesus is perfect.

We come to the Father through the Son by the Spirit—for if the Spirit didn't draw us, we'd never pray at all. "In me dwells no good thing," Paul declares (see Romans 7:18). That includes even the inclination to pray in more than a self-serving, superficial way. To pray in the Spirit means I come to the Father through the Son as the Spirit draws me.

A Pentecostal Application

Secondly, to pray in the Spirit refers ultimately to the Day of Pentecost. When the Holy Spirit came upon the disciples in the Upper Room, they began to pray in other tongues (Acts 2:4).

What does it mean to pray with other tongues? It means to pray with words, phrases, and—as Romans 8 indicates—with groanings that we have never learned, and that we don't understand intellectually.

> *For if I pray in an unknown tongue, my spirit prayeth, but my understanding is unfruitful.*
>   1 Corinthians 14:14

What is the benefit of "unfruitful" understanding? Simply this: We are commanded to pray without ceasing (1 Thessalonians 5:17), yet I cannot pray continually with my understanding. When I'm talking on the phone, driving a car, or shooting hoops, my mind is engaged in what I'm doing. But I can always pray in the Spirit—even while I'm preaching this sermon—because rather than using my mind to think about sentence structure and syntax, grammar and vocabulary, it's my heart that's praying.

I'm not on a tongues-speaking kick—but I do understand the validity of praying in the Spirit. There are so many situations about which I simply don't know how to pray intellectually. But I can pray in a prayer language and know I'm praying in perfect harmony with the Spirit. As I do, my own faith is strengthened (1 Corinthians 14:4; Jude 20). Who can pray in the Spirit? Anyone who desires to move in that dynamic, for Paul said, "I would that you all spake in tongues" (see 1 Corinthians 14:5).

A Transcendental Application

To pray in the Spirit carries with it a transcendental application. I'm not referring to the transcendental meditation of the '60s, or to the transcendentalists who gathered at Walden Pond with Thoreau, Emerson, and the boys. The word "transcendent" simply means "above"—a fitting description of praying in the Spirit, for when you engage in that kind of prayer, you transcend the limitations of the physical realm and move into the spiritual realm.

Warring against the nation of Israel, the king of Syria had cleverly set an ambush on the road he knew the king of Israel would travel. Just as the king of Israel was about to unknowingly walk into it, a messenger approached him, saying, "Proceed no farther! A message has come from the prophet in Dothan. There's an ambush ahead. Turn back."

Infuriated, the king of Syria set a second ambush. Again, as the king of Israel approached, a messenger came to him, saying, "Don't go that way. There's an ambush ahead." The king of Israel changed directions once again, leaving the king of Syria no choice but to try a third ambush—which also failed.

"There's a spy in our midst," said the king of Syria.

"Not so," said one of his advisors. "There is a prophet in the city of Dothan who knows everything you say."

With that, the king of Syria deployed thousands of soldiers to surround the city of Dothan and capture Elisha.

"We're dead!" cried Elisha's servant upon seeing the vast array of Syrian soldiers the next morning.

But Elisha, knowing what it meant to pray in the Spirit, to be transcendent, simply said, "Lord, open his eyes." And when Gehazi's eyes were opened, he saw that surrounding the Syrians were tens of thousands of angels in fiery chariots (2 Kings 6:17).

That's what it means to pray in the Spirit. You get above and beyond your present depressing, discouraging, physical limitations—and you begin to see what's happening in the Spirit even as you pray.

Jesus was in a seemingly impossible situation. His friend, Lazarus, had died. For four days, his body had been buried and was already beginning to decay.

"Roll away the stone," said Jesus. And then He lifted up His eyes and said, "Father, I thank Thee that Thou hast heard Me. Everyone else thinks the situation is impossible, but I thank Thee for what is about to happen" (see John 11:41, 42).

To pray in the Spirit means to transcend the stench and stink of death and despair. Let us quit our moaning, murmuring, and mourning and follow the example of Jesus, who said, "I see something about to happen, and I thank You, Father."

What would happen if we began to pray that way? Instead of going down a list during morning devotions, saying, "Bless Aunt Jane. Bless my dad. Bless my school teacher. Be with the president," we'd say, "Lord, I now see Your hand of blessing upon my son, and I thank You. I see provision being made for my neighbor. Thank You, Lord. I see Your Spirit speaking to my stubborn husband, or my rebellious daughter, or my hard-hearted boss. Thank You, Father."

The one who prays in the Spirit quits making speeches to God—going down a list of items to get it out of the way—and starts fellowshiping with God. His prayers slow down. His understanding opens up. His heart rejoices.

Perhaps the best example of what it means to pray in the Spirit is found in Luke 2.

Bludgeoned into submission by Rome, Israel was in bad straits. Nonetheless, a man whom tradition says was one hundred thirteen years old, upon whom Scripture says was the Holy Ghost, waited for the Messiah promised in Scripture. Day after week after month after year after decade went by, and still Simeon waited, having received revelation that he wouldn't die until his eyes had beheld Messiah.

Then came the word for which he had waited so long: "Today's the day."

No doubt Simeon shuffled as quickly as he could to the temple, expecting to hear the hoof beats of horses and the sound of soldiers marching as Messiah came with His army to set Israel free. But arriving at the temple, what did he see? Only a sixteen-year-old girl, her carpenter husband, and a baby.

Did Simeon say, "Let me get this straight. I've been hanging around for one hundred thirteen years, waiting for Messiah, anticipating the emancipation of our nation—and all I find is a *baby?* I'm out of here"?

No. He said, "Lord, now lettest thou thy servant depart in peace, according to thy word: For mine eyes have seen thy salvation, which thou hast prepared before the face of all people; a light to lighten the Gentiles, and the glory of thy people Israel" (Luke 2:29–32)

When you pray in the Spirit, believing God for a certain event or a specific situation, and the answer comes in an entirely different manner than you expected, you have a Simeon choice to make. You can either forget about praying in the Spirit and about believing God—or you can do what Simeon did. You can bless the Father.

If you choose to pray in the Spirit, I guarantee that your prayer lives will never be the same. While others are mourning and moaning, you'll be rejoicing. Where others are fearful, you'll be faithful. As others are bewildered, you'll be blessed.

May we be those who see the beauty and potency of "always praying with all prayer and supplication in the Spirit."

In Jesus' Name.

PHILIPPIANS

Background to Philippians

His mouth is most sweet: yea, he is altogether lovely.
Song of Solomon 5:16

What a wonderful description of our Lord, our Hero, Jesus Christ—for not only is He altogether lovely, He is simply All Together. He is at once:

- The Lion of the Tribe of Judah (Revelation 5:5)
- And the Lamb of God (John 1:29),

- The One who brings a sword (Matthew 10:34)
- And the Prince of Peace (Isaiah 9:6),

- The Man of Sorrows (Isaiah 53:3)
- And the Fullness of Joy (Psalm 16:11).

Truly, Jesus is the Man of Sorrows in order that He might identify with us, but also the Fullness of Joy that He might be attractive to us. There was something so radiant and full of joy about Jesus that people flocked around Him and listened to Him. Labeled a glutton and a winebibber by His enemies (Matthew 11:19), He was, in the best sense of the word, the Life of the party. "These things have I spoken unto you," He said, "that My joy might remain in you and that your joy might be full" (see John 15:11).

Christianity is to be a joyful religion—a relationship that experiences Jesus in such a way that there is, in fact, joy unspeakable. The idea that true spirituality is to be equated with misery is an idea completely contrary to Scripture, for truly, the nature of Jesus was such that people loved to be around Him. Thus, there should be a contagious joy within us.

Certainly such was the case with Paul, for in the four short chapters of his epistle to the Philippians, the word "joy" or "rejoicing" appears nineteen times—which is especially interesting in light of the fact that Paul penned his epistle from a Roman prison. Following the legal nightmare spoken of in Acts 21–28, Paul—chained to a guard—was awaiting trial, not knowing whether he would be befriended or beheaded by Caesar. If there was ever one who would be justified in writing a depressing and discouraging letter, it would be Paul. However, Paul took up pen and papyrus to do just the opposite, for Philippians is commonly known as "The Epistle of Joy." And if we grasp the basic message of Paul's letter to the church at Philippi, we, too, will be free to be joyful in Jesus—in spite of our external circumstances.

I am convinced that the joy Paul wrote about, the joy he lived out, was based not in his heart, but in his mind; not on how he felt, but on how he thought. The saying is true: Your attitude does, indeed, affect your altitude. How you think affects how you feel. And this epistle drives that point home: Fifteen times Paul talks about thinking, and ten times about remembering.

One of the most important components in understanding joyful, successful Christianity is this: You cannot change your heart—but you can change your mind. Conversely, God can change your heart, but He won't change your mind. Therefore, if I choose to change the way I think about a given situation, God will change my heart to follow suit. But if I do not choose to change my thoughts, God will not change my heart. That is why the wisest man on the face of the earth literally said, "As a man thinketh in his heart, so is he" (see Proverbs 23:7).

When people say, "I'm so depressed, so discouraged, so distraught," the only workable solution we can offer them is to tell them to change the way they think, for as they do, God will work in their hearts in due season. Even though he was in prison, Paul could rejoice and tell us to do so as well, for he was thinking clearly, singularly, rightly.

The four chapters of Philippians present four states of the mind. . . .

- Chapter 1 deals with a single mind.
- Chapter 2 deals with a submitted mind.
- Chapter 3 deals with a simple mind.
- Chapter 4 deals with a settled mind.

I believe if you take the time to study this epistle through, pray it in, and work it out, like Paul, you will be one who rejoices regardless of the trial facing you, the prison walls around you, or the guard chained to you.

PHILIPPIANS

1 **Philippians 1:1 (a)**
Paul and Timotheus, the servants of Jesus Christ, to all the saints in Christ Jesus which are at Philippi . . .

Philippi was a city in present-day Greece.

Philippians 1:1 (b)
. . . with the bishops . . .

"Bishop," "elder," and "pastor" are all interchangeable terms in the New Testament. *Episkopos*, or "bishop," describes the ministry as that of overseeing. *Presbuteros*, or "elder," describes the man as one who is mature. *Poimen*, or "pastor," describes the method as one who feeds the flock.

Philippians 1:1 (c)
. . . and deacons.

Deacons are those who serve in practical ways, as seen in those who served tables in Acts 6.

Philippians 1:2–5
Grace be unto you, and peace, from God our Father, and from the Lord Jesus Christ. I thank my God upon every remembrance of you, always in every prayer of mine for you all making request with joy, for your fellowship in the gospel from the first day until now.

Paul's initial path to Philippi was far from predictable. Perhaps you remember the story. . . .

Beginning his second missionary journey, Paul's plan was to go up into Asia. Stopping in Derbe and in Lystra, two small towns in present-day Turkey, he picked up Timothy—a young brother in the Lord who would become his protégé—and began to journey towards Asia. But there was a problem. Paul says in Acts 16 that every time they tried to go into Asia, "the Spirit forbade us" (see Acts 16:6). Doors slammed shut in his face. Unable to follow through with his plan, Paul backtracked until finally, at Troas—on the shores of the Aegean Sea—he was stuck.

The psalmist was right when he said, "The steps of a good man are ordered by the LORD" (Psalm 37:23a). Equally true, dear brothers and sisters, is this: The *stops* of a good man are ordered by the Lord as well. The Lord was stopping Paul from going into Asia because He had a different destination for Paul. It would do us well to tell ourselves and remind one another that if things don't work out, come through, or open up in the way we want—the failure for them to do so is in itself a clear answer—that stops are as valid as steps.

"Honey, come here," said the mother to her five-year-old daughter as cheerily as she could. Fido the family dog had died, and she didn't know the best way to break the news.

"Here, have some milk and cookies," she stalled.

Finally, able to put it off no longer, the worried mother said, "Honey, Fido died. And God took him to heaven"—to which her daughter replied, "What does God want a dead dog for?!"

That's just like us! We wonder what rationale we can give to someone when God doesn't answer the way we believed or prayed He would. Instead, we should forget the rationale; forget the sugar coating. God closed the door because He sees things we don't and knows things we can't.

Paul was in just such a spot. With his back to the sea, he wondered what to do. And then he had a vision in which he saw a Macedonian man saying, "Come over and help us" (Acts 16:9).

"That's it!" Paul must have said. "Here I was trying to go into Asia—but now I see the Lord has an entirely different plan for me. He wants me to go to Europe." So he sailed across the Aegean, and when he got to the other side, I'm sure Paul expected to find the Macedonian man he saw in his vision. Instead, he found a group of ladies gathered by the riverbank to pray. Again, the Lord's plan was different from Paul's—for it was when Paul shared the gospel with this group of ladies that the Philippian church was born.

Philippians 1:6
Being confident of this very thing, that he which hath begun a good work in you will perform it until the day of Jesus Christ.

Ten years passed since the day Paul first came across Lydia and the rest of the women praying by the riverbank. And here, in a Roman prison, thinking about what the Lord had done in and through them, Paul's heart is filled with confidence concerning the Philippian church. I believe that if Paul were alive today, he would exhibit the same confidence. Oh, I am aware of those who say, "What's wrong with the church? Why isn't the church on fire?"

But to those who say there needs to be revival, I say, "Don't you see it?" To those who call for radical renewal, I say, "Don't you get it? Look around and see what God is doing. It will blow your mind. It will warm your heart. It will cause you to applaud the Father for His faithfulness and goodness. What He's done for us personally and corporately blows me away totally."

Why is it the tendency among so many Christians to think that the Lord is always asking for more, more, more—that if they pray one hour, they should have prayed two; that if they witnessed to three people this month, they should have witnessed to four? It's my conviction that many, many, many Christians expect more out of themselves than God ever does.

How quick we are to beat up ourselves and other Christians. Yet if we would only open our eyes and see what the Lord is doing in the person sitting right next to us, we'd see a miracle—for the fact that God would mature and develop, build and use people like us is nothing short of miraculous. Like Paul, I thank God upon every remembrance of you. He's doing an awesome work in your lives. He's taking you through deep waters and tough times—and you're coming out the other side stronger than ever.

"Fear not, little flock, for it is the Father's good pleasure to give you the kingdom," Jesus said (see Luke 12:32). He's pleased with you. He's done a great and marvelous work through you. And I'm confident that He who began a good work in you shall complete it until the day of

Christ Jesus—when He comes back to take us all to heaven.

Philippians 1:7 (a)
Even as it is meet for me to think this of you all, because I have you in my heart . . .

If we were honest, to many of the people with whom we're linked, we would have to say, "You're on my nerves." Not Paul. He said, "You're on my heart."

Philippians 1:7 (b)
. . . inasmuch as both in my bonds, and in the defence and confirmation of the gospel, ye all are partakers of my grace.

Paul is in prison. He could have been pouting. He could have been pining. But, instead, he is "penning"—putting pen to papyrus to write a love letter to the Philippians.

Philippians 1:8
For God is my record, how greatly I long after you all in the bowels of Jesus Christ.

Rather than referring to the heart, Paul's culture referred to the intestines as the seat of deepest emotions. "I long for you greatly," said Paul, "not just superficially, but deep within me."

What gave Paul this kind of love? What caused him to pen this epistle rather than pout about his own situation? I believe it was because Paul utilized his prison time to pray. He cared about the Philippians because he prayed for them.

Who's on your nerves? Who's robbing you of joy? Maybe it's your boss or husband, a coach or teacher, a colleague or neighbor. Pray for them, for as you do, a couple of things will happen: First, because God answers prayer, they'll change. Second, and much more importantly, you'll begin to change. . . .

In Exodus 28, we read that on the ephod, the sacred vestment, the high priest wore a breastplate. And upon the breastplate were gems representing each of the twelve tribes of Israel. Thus, the people of Israel—those who were often stubborn, backslidden, unappreciative, and rebellious—were to be as gems on the heart of the high priest.

But that's only half the story. You see, inscribed on the shoulders of the high priest's ephod were the names of the tribes (Exodus 28:21). In other words, the high priest could not carry the gemstones of the tribes on his heart if the names of the tribes were not on his shoulders. Spiritually, the shoulder speaks of bearing burdens. Thus, as the high priest bore the bur-

den of intercessory prayer for the people, he would experience a change in his heart toward the people. He would view them not as dirt clods or pieces of coal—but as gems.

Gang, pray for the people who bug you. Pray God's blessing upon them. Pray for God's work to be flowing through them. Pray for good things to happen to them. Hold them up on the shoulders of intercession, and you will find that they will become gems in your heart. You cannot be angry or bitter toward someone for whom you're praying. That's why prayer is so important—not only because others will change, but because we ourselves will not be imprisoned by bitterness.

Philippians 1:9 (a)
And this I pray, that your love may abound yet more and more . . .

After patting them on the back, Paul says to the Philippians, "My prayer is that your love may abound more and more." Paul's was not a "sloppy *agape*"—where anything and everything was fine with him. No, he says, "I want you to do *better.*" How? Read on.

Philippians 1:9 (b), 10
. . . in knowledge and in all judgment; that ye may approve things that are excellent; that ye may be sincere and without offence till the day of Christ . . .

How will our love grow? Not by fault-finding, not by "sin sniffing," but by "excellence approving." That is, we grow by saying, "I can glean from that ministry, book, teacher, parent—from anyone who models any aspect of the nature of Christ, imperfect though they may be."

Philippians 1:11
Being filled with the fruits of righteousness, which are by Jesus Christ, unto the glory and praise of God.

When thou shalt besiege a city a long time, in making war against it to take it, thou shalt not destroy the trees thereof by forcing an axe against them: for thou mayest eat of them, and thou shalt not cut them down (for the tree of the field is man's life) to employ them in the siege.   Deuteronomy 20:19

"In besieging a city," God said, "be careful your axes don't fly indiscriminately, for you will rob yourself of fruit which could have nourished you."

So, too, Paul says, "Although there's a very real war in which you're involved, be very careful that in your battle mentality you don't start chopping this person, that group, or the other ministry. Don't pick on them; pick that which is helpful from them as fruit that can be used for your own growth."

Philippians 1:12
But I would ye should understand, brethren, that the things which happened unto me have fallen out rather unto the furtherance of the gospel.

Just as God used a sling in David's hand, a pitcher in Gideon's hand, and a rod in the hand of Moses, He used chains on Paul's hands. That's not surprising, for chains are what open the door to speak to people who would not otherwise give us the time of day. You see, it's when a wife hangs in there with her difficult husband; it's when an employee refuses to talk behind his boss's back; it's when a high-schooler willingly submits to his parents that people take note, thereby opening opportunity for the wife, the employee, the high-schooler to share the reason why.

I'm convinced that the troubles, challenges, and problems we face are custom-designed to do one thing: to allow us to draw others *to* Jesus Christ and to encourage them *in* Jesus Christ.

"But my burden is too heavy," you say.

Listen, God will not tempt you above what you are able (1 Corinthians 10:13). God doesn't play favorites—and if He has put you in a certain imprisonment, it's because He has prepared you for it and given you everything you'll need to go through it.

Philippians 1:13
So that my bonds in Christ are manifest in all the palace, and in all other places.

"My plan was to go to Rome," Paul said, "but God had a better idea. He brought Rome to me in the form of the soldiers chained to me round the clock. Every six hours, a different one comes on duty—and they're all getting saved! Members of the Praetorian Guard, they return to the palace, where they influence the very heart of the Roman system."

Philippians 1:14
And many of the brethren in the Lord, waxing confident by my bonds, are much more bold to speak the word without fear.

"In addition to the Roman soldiers who are getting saved, now that I'm no longer with you, others in Philippi are filling in and speaking out for the gospel," said Paul.

That's the way it's supposed to be, gang. What-

ever your arena of ministry, would to God there would be people who would step up and even take your ministry a notch higher in your absence.

Philippians 1:15 (a)
Some indeed preach Christ even of envy and strife . . .

"While some are preaching the gospel in my absence, others are exploiting the situation," said Paul, most likely referring to those who were preaching the rules and regulations of legalism.

Philippians 1:15 (b), 16
. . . and some also of good will: The one preach Christ of contention, not sincerely, supposing to add affliction to my bonds.

Since the word "contention" means "to canvass politically"—as when a candidate shakes hands in order to win votes—Paul is saying some preach Christ to increase their own influence.

Philippians 1:17, 18
But the other of love, knowing that I am set for the defence of the gospel. What then? notwithstanding, every way, whether in pretence, or in truth, Christ is preached; and I therein do rejoice, yea, and will rejoice.

"Even if some are preaching Christ from selfish motives, I rejoice anyway," says Paul, "because Christ is being talked about." What radical thinking!

Philippians 1:19, 20
For I know that this shall turn to my salvation through your prayer, and the supply of the Spirit of Jesus Christ, according to my earnest expectation and my hope, that in nothing I shall be ashamed, but that with all boldness, as always, so now also Christ shall be magnified in my body, whether it be by life, or by death.

Christ was magnified through Paul's difficulty. "Why does Christ have to be magnified?" you ask. "Isn't He big enough already?"

Think with me. . . .

Our sun is so big that, if hollowed out, it could hold 1,300,000 earths. The sun, however, is dwarfed by the star Antares, which could hold sixty-four suns. But Antares is a pipsqueak compared to Hercules, which could hold one hundred million Antares. Yet Hercules is a speck compared to Epsilon, the largest known star, which could hold three million Hercules.

These objects are *huge,* folks!
Why then, do they seem so small when we look at them in the night sky?
Because we are so far away.
So we use a telescope to magnify them and bring them closer to us.

People are far away from Jesus. What will make Him clear to them? Seeing Him walk with us and provide for us through the telescope of our difficulties. If this be true—if Christ is magnified in our hard times, the most logical thing for us to do in such times is to do what Paul did: rejoice.

Philippians 1:21
For to me to live is Christ, and to die is gain.

"For me to live is wealth, and to die is to leave it behind for my kids to fight over," some say.
"For me to live is pleasure, and to die is nothingness," others declare.
"For me to live is fame, and to die is to leave my mark," boast others.

There are three pyramids at Gaza, which the Pharaohs spent multiplied millions of dollars and multiplied millions of man-hours to erect in order that no one would forget them. Yet although the pyramids still stand, not one of us can name the men they were supposed to immortalize.

"For me to live is Christ," said Paul. "And to die is even better, for then I'll be with Him." This is the single mind we need, saints, if we're to think properly and live joyfully. Mr. Businessman, Mr. Athlete, anything else is going to be elusive and unsatisfying. Anything else will leave you on the short end of the stick. The only way to rejoice through life, to be happy about life, to be full of joy in life is to say, "My identity lies solely in Jesus."

Philippians 1:22–26
But if I live in the flesh, this is the fruit of my labour: yet what I shall choose I wot not. For I am in a strait betwixt two, having a desire to depart, and to be with Christ; which is far better: Nevertheless to abide in the flesh is more needful for you. And having this confidence, I know that I shall abide and continue with you all for your furtherance and joy of faith; That your rejoicing may be more abundant in Jesus Christ for me by my coming to you again.

"Although I want to go to heaven," says Paul, "I know it's important that I continue here on earth, sharing the gospel with you."

Philippians 1:27
Only let your conversation be as it becometh the gospel of Christ: that whether I come and see you, or else be absent, I may hear of your affairs, that ye stand fast in one spirit, with one mind striving together for the faith of the gospel.

"Whether I am set free and am able to come and see you again, or whether I remain in prison, I want to hear you are standing together in the Lord," says Paul.

Philippians 1:28
And in nothing terrified by your adversaries: which is to them an evident token of perdition, but to you of salvation, and that of God.

If you are being attacked, it's proof that the Enemy sees you as a worthy target, proof that you're making an impact.

Philippians 1:29
For unto you it is given in the behalf of Christ, not only to believe on him, but also to suffer for his sake.

Not only do the Enemy's attacks provide proof of our salvation, but a privilege for us to suffer for Christ. Jesus did so much for us and cares so much about us that the attacks of the Enemy provide rare opportunities in which we can show our allegiance to Him and our affection toward Him.

Philippians 1:30
Having the same conflict which ye saw in me, and now hear to be in me.

Thirdly, in addition to providing proof and a privilege, hard times and the Enemy's attacks are part of a process to make us more like Jesus. The Greek word translated "conflict" is *agon,* from which we get our word "agony."
There's no way to be deep in the Lord without going through some difficulties for the Lord. There's just no other way. So Paul says, "Don't be blown away; don't be taken aback; don't fall down because you're going through attacks and difficulties. They're proof that you're on target; they provide a privilege for you to suffer; and they're part of a process you must go through even as you see me go through it."
Even in hard times, even under the Enemy's attack, even throughout difficult days, we're to have a single mind: that to live is Christ, knowing that whatever comes our way will be used by Him for our good and for His glory.

2 In chapter 2, as he talks about Jesus willingly submitting Himself to the plan of His Father, Paul tells us not only are we to have a single mind, but a *submitted* mind. . . .

Philippians 2:1, 2
If there be therefore any consolation in Christ, if any comfort of love, if any fellowship of the Spirit, if any bowels and mercies, fulfil ye my joy, that ye be likeminded, having the same love, being of one accord, of one mind.

The Holy Spirit instructed our brother Paul to write these words: "If Christ has been good to you, if He's been there for you, if He's stood by you, fulfill my joy by being likeminded, of one accord"—surely a revelation of the heart of our Lord, the heart of our Father.

When my children were younger, nothing delighted me more than to pull into my driveway and see my teenage son, Peter-John, shooting hoops with his little brother, Benjamin. Even if they hadn't mowed the lawn or picked up the toys, love covers a multitude of sins! So, too, when our heavenly Father sees His children having one mind, being of one accord, loving one another, how it must bless Him.

"Fulfill my joy," Paul says, revealing the heart of our Lord, "by being of one accord." How does this happen? Read on.

Philippians 2:3 (a)
Let nothing be done through strife or vainglory . . .

There at the Pool of Bethesda, when the water was supposedly "stirred" by an angel, the first person in the pool would supposedly be healed. So there he sat month after year after decade—trying to win the competition, trying to win the prize. Suddenly, there stood a Man before him, saying, "Do you want to be healed?"
"I can't," he said. "I have no one to help me into the water."
"Take up your bed," Jesus replied, as though He were saying, "Let's not stick around here in the pool of competition, where people are striving to move up or to get ahead" (see John 5:8).

Let nothing be done through strife. Let nothing be done for vainglory. I'm sorry to say that much of the church has been infected and motivated by competition. It ought not to be. "Be of one mind, of one accord," said Paul. Not this church against that one, or this group versus the other one. We're all one in Christ."

Philippians 2:3 (b)
. . . but in lowliness of mind let each esteem other better than themselves.

This is the key: Let each one of you esteem others as being better than yourself. How does that happen? By simply realizing that every single person around you, that every single person you meet is better than you in some way or at some thing. And once we look into their lives and explore who they are, we must conclude, "It's a privilege to know you. I have no right to look down on you. You're better than me."

My natural, carnal mind doesn't work this way. My carnal mind wants to find fault with the person next to me so I can feel better about myself. But Paul says just the opposite: go around school tomorrow and look at every other student as being better than you—and treat them accordingly.

Gang, as we begin to develop the mind-set that we're privileged to be with everyone around us, the result will be joy. But it can't be done apart from our dependence upon the Lord day by day, moment by moment. It's a challenge, and yet it's something we can choose to do.

Philippians 2:4
Look not every man on his own things, but every man also on the things of others.

I believe verse 4 is really the key to verse 3. I will esteem others as better than myself to the degree that I listen to their stories and explore who they are—for if we knew the secret hurts and pains and suffering of even our worst enemy, we would find all of our animosity evaporating. If we looked into people instead of down on people, we would be filled with compassion for people.

Philippians 2:5 (a)
Let this mind be in you . . .

Again, notice over and over again, the emphasis in this epistle is not on how we feel, but on how we think.

Philippians 2:5 (b)
. . . which was also in Christ Jesus.

Now we come to holy ground. The following section of Scripture is one of the most profound, one of the most theologically important sections in all of the New Testament.

Philippians 2:6
Who, being in the form of God, thought it
not robbery to be equal with God.

"I and *my* Father are one," Jesus said (John
10:30). "He that hath seen Me hath seen the Father," He declared (John 14:9). Yet He wasn't
claiming something He had no right to claim. It
wasn't robbery for Jesus to claim equality with
the Father.

Philippians 2:7 (a)
But made himself of no reputation . . .

This phrase in Greek is *kenoo*, or, literally, "he
emptied himself." Jesus emptied Himself. Of
what? Of His divinity? No. When Jesus came as a
Man, He was still divine. Then of what did He
empty Himself? He emptied Himself of His divine powers.

The implications of the "doctrine of kenosis"
are huge because this means that everything
Jesus did—the miracles He ministered, the
prayers He prayed, the teachings He gave—
were not done in His own power. Jesus healed
and prayed and taught through the power of the
Holy Spirit as He followed the Father's directives.

Because I didn't know this for probably
twenty-plus years, when I read that Jesus
walked on water, I thought, Big deal. He's
Jesus; *when I read that He overcame tempta-*
tion, I thought, Big deal. He's Jesus; *when I*
read that He spent the night in prayer, I
thought, Big deal. He's Jesus. *Thus, the mira-*
cles and stories of the Gospels were irrelevant
to me as far as they related to being an exam-
ple or model for me.

I didn't understand *kenosis.* I didn't grasp Philippians 2. I didn't comprehend that when Jesus
came to earth, He emptied Himself of His divine
abilities—which means everything Jesus did, He
did as a man just like me. Before He did anything, Jesus had to be obedient to the Father, to
pray, to put Himself on the line, to be empowered
by the Spirit—or nothing would happen. That's
why He said, "Of my own self, I can do nothing"
(see John 5:30)—and neither can you.

When a man who is serious about loving and
serving God understands the *kenosis* of Philippians 2, he'll never look at Jesus the same way.
He'll see that Jesus' life is truly a model for anyone willing to be directed by the Father and empowered by the Spirit.

Philippians 2:7 (b)
. . . and took upon him the form of a servant,
and was made in the likeness of men.

Kenosis, tucked away in Philippians 2, is a doctrine of gigantic import as it relates to joy. This is
the mind that's to be in us—where we empty ourselves of our rights, where we became servants,
or, literally, slaves.

How do you know if you're a servant? There's
a very simple test: You'll know if you're a servant
by how you react when people treat you like one.
All of us like to think of ourselves as servants. "I
will serve You because I love You . . ." we sing. But
when someone treats me like a servant, I get offended.

Slaves are not noticed. Slaves are not thanked.
Slaves are not invited to dinner. No one compliments them. No one applauds them. They're expected to do their work and not be seen. And that
is the mind that is to be in me.

Why would anyone want to have such a mind?
Read on.

Philippians 2:8
And being found in fashion as a man, he
humbled himself, and became obedient unto
death, even the death of the cross.

Although Jesus was filled with the Spirit from
birth, He was not empowered by the Spirit until,
through His baptism, He said, "I am dying to Myself. Your will be done, Father."

Because Old Testament Scriptures teach that
every single sin must be atoned for, it is no wonder Jesus had to be slain before the foundation of
the world (Revelation 13:8). Jesus did not go to
the Cross simply for a few hours one April afternoon in A.D. 32. No, when He submitted Himself
to the Father's plan, a price was paid that we cannot understand until we see Him. Then, with
tears flowing down our cheeks and noses flattened as we fall on our faces, we'll say, "Truly,
Thou art worthy" (see Revelation 4:11).

Philippians 2:9
Wherefore God also hath highly exalted
him, and given him a name which is above
every name.

Peter put it this way: Humble yourself under
the mighty hand of God, and He will exalt you in
due time (1 Peter 5:6). If you exalt yourself and
demand your way, you will be abased. But if you
humble yourself, you'll be exalted. And Jesus is
the Perfect Example. God exalted Him because
He humbled Himself by becoming a slave to the
point of death for all humanity.

Philippians 2:10, 11
That at the name of Jesus every knee should bow, of things in heaven, and things in earth, and things under the earth; and that every tongue should confess that Jesus Christ is Lord, to the glory of God the Father.

Romans 10:9 declares that he who believes in his heart and confesses with his mouth that Jesus died for his sins and rose from the dead will be saved. Here we read that every tongue shall confess that Jesus is Lord. Does this mean that everyone will be saved eventually? No. There's coming a time when everyone will see Jesus and will bow before Him—but it will be too late. "Lord, Lord," they'll say in that day, only to hear Jesus say, "Depart from Me. I never knew you" (see Matthew 7:23).

But we who have said, "I'm flawed; I've failed; and I have all kinds of problems—but Jesus is my Lord, the Son of God who died for me"—we are saved. Our place in heaven is secure forever.

Philippians 2:12 (a)
Wherefore, my beloved, as ye have always obeyed, not as in my presence only, but now much more in my absence, work out your own salvation . . .

In addition to having a mind submitted to the will of the Father, Paul says that another key to joy is to work out your salvation. Notice he doesn't say, "Work *for* your salvation," or, "Work *on* your salvation." He says, "Work *out* your salvation." What does it mean to work out one's salvation? It's like going to the YMCA; it means you exercise it and strengthen it.

Notice also that Paul says we are to work out our *own* salvation . . .

What if Peter had said that day, "Hey, guys, look at me. I'm walking on water. You all should walk on water. Come on, guys. Get it together. Step out. Follow me. You can do it. Test your faith"?

We've all heard sermons along those lines, and I understand the intention, but they're terribly flawed. Peter walked on water not because he had faith. Peter walked on water because Jesus said, "Come." Jesus didn't tell James or John, Andrew or Bartholomew to come. The language is clear that His command was given to Peter singularly (Matthew 14).

Work out your own salvation. What's God working in your heart? What's He calling *you* to do?

In the course of a single evening, I read two outstanding books by two good Christian brothers. One said Christians should move into the city in order to minister to the multitudes. The other said Christians should move out of the city, as did the desert fathers. Unable to reconcile the two, I was troubled until the Lord spoke to my heart, saying, "Jon, what have I called you to do? What have I placed on your heart? I am the One who cared for the poor, and this brother is showing that side of Me. I'm also the One who moved to a solitary place and communed with the Father, and the other brother is showing that side. Let every brother reflect that which I have made clear to him."

That is why we need each other, gang. God manifests Himself through each of us a little differently.

Philippians 2:12 (b)
. . . with fear and trembling.

"With fear and trembling" means to give some real thought to what you're doing. Work out your salvation soberly and thoughtfully.

Philippians 2:13
For it is God which worketh in you both to will and to do of his good pleasure.

It's God who gives us the desires and the ability to do what He wants us to do.

Although he was only seventeen years old when he had a vision of the sun, moon, and stars bowing before him, Joseph knew it spoke of a position of authority he would assume over his brothers. And sure enough, as prime minister of Egypt, his brothers did, indeed, bow before him, asking help from him (Genesis 42:6). Joseph's dream came to pass—but not before he was thrown into a pit and tossed into prison.

Here's where a lot of us err. "I have a vision," we say. "It's in me to be a mother, so why am I not married?" or, "It's in me to be a missionary, so why isn't it happening?" or, "It's in me to work with kids, so why aren't the doors opening?" Understand this, dear brother and precious sister, concerning another man who had to go through a bunch of stuff before his vision was fulfilled: Scripture says it was not until he *patiently endured* that Abraham obtained the promise (Hebrews 6:15). You might land in a pit or two. You might go through a prison or three—but know this: God will fulfill that which He has placed in your heart if you patiently endure and don't give up.

I'm slowly but surely learning that what I really want, that what I truly desire, is His will. Why? Because I've demanded my will too many times and gotten it—only to be disappointed. Other times, I've watched the Lord work in ways I wasn't anticipating and seen that what came of it was wonderful.

Philippians 2:14
Do all things without murmurings and disputings.

A submitted mind doesn't murmur or make excuses, as the newer translations properly render the word "disputings."

As I tell my kids, "When you get good at making excuses, that's all you'll be good for."

That's why Paul says, "Don't make excuses and defend your positions. Don't murmur."

Murmuring was a real problem for the people of Israel. After God opened the Red Sea and crushed Pharaoh's army, the Israelites sang for a few moments, but then they started murmuring because they didn't have water to drink. When God gave them water, they murmured because they didn't have the right kind of food. And they murmured yet again when the land to which they were going seemed intimidating to them (Exodus 15, 16).

Scripture tells us the Lord hears us even as we murmur in our tents, even when we think no one is listening (Deuteronomy 1:27). "Do all things without murmuring," says Paul. Why? Read on.

Philippians 2:15, 16 (a)
That ye may be blameless and harmless, the sons of God, without rebuke, in the midst of a crooked and perverse nation, among whom ye shine as lights in the world; holding forth the word of life . . .

If you simply choose to say, "I will not murmur or excuse my behavior; I will not defend my position or dispute my situation," you will shine as a light in the world. Try it. Next time you're in line at the grocery store, tempted to murmur, "Can you believe how long these lines are? Can you believe how cold it is? I wish I lived in Hawaii . . ." and you'll fit right in. But, instead, say, "Can you believe how good the Lord is to give us this much food? Can you believe how wonderful a summer we're going to have because of all this rain?"—and without preaching a sermon, without passing out a tract, you'll shine like a light in the darkness.

Philippians 2:16 (b)
. . . that I may rejoice in the day of Christ, that I have not run in vain, neither laboured in vain.

Evidently, our brother Paul viewed himself as sort of a coach. He says, "I can't wait to see you guys at the judgment stand getting rewards because of the way you chose to shine like lights in the midst of a people who were always complaining and ungrateful. I coached you and you got the message."

Philippians 2:17, 18
Yea, and if I be offered upon the sacrifice and service of your faith, I joy, and rejoice with you all. For the same cause also do ye joy, and rejoice with me.

"If I end up losing my head here in Rome"—which he eventually would—"rejoice with me. I'm happy," said Paul.

The African impala can leap ten feet high when running at full speed. But when you go to a zoo, you'll see impalas kept in areas with only a four-foot fence.
Why?
Because if it can't see where it will land, an impala won't jump.

Here, Paul is jumping at the opportunity to go to heaven. Why? Because he had seen where he would land. Caught up into the heavens, he was given a sneak preview. And what he saw there was too good for him to even articulate (2 Corinthians 12:4). Paul's mind-set was like Christ's—submitted to the will of the Father. Whether he lived or died, it didn't matter to him, for he knew right where he'd land.

Philippians 2:19 (a)
But I trust in the Lord Jesus to send Timotheus shortly unto you . . .

Jesus is the Ultimate Example of a submitted mind. Paul, too, had a mind submitted to the will of the Father. And here Paul writes of another one who had a submitted mind: his young protégé, Timothy.

Philippians 2:19 (b)
. . . that I also may be of good comfort, when I know your state.

"I'm sending Timothy to you," Paul says, "that I might find out how you're doing."

Philippians 2:20
For I have no man likeminded, who will naturally care for your state.

Paul had a lot of men around him, but only one like Timothy.

Philippians 2:21–23
For all seek their own, not the things which are Jesus Christ's. But ye know the proof of him, that, as a son with the father, he hath served with me in the gospel. Him therefore I hope to send presently, so soon as I shall see how it will go with me.

Timothy was one who didn't have an agenda of his own, one who said, "I care about the people you care about, Paul. I'm going to serve you as a son would serve his father. And I'll go if you want me to go."

When Henry III, one of the great Bavarian kings, first came into power, he was burdened by the responsibilities and demands of being king. Feeling pressure on all sides, he finally walked away from the throne and went to a monastery.

"I want to contemplate God and worship the Lord," he said upon arrival.

"Understand this, Henry," said the abbot. "The first requirement of a monk is that he be in total submission. A monk's life is not his own. Can you submit yourself to the Lord by trusting me?"

"Yes," said Henry.

"Then go back to the throne. I am instructing you to rule and serve where God planted you."

Henry did, indeed, return to the throne, becoming one of the greatest German kings of history. The inscription on his tombstone gives the reason: Henry III, the king learned to rule by being obedient.

Such a man was Timothy.

Philippians 2:24–27 (a)
But I trust in the Lord that I also myself shall come shortly. Yet I supposed it necessary to send to you Epaphroditus, my brother, and companion in labour, and fellowsoldier, but your messenger, and he that ministered to my wants. For he longed after you all, and was full of heaviness, because that ye had heard that he had been sick. For indeed he was sick nigh unto death . . .

Epaphroditus was the man the Philippians sent to encourage and to bring financial assistance to Paul. "I'm sending him back your way," said Paul, "because he was concerned that you might be worried about his condition, having heard he had been sick."

What? Epaphroditus was sick when he was with Paul—Paul, the one whose sweatbands were used to bring healing to people; Paul, the one who laid his hands on people and they recovered; Paul, the one who was known for moving in the miraculous? Why didn't Paul heal Epaphroditus immediately?

For the same reason he didn't heal Trophimus (2 Timothy 4:20), or Timothy (1 Timothy 5:23), or even himself (2 Corinthians 12:7).

Ultimately, everyone will be healed, for by Jesus' stripes, we are all healed (Isaiah 53:5). The only question is timing. When they ask for healing, some are healed immediately; others, five years later; others, not until they get to heaven. Healing has nothing to do with a person's spirituality or faith. It has everything to do with God's sovereignty.

Three times Paul prayed for deliverance, only to hear the Lord say, "No, Paul. When you are weak, then My strength is manifested. My grace is sufficient for you" (see 2 Corinthians 12:9). Thus, I encourage those who are afflicted to follow Paul's model, to pray three times, thirty times, or three hundred times—until they receive what they're asking for, or until they have a peace in their heart that says, "This is what the Lord has for me, and I can embrace it."

Philippians 2:27 (b)
. . . but God had mercy on him; and not on him only, but on me also, lest I should have sorrow upon sorrow.

God healed Epaphroditus, and Paul was glad.

Philippians 2:28–30
I sent him therefore the more carefully, that, when ye see him again, ye may rejoice, and that I may be the less sorrowful. Receive him therefore in the Lord with all gladness; and hold such in reputation: Because for the work of Christ he was nigh unto death, not regarding his life, to supply your lack of service toward me.

This is a classic vignette because in it we see Paul making it easy for a homesick Epaphroditus to go home by saying, "When he gets there, honor him." Paul doesn't call Epaphroditus a wimp, a weasel, or the guy who couldn't hack it away from home. No, he calls him his brother, his companion, his fellow soldier. I like Paul's heart.

3 In chapter 1, we saw the single mind. In chapter 2, we saw the submitted mind. Here in chapter 3, we'll see the selfless mind.

Philippians 3:1 (a)
Finally, my brethren . . .

It would seem as though Paul is attempting to wrap things up when he uses the word "finally." In reality, he's only halfway done, for he'll go on for two more chapters—a typical preacher!

Philippians 3:1 (b)
. . . rejoice in the Lord. To write the same things to you, to me indeed is not grievous, but for you it is safe.

We are not commanded to rejoice in our circumstances, be they good or bad. No, we're to rejoice in the Lord. My circumstances may be bleak and brutal. But the Lord stands with me in those circumstances, and He will cause something good to come from them ultimately.

Philippians 3:2
Beware of dogs, beware of evil workers, beware of the concision.

The Jews referred to Gentiles as dogs. Yet here Paul is telling the Philippians to beware not of Gentiles, but of those who are of the concision, or, literally, "mutilators"—Jews who would follow behind Paul and say to the Gentiles, "If you're really serious about knowing God, what Paul said is okay as a beginning point, but you need to be circumcised if you want to be truly spiritual."
There are still those today who imply that to be spiritual, one must be miserable; those who say, "If you're truly spiritual, you'll do this and not do that; you'll go here, but not there . . ."
Of them, Paul says, "Beware."

Philippians 3:3
For we are the circumcision, which worship God in the spirit, and rejoice in Christ Jesus, and have no confidence in the flesh.

The true circumcision are not those who want to inflict pain. The truly spiritual man is one who worships God in the spirit, rejoices in Christ Jesus, and has no confidence in the flesh. True circumcision is not a mark on the flesh; it's a mark in the heart.

For topical study of Philippians 3:1–3 entitled "True Spirituality," turn to page 1287.

Philippians 3:4
Though I might also have confidence in the flesh. If any other man thinketh that he hath whereof he might trust in the flesh, I more.

"Regarding these dogs who undermine grace and boast of their external spirituality, I'll put my record against theirs any day," declares Paul.

Philippians 3:5 (a)
Circumcised the eighth day, of the stock of Israel . . .

"I was born a Jew and circumcised on the eighth day, according to the exact regulation of the law."

Philippians 3:5 (b)
. . . of the tribe of Benjamin . . .

Benjamin being the tribe of Israel's first king (1 Samuel 9:1, 2), and being the one tribe that remained loyal to the house of David when the ten northern tribes revolted under Jeroboam, Paul's lineage was admirable.

Philippians 3:5 (c)
. . . an Hebrew of the Hebrews; as touching the law, a Pharisee.

The Pharisees, numbering only six thousand, kept the minutest detail of the law and were known for their holiness and piety.

Philippians 3:6 (a)
Concerning zeal, persecuting the church . . .

"So zealous was I about Judaism," says Paul, "that I dragged Christians out of their homes, pulled them out of their churches, and incarcerated them in order that they might be put to death." Perhaps today's equivalent of Paul would be those who shoot abortion doctors in their zeal to protect the unborn, for Paul was ready to do whatever was necessary to protect the law.

Philippians 3:6 (b)
. . . touching the righteousness which is in the law, blameless.

Inspired by the Spirit, Paul could truthfully say, "Concerning the ordinances and requirements of the law, I kept them *all*." This doesn't mean Paul was faultless internally, for Romans 7:7 tells us he coveted. But externally, concerning the outward workings of the law, Paul was blameless.

Philippians 3:7
But what things were gain to me, those I counted loss for Christ.

"I let go of my standing as a Pharisee, my external piety, and everything else that looked good on my spiritual résumé—for none of it mattered compared to Christ," says Paul.

Philippians 3:8 (a)
Yea doubtless, and I count all things but loss . . .

Paul not only says, "I *counted* all things loss," but, "I continue to *count* all things loss."
It's not enough, gang, for you and me to revel in what we once counted as loss. It's not enough to say, "Yeah, fifteen years ago, I was witnessing to people, passing out tracts, knocking on doors, sharing my faith. Yep, back in the days of the revival, that was me." If what I did fifteen years ago, or what I gave up concerning the flesh one month ago doesn't translate into present practice, it's meaningless.

Philippians 3:8 (b)
. . . for the excellency of the knowledge of Christ Jesus my Lord . . .

Why did Paul count his impeccable religious pedigree as nothing? Because what He found in Jesus was infinitely superior to what he gave up.

Philippians 3:8 (c)
. . . for whom I have suffered the loss of all things, and do count them but dung, that I may win Christ.

Jesus told an interesting story in Luke 13 . . .

He spake also this parable; A certain man had a fig tree planted in his vineyard; and he came and sought fruit thereon, and found none. Then said he unto the dresser of his vineyard, Behold, these three years I come seeking fruit on this fig tree, and find none: cut it down; why cumbereth it the ground? And he answering said unto him, Lord, let it alone this year also, till I shall dig about it, and dung it: And if it bear fruit, well: and if not, then after that thou shalt cut it down. Luke 13:6–9

If you are one who appears outwardly spiritual, yet you lack the fruit of love and joy, peace and longsuffering, gentleness, goodness, meekness for your Master's pleasure—what are you to do? Let the Vinedresser come to you; let the Holy Spirit dig around your roots and expose sin. Then let Him expel it through the "dunging" process,

whereby we realize that glorying in anything we've done, any position we hold, or any credentials we've earned will keep fruit from being produced in our lives.

John the Baptist was right when he said a man cannot receive anything except it be given him from heaven (John 3:27). Whenever we think we've attained anything in our lives because of our dedication, our brilliance, or our good looks, there will be a dearth of fruitfulness in our lives.

Expose our sin, Lord. Expel our self. That way anything You want to do through us will be to Your glory.

Philippians 3:9 (a)
And be found in him, not having mine own righteousness, which is of the law . . .

"I let all my credentials go," said Paul, "for I see them for what they are: dung, fertilizer, pasture patties."

Philippians 3:9 (b)
. . . but that which is through the faith of Christ, the righteousness which is of God by faith.

When you become a Christian, not only did Christ Jesus come into your heart, but you were robed in Him, covered by Him, righteous through Him (1 Corinthians 1:30).

Philippians 3:10 (a)
That I may know him . . .

"In my legalistic, religious days, I knew about God theologically and intellectually," said Paul. "But now I want to know Him intimately." How does that happen? Read on.

Philippians 3:10 (b)
. . . and the power of his resurrection . . .

Jesus is not merely One who lived two thousand years ago, died, and that's the end of the story. He's a power; He's a Person; He's risen. And I will know Him intimately only through the power of His Resurrection.

Philippians 3:10 (c)
. . . and the fellowship of his sufferings . . .

When do you really know the Lord? When you realize He's alive. When do you really understand He's alive? When you go through tough times—the fellowship of suffering. When I'm cruising along on Easy Street, I don't know Jesus the way I often discover Him when I'm going through difficulty and problems, heartache or setbacks, tragedy or pain.

Here, in this book of rejoicing, Paul says, "Don't despise the difficulty, the tragedy, the tough time, the setback, the heartache—for those are the times you will understand that Jesus is truly risen. When the day is dark, the waters deep, the outlook grim—you'll see Jesus."

"Sure, I want to know the Lord," people say. "I just don't want to go through tough times. Of course I want to know His power, but I don't want to deal with the fellowship that comes through suffering."

The only way you can know the Lord intimately is through the power of His Resurrection. And the best way to experience the power of His Resurrection is through hard times.

"How many men did we throw in the fire?" asked Nebuchadnezzar.

"Three, your highness."

"Well, how is that I see four, and the fourth is like the son of God?"

So clearly did Shadrach, Meshach, and Abed-nego see Jesus in the fire of suffering that they chose to remain in the fiery furnace with Him rather than to walk free without Him (Daniel 3:26).

Philippians 3:10 (d)
. . . being made conformable unto his death.

We know the Lord by realizing He's with us in times of suffering, and by choosing to say, "Lord, I'll die to my self in order to have fellowship with You. As long as I try to protect myself, I'll not know You in the way I want to. So, Lord, I choose to conform myself to Your death. Do what You want in my life."

When Jesus started talking about the Cross, Peter's response was, "Be it far from Thee, Lord. It's not going to happen" (see Matthew 16:22).

And Peter's is a cry we utter as well. "Not the Cross," we say. "Not death, or bankruptcy, breakups, or leukemia. We want Cadillacs, miraculous healings, and holy laughter—that's our kind of Christianity, Lord."

We're just like Peter. But when, to one degree or another, we experience the fellowship of suffering, we begin to say, "I now choose death in order that I might know Jesus better."

Christians are the only people who can truly choose to rejoice and be happy when things on the outside seem so bleak because we're the only ones who know there will be a fellowship in suffering that will manifest the power of Jesus and His Resurrection, and which will, in turn, allow the intimacy with God that will make us deeply happy and truly blessed.

Philippians 3:11
If by any means I might attain unto the resurrection of the dead.

Paul isn't saying he hopes he goes to heaven when he dies. That's a given. Rather, he's speaking of the resurrection life—to live life here on earth through the power of Jesus' Resurrection.

Philippians 3:12
Not as though I had already attained, either were already perfect: but I follow after, if that I may apprehend that for which also I am apprehended of Christ Jesus.

On the Road to Damascus, Paul was on his way to persecute Christians when he was knocked to the ground. "Saul, Saul, why persecutest thou me?" said a voice from heaven.

"Who art thou, Lord?" asked Paul.

"I am Jesus whom thou persecutest. It's hard for you to kick against the goads, isn't it?"

"Lord, what would You have me to do?" Paul asked (see Acts 9:6).

And at that moment, Paul was apprehended— captivated by Jesus.

"I'm not there yet," said Paul. "I'll know I captured that for which I was captured when He calls me home."

Philippians 3:13–15 (a)
Brethren, I count not myself to have apprehended: but this one thing I do, forgetting those things which are behind, and reaching forth unto those things which are before, I press toward the mark for the prize of the high calling of God in Christ Jesus. Let us therefore, as many as be perfect, be thus minded . . .

Some people are always looking back. They can't get over what happened to them last year, five years, or twenty years ago. "She hurt me." "He fired me." "That company misused me," they say.

Paul says just the opposite. "This is what I do: I forget that which is behind. And the same mind is to be in you."

The sin we've committed in the past will condemn us to the place of paralysis. And the good stuff we've done by His grace will puff us up to the place of pride. Thus, our only option is to do what Paul did: Forget the past. We must be those who say, "I'm not going to dwell on that. I'm not going to be tripped up by that. I'm not going to glory in that. I'm not going to be confused about that. All of that is behind me. I'm moving on."

Philippians 3:15 (b)
. . . and if in any thing ye be otherwise minded, God shall reveal even this unto you.

If your mind is dwelling on the past, if you're defeated because of someone else's past, God will bring it to light.

Philippians 3:16
Nevertheless, whereto we have already attained, let us walk by the same rule, let us mind the same thing.

Where we have gone ahead, let's keep going.

Philippians 3:17, 18 (a)
Brethren, be followers together of me, and mark them which walk so as ye have us for an ensample. (For many walk, of whom I have told you often, and now tell you even weeping . . .

Here in his Epistle of Joy, we see Paul weeping. Is he weeping because of the prison in which he was confined?
No.
Is he weeping because of the guards to whom he's chained?
No.
He's not weeping over his brutal situation. He's weeping over potential deception . . .

Philippians 3:18 (b)
. . . that they are the enemies of the cross of Christ.

Who were these enemies of the Cross of Christ? We cannot say who they were individually, but we can see how they lived and what they taught contextually, for Paul goes on to tell us something about them.

Philippians 3:19
Whose end is destruction, whose God is their belly, and whose glory is in their shame, who mind earthly things.)

Concerning the enemies of the Cross of Christ, the end of their lives will prove to be destruction, or, literally, "a waste."

- Their god is their belly—they live for their fleshly appetites.
- They live for their own glory—they live to make a name for themselves.
- And they mind earthly things—they live for that which is temporal.

It is very likely these men were not unlike the prosperity teachers of today—the Name It/Claim It, Health/Wealth boys.
"Deny yourself? No way!" they proclaim. "God wants everyone to be totally healthy and totally wealthy here and now."

"What's the key to life?" he said. "Women!" So he gathered one thousand concubines—the most beautiful women in the region—only to discover they weren't the answer.
"Partying—that's the key," he decided. So he imported baboons and peacocks from Africa to entertain his guests, while he kept the wine flowing freely. But after partying for years, he found it empty.
"Power—that's what will satisfy a man," he surmised. So he expanded the boundaries of his empire farther than those of any other nation of antiquity. But even then he felt unsatisfied.
He studied philosophy and science—and garnered so much gold that silver was rendered worthless in his kingdom. And yet he declared it all empty.
At last he said, "Power, prosperity, fame, partying, women, wine, and education are not the answer. The only key to life is to fear God" (see Ecclesiastes 12:13). But by then, Solomon's most productive years were lost, wasted because his god was his belly; his glorying was in his own name; he minded earthly things.

Beware of those who try to get you focused on this life, worried about this life, caught up in this life. They're enemies of the Cross, for the Cross says, "Forget about yourself. Look toward eternity. Live for heaven."

Philippians 3:20
For our conversation is in heaven; from whence also we look for the Saviour, the Lord Jesus Christ.

Newer versions translate the word "conversation" as "lifestyle" or "citizenship." Why? Because a person's citizenship—be he English, French, or Australian—can be readily identified through his conversation, through the way he speaks. The same is true spiritually, for Scripture declares that out of the abundance of the heart, the mouth speaks (Matthew 12:34). What is your conversation, your lifestyle, your citizenship? It will be revealed in the heat of battle.

After civil war had broken out between the men from Gilead and the men from Ephraim, Jephthah, leader of the Gileadites, ordered his men to seal the passes lest the Ephraimites get away.

"But how will we identify them?" asked his men. "They're our brothers."

"Tell them to say the word "river," or "shibboleth," said Jephthah.

Why?

Because the men from Ephraim could not pronounce the sound of "sh." Thus, instead of "shibboleth," they said "sibboleth"—and were immediately betrayed by their speech (Judges 12).

The same holds true for you and me. In the heat of battle, how do we talk? When the accountant says, "You're bankrupt"; when the doctor says, "It's cancer"; when your boyfriend says, "Goodbye," what do we say? Our speech, our conversation will reveal whether we're men and women who live for the material, the temporal, the earthly—or whether we are those who live for heaven singularly.

Philippians 3:21 (a)
Who shall change our vile body, that it may be fashioned like unto his glorious body . . .

When we see Jesus, we shall be like Him (1 John 3:2). These vile bodies that are falling apart, which are prone toward sin, which give us problems in so many ways will be changed instantly. Hallelujah!

Philippians 3:21 (b)
. . . according to the working whereby he is able even to subdue all things unto himself.

Not only will our bodies be changed to be like His, but all things will be subdued, or "put in order." At last! All things will be subdued, reordered, made right.

Several years ago, a popular polling organization took a survey. According to the census, if

Michael Jordan had run for the US Senate in Illinois, he would have won by seventy percent. No one knew what he thought. No one cared where he stood. None of that mattered because, after all, he's Michael Jordan. And we want him to be our leader. Why? Because he can bounce a rubber ball filled with air and jump a few inches higher than the other guys who are also bouncing a rubber ball filled with air. And because he can jump a little higher, he can jump up and drop the rubber ball through a metal hoop.

Wow! Awesome! No wonder we want him to be our leader!

Our culture is topsy-turvy, gang—and the only answer is heaven, for in heaven people will not be abuzz about Michael Jordan—they'll be talking about Pearl Good . . .

Pearl Good cleaned houses to make enough money to be able to travel to wherever Billy Graham would be speaking, get a cheap motel room, and, unbeknownst to him, pray around the clock for the Crusade.

If you want a trading card that will be worth something in eternity, forget Michael Jordan's—get Pearl Good's!

We're all mixed-up, folks. Our society is confused. Our values are wrong. Do I despair over this? No, because everything will be made right in heaven.

- To the person complaining about cultural chaos, heaven is the answer.
- To the person who says life is unfair, heaven is the answer.
- To the Pearl Goods of the earth, heaven is the answer.

Heaven will solve every problem, answer every question, and right every wrong.

We're going to be there soon, gang—and I can't wait!

TRUE SPIRITUALITY
A Topical Study of
Philippians 3:1–3

A guest in a bed-and-breakfast outside of London, Archbishop Jonathan Kemple heard a woman robustly and repeatedly singing the hymn, "A Mighty Fortress Is Our God" in the kitchen.

"Your cook must be a very spiritual lady," he said to his host.

His host chuckled a bit and said, "Not really. It must be that we're having hard-boiled eggs for breakfast.

"Oh?" said the Archbishop.

"Yes," continued the host. "If the eggs are soft-boiled, she only sings 'A Mighty Fortress' three times. But hard-boiled eggs require six."

Sometimes we do the same thing. "We're going to sing three songs before the kids are dismissed and then two more songs before the sermon," we say. But that's not what worship in the Spirit is.

The Spiritual Man Worships God in the Spirit

Paul says one of the identifying marks of the spiritual man is that he worships God in the spirit. Oftentimes at worship conferences or in books about worship, discussion ensues concerning how to get people to be more expressive in worship. However, I don't believe this should be the emphasis. I believe that since true worship is the result of affection and commitment to the Lord, no amount of physical gyrations or carnal motivations will make a difference.

Suppose my wife, Tammy, and I weren't married. If she walked in, and though I had never met her, I went up to her, wrapped my arms around her, and started kissing her passionately—there would be a problem. I would get a slap across the face, and the ushers would come and take me away. The cops would show up, and I would have a jail ministry. Why? Because I would be trying to express affection without commitment. And that would be unacceptable.

Suppose, on the other hand, I look at her and say, "Would you go out to dinner with me?" We go out. And I take her out the next day and the day after that, and we're going out all the time. As we're cultivating a relationship, our commitment grows and deepens. So after taking her out for five months, I reach out and hold her hand for the first time. Is that acceptable? Sure! Because after five months of developing a relationship, such behavior would be acceptable, understandable, appropriate.

We then become more and more committed to each other—until we stand before the preacher, saying, "I'm committed to you for all of my life—for better or worse, for richer or poorer." And then it would be not only acceptable but laudable for us to be totally affectionate and intimate with each other because we would be committed to each other.

Here's the problem: Many times worship leaders try to get people to do things to express affection—but without true commitment, their efforts are little more than outward manipulation. The key to developing ever-affectionate and demonstrative worship is to take people deeper in their knowledge and commitment to Jesus Christ. Then you can get rid of all of the circus antics and maneuvering because as people are more deeply committed *to* Him, and have a greater knowledge *of* Him, there will be in their spirits a natural affection and display of love *for* Him.

Having said that, I feel I need to say this as well. . . .

When I kissed Tammy as I walked in the door one day, I should have been prepared for my kids' reaction.

"Eeeew! Not here," they said.

That's the way kids often respond when their parents are affectionate because it's distracting to them.

The same can be true in worship. To worship in the Spirit means to be completely intimate and totally affectionate. However, there are places where greater intimacy and affection can be displayed, and there are places where it's distracting to others. Thus, to worship in the Spirit is to say, "Lord, help me to know the right place and the right time to express myself in the right way that would honor You and not distract others."

If I am causing others to say, "Eeew! What's he doing?" I am no longer worshiping in the Spirit, but I am causing my brothers and sisters to be needlessly distracted from the Lord. Worship in the Spirit requires being sensitive to Him.

The Spiritual Man Rejoices in Christ Jesus

My entire Christian experience went through a radical, wonderful adjustment when I found myself freed up to rejoice in Christ Jesus. You see, I went through a season where my joy was somewhat lacking. . . .

Reading about how Jesus touched the leper (Mark 1:40, 41), I thought, *If I'm to be like Jesus, I must find people who are leprous, people who are being eaten up by sin, people who are falling apart—and touch them.*

But then I turned a few pages and read how Jesus put His fingers in the ears of a man who was deaf and dumb, causing the man to begin to speak (Mark 7:33), and I thought, *If I'm to be like Jesus, I must find dumb people and touch them that they might hear.*

But then I turned a few pages and saw Jesus feeding five thousand hungry men on a slope overlooking the Sea of Galilee (Mark 6:41). *To be like Jesus,* I thought, *I gotta feed the hungry.*

But then I turned a few pages and saw Jesus blessing the little children (Mark 10:14). *If I'm to be like Jesus,* I thought, *I've got to hang out with kids— all kids, every kid—because that's what Jesus did.*

But then I turned a few pages and saw Jesus forgiving the woman taken in the act of adultery (John 8:11). *That's what I'm to do,* I thought. *I must find people who are being picked on and set them free one at a time.*

On and on I went until finally I found myself totally exhausted.

Great is the day when, like John the Baptist, a man says, "I am not the Christ. Behold the Lamb. It's *Him,* not me" (see John 1:20).

It is wonderfully and gloriously liberating to say, "I'm not Jesus."

Then who am I?

I'm the leper being eaten by my own carnality. And the Lord comes to me every day and says, "I still love you. I'm here to cleanse you."

I'm the dumb one. My ears get clogged listening to the news, philosophy, and ideas of the world. Then Jesus sends a brother or a sister or a book or a radio program—and suddenly I hear Him again.

I'm the adulterer. My affections and priorities wander in all sorts of directions. Yet Jesus comes to me and says, "You've strayed from Me. But I don't condemn you. I'm here to stand by you. Go your way. Sin no more. You're free."

I'm the hungry one. And the Lord comes to me daily and nourishes me as I partake of the Bread of Life.

I'm the child of whom others say, "Don't bother with him," but of whom Jesus says, "Allow him to come to Me."

Gang, once this sinks in, you'll read the Gospels with new eyes. Instead of putting yourself in Jesus' place, you'll put yourself in the sinner's spot, where you belong, saying, "Look what *He* does. Look how good *He* is."

"Is it right to see ourselves in the place of the sinner? Aren't we commanded to be holy, as He is holy?" you ask.

John says that when we see Jesus, we shall be like Him without even trying (1 John 3:2). When I stop trying to *be* like Him and simply *like* Him—simply enjoy spending time with Him—then I become like Him. And I rejoice in Him all the more.

The Spiritual Man Has No Confidence in the Flesh

"I can't believe I did that," said a man who had stumbled badly, a tear falling down his cheek.

"I can," I said to his surprise.

You see, Paul tells us that in our flesh dwells no good thing (Romans 7:18). Therefore, if we're blown away or scandalized by a temptation to which we or someone else succumbs, it only means that we did, indeed, have confidence in our flesh.

When someone stumbles or falls, all a truly spiritual man can say is, "If it wasn't for God's grace, I would be in that same situation."

The truly spiritual man is one who realizes his weakness, but rather than mourning or moaning he says, "If anything good comes through me or from me, it comes from Christ. I'm weak, but He is wonderful. And I rejoice in Him."

True spirituality consists not in do's or don'ts, pain or piety, burdens or bondage. Paul says the spiritual man is one who worships God in the Spirit, rejoices in Christ alone, and has no confidence in his flesh.

And in that I can rejoice gladly and celebrate continually.

Philippians 4:1 (a)
Therefore . . .

Whenever you come to the word "therefore" in Scripture, it's wise to stop and ask what it's there for. Here at the outset of chapter 4, Paul refers to the end of chapter 3, wherein he tells us we don't have to be hopeless as we watch our culture crumble, for when Jesus returns He'll put all things in order.

Philippians 4:1 (b)
. . . my brethren dearly beloved and longed for, my joy and crown . . .

As was the case with Paul, the people God brings into the kingdom through our sharing with them or ministering to them will be our joy, our crown. In Daniel 12:3, we read that those who win souls are wise, for they shall shine as the stars forever. I think the shining refers to the glow radiating from the faces of people when, in heaven at last, they see those with whom they shared and for whom they prayed.

Philippians 4:1 (c)
. . . so stand fast in the Lord, my dearly beloved.

In light of the fact that the Lord's return is at hand, Paul tells the church at Philippi to stand fast, to stand confidently, to stand firmly in Him.

More and more, I'm convinced that heaven is the whole deal—just realizing that we're soon going to be there, and that we have a single job to do: to grab as many people as we can and say, "Come along with us to heaven."

I think we worry far too much about what we're doing or how we're feeling. We analyze ourselves endlessly. We scrutinize our situations continually. We ponder our circumstances tirelessly. But in reality, the joy, the crown lies in sharing with people who don't know Jesus, in praying for folks who will be cut off from Him unless they open their hearts to Him. I believe the reason Paul could talk so much about joy in this epistle— even while he was in chains—was because he was thinking about the people he knew would be in heaven with him eternally because he had shared with them personally.

Philippians 4:2
I beseech Euodias, and beseech Syntyche, that they be of the same mind in the Lord.

Who were Euodias and Syntyche? I believe their names indicate who they were: "You're Odious" and "Soon Touchy"! Notice, Paul doesn't say, "Let's find out who's right and who's wrong." He simply says, "The Lord's coming is near, so there's no time for squabbling."

Biblical counseling is amazingly simple. To those enmeshed in interpersonal conflicts, we can be like Paul and say, "Even if you're technically right in any given argument, you're spiritually wrong because the Lord wants you to be forgiving and gracious and merciful."

Philippians 4:3 (a)
And I intreat thee also, true yokefellow . . .

Tradition has it that this yokefellow has been identified as the Philippian jailer Paul led to the Lord, following the miraculous earthquake that set Paul free, but threatened the jailer's life (Acts 16).

Philippians 4:3 (b)
. . . help those women which laboured with me in the gospel . . .

This is in reference to Lydia and the other women who were so instrumental in the birth of the Philippian church.

Philippians 4:3 (c)
. . . with Clement also, and with other my fellowlabourers, whose names are in the book of life.

After ministering in various areas, the disciples returned to Jesus excited about what they had seen. "Lord," they said, "even the demons are subject unto us as we share in Your name. It's amazing what's happening!"

But what did Jesus say? He said, "Don't rejoice in what you've seen. Rather, rejoice that your names are written in the Book of Life" (see Luke 10:20).

We should be full of ecstasy and elated continually not because we cast out a demon or saw a healing or were used in ministry. We should be amazed constantly over one thing primarily: the fact that we're saved. Hell is real, gang. We don't understand it. It's still sort of fuzzy to us. But Jesus knew the reality of hell, even as He knew the reality of heaven. That is why He said to His disciples, "Here's what you should be excited about: Because your name is written in the Book of Life, you're not going to hell. You're going to heaven, where you will live with Me forever."

The knowledge that we're headed for heaven should keep a smile on our faces every day of our lives. Heaven alone should keep praise flowing from our lips perpetually.

- "I don't feel good," we groan.
  Who cares? We're not going to hell!
- "I'm not appreciated at work," we cry.
  Who cares? We're going to heaven!
- "I won the lottery!" we shout.
  So what? That's nothing compared to heaven!

Philippians 4:4
Rejoice in the Lord alway: and again I say, Rejoice.

I can't always rejoice in my circumstances, but I can *always* rejoice in the Lord.

Philippians 4:5
Let your moderation be known unto all men. The Lord is at hand.

The idea here is to avoid extravagance. Because the Lord is here among us, and because He's coming back for us, we don't need to get all caught up in earthly things.

Philippians 4:6 (a)
Be careful for nothing . . .

The idea of "careful" means "full of care or anxiety."

Philippians 4:6 (b)
. . . but in every thing by prayer and supplication with thanksgiving let your requests be made known unto God.

The way to remain in the place of rejoicing, the way to avoid being caught up in extravagance of any sort is to remain in prayer. In this context, prayer refers to communing with God, while supplication speaks of making specific requests to Him. Both are to be done with a spirit of thanksgiving for the abundance with which the Lord has *already* blessed us both materially and spiritually (Psalm 68:19).

Philippians 4:7
And the peace of God, which passeth all understanding, shall keep your hearts and minds through Christ Jesus.

The older I get, the more I'm learning that prayer is not a monologue. It's a dialogue. I'm discovering more and more that the real need in my life is not for God to hear from me, but for me to hear from Him. And I find that as I walk, drive, or get on my knees, if I will pray a phrase or two and then just rest and be quiet, the Lord will bring specific scriptures to my mind or will write His will upon my heart concerning how I am to pray.

But if I pray sentence after paragraph after page and then say, "Okay, that wraps it up for prayer time today," I really miss it. Oh, I know that even that kind of prayer has power. Any prayer is better than no prayer. But I suggest that if you learn to pause and listen in prayer, the Lord will show you how to believe on behalf of another, and how to pray specifically concerning any given situation.

———— ✦ ————

For topical study of Philippians 4:4–7 entitled "The Key to Being Carefree," turn to page 1294.

Philippians 4:8
Finally, brethren, whatsoever things are true, whatsoever things are honest, whatsoever things are just, whatsoever things are pure, whatsoever things are lovely, whatsoever things are of good report; if there be any virtue, and if there be any praise, think on these things.

Again, the theme of Paul's epistle to the Philippians is that the key to experiencing joy in your heart is to have the right thoughts in your mind. So how are we to think? Here's how: Think on things that are true, honest, just, pure, lovely, of good report, virtuous, and praiseworthy.

Even spiritual men and women become discouraged. You can see it in their eyes. And they wonder why. It's because they've been thinking thoughts that are not true and honest and lovely and good and pure. They stared at David Letterman before they went to bed, and they wonder why they wake up grumpy. If you are prone to depression, do not watch late-night TV. You'll wake up with a cynicism about life, a tainted twisted perspective on life. Instead, fill your mind with the goodness of God and the wealth of His Word, and, like Paul, you'll awake with a song in your soul.

Philippians 4:9 (a)
Those things, which ye have both learned,
and received, and heard, and seen in me,
do . . .

I like Paul's ministry: It was "Show and Tell."
Not only did he tell people what to do, but he
showed them by doing it himself.

Philippians 4:9 (b)
. . . and the God of peace shall be with you.

If you think rightly, if you rejoice in the Lord
continually, if you think on things that are pure
and lovely, the God of peace will be with you as
surely as He was with Paul.

Philippians 4:10
But I rejoiced in the Lord greatly, that now
at the last your care of me hath flourished
again; wherein ye were also careful, but ye
lacked opportunity.

This is in reference to the fact that the Philippians had sent Epaphroditus to Paul with a financial gift from them and news about their welfare.
But because Paul was always on the move,
Epaphroditus had a hard time catching up with
him.

Philippians 4:11
Not that I speak in respect of want: for I
have learned, in whatsoever state I am,
therewith to be content.

This is radical, gang. If you want to be a rejoicing, happy person, listen to what Paul is saying:
Contentment is learned. Because we are to learn
to be content in everything, I do not believe that
God uses restlessness or discontentment as a primary means of guidance. Wherever you're working now, you should learn to be content until God
makes it very clear to you that He wants to move
you or change your situation.

For topical study of Philippians 4:10–13 entitled
"Learning Contentment," turn to page 1298.

Philippians 4:12, 13
I know both how to be abased, and I know
how to abound: every where and in all
things I am instructed both to be full and
to be hungry, both to abound and to suffer
need. I can do all things through Christ
which strengtheneth me.

"The Lord is with me," says Paul, "And I can do
everything through Him—including being content in the situation I'm in." Either we believe
that, or we don't. Either we'll take advantage of
it, or we won't. The choice is ours.

Philippians 4:14, 15
Notwithstanding ye have well done, that ye
did communicate with my affliction. Now
ye Philippians know also, that in the begin-
ning of the gospel, when I departed from
Macedonia, no church communicated with
me as concerning giving and receiving, but
ye only.

All of the other churches Paul started and
tended forgot about him. To their commendation,
Paul says to the Philippians, "You remembered
me. You communicated with me. You stood by me
in the ministry."

Philippians 4:16
For even in Thessalonica ye sent once and
again unto my necessity.

"When I was in Thessalonica," continues Paul,
"you were the ones who came through for me."

Philippians 4:17
Not because I desire a gift: but I desire fruit
that may abound to your account.

There are a couple of areas I have found to be
very, very difficult in the ministry. One is to point
out other ministries, or TV evangelists, or teachers who are in error—whose entire ministry is
amiss. Yet if a shepherd only feeds the flock, but
never warns the flock about wolves, all he is doing is fattening them up for the kill (Acts 20:29–
31). So as a pastor, warn I must because I care
about the sheep.

A second area that is very difficult for me in
ministry is to address the subject of finances because it can appear to be so self-serving. Nevertheless, Paul hits this issue head-on by saying,
"It's not that I want a gift. It's that I want you to
have fruit."

When the person who gave the Lord's tithe
and offerings above and beyond that gets to
heaven, I guarantee he's not going to say,
"Phooey. I tithed faithfully. If I hadn't tithed, I
could have had a new patio set. And if I had only
saved that extra hundred dollars from that offering, I could have had a new barbeque." No. For
the next zillion years, you'll never regret what
you give to the Lord today—the tithes that are
His, and the offering beyond that—for they will
be fruit to your account.

The old adage is so true: You can't take it with

you, but you can send it ahead. And there will be some people in heaven who are incredibly wealthy. They'll have great rewards because they were wise investors on earth. They didn't rob God of the tithe. They didn't keep every penny for themselves.

Read the Book of Ezra. See the listing of the names verse after verse, page after page, recording the exact amounts people gave for the building of the temple. Why would God "waste" so many verses about what people were giving to that project? I believe it's because in it He is saying, "I notice what people give to Me, and record it forever."

Philippians 4:18
But I have all, and abound: I am full, having received of Epaphroditus the things which were sent from you, an odour of a sweet smell, a sacrifice acceptable, wellpleasing to God.

Paul calls the gift the Philippians gave him a sweet-smelling, well-pleasing sacrifice to God. We're all susceptible to believing the lie of the Enemy that we are excused from tithing if we don't agree with the manner in which the church is using our money. Therefore, I encourage you to find a church you can stand by and identify with—then bring your tithes and offerings through it to God.

Philippians 4:19
But my God shall supply all your need according to his riches in glory by Christ Jesus.

This verse is, indeed, a powerful and comforting promise—but notice to whom it's given.

Taken in context, Paul is saying, "Know this, you who are faithful in giving: God will supply all your need."

"Can I borrow your boat?" Jesus asked.
"Sure," said the fishermen.
So Jesus pushed out a little ways into the Sea of Galilee, and, using the water as a natural amplifier, He preached to the multitude gathered on the shore.
"Thanks for letting Me use your boat," He said to the fishermen when He was finished. "Go ahead and take it out now."
They did—and when they cast their nets into the water, the haul was so great it almost sunk their boat (Luke 5:3–6).

If we give, God will supply all of our needs because we just can't outgive Him. High-schooler, college student, start now. Develop a life of tithing—and you'll be just as amazed as were those fishermen by the Lord's provision in your life.

Philippians 4:20–22
Now unto God and our Father be glory for ever and ever. Amen. Salute every saint in Christ Jesus. The brethren which are with me greet you. All the saints salute you, chiefly they that are of Caesar's household.

The saints in Caesar's household were the guards who, after being chained to Paul, returned to Caesar's palace as believers.

Philippians 4:23
The grace of our Lord Jesus Christ be with you all. Amen.

And so Paul's epistle ends as it began—with the matchless grace of Jesus.

THE KEY TO BEING CAREFREE
A Topical Study of
Philippians 4:4–7

A godly man and a good king, Hezekiah loved the Lord and had a deep walk with Him. Nevertheless, he found himself in real difficulty when he heard that Sennacherib and his million-man Assyrian army were marching toward Jerusalem. The inventors of the siege strategy and the battering ram, the Assyrians had been unbeatable in battle, and unparalleled in brutality.

So what does Hezekiah do?

First, he tries to solve his problem financially by attempting to bribe Sennacherib with the gold of the temple. His plan, of course, backfired because the sight of the gold only increased Sennacherib's determination to plunder Jerusalem. (2 Kings 18)

Hezekiah's next plan was to build an alliance with Egypt. "You guys have horses and soldiers and military might at your disposal," he said. "Ally with us because if Sennacherib beats us, you'll be next."

At that moment, Isaiah the prophet comes on the scene and thunders a prophecy in the ears of Hezekiah:

Woe to the rebellious children, saith the Lord, that take counsel, but not of me; and that cover with a covering, but not of my spirit, that they may add sin to sin: That walk to go down into Egypt, and have not asked at my mouth; to strengthen themselves in the strength of Pharaoh, and to trust in the shadow of Egypt! For thus saith the Lord God, the Holy One of Israel; In returning and rest shall ye be saved; in quietness and in confidence shall be your strength: and ye would not.   Isaiah 30:1, 2, 15

In other words, "What God wants from you in this crisis, in this hour of need is to return to Him, to wait on Him, to be quiet before Him."

I wonder if there are good men and women sitting here today who, feeling pressure relationally or vocationally, in ministry or financially, are saying "Help me!" to this counselor, or "Save me!" to that group—when all along the Lord would say, "First and foremost, come to *Me*."

"Oh, I don't have time to pray," we say. "I'm late for my counseling appointment. I don't have time to seek the Lord. I've got to strip the temple of gold to pay off Sennacherib."

Yet all the while, Paul says we are not to be anxious, not to be full of care about anything. His, however, is not merely a "Don't worry, be happy" maxim, for he goes on to tell us *how*. . . .

Be careful for nothing; but in every thing by prayer and supplication with thanksgiving let your requests be made known unto God.   Philippians 4:6

"Prayer" refers to general communion with God; "supplication" to specific requests. Thus, Paul is saying, "Be anxious about nothing. Pray about everything. Give thanks for anything."

"That's easy for Paul," you say. "His prayers were always answered the way he wanted."

Really? Check out what he said to the Romans . . .

Now I beseech you, brethren, for the Lord Jesus Christ's sake, and for the love
of the Spirit, that ye strive together with me in your prayers to God for me;
that I may be delivered from them that do not believe in Judaea; and that my
service which I have for Jerusalem may be accepted of the saints; that I may
come unto you with joy by the will of God, and may with you be refreshed.

Romans 15:30–32

As he comes to the end of his letter to the Romans, Paul says, "Pray with me—first that I may be delivered from my enemies in Jerusalem; second, that my service may be accepted by the Christians; and finally, that I may come to you at Rome with joy."

But what happened? Paul was captured by his enemies in Jerusalem. His ministry was not readily accepted by the saints. And the only way he made it to Rome was as a prisoner.

Here's the deal, gang: God can say "Yes" to my prayers, or He can say "No." Either way, it's an answer. How many, many times I have said, "Here's my supplication, Father . . ." only to see that, down the road, what takes place is a whole lot better than what I asked for.

"If your child asks for bread, which of you would give him a stone?" asked Jesus. "Or if he wants a fish, who of you would give him a scorpion?" (see Luke 11:11, 12). Sometimes we think we're asking for salmon, but the Lord recognizes it as a scorpion. Sometimes we cry for bread, but the Lord sees it's a boulder—and He loves us too much to give us something that would hurt us.

So what are we to do? We're to make our request—and then rest in God's peace, a peace that passes our understanding (Philippians 4:7). We say, "Lord, I choose to not wring my hands and try to figure out how I can strip the temple or ally with Egypt. I choose to return to You, to rest in You, to worry about nothing, to pray about everything, and to be thankful for anything You decide to do."

And what happens may just blow your mind. Ask Hezekiah. . . .

"Seek the Lord," Isaiah said. And Hezekiah did just that—even as Sennacherib continued to march. Things looked ominous, when suddenly, hearing of a new war breaking out, Sennacherib diverted his troops to an uprising northeast of Jerusalem. But that didn't keep Sennacherib's general, Rabshakeh, from firing off a letter to Hezekiah that said, "If you think we're through with you, you're sadly mistaken. We will not be stopped from destroying Jerusalem" (see 2 Kings 18).

Ever get a letter like that? Intimidating, threatening, disheartening? "Service will be suspended in five days unless . . ."

This time, however, Hezekiah didn't say, "Oh no! What am I going to do? Who can I call?" No, having heard the Word from Isaiah, Hezekiah took Rabshakeh's letter, went into the temple, opened it before the Lord, and said, "Lord, I'm giving this to You," as he began to worship the One who dwells above all, the One who is greater than all (2 Kings 19).

Here on earth, things seem so big. Our mountains tower 29,028 feet above us, and the depths of the Mariana Trench plunge 36,198 feet below us. But from space, our planet looks perfectly smooth. In fact, if our earth was shrunk to the size of a bowling ball, a brand-new unused bowling ball would have more grooves and valleys and peaks than would our earth. It's all a matter of perspective.

When, like Hezekiah, you get above the situation, suddenly the problems that loomed so greatly and threatened so menacingly take on entirely different dimensions proportionately, for as the story goes on, Isaiah comes to Hezekiah, saying, "The Lord has spoken that not one person in Jerusalem shall be harmed. In fact, not one arrow shall enter the city."

The Assyrians did, indeed, come. As was their custom, they surrounded the city. All it would have taken to nullify Isaiah's prophecy was one soldier to take one arrow and fire it over the wall. But none did. The Assyrians set up their camp around the city, 185,000 soldiers strong. But that night, an angel of the Lord came and smote the Assyrians before even one man could string his bow. One hundred eighty-five thousand men were wiped out in a way Hezekiah could never have orchestrated or predicted, in a way no counselor could have directed, in a way no book would have addressed.

That's the way of the Lord. So what does He say to you and me today? "Take your cares and turn them into prayer." We all know this—but do we *do* it? Do we leave our anxieties and concerns with the Lord—or even as we read these words, are we wondering who we can get to help us in the problem facing us?

Right now, I ask you to find a scrap of paper and write on it that which concerns you today. It could be a relational stress, a ministry matter, a financial pressure, a family issue.

After you write it down, spread it before the Lord and say,

"Lord here it is. Like Hezekiah, I hear the footsteps and hoof beats of the mighty Assyrians headed my way. But instead of trying to take them on myself or ally with others, I choose to thank You for whatever You want to do in this situation. These are the matters that weigh me down, Lord. Free me of this burden as I lift it up to You."

Do this, saint, and you will experience the peace of God that comes not *from* your understanding, but which *passes* your understanding—a peace that will stop the Assyrians in their tracks, and that will leave you rejoicing in the goodness of your Father.

LEARNING CONTENTMENT
A Topical Study of
Philippians 4:10–13

O n our way to a mission base in Honduras, my brother Jimmy and I arrived at
the La Ceiba Airport. After making our way through Customs, we walked into
the small lobby, where before us stood an easel with a poster picturing a home for
sale, eight miles from the beautiful Roatan Peninsula. Upon closer inspection, we
could see that the home sat on its own one-and-a-half-acre island of white-sand
beach, ringed with coconut-bearing palm trees, and included a separate caretaker/
guest house. The price? One hundred fifty thousand dollars.

Hmm, I started thinking. *A guy could easily cash out here and buy his own
island. I wonder what it would be like to own your own island.*

There's something in each of us that desires to live in a different location, have
a different vocation, to be in a different situation—something in all of us that longs
for change. Advertisers know this and capitalize on it, parading an endless stream
of images before us that say, "*This* is where you long to live; *this* is what you want
to drive; *this* is how you desire to look," as they pull on the strings of discontent
which plague you and me.

Paul the apostle gives us a good piece of advice concerning this dilemma when
he says, "The key is to learn to be content no matter what state you're in." For, you
see, if we do not learn to be content in life, we will soon develop contempt for life.
So Paul says, "Whether I'm abounding or abased, full or hungry—it doesn't really
matter to me. Wherever I am, I have learned to be content."

We must learn that as well, for if we don't, we'll be dogged and devoured by
discontent. How do I know this? Because of the account in 1 Kings 21. . . .

Jezebel and Ahab

*And it came to pass after these things, that Naboth the Jezreelite had a vine-
yard, which was in Jezreel, hard by the palace of Ahab king of Samaria.*

1 Kings 21:1

Ahab, king of Israel, had a palace. Next to him lived Naboth. Next to the palace was Naboth's vineyard.

*And Ahab spake unto Naboth, saying, Give me thy vineyard, that I may have
it for a garden of herbs, because it is near unto my house: and I will give thee
for it a better vineyard than it; or, if it seem good to thee, I will give thee the*

worth of it in money. And Naboth said to Ahab, The Lord forbid it me, that I should give the inheritance of my fathers unto thee.   1 Kings 21:2, 3

"Give me your vineyard," said Ahab to Naboth.

"Sorry, King, the Lord forbids it," Naboth answered.

Naboth was right. Old Testament law required that inherited properties were to remain in the family (Leviticus 25; Numbers 36).

And Ahab came into his house heavy and displeased because of the word which Naboth the Jezreelite had spoken to him: for he had said, I will not give thee the inheritance of my fathers. And he laid him down upon his bed, and turned away his face, and would eat no bread.   1 Kings 21:4

His command refused, Ahab went to his palace and pouted.

But Jezebel his wife came to him, and said unto him, Why is thy spirit so sad, that thou eatest no bread? And he said unto her, Because I spake unto Naboth the Jezreelite, and said unto him, Give me thy vineyard for money; or else, if it please thee, I will give thee another vineyard for it: and he answered, I will not give thee my vineyard.   1 Kings 21:5, 6

Recounting the incident to Jezebel, Ahab conveniently left out the part where Naboth told him the vineyard was part of an inheritance and therefore couldn't be sold.

And Jezebel his wife said unto him, Dost thou now govern the kingdom of Israel? arise, and eat bread, and let thine heart be merry: I will give thee the vineyard of Naboth the Jezreelite. So she wrote letters in Ahab's name, and sealed them with his seal, and sent the letters unto the elders and to the nobles that were in his city, dwelling with Naboth. And she wrote in the letters, saying, Proclaim a fast, and set Naboth on high among the people.   1 Kings 21:7–9

Jezebel ordered the city fathers to call a special meeting, making sure Naboth was in attendance.

And set two men, sons of Belial, before him, to bear witness against him, saying, Thou didst blaspheme God and the king. And then carry him out, and stone him, that he may die.   1 Kings 21:10

Jezebel further instructed the men to hire two sons of Belial—or literally, "fools"—to lie and accuse Naboth of blasphemy.

And there came in two men, children of Belial, and sat before him: and the men of Belial witnessed against him, even against Naboth, in the presence of the people, saying, Naboth did blaspheme God and the king. Then they carried him forth out of the city, and stoned him with stones, that he died.

1 Kings 21:13

Falsely accused of blasphemy and treason, Naboth was stoned to death.

Then they sent to Jezebel, saying, Naboth is stoned, and is dead. And it came to pass, when Jezebel heard that Naboth was stoned, and was dead, that Jezebel said to Ahab, Arise, take possession of the vineyard of Naboth the Jezreelite, which he refused to give thee for money: for Naboth is not alive, but dead. And it came to pass, when Ahab heard that Naboth was dead, that Ahab rose up to go down to the vineyard of Naboth the Jezreelite, to take possession of it.

1 Kings 21:14–16

So it was that Ahab apparently got his way—but the plot thickens, for there was a prophet of God on the scene . . .

And the word of the Lord came to Elijah the Tishbite, saying, Arise, go down to meet Ahab king of Israel, which is in Samaria: behold, he is in the vineyard of Naboth, whither he is gone down to possess it. And thou shalt speak unto him, saying, Thus saith the Lord, Hast thou killed, and also taken possession?

1 Kings 21:17–19 (a)

Although Ahab didn't know anything about what Jezebel had done, God held him responsible for Naboth's death because it was his pining over Naboth's vineyard that caused Jezebel to implement her plan in the first place. Ahab couldn't be happy until he had his garden. He didn't know what it meant to be content in the state he was in as king of Israel. He just had to have something else, something more. And it drove his wife into a deadly activity for which he was held equally responsible.

And thou shalt speak unto him, saying, Thus saith the Lord, In the place where dogs licked the blood of Naboth shall dogs lick thy blood, even thine.

1 Kings 21:19 (b)

Dogged by discontent, Ahab was going down. But the prophecy didn't stop there. . . .

And of Jezebel also spake the Lord, saying, The dogs shall eat Jezebel by the wall of Jezreel.

1 Kings 21:23

Ahab's blood would be licked by dogs. Jezebel's body would be eaten by dogs. And in chapter 22, we begin to see it happen. . . .

And a certain man drew a bow at a venture, and smote the king of Israel between the joints of the harness: wherefore he said unto the driver of his chariot, Turn thine hand, and carry me out of the host; for I am wounded. And the battle increased that day: and the king was stayed up in his chariot against the Syrians, and died at even: and the blood ran out of the wound into the midst of the chariot.   1 Kings 22:34, 35

Ahab died in battle, his blood forming a puddle in his chariot.

So the king died, and was brought to Samaria; and they buried the king in Samaria. And one washed the chariot in the pool of Samaria; and the dogs licked up his blood; and they washed his armour, according unto the word of the Lord which he spake.   1 Kings 22:37, 38

Just as Elijah had prophesied, as Ahab's chariot was washed, the dogs weren't far behind.

Time passes.

Realizing that a man named Jehu had launched a coup to control Israel and knowing her life might be at risk, Jezebel had a plan. . . .

And when Jehu was come to Jezreel, Jezebel heard of it; and she painted her face, and tired her head, and looked out at a window.   2 Kings 9:30

When she heard her life was in danger, did Jezebel fall to her knees, did she lift her voice in prayer? No. She painted her face and fixed her hair.

And as Jehu entered in at the gate, she said, Had Zimri peace, who slew his master?   2 Kings 9:31

Zimri is one who came into power through a coup only to commit suicide seven days later, so Jezebel is trying to both seduce and intimidate Jehu.

And he lifted up his face to the window, and said, Who is on my side? who? And there looked out to him two or three eunuchs. And he said, Throw her down. So they threw her down: and some of her blood was sprinkled on the wall, and on the horses: and he trode her under foot. And when he was come in, he did eat and drink, and said, Go, see now this cursed woman, and bury her: for she is a king's daughter. And they went to bury her: but they found no more of her than the skull, and the feet, and the palms of her hands. Wherefore they came again, and told him. And he said, This is the word of

the Lord, which he spake by his servant Elijah the Tishbite, saying, In the
portion of Jezreel shall dogs eat the flesh of Jezebel.   2 Kings 9:32–36

What happened to Jezebel? Exactly what Elijah said would happen: Her body was devoured by dogs.

When a man or woman has not mastered the principle of learning to be content, he or she will ultimately be devoured by the dog of discontent. You've seen it happen. . . .

Because she's not happy, the wife walks away from her family. And it's not long before she's splattered emotionally.

Constantly looking for something better, the man changes jobs continually, until he's isolated and frustrated needlessly.

"Okay," you say. "I can see that if a person lives in a state of discontentment, it will destroy him. But how are we to avoid that?"

Look at Jesus

So in love with me was He, Jesus died on the Cross to save my soul in order that I might be His bride forever. Why He would love me in that way, I don't have the foggiest idea. But He does. And He proved it on the Cross. Therefore, if He loved me that much, I can be confident that He'll put me in the place financially, relationally, geographically that will make me into the man He sees I can be.

I am so concerned about my present comfort. God, however, is concerned about my eternal state. I pant after ministry or material things, fame or satisfaction. God, however, says, "I want you to be full and happy and useful and blessed for the next zillion years. Therefore, I will allow you to go through difficulties and challenges not because I'm being mean, but because I'm doing a deep work in you that you will never regret for all eternity."

If I invited people to come up after the service so I could slug them in the arm, there wouldn't be many takers. But if I invited people to come up after the service so I could slug them in the arm—after which they would receive a check for ten million dollars, people would be rushing to get in line.

So, too, God is saying, "Yes, you're going to take some hits. Yes, there will be some hurts, some setbacks, some disappointments. But, there's ten zillion dollars, so to speak, around the bend. And I have allowed you to be in the situation you're in because it's preparing you for what's to come. Will you trust Me? Will you not murmur about your condition? Will you not be always looking for some better situation? Will you learn to be content where you are right now?"

The story is told of a Swiss watch on the wrist of a lady in Zurich. It kept time perfectly and allowed her to keep her appointments punctually. One day, however, the watch said, "I'm doing a pretty good job. But why should I be limited to helping just one lady? I want to serve. I want to minister. A watch like me could help the whole city." So the watch found itself one day high, high above Zurich, fastened to the tallest building in the city. But no one could see it, for it was lost in the position of elevation.

Wise is the man or woman who says, "Lord, plant me where You see that I am designed to be. Be it on an island in Honduras, or a city in Oregon, place me in the spot wherein I can most glorify You presently, and that will prepare me for eternity. Teach me to be content, Lord."

And He will. He truly will.

COLOSSIANS

Background to Colossians

C. H. Spurgeon told of an event that took place in the glory days of Rome. During a severe famine in the North African colonies, Nero sent Roman galleons to the stricken area. When the starving people saw the ships on the horizon, they rejoiced greatly, saying, "Caesar has sent the ships! They're on the way! There's hope for us!" And then Spurgeon recounted the tragic end of the story. For when the ships sailed into port, the North Africans discovered they were full of sawdust to lay on the floor of the circuses Rome was exporting to the colonies. The people longed for food and got sawdust. They craved substance but got a circus.

Unlike what was exported from Rome, I'm happy to say that in the Epistle before us, we find a feast for our souls, hearty fare for our pilgrimage.

The Book of Colossians is a polemic epistle. That is, it argues for truth—a much-needed commodity in Colosse, a city invaded by untruths and subjective theology. "Be careful," Paul writes to the Colossian brothers and sisters. "Know the truth. Be grounded in truth." In chapter 1, he discusses the truth about Christ; in chapter 2, the truth about the cults; in chapters 3 and 4, the truth about the Christian in this wonderfully nourishing Epistle to the Colossians.

COLOSSIANS

1 Colossians 1:1–3
Paul, an apostle of Jesus Christ by the will of God, and Timotheus our brother, To the saints and faithful brethren in Christ which are at Colosse: Grace be unto you, and peace, from God our Father and the Lord Jesus Christ. We give thanks to God and the Father of our Lord Jesus Christ, praying always for you.

Although Paul had never been to Colosse, what he heard about the believers there caused his heart to rejoice and to respond by praying con-

tinual blessing upon them. I encourage you to do the same thing. When you hear something good about someone, pray for him. My tendency is to pray for people who are hurting or backsliding. While that is needed, indeed, we must also pray for people who are doing well because the Enemy will inevitably launch an attack against them in order to destroy their witness and tear down their testimony. Be like Paul. When you hear or see someone doing well, thank the Lord for him and intercede on his behalf.

Colossians 1:4 (a)
Since we heard of your faith in Christ Jesus . . .

The church at Colosse was characterized by three qualities—and it is my personal persuasion that these are the three marks of any solid church. The first mark of a mature fellowship is faith. The author of Hebrews tells us that without faith, it is impossible to please God. Therefore, the church that gathers together without believing God is going to do great things will not experience renewal, revival, or blessing.

Colossians 1:4 (b)
. . . and of the love which ye have to all the saints.

The second mark of a strong church is love, for it is love that identifies us as Jesus' disciples (John 13:35).

Colossians 1:5
For the hope which is laid up for you in heaven, whereof ye heard before in the word of the truth of the gospel.

Finally, a solid fellowship will have hope in its heart. The absolute expectation of coming good, hope says, "Sure it's tough down here, but this is the worst it will ever be. The coming of Jesus Christ is nigh. Life is short. We're going to heaven!"

I firmly believe that a church, family, or individual who is focused on faith, love, and hope will be stable, solid, and sure.

Colossians 1:6
Which is come unto you, as it is in all the world; and bringeth forth fruit, as it doth also in you, since the day ye heard of it, and knew the grace of God in truth.

The faith, hope, and love of the Colossian believers led not only to maturity and stability, but to fruitfulness as others were drawn into their midst.

Colossians 1:7, 8
As ye also learned of Epaphras our dear fellowservant, who is for you a faithful minister of Christ; Who also declared unto us your love in the Spirit.

I like Epaphras. He goes around speaking good things. I want to be like Epaphras—talking about how great someone is behind his or her back, for not only does this please the Lord, but it also has an impact on me as well. How? To a very real degree, you are the person I say you are when you're not around. You see, if when you leave church and, on your way home, talk about what an idiot the pastor is, he will become that

person to you the next time you meet. Talk negatively about him, and, even if those things are not totally true, that's what he will become in your sight. On the other hand, if you speak well of a person behind his back, that is the way you will tend to view him. The next time you see him, you will approach him with an entirely different mind-set than if you had come down on him. The power of words is awesome. For that reason, we must be very careful. Gossip about good stuff. That's what Epaphras did.

Colossians 1:9–13
For this cause we also, since the day we heard it, do not cease to pray for you, and to desire that ye might be filled with the knowledge of his will in all wisdom and spiritual understanding; That ye might walk worthy of the Lord unto all pleasing, being fruitful in every good work, and increasing in the knowledge of God; strengthened with all might, according to his glorious power, unto all patience and longsuffering with joyfulness; giving thanks unto the Father, which hath made us meet to be partakers of the inheritance of the saints in light: Who hath delivered us from the power of darkness, and hath translated us into the kingdom of his dear Son.

If you desire to be a prayer warrior, carefully consider this prayer. Notice how Paul prays for things we don't even think about. We pray, "Oh, Lord, help him to get over his arthritis," or, "Help her to be happy in her relationship," or, "Help them get the new car." But what does Paul pray? Under the inspiration of the Spirit, Paul prays that the Colossians would know the will of God and walk worthy of Him, that they would be fruitful and strengthened with His might, and that they would be patient and full of joy. Those are the important issues. Those are the issues of eternity. So if you want to know how to pray for your kids, grandchildren, parents, or husband—listen to Paul pray.

Colossians 1:14, 15 (a)
In whom we have redemption through his blood, even the forgiveness of sins: Who is the image of the invisible God . . .

People have had lots of ideas about what God is like. . . .

- The Hindu says, "God must be loving, benevolent, and gentle. Therefore, He must be a cow."

- The American Indian, watching an eagle soar majestically upon the wind currents, said, "God is an eagle."
- The ancient Egyptian saw the awesome power of the sun and says, "God is Ra. God is the sun."

Each culture spoke a partial truth, but all miss the total picture because they're blind. And so was all of humanity. So what did God do? He came and dwelt among us in the Person of Jesus Christ. Therefore, when I want to know what God is like, I don't have to try to figure out His nature on my own. I can study the life of Jesus Christ, for He alone reveals God in totality. He alone is the "image of the invisible God."

Colossians 1:15 (b)
. . . the firstborn of every creature.

"The firstborn of every creature" doesn't mean first in chronology, but rather first in priority. Jehovah's Witnesses and other cults will use this verse to erroneously say that, because Jesus was the firstborn, He was created, and therefore not eternal. But such is not the case, for God refers to Jacob and Ephraim as firstborn (Exodus 4:22; Jeremiah 31:9), even though both had older brothers. The Greek word *prototokos*, translated "firstborn," doesn't speak of chronology but of priority.

Colossians 1:16
For by him were all things created, that are in heaven, and that are in earth, visible and invisible, whether they be thrones, or dominions, or principalities, or powers: all things were created by him, and for him.

This, gang, is the secret of life. Jesus is not the created one; He is the Creator. "This is the day the Lord hath made," we sing. What does that mean? It means this day is made for Him, and the only way it will work is if I live for Him because, in so doing, I will be fulfilling the only reason it was created.

I could say, "I'd like to see the valley tonight. So I'll just rev up my Montero, drive up a mountain, hit the accelerator, and fly over the valley. It'll be great!" But the fact is, my Montero was not made to fly.

So, too, people say, "I'm going to fly high and live for myself." But they crash because they weren't made for any other purpose than to glorify God. *All* things were made by and for the Firstborn, the Preeminent One, Jesus.

Colossians 1:17
And he is before all things, and by him all things consist.

An interesting law of science known as Coulomb's Law of Electricity says that like charges repel. You can prove Coulomb's Law by pushing the positive ends of two magnets toward each other and feeling them repel each other. Opposite charges attract; like charges repel. But here's a great mystery: In the nucleus of the atom, protons are packed together that are *all* positive-charged particles.

What keeps these positive-charged protons from repelling like the magnets? What holds them together? Science doesn't know. You can study Quantum Physics and learn lots of hypotheses and theories, yet to this day, it's a mystery to scientists—but not to believers, for Scripture tells us the real answer. It is Jesus Christ who holds all things together. And the day is coming when suddenly He will let go.

But the day of the Lord will come as a thief in the night; in the which the heavens shall pass away with a great noise, and the elements shall melt with fervent heat, the earth also and the works that are therein shall be burned up.
2 Peter 3:10

This was written, of course, before man knew anything about nuclear physics or about things being dissolved instantaneously. But now we know if the "atomic glue" that holds the atom together were to suddenly disappear, everything would dissolve in zillion-degree "fervent heat" accompanied by a "great noise" so powerful and quick it wouldn't even be heard.

For, behold, I create new heavens and a new earth: and the former shall not be remembered, nor come into mind.　　Isaiah 65:17

Everything will vaporize and evaporate as if it never existed. Not only that, but in heaven, even the memory will be taken away. Think about that next time you're hammering, painting, or fixing your house. Of course, we should be good stewards of the things with which God has blessed us, but we must have the right perspective, always remembering that the things of this earth are temporary.

By Him all things are held together—not just physically, but in my life personally. My emotions, my family, my mental stability are held together by Jesus. By *Him* all things are held together. By *Him* all things consist.

Colossians 1:18 (a)
And he is the head of the body, the church: who is the beginning, the firstborn from the dead . . .

Others have risen from the dead—among them Lazarus, the son of the widow of Nain (Luke 7), and the widow's son in Elisha's day (2 Kings 4). But they all died again. Jesus alone is the First-born from the dead because He alone rose never to die again.

Colossians 1:18 (b)
. . . that in all things he might have the preeminence.

It is the Father's intent that in all things the Son should have preeminence over each day you begin and every decision you make.

Colossians 1:19
For it pleased the Father that in him should all fulness dwell.

All fulness is in Jesus. Therefore, the closer I am to Jesus, the fuller I will be as a man. Conversely, the further I pull away from Jesus, the emptier I'll feel inside. All of creation centers around Jesus, is held together by Jesus, points to Jesus, and finds its fulfillment in Jesus.

It's all about Jesus.

Some people compartmentalize their Christianity like a Swanson® TV Dinner. They've got their recreation section, their relationship section, their financial section, their hobby section, and their Christian section. So on Sunday they concentrate on church; Monday through Friday on money; evenings on relationships, and Saturday on sports and hobbies.

But ultimately, they find it frustrating and ineffective because God intended our lives to be not TV dinners, but chicken pot pies—all stirred together. In other words, when we're skiing, we're to be praising God for the beauty around us. When we're at work, we're to be praying, "Lord, help me use this as an opportunity to witness." When we're with family, we're to look for opportunities to serve. It's all mixed together.

If you continue to "TV-Dinner" it, you'll be depressed and discouraged. But it won't be because God is punishing you. It will simply be the result of your failure to understand that Jesus holds all things together and that in Him all fullness dwells.

Colossians 1:20, 21
And, having made peace through the blood of his cross, by him to reconcile all things unto himself; by him, I say, whether they be things in earth, or things in heaven. And you, that were sometime alienated and enemies in your mind by wicked works, yet now hath he reconciled.

What does "reconcile" mean? Simply this: If you planned to meet me at McDonald's® precisely at 7:45, it would be imperative that our watches be reconciled, or in agreement. Notice Paul says we are reconciled to God—not He to us. God didn't change His watch. No, *we* were the ones who were messed up and out of sync.

Colossians 1:22, 23 (a)
In the body of his flesh through death, to present you holy and unblameable and unreproveable in his sight: If ye continue in the faith grounded and settled, and be not moved away from the hope of the gospel, which ye have heard . . .

Because of Jesus' work on the Cross, we can be presented to God as holy and blameless if we continue on in faith. Therefore, I cannot in good conscience assure someone who walked forward at a crusade twenty years ago or was baptized six summers ago but has not continued in the faith that he will be presented to the Father as being holy and blameless.

Colossians 1:23 (b)
. . . and which was preached to every creature which is under heaven . . .

Paul reminds us that God makes Himself known to *every* creature. Creation around and conscience within the heart of every man are continual messages to people that there is a Creator. God is fair and will judge each man fairly, according to the knowledge given him (Romans 1—2).

Colossians 1:23 (c), 24
. . . whereof I Paul am made a minister; Who now rejoice in my sufferings for you, and fill up that which is behind of the afflictions of Christ in my flesh for his body's sake, which is the church.

Wait a minute, Paul. Are you saying that what Jesus did on the Cross is incomplete, that the reason you suffer is to fill up or complete that which He began on the Cross? It's a tricky verse because it is the basis for the Catholic doctrine of purgatory that says there must be a continuance of suffering, particularly by those who have not fully embraced the work of the Cross.

Is that what's being said here? No. Paul is saying it is not the completion *of,* but rather conformity *to* Christ's suffering. . . .

And after eight days again his disciples were within, and Thomas with them: then came Jesus, the doors being shut, and stood in the midst, and said, Peace be unto you. Then saith he to Thomas, Reach hither thy finger, and behold my hands; and reach hither thy hand, and thrust it into my side . . .   John 20:26, 27

In heaven, everything is made new, except for one thing: the scarred body of Jesus. Therefore, if we as His body are to be like Him, we must be scarred as well. "Make us like You, Lord," we pray.

And the Lord says, "Okay, but it cannot happen without suffering."

Suffering does some amazing things. . . .

First, suffering draws us closer to Christ.

"Take your only son and offer him as a sacrifice to Me," God said to Abraham.

What?! Abraham must have thought. Yahweh, You've been good to me, unlike the pagan gods who demand child sacrifices. But now You're asking me to offer my son?

Truly it must have been troubling and perplexing, yet Abraham obeyed as he took most likely a thirty-three-year-old Isaac up Mount Moriah to die.

Carrying the wood as they climbed, Isaac said, "Here's the wood, and, Dad, you've got the fire. But where's the sacrifice?"

"God will provide Himself a Lamb," Abraham replied.

Then Abraham took his son, laid him on the wood, raised the knife, and was ready to plunge it into the breast of his son when God said, "Stop. Now I know you love Me" (see Genesis 22).

Didn't God already know Abraham loved Him? Yes. But Abraham being one of the few men in the Bible called a friend of God, I believe God was saying,

"Abraham, My Son will carry His own wood up this same mountain. He will lie on the altar, and I will hurl the same fire you are carrying upon Him. You won't have to go through this, Abraham. But I will. At the moment when you think you're going to have to plunge that knife through Isaac's chest, you're going to feel something I'm not allowing many men in history to feel. You're going to know what it feels like to kill your son."

Precious people, God will allow suffering in your life in order that you can relate to Him in a deeper way than you ever would otherwise. But if you get thrown by it, you miss the opportunity for the fellowship of His suffering (Philippians 3:10).

You can say, "Lord, when I lost the promotion because I was a Christian, I felt a tiny bit of what You must have felt when they said, 'We will not have this man rule over us. Away with Him.'"

You can say, "Lord, when my girlfriend broke my heart, I could relate in a small way to how You must feel when people You love turn their back on You time and time again."

You can be a friend of God in a deeper way if you embrace suffering.

Second, suffering produces assurance in our hearts.

Remember the word that I said unto you, The servant is not greater than his lord. If they have persecuted me, they will also persecute you. . . .   John 15:20

Yea, and all that will live godly in Christ Jesus shall suffer persecution.   2 Timothy 3:12

If you're not suffering, it evidently means you're not living godly. It could even mean you're not a Christian. So when you suffer say, "Thank You, Lord! This is great! I know I'm one of Yours."

Third, suffering promises rewards in heaven.

For our light affliction, which is but for a moment, worketh for us a far more exceeding and eternal weight of glory.   2 Corinthians 4:17

I promise you, when you get to heaven, you won't say, "I suffered through cancer without murmuring. I accepted it as a way to bring You glory, Father. But now that I'm in heaven, I see it wasn't worth it."

No! When you get to heaven, you're going to say, "My goodness. I made such a big deal about my suffering on earth. But it was nothing compared to this! Even though I murmured, cried, and maybe even cursed, You loved me enough to allow suffering in my life. Thank You, Lord."

Fourth, suffering results in the salvation of others.

In Acts 28, Paul writes about a snake that fastened its fangs onto him. The islanders looked at the serpent hanging from his hand and thought, This guy's a murderer. That's why the snake has bitten him. *But when Paul*

didn't fall down dead and instead shook the snake off, the barbarians changed their minds, saying, "He's a god."

And Paul used the opportunity to say, "I'm not a god—but God in Christ Jesus lives inside me."

Why does God allow suffering? Because it gives us the opportunity to show skeptical barbarians the reality of faith. When the child is taken to heaven unexpectedly; when the doctor says, "It's malignant," when the boss says, "You're through"—people expect us to fall down dead. But we have the chance to shake it off and embrace the suffering. And if you make that choice, cynics change their minds about Christians because they see the reality of your faith.

Finally, suffering silences Satan.

Then Job arose, and rent his mantle, and shaved his head, and fell down upon the ground, and worshipped, And said, Naked came I out of my mother's womb, and naked shall I return thither: the LORD gave, and the LORD hath taken away; blessed be the name of the LORD. In all this Job sinned not, nor charged God foolishly.   Job 1:20–22

Job lost everything—his health, family, and wealth. Satan took everything but his wife—and even she said, "Curse God and die." But Job wouldn't, and Satan was defeated once again.

Colossians 1:25–27
Whereof I am made a minister, according to the dispensation of God which is given to me for you, to fulfil the word of God; even the mystery which hath been hid from ages and from generations, but now is made manifest to his saints: To whom God would make known what is the riches of the glory of this mystery among the Gentiles; which is Christ in you, the hope of glory.

The mystery is Christ living in you, not just telling you what to do.

I spent countless hours watching the same film loop over and over. I was attending Biola University, where I threw the discus. The film loop was of Jay Silvester's world-record discus throw. My teammates and I watched the way Silvester pivoted his feet. We watched the way he led with his hips. We watched the way he kept his arm behind him until the chest broke through the "glass wall" before it released the platter. Truly, it was a thing of beauty! But although I watched the film thousands of times and although I tried an equal number

of times to duplicate what Jay Silvester did, I never came close.

So, too, a lot of Christians are looking at the film loops. They study the Scriptures by the hour, which is wonderful, but it will ultimately lead to frustration until they understand the mystery. You see, if Jay Silvester could have left the film loop and taken up residence within my body, I would have pivoted perfectly, landed my feet just right, led with my hip, and tossed the discus for a world record.

"This is the mystery," writes Paul. "This is what I'm coming to share with you. It's not you being like Christ. It's Christ in you, showing you how to pray, what to do, and how to spend your time as He writes His will on your heart" (see Jeremiah 31:33).

It's not imitation. It's impartation. It's Christ *in* us—the hope of glory!

For topical study of Colossians 1:25–27 entitled "The Mystery of Life," turn to page 1310.

Colossians 1:28
Whom we preach, warning every man, and teaching every man in all wisdom; that we may present every man perfect in Christ Jesus.

Perfection in Christ is not based upon anything we can do, but rather upon all He has done. It's not dependent upon our works, but instead upon His work in us.

Colossians 1:29
Whereunto I also labour, striving according to his working, which worketh in me mightily.

Mom and Dad, that which you will most effectively communicate to your kids is that which works in you. Sunday-school teacher, youth worker, home group leader—what will ultimately be fruitful in your ministry is that which has personally been worked through and lived out by *you.* So many ministries lack power because they are based on sharing concepts that are true but lack impact because they haven't been worked out in the life of the teacher.

Gang, I'll tell you what to share with your kids, neighbors, Bible study group, or third-grade Sunday-school class: Share what works in *your* life. It's not how much you know; it's how well you know what you know. Has what you're teaching been worked through you? Has it become a part of you? If you share only what you've heard from others, your teaching will be dry. However, if, like Paul, you share that which "worketh in you mightily," your teaching will be anointed because it will truly be Christ *in* you, ministering the hope of glory.

THE MYSTERY OF LIFE
A Topical Study of
Colossians 1:25–27

When you come across the word "mystery" in your Bible, understand that it doesn't mean something that cannot be known, but rather something now made known that was previously incomprehensible.

> Many years ago I came into the kitchen and kissed my wife, Tammy. Observing the scene, my son Benjamin looked at me and said, "Ooh, Dad. Yuck!" because he can't figure out why any man would want to touch a woman, much less kiss her. So I stooped down, looked him in the eye, and said, "Ben, I know you think it's gross to kiss a girl. But not too many years from now, your perspective is going to change radically!"
>
> Indeed, one day, there was an unveiling, and suddenly Ben woke up and could say, "I get it. I understand. Yeah!"

That's the idea of biblical mystery. It's something that was talked about previously and prophesied historically, but was unable to be understood practically until the veil was lifted spiritually.

Such is the case with the mystery of which Paul writes, of Christ in us, the hope of glory. The Hebrew word for glory is *chabod*, a word signifying "weight" or "heaviness." *Chabod* is that which man has been craving ever since the Garden of Eden, when Adam and Eve enjoyed the visible, tangible presence of God as He walked with them in the cool of the day (Genesis 3:8). It was the glory, the *chabod*, which clothed Adam and Eve before they rebelled against God by eating the forbidden fruit.

The result of their rebellion was much more than physical nakedness. The result was a loss of the substance, the meaning, the heft of life. And so they took fig leaves and sewed them together to try to make up for the loss of the *chabod*. But Adam and Eve's fig leaves were no more effective than what people do today to try to fill their emptiness. People pursue relationships, houses, cars, boats, and trips. But none provide the weight they crave. It's all cotton candy. It looks good—but when they take a bite, they find nothing but air.

"Here's the hope of glory mankind has been craving since the Garden," Paul says. "Here's the mystery: It's Christ in you." We who have been around Christianity for a while have a tendency to think the idea of Christ in us is no big deal. But in reality, the concept is nothing short of radical.

> *Behold, the days come, saith the LORD, that I will make a new covenant with the house of Israel, and with the house of Judah: Not according to the covenant that I made with their fathers in the day that I took them by the hand to bring them out of the land of Egypt; which my covenant they brake, although I was an husband unto them, saith the LORD: But this shall be the covenant that I will make with the house of Israel; After those days, saith the LORD, I will put my law in their inward parts, and write it in their hearts; and will be their God, and they shall be my people. And they shall teach no more every man his neighbour, and every man his brother, saying, Know the LORD: for they shall all know me, from the least of them unto the greatest of them, saith the LORD; for I will forgive their iniquity, and I will remember their sin no more.*   Jeremiah 31:31–34

This is the New Covenant that was given to the people of Israel way back in the days of Jeremiah. But just like Benny seeing me kiss Tammy, they didn't get it. "We've got the Torah. We've got the law. We've got the Old Testament," they said. "What do you mean there's going to be something new?" So here comes Paul centuries later, explaining that Jesus Christ died for their sins, rose from the dead, ascended into heaven, and sent His Spirit to live inside those who believe. Once a person really understands this mystery, his entire thinking about Christianity changes significantly.

For many years I essentially made the New Testament the new law. My trinity was: God the Father, God the Son, and God the Holy Bible. In effect, I said, "The Old Testament was the Jewish law but the New Testament is our law." Thus, I found myself making new rules based not on the Old Testament, but on the New Testament. And my relationship with the Lord became legalistic, dry, boring, and predictable. But then the Lord began to bring people into my life and Scriptures to my heart that made me realize that if we merely trade the Old Testament for the New Testament, we remain a people under the law.

The most radical group of Christians who ever lived didn't have the New Testament. The early church never read Matthew, Romans, Colossians, or Revelation. Yet their lives impacted the world more than any other group of believers throughout history. How can this be? The answer is that, although they didn't have the New Testament Scriptures, they grasped New Covenant understanding. Thus, they acted upon the reality that Christ was in them, giving direction and inspiration moment by moment.

As they go to the temple in Acts 3, Peter and John see a man lame since birth lying by the Gate Beautiful. Suddenly, Peter's eyes fasten on him, and he says,

"Silver and gold have we none, but such as we have, we give to you. In the name of Jesus Christ of Nazareth, stand up and walk." So the man stands up, leaps, and praises God. Peter had perhaps walked by that man dozens of times before, but at this certain moment, Christ in him caused his eyes to "fasten" on the man and begin a conversation with him, thereby setting a miracle in motion.

That's New Covenant. That's the way the Lord wants you and me to walk. He wants to whisper in our ears. He wants our eyes to be fastened. He wants miracles to follow.

"Wait a minute," you say. "If all I need is Christ to direct me, why study the New Testament at all?"

Years after the birth of the church on the Day of Pentecost, letters from Paul began to circulate throughout the church—Colossians, Philippians, Romans, with the Gospels following even later. So, years and decades after early Christians had been turning the world upside down, they read letters from Paul and John, Luke and James and found them to either confirm or correct that which they were already doing.

The New Testament would confirm what the early church was doing—or it would correct them if they were out of line. In other words, the New Testament was not written as a legal document, but as confirmation or correction of what was already present in the hearts of believers. The present-day church is powerless to the degree we have lost hold of the mystery that every day, Christ will place on our hearts that which we should be doing.

> The storm was raging on the Sea of Galilee. The wind was howling. The waves were cresting. The disciples were fearful. Suddenly, they saw a Figure walking toward them.
>
> "It's a ghost!" they cried.
>
> Then they heard the words, "Be of good cheer. It is I. Be not afraid."
>
> "Lord, if that's You, bid me come," Peter said.
>
> "You come," Jesus literally answered. So Peter stepped out of the boat and began walking to Jesus. He wasn't walking to validate his ministry or to experience a Holy Ghost high. He was simply walking on water in order to get to Jesus. (Matthew 14)

If you've been a Christian very long, you've probably heard sermons based upon this story that say, "Peter took a step of faith. He walked on water. If *you* will leave your boat of comfort and take a step, you too will see great things happen."

And we say, "Okay."

A missionary shares his experience of leaving his comfort zone and "walking on water" to the mission field. "You should go, too," he says.

And we say, "Okay."

A person who prays eight hours a day talks about his step of faith and says, "You, too, should pray eight hours a day."

"Okay," we say. "But I thought I was supposed to be a missionary."

"No," he says. "You're supposed to pray."

Here's the question, gang. Peter walked on water. But what if John had said, "Wow, look at Peter. I'm going to walk on water, too"? What if Nathaniel, James, Thomas, or Andrew had? I suggest to you they would have sunk. Why? Because Jesus' invitation was issued only to Peter.

What does this mean? It means we don't have to let someone else's New Covenant experience put a weight on us. You see, when someone talks about fasting, I can say, "Good for you! I'm glad God told you to fast four days a week. I'm proud of you. But don't put that on me. Pass the burgers, please."

I can love people who have different ministries and perspectives without coming down either on them or on myself. This is what makes the New Covenant so cool. I can do what the Lord is telling *me* in my heart. If my perception is wrong, it will be corrected by Scripture. If it's right, it will be confirmed by Scripture.

If you come from a background like mine, I would encourage you to ask yourself these simple questions: Is my Trinity composed of God the Father, God the Son, and God the Holy Bible? Have I allowed other people to put their trips on me? Am I judging others because they don't see things my way? If your answer is yes, you need to rediscover the key to New Testament Christianity—the New Covenant— the fact that Christ is *in* you, and *He* will direct and guide you. Bible study will then become an adventure as you see how you're doing through the Scriptures. "Am I getting it, Lord? Am I hearing You correctly? All right! Terrific!"

Precious people, my prayer is that God will cause you to be Spirit-led—confirmed or corrected biblically as you follow the Son—for if you grasp this, you will experience exhilaration in your life and liberation in your love as you've never known before.

---

2 **Colossians 2:1, 2**
For I would that ye knew what great conflict I have for you, and for them at Laodicea, and for as many as have not seen my face in the flesh; that their hearts might be comforted, being knit together in love, and unto all riches of the full assurance of understanding, to the acknowledgement of the mystery of God, and of the Father, and of Christ.

Paul not only writes to the Colossians but agonizes for them. The Greek word translated "conflict" in verse 1 is *agon*, in Greek, from which we get our word "agony." Thus, Paul was saying, "I agonize for you, that you would be knit together, based on the fact that Jesus Christ is in you."

Colossians 2:3
In whom are hid all the treasures of wisdom and knowledge.

All wisdom, all knowledge is in—not from— Jesus. Whoever desires wisdom to navigate life successfully must come to the realization that there is nothing more, nothing less, nothing else than Jesus. All treasures of wisdom are in Him.

The story is told that one day William Randolph Hearst was looking through a book of famous artwork when a painting caught his eye. "I want this painting for my collection," he said to his aides. But after making some inquiries, they reported that they were unable to locate the particular work.

"If you value your jobs," Hearst said, "do whatever it takes to find that treasure, and secure it for me immediately."

Three and a half months later, the aides returned to Hearst. "Did you find the treasure?" he asked.

"Yes," they replied. "After much searching and painstaking research, we found it."

"Did you purchase it?" he asked.

"No."

"Why not?" Hearst asked.

"Because we found it in your warehouse."

So, too, Paul says to the Colossians, "You already have all the wisdom and knowledge you will ever need to get through life successfully. It's all in Christ. When you got Him, you got it all."

Colossians 2:4, 5
And this I say, lest any man should beguile you with enticing words. For though I be absent in the flesh, yet am I with you in the spirit, joying and beholding your order, and the stedfastness of your faith in Christ.

The story is told that in the days of the Roman Empire, a certain wealthy senator became estranged from his son. When he died unexpectedly, his will was opened. "Because my son does not appreciate what I've done, I leave all of my worldly possessions to my loyal slave, Marcellus," the will read. "However, because I am a man of grace, I bequeath to my son one of my possessions of his choosing."

"Sorry," said the testator to the son. "You can only take one of your dad's possessions. Which will it be?"

"I take Marcellus," said the son.

Brilliant! That's the idea. When you take Jesus Christ, you get all the treasures of wisdom and knowledge. When you open your heart to Him, you find everything you need. It's all in Him. Why is this understanding so important? Because it is the only way to keep from being sucked into "enticing words," cults, and other dead-end pursuits of pseudo-spirituality. That's what was happening in Colosse. People were coming on the scene, saying, "What Paul is preaching is fine, but there's much more."

"No," Paul says. "Be steadfast in your faith in Christ. All of the treasures of wisdom and knowledge are hidden in Him."

Colossians 2:6
As ye have therefore received Christ Jesus the Lord, so walk ye in him.

Over and over, the Scriptures tell us to walk. We're told to walk in light (Ephesians 5:8), in love (Ephesians 5:2), in wisdom (Colossians 4:5). And here we are told to walk in simplicity.

The banks of certain rivers are lined with a substance called "near quicksand." It's almost quicksand—but not quite. If you keep walking on this near-quicksand, you don't have a problem. But if you stop, you'll start sinking, and you'll eventually get sucked in completely.

So, too, if we don't keep walking in our Christian experience, we'll start sinking. The way to keep walking is not to seek some deeper truth. The way to keep moving is to do so in simplicity, to walk in the same way we received Christ.

Colossians 2:7
Rooted and built up in him, and stablished in the faith, as ye have been taught, abounding therein with thanksgiving.

The Church is truly an enigma, for we're the only people in the world who get together regularly to acknowledge that we're a bunch of sinners—all the while feeling wonderful about it. Because we recognize we're sinners saved by a wonderful Savior, we leave "abounding with thanksgiving." Every other group tries to convince itself how wonderful its members are, but they leave feeling miserable as they strive for increased sophistication and depth.

"Don't get sucked in to the quicksand of pseudo-sophistication," says Paul. "Walk in the simplicity with which you received Christ in the first place." And to underscore this, he goes on to enumerate four things of which to beware.

Colossians 2:8
Beware lest any man spoil you through philosophy and vain deceit, after the tradition of men, after the rudiments of the world, and not after Christ.

"Beware of intellectualism—of the philosophy and psychology the world values," warns Paul. "They're vain. They're empty. They don't work." I am concerned about the increasing number of believers who are wasting their money and time on unbelieving psychologists and psychiatrists when their problems are specifically dealt with in the Bible. Folks, if your car breaks down, I wouldn't tell you to read your Bible. I would tell you to read an automotive manual. If your arm breaks, I wouldn't tell you to read your Bible. I would tell you to go to a doctor or read a medical manual. But for matters of the heart and soul, I would implore you to read your Bible, for it alone contains the answers you need.

Colossians 2:9–13
For in him dwelleth all the fulness of the Godhead bodily. And ye are complete in him, which is the head of all principality and power: In whom also ye are circumcised with the circumcision made without hands, in putting off the body of the sins of the flesh by the circumcision of Christ: Buried with him in baptism, wherein also ye are risen with him through the faith of the operation of God, who hath raised him from the dead. And you, being dead in your sins and the uncircumcision of your flesh, hath he quickened together with him, having forgiven you all trespasses.

This is the key to biblical counseling and ministry. Paul says the issue is forgiveness of sin. What does man need? Forgiveness. It's so simple. We are forgiven because of Christ's work on the Cross. Therefore, we must forgive the person who bothers us, the parent who abused us, or the spouse who left us. We must realize that Jesus died for them, just as He died for us.

Colossians 2:14
Blotting out the handwriting of ordinances that was against us, which was contrary to us, and took it out of the way, nailing it to his cross.

The sins that have plagued you are written on a list. Santa Claus makes a list and checks it twice in order to find out who's naughty and nice. Our Father, on the other hand, makes a list and checks it once. Then He nails it to the Cross, where the blood of His Son covers it completely. The list of our sins, shortcomings, and stupidity is blotted out in totality by the blood of the Son of God.

Many Christians aren't healthy because they fail to understand this foundational and profoundly simple truth. They know they're forgiven—but they can't believe the one who hurt them is. "You can't ignore the abuse, the trauma, and the anxiety that have been inflicted upon you," they are told. "It must be dealt with." Wait

a minute! It *has* been dealt with by Jesus' blood on the Cross. He hung on the Cross of Calvary dying for the very sin that bugs us in others. Therefore, for us to say, "We must dig it up and talk it through," makes a mockery of what Christ did on Calvary. "It is *finished*," He cried. It's done. It's paid for. So be forgiven and forgive one another.

Colossians 2:15
And having spoiled principalities and powers, he made a shew of them openly, triumphing over them in it.

When a Roman general conquered an enemy, he would return to Rome in a triumphal procession. The general would ride in the lead chariot, followed by his soldiers. Behind the soldiers walked the conquered men, chained and often naked, to the derisive jeers of the crowds lining the streets. Paul borrows from this image in this verse.

The only toehold or handgrip a demon has on someone is his sin. But if the sin has been washed away by the blood of the Son, the demon has nothing upon which to cling. Once forgiveness is understood and blood is appropriated, the powers of darkness are rendered as powerless as a troop of chained and conquered soldiers. That's why Peter tells us that when Jesus died, He went into the lower parts of the earth and told the demonic spirits they no longer had authority over us (1 Peter 3:19).

If I understand and rejoice in the blood of Christ, demonic powers are nakedly impotent. But the funny thing about demonic powers is that they are squatters. They won't leave until I say, "I'm not going to listen to this depression you're whispering in my ear this morning. I'm not going to buy it because of the blood of Jesus Christ."

That's what is meant by pleading the blood. It's not a phrase you use; it's an understanding you have. Wherever I plead the blood of Christ, Satan doesn't have influence over me. Let this sink in, gang, and you will really be set free.

Colossians 2:16
Let no man therefore judge you in meat, or in drink, or in respect of an holyday, or of the new moon, or of the sabbath days.

Paul's second warning regards legalism. There were those in Colosse saying that the way to be more spiritual was to keep the Sabbath and festivals and to refrain from eating or drinking certain things.

Colossians 2:17
Which are a shadow of things to come; but the body is of Christ.

On occasion, people come to our churches and tell us that because we're worshiping on Sunday, we're worshiping the sun, not the Son. "Don't let anyone put those kinds of trips on you," says Paul, "because Sabbath days, festivals, eating and drinking are nothing more than shadows."

If I returned from a trip and Tammy fell to her knees and started kissing and hugging my shadow, I would say, "There's something shady about this, honey. Get up! I'm the reality. Hug me!"

That's what Paul is saying. These things people are hugging and kissing and founding movements upon are just shadows. The reality is Christ. *He* is the fulfillment of all Old Testament rules, regulations, and ordinances. Once you have the Reality, why kiss the shadows of legalism?

Colossians 2:18
Let no man beguile you of your reward in a voluntary humility and worshipping of angels, intruding into those things which he hath not seen, vainly puffed up by his fleshly mind.

Third, Paul says to watch out for mysticism. According to this passage, those who claim to be caught up in heavenly visions possess a cultlike mentality as they intrude into things they have not seen, puffed up by their fleshly mind.

Colossians 2:19
And not holding the Head, from which all the body by joints and bands having nourishment ministered, and knit together, increaseth with the increase of God.

Keep your focus on the Head, on Jesus, and beware of phony mysticism. How do you know when you're involved in a mystical group? You'll know when people get together at Bible studies or group sessions and say, "Well, what does this passage mean to you?" the supposition being that whatever the Bible means to you is valid.

The question is not "What does the Bible mean to you?" but "What does the Bible mean?"—period. That's why Paul instructed Timothy to study in order that he might *rightly* divide the Word of truth (2 Timothy 2:15). In questions of theology, people often say, "Let's agree to disagree." And we must tell them that the final word

is the Living Word, Jesus Christ, for He is the Head.

Colossians 2:20–22
Wherefore if ye be dead with Christ from the rudiments of the world, why, as though living in the world, are ye subject to ordinances, (Touch not; taste not; handle not; which all are to perish with the using;) after the commandments and doctrines of men?

Finally, Paul says to watch out for asceticism. A fourth group in Colosse was saying, "Discipline yourself in such a way that you deny your body, your family, your marriage partner. Deny. Deny. Deny. And in so doing, you will be showing true spirituality."

Colossians 2:23
Which things have indeed a shew of wisdom in will worship, and humility, and neglecting of the body; not in any honour to the satisfying of the flesh.

Denial appears to be wise, says Paul, but it's really will worship. What is will worship? It's saying, "Don't you wish you were strong and had will power like me?" Who else had incredible will power? The one who said, "I *will* ascend into heaven. I *will* sit above the stars. I *will* be like God"—Lucifer himself (see Isaiah 14).

Don't let people put trips on you. "If you're really serious about Christ, you'll eat lima beans," they'll say. Now, if you like lima beans, great. But don't make it a point of spirituality, for it's nothing more than will worship. Those who are focused on their flesh end up becoming obsessed with their flesh.

"Be careful," Paul says. "Intellectualism, legalism, mysticism, and asceticism are all snares that can rob you of your simple, joyful walk in Jesus Christ."

It's in Jesus that we have all the treasures of wisdom and knowledge. Therefore, keep everything focused on Him.

3 **Colossians 3:1, 2**
If ye then be risen with Christ, seek those things which are above, where Christ sitteth on the right hand of God. Set your affection on things above, not on things on the earth.

The only people who are truly happy on earth are those whose hearts are in heaven.

Peter-John came into the kitchen one day whistling and smiling. "Sixteen more days, Dad," he said. Sixteen more days until graduation, and he would be through with high school. He saw the finish line. Consequently, it caused him to go through the last couple weeks of school whistling.

I am thoroughly convinced from watching people and studying the Word that the people who are truly content are those who constantly realize that this world is not where it's at. On the other hand, those who try to find happiness here are perpetually frustrated. The possessions they purchase are never quite what they were supposed to be. The relationships they form are never as satisfying as they thought they would be. The dreams they pursue are never as fulfilling as they hoped they would be. Nothing is ever quite right until we realize, "Hey, it's not here!"

I believe this is why the Lord constantly tells us in the Word to set our hearts on things above. People are bogged down, with stomachs churning, brows furrowing, and hearts breaking because they are taking life on earth far too seriously. When a person finally understands that heaven is where it's at, he is free to enjoy life. It doesn't matter where he lives, what he does vocationally, what kind of car he drives, bike he rides, or skates he has. All of that is irrelevant because he sees the finish line—he realizes that graduation is only sixteen days away.

Set your heart on things above. It's a central message not only of Paul's, but throughout all of Scripture. Live for heaven and you'll enjoy life. How does that happen? Many ways, but I'll suggest three.

First, we live for heaven through that which we treasure. Jesus said, "Wherever your treasure is, there will your heart be also" (Matthew 6:21).

For one week, I had a crush on Denise Fuller and wanted to take her to our church youth group's Spring Banquet. In order to pay for it, however, I had to sell the one share of American Motors stock I had bought for twelve dollars. Now, I was really into my one share of stock—so much so that, although I was a big Giants fan, before I checked out the box scores to see how Mays, Cepeda, and McCovey were doing each day, I turned to the stock page to check on American Motors' progress. But when this banquet came up, I sold my one share of stock to take Denise Fuller to the banquet. And guess what. Once I sold my share, I never turned to the stock page again. I just lost interest.

When Jesus tells us to lay up treasure in heaven (Matthew 6:20), it's not God's way of raising money. Knowing that where our treasure is, our heart will follow, it's His way of raising our hearts and minds out of this world and up into heaven. You see, if you invest your treasure in American Motors, that's where your heart will be. If you put your treasure in your house or hobby, your heart will be there as well. Your heart follows your treasure. So one of the ways we get our hearts on things above is by investing in the kingdom.

Second, we live for heaven through our trials. I am convinced God will send a trial a day your way just to keep you homesick for heaven. If He didn't, we would become bound up in this earth and would miss out eternally on what He has in store for us.

A third way the Lord gets me to set my heart and mind on things above is by transfers—when the people we love precede us into heaven. This process is very important because when you have transferred friends, parents, and spouses into heaven, your heart longs to be there all the more keenly.

Treasures, trials, and transfers are three ways our hearts can be constantly set on things above.

Colossians 3:3
For ye are dead, and your life is hid with Christ in God.

Outside Warsaw, several Jews were hiding in a cemetery from the Nazis who had overrun Poland. Among them were a couple of pregnant women, who eventually gave birth in the cemetery. Thus, in the place of death, life was birthed.

How can we find safety and life in this world? By realizing that we're dead to this world and that a new life is being birthed in us through Christ.

Colossians 3:4
When Christ, who is our life, shall appear, then shall ye also appear with him in glory.

The days are going by rapidly, gang. We are going to see Jesus soon, and when we do, we will say, "This is it! This is what we've been craving and longing for all our lives." That is why I believe we can't talk too much about heaven. And that's why Paul tells us heaven is where our hearts should be. When Christ appears, it's going to be glorious.

Colossians 3:5 (a)
Mortify therefore your members which are
upon the earth . . .

Following Paul's exhortation concerning how
we should live for heaven in verses 1–4, in the remainder of the chapter, he turns our attention to
how we should live on earth.

Colossians 3:5 (b)–7
. . . fornication, uncleanness, inordinate af-
fection, evil concupiscence, and covetous-
ness, which is idolatry: For which things'
sake the wrath of God cometh on the chil-
dren of disobedience: In the which ye also
walked some time, when ye lived in them.

Our culture says, "Live for your earthly desires"—yet covetousness is the cause of wars
among nations and in relationships; pornography
is a major reason for the breakdown of families
and society; and evil desires have caused entire
countries to collapse. Read history and you will
find this to be so. Living for earthly desires
brings death. Putting to death our earthly desires, however, brings life.

Colossians 3:8 (a)
But now ye also put off all these; anger . . .

The Greek word translated "anger" is *orge*,
which refers to a slow, simmering emotion. It's a
festering, smoldering feeling—and it's got to go.

Colossians 3:8 (b)
. . . wrath . . .

The Greek word translated "wrath" is *thumos*,
which means "hot." Wrath is like a volcano. Put it
off, says Paul. Stuff a cork in it.

Colossians 3:8 (c)
. . . malice . . .

Malice is finding humor in another's misfor-
tune.

Colossians 3:8 (d)
. . . blasphemy, filthy communication out of
your mouth.

Defined as "contempt for God or anything sacred," blasphemy is to have no part of our thinking or speaking.

Colossians 3:9
Lie not one to another, seeing that ye have
put off the old man with his deeds.

The idea of lying here is that of bearing false
witness. What is a false witness? In Matthew 26,
we see the answer. . . .

Two false witnesses came forward and, referring to Jesus, said, "He said that if the temple
was destroyed, He would raise it in three days."
Did Jesus say that? Yes—but He was talking
about the temple of His body. Bearing false witness is giving the right information, but the
wrong implication.

Today's society is completely caught up in this.
"I technically told the truth." Yes, but did your
hearer understand what you were really saying—or did you hide behind rhetoric to conceal
the real implications? Scripture tells us that, like
blasphemy, anger, and malice, this is something
we are to choose to put off. No matter how tempting it is, we are not to use cleverness of speech or
intellectual prowess to conceal the truth.

Colossians 3:10–14
And have put on the new man, which is re-
newed in knowledge after the image of him
that created him: Where there is neither Greek
nor Jew, circumcision nor uncircumcision,
Barbarian, Scythian, bond nor free: but Christ
is all, and in all. Put on therefore, as the elect
of God, holy and beloved, bowels of mercies,
kindness, humbleness of mind, meekness,
longsuffering; forbearing one another, and
forgiving one another, if any man have a quar-
rel against any: even as Christ forgave you, so
also do ye. And above all these things put on
charity, which is the bond of perfectness.

"Put on the new man," says Paul. "Put on
mercy, kindness, and humility. Put on meekness,
longsuffering, and love." In short, put on Christ.

For topical study of Colossians 3:9–14 entitled
"Being a Put-On," turn to page 1320.
For topical study of Colossians 3:9–14 entitled "Being a Put-On," turn to page 1320.

Colossians 3:15
And let the peace of God rule in your hearts,
to the which also ye are called in one body;
and be ye thankful.

The word translated "rule" is a Greek word
that describes an official at an athletic event, similar to a present-day umpire. People ask, "Should
I move? Should I take that job? Should I marry
him?" I often answer with a question: "What does
your heart tell you? If you're walking with the
Lord, the peace of God will be an umpire in your
heart, calling Safe! or Out!"

Women, when he asks you to marry him, don't
say yes if there isn't a deep sense of peace in your

heart. "You just have cold feet," he'll say. But I suggest to you it is much more than that. I suggest it is God working deep within your soul, whispering, "Don't do it." Don't move, gang, without the peace of God umpiring and ruling in your heart.

The flip side is the man who says he has peace about divorcing his wife.

"Really?" I ask. "Why?"

"Well, I've prayed. I've fasted. I've sought God and I have peace."

In response, I'll say, "Jonah had peace, too. God told him to go to Nineveh, but he disobeyed and headed in the opposite direction to Tarsus. And guess what. There was a boat waiting for him because there's always a boat waiting to take you in the opposite direction of God's will—compliments of Satan. Such peace had Jonah about disobeying God that he even slept right through a storm.

Listening to our hearts can't be the only criteria for determining God's will because Jeremiah 17:9 says the heart is deceitful above all things and desperately wicked. That's where the Word comes in.

Colossians 3:16
Let the word of Christ dwell in you richly in all wisdom; teaching and admonishing one another in psalms and hymns and spiritual songs, singing with grace in your hearts to the Lord.

The Word is the final authority. When someone says they have peace about something that contradicts the Word, you must look him in the eye and say, "You're headed for a whale of a time. I don't care what ship is ready to take you away, or how peaceful you feel in the hull of the boat. What you're doing is contrary to the Word."

Yes, the peace of God rules in your heart, but it will never contradict the wisdom of God as revealed in His Word.

Colossians 3:17
And whatsoever ye do in word or deed, do all in the name of the Lord Jesus, giving thanks to God and the Father by him.

In other words, whatever you do, do everything in the nature and flavor of Jesus Christ.

Colossians 3:18
Wives, submit yourselves unto your own husbands, as it is fit in the Lord.

"Here's how you're to live on earth, wives," says Paul. "Submit to your husband." But notice Paul says wives are to submit to their *own* husband—not to submit to men generally, but to

their own husband specifically. Women, don't let anyone say, "Sister, I need to correct you on this, or deal with you on that," because, unfortunately, there are men who seem to feel it's their calling to go around the church correcting women. They have a "women's ministry," wherein they talk to women about the way to dress, behave, talk or think—and they are unscriptural in doing so, for Scripture says that wives are to submit to their own husbands exclusively.

Colossians 3:19
Husbands, love your wives, and be not bitter against them.

People become bitter whenever expectations are unrealistically high. Husbands, your wife is not going to be God for you. She will not satisfy your deepest longing. Only the Lord will satisfy you. And only the Lord will satisfy her. Truly, if you love the Lord with all your heart, you will have no reason to be bitter with your wife.

Colossians 3:20
Children, obey your parents in all things: for this is well pleasing unto the Lord.

This is written simply enough for any child to understand: Kids, obey your parents in all things. Don't argue with them, but do what they say, for by this is the Lord well pleased.

Colossians 3:21
Fathers, provoke not your children to anger, lest they be discouraged.

Similar to Paul's injunction to put away bitterness toward their wives, Paul warns fathers that unrealistic demands lead to anger and discouragement in the hearts of their children.

Colossians 3:22
Servants, obey in all things your masters according to the flesh; not with eyeservice, as menpleasers; but in singleness of heart, fearing God.

"What if I don't agree with my company's policy?" you ask. It might not be your flavor, or what you would do as a boss, but you are to obey those in authority over you unless what they demand is immoral—and then you better have Scripture and wise counsel to back your objection.

Colossians 3:23
And whatsoever ye do, do it heartily, as to the Lord, and not unto men.

The man God uses is a man who knows how to work.

It was when Moses was tending his father-in-law's sheep that God appeared to Him in the burning bush (Exodus 3).

It was when Elisha was plowing that Elijah cast the mantle of ministry upon him (1 Kings 19:19).

It was when Peter and Andrew were casting their nets that Jesus called them to be fishers of men (Matthew 4:19).

It was when Saul was laboring for the high priest on his way to Damascus that Jesus appeared to him and turned his life around (Acts 9).

Many people who want to be missionaries, ministers, or youth pastors are just sitting, "waiting on God." But they will still be sitting at age seventy. The answer is to work. Whatever you're doing, do it heartily unto the Lord—for it is then that God will tap you on the shoulder and give you even more significant tasks.

Colossians 3:24
Knowing that of the Lord ye shall receive the reward of the inheritance: for ye serve the Lord Christ.

Watching Mother Teresa care for people with their open sores, stinking bodies, and bleeding wounds, an observer said to her, "I wouldn't do what you do for a million dollars."

"Neither would I," Mother Teresa smiled.

The only motivation big enough for such service is an eternal reward.

Colossians 3:25
But he that doeth wrong shall receive for the wrong which he hath done: and there is no respect of persons.

If our sins are forgiven because of the finished work of Christ, what does it mean that "he that doeth wrong shall receive for the wrong"?

In Jeremiah 2:19, God says, "Thine own wickedness shall correct thee, and thy backslidings shall reprove thee: know therefore and see that it is an evil thing and bitter, that thou hast forsaken the Lord thy God . . ." thereby declaring that our own sin will one day track us down.

For example, for years, the proponents of premarital sex have used the logic that since "you wouldn't buy a car without test-driving it," if you're going to have a successful marriage, a "test drive" is in order. The problem is, coming together physically before marriage is like taking a test drive in a demolition derby. When the test drive is all over, you're shocked to find the car is beat up and doesn't work right anymore. And no doubt this explains why the most findings indicate that those who live together before they're married have a greater chance of divorce than those who don't.

Sin of any kind carries its own repercussions, and because God is neither a respecter of persons nor of parsons, none of us is exempt.

BEING A PUT-ON
A Topical Study of
Colossians 3:9–14

Shortly before his death, Cary Grant was interviewed on a television biography program. It caught my attention when the reporter asked him if he had always been a suave, sophisticated person. Grant chuckled, and then shared a little bit of his story. . . .

Cary Grant, the quintessential romantic leading man, was born Archibald Leach in 1904 in a rough section of Bristol, England. A ruffian with a cockney accent, he was anything but suave or sophisticated. But in his late teenage years, thinking acting might be the way to make an easy dollar, he went to the local theater and started to pick up some bit parts. And as he acted out these parts, he conjured up the kind of person he wished he was—a person of culture and sophistication, a romantic figure, a ladies' man.

And so convincingly did he portray this image that seventy films later, he was known as "Mr. Sophistication." That's why, when asked if he had always been so suave and sophisticated, Cary Grant chuckled. At the end of the interview, he said, "I played the part so frequently that it became me ultimately. I put on this character so often, that it became who I am."

In Colossians 3, Paul says we are to play a part as well. "Put on the new man," he writes. "Put on kindness and mercy, longsuffering and love"—as an actor puts on a role.

Most Christians say, "Accept me the way I am. I'm grumpy before I have my morning coffee, and that's just the way it's gonna be."

"Put off that old man," counters Paul. "And put on the new."

Oftentimes, people say to us, "You guys at church are a bunch of put-ons." And I have learned to respond, "You're right. We put on Jesus Christ as Romans 13:14 says we are to do. We put on the personality of Jesus to the best of our ability."

"Then you're play-acting," some argue. "You're a put-on, a phony."

But the fact is, every person on the stage of life is acting some part. You might be acting the part of a jock, a surfer, an entrepreneur, or a glamour girl. Everyone chooses a part, and in the end they become the role they choose. The question is, will they like the part they've chosen when the curtain comes down and the play is over.

Ask Cary Grant. The sophisticated star made millions, but how did his life end? After five failed marriages, he battled depression and became an alcoholic. While people were thinking he had everything, his life was empty.

Everyone is deciding who to be in the drama of life. If you're not careful, you'll make the wrong choice and pick the wrong part. Then you'll mess up like Cary Grant—or like me. . . .

I remember it as if it were yesterday. I saw her when I walked into the fellowship hall at church. I had noticed her for several weeks and finally got up the courage to fight through the crowd and introduce myself. But, you see, I realized there was a problem, for she was an older lady. After all, she was eighteen and I was only seventeen. Knowing I would have to approach her with maturity and sophistication, as I walked over to her, I tried to deepen my voice a bit.

"Hello," I said. "I'm Jon Courson."

"I'm Stephanie," she replied.

"Yes, I know. It's nice to officially make your acquaintance, ma'am."

She looked puzzled, but I went on. "Are you by any chance available for dinner this Saturday evening?"

"I guess so," she said.

"Then may I have the pleasure of escorting you to dinner at seven o'clock Saturday night?"

"Okay," she said.

"Delightful," I replied and walked away, proud of how debonair I had been.

Saturday finally came. I got up early to get my 1961 turquoise Ford Falcon ready for my big date. I washed, waxed, and vacuumed it. Then I took a shower, brushed my teeth, put on my one suit, and then called up the most exclusive restaurant on the wharf at Santa Cruz and reserved a table for two by the window, overlooking the ocean. Feeling quite dapper, I knocked on Stephanie's door.

"You look exquisite, Stephanie," I said as she appeared in the doorway. I gave her my arm as we walked out the door to my car. But as I opened the passenger door, it fell right off. So I borrowed a hammer and bolt from Stephanie's dad, jammed the door back on, and drove to Santa Cruz. When we reached the restaurant, the maitre d' seated us at the table I had reserved.

"Order whatever you want, Stephanie," I said—before looking at the menu. Having never eaten there before, as I studied the menu, I was shocked and chagrined to hear Steph order the most expensive item listed: Surf and Turf, $17.95. The problem was, all I had to my name was in my suit coat pocket—a $20 bill.

"I'll have the shrimp cocktail" (you know, those little shrimp things in ketchup that cost about $1.50) I quickly said to the waiter.

"Is that all you want?" asked Steph.

"Yeah," I assured her. "I sort of lost my appetite."

So there we sat—she, enjoying her Surf and Turf and me fishing little pieces of shrimp out of a sea of ketchup.

After dinner, I asked her if she would like to stroll down the wharf.

"Okay," she replied.

So we went outside and began to walk to the end of the pier. By this time, the sun had set on an unusually warm, beautiful, summer evening. And I was really impressed with this girl.

When we came to the end of the pier, Stephanie stopped and leaned against the railing. Wanting to show her I liked her without appearing too forward or tacky, this seemed the perfect opportunity. "I can just sort of put my hand on the railing," I said to myself. "It won't really be around her, and yet it kind of will, and I can leave the interpretation up to her." So I casually leaned over and put my hand on the railing—right in a big seagull mess. I immediately pulled my hand away to find gooey stuff running down my arm. Not knowing what else to do, I wiped it off on my dapper suit coat—which put an abrupt end to my sophistication.

Whenever we try to put on roles, the question will be: Will it work, or will you end up like me—with a mess on your hands? There is only one role that will ultimately satisfy any man. It is the role of putting on the Lord Jesus Christ (Romans 13:14).

What does it mean to put on Christ? In verses 12–14, Paul lists the following characteristics, traits also clearly seen in Jesus: Mercy, kindness, humility, meekness, longsuffering, forbearance, forgiveness, and love. Therefore, to put on Christ means to exhibit these same qualities.

> I was at Bi-Mart, and I was tired. It had been a long, tough week for me. I had hoped I could just blitz in with one of my kids and be out quickly. But a lady approached me in the aisle with a broken heart and a problem, so I listened, prayed, and spent some time interacting with her. Later, the child who was with me, insightfully asked, "Dad, you're tired. You've been frustrated. Was what you just did with that lady a put-on?"
> "Yep," I said. "It was. But not the way you think."

You see, all of true biblical Christianity is, in a sense, a put-on. It's a choice I make to put on Jesus Christ. It's a choice I make to ask, "What would Jesus do if He was tired and a woman came to Him with a problem?"

> As He sat by a well, exhausted, a woman who was living with a man and who had already had five husbands approached Him. Jesus began a dialogue with her that resulted not only in her salvation, but in the salvation of many (John 4:29, 30).

To put on Christ means to continually ask, "What would Jesus do in this situation?" And as you choose to put Him on, you will ultimately find yourself becoming the role and the role becoming you. Being grouchy or brusque, impatient or unforgiving because "that's just the way I am" is then no longer an option because God didn't save us to keep us the way we are. He saved us to change us into the image of His Son (Romans 8:29).

Perhaps more than anyone else, kids are the ones deciding what role they will play. Role models are paraded before them. Advertisers constantly barrage them. Peers tell them, "Be this, go there, wear the other." And it can be terribly confusing. . . .

> Six-year-old Benjamin played his first soccer game. The coach of the team asked Ben if he'd join mid-season because his team needed some reinforcement. So there Ben is, playing his first game without ever having practiced. As Tammy watched from the stands, she saw him doing great one minute, and then running to the wrong place the next; doing super again, and then in the worst possible position. After a while, she tuned in to what was going on. You see, the other team's key player was also named Benjamin. And when the opposing coach told his Benjamin to go forward, Benny would go forward. But when his own

coach told him to get back, he'd retreat. Not knowing that he was supposed to listen only to *his* coach, he ran in circles, totally confused.

At the first break, Tammy called, "Ben, come here."

"Whew," said an exhausted Ben. "You gotta run a lot in soccer!"

"Listen, honey," Tammy said. "When that other coach talks to Benjamin, he's not talking to you."

"He's not?"

"No. You don't have to listen to him."

"I don't? Great!" he said.

Like Ben, we hear voices from all sides telling us what to do, where to go, and how to act. Like him, we run in circles and become exhausted in the process. And like Tammy, the cloud of witnesses in the stands (Hebrews 12:1) would say to us, "Your role is singular. Put on Christ. As you go through the day ask yourself only what Jesus would do."

You're coming home from church and you're late again. As usual, the pastor has gone overtime, and the traffic is horrendous. As you drive into town, there's a guy waiting to cross the street to go to the bakery. Car after car passes him with no end in sight. And as you approach him, you have a choice to make, a question to ask: What would Jesus do? If you're convinced Jesus would hit the accelerator, you can proceed like everyone else.

But as I learn of Christ, I am convinced that if Jesus were driving a car through the center of town and a gentleman was waiting to cross the street, He would stop His car and let the man cross. The man would go his way thinking, *Wow! Whoever that was who just came from church is living what he's learning!*

The word "Christian" means "little Christ." That is the only role that will satisfy us presently and reward eternally. Put on kindness. Put on longsuffering. Put on mercy. Put on patience. Above all, put on love. But you'll fail miserably if you try to put them on without putting *Him* in.

You can say, "I admire Jesus' kindness and compassion, so I'm going to try to imitate Him." If you have Him in your heart, that's great. Without Him, you don't have a chance. You'll fail over and over again until finally you say, "This doesn't work!" and give up.

In this drama of life, Jesus is the Director in our hearts, saying, "Stop your car and let him cross." Or, "You can't talk to your son that way." Or, "You must not treat your wife unkindly." He's the One who whispers in our hearts and brings Scriptures to our minds, the One who enables us to play His part once we open our hearts to Him.

Other coaches will say, "Be this. Do that. Go there."

But you'll run in circles until you finally say, "The one thing I am is a Christian, and I'm going to play that part all the days of my life."

4 Heaven is the great reversal. Because man looks on the outward appearance (1 Samuel 16:7), those who know how to package and promote themselves are the most successful on this earth. But because God looks on the heart, everything will ultimately be judged not on external appearance, but on internal experience. Consequently, a lot of folks we might have brushed aside as weird or ugly on earth are going to be incredibly honored in heaven. And a lot of "beautiful people" on earth will take a backseat to those who were unnoticed here on earth.

In light of this, Paul opens chapter 4 with an injunction to those in positions of authority. . . .

Colossians 4:1
Masters, give unto your servants that which is just and equal; knowing that ye also have a Master in heaven.

"Bosses, make sure you're acting justly, lovingly, equitably. Sure, you might be in a place of power and prominence now, but never forget you will one day stand before your Master and give account of what went on through your life and in your heart."

Having said that, let me say this to those who are not masters, but employees. When things are done justly and equitably, sometimes it causes a problem in the hearts of the rank and file. "What's the big idea of him making as much as I do? He doesn't have nearly the education, experience, or work ethic that I have."

Jesus spoke to just such an issue. . . .

A master goes to the marketplace at nine o'clock in the morning and says, "I need some guys to help me bring in my crops. I'll pay one denarius to anyone who works for me." A denarius being the wage of a soldier, it was a good day's pay.

"We'll do it!" said some unemployed men looking for work. "We were wondering how we were going to feed our families today—and now we have the opportunity to make a good wage. We're so blessed!"

The master then goes back to the same marketplace at noon and finds more unemployed men whom he takes to his vineyard to join those he had hired previously. At three o'clock in the afternoon and again at five o'clock, one hour before quitting time, the master returns to the marketplace yet again and brings back more workers.

At the end of the day, he pays the laborers he had hired at five o'clock a denarius—a full day's wage. The first men hired immediately whis-per among themselves, "If he's paying those guys a full day's wage for only an hour's work, can you imagine what he's going to pay us?!"

But their dreams are abruptly cut short as the master pays them a single denarius.

"Unfair!" the nine o'clock group cries.

"Why?" the master asks. "I paid you the exact wage for which you welcomed the opportunity to work. Now, why is it a problem for you that I choose to be kind and treat everyone equally?" (see Matthew 20).

In this account, Jesus points out our tendency to be happy only until we see what someone else gets. The vineyard workers began the day excited and ended the day murmuring because they looked at the other guys. It's a problem with which we all struggle. So what's the key? Don't look around.

You see, once I start looking around, I inevitably get discouraged. I begin to say, "Hey, why is that guy getting the breaks?" or, "Why does that blessing go to him when I've been working harder and longer?" Gang, if you're going to be blue every time someone else is blessed, you really shouldn't be in the field of ministry or blessing.

Colossians 4:2 (a)
Continue in prayer . . .

Want to be a good master in the home or job? The only way I know to do it is to pray. "Father, Your Son taught us to ask You to give us our daily bread. And now, Lord, help me to properly distribute the bread You send."

Colossians 4:2 (b)
. . . and watch in the same with thanksgiving.

Be a thankful person. This applies to everyone—masters and servants, mothers and fathers, brothers and sisters.

One morning during an eclipse in the Middle Ages, people woke, expecting day to dawn. When it didn't, they cried. "Oh no! The sun didn't rise today." What was at first sort of a curiosity became a real concern—and they began screaming, wailing, and howling. When the sun did at last appear, the people cheered, clapped, and blessed God for the very sunshine they had previously taken for granted.

How good it would be for us to wake up and say, "Thank You for a new day, Father. I'm alive. The sun is out. There's air to breathe. I'm not a slug."

Personally, I don't think there's anything more abhorrent than grumpy believers. Don't they realize how good God has been to them? They're going to heaven. They have the Word. The Spirit indwells them. Thus, I don't think there's a single excuse for a rational person to be grumpy. Thanksgiving should be flowing from our lips constantly.

Colossians 4:3, 4
Withal praying also for us, that God would open unto us a door of utterance, to speak the mystery of Christ, for which I am also in bonds: That I may make it manifest, as I ought to speak.

This intrigues me. Paul says, "Pray for us—not that we'll get out of here, but that the Word will go forth from here." I think if I were writing this, I would say, "Please pray for me that I'll get out of here. I'm tired of being in prison." Not so Paul. He says, "My desire is that God's Word will go forth from here, that those around me will really see that Christ lives in me." Truly, this is the way to pray.

A few months ago, I saw a billboard that said: Pray. It works. And I thought, *True—but what if it doesn't work?* Most of the time we pray small prayers like, "Get me out of here." And when they don't work, we stop praying instead of learning what prayer really is. Prayer is not to get God to see things our way, but rather to get us to see things His way.

I read the story of an Arkansas woman who was confronted by a burglar who, after ripping the phone out of the wall, ordered her into the closet. After dropping to her knees, she asked the burglar if she could pray for him. "I want you to know that God loves you and I forgive you," she said. The burglar looked at her and apologized for what he had done. Then he yelled out the door to his partner in a pickup truck, "We gotta unload all this. She's a Christian lady. We can't do this to her!" The woman remained on her knees, and the burglar returned the furniture he had already taken from her home. Then he took the bullets out of his gun, handed her the gun, and walked out the door.

This lady could have prayed, "Get me out of here," but instead she prayed like Paul. "Could I pray for you?" she asked the burglar. *That's* in harmony with the heart of God. How do I know?

Because of what Jesus said on the Cross. He didn't say, "Get me out of here," He said, "Father, forgive them. They don't understand what's going on" (see Luke 23:34).

How I want to be more like Paul. I've got so much to learn in this arena—but I see the principle and the rightness of what Paul is modeling here as he prays not to get out of prison, but that he'll have boldness and wisdom in any situation.

Colossians 4:5
Walk in wisdom toward them that are without, redeeming the time.

Walk wisely because people are watching you. Time is moving rapidly, so redeem it. Somehow we think we're going to live a long time, but James was right when he said life is a vapor, a puff of steam (4:14). It's going so fast. Make it count. How? Redeem it.

According to those who study such things, the average American will spend six months of his life waiting at red lights. People say, "I just don't have time to pray"—but what if they decided that at every red light they would pray for people in their fellowships, for people in their communities who don't know Jesus, for people in the world who have never heard His Name? What if they decided to keep an open Bible on the seat next to them in order to read a verse or two during every red light? People say they don't have time to read, to pray, to memorize, to study. Yes they do. And I'm not even talking about getting up at three in the morning. I'm talking about just using the time they're at stoplights. Redeem the time!

Colossians 4:6
Let your speech be alway with grace, seasoned with salt, that ye may know how ye ought to answer every man.

Salty speech? Years ago, salty speech connoted swearing. That's not the salty speech Paul is talking about. No, the idea here is of salty French fries. I love salty French fries, but I've got to have a Coke to go with them, because they make me thirsty. So, too, the speech we use should create in people a thirst for the wine of the Spirit in our hearts.

Colossians 4:7
All my state shall Tychicus declare unto you, who is a beloved brother, and a faithful minister and fellowservant in the Lord.

Beloved brother, faithful minister, fellow-servant—what wonderful qualities Tychicus possessed.

Colossians 4:8

Whom I have sent unto you for the same purpose, that he might know your estate, and comfort your hearts.

Tychicus was sent to Colosse both to report to the believers there how Paul was doing and to bring word back to Paul how they were doing. This should not be surprising, for Paul was not only a soul-winner, but a friend-maker. As you read his letters, you'll find over one hundred people to whom he sends greetings.

Colossians 4:9

With Onesimus, a faithful and beloved brother, who is one of you. They shall make known unto you all things which are done here.

If you're a student of the Word, you know Onesimus plays a key role in the Book of Philemon. A runaway slave who ended up in prison as a cellmate of Paul, he got saved, was released, and now turns out to be a faithful friend and minister.

Colossians 4:10

Aristarchus my fellowprisoner saluteth you, and Marcus, sister's son to Barnabas, (touching whom ye received commandments: if he come unto you, receive him;).

Remember the story in Acts 13? Setting off on their first missionary journey, Paul and Barnabas took John Mark, Barnabas' nephew, with them. Then somewhere in the early part of the journey, John Mark went home. At the outset of their second missionary trip, Barnabas said, "I'll get John Mark and we'll be on our way."

"Hold on," Paul said. "John Mark flipped out and failed us last time. He's not coming again."

"Yes he is," said Barnabas, Son of Comfort.

"No way," said Paul. "There's work to do. We can't have this guy tag along with us. He just doesn't have what it takes."

"I'm taking John Mark," said Barnabas.

"Fine," said Paul. "Go your way. I'll take Silas, and we'll go in a different direction." (see Acts 15:36–41)

And they parted company.

Years later, we see that Barnabas' work was successful with John Mark, for here in Colossians, Paul salutes him.

So, too, you who feel like you "missed the mark," that God opened a door for you to do something, but you failed—take heart. I don't care how badly you messed up, He's not through with you.

Talk about failure! He had less than three years of formal education and failed in business in '31. He was defeated for State Legislature in '32 and failed again in business in '34. Finally elected to the State Legislature in '35, he ran for Speaker and lost in a landslide. He was defeated again for Elector in '40, and for Congress in '43. Elected in '46, he was tossed out of office two years later, defeated in a re-election attempt in '48. Failing in business once again, he ran for Senate, but was defeated in '55. He ran for Vice President in '56, was crushed, and was defeated for Senate another time in '58. And then in '60, 1860, Abraham Lincoln won—and went on to become perhaps the greatest political leader in American history.

Could it be that the wit, wisdom, and understanding of human nature he exhibited so powerfully came as a result of the setbacks, failure, and defeat Lincoln had experienced previously?

Don't despair, precious people. John Mark blew it badly but came through ultimately. So can you.

Colossians 4:11

And Jesus, which is called Justus, who are of the circumcision. These only are my fellowworkers unto the kingdom of God, which have been a comfort unto me.

Justus, Marcus, Aristarchus, Onesimus were all tremendous blessings to Paul.

Colossians 4:12, 13

Epaphras, who is one of you, a servant of Christ, saluteth you, always labouring fervently for you in prayers, that ye may stand perfect and complete in all the will of God. For I bear him record, that he hath a great zeal for you, and them that are in Laodicea, and them in Hierapolis.

Epaphras labored fervently in prayer. The idea here is one of giving birth, going through pain to bring forth prayer. Sometimes that's what it takes. Do you ever feel like not praying? Am I the only one who begins to pray, but then gets distracted and succumbs to the list of other things to tend to first? Such wasn't the case with Epaphras. He labored in prayer until there was a breakthrough, a birth of renewal and revival in the hearts and lives of those for whom he prayed.

Colossians 4:14 (a)
Luke, the beloved physician . . .

Why did Paul call Luke the beloved physician if Luke didn't even have enough faith to be a faith healer? Because Paul, the one who saw such powerful healing miracles happen that even the sweat bands and aprons he wore were used as instruments of healing (Acts 19:11, 12), knew the necessity of a physician given intellectual gifts and training to help people physically. And he welcomed Luke's presence on his missionary journey.

"If you have faith, you won't need a doctor. "Doesn't Psalm 90 declare that it is appointed for man to live threescore and ten years?" asks the televangelist. "If you die before seventy, it's because there's some sin in your life." If that be so, how does he explain Jesus' death at thirty-three?

Colossians 4:14 (b)
. . . and Demas, greet you.

In the Book of Philemon, which preceded the Book of Colossians by a couple of years, Demas is called a fellow-laborer (verse 24). Approximately six years after this, there's a third mention of Demas, where right before Paul dies, he says, "Demas has forsaken us, having loved this present world (2 Timothy 4:10). So Demas went from being a fellow-laborer to one who turned his back on the Lord because he loved the world.

How did this happen?

The Christian life is like a steam locomotive. When you're first saved and on fire, you stoke the boiler with the Word. You come to church; you're involved in ministry; and you're moving along in your faith. But there can come a time when you start to think, *Hey, I'm cruising along fine. I don't need to feed the fire so fervently. I don't need to study Scripture so consistently. I don't need to have devotions daily. I don't need to go to church regularly because, look, I'm really moving!* But once the fire stops being fed, the engine starts slowing down imperceptibly. Yes, the train keeps moving down the tracks for a time, and everything appears to be going fine, but little by little the engine goes slower and slower until finally it stops dead in its tracks. You might be able to go weeks, months, even years on the momen-

tum you gained in the early days—but if you don't continue to feed the fire, eventually you'll stop altogether. And, like Demas, you'll say, "What happened? How did I end up *here?*"

Colossians 4:15
Salute the brethren which are in Laodicea, and Nymphas, and the church which is in his house.

"The church which is in his house"—that's a great little phrase. If you have a family, you have a church.

Colossians 4:16
And when this epistle is read among you, cause that it be read also in the church of the Laodiceans; and that ye likewise read the epistle from Laodicea.

In other words, "Pass this letter on to the church at Laodicea, and they'll pass theirs on to you." We don't have the letter, but it was evidently written by Paul at this time to the Laodiceans.

Colossians 4:17
And say to Archippus, Take heed to the ministry which thou hast received in the Lord, that thou fulfil it.

"Do what God has told you, Archippus." It is a good word for us as well to do whatever it is God has told us, to keep on with whatever it is He has laid upon our hearts individually and corporately in order to bring it to completion.

Colossians 4:18 (a)
The salutation by the hand of me Paul. Remember my bonds.

This one who, at the beginning of the chapter instructed the Colossians to be thankful and who asked them to pray that he would be able to minister even in prison, tells them to remember his bonds not as a play for sympathy, but as a basis for his authority.

Colossians 4:18 (b)
Grace be with you. Amen.

Paul opened his epistle with the salutation of grace and now closes it with the benediction of grace. As it began, so it ends because grace is the whole deal.

1 THESSALONIANS

Background to 1 & 2 Thessalonians

A long with Paul's letter to the Galatians, his first letter to the Thessalonians is one of the two oldest of his letters. Written only twenty years after Jesus' Resurrection, it was addressed to the believers in Thessalonica, a mega-city of about two hundred thousand people. Renamed Salonika, the city thrives today.

Following his miraculous deliverance from a Philippian prison (Acts 16), Paul arrived in Thessalonica. There, he started a church, appointed elders, and helped the ministry to take root—all in the space of three weeks (Acts 17:2).

In this, I am reminded of the early days of Applegate Christian Fellowship.

> Our first youth pastor was a California-transplanted hippy who got saved and baptized at our first Bible study at Yale Creek. About two months later, he said, "Jon, I am so thrilled with what God is showing me that I want to teach kids."
>
> Smelling cigarettes on his breath, I said, "If you'll never smoke another cigarette, you can be our youth pastor."
>
> "Okay," he said.
>
> Dave stopped smoking that day and became our youth pastor. He is now pastoring a Four Square Church in Washington.

I look back now and wonder if I was crazy to put a guy on the ministry team who looked like Charles Manson and smoked constantly. Yet Dave was, and continues to be, an example of how the Spirit of the Lord can blow conventionality right out the window. I'm not suggesting we put every three-week-old Christian in a position of leadership. I am saying that in certain times and places, it can happen. Look at Paul. He was in Thessalonica only three weeks before he was driven out. But during that time, he saw people saved, discipled, and ordained for ministry.

Don't ever think you're too young in age or in the faith to be used for the kingdom. If your heart is right, the Lord has a place for you to serve Him.

Curious about how the Thessalonians were doing, and wanting to encourage them concerning the Lord's coming, Paul writes the letters before us, wherein he:

- Remembers the Thessalonians' past in chapters 1—3 as he recalls how he lived among them and shared with them in close communion;
- Refocuses their present in the first part of chapter 4 as he encourages them to love with brotherly affection;
- Reveals their future in the second half of chapter 4 and the first part of chapter 5 as he speaks to them of the Rapture and of heavenly expectation;
- Refines their walk in the last part of chapter 5 through a series of practical exhortations; and
- Reinforces his teaching concerning the Second Coming in 2 Thessalonians.

In these last days, as we study Paul's letters to the Thessalonians, may the Lord refocus our vision of the big picture—the hope of heaven.

1 THESSALONIANS

1 Thessalonians 1:1 (a)
Paul, and Silvanus, and Timotheus . . .

After their miraculous release from a Philippian prison by way of an earthquake, Paul and Silvanus—or Silas—traveled to Thessalonica, where there was "a synagogue of the Jews" (Acts 17:1).

1 Thessalonians 1:1 (b)
. . . unto the church of the Thessalonians which is in God the Father and in the Lord Jesus Christ.

The church at Thessalonica was comprised of Gentiles who had turned from idols to God, and of Jews who, recognizing their Messiah, believed in the Lord Jesus Christ.

1 Thessalonians 1:1 (c)
Grace be unto you, and peace, from God our Father, and the Lord Jesus Christ.

Paul begins his second epistle the same way he began his first (Galatians 1:3). It is also the way he would begin his subsequent epistles to the Corinthians, Ephesians, Philippians, and the Colossians. He links grace with peace. Man cannot experience peace until he receives God's grace because true peace is the result of an understanding that our salvation rests on what God has done rather than on what we must do.

1 Thessalonians 1:2, 3
We give thanks to God always for you all, making mention of you in our prayers; Remembering without ceasing your work of faith, and labour of love, and patience of hope in our Lord Jesus Christ, in the sight of God and our Father.

I believe a mature church will possess the same three characteristics Paul saw in the Thessalonian church.

First, a mature church demonstrates the work of faith.

"Master, what must we do to do the works of God?" the disciples asked in John 6.
"This is the work of God," Jesus answered, "that you believe on Him whom the Father has sent."

When a church says, "We believe in Jesus Christ and marvel at what He did on the Cross," that is the singular work of faith.

Second, a mature church labors in love. This is only logical, because whenever a person begins to comprehend how much the Lord has done for him, he can't help but love others.

During his visit to the Boys' Town orphanage in the 1940s, a reporter for Life *magazine observed a ten-year-old boy carrying a much older boy on his back.*
"Isn't he heavy?" asked the reporter.
"He ain't heavy," replied the younger boy.
"He's my brother"—giving rise to the song that would later be written about this true story.

It's not a burdensome obligation, but a labor of love that says, "God's been so good to me that I can't help but carry someone else."

Third, a mature church patiently hopes for the return of the Lord.

The night before Jesus' crucifixion, and after telling His disciples He would be betrayed, Jesus arose from the supper, girded Himself with a towel, and began to wash their feet. Why? Scripture says it was because He knew from whence He came and where He was going (John 13:3).

Knowing we're going to heaven is a key ingredient of maturity because heaven alone allows us to see the big picture. Only heaven puts everything in perspective.

1 Thessalonians 1:4
Knowing, brethren beloved, your election of God.

The election of God is not a matter of the Lord casting His vote on our behalf because He sees something that impresses Him. No, God elected us before the foundation of the earth apart from anything we have or haven't done (Ephesians 1:4). I agree with D. L. Moody when he said, "I'm glad the Lord chose me before I was born. I don't think He would have chosen me after I'd done some living!"

1 Thessalonians 1:5 (a)
For our gospel came not unto you in word only, but also in power, and in the Holy Ghost, and in much assurance . . .

"You shall receive power when the Holy Ghost comes upon you to be My witnesses," Jesus promised His disciples in Acts 1:8. Thus, the power to believe in Jesus, love others, and to patiently hope for the Lord's return—as seen in the Thessalonian church—was evidence of their being chosen by Him.

1 Thessalonians 1:5 (b), 6
. . . as ye know what manner of men we were among you for your sake. And ye became followers of us, and of the Lord, having received the word in much affliction, with joy of the Holy Ghost.

How can there be joy in the midst of affliction? When Cascade High School played football against St. Mary's High, the guys were battered—as evidenced by the teeth, hair, and blood left on the field. Yet even though bones were cracked and bodies were bruised, there was great joy at Cascade because of their victory.

The same thing happens spiritually. Sure, we get beat up. Sure, there are trials and tribulations. When we start to see the Lord's presence in the midst of the problem, we find joy in the big picture; joy in the knowledge that we're headed for heaven.

1 Thessalonians 1:7, 8
So that ye were ensamples to all that believe in Macedonia and Achaia. For from you sounded out the word of the Lord not only in Macedonia and Achaia, but also in every place your faith to God-ward is spread abroad; so that we need not to speak any thing.

Unlike the Pharisees who blew their own horns (Matthew 6:2), the Thessalonians trumpeted the sweet song of salvation to such a degree that everyone in the Greek peninsula heard about their radical faith.

1 Thessalonians 1:9, 10 (a)
For they themselves shew of us what manner of entering in we had unto you, and how ye turned to God from idols to serve the living and true God; and to wait for his Son from heaven . . .

Recounting verse 3, Paul says, "You turned to God from idols, which is the work of faith. You serve the living God, which is the labor of love. You wait for His Son from heaven, which is the patience of hope."

The idea of waiting does not infer apathy. In the Greek language, the word is used to describe what a mother does when she is anticipating the birth of her baby. She readies the nursery and eagerly prepares for his arrival.

So, too, we should say, "Jesus is coming. I must make sure my family and friends are ready."

1 Thessalonians 1:10 (b)
. . . whom he raised from the dead, even Jesus, which delivered us from the wrath to come.

Revelation 6—19 describes a time called the Tribulation, when God pours His wrath on a Christ-rejecting, sinful world. Scorpions are released. Hundred-pound hailstones come crashing down. Water turns to blood. Islands disappear. There is starvation, plagues, war, and famine. It's a hellish time, causing the people to cry, "Who shall save us from the day of the wrath of the Lamb?" (Revelation 6:16, 17).

Let me highly encourage you to miss that. Become a Christian today. Believe on Him whom the Father has sent, and, like the Thessalonians, you'll find yourself turning from the idols of our present day, laboring under the light burden of love, and waiting for the Son with joyful hope.

2 **1 Thessalonians 2:1–2**
For yourselves, brethren, know our entrance in unto you, that it was not in vain: But even after that we had suffered before, and were shamefully entreated, as ye know, at Philippi, we were bold in our God to speak unto you the gospel of God with much contention.

The contention of which Paul writes was due to the fact that the Jews hired "lewd fellows of the baser sort" to falsely accuse him of fanning the flames of revolution against Caesar (Acts 17:5).

1 Thessalonians 2:3, 4
For our exhortation was not of deceit, nor of uncleanness, nor in guile: But as we were allowed of God to be put in trust with the gospel, even so we speak; not as pleasing men, but God, which trieth our hearts.

The fear of God obliterates the fear of man. Because Paul answered to God rather than to man, he was free from the fear of man. God's antidote for young Jeremiah's timidity was to boldly speak the whole truth (Jeremiah 1:7, 8). The same is true today. If you're afraid of your audience and only speak those portions of truth that are easy to hear, you will be confounded in front of them. But if you "fully preach the gospel of Christ," you'll be strengthened (Romans 15:19).

1 Thessalonians 2:5, 6
For neither at any time used we flattering words, as ye know, nor a cloke of covetousness; God is witness: Nor of men sought we glory, neither of you, nor yet of others, when we might have been burdensome, as the apostles of Christ.

Whether it be in the business world, the sports world, or the arena of ministry, don't covet someone else's position. Don't say, "I want that cloak; I want that spot; I'll use whatever flattery or treachery it takes." I am reminded of the account in 1 Kings 22.

"Listen, Joe," said King Ahab of Israel to King Jehoshaphat of Judah, "I've got a problem with the Syrians. Let's form an alliance and battle them together."

Jehoshaphat agreed, and upon his arrival at Ramoth Gilead, he found Ahab waiting for him.

According to the Septuagint, Ahab suggested Jehoshaphat wear his royal robes.

Jehoshaphat agreed, and off they went into battle.

Unbeknownst to Jehoshaphat, however, the Syrian army had been instructed to spare everyone save the king of Israel. Consequently, imagine Jehoshaphat's surprise when he found the entire Syrian army heading straight for him, cloaked as he was in his kingly robes.

"Wait a minute! I didn't ask for this," you'll say as the arrows of criticism fly toward you. Oh, but you did when you coveted that position on the team or that space in the office. That's why Paul didn't come to the Thessalonians with flattery and manipulation, but with simplicity and honesty.

1 Thessalonians 2:7, 8
But we were gentle among you, even as a nurse cherisheth her children: So being affectionately desirous of you, we were willing to have imparted unto you, not the gospel of God only, but also our own souls, because ye were dear unto us.

Paul was like a nursing mother. As he remembers the Thessalonians' past, he doesn't complain about their crying but loves them as deeply as a mother loves her newborn baby.

1 Thessalonians 2:9
For ye remember, brethren, our labour and travail: for labouring night and day, because we would not be chargeable unto any of you, we preached unto you the gospel of God.

Secondly, Paul was like a working brother. He labored to support himself so as not to burden the Thessalonians.

1 Thessalonians 2:10–12
Ye are witnesses, and God also, how holily and justly and unblameably we behaved ourselves among you that believe: As ye know how we exhorted and comforted and charged every one of you, as a father doth his children, that ye would walk worthy of God, who hath called you unto his kingdom and glory.

Finally, Paul was like an encouraging father as he exhorted the believers to walk worthy of God.

Paul is a wonderful model for all who serve the Lord. Oh, that we might be like nursing mothers who aren't angry with the demands and cries of our children, like brothers who are working together and relating to one another, like fathers who are not afraid to speak the truth.

I see the same three traits in the Trinity. The ministry of the Spirit is to comfort, as does a nursing mother (John 14:15–17). The work of the Son is to labor among us, as does a working brother (Hebrews 2:11). The work of the Father is to exhort and challenge His children, as does an encouraging parent (Romans 8:16).

1 Thessalonians 2:13
For this cause also thank we God without ceasing, because, when ye received the word of God which ye heard of us, ye received it not as the word of men, but as it is in truth, the word of God, which effectually worketh also in you that believe.

How closely are the written Word and the living Word—Jesus Christ—related? Both are Truth (John 14:6; John 17:17). Both are Light (John 8:12; Psalm 119:105). Both are Bread (John 6:35; Matthew 4:4). People ask why we spend so much time teaching Bible studies. Why do we have retreats where we study Scripture? Why do we get together virtually every night of the week to open the Word? It is because we firmly believe that this is the very Word of God, and that it will radically alter and influence any person who spends time in its pages.

For topical study of 1 Thessalonians 2:13, see "Truly the Word of God" below.

1 Thessalonians 2:14–16
For ye, brethren, became followers of the churches of God which in Judaea are in Christ Jesus: for ye also have suffered like things of your own countrymen, even as they have of the Jews: Who both killed the Lord Jesus, and their own prophets, and have persecuted us; and they please not God, and are contrary to all men: Forbidding us to speak to the Gentiles that they might be saved, to fill up their sins alway: for the wrath is come upon them to the uttermost.

"You are following in the footsteps of the Jewish believers in Judaea who are also persecuted by their countrymen," Paul tells the Thessalonians. He would go on to tell Timothy that *all* who live godly in Christ Jesus shall suffer persecution (2 Timothy 3:12).

1 Thessalonians 2:17, 18
But we, brethren, being taken from you for a short time in presence, not in heart, endeavoured the more abundantly to see your face with great desire. Wherefore we would have come unto you, even I Paul, once and again; but Satan hindered us.

We err whenever we underestimate Satan's ability to hinder people from service, fellowship, or worship. Although greater is He that is in us than He that is in the world (1 John 4:4), we have a very real adversary who will do whatever it takes to thwart our ministry.

1 Thessalonians 2:19, 20
For what is our hope, or joy, or crown of rejoicing? Are not even ye in the presence of our Lord Jesus Christ at his coming? For ye are our glory and joy.

"Yes, we've been beaten up in the city," writes Paul. "Yes, we've been chased down by envious Jews. Yes, we're going through real persecution. But it's all worth it because you're getting saved."

The greatest joy in the world comes from seeing someone for whom you've been praying, and to whom you've been witnessing, receive Christ. No wonder Jesus tells us that when one person is saved, all of heaven breaks out in rejoicing (Luke 15:7). Truly, joy and evangelism go hand in hand. Thus, my prayer is that we would never lose sight of the privilege, priority, and pure joy of sharing the Good News with people who don't know Jesus.

TRULY THE WORD OF GOD

A Topical Study of
1 Thessalonians 2:13

There are those who say, "I believe that the Bible is inspired and that it contains God's Word," but with them I disagree. The Bible doesn't contain God's Word; the Bible *is* God's Word. Whenever liberal theologians say the Bible contains God's

Word, the implication is that it might also contain man's word. If I say, "Part of Scripture is God's Word, but part is man's ideas or myths," I become the ultimate judge, deciding what is God's Word and what are man's thoughts.

If I attribute to God "There is therefore now no condemnation to those who are in Christ Jesus," (Romans 8:1) and "The grace of our Lord Jesus Christ be with you all," (Philippians 4:23), but I attribute to Paul "Present your bodies a living sacrifice," (Romans 12:1) and "Those who live godly will suffer persecution" (2 Timothy 3:12), I judge the Bible rather than allowing the Bible to judge me.

Following, are four reasons I am theologically and academically convinced that every word of Scripture—even the "begats" and the genealogies—is inspired.

Internal Unity

The Bible is comprised of sixty-six books written by an extremely diverse group of forty human authors. We see a king in Solomon, a herdsman in Amos, a tax collector in Matthew, a scholar in Paul, a general in Joshua, a doctor in Luke, a poet in David, a prime minister in Daniel, and a building contractor in Jeremiah.

Not only did these men come from widely diverse backgrounds, but their writings span fifteen hundred years and are comprised of three different languages (Hebrew, Aramaic, and Greek).

Yet there is not a single contradiction from book to book, from author to author. I challenge you to find three men writing textbooks today on any subject who will completely agree. There is incredible unity in the Bible—unlike anything man could produce.

Archaeological Validity

"If My disciples are quiet, even the stones will cry out," Jesus declared (Luke 19:40). Guess what. The stones *are* crying out. What stones? The stones uncovered by the archaeologists' spades.

Julius Wellhousen made a huge impact on theology in the late 1800s when he said that, due to the fact that there were no kings near the Dead Sea at the time, the Bible could not be taken literally. He maintained that the battle between four kings from Mesopotamia and five kings from the Dead Sea region could not have taken place (Genesis 14). Poor Julius. Archaeologists in Egypt unearthed a library filled with tablets that contain a perfect description of the battle in which four Mesopotamian kings did indeed wage war against five kings near the Dead Sea.

Dr. John Gerstang, one of the primary excavators of Jericho, noted that, when an ancient city is excavated, the walls fall inward. The walls of Jericho actually fell outward and covered an unbelievable distance. "It was as though someone from the inside was shoving the walls out," said Gerstang, calling the force an "invisible hand."

According to Nelson Gluick, a brilliant Jewish archaeologist, "It may be categorically stated that no archaeological discovery has ever contradicted a single Bible reference."

Archaeology confirms the biblical account. I "dig" that!

Fulfilled Prophecy

In addition to the Bible, there is another book that contains prophecy. In the Koran, Mohammed says, "Before I die, I will go to Jerusalem." That's like me saying, "Before I die, I will return to Jacksonville." There is a great probability that will happen. Besides that single reference, the Koran does not address prophecy. Neither does any so-called "holy book." In the Old Testament alone, more than two thousand prophecies have come to pass. That's amazing!

Turn with me to Ezekiel. I never tire of this prophecy because it's fulfilled so beautifully and convincingly. It deals with the city of Tyre. Maybe that's why I never "tire" of it.

> *Therefore thus saith the Lord GOD; Behold, I am against thee, O Tyrus, and will cause many nations to come up against thee, as the sea causeth his waves to come up. And they shall destroy the walls of Tyrus, and break down her towers: I will also scrape her dust from her, and make her like the top of a rock. It shall be a place for the spreading of nets in the midst of the sea: for I have spoken it, saith the Lord GOD: and it shall become a spoil to the nations. And her daughters which are in the field shall be slain by the sword; and they shall know that I am the LORD.*   Ezekiel 26:3–6

In other words, "I'm going to flatten Tyre," said God.

Nebuchadnezzar destroyed Tyre in 586 B.C. However, he didn't "scrape her dust from her," as Ezekiel had prophesied. Two hundred and twenty-five years later, Alexander the Great besieged the city that had been rebuilt. For thirteen years, the people of Tyre didn't give up. When they could hold out no longer, they left out the back door and rebuilt the city on a little island a half mile off the coast. When Alexander finally broke in and found everyone gone, he ordered his men to throw every remaining stone, column, and bit of timber into the sea so that a bridge could be constructed to the island. Although the original city of Tyre was now "scraped clean," the prophecy was still not fulfilled because now there was a new city of Tyre.

Fast forward to A.D. 1290. When the Crusaders came to free the Holy Land from "Muslim infidels," they moved into the city of Tyre, which was now connected to the mainland. Eight years later, when the Crusaders were driven back to England, the Muslims said, "This city is so defiled that every stone must be thrown into the sea."

If you go to Tyre today, guess what you see. Nothing. It's flat like a rock and has become a place where fishermen park their boats—"like the top of a rock, a place to spread nets."

Because there is a spring in Tyre that produces one hundred thousand gallons of water every six hours, this area should be home to a huge city. It's not, however, because the people in the region think the area is cursed.

"I will make Tyre flat like a rock. The city will never be built again, and it will only be a place for fishing nets to be dried out upon," declared God. That's exactly what happened.

There are 221 prophecies concerning Jesus Christ. Chapter 7 of Isaiah tells us the manner of His birth. Daniel 9 declares the time of His birth. Micah 5 names the town of His birth. In Zechariah 11, we read how He would be sold for thirty pieces of silver, which would be thrown on the floor of the temple, and used to purchase a piece of property that would be used as a potter's field.

What is the statistical probability of these six prophecies being fulfilled? One in 10^{17}. Think of it this way:

Cover the entire state of California three feet deep in nuts and mark one nut with an X. Then go up in a plane with a flying squirrel named Rocky. Fly over the entire state and throw Rocky out at a random spot. Rocky comes down, sees the whole state covered in nuts and chooses one. The chances of him choosing the marked nut is one in 10^{17}.

That's only six prophecies. There are *221* Old Testament prophecies perfectly fulfilled in Jesus.

Jesus' Credibility

"Surely many of the Old Testament stories are nothing more than myths," scoffs the skeptic. Yet Jesus came on the scene and validated even the most controversial accounts when He talked about Lot's wife turning to salt (Luke 17:32), Jonah in the belly of the great fish (Matthew 12:40), and the prophecies of Daniel (Matthew 24:15). As the Son of God, Jesus' treatment of the above renders them true.

"Well, I don't know if He is the Son of God," some say.

"One sign I'll give to you," Jesus said. "Destroy this body and in three days I'll rise again" (John 2:18, 19). Thus, the inspiration question actually is answered by His Resurrection. If Jesus rose from the dead, then He is the Son of God. If He is the Son of God, what He says about even the most controversial Old Testament stories is true.

"Well, how do you know Jesus really rose from the dead?" some ask.

I've been to Jerusalem. I've seen His tomb. It's empty.

"Yeah, but the disciples could have stolen the body to perpetuate the hoax."

Really? They watched their sons and daughters killed, their wives raped, were crucified upside down, stoned with rocks, and sawn in half to perpetuate the hoax? Surely, *one* of them would have cracked. *One* of them would have said, "Wait a minute. This has gone far enough. We stashed His body behind the tree in the garden. You'll find it there." But no one did because the disciples knew they had seen the Resurrected Jesus.

"Okay, it wasn't the disciples. The Pharisees took Jesus' body."

If the Pharisees had stolen the body, they would only have had to produce it to halt the new religious "sect" of Christianity that threatened to undermine their authority.

"Then it was the Romans who took the body."

Really? The Romans were desperate to put Christianity down. They fed Christians to the lions. They dipped them in hot wax and ignited them as human candles. To destroy Christianity, they would only have had to produce the body.

So, who stole the body? It couldn't have been the disciples. It couldn't have been the Jews. It couldn't have been the Romans.

"Well, maybe the disciples just went to the wrong tomb."

Would no one have double-checked?

"Maybe Jesus wasn't really dead. Maybe He just swooned on the Cross. Maybe the sponge given to Him contained narcotics and He went into a coma."

This school of thought requires that a man beaten beyond recognition, nailed to a tree, and placed in a tomb would have come out of his coma, rolled away a two-ton stone, and taken on one hundred fifty Roman soldiers before walking throughout the city, saying, "I'm risen."

I'm sorry. I don't have enough faith to believe that. Jesus didn't swoon in the tomb. The women didn't go to the wrong gravesite. The disciples, Romans, or Jewish leaders didn't steal the body. No, the only intelligent position one can take is that Jesus rose from the grave just as He said He would.

"I'll rise from the dead. That's one sign I'll give to you that I am who I claim to be," Jesus declared (Matthew 12:39, 40).

Therefore, Jesus is the Son of God—rendering everything He said about Lot, Daniel, and Jonah equally true.

Spiritual Intimacy

For this cause also thank we God without ceasing, because, when ye received the word of God which ye heard of us . . .   1 Thessalonians 2:13 (a)

The word translated "received" is the Greek word *paralambano*, which means "to embrace intellectually."

. . . ye received it not as the word of men, but as it is in truth, the word of God, which effectually worketh also in you that believe.   1 Thessalonians 2:13 (b)

The Greek word *dechomai* is also translated "received," and it means "to embrace emotionally."

"Lo, I come to you in the volume of the book," says Jesus (Hebrews 10:7). Consequently, when you take in the Word, you're seeing the nature and person of Jesus. It's more than theology. You're embracing Him personally and emotionally.

- The Word is bread (Matthew 4).
- "I am the Bread of life," declared Jesus (John 6).
- The Word of God is truth (John 17).
- "I am the Truth," declared Jesus (John 14).

When you read the Scriptures, you embrace the Lord because the Word and the Lord are intimately bound.

But the Word just seems to go through me like a sieve, you might be thinking. *I can't even remember what we studied last Wednesday night.*

That's okay. It does the job. It doesn't return void (Isaiah 55:11). I don't remember the last time I had a Quarter Pounder® with cheese, but I know the proteins, vitamins, and other "nutritious" ingredients for which it is famous did the job and kept me going.

I've studied Genesis before. Why study it again? you might be wondering.

When my wife, Tammy, fixes Chicken Kiev, I don't say, "I ate that two months ago, so I think I'll pass on that tonight." No, I take in the same food again and again because it delights me every time. The same is true of the Word.

"I'm going to keep reminding you of the same truths over and over again," Peter said. "I don't care if you think I'm a creative teacher or not. You need to be established in truth" (2 Peter 1:12).

> *The prophet that hath a dream, let him tell a dream; and he that hath my word, let him speak my word faithfully. What is the chaff to the wheat? saith the* LORD.
> Jeremiah 23:28

Men's visions, ideas, and esoteric experiences are like chaff. They blow away. Not so the Word. It's wheat. It nourishes. It endures. Study the Word, dear people of God. It will produce faith in your life, joy in your heart, and sustenance for your soul.

---

3 **1 Thessalonians 3:1**
Wherefore when we could no longer forbear, we thought it good to be left at Athens alone;

Paul, Silas, and Timothy went to Berea after being driven out of Thessalonica. They taught the Word to the Bereans, who were good students. But the same people who drove Paul out of Thessalonica followed him to Berea, forcing them to leave for Athens.

1 Thessalonians 3:2 (a)
And sent Timotheus, our brother . . .

"We made it to Athens, but we couldn't wait to see how you were doing. We sent our brother Timothy to find out," writes Paul.

1 Thessalonians 3:2 (b)
. . . and minister of God . . .

Timothy was not only a brother, but also a minister. The word "minister" means "servant." As a true minister of God, Timothy's heart was not to be served, but to serve. He was not one who said, "Who cares if there's no room for the ambulance? I've got my clergy sticker, so I can park right in front of the hospital." No, Timothy did not take advantage of his position because he was a *true* minister.

1 Thessalonians 3:2 (c)
. . . and our fellowlabourer in the gospel of Christ, to establish you, and to comfort you concerning your faith.

The word "fellow-laborer" literally means "team player." People headed for ministry must be team players because they are to be linked to the rest of the body in submission and humility.

1 Thessalonians 3:3, 4
That no man should be moved by these afflictions: for yourselves know that we are appointed thereunto. For verily, when we were with you, we told you before that we should suffer tribulation; even as it came to pass, and ye know.

"Don't feel bad about our situation," Paul is saying. "Don't be surprised to hear people are chasing us around Greece, throwing rocks at us; trying to destroy us. Appointments with trouble are already on our calendars. We told you this would happen. It's all part of the program."

"Welcome this man," the Lord told Ananias concerning Paul, "for I'm going to show him he must suffer greatly for the sake of the kingdom" (Acts 9:16).

"Blessed be the Father of mercies, the God of comfort," Paul would later write to the Corinthians, "who comforts us in our troubles that we may be able to comfort others with the comfort we ourselves have received (2 Corinthians 1:4).

A. W. Tozer was right when he said, "Before God can use a person greatly, He must allow that person to be hurt deeply." This isn't because God is mean, but because He knows we can't comfort others unless we've been comforted ourselves.

Trials not only enable us to comfort others, but they purify our own faith. That's why Peter said,

"Don't think it strange concerning the fiery trials that come your way. They are sent to test and purify your faith" (1 Peter 4:12).

What happens when you are in a fiery trial? Shadrach, Meshach, and Abed-nego will tell you: Jesus shows up (Daniel 3:25). That's why James tells us to count it all joy when we fall into trials (James 1:2).

"Whoopee! A trial! How wonderful!" Crazy? Not really, because if you have this mind-set in your difficult times, you will see Jesus in a way that will blow your mind, warm your heart, and bless your socks off!

Trials don't make or break us, gang. They simply reveal what's inside. When I'm driving and hit a bump, the tea that splashes out of the mug on my dashboard was there before the bump. The bump doesn't put the tea in. It just shows what was already in the cup. That's what trials do.

"I'm angry because of what he or she did to me." No. The anger was already there. The bump just brought it out. Truly, the only way a man can really know how he's doing is through bumpy, discouraging, heartbreaking times, for they reveal his heart.

1 Thessalonians 3:5–8
For this cause, when I could no longer forbear, I sent to know your faith, lest by some means the tempter have tempted you, and our labour be in vain. But now when Timotheus came from you unto us, and brought us good tidings of your faith and charity, and that ye have good remembrance of us always, desiring greatly to see us, as we also to see you: Therefore, brethren, we were comforted over you in all our affliction and distress by your faith: For now we live, if ye stand fast in the Lord.

"The greatest joy I could possibly have," John wrote, "is to hear that those to whom I ministered are walking in truth" (3 John 4). Paul has the same heart. "Even though we're going through persecutions," he writes, "they're worth it if you're doing well."

1 Thessalonians 3:9
For what thanks can we render to God again for you, for all the joy wherewith we joy for your sakes before our God.

Paul went through problems that would make any of ours look like peanuts, yet he did well because he wasn't concerned for himself. "All I care about," he said, "are those with whom I've shared the gospel—my kids in the faith."

1 Thessalonians 3:10 (a)
Night and day praying exceedingly that we
might see your face . . .

Paul took advantage of sleepless nights to pray for these people whom he had only known for three weeks, but with whom his spirit was inextricably linked.

1 Thessalonians 3:10 (b)
. . . and might perfect that which is lacking
in your faith?

As proud as he was of the Thessalonian believers, Paul knew there were still areas in which they needed encouragement and guidance.

1 Thessalonians 3:11, 12
Now God himself and our Father, and our
Lord Jesus Christ, direct our way unto you.
And the Lord make you to increase and
abound in love one toward another, and to-
ward all men, even as we do toward you.

There come points in my walk when I say, "You know, I'm doing pretty good." I get comfortable as apathy begins to creep into my heart. Through Paul, the Spirit says to me, "I want you to increase. I rejoice in what's happening in your life, but may your love for Me grow to an ever-deepening measure."

"Moab has been at ease and settled in his lees. Therefore I will pour him out from vessel to vessel," said the Lord (see Jeremiah 48:11). The reference is to the way wine was made in Jeremiah's day. The winemaker would pick grapes, put them in a vat, and stomp on them to get the juice flowing. Then he would pour the juice into a vessel where the wine sat until the lees, or dregs, settled to the bottom. The winemaker would then pour the wine into another vessel, leaving the dregs behind, where it would sit while more dregs settled. This process was repeated up to six times, until the end result was wine without any dregs—wine that was pure and sparkling.

"I was just getting comfy," we cry, "when my boss said, 'You're through,'" when my girlfriend said, 'Goodbye,' when my coach said, 'On the bench.'"

"Great!" the Lord says. "I want to refine and use you as the wine of my Spirit flows through you. For that to happen, there will be regular seasons where you are poured. Otherwise you'll become cloudy and dull as you settle in your lees. I love you too much for that."

Instead of, "*Poor* me," we must be those who say, "*Pour* me, Father—that I may increase and abound in love."

1 Thessalonians 3:13
To the end he may stablish your hearts un-
blameable in holiness before God, even our
Father, at the coming of our Lord Jesus
Christ with all his saints.

"Regardless of the cost, I want you to abound and increase in love," Paul writes, "so that you will be ready for eternity."

---

4 **1 Thessalonians 4:1**
Furthermore then we beseech you, breth-
ren, and exhort you by the Lord Jesus,
that as ye have received of us how ye ought
to walk and to please God, so ye would
abound more and more.

The emphasis to this church doing well is: "Do better. Continue on. Mature even more in your faith."

1 Thessalonians 4:2–5
For ye know what commandments we gave
you by the Lord Jesus. For this is the will
of God, even your sanctification, that ye
should abstain from fornication: That every
one of you should know how to possess his
vessel in sanctification and honour; not in
the lust of concupiscence, even as the Gen-
tiles which know not God:

In chapter 4, Paul deals with the issue of love. "Your love is to be not lustful, sensual, or immoral—but pure," he says. Considering how young in the faith the church at Thessalonica was, it is easy to understand why they needed to be reminded not to fall into the immorality of the world that surrounded them.

1 Thessalonians 4:6, 7
That no man go beyond and defraud his
brother in any matter: because that the
Lord is the avenger of all such, as we also
have forewarned you and testified. For God
hath not called us unto uncleanness, but
unto holiness.

Verse 6 does not refer to business practices, but speaks of sexual matters. "I got a piece of her," the world says regarding sexual union. That's exactly right. Whenever sexual intimacy takes place outside of marriage, a piece of one's soul is taken away, simply to fulfill a lustful desire. You see, physical intimacy is not simply two bodies expressing passion. It's the essence, the souls of two people being made one. Consequently, if it's done outside of marriage, people are defrauded, deceived, and cheated out of what would have otherwise been theirs to enjoy. The repercussions go on and on.

When Absalom launched a coup against his father, David's trusted advisor Ahithophel sided with the rebellious Absalom. *Why? Why?* David must have wondered. *How can it be that Ahithophel—the brains behind all the political machinations in my kingdom—would rebel against me? Why would he side with my rebellious son?*

If you carefully read the genealogies, you'll find a possible answer. Ahithophel was the grandfather of a woman named Bathsheba (2 Samuel 23:34). Because David had defiled his granddaughter, animosity must have simmered inside Ahithophel year after year. Finally, when he saw his opportunity, he sided with Absalom.

"Be sure your sin will find you out," Moses writes (Numbers 32:23). It's not that *God* will find you out. When we accept Jesus as Savior, His blood completely washes us. God doesn't track us down; our sin does. In this case, if you defraud someone sexually, you'll reap a crop of destruction. The consequences might be immediate, or they might come a couple decades down the road. No one gets away with sin. Ask David.

"Aha!" you say. "I knew I was justified in being angry with that guy who defiled my wife," or, "I knew I was right to resent that girl who cheated on my brother. I'm never going to forgive him or her. Ahithophel didn't."

Look what happened to Ahithophel.

He hanged himself (2 Samuel 17:23).

No matter the extent of someone's sin, I must never be the one who commits the greater sin of bitterness. Ahithophel didn't forgive David, and what happened? War ensued. Ahithophel could have advised Absalom differently. His bitterness resulted in a worse tragedy than David's sin with Bathsheba. The war that followed brought about the deaths of twenty thousand (2 Samuel 18:7). Lest I sit here piously and think I have reason to be angry with my boss, spouse, or kids, I must realize the sin of unforgiveness will cause me to get hung up like Ahithophel. It will damage others in the process.

If, on the other hand, you are one who has defrauded someone, if you are one who has sinned, who has blown it—join the club. This church is packed with sinners because every one of us has had a point of failure in our lives. What are we to do? We're to say, "I failed, Father, but I confess my sin and turn from it. Use the scars of the repercussions I know are sure to follow to draw others to Your grace and forgiveness."

It was the wounds Jesus bore for our sin that convinced Thomas of the reality of His Resurrection (John 20:27, 28). So, too, the scars of our sin can witness to the reality of His grace in our lives.

For topical study of 1 Thessalonians 4:3–8 entitled "Pure Vessels," turn to page 1343.

1 Thessalonians 4:8
He therefore that despiseth, despiseth not man, but God, who hath also given unto us his holy Spirit.

"If you refuse this word," Paul says, "you're not rejecting us, but God."

1 Thessalonians 4:9–11 (a)
But as touching brotherly love ye need not that I write unto you: for ye yourselves are taught of God to love one another. And indeed ye do it toward all the brethren which are in all Macedonia: but we beseech you, brethren, that ye increase more and more; And that ye study to be quiet . . .

Most of us have difficulty following the admonition to be quiet.

Winston Churchill told the story of a man who was always chattering.
"Sir Winston," he chirped, "I haven't told you about my grandchildren yet."
"And for that," Churchill answered, "I am deeply grateful."

We can be conversationalists, but we shouldn't be chatty. We should study to be quiet.

1 Thessalonians 4:11 (b), 12
. . . and to do your own business, and to work with your own hands, as we commanded you; that ye may walk honestly toward them that are without, and that ye may have lack of nothing.

If you're not quiet, chances are you'll be talking about other people's business. What is Paul's solution? Get a job. If you're one who's prone to chatter, get to work. Find something practical to do.

"I don't need to work. I'm financially secure," you might be saying. Great! Volunteer to pull weeds at your church. It's real quiet where the weeds are growing, and you'll be minding your own business!

1 Thessalonians 4:13 (a)
But I would not have you to be ignorant, brethren, concerning them which are asleep . . .

Paul changes gears in this third and final section of his first epistle. After remembering their past and refocusing their present, Paul will reveal the future of the Thessalonians.

We are not to be ignorant concerning spiritual gifts (1 Corinthians 12:1). We are not to be ignorant of Satan's plans and strategies (2 Corinthians 2:11). We are not to be ignorant of the mystery that Israel will eventually be saved (Romans 11:25, 26). Here, Paul says we are not to be ignorant concerning the Rapture.

The following would be an especially comforting message to the Thessalonians, who, evidently, were concerned that fellow believers who had died would miss the Rapture.

1 Thessalonians 4:13 (b)
. . . that ye sorrow not, even as others which have no hope.

Mario, a father of six, was one of the pastors at a mission base in Honduras. Along with a bunch of other folks from the nearby town, Mario was watching a soccer game a couple of weeks ago. Suddenly, a lightning bolt hit the stands, claiming the lives of eighteen people. Mario was one. Reports came back that although Mario's wife was brokenhearted, she was full of joy because unbelievers began to open up to the gospel. They saw the hope of her joy and peace in the midst of her sorrow.

Occasionally, I have the opportunity to officiate at funerals where the family and friends are not believers. Such services are emotionally wrenching. When I officiate at services for believers—for those who see the big picture—there is incredible peace along with their sorrow.

1 Thessalonians 4:14
For if we believe that Jesus died and rose again, even so them also which sleep in Jesus will God bring with him.

In other words, "Believers who have died are presently in heaven." Some falsely teach that when believers die, they remain in the casket until the Rapture. What did Jesus say to the thief on the cross next to Him? He didn't say, "You will sleep for a couple thousand years and then you'll be resurrected." No, He said, "*Today* you'll be with Me in Paradise (Luke 23:43).

The moment someone leaves his body at death, an amazing thing happens. He moves into eternity where there is no time. There's no past, present, or future. It's just all one great big "Now" because eternity transcends time. How do I know this? Albert Einstein hypothesized about heaven without even knowing it. His the-

ory revealed that if one could ever travel at the speed of light, time would cease. Therefore, because God is light, time ceases in His presence. Thus, from the perspective of those in heaven, the Rapture has happened, and we're already with them in heaven.

How can this be? Think of it this way:

Here I am watching the Rose Parade on Colorado Boulevard. You find me watching the parade, and say, "Hey, Jon, good to see you. Listen, did the General Electric float go by?"

"Yeah. It was great," I say.

"Ooh, I missed it. I really wanted to see it," you say.

"Well, you can still see it if you go down Colorado Boulevard," I explain. "In other words, if you go to 'the past' that's already passed me, what's fresh for you will be something I've already seen."

If you came to me and asked what was coming up in the parade, I would say, "I don't know. You'll have to go to the future, to where the parade begins."

On the other hand, I could say, "Let's just get in the Goodyear blimp, and we'll be able to see the whole parade simultaneously—past, present, and future."

That is the best illustration I know to describe the concept of eternity. You see, we're down here on the curb watching the parade of life, wondering what's coming. From heaven's perspective, like the view from the Goodyear blimp—it's all one big Now. From heaven's perspective, the Rapture has already happened. From our perspective, however, we're still waiting on the curb.

I say this because many of us have dealt with the departure of loved ones. Personally, I do not believe that heaven could be heaven if a husband left his family behind and wondered how they would survive, or if a mother left her kids behind and worried about their well-being. That is why I suggest to you that heaven can only be heaven if we're all there simultaneously.

1 Thessalonians 4:15, 16
For this we say unto you by the word of the Lord, that we which are alive and remain unto the coming of the Lord shall not prevent them which are asleep. For the Lord himself shall descend from heaven with a shout, with the voice of the archangel, and with the trump of God: and the dead in Christ shall rise first.

There are those who contend that the trump of God mentioned here refers to the seventh trumpet of Revelation, which signals the Rapture

(Revelation 11:15). Thus, they reason the church will be present on earth during the Tribulation.

Such is not the case. The trumpets of Revelation 8—11 are blown by angels, whereas the trump of 1 Thessalonians 4 is the trump of *God*—the trump Paul refers to as "the last trump" (1 Corinthians 15:52). God sounded the first trump when He gathered the Jews at Mount Sinai (Exodus 19:16). He will sound the last trump before He gathers those who become believers during the Tribulation.

1 Thessalonians 4:17, 18
Then we which are alive and remain shall be caught up together with them in the clouds, to meet the Lord in the air: and so shall we ever be with the Lord. Wherefore comfort one another with these words.

"In this world you will have tribulation," declared Jesus (John 16:33)—from Satan, from the flesh, from the world. The Tribulation of Revelation 6–19 is the time when God pours out His wrath and judgment on a Christ-rejecting, sinful world. Certainly the Father is not saying, "Throughout your life, you'll face tribulation from Satan, the flesh, and the world—and then you'll experience Tribulation from Me." That's just not it. As believers, we will not go through the Tribulation. And that is a comforting word, indeed.

For topical study of 1 Thessalonians 4:15–17 entitled "Reasons for the Rapture," turn to page 1346.

PURE VESSELS
A Topical Study of
1 Thessalonians 4:3–8

As a pastor, one of the questions I am asked most frequently is, "How can I know God's will?" I'm glad I can answer that question with real certainty: God's will is that none should perish, but that all should come to repentance (2 Peter 3:9). God's will is that we continually give thanks (1 Thessalonians 5:18). As we see in our text today, God's will is that we possess our vessels in purity.

The word "vessel" means "container" or "pitcher." In the Old Testament, vessels contained wine for a drink offering to the Lord (Numbers 15). In the New Testament, we ourselves are earthen vessels, containing the treasure of Christ Jesus (2 Corinthians 4:7). Paul tells us we are to keep our vessels—our bodies—pure. In Daniel 5, we see what happens when a holy vessel is used in an immoral manner.

The year was approximately 539 B.C. Belshazzar partied in Babylon as thousands of Medes and Persians besieged the city.

"Hah! I'm not afraid," Belshazzar boasted. "After all, Babylon is surrounded by walls three hundred fifty feet high, eighty-seven feet thick." As the party continued, Belshazzar decided to drink from the holy temple vessels Nebuchadnezzar had taken when he conquered Jerusalem.

In the midst of the revelry, a hand appeared and wrote on the wall, "Mene, mene, tekel, upharsin," which meant "You've been weighed in the balance and have been found wanting. Tonight your kingdom will crash down upon you." Sure enough, after damming the Euphrates River, the Medes were able to crawl beneath the wall surrounding Babylon and into the city. Once there, they were able to capture Belshazzar's kingdom right out from under him.

Being baptized 20 years or 6 summers ago with no growth since then indicates a dubious commitment from the very beginning. Struggling, then failing to keep oneself pure, however, although it compromises ministry, joy, effectiveness, etc, does not jeopardize an already existing relationship with Christ.

How do we possess our vessel? I suggest three ways. . . .

Run to the Congregation

But in a great house there are not only vessels of gold and of silver, but also of wood and of earth; and some to honour, and some to dishonour. If a man therefore purge himself from these, he shall be a vessel unto honour, sanctified, and meet for the master's use, and prepared unto every good work.

2 Timothy 2:20, 21

Through Paul, God says, "You can choose to be a vessel of honor or dishonor. You can choose to be a beautiful vase or a spittoon. The key is to purge yourself from iniquity." How? Read on. . . .

Flee also youthful lusts: but follow righteousness, faith, charity, peace, with them that call on the Lord out of a pure heart.   2 Timothy 2:22

If you find yourself in a situation of temptation, do what Joseph did when Potiphar's wife grabbed him.

"Lie with me," she said. Joseph fled youthful lusts. He ran for his life (Genesis 39:12).

"But Joseph got thrown into prison," you say.

Yes—but then he became prime minister of Egypt, where he was "meet for the Master's use."

One day, I saw some Canadian geese flying overhead in a perfect "V." Why do geese fly in this formation? The reason is ingenious. You see, while the geese in the back are cruising, they're honking to the geese in the front, saying, "Keep it up in the front. You guys are doing great." Then, when the front boys get tired and drop to the back, the geese in the back work their way toward the front. The geese now in the back honk encouragement to them. For the geese to make it all the way to nice weather, they must encourage one another. They can't leave the flock, or they'll tire out.

If you say, "I'll flee from temptation, but I don't really need to be with other Christians," you're in for real problems because you'll never make it alone. Run from temptation to the congregation. Run to the place where there are people who love the Lord and want to walk with Him. Run from sin to the saints.

Receive the Bread of Heaven

Where were the Old Testament vessels of purity found?

They were on the table of shewbread (Leviticus 24:5, 6).

If you're struggling with lust or involved in immorality, go to the New Testament table of showbread—the table of Communion. Confess your sin and say, "Father, I'm struggling with these images. I'm struggling with these passions. I need Your Son to live in me as I eat of His body. As I take this cup, Lord, I thank You that I am forgiven by Your blood."

Perhaps you've been taught that if there is sin in your life, you cannot come to the Communion table. That's like a doctor saying to the emergency room patient, "Come back when you're not bleeding so much." Where else are we to find forgiveness but at the Lord's table?

The word "unworthily" in 1 Corinthians 11:29 doesn't refer to us, for we are never worthy of the privilege of Communion. It refers to the act of Communion. In other words, the one who takes the Cross lightly is the one who takes Communion unworthily. He who comes to the table saying, "Lord, I need You in my life. I confess that I have failed. Thank You for Your forgiveness. I choose to turn away from my sin. Give me Your grace, Lord. Help me this day," places great worth on Communion and will be forgiven completely: strengthened uniquely.

Each time you come to the Lord's table and confess your sin, you will find your struggle becoming a little easier. Watch. You'll see.

Refuse the Bread of Earth

Jesus said hellish temptations "do not come out but by prayer and fasting" (Matthew 17:21). Isaiah said the same thing.

> *Is not this the fast that I have chosen? to loose the bands of wickedness, to undo the heavy burdens, and to let the oppressed go free, and that ye break every yoke?*   Isaiah 58:6

Fasting is essential for those struggling with lustful temptations of the flesh. You see, my stomach is constantly saying, "It's burger time, buddy. You can't miss a meal. You can't deny your flesh." When I say, "I'm not giving in to you, stomach," self-denial spills over into other areas of my flesh as well.

Why could Jesus say, "I will not turn these stones into bread; I will not seek exaltation by jumping from the pinnacle of the temple; I will not receive the gift of all the earthly kingdoms?" He had been praying and fasting for forty days (see Matthew 4).

May I challenge you to consider fasting? During the time you would have been eating, pray. Whether you fast for a meal or a day, it is an absolute key to overcoming the flesh.

- Run to the congregation in the moment of temptation.
- Receive the bread of heaven at the table of Communion.
- Refuse the bread of earth through prayer and fasting.

If you do, you will be fulfilling God's will for your life. You will be exceedingly blessed in your marriage, your family, and your ministry.

REASONS FOR THE RAPTURE
A Topical Study of
1 Thessalonians 4:15–17

On July 20, 1969, astronaut Neil Armstrong left the Apollo Lunar Command Module and became the first human to set foot on the moon. Perhaps you recall his classic line, "One small step for man; one giant leap for mankind."

Let me tell you something, gang. The leap Armstrong referred to cannot hold a candle to the leap you'll be taking when the Lord comes in the clouds to rapture His church.

"Wait a minute," you say. "I have a problem with this because I don't see the word 'rapture' in the Bible."

That's because you're using the wrong Bible! You see, the New Testament was written in Greek. The phrase in verse 17, translated "caught up," is the Greek word *harpazo*, which means "to be grabbed by the collar and taken up with force." When the New Testament was translated into Latin, translators used the word *raptus* for *harpazo*—from which we get our word "rapture."

What is the purpose of the Rapture? I suggest there are four.

To Take up God's Children

Before World War II, Japan and Germany called their ambassadors away from America and back to their respective home countries. So, too, before the Lord declares war on the sin of our planet, He will take us—His ambassadors—home (2 Corinthians 5:20).

You can't pick up a newspaper or turn on TV without agreeing that the world is in a terrible state and needs to be judged. Before God judges our Christ-rejecting, sinful world, He will take His kids home to heaven.

If my house was infected with termites and I had to fumigate, even if my kids were being a bit rebellious or difficult, I would still make sure they were out of the house before the tent went up and the gas was pumped in.

If earthly parents are concerned about our children's safety, how much *more* is our heavenly Father concerned about the safety of His children?

To Shake up the Heathen

Not only will the Rapture ensure our safety, it will also bring about salvation. On the day of Pentecost, Peter spoke of the day when the sun shall be darkened, the moon shall turn to blood, and whoever shall call upon the name of the Lord shall be saved (Acts 2:17–21).

There are family members who have listened to you share Jesus, but don't believe in Him. There are friends who have heard your testimony and say, "That's all well and good—for *you*." There are co-workers with whom you've shared the plan of salvation who seem only to turn a deaf ear. The day is coming when we will be suddenly taken up and all your words will make perfect sense.

"Well, if that's the case," you say, "I'll just wait until you guys disappear. Then I'll know what you said is true, and I'll receive Jesus as my Savior."

If you cannot receive Jesus Christ in this day of grace, what makes you think you will be able to stand for Him in that time of intense persecution? Those who acknowledge Jesus as Lord in the Tribulation will be saved—but they'll lose their heads in the process (Revelation 20:4).

Lifesaving technique dictates that if a drowning person fights against him, a lifeguard must knock him out in order to save him. So, too, the Tribulation is God's knockout punch to the heathen in order to save them.

To Wake up a Nation

In referring to the Tribulation as *"Jacob's* trouble" (Jeremiah 30:7), Jeremiah makes it clear that it has a specific purpose for the nation of Israel. Israel will at last recognize her Messiah during the Tribulation.

> *When thou art in tribulation, and all these things are come upon thee, even in the latter days, if thou turn to the LORD thy God, and shalt be obedient unto his voice; (For the LORD thy God is a merciful God;) he will not forsake thee, neither destroy thee, nor forget the covenant of thy fathers which he sware unto them.*   Deuteronomy 4:30, 31

How will this come about? Two witnesses will preach in the streets of Jerusalem, which some commentators believe could be Elijah and Moses (Revelation 11). One hundred forty-four thousand Jewish Billy Grahams will preach throughout the world (Revelation 7). Angels will preach in the skies (Revelation 7).

When Jesus returns with ten thousand of His saints, all of Israel will lift up their eyes and say, "Where did You get those wounds?"

"In the house of My friends," He will answer (Zechariah 13:6).

Then the entire nation of Israel shall be saved (Romans 11). What a glorious day that will be!

To Make up the Millennium

At creation, God covered the earth with a blanket of water that filtered out the ultraviolet rays (Psalm 104:6). That is why Adam, Methuselah, and Enos lived nine hundred years or more. It was a perfect, wonderful environment. But when the world became so evil in the days of Noah that God had to flood it by breaking the protective water canopy, man's lifespan dwindled to only seventy to ninety years.

The Tribulation will purge the world of the depravity that permeates our planet to such a degree that even ecology will be restored in the Millennium. That is why the mountains shall break forth into song, and the trees of the field shall clap their hands (Isaiah 55:12); the wolf will lie down with the lamb (Isaiah 11:6); and men will live as long as they did in the days of Genesis (Isaiah 65:20).

> As the funeral procession made its way through the streets of Nain, Jesus had compassion on the bereaved mother. "Do not weep," He told her. Then, although it would have rendered Him ceremonially unclean, Jesus touched the coffin and said to the young man inside, "Arise" (Luke 7:11–15).

Gang, the day is coming when Jesus will say to us, "Arise! Come up here," (1 Thessalonians 4:16, 17). Up we'll go.

"Oh, but my heart is so hard," you say. "I'm a believer, but my heart is like stone."

It couldn't be harder than the heart of the young man in the coffin—he was dead! That didn't prevent him from rising and speaking at the sound of Jesus' voice. If you're a believer, you will not be left behind. Your heart will be softened; your lips will flow with praise; you will be free.

Maybe your heart is not heavy. Maybe it's broken.

The broken-hearted mother lost her only son. The ultimate "only Son," Jesus Christ, showed compassion to her.

> A man recently said to me, "Jon, I'm so sorry you lost your daughter."
> I had to say, "You know what? I didn't lose her. I know right where she is. She's in heaven, and I'll see her again."

You who are broken-hearted, be comforted. If you're missing a loved one, like the widow of Nain, rejoice. You will soon be reunited forever.

Jesus is coming, and He will soon call us to be with Him. Comfort one another with these words, gang. Keep talking about His coming. Keep looking for His coming. Whether we're hard or heavy-hearted, His coming is the ultimate answer for every heart.

5 **1 Thessalonians 5:1**
But of the times and the seasons, brethren, ye have no need that I write unto you.

People often ask why we spend so much time studying prophecy. There are two reasons. First, one-third of the Bible is prophetic, so we will inevitably encounter a great deal of prophecy as we journey through the Word. Second, we study prophecy because the present times and seasons point to the coming of Christ.

1 Thessalonians 5:2
For yourselves know perfectly that the day of the Lord so cometh as a thief in the night.

"Wait a minute," you say. "Doesn't verse 2—which says the Lord's return will come as stealthily as a thief in the night—contradict verse 1, which says the time of His return is predictable?" Read on.

1 Thessalonians 5:3–6
For when they shall say, Peace and safety; then sudden destruction cometh upon them, as travail upon a woman with child; and they shall not escape. But ye, brethren, are not in darkness, that that day should overtake you as a thief. Ye are all the children of light, and the children of the day: we are not of the night, nor of darkness. Therefore let us not sleep, as do others; but let us watch and be sober.

It is only the unbelievers who are in the dark concerning the Lord's return. Believers, on the other hand, know what's really happening. Comfort one another, says Paul, with the reminder that the Lord's coming is near. At the same time, realize the dark times and the seasons before the Rapture will become increasingly treacherous.

1 Thessalonians 5:7, 8 (a)
For they that sleep sleep in the night; and they that be drunken are drunken in the night. But let us, who are of the day, be sober, putting on the breastplate of faith . . .

Where do we get faith? Faith comes by hearing, and hearing by the Word of God (Romans 10:17). The only way we will be strong in faith is to stay in the Word.

1 Thessalonians 5:8 (b)
. . . and love; and for an helmet, the hope of salvation.

If you put on the breastplate of faith and love and the helmet of hope and salvation, you will constantly live in the hope that the Lord is coming soon.

1 Thessalonians 5:9, 10
For God hath not appointed us to wrath, but to obtain salvation by our Lord Jesus Christ, Who died for us, that, whether we wake or sleep, we should live together with him.

Paul says, "God has not appointed us to wrath." Why? Is it because we're so cool? Is it because we're so good? No. The wrath that should come down on us was poured out on Jesus Christ when He took our place on the Cross. Consequently, we are not ordained for the wrath of the Lamb, but for His marvelous, glorious work of salvation.

1 Thessalonians 5:11
Wherefore comfort yourselves together, and edify one another, even as also ye do.

As Paul begins to close his first letter to the Thessalonians, he does so with a series of practical exhortations intended to refine their walk.

1 Thessalonians 5:12, 13
And we beseech you, brethren, to know them which labour among you, and are over you in the Lord, and admonish you; and to esteem them very highly in love for their work's sake. And be at peace among yourselves.

We are to think highly of those who are called to instruct, admonish, or challenge us in the Name of the Lord—not because of their personalities, but because of their position; not because of who they are, but because of the invaluable work they do.

1 Thessalonians 5:14
Now we exhort you, brethren, warn them that are unruly, comfort the feebleminded, support the weak, be patient toward all men.

The four injunctions Paul gives provide a wonderful picture of true ministry: Clearly warn those whose behavior is out of line with the way of the Lord. Comfort those who have a hard time understanding the will of the Lord. Support those who are weak in the Lord. Show patience to all—even to those who don't know the Lord.

1 Thessalonians 5:15
See that none render evil for evil unto any man; but ever follow that which is good, both among yourselves, and to all men.

Don't be evil. Follow that which is good, both to those within the Christian community, and those without.

1 Thessalonians 5:16–18
Rejoice evermore. Pray without ceasing. In every thing give thanks: for this is the will of God in Christ Jesus concerning you.

What is God's will? Paul succinctly defines it as praying without ceasing, giving thanks in everything and rejoicing forevermore.

1 Thessalonians 5:19, 20
Quench not the Spirit. Despise not prophesyings.

Some scoff at the gift of tongues or words of wisdom. They do so to their own spiritual poverty because those who fail to acknowledge the manifestations of the Spirit actually quench His presence in their own lives.

1 Thessalonians 5:21, 22
Prove all things; hold fast that which is good. Abstain from all appearance of evil.

If you want to be used by the Lord, you must deal with the issue of appearances. You might be innocent, but if anything you're doing even *appears* evil, it can compromise your usefulness.

1 Thessalonians 5:23, 24, 25–28
And the very God of peace sanctify you wholly; and I pray God your whole spirit and soul and body be preserved blameless unto the coming of our Lord Jesus Christ. Faithful is he that calleth you, who also will do it. Brethren, pray for us. Greet all the brethren with an holy kiss. I charge you by the Lord that this epistle be read unto all the holy brethren. The grace of our Lord Jesus Christ be with you. Amen.

"I pray for you," writes Paul, "and I know God will see you through because He is faithful."

2 THESSALONIANS

1 A year after his first letter, Paul penned a second letter to the Thessalonians. This was done in order to clear up the confusion caused by those who preached after he left. They were saying that the persecution launched against the church in Thessalonica was proof that the Tribulation had already begun. Add to them a group who supposedly prophesied in the Spirit, and a forged letter from Paul saying the Tribulation had begun. It is easy to see why the Thessalonians were confused.

2 Thessalonians 1:1–3
Paul, and Silvanus, and Timotheus, unto the church of the Thessalonians in God our Father and the Lord Jesus Christ: Grace unto you, and peace, from God our Father and the Lord Jesus Christ. We are bound to thank God always for you, brethren, as it is meet, because that your faith groweth exceedingly, and the charity of every one of you all toward each other aboundeth.

In the first verse of his first letter to the Thessalonians, Paul had commended their work of faith, labor of love, and patience of hope. Here, in his second letter, he commends only their faith and love. Why? They had lost their hope because they were no longer living for Jesus' return.

Although of faith, hope, and love the greatest is love (1 Corinthians 13:13)—all three elements are essential because it is faith and hope that allow us to love. How? I'd be too ashamed to love if I were hung up over my past sins. Faith tells me my past failures were totally cleansed by the blood of Jesus. I'd be too afraid to love if I were worried about the future. Hope tells me He's coming again, so there's no need to fear.

2 Thessalonians 1:4
So that we ourselves glory in you in the churches of God for your patience and faith in all your persecutions and tribulations that ye endure.

Even as Paul wrote his epistles, Christians were being beat up and wiped out. "We're proud of you," says Paul. "You're enduring hard times."

2 Thessalonians 1:5
Which is a manifest token of the righteous judgment of God, that ye may be counted worthy of the kingdom of God, for which ye also suffer.

"The fact that you are persecuted and put down is proof that you're a part of the kingdom," declares Paul. He would say the same thing to Timothy by writing, "Yea, all those who live godly in Christ Jesus shall suffer persecution" (2 Timothy 3:12).

Hmm.

So often I pray to avoid pressure, problems, and persecution. In reality, it is those very things that would have produced Christlike qualities within me. There is really no other way. If you want to be like Jesus, hard times are inevitable.

"I want to shine like a diamond in the kingdom," we say. You know what a diamond is? It's a chunk of worthless coal that has undergone tremendous amounts of pressure over many, many years. So if your heart wants to reflect Jesus, know this: There is no other way that will happen than to go through fiery trials over great lengths of time. This is why Peter talks about our faith being purified by fiery trials (1 Peter 4:12), and why James says, "Count it all joy when you go through these trials" (James 1:2).

Although I know this in theory, I still find myself praying, "Lord, I don't want to deal with this. Lord, I don't want to go through that. Lord, do I have to go *there*? Lord, get me out of here!" In reality, such prayers are unwise because they can actually hinder the work the Lord was doing in me through these trials.

Consequently, I am praying less, "Lord, help me Yourself," and more, "Lord, help Yourself to me. I am tired of directing You. Put me wherever You see I'll be happy and most fruitful. You know best."

2 Thessalonians 1:6
Seeing it is a righteous thing with God to recompense tribulation to them that trouble you.

I personally believe this verse alludes to more than the tribulation the Thessalonians were experiencing. I believe it speaks of the bigger picture of the Tribulation of Revelation 6—19. Why? The phrase, "It is a *righteous* thing with God," takes me back to Genesis 18.

Concerning the impending doom of Sodom, Abraham asked God, "Shall not the Judge of all the earth do right?" (Genesis 18:25) God did, indeed, pour out His wrath on Sodom. Before He did, He raptured Lot and his family when He sent an angel to grab them by the hand and pull them out of the city.

And turning the cities of Sodom and Gomorrha into ashes condemned them with an overthrow, making them an ensample unto those that after should live ungodly; and delivered just Lot, vexed with the filthy conversation of the wicked: (For that righteous man dwelling among them, in seeing and hearing, vexed his righteous soul from day to day with their unlawful deeds;) The Lord knoweth how to deliver the godly out of temptations, and to reserve the unjust unto the day of judgment to be punished . . .   2 Peter 2:6–9

The word translated "out of" is the Greek word *ek. Ek* does not mean "to protect them while they are going through it." It means "to be taken out completely." Before God poured out His judgment on Sodom, He "took out" Lot and his family. God will take His children out before He pours out His wrath on a Christ-rejecting, sinful, corrupt world during the Tribulation.

2 Thessalonians 1:7–9
And to you who are troubled rest with us, when the Lord Jesus shall be revealed from heaven with his mighty angels, in flaming fire taking vengeance on them that know not God, and that obey not the gospel of our Lord Jesus Christ: Who shall be punished with everlasting destruction from the presence of the Lord, and from the glory of his power.

Are you getting picked on because of your faith in Jesus Christ? Relax, Paul says, because there's coming a day when the Lord will return with mighty angels to take vengeance on those who are purposefully, knowingly giving you headaches and heartbreaks because of your faith in Him.

2 Thessalonians 1:10–12
When he shall come to be glorified in his saints, and to be admired in all them that

believe (because our testimony among you was believed) in that day. Wherefore also we pray always for you, that our God would count you worthy of this calling, and fulfil all the good pleasure of his goodness, and the work of faith with power: That the name of our Lord Jesus Christ may be glorified in you, and ye in him, according to the grace of our God and the Lord Jesus Christ.

When Jesus comes, He will be glorified not among His saints—but *in* them.

I venture to guess that none of us bought the latest *Ladies Home Journal* expecting to see our names on the "Ten Most Admired People" list. Nor did we buy the latest edition of *Who's Who in America*, eager to see our names inside. That's because this is not our day. This is the "day of man" (Job 10:5)—"man" referring to fallen humanity. When Jesus returns, He will be glorified and admired in all who believe. This means we'll see Jesus in each other. "Wow, I thought you were a lightweight," we'll say; or, "I thought you were weird"; or, "I thought you were callous, cruel, pompous, or vain. Now look at you! I see *Jesus* in you!"

Oh, to have such a mind-set this side of eternity—to join Paul in "knowing no man after the flesh" (2 Corinthians 5:16), instead seeing Jesus glorified in His saints even now.

---

2 **2 Thessalonians 2:1**
Now we beseech you, brethren, by the coming of our Lord Jesus Christ, and by our gathering together unto him.

Writing of "our gathering together unto Him," Paul gets to the heart of his second letter as he deals with the Rapture.

2 Thessalonians 2:2 (a)
That ye be not soon shaken in mind, or be troubled, neither by spirit, nor by word, nor by letter as from us . . .

Referring to the false teachers that had descended upon the church at Thessalonica following his departure, Paul says, "Don't be troubled by spirit (false prophecies); word (false teaching), or by letter (forged)."

2 Thessalonians 2:2 (b)
. . . as that the day of Christ is at hand.

Although your King James Version translates this phrase "as that the day of Christ is at hand," more recent and correct translations render this verse "the day of the Lord has already come"

(NIV). As seen in the first and second chapters of the Book of Joel, the Day of the Lord is when the Lord intervenes in human history and brings about judgment and justice. It will begin with the Tribulation, extend through the Millennium, and culminate with the replacement of this earth by a new creation (Joel 2).

2 Thessalonians 2:3 (a)
Let no man deceive you by any means: for that day shall not come, except there come a falling away first . . .

The Greek word *apostasia* is translated "falling away." It is also where we get our word "apostasy." There are two equally valid translations of the word *apostasia*. The first translation is "turning one's back on truth." The second is a literal, physical "departure." Consequently, many Bible scholars have argued very passionately that the phrase "falling away" refers to a departure from earth—the Rapture. Others argue that the phrase simply means turning one's back on truth.

Which translation is correct? I believe it could be either one. The Tribulation will begin after the world continues to turn its back on truth (Matthew 24:12), and it will come after the church physically departs during the Rapture (1 Thessalonians 4:17, 18).

2 Thessalonians 2:3 (b)
. . . and that man of sin be revealed, the son of perdition.

The word "perdition" means "waste." The phrase "the son of perdition" is used twice in the Bible. Here, it is linked to Antichrist. The other time it is seen in Jesus' High Priestly prayer.

> While I was with them in the world, I kept them in thy name: those that thou gavest me I have kept, and none of them is lost, but the son of perdition; that the scripture might be fulfilled.
> John 17:12

Who is this "son of perdition"? Judas Iscariot. The same spirit that filled Judas Iscariot, making him the son of perdition, will also make Antichrist the "son of perdition."

> *When Mary broke her alabaster box and anointed Jesus in an act of worship, Judas said "To what purpose is this waste?" (Matthew 26:8; John 12:4, 5)*

Nothing given to the Lord is ever wasted. The young missionary martyred by the Auca Indians was right when he said, "He is no fool who gives what he cannot keep to gain what he cannot

lose."[1] Jim Elliot understood the big picture. Judas, the son of perdition, did not.

2 Thessalonians 2:4 (a)
Who opposeth and exalteth himself above all that is called God, or that is worshipped; so that he as God sitteth in the temple of God . . .

"Little children," wrote John, "it is the last time: and as ye have heard that antichrist shall come, even now are there many antichrists; whereby we know that it is the last time" (1 John 2:18).

The word "anti" does not only mean "against." It also means "in place of." Thus, the spirit of antichrist can be in the temple of my own body. I'm not talking about demons, but about the mind-set that leads me to say, "I don't need to rely on Christ. I don't need to pray about my kids today. I don't need to pray about how to use my time."

What will be the result? The same things that will follow the physical antichrist: I will experience "famine, wars and rumors of wars" (Matthew 24:4–8). I'll have problems in my marriage, my family, my ministry. The tribulation believers endure is often unnecessary. They could have been "raptured to heaven" by spending time seeking the Lord in the morning. They could have been "caught up in the clouds to meet Him in the air" and thus gained a heavenly perspective on the day before them. Instead, they chose to captain their own ship, plot their own course, and rely on their own wisdom instead of Christ's.

Oh, none of us are "anti-Christ" in the sense that we're against Him. We are, however, vulnerable to the subtle thinking that takes the place of Christ, whereby we make our own decisions and call our own shots. The spirit of Antichrist can pollute any of us. Let's be wise and say, "My temple is dedicated to only One: Jesus Christ. He will reign in my heart. He will rule my life. "

2 Thessalonians 2:4 (b)
. . . shewing himself that he is God.

After the "departure" of verse 3, Antichrist will demand to be worshiped as God in the temple in Jerusalem. This is really going to happen, gang. You can go to the Temple Treasury Museum in Jerusalem and see the garments already made for the priests, along with the utensils, tools, candles, mitres, and plans to replicate the ark of the covenant to Levitical standards.

"Wait a minute," you say. "How can the temple be rebuilt when the Mosque of Omar, the Dome of the Rock, the third most holy site of Islam sits on the very spot where the temple is to be rebuilt? To bulldoze it down would start a holy war of unbelievable proportions, as 850 million Muslims would rise up and crush the three million Jews in Israel."

Dr. Asher Kaufman is one of a number of Jewish archaeologists who contend the Dome of the Rock Mosque does not sit on the site of the Holy of Holies as previously believed. The actual Holy of Holies lies beneath a little gazebo-like structure called the Dome of the Tablets and the Dome of the Spirits.

Why would this spot be referred to as the Dome of the Tablets?
The Tablets were there.
What tablets?
The Ten Commandments that were in the ark of the covenant, which sat in the Holy of Holies.
Why would this spot be referred to as the Dome of the Spirits?
The Spirit of God, the shekinah glory, filled the Holy of Holies.
What stands on the temple mount in front of the Dome of the Spirits, the Dome of the Tablets?
Nothing.
"Let me solve this sticky issue, the Palestinian problem, the question of Jerusalem," Antichrist will say. "Jews, you build your temple on the true site of the temple. We'll build a wall to separate it from the Muslim Dome of the Rock Mosque." Ezekiel prophesied this very thing would happen (Ezekiel 42:20). In this way, Antichrist will seemingly solve the problem that has troubled and divided Jerusalem for centuries. The people will say, "He's wonderful. He's our hero!"

Then, in the midst of his popularity, Antichrist will walk into the temple and demand to be worshiped, "showing himself that he is God," and the horrific second half of the seven-year Tribulation will follow.
"Don't be shaken," Paul says to the Thessalonians. "You are not in the Tribulation. This is not the Day of the Lord. You did not miss the Rapture because the "son of perdition"—Antichrist—has not yet come."

2 Thessalonians 2:5
Remember ye not, that, when I was yet with you, I told you these things?

"Don't you remember that I explained these things when I was with you?" Paul asks the Thessalonian believers.

2 Thessalonians 2:6, 7 (a)
And now ye know what withholdeth that he might be revealed in his time. For the mystery of iniquity doth already work . . .

The "mystery of iniquity" refers to Satan's desire to take control of the world through Antichrist.

2 Thessalonians 2:7 (b)
. . . only he who now letteth will let . . .

A "let" in tennis is the term used when a served ball bounces off, or is deflected, by the net. In other words, the net keeps the ball from being a fair serve. So, too, there is a force deflecting Satan's attempt to control the world.

2 Thessalonians 2:7 (c)
. . . until he be taken out of the way.

Who is the force hindering Satan? The Holy Spirit. The only thing keeping any degree of sanity on this planet is the Spirit working in and through the church. When the Rapture takes place, the "net" is removed, and Satan's volleys will no longer be deflected.

2 Thessalonians 2:8 (a)
And then shall that Wicked be revealed . . .

"Wicked" refers to the wicked one, or Antichrist. After the church is raptured, Satan will fill a human vessel who will usher in the new economic system and world order preceding the Tribulation.
Come on, you may be thinking. *Do you really believe a literal, physical character claiming to be divine and godly, but actually filled with Satan, will appear on the scene?*
Yes. Little by little, even the world is unknowingly beginning to accept such a possibility. Through silly "X-Files" propaganda, the world is being prepped to explain away the disappearance of Christians in the Rapture. Through recent scientific advancements such as DNA cloning, the emergence of a "Christ figure" is, in the world's eyes, no longer a preposterous concept.

2 Thessalonians 2:8 (b)
. . . whom the Lord shall consume with the spirit of his mouth, and shall destroy with the brightness of his coming.

As intimidating as Antichrist may be, when Jesus comes back, His brightness will blast Antichrist into oblivion.

2 Thessalonians 2:9
Even him, whose coming is after the working of Satan with all power and signs and lying wonders.

May the Lord help us to be cautious so we are not taken in by so-called signs and wonders even in this day. They can indeed be false.

They saw the Red Sea part, and the waters collapse on the armies of Pharaoh. They saw a mountain shake; and heard a voice from heaven. They saw food fall every morning and the earth swallow people. They were led by a fiery pillar at night, and a cloud by day. They saw more signs and wonders than any group of people in history. Yet the children of Israel could not enter into the Promised Land because of their unbelief (Hebrews 3:19).

Signs and wonders do not produce faith. They only produce a craving for more signs and wonders. That's why, centuries later, the Jews were still asking for more (John 6:30).

As we approach the final days, there will be an increase in signs and wonders, along with vulnerability even within the body of Christ to chase after, and to be intrigued by them. Jesus said signs and wonders shall follow those who believe (Mark 16:17). The problem today is that those who believe are following after signs and wonders. There's a big difference. Miracles do not produce faith. Only the Word produces faith (Romans 10:17).

For topical study of 2 Thessalonians 2:8–10 entitled "Antichrist's Subtle Seduction," turn to page 1356.

2 Thessalonians 2:10–12
And with all deceivableness of unrighteousness in them that perish; because they received not the love of the truth, that they might be saved. And for this cause God shall send them strong delusion, that they should believe a lie: That they all might be damned who believed not the truth, but had pleasure in unrighteousness.

There are only two prayers a man can pray: Either *"Thy* kingdom come; *Thy* will be done"—or *"my* kingdom come; *my* will be done." He who prays the latter, says, "I am the king of my domain. I want to call the shots in my life." God gives us freedom to pray either prayer. To do so, it is necessary for Him to send "strong delusion," lest he who does not want to believe does so against his will.

Jesus touched on this same principle when He spoke in parables so that blind eyes would not see or deaf ears would not hear (Matthew 13:13). You see, the power of Jesus' words and life was so evident that had He not blinded the eyes and stopped the ears of those who did not want to believe. They would have had no choice but to believe. Thus, they would have followed Him out of coercion rather than out of love.

That's why when we witness to people, we find ourselves saying, "Don't you get it? God is so *good.* Who wouldn't want to be saved? Who wouldn't want to know his sins are forgiven, that he has a Friend closer than a brother, that he's going to live forever in heaven?"—only to hear people say, "No thanks."

Who wouldn't want to be saved?

Those who are deluded, those who believe a lie.

Even in the Tribulation, God will honor man's choice. He will allow those who don't want to see to remain blind.

2 Thessalonians 2:13, 14
But we are bound to give thanks alway to God for you, brethren beloved of the Lord, because God hath from the beginning chosen you to salvation through sanctification of the Spirit and belief of the truth: Whereunto he called you by our gospel, to the obtaining of the glory of our Lord Jesus Christ.

From the beginning, God chose the Thessalonian believers. From the beginning, He chose you. That's why you're in the Word even now. You could be at Rockin' Rodeo; you could be watching TV; you could be stuck in a world that is unsatisfying and destructive. The Lord, however, chose you to be saved.

"Wait a minute," you say. "Didn't we just read that God will not override our free will?"

Yes. God's sovereignty and man's free will dwell side by side throughout Scripture. It is only in our finite minds that the two cannot be reconciled. If you ignore God's tug on your heart, it will be because you are not chosen by God. If you choose God today, it will be because He already chose you.

Choose Him now, dear people. Surely it is His grace that has brought you this far.

2 Thessalonians 2:15
Therefore, brethren, stand fast, and hold the traditions which ye have been taught, whether by word, or our epistle.

Newer translations correctly render the word "traditions" as "ordinances." There are those who say, "Baptism is no longer necessary. The Lord's table is optional. There's no need to pray the Lord's prayer. Meeting together for Bible study is helpful, but not crucial."

Jesus was baptized in water. So was Peter. So was John. So was D. L. Moody, C. H. Spurgeon, and Billy Graham. I may not have the boldness of D. L. Moody, the fervency of C. H.

Spurgeon, or the anointing of Billy Graham, but I can stand exactly where they stood in the waters of baptism.

I can sit where the greatest Christians have sat through the ages, and have the same meal they had as I partake of Communion.

I can't preach like R. A. Torrey or Charles Finney, but I pray exactly as they did when I pray, "Our Father, which art in Heaven. . . ."

I don't have the power of the early church, but I do exactly as they did every time I meet with fellow believers to study the Word (Acts 2:42).

We have a glorious heritage, gang. Paul would say to us, even as he said to the Thessalonians, "Don't minimize traditions. Hold on to them.

Your faith will be the richer; your walk will be the surer for it."

2 Thessalonians 2:16, 17
Now our Lord Jesus Christ himself, and God, even our Father, which hath loved us, and hath given us everlasting consolation and good hope through grace, Comfort your hearts, and stablish you in every good word and work.

Used six times, "comfort" is the watchword of Paul's Epistles to the Thessalonians. The greatest comfort of all is the fact that Jesus could come even today and take us to heaven, where the forces of darkness will be obliterated by the "brightness of His coming."

ANTICHRIST'S SUBTLE SEDUCTION
A Topical Study of
2 Thessalonians 2:8–10

I spotted a deal on a billboard too good to pass up: A Big Mac® or Double Quarter Pounder® with Cheese for half price. Taking advantage of this Epicurean delight, I paid for my lunch with a twenty-dollar bill. The girl behind the counter looked at the bill, looked at me, and called for the manager. The manager looked at the bill, looked at me, pulled a yellow marking pen from his shirt pocket, swiped it across the bill, and said, "Okay."

"What was that all about?" I asked.

"We use this pen to check all twenty-dollar bills. If the ink had turned black, we would know this was a bogus bill. You see, we have a huge problem with counterfeiting."

Even today, the stage is set for the ultimate counterfeiter, Antichrist, to come on the scene and implement his new economic order. It will require no credit cards that can be lost, pin numbers that can be forgotten, or bills that can be counterfeited. It will simply be an innocent-looking number on one's forehead or hand (Revelation 14:9).

Counterfeiting is nothing new to Satan. Ever since he first appeared to Eve in the Garden of Eden, he has attempted to counterfeit God's work and His ways. Following are three questions that bring to light his "lying wonders."

Better or Worse?

"Thus saith the Lord," Moses said to Pharaoh. "Let My people go" (Exodus 8:1).

"Who is the Lord?" asked Pharaoh.

"Watch this," said Moses as he threw down his rod and it became a snake.

"We can do that, too," said Pharaoh's magicians as their sticks also became snakes—as if *more* snakes were just what Pharaoh needed.

"All of the waters of Egypt shall be turned to blood," declared Moses.

"We can do that, too," said Pharaoh's magicians—as if *more* blood was what Egypt wanted.

"Thus saith the Lord," declared Moses. "At this time tomorrow the whole land will be filled with frogs."

"We can do that, too," said Pharaoh's magicians—as if *more* frogs were desirable.

Whether through the occult or sleight of hand, Pharaoh's magicians were seemingly able to duplicate snakes, blood, and frogs. In so doing, they only made matters worse.

The same is true today. Satan's "lying wonders" can seem pretty impressive. Any time you or I get caught up in the world's system, when the special effects are turned off, when the smoke clears—all we are ultimately left with is a bunch of snakes and frogs.

Who Gets the Glory?

How are we to differentiate between the miracles of God and Satan's "lying wonders"? It's very simple. Look to see who's getting the glory.

Jesus said, "Let your light so shine before men that they might see your good works and glorify your Father which is in heaven" (Matthew 5:16).

Even Pharaoh's magicians had to eventually give glory to God when they admitted His work could not be duplicated (Exodus 8:19).

Nowhere is this principle more clearly seen than in the life of Jesus. Jesus raised the dead, healed the sick, and freed the captive. He went about constantly doing good, and without exception, He gave glory to the Father.

How can you tell whether a sign or wonder is of Christ or the spirit of antichrist—whether it's light, or only darkness camouflaged as light? Just watch who gets the glory, attention, applause, and exaltation. If it's a man, method, or idea—watch out. Satan the counterfeiter is not far behind.

As we head toward the last days, I believe there will be increased occurrences of demonic signs and wonders. Therefore, we must look carefully at any sign or apparent miracle and ask, "Who's getting the glory?"

Is Christ Preeminent?

While I do not believe most of you are vulnerable to Satan's tricks, there is something much more subtle to which we are all vulnerable. These are activities and pursuits that creep in and take the place of Christ in our hearts.

You see, the term "anti-Christ" not only means "against Christ," but "in place of Christ." Thus, the seduction of antichrist can be seen any time we substitute hobbies or relationships, ministries or occupations, pursuits or pleasure for the place only Jesus should hold in our lives.

Dear brother, precious sister: Don't allow anything—no matter how seemingly pure, productive, or profitable—to take the place of Christ in your heart. Don't allow anything—no matter how seemingly mystical, miraculous, or marvelous—to distract you from Jesus.

Expose the counterfeit by asking,

- "Are things getting better or worse?"
- "Who is getting the glory?"
- "Is Jesus still Lord?"

May we walk in wisdom in these last days.
In Jesus' Name.

3 **2 Thessalonians 3:1**
Finally, brethren, pray for us, that the word of the Lord may have free course, and be glorified, even as it is with you.

As he brings his second Thessalonian letter to a close, Paul says, "Pray for us." Notice that he doesn't say, "Pray for our programs." He doesn't say, "Pray for our projects." He says, "Pray for our preaching."

Last century, God did a mighty work in London through a giant of the faith named Charles Haddon Spurgeon. His sermons are studied to this day. The story is told that one Sunday afternoon, a contingency of ministers came to the massive Metropolitan Tabernacle to observe him. Assuming the stout man at the side of the building wearing bib overalls to be the janitor, they asked, "Sir, would you kindly show us the power plant of this huge structure?"

"Certainly," the man replied, leading them to the basement.

As he opened the door at the end of a hallway, the ministers expected to see a mighty furnace. Instead, they saw over two hundred men on their knees praying for the upcoming evening service.

"Prayer, gentlemen," he said, "is the power plant of the Metropolitan Tabernacle."

The man—Spurgeon himself—knew where the power lay.

2 Thessalonians 3:2
And that we may be delivered from unreasonable and wicked men: for all men have not faith.

Secondly, Paul asks that the Thessalonians pray that he would be delivered from "unreasonable"—or, as your margin renders it—"absurd" men. Who were these "absurd men"? Acts 17:5 describes them as "lewd fellows of the baser sort" who tried to get Paul in political hot water by saying he advocated Caesar's overthrow.

Was Paul preaching that there was another King besides Caesar? Certainly. He served the King of kings, Jesus Christ. He also argued that men were to be submitted to those in authority over them (Romans 13:1).

"Thou shalt not bear false witness," God declared in the ninth commandment (Exodus 20:16). These "absurd men" provide a classic example of what it means to bear false witness. You see, telling a lie is not the only way we bear false witness. We bear false witness whenever we simply misrepresent the truth.

How do I know this? There is another incident in the Word where we see false witnesses—at the trial of Jesus Christ.

Now the chief priests, and elders, and all the council, sought false witness against Jesus, to put him to death; but found none: yea, though many false witnesses came, yet found they none. At the last came two false witnesses, and said, This fellow said, I am able to destroy the temple of God, and to build it in three days.
Matthew 26:59–61

While Jesus had indeed said, "Destroy this temple and in three days, I'll rise again" (John 2:19) He was speaking of the temple of His own body. So, too, Paul preached the Lordship of Christ, but also that we should submit to earthly authority. In both cases, false witnesses gave the right information, but with the wrong implication.

Notice Paul doesn't say he wants to debate the

false witnesses. Rather, he simply asks to be delivered from them. Gang, there are those who will twist what you say to their own end. What are you to do? Do what Paul did. Don't complain. Don't explain. Instead, pray that God will take care of them in *His* time, and in *His* way because if you start defending yourself, you'll never stop.

A man and his son in need of money decided to sell their donkey at the marketplace. The townspeople shook their heads in disgust that the man would make his son walk while he rode the donkey. After hearing the criticism, the man quickly dismounted, and his son got on in his place. As they walked a little farther, they again heard the townspeople murmur, "How could that son be so disrespectful as to make his father walk while he rides the donkey?"

The man then joined his son astride the donkey, only to hear the townspeople down the road say, "How cruel of those two to ride that poor little donkey!" In response, both father and son dismounted the donkey and walked farther, amidst criticism that they were fools for failing to utilize their donkey.

At last, in desperation, the father and son picked the donkey up, and carried it the rest of the way.

Try to defend yourself, and, like the poor man and his son, you'll find yourself carrying a heavy burden. Instead, do what Paul did. Leave your defense to the Lord.

2 Thessalonians 3:3, 4
But the Lord is faithful, who shall stablish you, and keep you from evil. And we have confidence in the Lord touching you, that ye both do and will do the things which we command you.

"There are unreasonable, wicked men," says Paul. "But the Lord is faithful. That's how we know you'll do well."

I am often asked about our follow-up program for those we baptize every week. "We give them a Bible and a tape and pray for them," I answer, because, like Paul, I firmly believe that the Lord will establish those who are truly His.

If it's a philosophy or program we're pushing; if it's attendance we're trying to build—then, yes, we need a program. On the other hand, if it's simply Jesus we're preaching, He will, through His body, embrace those who come to Him. And He will tap some of you on the shoulder to allow Him to do just that.

2 Thessalonians 3:5
And the Lord direct your hearts into the love of God, and into the patient waiting for Christ.

Newer translations render "the patient waiting for Christ" as "the patience of Christ." I suggest to you that both translations are true, and both are linked together. The only way we can have the patience of Christ is by waiting for Him, knowing we'll soon be with Him. I have observed that the most peaceful, patient, and contented people are those who truly live in the expectation of Jesus' return.

2 Thessalonians 3:6–9
Now we command you, brethren, in the name of our Lord Jesus Christ, that ye withdraw yourselves from every brother that walketh disorderly, and not after the tradition which he received of us. For yourselves know how ye ought to follow us: for we behaved not ourselves disorderly among you; neither did we eat any man's bread for nought; but wrought with labour and travail night and day, that we might not be chargeable to any of you: Not because we have not power, but to make ourselves an ensample unto you to follow us.

The word "travail" refers to the pain of childbirth (John 16:21). In other words, Paul is saying it wasn't easy, but he and Silas worked hard to support themselves even as they ministered to the Thessalonians.

2 Thessalonians 3:10
For even when we were with you, this we commanded you, that if any would not work, neither should he eat.

Before Rush Limbaugh fans agree with this verse too quickly, notice it says, "If any man *would not* work . . ." It does not say, "If any man *cannot* work . . ." The Bible has much to say regarding compassion for those who cannot work, so be very careful before withholding food from someone who appears to be lazy.

2 Thessalonians 3:11
For we hear that there are some which walk among you disorderly, working not at all, but are busybodies.

Whenever a person who should and could be working is not, he will be a busybody. You see, when Adam fell in the Garden of Eden, it was God's mercy and wisdom that said to him, "You need to work" (see Genesis 3:17–19).

Evidently, the "unreasonable and wicked men" of verse 2 did not understand this, for they had enough time on their hands to endlessly discuss Paul's faults.

I once read an article about the shuttle *Discovery*. The article explained that its repaired fuel tank would be escorted to the launch pad by a six-eyed scarecrow. The scarecrow was intended to scare the woodpeckers that drilled 195 holes in the shuttle last month. The launch was delayed for two months due to the danger of ice forming in the holes and damaging the shuttle during liftoff.

The billion-dollar technological peak of man's abilities was grounded by two little woodpeckers. So, too, it only takes a couple busybodies poking where they ought not to damage the work of God.

2 Thessalonians 3:12–14
Now them that are such we command and exhort by our Lord Jesus Christ, that with quietness they work, and eat their own bread. But ye, brethren, be not weary in well doing. And if any man obey not our word by this epistle, note that man, and have no company with him, that he may be ashamed.

The best thing you can do with a busybody is to stay away from him or her—not out of rejection, but for restoration. If gossips and busybodies have no audience, they eventually stop.

For topical study of 2 Thessalonians 3:13, see "Be Not Weary in Well-Doing," below.

For topical study of 2 Thessalonians 3:13 entitled "Looking at Ministry," turn to page 1364.

2 Thessalonians 3:15
Yet count him not as an enemy, but admonish him as a brother.

The only people who have the right to point out the dirt on another's feet are those who have a towel about their waist, a basin of water in their hands, and are willing to wash them. If I'm not willing to come alongside someone in humility and love, I have no right to point out the dirt I see in him.

2 Thessalonians 3:16, 17
Now the Lord of peace himself give you peace always by all means. The Lord be with you all. The salutation of Paul with mine own hand, which is the token in every epistle: so I write.

Paul closes, saying, "Here's my own signature. This letter is not forged. It's the real thing. Grace be with you all."

2 Thessalonians 3:18
The grace of our Lord Jesus Christ be with you all. Amen.

So Paul's letter ends the way it began: with grace.

BE NOT WEARY IN WELL-DOING
A Topical Study of
2 Thessalonians 3:13

Sometimes we grow weary in serving, giving, sharing, and ministering. At the end of Paul's teaching concerning the Second Coming of Christ and the establishment of His kingdom, the Holy Spirit inspires Paul to give the Thessalonians a short exhortation with long-term implications.

Why were the Thessalonians not to be weary in well-doing?

I believe Numbers 7 gives us the answer.

It came to pass on the day that Moses had fully set up the tabernacle and had anointed it, that the princes of Israel, heads of the house of their fathers, who were princes over the tribes, brought their offerings before the Lord. And he that offered his offering on the first day was Nahshon, the son of Amminadab, of the tribe of Judah. And his offering was:

One silver charger, the weight thereof was an hundred and thirty shekels, one silver bowl of seventy shekels, after the shekel of the sanctuary; both of them were full of fine flour mingled with oil for a meat offering; one spoon of ten shekels of gold, full of incense; one young bullock, one ram, one lamb of the first year, for a burnt offering; one kid of the goats for a sin offering; and for a sacrifice of peace offerings, two oxen, five rams, five he goats, five lambs of the first year.

On the second day, Nethaneel, the son of Zuar, prince of Issachar, did offer:

One silver charger, the weight whereof was an hundred and thirty shekels, one silver bowl of seventy shekels, after the shekel of the sanctuary; both of them full of fine flour mingled with oil for a meat offering; one spoon of gold of ten shekels, full of incense; one young bullock, one ram, one lamb of the first year, for a burnt offering; one kid of the goats for a sin offering; and for a sacrifice of peace offerings, two oxen, five rams, five he goats, five lambs of the first year.

On the third day, Eliab, the son of Helon, prince of the children of Zebulun, did offer:

One silver charger, the weight whereof was an hundred and thirty shekels, one silver bowl of seventy shekels, after the shekel of the sanctuary; both of them full of fine flour mingled with oil for a meat offering; one golden spoon of ten shekels, full of incense; one young bullock, one ram, one lamb of the first year, for a burnt offering; one kid of the goats for a sin offering; and for a sacrifice of peace offerings, two oxen, five rams, five he goats, five lambs of the first year.

On the fourth day, Elizur, the son of Shedeur, prince of the children of Reuben, did offer:

One silver charger of the weight of an hundred and thirty shekels, one silver bowl of seventy shekels, after the shekel of the sanctuary; both of them full of fine flour mingled with oil for a meat offering; one golden spoon of ten shekels, full of incense; one young bullock, one ram, one lamb of the first year, for a burnt offering; one kid of the goats for a sin offering; and for a sacrifice of peace offerings, two oxen, five rams, five he goats, five lambs of the first year.

On the fifth day, Shelumiel, the son of Zurishaddai, prince of the children of Simeon, did offer:

One silver charger, the weight whereof was an hundred and thirty shekels, one silver bowl of seventy shekels, after the shekel of the sanctuary; both of them full of fine flour mingled with oil for a meat offering; one golden spoon of ten shekels, full of incense; one young bullock, one ram, one lamb of the first year, for a burnt offering; one kid of the goats for a sin offering; and for a sacrifice of peace offerings, two oxen, five rams, five he goats, five lambs of the first year.

On the sixth day, Eliasaph, the son of Deuel, prince of the children of Gad, did offer:

One silver charger of the weight of an hundred and thirty shekels, a silver bowl of seventy shekels, after the shekel of the sanctuary; both of them full of fine flour mingled with oil for a meat offering; one golden spoon of ten shekels, full of incense; one young bullock, one ram, one lamb of the first year, for a burnt offering; one kid of the goats for a sin offering; and for a sacrifice of peace offerings, two oxen, five rams, five he goats, five lambs of the first year.

On the seventh day, Elishama, the son of Ammihud, prince of the children of Ephraim, offered:

One silver charger, the weight whereof was an hundred and thirty shekels, one silver bowl of seventy shekels, after the shekel of the sanctuary; both of them full of fine flour mingled with oil for a meat offering; one golden spoon of ten shekels, full of incense; one young bullock, one ram, one lamb of the first year, for a burnt offering; one kid of the goats for a sin offering; and for a sacrifice of peace offerings, two oxen, five rams, five he goats, five lambs of the first year.

On the eighth day, offered Gamaliel, the son of Pedahzur, prince of the children of Manasseh:

One silver charger of the weight of an hundred and thirty shekels, one silver bowl of seventy shekels, after the shekel of the sanctuary; both of them full of fine flour mingled with oil for a meat offering; one golden spoon of ten shekels, full of incense; one young bullock, one ram, one lamb of the first year, for a burnt offering; one kid of the goats for a sin offering; and for a sacrifice of peace offerings, two oxen, five rams, five he goats, five lambs of the first year.

On the ninth day, Abidan, son of Gideoni, prince of the children of Benjamin, offered:

One silver charger, the weight whereof was an hundred and thirty shekels, one silver bowl of seventy shekels, after the shekel of the sanctuary; both of them full of fine flour mingled with oil for a meat offering; one golden spoon of ten shekels, full of incense; one young bullock, one ram, one lamb of the first year, for a burnt offering; one kid of the goats for a sin offering; and for a sacrifice of peace offerings, two oxen, five rams, five he goats, five lambs of the first year.

On the tenth day, Ahiezer, son of Ammishaddai, prince of the children of Dan, offered:

One silver charger, the weight whereof was an hundred and thirty shekels, one silver bowl of seventy shekels, after the shekel of the sanctuary; both of them full of fine flour mingled with oil for a meat offering; one golden spoon of ten shekels, full of incense; one young bullock, one ram, one lamb of the first year, for a burnt offering; one kid of the goats for a sin offering; and for a sacrifice of peace offerings, two oxen, five rams, five he goats, five lambs of the first year.

On the eleventh day Pagiel, the son of Ocran, prince of the children of Asher, offered:

One silver charger, the weight whereof was an hundred and thirty shekels, one silver bowl of seventy shekels, after the shekel of the sanctuary; both of them full of fine flour mingled with oil for a meat offering; one golden spoon of ten shekels, full of incense; one young bullock, one ram, one lamb of the first year, for *a burnt offering; one kid of the goats for a sin offering; and for a sacrifice of peace offerings, two oxen, five rams, five he goats, five lambs of the first year.*

On the twelfth day, Ahira, the son of Enan, prince of the children of Naphtali, offered:

One silver charger, the weight whereof was an hundred and thirty shekels, one silver bowl of seventy shekels, after the shekel of the sanctuary; both of them full of fine flour mingled with oil for a meat offering; one golden spoon of ten shekels, full of incense; one young bullock, one ram, one lamb of the first year, for a burnt offering; one kid of the goats for a sin offering; and for a sacrifice of peace offerings, two oxen, five rams, five he goats, five lambs of the first year.   Numbers 7

The longest chapter in the Bible is Psalm 119. There, the Word is portrayed as a teacher, a comforter, a lamp unto our feet, and a light unto our path. Extolling the power and beauty of the Scriptures, Psalm 119 is worthy of its length.

In contrast, Numbers 7—the second longest chapter in the Bible—redundant and a waste of time at first reading. The Bible is God's instruction manual for how to live. Why, then, does He seemingly waste paragraph after paragraph recording the gifts brought to the temple? Couldn't the Lord have simply said all of the princes gave exactly the same offering and used the leftover space to talk about things that really matter, things like marriage or child-rearing? Why does He list the offerings one at a time?

The author of Hebrews gives us the answer:

For God is not unrighteous to forget your work and labour of love, which ye had shewed toward his name, in that ye have ministered to the saints, and do minister.   Hebrews 6:10

In Numbers 7 and similar passages, God is saying, "I delight in individually listing what each one of these men has done for Me. Although it might be boring to you, it delights Me to record for all eternity the gifts each of My children has given Me. It doesn't bother Me a bit to take space in My Word to record what each man gave. To you, it might seem repetitive and redundant. To me, it's delightful and important. I will not forget."

Consequently, dear brothers and sisters, whatever you give in the Name of the Lord will not be forgotten. Others may not see what you've given or the sacrifices you have made in time and energy. The Lord sees. And He who sees in secret will reward you openly (Matthew 6:4).

If you are giving, loving, and sharing without any recognition, the Lord is delightfully and accurately recording your labor of love in eternity. He will not forget any good work you do—even if it is nothing more than giving a child a cup of cold water (Matthew 10:42). Don't be weary in well doing!

I have a problem with this exhortation, you may be thinking, *because I don't care about rewards in Heaven. I'd rather be rewarded now. I'd rather use my time and energy for my own recreation and pleasure. I don't care about treasures in Heaven. I want treasures now!*

When you see the Lord and He opens the books to determine what rewards He will be able to heap upon you, your heart will leap for joy if He finds your page full of sharing, giving, serving, and teaching. If your page is empty, your heart will break.

"Wait a minute," you say. "I thought there were no tears in heaven."

According to Revelation 7:17, God shall wipe away every tear—which some have suggested to mean that there will be tears in Heaven. If this is the case, I believe those tears will come on the day we stand before our Lord and give an account of all the blessings He heaped upon us, all the abilities He gave to us, all the opportunities He opened before us that we wasted because we grew weary in well-doing.

Think of it this way:

All year long we give financial contributions to this group; we help with that project; we donate to this ministry; we help fill that need—perhaps all the while saying, "Ouch, this hurts." On April fourteenth, it all changes to, "Whew! I'm glad I gave to that one. Oh, boy, I'm glad I shared with this one," as we see how our donations positively impact our tax return.

Right now we might be struggling or growing weary in well-doing. When we get to heaven, however, it's April fourteenth. We'll say, "Wow, Lord, I can't believe the rewards I receive simply because of the little service I did for You. I only wish I would have done more."

Brethren, be not weary in well-doing. Make sure you're investing in eternity with your time, money, abilities, and energy. God remembers, rewards, and delights in everything you do for Him.

LOOKING AT MINISTRY
A Topical Study of
2 Thessalonians 3:13; 1 Timothy 1:12

Flying home from Nampa, Idaho, our small plane was affected by the storms scattered all over the western portion of the country. With the hot dog I had gulped at the airport threatening to reappear, I looked out the window and for a fleeting moment wondered, *Why am I doing this?*

Perhaps as you've ministered, witnessed, or shared the gospel with people and found the way bumpy and brutal at times, you've wondered the same thing.

Following are seven reasons to join Paul in thanking Christ Jesus our Lord for allowing us to minister in His Name.

Looking Around

Over the years, I have come to the conclusion that the people I most respect wholeheartedly serve the Lord. There is solidity to people who have walked with the Lord for years, who speak about the Lord experientially, who have studied the Bible thoroughly.

On their way to the Promised Land, the children of Israel set up camp numerous times on their forty-year pilgrimage. Although the location changed, the layout was always the same: The tabernacle—wherein dwelt the shekinah glory of God—was always set up in the middle of the camp.

Guess who got to camp closest to the tabernacle, closest to the glory. It was those who were involved in service—the Levites (Numbers 2:17).

I have found that to be true even today. Those who are involved in serving the Lord and sharing the Word get to camp closest to the place where His glory is most clearly perceived and enjoyed. There is a richness and depth about them that stand in sharp contrast to the emptiness of the world.

Looking Within

"Give and it shall be given unto you," Jesus said, "good measure, pressed down, shaken together, running over. For with the same measure that you mete, it will be measured to you again" (see Matthew 7:2). In other words, to the degree you give out, you get back. As I look within, I know this to be true.

The same is true for whatever you do for others. When you do something for someone else—whether it's mowing a lawn, writing a check, or baking a cake—you receive as much joy as the recipient. I'm so thankful the Lord has ordained each of us to ministry (John 15:16), because as I look within, I realize how empty our lives would be if we weren't sharing, serving, or giving to others.

Looking Down

When I look down at the tactics of the Enemy, I'm thankful I'm in ministry.

Remember what Amalek did unto thee by the way, when ye were come forth out of Egypt; How he met thee by the way, and smote the hindmost of thee, even all that were feeble behind thee, when thou wast faint and weary; and he feared not God.   Deuteronomy 25:17, 18

On their way to the Promised Land, the enemies of the Israelites picked off those who were lagging behind. The same thing is true of you and me.

The most dangerous place to be in your Christian experience is in the back of the pack. That's where the Enemy attacks. Those who say, "Well, I'll make it to church if it's convenient for me," or, "I'll have devotions if I happen to wake up early," are the folks most prone to get picked off.

"Be sober," Peter says. "Be vigilant because your enemy goes about as a roaring lion, seeking whom he may devour" (see 1 Peter 5:8). He heads for the easy target—the stragglers.

I'm thankful I'm in ministry because I *have* to be here almost every day of the week. When the Lord saved me, He must have said, "You know, Jon, you're a bit flaky. How will I keep you in church? I know—I'll make you a pastor!"

I think the Lord wants every one of us in ministry so we cannot take the option of missing a week or two, a month or three. If you're locked into a Sunday school class, if you're helping with youth work, if you're parking cars or folding bulletins, it's for your own good! It keeps you at the front and protects you from falling prey to Satan.

Looking Back

I remember my Fourth Grade Sunday school teacher, Ernie Friesen. One afternoon, he stopped by my house for no real reason. He reached into the trunk of his car, pulled out a softball and glove and said, "Let's play catch."

There on Flamingo Drive in Campbell, California, we tossed the ball in front of my house for about half an hour. That's all he did. We just played catch for a while before he said, "Gotta go, Jon. Thanks a lot, buddy!" and drove away. For some reason, that simple game of catch really impacted me.

Years later, after I had finished teaching in a large convention in San Jose, a man came up to me with tears in his eyes and said, "Jon Courson, you don't remember me, but I'm so proud of you."

"Ernie Friesen!" I said. "I'm so grateful for *you!*"

As I look back, I have so many memories of people like Ernie who changed my life as they ministered to me. I look back and thank the Lord for godly parents, faithful Sunday school teachers, on-fire youth pastors, and for guys like Duane Davidson. He was a senior in high school who took me out witnessing with him when I was only a lowly freshman. I realize now it's *my* turn to be a father, to work with kids, to be a pastor.

Looking back, I am so grateful for the opportunity to do for others what so many others did for me.

Looking Ahead

As I look ahead to heaven, I'm thankful I'm in ministry. I can join the twenty-four elders and cast my crown at the feet of the One who alone is worthy of it (Revelation 4:10).

Who gave us our abilities? Who gave you the ability to be a mechanic, to have a sense for business, to play the guitar? Every good and perfect gift comes from above (James 1:17). A man can receive nothing except what's given to him from heaven (John 3:27).

Here's the way it works. God gives us abilities, opens the doors for us to use those abilities for Him, anoints us as we serve Him, empowers us as we minister for Him, blesses the fruit of our labor for Him, and then gives *us* a crown. Amazing!

If, as you were about to deposit your life's savings in the bank, the manager whispered to you, "Don't do it. We're shutting our doors tomorrow and claiming all deposits. You'll never get your money out," would you say, "Oh, well, I'll take my chances"? Of course not! Yet the Master says to us, "Put your treasure in heaven. Don't put it on earth. You'll never get it out" (see Luke 12:33). What do we so often say? "Oh, well, I'll take my chances."

Look ahead and be wise, dear saint. Invest your life in things that are eternal, and you'll never regret it.

Looking Out

"Lift up your eyes," Jesus said. "The fields are white with harvest" (John 4:35). As I look out, I see people all around us who are hurting and ready to receive Jesus.

> I read an account of a party at a civic center pool attended by two hundred lifeguards and their friends. They were celebrating the fact that, for the first time in city history, no one had drowned during the entire season in any of the city's lakes or public pools. It was not until almost everyone had gone home that a man was discovered dead at the bottom of the pool. In the midst of two hundred lifeguards enjoying their success, a man had drowned. No one knew it until the party was over.

So, too, as we come together and celebrate our salvation and God's goodness to us, we must also understand that people around us are drowning in sin, depression, confusion, and discouragement.

As wonderful as it would be to be a doctor who helps people physically, or a philanthropist who helps people financially, there's *nothing* like helping people get saved eternally by sharing the good news of the gospel with them.

Precious people, look and see a neighbor or friend, child or relative who is ready for harvest, ready to receive Jesus.

Looking Up

Finally, I'm glad I'm in the ministry when I look up and see Jesus on the Cross, dying for me. "It's the love of Christ," Paul said, "which constrains me" (2 Corinthians 5:14). Jesus' love is why we share with others, why we endure a turbulent plane ride or two, why we continue on in ministry.

Looking within, looking down, looking around, looking ahead are important. None, however, matches looking up at the Cross. Even if there were no heaven, even if people didn't respond, even if I didn't get to experience God's glory, I would still be in ministry because of the love Christ showed me when He rescued me from present disaster; when He snatched me from eternal darkness; when He saved my soul.

NOTE

[1]Elisabeth Elliot. *Through Gates of Splendor.* Tyndale House Publishers, Illinois, 1986.

1 TIMOTHY

Background to 1 & 2 Timothy

Along with Titus, 1 and 2 Timothy are referred to as the Pastoral Epistles because both Timothy and Titus were pastors. In his letters to them, the apostle Paul gives instruction and encouragement, wisdom and insight concerning the ministry. Anyone desiring to serve the Lord in any capacity would do well to study Paul's Pastoral Epistles carefully and to read them regularly.

In his first epistle to Timothy, Paul will deal with the church and its message in chapter 1, the church and its members in chapters 2 and 3, the church and its minister in chapter 4, the church and its ministry to itself in chapter 5, and the church and its ministry to the world in chapter 6.

1 TIMOTHY

1 Timothy 1:1
Paul, an apostle of Jesus Christ by the commandment of God our Saviour, and Lord Jesus Christ, which is our hope.

Paul often referred to himself as "an apostle by the will of God" (1 Corinthians 1:1; 2 Corinthians 1:1; Ephesians 1:1; Colossians 1:1). In this case, however, he says, "It's not just God's will for me, but His command that I am to be an apostle—one who is sent out, one who shares truth.

The things we have been commanded to do can sometimes become wearying when we find ourselves in situations we weren't anticipating—like prison. After all, it was from a Roman prison cell that Paul wrote to Timothy. And in this, I am reminded of another prisoner. . . .

"Oh, Lord, I cannot speak. I am but a child," Jeremiah protested when called to minister.

"Before you were born, I knew you and ordained you to be a prophet," the Lord replied. *"I will put My words on your lips—and you shall go."*

So Jeremiah did. And what happened? He eventually ended up in a dungeon.

"Okay, Lord," he said. *"Yes, You commanded me. Yes, You anointed me. But people aren't responding. No one is getting saved."*

So Jeremiah decided to quit prophesying, to quit sharing—until he realized that the Word of God was like fire in his bones and that he could not keep quiet (Jeremiah 20:9).

Maybe like Jeremiah, or perhaps like Paul, you feel imprisoned and are tempted to throw in the towel and to quit sharing the gospel with people, since none seem to respond. But if you do, the Word of God will burn in your heart as surely as it did in Jeremiah's, and, like Paul, you will realize you have no choice in the matter, for you are under the command of God.

1 Timothy 1:2 (a)
Unto Timothy, my own son in the faith.

Piecing the puzzle together, it seems that during his first missionary journey, Paul stayed in the home of Lois and Eunice, the mother and grandmother of Timothy. And it could very well be that at that time, Paul led a teen aged Timothy into a saving knowledge of Jesus Christ.

1 Timothy 1:2 (b)
Grace, mercy, and peace, from God our Father and Jesus Christ our Lord.

With few exceptions, Paul begins his letters pronouncing grace and peace upon his readers. But when he writes to Timothy and to Titus—another young man in the faith—he adds the word "mercy." Why? As parents, we know our sons are in need of great mercy! And evidently Paul knew the same thing about Timothy, his son in the faith.

1 Timothy 1:3, 4
As I besought thee to abide still at Ephesus, when I went into Macedonia, that thou mightest charge some that they teach no other doctrine, neither give heed to fables and endless genealogies, which minister questions, rather than godly edifying which is in faith: so do.

In verses 4 through 19, Paul will address four areas relating to doctrine: the loss of truth, the law of God, the love of Christ, and the life of faith. Here, we see the loss of truth. Leaving Timothy to continue the work in Ephesus while he traveled on to Macedonia, Paul's initial instruction to Timothy was to charge the Ephesian believers not to get caught up in any doctrine other than the simplicity of the gospel of Jesus Christ.

As we learn the Word and share with others, there is a danger of trying to find something in Scripture no one else has ever seen before. That's what some in Ephesus were doing as they looked into Old Testament genealogies, discussed the stories endlessly, and veered off into all sorts of vain speculations. In so doing, they missed out on solid teaching. To those who desire to be Bible teachers, I give this piece of advice: Give up trying to be creative and innovative. Instead, stick with the simple, powerful truth of the gospel—and you'll never go wrong.

1 Timothy 1:5
Now the end of the commandment is charity out of a pure heart, and of a good conscience, and of faith unfeigned.

After talking about the loss of truth, Paul speaks of the law of God—fulfilled simply and fully in love and faith.

1 Timothy 1:6, 7
From which some having swerved have turned aside unto vain jangling; desiring to be teachers of the law; understanding neither what they say, nor whereof they affirm.

"Let not many of you desire to be teachers," James declares, knowing that we who are teachers shall have the greater condemnation (see James 3:1). If God calls you to teach, that's terrific. But it shouldn't be a driving desire in any man or woman because with greater responsibility comes greater potential for condemnation should a teacher swerve from the simplicity of the Word.

1 Timothy 1:8
But we know that the law is good, if a man use it lawfully.

The law definitely has its place—not to lead people off on tangents, but to bring them to Jesus (Galatians 3:24).

1 Timothy 1:9–11
Knowing this, that the law is not made for a righteous man, but for the lawless and disobedient, for the ungodly and for sinners, for unholy and profane, for murderers of fathers and murderers of mothers, for manslayers, for whoremongers, for them that defile themselves with mankind, for menstealers, for liars, for perjured persons, and if there be any other thing that is contrary to sound doctrine; according to the glorious gospel of the blessed God, which was committed to my trust.

The law has one primary purpose: It's a schoolmaster to show us our need for a Savior and to drive us to Jesus Christ (Galatians 3:24). You see, contrary to the popular psychology of the day, I'm *not* okay—and neither are you! We're sinners in need of a Savior. Once, however, we come to that understanding, we are no longer under the demands of the law.

Sometimes people say to me, "Hey, you're laying the law down!"

"You're right!" I answer. "If you were walking righteously, I wouldn't need to. If you were loving the Lord and enjoying Him, there would be no need for the law. But not all are righteous. Not everyone wants to walk in the Spirit. Consequently, I have no other choice but to lay down the law."

As seen in the passage before us, any culture

or person involved in sin needs the law for its own welfare—for without it, sin runs unchecked.

1 Timothy 1:12–14
And I thank Christ Jesus our Lord, who hath enabled me, for that he counted me faithful, putting me into the ministry; who was before a blasphemer, and a persecutor, and injurious: but I obtained mercy, because I did it ignorantly in unbelief. And the grace of our Lord was exceeding abundant with faith and love which is in Christ Jesus.

Here, Paul speaks of the love of Christ. "I was sincere when I was persecuting Christians, dragging them out of their houses to incarcerate them," said Paul. "I was sincere—but I was sincerely wrong." Paul's admission sobers me greatly because the possibility exists that you and I can do wrong, all the while convinced we're doing right. What if we're wrong? Then God will do to us what He did to Paul: He'll knock us down and set us straight (Acts 9:4).

1 Timothy 1:15
This is a faithful saying, and worthy of all acceptation, that Christ Jesus came into the world to save sinners; of whom I am chief.

The closer Paul drew to the Lord, the more he understood the extent of his sin. But the Good News is that sinners are the very people Jesus came to seek and to save. Ever the Good Shepherd, Jesus specializes in finding the one in the back row, on the fringe, out to lunch, off the wall. This gives me great comfort and real hope. I must accept acceptance courageously. I must accept grace graciously. Jesus Christ came to save guys like me—and to keep saving me daily!

For topical study of 1 Timothy 1:15 entitled "The Chiefest of Sinners," turn to page 1372.

1 Timothy 1:16
Howbeit for this cause I obtained mercy, that in me first Jesus Christ might shew forth all longsuffering, for a pattern to them which should hereafter believe on him to life everlasting.

"If God saved Paul, He can save *anyone!*" said people of the man who had previously persecuted believers. That's why the Lord saved *you*, by the way—as a pattern, as an example, so that people can look at you and say, "If he's a Christian, I guess anybody can be one! If she can serve the Lord, I guess I can, too."

1 Timothy 1:17
Now unto the King eternal, immortal, invisible, the only wise God, be honour and glory for ever and ever. Amen.

Reflecting on the grace of God in turning him from a blasphemer into a believer, Paul has no other recourse but to burst forth in praise.

1 Timothy 1:18, 19 (a)
This charge I commit unto thee, son Timothy, according to the prophecies which went before on thee, that thou by them mightest war a good warfare; holding faith . . .

Finally, we see the life of faith. Words of prophecy are words of edification and exhortation, instruction and direction (1 Corinthians 14:3). "You heard such words," Paul reminded Timothy. "Now hold on to them, for they are vital in spiritual battle."

1 Timothy 1:19 (b)
. . . and a good conscience . . .

Some say the key to a good conscience is a bad memory. In reality, however, the key to a good conscience is understanding and embracing what Christ did on the Cross of Calvary.

1 Timothy 1:19 (c)
. . . which some having put away concerning faith have made shipwreck.

The loss of truth, the law of God, the love of Christ, the life of faith are four areas in which Timothy was schooled by Paul at the very outset of Paul's letter to him.

1 Timothy 1:20
Of whom is Hymenaeus and Alexander; whom I have delivered unto Satan, that they may learn not to blaspheme.

We don't know for sure what Hymenaeus and Alexander did, but Paul prayed that the Lord would remove His protective hedge from them, thereby exposing them to the Enemy. Why? His hope was that they would get burned out on their evil ways by getting a taste of the fires of hell. Paul's purpose was not punitive. It was restorative—that Hymenaeus and Alexander might be brought back to wholeness.

THE CHIEF OF SINNERS
A Topical Study of
1 Timothy 1:15

The book, *I'm OK, You're OK,* was written in 1967. Yet, it appeared on the *New York Times* bestseller list for two decades. Amazing. After twenty years, the book that is the prototype for the self-esteem movement was still selling like hotcakes.

Yet what does the Bible say? Scriptures declare we are sinners and that all we like sheep have gone astray (Isaiah 53:6), that there is none righteous no not one (Romans 3:10), that there is poison under our lips, blood on our hands, and our feet are swift to walk where they ought not to walk (Proverbs 6:17, 18). In other words, the diagnosis of the One who created us is that we are anything *but* okay!

No one understood this better than Paul. At the outset of his ministry, he declared himself to be the least of the apostles (1 Corinthians 15:9). Later on, he saw himself as less than the least of all saints (Ephesians 3:8). And here in our text, toward the end of his life, what does he say? Not, "I once was the chief of sinners," not, "I used to be the chief of sinners," but, "I *am* the chief of sinners."

Paul went from being the least of the apostles, to the least of all the saints, to the chief of sinners. How can this be? Did Paul become a worse and worse person the longer he walked with God? Did he sin more and more hideously, more and more frequently? No. Paul simply discovered that the closer he drew *to* the Lord, the more intimate he became *with* the Lord, the more he realized how far he was from the holiness *of* the Lord.

> When I play hoops with a first-grader, I am awesome. My hook shots, rebounds, and lay-ups are incredible—when I play against a first-grader. But if I went one on one with Shaquille O'Neal on the same court with the same ball, I would be the "chief of losers"! Why? Not because I had changed, but because my standard of excellence had changed.

If we compare ourselves with neighbors, friends, or even brothers and sisters in the congregation, we don't look too bad. But when we go one on one with Jesus Christ, as we draw closer to Him and spend more time with Him, we can't help but notice a huge difference between ourselves and the One we love.

> "Woe unto you, woe unto you, woe unto you," Isaiah proclaimed to the people of Israel and the surrounding communities (see Isaiah 1—5). But then in chap-

ter 6, we read, "In the year King Uzziah died, I saw the Lord high and lifted up. And I cried Woe is *me!*" In seeing the Lord, Isaiah also saw his own sin.

So, too, the longer I walk with Jesus, the clearer I see my own sin and inconsistencies. And this does several things for me . . .

Amazed by Him

The more I'm aware of my sin, the more I'm amazed by this One who came to save sinners.

The first time I saw the New York City skyline from an airplane, I wasn't as impressed as I thought I would be. But when I got off the plane, into a car, drove to Wall Street, and looked up, up, up at the buildings surrounding me, I was amazed because the closer I got to the buildings, the bigger they looked.

The same thing happens when I get close to Jesus. I just look at Him and say, "Wow, Lord, I'm amazed that in Your holiness and beauty and purity You would put up with a guy like *me!*"

Thankful for Him

The story is told of a rooster who arose early every morning of his life to crow. And every morning shortly thereafter, the sun would rise. As the months and years went by, the animals of the barnyard said, "Thank you for bringing the sun up every day. We're not worthy."

But one day, not feeling well, the rooster overslept. Yet the sun came up anyway.

"You fraud!" the animals said to the sleepy rooster. "You weren't even out here today. Yet the sun came up anyway."

Although at first, the rooster was embarrassed and depressed, he was eventually relieved when he realized that, because he didn't bring the sun up, the world didn't depend on him.

So, too, there comes a point in a believer's life when he realizes his Christian walk isn't dependent upon him, but solely upon Jesus. Happy is the day when he truly understands that his relationship with the Father has nothing to do with his attempts at being a spiritual rooster bringing the sun up. Instead, it has everything to do with admitting he would be in the dark were it not for the Son shining upon him all the days of his life.

Such a one joins the choir of those who say, "Alleluia; Salvation, and glory, and honour, and power" (Revelation 19:1). Why "Hallelujah"? Because *halal* speaks of "praise" and *Yahh* speaks of "God." Therefore, it's not "Hallelu-me" or

"Hallelu-you" but "Hallelu-*jah*" for it is God alone who saved and continues to save us from our sin, from our stupidity, from ourselves.

In Love with Him

If this Man is truly a prophet, He would know what kind of woman is washing His feet with her tears and wiping them with her hair, thought Simon.

"Simon," said Jesus, "let Me ask you a question: Two men are in debt to a third man. One owes fifty million dollars, the other fifty dollars. If their creditor erases both their debts, which will love him more?"

"The one forgiven millions," Simon answered.

"Right," said Jesus. "The one who is forgiven much loves much. You sit here at this table, robed in your Pharisaical spirituality. Yet this woman, a prostitute, is the one who washed My feet. Clearly, the one forgiven much loves much" (see Luke 7:47).

The person who is unaware of his sin and who thinks he's pretty good has, at best, a limited love for the Lord. But the one who is truly aware of that which goes on in his heart, of that which comes from his lips, and of that which runs through his mind says, "I love You, Lord, because I've been forgiven so much."

Pleasing to Him

The more clearly I see my sin, the more I desire to please Jesus. Paul tells us we are not to be those who grieve the Spirit (Ephesians 4:30). When I sin, it grieves the Spirit not because He's mad at me or disappointed in me, but because He knows how sin will hurt me.

When your kids make decisions you know are not wise, you don't turn your back on them—yet you know a painful process lies ahead of them. Such is the heart of our heavenly Father. And this causes me to say, "I want to walk with You, Lord. I want to do what You say because I know Your way is best."

Comfortable Around Him

According to our text, Jesus Christ came to save sinners. This makes me eminently qualified to be found by Him and to hang around Him. In His own mission statement, Jesus said He didn't come to find the self-righteous person, the one who thinks he has it all together. He came specifically for those who realize that they're sinners, that they're full of problems, that they're lost.

Jesus talked at length about the lost sheep, the lost coin, and the lost son (Luke 15) because it is His delight to find that which is lost. Let Him do what He came to do. Let Him do what He wants to do. Let Him find *you*.

Someone came to me once, brokenhearted about a serious sin in which he had been involved. "I want you to know that because Jesus Christ died on the

Cross, because the price has been paid for your sin, you are totally, completely, wonderfully cleansed," I said.

And when I was through with that conversation, the Lord whispered these words in my ear: "You believe that, don't you, Jon?"

"Yes, Lord, I do," I answered.

"Good," He said, "because it's true. But will you accept it for yourself?"

You see, it is far easier for me to tell someone else, "You're forgiven. The price is paid. You're free," than it is to accept it for myself. Yet Paul said, "Jesus came to the world to save sinners. This is a faithful saying and worthy of *all* acceptation." *Everyone* needs to accept it—including the preacher!

Will you embrace that which you share with others? It's not only for you to witness to the unbeliever, or to share with the hurting person. It's worthy of all acceptation. Will you accept it for yourself? So you missed devotions yesterday, for the last three days, or for the last three months. So you've been grumpy. Whatever your sin—be it big or small, subtle or obvious—I have good news for you: Your sin is forgiven!

Allow Jesus to forgive you of much—and then watch and see how *much* you'll love Him.

2 Having discussed doctrine in chapter 1, Paul moves on to discuss devotion in chapter 2. . . .

1 Timothy 2:1
I exhort therefore, that, first of all, supplications, prayers, intercessions, and giving of thanks, be made for all men.

First and foremost, we are to be a people who pray. The words "supplications," "intercessions," and "giving of thanks" refer to the various forms of prayer that we are to offer for all men.

1 Timothy 2:2 (a)
For kings, and for all that are in authority . . .

We are to pray for kings and even for presidents because they are in positions of authority only by the predetermined counsel of God.

No wonder he decreed that all the world should be taxed (Luke 2:1). He was, after all, Caesar Augustus—Caesar, the "august one," Caesar, "the highest." But wait a minute. While Caesar Augustus was breaking campaign promises and raising taxes, what was really going on? Carrying the Messiah in her womb, Mary resided in Nazareth. Yet hundreds of years

previously, the prophet Micah had declared that Messiah would be born in Bethlehem (Micah 5:2). Therefore, Mary and Joseph set out on the difficult and dangerous journey from Nazareth in the north to Bethlehem in the south not in response to an edict from Caesar, the "august one"—but in obedience to God, the Almighty One.

What if we looked at politics today believing that it is God who is truly on the throne? Wouldn't that be a radical concept for Christians? Yes, we have a responsibility to pray and to make supplications. But we are also to give thanks for all men no matter what side of the political spectrum they represent, for all rulers are used by God to fulfill prophecy and to accomplish His will ultimately.

1 Timothy 2:2 (b)
. . . that we may lead a quiet and peaceable life in all godliness and honesty.

I've noticed that those who are radically involved in the Christian political scene are rarely quiet or peaceful. On the contrary, there seems to be an anger about them. And sometimes I wonder if this is really what the Lord intends for us. How much better it would be, in my opinion, if we would do less talking and more praying concerning political matters.

In Jeremiah 29, we see the Lord saying to His people, "You're going to be held captive here in Babylon for seventy years. So go ahead and allow your kids to marry, build houses, plant gardens, and pray for the peace of Babylon. While you're here, make it better if you can. But don't get too rooted, because you're only here for seventy years."

So, too, we are only here in this Babylon called earth for seventy years or so. We're to pray, plant gardens, and leave it in a better condition than we found it—be that environmentally, politically, economically, or sociologically. Therefore, I do think it's important to vote and participate in the system, to be knowledgeable and wise. But in so doing, we must never forget that one day soon, this whole world is going to be folded up (Hebrews 1:12). Therefore, we need not take it too seriously.

1 Timothy 2:3, 4
For this is good and acceptable in the sight of God our Saviour; Who will have all men to be saved, and to come unto the knowledge of the truth.

After Paul tells us we should be talking to God about men—praying for people and leaders and politicians—he says we also have the responsibility to talk to men about God and to share with them the truth of the gospel.

1 Timothy 2:5
For there is one God, and one mediator between God and men, the man Christ Jesus.

When everything was going wrong and everything was coming down, Job said, "I wish there was a Daysman—an umpire, a mediator—between God and me" (see Job 9:33). And now Paul comes on the scene, using the same terminology, saying, "There is. There's a Mediator, a Bridge between infinite God and finite man because God Himself became a Man in Christ Jesus."

We are to follow the example of Jesus, who was willing to come and be the Daysman, the Mediator, the Savior between a holy God and sinful men. We're not to be fault-finders, political anarchists, people who are angry, or those who are bitter. We're to pray with thanksgiving and supplication and to follow the example of our Savior in the ministry of mediation.

1 Timothy 2:6
Who gave himself a ransom for all, to be testified in due time.

Although people repeatedly and flippantly call on God to damn others, nothing could be further from His heart. Because He desires that none should perish (2 Peter 3:9), He gave Himself a ransom for all.

1 Timothy 2:7
Whereunto I am ordained a preacher, and an apostle, (I speak the truth in Christ, and lie not;) a teacher of the Gentiles in faith and verity.

"I truly have been called to share with people and to pray for people," says Paul. And so have you.

1 Timothy 2:8
I will therefore that men pray every where, lifting up holy hands, without wrath and doubting.

Paul doesn't say, "I want men to clench fists and sign petitions." He says, "I want men to lift hands and pray."

I find it interesting that when the Bible talks about prayer, we see men raising their hands, lying prostrate on their faces, lifting up their eyes, and standing. What we never see throughout Scripture concerning prayer is someone folding his hands and closing his eyes. Yet that is precisely how we teach our kids to pray! I know why we do this. All parents do. Closed eyes and folded hands keep kids out of trouble! But now that we are adults, let's realize that there's great liberty in prayer. I often find myself prostrate before the Lord in times of intensity of prayer or worship. I also love to walk as I pray. I would encourage you to explore different postures of prayer—all the while remembering that it's not the position of the body that matters, but the position of the heart.

1 Timothy 2:9, 10
In like manner also, that women adorn themselves in modest apparel, with shamefacedness and sobriety; not with broided hair, or gold, or pearls, or costly array; but (which becometh women professing godliness) with good works.

"Shamefacedness" refers to blushing. Although we live in a culture that no longer blushes, the godly woman is one who is embarrassed by immodesty.

1 Timothy 2:11, 12
Let the woman learn in silence with all sub-
jection. But I suffer not a woman to teach,
nor to usurp authority over the man, but to
be in silence.

In the Book of Titus, Paul instructs older
women to teach younger women how to walk in
practical godliness. However, they are not to
teach men in matters of doctrine or theology, but
are to learn in silence. You might think this
sounds terribly chauvinistic. But Paul goes on to
give his reason. . . .

1 Timothy 2:13, 14
For Adam was first formed, then Eve. And
Adam was not deceived, but the woman be-
ing deceived was in the transgression.

"Eat of the tree of the knowledge of good and
evil, and your eyes will be opened. You'll be like
God," Satan promised Eve (see Genesis 3:5).
Thus, Eve was deceived not by a desire to do
something illicit, but by a desire to be godly.
I firmly believe women have an innate desire
to be spiritual. They want to extract all they can
from Scripture. They want to know what it really
means to worship. They want their eyes to be
opened, to know how to be lovers of God. Satan
took advantage of this, and the woman was
thereby deceived. Therefore, it is men who are to
instruct the church in doctrine.
What are the women to do?
Paul goes on. . . .

1 Timothy 2:15
Notwithstanding she shall be saved in child-
bearing, if they continue in faith and char-
ity and holiness with sobriety.

The Greek word *sozo,* or "saved," meaning
"the full orb of God's blessing"—that women will
be "saved in childbearing"—does not refer only
to the fact that they won't die bearing children,
but that they will experience the full orb of God's
blessing in raising children. Although there are
exceptions, although there are women who are
uniquely called to separate themselves for service to the Lord, the rule of thumb for the church
is that women are to pour themselves into their
kids, for there they will find their greatest
blessing.
If a woman must work, she should carefully
make her job selection in such a way that her job
does not in any way pull her emotions or her energy away from her family. You see, Moms, by the
time people come to me as a pastor, they've usually been beaten up by life. Moms, on the other

hand, have the opportunity to love and shape
fresh, new lives that haven't been messed up by
the world. This is not a popular position. But look
at our culture. We're paying the price for turning
away from these very simple and basic premises.
Everyone is trying to figure out why our kids
have gone so awry. But God has already told us:
Men should lead the church. Women should lead
the kids.
So, too, as the bride of Christ, where will I also
be saved? Where will I most fully experience
God's blessing? In child-bearing. There is no joy
like that of seeing someone born again. That's
why Jesus said when one sinner comes into the
kingdom, there's a party in heaven (Luke 15:10).
Has it been a while since you shared the Lord
with someone? If you haven't led someone to
Jesus, you're missing out, for all of us will discover that the full orb of salvation is, indeed,
found in seeing other folks born again.

───────── ✎ ─────────

3 In chapter 3, the apostle Paul talks to Pastor
Timothy about those involved in church
leadership. . . .

1 Timothy 3:1 (a)
This is a true saying, If a man desire the
office of a bishop . . .

Because the words "bishop," "pastor," and "elder" are used interchangeably throughout the
New Testament, Paul's instructions concerning
bishops apply to anyone who wants to be used by
the Lord.

1 Timothy 3:1 (b)
. . . he desireth a good work.

If a man desires to be involved in a greater degree of ministry, he desires a good work—not a
good position, not a good salary, not a good retirement plan, but a good *work.* The ministry is not a
profession one enters into, saying, "These are my
office hours. These are my off hours. My phone
number is unlisted." Ministry is a good work indeed—but it's work.

1 Timothy 3:2 (a)
A bishop then must be blameless . . .

If "blameless" meant "flawless," we'd all be
disqualified from ministry at Step One! Fortunately, the idea of blamelessness implies a heart
that says, "Lord, I know I'm not perfect. But
there's nothing in my life I'm clinging to or holding on to which I know is contrary to You."

1 Timothy 3:2 (b)
... the husband of one wife ...

The Greek culture, a powerful influence on society in Paul's day, held that every man should have three women in his life: a mistress for conversation, a concubine for pleasure, and a wife to bear his children. "Tilt!" says Paul. "Those in the ministry must be one-woman men."

There are those who, on the basis of this verse, say that a bishop, pastor, or elder must be married. But the ultimate minister was Jesus of Nazareth. And He was single. Therefore, this verse doesn't mandate marriage. It does, however, mandate complete faithfulness for those who are married.

1 Timothy 3:2 (c)
... vigilant ...

"Watch and pray," Jesus said to His disciples (Matthew 26:41). Sadly, it seems increasingly difficult to motivate men in the ministry to be men of vigilant prayer. This ought not be.

1 Timothy 3:2 (d), 3 (a)
... sober, of good behaviour, given to hospitality, apt to teach; not given to wine ...

If you hold the position of elder, bishop, or pastor, you are not to drink anything intoxicating. Ever. Why? "It is not for kings, O Lemuel, to drink wine or princes to drink strong drink lest they forget the law and pervert the judgment" (see Proverbs 31:4, 5). We forget the Word easy enough when we're sober, gang. Therefore, we can't afford to have leaders who are less than sober. I feel very strongly about this because I believe the times are influencing the ministry rather than the other way around.

1 Timothy 3:3 (b)
... no striker, not greedy of filthy lucre; but patient ...

A man in Seattle was known for his punctuality. One morning, however, he slept a little too long. Realizing his mistake, he ran out to his car, raced across town, and made it to the dock just in time to see the ferry he usually rode to work pulling away from the pier. Slamming his car into park, he grabbed his briefcase, and jumped over the railing, narrowly landing on the deck of the ferry.

"What a jump!" said the captain. "I've never seen such an effort! But if you would have waited another minute, we would have been at the dock."

Like this man, patience is hard for me. I jump off in one direction and crash down in another—only to discover that had I waited another minute or two, everything would have gone a lot more smoothly.

1 Timothy 3:3 (c)
... not a brawler ...

Those in the ministry are easy targets for people who have an axe to grind because they think if they can pull a minister down, they will feel better about their own sin. Yet although the tendency is to want to strike back, we must follow the example of Jesus Christ who, even on the Cross, said, "Father forgive them. They don't know what they're doing."

1 Timothy 3:3 (d)–5
... not covetous; One that ruleth well his own house, having his children in subjection with all gravity; (For if a man know not how to rule his own house, how shall he take care of the church of God?)

"Your mother and Your brothers want to see You," they said to Jesus in the midst of His teaching.

"Who is My mother? Who are My brethren?" He answered. "Are not these who hear the Word of God, are not they My mother and My brothers?" (see Matthew 12:48–50)

Jesus' disciples were His family. Conversely, your family members are your disciples. The validation of your ministry will not be the size of your church or the degrees after your name. According to Paul's charge to Timothy, the validity of ministry lies in the family. If a man cannot rule, lead, or direct his home in spiritual matters, then he shouldn't try to oversee the church. Such a stand is not legalism—it's wisdom.

1 Timothy 3:6
Not a novice, lest being lifted up with pride he fall into the condemnation of the devil.

Why was the devil—Lucifer—initially condemned? Because of pride (Isaiah 14:12–15). Thus, Paul warns Timothy not to place a novice in a position of leadership because novices tend to think that if anything good happens through them it's because they're a skilled speaker or a clever person. Only someone who has walked with the Lord awhile understands that if anything good happens through him it's not *because* of him, but rather *in spite* of him!

1 Timothy 3:7
**Moreover he must have a good report of
them which are without; lest he fall into
reproach and the snare of the devil.**

I think it's a tragedy when Christians are
known as terrible credit risks, and pastors are
known as the worst. This doesn't mean good pastors won't have critics. It does mean, however,
they won't provide reasons for their critics to find
fault with them.

1 Timothy 3:8 (a)
Likewise must the deacons . . .

Deacons are those involved not so much in
overseeing, teaching, or pastoring—but in practical service, in tending physical needs like waiting
on tables (Acts 6).

1 Timothy 3:8 (b)
. . . be grave, not doubletongued . . .

A deacon with a double tongue is dangerous
because anyone involved in spiritual leadership
who can't control his tongue will say things that
distract people from Jesus Christ.

1 Timothy 3:8 (c)
. . . not given to much wine . . .

Because judgment is not as greatly needed in
the ministry of a deacon as it is in that of a pastor
or elder, wine is not forbidden for a deacon—although in our culture, I personally think the wisest choice is always to stay away from
intoxicants.

1 Timothy 3:8 (d)
. . . not greedy of filthy lucre.

If you're involved in the physical needs of the
fellowship—whether it be waiting on tables or
tending to business matters—you cannot be one
who has sticky fingers.

1 Timothy 3:9, 10
**Holding the mystery of the faith in a pure
conscience. And let these also first be
proved; then let them use the office of a
deacon, being found blameless.**

Those who volunteer to help the body in any
way they can—be it teaching Sunday school, watering plants, or parking cars—prove themselves
as those who are potential deacons or pastors.

1 Timothy 3:11
**Even so must their wives be grave, not slan-
derers, sober, faithful in all things.**

Because the words "must their" are in italics
and therefore not in the original text, because the
phrase translated "even so" is *hosautos* in
Greek—a word always used to start a new list,
and because the word "wives" is *gune*, which simply means "woman," I believe this verse could refer to deaconesses—women who serve the
practical needs of the church.

1 Timothy 3:12, 13
**Let the deacons be the husbands of one wife,
ruling their children and their own houses
well. For they that have used the office of a
deacon well purchase to themselves a good
degree, and great boldness in the faith
which is in Christ Jesus.**

"If you use the office of a deacon well, you purchase boldness," says Paul. He's right—Stephen,
the first martyr, was a deacon. And Philip, the
first evangelist, was a deacon. These guys were
dynamic. They were bold. And they began simply
by serving tables (Acts 6).

1 Timothy 3:14, 15
**These things write I unto thee, hoping to
come unto thee shortly: But if I tarry long,
that thou mayest know how thou oughtest
to behave thyself in the house of God, which
is the church of the living God, the pillar
and ground of the truth.**

In a debate with Dennis Praeger, a believer,
atheist Oxford University professor Jonathan Glover, said, "It doesn't really matter
whether a person has a belief system that is
biblical or godly. The important thing is that
they believe in something."
    Praeger replied, "Imagine, Professor
Glover, that you're in downtown Los
Angeles. It's two o'clock in the morning. Your
car breaks down. You get out. You hear footsteps. You turn around to see ten big young
men walking toward you. Would it make a
difference if you knew they had just come
from a Bible study?"

It *does* matter what people believe! And praise
be to the Lord that we are a part of the church of
the living God, the pillar and ground of truth.

1 Timothy 3:16 (a)
**And without controversy great is the mys-
tery of godliness.**

At this point, your spirits might be sagging as you think, *Oh, my, as I go through this list, I realize I'm so far off from where I should be.* But then we read of the mystery of godliness. . . .

1 Timothy 3:16 (b)
God was manifest in the flesh, justified in the Spirit, seen of angels, preached unto the

Gentiles, believed on in the world, received up into glory.

Every other philosophy and religion tells people how to live and can only say, "Good luck." But great is the mystery that God came, dwelt *among* us, died *for* us, and sent His Spirit to live *within* us.

THE MYSTERY OF GODLINESS
A Topical Study of
1 Timothy 3:1–7, 16

S ometimes life can seem almost overwhelming. Perhaps Timothy felt that way when he received instructions from the apostle Paul concerning those who were qualified to be involved in ministry, for who could ever qualify? Who could say, "I am vigilant in prayer, patient, hospitable, and blameless. And so are my kids. Yes, these qualifications fit me to a T'"?

In reality, we say, "Oh, I see the validity of the list before me, but I could never qualify because of the sins and mistakes I carry with me."

As I arrived at the Medford Airport one morning years ago, to my good fortune, I bumped into my mom and daughter, who were waiting to board a plane to the Mission at Carmen Serdan, Mexico. So we decided to have breakfast together. As we talked, a baggage cart being pulled by a tractor caught Mary's eye.

"I bet our bags are right there on that little cart," my mom said to her.

"Wow!" gasped Mary. "That guy's going to drive all the way to Mexico?!"

That's a lot like me! "My, oh, my," I say, "the journey to godliness is so far, and my baggage is so great. I'll never get there just putt-putt-putting along the road."

But the text before us reminds me that there's a better way than just plodding away through item after item—trying to be blameless, trying to get my house in order, trying not to brawl, trying to fulfill the requirements that would make it an arduous journey at best. Paul calls it the mystery of godliness and talks about it not as it relates to a procedure, a process, or a program. He talks about godliness as it relates to a Person.

Paul could have given us fifteen guidelines to godliness, or twenty hints about holiness. Instead, he just starts talking about Jesus. . . .

And without controversy great is the mystery of godliness: God was manifest in the flesh . . .

God became a Man when Jesus Christ was born in Bethlehem, when the Word became flesh and dwelt among us. Therefore, concerning an answer to any question I have about the way life should be lived, I don't have to wait for inner revelation or sign up for a seminar to get instruction. All I have to do is look at Emmanuel, God With Us, Jesus. Too many people are looking for a manual on how to raise kids, how to be a better husband, how to live successfully. Forget the manuals. We have Emmanuel.

. . . Justified in the Spirit . . .

Jesus was justified in the Spirit when, following His baptism in the Jordan River, the Holy Spirit came upon Him in the form of a dove (Matthew 3:16). When He was thus empowered for service, His public ministry began and miracles followed. The same holds true for you. Just as anything you want to know about godliness can be seen in the Person of Jesus Christ, whatever you accomplish in ministry will be done solely through the power of the Holy Spirit.

. . . Seen of Angels . . .

Following His baptism, Jesus was led to the wilderness, where He was tempted by Satan with the same temptations that bug, plague, and hassle you. At the end of forty days, Jesus was victorious and was ministered to by angels (Matthew 4:11). When a bright light shines in your eyes, you instinctively shield your face. Can you imagine the brightness of He who is light? Thus, it is highly possible that angels never saw God before the Incarnation. Only when He became a Man could they look at Him. And so can we.

. . . Preached unto the Gentiles . . .

Jesus marveled at the faith of only two people. Both were Gentiles. . . .

"You don't even need to come to my house," said the Roman centurion to Jesus. "Just speak the word and my servant will be healed long distance" (see Matthew 8:8).
    "Lord, help me," said the Syro-Phoenician woman on behalf of her demon-possessed daughter (see Matthew 15:25).

At a time when Gentiles were considered by Jews to be nothing more than fuel for the fires of hell, Jesus not only talked to Gentiles, but commended them uniquely. So, too, you might feel like the least likely candidate to deserve a word from Jesus. Take heart! He marvels at the faith of people like you!

. . . Believed on in the World . . .

"Truly this was the Son of God," the centurion proclaimed as He saw Jesus on the Cross (Matthew 27:54). Believed on by the centurion who stood below Him and by the thief who hung beside Him, Jesus was further believed on by the hundreds who were eyewitnesses of His resurrection.

. . . Received Up into Glory . . .

Jesus is in heaven where He lives to make intercession for you and me (Hebrews 7:25). In other words, Jesus went to heaven where He's talking to the Father nonstop about *you.*

> "Peter, Satan desires to sift you like wheat, but I have prayed for you," Jesus said. "Therefore, when you are converted—not *if* you are converted, but *when* you are converted—strengthen the brothers" (see Luke 22:32). In other words, "You're going to make it, Peter, because I'm praying for you."

I have great news for you as well: All those of you who know Jesus are going to make it. You're going to be godly because Jesus is praying for you—and His prayers are always heard and heeded by the Father.

> If we could understand baby talk, we would know what babies fuss about. We might hear one say, "You know I'm just never going to get this walking thing down. All I do is stumble around, fall down, and land on my bottom."
>
> And maybe another says, "I don't think I'll *ever* figure out how to eat with a spoon. . . ."
>
> Yet, as adults, if we could understand them and they us, we'd say, "It's all going to work out, kids. You're going to walk, you'll see. You'll get that spoon thing down. It *will* work!"

And that's what the Lord would say to you. Great is this mystery of godliness. Jesus has walked where you walk. He knows what you're going through, and now He's at the right hand of the Father, praying for you.

Not only does Jesus pray for you, but He lives in you. "It's expedient I go away," He said, "for if I go away, I will send you another Comforter" (see John 14:16). Not only is Jesus praying for us, but by His Spirit, He lives in us.

> Your co-workers are telling a dirty joke. An opportunity is before you to cheat on your income tax. Your friends are gossiping and expect you to join in. But there is a voice in your ear saying, "Don't do it. It will hurt you." *That's* the voice of God within you.

The mystery of godliness is so simple. It's not a matter of working hard on the list in 1 Timothy 3. It's a matter of saying, "Lord, whatever You say, that's what I'll do." Finally, not only is Jesus praying for us and living within us, He's coming to get us. "Let not your heart be troubled," He said, "I go to prepare a place for you" (see John 14:1, 2).

It was time for my mom and daughter to check in for their flight.
"Which one of you is Mary Courson?" asked the attendant.
They both raised their hands.
"Which one of you is Mary *Elizabeth* Courson?" she asked again.
They both raised their hands.
"Which one of you is Mary Elizabeth Courson related to Jon Courson?"
Two hands went up.

When Jesus comes back, all those who opened their hearts to Him will go with Him. Like Mary, compared to another, you might feel your faith is too small or too young—but we're *all* going because we all bear Jesus' Name. It's a *fabulous* hope!

Dear saint, please understand that we don't have to drive our baggage all the way to Mexico—or to heaven. Because Jesus became a Man who walked in our steps, died in our place, and lives in our hearts, we can soar to the heavenlies in Him. And *that* is the great and glorious mystery of godliness.

4 After talking about the church and her message in chapter 1, and the church and her members in chapters 2—3, here in chapter 4, Paul will talk about the church and her ministry. And in so doing, he will exhort young Timothy to be a good minister in verses 1–6, a godly minister in verses 7–11, and a growing minister in verses 12–16.

1 Timothy 4:1 (a)
Now the Spirit speaketh expressly, that in the latter times some shall depart from the faith . . .

The same is true in our times. There are those who falsely teach that it is impossible to depart from the faith. But our text says otherwise. While I do not believe that one can lose his salvation (John 10:29), I do believe one can leave his salvation. That is, if a man is truly intent on turning his back on the Lord and spending eternity in hell, God will not force him to remain in His family.

1 Timothy 4:1 (b)
. . . giving heed to seducing spirits . . .

I believe ours are difficult days in which to be a Christian. Although the early church experienced persecution to such a degree that, by conservative estimates, six million of our brothers and sisters in Christ were martyred by Rome, Satan had a problem because the blood of the saints proved to be the seed of the church. The church grew. So Satan changed strategies. Unable to beat the church, he decided to join it and seduce it into lethargy and sleepiness.

Thus, I suggest to you it is tougher to be a Christian in the days of pleasure and prosperity than in the days of persecution. Persecution necessitates a stand, a declaration, an identification. But in our day, people can come to church on Sunday morning and watch HBO on Sunday evening. And in so doing, they unknowingly fall prey to the seducing spirits that lure them away from the faith.

1 Timothy 4:1 (c), 2
. . . and doctrines of devils; speaking lies in hypocrisy; having their conscience seared with a hot iron;

"If you will contribute just a little more money to my television ministry, I guarantee you'll be healed," televangelist Bob Tilton's letters promised the man diagnosed with cancer. The problem was, the letters were sent six months after the man had been buried. Consequently, it was reported that Bob Tilton lost a lawsuit filed by the widow of the deceased.

The only explanation for corruption such as this is the demonic doctrines given to men whose consciences are seared, to men who no longer have any sensitivity to people or to the Lord.

1 Timothy 4:3
Forbidding to marry, and commanding to abstain from meats, which God hath created to be received with thanksgiving of them which believe and know the truth.

Diabolical doctrine results not only in a seared conscience but also in legalism that parades as piety.

1 Timothy 4:4, 5
For every creature of God is good, and nothing to be refused, if it be received with thanksgiving: For it is sanctified by the word of God and prayer.

The Levitical dietary laws are pictures pointing to spiritual truth meant to drive us to Christ. But they are not to be embraced legalistically today. "Let no man judge you in meat or in drink or Sabbath days or new moons," Paul said (see Colossians 2:16). Instead, we are to celebrate our liberty, pray constantly, and give thanks continually."

1 Timothy 4:6 (a)
If thou put the brethren in remembrance of these things, thou shalt be a good minister of Jesus Christ . . .

Here's how to be a good minister: Stay away from esoteric posturing, dietary discussions, and legalism. Keep the main thing the main thing. And the main thing is Jesus.

1 Timothy 4:6 (b), 7
. . . nourished up in the words of faith and of good doctrine, whereunto thou hast attained. But refuse profane and old wives' fables, and exercise thyself rather unto godliness.

In Paul and Timothy's day, people were caught up in Greek and Roman mythology and genealogies—trying to figure out to which god they were linked and from which god they descended. Paul told Timothy to stay away from all such questions and to instead study godliness.

1 Timothy 4:8 (a)
For bodily exercise profiteth little . . .

The Greek culture put tremendous emphasis on the physique. But Paul says, "Timothy, understand this: I'm an older man and I'm telling you that bodily exercise profits little—or, as your margin may read, "a little while."

According to a recent study, for every hour one spends working out, he will live one hour longer. But think about it: The hour he gained was wasted in a hot, sweaty, stinky gym!

There is, indeed, a little profit in bodily exercise. It's a good thing—but not nearly as important as exercising oneself in godliness. If you have to choose between working out and worshiping, opt for worship every time. If you have to choose between Bible study and bodybuilding, always go with Bible study. It's good to jog and to do deep knee bends, presses, and curls. But I wish people would put the same emphasis on jogging their memory of Scripture, bending their knees in prayer, pressing on in the faith, and curling up with a good Book—the Word of God.

1 Timothy 4:8 (b)
. . . but godliness is profitable unto all things, having promise of the life that now is, and of that which is to come.

A life of godliness is a win/win situation because those who choose to follow such a life will be blessed both presently and throughout eternity.

1 Timothy 4:9, 10 (a)
This is a faithful saying and worthy of all acceptation. For therefore we both labour and suffer reproach, because we trust in the living God . . .

Suppose our government suddenly collapsed, and a godless dictator appeared on national TV calling for the immediate arrest of all those allied with and linked to Jesus Christ. Would your neighbors rise up in one accord and identify you as a Jesus Person? Would the people on your campus label you as a Christian? It's a probing question because Paul says reproach is inevitable for those who truly live out their faith.

1 Timothy 4:10 (b)
. . . who is the Saviour of all men, specially of those that believe.

The result of godliness is persecution. "But keep in mind, Timothy," writes Paul, "that Jesus is the Savior of all men—even of those who persecute you."

1 Timothy 4:11
These things command and teach.

Timothy was to be a good minister, reminding people of simple truth. He was to be a godly minister, exercising spiritual disciplines. And now we come to the third section, where we see that Timothy was also to be a growing minister. . . .

1 Timothy 4:12
Let no man despise thy youth; but be thou an example of the believers, in word, in conversation, in charity, in spirit, in faith, in purity.

What if the spiritual walk of everyone in your fellowship was exactly like yours? What if everyone gave financially to the degree you give every week? What if everyone prayed for missions to the same degree you do? What if everyone in the Christian community witnessed as much as you do? Where would we be?

It's easy to exhort others. Being an example ourselves, however, is much more difficult. . . .

"Son," said the concerned father, "you're not studying the way you could. When Abraham Lincoln was your age, he didn't have computers or electric lights. He walked fifteen miles through the snow to check out books at the library—and then walked fifteen miles home so that he could read them by the light of the fireplace. When he was your age, that's what he did."

"Well," replied the son, "when Abraham Lincoln was your age, he was President of the United States!"

It's easy to want to exhort someone else! But Mom and Dad, if you want to see your kids be more spiritual, you be more spiritual. Pastors, if you want your congregations to be more radical, you be more radical. The key lies in being an example.

For topical study of I Timothy 4:12 entitled "Be Thou an Example," turn to page 1386.

1 Timothy 4:13
Till I come, give attendance to reading, to exhortation, to doctrine.

"Make sure you're reading the Word, Timothy. Make sure you're growing in faith." I feel one of the most neglected practices in the church today is the simple reading of the Word both corporately and personally. There's power in the reading of Scripture.

1 Timothy 4:14
Neglect not the gift that is in thee, which was given thee by prophecy, with the laying on of the hands of the presbytery.

Each of us has been given gifts by the Spirit. But here's the problem: We spend far too much time trying to strengthen our weaknesses—only to find that in so doing, we weaken our strengths! Go where you're strong. If you are gifted as a worship leader, then lead worship. If you're gifted with kids, plug into children's ministry. If you're gifted in one-on-one situations, don't try to preach before thousands. Go with your strength, gang. Whatever God has called you to do, go for it with intensity and tenacity.

1 Timothy 4:15
Meditate upon these things; give thyself wholly to them; that thy profiting may appear to all.

Find a quiet place at a quiet time where you can meditate with a quiet heart.

Moses spent forty days communing with God. But the congregation grew restless (Exodus 32:1).

"Where's Moses?" they said. "We have Sunday-school committee meetings for him to attend, trustee obligations for him to address, denominational by-laws for him to discuss, retirement plans for him to consider. Where is he?"

I appreciate this about Moses' example: He did not come down from the mountain until he had the Word of the Lord in His hand. And because of this, when he did come down, he could say with authority, "Thus saith the Lord. . . ."

1 Timothy 4:16
Take heed unto thyself, and unto the doctrine; continue in them: for in doing this thou shalt both save thyself, and them that hear thee.

Why do I teach the Bible? Because *I* need to hear it. Every time I teach, I am reminded of the basics over and over again. And how greatly I need to know them!

BE THOU AN EXAMPLE
A Topical Study of
1 Timothy 4:12

I remember it as if it were yesterday. Tom McKee, my youth pastor, came to me, a freshman in high school, and said, "Jon, how would you like to preach this Monday night?"

Honored, flattered, and excited, I said, "Yeah, okay!" And Tom went on to say he would be taking me with him on Monday night to the San Jose Rescue Mission. I had never been to a Rescue Mission before. I didn't really even understand what they were about. I just knew it was an opportunity to preach.

For my preaching debut, I chose the story of Zacchaeus and wrote a fifteen-page manuscript in which I proposed that Zacchaeus represented the people of Israel and the sycamore tree he climbed represented the Gentile nations. I went on to propose that just as Jesus told Zacchaeus He would come to his house, Jesus would draw His people out from the Gentile nations to come and once again have fellowship with Him.

Monday night finally came. Dressed in suit and tie, I stood up to preach to a couple hundred of San Jose's most down and out. Most were homeless, some just drunk—and I realized as I began to teach that they weren't listening to a word I was saying. I didn't find out until later that the rule at the Rescue Mission was that those who wanted to eat had to first attend the service.

So there everyone was. Their stomachs were growling, and their mouths salivating as I went on and on and on, enlightening them concerning the eschatological nuances of Zacchaeus and the sycamore tree. At about page eight, I felt the blush of embarrassment rise to my face and proceed all the way to my red hair. Just then, a guy stood up in the back and yelled, "Sit down, you overgrown tomato!" I sat down on page nine.

It's hard to serve the Lord to any degree when you're young because people have a tendency to look down on you. "Who are you, you overgrown tomato?" they jeer. "Who are you, you high-school junior?" "Who are you, you college freshman?" "Who are you, you twenty-five-year-old?"

Paul takes this tendency to task when he tells Timothy, "Let no man despise thy youth."

Neotes, the Greek word translated "youth," is an interesting one. It was a term used for anyone of military age. In Paul's day, a man was eligible for the draft in the Roman army through the age of forty. So the word "youth" here can refer to anyone up to and through the age of forty. Does this mean Timothy was forty years old when Paul wrote to him? Probably not. Most likely, Timothy was in his late teens or early twenties at this point. Yet even if Timothy had been forty years old, his age would have been problematic for some, for not too many years after Paul had written this letter, writings known as "The Apostolic Canons" circulated throughout the early church, declaring that a man should not be appointed pastor until he was past thirty years of age, at which time he would be past "youthful disorders."

"Don't let anyone put this trip on you, Timothy," countered Paul. "Let no man despise your youth."

So, too, I say to you who are eighteen, sixteen, or fourteen years old—"don't let people say you can't be used in ministry, that you can't be used in the work of the kingdom because you're too young—for now is the very time for you to get going, to get engaged, to get involved. I have noticed that as people get older, they no longer have the courage to step out because their lives become too complicated. All too often, they say, "First I have to take care of this and do that"—but the years slip by and they miss out on so many opportunities.

If the Lord has placed a calling within you, how I encourage you to begin serving and ministering regardless of those who say, "You don't know enough yet."

"There will be those who say you're too young, Timothy," warned Paul. "Don't argue *with* them, but instead, be an example *to* them. Live your life in such a way that they will see there's something deep and rich about you."

Paul then goes on to present six characteristics that would silence those who sought to criticize Timothy. And it should come as no surprise that these six characteristics are seen most clearly in the life of the One who is our ultimate Example—Jesus Christ. The account in Luke 2 is the only one in the Bible that shows us Jesus as a young Man. Yet in the one story we have, we see all six of these characteristics modeled perfectly. . . .

. . . be thou an example of the believers, in word . . .

And it came to pass, that after three days they found him in the temple, sitting in the midst of the doctors, both hearing them, and asking them questions.

Luke 2:46

Teenager, notice that Jesus wasn't preaching to the elders in the temple. He was listening to them and asking questions of them. Let me suggest that if you want to be an example of the believer, your speech is to be based upon your listening to those who are older than you.

"But they don't know as much as I do," you may say.

Don't you think Jesus knew more than those men in the temple? Yet He engaged in meaningful conversation with them for days.

George Washington was right when he said, "When a younger man and an older man are conversing, the older man must never mention that he is older, but the younger man must never forget it."

You who are younger than forty, be an example of the believer in speech by listening, by asking questions, and by engaging in meaningful conversation—because after He listened to them and asked questions of them, Jesus astonished the learned men in the temple with His understanding (Luke 2:47).

. . . in conversation . . .

And it came to pass, that after three days, they found him in the temple . . .

Luke 2:46 (a)

The Greek word translated "conversation" means "lifestyle," or "conduct." Teenager, if you were suddenly discovered to be missing, would Mom and Dad say, "No doubt he's at church"? In your free time, where do you go? Jesus' lifestyle was centered around the temple, around the things of the kingdom. It wasn't part of His life. It *was* His life.

If, as a fifteen-year-old, you decide that church will have priority over volleyball, football, delivering newspapers, or watching TV—just watch and see how God will bless you as you seek first the kingdom.

. . . in charity . . .

And when they saw him, they were amazed: and his mother said unto him, Son, why hast thou thus dealt with us? behold, thy father and I have sought thee sorrowing. And he said unto them, How is it that ye sought me? wist ye not that I must be about my Father's business? And they understood not the saying which he spake unto them.

Luke 2:48–50

Of Joseph, Jesus could have said, "He's not my dad." Instead, He corrected His mother so tenderly that neither she nor Joseph understood what He was saying. Jesus didn't say, "Let Me clarify." He simply spoke the truth, and then He backed off. Mary and Joseph didn't understand—but Jesus didn't press His point.

So, too, while we are not to compromise truth, neither are we to strive, fight, or argue (2 Timothy 2:24).

. . . in spirit . . .

. . . wist ye not that I must be about my Father's business?

Luke 2:49

As a teenager, Jesus didn't say, "I'll try to be about My Father's business." He didn't say, "I should be about My Father's business." He didn't say, "I want to be about My Father's business." He said, "I *must* be about My Father's business."

As an adult, He would say, "I must go and preach the gospel of the kingdom (see Luke 4:43). I must go through Samaria (see John 4:4). I must be lifted up on the Cross" (see John 3:14).

Young man, young woman, be one who says, "I *must* tithe—no matter how the bills are stacking up. I *must* pray—no matter how busy my day. I *must* serve faithfully. I *must* stay married to my husband. I *must* love my wife." Show me a dad who says, "Family devotions are not optional." Show me a teenager who says, "If the game interferes with church, I'm not going to the game." Show me a man, a woman, a teenager, a married couple like that, and I'll show you people God will use profoundly.

. . . in faith . . .

And he went down with them, and came to Nazareth, and was subject unto them . . .   Luke 2:51 (a)

Jesus submitted Himself to His mother and stepfather. It took faith to say, "I choose to submit to you. Even though you don't understand what I'm saying, even though you don't fully realize who I am, I choose to submit Myself to you because My Father in heaven has placed Me in this home, and I have faith that He has ordained this to be."

Whether at work or home, in school or in marriage, the key to submission is faith. The key to submission is saying, "Lord, I know that You are on the throne, that you put me in this home, that You placed me in this position."

. . . in purity . . .

And it came to pass, that after three days they found him in the temple . . .   Luke 2:46 (a)

Left alone in the city, Jesus kept Himself pure. Although He was tempted in all points like as we are, although He felt the same temptations and tugs of the flesh we do (Hebrews 4:15), He didn't try to sneak into a movie. He remained in the temple.

In his second letter, Paul will tell Timothy to flee youthful lusts by hanging out with those who love God (2 Timothy 2:22). Seventeen-year-old, twenty-three-year-old, listen: There are "hot spots" all over—places that will burn you out. Run from them and run to those who are gathering together to worship the Lord and to study His Word.

Why should you be an example of the believers? Why should you follow the Example of Jesus? Look at the last verse of Luke 2. . . .

And Jesus increased in wisdom and stature, and in favour with God and man.   Luke 2:52

If you choose to walk in humility, love, zeal, faith, and purity, you'll increase in wisdom and stature. You'll grow in favor with God and man.

The choice is yours.

5 In chapter 5, dealing with the church and her ministry to herself, Paul will address three areas: the church family, widows specifically, and leaders practically. . . .

1 Timothy 5:1 (a)
Rebuke not an elder, but intreat him as a father . . .

Paul's word to young Timothy is an important word for all younger men, for, in their zeal, young men have a tendency to feel as if they know all the answers. But in reality, as we go through life with the Lord, we realize we don't know as much as we thought we did. I know I, for one, was a whole lot smarter when I was twenty-two than I am now, twenty-five years later!

1 Timothy 5:1 (b), 2
. . . and the younger men as brethren; the elder women as mothers; the younger as sisters, with all purity.

Within the church family, we're to treat older men with respect, older women with devotion, contemporaries as brothers, and younger women as sisters.

1 Timothy 5:3
Honour widows that are widows indeed.

In Acts 6, we read of division in the early church due to tension arising concerning the care of the Greek and Hebrew widows. Thus, from the very beginning—in the days before Social Security, retirement plans, or life insurance—the church realized her responsibility to care for those who would otherwise have been in financial straits.

1 Timothy 5:4
But if any widow have children or nephews, let them learn first to shew piety at home, and to requite their parents: for that is good and acceptable before God.

If a widow had children, or grandchildren, it was not the church's responsibility to care for her. There were those who were saying, "We don't have to worry about Mom because the church will take care of her."

"No," said Paul. "The first place to show piety is with the older members of your own family who are in need." Thus, one of the characteristics of a "widow indeed" (verse 3) was being one who didn't have children or grandchildren to care for her.

1 Timothy 5:5
Now she that is a widow indeed, and desolate, trusteth in God, and continueth in supplications and prayers night and day.

"Widows indeed" were women who gave themselves to constant prayer. I like the order—night and day. When one is suddenly single, sometimes it's hard to sleep. I've been there—but I'll tell you this: Such times provide wonderfully rich opportunities for prayer. When you can't sleep, don't watch TV. Pray. Go to your knees and intercede for those who are hurting. There's something about the nighttime hours that often cause them to become the matrix of miracles, the womb of wonder. There's something about being in the dark with the Lord that allows you to focus on Him, to do battle against the Enemy, to receive insight from Him in a way unlike at any other time of the day.

1 Timothy 5:6
But she that liveth in pleasure is dead while she liveth.

If an older woman is living for pleasure in her later years, she's doing nothing more than going through the motions of life.

1 Timothy 5:7, 8
And these things give in charge, that they may be blameless. But if any provide not for his own, and specially for those of his own house, he hath denied the faith, and is worse than an infidel.

It's up to you as a child or a grandchild to take care of your parents and grandparents. Don't leave it to the church. I believe this principle applies down the line. Mom, Dad, the church should not be expected to foster your teenager's spirituality or your preschooler's introduction to Jesus. Oh, the church gets to partner with you in seeing Junior taught the things of God— but nothing the church can do is as effective as what children learn from their parents on a daily basis.

1 Timothy 5:9, 10
Let not a widow be taken into the number under threescore years old, having been the wife of one man, well reported of for good works; if she have brought up children, if she have lodged strangers, if she have washed the saints' feet, if she have relieved the afflicted, if she have diligently followed every good work.

A woman at least sixty years of age, who had been a faithful wife and a good mother, who had been given to hospitality and who had refreshed the saints, who had helped those who were hurting, but who had no family to care for her was a "widow indeed" and therefore qualified to be cared for by the church.

1 Timothy 5:11, 12
But the younger widows refuse: for when they have begun to wax wanton against Christ, they will marry; having damnation, because they have cast off their first faith.

"Don't let younger women join the community of widows," said Paul, "because when they remarry, they'll condemn themselves, wondering if they should have remained singularly devoted to the Lord and to prayer."

1 Timothy 5:13, 14
And withal they learn to be idle, wandering about from house to house; and not only idle, but tattlers also and busybodies, speaking things which they ought not. I will therefore that the younger women marry, bear children, guide the house, give none occasion to the adversary to speak reproachfully.

Paul instructs Timothy to make sure the women of the church don't give the enemy opportunity to speak negatively in the community about Christians due to the neglect of their own households.

1 Timothy 5:15, 16
For some are already turned aside after Satan. If any man or woman that believeth have widows, let them relieve them, and let not the church be charged; that it may relieve them that are widows indeed.

After dealing with the state of widows in the church, Paul will go on to delineate some standards of leadership for the church. . . .

1 Timothy 5:17
Let the elders that rule well be counted worthy of double honour, especially they who labour in the word and doctrine.

In this, we see that the church is to financially support those who labor in the teaching ministry.

1 Timothy 5:18
For the scripture saith, Thou shalt not muzzle the ox that treadeth out the corn. And, The labourer is worthy of his reward.

Paul supports his previous assertion both with the law that said, "While an ox grinds meal for others to eat, he is to be supported as well" (see Deuteronomy 25:4) and with Jesus' instruction to the disciples He sent out that those to whom they ministered would provide for them (Matthew 10:10).

1 Timothy 5:19
Against an elder receive not an accusation, but before two or three witnesses.

Do not listen to slander against spiritual leaders unless there are two or three witnesses willing to go on record to discuss the situation. Why does Paul say this? Because the Enemy wants to destroy churches, and he will do that most significantly and successfully by attacking leaders.

The Book of Proverbs says, "Where there is no wood, the fire goes out" (see Proverbs 26:20)—a good principle to grasp not only for the church but also for life in general. As long as you give ear to gossip, you encourage the gossiper to continue in his or her sin. Don't listen to gossip ever—not even if it's couched in a "prayer request"—for it will hurt the church corporately and your own walk personally.

1 Timothy 5:20
Them that sin rebuke before all, that others also may fear.

On the other hand, if there is legitimate sin, it needs to be rebuked in order that all may learn to be in awe of God.

1 Timothy 5:21, 22
I charge thee before God, and the Lord Jesus Christ, and the elect angels, that thou observe these things without preferring one before another, doing nothing by partiality. Lay hands suddenly on no man, neither be partaker of other men's sins: keep thyself pure.

Paul warns Timothy not to have favorites and not to bestow leadership on anyone too quickly—a charge of which I need to be more mindful. . . .

Years ago, I baptized a young man who had previously dabbled in Rastafarian religion. Articulate and insightful, he had so much going for him that I turned over a Monday night Bible study to him only eight months later. It proved to be a total disaster, however, when I found out that for inspiration before the study, he would get high on marijuana.

As is too often my tendency, I laid hands on someone too quickly. I like to give people an opportunity to serve—but I am learning to listen to Paul when he advised Timothy to go slowly in appointing leaders.

1 Timothy 5:23
Drink no longer water, but use a little wine for thy stomach's sake and thine often infirmities.

Earlier, in chapter 3, Paul told Timothy an elder was not to be given to wine. Yet here in chapter 5, he's telling Timothy, an elder, to use a little wine—the medicine of the day—for his stomach. I find this intriguing on a number of counts. . . .

As one who moved powerfully in the arena of healing, Paul obviously had prayed for Timothy. Yet Timothy was not healed right then. Does this mean God was unable to heal Timothy or that He didn't hear Paul's prayer? No. God *will* heal everyone who believes in Him (Isaiah 53:5). When? It might be immediately. It might take a year or ten. Or it might not happen until the person goes to heaven.

Prayer doesn't heal. Faith doesn't heal. Medicine doesn't heal. Our own bodies don't heal themselves. *God* heals (Exodus 15:26). And He can use prayer. He can use medicine. He can use faith. He can use our own bodies. Therefore, because God heals, I pray for His direct healing, as well as thanking Him for His gift of medicine—knowing that His method and His timing will be perfect.

1 Timothy 5:24, 25
Some men's sins are open beforehand, going before to judgment; and some men they follow after. Likewise also the good works of some are manifest beforehand; and they that are otherwise cannot be hid.

Referring to the fact that Timothy would be open to criticism if he followed Paul's advice and took some wine for his stomach, Paul advised his young protégé to ignore the innuendoes of his critics.

If you are one who will not "take your medicine" because you're living in fear of being misunderstood or if you are one whose entire life is governed by what people think or say, you'll be tripped up in your Christian walk because the fear of man is indeed a snare (Proverbs 29:25).

If, on the other hand, like Jesus, you let go of your reputation (Philippians 2:7) and seek only to please the Father, you'll find an easy yoke upon you and a clear path before you.

〰️

6 In chapter 6, Paul addresses the ministry of the church to the world vocationally, materially, and intellectually.

1 Timothy 6:1
Let as many servants as are under the yoke count their own masters worthy of all honour, that the name of God and his doctrine be not blasphemed.

Employees—those who are under the yoke—are to be "good eggs." When the whistle blows, they're not to "scramble." When things get hot, they're not to get "fried."

I have gotten calls not infrequently from people saying, "I don't even go to your church, but I need an honest plumber or a trustworthy mechanic, and I know I can find one at your church." Be a witness for Jesus Christ by being the best worker, the best athlete, the best student you can be. The world is looking for reasons not to believe in God. Don't give them one.

1 Timothy 6:2
And they that have believing masters, let them not despise them, because they are brethren; but rather do them service, because they are faithful and beloved, partak-

ers of the benefit. **These things teach and exhort.**

If your boss is a Christian, be careful you don't exploit your relationship by saying, "He'll understand if I don't show up today because I have to pray with my wife," or, "I can't keep my commitment at work because the Spirit is calling me to go to the lake and meditate." Don't be one who takes advantage of a boss who is a brother or sister in the Lord. Instead, take care to esteem them even higher.

1 Timothy 6:3–5
If any man teach otherwise, and consent not to wholesome words, even the words of our Lord Jesus Christ, and to the doctrine which is according to godliness; he is proud, knowing nothing, but doting about questions and strifes of words, whereof cometh envy, strife, railings, evil surmisings, perverse disputings of men of corrupt minds, and destitute of the truth, supposing that gain is godliness: from such withdraw thyself.

"Gain is godliness," said some in Paul's day. "Don't worry about being faithful at work, but rather learn to work the faith. You don't need to work hard. Just Name It and Claim It." Ever hear teaching like that?

1 Timothy 6:6
But godliness with contentment is great gain.

Today's "faith teachers" say "Godliness will bring gain which will make you content."
That's not what Paul said. He said, "Gain lies in godliness with contentment." Why? Because no good thing will God withhold from them that walk uprightly (Psalm 84:11).
"I don't think that's true," you say. "I'm walking with the Lord and I don't have a new car." If that is the case, a new car would not be good for you. God knows that toys and hobbies and bigger houses would be distractions for too many of us. So if things that seem wonderful don't come your way, you can trust that He knows they wouldn't be good for you.

1 Timothy 6:7, 8
For we brought nothing into this world, and it is certain we can carry nothing out. And having food and raiment let us be therewith content.

If you have something to eat and a shirt on your back, be content. This is neither a suggestion nor a principle. It's a command.

In the mountains of Mexico lie two adjacent springs. One sends forth hot water, the other cold.
"Your people must thank Mother Nature for hot and cold water right next to each other," said a travel guide to an Indian as he washed his clothes in the springs.
The Indian wisely answered, "No, we grumble because she didn't supply soap."

God is so good to us, gang. Statistically, the poorest person in this congregation is wealthier than 90 percent of the world's population. Think about that next time you feel inclined to grumble about a lack of soap!

1 Timothy 6:9, 10
But they that will be rich fall into temptation and a snare, and into many foolish and hurtful lusts, which drown men in destruction and perdition. For the love of money is the root of all evil: which while some coveted after, they have erred from the faith, and pierced themselves through with many sorrows.

The love of money can lead to pointless pursuits and persistent pain because those with money can indulge themselves with possessions and in places they wouldn't otherwise be. God's Word says wanting to be rich, many people get wiped out.

1 Timothy 6:11 (a)
But thou, O man of God . . .

Although we use the phrase "man of God" rather freely, the Bible uses it quite sparingly. Therefore, Timothy must have been something really special.

1 Timothy 6:11 (b), 12
. . . flee these things; and follow after righteousness, godliness, faith, love, patience, meekness. Fight the good fight of faith, lay hold on eternal life, whereunto thou art also called, and hast professed a good profession before many witnesses.

Man of God, keep eternity's values in view. Lay hold on eternal life. Keep focused on the fact that you're going to heaven.

1 Timothy 6:13
I give thee charge in the sight of God, who quickeneth all things, and before Christ Jesus,

who before Pontius Pilate witnessed a good confession.

"Art thou a king?" Pilate asked Jesus.
"You said it, Pilate," answered Jesus. "And if you really desire to hear truth, you too will hear My voice" (see John 18:37).

1 Timothy 6:14–16
That thou keep this commandment without spot, unrebukeable, until the appearing of our Lord Jesus Christ: Which in his times he shall shew, who is the blessed and only Potentate, the King of kings, and Lord of lords; Who only hath immortality, dwelling in the light which no man can approach unto; whom no man hath seen, nor can see: to whom be honour and power everlasting. Amen.

In light of who God is and where we're going, it's ludicrous to think highly of ourselves.

1 Timothy 6:17 (a)
Charge them that are rich in this world, that they be not highminded, nor trust in uncertain riches . . .

Unlike the game of musical chairs—wherein there's only one chair too few—if the music in the financial world stopped today and every government, corporation, financial institution, and private individual called in their debts, only three out of ten would get a chair. In other words, the entire world economy is built on faith that the music's not going to stop. But when it does—and it will—the world will be shocked to realize how many chairs are missing. Thus, the reason the Bible calls riches uncertain is because they are!

1 Timothy 6:17 (b)
. . . but in the living God, who giveth us richly all things to enjoy.

I could tell you story after story of things I thought I just had to have. So I bought them—only to find that they bought me as I was held captive paying them off and maintaining them. Possession brings problems, indeed. Yet Americans persist in thinking they must own something in order to enjoy it. Not so. A walk on the beach, a picnic by a stream, and a bike ride through the park are all free. Thus, God has given us freely the *best* things to enjoy.

1 Timothy 6:18
That they do good, that they be rich in good works, ready to distribute, willing to communicate.

If God blesses you with wealth, become the most generous, magnanimous person you possibly can be, for the funny thing about money is that often the more wealth a person amasses, the more stingy he becomes. I have a sneaking suspicion that God desires to bless us even more in the realm of finances if we would learn to be channels through which His blessing would flow.

How do we learn this? The best way is to do what God says: to tithe. The first tenth of every single penny that comes your way is God's. If God has made you a millionaire, you need to tithe on that million. It's His. If God has given you one dollar per year, then a dime of that is His. Become people who tithe, for with every tithe, you give far more than money. You give away a part of your selfishness.

1 Timothy 6:19
Laying up in store for themselves a good foundation against the time to come, that they may lay hold on eternal life.

The old adage is true: You can't take it with you. But you can send it ahead through tithing, giving, and sharing. Oh, that we would understand the truth of this!

1 Timothy 6:20, 21
O Timothy, keep that which is committed to thy trust, avoiding profane and vain babblings, and oppositions of science falsely so called: Which some professing have erred concerning the faith. Grace be with thee. Amen.

After telling us that professionally, we're to be good workers, and financially, we are to be content and generous, Paul moves to his third and final exhortation concerning the church and her ministry to the world when he says that intellectually, we are to be true to the Word.

If you want to navigate life now and eternally without being embarrassed, study the Scriptures and do what they tell you to do. Without exception, the times of which I'm ashamed are the times I didn't do what the Word said to do. When I violated the Word, when I did my own thing, when I chose to ignore a command or a principle, my actions always resulted in error and shame.

May the Lord continue to help us walk wisely

in these dark and treacherous days. May the Lord give us a heart to continue to study the Word—not academically only, but with a determination to obey it practically.

SCIENCE FICTION
A Topical Study of
1 Timothy 6:20–21

As a sophomore in high school, I listened as Mr. Flanner, my science teacher, gave us reason after reason why evolution is so certain, so factual, so undeniable. This intrigued me because at the beginning of the semester, he had taught us that all of science is built not upon a theory, not upon a hypothesis, but upon a law—the Second Law of Thermodynamics, which says that everything goes from order to disorder, that everything is winding down.

We know this to be so. Every second of every minute, the sun loses 1,200,000 tons of mass. As a result, scientists tell us that eventually the sun will burn out. This means that if we go back fifteen million years—the length of time required by the evolutionary process to bring life as we know it to our planet—the sun would be substantially larger than it is now, causing the average temperature on earth to exceed three hundred degrees—which would kill the very life forms that were supposedly evolving into men.

It just doesn't add up! And scientists are increasingly coming to this conclusion. A best-selling book in England, entitled, *The Facts of Life: Shattering the Myth of Darwinism,* was written by an eminent scientist who doesn't believe in God but who, nonetheless, says there are too many problems with Darwinism to make it a viable theory. Among them are the following. . . .

Dating

Scientists at the Hawaiian Institute of Geophysics collected rocks from a lava flow that had hardened and dated them according to the most sophisticated, scientific systems. According to the most advanced computer models, the sample was said to be three billion years old. The problem, however, was that the scientists at the Hawaiian Institute of Geophysics had actually seen the volcano from which the rocks were taken erupt only two years previously.

Fossils

There are fossilized trees in Indonesia that are forty feet high. Because it has been established that it takes centuries to produce a fossil only one inch thick, it would take countless centuries to fossilize an entire tree. The problem is that the tree couldn't stand that long without breaking down under its own decaying process. Therefore, for the tree to be fossilized to a height of forty feet, it had to be fossilized in a way other than the evolutionist suggests. There had to be an instant cataclysmic event—like, for example, a flood.

Transitional Forms

When Darwin wrote his theory, he stated categorically that paleontology—the study of fossils—would verify the theory of evolution because in them we would see transitional forms linking together two distinct species. The problem is that since Darwin presented his theory, scientists have studied fossils by the ton. And they have yet to find a single transitional form.

One Gallup poll found that only 9 percent of Americans believe man came into being apart from God. Why, then, do scientists continue to propagate the theory of evolution? Why do academicians continue to stand by evolution? Why does our public school system continue to teach evolution when it clearly violates the Second Law of Thermodynamics and other empirical evidence?

The Bible gives us the answer in Romans 1. . . .

For the invisible things of him from the creation of the world are clearly seen, being understood by the things that are made, even his eternal power and Godhead; so that they are without excuse.   Romans 1:20

God's attributes, His power, His creative ingenuity, and His presence are seen in all of creation—from the circulatory systems within us to the stars above us.

Because that, when they knew God, they glorified him not as God, neither were thankful; but became vain in their imaginations, and their foolish heart was darkened. Professing themselves to be wise, they became fools, and changed the glory of the uncorruptible God into an image made like to corruptible man, and to birds, and fourfooted beasts, and creeping things.   Romans 1:21–23

Even though nature attests to God's reality, man chose to believe a lie and to change the glory of the incorruptible God into man, birds, four-footed beasts, and creeping things—which, interestingly, is the evolutionary order in reverse.

Wherefore God also gave them up to uncleanness through the lusts of their own hearts, to dishonour their own bodies between themselves: Who changed the truth of God into a lie, and worshipped and served the creature more than the Creator, who is blessed for ever. Amen.   Romans 1:24, 25

"Because there is no God; because we came from slime, we can act like slime," says the unbeliever.

And *that's* the issue, gang. The issue is not scientific, academic, or intellectual. The issue is moral. People innately know there is a divine design to the universe. They know it in their hearts. They see it in the sky. It rings true in their souls. But because the so-called intellectuals don't want to be accountable to a Creator, they simply remove God from the picture.

Guns, rape, and profane behavior of every type have replaced chewing gum, un-tucked shirts, and talking in class as the prevalent problems in our high schools. And educators are stymied. "What's wrong with the culture?" they ask. They give lectures and bring in motivational speakers to try to instill values in their students—all the while blind to the obvious fact that if kids are taught they came from animals, they're bound to act like animals. Understanding what they innately know to be true—that they were created by God—would affect the way students would view life, one another, and themselves. But take away that underpinning—and we are currently reaping the result.

And if you are one who says, "I know God created the earth and everything in it," my question to you is this: Do you live as though that were true?

God created you for one reason: To bring Him pleasure (Colossians 1). Therefore, if you please God this week, you will fulfill the very reason for your existence. It is in bringing joy and pleasure to the heart of God through worship, Bible study, family devotions, personal contemplation, prayer, meditation, and submission that we disarm Darwin, expose evolution, and silence the skeptic.

Mr. Flanner had a Master's Degree, but I, a lowly sophomore, understood the Decree of the Master—and that made all the difference.

2 TIMOTHY

1

2 Timothy 1:1 (a)
Paul, an apostle of Jesus Christ by the will of God . . .

As you may recall, Paul endured two periods of imprisonment. . . .

The Book of Acts closes with Paul under house arrest in Rome. Although he was linked to a guard at all times, he lived in his own quarters and was able to have visitors. After his release from house arrest, Paul embarked on yet another missionary journey, probably into Spain. Upon his return to Rome, he was arrested a second time. This time, however, Paul was put in a dark, damp dungeon. Why? The reason most probably lies with the then-emperor of Rome—Caesar Nero. . . .

According to historical evidence, such a megalomaniac was Caesar Nero that he desired to burn Rome in order to rebuild it and become known as the supreme architect of a rebuilt Rome. Thus, the majority of historians believe that Caesar Nero was the one who set the fire that did, indeed, burn the city in A.D. 64. Needing a scapegoat for the fire, Nero chose to blame Christians. "These Christians are always talking about being the light of the world," he said, "but really they're nothing but a bunch of arsonists and cannibals"—referring to Communion. Eventually, Caesar Nero would ride through his palace grounds, shrieking with glee, as he watched Christians lit as human torches.

Why did Nero descend to such depths of insanity? Historical evidence points to the fact that Nero went insane after he had a discussion with Paul the apostle. Church history indicates that Paul was indeed brought into a discussion with Nero before he was beheaded. Thus, it was at the point that Nero rejected the gospel that he seemingly lost his mind.

Awaiting trial before Caesar Nero, Paul picks up his pen for the last time. . . .

2 Timothy 1:1 (b)
. . . according to the promise of life which is in Christ Jesus.

I love this opening salutation. Knowing he's probably only days away from his death, Paul talks about life. What kind of life? Eternal life. He's ready to pull up stakes and move on. He's not downcast or depressed because he sees the bigger picture—the promise of life.

If you believe in Jesus, I have good news for you: You're never going to die. You're just going to "move" on to heaven. God is so good to allow these tents we inhabit to fall apart through the aging process because, in so doing, He's getting us ready to move into the fabulous home He is preparing for us, and for the new bodies He will give us that are designed for eternity, custom-made for the cosmos.

2 Timothy 1:2 (a)
To Timothy, my dearly beloved son:

As noted in 1 Timothy, it seems Paul led Timothy to a saving knowledge of Jesus Christ during his first missionary journey. On his second journey, Paul again encountered Timothy, and this time invited Timothy to travel with him.

I like that! We need to include younger people on the journey we're on, in the ministry to which we're called. Whatever might be your calling, say, "Lord, show me those who I can bring alongside me to travel with me"—and then begin to entrust to them an even greater degree of ministry. I'm so thankful there were people in my life who took chances with me when I was young.

But what if the younger Christians mess up? Sometimes they will, but, as Solomon said, "Although an empty stable stays clean, an empty stable brings no profits" (see Proverbs 14:4). We need to make way for those who are younger because along with the potential for an occasional mess in the stable, there is about them a vitality and an ability to relate sometimes lacking in those of us who are older. Paul took a chance on Timothy—and Timothy profited Paul greatly.

2 Timothy 1:2 (b)
Grace, mercy, and peace, from God the Father and Christ Jesus our Lord.

In his usual fashion, Paul uses the traditional Greek greeting of *charis,* or "grace," coupled with the traditional Hebrew greeting of *shalom,* or "peace." But he wisely adds mercy as he thinks of the vulnerabilities of young Timothy.

2 Timothy 1:3
I thank God, whom I serve from my forefathers with pure conscience, that without ceasing I have remembrance of thee in my prayers night and day.

No doubt unable to sleep well in a dungeon, what did Paul do? Grumble? No. Complain? No. He saw his prison as a place of prayer.

Perhaps you feel imprisoned by past decisions. "I can't believe I married him. The Lord could have used me on the mission field. I could have done great things for the kingdom. But here I am, stuck washing his underwear and socks." What can you do? Do what Paul did. Use the opportunity of folding laundry to pray night and day, for that's the most powerful ministry there is.

If you're stuck in a boring job or difficult relationship, don't try to find a way out. Instead, say, "The dungeon I'm in gives me opportunity to do what I might never have done were I in another place or another ministry: I can pray night and day." Eternity will reward those who, because they are in seeming dungeons on earth, lift themselves and others up in prayer to the very gates of heaven.

Wouldn't you love to have Paul praying for you night and day? But wait. Jesus Christ Himself is at the right hand of the Father, praying for you and me even now (Hebrews 7:25). And unlike me, unlike Paul, He never grows weary in prayer (Psalm 121:3). Oh, to truly believe and firmly embrace the fact that Jesus, our faithful High Priest, is at the right hand of the Father, saying, "Jon needs You desperately. Let's bless him."

2 Timothy 1:4
Greatly desiring to see thee, being mindful of thy tears, that I may be filled with joy.

One of the few called a "man of God" in the Bible (1 Timothy 6:11), Timothy was, nonetheless, sickly. He fought timidity. And he cried.

Thus, he was not necessarily the kind of guy of whom I would have said, "Here's my man." But although he was sickly and timid, young and emotional, Paul saw in Timothy one who had a desire to serve the Lord with all his heart, one whose priority was the kingdom.

The Lord delights in using the foolish things of the world to confound the wise, and the weak things to show up the strong because when He uses people like Timothy—people like you and me—He gets all the glory!

2 Timothy 1:5
When I call to remembrance the unfeigned faith that is in thee, which dwelt first in thy grandmother Lois, and thy mother Eunice; and I am persuaded that in thee also.

In Lois, I am reminded of my own grandmother who, although she "moved" to heaven when I was only three years old, impacted my life so greatly that I still clearly remember her teaching me Bible verses and stories.

2 Timothy 1:6
Wherefore I put thee in remembrance that thou stir up the gift of God, which is in thee by the putting on of my hands.

"Your heritage is godly, Timothy. Now, stir up the gift within you," says Paul. Why do people let their gifts go dormant? I'm convinced it's because of fear.

- "If I share that word of prophecy—what if people don't understand?"
- "If I give that utterance in tongues—what if there's no interpretation?"
- "If I witness on my campus or at my job— what if people think I'm a Holy Joe?"
- "If I lay hands on that sick person and he's not healed—people will think I'm a failure."

My experience, however, has shown the opposite to be true. For example, in praying for healing, I've seen people healed immediately; I've seen people healed later on down the road; I've seen people get sicker; I've seen people die. But never once in the multiplied hundreds of times that I've prayed for Christians and non-Christians alike have I ever heard someone say, "I'm angry that you prayed for me." People always say, "Thank you," and mean it.

2 Timothy 1:7
For God hath not given us the spirit of fear; but of power, and of love, and of a sound mind.

This is a great verse to teach your kids at a young age. After all, if they have power, love, and a sound mind—they're in pretty good shape!

2 Timothy 1:8, 9
Be not thou therefore ashamed of the testimony of our Lord, nor of me his prisoner: but be thou partaker of the afflictions of the gospel according to the power of God; Who hath saved us, and called us with an holy calling, not according to our works, but according to his own purpose and grace, which was given us in Christ Jesus before the world began.

Although we know we're saved by grace, why is it that we have a tendency to think we can only be blessed through works? Yes, James says faith without works is dead (James 2:20). However, blessing comes neither from faith *and* works, nor from faith *or* works, but from faith *that* works in response to the grace God has already bestowed upon us.

2 Timothy 1:10 (a)
But is now made manifest by the appearing of our Saviour Jesus Christ . . .

Where is the grace of God, the love of God, the goodness of God manifested? In Jesus Christ.

"I don't need to go to church because I just go out into the woods on Sunday and feel really close to God," some say. Or, "I sense God's presence most clearly under the blue sky on a golf course." I don't doubt there is truth in that, for Psalm 19 says the heavens declare the glory of God, and Romans 1 declares that all of creation testifies of the ingenuity, power, and creativity of the Father. The heavens, trees, mountains, and oceans, indeed, speak of God's power and creativity. But not of His love and grace.

"I'm going to walk on the beach tonight instead of going to church," a Floridian might say—unaware that the biggest storm in thirty years is rumbling through the beaches of Pensacola. With winds blowing at one hundred nineteen miles per hour, roofs are blowing off houses and people are getting hurt.

Yes, nature gives witness to the reality of God, but it is a limited witness and can be a confusing message. That's why pagan cultures tried to appease the god of nature with human sacrifices, hoping that they would not be swallowed up in earthquakes or burned up in lava floes.

The only way to understand the grace and goodness of God is not by going hunting on Sunday, but by remembering what Jesus did on Calvary, opening up the Scriptures with your brothers and sisters corporately, and worshiping Him in unity.

2 Timothy 1:10 (b)–12 (a)
. . . who hath abolished death, and hath brought life and immortality to light through the gospel: Whereunto I am appointed a preacher, and an apostle, and a teacher of the Gentiles. For the which cause I also suffer these things . . .

"I'm a preacher," said Paul, "but I'm also a teacher." Preaching and teaching are different ministries. Preaching is proclaiming the Good News of the gospel to a world lost and headed for destruction. Teaching, on the other hand, is grounding believers in the full orb of Scripture.

Concerning marriage, Paul simply said, "In light of the times, let those that are married be as though they're not." In fact, he went on to say, "Let those that weep be as though they wept not; those that buy, be as though they possessed not" (see 1 Corinthians 7:29, 30). Thus, I find it interesting that the three subjects people most want to deal with in the church are marriage, emotions, and money matters—subjects Paul addressed very lightly.

What did Paul emphasize? The same themes Jesus did. He emphasized the huge, overarching themes of the kingdom—eternity, redemption, justification, sanctification, walking in the Spirit, the nature of the Father. Why does he emphasize those things? Because when they are understood, everything else falls into place (Matthew 6:33).

If I didn't teach through the Bible, I would have a tendency to choose certain subjects and ride them indefinitely. But as I teach through the Word, I find subjects are addressed in the right proportion at precisely the right time. If you're in ministry, teach the Bible from cover to cover. Avoid the temptation to talk about the issues people think they want to hear. Be like Paul, a preacher to non-believers, and a teacher of the full orb of Scripture to those who believe.

2 Timothy 1:12 (b)
. . . nevertheless I am not ashamed: for I know whom I have believed, and am persuaded that he is able to keep that which I have committed unto him against that day.

I know whom I have believed. Circle the word "whom." Underline it. Meditate on it. Paul doesn't say, "I know *what* I believe." He says, "I know *Who* I believe." That's the key. What gets you through the dark, damp, dungeons of life? Not what you believe. It's who you believe.

Many people know what they believe doctrinally. They know what they believe theologically. But they don't know Jesus personally. Others may not be all that familiar with the theology, but they know Jesus intimately—and they're a joy to be around.

"What" will never see you through dark, damp dungeon days. It will only say, "Wait a minute. This doesn't figure in to my theology."

But if you know *Who* you believe, you'll join Paul in saying, "Lord, if You have me here in this dungeon, that's okay with me. After all, when I remember what You did for me on the Cross, how could I not trust You?"

2 Timothy 1:13–15
Hold fast the form of sound words, which thou hast heard of me, in faith and love which is in Christ Jesus. That good thing which was committed unto thee keep by the Holy Ghost which dwelleth in us. This thou knowest, that all they which are in Asia be turned away from me; of whom are Phygellus and Hermogenes.

I believe Paul models the principle of specifically identifying false teachers who knowingly and poisonously peddle heresy.

2 Timothy 1:16–18
The Lord give mercy unto the house of Onesiphorus; for he oft refreshed me, and was not ashamed of my chain: But, when he was in Rome, he sought me out very diligently, and found me. The Lord grant unto him that he may find mercy of the Lord in that day: and in how many things he ministered unto me at Ephesus, thou knowest very well.

In contrast to Phygellus and Hermogenes, Paul writes of Onesiphorus as one who truly cared about him. Interestingly, all of Paul's allusions to Onesiphorus are in the aorist, or past tense, including a reference at the end of this letter (4:19). Therefore, we can conclude that Onesiphorus had died, "moved on" to his heavenly home. In this, we are given interesting insight into Paul's heart for this one to whom he felt

uniquely linked at a time when everyone else had abandoned him—a link that transcended the temporary separation that exists between we who are looking forward to the day when we will be in heaven and those who are already there.

2
2 Timothy 2:1
Thou therefore, my son, be strong in the grace that is in Christ Jesus.

"Sickly, emotional, young, timid one, be strong in grace," said Paul to Timothy. I would have said, "Timothy, be strong emotionally. Get it together." Or, "Quit your bellyaching and be strong physically." But that's not what Paul said. He said, "Be strong in *grace*."

So, too, the Lord wants you who, like Timothy, feel you're a little lacking in personality, somewhat weak emotionally, or less than impressive intellectually to be strong in grace—to expect the Lord to bless you not because of who you are, but in spite of who you are! God is looking for men and women He can bless not because of their prayer, their talent, their piety, or their devotion, but simply because of His grace—for they will be those through whom He is most glorified (1 Corinthians 1:27).

2 Timothy 2:2
And the things that thou hast heard of me among many witnesses, the same commit thou to faithful men, who shall be able to teach others also.

In our educational system, there are few greater sins than that of plagiarism. "Be innovative, creative, and original," our teachers say—which is fine for schoolwork, but not for ministry. Because there is no such thing as plagiarism in ministry, Paul told Timothy to take the very things he had heard Paul teach and pass them on to others.

2 Timothy 2:3, 4
Thou therefore endure hardness, as a good soldier of Jesus Christ. No man that warreth entangleth himself with the affairs of this life; that he may please him who hath chosen him to be a soldier.

Knowing they would be mowed down by Nazi machine guns, the first soldiers off the landing craft at Omaha Beach charged valiantly. Those who miraculously made it to shore safely began to climb the cliffs, knowing they were most likely climbing to their deaths. What would cause a man to hit the beach or to climb a cliff, knowing he would be gunned down in the process? Subsequent studies have shown that the heroes of D-Day did so out of respect and appreciation for their commanding officer and fellow soldiers. The concept of fighting for one's country is sometimes too big, too abstract. But risking one's life for the safety of one's commander or for the safety of the soldiers right beside him makes sense.

Paul didn't give Timothy ten theological reasons why he should serve the Lord. Rather, he gave him only one: to please the commanding officer and fellow soldier who had laid down His life for him.

2 Timothy 2:5
And if a man also strive for masteries, yet is he not crowned, except he strive lawfully.

Paul changes his analogy from warfare to athletics when he says, "You're not going to get the gold medal if you break the rules." So, too, we must know and abide by the principles found in the Scriptures.

2 Timothy 2:6
The husbandman that laboureth must be first partaker of the fruits.

In his third analogy, Paul challenges Timothy to be like a farmer—to wait patiently.

I have seen a bunch of churches and people who were on the verge of seeing some wonderful things happen in their ministries give up prematurely. Whether it be in ministry, marriage, witnessing at the job, or on the campus, hang in there. The great need in many cases is just to be patient.

It wasn't too many years ago that we met in a circle of about fifteen chairs for Sunday night service. For many years, Sunday night attendance at Applegate Christian Fellowship just never seemed to grow numerically. Many were the nights I would come home and wonder if we should just pull the plug on it completely. But I knew in my heart we had to keep on, for it was on Sunday nights that prayer was offered most deeply, where the gifts were expressed most freely, where Communion was served regularly. We did, indeed, keep on— and finally people realized the blessing of meeting together in that kind of atmosphere. So many things that have happened at the fellowship are like that. People who don't know the background see them as overnight suc-

cesses. But more often than not, there were years and years of just planting, watering, and waiting before any fruit was seen.

"Like a soldier, Timothy, please your commander," said Paul. "Like an athlete, compete lawfully. Like a farmer, be patient—and you will see fruit eventually."

2 Timothy 2:7
Consider what I say; and the Lord give thee understanding in all things.

In this verse we see a direct link between considering and understanding. "I don't understand the Bible," people say. "I just can't get it."

"Have you ever considered what you're reading?" I ask. "Have you ever slowed down and talked to the Lord about what you're reading? Have you ever waited quietly for Him to inspire your thoughts and touch your heart?"

We know that if we meditate on God's Word, we will have prosperity and good success (Joshua 1:8; Psalm 1:2). But what does the Bible mean by meditation?

The goal of Eastern meditation is to empty oneself of all thoughts until he becomes one with the universe. Biblical meditation is just the opposite. The Hebrew word for "meditation" is linked to what a cow does when it chews its cud. A cow constantly re-chews its food as it sends it to each of its seven stomachs.

That's what we're to do with Scripture. We're to read a passage, stop and consider it, meditate on it, chew on it, think through it, and pray about it. If I just read a chapter or five verses and say, "I don't get it"—I won't! But if I wait on God, if I stop and consider it, if I meditate on it, the Lord has promised to give understanding.

2 Timothy 2:8
Remember that Jesus Christ of the seed of David was raised from the dead according to my gospel.

"Be strong in grace, Timothy," exhorts Paul. "Be like a soldier, an athlete, a farmer. Meditate, slow down, and above all, remember Jesus Christ."

Paul's is a powerful and important exhortation: Don't become so enamored with ministry and so caught up in theology that you forget that Jesus is risen.

How do we remember Jesus? "Do this in remembrance of Me," Jesus said as He served His disciples Communion (Luke 22:19). Come to the

Table, saint, and remember both the work Jesus did for you on the Cross and that He is risen and lives in you right now.

2 Timothy 2:9, 10
Wherein I suffer trouble, as an evil doer, even unto bonds; but the word of God is not bound. Therefore I endure all things for the elect's sakes, that they may also obtain the salvation which is in Christ Jesus with eternal glory.

"Even though I'm in prison, the Word is not bound, for I'm still sharing through the epistles I'm writing," says Paul.

2 Timothy 2:11
It is a faithful saying: For if we be dead with him, we shall also live with him:

If we're dying for Jesus, we will also live with Him—not only in heaven, but presently—because for the extent to which we die to ourselves is the extent to which we will experience life abundantly. When I choose to die to my reputation, my rights, my ideas, and my pleasures—when I choose to take up the Cross and die daily as Jesus told me to, I live.

What does it mean to take up the Cross? Fighting the flu is not taking up the Cross. Grieving over the loss of a loved one is not taking up the Cross. Taking up the Cross is something we *choose* to do. Taking up the Cross means choosing to sacrifice something of yourself for the redemption of someone else.

What are you choosing to do for someone else's redemption, for someone else's spiritual growth? What are you choosing to let go of, to give up, to die to? Let go of self, and you'll find life abundant. That's a promise.

2 Timothy 2:12
If we suffer, we shall also reign with him: if we deny him, he also will deny us.

"I never knew the man," Peter cursed vehemently (Matthew 26:74). Yet after His Resurrection, Jesus found Peter personally and ministered to him tenderly (John 21:16). Thus, this verse doesn't refer to those who stumble like Peter, but to those who decide repeatedly that they want nothing to do with Jesus.

2 Timothy 2:13 (a)
If we believe not . . .

This is talking not about believing for salvation, but of the times when our faith is faltering,

when we're struggling, when we're slipping and sliding.

2 Timothy 2:13 (b)
. . . yet he abideth faithful: he cannot deny himself.

Imagine that you travel with me halfway across the country to Yellowstone National Park. There we are, standing by the fence waiting for Old Faithful to erupt—as it does approximately every ninety minutes. But after about thirty minutes, you become bored and you see a goose that you follow into the woods. I remain by the fence and see the spectacle of Old Faithful's geyser. You, on the other hand, miss out because you're on a wild goose chase. Finally, you say, "This is dumb. I'm going back and position myself near Old Faithful again."

Now, when Old Faithful sees you coming, it doesn't say, "Well, well, well. Look who's finally decided to show up. There's no way I will erupt for you. You've been on a wild goose chase." No, Old Faithful erupts regularly, faithfully no matter your position.

Paul is saying that God is, in the best sense of the word, like Old Faithful because His blessings are continually flowing. If I go off on a wild goose chase, I won't be blessed—not because the blessings aren't there, but because I've moved away. But once I realize I'm in the woods on some crazy excursion and return to the geyser of the goodness of God's grace, I find that God is faithful still.

For years, I thought God had to be "primed" through praise, prayer, and devotion. And I thought if I could just pump the handle of His blessings hard enough, blessing would start coming my way. But then I realized His grace is there anytime I choose to come back to my senses and return to Him.

God cannot deny Himself, gang. He's not faithful one day and frustrated the next. He's not generous one day but stingy the next. He is continually and completely *faithful.*

2 Timothy 2:14, 15
Of these things put them in remembrance, charging them before the Lord that they strive not about words to no profit, but to the subverting of the hearers. Study to shew thyself approved unto God, a workman that needeth not to be ashamed, rightly dividing the word of truth.

We are to understand how the Word is divided and then allow the Word to divide us (Hebrews 4:12).

For topical study of 2 Timothy 2:15 entitled "Rightly Dividing the Word," turn to page 1405.

2 Timothy 2:16
But shun profane and vain babblings: for they will increase unto more ungodliness.

Herein lies a perfect description of American television talk shows!

2 Timothy 2:17, 18
And their word will eat as doth a canker: of whom is Hymenaeus and Philetus; Who concerning the truth have erred, saying that the resurrection is past already; and overthrow the faith of some.

Hymenaeus and Philetus were saying, "There is no real resurrection. Forget the Rapture. It's all symbolic and not to be taken literally." They claimed to be insightful, but because of their vain discussion of these things, the faith of some was hurt badly.

2 Timothy 2:19
Nevertheless the foundation of God standeth sure, having this seal, The Lord knoweth them that are his. And, Let every one that nameth the name of Christ depart from iniquity.

Quoting from Numbers 16, Paul says, "Even though there are men causing problems with their erroneous teaching, the Lord will keep those that are truly His."
Numbers 16 is indeed an appropriate parallel. . . .

"Who gave you the right to rule over us?" Korah, Dathan, and Abiram asked Moses.
And Moses wisely responded by saying to the two hundred fifty men with them, "If I were you, I would depart from them. They're causing division. They're a big problem. Stay away."
But Moses' warning went unheeded. So the earth swallowed them all (Numbers 16:32).

If you want to find yourself swallowed up by despair or confusion, hang around those who cause problems. I have yet to see a man or a woman prosper who causes division and problems in a church.

2 Timothy 2:20, 21
But in a great house there are not only vessels of gold and of silver, but also of wood and of earth; and some to honour, and some to dishonour. If a man therefore purge himself from these, he shall be a vessel unto honour, sanctified, and meet for the master's use, and prepared unto every good work.

"Consider the church a great house," said Paul to Timothy. "Within it you will find many containers: Some are beautiful vases, others are garbage cans." In reference to both the passage that precedes this as well as the passage that follows, Paul says, "Separate yourself from those who pollute or cause problems in the body—or you will end up as a garbage can rather than as a beautiful vase."

2 Timothy 2:22 (a)
Flee also youthful lusts . . .

This doesn't mean if you're young, you're to flee lusts. It means regardless of your age, you're to flee youthful lusts. "I can watch HBO because I'm fifty and it doesn't affect me," some say. Or, "I can go in there because I'm not a kid anymore." Those who think this kid themselves. For the lusts that were real when they were younger are real all the days of their lives.

2 Timothy 2:22 (b)
. . . but follow righteousness, faith, charity, peace, with them that call on the Lord out of a pure heart.

When you're struggling, if you don't flee and run to those who call upon the Lord, you're going to be tempted a second time even more heavily than you were the first time.

2 Timothy 2:23–26
But foolish and unlearned questions avoid, knowing that they do gender strifes. And the servant of the Lord must not strive; but be gentle unto all men, apt to teach, patient, in meekness instructing those that oppose themselves; if God peradventure will give them repentance to the acknowledging of the truth; and that they may recover themselves out of the snare of the devil, who are taken captive by him at his will.

Sometimes the hardest thing to do in ministry is to be gentle with people who "oppose themselves"—with people who continue to be at cross-purposes with their own welfare—not because they hurt us, but because they hurt themselves. Yet Paul says we must be gentle and patient with *all* men—even those who are their own worst enemies.

If you are one who blindly or foolishly opposes yourself, my prayer is that you will see the vanity, the foolishness of doing so. May you choose, instead, like a soldier, to obey your Commander. May you choose, instead, like an athlete, to live according to the principles of Scripture. May you choose, instead, like a husbandman, to not grow weary in well-doing.

In short, may you grow strong in the grace of our Lord Jesus Christ.

RIGHTLY DIVIDING THE WORD
A Topical Study of
2 Timothy 2:15

O ver the years, I have observed that many people who love the Lord Jesus deeply are, nonetheless, embarrassed occasionally when unbelievers raise questions like the following. . . .

"How could a God of love order the extermination of the Canaanite civilization?"
"How could a God of love mandate the slaughtering of bulls and goats and little lambs and pigeons for sacrifices?"
"Why does the Bible set guidelines for slavery rather than abolishing it altogether?"

On and on, questions come our way that cause some who love the Lord to feel embarrassed about parts of the Bible.

The problem isn't with the Bible. The problem is with our inability to rightly divide it. The Greek word for "divide" means to cut a straight line, to make an incision. In order to rightly divide the Word, we need to understand first of all that the Bible is not simply a book of theology, but rather a drama through which we see the unfolding of God's redemption of mankind. Viewed as a drama, we see seven scenes, or "dispensations," into which all of Scripture is divided. . . .

Scene I
The Dispensation of Innocence

Psychologist B. F. Skinner voiced the belief of many when he said, "If you can change the external environment of a group of people, they will live at peace." Scripture, however, says otherwise, for when God placed man in the perfect environment in the Garden of Eden, what did man do? He chose to rebel in the one and only way possible. He chose to eat of the tree of the knowledge of good and evil that was placed in the Garden as a way for him to choose for or against God's love.

B. F. Skinner was wrong. Man chose to rebel. Consequently, those who say it's okay to smoke marijuana because God created it don't rightly divide the Word, for it was only during the age of innocence that God declared that which He had made to be good. But because the first dispensation came to a close when man fell, the Bible says at that point, all of creation entered into a fallen condition—groaning, aching, and longing for the day of restoration (Romans 8:22)

Scene II
The Dispensation of Conscience

Many think that if everyone simply followed their conscience, the world would be right. So in the period between Adam and Eve's fall in the Garden of Eden and the Flood that covered the earth, God declared "If you do well, you'll be accepted" (see Genesis 4:7). But it didn't work, for the dispensation began with Cain killing Abel and ended with the imagination of man being evil continually (Genesis 6:5).

Scene III
The Dispensation of Government

Mankind still has a tendency to think that if we could only elect good leaders, the problems of the world would be solved. Following the Flood, based upon the right and responsibility of capital punishment given to Noah, mankind was to govern himself.

Yet the "Dispensation of Government" began and ended dismally. No sooner had God given Noah responsibility to govern the world than, unable to govern even himself, Noah ended up drunk in his tent, fathering two peoples who would be problematic to the people of God throughout their history. The end of the dispensation is typified by the Tower of Babel—a government project constructed of mud and slime whose end result was total confusion.

Scene IV
The Dispensation of Promise

"We need a promise, a hope that good is coming," says man. God gave Abraham such a promise when He said He would make of Abraham a great nation (Genesis 12:2). Yet when famine hit, Abraham's descendants lost hope, disobeyed God, and headed for Egypt (Genesis 26:2).

Scene V
The Dispensation of Grace

"You tried a perfect environment. You tried to live by your conscience. You've given human government a whirl. You tried rules and regulations. Now," says God, "try this: For by grace are you saved, not of works. It's a gift of God" (see Ephesians 2:8, 9).

All of the previous dispensations lead to the one we are in right now—grace. We admit that government isn't the answer, that environment won't solve the problem, that our consciences are corrupt and seared. We admit we're sinners in desperate need of a Savior.

But some say, "I don't really know if I can believe in the idea of a free gift of salvation. I want to see some proof." And this leads to the next scene. . . .

Scene VI
The Tribulation

After the church is taken to heaven, God will begin to make himself known powerfully and visibly to those who don't believe on Him, to those who want nothing to do with Him. Hundred-pound hailstones will pelt the earth, and blood will fill valleys two hundred miles long as God employs terrible tragedy in a wake-up call to earth.

Scene VII
The Kingdom Age

At the end of the Tribulation, Jesus Christ will come back to rule and reign in Jerusalem for one thousand years. It seems all would be well at last. But in Revelation 20, we read an amazing thing: After one thousand years of such peace that the lion will lie down by the lamb, after one thousand years of such health that those who are one hundred years of age are considered children, after one thousand years of perfect conditions for humanity, guess what happens? Man rebels against God once again. Not you and me—but many of those who are on the earth in a human state will turn away from Jesus, ushering in the creation of a new heaven and earth.

Truly, there's a flow, a drama that unfolds throughout Scripture, which is not seen by those who simply focus on one section. That's why Paul said to Timothy, "Study." That's why we meet together regularly to study. And in so doing, we are able to say to the Jehovah's Witness, for example, that the 144,000 among which he numbers himself are part of a dispensation yet to come. And we are able to tell the Adventist that keeping the Sabbath in the "Age of Grace" is impossible if for no other reason than the fact that attending church on the Sabbath is in direct violation of the law that prohibits travel beyond one hundred yards.

An understanding of God's unfolding plan of redemption will cause one to read the Scriptures with an awareness of the scope and purpose of any given dispensation. However, one can rightly divide the Word and still miss the point if the Word of God doesn't divide him (Hebrews 4:12). That is, the Word of God must not only lodge in our minds—it must touch our hearts.

How can we know if the Word is touching our hearts? In Revelation 10:10, we read that when John ate of the scroll, signifying the Word, it was sweet to his mouth, but bitter to his belly. So, too, when I study theology—the promise of heaven, the assurance of salvation, the doctrine of justification—I find them oh, so sweet. But I know the Word is truly accomplishing its work within me when, upon further contemplation, I find them bitter as I realize the plight of those around me who don't yet know Jesus. In other words, I know the Word is having its intended effect when it not only satisfies my spirit, but when it motivates my soul to ministry, to service, to prayer, and to love.

May we be those who, like a skilled surgeon, rightly divide the Word. And may we be those who, like a willing patient, allow the Word to divide us, and to make us more like Jesus.

3 Hours before His death, Jesus told His disciples that the time would soon come when they would be persecuted even to the place of execution. "I'm telling you these things so you won't be offended," He said (John 16:1). The Greek word translated "offended" is *skandalizo,* from which we get our word "scandalize." In other words, not wanting His disciples to be scandalized, Jesus said, "The religious community will come after you. The political authorities will order your execution. But know this: In My Father's house are many mansions. And I'm going to prepare a place for you. Therefore, although in this present age you will experience great difficulty, you will ultimately be blessed incredibly because you're going to heaven" (John 14:1).

Coming to the end of his own life, the apostle Paul picks up this same theme as he warns Timothy of difficult days to come. And what he shares with Timothy has application for you and me specifically. . . .

2 Timothy 3:1
This know also, that in the last days perilous times shall come.

Knowing his death was imminent, I believe Paul nonetheless thought the Rapture would happen either in his lifetime or shortly thereafter. So do I. I believe the Rapture will happen in my lifetime.

"Well," you say, "if Paul thought the Rapture would happen in his lifetime, and it didn't—and if men of God throughout the ages have felt as though they were living in the last days and the Rapture would happen in *their* lifetimes, and it didn't—doesn't it seem foolish to think the Rapture will happen in *your* lifetime?"

Not at all. Throughout the history of the church, the greatest men and women of the faith have all lived their lives believing that the Lord's coming was nigh. And even though the Lord didn't come when they thought He would, looking for His return impacted their lives in such a way that they left their mark on history and will be rewarded greatly in eternity (2 Timothy 4:8). Luther, Calvin, Spurgeon, Finney, Moody, Torrey all felt the Lord's coming was close at hand. Put me in their company any day!

I choose to live my life looking for the Lord's coming. And if I am wrong, even if He doesn't come back for another five hundred years, I would rather go through the days I have left looking for the sudden appearing of Jesus Christ because I know the effect it has upon the life of any man or woman who believes He could come today: One's heart does not get troubled as easily. One is not prone to sin so readily. If you want to live a zealous, exciting, fulfilling, pure Christian life, live it looking for the Lord's coming (1 John 3:3).

2 Timothy 3:2 (a)
For men shall be lovers of their own selves . . .

Of the students in the ten leading industrialized nations, American high-school students scored either ninth or tenth in every academic category. But in the category of self-esteem, they came in first. In other words, our culture is very good at teaching our kids to say, "I'm okay. I'm somebody. I'm proud."

2 Timothy 3:2 (b)
. . . covetous, boasters . . .

The Greek word translated "boasters" is *alazon,* which speaks of a claim made by a quack promising something but unable to deliver that which was promised.

2 Timothy 3:2 (c)
... proud, blasphemers ...

The idea of blasphemy literally refers to those who use the Lord's name in vain. People say "God" constantly—but seldom with reverence. Even by people interviewed on news programs, the Lord's name is used in vain constantly.

2 Timothy 3:2 (d), 3 (a)
... disobedient to parents, unthankful, un-holy, without natural affection ...

I believe nothing identifies us more clearly as those who have fallen into unnatural affection than the sad statistics relating to abortion. We're horrified when we read that the Canaanites placed their babies on the incandescent arms of idols. *How can this be?* we wonder. And yet we burn our babies with saline solutions in the wombs of mothers—a practice even more hor-rific, a practice that goes against every natural instinct to protect one's offspring.

2 Timothy 3:3 (b)
... trucebreakers ...

The idea here is of people ignoring covenants or contracts.

2 Timothy 3:3 (c)
... false accusers, incontinent, fierce ...

After being confronted by a student upset with an assignment, the teacher of an anger man-agement class lost his temper and hit the stu-dent in the face. Now, if even teachers of anger management are hitting people, without the Lord, what hope is there for the rest of our an-gry world?

2 Timothy 3:3 (d), 4
... despisers of those that are good, traitors, heady, highminded, lovers of pleasures more than lovers of God.

People love pleasure. But it's a love that leads only to the "Been there, done that, now what?" mentality, as they find they have to continually do something bigger, better, farther, faster, and higher in order to get the same thrill they once did.

2 Timothy 3:5
Having a form of godliness, but denying the power thereof: from such turn away.

We're to turn away from those who are without natural affection, from those who despise things that are good, from those who love pleasure more than God, from those who talk about NewAge spirituality but who know nothing of the power of the Holy Spirit and the Resurrected Jesus.

2 Timothy 3:6, 7
For of this sort are they which creep into houses, and lead captive silly women laden with sins, led away with divers lusts, ever learning, and never able to come to the knowledge of the truth.

Those who propagate a form of godliness not based upon the Resurrection creep around neighborhoods looking for people who have time on their hands to whom they can say, "Let us hold a class in your house so we can share our interest-ing insights and esoteric experiences."

2 Timothy 3:8
Now as Jannes and Jambres withstood Mo-ses, so do these also resist the truth: men of corrupt minds, reprobate concerning the faith.

As proof to Pharaoh that God had indeed sent him, Moses threw down his rod and it became a serpent. Jannes and Jambres, magicians in Pha-raoh's court, threw down their rods—which also became snakes. When Moses caused all of the water to turn to blood, Jannes and Jambres said, "We can do that, too." And they did. When Moses called for frogs to cover the land, Jannes and Jambres were able to counterfeit that miracle as well (Exodus 7). Here, Paul likens those who live for pleasure, ignore the Lord, and resist truth to these two magicians of the occult in Pharaoh's court.

2 Timothy 3:9
But they shall proceed no further: for their folly shall be manifest unto all men, as theirs also was.

What folly was manifest in Jannes' and Jam-bres' situation? Their counterfeiting Moses' mir-acles was foolish because all they could do was make matters worse. All they could do was make *more* blood, *more* frogs, *more* snakes. That's the way it always is with Satan's counterfeits be-cause all he ever does is make things worse. Yes, there is power in the occult. Surely demons can counterfeit miracles. And perhaps there are strange things that happen when palms or tarot cards are read. But they will only make things worse, for Satan will never make things better. Ever.

Contract breakers, pleasure seekers, false spiritualists, lovers of self—these indicators of the last days don't discourage me for a couple of reasons . . .

First, bad times are made for good people. That is, when times get tough, good things start happening in our lives. What takes the wrinkles out of the shirt I wear? The heat and pressure of an iron. What turns a lump of coal into a sparkling diamond? Heat and pressure. So, too, I have noticed that the tougher the times— whether it be financially, spiritually, relationally—the more wrinkles are smoothed out, the more the brilliant light of Jesus shines, the more people grow in their walk with God.

Second, good people are made for bad times. Shadrach, Meshach, and Abed-nego were three kids who refused to bow the knee to Nebuchadnezzar's statue. "Throw us into the fiery furnace," they said. "If God chooses to deliver us, so be it. But if not, that's okay, too" (see Daniel 3:17, 18). When were Shadrach, Meshach, and Abednego seen in this light? When times were dark.

The darker your campus or your office, the easier it will be for you to shine for Jesus Christ. Perhaps it was tougher in some ways in the fifties when everything was white picket fences, homecooked meals, and Ike. Perhaps it was tougher in some ways to stand out or stand up because the contrast may not have been as great. On the other hand, in these times when things are so perverse and polluted, we can stand out without even trying!

2 Timothy 3:10, 11
But thou hast fully known my doctrine, manner of life, purpose, faith, longsuffering, charity, patience, persecutions, afflictions, which came unto me at Antioch, at Iconium, at Lystra; what persecutions I endured: but out of them all the Lord delivered me.

"You know me, Timothy," said Paul. "These false teachers are charlatans. They do magic tricks. They talk in riddles. They're impressive for a moment or two, but you know what I've been through on behalf of the gospel. You know what kind of man I am."

What a statement! How I pray that we, like Paul, might be able to say to our kids and to younger men and women, "You know my lifestyle. You know my purpose. You know my faith."

2 Timothy 3:12
Yea, and all that will live godly in Christ Jesus shall suffer persecution.

Here's a promise you're not likely to find in your Precious Promise box! Yet Paul gave this as the reason for what he was going through and the reason he was not surprised or discouraged by it.

2 Timothy 3:13, 14 (a)
But evil men and seducers shall wax worse and worse, deceiving, and being deceived. But continue thou in the things which thou hast learned and hast been assured of . . .

"Continue in what you *have* learned, in what you *have been* assured of." Paul isn't saying, "Learn more; dig deeper." No, he's telling Timothy to stay away from false spirituality and to stick with the basics.

2 Timothy 3:14 (b)
. . . knowing of whom thou hast learned them.

The word translated "whom" being plural, Paul most likely is alluding to Timothy's mother and grandmother as those who, in addition to himself, had spiritually impacted Timothy's life.

I'm always a little skeptical and somewhat suspicious when a person says, "I only learn from this guy," or, "I'm only a follower of that man." Wise is the man or woman who will learn from the many people the Lord places in their lives to reinforce and undergird their faith.

2 Timothy 3:15
And that from a child thou hast known the holy scriptures, which are able to make thee wise unto salvation through faith which is in Christ Jesus.

"Ever since childhood, you've been taught the Word, Timothy. And it is the Word that will make you wise."

2 Timothy 3:16, 17
All scripture is given by inspiration of God, and is profitable for doctrine, for reproof, for correction, for instruction in righteousness: That the man of God may be perfect, thoroughly furnished unto all good works.

The Greek word translated "all" is an interesting one. It means *all.* There are critics and commentators who say this verse would be rendered, "All Scripture which is by inspiration of God is profitable for doctrine . . ."—the implication being that not all Scripture is inspired. If I adopt this stance, however, I have to decide what's inspired and what isn't. And in so doing, I become the judge of the Bible rather than allowing the Bible to judge me. Jesus said, "Man shall not live by bread alone but by *every* word which proceeds out of the mouth of God" (see Matthew 4:4). Here in Timothy, we see that it is because *all* Scripture is inspired that we can be furnished unto *all* good works.

━━━━━━━━━━━ ✆ ━━━━━━━━━━━

2 Timothy 4:1–4
I charge thee therefore before God, and the Lord Jesus Christ, who shall judge the quick and the dead at his appearing and his kingdom; Preach the word; be instant in season, out of season; reprove, rebuke, exhort with all longsuffering and doctrine. For the time will come when they will not endure sound doctrine; but after their own lusts shall they heap to themselves teachers, having itching ears; and they shall turn away their ears from the truth, and shall be turned unto fables.

Most pastors evidently thinking that the day of Bible study has long since come and gone, only 3 percent of evangelical, fundamental churches in America have midweek Bible studies. As sad as this is, it should come as no surprise, for Paul told Timothy that in the end times, people would not have a desire for sound doctrine.

2 Timothy 4:5, 6
But watch thou in all things, endure afflictions, do the work of an evangelist, make full proof of thy ministry. For I am now ready to be offered, and the time of my departure is at hand.

The Greek word translated "departure" is a great one. It can refer to the taking up of an anchor, the unyoking of an ox, or the folding of a tent. Thus, in using this word, Paul is saying, "I'm ready to take up the anchor and sail into heaven. I've been plowing long enough on earth. It's time to move on!"

2 Timothy 4:7, 8
I have fought a good fight, I have finished my course, I have kept the faith: Henceforth there is laid up for me a crown of righteousness, which the Lord, the righteous judge, shall give me at that day: and not to me only, but unto all them also that love his appearing.

If you are one who says, "I love life. God has been good to me. But I know I'm only a pilgrim because I'm headed for heaven and looking for His coming,"—you are guaranteed a crown of righteousness, which will determine your ministry in the ages to come.

According to Luke 12, Jesus will actually serve a meal to those who are watching for His coming. What a day that will be!

Oh, but I've blown it so badly. There's no way the Lord would serve me, you might be thinking. Ask Peter about that. After denying the Lord, he went back to his old occupation of fishing. But even when he was out at sea and out to lunch, when he saw Jesus on the beach, he swam to shore, wanting to be with Him. And what did Jesus do? He served Peter a meal (John 21:12)—just as He had promised.

2 Timothy 4:9, 10 (a)
Do thy diligence to come shortly unto me: For Demas hath forsaken me . . .

In his letter to Philemon, Paul referred to Demas as his fellow labourer (Philemon 24). A few years later in his letter to the Colossians, Paul would say, "Demas greets you" (see Colossians 4:14). Having gone from being a fellow labourer to simply one who said, "Hi," here in 2 Timothy, we read that Demas had forsaken Paul altogether.

There exists the very real possibility of slowly drifting away from the Lord even by those who are at one time used by Him. It happened to Demas. Don't let it happen to you. How? Read on.

2 Timothy 4:10 (b)
. . . having loved this present world, and is departed unto Thessalonica.

Don't get caught up in the entertainment, the distractions, the baubles, or the frivolity of the world—for such will only distract and pull you away from serving the Lord.

2 Timothy 4:10 (c), 11
Crescens to Galatia, Titus unto Dalmatia. Only Luke is with me. Take Mark, and bring him with thee: for he is profitable to me for the ministry.

Mark is John Mark—the one who Barnabas wanted to bring on Paul's second missionary journey, but whom Paul refused due to the fact that John Mark had bailed out on their first missionary journey. After having "no small dispute" concerning John Mark (Acts 15), Paul and Barnabas split company. Barnabas, whose name means "son of consolation," continued on, focusing on the rehabilitation of his nephew, John Mark. Paul, on the other hand, focused on the work at hand, replacing Barnabas with Silas.

Who was right—Paul who said, "The work is too important to take a risk on someone who might turn away," or Barnabas who said, "We need to work with anyone who shows even a little potential"?

They both were. There are those who have a vision and passion for the work at large, and there are those who have a heart for each individual. And although these two groups will not always see eye to eye, both are needed. Here, at the end of his life, Paul sends for John Mark, for evidently Barnabas had indeed accomplished a good work in him.

2 Timothy 4:12, 13 (a)
And Tychicus have I sent to Ephesus. The cloke that I left at Troas with Carpus, when thou comest, bring with thee, and the books . . .

"The books," or *biblion*, could very well refer to the Gospels. "Bring me the Gospels," Paul said. "My days are limited here. Final exams are coming up!"

You'll know what a man's passion is by what he does when he doesn't have to do anything. Paul didn't have to do anything. He had no teaching to prepare, no sermon to outline. Yet he said, "Even though the hour is come to hoist up the anchor, to take off the yoke, to fold up the tent, I want to know more about Jesus."

2 Timothy 4:13 (b)
. . . but especially the parchments.

The Greek word translated "especially" meaning "also" and parchments most likely referring to the Old Testament scrolls, Paul was requesting the Old Testament as well as the Gospels.

2 Timothy 4:14
Alexander the coppersmith did me much evil: the Lord reward him according to his works.

All of us will have an Alexander the coppersmith or two in our lives—people who are just out to get us. Notice that of Alexander, Paul did not fret and fume, saying, "Get him, Lord." Rather, he simply said, "I know the Lord will deal justly with him."

2 Timothy 4:15, 16
Of whom be thou ware also; for he hath greatly withstood our words. At my first answer no man stood with me, but all men forsook me: I pray God that it may not be laid to their charge.

In accordance with Matthew 5:44, Paul prayed, "Lord, forgive those who didn't have the courage to stand by me or to stay with me."

2 Timothy 4:17 (a)
Notwithstanding the Lord stood with me, and strengthened me . . .

Forsaken by many, Paul said it was when he was alone that he had an awareness of the Lord's presence. How often that is the case. It's when we feel let down by a friend who ignores us, disheartened by an illness that strikes us, or abandoned when a loved ones leaves us that the Lord becomes most real to us.

Over and over again, I have found that when I felt most alone, the Lord became most real. You have found the same to be true, for when there are people around us, we have a tendency to rely on them. But when we're alone, we find ourselves walking with the Lord in ways we wouldn't have otherwise.

2 Timothy 4:17 (b)
. . . that by me the preaching might be fully known, and that all the Gentiles might hear . . .

Even in prison, Paul continued to preach. How? Through the epistles he wrote and through the conversations he shared with his jailers.

2 Timothy 4:17 (c)
. . . and I was delivered out of the mouth of the lion.

Some believe Paul was placed in the coliseum before he was beheaded, and a miracle took place when, like Daniel, he was delivered from the mouth of the lion. Others believe this reference is to Satan, who walks about as a roaring lion, seeking whom he may devour (1 Peter 5:8). But whether Paul was referring to an actual lion or to Satan, the fact is, God came through. God delivered him.

2 Timothy 4:18
And the Lord shall deliver me from every evil work, and will preserve me unto his heavenly kingdom: to whom be glory for ever and ever. Amen.

Some have suggested that Paul thought he was so close to the time of the Rapture that he would be delivered from being beheaded by Nero.

Whether or not that be so, Paul knew that one way or the other, he would soon be in the presence of the Lord.

2 Timothy 4:19, 20
Salute Prisca and Aquila, and the household of Onesiphorus. Erastus abode at Corinth: but Trophimus have I left at Miletum sick.

Concerning Trophimus, Paul didn't say, "Why are you sick? Where's your faith?" No, some were healed when Paul prayed for them; some weren't. Trophimus was one who wasn't. Those who say God wants everyone healed immediately have not read this verse.

2 Timothy 4:21, 22
Do thy diligence to come before winter. Eubulus greeteth thee, and Pudens, and Linus, and Claudia, and all the brethren. The Lord Jesus Christ be with thy spirit. Grace be with you. Amen.

As we come to the end of Paul's second letter to Timothy, we come as well to the last of Paul's recorded words. His final utterance was, "Timothy, after all is said about the end times in which you'll be living and the challenge of the ministry you're undertaking—everything is summed up in one word: Grace.

And that's the word for us as well.

TITUS

Background to Titus

Written in approximately A.D. 64, between his first and second letters to Timothy, Paul's letter to Titus was written to instruct and encourage this young man as he ministered on the island of Crete. Crete, an island in the Mediterranean 135 miles long and 30 miles wide, is a mountainous island and was quite heavily populated according to the demographics of Paul's day. As we shall see, the inhabitants of Crete were a difficult, problematic people. In fact, it's interesting to note that the Philistines—they who were always hassling the people of Israel—originally came from Crete. Crete was an island steeped in Greek mythology, Zeus having supposedly been born on Crete's own Mount Ida.

Commissioned to preach to a problematic people who were believers in Greek gods, Titus had his work cut out for him.

TITUS

1 **Titus 1:1 (a)**
Paul, a servant of God, and an apostle of Jesus Christ . . .

It was after he had been released from his first imprisonment in Rome that Paul most likely traveled to Crete and left Titus there to establish a work on the island.

Titus 1:1 (b)
. . . according to the faith of God's elect . . .

The Greek phrase translated "according to the faith" is better translated "for the furtherance of the faith." Paul is saying, "I just want to see God's people go farther, and do better. I want to see the kingdom expanded and people deepened." Such was Paul's heart.

Titus 1:1 (c)
. . . and the acknowledging of the truth which is after godliness.

Although the King James Version reads, "truth which is after godliness," the idea here is "truth which produces godliness."

Titus 1:2
In hope of eternal life, which God, that cannot lie, promised before the world began.

Paul's intent is that people do better and go farther in the glorious hope of eternal life. "And this is eternal life," Jesus prayed in His High Priestly prayer, ". . . that they might know thee the only true God, and Jesus Christ, whom thou hast sent" (John 17:3).

We usually think of eternal life as existing someday far away in heaven. But that's only part of it. According to Jesus' prayer, eternal life is to know the Lord here and now in our hearts. Thus, the farther I get from the Lord, the more hellish things become. But in the days I spend time with the Lord, I experience something of heaven on earth. The closer I walk to the Lord, the more heavenly my days will be.

It was after Enoch fathered his son, Methuselah, that Scripture records he began to walk with God (Genesis 5:22). Kids will make one walk with God—especially a kid like Methuselah. Living to the age of 969, he must have been home for five hundred years!

"Enoch walked with God: and he was not; for God took him" (Genesis 5:24). I can almost hear the Lord saying, "You know, Enoch, this walk we've enjoyed together has been so wonderful. You've walked with Me so closely that now we're closer to My house than yours. Come on Home."

"This is eternal life," Jesus prayed, "that they may know You, Father—not out there geographically, but here and now intimately."

Titus 1:3
But hath in due times manifested his word through preaching, which is committed unto me according to the commandment of God our Saviour.

In his first letter to the Corinthians, Paul talks about the foolishness of preaching (1 Corinthians 1:21). So, too, when people hear that you drive to church to sit in a pew for a couple of hours, they say, "That's foolish." But the preaching of the Word causes our hearts to be happy, our spirits to be warmed. Let the world call it crazy, but to those of us who are a part of the kingdom, there's nothing like it.

Titus 1:4 (a)
To Titus . . .

Like Timothy, Titus was one who was probably led to Jesus by the apostle Paul. We know from Galatians 2 that Titus, a Greek, traveled with Paul to the Jerusalem council, wherein it was decided that, because salvation came by grace through faith alone, circumcision was not a requirement for salvation (Acts 15). We see Titus again in 2 Corinthians 8, where he is instrumental in the raising of money by the Corinthian church to help those who were hurting in Jerusalem. After that, Paul sent Titus to the island of Crete, and later to the region of Dalmatia, or present-day Bosnia.

When you put Titus' travel log together, you realize he went down to Jerusalem to deal with the controversy over circumcision, then to Corinth, which was a difficult ministry, then to Crete, where there was no shortage of problems, and finally on to Bosnia. It was an arduous program, but Paul had great confidence

in Titus, for like Timothy, Paul esteemed him highly.

Titus 1:4 (b)
. . . mine own son after the common faith.

As he did with Timothy, Paul evidently was the one who brought Titus to a saving knowledge of Jesus Christ.

Titus 1:4 (c)
Grace, mercy, and peace . . .

To his usual salutation of grace and peace, Paul adds mercy in his letters to Timothy and Titus because they're his sons in the faith—and all fathers know their sons need mercy!

Titus 1:4 (d)
. . . from God the Father and the Lord Jesus Christ our Saviour.

As in his usual salutations, Paul bestows grace and peace from God the Father and the Lord Jesus Christ. Have you ever wondered why the Third Person of the Trinity—the Holy Spirit—is not mentioned? In John 16, Jesus taught us that when the Spirit came, He would not speak of Himself. Therefore, as He inspires Paul, the Holy Spirit does not mention Himself in the opening credits because His ministry is not to speak of Himself. The ministry of the Holy Ghost is singular: to point people to Jesus Christ. When churches, people, or movements are centered on the Holy Spirit, I am suspicious because the ministry of the Spirit is to spotlight Jesus.

Titus 1:5 (a)
For this cause left I thee in Crete, that thou shouldest set in order the things that are wanting . . .

Because Titus was to set the church of Crete in order, we can assume Paul didn't start the church there. Who did? We can't be sure—but this we do know: When the Holy Spirit came upon the believers in the Upper Room, men from Crete are listed among those who heard the gospel in their own tongue (Acts 2:11). Thus, it could very well be that those who heard the message of salvation on the Day of Pentecost got saved and returned to Crete.

At Babel, languages and culture groups were separated (Genesis 11). The great reversal of Babel happened at Pentecost when suddenly different language groups and cultures were brought together through the power of the Holy Spirit. Whatever attempts man makes in the flesh toward unity are doomed to fail. It is only in the Spirit where the effects of Babel are reversed.

Titus 1:5 (b)
. . . and ordain elders in every city, as I had appointed thee.

There's no room for political maneuvering in spiritual leadership. "You are to ordain elders," or literally "You are to appoint elders," Paul instructed Titus.

"Choose you out men, Moses, whom you know to be elders and appoint them to be rulers over tens, fifties, hundreds, and thousands" (see Exodus 18:21–25). The very first time we see elders in Scripture, they weren't voted into office. They were appointed. In the same way, Paul says to Titus, "You appoint elders as I appointed you."

Titus 1:6 (a)
If any be blameless . . .

This doesn't mean that to be an elder a man must be perfect, or we're all in big trouble! No, the idea here is that an elder must be one who's not pointed at in derision.

Titus 1:6 (b)
. . . the husband of one wife, having faithful children not accused of riot or unruly.

Ministry must be established at home before one can have credibility in the church. I once read an article about the first man to scale Mount Everest without oxygen. He was recovering in a hospital after falling off a wall at his home because he had locked himself out of his house. Here's a guy who conquers every mountain in the world. But where does he fall? At home. There are men who can conquer mountains on the job or with finances, but as far as ministry is concerned, if a man can't keep his balance at home, Scripture says he is disqualified from ministry in the church. That's not a word of condemnation. It's a word of re-prioritization.

Get your home squared away, Dad. Get your kids grounded and walking with the Lord. Whatever you want to do in ministry, you can do with your kids. You can lead them in worship; you can serve them Communion; you can preach as long as you want! True ministry may one day extend beyond your family, but not before it is established within your family.

Now that my kids are grown up and beginning

to leave home, I don't regret one moment I spent having devotions with them. I only wish I had done it more. I don't wish I had taken them to more baseball games or more movies. I'm just thankful for the time we logged together talking about the Lord, learning His ways, studying His Word.

Train up your kids, Mom and Dad. Other ministry will come, but that's where it all starts.

Titus 1:7 (a)
For a bishop must be blameless, as the steward of God . . .

"Steward" simply means "servant." There's a lot of talk about the need for *men of faith*. But an even greater need is for *faithful men* to simply and consistently direct traffic, change diapers, or put away chairs at their fellowships if that's what the Lord has called them to do.

Titus 1:7 (b)
. . . not selfwilled, not soon angry . . .

As a spiritual man desiring to be used by the Lord to any degree, you can't be one who loses your temper.

Titus 1:7 (c), 8 (a)
. . . not given to wine, no striker, not given to filthy lucre; but a lover of hospitality . . .

Whereas Paul told Timothy an elder should be hospitable (1 Timothy 3:2), here he tells Titus that an elder must be one who loves hospitality. I suggest the reason we don't love hospitality is because we fall into the "Martha mentality" . . .

"Tell Mary to help me prepare this meal," said Martha to Jesus.

"Martha, you're troubled about many things, but only one thing is needful," Jesus answered.

Most people think the one needful thing Jesus referred to is sitting at His feet as Mary was doing. While that is important, indeed, I believe Jesus was also saying, "You're cooking this big meal, Martha. Pots are boiling, toast is burning, stuff is spilling, but all I wanted was just one simple thing to eat" (see Luke 10:42).

The key to loving hospitality is just being real, not trying to impress people, but simply enjoying one another's company.

Titus 1:8 (b), 9 (a)
. . . a lover of good men, sober, just, holy, temperate; holding fast the faithful word as he hath been taught . . .

In this, I am reminded of one of David's men—
a man named Eleazar.

The Israelites were fleeing from the Philis-
tines. But Eleazar, whose name means "God
is my help," grabbed his sword and stood
his ground. Samuel's account says his
hand "clave unto the sword," and that the
Lord brought a great victory (see 2 Samuel
23:9, 10).

May we be those whose hands cleave to the
sword of the Word (Hebrews 4:12), who don't let
it go, who pack it around with us. A Bible that's
falling apart usually belongs to someone who
isn't. Get in the Word. Stay in the Word, gang.
Make it a nonnegotiable priority in your daily
life.

Titus 1:9 (b)
. . . that he may be able by sound doctrine
both to exhort and to convince the gain-
sayers.

"To establish this work on the island of Crete,
you must be a man who's in the Word," Paul instructs Titus, "in order for you to deal with the
challenges that are sure to come your way."

Titus 1:10
For there are many unruly and vain talkers
and deceivers, specially they of the circum-
cision.

"The Judaizers with whom we dealt in Jerusalem are going to come your way, Titus—those
who will try to place regulations and burdens
upon others," said Paul. "The only way you'll fend
them off is by sound doctrine."

Titus 1:11 (a)
Whose mouths must be stopped . . .

The mouths must be stopped of those who
preach legalism and who put people in bondage
about what day they should or shouldn't worship,
how they should dress, what they should or
shouldn't eat.

Titus 1:11 (b)
. . . who subvert whole houses, teaching
things which they ought not, for filthy lu-
cre's sake.

I often wonder how many ministries would
continue if there was no money coming in.

Titus 1:12, 13 (a)
One of themselves, even a prophet of their
own, said, The Cretians are alway liars, evil
beasts, slow bellies. This witness is true.

A Cretan poet named Epimenides called his
own people liars and gluttons, and Paul agreed.
Talk about politically incorrect! I like Paul's courage and his honesty, as he was not afraid to go on
record saying that the false teachers were in ministry simply for money, and that the Cretans
were prone to lies and laziness.

Titus 1:13 (b)
Wherefore rebuke them sharply, that they
may be sound in the faith.

"If the Cretans behave according to stereo-
type," Paul says, "rebuke them."

Titus 1:14
Not giving heed to Jewish fables, and com-
mandments of men, that turn from the truth.

Whether ministering to the Cretans with their
laziness or the Jews with their tendency to get
wrapped up in fables that distract people from
the truth, Paul exhorts Titus to keep focused and
centered on the Scriptures.

Titus 1:15
Unto the pure all things are pure: but unto
them that are defiled and unbelieving is
nothing pure; but even their mind and con-
science is defiled.

"I want you to be wise, knowledgeable in the
things that are good, but naive in the things
which are evil," Paul told the church at Rome
(Romans 16:19)—a needed word for our culture
as well. Believers should be those who know
Scripture like the back of their hands, but are
clueless regarding the double entendres and
jokes of the world.

Titus 1:16
They profess that they know God; but in
works they deny him, being abominable, and
disobedient, and unto every good work rep-
robate.

"Don't judge me," the world says to us. "Didn't
Jesus tell you to judge not lest you be judged?"
Yes, Jesus did say that (Matthew 7:1). But the
Greek text renders the word "judge" as *krino,*
which means "judging to condemnation." In the
same chapter, Jesus went on to say, "You'll know

false teachers and false prophets by their fruit" (see Matthew 7:16).

In other words, we're not to judge others for purposes of *condemnation*, but we are to judge the fruit of others for purposes of *identification*. That is why Paul tells young Pastor Titus to beware of the religionists and mystics whose works prove they don't know God.

§

2 Titus 2:1
But speak thou the things which become sound doctrine.

As he continues to give instruction and encouragement concerning the ministry on the island of Crete, Paul tells Titus to teach sound doctrine. At this point, I would think Paul would go on to define sound doctrine in terms of pneumatology, eschatology, soteriology, and all kinds of other big words. But that's not what he does.

Titus 2:2
That the aged men be sober, grave, temperate, sound in faith, in charity, in patience.

The Lord is not interested in us becoming people who have theories of theology. He wants the understanding of the Word to be translated through our lives into daily practicality. "This is sound doctrine, Titus," he says, "that the older guys are to be sober." That is, they shouldn't be caught up in silliness or frivolity.

Sound doctrine also dictates that older men are to be grave. This doesn't mean they're dour, or that they don't know how to have a good time. It means they don't take life lightly. They live for eternity, and they see the big picture.

Titus 2:3 (a)
The aged women likewise, that they be in behaviour as becometh holiness . . .

Sound doctrine for older women is that they exhibit holy, whole, together lives.

Titus 2:3 (b)
. . . not false accusers . . .

We see the same word used with regard to Satan as he accuses us day and night (Revelation 12:10). False accusers categorize people, saying, "Isn't that just like her?" or, "He always does that," with the intent of subtly slandering others.

Titus 2:3 (c)
. . . not given to much wine, teachers of good things.

Godly women don't categorize people. Instead, they teach good things like the following . . .

Titus 2:4, 5 (a)
That they may teach the young women to be sober, to love their husbands, to love their children, to be discreet, chaste, keepers at home, good, obedient to their own husbands . . .

I am firmly convinced that this is the ideal curriculum for a women's ministry. I know there are lots of women's study groups that study doctrinal issues. While that is fine, I suggest a higher, better way: to teach younger women how to be keepers of their homes and lovers of their kids and husbands.

Titus 2:5 (b)
. . . that the word of God be not blasphemed.

Notebooks full of theological insights are useless if they come at the expense of a well-ordered home and a well-loved family.

Titus 2:6, 7 (a)
Young men likewise exhort to be sober minded. In all things shewing thyself a pattern of good works . . .

Young men, you are not to simply tell others what they should be doing, but rather you are to be a pattern to others. Just as Moses was to make all things according to pattern regarding the construction of the tabernacle (Exodus 25:9), young men are to pattern their lives after the One who lived, or "tabernacled," among us—Jesus Christ (John 1:14).

Titus 2:7 (b)
. . . in doctrine shewing uncorruptness, gravity, sincerity.

The word "sincerity" means "without wax," referring to the ancient practice of the sculptors who patched their mistakes with wax—unseen until the noonday sun shone on the sculpture after the unsuspecting customer had taken it home. Thus, sincerity refers to a quality of reality and honesty that doesn't "melt" in the heat of adversity.

Titus 2:8
Sound speech, that cannot be condemned; that he that is of the contrary part may be ashamed, having no evil thing to say of you.

Sound doctrine for young men is that they live in such a way that those who are eager to put

Christians down will find nothing to hold against *them*.

Titus 2:9 (a)
Exhort servants to be obedient unto their own masters, and to please them well in all things . . .

In our day, the word "servants" refers to employees.

Titus 2:9 (b), 10 (a)
. . . not answering again; Not purloining, but shewing all good fidelity . . .

Christian employees are not to talk back or steal from their employers in either time or money.

Titus 2:10 (b)
. . . that they may adorn the doctrine of God our Saviour in all things.

By being obedient and serving your employer well, you'll make salvation attractive to the boss who may not yet be a believer.

Titus 2:11, 12
For the grace of God that bringeth salvation hath appeared to all men, teaching us that, denying ungodliness and worldly lusts, we should live soberly, righteously, and godly, in this present world.

Once a person chooses to receive the free gift of salvation, he knows intuitively, innately, and immediately that he is to live righteously. And the next verse tells us how.

Titus 2:13
Looking for that blessed hope, and the glorious appearing of the great God and our Saviour Jesus Christ.

If you really believe Jesus is coming soon, it will affect everything you do.

For topical study of Titus 2:11–13 entitled "Looking for Our Lord," turn to page 1420.

Titus 2:14 (a)
Who gave himself for us, that he might redeem us from all iniquity, and purify unto himself a peculiar people . . .

"Peculiar" doesn't mean "odd." It means "awed." That is, people will be awed by the fact that while everyone else at work is panicking,

you're peaceful; while everyone else is gossiping, you're gracious; while everyone else is bitter, you're doing better.

Titus 2:14 (b)–15; 1:16
. . . zealous of good works. These things speak, and exhort, and rebuke with all authority. Let no man despise thee. They profess that they know God; but in works they deny him, being abominable, and disobedient, and unto every good work reprobate.

Telling the truth to his contemporaries as well as those younger and older than him would probably not have been easy for Titus. And it may not always be easy for you. But if you're a boss, a Bible study teacher, a parent, or a coach, there are times when you need to speak the truth, as hard as it may be.

Then said I, Ah, Lord GOD! behold, I cannot speak: for I am a child. But the LORD said unto me, Say not, I am a child: for thou shalt go to all that I shall send thee, and whatsoever I command thee thou shalt speak. Be not afraid of their faces: for I am with thee to deliver thee, saith the LORD. See, I have this day set thee over the nations and over the kingdoms, to root out, and to pull down, and to destroy, and to throw down, to build, and to plant.
                                                  Jeremiah 1:6–8, 10

That's what moms and dads, pastors and grandparents, bosses and coaches have to do sometimes. We're called to pull down in order that we may build up.

Purge me with hyssop, and I shall be clean: wash me, and I shall be whiter than snow. Make me to hear joy and gladness; that the bones which thou hast broken may rejoice.
                                                  Psalm 51:7, 8

As a shepherd, David understood the meaning of broken bones. You see, when a lamb would stubbornly and rebelliously continue to wander away from the flock, the shepherd would break its legs and place the lamb on his shoulder where it would remain until its bone was healed. When the lamb could again walk, so bonded was he with the shepherd, he would never stray again.

Like sheep, we all go astray (Isaiah 53:6). Therefore, in His love, the Good Shepherd breaks a bone or two and carries me while I whine and cry and wonder what He's doing. But as the days and weeks and months go by, I find myself closer to Him than I had ever been previously, and all I can say is, "Thank You, Lord."

Part of shepherding means breaking a bone or two. Thus, Titus would have to speak words that could cause tears to flow or bones to snap. But he could do so with authority, knowing it was an opportunity for the wounded sheep to one day walk with its Shepherd more intimately.

LOOKING FOR OUR LORD
A Topical Study of
Titus 2:11–13

Jesus spoke of the eye as being the light of the entire body (Matthew 6:22, 23). And Paul tells us that we are to think on whatsoever things are true, honest, just, pure, lovely, virtuous, praiseworthy, and of good report (Philippians 4:8). But because our society no longer believes in the authority of the Bible, our culture continues to crumble—which is exactly what Jesus said would happen.

> *And as it was in the days of Noah, so shall it be also in the days of the Son of man. They did eat, they drank, they married wives, they were given in marriage, until the day that Noah entered into the ark, and the flood came, and destroyed them all. Likewise also as it was in the days of Lot; they did eat, they drank, they bought, they sold, they planted, they builded; but the same day that Lot went out of Sodom it rained fire and brimstone from heaven, and destroyed them all.*   Luke 17:26–29

Once we're saved, we need no one to tell us that, like Noah, we are to be those who are different from the times in which we live, that we are to live soberly, righteously, and godly. But here's the question for you and me: How? How can we live soberly, righteously, and godly in a world full of iniquity? According to our text, the answer is that we are to be looking for Jesus constantly.

You never drive so carefully as the day you discover your driver's license has expired. So, too, we will live soberly, righteously, and godly when we understand that because our culture is as it was in the days of Noah and as it was in the days of Lot, time itself is nearly expired, and we must live very carefully.

The apostle John knew this to be true. . . .

> *Beloved, now are we the sons of God, and it doth not yet appear what we shall be: but we know that, when he shall appear, we shall be like him; for we shall see him as he is. And every man that hath this hope in him purifieth himself, even as he is pure.*   1 John 3:2, 3

Thinking the Lord could come back today will affect everything I do—how I talk, what I watch, where I go. On the other hand, Jesus taught us that if you sit here today, and even as I'm teaching, you're thinking, *The Lord is not coming back any time soon*, that too will have a very real effect upon your life.

> *Therefore be ye also ready: for in such an hour as ye think not the Son of man cometh. Who then is a faithful and wise servant, whom his lord hath made ruler over his household, to give them meat in due season? Blessed is that servant, whom his lord when he cometh shall find so doing. Verily I say unto you, That he shall make him ruler over all his goods. But and if that evil servant shall say in his heart, My lord delayeth his coming; and shall begin to smite his fellowservants, and to eat and drink with the drunken; the lord of that servant shall come in a day when he looketh not for him, and in an hour that he is not aware of, and shall cut him asunder, and appoint him his portion with the hypocrites: there shall be weeping and gnashing of teeth.*
>
> Matthew 24:44–51

The Greek word translated "evil" is *kakos* and refers to that which was once good but has gone bad—like a piece of fruit, or a musical instrument that was once in tune but is now out of tune. Thus, Jesus is saying the once-good servant became sour, slipped out of tune, because he said, "The Lord delays His coming." And Jesus says the result of such a viewpoint is twofold.

Brutality

> *And he shall begin to smite his fellowservants . . .*

He who doubts the nearness of the Lord's return will gossip about people, be cynical toward people, and will be harsh with people. Whereas if he really thought today could be the day the Lord comes back, he wouldn't scream at people, find fault with people, or be bitter toward people. In short, he wouldn't smite his fellow servants.

Carnality

> *. . . and to eat and drink with the drunken . . .*

He who doubts the Lord's soon return will begin to eat and drink with the drunkards. "It's party time," he'll say. "The Lord isn't coming back for a while—probably not even in my lifetime—so let's party. I'll only go to church if there's nothing else to do. I'll only study the Word if there's nothing on TV."

The servant who was once good and who has now gone bad is not one who denies the coming of Christ. Rather, he's one who simply believes He's not coming soon. In Exodus 32, we see an Old Testament parallel to the evil servant parable. . . .

> *And when the people saw that Moses delayed to come down out of the mount, the people gathered themselves together unto Aaron, and said unto him, Up,*

make us gods, which shall go before us; for as for this Moses, the man that
brought us up out of the land of Egypt, we wot not what is become of him.

Exodus 32:1

The people became *kakos*. They went bad. Why? Because they thought Moses, their leader, delayed his coming. The result? Exactly what Jesus said it would be: Carnality when they danced around a golden calf and brutality when three thousand of them were killed (Exodus 32:28).

The way to live godly, soberly, and righteously is to look for the blessed hope of the coming of Jesus Christ in any given day. But what if He doesn't come that day? You had a great day! You walked righteously, soberly, and godly. Your family was blessed. Your heart was full. God's blessings were celebrated and enjoyed because you lived looking for the blessed hope of His return.

The majority of us fail to look for the Lord's coming today not because we deny its reality nor because we think it will be delayed chronologically, but because we are afraid emotionally. "I see things falling apart, and I know the only solution is for the Lord to come back. Yet when He comes back, I don't know where I will stand. I love Him. I believe in Him. But I haven't done as much as I wanted to for Him," we say.

If this is how you feel, there is good news for you in Luke 12. . . .

Blessed are those servants, whom the lord when he cometh shall find watching:
verily I say unto you, that he shall gird himself, and make them to sit down
to meat, and will come forth and serve them.   Luke 12:37

Leaving the kids with a babysitter, my wife, Tammy, and I returned home a few hours later.

"The kids did great," said the babysitter. "But the whole time you were gone, Benjamin sat on the couch and looked out the window, just waiting for you guys to come back."

Upon hearing this, I didn't say to three-year-old Benny, "What's the big idea sitting on the couch looking for my coming?" Nor did I say, "Why weren't you in the backyard raking the leaves and picking up after Sam?" Instead, I just took him in my arms and gave him a great big hug because I knew how much he just wanted to be with me.

The same is true of Jesus. To the one who says, "Life is good, but what I'm really looking for and craving is You, Lord," He won't say, "Why didn't you do more?" According to our text, He'll say, "Let's have lunch."

But I haven't been a very good person, you might be thinking. Join the club. Like me, you may have done things you didn't want to do, said things you shouldn't have said, gone where you shouldn't have gone. But the Lord still has a place for you at His table. How do I know? Because of what I see in the life of Joseph. . . .

One of the clearest pictures of Jesus is seen in the person of Joseph—a man of whom there is no recorded sin, a man who was betrayed by his brothers for twenty pieces of silver, a man whose public "ministry" began at age thirty when he became prime minister of Egypt, a man who took a Gentile bride. As his brothers gathered before him, their hearts must have been filled with fear concerning what they had done to him. Yet what does Joseph say?

> *But as for you, ye thought evil against me; but God meant it unto good, to bring to pass, as it is this day, to save much people alive. Now therefore fear ye not: I will nourish you, and your little ones. And he comforted them, and spake kindly unto them.*
>
> Genesis 50:20, 21

When Jesus comes, you will be as blown away and amazed as Joseph's brothers were—amazed by how kind He is to you, by the comfort He shows to you, by the meal He provides for you. But you can experience His love and kindness, His grace and forgiveness even before then by simply watching for His coming every day.

My desire and prayer is for us to be a people who look for the blessed hope—the coming of our Lord Jesus Christ. The lives of those who do will be ordered and fruitful, righteous and godly. May we learn the lesson of Exodus and listen to the parable of Jesus. May we live our lives looking for His coming, knowing that in doing so, we will be blessed not only in that day, but in this day as well.

3 Titus 3:1
Put them in mind to be subject to principalities and powers, to obey magistrates, to be ready to every good work.

We are to be a people who live under authority.

Titus 3:2 (a)
To speak evil of no man . . .

I learned this the hard way a few years ago . . .

Walking into the YMCA, I saw a young guy I recognized as Marty, a high-school student from Applegate, dribbling a basketball on the gym floor. As he took a shot from half-court, the ball went up in the air—and missed everything.

"Way to go! Nice shot!" I kidded.

He got the ball, took a hook shot, and missed again.

"Keep it up, buddy. Looking good!" I jeered.

But as I walked closer, I realized it wasn't Marty at all. Some high-school kid was shooting hoops, and here I was just railing on him!

How I wish I had read this verse before I went to the YMCA that day!

Titus 3:2 (b), 3
. . . to be no brawlers, but gentle, shewing all meekness unto all men. For we ourselves also were sometimes foolish, disobedient, deceived, serving divers lusts and pleasures, living in malice and envy, hateful, and hating one another.

Paul tells Titus to appoint meek men to the position of elder.

After speaking at a men's retreat one weekend, I was driving to the airport feeling pleased with how well it had seemed to go. "What a blessing," I said to myself. "Maybe I should do more of this type of retreat. I wonder what's ahead for me?"

That thought had no sooner entered my mind than a sign on the roadside caught my eye. In better days, it had read: WORLD'S BIGGEST JERKY AHEAD. Now, however, the

*"Y" having fallen off, it read: WORLD'S BIG-
GEST JERK AHEAD.*
  *And all I could say was, "I get the message,
Lord!"*

Oh, that we would be meek—always keeping in
mind what we once were, and what we still have
a tendency to be!

Titus 3:4–6
**But after that the kindness and love of God
our Saviour toward man appeared, not by
works of righteousness which we have done,
but according to his mercy he saved us, by the
washing of regeneration, and renewing of
the Holy Ghost; which he shed on us abundantly through Jesus Christ our Saviour.**

Although we still have fleshly tendencies, we
have been washed and renewed—not because of
our righteousness, but because of what Jesus did
on the Cross in our place. And because we're a
forgiven people, we are to forgive others.
  It's as if Paul is saying, "Yes, Titus, you must
speak truth. You must tell your congregation
both young and old how to live. However, you
must do so with great meekness, remembering
that the Lord washed you, renewed you, and
saved you not by any works of righteousness you
did, but according to Jesus' "abundant mercy."

Titus 3:7
**That being justified by his grace, we should
be made heirs according to the hope of eternal life.**

This doctrine is so important in relation to
what Paul had told Titus to do. "Keep everything
in perspective, Titus. Remember what you once
were and how you've been washed, renewed, and
justified not by your discipline, dedication, or devotion—but solely by God's grace."

Titus 3:8
**This is a faithful saying, and these things I
will that thou affirm constantly, that they
which have believed in God might be careful
to maintain good works. These things are
good and profitable unto men.**

Bible teachers and parents, it's not how much
you know that matters. It's how well you know
what you know. How do people get to know things
well? By hearing them over and over again. That
is why we are to affirm constantly and remind
continually.

Titus 3:9 (a)
**But avoid foolish questions, and genealo-
gies . . .**

Mormons spend multiplied millions of dollars
and countless man-hours researching genealogies in order that they might baptize for the
dead. That is, they believe benefits of baptism
can be experienced by those who are already
deceased. Cult leader Garner Ted Armstrong
tries to prove through genealogies that
America constitutes the lost tribes of Israel.
It's all foolishness. Stay away from these tangents. The main thing is to keep the main thing
the main thing. And the main thing is Jesus.

Titus 3:9 (b)
**. . . and contentions, and strivings about the
law; for they are unprofitable and vain.**

People constantly confront me who want to
strive about the law, about diet, or about Sabbath
days. Maybe you are too. Paul's word to Titus
concerning such people is not to dialogue with
them, but to avoid them.

Titus 3:10, 11
**A man that is an heretic after the first and
second admonition reject; knowing that he
that is such is subverted, and sinneth, being
condemned of himself.**

"Warn them once, talk to them a second time,
but don't continue dialoguing with those who are
into heresy." Why? You'll waste your time. You'll
spin your wheels. You'll get nowhere. Satan
knows your endless talking with someone who's
in a cult will prevent you from witnessing to your
next-door neighbor. There are those who waste
tons of time trying to convert heretics. Don't do
it. Paul's instruction is to tell them the truth once.
Tell them a second time. Then reject them, knowing they've condemned themselves.

Titus 3:12
**When I shall send Artemas unto thee, or
Tychicus, be diligent to come unto me to
Nicopolis: for I have determined there to
winter.**

Nicopolis was a city on the west side of the
Greek islands. "Once help arrives for you, come
and meet me in Nicopolis," said Paul.

Titus 3:13 (a)
Bring Zenas the lawyer . . .

Paul was in jail a lot. No wonder he called for a lawyer!

Titus 3:13 (b)
. . . and Apollos on their journey diligently, that nothing be wanting unto them.

Apollos was a powerful orator, a preacher skilled in rhetoric, and a good man.

Titus 3:14
And let ours also learn to maintain good works for necessary uses, that they be not unfruitful.

"To maintain good works" is better translated "to possess honest trades." That is, the men with whom Titus was ministering were to be those who had the ability to support themselves by the work of their hands in order that they wouldn't be a burden financially.

Titus 3:15
All that are with me salute thee. Greet them that love us in the faith. Grace be with you all. Amen.

Thanks to Paul's letter to Titus, we have just completed Doctrine 101—practical things we need to think through, pray in, and remind one another of. I encourage you to take some time to go through Paul's lists again. If you're an older man, read the verses addressed to older men. If you're an older woman, read the verses written for you. If you're a young man or woman, read the verses concerning you, and say, "Lord, how am I doing in these areas?" And as you do, begin and end your study as Paul did his letter. Begin and end it not with determination or discipline, work ethic or will power. Begin and end it with an appreciation of God's undeserved, unearned, unmerited favor poured out upon you.

In other words, begin and end it with grace.

PHILEMON

Background to Philemon

O n a trip once, I came across a shop containing correspondence of famous people. There was a handwritten note from Abraham Lincoln written to a lady who had invited him and his wife for dinner. Framed and carefully preserved, it was selling for tens of thousands of dollars. There was also a handwritten note from Harry Truman—a very terse note to someone who had criticized his daughter's piano playing. And there was a note from Sirhan Sirhan, the assassin of Robert Kennedy. Although each of these letters was being sold for a great sum of money, I'm sure that when they were written, their authors had no idea they would be so valuable.

So, too, I'm sure the apostle Paul would be surprised to discover just how valuable this little note he wrote to his friend Philemon has proven to be. It was, after all, a personal letter to a personal friend about a personal problem. Unlike his other letters, written to instruct churches or to exhort pastors, this letter was not intended to be read publicly.

Yet as we read it, we will see why it is included in the canon of Scripture, for not only does it give us unique insight into the heart of Paul, it is also a powerful portrayal of one of the great doctrines of our faith.

PHILEMON

P hilemon 1 (a)
Paul, a prisoner . . .

The year is A.D. 62. Paul is under house arrest in Rome. That is, although he's chained to a guard at all times, he can evidently leave his rented room as long as the guard goes with him.

Philemon 1 (b)
. . . of Jesus Christ . . .

Paul usually begins his letters by identifying himself as an apostle of Jesus Christ. This time,

however, he's a prisoner of Jesus Christ. Would to God that I would be more like Paul—that when I feel chained by circumstances or imprisoned by problems, I would realize I would not be there were it not the Lord allowing me to be there for His purposes. Paul was used powerfully because he had the understanding that wherever he might have been was not due to the politics of man, but to the sovereignty of God.

Philemon 1 (c)
. . . and Timothy our brother . . .

Paul adds Timothy's name because, growing older, he was in the process of preparing people

to accept the ministry and authority of his young
protégé.

Philemon 1 (d), 2 (a)
... unto Philemon our dearly beloved, and
fellowlabourer, and to our beloved Apphia,
and Archippus our fellowsoldier ...

Apphia, very possibly Philemon's wife, and Archippus their son, Paul is greeting the whole family here.

Philemon 2 (b)
... and to the church in thy house.

I like this phrase! People say to me, "I wish I
were in the ministry."
And I say, "You can be tonight! Train your kids
in the ways of God. Minister to them. Teach them
the Word. Pray with them. Serve Communion to
them. Build your family. Your house is your
church."
"But I'm just a teenager," you say.
Then be nice to your little brother or sister and
talk to them about the Lord!
Listen, gang, everyone should be in the ministry because the ministry needed most is right
there under your own roof. Philemon's family
was one dedicated to the Lord. And evidently,
Philemon and Apphia not only ministered to their
own family but also opened their house and ministered to others.

I recently visited the Mission at Carmen Ser-
dan—the orphanage for handicapped kids in
Mexico—run by my brother Jimmy and his
wife, Julie. The work at the Mission is always
amazing to me, but this time I was particu-
larly blessed by hearing Jimmy and Julie's
kids say their ABC's. As are all of the mission
staff kids, Abby, David, and Ellie are home-
schooled. And the way Jim and Julie taught
them their alphabet was with a verse for each
letter... And we know all things work together
for good ... Believe on the Lord Jesus Christ
and thou shalt be saved ... Casting all your
care upon Him for He careth for you ... De-
light thyself in the Lord and He shall give thee
the desires of thine heart ...

Every one of us can follow the example of Philemon. Every one of us can teach our kids the
things of the Lord, and then open our homes to
share with others.

Philemon 3–5
Grace to you, and peace, from God our Fa-
ther and the Lord Jesus Christ. I thank my
God, making mention of thee always in my

prayers, hearing of thy love and faith, which
thou hast toward the Lord Jesus, and to-
ward all saints.

There's lots of talk today about preventive
medicine—keeping people healthy rather than
merely taking care of them when they're sick.
Paul here models not preventive medicine, but
preventive ministry, when he says to Philemon,
"Hearing that your family is walking with the
Lord and that there's a church in your house
causes me to pray for you constantly."
We generally only pray for people when we
hear they're sick or struggling, going through
tough trials, or facing hard times. And pray we
must. But in addition to that, I suggest we pray
like Paul. I suggest we pray for those who are doing well that they might do even better.
It's when the Enemy sees people doing well
that he decides to launch an attack against them.
Why? He knows he's lost their souls, but if he can
pull them down in depression or discouragement,
he knows they'll be unable to impact others
whose souls he's not yet lost. Satan doesn't spend
his time on the lost. You will never read in the
New Testament where Satan himself is warring
against an unbeliever. Yes, as the prince of darkness, he blinds the eyes of unbelievers (Ephesians 2:2; 2 Corinthians 4:4), but as far as
spiritual attacks, he saves himself totally and exclusively for those who are in Christ, for those
who are walking with God. In every instance
where you see Satan in the New Testament, you
will always see him coming against believers in
order to minimize their effectiveness for the
kingdom. This makes it all the more important
for us to pray for those doing well, for they are
sure targets of the Enemy.

Philemon 6
That the communication of thy faith may be-
come effectual by the acknowledging of every
good thing which is in you in Christ Jesus.

"I thank God for you," says Paul, "and I pray
that you'll be even more effective in communicating the faith as people around you see the good
things that are happening within you."
Let me ask you this question: Do you think the
people at your job, on your campus, or in your
neighborhood see in you such joy, peace, and love
that they wish they knew your secret? Such was
the case with Philemon.

Philemon 7
For we have great joy and consolation in thy
love, because the bowels of the saints are re-
freshed by thee, brother.

The bowels being the seat of emotion in Greek thought, Paul and others were deeply refreshed by news of Philemon's love.

Philemon 8 (a)
Wherefore . . .

After affirming Philemon, Paul moves on to the reason for his letter . . .

Philemon 8 (b), 9
. . . though I might be much bold in Christ to enjoin thee that which is convenient, Yet for love's sake I rather beseech thee, being such an one as Paul the aged, and now also a prisoner of Jesus Christ.

"Philemon, I've got a problem," Paul says. "I could enjoin you to help me, but instead I entreat you. I could command you, but instead I ask you."

Philemon 10
I beseech thee for my son Onesimus, whom I have begotten in my bonds.

While chained to a Roman guard, Paul encountered a man named Onesimus who was a fugitive in the city of Rome, a runaway slave who had stolen goods from his master. It is possible that Paul somehow bumped into Onesimus in the marketplace and began to dialogue with him. It is also possible that Onesimus was apprehended and chained to the same guard as Paul. We are not exactly sure how the paths of Onesimus and Paul crossed, but cross they did.

Onesimus found there is no freedom in freedom itself, for although he was free from his master, he was still a slave to his own conscience, to his own sin. But Onesimus was to discover that although there is slavery in freedom, there is also freedom in slavery. How? Jesus calls all who are weary and heavy laden to take His yoke upon them, to be chained to Him, so to speak (Matthew 11:28, 29). But He is a good Master, and all do find freedom in "slavery" to Him. That's why Paul said, "I am a bondslave"—a slave by choice (see Romans 1:1). Marriage proves this point, for it is, in a sense, slavery. And it can either be glorious or miserable, depending on with whom you are linked!

The question in this life is not whether or not you're yoked, but to Whom are you yoked? If we are yoked to Jesus, we are yoked to the quintessentially excellent Master, to the One who loves us so much, to the One who's so good *for* us, and so good *to* us.

Realizing that although in chains, Paul was free, and although he was free, he was enslaved to his own sin, Onesimus was led to a saving knowledge of Jesus Christ by Paul the apostle.

Philemon 11
Which in time past was to thee unprofitable, but now profitable to thee and to me.

I can see a twinkle in Paul's eye as he writes this, for he employs a play on words that Philemon was sure to appreciate. You see, "Onesimus" means "profitable." Although he had been a most unprofitable slave to Philemon when he stole from him and ran away, Paul knew the born-again Onesimus would now be highly profitable to Philemon because his friendship and help were already of great value to Paul.

Philemon 12, 13
Whom I have sent again: thou therefore receive him, that is, mine own bowels: Whom I would have retained with me, that in thy stead he might have ministered unto me in the bonds of the gospel.

"I would love to keep him," Paul tells Philemon. "If you could be here to help me, I know you would. But Onesimus has already been of great help to me, as well as being a comfort to me."

Philemon 14
But without thy mind would I do nothing; that thy benefit should not be as it were of necessity, but willingly.

"I don't want to do something that would interfere with your relationship with Onesimus," said Paul. "You're his master. He's your slave."

Philemon 15, 16
For perhaps he therefore departed for a season, that thou shouldest receive him for ever; not now as a servant, but above a servant, a brother beloved, specially to me, but how much more unto thee, both in the flesh, and in the Lord?

"Although he didn't know it, perhaps the reason Onesimus ran away was so he could be with you forever in heaven as a brother," Paul tells Philemon.

Philemon 17
If thou count me therefore a partner, receive him as myself.

"Philemon, if our relationship has meant anything to you, if you count me as a partner, receive Onesimus as you would receive me," Paul writes.

Philemon 18, 19 (a)
If he hath wronged thee, or oweth thee ought, put that on mine account; I Paul have written it with mine own hand, I will repay it ...

And here is the reason I believe this personal little postcard of Paul's was included in the canon of Scripture: Nowhere is the glorious "Doctrine of Imputation" seen more clearly.

For topical study of Philemon 17, 18, see "Paul the Peacemaker," below.

Philemon 19 (b)
... albeit I do not say to thee how thou owest unto me even thine own self besides.

"I'll pay Onesimus' debt," says Paul, "and I won't even bring up the fact that, as your spiritual mentor, you owe me your very life!"

Philemon 20, 21
Yea, brother, let me have joy of thee in the Lord: refresh my bowels in the Lord. Having confidence in thy obedience I wrote unto thee, knowing that thou wilt also do more than I say.

There are those who can't understand why Paul would send Onesimus back into slavery, but I believe this passage more than hints that Paul knew Philemon would set Onesimus free.

Philemon 22
But withal prepare me also a lodging: for I trust that through your prayers I shall be given unto you.

Catch the flow here: Having said, "I'm confident you'll do even more than I ask concerning Onesimus," Paul goes on to say, "As soon as I am released from prison, I'm coming to visit you." In other words, Philemon most likely understood that Paul didn't expect Onesimus to still be a slave in Philemon's house when he arrived!

Philemon 23–25
There salute thee Epaphras, my fellowprisoner in Christ Jesus; Marcus, Aristarchus, Demas, Lucas, my fellowlabourers. The grace of our Lord Jesus Christ be with your spirit. Amen.

As always, as we come to the end of this personal letter, Paul leaves us in the place of grace.

PAUL THE PEACEMAKER
A Topical Study of
Philemon 17, 18

Whether it was in a crowded Roman marketplace, or through an armed Roman guard, we can't be sure. But this much we do know: The "aged apostle" and the runaway slave met, resulting in the letter before us. Why was this personal postcard of Paul's included in the canon of Scripture? I suggest the following possible reasons. . . .

Biographical Value

For a man to go to bat for a slave was unheard of in Paul's day. Greek historian, Pliny, recounts an incident concerning a slave who accidentally tipped a dish he was carrying, causing a bit of food to spill on his master's table. His punishment? He was immediately thrown into the courtyard pond stocked with bloodsucking lampreys and was devoured. According to Pliny, this was not unusual treatment because slaves were thought of as less than human. Yet here is Paul saying, "I care deeply about Onesimus."

Most people think of Paul as harsh and austere. His letter written on behalf of a runaway slave clearly says otherwise.

In the little book before us, we also see in Paul a man who not only had a compassionate heart, but one who didn't pull rank. To Philemon he says, "I'm going to talk to you as a brother. I'm praying for you. I have confidence in you. I'm going to give a suggestion to you that you would be wise to consider, but I'm not going to force this upon you."

His letter to Philemon allows us to see in Paul a heart, an attitude, a tactfulness, a grace that helps round out our understanding of our wonderful brother, Paul.

Ethical Value

Onesimus is saved. He's born again. But what does Paul do? He tells him he must go back and pay his debt. Why is this important? Because many people say, "There's no need for restitution, no need for meeting my obligation because I wasn't a Christian when I ran up my credit cards to forty thousand dollars." Or, "I signed that contract before I was born again; therefore, it doesn't matter now." This little book is important because it says a new life does not release one from old debts. Yes, we have a new life in Christ, and He looks at us as being without spot or wrinkle positionally, but we have an obligation to the people around us practically to pay old debts and make things right.

Mom and Dad, please teach your kids that once confession is made, there is immediate and total forgiveness from God, but they still have an obligation to make things right in man's sight. The world looks at Christians, wanting to find a reason not to believe. Let's not give them one. Onesimus shows us that we have an ethical obligation to pay debts—be they financial, relational, or societal.

Theological Value

Under the inspiration of the Spirit, Paul told Philemon that perhaps it was part of God's plan for Onesimus to rip him off and run away in order that Onesimus would come to a saving knowledge of Jesus. But notice Paul says, "Perhaps."

Growing up, I would hear testimonies of guys who came to the Lord after years of doing drugs or being involved in gangs. And I erroneously concluded that the only way to be really used by God was to first go through perversity. God may perhaps work that way, but it's not the only way. I am so thankful I was raised in a Christian home. Oh, it might not make for a very exciting testimony, but it shows that God is not limited to any single methodology.

Political Value

Paul doesn't use this situation to kick off an antislavery campaign. He doesn't say, "We'll start the Onesimus Coalition. Get our newsletter, and for only thirty-five dollars a month, you, too, can lead a movement to abolish slavery." No, Paul masterfully and insightfully says, "Philemon, I trust God's work in your life, and I know you'll do even more than I'm suggesting to you," the implication being that Philemon would set Onesimus free of his own accord.

Paul was not trying to legislate morality, but rather he was trusting in the work of the Holy Spirit to transform a man's heart internally. The problem with the Christian political movement is that so often it tries to clean the fish before it catches it; it attempts to change people before saving them.

Paul makes a suggestion here, saying, "Do more than what I say." Centuries go by. The gospel does its work through Wilberforce in England, through Lincoln in America. Hearts are changed. People come to understand that the institution of holding another man down is not right, and the work Paul begins is finally complete. Cultures and communities only truly change when people are born again, when they're changed from within.

Doctrinal Value

As important as the biographical, ethical, theological, and political implications of Paul's Epistle to Philemon are, I believe the doctrinal value inherent in this seemingly insignificant little postcard is the reason we hold in our hands Paul's letter as part of the canon of Scripture. Herein we see the glorious "Doctrine of Imputation," as Paul says to Philemon, "If Onesimus wronged you, if he owes you anything, charge it to my account."

Blessed is the man to whom the Lord will not impute sin.   Romans 4:8

To whose account is our sin imputed, or charged?
To the account of the One who was pinned to a Cross in our place.

Therefore being justified by faith, we have peace with God through our Lord Jesus Christ . . .   Romans 5:1

The incredible fact of justification means God not only forgives our sin but also chooses to forget we're sinners.

For all have sinned, and come short of the glory of God; being justified freely by his grace through the redemption that is in Christ Jesus: Whom God hath set forth to be a propitiation through faith in his blood, to declare his righteousness for the remission of sins that are past, through the forbearance of God . . .
                                                                   Romans 3:23–25

Imputation is based upon justification, which can only come about through propitiation. Propitiation means that the righteous wrath God should hurl on me, the righteous anger He should feel toward you, was absorbed by His Son.

I remember reading the story of a man who, on his way to the kitchen late at night, noticed the top of the terrarium in which he kept his eight-foot boa constrictor was ajar. As he glanced around the room for the snake, he was suddenly gripped by a horrifying thought. He ran to the nursery, where he found the snake in his son's empty crib. Racing to his garage, he grabbed an ax and began chopping the snake, hoping to pull his baby to safety. But it was too late. No one arrested this dad for killing the boa constrictor. No one called the animal rights people. No, everyone identified with the righteous anger in his heart concerning the fate of his son.

So, too, it is a loving Father who feels a holy indignation, a righteous anger when He sees every one of His children being eaten up by the snake of sin. He is right in taking up the ax and saying, "I can't stand what sin has done. It's swallowed up, ripped off, and ruined people's lives."

Yet as willing participants, we become not only the victims of sin, but propagators of it. So to destroy sin, God would have to destroy mankind. Instead, He comes up with an unbelievable third alternative. He took the ax of His indignation and didn't thrust it in the snake, but buried it in Himself. He who knew no sin became sin (2 Corinthians 5:21). God's understandable, justifiable, righteous anger was released, His justice meted out when He slaughtered Himself to become the propitiation for my sin.

What does this mean? It means that reconciliation is based upon imputation by means of justification through the work of propitiation. Simply said, reconciliation between God and us meant Jesus had to die. Reconciliation always means someone has to die.

Husband, if you're distanced from your wife; Wife, if you're estranged from your husband; Kids, if you feel as though there's a problem between you and your parents, the only way there will be reconciliation is if someone dies. Will you choose to die, Husband? Will you choose to end the war between you and your wife by laying down your point of view, your way of thinking, your anger, bitterness, or hostility?

Will you choose to die, Wife, by laying down your hurts and your fears, your cares and concerns in order to make peace with your husband?

Will you choose to die, Kids, to your own demands and needs and, instead, honor your parents?

At work, on the ball field, in the classroom, at home, the only way there can be reconciliation is if someone dies. The question is, will it be you?

"But he has to pay for what he said about me," or "She has to pay for what she did to me," or "They have to pay for how they hurt me."

"It's already been paid," Jesus says. "As I bled on the Cross of Calvary, I absorbed that sin specifically."

Therefore, all that remains is for us to say, "Thank You, Lord. I'm free."

As I consider this, I wonder who you are.

Some are Onesimus. If you're Onesimus, open your heart anew to the Lord, and do what's right. If you're not paying child support, pay it. If you're cheating your workplace, make restitution. I admire Onesimus because instead of refusing to go back, he returned and made things right. If you're Onesimus tonight, I have good news for you: God can do something wonderful with your life if you'll choose to do what's right.

Some are Philemon. If you're Philemon, you need to say, "I have no right to hold this debt, this unforgiveness, this bitterness toward that person. And even though I might not agree with him or have been hurt badly by her, I am going to see Christ dying for that sin and embrace that person once again."

Others are like Paul, looking for ways to make peace. If you're making peace between people at war with one another, good for you! In humility, you are not pulling rank, not preaching, but simply willing to not only point out the problem but also ready to get your own hands dirty to help pay the price.

Who am I?

I suppose I'm all three. Sometimes, though not often enough, I'm Paul. Other times, needing to make things right, I'm Onesimus. Often, I'm Philemon, needing to forgive. Yet this powerful postcard of Paul ministers to me on all three levels. And I pray it will do the same for you.

May you, like Onesimus, celebrate the freedom of your salvation. May you, like Philemon, embrace others, knowing their sin has been imputed to our Lord's account. And may you, like Paul, be a peacemaker.

In Jesus' Name.

HEBREWS

Background to Hebrews

By way of introduction, I would like you to note three things about this fabulous Book of Hebrews: its author, its audience, its argument. . . .

Author

Debates have raged for almost two thousand years concerning the author of this book. Many scholars believe it has the fingerprints of Dr. Luke all over it. Others insist the eloquence of the Book of Hebrews argues for the orator Apollos, the powerful speaker mentioned in the Book of Acts, and also alluded to in the first Corinthian Epistle. It could be Apollos; it could be Luke. One thing, however, is certain: Whoever penned this epistle had an intense understanding of theology combined with an immense Greek vocabulary. And these two factors point me personally to the apostle Paul. Not only did Paul's brilliant mind give him a greater grasp of the Greek language than any other man throughout history, but his understanding of Old Testament theology was unrivaled as well.

In a greater sense, though, the question of authorship doesn't really matter, for, truly, God is the author of Hebrews ultimately. In reality, the entire Bible is the autobiography of God—all the way from Genesis to Revelation. And when a person writes an autobiography, he doesn't try to prove his authorship or existence. Therefore, those who engage in endless debates trying to prove the existence of God do something that God felt no need to do—for from Genesis 1:1 to Revelation 22:21, the underlying premise is that God is, and that He Himself wrote His Autobiography, His Word.

Audience

The Book of Hebrews was addressed to Jewish believers who were being pulled back into Judaism. Living in Jerusalem, no doubt each time they heard the trumpets sounding from the courtyard of the temple, reminded of their heritage and history, they found themselves drawn back into the religion and rituals of the

Levitical system. Jesus came to establish a *New* Covenant, the *New* Testament. That is why there are very sober warnings throughout the book, saying, "If you go back to the old religion and ritual, you nullify the work Christ did on the Cross for you. Don't complicate your faith. Keep it simple. Keep it focused. Keep it centered on Jesus."

Argument

The argument of the Book of Hebrews is that Jesus Christ is superior to the old way of religion. He is superior in His majesty because, as the Son of God, He is superior to angels, to Moses, to Joshua, and to the entire Levitical system. And He is superior in ministry because, as the Son of Man, He died for us. He relates to us. He works with us.

I think we're going to be blessed greatly in the study of this book because the theme and message is to point out the sufficiency and beauty of Jesus—always a grand endeavor.

HEBREWS

1 Hebrews 1:1 (a)
God . . .

Hebrews opens with the name of its Author—not Apollos, not Luke, not Paul—but God.

Hebrews 1:1 (b), 2 (a)
. . . who at sundry times and in divers manners spake in time past unto the fathers by the prophets, hath in these last days spoken unto us by his Son . . .

God did indeed speak in times past in many ways. . . .

The psalmist writes that the heavens declare the glory of God (Psalm 19).
Paul makes it clear that not only creation around, but also conscience within every man verifies the existence of God (Romans 1).
Throughout Scripture, angels have attested to the reality of God.
Prophets have spoken clearly and unmistakably of God's verity.

Yet in none of these ways—creation above, conscience within, angels from on high, prophets in our midst—was the message complete. It was not comprehensible. It was difficult to grasp. So God sent His Son, His final Word to humanity. There's nothing more to be said. There's nothing left unsaid. It's all said in Christ.

Well, then, you wonder, *why didn't God just send His Son in the first place? Why did He bother with the lengthy process of sending prophets, of speaking through creation? Why didn't He just send Jesus immediately?*

I suggest our pride is the answer. "Now, Father, You didn't have to send Your Son," we would have said. "We could have figured You out by looking at the stars. Or if You would have just blessed a prophet, we would have gotten Your message from Him. Or surely an angel would have been sufficient."

It's almost as though the Father has to constantly let us play out all of our options before we realize our stupidity, before we say, "We're sinners. We're not capable of figuring things out. Father, we *need* Jesus." You see, had we not gone through the entire process in human history, I believe we would be arguing perpetually. "Oh, Father, You didn't have to become a Man and dwell among us. And You certainly didn't have to die for us. You could have just given us ten rules, and we could have lived by them." That's the tendency of humanity—to feel like we can do it. So God has to allow history to unfold in such a way that we see we are losers, failures, blockheads, idiots—until finally we say, "We're stuck. We need Your Son to dwell among us. We need a Savior to die for us. We *need* Jesus."

For topical study of Hebrews 1:1, 2 entitled "God Has Spoken," turn to page 1439.

Hebrews 1:2 (b)
. . . whom he hath appointed heir of all things . . .

Jesus Is the Inheritor

The Father has willed everything to the Son, and *we* are His inheritance (Ephesians 1:11). This explains the parable Jesus told in Matthew 13 about a man who walked through a field, found a treasure, and bought the field in order to take out the treasure. What is that parable about? It's not about us selling everything to buy the treasure of the gospel. No, for in an earlier parable in the same chapter, Jesus says the field is the world. Jesus bought the world with His own blood. Why? Because He wanted the world? No, because He wanted the treasure. What is the treasure? We are. *We* are His inheritance. Amazing!

Hebrews 1:2 (c)
. . . by whom also he made the worlds.

Jesus Is the Creator

People get confused. They say, "Genesis 1 says that in the beginning God created the heavens and the earth, but John 1 says that without the Son nothing was made that was made. So who created the earth—the Father or the Son?"

I suggest you think of creation this way: The Father as the Architect (Genesis 1:1), the Son as the Contractor (John 1:1), and the Holy Spirit as the Carpenter (Genesis 1:2). The analogy is far from perfect, but the fact is all three Persons of the Godhead were involved in the creative process. Creation occurred *from* the Father, *by* the Son, *through* the Holy Spirit.

Hebrews 1:3 (a)
Who being the brightness of his glory . . .

Jesus Is the Radiator

A reflector is something that bounces light off itself. For example, the moon is a reflector of the glory of the sun. When you see the moon, you're not seeing its own light. You're seeing a reflection of the sun. Not so with Jesus, for He not only reflects the glory of the Father, but He radiates the glory of the Father. That is why there is neither sun nor moon in heaven. Jesus is the Radiator. He's all the light we need.

Hebrews 1:3 (b)
. . . and the express image of his person . . .

Jesus Is the Representer

The literal translation of the term "express image" refers to the method used to imprint coins in biblical times, whereby a piece of metal would be pounded against a stamp of the head of Caesar, making an "express image." Although the stamp and the coin were two separate entities, both bore the same image.

"Show us the Father and it will suffice us," said Philip.

"Don't you understand that he who hath seen me hath seen the Father?" answered Jesus (see John 14:9). In other words, "I'm the express image."

Hebrews 1:3 (c)
. . . and upholding all things by the word of his power . . .

Jesus Is the Sustainer

What holds the atom—the very building block of all matter—together? Nothing other than Jesus Christ and His Word. What's going to hold your marriage together, your parenting, your sanity—what's going to keep your world from falling apart? Only one thing: the Word of His power.

For topical study of Hebrews 1:3 entitled "Holding Your World Together," turn to page 1444.

Hebrews 1:3 (d)
. . . when he had by himself purged our sins . . .

Jesus Is the Purifier

The phrase "by himself" is interesting. It means two things: It means through Himself, that is, with His own body, Jesus purged my sins. But it also means He alone purged my sins. The Hebrew Christians to whom this book is addressed would know that on the Day of Atonement, the high priest alone made sacrifice for the sins of the entire nation. The Levitical high priest expended great energy. Yet that was nothing compared to the energy expended when our High Priest, Jesus Christ, gave His entire life in order to purify me from my sin.

Hebrews 1:3 (e)
. . . sat down on the right hand of the Majesty on high.

Jesus Is Our Ruler

What does He do on the right hand of the Majesty on high? Romans 8:34 says He prays for you and me. Thus, His rule over us is based on His intercession on behalf of us.

For topical study of Hebrews 1:3 entitled "Heaven Ain't that Far Away," turn to page 1449.

Meditate on any one of these seven traits of the incomparable Christ and your view of Him will be changed. . . .

In C. S. Lewis' book *The Chronicles of Narnia*, when Lucy finally sees Aslan the Lion—a picture of the Lion of Judah, Jesus Christ—she cries, "Aslan! Aslan! You've grown so much bigger."

"No, Lucy, *you've* grown so much bigger—and the bigger you grow, the bigger I'll seem to you," replied Aslan.

Gang, the older we get, the smaller our heroes—be they sports figures, Santa Claus, or Disney characters—become. Not so with the Lord. The longer I walk with Him, the more I think on Him, the more I learn of Him, unlike anything else in this world, He just gets bigger in my eyes.

Hebrews 1:4
Being made so much better than the angels, as he hath by inheritance obtained a more excellent name than they.

According to Deuteronomy 33:2, it would seem as though when Moses received the law on Mount Sinai, it was given to him by God through angels—perhaps thousands of angels. Certainly that's what the Jewish people have always believed. Thus, due to their high esteem of the law, the Jews esteemed angels highly as well. Yet here the Book of Hebrews makes it clear that Jesus is superior to the angels.

There are those who will knock on your door and say that Jesus Christ is not ultimately superior to the angels, but that He is one of the angels. . . .

Jehovah's Witnesses teach that Jesus is the brother of the archangel Michael. But it's absolute heresy—not because we're splitting doctrinal hairs, but because if, like angels, Jesus Christ was created by the Father, it greatly cheapens the sacrifice God made on the Cross of Calvary. If Jesus is not God of very God, then God merely sent an angel to die on the Cross and take the rap for humanity. That's not what happened. Paul would say great is the mystery of godliness that God was manifested in the flesh (1 Timothy

3:16). God Himself bore our sin. God Himself died on the Cross.

Mormons also deny Jesus is superior to the angels. Although they don't talk about it very readily, if you press them on the point, they'll admit they believe Jesus is the brother of Lucifer. You see, according to Mormon theology, God called Jesus and Lucifer together and said, "We need to redeem humanity." And the two created beings—Jesus and Lucifer—both gave their suggested plan. The Father went with Jesus' suggestion. Lucifer got ticked, and from that time has been determined to undermine his brother's work.

Gang, turn the cultist to Hebrews 1 and say, "Jesus is not in the same category as any angel—Michael, Lucifer, or the devil. He's superior." A lot of people have the idea that there's a cosmic contest between God and the devil—that they're equals and they're battling it out. Oh, they know eventually God's going to win—but it's going to be tough. Not so! It's not God and Satan battling it out. God is in an entirely different realm. Now, if Satan and Michael, or Satan and Gabriel fought—then you would have an interesting contest. Satan, however, is no match for God, Jesus, or the Holy Spirit, for they are far superior to any angel.

Hebrews 1:5, 6
For unto which of the angels said he at any time, Thou art my Son, this day have I begotten thee? And again, I will be to him a Father, and he shall be to me a Son? And again, when he bringeth in the firstbegotten into the world, he saith, And let all the angels of God worship him.

The cultist, the heretic uses this verse as "proof" that because Jesus is "begotten" He's not eternal. In Jeremiah 31:9, however, we find a reference to Ephraim being the firstborn of Joseph. Was Ephraim Joseph's firstborn? No, Manasseh was. Why, then is Ephraim called the firstborn? Because firstborn or first begotten in Scripture does not simply speak of precedence. It can also speak of priority. In this case, even though Ephraim wasn't born first in precedence, he had priority in blessing.

Hebrews 1:7
And of the angels he saith, Who maketh his angels spirits, and his ministers a flame of fire.

Truly, angels are like the wind, like a flame of fire—as seen clearly in the story of Manoah and his wife. After an angel appeared to them, they offered a sacrifice, and the angel went up in a flame of fire like the wind and disappeared (Judges 13).

Hebrews 1:8 (a)
But unto the Son he saith, Thy throne, O God, is for ever and ever . . .

In this verse—quoting Psalm 45:6, 7—God calls Jesus "God." Now, if God refers to Jesus as God, Jesus is God. End of discussion.

Hebrews 1:8 (b)
. . . a sceptre of righteousness is the sceptre of thy kingdom.

I like this! Speaking to the Son, God says, "You're on the throne and You rule righteously." How is God going to rule? How is He going to judge the man in Africa who never heard the gospel back in 1426? How is He going to decide what to do? Beats me. All I know is this: Around the throne of the Lamb in heaven, the cry goes up, "Righteous and true are Your judgments, Lord" (see Revelation 16:7). In other words, "Good for You! Perfect! You haven't compromised integrity. But You show compassion and love perfectly."

Hebrews 1:9
Thou hast loved righteousness, and hated iniquity; therefore God, even thy God, hath anointed thee with the oil of gladness above thy fellows.

"Because You've loved righteousness and hated iniquity," said the Father to the Son, "You are anointed with the oil of gladness above all others." Did you know that gladness is directly proportional to holiness? Happiness and holiness go hand in hand. That is why crowds flocked to Jesus. Wasn't He the Man of Sorrows (Isaiah 53:3)? Certainly. But there was also a gladness and joy about Him unlike that of any other human being in history. Jesus was immensely attractive to the crowds because holiness and happiness are directly proportional.

Some folks don't see this until they're fifty or sixty years old. And some never see it at all. They think holiness is drudgery. They think if they're righteous they won't be happy, that they'll just have to endure the pain of Christianity. Nothing is further from the truth. To the extent you choose to be holy is the extent to which you will be happy. Conversely, to the extent you compro-

mise holiness is the extent to which you diminish happiness. It's just that simple.

Hebrews 1:10–12
And, Thou, Lord, in the beginning hast laid the foundation of the earth; and the heavens are the works of thine hands: They shall perish; but thou remainest; and they all shall wax old as doth a garment; and as a vesture shalt thou fold them up, and they shall be changed: but thou art the same, and thy years shall not fail.

Still quoting the Old Testament as proof that Jesus is in a different category than the angels, the author makes reference to Psalm 102, wherein, concerning the Son, it is said, "In the beginning, You laid the foundation of the earth and, even when it's gone, folded up like an old garment, You'll remain." Did you know that the One who sustains all things is someday going to let them all go? Like the Nehru jackets of the seventies, the heavens and earth will one day disappear—but Jesus will remain.

Hebrews 1:13
But to which of the angels said he at any time, Sit on my right hand, until I make thine enemies thy footstool?

Again, quoting Psalm 110, only to Jesus did God say, "Sit on My right hand."

Hebrews 1:14
Are they not all ministering spirits, sent forth to minister for them who shall be heirs of salvation?

Angels are everywhere these days. There have been best-selling books about angels. There are entire stores devoted to angels. And yet angels are nothing more than servants. Whose servants? Ours, for we are the heirs of salvation. . . .

- In Psalm 91:11 we read of their protective work.
- In Luke 15, we see them rejoicing over saved sinners.
- In Luke 16, we see them carrying people to their eternal state.
- In Acts 5 and 12, we see them delivering Peter and other apostles from prison.

Angels do, indeed, have a ministry, but the ministry is to us. They're not to be exalted or worshiped by us. That is why in Colossians 2, there is a warning concerning the worship of angels. Our focus is to be on Jesus—and on Him singularly.

GOD HAS SPOKEN
A Topical Study of
Hebrews 1:1, 2

Ingmar Bergman, the famous Swedish filmmaker of a generation ago, writes in his autobiography the story behind one of his most critically acclaimed and successful pictures. He tells of how one day, discouraged and depressed, he found himself strolling into a large cathedral. Inside, he saw a stained-glass window depicting the Good Shepherd. "Talk to me. Talk to me," he said to the window. But the cathedral remained silent. Bergman walked out, went back to his room, and began to write the script for a movie called "The Silence"—a film that captured the attention of his day due to its portrayal of despairing, depressed people who hear only silence from God.

Does God really speak—in my situation, in my depression, in my consternation? Like Bergman, most people today say God doesn't speak. But our text shouts out, "Yes, He does!"

How? Four ways.

Creation Around Us

Johannes Kepler, the father of modern astronomy, the man who coined the word "satellite" and wrote the foundational *Planetary Law Of Motion,* said this: "Any astronomer who is undevout is mad." Truly, when you study the heavens, the cosmos, the galaxies, you have no choice but to be impressed with the necessity, the reality of a Creator.

This ball we're sitting on right now is spinning at the rate of 100,000 mph. As it's spinning, it's moving around the sun at 67,000 mph, while the sun itself is moving at 64,000 mph. And the whole galaxy in which the sun and planets are moving is speeding through space at 450,000 mph. Multiply that, and you come to 1,350,000 mph. No wonder your hair won't stay in place!

While all this is happening, there are multiplied billions of other stars and multiplied millions of other galaxies also moving in all directions. Who keeps the whole thing from colliding? Kepler was right. There has to be an Orderer.

God does, indeed, speak through creation (Psalm 19). Yet the message sometimes seems contradictory, for although the stars overhead are magnificent, down here where we stand, the earth quakes, hurricanes rage, and volcanoes erupt. Yes, nature is beautiful and serene—but it can also be brutal and severe. Why? Because when Adam fell, creation was affected as well (Romans 8:22). Consequently, while it's true that God speaks through creation around us, the message is seemingly inconsistent.

Prophets Among Us

God told the prophet Ezekiel to chop off his hair and burn it in a fire and to lie on his side without moving for one thousand days. Malachi came on the scene not with bizarre actions, but with many questions. Amos came with a straightahead, in-your-face approach. Zechariah had apocalyptic visions and dreams. And God used each of these men to achieve His purpose. Yet if creation's message is inconsistent, the prophet's message is incomprehensible, for even the prophets themselves did not fully understand what they were saying (1 Peter 1:9–12).

You see, on one hand, they talked about the Messiah who would come to rule and reign with a rod of iron. On the other hand, they talked about the same Messiah being despised and rejected. They prophesied of suffering and glory but couldn't put it all together. Thus, their message was often incomprehensible.

Conscience Within Us

The third way God speaks is through the conscience within every man that tells us innately and intuitively that there must be a God (Romans 1). But people suppress this knowledge. Why? Because, according to 1 Peter 4:2, men don't want to acknowledge there is a God lest they are forced to obey Him. And even to those who do listen to their conscience, what they hear can be confusing, as Satan accuses us continually (Revelation 12:10). Thus, our conscience plays tricks on us. We can repress it, it can be seared by our own stubbornness, and Satan can employ it to cause confusion within us.

Consequently, we have a problem. God speaks through creation around us— but the message is seemingly inconsistent. He speaks through prophets among us—but what we hear is at times incomprehensible. He speaks through conscience within us—but the signal is somewhat inconclusive. So what did God do? He solved the problem through Incarnation. The message became the Messenger. And the Messenger was the message. God became one of us.

I see them coming, marching rather orderly up the steps. The ants are definitely headed this way.

"Slow down," I say. "Back off. Run! I know after third service, the boys will bring the vacuums out, and you'll be sucked up and cast into outer darkness. You'll go into that black bag, where there is weeping and wailing and gnashing of ant teeth. Turn away! Flee while you can!"

But not a single ant heeds my warning. Why? Because I'm so big they don't even acknowledge my presence.

So I go backstage and start flicking the lights on and off. Thus, the heavens declare to them that someone is masterfully working the controls. But the ants just look up and don't get it.

So I grab a couple of them and say, "You have to speak to your brothers. You have to tell them that a vacuum is on the way and that destruction is imminent. But even these prophet ants don't clearly understand my message.

My next plan is to hope that maybe some of them will come to their senses and their consciences will stir them to see that they belong not in the sanctuary, but outside. Some do, and they say, "You know, guys, we really shouldn't be in here."

"Oh, come on," the others say. "That's old-fashioned."

So I see I have only one option left to bring about their salvation: I need to become one of them. As an ant, I need to go into their midst and say, "Listen, guys. I know where I'm coming from. I know what happens in this sanctuary on Sunday afternoon. I'm the boss. You're going to get sucked up. But if you follow me, I know where the back door is. I'll lead you to salvation."

That is the Incarnation—God becoming Man, the Word becoming flesh.

The Son Sent to Us

The fourth way, the final way, the full way God speaks is in His Son sent to us. God has spoken in His Son. There's nothing more to say.

When Peter John and I were in Washington D.C. a number of years ago, we saw some original Rembrandts on display in the National Gallery of Art. Now, if, thinking the paintings needed a little more color, we started to spray them with red, green, and orange paint, we would have been arrested immediately.

"What in the world were you doing?" I would no doubt have been asked.

"I was adding a little color, a little sparkle to the masterpieces," I could have answered.

"You're crazy!" I would have been told. "Those are masterpieces, completed works, finished."

So, too, the masterpiece of all that God wanted to say, needed to say, intended to say was said when the Word became flesh and dwelt among us. God *has* spoken. Therefore, Mormons who say, "Call our 800 number in Salt Lake City for another gospel," Jehovah's Witnesses who say, "We'll send you our magazine that will show you that in 1914 more was added to the gospel message," New-Agers who say, "God speaks through crystals and pyramids," and even Christians who say, "There must be more"—all miss the point completely, for God said, "I have spoken perfectly. I have spoken completely. I have spoken fully in the Person of My Son. All you will ever need to know you'll know by looking at Him, focusing on Him, and learning of Him."

What does this mean?

Understanding God's Word

You'll never be a good Bible teacher until you realize that God speaks in His Son.

> In Genesis 3, after Adam and Eve sinned in the Garden of Eden, God said, "Adam, where art thou?" How is this to be read? Was God like an angry policeman, searching for Adam in order to bust him because of his sin? Such is what a lot of Bible teachers would have us believe. But seen through the Son, this account must be viewed differently, for in another garden, the Garden of Gethsemane, we see Jesus calling His worst enemy "Friend" (Matthew 26:50). Now if Jesus called Judas—a far more despicable character than Adam— "Friend," certainly when God called to Adam in the Garden of Eden, it wasn't as an angry cop, but as a loving Father.

Gang, you will never understand the Old Testament, Paul's epistles, or the Revelation of John if you don't understand the language in which they were written. And the language is "in the Son." This is where Bible teachers and students really miss the boat in many cases. They let the apostle Paul or the prophets interpret Jesus. Wrong. Jesus interprets the law. Jesus interprets Paul. Jesus interprets the Old Testament prophets. If you want the Bible to have a full message and if you want to share it effectively, you've got to understand that it's written in the Son. That's the key to unlocking the whole Bible. Any interpretation of any passage of Scripture that contradicts the nature of the Son as seen in the gospels is amiss. But those who look at everything in the Word through the lens of Jesus will be amazed at how clear the Word becomes.

Understanding God's Ways

Knowing God speaks in His Son affects not only my understanding of His Word but also my understanding of His ways. As I look at Jesus Christ, God's Final Word, I see He had compassion on the lame man. I see Him defending a blind man. And I see Him healing them both. So to those who wonder why cancer, Alzheimer's, or even the flu is besetting them, I say that in the fullness of time God sent forth His Son (Galatians 4:4). And in the fullness of time—at just the right time—He will heal all who come to Him. That "right time" might be today. It might be next month. It might be ten years from now. It might not be until they're in heaven. But all of His children will be healed ultimately.

Therefore, to the one dealing with pain, I say, "I don't know why you're still struggling with that disease or that infirmity, but in the fullness of time, God sent forth His Son. And He's going to do it again in your situation. You'll see."

Truly, I understand God's ways if I look at the Son, for I never hear Jesus say, "Your lack of faith is the reason you're not healed." I never hear Jesus say, "Your great sin is the reason for your condition." I never hear Him say many of the things I hear from too many pulpits and preachers who speak a language other than the language of the Son.

Understanding God's Will

God has spoken. Everything you need to know about any financial, vocational, or relational situation has already been addressed. Where? In the Son. The answer to any question is packed into twenty-five pages called the Gospels.

Grab Matthew, Mark, Luke, or John. Study the life of the Son, and you will find God's will for every situation.

"But I just wish God would speak to me," we blubber. "I wish I could hear Him audibly."

In Exodus 19, God did speak audibly. Thunder boomed. A mountain shook. Smoke bellowed. And the people said, "*You* go talk to Him, Moses. Tell us what He's saying, and we'll do it. But if we talk to Him, we'll die!" So two thousand years later, God said, "I'll speak again—not on Mount Sinai, but on Mount Calvary. The people won't die. I will."

Gang, when you come to a crossroads of wondering what God's will is, look at Calvary and be reminded once again that if God loved you enough to die for you, there is no doubt He will do what's best for you.

"Why aren't I hearing from God?" people ask. "I'm going to prayer meetings. I'm reading lots of good books. I'm reading the Bible."

The answer could be they're not listening for Him through the Son.

Amazed to be standing in the presence of the miracle-worker and the lawgiver on the Mount of Transfiguration, Peter said, "Let's build booths for Elijah and Moses—and one for Jesus, too."

But God interrupted Peter and said of Jesus, "This is My beloved Son. Hear ye *Him*." And when Peter looked around, he "saw no man save Jesus only" (see Matthew 17:8)—for as vital as the law and the prophets might be, they are inconsequential in comparison to the Word made flesh.

Therefore, as you study the Law and the Prophets, the Gospels and the Epistles, look for Jesus in every passage. For truly in these last days, God has spoken. He has spoken in His Son.

HOLDING YOUR WORLD TOGETHER
A Topical Study of
Hebrews 1:3

In the second verse of the first chapter of this glorious letter—written to Jewish believers who were being drawn back into the rules and regulations of Judaism—we read that Jesus is the "heir of all things, by whom also He made the worlds." That is, Jesus is not only the Inheritor of all things but also the Creator of all things as well. You see, when God created everything, He did so by divine fiat. What is divine fiat? The word "fiat" simply means "spoken command." Translated literally, for example, "Let there be light" in Hebrew reads, "Light be, light was." Thus, God spoke the worlds into existence via the Word. Who is the Word? Jesus (John 1:1). God spoke the worlds into existence through His Son, by His Son, and for His Son.

In our text, I find something that intrigues me further, for not only is Jesus the Creator, He's the Sustainer. He holds everything together by the word of His power. When you look at creation, you encounter a major problem because, according to Coulomb's Law of Electricity, the positive-charged protons within the atom—from which all matter is composed—should repel each other. As a fourth-grader, I proved Coulomb's Law of Electricity when I bought two little plastic dogs—one black, one white—in a souvenir shop in San Francisco. Due to the magnets glued to their feet, I could push them around the table and, faced one way, they would chase each other. But if I turned them the other way—that is, if the positive sides of the magnets faced each other, although I could flex my fourth-grade muscles and summon the energy to hold those two little dogs together, if I let go, they would push away from each other.

I have proven Coulomb's Law personally. You have too. Every person in here knows magnets have the tendency to push away from each other. But on a larger scale, if you put a tablespoon full of positive charges on the North Pole, and a tablespoon of positive charges on the South Pole, the repellent force even at that distance would be so great that it would take thirty thousand tons of pressure on each of those tablespoons to keep them from pushing away from each other.

So, too, it takes a tremendously powerful force to keep the protons in the nucleus of the atom from repelling each other. How powerful? Those who survived Hiroshima or Nagasaki know because the principle of the atom bomb is to upset the nucleus of the atom, thereby releasing a force so powerful that it results in an atomic explosion of unbelievable proportion.

Everything we see is made up of atoms that, in turn, are made up of protons that want to repel each other. Yet something is holding it all together. Baffled by what it is that keeps the positive-charged protons packed together in the nucleus of the atom, scientists have coined a term to describe this mysterious force. They call it "atomic glue." In Colossians 1, we'll see what this atomic glue actually is. . . .

And he is before all things, and by him all things consist. (Colossians 1:17)

There it is. Jesus creates everything, and He is the atomic glue that holds everything together.

"Thanks, Jon," you may be saying, "but I didn't come for a lecture on the atomic structure, Coulomb's Law, or your fourth-grade science experiment."

Listen, gang, there is no verse of Scripture more practical for you and me than the one before us presently because Jesus not only holds all things together physically by the power of His Word—He holds all things together personally and practically as well. Let me explain. . . .

> During a retreat several years ago, a couple of guys cornered me and said, "Jon, if we had to go through what you went through in this past year, we couldn't have done it. Our worlds would have fallen apart. We would have been blown away."
>
> "I hear you," I said to them. "But you're failing to factor in one key component to the equation: He holds all things together by the word of His power—not only the world we walk on physically, but the world we walk through emotionally."

Truly, if I didn't have the Word, my life would be scattered, blown away, disorganized, formless, and wiped out. And so would yours. Life is full of difficulties and challenges, tragedies and trials for every one of us. But there's a mysterious force at work that holds us together because all things are held together by the Word of His power. Consequently, our lives will be held together to the degree we are centered and focused on His Word.

The Word of God's power and the power of His Word are perhaps seen nowhere more clearly than in the longest chapter in the Bible: Psalm 119. . . .

> *Blessed are they that keep his testimonies, and that seek him with the whole heart.* Psalm 119:2

The psalmist declares that blessed, or happy, is the man who keeps the Word. Therefore, if a person is depressed or defeated, it is usually because he is not in the Word.

I will praise thee with uprightness of heart, when I shall have learned thy righteous judgments.   Psalm 119:7

"Uprightness of heart" literally means "fervency of heart." Who will praise the Lord fervently? The one who learns His righteous judgments, His Word. "Do we have to sing *another* praise song?" some ask. People who don't like to worship are people who are not in the Word. Get into the Word and you can't help but discover the nature, the character, and the goodness of God, which will, in turn, create in you a heart overflowing with praise.

Wherewithal shall a young man cleanse his way? by taking heed thereto according to thy word. Thy word have I hid in mine heart, that I might not sin against thee.   Psalm 119:9, 11

The only way for a young man to cleanse his ways is to be in the Word. If your world is falling apart because of sin, temptations, habits, or addictions, there's something better than a nicotine patch or an AA meeting. Get into the Word and let the Word get into you, for therein is power.

I will meditate in thy precepts, and have respect unto thy ways.   Psalm 119:15

"I don't understand what's happening. What's God doing? Where is He when I call out to Him?" we snivel and whine. People who are not in the Word will not understand His ways. But if you meditate in His precepts, you see a bigger picture framed by the future of eternity and the past of Calvary.

Thy testimonies also are my delight and my counsellors.   Psalm 119:24

You can spend fifty dollars an hour on a psychiatrist for psychiatric counsel— or you can spend fifteen dollars on a Bible and get the greatest counsel you'll ever receive.

"But the Bible's so big," people complain. "There's too much to read."

Listen, the Bible can be read aloud from cover to cover in seventy-one hours. That's only twelve-and-a-half minutes a day for one year.

Make me to understand the way of thy precepts: so shall I talk of thy wondrous works.   Psalm 119:27

Here's a verse for those who don't know what to talk about when you get together with other believers, for those of you who are shy. If you're in the Word, you'll always have something to talk about because there's so much within its pages to ponder, to think through, and to share.

*Turn away mine eyes from beholding vanity; and quicken thou me in thy
way.*   Psalm 119:37

The word translated "vanity" literally means "emptiness." How can you turn
your eyes from emptiness? Read your Bible. If you're reading your Bible, you won't
be watching junk on the screen because the two just don't mix.

*So shall I have wherewith to answer him that reproacheth me: for I trust in
thy word.*   Psalm 119:42

You can answer those who accuse, question, or argue with you if you trust in
the Word.

I will speak of thy testimonies also before kings, and will not be ashamed.
                                                                Psalm 119:46

I can talk about the Word boldly to a king, to my boss, or to anyone else because it makes so much sense. It's pragmatic. It's practical. It's powerful. It's unas-
sailable.

*My hands also will I lift up unto thy commandments, which I have loved; and
I will meditate in thy statutes.*   Psalm 119:48

Who are those people who so expressively lift their hands to the Lord? They
are those who have seen the goodness and grace of God. They are those who have
been in the Word.

Thy statutes have been my songs in the house of my pilgrimage.
                                                                Psalm 119:54

Is there a funeral dirge in your heart today? This verse says the Word of God-
will put a song in your heart as an accompaniment to your earthly pilgrimage.

It is good for me that I have been afflicted; that I might learn thy statutes.
                                                                Psalm 119:71

It's good for me to be afflicted, writes the psalmist, because it is then that I
get back into the Word. When times are easy, we usually don't take the time to
search God's mind or to hear His heart. It's in affliction, difficulty, or problems that
we tend to open the Scriptures much more.

*They that fear thee will be glad when they see me; because I have hoped in thy
word.*   Psalm 119:74

What's the key to popularity? It doesn't lie in any man-made program or theory. The Scriptures declare those who hope in the Word make people glad because they have something substantial to say. Whatever the conversation, their perspective is based on a biblical foundation. Thus, their insights are rich and solid.

For ever, O LORD, thy word is settled in heaven.   Psalm 119:89

Fads come and go. Politicians are here today and gone in November. But the Word remains unchangeable, immutable. This Book is not going out of print, gang. It will never be out of style. It will never need revision. It's settled. You can build your life upon it with confidence. It will bless you. It will keep your life together. The Word is settled forever and ever.

Unless thy law had been my delights, I should then have perished in mine affliction.   Psalm 119:92

Without the Word, we would perish in the afflictions of life. Nothing would make sense.

Through thy precepts I get understanding: therefore I hate every false way.
                                                              Psalm 119:104

The best way to identify a cultist is not to study the cult, but to be in the Word because then when a cultist knocks on your door or tries to sell you his magazine, you'll know what he's saying doesn't ring true.

Thou art my hiding place and my shield: I hope in thy word.   Psalm 119:114

Lord, You're my safety and my security because of the Scripture You've given to me.

The entrance of thy words giveth light; it giveth understanding unto the simple.
                                                              Psalm 119:130

The word "simple" literally means "stupid." We qualify, gang! The Word gives understanding to the simple or stupid, unlearned or uneducated. Thus, you are wiser and smarter than any professor on any university campus who doesn't believe in the Word and doesn't walk according to the light of the Word.

Rivers of waters run down mine eyes, because they keep not thy law.
                                                              Psalm 119:136

Do you want compassion for those who are lost? The psalmist found himself weeping for those who were without the Word.

Great peace have they which love thy law: and nothing shall offend them.
Psalm 119:165

Why shall no one offend those who are in the Word? Because students of the Word see things from an entirely different perspective. They realize it's not people, but spiritual forces that are the problem (Ephesians 6:12). They know that even if people throw rocks at them, the Lord has allowed it in order to produce humility within them.

Let my cry come near before thee, O LORD: give me understanding according to thy word.
Psalm 119:69

Prayer makes sense when it's enveloped in the Word. Prayer and the Word go hand in hand.

My lips shall utter praise, when thou hast taught me thy statutes.
Psalm 119:171

I am so very thankful the Lord has given us this Word. Without it, our lives would be frazzled. Without it, we would be blown apart emotionally. Without it, we would be lost.

Precious people, Jesus is the Sustainer not only of the physical world, but of your soul. Keep reading your Bible. Keep studying the Scriptures. Your life will be held together to the extent that you are in the Word—for truly all things are upheld by the Word of His power.

HEAVEN AIN'T THAT FAR AWAY
A Topical Study of
Hebrews 1:3

The central message of the Book of Hebrews is "Consider Jesus." In the first half of Hebrews 1:2, consider why He came. That is, He is God's final word. Then, in the second half of verse 2 and on into verse 3, we see who He is through seven characteristics of the incomparable Christ.

In the text before us, the author continues to consider Jesus. . . .

Where He Is

> ... *when he had by himself purged our sins, sat down on the right hand of the Majesty on high* ...
>   Hebrews 1:3 (b)

If you were in the sandals of the Hebrew Christians to whom this book was written, this statement would be shocking, even scandalous. Why? Because the priests in the tabernacle and the temple never sat down. If you went into either place, you would see the brass altar, the laver, the table of showbread, the altar of incense, the golden candlestick, the ark of the covenant—but not a single chair because the work of a priest was never done. You see, the sacrifices made by the priests could never take away sin. That's why they had to be offered again and again. Yet this Man, Jesus, the High Priest, sits down.

Why?

Because when He cried, "It is finished," on the Cross, it meant the work was done. Thus, when He went to heaven, He sat down—not out of exhaustion, nor out of frustration, but out of complete and total relaxation, knowing the price had been paid for all of our sins—past, present and future.

What He's Doing

> *Wherefore he is able also to save them to the uttermost that come unto God by him, seeing he ever liveth to make intercession for them.*   Hebrews 7:25

What's our Great High Priest doing? He's talking to the Father about your situation. Think with me about the intercessory ministry of Jesus. . . .

Only hours away from His crucifixion, looking at Peter, Jesus said, "Simon, Satan has desired to sift you like wheat. But I have prayed for you. And when you get through this trial, strengthen the brothers" (see Luke 22:31, 32). In other words, "Satan desires to rip you apart, to wipe you out, to do you in. But I have prayed for you and when you get through—and you *will* get through—help others." In Philippians 1:6, the promise is given to us that He who has begun a good work in us will continue to perform it until the end. It's a done deal. Jesus is not pacing. He's sitting in heaven, talking over your situation with the Father with complete confidence that He will see you through ultimately, completely and totally. That's His ministry. . . .

There I am at what used to be Candlestick Park. The Niners are playing the Cowboys. It's a close game. The battle has been brutal. The score has seesawed back and forth. With time running out in the fourth quarter, the Niners are trailing by six. There's sixty yards to go to score. Steve Young calls the play, sets the team down, takes the snap, drops back. Deep, deep goes Jerry Rice, and running alongside him step for step is Neon Deion Sanders. Rice runs a perfect post pattern. He breaks away—but Sanders catches up. The ball is in the air. It's a beautiful pass. Both men go up for it; both have their hands on it. They come down, and it looks like Jerry Rice has it—but what's this? We can't believe what we're seeing as a little red flag comes out of the hip pocket of the referee. We stand to our feet in anxiety. Who's it against? The referee makes the call against Sanders! The Niners win!

Later on that evening, my wife, Tammy, and I watch highlights of the game on CNN. I see Steve Young's pass. I see Sanders and Rice both go for it. I see Rice come down. I see the flag drop—yet I am totally at rest.

Why?

Because I know the outcome.

So does our Lord. He knows how it's all going to come out. He promises to see us through. He will complete that which He's begun. That's why He can say, *"When you make it through, strengthen others."*

Jesus is seated at the right hand of the Father—but He's not always seated. . . .

When Stephen began preaching about the reality of Jesus Christ, the crowd became so incensed that people began throwing rocks at him. And as the stones begin to strike him, Stephen said, "I see heaven opening and the Son of God standing" (Acts 7:56).

I would have thought it would have been just the opposite. I would have thought Jesus would stand as we go through life. Then, when we finally get to heaven, He would say, "Whew. You made it. I can sit down now."

But, as is true in all areas of spiritual life, Jesus does just the opposite of what I would do. He's sitting down when we're going through life because He's sure we're going to make it. But when we get to heaven, He stands up to welcome us, saying, "Enter into My joy!"

Here's the challenge for me: I tend to think, *Well, somewhere way up there beyond the blue, the Lord is sitting at the right hand of the Father, thinking about me, interceding for me.* But I suggest to you that nothing could be further from the truth. Think with me. . . .

Scientists have been telling us for a number of years that atoms are composed primarily of space. In fact, if I were to squeeze out all the space between the nucleus of the atoms and the electrons within your own body, you would be reduced to the size of a speck of dust. That's why scientists say it is theoretically very possible that there could be an entirely different material world in this place right now that we can't see or hear. In other words, a tree could be growing through the roof of the sanctuary right now if the space of its atoms coincided with the solid part of the atoms of everything we see. Theoretically, then, due to the fact that if a single atom here in Jacksonville was enlarged to the size of a basketball, its electron, proportionately, would be in Philadelphia—there would be ample space for people, trains, planes, even armies to pass through our midst unnoticed.

What does this have to do with the ministry of Jesus, with Him praying for me, with Him being seated at God's right hand? Everything. You see, Jesus said something radical when He said that the kingdom of God is among you (Luke 17:21).

The word translated "among" is *entos* in Greek—a word referring to location. Thus, Jesus said the kingdom of God is not out there beyond the blue. It's among you right here, right now.

"But, Jon," you protest, "haven't you always taught that when the Rapture comes, Jesus will come in the clouds?"

Yes, but I suggest we're looking at clouds in the wrong way. Hebrews 12:1 says we are surrounded by a cloud of witnesses. Who are these witnesses? Hebrews 11 identifies them as Abraham, Moses, Samson, Gideon, Jephthah—the heroes of faith. So perhaps when Jesus comes, it won't be in a nimbus or a cumulus cloud. It will be, as Jude says, with ten thousand saints, in a cloud of witnesses. Where are these witnesses right now? They're not "out there." They're right here. Ask Gehazi. . . .

"Master, we're in trouble," he cried. "The Syrians are surrounding our city.

His master, a man of miracles named Elisha, prayed the Lord would open Gehazi's eyes. When He did, Gehazi said, "Whoa! There are angels everywhere—and they're surrounding the Syrians" (see 2 Kings 6).

You see, angels were there all along. It's just that Gehazi was allowed to see a different dimension.

"Things like that only happen in the Old Testament," you say.

Turn, then, to 1 Corinthians 11, where Paul says, "When you come together in worship meetings where gifts are flowing, where the body is interacting, be careful about certain issues because angels are present in the midst of the congregation."

Why don't we see them?

Because they're in a different dimension. The cloud of witnesses, heroes of faith, loved ones who have gone ahead of us are not way out there. They're surrounding us. Could it be, then, that when we die or go to be with the Lord in the event called the Rapture, we don't go somewhere way out there? Could it be that we simply step into the next dimension?

Ask Peter, James, and John. Jesus gave them a sneak preview of the coming dimension when, on the Mount of Transfiguration, they suddenly saw Elijah and Moses in their midst. Like Gehazi before them, they were allowed to see into a different dimension and thereby made aware of the fact that Elijah and Moses were present, although unseen previously.

If this is true, if heaven's just stepping into a different dimension and it's right here—what does this mean to me? It means when I pray to my faithful friend, my High Priest, Jesus Christ, I'm not saying, "Hello-lo-lo. Can You hear me way up there-ere-ere?" No, the Lord is not somewhere way beyond the blue. He is with us always (Matthew 28:20). The kingdom of heaven is among us. The great cloud of witnesses are presently around us. Ministering spirits are in the midst of us. Jesus Himself is in the midst of the congregation. And all of a sudden I realize that heaven isn't that far away—not only because we'll be there soon chronologically, but also because the kingdom surrounds us presently.

I don't see it because, like Paul, I see through a glass darkly (1 Corinthians 13:12). And, like Gehazi, I can't see what's going on. But I understand there is a dimension of the kingdom round about me, and I know with certainty that the Lord is seated at the right hand of the Father, at rest, praying for me.

And He's praying for you, too.

---

2 I was amazed. The Christmas season was in full swing, and it was only November. At first I thought I would just "bah, humbug" it for a week or two more. But it doesn't work that way. There's a flow that kicks in, and, like it or not, one finds himself being caught up and carried away in the momentum of Christmas tradition because traditions have real power.

And that's the dilemma here in the Book of Hebrews. You see, the people to whom it is addressed were Christians who had come from a Jewish heritage. Yes, they had been converted to Christianity, but because they had grown up in Judaism, whenever they heard the trumpets sounding from the temple, whenever they smelled the incense, whenever they heard the swishing of the priests' robes, memories and tradition tugged on their minds and hearts.

Taking up where he left off in chapter 1, Paul continues his discussion of angels, whom the Hebrews traditionally held in high regard.

Hebrews 2:1, 2
Therefore we ought to give the more earnest heed to the things which we have heard, lest at any time we should let them slip. For if the word spoken by angels was stedfast, and every transgression and disobedience received a just recompence of reward.

In other words, if you broke the law given to Moses on Mount Sinai by the hand of angels, there would be serious repercussions.

For topical study of Hebrews 2:1 entitled "The Danger of Drifting," turn to page 1456.

Hebrews 2:3 (a)
How shall we escape, if we neglect so great salvation . . .

How can we escape the severe consequences of breaking the law if we refuse the salvation offered to us by Jesus Christ—He who is greater than any angel?

Hebrews 2:3 (b), 4 (a)
. . . which at the first began to be spoken by the Lord, and was confirmed unto us by them that heard him; God also bearing them witness . . .

God also bore witness to those who came after Jesus—to Peter and James, to John and Andrew—as they spread the Good News of the gospel into further regions.

Hebrews 2:4 (b)
. . . both with signs and wonders, and with divers miracles . . .

Signs and wonders confirmed the Word that was shared evangelistically. I believe this is the way it needs to be, the way it's supposed to be, the way it still can be. "Why aren't we seeing greater expression of signs and wonders?" people ask.

I believe the answer is found in Mark 16, where Jesus said, "Go into all the world and preach the gospel, and these signs shall follow: In My Name you shall cast out demons, speak with new tongues, and heal the sick." About whom is Jesus talking? Not those who get together in the back hills of Kentucky to handle snakes, those who pass around a cup of poison, or those who say, "It's Miracle Monday. Let's all see signs and wonders."

Dealing with poisons, overcoming snakebites, casting out demons, healing sickness are all linked to people who are on the mission field, people who are involved in ministry, people who are risking their lives and taking a stand.

How do I know this is the correct application? Because when I read the Book of Acts, I see the apostles out on the front lines—not in meetings surrounded by Christians where it was safe. As they were out in the streets, the Lord would bless them with miracles, signs, and wonders to confirm His Word in their missionary endeavors.

So, too, if you put yourself in a place of vulnerability for ministry, you'll see God work with you. Personally, I am a bit appalled by those who say, "Signs and wonders are going to happen at our Signs and Wonders Convention. Pay a hundred dollars. Come and get your notebook, hear our speakers, and then we'll all start shaking."

I don't buy it because I don't see that anywhere in the Word. God will work with you. He'll be a protection to you, and great things will happen around you—but not necessarily in the safety of the sanctuary or in the confines of a convention.

Hebrews 2:4 (c)
. . . and gifts of the Holy Ghost, according to his own will?

A teaching presently making the rounds today says God will give you any gift you claim—that you can have any gift you wish to use in a given situation. But that's not what the text says. That's not what Paul teaches. Rather, the Holy Spirit gives gifts according to His will as He wishes.

Hebrews 2:5
For unto the angels hath he not put in subjection the world to come, whereof we speak.

Which of the angels is going to be in charge of the world? None. First Corinthians 6:3 says you and I will judge the angels. Therefore, they are not to be exalted in the way today's society exalts them.

Hebrews 2:6
But one in a certain place testified, saying, What is man, that thou art mindful of him? or the son of man, that thou visitest him?

In Psalm 8, from which Paul quotes, David says, "When I consider the sun, thy moon, thy stars and the works of thy fingers, what is man that thou art mindful of him?" Perhaps out in a field on a clear evening, watching his sheep as a young man, David looked up, saw a canopy of stars, and said, "When I see all of this, who am I that You would visit a guy like me?"

Hebrews 2:7, 8 (a)
Thou madest him a little lower than the angels; thou crownedst him with glory and honour, and didst set him over the works of thy hands: Thou hast put all things in subjection under his feet.

God has not only put the works of His fingers—the sun, moon, and stars—but the works of His hands in subjection to man. In other words, man was given an awesome cosmic responsibility. But what happened? Crowned with glory, given fabulous responsibility and endless opportunity in the Garden of Eden, man blew it and lost it all. Thus, the world of which man was put in charge was turned over to the one who tricked him.

Why is there war? Why is there rape? Why is there disease? Because, in a very real sense, Satan is presently in charge of this world. While Jesus is coming back to take that which He purchased with His own blood, Satan is presently exercising squatter's rights. He's causing hell on earth. Don't blame the Father. Man blew it. We turned this world over to the Enemy. Yet we continue to watch his junk, listen to his music, think the way he would have us think—and then wonder why we walk in darkness.

Hebrews 2:8 (b), 9 (a)
For in that he put all in subjection under him, he left nothing that is not put under him. But now we see not yet all things put under him. But we see Jesus . . .

The first Adam blew it, and all of us followed in his footsteps. Then came the Last Adam—Jesus. What do we see with Jesus? "Wind be muzzled," He said. And the wind stopped. "Waves be still," He said. And the sea was glassy (Mark 4:39). "Beasts, be at rest," He said. And they lay down next to Him (Mark 1:13). If you want to see how the earth was supposed to be, look at Jesus and you'll see Man living in harmony with the Father, exercising authority over nature.

Hebrews 2:9 (b)
. . . who was made a little lower than the angels . . .

Anything you want to know about the way man was created to be, you can find in studying the life of Jesus.

Hebrews 2:9 (c)
. . . for the suffering of death, crowned with glory and honour; that he by the grace of God should taste death for every man.

The reference here is to the position of cupbearer. You see, in Old Testament days, whenever a king was given something to drink, his cupbearer took the first sip. That way, if the winemaker had it in for his royal boss, the cupbearer would drop dead instead of the king.

Jesus is our Cupbearer—which is why He prayed, "Father, if it be possible, let this cup pass from me. Nevertheless not My will, but Thy will be done" (see Matthew 26:39). He tasted death so that we might live.

Hebrews 2:10
For it became him, for whom are all things, and by whom are all things, in bringing many sons unto glory, to make the captain of their salvation perfect through sufferings.

A cartoon in the newspaper depicted President Clinton bidding farewell to U.S. troops leaving for Bosnia. "Don't do anything I wouldn't do," he calls. The next frame is of one soldier saying, "We already are."

Our Lord doesn't simply say, "Good luck down there. Don't do anything I wouldn't do." No, He says, "I've marched down the same road you're marching. I've fought the same battle you're now fighting." That's what it means to be made perfect through suffering. Jesus was always perfect, but the fact that He suffered like us makes Him the perfect captain for us.

Hebrews 2:11
For both he that sanctifieth and they who are sanctified are all of one: for which cause he is not ashamed to call them brethren . . .

We can be one with Jesus not because of anything we have achieved but because He chooses to identify with us.

Hebrews 2:12
Saying, I will declare thy name unto my brethren, in the midst of the church will I sing praise unto thee.

When we come together to worship—be it for an hour on Friday night, a couple of hours on Sunday evening, or for a song or two before a Bible Study on Tuesday—Jesus is not only the object *of* our worship. He is also a participant *in* our worship—singing praise to the Father right alongside us. Amazing!

Hebrews 2:13–15
And again, I will put my trust in him. And again, Behold I and the children which God hath given me. Forasmuch then as the children are partakers of flesh and blood, he also himself likewise took part of the same; that through death he might destroy him that had the power of death, that is, the devil; and deliver them who through fear of death were all their lifetime subject to bondage.

As our Captain, Jesus relates to us. As our Brother, Jesus sings praise with us. As our Savior Jesus died for us—that we might be delivered from the deathly fear that haunted us.

You see, life is like reading a murder mystery. All through their journey of life, people know they're going to get murdered—maybe not in the physical sense, but they know the relationship is going to die, that they'll be fired, or that the cancer will return. Thus, there is an understandable fear that haunts everyone.

Jesus came to set us free from the fear of death. "Let Me put you out of your misery," He says. "Die."

"What?"

"Die. If any man come after Me, let him deny himself, take up his cross daily, for this is the way to be free" (see Matthew 16:24, 25).

And, as always, He's right. If you don't believe me, go to a funeral home, and sneak around the viewing rooms. Whisper into the ears of the corpses, "You're going to get killed. The relationship isn't going to work out. The finances aren't going to come through. You're not going to get the promotion"—and you'll find it won't bother them a bit because they're already dead.

Hebrews 2:16 (a)
For verily he took not on him the nature of angels . . .

Listen carefully, Jehovah's Witnesses. Jesus did not take on the nature of angels. He is not Michael. And dear Mormon, He is not the brother of Lucifer.

Hebrews 2:16 (b), 17 (a)
. . . but he took on him the seed of Abraham. Wherefore in all things it behoved him to be made like unto his brethren . . .

Jesus chose to be like *us*. Incredible!

Hebrews 2:17 (b)
. . . that he might be a merciful and faithful high priest in things pertaining to God, to make reconciliation for the sins of the people.

He became like us that He might be a merciful Priest. "I know what you're going through," He says. "I was just like you. I never sinned—but I understand your struggle."

Hebrews 2:18
For in that he himself hath suffered being tempted, he is able to succour them that are tempted.

What does it mean that He Himself suffered being tempted? Could Jesus really be tempted?

If you put a hot fudge sundae in front of me, it would draw me, entice me, intrigue me. It would be a real temptation. And I would suffer with that. On the other hand, if you took me to a sewage treatment plant and told me to stand there all day and look at it, I would also suffer—not because I would be tempted to dive in, but because I would be sickened by what was in front of me.

In this admittedly simplistic analogy, you have the argument that has raged for a couple thousand years. Was it the seeming sweetness of sin that caused Jesus to suffer being tempted, or was He tempted to just walk away from the stench of sin altogether? While there is good argument on both sides, in a later study, I'll weigh in with my opinion. . . .

THE DANGER OF DRIFTING
A Topical Study of
Hebrews 2:1

"**Q**uick!—throw out the anchor!" my brother Dave yelled to my sister as the boat motor coughed its last breath. She did. But with no rope attached, it sunk to the bottom of the Colorado River as the three of us drifted ever closer to Hoover Dam. Although we made it safely to shore, and although I was only thirteen years old at the time, I'll never forget the feeling of drifting down the river, wondering what would happen.

It's important to have an anchor connected to the boat if you're on the Colorado River—or the Wellington River. Perhaps you have never heard of the Wellington, but I guarantee you've heard of the river into which it flows: the Niagara. Posted at the point where the Wellington empties into the Niagara, is this sign: DO YOU HAVE AN ANCHOR? DO YOU KNOW HOW TO USE IT?

Do you have an anchor, and do you know how to use it? That's the subject of our text, as the writer of the Book of Hebrews employs a nautical nuance in the first verse of the second chapter. In the first phrase of the verse, the word translated "earnest heed" is the Greek word *prosecho*, which means to anchor, or to moor a ship or a boat. Notice, too, the last word of the verse. If you have a newer translation, it probably renders it properly, for the Greek word is *pararrhueo*, or "drift."

Thus, the writer here is saying we ought to carefully anchor ourselves to the things we have heard lest at any time we find ourselves drifting.

Cognizant of this concept, there were three symbols used by the early church: One was a fish, symbolic of the acronym for Jesus Christ, God's Son, Savior. Another was a boat because the disciples were fishermen before Jesus called them to be fishers of men. But the most common symbol was an anchor. In early Christian drawings and literature, the anchor is seen more than the fish or boat.

And the anchor, although not popular as a symbol to us today, is still a concept vital for us. You see, most of us are not in danger of plunging into the sea of carnality. This week, next month, or in the upcoming year, most of us are not going to be tempted to become murderers or drug addicts. So, too, the writer of this Book was talking to a group of people who were not only Christians, but Hebrews with a religious tradition and heritage. And he says, "The danger is not plunging into the ocean of perversity, but rather drifting away almost imperceptibly."

Like the Hebrews, we have heard the Word. We believe the Word—and yet perhaps the anchor that was once firmly set in the rock of Scripture is no longer tethered to our boat in the way it once was. Why? It could be because of busyness. Or it could be because of a problem with carnality. But let me suggest to you what I think is the primary reason people like you and me who love the Lord, who've been in church, who have a spiritual heritage and tradition drift: familiarity.

"I already know the Scriptures," we say. "I've led a Bible Study," or, "I've gone to Bible College," or, "I listen to Christian radio. I've heard the Word."

I used to live about thirty minutes from the magic kingdom of Disneyland. When we lived near Disneyland, I went there a lot. The first time I went, it was magical. The second time, it was intriguing. The third time, it was exciting. And the fourth time was wonderful. The fifth time was fine. And the sixth was okay. But after the tenth, twenty-fifth, and thirty-ninth time, I finally said, "I've been on the submarine ride a lot. I know every twist and turn of the Matterhorn; I could give you the jungle cruise spiel verbatim." Now, at that point, if someone asked me if I liked the magic kingdom, I would say, "Sure. Go. It's great." But if he asked me if I would come along, I'd say, "No thanks—but you should go!"

The same is true in the arena of Bible study or any other area of spirituality. "You should go there," we say. "You should plug in," we insist. But when asked if we're going to come, we say, "Well, I've been down the Main Street of Matthew a bunch of times already. I've strolled through the Tomorrowland of Revelation on numerous occasions. I don't need to go. I'm familiar with the story. But you should go. You should plug in. Me? I'm all for it, but . . ."

Familiarity—that's the problem.

There you are, shoveling coal into the boiler, chucking wood into the fire, making sure the train of which you are the engineer reaches its destination—until you say to yourself, "We're cruising fine. We're making good time. Why should I keep shoveling this coal and splitting this wood for the fire?" So you stop. And guess what happens? The train goes just fine. "This is great," you say. "I don't need to keep feeding the fire. We're cruising!" But unbeknownst to you and imperceptible to your family and friends in the passenger cars behind you, the train is slowing down at such a slow rate that no one realizes what's happening.

Finally, ten miles down the track, the train slows to a stop.

"What's going on?" your family and friends holler.

"The train stopped," you reply.

"Why?" they ask.

And if you're honest, you'd have to say, "The problem isn't the present location—it's what I stopped doing twelve miles back when I stopped feeding the fire, thinking I could just cruise."

"Jon, our marriage has blown up. She walked out on me. How did this happen?"

It didn't start happening today or yesterday. It started way back when you stopped feeding the fire, when you thought you could cruise on the momentum of previous history. You thought you didn't need to pray. You thought you didn't need Bible study. Church became something you did occasionally on Sunday if there was nothing else to do.

And now your train is at a standstill—or, worse, your boat is drifting dangerously toward Hoover Dam.

Jonah found himself in a similar situation as he drifted along in the middle of the ocean in the belly of a whale. Why was he drifting? Familiarity. You see, according to Jonah 4:2, the reason Jonah headed to Tarshish in the first place was because he knew God would save the Ninevites. And he wanted no part of it. "I knew You were like this," Jonah said. "That's why I chose to go to sleep in the hold of the boat and drift toward Tarshish in the opposite direction."

"I know that preacher," we say. "He's going to talk about the importance of loving God, tithing, or prayer. That's why I'm going fishing. That's why I'm going to drift down the Rogue River on Sunday. *You* should go to church," you tell others. "*You* should go to that Bible Study. It will be good for you. Me? I'm going to drift for salmon on Sunday because I already know all that stuff anyway."

What's the solution?

Back to Disneyland.

After I had been forty times or so, a friend of mine said, "Let's take our wives out to dinner at Disneyland."

"I'm kind of busy," I said. "But you go. It's a great place. You'll love it."

"No," he said. "You don't get it. My dad has connections with Walt Disney. I'm inviting you to dinner in Walt's private dining room above Main Street."

So we went, and sure enough, after climbing a flight of stairs to the upper level of Main Street, we were ushered into a beautiful teakwood dining room. As we found our places at the table, I noticed a waiter standing discreetly behind each couple. And as the meal progressed, every time we took even a sip of water or a pat of butter, these waiters replaced whatever was taken so that there was never anything half-full. I've never been in any place like it before or since.

Now, if my friend had said to me, "Come back next week. Walt's going to be here, too," I would have accepted his invitation gladly. I would talk to Walt, and he would tell me the inside story about Mickey and Minnie and give me the history of Disneyland. And if Walt invited me back a second time—to get my opinion on future projects—I would jump at the chance because I wouldn't merely be cruising through the magic kingdom. I would be talking to the king!

The same is true in spiritual life. Whenever we've seen the sights of Genesis or strolled the streets of Matthew, we can say, "I don't need to go to Bible study. I know the stories; I've heard the applications." And, not taking earnest heed unto the Word, we can drift our way to the falls, wondering how we got there.

Or—we can say, "I know the Scriptures; I've heard the sermons; I've sung these songs over and over. But I get to talk to the King as the message unfolds; I get to ask for forgiveness as I am convicted; I get to give thanks for grace and mercy as I am instructed." That's what makes devotions come alive. That's what makes church services meaningful. That's what makes us come to this place year after year. Not ritual—but *relationship;* not cruising through the kingdom, but talking to the *King.*

This is what Jonah should have done. When the Lord first told him to go to Ninevah, he should have said, "I hear Your Word, Lord. I know Your nature. But here's my problem: I don't want to go to the Ninevites. I can't stand what they say about You and what they've done to Your people." Had Jonah done this, the Lord could have worked with him right then, sparing him a swim in the sea, the loss of his hair, the fragrance of the inside of a whale.

So, too, any man or woman who comes to their private devotions or corporate worship with the single intent of talking to the King will never find time spent with Him a discipline, an obligation, or a burden. It will be the delight of their lives.

If you're forty years of age or older, watch out. Most likely, you do, indeed, know the Word. Main Street, Tomorrowland, Adventureland are extremely familiar to you. Thus, you are particularly vulnerable not to partying, but to drifting.

There are two types of people at Bible studies: those who give earnest heed, drop the anchor, and say, "I'm engaged in this service; I'm a part of this song; I'm embracing this message"—and those who sit and drift. Precious people, none of us can afford to drift. God wouldn't say, "Be careful. Sink your anchor into My Word," if we didn't need to heed it.

Niagara lies dead ahead, gang. Be certain you have an anchor. And make sure you know how to use it.

3 In his first two chapters, the writer of the Book of Hebrews argues that, although for a season Jesus was made lower than the angels in order to relate to us and die for us, in reality, He is greater than any angel. Yet there would be those who would have said, "Well, maybe Jesus is greater than angels, but He can't be greater than the great lawgiver, Moses."

Consequently, chapter 3 addresses this question. . . .

Hebrews 3:1, 2
Wherefore, holy brethren, partakers of the heavenly calling, consider the Apostle and High Priest of our profession, Christ Jesus; Who was faithful to him that appointed him, as also Moses was faithful in all his house.

The word "house" means either "a place to live" or "a people." In 2 Samuel 7, David prayed, "I want to build You a house, a temple."

"No, David," God replied through the prophet Nathan. "You can't build Me a house because you're a man of war. But I'm going to build *you* a house, a family from which will come Messiah." Thus, we see in the Scriptures "house" used both ways. Here we read Moses was faithful in his house—that is, to the people to whom he ministered.

For topical study of Hebrews 3:1, 2 entitled "It's Not About You!" turn to page 1462.

Hebrews 3:3–6 (a)
For this man was counted worthy of more glory than Moses, inasmuch as he who hath builded the house hath more honour than the house. For every house is builded by some man; but he that built all things is God. And Moses verily was faithful in all his house, as a servant, for a testimony of those things which were to be spoken after; But Christ as a son over his own house . . .

Truly, Moses was without peer as a servant in the house. But the Son is the Builder of the house and therefore deserves more honor than Moses.

Hebrews 3:6 (b)
. . . whose house are we . . .

Where does the Lord choose to dwell? In us. Amazing.

Hebrews 3:6 (c)
. . . if we hold fast the confidence and the rejoicing of the hope firm unto the end.

In other words, we are His house *if* we hold on to the confidence of the hope of the gospel. But if we return to traditionalism, rules, regulations, or our own efforts at spirituality, there's no guarantee.

Hebrews 3:7–11
Wherefore (as the Holy Ghost saith, To day if ye will hear his voice, Harden not your hearts, as in the provocation, in the day of temptation in the wilderness: When your fathers tempted me, proved me, and saw my works forty years. Wherefore I was grieved with that generation, and said, They do alway err in their heart; and they have not known my ways. So I sware in my wrath, They shall not enter into my rest.)

Quoting Psalm 95:7–11, a key passage in Scripture, the writer alludes to the account found in Numbers 13. . . .

The spies returned from the Land of Promise, saying, "It's a fabulous land—a land flowing with milk and honey. But there's a huge problem. There are giants there and we look like grasshoppers to them."

"Oh no," the people said. "We're toast."

And although Joshua and Caleb said, "If God is with us, it won't be a problem," the ten other spies convinced the congregation they couldn't simply believe that God would give them the Land.

*"Because you don't believe the simple word
I gave you," God said, "you're not going in."*

And the longest death march in world history
ensued as the Israelites wandered around for
thirty-eight years until an entire generation
died—including Moses.

Hebrews 3:12–16 (a)

**Take heed, brethren, lest there be in any of
you an evil heart of unbelief, in departing
from the living God. But exhort one another
daily, while it is called To day; lest any of
you be hardened through the deceitfulness
of sin. For we are made partakers of Christ,
if we hold the beginning of our confidence
stedfast unto the end; while it is said, To
day if ye will hear his voice, harden not your
hearts, as in the provocation. For some,
when they had heard, did provoke. . . .**

Watch out, warns the writer of Hebrews, that
you don't make the mistake your fathers made at
Kadesh Barnea when they looked to their inadequacy rather than at God's inerrancy.

Hebrews 3:16 (b)

**. . . howbeit not all that came out of Egypt
by Moses.**

How were the children of Israel delivered from
Egypt? By blood and water—the blood that they
applied to the doorposts before Passover and the
water of the Red Sea which drowned the chariots
pursuing them.

So, too, we are delivered from "Egypt"—from
damnation and destruction—by the blood and
water that flowed from Jesus' side on the Cross
of Calvary. Yet, like the children of Israel, although they are delivered from Egypt, too many
Christians spend their whole lives wandering between Egypt and the land of abundance. Year after year, they trudge through life, thinking, *Well,
this is as good as it can get until I die and go to
the Promised Land of heaven.*

That's not what God intended for us, gang. He
intended to take us out of Egypt, through the wilderness quickly, and into the Promised Land of
the Spirit-filled, abundant life. You see, the Promised Land in Bible typology is not a picture of
heaven. It's a picture of life in the Spirit. How do
I know? Because while there are neither giants
nor battles in heaven, the Spirit-filled life is filled
with many a giant to wrestle and many a battle to
wage.

Only Joshua and Caleb realized that giants,
battles, wars notwithstanding, God would, indeed, give them the Promised Land. And thus,
they did not provoke God.

Hebrews 3:17–19

**But with whom was he grieved forty years?
was it not with them that had sinned, whose
carcases fell in the wilderness? And to
whom sware he that they should not enter
into his rest, but to them that believed not?
So we see that they could not enter in because of unbelief.**

To whom did God say, "You shall not enter into
the rest, the Promised Land, the abundance of
milk and honey"? I would have thought it would
have been to those who worshiped idols or to
those who didn't have morning devotions. I would
have thought it would have been to immoral men
or to those who didn't offer sacrifices. Yet, in reality, the only thing that kept the children of Israel
from the Promised Land was their lack of faith.

This is critically important theology, for the
singular sin that kept them from blessing was
simply thinking God's promise was just too good
to be true. Precious people, you can live the abundant, Spirit-filled, successful, exciting, thrilling
Christian life if, instead of thinking that God can't
bless you because you haven't been to Bible
study, because you've been yelling at your
husband, or because you haven't had morning devotions regularly, you say, "I'm a spiritual grasshopper, Lord. But if You want to bring me into
this great land of blessing, I'll gladly go in!"

The sin of Hebrews 3 is singular. It's not fornication, as destructive as that sin may be. It's not
idolatry, as sad as that sin is. Rather, it's simply
not believing how good God is.

*When he came home from Bible School, my
son Peter-John shared with me how passionate he and his friends were about seeing their
generation brought into the kingdom. "So I get
up early in the morning and pray and spend
time in the Word. I do so well for about three
or four days," he said. "But then I get tired. I
sleep in. I miss my devotional time. And I
don't go to prayer meeting." With tears running down his cheeks, this football-playing son
of mine said, "Dad, I want to do so well. But
I'm not."*

*"Peter," I said, "when you learn the lesson
that took me years and years to understand,
you'll be on your way. And that lesson is simply this: Blessing, anointing, ministry, fruitfulness, and victory are not about you. It's not
about the work you do for the Lord; it's about
the work He did for you. It's not about your
prayer to the Lord; it's about His intercession
for you. It's not about your faith in the Lord;
it's about His being faithful when you falter.*

It's all about Him being the hero, the prayer warrior, the victor, the friend, the faithful One."

The key not only to ministry but to every area of spirituality is found in John 10. . . .

Of John the Baptist, Jesus said, "This is the greatest man who ever lived." Yet Scripture also records John did no mighty miracles (John 10:41). So what made John the greatest man who ever lived? One thing: He didn't preach on power in prayer. He didn't propagate victory through discipline. He simply said, "Behold the Lamb. Check Him out. Follow Him."

Happy is the day when a woman grasps the fact that spiritual life has nothing to do with her and everything to do with God. Happy the day when a man finally realizes all he has to say is, "I don't know why You put up with a grasshopper like me, but, Lord, if You want to allow me to be in ministry, if You want to give me a family, if You want to bless me in countless ways—that's okay with me!"

Don't let anyone sell you a bill of goods, saying, "The reason I'm so successful is because I pray night and day. And the reason you will never be part of the chosen few is because you don't."

Any man or woman can leave here tonight to be used mightily and blessed exceedingly beyond anything they could ask or even think if they would just learn to say, "I believe You, Lord."

Contrary to many sermons, the deceitfulness of sin is one thing. It's saying, "I've got to do more. I've got to be bigger, stronger, better in my spiritual walk so that I can battle the giants ahead of me." God says that's the very sin that will keep you out.

Dear saint, it's all about God's work for you, not your work for Him. Fix your eyes on Jesus. Be blown away by Him. Behold the Lamb!

IT'S NOT ABOUT YOU!
A Topical Study of
Hebrews 3:1, 2

The longer I walk with the Lord, the more at rest I am in the Lord. But rather than lead me into a lethargic kind of apathy, the rest of which I speak causes me to step out in victory and to walk with my Father confidently. To this end, I want to share a truth with you that is simple, but I believe profoundly so.

Keep in mind that the Book of Hebrews was written to Christians who had come out of a Hebrew, or Jewish, culture. They were believers in Christ; they were converted to Christ; they recognized Jesus as Messiah—but as the years went on, these Hebrew Christians were being drawn back to Judaism. After all, there in Jerusalem they could see the temple. They could hear the trumpets. They could smell the incense. And the pull of tradition, nostalgia, and memories is a strong one.

"Don't go back," writes the author of this book. "Even though it's tempting, even though traditions have a powerful pull, keep the foundation of your faith basic. Keep it focused. Keep it simple. It's Jesus—nothing more, nothing less, nothing else." That is why he says in chapter 3, "Consider the Apostle of our profession." The word "apostle" meaning "sent one," upon reading this, the mind of the Jewish reader would immediately race to the Apostle of Israel, the one sent to deliver them from the bondage of Egypt. . . .

After baking bricks in the blistering Egyptian sun for four hundred years, the people of Israel finally came to their wits' end and cried to the Lord to send a deliverer. Therefore, sent *by* the Lord on a mission *for* the Lord, Moses was an apostle in the truest sense of the word.

"Thus saith the Lord, Let My people go," he declared to Pharaoh. And you know the story. This apostle, this leader, Moses, led a congregation of perhaps three million Jews to the Land of Promise.

Notice they are told to consider not only the apostle, but the High Priest of their profession. Upon reading this, the Jewish mind would think of the first high priest, Moses' older brother, Aaron. So beginning in chapter 5, the author reminds his audience that not only did Moses fail to enter the Promised Land but also that Aaron failed to enter in as well. . . .

In Numbers 20, the children of Israel were once again murmuring against Moses and Aaron, saying,

> *Would God that we had died when our brethren died before the LORD! And why have ye brought up the congregation of the LORD into this wilderness, that we and our cattle should die there? And Moses and Aaron went from the presence of the assembly unto the door of the tabernacle of the congregation, and they fell upon their faces: and the glory of the LORD appeared unto them. And the LORD spake unto Moses, saying, Take the rod, and gather thou the assembly together, thou, and Aaron thy brother, and speak ye unto the rock before their eyes; and it shall give forth his water, and thou shalt bring forth to them water out of the rock: so thou shalt give the congregation and their beasts drink. And Moses took the rod from before the LORD, as he commanded him. And Moses and Aaron gathered the congregation together before the rock, and he said unto them, Hear now, ye rebels; must we fetch you water out of this rock? And Moses lifted up his hand, and with his rod he smote the rock twice: and the water came out abundantly, and the congregation drank, and their beasts also. And the LORD spake unto Moses and Aaron, Because ye believed me not, to sanctify me in the eyes of the children of Israel, therefore ye shall not bring this congregation into the land which I have given them.*
>
> Numbers 20:3 (b), 4, 6–12

With this passage in mind, if you came from a Jewish background and are told to consider the Apostle and High Priest of your confession, the implication might trouble you because you would say, "Uh-oh. I know our national history. We were given a fine apostle and a wonderful high priest, two of the best of men. But we drove them crazy. I wonder, therefore, if I will do the same thing to this great Apostle and High Priest, Jesus Christ."

The fact is, one need not be a Jew to feel this way. I've been a Christian for almost fifty years, and as I watch my life unfold year after year, as I hear myself murmuring, as I see my lousy attitudes, as I succumb to sin and carnality, my tendency is to say, "At fifty years old in the faith, I should be a lot further along than I am. No doubt I'm frustrating my Great High Priest and Apostle Jesus Christ much more than the children of Israel frustrated Moses and Aaron. Any day now, He's bound to say, "Jon, how long will it take for you to get it right? I'm out of here." But such is not the case, for look at our text. . . .

Who was faithful to him that appointed him, as also Moses was faithful in all his house.

Hebrews 3:2

To whom is our High Priest faithful? Not to you, not to me, not to your congregation. He is faithful to the One who appointed Him. He is faithful to the Father.

The overwhelming majority of Christians think that God the Father was holy and awesome and powerful. But He was understandably angry. So Jesus shed His blood on the Cross, went to heaven, and said, "Take it easy, Father. Here's My blood. It's okay now."

Truly, the basic understanding of most people is that, because God was frustrated with mankind, Jesus came on the scene to calm Him down. But such is not true biblical theology. Jesus came to earth not primarily for you or me. He came to do the will of His Father. And it was the Father's will to save you.

Biblical Christianity is not about us, gang. It's not about our prayer. It's not about our devotion. It's not about whether we're good or bad, obedient or disobedient. It's not about how much we pray or how little we pray. It's not about where we go or don't go, what we do or don't do. It's about Jesus' faithfulness to His Father. And our failures only make His ministry to the Father that much more impressive.

"If that's true," you say, "if my relationship with God is not about my prayer life, my worship, my anointing, my ministry, then how do I fit in at all? Am I just a pawn, just a piece of the puzzle in this demonstration of the faithfulness of the Son to the Father?"

For the answer, turn to John 17. . . .

I in them, and thou in me, that they may be made perfect in one; and that the world may know that thou hast sent me, and hast loved them, as thou hast loved me.

John 17:23

What if we believed this? What if we really believed that the Father loves us as much as He loves His own Son? We would pray with confidence. We wouldn't have to prove anything to Him or to ourselves. We would be at peace.

The repercussions? We would pray more. We would study the Word more.

We would worship more—not to earn spiritual brownie points, but just to enjoy our Father.

Our Apostle and High Priest, Jesus Christ, will not fail—no matter how many times we do—because His ministry is to the Father. And the Father will never frustrate Him.

Hebrews 4:1
Let us therefore fear, lest, a promise being left us of entering into his rest, any of you should seem to come short of it.

What should we be afraid of? Simply of limiting the Holy One of Israel due to unbelief (Psalm 78:41). Israel did not believe God would lead them into the Promised Land and give them victory over the giants that roamed therein. "Fear that," warns the author of Hebrews. "Be afraid of being one who doesn't believe God is good and that He has provided rest in His Son."

Hebrews 4:2
For unto us was the gospel preached, as well as unto them: but the word preached did not profit them, not being mixed with faith in them that heard it.

The word "gospel" meaning "good news," the good news for the children of Israel was that there was a land flowing with milk and honey. Yes, there were obstacles. But God promised them victory if they simply believed.

"Oh, but we're only grasshoppers," they said. And the grasshopper mentality still paralyzes us today. "I'm not a man of this," we say, or, "I'm not doing that. I can't receive God's blessing on my life because I'm blowing it here, or I must be bugging God there."

No. According to our text, it was not their shortcomings that kept the children of Israel from entering the Land of Promise. It was their failure to mix God's promises with faith. What will keep you from enjoying the best blessings in your family or in your ministry? Simply not believing what God says. Maybe you have the Promise Box on your breakfast table or *The Jesus Person Pocket Promise Book* in your back pocket. You know God said He would provide for all of your needs (Philippians 4:19), that all things are working together for good (Romans 8:28) and that He is with you even unto the end of the world (Matthew 28:20). But these promises will not do you any good until you stop saying, "What's the catch? This can't be true for me. I'm nothing but a grasshopper."

What does it mean to mix the gospel with faith? The answer is seen in Acts 12. . . .

When Herod put Peter in prison, Scripture records that the church got together and prayed fervently. God sent an angel to Peter as he slept between two guards.

"Arise," said the angel. And the chains fell off Peter's wrists and legs. So Peter got up and followed the angel into the city—even though Scripture tells us he thought it was nothing more than a vision. Walking through the streets of the city, however, he realized it was no dream.

Now, had Peter not stood up and stepped out, had he not started moving, but instead said, "This is a neat thought, an interesting insight," had he not mixed the angel's command with faith—even though the chains were off and the door was opened, he would have remained in jail.

What about us? God gives a promise to us, and we say, "It's a vision. It sheds some esoteric light on theology. But it can't really mean I can step out. So I'll just stay in my prison, wait for my execution, and be comforted with this thought." No! Get up! Step out! Go for it! And you might discover it's reality. Listen, folks, the Word being mixed with faith means we stand up and start moving. . . .

You pray for your teenage son, "Lord, revive him. Bless him. Help him." Get up and expect him to do well. Start treating him like he is doing well. And you'll find the promise is true. But if you stay in your cell, theorizing and saying, "I need to study deeper on this matter," you'll never enter the Land of Promise regarding your situation.

How much faith does it take? Look at the believers in Acts 12. . . .

Knock. Knock. Knock. "It's Peter."

"No, it can't be Peter. Lord, we pray that You would free Peter."

Knock. Knock. Knock. "It's Peter."

"No, it can't be Peter. Lord, we pray You would free Peter. . . ."

How much faith did they have? About a mustard seed's worth. But Jesus said that's all it takes to move a mountain. I'm convinced that if you have only enough faith to pray, that's enough to start things happening, to start doors opening. It doesn't take much. The promises, the blessings, the good things of God happen when you take the Word and mix it with faith.

Hebrews 4:3 (a)
For we which have believed do enter into rest . . .

"Wait!" the Jew would protest. "We already have rest. On the Sabbath, we rest one day in seven." But the rest talked about here is something much bigger than a one-day vacation or a one-day Sabbath. . . .

Hebrews 4:3 (b)–6
. . . as he said, As I have sworn in my wrath, if they shall enter into my rest: although the works were finished from the foundation of the world. For he spake in a certain place of the seventh day on this wise, and God did rest the seventh day from all his works. And in this place again, If they shall enter into my rest. Seeing therefore it remaineth that some must enter therein, and they to whom it was first preached entered not in because of unbelief.

Although there was a Sabbath day established in the first creation week, here—thousands of years later—God says, "It remaineth that some must enter in," as though it were a future event. Therefore, this speaks not of creation but of Canaan. . . .

Hebrews 4:7, 8 (a)
Again, he limiteth a certain day, saying in David, To day, after so long a time; as it is said, To day if ye will hear his voice, harden not your hearts. For if Jesus . . .

The Greek form of "Jesus" being *Yeshua,* or Joshua—the word "Jesus" in this text refers not to Jesus Christ, but to Joshua—the one who led the children of Israel into the physical Promised Land.

Hebrews 4:8 (b), 9
. . . had given them rest, then would he not afterward have spoken of another day. There remaineth therefore a rest to the people of God.

Although Joshua led the people into the Promised Land, God still promised a rest to come *after*

they were in the Land of Promise. Thus, there's a promise given of rest, real rest. It is not the Sabbath day. It is not the Promised Land. It is not creation rest. It is not Canaan rest. It is Christ's rest.

Hebrews 4:10
For he that is entered into his rest, he also hath ceased from his own works, as God did from his.

The rest spoken of is the rest that occurs when you give up trying to earn salvation or blessing—when you realize it's not through your works, by your energy, because of your righteousness, or due to your prayer life. True rest occurs when you realize your salvation is not dependent upon anything you do but rather upon who Jesus is, and what He's done.

Hebrews 4:11 (a)
Let us labour therefore to enter into that rest . . .

What does it mean to labor to enter into rest? It means just to rest in God and relate to Him. It's like riding a bike. When you begin learning, you wobble around and maybe skin your knees a time or two. But then once you get it, riding a bike is the easiest, most relaxing thing in the world. The same thing is true with spiritual rest. Initially, we wobble all over the road, saying, "What about?" and, "How come?" and, "That can't be . . ." as we try to figure it out. But when we finally learn the Christian walk is not about us, but about Jesus—not about what we must do, but about what He's already done—we start to cruise.

Hebrews 4:11 (b)
. . . lest any man fall after the same example of unbelief.

If we don't enter into His rest, like the children of Israel, we will wander year after year in the wilderness of dryness and drought, never blessed because we're trying to work our salvation out in our own energy, never at peace because we just can't believe God is as good as He promises to be.

Hebrews 4:12
For the word of God is quick, and powerful, and sharper than any two-edged sword, piercing even to the dividing asunder of soul and spirit, and of the joints and marrow, and is a discerner of the thoughts and intents of the heart.

I always thought the Word was quick and powerful and sharper than any two-edged sword because it would bring to light and deal with my failures. Not true. Look at the context of the verse. The Word pierces the heart as it recounts stories of people who were robbed because they just didn't believe how good God is. It's all about *Him*.

Hebrews 4:13
Neither is there any creature that is not manifest in his sight: but all things are naked and opened unto the eyes of him with whom we have to do.

Not only does God's Word pierce, but His eyes pierce as well. Yes, the Lord sees my inadequacies, my unbelief. But look at the next verse. . . .

Hebrews 4:14, 15
Seeing then that we have a great high priest, that is passed into the heavens, Jesus the Son of God, let us hold fast our profession. For we have not an high priest which cannot be touched with the feeling of our infirmities; but was in all points tempted like as we are, yet without sin.

I have a tendency to doubt, to fear, and to focus on my inadequacy rather than God's sufficiency. But I have a Great High Priest who understands. How does He know how I'm feeling? Our text says He was tempted as we are. And I suggest a temptation that would cause Him to be a compassionate High Priest, a temptation that would cause Jesus to empathize with me would have to be a genuine temptation for Him. . . .

If a trusted congregant pulled out an Uzi machine gun from under the pew and began spraying bullets everywhere, leaving 458 people wounded, I would not go to the jail the next day and say, "I understand what you're going through, Friend. I have the same feelings."

No, I would be mad at him, disappointed in him, wouldn't want anything to do with him. However, if the congregant reached under the pew and pulled out not an Uzi machine gun but a hot fudge sundae and started eating it, when the service was over, I would say, "I understand, my friend."

So, too, I suggest that for Jesus to be the compassionate, faithful High Priest the Book of Hebrews tells us He is, the temptations He endured had to be genuine temptations for Him. For Him

to be touched with the feeling of our infirmities and to understand what we're going through, He had to be where we've been. Therefore, even though the Word pierces me when I see stories of unbelief and I realize the same kind of unbelief resides in me, I have a High Priest who says, "I understand. I've been tempted in all points—even the points of unbelief with which you struggle."

And what does that make me do? Read on.

Hebrews 4:16
Let us therefore come boldly unto the throne of grace, that we may obtain mercy, and find grace to help in time of need.

The Greek word translated "may" does not mean "might." It means "will." Thus, this is not an invitation to "Come boldly and we'll see how you're doing." No, it's to "Come boldly and you *will* obtain mercy and find grace." The definition of mercy is "not getting what you deserve." The definition of grace, on the other hand, is "getting what you don't deserve." What do we deserve? We deserve to have a trusted friend take an Uzi and start splattering every one of us. That's what we deserve—and worse. But grace is God saying, "Hot fudge sundaes for everyone!"

When you come to the throne boldly—not tentatively, not reluctantly, but boldly because the price has been paid and the work done—you find mercy and grace.

When?

Whenever you have need.

5 ### Hebrews 5:1
For every high priest taken from among men is ordained for men in things pertaining to God, that he may offer both gifts and sacrifices for sins.

The Jewish reader would have been very familiar with the concept, if not the Person, of the high priestly ministry of Jesus Christ, believing as he did, that one could relate to God only through a priest.

Hebrews 5:2–4
Who can have compassion on the ignorant, and on them that are out of the way; for that he himself also is compassed with infirmity. And by reason hereof he ought, as for the people, so also for himself, to offer for sins. And no man taketh this honour unto himself, but he that is called of God, as was Aaron.

The high priest had compassion on people because he himself knew his own failings and shortcomings. He was aware of his own struggles. If you've had struggles and setbacks, failures and hurts, pains and problems, know this: Once you turn those things over to the Lord, you will have compassion on people you wouldn't have had otherwise. In the service of the Lord—be it as a Bible study teacher, deacon, children's worker, pastor, or missionary—we're not the doctors. There's only one great Physician, only one Healer—Jesus Christ. As a pastor, then, who am I? I'm just a guy who has been in the hospital for a lot of years. And because I know where the bathroom is, where the cafeteria is, where the gift shop is, who the orderlies are, I can help others find their way around the hospital.

People get mixed up about this when they begin to think, *That missionary, singer, Bible teacher, or pastor is the answer.* No. They're walking around in the same blue gowns that tie in the back that you are. I'm still getting patched up myself. I'm still getting operated on regularly. I'm still terminal—but I've found a *great* Doctor. Such *is* the essence of true ministry.

Hebrews 5:5–8
So also Christ glorified not himself to be made an high priest; but he that said unto him, Thou art my Son, to day have I begotten thee. As he saith also in another place, Thou art a priest for ever after the order of Melchizedek. Who in the days of his flesh, when he had offered up prayers and supplications with strong crying and tears unto him that was able to save him from death, and was heard in that he feared; Though he were a Son, yet learned he obedience by the things which he suffered.

When Jesus was about to be taken away in order to be tried before Pontius Pilate and ultimately crucified on Golgotha, He cried strong tears and sweat drops of blood in the Garden of Gethsemane.

In this, I find two points of which we are to be very cognizant. . . .

First, in His most intensive moment of prayer, Jesus shows us the purpose of prayer is not to get God to do what we want. It's to get us in harmony with what *He* wants. Not our will, but *His* be done.

Now, here's the amazing thing. When I get in harmony with what God wants, guess what I find. I find ultimately it's what I truly wanted all along. Oh, there might be a Cross to endure. There might be blood and pain and suffering for

a season. But on the other side of the Cross, there is joy (Hebrews 12:2). Prayer is to get me in harmony with the Father. If you don't get this lesson down, prayer will always be a mystery to you and a problem for you. And you will ultimately stop praying as a result.

"I prayed for that and nothing happened." "I prayed for the other, but it didn't work out." Wait a minute. If you gave the matter to God, God will do what's best. Prayer is not to get God to do my bidding. Prayer is for me to get in line with Him. Although it's a struggle, it's in prayer when I finally find myself getting to the place where I say, "Okay, Father, *Your* will be done."

Second, it was God who sent Jesus to die for us. Most people have the view that God the Father is angry with man. That's not it. God so loved the world—loved *you*—that He sent His Son (John 3:16).

"The Father sent His Son to pay the price?" you say. "I'm not sure it's really loving for the Father to send someone else to accomplish His purpose of redemption."

Wait a minute. "His name shall be called Wonderful, Counselor, Mighty God, Everlasting Father" (see Isaiah 9:6). To whom does this refer? To Jesus. Great is the mystery, declared Paul, that God Himself became a Man (1 Timothy 3:16).

Hebrews 5:9
And being made perfect, he became the author of eternal salvation unto all them that obey him.

Always perfect in Person, Jesus became perfectly suited and prepared through the things He suffered to be called our Friend and our faithful High Priest.

Hebrews 5:10, 11 (a)
Called of God an high priest after the order of Melchizedek. Of whom we have many things to say, and hard to be uttered . . .

"There are so many things I would like to teach you," the writer laments, "but you don't hear as you once did because you're back into swishing robes, blaring trumpets, and religion once again. I want to dive into the fantastic implications of the Melchizedekian ministry, but I can't because you're not ready."

Hebrews 5:11 (b)
. . . seeing ye are dull of hearing.

The term translated "dull of hearing" is the word for "ignorant" in Greek. But the ignorance spoken of is not due to never hearing. Rather, the ignorance spoken of is the result of ignoring. In other words, when truth was shared, the response was, "Big deal. I don't care what you say. I have my own perspective."

There are those who say, "I'm just not getting anything out of Bible study. I go to church, but nothing registers with me. I read the Bible, but it just seems like ink on paper." Why? It could very well be because they are those who are dull of hearing. That is, God spoke to them a week, a month, or a year ago concerning something they were to do. But they ignored it. Why, then, would God keep speaking to them if they refused to do those things He already made clear to them?

It is a loving Father who says, "Jon, I'm going to make it real simple. When you do step one, I'll take you to step two. When you do what I ask, when you incorporate what I show you—then I'll take you farther down the road. But I'm not going to keep on heaping instruction and insight upon you if you're only going to ignore what I've already told you."

Dear saint, what is the last thing God told you to do?

Have you done it?

Hebrews 5:12, 13
For when for the time ye ought to be teachers, ye have need that one teach you again which be the first principles of the oracles of God; and are become such as have need of milk, and not of strong meat. For every one that useth milk is unskilful in the word of righteousness: for he is a babe.

I'm sorry to say that in many churches, sermons cannot be longer than twenty-five minutes. And during those twenty-five minutes, the preacher better have lots of stories and jokes because people choke on meat. But once you start studying Scripture seriously, you start gaining strength, your spiritual muscles start bulging, and you hunger for more than pablum week after week.

Hebrews 5:14
But strong meat belongeth to them that are of full age, even those who by reason of use have their senses exercised to discern both good and evil.

I had a big chunk of prime rib one night on the Rogue River in Oregon. When I finished it, I thought I would never have prime rib again. But you know, a day later I was ready for another piece! So, too, you might leave a Bible study, saying, "That was sure a long study,"—but if you're

walking, exercising, growing in the Lord, you'll be back for more on Sunday, saying, "Serve it up again. I'm hungry!"

6 I'm convinced Hebrews 6 is one of Satan's favorite passages, for he has used this passage to cause dismay, despondency, and depression in more Christians than perhaps any other single passage in the Bible. Make no mistake about it—the devil is a Bible scholar. . . .

TIME *magazine may have thought they were on the cutting edge of society with their "Is the Bible Fact or Fiction?" cover one week, but in reality, they fell prey to the oldest trick in the book. After all, way back in the Garden of Eden Satan did the same thing when he said to Eve, "Did God really say . . . ?"*

In Matthew 4, he quoted Psalm 91:12, saying to Jesus, "Is it not written that the Father shall give His angels charge over thee lest You dash Your foot against a rock?" Yes, he quoted Scripture—but he conveniently left out the part that says, "to keep thee in all thy ways"— for God's ways don't include jumping from the temple.

Satan still uses these tactics today. As he did with Eve, he'll either question or contradict the Word. As he did with Jesus, he'll quote it and omit part of it. Hebrews 6 is one of those passages a lot of believers read and say, "Uh-oh. I'm in a heap of trouble," because Satan is all over it, saying, "You've fallen away. You've lost your salvation. There's no hope for restoration."

While Hebrews 6 is, indeed, meant as a warning, the question is: Does it apply to you and me? Let's see. . . .

Hebrews 6:1–3
Therefore leaving the principles of the doctrine of Christ, let us go on unto perfection; not laying again the foundation of repentance from dead works, and of faith toward God, of the doctrine of baptisms, and of laying on of hands, and of resurrection of the dead, and of eternal judgment. And this will we do, if God permit.

Here the author lists six basic foundational principles every believer should understand:

- Repentance—both from sin and from trying to earn salvation through works
- Faith
- Baptism—both water baptism and the baptism of the Holy Spirit

- Laying on of hands—finding your spiritual gift and being empowered for service
- Resurrection—including end-times teaching, the Rapture of the Church, and the millennium
- Eternal judgment

If you're a teacher, these are six areas you should be teaching new believers. And if you are a new believer, I encourage you to explore these very important principles of our faith.

After addressing these foundational principles, the author moves on to the section so often misinterpreted. . . .

Hebrews 6:4–6

For it is impossible for those who were once enlightened, and have tasted of the heavenly gift, and were made partakers of the Holy Ghost, and have tasted the good word of God, and the powers of the world to come, if they shall fall away, to renew them again unto repentance; seeing they crucify to themselves the Son of God afresh, and put him to an open shame.

"If you ignore these foundational truths and return to your old ways, it is impossible to renew you to repentance," writes the author of Hebrews. And that's why this Scripture is so troubling.

I often become involved in conversations where someone says to me, "I'm lost," or, "I've committed the unpardonable sin," or, "It's hopeless."

"Why?" I ask.

"Because, after I went back to the old scene, I heard a sermon on Hebrews 6 that said it's impossible for me to return to salvation. I'm doomed."

There are those who say Hebrews 6 is talking about people who were never saved—about people who just sort of dabbled in Christianity. They came to church occasionally on Sundays. They had devotions if they weren't too busy. But they weren't really plugged in. They were on the periphery—dabbling in Christianity, dabbling in mysticism, dabbling in materialism, dabbling here and there. Yes, they tasted of the heavenly gift and of the Word, but they never really sank their teeth into it, never digested it. Consequently, certain Bible teachers maintain that Hebrews 6 does not even apply to a born-again believer.

I have difficulty with this argument because in a previous chapter, we read how Jesus Christ tasted death for all men (2:9). Does that mean Jesus merely dabbled in securing our salvation, that He didn't pay the full price? No. When Scripture says Christ tasted death for all men, it means He took the poison; He died in our place; He who knew no sin became sin for us. Thus, I believe those who use the word "taste" lightly in reference to Hebrews 6 have problems in their position.

A second group says that, based on the word "if" in verse 6, Hebrews 6 presents nothing more than a hypothetical situation. In other words, *if* there was someone who really experienced the Holy Spirit and tasted of the good Word of God, and *if* it were possible that they would fall away, then they would re-crucify Christ and put Him to open shame. But I find such an argument stretching the language to an illogical conclusion.

I believe Hebrews 6 is not about an unbeliever who was never really saved. Nor is it presenting a hypothetical situation. I believe it speaks of those who leave the simplicity of Jesus Christ. So when a person says, "Oh, Jon, I went back into the party scene for three years," or, "back into that religious trip and depended upon my own efforts and my own goodness," on the basis of this passage, I have to say to him, "It's impossible to renew your salvation—but there is a story you must remember. . . ."

He had everything going for him. Rich, young, and powerful, he was one of People *magazine's "Twenty-Five Most Intriguing People." In a moment of desperation, however, he came to Jesus and said, "Good Master, what must I do to inherit eternal life?"*

Jesus listed several of the commandments, of which the young man said, "I've kept them all."

"Right," Jesus said. "Now go sell your goods and you'll be free to follow Me."

"I can't," said the rich young ruler as he walked away.

"I tell you the truth," Jesus said sorrowfully, "it is easier for a camel to go through the eye of a needle than for a rich man to enter into the kingdom."

"Then who can be saved?" asked His disciples, who were under the impression from generations of rabbinical teaching that riches were a sign of God's blessing. "If a rich man can't be saved, who can be?"

And Jesus said, "With man it is impossible, but"—and here is the glorious but—"with God all things are possible" (see Mark 10:27).

You've walked away, sister? You've walked away, brother? It is impossible in your own energy, in your own strength, by your own efforts to renew yourself again to repentance. But guess what? Even now God is doing a miracle. He's brought you into this understanding. He's made you see the stupidity of what you've been doing. And He has done the impossible. He has brought you back once again. But understand that if it weren't for His miraculous power and matchless mercy, it would be impossible for you to return to Him.

A glorious truth—yet a sobering one as well, for Scripture indicates it is possible to wander away once too often. Like the rich young ruler, there can come a day when you just can't return. The job's too demanding; the movie's too enticing; the guy's too handsome. There can come a day when a person can wander away to the point where his heart becomes hardened.

You cannot lose your salvation—but you can leave it because God won't force eternal life on anyone. What can separate us from the love of God? Neither height nor depth nor principalities nor power nor things present nor things to come. No outside force can separate you from the love of God which is in Christ Jesus (Romans 8:38, 39). Only you can. And that's the warning of this passage.

Hebrews 6:7, 8
For the earth which drinketh in the rain that cometh oft upon it, and bringeth forth herbs meet for them by whom it is dressed, receiveth blessing from God: But that which beareth thorns and briers is rejected, and is nigh unto cursing; whose end is to be burned.

Just as rain falls on both briars and fruit-bearing plants, the glorious news of salvation would have been refreshing and renewing to those who understood that salvation is based solely and completely on the finished work of the Cross. But to those who insisted on returning to a works-based relationship with God, the same Word would be damning.

Hebrews 6:9
But, beloved, we are persuaded better things of you, and things that accompany salvation, though we thus speak.

This is how I feel about you. I'm persuaded of better things because you're interested in salvation. How do I know? Because you're here; because you worship; because you pray; because you want to take in the Word.

Hebrews 6:10
For God is not unrighteous to forget your work and labour of love, which ye have shewed toward his name, in that ye have ministered to the saints, and do minister.

Faith without works is dead (James 2:26). It's not faith *and* works. It's not faith *or* works. It's faith *that* works. True faith works. When you're madly in love with someone, you do things you would never have done otherwise. True faith works because true love works.

The idea in this verse is intriguing. God will not forget the works we've long since forgotten. Conversely, I don't believe there will be a lot of rewards for the works we haven't forgotten. "Look at the guys on the street corner," Jesus said. "They want to be acknowledged. They want to be applauded. But I say unto you, they have already had their reward" (see Matthew 6:5).

Jesus wasn't being spiteful—just truthful. Therefore, minister secretly whenever you can. Bless people in a way they don't even know from whence it came, and you will have reward in heaven.

Hebrews 6:11, 12
And we desire that every one of you do shew the same diligence to the full assurance of hope unto the end: That ye be not slothful, but followers of them who through faith and patience inherit the promises.

Keep ministering. Keep believing that the promises of God work for you, in you, and through you.

Hebrews 6:13–15
For when God made promise to Abraham, because he could swear by no greater, he sware by himself, Saying, Surely blessing I will bless thee, and multiplying I will multiply thee. And so, after he had patiently endured, he obtained the promise.

In addition to the swishing of priestly robes and the sounding of temple trumpets, there was another reason the Hebrews were being drawn back to religiosity. The early church lived in anticipation of the return of Jesus. But weeks, months, and years passed. And Jesus had not come back. "The temple we can see," the Hebrews must have said. "The incense we can smell. Jesus left us with His promise—but *where is He?*" Consequently, many grew weary, wondering if they could trust the promise of His coming.

Throughout Scripture, there is inevitably a gap of time between the giving of a promise and the performance of the promise. Abraham "patiently endured." How long? Twenty-five years. In your case, maybe the same will be true because in the period of waiting, in the gap between the giving of the promise and the performance is when God does His best work.

For topical study of Hebrews 6:15 entitled "Waiting for His Working," turn to page 1473.

Hebrews 6:16, 17
For men verily swear by the greater: and an oath for confirmation is to them an end of all strife. Wherein God, willing more abundantly to shew unto the heirs of promise the immutability of his counsel, confirmed it by an oath.

Today, when people swear to strengthen their credibility, they swear by something greater than themselves. They don't say, "I swear by my guinea pig," but rather, "I swear on a stack of Bibles."

"Let your yes be yes, and your no be no," Jesus taught in reference to the hypocrisy of this mentality (see Matthew 5:37). And yet—realizing man is slow to believe and prone to suspicion, here God takes an oath to verify His promise. He meets us on our level.

Hebrews 6:18
That by two immutable things, in which it was impossible for God to lie, we might have a strong consolation, who have fled for refuge to lay hold upon the hope set before us.

Determined to show you and me that He will keep His promise as we're waiting impatiently, God takes an oath. And thus there are two proofs that His promise will come to pass (Psalm 110): His Word that He cannot lie and His oath that He need not take, but does for our sake.

Hebrews 6:19 (a)
Which hope we have as an anchor of the soul, both sure and stedfast . . .

In the catacombs of Rome, where Christians hid in times of persecution, one symbol can be seen more than any other: the anchor. No matter what storms come our way, we are anchored in the Word of God, in the promises He made. We have this sure hope that He will do what He says. So don't go back to temple worship, entreats the author. Don't go back to heathen practices, to partying, to wherever else you came from. Be anchored in the immutable, unchangeable, sure, and steadfast Word of God.

Hebrews 6:19 (b)
. . . and which entereth into that within the veil.

The writer goes on to say that our Anchor, our Hope, entered the veil—a reference that his Jewish audience would have readily understood . . .

The temple veil that separated the people from the shekinah glory of God measured sixty by thirty feet, was ten inches thick, and was so heavy it took one hundred priests to move it. Although the priests could minister on the side of the veil where the table of showbread, the altar, and the incense were, only the high priest on the Day of Atonement could go behind the veil to the ark of the covenant and the glory of God. But when Jesus paid the price for our sin, and cried, "It is finished," the veil was rent from top to bottom, thereby declaring, "Open House! Any day, any one, come on in!"

We're steeped in this knowledge. But if you can put yourself in the mind-set of the Hebrew, you'll see this would have been a radical understanding.

Hebrews 6:20 (a)
Whither the forerunner is for us entered . . .

It's the big high-school game. Between the goalposts, the cheerleaders have stretched a paper banner that says something clever like, "Win!" And what happens? The forerunner—the first guy out on the field—breaks through the banner, and the rest of the team follows behind him.

Jesus is our Forerunner. He's the first one through the veil. And the whole team—you and I—get to come charging in behind Him.

Hebrews 6:20 (b)
. . . even Jesus, made an high priest for ever after the order of Melchizedek.

"Wait a minute," the Jew would say. "You're saying Jesus broke through the veil and leads the way for the rest of us? Tilt. Problem. Only the high priest could go behind the veil—only those of the tribe of Levi could be priests—and only direct descendants of the first high priest, Aaron, could be high priest. If Jesus is from the tribe of Judah, how could He be the Forerunner into the Holy of Holies if He wasn't even a Levite?"

To answer this objection, the writer reaches back two thousand years and pulls out the story of Melchizedek. Who is Melchizedek? He's quite an important figure, for according to Hebrews 5:10, one's understanding of Melchizedek is an indication of how well versed one is in Bible doctrine. You see, a chapter and a half earlier, the writer said he wanted to explain the Melchizedekian ministry but couldn't because the Hebrews weren't ready to take it in. But here and on into the next chapter, he raises the subject of Melchizedek anyway. It's as though he couldn't resist.

WAITING FOR HIS WORKING
A Topical Study of
Hebrews 6:15

After anticipating this day for months, Paul and Penny stand before the pastor promising they'll be faithful and true in sickness and in health, in riches or rags, until death separates them. But five years later, Paul comes home and says, "I'm out of here, Penny. You no longer meet my needs. You no longer captivate my heart." And he walks away from the promises he made, leaving his wife and family behind.

The Bible you hold in your hands is packed full of promises—more than three thousand in number. Many of you have promise boxes sitting on your kitchen table or promise books stuffed in your back pocket. But today, there are those in our midst who would say, "My heart is broken because I don't think the Lord has kept His promise to me. I claimed the promise. I prayed it in. I wrote it on a three-by-five card and stuck it on my mirror. But nothing happened."

Maybe, like Penny, you're in that place today. If so, this is a highly important text for you to consider. If you're not, certainly you're living near or linked to those who wonder why things don't work as Scripture promises.

In verse 12, we are exhorted to follow those who went before us and obtained the promise by faith. The author of Hebrews uses one man specifically as an illustration—Abraham, the father of faith. After Abraham patiently endured, he obtained the promise. What promise? You know the story. . . .

> Abraham was seventy-five years old when, in Genesis 12, he was told to leave his home and father to go to a new land where God would give him offspring as the stars overhead. This must have blown Abraham's mind, for he and his wife, Sarah, had no children at that time. Off he goes on his journey, this father of faith, and sure enough, God gave him a son from whom an entire nation was born. But it didn't happen immediately. In fact, it took twenty-five years.

And in this there is a hugely important spiritual principle that needs to be part of your life. That is, there is very often a gap of time between the promise and the performance of the promise. In Abraham's case, the gap of time was twenty-five years. We read that after Abraham patiently endured, he obtained the promise. I love the New Testament because it is so wonderfully gracious in that it never once mentions the sins or failings of the Old Testament saints. And that's the way God looks at you and me under the New Covenant. "Your sins and iniquities will I remember no more," He says, (see Hebrews 8:12).

If you only read the New Testament account of Abraham, you wouldn't know the rest of the story. For while it is true that Abraham patiently endured and obtained the promise, it is also true that when he was in his mid-eighties, Sarah said, "I know God promised you we would produce a nation. But let's be reasonable. Ten years have come and gone since we heard from Him—and nothing's happened. I'm long past the age of child-bearing, so have relations with my handmaid, and the child produced will count as ours." Abraham agreed to Sarah's suggestion, and a baby named Ishmael was the result. Ishmael was not the promised child—but rather an attempt by Abraham and Sarah to try to help God fulfill His promise. And as is always the case whenever we try to help God out, Ishmael only made matters worse, for Ishmael became the father of the Arab nation. The promised son, Isaac, would come through Sarah thirteen years after Ishmael was born.

"This raises an interesting question," you say. "What kind of father would give a promise to his kids and then wait twenty-five years to fulfill it? Why does God make us wait?" Following are three reasons why God our Father tells us to patiently endure. . . .

To Produce Endurance

Jeremiah was getting a bit weary of the ministry to which God called him. *When are You going to come through, Lord?* he wondered. And God answered him by saying,

> *If thou hast run with the footmen, and they have wearied thee, then how canst thou contend with horses? and if in the land of peace, wherein thou trustedst, they wearied thee, then how wilt thou do in the swelling of Jordan?*
>
> Jeremiah 12:5

In other words, "You may think it's tough now, Jeremiah, but I know what's ahead. There are some real difficulties coming your way, some tremendous challenges heading in your direction."

Jesus made it clear that it rains on the just and the unjust alike (Matthew 5:45). Because of the fallen condition of the world in which we live, death, disease, poverty, tragedy, and heartache abound. Consequently, God says, "Due to the repercussions of the fall of this planet, due to the repercussions of the depravity of the race, storms are coming."

"Change the weather," we say.

"No," says God. "I am going to change *you*—through the trials you're going through right now, through the promises you're claiming but have not yet seen come to fruition."

If someone had told me twenty years ago the things that would come down in my life, I would have said, "I can't deal with that. I won't be a part of that. No way." But my Father has been so good, so faithful to prepare me all along the way through difficulties and challenges. Yes, there were promises—but yet there were gaps between the promise and performance that tested my faith—not because God was cruel to me, but because He cared about me. "I'm training you for what I see is coming down the path," He said. "It's all part of the plan, Son."

To Perfect Blessing

"I'm going to do exceeding abundantly above all you could ask or even think," the Lord says (see Ephesians 3:20)—"but it's going to take time."

> Due to his allergies, when Peter-John was a baby, he required a special formula. On one of the very rare occasions I, rather than my first wife Terry, was up at night with him, he started crying as I impatiently heated his bottle. I can remember saying, "Calm down, buddy. It's coming. You won't want it cold."
>
> But you know what? He continued to howl because he couldn't understand what I was saying. And the Lord whispered in my ear that night, "Jon, that's you. I'm cooking something up; I'm getting something ready. But you're crying, 'Where is it?' because you don't understand the language of faith."

And that's all of us. "Wah, wah," we cry. "It's been twenty-five days or two years or fifteen years. Where's the promise?" And all along, the Father is saying, "I'm getting it ready. I'm going to do something better than you could even imagine. But it's going to take some time."

> Zacharias and Elizabeth were well beyond the years of bearing children. No doubt they had stopped asking for children decades ago. But God heard their prayers and knew He wanted not only to give them a baby, but to give them the greatest prophet who had ever lived, one who would prepare the hearts of Israel for the coming of His Son (Luke 1:16).

The same is true for you and me today. God says, "I want to do things beyond anything you could dream or imagine. So hang on, folks, the bottle's getting warm."

I have discovered that the longer God takes to fulfill a promise in my life, oftentimes the better it will be.

"I want a man who loves God passionately," she says. "Doesn't God say to delight in Him and He'll give us the desire of our hearts? Well, I'm praying for a man who loves God, who's six feet four inches tall with dark hair, a big smile, a good business head, who loves to talk about the Lord, who cares about people, who is a good athlete with a great sense of humor, who's sensitive and considerate, and who has eyes only for me. That's what I want."

So the Lord begins shaping and developing her to make her the woman who would be attractive to such a man.

But what happens?

"I've waited two months," she says as she heads off to Rockin' Rodeo to scope out the situation. And then she wonders why she ends up with Tex.

After Abraham patiently endured, he obtained the promise. We know the inside story. He wasn't patiently enduring perfectly. But he learned his lesson, and the promise eventually came his way.

To Prepare Us

The language of eternity is faith. When the Lord has us ruling and reigning at His side, under His command, doing His bidding—whatever that means in the ages to come—He's going to need men and women like you who are not second-guessing, not doubting, not faltering. Jesus taught about the faithful in this life who will be rulers over five and ten cities in the kingdom (Luke 19). In other words, Jesus is saying there is a destiny far beyond what any of us know or can imagine awaiting us in the next zillion years to come.

And the language that must be fluently spoken by us if we are going to be ambassadors for Him in the realms and regions beyond is the language of faith.

She was the best teacher I ever had. We walked into our sophomore Spanish class and Señorita Thomas greeted us that first day, saying, "Listen, carefully. These are the last words of English you're going to hear this entire year in this class." And that was it. From then on, everything she spoke was Spanish. It was miserable initially. But it forced us to think in a way we never would have had we been able to fall back on English.

And that's what the Father's doing. "Kids," He says, "the only way you'll be prepared for what's coming is if I force you to learn the language of faith now because that's the language you'll be speaking for the next billion years to come."

If I were God, you know what I'd do? Once a year, I'd go to every church and appear with a great display of power and fire and smoke. That would probably get everyone by for a year or so. But God knows such a thing would actually undo what He desires to do—for the growth of faith would be retarded. We would depend on what we could see physically or hear audibly—and consequently, we would not be fluent in the language of eternity.

All the promises will come about in due season. In the meantime, precious people, realize God's heating the bottle. Understand that He's forcing you to develop a whole new way of thinking and living.

And remember, Scripture says it was after he *patiently endured* that Abraham obtained the promise.

7 Maybe you remember June 27, 1976, when the world was stunned as El Al Air, Israel's national airline, was boarded by hijackers who took the plane and its one hundred thirteen passengers into Idi Amin's Uganda. And maybe you recall that after Israeli soldiers loaded themselves into three C-3 cargo planes, landed at Entebbe, snuck into the airport, and rescued one hundred ten of the one hundred thirteen hostages, it was considered to be the greatest covert military operation in history.

But there was a greater one. In Genesis 14, Chedorlaomer, Tidal, and a couple other kings invaded the area around Sodom and Gomorrah, conquering five city-states in the process. Four kings whipped five and carried away hosts of hostages and all kinds of goods. One who happened to be swept up in Chedorlaomer's attack was a man named Lot, Abraham's nephew. So Abraham trained his three hundred eighteen servants to rescue Lot—three hundred eighteen vs. the combined armies of four kings. Yet Scripture records that not only did Abraham's men rescue every single person—they also reclaimed all of the material goods. In so doing, Abraham made the raid at Entebbe look like child's play. On his way back home, Abraham was met by a mysterious person named Melchizedek. . . .

Hebrews 7:1 (a)
For this Melchizedek, king of Salem . . .

Melchizedek was king of "Salem"—or Jerusalem. Jerusalem is called the city of the Great King. Thus, Melchizedek was King of the Great King.

Hebrews 7:1 (b)
. . . priest of the most high God . . .

Melchizedek was also priest of the Most High God. "How could that be?" the Jew would ask,

since Jewish law forbids any one man to be both king and priest. . . .

There was a man in 2 Chronicles 26 who tried it—a good man named Uzziah. After being blessed by God, after ushering in revival, after expanding the borders of Israel, he said, "I'm going into the temple to burn incense unto the Lord." Now, a man could be a king and a prophet—like David. Or a priest and a prophet—like Aaron. But he could not be a king and a priest.

"I don't think that applies to me," Uzziah said as he went into the temple, only to be smitten immediately with leprosy.

God does not want the priesthood involved in politics. I look at good men who have been eaten up trying to mix ministry and politics. Jerry Falwell has gone on record saying, "I regret the years I spent activating people politically when I was called to preach the gospel in simplicity." I've heard Billy Graham in an interview say that his mistake that stands out most clearly was his close involvement with the Nixon Administration.

It is a dangerous thing to mix politics and preaching. It will eat you up. Ask Uzziah. But Melchizedek is an entirely different case. He's the priest of the Most High, and he's also the King of Salem.

Hebrews 7:1 (c), 2 (a)
. . . who met Abraham returning from the slaughter of the kings, and blessed him; to whom also Abraham gave a tenth part of all . . .

Who is Melchizedek? According to this passage, he doesn't have a father or a mother; he doesn't have a beginning or an end. He is like the Son of God, abiding a priest continually. Thus, I personally believe Melchizedek of Genesis 14 is none other than Jesus Christ—a Christophany, an appearance of Jesus in the Old Testament before He appeared as Jesus of Nazareth.

Others say, "No, this idea of not having a father or mother simply means that there's no genealogical record of his parents." I don't argue that point, but I take this literally, for, in addition to his unique genealogy, I see Abraham bowing before Melchizedek and giving tithes to him.

Hebrews 7:2 (b), 3
. . . first being by interpretation King of righteousness, and after that also King of Salem, which is, King of peace; without father, without mother, without descent, having neither beginning of days, nor end of life; but made like unto the Son of God; abideth a priest continually.

There's only One who truly can be called King of Peace—that is the Prince of Peace, Jesus Christ. And there's only One whose name shall be called the Lord our Righteousness (Jeremiah 23:6)—Jesus Christ.

Note that He is first called the King of Righteousness before He is called the King of Salem, or Peace, because there cannot be peace until there is rightness. You cannot have peace by compromise—only by consecration. You cannot have peace by working deals with your enemy, for there is no peace with the wicked (Isaiah 48:22). One must have righteousness before one can have true peace—be it internally or internationally.

Hebrews 7:4
Now consider how great this man was, unto whom even the patriarch Abraham gave the tenth of the spoils.

"I don't believe in tithing," people say, "because it's part of the law." No, Abraham was on the scene well before the law was given—and yet he intuitively knew that the tithe of all he had that day belonged to Melchizedek. Tithing precedes the law, is talked about in the law, and was in effect after the law as seen by Jesus' words when He said, "Don't be like the Pharisees who tithe their mint and cumin and all their spices, but ignore the weightier matters of justice and righteousness and mercy" (see Matthew 23:23).

I recently read that to figure out your financial needs, the rule of thumb is to add ten percent to your income. In the tithe, God is essentially saying, "Add up all your income and give Me ten percent"—which, according to the financial rule of thumb doesn't make sense. But I suggest this is precisely the reason the only time God ever says to test Him is when He says, "Bring Me the tithe

and see if I will not bless you so much that you'll need added barns to contain the blessings that will come your way" (see Malachi 3:10).

Hebrews 7:5–10
And verily they that are of the sons of Levi, who receive the office of the priesthood, have a commandment to take tithes of the people according to the law, that is, of their brethren, though they come out of the loins of Abraham: But he whose descent is not counted from them received tithes of Abraham, and blessed him that had the promises. And without all contradiction the less is blessed of the better. And here men that die receive tithes; but there he receiveth them, of whom it is witnessed that he liveth. And as I may so say, Levi also, who receiveth tithes, payed tithes in Abraham. For he was yet in the loins of his father, when Melchizedek met him.

Not only did Abraham pay tithes to Melchizedek, but, Abraham being the father of the nation of Israel, the entire Levitical priesthood did as well—further proof that Melchizedek was, indeed, worthy of great honor.

Hebrews 7:11
If therefore perfection were by the Levitical priesthood, (for under it the people received the law,) what further need was there that another priest should rise after the order of Melchizedek, and not be called after the order of Aaron?

After Abraham bowed and worshiped him, nothing is heard of Melchizedek for another thousand years—until Psalm 110, where we read a priest would come not from Aaron and the Levites but from the order of Melchizedek (verse 4).

Hebrews 7:12
For the priesthood being changed, there is made of necessity a change also of the law.

If there's now a new priesthood on the scene greater than Aaron and the Levites, then there must be a change of the law as well, reasons the author of Hebrews. In other words, the rules of the entire game are changing.

Hebrews 7:13–17
For he of whom these things are spoken pertaineth to another tribe, of which no man gave attendance at the altar. For it is evident that our Lord sprang out of Juda; of which tribe Moses spake nothing concerning priesthood. And it is yet far more evident: for that after the similitude of Melchizedek

there ariseth another priest, Who is made, not after the law of a carnal commandment, but after the power of an endless life. For he testifieth, Thou art a priest for ever after the order of Melchizedek.

Neither Melchizedek nor Jesus was of the tribe of Levi. Yet the Father, talking to the Son in Psalm 110, identified Jesus as a Priest after the order of Melchizedek.

Hebrews 7:18, 19 (a)
For there is verily a disannulling of the commandment going before for the weakness and unprofitableness thereof. For the law made nothing perfect . . .

The only thing the law makes perfect is the understanding that no one can keep it. Therefore, Aaron and the Levites were part of a system unable to make you, me, or anyone perfect.

Hebrews 7:19 (b)
. . . but the bringing in of a better hope did; by the which we draw nigh unto God.

The better Hope, the Anchor who makes us perfect is Jesus Christ.

Hebrews 7:20, 21 (a)
And inasmuch as not without an oath he was made priest: (For those priests were made without an oath . . .

In the Levitical system, there was no swearing-in ceremony. One became a priest by being born into the tribe of Levi and a high priest by being born into the direct line of Aaron.

Hebrews 7:21 (b)
. . . but this with an oath by him that said unto him, The Lord sware and will not repent, Thou art a priest for ever after the order of Melchizedek:)

Unlike the Levitical priesthood, Jesus had a "swearing-in ceremony," recorded in Psalm 110, as the Father "swears in" the Son after the order of Melchizedek.

Hebrews 7:22, 23
By so much was Jesus made a surety of a better testament. And they truly were many priests, because they were not suffered to continue by reason of death.

Because every priest died, the Levitical priesthood was constantly changing.

Hebrews 7:24
But this man, because he continueth ever, hath an unchangeable priesthood.

According to the Talmud, there were eighteen high priests before the destruction of the first temple and three hundred-plus before the destruction of the second. In the Levitical system, there was a bunch of priests. In the Melchizedekian order, there was only One.

Hebrews 7:25 (a)
Wherefore he is able also to save them to the uttermost that come unto God by him . . .

The implication in the Greek language is that He is able to save continually.

Hebrews 7:25 (b)
. . . seeing he ever liveth to make intercession for them.

When most people think of intercession, here's what they picture: I sinned again. And Jesus, my Intercessor pleads my case before the Father.
"Okay, I hear Your presentation, Son," the Father says. "So because You are the Intercessor, the charges against Jon are dropped."
But wait. That's not what happens. In chapter 1, we saw that after He purged our sins, Jesus went to the right hand of the throne of God and sat down. Therefore, although Romans 8 declares He's at the right hand of the Father making intercession, He's doing so not with His words, but with His wounds.

Both Johnnie Cochran and Marcia Clark stood when they made their cases in the O. J. Simpson trial because they were trying to persuade a jury. Neither side felt their case was secure enough to sit. On the other hand, if you walked into the home of another football legend, Jim Plunkett, and heard him say, "I was a great quarterback," there would be no discussion, no debate, no argument. The Heismann trophy on his mantel would be absolute evidence of the fact that Jim Plunkett was a great football player.

So, too, Jesus sits at the right hand of the Father, and the wounds in His hands and feet, the scars on His brow, the hole in His side settle the issue. Jesus isn't talking the Father into being merciful to me. He's not asking the Father to be lenient with me. His scars alone are sufficient. That's why when Thomas finally saw Jesus, Jesus didn't say to him, "Let's talk doctrine. He said, "Touch My wounds" (see John 20:27).

Hebrews 7:26–28 (a)
For such an high priest became us, who is holy, harmless, undefiled, separate from sinners, and made higher than the heavens; Who needeth not daily, as those high priests, to offer up sacrifice, first for his own sins, and then for the people's: for this he did once, when he offered up himself. For the law maketh men high priests which have infirmity . . .

The author makes a case saying the Levitical priesthood was flawed. The Levites had infirmities physically, problems spiritually, and they kicked the bucket eventually.

Hebrews 7:28 (b)
. . . but the word of the oath, which was since the law, maketh the Son, who is consecrated for evermore.

The fact that the Aaronic priesthood was flawed does not diminish the fact that in chapter 5, when the author discussed the priesthood of Aaron, he listed three characteristics that point to Jesus. . . .

First, He's chosen from among men.
For every high priest taken from among men is ordained for men in things pertaining to God, that he may offer both gifts and sacrifices for sins . . .   Hebrews 5:1 (a)

Wherefore in all things it behoved him to be made like unto his brethren, that he might be a merciful and faithful high priest in things pertaining to God, to make reconciliation for the sins of the people.   Hebrews 2:17

Second, He offered sacrifice for sins.

And by reason hereof he ought, as for the people, so also for himself, to offer for sins.
Hebrews 5:3

Who needeth not daily, as those high priests, to offer up sacrifice, first for his own sins, and then for the people's: for this he did once, when he offered up himself.   Hebrews 7:27

Third, He attained the position through lineage.

And no man taketh this honour unto himself, but he that is called of God, as was Aaron.
Hebrews 5:4

So also Christ glorified not himself to be made an high priest; but he that said unto him, Thou art my Son, to day have I begotten thee.
Hebrews 5:5

Thus, Jesus completely fulfills the picture and the type of Aaron's priesthood. But He is represented more fully in the Melchizedekian order.
Why is this important?
Because every one of you is relating to Jesus in one of those two ways. . . .
Many people relate to Jesus only as the fulfillment of the Aaronic priesthood. And what they see is this: a Man who became like us, who laid down His life for us, who did not choose that position for Himself but only sought to glorify the Father and to obtain our salvation through His sacrifice for us. And for them, that's as far as it goes. They do not understand that Jesus is not only the fulfillment of the Aaronic priesthood, but that He is Melchizedek. Melchizedek's ministry is not to obtain salvation. It is to maintain salvation. That is why Jesus ever lives to make intercession (Hebrews 7:25).
The Melchizedekian order is a ministry of maintaining my salvation based upon His wounds—and it's a done deal. That means that as I drive home tonight, and I have something I need to pray about or a promise I wish I could claim, I don't have to say, "I can't claim this promise because I haven't prayed with the kind of intensity I should," or, "I can't pray now because I haven't read my Bible in three months." No, I can simply say, "Jesus continues to save me because His ministry is intercession based upon what He once offered, upon the wounds He now has. There's no discussion about my worthiness. I am free. I am completely and totally free."
Aaron's line was always busy working, always pleading, always sacrificing. In the Melchizedekian order, however, there's nothing more to be said, nothing more to do. It was done once and for evermore when our Great High Priest, Jesus Christ, offered Himself as a sacrifice on the Cross of Calvary.

8 **Hebrews 8:1 (a)**
Now of the things which we have spoken this is the sum:

Chapter 8 begins with a summary of the previous seven chapters . . .

Hebrews 8:1 (b)
We have such an high priest, who is set on the right hand of the throne of the Majesty in the heavens.

What Jesus did for me on the Cross of Calvary opened the way for me to fellowship with the Father regardless of whether I have morning devotions, regardless of whether I made it to church last Sunday, regardless of whether I've been tithing or worshiping. Those are not the issues. Yes, it benefits me greatly to cultivate my walk with the Lord through prayer and worship, through tithing and devotions. But my relationship with the Father is not based on any of these things. It's based on the High Priestly work of Jesus Christ.

So, if you have need in any way, you can come boldly before the Father—even if you haven't prayed in the past ten years. You can come boldly before Him because of one thing and one thing only: the High Priestly work of Jesus Christ and what He accomplished on Calvary. Nothing must be added to that; indeed, nothing can be added to that.

Hebrews 8:2–4
A minister of the sanctuary, and of the true tabernacle, which the Lord pitched, and not man. For every high priest is ordained to offer gifts and sacrifices: wherefore it is of necessity that this man have somewhat also to offer. For if he were on earth, he should not be a priest, seeing that there are priests that offer gifts according to the law.

In other words, Jesus was of a higher priesthood than the Levitical priesthood. He was of the order of Melchizedek, a superior priesthood.

Hebrews 8:5
Who serve unto the example and shadow of heavenly things, as Moses was admonished of God when he was about to make the tabernacle: for, See, saith he, that thou make all things according to the pattern shewed to thee in the mount.

"Moses," God said, "be sure you make the tabernacle precisely according to the pattern I give you because the pattern of the earthly tabernacle is a shadow of the true tabernacle which is in heaven."

Hebrews 8:6, 7
But now hath he obtained a more excellent ministry, by how much also he is the mediator of a better covenant, which was established upon better promises. For if that first covenant had been faultless, then should no place have been sought for the second.

After the 49'ers win the Super Bowl, their owner is not going to fire the offensive and defensive coordinators. No, once you win the championship, you stay with the team. But there will be a whole lot of defensive and offensive coordinators of other teams canned in January because

they didn't do well enough, because they didn't win the championship, because their record was not satisfactory.

So, too, the author of Hebrews says, "If the first covenant—the law—was a winner, there would be no talk of a second covenant, a New Covenant. But because the Old Testament itself speaks of a New Covenant, it can only mean the first one wasn't sufficient."

Hebrews 8:8 (a)
For finding fault with them, he saith . . .

Here begins the prophecy of Jeremiah 31—the same one repeated in Ezekiel 36—the prophecy of the New Covenant, the new agreement, the New Testament.

Hebrews 8:8 (b), 9
Behold, the days come, saith the Lord, when I will make a new covenant with the house of Israel and with the house of Judah: Not according to the covenant that I made with their fathers in the day when I took them by the hand to lead them out of the land of Egypt; because they continued not in my covenant, and I regarded them not, saith the Lord.

The Old Covenant said, "Do this and live" (see Deuteronomy 4:1), and, by implication, "if you don't, you're dead." The Old Covenant was based upon your success, my obedience, our keeping the rules and regulations. And therein lies the problem, for, like the house of Israel, we are unable to keep the law, the Old Covenant.

Hebrews 8:10
For this is the covenant that I will make with the house of Israel after those days, saith the Lord; I will put my laws into their mind, and write them in their hearts: and I will be to them a God, and they shall be to me a people.

Jeremiah 31 is pivotal to understanding Christianity in the truest sense because it is there God declares that, rather than writing His will on tablets of stone as He did with the Old Covenant, He would write the New Covenant on the tablets of our hearts. No longer external, His will would be internal. In other words, grace would put into us everything God wants out of us. . . .

Go to the YMCA today, and you'll find it full of people who made New Year's Resolutions to get in shape. Go back in June or July, however, and you'll find it far less crowded because although people want to, although they mean to, they're unable to live up to their resolutions.

So, too, you can read the Scriptures and say, "I want to do that. That's how I want to be"—but inevitably you'll find your flesh incapable. So God says, "I'm going to do something new. I'm going to write My will in your heart. I'm going to put My thoughts in your mind. I'm going to put My Spirit in your spirit."

Hebrews 8:11
And they shall not teach every man his neighbour, and every man his brother, saying, Know the Lord: for all shall know me, from the least to the greatest.

One day, someone said, "Jon, I haven't been in church lately."

"I know," I said.

"Well, why didn't you come and tell me to get back to church?" he asked.

"That's not my job," I answered. "The New Covenant says you already know what you should have been doing because the Lord wrote His will on your heart."

Gang, we don't need anyone to put rules on us or regulations around us because the Lord lives in us. And that's the great thing about Christianity. When you're walking with the Lord, when you're living in the New Covenant, you don't have resolutions and regulations, stipulations and obligations. Those are the way of the law.

Instead, you just do what the Lord is writing on your heart, telling you in your mind, whispering in your ear moment by moment. . . .

"Talk to that guy over there," or;
"Go to the Mission," or;
"Make her some chocolate chip cookies. . . ."

And all you have to do is say, "Okay. Far out!"—and do it. That's what it means to be a born-again New Covenant, Spirit-led Christian, for whatever God wants from you, by His grace, He will work within you (Philippians 2:13).

Our brothers and sisters in the first-century church were the most radical Christians in all of history. They sold all of their possessions. They spread throughout the world. They lived for the kingdom. But you know what? They didn't get together and study Hebrews, because Hebrews wasn't yet written. They didn't study the theological implications of Romans because Romans wasn't written. They didn't scrutinize the teachings of Jesus as recorded in John's Gospel because John's Gospel wasn't written.

They didn't have the written New Testa-

ment—but they did understand the reality of the New Covenant. They obeyed what the Lord was writing in their hearts. And as a result, they turned the world upside down (Acts 17:6). Then, when the New Testament was written and began to circulate through the church, it was a confirmation of what they were already doing because it was the same Lord who had been writing His will for them upon their hearts.

Today, sad to say, many don't understand the New Covenant. Our Trinity is God the Father, God the Son, and God the Holy Bible. We've lost touch with how the Holy Spirit speaks to us moment by moment because we've replaced His voice with the written Word. Many churches and organizations study the Bible and are right in their theology—but they're dead right because theirs is knowledge for knowledge's sake. The New Testament was never intended to be an esoteric, intellectual, theological trip for people who like to fill notebooks, answer questions, and work on workbooks. That was never the intent of the New Testament writer. What was the intent? To provide a way believers could be confirmed or corrected in what they were already living out as a result of obeying the still, small voice of the Spirit.

The person who's really used by the Lord is one who simply says, "You're going to tell me moment by moment what I should do, and, Lord, I will just say, 'Yes,' to whatever You say." A whole lot of people have made the New Testament writings the new law. Like Pharisees searching for jots, tittles, and interesting insights, they fail to see that the Word was simply written to nudge them along in their walk and to confirm the voice of the Lord in their heart.

Hebrews 8:12, 13
For I will be merciful to their unrighteousness, and their sins and their iniquities will I remember no more. In that he saith, A new covenant, he hath made the first old. Now that which decayeth and waxeth old is ready to vanish away.

What makes me want to know God and walk with Him? Why do I start my day wanting to touch base with the Lord and be in the Word? Why am I here tonight? One reason: God's mercy. I am such a jerk. I have failed so miserably. I have missed the mark so greatly. I have been so inconsistent and stubborn. I've been such a sinner. And yet God keeps blessing me; He keeps putting up with me; He keeps allowing me to know Him.

I look at my life, my family, this church, the nation, the world—and I say, "Lord Your mercy is incredible. How good You've been to me. I don't pray the way I could or should. I don't know as much as I should know at this point in my walk with You. I don't serve You with the kind of faithfulness You're worthy of. But, Lord, You just keep blessing. You keep showing mercy. You keep forgiving—and I have no other choice but to want to know You more."

9

Hebrews 9:1, 2 (a)
Then verily the first covenant had also ordinances of divine service, and a worldly sanctuary. For there was a tabernacle made . . .

The Lord instructed Moses to establish a place of meeting between Him and the people, wherein a courtyard one hundred fifty feet long and seventy-five feet wide was to be cordoned off with white linen. I'm sure when Moses heard these dimensions, he thought, *Wait a minute. There are three million of us. We'll never fit in such a small place.*

But it's almost as if the Father was saying, "That will be sufficient because, at any given time, there won't be that many who will want to spend time with Me."

Hebrews 9:2 (b)
. . . the first, wherein was the candlestick, and the table, and the shewbread; which is called the sanctuary.

Beyond the courtyard was the sanctuary, or tabernacle. It looked just like the tents the people lived in as they wandered through the wilderness, and was covered with badger skins. Forty-five feet long, fifteen feet high, and fifteen feet wide, it was divided into two compartments. The first compartment was thirty feet long and was called the Holy Place. In this Holy Place stood the table of showbread to the right, upon which twelve loaves of bread sat. To the left, was the golden candlestick, comprised of seven oil lamps. Straight ahead was the altar of incense, wherein incense would be offered to the Lord. And behind the altar of incense hung a massive veil, held up by four golden columns that rested in silver sockets—a beautiful picture in itself, silver being the metal of redemption.

Hebrews 9:3–5
And after the second veil, the tabernacle which is called the Holiest of all; which had the golden censer, and the ark of the covenant overlaid round about with gold, wherein was the golden pot that had manna, and Aaron's rod that budded, and the tables

of the covenant; and over it the cherubims of glory shadowing the mercyseat; of which we cannot now speak particularly.

Behind the veil was the ark of the covenant—a three-foot-by-two-inch box containing the Ten Commandments, Moses' rod, and a pot of manna. Covering the ark was a lid called the mercy seat. And above the mercy seat were two golden angels whose wings met and whose eyes looked down upon the mercy seat.

I draw your attention to verse 4, where mention is made of a golden censer, or altar of incense. According to Exodus, this altar of incense was in front of the veil. But here in verse 4, the author puts it behind the veil, in the same room as the ark of the covenant. Is the Bible contradicting itself?

No, I suggest that somehow the altar of incense was moved. Somewhere along the way, someone put the altar where it wasn't supposed to be. Yet God still worked—which is a great relief to me because in my heart, at my house, in this church, things get messed up. Furniture gets out of place—but God can handle it.

So, too, I'm amazed at how God has worked through the Church. Some churches are led by men in pointy hats, scarlet robes, backward collars—and I wonder how God could work through guys dressed like that. Other churches have pastors who wear sweatshirts, Birkenstocks, and sit on stools. How could God work through them? Some churches have big programs. Other churches have none. It's amazing to me that all of us haven't so messed it up that no one can find the Lord. Yet somehow God breaks through and works through us all to draw people to Himself. Amazing!

Hebrews 9:6
Now when these things were thus ordained, the priests went always into the first tabernacle, accomplishing the service of God.

As he prepares for ministry, the young Levite goes into the courtyard and sees his dad offering sacrifices. Finally allowed to minister himself, he goes into the Holy Place, where every morning and evening he would trim the wicks, refill the oil in the lamps, and replace the incense on the altar of incense. Once a week, he would replace the twelve loaves upon the table of showbread.

Hebrews 9:7 (a)
But into the second went the high priest alone once every year . . .

Once a year on the Day of Atonement, Yom Kippur, it would be the high priest's privilege to go alone into the Holy of Holies to sprinkle blood on the mercy seat and catch a glimpse of the Shekinah glory of God.

In Jesus' day, here's what would transpire: The week before Yom Kippur, the high priest would never leave the temple ground, for every day of that week, he would rehearse what he would do on the Day of Atonement. When that day finally came, arrayed in his high priestly robes, he would sacrifice a bull on the brass altar in the courtyard as a dedicatory offering. That done, he would take off his high priestly garments and put on his linen garments—long underwear, really, covered by a tunic and sash. Then he would sacrifice another bull as a sin offering for himself. At this point, two goats would be chosen by lot and a red scarlet cord would be tied around one, signifying it was the sacrificial goat. The other goat—the scapegoat—would be carried into the wilderness. Why two goats? Because our sins are not only forgiven—they are forgotten, carried away as far as the east is from the west (Psalm 103:12).

The priest would then take the coals from the outside altar with two handfuls of incense into the Holy Place. And as he put them on the altar of incense, a cloud would fill the room. Returning to the brass altar, he would carry the blood that had drained from the bull back into the Holy Place, and this time he would go through the veil into the Holy of Holies, where he would sprinkle the blood seven times on the ground and seven times on the mercy seat. After that, he would sacrifice the sacrificial goat and take its blood back into the Holy of Holies, where he would sprinkle it again seven times on the ground and seven times on the mercy seat. Finally, after sacrificing the bull and going into the Holy of Holies, and after sacrificing the goat and going into the Holy of Holies, he would come back out and place his hand upon the living goat, saying, "Bear and be gone." In other words, "Bear the sin and take it away."

Then, at last, the priest would stand before the people. With both hands, he would pronounce, "Forgiven," and the people would begin to hoop and holler and celebrate because if the priest was not purified properly, if he went into the Holy Place presumptuously, his resulting death would signify that they weren't forgiven. So the people always waited to see if the high priest would make it out of the Holy of Holies. *Are we forgiven?* they wondered. *Did the sacrifices work? Is God pleased? Are we okay?*

Don't you see what happened concerning our High Priest? The whole world was watching—without even knowing for what they were watching. And our Great High Priest, wrapped in white linen, emerged from the Holy of Holies on Easter Sunday. The tomb was the Holy of Holies? Certainly, for when the disciples peeked in that morning, they saw a bench sprinkled with blood—His blood where His body had lain. And we are told by the Gospel writer that on either end of the bench sat an angel. Thus the picture of a blood-sprinkled mercy seat was complete. When Jesus emerged from the tomb on the third day, it was a declaration of forgiveness—not just for a year, but for eternity.

Therefore, because of the Resurrection, we are confident that our sin—whatever it is, whatever it was, whatever it will be—is forgiven, forgotten, no longer an issue. The Resurrection is crucial because if Jesus had not come back from the dead, we would never know if the offering took. And we had no other Priest to send in.

"Show us the Father and it will suffice us," said Philip (see John 14:8). And he was right, for the *chabod,* the glory of God as seen in the Holy of Holies, is what the heart of every man craves.

Here's the question: Where are you in your walk with the Lord?

Maybe you're in the courtyard, saying, "I'm saved. The sacrifice was made for me. Praise the Lord, I'm forgiven!" Many of you are in that place, and that's terrific—but there's more. . . .

Move out of the courtyard and into the Holy Place, where you can serve—where you're trimming the lamps, that is, letting your light shine for others; where you're changing the showbread, that is, feeding others; where you're involved in offering incense, that is, praying for others. The outer courtyard is the place of salvation. The Holy Place is the place of service. Most of us in this room have realized and celebrated our salvation and are now engaged in service. But there's a deeper, better place. It's called the Holy of Holies—it's being in the presence of the Lord.

"Tell Mary to come and help me, Lord," cried Martha.

"Oh, Martha, Mary has chosen the better part—sitting in My presence," answered Jesus (see Luke 10:40–42).

"What a waste," complained Judas as Mary anointed Jesus' head with costly perfume. "That money could have been used to feed the poor."

"On the contrary," said Jesus. "What she has done will be spoken of throughout the world for all time" (see Matthew 26:13).

Gang, the highest, deepest, richest place to be is sitting in the presence of the Lord. I believe there may come a day when we as Christians finally understand that it's not what we're doing for Him in the Holy Place, but being with Him in the Holy of Holies that matters. There is nothing that more closely approximates heaven than being in the presence of the Lord.

"But there's a problem," you might be saying. "When I go into the Holy of Holies, when I spend time in the presence of the Lord, my sin is ever before me. I see huge splotches on the garments I thought were fairly white."

You're in good company, for when did Isaiah cry, "Woe is me. I am a man of unclean lips"? When he was in the presence of the Lord (see Isaiah 6). But the good news is this: An awareness of sin ushers in repentance. "Lord, I'm not what I thought I was, and I'm not who I want to be." You know, I never have those thoughts when I'm playing racquetball. So if I fill my life with enough activity, I never have to deal with the splotches. People immerse themselves in hobbies, recreation, or even ministry because if they stay busy enough, they can walk around feeling pretty clean.

It's only when I come with you and sit before the Lord or have a quiet time in the morning hour that I say, "I'm dirty." And conscious repentance results in unconscious holiness. For although we leave the Holy of Holies feeling as though we're not worthy, as though we're inadequate, as though we're inconsistent—others see in us a holiness of which we are not even aware.

When Moses descended from Mount Sinai after receiving the Ten Commandments, although he didn't realize it, his face glowed (Exodus 34:29). Likewise, there are young men, older women, middle age guys in this room tonight who will choose to go deeper in the Lord, saying, "I'm not going to be satisfied in the courtyard celebrating salvation. And I'm not even going to be satisfied trimming wicks, changing bread, and offering incense. I'm going to be one who goes into the Holy of Holies."

If you make that decision, God's greatness, grace, and glory will cause you to repent and say, "I'm nothing."

But people around you will say, "Man, you're glowing. Share with us. Help us."

Truly, a man who has been in the presence of God will, like Isaiah, say, "Woe is me." But he'll be used. He'll be blessed. He'll glow because conscious repentance leads to unconscious holiness.

Hebrews 9:7 (b)
. . . not without blood, which he offered for himself, and for the errors of the people.

The word translated "errors" literally means "ignorance." Thus, the blood only covered sins done in ignorance, or unintentionally. You see, the only sins forgiven in the old economy were sins in which one was caught up without knowing what he was doing. That is why, after taking Bathsheba and then killing her husband, David cried, "For thou desirest not sacrifice; else would I give it: thou delightest not in burnt offering" (Psalm 51:16). In other words, "There's no sacrifice, no burnt offering I can give for my sin because my sin was intentional. I knew what I was doing."

But then, looking beyond the sacrificial system and prophetically to the Cross, David goes on to say, "The sacrifices of God are a broken spirit: a broken and a contrite heart . . . thou wilt not despise" (Psalm 51:17). "Sacrifices won't work," he said, "not for *my* sins. But, Lord, You know I'm sorry. I'm broken within. So somehow, some way, someday You'll make a way that I will be forgiven."

Hebrews 9:8–10
The Holy Ghost this signifying, that the way into the holiest of all was not yet made manifest, while as the first tabernacle was yet standing: Which was a figure for the time then present, in which were offered both gifts and sacrifices, that could not make him that did the service perfect, as pertaining to the conscience; Which stood only in meats and drinks, and divers washings, and carnal ordinances, imposed on them until the time of reformation.

The problem with the Old Testament priesthood was that it provided limited access and limited effectiveness. It was limited in access because only one man (the high priest) could enter into the presence of God only one day (the Day of Atonement) each year. It was limited in effectiveness because the high priest was himself a sinner.

Hebrews 9:11, 12
But Christ being come an high priest of good things to come, by a greater and more perfect tabernacle, not made with hands, that is to say, not of this building; neither by the blood of goats and calves, but by his own blood he entered in once into the holy place, having obtained eternal redemption for us.

Once again, keep in mind this epistle was written to Hebrew Christians who were being drawn back to the sacrificial system. And here again, the author is saying, "Don't go back. Why would you want to return to rules and regulations when the work of salvation has been completed by Jesus Christ, the only perfect Lamb of God?"

When a Jewish person went to the temple to worship, he would bring a lamb to offer on the altar. After careful examination by the priest, if the lamb was found to be without spot or blemish, the worshiper could worship confidently. You see, the priest never inspected the person—only the lamb. Satan will try to whisper in your ear, "You're blemished. You've dropped the ball. You haven't been a woman of prayer. You haven't been a man of integrity. You can't worship. You can't talk to the Father. You can't be blessed."

But he's wrong. At the temple, the priests didn't inspect the worshiper. They inspected the lamb. The same is true of you and me. "Behold the Lamb of God who takes away the sin of the world," declared John the Baptist—which is why three days before His crucifixion, Jesus Himself was scrutinized as the scribes and Pharisees, Sadducees, and Greeks questioned His theology, His morality, and His integrity (Matthew 22). Pilate's declaration that he found no fault in Jesus meant He passed even their inspection perfectly.

Therefore, we can come to the Father confidently and talk to Him freely based not upon our righteousness, but solely on the perfection of the Lamb.

Hebrews 9:13, 14

For if the blood of bulls and of goats, and the ashes of an heifer sprinkling the unclean, sanctifieth to the purifying of the flesh: How much more shall the blood of Christ, who through the eternal Spirit offered himself without spot to God, purge your conscience from dead works to serve the living God?

The reference to the ashes of a heifer is found in Numbers 19, wherein we read that when a person came into contact with a corpse, ashes of a heifer were to be sprinkled in water and poured over him to ceremonially cleanse his flesh in order that he could continue in tabernacle or temple worship. The author asks how much better is the blood of Christ—which doesn't only deal with the external, but with the internal as well.

Suppose, late to an appointment, I speed through Medford, Oregon, at 85 mph. Glancing in the rearview mirror, I see red lights flashing and realize I've been caught breaking the law.

"Sorry, Officer," I apologize to the policeman who pulls me over. "I didn't know I was going that fast."

Nonetheless, he writes me a five thousand dollar ticket. As he hands it to me, it drops in

the gutter, but he picks it up, shakes it off, and says, "I'll see you in court."

When my trial date arrives, the judge looks at my ticket and says, "This is a citation for something, but I can't make out what it's for because it's covered with mud. Therefore, I guess you're free to go."

So I go my way—not because my offense was taken away, but because it was covered.

In a similar way, the blood of bulls and goats would cover sin—not remove it, but cover it.

Now suppose the ticket hadn't fallen in the mud. The judge would read the ticket and say, "Okay, Pastor Courson, you were going eighty-five through Medford. That will be five thousand dollars."

Then I would be in a heap of trouble because I certainly don't have five thousand dollars. But imagine just then my brother Jimmy walks in, whips out his hefty wallet, and pays my fine without even denting his billfold. Then I would be free because the price of my offense was not just covered by mud, but truly paid.

The soul that sinneth shall surely die (Ezekiel 18:20). Although ashes of heifers and blood of goats and bulls could cover sin, they could not pay for it because payment required the death of a man. Jesus came on the scene and died for me. Yes, I've sinned. Indeed, I've blown it. But I'm free—not because of some technicality but because God Himself became a Man and died in my place.

So what does the Enemy do? Revelation 12:10 says he accuses us day and night. "You blew it. You didn't do that. You should've done this. You dropped the ball again." But when you really understand the idea of God becoming a Man and dying in your place, you don't go around with the baggage of a guilty conscience because when Satan reminds you of your shortcomings, your past failings, or your present weaknesses, you can say, "That's only half the story, Satan. I'm a worse sinner than you even know. But your reminding me of these things only makes me all the more amazed by what Jesus did on my behalf."

Hebrews 9:15–17

And for this cause he is the mediator of the new testament, that by means of death, for the redemption of the transgressions that were under the first testament, they which are called might receive the promise of eternal inheritance. For where a testament is, there must also of necessity be the death of the testator. For a testament is of force after

men are dead: otherwise it is of no strength at all while the testator liveth.

Jesus is the Mediator, the Executor of the will. But He's also the Testator. In other words, He's got to die before the will kicks in. On earth, this would be a dilemma. . . .

Suppose eighty years from now, my mom goes to heaven and the family meets to read her will. "Look what I get," says Jimmy. "I get the electric grill!"

"Wait a minute," I say, "I get the electric grill"—and an argument ensues. All the while, Mom is up in heaven. She knows what she meant. Jimmy's right. He did get something electric. But it's not the electric grill. It's the electric bill. Because she's in heaven, however, she can't do anything about it.

In Jesus, such a problem doesn't exist. You see, Jesus being the Fulfillment of the Old Testament law, when He died, the new will, the New Covenant came into effect. And when He rose again, He became the Executor of the New Testament, who, by the Holy Spirit, lives in our hearts and tells us how it is to work out in our lives. Fabulous! He not only is the Testator who *gives* us the New Covenant—but He is the Mediator who *guides* us in the New Covenant.

Hebrews 9:18–22 (a)
Whereupon neither the first testament was dedicated without blood. For when Moses had spoken every precept to all the people according to the law, he took the blood of calves and of goats, with water, and scarlet wool, and hyssop, and sprinkled both the book, and all the people, saying, This is the blood of the testament which God hath enjoined unto you. Moreover he sprinkled with blood both the tabernacle, and all the vessels of the ministry. And almost all things are by the law purged with blood . . .

Referring to Exodus 24, when the Old Covenant came into effect, when the tabernacle was erected and the priesthood established, everything was sprinkled with blood Why? Read on.

Hebrews 9:22 (b)
. . . and without shedding of blood is no remission.

Someone once said to me, "That book in your hands is full of blood and war, sin, greed, and lust. And they call it *Holy* Bible?"

"Yes," I said. "It is full of sin and death. But it also tells the truth about the solution for all of those terrible situations. It's blood. Why blood? Because how else could God so clearly illustrate to humanity the severity of sin? What else could He do? How else could He proclaim to our culture that sin is serious? You don't wink at it. You don't make jokes about it. You don't pay five bucks to see it on the screen."

Why is God so deadly serious about sin? It's not because He's prudish and can't handle violence or sex. It's because He knows what sin does. Sin kills. It kills happiness, joy, health, and life. It kills kids, families, societies, and cultures. That's why the only way there can be forgiveness is by the shedding of blood. There's no such thing as Forgiveness Lite. Forgiveness only comes through blood.

Hebrews 9:23
It was therefore necessary that the patterns of things in the heavens should be purified with these; but the heavenly things themselves with better sacrifices than these.

The earthly tabernacle is a pattern of the heavenly tabernacle, so if the earthly tabernacle was purified with blood, then the heavenly tabernacle must be purified with a much better sacrifice than the blood of bulls and goats.

Hebrews 9:24
For Christ is not entered into the holy places made with hands, which are the figures of the true; but into heaven itself, now to appear in the presence of God for us.

I believe personally that between the time Jesus died on the Cross and the time He rose again, He sprinkled His blood in the heavenlies. Why would heaven need purifying? For one, Satan's been there and still has access to heaven (Job 1:6). Not only that, but we're there—seated with Christ (Ephesians 2:6). Thus, the blood of Jesus Christ is necessary to purify and sanctify heaven.

Hebrews 9:25, 26
Nor yet that he should offer himself often, as the high priest entereth into the holy place every year with blood of others; for then must he often have suffered since the foundation of the world: but now once in the end of the world hath he appeared to put away sin by the sacrifice of himself.

There are those who teach that there's a continual sacrifice taking place, that the perpetual suffering of Christ goes on each time the mass is celebrated and the Eucharist served. No, the

Scripture says clearly Christ offered His Body *once.*

Hebrews 9:27
And as it is appointed unto men once to die, but after this the judgment.

Man dies *once.*

After she had been dead one thousand years, Jesus declared the Queen of Sheba would rise up in judgment (Matthew 12:42). He didn't say, "The Queen of Sheba would rise up in judgment if she was still around—but now she's Elizabeth Taylor or Shirley MacLaine or someone else."

When Elijah and Moses appeared on the Mount of Transfiguration, Jesus didn't say to Peter, James and John, "Meet Rajneesh. He used to be Moses." No, he was still Moses.

Take those who say the Bible doesn't teach against reincarnation to this passage—and wallop 'em!

Hebrews 9:28
So Christ was once offered to bear the sins of many; and unto them that look for him shall he appear the second time without sin unto salvation.

Jesus is not coming back to bear our sin. That was done once, and once is enough. No, He's not coming back bearing a Cross. He's coming back wearing a crown.

Hebrews 10:1-4
For the law having a shadow of good things to come, and not the very image of the things, can never with those sacrifices which they offered year by year continually make the comers thereunto perfect. For then would they not have ceased to be offered? because that the worshippers once purged should have had no more conscience of sins. But in those sacrifices there is a remembrance again made of sins every year. For it is not possible that the blood of bulls and of goats should take away sins.

You make your way to the tabernacle, bringing your little lamb with you. Watching the blood flow as it is offered as a sacrifice, you're reminded once again that you're still a sinner, still a sinner year after year after year. When Jesus came on the scene, however, what did He say? "Do this in remembrance of *Me.*" In other words, He didn't

say, "Remember your sin." He said, "Remember your Savior" (see Luke 22:19).

The same is still true today. I have a tendency to keep returning to my own little sacrificial system, asking myself, "How long did I pray today?" or, "How many chapters have I read this year?" But, due to our inability to keep our own rules, rituals, and regulations, our promises and pledges only continually remind us that we're failures. That is why Jesus said, "I don't want you to remember your sin by continual sacrifice. I want you to remember your salvation by continual celebration."

The price has been paid. The blood has been shed. The work is done. Jesus left us with Communion, not that we would say, "Oh, we're such sinners," but that we would say, "Oh, what a Savior!"

"But doesn't 1 Corinthians 11 say that if we eat or drink unworthily, we're eating to our damnation?" you ask.

Yes. But what is meant there is if you don't give worth to the work that was done, you're going to keep damning yourself. If, however, you say, "I remember again, Lord, that You paid the price completely"—then Communion becomes what it was meant to be: a celebration of the finished work of the Cross of Calvary.

Hebrews 10:5 (a)
Wherefore when he cometh into the world, he saith, Sacrifice and offering thou wouldest not . . .

From my own study, I am convinced that verses 4–6 are a record of the conversation that very likely took place on Christmas Eve between the Father and Son.

Hebrews 10:5 (b), 6
. . . but a body hast thou prepared me: In burnt offerings and sacrifices for sin thou hast had no pleasure.

Even as Adam became a living soul when life was breathed into him (Genesis 2:7), so, too, life entered the Last Adam, the Babe of Bethlehem. And He said to His Father, "You have prepared a body because You have no pleasure in sacrifices."

Hebrews 10:7, 8
Then said I, Lo, I come (in the volume of the book it is written of me,) to do thy will, O God. Above when he said, Sacrifice and offering and burnt offerings and offering for sin thou wouldest not, neither hadst pleasure therein; which are offered by the law.

If the Father has no pleasure in sacrifices, why did He establish the system in the first place? Simply put, the bulls and rams, goats and lambs were a promissory note. . . .

The one-dollar bill in your pocket would be a worthless piece of paper if not for the government in Washington D.C. putting its weight behind it, guaranteeing its value. Suppose, however, you opened your great-grandmother's trunk and found stacks of thousand-dollar bills. Upon closer inspection, you see upon them the image of Jefferson Davis. Now, although an antique dealer might buy them from you, the bills wouldn't be worth nearly their original value because the Confederate government no longer exists.

The same is true of the sacrificial system. At one time, it had some weight because it represented the blood of the coming sacrificial Lamb of God. But once the new government, the New Testament, the New Covenant took effect, the sacrifices of the Old Covenant became confederate money—as worthless as any sacrifice you're presently making to try to earn God's blessing or to get Him to listen to you.

God has pleasure in only one Sacrifice. And once you see this, once it really sinks into your heart, you are free because you are in a position to receive blessing from the Father based solely upon *His* provision.

Hebrews 10:9, 10
Then said he, Lo, I come to do thy will, O God. He taketh away the first, that he may establish the second. By the which will we are sanctified through the offering of the body of Jesus Christ once for all.

The first sacrificial system is gone—replaced by the New Covenant.

Hebrews 10:11
And every priest standeth daily ministering and offering oftentimes the same sacrifices, which can never take away sins.

If you feel like you're in a rut, doing the same things every day to try to impress God, you're under the old system. And like the priests of old, your work is never done.

Hebrews 10:12
But this man, after he had offered one sacrifice for sins for ever, sat down on the right hand of God.

Jesus isn't standing or pacing, running or fretting. He's totally at rest concerning you.

Hebrews 10:13, 14
From henceforth expecting till his enemies be made his footstool. For by one offering he hath perfected for ever them that are sanctified.

That's you. He has perfected you forever because the work of salvation is complete.

Hebrews 10:15–20 (a)
Whereof the Holy Ghost also is a witness to us: for after that he had said before, This is the covenant that I will make with them after those days, saith the Lord, I will put my laws into their hearts, and in their minds will I write them; and their sins and iniquities will I remember no more. Now where remission of these is, there is no more offering for sin. Having therefore, brethren, boldness to enter into the holiest by the blood of Jesus, By a new and living way . . .

Because the veil was rent, we can come into the Holy of Holies. In the Holy of Holies stood the ark of the covenant. And in the ark of the covenant are the Ten Commandments that we've broken, Aaron's rod that budded as a sign to a people who chafed under God's leadership, and a pot of manna given to a people who grumbled about God's provision. In other words, the ark held reminders of failure. But guess what. Covering the ark—hiding the broken commandments, the rod of rebellion, the manna of unthankfulness—was the mercy seat. No wonder Jesus said, "Go your way and learn of this that you might learn mercy" (see Matthew 9:13). The one course of education prescribed by Jesus is mercy because it is at the mercy seat that God meets us.

Hebrews 10:20 (b)
. . . which he hath consecrated for us, through the veil, that is to say, his flesh.

We have a High Priest interceding for us not with words on His lips, but through the wounds of His flesh.

Hebrews 10:21, 22
And having an high priest over the house of God; let us draw near with a true heart in full assurance of faith, having our hearts sprinkled from an evil conscience, and our bodies washed with pure water.

Let us draw near with a true heart—not a pure heart, or a clean heart, but a *true* heart, saying, "I know I'm a sinner. But I also know what Jesus did is sufficient." So I come boldly to Him, even if I haven't prayed in ten minutes, ten days, or ten years. Once I come with a *true* heart, the effectiveness of the sacrifice of Calvary takes effect.

Hebrews 10:23 (a)
Let us hold fast the profession of our faith without wavering; (for he is faithful . . .

Jesus is our faithful High Priest. To whom is He faithful? He is faithful to His Father (Hebrews 3:1, 2). Could we exhaust His patience? Possibly. Could the Father exhaust His patience? Impossible.

Hebrews 10:23 (b)
. . . that promised;).

Jesus is faithful to His Father to do what? To keep those who had been committed to Him (John 17:12).

Hebrews 10:24, 25
And let us consider one another to provoke unto love and to good works: Not forsaking the assembling of ourselves together, as the manner of some is; but exhorting one another: and so much the more, as ye see the day approaching.

Encourage one another as the day of the coming of the Lord draws near.

Hebrews 10:26–29 (a)
For if we sin wilfully after that we have received the knowledge of the truth, there remaineth no more sacrifice for sins, but a certain fearful looking for of judgment and fiery indignation, which shall devour the adversaries. He that despised Moses' law died without mercy under two or three witnesses: Of how much sorer punishment, suppose ye, shall he be thought worthy, who hath trodden under foot the Son of God . . .

Like Hebrews 6, this next section has caused terror in the hearts of many. But in actuality, as we shall see, it's a wonderful warning.

For topical study of Hebrews 10:26–31 entitled "A Wonderful Warning," turn to page 1491.

Hebrews 10:29 (b)
. . . and hath counted the blood of the covenant, wherewith he was sanctified, an un-

holy thing, and hath done despite unto the Spirit of grace?

The Spirit of grace refers to the Holy Spirit (Zechariah 12:10). "Doing despite to the Spirit of grace" means returning to the sacrificial system of offering bulls or goats or anything else to try to make things right with the Lord.

Hebrews 10:30, 31
For we know him that hath said, Vengeance belongeth unto me, I will recompense, saith the Lord. And again, The Lord shall judge his people. It is a fearful thing to fall into the hands of the living God.

The warning isn't that if you sin or struggle with sin, there's no hope for you. No, the sin of backsliding here in Hebrews 10 is not going back into sin, but rather turning your back on the Provision *for* sin. If I say, "Jesus didn't really pay the price sufficiently, so I've got to contribute my own effort," I mock the broken Body and fail to give worth to the shed blood. That's the warning here.

So what does this mean? It means I'm free. It means I know there's nothing else I can do or must do or should do. It's all been done, and I rest in that fact.

Hebrews 10:32–34
But call to remembrance the former days, in which, after ye were illuminated, ye endured a great fight of afflictions; partly, whilst ye were made a gazingstock both by reproaches and afflictions; and partly, whilst ye became companions of them that were so used. For ye had compassion of me in my bonds, and took joyfully the spoiling of your goods, knowing in yourselves that ye have in heaven a better and an enduring substance.

Part of the reason the Hebrews were returning to the sacrificial system was because, in so doing, they were no longer alienated from the community. "Why go back to the old way?" Paul asks. "They've already called you Jesus freaks. You've already been beaten up. So why, after suffering so much, would you return to the system from which this punishment came? The best is still ahead. Keep your hope in heaven."

Hebrews 10:35–37
Cast not away therefore your confidence, which hath great recompence of reward. For ye have need of patience, that, after ye have done the will of God, ye might receive the

promise. For yet a little while, and he that shall come will come, and will not tarry.

Don't worry about fitting in with the old gang. Keep going. Keep living for heaven.

A certain sheik in Saudi Arabia wanted to give his stockbroker a gift above and beyond her commission. "I can't take anything from you," she protested. But finally after much badgering and pressure, she relented, saying, "I'm kind of getting into golf. If you want to get me a couple clubs, that would be fine."

The sheik came back a few months later, saying, "I got you five golf clubs—but only four of them have pools and tennis courts. I hope that's okay."

That which the Lord has in store for you and me makes the gift of any sheik look like a golf tee in comparison. So be patient, gang. Eyes have not seen, nor ears heard the wonderful things He's preparing for those who love Him (1 Corinthians 2:9).

Hebrews 10:38, 39
Now the just shall live by faith: but if any man draw back, my soul shall have no pleasure in him. But we are not of them who draw back unto perdition; but of them that believe to the saving of the soul.

"Perdition" means "waste"—a perfect word choice for the frustratingly pointless existence under the law of self-help and self-effort.

A WONDERFUL WARNING
A Topical Study of
Hebrews 10:26–31

A sign posted near a convent reads:

ABSOLUTELY NO TRESPASSING
VIOLATORS WILL BE PROSECUTED
TO THE FULL EXTENT OF THE LAW
—Sisters of Mercy

—and the passage before us hits many people the same way. I mean, here we've been reading of our faithful and merciful High Priest, Jesus Christ, who was touched with the same feelings with which we wrestle, and tempted by the same things that tempt us. We've been reading that we can come boldly unto His throne of grace and that the veil has been rent, giving us access to the very Holy of Holies of the goodness and grace of God. And then we come to chapter 10, where we read that if we sin willfully, there's no more sacrifice for sins; that if we sin, we trample under foot the Son of God; that it's a fearful thing to fall into the hands of the living God.

Thus, this passage seems, upon first reading, to be somewhat contradictory to the entire spirit of the rest of the epistle. But it's not.

You see, warnings can affect people two ways: They can either be intimidating or they can be inviting.

Go to Makaha on the island of Hawaii, and you'll find a sign reading: WARN-ING: HEAVY SURF! Now, if you're a parent and you brought your little kids to the beach, this sign would be intimidating. But if you're a surfer and you brought your surfboard, this sign would be inviting.

Intimidation

Throughout church history, Satan has used the passage before us to intimidate the hearts of people like you and me. Indeed, Satan has and will use the Word for his purposes. . . .

"Did God really say you can't eat of every tree of the garden?" he asked Eve, implying God's command was of questionable motive (see Genesis 3).

"Jump off the temple," he taunted Jesus (see Matthew 4). "Isn't it written that God will take care of You?" he said, misquoting Psalm 91.

Truly, Satan has misused the Word to cause confusion and consternation in the lives of those who love the Lord.

But wait a minute. The Epistle to the Hebrews was written to Jewish believers who were being pulled back to temple worship and the sacrificial system. There-fore, the warning is this: If you return to the temple to offer sacrifices for your sins, you are missing the point totally because the price was paid completely when Jesus died in your place. There are no more sacrifices that can be, need be, or should be offered. The Way is open. The Work is complete. Going to confession, getting rebap-tized, making a promise, or signing a pledge will not make you right with God.

None of these sacrifices will do any more than the sacrifice of bulls, rams, or goats. You can't add to what Jesus did on the Cross by promise keeping, confessing, working, or giving. Don't fall into that mind-set, for if you do, you tread on what the Lord has already done.

Thus, contrary to many well-intentioned sermons, the warning in Hebrews 10 is not so much in reference to backsliding as it is to back-turning—turning one's back on what Jesus did on our behalf. Certainly, this is what the writer intended, for every one of us fails. Every one of us is increasingly aware of our shortcomings the closer we get to the Lord. Every one of us joins Paul in saying, "I am the chief of sinners" (see 1 Timothy 1:15).

Jesus died not only for our sins—but for the sins of the whole world. How dare we, then, say that what He did on the Cross is insufficient or inadequate? How dare we trample the body of Christ? If you want to see the anger of the Father, say that what Jesus did at Calvary is inadequate without your additional efforts.

The author is right. It *is* a terrible thing to fall into the nail-pierced hands of the living God if we fall into them with any sacrifice of our own, suggesting that His was not enough.

Invitation

We're surfers, gang. The warning of Hebrews 10 is not intimidating. It's inviting! It's great news!

"You mean Your warning, Father, is to not go back to self-efforts or religious activities to try to earn Your favor? You mean I'm free to just remember what *You've* done, and to *celebrate* my salvation? Wonderful!"

The warning here in chapter 10 does not cause me to be intimidated, folks. Rather, it invites me to keep my walk simple, and to *enjoy* my salvation. There is no more sacrifice for sins. Jesus has done it all. Surf's up—so boldly enter in!

11 In writing his epistles, Paul's typical method at the outset was to address issues of doctrine and to follow with exhortations to duty. He would talk about position—who we are in Christ—before he would deal with practice—how we should live and behave. And such is the case in this epistle to the Hebrews. The first ten chapters have been concerned with doctrine, position, and what Christ has done for us. In the remaining three chapters, the author will make practical application. In fact, in each of the three remaining chapters, he will address one of the three great virtues . . .

- In chapter 11, we read about the walk of faith.
- In chapter 12, we are reminded of the wisdom of hope.
- In chapter 13, we see the way of love.

It's not that the author of this letter is suddenly saying, "Okay, now we're done with doctrine, so let's switch gears and talk about something practical." No it all flows together. Keep in mind the Epistle to the Hebrews was written to keep Jewish believers from being sucked back into religious traditions. That's why chapter 11 is so essential to the discussion of the first ten chapters. "I know it's tempting to go back to that which you can see with your eyes, smell with your nose, and touch with your hands. But don't do it," the author pleads, "for now you are called to something entirely different. You are called to walk by faith."

Hebrews 11:1
Now faith is the substance of things hoped for, the evidence of things not seen.

The phrase "things not seen" is literally "things not *yet* seen." Faith is the substance of what you know is coming your way, even though it is not *yet* seen. Faith isn't wishful thinking. No,

based upon the Word of God, faith says, "Whether I see it presently, understand it intellectually, or experience it immediately, I *know* what God says He'll do, He *will* do."

Hebrews 11:2
For by it the elders obtained a good report.

While faith may sound somewhat impractical, in reality, every single one of us exercises faith constantly.

Upon entering church on Sunday, you exercised great faith that the architect and the engineer knew what they were doing. If you didn't have faith, you'd be hiding under the pew. But even then, you'd be trusting the pew maker—that he knew how to design a pew to support not only your weight, but the weight of all of the people on it. That's faith, folks!

If you drive your car sixty-five miles per hour, you do so trusting the engineers who drew the plans and the workers on the assembly line are men of responsibility and integrity, that the system will work, that when you hit the brake, the car will stop.

It's an amazing thing, this world of faith in which we live. But the irony is that, although we have faith in the boys at Ford and in the maker of the pew; when it comes to God, we get a little iffy and a little shaky. This ought not be. Even though we don't know how it works or when it will come to pass, we're to be those who, like the elders in our text, have faith that God's will shall be worked out ultimately—and that it will be good.

On the other hand, a lot of teachers in the "positive confession" or "hyper-Pentecostal" movement are in great error when they suggest that faith is a force you use to get your will done; that if you learn how to use the force by spoken word, by positive confession—like rubbing a genie's lamp—you can control your destiny. That is faith in faith—and it is foolishness.

Faith is in the Father. Faith says, "I trust You, Lord, in whatever You choose to do in this situation."

Hebrews 11:3 (a)
Through faith we understand that the worlds were framed by the word of God . . .

If you believe God spoke the worlds into existence, you lead the parade of those who obtain a good report.

Hebrews 11:3 (b)
. . . so that things which are seen were not made of things which do appear.

The author of this epistle was two thousand years ahead of his time because we now know that everything that exists materially is made of atoms that cannot be seen.

"Not so," you argue, "because now we have electron microscopes and can see all kinds of things previously invisible."

Yes, but when you break down the atom, you enter into the area of energy—which is not material at all. So guess what. The further you get into science, the more you realize everything is made out of that which cannot be seen. Everything is made out of energy. Consequently, the man of faith was thousands of years ahead of the man of science.

Hebrews 11:4
By faith Abel offered unto God a more excellent sacrifice than Cain, by which he obtained witness that he was righteous, God testifying of his gifts: and by it he being dead yet speaketh.

Not only was Cain's sacrifice of vegetables unacceptable because rather than pointing to the Lamb of God, it spoke of his own effort—it was unacceptable because, unlike Abel, Cain did not offer his sacrifice by faith. This realization would stab the Jewish heart because the Jews took great pride in their ceremonies, traditions, and attempts at spirituality.

Hebrews 11:5 (a)
By faith Enoch was translated that he should not see death; and was not found, because God had translated him . . .

Those who believe the church will go through the Tribulation—the period of time when God pours out His wrath on a Christ-rejecting world—use Noah as their proof. "Although judgment fell with the rain," they say, "Noah and his family were protected in the ark—just as the church will be protected in the Tribulation."

Not so. Noah is a picture of the Jewish people going through the Tribulation, for truly, they will go through it (Revelation 7) and be saved in it. The church, on the other hand, is pictured by Enoch, who, a few verses before the story of Noah, was "translated"—or raptured—*before* the rain came down, *before* judgment took place.

Hebrews 11:5 (b)
. . . for before his translation he had this testimony, that he pleased God.

"What must we do to do the works of God?" they asked Jesus.

"This is the work of God," He answered, "that you believe on Him whom the Father hath sent," answered Jesus (see John 6:29).

How do you please the Father?
You believe on the Son.

Hebrews 11:6
But without faith it is impossible to please him: for he that cometh to God must believe that he is, and that he is a rewarder of them that diligently seek him.

Here are two keys to faith. The first is to believe that God is.

"Who do I say You are?" Moses asked God.
"I AM THAT I AM," God answered (see Exodus 3:14).

In other words, God said, "I am whatever you need." Are you lonely tonight? God is the friend who's closer than a brother. Are you confused about what to do? He is the door. Are you feeling like you're walking in a haze? He's the Good Shepherd. Faith hopes for the unseen because it believes God is.

Secondly, faith believes God is the One who will meet the needs deep within my heart. There are those who believe God is—but they don't really seek Him. Why must we diligently seek God? Why isn't it enough just to believe He is whatever we have need of? Because God knows if we diligently seek Him, the very things about which we seek Him will fade in importance as we realize it's Him we want all along.

I believe most of us have no problem with the first of these two keys to faith. We believe God is. But because we don't believe He rewards those who seek Him, we seek Him haphazardly or half-heartedly if at all.

I long for the day when retreat centers are full of people saying, "Lord, we seek Your blessing and Your direction, Your leading and Your provision because we understand You reward those who diligently seek You."

"I don't have time," you might be saying. Not true. We have time to golf, time to see the Blazers play, time to water ski, fix the plumbing, and go to the dentist. Every single one of us without exception has time. We do what we want and make time for what is of value to us.

Throughout history, the common denominator in the lives of those who have been blessed is that they have all been those who realize God enjoys our company. And when we seek Him, we're rewarded—not because we're trying to earn brownie points—but just because hanging out with the Lord opens the door to fabulous blessing from Him.

Hebrews 11:7
By faith Noah, being warned of God of things not seen as yet, moved with fear, prepared an ark to the saving of his house; by the which he condemned the world, and became heir of the righteousness which is by faith.

Twenty years before his first child was born, Noah planned the construction of the ark with rooms for his sons and his sons' wives. In other words, by faith, he said, "My sons and their wives are going to be saved. And I'm providing a place for their salvation."

Every parent should have this verse underlined and by faith say, "With the hammer of intercession in one hand and the nail of instruction in the other, I believe You will use my meager labor, Lord, to save my family."

Hebrews 11:8
By faith Abraham, when he was called to go out into a place which he should after receive for an inheritance, obeyed; and he went out, not knowing whither he went.

Abraham didn't know where he was going—he just started moving. Most of us in his position would say, "Father, I know You're calling me to leave Ur, and I'll be happy to go as soon as You give me a map of Mesopotamia."

But the Lord doesn't work that way in the arena of faith. "Start moving one step at a time," He says. "I'll direct you, but I will not give you directions for Step 2 until you first take Step 1. A step of faith is the prerequisite for a man or woman to be used by God. He's looking for those who will come to the Jordan and get their feet wet (Joshua 3:15). My tendency, however, is to say,

"Here I am, Lord. Right near the edge, just like You told me to be. Now, Lord, this ark is important cargo. You don't want to see it get dropped into the river and carried downstream, do You? That's not practical. So in order to help You protect Your good Name, whenever you part the water, I'll be thrilled to go across. Here I am, Your man of faith, ready to serve You on the spot."

But without faith, it's impossible to please God. "Why?" you ask. "Why does God take me to the edge of the Jordan, tell me to put my foot in, and risk my looking like a fool or the ark floating down the river? I don't get it."

Guess what. You will—because faith is the lingua franca of eternity. God's not saying, "I'm going to put you to the test for the fun of it. Let's see if you step in or not." The Father has no joy in seeing His kids agonize at the edge of the Jordan. "If this causes you agony," He says, "it's because you yet need to become a man of faith. After all, it's who you are in the arena of faith that will affect how I will use you in the next billion years to come."

You see, gang, if you take eternity out of the equation, the whole life of faith seems like a bad joke. But once you understand that life on earth is to train and stretch, develop and mature you for heaven and the ages to come, you start looking at everything differently. "Okay, Father," you'll say, "this is a stretch for me. It's uncomfortable. It's not easy. But because You told me to be like Abraham, even if I don't know where I'm going, I trust You."

Hebrews 11:9, 10
By faith he sojourned in the land of promise, as in a strange country, dwelling in tabernacles with Isaac and Jacob, the heirs with him of the same promise: For he looked for a city which hath foundations, whose builder and maker is God.

Why did Abraham embark on such a venture, such a journey? Because he was looking for a city that had foundations, whose builder and maker was God—all the while knowing that what he was looking for would never be found anywhere on the face of this earth.

Why is this so important? Because when I moved from San Jose to Applegate, for example, if I had been looking for a city on earth to satisfy me, I would have been paralyzed by fear. I would have said, "What if I get there and discover Applegate's not it?" But since the longing of my heart was for a city without foundations, I already knew Applegate wouldn't be it!

- "What if I go there, and it doesn't work out?" you ask.
  Don't worry—it's not going to work out!
- "What if I marry her, and she doesn't fully satisfy me?" you ask yourself.
  Don't worry—she won't!
- "What if I take that job and it's not what I hoped?" you speculate.
  Don't worry—it won't be!

You'll never be a man or woman of faith if you're looking for fulfillment here. No matter your ministry, your geographic location, your job, or who you marry—you'll not find it here. Like Abraham, don't look for a city that has foundations on earth. Look for eternity, and you'll experience heaven in your heart, and you'll be blessed in your soul wherever you are.

Had Abraham looked for a city on earth, he would have been stuck in Ur forever. But at some point, God by His grace allowed Abraham to understand that everything on earth is in preparation for heaven. If you don't see Abraham as a model of faith, you'll be perpetually paralyzed and completely frustrated. You must understand that God only leads you one step at a time. He doesn't tell you what lies around the bend. And even when you get around the bend, you must understand it's not going to be what you were hoping for because what you really crave is heaven.

In spiritual life, the Lord will take you as far as you want to go—and not one step further. If you choose to take one baby step and stop, God will still love you because His love for you is not based on anything you do or don't do. But if you choose to walk by faith from Ur of the Chaldees all the way to the land flowing with milk and honey, He'll be with you every step of the way.

People wonder why some folks are so spiritual, why others seem particularly blessed, why others are mightily used. It's not that God is playing favorites. It's just that those who seem to have a special relationship with God are simply those who chose to keep going. Whether it's in expression of praise, gifts of the Spirit, or aspects of ministry—however far you want to go in spiritual life, God will never say to you, "You're going

a little too far. You're getting a little too spiritual." Never.

Hebrews 11:11, 12
Through faith also Sara herself received strength to conceive seed, and was delivered of a child when she was past age, because she judged him faithful who had promised. Therefore sprang there even of one, and him as good as dead, so many as the stars of the sky in multitude, and as the sand which is by the sea shore innumerable.

When the Lord and two angels came to Abraham's tent and told him his wife would conceive, what did the wife of the father of faith do? She laughed (Genesis 18:12). This encourages me a whole bunch because Sarah's faith was not real strong. Yet Jesus taught that if we have just a tiny bit of faith—the size of a grain of mustard—mountains of barrenness could be removed and miracles could take place (Matthew 17:20).

Sarah's story encourages me greatly because sometimes I sense a promise from the Lord being written on my heart, or I read a promise in the Word and I kind of chuckle in disbelief. So did Sarah. Yet the Lord honored the seed of faith within her, and a child whose name means "laughter" was born to her (Genesis 21:5, 6).

Hebrews 11:13 (a)
These all died in faith, not having received the promises, but having seen them afar off, and were persuaded of them, and embraced them . . .

Although Abraham never saw his offspring number more than the stars in the heavens, in Isaac he saw the beginning of the fulfillment of this promise.

Hebrews 11:13 (b)
. . . and confessed that they were strangers and pilgrims on the earth.

Abraham was one who was characterized by two objects: a tent and an altar. He was a wanderer and a worshiper, a pilgrim and a priest. So, too, as I look around this world, I feel like I fit in less and less. Like Abraham, we are strangers because it's strange around here. And, like him, we realize what we're looking for and craving is not to be found here.

Hebrews 11:14–16
For they that say such things declare plainly that they seek a country. And truly, if they had been mindful of that country from

whence they came out, they might have had opportunity to have returned. But now they desire a better country, that is, an heavenly: wherefore God is not ashamed to be called their God: for he hath prepared for them a city.

If Abraham had been thinking about the stuff he left behind in Ur, he might have gone back. But those things weren't what he looked for or lived for. He looked for, lived for, longed for a *better* country.

Hebrews 11:17
By faith Abraham, when he was tried, offered up Isaac: and he that had received the promises offered up his only begotten son.

Since Abraham had two sons, why is Isaac referred to as his only begotten son? For the same reason God referred to Isaac as Abraham's only son in Genesis 22 as they climbed Mount Moriah: God didn't acknowledge Ishmael.

This is great news for us, gang, because every one of us has a bunch of Ishmaels—a bunch of reminders of our flesh—running around. But God doesn't even acknowledge them. Our sins and iniquities He remembers no more (Hebrews 8:12).

Hebrews 11:18, 19
Of whom it was said, That in Isaac shall thy seed be called: Accounting that God was able to raise him up, even from the dead; from whence also he received him in a figure.

How many people had been resurrected from the dead in Abraham's day? Zero. Therefore, in saying to the servants who waited for him at the base of Mount Moriah, "You stay here while I and the lad go up to the mountain and worship, and *we* will return again unto thee," Abraham's faith was great, indeed (see Genesis 22:5).

Hebrews 11:20, 21
By faith Isaac blessed Jacob and Esau concerning things to come. By faith Jacob, when he was a dying, blessed both the sons of Joseph; and worshipped, leaning upon the top of his staff.

As we see Isaac and Jacob bless their sons and grandchildren, please note three components of biblical blessing. . . .

First, we see tender affection. A blessing was pronounced while laying a hand upon the child's head.

After investigating the lives of four hundred women who had given birth four or more times outside of marriage, a college professor discovered one common denominator among them. This common denominator was not income, education, race, or religion. The common denominator was that in their childhoods, each lacked being embraced properly and lovingly by a father or grandfather. How important it is, Dad, to consistently, tenderly, lovingly embrace your kids.

Second, we see present affirmation. Biblical blessings always contained fitting words of description. One child would be likened to a fruitful vine overflowing its walls. Another would be likened to a lion crouching in strength. And through these meaningful words, children gained access into how their parents saw them.

Finally, we see future direction. Kids still need this today. . . .

In Orthodox Jewish homes, you might hear the parents say, "Meet my son, Jacob, the lawyer," or, "Meet my daughter, Sarah, the doctor,"—regardless of the fact that Jacob's eight and Sarah only five.

We have the privilege of saying, "You know, son, it wouldn't surprise me if God uses you in days to come to teach the Bible." Or, "You have a spirit of adventure about you. It wouldn't surprise me if you end up being a missionary." I believe it is imperative for parents and grandparents to dispense blessing constantly. Yes, it takes faith—especially when there's not a whole lot to bless in your kids. But without faith, it's impossible to please God—so bless your kids in faith!

Hebrews 11:22
By faith Joseph, when he died, made mention of the departing of the children of Israel; and gave commandment concerning his bones.

Even though he himself died in Egypt, Joseph *knew* his people would make it back to the Promised Land. By faith, he *knew* good things would happen not only for his family but also for the entire nation.

Hebrews 11:23
By faith Moses, when he was born, was hid three months of his parents, because they saw he was a proper child; and they were not afraid of the king's commandment.

I suggest it was through the eyes of faith that Jochebed and Amram said of their son, Moses,

"This child is going to be special" (see Exodus 2:2). So, too, Mom and Dad, if you think your child will never amount to much, that he'll always struggle or that she's not quite up to par—that's simply a lack of faith because faith is the substance of things not *yet* seen. If you see your kid as a problem child, this will be understood within his soul, and it will greatly hinder what God can do in and through his life. Such was not the case with Amram and Jochebed. Knowing Moses was special, they went to great lengths to make sure his life was spared.

Hebrews 11:24 (a)
By faith Moses . . .

Not only was he the lawgiver, the deliverer, and the historian of the nation of Israel, Moses was also the meekest man on the face of the earth (Numbers 12:3). No wonder, then, that the Jewish people to whom this book is written esteemed Moses higher than the angels. In the following five verses, please note seven characteristics of this remarkable man of faith . . .

Hebrews 11:24 (b)
. . . when he was come to years, refused to be called the son of Pharaoh's daughter.

Moses chose humility.

In the original text, the article "the" is absent, rendering it, "he refused to be called son of Pharaoh's daughter." Why is this important? Because "Son of Pharaoh," a title like "Queen of England" or "Duke of York," carried with it the understanding that the bearer was next in line to the throne.

"I'm not interested," said Moses, "in the prestige or the power, the prominence or the prosperity."

Hebrews 11:25
Choosing rather to suffer affliction with the people of God, than to enjoy the pleasures of sin for a season.

Moses chose to suffer.

There *is* pleasure in sin for a season—but with every kick comes a kickback that causes great heartache and confusion. You can either give in to your flesh now and have a lifetime of pain—or you can say no to your flesh, say no to that guy, say no to that thing and experience a little pain now, but a lifetime of pleasure later. That's the choice.

Having been in the ministry over twenty years, I have never once heard anyone say, "I'm sure glad about the sins I committed in college," or,

"I'm so grateful for my adulterous experience." I have, however, talked to literally hundreds who have said, "I wish I could go back and do it over. I wouldn't give in. I wouldn't succumb. I would choose differently."

Hebrews 11:26
Esteeming the reproach of Christ greater riches than the treasures in Egypt: for he had respect unto the recompence of the reward.

Moses invested in things eternal.

Did you see the miracle that took place when the offering was taken at church on Sunday? Baskets were passed, and, contrary to human nature, people put money *in* rather than grabbing money *out.* "The tithe is mine," says the Lord (Malachi 3:8). And those who obey, like Moses, discover riches greater than the treasure of Egypt.

Hebrews 11:27 (a)
By faith he forsook Egypt, not fearing the wrath of the king . . .

Moses walked out with the world's wrath.

Because Moses grew up in the palace, Pharaoh and his court were actually Moses' colleagues. The people with whom we are the most familiar are often the people before whom it is hardest to take a stand. Not so with Moses.

Hebrews 11:27 (b)
. . . for he endured, as seeing him who is invisible.

Moses developed spiritual eyesight.

"I don't believe in blind faith," the skeptic says. And I agree! Our faith is not blind, folks. On the contrary, we see *more* than the unbeliever sees, for, like Moses, we see the invisible.

Hebrews 11:28
Through faith he kept the passover, and the sprinkling of blood, lest he that destroyed the firstborn should touch them.

Moses kept Passover.

The Greek word translated "kept" denotes continual action. In other words, Moses "kept on keeping" Passover. Why? To keep the death angel away.

Because Christ is our Passover (1 Corinthians 5:7), Paul would write, "For this cause many are sick and weak and dying, not giving worth to the Lord's table" (see 1 Corinthians 11:29, 30). Why does Applegate Christian Fellowship serve Communion every morning at 6:30 A.M.? And why do people come? For the same reason Moses kept on keeping Passover: To keep away the death angel who would creep into our families spiritually and into our hearts personally.

Hebrews 11:29
By faith they passed through the Red sea as by dry land: which the Egyptians assaying to do were drowned.

Moses kept the ordinance of baptism.

Not only did Moses keep the ordinance of Passover, but he kept the ordinance of baptism. You see, according to 1 Corinthians 10:2, the parting of the Red Sea was a picture of baptism. The same waters that parted for the Israelites buried the Egyptians. So, too, by entering the waters of baptism, we say, "Bury the Egypt in me, Lord. Drown out the old, the flesh, the world. I'm headed for a new land and a new way of living."

Hebrews 11:30
By faith the walls of Jericho fell down, after they were compassed about seven days.

To claim the Promised Land, God's strategy for His people was fairly simple: Drive a wedge through the middle, dividing the north from the south. There was only one problem, however. To do this, they had to take Jericho—a city that seemed absolutely impenetrable because of the thick double walls surrounding it. Certainly as the Israelites marched around the walls once a day for six days, the people in Jericho must have looked down on them and laughed. "*That's* their army?" they must have scoffed. "*That's* their strategy?" On the seventh day, however, the heretofore-impenetrable walls came down.

And the walls came down not brick by brick but by faith.

"There's a wall between my eighteen-year-old daughter and me," cries the brokenhearted mother. "We've gone to counseling. We've followed the workbooks. We've tried all the techniques. Yet, although a brick or two might get chipped away, within a month there are three more in their place."

"The walls between me and my son are keeping me out of the Promised Land of what I know a Christian family should be," says the weary father. "I tried to reason with him, but there's a wall between us."

Perhaps you are looking at a wall in your own family that seems impenetrable, a wall that appears as though it will never come down. The key isn't counseling, dialoguing, or role-playing. The key is faith.

"But I've been marching around, working on,

going through this situation for a long time," you say.

Great—because the longer the wall has been up between you and your husband, you and your father, or you and your daughter—the more you know it can't be brought down by your own effort. Walls come down when God moves in. But until God moves in, you'll just chip away, and frustration will fill your heart. Have faith in *God*, for when you finally realize that human skill or ability is insufficient, when you finally say, "Lord, if anything's going to happen, it's going to be because of *You*"—that's when the wall will fall.

Oh, it might take a week or a month, a year or a decade. But by faith in God, the wall *will* come down. How? In a way you would never have guessed, planned, or predicted. The older I get, the less impressed I am with people's abilities to solve problems and the more amazed I am at God's faithfulness if we'll just believe Him. If you think that's a cop-out, join the jeerers of Jericho. But if you want to see a miracle, march with the Lord, and see what *He'll* do.

Hebrews 11:31
By faith the harlot Rahab perished not with them that believed not, when she had received the spies with peace.

Here, alongside the names of Moses and Joshua, we find a seemingly unlikely member of the Hall of Faith. But I find Rahab's inclusion particularly pertinent to the culture in which we live . . .

For topical study of Hebrews 11:32–35 entitled "Rahab: Holy or Hypocrite?" turn to page 1500.

Hebrews 11:32–35 (a)
And what shall I more say? for the time would fail me to tell of Gedeon, and of Barak, and of Samson, and of Jephthae; of David also, and Samuel, and of the prophets: Who through faith subdued kingdoms, wrought righteousness, obtained promises, stopped the mouths of lions, quenched the violence of fire, escaped the edge of the sword, out of weakness were made strong, waxed valiant in fight, turned to flight the armies of the aliens. Women received their dead raised to life again . . .

The dead were raised. The fire was quenched. The lions' mouths were stopped. There was victory, power, and deliverance—all because of faith. But watch out because so-called "faith teachers" will quote this verse saying, "You too can see your dead raised, your sick healed, your bank accounts swell." The problem is, they conveniently don't finish the passage, for it goes on. . . .

Hebrews 11:35 (b)–38
. . . and others were tortured, not accepting deliverance; that they might obtain a better resurrection: And others had trial of cruel mockings and scourgings, yea, moreover of bonds and imprisonment: They were stoned, they were sawn asunder, were tempted, were slain with the sword: they wandered about in sheepskins and goatskins; being destitute, afflicted, tormented; (Of whom the world was not worthy:) they wandered in deserts, and in mountains, and in dens and caves of the earth.

In verses 33–35, faith gave people victory over their circumstances. But in verses 35–38, faith gave others victory *in* their circumstances. The latter were those who, because they saw the big picture of eternity, left a lasting impression on the world.

Hebrews 11:39
And these all, having obtained a good report through faith, received not the promise.

The promise referred to, of course, is the central promise of the Book of Hebrews, the promise of the New Covenant, the promise of salvation by faith.

Hebrews 11:40 (a)
God having provided some better thing for us . . .

"Oh, to have seen the lions' mouths stopped, the parting of the Red Sea, or fire falling from heaven," we say. But in reality, we have experienced something far greater than any of these miracles. The Lord lives in our hearts. He walks with us every moment of every day. He gives direction to us whenever we take time to stop and listen. Although we take all of these things for granted, any one of them would have astounded the Old Testament saints.

Hebrews 11:40 (b)
. . . that they without us should not be made perfect.

The heroes of faith who preceded us didn't experience the perfection or the maturity we enjoy in the New Covenant. How do you receive this New Covenant? By faith, saying, "Lord, I, too, am looking for a better country. And by faith, I'll see greater things than even these heroes and heroines did because, although they saw awesome events externally, I've experienced Your miraculous grace internally, the promise of Your kingdom ultimately, and the promise of Your presence eternally."

RAHAB: HOLY OR HYPOCRITE?
A Topical Study of
Hebrews 11:31

One of the best-known chapters in the entire Bible, Hebrews 11 is known as God's Hall of Faith. I find this Hall of Faith amazing—as much for who's not in it as who is. I mean, think who's missing: Elijah and Elisha, Jehoshaphat and Jeremiah. I would have thought they would have been shoo-ins! But, instead, we find Sarah and Samson, Jacob and Jephthah . . . and Rahab.

Interestingly, Rahab and Sarah—the only two women in the seventeen-member Hall of Faith—are both linked to Abraham. Sarah was his helpmate. But, according to James 2, Rahab was his soulmate, for she, like Abraham, had faith that showed itself not just theoretically, but practically.

As we look at Rahab, I want you to see her in two ways: both as a picture of the believer, and as a problem for the believer.

A Picture of the Believer

After wandering in the wilderness for forty years, the children of Israel were ready to claim the Promised Land. Their first obstacle was Jericho—a double-walled city that seemed impregnable. So Joshua sent spies into Jericho, who ended up lodging in the house of a harlot named Rahab. After hearing of the king's intent to capture them, Rahab hatched a plan to protect the spies. Why? "I know the Lord, Yahweh, hath given you the land," she said. "We have heard what you did to the two kings of the Amorites. And as soon as we heard these things, our hearts did melt. For the Lord, your God, He is God in heaven, and He is God in earth" (see Joshua 2:9–11).

Faith comes by hearing and hearing by the Word (Romans 10:17). Thus, even though Rahab neither saw the Red Sea part nor the Amorite kings get wiped out, she heard the Word and she believed. Way back in the Book of Exodus, after the Red Sea parted miraculously, Moses was so thrilled he wrote this song:

Who is like unto thee, O LORD, among the gods? who is like thee, glorious in holiness, fearful in praises, doing wonders? Thou stretchedst out thy right hand, the earth swallowed them. Thou in thy mercy hast led forth the people which thou hast redeemed: thou hast guided them in thy strength unto thy holy habitation. The people shall hear, and be afraid: sorrow shall take hold on the inhabitants of Palestina. Then the dukes of Edom shall be amazed; the mighty men of Moab, trembling shall take hold upon them; all the inhabitants of Canaan shall melt away. Fear and dread shall fall upon them . . .

Exodus 15:11–16

And that's exactly what happened to Rahab. Not only did Rahab hear the Word *about* God, she believed *in* God, and risked her life to serve Him. That is why in the next scene, we see her hiding the spies among the flax on her roof. Perhaps the mention of flax rings a bell, for it is also used in the classic Proverbs 31 description of the virtuous woman. Now if *virtuous* women worked with flax, what was Rahab doing with it on her roof? I suggest that after hearing about God, she who was previously a prostitute had given up her former occupation. She heard *about* God. She believed *in* God. And she was changed *by* God.

"We'll take care of you and your family," said the spies. "Behold, when we come into the land, thou shalt bind this line of scarlet thread in the window which thou didst let us down by: and thou shalt bring thy father, and thy mother, and thy brethren, and all thy father's household, home unto thee."

"According unto your words, so be it," answered Rahab (see Joshua 2:18–21).

When at last Joshua led the people of Israel to march around Jericho and the walls came down, one part of the wall remained: the portion that held a scarlet thread—the scarlet thread of redemption, whereby Rahab's house was saved.

Truly, Rahab is a beautiful example of the believer, for hers was a saving faith in-deed—not only for her but also for her family.

But think with me about another aspect of Rahab—for while she's a picture of faith, she also poses a problem. . . .

A Problem for the Believer

Rahab presents a problem for the believer because instead of just trusting in the Lord by saying to the soldiers concerning the spies, "Kill me if you wish, but my lips are sealed," she said, "They're not here. They went that-a-way." In other words, she intentionally, purposefully told a whopper of a lie.

En route to Seattle one weekend, I had an intriguing conversation with a well-known author. After interviewing a number of Christian leaders, he came to the conclusion that they're all hypocrites.

Oh no, I thought. *Not the age-old hypocrite argument again.*

"You know, it's interesting," I said. "Even though he's repented of wrong theology and foolish financial decisions, you'd call Jim Bakker a hypocrite—yet you'd never say that of Hugh Hefner. Why? Because Mr. Hefner doesn't have any standards to violate."

Gang, if anyone knows you're a believer, sooner or later they'll see you strug-gle in some area or fail at some point and call you a hypocrite. "Watch me," you need to say, "and you'll see me fail. I'm not what I should be, but I praise God I'm not what I used to be, and not what I would be if I had no standards whatsoever."

You see, the higher your standards, the more vulnerable you'll be to what the world calls hypocrisy. The problem is, the world's definition of hypocrisy is totally amiss. Who did Jesus identify as hypocrites? Not Rahab, who, in spite of her new-found belief in God lied openly. Not Jim Bakker, whose excesses caused heartache and tragedy. Jesus labeled only one group as hypocrites: Those determined to keep others from the kingdom (Matthew 23) don't fall into that category. Neither does Rahab.

What did God do with Rahab? "Let the critic, the cynic, the skeptic point out her failings, shortcomings, and flaws," He would say. "But she is one of only seven-teen I have chosen to be in My Hall of Faith."

That's the kind of God we serve. The world finds flaws. Our God finds faith. I know this because when He became a Man in Jesus Christ, He found another loose woman, called her *gune*—a term of respect—and said, "Go call your husband."

"I don't have a husband," she answered.

He didn't call her a liar. He said, "Thou hast spoken well. You don't have a hus-band. You've had five. And the one you're living with now is not your husband" (see John 4:16–18).

Only Jesus has the ability to extract the precious from the vile (Jeremiah 15:19). The world does just the opposite. The world sniffs out the vile in the precious. The world is quick to point to the failures, shortcomings and inconsistencies in the lives of believers. Why? Because the world is determined to keep people out of the kingdom of God.

Thus, by Jesus' definition, it is the world rather than the believer that is hypocritical. Please remember this, gang, the next time the label of hypocrite is bandied about. It is not the breaking of one's standards that defines one as a hypocrite but rather the breaking of God's heart by those whose goal is to keep people from Him.

May we learn the lesson of Rahab. And may we all celebrate the grace and mercy of the One who looks past our flaws to find our faith.

12 In chapter 11, looking at the men and women who tapped into the blessing of God by believing God is who He claims to be and that He does what He says He will do, we saw the walk of faith. Here in chapter 12, we'll see the wisdom of hope. And in chapter 13, we'll see the way of love. . . .

Hebrews 12:1 (a)
Wherefore seeing we also are compassed about with so great a cloud of witnesses . . .

We are in a race, folks, observed and cheered on by a cloud of witnesses. Who are these spectators? They are the ones spoken of in chapter 11, the heroes of faith. . . .

Shortly before He was to die outside Jerusalem on a hill called Calvary, Elijah and Moses appeared with Jesus on Mount Hermon (Matthew 17). They had come, if you would, to cheer Him on.

So, too, it is my firm conviction that right now, you and I are being cheered on by those in heaven. Furthermore, I believe the clouds spoken of in 1 Thessalonians 4:17, in which we will be caught up during the Rapture, are not of the cumulus or nimbus variety. Rather, they're clouds of those who have gone before us. Therefore, next time you feel you're being "wailed on," think of Jonah. He's up there cheering you on. Next time you feel like you're in a fiery trial, look for Shadrach, Meshach, and Abed-nego in the stands. Next time you feel like you're up against a giant of a problem, remember David, the giant-slayer, and take heart.

Hebrews 12:1 (b)
. . . let us lay aside every weight, and the sin which doth so easily beset us . . .

"Weight" is not necessarily sin—it's just stuff.

A woman dreamed the Rapture was taking place. But much to her consternation, while everyone else was zooming up, it was a struggle for her to get even twenty feet off the ground. Looking down, she saw the problem. Around her ankle was a rope, the end of which was tied to all her furniture. When she awoke, she realized the Lord was telling her she was tied down by all her possessions.

Hebrews 12:1 (c)
. . . and let us run with patience the race that is set before us.

The race before us is not a sprint. It's a marathon. We're in it for the long haul, gang.

Hebrews 12:2 (a)
Looking unto Jesus the author and finisher of our faith . . .

For an example of One who ran the race with patience, look to Jesus.

Hebrews 12:2 (b)
. . . who for the joy that was set before him endured the cross, despising the shame, and is set down at the right hand of the throne of God.

The course Jesus ran wasn't easy, but He knew on the other side of the finish line, joy awaited Him. I believe the Father gave His Son a sneak preview of this joy even as He hung on the Cross.

You see, when one of the two thieves who hung on either side of Jesus said, "Remember me when You come into Your kingdom" (see Luke 23:42) it was as if the Father gave His Son a taste of the joy that would be His when an entire world would have the opportunity to follow the thief's example.

Hebrews 12:3
For consider him that endured such contradiction of sinners against himself, lest ye be wearied and faint in your minds.

Consider Jesus, who endured the opposition of sinners. He was drenched in their spittle, pelted with their curses, beaten with their fists, and crowned with their thorns.

Hebrews 12:4
Ye have not yet resisted unto blood, striving against sin.

We sweat at times because of things we go through. But we have never sweat like Jesus did, for in the Garden of Gethsemane, knowing the Cross awaiting Him and the challenge before Him, Jesus prayed with such intensity that the capillaries in His forehead burst, causing blood to flow down His face. Had He so chosen, He could have backed out at this point. Instead, He prayed, "Not My will, but Thine be done." Therefore, because He wrestled with His own ability to choose, perhaps the pain of Gethsemane was, in some ways, even greater than the pain of the Cross.

Hebrews 12:5-9
And ye have forgotten the exhortation which speaketh unto you as unto children, My son, despise not thou the chastening of the Lord, nor faint when thou art rebuked of him: For whom the Lord loveth he chasteneth, and scourgeth every son whom he receiveth. If ye endure chastening, God dealeth with you as with sons; for what son is he whom the father chasteneth not? But if ye be without chastisement, whereof all are partakers, then are ye bastards, and not sons. Furthermore we have had fathers of our flesh which corrected us, and we gave them reverence: shall we not much rather be in subjection unto the Father of spirits, and live?

Quoting Proverbs 3:11, 12, the author seems to change metaphors from running a race to disciplining children. But in reality, the best coaches are like dads. Yes, they get in the faces of their athletes from time to time—but it's because they want them to succeed, to excel, and to finish the race set before them.

"Wait a minute," you protest. "If the first eleven chapters of Hebrews are true, how can it be that here in chapter 12, all of a sudden we're talking about a Father who scourges His son? If it is true that He doesn't remember our sins and iniquities (8:12), and if it is true that we are completely sanctified through our High Priest, Jesus Christ (10:10), then how can God punish us for sin He doesn't remember or doesn't see?"

I submit two points for your consideration in this very important matter of the chastening hand of God. . . .

First, God's chastening is never punitive. It's corrective.

People would often travel great distances to worship in the temple. Upon their arrival, a priest would most likely meet them at the door, saying, "I'm sorry, but that ox you're bringing as a sacrifice has a problem—a little splotch under his left ear. But this is your lucky day. We just happen to have on hand preapproved oxen you can buy." Or worshipers would bring money to place in the offering, only to hear the priest say, "I'm sorry, but that money is not temple currency. You're in luck, however, because one of our moneychangers will be happy to take your money and give you temple currency—for a price, of course." Thus, the priests were becoming millionaires by ripping off people who had come to worship the Father.

In John 2, Jesus went into the temple, and finding pollution and corruption within, with scourge in hand, He overthrew tables, chased out livestock, and drove out moneychangers. So, too, we being the temple of the Holy Ghost (1 Corinthians 6:19), Jesus has every right and reason to come into our lives and throw out anything and everything that would hinder ours or anyone else's access to Him. His goal isn't punitive. It's corrective. His goal is to get rid of the stinky cattle, bleating sheep, and rip-off moneychangers who pollute our temples.

Second, God's chastening is never confrontational. It's consequential.

If you're a Christian, God does not confront you in a disciplinary manner for the sins that you have done or ever will do. Your sin is forgiven—past, present, and future. However, in Numbers 32:23, we read: "Be sure your sin will find you out." Notice it's not God finding us out—it's our sin. God is not sniffing around, searching for our failings and shortcomings so that He can have reason to punish us. No, the sin itself will track us down and deal with us in every single instance.

"Be not deceived," Paul says, "whatever a man sows, that will he reap" (see Galatians 6:7).

How many sins have repercussions?

Every single one.

How do I know? Check out Jeremiah 2. . . .

When the people of Israel were getting involved with all kinds of sin, God said, "Thine own wickedness shall correct thee, and thy backslidings shall reprove thee. . . ." (Jeremiah 2:19).

Did you catch that? *Thine own* wickedness shall correct thee. *Thy* backslidings shall reprove thee. It's not God, gang. It's the consequences of our own sin that bring their own tragic repercussions.

After slaying his brother, it seemed as though Cain got away with murder. After all, God even marked him for his own protection. Nonetheless, Cain was a fugitive all the days of his life, shunned and ostracized by the community that had once embraced him, because sin brings about its own repercussions.

Fearing for his own life, Abraham told Pharaoh his wife, Sarah, was his sister. Pharaoh in turn added Sarah to his harem. When Pharaoh released Sarah untouched, adding all kinds of servants, livestock, and possessions to pay for his error—it seemed as though Abraham got away with his lie. But among the servants given him by Pharaoh was a woman named Hagar, who would eventually bear the son who would shatter Abraham's family.

Although David was forgiven his sin of murdering Uriah following his adultery with Bathsheba, blood and tragedy flowed in David's family from that point on.

Sin stinks. God forgives it and doesn't even remember it. But the sin itself searches us out and has terrible repercussions.

After a game of hoops at the YMCA, you stop off for some drinks with the guys. On your way home, you plow into a wall. Your sin of drunkenness is forgiven and forgotten. But that doesn't change the fact that you're crippled for the rest of your life.

Truly, the work of forgiveness is finished. But the sin itself will be the scourging.

"Give me my inheritance," said the foolish son to his good father before heading to a far country where he spent freely on wine and women. He thought he was getting away with it—until the money ran out and he found himself living

in a pigpen (Luke 15). The father didn't put him in the pigpen. The father didn't send the police after him. The father just let it play out, knowing his son's own sin would correct him.

As believers, every sin we commit is forgiven. But even as believers, every sin we commit brings repercussion. Ask David or Moses, Abraham or Cain. So what do we do with the scars from our sin? The same thing Jesus did. After He was scarred in the process of absorbing our sin, He said to Thomas, "You who are cynical and skeptical, touch My wounds." And, in seeing the scars sin caused in Jesus, Thomas was rescued from his own sin and unbelief (see John 20:27, 28).

You may have blown a marriage. You may have lost your health. You may have bottomed out financially. Who knows what it might be that has scarred you permanently. I wish I could tell you your scar will go way. It won't. But if you say, "Lord, I give these scars that were brought on because of my sin to You to use," He will.

Hebrews 12:10 (a)
For they verily for a few days chastened us after their own pleasure . . .

The idea here is that our earthly fathers corrected us lest we be an embarrassment to them.

Hebrews 12:10 (b)
. . . but he for our profit, that we might be partakers of his holiness.

Everything God does in correcting us is not because we are an embarrassment to Him, but because He wants the best for us. And the best for us is that we drink deeply of His holiness, His wholeness.

Hebrews 12:11
Now no chastening for the present seemeth to be joyous, but grievous: nevertheless afterward it yieldeth the peaceable fruit of righteousness unto them which are exercised thereby.

No child says, "Oh, boy, I'm being disciplined!" No, it's grievous. Nevertheless, the fruit, the result of discipline is sweet indeed.

Hebrews 12:12, 13
Wherefore lift up the hands which hang down, and the feeble knees; and make straight paths for your feet, lest that which is lame be turned out of the way; but let it rather be healed.

This is great! The exhortation here is, "You've been disciplined. You've been injured and sidelined by your sin. But you've been healed by your Father. Now wipe away your tears and get back into the race, where you'll be able to run better than before."

Hebrews 12:14
Follow peace with all men, and holiness, without which no man shall see the Lord:

The word "follow," which can also be translated "pursue," gives further insight into the race we run. All athletes pursue something—be it health, wealth, or fame. Ours is a far more glorious prize, for ours is a pursuit of peace.

Hebrews 12:15
Looking diligently lest any man fail of the grace of God; lest any root of bitterness springing up trouble you, and thereby many be defiled;

A more proper rendering of this text would be: "Looking diligently lest any man fail *because* of the grace of God." Follow the flow here, gang, because it's intriguing. We're in a race, surrounded by witnesses cheering us on. We're to keep our eyes on Jesus, who is our example of how to run. We're to lay aside the stuff that slows us down. We're to realize the Father so loves us and wants us to win that, when necessary, He will discipline us. And we are to be careful of bitterness. Why? Because after we've been disciplined, we're vulnerable to bitterness toward those who enjoy God's grace.

"How come he's getting away with that? Why is she being blessed? They haven't been to church in three years, while I haven't missed a service in ten! How come I'm getting busted and they're not?" In this way, if we're not careful, the grace of God in the lives of others can actually produce the root of bitterness within us. Jesus knew this would happen. . . .

In need of laborers, the owner of the vineyard went to the town square early in the morning and hired some workers. Still needing more help, he returned at noon to hire more. At three o'clock in the afternoon he did the same thing, and again at five o'clock. At the end of the day, he paid the last hired a full day's wage. If those guys got that much" thought the men hired first, just think what we'll get! But when they were paid the same full day's wage, they became bitter.

"Didn't we agree on this?" asked the owner.
"Well, yeah," said the disgruntled laborers.

"But what about those guys? They only worked one hour."
"Why are you upset because someone else was the recipient of grace and mercy?" asked the owner (see Matthew 20).

Truly, the tendency for us, like the prodigal son's older brother of another parable, is to murmur and complain when grace and mercy are lavished on those whom we deem undeserving. And it ought not be—for the root of bitterness is far more deadly than it appears. . . .

Hebrews 12:16
Lest there be any fornicator, or profane person, as Esau, who for one morsel of meat sold his birthright.

Following the flow, Esau is cited as the biblical example of the fruit of the root of bitterness. Why did Esau sell his birthright—that which would have given him leadership spiritually and a double portion financially? Could it be because Esau was bitter over the fact that before he was born, God had said, "The elder, Esau, shall serve the younger, Jacob" (see Genesis 25:23)?

"It's not fair," Esau must have thought. And as a result, he sold his birthright for a bowl of beans. Consequently, Esau became a fornicator—a profane man.

"The first shall be last, and the last first," Jesus would say centuries later (see Matthew 19:30). Therefore, could it be that Esau had the potential to be even greater than Jacob in the eternal economy if he had accepted his role and embraced his lot? Perhaps. But he became bitter.

And that's just what happens today. People say, "Why should I live godly if those guys are getting blessed anyway? Why not just live a life of compromise?" And like Esau, their lives become a mess because of bitterness.

Hebrews 12:17
For ye know how that afterward, when he would have inherited the blessing, he was rejected: for he found no place of repentance, though he sought it carefully with tears.

This intrigues me, for this man who was initially a party animal, who initially tossed away his birthright without a second thought, later wept over the lack of his father's blessing. Truly, whether a man is spiritual or carnal, whether he is perceptive of the things of God or whether he walks away from God, every single son and daughter craves the blessing of their father.

Now think with me: Just as blessing could not be given because Esau was not interested in the birthright, so, too, we cannot despise our birthright if we expect to receive the blessing of our heavenly Father. "I want that blessing," people say as they read of the righteous never begging for bread (Psalm 37:25), of the Lord delivering those that fear Him (Psalm 34:7), or of the Lord upholding those who fall (Psalm 37:24).

But if they despise the birthright, if they don't see the need to be born again, the blessings will not be bestowed. The Book of Hebrews was written for those who desperately desired blessing but were unable to receive it because they wanted to earn it through rules and religion instead of relationship.

Hebrews 12:18–21
For ye are not come unto the mount that might be touched, and that burned with fire, nor unto blackness, and darkness, and tempest, and the sound of a trumpet, and the voice of words; which voice they that heard intreated that the word should not be spoken to them any more: (For they could not endure that which was commanded, And if so much as a beast touch the mountain, it shall be stoned, or thrust through with a dart: And so terrible was the sight, that Moses said, I exceedingly fear and quake:)

The law is awesome. Like the mount from which it was given, it quakes and shakes and is laden with power and possibility. But no one can keep it. And therein lies the problem, for all the blessings connected to it are impossible to touch or to receive.

Hebrews 12:22–24 (a)
But ye are come unto mount Sion, and unto the city of the living God, the heavenly Jerusalem, and to an innumerable company of angels, to the general assembly and church of the firstborn, which are written in heaven, and to God the Judge of all, and to the spirits of just men made perfect, and to Jesus the mediator of the new covenant . . .

Like Esau, you can try to gain the blessings of God with tears, by futilely trying to keep the law given on Mount Sinai—or you can go to Mount Zion, the heavenly mountain, the city of the Living God, and enter in to the New Covenant.

Hebrews 12:24 (b)
. . . and to the blood of sprinkling, that speaketh better things than that of Abel.

When Cain killed Abel, God said, "Abel's blood cries out to me" (see Genesis 4:10). What did Abel's blood cry? Justice. Judgment. Revenge.

Jesus' blood also cries out—not justice, but mercy; not judgment, but forgiveness; not revenge, but grace. Thus, the blood of Jesus Christ, the New Covenant, makes the birthright *and* the blessing available to me.

Hebrews 12:25–27
See that ye refuse not him that speaketh. For if they escaped not who refused him that spake on earth, much more shall not we escape, if we turn away from him that speaketh from heaven: Whose voice then shook the earth: but now he hath promised, saying, Yet once more I shake not the earth only, but also heaven. And this word, Yet once more, signifieth the removing of those things that are shaken, as of things that are made, that those things which cannot be shaken may remain.

"In the year King Uzziah died, I saw the Lord," wrote Isaiah (6:1). Under the reign of Uzziah—one of the greatest kings in the history of Judah—wealth flowed throughout the Jewish empire, and the borders of the nation were not only protected but expanded. So powerful was he, it was said that his name was on the lips of everyone from Babylon in the north to Egypt in the south. But when did Isaiah see the Lord? In the year Uzziah *died*.

So, too, in each of our lives there are Uzziahs: good things, wonderful things—but things in which we trust and upon which we depend instead of trusting in and depending upon God. And because He loves us and wants the best for us, our Father says, "As good as Uzziah might be, he's not Me. As secure as you might feel because of his weaponry, it's not nearly as secure as you would be if you were looking to and leaning on Me."

Because we are so prone to put our trust in things that are not trustworthy, God shakes our world as surely as He shook Mount Sinai in order to knock away anything we are trusting in and living for. Gang, He loves you enough to say, "If year after year I let you trust in that, lean on him, or live for her, you will be a spiritual midget. I don't want that for you. You don't want that either. So, I've got to shake it to remove it, that you might again lean on Me, look to Me, and walk with Me—for then you'll be blessed, strengthened, and ready for eternity."

Hebrews 12:28 (a)
Wherefore we receiving a kingdom which cannot be moved . . .

I like this! Even though it takes some shaking to get us there, we eventually receive a kingdom that is stable and solid.

Hebrews 12:28 (b)
. . . let us have grace . . .

The author of this letter addressed to Jewish believers who had a tendency to lean on their traditions, their priests, and their sacrifices never misses an opportunity to draw their attention back to the finished work of the Cross, to the New Covenant, to *grace*.

Hebrews 12:28 (c), 29
. . . whereby we may serve God acceptably with reverence and godly fear: For our God is a consuming fire.

Serve Him with reverence and godly fear, for our God is indeed a consuming fire who will consume anything which distracts you from your relationship and dependency upon Him. If you are at a place where you're experiencing the fire of God, fear not, for if allowed to burn, the warmth and brightness of His love will, indeed, burn away all that is unfruitful and distracting in your walk with Him.

13 In chapter 11, we saw the walk of faith and in chapter 12, the wisdom of hope. Here in chapter 13, we'll see the way of love. Notice seven characteristics of this most important virtue. . . .

Hebrews 13:1
Let brotherly love continue.

Love flows among the saints.
The implication linguistically is that this love is not something you have to work at, pump up, or rally around. It's already there.
A man gave the following account. . . .

I was walking across the Golden Gate Bridge when I saw a man about to jump off. I tried to dissuade him from committing suicide and told him simply that God loved him. I noticed a tear came to his eye. "Are you a Christian?" I asked.
"Yes," he said.
"Me too! What a small world. Protestant or Catholic?"
"Protestant."
"Me too! What denomination?"
"Baptist."

"Me too!" I said. "Northern Baptist or Southern Baptist?"
"Northern Baptist."
"Northern Conservative Baptist or Northern Liberal Baptist?"
"Northern Conservative Baptist."
"Amazing!" I said, "Call Ripley. This is incredible! Northern Conservative Fundamentalist Baptist or Northern Conservative Reformed Baptist?"
"Northern Conservative Fundamentalist Baptist."
"Remarkable! Northern Conservative Fundamentalist Baptist Great Lakes Region or Northern Conservative Fundamentalist Baptist Eastern Region?"
"Northern Conservative Fundamentalist Baptist Great Lakes Region."
"This is a miracle!" I said. "Are you Northern Conservative Fundamentalist Baptist Great Lakes Region Council of 1879 or are you Northern Conservative Fundamentalist Baptist Great Lakes Region Council of 1912?"
"Northern Conservative Fundamentalist Baptist Great Lakes Region Council of 1912."
"Die, you heretic," I said—and pushed him over the rail.

Rather than dividing the body of Christ with labels and factions, we are to let brotherly love flow to the person sitting next to us, to our Baptist brothers, to our Episcopalian sisters, to the entire scope of Christianity.

Hebrews 13:2
Be not forgetful to entertain strangers: for thereby some have entertained angels unawares.

Love shows itself to strangers.
When the angels approached Abraham as he sat in front of his tent, he realized there was something supernatural about them (Genesis 18:2). There are those who take this verse to mean they should pick up every hitchhiker they see in the event he might be an angel. But such is probably not the case. As I read the Word, I am aware that when angels do appear, there's a sense within the hearts of those showing hospitality that they are entertaining someone unique.

Hebrews 13:3
Remember them that are in bonds, as bound with them; and them which suffer adversity, as being yourselves also in the body.

Love cares about suffering.

Love not only flows among the saints and shows itself to strangers but also cares about those in bonds, and those hurting physically.

Hebrews 13:4 (a)
Marriage is honourable in all, and the bed undefiled. . . .

Love clings to one's spouse.

Perhaps to counter the teaching of the Essenes, who abstained from marriage, as well as that of the gnostics, who discredited it, the author defends the divine design of marriage.

Hebrews 13:4 (b)
. . . but whoremongers and adulterers God will judge.

The Book of Proverbs makes it plain that if you give yourself outside of marriage, you will experience a destruction of your soul due to the fact that when two people come together physically, it is not only the melding of two bodies, but of two souls (Proverbs 6:32).

Hebrews 13:5, 6
Let your conversation be without covetousness; and be content with such things as ye have: for he hath said, I will never leave thee, nor forsake thee. So that we may boldly say, The Lord is my helper, and I will not fear what man shall do unto me.

Love brings satisfaction.

We can practice the admonition of verse 5 to be content because of the promise in verse 6 that Jesus will never leave us. You see, the degree to which I realize the Lord is with me, the degree to which I enjoy His fellowship intimately is the degree to which I will be content continually.

When you're newly married—living on beans and decorating with bookshelves made of bricks and boards—you have very little materially. But you don't even notice it because you're in love, and love brings true contentment and satisfaction. So, too, if I'm in love with the Lord, I will not covet. I will be content with whatever I have simply because He is with me.

Hebrews 13:7
Remember them which have the rule over you, who have spoken unto you the word of God: whose faith follow, considering the end of their conversation.

Love is seen in submission.

"How can I get my kids to respect the authority I have been given over them?" The answer is to base your words with your kids upon Scripture. Tell them not only what to do, but *why*—based upon the stories of the Old Testament, the parables of Jesus, the teachings of Paul. If I only tell my kids what to do and never why, they will ultimately rebel against what they will perceive as legalism. But if what I'm saying is based upon and illustrated by the Word, submission is not nearly the problem it would be otherwise.

It's amazing what God will bring to your memory as you're talking with your kids during devotions or over dinner. After all, didn't Jesus promise the Holy Spirit would bring all things to our remembrance? (John 14:26) Nothing, however, can be brought to your remembrance that was never stored in your memory. Read the Word, dear Mom and Dad—and teach it to your kids.

Hebrews 13:8
Jesus Christ the same yesterday, and to day, and for ever.

Love's source is Jesus.

The fact that love flows among the saints and shows itself to strangers; that it cares about suffering and cleaves to one's spouse; that it brings satisfaction and is seen in submission is all based upon the singular presupposition that Jesus is the source and that He'll never change.

Hebrews 13:9 (a)
Be not carried about with divers and strange doctrines.

On the Cross, Jesus didn't say, "To be continued." He said, "It is *finished*." Sacrifices, self-effort, works of the flesh, or anything else that diminishes this is a strange doctrine.

Hebrews 13:9 (b)
For it is a good thing that the heart be established with grace; not with meats, which have not profited them that have been occupied therein.

The author enjoins his readers to stay away from doctrines based upon rules and rituals, meats and sacrifices and, instead, keep their walk with the Lord based on grace. "But we miss the texture and tradition of the temple," some might have protested. "How can we truly worship without incense or an altar?" Read on.

Hebrews 13:10, 11
We have an altar, whereof they have no right to eat which serve the tabernacle. For the bodies of those beasts, whose blood is

brought into the sanctuary by the high priest for sin, are burned without the camp.

"Oh, but we do have an altar," maintains the author. "It's just outside the camp" . . .

Hebrews 13:12
Wherefore Jesus also, that he might sanctify the people with his own blood, suffered without the gate.

Leviticus 14, 16, and Exodus 29 are three Old Testament passages that speak of sacrifices on the Day of Atonement for the cleansing of leprosy and for the consecration of the priesthood that were offered outside the city.

So, too, Jesus left the temple, left the city, left all the traditions and regulations, all of the priestly robes and fragrant incense, all of the rituals with which people are enamored to be taken "without the gate" to a hill called Calvary.

Hebrews 13:13
Let us go forth therefore unto him without the camp, bearing his reproach.

"Get out of the camp," admonishes the author. "Leave the city. Leave religion. Leave traditionalism. Leave rules, rituals, incense, and candles. Leave it all." Contrary to the present fascination with icons and old pictures of Jesus and the disciples, the call of the entire New Testament is to walk by faith and *not* by sight.

Hebrews 13:14
For here have we no continuing city, but we seek one to come.

Like Abraham who searched for a city whose Builder and Maker is God, we don't have a city here. Thus, we have no reason not to follow Jesus outside the city, outside the restrictions of religion all the way to Calvary.

Hebrews 13:15
By him therefore let us offer the sacrifice of praise to God continually, that is, the fruit of our lips giving thanks to his name.

"I don't feel like praising the Lord," some say, "because the traffic bugs me," or, "because the dishes are getting to me." Gang, those are the *best* times to praise Him—for then it's a sacrifice of praise as you worship the Lord in spite of your own fleshly inclinations.

I talked to a young man at church who said,
"I don't know what's wrong. For several days I haven't felt close to the Lord."

"That's nothing," I said. "I've gone months feeling distant from Him."
"You have?" he asked incredulously.
"Yep."
"Doesn't that freak you out?"
"It used to," I answered—"until I understood that the Scriptures have much to say about ministering in season and out of season."

You see, in my Christian walk, I find myself going through seasons. There's springtime—when, with new understandings and fresh growth, I sense the Lord's presence in my heart. Springtime leads to summertime—those warm, wonderful days when the new growth bears fruit from which people glean. Summertime leads to fall—when the winds blow and shake the leaves off my tree. Fall leads to winter—when the fall winds give way to a cold, wintry, silence. I used to freak out in wintertime. Then I learned that if I am going to be a man who walks by faith and not by sight, I must not constantly monitor my feelings because feelings are fickle. The Lord allows you and me to go through regular seasons of wintertime, asking us, "Are you going to walk by the state of your emotions—or by the promises of My Word?"

This has allowed me the privilege of being a minister of the gospel regardless of any tragedy or heartache in my own life. Truly, if I hadn't learned the lessons of the winter season, I wouldn't be where I am right now. But the good news is this: Winter doesn't last forever. It gives way to spring.

During worship, some are elated, caught up in an overwhelming sense of the Lord's presence. And that's good. Others say, "I'm here. But I don't feel anything. However, I'm still going to lift my hands and my voice in a sacrifice of praise to the One who has done so much for me in the past, to the One whose touch I know I will feel again in the future." And that, in some ways, is even better.

Hebrews 13:16
But to do good and to communicate forget not: for with such sacrifices God is well pleased.

Not only is the expression of our love to the Lord sometimes a sacrifice, but the communication of encouragement can be a sacrifice as well. Have you ever witnessed the miracle of one of your kids thanking another of your kids? Doesn't it just blow your mind? Truly, few things are more delightful. So, too, don't forget to write that note of thanks to your sister in the Lord or to speak that word of encouragement to your brother in the Lord, because thereby our heavenly Father is well pleased.

Hebrews 13:17–19

Obey them that have the rule over you, and submit yourselves: for they watch for your souls, as they that must give account, that they may do it with joy, and not with grief: for that is unprofitable for you. Pray for us: for we trust we have a good conscience, in all things willing to live honestly. But I beseech you the rather to do this, that I may be restored to you the sooner.

There are leaders and mentors, pastors and teachers watching over us. And each must give an account before the Lord concerning their ministry to us.

Hebrews 13:20, 21

Now the God of peace, that brought again from the dead our Lord Jesus, that great shepherd of the sheep, through the blood of the everlasting covenant, make you perfect in every good work to do his will, working in you that which is wellpleasing in his sight, through Jesus Christ; to whom be glory for ever and ever. Amen.

The blood of Jesus has the ability to make us complete and whole. Truly, there is *power* in the blood.

For topical study of Hebrews 13:20, 21, see "There Is Power in the Blood," below.

Hebrews 13:22

And I beseech you, brethren, suffer the word of exhortation: for I have written a letter unto you in few words.

The fact that the author calls his thirteen-chapter letter only "a few words" long makes him a man after my own heart!

Hebrews 13:23–25

Know ye that our brother Timothy is set at liberty; with whom, if he come shortly, I will see you. Salute all them that have the rule over you, and all the saints. They of Italy salute you. Grace be with you all. Amen.

"Blessed are the poor in spirit," Jesus said, "for theirs is the kingdom" (Matthew 5:3). Who are the poor in spirit? People like you and me who realize that blessing can't be based on our devotion or diligence, sincerity, or spirituality due to the fact that we have none. It's *gotta* be grace because we're sinners. Our motives are mixed. Our flesh gets in the way. The kingdom belongs to the poor in spirit because they don't try to earn it. They just marvel at God's goodness in opening the Way.

So it is that I echo the author of this wonderful epistle and say, Grace be with you *all!*
Amen.

THERE IS POWER IN THE BLOOD
A Topical Study of
Hebrews 13:20, 21

Driving Santa Cruz's Highway 9 on my way home from a men's retreat, my mind was flooded with memories of numerous family camping trips to Big Basin—a beautiful state park situated in the midst of the Santa Cruz mountains in California. As my thoughts traveled back to those family vacations, I pictured all six of us climbing into our VW Bug—with luggage and our German Shepherd, Sam, in tow. And I could hear my mom praying, as she did before every trip, asking the Lord to bless our time together, pleading the blood to cover our car as we drove.

Sadly, the phrase "pleading the blood" is out of fashion in our day. And we are the poorer for it. But in the text before us, we see the power of the blood that can make us "perfect in every good work."

The phrase translated "make you perfect" is *katartizo*, a Greek word used in reference to the setting of a broken bone, to the mending of a fishing net, to the readying of a ship for a journey, and to the equipping of an army for battle.

Thus, it is through the blood that the broken bones of our bodies, our relationships, and our fellowship are set right. It is through the blood that the holes are mended in the nets of our vocation and finances. It is through the blood that we journey on toward heaven. It is through the blood that we battle against the Enemy. Physically, relationally, vocationally, spiritually, and eternally we are made perfect not by studying, counseling, or seminars. We're made perfect by one thing only: the blood of the everlasting covenant.

The blood has been supplied. The question is, is it being applied? "Sure, I'd like my family to do well, my home to be blessed," you say. "But how does it happen?"

The Blood Supplied

Leviticus 14 presents wonderful instruction concerning the blood as seen in the law of the leper. You see, throughout the Bible, leprosy served as an illustration of sin. Like sin, leprosy manifested itself insignificantly at first—just a little spot under the skin. But it went on to spread so insidiously that the afflicted one would be cast out of the community. According to Leviticus 14, anyone healed of leprosy was to be brought before a priest outside the camp. If the priest found him healed, indeed, the former leper was instructed to bring two sparrows, cedar wood, scarlet and hyssop. One of the birds was then killed in an earthen vessel. The other bird, along with the cedar wood, scarlet and hyssop, was dipped in the blood of the slain bird. Finally, the blood was also sprinkled seven times on the healed leper.

The picture of redemption is absolutely perfect. Like the leper of Leviticus 14, we come to our great High Priest, Jesus Christ and follow Him "outside the camp." Like the leper, the sacrifice our Savior made on our behalf consisted of the cedar wood of the Cross, the offering of His own Life, the scarlet of His blood, and the hyssop upon which He was offered drink (John 19:29). The earthenware vessel wherein the sparrow was killed speaks of humanity, while the released bird soaring to heaven speaks of deity. The blood sprinkled seven times speaks as much of completion as it does of the seven places from whence Jesus bled. . . .

- from His forehead in the Garden of Gethsemane,
- from His back due to the flagellum,
- from His brow due to the crown of thorns,
- from His face as His beard was plucked,
- from His hands nailed to the Cross,

- from His feet nailed to the Cross,
- from His side due to the soldier's spear.

Seven times Jesus' blood flowed, providing complete forgiveness for my sin, complete healing of my leprosy, and complete victory over the Enemy. . . .

In Revelation 12, we see a battle waged in heaven between the archangel Michael and the dragon, or Satan. Michael wins. The dragon is eventually cast out of Heaven. How? By the blood of the Lamb and the word of testimony which says,

And I heard a loud voice saying in heaven, Now is come salvation, and strength, and the kingdom of our God, and the power of his Christ: for the accuser of our brethren is cast down, which accused them before our God day and night.   Revelation 12:10

"Thy kingdom come. Thy will be done in earth as it is in heaven," Jesus prayed (Matthew 6:10). How do we overcome the dragon, our accuser, the devil? The same way it's done in heaven: Through the blood of the Lamb.

The way to overcome the Enemy in your children, your marriage, and your home, as seen in Revelation 12, Leviticus 14, and here in Hebrews 13, is not by counseling, not by attending workshops, and not by establishing support groups. The Enemy is overcome by the blood—for nothing else is powerful enough.

You see, in the Garden of Eden, in giving Adam dominion over the earth (Genesis 1:26), God, in effect, handed Adam the title deed to the planet. Adam, in turn, transferred ownership to Satan when he knowingly bought into Satan's lie. That's why Jesus calls Satan the prince of this world (John 12:31). That's why there are wars, famine, and heartache. That's why there is murder, disease, and death. These things are not God's fault. They are the consequence of man's rebellion.

But God had a plan. "I'm going to buy back the world by sending My Son, the sparrow, the Lamb, to die and pay the price for the sin of Adam and all humanity," He said. So He did. Pinned to the Cross, Jesus' blood was shed as payment for our sin. Truly, the world has been purchased back by the blood of the Son on Calvary. Therefore, Satan's days are numbered, and He will be dealt with in due season. Presently, however, he's exercising squatter's rights in this world—and possibly in your home.

Suppose while I'm at church, someone moves into my house. Finding this guy sitting in my living room, I dejectedly head to the market, get a shopping cart, and start walking the streets.

"What are you doing, Jon?" you would ask me.

"I'm homeless," I would say. "I went to church, and somebody moved into my house. I'm defeated. I'm discouraged."

"Let me get this straight," you'd say. "Someone moved into the house you bought—and you just let him have it?"

"Yeah," I would answer. "I don't know what else to do."

"Do you have a title deed to the house?" you'd ask.

"Yes."

"Well, go get the authorities. Show them the title deed, and move back into your house. It's yours."

The same thing happens spiritually. Satan has no authority, no right, no hold on you. All he can do is claim squatter's rights and say, "This depression will never lift. This addiction will never leave. Your daughter's going to blow it. Your son's going to rebel. Divorce is inevitable." And what do we do? We get our shopping carts and wander the streets in despair.

Satan the squatter takes up residence by falsely accusing us in three areas. Of our past sin, he accuses us day and night, saying, "You've fallen in this area so many times. You'll never make it." But the way we overcome past sin is by the blood.

"Wait a minute, Satan," we must say, "I may have failed a billion times, but the blood of the Lamb is absolutely inexhaustible. You might accuse me night and day, but the blood of Jesus Christ covers me completely, for where sin abounds grace abounds even more (Romans 5:20).

Concerning our present struggles, Satan cannot grasp, grip, or dominate any area to which the blood has been applied. I can choose to give in if I wish; I can succumb if I want. But in reality, the Enemy has no authority whatsoever because of the cleansing power of the blood.

Regarding future salvation, I think of Noah, who, in construction of the ark, provided a place of salvation for his sons and their wives twenty years before his sons were even born. "Believe in the Lord Jesus Christ and thou shalt be saved— and thy house," declared Paul (Acts 16:31). Am I suggesting salvation is inherited? No, everyone must make his own decision. But, like Noah, I can provide a place in which Satan will not be able to seduce my son or my daughter into walking away from the Lord if I apply the blood to my house.

How?

I suggest three ways. . . .

The Blood Applied

First, the blood is to be applied to our homes corporately.

After being held in bondage for four hundred years, the children of Israel prayed to the Lord and He raised up a deliverer named Moses.

"Thus saith the Lord," he announced. "Let My people go."

But reluctant to do so, Pharaoh subjected the nation of Egypt to a series of plagues—the last of which was the death of every firstborn son whose house was not marked with blood.

How were the houses to be marked? Each household was to kill a lamb, dip the brushlike hyssop plant into the blood and mark the top, sides, and threshold of the door—thereby forming a picture of a cross. Houses so marked were "passed over" by the death angel (Exodus 12:22, 23).

Why was the blood applied to the doorway? Because in that culture, the doorway was the most prominent part of the home. Entrances and exits were always made through the front door. Thus, the picture of a Cross was ever before them.

So, too, all who enter and leave our homes should be cognizant of a redemptive environment within—a place where the death angel is noticeably absent from the conversation and decor, from what we watch on TV and listen to on the radio.

Second, the blood is to be applied to our bodies individually.

In Leviticus 14:10–18, we see the remaining sequence of the law of the leper. That is, on the eighth day, a trespass offering was made in which some of the blood of the lamb slain was applied to the tip of the right ear, right thumb, and right big toe of the one who had been healed of leprosy. In other words, the blood was applied to the man's hearing, to his activity, and to his direction. Oil was then applied to those same three places.

"I want power to hear properly, to work effectively, to walk uprightly," we say. Oil being symbolic of the Spirit, the power of the Spirit can flow only where the blood has first been applied. Thus, there are those who long for the empowering of the Spirit without realizing that they first need the cleansing of the blood.

The blood has been supplied. The question is, will I apply it?

Will I go into my son Benjamin's room as he's sleeping, kneel beside his bed, lay my hand upon him, and plead the blood over him? It's powerful. It's potent. And you can do it, Dad and Mom. Teenager, you can kneel by your bed, lift your hands to heaven, and say, "Lord, thank You that the blood cleanses me from past failings, that it thwarts the attack of the Enemy, and that it secures my salvation."

Finally, the blood is applied in Communion practically.

"This is My blood shed for you," Jesus said. "Do this in remembrance of Me" (see Luke 22:19). Every morning in the sanctuary at Applegate Christian Fellowship, people can come, bow the knee, and plead the blood over themselves and their families at the Lord's table. It's available. It's supplied. But will it be applied? That's the only question.

Plead the blood, precious people—and as you do, realize pleading the blood of the Lamb is not a magical incantation. It's not "Open Sesame," or "Abracadabra." It's not a phrase or a mantra. It's understanding that the victory has already been won, that the price has been paid, that the work of the Cross is complete.

Put your shopping cart away, saint, and reclaim your house.

In Jesus' Name.

JAMES

Background to James

The author of the book before us is not James the brother of John, but James, the son of Joseph and Mary; James, the half brother of Jesus. Growing up in the same household with Him, no doubt Jesus' brothers had a hard time getting a handle on Him. This much we know from the Gospel account: Jesus' brothers didn't believe on Him until after His Resurrection—an event that was, even for them, irrefutable and undeniable. In fact, James was so convinced that his Brother was the Son of God that he went on to become a leader in the early church—as evidenced by the account in Acts 15, wherein we see him leading the council in Jerusalem.

As seen in their writings, the Jerusalem believers—James, Peter, and, to a lesser degree, John—tended to behave a bit more strictly than did Paul, Barnabas, and the Antioch believers who were primarily students and scholars of grace. Both groups were—and still are—very definitely needed in the body. It's sort of like a trampoline—pressure from both sides is needed if the trampoline is to stay taut. So, too, with discipline and grace—both are essential.

As we read, we'll see James make reference to the Old Testament forty-five times in this relatively short book, for not only was he related to the Living Word, but he was a man greatly given to the written Word.

JAMES

1 James 1:1 (a)
James, a servant of God and of the Lord Jesus Christ . . .

James certainly doesn't begin his epistle the way I would have. If I were James, I'm afraid I would have identified myself not as James, a servant of the Lord Jesus Christ, but as James the *brother* of the Lord Jesus Christ! James, however, was a man who, although he was very straightforward, as we shall see, was also known as a man of tremendous humility. He doesn't pull

rank; he doesn't drop names; he simply considers himself a servant.

James 1:1 (b)
. . . to the twelve tribes which are scattered abroad, greeting.

"The twelve tribes" is a reference to the Jewish people scattered throughout the world, who had come to a knowledge of the true Messiah and had become believers in Jesus.

James 1:2
My brethren, count it all joy when ye fall into divers temptations.

Newer translations render this verse "Count it all joy when ye fall into various *trials.*" Why? Because the Greek word for both "trial" and "temptation" is the same. You see, what God will send or allow as a trial to strengthen our faith, Satan will seek to exploit to get us to sin. Conversely, what Satan throws our way as a temptation, God allows to be a trial. Satan wants to use the event to tear us down and wipe us out; God wants to use the same event to show us how faithful He is and how real He can be.

Think of it this way: If Jerry, a master woodworker, invited me to sit in a chair he had made, I wouldn't do so wondering if it would hold me up, but rather I'd marvel at how well it was crafted. If, on the other hand, a prankster invited me to sit in a chair, I would be leery, knowing it would probably either be pulled out from under me, or collapse underneath me. So, too, the chair that Satan seeks to pull out from under us is the very one God uses to show just how strong He can be.

In the Book of Job, we see Satan trying to wipe Job out by afflicting him physically, causing him to lose his family, and ruining him financially. But God was proving something else. God was showing how faithful He would be. As a result, all of history would marvel in studying how, in the midst of what Satan meant for evil, God used it for good as He sustained Job all the way through and rewarded him ultimately.

When a trial comes your way, Satan will be there the same day to try to get you to do what Mrs. Job suggested her husband do—to curse God and die (Job 2:9). But God will be there as well, waiting to show you His strength in seeing you through.

James 1:3, 4
Knowing this, that the trying of your faith worketh patience. But let patience have her perfect work, that ye may be perfect and entire, wanting nothing.

Like the Jewish believers who were scattered throughout the Roman Empire and beyond, we're to count it joy when we go through trials and face temptations. Why? Because seeing God's faithfulness manifested in the situation, we'll be made entire and complete; we'll become mature. Maturity only comes through testing. Faith is made pure only when fiery trials burn away the dross.

James 1:5–8
If any of you lack wisdom, let him ask of God, that giveth to all men liberally, and upbraideth not; and it shall be given him. But let him ask in faith, nothing wavering. For he that wavereth is like a wave of the sea driven with the wind and tossed. For let not that man think that he shall receive any thing of the Lord. A double minded man is unstable in all his ways.

If you lack wisdom, ask God in faith, and He will give it to you.

For topical study of James 1:5–7 entitled "How to Know What to Do," turn to page 1520.

James 1:9–11
Let the brother of low degree rejoice in that he is exalted: But the rich, in that he is made low: because as the flower of the grass he shall pass away. For the sun is no sooner risen with a burning heat, but it withereth the grass, and the flower thereof falleth, and the grace of the fashion of it perisheth: so also shall the rich man fade away in his ways.

The Jewish Christians to whom James is writing would be well aware of an enemy that posed a threat to the people of God throughout their history. Led by giants like Goliath, the Philistines hassled the Jews continually. In our day, we don't fear Philistines, but it seems that finances bring us into as many trials and testing points. I don't know of a man or a woman who either at some point or regularly doesn't deal with a financial trial, wondering how to make ends meet. Whether individually, or as a church family corporately, finances have proven to be the Philistine that stomps and threatens us continually.

Knowing this, James reminds us that regardless of our financial situation on earth, we're exalted, elevated above the world system because we're part of a kingdom whose streets are paved with gold. Thus, whether we're worried about poverty or weighed down with riches, we can be absolutely free if we keep a heavenly perspective.

James 1:12
Blessed is the man that endureth temptation: for when he is tried, he shall receive the crown of life, which the Lord hath promised to them that love him.

Trials result not only in spiritual maturity but also in crowns eternally. Granted, you may not think crowns are a big deal now—but I guarantee you will in heaven, for your crown will determine whether you'll rule over ten cities, five cities, or no cities in heaven (Luke 19:11–27).

When you face trials and temptations, if you stay close to the Lord, you will hear Him say, "Well done, good and faithful servant," (see Matthew 25:21) and you will receive the crown of life specifically reserved for those who don't walk away from Him in trials or temptations.

James 1:13
Let no man say when he is tempted, I am tempted of God: for God cannot be tempted with evil, neither tempteth he any man.

Regarding the entire arena of trials and temptations, understand this: God will allow a trial; Satan will come with a temptation. The trial may be financial; the temptation may be cocaine to escape the pressure. It's not God who brings the cocaine your way. It's not God who tempts you with pornography. No, God simply allows the trial to come. It's Satan who brings the temptation.

Never, ever be mistaken on this point. The trial of our faith is to prove the faithfulness of God. It is never a temptation or an enticement to sin. Therefore, if you're half-drunk in a bar, the guy offering you free drugs is not God's way of saying, "I'm going to prove how faithful I am by sending this guy your way." No! That's a temptation you brought on yourself by placing yourself in that situation in the first place.

James 1:14, 15
But every man is tempted, when he is drawn away of his own lust, and enticed. Then when lust hath conceived, it bringeth forth sin: and sin, when it is finished, bringeth forth death.

Sin always brings forth death. Every time. Sin will kill relationships. It will destroy happiness. It will ruin health. When you want to tell kids how serious sin is and what sin does, the best thing you can do is take them to the Cross of Calvary and say, "Look at this wonderful, perfect, loving Person and see Him on the Cross in agony and pain and blood. It was when Jesus became sin for us that He died, for sin *always* brings death."

James 1:16
Do not err, my beloved brethren.

"Don't make a mistake about this," James says. Sin always results in death and tragedy. Paul would put it this way: Be not deceived. God is not mocked. Whatever a man sows, that shall he also reap (see Galatians 6:7).

James 1:17 (a)
Every good gift and every perfect gift is from above, and cometh down from the Father of lights . . .

The good gifts, the perfect things, and the cool stuff that come your way are solely because of God's grace and kindness and benevolence. You might be a gifted musician, an intelligent person, a hard worker. Those are gifts from God, by grace, that have nothing to do with your earning them. Therefore, there's no room for us to take credit for anything we are able to perform or achieve. Everything that is wonderful in your life is because of God's grace to you.

James 1:17 (b), 18
. . . with whom is no variableness, neither shadow of turning. Of his own will begat he us with the word of truth, that we should be a kind of firstfruits of his creatures.

Not only is God good in the gifts He gives, but in who He is. In Him there is no variableness or shadow of turning. That is, He's not moody. He doesn't have bad days. He's not generous with me one day, but grouchy the next—as I can so often be.

We're variable. We go up and down. God doesn't. He can be nothing but good. He doesn't react to me according to how I'm doing with Him. He is faithful when I am faithless (2 Timothy 2:13). He is good when I am grumpy. He doesn't change. He's locked into His nature.

That's why I love the Lord so much. He's solid as a Rock. And I can just enjoy Him without worrying about Him being ticked with me or tired of me. He gives nothing but good gifts, for He is a good God.

James 1:19
Wherefore, my beloved brethren, let every man be swift to hear, slow to speak, slow to wrath.

In talking to the believers dispersed throughout the Roman Empire, undergoing unbelievable persecution, James says, "Don't forget that God is good. And what's happening in you is going to work for good ultimately. Therefore, don't be cynical; don't be quick to complain about your situation. Instead, stop speaking and start listening—and you'll hear God's voice in your trial."

James 1:20
For the wrath of man worketh not the righteousness of God.

I hope you have this verse underlined—at least mentally—for being ticked-off and hot under the collar doesn't accomplish anything that proves to be right. Ever.

James 1:21 (a)
Wherefore lay apart all filthiness and superfluity of naughtiness . . .

Referring to the Word of God, "Let every man be swift to hear," James instructed us in verse nineteen.

"But I can't hear God's Word to me," we say.

Perhaps you can't hear the Word of God for you because your ears are clogged up with "filthiness and superfluity of naughtiness"—plain old sin. If I'm filling my ears with the music and the scenes, gossip, and junk of the world, I can't hear properly. I need to get rid of that stuff before I can really be tuned in to God's frequency.

James 1:21 (b)
. . . and receive with meekness the engrafted word, which is able to save your souls.

Perhaps I can't hear the Word of the Lord because my mind is made up. James tells us we are to receive the Word with meekness, the implication being, "Lord, I'm in this trial or temptation or difficulty, and I need direction from You. I need Your Word to direct me, or I'm not going to do well. Therefore, I come to You not with my own agenda or plan, but meekly. Whatever You say, that's what I'll do."

Many people don't hear from the Lord when they read the Word of God because they lack a spirit of meekness before Him.

James 1:22–25
But be ye doers of the word, and not hearers only, deceiving your own selves. For if any be a hearer of the word, and not a doer, he is like unto a man beholding his natural face in a glass: For he beholdeth himself, and goeth his way, and straightway forgetteth what manner of man he was. But whoso looketh into the perfect law of liberty, and continueth therein, he being not a forgetful hearer, but a doer of the work, this man shall be blessed in his deed.

Third, perhaps we can't hear from the Lord because we are mixed up. You see, so many times our tendency is to think that just because we're reading the Word, we're obeying it—at least that's the way it is with me. A lot of times I'll hear a sermon or read a book and I'll say, "Right on. I agree with that." But I deceive myself if, having seen what needs to be taken care of in the mirror of the Word, I then don't do it. One of the great dangers for us who love the Word is to falsely assume that simply agreeing that we should pray means we're praying; or knowing we should worship makes us worshipers.

James clearly warns us not to think that seeing our reflection properly means we're doers of the Word automatically. If the Lord shows you in the Word that you need to praise Him, don't say, "Good point"—but start praising Him right then! If the Lord shows you in the Word that you need to get right with a brother, don't say, "Someday"—do it right then. Be a *doer* of the Word.

With ears clogged up, mind made up, or all mixed up, we won't hear from the Lord. But reading the Word with meekness and then obeying it is the best hearing aid there is.

James 1:26
If any man among you seem to be religious, and bridleth not his tongue, but deceiveth his own heart, this man's religion is vain.

There's a teaching currently making the rounds that says, "Be honest with God. Tell Him what you really feel. Tell Him you're ticked off." I shudder at such teaching. Oh, it might be popular psychologically, but it's not right biblically. A truly religious man, a deep man, does not pop off and throw temper tantrums at God. God is God, and we're not. God is good, and we're not. If there are problems in our lives, He's not wrong. We are.

James 1:27
Pure religion and undefiled before God and the Father is this, To visit the fatherless and widows in their affliction, and to keep himself unspotted from the world.

This verse is Applegate Christian Fellowship's mission statement for its ministry to handicapped orphans in Mexico. I pray it is a practical mission statement for our own lives as well—for James cuts to the bottom line here when he says that rather than being a matter of compromise and verbosity, true religion is a matter of purity and humility.

HOW TO KNOW WHAT TO DO
A Topical Study of
James 1:5–7

His father, who had been deeply loved and mightily used would be sorely missed. One of the greatest men in all of history, his father was a man who, in addition to being able to leap over walls physically, was so gifted musically that he not only composed songs, but he invented the instruments to play them. So courageous of heart was he that when he was but a teenager, he conquered a giant in battle, making him so popular that women sang songs about him in the streets. This one's father, of course, was David.

And now that David had passed from the scene, Solomon would step up and try to fill his father's shoes—a seemingly impossible task. After learning of his father's death, Scripture tells us that Solomon headed for Gibeon, for in Gibeon was a tabernacle, a place to meet God. That night, the Lord appeared to Solomon in a dream, saying, "Whatever you ask of Me, I'll do for you" (see 2 Chronicles 1:7).

"Lord," said Solomon, "I ask of You wisdom. I need to know how to go out and come in amongst these, Your people."

By God's grace, this young man, who had tremendous responsibility suddenly placed upon him and very difficult obligations looming before him, was given the wisdom to ask for wisdom.

So pleased was God with Solomon's request that He said, "I will not only grant you wisdom greater than any other man—but I will give to you more wealth and fame than any other person has ever enjoyed, victory over your enemies, and length of days" (see 2 Chronicles 1:11, 12). In other words, by asking for wisdom, Solomon got everything else thrown in.

Personified as a woman, wisdom says this:

> I love them that love me; and those that seek me early shall find me. Riches and honour are with me; yea, durable riches and righteousness. My fruit is better than gold, yea, than fine gold; and my revenue than choice silver. I lead in the way of righteousness, in the midst of the paths of judgment: That I may cause those that love me to inherit substance; and I will fill their treasures.
>
> Proverbs 8:17–21

Wisdom cries out to simple men—dumb, unsophisticated, naive, common people like you and me, saying, "If you walk with me, I will cause you to have riches and success in all that you do" (see Proverbs 8:5).

How do we get wisdom? The text before us says if any man lacks wisdom, let him ask of God who gives to all men generously. What does it mean to ask of Him?

In Solomon's day, in Old Testament times, if someone needed wisdom, for example concerning who to marry, where to move, what job to take, he would go to Jerusalem where he would find the high priest. As part of his vesture, the high priest wore a pouchlike breastplate upon which were twelve gems, each representing one of the tribes of Israel. It seems that these gems were instrumental in the dispensing of wisdom. You see, according to Exodus 28:30, if one had need of wisdom or direction personally, or if the people had need corporately, the high priest would consult the Urim and the Thummim. Although we can't say dogmatically what the Urim and the Thummim were, we do know what the words mean: "urim" means "light"; "thummim" means "perfection"—perfect light to give direction.

How did they work?

It would seem as though the stones on the breastplate of the high priest that were linked to the Urim and the Thummim would light up in such a way that, using the letter of the tribe each represented, an answer would be spelled out. The problem was that, with only the high priest having the Urim and the Thummim, anyone having a question would have to travel all the way to Jerusalem and make an appointment with him to get an answer. Getting wisdom was not an easy thing to do!

There's an infinitely better way for you and me to get light and perfection, for Jesus said, "I am the Light of the world" (John 8:12); and Paul said in Him are hidden all the treasures of wisdom and knowledge (Colossians 2:3). Thus, Jesus fulfills the Urim and Thummim perfectly. We go to the One who is Light personified, who is Wisdom incarnate, and say, "Lord, what should I do in this situation?"

How does He answer? I suggest three ways. . . .

Through His People

It was God's people—the twelve tribes of Israel—who symbolically flashed the message on the breastplate of the high priest. So, too, Scripture says God's people are jewels in His crown (Zechariah 9:16). You may not feel like a gem; you may not think the person sitting next to you is of very much value—but on the heart of our High Priest, Jesus Christ, we are just that.

Where no counsel is, the people fall: but in the multitude of counsellers there is safety.   Proverbs 11:14

Where there is no counsel, people fall—or literally, stumble—in the dark. But as I talk with my brothers, as I share with God's people, the light shines through them in the counsel they give to me.

Through His Word

Thy word is a lamp unto my feet, and a light unto my path. The entrance of thy words giveth light; it giveth understanding unto the simple.

Psalm 119:105, 130

I can't tell you how many times when, wondering what I should do or which way I should go, I'll hear someone share from the Word on the radio, and it speaks directly to my situation. Or I'll open the Scriptures, a commentary, or a devotional book and find the Word of God giving perfect light to me.

Upon Our Hearts

But this shall be the covenant that I will make with the house of Israel; After those days, saith the LORD, I will put my law in their inward parts, and write it in their hearts; and will be their God, and they shall be my people.

Jeremiah 31:33

Paul picks up this same idea when he says, "Let the peace of Christ rule in your heart" (Colossians 3:15). The word translated "rule" is an interesting one. A term linked to sports, it was used with regard to officiating or umpiring. In other words, the peace of Christ will call "Safe!" or "Out!" in your heart, giving you light and direction.

I find that these three avenues work together very harmoniously: Through God's people there is safety. In God's Word there is light. Upon my heart, He'll write His will. So I can know whether I should make that move or take that job by simply asking the Lord, knowing He'll make His will known to me through His people, in the Word, or upon my heart if I ask in faith.

What does it mean to ask in faith?

The integrity of the upright shall guide them . . .   Proverbs 11:3

The Hebrew word translated "integrity" is *tummah*—from the same word as *thummim*. In other words, direction and integrity are linked together. What does the word "integrity" mean? It means "integrated" or "single." Thus, the single-minded man of integrity says, "Father, I'm not asking for wisdom out of curiosity. I'm committed to doing what You tell me."

Anyone who's not sure if he's really going to follow through is double-minded and should not expect to receive direction from the Lord. But to the man who asks in integrity, the man who is single in purpose and heart, God will give wisdom generously.

"But what if I misinterpret His will on my heart, through His people, or in the Word?" you ask.

I believe the answer lies in Genesis 20—where we see the first mention of integrity in the Bible.

> Eager to become acquainted with the newest acquisition to his harem, Abimelech looked forward to meeting Sarah—until God appeared to him in a dream, saying, "The woman you've taken is another man's wife."
>
> "In the integrity of my heart I have done this," Abimelech answered.
>
> "Yea, I know thou didst this in the integrity of thy heart, for I also withheld thee from sinning against Me. Therefore I allowed thee not to touch her," the Lord replied.

What's being said here is wonderful, for God is saying, "Abimelech, you made a mistake. But your heart was right, so I protected you in the decision you made."

This means that when I ask God to give me wisdom, He gives me direction through His people, in His Word, and upon my heart. But even if I don't hear correctly and make a wrong decision, if my heart is right, the Lord will protect me and correct me just as He did Abimelech.

So many people never move out because of the paralysis of analysis. That is, they're always analyzing a situation to determine what they should do. The Genesis 20 account frees us from this, for if our hearts are right, we can move ahead, knowing that He will protect us even if we're moving in the wrong direction.

Dear saint, as you pray today, I encourage you to do what you know, and you'll know what to do. You know that you should be in fellowship Sunday morning, studying the Word with your brothers and sisters. I don't know what I'm to do tomorrow. I don't know what's ahead for me next month or next year. I simply know what I'm supposed to do today. So I do what I know today, and when tomorrow comes, I'll know what to do then. You will too.

If you lack wisdom, ask of God. And if you do that in faith, you'll be doing what you know. Then through His people, through His Word, and through His will upon your heart, you'll know what to do as you walk in the Light of the Perfect One, Jesus Christ.

---

2 **James 2:1–4**
My brethren, have not the faith of our Lord Jesus Christ, the Lord of glory, with respect of persons. For if there come unto your assembly a man with a gold ring, in goodly apparel, and there come in also a poor man in vile raiment; and ye have respect to him that weareth the gay clothing, and say unto him, Sit thou here in a good place; and say to the poor, Stand thou there, or sit here under my footstool: Are ye not then partial in yourselves, and are become judges of evil thoughts?

If you knew that in ten minutes you would have a half-hour meeting with Donald Trump, would you comb your hair, brush your teeth, think about what you would say? What if you knew that in ten minutes you would meet with a homeless man? Would you expend the same kind of energy?

This is what James is getting at. We're all vulnerable; we're all guilty of treating people differently, depending on how we view them outwardly. But almost without exception, the irony is that the people we try to impress the most are those who care about us the least—while the people who really would be open to receiving from us are those for whom we think we don't have time.

On the high-school campus, so often the goal is to see the quarterback or the head cheerleader saved. The real key, however, is to go for the kid who sits in the back of the cafeteria all alone, for he's the one who is most often the one ready to listen. The same holds true where you work. We tend to get all excited about the people we highly esteem financially or professionally, economically or intellectually. But it's the poor people who will be most responsive to the gospel and most welcoming of us. Because we so often waste our time trying to impress people who are impressed with themselves, we need to change our perspective.

That is what James is championing. "Why is it," he asks, "that when someone comes into your congregation who is dressed in fine clothes, who has a name, or who is esteemed highly, you give him the best seat in the house?" Oh, how we need to be aware of our own fleshly tendencies.

James 2:5–9
Hearken, my beloved brethren, Hath not God chosen the poor of this world rich in faith, and heirs of the kingdom which he hath promised to them that love him? But ye have despised the poor. Do not rich men oppress you, and draw you before the judgment seats? Do not they blaspheme that worthy name by the which ye are called? If ye fulfil the royal law according to the scripture, Thou shalt love thy neighbour as thyself, ye do well: But if ye have respect to persons, ye commit sin, and are convinced of the law as transgressors.

It would seem as though whenever certain wealthy people who weren't part of the body made a guest appearance at church, they were ushered to the front and given the best seats. James, however, was not impressed.

James 2:10, 11
For whosoever shall keep the whole law, and yet offend in one point, he is guilty of all. For he that said, Do not commit adultery, said also, Do not kill. Now if thou commit no adultery, yet if thou kill, thou art become a transgressor of the law.

James goes on to say it's not only how we view others externally, but how we think about ourselves internally that matters. "Don't you realize," he asks, "that because the law is a single unit, if you say you've never committed adultery, yet you've murdered someone, you're guilty of adultery, too?"

It's like the space shuttle. The space shuttle is designed to go up into the heavenlies. But if any one part of it is not functioning properly or is flawed in any way, it won't lift off. So, too, you may not have killed anyone or committed adultery. But if you've lied, your shuttle is grounded.

James 2:12, 13
So speak ye, and so do, as they that shall be judged by the law of liberty. For he shall have judgment without mercy, that hath shewed no mercy; and mercy rejoiceth against judgment.

Luke 6:38 is a verse often used in relation to the giving of tithes and offerings. But from the context, we know that when Jesus said, "Give, and it shall be given unto you; good measure, pressed down, and shaken together, and running over, shall men give into your bosom. For with the same measure that ye measure it shall be measured to you again," He was speaking not of money but of mercy.

In other words, if you are merciful to others, if you are forgiving toward others, if you are kind and compassionate with others, then when you need mercy and grace and kindness—and you will—it will be given to you. But if you have been harsh and judgmental, if you have been fault-finding and sin-sniffing, when you need mercy from others, there will be none for you.

James 2:14–26
What doth it profit, my brethren, though a man say he hath faith, and have not works? can faith save him? If a brother or sister be naked, and destitute of daily food, And one of you say unto them, Depart in peace, be ye warmed and filled; notwithstanding ye give them not those things which are needful to the body; what doth it profit? Even so faith, if it hath not works, is dead, being alone. Yea, a man may say, Thou hast faith, and I have works: shew me thy faith without thy works, and I will shew thee my faith by my works. Thou believest that there is one God; thou doest well: the devils also believe, and tremble. But wilt thou know, O vain man, that faith without works is dead? Was not Abraham our father justified by works, when he had offered Isaac his son upon the altar? Seest thou how faith wrought with his works, and by works was faith made perfect? And the scripture was fulfilled which saith, Abraham believed God, and it was imputed unto him for righteousness: and he was called the Friend of God. Ye see then how that by works a man is justified, and not by faith only. Likewise also was not Rahab the harlot justified by works, when she

had received the messengers, and had sent them out another way? For as the body without the spirit is dead, so faith without works is dead also.

Arguing that faith without works is dead, the Book of James so incensed Martin Luther that the reformer called it "a veritable straw Epistle that should be thrown into the Rhine River." Yet James proves that faith without works is dead by pointing to the example of Abraham. It's not that Abraham was saved by taking Isaac up the mountain to sacrifice him in obedience to God. No, James says the work that saved Abraham took place years before that when he simply believed in God (verse 23).

When was Abraham declared righteous? As James quotes Genesis 15:6, we understand that Abraham was declared righteous when he simply believed God would do what He said He would do when He told Abraham He would make his descendants more numerable than the sand on the seashore. Interestingly, Paul would also point to Abraham as proof that man is justified by faith apart from works (Romans 4:3).

James and Paul are in full agreement because they both maintain that the moment Abraham simply believed God was the moment God imputed righteousness unto him.

It is not faith *and* works that saves a man. It is not faith *or* works. It is faith *that* works. All Abraham was doing on Mount Moriah was showing the reality of what had taken place in his life years earlier when he simply believed God.

If your faith is real, it will show itself. How? By obeying the Word of God and following the leading of the Lord, even though you may not understand where it will lead. At the time, Abraham could not have understood the significance of what he had done on Mount Moriah. But this side of Calvary, we see it was a perfect picture of what God the Father would do in sending His Son to that same mountain to die for the sins of the world.

You know you're truly born again when you find yourself obeying God. We're not saved by obedience. But our obedience proves we're saved, for true faith works.

❧

3 In chapter 2, James stressed that mere words are not the issue. The proof of one's salvation is seen in works. Yet here in chapter 3, we'll see him plunge into a discussion about the tongue. Why? I suggest the reason is that, although it is true that it is our works and not our words that validate and verify our salvation, this does not mean words are not important in our spiritual life . . .

James 3:1, 2 (a)
My brethren, be not many masters, knowing that we shall receive the greater condemnation. For in many things we offend all.

James begins his discussion by saying, "Don't be eager to be a teacher because teachers can receive greater condemnation." Because it is inevitable that sooner or later we offend people with the words we say, the more a person says, the greater his chances of offending someone. Jeremiah certainly found this to be true. . . .

When the people of Israel didn't like what Jeremiah was saying, they threw him into a prison—at which time Jeremiah decided he would speak no more. But there's a problem with those who are called to teach. As Jeremiah discovered, the Word of God burned in his heart, and he could not keep quiet (Jeremiah 20:9).

If, like Jeremiah, you are called to teach the Word, you will be unable to keep quiet, even though it might mean you're tossed into a storm of controversy or a dungeon of condemnation.

I wish I could say that all of the problems teachers encounter are due to the powerful messages we bring and the conviction they cause in the hearts of people. But that's not the whole story—not by a long shot! You see, greater condemnation comes to teachers because in the multitude of words there lacketh not sin (Proverbs 10:19). We who are always speaking inevitably say things we wish we hadn't said or in a way we wish we hadn't said them.

Thus, condemnation comes not only from other people, but from within our own hearts when we realize our inadequacy to communicate the Word properly.

"Be careful," says James. "Don't be too eager to be a teacher, knowing that you'll receive greater condemnation from within and without than if you sat quietly in a pew, taking it all in."

The longer I walk with the Lord, the more I see that the key to life is to learn to be content where God has placed you (Philippians 4:11). If you're called to teach, that's great! If you're called to listen, that's wonderful! In either place, contentment is the key.

James 3:2 (b)
If any man offend not in word, the same is a perfect man, and able also to bridle the whole body.

Whoever does not offend in word is a mature person whether he is a teacher or not, for he who controls his tongue controls his life.

James 3:3–6
Behold, we put bits in the horses' mouths, that they may obey us; and we turn about their whole body. Behold also the ships, which though they be so great, and are driven of fierce winds, yet are they turned about with a very small helm, whithersoever the governor listeth. Even so the tongue is a little member, and boasteth great things. Behold, how great a matter a little fire kindleth! And the tongue is a fire, a world of iniquity: so is the tongue among our members, that it defileth the whole body, and setteth on fire the course of nature; and it is set on fire of hell.

Just as surely as an insignificant-looking rudder controls an entire ship, or a little piece of metal controls a powerful horse, so the tongue, weighing a mere twenty ounces, can either bring direction or destruction—for truly the power of life and death is in the tongue (Proverbs 18:21).

What can we do to keep our tongues from being ignited by the fires of hell?

In Acts 2 we read of another tongue of fire, one which led to worshiping and witnessing. Therefore, I suggest that the more time we spend praying in tongues, the less time we'll spend preying on others with our tongues.

Where no wood is, there the fire goeth out: so where there is no talebearer, the strife ceaseth.
Proverbs 26:20

When you hear gossip, pray silently in the Spirit to keep your tongue busy lest you join in the hellish discussion. If I listen to gossip, to put-downs, I am actually an accomplice in that fire ignited by hell. But if I refuse to listen and pray instead, the water of the Spirit douses the fire of hell, and the conversation dies.

James 3:7, 8
For every kind of beasts, and of birds, and of serpents, and of things in the sea, is tamed, and hath been tamed of mankind: But the tongue can no man tame; it is an unruly evil, full of deadly poison.

Here's the problem: In our own energy, we cannot tame our tongues. We need the Lord.

James 3:9, 10 (a)
Therewith bless we God, even the Father; and therewith curse we men, which are

made after the similitude of God. Out of the same mouth proceedeth blessing and cursing . . .

"Cursing" implies any words that bring hurt to someone.

James 3:10–12 (b)
My brethren, these things ought not so to be. Doth a fountain send forth at the same place sweet water and bitter? Can the fig tree, my brethren, bear olive berries? either a vine, figs? so can no fountain both yield salt water and fresh.

"We live in a pleasant area," said the men of Jericho to the newly anointed prophet. "But our crops are dying because our water is poisoned."

So what did Elisha do? He poured salt into the water, and the water became sweet once again (2 Kings 2:21).

Salt was to be poured into polluted water? Yes, because Paul tells us our speech is always to be seasoned with salt, that is grace (Colossians 4:6). What does this mean? It means that in any given moment I can bring healing to an otherwise poisonous situation by speaking grace. If I keep talking about how gracious God has been to me, and how gracious He'll be toward others, the polluted puddles of put-downs and pettiness will become pools of purity and praise.

I want this in my life so badly I can taste it. Oh, I'm far from what I should be—but I see the wisdom of James, for I've known people who have refused to listen to gossip and who have, instead, learned to speak graciously. There is a beauty about their lives and refreshment from their lives I so desire. If you want to be the man or woman God uses, join me in praying that we will be those who add the salt of grace to everything we say.

James 3:13, 14
Who is a wise man and endued with knowledge among you? let him shew out of a good conversation his works with meekness of wisdom. But if ye have bitter envying and strife in your hearts, glory not, and lie not against the truth.

Come to terms with the fact that if your words are bitter, it's because your heart is bitter. Out of the abundance of the heart, the mouth speaks (Matthew 12:34). Bitter words come from a bitter heart.

James 3:15–18
This wisdom descendeth not from above, but is earthly, sensual, devilish. For where envying and strife is, there is confusion and every evil work. But the wisdom that is from above is first pure, then peaceable, gentle, and easy to be intreated, full of mercy and good fruits, without partiality, and without hypocrisy. And the fruit of righteousness is sown in peace of them that make peace.

I have this verse underlined because it is a grid through which I can run any conversation, teaching, or any word of instruction. If there is envy and strife, tension and confusion in what I hear, then I know it's from hell. But if there is purity and peace, righteousness and mercy in what I hear, I embrace it as being from the Lord.

May God give us wisdom, and may our words as well as our actions reflect His goodness, His gentleness, His grace.

4 James is not interested in how great we talk. He's interested in how straight we walk. After establishing this firmly in chapters 1 and 2, we saw him back up somewhat in chapter 3 to say that although what we say does not eclipse what we do—our words still make an impact.

"Out of the abundance of the heart, the mouth speaks," Jesus declared (Matthew 12:34). So here, in chapter 4, we'll see James deal with the issue of the heart.

James 4:1, 2
From whence come wars and fightings among you? come they not hence, even of your lusts that war in your members? Ye lust, and have not: ye kill, and desire to have, and cannot obtain: ye fight and war, yet ye have not, because ye ask not.

The reason we put down other people, gossip about other people, fight with other people is because we want something from other people. It can be as stupid as thinking, *Talking about that guy will make me look better to this guy.* Yet the only way to get what our heart really craves is not to prey on others, but to pray to the Father.

James 4:3
Ye ask, and receive not, because ye ask amiss, that ye may consume it upon your lusts.

"I do pray," you may say. "But I don't get what I ask for."

That's because you're asking amiss. Prayer is

not giving orders. It's reporting for duty. And once a person finally understands that prayer is not man saying, "Bless the business; bring in the money; solve the problem," and God saying, "Aye, aye, Captain," his prayer life will be revolutionized.

Prayer is saying, "Father what do *You* want to do in my life? I want You to do what You see is best for me because I get mixed up so easily."

I walked into his room during his nap to find one-year-old Peter-John lying on his back, eagerly reaching for an object dangling just inches above his head. Living in a rustic cabin in the woods at that time, we were sometimes surprised by the visitors we would have. And this particular afternoon was no exception, for I was surprised indeed to see the object for which Peter was so intently reaching was a black widow spider.

We're just like Peter-John. We lie on our beds or kneel beside them and, through prayer, grab for things we think would be so wonderful, failing to realize they are nothing but black widows. Therefore, every bit as exciting to me as prayers God does answer are those He doesn't answer because I know I'll see that what I thought was so intriguing and tantalizing will prove to be poisonous and deadly. Oh, may we learn not to give orders or grab spiders, but to do what Jesus did in the Garden: to submit to whatever the Father has for us.

James 4:4
Ye adulterers and adulteresses, know ye not that the friendship of the world is enmity with God? whosoever therefore will be a friend of the world is the enemy of God.

Because the Father looks at the world system and sees corruption and danger, pollution and problems—if we continue to reach for the trinkets of the world, we'll be at odds with God.

James 4:5
Do ye think that the scripture saith in vain, The spirit that dwelleth in us lusteth to envy?

"Lusteth to envy" means "guards jealously." In other words, the Spirit of God that dwells within us wants the very best for us. When we talk about grieving the Holy Spirit, we must understand the Spirit is grieved not because we've hurt Him, but because—seeing what's ahead for us if we continue on the path we're on—He hurts for us.

If you're a dad, you can understand this. . . .

Your sixteen-year-old daughter can't stop talking about him. So finally a week or two later, he shows up on his Harley in black leathers, a marijuana joint hanging out of his mouth, a swastika tattooed on his arm, a patch over his eye, a flask of whiskey in his pocket, a Playboy bunny on his shirt, saying, "I like your daughter."

Although your daughter says, "Isn't he dreamy?" you know he's nothing but a nightmare—and that she'll be hurt badly if she gets on his Harley and goes down the road of life with him.

That's how the Holy Spirit feels when He sees us getting on the back of some Harley we think is dreamy. He's not mad *at* us, not disappointed *in* us, not hurt *by* us, but jealous *for* us as a dad is for his daughter.

James 4:6 (a)
But he giveth more grace.

Even when I'm asking for the wrong things—grabbing for spiders or dreaming of Harleys—God gives more grace to resist the temptation and/or to recover from the situation because where sin abounds, grace abounds more (Romans 5:20).

James 4:6 (b)
Wherefore he saith, God resisteth the proud, but giveth grace unto the humble.

Although God has grace to give to us to resist the temptation or to recover from the situation, there's no room for pride. Who is the proud person? Barometers predict storms by measuring air pressure. Prayer-ometers indicate pride by measuring prayer pressure.

If I don't pray in a given day, it is the ultimate indication of pride because it is the proud person who says, "I don't need to pray about it. I can handle it." Oh, I may not be cocky like Dennis Rodman or Mike Tyson, but if I'm not praying, I'm every bit as proud as they are because prayerlessness is the truest indicator of pride.

James 4:7
Submit yourselves therefore to God. Resist the devil, and he will flee from you.

How many of you have ever had a hard time getting to Bible study, but somehow got there? I commend you because had you succumbed to those pressures, you would have faced them again and again. You see, gang, because Satan isn't omniscient, because he can't read your mind or see into your heart, he's dependent solely upon

trial and error to see what works. Therefore, if he sees that a headache will keep you from worship and Bible study, guess what will happen. You'll have headaches perpetually. If he sees that your kids acting up causes you to pull back, stay home, and not be where you should be, he'll have found the key to slowing down your walk.

I am convinced that many people experience unnecessary hell in their homes or trials in their lives because they don't understand this verse. They don't realize that if they resist the devil, he will indeed flee.

Behind the cyclone fence of a house I used to jog by regularly was a little mousy dog. Every time I ran by, this little yapper would start at one corner of the yard and snap and bark at me the entire length of the fence. He's crazy! I used to think—until it hit me one day that the only reason he was running alongside me barking noisily was because he thought he was winning. He thought he was chasing me away. So he did this over and over again because he thought it was working.

Satan is the same way. The Bible says that when we see him, we'll say, "Is this little yapper the one who troubled the whole earth?" (see Isaiah 14:16).

How can we stop him? By resisting him.

One day, I just stopped and roared at the yappy little dog. He put his tail between his legs, rolled over on his back, and started shaking. At that point, the front door opened, and a lady peeked out, saying, "Pastor Jon?"!

Resist the devil and he will flee from you—just as surely as did that little mouse of a dog!

James 4:8 (a)
Draw nigh to God, and he will draw nigh to you.

One of my favorite verses in all of the Bible: Draw nigh to God, and He might draw nigh to you. No. Draw nigh to God, and He will sometimes draw nigh to you. No. Draw nigh to God, and He *will* draw nigh to you. That's a promise! Don't let anyone cast aspersions on God's goodness or nature by saying, "I tried to get close to the Lord, but He is just so far from me." The Bible says He will draw nigh—always.

People say to me, "I've tried, but I can't seem to connect with God."

"I don't believe you," I lovingly answer, "because God's Word says He will always draw near to us if we draw near to Him. And I have found this promise to be true, for, without fail, every time I have been serious about seeking God, He has made Himself known to me through a Scripture, in my heart, or through the body of Christ."

Sometimes, gang, we need to lovingly say to those who whine about feeling far from God, even though they claim they have tried to draw near to Him, "You're deceiving yourself, or you're trying to deceive me because God's Word says that if you take the time and expend the energy to draw near to Him, He *will* draw near to you."

James 4:8 (b)–10
Cleanse your hands, ye sinners; and purify your hearts, ye double minded. Be afflicted, and mourn, and weep: let your laughter be turned to mourning, and your joy to heaviness. Humble yourselves in the sight of the Lord, and he shall lift you up.

Draw near to God, and He will draw near to you. When? When you're serious about seeking Him. The idea is to be serious about it, to turn off the TV, to take some time and make an effort. Why? Not because God is saying, "Only when you mourn and are afflicted will I speak to you." That's not it at all. The purpose of mourning and cleansing is not so that God will speak—but to get me tuned in to the right frequency so I can hear Him already speaking. Think of it this way. . . .

Right now, Channel 10 is broadcasting all sorts of words and images. But we aren't tuned in to the frequency. To get the picture, we'd have to take some time, bring in a TV, and put up the antenna. Would we do that to impress Channel 10 to send pictures our way? No. They're already doing that constantly. We'd have to bring in a TV and put up an antenna simply to get us in the position to receive what's already being broadcast from Channel 10 continually.

If people don't read this passage right, they begin to say, "If we afflict ourselves like the prophets of Baal on Mount Carmel, if we slash our bodies and dance in a frenzy, God will speak" (see 1 Kings 18). That's not the heart of the Father. That's the heart of a false god. The purpose of washing your hands and humbling your heart implies quitting your normal activities and taking some time to get tuned in to the proper frequency. Go to the park. Get away. Do whatever it takes to change your setting and say, "Lord, I've been tuned in to work. I've been dialed in to parenting. I've been positioned to pursue my hobbies. But now I'm taking time to hear from You

because I know You're broadcasting twenty-four hours a day, and I want to hear what You say."

James 4:11
Speak not evil one of another, brethren. He that speaketh evil of his brother, and judgeth his brother, speaketh evil of the law, and judgeth the law: but if thou judge the law, thou art not a doer of the law, but a judge.

What law is James talking about? The law of love. Galatians 5:14 says, "All the law is summed up in this one word: love." Jesus said, "Upon loving God and loving our neighbor hang all the law and the prophets (see Matthew 22:40). So here James is saying, "Don't speak evil of any brother or sister. If you do that, you're not obedient to the law of love."

James 4:12
There is one lawgiver, who is able to save and to destroy: who art thou that judgest another?

One of the greatest days in my own Christian walk was the day the Lord whispered a very simple truth into my heart that changed my entire approach to ministry and to life. He said, "Jon, you love 'em, and I'll judge 'em." You see, before that, I had it the other way around. I thought it was the Lord's job to love people and my job to judge them. I can't tell you how freeing it was to discover that I had it backward!

James 4:13–15
Go to now, ye that say, To day or to morrow we will go into such a city, and continue there a year, and buy and sell, and get gain: Whereas ye know not what shall be on the morrow. For what is your life? It is even a vapour, that appeareth for a little time, and then vanisheth away. For that ye ought to say, If the Lord will, we shall live, and do this, or that.

There are people who have tremendous confidence in what they're going to do because they think they have their future all worked out. But in reality, of a group this size, statistics indicate that two of us will not be here next year. Life is a vapor. It goes oh, so quickly.

James 4:16
But now ye rejoice in your boastings: all such rejoicing is evil.

Putting my hope in my plans, projections, or portfolio instead of in the Lord is not only foolish. James tells us it's evil.

James 4:17
Therefore to him that knoweth to do good, and doeth it not, to him it is sin.

There are those who say, "I'm going to do this. I'm going to retire there. I've got my future all worked out." But when asked if they're going to church on Sunday or if they'll have devotions tomorrow, they say, "If the Lord wills." Do you see the irony?

"I'm going skiing next week, or on vacation in July," we say. But regarding church tomorrow night, we say, "We'll see what God has in store." We have it backward! We should be saying, "I may go skiing next week if God wills. Or, I may take a vacation in July if that's what the Lord has for me. But as for going to church on Sunday? I'll be there absolutely!"

That's why James says, "If you know what's right, but hide behind the excuse of waiting for God's leading before doing it, it's sin."

5 Continuing where he left off in chapter 2, here in chapter 5, James attempts to do what his half Brother had done when He cleansed the temple, as he cleans house concerning wealthy people who had no real relationship with the Lord, but who simply liked to be seen in the midst of the believers....

James 5:1–3
Go to now, ye rich men, weep and howl for your miseries that shall come upon you. Your riches are corrupted, and your garments are motheaten. Your gold and silver is cankered; and the rust of them shall be a witness against you, and shall eat your flesh as it were fire. Ye have heaped treasure together for the last days.

Because the language in verse seven makes it clear that he is addressing the true believer, James' harsh words here in verse three are not directed to true brothers, but to those who were only playing church. They are directed to those who thought they would be saved in the last day because of their wealth. They are directed to those who were using their money to be esteemed highly in the church.

James 5:4–6
Behold, the hire of the labourers who have reaped down your fields, which is of you

kept back by fraud, crieth: and the cries of them which have reaped are entered into the ears of the Lord of sabaoth. Ye have lived in pleasure on the earth, and been wanton; ye have nourished your hearts, as in a day of slaughter. Ye have condemned and killed the just; and he doth not resist you.**

"You've made your money because you paid poor wages. You've made your fortunes at the expense of others," says James. "But know this: The Lord is hearing the cries of those you have exploited."

James 5:7, 8
Be patient therefore, brethren, unto the coming of the Lord. Behold, the husbandman waiteth for the precious fruit of the earth, and hath long patience for it, until he receive the early and latter rain. Be ye also patient; stablish your hearts: for the coming of the Lord draweth nigh.

Shifting gears and addressing the true believer, James says, "Yes there will be injustice, rip-offs, and unfairness, but keep this in mind: The Lord is coming. He sees what's going on, and *He* will settle the score."

James 5:9
Grudge not one against another, brethren, lest ye be condemned: behold, the judge standeth before the door.

Salvation is not going to come through union participation or a Christian coalition organization. Salvation is going to come when Jesus Christ comes back. Stick to the big picture. Live for the kingdom. Be looking for His coming.

James 5:10, 11
Take, my brethren, the prophets, who have spoken in the name of the Lord, for an example of suffering affliction, and of patience. Behold, we count them happy which endure. Ye have heard of the patience of Job, and have seen the end of the Lord; that the Lord is very pitiful, and of tender mercy.

Job was a wealthy man. Then he lost everything. But if you read the last chapter of the book that bears his name, you see that he ended up with twice as much as he had before his difficulties began. Even his family was replenished. Why? Because he was patient. Yes, he had periods where he doubted and questioned God. But he's an example of a man who endured difficulty and of one who was rewarded greatly. So, too, we are to wait patiently for the Lord's return.

James 5:12
But above all things, my brethren, swear not, neither by heaven, neither by the earth, neither by any other oath: but let your yea be yea; and your nay, nay; lest ye fall into condemnation.

I know of a man who was so determined to learn this lesson that once a week for over forty years, he took one day to fast from talking.

Truly, the Bible tells us that in the multitude of words there lacketh not sin (Proverbs 10:19). The more I talk, the more trouble I can get in. So James very practically says we are to keep our speech as simple and straightforward as possible.

James 5:13 (a)
Is any among you afflicted? let him pray.

What if we really believed this? What if we said, "I'm not going to speak so much or so quickly. I'm not going to hold a grudge against people even if I feel they're afflicting me. Instead, I'm going to pray"? What a simple, workable, radical idea James presents to us.

This is hard for me because I want to mix it up verbally with those who afflict me and give them a piece of my mind. But I'm wrong every time I do because our fight is not against flesh and blood, but against principalities and powers (Ephesians 6:12).

There's no way we can continue to justify our tendency to fault folks or to war against them with words when James clearly tells us that the only solution to oppression is to look for the Lord's coming. In the meantime, when we're afflicted, we're to watch our words. Let them be yea, nay, and by all means—pray.

James 5:13 (b)
Is any merry? let him sing psalms.

There are psalms for every occasion. That's what's so great about the one hundred fifty psalms in the center of our Bibles. For every occasion, for any situation, there is a psalm for us to sing.

James 5:14 (a)
Is any sick among you? let him call for the elders of the church; and let them pray over him . . .

The affliction of verse thirteen is a mental, spiritual, or emotional affliction. The responsibil-

ity of the afflicted person is to pray. But the responsibility of the person who is sick physically is to call for the elders of the church.

"I was sick and none of the elders came to pray for me," you say.

Did you call for them?

James says it is the responsibility, the privilege, the opportunity, the command, for the sick person to humble himself and to call for the elders. Notice the word "elders" is plural. When the sick are being prayed for, it is always to be by a group of men corporately rather than one man individually. Why? There are few things more potentially dangerous than for a person to be used in the ministry of healing because what begins as a simple desire to be used by the Lord can so easily end up in book-signings and a speaking tour. To keep this tendency in check, James says when someone is sick, a group of men is to pray so that no one man will get the credit.

James 5:14 (b)
. . . anointing him with oil in the name of the Lord.

What does it mean to anoint with oil? In Scripture, we see oil used symbolically, when, as an illustration of the anointing of the Holy Spirit, prophets, priests, and kings were anointed with oil before they assumed their positions of authority. We also see oil used medicinally, as in the story of the Good Samaritan who put oil on the wounds of the man left for dead (Luke 10:34).

I suggest that the anointing of oil spoken of by James refers to both the symbolic and the medicinal realms. It speaks of a person saying, "I'm looking to the Lord for healing. I'm submitted to His will being done in my life; I believe in His power and presence—and I'm going to use His gift of medicine as well." There are two streams of healing: prayer and medicine. But it's the same God who works through both streams. Medicine does not heal. Prayer does not heal. God heals.

James 5:15 (a)
And the prayer of faith shall save the sick, and the Lord shall raise him up . . .

What is the prayer of faith? It is not prayer offered due to working up feelings emotionally or hyping a congregation into a frenzy, but as a result of responding to the Lord personally.

No doubt Peter and John had passed him hundreds of times as he sat by the Gate Beautiful outside of the temple, begging for money. But one day as they walked by him, something unique happened within them that caused them to stop, look at him, and say, "Silver and gold have we none, but such as we have give we you. In the name of Jesus, rise up and walk" (see Acts 3:6). In the moment of the miraculous, Peter and John experienced faith unlike at any other time they had walked by this man previously.

So, too, there will come times when you're praying for your friends, family, or yourself when you'll suddenly sense God at work in a unique way, and you'll know a miracle is about to take place.

But what if you don't experience this kind of faith? Pray anyway.

I've prayed for perhaps thousands of sick people over the years. A few were healed immediately. Others continued in their sickness. Many weren't healed until they got to heaven. Yet even if it doesn't bring about the full healing we anticipate, something wonderful always happens whenever a group of people talk to the Father.

It's good for a person going through physical suffering to call for the elders of the church to pray for healing—and to continue seeking healing until he is healed. Or until, like Paul, he is at peace, knowing that God's will is being worked out in his condition, and that even in weakness, God is made strong (2 Corinthians 12:9).

James 5:15 (b)
. . . and if he have committed sins, they shall be forgiven him.

Sometimes, sin brings sickness. How do I know this? Because after He healed the lame man in John five, Jesus said, "Be careful that you don't sin lest a worse thing happen to you" (see John 5:14), implying that his paralysis was the result of a previous sin. So, too, when the four guys lowered their paralyzed buddy through a roof in the home wherein Jesus was teaching, Jesus linked the man's paralysis to sin (Mark 2:5–11).

Does this mean sin is always the reason for sickness?

No. When asked whether it was his own or his parents' sin that made a man blind, Jesus answered that neither his or his parents' sin was the reason (John 9:3). While sickness can indeed be a repercussion of a sin or a lifestyle, this doesn't mean that every sickness is the result of an individual's sin.

James 5:16 (a)
Confess your faults one to another, and pray one for another, that ye may be healed.

Many of us have an obsession with confession. That is, we think that if there is any unconfessed sin in our lives, God will not hear our prayer. But I have good news for us today, for to us who understand that Jesus died for our sins past, present and future, regarding His work on the Cross, He doesn't say, "To be continued if you confess." No, He says, "It is *finished*."

For topical study of James 5:16 entitled "True Confession," turn to page 1534.

James 5:16 (b)–18
The effectual fervent prayer of a righteous man availeth much. Elias was a man subject to like passions as we are, and he prayed earnestly that it might not rain: and it rained not on the earth by the space of three years and six months. And he prayed again, and the heaven gave rain, and the earth brought forth her fruit.

"Well, that knocks me out," you say, "because I'm not Elijah; I'm not a righteous man, and I'm not an effectual, fervent pray-er."

You might be surprised. . . .

For topical study of James 5:16 entitled "Effective Prayer," turn to page 1536.

James 5:19, 20 (a)
Brethren, if any of you do err from the truth, and one convert him; let him know, that he which converteth the sinner from the error of his way shall save a soul from death . . .

The Greek word translated "err" is *planao*, from which we get our word "planet." It literally means "heavenly wanderer" and in this context refers to one who is headed for heaven ultimately, but is wandering presently. Those who "err from the truth" may, indeed, be born again. They may, indeed, have a relationship with the Lord. But it's distant because it lacks the connection that was there previously.

What causes a person to become *planao*, to become spiritually spaced-out?

Because at the heart of every problem lies a problem of the heart, I believe a person stops traveling with the body of Christ when a problem in his heart causes him to be uncomfortable in the presence of God's people. Such was the case with Demas. "Demas has forsaken us," said Paul.

Why? Because "he has loved this world" (see 2 Timothy 4:10).

If you asked Demas about his absence, he might have been able to justify it doctrinally, saying, "I'm having a problem with Paul's doctrine of justification. I find it to be too grace-oriented. So now I'm just seeking God and getting instruction on my own."

Just as he did with Demas, Satan wants to see us disconnected, out in space, cut off. But James says that if we convert such a one, if we get him to turn back and get involved once again, we have actually saved him from death.

What kind of death?

First, we have saved him from physical death (1 John 5:16). There is a sin, in which, if a man or woman continues to persist, God will take him or her home prematurely. If a person is rebelling against the Lord and walking farther and farther away from Him, such a one is in danger of being blown out into outer darkness. So God in His mercy may say, "It's time to take this person to heaven." While this obviously doesn't mean that anyone who dies before the age of ninety is out of fellowship, the Word does, indeed, declare that there is sin that will cause a person's life to end sooner than it would have had he continued walking in fellowship.

"Why should we try to convert such a one if he's headed to heaven anyway?" you ask.

The answer is that, although he will make it to heaven, he will enter in as though by fire, bankrupt spiritually, lacking the rewards that will affect his ability to enjoy heaven eternally (1 Corinthians 3:15).

Second, if we convert a brother who errs, who has wandered away, we save his soul from spiritual death. Because the wages of sin is always death, as you watch people who aren't plugged in, who aren't walking with the Lord as closely as they once did, you see death in their lives—the death of joy, the death of purpose, the death of peace. Their eyes become dull. Their faces become drawn. They start looking sad as they trade vitality for mortality.

Third, saving an erring brother from death could mean saving him from eternal death. The reason the debate has gone on for centuries concerning whether a Christian can go so far that he ends up forfeiting his salvation is because Scripture can be used to argue both sides. If this issue were cut and dried, a lot of people would drift farther and farther out in space. But because it is not, we have to realize that one's eternal destiny is at stake.

James 5:20 (b)
. . . and shall hide a multitude of sins.

The interesting thing about this phrase is that, linguistically, one can't be sure if it's the sins of the sinners that are covered, or those of the person who converts him. Commentators are divided on this question, yet all I know is this: Every time I talk to someone who has wandered away, every time I see the unhappiness and emptiness of his life, I find myself turning, repenting, and hating sin all over again. Conversely, like the shepherd who found the one sheep that was lost, when I am able to return to the fold someone who was lost and wandering, I experience an explosion of joy within my own heart.

How are we to convert those who err, those who wander away?

First, we're to be men and women of prayer—we're to talk to God about people. Second, we're to be men and women who share—we're to talk to people about God.

After engaging in a real estate deal that resulted in the death of an innocent man, Ahab, king of Israel, was confronted by Elijah the prophet. "Because of what you've done, because the dogs have licked the blood of the man you killed, the dogs will lick your blood and the blood of all of your children," Elijah declared. "If they die in the city, the dogs will lick their blood. If they die in the fields, the birds will peck their flesh. You crossed the line, Ahab. You went too far. And your family's going down as a result" (see 1 Kings 21:19).

The account in 1 Kings goes on to say that after Ahab heard Elijah, he rent his clothes, wore sackcloth, and walked softly, stooped over, broken. Because Ahab humbled himself, God instructed Elijah to tell him that his family wouldn't be annihilated.

So here's the wickedest man in the history of the nation Israel, and what does God do? Because Elijah talked to him, he repented and God was able to show him mercy.

Talk to the Lord about people. Then talk to people—even if they're Ahab-like—about the Lord. Your own sin will be covered in the process—and you will save from death the soul of the one with whom you share. It's a tall order to be involved in the restoration of a sinner who was once part of the kingdom. It's also a great privilege.

The Epistle of James ends in a most unusual, but not very surprising manner. Most New Testament Epistles end with a closing benediction. Not

James. There is no closing benediction. There is
no doctrinal conclusion. There is not even a
prayer of intercession. In fact, in closing his book
simply with a practical and pointed exhortation,
it's as though James is saying, "I've given to you
the Word of the Lord. Now go do it."

TRUE CONFESSION
A Topical Study of
James 5:16

If we confess our sins, he is faithful and just to forgive us our sins, and to
cleanse us from all unrighteousness.   1 John 1:9

I think many of us coming from church backgrounds have a misconception of
the idea of confession. I know I did. For many years, I believed that if there was any
unconfessed sin in my life, God would not hear my prayers. Consequently, I went
through decades gripped by the "paralysis of analysis." I knelt at my bed or by my
desk trying to confess everything I did or thought that day or that week, wondering
all the while if there was anything I left out, any unconfessed sin that would keep
me from being heard by my Father in heaven—or, worse yet, which would prevent
me from being forgiven by Him.

If, like me, you were ever under that impression, I have good news for you today: According to the context, 1 John 1:9 is not talking about you, but about those
who don't even acknowledge that they're sinners. You see, in John's day, a school of
thought called Gnosticism propounded that because the material realm is not eternal, it doesn't matter what a man does with his flesh. He can eat, drink, and be
merry because only the spiritual is eternal.

This is the issue John was dealing with when he said, "If you say you have no
sin, you deceive yourselves and the truth is not in you. But if you confess your sin—
if you admit that you're a sinner—God will be faithful and just to forgive your sin
and to cleanse you from all unrighteousness." In other words, "You cannot be forgiven, you cannot be born again, you cannot be saved until you admit you're a sinner
in need of a Savior."

I don't think many of us are involved in the gnostic heresy. We know we've
sinned; we know we've blown it; we know at least one time somewhere we dropped
the ball and messed up. And once we acknowledge this, our sin is forgiven—for on
the Cross, Jesus didn't say, "To be continued if you continue to confess." No, He
said, "It is *finished*" (John 19:30).

This means that we can stand confidently in the presence of God—not because
of who we are, but because of what He did for us on the Cross of Calvary.

"Okay, then," you say, "if that's true, then how do you explain the text before us: 'Confess your faults one to another, and pray one for another, that ye may be healed'"?

Confession is not for the purpose of restoration to our Savior. Confession is for liberation from our sin. We don't have to worry about being restored to the Lord once we believe in Him because He paid for every sin we've ever done, are doing, or ever will do. The veil is rent. The way is open. The invitation is given to us to come boldly to the throne of grace to find mercy and help in time of need (Hebrews 4:16). It's a done deal. Thus, the purpose of confession is not for God's sake. It's for ours. It's not for restoration, but for liberation—to set us free.

Consider four ways confession liberates us from sin. . . .

Confession Promotes Prayer

Confession promotes prayer. How? Confession produces compassion, and compassion produces intercession. Human nature is such that most of us don't pray very intensely for people we think are doing well. But because our hearts go out to those we think are hurting or struggling, we find ourselves praying on their behalf. Therefore, if you want people to pray for you, one of the most practical things you can do is confess your faults to someone or to a small group of people. Then watch how they'll pray for you.

Confession Provides Protection

Confession provides protection from potential hostility. The Enemy seeks to cause whatever I'm struggling with, whatever you're wrestling with to be exposed. That's his method of operation. He sucks us into sin, then publicizes our sin to bring consternation, embarrassment, and division.

> As Peter preached on the Day of Pentecost, Luke records that the other eleven disciples stood with him (Acts 2:14). Keep in mind, it had only been a month or so since Peter had denied even knowing Jesus. Thus, by standing with him, the other disciples were in effect saying, "We know Peter's history. Yet we continue to stand by him. So pipe down, you who would be hostile and critical of him."

That's what confession does. It disarms the Enemy.

Confession Prohibits Pride

> In the interest of accountability, three ministers gathered to confess their faults to one another.
>
> "I'm sad to say this," said the first minister, "but I've been struggling with whiskey. I just keep hitting the bottle after every service and every evening."

The second minister said, "I must confess quite frankly that I've been struggling with women."

The third minister said, "I confess I have a problem with gossip, and if you'll excuse me, I've got to make some phone calls. . . ."

People say, "If I confess my faults to another, what will happen if they leak out?"

You know what will happen? Your pride will be destroyed, and that's the best thing that could happen! Although we're so careful to cultivate a certain image, the Lord has ways of making sure it never lasts because pride leads to destruction and a haughty spirit to a fall (Proverbs 16:18). Ask Lucifer. It was when pride filled his heart that he was cast out of heaven (Isaiah 14:12–15).

Confession prohibits pride, and in so doing, it breaks our otherwise tragic fall.

Confession Produces Praise

The church of Jesus Christ is the only place I know where people come together and admit they're a bunch of losers who have problems. Go to the Elks Club or Rotary or the GOP fundraisers, and you're not going to see a group of people saying, "We're idiots. We failed again. We dropped the ball." It just doesn't happen that way! In every other organization, people get together to say, "Aren't we great?" But we, the church, come together to say, "Isn't God gracious? That He would use people like us with all our faults and failings is nothing short of amazing!"

Sin will lose its grip if you take seriously this command, this invitation to confess and pray for one another. Whatever you do, know this: You are forgiven and you can experience liberation if you confess your faults one to another.

I love the Lord. I love the theology of being forgiven. I love the practicality of confession. I'm so glad I'm saved. And I'm glad you are too.

EFFECTIVE PRAYER
A Topical Study of
James 5:16–18

All of us know there is power in prayer. Most of us understand that our priority is to be prayer. After all, we know that although the disciples observed Jesus raising the dead, healing the sick, feeding the multitudes, preaching the Word, walking on water, and casting out demons, they asked Him to teach them how to do only one thing. They asked Him to do the one thing they understood to be foundational to everything else He did. They asked Him to teach them to pray (Luke 11:1).

We, too, understand that there is power in prayer, that our priority is to be prayer—yet most of us have a problem with prayer because simple exhortations like the one before us become subtle intimidations to us.

In our text, I suggest the problem lies in three words. . . .

Effectual

James tells us very clearly that it is *effectual* prayer that avails much—and uses a man named Elijah as an example of effectual prayer. . . .

The first time we meet Elijah, he's storming into King Ahab's court, saying, "It's not going to rain but according to my word." Scripture records that the clouds, indeed, went away and no rain fell on Israel for three and a half years (1 Kings 17:1).

How could Elijah speak with such boldness? James tells us something we wouldn't know from reading the Old Testament account when he tells us Elijah prayed earnestly.

What does it mean to pray earnestly? The Greek word translated "prayer" is *deesis*, which means "to bow down." The Greek word translated "earnestly" is *proseuche*, which means "to pray." This means Elijah could speak to Ahab with certainty and could pray effectively because he was bowed down, submitted to the Scriptures.

You see, Deuteronomy 11:16, 17—a text Elijah would surely have known—says this:

> Take heed to yourselves, that your heart be not deceived, and ye turn aside, and serve other gods, and worship them; and then the LORD's wrath be kindled against you, and he shut up the heaven, that there be no rain, and that the land yield not her fruit; and lest ye perish quickly from off the good land which the LORD giveth you.

Aware of this promise, Elijah could say to Ahab, "Because of what you have done in this land by introducing Baal worship, it's not going to rain."

Time passed, and in a confrontation with Elijah, the prophets of Baal found themselves on Mount Carmel praying hour after hour for their god to send fire as they danced and screamed and slashed their bodies. Finally, Elijah said, "You've been going all day, boys. Your god has baal-ed out. Now it's my turn."

> And it came to pass at the time of the offering of the evening sacrifice, that Elijah the prophet came near, and said, LORD God of Abraham, Isaac, and of Israel, let it be known this day that thou art God in Israel, and that I am thy servant, and that I have done all these things at thy word. Hear me, O LORD, hear me, that this people may know that thou art the LORD God, and that thou hast turned their heart back again.   1 Kings 18:36, 37

And, after praying this prayer that takes about seven seconds to utter, fire came down.

"Do not be like the heathen who think they are heard because of their much speaking," Jesus said (Matthew 6:7)—and then gave us for a model a prayer sixty-five words long that takes less than fifteen seconds to say slowly. We think we have to impress God with lengthy prayers and fancy words. Jesus says, "No, that's the way of the prophets of Baal, the way of the heathen. Just talk to Me simply."

Elijah knew the Word, was submitted to the Word, and prayed according to the Word. So, too, we must understand that to pray effectively is to combine prayer with reading the Word. You will never again snooze through a service or doze off during devotions if you are praying while you're listening. That is, when a point comes to you that you know is convicting you, talk to the Lord about it *right then.*

> For years, I didn't know this. I thought the right way to fellowship with God
> was to read a chapter or two in the Word and then pray. But that is as silly as
> if I called Tammy and said, "We've got to talk," and then I proceeded to talk
> for ten minutes straight—talk, talk, talk, talk, talk—before saying, "Now you
> talk"—at which point she'd talk, talk, talk, talk to me.

That's the way I thought I was supposed to communicate with the Lord. "Okay, Father, I know You speak to me through Your Word, so I'll listen, listen, listen, listen. Done. Now it's my turn. Pray, pray, pray, pray, pray."

I'm not saying you can't do it that way, but there's a much better way. That is, as you are reading the Word, a phrase or two will strike you, and you pause right then to talk it over with the Father. You pray about it *right then.* Then you read a verse or two or three more until something else stirs your thinking or strikes your heart. You pause, then talk to the Lord again. With tens of thousands of precepts, principles, and promises in this book, I guarantee you'll never have a boring devotional time if you pause, then talk to the Lord again. With tens of thousands of precepts, principles, and promises in this book, I guarantee you'll never have a boring devotional time if you pray with open Bible and talk to the Father about you read.

So, too, if you go to church on a Sunday morning or Wednesday evening and say, "Every time a point hits me, confuses me, or stirs me, I am going to pray about it right then." Bible studies will never, ever again be drowsy for you because it's just impossible to talk to the Father as you're taking in the Word and find yourself bored and slumbering.

"If you abide in Me—stay close to Me—and My words abide in you," Jesus declared, "you shall ask whatever you will and it shall be done" (see John 15:7). "If My Word is stirring in you and you're staying close to Me, you'll be able to ask whatever you want as you pray biblically, and it will happen. You'll see."

To pray effectually is to pray biblically.

Fervent

James tells us that it is not only effectual prayer that avails much, but *fervent* prayer. And, again, Elijah is our model. . . .

After calling down fire with a prayer that took only five or six seconds to utter, and after telling Ahab it was going to rain, Scripture records that there, on the top of Mount Carmel, Elijah placed his head between his knees and prayed for rain.

"Any clouds coming?" he asked his servant.

"There's not a cloud in sight. It's clear and sunny," his servant answered.

So Elijah put his head between his knees again and prayed some more.

"Any clouds yet?" he asked.

"It's as clear as a bell," his servant answered.

So Elijah put his head between his knees and prayed a third time.

"Any clouds yet?"

"Nothing."

Elijah did this a fourth time, a fifth time, a sixth time. But when he popped up the seventh time, his servant said, "There's a little tiny cloud the size of a man's fist on the horizon."

"Great!" said Elijah. "Batten down the hatches! A storm's coming!"

And indeed it did (1 Kings 18:45).

If you lived in Bible times, you would know that to give birth, a woman would place her head between her knees. That's exactly what Elijah was doing. Prior to this, we saw him standing serenely and praying expectantly. Now we see him praying with fervency, with his head between his knees.

"But I thought we didn't have to go through contortions when we pray," you say. "I thought prayer was to be simple."

It is.

Then what's Elijah doing?

There come times, gang, when in prayer I will go to the Father and I will pray like Elijah in the first example. I'll pray simply, casually, and comfortably. But the fire doesn't come down or the heavens don't open up, and I wonder why. I have learned that during such seasons, the Father is saying, "Pray fervently. Come back a second time and a third time, an eighth time and a twelfth time. Why? Because I know what's ahead."

You see, as the story unfolds, on the heels of his incredible victory on Mount Carmel, we will see Elijah fall into such depression and despondency that he will despair even of life itself (1 Kings 19:4). Knowing this, God says to Elijah, "What you need, Elijah, is not for Me to respond immediately, but to come into My presence repeatedly. I know what's coming—and you need to log in time with Me."

So, too, sometimes I pray, "Father, Your Word promises this . . ." and boom! It happens immediately. Other times, God says to me, "You think you need that relationship resolved or that ministry opened, or that financial matter worked out. But

I see where you're going to be tomorrow. I see that what you're really craving is not what you're asking. You're craving Me. So come back three times, seven times, twenty-seven times, forty-two times and spend time with Me."

And you know what I have discovered, dear precious people? In coming back over and over with my head between my knees, so to speak, laboring and wondering, I find that what I was so concerned about fades from importance, for I find in Him everything my heart desires.

What was birthed by Elijah that day on the mountain wasn't a rain cloud. It was a relationship. That's what it means to pray fervently—not to get God's attention, but to birth a deeper relationship with Him.

Righteous

James tells us it is not only effectual and fervent prayers that avail much, but effectual and fervent prayers prayed by a *righteous* man. Again, Elijah is our example. . . .

James calls Elijah a man of like passions—a man with the same vulnerabilities we have. That explains why, after calling down fire from heaven, and hacking up four hundred fifty prophets of Baal single-handedly, frightened by the words of a woman, Elijah ran seventy miles like a chicken with his head cut off only to end up in a cave depressed, discouraged, and defeated.

Here's a guy who's just like me. One minute he's up on the mountain; the next minute he's in a cave. One minute, he's victorious over Baal; the next minute, he's done in by despair. Yet James refers to Elijah as a righteous man. Why? Because in the New Testament particularly, righteousness is not dependent upon the way we behave. It is dependent upon what we believe.

How do I know this?

In Romans 4, Paul reaches back through the tunnel of time and grabs a name for our consideration: Abraham. Simply because Abraham believed God would do what He said He would, that God is who He declared Himself to be, Abraham was declared righteous (Romans 4:3).

Do you believe God? Do you believe the foundational fact of faith—that Jesus Christ, the Son of God, died on the Cross for your sin and after three days rose again? Do you believe He is your Savior? If so, you are righteous.

"Oh, but you don't know where I was last year," you say.

Second Corinthians 5:17 says that if any man be in Christ—and you are—he is a new creation. Old things are passed away, behold all things are become new. Therefore, regardless of where you've been or what you've done, you're a new creation in Christ. You're righteous.

"Yes, but I have sinned greatly even after becoming a new creation, a believer."

Paul goes on to say, "And He made Him who knew no sin to be sin that we might be the righteousness of God in Christ Jesus" (see 2 Corinthians 5:21). That means God put our sin—past, present, and the stuff we haven't even done yet—on the Son. Therefore, if you are a believer, you are surrounded by Christ, covered with Christ, and washed by the blood of Christ. And you can't get any more righteous than that.

The effectual, fervent prayers of a righteous man availeth much. "Effectual," "fervent," and "righteous" are words that, unless understood biblically, can intimidate us and keep us from praying consistently. But once we understand their meaning, all that remains is to understand the word "much"—for "much" is what God has done and wants to continue to do in our lives as we walk with Him and wait on Him in effectual, fervent prayer.

Amen.

1 PETER

Background to 1 & 2 Peter

In the year A.D. 63 or 64, Peter wrote 1 Peter. As obvious as that may sound, in 1947, a school of thought developed that declared it would have been impossible for a fisherman like Peter to employ the complex sentence structure and sophisticated vocabulary found in the letter before us.

Yet 1947 was hardly the first year in which Peter's credentials were called into question. Luke records that after hearing Peter speak, the learned men of the day wondered how he was able to speak with such clarity and authority—until they realized he had been with Jesus (Acts 4:13).

I like that! Hanging out with Jesus will make a smart man out of anyone! Peter had listened to, eaten with, and traveled alongside Jesus for three years. The result was obvious.

So, too, as we spend time hanging out with one who hung out with Jesus, my prayer is that we will take on His characteristics just as noticeably, as readily, as wonderfully as did the fisherman-turned-scholar: the apostle Peter.

1 PETER

1
1 Peter 1:1 (a)
Peter, an apostle of Jesus Christ . . .

Peter and Paul were two apostles who had a major impact on the early church. In fact, when you read the New Testament, you see Peter's name two hundred ten times and Paul's one hundred sixty-two times—while all of the other apostles combined are mentioned only one hundred fourteen times.

However, there is a third man who figures prominently in the early church. That man is John. As you look at these three—Peter, Paul, and John—you must conclude that Peter is the "apostle of hope." More than anyone else, Peter stresses hope as the answer to persecution and difficulty. Paul is the "apostle of faith," as he articulates more clearly than any other writer the doctrine of justification by faith. John is known both through his person and writing as the "apostle of love." Faith, hope, and love are personified in Paul, Peter, and John—all apostles of Jesus Christ.

1 Peter 1:1 (b)
. . . to the strangers . . .

The idea of "stranger" referring to one who is displaced, Peter could be addressing the Jewish Christians who were dispersed—as well as speaking to any Christian feeling displaced or lost.

This side of heaven, we're part of an empire in which we don't fit, part of a system with which we can't agree. This is why Peter's words are as needful for us now as they were for the early church.

1 Peter 1:1 (c)
. . . scattered throughout Pontus, Galatia, Cappadocia, Asia, and Bithynia.

Nine or ten months after Peter wrote his letter, the persecution against Christians that had been simmering for quite some time came to a full boil. On July 19, A.D. 64, Caesar Nero set fire to the Imperial City of Rome. You see, determined to stamp his image upon a new Rome, Caesar hired arsonists to destroy the old one. Maybe you remember stories of Caesar fiddling while Rome burned. While that may not have happened literally, Caesar was fiddling around very definitely! The ensuing devastation gave him justification to rebuild structures like the Circus Maximus. Seating over one hundred thousand people, the existing Circus Maximus wasn't big enough for Nero. So he had it burned along with most of the city and rebuilt it to give three hundred thousand spectators the opportunity to witness sporting events, gladiatorial bouts, and, eventually, Christians being thrown to lions.

Due to the immediate suspicion that he had a part in the fire, Nero knew he had to quickly find a scapegoat. He conveniently found one in the Christian community. "It's not I who burned the city," he said. "It's these who speak of the unquenchable flames of hell." Coupled with the absurd misconception that, due to their observance of Communion, Christians were cannibalistic, and combined with the fact that because Christians stressed love and purity, they were a threat to the rampant perversity of the day, the populace was eager to blame Christianity for their crumbling families and charred capital city.

Consequently, only months after Peter's Epistle was penned, persecution would come that would result in the annihilation of six million Christians as they were lit as candles or fed to lions. So Peter addresses this issue as he writes to people who would be understandably vulnerable to confusion and depression as they questioned the reason for their relentless persecution.

1 Peter 1:2 (a)
Elect . . .

Here in verse 2, Peter will refer to the Trinity at the very outset of his letter to remind his readers that they are a chosen community.

1 Peter 1:2 (b)
. . . according to the foreknowledge of God the Father . . .

Because God elected us before the world began, He sees us as already glorified. People look at us and they say, "Glorified? *Them?!*" The Father, however, knows better. . . .

Suppose you suddenly found yourself tumbling down a time tunnel, where you end up in the year 1992. There you are. The Gulf War has just ended. The country is celebrating victory. And with a 91 percent approval rating, George Bush is a shoo-in to be reelected president. If you find a bookie, and against unbelievably high odds, you place a bet that a governor from Arkansas will beat him in the upcoming election, you would walk away a rich man because you would have foreknowledge. Therefore, you would have put your money down not as a gamble, but with certainty because you would have known the outcome.

The same is true with the Father. He sees the end from the beginning. He understands what no other person can comprehend. He knows we are going to make it. As bad a bet as we might seem to ourselves or to others, as steep as the odds against us may be, He calls us already glorified. Therefore, we can approach Him boldly. We can enjoy Him intimately. We can ask of Him expectantly because we have been elected eternally.

1 Peter 1:2 (c)
. . . through sanctification of the Spirit . . .

For me, the sanctification of the Spirit took place not before the foundation of the world, but on a summer evening in 1957, when, in a little church called Calvary Temple, Pastor Kermit Jeffries was preaching about hell. Almost four years old, I wasn't coloring or sleeping on my mom's lap as I usually did in church, but was listening intently. I knew I needed to receive Jesus personally if I didn't want to fry in hell eternally. When Pastor Jeffries gave an invitation, I was the first one down the aisle. That was the hour of my sanctification, my being set apart, my salvation.

1 Peter 1:2 (d)
. . . unto obedience and sprinkling of the blood of Jesus Christ.

As far as the Son is concerned, I was saved when, two thousand years ago on a hill called Calvary, He shed His blood to cleanse me. Like the thief hanging next to Him, a way was made for me to be with Him in paradise that very day (Luke 23:43).

1 Peter 1:2 (e)
Grace unto you, and peace, be multiplied.

The usual Pauline greeting is "Grace and peace." Peter seems to borrow this phrase of Paul's, and then makes it his own.

1 Peter 1:3, 4 (a)
Blessed be the God and Father of our Lord Jesus Christ, which according to his abundant mercy hath begotten us again unto a lively hope by the resurrection of Jesus Christ from the dead, to an inheritance incorruptible, and undefiled, and that fadeth not away . . .

To these who are feeling discouraged, displaced, depressed, or in danger, Peter addresses the issue right away, saying, "We have a living hope based upon the resurrection of our Lord and Savior."

Unlike living hope, human hope tends to get weaker and dimmer, and finally dies altogether the farther one goes down the road of life.

I was an awesome pitcher. As I stood in the street and pitched a tennis ball against my garage door, you wouldn't believe my split finger fastball, my curve, my sinker. I knew even Hank Aaron would strike out if he ever faced me at the plate. Oh, I might go to the full count, but I would always come through—every single time. In my imagination, I pitched perfect game after perfect game as a nine-year-old. But it finally hit me about two years ago that, in reality, I'll never pitch for the San Francisco Giants. Even if I practice really hard, I now know it's just not going to happen. My hope that once shone so brightly is now gone altogether.

The same is true for all of us. As we go down the road of life, we check off more and more things we thought we would one day do or be. Regarding spiritual life, however, the opposite is true. The farther down the road we walk with Jesus, the more we realize our hope doesn't lie on this earth, but in heaven. We don't need to be a people who wrestle with midlife crises because our hope is not to make the San Francisco Giants or to make ten million bucks. Our hope is in heaven. And heaven's getting closer every day.

1 Peter 1:4 (b)
. . . reserved in heaven for you.

"Even if there is an inheritance reserved for me in heaven, it won't do me any good if I never get there," you say. "What if I don't make it?" Read on.

1 Peter 1:5 (a)
Who are kept by the power of God . . .

We are kept by the power of God. It's not us holding on to Him. It's Him holding on to us.

"Hold on to Daddy's hand," I would say to my kids as we crossed the street. And they would. But if, out of forgetfulness or fatigue, they loosened their grip, it wouldn't matter because, although they thought they were holding my hand, in reality, I was holding theirs—and I would never let go.

So, too, we think we're holding on to the Lord, but in reality, He's holding on to us. We're kept by *His* power.

1 Peter 1:5 (b)
. . . through faith unto salvation ready to be revealed in the last time.

A young man who was being hazed by a college fraternity was taken to a secluded spot where he was told to hold on to a knot at the end of a greased rope as his fraternity brothers lowered him into a dark well. Thinking they would pull him up after a few minutes, he was terrified to see them tie their end of the rope to the bar across the top of the well, leaving him suspended in midair.

This can't be! he thought as he called for help. But none came.

As he approached the fifteen-minute mark, his arms aching unbelievably, and his shoulders feeling as though they were on fire, he started to cry.

Finally, after about twenty-five tortuous minutes, able to hang on no longer, he let go—and fell two inches—just as his fraternity brothers had calculated.

Isn't that just like us? "Where are You, God? I don't know if I'm going to make it," we cry. We fret, blubber, and scream until we finally let go. And guess what we find. We discover that our Solid Rock, Jesus Christ, was there all along.

A bunch of us have burning shoulders and aching arms for absolutely no reason. We're trying to hang on through our own efforts, by our own spirituality. We get disgusted with ourselves and worried we're not going to make it. If we would just let go of the rope and rest in what Jesus did on the Cross of Calvary, we would realize it's not our puny efforts that will see us through, but the power of God.

This is what Peter is telling the believers who, no doubt, were wondering if, when the temperature rose and persecution came down, they would be able to hang in there.

"I want you to know something," Peter said. "You have an inheritance waiting for you that can't be taken from you. You are kept by the power of God, and He is committed to seeing you through. All that remains for you to do is believe."

1 Peter 1:6
Wherein ye greatly rejoice, though now for a season, if need be, ye are in heaviness through manifold temptations.

In using the word "heaviness"—the same word used to describe what Jesus felt in the Garden of Gethsemane when He sweat great drops of blood (Luke 22:44)—Peter isn't minimizing the reality of what his readers were fearing or feeling. "I know what you're going through is heavy," he says. "But it's only for a season. Rejoice greatly because you're going to heaven."

Think of it this way:

You go to the United Airlines counter at the airport, and the ticket agent says, "Your flight to San Francisco is on time. There's been some turbulence, but we absolutely guarantee that you'll get there. Our plane is in great shape. Our pilot is fully qualified. You might experience a bump or two, but you're going to get there just fine."

"Hang on to my ticket," you say as you make your way to a different ticket counter.

"Are there any seats available for the flight to San Francisco?" you ask.

"You bet," says the agent. "And we guarantee you'll have a smooth ride. No bumps, no jolts, no airsickness. Guaranteed smooth sailing all the way. It's the landing we're not so sure about. You see, our landing gear is not working quite right, and we seem to have a problem with occasionally landing nose-first. Also, the brakes haven't been serviced recently. But we guarantee the flight will be smooth— even if the landing is a little iffy."

If you have to choose between a smooth flight with a crash landing, or a bumpy flight with a safe landing, you'll no doubt opt for the bumpy flight. There are those who say, "I don't want trials. I

don't want to go against the world's system. I don't want to deal with all of those church disciplines you talk about. I just want smooth sailing." They are fools, for although they might escape a bump or two presently, they're ultimately headed for a fiery crash landing. On the other hand, those of us who presently deal with a bump or two along the way, will make a safe landing in heaven.

That's what Peter will emphasize over and over throughout his epistle as he sets our sights on the big picture, on heaven.

Jesus said it best: "Seek ye first the kingdom of God and His righteousness, and all these things will be added unto you" (Matthew 6:33).

1 Peter 1:7 (a)
That the trial of your faith . . .

When they go through hard times or difficult days, people sometimes say, "I don't see anything good coming out of this trial." Does the Bible say, "We see all things work together for good to those who love God"? No. It says, "We *know* all things work together for good" (see Romans 8:28). We may not see things working together for good this month or this year or even in our lifetime. The Bible doesn't say we see it. The Bible says we know it. That's what Peter is reminding the believers to whom he is writing.

1 Peter 1:7 (b)
. . . being much more precious than of gold that perisheth, though it be tried with fire, might be found unto praise and honour and glory at the appearing of Jesus Christ.

"I know you're going through exceedingly difficult days, with even tougher times coming your direction," says Peter, "but you can choose to rejoice. Why? Because trials strengthen faith."

In likening faith to gold tried by fire, Peter reaches back to a statement made by a man who knew uniquely what it meant to go through trials and difficulties.

But he knoweth the way that I take: when he hath tried me, I shall come forth as gold.
Job 23:10

In Bible times, when a man wanted to make something of fine gold, he would subject the ore to such intense heat that all of the impurities would be burned out. The goldsmith would know that the work was done when he could see the reflection of his own face in the liquefied gold.

The same thing is true with us. The Lord says,

"I've got big plans for you, huge plans. I've got plans not for this life only, but for eternity. Therefore, I may need to turn up the heat a bit to work out the impurities. But My hand is on the thermostat. I know exactly what I'm doing. Although at the present moment, it might not be easy, you'll thank Me for the next billion years to come because what I'm after is to see the reflection of My face in your life."

Why?

God doesn't want to see His reflection in our lives because He's on some sort of an ego trip, but because He knows that although we may not realize it, what we really want is to be like Him. There are things in our lives that keep that from happening, so the way He deals with them is to turn up the heat a bit in order that we'll come out of the fire stronger in faith and more like the Lord.

> . . . but we glory in tribulations also: knowing that tribulation worketh patience; and patience, experience; and experience, hope: And hope maketh not ashamed; because the love of God is shed abroad in our hearts by the Holy Ghost which is given unto us.   Romans 5:3–5

When you finally understand this, you'll rejoice in difficulty rather than rebel because you'll see it as a purifying process that will work wonderful things into your life. Tribulation works patience. When you're going through difficulty, there's not a lot you can do other than wait for the master goldsmith to finish the process. Patience, in turn works experience as we learn that God truly knows what He's doing. Experience works hope—the absolute expectation of coming good.

1 Peter 1:8
Whom having not seen, ye love; in whom, though now ye see him not, yet believing, ye rejoice with joy unspeakable and full of glory.

Not only do trials strengthen our faith *in* the Lord, but they deepen our love *for* the Lord. Although those to whom Peter was writing had never seen Jesus physically, such was not the case with Peter. Peter had not only seen Jesus daily in His humanity, but he had actually seen a sneak preview of His deity. Yet Peter's joy was not unspeakable on the Mount of Transfiguration, for he merely said, "Lord, it is good for us to be here" (Matthew 17:4). Therefore, I suggest that even though Peter had beheld Jesus physi-

cally, those to whom Peter was writing would experience an even deeper love and keener perspective due to the trials they faced.

Certainly Shadrach, Meshach, and Abed-nego found this to be true.

> *Inside a furnace seven times hotter than it had ever been heated, these guys were in a fiery trial indeed. Yet because a "fourth Man"—the Son of God—was in the fire with them, they didn't come out of the furnace until they were commanded to do so (Daniel 3:26).*

A lot of us are getting to the place where we say, "Lord, keep me in the fire continually if that's what it takes for me to see You more clearly."

"Your joy is unspeakable," Peter says, "because you've seen Jesus in ways that far transcend seeing Him physically—even when He was transfigured in glory."

1 Peter 1:9–11
Receiving the end of your faith, even the salvation of your souls. Of which salvation the prophets have inquired and searched diligently, who prophesied of the grace that should come unto you: Searching what, or what manner of time the Spirit of Christ which was in them did signify, when it testified beforehand the sufferings of Christ, and the glory that should follow.

"What you're experiencing," Peter says, "is something by which the prophets were intrigued, interested in, but couldn't get a handle on." You see, the prophets wrote about things they just couldn't figure out, for they saw the glory of Psalm 2. However, they also saw the suffering of Isaiah 53. They saw the triumph on the Mount of Olives, where the returning Messiah will stand; but they also saw the blood on Mount Calvary upon which Messiah died. *How can it be,* they must have wondered, *that He will be despised, rejected, and smitten; suffering, yet also ruling and reigning? This doesn't make sense.*

They saw Mount Calvary. They saw the Mount of Olives. But what they didn't see was the valley between the two—a valley of about two thousand years. They didn't understand that they were writing of two comings—that Messiah would come as a suffering Savior before returning as a conquering King.

Some today might say, "I hear all of the promises, but I don't see any glory." That's because there's a valley between them that might last a week, a month, a decade, a lifetime. But God's plan is being unfolded nonetheless, for glory always follows suffering. Always.

1 Peter 1:12
Unto whom it was revealed, that not unto themselves, but unto us they did minister the things, which are now reported unto you by them that have preached the gospel unto you with the Holy Ghost sent down from heaven; which things the angels desire to look into.

The phrase translated "look into" is the same phrase used to describe what Peter did when he peered into the tomb on Easter Sunday (Luke 24:12). Just as the disciples wondered about the meaning of the empty tomb, angels stoop down and look at you and me in wonder. "What does this mean," they ask, "that God has chosen *these* people to be His family? Is that the best He could do?!"

1 Peter 1:13
Wherefore gird up the loins of your mind, be sober, and hope to the end for the grace that is to be brought unto you at the revelation of Jesus Christ.

Because we understand those things that were only a mystery to the prophets and angels, we're to think soberly. What does it mean to "gird up the loins of your mind"? In Bible days, men would wear ankle-length robes. But if they wanted to move quickly or freely, they would loop the bottom of their robes over their belts. Thus, Peter is saying, "Don't walk around with long robes or long faces. Pull up the mental garments that are tripping you up. Change your way of thinking concerning your situation."

It's such an important principle. You cannot change your heart, but you can change your mind. God can change your heart. He won't change your mind, but if you choose to change your mind, God will change your heart.

1 Peter 1:14–16
As obedient children, not fashioning yourselves according to the former lusts in your ignorance: But as he which hath called you is holy, so be ye holy in all manner of conversation; because it is written, Be ye holy; for I am holy.

When people go through difficulty, there is a tendency for them to drift into carnality. "Oh, what's the use," they say. "Let's just watch a video."

As we face trials and difficulties, Peter tells us we're to gird up the loins of our minds, to think

soberly, and hope to the end. Whatever we do, we're not to return to our old fleshly inclinations, for God says we're to be holy, to be whole. In other words, we're not to tear ourselves apart or wear ourselves down with sin and sloth, laziness and iniquity. Instead, we're to choose in the midst of our difficulty to think rightly.

1 Peter 1:17
And if ye call on the Father, who without respect of persons judgeth according to every man's work, pass the time of your sojourning here in fear.

Keep the context in mind. Peter says to a group of people going through really tough times, "In the midst of this difficulty you can either experience unspeakable joy, or you can feel sorry for yourself and drift back into carnality. If you return to carnality, know the repercussions are going to be heartbreaking. Therefore, pass the time in fear—not fear of the Father, but fear of the repercussions of your sin."

1 Peter 1:18, 19 (a)
Forasmuch as ye know that ye were not redeemed with corruptible things, as silver and gold, from your vain conversation received by tradition from your fathers; but with the precious blood of Christ . . .

"If you have a tendency to return to your carnal lifestyle, I want you to remember that you were purchased with the blood of Christ," Peter says.

Why did it take the blood of Christ to purchase us?

The wages of sin is always death. Look carefully at the blood pulsing from the veins of Jesus Christ. See the thorns smashed into His skull. Listen to the crowd around Him mocking and cursing Him. Understand that is what sin does. The only way we, our kids, or our friends and neighbors will understand the result of sin is to look at the Cross.

1 Peter 1:19 (b), 20
. . . as of a lamb without blemish and without spot: Who verily was foreordained before the foundation of the world, but was manifest in these last times for you.

In the infamous work *The Passover Plot*, it is suggested that the disciples drugged Jesus on the Cross, which caused Him to swoon until He "came to" in the tomb, appearing to come back to life. While visiting a college campus, I noticed that this book is still being sold and is required reading for a certain course on religion.

I, too, believe in the Passover plot—that it was plotted before the foundation of the world. Jesus Christ would be sent to die as a Passover Lamb for my sin. In looking on Him as a Lamb slain, I see not only His grace and mercy, but a graphic picture of what sin does.

1 Peter 1:21, 22
Who by him do believe in God, that raised him up from the dead, and gave him glory; that your faith and hope might be in God. Seeing ye have purified your souls in obeying the truth through the Spirit unto unfeigned love of the brethren, see that ye love one another with a pure heart fervently.

"They're going to persecute you," Jesus told Peter. "They're going to stretch out your arms and take you where you don't want to go," He said, speaking of the manner of his death (see John 21:18, 19).

"What about this man?" Peter asked as he pointed to John.

"What is that to thee?" Jesus answered. "Follow thou Me."

When pressure rises, when persecution comes down, when things are tough, like Peter, we say, "How come he's not going through it?" or, "How come she's got it made in the shade?" If we're not careful in the time of difficulty, we can raise questions about one another and even experience a certain degree of animosity. Perhaps because he himself felt this, Peter said the solution is to love one another fervently—and then goes on to give us four reasons why we should.

1 Peter 1:23–25
Being born again, not of corruptible seed, but of incorruptible, by the word of God, which liveth and abideth for ever. For all flesh is as grass, and all the glory of man as the flower of grass. The grass withereth, and the flower thereof falleth away: But the word of the Lord endureth for ever. And this is the word which by the gospel is preached unto you.

The first reason we are to love one another fervently is because we are children in the same family, born not of man but by the explosive power of the Word of God.

THE EXPLOSIVE POWER OF THE WORD

A Topical Study of
1 Peter 1:24

I was waiting to buy a book that had been on the bestseller list for about six months, but I thought the list price of $29.95 was a bit high. While in San Francisco, I saw it on the bargain table—for $1.88. That's the way it always is. The bestsellers of today will be on the bargain table six months from now. Watch and see!

I find it interesting that the fastest-growing category of books deals with the human growth, or human potential movement (we used to call them self-help books). These are books that help people be better, like Tony Robbins' *Awakening the Giant Within,* or John Gray's *Men Are From Mars, Women Are From Venus,* or Steven Covey's *Seven Habits of Highly Effective People.* One that quickly climbed the charts was *The High Fat Diet,* in which the author maintains that our country is headed for serious health problems unless we get back to hot fudge sundaes and cherry pie. I can't wait to get that book!

Diet books, relationship books, and leadership books will all end up on the bargain table eventually and ultimately fade into oblivion for one simple reason: They don't work.

One hundred years ago, the best-selling book in our country was a book on phrenology. It said one could discover his personality strengths and weaknesses, and also predict his future by feeling the lumps on the top of his head. Phrenologists were serious people who would feel the lumps on people's skulls and tell them how to get "ahead." It sounds crazy now, but one hundred years ago, phrenology swept the nation.

Solomon was right when he ended Ecclesiastes saying, "Of the making of many books there is no end" (Ecclesiastes 12:12). Our text goes on to say that although men's ideas and philosophies spring up like grass and bud like flowers, as time passes, they fade away into oblivion and are ultimately forgotten. Perhaps no one epitomizes this truth better than Voltaire, the famous French infidel of the eighteenth century.

Voltaire was seemingly a deep thinker, a persuasive orator, a well-known figure. He called his rival, Sir Isaac Newton, a "doddering fool" because of Newton's contention that there would come a day when men would travel around the world. Newton knew this because, as a believer, he had read in the Book of Daniel that men would go "to and fro"—an idiom for global travel.

"For men to travel globally, they would have to travel at speeds in excess of sixty miles per hour," scoffed Voltaire. "Any thinking man knows speed that high would cause one's heart to stop beating."

That isn't the only time Voltaire proved to be wrong. On his deathbed in 1778, he declared that within one hundred years of his death, the Bible would only be found in museums and in the archives of libraries. How fitting, then, that Voltaire's house was purchased by the European Bible Society to produce thousands of Bibles annually—even to this day.

Voltaire passed away like the grass, like a flower. The Word of God endures forever. Why? It is unique among all books in that it's the only book that is living.

For the word of God is quick, and powerful, and sharper than any two-edged sword, piercing even to the dividing asunder of soul and spirit, and of the joints and marrow, and is a discerner of the thoughts and intents of the heart.

Hebrews 4:12

The Word of God is living, folks. It's not just alive metaphorically, but it is living in reality. Every book of the Bible, all 66; every chapter, all 1,118; every verse, all 774,746; every word, all 3,500,034 are inspired.

"Man shall not live by bread alone," Jesus declared," but by every word which proceeds out of the mouth of God" (see Matthew 4:4). Every part of the Word is living. None can be ignored. All must be embraced.

Every word is inspired—not just poetically or theologically—but physically. How do I know? Look at our text. . . .

Being born again, not of corruptible seed, but of incorruptible, by the word of God, which liveth and abideth for ever.   1 Peter 1:23

The phrase "incorruptible seed" is a Greek term that speaks of sperm. This should not be surprising, for by definition, any living thing has the capability to reproduce itself. The Word of God is no exception, for by it we are born again.

"The words which I speak are spirit and life," Jesus declared (see John 6:63).

"Master, we know that You must be from God, for no man can do the works You do unless God be with him," Nicodemus said to Jesus one night.

"Verily, I say unto you, you must be born again," Jesus said.

Perhaps scratching his head, Nicodemus said, "How can this be? How can a man enter into his mother's womb a second time? What do You mean?"

"That which is born of flesh is flesh," Jesus said, "but that which is born of spirit is spirit. Marvel not that I say you must be born again. The wind bloweth where it wants, and you hear the sound, but no man knows from whence it comes and no man knows where it goes" (see John 3:1–8).

A teacher of Israel, Nicodemus should have understood the reference. Born again, wind blowing? His mind should have raced immediately to Ezekiel 37, a passage familiar to every rabbi and teacher in Israel. . . .

One day, the spirit of the Lord took Ezekiel to a valley full of dry, dead bones and told him to preach to the bones. As Ezekiel began to preach the Word, something amazing began to happen. The bones started to move. Before long, they had joined together like a great army, yet zombielike because they were without life.

"Prophesy to the wind," the Lord said to Ezekiel.

So Ezekiel prophesied unto the wind even as he had done to the bones, and the wind—the *ruwach*—the spirit moved into them and the bones came to life.

If Nicodemus had made the connection between this story and what Jesus was telling him that night, he would have understood that to be born again means to be made alive by the Spirit and the Word, just as the bones became alive when Ezekiel preached the Spirit and the Word.

Perhaps, like me, you have known for years that when the seed of the Word and the Spirit of God penetrate our being, we "dry bones" come to life. I want you to see that the same dynamic that caused us to be born again can continually impact us in any arena where there are dry bones in our lives.

"Our marriage is as dry as a bone," you might be saying. Or, "I respect him immensely, but my dad is spiritually as dry as a bone." Or, "My seventh-grade daughter is not walking with the Lord as closely as she could be."

I have great news for you. The Word of God has the unique ability to impact and change your teenage son or daughter, your grandchildren, your mother, your co-worker, your friend, your husband, your neighbor.

How?

For as the rain cometh down, and the snow from heaven, and returneth not thither, but watereth the earth, and maketh it bring forth and bud, that it may give seed to the sower, and bread to the eater: So shall my word be that goeth forth out of my mouth: it shall not return unto me void, but it shall accomplish that which I please, and it shall prosper in the thing whereto I sent it.

Isaiah 55:10, 11

God is saying, "Just as rain coming down causes growth to take place on a barren hillside, so My Word will accomplish the purpose I sent it to do."

Hear, O Israel: The LORD our God is one LORD: And thou shalt love the LORD thy God with all thine heart, and with all thy soul, and with all thy might. And these words, which I command thee this day, shall be in thine heart: And thou shalt teach them diligently unto thy children, and shalt talk of them when thou sittest in thine house, and when thou walkest by the way, and when thou liest down, and when thou risest up.   Deuteronomy 6:4–7

When you're driving in your car; when you're having breakfast together; when you tuck your kids into bed, don't talk to them about your ideas on dating or your philosophy on politics. Talk to them about Scripture. Share Bible verses with them over and over again.

You see, the verse itself has power. It is the incorruptible seed that has the power to produce spiritual life: in your husband who seems to be a dry bag of bones; in your wife who seems to be unresponsive to spiritual things. The power is in the Word itself. It is a seed that will not return void but will permanently impact and powerfully affect anyone who hears it.

If we really believed this, folks, we would be sharing Bible verses constantly— as we drive, as we have a meal, as we go on vacation, in the office, on the ball field, in the neighborhood. There would be a steady stream not of our thoughts, but of the living Word of God. Now, we may not see its effect immediately, but, according to Isaiah 55:11, it will take root and blossom ultimately.

I challenge you today, Mom, Dad, Friend, Teenager, Grandfather, Neighbor—to take a verse—any verse—and plant it in the ear of your granddaughter. Use it in your conversation as you talk on the phone. Say it in passing to the guy at the gas station. The impact will be huge because God honors His Word even above His name.

"That may be true," you sigh. "but you must understand. It's not just that I am surrounded by dry bones; I myself am dry."

If you feel this way, turn to 2 Kings 13. . . .

During an invasion in Israel, a Moabite soldier died. Midway in the process of burying him, his fellow soldiers caught sight of their enemies headed right at them. To save time, they tossed their dead buddy into a grave that was already occupied by the body of the prophet Elisha. When the corpse hit the bones of Elisha, it immediately came back to life—revived, resurrected, born again!

This story never ceases to amaze me. It tells me that if our lives have been permeated with the Word of God, even when we go through dry days or dark nights, life will come from us as the Word of God flows through us to those around us.

It's not how we're doing or how we're feeling that matters. Whether we feel high or dry is irrelevant. It's the power of the Word that works.

Therefore, your assignment this week is to share a verse with your son, daughter, schoolmate, or co-worker.

"I don't know any verses," you say.

Come to Bible study and learn one! Learn one verse a week and then plant it in the heart of someone else to bring life to them. Speak Scripture, gang, and watch what happens.

---

2 **1 Peter 2:1–3**
Wherefore laying aside all malice, and all guile, and hypocrisies, and envies, and all evil speakings, as newborn babes, desire the sincere milk of the word, that ye may grow thereby: If so be ye have tasted that the Lord is gracious.

Peter closed the first chapter of his epistle by saying we should love one another fervently because we're members of the same family. Just as we were all conceived *by* the incorruptible Word of God, as newborn babes, we're to continue *in* the Word of God.

If you're a parent, you know how newborn babes crave milk. In the middle of the night, they want milk. When you're trying to study, they want milk. Every few hours they want milk. Peter says we're to be the same way. He doesn't say

if we're newborn babes, or *when* we're newborn babes, but rather we're to continue all the days of our lives *as* newborn babes, craving the sincere milk of the Word.

If we are all in the Word together, the result will be unity. If you don't believe me, take a look around. This group of people would never get together for any other reason except the Word. We have different interests, political inclinations, ideas, philosophies, and backgrounds. However, as we study the Word, we are knit together in unity.

That is why we are to lay aside the slow-burning anger of malice, the trickery of guile, and the divisiveness of hypocrisy, envy, and evil speaking. The degree to which those attributes exist in our lives will be the degree to which our hunger for the Word will be diminished.

No matter how good the meal my wife, Tammy, prepares for me, if I stop off at McDonald's on the way home and score a couple of Quarter Pounders with large fries—and super-size the whole deal—when I get home, I won't be interested in what she's made.

When people stop reading or studying the Word, it's because they're eating the junk food of the world. That's why Peter says, "First lay aside the junk and then you will desire the milk of the Word."

1 Peter 2:4, 5 (a)
To whom coming, as unto a living stone, disallowed indeed of men, but chosen of God, and precious, ye also, as lively stones . . .

Peter says not only are we children in the same family, but we are stones in the same building. Several years ago, there was a mini controversy at Applegate Christian Fellowship for a few days relating to whether young men should be allowed to wear hats in church. While I understand the concern for respect, the issue wasn't that guys were wearing hats in church. The issue was that the church was wearing hats. The building isn't the church—the body is! We are the living stones.

People like to be on the church grounds at Applegate Christian Fellowship. They enjoy the amphitheater, the sanctuary, the mountaintop. I like to be there, too. Why? It's not because the grounds are anything special. It's because the fragrance of the church is left behind. These buildings are nothing more than buildings. But because the church is here worshiping and praying, studying and fellowshiping with the Lord, the environment is filled with the fragrance of Jesus.

1 Peter 2:5 (b)
. . . are built up a spiritual house . . .

That we are living stones who are being built up, or fit together, as a spiritual house brings to mind a most interesting Scripture. . . .

And the house, when it was in building, was built of stone made ready before it was brought thither: so that there was neither hammer nor axe nor any tool of iron heard in the house, while it was in building.   1 Kings 6:7

When Solomon's temple was being constructed, all of the chiseling, hammering, cutting, and chipping was done underneath the old city of Jerusalem. When the stones were taken to the temple mount, they could be fit together in silence.

We're living stones being fit together for an eternal temple in heaven. This life is the quarry, which explains why we always feel like we're being chipped and chiseled. "Why am I next to this blockhead?" you ask, or, "Why are they part of the family?" You know why? As *living* stones, we constantly rub against one another, knocking rough edges off one another in the process. You see, God puts us right next to the very people He knows will smooth us down so He can build us up into a temple for His glory.

The problem is, I try to get away from the blockhead I'm rubbing against. But because God puts us in fixes to fix us, He puts us with people and in situations He knows will shape us most effectively. So if I try to fix the fix God put me in, He will be faithful to put me in another fix to fix the fix He wanted to fix in the first place! If we don't learn this, we'll go from fix to fix until finally we say, "Okay, Lord. I'm not going to try to fix this, or wiggle out of that, but I'm going to embrace and accept where You have me because I know You're doing a work on me, shaping me for eternity."

1 Peter 2:5 (c)–8
. . . an holy priesthood, to offer up spiritual sacrifices, acceptable to God by Jesus Christ. Wherefore also it is contained in the scripture, Behold, I lay in Sion a chief corner stone, elect, precious: and he that believeth on him shall not be confounded. Unto you therefore which believe he is precious: but unto them which be disobedient, the stone which the builders disallowed, the same is made the head of the corner, and a stone of stumbling, and a rock of offence, even to them which stumble at the word, being disobedient: whereunto also they were appointed.

According to tradition, during the construction of Solomon's temple, work went smoothly until the builders were unable to locate the cornerstone. Word was sent to send the missing stone up to the temple mount.

"We sent that stone a long time ago," the quarriers replied.

The builders were confused until one of them remembered a perfectly cut stone that was tossed over the gully into the Kidron Valley because no one knew what to do with it.

The rejected cornerstone is a biblical allusion that shows up again and again throughout Scripture (Isaiah 28:16–18; Psalm 118:22; Acts 4:11).

"It was a mistake to marry him," she cries.

"I can't figure her out," he sighs.

"This is unworkable. Let's quit," they say.

The same thing happened to Jesus. . . .

"How can this carpenter, this peasant, be the Messiah?" they scoffed. "He leads no army. He has no credentials. Let's get rid of Him," they said.

Instead of saying, "Dump them," you and I must be those who look at people and situations and say, "I bet this is the Cornerstone working in my life. Jesus is using this situation in some way I can't figure out. It doesn't fit in with my thinking. It doesn't work according to my calculation or design—but somehow, even as He was rejected, this could very well be a key to what He is doing in my life."

1 Peter 2:9 (a)
But ye are a chosen generation, a royal priesthood . . .

Not only are we children in the same family and stones in the same building, but we are priests in the same temple. . . .

For topical study of 1 Peter 2:9 entitled "The Power of Sacrifice," turn to page 1555.

1 Peter 2:9 (b), 10
. . . an holy nation, a peculiar people; that ye should shew forth the praises of him who hath called you out of darkness into his marvellous light: Which in time past were not a people, but are now the people of God: which had not obtained mercy, but now have obtained mercy.

As children of the same family, stones in the same building, priests in the same temple, we are also citizens of the same nation. People look at us and say, "What a peculiar group you are." Any nation that would heavily fine a person for destroying an eagle's egg, yet actually encourage the destruction of a human embryo is peculiar indeed. Therefore, I'm *glad* they look at us as being strange!

1 Peter 2:11 (a)
Dearly beloved, I beseech you as strangers and pilgrims, abstain from fleshly lusts . . .

As a body, we are to do three things in light of our unity. First, we are to live in purity. Having talked about trials and persecution from without, Peter seems to shift gears here and address the potential danger from within. "I beseech you," he says. "I beg you. I plead with you. Hear the cry of my heart: Abstain from fleshly lusts that war against your soul."

In times of difficulty, people sometimes say,

"Why should I refrain? Why should I abstain? I just can't take it anymore."

Peter answers, "Even as things get tough, whatever you do, don't give in to your fleshly lusts. Be careful. You're vulnerable." Perhaps better than anyone else, Peter knew what he was talking about, for he was one who succumbed to his fleshly lusts when things got tough.

"Watch and pray," Jesus told him specifically, "lest you enter into temptation" (Matthew 26:41).

Peter listened to his flesh, saying, "This Passion Week has been pretty intense. You need a break. Kick back. Relax."

So he did.

A few hours later, standing by the fire not of persecution, but of temptation, Peter ended up denying Jesus three times. Shaken in his soul, he wept bitterly (Luke 22:62).

Peter knows what he's talking about when he says to the early believers, to you, and to me, "I beseech you as strangers and pilgrims. Abstain from the lust of this world." Notice Peter doesn't say, "Refrain temporarily," or, "Know when to say when," or, "Be sure you have a designated driver." No, he simply says, "Abstain completely."

1 Peter 2:11 (b), 12
. . . which war against the soul; having your conversation honest among the Gentiles: that, whereas they speak against you as evil-doers, they may by your good works, which they shall behold, glorify God in the day of visitation.

The Greek word translated "war" is *strateuomai*, from which we get our word "strategy." The Enemy has a strategy to war against your soul—your personality, your emotions, your will, your volition. The strategy of Satan is simply to say, "Abstinence is too old-fashioned, too legalistic, too unrealistic, too harsh. Just know when to say when. Be wise in what you're doing."

You see, gang, Satan won't come blasting into your life with a drug dealer in tow. No, his strategy is much more subtle. He simply wants you to compromise a little here and a little there, until there is nothing left of your purity. The problem with lust is not that it hurts God or others. The problem with lust is that it wars against *us*. It tears us down as it wears us down.

1 Peter 2:13–20
Submit yourselves to every ordinance of man for the Lord's sake: whether it be to the king, as supreme; or unto governors, as unto them that are sent by him for the pun-

ishment of evildoers, and for the praise of them that do well. For so is the will of God, that with well doing ye may put to silence the ignorance of foolish men: As free, and not using your liberty for a cloke of maliciousness, but as the servants of God. Honour all men. Love the brotherhood. Fear God. Honour the king. Servants, be subject to your masters with all fear; not only to the good and gentle, but also to the froward. For this is thankworthy, if a man for conscience toward God endure grief, suffering wrongfully. For what glory is it, if, when ye be buffeted for your faults, ye shall take it patiently? but if, when ye do well, and suffer for it, ye take it patiently, this is acceptable with God.

We are to walk in purity and humility. At the time of Peter's writing, a majority of Rome's population were slaves. They were treated as less than human. Peter instructs them to not only honor the king, but to submit to their masters. How, then, can we have the audacity to snivel about our president or whine about our bosses when our brothers and sisters served cruel masters and honored a demented king whose main objective was to annihilate them?

Lord, forgive us.

1 Peter 2:21–25

For even hereunto were ye called: because Christ also suffered for us, leaving us an example, that ye should follow his steps: Who did no sin, neither was guile found in his mouth: Who, when he was reviled, reviled not again; when he suffered, he threatened not; but committed himself to him that judgeth righteously: Who his own self bare our sins in his own body on the tree, that we, being dead to sins, should live unto righteousness: by whose stripes ye were healed. For ye were as sheep going astray; but are now returned unto the Shepherd and Bishop of your souls.

We are to walk in purity, humility, and we are to walk in conformity to the Lamb. Facing persecution, the early believers were not left on their own without a model to follow, for "Christ also suffered for us, leaving an example, that we should follow in his steps."

When my son Peter-John was about three years old, we were playing in the snow, and I said, "Come on, PJ, follow in my footprints if you can." He couldn't. My stride was too big.

To be frank, folks, I look at a verse like this and read that when He was being wrongly, cruelly, terribly treated, Jesus didn't answer back. I am to follow His steps. Yet I know I can't do this because I want to fight back; I want to let my opinion be known; I want to make sure I'm heard. Here's the good news: Jesus not only is our example; He is our enabler. He is not only the Lamb He is the Shepherd of our souls.

Peter-John did indeed follow in my steps that day—as I lifted him into the air and back down again and again so that he could put his feet in each one. He followed in my footsteps not only because I gave him steps to follow, but because I also enabled him to do so by lifting him up.

That's what our Lord does. He's the One who hoists me up and allows me, if I'll let Him, to follow in His footsteps.

And He'll do the same for you.

THE POWER OF SACRIFICE
A Topical Study of
1 Peter 2:9

As I read page after page of Richard Scarry's *What Does Daddy Do?* to then three-year-old Peter John, he discovered that some daddies are bakers; some are carpenters. Some are policemen, others firemen. When we finished the book, I said, "Peter, do you know what your daddy does?"

Peter thought for a minute and said, "You're a screecher!"

"No," I said.

"A creature?" he tried again.

"No, Peter," I laughed. "I'm a preacher."

There's nothing I'd rather be, for there is nothing as fulfilling as being in ministry. As minister, I get to see people's eternal destiny changed. I get to share the Good News of what Jesus did on the Cross of Calvary with people who are not sure where they will spend eternity. I get to see marriages turn around and families discover a foundation upon which they can build successfully. There's nothing I would rather do than be in the ministry.

Guess what. Our text tells us you are in the ministry every bit as much as I am—for we are *all* chosen to be a royal priesthood.

"Wait a minute," you say. "How can I be in the ministry? I've never been ordained."

Really? Didn't Jesus say, "You have not chosen Me, but I have chosen you and *ordained* you that you should go and bring forth much fruit" (see John 15:16)?

"Well," you say, "if I'm an ordained minister, where's my office?"

If you work at a bank, your office is in a bank. If you work at Wal-Mart, it's at Wal-Mart. If you go to school, your office is your campus. You see, the Lord ingeniously has positioned his pastors in places "professional pastors" like me could never go.

When we understand this, it changes everything because we see ourselves not as a banker, a student, or a truck driver, but as a minister of the gospel who has been subversively placed in a given arena to make an impact for the kingdom. Truly, we are a royal priesthood, ordained and assigned by no less than the King of kings.

What is a priesthood? In the Old Testament, the priesthood consisted of a specific group of men who would stand before God on behalf of the people, and before the people on behalf of God. In New Testament times, the entire church is a priesthood.

"If that's the case," you say, "it was the job of the Old Testament priests to offer sacrifices to the Lord. How does that apply to us?"

Consider the following five sacrifices we, the New Testament priesthood, are instructed to offer. . . .

The Sacrifice of Self

I beseech you therefore, brethren, by the mercies of God, that ye present your bodies a living sacrifice, holy, acceptable unto God, which is your reasonable service.   Romans 12:1

The first sacrifice we offer as New Testament priests is that of ourselves. Because living sacrifices tend to wiggle off the altar, we must continually lay our lives down. Thus, daily, even hourly, we pray,

"Today, Father, I give my eyes to You. May I look at people the way You do. I give My lips to You. May I speak words that are in harmony with Your heart. I give my hands to You. May they reach out in love. I give my feet to You. Please guard and guide my steps. I give my body to You, Lord, a living sacrifice."

The Sacrifice of Souls

That I should be the minister of Jesus Christ to the Gentiles, ministering the gospel of God, that the offering up of the Gentiles might be acceptable, being sanctified by the Holy Ghost.   Romans 15:16

When you witness at Wal-Mart, the bank or around your neighborhood, when you speak in such a way that people can see you're a Christian—be it as you give a word of testimony, or as you turn the conversation in some way to the goodness and grace of God—you are offering a well-pleasing sacrifice to the Father.

The Sacrifice of Stuff

But I have all, and abound: I am full, having received of Epaphroditus the things which were sent from you, an odour of a sweet smell, a sacrifice acceptable, well-pleasing to God.   Philippians 4:18

As in Old Testament days when the aroma of barbequed bulls and lambs was well-pleasing to the Father, the material stuff we share is delightful to His senses as well. Why? He knows our tendency to buy things we can't afford with money we don't have in order to impress people we don't like. Therefore, He says, "I want you to give—not because I need the money, but because you need to be released from the bondage of materialism."

When you give to the Lord, gang, you're not just supporting a ministry, but you are giving away a bit of your selfishness and greediness. Doing so is pleasing in God's sight.

The Sacrifice of Song

By him therefore let us offer the sacrifice of praise to God continually, that is, the fruit of our lips giving thanks to his name.   Hebrews 13:15

The Father is delighted when His children come together to praise Him. This is not surprising. Gifts of thanksgiving and love and praise delight the heart of any father.

Tammy and I were sitting in the backyard. "Mommy! Mommy!" we heard our then six-year-old call at the top of her lungs.

"Mary," said Tammy, "if you want to talk, you're going to have to come back here."

The next thing we heard was an odd noise working its way through the house. Wearing her rollerblades, Mary then appeared in the backyard. At this point, I was all ready to lecture her about why she shouldn't have been yelling in the first place, much less wearing her rollerblades in the house, when suddenly she took from behind her back a beautiful hand-picked bouquet. You know what? I forgot all about my lecture.

You, too, might feel like you've messed up. But when you come before the Father with a bouquet of praise, saying, "Lord, I know I left rollerblade tracks behind me, but I love You," His heart is touched.

Maybe singing praise songs isn't your thing. If you choose to lift hands, or bow the knee, or sing anyway, you're sacrificing your own comfort, shyness, image or feeling of inadequacy. Then it becomes a true sacrifice of praise.

As is the case with the sacrifice of our stuff, God doesn't need to be praised. We need to praise. God doesn't need affirming. He doesn't suffer from low self-esteem. He's not saying, "Am I really the Holy and Anointed One? Am I really sweeter than honey? Thanks for reminding Me because I was questioning that this morning." No! That's not it! God knows who He is, and He also knows we need to acknowledge who He is in order that *we* might be reminded.

The Sacrifice of Service

But to do good and to communicate forget not: for with such sacrifices God is well pleased.   Hebrews 13:16

When you write a thank-you note to someone, when you tell a brother you see the Lord in him, or when you affirm a sister in her faith, you offer the sacrifice of service. When you mow someone's lawn or bake someone cookies, you're doing good and offering a sacrifice which is well-pleasing to God.

"Okay," you might be saying, "I understand I'm in the priesthood, and I understand the sacrifices I am supposed to offer. To be honest, however, the idea of sacrifice just doesn't appeal to me."

Sacrifice may not appeal to you, but I'll bet success does. Sacrifice secures success because sacrifice releases power, and great sacrifice releases great power. This is one of those pivotal, essential, and foundational understandings for success in spiritual life. The reason God is calling you and me to be a priesthood that offers sacrifices is because He knows that sacrifice secures success. Sacrifice releases power, and great sacrifice releases great power.

For a story which illustrates this point, turn to 2 Kings 3. . . .

The nations of Judah and Israel had allied with the nation of Edom for one reason: to engage the murderous Moabites in battle. On their march across the blistering, burning desert, they ran out of water. In trouble, they called for a prophet. Elisha was dispatched and told them in the name of the Lord to do something rather odd. He told them to dig ditches. So they dug the ditches— even though it seemed impractical, illogical, and a waste of their rapidly diminishing energy.

The next morning, the ditches were miraculously filled with water, and they were saved. The miracle continued. Not only was their thirst quenched, but when the rising sun shone on the water, it appeared as blood to the Moabites.

"The three nations have taken up arms against one another!" the Moabites said. "Their alliance has crumbled. They've killed one another!"

Thinking all they had to do was march in and pick up the spoils, the Moabites were sorely surprised to discover that the Edomites and Jews weren't dead at all. Proving to be no match for their combined forces, the Moabites fled before them. But Israel pursued them to their city.

Surrounded by the Israelites, and sensing he and his people were doomed, indeed, the king of Moab did something unbelievable when he offered his eldest son as a burnt offering upon the wall of his city. When the men of Israel saw the prince hanging from the wall, they returned to their own land.

The king of Moab saved his people through a great sacrifice. He sacrificed his son, and in humiliation, the son hung for all to see. I'm sure you understand the analogy. We were about to be wiped out because of our own sin. Yet the Father stepped in and sacrificed His Son, hanging Him on a tree in humiliation, pain, and suffering to die for you and me. The Enemy that was about to chase us down and damn us eternally can no longer fight against such a sacrifice.

Sacrifice releases power. Great sacrifice releases great power. The greatest sacrifice ever offered was when God gave His Son. The greatest power ever released is that which secures our salvation. May God help you and me to understand that sacrifice is not something that is simply to cause us pain or agony. The sacrifice God calls us to is to set us free in order that we might be successful and powerful in life and ministry.

If you want little success or little power, give little sacrifices. But if you want great success and great power, say, "I'm going to praise the Lord even if it means getting less sleep." Or, "Instead of gossiping in the lunchroom at work, I'm going to slip away to a quiet spot and thank the Lord for His goodness to me." Or, "I'm going to share the Lord with kids at school." Or, "I'm going to give to someone in need."

The Father will breathe deeply of such sweet-smelling sacrifice to Him—as you take your place in the royal priesthood.

3 We should not be surprised that in the middle of his epistle in which the word "suffering" appears sixteen times, Peter addresses the subject of marriage. In days of difficulty, marriages will either grow stronger or collapse under the strain. Thus, it is fitting that Peter would address the issue of marriage within the overarching theme of the believer and suffering.

Why is it that in our day—when there are countless seminars and books, tapes and videos available concerning marriage—we're seeing even Christian marriages unraveling to an unparalleled degree?

Perhaps part of the answer lies in the same reason the Bible keeps its teaching on marriage very simple. The real issue is not knowing what to do—it's doing what we know. You see, many people believe that if people had more information on how to be better wives or husbands, everything would be fine. Yet it only takes a few minutes to study everything Jesus said concerning marriage.

I find Peter's instructions to be succinct, simple, and wonderfully workable.

1 Peter 3:1, 2
Likewise, ye wives, be in subjection to your own husbands; that, if any obey not the word, they also may without the word be won by the conversation of the wives; While they behold your chaste conversation coupled with fear.

As a pastor, I have found that, when a man gets saved, his wife and his kids follow him in faith. Such was the case in the house of Cornelius (Acts 10), as well as in the family of the Philippian jailer (Acts 16). When a woman is saved first, however, I have found she tends to come alone. This is partly due to a phony sense of male superiority that says, "If she found it first, how right can it be?" Or, "This church stuff doesn't fit in with the macho image I've cultivated so carefully."

Consequently, Peter is saying to wives, "Even if your husbands aren't saved, don't preach at them. Don't put tracts in their lunchbox when you send them off to work. Don't turn on the Christian radio station when you go to bed. You are to win your husbands simply by submitting to them."

1 Peter 3:3, 4 (a)
Whose adorning let it not be that outward adorning of plaiting the hair, and of wearing of gold, or of putting on of apparel; but let it be the hidden man of the heart, in that which is not corruptible . . .

The Greek word translated "adorn" is *kosmos,* which means "ordered universe," and from which we get our word "cosmetic," so here Peter is speaking of an order not of the outward appearance, but an order in the inner person. "Don't make clothes, jewelry, or the way you fix your hair the center of your universe or your top priority," says Peter. If you do, you're missing God's best for you.

1 Peter 3:4 (b)
. . . even the ornament of a meek and quiet spirit, which is in the sight of God of great price.

Derived from the idea of a powerful horse brought into submission, the Greek word translated "meek" is *praus,* which means "strength under control." Thus, a meek person is one who is centered, grounded, one who knows what he or she is about, who has a godly perspective on life. It is no wonder, then, that to the Lord, a meek and quiet spirit is never out of style.

I believe heaven will prove to be the great reversal. That is, many of those who appear on the cover of *People* magazine today will, in eternity, be shriveled, insignificant, or absent altogether—while many of those on earth who are today thought of as unattractive, unimportant, and insignificant will be beautiful in heaven because of their inner person. For the next billion years, no one will care about your hair or biceps, your wardrobe or your tan. All that will matter is whether you cultivated a meek and quiet spirit.

1 Peter 3:5, 6
For after this manner in the old time the holy women also, who trusted in God, adorned themselves, being in subjection unto their own husbands: Even as Sara obeyed Abraham, calling him lord: whose daughters ye are, as long as ye do well, and are not afraid with any amazement.

Not only are wives to be attractive inside, they are to stand by their husbands' side. The example used here is an interesting one, for Peter reaches back to the Old Testament and singles out Sarah as the model of a submitted woman.

Catch the scene:

Sitting in front of his tent, Abraham saw three men headed his way. As they drew nearer, he realized they were unique—and indeed they were, for they were two angels and the Lord. Running out to greet them, he fell at their feet, saying, "Come to my tent and be refreshed."

Over dinner, the Lord said to Abraham, "Sarah will bear a son"—a reiteration of the promise given to him years before (see Genesis 12:2).

Hearing this, Scripture says Sarah laughed within herself (Genesis 18:12).

The story is pertinent because in reaching back to this particular event, Peter is saying that Sarah called Abraham "lord" at the very point she was having a hard time believing his vision. How needed is the submissive spirit of Sarah today. The wife who hears the vision, the dream, the call of her husband, is tempted to say, "No way. You're too old. You're untrained. You're not qualified enough. You're not smart enough. You're not skilled enough. Forget it!"

A dear friend of mine loved the Word and felt called to start a ministry. "That's impractical," said his wife. "Get your head out of the clouds and your feet back on the ground. This is just not going to happen." He let go of the vision. Today they're divorced, and their kids are heartbroken.

How much better it would have been had this wife taken Peter's simple, practical word and said, "Here's my perspective, honey, but whatever the Lord leads you to do, I'll travel with you." How much better it would have been if, like Sarah, in the moment of her own doubting, she chose to honor her husband, even though his vision didn't make sense to her.

"I would be happy to believe in my husband's vision," you say. "But let me tell you, my husband's no Abraham!"

For that, you can be glad—for you recall the story. . . .

To escape famine in the land, Abraham headed to Egypt. He took Sarah with him. Once there, Abraham instructed Sarah to tell people they were brother and sister, knowing Pharaoh would kill him in order to add Sarah to his harem. This amazes me until I remember that, although Abraham is indeed a giant of the faith, he is still a man with flaws and weaknesses.

"Take these camels, goods, and servants," said Pharaoh to Abraham. "Your sister is one pretty lady." So Abraham became a wealthy man. What about Sarah? Even though Abraham had let her down, God didn't. He protected her when He plagued the house of Pharaoh, rendering Pharaoh unable to touch her (see Genesis 12:17).

Even though Abraham was going in the wrong direction, God protected Sarah and enriched the family as a result of her obedience. As for Abraham, he suffered the consequences of his sin. His heart was later broken when he had to let go of the son born to him through his union with one of the servants given him by Pharaoh (Genesis 16:3, 4).

When I lead my family in the wrong direction, God deals with me directly. Because Tammy travels with me, God protects her and enriches our family through her submission. As you study Abraham's life, you see that a key component to his greatness was having Sarah for his wife—one who traveled with him, one who trusted in God, one who called him lord.

Wives, don't strive with your husbands. If he has a dream, if there's something on his heart, if he senses a calling stirring within him—even if it doesn't make sense to you, even if you might be worried about the financial repercussions, don't get in his way. Travel with him. If you don't, he will become quenched spiritually, your family will be fractured unnecessarily, and years will be tragically lost. Be like Sarah—even if you have to stifle a chuckle or two—and watch the Lord bless abundantly.

1 Peter 3:7 (a)
Likewise, ye husbands. . . .

Of his seven verses dealing with marriage, Peter spends six of them addressing women. I think there's a reason for that.

If you went to a pet store to buy a pet turkey, you would pick up a cage, food, water bowl, and a booklet, wherein you would find lengthy instructions on how to care for your pet. The turkey, on the other hand, wouldn't need a book telling him how to live with you because the smarter one gets the instructions.

I think you see the analogy! Women are given a greater amount of instruction because their challenge to live with men can be much more difficult! Peter makes it as simple as he can for husbands when he tells them they are to do three things. . . .

1 Peter 3:7 (b)
. . . dwell with them according to knowledge . . .

As a husband, I am to know my wife deeply, profoundly, in the way she deserves to be known. How does this happen? I believe the answer can be seen in the way our Bridegroom, Jesus Christ, relates to His bride.

At the outset of His public ministry, Jesus called Philip to follow Him. So impressed was Phillip with Jesus that he told his friend Nathanael he had found the Messiah.

"Can any good thing come out of Nazareth?" Nathanael asked.

"Come and see," said Philip.

So Nathanael did.

"Behold, an Israelite in whom is no guile," said Jesus of Nathanael.

"How do you know me?" asked Nathanael.

"Before you came to meet Me, when you were sitting under the fig tree, I saw you," Jesus said.

"Truly You must be the Master," Nathanael said.

"Stick around, Nathanael," said Jesus, "for you will see angels descending and ascending from heaven."

And Nathanael followed Jesus from that moment on (see John 1:43–51; 21:2).

Rabbinical literature indicates that studying was often done under a fig tree, the national symbol of Israel. Thus, Nathanael was studying when Jesus saw him. I suggest he was reading the account in Genesis 28. Jacob, a man whose name meant "guile," was in a place he thought was forsaken by God. Yet in his sleep, Jacob saw a ladder come down from heaven with angels ascending and descending upon it. Thus, it could be that when Jesus referred to him as an Israelite in whom there was no guile, no "Jacob"—and then went on to refer to Himself as the Ladder upon which the angels ascend and descend, Nathanael might have thought, *That's the story I was just reading a few moments ago!* (see John 1:43–51)

Jesus, the Bridegroom, knew His bride, Nathanael, because Nathanael was studying the Word. The best way for you to have knowledge of your wife, husband, is to spend time with her in the Word.

1 Peter 3:7 (c)
. . . giving honour unto the wife, as unto the weaker vessel . . .

Not only are we to have knowledge of our wives, but we are to honor them as weaker vessels. The idea of her being the weaker vessel does not mean she is intellectually, morally, or spiritually inferior. On the contrary, her weakness stems from her innate desire for spirituality. In the Garden of Eden, it was Eve Satan seduced—not to party, but to be more spiritual. Eve was the weaker vessel in the sense that she was more vulnerable to Satan's suggestion that she eat of the fruit of the tree of the knowledge of good and evil in order to be more like God (Genesis 3:5).

This helps me understand that my wife will innately have a desire for the Lord that will perhaps transcend my own. Thus, I can be blessed by her relationship with Him. On the other hand, she will also be more vulnerable to some of Satan's subtle seductions. So we need each other.

After the Fall, the situation worsened due to the curse which said that although the desire of the woman would be for the man, it would be the lot of the man to work hard for a living (Genesis 3:16–19). That is why husbands hear their wives saying, "I just want to be with you," and why wives hear their husbands saying, "I just want to provide for you." It's the curse that affects every marriage to one degree or another.

1 Peter 3:7 (d)
. . . and as being heirs together of the grace of life . . .

Not only are husbands to have knowledge of and give honor to their wives, they are to be enriched by their wives. Suppose you inherited ten thousand dollars, but your wife inherited ten million dollars. Would you choose to have a joint checking account? Would you choose to be joint heirs? I think so!

Husband, you can enjoy the *charis*, the grace, the "beauty of life" if you see your wife as being rich in the things of God.

"Oh, but I don't need my wife spiritually," you might be thinking. "I'm a mighty man of God."

So was Moses.

God had called Moses to set His people free. Yet after hearing the Word of the Lord, he found himself pinned down by Lord's strength. Intuitively realizing what was happening, his wife, Zipporah, grabbed a sharp rock and circumcised their son. The Lord then released Moses to go on to become the leader of the nation of Israel (Exodus 4:25).

You see, God had told Moses that the eldest sons of the Egyptians would die. Moses had a problem in that his own son was not circumcised according to the covenant of God. Zipporah knew this. Oh, others might have been in awe of Moses. Others might have been impressed with Moses. Others had certainly been led by Moses. Zipporah knew that God would not continue to use Moses if he failed to tend to his own son.

So often, it's the wife who will say, "Others

might think you're Mr. Wonderful, but because I want to see you become what I know God has called you to be; because I want you to be the leader of our family; because I want our sons and daughters to do well, this is what needs to happen. . . ."

Husband, God put your wife in your life to enrich you. Listen to her. Honor her. Know her. My wife has a huge part to play in my life and ministry. She's a joint heir. I will enjoy the *charis*, grace, the "beauty of life" to the degree that I know, honor and listen to her.

1 Peter 3:7 (e)
. . . that your prayers be not hindered.

Husband, more than success in ministry, more than professional accolades, more than material wealth, God wants you to experience the joy of seeing your wife as a joint heir with Christ. He wants you to see your kids grow up serving Him wholeheartedly. To that end, as He did with Moses, He'll stop you if your priorities are amiss. If you notice a dryness in your walk or a brass ceiling that causes your prayers to bounce back to you, could it be that something is wrong at home? The Father loves us too much to let us go about our business for Him if things aren't right with our families. If our faith doesn't work at home, it doesn't work anywhere.

1 Peter 3:8–10 (a)
Finally, be ye all of one mind, having compassion one of another, love as brethren, be pitiful, be courteous: Not rendering evil for evil, or railing for railing: but contrariwise blessing; knowing that ye are thereunto called, that ye should inherit a blessing. For he that will love life, and see good days, let him refrain his tongue from evil . . .

After talking about marriage and "love life," Peter talks about loving life. Even in the midst of the persecution where believers were being crucified upside down, Peter encourages his readers to love life.

It is when the hard times come that we need to watch our tongues. It's very easy to begin complaining, "Why me? Why this? Why now?" Peter tells us that if we want to love life and see good days, we are to refrain our tongue from evil—literally to keep from complaining.

1 Peter 3:10 (b)
. . . and his lips that they speak no guile.

While speaking evil implies speaking against God, "speaking guile" means manipulating situa-

tions to make it easier on oneself. This happens most easily when times get tough, as we begin to twist the truth, saying things that put us in a better light. We manipulate the situation to our own advantage.

1 Peter 3:11 (a)
Let him eschew evil, and do good . . .

In other words, "Turn your back on evil and, instead, do good." This is the idea that we are to do good for others. When hard times come, it's easy to think that it's not our fault. Peter tells us that if we want to love life and see good days, we must not let our guard down. This isn't meant to put a legalistic burden *upon* us, but rather to be a wise and loving guide *for* us.

1 Peter 3:11 (b), 12
. . . let him seek peace, and ensue it. For the eyes of the Lord are over the righteous, and his ears are open unto their prayers: but the face of the Lord is against them that do evil.

Peter continues quoting another who experienced brutal days.

What man is he that desireth life, and loveth many days, that he may see good? Keep thy tongue from evil, and thy lips from speaking guile. Depart from evil, and do good; seek peace, and pursue it. The eyes of the LORD are upon the righteous, and his ears are open unto their cry. The face of the LORD is against them that do evil, to cut off the remembrance of them from the earth.　　　　Psalm 34:12–16

With Saul out to kill him, David found himself seeking refuge in the Philistine city of Gath. When he realized that he was recognized as the one who had slain Goliath, David knew he was again in danger. In order to make it out of Gath alive, he clawed at the gates of the city, ranting and raving like a lunatic as he feigned insanity. When the king heard there was a crazy man within his gates, David was allowed to go his way. (1 Samuel 21:10–15)

Psalm 34 was written while David was running for his life. Yet he says, "I will bless the Lord at all times. His praise shall continually be in my mouth, for I have tasted and seen in the midst of this difficulty that the Lord is good."

Who will love life and see good days? Society says it's the one who can make his life problem-free, who insulates himself from difficulty, who escapes adversity. David says just the opposite. He says it's when you're wondering how the next bill will be paid, or if the marriage will work out that the Lord makes Himself most real to you. He says it's when you're trapped in Gath that suddenly you see God.

If we really embraced what Peter is saying, what David is declaring, and what James' injunction to "Count it all joy when you fall into various trials" (see James 1:2), we would not try to make our life easier. Instead, we would be those who say, "It's in the day of difficulty, in the years that are hard for me that I'm going to have the opportunity to taste and see that the Lord is good."

We all know people who are insulated from problems, who don't have challenges, who succeeded in making their lives as easy as they possibly could. Yet the easier it gets for them, the less joy there is within them.

Peter says something absolutely shocking—at least to the ears of our culture: "In the midst of suffering, difficulty, and challenges, don't seek to fix the problem. Don't make it easier. Instead, choose to do good and seek peace. Don't murmur; don't complain. You'll find that you love life because God will meet you in the midst of your difficulty."

1 Peter 3:13
And who is he that will harm you, if ye be followers of that which is good?

To the early church, Peter says, "If you choose to do good in hard times, who can really harm you? Oh, people might hurt you, but they can't harm you. They might tie you to a tree and ignite you. They might throw you to lions that devour you. But they can't harm you because you'll end up in heaven."

Those who live for heaven have an entirely different perspective on life because they're able to take a lot more things a lot less seriously. If you're living for earth, for an easy life, you'll be miserable. If you seek first the kingdom of God, if you live for heaven, you'll find that, although people may hurt you, no one can harm you.

1 Peter 3:14 (a)
But and if ye suffer for righteousness' sake, happy are ye . . .

"Blessed are you when men revile you and persecute you and say all manner of evil against you falsely for My name's sake. Rejoice and be exceedingly glad, for great is your reward in heaven" (see Matthew 5:11, 12).

Echoing Jesus, Peter says, "Be happy in suffering, in difficulty, in persecution." Why? Suffer-

ing, difficulty, heartache, and tragedy set our sights on heaven.

Although I long to go oh, so much further, I'm not sure that had I not been given the privilege of going through some heartaches and tragedies, I would be where I am presently. And the same is true for you. The aching back, the kids that break your heart, the career advancement that didn't work out—are all necessary to sever the cords that bind us to this earth.

1 Peter 3:14 (b), 15 (a)
. . . and be not afraid of their terror, neither be troubled; but sanctify the Lord God in your hearts . . .

After quoting David and Jesus, Peter quotes Isaiah.

With the dreaded Assyrians headed their way, the kings of Syria and Israel asked Ahaz, the king of Judah to join them. However, being warned through Isaiah by the Lord not to, Ahaz refused. This put him in a position in which Assyria, Syria, and Israel were now all against him.

> For the LORD spake thus to me with a strong hand, and instructed me that I should not walk in the way of this people, saying, Say ye not, A confederacy, to all them to whom this people shall say, A confederacy; neither fear ye their fear, nor be afraid. Isaiah 8:11, 12

"Do not be afraid of confederacies," Isaiah said. In other words, "Focus on the Lord."

Peter was talking to a group of people who were, indeed, the object of a conspiracy, as the Roman Empire conspired against Christians. Yet because he knew the Word, Peter was able to draw on Old Testament illustrations to encourage them in their situation.

1 Peter 3:15 (b)
. . . and be ready always to give an answer to every man that asketh you a reason of the hope that is in you with meekness and fear.

The idea here is not primarily to defend a theological position. Rather, it is to give a very simple explanation for your hope. This is another good thing about hard times: they give us an opportunity to shine brightly in what would otherwise be darkness.

For topical study of 1 Peter 3:14–15 entitled "The Reason for Hope," turn to page 1567.

1 Peter 3:16, 17
Having a good conscience; that, whereas they speak evil of you, as of evildoers, they may be ashamed that falsely accuse your good conversation in Christ. For it is better, if the will of God be so, that ye suffer for well doing, than for evil doing.

Why is it important to have a good conscience? Without one, we will not speak boldly when people ask about the hope within us.

If you stagger out of a tavern, get in your car, and hit fifteen cars on your way down the street, when the policeman pulls you over and the newspaper puts your picture on the front page the next day, how bold a witness would you be?

The Bible speaks specifically about our conscience.

In Titus 1:15, we are warned about the danger of a defiled conscience. The word "defiled" speaks of the way an unwashed window gets dirtier and dirtier, making things appear darker and darker. It's an excellent illustration, for if I expose my mind to sin, my conscience becomes dirtier and dirtier, allowing less and less light to break through. Bible study becomes increasingly difficult, and my heart feels heavy and dark.
In 1 Timothy 4:2, we read of a seared conscience—one no longer sensitive to that which once troubled it.
Hebrews 10:22 speaks of an evil or a poisoned conscience within those who twist Scripture not only to justify their own sin, but to draw other people in as well.

Because it sounded like a woman's voice, the owner of a Lincoln Town Car deluxe edition called the computer-generated voice that notified him of any problems "the little lady." One day, as he was driving, the little lady said, "You're running low on fuel. You're running low on fuel."
No way, thought the man. *I have almost half a tank left.*
Every thirty seconds, the voice said, "Stop for gas. Stop for gas. Stop for gas."
Frustrated, he stopped his car, reached under the dashboard, and ripped out the wiring. When he drove a little farther, however, his car sputtered before stopping altogether—for, indeed he was out of gas. The little lady wasn't wrong. It was his gas gauge that was broken.
Man was created with a voice inside of him that

says, "You're running low on fuel," or, "Stay away from there," or, "Watch out for that." Those with a seared or evil conscience say, "No problem," as they begin ripping away the wires of their conscience until they no longer can hear the voice within.

1 Peter 3:18
For Christ also hath once suffered for sins, the just for the unjust, that he might bring us to God, being put to death in the flesh, but quickened by the Spirit.

A good conscience is not dependent upon what we do or don't do, but upon what Jesus did. I can truly have a good conscience if I understand that the sins, shortcomings, and failings that are part of my history were completely paid for by Christ. No one knew this better than Peter.

Cursing vehemently, he swore he didn't know Him, as he stood in the courtyard of Caiaphas—for just as Jesus said he would, Peter denied Christ. Aware of his failing, he wept bitterly (Luke 22:62).

Peter went on from there to become a man who was mighty in ministry, a man who was totally restored because he understood that Jesus Christ died for his sins of betrayal, rebellion, and blasphemy.
The same evening Peter openly denied Jesus, another disciple secretly betrayed Him. . . .

After selling Him out for thirty pieces of silver, Judas' conscience bothered him greatly. "I have betrayed innocent blood," he said as he threw the money on the floor of the temple, wanting to reverse the deal. But realizing that the priests would not allow him a way out, Judas hung himself (see Matthew 27:5).

Both men failed Jesus in the same evening. One went to hell, the other went on to great things. What was the difference? They each chose a tree. Judas chose a tree from which to hang himself. Peter chose a tree upon which to look. Truly, there is great power in seeing the Cross.
"I'm so poisoned," you say.
So were the Israelites. . . .

By the tens of thousands, they were bitten by snakes that sent poison coursing through their veins. The cure? God told Moses to put a brass serpent upon a brass pole in the middle of the camp—and whoever would look upon it would be healed (Numbers 21:8). Those who took this to be trivial and simplistic died in the desert.

Those who simply lifted up their eyes and looked upon the serpent were completely healed. This served as a sneak preview of what would happen when the Son of God became a serpent, became sin, and hung on the Cross in our place (2 Corinthians 5:21).

So, too, there are people who say, "Guilt will not dissipate simply by looking to the Cross. What's needed is years of analysis followed by years of counseling." Peter says otherwise. Because he looked to the One hanging on the tree— even though he had been bitten by his own sin— Peter was forgiven immediately and went on to great ministry.

1 Peter 3:19, 20
By which also he went and preached unto the spirits in prison; which sometime were disobedient, when once the longsuffering of God waited in the days of Noah, while the ark was a preparing, wherein few, that is, eight souls were saved by water.

"I believe Christ died for my sin," you may say, "but why am I always thinking about my failure? Why am I always aware of my sin and rebellion?"

You have an adversary who perches on your shoulder and whispers in your ear, "You're a sinner. You failed here. You dropped the ball there. You're going to need lots and lots of psychological work to have any hope of recovery because you're a rotten loser" (see Revelation 12:10). Satan, the accuser of the brethren, is not omnipresent. He cannot be everywhere at once. But he can dispatch demons. Therefore, Jesus not only died for our sins, but after He died, He "preached unto the spirits in prison." That is, He went to hell.

We know from the account in Luke 16 that before Jesus rose from the dead, hell was divided into two compartments: Paradise was where the Old Testament saints waited for the work of the Cross. That is why Jesus said to the thief on the cross, "This day you'll be with Me in paradise" (see Luke 23:43). Those who didn't believe on the Lord were on the other side of hell—a place of torment.

In our text, we read that Jesus preached to the spirits who were disobedient in the day of Noah. Who were these spirits? Genesis 6 tells us they were particularly disobedient and diabolical. The most wicked of all demons, they actually had relations with women, from which a race of giants was produced. It was to these spirits that Jesus preached. Why? They were the "big guns," the most terrible, the ones that will be released during the Tribulation, where they will cause unparalleled pain and problems for people on the earth.

What did Jesus say to them? He said, "Your authority to keep a grip on Jon Courson has been broken. The blood I shed washed away every sin he has done, is doing, or ever will do. The perfect provision I have made now absolutely, completely frees him from your authority."

You see, it is only through sin that Satan's demons have authority in our lives. When we sin, we essentially rebel against God and open ourselves to the devil and his demons. They can do whatever they want because the sin in our lives gives them a handle upon which to hold. However, the blood of Jesus is so powerful that it eradicates the sin, thereby obliterating the handle.

Without that handle, what can Satan and his henchmen do? All they can do is lie to you and me, saying, "There's no hope for you. You've blown it too badly. You've gone too far. You're through."

Is your conscience bothering you? Peter says, "Look to the Cross." If you still feel condemned, realize it's a lie from the Enemy telling you that you're not forgiven, that you're unworthy, that you can't be used, that you've gone too far, that you've been too bad. Realize that Jesus told the very worst of the demons that they no longer have power over you.

1 Peter 3:21, 22 (a)
The like figure whereunto even baptism doth also now save us (not the putting away of the filth of the flesh, but the answer of a good conscience toward God,) by the resurrection of Jesus Christ: Who is gone into heaven, and is on the right hand of God . . .

The Cross provides forgiveness. The demons have been put on notice. If you still are struggling with your conscience, the solution is found in the same place it was in Noah's day, when the Flood washed away the memory of the sinful world. Just as the Flood drowned out the world and washed away the problem, when a person is baptized, the world's pull is reduced, washed away, drowned out due to the realization of what Christ did on the Cross and the proclamation He made to the demons in hell.

1 Peter 3:22 (b)
. . . angels and authorities and powers being made subject unto him.

"Angels and authorities and powers" refer to demons. They cannot rebel against Jesus. They cannot contradict Jesus. They must submit to Jesus because they were rendered ineffective by Jesus.

THE REASON FOR HOPE
A Topical Study of
1 Peter 3:14, 15

Astronomers tell us that at this moment there are 1,096 stars visible to the naked eye. Yet in the morning, you can't see even one of them because the brightness of the sun obscures the beauty of the stars. It is only when darkness falls that the stars become visible.

The people to whom Peter was writing were living in troubled times, in dark days. Persecution against them had already begun and would only intensify in the days to come as six million of them would be fed to lions, nailed to crosses, ignited as human torches, or boiled in oil. But Peter knew that just as in the heavens above, the darker the sky became around the Christians, the greater light shining from them would be.

Although we don't experience physical persecution in our own country, none can deny that the culture is growing darker and darker all around us. In light of this, what does Peter tell us to do?

Be happy. Personal difficulties, hard times, and suffering allow one the opportunity to give an answer for his hope. Be it cultural or personal difficulty, you can shine more brightly when people look at you—even as they looked at those to whom Peter was writing who seemed to be living in a hopeless situation—and ask, "How can you have such hope?"

You must be ready to give an answer—not primarily concerning the theological position you hold, but rather concerning the spiritual hope you have—for people are hopeless in four ways.

Essentially Empty

Augustine was right when he said, "Our hearts are restless until they find their rest in Thee, O Lord."

Pascal put it this way: There is a God-shaped vacuum in the heart of every man that cannot be satisfied by anything but God.

Paul said it best when he said God created us subject to emptiness (Romans 8:20).

Suppose you go to the Ford dealership today and see the new Ford Explorers all lined up, gleaming in the sun. You can open the door of one, take your seat behind the wheel, shift the gears, and pump the brake. But you won't go anywhere because there's a hole in the car that must be filled. It's called the ignition. Is the Ford dealership mean to put those cars out on the lot with holes in them? No. They simply want a relationship with you. The hole in the car keeps you from cruising away because they want you to come into their showroom and to sit across the table from them as they draw up papers for you to sign.

God created every single human being in such a way that his life won't work until the hole in it is filled with Jesus. God is good. There's nothing about Him that's capricious. Because He created a hole within the heart of every person you go to school with, every person you work with, every person you live near—they're all essentially empty, curious about the reason for the hope within you.

Desperately Lonely

Not only are people essentially empty, but adults, teenagers, and even children are desperately lonely. They are seeking a solution for their loneliness in some earthly relationship, not knowing it will only be solved by discovering the greatest Friend anyone can have—a Friend who sticks closer than a brother, a Friend who will never leave them—Jesus Christ.

On the mountaintop one morning, talking things over with the Lord, I was reminded how fabulous it is to have a Friend who's always there. This realization keeps me from clinging to others, from being a burden to others, from taking advantage of others. It's a relationship for which the world longs, even though they don't know it.

Painfully Guilty

In addition to being essentially empty and desperately lonely, every person is painfully guilty. No matter how we try to deny it, every one of us knows we've dropped the ball; we've hurt people; we've messed up. Every single person you talk to is aware that he has failed, for all have sinned and fallen short of the glory of God. There is none righteous, no not one (Romans 3:10, 23). We can be righteous not by trying to be good little boys or girls—but only by realizing we're sinners and that Jesus took our place when He died.

Filled with Anxiety

Finally, every person on this planet is filled with anxiety. The writer to the Hebrews tells us that Jesus came to deliver those subject to bondage of the fear of death (Hebrews 2:15). The fear of death holds every single person in bondage all the days of his life.

I'm so glad I'm a Christian. I'm so glad you're saved. I'm so thankful we know that to be absent in the body is to be present with the Lord (2 Corinthians 5:8). I'm so grateful we don't have to be fearful about our own situation, or angry when a loved one is taken from us because we know that what Jesus said is true. "Let not your heart be troubled," He said. "You believe in God. Believe also in Me. In My Father's house are many mansions. If it were not so, I would have told you. I go to prepare a place for you. And if I go to prepare a place for you, I will come again and receive you unto Myself, that where I am there you may be also" (see John 14:1–3).

When days grow darker, when depravity intensifies, when persecution comes, when people want to hear the reason for your hope, you can simply tell them, "The reason I have hope in my heart is because of Jesus Christ. He's the key to the emptiness that was inside me. I no longer am haunted by my past mistakes because they've been washed away by His blood at Calvary. I have a Friend I can talk to continually. And I know I'll live with Him eternally."

You see, it all gets down to Jesus.

When asked who had healed him, the once-blind man answered, "A Man named Jesus."

"How did this happen?" asked the Pharisees some time later.

"He's a Prophet," the man explained.

"Do you believe in the Son of God?" Jesus asked him even later.

"I believe, Lord," came the reply (see John 9:38).

Notice the progression. To the man born blind, Jesus was first a man, then a prophet, and finally Lord.

When questioned about the event, his parents, fearing excommunication, said of their son, "He's of age. Ask him."

So when pressed for the reason Jesus healed him on the Sabbath day, the man simply and powerfully said, "I can't answer your questions. I can't give you a full explanation. All I know is this: Once I was blind, but now I see" (see John 9:25).

That's the hope Peter says we must share. You may not be able to answer another's questions theologically, but when difficulties come your way, you can say, "Here's my story: I was blind once. I was empty. I was lonely. I was guilty. I had anxiety just like you. But now I see. Jesus came into my life, and He's completely changed me. I can't explain it. I can't defend it intellectually, but I can share with you something you cannot refute. Jesus saved me. Therefore, even though I'm not what I should be, I'm not what I used to be."

When times are hard, when catastrophe comes, when setbacks arise, be ready. They will give you opportunity to shine brightly. May God give us boldness and wisdom to see that the reason for the hope within us lies solely in the One who opens our eyes to see Him, even in the darkest day of difficulty.

4 Having told us how to have a clear conscience in chapter 3, here in chapter 4, Peter tells us how to think clearly in days of difficulty,

1 Peter 4:1 (a)
Forasmuch then as Christ hath suffered for us in the flesh, arm yourselves likewise with the same mind . . .

"Tough times are coming," says Peter. "Therefore, arm yourselves with clear thinking." He goes on to give us seven benefits of suffering. . . .

1 Peter 4:1 (b)–3
. . . for he that hath suffered in the flesh hath ceased from sin; that he no longer should live the rest of his time in the flesh to the lusts of men, but to the will of God. For the time past of our life may suffice us to have wrought the will of the Gentiles, when we walked in lasciviousness, lusts, excess of wine, revellings, banquetings, and abominable idolatries.

When you go through tough times, realize, first, that suffering loosens sin's grip on us. That is, when you go through suffering, you no longer give in to the lusts of the flesh; you no longer succumb to sin with the same ease, the same vulnerability you experienced previously. Why? Perhaps the story of a man in the Rogue Valley provides the best answer. . . .

> Known as the life of the party, he played on the local softball team and would often supply the keg. When his three-year-old daughter was killed by a drunk driver, he lost his heart for partying. He was no longer interested in the keggers after the softball games. He found himself despising the places to which he was once attracted when he saw the reality of what drunkenness and partying did to his own family.

That's what suffering does. That's what trials do. The ugliness of sin is seen when it begins to touch your own life. That is why Peter says, "If you've suffered in the flesh—either due to your own sin or sin by the hands of others—you see the result of sin and realize that rather than being something to wink or chuckle at, sin stinks."

1 Peter 4:4
Wherein they think it strange that ye run not with them to the same excess of riot, speaking evil of you.

Not only do you look at life more soberly, but, secondly, suffering causes others to see you differently. Tragedy, persecution, and difficulty make you a marked man. Because of what you've gone through, you no longer can spend your life in trivial pursuits.

1 Peter 4:5
Who shall give account to him that is ready to judge the quick and the dead.

Those who choose to continue in sin will one day stand before the Lord. Peter is not saying this out of condemnation, but rather out of compassion, for he realizes they're in grave danger.

1 Peter 4:6
For this cause was the gospel preached also to them that are dead, that they might be judged according to men in the flesh, but live according to God in the spirit.

In addition to loosening sin's grip on us and causing others to look at us differently, suffering places us in good company—the company of the martyred. Some cults use this verse to say, "When a person dies, they'll have a second opportunity to accept the gospel." However, taken in context, it's clear Peter is talking about those who suffered to the point of death and are now living in heaven.

"Blessed are you when men revile, persecute, and say all manner of evil against you falsely for My name's sake," Jesus said. "Rejoice and be exceedingly glad, for great is your reward in heaven. So did they unto the prophets who were before you" (see Matthew 5:11, 12). In other words, when you're suffering, being put down, or mocked because of your belief in Christ, rejoice because you're in the company of the prophets—of Jeremiah and Isaiah, Ezekiel and Hosea.

"Yea, all those who live godly in Christ Jesus shall suffer persecution," Paul told Timothy (see 2 Timothy 3:12). In other parts of the world, such persecution results in death. In our present culture, it results in ostracism or rejection. One way or another, those who live godly lives suffer persecution sooner or later. When it happens, we're to rejoice because, according to Peter, we're in the company of the martyrs. According to Paul, we're in the company of the godly. And according to Jesus, we're in the company of the prophets—good company, indeed!

1 Peter 4:7
But the end of all things is at hand: be ye therefore sober, and watch unto prayer.

Fourth, suffering keeps us focused on eternity. It's when you're going through tough times, difficult days, seasons of suffering, pressures and persecution that you long for heaven. The good times, the nice things, and the easier days have a tendency to shift our focus off of eternity. It's when the tough times come—when the body hurts, the heart breaks, or the wallet is empty that we say, "I don't belong here. I'm longing for heaven."

1 Peter 4:8–11
And above all things have fervent charity among yourselves: for charity shall cover the multitude of sins. Use hospitality one to another without grudging. As every man hath received the gift, even so minister the same one to another, as good stewards of the manifold grace of God. If any man speak, let him speak as the oracles of God; if any man minister, let him do it as of the ability which God giveth: that God in all things may be glorified through Jesus Christ, to whom be praise and dominion for ever and ever. Amen.

Fifth, suffering frees us to participate in ministry. With persecution heightening, no doubt Peter's readers had already begun to scatter. Some would leave everything to hide in catacombs. Others would open their homes to those fleeing persecution. All would be called to love one another fervently, especially in those dark days of difficulty. So much of my time is absorbed with "stuff." When my material, emotional, or relational "stuff" is taken away, I find I am free to share with and care for others in ways I never had previously.

1 Peter 4:12
Beloved, think it not strange concerning the fiery trial which is to try you, as though some strange thing happened unto you.

"Why me?" we ask when fiery trials come upon us. The real question is, "Why not?" If suffering loosens sin's grip on us and causes others to see us differently, if it places us in good company, keeps us focused on eternity, and frees us to participate in ministry—why *wouldn't* we embrace it as a necessary part of our growth?

1 Peter 4:13, 14
But rejoice, inasmuch as ye are partakers of Christ's sufferings; that, when his glory shall be revealed, ye may be glad also with exceeding joy. If ye be reproached for the name of Christ, happy are ye; for the spirit of glory and of God resteth upon you: on their

part he is evil spoken of, but on your part he is glorified.

Sixth, suffering allows us to experience glory. Jesus gave us a wonderful illustration concerning suffering when He reminded us that after a woman endures pain and suffering to give birth, she forgets about the agony when her baby is born because the suffering is transformed into glory. The same baby who causes pain brings joy.

The heartache, setback, or difficulty that is causing you pain and agony will be the very thing that will ultimately bring joy. That which is breaking your heart right now will soon be the delight of your soul—watch and see!

For topical study of 1 Peter 4:12–14 entitled "Suffering into Glory," turn to page 1572.

1 Peter 4:15
But let none of you suffer as a murderer, or as a thief, or as an evildoer, or as a busybody in other men's matters.

I find it interesting that Peter places busybodies and murderers in the same category.

1 Peter 4:16 (a)
Yet if any man suffer as a Christian . . .

The word "Christian" only appears three times in the Bible: twice in the Book of Acts (11:26; 26:28) and once here. Meaning "little Christ," it was initially a put-down. The early church, however, said, "That's okay. We'll wear with pride what the world intends as derision." Believers have claimed it ever since.

1 Peter 4:16 (b)
. . . let him not be ashamed; but let him glorify God on this behalf.

If we're suffering, our attitude should be "Thank You, Lord, that I'm found worthy to suffer. I'm in good company. You're freeing me from the sins that used to strangle me. My vision is refocused on eternity."

1 Peter 4:17 (a)
For the time is come that judgment must begin at the house of God . . .

Writing this epistle from Rome, Peter is accurately discerning the situation. As he watches the bizarre behavior of Nero and reads the winds of change, he knows that the judgment that has begun will continue. The judgment he speaks of is not from God, for the judgment we deserve was poured out on Christ. Rather, it is Satan who wars against the church.

1 Peter 4:17 (b)
... and if it first begin at us, what shall the end be of them that obey not the gospel of God?

If you think times are tough now, wait until God moves upon a Christ-rejecting world during the Tribulation described in Revelation 6—19. Yes, it's hard being a Christian—but it's a whole lot harder being a pagan. The pagan will endure unbelievable difficulty only to end up in hell.

Life is hard. That's just the way it is. It's hard for everyone. You're not being picked on. I'm not being singled out. It's just life. Even though it's hard, and even though we have problems, we have access to the problem-solver, Jesus Christ. We can cast our care upon Him.

1 Peter 4:18
And if the righteous scarcely be saved, where shall the ungodly and the sinner appear?

"I tell you the truth," Jesus said, "it is easier for a camel to go through the eye of a needle than for a rich man to enter into the kingdom. But with God all things are possible" (see Matthew 19:24–26). Because the rich were considered to be especially blessed, the idea is not that the rich can't be saved. The idea is that any man getting saved is impossible. It is only with God that all things are possible. Only God can squeeze sinners like us through the eye of a needle (Matthew 19:24).

1 Peter 4:19
Wherefore let them that suffer according to the will of God commit the keeping of their

souls to him in well-doing, as unto a faithful Creator.

Finally, suffering reminds us to faithfully commit our soul unto our Creator. Of all the titles for God, Peter could have employed in this section dealing with suffering, he says, "When you suffer, commit your soul to your Creator."

Why Creator?

God is the Creator of everything, including the situation in which you're suffering. Nothing can happen that God doesn't allow. He's the Creator of the person to whom you're married, the person with whom you work, and the neighbor by whom you live. He's the Creator of *every* situation.

After tossing and turning concerning a certain aspect of ministry, I slipped out of bed, thinking, How am I going to deal with this? As I stepped outside, I immediately felt the unmistakable, all too familiar sensation of cold ooze flowing through my toes. Yes, I had stepped squarely on a giant slug. Although I immediately recoiled, the slug stuck to the bottom of my foot so firmly that I had to shake it off—causing it to hit the side of my house. As I watched it slide down the wall, I suddenly realized that, although God could have made me a slug, He, instead, created me in His own image. Because He's my Creator, because He made the situations and the challenges around me, I must trust Him with them all.

Dear, precious people, may we be those who slowly but surely learn to embrace suffering. May we begin to understand that it truly loosens sin's grip on us personally, causes others to see us differently, places us in good company, keeps us focused on eternity, frees us to participate in ministry, allows us to experience glory, and reminds us to commit our souls unto our Creator faithfully.

SUFFERING INTO GLORY
A Topical Study of
1 Peter 4:12–14

Suffering and glory are the twin truths woven into the fabric of Peter's first epistle. This should not be surprising, since suffering and glory truly walk hand in hand. Whether or not they realize it, everyone craves glory. The biblical definition of "glory" is seen in the Hebrew word *chabod*, which means "weighty" or "substantial." Glory is a top sirloin steak as opposed to cotton candy—something one can sink his teeth into as opposed to something composed simply of sugar and air.

Man was originally clothed with this glory—the weight of the reality of God. When Adam sinned, the *chabod* departed, leaving him empty and exposed (Genesis 3:7). Yet according to our text, the day is coming when our suffering will be translated into glory for all eternity.

> *But rejoice, inasmuch as ye are partakers of Christ's sufferings; that, when his glory shall be revealed, ye may be glad also with exceeding joy.*
> 1 Peter 4:13

"But that's in the sweet by-and-by," you say. "What about *now?*"
Look at the next verse.

> *If ye be reproached for the name of Christ, happy are ye; for the spirit of glory and of God resteth upon you.*   1 Peter 4:14

Peter declares that the presence of suffering brings glory. I want you to see this because it's radical—completely contrary to everything our flesh tells us.

"If I didn't have to suffer and go through trials, life would be glorious," we say. Not true. Check out *Lifestyles of the Rich and Famous* and see if those people are experiencing glory, substance, or joy. The world insists that the absence of suffering brings glory. The Word says the presence of suffering brings glory.

In our fallen, depraved condition, we are unable to differentiate between what is truly good and bad. What we think is good and wonderful is often bad and brutal. What we think is suffering and pain is actually that which brings happiness, joy, and glory.

> Suppose I had said to my son Benjamin when he was young, "Benny, you must keep your room immaculate because each day I'm going to give you an eight-inch-by-twelve-inch piece of paper to take care of."
>
> "Oh," he would probably have said. "Why is Dad giving me this hard job? Oh, pain, agony and suffering!"—until the day in college he decides to look more closely at the stack of paper I've given him and discovers that each one represents one hundred shares of preferred IBM stock. He's now a billionaire.

Turn to John 16, where we see Jesus give an infinitely better illustration of suffering being transformed into glory. . . .

> *A woman when she is in travail hath sorrow, because her hour is come: but as soon as she is delivered of the child, she remembereth no more the anguish, for joy that a man is born into the world.*   John 16:21

When someone tells you she's pregnant, do you say, "Oh no! That's going to be awful! You're going to start gaining weight and stretching in unbelievable ways. You'll have to go to the hospital, where you'll sweat and strain. Oh, I'm so sorry you're pregnant"? Of course not! We look at childbearing as a great privilege and a real joy because we know that the same baby who brings pain for a short time brings joy for a lifetime.

Peter echoes Jesus in saying that the very thing that causes discomfort—be it a marriage, job, illness, or finances—is precisely that which will bring glory and unspeakable joy.

What if we really believed this? If we truly understood what Jesus taught and what Peter reiterated, we would look at each obstacle and disappointment as a "preferred stock certificate" that will one day be transformed into great wealth. Whether it takes nine months or nine years, I have God's word that the very thing causing me pain will be that which brings substance and joy.

Jesus modeled this for us perfectly. You see, He knows what He's talking about when it comes to joy.

Looking unto Jesus the author and finisher of our faith; who for the joy that was set before him endured the cross, despising the shame, and is set down at the right hand of the throne of God.   Hebrews 12:2

Jesus endured the Cross because He knew it was the Cross that would bring joy. In the pain of the Cross, a baby was birthed. . . .

To hasten death, the legs of one being crucified were broken. No longer able to displace the weight of his body from his wrists and draw air into his lungs, the victim would die by suffocation. When the soldiers came to Jesus, however, there was no need to break His legs, for He had already released His spirit. Instead, a soldier pierced His side. As a result of this seemingly capricious act, blood and water—the fluids of birth—flowed from His side.

Compare this with the account of Genesis 2. . . .

After causing a deep sleep to fall upon Adam, God opened his side and removed a rib, with which he formed a bride for Adam.

You see, just as Adam's bride came from his side, a bride came from the blood that flowed from the side of the Last Adam—Jesus Christ.

- Who is this bride?
  You and me (Ephesians 5:25–27).

For the joy set before Him, Jesus endured the Cross.

- What joy?
  The joy of birth.

Jesus knew that the pain and suffering He endured on the Cross would be transformed into joy. Likewise, the struggle you face today—emotional or financial, spiritual or physical—has the potential to birth something wonderful in your life.

"Count it all *joy* when ye fall into temptation, into trials, into suffering," James wrote (see 1:2). May we be those who do just that.

May we be those who celebrate even the difficulties that come our way, knowing they are the materials from which the Lord will fashion joy.

May we realize suffering and glory are two sides of the same coin. And, preferred stock that they are, may we invest wisely and spend freely.

5 Peter understood that fiery trials would begin at the house of God (4:17). He also knew that the house of God had better be in order. That is why here in chapter 5, he ends his letter talking about the leaders and structure of the church.

1 Peter 5:1 (a)
The elders which are among you I exhort . . .

The words "elder," "bishop," and "pastor" are used interchangeably in the New Testament.

Presbuteros, *the Greek word translated "elder," describes the man as—one who is to have some maturity, experience, and history with God.*
Episkopos, *the Greek word translated "bishop," describes the ministry—not as overlording or overburdening, but as overseeing.*
Poimen, *the Greek word translated "pastor," describes the method—as that of feeding the flock of God.*

The following words directed toward elders also apply to every one of you who is involved in caring for or overseeing your family or others.

1 Peter 5:1 (b)
. . . who am also an elder . . .

Notice, Peter doesn't identify himself as the first pope. Rather, he says, "I'm an elder just like you."

1 Peter 5:1 (c)
. . . and a witness of the sufferings of Christ, and also a partaker of the glory that shall be revealed.

"I'm one of you," says Peter, "but I've also had a little more history with Jesus than you. I saw His sufferings and His glory on the Mount of Transfiguration" (see Matthew 17).

1 Peter 5:2 (a)
Feed the flock of God . . .

Although he knew tough times were coming, Peter says, "Don't neglect your singular responsibility to feed the flock of God." We don't need to be plugged in to a lot of activities or Christian recreation. What we need is the Word of God.

1 Peter 5:2 (b)
. . . which is among you, taking the oversight thereof . . .

Although Peter was one with the people, he was responsible to oversee them. Such is the tension for any leader—as a pastor, a parent, or a youth leader. Sometimes it can be extremely difficult. If I am simply overseeing but am not among the people to whom I'm ministering, I will become aloof and untouchable. If, on the other hand, I'm just one of the gang, shooting pool and joking around every night, I probably won't have the authority to oversee as I'm told to do.
What is Peter's solution?
We'll see it in verse 3.

1 Peter 5:2 (c)
. . . not by constraint, but willingly . . .

You shouldn't have to be prodded to pastor, to parent, or to work with the fourth-graders in Sunday school. In other words, your motivation should not stem from someone relentlessly badgering you, but from the internal call of God.

There are two inherent dangers in the ministry. The first is laziness, when people do the very least they possibly can. There's no room in the ministry for laziness because, to a large degree, the well-being of the flock depends upon the care of those in positions of authority.

1 Peter 5:2 (d)
. . . not for filthy lucre, but of a ready mind.

The second inherent danger in ministry is that of covetousness.

1 Peter 5:3 (a)
Neither as being lords over God's heritage . . .

As pastor, I'm not the Reverend Right Most Holy Bishop. Rather, I'm just one of the sheep. Why am I up front? If the church were likened to a hospital, I am up front simply because I've been a patient a little longer than most of you in the Hospital of God's Grace and Goodness. Thus, I know where the cafeteria is and where the restrooms are. I know which orderlies to watch out for, and which doctors have big needles. We're all in this thing together. We're *all* sheep. Therefore, no one in the body of Christ can lord it over anyone else.

1 Peter 5:3 (b)
. . . but being ensamples to the flock.

Here is the solution to verse 2. In parenting, pastoring, or anything else concerning working with people, the bottom line is this: Be an example. That's how you can be among people and oversee them, as well. Whether raising my kids or serving at Calvary Chapel, I am not to be a lord. I'm to be an example.

There's a big difference between dictatorship and leadership. Dictatorship says, "Go." Leadership says, "Let's go." Whether parenting or pastoring, the true leader is involved in whatever he's teaching or helping others to do. Paul put it this way to his young protégé, Timothy: "Be thou an example of the believer" (see 1 Timothy 4:12). In other words, be a man of prayer, a man of compassion, a man who worships. Let people see this first in you.

Let me ask you this question: If everyone at Calvary Chapel was exactly like you, what kind of church would we have? If everyone prayed for the body of Christ as much as you do, how much prayer would we have? If everyone tithed exactly like you, how much would we be able to invest for the kingdom? If everyone came to morning worship as much as you, how many would come? If everyone helped in Sunday school to the degree you do, would the church be bigger, stronger, and healthier? Or would we be meeting in the park at Picnic Table Number Three? It's a very important question because that which each of us does or doesn't do affects the rest of us very definitely.

1 Peter 5:4
And when the chief Shepherd shall appear, ye shall receive a crown of glory that fadeth not away.

If you're an example—if you're feeding people and caring for them—the day is coming when all of those things that were unnoticed will be greatly rewarded. A time is coming when all of the things I have done are going to be tested by fire. I will stand before the Lord, realizing I could have given more generously and served more freely.

The crowns of which Peter speaks are not just to parade around in. No, they are to cast at Jesus' feet in gratitude and adoration—as well as determining our function in eternity. If you're tired of where you're at now, be one who says, "I might not be where I wanted to be on earth, but I'm praying, giving, worshiping and serving as if the chief shepherd is coming. My efforts will be known to Him, and I will be fulfilled in ways I never was on earth."

1 Peter 5:5 (a)
Likewise, ye younger, submit yourselves unto the elder. Yea, all of you be subject one to another, and be clothed with humility . . .

Peter reminds us we are called to humility. Humility means that even if the elder over me—be it Mom and Dad, or the spiritual brothers overseeing my ministry—makes the wrong decision, I must be the right person. This applies to marriage, parenting, church, the job site—anywhere people are. Our responsibility is not to make sure that those in authority over us make the right decision. Our responsibility is to make sure we're the right people.

Why? Read on.

1 Peter 5:5 (b), 6
. . . for God resisteth the proud, and giveth grace to the humble. Humble yourselves therefore under the mighty hand of God, that he may exalt you in due time.

Those who are humble will be exalted. Immediately? No. They will be exalted in due time, at the perfect time.

1 Peter 5:7
Casting all your care upon him; for he careth for you.

The Greek word *epirrhihipto*, translated "casting," is interesting because it means to roll something that will most likely roll back upon you. Have you found that after casting your care on the Lord, you feel okay for a day or two, but then the burden rolls right back on you? If so, know that's the way of the Lord. Why? He wants us to stay in close touch with Him, and if we cast our care upon Him never to feel the pressure, the anxiety, the tension, the worry again, we would not be people who pray.

You see, the Father wants to do something bigger than merely taking our burdens from us. He wants to develop a relationship with us. Thus, the burdens and struggles that repeatedly roll upon us cause us to become linked to Him in continual prayer. That's infinitely more important than the solution to the burden for which we were praying in the first place. So cast your care upon Him—and keep doing it over and over and over again, knowing how deeply He cares for you.

1 Peter 5:8, 9
Be sober, be vigilant; because your adversary the devil, as a roaring lion, walketh about, seeking whom he may devour: Whom resist stedfast in the faith, knowing that the same afflictions are accomplished in your brethren that are in the world.

Even as you cast your care upon God, know the Enemy is out to destroy you.

For topical study of 1 Peter 5:8–9 entitled "Running to the Roar," turn to page 1578.

1 Peter 5:10, 11
But the God of all grace, who hath called us unto his eternal glory by Christ Jesus, after that ye have suffered a while, make you perfect, stablish, strengthen, settle you. To him be glory and dominion for ever and ever. Amen.

As both a pastor and a parent, I go through the previous nine verses and realize how greatly I have failed and how far short I fall of this standard. That's why I believe verse ten is the key to this whole section. You see, the Christian life is all about grace. No one knew this better than Peter.

In verse 1 Peter declared himself a witness of the sufferings of Christ. Yet when we read the

Gospel account, we see that Peter was not present when Christ was led away to be tried by Caiaphas. He was following far off in the shadows. When Christ was on the Cross, he viewed His suffering from a distance, if at all, for of all the disciples, only John was at the foot of the Cross (John 19:26).

Peter also says he was a partaker of glory. He fails to mention, however, that he was reprimanded by God for placing Jesus on the same plane as Moses and Elijah on the Mount of Transfiguration (Matthew 17:5).

In verse 2, Peter says pastors are to feed the flock of God. Yet when he initially heard these words, Peter wasn't waiting for the empowering of the Spirit with God's people as he was supposed to be. Instead, he was fishing on the Sea of Galilee (John 21:3).

Peter also tells pastors not to be lazy. When Jesus asked Peter to pray with Him in the Garden of Gethsemane, what did Peter do? He fell asleep (Mark 14:37).

In verse 3, Peter tells us we are not to be lords over God's heritage. We are to be an example. Yet in the garden, what did Peter do? Far from being an example, he took out a sword and chopped off the ear of Malchus (Mark 14:47).

"Submit yourself unto the elder," Peter says in verse 5. When Jesus said He had to suffer many things in Jerusalem, Peter rebuked Jesus, saying, "Be it far from thee, Lord" (see Matthew 16:22). Submission? Hardly.

Peter went on to say we are to be clothed with humility. Yet as he sat in the Upper Room with the other disciples, it was not Peter but Jesus who humbled Himself to wash feet (John 13:3, 4).

In verse 7, Peter tells us we are to cast our care upon God. It is an interesting choice of words, for when Jesus told Peter to cast his net on the other side of the boat, Peter was fishing for fish rather than fishing for men as he had been called to do (Matthew 4:19; John 21:6).

In verses 8, 9, Peter tells us to be sober and vigilant in light of our adversary. Yet when Jesus warned him that Satan desired to sift him like wheat, what did Peter say? "Not me, Lord. I am ready to go to prison with You. These other guys might fail you, but You can count on me." Hours later, seduced by Satan, Peter denied Jesus three times (Matthew 26:69–74).

Peter failed at every point. But here's the good news—he was used mightily even after all his failings, because he understood that which he shares with us in verse 10: It's not impeccability that is necessary. It's "teachability." I have failed.

You have failed. Yet if, like Peter, we learn lessons from our failures, we can speak with authority. We can say to others, "I've been there. I've done that. I've made mistakes. You don't have to."

If as a dad or mom, a Sunday-school teacher, elder, or leader at work, you are aware of your shortcomings, if you're not careful, you will think they disqualify you from sharing with others. Take hope from Peter. He failed at every point. Yet when he learned his lesson, he didn't fall again. It's God's grace that will establish, settle, and strengthen you as long as you learn the lessons God has for you.

1 Peter 5:12, 13
By Silvanus, a faithful brother unto you, as I suppose, I have written briefly, exhorting, and testifying that this is the true grace of God wherein ye stand. The church that is at Babylon, elected together with you, saluteth you; and so doth Marcus my son.

No doubt Marcus is John Mark, who, after failing in a previous missionary endeavor (Acts 13:13), was later encouraged by Barnabas and went on to be useful to both Peter and Paul (2 Timothy 4:11).

1 Peter 5:14
Greet ye one another with a kiss of charity. Peace be with you all that are in Christ Jesus. Amen.

To a people going through persecution, Peter ends his letter not with a promise of ease, but with a benediction of peace, knowing that harder times were ahead.

RUNNING TO THE ROAR
A Topical Study of
1 Peter 5:8, 9

O f all the disciples, the most relatable—at least to me—is Simon Peter, the fisherman from Galilee. How right Jesus was when, seeing Peter sleeping in the Garden of Gethsemane, He said, "The spirit is willing, but the flesh is weak" (see Matthew 26:41). I think that's why we readily identify with Peter.

"Follow Me," Jesus said when He first called Peter. Peter dropped his nets on the spot. Three years later, after being with Jesus daily, we see Peter still following—but now from afar (see Matthew 26:58).

"If it's You, Lord, beckon me to come," Peter cried in the midst of the storm. When Jesus did, Peter miraculously walked on water—until he took his eyes off the Lord and began to sink (see Matthew 14:30).

"Thou art the Christos, the Messiah, the Son of the Living God," Peter declared. Five verses later, Peter opposes Jesus to such a degree that Jesus calls him Satan (see Matthew 16:23).

That's why I can relate to Peter. "Follow Me," Jesus said, but Peter followed from a distance. "Walk on water," Jesus said. Peter sank. "You are the Christ," Peter said boldly, but he argued with Jesus anyway.

Peter had such great moments, followed by such deep defeats. His heart was willing, but his flesh was weak.

It shouldn't surprise us that Peter went through those kinds of times. After all, Jesus had told him directly, "Satan desires to sift you like wheat, to grind you up, to wipe you out. I have prayed for you, Peter, and when you are converted—not if but *when* you make it through—strengthen the brethren" (see Luke 22:32). Guess what. In our text, Peter's doing just that, for we're sitting here almost two thousand years later, listening to Peter telling us to be sober and vigilant because our adversary, the devil, goes about as a roaring lion.

Peter would say to us, "I've been there. I desired to walk with, be used by, and be faithful to the Lord. He was right when He told me Satan was trying to sift me like wheat. Our adversary is real."

"Why does Satan want to pick on me?" you ask. Many theories have been presented concerning what motivates our adversary. Among them is the hostage theory that says that Satan seeks to gather as many people as possible into his kingdom of death and darkness in order to use them as a bargaining chip with the Father at the end of time, saying, "These people are in my domain. I will let them go if You let me go." Although there are some obscure references to this in the Word, I don't personally believe this to be true.

Why does Satan bother with us? I think he simply does it because of his perverse nature. I think he's doing just what we do in our own perversity.

There you are—standing by the edge of the pool—when out of the corner of your eye, you see a group of guys headed your way. By the look on their faces, you know what they're about to do. Because you're perverse and depraved, what do you do? You do just what I do. You say, "If I'm going in, you're going too," as you grab as many arms and legs as you can.

Because Satan is innately perverse, I believe he's grabbing as many people as he can to pull into the lake of fire with him.

"I've already given my heart to Jesus," you say, "so why would Satan pick on me when he knows he's already lost me?"

Although he can't take you to hell, he can make you feel so discouraged, so defeated in your own walk that you won't be able to effectively impact others for the kingdom.

Peter was firmly in the camp of the Lord, yet Satan came against him just as Jesus said he would. Peter, however, made it through. And you can, too.

How?

Peter gives a singular answer when he tells us we are not to run, but to resist; we are not to fear, but to resist; we are not to give in, but to resist. James says the same thing when he says, "Resist the devil and he will flee from you" (4:7). Inspired by the same Spirit, James and Peter are in agreement concerning the strategy of dealing with Satan.

Because we have the helmet of salvation, the shield of faith, the sword of the

Spirit, the breastplate of righteousness, our loins girded with truth, and the gospel of peace for shoes, there is only one part of our anatomy vulnerable to the Enemy: our backs (Ephesians 6:13–17).

Why?

It's never the strategy of the Lord to run from the Enemy. Rather, we are equipped to resist and even attack with such power that not even the gates of hell can withstand the onslaught (Matthew 16:18).

We have an Enemy who wants to take us down, wipe us out, make us miserable, and nullify our effectiveness. Peter calls this one a roaring lion.

> The roaring lion, known in Bible times and even to this day, is the king of the pride of lions—not because he is the most powerful lion in the family, but because of what he once was. You see, the roaring lion is the oldest lion in the pride. His teeth are worn. His feet are slow. He's not as quick as he once was, nor as powerful as he used to be. Therefore, his assignment is to hide in the grass until an unsuspecting impala or deer comes walking through. Then he is to stand up and roar. Hearing this, the deer or impala runs away from the roar of the lion—right to the place where all of the young, virile lions are waiting. In so doing, he runs to his death.

> If you could give counsel to the impala or the deer in the savannahs of Africa, you'd say, "If you walk through a grassy area and hear a roar, whatever you do, don't run. Don't be afraid. Just go toward the roar. Resist, resist, resist. Don't run."

The devil is a roaring lion. He had his teeth kicked out at Calvary. Yet he can still roar. "YOU'RE GOING TO FAIL," he roars, and we run right into failure. "YOU'RE GOING TO GIVE IN," he roars, and we do just that. So how are we to withstand his roars?

The Old Testament picture of what it means to resist rather than run is found in 2 Samuel.

> *And Benaiah the son of Jehoiada, the son of a valiant man, of Kabzeel, who had done many acts . . .*
>
> 2 Samuel 23:20 (a)

Benaiah, whose name literally means "built by God," was one of David's mighty men who stood by and traveled with him.

> *. . . he slew two lionlike men of Moab . . .*
>
> 2 Samuel 23:20 (b)

Benaiah took on a couple of strong, bushy-bearded or long-haired men of Moab.

> *. . . he went down also and slew a lion . . .*
>
> 2 Samuel 23:20 (c)

After doing battle with lionlike men, Benaiah was ready to take on the lion itself. I find it to be true oh, so often, that the temptations, difficulties or challenges that come my way in any given day are simply to prepare me for the battles coming eventually.

> . . . *in the midst of a pit in time of snow.*   2 Samuel 23:20 (d)

Maybe you've felt cold in your spirit recently. What did Benaiah do at such a time? He went on the offensive and went into the pit itself to deal with the lion directly. Even in the snowy times, on a cold day, he attacked the Enemy.

> *And he slew an Egyptian, a goodly man . . .*   2 Samuel 23:21 (a)

Being an Egyptian meant this man was a type of the world. Being a "goodly man" meant that he was a big guy.

> . . . *and the Egyptian had a spear in his hand; but he went down to him with a staff, and plucked the spear out of the Egyptian's hand, and slew him with his own spear.*   2 Samuel 23:21 (b)

After being prepared by battling the lionlike men and the lion in the pit, Benaiah now takes on a big chunk of the world and kills him with his own spear. In this brief vignette, I begin to understand what it means to resist the devil. I begin to realize that the skirmishes I'm going through presently are preparatory for what is headed my way in the snowy day. I realize my call is to go into the pit itself, to storm the gates of hell and do battle with the Enemy.

"I try to battle the Enemy," you say, "but I lose every time. I have such a terrible time with my thought life. I'm driving down the street, worshiping the Lord when suddenly a lady gets out of her car and walks down the street. My mind strays, leaving me wondering where in the world those thoughts come from."

Those thoughts don't come from the world. They are fiery darts shot in your direction from hell itself in an attempt by the Enemy to discourage, depress, and defeat you.

Someone else says, "What can I do? It seems like whenever I'm with the girls and I just want to talk about the Lord, the conversation centers on gossip. I try not to get caught up in it, but it just seems to take control of the moment and I succumb."

Simply telling people not to think about lust or gossip is about as effective as telling you not to think about a pink elephant. The harder you try not to think about something, the more you will! Telling people to put depression, gossip, lust, or whatever else they struggle with out of their minds will only lead to frustration because it can't be done.

What are we to do?

Follow the Benaiah model. Resist Satan by going into the pit itself, by taking the weapon of the Egyptian and turning it against him.

How?

You're driving down the road and your mind is playing games with you. Here's what to do: Go on the offensive. Say to the Enemy, "I'm going to run right in your direction. Go ahead and fire that arrow at me as much as you want. Put those thoughts in my mind. Play those games. I want you to know, however, that every time you fire one of those arrows into my mind, I'm not going to come down on myself or try to talk myself out of thinking about a pink elephant. I'm simply going to take that same arrow and turn it against you. I'm going to pray for fifteen people I know who also struggle with this difficulty. Take that."

What happens?

The Enemy begins to see that every time he fires one of his arrows at you, he inadvertently causes you to pray for others. Since prayer binds Satan, he suddenly realizes his plan is backfiring and he flees.

"I'm so depressed," you say. What do you do? Grab the weapon of the Enemy and turn it against him. Go into the pit and say, "You can depress me as much as you wish, but every time you do, Satan, I am going to stop what I'm doing, and, by faith, give thanks to God for all the good things He's done for me. I'm going to worship Him."

Now, because Satan used to be the worship leader in heaven before being demoted to a snake in the dust, the sound of worship is like fingernails on a chalkboard in his ears. So he flees.

"I just can't quit gossiping," you say. You can if you go on the offensive and say ten good things about the person whose name has come up in the conversation. Seeing that tempting you to tear people down only results in you building them up will send Satan running every time.

To resist the devil doesn't mean you try to ignore the reality of the temptation. It means you take the very weapon fired against you and turn it against Satan through intercession, worship, or praise. Do that and Satan will flee from you. He'll leave you alone—at least for a season.

How do I know?

That's what Jesus did. When the Spirit drove Him into the wilderness to be tempted by the Enemy, Satan came to Him, trying to get Him to doubt the character, the provision, and the plan of the Father. What did Jesus do? Did He run? No, He gave Satan a Bible study each time the lion came His way (Matthew 4:4–10).

I don't know what your area of vulnerability is. I don't know where the roaring lion yells at you. This I do know: Whatever your area of weakness, don't run from it. Be Benaiah. Take the offensive. Resist.

Peter was a man who dealt with the Enemy. Now he comes with this word to strengthen you and me. Run toward the roar and watch the toothless old lion flee.

2 PETER

1

2 Peter 1:1 (a)
Simon . . .

As we read the Gospel accounts, we see Peter talking when he should have been listening (Matthew 16:21, 22), sleeping when he should have been praying (Mark 14:37), stepping out when he should have held back (John 18:10), and holding back when he should have stepped out (John 13:8).

That's why Peter is such a favorite of mine—I see his characteristics and tendencies in my own walk and history. Maybe you see them in yours as well. But here's the great news, the amazing truth, the glorious fact: Even with all of his failures and denials, even with all of his setbacks and stumbles, Simon made it through.

Why? Because he was such a great guy?

No. Simon made it through because Jesus prayed for him (Luke 22:32). And guess what. The same thing is true of you and me. We're all people who want to do right, but who invariably mess up. We're all people whose spirits are willing, but whose flesh is unbelievably weak. Yet even right now, Jesus knows the temptation we're facing, the fears we're feeling, the questions that are churning. He knows them all, and He's praying for us (Hebrews 7:25)—not because we're worthy, but because He's faithful.

2 Peter 1:1 (b)
. . . Peter . . .

When Jesus first called Peter, He said, "You are Simon, but you shall be Petros, Peter, Rock," as if to say, "You're shifting sand now, but I know what I'm going to do with you, and I know what will be accomplished in you."

When was Simon's name officially changed to Peter? It happened in Caesarea Philippi. . . .

"Whom do men say that I am?" Jesus asked His disciples.

"Some say You're Elijah; some say You're John the Baptist; some say You're Jeremiah; some say You're the promised prophet of Deuteronomy 18," they answered.

"Yes, but who do you say that I am?" He asked His boys.

It was Peter who said, "Thou art the Christ, the Son of the Living God."

"Blessed are you, Simon," Jesus said, "for flesh and blood has not revealed this to you, but My Father which is in heaven. Thou art Peter. Upon the rock of your confession, I will build My church. And the gates of hell shall not prevail against it" (see Matthew 16:18).

Peter discovered his identity. Peter was changed from shifting sand to rock when he understood who Jesus was. And the same is still true today. I know men fifty years old who are still trying to figure out their identities. Confused about who they are, they try to drive the newest car, marry the youngest wife, and line up the easiest job. But they remain unhappy and unstable because it's only when a man, woman, or teenager finally realizes who Jesus Christ is that life begins to make sense. It's only when we understand that God doesn't exist for us, but that all things were made by and for the One who died for us (Colossians 1:16) that we see who we are in Him.

Show me a teenager who realizes that Jesus does not exist to give him a girlfriend, but that he exists to please Jesus Christ; show me a mom who understands that her purpose is to please Christ even more than pleasing her family; show me a businessman climbing the ladder vocationally who knows his job simply gives him opportunity to please Christ in the workplace—and I'll show you a teenager, a mom, a businessman who knows their true identity.

Please note with me one other element of Peter's introduction. In his first epistle, he referred to himself simply as Peter. In this, his second epistle, coming to the very last days of his life, he refers to himself as *Simon* Peter.

Samuel Chadwick, powerful preacher of generations past, was known as the "Preacher of Passion." This was due to the fact that at some point in every sermon, tears would fill his eyes. His writings reveal the reason why week, after week, year after year he felt such compassion for people. He recounts how every Saturday night, after his sermon was prepared, he would go into his study, close the door behind him, and reflect on what a sinner he had been before he met Christ and how good God was to save him. Remembering the pit from which he had been rescued caused him to break down in gratitude. Then, looking out at his congregation the next morning, realizing many of them were in the same place he had been, he wept for them.

For we who have been saved for over ten years, the danger lies in forgetting the emptiness, the shattered relationships, the broken promises, the valleys that defined our days before the Lord saved us. What was good for Samuel Chadwick and Simon Peter is good for you and me as well—as we reflect on who and where we would be if it wasn't for Jesus in our lives.

2 Peter 1:1 (c)
... a servant ...

The Greek word translated "servant" is *doulos*, or bondservant. After six years of service, slaves were set free. But if a slave wanted to remain in his master's service, an earring would be placed in his ear, signifying that he was a slave by choice.

Such is what Peter was. Why?

Because although the *doulos* was committed to serve his master for life, the master was equally committed to provide for the slave. Now, if you know Jesus at all, it makes all the sense in the world that Peter would want to be a servant of His because who would care for him, who would provide for him better than Jesus?

2 Peter 1:1 (d)
... and an apostle of Jesus Christ ...

"Apostle" means "sent out one." Of the hundreds of disciples, or "disciplined ones," who followed Him, Jesus chose twelve apostles to bring into His inner circle, and then to send out into ministry. Peter was one of those twelve.

2 Peter 1:1 (e)
... to them that have obtained like precious faith ...

I find it intriguing that throughout his writing, Peter uses the word "precious." In his first epistle, he wrote of precious blood (1:19). Here in verse 1 of his second epistle, he speaks of precious faith. In verse 4, he'll talk about precious promises. In chapter 2, he'll speak of the precious stone. Although it's not a word we would expect to find in the vocabulary of a big fisherman, "precious" is a perfect choice because it literally means "beyond calculation." And truly, the faith, blood, and promises of our Lord are of incalculable worth.

2 Peter 1:1 (f)
... with us ...

Peter isn't saying, "I'm flying First Class because I'm an apostle, but the rest of you are in Coach." No, he says, "You have the same precious faith I do. It's common to us all."

2 Peter 1:1 (g)
... through the righteousness of God and our Saviour Jesus Christ.

The Greek phrase translated "of God and our Savior Jesus Christ" is literally "of our God and Saviour Jesus Christ." This means Peter is calling Jesus—with whom he lived and walked for three years—God.

2 Peter 1:2
Grace and peace be multiplied unto you through the knowledge of God, and of Jesus our Lord.

The more knowledge you have of Jesus Christ, the greater understanding you'll have that our God is truly a God of grace.

At the outset of his ministry, Billy Graham was referred to as "God's Machine Gun." But as he went on in his knowledge of the Lord, he found himself becoming more and more oriented toward grace—so much so that many Christians today scratch their heads and wonder how he can be open to so many. "*That* denomination can't be Christian," they scoff. Or, "Surely, *those* people can't be saved." But Billy has a way of being incredibly embracive without compromising. And in his own writings, he explains that as he grows older in the Lord, he's more and more amazed by the grace of the Lord.

The older you grow in the Lord, the more grace-oriented you'll be as you realize the

Christian life is all about Jesus and the undeserved, unearned favor He lavishes upon us so freely due to the finished work of Calvary. The result? Unmistakable, undeniable, unshakable peace. Grace and peace walk hand in hand.

2 Peter 1:3 (a)
According as his divine power hath given unto us all things that pertain unto life and godliness . . .

Notice that Peter is not telling us that everything we have need of pertaining to life and godliness *will be* given to us. No, he says everything we need to live an abundant, fulfilled life—and everything we need to live like Christ—has *already been* given to us.

This is radical because many of us don't have this understanding. We think we're still pursuing some key and if we can find it, then we'll be able to unlock the secret of life. We're looking for the combination on the padlock of godliness. But Peter says something wonderful when he says God has already given us all things—not most things, not a bunch of things—but *all* things that pertain to life and godliness.

When my son Benjamin was born, although he wasn't all that he will be one day, everything he needed was already packed into his little body. His job, then, was not to find additional body parts to add to himself. His job was simply to grow.

"That's obvious," you say. But a whole bunch of Christians do what I did for some years in my walk—they read, search, look for what's missing in their faith, instead of simply taking God's Word at face value, which says His divine power has given us everything we need for godliness and all we need for abundant life. This understanding can save us a bunch of time and a lot of money. For instead of searching bookstores and infomercials to find the seven secrets of effective people, or the way to "awaken the giant within," we can simply grow in the knowledge that we've already been given everything we need to live abundantly and godly.

How do we grow? Read on.

2 Peter 1:3 (b)
. . . through the knowledge of him that hath called us . . .

We grow as we get to know the Lord Jesus through prayer, through the Word, through worship morning by morning, day by day, evening by evening. For the better we know Him, the better we understand how all things that pertain to life and godliness can function within us.

2 Peter 1:3 (c)
. . . to glory and virtue.

The Hebrew word translated "glory" is *chabod,* meaning "weight" or "heaviness." The opposite of a cotton candy-type froth, He who calls us has called us to a substantial, meaningful life.

2 Peter 1:4 (a)
Whereby are given unto us exceeding great and precious promises . . .

"She shows great promise," the teacher says of the child prodigy.

"He shows so much promise," the press says of the NFL rookie.

The question is—will they live up to it?

The same is true of us, for in addition to giving us everything we need to live godly, God also makes amazing promises available to you and me. The question is: Are we living up to them?

2 Peter 1:4 (b)
. . . that by these ye might be partakers of the divine nature . . .

We partake of the divine nature through the promises He's given to us and through the knowledge of Him who gave Himself for us.

2 Peter 1:4 (c)
. . . having escaped the corruption that is in the world through lust.

The craziness of the world can be traced directly to lust. Whether regarding money, sex, esteem, or approval, lust simply says, "I've got to have more." And it is from such a mind-set that we have been delivered.

2 Peter 1:5 (a)
And beside this . . .

"Beside this" could be translated "in light of this." In other words, in light of the fact that we have everything we need to enjoy life fully and to live godly; in light of the fact that we have been given hundreds of promises so graciously; in light of the fact that we are free of the grasp of lust, we are to be those who add to their faith diligently. . . .

2 Peter 1:5 (b)
. . . giving all diligence, add to your faith
virtue . . .

"You have faith," says Peter. "Now go for virtue, or moral excellence." This means that the darkness of our culture as portrayed on the screen or in print, in song lyrics or in the questionable jokes around the water cooler has no place in our lives.

2 Peter 1:5 (c)
. . . and to virtue knowledge.

Why are we to add virtue before knowledge? I believe it's because if my mind is cluttered with pornography and violence, I won't be able to extract knowledge about life from the Word because I've filled my spirit with the junk food of the world. Moral excellence is that which makes room for us to take in the Word and gain knowledge of the Lord.

2 Peter 1:6 (a)
And to knowledge temperance . . .

Why is temperance, or self-control, to be added to knowledge? Because as I gain knowledge, if I'm not very, very careful, I will begin to say, "Now that I have knowledge about this, I can handle it."

A dear pastor friend of mine who had been mightily used by the Lord began to say, "My studies have convinced me that Jesus drank alcohol." And he went on to develop an extensive argument for why Christians should be able to drink. This led him and his wife to wine-tasting events, which led to nightclubs, which led to dancing with other people, which led to divorce. In the name of knowledge, this dear brother sacrificed temperance—and lost his family and ministry as a result.

Peter warns us that as we add knowledge, we must be sure we don't get caught up in a pharisaical pseudo-intellectualism that makes us feel that, because we're a cut above others, we can indulge ourselves in ways that will destroy us.

2 Peter 1:6 (b)
. . . and to temperance patience . . .

Although I'm temperate, disciplined, self-controlled, if I'm not careful, I can become impatient with those who aren't. Therefore, I must add patience to my temperance.

2 Peter 1:6 (c)
. . . and to patience godliness.

Yes, I must be patient—but not to the point where I no longer stand for righteousness and godliness.

2 Peter 1:7 (a)
And to brotherly kindness . . .

Brotherly kindness keeps godliness from being harsh, for brotherly kindness dictates that we be as magnanimous as we possibly can to as many as we possibly can.

2 Peter 1:7 (b)
. . . charity.

Because John tells us that love is the proof that we have passed from death to life (1 John 3:14), it is easy to see why He places charity, agape, perfect love at the top of the list.

2 Peter 1:8
For if these things be in you, and abound, they make you that ye shall neither be barren nor unfruitful in the knowledge of our Lord Jesus Christ.

If you feel barren or unfruitful spiritually, if you're going through a dry season in your walk, the Holy Spirit inspired Peter to tell you to start working on these things. Start being kind to people. Start adding temperance to your life. Be patient with folks. Go for moral excellence. The degree to which you add these qualities to your life will be the degree to which you will be fruitful and productive in your knowledge of the Lord.

"Abide in Me," Jesus said, "and I in you. As the branch cannot bear fruit of itself except it abide in the vine, neither can ye except ye abide in Me" (John 15:4). It is as we abide in the only One whose nature contains all of these traits, the only One who lived them out daily, that we will be able to incorporate them into our own lives.

2 Peter 1:9
But he that lacketh these things is blind, and cannot see afar off, and hath forgotten that he was purged from his old sins.

The idea of purging, or pruning, takes us back to the abiding, the fruitfulness of John 15.

2 Peter 1:10
Wherefore the rather, brethren, give diligence to make your calling and election sure: for if ye do these things, ye shall never fall.

"I'm worried I'm going to lose my salvation," some say. Not if you do these things. "I'm worried I'll stumble," some say. Not if you do these things. According to Peter, if you do these things, your calling, your election is sure and you'll not fail.

2 Peter 1:11
For so an entrance shall be ministered unto you abundantly into the everlasting kingdom of our Lord and Saviour Jesus Christ.

If you do these things, you'll not only be fruitful in this life, but you will be rewarded eternally. I find it amazing and wonderful that Peter doesn't give us a fifteen-volume set of books on how to be fruitful. Rather, he gives us two verses. If I don't pursue knowledge, I may fall. If I don't add virtue, I may fall. If I don't seek after godliness, I may fall. But if I do these things I will never fall—and I will be rewarded eternally on top of that.

2 Peter 1:12, 13
Wherefore I will not be negligent to put you always in remembrance of these things, though ye know them, and be established in the present truth. Yea, I think it meet, as long as I am in this tabernacle, to stir you up by putting you in remembrance.

Very likely in prison even as he writes this letter, Peter knows he's about to die. And he uses whatever life he has left to say, "I know you know this stuff. But I will not be negligent to put you in remembrance of it until you are established in it."
If you are a Sunday-school teacher, parent, elder, or anyone else who wants to be used in service, this is a huge point, for the key to ministry is putting people in remembrance of things they already know. You see, because our minds have been affected by sin, we forget the things we should remember and remember the things we should forget. Therefore, your job as a dad, my job as a pastor is to say the same things over and over and over until those in our charge are established in them.
It's not how much you know that counts, gang. It's how *well* you know what you know. What matters is how *well* you understand the basic truths, and how deep they sink into the soil of your soul.

2 Peter 1:14
Knowing that shortly I must put off this my tabernacle, even as our Lord Jesus Christ hath shewed me.

Peter knew his death was imminent. But rather than producing panic, this knowledge produced peace.

For topical study of 2 Peter 1:14 entitled "Peter's Perfect Peace," turn to page 1590.

2 Peter 1:15
Moreover I will endeavour that ye may be able after my decease to have these things always in remembrance.

The Greek word translated "decease," is *exodos*. I like that! Just as the children of Israel left Egypt for the Promised Land, Peter knew he'd soon leave earth for the ultimate Promised Land: heaven. But before he does, he reminds us of three important truths concerning the Word. First, he reminds us that men die, but the Word lives.

2 Peter 1:16
For we have not followed cunningly devised fables, when we made known unto you the power and coming of our Lord Jesus Christ, but were eyewitnesses of his majesty.

"We're not following fables and myths, super heroes and zodiac signs, fads or theories," says Peter, "for we were actual eyewitnesses of the majesty of Jesus Christ."

2 Peter 1:17, 18
For he received from God the Father honour and glory, when there came such a voice to him from the excellent glory, This is my beloved Son, in whom I am well pleased. And this voice which came from heaven we heard, when we were with him in the holy mount.

The event to which Peter refers is the Transfiguration—when Jesus' deity shone through His humanity. Wouldn't it be radical to hear a voice from heaven and to see the Lord glowing, talking with Elijah and Moses? Yet Peter, who had experienced all of this, says there's something even better. . . .

2 Peter 1:19 (a)
We have also a more sure word of prophecy . . .

If someone offered you the choice of either being on Mount Hermon with Jesus, seeing Moses and Elijah, hearing a voice from heaven—or having the Old Testament, most of us would choose to see the Lord glowing, to see Moses and Elijah, to hear a voice from heaven. But Peter would choose otherwise. Why? Because experiences fade, but the Word endures.

The problem with experiences is that all they produce is a craving to see more. How do I know? Because the people who saw more experiences than any other were the children of Israel. They saw God part the Red Sea miraculously. They were fed from heaven daily. They saw miracles constantly. Yet why couldn't they enter into the Promised Land? Because of unbelief (Hebrews 3:19).

Having been around for a while, I would rather hear a great Bible study and be fed from the Scriptures than see a bunch of experiences unfolding. There was a time when this was not true in my life. But the longer I walk with the Lord, the more I realize that experiences fade—even the valid ones, even the wondrous ones. Only the Word endures.

2 Peter 1:19 (b)
. . . whereunto ye do well that ye take heed, as unto a light that shineth in a dark place, until the day dawn, and the day star arise in your hearts.

Finally, the world gets darker, but the Word shines *brighter*. The Greek word translated "dark" is literally "murky." "Thy Word is a lamp unto my feet and a light unto my path," the psalmist declared (119:105). The darker or murkier the world gets—or the darker or murkier your situation becomes in your marriage, your family, at school, or on the job—the brighter the Word will shine and be more precious to you than ever.

2 Peter 1:20
Knowing this first, that no prophecy of the scripture is of any private interpretation.

"Make sure you understand that no prophecy is of private interpretation," Peter warns. That is, there is no such thing as a private interpretation of Scripture that someone can sell you "for only $29.95." I love hearing teachings and reading commentaries because it's wonderful to see how, regarding basic truths of the faith, godly men always line up in agreement.

Not only is interpretation never given to individuals exclusively, but Scriptures are linked together perfectly. That is, doctrine or theology cannot be built upon an isolated Scripture, but only upon the full counsel of God.

I would be sadly mistaken if I said, "Folks, I've just been reading Daniel and now I understand how to pray. We are to pray three times a day—morning, noon, and night. We are to face Jerusalem. And we are to pray with our windows open." Now, if I read a little further, I'd see Jesus specifically telling us to pray in a closet so that we wouldn't be seen of men (Matthew 6:6). And Paul instructed us not to pray three times a day, but unceasingly (1 Thessalonians 5:17).

No Scripture stands by itself in isolation. That is why, at Calvary Chapel, we are absolutely committed to going through the Bible cover to cover. In your own devotional life, I would encourage you to do the same.

2 Peter 1:21
For the prophecy came not in old time by the will of man: but holy men of God spake as they were moved by the Holy Ghost.

The Word is inspired, indeed. One thousand years before Jesus Christ came, men of old were moved by the Holy Ghost to post prophetic signposts that would point to Him as Messiah. . . .

David prophesied that Messiah's hands and feet would be pierced (Psalm 22:16).

Isaiah prophesied that Messiah would not open His mouth to defend Himself when tried on false charges (53:7), and that although He initially would be destined for burial with the wicked, He would ultimately be buried in the tomb of a rich man (53:9).

Micah prophesied that Messiah would be born in the town of Bethlehem (5:2).

Zechariah prophesied that He would ride into the Holy City on the back of a donkey (9:9), that He would be betrayed by a friend for thirty pieces of silver (11:12), and that the silver would be used to buy a potter's field (11:13).

Malachi prophesied that He would have a forerunner announcing His coming (3:1).

What is the chance that those eight prophecies would be fulfilled in the life of one individual? The "Law of Compound Probabilities" tells us the chance is 1 in 10^{28}. In other words . . .

You cover the entire state of Texas two feet deep in silver dollars, one of which has a red mark on it, and tell your friend to walk through the entire state—through the Panhandle down to the Gulf, through Dallas, Houston, and Corpus Christi, from north to south, east to west—and choose one silver dollar. The statistical probability that he will choose the one with the red mark is 1 in 10^{28}.

But there are not three prophecies given in the Old Testament concerning Messiah. There are *three hundred!* And the probability of one individual perfectly fulfilling all three hundred is beyond the ability to illustrate.

No other so-called holy book dares to deal with prophecy. Only this book we hold in our hands has the boldness, the courage to deal with future events.

That is why, although men die, the Word lives.

That is why, although experiences fade, the Word endures.

That is why, although the world gets darker, the Word shines brighter.

How I thank God for the Scriptures. I'm *so* glad we have this Book.

PETER'S PERFECT PEACE
A Topical Study of
2 Peter 1:14

An old man, Peter said, "I'm about to die." Although this is the first time Peter makes such a statement, it wasn't the first time he could have had reason. You recall the story. . . .

Eager to gain favor with the Jewish community, Herod killed James, the brother of John. And when he saw this pleased the Jews, he imprisoned Peter as well. Scripture tells us that on the night before his execution, Peter slept between two soldiers (Acts 12:6). Peter's heart should have been filled with fear. Instead, his eyes were heavy with sleep. Why? Some suggest it was because Peter was one who fell asleep easily and often. . . .

One of only three men who accompanied Jesus to the Mount of Transfiguration, you'd think Peter would be curious about what would transpire. In reality, however, such was not the case, for Luke tells us that when Moses and Elijah appeared, and when Jesus started shining, Peter was sleeping (Luke 9:32).

It was to Peter and James and John that Jesus said, "My soul is troubled. Come to the Garden and pray with Me." But after having gone a short distance from them, when Jesus returned to His boys, He found them sleeping.

"Could you not watch and pray but one hour with Me?" He said before returning to His place of prayer.

Jesus came back a second time to find His disciples asleep again.

And, after a third time, He finally said, "Sleep on" (see Mark 14:37–41).

Why was Peter sleeping in prison? Perhaps it was because he was a sound sleeper. But I don't think that's the reason. I don't think anyone sleeps the night before his execution.

Others propose Peter could sleep because prayer had been made. That could be the case, for evidently having seen what had happened to James, Luke tells us the church prayed without ceasing for Peter (Acts 12:5).

Yet, I think there's a more profound and practical explanation for why Peter was sawing logs the night before he was ordered to die. I suggest Peter could sleep because he knew that, although he was indeed chained to Roman guards, he could not be executed at that time. How did he know? I believe the answer is found in John 21. . . .

After dying on the Cross and rising from the dead, Jesus sought out the one who had thrice denied Him. "I'll stand for You, Lord," Peter had declared. "I'll never turn my back on You. You can count on me." After failing miserably, thinking he had no choice but to return to his former occupation, Peter was fishing when Jesus came to him. Realizing it was the Lord calling him, Peter quickly swam to shore—where Jesus would re-commission him for service (see John 21:15–17).

Then, after re-commissioning him, Jesus went on to tell him,

> *Verily, verily, I say unto thee, When thou wast young, thou girdedst thyself, and walkedst whither thou wouldest: but when thou shalt be old, thou shalt stretch forth thy hands, and another shall gird thee, and carry thee whither thou wouldest not.*   John 21:18

Jesus spoke of crucifixion—the very way Peter did, in fact, die, upside down on a cross outside of Rome. So because Peter had heard Jesus say, "When you're old, you're going to die in this manner," chained between two guards as a young man, Peter knew it wasn't his time to die.

Whether you feel like you're on a merry-go-round at work, or like you're being driven crazy by your parents or kids; whether you're not finding what you thought you would find in that relationship, or whether your bills are threatening to bury you, you can be at total peace if you want to be.

How? By doing the same thing Peter did—by simply believing the promise Jesus gives to you even as Peter believed the promise Jesus had spoken to him. What promise? Take your pick. . . .

> *But my God shall supply all your need according to his riches in glory by Christ Jesus.*   Philippians 4:19

> *Delight thyself also in the LORD; and he shall give thee the desires of thine heart.*   Psalm 37:4

> *And we know that all things work together for good to them that love God, to them who are the called according to his purpose.*   Romans 8:28

> *I will never leave thee, nor forsake thee.*   Hebrews 13:5

> *Casting all your care upon him; for he careth for you.*   1 Peter 5:7

God makes promise after promise to you and me throughout His Word. Therefore, in any given situation, we can either become hostile and tense—or, like Peter, we can sleep like a baby, saying, "I don't know how this is going to work out. I don't see a solution. But God has said that He would provide for me, give guidance to me, and would always be right beside me. And He is all I need."

"Wait a minute," you say. "The promise given to Peter was that he would eventually be crucified. What kind of a promise is that?"

To Peter, it must have been a wonderful promise. You see, Peter was a great big fisherman who had said to Jesus, "I'll stand with You. I'll stay by You. No matter what happens, You can count on me"—only to fail miserably and deny Him completely. So when Jesus told him he would be crucified, Peter's heart must have been warmed, knowing that he would at last be able to lay down his life for his Lord—something he had wanted to do all along.

"Yea, all those who live godly in Christ Jesus shall suffer persecution," we read (see 2 Timothy 3:12). What kind of a promise is that? We wonder. But knowing we want to be a people who truly do come through and stand strong, the Lord says, "You who live godly will have the opportunity to suffer persecution in some form or another. And as you do, I'm going to come through for you."

Know this, precious people—if you're upset by the prison of a situation in which you find yourself, you can either remain in a state of confusion, or you can sleep like Peter in peace. I suggest you choose peace—for whatever you're going through, there's a promise in Scripture just waiting for you to embrace it.

2 Although Peter was a fisherman by occupation, Jesus commissioned him to be a shepherd by vocation when He said, "Feed My sheep; tend My flock; tend My lambs (see John 21:15–17). And as a shepherd, Peter knew his responsibility was twofold: to feed the flock, even as Paul instructed the Ephesian elders to do in Acts 20:28; and, secondly, to warn the flock as Paul instructed two verses later in Acts 20:30—for if a shepherd feeds the flock without warning it, he is only fattening it for the kill.

So here in chapter 2, as we come to the heart of Peter's last epistle, we will see him issue a heartfelt word of warning to those he cares about so deeply. . . .

2 Peter 2:1
But there were false prophets also among the people, even as there shall be false teachers among you, who privily shall bring in damnable heresies, even denying the Lord that bought them, and bring upon themselves swift destruction.

Just as there were false prophets amidst the "holy men of God who spoke as they were moved by the Holy Ghost" (see 1:21), Peter knew that, following his "exodus," false teachers would move in who would seek to destroy the work of God.

2 Peter 2:2 (a)
And many shall follow their pernicious ways . . .

"Pernicious" means "lascivious" or "loose." False teachers are loose with the truth, loose with their morals.

2 Peter 2:2 (b)
. . . by reason of whom the way of truth shall be evil spoken of.

Peter prophesied that, due to their loose lifestyles, false teachers would give a black eye to the Christian community, making it fodder for jokes on late-night television.

2 Peter 2:3 (a)
And through covetousness shall they with feigned words make merchandise of you . . .

What motivates these false leaders, these false teachers? Making merchandise of God's people, their desire is not to feed the flock, but to fleece the flock.

2 Peter 2:3 (b)
. . . whose judgment now of a long time lingereth not, and their damnation slumbereth not.

Throughout history, there has been no shortage of gimmicks to make money in the name of spirituality. For example, certain ministries sell "holy water" from the Jordan River for a donation of twenty-five dollars. But if you go to Israel, you'll see the same little vial selling for one dollar. This tendency so grieved Jesus that it caused Him to overturn tables in the temple rather than allow His Father's house to remain a den of thieves (Matthew 21:12, 13).

2 Peter 2:4
For if God spared not the angels that sinned, but cast them down to hell, and delivered them into chains of darkness, to be reserved unto judgment.

"Wait a minute," you say. "I know some of these preachers get a little carried away with their merchandising, but they're really angels at heart."

"I don't care if he, she, or they appear angelic," Peter counters. "The fact is, God didn't spare even angels who sin."

2 Peter 2:5
And spared not the old world, but saved Noah the eighth person, a preacher of righteousness, bringing in the flood upon the world of the ungodly.

Not only were angels cast down, but the world was washed up when, seeing a world polluted beyond redemption, God flooded it to put it out of its misery.

2 Peter 2:6
And turning the cities of Sodom and Gomorrha into ashes condemned them with an overthrow, making them an ensample unto those that after should live ungodly.

Whether it be in a worship leader like Lucifer, or a prosperous community like Sodom, God does not look lightly on falsity. The wheels of His judg-

ment may turn slowly—but they grind thoroughly.

"Look at history," Peter says. "See what happens to angels, to people, to communities who manipulate, exploit, and play games spiritually."

2 Peter 2:7, 8
And delivered just Lot, vexed with the filthy conversation of the wicked: (For that righteous man dwelling among them, in seeing and hearing, vexed his righteous soul from day to day with their unlawful deeds).

When Abraham left Ur of the Chaldees for the land to which God called him, he took his nephew with him. But as they traveled, problems arose when their flocks increased to the point that tension arose between the herdsmen over water rights and pastureland. "The world is watching us," Abraham said. "It's not good that our men are fighting. Therefore, choose where you want to settle. If you go to the left, I'll go to the right; if you go to the right, I'll go to the left."

We are told in Genesis 13, that Lot lifted up his eyes and, seeing grassy green hills, he said, "That's where I want to take my flock." And so it was that Lot chose to settle in the green hills surrounding Sodom and Gomorrah—a great place for cattle, but a lousy place for kids; a great place economically, but a dangerous place for his family; a great place materially, but a dark place spiritually. Lot lifted up his eyes—but he didn't lift them high enough. Whenever you're considering a move, if you lift your eyes only high enough to analyze the situation economically, you might end up on the hills of Sodom and Gomorrah that will destroy your family eventually. Look higher. Ask God who gives wisdom to all men generously (James 1:5).

After looking toward Sodom, in Genesis 14 we see Lot living in Sodom. "It's closer to the schools and to soccer practice," he may have said. "We can save gas money." So they moved to Sodom—where the situation worsened, for in chapter 19, we see Lot sitting in the gate as a leader of Sodom. Following God's judgment of Sodom, Lot ended up in a cave outside the city, where, after being seduced by his two daughters, he fathered Moab and Ammon— two nations who would be perpetual enemies of the children of Israel.

In light of this sad, sordid story, I would think Lot was at best a marginal believer. But Scripture says otherwise, for Peter calls him a righteous man who was vexed, grieved, bothered by the pollution and sin surrounding him. This tells me a couple of things. . . .

First, we don't know what's going on in the heart of a man. We may think, *That guy's in Sodom. She's in sin.* But because we don't know what's going on deep within them, we mustn't judge them.

"The heart is deceitful," Jeremiah tells us, "and desperately wicked above all things. Who can know it?" (see Jeremiah 17:9). That's why the psalmist would say, "Search my heart, Lord, and see if there be any wicked way in me" (see Psalm 139:23). We don't even have the ability to know our own hearts, much less the hearts of others.

Second, Peter's account of Lot reminds me that the sins of believers are never mentioned once in the New Testament. In the Old Testament, we see, for example, Abraham lying about his wife in order to protect his own skin, Lot's foolish mistake in moving his family to Sodom, David's murder of Uriah and adultery with Bathsheba. But in the New Testament there is no record of a believer's sin.

Why?

Because under the New Covenant, the work of the Cross renders sin forgiven and forgotten (Hebrews 10:17). The Good News of the gospel is that if you are born again, you are justified—just as if you never sinned. Christianity is not based on good ideas or good views. It's Good *News.* And I like that—a Lot!

2 Peter 2:9
The Lord knoweth how to deliver the godly out of temptations, and to reserve the unjust unto the day of judgment to be punished.

I believe this passage to be one of the most powerful proofs that believers will not go through the Tribulation—that period in history described in Revelation 6—19 when God will pour out His wrath upon a Christ-rejecting, sinful world.

Peter's words refer to a story we know well. . . .

"Abraham, we have come to judge Sodom," said the Lord.

Knowing his nephew, Lot, was living in the midst of Sodom with his family, Abraham said, "Shall not the judge of all the earth do righteously? Will You destroy the righteous with the wicked? If there are fifty righteous men in the city, will You spare the city?"

"I'll spare the city for fifty righteous men," the Lord answered.

"On second thought," said Abraham, "if there are forty-five righteous men living in Sodom, will You spare the city?"

"I'll spare it for forty-five," said the Lord.

"Thirty?" ventured Abraham.

"Okay," said the Lord.

"What if there are twenty righteous men living in Sodom?"

"I'll spare Sodom if there are twenty righteous men within," said the Lord.

"I hate to ask this," Abraham finally said, "but will You spare it for only ten?"

"Yes," said the Lord.

At that point, Abraham stopped negotiating. After all, Lot, his wife, two daughters, and two sons-in-law lived in Sodom. Surely they had influenced at least four others.

However, as it turned out, Lot, his wife, and his two daughters were the only ones who escaped destruction, as the angels literally pulled them out of the city (Genesis 19:16).

The Lord does, indeed, know how to deliver the godly out of temptation, out of judgment, out of destruction. And, just as He did Lot and his family, He will deliver believers before He pours out His wrath in the Tribulation. Before the Tribulation breaks forth, He will snatch us up, take us out, call us home in the event called the Rapture, described in 1 Thessalonians 4.

2 Peter 2:10
But chiefly them that walk after the flesh in the lust of uncleanness, and despise government.

The idea of "despising government" does not speak politically, but spiritually. That is, those who despise government are those who refuse to believe in the unseen spiritual realm.

2 Peter 2:10
Presumptuous are they, self-willed, they are not afraid to speak evil of dignities.

Again, the idea of dignitaries speaks not of human dignitaries, but of the demonic hierarchy seen in Ephesians 6.

2 Peter 2:11
Whereas angels, which are greater in power and might, bring not railing accusation against them before the Lord.

In the Book of Jude, we read that after Moses died, Satan wanted his body (Jude 9). Knowing Scripture as he does, perhaps this was because Satan is aware of the fact that Moses will most likely be one of the two witnesses spoken of in the Tribulation period (Revelation 11:3)—and he wanted to prevent this from happening. Be that as it may, as Michael the archangel protected the body of Moses, Jude tells us he did not dare bring railing accusation against Satan, but rather called upon the Lord to rebuke him (Jude 9).

As they rant and rave against the devil, I have seen some evangelists talk to and about Satan in ways Michael dared not speak. Peter and Jude say this ought not to be. Why? If you've played football you know the answer. . . .

As a football team, the last thing you want to do is mock your upcoming opponent in an interview because the opposing coach will gladly clip the article and put it on his team's locker room bulletin board, knowing your comments will fire up his team better than he himself could. "They call us wimps and losers? We'll see about that. . . ."

So, too, anyone who tries to incite believers to action by mocking Satan and his demons is making a big mistake. Wise is the man who, like Michael, puts the Lord between himself and the Enemy.

2 Peter 2:12, 13 (a)
But these, as natural brute beasts, made to be taken and destroyed, speak evil of the things that they understand not; and shall utterly perish in their own corruption; and shall receive the reward of unrighteousness, as they that count it pleasure to riot in the day time.

The riot spoken of here is not one of throwing rocks or bottle rockets against government buildings. No, it speaks of false teachers who flaunt their sinful lifestyles in the name of liberty.

2 Peter 2:13 (b)–16
Spots they are and blemishes, sporting themselves with their own deceivings while they feast with you; having eyes full of adultery, and that cannot cease from sin; beguiling unstable souls: an heart they have exercised with covetous practices; cursed children: Which have forsaken the right way, and are gone astray, following the way of Balaam the son of Bosor, who loved the wages of unrighteousness; but was rebuked for his iniquity: the dumb ass speaking with man's voice forbad the madness of the prophet.

Hearing what the three million Israelites who were headed his way had done to Kings Sihon and Og, a worried King Balak sent for a prophet named Balaam to curse them.

"The king wants to see you," said Balak's emissaries to Balaam.

So Balaam asked God if he should go. When God said, "No," Balaam said to the emissaries, "Sorry, guys. God says I can't go."

Hearing this, Balak sent more powerful men to Balaam's house.

Again, Balaam prayed. "The Lord said I can't go. In fact, even if you gave me a houseful of gold, I couldn't go with you (hint, hint, hint)."

After returning to Balak, they appeared a third time to Balaam—this time with a houseful of gold. At this point, Balaam prayed again. And this time, God said, "If you're going to keep pressing the point and wanting your way, go—but don't say anything I don't tell you to say." So Balaam got on his donkey and set off to see Balak.

On his way, God intervened three times, sending an angel to stand in Balaam's path. But only his donkey saw the angel, causing Balaam to become so angry that the donkey had to finally speak in self-defense.

Balaam finally reached Balak and, although God didn't allow him to pronounce a curse on the people of Israel, Balaam was instrumental in their bringing a curse upon themselves (Numbers 22—24).

In reaching back to this Old Testament account, Peter says the same greed that motivated Balaam motivates false teachers.

2 Peter 2:17–19
These are wells without water, clouds that are carried with a tempest; to whom the mist of darkness is reserved for ever. For when they speak great swelling words of vanity, they allure through the lusts of the flesh, through much wantonness, those that were clean escaped from them who live in error. While they promise them liberty, they themselves are the servants of corruption: for of whom a man is overcome, of the same is he brought in bondage.

The liberty promised by false teachers is like the Judas tree of the Middle East. . . .

The Judas tree has a beautiful red flower that attracts bees by the millions. But the nectar inside contains an opiate that is deadly to them—as evidenced by the piles of dead bees at the base of every Judas tree.

Peter's clear warning is extremely appropriate for us today because in the last days more and more will teach from their own imaginations, following their own agendas. And if you think Peter's warning doesn't apply to you, perhaps you are in the gravest danger because you will eventually buy into some new idea or practice that, although it's not seen in the life of Christ, throughout the Book of Acts, or taught in the Epistles, will seem so spiritual, so logical. Oh, it may not be the current fad of "holy barking" or "holy laughter." It may be something much more intellectual, much more subtle, but no less dangerous.

2 Peter 2:20–22 (a)
For if after they have escaped the pollutions of the world through the knowledge of the Lord and Saviour Jesus Christ, they are again entangled therein, and overcome, the latter end is worse with them than the beginning. For it had been better for them not to have known the way of righteousness, than, after they have known it, to turn from the holy commandment delivered unto them. But it is happened unto them according to the true proverb, The dog is turned to his own vomit again . . .

Peter likens false teachers to dogs and defines such dogs as those who said, "It's not enough to simply believe on the Lord Jesus Christ. You must also be circumcised as Old Testament law prescribes. Christianity should be painful. Misery proves spirituality" (see Philippians 3:2). So important is this issue that Paul will write an entire book—the Book of Galatians—dealing with it.

Why do people become legalistic? I believe it's because they themselves are miserable. They've given up certain things and therefore say, "If I'm in pain, you should be, too. If I'm under the law, you should be as well. If I can't go there, I'm going to make sure you can't either."

But if you watch a legalistic preacher, a legalistic parent, a legalistic person, you'll see the truth of Peter's analogy, for, although they bark and yap at others, they eventually return to those tendencies or activities against which they preach most vehemently.

2 Peter 2:22 (b)
. . . and the sow that was washed to her wallowing in the mire.

In addition to the dogs of legalism, we're to beware of the hogs of hedonism. To be hedonistic is to live for pleasure.

You can give a pig a bath, blow-dry her hair, put a bow on her tail and blush on her face. But, although she'll look fine for a short time, she will eventually make her way back to that which pleases her—mud.

So, too, any teacher or religion that encourages people to wallow in sin is piglike in nature. And wise is the one who is able not only to identify those tendencies in false teachers, but is aware of them within himself.

3 As we have seen, Peter knew his days were numbered. And from this final chapter of his last epistle, it would also seem as though he knew that following his departure, men would prey on the church with false teaching that would stem from a denial of the Second Coming of Christ and of the Rapture of the church—for in verses 1–9, Peter addresses the subject of the Lord and His delay; and in verses 10–18, he writes of the Lord and His Day.

2 Peter 3:1
This second epistle, beloved, I now write unto you; in both which I stir up your pure minds by way of remembrance.

Reminiscent of his commitment to "put you always in remembrance of these things" (see 1:12), Peter says, "I'm writing to you to stir up your minds, to bring to your remembrance that which I've already taught you."

2 Peter 3:2
That ye may be mindful of the words which were spoken before by the holy prophets, and of the commandment of us the apostles of the Lord and Saviour.

Because he places his writings alongside those of the holy prophets, Peter is evidently aware of the inspiration of the Spirit flowing through him as surely as it had flowed through Isaiah and Jeremiah, Ezekiel and Daniel.

2 Peter 3:3 (a)
Knowing this first, that there shall come in the last days scoffers . . .

"Things are going on just as they always have," says the skeptic. "We've heard the prophecy update tapes. We've read *The Late Great Planet Earth*. But where is this Second Coming everyone keeps talking about?"—little knowing that his very scoffing fulfills Bible prophecy.

2 Peter 3:3 (b), 4
. . . walking after their own lusts, And saying, Where is the promise of his coming? for since the fathers fell asleep, all things continue as they were from the beginning of the creation.

The root of skepticism and cynicism lies in a desire to follow one's flesh and fulfill one's lust. A denial of the return of Jesus allows people to live however they want because it removes accountability to the God who made them and who will return for them.

2 Peter 3:5, 6
For this they willingly are ignorant of, that by the word of God the heavens were of old, and the earth standing out of the water and in the water: Whereby the world that then was, being overflowed with water, perished.

There was another time in human history when men scoffed. Day after day, decade upon decade, as Noah constructed a prophetic illustration of gigantic proportion, the laughter of his friends and neighbors accompanied the sounds of his saw and hammer. But eventually, the collapse of the water canopy that surrounded the earth in days of antiquity caused rain to fall, resulting in a world-wide flood—as evidenced to this day not only by geological data, but by its appearance in the written or oral history of virtually every culture.

2 Peter 3:7
But the heavens and the earth, which are now, by the same word are kept in store, reserved unto fire against the day of judgment and perdition of ungodly men.

Just as the world was destroyed in the days of Noah, Peter says it will be destroyed again—not by water, but by fire. Let the cartoonists draw their caricatures of prophets of doom. Let the world make its jokes. But you can go to the bank on the fact that just as the world was flooded with water in days of old, it will one day be burned with fire.

2 Peter 3:8
But, beloved, be not ignorant of this one thing, that one day is with the Lord as a thousand years, and a thousand years as one day.

After addressing the ridicule of the lost concerning the Lord and His delay in verses 1–7, Peter goes on to speak about the restraint of the Lord in verses 8–9—an understanding based upon the fact that the Lord completely transcends time. . . .

For topical study of 2 Peter 3:8 entitled "Daylight Saving Time," turn to page 1601.

2 Peter 3:9
The Lord is not slack concerning his promise, as some men count slackness; but is longsuffering to us-ward, not willing that any should perish, but that all should come to repentance.

As far as I understand prophecy, Jesus could have come back in 1967, following Israel's Six Day War, when Jerusalem was at last united. Why didn't He? If you are among those who didn't get saved until after 1967, He delayed His coming for *you*. Although we want the Lord to come back so desperately, we must never forget what this would mean to those who don't yet know Him.

2 Peter 3:10 (a)
But the day of the Lord . . .

After discussing the Lord's delay, Peter goes on to talk about the Lord's Day.

For prophecy to make sense to you, there are four days you need to know:

The Day of Man began in the Garden of Eden when God gave man the privilege, the opportunity to steward this planet (Genesis 2:15). But when Adam and Eve chose to listen to Satan rather than to obey God, the Day of Man became a total, unmitigated disaster characterized by famine and starvation, disease, war, and death.

The next day on the calendar is the Day of Christ—which will begin when Jesus appears in the clouds to meet His bride in the air and take us to heaven for a seven-year honeymoon with Him (1 Thessalonians 4:17).

The third day is the Day of the Lord when, beginning with the Tribulation, God will intervene in human affairs (Joel 2; Revelation 6). Extending through the period of time called the millennium, the Day of the Lord starts dark, but gets brighter and brighter—just as the Jewish day begins at sundown and works its way to dawn. I like that!

The fourth day, seen here in verse 12, is the Day of God, which begins after the millennium, when, because heaven and earth have been polluted by the presence of Satan, the present heaven and earth are done away with, replaced by a new heaven and earth.

2 Peter 3:10 (b)
. . . will come as a thief in the night . . .

Because it is the Day of the Lord rather than the Day of Christ that will come as a thief in the night, the scoffer, the unbeliever will be caught off guard—but not the believer who is watching for His coming (I Thessalonians 5:4).

2 Peter 3:10 (c)
. . . in the which the heavens shall pass away with a great noise . . .

The Greek word translated "great noise" is *rhoizedon,* which speaks of a great roar and the wind of a fire.

2 Peter 3:10 (d)
. . . and the elements shall melt with fervent heat . . .

The Greek word translated "element," is *stoicheion* and refers to the letters of the alphabet—alpha, beta, gamma, delta, etc. If a great noise, wind of fire, and melting of gamma rays sound familiar, it's because these are all terms associated with nuclear radiation.

2 Peter 3:10 (e)
. . . the earth also and the works that are therein shall be burned up.

On December 2, 1942, this scripture suddenly had new meaning for many who were reading with understanding—for on that cold winter day on the University of Chicago's Stagg Field, Robert Oppenheimer, Enrico Ferme, and Albert Einstein tested their theory that if Uranium 235 was bombarded with neutrons, energy would be released. And indeed it was.

Moving the experiment to a desert in New Mexico, on July 16, 1945, engineers were shocked when the ten-inch rail metal used to drop the first nuclear device was immediately vaporized, shooting debris seven miles into the air and eighteen hundred feet in every direction. With heat so intense that the surrounding sand was turned into glass, it was clear something ominous was taking place. The Nuclear Age was born.

Finally, in August of the same year, the A-bomb was dropped over the cities of Hiroshima and Nagasaki.

Many who read these verses said, "Impossible! Elements can't melt. The whole earth can't be burned up." But in the events of 1945, they were suddenly silenced.

While the Day of the Lord will indeed usher in the destruction spoken of here, I believe Peter's reference is to something even more devastating.

What could possibly be more devastating than nuclear warfare?

Concerning Jesus Christ, Colossians 1 tells us that all things were made and are held together by Him. Now, because Coulomb's "Law of Electricity" says that like charges repel, what keeps the positive-charged protons in every atom from pushing apart? With no better explanation, scientists call it "atomic glue." We, however, know that by *Him* all things hold together, that *He* upholds all things with the Word of His power (Hebrews 1:3). But there will come a day when He lets go—and with one gigantic boom everything will be wiped out, obliterated, done away with in the Day of the Lord.

2 Peter 3:11
Seeing then that all these things shall be dissolved, what manner of persons ought ye to be in all holy conversation and godliness.

If everything we strive for materially will explode eventually, what should be our priority?

Rabbi Chaim Herzog, a prominent scholar and lover of the Torah lives in the old section of Jerusalem in a small apartment containing only a chair, desk, and bed.

"Rabbi, is *this* your house?" asked a lady from New York who had come to visit him.

"Yes," replied the Rabbi.

"Well, where is your furniture?"

The Rabbi looked at this wealthy American lady and said, "Where's *your* furniture?"

"I didn't bring my furniture," she said. "I'm just traveling."

"Ah," the Rabbi smiled, "so am I."

The message of Scripture from cover to cover is that we're pilgrims and sojourners on this earth. Yes, God can bless us with cars and houses—but we're not to make them high priorities because they're just going to burn, dissipate, and dissolve. "Keep your eyes on the big picture," says Peter. "Look for the coming Day of God."

2 Peter 3:12
Looking for and hasting unto the coming of the day of God, wherein the heavens being on fire shall be dissolved, and the elements shall melt with fervent heat?

The flavor of the Greek text is that we don't look for the Day of God passively, but that we actually have the ability to speed it along.

"I thought God was sovereign," you say.

He is, but in Scripture we see a sovereign God affected and impacted by His people and their cooperation. . . .

Before entering the Promised Land, the children of Israel sent twelve spies to check it out. And because they chose to retreat in fear rather than advance in faith, they were destined to wander in the wilderness for forty years (Numbers 13).

The children of Israel actually slowed down God's timetable by forty years.

"Yet forty days and Nineveh shall be destroyed," Jonah declared. But the people repented, and God chose not to destroy the city (see Jonah 3).

Yes, God is sovereign. Yes, God is in control. But He factors in to His sovereign plan the attitudes and cooperation of man. Knowing this, Peter says we can hasten His return.

Are you tired of death and disease and depression? Have you had your fill of sadness and sickness and sin? If so, there are two ways you can hurry the day when righteousness will rule the earth.

First, the Day of God is hastened by our prayer. In teaching us to pray, Jesus taught us to ask that His kingdom come (Matthew 6:10). This is precisely what one who heard Him teach that prayer did. At the end of the Book of Revelation, Jesus said, "Behold, I come quickly"—to which John responded in prayer, "Even so, Lord, come quickly." The same is still true. Prayer influences the timing of God—including the coming of the kingdom.

Second, the Day of God is hastened as we share. According to Acts 2:47, the Lord adds daily to the church such as should be saved. Thus, there is someone who is the last one to be added to the church to complete the bride of Christ. And when that last one gets saved, the body of Christ will be complete, and we'll go up.

Consequently, as we witness, share, and invite people to be a part of the family and make a decision for Jesus Christ—we actually bring closer the day of His return. But the benefits of hastening the day are not limited to future times. Rather, this kind of living and thinking has benefits now, as it produces within us three important qualities. . . .

Purity. First John 3:3 tells us that he who looks for Jesus' coming purifies himself. It's amazing how careful a person drives when he looks in his wallet and realizes his license has expired. So, too, it's amazing how purity will characterize the life of one who believes this could be the day, this could be the hour of Christ's return.

Peace. The one who looks for the Lord's coming takes a whole lot more things a whole lot less seriously. In other words, the one who looks for the Lord's coming is not uptight

about the scratch in his car, the bruise to his ego, or the slight at the office because he sees the bigger picture of eternity.

Purpose. The life of the one who looks for the Lord's coming, who is involved in the work of the kingdom, is neither boring, predictable, nor routine. If you feel that your life is simply going in circles, it could be because you've lost sight of your purpose.

Hasten the day, gang, by your prayer and as you share. Live for eternity, and you'll find unparalleled purity, purpose, and peace.

2 Peter 3:13
Nevertheless we, according to his promise, look for new heavens and a new earth, wherein dwelleth righteousness.

Taken from Isaiah 65:17, the Hebrew word translated "create" is *bara* and refers to the act of creating something from nothing. The new heavens and new earth are not a remodeled or renovated version of the present. No, they're brand new.

For topical study of 2 Peter 3:13 entitled "Flight to Heaven," turn to page 1604.

2 Peter 3:14
Wherefore, beloved, seeing that ye look for such things, be diligent that ye may be found of him in peace, without spot, and blameless.

We know Jesus is coming back, but there are many who don't have a peace about His coming because they know they are not spotless and blameless. Understand, dear saint, that in Luke 12:37 we hear Jesus saying, "Blessed are those servants whom the Lord when He cometh shall find watching." Therefore, if you are simply watching for His coming, if you are tired of this world system's sin and corruption and want to see the Lord rule and reign at last—it is you the Lord calls blessed.

Many years ago when we went to see the Oakland A's play, upon entering the stadium, Ben, seven, and Mary, eight, were given free wristbands with their names and seat numbers on them. As we made our way into the stands, we turned around to see Mary wasn't with us. We looked and looked for her until—after about ten minutes—one of the ushers brought her to the seat number printed on her wristband.

When we were reunited, did we yell at her? No.

Did we come down on her?
No.
Did we say, "Mary, you are spotted and full of blame. Depart, Mary. Away with you!"
No.
For although she had wandered off, although she had become mixed up, all she really wanted was to be with Mommy and Daddy. So with tears in her eyes, we embraced her, sat her down between us, and bought her some popcorn, a hotdog, and a some cotton candy.

So, too, if your heart is like Mary's, if you simply say, "Yes, I wandered away, but what I really want is to be with You, Father"—don't you know He is going to embrace you as tightly as we embraced Mary?

"Wait a minute," you say. "The text says not only are we to look for Him, but we are to be found of Him in peace, without spot and blameless."

That's true. And the only way we can be found *of* Him in peace without spot and blameless is to be found *in* Him. The great news of the gospel is that the moment you became a Christian, you were positioned in Christ (2 Corinthians 5:17). Consequently, when the Father looks at you, He doesn't see you. He sees the spotless and blameless One, Jesus Christ.

And no one embodied the reality of this truth better than Peter . . .

When Jesus called to Peter fishing on the Sea of Galilee in direct violation of the command He had given him to remain in Jerusalem, Peter couldn't swim to shore fast enough. And when he got there, did Jesus lecture Peter, berate Peter, humiliate Peter? No. He served Peter (John 21:12, 13).

Will Jesus be mad at you when He comes? Not if, like Peter, you're saying, "Lord, even though I'm out to lunch, drifting out to sea, fishing where I ought not be, I still want to be with You."

2 Peter 3:15, 16 (a)
And account that the longsuffering of our Lord is salvation; even as our beloved brother Paul also according to the wisdom given unto him hath written unto you; as also in all his epistles, speaking in them of these things; in which are some things hard to be understood . . .

Peter and Paul had an interesting relationship. In Galatians 2, we read that Paul rebuked Peter for his failure to fellowship with Gentiles when fellow Jews were present. Here, Peter tells us that Paul's writings are hard to understand. With different callings and different methods—Peter called to primarily minister to Jewish believers, Paul to Gentiles—Peter and Paul illustrate what is to take place in and through the body of Christ as we find both unity and diversity in Him.

2 Peter 3:16 (b)
. . . which they that are unlearned and unstable wrest . . .

"Wrest" means "to torture" or "to distort." Those who twisted Paul's words were his enemies, the legalists, who accused Paul of telling people to sin in order that grace might abound (Romans 6:1).

2 Peter 3:16 (c)
. . . as they do also the other scriptures, unto their own destruction.

There are those who contend that it was not until centuries later that the church recognized Peter's, James', or Paul's writings to be inspired. But such is not the case, for in placing Paul's writings on the same plane as "the other Scriptures," Peter knew they were equally inspired.

2 Peter 3:17
Ye therefore, beloved, seeing ye know these things before, beware lest ye also, being led away with the error of the wicked, fall from your own stedfastness.

While it is true that belief affects behavior, it is equally true that behavior affects belief. For example, the more you study evolution, the more you become aware of its scientific absurdity. But people continue to buy into it because believing they are nothing more than animals allows them to justify their own animal behavior.

Peter says, "I know you know the truth. But be careful because if you choose to live in carnality, you will eventually change your theology to justify your sin."

2 Peter 3:18
But grow in grace, and in the knowledge of our Lord and Saviour Jesus Christ. To him be glory both now and for ever. Amen.

Peter closes not by saying, "Grow in devotion," or, "Grow in zeal," or "Grow in holiness." He closes by saying, "Grow in grace" because grace is not the starting point. Grace is the only point.

For topical study of 2 Peter 3:18 entitled "Grow in Grace," turn to page 1606.

DAYLIGHT SAVING TIME
A Topical Study of
2 Peter 3:8

Twelve to fifteen years ago, those who study such things predicted that by the year 2000, due to the technological advances that would so lighten our workloads that they would usher us in to a veritable Age of Leisure, most Americans would work only three days a week. In reality, however, the inventions that were supposed to make our lives easier have had just the opposite effect. But if you are one who is growing increasingly weary of the whir of the fax machine, the beep of the pager, the ring of the cell phone, I have good news for you today because the passage before us contains not only prophetic implications, but practical application for you and me. . . .

Practical Application

But, beloved, be not ignorant of this one thing, that one day is with the Lord as a thousand years . . .   2 Peter 3:8 (a)

"We're in trouble," said the Gibeonites to Joshua. "We're about to be wiped out by the five Amorite kings who are besieging our city."

Therefore, keeping his end of the treaty he had made with them, as recorded in Joshua 9, Joshua and his troops rescued the Gibeonites. And as the Amorites fled in retreat, the Israelites were poised to finish them off—when the sun began to set. So with time running out and the job still undone, Joshua commanded the sun to stand still. And Scripture records that the sun did, indeed, stand still until the people had avenged themselves upon their enemies (Joshua 10:13).

"Ha!" scoffs the cynic. "Everyone knows it is the earth that rotates around the sun—not vice versa. The Bible is wrong once again."

But I remind such a one that even the most brilliant scientists of our day speak of sunrises and sunsets, employing the same universal concept to paint a picture.

What does this have to do with us practically? Understand this: Although in fighting the Amorites Joshua was doing something that would not be easy for him to do, because he was obedient to the Lord, he was able to get the job done. So, too, there are things the Lord might have us do this week that aren't easy—about which we might find ourselves saying, "I don't want to call her," or, "I don't want to be kind to my neighbor," or, "I don't want to do that or go there." So, instead, we'll go our own way, follow our own agenda, and what will happen? We'll run out of time to do the things we mistakenly thought we were supposed to do rather than those things the Lord had directed us to do.

On the other hand, if, like Joshua, we speak to the Son and are obedient to Him, we find we have time to accomplish that which He would have us do. This is the greatest piece of time management advice there is. Do what the Lord is telling you to do. Don't put it off. Don't say, "Later." Don't say, "Sometime." Do what He's showing you to do *now*—and you will find the sun standing still. You'll find you have plenty of energy, plenty of opportunity because, having given God your day, you can't outgive Him.

When we walk with the Lord, something happens. When we give a day to the Lord, something happens. When we're obedient to the Lord something happens. Our days seems to expand. If you say, "Even though my flesh doesn't want to, even though I think I'm too busy, whatever You say, Lord, I'll do"—you will find your day elongated.

Prophetic Implication

> . . . *and a thousand years as one day.*   2 Peter 3:8 (b)

"Surely I come quickly," Jesus said (see Revelation 22:20), to which the cynics and scoffers reply, "*Quickly?* It's been two thousand years!" But in the Lord's economy—one thousand years being a day—He's only been gone two days. And He's coming back on the third. . . .

> *Come, and let us return unto the LORD: for he hath torn, and he will heal us;*
> *he hath smitten, and he will bind us up. After two days will he revive us: in*
> *the third day he will raise us up, and we shall live in his sight.* Hosea 6:1, 2

Two thousand years ago, Israel was destroyed as a nation when, under General Titus, the Romans decimated the city of Jerusalem, burned the temple, and scattered the people. But after two days—or two thousand years—a miracle took place when, inconceivable by human design but prophesied throughout the Old Testament, Israel was revived as a nation in 1948.

Many Bible scholars concur with Archbishop Usher's conclusion that, according to Old Testament genealogy, Adam came on the scene four thousand years before Christ. If that is true, this is most intriguing, because in Bible numerology we see a consistent pattern. . . .

> After six days of struggle, strain, and sweat there was to be a seventh day of
> rest (Exodus 20:9–10).
>   After six years of tilling the ground and planting crops, the seventh year
> was to be a sabbatical in which the land was to rest for a year (Leviticus 25).

After serving as a slave for six years, a man was to be set free (Deuteronomy 15).

For six thousand years, or six days, we've been sweating and struggling and straining. We're headed for the seventh day, the seventh millennium—one thousand years of rest, peace, and prosperity when Jesus comes back to establish His kingdom in the city of Jerusalem.

I am personally persuaded that the typology of the Old Testament, as it points to the prophecies of the kingdom, places us on the verge of the seventh day. We've gone through six days of struggle and strain, six years of slavery to sin and the flesh. And now it's time for the seventh day.

Then why are we still here? We're in overtime.

Personal Invitation

The Lord is not slack concerning his promise, as some men count slackness; but is longsuffering to us-ward, not willing that any should perish, but that all should come to repentance.   2 Peter 3:9

Not only did the sun stand still, but it actually disappeared as Jesus hung on the Cross to pay for the sins of humanity (Mark 15:33). Fulfilling Old Testament typology, He bore each of our sins specifically because He loves us passionately. Therefore, He delays His coming for us in order to give everyone abundant opportunity to come to Him. But He will not delay forever. The third day is soon to dawn—beginning with the seven-year period known as the Tribulation—when God will pour out His wrath on a Christ-rejecting, sinful world. The Tribulation, described in Revelation 6—19, will be a time of unparalleled destruction and difficulty. But the good news is that many who are doubting, skeptical, lukewarm toward the gospel will see God's reality and will be saved in that day.

"I'll just wait until then to make my decision," you say.

You can. But here's the question: If, because of what your friends will think, or your colleagues will say, it's too difficult for you to make a decision for Jesus today in this time of peace and safety, what makes you think you'll suddenly have the courage to refuse the mark of the beast—to turn your back on any ability to buy food, gas, electricity or oil to keep warm—in the day of Tribulation? What makes you think you'll be able to stand against an entire new world order, face unbelievable pressure and imminent death then if you're worried about what others will say today?

Precious people, *now* is the accepted time; *today* is the day of salvation (2 Corinthians 6:2). Therefore, may the Lord give understanding of His working and of His ways to you who seem to have more to do than time to do it, to you who increasingly long for Jesus' return, to you who have yet to come to Him. And may you daily find your place in the Son.

FLIGHT TO HEAVEN
A Topical Study of
2 Peter 3:13

I f heaven is real, then that is all that really matters; but if heaven is not real, then nothing really matters at all. It's all about heaven. That's not just my conclusion. Inspired by the Spirit, Paul said, "If in this life only we have hope in Christ, we are of all men most miserable" (see 1 Corinthians 15:19).

The passage before us deals with heaven, even as the events one week dealt with heaven. . . .

I had decided to teach on the subject of the shortness of life to the one hundred or so in attendance at Applegate Christian Fellowship's Family Camp on Washington's beautiful San Juan Islands. So we joined the children of Israel on their camping journey as we looked at Exodus 12—17. . . .

Following their release from Egypt, the first place the Lord directed the children of Israel to stop was Succoth, or "Tent Town"—a place that would have reminded them not to take this life too seriously because they were only passing through.

It was at stop number two, Etham, which means "sea bound," that God told them He would lead them with a cloud by day and a fire by night.

Stop number three found them camped between Mount Pi-hahiroth and Migdol with their backs to the Red Sea. It was there that God said, "You might complain and wonder, question and murmur, but I will put you in whatever box you need to be in to let other people see My reality and My power" (see Exodus 14:3).

After crossing the Red Sea, the children of Israel stopped at Marah, or "Bitter," where, after drinking bitter water, they were instructed by God to throw a tree into the water—whereby it became sweet. The tree in Scripture being a picture of the Cross of Calvary, this account leads me to say, "Although the situation I'm in might seem bitter presently, I know the Lord will make it sweet eventually."

Stop number five was at Elam, where seventy palm trees and twelve wells provided an oasis for no other reason than simply to bless the children of Israel.

Stop number six led from the place of blessing to the "Wilderness of Sin," from which we get the word "Sinai." With nothing to eat, the children of Israel murmured and complained, until the Word—the manna—came down and fed their souls. This is a potent reminder that even when we journey through the wilderness, it's the Word, the Word, the Word that feeds our souls.

At stop number seven, Rephidim, a war broke out between the Israelites and the Amalekites. As Moses went to the mountain and held up his hands in prayer, Joshua and the Israelite solders were victorious. But when his hands became heavy, the Amalekites would gain the advantage. So, standing on either side of Moses, Aaron and Hur held up his hands, and the Israelites prevailed.

"Life is short," I said, concluding my teaching that Friday morning. "We're just passing through. We don't belong here. We're going to heaven. And we need one another to hold up our hands along the way."

Five minutes later, we heard the news that in the early morning hours, Kelly— a wonderful brother whose smile lit up any room he entered—had taken off in his plane in order to get home before the predicted clouds rolled in. And twenty-year-old Ryan—an incredibly gifted young man—felt compelled to accompany him. But for reasons we don't understand, the plane exploded mid-flight.

So there we sat—Kelly's widow and Ryan's parents—on the bench where I had only moments earlier concluded our time together in the Word.

Suddenly, all of the studies I had shared concerning life being short, the mystery of the Red Sea for God's sovereign purposes and plan, the clouds and the pillar of fire, experiences that could produce bitterness if we allowed them to, and hands that hang down unless propped up in intercession, were no longer theoretical.

Driving home through the night with Ryan's parents, I thought, *Lord, what do I say this morning in Applegate's amphitheatre to a group of people who are hurting?*

But as I opened the text, the answer was in front of me, for I realized that in the fire and explosion of the previous night, Kelly and Ryan had simply taken an early flight to heaven.

Heaven. Peter tells us we are to look forward to heaven. Yet the Bible doesn't really say much about it. I suggest a couple of reasons for this. . . .

The strongest instinct in man is survival. But the beauty of heaven can overcome and overpower even that strongest of instincts. Therefore, I believe Christians would be committing suicide to get there if heaven were understood clearly.

I believe the second reason the Bible doesn't speak very much about heaven is because it's impossible for us to comprehend the fifth dimension (1 Corinthians 2:9).

Suppose I gave you a blank piece of paper with a dot on it. How long would it hold your attention? Maybe a second. A dot is boring because it's one-dimensional. But suppose I make it two-dimensional. Suppose I add a series of circles and lines so that it resembles the face of a man. That would be a little more interesting, but you'd still be bored with that after a short time. But what if I made it three-dimensional, not just a dot or a picture, but a statue—a Michelangelo statue of David. Although that would definitely be more intriguing, you would eventually tire of it. But how much more interesting than three dimensions is the fourth one—time and space. If you could actually talk to Michelangelo, your interaction with him would be infinitely more interesting than any picture or statue could be.

But there's a fifth dimension—a dimension we have not seen, cannot hear, and do not understand. It's called eternity, and it's going to make this life look like a dot on a piece of paper.

Paul was given a sneak preview of coming attractions. And it was after he was given a glimpse of heaven that he declared, "For to me to live is Christ, and to die is gain" (see Philippians 1:21, emphasis mine). This one, who had perhaps the greatest command of language in history, was left speechless in his attempt to describe what he had seen there (2 Corinthians 12:4).

Therefore, on the basis of the Word of God, I promise you that Kelly and Ryan are not saying, "Is this it?" No, they're saying, "This is it!" They're not saying, "Why?" They're saying, "Wow! Truly, this is the place of righteousness—for this is the right way, the right moment, and the right place for us to be."

GROW IN GRACE
A Topical Study of
2 Peter 3:18

This article in the paper caught my attention. . . .

"Author Hyason Has Bummer of a Summer"

This hasn't been the best of summers for Carl Hyason, the most acclaimed novelist from South Florida since John D. McDonald invented the place thirty years ago. First, there were critical slams and sparse audiences for a much-hyped film of one of his novels. Then Warner Books printed 530,000 paperbacks of his latest crowd-pleaser, *Stormy Weather,* and left out the epilogue. Many of these copies have been sold over the past month. Hardly anyone has complained that this well-received comic novel about a major hurricane hitting Florida was lacking a certain something, according to the publisher. But Hyason pointed out in a phone interview from his Florida Keys home, "How could they complain if they didn't know the epilogue was supposed to be there in the first place?"

Hyason's frustration is understandable in light of how much consideration authors give to a closing chapter, a final sentence, a last word.

As an author, Peter was no exception. And what does this physical and spiritual giant of a man say in the final words he ever penned? He says, "Grow."

"Good admonition, Peter," I would say. "Good closing. Tell the people to grow in holiness, to grow in discipline, to grow in theological knowledge, to grow in zeal."

But that's not what Peter says. He says, "Grow in *grace.*"

Why? Because such is the heart of the Holy Spirit.

Paul said something similar when, in his own last words to the church, he said, "Grace be with you" (2 Timothy 4:22).

In fact, the last words of the entire Bible being, "the grace of our Lord Jesus Christ be with you all" (Revelation 22:21), whether in Peter's epistles, Paul's letters, or the Bible in its entirety—the final word is grace.

What is grace?

Grace is unmerited favor, undeserved kindness, unearned blessing. Grace is God giving to us not because of what we do, but in spite of what we've done.

> *For by grace are ye saved through faith; and that not of yourselves: it is the gift of God: Not of works, lest any man should boast.*   Ephesians 2:8, 9

> *As it is written, "There is none righteous, no, not one: There is none that understandeth, there is none that seeketh after God."*   Romans 3:10, 11

> *But as many as received him, to them gave he power to become the sons of God, even to them that believe on his name: Which were born, not of blood, nor of the will of the flesh, nor of the will of man, but of God.*   John 1:12, 13

Grace is ours not because we earned it, not because we willed it, not because we were born into it, but because God chose to be kind to us for no reason whatsoever. Too many people think that after they're saved by grace, it's up to them to earn God's blessings. But the heart of Peter, as seen here at the end of his epistle, says otherwise.

Why?

Perhaps it is because of the grace he himself received . . .

"Lord, though all others forsake you, I never will," he declared, cock-sure of himself.

"Before the cock crows twice, you'll deny me three times," Jesus answered (Mark 14:72).

"I'm going to Jerusalem, where I will be crucified," Jesus said.

"Not so," argued Peter.

"Get thee behind me, Satan," Jesus replied (see Matthew 16:23).

"Bid me come unto Thee on the water," said Peter to Jesus in the storm.

"Come," said Jesus.

"Lord, save me," said Peter when he began to sink (see Matthew 14:28–30).

"I'm going fishing," Peter said in direct opposition to the Lord's command to stay in Jerusalem (see John 21:3).

"Feed My sheep," Jesus said nonetheless (see John 21:17).

During the three and a half years he lived and walked with Jesus, Peter was a recipient of repeated, continual, abundant grace. And as a result, he tells us to grow in grace.

How?

Peter gave us the answer in chapter 2 of his first epistle when he said, "Desire the sincere milk of the Word that you may grow thereby" (1 Peter 2:2). The writer to the Hebrews tells us that milk, unlike meat, deals with the first principles of salvation (Hebrews 5:12). Thus, the implication is that although our knowledge of the Word and of the Lord is to expand, we are not to leave the basics of our salvation; we are not to forget what Jesus did on the Cross; we are not to forsake the table of Communion, where we are reminded over and over and over again that Jesus died for us. We grow by remembering what Christ did for us continually. We grow by partaking of grace daily.

In 2 Kings, we see an Old Testament picture of the New Testament principle of grace. . . .

> When he came into power as the nineteenth king of Judah, Jehoiachin was eighteen years old. Although his name meant "The Lord Will Establish," Jehoiachin did exceedingly evil in the eyes of the Lord—so much so that the prophet Jeremiah thundered this curse upon him: "Coniah (another name for Jehoiachin) shall have no descendants sit upon the throne forever and ever" (see Jeremiah 22:24–30).
>
> In the third month of Jehoiachin's reign, Nebuchadnezzar marched on Judah, captured Jehoiachin, and threw him into a Babylonian prison, where he remained for thirty-six years—until Nebuchadnezzar was succeeded by a man named Evil-Merodach, whose name means "Rebellion Is Foolish." And Scripture records that Evil-Merodach spoke *graciously* to Jehoiachin. "I'm going to replace your prison stripes with royal robes," he said. "You will sit with me in the palace, dine with me at my table, and receive money from my hand" (see 2 Kings 25:29–30).
>
> And that's where the story, as well as the Book of 2 Kings ends.

What caused Evil-Merodach to speak graciously, to robe Jehoiachin royally, to provide food for him daily? Some scholars suggest it was because he himself had been a prisoner. Others surmise that he acted graciously because of his belief in the God of Daniel, who was also on the scene at the same time. I, however, believe the fact that the Bible is silent concerning the reason for Evil-Merodach's kindness is because there wasn't a reason. It was pure grace.

You see, we are Jehoiachin. Over and over, we turn our backs upon our good, gracious Lord and end up imprisoned by the very things we thought were so cool. But God in His matchless grace comes to us, provides for us, and welcomes us into His presence.

Why does the Lord speak kindly to us? Why would He robe us with His righteousness? Why will He lift us up and allow us to rule and reign with Him? There is no other reason than grace. We were foolish in rebellion, yet He establishes us in grace.

And all that remains is for us to say, "Thank You, Lord, for being so kind to me. Thank You for providing so graciously. Thank You for Your promises to me. To You be the glory."

The Christian life is all about grace, grace, amazing grace. Therefore, may the grace of our Lord be with *you*.

Amen.

1 JOHN

Background to 1 John

F irst John is a very powerful epistle, written by a very old apostle. Along with the rest of Jesus' disciples—with the exception of Judas—John was sentenced to a martyr's death. But unlike the other disciples, even after being placed in a cauldron of boiling oil and banished to the seemingly God-forsaken island of Patmos, John lived a full life—so full, in fact, that he was probably one hundred years old when he penned the epistle before us.

Some commentators, with whom I am inclined to agree, maintain that 3 John is actually the last book to be written of all sixty-six books in the Bible.

According to historians, at one hundred years of age, John was taken from church to church throughout the region of Asia Minor, or present-day Turkey. Upon hearing news of his arrival, people would gather full of anticipation. After all, John was the last surviving member of the band of twelve men hand-picked by Jesus. Surely he would have indelible memories to share with them and incredible insights to encourage them. Yet time after time, in place after place, John would stand to his feet, look out at the assembled congregation, and simply utter one sentence: "Little children, love one another."

This should come as no surprise, for truly John was known as the "apostle of love," referring to himself throughout his Gospel account as "the disciple Jesus loved" (see 13:23). Was this because John saw himself as the one Jesus loved above the others? No, I suggest it was because he was amazed that Jesus would love one like him.

"Lord, let's call down fire from heaven and blast them," John had said after the people of a certain region in Samaria failed to respond to the ministry of Jesus and the disciples (Luke 9:54). The one-time son of Boanerges—or thunder—John was evidently a highly flammable hothead (Mark 3:17). But something happened to him, for as he spent time with Jesus, he became like Jesus.

And that same thing is happening to you and me. Slowly but surely, as we hang out with the Lord, we begin to become more and more like the Lord.

John's first epistle divides itself into three main sections as he discusses the light of God in chapters 1 and 2, the love of God in chapters 3 and 4, and the life of God in chapter 5.

Not only does John's first and longest epistle divide itself into three sections, but John gives four reasons why it should be read. . . .

First, John tells us his first epistle was written that our joy might be full (1:4). Joy is different from happiness. Happiness deals with one's mind and emotions in the realm of the soul. Joy, on the other hand, resides in the spirit—the part of us that will live forever, the essence of our being. Based upon outward circumstances, happiness comes and goes. Independent of circumstances, joy can be constant.

The old acrostic is true. . . .

J stands for Jesus. Because Jesus is the Fountainhead of joy, He is to have first place in our lives.

O stands for others. As we have all discovered, the way to be miserable is to focus on ourselves, cater to ourselves, analyze ourselves, and worry about ourselves. The way to find joy is to lay down our lives for the sake of others.

Y stands for you—last in the equation. When you're not thinking about yourself, talking about yourself, or burdening others with your situation, but rather saying, "What can I do today to die to myself and help others along the way?"—joy will reign in your spirit.

We will see John exhorting us to walk with Jesus and to care for others, knowing this is the secret of joy.

Second, John wrote his Epistle in order that we sin not (2:1). Are you struggling with sin? Are you battling a specific habit, problem, or addiction? Get into the Word, for David declared he hid the Word in his heart in order that he might not sin against God (Psalm 119:11).

"How shall a young man cleanse his way?" David asked.
"By having his pastor pray for him?
No.
By going to a Christian counseling clinic?
No.
By taking heed unto the Word (Psalm 119:9).

If you don't feel a need to come to Bible study or engage in morning devotions, it could be because you're filling your soul with the junk food of carnal entertainment or frivolous activities. But if you say, "Lord, today I choose to give my life to You once more and dig into Your Word," victory over sin will be yours.

The third reason John wrote his first epistle was as a warning about false teachers who would seek to seduce us (2:26). "I have meditated in Thy precepts," David declared. "Therefore I hate every false way" (see Psalm 119:104). How do you deal with those who try to trip you up in your faith? Stay in the Scriptures, and that which is false just won't ring true. It's sad to see wonderful folks who have been pulled away into false doctrines and cultic activities because they didn't know the Scriptures, because they didn't learn the Word.

The fourth and final reason John gives for writing his epistle is that we might believe on the name of the Son of God and that we might know we have eternal life (5:13). People often say, "I just don't know if I'm saved." The solution to their struggle is to stay in the Word, to let it soak into their spirit. If they do, they will have fullness of joy. They will be set free from sin. They will be kept from false teaching. And they'll know they have eternal life.

May the Lord bless us in this season as we look into this potent and practical section of Scripture penned by the one-time Son of Thunder, the apostle whom Jesus loved.

1 JOHN

1 John 1:1–3
That which was from the beginning, which we have heard, which we have seen with our eyes, which we have looked upon, and our hands have handled, of the Word of life; (For the life was manifested, and we have seen it, and bear witness, and shew unto you that eternal life, which was with the Father, and was manifested unto us;) That which we have seen and heard declare we unto you, that ye also may have fellowship with us: and truly our fellowship is with the Father, and with his Son Jesus Christ.

Claiming to possess super intellects, to be true thinkers, they were known as gnostics—or "the knowledgeable ones." And these "knowledgeable ones," these "enlightened ones" maintained that even if His followers claimed Jesus was God, they were embarrassingly naive to think He had a body physically, for anyone with any intelligence understood that anything in the material realm was inherently evil.

Why did they make this claim?

By arguing that everything material is evil, the gnostics absolved themselves of any responsibility for the activity of their bodies. In other words, their logic allowed them to position themselves as deep thinkers while behaving themselves as party animals.

"It is impossible that God actually became a Man," the gnostics declared. "Jesus was an ema-

nation of God, but not God Incarnate." And such thinking is the common denominator of all cults to this day.

Here at the outset of his epistle, John says, "Wait a minute. Jesus wasn't a phantom, an emanation, or a vision. We walked, hung out, and lived with Him. And we want you to have the same kind of fellowship with Him."

How can this happen?

The same way it did for two men on their way to the town of Emmaus. . . .

"Why are you so sad?" asked the Stranger walking with them.

"Don't you know what's happened?" they replied, not realizing it was the Lord. And they went on to recount to Him how Jesus had died on the Cross just a few days before.

Then, beginning with Moses and working His way through the Old Testament, Jesus opened the Word to them, explaining how it all pointed to Him.

Upon reaching their destination, yet wanting to hear more, the two men invited Jesus to dine with them. And it was when they saw Jesus break bread that their eyes were opened to recognize Jesus in their midst (Luke 24).

Two things took place on the Road to Emmaus: Jesus opened the Word to the disciples, and the eyes of the disciples were opened to Jesus. Haven't you experienced the same thing? "Lo, I come in the volume of the book," Jesus says (see Psalm 40:7). And truly this book causes us to have an awareness of the nearness of the Lord. When I don't get into the Word, I miss Him. Oh, He's still here, but, like the men on the Road to Emmaus, I don't recognize Him as readily or see Him as clearly.

Secondly, we see Jesus in the breaking of the bread at the table of Communion. "Take eat. This is My body broken for you," He said (see 1 Corinthians 11:24). That's why Communion is so very, very important. It's not just a little cracker-and-juice-monthly ritual. It is infinitely more than that, for it is at the table that we are given the unspeakable privilege of seeing Jesus clearly once again.

1 John 1:4
And these things write we unto you, that your joy may be full.

John says that the reason to touch the Lord at the table of Communion and see Him in the pages of the Word is in order that we might be full of joy. Elton Trueblood, classic preacher from a generation past, put it this way: "The Christian is joyful not because he is blind to injustice and suffering, but because he is convinced that these, in the light of Divine Sovereignty, are never ultimate. The humor of the Christian is not a way of denying the tears but rather a way of affirming something that is deeper than tears."

We're full of joy not because we're trite or frivolous, but because there's a deeper reality than the temporary separation from a loved one, the problem with the car, or the bankruptcy of the business. None of those things need rob us of joy because we know there's a much bigger picture.

For topical study of 1 John 1:4 entitled "The Wine of Joy," turn to page 1614.

1 John 1:5
This then is the message which we have heard of him, and declare unto you, that God is light, and in him is no darkness at all.

People who are depressed in their spiritual lives because they think being a Christian is so hard, don't match up with true biblical Christianity because John says there's no dark side to God; there's nothing negative about Him; there's not a mean bone in His body. Therefore, a sour, dour, dark, and discouraged Christian is an oxymoron, a contradiction of terms.

"Wait a minute," you say. "Wasn't Jesus the Man of Sorrows?" (see Isaiah 53:3).

Yes. Jesus wept over Jerusalem (Luke 19:41). He wept at the tomb of Lazarus (John 11:35). When Jesus wept, however, it was always for others.

"What about when He wept in the Garden of Gethsemane?" you ask.

The night before He would go to the Cross, Jesus sweat blood because He was terrified not by the pain of the Cross, the spittle that would run down His face, or the flagellum that would rip into His back. Jesus was almost literally scared to death by the thought of being temporarily separated from His Father when He would be made sin on our behalf.

"What if I can't pay the bills?" we ask. "What if the car doesn't work?" "What if I lose a loved one?" These are the things that frighten us. But separation from the Father? We don't even give it a second thought. God have mercy on us. We're terrified of all the wrong things.

1 John 1:6
If we say that we have fellowship with him, and walk in darkness, we lie, and do not the truth.

We cannot say, "I'm close to the Lord and I'm miserable. I'm walking with Jesus; I'm at the table; I'm in the Word—and am I ever depressed." We're kidding ourselves if we say we have fellowship with Jesus but walk around in darkness.

1 John 1:7 (a)
But if we walk in the light, as he is in the light, we have fellowship one with another . . .

One of the ways we know we have fellowship with the Lord is that we have fellowship with other people. That is, if we're truly in the light, our hearts will be full of joy. Therefore, we won't gossip about, find fault with, or put down others.

1 John 1:7 (b)
. . . and the blood of Jesus Christ his Son cleanseth us from all sin.

The Greek word translated "cleanseth" clearly speaks of a continual cleansing.

If we're continually cleansed, shall we continue to sin? "God forbid," says Paul (Romans 6:2) because even though we are cleansed from the penalty of sin, the repercussions of sin remain. Whatever a man sows, that shall he also reap (Galatians 6:7). And there are no exceptions to this rule.

"Be sure your sin will find you out," Numbers 32:23 declares—not "sometimes it will find you out," not "perhaps it will find you out," but "it *will* find you out," bringing with it terrible, painful, and sometimes lifelong repercussions.

1 John 1:8
If we say that we have no sin, we deceive ourselves, and the truth is not in us.

Who was saying they had no sin? The gnostics. "It's not me sinning," they said. "It's just my body."

So, too, there are people today who say, "There are no absolutes. What's wrong for you isn't wrong for me. I may not be perfect, but I'm not a sinner."

John, however, says any person at any time in any culture who says, "I'm not a sinner," is deceiving himself. He just doesn't get it.

1 John 1:9, 10
If we confess our sins, he is faithful and just to forgive us our sins, and to cleanse us from all unrighteousness. If we say that we have not sinned, we make him a liar, and his word is not in us.

For a number of years in my own walk, this passage kept me in bondage. You see, somewhere along the line, I picked up the idea that if there was one unconfessed sin in my life, God would not hear my prayers. As a result, I would spend time

at night on my knees by my bed trying to remember if there was any sin I hadn't confessed that would keep me out of fellowship. I knew I could be forgiven; I knew I could talk to the Father—but only if I first confessed my sin.

The problem with this kind of thinking is that it adds to what Christ did on the Cross. And in so doing, it is heresy. How are we saved? How do we walk with God? How are we allowed to enter heaven?

Cults answer, "Believe on Jesus Christ, *and . . .*"

"Believe on Jesus Christ and follow this teaching . . ." or, "Believe on Jesus Christ and knock on doors . . ." or, "Believe on Jesus Christ and wear holy underwear . . ."

And I suggest that "Believe on Jesus Christ and make sure you confess every sin" falls into this category. When Jesus died on the Cross, He didn't say, "To be completed." He said, "It is *finished.* The price is paid. The veil is rent. The way is open."

Am I suggesting we are no longer to confess our sin? Not at all. Confession of sin is a needful practice because in constantly confessing our sin to the Lord, we allow the Holy Spirit to readjust our thinking and set us free. Do I confess sin? Constantly—not to earn forgiveness, but because I want to be free. And each time I confess my sin, I find myself celebrating, saying, "Thank You, Lord. As I talk with You about this sin, I'm even more amazed by Your finished work on the Cross of Calvary."

THE WINE OF JOY
A Topical Study of
1 John 1:4

Having spent three years in the physical company of Jesus, no doubt John had countless memories of time spent with Him. After all, it was John who said that even the world itself could not contain the books that could be written about Him (John 21:25). Therefore, I wonder if, in writing about joy, John's mind went back to an unforgettable day in Galilee, an account of which he was the only Gospel writer to record. . . .

The Production of Wine

And the third day there was a marriage in Cana of Galilee; and the mother of Jesus was there: And both Jesus was called, and his disciples, to the mar-

riage. And when they wanted wine, the mother of Jesus saith unto him, They have no wine. Jesus saith unto her, Woman, what have I to do with thee? mine hour is not yet come. His mother saith unto the servants, Whatsoever he saith unto you, do it. And there were set there six waterpots of stone, after the manner of the purifying of the Jews, containing two or three firkins apiece. Jesus saith unto them, Fill the waterpots with water. And they filled them up to the brim. And he saith unto them, Draw out now, and bear unto the governor of the feast. And they bare it. When the ruler of the feast had tasted the water that was made wine, and knew not whence it was: (but the servants which drew the water knew;) the governor of the feast called the bridegroom, And saith unto him, Every man at the beginning doth set forth good wine; and when men have well drunk, then that which is worse: but thou hast kept the good wine until now.

John 2:1–10

What was the reason for this miracle? Wine being the symbol of joy throughout the Bible, I suggest Jesus chose to do His first miracle behind the scenes, out of sight of most people, simply to add joy to a marriage ceremony.

Now, if I were the Lord, I would have chosen as my first miracle to resurrect someone from the dead, cleanse someone from leprosy, or cast out a demon—something spectacular or necessary. But Jesus chose to do His first miracle in a way that says very clearly to you and me, "I want people to be full of joy. Whether it's a marriage that's watered down or a life that's washed up, I want to bring in one hundred eighty gallons of sparkling, bubbling joy—better than anything you've ever tasted before, better than anything the world can offer. I want to do something to bring you joy—joy in your parenting, joy in your profession, joy in your hearts."

Whenever people are with Jesus, close to Jesus, learning about Jesus, joy abounds. "If that be true," you say, "how do you explain what I'm going through this week? How can you explain what I've experienced this month? If I John was written in order that our joy might be full, if Jesus declared He wants us to be filled with joy, why has the last week, month, or year been anything but joyful for me?"

For the answer, turn to the Book of Jeremiah. . . .

The Purification of Wine

Moab hath been at ease from his youth, and he hath settled on his lees, and hath not been emptied from vessel to vessel, neither hath he gone into captivity: therefore his taste remained in him, and his scent is not changed.

Jeremiah 48:11

In Old Testament times, wine was made by pouring the juice of crushed grapes into a large vessel and allowing it to sit until the lees—the dregs, the impurities—

settled to the bottom. At just the right time, the winemaker would pour the wine into another vessel, leaving the dregs behind. This process would be repeated sometimes twelve to fifteen times.

Why?

If the wine wasn't poured from vessel to vessel, it would begin to take on the bitter taste of the lees. So in order to make wine that was pleasing to the taste, smell, and sight, the winemaker would pour the wine again and again until there were no dregs left.

When I begin to understand that this is God's process for purifying people as well as wine, my life makes a lot more sense. You see, the Lord says, "I want to flood you and fill you with the wine of the Holy Ghost. This means that not only will I provide the wine of My joy in your life—but that I will purify it as well."

Thus, when everything is relaxed and peaceful and wonderful, when I get settled, lethargic, and comfortable, the winemaker will stir up my life as He overturns my vessel. "Poor me!" I cry. "How could You do this? Why is this happening?"

The Lord knows that what I truly desire is to be filled with the sparkling, bubbly, pure wine of joy, a wine that is pleasing to Him, a wine that is contagious for others. He also knows that stagnation and comfort will circumvent the purification process because when I get comfortable, all too often, I stop seeking God; I don't go to church; I don't read the Word. And as I am cut off from the One who is the source of joy, my life gets shallower, narrower, and smaller. And I become bitter as a result.

So the Lord says, "Because I love you too much to leave you in the dregs and let your life become a drag, I'm going to overturn it regularly."

And finally, after being poured from vessel to vessel to vessel each time I get comfortable, instead of, "Poor me," I hear myself saying, "Pour me, Lord. Pour me," as I begin to learn that it is a process that produces in me a joy unspeakable and full of glory. It is a process that matures, deepens, and purifies me; a process that keeps me from becoming polluted and defiled by the dregs of my own complacency.

My teenagers, Ben and Mary, are very different—Mary is as feminine as Ben is tough. But there's one exception. At the Santa Cruz boardwalk and Great America years ago, I was reminded of this exception once again. You see, my daughter Mary always loved scary rides—the ones that spin and drop, the ones from which everyone exits with a green hue to their faces. On the other hand, my tough guy, Ben, was terrified by the Pirates of the Caribbean—not by the pirates, but by the little dip at the beginning of the ride. So here was Mary spinning around on all these huge rides—while Ben rode the kiddy cars.

Mary knew something that Ben didn't understand. Ben was convinced that scary rides were deathtraps. Mary, on the other hand, had total confidence that whoever engineered them did so in such a way that they would be thrilling, unpredictable, and exciting—but safe. Mary knew the rides were designed to provide a thrill—but not to kill.

Why, when they go through the twists and turns and "pourings" of life, do some people say, "Whoopee!" while others say, "Woe is me"? I believe it all has to do with trust. Regardless of the dips and turns in the career, the family, the sports field, or the classroom, one person says, "Although my stomach's a bit queasy, I trust that God knows what He's doing perfectly."

The other person—even though he may know God's in control theoretically—says, "This is it. It's all over. I'm doomed. I'm going to crash."

Why?

Because of his basic fear that God cannot be trusted in the pouring process, that His timing is wrong, that His pouring is too severe. What's the solution? I suggest it's found in the Book of Exodus. . . .

With the Egyptians barreling down upon them, they would have stoned Moses had God not parted the Red Sea. And when they had crossed over to the other side, Miriam grabbed a tambourine and led the children of Israel in a song of praise. "Our Lord has done gloriously. Horse and rider He has thrown into the sea."

As fitting as their praise was, how much better it would have been had the Israelites grabbed the tambourine *before* the water parted, saying, "We trust You wholeheartedly, Lord. We're going to celebrate, sing, and dance right now—*before* we understand how You're going to come through" (see Exodus 15:20, 21).

There are those of us who shake the tambourine when the Red Sea parts—but not until. Others of us are learning to sing praise *before* the Red Sea parts, to say, "Lord, I trust You."

Precious people, we can trust God to purify the wine within us because of the cup of wine on the table of Communion. You see, in saying, "This is My blood shed for you," Jesus is saying, "I'm deadly serious about My commitment to you. I'm totally and completely in love with you. I only want the best for you. And I prove it absolutely with the wine of My blood before you."

It's impossible for anyone to go to the table of Communion in sincerity and contemplation without coming away, saying, "Lord, I don't understand all the whys, but I trust You. The blood You shed for me, Your body broken on behalf of me proves absolutely to me that you're in love with me and will only do what's best in me."

Allow the Lord to have His way in your life. The pouring process He puts you through, the seemingly wild ride He takes you on won't cause you to crash. Oh, it might be a bit interesting from time to time—but rather than wiping you out, it will fill you up with the wine of great, great joy.

2

1 John 2:1
My little children, these things write I unto you, that ye sin not.

At nearly one hundred years of age, John has the right to address us as "little children"—as well as to speak with authority concerning the sin that threatens to wipe us out and do us in.

1 John 2:1 (a)
And if any man sin . . .

"I write to you that you sin not," John said. But knowing personally the frailty of humanity, he continued, "but if you sin . . ."

1 John 2:1 (b)
. . . we have an advocate with the Father, Jesus Christ the righteous.

If we sin, we're not written off the list or kicked out of the family, for we have an advocate, a defense attorney in Jesus Christ.

1 John 2:2 (a)
And he is the propitiation for our sins . . .

The tactic of our defense attorney is not to manipulate the evidence for us or to make excuses for our sin. No, our advocate bases His entire case upon the fact that He is the propitiation for our sins. That is, He took upon Himself the righteous indignation of the Father that should have been hurled on us.

Think of it this way. . . .

While driving eighty miles an hour through downtown Medford, Oregon, I'm pulled over by an officer of the law and taken into a courtroom. But although I walk in with knees knocking and forehead perspiring, I am greatly relieved to discover that the presiding judge is my dad. That is why there is a smile on my face even after the evidence against me is presented. After all, the judge is my dad—and he knows boys will be boys.

Imagine my surprise, then, when I hear his voice thunder, "Guilty. The fine is five thousand dollars or five years in jail."

"How can this be?" I cry. "You're my dad."

"Sir," he answers, "in this courtroom I am your judge. And justice must be done."

So I open my wallet to pay the fine, but all I find is a crumpled dollar bill and some change. And just as the bailiff is about to slap cuffs on my wrists and haul me to jail, the judge stands up, deliberately takes off his robe, and leaves the bench to stand beside me and

to pay my fine. Thus, justice is served because the price for the sin of speeding was paid—not by me but by my father who paid a debt I was completely unable to pay.

And that's exactly what happened when Jesus Christ became the propitiation, the payment for my sin.

1 John 2:2 (b)
. . . and not for ours only, but also for the sins of the whole world.

Jesus not only paid the price for my sin, but for the sins of the whole world. "All manner of sin is forgiven all men, He said, except for one: the blasphemy of the Spirit" (see Matthew 12:31). The one sin that will separate man from God presently and that will damn him eternally is the repeated refusal to listen to the Spirit speaking to one's heart, saying, "You need a Savior. Jesus paid the price for your sin. Accept His free gift of salvation."

1 John 2:3, 4
And hereby we do know that we know him, if we keep his commandments. He that saith, I know him, and keepeth not his commandments, is a liar, and the truth is not in him.

After talking about enjoying communion *with* God in the first section of his epistle, in verses 3–11, John goes on to talk about obeying the commandments *of* God. The second appearance of the word "know" in this passage is the Greek word *ginosko*, which speaks of intimacy. Thus, we know we are walking in intimacy with God if we keep His commandments.

1 John 2:5
But whoso keepeth his word, in him verily is the love of God perfected: hereby know we that we are in him.

We have the privilege of saying, "Lord, even though I struggle and fall, I see the beauty of holiness and the rightness of Your ways—and I desire with all of my heart to do what You say." If that is your heart, you are in Him.

1 John 2:6
He that saith he abideth in him ought himself also so to walk, even as he walked.

Is it a burdensome obligation to keep His commandments and to walk as He walked? Read on.

1 John 2:7

Brethren, I write no new commandment unto you, but an old commandment which ye had from the beginning. The old commandment is the word which ye have heard from the beginning.

"I'm not laying legalism on you," says John. "I'm not giving new rules to you. That which I'm telling you to do you've heard all along from the very beginning."

1 John 2:8

Again, a new commandment I write unto you, which thing is true in him and in you: because the darkness is past, and the true light now shineth.

Having said, "I write no new commandment to you," in verse 7, the word "new" John uses in verse 8 doesn't refer to something that hasn't been heard before, but rather to something that is fresh. In other words, although it's an old commandment, it's neither stale nor archaic. The old commandment is as fresh as the day it was given.

1 John 2:9–11

He that saith he is in the light, and hateth his brother, is in darkness even until now. He that loveth his brother abideth in the light, and there is none occasion of stumbling in him. But he that hateth his brother is in darkness, and walketh in darkness, and knoweth not whither he goeth, because that darkness hath blinded his eyes.

The new commandment of which John speaks is the greatest commandment of all. The new commandment is to love.

"What is the greatest commandment?" the young lawyer asked the Master.
*   And Jesus said, "How do you read it?"*
*   "Love the Lord thy God with all thy heart and soul and mind and strength," the lawyer answered.*
*   "That's it," Jesus said. "And the second is like unto it: Love thy neighbor as thyself" (see Matthew 22:36–39).*

The fresh word for you and me is that we are to love, for if we say we're walking with the Lord and are close to the Lord but have hatred in our hearts toward our brother, then something is not right. It's a wonderful thing to be able to say, "To

the best of my knowledge, I'm not bitter toward anyone, mad at anyone, or angry with anyone because I know what a sinner *I* am. I know how much *I've* failed. I know how gracious God has been to *me*." When that's our heart, we know things are right.

1 John 2:12–14

I write unto you, little children, because your sins are forgiven you for his name's sake. I write unto you, fathers, because ye have known him that is from the beginning. I write unto you, young men, because ye have overcome the wicked one. I write unto you, little children, because ye have known the Father. I have written unto you, fathers, because ye have known him that is from the beginning. I have written unto you, young men, because ye are strong, and the word of God abideth in you, and ye have overcome the wicked one.

Although there are four stages in our physical life (childhood, youth, adulthood, and, "My, you're looking wonderful"), John tells us there are three stages of spiritual life: little children, young men, and mature fathers.

Two things are characteristic of the little child: He realizes his sins are forgiven (verse 12), and he knows the Father (verse 13). While this is an excellent starting point, the child must go on to become a young man.

The young man in the faith not only knows the Father and knows his sins are forgiven, but he has overcome the wicked one (verse 13). How? By the Word of God (verse 14). In His wilderness temptation, it wasn't the Word quoted three times by Jesus that defeated the Enemy. It was His submission to it. . . .

• When Jesus said, "It is written that man shall not live by bread alone, but by every word that proceeds from the mouth of God," His implication was, "therefore I will not turn stones to bread, but will live by God's Word" (see Matthew 4:4).
• When Jesus said, "It is written that thou shalt not tempt the Lord thy God," His implication was, "therefore I will not jump off this pinnacle and tempt My Father to save me" (see Matthew 4:7).
• When Jesus said, "It is written that thou shalt worship the Lord thy God," His implication was, "therefore, I won't bow down to you, but will worship My Father exclusively" (see Matthew 4:10).

Believers who think power lies in merely quoting Scripture are mistaken. It's not the quoting of the verse, but rather submission to the Father that overcomes the Enemy. The wicked one flees when he hears a man or woman say, "I don't care what my fleshly tendencies are, here's what God's Word says—and with His help and by His grace, His Word is what I choose to follow."

The third category of spiritual life is that of fathers, or mature ones. Like little children, fathers know their sins are forgiven and understand the nature of their Father. Like young men, they overcome the wicked one by being submitted to the Word. And as a result, they have a simple, singular passion: To know Him that is from the beginning (verse 13)—to know Jesus (John 1:1).

As you walk with Jesus, spiritual life gets simpler and simpler because the longer you walk with Him, the fewer principles there are. I used to have notebooks full of principles concerning success in ministry, theology, and family. But the more time that passes, the more I say, "Jesus, You're my life—not ministry, not theology, not success as a family, but just *You.* I love being with You; I love talking with You; I just love *You.*"

That's when you know you're reaching the state of spiritual fatherhood. And the interesting thing about fathers is that there's reproduction. In the office, on the campus, around the neighborhood, others sense the Lord in you and are inspired to follow in your footsteps.

Children, young men, spiritual fathers—John commends them all.

1 John 2:15 (a)
Love not the world . . .

The Greek use of the word "world" is clear: It doesn't refer to people, but rather to the philosophy and mentality of the world system.

1 John 2:15 (b), 16
. . . neither the things that are in the world. If any man love the world, the love of the Father is not in him. For all that is in the world, the lust of the flesh, and the lust of the eyes, and the pride of life, is not of the Father, but is of the world.

If the San Francisco 49'ers approached their game next week with only three plays in their playbook—a sweep around the left, a run up the middle, and a screen pass to the right—and the opposing team knew they had only three plays, I guarantee they wouldn't win.

From the beginning of time, Satan has had only three plays: the lust of the eyes, the lust of the flesh, and the pride of life. . . .

In Genesis 3:6, we read that Eve saw that the tree of the knowledge of good and evil was good for food (the lust of the flesh), pleasant to the eyes (the lust of the eyes), and would make one wise (the pride of life).

In Matthew 4, we read that Satan tried to tempt Jesus to turn stones into bread (the lust of the flesh), to look at the kingdoms that could be His (the lust of the eyes), and to prove Himself to the people by jumping from a pinnacle (the pride of life).

To this day, every temptation, every attack from the Enemy and every worldly seduction falls into one of these three categories because Satan has no other plays. Therefore, to counter the lust of the flesh, do what Paul did when he said, "I don't allow my body to have mastery over me" (see 1 Corinthians 9:27). To counter the lust of the eyes, do what David did when he said, "I will set no wicked thing before my eyes" (see Psalm 101:3). To counter the pride of life, do what Jesus did when He humbled Himself and made Himself of no reputation (Philippians 2:7).

1 John 2:17
And the world passeth away, and the lust thereof: but he that doeth the will of God abideth for ever.

All that is in the world is based upon the lust of the flesh, the lust of the eyes, and the pride of life. But it's all going to pass away.

1 John 2:18 (a)
Little children, it is the last time . . .

In the beginning of the chapter, John talked about the light of God. Here in the second half of chapter 2, he gives us a warning about the darkness of the Enemy. . . .

1 John 2:18 (b)
. . . and as ye have heard that antichrist shall come, even now are there many antichrists; whereby we know that it is the last time.

Literally translate, "against Christ" or "in place of Christ," the term "antichrist" carries with it a three-fold meaning. . . .

- First, Antichrist is a person (Revelation 13; 16; 19). A world leader will come on the scene who will be so cunning, so clever, and so charismatic that he will actually take the place of Christ in the minds of many people.

- Second, there is such a thing as the spirit of antichrist (1 John 4:3). The spirit of antichrist has pervaded human history. For example, as the atrocities of Hitler and Stalin continue to come to light, the only explanation for their murderous insanity is the spirit of antichrist attempting to destroy God's people, and, in Stalin's own words, to become "the new Christ."
- The third meaning of the term "antichrist" is seen here in our text in reference to teachers who, in denying Jesus' deity, make Him out to be less than He declared Himself to be when He claimed to be God Himself (John 10:30).

1 John 2:19
They went out from us, but they were not of us; for if they had been of us, they would no doubt have continued with us: but they went out, that they might be made manifest that they were not all of us.

John tells us we can recognize those who have been seduced by the spirit of antichrist as those who say, "Forget the church. I'm not interested in the body of Christ. I can experience Christ on my own." Linked to no one, accountable to no one, they not only depart from the fellowship, but, as seen in verses 20–25, they deny the faith. . . .

1 John 2:20
But ye have an unction from the Holy One, and ye know all things.

The Greek word translated "know" is *eido*, which means "to know intuitively," so John is saying, "Because you have an anointing from God, there are certain things you know—not because you have mentally figured them out, but because you intuitively know they're wrong." That which false teachers propagate falls into this category because their words simply don't ring true in our hearts.

1 John 2:21–23
I have not written unto you because ye know not the truth, but because ye know it, and that no lie is of the truth. Who is a liar but he that denieth that Jesus is the Christ? He is antichrist, that denieth the Father and the Son. Whosoever denieth the Son, the same hath not the Father: (but) he that acknowledgeth the Son hath the Father also.

To deny the Father and the Son means to make a differentiation in their elevation. Jehovah Wit-

nesses, Mormons, and all other cults have their roots in gnostic heresy because all of them diminish the Son.

"Jesus is great," they say.
"Is He God?" I ask.
"He is great and by Him you must be saved," they say.
"Is He God?" I ask.
"He's the first begotten, the Son of God," they say.
"Is He God?" I ask.
"Well . . ."

"Why does John get so uptight about cultists who diminish the Son?" you ask. "Mormons love the Lord. They always talk about Jesus. What's the big deal?"

I answer this way. . . .

You're in my house when suddenly a man comes up my walkway, kicks down the door, and rolls a live grenade in your direction. As you sit glued to your seat, paralyzed with fear, I spring into action. I run down the hall, grab my nine-year-old son, Ben, and—just as the grenade is about to go off—I throw him on the grenade, saving you in the process.

Such is the damnable and erroneous picture the cultist paints concerning the Father. They say Jesus was not God, not equal to the Father, but rather a created being God the Father sent to take the blow while He watched. You see, unless I understand that Jesus is Himself the Wonderful Counselor, the Everlasting Father (Isaiah 9:6)—unless I understand that Jesus is who He claimed to be when He said I and the Father are one (John 10:30), unless I take Paul's words at face value when he said that God was in Christ reconciling the world to Himself (2 Corinthians 5:18–19), my perception of the Fatherhood of God and the sacrifice of the Son will be terribly skewed.

"Great is the mystery that God became a man," Paul told Timothy (see 1 Timothy 3:16). This is infinitely more than a doctrinal discussion, for if you do not say that Jesus is God, then you make God a very cruel, awful Person who created a Son to take the hit because He was unwilling to do so Himself. If, on the other hand, Jesus is indeed God, then God Himself absorbed the blow, took the hit, and was pinned to the Cross personally. No wonder those who teach anything else are damned.

1 John 2:24, 25
Let that therefore abide in you, which ye have heard from the beginning. If that

which ye have heard from the beginning shall remain in you, ye also shall continue in the Son, and in the Father. And this is the promise that he hath promised us, even eternal life.

The mystery of God in Christ reconciling the world unto Himself is the key to eternal life.

1 John 2:26
These things have I written unto you concerning them that seduce you.

False teachers not only depart from the fellowship and deny the faith, but they also try to deceive the family in their attempt to cloud people's understanding of the true nature of the Son.

1 John 2:27
But the anointing which ye have received of him abideth in you, and ye need not that any man teach you: but as the same anointing teacheth you of all things, and is truth, and is no lie, and even as it hath taught you, ye shall abide in him.

John is saying, "If you listen to the Holy Spirit, you'll recognize false teaching as foolishness."

I've heard people use this verse to say, "If we need not that any man teach us, we don't need to come to Bible study." However, because God gave teachers to the church (Ephesians 4:11), because Paul himself taught daily in the school of Tyrannus (Acts 19:9), and because the early church devoted herself to teaching (Acts 2:42), we know John is not denying the necessity of true teaching. Rather, he is denying the validity of false teaching.

1 John 2:28, 29
And now, little children, abide in him; that, when he shall appear, we may have confidence, and not be ashamed before him at his coming. If ye know that he is righteous, ye know that every one that doeth righteousness is born of him.

Those who have made Jesus less than He is will be ashamed at His coming when they find themselves face to face with His deity.

※

3 After telling us how to experience the light of God in chapters 1 and 2, we begin a new section here in chapter 3 as John calls us to experience the love of God—love that is pure (verses 1–9), love that is practical (verses 10–24), and love that is perfect (chapter 4).

1 John 3:1
Behold, what manner of love the Father hath bestowed upon us, that we should be called the sons of God: therefore the world knoweth us not, because it knew him not.

In his Gospel, John tells us that as many as received Jesus were given power, or authority, to become the sons of God (1:12). Here, he picks up on the same theme.

Paul further develops this idea of sonship when he writes of the "doctrine of adoption" in his epistles to the Ephesians and Romans. Seen in light of our position as sons of God, the Greek word for adoption is interesting indeed. *Huiothesia* comes from *huios,* or "son," and *thesis,* or "position." Thus, Jesus Christ took our position on the Cross in order that we might take the position of the Son in heaven. He who was rich became poor for our sakes that we might enjoy the riches of God (2 Corinthians 8:9).

The story is true, I'm told, of the brothers who wanted to play Little League. As they signed up, the registrar was puzzled when, according to their papers, he noticed they were six months apart.

"You're brothers?" he asked.

"Yep," they answered.

"But you're only six months apart," the puzzled official countered.

"Well, one of us was adopted," said one of the boys.

"Which one?" asked the registrar.

"We ask our dad all the time," said the boys, "but he says he can't remember."

I in them, and thou in me, that they may be made perfect in one; and that the world may know that thou hast sent me, and hast loved them, as thou hast loved me.   John 17:23

I studied this verse a year ago, and have been in somewhat of a daze ever since, for the word "as" means "to the same degree." In other words, Jesus says that the Father loves me, His adopted son, to the same degree that He loves Jesus, His only begotten Son. Amazing!

1 John 3:2
Beloved, now are we the sons of God, and it doth not yet appear what we shall be: but we know that, when he shall appear, we shall be like him; for we shall see him as he is.

We don't always act like sons of God or look likes sons of God, but John says when He shall appear, we shall be like Him. Do I like that? Yes, because I like Him! After all, Jesus Christ is the Man everyone desires to be like . . .

So gentle was He that little children flocked to Him (Matthew 19:14).

Yet so commanding was He that a single look from Him parted the angry crowd intending to do Him in (Luke 4:29, 30).

So authoritative was He that fierce storms would be quieted by His word (Mark 4:39).

Yet so tender was He that He stilled the storm of criticism that swirled around the adulterous woman (John 8:11).

So embracive was He that sinners called Him friend (Matthew 11:19).

Yet so righteous was He that His blood could wash away the sin of the entire world (1 John 2:2).

Jesus is, indeed, the Perfect Man. He's everything every one of us innately wants to be.

The more you read the Gospels carefully and thoughtfully, prayerfully and contemplatively, the more you will develop a profound appreciation of the personality, character, integrity, wisdom, and strength of Jesus. When I didn't know as much about Jesus as I know now, I wasn't as impressed with Him as I am today. And this is amazing because in every other case, the better you know people, the more disillusioned you become as you begin to see their cracks and flaws.

Not so with Jesus. The longer you walk with Him and the more you learn about Him, the more you will be impressed by Him, and the more you will long to see Him. Even though now we only see Him through a glass darkly (1 Corinthians 13:12), I like what I see!

1 John 3:3
And every man that hath this hope in him purifieth himself, even as he is pure.

Every man who has the hope of seeing Jesus, everyone who looks for His coming walks with a greater degree of purity than with which he would otherwise walk. Living in the constant awareness that the Lord's coming is at hand has a definite effect on the way one lives.

Whether you subscribe to a Pre-Tribulation, Mid-Tribulation, or Post-Tribulation Rapture, when you read Jesus' words concerning the end times, you cannot come to any other conclusion than to say He wants us living each and every day looking for His coming.

"I've been hearing you talk about the soon coming of Jesus for twenty years now," you say. "Before that, I heard Billy Graham talk about it.

And isn't it true that one hundred years ago D. L. Moody also believed Jesus would come shortly? C. H. Spurgeon said the same thing one hundred and fifty years ago. And it *still* hasn't happened."

That's okay. Even if the Lord doesn't come back in my lifetime, put me in the company of men throughout history who have lived their lives expecting the soon coming of Christ. Put me in the company of St. Francis of Assisi and Thomas ' Kempis, Spurgeon and Moody, Torrey and Finney. I would much rather be with those men throughout the ages—including the first-century church—who were living the true expectancy of the coming of Christ than to be in the company of those who say, "It can't be today."

1 John 3:4
Whosoever committeth sin transgresseth also the law: for sin is the transgression of the law.

The Greek word translated "committeth" is in the present perfect tense that speaks of continual action. Thus, this verse does not refer to one who falters in sin, struggles with sin, or falls because of a struggle with a certain sin. It refers to one who blatantly, habitually, and continually practices sin.

I used to watch my son Benny in the backyard with his baseball bat, practicing his swing over and over again. So, too, there are those who practice sin in order to get good at it.

1 John 3:5, 6
And ye know that he was manifested to take away our sins; and in him is no sin. Whosoever abideth in him sinneth not: whosoever sinneth hath not seen him, neither known him.

In verses 5–8, and in verse 4 of chapter 4, John will give us three reasons why Jesus came. As seen here in verse 5, the first reason was to take away our sin.

1 John 3:7, 8 (a)
Little children, let no man deceive you: he that doeth righteousness is righteous, even as he is righteous. He that committeth sin is of the devil; for the devil sinneth from the beginning.

We need to remind those who claim to be believers yet habitually, continually practice sin that, in the life of a true believer, the Lord came to take *away* sin."

1 John 3:8 (b)
For this purpose the Son of God was mani-
fested, that he might destroy the works of
the devil.

Here we see the second reason Jesus came: to
destroy the works of the devil. In taking away our
sin, Jesus paid the price for sin. In destroying the
works of the devil, He destroyed the power of sin.
That is, He destroyed the power of the Enemy to
entangle us in those things that compromise our
ability to impact the world for the kingdom.

1 John 3:9 (a)
Whosoever is born of God doth not commit
sin . . .

Because Jesus came to take away sin and to
destroy the works of the devil, he who is truly
born again doesn't practice sin.

1 John 3:9 (b)
. . . for his seed remaineth in him: and he
cannot sin, because he is born of God.

The seed spoken of here in verse 9 could either
refer to the life of Christ within the life of the believer (John 1:13) or to the Word of God (1 Peter
1:23). Which is it? I believe it's both. When the
Spirit of Christ comes into a man and when the
Word of God stirs within him, he cannot continue
sinning indefinitely. Oh, he might struggle with
sin. He might even be ensnared at times by sin.
But he's not comfortable in sin. That's why a
Christian involved in sin is the most miserable
person in the world. He has too much of the Lord
to enjoy sin, and too much sin to enjoy the Lord.
The seed—be it the Person of Christ, the Word of
God, or both—does not allow a person to habitu-
ally, continually practice sin.

1 John 3:10
In this the children of God are manifest,
and the children of the devil: whosoever do-
eth not righteousness is not of God, neither
he that loveth not his brother.

In the lives of those who are born again, there
is not only the absence of something negative but
also the presence of something positive. That is,
there is not only an absence of habitual, constant
sin, but there is the presence of love.

1 John 3:11, 12 (a)
For this is the message that ye heard from
the beginning, that we should love one an-

other. Not as Cain, who was of that wicked
one, and slew his brother.

John points to Cain as a picture of one who
could not claim to be a believer.

1 John 3:12 (b)
And wherefore slew he him? Because his
own works were evil, and his brother's righ-
teous.

The Book of Hebrews tells us Abel's sacrifice
was offered to God in faith. Cain's, on the other
hand, was the work of his hands, the fruit of his
own energy, and was therefore rejected. This
produced a bitterness and jealousy so deep
within Cain that it caused him to kill his brother.
The more successful a person is, the more vulnerable he, like Cain, is to jealousy or envy and
the more likely he is to make a snide remark
about the one of whom he's jealous. Oh, it might
be just a word or two, a wink or a chuckle, a nod
or a smile. But when I engage in such activity
concerning a brother, I know in my heart what
I'm doing. I'm murdering him.

1 John 3:13
Marvel not, my brethren, if the world hate
you.

Even though you're called to love all people—
especially the brothers and sisters in the Christian community—don't expect to be loved in return.

1 John 3:14
We know that we have passed from death
unto life, because we love the brethren. He
that loveth not his brother abideth in death.

"I'm not sure I'm a Christian," someone says.
John says one of the primary ways a person
knows he's born again is if he loves his sisters and
brothers in the Lord. If you find yourself caring
about your brothers and sisters in Christ and
wanting to stand up for them, you can be sure
something unusual has taken place in your heart
because such feelings are contrary to human nature.

1 John 3:15
Whosoever hateth his brother is a murderer:
and ye know that no murderer hath eternal
life abiding in him.

Jesus said, "You've heard it said of old that
you're not to commit murder, but I say unto you
if you're angry with your brother, you're guilty of
murder" (see Matthew 5:21, 22). If I'm angry

with someone, I am guilty of murder. Why? Because I will be killing him with my comments and cynicism (Proverbs 18:21).

The message of 1 John is that we are to *love*. An on-fire group of young believers in Germany end each of their petitions to the Lord with, "No matter the cost." I like that. Ask the Lord to make you a lover of people—no matter the cost.

1 John 3:16

Hereby perceive we the love of God, because he laid down his life for us: and we ought to lay down our lives for the brethren.

There is no reconciliation apart from death. For us to be reconciled to God, someone had to die—and it wouldn't be us. God initiated the process of reconciliation by laying down His own life.

So, too, the only way there will ever be reconciliation between you and the person with whom you are at odds with or toward whom you feel tension is if someone dies. Either you will lay down your life and quit proving your point—or the other person will be the bigger person and choose to do so. If there's someone with whom you want to be reconciled—be it a parent, child, spouse, or ex-spouse—the only way it can happen is through death. Somebody's gotta die.

1 John 3:17, 18

But whoso hath this world's good, and seeth his brother have need, and shutteth up his bowels of compassion from him, how dwelleth the love of God in him? My little children, let us not love in word, neither in tongue; but in deed and in truth.

It's very easy to talk about love and even easy to wax poetic about it. But John says, "Don't talk about it, kids—just do it."

1 John 3:19, 20

And hereby we know that we are of the truth, and shall assure our hearts before him. For if our heart condemn us, God is greater than our heart, and knoweth all things.

If your heart is attacking you, don't worry. God is greater than your heart, for He knows more about who you are than your heart ever could....

For topical study of I John 3:20 entitled "Heart Attacks," turn to page 1626.

1 John 3:21, 22

Beloved, if our heart condemn us not, then have we confidence toward God. And whatsoever we ask, we receive of him, because we keep his commandments, and do those things that are pleasing in his sight.

We have confidence with God because we do things that are pleasing in His sight. What things are pleasing in His sight? To the Jews, it was the six hundred thirteen commandments—three hundred sixty-five that are negative, two hundred forty-eight that are positive—they are found in the Old Testament law. But six hundred thirteen being quite a heavy load, David reduced the number to twelve....

LORD, who shall abide in thy tabernacle? who shall dwell in thy holy hill? He that walketh uprightly, and worketh righteousness, and speaketh the truth in his heart. He that backbiteth not with his tongue, nor doeth evil to his neighbour, nor taketh up a reproach against his neighbour. In whose eyes a vile person is contemned; but he honoureth them that fear the LORD. He that sweareth to his own hurt, and changeth not. He that putteth not out his money to usury, nor taketh reward against the innocent. He that doeth these things shall never be moved.   Psalm 15

And if a dozen is too many, Micah reduced the number to three when he said,

He hath shewed thee, O man, what is good; and what doth the LORD require of thee, but to do justly, and to love mercy, and to walk humbly with thy God?   Micah 6:8

Yet if three is too hard, Jesus reduced the number to two when He said,

Thou shalt love the Lord thy God with all thy heart, and with all thy soul, and with all thy mind. This is the first and great commandment. And the second is like unto it, Thou shalt love thy neighbour as thyself. On these two commandments hang all the law and the prophets.   Matthew 22:37–40

How do we have an assured heart, a free heart? By loving the Lord and His people—not in word and tongue, but in deed and truth (3:18).

When I don't live up to my own expectations, I tend to say, "I'm such a loser, why should I even bother to ask the Lord for anything?" But when my heart is not condemning me, I find I have a beautiful freedom with the Lord. From His perspective, it's there all the time. But I only recognize it when I am free from the heart attacks of condemnation.

1 John 3:23
And this is his commandment, That we should believe on the name of his Son Jesus Christ, and love one another, as he gave us commandment.

"Master," they said, "what must we do to do the *works* of God?"
Jesus answered, "This is the singular *work* of

God: That you believe on Him whom the Father hath sent" (see John 6:28, 29).

1 John 3:24
And he that keepeth his commandments dwelleth in him, and he in him. And hereby we know that he abideth in us, by the Spirit which he hath given us.

We know Jesus lives in us when the fruit of His work in and through our lives is the fruit of the Spirit, or love (Galatians 5:22).

HEART ATTACKS
A Topical Study of
1 John 3:20

How glorious it is to be free from condemnation. It happened to me one morning when I looked on the front page of the paper and saw this headline: "Chocolate Good In Fight Against Bad Cholesterol." The article went on to say that, according to researchers, while chocolate may be the despair of dieters, it also contains certain chemicals that help lower the risk of heart disease. No more condemnation!

But how much more glorious it is to be free from condemnation spiritually, for when our heart is free from condemnation, we have confidence toward God and effectiveness in prayer. This doesn't mean we dictate to or demand from God. However, when there's not a lot of junk in the way of our relationship with Him, we find the desires of our heart coming closer and closer in line with His will for our lives. Consequently, when we pray for the desires of our heart, we're praying for that which is God's will because it was God who put the desires in our heart in the first place.

If, on the other hand, you don't have confidence with God because your heart condemns you, John has good news for you as well. "God is greater than our heart," he says, "and He knows all things."

What does God know?

He knows a lot. . . .

Like as a father pitieth his children, so the LORD pitieth them that fear him.
                                                           Psalm 103:13

When my heart reminds me that I'm not doing what I could be and that I'm not as loving as I should be, God reminds me that He knows I'm only made of dust.

Nevertheless the foundation of God standeth sure, having this seal, The Lord knoweth them that are his. And, Let every one that nameth the name of Christ depart from iniquity.   2 Timothy 2:19

Immediately after a mother penguin lays her egg, she heads out to sea for a three-month eating binge, leaving Dad on the ice floe to stand on the egg and keep it warm until she returns. Then it's Dad's turn to take to sea and grab a bite to eat. By the time he returns, the egg has hatched. Yet, although there are millions of penguins on the ice floe dressed exactly alike, and although he has never even seen his offspring, he'll go directly to his own baby.

So, too, God says, "I know those who are Mine."

If you've ever been in a public place in a time of confusion and commotion, you've seen parents act the same way as they immediately, instinctively, intuitively gather their kids around them. They don't say, "Peter, you've been good, so I'm going to find you. Christy, you're on your own." No, when there's danger, disaster, or difficulty, a parent gathers every one of his kids around him. He gathers them *all.* Even though your heart may condemn you, God knows you are His, and He will gather you as well.

Now when he was in Jerusalem at the passover, in the feast day, many believed in his name, when they saw the miracles which he did. But Jesus did not commit himself unto them, because he knew all men, and needed not that any should testify of man: for he knew what was in man.   John 2:23–25

Jesus was in Jerusalem at Passover and many believed in His name when they saw the miracles He did. But Jesus did not commit Himself unto them because He knew they wouldn't be able to keep their commitment to Him. Although they were impressed with His miracles, although they were blown away by His presence and power, knowing they didn't understand what was asked of them, He didn't hold them to their commitment.

O LORD, thou hast searched me, and known me. Thou knowest my downsitting and mine uprising, thou understandest my thought afar off. Thou compassest my path and my lying down, and art acquainted with all my ways. For there is not a word in my tongue, but, lo, O LORD, thou knowest it altogether. Thou hast beset me behind and before, and laid thine hand upon me. Such knowledge is too wonderful for me; it is high, I cannot attain unto it.   Psalm 139:1–6

The Lord knows my ups and downs, my failings, vulnerabilities, and shortcomings. He knows all about me. And He knows everything about you, for He put you together. He knows how you are, what you are, who you are.

For I know the thoughts that I think toward you, saith the LORD, thoughts of peace, and not of evil, to give you an expected end.   Jeremiah 29:11

When did God say this? When His people were headed into captivity. For seventy years, the Jewish people would go through difficult days and tough times in Babylon. Yet the Lord said, "I know what I'm doing. It might look brutal and bleak to you—but it's all to bring you to a glorious end."

And the same is true for you and me.

When our hearts condemn us, God is greater than our hearts. He knows all things. He knows we are made of dust, that we make promises we can't keep, and that we are bound to fall and fail. Yet He also knows that we are His and that He has a glorious plan for our lives.

The One who knows us best loves us most.

What a miracle!

4 Having written about pure love in chapter 3, verses 1–9, and practical love in verses 10–24, here in chapter 4, John will write of perfect love. . . .

1 John 4:1
Beloved, believe not every spirit, but try the spirits whether they are of God: because many false prophets are gone out into the world.

Perfect, mature love requires discernment. Perfect love requires that we test the spirits in order that we don't fall prey to those who would seek to lure us away from the simplicity of the gospel. How do we test the spirits? Read on.

1 John 4:2, 3
Hereby know ye the Spirit of God: Every spirit that confesseth that Jesus Christ is come in the flesh is of God: And every spirit that confesseth not that Jesus Christ is come in the flesh is not of God: and this is that spirit of antichrist, whereof ye have heard that it should come; and even now already is it in the world.

If a teaching, suggestion, or thought is of the spirit of God, it will affirm both the deity and the humanity of Christ.

The question in the early church never concerned the deity of Christ. The debate was over His humanity. Church councils would convene in the second century and argue vehemently over this issue because gnostic thought had penetrated the church. Two thousand years later,

however, it is the deity of Christ that is continually called into question. John says the Spirit of God attests to both the humanity and deity of Christ. Such is the test by which we recognize Him.

1 John 4:4
Ye are of God, little children, and have overcome them: because greater is he that is in you, than he that is in the world.

The walls of the submarines that descend two miles into the Mariana Trench of the Pacific Ocean are constructed of thick steel plates to withstand the tremendous pressure placed upon them. But the pictures taken from such heavily protected submarines reveal fish swimming two miles below the surface of the water with scales no thicker than that of any other fish. How can this be? The answer is simple: The pressure on the inside of those fish is equal to the pressure of the water around them.

That's the beauty of Christianity. Some people erect massive walls to insulate themselves from the attacks of the Enemy—only to find themselves filled with the frustration of isolation. The key is not to put up massive walls to protect you from the Enemy—but to realize the One inside you is greater than whatever pressure threatens to attack you. When we understand that He that is in us is greater than any temptation, problem, trauma, or difficulty that could come against us, we can move through life freely.

1 John 4:5, 6 (a)
They are of the world: therefore speak they
of the world, and the world heareth them.
We are of God: he that knoweth God heareth
us; he that is not of God heareth not us.

Inspired by the Spirit, John declares those
who truly know God know the Word. Those who
don't know God don't listen to the Word.

1 John 4:6 (b)
Hereby know we the spirit of truth, and the
spirit of error.

In this simple section, John has told us all we
need to know to identify the cultist. That is, if a
person draws people closer to God, if he embraces both the deity and humanity of Jesus
Christ, if he encourages folks to read the Scriptures, he is of the Spirit. On the other hand, if he
diminishes either the deity or humanity of Christ,
if he makes people feel distant from God, or if he
makes light of the Word, he is in error.

1 John 4:7, 8
Beloved, let us love one another: for love is
of God; and every one that loveth is born of
God, and knoweth God. He that loveth not
knoweth not God; for God is love.

As John puts the clutch in and changes gears a
bit, he tells us that even though we are to test the
spirits, we must not become cynical. Although we
are to be able to identify heresy and pseudo-
spirituality, we must also be those who love, for
God is love.
Earlier, John told us God is light (1 John 1:5).
Moses tells us He is a consuming fire (Deuteronomy 9:3). Taken together, these descriptions of
God paint a powerful portrait—for fire can either
be very lovely or it can be terrifying. It all depends on one's relationship with the fire. Fire in
the fireplace is light and love. But outside of the
fireplace, raging through one's house, fire is terrifying.
So, too, he who embraces what God did for him
on the Cross of Calvary will be one who basks in
His love, one who glows in His light. On the other
hand, he who doesn't accept God's free gift of salvation will feel the heat of His wrath because the
sin of unbelief abides on him (John 3:36).

1 John 4:9, 10
In this was manifested the love of God to-
ward us, because that God sent his only be-
gotten Son into the world, that we might
live through him. Herein is love, not that
we loved God, but that he loved us, and sent
his Son to be the propitiation for our sins.

Scripture declares that no man seeks God (Romans 3:11). He seeks us. And He pulls us into His
kingdom by the provision He made for us on Calvary. *He* does the whole thing.
I don't know what happens to us. Why is it that,
when we get saved, we accept grace so easily—
but then after we walk with the Lord for a season, we begin to think we can add to grace?
"Even as you have received Christ, so walk ye in
Him" Paul declares in Colossians 2:6.
"Herein is love," John says—"not that we
loved God, not that we had devotions, not that we
were involved in missions—but that God loved us
and sent His Son to be the propitiation for our
sins."

1 John 4:11
Beloved, if God so loved us, we ought also
to love one another.

If God so loved us—and keeps on loving us—
then we have no other recourse but to forgive
people who have knowingly or unknowingly offended us. If you're having a hard time forgiving
someone, ask the Lord to give you a glimpse of
your own sin, a peek at how much He has forgiven you.

1 John 4:12, 13
No man hath seen God at any time. If we
love one another, God dwelleth in us, and
his love is perfected in us. Hereby know we
that we dwell in him, and he in us, because
he hath given us of his Spirit.

How do you know if you're really walking with
the Lord and dwelling in the Lord? Because you
have His Spirit. How do you know if you have His
Spirit? The fruit of the Spirit being love, I know I
am walking close to the Lord to the degree that I
am loving people.

1 John 4:14, 15
And we have seen and do testify that the
Father sent the Son to be the Saviour of the
world. Whosoever shall confess that Jesus
is the Son of God, God dwelleth in him, and
he in God.

We must confess that Jesus came in the flesh
to be the Savior of the world. And we must confess that He is the Son of God. These are the two
components that will keep us free of heresy.

1 John 4:16, 17
And we have known and believed the love
that God hath to us. God is love; and he that
dwelleth in love dwelleth in God, and God
in him. Herein is our love made perfect, that

we may have boldness in the day of judgment: because as he is, so are we in this world.

God is love. Therefore, if we are His, if we are
abiding in Him, we will, like Him, love others.

1 John 4:18
**There is no fear in love; but perfect love
casteth out fear: because fear hath torment.
He that feareth is not made perfect in love.**

Perfect love casts out fear. How so? If I understand that God really, truly loves me, I can have
absolute confidence that whatever happens at
any given moment is the best for me. Regardless
of what the doctor may say, what the IRS may declare, or who wins the election—when you are
sure of God's love for you, you don't have fear.
The answer to anxiety and fear is not to face
your fears or to figure out your phobias. The answer to fear is to become saturated in God's love
because His perfect love casts out fear. Grumpiness and cynicism, doubt and despair wash over
me whenever I take my mind off God's perfect
love—so undeniably demonstrated at Calvary.

1 John 4:19–21
**We love him, because he first loved us. If a
man say, I love God, and hateth his brother,
he is a liar: for he that loveth not his brother
whom he hath seen, how can he love God
whom he hath not seen? And this commandment have we from him, That he who loveth
God love his brother also.**

Forgiveness doesn't have to do with feelings.
Forgiveness is a decision we make. If we decide
to forgive, feelings will follow in due season. Who
can choose to forgive? Only one who's living in
love. Who is living in love? The one who realizes
that, although he's a sinner and a failure, because
God has been so good to him, he has no reasonable option but to love his brother.

5 In chapters 1 and 2, John wrote of walking
in God's light. In chapters 3 and 4, he discussed living in God's love. Here, in the final
section of his epistle, he talks about experiencing
God's life. . . .

1 John 5:1
**Whosoever believeth that Jesus is the Christ
is born of God: and every one that loveth
him that begat loveth him also that is begotten of him.**

Everyone who loves the Father will also love
the Son. It is the spirit of antichrist that says, "I
love God, but the Son is on a different level."

1 John 5:2
**By this we know that we love the children
of God, when we love God, and keep his commandments.**

Because God is love, the closer I get to the
Lord, the more His love will rub off on me and the
more I will love His children. Those who think
they don't need fellowship with the body or those
who call Christians hypocrites are not truly close
to the Father because John says he who loves
God loves His kids.

1 John 5:3
**For this is the love of God, that we keep his
commandments: and his commandments
are not grievous.**

God's commandment to love Him with all our
heart, soul, mind and strength and to love our
neighbor as ourselves is neither hard to discern
nor, by the power of His Spirit, hard to follow.

1 John 5:4, 5
**For whatsoever is born of God overcometh
the world: and this is the victory that overcometh the world, even our faith. Who is
he that overcometh the world, but he that
believeth that Jesus is the Son of God?**

How do we overcome the seductions, temptations, and attractions of the world? Not by a program, but through a Person. "In the world you
will have tribulation," Jesus said, "but be of good
cheer, for I have overcome the world" (John
16:33).
I was often asked what Applegate Christian
Fellowship's follow-up program was for all of the
people who are baptized there Sunday after Sunday. My answer was that Jesus Christ—the One
who overcame the world, the One who dealt with
every temptation successfully, the One who
stared down the Enemy—lives in every one of
them and in Him lies victory.

1 John 5:6
**This is he that came by water and blood,
even Jesus Christ; not by water only, but by
water and blood.**

Keep in mind that throughout his entire epistle, John is doing battle with gnostics who taught
that because the material realm is evil, if Christ
was, indeed, who He claimed to be, He couldn't
really have had a material body.

1 John 5:6, 7
And it is the Spirit that beareth witness, because the Spirit is truth. For there are three that bear record in heaven, the Father, the Word, and the Holy Ghost: and these three are one.

Perhaps this verse is footnoted in your Bible as not being in the original manuscript. In this way, one of the most powerful statements of the Trinity takes its place with other passages whose validity is questioned in many good translations. Among them are John 8—the story of the woman taken in adultery—Mark 16:15, and Romans 8:1.

But remember, we not only have copies of the original texts—we also have sermons of church fathers that are older than the oldest texts we have. And guess what. The messages of the early church preachers refer to John 8, Mark 16, Romans 8, and 1 John 5:7. So whatever texts they had in their hands contained the very passages that newer translations question. If these texts were not so pivotal, I wouldn't think so much about the controversy. But I see something more than coincidental in attacking such powerful passages.

1 John 5:8
And there are three that bear witness in earth, the spirit, and the water, and the blood: and these three agree in one.

Just as the Father, the Word, and the Spirit bear witness in heaven, the Spirit, the water, and the blood bear witness on earth. . . .

- First, the Spirit bears witness that Jesus Christ is in us. Paul put it this way: His Spirit bears witness with our spirit that we are the sons of God (Romans 8:16). No matter how many people argue with me or point out my faults accusingly, I *know* I'm a child of God because His Spirit bears witness with my spirit.
- Second, water bears witness that Jesus Christ is in us. When Satan says, "You're not saved," think back to the day you went into the water of baptism and came out looking like a drowned rat. What would make you do that? The Spirit drew you—and the water is a confirmation or reminder to you.
- Third, the blood bears witness that Jesus Christ is in us. I come to the table of Communion, and as I drink of the cup, I absorb and embrace, commemorate and celebrate the work of Christ on my behalf.

The Spirit inside you, the baptism you went through, and the blood shed for you work to-

gether as one proof that you truly are a Christian.

1 John 5:9
If we receive the witness of men, the witness of God is greater: for this is the witness of God which he hath testified of his Son.

"This is My beloved Son in whom I am well pleased," said God of Jesus (Matthew 3:17). If we believe the information given to us by mere people, how can we not believe the statements made by God?

1 John 5:10, 11
He that believeth on the Son of God hath the witness in himself: he that believeth not God hath made him a liar; because he believeth not the record that God gave of his Son. And this is the record, that God hath given to us eternal life, and this life is in his Son.

Sorry, Islam. Sorry Watchtower Society. Sorry Salt Lake City. The fact of the matter is this: Life is in the *Son*.

1 John 5:12
He that hath the Son hath life; and he that hath not the Son of God hath not life.

In his Gospel, John added a phrase to this verse for greater emphasis when he wrote, "But the wrath of God will abide on him" (see 3:36).

1 John 5:13–15
These things have I written unto you that believe on the name of the Son of God; that ye may know that ye have eternal life, and that ye may believe on the name of the Son of God. And this is the confidence that we have in him, that, if we ask any thing according to his will, he heareth us: And if we know that he hear us, whatsoever we ask, we know that we have the petitions that we desired of him.

"I'm going to pull your hair, Mary," Benjamin would threaten.

"Benny," I would say, "I didn't hear what I thought I heard, did I?"

So, too, if we ask for things or situations that are not God's will, He's good enough and kind enough and loving enough to say, "I didn't hear that, did I?" We ask for the dumbest things! Think back to that for which you prayed passionately when you were eighteen, twenty-four, or sixty years old. So good is God to you and me that He says, "I'm not going to hear prayers that are not My will—not because I'm mean, but because I want the best for you."

On the other hand, if we ask anything according to His will, God hears us. . . .

"Lord, help me to love people," we say.
"I hear you," He answers.
"Help me to forgive people I feel have wronged me," we pray.
"I hear your prayer," He replies.

John tells you and me that if we ask anything according to His will, God hears us. And if He hears us, we have confidence that He will give us that for which we ask. So if your prayers are crashing before they make it to heaven, do some investigation as to why. . . .

If I regard iniquity in my heart, the Lord will not hear me.   Psalm 66:18

If I'm living in rebellion and sin, my prayers will not be answered. Why? Because God is mad at me? No, it's because it's a sign that I'm involved in some sin that, if not dealt with, will wipe me out. Thus, God's failure to answer my prayer is not punishment but protection.

Likewise, ye husbands, dwell with them according to knowledge, giving honour unto the wife, as unto the weaker vessel, and as being heirs together of the grace of life; that your prayers be not hindered.   1 Peter 3:7

Because God wants husbands and wives to walk in unity and love, if a husband is not honoring or loving his wife, his prayers will be hindered as an incentive for him to make things right.

Therefore if thou bring thy gift to the altar, and there rememberest that thy brother hath ought against thee; Leave there thy gift before the altar, and go thy way; first be reconciled to thy brother, and then come and offer thy gift.   Matthew 5:23, 24

When you come to the altar—to the place of worship and petition—and there the Holy Spirit taps you on the shoulder, saying, "This person is deeply and greatly offended with you," you need to make things right with him before you continue in prayer.

If ye abide in me, and my words abide in you, ye shall ask what ye will, and it shall be done unto you.   John 15:7

If we're not in the Word, we can't pray in harmony with the heart of Jesus because we won't know what His will is. Consequently, our prayers won't be heard.

Is there a sin you're harboring? Are there problems in your marriage? Is there a relationship that needs to be repaired? Are you neglecting the Word? These are the issues that will hinder our prayers.

1 John 5:16
If any man see his brother sin a sin which is not unto death, he shall ask, and he shall give him life for them that sin not unto death. There is a sin unto death: I do not say that he shall pray for it.

"If you see a brother sinning, pray for him that the Lord will convict him and that he will choose to do what is right," says John. "But if he is sinning unto death, do not pray for him." The sin unto death is the rejection of Jesus Christ—the blasphemy of the Spirit (Matthew 12:31).

"My spirit will not always strive with man," God declared (Genesis 6:3). Thus, there comes a point in time when a man says, "No," to the prompting of the Spirit so many times that he cannot be born again. If a man has done this, we are not to pray for him.

How can we know if someone has come to that point?

We can't. Therefore, we're to keep praying.

Before Jeffrey Dahmer died in prison, he had a true, born-again experience and shared the gospel with every prisoner he could. When I read his story, I thought, *Wait a minute. This guy kills people, cuts up their bodies, puts them in his freezer, and has them for lunch. Then he goes to prison, hears the gospel, gets saved—and now everything's okay?* Yes. As shocking as that seems, the power of the Cross of Calvary, the matchless mercy of the Master, the unfathomable potency of the blood makes such a miracle possible. And although at first it seems disquieting and troubling, in reality it gives me great hope because I know if the Lord can save Jeffrey Dahmer, He can save me.

1 John 5:17, 18 (a)
All unrighteousness is sin: and there is a sin not unto death. We know that whosoever is born of God sinneth not . . .

That is, whoever is born of God does not practice sin, does not work on getting better at sinning.

1 John 5:18 (b)
. . . but he that is begotten of God keepeth himself . . .

The original Greek text makes it clear that the word "he" refers to Jesus, and the word "himself" is actually "him." Thus, Jesus—who is begotten of God—keeps him. Keeps who? You and me (Jude 24).

1 John 5:18 (c)
. . . and that wicked one toucheth him not.

I love this! Jesus keeps me, and the wicked one cannot do anything to me. Demon possession in a Christian is impossible because we're kept by Jesus—and greater is He in us than he that is in the world (1 John 4:4).

1 John 5:19
And we know that we are of God, and the whole world lieth in wickedness.

This is truth—but it isn't despair. Things will not be right until Jesus Christ comes back to rule and reign. Until then, it's pointless to pin our hopes to anything but that fact.

1 John 5:20, 21
And we know that the Son of God is come, and hath given us an understanding, that we may know him that is true, and we are in him that is true, even in his Son Jesus Christ. This is the true God, and eternal life. Little children, keep yourselves from idols. Amen.

John ends his epistle with a word of warning that, while it at first seems out of sync with the rest of the book, is, in fact, most appropriate. You see, taken in context, the idols of which John writes are not movie stars or sports heroes, fancy homes or opulent lifestyles. No, the idols to which he alludes throughout his entire epistle are those who embrace and propagate the spirit of Gnosticism.

Gnosticism can be seen in anyone who worships his own concept of Christ, in anyone who idolizes his own intellectual theology about God. And it will always manifest itself in a pulling away from the body of Christ. The end result of the subtlety of such idolatry can be seen in a story found in Judges 17—18 of a man named Micah. . . .

Using her life savings, Micah's mom bought two idols for her son—a "graven image," which was very possibly a silver calf like the golden calf of Exodus 32, and a "molten image," which was possibly a poor replica of the ark of the covenant, containing a copy of the Ten Commandments. After constructing a shrine for his idols, Micah made an ephod—an article of clothing worn by priests. And after fashioning terraphim—family gods—he consecrated one of his sons to be his priest. Although this sounds strange to us, Micah was emblematic of a problem in the entire nation of Israel, a nation wherein "everyone did right in his own eyes" (see Judges 21:25).

When a Levite passed through his region, Micah jumped at the opportunity to add a bona fide priest to his designer religion and employed the Levite. At this point, Micah had a religion with four attractive elements:

Practical convenience. With his shrine conveniently located in his backyard, Micah had no journey to make, no traffic to fight.

Family involvement. His mom having financed the whole enterprise and his son being the priest, Micah could have "family time" even as he worshiped.

Biblical components. With his ephod, miniature ark, copy of the Ten Commandments, and a replica of the idol the first high priest had made, Micah incorporated biblical components into his backyard religion as seamlessly as those who think a recitation of the Lord's Prayer at family gatherings or the display of a nativity scene at Christmas is an alternative to fellowship with the body of Christ.

Cultural tolerance. Mixing terraphim with the ark of the covenant made Micah inclusive and politically correct.

But Micah's custom-made religion toppled around him when the men of Dan ripped off his idols and lured away his priest. And, as a result, Micah's do-it-yourself belief system that had nobly included practical convenience, family involvement, biblical components, and cultural tolerance was, in the end, tragically impotent.

"Forsake not the assembling of yourselves together," warns the writer of Hebrews (see Hebrews 10:25). We are to worship as a family corporately. If we don't, when trouble strikes and when disaster comes, we'll run to our custom religion, but it will not save us no matter how loudly we cry. Any who have been through difficulties and tragedies know that blessing and strength come from being part of the body, submitting to the principles and precepts of the Lord, and continuing in the ordinances faithfully.

In Shiloh—only a few miles away from Micah's house—stood the tabernacle containing the true ark of the covenant, the true Word of God, the true priesthood. While Micah dabbled in deception and idolized imitations, reality was right up the road.

May such never be said of us. May we continue to be those who exchange the subtlety of idolatry for the surety of Shiloh as we renew our commitment to be a people whose God is the Lord.

2 JOHN

Background to 2 & 3 John

Because they were written as personal correspondence rather than as doctrinal statements or historical records, John's second and third epistles afford us the opportunity to eavesdrop on the early church, to read mail addressed to the group who "turned the world upside down" (see Acts 17:6). And in so doing, we see that the old adage is indeed true: Wherever there are people, there are problems. So it is that in 2 and 3 John, John deals with people problems in the early church. In 2 John, He deals with them generically; in 3 John, he deals with them specifically.

There are times when we must speak the truth generally and let the Holy Spirit make application specifically. But there are also times when, like John, we must speak the truth to people individually and personally.

The lessons seen in John's last two epistles have great application to us congregationally, as families, and as individuals.

2 JOHN

2 John 1 (a)
The elder . . .

John refers to himself as "the elder" because in addition to being the last surviving apostle, at the time he wrote this letter, he was most likely close to one hundred years old. That's the great thing about ministry. A thirty-three-year-old player in the NFL is considered an old man. But in the things of God, a man that age is just beginning. Because our lives become richer and deeper the longer we walk with the Lord, there is no disqualification for age.

2 John 1 (b)
. . . unto the elect lady and her children . . .

There is debate about whether the "elect lady" to whom John wrote was a literal lady, an ac-

quaintance of John's—or a church, the church being the elect as well as the bride of Christ.

Why didn't John identify the elect lady? If, indeed, she was an individual, I believe it is very likely John kept her identity hidden in order to spare her from the persecution aimed at believers when this letter was written. John commends the elect lady in verses 1–4, commands her in verses 5–6, cautions her in verses 7–11, and, lastly, comforts her in verses 12, 13.

2 John 1 (c)–3
. . . whom I love in the truth; and not I only, but also all they that have known the truth; for the truth's sake, which dwelleth in us, and shall be with us for ever. Grace be with you, mercy, and peace, from God the Father, and from the Lord Jesus Christ, the Son of the Father, in truth and love.

Although John talks about love more than any other writer in Scripture, he also emphasizes truth more than any other writer—using the word "truth" twenty times in his Gospel, nine times in 1 John, five times in these opening verses of 2 John, and five more times in 3 John.

I find it interesting that it was the "apostle of love" whom the Lord tapped on the shoulder to also be the one who stressed truth, because when you talk about love, it's very easy to get mushy, to become sentimental, to begin to say, "I'll just love that person rather than be honest with him." Such is not the case with John. And his example is a needful one in a day when the economy has eclipsed integrity as our nation's top priority, in an age where what is true for one person may or may not be true for another, in a culture that embraces Pilate's question, "What is truth?" (John 18:38), rather than Jesus' declaration, "I am the truth" (John 14:6).

While I don't want to be one who causes people to batten down the hatches whenever they see me coming, neither do I want to let the church or my kids walk in ways I know will be destructive. Our relationships with our kids, our spouses, and our sisters and brothers in the Lord cannot survive without truth. That's why Paul says we are to speak the truth in love (Ephesians 4:15)—for both are vital.

2 John 4
I rejoiced greatly that I found of thy children walking in truth, as we have received a commandment from the Father.

Mom and Dad, make sure you model absolute integrity to your kids. Never let them see you compromise truth even in little, seemingly insignificant ways—for such actions will plant seeds in their hearts that will take root, causing them to be people who do not walk in integrity or deal with others honestly.

For topical study of 2 John 4 entitled "Children Walking in Truth," turn to page 1637.

2 John 5, 6
And now I beseech thee, lady, not as though I wrote a new commandment unto thee, but that which we had from the beginning, that we love one another. And this is love, that we walk after his commandments. This is the commandment, That, as ye have heard from the beginning, ye should walk in it.

After commending her for walking in truth, John reminds the elect lady of the command to love. Truth and love are an unbeatable team, a winning combination, a dynamic duo. Truth without love makes a person harsh. But love without truth makes a person dangerous because he will allow cancers to grow and problems to take root in his life, in his family, on the job, or in the church.

"I commend you for walking in truth," said John, "and I command you not to forget love." And then he issues a word of caution. . . .

2 John 7, 8
For many deceivers are entered into the world, who confess not that Jesus Christ is come in the flesh. This is a deceiver and an antichrist. Look to yourselves, that we lose not those things which we have wrought, but that we receive a full reward.

The Greek word translated "come" being a present participle, newer translations are correct in rendering verse 7: "For many deceivers are entered into the world, who confess that Jesus Christ is not coming in the flesh."

"Watch out," John says, "for people who say or imply that Jesus isn't coming in the flesh, who tell you not to get too serious about prophecy and not to look for Jesus to return physically." Who says this? Jehovah's Witnesses, for one. They say Jesus came—but not in the flesh. He came secretly in the Spirit and revealed Himself only to the Watchtower Society. According to the passage before us, this puts Jehovah's Witnesses in the camp of the Enemy.

2 John 9–11
Whosoever transgresseth, and abideth not in the doctrine of Christ, hath not God. He that abideth in the doctrine of Christ, he hath both the Father and the Son. If there come any unto you, and bring not this doctrine, receive him not into your house, neither bid him God speed: For he that biddeth him God speed is partaker of his evil deeds.

This is a strong word. We are not to get involved with people who don't believe in the literal, physical return of Jesus. We are not to say, "God bless you," to such people, or to invite them into our homes. Those who reject Jesus Christ, those who are not looking for Jesus Christ, those who have diminished the Person of Jesus Christ are to be shunned.

It's a good thing these strong words come from the pen of John—for if Paul had written them, this severe warning could simply be attributed to his forceful personality. But the fact that this warning comes from the "apostle of love" makes it all the more imperative.

2 John 12, 13
Having many things to write unto you, I
would not write with paper and ink: but I
trust to come unto you, and speak face to
face, that our joy may be full. The children
of thy elect sister greet thee. Amen.

Finally, after commending, commanding, and cautioning, John comforts. "I'd like to deal with many more things," he says, "but I'll do it face-to-face rather than with pen and paper." Why would this be a comfort? Because keeping a balance between truth and love often raises more questions than it answers. So John simply says, "Do those things you understand, and I'll explain the rest when I come."

We have a tendency to get tripped up by that which we don't understand. For example, we wonder what will God do with those who are seemingly sincerely tricked by the cults or iso-lated in regions of the world where they never hear the gospel.

In answer to such questions, the Lord says to you and me through the apostle John, "Hold on. I'm coming soon. Everything will make sense when you see Me face-to-face."

In the meantime, we are to do what we under-stand. We are to stay away from those who propa-gate heresy and we are to preach Christ to people with a sense of urgency. We must do what the Word says and let God do what He wants to do rather than say, "I don't have to witness to him. I don't have to share with my neighbor. They'll probably make it to heaven, anyway. My kids are probably saved; I don't want to bother them."

In John's second letter, I hear an urgent heart. The "apostle of love" is one who draws a very real dividing line in the sand between Christ and anti-christ, light and darkness, truth and heresy. "Stay away from heretics," he writes, "Walk in truth. And don't forget love."

CHILDREN WALKING IN TRUTH
A Topical Study of
2 John 4

I rejoiced greatly that I found of thy children walking in truth . . .
                                                          2 John 4 (a)

I have no greater joy than to hear that my children walk in truth.   3 John 4

At this point in my life, at the ripe old age of forty-three, I have concluded that John is right: There is no deeper delight, no greater joy than seeing my children walk in truth. Whether you're a parent or involved in discipling someone, please take note of these five scriptures that tell us how to see our kids walk in truth. . . .

Walking Together with Them

Hear, O Israel: The LORD our God is one LORD: And thou shalt love the LORD thy God with all thine heart, and with all thy soul, and with all thy might. And these words, which I command thee this day, shall be in thine heart: And thou shalt teach them diligently unto thy children, and shalt talk of them when thou sittest in thine house, and when thou walkest by the way, and when thou liest down, and when thou risest up.   Deuteronomy 6:4–7

I know you're busy, Mom and Dad. I know there are innumerable demands on your time. But they need not prevent you from talking to your kids as you drive them to soccer practice, take them grocery shopping, or head out for a family vacation.

When John was caught up into heaven, an elder approached him and said, "Who are these arrayed in white robes?"

"I don't know," answered John.

The elder then went on to explain they were those who had come out of the Great Tribulation and had washed their robes in the blood of the Lamb (Revelation 7:14).

The interesting thing about this dialogue is that it was not initiated by John, but by the elder. So, too, as moms, dads, mentors, or disciplers—like the elder in heaven, we have both the opportunity and responsibility of initiating meaningful discussion with our kids—for if we wait for them to ask us about the danger of pornography or the question of predestination, we'll wait forever. We must be the ones who get the ball rolling.

"They'll think I'm crazy," you say.

And so they may. But they won't think you're boring. If you are one who initiates discussion by telling them what you're learning—not preaching at them, but sharing with them the things you're learning—you'll be surprised by their eagerness to listen.

Walking Ahead of Them

And there was yet a battle in Gath, where was a man of great stature, that had on every hand six fingers, and on every foot six toes, four and twenty in number; and he also was born to the giant. And when he defied Israel, Jonathan the son of Shimea the brother of David slew him. 2 Samuel 21:20, 21

Because David killed a giant named Goliath, those who followed him killed giants as well—even though they were too young to have seen him kill Goliath.

So, too, when David confessed his acts of murder and adultery, he was forgiven completely. But murder and immorality would crop up in the lives of his children (2 Samuel 13).

Thus, the principle is clear: Whether or not our kids or those we disciple see what we do, they will inevitably become like us as they follow us in ways we don't think they even know about. If, Mom, you are a woman of prayer, your children will pray. Dad, if you're doing battle with the giants of selfishness and darkness, your kids will too. Whether we know it or not, who we are and how we walk even when we think no one is watching will directly affect those we're parenting, mentoring, and discipling.

Walking Honestly Before Them

Therefore the children of Israel eat not of the sinew which shrank, which is
upon the hollow of the thigh, unto this day: because he touched the hollow of
Jacob's thigh in the sinew that shrank.   Genesis 32:32

About to face the brother he had tricked out of his birthright and blessing, Jacob feared for his life. So it was that when the angel appeared to him, he was desperate for a genuine blessing. After wrestling with the angel all night, it was when Jacob's hip was dislocated that the angel said, "No longer are you Jacob—or Tricky One. Now you shall be Israel—Governed by God."

Limping into the camp where he had stationed his family, Jacob explained to them what had happened to him. And so impressed were his children by hearing of what had transpired in the life of their father that to this day they honor that event.

Gang, when a dad, a mom, a teacher, or a mentor says, "Let me tell you about what I went through. Here's the difficulty I encountered. Here's what I learned the hard way. I limp to this day; I can never walk as quickly as I once did; but I'm changed,"—those who follow in his or her footsteps will be changed themselves. Walk honestly before your kids, and they will not be disappointed in you, but will thank you and honor you. Walk honestly and you will not only earn the respect of those who follow you, but you will keep them from making the same mistakes that plagued you.

Walking Away from Them

And when she had weaned him, she took him up with her, with three bullocks,
and one ephah of flour, and a bottle of wine, and brought him unto the house
of the LORD in Shiloh: and the child was young.   1 Samuel 1:24

"Lord, if You give me a child, I will give him to You," Hannah prayed.

"That's what I was waiting for," said the Lord, "because I want to bless you with a special child"—which He did in Samuel.

True to her promise, after Samuel was weaned, Hannah took her son to the tabernacle at Shiloh—and left him in the care of Eli, the priest. How could she do this? She realized her son was the Lord's and her hovering over him would only diminish or restrict what God wanted to do in and through his life.

There are times when a parent who wants to see his kids walk in truth must walk away from them in order to allow God to do what He wants to do in and through them. As prone as we are to hover and smother, we must let God be God in the lives of those who follow in our steps.

Seeing a cocoon swaying from the limb of a tree, you decide to help the butterfly by carefully cutting a slit in the cocoon. Yet although your cut allows the butterfly to escape with ease, it inevitably kills him because it's in the very struggle to escape the cocoon that the butterfly gains the strength and ability to use his wings.

Thus, it was the wise father who, hearing his son was eating pig slop in the city, didn't go and rescue him, but rather let the process play out. And when it did, his son came to his senses and returned home a new man (Luke 15).

There are many times when we must walk away from our kids not in apathy or anger, but in the realization that they are the Lord's and that He must be given a free hand to work in their lives.

Walking Closely Behind Them

And it was so, when the days of their feasting were gone about, that Job sent and sanctified them, and rose up early in the morning, and offered burnt offerings according to the number of them all: for Job said, It may be that my sons have sinned, and cursed God in their hearts. Thus did Job continually.

Job 1:5

Knowing that on feast days his sons would be tempted, Job offered a sacrifice every day on their behalf. In so doing, he was saying, "I want to walk behind my sons to make sure they're covered."

So, too, I know my kids are vulnerable to sin—because they're just like me. What can I do? I can cover them daily in prayer.

What would happen if we got up every morning and truly sacrificed in prayer—not just "Bless my kids, Amen"—but talked to and waited on the Father on behalf of each one of them? We can cover their vulnerable spots, the places we know they are likely to be attacked. We can walk behind them protectively and prayerfully if we are willing to take the time and expend the same energy Job did.

As we walk together, with, ahead of, away from, honestly before, and close behind our kids and those whom we disciple, as is the case in every area of spiritual life, we have the example to follow of One who walked in each and all of these ways. . . .

Jesus walked with the otherwise-saddened disciples on the road to Emmaus and opened the Scriptures to them, explaining all things concerning Himself (Luke 24:27).

Jesus walked ahead of John's disciples in such a way that caused the Baptist to proclaim, "Behold the Lamb of God!" (John 1:36)

Jesus walked honestly before the skeptic, not saying, "Listen to My sermon," or, "Watch My miracle," but, "Touch My wounds" (see John 20:27).

Jesus walked away from His disciples when He sent them out to preach about the kingdom (Matthew 10). And while they were gone, what did He do? He preached in their hometowns (Matthew 11:1). Had they not gone, Jesus wouldn't have moved in. So, too, do what the Lord tells you to do and watch and see how He moves into your city, how He touches and teaches your family.

Jesus walked behind His disciples as He prayed for them constantly—not only as they toiled in the storm on the Sea of Galilee (Matthew 14:23), but even as they slept in the Garden of Gethsemane (John 17).

Jesus shows us what it means to walk with people, to walk ahead of people, to walk honestly before people, to walk away from people, and to walk prayerfully behind people. He does that with me. He's done that with you. Now let's do the same thing for those we're discipling and parenting.

If you do, because God doesn't violate the free will of any of His children, there is no guarantee that your kids will be godly—but it increases the odds radically. And this is the promise you can bank on: Even if they do go through seasons or years or even decades of rebellion, the Bible says, "Train up a child in the way he should go and when he is old, he will not depart from it" (Proverbs 22:6).

Do what you're supposed to do, Mom and Dad—and even if your child rebels initially, he'll come around ultimately as he remembers the training, the example, the teaching, and the prayer you lived out before him. Do these things and, like John, your joy will be great when you see your children walk in truth.

3 JOHN

3 **John 1**
The elder unto the well-beloved Gaius, whom I love in the truth.

In this final epistle in which John deals with specific problems in the church, he'll refer to three personalities. The first is an encourager named Gaius, seen in verses 1–8. The second is an egotist named Diotrephes, seen in verses 9–11. The third is an example named Demetrius, seen in verse 12.

3 John 2
Beloved, I wish above all things that thou mayest prosper and be in health, even as thy soul prospereth.

"Name It And Claim It" teachers love to camp on this verse. The prosperity teachers refer to it, saying, "God wants everyone to be healthy and to prosper financially." But in so doing, they fail to understand that John is not propounding a principle, but offering a prayer.

Because I want my kids to be blessed, because I want you to be blessed, I pray this prayer as well. But I also understand that God's ways are not my ways, and sometimes it is only through brokenness and pain that blessing and ministry are born.

Some of us preach sermons. Others *are* sermons as they continually deal with pain and loss. Therefore, it is a damnable heresy for anyone to imply that those who are sick lack faith or that those who are poor are second-rate believers.

3 John 3–7
For I rejoiced greatly, when the brethren came and testified of the truth that is in thee, even as thou walkest in the truth. I have no greater joy than to hear that my children walk in truth. Beloved, thou doest faithfully whatsoever thou doest to the brethren, and to strangers; which have borne witness of thy charity before the church: whom if thou bring forward on their journey after a godly

sort, thou shalt do well: Because that for his name's sake they went forth, taking nothing of the Gentiles.

In the days before Motel 6, Gaius would not only house itinerant preachers, apostles, and prophets, but he would provide for them financially so that, as they journeyed, they wouldn't have to take anything from the Gentiles. So, too, for us to walk in truth and love means we assist people on their journey toward heaven by reminding them of the faithfulness of God and the nearness of heaven.

It is our privilege and our responsibility to say to people, "God will do what He promised. He will never leave you. He will see you through here on earth." And it is also our privilege and responsibility to direct their eyes to heaven. After all, it was by immediately directing their hearts to heaven that Jesus could calm the disciples' troubled hearts on earth (John 14:1–2). If one takes heaven out of the equation, he's left with desperate, disturbed, depressed people. Heaven in the equation changes everything.

3 John 8
We therefore ought to receive such, that we might be fellowhelpers to the truth.

Whereas previously John had said, "Don't let deceivers into your house" (see 2 John 10), here he says, "Don't become so skeptical that you keep everyone out."

3 John 9
I wrote unto the church: but Diotrephes, who loveth to have the preeminence among them, receiveth us not.

In his quest to be the big shot, Diotrephes not only spoke malicious words against John, but he excommunicated from the church anyone connected with John.

3 John 10 (a)
Wherefore, if I come, I will remember his
deeds which he doeth ...

"Open rebuke is better than secret love," Solomon declared (Proverbs 27:5). True love cares enough to confront, to speak the truth, and to deal with issues that would otherwise cause decay or destruction. Such was the love within the heart of John.

3 John 10 (b), 11
... prating against us with malicious words:
and not content therewith, neither doth he
himself receive the brethren, and forbiddeth
them that would, and casteth them out of
the church. Beloved, follow not that which
is evil, but that which is good. He that doeth
good is of God: but he that doeth evil hath
not seen God.

The meaning of the Greek word translated "prating" refers to bubbles underwater that burst when they reach the surface. Diotrephes was one who stirred up bubbling accusations against John that were without substance but which caused undercurrents of turmoil.

3 John 12
Demetrius hath good report of all men, and
of the truth itself: yea, and we also bear
record; and ye know that our record is true.

Although John doesn't record what he did specifically, Demetrius goes down in history for all

eternity as being one who was a good example of what it means to be a believer. Oh, how glorious to be remembered as one who was an example of how to walk through difficult days, of how to live by faith, of how to embrace grace.

For topical study of 3 John 9–12, see "Dealing
with Diotrephes," below.

3 John 13, 14
I had many things to write, but I will not
with ink and pen write unto thee: But I trust
I shall shortly see thee, and we shall speak
face to face. Peace be to thee. Our friends
salute thee. Greet the friends by name.

And there are also many other things which Jesus did, the which, if they should be written every one, I suppose that even the world itself could not contain the books that should be written. Amen.   John 21:25

Having many things to write unto you, I would not write with paper and ink . . . 2 John 12 (a)

I had many things to write, but I will not with ink and pen write unto thee.   3 John 13

I find it more than coincidental that John closes three of his four books, saying, in essence, "There's so much more to say." Because love bears all things, believes all things, hopes all things, and endures all things, it should be no surprise that the "apostle of love" would have a heart too full for mere paper to contain.

DEALING WITH DIOTREPHES
A Topical Study of
3 John 9–12

He was a man who had so much going for him that he stood figuratively as well as literally head and shoulders above the rest. Not only was Saul handsome physically, but his heart was full of such humility that he had to be coaxed out of hiding to present himself before the people of Israel as their king (1 Samuel 10:22). And in addition to possessing an attractive appearance and a humble heart, he was empowered by the Spirit to such a degree that he began to prophesy (1 Samuel 10:10).

So here was this good-looking, tall, humble, spiritual, anointed man who seemed to have it all. But he was a man who would fall brutally because, like Diotrephes, he grew to love preeminence and was determined to remain in power.

We see this tendency beginning to surface soon after he ascended the throne. . . .

Engaged in a protracted battle with the Philistines, Saul led one thousand men, while his son, Jonathan, led another thousand. Although it was Jonathan's men who overcame the Philistines, Scripture says it was Saul who blew the trumpet, Saul who claimed the victory (1 Samuel 13:3, 4).

In a subsequent skirmish, Saul was instructed not to engage in battle until after Samuel offered a sacrifice to the Lord. So Saul waited. But when Samuel didn't show up, Saul decided to offer the sacrifice himself. And because of that, when Samuel did at last arrive, he looked at Saul and said, "Because you have taken matters into your own hands and haven't been obedient to the Lord, you have forfeited your right to rule the nation" (see 1 Samuel 13:13).

Still later, we see how Saul was told by Samuel to wage war against the Amalekites and take no hostages, to leave no survivors. So Saul went off into battle and won the battle. Upon his return, Saul encountered Samuel.

"How did it go, Saul?" asked the prophet.

"I have obeyed the Lord," answered Saul.

"Then what's the bleating I hear?" asked Samuel.

"Well, I did save a couple of sheep to sacrifice to the Lord," said Saul.

"And who's that?" asked Samuel, pointing to the man standing beside Saul.

"Oh, that's Agag, king of the Amalekites," said Saul. "I saved him as a trophy."

So once again, Samuel told Saul, "You have been a man who does what you want to do, who does not take into consideration what God says. Consequently, you have no authority in God's sight" (see 1 Samuel 15:26). Yet although Saul realized he had been rejected, he remained determined to hang on to power regardless of the fact that God's anointing had been given to another—a young man named David.

When, in a depressed state, Saul threw a javelin at David. David, a champion, an athlete, one who bounded over walls (Psalm 18:29), could have chucked it right back at Saul. Instead, he did a very wise thing: He ducked.

And even when Saul's determination to kill him intensified, David refused to retaliate. . . .

Running from Saul in the Dead Sea region of En Gedi, David's men were jubilant when Saul unknowingly took refuge in the very cave in which they were hiding.

"Here's your chance!" they said to David. "Lop off his head and claim the throne that is rightfully yours."

So, as Saul lay sleeping, David did, indeed, unsheathe his sword—but only to cut off a piece of Saul's skirt as proof to Saul that he could have taken his life. Yet even this seemingly minor gesture weighed heavily on David.

"I shouldn't have even touched the Lord's anointed," he said (see 1 Samuel 24:5, 6).

Why did David say this? Because he recognized Saul as the instrument God had allowed in his life to prepare him for becoming king. He realized he was not to grab the reins of power, or strive for preeminence. In short, he was not to be like the one who sought his life.

Saul's life was a tragedy. Humble, spiritual, charismatic, and anointed, he had everything going for him. But, like Diotrephes, he loved preeminence. His refusal to place himself in a position of submission cost him his life, for he was killed by an Amalekite (2 Samuel 1:6–8)—the very people God had told him to destroy (1 Samuel 15:3).

What about you? Are you a Saul or a David? Are you a Diotrephes or a John? Like Saul, is your intent to control? Like Diotrephes, do you seek preeminence? Or, like David, do you choose to submit to God? Like John, is love your aim?

If you're a David, you'll not be one who throws spears—even when spears are thrown at you. It's always the troubled individual who finds fault and fires away. David ducked. He didn't fire back. And therein lies great wisdom.

Are you one who subtly puts down other people, hoping that by doing so you'll elevate yourself? It might work for a while—as it did for Saul and Diotrephes. But ultimately your words will come crashing down around you. "Be not deceived," Paul says. "God is not mocked. Whatever a man sows, that shall he also reap" (see Galatians 6:7).

Regardless of how long you have walked with the Lord or how close you are to the Lord, every one of us has to deal with our flesh. Thus, although part of me wants to be humble, although part of me does not want to manipulate or strive, find fault, or gossip, another part of me has a tendency to listen to prating words or malicious talk, to revel in the fact that someone else has fallen short or is not doing well.

Even Paul would say, "What I want to do, I don't do. And what I don't want to do, I end up doing. Oh, wretched man that I am" (see Romans 7:15–24).

So what are we to do?

Think of it this way. . . .

Inside each of us are two dogs—the black dog of our sin nature and the white dog of our new nature in Christ. The more I try to manipulate situations and seek preeminence, the bigger the black dog will grow, and the smaller the white dog will become. Such is what happened to Saul. Rather than repenting or praying, he fed his flesh. On the other hand, I can choose to feed the white dog and starve the black dog. I can choose to worship the Lord and live in obedience to His Word. I can choose to submit to fellow believers and to walk in humility. And if I do, the black dog becomes as small as a Chihuahua, while the white dog grows as big as a St. Bernard. It all depends on which dog I feed.

If I walk in the flesh, like Saul, I'll be done in by the very things I should have destroyed. And like Diotrephes, I'll be known as one who strives for preeminence. But if I walk in the Spirit, like David, I'll be exalted in due time. And like John, my life will be characterized by love.

Background to Jude

T he story is told of a preacher who, after getting ready for services one Sunday morning, emerged from the bathroom with a large bandage on his face.

"What happened to you?" asked his wife.

"I cut myself shaving while concentrating on my sermon," he said.

"Honey," she replied, "you should have been concentrating on your shaving while cutting your sermon!"

Such is the challenge with the Book of Jude, for while there are only six hundred thirteen words and twenty-five verses within the single chapter in the short book before us, there are eight illustrations from the Old Testament—each one containing fascinating implications and practical applications.

Thus, it is, indeed, tempting for me to spend a long time in this wonderful epistle. And yet, I would like us to look at Jude in one sitting—no doubt the way it was intended to be read—in order that we might gain a feel for the Book of Jude in its totality and grasp its message personally.

So let's begin.

JUDE

J ude 1, 2
Jude, the servant of Jesus Christ, and brother of James, to them that are sanctified by God the Father, and preserved in Jesus Christ, and called: Mercy unto you, and peace, and love, be multiplied.

Jude was the brother of James, and both Jude and James were half brothers of Jesus (Mark 6:3). James was a leader in the early church, as seen in Acts 15, concerning the argument as to whether or not Gentiles converted to Christianity were required to undergo the rite of circumcision. The ques-

tion was debated until James stood, and quoting the prophet Amos (9:11–12), said Gentiles did not need to become Jews first and did not need to be circumcised in order to become Christians because God has His called ones even among the heathen.

Perhaps the reason James grasped this kind of grace so firmly is that, although he had grown up in the same household as Jesus, initially he did not believe His Brother was the Son of God (John 7:5).

What changed James' and Jude's minds? What turned them from skeptics to leaders of the faith? Nothing short of the Resurrection, for it is after that event that we see them numbered with the disciples in the Upper Room (Acts 1:14).

Sometimes we think that by being nice—mowing our neighbor's lawn, baking him cookies, or smiling when he drives by—we will convert him. Not true. There was no lovelier person than Jesus Christ. Yet, His brothers did not believe on Him until the Cross and the Resurrection. That is why it is imperative to preach Christ crucified (1 Corinthians 1:23). You can wave to your neighbor for twenty years, and wave him right into hell. Or you can take the time at some point to say, "You know what? Jesus Christ died for your sins and rose from the dead, and you must believe on Him."

Jude 3
Beloved, when I gave all diligence to write unto you of the common salvation, it was needful for me to write unto you, and exhort you that ye should earnestly contend for the faith which was once delivered unto the saints.

It seems Jude's original intent was to write about our "common salvation." That is, his was to be a letter celebrating the grace and goodness of God. But it took a different turn when an issue arose that he felt pressed to address.

Jude 4
For there are certain men crept in unawares, who were before of old ordained to this condemnation, ungodly men, turning the grace of our God into lasciviousness, and denying the only Lord God, and our Lord Jesus Christ.

False teachers had crept into the early church, seeking to rob and rip off God's people, seeking to pervert their understanding and keep them from enjoying God's blessing.

Jude 5 (a)
I will therefore put you in remembrance, though ye once knew this. . . .

The foundational theme of this wonderful epistle, as found in verse 21, is an exhortation to keep ourselves in the love of God. Underline this phrase because it is the hinge upon which the Book of Jude swings. Jude's heart is, "Yes, there are heretics and deceivers, but you, beloved, keep yourselves in the love of God."

Keeping yourself in the love of God does not mean earning God's love by being a "good little boy or girl." God's love is unconditional—so much so that in Romans 5:8, Paul declares that God demonstrated His love toward us in that while we were yet sinners, Christ died for us. When did God demonstrate His love for you and me? Not when we were trying to be good Christians, but when we were pagans, heathens, and rebels.

When you couldn't have cared less about Him, God looked at you and said, "I love you deeply."

Never buy into the thinking that you earn God's love by being good. Many Christians look at God as being like Santa: He's making a list, checking it twice, and He's going to find out who's naughty and who's nice. If you've been good, you'll get gifts; if not, you'll be lucky to get a lump of coal.

But nothing could be further from the nature of our Father. Making a list? Checking it twice? Paul tells us the list of our failings was blotted out by the blood of Christ (Colossians 2:14). The list of my sins was pinned to the Cross of Calvary and cleansed so thoroughly by the blood of the Lamb that the writing became completely illegible. God's love for us is not based upon anything we do or don't do, for His love is unconditional.

What, then, does it mean to keep yourself in the love of God? It simply means to keep yourself in the place where you can receive His blessings. In other words, God is constantly showering us with blessings, love, and grace. He's not saying, "Hmm, you've been bad today, so I'm turning off the spigot." No, God's blessings are always coming down (Lamentations 3:23).

"Then why aren't I being blessed?" you ask. The answer is easy: You're not under the spout where the blessings come out. You have wandered away. God didn't close the spigot—because even when we are faithless, He is faithful still (2 Timothy 2:13). God doesn't monitor the flow of blessings depending on how we're doing. No, the spigot is on full blast all the time. Therefore, the only thing we have to do is to make sure we're in the place where we enjoy God's blessings—that we're standing under the spout where the blessings come out.

Am I suggesting it is possible for a person to remove himself from the place of God's blessings? Yes. And Jude gives us three examples of those who did.

Jude 5 (b)
. . . how that the Lord, having saved the people out of the land of Egypt, afterward destroyed them that believed not.

First, Jude brings to remembrance the people delivered by God. You know the story. In bondage for four hundred years, the Israelites cried out to the Lord. The Lord raised up Moses as a deliverer and worked powerfully through him. After He smote Egypt with ten plagues, the Israelites were finally released. They made it to the edge of the Red Sea, where God not only parted the water but also unleashed the very same water on their enemies.

Then what happened? They came to the border of Kadesh Barnea and sent twelve spies to scope out the land. "Wow!" said the spies upon their return. "It's beautiful. It's prolific, productive, and perfect! There's only one problem: Tens of thousands of Anakim, giants—Shaquille O'Neals—occupy the land. We're nothing but grasshoppers in their sight, and we're sure to be squished."

Joshua and Caleb, two of the twelve spies, countered, saying, "Hey, we might be grasshoppers in their sight, but they're grasshoppers in God's sight. Therefore, they pose no problem. They'll be bread for us. We can eat them up!" (see Numbers 14:9)

But the people chose to listen to the other ten spies instead of to Joshua and Caleb—a choice that led God to say, "Okay, because you don't believe what I intended to do for you, you're going to have to wander in the wilderness until a new generation is raised up" (see Numbers 14:22, 23).

Thus, because God's people, who were delivered by Him, did not keep themselves in the assurance of His love and provision, they ended up dying in the desert.

Jude 6
And the angels which kept not their first estate, but left their own habitation, he hath reserved in everlasting chains under darkness unto the judgment of the great day.

Second, not only can those delivered by God fail to keep themselves in the love of God, but so can those who are worshipers of God. Lucifer was the leader of all the worshipers of heaven. The one the Bible calls the "Anointed Cherub" (Ezekiel 28:14) had a voice like a pipe organ and hands like tambourines. He wasn't just a worship leader, he was a full on orchestra until the day he said, "I will be like God," and launched a rebellion in which one third of the angels followed him.

Amazing. Here, the worshipers of God in heaven became demons in hell because they did not keep themselves in the love of God.

Jude 7–10
Even as Sodom and Gomorrha, and the cities about them in like manner, giving themselves over to fornication, and going after strange flesh, are set forth for an example, suffering the vengeance of eternal fire. Likewise also these filthy dreamers defile the flesh, despise dominion, and speak evil of dignities. Yet Michael the archangel, when contending with the devil he disputed about the body of Moses, durst not bring against him a railing accusation, but said, The Lord rebuke thee. But these speak evil of those things which they know not: but

what they know naturally, as brute beasts, in those things they corrupt themselves.

Third, Jude says, "Not only can you be delivered by God and be a worshiper of God, but you can receive blessing from God and still fail to keep yourself in His love." You see, at one time, Sodom and Gomorrah were cities uniquely blessed by God. In the agrarian economy of the day, the place to be was Sodom or Gomorrah.

We read in Genesis 13 that after leaving Egypt, Abraham and Lot had so much livestock between them that the land could no longer support them. "We're going to have to separate," Abraham said to Lot. "Wherever you want to go, I'll go in the opposite direction." So, after checking out the situation, Lot found the best pasture land, the ideal place to raise livestock, the perfect place to get rich: the plain of Jordan, wherein lay Sodom and Gomorrah.

At one time, Sodom and Gomorrah were truly blessed by God. Yet, what happened? They turned their backs on the Lord and were eventually destroyed. This is very sobering to me because it says,

- So you've been saved—so were they who wandered in the wilderness.
- So you've been a worshiper—so were they who are now in hell as demons.
- So you've been blessed—so were they who were destroyed by their own depravity.

Gang, it is possible to experience deliverance by God, to partake in worship to God, to receive blessing from God, and still not keep yourself in the love of God.

How can this happen? After giving us three examples, Jude goes on to provide three explanations.

Jude 11 (a)
Woe unto them! for they have gone in the way of Cain . . .

The first explanation for why people no longer experience the love of God in their lives is that they've gone the way of Cain. The way of Cain is anger. Cain was angry with his brother, Abel, because God blessed Abel, but He didn't bless Cain. *It's not fair,* Cain must have thought. *We both offered sacrifices to God. Abel brought a lamb, and I brought the fruit of my labor from the garden, but God blessed my brother's and not mine* (see Genesis 4:4, 5). And such anger took root in Cain's heart that he killed his brother.

If you're angry with your spouse, bitter toward your boss, unforgiving of your brother, you have gone the way of Cain. Watch out for anger, gang. It'll pull you away from the place where you just enjoy God's love. It will draw you away from the spout where the blessings come out.

Jude 11 (b)
. . . and ran greedily after the error of Balaam for reward . . .

Jude draws our attention not only to the anger of Cain but also to the greed of Balaam. You know Balaam's story. The children of Israel, all three million of them, were on their way to the Promised Land. "Whoa," said Balak, king of the Moabites. "There's a horde of people coming our way, and unless we do something, we're going to get trampled."

Knowing of a prophet in the area named Balaam, Balak sent messengers asking him to curse the approaching Israelites. "Wait here," Balaam said to the messengers, "I must talk to God about this." Even before Balaam asked, the Lord told him not to curse the Israelites (Numbers 22:9–12). So the messengers returned to Balak with word of Balaam's refusal to join them. Balak, in turn, sent some VIPs to Balaam.

They arrived in their Mercedes and their flashy clothes, saying, "Come with us, and you'll be blessed."

"Listen, guys," said Balaam, "even if you offered me a house full of silver and gold (hint, hint), I wouldn't go with you."

So once again, the messengers returned empty-handed. And yet, a third time they appeared before Balaam, this time offering him a portion of wealth and honor. A third time, Balaam said he would seek the Lord. But this time, God gave him permission to go, so off Balaam went. En route, however, an angel appeared to his donkey, causing the donkey to crash into a wall, smashing Balaam's foot in the process. "You dumb donkey. You crushed my foot," Balaam cried as he beat his donkey.

"Why are you beating me?" asked the donkey. "Haven't I been a good donkey all these years? I've never given you any problems. Don't you see there's an angel standing right here, preventing me from taking you where you ought not go?"

Yet even a talking donkey could not deter Balaam, so he continued on, until at last he reached the mountain overlooking the Israelite camp. Opening his mouth to curse them, all that came out was blessing. "Hey!" said Balak, "I hired you to curse them, not to bless them! Maybe we should change locations." So they built another altar in a different location. Once more, Balaam stood to curse. And once more, all that came from his lips were words of blessing.

The error of Balaam lay in the fact that he didn't understand God's grace. Balaam thought that because His people were rebellious and evil, God would surely want to destroy them. Consequently, knowing that even though he could not curse the Israelites, the Israelites could bring a curse upon themselves, Balaam told Balak to have the Moabite women parade themselves in front of the Jewish men. And during the romantic interludes that were sure to follow, the Moabite women would be able to introduce the Jewish men to their idols.

Balaam was right. In the Book of Numbers, we read "the people did eat, and bowed down to their gods." The anger of the Lord was kindled against Israel, and twenty-four thousand died as a result (Numbers 25:1–9).

Why did Balaam, who spoke some of the most beautiful prophecies in all of the Old Testament about the coming of Messiah, end up a heretic and a loser? Because he did not keep himself in God's love. Why didn't he keep himself in God's love? Greed. What is greed? Never being satisfied, never being thankful, always wanting just a little more. Watch out, precious people. Greed will remove you from the spout where the blessings come out.

Jude 11 (c)
. . . and perished in the gainsaying of Korah.

Korah's sin was envy. We find his story in Numbers 16: "Moses, who made you the big enchilada? I have just as much right to determine direction for this nation as you do." So saying, Korah led a rebellion that resulted in the deaths of nearly fifteen thousand of God's people. Beware of envy—of wanting someone else's position.

Joseph's brothers were jealous. Joseph had a coat of many colors, or literally, a coat of "big sleeves." In Joseph's day, working men wore sleeveless coats, like vests, in order that their arms would be free to labor. But the bosses, the supervisors, the head honchos wore coats with big sleeves in which they could keep money and supplies—sort of like briefcases.

Sometimes we look at someone else's big sleeves and say, "Boy, that guy's got it made." But Joseph's big sleeves were hardly an asset. You see, envious of Joseph's position, his brothers sold him as a slave to a group headed for Egypt. There, Joseph was eventually promoted to the position of head slave. No doubt some of his fellow prisoners looked at him and said, "Boy, I wish I had the coat of a head slave"—little knowing that even this coat

*would get him in trouble as he shed it to flee
Mrs. Potiphar's advances (Genesis 39:12).*

Just rest in the place God has you, gang. He'll put you right where you should be. This doesn't mean we shouldn't want to be all that the Lord would have us be. But there comes a point when we're no longer saying, "Lord, I want to develop the talents and abilities you've given me to the fullest degree," but rather, "I've got to do whatever it takes to gain that guy's position. I've got to be the guy with the big sleeves."

What happened to Korah? The ground opened up and sucked him in (Numbers 16:31–33). Here's an easy way to find yourself in the pit: Be envious of another's position. You don't know what you're headed for; you don't see what you're getting into; and before you know it, your world will come crashing down upon you.

I wouldn't have chosen anger, greed, and envy as the three reasons people move away from God's blessings. I would have listed cocaine, pornography, and larceny. Why? Because those things are not my problem. You see, we tend to think the sins that will take a man away from the spout where God's blessings come out are the biggies we don't do. Not true. God has an entirely different way of looking at things. And in His Word, He says through Jude to me and to you, "These are three specific areas that will keep you from enjoying and experiencing My love."

Jude 12 (a)
These are spots in your feasts of charity, when they feast with you, feeding themselves without fear . . .

The "certain men who crept in unnoticed" (verse 4) were those who, like Korah, Cain, and Balaam, endangered God's people, seeking to woo them away from the simplicity of God's grace. Jude calls them "spots." They're like hidden rocks, he says. They join in your fellowship, in your potluck dinners, in your celebration of the grace and goodness of God—but with a hidden agenda. Like hidden rocks, they blend in presently, but they will cause you to crash eventually. And then he goes on to use even stronger metaphors to describe these false teachers.

Jude 12 (b)
. . . clouds they are without water, carried about of winds . . .

They're waterless clouds. That is, they *seem* to say all sorts of wonderful things, but their teaching leads only to dry, discouraging days.

Jude 12 (c)
. . . trees whose fruit withereth, without fruit, twice dead, plucked up by the roots.

Because they're dead trees, they bear no fruit.

Jude 13 (a)
Raging waves of the sea, foaming out their own shame . . .

They're wild waves. They have lots of motion, but erratic, meaningless, and wasted energy.

Jude 13 (b)
. . . wandering stars, to whom is reserved the blackness of darkness for ever.

Finally, Jude likens the false teachers to wandering—or shooting—stars. Even in our little valley, I have seen people come on the scene with all sorts of fantastic promises, all kinds of interesting doctrines, shining brightly for a month or two or three. Then when hard times came, or things didn't work out, like shooting stars, they fizzled, faded, and moved on to the next unsuspecting community.

Jude 14–16
And Enoch also, the seventh from Adam, prophesied of these, saying, Behold, the Lord cometh with ten thousands of his saints, to execute judgment upon all, and to convince all that are ungodly among them of all their ungodly deeds which they have ungodly committed, and of all their hard speeches which ungodly sinners have spoken against him. These are murmurers, complainers, walking after their own lusts; and their mouth speaketh great swelling words, having men's persons in admiration because of advantage.

The same problems Jude is addressing affect the body of Christ today. False teachers, "mouthing great swelling words," continue to peddle their phony doctrines to anyone who will listen. If you've been walking with the Lord very long, you know that as soon as one strange wind of doctrine blows through, another is sure to follow.

Jude 17–19
But, beloved, remember ye the words which were spoken before of the apostles of our Lord Jesus Christ; how that they told you there should be mockers in the last time, who should walk after their own ungodly lusts. These be they who separate themselves, sensual, having not the Spirit.

Happy is the man or woman who understands that the gospel message is profoundly simple and simply profound. It's Jesus—nothing more, nothing less, nothing else.

After giving us three examples of people who walked away from God's love and three explanations of why they did so, Jude now gives us three exhortations to keep ourselves in the love of God.

Jude 20 (a)
But ye, beloved, building up yourselves on your most holy faith . . .

The first way to keep yourself in the place where you're being drenched in the love of God is to build up your faith. How are we built up in faith? The Bible tells us very simply that faith comes by hearing and hearing by the Word of God (Romans 10:17). That's it. To keep yourself in the love of God means that you continue to be a student of the Word. You build up your faith by taking in God's Word, by daily making the practice of spending time in Scripture a priority, by assembling with other believers to study the Word corporately (Hebrews 10:25).

Jude 20 (b)
. . . praying in the Holy Ghost.

What does it mean to pray in the Holy Ghost? It means allowing the Holy Spirit to inspire your prayers, saying, "Lord, I don't want to come to You with my ideas and my agenda because I don't know what these things might lead to if You grant them to me. So I come to You, Lord, asking for Your Spirit to inspire me to pray. Guide my conversation, Lord. Help me to pray biblically, to be guided by Your Spirit even as I talk with You right now."

To pray in the Spirit means the Spirit is inspiring prayer. To pray in the Spirit also sometimes means just groaning. "Oh, Lord, I don't know what to do about this. I don't know how to handle that." Ever just groan? Paul did, for in Romans 8 he writes that the Spirit Himself makes intercession for us with groanings that cannot be uttered (verse 26). Praying in the Spirit says, "Lord, I can't even articulate my situation without You."

Second, praying in the Spirit means praying in tongues. Speaking specifically of praying in tongues, Paul says, "I will pray with the Spirit and I will pray with understanding also. I'm going to allow this miraculous, mysterious process of the Spirit praying through me with words I do not understand intellectually and have not learned academically" (see 1 Corinthians 14:15).

I encourage those of you who have exercised this particular manifestation to continue to develop it. Your mind will rebel against it. You mind will ask, "Why do it? What good is it?" But Paul says, "I would that you all spoke with tongues" (see 1 Corinthians 14:5). That is why I am personally strongly persuaded that if you read 1 Corinthians 12 and 14 carefully, you will conclude that, while placing severe restrictions around the public utterance of tongues, Paul encourages the private, devotional use of the prayer language.

Being led *by* the Spirit, groaning *in* the Spirit, using a prayer language *from* the Spirit are all aspects of what it means to pray in the Holy Ghost.

Jude 21
Keep yourselves in the love of God, looking for the mercy of our Lord Jesus Christ unto eternal life.

Finally, we are to keep ourselves in the love of God by looking for the coming of Jesus. How it affects my priorities, how it changes my perspective, how it alters my emotions when I say, "Lord, today I'm going to look for Your coming." Today might be the day, dear saints. What a difference it makes when we remember this.

Stay in the Word. Pray in the Spirit. Look for Jesus' coming—three things you can do to keep yourself under the spout where the blessings come out. They're practical, workable, doable—and, interestingly, we see in them faith, love, and hope: Faith, by being in the Word (Romans 10:17); love, by praying in the Spirit whose fruit is love (Galatians 5:22); and hope, by looking for the blessed hope of our Lord's return (Titus 2:13).

"All you guys at Calvary Chapel ever talk about is being in the Word, looking for His coming, and praying," some charge.

"Right. Exactly. You got it!" I say—for that's exactly what Jude tells us to do in order to keep ourselves in God's love.

Jude 22, 23 (a)
And of some have compassion, making a difference: And others save with fear, pulling them out of the fire . . .

What about those who have been affected by false teachers, who are caught up in wrong doctrine? What are we to do with them? Jude gives two approaches. To some, show compassion. Be very gentle with them as you patiently wait for them to see the light. Others, however, you have to grab by the nape of the neck and yank them out of the destructive stuff with which they're involved.

*The Great Awakening in America was ush-
ered in by a man who spoke in a monotone
voice, and who had such bad eyesight that he
could only occasionally squint at his congregation from above the manuscript he held
inches from his face. He preached a sermon
many of you have studied in literature class
entitled, "Sinners in the Hands of an Angry
God" in which he likened mankind to a spider
dangling over a fire with only one thread separating it from damnation. And when he was
finished, people began to weep under the conviction of the Spirit.*

Some people you can minister to with compassion, stressing the goodness of God, for doesn't
Paul say in Romans 2:4 that it's the goodness of
God that leads men to repentance? Others, however, you have to grab by the collar, and like Jonathan Edwards, dangle them over hell.

Jude 23 (b)
**. . . hating even the garment spotted by the
flesh.**

In the Old Testament, whenever a man was
cleansed from leprosy—a picture of sin—his garments were to be burned (Leviticus 13:52). Jude
uses this as an analogy to say, "When you're dealing with folks who are caught up in perversity,
make sure you yourself are not affected." In
other words, "Save the man, but burn the garment."

Jude 24, 25
**Now unto him that is able to keep you from
falling, and to present you faultless before
the presence of his glory with exceeding joy,
to the only wise God our Saviour, be glory
and majesty, dominion and power, both now
and ever. Amen.**

Finally, after all of his warning, Jude leaves us
in a place of rest, saying *God* is the One who will
keep us from falling.
God's love is unconditional, never turned off,
never diminished. The only question is: Will you
plant yourself in the place where you can be
drenched with it?
Jude tells us exactly how to do that as he exhorts us to stay in the Word, pray in the Spirit,
and look for our Lord's coming. "If you know
these things, happy are you if you do them,"
Jesus said (see John 13:17).
I love the simplicity of the Word! May the Lord
build your faith as you study it. May He fill you
with love as you pray in the Spirit. May He give
you hope as you look for His coming.
Amen!

GOD IS ABLE
A Topical Study of
Jude 24

I love the Scriptures. And I especially enjoy those passages that deal with God's
ability. Such is the text before us today. Indeed, the Word is full of passages that
talk about God's ability—His "able-ness."

*If it be so, our God whom we serve is able to deliver us from the burning fiery
furnace, and he will deliver us out of thine hand, O king.*   Daniel 3:17

You know the story. King Nebuchadnezzar ordered his subjects to bow down
to the golden image he had constructed. All complied—except three young Jewish
men named Shadrach, Meshach, and Abed-nego.
Threatened with death in a fiery furnace stoked seven times hotter than normal for their insubordination, they answered, "No matter how hot that furnace may
be, God is able to deliver us."

And think not to say within yourselves, We have Abraham to our father: for I say unto you, that God is able of these stones to raise up children unto Abraham. Matthew 3:9

To the Pharisees and Sadducees, John the Baptist said, "Being a Jew is nothing special. God is able, if He so chooses, to raise up stones and make them Jewish children." What does this have to do with us today? Maybe your teenage son or daughter is falling into the "stoner" scene. Take heart! God is able to take "stoners" and make them children of faith. God is able!

He staggered not at the promise of God through unbelief; but was strong in faith, giving glory to God; and being fully persuaded that, what he had promised, he was able also to perform. Romans 4:20, 21

Even though he was one hundred years old and still childless, Abraham was strong in faith, knowing God was yet completely able to keep His promise. God is able!

Every man according as he purposeth in his heart, so let him give; not grudgingly, or of necessity: for God loveth a cheerful giver. And God is able to make all grace abound toward you; that ye, always having all sufficiency in all things, may abound to every good work. 2 Corinthians 9:7, 8

The Greek word translated "cheerfully" actually means "hilarious," joyful abandon. In other words, God loves those who give to Him with hilarious, joyful abandon. And He is able to bless and grace them in every area—including seeing them through their financial obligations.

Now unto him that is able to do exceeding abundantly above all that we ask or think, according to the power that worketh in us, unto him be glory in the church by Christ Jesus throughout all ages, world without end. Amen. Ephesians 3:20, 21

God is able to do more than we can ask or even imagine. Truly, God is able!

For the which cause I also suffer these things: nevertheless I am not ashamed: for I know whom I have believed, and am persuaded that he is able to keep that which I have committed unto him against that day. 2 Timothy 1:12

It's not so much knowing what you believe as knowing in *Whom* you believe. "I know Who I believe," said Paul. "I can count on Him." So can we. He's able to keep that which we've committed to Him—be it our lives, our spouses, our businesses, our children, and our grandchildren. God is able!

For in that he himself hath suffered being tempted, he is able to succour them that are tempted.   Hebrews 2:18

God is able to see you through times of temptation. He knows what you're feeling. He suffered too. Yet, He can see you through because He came through without sin. He is able!

Wherefore he is able also to save them to the uttermost that come unto God by him, seeing he ever liveth to make intercession for them.   Hebrews 7:25

A generation ago, baseball player-turned-evangelist, Billy Sunday, preached from this text, saying, "God can save to the guttermost." Maybe you feel like you're in the gutter today. Take heart. God can save you. He can save me. He is able!

Now unto him that is able to keep you from falling . . .   Jude 24

Here, in our text, we read that God is able to keep us from falling. Kids, your parents can't keep you from falling. Wives, your husbands can't keep you from falling. Husbands, your wives can't keep you from falling. Precious people, the church can't keep you from falling. And I certainly can't keep you from falling. After all, I couldn't even keep my own brother from falling.

I was about six years old when, on a family camping trip to Big Basin State Park, I was shocked to hear my brother Dave say, "Jonny, tomorrow, bright and early, I'm taking you fishing." This was highly unusual because Dave, being six years my senior, didn't normally do that kind of stuff with me. Well, that night, I got my tackle box out and my worms all ready to go. I could hardly wait!

The next morning, with tackle boxes and lunches in hand, I asked Dave where we were going.

"I know a secret place," Dave said.

Dave always knew about secret places. He had a tree house, or so he told me, in the backyard, which had seven bedrooms, a den, a pool, and a television. When I was little, I would gaze up at Dave's tree house. "It's awesome up here," he would call to me down below. But whenever I would grab even the first rung of the rope ladder, it would be raptured without me. So I'm not sure to this day if it did have seven bedrooms. All I know is that Dave always knew about secret places and special stuff.

After walking a mile or so, we came to a spot on the trail, which the winter rains had washed out. "We better go back, Dave," I said.

"No, we don't have to go back," he said.

"Well, how are we going to get around this big hole?" I asked.

"Simple," he said. "It's only about nine feet. You hold my pole, my lunch bag, and my tackle box, and I'll jump across. When I make it, I'll reach over and pull you across."

So I held his stuff, and he reared back and took off like Carl Lewis into the air. Although he made it across the gap beautifully, when he reached the other side, the ground beneath his feet gave way—and I watched him tumble about sixty feet down the cliff head over heels until he hit a stump.

"Are you okay?" I called.

"Ohhhhhhh," he moaned. "Go get Mom."

Like a flash of lightning, I immediately bolted back toward camp. But after about one hundred yards, I stopped dead in my tracks. "I bet he's tricking me. I'm going to run all the way back to camp, and when I bring Mom back, he'll be standing there, saying, 'Where did you go, Jon?'" So I returned to the ledge, and looked down. There was Dave—still wrapped around a tree with his leg sticking up behind him. Just to make sure he wasn't faking, however, I picked up a small rock and pitched it at him.

"Ohhhh," he groaned as it hit him.

"Hmmm," I said. "Maybe he really is hurt, but I don't know for sure." So I grabbed a bigger rock, and threw it down the cliff.

"Ohhhh," he groaned. "Get Mom."

Still dubious, I took a boulder and rolled it down toward him. Direct hit—and he still didn't get up.

"Okay. He's definitely hurt," I said. So I headed toward camp once again, told my mom what happened, and a rescue team was sent to extract him.

I could not keep my brother from falling. None of us can. No matter who we might be, the fact is, we cannot keep others from falling. But there is good news for you, good news for me. The Bible tells us, "Now unto Him who *is* able to keep us from falling be glory."

"Wait a minute," you say. "If God is able to keep us from falling, then why did I fall last week, last year, or five years ago? If He is able to keep me from falling, why didn't He?"

Based on Jude 24, I believe it is impossible for Christians to fall.

"But I'm a Christian, and I fell into sin," you say.

No you didn't. You walked into sin one step at a time. And God was there every step of the way, warning you to turn, providing a way of escape (1 Corinthians 10:13).

"I can handle this," we say. "I can go to that party. I can take in that movie. I can talk to that lady. I'm not going to have a problem. Not me." In the Book of 2 Kings, we see what happens so often, so tragically, so needlessly as a result.

In the second year of Joash son of Jehoahaz king of Israel reigned Amaziah the son of Joash king of Judah.   2 Kings 14:1

In 2 Kings 14, we meet a man named Amaziah, king of Judah.

And he did that which was right in the sight of the LORD, yet not like David his father.   2 Kings 14:3

Although Amaziah did that which was good, he didn't have a heart for the Lord like David did.

Howbeit the high places were not taken away: as yet the people did sacrifice and burnt incense on the high places.   2 Kings 14:4

The high places being mountaintops where idols were worshiped, idolatry was allowed under Amaziah's reign.

He slew of Edom in the valley of salt ten thousand, and took Selah by war . . .   2 Kings 14:7

This guy who did that which was right in the sight of the Lord, but didn't have a tender heart for the Lord as David did, experienced an impressive victory over the Edomites.

Then Amaziah sent messengers to Jehoash, the son of Jehoahaz son of Jehu, king of Israel, saying, Come, let us look one another in the face.   2 Kings 14:8

"To look one another in the face" means to have a face-to-face confrontation. Feeling invincible, Amaziah sent messengers to Jehoash, king of Israel, saying, "Come on, let's mix it up."

And Jehoash the king of Israel sent to Amaziah king of Judah, saying, The thistle that was in Lebanon sent to the cedar that was in Lebanon, saying, Give thy daughter to my son to wife: and there passed by a wild beast that was in Lebanon, and trode down the thistle.   2 Kings 14:9

Jehoash answered Amaziah, saying, "Amaziah, you're a little thistle. I'm a big tree. What do you want to mix it up with me for? You're going to get crushed."

Thou hast indeed smitten Edom, and thine heart hath lifted thee up: glory of this, and tarry at home: for why shouldest thou meddle to thy hurt, that thou shouldest fall, even thou, and Judah with thee?   2 Kings 14:10

"Why are you doing this?" asks Jehoash. "Celebrate your victory over the Edomites, but don't get over your head in dealing with me. You're headed for trouble."

But Amaziah would not hear. Therefore Jehoash king of Israel went up; and he and Amaziah king of Judah looked one another in the face at Beth-shemesh, which belongeth to Judah. 2 Kings 14:11

Amaziah was warned directly, but he wouldn't listen. So he engaged in battle with Jehoash. And guess what happened?

And Judah was put to the worse before Israel; and they fled every man to their tents. 2 Kings 14:12

Judah got stomped, just as Jehoash had predicted. Amaziah didn't fall into defeat. Having been warned directly, having been spoken to plainly, he *walked* into defeat.

"I can do that," we say. "I can go there. I'm strong. She won't affect me. That group won't taint me. I just gave myself to the Lord. I've had great victory. I'm okay." And, like Amaziah, we "meddle to our own hurt."

Please note three things that happened to Judah as a result of Amaziah's stroll into sin.

And Jehoash king of Israel took Amaziah king of Judah, the son of Jehoash the son of Ahaziah, at Beth-shemesh, and came to Jerusalem, and brake down the wall of Jerusalem from the gate of Ephraim unto the corner gate, four hundred cubits. 2 Kings 14:13

First, defenses were broken. When you meddle where you ought not meddle, the first thing that happens is that defenses are broken down. Before, when we flirted with that kind of activity, that kind of language, that kind of visual presentation, we were offended and uncomfortable with them. But when we say, "I'm strong. I can take that in. I can go there. It's not going to hurt me"—the first thing that happens is our walls are broken down.

It's the proverbial story of the frog in the kettle: Put a frog in a kettle of boiling water, and he will jump out immediately. But put him in a kettle of cool water and slowly heat it up, and he'll die in the boiling water, never noticing it becoming hotter and hotter.

So, too, if we get involved in battles we should stay away from, if we go to places we know better than to go, saying, "It's no big deal," we won't even notice our defenses disappearing.

And he took all the gold and silver, and all the vessels that were found in the house of the LORD, and in the treasures of the king's house . . . 2 Kings 14:14

Second, treasure was lost. After Jehoash tore down the walls of Judah, he took precious treasure. So, too, when our defenses are down, we become susceptible and vulnerable. Treasure is lost, never to be returned. Precious people, whenever we sin, certain precious treasures are lost permanently. Oh, we can be forgiven totally, but treasure is lost—be it innocence, health, perspective, holiness—never to be returned this side of eternity.

. . . And hostages, and returned to Samaria.   2 Kings 14:14

Finally, hostages were taken. When walls are broken down because I'm no longer sensitive to sin as I once was, not only is treasure lost, but hostages are taken, as I find myself prisoner to the very sin I thought was no problem. It has been rightly said that the chains of sin are too light to be felt until they are too strong to be broken.

If I wrapped some thread once around your wrists and said, "Get out of that," you would have no problem doing so. But if I kept wrapping that same thread around your wrists over and over again, the same thread you could snap so easily before would eventually bind your wrists totally.

"I can go there. It won't affect me," a kid says.
"I just drink socially," an adult says.
"Don't be so legalistic," we all say.
But before we know it, we're wrapped up, held hostage.
That is why I suggest to you that no one falls into sin, for every step of the way, God is saying, "Don't go in. Don't do that. Turn away. Get out of there."
But we say, "I'm strong. I can handle it. No problem," as we walk into sin one tragic step at a time.
Maybe you're saying, "I've done just that. I knew when I started what I was doing could cause a problem, but I thought I was strong enough. I thought I could handle it. And now, just like Amaziah, walls are broken, treasure's taken, and I'm held hostage. What hope is there for me?"
Back to Jude . . .

Now unto him that is able to keep you from falling, and to present you faultless before the presence of his glory with exceeding joy . . .   Jude 24

The first part of the verse deals with our temporal situation. But here's the good news: The second part of the verse deals with our eternal position.
You see, God is, indeed, able to keep us from falling—but if we do fall, He is still able to present us faultless before the presence of His glory.

This means, when I get to heaven, the Lord is going to say, "Father, here's Jon, and he is faultless. He is spotless."

And I'm going to say, *"Amazing!"* because I know that I've sinned, that I've meddled where I ought not to have meddled. I know walls have been broken and treasure has been lost. I know what it feels like to be held in bondage. We all do. But the fact is, when we get to heaven, He will call us faultless.

Why?

Back to Big Basin . . .

After the park rangers lifted Dave from the pit, I had to accompany my mom to the infirmary where he was recovering from the injuries to his leg and from all of the mysterious bruises on his back. *He's going to kill me,* I thought as I walked in and weakly asked him how he was. But to my great astonishment, Dave just smiled. Why? Because he didn't remember a thing. A mild concussion had wiped away all memory of my brutality!

Dear saint, the good news for you and me is that God has, if you would, chosen to have a concussion, causing Him to say, "And their sins and iniquities will I remember no more" (Hebrews 10:17). That is why, when Jesus died on the Cross, He declared, "It is finished. You are forgiven. Your sin is forgotten."

God is able to keep me from falling. I can choose to meddle where I ought not meddle, and I can walk into sin one step at a time. If I do, walls will be broken, treasure will be lost, and I will be held hostage.

But even then, there is still good news for me. For He is not only able to keep us from falling, but in the light of Calvary and because of the blood He shed for you and me, He is able to present us faultless with exceeding joy.

"Oh, but I've been such a terrible sinner," you say.

That just makes Him present you with more joy. How so? Which fish does the fisherman choose to mount on his wall—the little four-inch minnow, or the great big fifty-pound salmon he hauled in? He saves the big fish, the one that struggled, the one that took the most effort to reel in.

So, too, if you'll respond to God and allow Him to reel you in, you'll be a great big trophy of His grace because where sin abounds, grace abounds even *more* (Romans 5:20).

Precious people, God is able to keep you from falling. But even if you do fall, as we all have, the day is coming when you will hear Him say, "I see you as faultless. I don't remember any failure, any sin. The concussion of the Cross has wiped out all memory."

And there will be exceeding joy. God is able. What a *glorious* promise.

REVELATION

Background to Revelation

The year was A.D. 95. Domitian had just ascended to the throne of Rome. Like his predecessor, Caesar Nero, Domitian was an egomaniac, claiming deity and demanding the worship of his subjects. Refusing to worship this madman, a second wave of persecution is launched against the Christians, including the disciple "whom Jesus loved"—John. Following a failed attempt to boil him alive, Domitian banished John to the rocky, barren, seemingly God-forsaken island of Patmos. And it is here on Patmos that John was given the Revelation of Jesus Christ.

That's the way it always is. Truly, the things I know about the Lord weren't learned in Bible school, a teaching tape, or a Bible commentary. The things I know about the Lord were learned on my own "Patmoses," my own tribulations, my own difficulties. And the same is true for you. When you are given a medical report that doesn't look good, when divorce papers are sent your way, your business goes belly-up, when the relationship doesn't work out, when the child runs away—you will have a choice on that seemingly forgotten and forsaken island whether to launch out in spiritual rebellion, or whether to await fresh revelation.

"Why? Why would You do this, Father?" Abraham must have wondered as he climbed Mount Moriah with his son, Isaac.

Ready to plunge a knife through his only son's chest in obedience to the Lord's command, Abraham stopped abruptly when the Lord said, "Stop, Abraham. I know you love Me. See that ram over there? Put it on the altar in place of Isaac for I am Jehovah-Jireh: The Lord who sees and provides" (see Genesis 22:14).

A quality of God never known before was revealed to Abraham. When? When he was about to lose his son, but chose to obey anyway.

"I'm sure I'm forgotten," Jacob must have thought as he grabbed a rock for a pillow and laid his head down in Luz. "Certainly God's turned his back on me. After all, I've ripped off my brother all my life." That night, however, after the

Lord appeared to him in a vision, Jacob awoke, saying, "Wow! Truly God is in this place, and I knew it not" (see Genesis 28:16).

Luz became "Bethel" or "House of God" when God appeared to Jacob with fresh revelation at the very point he felt most alone.

"The people have been without water for three days and are about to kill me," cried Moses to the Lord.

"See that tree over there, Moses?" the Lord answered. "Chop it down, throw it into the water, and that which was bitter will become sweet because I am Jehovah-rappah—the God who healeth thee" (see Exodus 15:23–27).

When did this revelation come? When Moses was about to lose his life at the hands of an angry mob.

Read your Bible, and you will discover that every time someone had fresh vision, new understanding, clear revelation of the Lord, it was received when, like John, they were on Patmos. Precious saint, the tribulation you may be going through even now is for one purpose: to bring you a fuller revelation of Jesus.

As we embark on our journey through this Book of Revelation, we are truly about to be blessed, for of the sixty-six individual books that make up the Bible in its entirety, this book alone has a unique promise attached to it. Look at verse 3 of chapter 1: "Blessed is he that readeth (that's me) and they that hear (that's you) the words of this prophecy and keep those things which are written therein." This book alone promises anyone who reads it or even hears it receives a blessing.

I have found this to be true personally. In my study of the Word, Revelation always brings a blessing in a unique way to me. And I've also seen it to be true congregationally. "Do yourself and your people a favor," I tell young pastors. "If you want your congregation to be blessed and your own heart to be touched, teach Revelation."

I find it ironic that pastors are reticent to teach the Book of Revelation and that believers are hesitant to read it because they think it is hard to understand. Nothing could be further from the truth, for not only does this book have a blessing attached to it—it also comes with its own outline in chapter 1, verse 19 where Jesus tells John to "write the things which thou hast seen, and the things which are, and the things which shall be hereafter."

Thus, the flow of the book is as follows:

- Section I (chapter 1) presents Him whom John has seen—the Lord's Person.
- Section II (chapters 2—3) addresses the things that are—the Lord's people.
- Section III (chapters 4—22) details the things yet to come—the Lord's program.

Chapter 1 is the revelation of the glorified Christ. In chapters 2 and 3, we see the entire scope of church history. In chapters 4 and 5, we see the church taken up to heaven. In chapters 6 through 19, we see the Tribulation. In chapter 20, we see the Millennium. In chapters 21 and 22, we see the new heaven and the new earth.

As you read through this book, always bear in mind that it was given not because believers were trying to figure out the nuances of eschatology, but because they were watching their brothers and sisters dying as a result of inconceivable persecution. "Where is the Lord?" they must have cried. "We believe in Him. We've given our lives to Him, but what's happening?" They needed a revelation of Jesus Christ to see that Jesus Christ is in control, that He is on the throne. Thus, this message coming from John would give great comfort to their hearts.

The overarching theme of this book is that Jesus Christ is on the throne and is in control. Things are going according to plan, and He's coming back.

> In the 1300s Richard I left England to do battle in the Middle East. While he was gone, his brother, Prince John, took over the reins of power. So evil was John that men like Robin Hood rose up as a result of his corrupt rule. But the day came when finally Richard—the Lionhearted—finished his crusade and worked his way back up into Europe and toward England. When word traveled through the land that Richard was returning, Prince John erected a series of castles and defenses to keep his brother from regaining control. But as Richard and his men arrived on the shores of England, they mowed down the lines of defense and took control of the castles as easily as a hot knife goes through butter. And in each village and hamlet on his way back to power, church bells pealed, and people shouted, "The king is coming! The lion has returned!"

Such is the message of the Book of Revelation. The King is in control. The Lion of the Tribe of Judah has prevailed. Jesus is on His way.

OUTLINE

Many people are afraid of the Book of Revelation because they think it's a difficult book to comprehend. Not so. The word "revelation" means just the opposite: the revealing, the unveiling.

The Book of Revelation is very simple—particularly because it's the only Book with its own divine outline, found in chapter 1 verse 19, where Jesus told John to "write the things which thou hast seen, and the things which are, and the things which shall be hereafter."

If you follow this divine outline, the Book unfolds very easily. . . .

   I. The things which thou hast seen—chapter 1
      The reality of the Resurrected Jesus

II. The things which are—chapters 2—3

Jesus gives seven messages to seven churches, wherein lies the chronological flow of church history from the beginning of the early church to the present.

III. The things which shall be hereafter . . .

Chapters 4—5

The church is raptured and taken to heaven for a seven-year "honeymoon" with the Lord.

Chapters 6—19

The Tribulation occurs on earth as God pours out His wrath on a Christ-rejecting, sinful world.

Chapter 19

At the end of chapter 19, the Lord comes back to Jerusalem with His church to establish His kingdom.

Chapter 20

The Millennium—a thousand-year period of peace and prosperity—follows as the Lord rules and reigns from Jerusalem. At the end of the Millennium, Satan is loosed. A final rebellion ensues before Satan is put away permanently.

Chapters 21—22

A new heaven and a new earth are created wherein we will live oh, so *happily* ever after.

REVELATION

1

Revelation 1:1 (a)
The Revelation of Jesus Christ . . .

As you open the Book of Revelation, perhaps the title in your Bible reads: The Revelation of St. John the Divine. You must understand that the title, chapter, and verse delineation in the Bible were not in the original text, and are, therefore, not inspired. This is the revelation not of John, but of Jesus Christ.

Revelation 1:1 (b)
. . . which God gave unto him . . .

The pronoun "him" in this verse refers back to Jesus Christ. This whole Book—the revelation of how the Lord is ruling and reigning, of how all things are going according to plan—was given to Jesus. "I don't know the time of the coming of the kingdom," said Jesus. "Only My Father has the

full plan" (see Mark 13:32)—which raises a very intriguing question: Did Jesus know everything?

In Luke 2:52, we read that Jesus grew in stature and wisdom. In other words, He went through life learning. That is why His baptism is so significant, for it was then that His Father's voice thundered from heaven, "This is My beloved Son in whom I am well pleased." It was then, at thirty years of age, that Jesus fully realized He had come to die.

Revelation 1:1 (c)
. . . to shew unto his servants things which must shortly come to pass . . .

The Father gave revelation to the Son. The Son gave revelation to John. And John gave revelation to us that we might understand the things that must shortly come to pass. "*Shortly* come to pass?" you say. "This book is over two thousand years old!" The Greek word translated "shortly" is *en tachei*, meaning "must come to pass with rapidity." It's the same Greek word from which we get the word "tachometer"—the instrument used to determine the speed of an engine. Thus, the Lord is telling us in this verse that when end-time events begin to happen, they'll increase their rpms and happen with greater rapidity.

Heading south from Medford, Oregon on I-5 toward San Diego, I don't see a single sign that says San Diego until I get past Chico, where I see only one. Then I don't see another one until I get to San Jose. But as I go farther south, the signs start appearing a little more frequently, until I get to Ventura. Suddenly, the signs appear every fifty miles. When I get past LA, the signs appear with even greater rapidity until I finally see the sign reading, "Welcome to San Diego."

That's the idea here, folks. Things begin slowly. One sign appears. Then, maybe one hundred years pass before another sign is seen. But one day, all of a sudden, the tachometer will show the engine revving up and sign upon sign will be seen.

Revelation 1:1 (d)
. . . and he sent and signified it by his angel . . .

The word "signified" means "written with signs"—which explains why people read the Book of Revelation and say, "It seems to be written in code." Why was it written this way? I suggest three reasons:

First, the Book of Revelation was written with signs to provide protection. At the time John wrote this letter, there was a tremendous wave of persecution afflicting the church. Consequently, this letter was written in such a way that, although it would make no sense to the enemies of the church, those who knew Scripture would find it relatively easy to understand.

Second, the Book of Revelation was written with signs to convey information. Language changes with time. Read your King James Bible, written in 1611, and the changes in language that have taken place since it was written are obvious. Pictures and symbols, on the other hand, are timeless and thus convey more clearly the thoughts and intent of the writer.

Finally, the Book of Revelation was written with signs in order to arouse emotions. It's one thing to say, "There's a world political leader coming." It's something else to say, "The Beast is coming." It's one thing to refer to a commercial system. It's something else to call it Babylon the Whore. It's one thing to say "Christians," and another to say, "the bride of Christ." It's one thing to talk about authority and something else to talk about the Lion of the Tribe of Judah. These images are powerful, vivid, indelible.

Revelation 1:1 (e)
. . . unto his servant John.

John, the "disciple whom Jesus loved," was used by the Lord to author five books. The Gospel of John was written that we might believe that Jesus is the Christ, the Son of God (John 20:31). First, 2, and 3 John were written that we might know we have eternal life (1 John 5:13). Thus, John wrote his Gospel that we might believe, his epistles that we might be sure, and the Book of Revelation that we might be ready.

Revelation 1:2
Who bare record of the word of God, and of the testimony of Jesus Christ, and of all things that he saw.

Revelation was entrusted to John because he bore record of the testimony of Jesus and of all the things he saw. People who say, "I don't seem to be growing in the Lord," must understand that when it comes to revelation, information, or inspiration, the Lord has a very definite prerequisite: Are we going to personally receive it in our heart and freely release it to others?

After visiting with Abraham, the Lord said to His angels, "I'm going to tell Abraham what is going to come down in Sodom because I know he will not only receive but share it" (see Genesis 18:17, 19).

Jesus put it this way: Take heed how you hear—for the one who has shall be given more (Mark 4:24, 25). In other words, if you come to Bible study or your morning devotions saying, "Entertain me," or, "I'm curious about prophecy," you won't receive. But if you are hearing, studying, learning, praying, and reading for the purpose of embracing what you receive and sharing it with others, the Lord will give you continual revelation.

Revelation 1:3 (a)
Blessed is he that readeth . . .

The Greek word translated "readeth" literally means "to read out loud." I often encourage people to read their Bibles out loud. Why? Because I find if I don't read my Bible aloud, I have a tendency to read only the passages I've highlighted—which are usually promises like: "Delight yourself in the Lord, and He'll give you the desires of your heart." "My God shall supply all your needs according to His riches." "All things work together for good to those who love God." What I don't have underlined are verses like, "All those who live godly in Christ Jesus shall suffer persecution." "Blessed are you when men shall revile you, persecute you, and speak all manner of evil against you." Sometimes we need to study the passages *not* underlined in our Bibles. And the way this can be done practically is by reading aloud.

Revelation 1:3 (b)
. . . and they that hear the words of this prophecy, and keep those things which are written therein: for the time is at hand.

I find that hearing the Word spoken audibly has a powerful impact on my heart. That is why I also encourage people to pray out loud. It's not for God's sake—but to keep *us* focused and engaged.

Revelation 1:4 (a)
John to the seven churches . . .

Why are there seven churches? Because seven is the biblical number of completion.

Revelation 1:4 (b)
. . . which are in Asia.

Asia does not refer to Korea, Japan, or Viet Nam. It refers to present-day Turkey. Why was this letter written to the church in Turkey rather than to the church at Jerusalem, or Rome, Colosse, or Antioch? After all, it seems those would have been much more appropriate choices. Why was this letter written to seven churches in Turkey? Because no other churches could have so perfectly painted the picture they portray.

Revelation 1:4 (c)
Grace be unto you, and peace . . .

"Grace and peace be unto you," is not the equivalent of "Yo, dude." It has a depth of meaning. You see, "grace," or *charis*, was a Greek greeting. *Shalom*, or "peace," was a Hebrew greeting. The combination of the two is powerful because man can't have peace until he understands the favor God has given to him in and through the grace of Christ Jesus.

Revelation 1:4 (d), 5 (a)
. . . from him which is, and which was, and which is to come; and from the seven Spirits

which are before his throne; and from Jesus Christ, who is the faithful witness . . .

Here we see the Trinity. . . .

"Him which is, and was, and is to come" is God the Father.
"What's Your name?" asked Moses of God in Exodus 3.
"I Am that I Am," God answered—the Tetragrammaton that became so sacred to the Jews that they would only write the consonants: YHWH.

The seven Spirits refer to the seven-fold ministry of the Holy Spirit as seen in Isaiah 11:2.

Jesus Christ is indeed the faithful Witness.
"Show us the Father," Philip said, "and it will suffice us."
"Don't you know that he that hath seen Me hath seen the Father?" answered Jesus (John 14:9).

Revelation 1:5 (b)
. . . and the first begotten of the dead . . .

"Aha!" the cultist says. "Jesus is begotten. Therefore, He didn't always exist." Wrong. We refer to Laura Bush as the First Lady. Does this mean she's the first lady who ever lived? No. "First Lady" refers to her position. So, too, in Jeremiah 31:9 God calls Ephraim His firstborn. Was Ephraim the firstborn? No. Although he was the younger brother, however, Ephraim had prominence. Thus, "first begotten" in Scripture speaks not of precedence—but of preeminence.

Revelation 1:5 (c)
. . . and the prince of the kings of the earth. Unto him that loved us, and washed us from our sins in his own blood.

I'm so thankful the Lord doesn't just whitewash our sins, but rather, through the shedding of His own blood, washes us white.

Revelation 1:6 (a)
And hath made us kings and priests unto God and his Father . . .

In the Millennium, we'll rule and reign on the earth as kings and priests (Revelation 5:10).

Revelation 1:6 (b)–7
. . . to him be glory and dominion for ever and ever. Amen. Behold, he cometh with clouds; and every eye shall see him, and they also which pierced him: and all kindreds of

the earth shall wail because of him. Even so, Amen.

When the final battle in the Valley of Megiddo is being fought, when the nations of the world come against the Jews to annihilate Israel, suddenly when it looks so bleak, the Lord will come back. And the Jews will say, "Where did You get those wounds?"

"In the house of My friends," He'll answer (Zechariah 13:6).

And all the people shall wail, "We fought against Him. We didn't believe in Him. And now He's here."

Revelation 1:8 (a)
I am Alpha and Omega, the beginning and the ending . . .

In the original text, it is plainly seen that, under the inspiration of the Spirit, John writes out the word "Alpha"—the first letter of the Greek alphabet. But when it comes to Omega, he uses only the letter. Why? I suggest it is because the Lord is the beginning and the end without end. In other words, Omega is never written out fully because the Lord never ends. We'll spend eternity exploring His nature.

Revelation 1:8 (b)
. . . saith the Lord, which is, and which was, and which is to come, the Almighty.

Ask a Jehovah's Witness or Mormon the identity of the speaker in this verse, and he'll say it's Jehovah, or God the Father.

Turn him to Isaiah 41:4, which reads: "Who hath wrought and done it, calling the generations from the beginning? I the Lord, the first, and with the last: I am he," and ask of whom it speaks.

"Jehovah," he'll say.

Then turn him to Isaiah 44:6, which reads: "Thus saith the Lord the King of Israel, and his redeemer the Lord of hosts; I am the first, and I am the last; and beside me there is no God," and ask of whom it speaks.

"Jehovah," he'll say.

Then turn him to Isaiah 48:12, which reads: "Hearken unto me, O Jacob and Israel, my called; I am he; I am the first, I also am the last," and ask of whom it speaks.

"Jehovah," he'll say.

Then turn him to Revelation 21:6, 7, which reads: "And he said unto me, It is done. I am Alpha and Omega, the beginning and the end. I will give unto him that is athirst of the fountain of the water of life freely. He that overcometh shall inherit all things: and I will be his God, and he shall be my son," and ask him who it is who cries out "It Is Finished," and who says He will give the water of the fountain of life freely?"

"Jehovah," he'll say—even though it was Jesus who cried out on the Cross, "It is Finished," and who said, "If any man thirst, let him come to Me" (John 7:37).

Then turn him to Revelation 22:12, 13, which reads: "And behold, I come quickly; and my reward is with me, to give every man according as his work shall be. I am Alpha and Omega, the beginning and the end, the first and the last," and ask of whom it speaks

"Jehovah," he'll say—even though verse 16 identifies the Speaker of verses 12, 13 as Jesus.

And now he has a problem, for the reference in Revelation clearly being to Jesus, either there are two firsts and two lasts, two alphas and two omegas, two beginnings and two endings—or else Jesus and the Father are one.

Revelation 1:9 (a)
I John, who also am your brother, and companion in tribulation . . .

Keep in mind that John is writing as pastor of the seven churches under his care, as a pastor of people who are being tortured, persecuted, and slaughtered. That is why he identifies himself as their brother and companion in difficulty. Still today, the effective pastor, parent, or mentor is one who realizes we're all in this together—that we're all brothers and sisters, companions and fellow-pilgrims.

Revelation 1:9 (b)
. . . and in the kingdom and patience of Jesus Christ, was in the isle that is called Patmos, for the word of God, and for the testimony of Jesus Christ.

John was not only a pastor but also a theologian. Banished to Patmos, the Word put him where he was. But the Word also made him who he was. John is a giant of Christendom because he was a man of the Word.

Revelation 1:10 (a)
I was in the Spirit on the Lord's day . . .

Not only a pastor and a theologian, John was a poet. Under the inspiration of the Spirit, John painted pictures to impact the emotions of a people going through tough times and tremendous difficulties. John wanted his people to have more than dead doctrine. He wanted them to feel the reality of the Lord's coming burning in their hearts and illuminating their imaginations.

I say this because if you don't read this book as poetry—if you read it only intellectually or academically—you'll miss a key component. You've got to keep reminding yourself that the people to whom John was writing were watching their kids die, their wives being dragged off, their husbands disappear. The people to whom John was writing weren't saying, "What can we learn about the latest rap on the mark of the beast?" No, they were saying, "What's going on? Why aren't things working out? Is there hope?"

"Yes!" answers John, the poet. "I want you to feel the drama, see the picture, taste the reality—for then your heart will be stirred, your faith strengthened."

Revelation 1:10 (b), 11 (a)
. . . and heard behind me a great voice, as of a trumpet, saying, I am Alpha and Omega, the first and the last . . .

Why is this repeated? After all, John said the same thing just two verses earlier. I suggest it is because most people don't struggle with the Alpha or the Omega. They know God looked at creation and declared it good. And they know in the end, in heaven, things will be good. But where people have a hard time is in the middle. They question and struggle with the things going on presently. "Why is this happening? Why didn't God do this? Where was God when that happened?" they cry.

So what does a pastor, a theologian, a poet do? He whispers in people's ears over and over again that God is in control, that God is on the throne, that the same God who did the good work in the beginning is here in the middle and will come through in the end.

And that's what we must do. We must whisper over and over in the ears of our teenagers, our friends, our neighbors, "God is here, and He's going to see you through."

Revelation 1:11 (b)
. . . and, What thou seest, write in a book, and send it unto the seven churches which are in Asia; unto Ephesus, and unto Smyrna, and unto Pergamos, and unto Thyatira, and unto Sardis, and unto Philadelphia, and unto Laodicea.

As we will see in chapters 2 and 3, these seven churches speak of the seven epochs of the church age. Each church speaks of a period in church history chronologically and consecutively.

Revelation 1:12
And I turned to see the voice that spake with me.

When John heard a voice behind him, he turned to see what it meant. And in this, I am reminded of other who "turned to see the voice that spake with them."

When an angel appeared to them, telling them to go to Bethlehem, the shepherds could have said, "Forget it. It's the middle of the night. Why go to Bethlehem now?" But they didn't. They went. And they ended up rejoicing (see Luke 2).

When they saw a star they'd never seen before, the wise men could have been reticent to embark on the nearly two-year journey. But they got on their camels, set out across the desert—and ended up worshiping the King of kings (see Matthew 2).

When an angel appeared to him, saying, "Your betrothed has conceived miraculously, the young carpenter from Nazareth could have said, "The engagement's off." But, like the shepherds and the wise men, Joseph responded to the revelation given to him, thereby becoming and integral part of the earthly life of the Son of God (see Matthew 1:24).

After the Spirit told an old prophet that he would see the Messiah, no doubt Simeon was waiting to hear the rumble of chariot wheels and the footsteps of soldiers escorting the King of the Jews to the temple. Instead, he heard the cry of a baby in the arms of a sixteen-year-old girl. And he beheld the Savior (Luke 2:26–28).

There was one group, however, who did not "turn to see" and thus missed the Incarnation. . . .

When the wise men arrived in Jerusalem and asked, "Where is Messiah to be born?" the Bible scholars were quick to answer, "Bethlehem." You see, they knew Bible prophecy like the backs of their hands. They knew the obscure verses in Micah 5 that foretold the place of His birth; the portions of Daniel 9 that foretold the time of His birth; the passages in Isaiah that prophesied He would be born of a virgin and sojourn in Egypt. They were the Bible students, the Wednesday nighters, the pastors, the elders, the note-takers. These were people who, if we're not careful, we could be.

*They knew the Word—and yet they never
made the five-mile walk from Jerusalem to
Bethlehem in pursuit of a personal, real encounter with God. And, gang, we are vulnerable to the same mentality. We can read the
Book of Revelation academically. We can
search for clues of typology. We can draw parallels to current events internationally—all
the while missing the revelation of Jesus personally. Not so John. When he heard a voice,
he didn't say, "I know the Bible. After all, I
wrote a good part of it." No, he turned to see—
and saw Jesus in the process.*

Finally, I am reminded of One who lived His
life "turning to see." "What I see the Father do,
that I do," declared Jesus in John 5:19—nothing
more, nothing less, nothing else.

Wouldn't it be radical for us to base all of our
analyses, judgments, and evaluations solely on
what we see of the Father?

"The judgment I make is right because I judge
on the basis of what I hear from the Father,"
Jesus said (see John 5:30).

What if we did the same? What if, before I gave
my two cents' worth about a person, I chose instead to withhold evaluation or judgment until I
talked to the Father? May we be a people who
love the Lord and are led by the Spirit in a fuller,
fresher measure—"turning to see" and obeying
what He tells us to do.

Revelation 1:12
**And being turned, I saw seven golden can-
dlesticks.**

The seven golden candlesticks refer to the
golden lamp stand of Exodus 25, which, with
three lamps on each side of a main stem, speak
both of John 15, where Jesus said, "I am the Vine
and you are the branches," and of John 8 where
He declared Himself to be the Light of the world.
As seen in Matthew 5, we are to let our light shine
as well—which can only happen as we stay connected to the Stem of the candlestick, the true
Vine, Jesus Christ.

Notice also the candlestick is made of gold,
which speaks of divinity. But it was not molten
gold, it was one piece of beaten gold because
Jesus was beaten that we might be included with
Him in the lamp stand.

Revelation 1:13 (a)
**And in the midst of the seven candlesticks
one like unto the Son of man . . .**

Perhaps it was because it spoke of His ability
to relate to people that the term "Son of man"

was the term Jesus used most often to speak of
Himself. The term also has prophetic implication,
for in Daniel 7:13, we read of the Son of Man coming with the clouds of heaven.

Revelation 1:13 (b)
**. . . clothed with a garment down to the
foot . . .**

The Son of Man is clothed to His feet—which
speaks of the priesthood (Exodus 28:42). His entire body is covered. Who is the body of Christ?
We are. We're covered with the robe of His righteousness (Isaiah 61:10).

Revelation 1:13 (c)
**. . . and girt about the paps with a golden
girdle.**

In Old Testament times, priests would normally wear girdles, or beltlike sashes, around
their waists. But in this case we see the girdle
around the chest—which would speak of the One
who's in the midst of His church. You see, when
Jesus was on earth, He wept for Lazarus, and for
a lost world. But now there's a sash binding His
heart. There's no weeping because He is in control. He's on the throne. Everything is going according to plan.

Revelation 1:14 (a)
**His head and his hairs were white like wool,
as white as snow . . .**

I've seen frightening pictures based on this
chapter, depicting a white-haired Jesus with eyes
blazing and a sword protruding from His mouth.
But that's not the picture John was painting.
John's poetry must be seen in conjunction with
scriptures given previously. What does "white as
snow" bring to mind? Isaiah 1:18, where we read,
". . . though your sins be as scarlet, they shall be
as white as snow. . . ." Thus, white hair represents
the forgiveness and mercy that permeate Jesus'
mind. "I know where you've been," He says. "But
you are cleansed. You are forgiven. You are white.
That's the way I see you."

Revelation 1:14 (b)
. . . and his eyes were as a flame of fire.

Fire can be frightening, but in a fireplace,
there's nothing more inviting or comforting. I
suggest we see both aspects in the eyes of
Jesus. . . .

*When we stand before the judgment seat of
Christ, He's going to look at all of our works.*

The wood, hay, and stubble—all of our fleshly, futile efforts—will ignite under His gaze of fire, leaving only the gold, silver, and precious stones—that which He did through and in spite of us. Then, with eyes of warmth and love, He will look at us and say, "Well done!"

To me, this is a tremendous relief because I know I have a whole lot of wood, a huge pile of hay, and all sorts of stubble. But in that day, it will all disappear under His gaze.

Revelation 1:15 (a)
And his feet like unto fine brass, as if they burned in a furnace . . .

The mention of furnace would bring to the minds of the persecuted believers to whom John was writing the story of three others who endured the fire of persecution. But guess who was in the fire with Shadrach, Meshach, and Abednego. Jesus was (Daniel 3:25). His feet are burned because He's been through the same furnaces we have.

Revelation 1:15 (b)
. . . and his voice as the sound of many waters.

"I don't hear the Lord," we sometimes say. Yet if we listen carefully, we'll hear a little creek on the radio, or a small stream in our devotions. We'll hear a river through a conversation with a friend. We'll hear a brook as we observe nature. And suddenly these little creeks and rivers and brooks and streams flow together until finally, at the end of the day, we say, "Hey, I *have* heard You, Lord."

Revelation 1:16 (a)
And he had in his right hand seven stars: and out of his mouth went a sharp two-edged sword . . .

Again, don't miss the poetry here. It's not as though Jesus opens His mouth to smile and a big sword emerges. Rather, the sword symbolizes the Word He speaks—full of grace and truth (John 1:14).

Revelation 1:16 (b)
. . . and his countenance was as the sun shineth in his strength.

Reminiscent of the blessing in Numbers 6, the allusion here is to graciousness and peace.

Revelation 1:17 (a)
And when I saw him, I fell at his feet as dead.

Some use this Scripture as biblical justification for being slain in the Spirit. But I want you to notice John did not fall backward. He fell at Jesus' feet. There's only one place in the Bible where people fell backward: the Garden of Gethsemane, when two words—I AM—knocked the feet out from under the soldiers sent to arrest Jesus (John 18:6).

Revelation 1:17 (b)–18 (a)
And he laid his right hand upon me, saying unto me, Fear not; I am the first and the last: I am he that liveth, and was dead; and, behold, I am alive for evermore, Amen . . .

Notice the order: John heard. He saw. He fell. Then he was touched, revived, and commissioned into ministry to write "the things which he had seen, and the things which are, and the things which shall be hereafter."

John turned to see what he heard and found it led to a deeper understanding and renewed appreciation of Jesus Christ. And that, gang, is what this book before us is all about. Revelation is not given primarily to give us information about Bible prophecy, but to bring to us a revelation of Jesus Christ personally.

Revelation 1:18 (b)
. . . and have the keys of hell and of death.

The keys of hell and death are not to lock people up but to set people free. "I can get you out of your damnable, hellish situation if you'll let Me," Jesus says. "I can save you from hell eternally if you'll receive Me. My desire is to set you free" (see Luke 4:18). The Lord holds the keys to that which is imprisoning you, gang. Let this One with the eyes of a warm fire set you free.

Revelation 1:19, 20
Write the things which thou hast seen, and the things which are, and the things which shall be hereafter; the mystery of the seven stars which thou sawest in my right hand, and the seven golden candlesticks. The seven stars are the angels of the seven churches: and the seven candlesticks which thou sawest are the seven churches.

Angelos, the word translated "angel," also means "messenger" and is referring to the pastors, the leaders of the seven churches. Why are they likened to stars? Because according to Daniel 12, those who turn many to righteousness will shine as stars forever. Truly, once you start sharing your faith, once you start reflecting the goodness and grace of God, there will be a radiance about you that will draw others to your Savior. Try it and see!

2 We come now to the second section of the Book of Revelation, which deals with "the things which are" (Revelation 1:19). As he addresses the seven churches of which he was an overseer, John paints a portrait of church history in its entirety. The seven messages that follow have a four-fold application. . . .

First, they are to be applied locally. The cities of the seven churches are given in the order of an ancient Roman postal circuit. Thus, they could be easily circulated among the churches addressed.

Second, they apply ecclesiastically. Anyone who cares about the church or is involved with the church needs to study these letters because every problem, difficulty, and challenge facing the church is addressed in these seven letters.

Third, they apply personally. These letters apply to us individually. How do I know? Because each letter ends with "Let he that hath an ear, hear what the Spirit saith." Thus, this applies to anyone who has an ear. If you have two ears, it's a double directive!

Fourth, the letters apply prophetically. For us today, most of the events are history because we're approaching the end of the church age. But for John, at the beginning of the church age, the events of which he wrote had not yet transpired.

In addition to a four-fold application, there is also a four-element pattern seen in each letter. . . .

First, there is positive affirmation, where Jesus finds something to affirm in the churches. Second, there is corrective exhortation. Third, there is an eternal motivation. And finally, there is partial revelation—as each of the churches reveals something of the nature of Christ. You see, the only way we're going to see the complete picture is to embrace the church in totality. That's what is so important about the body of Christ. As I look at the body, each person exhibits a unique aspect of Jesus Christ. It takes the whole body to truly magnify the Lord. That's why the psalmist said, "O magnify the Lord with me" (see Psalm 34:3).

May we be those who embrace other believers and other churches because they each reveal something of Him.

Revelation 2:1 (a)
Unto the angel . . .

Meaning "messenger," it is most likely that the word *angelous* used here speaks of a pastor, or leader.

Revelation 2:1 (b)
. . . of the church of Ephesus . . .

The church of Ephesus speaks of the period of church history from A.D. 33 to A.D. 100. By A.D. 97—the year John recorded this book—the church was already a mess. The Book of Acts presents the model of the way the church was supposed to function. But Acts only covers a span of thirty years. By the time John penned Revelation a mere sixty years later, the purity of the church had been compromised to such a degree that they were in a position to hear the Lord say, "Unless you repent, I'll not stay in your midst" (see verse 5).

Those caught up in some of the so-called revivals of today say, "We can't explain from the Bible what is happening in our church, but in earlier days, we read of people barking or shaking . . ." as they turn not to the Scriptures but to church history for justification of aberrant behavior.

Let it be noted, precious people, that we can't appeal to church history for practices of doctrine because the church has had problems from the very outset. I don't ever defend church history. But I do defend the church as seen in the Book of Acts. Appeal only to the Bible, gang, because that's where you find safety and sanity. You're always on solid ground if you stick with Scripture.

Revelation 2:1 (c)
. . . write; These things saith he that holdeth the seven stars in his right hand . . .

Who are the seven stars? The leaders of the seven churches.

Revelation 2:1 (d)
. . . who walketh in the midst of the seven golden candlesticks.

Where is Jesus walking? In the midst of the church. You will meet Christians who say, "Well, I'm not into church." That's too bad, because Jesus is. "Yeah, but the churches around here are really hurting," they'll say. So were these. And yet Jesus was in their midst.

Revelation 2:2, 3
I know thy works, and thy labour, and thy patience, and how thou canst not bear them

which are evil: and thou hast tried them which say they are apostles, and are not, and hast found them liars: And hast borne, and hast patience, and for my name's sake hast laboured, and hast not fainted.

Here, Jesus gives His affirmation. He says, "First of all, I affirm you for staying with the task. That is, you've worked hard. You haven't fainted. Secondly, you've stood with the truth. You've rooted out the deceivers who have come into your midst."

On occasion, people will say to us as Christians, "Don't judge me. Didn't Jesus say to judge not lest ye be judged?"

And I tell them He did. But I also remind them that fifteen verses later, He said, "Beware of false prophets who will come into your midst as wolves in sheep's clothing. By their fruit you shall know them" (see Matthew 7:15, 16).

So what is Jesus saying? In Matthew 7:1, He says we're not to judge for condemnation. In verse 15, however, we are instructed to judge for identification. If we only teach the Word, but don't warn the flock about liars and deceivers, then we simply fatten people up for the kill. Part of the job of parenting and pastoring, part of the responsibility of any believer is to warn of false doctrine and false teachers.

Revelation 2:4
Nevertheless I have somewhat against thee, because thou hast left thy first love.

The corrective exhortation concerns the fact that, although they labored faithfully and showed discernment theologically, they had left their first love.

Notice He doesn't say they *lost* their first love. He says they *left* it. . . .

While chopping trees for the expansion of their facility, the axe head of one of Elisha's students flew into the Jordan River. Ever feel like the cutting edge is gone from your ministry, like the power is absent from your life? Since wood is biblically symbolic of the flesh, this guy with the wooden handle still in his grasp could have said, I can still make noise banging trees with the handle. Maybe no one will notice that nothing's happening in the way of effective ministry." But he didn't. Instead, he did what Jesus tells you and me and those at Ephesus to do: he cried, "Master, it's not there anymore. The cutting edge is gone."

"Take me to the place you had it last," said Elisha. And the young man took Elisha to the edge of the river where he had last seen the axe head. Elisha ripped off a limb from a nearby tree, put it in the river, and miraculously, the axe head floated to the top.

"There it is, son," said Elisha. "Now reach in and grab it" (see 2 Kings 6:1–7).

It's a perfect picture of what Jesus is about to say to those at Ephesus and to those of us who have left our first love. . . .

Revelation 2:5 (a)
Remember therefore from whence thou art fallen . . .

Remember how it felt to have the cutting edge, when you were passionate, when your walk was vibrant. Remember how it used to be when you had it last.

Revelation 2:5 (b)
. . . and repent . . .

"Repent" simply means "change direction."

Revelation 2:5 (c)
. . . and do the first works. . . .

What were you doing when you were on fire for the Lord?
"I was going to church."
Go again!
"I was getting up early for morning devotions."
Do it again!
"I sang praise to the Lord as I drove down the street."
Sing again!
Remember how it used to be when you were amazed by the Lord's goodness—do again what you were doing then, and you will see the cutting edge return. The injunction of Jesus is simple: Remember, repent, and return.

Revelation 2:5 (d)
. . . or else I will come unto thee quickly, and will remove thy candlestick out of his place, except thou repent.

You may have lots of programs and lots of activities. You may even have doctrinal purity. But Jesus will not stay in a church where there is not true love because without love, nothing else matters (1 Corinthians 13:2).

Revelation 2:6
But this thou hast, that thou hatest the deeds of the Nicolaitans, which I also hate.

"Nicos" meaning "conquest" and "laity" meaning "people of the church," the Nicolaitans were evidently those who came on the scene, saying, "I will tell you who to marry, where to live, and what to do because I am your spiritual leader."

But what did Paul say? He said, "We do not seek to have dominion over you, but we are helpers of your joy" (see 2 Corinthians 1:24).

Sometimes people say, "Jon, I want you to know I'm submitted to you." While I hear their heart, I say, "Don't submit to me. I've got a tough enough time trying to figure out what *I* should do! I'd love to share with you from the Word and pray for you each day. But it's Jesus alone to whom you must submit."

Revelation 2:7
He that hath an ear, let him hear what the Spirit saith unto the churches; To him that overcometh will I give to eat of the tree of life, which is in the midst of the paradise of God.

What did the Ephesians lack? Love. What would they get if they changed their ways? The fruit of the tree of life, the fruit of the Spirit: love. Thus, the eternal motivation for the Ephesian church perfectly answered their greatest need.

Revelation 2:8, 9 (a)
And unto the angel of the church in Smyrna write; These things saith the first and the last, which was dead, and is alive; I know thy works, and tribulation, and poverty, (but thou art rich) . . .

The church in Smyrna represents the period in church history from A.D. 100 to A.D. 312. The word "smyrna" comes from myrrh—a fragrance released only when crushed.

At His birth, Jesus was presented with gold, frankincense, and myrrh. Gold was for kings, frankincense for priests. But myrrh was a burial spice. Jesus is a King, yes. He is a Priest, indeed. But He's also the Prophet who said, "Destroy this body and in three days, I will rise again" (see John 2:19).

On the Cross, Jesus was presented with myrrh when a soldier offered it to Him to deaden His pain. Let Jesus' refusal of the myrrh offered to Him on the Cross be an example to us in a culture that says, "Depressed? Take an antidepressant. Feel pain? Try this drug." May we be those who, when the process of crushing takes place, let the Cross do its job.

Myrrh was offered to Jesus a third time— when the women came Easter Sunday to put burial spices on His body. But He wasn't there. He had risen.

So, too, when Jesus returns in His Second Coming, Isaiah writes "all they from Sheba shall come: they shall bring gold and incense; and they shall shew forth the praises of the Lord" (see 60:6). The people of Sheba will bring gold for the King; frankincense for the Priest. But they won't bring myrrh because when Jesus comes back, He's not coming to die. He's coming to rule and reign.

Revelation 2:9 (b)
. . . and I know the blasphemy of them which say they are Jews, and are not, but are the synagogue of Satan.

In Smyrna, as in other places, Jews would sometimes take the heat of persecution off themselves by inciting the Romans against the Christians. They would present Communion in a wrong light by accusing believers of drinking blood and eating broken bodies. Thus, in God's economy they were no more His people in reality than were the Christians who, in the Name of Christ, slaughtered Jews by hundreds of thousands during the Crusades.

The pastor of the church at Smyrna was a man named Polycarp, the last man personally discipled by John. At eighty-six years of age, amidst one of the numerous waves of persecution, Polycarp was ordered to burn incense at the altar of Caesar. "How can I deny Him who has been faithful to me these six and eighty years?" he asked. Consequently, he was sentenced to burn at the stake. When the fire failed to come near him, however, a frustrated guard pierced Polycarp's shoulder with his sword—inadvertently drawing blood, which put out the flame.

At times, the only substance powerful enough to extinguish the fire of persecution was the blood of the saints.

Revelation 2:10 (a)
Fear none of those things which thou shalt suffer: behold, the devil shall cast some of you into prison, that ye may be tried; and ye shall have tribulation ten days . . .

In the years A.D. 100 through A.D. 313, there were ten Roman emperors who correspond to the ten days spoken of here. They launched such massive attacks against the believers that between five and seven million Christians were killed during their rule.

Revelation 2:10 (b)
. . . be thou faithful unto death, and I will
give thee a crown of life.

Notice that for this group, Jesus doesn't have
a corrective exhortation. Perhaps this is because
by enduring persecution, they remained pure.
But notice also that Jesus makes no promise to
lighten their affliction. On the contrary, He says,
"Go through the pain and crushing. Be faithful
unto death."

Revelation 2:11
He that hath an ear, let him hear what the
Spirit saith unto the churches; He that over-
cometh shall not be hurt of the second
death.

What is the second death? At the end of the
Millennium, the unbeliever will be resurrected to
stand before the Lord at the Great White Throne
Judgment. There, his failure to believe on the
Lord and his refusal to accept God's payment for
his sins will condemn him to outer darkness
(Revelation 20:6). But for those who, like the
church at Smyrna, stay true, the second death
will have no effect.

Revelation 2:12 (a)
And to the angel of the church in Pergamos
write:

The Greek prefix *per,* seen in words like "pervert," means opposition. The suffix *gamos,* seen
in words like "monogamy" or "bigamy," means
"marriage." *Pergamos,* then, means "objectionable marriage"—a fitting description of the next
phase of church history. . . .

The year was A.D. 312. The last of the ten Roman emperors who had persecuted the church
was dead, ushering in a power play for the
reins of the empire. To this end, one young
hopeful prepared to engage in a huge battle.
According to legend, he saw a cross in the heavens and heard a voice saying, "In this sign conquer." And as a result, young Constantine fell
to his knees and became a born-again believer.

According to history, however, what really
happened was that, substantially outnumbered, Constantine noticed that Christians
were not enlisting in anyone's army. Realizing
that if he converted to Christianity, he would
have access to a potential infusion of new
troops, he became a Christian. And the Christians responded by siding with him.

But it would turn out to be an unmitigated
disaster. As a result of Constantine's Edict of

Toleration, which forbade persecution of Christians, Christianity became the official religion
of Rome. In fact, soon all Roman babies would
be legally required to be baptized into the
Christian faith. Yes, the Christians were in
power, but, understanding the political expedi-
ency of concession, Constantine compromised
with the pagan priests and traditions that permeated Rome.

"I feel your pain," he said. "Let's find common ground. Let's meet halfway." So a marriage took place that was perhaps most clearly
illustrated by the coin issued shortly thereafter. Christian symbols were stamped on one
side of the coin and pagan symbols on the other.
From A.D. 313 to A.D. 600, church and state
worked together as a political power—and as a
result the church began a downward spiral
from which she has yet to recover, as we shall
see.

Revelation 2:12 (b), 13 (a)
These things saith he which hath the sharp
sword with two edges; I know thy works,
and where thou dwellest, even where Sa-
tan's seat is . . .

According to Greek mythology, Pergamos was
the birthplace of Zeus. "Satan's seat" is in reference to the one hundred-fifty-foot-high structure
dedicated to Zeus in the middle of the city of Pergamos.

Revelation 2:13 (b)
. . . and thou holdest fast my name, and
hast not denied my faith, even in those days
wherein Antipas was my faithful martyr,
who was slain among you, where Satan
dwelleth.

The historian Tertullian tells us that, because
Antipas, a physician in the city of Pergamos,
wouldn't renounce his faith, he was fried to
death.

Revelation 2:14
But I have a few things against thee, be-
cause thou hast there them that hold the
doctrine of Balaam, who taught Balac to
cast a stumblingblock before the children
of Israel, to eat things sacrificed unto idols,
and to commit fornication.

You remember the story of Balaam. Asked by
Moabite King Balak to pronounce a curse on the
people of Israel, God forbade the prophet Balaam
to go. But Balaam went anyway, and after a short

discussion with a donkey, he wound up on a mountain overlooking the encamped Israelites upon whom he was to issue a curse. After three failed attempts, realizing he couldn't curse them, Balaam resorted to an alternate plan. "If your women seduce the Israelite men," he said to Balak, "they can introduce idol worship to them through which Israel will thereby bring a curse upon herself" (see Numbers 22).

What, then, is the doctrine of Balaam? It is Pergamos: objectionable marriage with the world.

Revelation 2:15
So hast thou also them that hold the doctrine of the Nicolaitans, which thing I hate.

Not only had the church in Pergamos embraced the marriage of church and state, but they embraced the Nicolaitans—the priests, pontiffs, and people who think they are infallible.

Revelation 2:16
Repent; or else I will come unto thee quickly, and will fight against them with the sword of my mouth.

How do you know who's who or what's what in a world so prone to the Pergamos tendency? Stick with the Word—with that which divides sin's mind-set from that which is right eternally (Hebrews 4:12).

Revelation 2:17 (a)
He that hath an ear, let him hear what the Spirit saith unto the churches; To him that overcometh . . .

Since the Pergamos mind-set was a mixture of political power and religious mystery, it is interesting to note the three things the Lord promised to those who overcome this tendency. . . .

Revelation 2:17 (b)
. . . will I give to eat of the hidden manna . . .

A young man in a hotel on the corner of Chicago's 5th and Broadway prayed, "Lord, I'm not going to leave this room until you empower me." Four days later, the Holy Spirit came upon him and D. L. Moody was empowered in such a way that he said, "Lord, if You don't back off, I'm going to die of ecstasy."

Revelation 2:17 (c)
. . . and will give him a white stone . . .

The secret ballot of John's day was a stone. A black stone was "no"; a white stone "yes." We still

refer to this practice when we say someone was "blackballed." Thus, Jesus was saying, "If you turn away from paganism, compromise, and the Pergamos mentality, I'll give you a white stone, which means you're not guilty; you're righteous; you're free."

Revelation 2:17 (d)
. . . and in the stone a new name written, which no man knoweth saving he that receiveth it.

"If you're looking for mystery," says the Lord, "don't look to worldly traditions. Look to Me, and I will give you hidden manna, a white stone, and a secret, pet name."

Watch out for the Pergamos mentality, gang. It's tempting to seek political change—to make our voice heard, to get our candidates in, to make our agenda happen. But history proves that strange things happen when church and politics get in bed together. If we think the key is to engage ourselves in political activism in the Name of Jesus Christ, we are in danger of committing the same historic error. Watch out. Keep your focus on the kingdom. Keep your passion for Jesus. Keep true to the Word, and God will bless you with the manna of salvation, the white stone of acquittal and approval, a new name of special affection.

On the island of Patmos, the Lord told John to write seven letters that were to be delivered to seven churches in Asia Minor. But evidently these churches did not receive or respond to the messages, for if you look at Asia Minor, or present-day Turkey, you see one of the most spiritually dark regions in the world. May the Lord help us and be merciful to us that we don't simply take in these messages without personally embracing them.

We now come to the fourth period—a period of time that begins in A.D. 600 and goes to the present. The following four churches—Thyatira, Sardis, Philadelphia, and Laodicea—all represent churches on the earth today. How do we know this? Because it is to these churches that Jesus talks about His coming and about the Tribulation.

Revelation 2:18 (a)
And unto the angel of the church in Thyatira write:

In Thyatira, we see a church emerge in the year A.D. 600, which will exert major influence on Martin Luther and the Reformers through A.D. 1500. This church still exists presently.

Revelation 2:18 (b)
These things saith the Son of God, who hath his eyes like unto a flame of fire, and his feet are like fine brass.

This is the only time in the entire Book of Revelation that Jesus identifies Himself as the Son of God rather than as the Son of Man. He chooses this reference because fire and brass speak of judgment.

Revelation 2:19
I know thy works, and charity, and service, and faith, and thy patience, and thy works; and the last to be more than the first.

Although Jesus is about to give a heavy word of judgment to the church at Thyatira, He first finds six areas in which to commend them.

Revelation 2:20
Notwithstanding I have a few things against thee, because thou sufferest that woman Jezebel, which calleth herself a prophetess, to teach and to seduce my servants to commit fornication, and to eat things sacrificed unto idols.

Based on the account in Acts 16, wherein we read that Paul encountered a group of women worshiping by a riverside, it is very possible that the church at Thyatira was founded by a woman. However, in addition to being founded by a woman, the church at Thyatira was floundering because of a woman. A woman who called herself a prophetess had persuaded people to eat food sacrificed to idols. Her influence upon the church was reminiscent of one of the most ungodly women in Israel's history. . . .

Jezebel, daughter of Ethbaal, king of the Zidonians, was given to King Ahab of Israel, in marriage. Since Ethbaal was the high priest of Ashtaroth—goddess of sensuality and fertility—Jezebel's background adversely influenced God's people. For example, finding Ahab weeping one day, Jezebel asked the reason. "Our power is growing and our influence is increasing," answered Ahab. "But a man named Naboth won't sell me his property."

"If you're the king, you should have it," answered Jezebel. "Leave it to me." So saying, she hired some men to falsely accuse Naboth of cursing God. And, following an inquisition and mock trial, Naboth was put to death (1 Kings 21).

Thus, Ahab and Jezebel inherited the land in a power play and an inquisition—a microcosm of the grander scale we will see as the story of church history unfolds.

Revelation 2:21
And I gave her space to repent of her fornication; and she repented not.

Keep in mind that fornication does not refer exclusively to physical relationships. It can refer, as it often does in the Old Testament, to a spiritual relationship with idolatry. This New Testament woman, following in the footsteps of her predecessor of old, was encouraging idolatry in the church at Thyatira.

Revelation 2:22
Behold, I will cast her into a bed, and them that commit adultery with her into great tribulation, except they repent of their deeds.

If the Jezebel spirit, prone to idolatry, is not rejected and turned from, this church—representing not only a local congregation but an epoch in church history—will go into the Tribulation period.

Revelation 2:23
And I will kill her children with death; and all the churches shall know that I am he which searcheth the reins and hearts: and I will give unto every one of you according to your works.

Not only Thyatira, but her offspring will also go through judgment and death as well.

Revelation 2:24
But unto you I say, and unto the rest in Thyatira, as many as have not this doctrine, and which have not known the depths of Satan, as they speak; I will put upon you none other burden.

The "depths of Satan" speaks of the esoteric mystery of the false, cultic Babylonian religion. "We alone know the mysteries, the deep things," said the Babylonian priests. But those who didn't buy their line were exempt from God's judgment.

Revelation 2:25
But that which ye have already hold fast till I come.

"Till I come" is the first promise of Jesus' return found in these letters to the seven churches. That's how we know this church goes on to Jesus' Second Coming.

Revelation 2:26, 27
And he that overcometh, and keepeth my works unto the end, to him will I give power over the nations: And he shall rule them with a rod of iron; as the vessels of a potter shall they be broken to shivers: even as I received of my Father.

"Those in Thyatira," says Jesus, "who have not bought into the seductive teachings of Jezebel will be given nations to rule." What was Jezebel's goal? Ahab and Jezebel united in marriage to increase their power by merging countries and joining religions. The result? As seen in the story of Naboth's vineyard, they wielded power and gobbled up land.

"If you're not a part of the Jezebel mentality, you will rule and reign with Me," Jesus says. "But if you try to do it in the spirit of Jezebel—through inquisition and manipulation—you'll be cast into a bed with other harlots in the great Tribulation."

Revelation 2:28
And I will give him the morning star.

The Old Testament image of Jesus is as the Sun of Righteousness (Malachi 4:2). Here in the New Testament, He's seen as the Morning Star.

Revelation 2:29
He that hath an ear, let him hear what the Spirit saith unto the churches.

I believe the church at Thyatira refers to the Catholic Church because "Thyatira" speaks of "continual sacrifice." You see, the Catholic Church traditionally, historically, and presently embraces the idea that in Communion, the elements are transformed into the literal, physical body of Christ in a process called transubstantiation. Thus, Catholic priests ensure that during the Mass, all of the wine is drunk and all of the bread eaten because they believe the elements are the actual body of Christ and, therefore, cannot be poured down the drain or thrown out. They think that the continual sacrifice of Christ is what really brings grace, or salvation—which is in direct contrast to what Jesus declared from the Cross when He cried, "It is finished" (John 19:30). The price is paid. The work is *done.*

During the Inquisition Period from A.D. 600–A.D. 1500, the Catholic Church amassed great amounts of wealth through political power plays. Consequently, the Catholic Church is extremely wealthy due to their land holdings and banking system. Please hear my heart, folks,

I'm not Catholic-bashing. This is history. For nine hundred years, vast amounts of money, property, and treasures were accumulated by keeping people in spiritual darkness. . . .

For example, if you were going to a party on Saturday evening, you could buy an indulgence from a priest, and thus be "preforgiven" of any ensuing sin. During this time, the "doctrine of purgatory" was also developed, which stated one could speed up the process of the purging of a deceased loved one's soul by buying candles and lighting them on his behalf.

And even as Naboth was killed, so were tens of millions of believers—including Hugh Latimer and John Hus, followers of John Wycliffe. What did Wycliffe want to do? He said it wasn't right that one had to go through a priest to get his sins forgiven. He said purgatory and the selling of indulgences were an abomination. He said the Mass being held in Latin—a language people couldn't understand—was nothing of what Jesus was about. As the fire that would burn them at the stake was lit, John Hus turned to Hugh Latimer and said, "Today they are igniting a candle that will never go out."

Presently there are excellent Catholic churches and wonderful Catholic pastors. There are those who have not bought into the deception of Jezebel. There are substantial segments of the Catholic Church who love Jesus Christ and are not into the hocus-pocus imagery and idolatry that keep people away from knowing the Lord personally.

On the other hand, much of the Catholic Church still has the Thyatira mentality—just as much of the Protestant Church is deader than a doornail, as we'll see in the next chapter.

What does this have to do with us? I think a whole lot because the error of Thyatira is possible today. We can also have idols. We can look to a church, a person, a program and say, "I'm going to put all my hope in that structure, or those guys"—no longer just loving the Lord, staying close to the Lord, getting our cues and directions from the Lord, but leaning on idols and structures and people.

Likewise, there can be those who imply that the common people can't understand the Bible because they have not attended seminary and therefore cannot grasp the intricacies of theology. Not true. While Greek and Hebrew can, indeed, help give illumination, the Book we hold in our hands was written for you and me, for the man and woman on the street. Don't let anyone tell you that you can't know God's will or His heart, His ways or His Word.

We must make sure we say no to idolatry, to systems of religion, to spiritual hierarchies. May God give us wisdom. May God help us to keep the focus on Jesus. May God give us the grace to keep it simple.

REVELATION IN THE CONGREGATION
A Topical Study of
Revelation 2—3

R ugged individualism is highly esteemed by our culture, but not by God. . . .

Of all God created, the only thing He declared "not good" was the fact that Adam was alone (Genesis 2:18).

When God called Abraham, His promise was not to make him a great man, but to make of him a great nation (Genesis 12:2).

Jesus taught us to pray, "*Our* Father . . ." (Matthew 6:9).

"Bear one another's burdens" Paul would write (see Galatians 6:2).

"Forsake not the assembling of yourselves together," the writer of Hebrews would echo (see Hebrews 10:25).

The Christian walk is all about togetherness, community. It's all about being a holy nation, a corporate entity because God is not into spiritual Lone Rangers.

Jesus Is Seen in and Through the Church

At the outset of this Book, John was not instructed to lock away in his private journal a record of that which he would see. On the contrary, he was to circulate it throughout the churches to whom he ministered. In other words, the vision is for the church in its entirety. Each part of the church has a certain revelation. And we don't see the whole picture unless we're in the congregation.

This troubles me. You see, my natural inclination is to go from chapter 1 to chapter 4. Why? The mysteries of the Lord revealed in chapter 1 intrigue me endlessly. And the glories of heaven revealed in chapter 4 delight me deeply. But I can't go from chapter 1 to 4 without going through chapters 2 and 3—which deal with the church, with people.

One day, I was reading about a lady who grew tired of ugly architecture, off-key singing, silly sermonizing, and hypocritical Christians dozing. She stopped going to church for thirty years. As I was reading, my dog Sam plopped himself outside my door. I invited him in, where he curled up at my feet, but after five or six minutes, he started scratching. Fleas. I immediately opened the door and cast him into outer darkness.

Listen, folks, problems come with people as sure as fleas come with dogs. But sibling rivalries, difficulties, pressures, and tensions are all part of the process of raising children into mature adults. And that's what the Father is doing. The lady who stopped attending church came to the realization in her mid-fifties that she had huge gaps in her understanding of God's nature that would have been filled had she remained in church.

Jesus Speaks to and Through the Church

Notice each of the seven letters in chapters 3 and 4 ends with the phrase: "He that hath ears to hear, let him hear what the Spirit says"—not to the mystic, the poet, or the isolated brother, but—"to the *churches*." Therefore, if you want to hear from the Lord, walk with the Lord, and know more about the Lord, you've got to put up with the fleas—people like me and the ones sitting next to you.

Although Jesus said, "If your right hand offends you, cut it off; if your eye offends you, pluck it out" (see Matthew 5:29), He didn't say, "If your ear offends you, cut it off." You can do without your hand. You can do without your eye. But you can't do without your ear because faith comes by hearing (Romans 10:17).

We have eyelids to shut out the world around us but not "earlids." God designed us so that we're always in a state of hearing. I can be asleep, but if someone comes into my house, it is my ears that open my eyes. This is also true in spiritual life. That's why the ear is so essential.

There's no better place to hear the Word of the Lord than the church. Why? Because as we go through the Word together, we receive positive affirmation, corrective exhortation, eternal motivation—as clearly seen in each of the seven letters.

If you work with people—as a mom or dad, schoolteacher or employer—these are the three vital elements of your job. Because no one is all bad, there is something to affirm in everyone. Because no one is all good, there is something to correct in everyone. And because we all get weary, there is the need of motivation for everyone.

A married couple wants to throw in the towel and call it quits. Saying, "Hang in there, and your marriage will get better," doesn't work, because maybe it won't. A teenager wants to compromise his walk. Saying, "Just wait, and you'll outgrow that desire," doesn't work, because maybe he won't. A young woman struggles with sickness. Saying, "Don't give up, you'll get better," doesn't work, because maybe she won't.

That's why the singular motivation Jesus used was heaven. "Stay the course. Keep the faith because of heaven," He said to those in Pergamos, in Thyatira, in Laodicea. "There's a tree of life up there, a crown for you, a new name."

As a dad, if I'm only helping my kids get through their teenage years, I'm a failure. If I'm only helping them be successful adults, I'm missing the point. If I'm only making sure they're set up for retirement, I've shirked my responsibility. What does it matter if our sons and daughters navigate life successfully—if they have a bank account, a retirement plan, or win an award—but are paupers in heaven eternally?

On the other hand, making the team or making money will shrink in importance if we're constantly talking to people about the bigger, overarching principle of eternity. Life is truly a vapor, gang. Heaven is where it's at. And it's in and through the church that we are reminded of this daily.

Affirmation, exhortation, motivation—nowhere else are these components so powerfully and beautifully balanced as, fleas notwithstanding, in the church.

3 Looking at church history, we now come to the Reformation. The age of Medieval Catholicism became so dark that when Sergius III became Pope (A.D. 904–A.D. 967), he ushered in what history calls the Rule of Harlots, during which time his mistress publicly accompanied him to the papal palace. Sergius' grandson, John X, continued this legacy until he was actually killed in his bedroom while committing adultery. Next came Benedict IX, who assumed the position of pope at twelve years of age through the practice of simony—selling positions within the church to the highest bidder. Benedict IX was so corrupt that the citizens of Rome drove him out of the city, replacing him with Clement III, who was appointed by Henry III. Clement III was not a Roman because, in the words of Henry III: "I appoint no one from Rome because no priest can be found in this city who is free from the pollution of fornication and simony."

Times were dark, diabolical, and depressing—which caused some stirring to take place in the hearts of good Catholic people. In 1330, a giant of the faith named John Wycliffe was born in England. An Oxford scholar and Catholic priest, he began to write about the need to get away from papal edicts and back to the Bible. He began to publicly question doctrines such as transubstantiation and continual sacrifice so much so that he was excommunicated by the powers in Rome. Although he himself was safe at Oxford, his disciples—men like John Hus and Hugh Latimer—were burned at the stake. But their deaths caused a spark of Reformation that would burn throughout England.

A glorious move took place, culminating in the year 1483 in Eiselben, Saxon Germany, when a coal miner and his wife gave birth to a baby boy they named Martin. "This boy is not to follow me into the mineshafts," said Martin's father. So Martin enrolled in the university to study law. While walking on campus one day, a thunderstorm arose unlike anything he had ever seen. Petrified, Martin cried out to St. Anne, the patron saint of coal miners, "If you save me from this lightning, I will become a monk." Spared, and true to his word, Martin Luther enrolled in seminary.

After two years, he earned his Doctorate, but the more he studied theology, the more he knew he could never be righteous enough to earn God's favor. To this end, he regularly beat himself, slept outside in freezing temperatures, and fasted for long periods. Still not experiencing the reality of God in his life, he decided to journey to Rome for an audience with the pope. On his way to Rome, however, he contracted a dangerous fever. While recovering in an Alpine monastery, one of the monks, sensing Luther's struggle, told him to read the Book of Habakkuk.

Why Habakkuk? Habakkuk was also one who wrestled with issues. Luther took his advice and when he came to the fourth verse of the second chapter, "The just shall live by faith"—he finally understood.

"That's it!" he cried. "If I'm going to be just, it's not because of what I do or who I am, but by faith in what God's done and who He is." However, upon arriving in Rome, with his heart full of excitement, Luther was shocked by the abuses and hypocrisy he found there.

Returning to Germany, he realized he had to take a stand. So in 1517, he nailed a parchment containing ninety-five theses challenging the pope to the university door in Wittenburg. Three and a half years later, Rome answered, "Retract or die." After burning this response, Luther was summoned to Rome. In 1521, the Diet of Worms was convened, at which the Church realized, that due to his popularity, they had a problem in Luther. "We're giving you a second opportunity to recant," they said—to which Martin Luther gave his classic reply: "Here I stand. I can do no other, so help me God."

Luther's stand gave rise to the birth of the Jesuits—an order dedicated to enforcing papal power no matter the cost. Meanwhile, the Reformation swept across Europe. Luther in Germany, Zwingli in Switzerland, Knox in Scotland all called for a return to the Bible—which strengthened the determination of the Jesuits to stand by the pope and stem the tide of what they perceived to be heresy. . . .

Of the four million people living in Bohemia in 1600, 80 percent were "Protest-ants"—sympathizers of the Reformation. Two years later, the population of Bohemia numbered a mere eight hundred thousand. Austria and Hungary were also early hotbeds of the Reformation.

Today, when we think of these countries, we think Catholic. Why? Because the worst bloodshed in history took place in the wake of the Reformation—even worse than the persecution of Christians under the Roman emperors and the holocaust of Nazi Germany under Hitler. This upheaval and bloodshed was so far-reaching that the seeds of the events in Bosnia and Northern Ireland today have their roots in those terrible, brutal times.

And understanding this context of the Reformation is vital to understanding the meaning of the text before us. . . .

Revelation 3:1 (a)
And unto the angel of the church in Sardis write:

Meaning "remnant," Sardis is a fitting name. Built on a one thousand-foot bluff, Sardis was an extremely wealthy city that seemed invincible—until the year 549 B.C. when Cyrus, conqueror of the city of Babylon, also conquered Sardis. Sardis was conquered again three hundred years later, a fact to which Jesus will allude. . . .

Revelation 3:1 (b)
These things saith he that hath the seven Spirits of God, and the seven stars . . .

As you read this section, you will notice that all of the references about Christ in chapter 1 are repeated again in chapters 2 and 3. We saw in verse 4 of chapter 1 that the "seven Spirits of God" refers to the seven-fold nature of the Holy Spirit as seen in Isaiah 11:2. Why would this description be repeated in conjunction with Sardis? Because, while most traditional mainline Protestants like Lutherans, Presbyterians, Wesleyans, Methodists, and Congregationalists champion everything from homosexuality to environmental issues—they are wary of the ministry of the Spirit.

Revelation 3:1 (c)
. . . I know thy works, that thou hast a name . . .

The word translated "name" is *onoma* in Greek, from which we get our word "denomination."

You can go out tonight and behold the beauty of the North Star. In reality, however, you don't know if it's there. Thirty-three light years away, it could have blown up thirty-two years ago, and we wouldn't know it until next year.

So, too, there are those who proudly say, "Look at this group, or that denomination." And the Lord says, "You're depending on reputation, on history, on what it used to be. You're resting in tradition, not relationship."

Revelation 3:1 (d)
. . . that thou livest, and art dead.

Although Jesus had much to correct in Thyatira, He commended them in verse 19 for their works and charity, service, faith, and patience. But here at Sardis, He simply says, "You're dead."

Revelation 3:2 (a)
Be watchful . . .

Why should Sardis be watchful? Because their city fell when they weren't watching. So, too, spiritually, they were saying, "We're on solid ground. No one's going to knock us down."

"You guys in Sardis should know better than that," Jesus says. "Your own history should tell you the results of being haughty and arrogant, of resting in a false sense of security."

Revelation 3:2 (b), 3
. . . and strengthen the things which remain, that are ready to die: for I have not found thy works perfect before God. Remember therefore how thou hast received and heard, and hold fast, and repent.

What was received initially? The Bible—from Wycliffe, Calvin, Knox, Luther. "Remember how it was received initially," Jesus is pleading. "And repent for how far you've come from that foundation."

Tragically, the Jesus Project—the group of theologians who concluded that "It is more blessed to give than to receive" is the only verifiable phrase uttered by Jesus—is comprised of mainline Protestants. And their sin is greater in God's economy than the abuses of the Roman Church with her bloodshed and immorality because they have bought into liberal theology. What's worse, they are undermining people's beliefs by muddying even the clearest statements of Christ.

Revelation 3:3
If therefore thou shalt not watch, I will come on thee as a thief, and thou shalt not know what hour I will come upon thee.

Jesus says, "If you don't get back to basics, I'm going to come to you as a thief."

This is where mainline denominationalism increasingly finds itself. Proponents of such do not believe in a Rapture, or even a Millennium. They teach that the promises of the kingdom, the sayings of Isaiah, the teachings of Revelation are simply allegorical. "Don't look for the Rapture," they say, "and don't look for a real kingdom established on earth." Thus, they will be totally caught off guard by Jesus' return.

Revelation 3:4, 5 (a)
Thou hast a few names even in Sardis which have not defiled their garments; and they shall walk with me in white: for they are worthy. He that overcometh, the same shall be clothed in white raiment . . .

In other words, those in Sardis—or in this epoch of church history that began in A.D. 1500 and goes on until the kingdom comes—who have stayed true to the Word will be overcomers.

Revelation 3:5 (b)
. . . and I will not blot out his name out of the book of life, but I will confess his name before my Father, and before his angels.

When someone comes to me broken-hearted about his sin, I take him to John 10:28, wherein Jesus says we are eternally secure in His hand, to Romans 8:38, 39 where we read that nothing can separate us from the love of God, and to 2 Timothy 1:12, where we are reminded that He is able to *keep* that which is committed to Him.

But when someone comes to me and says, "I don't care what you think. I'm going to do this anyway. It's none of your business," I take him to a different set of Scriptures—to 1 Corinthians 6:9, 10; Galatians 5:19–21; Ephesians 5:3–5; and here to Revelation 3:5—because if there's no repentance month after year after decade, his salvation is not on very solid ground.

Revelation 3:6
He that hath an ear, let him hear what the Spirit saith unto the churches.

Every generation needs its own Reformation, its own renewal, its own revival. It's not enough for a generation to hear about how it was in their parents' day. The Jesus Movement of the '60s was wonderful—but the days to come are going to be grander still because God's heart is to go from glory to greater glory whenever we get out of the way and don't fall prey to the Sardis Syndrome.

Revelation 3:7 (a)
And to the angel of the church in Philadelphia write:

In this next phase of church history, we see a stirring in the dead denominationalism that had strayed from the simplicity of the gospel.

Two books sat in the London shop of a young cobbler: a well-worn Bible and Captain Cook's journal. As the days went by, the cobbler found himself losing interest in working on the soles of shoes, and caring more about the souls of people in far regions. So deep was the passion that stirred within him that on May 31, 1793, he walked into the little Protestant church he attended and said, "Could I please share?" Allowed to speak a word, he read Isaiah 54:2, 3. "We must lengthen the cords; we must strengthen the stakes," he preached passionately. "We must include others who have never heard. I want to go. Send me to India."

His request stunned his congregation. After all, it had been one thousand years since anyone had launched a foreign missionary endeavor. But their surprise didn't stop Carey's congregation from sending him to India. In his first ten years, he became fluent in twelve languages. One of his works, the

Bible he translated in Sanskrit, is still used to this day.

William Carey goes down in history as the father of the modern missionary movement—as suddenly the church awoke from her lethargy. Carey set the example that one doesn't have to be skilled, gifted, or special to be used in the kingdom. God is simply looking for men who are willing to go.

The church at Philadelphia speaks of this age of church history beginning in the 1800s, for it was through men like Carey in India and Hudson Taylor in China, D. L. Moody in America and C. H. Spurgeon in London that evangelism was taking place and missionaries were being sent out.

The letter to Philadelphia is one of only two letters of the seven in which Jesus has nothing critical to say. Why? Perhaps it is because the Philadelphians were involved in evangelism. They were loving the lost—and love covers a multitude of sins (1 Peter 4:8).

There are three Greek words for love. *Eros* is erotic or sensual love. *Phileo* is brotherly love. *Agape* is God's love. The city of Philadelphia was founded in 189 B.C. by a man named Eumanes II. When he died, he was succeeded by his younger brother, Attalus II, who named buildings after his older brother, minted coins bearing his brother's image, and talked about his brother constantly. Consequently, the people of the town began to call this place Philo-delphia, or the city of brotherly love.

Nothing is coincidental in the Scriptures. I believe it is true that every book of the Bible is inspired. And every chapter of every book is inspired. And every verse of every chapter is inspired. And every word of every verse is inspired. And every letter of every word is inspired. In fact, I agree with the Rabbis that every space between every word is inspired! Thus, it is no surprise that Philadelphia, the city of brotherly love is the center of evangelism.

Revelation 3:7 (b)
These things saith he that is holy, he that is true, he that hath the key of David . . .

In chapter 1, we read that Jesus holds the keys of hell and death (1:18). To this missionary church, He says He holds an additional key: the key of David—which takes one back to the key of David spoken of in Isaiah 22, wherein we read of a man named Shebna, who was the treasurer in the kingdom of Judah during the reign of Hezekiah. After Shebna used temple money to purchase a sepulcher and chariots for himself, Isaiah

came on the scene and said, "What are you doing? You had opportunity, but you abused it." So the key to the treasury was taken from off Shebna's shoulder, where the key was traditionally worn, and given to a godly man who wore it wisely. Isaiah went on to speak of this one who used the keys properly as being "fastened like a nail," or steadfast and dependable. Of course, we think of another who was fastened—not *like* a nail, but *with* a nail. We think of another who perfectly carried the key of the government upon His shoulder (Isaiah 9:6). We think of Jesus.

Revelation 3:7 (c)–8 (a)
. . . he that openeth, and no man shutteth; and shutteth, and no man openeth; I know thy works: behold, I have set before thee an open door, and no man can shut it . . .

Jesus is the One who opened the doors for William Carey in India, Hudson Taylor in China, for us in the United States, in Mexico, in Honduras, in Vanuatu. But He also shuts doors that can't be opened. If a man continually says, "No," to the Lord, there will come a time when he will be unable to say, "Yes"—at which point he's locked in to his eternal decision and destruction.

Revelation 3:8 (b)
. . . for thou hast a little strength . . .

There are those who teach that in the last days there will be a major manifestation of the sons of God; that miracles will happen, wherein every sick person is healed and glorious things will occur. But I believe that's hype and hyperbole. Yes, there are some good things happening. But it's the time of little strength. Jesus does not say this condemningly. He merely says that's the way it is during the age of Philadelphia. Thus, it's not an indictment, but rather an honest assessment of the "last days" church at Philadelphia.

Revelation 3:8 (c)
. . . and hast kept my word . . .

Besides having little strength, the "last days" church at Philadelphia is a church that has returned to the Word, has a desire for the Word and studies the Scriptures constantly.

Revelation 3:8 (d)
. . . and hast not denied my name.

The idea here is "You have not denied My deity. You recognize I am who I claim to be—not just an interesting teacher, not just a model of how to live successfully, of how to have prosperity, or of how to be happy. I am the Christ."

Revelation 3:9
Behold, I will make them of the synagogue of Satan, which say they are Jews, and are not, but do lie; behold, I will make them to come and worship before thy feet, and to know that I have loved thee.

In this end-times church there is a synagogue of Satan—those who say they are Jews but aren't. Who are these people? In John's day, the reference would have been to the Jews who persecuted believers. Jesus said previously and reiterates here, "They're not true Jews, any more than Christians who persecute Jews are true Christians." In our day, I believe the reference is to the growing number of people in the Christian community who say, "Because God is through with the Jew, *we* are Israel."

In *The Road to the Holocaust,* Hal Lindsey proves that the deaths of six million Jews did not begin with the Third Reich. They began one hundred years earlier, when Bible teachers began to teach that God is through with the Jew. Anti-Semitism is always the mark of a people who fail to read their Bibles, for in Romans 9—11 God declares He is not through with Israel.

There are three categories of people in the Bible: Jews, Gentiles, and the church. Who makes up the church? Former Jews and former Gentiles. This is important to understand because we need to realize that the reason for the Tribulation is the fact that God is not through with Israel.

The Rapture is when Jesus comes to get us—but the Second Coming is when Jesus comes back to rescue Israel. May God help us to never lose our understanding of Israel's importance.

Revelation 3:10 (a)
Because thou hast kept the word of my patience . . .

What is the word of His patience? In 2 Thessalonians 3:5, we are told that God is establishing us in the patience of waiting for Jesus Christ. I point this out because the church at Philadelphia is the church interested in Bible prophecy. Although in the first two centuries, the topics of Jesus' Second Coming and the Rapture of the church were central themes of preaching and writing, Bible prophecy was lost as an interest in the church until the 1800s because people said, "It's impossible

for a nation to come back from the dead. "It's unthinkable that the Jewish people could have a national identity again. It's gotta be an allegory. Why would the Middle East be the focal point of a battle? Who cares about the Middle East?" We now understand why that region of the world is so strategic: oil. Economically, militarily, politically, the attention of the whole world is constantly focused on the Middle East.

Revelation 3:10 (b)
. . . I also will keep thee from the hour of temptation . . .

The Greek word translated "from" is *ek*, which means "out of." In other words, Jesus says, "You at Philadelphia, you of little strength, you've kept My Word and you haven't denied My Name. You've gone through the open door, and you've been patiently awaiting My coming. Because of this, I will take you out of the time period of temptation yet to come."

Revelation 3:10 (c)
. . . which shall come upon all the world, to try them that dwell upon the earth.

I believe the church is the group of people who will be taken out of the hour of temptation that shall come upon all the world. This is not simply local persecution in Philadelphia, but a time of difficulty that encompasses the entire globe. And there's only one event that fits this description: the Tribulation.

For topical study of Revelation 3:10 entitled "The Rapture Controversy," turn to page 1687.

Revelation 3:11 (a)
Behold, I come quickly . . .

Tachu, the Greek word translated "quickly," actually means "suddenly." Thus, the Lord could come at any moment. Only we who believe in a pre-Tribulation Rapture can say, "It could be today." Mid- and post-Tribulationists, on the other hand, have no recourse but to say, "The Lord can't come back today because the Tribulation hasn't begun yet."

But we say, "It could be today." And such is the throbbing heartbeat of Bible prophecy.

Revelation 3:11 (b)
. . . hold that fast which thou hast, that no man take thy crown.

This is intriguing. "I'm coming suddenly," Jesus says, "so hold fast in order that you don't lose your crown."

"Crown?" you say. "I don't have one yet. What does this mean?"

I believe the answer is found in 1 Thessalonians 2:19, 20, where Paul identifies the crown as people—people with whom we've shared, people for whom you've prayed. "Stay with them," says Jesus. "Keep praying for them. Don't give up on them."

Revelation 3:12 (a)
Him that overcometh will I make a pillar in the temple of my God, and he shall go no more out . . .

"Hold fast to your crown, look for My coming, and you will be planted firmly as a pillar in My kingdom," says Jesus.

Revelation 3:12 (b)
. . . and I will write upon him the name of my God . . .

The best part about making the team was that I got to wear the jacket. You see, the Hornets were the #1 Pop Warner football team in the nation five years out of six. So the word "Hornets" emblazoned across the jacket I wore every day to fifth grade made me feel like I had arrived—regardless of the fact that the year I played as third-string quarterback our record was two wins, seven losses. Even though I was terrible and our team stunk, I still got to wear the jacket.

So, too, the Lord says, "I'm going to put the name of My Father on your jacket. His will be the Name you wear for eternity."

Revelation 3:12 (c)
. . . and the name of the city of my God, which is new Jerusalem, which cometh down out of heaven from my God . . .

You're not only going to have the glory of God emblazoned upon you, but you're going to have the government of God given to you. The New Jerusalem is going to make any city on this planet look insignificant. And we will be residents therein.

Revelation 3:12 (d)
. . . and I will write upon him my new name.

Proverbs 25:2 says it is the glory of God to conceal or to hide His name, but the honor of kings to search it out. Because we are a nation of kings and priests (Revelation 1:6), we will be those who search out His name. It's as if the Lord is saying,

"There are aspects of who I am of which you have no idea on this earth, for it will take eternity for you to perceive and enjoy the aspects of My being. It's My glory to conceal a thing. It's your privilege to search it out."

When we get to heaven, we're truly going to be the bride of Christ. I pity our poor brides, guys, because as time goes on, it must be disappointing, disheartening, disillusioning, and depressing to them to see our flaws become ever more evident. Not so with God. Unlike any relationship on earth, this one will only produce greater and greater ecstasy, greater and greater delight as we explore the nooks and crannies of His nature for all eternity.

Revelation 3:13
He that hath an ear, let him hear what the Spirit saith unto the churches.

Brotherly love, evangelism, holding fast are all characteristics of this church at Philadelphia—which is perhaps best typified by Francis of Assisi when he said, "Witness wherever you go, and if absolutely necessary, use words." Truly, evangelism is directly connected to love.

Revelation 3:14 (a)
And unto the angel of the church of the Laodiceans write:

Six miles south of Philadelphia, the city of Laodicea was the banking center of the region. Consequently, it had ample money to spend on entertainment—as evidenced by the thirty thousand-seat amphitheatre whose ruins still stand.

In addition, Laodicea was known throughout history as being very tricky politically because the city was built in a way that it could not defend itself militarily—a very unusual trait for an ancient city. The only way Laodicea could survive was by making compromises with her enemies.

Finally, even as Aristotle noted, Laodicea was known for the eye salve manufactured there, highly valued in the ancient world. All of these factors figure in to what Jesus will say to this group.

Take note that the address is not to the church *at* Laodicea, but to the church *of* the Laodiceans. The Greek word *laos*, from which we get our word "laity," means "people." *Diece* means "decision" or "rule." Thus, the church of the Laodiceans was directed by the people rather than guided by the Lord. The Laodicean mentality remains. I'm amazed at the influential churches whose services regularly include interviews with celebrities who are not living godly lives, who have not taken a stand for Jesus Christ, who have little more than positive stories to share— churches where people rule; wherein "Smile, be happy," has replaced the message of repentance.

Revelation 3:14 (b)
These things saith the Amen . . .

Why does Jesus refer to Himself as "the Amen"? "Amen" meaning "so be it," Jesus identifies Himself to this group so prone to compromise, saying, "There is certainty. It's Me."

Revelation 3:14 (c)
. . . the faithful and true witness . . .

The Greek word translated "witness" is *martus,* from which we get our word "martyr." What is a witness? One who lives so much like Jesus Christ and is so in love with Jesus Christ that he ends up being crucified even as Jesus Christ was crucified. The Bible puts it this way: Yea, all those who live godly in Christ Jesus shall suffer persecution (2 Timothy 3:12).

"Don't talk about suffering," the Laodicean would say. "We just want to be positive and happy." You'll never hear a message about suffering, persecution, or martyrdom in a Laodicean church. They don't want to think about those things. The truth, however, is that if we're living godly, we're going to get nailed. No question.

Revelation 3:14 (d)
. . . the beginning of the creation of God.

Cultists often use this verse to say that Jesus is created and therefore not coequal with the Father. But the Greek word translated "beginning" is *arche,* which actually means "the origin." You see, God the Father created all things through the Son (Colossians 1:16) by the power of the Spirit (Genesis 1:2). In the last days, the question is, and will continue to be, "Who is the Creator?" Evolution being part of the end-time deception, it is no surprise that in the church of the Laodiceans there will be questions concerning creation.

Revelation 3:15, 16
I know thy works, that thou art neither cold nor hot: I would thou wert cold or hot. So then because thou art lukewarm, and neither cold nor hot, I will spue thee out of my mouth.

In Laodicea's sister city of Hieropolis were hot springs—from which the present-day Turkish government is trying to extract geo-thermal power. To take advantage of this, an aqueduct was constructed that carried the hot water from Hieropolis through Laodicea and on to Colossae. In theory, it was a good idea. But in reality, by the time the water reached Laodicea, it was lukewarm. Thus, as lukewarm water flowed through their city, the Laodiceans would know hot water was useful, cold water was refreshing, but lukewarm water was not good for much.

The Lord says the same thing about His people. "If you're hot, I can use you. If you're cold, I can deal with you. But if you're lukewarm, you'll neither be hot enough to use nor cold enough to correct."

Revelation 3:17
Because thou sayest, I am rich, and increased with goods, and have need of nothing; and knowest not that thou art wretched, and miserable, and poor, and blind, and naked.

To this Laodicean church, which wasn't talking about the reality of sin, the need for repentance, or the Cross of Christ; which didn't speak of witnessing, standing, and living for eternity, Jesus said, "You think you're rich—but you're impoverished. You think you're doing well, but you're miserable."

Revelation 3:18 (a)
I counsel thee to buy of me gold tried in the fire, that thou mayest be rich . . .

In Bible days, smelters would take the gold brought in from the mines and heat it by fire until it liquefied. After stirring it until the impurities were burned out, they would know the process was complete when the smelter could look into the pot of liquid gold and see the reflection of his own face. Because Jesus is the Master Smelter, He uses heat as well. So, to these people who were impure, carnal, vacillating, and lukewarm, He says, "Get into the fire. Get into the battle. Engage yourself like you once did in ministry."

Before the Battle of Trafalgar, knowing this particular battle would determine the fate of Europe, Lord Nelson assembled his men and said, "In the event you cannot see or read the signals in the heat of battle, know this: No captain in this fleet can do wrong if he places his ship alongside that of an enemy."

I like that! "Captains, if you can't read my signals, and you don't know what to do, the answer is very simple: Engage in battle the first enemy you can find." So, too, when you feel yourself becoming complacent, get involved in service, in sharing, in ministry. Determine in your heart to engage yourself once more in the fire of ministry—not because God wants to watch you burn, but because He wants to warm your heart and get you going again.

Revelation 3:18 (b)
... and white raiment, that thou mayest be clothed, and that the shame of thy nakedness do not appear ...

The Laodiceans were not only to get back into the race, but also to get back to grace. Throughout Scripture, white raiment speaks of the robe of righteousness (Isaiah 61:10) given to those who are in Christ. The Laodiceans were known for a unique kind of wool taken from black sheep, yet the Lord says to them, "You might be fashion plates with your black garments, but you need garments of *white*—righteous garments, the covering of My grace."

Revelation 3:18 (c)
... and anoint thine eyes with eyesalve, that thou mayest see.

The same Jesus who says, "Anoint your eyes with eye salve," is the One who put mud in the blind man's eyes in John 9. The way of the Great Physician is to allow irritation to produce illumination. "You're seeing everything in a carnal way," He says, "and you need to humble yourself before Me and deal with the mud."
"Ouch," we say. "That mud hurts." But in reality, there must be an awareness of the problems in our hearts and the trouble in our souls before we can see.
"Search me, O God," cried David, "and see if there be any wicked way in me" (see Psalm 139:23, 24). Listen, if you're feeling Laodicean, if you feel lukewarm, you need to ask the Great Physician to search you, for that will be the eye salve that will allow you to see clearly. How long has it been, dear saint, since you've been on your face before the Lord saying, "Search me concerning the words on my lips, the bitterness in my heart, and the thoughts on my mind"?
Truly, confession precedes vision as surely as irritation precedes illumination.

Revelation 3:19
As many as I love, I rebuke and chasten: be zealous therefore, and repent.

If you feel miserable and blind, wretched and troubled, the Lord would say to you, "Terrific. This just proves to you conclusively how much I love you." A coach will always be the harshest on those in whom he sees the most promise. If he

sees you as a benchwarmer, he'll never criticize you. But if you have potential, he'll have a great deal to say to you.

For topical study of Revelation 3:20 entitled "Jesus at the Door," turn to page 1691.

Revelation 3:20 (a)
Behold, I stand at the door, and knock: if any man hear my voice, and open the door, I will come in to him ...

While this verse has been used as a powerful illustration of the invitation for personal salvation, Jesus is primarily speaking to the church. Tragically, some people go to church all their lives but never hear a message on repentance, on the fact that there is sin, or that there is a hell. To such a church, Jesus says, "I love you and care about you. That's why I give this invitation to you."

Revelation 3:20 (b)
... and will sup with him, and he with me.

In every account of Christ's post-resurrection appearances He's eating. I like that! That's where we really find the answer to our Laodicean condition—at His table. As Solomon tells us in Ecclesiastes 3, there's a season for everything— a time to weep and a time to rejoice. The Lord's table has a unique way of bringing us into the full orb of just such diverse emotional reactions and responses because we leave saying, "I'm sobered by my sin, yet elated by the fact that it's washed away."

Revelation 3:21
To him that overcometh will I grant to sit with me in my throne, even as I also overcame, and am set down with my Father in his throne.

"Open your heart to Me," Jesus would say, "and I'll open heaven to you."

Revelation 3:22
He that hath an ear, let him hear what the Spirit saith unto the churches.

It's one thing to have Jesus as a Model or a Mascot. That's what they were doing at Laodicea. They were "good Christians." But Jesus is not to be a Model or a Mascot. He is to be our Master. That's what He was asking of that congregation. And that's what He's asking of you and me.
May this church not be a place that is popu-

lar—full of people who have good mottoes and good intentions. May it be a place where we realize that, although we're sinners who have failed miserably, God has provided Jesus Christ, and He will come in to our hearts to rule and reign within if we simply open the door.

THE RAPTURE CONTROVERSY
A Topical Study of
Revelation 3:10

The Book of Acts tells us the Berean believers were more noble than their neighbors in Thessalonica because the Bereans searched the Scriptures to validate what Paul taught them (17:11). So, too, I want our church family to be able to say, "Here's *why* we believe what we do." To this end, I would like to submit to you thirteen reasons why I believe the church will be raptured before the Tribulation.

"Well, I have friends who say the church will go through the Tribulation. Why get all concerned about this issue?" you might say. My answer is because I believe one's view on Bible prophecy and the timing of the Rapture will affect the way one lives out his faith. Why does the debate continue concerning the timing of this event? I believe it is due to misunderstanding in three areas:

The Elect

> For then shall be great tribulation, such as was not since the beginning of the world to this time, no, nor ever shall be. And except those days should be shortened, there should no flesh be saved: but for the elect's sake those days shall be shortened.
> Matthew 24:21, 22

On the basis of this verse, people say "Aha! Here we see the elect in the Tribulation"—failing to realize that the term "elect" refers to three groups of people: Christians (Colossians 3:12), Israel (Isaiah 45:4), and those who will be saved in the Tribulation (Matthew 24:21, 22).

To which of the elect does Jesus refer in Matthew 24:21? I believe the answer lies in the verse preceding it. . . .

> But pray ye that your flight be not in the winter, neither on the sabbath day.
> Matthew 24:20

Even to this day, transportation in Israel is shut down on the Sabbath. Since the Sabbath means nothing to Gentile nations, the application to Israel is clear.

The Trumpets

In a moment, in the twinkling of an eye, at the last trump: for the trumpet shall
sound, and the dead shall be raised incorruptible, and we shall be changed.

1 Corinthians 15:52

On the basis of this verse, people say, "Aha! According to Revelation 11, the seventh, or last trump signaling the Rapture, will take place midway through the Tribulation." But wait a minute. The seventh trumpet of Revelation 11 is sounded by angels, whereas 1 Thessalonians 4:16 makes it clear that the last trump is sounded by God.

In Exodus 19, God sounded the first trump when the Jews were gathered at the foot of Mount Sinai to hear the law. The last trump will sound when the church is gathered to meet the Lord in the air and taken to heaven. Thus, the Jews hear the first trump; the church hears the last. The following thirteen reasons are why I believe this trump of God will sound before the Tribulation. . . .

1. The doctrine is to be a comforting one (1 Thessalonians 4:18). The belief that the Rapture happens after or in the middle of the Tribulation is anything but comforting because it means believers must endure unbelievable agony before they are taken to heaven.

2. The Tribulation is the outpouring of the wrath of the Lamb—and God has not appointed us to wrath (1 Thessalonians 5:9–11). The wrath that should have been hurled at you and poured out on me was absorbed by our Hero, our Lord, our Savior on the Cross of Calvary.

3. Rapture before the Tribulation is illustrated in Genesis 19, where we see angels delivering Lot and his family before the destruction of Sodom. How do I know this is a picture of the Rapture? Because in reference to this, Peter writes, "The Lord knoweth how to deliver the godly out of temptations" (2 Peter 2:9). The word translated "temptations" is the same word translated "tribulation."

4. Rapture before the Tribulation is illustrated in Enoch, who was taken to heaven prior to the Flood (Genesis 5:24). "Wrong analogy," some protest. "The correct picture is Noah who went through the tribulation of the Flood." But wait a minute. Noah is not a picture of the church, but of Israel, who will indeed go through the Tribulation—and will at last come to Jesus as a result.

5. Rapture before the Tribulation is illustrated in Daniel 3. When Shadrach, Meshach, and Abed-nego refused to worship Nebuchadnezzar, they were thrown into a fiery furnace. But where was their friend Daniel? Either he did, indeed, bow to Nebuchadnezzar—which is completely contrary to the rest of the book—or, his omission is in itself a picture of the Rapture. Bible scholars believe that, very likely, he was away on official business as an emissary. All we know with certainty, however, is that he was taken out of the scene.

6. Jesus told us to pray that we would be raptured before the Tribulation. In

speaking of the Tribulation in His Olivet Discourse, Jesus said, "Watch and pray always that you may be accounted worthy to escape all these things" (see Luke 21:36). How are we accounted worthy? One way: We are worthy because of what Jesus did for us on the Cross of Calvary.

7. Pre-Tribulation Rapture makes sense historically and scripturally. In accordance with Jewish custom, when a man came of age to marry, he would add a room on to his father's house for himself and his bride. When the addition was complete, and when the father gave the go-ahead, a trumpet would sound, and the bridegroom would go to meet his bride. Following the wedding ceremony, the bridegroom would take his bride to his father's house, where they would be tucked away for seven days in the newly completed "bridal suite." At the end of seven days, the bridegroom would come out with his bride and introduce her to the community.

That's exactly what's going to happen with us. Jesus, our Bridegroom, is preparing a place for us in heaven, His Father's house (John 14:2). At the appointed time known only by the Father, a trumpet will sound and Jesus will meet us, His bride, in the air to escort us up to the "Bridal Suite" He has prepared for us. We will remain with Him in heaven for seven years before we are presented to the world, where we will rule and reign with Him.

8. Pre-Tribulation Rapture follows the outline of the Book of Revelation. If you don't embrace a Pre-Tribulation view, your understanding of Revelation becomes as twisted as a pretzel because you've got to put chapters 4 and 5 after chapter 11, if you hold to a Mid-Tribulation stance; after chapter 19 if you take a Post-Tribulation point of view. Only a Pre-Tribulation placement of the Rapture allows for a consistent flow of the Book of Revelation.

9. Pre-Tribulation Rapture allows for the conditional aspect of the Tribulation. To the church at Thyatira, Jesus said, "If you don't repent, you will experience Tribulation" (see Revelation 2:22). If the Rapture won't occur until after the Tribulation, what would be the reason for this warning of Jesus?

"Well, didn't Jesus say in this world we would have tribulation?" you ask.

Yes, but the crushing the believer goes through in the world is from Satan. The Tribulation of chapters 6—19, on the other hand, is from God as He pours out His wrath on a Christ-rejecting world. Folks, God will not allow anyone to get hit from both sides. If we experience tribulation in the world because of our faith, we will not experience the Tribulation of those who have none.

10. Pre-Tribulation Rapture allows for the unknown time of the Lord's return. According to Daniel's prophecy, three and a half biblical years (a Biblical year being three hundred sixty days) from the day Antichrist enters the temple and demands worship midway through the Tribulation, the Lord will return. Consequently, if believers were on earth during the Tribulation, they would be able to predict the exact time of the Second Coming—three and a half biblical years, or forty-two months, or one thousand two hundred sixty days after Antichrist enters the temple. The

problem is, 1 Thessalonians 5:2 and Matthew 24:36 make it clear that no one knows the hour of His coming. Therefore, it follows that believers must be absent at this time.

11. The Tribulation is unnecessary for the church. Referred to as the time of Jacob's trouble, the Tribulation targets Israel, for through it she will be awakened and at last see Jesus as the Messiah (Deuteronomy 4:29, 30). The promises God made to Abraham and to the Jewish people have not been forgotten, gang. God will work with Israel in the days of the Tribulation. He will make Himself known to them—and they shall indeed be saved.

12. Pre-Tribulation Rapture squares with the prophecy of Daniel. At the end of Daniel 9, Daniel was given the timetable for all of Jewish history in units of *heptads,* or weeks. It is clear from this all-important passage of Scripture that the sixty-nine weeks of Daniel refer to the time between the commandment to rebuild the temple, given in 445 B.C. by Artaxerxes, and the coming of Messiah, fulfilled perfectly on Palm Sunday when Jesus rode into Jerusalem on the back of a donkey. But Daniel was also told, "Seventy weeks are determined upon Israel." To what does the seventieth week of Daniel refer? To the Tribulation. You see, the seventy weeks of Daniel refer to Israel. The church was not present for the first sixty-nine weeks. And the seventieth week doesn't begin until after the church is raptured. In other words, if the church was not present in the first sixty-nine weeks, why would she be present in the last week? She won't. She'll be in heaven.

Those are twelve reasons I believe the Rapture will occur before the Tribulation. But the most important one is the following:

A Pre-Tribulation Rapture viewpoint makes one seek first the kingdom. "Who then is a faithful and wise servant, whom his lord hath made ruler over his household, to give them meat in due season? Blessed is that servant, whom his lord when he cometh shall find so doing" (Matthew 24:45, 46). Who is the one who will have authority and purpose in eternity? He who is watching for Jesus' coming. But this is impossible for those who believe the Tribulation precedes the Rapture because they must first watch for Antichrist, then the rebuilding of the temple, and finally the Abomination of Desolation when Antichrist demands to be worshiped as God.

Two factors kept the early church on fire: the empowering of the Holy Ghost and the belief that Jesus would return during their lifetime. "But He didn't come back in their day," you say. And you're right—but do you think those early believers are in heaven now, saying, "We didn't get bogged down in materialism or trivial pursuits. We sought the Lord. We witnessed fervently. We lived for the kingdom. If only we knew He wasn't coming, we could have played more racquetball"? No! They're ecstatic that they chose to do what Jesus says to do in every generation—to watch, to be ready, to live for His coming.

Whether or not you believe in a pre-Tribulation Rapture will not affect where you'll ultimately end up. If you're a believer, you'll be in heaven no matter what position you hold. But your viewpoint concerning the Rapture very definitely affects how you live your life this side of eternity. If you do not believe in a pre-Tribulation Rapture, you cannot look for Jesus Christ because, according to your eschatological viewpoint, Antichrist must appear first. Therefore, you find yourself scanning the news, checking out current events, watching the global scene for Antichrist rather than for Jesus. And this puts believers in a "survivalist" mentality. "We're going through the Tribulation," they say. "We better get ready." Is this what Jesus meant? Does He want us storing gold and guns? Or does He want us living every day in hopeful anticipation that today could be the day we go to heaven?

"I want you looking for Jesus every day," John said, "because he who has the hope of the imminent, sudden appearing of Christ and the Rapture of the church purifies himself" (see 1 John 3:3). That is why I believe your view on the Rapture is of utmost importance. Live in constant expectancy of Jesus' return, gang. Be watching and be ready.

JESUS AT THE DOOR
A Topical Study of
Revelation 3:20

No doubt you've seen the classic picture by Holman Hunt of Jesus knocking on a door. Now hanging in St. Paul's Cathedral in London, upon its first unveiling, it is said that a certain critic said, "You've made a mistake, Mr. Hunt. There's no handle on the door."

"That was intentional," the artist is said to have replied. "The door opens only from the inside."

If this story is true, Holman Hunt was right, for it's up to you and me to let the Lord into our lives. He won't kick the door down. He won't force His way into our hearts.

Yet although we use this verse as a call to individual salvation, it was actually written to a self-satisfied congregation.

Is Jesus talking to people meeting in His Name who are supposed to be Christians? Yes. And is He saying He's on the outside and wants to come in? Yep.

Well, how does one get to the point where the Lord is on the outside? How does a church get to the place where it thinks it's doing fine but is spiritually bankrupt? If it happened at Laodicea, can it happen to us?

Because Scripture is the best interpreter of Scripture, turn with me to the Song of Solomon for the answer. The story is of a king, a bridegroom in love with his new bride. After experiencing intimacy with her, the next morning finds him outside her door. . . .

> *My beloved spake, and said unto me, Rise up, my love, my fair one, and come away. For, lo, the winter is past, the rain is over and gone; the flowers appear on the earth; the time of the singing of birds is come, and the voice of the turtle is heard in our land; the fig tree putteth forth her green figs, and the vines with the tender grape give a good smell. Arise, my love, my fair one, and come away. O my dove, that art in the clefts of the rock, in the secret places of the stairs, let me see thy countenance, let me hear thy voice; for sweet is thy voice, and thy countenance is comely. Take us the foxes, the little foxes, that spoil the vines: for our vines have tender grapes.*   Song of Solomon 2:10–15

"Come away with me," says the bridegroom. "The rain has stopped. The birds are singing. I want to hear your voice. I long to see your countenance. Watch out for the little foxes—the subtle little temptations that could hinder our love."

After hearing his invitation and warning, the bride responds. . . .

> *My beloved is mine, and I am his: he feedeth among the lilies. Until the day break, and the shadows flee away, turn, my beloved, and be thou like a roe or a young hart upon the mountains of Bether.*   Song of Solomon 2:16, 17

Here is the bridegroom outside the door, saying, "Honey, come on. It's a glorious morning. I want to take you to new heights, to hear wonderful songs, to be on guard against the little foxes."

And what does his bride say?

"It's too early. You go play on the hills, and I'll catch up with you later."

Doctrinal Drowsiness

> *By night on my bed I sought him whom my soul loveth: I sought him, but I found him not. I will rise now, and go about the city in the streets, and in the broad ways I will seek him whom my soul loveth: I sought him, but I found him not.*   Song of Solomon 3:1, 2

What happened here is something that can happen to us corporately or to you and me individually. It's the danger of doctrinal drowsiness that says, "Lord, I know You're calling me to come away this morning and seek You. But I'm yours and You're mine. I'm robed in Your righteousness, and my name is written in Your book (yawn), so I'll meet with you a little later . . . zzz . . . ."

As the day progresses, however, and the trials arise, we cry, "Lord, Lord! Where are You?" Like this bride, how often we say, "I don't feel the Lord anymore. My day is empty. My night is dark. Where is He?" The answer is, when He called to us we chose to say, "I don't need to go to Bible study. I don't need devotions this morning. I don't need to expend the energy because I'm His and He's mine."

As the story unfolds, we see that as the bride seeks her bridegroom she does, indeed, find him. But it takes energy. So, too, Jeremiah 29 says, "You shall seek Me and find Me when you search for Me with all of your heart." There's no room for laziness in our relationship with the Lord.

"But I'm saved," you say.

Yes, you are.

"The Lord is mine and I am His."

That's true, too.

"And I can just be at peace and rest in the finished work of the Cross."

Absolutely.

But watch out for a dangerous doctrinal drowsiness that keeps you from responding when the Lord pulls on the strings of your heart during your lunch hour, saying,

> "Come away, My beloved. There are some mountains I want to show you, some songs I want to share with you."

You see, the Lord comes to us constantly, saying, "Drop what you're doing and take five minutes and talk to Me," or, "Take ten minutes and worship Me," or, "Take fifteen minutes to pour out your heart to Me."

"The Spirit is like the wind," said Jesus. "No man knows from whence it comes or where it goes" (see John 3:8). Hang gliders understand this. When they get a report that the thermals are perfect, they don't say, "I can't go today, but maybe tomorrow I can fit it in"—because there's no guarantee the winds will blow the same way tomorrow. Avid hang gliders move when the wind is blowing. So do surfers. When the swells are five feet, they don't say, "Thanks for the invitation. I can't go this week, but next week I'll be there"—because there's no guarantee what they'll find the following week.

The same is true in spiritual life. When the thermal of the Spirit, when the wave of the Holy Ghost is rolling in, I must respond immediately. "But that's irresponsible," you say. "What about obligations or family responsibilities?"

Let me tell you something: The Holy Spirit knows about those. He's not going to say, "Oh, I forgot. You have that meeting," or, "Forgive me, I didn't know about your business obligation or your family commitment."

No, the Holy Spirit knows our schedules. Thus, it's not the conflicts that are the problem. It's the times we think we deserve to watch CNN for an hour, to watch a 49'ers game, or to read *Newsweek*—for those are the times the Lord calls us to come away.

Spiritual Self-Centeredness

I sleep, but my heart waketh: it is the voice of my beloved that knocketh, saying,
Open to me, my sister, my love, my dove, my undefiled: for my head is filled
with dew, and my locks with the drops of the night.　　　Song of Solomon 5:2

"Foxes have holes, birds have nests, but the Son of Man hath nowhere to lay His head" (see Matthew 8:20). The hair of the King of kings was full of dew because He came to enter the dark night of human sin. Yet how does the bride respond to her bridegroom?

I have put off my coat; how shall I put it on? I have washed my feet; how shall
I defile them? My beloved put in his hand by the hole of the door, and my
bowels were moved for him. I rose up to open to my beloved; and my hands
dropped with myrrh, and my fingers with sweet smelling myrrh, upon the
handles of the lock. I opened to my beloved; but my beloved had withdrawn
himself, and was gone: my soul failed when he spake: I sought him, but I could
not find him; I called him, but he gave me no answer.

Song of Solomon 5:3–6

"I am perfumed," the bride says. "My feet are washed. Why should I defile myself opening the door for you?"

Follow the analogy, gang. Jesus came to seek and save those who were lost. Without a home, His locks are full of dew. His hands are soiled from touching humanity. He gave everything. He bled. He died. He who knew no sin became sin for us. If we're not careful, however, like the bride, we can say, "I don't want to soil my hands. I just want to be mystical. I want to stand in the midst of the candlesticks with incense wafting over my head."

"That's not where I'm at," says our Bridegroom. "My head is wet because I came to impact the world. Forget your clean hands and feet. There is practical ministry to do. There are people to touch."

There's a tragic self-centeredness to which the bride is vulnerable—especially after she's been a bride for a while. It's not about how *we're* doing. It's about how willing we are to dirty our feet, open the door, and give to others.

This account is interesting because I wouldn't have chosen doctrinal drowsiness and spiritual self-centeredness to characterize those who don't open the door to Jesus. If I were writing the Bible, I would have said, "That which will separate you from intimacy with Jesus is a specific sin, or a particular problem." But Jesus says it is our failure to respond to the prompting of His Spirit and our being enamored with our own holiness that separate us from Him.

I also find it extremely interesting that the bride located her bridegroom by giving a detailed description of him to her friends (5:10–16). In other words, she realized where to find him not when she sat in her room with her clean hands and feet, but when she ran out into the city and said, "Let me tell you about this one whom my soul loves." The same thing happens to me. I'll be wondering where the Lord is and why I'm not sensing His presence, when suddenly there's someone for me to tell about Him. And sure enough, as I talk about Him, I experience intimacy with Him.

Dear sisters, precious brothers—the key to intimacy in your Christian walk, the source of enough spiritual energy to skip on the mountains of fellowship, and share with your neighbors in Jerusalem is to say, "YES," when the Bridegroom knocks at your door.

The waves are perfect. Get out of bed, grab your board, and open the door!

4 In chapter 4, we begin the third and final section of the Book of Revelation, as John writes of "the things which shall be hereafter" (see Revelation 1:19).

Revelation 4:1 (a)
After this . . .

The Greek words here are *meta tauta*. It's the same phrase used in the divine outline, where John was instructed to write of the things which he had seen, the things which are, and the things which shall be hereafter (1:19). After what? After chapters 2 and 3—after church history. I find it interesting that in the first three chapters of the Book of Revelation, the word "church" appears nineteen times. From chapter 4 on, however, it never appears. Why? Because in chapter 4, the church is taken off the scene and into heaven.

Revelation 4:1 (b)
. . . I looked, and, behold, a door was opened in heaven . . .

I like this! In verse 20 of chapter 3, we saw Jesus knocking at the door. Anyone who opens the door of his heart to the Lord will have the door of heaven opened to him.

Revelation 4:1 (c)
. . . and the first voice which I heard was as it were of a trumpet . . .

This trumpet sound draws my mind back to 1 Thessalonians. . . .

For the Lord himself shall descend from heaven with a shout, with the voice of the archangel, and with the trump of God: and the dead in Christ shall rise first: Then we which are alive and remain shall be caught up together with them in the clouds, to meet the Lord in the air: and so shall we ever be with the Lord. Wherefore comfort one another with these words.   1 Thessalonians 4:16–18

Obviously this is speaking of the Rapture—when the Lord appears in the clouds to take us, His bride, to heaven.

Revelation 4:1 (d)
Come up hither . . .

When I hear the Lord saying, "Come up here"—I'm going—and so are you! This is a phrase I can't wait to hear!

Revelation 4:1 (e)
. . . and I will shew thee things which must be hereafter.

Meta tauta—hereafter. Why do you suppose this phrase is used twice in this verse? I suggest it is because the Lord doesn't want us to miss it. After these things, after church history—when the last person gets saved; when the last one is added to the kingdom; when the bride of Christ is complete—we're going up!

Revelation 4:2 (a)
And immediately I was in the spirit . . .

I'm really looking forward to being in the spirit, to being immediately changed. How many of you today found yourself thinking a fleshly thought, reacting in a fleshly way, or doing something in the flesh? We all struggle with this constantly. We all fail continually. But there's coming a day when we will no longer struggle with the flesh because when we see Him, we shall be like Him (1 John 3:2). I'm *really* looking forward to that.

Revelation 4:2 (b)
. . . and, behold, a throne was set in
heaven . . .

The first thing that captures John's eye is a
throne set, or literally "planted" in heaven. I suggest this was a vital concept for Pastor John to
pass on to his flock in the midst of terrible persecution. "I saw a throne *set*," said John.

Just as the altars whereupon the children of Israel worshiped Baal or Ashtaroth in Old Testament times were portable—able to be moved
from one "high place" or grove to another—the
high places and altars of today's pagan deities
are constantly in flux. If you're worshiping at the
altar of materialism, you get the house or buy the
car and worship there for a week or two, a year
or ten—but then it doesn't work anymore. You
have to have a newer house or better car. So you
move.

Or, if you're worshiping at the altar of sensuality, you worship there for a while—until that altar
doesn't work anymore and you have to find someone else. If you worship at the altar of intellectualism and immerse yourself in the study of this
philosophy or that concept, a month or a year
later, you're bored with it.

That's why we live in a culture that says, "Been
there, done that, now what?" Not so with the
Lord. I've been walking with Him for forty years,
and I'm not at all bored. My relationship with
Him just gets better and more interesting, more
challenging and more intriguing because His
throne is *set*.

Revelation 4:2 (c)
. . . and one sat on the throne.

John likens the One on the throne to precious
stones. . . .

Revelation 4:3 (a)
And he that sat was to look upon like a
jasper . . .

The jasper stone was a clear stone—probably
a diamond—and speaks of light. Because God is
light (1 John 1:5), He's not in the dark about your
disappointing marriage, your distressing physical affliction, or your depressing financial situation.

"Then why doesn't He do anything about it?"
you ask.

He has. . . .

Revelation 4:3 (b)
. . . and a sardine stone . . .

The sardine stone was most likely a ruby,
which of course, is red. Truly, the ruby-red blood
of Christ flowed from His veins as the nails
pierced His hands, as the crown of thorns was
clubbed into His skull, as the spear sliced into His
side. And through it all, He would declare,
"There's nothing more I could ever do or say to
prove to you I am in love with you" (see Romans
5:8).

Therefore, when people get angry with God or
arrogantly put God on trial, be one who says, "I
understand what you're saying, but you're wrong
because God proved His love for you. What else
could He possibly do to show you He's in love
with you and wants the best for you? He laid
everything on the line and was slaughtered in
your place with you on His mind and on His
heart."

In Exodus 28, we read that the high priest
wore a breastplate upon which were twelve
stones—one for each tribe. The first of the twelve
sons of Jacob was Reuben. Reuben's name means
"behold" or "see, a son." His stone was the sardine stone. The last of the twelve sons was Benjamin, whose name means "son of my right hand."
Benjamin's stone was a jasper. Thus, this One on
the throne is, "Behold, the Son of My right hand."
It's Jesus.

Revelation 4:3 (c)
. . . and there was a rainbow round about
the throne, in sight like unto an emerald.

The throne of God is not surrounded by danger
signs or warning lights. It's surrounded by a
rainbow emblematic of grace (Genesis 9:16). That
is why we are not instructed to come boldly unto
the throne of service, intense worship, or clean
living. We are invited to come boldly unto the
throne of *grace* (Hebrews 4:16).

I am totally convinced that grace is not the beginning thing—it's the whole thing. God is looking for people to bless who won't take credit by
saying, "It's my praying or witnessing, my disciplined spirituality or intense study," but rather,
"It's only grace that has brought me thus far."
You see, grace is the only thing that truly allows
the Lord to get all the glory. That's why His is a
throne of grace. *Amazing* grace.

Revelation 4:4
And round about the throne were four and
twenty seats: and upon the seats I saw four
and twenty elders sitting, clothed in white

raiment; and they had on their heads crowns of gold.

Because the Old Testament priesthood was divided into twenty-four groups (1 Chronicles 24), and because the church is called a kingdom of priests (Revelation 1:6), some suggest that the twenty-four elders speak of the church, with their white garments symbolizing the righteousness given to us in Christ.

In my opinion, however, the twenty-four elders refer to the twelve patriarchs and the twelve apostles because on each of the twelve gates into the New Jerusalem is the name of one of the patriarchs; and on each of the foundations is the name of an apostle (Revelation 21). If this is the case, the twenty-four elders would symbolize God's people in entirety—the patriarchs representing the Old Testament believers, the apostles representing the New Testament believers.

While we cannot be dogmatic regarding the identity of the twenty-four elders, we can be certain of their ministry, for as the Book of Revelation progresses, we'll see what these elders do in heaven. They don't have board meetings. They don't run programs. They don't pursue higher office. What do they do? Here we see them sitting in God's presence. In the next chapter, they seek out John, saying, "Weep not. The Lion of the Tribe of Judah has prevailed." Later, we see an elder ask John questions to spark spiritual discussion and to provide information and enlightenment. We'll also see the elders singing a new song.

So, too, if we want to be elders, ministers, or servants here on earth, we must be those who sit in God's presence, those who seek out people who are hurting and point them to the Lord. We must be those who share truth; and those who sing a new song of something God is doing today, in this hour.

Revelation 4:5 (a)
And out of the throne proceeded lightnings and thunderings and voices . . .

When you see lightning and hear thunder, you know a storm is coming. Keep in mind that John is addressing people going through terrible times and dark days. "Why doesn't God do something?" they must have wondered.

"You can't hear it yet," John would answer, "but a storm is coming—through which God will pour out justice upon the earth."

Revelation 4:5 (b)
. . . and there were seven lamps of fire burning before the throne, which are the seven Spirits of God.

In reference to Isaiah 11:2, this speaks of the seven-fold nature of God's Spirit.

Revelation 4:6 (a)
And before the throne there was a sea of glass like unto crystal . . .

When you get to heaven, the throne will catch your eye, the One on the throne will warm your heart, and the crystal sea before the throne will bring you peace. If you haven't done so lately, I encourage you to take time to sit in the presence of the Lord. Think on Him, talk to Him—and you will find the troubled waters of your heart and soul become like glass. Why is it we would sooner run out and try to make things right than sit before the Lord? We try to solve this and take care of that—only to find ourselves troubled and upset, fatigued and frustrated. Don't wait until you get to heaven physically to experience the glassy sea of peace. Make time daily to take a trip to heaven in your spirit, to sit in the throne room. The opportunity is yours for the taking.

Revelation 4:6 (b)
. . . and in the midst of the throne, and round about the throne, were four beasts full of eyes before and behind.

The Greek word translated "beasts" actually means "creatures." These living creatures are described in greater detail in Ezekiel 1 and 10, where we are told they are cherubim. Cherubim are first seen in the Garden of Eden. After driving Adam and Eve out of the Garden after they had sinned, God employed cherubim with flaming sword to keep Adam and Even from eating of the tree of life and living forever in their fallen condition (Genesis 3:24).

In the Book of Exodus, cherubim are seen again on the mercy seat—a fitting place for them to be, as we shall see. . . .

Revelation 4:7
And the first beast was like a lion, and the second beast like a calf, and the third beast had a face as a man, and the fourth beast was like a flying eagle.

Since the early days of church history, Iranius and others recognized that the four faces of these cherubim correspond with the four Gospels: Matthew presents Jesus as King, typified by a lion. Mark presents Him as a Servant, the ox representing servitude. Luke presents Jesus in His Humanity, seen in the face of a man. And John presents Jesus as the Son of God, pictured by the eagle who not only soars higher than any other creature, but is the only animal able to look directly into the sun, even as only the Son of God beholds the glory of the Father.

But there's something else about these four faces that intrigues me. That is, in chapters 1 and 2 of the Book of Numbers, God declares that His people were to camp in a certain order as they traveled through the wilderness.

He told the Levites to surround the tabernacle on the north, south, east, and west sides. Why? Those serving the Lord—whether in their neighborhood, on their campus, or in their church always end up camping closest to where God's glory is. That's the beauty of serving the Lord: You get to camp out closest to His glory because when you're serving Him, sharing your faith, praying for others, teaching Sunday school you experience most fully the *chabod*—the glory of God. That's why God lets us serve Him. He doesn't need us. Rather, He allows us the privilege to serve because in so doing we draw closest to Him.

Numbers 2 goes on to say that on each of the four sides were to be three tribes. Judah, Issachar, and Zebulon, numbering 186,400, were to camp on the east side and were known as the Camp of Judah. What is the symbol, the ensign of Judah? The Lion. Why were they on the east side? Because when Jesus comes back, roaring with authority, He's going to come from the East.

Ephraim, Manasseh, and Benjamin, numbering 108,100, were to camp on the west side, and were known as the Camp of Ephraim. Their symbol was an ox.

Reuben, Simeon, and Gad, numbering 151,400, were to camp on the south side and were known as the Camp of Reuben, whose symbol was a man.

Dan, Naphtali, and Asher, numbering 157,600, were to camp on the north side and were known as the Camp of Dan, signified by an eagle.

With the largest number of people camped on the east, the smallest number on the west, and an almost identical number of people on the north and south sides of the tabernacle, the configuration is that of a Cross—which is as applicable practically as it is significant spiritually. . . .

Fearing the approaching Israelites, Balak, king of Moab, hired a prophet named Balaam to curse them.

No problem, *Balaam must have thought. These people have been idolatrous and rebel-*

lious, ungrateful and immoral. Surely God will curse them.

But Balaam erred greatly in thinking God was angry with His people, for when he attempted to utter a curse over them, all that came out of his mouth was a blessing (Numbers 23—24). Why? Because as he looked over the camp of Israel from the high places of Baal, what did Balaam see?

A Cross.

So, too, we think we deserve to be cursed because we rebel, murmur, and complain. We think we deserve to be cursed because we don't do what we should and, instead, do what we shouldn't. But God looks upon us and sees us in light of the Cross. Therefore, all He desires to do is bless us.

Revelation 4:8 (a)
And the four beasts had each of them six wings about him . . .

How bizarre! you must be thinking. *Creatures with four faces and six wings.* Listen—what seems bizarre to us living in our little corner of time and space will make perfect sense when we get to heaven.

Revelation 4:8 (b)
. . . and they were full of eyes within . . .

Oftentimes, the more insight one has or the more vision one has been given, the more one says, "I thought marriage would be it—but it isn't." Or, "I thought this person would change—but he didn't." Or, "I thought my ministry would blossom—but it hasn't." Truly, the more you see, the more you know, the more disillusioned or disappointed you can become. Not so the cherubim. Even though they are full of eyes, they find someone completely worthy of their gaze.

Revelation 4:8 (c)
. . . and they rest not day and night, saying, Holy, holy, holy, Lord God Almighty, which was, and is, and is to come.

Why do the cherubim say, "Holy, Holy, Holy"? Because God is Triune—Father, Son, and Spirit. The word "holy" means "whole"—not eroded by sin, not falling apart at the seams, not hypocritical or flawed in any way. And it is this holiness, this wholeness, which causes the cherubim to fall down in worship. Then, rising to go their way, they see Him again and bow again in ecstasy and awe. And on and on it goes perpetually—not because the cherubim are some kind of wind-up angels programmed to do this, but because they are totally overwhelmed by the beauty of holiness (Psalm 29:2).

Truly, there is nothing as lovely as holiness in a man or woman, in a church or family—for, without even being able to identify it, people are attracted to it. Oh, they might be enamored or seduced by evil or darkness for a season—but when judgment comes, people hate it. Holiness, on the other hand, never becomes disillusioning or disappointing. The more holy a person, family, or congregation is—the more satisfying they are.

Full of vision and insight, the cherubim understand this. And that's why they can't take their eyes off this One who is holy.

Revelation 4:9, 10 (a)
And when those beasts give glory and honour and thanks to him that sat on the throne, who liveth for ever and ever, the four and twenty elders fall down before him that sat on the throne, and worship him that liveth for ever and ever, and cast their crowns before the throne . . .

As the cherubim worship, the twenty-four elders join in, casting their crowns before the throne. The Bible speaks of five crowns available to you and me. . . .

The crown of righteousness is given to those who love His appearing (2 Timothy 4:8). A person who lives in constant expectation of Jesus' return is going to live righteously (1 John 3:3) because one of the most purifying truths in all of the Bible is the fact that Jesus could come back at any moment.

The crown of life is given to those who love Him (James 1:12). If you love the Lord, you're going to hang out with the Lord; and if you hang out with the Lord, you're going to have life abundantly. The degree to which you spend time with the Lord is the degree to which you'll have abundant life.

The crown of glory is given for servanthood (1 Peter 5:4). One experiences the glory, the weight, and the reality of God to the extent that one serves Him.

The soul-winners crown is given to those who share their faith (1 Thessalonians 2:19).

The martyr's crown is for those who lay down their lives (Revelation 2:10). It is my opinion that this refers not only to those who die a martyr's death, but also to those who lay down their lives in obedience to what they know is right. Sure, it might seem easier to leave him, to walk out on the marriage, to do your own thing, but I believe those who say, "I'm going to die to self and do what the Lord would have me do even if it kills me," will receive a crown because they chose to

lay down their lives rather than give in to their own fleshly inclinations.

Well, I'm not into crowns, you might be thinking. *As long as I'm in heaven, I'll be happy.* But think of it this way. . . .

You're drafted into the army. As you're getting your hair buzzed, the President of the United States, your Commander in Chief walks in and says, "I have something for you," handing you a hat covered with gold braid and five stars.

"Thanks," you say, "but I'm not into hats. I'll just take one of the khaki caps like everyone else has."

"You don't understand," he would say. "The five stars on this hat open incredible doors. You don't stay in the barracks—you have the great big mansion on the hillside. You have a staff to iron your uniforms, feed you the finest food, and give you whatever you need. It all comes with the hat."

Bunches of Christians don't get this. The purpose of crowns is not to make a fashion statement. They're highly significant. And this life is the only chance we have to get them. There is no other opportunity for the next thousand, ten thousand, one hundred million years. Therefore, what I'm doing now with my time, money, or energy will directly determine whether I am in the General's mansion or on kitchen duty for all eternity. No wonder Paul tells us to run the race so that we may win the prize (1 Corinthians 9:24).

Revelation 4:10 (b), 11 (a)
. . . saying, Thou art worthy, O Lord, to receive glory and honour and power . . .

Because it is the Lord who gives us the ability to witness, to love Him, to lay down our life in ministry, when we get to heaven, we'll say, "*You* are worthy, Lord. Anything good in my life wasn't accomplished by my own energy or power. It was all *You.*"

Revelation 4:11 (b)
. . . for thou hast created all things, and for thy pleasure they are and were created.

Why is worship so important?

First, worship is the program in heaven. If you want heaven in your heart or home tonight, if you feel as if you're trapped in a hellish situation at work or in a terrible situation in a relationship, you can bring heaven into it by worshiping.

Second, worship is the purpose of creation. You see, everything exists for one reason: to please God. Therefore, to the extent you please Him is the extent to which you will experience fulfillment in the deepest part of your soul.

How do we worship? The word itself tells us. *Proskuneo* in Greek means "to turn and kiss." Thus, true worship is any sincere expression intended for the Lord's pleasure. Worship is the program in heaven, the purpose of creation on earth. May His will be done in our lives, as it is in heaven.

5 In chapters 1 through 3 of the Book of Revelation, John sets the stage as he takes pen in hand to record what is about to transpire.

In chapter 4, the curtain rises, as he describes the throne room of the King.

And in chapter 5, the drama begins. . . .

Revelation 5:1
And I saw in the right hand of him that sat on the throne a book written within and on the backside, sealed with seven seals.

The "book" John sees is actually a scroll. If similar to other scrolls in John's day, it was made of eight-by-ten-inch sheets of papyrus, which were connected horizontally and wound around a wooden handle. Epistles the size of Jude, Philemon, and II and III John would all be written on one single piece of papyrus. The Book of Revelation, on the other hand, would require a scroll fifteen feet long. Due to the coarse back of the papyrus, the three-inch-wide columns of writing were penned on only the smooth side. Here, however, we see a scroll written on *both* sides and sealed with seven seals, which can be perplexing until one studies Jewish history—wherein are found numerous examples of a certain kind of document with writing on both sides and sealed with seven seals: a title deed to a piece of property.

Initially, a title deed would be written only on the smooth side and sealed with a single seal (Jeremiah 32:6–29). But if the owner became unable to meet his financial obligations, he would have to relinquish his title deed—upon the backside of which would be written his debts and upon which would be placed seven seals. If at any time during the ensuing seven years he could pay off his debts, the seals would be broken and the title deed returned.

All of this explains what is in the hand of the One who sits on the throne here in chapter 5: It's the title deed to planet earth. The title deed to this planet was originally given to Adam in the Garden of Eden when God told him to subdue the earth (Genesis 1:28). But Adam forfeited his right to ownership when he ate of the fruit of the tree of the knowledge of good and evil. You see, although Eve was tricked into eating the forbidden fruit, Adam's was an overt, calculated act of rebellion, which is why the Bible speaks of Adam's sin as that which transferred to Satan the title deed of our planet (Romans 5:14). This explains why Paul called Satan the god of this world (2 Corinthians 4:4) and why Jesus referred to him as the prince of this world (John 12:31).

Therefore, when people say, "Well, if God is so good, why are there wars, cancer, floods, AIDS, depression, rape, and injustice?"—they're blaming the wrong person. The planet God gave man was absolutely perfect. *Man* is to blame for turning the planet over to Satan. And he is the reason the people to whom John was writing were watching their brothers and sisters incarcerated or fed to the lions, crucified, or dipped in hot wax. This book was written not only to deal with prophecy, but primarily to deal with the questions with which John's flock wrestled—and the questions with which Christians have wrestled ever since.

Revelation 5:2
And I saw a strong angel proclaiming with a loud voice, Who is worthy to open the book, and to loose the seals thereof?

In other words, "Who is able to meet the requirements, to pay off the debt?" Notice he does not say, "Who is *willing?*" Alexander the Great was willing. Genghis Khan was willing. Charlemagne was willing. Napoleon was willing. Hitler was willing. There have been lots of people who have said, "I want to be in power. Give me a crack at it. Let me see what I can do." But the angel doesn't ask, "Who is willing?" The angel asks, "Who is *worthy?*"

Revelation 5:3
And no man in heaven, nor in earth, neither under the earth, was able to open the book, neither to look thereon.

When no one comes forward to reclaim earth's title deed, something happens that probably never happened before in heaven throughout all eternity past: tears begin to flow.

Revelation 5:4
And I wept much, because no man was found worthy to open and to read the book, neither to look thereon.

The Greek word translated "wept much" actually means "sobbed convulsively." John is overcome with grief when he realizes the earth would remain in Satan's grasp forever. And I understand. I look at Benjamin and Mary, and think, *What's it going to be like for them if things continue on the way they have for the past forty years?* If I didn't have this book and know this story, I would be distraught, indeed.

Revelation 5:5 (a)
And one of the elders saith unto me, Weep not: behold, the Lion of the tribe of Judah...

The "Lion of the tribe of Judah" takes us back to Genesis 49, where Jacob calls his twelve sons together to pronounce a blessing upon them. As he comes to Judah, Jacob likens him to a lion's whelp, and then says that power and authority would be his until the coming of Messiah...

The year is A.D. 12. In the springtime, the Romans issue a decree declaring that the Jewish people would no longer be able to carry out capital punishment. The rabbis' response to the decree was immediate because they believed capital punishment was the cornerstone of government as defined in the Noahic Covenant. When they were denied this fundamental right of government, and thereby rendered powerless as a nation, the rabbis rushed into the streets of Jerusalem, rending their clothes and smiting their breasts.

In fact, we are told the whole city was filled with the wailing of rabbis who understood that something terrible was happening. The scepter had departed. The authority was gone. Yet Messiah had not come—or so they thought. For on that very day, guess who was sitting in the temple in Jerusalem as a twelve-year-old confounding the scribes and thinkers of the day: The Lion of the Tribe of Judah—Jesus Christ.

So, too, how often we throw dirt in the air and wail and moan, ripping our clothes and crying, "Where are You, Lord?"—when He's right in our midst, working everything out perfectly.

Revelation 5:5 (b)
... the Root of David, hath prevailed to open the book, and to loose the seven seals thereof.

Jesus was born of the house and lineage of David, but because He preceded David by all eternity, He's the Root *of* David, as well as a Branch *from* David. "I understand why you're weeping,

John," said the angel. "But this won't go on forever. The Lion of the Tribe of Judah, the Root of David has prevailed."

At this point, John turns around, expecting, no doubt, to see a massive figure, a roaring lion. . . .

Revelation 5:6 (a)
And I beheld, and, lo, in the midst of the throne and of the four beasts, and in the midst of the elders, stood a Lamb . . .

The Greek word translated "Lamb" is in the diminutive form—meaning a pet lamb.

Revelation 5:6 (b)
. . . as it had been slain . . .

According to Isaiah 52, Jesus' visage is marred more than that of any other man. Marred more than a man in a train wreck, a plane crash, Hiroshima? Yes. You see, it's not only that Jesus' beard was plucked out, His back beaten, His side pierced, and His wrists nailed. It's the psychological and spiritual stress He experienced in the Garden of Gethsemane that caused the blood vessels in His face to burst. Jesus experienced marring and scarring in ways we'll never understand until we see Him.

But here is the interesting thing: The terror that would mar Him psychologically and physiologically was due neither to the physical suffering He would endure nor to the blood He would shed. The one thing that terrorized our Hero was that He knew He would, for a time, lose contact with His Father as He who knew no sin became sin for us.

We shudder at the thought of hearing our boss say, "You're through," or of our girlfriend saying, "Goodbye." But if someone were to say, "You're going to lose fellowship with the Father for a day," we wouldn't care. Why is it that we are nonchalant about that which terrified Jesus—and we are fearful about that which He said, "Let not your hearts be troubled"?

Jesus was close to His Father, drew His life from His Father, was in love with His Father. That's why He bled from His face at the thought of being out of fellowship with His Father for even a short period of time. That's why He asked that this particular cup be taken from Him. That's why He was marred more than any other man in history. Truly, when we see Jesus, we'll be awed, amazed, and broken by what He did to get us to heaven.

Revelation 5:6 (c)
. . . having seven horns . . .

This speaks of perfect power.

Revelation 5:6 (d)
. . . and seven eyes . . .

This speaks of perfect insight.

Revelation 5:6 (e)
. . . which are the seven Spirits of God sent forth into all the earth.

This doesn't mean the Lamb literally had seven eyes. Rather, this speaks of the fullness of God's Spirit.

Revelation 5:7
And he came and took the book out of the right hand of him that sat upon the throne.

The Lion of the Tribe of Judah, the Root of David, the Lamb slain is the only One worthy to pay the price for the bankruptcy of mankind.

Revelation 5:8 (a)
And when he had taken the book, the four beasts and four and twenty elders fell down before the Lamb, having every one of them harps . . .

Since the harps of John's day were ten-stringed, the number brings to mind the Ten Commandments, the law.
"I'm not under the law," some boast.
To them, I say, "Tell me, which part of the law don't you like? The fact that God says we're to love Him and to be kind and considerate to people? That we're to walk in purity so that we might have peace? Exactly with which part do you have such a hard time? Do you really want to live like a pig in the name of being free from legalism?"

In Deuteronomy 23, God gave His people a peculiar set of instructions. "When you have to use the restroom," He said, "go outside the camp, dig a hole, and bury it." Although this is common sense to us, it was unheard of to the people of that day.
Well, what kind of legalism is this? they must have wondered. We're under grace, aren't we, Moses?
Now obviously, bacteria, germs, and diseases would be passed on from person to person if they just continued to do what everyone else was doing. Yet God never gave the reason. He simply said, "I'm in the camp. And this is what I desire."

So, too, you may say, "Drinking's okay," or, "Everyone's going to those shows," or, "Everyone's downloading this . . ." It's not legalism that tells you otherwise. It's the music of heaven being played on the ten-stringed harp. The harp is emblematic of the beauty of a man or woman who says, "The law of the Lord is wisdom—even if I don't initially understand it."

Revelation 5:8 (b)
. . . and golden vials full of odours, which are the prayers of saints.

An angel appeared to Zacharias, saying, "Your prayer is heard. Your wife, Elisabeth, is going to conceive" (see Luke 1:13).
What do you mean? Zacharias must have thought. *I haven't prayed that prayer in decades*—which shows us even the prayers we forget about are still in God's "Active" box. Therefore, I'm convinced that many of the blessings in our lives are answers to prayers we prayed years previously. According to our text, our prayers are kept in vials, or bowls. How full is yours?

Revelation 5:9, 10
And they sung a new song, saying, Thou art worthy to take the book, and to open the seals thereof: for thou wast slain, and hast redeemed us to God by thy blood out of every kindred, and tongue, and people, and nation; and hast made us unto our God kings and priests: and we shall reign on the earth.

Who is the only group of people who can say, "Out of every kindred and tongue, nation and people, we have been redeemed by the blood"? Only the church—which means the church is in heaven in chapter 5 before the Tribulation begins in chapter 6.

Revelation 5:11, 12
And I beheld, and I heard the voice of many angels round about the throne and the beasts and the elders: and the number of them was ten thousand times ten thousand, and thousands of thousands; saying with a loud voice, Worthy is the Lamb that was slain to receive power, and riches, and wisdom, and strength, and honour, and glory, and blessing.

When does true worship take place? When a worship leader is giving an exhortation? No. When someone is trying to manipulate the heavenly scene to praise? No. It happens when those in heaven see the slain Lamb. So, too, who are vibrant worshipers today? Not those who are manipulated by a worship leader or pastor, but those who understand that Jesus really died for them. Anyone who truly sees the slain Lamb cannot help but worship.

Revelation 5:13 (a)
And every creature which is in heaven . . .

Will there be dogs and cats and pets in heaven? I don't know. However, this I do know: Jesus comes back to earth riding a horse (Revelation 19).

Revelation 5:13 (b), 14 (a)
. . . and on the earth, and under the earth, and such as are in the sea, and all that are in them, heard I saying, Blessing, and honour, and glory, and power, be unto him that sitteth upon the throne, and unto the Lamb for ever and ever. And the four beasts said, Amen.

"Amen" simply means "Yes." In 2 Corinthians 1:20, Paul writes that the promises of God are in Christ Yea and Amen, for Jesus *is* the Amen (Revelation 3:14).

Revelation 5:14 (b)
And the four and twenty elders fell down and worshipped him that liveth for ever and ever.

Because the Lamb slain has taken control of the Book—the scroll, the title deed to earth—worship abounds.

6 In chapter 6, we continue in the third and final section of the divine outline given in chapter 1 verse 19, when John was instructed to write the things that he had seen, the things that are, and the things that shall be hereafter.

Revelation 6:1
And I saw when the Lamb opened one of the seals, and I heard, as it were the noise of thunder, one of the four beasts saying, Come and see.

Chapters 6 through 19 describe the seven-year period of the Tribulation—result of the rebellion and sin of mankind.

Hast thou not procured this unto thyself, in that thou hast forsaken the Lord thy God, when he led thee by the way? Thine own wickedness shall correct thee, and thy backslidings shall reprove thee . . .   Jeremiah 2:17–19 (a)

To the people of Jeremiah's day, to those who rebelled against the Lord and found themselves threatened by external enemies and internal problems, the Lord said, "It's not that I will punish you. Rather, it will be your own sin that will come back to bite you."

So, too, the world has declared corporately, "We will not allow this Man to rule us (John 18:40). We want to do our own thing. We want to call our own shots. We want to live our own life."

And in response, God says, "Be not deceived. God is not mocked. Whatever a man sows, that shall he also reap" (see Galatians 6:7).

Our sin will track us down, gang. Which sins? Every sin—every white lie, every questionable late night TV show, every bit of fudging on our income tax. Yes, if we have confessed them, they have all been forgiven and forgotten. But whatever sin in which a man indulges will track him down like a hound dog until it eventually catches up with him and bites into him. There is no exception.

I don't know how old a man has to get or how much he has to go through before he finally realizes God's Word is right. "Be *sure* your sin will find you out" (Numbers 32:23). There is no exception. None.

Chapter 6 is the account of mankind's sin coming back to bite him—for although Jesus is reclaiming the title deed to earth, sin still brings repercussions, still exacts a price.

Revelation 6:2 (a)
And I saw, and behold a white horse . . .

In chapter 19, we will see a Man on a white horse, who is clearly the Son of Man, Jesus Christ. But we know by the company he keeps that the man on the white horse here in chapter 6 is not Jesus. . . .

Revelation 6:2 (b)
. . . and he that sat on him had a bow . . .

The word "bow" tends to conjure up an image of a bow and arrow. But I'm not sure that's correct. The first time a bow is mentioned in the Bible, it refers to a rainbow—the token of God's promise that He would not destroy the world with a flood (Genesis 9:13). Now think with me: Right after the church is raptured, Daniel says a man will come, making a covenant with Israel—a seven-year peace treaty. And the whole world will say, "Hooray! At last someone has solved the problem of Jerusalem. There's peace between the Israeli and the Palestinian, between the Arab and the Jew." Thus, this bow could be the same type God displayed to Noah—a rainbow.

Revelation 6:2 (c)
. . . and a crown was given unto him . . .

The Greek word translated "crown" is *stephanos*. A diadem is a permanent crown. A *stephanos*, on the other hand, is a wreath made of olive branches that only lasts a short while.

Revelation 6:2 (d)
. . . and he went forth conquering, and to conquer.

How will this one riding a white horse, carrying a bow, and wearing a crown of olive branches conquer? As a peacemaker (Daniel 8:23–25). Isn't this exactly what Jesus prophesied when He proclaimed, "I come in My Father's name, and you receive me not. But another will come in his own name, and him you shall receive" (see John 5:43)?

- How did Jesus come?
  Meekly riding on a donkey.
- What did the world say?
  "We will not have this Man rule over us."
- So who will the world get instead?
  Antichrist.

And look who Antichrist brings with him. . . .

Revelation 6:3, 4
And when he had opened the second seal, I heard the second beast say, Come and see. And there went out another horse that was red: and power was given to him that sat thereon to take peace from the earth, and that they should kill one another: and there was given unto him a great sword.

The red horse following the white horse of Antichrist is war. Anyone who thinks there can be true political solutions to the world's problems is sadly mistaken. Politics is solely about gaining and maintaining power. "From whence come wars and fightings?" James asks. "Come they not even from your own lusts?"—from wanting power, wanting property (see James 4:1, 2).

Truly, any man who thinks he can bring about peace politically, or any church that looks to the government for a solution to our country's problems will be disappointed. Power always brings war. And war is always disguised to look acceptable.

I think of the recent Gulf War. It was covered in patriotism and heroism, with the waving of the flag, the singing of the song, the colorful parade. The ugliness and hellishness of war is so heavily disguised that people begin to think war is acceptable, justifiable, okay—but it's not. Jesus refused to be pulled into politics when the mul-

titude wanted to make Him king (John 6:15). And when Peter unsheathed the sword to fight a "righteous war," He said, "Put it away. That's not My way" (Matthew 26:52).

Revelation 6:5 (a)
And when he had opened the third seal, I heard the third beast say, Come and see. And I beheld, and lo a black horse . . .

As we shall see, the black horse symbolizes famine—with reference to an imbalance in nature as well as physical famine. We're out of balance, gang. People work at machines that pollute the air to purchase machines that travel at lethal speeds over blacktop so they can come home to sit before high-priced boxes that flicker images telling them what to buy. Then they get up the next morning to repeat the process—all the while living in a state of spiritual famine.

Revelation 6:5 (b), 6 (a)
. . . and he that sat on him had a pair of balances in his hand. And I heard a voice in the midst of the four beasts say, A measure of wheat for a penny, and three measures of barley for a penny . . .

"A measure of wheat for a penny" means that the time of the Tribulation will be so economically oppressive that the masses will exist on rations. A full day's wage will only buy a little wheat or barley because of Antichrist's system that is based on the mark of the beast.

Revelation 6:6 (b)
. . . and see thou hurt not the oil and the wine.

Biblically, oil and wine symbolize luxury. You see, the wealthy of the world somehow continue to get wealthier even in times of war and famine.

Alfred Nobel, of the Peace Prize fame, made his fortune manufacturing explosives. When his father, also named Alfred, died, an obituary mistaking father for son stated that "he was a rich industrialist who made his fortune in war."

"This is my legacy?" asked a horrified Nobel. And from that day on, he set apart a substantial sum of money to fund prizes for peace and science, medicine and literature.

Nobel is the rare exception, for the famine that follows war never seems to affect the oil and wine of the wealthy.

Revelation 6:7, 8 (a)
And when he had opened the fourth seal, I heard the voice of the fourth beast say, Come and see. And I looked, and behold a pale horse . . .

Chloros, the Greek word translated "pale," is the same word from which we get the word "chlorine"—or bleached—and "chlorophyll"—or green. In other words, this horse is really ugly.

Revelation 6:8 (b)
. . . and his name that sat on him was Death, and Hell followed with him. And power was given unto them over the fourth part of the earth, to kill with sword, and with hunger, and with death, and with the beasts of the earth.

The phrase translated "beasts of the earth" is *therion* in Greek. *Therion* does not mean gigantic or monstrous. It means something frightful of any size—even, I suggest, microscopic, as are the HIV and e-coli viruses.

Each of the three preceding horsemen appeared in disguise. Deception appeared as a peacemaker on a white horse; war as patriotism on a red horse; famine as luxury on a black horse. And this fourth horseman is no exception, for what does it say about a culture like ours whose number one industry is health care?

"We're so advanced!" we think.

No, we're sick!

Revelation 6:9–11
And when he had opened the fifth seal, I saw under the altar the souls of them that were slain for the word of God, and for the testimony which they held: And they cried with a loud voice, saying, How long, O Lord, holy and true, dost thou not judge and avenge our blood on them that dwell on the earth? And white robes were given unto every one of them; and it was said unto them, that they should rest yet for a little season, until their fellowservants also and their brethren, that should be killed as they were, should be fulfilled.

Things are going badly. The bow of the horseman on the white horse is broken. Blood flows. Famine follows. Disease and sickness run rampant. So who does the world blame? The believers who come to Christ during the Tribulation. This is not new. In the days of the Black Plague, one of every four people died. The one group of people spared was the Jews. Today, we know it is because they were simply following the biblical principles of hygiene. But their contemporaries,

convinced the Jews were the reason for the plague, persecuted them.

The same will be true in the Tribulation. Amid sickness and blood, economic disharmony and war—believers will be martyred. And this is where the Lord seems to intervene.

Revelation 6:12, 13
And I beheld when he had opened the sixth seal, and, lo, there was a great earthquake; and the sun became black as sackcloth of hair, and the moon became as blood; and the stars of heaven fell unto the earth, even as a fig tree casteth her untimely figs, when she is shaken of a mighty wind.

There's a cataclysmic, catastrophic shaking going on. Why? Some suggest this describes a nuclear winter—the result of a nuclear exchange in which the sun would be darkened, the stars would fall, and the tectonic plates would shift. But I suggest the shaking and quaking is the result of God Himself getting involved when He sees His kids being attacked.

Revelation 6:14
And the heaven departed as a scroll when it is rolled together; and every mountain and island were moved out of their places.

Isaiah 42:5 says that God stretched out the heavens. Isaiah 34:4 says the heavens will be rolled up like a scroll. Skeptics laughed at this for years—until now. Recent findings not only verify that the universe is indeed expanding, but quantum physics and the findings of the Hubbell spacecraft verify that the universe is indeed curved, or scroll-like in shape.

Revelation 6:15, 16 (a)
And the kings of the earth, and the great men, and the rich men, and the chief captains, and the mighty men, and every bondman, and every free man, hid themselves in the dens and in the rocks of the mountains; and said to the mountains and rocks, Fall on us, and hide us from the face of him that sitteth on the throne . . .

Refusing to call on the Rock of Ages, men have no other choice but to cry to the rocks of the earth.

Revelation 6:16 (b)
. . . and from the wrath of the Lamb.

There are those who say the wrath of the Lamb, the real Tribulation, does not happen until midway into this seven-year period. They believe the church is raptured immediately before Antichrist enters the temple, demanding to be worshiped as God. Adherents to this view, called the Mid-Tribulation or Pre-Wrath Rapture, would do well to read Revelation 6 more carefully, because verse 16 makes it clear that the wrath of the Lamb occurs at the beginning of the Tribulation, not halfway through.

"Pray you may be found worthy to escape all of these things," Jesus taught in His Olivet Discourse—not "that you may be found worthy to escape halfway through" (see Luke 21:36).

How is one found worthy?

Simply by being in Christ (Jude 24).

Revelation 6:17
For the great day of his wrath is come; and who shall be able to stand?

Who can stand? We can. Because God has not appointed us unto wrath, but unto salvation (1 Thessalonians 5:9), we'll be standing in heaven. But we're not the only ones standing. In chapter 7, we'll see three other groups who stand in the day of the wrath of the Lamb. . . .

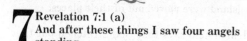

7 **Revelation 7:1 (a)**
And after these things I saw four angels standing . . .

Who can stand in the Tribulation? We can because we'll be in heaven. But there are two other groups who will also stand—one of which is comprised of four angels.

Revelation 7:1 (b)
. . . on the four corners of the earth . . .

"Aha!" you say, "The Bible can't be taken literally because everyone knows the earth is round. How, then, can it have four corners?" Tell that to the Pentagon. The U.S. Marines ran an advertising campaign a few years back that said "Our Marines are stationed on the four corners of the earth." Thus, it's a figure of speech we still use today.

Revelation 7:1 (c)
. . . holding the four winds of the earth, that the wind should not blow on the earth, nor on the sea, nor on any tree.

In Bible typology, wind speaks of the judgment of God (Jeremiah 49:36; 51:1, 16). The seals have been opened—and suddenly it is eerily quiet.

Revelation 7:2 (a)
And I saw another angel ascending from the east, having the seal of the living God . . .

The idea of sealing refers to the process whereby a builder would seal with wax the lumber he chose before it was shipped across the Aegean Sea. Arriving at the port nearest him, the builder would carry away whichever trees had his seal upon them.

So, too, the Master Carpenter, Jesus Christ, has chosen us to be the material of His eternal temple. Therefore, He has sealed us with His Spirit (Ephesians 4:30).

Revelation 7:2 (b)–4
. . . and he cried with a loud voice to the four angels, to whom it was given to hurt the earth and the sea, saying, Hurt not the earth, neither the sea, nor the trees, till we have sealed the servants of our God in their foreheads. And I heard the number of them which were sealed: and there were sealed an hundred and forty and four thousand of all the tribes of the children of Israel.

One hundred forty-four thousand will be marked by God as His servants during the Tribulation. And guess what. In chapter 14, verse 1, we see every single one of them surviving the Tribulation to stand with the Lord. Who *is* this second group who will stand in the Tribulation?

Many groups claim to be the 144,000. Jehovah Witnesses are one, even though they had to change their stance a bit when their group grew to number more than 144,000. Historical Mormonism also claimed to be the 144,000. Ellen G. White and the Seventh Day Adventists claim to be the 144,000. Garner Ted Armstrong and his Worldwide Church of God claim to be the 144,000.

Why would such groups *want* to be these 144,000, considering that during the Tribulation, the world will be falling apart around them?

Because in so doing, they conveniently write the Jews out of prophecy.

You see, throughout history, Christians and cult members alike have attempted to take Israel out of the eschatological equation. Doctrines such as "Replacement Theology," "Reconstructionism," and "Kingdom Now" propound that all of God's promises to Israel were passed on to the church because the Jews rejected Jesus. This is anything but a new idea. . . .

Following Constantine's conversion in A.D. 312, Christianity became the official religion of the Roman Empire. At this point, Christian teachers, thinkers, and theologians said, "Uh-oh. We've been teaching the kingdoms of this world are going to fall—but now we've got a Christian in power in the person of Constantine."

So, Origen, a heavyweight Bible teacher and philosopher of the day said, "I think we've been reading the Scriptures wrong. All of the promises given to Israel are simply allegories and illustrations." And as a result, the power and potency, the effectiveness and impact of the church decreased steadily.

Origen left the scene and was followed by Augustine, who was such a gifted proponent of the case for the allegorizing of the Old Testament, that even in some of today's King James Bibles, headings of the sections that speak of blessings upon Israel read "Blessings to the Church," while sections that speak of curses upon Israel read "Cursing Upon Israel" (Micah 6—7).

Augustine was eventually followed by Martin Luther. And Luther, although a giant of the faith, was terribly wrong on one issue: He hated the Jews. That's why many Protestant pastors supported Hitler well into his regime.

God is not through with His people. His promises to them are firmly rooted in the five covenants He made with them—four of which are unconditional. . . .

In the Abrahamic Covenant, God promised to bless Abraham regardless of what Abraham did or didn't do (Genesis 12:1–3).

In the Palestinian Covenant, God gave three hundred thousand square miles of land—from the Euphrates River to the Nile—to the Jews, even though at the height of their rule under Solomon, they only possessed thirty thousand square miles (Genesis 13:14).

In the Mosaic Covenant, otherwise known as the Law, God promised to bless Israel if they followed His commandments (Deuteronomy 28). Of the five covenants, only the Mosaic Covenant is conditional.

In the Davidic Covenant, God promised that an eternal King would come from David's lineage—fulfilled, of course, in Jesus (2 Samuel 7).

In the New Covenant, God promised to give Israel a new heart upon which He would write His will (Jeremiah 31:31–33).

God is *not* through with the Jew. Because the promises He made to them were *un*conditional, they cannot be forfeited.

"But Israel failed," you say.

So do I.

"But Israel was fickle," you protest.

So are you.

"But Israel faltered," you whisper.

So do we.

That's why in Romans 9—11, God says, "Look at Israel. I have not turned My back on them—and I'll not turn My back on you."

Revelation 7:5–8 (a)
Of the tribe of Juda were sealed twelve thousand. Of the tribe of Reuben were sealed twelve thousand. Of the tribe of Gad were sealed twelve thousand. Of the tribe of Aser were sealed twelve thousand. Of the tribe of Nepthalim were sealed twelve thousand. Of the tribe of Manasses were sealed twelve thousand. Of the tribe of Simeon were sealed twelve thousand. Of the tribe of Levi were sealed twelve thousand. Of the tribe of Issachar were sealed twelve thousand. Of the tribe of Zabulon were sealed twelve thousand.

Listed by tribe, the 144,000 refer to 144,000 Jews who will preach throughout the world during the Tribulation.

Revelation 7:8 (b)
Of the tribe of Joseph were sealed twelve thousand. Of the tribe of Benjamin were sealed twelve thousand.

Joseph's two sons, Ephraim and Manasseh, step in and take the place of Joseph. But if Joseph is replaced by two in this list and yet the number of tribes remains twelve, a tribe must be missing. The missing tribe is Dan.

Why? The Rabbis have consistently interpreted the ominous word in Genesis 49:17 to mean that a false Messiah, or Antichrist, will come from the tribe of Dan. That could indeed be true. But Dan's exclusion may also be the result of something else. You see, God specifically says in Deuteronomy 29 that any tribe involved in idolatry would be separated from the remaining tribes of Israel. This is exactly what happened to Dan. When they came into the Promised Land, the people of Dan were given coastal territory. But they weren't happy. They soon migrated north in search of new land, finally settling above the Sea of Galilee in close proximity to the pagans. Because of their geographic location, Dan fell into idolatry.

Consequently, just as Deuteronomy 29:21

prophesied, Dan was blotted out as a tribe. But when the Lord comes back and establishes His kingdom in Israel, guess who is the first tribe given their allotment. Dan (Ezekiel 48:1–3). Such is the incredible grace, mercy, and forgiveness of our God.

Revelation 7:9–11

After this I beheld, and, lo, a great multitude, which no man could number, of all nations, and kindreds, and people, and tongues, stood before the throne, and before the Lamb, clothed with white robes, and palms in their hands; and cried with a loud voice, saying, Salvation to our God which sitteth upon the throne, and unto the Lamb. And all the angels stood round about the throne, and about the elders and the four beasts, and fell before the throne on their faces, and worshipped God,

This company causes the angels to hold a heavenly hallelujah hoe-down, giving worship and adulation, praise and glory. . . .

Revelation 7:12

Saying, Amen: Blessing, and glory, and wisdom, and thanksgiving, and honour, and power, and might, be unto our God for ever and ever. Amen.

What would cause these angels, elders, and living creatures to burst forth in such ecstasy? The company described in verse 9. Who are they? Read on.

Revelation 7:13

And one of the elders answered, saying unto me, What are these which are arrayed in white robes? and whence came they?

I find it intriguing that one of the elders answered—even though no one was asking. That's exactly what an elder, a mature brother or sister, is supposed to do: answer even though no one's asking. If you go to work or school, saying, "Lord, use me. Bring me someone today who will ask me about the meaning of life—it's possible that will happen, but more than likely you'll wait a long time for that to occur. An elder is one who doesn't wait for someone to ask. Just as this elder did, he initiates spiritual discussion.

Revelation 7:14 (a)

And I said unto him, Sir, thou knowest.

In chapters 4 and 5, John recognized the church. Yet he doesn't recognize this multitude before the throne. Therefore, they cannot be the church.

Revelation 7:14 (b)–17

And he said to me, These are they which came out of great tribulation, and have washed their robes, and made them white in the blood of the Lamb. Therefore are they before the throne of God, and serve him day and night in his temple: and he that sitteth on the throne shall dwell among them. They shall hunger no more, neither thirst any more; neither shall the sun light on them, nor any heat. For the Lamb which is in the midst of the throne shall feed them, and shall lead them unto living fountains of waters: and God shall wipe away all tears from their eyes.

Who is this company? First of all, keep in mind the angels are thrilled to see them arrive in heaven. Jesus said that when one lost person is found, all of heaven breaks out in a fabulous chorus of praise (Luke 15:7,10). Therefore, these are people who were lost, but who have come to believe in Jesus during the Tribulation. Be faithful in sharing, precious people—even if you're not presently seeing people respond. Keep proclaiming the Word because the greatest revival in world history will take place *after* the Rapture.

As we read through the book, we'll see angels flying across the sky, and two witnesses preaching in Jerusalem. Then suddenly, a "great multitude which no man could number" will turn to the Lord. But their repentance could very well cost them their lives, as Antichrist declares war on those who refuse his mark.

"I'll wait to get saved until I see the Tribulation really happen," some say. "So what if I'm martyred in the process? It will be worth it."

I answer, "You must understand that people saved during the Tribulation are not the church, and therefore are in an entirely different position than the church. . . .

- This company stands before the throne (verse 9).
- The bride of Christ sits *on* the throne (Revelation 3:21).
- This company serves the Lord (verse 15).
- The bride of Christ is served *by* the Lord (Luke 12:37).

Precious people, *today* is the day of salvation (2 Corinthians 6:2). Don't wait until you see everything happen with your physical eyes. Be a man or woman of faith, and come, be part of the bride of Christ.

8 Revelation 8:1
And when he had opened the seventh seal, there was silence in heaven about the space of half an hour.

As the prayers of the saints, mixed with the incense of Christ's intercession rise to the ears of the Father, God silences everything in heaven to zero in on the prayers being offered to Him.

For topical study of Revelation 8:1 entitled "The Hush of Heaven," turn to page 1710.

Revelation 8:2–4
And I saw the seven angels which stood before God; and to them were given seven trumpets. And another angel came and stood at the altar, having a golden censer; and there was given unto him much incense, that he should offer it with the prayers of all saints upon the golden altar which was before the throne. And the smoke of the incense, which came with the prayers of the saints, ascended up before God out of the angel's hand.

"Make everything according to pattern," God told Moses concerning the tabernacle (Exodus 25:9). It was imperative Moses followed God's plan because the tabernacle was an earthly shadow of heavenly reality . . .

- Just as heaven has a door, so did the tabernacle.
- As heaven has a sea, the tabernacle had a brass laver, or "molten sea."
- As heaven has a lampstand, the tabernacle had a candlestick.
- As heaven has an altar of incense, so did the tabernacle.
- And as heaven has a throne of grace, the tabernacle had a seat of mercy.

Revelation 8:5
And the angel took the censer, and filled it with fire of the altar, and cast it into the earth: and there were voices, and thunderings, and lightnings, and an earthquake.

We see the impact and power of answered prayer as the prayers of the saints are hurled back to earth.

Revelation 8:6, 7
And the seven angels which had the seven trumpets prepared themselves to sound. The first angel sounded, and there followed hail and fire mingled with blood, and they were cast upon the earth: and the third part of trees was burnt up, and all green grass was burnt up.

It is very possible that these trumpet judgments that include flowing blood, pelting hail, and consuming fire describe what would happen in a nuclear holocaust. Keep in mind, history verifies that weapon systems have never been developed that have not been used. Therefore, it would be an aberration of history if all of the countries that presently have nuclear weapons—including Russia, France, England, Israel, India, China, the U.S., and a host of others—failed to use them.

I am not saying this passage can only refer to a nuclear holocaust. However, the fact remains that upon the detonation of a nuclear warhead, two hundred fifty-mph winds of fire follow. In addition, aboveground nuclear tests on the island of Bikini caused the surrounding water to shoot thousands of feet into the air, where it froze and returned as hailstones big enough to destroy the equipment intended to monitor it.

Revelation 8:8 (a)
And the second angel sounded, and as it were a great mountain burning with fire was cast into the sea . . .

"As it were" is the operative phrase. Therefore, the text does not refer to a literal mountain, but to something that looked like a mountain. Again, it could be the mushrooming of a nuclear cloud.

Revelation 8:8 (b), 9
. . . and the third part of the sea became blood; and the third part of the creatures which were in the sea, and had life, died; and the third part of the ships were destroyed.

Water covers three-fourths of the earth, one-third being the Atlantic Ocean. Interestingly, one-third of the ships afloat today are in the Atlantic region. Thus, this passage may refer to one specific site where the firing of weapons causes ecological catastrophe.

"Come on," some say. "These judgments are allegories. You can't take them literally." In response, I challenge them to compare the trumpet judgments with the plagues that befell Egypt (Exodus 7—12). Were those plagues allegorical or literal? Ask Pharaoh.

Revelation 8:10
And the third angel sounded, and there fell a great star from heaven, burning as it were a lamp, and it fell upon the third part of the rivers, and upon the fountains of waters;

Aboveground nuclear testing has been banned largely due to the discovery of radioactive Strodium 90 in fresh-water supplies surrounding the areas of detonation.

Revelation 8:11 (a)
And the name of the star is called Wormwood . . .

Perhaps coincidentally, perhaps not—the Russian word for "wormwood" is "cherynobyl."

Revelation 8:11 (b)
. . . and the third part of the waters became wormwood . . .

"Wormwood" alludes to prophecy. But I believe it also speaks of Jesus, who became a worm as He became sin for you and me (Psalm 22:6).

Revelation 8:11 (c)
. . . and many men died of the waters, because they were made bitter.

After the Israelites traveled through the wilderness for three days without water, it is no wonder they dove into the first pool of water they encountered. But discovering it bitter, they called it "Mara" or "bitter." To remedy the situation, the Lord directed Moses to cast a nearby tree into the water—whereupon the water became sweet. It is interesting that in the Exodus 15 account it is a tree that makes the water sweet. The tree is always a picture of the Cross. When you add the Cross to the bitter water in your life, the result will be sweetness. In this passage, however, just the opposite transpires because those who reject

Christ's work on the Cross will drink the bitter water of the Tribulation.

Revelation 8:12
And the fourth angel sounded, and the third part of the sun was smitten, and the third part of the moon, and the third part of the stars; so as the third part of them was darkened, and the day shone not for a third part of it, and the night likewise.

When Mount St. Helens erupted, the dust that shot into the air made the sky hazy for weeks. Can you imagine what would happen if nuclear warheads were being detonated all over the world? If a nuclear exchange took place in the summertime, scientists tell us the high temperature on the west coast of the United States would be fifteen degrees. Obviously, crops would not grow, and starvation would result. Thus, when Scripture talks about a thirty-three percent reduction in the light of sun, moon, and stars, it could be speaking of what scientists ominously term "nuclear winter."

Revelation 8:13
And I beheld, and heard an angel flying through the midst of heaven, saying with a loud voice, Woe, woe, woe, to the inhabiters of the earth by reason of the other voices of the trumpet of the three angels, which are yet to sound!

In other words, the angel is saying, "The worst is yet to come because the last three trumpets are worse than the first four."

As we will see in chapter 9, the next three trumpets to blast judgment upon the earth are much more devastating than the first four. The first four trumpets dealt with the arena of the natural. The last three deal with the supernatural—specifically demonic activity.

THE HUSH OF HEAVEN
A Topical Study of
Revelation 8:1

The apostle John is writing to a group of people who are picked on, put down, beat up, and persecuted as they are fed to lions, crucified upside down, and ignited as candles by the hand of the Roman Empire. As you read the Book of Revelation, keep this backdrop in mind. The temptation is to view this book only in the context of current events and eschatology. Although current application is important, we must listen to John's heartfelt words to his readers in A.D. 96—people who had no prestige, power, or prominence—people who perhaps wondered if they even had a prayer.

"Yes! You do!" John would say resoundingly. "These winds of persecution do not have to blow you away because you *do* have a prayer."

I was in the Spirit on the Lord's day . . .   Revelation 1:10 (a)

"I was *on* the island of Patmos due to persecution," writes John, "but I was *in* the Spirit. *Ginomai en pneuma* in Greek translates literally "I *came* to be in the Spirit." Not, "I was sitting in a pew, when I suddenly found myself in the Spirit"—but "I *came to be* in the Spirit. I actively pressed in."

How did John press in?

He prayed.

The entire Book of Revelation is a mixture of vision and prayer. And here in chapter 8, John deals with this issue in a most powerful, picturesque, practical way as he reminded his persecuted people to pray.

According to church historians, the distinctive feature of early Christian prayer is the certainty of being heard. In other words, when the early church prayed, they believed God was actually listening.

And when he had opened the seventh seal, there was silence in heaven about the space of half an hour.   Revelation 8:1

Commentator after commentator will tell you the silence in heaven of Revelation 8:1 is a mystery. But I suggest to you our text indicates that as the prayers of the saints ascend before Him, it's as though God says, "Hush." To the living creatures who cry, "Holy, Holy, Holy," He says, "Hush"; to the twenty-four elders who praise Him continually, He says, "Hush"; to the thousands of angels who serve Him perpetually, He says, "Hush"—rendering heaven completely, totally silent.

It's as though God says, "At this moment in time, nothing else has My attention like this prayer being offered to Me. I don't want to miss a single word."

Because our days are filled with a cacophony of noise, we don't hear each other very well. We talk, but we don't listen. We converse, but we don't understand. There is, however, one exception: Two people who are totally in love can sit in a crowded, noisy restaurant and converse as though there's no one else around. And that's the idea here. "I am passionately in love with the child speaking to Me," says God, "and I don't want to miss a word he's saying." So, like a laser, fixing His full attention on the person offering even the simplest of prayers, God listens.

People spend thousands of dollars on psychiatrists, or months waiting for a pastoral appointment—yet God gives His undivided, complete, total attention to the prayers of anyone going through tribulation or trouble. The key is simply to pray.

And another angel came and stood at the altar, having a golden censer; and there was given unto him much incense, that he should offer it with the prayers of all saints upon the golden altar which was before the throne.

Revelation 8:3

The prayer that causes silence throughout heaven is mixed with much incense. Throughout Scripture, incense speaks of intercession. Hebrews 7:25 says that Jesus Christ, our Great High Priest, ever lives to make intercession for the saints. In other words, the incense of Jesus' intercession on our behalf sweetens our prayers. You see, my prayers stink because they're tainted by my flesh. I ask for something I think is good, but Jesus, knowing my request would have disastrous results says, "Father, this is how Jon is praying, but what he really means is . . ."

Knowing our hearts, Jesus perfumes our clumsy and faulty prayers through His intercessory ministry.

And the angel took the censer, and filled it with fire of the altar, and cast it into the earth: and there were voices, and thunderings, and lightnings, and an earthquake.

Revelation 8:5

The angel takes the censer of prayer, perfumed with intercession, and casts, or literally "hurls" it back to earth. As the answer reenters earth's atmosphere, the whole world is shaken with incalculable effect. These guys being beat up and persecuted are told through this prophecy that their prayers are heard, and that, in due season, the answer will shake their world.

And the seven angels which had the seven trumpets prepared themselves to sound.

Revelation 8:6

What was the answer? It was music to the ears of the persecuted, for when these first-century believers studied the Bible, they studied the Old Testament. And when they did, they read of trumpets. . . .

The blast of seven trumpets preceded the collapse of the seemingly impregnable walls of Jericho (Joshua 6).

The alarm of two trumpets reminded the children of Israel that the Lord their God would bring them victory (Numbers 10:9).

The sound of the trumpet signaled the year of Jubilee—in which all debts were canceled, all slaves set free (Leviticus 25:9).

Thus, the answer to their prayers was truly music to the ears of John's congregation, for the sound of the trumpet promised victory, liberation, and the collapse of a city stronger even than Rome.

"Interesting study," you may say, "but I've been saved for a while, and I know differently. Oh, I'm not saying God doesn't listen to prayer generally—just that He doesn't hear My prayer specifically. My marriage was on the rocks," or, "My daughter had cancer," or, "My business was going bankrupt, so I prayed and prayed and prayed—and nothing happened. You talk about blaring trumpets, about a fireball of an answer hurled from heaven. That's fine theoretically, but it doesn't play that way for me personally."

If you feel this way, you're not alone. . . .

There was in the days of Herod, the king of Judaea, a certain priest named Zacharias, of the course of Abia: and his wife was of the daughters of Aaron, and her name was Elisabeth. And they were both righteous before God, walking in all the commandments and ordinances of the Lord blameless. And they had no child, because that Elisabeth was barren, and they both were now well stricken in years.   Luke 1:5–7

Because barrenness was considered a curse, Zacharias and Elisabeth were considered sinful in the eyes of their community. Although God deemed them righteous, others believed there was a defect in their piety. This being the case, perhaps Zacharias and Elisabeth lived their lives brokenhearted, wondering what was wrong.

And there appeared unto him an angel of the Lord standing on the right side of the altar of incense. And when Zacharias saw him, he was troubled, and fear fell upon him. But the angel said unto him, Fear not, Zacharias: for thy prayer is heard; and thy wife Elisabeth shall bear thee a son, and thou shalt call his name John.   Luke 1:11–13

"*What* prayer?" Zacharias must have asked. "Prayer for a son? I stopped praying for a son thirty years ago!"

Do you understand the implication? This verse tells us that God remembers even the prayers we forget. "Give us a son," prayed Elisabeth and Zacharias. But they heard nothing day after week after month after year because God wanted to give them more than just a son. His plan was to give them the herald for His own Son (Matthew 11:11).

Slowly, I begin to understand that my prayers remain in the Lord's "To Do" box, even though I may have given up hope long ago. Mixed with the sweet incense of Christ's intercession, they simmer on the altar until God answers them in a way I would never have dared dream (Ephesians 3:20).

Thus, the delay in answered prayer is not due to God's procrastination, but to His desire to exceed even our wildest imagination.

"Shhh," says God. "My child is praying." And at the right time—maybe that day, maybe next week, maybe ten years down the road, maybe half a century later—the answer will quake his world.

Every time you pray, dear saint, you have your Father's full attention. And one day, trumpets will sound; walls will fall; debts will be canceled; victory will abound.

May God help us to be people who pray.

9

Revelation 9:1 (a)
And the fifth angel sounded, and I saw a star fall from heaven unto the earth . . .

In the original Greek text, the word "fall" is in the past tense. Thus, newer translations properly render this verse, "I saw a star which had fallen to the earth"—an event that has already taken place. Who is this star? Lucifer, or Satan, who also bears the name "Shining One."

There was Another who also saw Satan fall from heaven. . . .

"Master," said the excited disciples, returning from their first missionary venture, "even the demons are subject to us as we minister in Your Name."

"I saw Satan fall from heaven like lightning," answered Jesus. In other words, "You guys are so excited about the power you're experiencing in ministry, but be careful: I saw Satan fall from heaven because he got wrapped up in the power he possessed as heaven's worship leader. No longer a servant, he wanted heaven to serve him. Therefore, do not rejoice in what you are doing or what you have seen happen in your service for Me. Rejoice instead in the fact that your names are written in the Book of Life—that you're saved by the goodness and generosity of God" (see Luke 10:20).

The sober warning to anyone in ministry is to make sure that seeing demons flee or lives changed doesn't become your passion. Rejoice, instead, in what God has done for you in rescuing you from the fires of hell.

Revelation 9:1 (b)
. . . and to him was given the key of the bottomless pit.

When Lucifer fell from heaven, Isaiah 14, Ezekiel 28, and Revelation 12 tell us one-third of the angels went with him and became demons. The worst of these demons—those who "left their first estate" (Jude 6) and had the audacity to have relations with women, producing the "nephilim," or giants, seen in Genesis and Numbers—God cast into the *abussos*, or bottomless pit. But now watch what happens as the plot thickens. . . .

Revelation 9:2 (a)
And he opened the bottomless pit . . .

Can you imagine what will happen when the worst demons presently chained are suddenly released? If every prison in our nation was opened and all the inmates immediately released, it would be Romper Room compared to what will happen when these demons are free.

Revelation 9:2 (b)
. . . and there arose a smoke out of the pit, as the smoke of a great furnace; and the sun and the air were darkened by reason of the smoke of the pit.

If you were transported to seventeenth-century London, you would find yourself enveloped in the smoke of cannons and fires burning day and night. You would soon learn that the intelligentsia of the day had identified fresh air as the cause behind the epidemic claiming one out of four lives. You alone would know the culprit was not fresh air, but rather the fleas on the rats that carried the Bubonic Plague. However, were you to target fleas as the problem, you would be laughed to scorn.

So, too, educated people today scoff at the very idea of demons. "You don't really believe in demons, do you?" they chide. "We now know that demons are only another name for fears, phobias, and psychological imbalances." Gang, they were blowing smoke in 1666, and they're blowing smoke today. The Bible says demons are at work presently causing people to experience depression, emotional distress, and relational trauma.

Inspired by the Spirit of God, Paul said we do not wrestle against flesh and blood but against the very real entities of principalities and powers, against spiritual wickedness in high places (Ephesians 6:12).

Revelation 9:3, 4
And there came out of the smoke locusts upon the earth: and unto them was given power, as the scorpions of the earth have power. And it was commanded them that they should not hurt the grass of the earth, neither any green thing, neither any tree; but only those men which have not the seal of God in their foreheads.

As we have seen, the sounding of the trumpets would have been especially significant to John's congregation—bringing to mind the victory of Jericho, the freedom of the Year of Jubilee, the call to worship from the temple in Jerusalem. In fact, some of John's readers would have been on the scene when Jesus Himself talked about the angel who would blow his trumpet to gather the elect (Matthew 24). Jerusalem, Jericho, Jubilee, Jesus—all these images would stir the hearts of John's flock as he told them of the trumpets which would sound. But there's another image that would enter their minds as well: Joel....

Revelation 9:5, 6
And to them it was given that they should not kill them, but that they should be tormented five months: and their torment was as the torment of a scorpion, when he striketh a man. And in those days shall men seek death, and shall not find it; and shall desire to die, and death shall flee from them.

Due to these scorpionlike locusts, men will try to take their own lives.

For topical study of Revelation 9:6 entitled "Euthanasia," turn to page 1717.

Revelation 9:7–10
And the shapes of the locusts were like unto horses prepared unto battle; and on their heads were as it were crowns like gold, and their faces were as the faces of men. And they had hair as the hair of women, and their teeth were as the teeth of lions. And they had breastplates, as it were breastplates of iron; and the sound of their wings was as the sound of chariots of many horses running to battle. And they had tails like unto scorpions, and there were stings in their tails: and their power was to hurt men five months.

Even this description of bizarre and horrific demons would remind John's congregation of God's promise. You see, in Joel 2, we find a parallel passage to Revelation 9....

Historically, the prophecy of Joel 2 was fulfilled in Joel's day when Israel was besieged with locusts.

Symbolically, the prophecy was fulfilled in 722 B.C. when the Assyrians marched south and carried the ten northern tribes into captivity.

Prophetically, the locusts speak of the demons that will be released from the abussos in Revelation 9.

But nestled among the dire warnings of this terrible invasion is a wonderful promise....

And I will restore to you the years that the locust hath eaten, the cankerworm, and the caterpiller, and the palmerworm, my great army which I sent among you. And ye shall eat in plenty, and be satisfied, and praise the name of the LORD your God, that hath dealt wondrously with you: and my people shall never be ashamed.   Joel 2:25, 26

Gang, whenever we obey Scripture—when we listen to the trumpet, repent, and seek the Lord with sincerity—the Lord not only forgives us but makes up to us what was lost. Amazing! I would have thought it would be enough for God to forgive us. But He says, "No, I'm going to do more than that. I will restore to you what the locusts ate."

You might be fifty, sixty, or seventy years old, and you might be saying, "There's a big chunk of my life eaten away by grasshoppers." Good news for you: Whenever you choose to humble yourself and call out to the Lord, He'll make up for lost time.

Revelation 9:11
And they had a king over them, which is the angel of the bottomless pit, whose name in the Hebrew tongue is Abaddon, but in the Greek tongue hath his name Apollyon.

Both names mean "destroyer." No matter what your language or culture, the devil always does the same thing: He's an equal opportunity destroyer. He destroys everyone.

Revelation 9:12–14 (a)
One woe is past; and, behold, there come two woes more hereafter. And the sixth angel

sounded, and I heard a voice from the four horns of the golden altar which is before God, Saying to the sixth angel which had the trumpet, Loose the four angels . . .

According to Joel 2, the priests were to lead the people in repentance. We see the same thing happen in heaven. Who is the Priest at the altar of intercession here in Revelation 9? Who speaks to the sixth angel as He orchestrates the judgment of the Tribulation? It's none other than Jesus Christ. You see, God desperately desires to see people who have rejected salvation wake up. Therefore, He will do whatever it takes in their families, financial situations, health, or marriages to get them on their knees where they can finally call out to Him. The question is, what kind of locusts will God have to allow in our lives to wake us from our lethargy, to wake us from our apathy? Whatever it takes, He loves us enough to let it happen.

Revelation 9:14 (b)
. . . which are bound in the great river Euphrates.

The Euphrates was part of the original boundary of the Garden of Eden (Genesis 2:14). It also marked the east boundary of the Promised Land God deeded to Abraham (Genesis 15:18).

Revelation 9:15
And the four angels were loosed, which were prepared for an hour, and a day, and a month, and a year, for to slay the third part of men.

When the demons that reside in the Euphrates are loosed, they will kill one-third of humanity. Added to the number of those already killed, 50 percent of humanity will be dead. How will this take place? Read on.

Revelation 9:16–19
And the number of the army of the horsemen were two hundred thousand thousand: and I heard the number of them. And thus I saw the horses in the vision, and them that sat on them, having breastplates of fire, and of jacinth, and brimstone: and the heads of the horses were as the heads of lions; and out of their mouths issued fire and smoke and brimstone. By these three was the third part of men killed, by the fire, and by the smoke, and by the brimstone, which issued out of their mouths. For their power is in their mouth, and in their tails: for their tails were like unto serpents, and had heads, and with them they do hurt.

What *is* this army? John's readers must have thought, *Oh, no, the armies of Rome will march once again*—as indeed they would. Yet read carefully, there is reason to agree with many commentators who say this is John's attempt to describe guns and tanks, troop personnel carriers, and missile launchers—a description of what we know today as modern weaponry.

But because this army is set in motion by the four fallen angels of verse 15, it's comprised of much more than military generals or political coalitions. From his heavenly vantage, John sees that the demonic realm directly affects nations.

The demons are stinging. The armies are marching. Jesus is interceding. What's the response of the people? Read on.

Revelation 9:20
And the rest of the men which were not killed by these plagues yet repented not of the works of their hands, that they should not worship devils, and idols of gold, and silver, and brass, and stone, and of wood: which neither can see, nor hear, nor walk.

"Well," you say, "this can't apply to us today. We don't have idols of brass, metal, or gold." But have you looked in your garage lately?

Revelation 9:21 (a)
Neither repented they of their murders . . .

As bills to stop funding for human cloning fly through the House and Senate even as abortion runs rampant, we launch into frontiers that frighten not only the Christian community, but those in the political arena as well.

Revelation 9:21 (b)
. . . nor of their sorceries . . .

The word translated "sorceries" is *pharmakeus* in Greek, from which we get our word "pharmacy." And now we begin to see the access point into an individual, a people, a generation, a nation. When a person smokes marijuana, drinks alcohol, uses cocaine, it's a spiritual issue. Why did hippies in the '60s shout, "I am Jesus Christ!" as they dropped acid? Because drugs and mysticism are related. The world thinks drugs tamper only with the mind, but they're about much more than that. They affect the soul.

Revelation 9:21 (c)
. . . nor of their fornication . . .

This is why many of your friends and coworkers are going through their own tribulation right now. "Oh, but I haven't hurt anyone," they say. Wrong. There is a demonic component to pornography, to fornication, to adultery that puts a hook into one's soul.

Revelation 9:21 (d)
. . . nor of their thefts.

It's tax time, folks. "Oh, well, everyone steals," we say. Maybe that's why so many folks are experiencing tribulation today. Is giving Satan access to your world worth twenty dollars?

"I'm confused," you say. "I thought you taught demons cannot possess believers." They can't. You'll never see a demon possess a believer in Scripture because He that is in us is greater than he that is in the world (1 John 4:4). For a believer, there's no such thing as demon possession. But there is such a thing as demon oppression. Your life and family will be oppressed continually if you allow demons entry points through drugs or alcohol, pornography or thievery.

The Jews returned to Israel following their Babylonian captivity and rebuilt the temple under Ezra's leadership. As the temple was a picture of the spirit, and the Land representative of the body, physically, and spiritually the Jews were okay. But the walls—emblematic of the soul, the place where decisions are made—were in ruins.

And we've all been there. Our spirit is born again. Our body is functioning. But our soul is constantly attacked by the Enemy. Perhaps it's lust; maybe it's just lousy attitudes. We know we're saved; we know we're going to heaven, but our soul—the seat of government in our life—is vulnerable to attack. And that's where Nehemiah comes in.

You see, Ezra built the temple. But the repair of the walls—the soul—was left to Nehemiah. This one whose name means "comforter" rode around the city for three days, saying nothing to anyone. A picture of the Holy Spirit, Nehemiah looked around and saw destruction. Then he began speaking. And the people had a choice to make. They could either listen to what Nehemiah was saying about their broken-down condition, or they could say, "Beat it, Comforter. We'll put up with the attacks of the enemy."

The people wisely heeded Nehemiah's cry, and Scripture says they "had a mind to work" (Nehemiah 4:6). They got busy and rebuilt the walls that were destroyed. It wasn't easy. There were attacks from within as when Judah, the strongest tribe said, "Let's give up." And there were attacks from without, as they were taunted, harassed, and harangued. But Nehemiah set the example—as the Holy Spirit always will—and kept on working. The people responded and the wall was rebuilt.

Tonight, the Holy Spirit may be speaking to you, saying, "You're being stung badly. You need to repent." If you listen to His voice, He will begin to rebuild and restore the walls of your soul.

EUTHANASIA
A Topical Study of
Revelation 9:6

For a few years, Jack Kevorkian, also known as "Dr. Death," seemed to show up on the news every few weeks. Up to this point, he has helped at least forty people take their lives. Although he paints himself as a man of compassion, his paintings on canvas, with titles like "Coma" and "Nausea," depict the macabre. His view that the organs of those who die should be auctioned to the highest bidder for use as transplants resulted in the loss of his medical license. And his statement that, "Jesus would have died a much more dignified death in the back of my van than on that Cross," sends chills down the spine. Of the forty-plus suicides he has assisted, autopsies show twenty-four were of people without terminal illness, three without any illness at all.

Jack Kevorkian has asked a question that the second highest court in the land has answered with this judgment: Assisted suicide is not only legal, but Americans have a Constitutional right to seek help in the taking of their lives. Oregon passed a referendum legalizing assisted suicide. No doubt, voters were swept up in the argument that people have a right to die with dignity.

In fact, proponents of assisted suicide point to passages like the one before us and say our God is mean-spirited. Why else would He allow people to be tormented, stung by demon-scorpions, unable to put an end to their pain?

Is it true? As seen here in chapter 9 of Revelation, is God mean? And are we as believers hard-hearted and calloused because we do not agree with the three out of four Americans who maintain that a person has the right to determine the time of his death? Our text says God does not want people taken out of their tribulation so readily. Why? In every single case where suicide is seen in the Word, it is linked to spiritual collapse—Judas Iscariot being the clearest example. But even assisted suicide is seen as a spiritual collapse. . . .

> Wounded in battle on Mount Gilboah, King Saul lay on the ground. "Kill me," he said to an Amalekite passing by. The Amalekite did so and then rushed to tell David the news, thinking David would be thrilled that he could now ascend the throne.
>
> But David looked at this man and cried, "How could you touch the Lord's anointed?"—the implication being that he had interfered with God's plan. And David ordered him executed on the spot (see 2 Samuel 1:14, 15).

Why was David upset? Why is it wrong to assist in suicide? I suggest five reasons. . . .

First, God has established the day of death (Job 14:5).

"It's *my* body," people say. "I have a right to do whatever I want." Tilt. Wrong. Not true. Our bodies have been bought with a price (1 Corinthians 6:19, 20). Asked who determines right from wrong in the area of assisted suicide, Jack Kevorkian answered, "*I* know what is right." Yet Proverbs 14:12 says there is a way that seems right to a man, but the end is death.

Second, pressure is put on the elderly to stop burdening society.

In Holland, where assisted suicide is legal, once a man sees white in his hair, he begins to feel selfish for continuing to live—even though, due to his wisdom and experience, his greatest contributions may be ahead of him.

Third, selfish motives arise.

In a news story years ago, a medical doctor was diagnosed with Alzheimer's disease. His wife suggested he take his life. But wrangling between mother and son over custody of the man resulted in the discovery of a large estate at stake.

Fourth, irreversible mistakes will be made once suicide is condoned.

Shortly after the fall that broke his spinal cord, actor Christopher Reeve fought off the temptation to seek assisted suicide. In years since, such advances have been made in spinal cord restoration, it is no longer inconceivable that he will walk again.

Finally, assisted suicide dries up resources.

Only two hospices exist in Holland today, and medical technology is at the lowest point it has ever been, compared to the rest of the European community. Why? The money once spent on saving lives is now spent extinguishing them.

But none of these reasons address this foundational error of euthanasia: Although man is concerned about his present comfort, God is concerned about his eternal state. Never forget this. You see, if these people of Revelation 9 had the "right to die," they would not have seen the angel fly across the sky preaching salvation. They would not have heard the 144,000 call for repentance. They would not have seen the two witnesses—most likely Moses and Elijah—doing miracles in the streets of Jerusalem. It won't be God's meanness that will keep them from killing themselves. It will be His mercy.

The world says, "Eat, drink, and be merry, for tomorrow you die. And if you can't eat drink and be merry, then die today." But this is fallacious because we don't die tomorrow. We move into eternity.

It's the loss of a loved one, the struggle with cancer, the dealing with depression, the aging of the body that causes people to say, "I had better develop a relationship with God, or I'm not going to make it through this tribulation." In so doing, they are strengthened and deepened. The people you admire most, the people who impact you the greatest are undoubtedly those who have gone through "the fellowship of suffering" (Philippians 3:10).

Strolling through the forest, you spy a cocoon hanging from a tree. Upon closer examination, you see it move. "Bobby Butterfly is trying to get out," you say.

"He's struggling. He must be hurting. Poor Bobby." And so, in the name of compassion, you take out your Swiss Army knife and clip the bottom of the cocoon, whereupon Bobby Butterfly falls to the ground. You're so proud. After all, you saved him from the struggle and pain of breaking out of his cocoon. But look at him. He's dead—because the wings of a butterfly are strengthened only through struggle.

"I'm just trying to put her out of her misery," someone might say. But there's a struggle going on in that person's soul that will cause her to fly eternally. How dare we interfere.

"But he seems to know so little." Ah, but you cannot see what God is doing in his soul, in the deepest recess of his being. How dare we claim to know.

I am not arguing that we should sustain life when the time to die arrives. But to assume that we have the right to shorten a life span is biblically and morally wrong.

Life isn't easy, gang. There are sad times. There are struggles. But don't short-circuit them because those times will make you rich in heaven. It's all about eternity, precious people. Don't lose sight of that. There are bigger issues than comfort and ease and freedom from pain. Be wise in these last days.

10

In contrast to chapter 9, which was dark and dismal, chapter 10 is bright and uplifting as we see what follows the demons' release from the bottomless pit. . . .

Revelation 10:1 (a)
And I saw another mighty angel come down from heaven . . .

After the darkness comes light as an awesome angel, an ambassador from heaven, descends.

Revelation 10:1 (b)–3
. . . clothed with a cloud: and a rainbow was upon his head, and his face was as it were the sun, and his feet as pillars of fire: And he had in his hand a little book open: and he set his right foot upon the sea, and his left foot on the earth, and cried with a loud voice, as when a lion roareth: and when he had cried, seven thunders uttered their voices.

Many good Bible teachers believe this angel is Jesus Himself because the angel's description is very similar to the description of Jesus in chapter 1. In addition, "angel," or *aggelos* in Greek, means "messenger"—a term that could theoretically apply to Jesus. But I have a problem with this view because the appearance of Jesus on the

earth at this time would interrupt the flow of the book. I suggest this is an angel of importance who, like Moses in Exodus 34, takes on characteristics of the Lord because he is in the presence of the Lord. This encourages me because the same thing is true for us. If we spend time with the Lord, we begin to sound like Him, look like Him, and act like Him a little more each day.

Revelation 10:4
And when the seven thunders had uttered their voices, I was about to write: and I heard a voice from heaven saying unto me, Seal up those things which the seven thunders uttered, and write them not.

Seven thunderous voices roar in response to the angel. What did they utter? We don't know.

For topical study of Revelation 10:4 entitled "The Blessing of Not Knowing," turn to page 1722.

Revelation 10:5, 6
And the angel which I saw stand upon the sea and upon the earth lifted up his hand to heaven, And sware by him that liveth for ever and ever, who created heaven, and the

things that therein are, and the earth, and the things that therein are, and the sea, and the things which are therein, that there should be time no longer.

The Greek word translated "time" is *chronos* and means either "time" or "delay." Delay is what is meant here. "Thy kingdom come," we pray. "But where are You, Lord?"

"I'm on the way, but I have chosen to delay," He says.

Why? I believe Peter gives us the reason: The Lord is not slack concerning His promise, but is longsuffering, not willing that any should perish, but that all should come to repentance (2 Peter 3:9).

Truly, the Lord is longsuffering, waiting for people to receive Him, to hear the Good News, to be part of the kingdom. But there's coming a time when there will be no more delay.

Revelation 10:7
But in the days of the voice of the seventh angel, when he shall begin to sound, the mystery of God should be finished, as he hath declared to his servants the prophets.

Because John's readers were seeing family members killed, friends beat up, terrible things take place, he writes, "There's coming a time when all of the questions you have and all of the pain you're experiencing will be alleviated."

Revelation 10:8, 9 (a)
And the voice which I heard from heaven spake unto me again, and said, Go and take the little book which is open in the hand of the angel which standeth upon the sea and upon the earth. And I went unto the angel, and said unto him, Give me the little book. And he said unto me, Take it, and eat it up . . .

The angel's command to eat the book may sound odd to us, but it shouldn't. We often talk about people who "devour" books. The only difference is, John does so literally.

Revelation 10:9 (b), 10
. . . and it shall make thy belly bitter, but it shall be in thy mouth sweet as honey. And I took the little book out of the angel's hand, and ate it up; and it was in my mouth sweet as honey: and as soon as I had eaten it, my belly was bitter.

Like the book the angel gave John, the Word is sweeter than honey (Psalm 19:10; 119:103). But if the sweet Word we take in through devotions or Bible study doesn't create a sour taste, something's wrong. You see, the fact that we're saved is sweet indeed—but the fact that people we love are going to hell is bitter.

It was only after Ezekiel ate the book that was sweet to his mouth but bitter to his belly that he was able to share boldly with those of whom he had previously been afraid (Ezekiel 3:3, 14). The bitterness in his belly motivated Ezekiel to share truth.

Revelation 10:11
And he said unto me, Thou must prophesy again before many peoples, and nations, and tongues, and kings.

The idea of "must" here is not a command, but a statement of what will inevitably happen when one takes in the Word. How do you know you've really heard the Word? When you have compassion for the sinner and conviction of your own sin.

"Then why go to Bible study?" you ask. "Who wants a bitter belly? I want sweetness." And I understand this. . . .

I'm watching CNN on TV when a commercial for Compassion International suddenly appears: Sally Struthers showing starving kids in Africa or Southeast Asia.

"Oh no," I say to myself. "I don't want to deal with this now." Click. Sally disappears. So do the kids.

That's what people do with church and devotions and witnessing. "I don't want to go anymore," they say. "It makes my belly hurt." Click, Wednesday night Bible study, gone. Click, Thursday morning worship, gone. Click, devotions gone. "I don't want to deal with this sin, these attitudes, that cynicism. Just give me the sweet stuff."

But you know what happens to those people? Their lives begin to unravel because staying in the Word is the only way to experience prosperity and success (Joshua 1:8). Yes, it will trouble you. No doubt it may upset you. But as time goes on, you will begin to see that your life is centered and grounded, fruitful and prosperous because the Word always does its work.

My prayer is that we will be those who, like John, devour and digest Scripture—the bitter portions as well as the sweet—in order that we, like John, would impact our world for the kingdom.

THE BLESSING OF NOT KNOWING
A Topical Study of
Revelation 10:4

Although the purpose of Revelation is to reveal, we find a concealing in our text as John is forbidden to record the response of the seven thunderous voices to the roaring of the angel in verse 3. Why was John not allowed to record it? After careful study, I have come to the conclusion that I don't have a clue.

Not so Ellen G. White, founder of the Seventh Day Adventist movement. She has much to say about what these voices uttered. So do the Mormons and many other cults who have built entire doctrines upon this mysterious section of Revelation 10.

But Scripture makes it clear that the message of the seven thunderous voices was to be hidden—which raises a very interesting question: Why is it even mentioned? It's like someone saying, "I know something, but I'm not going to tell you." Is the Lord just teasing us here?

No. I suggest to you it's a very simple but significant reminder placed in the middle of the book that there are some things we simply are not going to know.

When I was younger, I thought I had to solve every problem, unknot every difficult situation. I was burdened by my need for answers. However, as I get older, I have discovered a real blessing in *not* knowing. "The secret things belong to Me," declares the Lord (see Deuteronomy 29:29). Why would He want to keep things away from you? Why would He want to keep me in the dark about certain issues?

Not Knowing Keeps Us Humble

When I think I have all the answers in any area, I become puffed up, self-sufficient. Conversely, not knowing the answers, not having the solutions, produces within me a humility that ultimately makes me very happy because it takes all the pressure off. Even as the psalmist said, "Lord, I do not look into things too great for me, but like a weaned child, I just put my trust in You" (see Psalm 131:1, 2), I say, "I don't get this, Lord. So I'll just trust You."

In the wee hours of the morning, a dozen of us freshman guys at Biola were discussing theology in my dorm room. Dave Hong brought up the question,

"Can God make a rock so big He can't lift it?"—which I pondered throughout my classes the next day.

It sounds funny, but it really threw me. I thought, *Oh no! Maybe God can't do everything. Maybe He can't make a rock so big He can't lift it. What does this do to my theology?*

When Sunday finally arrived, we piled into my roommate's Mustang and drove to church in Costa Mesa where, late, we slipped into the back pew. Pastor Chuck was teaching on Deuteronomy 29:29. "You know," he said, "the apostle Paul tells us we are to avoid foolish and ignorant questions like: Can God make a rock so big He can't lift it—because such questions are just dumb."

Suddenly I realized I no longer needed an answer.

Not Knowing Keeps Us Useful

The son of ex-slaves, George Washington Carver had a keen intellect that afforded him a college education. After graduating from Simpson College right before the turn of the century, Carver was invited to remain at his alma mater as a science professor. Perhaps feeling overwhelmed by the prospect of this new responsibility, he prayed, "Lord, show me something of the mysteries of the universe." But there was no response.

"Maybe I'm asking for something a little too big for me," he thought. "Lord, show me the mysteries of our earth," he prayed. But again, there was no response. "Lord, show me something about our bodies," he then prayed— to no avail. Finally, he prayed, "Lord, show me something about a peanut." And he writes that he experienced a strange sense of God's presence.

So George Washington Carver began to study the peanut, which, up to that time was thought to be a fairly useless commodity. In the ensuing years, he discovered three hundred uses for the lowly peanut: soap, shoeshine, ink, and, of course, peanut butter, for which I am very thankful—and thus began diversification of the crippled economy of the South.

Sometimes I am asked how I know what I do about the Bible. And the answer is very simple: I don't know anything else. If you come to my house, you'll never see me working on my transmission. Is this because I'm so spiritual? No, it's because I tried it once. I took the engine of my 1960 Ford Falcon apart, put it back together, and it never ran again. "Why don't I have the skills other guys have?" I used to ask myself. "How cool it would be to be able to build a house or fix a car!" Yet, the Lord has shown me that because I'm to be focused on the one thing He wants me to be about, I won't be able to do a whole bunch of other stuff.

It's a peanut thing. I know what my calling is, and I can focus on that singularly. So can you. Whatever He's placed in your hand, whatever He's called you to do—the gifts, the skills, the interests He's given you—that's what you should be about for His glory.

Not Knowing Keeps Us Stable

Over the years, I have seen in my own life and in the lives of others a vulnerability to instability when life gets difficult, a tendency to ask, "Why, God? How come, Lord? What's going on here?"

Yet, knowing we would invariably argue with Him if He answered our questions, the Lord chooses to give us a peace that *passes* our understanding (Philippians 4:7).

You won't find a single verse in Scripture that promises we'll understand. Therefore, happy is the day when a man says with Paul, "I only know in part" (see 1 Corinthians 13:12).

> The sixteen-year-old daughter of G. Campbell Morgan, one of my heroes of the last generation, lay on her deathbed. As he prayed, the Lord gave him the Scripture about Jairus. "Come quickly," said Jairus to Jesus, "my daughter is sick even to the point of death."
>
> "I will come," Jesus said. But on the way, another need arose, and He was delayed in reaching the house of Jairus. When He finally arrived, messengers said, "Don't bother to come in, Master. She's dead." But Jesus took the hand of Jairus' daughter, said, "Daughter arise," and she was healed (see Mark 5:41).
>
> G. Campbell Morgan embraced the promise and knew his daughter would also be healed. Three days later, she died. "Wait a minute, Lord," he cried, "You gave me this Scripture: Daughter, arise."
>
> And the Lord gently whispered, "That's exactly what happened. I took her hand, said, 'Daughter arise,'—and took her to heaven."

After observing and enduring tragedies and difficulties as we all have, I have concluded this: If you think you have to know why things happen or don't happen, you'll go up and down like a roller coaster. "How come she left me?" "Why didn't the business work out?" "Why didn't the college accept me?"

But when you reach the place of saying, "I don't know why; I don't know how; but I know who"—your roller coaster ride will even out.

"Trust Me," thunders a voice from Calvary in the midst of the unsettling earthquake and the mysteriously dark sky. "I'm laying down everything for you. I'm dying in place of you. I love you. If I gave everything for you, you can trust Me in the situation you're going through."

I might not know what or how or why—but I know whom I have believed, and am persuaded He'll do what's best for me (2 Timothy 1:12).

"We know all things work together for good," said Paul (see Romans 8:28). He didn't say, "We *see* all things work together for good," because we might not see that happen this side of eternity. But when we get to heaven, we'll say, "Thank You,

Lord, for Your goodness and grace in allowing that trial. I thought it was a tragedy. But now I see that righteous and true are Your judgments, O Lord."

I stopped asking "Why?" a long time ago. I don't even think about it. I just know God loves me. And I know He loves you. I like what Jesus told Peter when He washed Peter's feet: "What I do now you understand not, but you shall hereafter" (see John 13:7). In other words, "What I'm doing now, you don't understand. But you will ... down the road."

Such is the Word of the Lord for many of us today.

11

We are at the halfway point of the Tribulation, and this is quite an incredible section.

Revelation 11:1 (a)
And there was given me a reed like unto a rod . . .

A measuring instrument in John's day, a "reed like unto a rod" would probably be approximately ten feet high.

Revelation 11:1 (b)
. . . and the angel stood, saying, Rise, and measure the temple of God, and the altar, and them that worship therein.

Midway into the Tribulation, John is told to measure the temple, which presupposes there is, indeed, a functioning temple at this point.

Throughout Scripture the temple plays a key role. . . .

Solomon built the first temple on Jerusalem's Mount Moriah in 1050 B.C. More than four hundred years later, the Babylonians destroyed Jerusalem and decimated the temple in 586 B.C.

About seventy years after Babylon's first invasion of Israel, Zerubbabel rebuilt the temple in 536 B.C.

A "third" temple was built in 20 B.C. However, not all scholars deem this the third temple because it was simply an expansion of the old. Wanting to obtain the favor of the Jewish people, King Herod enlarged and expanded the temple—a project that took decades to complete. Jesus referred to this temple when He said, "There shall not be left one stone standing" (see Matthew 24:2).

Forty years after Jesus' resurrection, His prophecy came to pass. While sacking the city of Jerusalem in A.D. 70, a Roman soldier disobeyed the orders of General Titus and threw a torch into the temple. The ensuing fire was so hot that it caused the gold to melt and run down the temple walls into the cracks of the hundred-ton stones. The soldiers pulled down every stone from the walls to extract the gold—fulfilling Jesus' prophecy to the letter.

But there is a fourth temple, yet to be built. In the Institute of Temple Treasures in Jerusalem, you can see preparations for this fourth temple being made even now. Sixty percent of all instruments needed for temple worship, according to Old Testament regulations, are completed. And two yeshivas, or schools, are training young men with the last name of Cohen—Cohen meaning "priest"—to sacrifice animals in the temple tradition.

Why? Because the Orthodox Jewish community understands that without the shedding of blood there is no remission of sin (Leviticus 17:11; Hebrews 9:22). And since they do not believe Jesus is the Messiah who died for their sins, they realize they must make sacrifices for the forgiveness of their sins. Does this mean we will see the temple rebuilt before the Rapture? Not necessarily, for there's a rather large obstacle in the way: A mosque known as the Dome of the Rock. . . .

Revelation 11:2 (a)
But the court which is without the temple leave out, and measure it not . . .

In the late 600s, a man named Omar built a mosque on the thirty-five-acre platform over the rock believed to be the site of the Holy of Holies. This renders a temple rebuilding on this site impossible because the Muslims would immediately invade Israel if anything happened to the mosque.

But twenty years ago, after spending sixteen years studying the temple mount area, a physicist and archaeologist at Hebrew University named Dr. Asher Kaufman came to some remarkable conclusions. In his landmark article in the March/April 1983 issue of *Biblical Archaeological Review,* Dr. Kaufman declares that while the Mosque of Omar has been assumed to sit on the Holy of Holies site, the true location is actually one hundred meters north.

What is one hundred meters north of the Dome of the Rock? A small gazebo-like structure, below which is the only other place the original bedrock of the temple is exposed. As opposed to the jagged rock in the Dome of the Rock, however, the stone one hundred meters to the north is flat—providing a much more likely setting for the ark of the covenant within the Holy of Holies.

Not only more logical, this site seems more historical. You see, according to the Mishna—the highly esteemed book of Jewish oral traditions—when the priest stood in the Holy of Holies on the Day of Atonement, he could look through the veil, through the door, and see the Eastern Gate directly before him.

The results of a secret excavation in 1970 confirmed that the original Eastern Gate is directly below the present Eastern Gate. This makes Kaufman's assertion even more intriguing. For if you stand one hundred meters north of the Dome of the Rock, the Eastern Gate is in plain view.

In addition, when the Muslims built the gazebo-like structure in A.D. 680, they gave it two names: The Dome of the Spirit, and the Dome of the Tablets. Thus, even Islam recognized this site as the spot where the tablets (the Ten Commandments within the ark of the covenant) and the Spirit (the *shekinah, chabod,* glory of God over the ark of the covenant) had been.

So, according to Kaufman and most scholars, the temple could be rebuilt and the Dome of the Rock would remain standing. But the Dome of the Rock would be in the outer courtyard of the temple—which brings us to the rest of verse 2. . . .

Revelation 11:2 (b)
. . . for it is given unto the Gentiles: and the holy city shall they tread under foot forty and two months.

During the Six-Day War of 1967, the Israelis launched a preemptive strike against the Arabs and recaptured the city of Jerusalem.

General Moshe Dayan could have easily booted the Muslims off the temple mount at this point, saying, "You lost. Too bad." But he didn't. In a gesture he himself never fully explained, he let them retain control of the thirty-five-acre parcel. Thus, the outer court of the temple remains "given to the Gentiles" to this day.

Revelation 11:3
And I will give power unto my two witnesses, and they shall prophesy a thousand two hundred and threescore days, clothed in sackcloth.

Why are there two witnesses? Because "in the mouth of two witnesses every word shall be established" (2 Corinthians 13:1). Thus . . .

- Two spies of the twelve commissioned were correct (Numbers 13).
- Joshua sent in two spies to scope out the land (Joshua 2:1).
- There were two angels in the tomb on Easter morning (John 20:12).
- Jesus sent out His witnesses two by two (Mark 6:7).

Revelation 11:4
These are the two olive trees, and the two candlesticks standing before the God of the earth.

The two witnesses are likened to the two olive trees in Zechariah 4 that provide a perpetual supply of oil and are emblematic of the Spirit's anointing in ministry (Zechariah 4:3–6).

Revelation 11:5, 6 (a)
And if any man will hurt them, fire proceedeth out of their mouth, and devoureth their enemies: and if any man will hurt them, he must in this manner be killed. These have power to shut heaven, that it rain not in the days of their prophecy . . .

Who are these men hinted at in Zechariah 4, clothed in sackcloth in Revelation 11, with power to bring about drought and scorch anyone who hassles them?

- Elijah called down fire from heaven that destroyed one hundred soldiers (2 Kings 1).
- Elijah prayed, and the heavens yielded no rain for three and a half years (James 5:17).
- Elijah never died, but instead rode to heaven in a fiery chariot (2 Kings 2:11).
- The Old Testament ends promising Elijah's return (Malachi 4:5).

Thus, I believe Elijah is one of the two witnesses, who, anointed with the oil of the Holy Ghost, will shine as brightly as candlesticks in the midst of the Tribulation.

Revelation 11:6 (b)
. . . and have power over waters to turn them to blood, and to smite the earth with all plagues, as often as they will.

While some have suggested Enoch or Zerubbabel as the second witness, I believe it is Moses.

At Moses' command, Egypt was plagued with darkness, frogs, and death; at his command, the water of the Nile turned to blood (Exodus 7—12).

Moses, representing the law, appeared with Elijah, representing the prophets, on the Mount of Transfiguration (Matthew 17).

Satan and Michael the archangel argue over the body of Moses (Jude 9)—very likely in order to prevent his resurrection as the second witness.

Revelation 11:7, 8
And when they shall have finished their testimony, the beast that ascendeth out of the bottomless pit shall make war against them, and shall overcome them, and kill them. And their dead bodies shall lie in the street of the great city, which spiritually is called Sodom and Egypt, where also our Lord was crucified.

Jerusalem, the only city God calls His own, the city over which Jesus wept compassionately, is now likened to Egypt and Sodom because she has rejected Christ.

Revelation 11:9
And they of the people and kindreds and tongues and nations shall see their dead bodies three days and an half, and shall not suffer their dead bodies to be put in graves.

For hundreds of years, commentators did not understand how the whole world could see this event. Then enter CNN, *20/20*, and Tom Brokaw. I have a piece of advice for Brokaw and the boys: When this story breaks, leave your camera crews in place because it's not over yet. . . .

Revelation 11:10
And they that dwell upon the earth shall rejoice over them, and make merry, and shall send gifts one to another; because these two prophets tormented them that dwelt on the earth.

The only time people rejoice in the Tribulation is over the death of the two witnesses. "Hey, the guys who made us feel uncomfortable, who talked to us about stuff we didn't want to hear are dead! Leave them in the gutter, and let's celebrate!"

If you've been beaten down or left out, rejoice. You're in good company.

Revelation 11:11, 12
And after three days and an half the Spirit of life from God entered into them, and they stood upon their feet; and great fear fell upon them which saw them. And they heard a great voice from heaven saying unto them, Come up hither. And they ascended up to heaven in a cloud; and their enemies beheld them.

These witnesses are examples of what you can be in the last days in which we live. You're to share the gospel with people. Yes, you'll be beat up emotionally and verbally, ostracized, left out, not invited to the party. But you know what will happen? Three and a half days later, you'll rise. There will be a spring in your step and joy in your heart as you find yourself soaring emotionally. Truly, gang, there is nothing, nothing, nothing like sharing your faith. Even if you're put down, beat up, left out, you'll find yourself revived.

If you feel your relationship with the Lord is stagnant or tedious—witness. I guarantee, like the two witnesses in Revelation 11, you'll be caught up into heavenly places. Witnessing is the single most important way I have found to see my own faith revived and renewed.

Jesus didn't tell us to preach the gospel because He wants us to be miserable. On the contrary, He said, "Give, and it shall be given unto you; good measure, pressed down, shaken together, and running over, shall men give into your bosom. For with the same measure that ye mete withal it shall be measured to you again" (see Luke 6:38).

Revelation 11:13 (a)
And the same hour was there a great earthquake . . .

Not only is the world shaken up emotionally by the resurrection of the two witnesses but it is shaken physically in a great earthquake.

Revelation 11:13 (b)
. . . and the tenth part of the city fell, and in the earthquake were slain of men seven thousand . . .

The notes in the margins of newer translations correctly render this phrase "seven thousand men of names." If this earthquake, originating in the fault of the Rift Valley that runs through Israel to North Africa, claims the lives of seven thousand notables, it must also take the lives of multiplied thousands of unknowns in Jerusalem.

Revelation 11:13 (c)–15 (a)
. . . and the remnant were affrighted, and gave glory to the God of heaven. The second woe is past; and, behold, the third woe cometh quickly. And the seventh angel sounded . . .

Here is the last of the seven trumpets, sounded not by God—as those who espouse a mid-Tribulation Rapture view suggest—but by an angel.

Revelation 11:15 (b)–17
. . . and there were great voices in heaven, saying, The kingdoms of this world are become the kingdoms of our Lord, and of his Christ; and he shall reign for ever and ever. And the four and twenty elders, which sat before God on their seats, fell upon their faces, and worshipped God, saying, We give thee thanks, O Lord God Almighty, which art, and wast, and art to come; because thou hast taken to thee thy great power, and hast reigned.

"See," say those who believe in a mid-Tribulation Rapture, "the seventh trumpet sounds and the kingdoms of this world become the kingdoms of our Lord." But they don't take into account the fact that the verb translated "are become" is in the aorist active indicative tense, which means the kingdoms of this world *are becoming* the kingdoms of our Lord. It is what is referred to as a proleptic statement. That is, it is an event so certain that it is spoken of as if it has already taken place.

In Isaiah 53:5, we read, "He was wounded for our transgressions. He was bruised for our iniquities." Of whom is this speaking? Jesus. Had this already happened when Isaiah penned these words? No. But Isaiah wrote it in the past tense because it was as certain as if it had already happened.
    In Romans 8:17, we read that we were glorified because one day, we, indeed, will be.

How do you speak? Those who are spiritually dyslexic say, "I can't make sense of what's going on. Everything's backward. Why even worship? What's the point of praying?" On the other hand, those who are proleptic say, "Even in the middle of my tribulation, the midst of my difficulty, the center of my pain, I know God is on the throne and He is good."

A baby girl was born thirty-one days prematurely to Matt and Cyndy McCollum, missionaries in Honduras. Little Maria Nicole stopped breathing and began to turn blue. Since the tiny airport at La Ceiba was closed, it was doubtful whether she would survive. But I was so blessed talking with Matt's dad, Jerry, the next morning because before he even knew the outcome, he said, "Certain members of Cyndy's family who aren't interested in the things of God are now praying and seeking Him about this situation. And the health care official in Honduras has rededicated her life to Christ watching Matt and Cyndy go through this trial. Great things are happening."

Jerry could have said, "My kids are serving God, and *this* is what He does?" Instead, he was proleptic.

It was after they made it through the Red Sea on dry ground that Miriam led the multitude—who moments before had wanted to kill Moses—in worship (Exodus 15:20). While praise is always fitting, how much better if they had praised God before the Red Sea parted?

The kingdoms of this world *are become* the kingdoms of our Lord. Such is the language of heaven. If you want heaven in your heart or home, speak proleptically as you praise God prolifically.

Revelation 11:18 (a)
And the nations were angry . . .

As the earth quakes, are people repentant? No, they're angry.

Revelation 11:18 (b)
. . . and thy wrath is come, and the time of the dead, that they should be judged, and that thou shouldest give reward unto thy servants the prophets, and to the saints, and them that fear thy name, small and great; and shouldest destroy them which destroy the earth.

Those who destroy—or, literally, "corrupt or pollute" the earth will be destroyed, while those who serve God will be rewarded.

Revelation 11:19 (a)
And the temple of God was opened in heaven, and there was seen in his temple the ark of his testament . . .

Sometimes I am asked if the "ark of his testament," or the ark of the covenant, will be found. I don't think so because Jeremiah 3:16 says in the last days the ark will not be mentioned—probably because no one remembers it. But as the temple is merely a shadow of the reality in heaven, the true ark will be seen in heaven.

Revelation 11:19 (b)
. . . and there were lightnings, and voices, and thunderings, and an earthquake, and great hail.

The "great hail" in the last verse of chapter 11 sets the stage for the parade of great beings and events John is about to witness in chapter 12. . . .

---

12 Chapter 12 is a great chapter, for we find a great wonder in verse 1, a great dragon in verse 3, a great wrath in verse 12, a great eagle in verse 14. In it, we also find great help, for it is here we find great insight about our Enemy.

Revelation 12:1, 2
And there appeared a great wonder in heaven; a woman clothed with the sun, and the moon under her feet, and upon her head a crown of twelve stars: And she being with child cried, travailing in birth, and pained to be delivered.

Who is this woman? Throughout history, there have been a number of suggestions. . . .

Many believe this is the Virgin Mary. But I disagree because if this was Mary, she wouldn't experience birth pains in heaven—a skewed image on many counts.

Others believe this is Mary Baker Eddy, and Christian Science is the birthed child.

Others believe it's the church. But again, this interpretation paints a twisted picture of the church giving birth to the One who will rule and reign. The church doesn't give birth to Jesus. Jesus gives birth to the church. How so? It was the rib taken from Adam's side that birthed Eve. So, too, as He hung on the Cross, it was the blood and water flowing from the side of the Last Adam (1 Corinthians 15:45) that birthed the church.

I believe the only contextual and theological solution to the question of the identity of this woman in Revelation 12 is Israel.

Contextually, while the church is the bride of Christ, Isaiah and Hosea identify Israel as the wife of Jehovah.
Theologically, the answer to questions regarding any particular issue can most often be found by looking to its first mention in Scripture. Employing this principle of first mention, we first see sun, moon, and stars in a dream that pertains directly to Israel (Genesis 37).
And it is Israel who births the One who will rule with righteousness, for Jesus was born of the tribe of Judah.

Revelation 12:3 (a)
And there appeared another wonder in heaven; and behold a great red dragon. . . .

Throughout the remainder of Revelation, the dragon refers to Satan, as it does elsewhere in Scripture (Isaiah 27:1; 51:9).

Revelation 12:3 (b)
. . . having seven heads . . .

The seven heads refer to the city from which Antichrist will reign—the city referred to throughout history as the City of Seven Hills: Rome.

Revelation 12:3 (c)
. . . and ten horns, and seven crowns upon his heads.

While the seven heads refer to a geographical place, the ten horns refer to Satan's political base. The horns, like the ten toes of Daniel 2, typify the ten-nation confederation that will emerge from the old Roman Empire.

Revelation 12:4 (a)
And his tail drew the third part of the stars of heaven, and did cast them to the earth . . .

Lucifer was chief of all created beings in heaven. When he launched a rebellion against God, one third of the "stars"—a biblical term that refers to angels—were cast out of heaven with him.

Revelation 12:4 (b)
. . . and the dragon stood before the woman which was ready to be delivered, for to devour her child as soon as it was born.

Satan's attempt to annihilate Israel is an overriding theme throughout both biblical and secular history. Whether it be through Cain or Pharaoh, Haman, Herod, or Hitler, Satan has been so relentless in his drive to destroy God's people that at one point, only one son of the house of David was left alive.

Why have the Jews been perpetually persecuted? The only explanation must be the one we see here in Revelation 12: The dragon is determined to devour the child of the woman. You see, if there is no Jerusalem, if there is no Israel, if there are no Jewish people, how could Jesus fulfill the prophecies of His return to rule and reign His people in Jerusalem? Consequently, the plan of the dragon is to keep Messiah from returning to Israel by annihilating the Jews. If you don't grasp this, you'll never have a satisfactory answer for the mystery of anti-Semitism.

Revelation 12:5
And she brought forth a man child, who was to rule all nations with a rod of iron: and her child was caught up unto God, and to his throne.

This One who will rule all nations, who ascended into heaven, is, of course, Jesus.

Revelation 12:6
And the woman fled into the wilderness, where she hath a place prepared of God, that they should feed her there a thousand two hundred and threescore days.

As we shall see, when Antichrist enters the temple and demands to be worshiped, the great Tribulation Jesus spoke of in Matthew 24 begins. And 1,260 days, or 3.5 biblical years, of unparalleled hostility will break loose against the Jews. That is why Jesus told the Jews to flee to the wilderness when they see this day dawn (Matthew 24:15). Isaiah tells us exactly where this wilderness is:

Send ye the lamb to the ruler of the land from Sela to the wilderness, unto the mount of the daughter of Zion. For it shall be, that, as a wandering bird cast out of the nest, so the daughters of Moab shall be at the fords of Arnon. Take counsel, execute judgment; make thy shadow as the night in the midst of the noonday; hide the outcasts; bewray not him that wandereth. Let mine outcasts dwell with thee, Moab; be thou a covert to them from the face of the spoiler: for the extortioner is at an end, the spoiler ceaseth, the oppressors are consumed out of the land.   Isaiah 16:1–4

As your margin might say, "Sela" means "Rock" or "Petra." Petra is truly an amazing city. Located in Moab, or present-day Jordan, this city carved of stone has stood for centuries, preserved largely because the sole entrance is a passageway only twelve feet wide.

Revelation 12:7, 8
And there was war in heaven: Michael and his angels fought against the dragon; and the dragon fought and his angels, and prevailed not; neither was their place found any more in heaven.

"Wait a minute," you say. "I thought Satan was already cast out of heaven." He was, but as seen in Job 1, he still has access to heaven.

Revelation 12:9
And the great dragon was cast out, that old serpent, called the Devil, and Satan, which deceiveth the whole world: he was cast out into the earth, and his angels were cast out with him.

The word "devil" means "accuser" or "slanderer." "Satan" means "adversary" or "one who lies in wait."

Revelation 12:10
And I heard a loud voice saying in heaven, Now is come salvation, and strength, and the kingdom of our God, and the power of his Christ: for the accuser of our brethren is cast down, which accused them before our God day and night.

When rewards are given to believers at the judgment seat of Christ, Satan—the accuser of the brethren—says, "What? *Him? Her?!* Why are *they* getting rewards?"

And what happens in heaven occurs every day on earth as Satan whispers in your ear, "You're not worthy to be blessed. You're not good enough to be used." Please understand the difference between condemnation—which is from Satan, and conviction—which is from the Holy Spirit. The condemning work of Satan always pushes you away from God. The conviction of the Holy Spirit, on the other hand, always draws you closer to God. The condemnation of Satan is always about self, about never measuring up, about hopelessness. The conviction of the Spirit is always about forgiveness, about going on, about God's glory and grace.

Revelation 12:11, 12
And they overcame him by the blood of the Lamb, and by the word of their testimony;

and they loved not their lives unto the death. Therefore rejoice, ye heavens, and ye that dwell in them. Woe to the inhabiters of the earth and of the sea! for the devil is come down unto you, having great wrath, because he knoweth that he hath but a short time.

Satan is overcome in heaven. He can be overcome on earth the same way. . . .

For topical study of Revelation 12:11 entitled "Overcoming the Enemy," turn to page 1732.

Revelation 12:13
And when the dragon saw that he was cast unto the earth, he persecuted the woman which brought forth the man child.

Unable to accuse the believers in heaven, Satan makes his last attempt to thwart fulfillment of the prophetic plan as he spews his anger upon God's people.

Revelation 12:14
And to the woman were given two wings of a great eagle, that she might fly into the wilderness, into her place, where she is nourished for a time, and times, and half a time, from the face of the serpent.

What are these two wings? The eagle being the symbol of America, some suggest this could be a reference to United States military power. Could it be America, the only country who has consistently stood by Israel since her return to the Land in 1940?
Could it be the firepower of the sixth fleet stationed off the Mediterranean Sea? Could it be that the United States will airlift the people of Israel to Petra?
I don't know. I don't think so. But somehow the Lord will take His people to the place He has prepared for them in the wilderness. Although we can't be certain of the identity of the two wings of the eagle, this much we do know: God has used this terminology before. . . .

Ye have seen what I did unto the Egyptians, and how I bare you on eagles' wings, and brought you unto myself.   Exodus 19:4

For the LORD's portion is his people; Jacob is the lot of his inheritance. He found him in a desert land, and in the waste howling wilderness; he led him about, he instructed him, he kept him as the apple of his eye. As an eagle stirreth up her nest, fluttereth over her young, spreadeth abroad her wings, taketh them,

beareth them on her wings: So the LORD alone did lead him, and there was no strange god with him.   Deuteronomy 32:9–12

After choosing a site on a rocky cliff sometimes thousands of feet above the ground, a mother eagle constructs her nest. For protection, she arranges sharp sticks along the perimeter. But inside, the nest is soft and comfortable for the eggs. So, when Ernie Eaglet pops out of his shell, he finds his accommodations quite to his liking. "Wow! What a view!"
And with Mama Eagle dropping breakfast, lunch, dinner, and an after-dinner mint into his beak every day, he's a happy eaglet indeed—until his girth increases and he begins to bump into the sharp sticks Mama purposefully placed around the nest. Suddenly, the once-cozy abode becomes a little uncomfortable.
The same goes for us. When what was once so cozy—that group you were in, those people you were linked to, the job you had—gets a little irritating, you may have a tendency to grumble. But you must realize God does this intentionally because He will not allow you to perpetually nest in a place of fatness and flightlessness.
Then, just when Ernie thinks he can't stand one more poke, Mama Eagle comes and, with her powerful wings, bumps the nest—sending Ernie tumbling out. Flapping his little wings frantically yet futilely, he falls hundreds of feet and is about to crash when Mama Eagle scoops him up on her wings and takes him back to the nest. "Whew! What was *that* about?" Ernie wonders.
And for a couple of days, he's happy again, being served breakfast, brunch, lunch, and dinner. But then the pesky sticks begin to bother him again, and after a couple of days—bump goes the nest and out he falls. Once more, right when he thinks his life is over, there's Mom bearing him on her wings, returning him to the nest. Now Ernie's really wondering. "Every time I get comfortable, every time I settle back in, Mama comes and turns my nest over. What kind of parent is she, anyway?" Yet the process is repeated five or six times, until one day—Ernie soars. And as he does, he understands that the pokes, the overturned nest, the perilous plummeting were all about spurring him to do what he never would have done on his own. They were all about teaching him to fly.
Precious saint, if you've been flapping or squawking or crying, this word is for you: God says, "I found you in a wasteland. You are the apple of My eye. I've got nothing but the best in My heart for you. You're not going to crash. I'll always be there to catch you. But I'm going to continue working with you that you might fly."

As a result, I am slowly learning not to be quite so squawky, quite so angry, quite so fearful—but to remember the plan of the Father to bear me on eagles wings. The pokey sticks are preparatory for the overturning of the nest. And the overturned nest is absolutely essential to teach me to fly.

Revelation 12:15
And the serpent cast out of his mouth water as a flood after the woman, that he might cause her to be carried away of the flood.

Satan, through Antichrist, spews his hostility and anger upon the Jewish people, chasing them like a flood. How many Jews will survive? According to Zechariah 13:9, two out of three will die. But the end result will be that one-third of Israel will finally acknowledge the Lord and will enter the kingdom, the Millennium, the thousand years of peace.

Revelation 12:16, 17
And the earth helped the woman, and the earth opened her mouth, and swallowed up the flood which the dragon cast out of his mouth. And the dragon was wroth with the woman, and went to make war with the remnant of her seed, which keep the commandments of God, and have the testimony of Jesus Christ.

In the Book of Numbers, we find another account of the earth ingesting someone. After rebelling against Moses, the ground "clave asunder" under the feet of Korah, Dathan, and Abiram, swallowing not only them, but their possessions and allies (Numbers 16).

"That may be," you may say, "but the text before us is not the account of a few men, tents, and camels being swallowed. This is about an entire *army* complete with bombers and missiles, troop carriers and helicopters. How could this be?"

Look at recent history. . . .

When diplomacy failed to bring about the release of Americans held hostage in Iran in the 1980s, we decided to unleash our military prowess. After months of planning, we sent our most advanced technology and our finest fighting men to Iran. However, as they approached the Iranian Embassy, a sandstorm broke loose so severe that it shut the mission down—and, in so doing, eventually contributed to the demise of the Carter Administration.

The Middle East is a tricky place, folks. The earth could easily swallow an army through a sandstorm or a multiplicity of other events. However it transpires, this much is sure: The army of Antichrist will be thwarted in its attempt to decimate the Jews.

OVERCOMING THE ENEMY

A Topical Study of
Revelation 2:11

. . . for we are not ignorant of his devices.   2 Corinthians 1:10

Because far too many believers are ignorant of who our foe is and the way he works, we're going to join the apostle John as he looks at our enemy. . . .

Past History

Before our enemy was called the devil, his name was Lucifer, or "Shining Star." But he developed an "I" problem. . . .

For thou hast said in thine heart, I will ascend into heaven, I will exalt my throne above the stars of God: I will sit also upon the mount of the congregation,

in the sides of the north: I will ascend above the heights of the clouds; I will
be like the most High.   Isaiah 14:13

According to the Book of Ezekiel, which describes Lucifer as the power behind the king of Tyre, Lucifer was not only a worship leader in heaven, but he was unparalleled in beauty and uniquely anointed. . . .

Son of man, take up a lamentation upon the king of Tyrus, and say unto him,
Thus saith the Lord GOD; Thou sealest up the sum, full of wisdom, and perfect
in beauty. Thou hast been in Eden the garden of God; every precious stone
was thy covering, the sardius, topaz, and the diamond, the beryl, the onyx,
and the jasper, the sapphire, the emerald, and the carbuncle, and gold: the
workmanship of thy tabrets and of thy pipes was prepared in thee in the day
that thou wast created. Thou art the anointed cherub that covereth; and I have
set thee so: thou wast upon the holy mountain of God; thou hast walked up
and down in the midst of the stones of fire. Thou wast perfect in thy ways
from the day that thou wast created, till iniquity was found in thee.
                                                          Ezekiel 28:12–15

Lucifer wasn't merely a good musician; he was a musical instrument—with tambourines for hands and a pipe organ for a voice. And there he was, year after decade after millennia leading all of heaven in worship—until the day he began to wonder why all of the praise was going to someone else.

Those who serve the Lord must keep this in mind, for that same tendency can creep in anytime we think, *Here I am doing this, but no one seems to appreciate what I'm doing; no one acknowledges what I've done.* Be careful. That's the iniquity of Lucifer.

Lucifer was cast out of heaven and became Satan, or "Adversary"; the Devil, or "Accuser." And to this day, like fingernails on a blackboard, praise and worship drive him crazy because they remind him of what he once was, but will never be again.

King Jehoshaphat was surrounded by the Edomites, Ammonites, and Moabites—just as you may have been surrounded by depression, discouragement, and defeat.

After the Spirit of the Lord came upon him, a man named Jahaziel stood up and said, "Don't fear, Jehoshaphat. The battle is not yours but the Lord's. There is no need to fight. Stand still and see the salvation of the Lord." So, instead of soldiers, Jehoshaphat sent the choir into battle, and as they began to sing, the Ammonites, Moabites, and Edomites, became so confused that they began to fight among themselves—leaving the Israelites the victors (2 Chronicles 20).

There is *power* in praise!

Future Hostility

Following the loss of his position in heaven, Satan will spew his anger upon God's people on earth in the Tribulation as he continues to accuse the believers in heaven.

"What's he doing in heaven?" you say. "I thought he was cast out." He was. But as we read in Job 1, he still has access to heaven. Consequently, in the middle of the Tribulation, Michael the archangel wages war against Satan in heaven. It is possible that Michael, whose name means "Who is like God?" took the place of this one who claimed, "I will be like God." Be that as it may, Michael and the angels prevail over Satan and his demons.

In his anger, Satan continues his campaign against the church as he "accuses the brethren day and night" (see Revelation 12:10). Of what does he accuse the believers? Of not deserving the rewards they are given. You see, here in the middle of the Tribulation, believers stand before the judgment seat of Christ. Called the *bema* because that was the term used for the place where rewards were given for athletic events, the judgment seat of Christ is not where we will be judged for our sin because our sin was completely forgiven—past, present, and future—through the finished work of the Cross. Rather, the judgment seat of Christ is the place where rewards are given—crowns that will determine our position, our ministry in eternity.

And who's on the sidelines, hooting and hollering, "What?! You're giving *Mike* a reward? I know him. I've been watching him for years. He's done this and that and he failed to do the other. Why is *he* getting a crown?" Satan will not only do this in the middle of the Tribulation, but he will appear in your present situation. . . .

Present Strategy

As he does in heaven, Satan will try to keep you from being used and blessed by accusing you night and day, saying, "You're not worthy to be in ministry. You're not good enough to have your family blessed. You're not spiritual enough to have your prayers answered."

But he can be overcome on earth the same way he's overcome in heaven: by the blood of the Lamb, the word of testimony, the dying to self.

The Blood of the Lamb

It was the blood applied to the door in the shape of a Cross that spared the firstborn as the death angel flew over Egypt (Exodus 12). So, too, God will bless your home, marriage, family not on the basis of how much you've prayed or how good you've been, but on your understanding of the potency and the sufficiency of the blood of Calvary.

First John 2:1 says if any man sin, he has an advocate, a defense lawyer in the person of Jesus Christ. Satan is the prosecuting attorney, accusing and condemning us endlessly. Jesus, however, is our defense attorney, our advocate. And what would our defense attorney have us do? He would have us agree with our adversary—a truly brilliant strategy. The word "Satan" means "adversary." And what did Jesus tell us to do with our adversary?

Agree with him (Matthew 5:25).

When Satan condemns you, don't fight him. Don't say, "I didn't really mean it" or, "I'm not that bad," or, "I can't help it." Say, "You're right. In fact, I'm a lot worse than you even know because, since you're not omniscient, Satan, you can't see the deceitful and desperately wicked state of my heart (Jeremiah 17:9). But the blood of my defense attorney has cleansed me from my sin—past, present, and future. Therefore, it's not about anything I do or don't do. It's all about what *He's* done on my behalf. It's all about the blood."

The Word of Their Testimony

What is my testimony? What has the Lord done for me? As He did with David, He rescued me from a horrible pit, brought me out of miry clay, and set my feet upon the Rock (Psalm 40).

Every cult, every false religious system has man reaching up to God. Whether it be through knocking on doors, selling Watchtower magazines, or being baptized in holy underwear—all religions say, "I can make it to heaven's gate by my own efforts, my own wisdom."

Only the Christian says, "I didn't seek after God (see Romans 3:11). *He* reached down to me."

The accuser of the brethren is silenced when the blood is applied and the testimony of grace is shared. If you are still trying to impress God with anything you do or don't do, the Enemy will beat you every time. It's when you come to a place where you say, "The word of my testimony is simply grace—amazing grace."

Dying to Self

Many Christians aren't blessed because they constantly monitor their own spiritual condition. "Am I spiritually fit enough for God to bless me? Is my spiritual temperature high enough for God to use me on the job or with my kids?" Yet Jesus taught us to deny ourselves (Matthew 16:24), which is why Paul didn't judge even himself (1 Corinthians 4:3). Here's the key: Forget yourself and let God bless you for no reason. Let Him use you regardless of what you think or how you feel. And in so doing, you'll overcome the Enemy.

In Isaiah 7, we see this all come together. . . .

"Ask a sign of God," said Isaiah to wicked King Ahaz.

"I will not ask a sign. I don't want to tempt God," Ahaz answered.

Although Ahaz's response sounds pious, the real reason behind his refusal was that he was looking to the Assyrians for help. Thus, Isaiah responded, "Hear ye now, O house of David; Is it a small thing for you to weary men, but will ye weary my God also?" (see Isaiah 7:13).

It's not our asking that wearies God, gang. It's our refusal to ask.

That's why in the original language, Jesus' words in Matthew 7:7 are, "Keep asking and it shall be given you; keep seeking and you shall find; keep knocking and it shall be opened unto you."

Perhaps you're saying, "I'm not going to ask God for that job, for that healing in my marriage, for that miracle."

And it sounds so pious, so selfless—but in reality, it's the result of listening to the accuser of the brethren saying, "You're a failure. God can't work in your life until you study harder, pray longer, do better."

> *Behold, a virgin shall conceive, and bear a son, and shall call his name Immanuel.*
> Isaiah 7:14

God gave Ahaz the greatest sign of all in spite of the fact that Ahaz refused to even ask.

Truly, God draws grace from a bottomless well. "Come boldly to My throne," He says, "for there you will find grace to help. When? Every time you have need" (see Hebrews 4:16).

There is no measure of what God can do in the lives of those who overcome the Enemy as they love not their own lives but instead rejoice in the blood of the Lamb and cling to His amazing grace.

May we be those people.

13 Twenty-nine years before Christ came as the Babe of Bethlehem, the worship of Caesar had been instituted throughout the Roman Empire. Initially, the Caesars viewed this as little more than a way to stir up feelings of patriotism within the people of the empire. But at the end of the first century, Caesar Nero actually believed his press clippings and truly believed he was God in the flesh. Thus, beginning with his reign, every subject within the Roman Empire was required to go to one of the pagan temples, stand before a priest, and confess on a yearly basis that Caesar was Lord.

For most, it was merely an annoyance. Not so for the believers. They wouldn't play the game. As a result, most historians believe that the number of Christians killed in the ten waves of persecution that followed exceeded six million. Consequently, what John writes about here is not only for us in these last days in terms of prophecy and eschatology—but for the hearts of his flock, who themselves were face-to-face with the beast of Roman persecution.

You see, John the prophet is also John the pastor—sharing his heart with any and all facing hard times. . . .

Revelation 13:1 (a)
And I stood upon the sand of the sea, and saw a beast . . .

The beast John sees is Antichrist. "Antichrist" literally meaning "in place of Christ," John would go on to write that there are many antichrists—not *the* Antichrist, but anything that takes one's focus off Jesus (1 John 2:18). Here in Revelation 13, however, the reference is to *the* Antichrist.

Revelation 13:1 (b)
. . . rise up out of the sea . . .

"The sea" in Bible typology always referring to Gentile nations as opposed to "the land" referring to Israel, the mention of the sea here indicates that Antichrist will not come from Israel. In fact, chapter 17 goes on to say that the beast will come from the ten Gentile nations that stem from the old Roman Empire and that make up the last world empire. But this doesn't necessarily mean Antichrist will be a Gentile, for he could be a European Jew.

Revelation 13:1 (c)
. . . having seven heads . . .

Revelation 17 identifies the seven heads as the seven mountains of Rome. Thus, Antichrist's government will initially be based in the city of Rome.

Revelation 13:1 (d)
. . . and ten horns, and upon his horns ten crowns . . .

There are ten crowns on only seven heads because, according to Daniel 2 and 7, when Antichrist comes to power, he will initially grab the reigns of three nations from the ten-nation confederation. As you study history, you catch glimpses of men who wanted to revive the glory of Rome. But it won't happen until Antichrist comes, for he alone will be able to reignite the fire of the Roman Empire.

Revelation 13:1 (e)
. . . and upon his heads the name of blasphemy.

The beast has blasphemy upon his heads because he has rebellion on his mind. The image of a seven-headed, ten-horned beast is meant to be monstrous and hideous, for such is the nature of the one who is rebellious, who is blasphemous, who is—as we shall see—the devil incarnate.

Revelation 13:2
And the beast which I saw was like unto a leopard, and his feet were as the feet of a bear, and his mouth as the mouth of a lion: and the dragon gave him his power, and his seat, and great authority.

The four successive empires that would rule during the time Israel was a nation are described as a glorious statue in Daniel 2. Such is man's perspective. God's perspective, however, is seen in Daniel 7 through a series of monstrous beasts—the same beasts described here, although in inverse order: the leopard symbolizing Alexander the Great's ability to pounce; the bear symbolizing the Medes and the Persians, the lion symbolizing Babylon. Why is the order inversed in Daniel? Because Daniel is looking ahead, while John is looking back.

Revelation 13:3
And I saw one of his heads as it were wounded to death; and his deadly wound was healed: and all the world wondered after the beast.

At this point in the Tribulation, Antichrist is mortally wounded. According to Zechariah 11:17, there will be an assassination attempt on Antichrist that will evidently cause his eye to be poked out and his right arm to be paralyzed. Because the Greek text can either be rendered "wounded to death" or "wounded to the appearance of death," there are those who believe Antichrist will only appear to be dead as a result of this wound. My opinion, however, is that he truly will die and descend to hell (Revelation 17:8).

Revelation 13:4
And they worshipped the dragon which gave power unto the beast: and they worshipped the beast, saying, Who is like unto the beast? who is able to make war with him?

At the point this popular, powerful figure—who captures the affection and imagination of the entire world with all of his grand ideas and peace programs—ascends from hell, he truly is the incarnation of Satan. Just as Jesus Christ comes from heaven and is God, it would seem as though Antichrist will truly be the incarnation of the dragon, of Satan. Put yourself in the shoes of those who will see this great leader come back to life after being assassinated, and you will understand why they will give Satan what he has desired ever since he was cast out of heaven before the fall: worship.

Revelation 13:5 (a)
And there was given unto him a mouth speaking great things and blasphemies . . .

Antichrist is on a roll. He's on *Larry King, Oprah, World News Tonight* declaring that he truly is deity.

Revelation 13:5 (b)
. . . and power was given unto him to continue forty and two months.

How long is forty-two months? Three and a half years, 1,260 days, or "a time, times and a half time." All of these phrases pop up throughout Revelation and describe the last half of the Tribulation—the Great Tribulation. And now begins the hellish last half of Antichrist's seven-year reign. . . .

Revelation 13:6, 7 (a)
And he opened his mouth in blasphemy against God, to blaspheme his name, and his tabernacle, and them that dwell in heaven. And it was given unto him to make war with the saints . . .

Some people believe that the church must be on earth during the Tribulation in order for Antichrist to "make war with the saints." But they fail to understand that there are three groups of people in the Bible referred to as saints: Simply meaning "separated one," throughout the Old Testament the word "saints" refers to Israel. In the New Testament it refers to the church. And after the church is raptured, it refers to those who are saved in the Tribulation.

Revelation 13:7 (b)
. . . and to overcome them . . .

"I will build My church and the gates of hell shall not prevail against it," Jesus said (Matthew 16:18). The church will not be overcome. Therefore, this passage cannot refer to the church.

Revelation 13:7 (c), 8 (a)
. . . and power was given him over all kindreds, and tongues, and nations. And all that dwell upon the earth shall worship him . . .

"Dwell" meaning "to be at home with," and earth referring to the world system, those who are comfortable with the worldly scene will end up worshiping Antichrist.

Revelation 13:8 (b)
. . . whose names are not written in the book of life . . .

The book of life includes the names of those who get saved during the Tribulation.

Revelation 13:8 (c)
. . . of the Lamb slain from the foundation of the world.

The book of life belongs to the Lamb slain from the foundation of the world—or from *before* the foundation of the world, as the newer translations render this verse. Too many people have far too small a view of what Christ did in dying for the sin of humanity—including me.

Growing up, I was under the distinct impression that Jesus died on the Cross and remained there for six hours, paying the price for my sin. While that is true, it's not the full picture. You see, the Old Testament makes unmistakably clear the fact that every sin needs to be dealt with individually. That is why Old Testament believers were required to lay their hands on the animals they sacrificed and confess their sins specifically (Leviticus 1:4). Yes, there was Yom Kippur, the Day of Atonement for the nation, but every individual was still required by the law to make sacrifice for his personal transgressions in the trespass offering. Multiply all of the sins of those in your church—add to that the sins of all of the people in our country, all of the folks who have lived throughout history—and the amount of sin staggers the imagination.

That is why I believe that when the Word speaks of Christ being slain before the foundation of the world, only heaven will allow us to understand that He was slaughtered and slain in a way we cannot understand in the time/space continuum in which we live. Consequently, when we see Him, we will worship Him with an intensity and an explosion of praise never before experienced because we will at last see Him as a Lamb having been slain—newly slain. "I thought He was on the Cross for a few hours one Friday," we'll say. "I had no idea what *my* sin cost Him."

Revelation 13:9, 10 (a)
If any man have an ear, let him hear. He that leadeth into captivity shall go into captivity: he that killeth with the sword must be killed with the sword.

What is John saying? I can hear his heart, can't you? He's saying to those in his day, just as he would say to me and you today who are in tribulation or difficulties, "The one putting you in prison, unsheathing the sword, marching you into the coliseum is himself going down."

Revelation 13:10 (b)
Here is the patience and the faith of the saints.

Do you realize how blessed we are because we know the end of the story? You may be in a difficult marriage, persecuted on the job, fighting illness, undergoing severe pressures financially, or weary of your flesh that rears its ugly head constantly. But we know one day it will all be solved. That's what John told his people. And that's what the Spirit would say to us. We who have been saved awhile take this for granted. But what if this was the first time you understood that everything that plagues you presently will be gone in a heartbeat; that you're going to heaven, where everything will be wonderful forever and ever?

"If any man has an ear, let him hear. Listen up," says Pastor John. "I don't care if you miss everything else, get this: The forces against you are soon going to be done away with: The beast, persecution, problems, will undo themselves."

That's why I need to read the Book of Revelation over and over again. It's not about deciphering the mark of the Beast. It's not written to help us figure out who the false prophet or Antichrist is. It's written to give us hope and to bring us back constantly to the fact that life is short and we'll be in heaven soon.

The person who doesn't understand the Book of Revelation will go through life in his own personal tribulation. The person who grabs hold of Revelation, on the other hand, will live in a state of anticipation and celebration. Every single one of us will either go through this week in tribulation or celebration.

Life is short. The Lord is in control. We're going to heaven. That's what this book is about.

Revelation 13:11 (a)
And I beheld another beast coming up out of the earth . . .

When Jesus ascended to heaven, He promised to send the Holy Spirit, the third Person of the Trinity (John 14:16). The other beast named here—the false prophet, as we shall see—is to Antichrist what the Holy Spirit is to Jesus.

Revelation 13:11 (b)
. . . and he had two horns like a lamb, and he spake as a dragon.

Minus the horns or crowns of Antichrist, the false prophet comes across like a lamb. He seems to be so humble and gentle. Whereas Antichrist is the political leader, the false prophet is the religious leader who will unify the world religion as the public relations man for Antichrist.

Revelation 13:12
And he exerciseth all the power of the first beast before him, and causeth the earth and them which dwell therein to worship the first beast, whose deadly wound was healed.

Who's the first beast? Antichrist. The ministry of the Spirit is to put the focus on Jesus. The ministry of the false prophet is to put the focus on Antichrist. The parallel is exact.

Revelation 13:13, 14
And he doeth great wonders, so that he maketh fire come down from heaven on the earth in the sight of men, and deceiveth them that dwell on the earth by the means of those miracles which he had power to do in the sight of the beast; saying to them that dwell on the earth, that they should make an image to the beast, which had the wound by a sword, and did live.

Although this false prophet will appear to be as gentle as a lamb, he'll also have the ability to call fire down from heaven. This should be a practical word of warning to you and me. You see, there are those who come on the scene appearing to be so spiritual and so "on fire." But Pastor John the Revelator would have us be aware of the very real ability of Satan to transform himself into an angel of light and to perform all kinds of miracles.

Gang, whenever someone comes on the scene pointing to some movement, man, mantra, or method, saying, "This is the hot thing"—I would encourage you to run in the opposite direction. When a person or group is more excited about what's happening in Canada or Korea than they are about the character, work, or Person of Jesus—stay away. You can always spot a counterfeit. Like the false prophet, a counterfeit calls attention to "Antichrist," to something "in place of Christ."

Revelation 13:15
And he had power to give life unto the image of the beast, that the image of the beast should both speak, and cause that as many

as would not worship the image of the beast should be killed.

What is this statue evidently erected in the rebuilt temple in Jerusalem? Computer chips are presently based on sand, on silicon. But the new computer chips will be based on living matter, on protein. When these protein-based computer chips finally get perfected, the computing power will immediately increase fifty thousand times. So it could be that this image is a sophisticated automaton. Or it could be an image that is powered demonically. Whatever it is, it will appear to have life.

Revelation 13:16, 17
And he causeth all, both small and great, rich and poor, free and bond, to receive a mark in their right hand, or in their foreheads: And that no man might buy or sell, save he that had the mark, or the name of the beast, or the number of his name.

"Hear, O Israel: The Lord our God is one Lord." This is the "shema" of Deuteronomy 6:4 that is so essential to Jewish belief that it is placed in phylacteries and worn on the head and arms of Orthodox Jews to this day.

I find it interesting that even as Satan, Antichrist, and the false prophet counterfeit the Trinity, so their mark worn on the head and arm counterfeits the command of God in Deuteronomy 6:4–8.

Hear, O Israel: The LORD our God is one LORD: And thou shalt love the LORD thy God with all

thine heart, and with all thy soul, and with all thy might. And these words, which I command thee this day, shall be in thine heart: And thou shalt teach them diligently unto thy children, and shalt talk of them when thou sittest in thine house, and when thou walkest by the way, and when thou liest down, and when thou risest up. And thou shalt bind them for a sign upon thine hand, and they shall be as frontlets between thine eyes.

Deuteronomy 6:4–8

I am reminded of Pharaoh's magicians who could do no more than mimic the miracles God did through Moses. Because God is the only Creator, Satan is left to do no more than copy.

Revelation 13:18
Here is wisdom. Let him that hath understanding count the number of the beast: for it is the number of a man; and his number is Six hundred threescore and six.

Throughout the Old Testament when God gave dietary regulations and health procedures to His people, He never explained His reasons. He simply said, "I am the Lord" (Leviticus 11:44). In the ensuing centuries, as scientific and medical knowledge caught up, man slowly understood the wisdom behind God's commands. So, too, the reason God's command in Leviticus 19:28 not to mark our bodies becomes ever clearer in light of the demand of Antichrist to receive his mark in one's body.

"Trust Me," says the Lord. "I love you passionately and want nothing but the best for you eternally." Truly, here is wisdom.

THE BEAST WHO WAS MARKED
A Topical Study of
Revelation 13:16–18

John wrote this Book of Revelation while on an isolated island, wearing clothing that looked more like a towel than what we wear today, during a period in history when the highest form of technology was a mule, and when the world's economy was based on bartering. Therefore, what makes this passage so absolutely intriguing is that John describes precisely that which is upon us economically and culturally.

For centuries, this passage confused Bible scholars. While they knew it was true, exactly how it would happen was beyond their wildest imaginations.

But for us, this is no big deal, for we are accustomed to buying and selling numerically.

> The banking industry has been pushing hard for a cashless society for many decades. Why? Every check costs a bank between thirty-five and sixty cents to process. Electronic transactions, on the other hand, cost one cent. Banks have a very real interest in seeing us move toward an electronic funds transfer system. So do small business owners, due to the multimillion-dollar price they pay for employees who steal from the till.
>
> Not only are banks and businesses eager to see a cashless society, but the IRS is as well. The government loses what is estimated to be one trillion dollars a year in the "underground" economy—the system whereby employees are paid in cash in order to avoid the paper trail that would require them to pay taxes.

Technology for a cashless society has been around for decades. The only reason we have not seen it implemented until recently is not due to a lack of technology, but rather to a phobia with technology. Because people my age and older are somewhat techno-phobic, we have been reluctant to embrace technology. But that's changing. Why? It is partially due to the fact that the older generation is dying. You see, the kids who have grown up with Nintendo are not intimidated by technology in the least.

Even more than this, our culture has changed in such a way that even we who are older are feeling a need to move into a cashless society. Consider the reasons why. . . .

> Crime. So many people are being ripped off after withdrawing money from Automated Teller Machines, that cities like Berkeley, California, are passing ordinances making it illegal to stand within one hundred fifty feet of an ATM unless making a transaction.
>
> Drugs. Drug lords don't write checks. The entire drug culture is based on the exchange of cash, rendering a record of such transactions nonexistent. Consequently, the most effective way to curb drug traffic would be to get rid of all cash.
>
> Taxes. On television one week was a story on the various ways the wealthy in our society legally avoid paying one penny on their vast amounts of income—one of which is to deal solely with cash. Because the taxes of commoners like you and me go up radically as a result, people are demanding something be done to restore equity in our tax system. How can this happen? One of the easiest ways is to get rid of cash.

Enter the debit card. VISA alone has issued one million combination credit/debit cards worldwide to people using numbers to buy and sell, just as John prophesied.

But it gets even more amazing. There is a MARC card. MARC stands for Multi-technology Automated Reader Card. It's given to Armed Forces personnel. In addition to accessing economic transactions a la a VISA card, the MARC card contains a computer chip with the medical and personal history of the holder, giving him clearance for all sorts of weapons and other technology.

But more than that, his location can be pinpointed anywhere in the world in a matter of seconds. The practicality of this in times of war is understandable—but so are the problems. Because like a VISA card, a MARC card can be easily lost or stolen, the solution to this problem has been biometrics—where clearance to a secured area is obtained by the scanning of one's palm. But due to even the most undetectable interference (like hand cream) biometrics has not proven to be as practical as originally hoped. Such is the reason for the introduction of an ATM that would identify customers simply by reading the iris of their eyes. However, even these can run into problems due to something as simple as a contact lens.

The only solution seems to be what John prophesied two thousand years ago when he wrote that Antichrist will require everyone to receive a mark in his right hand or forehead. Certainly we're not far from this. A recent newspaper article I read addressed the fact that we are approaching the time when the key to all transactions will be a computer chip imbedded in the hand. Already, horses in St. Louis are required to have such a chip under their manes for identification purposes. Cats in San Francisco carry such chips containing their vaccination records and identification so that if lost, their owners can be notified. There is even a proposal to use such technology on convicted felons in Southern California.

Although horses in St. Louis, cats in San Francisco, and felons in Orange County might seem a world away, one's children don't. With the growing threat of kidnappings, parents will be much more likely to welcome such technology.

There's only one problem: John tells us the mark of the beast will seal the fate, will doom the one who accepts it. You see, with the acceptance of his number, one pledges total allegiance to Antichrist. That is why the Lord warns people—not only in the Word, but with two prophets in Jerusalem, 144,000 Jewish Billy Grahams spanning the globe, and an angel flying across the sky, saying, "Don't take the mark." But most will. Most will say, "It makes too much sense not to."

> *Here is wisdom. Let him that hath understanding count the number of the beast: for it is the number of a man; and his number is Six hundred threescore and six.*   Revelation 13:18

Knowledge is one thing, but wisdom is another. Knowledge is information. Wisdom is application. Theories abound as to what the number 666 refers. Some believe it refers to a type of UPC code. Others suggest that because in both Greek and Hebrew, letters are used as numbers, the letters in Antichrist's name add up to 666. But I don't believe this is the primary point John is making.

The best commentary on the Bible being the Bible, when you want to know what a verse or phrase means, look to the Bible for the interpretation. And in Genesis 4, we find the account of someone else who was marked with "the number of man."

And Adam knew Eve his wife; and she conceived, and bare Cain, and said, I have gotten a man from the LORD.   Genesis 4:1

The Scofield Bible correctly renders this verse: "I have gotten a man, even Jehovah, the Lord." Why would Eve say this? Because after she and Adam sinned in the Garden of Eden, God promised that her seed would crush the head of Satan (Genesis 3:15). Consequently, when Cain was born, she believed him to be the one who would free mankind from the power of Satan. It wasn't long until she realized Cain was not the deliverer, as evidenced by the name she gave her second son: Abel, or literally, "hopeless." You know the story. After his self-sufficient sacrifice was rejected by God, Cain killed Abel. As a result, Cain was banished to the wilderness, with a mark to protect him.

Follow this with me. Abel is thought to be hopeless, unimportant, nothing. Cain was thought to be the Promised One. But Cain proves to be antichrist, that is, "in place of Christ"—while Abel is a picture of Christ. . . .

- Abel was a shepherd (Genesis 4:2).
- Jesus is the Good Shepherd (John 10:11).

- Abel brought a lamb to sacrifice to God (Genesis 4:4).
- Jesus offered Himself as the Lamb of God (John 1:29).

- Abel was hated by his brother (Genesis 4:5).
- Jesus came to His own and His own received Him not (John 1:11).

- Abel was slain by his brother (Genesis 4:8).
- Jesus was crucified by His brethren (John 19:6).

- The blood of Abel cried out to God (Genesis 4:10).
- The blood of Jesus speaks of better things (Hebrews 12:24).

- Abel submitted to the directive of the Father (Hebrews 11:4).
- Jesus always does the things that please the Father (John 8:29).

What does this have to do with you?
Everything.

"Understand," said John, "the number of the beast is the number of man: 666." Throughout Scripture, six is the number of the flesh. The fleshly Cain mentality can rise up in you and me. How? By saying,

"The sweat I pour out, the good I do, the things I accomplish are going to be more impressive to God than just killing a bloody lamb. Through my energy, my initiative, my efforts I will impress God."

Some today say, "I'm a Rotarian; I'm a Republican; I attend PTA; I coach Little League. I'm putting together a pretty good basket of fruit. I don't need this bloody stuff: Christianity, Bible study, Communion. I can do something much more intellectually creative, much more beautiful. I can do it. I can pull it off."

But the Bible says,

"*All* have sinned and fall short of the glory of God (Romans 3:23). And because you're marked with your own efforts, you're marked for damnation. You've fallen short. You need a Savior, a Sacrifice to die in your place."

Even believers can be caught up in the spirit of 666 when they say,

"I don't need to pray. I can figure out my career on my own. I'm reading books. I'm attending seminars. I know what's best for my kids, my family, my future."

We're either of the spirit of Cain, saying, "I'm a hard worker. I'm a creative thinker. I'm a good guy"—or of Abel who's humble, broken, and dependent upon God.

Here's the good news. God has one simple thing to say to you who are struggling in marriage, in parenting, in relationships, in school:

"Talk to Me. Spend time with Me. Humble yourself before Me. Seek My face. Wait and see what I'll do in your life. Fight the tendency to be Cain, and watch how I'll bless you."

May God keep you from the number of man, the mark of Cain, the mark of the beast. May this be a time in your life when you are recommitted to dependency and brokenness before the Lord. Herein is wisdom, gang: Seek first the kingdom, and everything else will fall into place (Matthew 6:33).

14

Revelation 14:1
And I looked, and, lo, a Lamb stood on the mount Sion, and with him an hundred forty and four thousand, having his Father's name written in their foreheads.

In chapter 7, we read of twelve thousand from each of the twelve tribes of Israel who will go throughout the world preaching the gospel. Although they will be targets of Antichrist's perse-

cution, here in the middle of the Tribulation, we see not 143,999 witnesses, but 144,000. In other words, they all make it through.

Revelation 14:2, 3
And I heard a voice from heaven, as the voice of many waters, and as the voice of a great thunder: and I heard the voice of harpers harping with their harps: And they sung as it were a new song before the throne,

and before the four beasts, and the elders: and no man could learn that song but the hundred and forty and four thousand, which were redeemed from the earth.

Why could no one else sing the song of the 144,000? Because they alone went through testing and Tribulation—yet maintained their integrity. Thus, they alone could sing of what they were able to observe the Father do on their behalf in the time of Tribulation. Every one of us goes through times of tribulation. God's intention is that they might produce in us "as it were, a new song"—a symphony.

There they were—in a damp, dark dungeon— without even a crust of bread to eat or the ACLU to plead their case. Yet what were they doing? They were singing. At midnight—in the darkest hour—Paul and Silas sang. They weren't singing to try to get God to do something. They sang simply because the Lord was with them (Acts 16:25).

"Well, that hasn't been my experience," you might be saying. "My marriage," or "my job," or "my health is a dungeon to me, and I'm not happy."

Precious brother, dear sister—God's intent is to give you a new song. But there's one thing that will stand in the way: sympathy. You see, I can either go through challenges and hard times with a symphony in my heart because the Lord has promised not only to strengthen me in them (Isaiah 41:10), but to walk with me through them (Matthew 28:20)—or I can choose to get sympathy from people. If I choose to tap into sympathy, it will always be at God's expense because the underlying though unspoken implication is that what is happening in my life is out of God's control.

God is totally, absolutely, completely faithful to meet us in every trial, in every difficulty. Don't let His plan get short-circuited by those who say, "I feel sorry for you." Instead, say, "God is good. Sure, what I'm dealing with right now is a challenge. But I am discovering the Father is exactly who He claimed to be—a God who comforts me completely."

It's tempting to let people feel sorry for us, but we mustn't, because it puts God in a bad light. Don't settle for sympathy, gang. Go for the symphony.

Revelation 14:4, 5
These are they which were not defiled with women; for they are virgins. These are they which follow the Lamb whithersoever he goeth. These were redeemed from among

men, being the firstfruits unto God and to the Lamb. And in their mouth was found no guile: for they are without fault before the throne of God.

These 144,000 are blessed. They speak with authority They have the Lord on their minds constantly. They have a song in their heart personally. They see the Lamb's directives very clearly. It's all built and based on the fact that they are virgins—people of purity.

For topical study of Revelation 14:4, 5 entitled "Purity Pays," turn to page 1748.

Revelation 14:6 (a)
And I saw another angel fly in the midst of heaven, having the everlasting gospel to preach unto them that dwell on the earth ...

The 144,000 have been the infantry. Now here comes the air support: angels. I believe angels have been itching to get into the fray, to preach. Why? Because they've been going to school for a long time to get ready for this ministry. Peter says that the angels are studying, earnestly looking into the things of salvation (1 Peter 1:12).

Paul goes on to say that when we meet together, we need to be sensitive to the angels in our midst (1 Corinthians 11:10). I truly believe angels are studying right along with us. Studying what? The Scriptures? No. They already know Scripture. They're studying us. Why? They're trying to figure out this thing called grace. Having never fallen into sin, how are they to learn about grace? By watching us. *How could God use Jon? Why would He put up with Linda? How could Kent be part of His chosen priesthood?* they wonder. But the time is coming when their schooling will be over, and they'll be released in the Tribulation to preach the everlasting gospel.

Revelation 14:6 (b)
. . . and to every nation, and kindred, and tongue, and people,

Jesus declared that the end of the world as we know it will come after the gospel of the kingdom is preached to the entire world. Consequently, you will hear people say, "We've got to get out there and preach to every nation so the Lord can come to rapture the church." Not true. The Lord can rapture the church today, even though there are people groups who have not heard the gospel directly because the angels will preach the gospel to every nation, every tongue, every kindred, every people.

Revelation 14:7
Saying with a loud voice, Fear God, and give glory to him; for the hour of his judgment is come: and worship him that made heaven, and earth, and the sea, and the fountains of waters.

"Worship the One who made everything you see," the angel will declare—putting a conclusive end to the evolution/creation debate.

Revelation 14:8
And there followed another angel, saying, Babylon is fallen, is fallen, that great city, because she made all nations drink of the wine of the wrath of her fornication.

Two Babylons are spoken of in Revelation: religious Babylon and commercial Babylon—the false religious system and the oppressive economic system. The second angel declares both are powerless.

Revelation 14:9, 10 (a)
And the third angel followed them, saying with a loud voice, If any man worship the beast and his image, and receive his mark in his forehead, or in his hand, the same shall drink of the wine of the wrath of God, which is poured out without mixture into the cup of his indignation . . .

The third angel says, "Don't take the mark of the beast." But the world, by and large, will buy into Antichrist's diabolical plan.

Revelation 14:10 (b), 11
. . . and he shall be tormented with fire and brimstone in the presence of the holy angels, and in the presence of the Lamb: And the smoke of their torment ascendeth up for ever and ever: and they have no rest day nor night, who worship the beast and his image, and whosoever receiveth the mark of his name.

Those who suggest either that hell is not a literal place or that it won't last for eternity haven't read the Bible. In fact, Jesus taught more on the subject of hell than on the subject of heaven. That is why this angel cries with a loud voice, warning people to reject the mark of the Beast. There's lots of talk about angels these days as cute, cuddly creatures. But when you read this passage, you realize they are creatures who plead passionately, proclaim loudly, and preach vehemently because hell is real. It's not a game. I think of the twentieth chapter of Isaiah, where a most amazing thing happens. . . .

Although the Assyrians were headed in their direction, the people of Israel didn't take the threat seriously. Oh, come on, they thought. Certainly we won't be wiped out by the Assyrians.

So God said to Isaiah—the eloquent orator, the educated, articulate prophet—"The stakes are high. But the people aren't listening. So I want you to take off your sandals, take off your clothes, and walk naked throughout this region for three years."

Now, whether this was three years continually or three years sporadically, Bible scholars disagree. But the fact remains that stately Isaiah did, in fact, obey. Why was he told to do this? Because the people had grown so calloused to the prophets' words, they weren't heeding the message. So God used this bold move to get their attention and to illustrate the fact that, as captives of the Assyrians, the Israelites would be led naked across the desert into captivity.

Like Isaiah, we, too, live in crucial times, gang. You have relatives. I have friends. We have co-workers who are going to hell because, like the Israelites, they have become calloused to the threat of hell. But the stakes are too high for us just to say, "Well, whatever." No, we must share the naked truth with them—not baring our bodies, but baring our souls.

"But they'll laugh at me," you say.

What do you think they did to Isaiah?

Here in Revelation, the angels preach with a loud voice, "Don't take the mark. You'll be tormented forever." People are in tribulation even today. Share the everlasting gospel with them, and, like the angels, you'll soar in the heavenlies. I guarantee it!

Revelation 14:12
Here is the patience of the saints: here are they that keep the commandments of God, and the faith of Jesus.

"Be patient" is the word given to those who become Christians during the Tribulation—to those who respond to the evangelism of the 144,000, the message of the angels, the powerful testimony of the two witnesses in Jerusalem.

Revelation 14:13
And I heard a voice from heaven saying unto me, Write, Blessed are the dead which die in the Lord from henceforth: Yea, saith the Spirit, that they may rest from their labours; and their works do follow them.

The voice saying, "Blessed are those who die after they become believers during the Tribulation, because they will have rest from the hell on earth surrounding them," would be unnecessary if the church is to go through the first part of the Tribulation, as some believe. If that were the case, the word would not be, "Blessed are you if you die," but, "Blessed are you who hang on because the Rapture is about to occur."

For topical study of Revelation 14:14 entitled "Rest In Peace," turn to page 1752.

Revelation 14:14 (a)
And I looked, and behold a white cloud, and upon the cloud one sat like unto the Son of man, having on his head a golden crown . . .

Clouds are significant throughout Scripture because they represent the visible presence of God. . . .

- When the law was first given, a cloud covered the mountain (Exodus 19:16).
- When the law was given a second time, a cloud again appeared (Exodus 34:5).
- Upon its completion, a cloud covered the tabernacle (Exodus 40:34).
- Whenever the Israelites were to break camp on their journey to the Promised Land, a cloud led the way (Numbers 9:17).
- When the temple was dedicated, a cloud filled the holy of holies (1 Kings 8:10).

What a tragic sight it must have been for the Jews to see the glory of God leave the temple, the city of Jerusalem, the land of Israel because of their sin (Ezekiel 9:3).

But wait. God is never through with Israel. The cloud reappears in Israel when Jesus was on the Mount of Transfiguration (Matthew 17:5) and again when He ascended to heaven (Acts 1:9).

Revelation 14:14 (b)–16
. . . and in his hand a sharp sickle. And another angel came out of the temple, crying with a loud voice to him that sat on the cloud, Thrust in thy sickle, and reap: for the time is come for thee to reap; for the harvest of the earth is ripe. And he that sat on the cloud thrust in his sickle on the earth; and the earth was reaped.

According to this passage, it would seem that there comes a point in the Tribulation when salvation is no longer possible. The 144,000 have been called to heaven. The angels have made

their proclamation. And now there will be a separation between those who become Christians in the Tribulation and those who don't.

So, too, in your own tribulation you need to understand there comes a time when your own heart—even as a believer—can become hardened. The Bible speaks of a root of bitterness that can take hold in the soil of a man's soul (Hebrews 12:15). I've seen believers go through tribulation, and rather than allow the Lord's work of grace to take place in their hearts, they choose, instead, to be bitter and unforgiving. Don't let that happen. Don't be unforgiving. Don't be cynical. Don't be bitter. Don't play that game because if you let bitterness and unforgiveness continue, there will come a point in your own tribulation when it will become an irreversible part of who you are.

Revelation 14:17, 18
And another angel came out of the temple which is in heaven, he also having a sharp sickle. And another angel came out from the altar, which had power over fire; and cried with a loud cry to him that had the sharp sickle, saying, Thrust in thy sharp sickle, and gather the clusters of the vine of the earth; for her grapes are fully ripe.

Referring to the parable of the wheat and tares in Matthew 13, the previous passage spoke of a harvest of grain. The second harvest here in verse 18 speaks of a harvest of grapes.

Revelation 14:19, 20 (a)
And the angel thrust in his sickle into the earth, and gathered the vine of the earth, and cast it into the great winepress of the wrath of God. And the winepress was trodden without the city . . .

At this point, the harvest of separation has begun; the end of the world is at hand. "The city" in Scripture always referring to Jerusalem, it is fitting that the grapes are pressed "without the city," for it was "without the city" that the True Vine, Jesus Christ, was pressed to the Cross for our sin (John 19:17).

Revelation 14:20 (b)
. . . and blood came out of the winepress, even unto the horse bridles, by the space of a thousand and six hundred furlongs.

The blood resulting from the second—and last—harvest will flow from the valley of Armageddon down Jordan's Rift Valley past

Jerusalem one hundred eighty miles to the city of Bozrah. . . .

Who is this that cometh from Edom, with dyed garments from Bozrah? this that is glorious in his apparel, travelling in the greatness of his strength? I that speak in righteousness, mighty to save. Wherefore art thou red in thine apparel, and thy garments like him that treadeth in the winefat?   Isaiah 63:1, 2

Who is this One?

None other than Jesus Christ.

And now I begin to understand that I have two options: I will either drown in the horrific bloodbath of Armageddon, or I will bathe in the gracious Blood of the Lamb. Truly, the greatest bloodshed in all of history took place not in a world war, but when Jesus died on the Cross in order to wash us in His blood.

PURITY PAYS
A Topical Study of
Revelation 14:4, 5

Over the years, I have noticed that when people go through trials and tribulations, one of two things inevitably happens. Either their faith ignites and burns bright, or their faith is quenched and burns out. We see this same principle in Scripture. . . .

Standing near the fire, he couldn't believe what was happening. He had left his business, his family, everything to follow the Rabbi from Galilee. And now, after three years, the One he was looking to, believing in, depending on was being carried off to be crucified. When asked if he was a disciple of this One, Peter swore, "I don't even know Him"—as the flame of his faith turned to embers (Matthew 26:74).

"If you don't bow down to my idol, you'll be cast into a fiery furnace," declared the king.

"So be it," answered three Jewish young men. "God is able to deliver us. And even if He doesn't deliver us, we will not bow to your idol." So it was that Shadrach, Meshach, and Abed-nego were thrown in the fiery furnace where— rather than burning out, their faith burned bright as they walked through their trial unharmed (Daniel 3).

Burning out or burning bright, which will it be? Here in Revelation, Pastor John's desire is that the faith of those in the seven churches under his care would burn hot amidst the persecution that threatened to extinguish it.

You see, like Shadrach, Meshach, and Abed-nego, John's flock was commanded to annually declare the lordship of Caesar. Failure to do so resulted in a loss of their livelihoods economically—or the loss of their very lives physically as they were burned as candles or fed to lions by the thousands. Because some of his congregants would be tempted to give in and burn out under such pressure, Pastor

John was given a vision of 144,000 whose faith would not falter even in the overwhelming persecution of the great Tribulation.

We first met these 144,000 in chapter 7—twelve thousand evangelists from each of the twelve tribes of Israel who fan out throughout the globe sharing the gospel. Here in chapter 14, we find all 144,000 standing with the Lord on Mount Zion. In other words, they made it through the Tribulation without collapsing, without caving in, without giving up.

How? I believe the answer is crucial for us because Jesus said in the world we all will have tribulation (John 16:33). When the job we count on doesn't open up, when the marriage we long for doesn't pan out, when the kids we wait for don't turn around, when the money we hope for doesn't come in—we will be tempted to think that, because the Lord didn't seem to do what He said He would do, we're justified in downing a couple cold ones at Mutt's, logging on to a pornographic website, or dating an unbeliever. It's in the time of tribulation that the pressure is greatest to bow before the idol and say, "It's okay if I get my mind off my problems for a while because I'm in Christ. I'm forgiven."

"Wait," says Pastor John to his congregation, "there are 144,000 who will not get sucked into compromise, 144,000 who won't defile themselves. Therefore, you can make it as well."

So can we. We're living in dark days. The temptations are intense. It would be so easy to let down and give in. But in our text, John gives us six reasons why we shouldn't. . . .

The Lord on Our Mind

And I looked, and, lo, a Lamb stood on the mount Zion, and with him an hundred forty and four thousand, having his Father's name written in their foreheads.   Revelation 14:1

Choose to walk in purity, and the Lord will be on your mind constantly. As a result, you will have peace of mind continually. Why? Because God will keep the one whose mind is stayed on Him in perfect peace (Isaiah 26:3). That is why Paul says, "I would have you be wise concerning that which is good but simple concerning that which is evil" (Romans 16:19). The word he uses for "simple" is literally "stupid." In other words, "When everyone else is laughing at the off-color joke, you be the one who doesn't get it."

A number of Christmases ago, I was given a footstool with a wonderful handpainted bear on it. Unfortunately, it was the same Christmas that then-three-year-old Peter John received his first tool set—which was why Christmas afternoon found an unattended Peter John with hammer in hand and eight nails in the bear stool. Knowing he had done wrong, he said, "Pray for me, Daddy," as I walked into the room.

"Okay, Peter," I said. "Lord, thank You that You forgive our mistakes."

And Peter felt a lot better. As I pulled the nails out of the bear, Peter grew more relieved with each one. But the problem was, that although the nails were gone, the holes remained. I still have that footstool. It's a wonderful reminder to Peter John—and to me!

Yes, you can log on to the Internet. You can tune into HBO. You can go to the tavern and then say, "Father, forgive me. I did that in a moment of depression." And you'll be forgiven right then. Your sin will be forgotten by the Father—but not by you because, although the nails will be gone, the holes will remain. That is why David, a man who knew something about looking where he shouldn't have, and doing something he shouldn't have, says in Psalm 101:3, "I will set no wicked thing before mine eyes."

Authority in Our Voice

And I heard a voice from heaven, as the voice of many waters, and as the voice of a great thunder: and I heard the voice of harpers harping with their harps.

Revelation 14:2

The voices of the 144,000 were like thunder—earth-shaking and impacting. Truly, the voice of a grandparent, a parent, or a high-schooler living in purity is like thunder because authority and integrity are linked together inextricably. You cannot separate the two. If you think, *My kids will never know; my grandchildren will never hear; the guys at work don't have a clue what I do late at night,* you underestimate the discerning ability of the human spirit. Even if people don't know your story, they can sense in your voice, see in your face, discern in their hearts whether or not you are a person of integrity. That is why the voices of the 144,000 are likened to thunder.

A Song on Our Lips

And they sung as it were a new song before the throne, and before the four beasts, and the elders: and no man could learn that song but the hundred and forty and four thousand, which were redeemed from the earth.

Revelation 14:3

A new song in Scripture always implies a song of rejoicing or happiness. It may come as a shock to you if you're new in the things of the Lord that God is a happy God. It's true. The reason people left everything to follow Jesus, the reason they traveled great distances to see Him and even went days without food to listen to Him was because there was something about Him so joyful, so happy, so abundant.

Concerning Jesus, Hebrews 1:9 declares, "Because thou hast loved righteousness and hated iniquity thou art anointed with the oil of gladness above thy fellows."

In other words, "The happiest Man in history was the One who hated sin." In that, I understand happiness in life is directly proportional to holiness in life.

Happy is the people whose God is the Lord (Psalm 144:15). The holier we choose to be, the happier we will be because happiness and holiness travel together.

The Lamb in Our Sight

These are they which were not defiled with women; for they are virgins. These are they which follow the Lamb whithersoever he goeth.   Revelation 14:4

Wherever the Lamb goes, the 144,000 follow.

The sun is so big its interior could hold 1,300,000 earths. Yet I can block the entire sun out of my sight with only my thumb.

The same is true concerning God. He'll never leave or forsake us, but the "thumb" of our sin blocks Him from our sight. The 144,000 follow the Lamb easily because their purity allows them to see Him clearly.

Sweetness in Our Mouth

And in their mouth was found no guile: for they are without fault before the throne of God.   Revelation 14:5

In Ephesians 5:3, 4, Paul makes an interesting point when he says, "Let not fornication, uncleanness, or covetousness be named among you; neither filthiness, foolish talking, nor coarse jesting." The first list is like the engine of a train—the second like the cars that follow.

The Bible always links purity with speech because out of the abundance of the heart the mouth speaks (Matthew 12:34). Thus, when a person is always telling coarse jokes, or involved with foolish jesting, it means that he or she is partaking of immorality in some way. The words are merely the cars that follow the engine. That is why the mouths of the 144,000 were filled with sweetness.

Fruit for Our God

These were redeemed from among men, being the firstfruits unto God and to the Lamb.   Revelation 14:4

John's admonition to those in the first century is as vital to us as it will be to those in the Tribulation: Choose holiness—for the result of holiness is that the Lord will be on your mind, authority will be in your voice, a song of happiness will be on your lips, Jesus will be in your sight, and sweetness will be in your mouth. But above all, holiness in your life will produce fruit for your God.

You might not care about being happy, about being blessed, about having direction for your life personally, or speaking with authority presently. But perhaps you really do care about what God thinks of you eternally. And of the 144,000 who walk in purity, He says, "They've made a tough choice, and I regard them as the finest fruit."

And even if you have failed—as we all have—if you are one of His, God still finds you faultless.

Where?

Before the throne (verse 5).

Why?

Because the blood of Jesus cleanses us from all our failings (1 John 1:7).

So it is that God says, "Not only are you faultless before the throne, but I will keep you from falling on earth" (see Jude 24). You're faultless positionally, but I can keep you from falling practically if you'll allow Me."

Choose holiness, gang. You'll never regret it. Choose holiness, for if you do, you will be happy presently and blessed eternally.

REST IN PEACE
A Topical Study of
Revelation 14:13

I read an article about an intern in San Francisco who carries a cell phone, a laptop computer, and a handheld computer organizer to stay on top of his daily schedule. He even wears a pager under his wetsuit while surfing. No wonder psychologists are seeing more and more cases of stress and fatigue caused by a syndrome that has come to be known as "information overload." After all, a single weekday edition of the *New York Times* contains more information than the average person in the seventeenth century would have encountered in his entire lifetime.

That's why I love what Jesus said when He said,

Come unto me, all ye that labour and are heavy laden, and I will give you rest. Take my yoke upon you, and learn of me; for I am meek and lowly in heart: and ye shall find rest unto your souls.   Matthew 11:28, 29

It is interesting to me that Jesus doesn't promise rest from a difficult relationship, rest from the pressure of a job, or rest from the expectation of a college professor. He promises rest in one's soul. Fellow fatigued Christian—as we learn of Him, we find that the commands and demands, frustrations and expectations, the whirling and swirling of information all around us is actually redemptive. That is, it can serve a purpose.

> Due to a previous commitment, my wife, Tammy, and I weren't able to see our son Benny's Little League game one Friday. "How did it go, Ben?" we eagerly asked upon our return.
>
> "Well," he answered, "before I got up to bat the first time, I went to the end of the dugout and I got on my knees and prayed."
>
> "That's great!" I said. "You probably parked it over the fence, huh?"
>
> "No," he said as a huge grin spread across his face. "I struck out. But I got to *pitch* the next inning!"

How often we pray, "Lord, change my husband," or, "Lord, help my boss see the talent latent within me," or, "Lord, let me get an 'A.'" Like Benjamin, we pray with faith and fervency—only to strike out. But there's a next inning, folks—a big inning, a new, big inning, a new beginning. It's called heaven.

And because Jesus is preparing a place for us there (John 14:2), it is necessary that He prepare us for the place. But here's the problem: We keep getting sidetracked. God desires us to focus on the big inning, the big picture of eternity—but we remain glued to home plate—continually intrigued, interested, tempted by the things of earth. I'm not talking about sin necessarily; but about getting stuck in the world's trappings and priorities. To counter this, the Lord instructed His people to put a ribbon of blue on the borders of their garments, since blue in Scripture is the color of heaven (Numbers 15:38). But over the years, people became so accustomed to seeing blue, they didn't notice it any more than you would notice someone coming in here wearing a pair of Levi 501s.

So how does God choose to free us from the pull of the world? Our text tells us. . . .

> *And I heard a voice from heaven saying unto me, Write, Blessed are the dead which die in the Lord from henceforth: Yea, saith the Spirit, that they may rest from their labours; and their works do follow them.*   Revelation 14:13

Who is the Lord speaking to here?

To those who become believers during the Tribulation.

With the wrath of God toward a Christ-rejecting, sinful world being poured out all around them, these Tribulation saints are weary beyond anything we can imagine. And what do they hear in heaven? "Happy are you who die in the Lord." Why? "Because, at last, you will rest from your labor."

Fellow baby boomers, the older generation understood this in ways we don't, as evidenced by the inscription seen on so many headstones in generations past: Rest In Peace. Perhaps it was the hardship of their lives that made them so much more aware of the true rest awaiting them in heaven than are we with our cars and computers and compactors.

Our text helps me begin to understand that the gravitational pull of the world—to get me to trivialize my life, to waste my time, to throw away the limited days given me on earth to prepare for heaven—is weakened through my own personal struggles and trials, fatigue and disappointments, heartaches and tribulation. And unlike a blue ribbon that's easily forgotten or becomes an item of superstition, the weight of weariness or worry, sadness or stress causes me to say, "I'm *really* looking forward to heaven."

Why do I go through this struggle year after year? you wonder. The reason is that it's absolutely necessary—to get you uncoupled from the world, to set you free from the pull of the temporal, to get you to long for heaven.

If the people to whom our text was initially written were living on an island in Hawaii, being waited on hand and foot under swaying palm trees and setting sun with no money problems, no physical pain, no marital stress, no child-rearing difficulties, they would probably say, "My butler should be here any minute with my filet mignon, so could You hold off Your return for a little while longer, Lord?"

Hard times will never come to an end, gang, because God knows they're the only way we'll long for heaven and thus fix our eyes on eternity. Jesus didn't talk about heaven while sitting on the beach, overlooking the ocean, sipping a Coke. He talked about heaven in the same passage in which He told His disciples one of them would betray Him, one of them would deny Him, and He Himself would die (John 13—14).

We don't sense the bleakness the disciples must have felt because we know the whole story. They didn't. They thought their whole lives were coming to an end. After all, they had left *everything* to follow this Rabbi.

"Blessed are they," Jesus would say, "who see the bigger picture, the scope of eternity, the kingdom of heaven—for they will have rest not from their problems, but in their soul. Precious brother, dear sister, you can get on your knees every night and pray, "God, solve this problem," or, "Take away that pain," or, "Get me out of this situation"—but it could be that those are the very things God is using to make you a man or woman who lives for heaven.

You might pray passionately and strike out on three pitches—but never lose sight of the new, big inning just ahead.

Batter up!

15

Revelation 15:1 (a)
And I saw another sign in heaven,
great and marvellous, seven angels
having the seven last plagues . . .

Chapter 15 unfolds in the period of time known as the Tribulation—the seven-year period following the Rapture of the church. In chapter 15, we'll begin to see God pour out His wrath on the world that rejected His payment for their sin—an understanding vital to the events that follow, for it is only a clear understanding of Revelation 15 that keeps us from thinking God unfair in chapters 16 through 19.

Revelation 15:1 (b)
. . . for in them is filled up the wrath of God.

In Revelation 15, God says, "I have been patient with human rebellion and depravity—and now the bowls are full." In Genesis 15:13–16, God says to Abraham, "You're going to be the father of a nation that will sojourn in another country for four hundred years. Your people will be afflicted and enslaved because the iniquity of the Amorites is not yet full." In other words, while Israel was held captive in Egypt for four hundred years, God was giving the Canaanites an opportunity to repent and turn to Him. Tragically, however, they didn't.

"Destroy the Amorites," God commanded Joshua upon the Israelites' entry into Canaan (see Deuteronomy 20:17). This only seems extremely unfair and brutal when one fails to take into account the fact that God waited four hundred years for these same Amorites to turn from the horrific perversion and cruelty that defined their culture and destroyed their souls.

Four hundred years is a long time. For twice as long as our nation has existed, while Israel was held captive in Egypt, God waited for the Amorites to turn from their bizarre, evil practices. But they didn't. So finally, when the iniquity of the Amorites was full, God said, "Enough is enough. Destroy them." Did He do so because He is cruel? No. The Amorites were already doomed, damned, lost, gone, toast, curtains, dust. They were so sick that in ordering their annihilation, God was simply putting them out of their misery.

I camp on this point because people who read the Bible casually or hear a story in a Sunday sermon occasionally can think God is cruel. We must explain to them how patient God is—but that we must not mistake His patience for apathy, impo-

tence, or approval of sin. For while the wheels of God's judgment turn slowly, they do, indeed, grind thoroughly.

Revelation 15:2 (a)
And I saw as it were a sea of glass mingled with fire . . .

In addition to seeing the seven angels about to pour out the fullness of God's wrath, John sees a sea of glass. Because the tabernacle was a shadow of the reality of heaven (Hebrews 8—9), I believe the sea of glass is actually a glassy sea of literal water, of which the laver in the temple was a picture (Exodus 30:18).

Revelation 15:2 (b)
. . . and them that had gotten the victory over the beast, and over his image, and over his mark, and over the number of his name, stand on the sea of glass, having the harps of God.

It is intriguing to me that those who lose their lives in the Tribulation because they choose to listen to the message of the 144,000 and believe God rather than take the mark of the Beast or bow before the image are seen not around, but *on* the sea of glass.

Why does this intrigue me? Because it reminds me of another tribulation. . . .

Out on the sea with the wind blowing and the waves rolling, the disciples were understandably terrified. Seeing the Lord walking toward them, Peter cried, "Lord, if that's really You, bid me come."

Jesus said, "Come," and Peter did just that (Matthew 14:28).

So, too, in our text, these guys are walking on water. On earth they didn't. Having been persecuted and destroyed by Antichrist, on earth they would have been seen as losers. Not so in heaven. In heaven, they're water-walkers.

If you don't factor in heaven, none of biblical Christianity works. Without heaven, folks, you're going to go down the wrong path in your experience of spiritual life. You've got to factor heaven into every single equation. If you get nothing else out of the Book of Revelation, my prayer would be that you would first of all see Jesus Christ on the throne in control, and, secondly, that you'd understand it's all about *heaven*.

Revelation 15:3 (a)
And they sing the song of Moses the servant of God . . .

The song of Moses, recorded in Exodus 15, is the first song in the Bible. With their backs to the Red Sea, three million Jews looked up to see Pharaoh's army barreling down on them. "Moses, you've led us into a trap!" they cried because not one of them knew that God was about to do something totally unexpected, unpredictable, unprecedented. So it was not until after God intervened, after the Red Sea parted, after the children of Israel crossed safely to the other side that they sang, "The Lord has triumphed gloriously."

Revelation 15:3 (b)
. . . and the song of the Lamb, saying, Great and marvellous are thy works, Lord God Almighty; just and true are thy ways, thou King of saints.

- The song of Moses was sung near the Red Sea.
- The song of the Lamb is sung near the glassy sea.

- The song of Moses dealt with rescue.
- The song of the Lamb deals with Rapture.

- The song of Moses was sung by those brought out of Egypt.
- The song of the Lamb is sung by those brought into heaven.

Revelation 15:4
Who shall not fear thee, O Lord, and glorify thy name? for thou only art holy: for all nations shall come and worship before thee; for thy judgments are made manifest.

"All nations shall come and worship before thee," sing the overcomers in Revelation 15, fulfilling Zechariah's prophecy. . . .

And it shall come to pass, that every one that is left of all the nations which came against Jerusalem shall even go up from year to year to worship the King, the LORD of hosts, and to keep the feast of tabernacles. Zechariah 14:16

When the Lord comes back, the Feast of Tabernacles—the week-long celebration, wherein throughout history the Jews commemorated how God brought them through the wilderness—will be reinstated. Instead of commemorating how the Lord brought His people through the wilderness, however, it will celebrate how He brought His people through the world.

Everyone will be invited, but not everyone will come . .

And it shall be, that whoso will not come up of all the families of the earth unto Jerusalem to worship the King, the LORD of hosts, even upon them shall be no rain. Zechariah 14:17

Those who don't come will experience drought, limited fruit, restricted harvest.

The Lord says the same thing to you and me today, "Come and dine. Worship Me."

And we say, "Well, I'm kind of busy."

We don't *have* to come, gang. But I'll tell you this: When I don't come, I get real dry because God is into corporate worship. Those of you who say, "But I've heard Revelation already," or, "Why should I hear the Book of Acts being taught again? I studied it a year ago," consider this. . . .

I talked with a precious couple from Missouri who said, "When your daughter, Jessie, went to heaven, we ordered the videotape of her memorial service. After watching it, we decided to hang on to it because we knew someone would need to see it. Almost a year to the day after Jessie went to heaven, our son was killed in an automobile accident. We pulled out the video, and you know what? It was for us."

It had only been a year since their son went to heaven, yet they shared with me maturely, wisely, deeply because, you see, although they had heard about heaven many times before, now they truly had the bigger picture of heaven burned into their hearts.

Saying, "We don't need to go to Bible study because we've heard that before and have been there already," is really foolish because we don't know what lies right around the bend. . . .

King Asa was wise. During the ten years of peace and prosperity under his reign, he built up the walls of his kingdom. He put bars on the gates. He raised up 280,000 men from Judah and gave them shields and spears. He raised up another 200,000 men of Benjamin and armed them as well. Why? Because knowing there would be a battle ahead, he used the time of peace and prosperity not to kick back, but to build up (2 Chronicles 14).

This world isn't a playground, dear saints. It's a battlefield. And wise is the one who, over the weeks and months and decades, says, "I'm going to build the walls of my faith. I'm going to fortify the city. I'm going to get the shields and weapons ready because I know sooner or later there will come trials and difficulties through which the Enemy desires to make my faith collapse. I need to be forewarned that I might be forearmed, prepared that I may be preserved."

Revelation 15:5, 6 (a)
And after that I looked, and, behold, the temple of the tabernacle of the testimony in heaven was opened: And the seven angels came out of the temple, having the seven plagues, clothed in pure and white linen . . .

As the period of the Tribulation begins here in chapter 15, we see the angels dressed in spotless white linen—like a surgical team, if you would.

Revelation 15:6 (b)
. . . and having their breasts girded with golden girdles.

The girdles of gold across their breasts symbolize the heart of gold within. That is, the judgment they are about to administer to the earth stems not from cruelty but from love.

Revelation 15:7, 8
And one of the four beasts gave unto the seven angels seven golden vials full of the wrath of God, who liveth for ever and ever. And the temple was filled with smoke from the glory of God, and from his power; and no man was able to enter into the temple, till the seven plagues of the seven angels were fulfilled.

Knowing that sin bites, burns, brutalizes, and butchers His children (Romans 6:23), God sends His surgical team of angels with vials of the bitter medicine of judgment in their hands in order to deal with the sin that destroys humanity.

In a parallel passage, we see David dealing with the repercussions of his own sin following his adulterous relationship with Bathsheba, and the subsequent murder of her husband, Uriah. . . .

Purge me with hyssop, and I shall be clean: wash me, and I shall be whiter than snow. Make me to hear joy and gladness; that the bones which thou hast broken may rejoice.
Psalm 51:7, 8

When a lamb repeatedly jeopardized his own safety by continually wandering away from the flock, the shepherd would break its leg. Then, throughout the healing process, the shepherd would carry the heretofore straying lamb on his shoulder, during which time something amazing transpired in the lamb. You see, when after five

or six weeks, his bone could again support his weight, the lamb remained close to the shepherd, never to wander again—not because he feared another broken bone, but because he had become attached to the shepherd. So it is as a shepherd that David cries, "Lord, I know that the bones which Thou hast broken shall rejoice again."

Precious people, if we wander away and continue in sin, the Good Shepherd will do what He did with David and what David did with his own sheep: He'll break the bone of our self-sufficiency in order to force us to draw close to Him in ways we never would have otherwise.

But lest you think the vials of judgment about to be poured out in the Tribulation are still unfair, take another look at our Shepherd, and you'll realize that the Good Shepherd is also the Lamb of God who suffered not a broken bone, but a broken body and a broken heart as He died for our sin.

16

Revelation 16:1
And I heard a great voice out of the temple saying to the seven angels, Go your ways, and pour out the vials of the wrath of God upon the earth.

The world is not well, folks. It's suffering from the cancer of carnality, the plague of perversion, the sickness of sin. Therefore, in the period of the Tribulation, the Father will deal with the sin that permeates and pollutes our world. Now, you can either undergo the brutal and bloody radical surgery of the Tribulation—or you can undergo open-heart surgery in this day of grace by opening your heart to Jesus Christ. You see, sin *must* be judged one way or another. I highly recommend bypassing the Tribulation and letting the Lord do surgery on your heart today!

Revelation 16:2
And the first went, and poured out his vial upon the earth; and there fell a noisome and grievous sore upon the men which had the mark of the beast, and upon them which worshipped his image.

The first strong medicine poured out upon the earth results in "grievous sores" upon those who take the mark of the Beast. Initially, taking the mark of the Beast would seem to be so logical, so technologically sophisticated, so wise. I mean, why deal with credit cards that can be stolen, checks that can be forged, or cash that can be lost when you can enter into a brand-new economic order where you can buy and sell with simply a number?

"Don't take the mark of the Beast!" the angels will cry as they fly across the sky. "Don't take his number," the 144,000 Jewish evangelists will preach on the streets. But most will not heed the message. And their refusal to do so will bring about its own pain.

That's always the way it is with sin. "The reason you have so many problems and pains and difficulties is because of your own sin. It's not Me punishing you," says God. "It's the result of your own backsliding" (see Jeremiah 2:19).

Revelation 16:3
And the second angel poured out his vial upon the sea; and it became as the blood of a dead man: and every living soul died in the sea.

An abnormal multiplication of plankton causes not only a depletion of the oxygen supply in the surrounding water, but ushers in a phenomenon known as "red tide"—wherein the phosphorous in the plankton causes the water to turn red as blood. It could be that this is a "red tide" taken to the extreme. I don't know. But whatever it is, it will be absolutely horrible.

Revelation 16:4
And the third angel poured out his vial upon the rivers and fountains of waters; and they became blood.

As hard as it is to imagine, every creek, lake, and river will turn to blood. Every faucet, every hose, every drinking fountain will run blood instead of water. If you think that's a bit extreme, read on.

Revelation 16:5, 6
And I heard the angel of the waters say, Thou art righteous, O Lord, which art, and wast, and shalt be, because thou hast judged thus. For they have shed the blood of saints and prophets, and thou hast given them blood to drink; for they are worthy.

Through the centuries, people have questioned how He who is supposed to be love can be so judgmental, so brutal, so bloody. Yet here in verse 5, we hear the angel say that the very turning of the water to blood is an act of righteousness.

Why?

Think with me. . . .

As Jesus hung on the Cross, praying forgiveness upon those who nailed Him there, water and blood flowed from His side (John 19:34). Medically indicative of a broken heart, the water and blood meant nothing to the crowd at Golgotha

who cursed Him, spat upon Him, and turned their backs on Him. Thus, here in Revelation, the water is turned to blood physically because mankind rejected the blood that flowed with water redemptively.

Revelation 16:7
And I heard another out of the altar say, Even so, Lord God Almighty, true and righteous are thy judgments.

The phrase "another out of" does not appear in the original Greek text. Thus, newer translations correctly render this verse: "And I heard the altar say, even so, Lord God Almighty, true and righteous are thy judgments." Now, whether this voice be figurative or literal, I cannot say. But this much is sure: The voice that cries, "True and righteous are thy judgments, O Lord," originates at the altar.

In our own times of trial and tribulation, there can be a tendency within us to question the fairness of the Father. But the altar, the place of sacrifice, the Cross speaks just the opposite. If you don't see this, you'll go through life one day blessing the Lord in the amphitheater and the next day cursing Him because of your troubles at work. God demonstrated His love for you in that while we were yet sinners Christ died for us (Romans 5:8). Therefore, it is through the lens of God's love as demonstrated on the altar of Calvary that I must look at every trial I face and every hard time I endure.

"What shall we say then? He that spared not his own Son, but delivered Him up for us all, how shall He not with Him also freely give us all things?" (see Romans 8:32) Because God loved me enough to hang on the Cross in my place, to pay for my sin, to die for me, I know everything He does in my life—whether or not I understand it at the time—is *right.*

Complaining about my job, boss, paycheck, kids, singleness, or employees only means I am not listening to the cry of the altar, that I have forgotten Calvary. Allow the Cross to "altar" your view, precious people, as you look at everything in the light of Calvary.

Revelation 16:8
And the fourth angel poured out his vial upon the sun; and power was given unto him to scorch men with fire.

This could be referring to a supernova—the stage directly preceding the death of a star, wherein the star becomes intensely hot. Be that as it may, because men turned their backs on the Son, they will experience the burning of the sun.

Revelation 16:9
And men were scorched with great heat, and blasphemed the name of God, which hath power over these plagues: and they repented not to give him glory.

The judgments poured out upon the earth in rapid succession result in blistered bodies, stinking seas, blood-red rivers, and a scorching sun. Yet man chooses through it all to blaspheme rather than repent. This is vital to understand because it answers the charges of those who say, "If God is a God of love, wouldn't one thousand, ten thousand, or even one million years be sufficient punishment for mans' sin and rebellion? Be reasonable. What kind of God would allow someone to burn in hell *forever?*"

In Matthew 25:41, Jesus speaks of everlasting fire and in Mark 9:43–45 of hell as being a place where the fire is not quenched. Hell is eternal. Why? Because men are eternally unrepentant. As we see in our text, no matter how hot the sun becomes or how red the rivers run, man refuses to repent.

"Oh, but I repented," you say. Yes—but it was only by God's grace because there is none righteous (Romans 3:10). That is why you and I must be forever grateful that the Lord, by His grace, initiated His work of salvation in us.

Revelation 16:10 (a)
And the fifth angel poured out his vial upon the seat of the beast; and his kingdom was full of darkness . . .

The seat of Antichrist's government is Babylon—the city constructed on the same site as the tower of Babel. "We don't need God. We'll build a tower, study the stars, and let our horoscopes run our lives," declared Nimrod and his fellow inhabitants of Babel.

Revelation 16:10 (b)
. . . and they gnawed their tongues for pain.

At the tower of Babel, men's tongues were affected in that they no longer spoke the same language. In the city of Babylon, men's tongues will again be affected when they are gnawed as a result of pain.

Revelation 16:11
And blasphemed the God of heaven because of their pains and their sores, and repented not of their deeds.

Even though they can barely speak due to the pain that overwhelms them, men still find it in their hearts to blaspheme God.

Revelation 16:12 (a)
And the sixth angel poured out his vial upon the great river Euphrates . . .

Referred to twenty-five times in Scripture, the Euphrates River is highly significant. The Euphrates formed the northernmost boundary of the land promised to Abraham in Genesis 15, the Nile forming the southern boundary. Although the land promised to the Jews comprised a substantial chunk of real estate, only during Solomon's reign would the Jews actually possess even a measurable percentage of this vast region.

Revelation 16:12 (b)
. . . and the water thereof was dried up . . .

Because the Euphrates is eighteen hundred miles long, an average of thirty feet deep, and three to twelve hundred feet wide, people used to scoff at this Scripture. "How could such a massive river dry up?" they chuckled. But in 1994, the site manager of the Ataturk Dam, located at the headwaters of the Euphrates, was quoted in *The Atlantic* as saying, "It is true that we can stop the flow of water into Syria and Iraq for up to eight months in order to regulate their political behavior."

Revelation 16:12 (c)
. . . that the way of the kings of the east might be prepared.

The phrase translated "kings of the east" is literally "kings of the rising sun" in the original text. The "land of the rising sun" traditionally and historically referring to both Japan and China, the pieces of the puzzle of prophecy begin to fall into place—for the technology of Japan and the sheer manpower of China could easily produce the two-hundred-million-man army prophesied in Revelation 9:14–16.

Why would China want to go to war? China has a problem: One and one-half billion people—that is, one of every four people on earth—will live in China. To address this situation, the Chinese government imposed a fifteen-year prison sentence on couples with more than a single child. As a result, due to the massive abortion of baby girls, sending their boys to war could be seen differently.

Revelation 16:13, 14
And I saw three unclean spirits like frogs come out of the mouth of the dragon, and out of the mouth of the beast, and out of the mouth of the false prophet. For they are the spirits of devils, working miracles, which go forth unto the kings of the earth and of the whole world, to gather them to the battle of that great day of God Almighty.

As the Tribulation nears its end, three froglike demons croak, "GotoMegiddo, GotoMegiddo," in the ears of world leaders. It's a demonically induced suggestion because Satan is actually orchestrating the entire scenario.

Revelation 16:15
Behold, I come as a thief. Blessed is he that watcheth, and keepeth his garments, lest he walk naked, and they see his shame.

Because of the admonition given to us in 1 Thessalonians 5:1–4, we know what's ahead. We're looking for the Rapture. But these left behind, having been in darkness, receive this word of encouragement in verse 15: "Take hope. Even though the armies are marching, I'm on My way. My coming is not only imminent—it's immediate."

Revelation 16:16
And he gathered them together into a place called in the Hebrew tongue Armageddon.

Located sixty miles north of Jerusalem, the Jezreel Valley has been filled with warfare. When Gideon and three hundred men overcame the Midianites, it was at the valley below a little hill called Megiddo. When Samson took on the Philistines, one of the key battles was at Megiddo. King Josiah was killed at Megiddo. Deborah and Barak defeated Sisera at Megiddo.

The Turks, Muslims, Syrians, Egyptians, and the Europeans have all waged war in this valley. In his disastrous excursion into Egypt, Napoleon passed through the Jezreel Valley. "If ever there is a place on earth where the last war must be fought," he declared, "it is here."

The armies of the world will indeed gather at Armageddon. And Antichrist, the false prophet, and Satan himself will meet them there.

Why?

First, to devour Israel. The ultimate anti-Semite is Satan. If He can destroy Israel, Bible prophecy will fail, for how can Jesus return to rule and reign from Israel if Israel ceases to be?

Second, to destroy believers. Having wiped out the nation Israel, Satan would then wipe out all who oppose him.

Finally, to determine who will rule. Satan knows he will ultimately encounter God at Megiddo. Daniel 11:40–45 outlines the actual strategy that will be used in this final battle: While Antichrist is headquartered at Babylon, the king of the south—Egypt and the northern African nations—will launch an insurrection against him. At the same time, the king of the north—Russia—will come south in order to assist the Egyptians and the northern African nations in their rebellion against Antichrist. But the Russians will fool the king of the south, continue on into Egypt, and carry off the treasures of Egypt.

So we see Egypt coming north, Russia coming south, Antichrist coming from the east—and they all converge in Megiddo.

Revelation 16:17
And the seventh angel poured out his vial into the air; and there came a great voice out of the temple of heaven, from the throne, saying, It is done.

Two mountains come to mind. . . .

Both deal with the wrath of God as He pours out His wrath on men at Megiddo and upon His Son at Calvary.

Both deal with the rebellion of man as they blaspheme God at Megiddo and His Son at Calvary.

Both are bloodbaths as blood flows to the horses' manes at Megiddo and from the Son's veins at Calvary.

Both are completions, as "It is done," cries a voice from heaven at Mount Megiddo while "It is finished," cries a voice from Mount Calvary.

Will you endure the final wrath of the Father at Megiddo—or will you embrace the finished work of the Son on Calvary? The choice is yours.

Revelation 16:18–20
And there were voices, and thunders, and lightnings; and there was a great earthquake, such as was not since men were upon the earth, so mighty an earthquake, and so great. And the great city was divided into three parts, and the cities of the nations fell: and great Babylon came in remembrance

before God, to give unto her the cup of the wine of the fierceness of his wrath. And every island fled away, and the mountains were not found.

The armies gather. The earth shakes. The blood flows in this event in which the topographical changes described in this passage are consistent with the effects of nuclear warfare.

Revelation 16:21 (a)
And there fell upon men a great hail out of heaven, every stone about the weight of a talent . . .

One of the surprising results of the 1950s nuclear testing on the Bikini Islands were the hailstones that formed when the surrounding water shot so high into the atmosphere that it froze before returning to earth. The bombs detonated at Nagasaki and Hiroshima are BB guns in comparison to the power of the bombs presently in the arsenals of numerous nations, so one talent—or one-hundred-pound—hailstones are certainly possible.

Revelation 16:21 (b)
. . . and men blasphemed God because of the plague of the hail; for the plague thereof was exceeding great.

What was the Old Testament punishment for blasphemy? Stoning (Leviticus 24:16). What's happening here? Stoning by hundred-pound hailstones.

17 A few days ago, during one of my rare stops at McDonalds, I engaged in a delightful conversation with a couple in the next booth. We talked for twenty minutes about prophecy and world events before the lady asked me the question I dread hearing: "What do you do for a living?"
"I'm a teacher," I said.
"Oh?" she said. "What do you teach?"
"I'm a Bible teacher," I said, somewhat reluctantly.
Driving back from McDonalds®, I wondered why, although I love to share the gospel, I am so hesitant to admit I'm a pastor. Then it hit me: I'm just not a "religious" guy.
Jesus came on the scene, saying, "The truth shall set you free" (see John 8:32). But the very word "religion" means "to bind." Here in our text, we see the subject of religion addressed very clearly. . . .

Revelation 17:1 (a)
And there came one of the seven angels which had the seven vials, and talked with me, saying unto me, Come hither; I will shew unto thee the judgment of the great whore . . .

At this point in the Book of Revelation, although the church is in heaven, the structures, systems, and stuff of religion—referred to here as the great harlot—remain intact on earth.

Revelation 17:1 (b), 2
. . . that sitteth upon many waters: With whom the kings of the earth have committed fornication, and the inhabitants of the earth have been made drunk with the wine of her fornication.

Note the universal power of the false religious system as the harlot consorts with the political leaders of "many waters," or many nations.

Revelation 17:3
So he carried me away in the spirit into the wilderness: and I saw a woman sit upon a scarlet coloured beast, full of names of blasphemy, having seven heads and ten horns.

Note the unique position of the false religious system as the harlot is seen riding the Beast, or Antichrist. At this point, all true believers—be they Baptists or Catholics, Episcopalians or Pentecostals—are in heaven. This leaves only the trappings of religion atop the Beast.

Revelation 17:4 (a)
And the woman was arrayed in purple and scarlet colour, and decked with gold and precious stones and pearls . . .

Note the unlimited prosperity of the false religious system as seen in the purple robes and precious jewels with which the harlot is attired.

Revelation 17:4 (b)
. . . having a golden cup in her hand full of abominations and filthiness of her fornication.

Note the unholy passion of the false religious system as seen in the golden cup in the hand of the harlot, full of the fruits of her fornication.

Revelation 17:5
And upon her forehead was a name written, MYSTERY, BABYLON THE GREAT, THE MOTHER OF HARLOTS AND ABOMINATIONS OF THE EARTH.

The Bible could rightly be called The Tale of Two Cities, for from cover to cover, two cities pop up over and over again: One is Jerusalem, the city of God. The other is Babylon, the city of rebellion.

Mentioned more than three hundred times in Scripture, Babylon was founded on the plain of Shinar near the Euphrates River by Nimrod, a man whose name literally means "we will rebel." Babylon was centered around the tower of Babel—a ziggurat used for the practice of astrology.

Revelation 17:6 (a)
And I saw the woman drunken with the blood of the saints, and with the blood of the martyrs of Jesus . . .

Note the unsettling persecution perpetrated by the false religious system. Bear in mind that John wrote the Book of Revelation in the midst of ten waves of persecution that would ultimately claim the lives of six million believers.

Revelation 17:6 (b), 7
. . . and when I saw her, I wondered with great admiration. And the angel said unto me, Wherefore didst thou marvel? I will tell thee the mystery of the woman, and of the beast that carrieth her, which hath the seven heads and ten horns.

Initially, we saw the woman riding the Beast (verse 3). Here, we see the Beast carrying the woman—a small, but I believe, important change of terminology as Antichrist employs the false religious system to serve his own agenda.

Revelation 17:8
The beast that thou sawest was, and is not; and shall ascend out of the bottomless pit, and go into perdition: and they that dwell on the earth shall wonder, whose names were not written in the book of life from the foundation of the world, when they behold the beast that was, and is not, and yet is.

John gives a seemingly enigmatic description of the beast carrying the woman when he writes of the "beast that was seen and is not, and yet is." But then he goes on to give further illumination. . . .

Revelation 17:9
And here is the mind which hath wisdom. The seven heads are seven mountains, on which the woman sitteth.

Only one city in history is known as "The City of Seven Mountains": Rome.

Revelation 17:10 (a)
And there are seven kings . . .

At the time John wrote this, there had been seven Roman emperors: Julius Caesar, Caesar Augustus, Tiberias, Caligula, Claudius, Nero, and Domitian.

Revelation 17:10 (b)
. . . five are fallen . . .

Of the original emperors, the lives of five were cut short. Julius Caesar was assassinated. Tiberias was poisoned. Caligula was stabbed. Claudius was smothered. And Nero committed suicide.

Revelation 17:10 (c)
. . . and one is . . .

When John penned this book, Domitian was on the throne.

Revelation 17:10 (d)
. . . and the other is not yet come; and when he cometh, he must continue a short space.

This is a reference to Antichrist.

Revelation 17:11
And the beast that was, and is not, even he is the eighth, and is of the seven, and goeth into perdition.

The Beast yet to come is "of the seven." In other words, Antichrist is one of the original seven emperors. Consider with me Caesar Nero—the sixth of the original Roman emperors. . . .

It was to Caesar Nero that Paul appealed (Acts 25:11). History verifies that it was after meeting with Paul that Caesar Nero went on a rampage that resulted in the martyrdom of tens of thousands of believers. This coupled with the fact that the Hebrew numeric value of the letters of his name equal 666, I personally believe Caesar Nero will one day reappear as Antichrist. Oh, he'll not come wearing a toga, playing a fiddle, saying, "I'm back." Rather, the perverted spirit of Caesar Nero that caused massive bloodshed under his reign will reappear in Antichrist.

Revelation 17:12, 13
And the ten horns which thou sawest are ten kings, which have received no kingdom as yet; but receive power as kings one hour

with the beast. These have one mind, and shall give their power and strength unto the beast.

Daniel 7 tells us that the ten horns of the beast signify the ten nations of the revived Roman Empire. Since the Rapture has happened at this point, Antichrist and this ten-nation federation will be of one mind.

Revelation 17:14 (a)
These shall make war with the Lamb . . .

The bottom line, the only goal, the one objective of Antichrist is to destroy Jesus.

Revelation 17:14 (b)
. . . and the Lamb shall overcome them: for he is Lord of lords, and King of kings: and they that are with him are called, and chosen, and faithful.

Because Jesus is the Lord of lords and the King of kings, Antichrist will be unsuccessful in his attempted coup.

Revelation 17:15, 16
And he saith unto me, The waters which thou sawest, where the whore sitteth, are peoples, and multitudes, and nations, and tongues. And the ten horns which thou sawest upon the beast, these shall hate the whore, and shall make her desolate and naked, and shall eat her flesh, and burn her with fire.

Once the Beast has used the false religious system to gain power, he will then turn against her. So, too, we will be disgraced, denuded, and devoured by any sin we attempt to control rather than confess. Oh, perhaps, like the harlot, we can ride the sin for a season, arrayed in the pearls, precious stones, and purple robes of confidence—but eventually, like the harlot, we will be burned and eaten up by the very sin we thought we controlled. I believe the language in this verse is purposely horrific because, truly, the wages of sin is death (Romans 3:23).

Revelation 17:17
For God hath put in their hearts to fulfil his will, and to agree, and give their kingdom unto the beast, until the words of God shall be fulfilled.

According to His own will, God will use the Beast to destroy the false religious system.

Revelation 17:18
And the woman which thou sawest is that great city, which reigneth over the kings of the earth.

This chapter has dealt with all of so-called Christendom being united by the power and potency of Rome. But one must not equate Rome with Catholicism. There are wonderful brothers and sisters in the Catholic Church, just as there are wonderful brothers and sisters in the Baptist, Lutheran, Episcopalian, Methodist, and Orthodox church. But after these brothers and sisters are raptured, the remaining power and prestige of the church in Rome will be manipulated by Antichrist. And although the Roman Church will think she's in control, she'll inevitably suffer the same fate as that of her own Pope Pius. . . .

In 1804, Napoleon summoned Pope Pius VII to leave Rome and to come to Paris in order to crown him emperor of France. Knowing the one who crowns the emperor will always have a voice of power with the emperor, Pius showed up with crown in hand. But just as he was about to place the crown on Napoleon's brow, Napoleon grabbed it from Pope Pius and crowned himself. Horrified, Pius immediately understood the implication: Napoleon had wrested all power from Rome.

And the day is coming when Antichrist will do the same.

18

Revelation 18:1 (a)
And after these things . . .

After what things? After the destruction of Babylon (Revelation 17:15). What is left of the one-world religious system will join with Antichrist and the ten-nation confederation of Europe. Playing right into his hands, the religious system will initially work with Antichrist and the European Union—the revived Roman Empire.

The religious system based in Rome will appear to control the European coalition of the revived Roman Empire—but only for a certain season, for these kings will ultimately turn against Rome and, after using her to gain control of the reigns of world power, will trash her. That's why Babylon is called a harlot in chapter 17. She's used, abused, and thrown away.

Revelation 18:1 (b), 2 (a)
. . . I saw another angel come down from heaven, having great power; and the earth was lightened with his glory. And he cried

mightily with a strong voice, saying, Babylon the great is fallen, is fallen . . .

Why do we see Babylon again in chapter 18 after seeing her destroyed in chapter 17? Because chapter 17 deals with the false religious system Babylon represents, while chapter 18 deals with the literal city of Babylon. Chapter 17 deals with religious Babylon. Chapter 18 deals with political and economic Babylon.

This explains the seeming discrepancy between 17:16, which reads: ". . . and the ten horns which thou sawest upon the beast, these shall hate the whore . . ." and 18:9, which reads: ". . . and the kings of the earth, who have committed fornication and lived deliciously with her, shall bewail her, and lament for her . . ." You see, although the kings of the earth hate the religious system, they love and embrace the economic system of Babylon.

Revelation 18:2 (b)
. . . and is become the habitation of devils, and the hold of every foul spirit, and a cage of every unclean and hateful bird.

As also seen in Jeremiah 51, the utter destruction of Babylon is reiterated in the Book of Isaiah . . .

And Babylon, the glory of kingdoms, the beauty of the Chaldees' excellency, shall be as when God overthrew Sodom and Gomorrah. It shall never be inhabited, neither shall it be dwelt in from generation to generation: neither shall the Arabian pitch tent there; neither shall the shepherds make their fold there. But wild beasts of the desert shall lie there; and their houses shall be full of doleful creatures; and owls shall dwell there, and satyrs shall dance there. And the wild beasts of the islands shall cry in their desolate houses, and dragons in their pleasant palaces: and her time is near to come, and her days shall not be prolonged
Isaiah 13:19–22

Although destroyed by Alexander the Great in 330 B.C., there have always been small communities of inhabitants in Babylon. Isaiah, however, prophesied that not even shepherds and their flocks would hang out there, that it would simply be a place for weird birds and wild animals. Thus, Isaiah's prophecy concerns a future destruction, which will come to further light as Revelation 18 unfolds. . . .

Revelation 18:3
For all nations have drunk of the wine of the wrath of her fornication, and the kings

of the earth have committed fornication with her, and the merchants of the earth are waxed rich through the abundance of her delicacies.

Here we see interaction and commercial intercourse with Babylon. And because every nation has interaction with Babylon, every nation is affected by Babylon. *All* nations have drunk of the wine of the wrath of her fornication.

Revelation 18:4
And I heard another voice from heaven, saying, Come out of her, my people, that ye be not partakers of her sins, and that ye receive not of her plagues.

The voice from heaven speaks to those who become believers during the Tribulation. The church is already in heaven, but the Lord will still save souls—so many that in the Tribulation there will be a large number of people who finally understand the gospel message and are converted to Christ. To them, this clarion call comes from heaven, saying, "Stay away from Babylon."

Revelation 18:5
For her sins have reached unto heaven, and God hath remembered her iniquities.

The goal of the builders of the Tower of Babylon's birthplace was to "build a tower whose top may reach unto heaven" (Genesis 11:4). In reality, the only thing that reached to heaven was their iniquity.

Revelation 18:6
Reward her even as she rewarded you, and double unto her double according to her works: in the cup which she hath filled fill to her double.

In other words, Babylon is about to receive twice the wrath and destruction ever perpetrated by her.

Revelation 18:7 (a)
How much she hath glorified herself, and lived deliciously, so much torment and sorrow give her: for she saith in her heart, I sit a queen, and am no widow . . .

She who has had interaction with all nations and with whom all nations have been involved in fornication now says, "I'm a queen, not a widow. I'm neither impoverished nor in need of anything."

Revelation 18:7 (b)
. . . and shall see no sorrow.

This doesn't mean Babylon will not experience sorrow—but that she refuses to see it. Consumed with a "let them eat cake" mentality, Babylon is so absorbed in her own delicacies, her own materialism, her own economy that she does not see the sorrow of people even within her own boundaries.

Revelation 18:8
Therefore shall her plagues come in one day, death, and mourning, and famine; and she shall be utterly burned with fire: for strong is the Lord God who judgeth her.

"You claim to be a queen and you see no sorrow. But I look at you differently," declares God. "You're going to be judged thoroughly."

Revelation 18:9, 10 (a)
And the kings of the earth, who have committed fornication and lived deliciously with her, shall bewail her, and lament for her, when they shall see the smoke of her burning, standing afar off for the fear of her torment, saying, Alas, alas, that great city Babylon, that mighty city . . .

Not wanting to be tormented with the same torment with which Babylon is tormented, the kings of the earth will lament and mourn—but "standing afar off"—at a safe distance.

Revelation 18:10 (b)
. . . for in one hour is thy judgment come.

The utter destruction of a city like Babylon taking place in one hour would most likely be the result of a nuclear exchange—the fallout of which would help explain why the kings of the earth "stand afar off."

Revelation 18:11
And the merchants of the earth shall weep and mourn over her; for no man buyeth their merchandise any more.

No one is saying, "Oh, those poor people in Babylon." No, they're saying, "Oh no, the world economy is wiped out." And as the results of the destruction of Babylon are described, it feels as if we're on a floor-by-floor tour of a huge department store like Saks Fifth Avenue or Bloomingdale's. . . .

Revelation 18:12 (a)
The merchandise of gold, and silver, and precious stones, and of pearls . . .

First floor: Jewelry

Revelation 18:12 (b)
. . . and fine linen, and purple, and silk, and scarlet . . .

Second Floor: Clothing

Revelation 18:12 (c)
. . . and all thyine wood, and all manner vessels of ivory, and all manner vessels of most precious wood, and of brass, and iron, and marble.

Third Floor: Home Furnishings

Revelation 18:13 (a)
And cinnamon, and odours, and ointments, and frankincense . . .

Fourth Floor: Cosmetics

Revelation 18:13 (b)
. . . and wine, and oil, and fine flour, and wheat, and beasts, and sheep . . .

Fifth Floor: Food Court

Revelation 18:13 (c)
. . . and horses, and chariots . . .

Sixth Floor: Automotive

Revelation 18:13 (d)
. . . and slaves, and souls of men.

The word "slaves" literally meaning "bodies," this is the basement—the Adult Bookstore.
Please note not one of the aforementioned deals with life's necessities. They're all luxuries. Babylon specializes in materialism gone mad.

Revelation 18:14–17 (a)
And the fruits that thy soul lusted after are departed from thee, and all things which were dainty and goodly are departed from thee, and thou shalt find them no more at all. The merchants of these things, which were made rich by her, shall stand afar off for the fear of her torment, weeping and wailing, and saying, Alas, alas, that great city, that was clothed in fine linen, and purple, and scarlet, and decked with gold, and precious stones, and pearls! For in one hour so great riches is come to nought.

Babylon is the city that drives world economy, so everyone who exported from or imported to her is saying, "Oh no! How will we buy and sell now?"

For topical study of Revelation 18:17 entitled "It's All Going to Burn," turn to page 1768.

Revelation 18:17 (b)–20
And every shipmaster, and all the company in ships, and sailors, and as many as trade by sea, stood afar off, And cried when they saw the smoke of her burning, saying, What city is like unto this great city! And they cast dust on their heads, and cried, weeping and wailing, saying, Alas, alas, that great city, wherein were made rich all that had ships in the sea by reason of her costliness! for in one hour is she made desolate. Rejoice over her, thou heaven, and ye holy apostles and prophets; for God hath avenged you on her.

The peoples' response to the destruction of Babylon is to weep and wail. But heaven's response is to rejoice.

Revelation 18:21–23 (a)
And a mighty angel took up a stone like a great millstone, and cast it into the sea, saying, Thus with violence shall that great city Babylon be thrown down, and shall be found no more at all. And the voice of harpers, and musicians, and of pipers, and trumpeters, shall be heard no more at all in thee; and no craftsman, of whatsoever craft he be, shall be found any more in thee; and the sound of a millstone shall be heard no more at all in thee; and the light of a candle shall shine no more at all in thee . . .

The entire life of the city comes to a complete, abrupt halt in the aftermath of what is most likely a nuclear exchange. To John, the destruction in a single hour of the economic capital of the world would have been unimaginable. To our culture, having seen even the infancy of nuclear warfare demonstrated at Hiroshima and Nagasaki, this is completely possible.

Revelation 18:23 (b)
. . . for thy merchants were the great men of the earth . . .

Who, where, what is this city of Babylon? The first clue is that her merchants were the great, or wealthiest, men on earth.

Our government's historic and continued support and subsidy of the tobacco industry is an example of the "get rich at all costs" mentality that will do anything for a dollar—even if it means hiring Joe Camel to sell cigarettes to our own children.

Revelation 18:23 (c)
. . . for by thy sorceries were all nations deceived.

The word translated "sorceries" being *pharmakeia*, or "drugs," the second clue concerning Babylon's identity is that this city has caught the entire world in her web of drug traffic.

The evidence is conclusive that due to the availability of money and to the demand of a culture that sinks so low as to glorify heroin addiction on its fashion models, the country that drives the drug industry today is unquestionably the United States.

Revelation 18:24
And in her was found the blood of prophets, and of saints, and of all that were slain upon the earth.

The third clue concerning Babylon's identity is that: The blood of the saints is on Babylon's head.

Since 1900, an average of 250,000 born-again believers have been martyred every year. This issue is presently before our own Congress as the Christian community is saying the U.S. must take a stand—particularly as it relates to the nation of China, where the highest percentage of this type of persecution has taken place. But our country refuses to do this, instead granting China Most Favored Nation status in order that her 2.5 billion people can buy our cars and computers.

Am I suggesting the Babylon of Revelation 18 is actually America?
There are those who think so.
Turn to the Book of Isaiah, written by another prophet who foretold the destruction of Babylon (21:9). . . .

Woe to the land shadowing with wings, which is beyond the rivers of Ethiopia.   Isaiah 18:1

"Beyond the rivers of Ethiopia is a term to describe an unknown region—certainly what America would have been to Isaiah. In addition, some suggest the "shadowing with wings" reference is to the eagle, our country's insignia.

That sendeth ambassadors by the sea, even in vessels of bulrushes upon the waters . . .
Isaiah 18:2 (a)

Isaiah's point of reference being the Middle East, her ambassadors could only have reached America by crossing the sea.

. . . saying, Go, ye swift messengers, to a nation scattered and peeled, to a people terrible from their beginning hitherto . . .   Isaiah 18:2 (b)

The original Hebrew meaning of this passage is: "Go ye swift messengers to a nation, wide and polished, to a people awesome from their beginning."

. . . a nation meted out and trodden down . . .
Isaiah 18:2 (c)

Some suggest this is a precise description of our own history in light of our "manifest destiny" to claim our land from coast to coast, from "sea to shining sea," regardless of the indigenous people groups in the way.

. . . whose land the rivers have spoiled!
Isaiah 18:2 (d)

Some suggest this refers to the pollution of our rivers.

In his description of Babylon, the prophet Jeremiah writes of "the mingled people" in the midst of a land "that dwellest upon many waters" (see Jeremiah 50:37; 51:13). Inhabited by a mono-ethnic people and situated on only the Euphrates River, Jeremiah's reference does not describe historic Babylon. America, on the other hand, is a melting pot of people and surrounded by oceans and rivers—not to mention the Great Lakes that alone contain one-quarter of the world's fresh water.

Add to this the fact that Babylon will "mount up to heaven, and fortify the height of her strength" (see Jeremiah 51:53) in a seeming reference to a space program, the case made by those who believe the Babylon of Revelation 18 is actually America—New York City, in particular—is a strong one.

Do I agree with this?

I don't know.

You see, it could very well be that present-day Babylon will become the center of world com-

merce during the Tribulation. Once surrounded by walls wide enough that six chariots could race atop them and containing hanging gardens so magnificent that they were one of the seven wonders of the world, after its destruction in 330 B.C. by Alexander the Great, Babylon was a rather unimportant place for many centuries—until Saddam Hussein came to power. Fifteen years ago, he commissioned a team of brilliant Japanese architects to mastermind the rebuilding of the once-awesome city. Today, the palace of Nebuchadnezzar, the gate of Ishtar, and the royal paveway are complete. The wall is near completion.

Why is Hussein investing hundreds of millions of dollars on this building project? Partly as a nod to the past, an homage to his hero, Nebuchadnezzar—the last king of Babylon able to control Israel; partly as an understanding of the present, as a way to compete for the much-needed tourist dollar; and partly as a hope for the future—the first part of a plan to establish Babylon as the center of the Arab world.

So it could well be that after Rome is devoured in the Tribulation (Revelation 17:14), Antichrist will choose to move his base of operation to Babylon in Iraq. Interestingly, in the first Gulf War, due to its archaeological, historical, and cultural significance, orders were issued by the Gulf War Coalition that under no circumstances was Babylon to be touched. Thus, the possibility certainly exists that Babylon was preserved not only for her archaeological, historical, and cultural significance—but, unknowingly, for her prophetic significance.

Whether the Babylon of Revelation 18 is actually present-day Babylon or present-day America, the fact remains that although a revived Roman Empire, a restored Russia, a Chinese-Asian coalition, and Israel are all clearly seen in the end times—America is strangely absent. While this could be due to the fact that she truly is devastated in the nuclear exchange described in Revelation 18, it could also be due to the fact that the percentage of Christians in our nation—be they strong or weak or vacillating—is so high that America is disabled as a result of the void they leave after the Rapture. You see, if I were to go to Hawaii tomorrow, my whole body would go—even if my arm was broken, my back was sore, my knee was bruised. The same is true of the Rapture. The *entire* body of Christ will go—comprised of any who simply believe that Jesus died for their sins and rose again, of all who embrace His gift of salvation.

While we will have to wait for a definitive answer to the question of Babylon's identity in the last days, however, our brother James has a particular word for us this day. . . .

Go to now, ye rich men, weep and howl for your miseries that shall come upon you. Your riches are corrupted, and your garments are motheaten. Your gold and silver is cankered; and the rust of them shall be a witness against you, and shall eat your flesh as it were fire. Ye have heaped treasure together for the last days.
James 5:1–3

In other words, our garages full of stuff we can't get rid of because we're sure that someday we'll actually use that electric toothbrush and our closets full of clothes we can't give away because we're also sure that someday we'll lose those twenty pounds and wear them again, witness against us.

Behold, the hire of the labourers who have reaped down your fields, which is of you kept back by fraud, crieth: and the cries of them which have reaped are entered into the ears of the Lord of sabaoth.   James 5:4

The cries from the people you've cheated by cutting corners, from the employees you're tricked, from the system you've "beat" all enter the ears of the Lord.

Ye have lived in pleasure on the earth, and been wanton; ye have nourished your hearts, as in a day of slaughter. Ye have condemned and killed the just; and he doth not resist you.
James 5:5, 6

In taking care of your own business and pleasure, you've forgotten everyone else.

Be patient therefore, brethren, unto the coming of the Lord. Behold, the husbandman waiteth for the precious fruit of the earth, and hath long patience for it, until he receive the early and latter rain. Be ye also patient; establish your hearts: for the coming of the Lord draweth nigh. Grudge not one against another, brethren, lest ye be condemned: behold, the judge standeth before the door.   James 5:7–9

Don't cheat one another. Instead, be as generous as you can, realizing the nearness of the Lord's return.

Truly, James is "another voice from heaven, saying, Come out from Babylon, my people, that ye be not partakers of her sins, and that ye receive not of her plagues" (see Revelation 18:4).

It's a convicting word for me—one I need to hear, one I need to heed.

IT'S ALL GOING TO BURN
A Topical Study of
Revelation 18:17

I am about to give you, free of charge, the best investment advice you will ever receive.

Look with me at Luke 12. . . .

And one of the company said unto him, Master, speak to my brother, that he divide the inheritance with me.   Luke 12:13

Jewish tradition contained a brilliant way of dividing an inheritance. If there were two brothers, it was the responsibility of the eldest to divide the inheritance in two, and the privilege of the youngest to have first choice. This way everything was fair.

In this case, however, something went wrong, and the inheritance was not correctly divided.

And he said unto him, Man, who made me a judge or a divider over you?
Luke 12:14

"That's not what I'm about," answered Jesus, knowing that the real problem wasn't financial, technical, or legal. It was spiritual. The issue was not a matter of money. The issue was a matter of the heart because both brothers were covetous.

"I have heard confessions of every sin imaginable," wrote Francis of Assisi, "but I have never heard a man confess the sin of covetousness."

Scripture, however, records such a confession by one who was otherwise "blameless concerning the law." In Romans 7, the apostle Paul says the sin that damned him was covetousness.

What is covetousness?

Wanting more of that of which you already have enough.

Whether with regard to power or pleasure, clothes or cars, houses or hobbies, covetousness is any attitude that says, "Just a little more, and I'll be happy." Knowing this, Jesus said,

Take heed, and beware of covetousness: for a man's life consisteth not in the abundance of the things which he possesseth.
Luke 12:15

It has been rightly said that small men seek to get a little more, while great men seek to be a little more.

"I can't promise you a yacht or a big house or a Rolex or a Rolls Royce as Johnny Green could," said the young man to his girlfriend. "But I can promise you all my love."

"I love you too," answered his girlfriend, "but tell me more about Johnny Green. . . ."

Life is not about possessions; so Jesus continued on with a parable to drive this point home. . . .

The ground of a certain rich man brought forth plentifully: and he thought within himself, saying, What shall I do, because I have no room where to bestow my fruits? And he said, This will I do: I will pull down my barns, and build greater; and there will I bestow all my fruits and my goods. And I will say to my soul, Soul, thou hast much goods laid up for many years; take thine ease, eat, drink, and be merry. But God said unto him, Thou fool, this night thy soul shall be required of thee: then whose shall those things be, which thou hast provided? So is he that layeth up treasure for himself, and is not rich toward God.
Luke 12:16–21

A story was told of Dietrich Reinhold, a man known throughout his community to be very wealthy. One night he went to sleep in his huge mansion, only to wake up a couple hours later in a cold sweat, frightened by a dream in which an angel appeared to him, saying, "At midnight, the richest man in the valley shall die."

That's me, thought Reinhold, and he sent a servant to quickly fetch the doctor.

The doctor came hastily, listened to Dietrich's story, and sat with him until the clock struck twelve. When the last bell sounded, just as Dietrich was breathing a huge sigh of relief, he heard a pounding on his door. He opened it to find one of his servants.

"Master! Master Reinhold! Hans has just died!"

And suddenly Dietrich Reinhold understood that Hans, the servant who was known throughout the region as one who loved the Lord, was the richest man in the village.

Dear friend, in one hour—and the hour could be very soon—your entire empire, however big or small it might be, could burn. That is why Jesus said we are fools if we're rich on earth but paupers in heaven.

One hundred years ago, a sailor shipwrecked in the South Seas found himself washed to the shore of a small island. The natives took one look at his white skin and made him their god. "This is my lucky day!" thought the sailor. But after six months of being treated like a king and learning the customs of the people, he was shocked to discover that each god served for one year, only to be sacrificed at the end of the year to the next god.

So seeing a bigger picture than living the life of luxury for the next six months, what did this guy do? He set his subjects to work on building a boat. When it was completed five and a half months later, he got on it and sailed away.

What would happen if we said, "Since Babylon is all going to burn, why don't I do something radical and spend the six months I have left to prepare for eternity? I'll use whatever I have on this earth for God's glory by giving it away or sharing it with others"? If that were truly our mind-set, we'd gladly lend our little brother our new CD player or our friend our new car. You see, the problem doesn't lie with material possessions. The problem only arises when we grasp them too tightly or when they keep us from fellowshiping with our Lord or loving our neighbor.

This is a hard message to give to young people because they think they can wait to get radical until they're older. But if you're in your fifties, like me, or older, you know that wrinkles and gray hair are constant reminders that life is short.

But all too often what do we do? We buy hair dye and cactus root extract from Arizona that promises to give us an extra ten minutes of life.

And he said unto his disciples, Therefore I say unto you, Take no thought for your life, what ye shall eat; neither for the body, what ye shall put on. The life is more than meat, and the body is more than raiment.   Luke 12:22, 23

Don't make styles or health food your focus to the point that when people see you coming, they know you're going to try to get them caught up in the latest fad.

Consider the ravens: for they neither sow nor reap; which neither have store-house nor barn; and God feedeth them: how much more are ye better than the fowls? And which of you with taking thought can add to his stature one cubit? If ye then be not able to do that thing which is least, why take ye thought for the rest? Consider the lilies how they grow: they toil not, they spin not; and yet I say unto you, that Solomon in all his glory was not arrayed like one of these. If then God so clothe the grass, which is to day in the field, and to morrow is cast into the oven; how much more will he clothe you, O ye of little faith? And seek not ye what ye shall eat, or what ye shall drink, neither be ye of doubtful mind. For all these things do the nations of the world seek after: and your Father knoweth that ye have need of these things. But rather seek ye the kingdom of God; and all these things shall be added unto you.

Luke 12:24–31

"Consider the ravens. . . ." This passage doesn't mean you don't have to do any-thing because God will take care of you. Even the birds know better than that. No, they do what they can to provide for themselves, but they don't develop ulcers in the process.

Fear not, little flock; for it is your Father's good pleasure to give you the kingdom.   *Luke 12:32*

What is the kingdom? Paul defines it not as meat or drink, but as righteous-ness, peace, and joy (Romans 14:17). Righteousness, peace, and joy—these are what God promises us if we seek first the kingdom.

Sell that ye have, and give alms; provide yourselves bags which wax not old, a treasure in the heavens that faileth not, where no thief approacheth, neither moth corrupteth. For where your treasure is, there will your heart be also.

Luke 12:33, 34

How do we disentangle our hearts from the things of Babylon and focus on the things of heaven? By putting our treasure there, by giving stuff away, by helping people out, by doing whatever we can to be as generous as we can possibly be. We set our hearts on heaven not by building bigger barns, but by becoming bigger peo-ple in light of eternity.

As opposed to the current health and wealth teaching that propounds that godliness with great gain makes for contentment, Paul wrote to Timothy,

But godliness with contentment is great gain. For we brought nothing into this world, and it is certain we can carry nothing out. And having food and raiment let us be therewith content. But they that will be rich fall into temptation and a snare, and into many foolish and hurtful lusts, which drown men in destruction and perdition.   1 Timothy 6:6–9

A Confederate spy during the Civil War, Rose O'Neal Greenhow received two thousand dollars in gold as payment for her memoirs and boarded a ship home with the gold sewn into the hem of her dress and petticoats. Sailing on the blockade-runner Condor, she reached the mouth of the Cape Fear River just outside Wilmington, North Carolina, when a Union ship gave chase, forcing the Condor aground. Rose, fearing capture and reimprisonment, persuaded the captain to send her and two companions ashore in a lifeboat; but in stormy seas, the small vessel overturned. The ship sank, and so did Rosie.[1]

Paul's right—gold can drown men. So what's the solution?

The one Paul gave to Timothy. . . .

Charge them that are rich in this world . . .   1 Timothy 6:17 (a)

I believe this verse applies to every single one of us in some respect. Why? Because having a roof over our heads, food on the table, and even a single car in our garage makes us rich, indeed, compared to the rest of the world.

. . . that they be not high-minded, nor trust in uncertain riches, but in the living God, who giveth us richly all things to enjoy.   1 Timothy 6:17 (b)

Don't trust in your money; don't live for it, but rather trust God who gives us all things to enjoy and live for Him.

That they do good, that they be rich in good works, ready to distribute, willing to communicate.   1 Timothy 6:18

The word translated "communicate" literally means "be sociable." In other words, open up your home, heart, and possessions. Give them away; let them go; be as generous as you can possibly be with everyone the Lord sends your way on any given day. The key to enjoying that which God has given us is employing it for His glory.

I join Paul in promising you that when you get to heaven, whatever you did on earth in response to God guiding you to—support a ministry, give to a homeless person on the street, or share a meal with someone in need—will not cause you to say, "Phooey. I could have built a bigger barn. Why did I give so much away?"

You'll never say that!

Laying up in store for themselves a good foundation against the time to come, that they may lay hold on eternal life.   1 Timothy 6:19

Gang, even if the Rapture doesn't happen in our lifetime (which I am convinced it will), the riches you have generously dispensed on earth in obedience to the Spirit will make you rich in heaven because you've been obedient to the Spirit of God.

Lay up for yourselves a good foundation.

How?

By letting go; by sharing with people; and by obeying the Lord.

Let us be glad and rejoice, and give honour to him: for the marriage of the Lamb is come, and his wife hath made herself ready.   Revelation 19:7

19 Here's the question: Would you rather *have* dinner or *be* dinner—for that, ultimately, is the issue raised here in chapter 19 in the account of the Marriage Supper of the Lamb in heaven, and the feast of the fowls at Armageddon. One is glorious and beautiful, the other bloody and brutal. Reservations are now being taken. You will be at one or the other. I highly recommend the first. . . .

Revelation 19:1 (a)
And after these things . . .

Chapter 19 takes place after the destruction of Babylon—the political and commercial epicenter of the world.

Revelation 19:1 (b)
. . . I heard a great voice of much people in heaven, saying, Alleluia; Salvation . . .

The world says there's an alternative to salvation. They call it optimism. "There's a great big beautiful tomorrow," they sing. "Inch by inch, anything's a cinch," they say. "If it's to be, it's up to me," they declare—not realizing that nothing short of salvation will truly alter the tribulation that threatens them daily.

Revelation 19:1 (c), 2
. . . and glory, and honour, and power, unto the Lord our God: For true and righteous are his judgments: for he hath judged the great whore, which did corrupt the earth

with her fornication, and hath avenged the blood of his servants at her hand.

The people on earth wail following the destruction of Babylon. But heaven rejoices. Why? Because, although the natural tendency of people is to say, "Wasn't that a bit brutal, Lord? Did You really have to drop hundred-pound hailstones? Wouldn't thirty-pounders have done the job? What are You doing, Lord? Why do You allow such difficulty, tragedy, pain?" chapter 19 shows us there is no such questioning in heaven. It's not because there's a "No Questioning Allowed" sign in heaven—but because in heaven, the full picture becomes clear. And that which seemed to be so terrible, painful, and unnecessary on earth will seem brilliant, perfect, and righteous from the vantage of heaven.

The same is true regarding trials in our lives presently. Why doesn't the Lord just show us the whole story now? Because He is teaching you and me to walk by faith and not by sight. Why? Because He knows that developing faith in you and me is absolutely necessary in light of what we will be doing throughout eternity.

Revelation 19:3, 4
And again they said, Alleluia. And her smoke rose up for ever and ever. And the four and twenty elders and the four beasts fell down and worshipped God that sat on the throne, saying, Amen; Alleluia.

"Amen" means "so be it." "Alleluia" means "praise the Lord." Interestingly, "Amen" and

"Alleluia" are the only universally known words. That is, they are understood in every language, by every culture. The elders—or mature ones—are those who say, "So be it. Praise the Lord."

Revelation 19:5, 6
And a voice came out of the throne, saying, Praise our God, all ye his servants, and ye that fear him, both small and great. And I heard as it were the voice of a great multitude, and as the voice of many waters, and as the voice of mighty thunderings, saying, Alleluia: for the Lord God omnipotent reigneth.

Handel's inspired and glorious Hallelujah Chorus draws from this text.

Revelation 19:7
Let us be glad and rejoice, and give honour to him: for the marriage of the Lamb is come, and his wife hath made herself ready.

It's not a list of things to do that prepares us for the Marriage Feast. It's an embracing of what the Lamb has done.

For topical study of Revelation 19:7 entitled "The Wedding Feast," turn to page 1777.

Revelation 19:8
And to her was granted that she should be arrayed in fine linen, clean and white: for the fine linen is the righteousness of saints.

In the Book of Isaiah, we see what "the righteousness of saints" is. . . .

I will greatly rejoice in the LORD, my soul shall be joyful in my God; for he hath clothed me with the garments of salvation, he hath covered me with the robe of righteousness, as a bridegroom decketh himself with ornaments, and as a bride adorneth herself with her jewels.   Isaiah 61:10

It's not *my* righteousness that saves me, for Isaiah goes on to say that my righteousness is as filthy rags (64:6). No, it's the robe of righteousness the Lord places around me that affords me entrance to the Marriage Feast of the Lamb.

Revelation 19:9, 10 (a)
And he saith unto me, Write, Blessed are they which are called unto the marriage supper of the Lamb. And he saith unto me,

These are the true sayings of God. And I fell at his feet to worship him.

At this point, John is so blown away by seeing the bride, that he falls at the feet of the angelic messenger.

Revelation 19:10 (b)
And he said unto me, See thou do it not: I am thy fellowservant, and of thy brethren that have the testimony of Jesus: worship God: for the testimony of Jesus is the spirit of prophecy.

"Don't worship me. I'm just a fellow servant," the angel declares. Throughout the Gospels we see people worshiping Jesus. . . .

Peter fell down and worshiped Him, saying, "Depart from me. I'm a sinful man" (see Luke 5:8).
    Thomas said, "My Lord and my God" (John 20:28).

Yet Jesus never says, "Don't worship Me. I'm just an angel." Therefore, the contention of the Mormon or Jehovah's Witness that Jesus is nothing more than an angel is completely erroneous. Jesus receives worship because He is more than an angel. He is God Incarnate.

Revelation 19:11 (a)
And I saw heaven opened . . .

It is only in the Book of Revelation that we see the door of heaven open. In chapter 4, verse 1, the door is opened for the entrance of the raptured church. Here in chapter 19, the door is opened for the exit of the church seven years later when she returns to earth with Jesus at His Second Coming.

Revelation 19:11 (b), 12 (a)
. . . and behold a white horse; and he that sat upon him was called Faithful and True, and in righteousness he doth judge and make war. His eyes were as a flame of fire . . .

Based on 1 Corinthians 3:12, 13, I used to think there would be a great big oven in heaven, a kiln of some sort into which all my works would be shoveled. The wood, hay, and stubble would burn while the gold, silver, and precious stones would remain. But in light of our text, I no longer expect an oven. Instead, I expect Jesus will just look at me, and everything in my life that is worthless will ignite and disappear. I've got cords of wood, bales of hay, truckloads of stubble—and I'm so thankful that with one look from my Lord, they will all go up in smoke.

"Take your only son to Mount Moriah," God commanded Abraham (see Genesis 22:2). God didn't even acknowledge Ishmael as Abraham's son because, while Isaac was the product of God's faithfulness, Ishmael was a product of Abraham's flesh. I love this because most of us have a bunch of Ishmaels running around—things we've done in our flesh, trying to help God. But God doesn't even acknowledge them. Glorious, indeed, will be the day when He'll look at me with His eyes of fire, warming my heart and melting the junk.

Revelation 19:12 (b)
... and on his head were many crowns ...

Perhaps the "many crowns" in this passage signify all of the denominations within the church who crown Jesus Lord. After all, the leaders of some churches wear big hats and sprinkle water on people. The leaders of other churches wear fancy suits and slicked-back hair. The leaders of other churches wear baseball hats and Birkenstocks. But guess what. God has His people in the congregations of every one of them as He breaks through the barriers that divide them and makes Himself known.

Revelation 19:12 (c)
... and he had a name written, that no man knew, but he himself.

Name speaks of nature. Thus, this verse suggests that, due to the fact that there's a part of Him that is not understood by any but Himself, we will be amazed when we see Jesus because none of us knows Him presently the way we will know Him eventually. The neat thing is that we will spend eternity exploring the nuances of His nature, astounded by His beauty, awed by His holiness, amazed at His love that we only see "through a glass darkly" this side of heaven (1 Corinthians 13:12).

Revelation 19:13
And he was clothed with a vesture dipped in blood: and his name is called The Word of God.

It's His blood that cleanses me from my impurity and washes me from my stupidity. I am pure not because of my efforts, but because Jesus died for me.

Revelation 19:14
And the armies which were in heaven followed him upon white horses, clothed in fine linen, white and clean.

The door in heaven is open and, clothed in white linen, here we come with the Lord—not to fight, but rather to observe Him secure the victory.

Revelation 19:15
And out of his mouth goeth a sharp sword, that with it he should smite the nations: and he shall rule them with a rod of iron: and he treadeth the winepress of the fierceness and wrath of Almighty God.

I've seen artists render this scene with a literal sword protruding from the mouth of the Lord. I don't believe such is the proper view. I believe the "sharp sword" that comes forth from His mouth is simply the Word He speaks—sharper than any two-edged sword (Hebrews 4:12).

Revelation 19:16–18
And he hath on his vesture and on his thigh a name written, KING OF KINGS, AND LORD OF LORDS. And I saw an angel standing in the sun; and he cried with a loud voice, saying to all the fowls that fly in the midst of heaven, Come and gather yourselves together unto the supper of the great God; that ye may eat the flesh of kings, and the flesh of captains, and the flesh of mighty men, and the flesh of horses, and of them that sit on them, and the flesh of all men, both free and bond, both small and great.

Here is Dinner Number Two. If you don't want to take part of the Marriage Feast of the Lamb, you'll be part of this horrendous "supper of the great God."

Revelation 19:19
And I saw the beast, and the kings of the earth, and their armies, gathered together to make war against him that sat on the horse, and against his army.

The armies of the world gather in the plain of Jezreel, the valley in northern Israel called the Valley of Megiddo—the place we know as Armageddon. Two hundred million men have come from the East; Antichrist is storming into Jerusalem to secure his power base. According to Daniel 11, the South, which would include the Pan African nations and the Arab states banded together, also head toward Israel, to which the Northern armies come from Europe. They all converge to fight one another. But as the battle begins, everyone looks up and sees One whose eyes are like fire, crowned with many crowns, riding a white horse, leading an innumerable army. And suddenly, all of the weapons of all earth's armies are turned upon this One—which was Satan's intention all along.

Revelation 19:20, 21

And the beast was taken, and with him the false prophet that wrought miracles before him, with which he deceived them that had received the mark of the beast, and them that worshipped his image. These both were cast alive into a lake of fire burning with brimstone. And the remnant were slain with the sword of him that sat upon the horse, which sword proceeded out of his mouth: and all the fowls were filled with their flesh.

Reading this chapter, I realized if it were up to me, I would have spent more time on Jesus' Second Coming. I mean, we have been building up to this moment for a long time. Chapters 6, 7, 8, 9, 10, 11, 12, 13, 14, 15, 16, 17, and 18 all were about tribulation. You've read through studies on seven seals followed by seven trumpets followed by seven vials. You've studied plagues, pests, and problems; suffering, scorching, and sorrow; heartache, earthquakes, and death. And finally we come to the culmination of the Tribulation— the glorious Second Coming—only to have it wrapped up in one short chapter. If I were writing this, I would have reversed it. I would have described the Tribulation in one chapter, and the second coming in thirteen.

Why didn't John do this?

Because, although the Book of Revelation does, indeed, deal with the mark of the Beast, the Common Market, and everything else that relates to current events—we must never forget it was written by a real-life pastor named John who ministered to the people of seven real churches who were being fed to lions, dipped in hot wax, sawn in half lengthwise, and crucified upside down. By conservative estimates, six million would die before the persecution ended. In light of this, through seal after trumpet after vial, Pastor John assures his congregation that life is brutal, painful, and bloody. Why? Because when Adam and Eve fell, the whole world fell with them.

For we know that the whole creation groaneth and travaileth in pain together until now.
Romans 8:22

We look at the mountains in awe and are enraptured by the beauty of a wooded stream. Nature, on the other hand, groans, knowing what it was before the Fall. That is why when the King comes back the mountains will break forth into song, and the trees of the field shall clap their hands (Isaiah 55:12).

It used to be that man would walk with God in the cool of the day, talking to Him without having to break through, press in, or hold on. Everything was right. Then came the Fall, and nothing was ever right again. There is a solution, however. It's called salvation. And nowhere is salvation more clearly framed than at the table of Communion.

I believe Pastor John was warning his people that even in the midst of their own tribulation, if they ate of the marriage feast as seen in the first half of chapter 19, they would be able to navigate the Armageddon of the second half. David said the same thing when he said, "Thou preparest a table before me in the presence of mine enemies" (Psalm 23:5).

So, too, even though you may be surrounded by disappointments, pain, and the presence of enemies—there's a table set before you that will restore your soul and allow you to face tribulation without being shot down or wiped out. Many Christians are unable to navigate tribulation well because, although they have knowledge of the Word, they lack the intimacy with the Lord that takes place at the Communion table.

While the techniques of teaching and ways of worship have changed, one thing has remained constant for all believers throughout church history: communion. Century after century, the church has understood that the Eucharist is vital for survival. Presently, however, we come dangerously close to substituting Bible study for the Lord's table.

The solution to catastrophe is not optimism. It's salvation. And the way to salvation is not through intellectual understanding. The way to salvation is through spiritual intimacy, illustrated most clearly when we eat and drink of Jesus—the most intimate kind of worship possible.

Whether you partake of the Lord's table with your family at home or at the church, don't ignore Communion, dear saint. Being one with Jesus is that which will see you through any Armageddon that lies right around the bend.

In due season, our Lord will, indeed, come again, and there will be no more battle whatsoever. In the meantime, He prepares a table before us in the presence of our enemies. Surely goodness and mercy shall follow us all the days of our lives, and we will dwell in the house of the Lord *forever*.

THE WEDDING FEAST
A Topical Study of
Revelation 19:7

This being June, we find ourselves well into another wedding season. But no wedding can hold a candle to the wedding in the passage before us. Following the description of the Tribulation in Revelation chapters 6—19, we come to the Marriage Supper of the Lamb.

"Wait a minute," you say, "if the Book of Revelation does, indeed, flow in chronological order, since the church is raptured in chapter 4 to begin her seven-year honeymoon with the Lord, why does the marriage feast not take place until chapter 19?"

The answer lies in an understanding of the Jewish marriage tradition, which comprised three stages. . . .

The Engagement

Historically, Jewish children would often be engaged by the age of two or three—sometimes before they were even born. That is, families that shared the same values and social standing would say, "If you have a daughter and I have a son, let's agree right now that they will marry each other." You see, the Jewish people looked at marriage as far too important to be left up to the decision-making skills of young adults. So it was up to the father specifically to arrange with other fathers to whom his son or daughter would be engaged.

Scripture does record a few cases when men chose their own brides. But each of these marriages ended in heartache or disaster. . . .

> Against his father's wishes, Esau married an Ishmaelite (Genesis 28:8, 9).
> Jacob fell in love with Rachel at first sight, but ended up working for her for seven years before unknowingly marrying her sister (Genesis 29).
> Samson "loved a woman in the valley of Sorek, whose name was Delilah" (Judges 16:4).

Since the result of a man choosing his own wife without the directive of his father often resulted in tragedy or difficulty, it became the norm for the father to select his child's spouse.

Betrothal

The engagement led to the betrothal—usually between the ages of twelve and fifteen for a young lady. At this point, bride and groom would perhaps meet for the first time, as the father of the groom would negotiate the bride price. The price would be based upon three variables.

First, it would be predicated upon the father's wealth. If the father of the groom was a rich man, he would pay a high price so as not to look like a cheapskate.

Second, the price would be determined by the bride's worth. If she was attractive or otherwise gifted, her bride price would be higher.

Thirdly, the price was based upon the groom's work. That is, in some cases it was up to the groom to pay the price. . . .

Because Jacob chose his own bride, he paid for her himself with seven years' labor (Genesis 29:18).

"He who marries my daughter must conquer the enemy city of Kirjath-sepher," declared Caleb. Othniel took the challenge and won (see Joshua 15:16, 17).

A Gentile named Shechem who fell in love with Jacob's daughter, Dinah, was informed her price would be the circumcision of himself and all of the men in his city as a sign of identification with the Jews (Genesis 34:15, 16).

A portion of the bride price would go to the bride to use as security in the event she was widowed or divorced. This explains why Rachel and Leah accused their uncle, Laban, of "devouring their money" (see Genesis 31:15).

The remainder of the bride price went to the bride's father in compensation for the fact that, unlike a son, his daughter wouldn't be able to carry on his name, help defend him, or take over the family business.

After at least a portion of the bride price was laid upon the table, a contract would be signed to further validate the agreement. Then, the prospective bride and groom would sip from a single cup of wine, at which point they were legally betrothed.

For the following year, the couple would not drink of the vine nor live together. The bride would begin to wear a veil, signifying that she was "taken." She would also begin to prepare her wedding dress, sometimes from material provided by the groom (Ezekiel 16:10).

Meanwhile, the groom would begin construction on what is called in Hebrew "a little mansion"—a room built onto his father's house. When the father decided the preparations were complete, his son, wearing a crown, would be sent off to his wedding (Song of Solomon 3:11).

Wedding

Although the bride didn't know the exact day of her wedding, she knew it would most likely be in autumn to allow for the completion of harvest, and that it would most likely be on a Wednesday. Wednesday was the day couples got married because Thursday was the day the courts were opened. If it was discovered on her wedding day that the bride was not a virgin, she could easily be divorced the next day.

As the preparation of her "little mansion" neared completion, the bride would begin to gather her friends to await the arrival of her groom.

On the day of his wedding, the groom and his friends—particularly his best man—would walk through the streets with trumpets blaring, taking the most circuitous route to the bride's house. Already attired in her wedding dress, when the bride heard the sounding of the trumpet, she would arise and receive a blessing from her father. Then she would run out the door to be met by the groom in the streets.

Together, they would make their way to the four-postered canopy under which they would be married. The ceremony itself consisted not of vows, which were Roman and Greek in tradition, but simply a reading of the contract that had been drawn up a year before, along with a blessing.

The procession would then continue on to the "little mansion," where the best man would stand outside the door while the marriage was consummated. Why would he stand outside the door? To wait for word from the groom that the bride was a virgin—as evidenced by a blood-spotted bed-sheet. If the bride were, indeed, a virgin, the wedding celebration would continue for seven days. If not, the guests would go home, and the bride would face either divorce or death by stoning.

Although seven days spent in an addition to one's father's house while friends and family partied just outside the door may not sound like the ideal honeymoon to us, but in the Jewish culture, being waited on for a week was glorious. You see, this would be the only time in their entire lives when the bride and groom would do no labor. Remember, there were no vacations in those days—no holiday cruises, no jets, no Maui. The one and only time people were able to kick back was during their marriage week. During this week, the bride would never be seen. The groom, on the other hand, would occasionally come out and greet the guests before bringing back food and gifts to his bride.

After seven days, the groom would present his bride to his family, friends, and community—at which time the marriage feast would begin.

Looking again at this process, it becomes a picture-perfect analogy of our Bridegroom's relationship with us. . . .

Just as the Jewish father chose whom his child would marry, it's mind-boggling to realize that our heavenly Father elected us to be the bride for His Son (1 Peter 1:2). As proof of this intent, He paid the bride price, based first upon His wealth. How rich is God? Neither all the gold in the world nor all of the galaxies in the universe would begin to reflect His wealth. Instead, the "bride price" God paid for us was something of which He had only one: His Son (John 3:16).

Second, the price had to be according to the bride's worth.

The story is told of an Arabian man who had one daughter so plain he doubted anyone would ever want to marry her. One day, however, he received word that a man from a distant village was so taken with her that he was coming to see him with bride price in hand. Prepared to take whatever he was offered, imagine the father's surprise when the visitor offered him six cows for his daughter's hand.

Six cows! thought the father in amazement. "The highest price ever paid in this village has been three cows!"

So it was that the father gave his daughter's hand in marriage.

Two years later, the daughter and her husband returned to her home village, where everyone was startled by her exquisite beauty.

"How is she so beautiful?" they wondered.

The answer was simple: Because her husband saw her as worth six cows, a six-cow beauty is what she became.

That's how God views me. I don't understand it, but I rejoice in the fact that God looks at me and says, "I am in love with you so passionately that I'll give everything to bring you into the kingdom in order that you might live with Me forever and ever throughout eternity." To this end, God gave not six cows or even six galaxies—He gave Himself.

Third, the bride price was determined by the groom's work. Jesus outdid Jacob five-fold when He labored on earth as a Man for thirty-three years. And He not only conquered a city, as did Othniel, but He conquered the whole world when He thrust Himself into the very heart of hell to pay the price for my sin (Ephesians 4:9). Finally, when God became Man to identify with us in the Incarnation, it was an infinitely greater step than Shechem took to identify with the Jews, for Jesus was not only afflicted momentarily, but was slain before the foundation of the world (Revelation 13:8).

The bride price paid, just as a contract was signed and a cup of wine shared by the bride and groom in a Jewish betrothal, we hold in our hands the "contract" of the Word of God, along with Jesus' promise that He would not drink of the cup again until He did so with us in the kingdom (Matthew 26:29). And as a bride wore a veil that, although it obscured her vision, signified her relationship with the groom, so at present we see through a glass darkly, but shall one day see our Bridegroom clearly (1 Corinthians 13:12).

Like the Jewish bride whose wedding dress was made from material provided by her groom, we are invited to "put on the Lord Jesus Christ" (Romans 13:14) and robe ourselves in His righteousness (Isaiah 61:10).

Like the groom who added a "little mansion" to his father's house, Jesus went to His Father's house to prepare a place for us (John 14:2). Then, at the time appointed by the Father, the Son, wearing many crowns (Revelation 19:12), will come for us, His bride (Mark 13:32). Like the Jewish bride, we don't know the day or hour of His return, but like her, we know the season (1 Thessalonians 5:1). We understand the place of Israel, the problems in Jerusalem, the coming together of the

European Union. We understand from Bible prophecy that the Lord's coming is near, even at the very door (Mark 13:29). Thus, like the Jewish bride, we ready ourselves for the day we will hear the trumpet and the shout (1 Thessalonians 4:16), before we are caught up to meet the Lord, not on earth, but in the clouds (1 Thessalonians 4:17).

In the context of a Jewish wedding, John's position as "friend of the bridegroom" (John 3:29) and his message of repentance in preparation for the coming Bridegroom (Matthew 3:3) becomes clear.

"Therein lies the problem," you say. "If the marriage is to be validated on my purity, I deserve only divorce or stoning because I sin miserably; I mess up constantly; I fail continually."

Good News! The validation of our relationship with our Bridegroom doesn't depend on our sinlessness, but on His. It is the vesture dipped in *His* blood (Revelation 19:13) that allows us to be presented to Him without spot or wrinkle (Ephesians 5:27).

You mean we don't have to clean up our act, do this, or accomplish that? No, Jesus said blessed are those who are simply watching for His coming (Revelation 16:15), blessed are those who realize the price has been paid, the work done.

Precious people, that's what true Christianity consists of, marveling at the love of the Father and of the Son for me and for you.

We then are afforded a glorious honeymoon with Him—not for seven days, but for seven years as He serves us, His bride, in heaven (Luke 12:37). At the end of seven years, we come back to earth with Him in the Second Coming (Revelation 19:14) where, at the marriage feast of the Lamb, we are presented as His bride forever and ever.

And that is why we see the marriage feast in Revelation 19 rather than in chapter 4. The analogy is perfect.

Dear friend, if you have said, "Lord, I know I have sinned and failed, but I believe You love me and that You paid the price for me," Rejoice! Be glad! Celebrate! In the Lord's sight, you are a six-cow woman, a beautiful, glorious bride.

20

The Lord has come back. The final, climactic battle of Armageddon is over. The Millennial kingdom has begun. . . .

Revelation 20:1, 2
And I saw an angel come down from heaven, having the key of the bottomless pit and a great chain in his hand. And he laid hold on the dragon, that old serpent, which is the Devil, and Satan, and bound him a thousand years.

Satan is bound not by the Lord, not by a host of angels, not even by Michael the archangel—but by

a single, unnamed angel. We often imagine a huge cosmic struggle going on constantly between God and Satan. Oh, we know God will win ultimately—but for now, we assume it's touch and go.

Not true. Satan is not the evil counterpart of God. God is God. There is none like Him, none who can even begin to challenge Him (Deuteronomy 4:39). Satan, previously known as the archangel Lucifer, has always been a created being. Thus, if there is a counterpart to Satan, it would be an archangel like Michael or Gabriel—but not God.

That is why when we see Satan from a heavenly perspective, we will say, "Is *this* the one who troubled the whole world?" (Isaiah 14:16) Holding a chain in his other hand, it only takes one hand of a single angel to detain Satan.

For topical study of Revelation 20:1, 2 entitled "Binding Satan," turn to page 1785.

Revelation 20:3 (a)
And cast him into the bottomless pit . . .

The bottomless pit, or *abussos* into which Satan is tossed is the place wherein the worst demons are presently incarcerated—a place so horrific that the demons of Matthew 8 begged to be cast into a herd of swine rather than be sent there.

Revelation 20:3 (b)
. . . and shut him up, and set a seal upon him, that he should deceive the nations no more . . .

What did Satan try to do to Jesus? He tried to seal Him in a tomb (Matthew 27:66). But Jesus didn't stay there. Now the tables are turned.

Revelation 20:3 (c)
. . . till the thousand years should be fulfilled . . .

Satan will be in the *abussos* for one thousand years. This explains how the wolf can lie down by the lamb, how the lion and bullock shall graze together, how snakes shall eat only dust—how peace will reign (Isaiah 65:25). It explains how every man will abide under his own vine (Micah 4:4), how no one will have to work for anyone else (Isaiah 65:23)—how prosperity will abound. The Millennium will be a fantastic time of unparalleled peace and total prosperity because Satan will not be on the scene.

Revelation 20:3 (d)
. . . and after that he must be loosed a little season.

Rather than being cast into outer darkness, or *Gehenna*, Satan is held in the *abussos*, the bottomless pit, for one thousand years because God will still have a job for him to do—as we will see in verse 7. . . .

Revelation 20:4 (a)
And I saw thrones, and they sat upon them, and judgment was given unto them . . .

The "sheep" of Matthew 25 are the remaining one-third of the nation of Israel who don't die in the Tribulation, along with those who stand by her during the Tribulation. When Jesus returns at His Second Coming, this remnant of Israel will ask Him, "Where did You get those wounds?"

"In the house of My friends," He will answer, (Zechariah 13:6). And at this moment, Israel will at last acknowledge Him as her Messiah—and all of the remaining house of Israel will be saved (Zechariah 13:9).

These are they whom we, the bride of Christ, will judge (Luke 19:15–19). You see, even though those living in the Millennium won't be influenced by Satan, they still will have their human nature to deal with. So when they think of ripping off a Butterfinger, we will be those who enforce Christ's righteousness. That is, before the guy can even develop the plan to steal the Butterfinger, we'll say, "Don't even think about it." It will be an enforced righteousness that governs the Millennial kingdom and that allows a glorious time of peace on earth.

"I don't like this idea of ruling or of judging," you might be saying. But let me tell you something: Jesus would not have taught us to be seizing opportunities to use our time and treasure wisely here on earth if He thought we wouldn't like the reward for doing so. And Paul would not have told us to run so that we might win the prize (1 Corinthians 9:24) if the prize was not something to be greatly desired.

Revelation 20:4 (b), 5
. . . and I saw the souls of them that were beheaded for the witness of Jesus, and for the word of God, and which had not worshipped the beast, neither his image, neither had received his mark upon their foreheads, or in their hands; and they lived and reigned with Christ a thousand years. But the rest of the dead lived not again until the thousand years were finished. This is the first resurrection.

The first resurrection is not a single point in time. Rather, the first resurrection begins with the Resurrection of Jesus Christ as the firstfruits (1 Corinthians 15:20, 23). It continues on to include those who believe in Jesus but died before the Rapture (1 Thessalonians 4:14), believers who are alive at the time of the Rapture (1 Thessalonians 4:17), those who are martyred in the Tribulation for their refusal to take the mark of the beast (Revelation 20:4), and the Old Testament saints who believed in Yahweh but did not have opportunity to be a part of the church because they died before Jesus came.

Thus, the first resurrection speaks of all those who are included in the grand plan of salvation.

Revelation 20:6 (a)
Blessed and holy is he that hath part in the first resurrection . . .

Gang, even if nothing else in your life goes right, you are so blessed because you are part of the first resurrection. You are going to heaven.

Revelation 20:6 (b)
. . . on such the second death hath no power, but they shall be priests of God and of Christ, and shall reign with him a thousand years.

The first death is physical. The second death is eternal. Yes, we will die physically unless the Lord raptures us first. But the second death is for those who are damned eternally. Glory be to God, over us this second death has no power.

Revelation 20:7, 8 (a)
And when the thousand years are expired, Satan shall be loosed out of his prison, And shall go out to deceive the nations which are in the four quarters of the earth . . .

Who will Satan try to deceive? Those born in the Millennium—those living in enforced righteousness and peace because there's no other choice, those who never had an opportunity to decide whether or not they would follow the Lord. You and I have made such a choice. We have "chosen to be chosen." We have "selected to be elected." Here, those born during the Millennium are also given this choice.

I am blown away by the fact that somehow Satan will be able to persuade a great number of people to rebel against the One who will have done nothing but good for them and who will have given them a perfect environment wherein plenty, prosperity, peace, and perfection prevail. But I am only blown away until I stop to realize how good the Lord has been to me; how He gave His life for me; how He provides for me, walks with me, blesses me—and how often I turn my back on Him, fail to learn of Him, refuse to talk to Him.

And then I understand how Satan will be able to get a number of those living in the Millennium to echo the cry of Jerusalem: "We will not have this Man to reign over us" (Luke 19:14).

Why will the Lord allow this to happen? Because God is love, and love requires a choice.

If my wife, Tammy, agreed to marry me simply because I was the only man on earth or only because I held a gun to her head—our relationship wouldn't be based on love, but on the absence of any other choice.

So, too, God lets Satan loose for a short season in order to give people a choice.

Revelation 20:8 (b)
. . . Gog and Magog, to gather them together to battle: the number of whom is as the sand of the sea.

At this point, Russia already having been destroyed on the hills of Israel (Ezekiel 38—39), I believe the usage of "Gog and Magog" in this passage is similar to our usage of "Waterloo." Because Napoleon was defeated by Wellington in the Battle of Waterloo, the term "Waterloo" has come to signify a decisive battle or turning point. So, too, I believe the reference to Gog and Magog in this passage speaks of a cataclysmic, monumental battle in which Satan attempts a final rebellion.

Revelation 20:9 (a)
And they went up on the breadth of the earth, and compassed the camp of the saints about, and the beloved city . . .

The rebellious group led by Satan encircles the city of Jerusalem in a futile attempt to wrest power from the One who reigns within.

Revelation 20:9, 10 (a)
And they went up on the breadth of the earth, and compassed the camp of the saints about, and the beloved city: and fire came down from God out of heaven, and devoured them. And the devil that deceived them was cast into the lake of fire and brimstone, where the beast and the false prophet are . . .

Satan's purpose in God's plan having been accomplished, he is cast into the lake of fire to join the Beast and the false prophet.

Revelation 20:10 (b)
. . . and shall be tormented day and night for ever and ever.

The cartoons are wrong, and Hollywood is terribly mistaken in portraying hell as a hot place where people play poker and talk to one another amidst flickering flames and an occasional jab by

Satan's pitchfork. You see, in addition to being called a lake of fire, hell is called a place of outer darkness (Matthew 8:12). Consequently, the torment in a place so dark even the flames of the lake of fire don't shed any light is exceeded only by the inner torment people feel throughout eternity as they recall the sermons they heard and the invitations to salvation they ignored.

Jesus said specifically that hell was not created for people, but for the devil and demons (Matthew 25:41). Peter said God is not willing that *any* should perish (2 Peter 3:9). Yet, God, being Light, if man says, "I don't want God," he will be consigned to darkness. God, being health, if man says, "I don't want God," he will be relinquished to a place of pain. God, being a Father, if man says, "I don't want God," he will spend eternity in isolation.

God, on the other hand, says, "I would rather die than live without you." And He did just that when He died on the Cross in order that, forgiven of our sins, we might live with Him forever.

Revelation 20:11, 12 (a)
And I saw a great white throne, and him that sat on it, from whose face the earth and the heaven fled away; and there was found no place for them. And I saw the dead, small and great, stand before God . . .

Will believers stand before God at this White Throne Judgment?

No.

If you're a Christian, this judgment doesn't apply to you, for you were judged when Christ was on another throne—not a white one, but a wooden one; when He wore a crown not of gold, but of thorns as He died to cleanse you from every sin you ever have or ever will commit.

Revelation 20:12 (b), 13
. . . and the books were opened: and another book was opened, which is the book of life: and the dead were judged out of those things which were written in the books, according to their works. And the sea gave up the dead which were in it; and death and hell delivered up the dead which were in them: and they were judged every man according to their works.

If you're a Christian, your name is written in the Book of Life. The names of those who said, "I didn't buy into that Christian stuff they were always trying to cram down my throat," or, "I needed my space," or, "I had to explore various aspects of spirituality," aren't.

"But I lived a pretty good life," they'll protest.

Yet the books wherein are recorded the reasons for everything they ever did will prove otherwise. . . .

"I was an outstanding member of Rotary."
Yes—but the books indicate it was to make some business contacts.
"Oh, but I gave blood."
Perhaps—but the books indicate you were paid twenty-five dollars in return.
"But I saved the whales, marched for peace, built homes for the homeless."
All well and good—but you did so to hear the applause of men.

You see, God made us in such a way that we are spared from remembering the sins we have committed. He let us remember enough sin to make us aware of our need for salvation—but not every motive, every word of gossip, every cutting comment, every angry feeling. When the books are opened, the utter weight of all one's sin will come to light. God sends no one to hell. By the time Volume 167 of one's sins is opened, it's as if he will cry, "Depart from me for I am a sinful man," and will send himself to the lake of fire.

That's why I am so glad I'm saved. The Bible says the "handwriting of ordinances that was against us"—all of our mistakes, sins, and failures—were blotted out by the blood of Jesus Christ (Colossians 2:14). In other words, the pages and pages containing my sin are all illegible because they're covered with the red blood of Jesus.

Revelation 20:14, 15
And death and hell were cast into the lake of fire. This is the second death. And whosoever was not found written in the book of life was cast into the lake of fire.

Maybe you're saying, "What will happen at the end of the world is all very interesting, but the bottom line is that I'm a believer, and I know I'm going to heaven. I'm far more concerned about the problems facing me right now."

So was John. The Book of Revelation was written specifically to a group of people facing far greater problems than you'll ever face. And the message it contains is as vital for us as it was to them: It's not over yet. Satan and death itself will be cast into the lake of fire. They lose. And all who embrace what Jesus did on the Cross when He plunged into hell on their behalf—all whose names are written in the Book of Life—win.

BINDING SATAN
A Topical Study of
Revelation 20:1, 2

Said one third-grader to another:
"Do you *really* think there is a devil?"

"No," answered his friend. "The devil's just like Santa Claus. He's really your dad."

Lots of people think of the devil as an "anti-Santa." Whereas Santa stands for kindness and good cheer, Satan stands for evil—but, like Santa, he's not a real person.

Jesus would disagree, for He identifies Satan as the prince of this world (John 12:31). So would the apostle Paul, calling him the "god of this world" (2 Corinthians 4:4). The terminology employed by both Jesus and Paul indicates that not only is Satan very real, but that he is actually the reason for some of what happens in the world today. You see, when famine, war, earthquake, or ecological disasters erupt, people are prone to say, "Why did God do this?" But the Bible indicates very clearly that they are the acts not of God, but of "the prince of this world." Thus, Satan is very real.

He is, however, not very powerful. In the passage before us, we see a single angel binding him. And since we are to rule over angels, this gives us definite authority over Satan. Maybe there's a hellish quality in your marriage or family, on the job site or in your emotions—a persistent, painful problem over which you think you have no control.

"There's nothing I can do about this," you sigh. "I just have to live with this pull toward pornography, the depression that plagues me night and day, or the problem in my marriage that won't go away until I get to heaven."

Not true! Our text suggests otherwise.

And Simon Peter answered and said, Thou art the Christ, the Son of the living God. And Jesus answered and said unto him, Blessed art thou, Simon Barjona: for flesh and blood hath not revealed it unto thee, but my Father which is in heaven. And I say also unto thee, That thou art Peter; and upon this rock I will build my church; and the gates of hell shall not prevail against it.

Matthew 16:16–18

That the gates of hell "shall not prevail" doesn't mean that the gates of hell will dog us all our days on earth until we eventually outrun them and barely make it to heaven. Folks, when was the last time you were walking down a street and you were attacked by a gate? Gates are inanimate objects. Thus, in Matthew 16, Jesus is not talking about the inability of the gates of hell to track you down, but about their inability to keep you out.

In other words, we can storm territory that seems to be controlled by hell. In Matthew 12, Jesus further illuminates this matter by saying,

> *Or else how can one enter into a strong man's house, and spoil his goods, except he first bind the strong man? and then he will spoil his house.*
>
> Matthew 12:29

Breaking into a house to steal a TV does no good unless you first tie up whoever's inside. So, too, Satan being the "strong man," if you're going to take that which is in his control presently, you'll first have to bind him.

"I'm just not getting the goods," you say. "I go to church; I sing; I pray—but it seems as if I'm getting nowhere." Jesus said unless the strong man is bound, we're unable to get the goods. Has the strong man been bound in your life, in your family, in your emotions?

How is the strong man bound?

The Example of Elisha

In 2 Kings 6, we find the New Testament principle for this Old Testament picture. . . .

Led by their king, Ben-Hadad, Syria did battle with Israel. "Ben-Hadad" meaning "shouter," he is a fitting picture of Satan, the one who shouts accusations at the brethren day and night (Revelation 12:10).

"I'm going to ambush God's people," declared Ben-Hadad, much the same way Satan taunts us. Knowing this, Elisha warned the king of Israel of the ambush, and Ben-Hadad was thwarted in his attempt to destroy Israel.

After this happened two more times, Ben-Hadad was determined to root out the traitor from his ranks. When it was told him that an Israelite prophet named Elisha was the reason for his failed attempts, Ben-Hadad deployed troops to the city of Dothan—either to destroy or employ Elisha. When Gehazi, Elisha's servant, awoke to find the city encompassed by the enemy, he was understandably fearful. Maybe you know the feeling when Satan seemingly does the same to you.

"Don't worry," said Elisha, "for they that are with us are more than they that are with them."

What? Gehazi must have thought. *It's just you and me, Elisha—and you're old. This* isn't *a good situation.*

No doubt knowing the same thing David knew when he wrote, "The Lord encamps his angel around them who fear him" (Psalm 34:7), Elisha prayed that the Lord would open Gehazi's eyes. The Lord did—and Gehazi saw that the Syrians were themselves surrounded with horses and chariots of fire.

Unaware that they were surrounded, the Syrians moved toward Elisha. As they did, Elisha prayed they would be blinded. Then, in their blinded state, they heard Elisha say, "This isn't where you want to be. I will bring you to the man whom you seek." Who were they seeking? Before Elisha blew the whistle on their ambushes, the original intent of the Syrians was victory over Israel. Thus, they were seeking Israel's king.

When the Lord opened the eyes of the blinded Syrian army, they couldn't believe that Elisha had, indeed, led them into Samaria—the city of the king of Israel. Seeing his enemy delivered into his hand, the king of Israel said, "shall I smite them?"

"No," answered Elisha and ordered, instead, that a meal be set before them.

When they had eaten and drunk, the Syrian army was set free—and they never bothered the king of Israel again (2 Kings 6:8–23).

Gang, that's how Satan is bound. Elisha didn't pace the floor, shake his fist, and say, "In the name of Jesus, I bind you, Ben-Hadad."

No, Elisha bound Satan in an entirely different way when he fed rather than fought his enemies.

The Pen of Paul

Paul summed up Elisha's methodology when he wrote—

Therefore if thine enemy hunger, feed him; if he thirst, give him drink: for in so doing thou shalt heap coals of fire on his head.   Romans 12:20

In Bible days, before the advent of matches or propane, if the fire went out in their homes, rather than reigniting it with flint and spark, women would get live coals from their neighbors that they could carry back in earthen pots on their heads in order to rekindle their own fire. Thus, "heaping coals on his head" is a display of generosity and kindness.

Be not overcome of evil, but overcome evil with good.   Romans 12:21

Overcoming evil, binding Satan is not a phrase we say—it's a deed we do.

The Joy of Jesus

Directly preceding His discourse on binding the strong man, Jesus gave opportunity to see the practicality of this premise. . . .

Then was brought unto him one possessed with a devil, blind, and dumb: and he healed him, insomuch that the blind and dumb both spake and saw.

Matthew 12:22

Jesus didn't grill the demonized man about unconfessed sin or lack of faith. He didn't accuse the demonized man of being into ouija boards, crystals, or drugs. He didn't march around the demonized man shouting, "I bind you, Satan." What did Jesus do? He did good to the demonized man. He healed him.

Jesus models aggressive goodness, for that's how Satan is bound.

And we must do the same.

Bring candy to the boss who's stingy. Make dinner for the wife who's cranky. Buy a shirt for the husband who's moody. The Enemy is bound whenever we do good things, kind things, generous things. The Enemy is bound when we stop criticizing, backbiting, and judging. The Enemy is bound when we start praying, giving, blessing.

May each of us have ears to hear what the Spirit would say to us today.

21

It is true that the church is to be a hospital where people who are hurting can come and be healed through the body of the Great Physician, Jesus Christ (Matthew 9:12). It is also true that the church is to be a school where we can study to show ourselves approved unto God (2 Timothy 2:15). It is also true that the church is to be a gymnasium wherein we work out our own salvation (Philippians 2:12) and exercise unto godliness (1 Timothy 4:7). But perhaps most importantly the church is to be a travel agency, booking people on an eternal excursion to heaven.

Revelation 21 and 22 constitute a travel brochure for just such a journey. . . .

Revelation 21:1 (a)
And I saw a new heaven and a new earth . . .

Due to the pollution and destruction of our planet, we understand the need for a new earth. But what is the reason for a new heaven? According to Job 15:15, the heavens are not clean in God's sight. Why? Because Satan's presence has polluted them (Revelation 12:10).

Revelation 21:1 (b)
. . . for the first heaven and the first earth were passed away . . .

Some teachers and commentators declare that rather than passing away, the present heaven and earth will simply be refurbished. Due to Isaiah's

account of this event, however, I don't believe that's the case. . . .

For, behold, I create new heavens and a new earth: and the former shall not be remembered, nor come into mind.   Isaiah 65:17

The word translated "create" is the Hebrew word *bara*—the same word used in Genesis 1:1, which means "to create from nothing." The fact that God creates from nothing continues to be a stumbling block to the evolutionist. . . .

Knowing this first, that there shall come in the last days scoffers, walking after their own lusts, and saying, Where is the promise of his coming? for since the fathers fell asleep, all things continue as they were from the beginning of the creation.   2 Peter 3:3, 4

Because evolution is based on a closed environment, it excludes the possibility of divine intervention. Thus, the evolutionist and scoffer is usually the same person. And the denominations who question biblical prophecy are usually the same ones who question the creation account because they don't understand that just as God was active in the creative process, so He will be in the prophetic context.

For this they willingly are ignorant of, that by the word of God the heavens were of old, and the earth standing out of the water and in the water: Whereby the world that then was, being overflowed with water, perished.

2 Peter 3:5, 6

Peter goes on to say that those who scoff at the biblical accounts of the beginning and the end of time are willingly ignorant of the fact that the first earth was destroyed by water, and the second will be destroyed by fire. We know the first earth was flooded in the days of Noah. But what about the fire that will destroy the second earth? Peter continues. . . .

But the heavens and the earth, which are now, by the same word are kept in store, reserved unto fire against the day of judgment and perdition of ungodly men.   2 Peter 3:7

The word translated "reserved" means "stored." That is, fire—or energy—is stored in the world.

But the day of the Lord will come as a thief in the night; in the which the heavens shall pass away with a great noise, and the elements shall melt with fervent heat, the earth also and the works that are therein shall be burned up. Seeing then that all these things shall be dissolved . . .   2 Peter 3:10, 11 (a)

Albert Einstein, Robert Oppenheimer, and others ushered us into the atomic age. Therefore, unlike previous generations, we understand what happens when an atom is split. Consequently, when Jesus lets go His hold of the atom, it should be no surprise to us that the explosion caused will be followed by a "fervent heat" so great that everything will dissolve. Following this mass atomic destruction, God will create from nothing (*bara*) yet another heaven and another earth— which is how Isaiah could write,

For, behold, I create new heavens and a new earth: and the former shall not be remembered, nor come into mind.   Isaiah 65:17

—and why Paul would write of the third heaven (2 Corinthians 12:2). You see, while it has often been suggested that the first heaven is the atmosphere where birds fly, the second is where the stars shine, and the third is where God's presence is—I believe the term "third heaven" refers to the new heaven God will create after the second one is dissolved.

Revelation 21:1 (c)
. . . and there was no more sea.

This speaks of a new creation. . . .

For topical study of Revelation 21:1 entitled "What?! No Beach?" turn to page 1793.

Revelation 21:2
And I John saw the holy city, new Jerusalem, coming down from God out of heaven, prepared as a bride adorned for her husband.

Here is the new capitol of the new creation.

Revelation 21:3
And I heard a great voice out of heaven saying, Behold, the tabernacle of God is with men, and he will dwell with them, and they shall be his people, and God himself shall be with them, and be their God.

This speaks of a new communion. Presently, as we partake of the bread and drink of the cup at the Lord's table, we long to have close communion with Him. But Paul was right when he said we only see through a glass darkly (1 Corinthians 13:12). In the New Jerusalem, however, we'll at last see the visible glory of God. It won't be fuzzy any longer. My vision of the Lord won't be different from yours, for we'll all be in His presence.

Revelation 21:4
And God shall wipe away all tears from their eyes; and there shall be no more death, neither sorrow, nor crying, neither shall there be any more pain . . .

"Being with the Lord in a new heaven and new earth sounds wonderful," you might say. "But if my daughter or dad or husband or son isn't there, won't I weep eternally?" No, because when God creates the new heaven and earth, "the former shall not be remembered, nor come into mind" (Isaiah 65:17). That is, when we get to heaven we will not have memory of those who aren't there.

Revelation 21:4 (b), 5 (a)
. . . for the former things are passed away. And he that sat upon the throne said, Behold, I make all things new.

There may be believers about whom you presently say, "I don't want to spend eternity with *her*," or "I don't want to see *him* in the mansion next door to mine forever and ever"—but when we get to heaven we will find ourselves blown away by the very people who bugged us. The former things are passed away. There will be a glorious transformation of every believer, for when we see Jesus we shall *all* be like Him (1 John 3:2). The things that irritate you now about your spouse or neighbor will be eradicated in heaven. That is why Paul said, "I know no man after the flesh" (see 2 Corinthians 5:16). The flesh will be absent from heaven.

Revelation 21:5 (b)
And he said unto me, Write: for these words are true and faithful.

Why would John be told to write that these things are true and faithful? Because what he's writing sounds too good to be true!

Revelation 21:6
And he said unto me, It is done.

"It is done," is the statement of a carpenter who has completed his work. Two thousand years ago, our Master Carpenter said, "I go to prepare a place for you." Here in verse 6, He doesn't say, "The place I prepared is a fixer-upper," or, "It's a good starter home," or, "It's got charm." He says, "It is *done.*"

How many of us have bought our dream house only to say a little while later, "If we knock out a wall there, add another bathroom here, take out this counter, and reshape the patio, this place will be a lot better"? Such will not be the case in heaven. Not one person will say, "This is great—but it could use a skylight or two. . . ." No, we'll say, "This was designed perfectly for me. It's *exactly* what I've been craving but could never articulate. It's *done.*"

Revelation 21:6
I am Alpha and Omega, the beginning and the end. I will give unto him that is athirst of the fountain of the water of life freely.

There are three elements essential to any community. Here we see the first: resources. The water in the city of the new Jerusalem flows freely.

Revelation 21:7 (a)
He that overcometh shall inherit all things . . .

Second, we see responsibility. The inheritance here is that of a father who's sharing the family business with his son. Thus, the inheritance spoken of incorporates not only acquisition but also administration. That is, in eternity, there will not only be stuff to acquire but also things to do. In Luke 19, Jesus says if we're faithful in our re-

sponsibilities here on earth, we'll be given cities to rule over in the ages to come eternally.

I'm not really into ruling, you might be thinking.

Listen, the things you really wish you could do here but can't will, I believe, be your area of rule, your responsibility in heaven. Some of you are master mechanics and find total satisfaction in tearing down and rebuilding an engine. Others are authors, artists, or athletes who never seem to have enough time to do what you love because of your responsibilities here on earth. I believe those are the very areas with which you will be involved eternally—or else why would God have given you those desires and gifts in the first place?

Those of you who feel life has passed you by without your ever being able to do what you really loved—take heart! I believe the time is coming when you will be ruling in heaven in the very arena that intrigues you here on earth.

Revelation 21:7 (b)
. . . and I will be his God, and he shall be my son.

In addition to resources and responsibility, there will be a relationship in heaven unlike anything we've known on earth. In John 3:16, we read that God gave us His Son. In Luke 11:13, we read He gives us His Spirit. Here in Revelation 21:7, He gives us *Himself.*

Revelation 21:8
But the fearful, and unbelieving, and the abominable, and murderers, and whoremongers, and sorcerers, and idolaters, and all liars, shall have their part in the lake which burneth with fire and brimstone: which is the second death.

Vastly more comforting than the fact that murderers and sorcerers and liars won't be in heaven is the fact that I will be. You see, all of these tendencies are inherent within me, but they will be burned up, not allowed in my eternal destination. There's coming a time when I will truly be set free from the flesh of which I grow ever wearier as I grow older. Heaven will be a safe place because the flesh within me will be cast away. And for that I am so grateful.

Revelation 21:9, 10
And there came unto me one of the seven angels which had the seven vials full of the seven last plagues, and talked with me, saying, Come hither, I will shew thee the bride, the Lamb's wife. And he carried me away in the spirit to a great and high mountain, and

shewed me that great city, the holy Jerusalem, descending out of heaven from God,

The New Jerusalem descends from heaven. But the language implies it doesn't land on earth. Rather, it hovers above the earth, suspended between heaven and earth.

Revelation 21:11
Having the glory of God: and her light was like unto a stone most precious, even like a jasper stone, clear as crystal.

Due to its description as being clear as crystal, most scholars believe the jasper of verse 11 is actually a diamond. A diamond would be a fitting description of the city wherein dwells the church—not because as the bride of Christ we deserve diamonds, but because, like diamonds we are simply chunks of worthless coal made brilliant by heat and pressure (1 Peter 4:12, 13).

Revelation 21:12, 13
And had a wall great and high, and had twelve gates, and at the gates twelve angels, and names written thereon, which are the names of the twelve tribes of the children of Israel: On the east three gates; on the north three gates; on the south three gates; and on the west three gates.

Regardless of what you've heard, there's not one mention of Peter at the gates of heaven. Instead, there are the names of the twelve tribes of Israel. As Gentiles, we were lost without the covenants, without any understanding of Yahweh before we were grafted into the olive tree of the faith (Romans 11:17). Thus, the names of the twelve tribes remind us that we are indebted to the people of Israel as we are to no other people.

Revelation 21:14 (a)
And the wall of the city had twelve foundations . . .

Because Abraham looked for a city with foundations (Hebrews 11:10), because he understood that what he longed for would not be found on earth, he lived his whole life in a tent. Like Abraham, we will be truly free when we understand that what we really crave is not a better car or a bigger house, but rather the city with not one foundation but twelve: the New Jerusalem, heaven.

Revelation 21:14 (b)
. . . and in them the names of the twelve apostles of the Lamb.

The names of the twelve apostles remind us that although we were originally granted access to an understanding of God through the gate of our Jewish heritage, our faith is founded on the message committed to the apostles: the gospel of Jesus Christ.

Revelation 21:15, 16
And he that talked with me had a golden reed to measure the city, and the gates thereof, and the wall thereof. And the city lieth foursquare, and the length is as large as the breadth: and he measured the city with the reed, twelve thousand furlongs. The length and the breadth and the height of it are equal.

The New Jerusalem is a fifteen-hundred-mile cube with twelve foundations or levels. This means it's three billion square miles in size. The present population of earth is 5.3 billion people. With 90 percent of the people who have ever lived in history alive today, if even three billion people are in heaven, there will be enough room for each person to have one square mile. It's huge!

Revelation 21:17, 18 (a)
And he measured the wall thereof, an hundred and forty and four cubits, according to the measure of a man, that is, of the angel. And the building of the wall of it was of jasper . . .

Two hundred sixteen feet is a high wall—but not in comparison to a city fifteen hundred miles high. At times, due to a misunderstanding or breakdown in communication, you might feel like there's a wall between you and someone else. You won't in heaven. The wall around the New Jerusalem speaks of safety and security, but not of secrecy.

Revelation 21:18 (b)
. . . and the city was pure gold, like unto clear glass.

The city is brilliant like a diamond but also like transparent gold.

Revelation 21:19, 20
And the foundations of the wall of the city were garnished with all manner of precious stones. The first foundation was jasper; the second, sapphire; the third, a chalcedony; the fourth, an emerald; the fifth, sardonyx; the sixth, sardius; the seventh, chrysolite; the eighth, beryl; the ninth, a topaz; the tenth, a chrysoprasus; the eleventh, a jacinth; the twelfth, an amethyst.

In Old Testament times, if one had a question regarding what he should do, he would go to the high priest, who would, in turn, seek God through the Urim and the Thumim, or literally, "lights and perfections" (see Numbers 27:2; Nehemiah 7:65).

Most Orthodox rabbis teach that the twelve stones that represented the twelve tribes of Israel on the breastplate of the high priest would light up in such a way that direction would be given. Some have suggested it was through the lighting of the twelve stones that the desired answer would be given, perhaps through the letter associated with the tribal name each stone represented.

A fundamental element of this Old Testament practice—the stones of which, I believe, are seen in the foundations of the walls in the New Jerusalem—is equally valid today. That is, you'll know God's will for your life if you hang out with God's people. Believers are vulnerable when they are no longer in fellowship with other "tribes," when they try to figure things out on their own independently from of the rest of the body. Satan's plan is always the same: to isolate believers. Therefore, the safest place to be is surrounded by the "walls" of God's people.

Revelation 21:21 (a)
And the twelve gates were twelve pearls; every several gate was of one pearl . . .

The pearl represents God's people. How do I know? In Matthew 13, Jesus told the story of a man who sold everything to purchase a pearl. That's just what Jesus did. He gave everything He had—even His very life—to purchase us. This makes us the pearl—a fitting description, since a pearl is nothing more than an irritating grain of sand or a tiny parasite coated by the lustrous nacre of an oyster. We're irritating indeed, parasitic beyond question. But God robes us and covers us and thereby makes us trophies in order that all of creation throughout eternity might marvel at His grace.

Revelation 21:21 (b)
. . . and the street of the city was pure gold, as it were transparent glass.

So highly valued is gold on earth that throughout history, man has lived by the golden rule: He who has gold rules. Such is not the case in heaven, where gold is used as casually as asphalt. Gang, whatever you value most on earth will be as commonplace as asphalt in comparison to the glory of the New Jerusalem.

Revelation 21:22
And I saw no temple therein: for the Lord God Almighty and the Lamb are the temple of it.

Have you ever been at a camp or a worship service or a Bible study where you sensed God's presence so powerfully that you didn't want to leave? That's the way heaven will be all of the time. That's why there's no need for a temple.

Revelation 21:23, 24 (a)
And the city had no need of the sun, neither of the moon, to shine in it: for the glory of God did lighten it, and the Lamb is the light thereof. And the nations of them which are saved shall walk in the light of it . . .

In the Millennium of chapter 20, the moon will be as bright as the sun is presently, and the sun will be seven times brighter than it is now (Isaiah 30:26). But in the New Jerusalem, there will be no need for the sun or moon at all because the glory and brilliance of the Lord will illuminate the entire city.

Revelation 21:24 (b), 25
. . . and the kings of the earth do bring their glory and honour into it. And the gates of it shall not be shut at all by day: for there shall be no night there.

As freshmen at Biola University, we were excited to go to Disneyland® one fall evening. Cruising into the parking lot at 5:59 P.M., we were disappointed to learn that the gates of the Magic Kingdom™ closed at 6:00. This is not true of the gates of the true kingdom. They never close.

Revelation 21:26, 27
And they shall bring the glory and honour of the nations into it. And there shall in no wise enter into it any thing that defileth, neither whatsoever worketh abomination, or maketh a lie: but they which are written in the Lamb's book of life.

As chapter 21 draws to a close, I hear Pastor John, by the inspiration of the Spirit, saying to his flock in the midst of tribulation and persecution, "The key to victory, the antidote to despondency is one thing: heaven."

Let not your heart be troubled: ye believe in God, believe also in me. In my Father's house are many mansions: if it were not so, I would have told you. I go to prepare a place for you.   John 14:1, 2

Saint, if you take your focus off eternity and get caught up in the present world, like Peter on the water, you'll sink into the ocean of depres-sion. But the extent to which you set your heart on things above is the extent to which you will be free from defeat and discouragement.

May we be a heavenly minded people as we book ourselves and as many others as we can on the flight to the New Jerusalem.

WHAT?! NO BEACH?
A Topical Study of
Revelation 21:1

And I saw a new heaven and a new earth: for the first heaven and the first earth were passed away; and there was no more sea.

Revelation 21:1

Quite frankly, our text is a bit disconcerting, even somewhat disappointing to me—a brand-new city, but no more sea? If I were creating the new heaven and the new earth, I would have said, "There shall be no more cities and lots and lots of oceans, beaches, sand, and surf!" After all, cities aren't spoken of very favorably, even in Scripture. . . .

- The first city in the Bible was founded by a brother-hating Cain (Genesis 4:17).
- The second city in the Bible was built by a God-defying Nimrod (Genesis 10:9).
- The holy city of Jerusalem was filled with a prophet-killing people (Matthew 23:37).

Truly, cities are not valued in Scripture. The same is true today. When we think of cities, we think of pollution, perversion, and problems. So why does the new heaven and the new earth consist of a city—with no beach?

In the sixties, it seemed to me as though everyone in the whole country was singing "Let's Go Surfin'" along with the Beach Boys. As a sophomore at Del Mar High School, about fifty miles north of Santa Cruz, "surf city," California, I dressed the part along with everyone else in my school: huarache sandals with tire tread bottoms, powder blue Levi's with a block of surf wax in one pocket and a copy of *Surfer Magazine* in the other, either a red or blue and white wide-striped T-shirt, and hair parted in the middle. Walking down the hall, a "thumbs up" sign meant we had just caught the surf report on KLIV—1260 on the AM radio dial—and Pleasure Point was breaking big.

One day in May, all decked out in my huaraches, powder blue Levi's, etc., on my way to fifth period Spanish class, I ran into Lindsay, Chuck, and Bob going the opposite direction. "Hey, Jon," they said. "We heard it's monster stuff at Steamer Lane. We saw the Turtle in the parking lot. Let's go!"

Now, the "Turtle" to which they referred was the shortened name for the "Turquoise Turtle," my 1961 Ford Falcon—so named partly because of its color and partly because it went 0–60 mph in 2.5 hours.

"I can't go, guys," I said. "I've got a Spanish test."

"Come on, Jon," they begged. "You're the only one of us with a car."

Feeling the pressure mounting, I relented. After grabbing my lunch out of my locker, I headed out to the car with Lindsay, Chuck, and Bob—a feeling of dread beginning to wash over me. With Lindsay riding "shotgun" and Bob and Chuck in the back, I swung by their houses to get their boards. No need to get mine. My 9'6" O'Neill was always on the rack on top of my car.

Wending our way over Highway 17, Lindsay looked at me and said, "You don't look so good. You must be carsick." Little did he know it wasn't the curves in the road causing me to sweat. It was the fact that although I was a charter subscriber to *Surfer*, had a great board, and knew how to dress, unbeknownst to anyone else, I had never surfed before.

When we arrived at the Henry Cowell State Park parking lot, from which point we'd hike down to the beach and paddle out, Lindsay, Chuck, and Bob grabbed their boards. "Listen, guys," I said. "I'm not feeling so good. I'll just have my lunch and join you later."

"Okay," they called over their shoulders as they ran toward the trail.

Opening my lunch, I was happy to see that my mom had packed two peanut butter, mayonnaise, and pickle sandwiches—my favorite—along with about ten homemade chocolate chip cookies, an apple, and a carton of milk. After finishing the last cookie, I knew I could stall no longer. So I trekked on down to the beach and saw Lindsay, Chuck, and Bob all doing great. Bob came in. "Come on, Jon," he said, "it's excellent out there!"

I walked down to the water's edge, reached into the back pocket of my jams, took out my wax, and began to wax my board. Seeing Bob was looking at me rather quizzically, I realized I was waxing the wrong side. You see, I thought you were supposed to wax the bottom of the board so you could cut through the water. But I came to find out that you wax the top of the board for traction. "I'm just trying something new," I said, attempting to cover my blunder.

"Come on, Jon. Quit fooling around. Let's go," Bob said as he knee-paddled out. I followed at a safe distance—hoping he wouldn't turn around and see me paddling on my belly. (Knee-paddling takes practice and coordination. I had neither.) Finally, after I had sat on my board for about half an hour, Lindsay called, "Take this one, Jon." I looked back, and sure enough, there was a beautiful swell coming right in my direction that appeared to be forty-to-fifty feet high. At that point, I had no other choice but to lie down and paddle for all I was worth. Then a miracle happened. I actually got to my feet and stood on my board—for about a second and a half. But being too close to the nose, I "pearled." That is, the nose of the board went underwater, causing the rest of the board to become a catapult that launched me into the air. I landed in front of the wave that proceeded to break right on top of me.

After tossing and turning underwater for what felt like forever, I finally figured out which way was up, shot toward the surface of the water for a desperately needed gasp of air, inadvertently sucking in a huge piece of kelp in the process. Grabbing my board as it floated by, there I was—clinging to my board for dear life, with seaweed hanging out of my mouth. It was at this point that the peanut butter and pickle sandwiches began to work their way up. Suddenly, with Lindsay, Chuck, and Bob looking on in utter disbelief, I barfed on my board.

Needless to say, the entire area cleared out immediately. Although I did learn to surf later on, I was set free that day from the image I was so desperately trying to cultivate.

As this incident came to mind, I was reminded that, along with the beautiful waves, salt air, and cool breeze of the beach scene, there's also a preponderance of phoniness and jealousy, of taunting and flaunting. All kinds of things take place at the beach that we feel pressured to fit into. The same is true of the football field, basketball court, or even the business office.

Therefore, I suggest to you that one of the grand and glorious things the Lord says through our text is, "In the new heaven and earth, I'm going to liberate you from all of the things you think appear to be so cool on the outside but which hide a dark side underneath." You who are trapped in the business gig, the materialistic stuff, the sports scene—the Lord calls you to something bigger, something grander, something better. In the new heaven and the new earth, the sea shall be replaced by a city.

"A city?" you say. "That's exactly where I wouldn't want to be!" Listen, those to whom John addressed the Book of Revelation were those who lived in cities. Thus, John is telling them, "Heaven doesn't eliminate your situation. It transforms it."

Gang, heaven is not "other." It's "more." Therefore, if you want heaven in your home, in your life, or in your city—it will come not by elimination, but by transformation. If any man be in Christ, he is—not "will be"—a new creation. Old things are passed away. Behold all things are become new (2 Corinthians 5:17).

To experience eternal, abundant life this side of heaven, see yourself as a new creation rather than as a businessman; a child of God rather than as a sports star; a follower of Jesus rather than as a supermom; a fisher of men rather than as an image-conscious surfer. If you do, you'll find yourself free from having to know the language, dress the part, or fit the image.

Find your identity in Jesus, fellow city-dweller, and you won't miss the beach at all. I guarantee it!

22

Revelation 22:1
And he shewed me a pure river of water of life, clear as crystal, proceeding out of the throne of God and of the Lamb.

According to Zechariah 14, as Jesus comes back to earth, He will set foot upon the Mount of Olives—which will usher in a radical topographical change in Israel. The Mount of Olives will split in two from north to south, causing a river to flow to both the Dead Sea and the Mediterranean Sea. The infusion of fresh water into the Dead Sea will, in turn, cause it to come back to life to such a degree that a fishing industry will thrive in the region (Ezekiel 47).

It is fascinating to me that Ezekiel's account provides not only prophetic information, but practical application. . . .

As Ezekiel was given this vision, a man appeared to him, saying, "Step into the river." Ezekiel did, and the water was up to his ankles. "Come out," said the man and took Ezekiel downriver one thousand cubits or so, where Ezekiel was told to go into the river once more. This time the water was up to his knees. "Come out," said the man and took Ezekiel one thousand cubits farther downriver, where he told Ezekiel to go into the river yet again. This time the water was up to Ezekiel's waist. When he was told a fourth time to go into the river, the water was over his head, and Ezekiel was caught up in its flow.

Dear saint, the Lord won't force us to go any deeper in Him than we choose—but He will take us as deep as we wish. . . .

Some get their feet wet up to their ankles. They are standing on the promises, born again, saved.

Others, wanting to go deeper, go up to their knees—that speaks of prayer. "I want to do more than get my feet wet, Lord," they say. "I want to be part of what You are doing. Use me in prayer." And they get involved in intercessory ministry—praying in the Spirit.

Others, wanting to go deeper still, wade in to their waists—signifying reproduction. Not only are they standing on the promises, or up to their knees in intercessory ministry, they

are adding to the kingdom by witnessing to their family, friends, and neighbors.

But there comes a point where some are just over their heads, saying, "Lord, I'm going to just let go. Have Your way in my life. I'm giving it to You without reservation. I don't know where this will take me, but I'm Yours totally. Do what You want to do in and through me for Your glory."

Maybe right now you're in the doldrums in your walk. If so, I encourage you to launch out into the deeper waters of faith. Oh, maybe your kayak will get overturned in the rapids a few times and maybe you won't know exactly where you'll land. But I guarantee you won't regret it. I'm so glad that the water of life flows right through heaven because it means that the Lord's Spirit is on the move even there and that we can continue going deeper and deeper in Him throughout eternity.

Revelation 22:2 (a)
In the midst of the street of it, and on either side of the river, was there the tree of life, which bare twelve manner of fruits, and yielded her fruit every month . . .

Is this good news or what? People ask, "Are we going to eat in heaven?"
My answer is, "I am!"

"Have you any meat?" asked the resurrected Jesus of His disciples. When they gave Him a piece of fish and some honey, and saw Him eat it, they knew He was not a phantom (Luke 24:37–43).

Following His Resurrection, Jesus ate. Therefore, I believe we'll be eating the fruits of this amazing evergreen, twelve-fruit-bearing tree in heaven.

For topical study of Revelation 22:2 entitled "The Tree of Life," turn to page 1799.

Revelation 22:2 (b)
. . . and the leaves of the tree were for the healing of the nations.

"Wait a minute," you say, "if the leaves are for healing, does that mean there will be sickness in heaven?"

No. The Greek word translated "healing" is literally *therapeia*, from which we get our word "therapy." It doesn't mean healing from sickness, but rather a maintaining of health. In fact, the original language also implies exhilaration and invigoration.

Do you ever get tired of being tired? I do. What a grand day it will be when we are in heaven, shooting the rapids of the river of life, eating of the fruit of the Spirit, revived eternally by the leaves of the Tree of Life.

Revelation 22:3 (a)
And there shall be no more curse: but the throne of God and of the Lamb shall be in it . . .

The fallout of Adam's bomb in the Garden of Eden is felt to this day as a result of the curse that followed (Genesis 3:17–19). In heaven, however, the curse is gone, replaced by the throne of God and of the Lamb.

Revelation 22:3 (b)
. . . and his servants shall serve him.

The interests and inclinations that the Lord built into each of us will at last be fully utilized in heaven, where, free from time limitations or financial obligations, we'll use them to serve the Lord. Ours will not be the service of one who drags into work at the last moment, dreading the day ahead. No, ours will be the service of one who says, "Oh, boy! This is what I always wanted to do!"

Revelation 22:4 (a)
And they shall see his face . . .

What will happen when we see His face? Like David, we shall at last be truly satisfied (Psalm 17:15) because when we see Him, we'll be like Him (1 John 3:2).

Revelation 22:4 (b)
. . . and his name shall be in their foreheads.

I'll see the Lord's name on all of you—but not on myself because no one can see his own forehead. That's the way it should be here on earth as well. "I know no man after the flesh," said Paul (see 2 Corinthians 5:16). In other words, he chose to see past the fleshly tendencies of others and, instead, saw others positioned in Christ. What do I do? All too often, just the opposite. Far too fre-

quently, I see myself as forgiven and robed in God's righteousness but others as a disgrace to the body of Christ.

Revelation 22:5
And there shall be no night there; and they need no candle, neither light of the sun; for the Lord God giveth them light: and they shall reign for ever and ever.

There will be no need for the sun because warmth and illumination will come from the Son.

Revelation 22:6 (a)
And he said unto me, These sayings are faithful and true . . .

The glorious garden city, the time when things are right at last, the pure river that flows, the fruit-bearing trees—they're not too good to be true. They are true!

Revelation 22:6 (b)
. . . and the Lord God of the holy prophets sent his angel to shew unto his servants the things which must shortly be done.

"*Shortly?* This was written two thousand years ago!" you might say to yourself.

"Things which must shortly be" doesn't mean these things would transpire in John's day. Rather, it means once the end-time events begin, they will rev up like an engine and increase in speed.

In New York City, you can stand on the street for a relatively long period of time hailing a taxi as cab after cab passes you by. But once one stops and you get in—hold on, because once you're in, you're on your way!

Folks, we've seen Israel become a nation again. We're in the taxi. Hold on! We're on our way!

Revelation 22:7
Behold, I come quickly: blessed is he that keepeth the sayings of the prophecy of this book.

To us, a period of two thousand years doesn't seem "quickly," but since to the Lord, one thousand years is as a day (2 Peter 3:8), according to His timetable, He's only been gone two days.

Revelation 22:8, 9
And I John saw these things, and heard them. And when I had heard and seen, I fell down to worship before the feet of the angel which shewed me these things. Then saith

he unto me, See thou do it not: for I am thy fellowservant, and of thy brethren the prophets, and of them which keep the sayings of this book: worship God.

I find it interesting that the same thing happened just a couple pages earlier in chapter 19. After he fell down and worshiped an angel, the angel said to John, "See thou do it not." So how could John worship an angel *again?* The same way we make the same mistakes and commit the same sins over and over and over again. But the good news is that the Lord taught us to forgive so many times that we lose count (Matthew 18:22). And if He taught us to forgive to that degree, how much more will He!

"Oh, Lord, I blew it again," I cry.

"Again?" He says. "What are you talking about? I don't remember you blowing it before" (see Hebrews 8:12).

If someone suddenly charged up the platform steps and punched me in the nose while I was preaching, that I could forgive that person is within the realm of possibility. But I would never, ever forget it. I don't have that capability. Only God can say, "I'll not only forgive you, but I won't remember your sin."

You see, so precious, so powerful is the blood of Jesus to the Father, that it obliterates every trace and memory of sin. I love that! It's what gives me such boldness to come before the throne of grace so that I may obtain mercy and find grace to help in time of need (Hebrews 4:16).

Revelation 22:10
And he saith unto me, Seal not the sayings of the prophecy of this book: for the time is at hand.

There are preachers, professors, authors, commentators, and sincere brothers and sisters who say, "Don't read Revelation. It's too complicated. There are too many interpretations. Seal it up." But here is a direct command from heaven: "Don't shut it."

People think Revelation is a hard book to understand. But if you follow the divine outline given in chapter 1, verse 19, it becomes crystal clear. . . .

- Chapter 1   Jesus resurrected
- Chapters 2—3   Church History
- Chapters 4—5   The Rapture
- Chapters 6—19   The Tribulation
- Chapter 20   The Millennium
- Chapters 21—22 The new heaven and new earth

This book is to be kept open. And the same holds true for us. When you're done reading it, don't say, "Well, that about wraps up the Book of Revelation for the next fourteen years. . . ." Because this book has a unique blessing attached to it that says, "Blessed are they that hear these words of this prophecy" (see Revelation 1:3), if we seal it up, or put it aside, we will be the poorer for it.

Revelation 22:11
He that is unjust, let him be unjust still: and he which is filthy, let him be filthy still: and he that is righteous, let him be righteous still: and he that is holy, let him be holy still.

If you choose to be unjust after reading this prophecy, be unjust still. If you choose to be filthy after reading this prophecy, be filthy still. In other words, if you cannot be convinced of the truth of the Word by the revelation of Jesus Christ and the fulfilling of Bible prophecy, what could possibly convince you? After reading this book, you have no other logical option, no other rational recourse than to say, "Jesus is Lord, and I'm going to live for His kingdom."

Revelation 22:12–14
And, behold, I come quickly; and my reward is with me, to give every man according as his work shall be. I am Alpha and Omega, the beginning and the end, the first and the last. Blessed are they that do his commandments, that they may have right to the tree of life, and may enter in through the gates into the city.

"What must we do to do the works of God?" the multitude asked Jesus.

"You're asking about works," Jesus answered, "but this is the singular work: That you believe on Him whom the Father hath sent" (see John 6:28, 29).

People make following the Lord so complicated. "You gotta do this," they say, "and keep away from that. Wear these clothes and don't eat those foods." But that's not what Scripture teaches. . . .

Nine simple words is all it took for a death-row thief to enter the kingdom: "Lord, remember me when You come into Your kingdom" (see Luke 23:42, 43).

But it's even simpler than that. Peter expressed the same thing in only three words: "Lord, save me" (Matthew 14:30).

But it's even simpler than that. John says only one word is necessary to assure an eternity in heaven: "Lord" (Romans 10:9).

Revelation 22:15

For without are dogs, and sorcerers, and whoremongers, and murderers, and idolaters, and whosoever loveth and maketh a lie.

The word "dogs" refers to legalists (Philippians 3:2). The Greek word translated "sorcerers" is literally "drug-takers."

Revelation 22:16

I Jesus have sent mine angel to testify unto you these things in the churches. I am the root and the offspring of David, and the bright and morning star.

Jesus says, "I am both root and offspring of David. David comes from Me, and I from Him." How can this be? As the babe of Bethlehem, Jesus was the offspring of David; but as the Christ of eternity, He existed before David.

Revelation 22:17

And the Spirit and the bride say, Come. And let him that heareth say, Come. And let him that is athirst come. And whosoever will, let him take the water of life freely.

The invitation to come is given to a world that is lost and dying, doomed and damned. It is the Spirit who woos people to Jesus; but we, as the bride, have the privilege of issuing the invitation. Throughout Scripture, "Come" has always been the invitation . . .

- "*Come* now, and let us reason together, saith the Lord . . ." (Isaiah 1:18).
- "Ho everyone that thirsteth, *come* ye to the waters . . ." (Isaiah 55:1).

- "*Come* unto Me, all ye that labour and are heavy laden . . ." (Matthew 11:28).
- "Suffer the little children to *come* unto Me . . ." (Mark 10:14).
- "*Come* and see . . ." (John 1:39).

Revelation 22:18

For I testify unto every man that heareth the words of the prophecy of this book, If any man shall add unto these things, God shall add unto him the plagues that are written in this book.

If you're tempted to add to this book, you might want to review "the plagues that are written" in chapters 6 through 19.

Revelation 22:19–21

And if any man shall take away from the words of the book of this prophecy, God shall take away his part out of the book of life, and out of the holy city, and from the things which are written in this book. He which testifieth these things saith, Surely I come quickly. Amen. Even so, come, Lord Jesus. The grace of our Lord Jesus Christ be with you all. Amen.

The last phrase in the Old Testament is, "Lest I come and smite the earth with a curse" (Malachi 4:6). That's the law. "God is upset. You should be doing more. What's wrong with you?"

But the New Testament ends this way: "The grace of our Lord Jesus Christ be with you all." *Grace* is the final word of the New Testament.

Seek first the kingdom, gang. Set your heart on things above. His coming is nigh.

And I can't wait!

THE TREE OF LIFE

A Topical Study of

Revelation 22:2

I t could rightly be said that the Bible is an account of three trees. . . .

The Tree of Life

The Tree of Life was seen at the beginning of human history. It will be seen again at the end of human history.

It was originally planted in the Garden of Eden.
It will be transplanted into the gardenlike city of the New Jerusalem.

Man chose not to eat of the Tree of Life in the Garden of Eden.
Man will eat freely of the Tree of Life in the New Jerusalem.

The Tree of the Knowledge of Good and Evil

Also introduced in the opening chapters of Genesis, the Tree of the Knowledge of Good and Evil was the one tree of which Adam and Eve were not to partake. When they disobeyed and ate of the forbidden tree, death and damnation were the result.

The question arises as to why God would place a forbidden tree in the Garden in the first place. I suggest the following reasons. . . .

Choice. Because God is love, He wants a loving relationship with humanity. But true love always demands a choice. Therefore, God said to Adam and Eve, "Because I want to live with you in a love relationship, I will provide you the opportunity to reject Me, to turn your back on Me. Eating from the Tree of the Knowledge of Good and Evil will be a sign to you and to Me that you don't want to maintain a loving relationship with Me." Simply put, without the Tree of the Knowledge of Good and Evil, there would be no choice. And without choice love is questionable.

Dependence. Before they ate of the Tree of the Knowledge of Good and Evil, Adam and Eve knew only good, because any time they had a question, they went directly to God for the answer. This is the way God created them—not because He wanted to cripple man, but because He wanted to bless man. Yet when man ate of the Tree of the Knowledge of Good and Evil, he knew good and evil apart from God. He no longer realized he needed a moment-by-moment reliance on the Father. Thus, he became independent—cut off from all the resources and blessings of his Creator.

The same thing happens to us. Even we who love the Lord are vulnerable to saying, "I don't need to be in close communication with the Lord because I've walked with Him for years. I know my Bible; I understand theology; I have experience.

Such was recently the case with me. Feeling I had already heard the word of the Lord regarding an upcoming decision, I was already moving in a certain direction when the Lord stopped me dead in my tracks with the account found in Genesis 22. . . .

Surely you're not that kind of God, Abraham must have thought when he was told to sacrifice his son Isaac on Mount Moriah. But knowing he had heard the word of the Lord, Abraham did, indeed, lay Isaac on the altar and take knife in hand, ready to plunge it into his son's chest.

Suddenly, "The angel of the Lord called unto him out of heaven and said, Lay not thine hand upon the lad . . ." (see 22:11, 12).

Perhaps, like me, a number of you have heard the word of the Lord clearly in a Bible study or prayer meeting, through corporate worship, or private devotions.

You wrote it in your journal and are now moving in a certain direction in obedience to His word to you. But you must realize that what the Lord wants from you is *constant* communion with Him. You see, if Abraham hadn't heeded the second word of the Lord—if he had stubbornly sacrificed his son in obedience to the first word of the Lord—he would have made a bloody mess and a very grave mistake.

"Got the word. I'm on my way," we so often say, failing to realize it might change the very next day. How many unnecessary grave mistakes I've made that could have been avoided had I said, "Lord it's not enough to act on what You spoke to me three days ago. I must hear from you constantly."

"But what if I've already made a grave mistake?" you ask.

Go to the third tree. . . .

The Tree of Calvary

The Tree of Calvary covers my mistakes, washes away my arrogance, and cleanses my sin. You see, after offering the sacrifice of His own body for the bloody messes I have made, Jesus arose from the grave to obliterate the grave mistakes I have made.

The word of the Lord for us today is this, precious people: On the path to heaven, we must keep current with the Lord. We can't rely on what we heard yesterday, last week, or a year ago. If you're not receiving what the Spirit says to you *today*, like Abraham, you could end up making a big mistake.

Turn away from the Tree of the Knowledge of Good and Evil—from what you think you know—and begin to feast on the Tree of Life by saying,

- "Before I make my plans for the afternoon, what's *Your* agenda, Lord?"
- "Lord, how do *You* want me to parent my five-year-old son today?"
- "Lord, what do *You* want me to do about the situation at work this morning?"

Let us who love the Bible be those who seek the Lord intimately even as we take in knowledge intellectually. Because of the Tree of Calvary, when we get to heaven, we won't see the Tree of the Knowledge of Good and Evil—only the Tree of Life, from which we will partake freely, enjoying the fruit that will keep us in perfect health and total harmony with our King, our Savior, our Lord Jesus.

But you don't have to wait until then, saint. Heaven can be in your heart today if you'll choose to eat daily from the tree of *His* direction.

NOTES

[1]Source: "Historical Times Encyclopedia of the Civil War" edited by Patricia L. Faust. New York Harper & Row, New York, 1986.